Spinoza, Life and Legacy

Frontispiece: *Portrait of Spinoza*, anonymous. Museum: Herzog August Bibliothek Wolfenbüttel. Reproduction courtesy of Album/Alamy Stock Photo.

Spinoza, Life and Legacy

JONATHAN I. ISRAEL

OXFORD
UNIVERSITY PRESS

Great Clarendon Street, Oxford, OX2 6DP,
United Kingdom

Oxford University Press is a department of the University of Oxford.
It furthers the University's objective of excellence in research, scholarship,
and education by publishing worldwide. Oxford is a registered trade mark of
Oxford University Press in the UK and in certain other countries

© Jonathan I. Israel 2023

The moral rights of the author have been asserted

All rights reserved. No part of this publication may be reproduced, stored in
a retrieval system, or transmitted, in any form or by any means, without the
prior permission in writing of Oxford University Press, or as expressly permitted
by law, by licence or under terms agreed with the appropriate reprographics
rights organization. Enquiries concerning reproduction outside the scope of the
above should be sent to the Rights Department, Oxford University Press, at the
address above

You must not circulate this work in any other form
and you must impose this same condition on any acquirer

Published in the United States of America by Oxford University Press
198 Madison Avenue, New York, NY 10016, United States of America

British Library Cataloguing in Publication Data

Data available

Library of Congress Control Number: 2022950227

ISBN 978–0–19–885748–8

DOI: 10.1093/oso/9780198857488.001.0001

Printed and bound by CPI Group (UK) Ltd, Croydon, CR0 4YY

Links to third party websites are provided by Oxford in good faith and
for information only. Oxford disclaims any responsibility for the materials
contained in any third party website referenced in this work.

Preface

No account of Spinoza's life and legacy can have much value unless it rests on an exhaustive analysis of his works and correspondence. But this in turn inevitably involves delving into the wider debates and polemics of his age, personages and texts he praised and (more often) against whom he aimed his critical barbs as well as friends and sparring partners with whom he debated during his life. Equally, there cannot be a comprehensive biography of Spinoza not enmeshed in analysis of the deep-seated religious and political tensions and conflicts of the Dutch Golden Age as well as the central issues debated by its philosophers, scientists, religious leaders, and statesmen. All considered, a great deal of preliminary research and publication of other documents and surviving material is requisite before it is at all feasible to attempt a comprehensive, documents-based biography that, hopefully, adds to the earlier picture that Steven Nadler, in particular, has given us. There is thus good reason to emphasize here the crucial role of the marked revival of interest, and surge of new research, in all aspects of Spinoza's life and writings that followed in the wake of Nadler's biography which appeared in 1999 in making possible a more detailed account of Spinoza's contribution to the history of philosophy, the Enlightenment and of his age.

"Given Spinoza's continuing relevance and pervasive influence," commented Frederick Beiser, in 1999, in response to Nadler's *Spinoza: A Life* which he reviewed together with another less significant biography, Margaret Gullan-Whur's *Within Reason*, both published in 1999, "it is surprising to find that there have been so few biographies of him."[1] It is indeed "surprising," and a phenomenon not easily explained, but certainly one factor, until recently, was the relative inaccessibility and where published, elusiveness, of much of what solid documentary material was available. In 2018, the Cambridge University Press brought out the revised edition of Nadler's masterful biography which reflects many though not all the recent finds relating to Spinoza's life. Nadler's biography and mine present a different picture in some regards though not in others, and while I have tried to fill in more of the historical and cultural context of Spinoza's life and early impact, I have remained conscious throughout of my enduring debt to Steve, my continuing debate with him, and the formidable and lasting value of his achievement.

---

[1] Beiser, "Homesick Hidalgo," 4.

As Nadler mentions in his preface to the second edition of his biography, the completion of Edwin Curley's landmark two-volume English edition of Spinoza's writings with the appearance of the second volume in 2016 not only provides a fresh store of valuable notes and commentary on the writings but enables one to refer the reader to a single complete, consistent, and mostly reliable English rendering of Spinoza's texts and letters. Curley's edition of Spinoza's *Collected Works* (2 vols., Princeton 1985 and 2016) the reader will find frequently referred to throughout. However, the best way of rendering into English Spinoza's meaning from the original Latin or Dutch still often remains elusive or debatable and there are numerous points throughout this biography where, after careful consideration, I have opted to render some of Spinoza's phrases and expressions rather differently from Curley and a great many slightly differently. The reader's attention is drawn to this point. Rather than quoting Curley's, or another translator's rendering exactly, my policy throughout has been to refer back to the original Latin and compare the various renderings, frequently arriving at wording that diverges, sometimes significantly, from the wording in the sources quoted. Where I have preferred to avoid Curley's understanding of the Latin, I have indicated this by referring to the Akkerman Dutch rendering or Maxime Rovere's excellent recent French translation.

Where this divergence seems significant I have indicated this either by referring directly to Carl Gebhardt's classic four-volume Latin edition of Spinoza's *Opera* (Heidelberg, 1925) or by referring to the extremely exacting scholarly bilingual Latin-French PUF editions of the texts by the team that produced the *Traité Théologico-Politique* (1999), Fokke Akkerman, Jacqueline Lagrée, and Pierre-François Moreau, the *Traité Politique* (2005), Omero Proietti and Charles Ramond, the *Premiers Écrits* (2009), Filippo Mignini, M. Beyssade, and J. Ganault, and the *Éthique* (2020), Akkerman, Moreau, and Piet Steenbakkers. Since much of Spinoza's correspondence was in Dutch, as also is the earliest surviving version of Spinoza's *Short Treatise on God, Man and his Well-Being*, some of my translations of Spinoza's remarks and expressions have relied on the modern Dutch editions of Spinoza's letters by Akkerman, H. G. Hubbeling, and A. G. Westerbrink, of 1992 and of the early writings by Akkerman, Hubbeling, Mignini, M. J. Petry, and N. and G. van Suchtelen of 1982. However, though guided or influenced by these scholars, all the many English renderings in this volume wherever they do noticeably diverge from Curley's wording, are my own.

Steve Nadler has himself painstakingly continued adding to the research he originally did for his 1999 biography, and also since the appearance of the revised edition, and for the opportunities I have had to exchange information and views with him since (as well as before) 2018, I feel much additional gratitude. Meanwhile, a great deal of the most important and valuable research since the 1990s has been carried on in the archives and libraries of the Netherlands by Jeroen van de Ven, Piet Steenbakkers, Frank Mertens, Henri Krop, Wiep van Bunge,

Eric Jorink, and Albert Goosjes. I am especially indebted for the opportunity to correspond frequently and exchange information with Van de Ven whose efforts to find new material and willingness to discuss his finds with others has proved inexhaustible and who has been of enormous help to me for which I shall always remain extremely appreciative. Van de Ven's impressive bibliographical history of Spinoza's writings, their clandestine publication, distribution, variant editions and translations is already proving a landmark event in Spinoza studies and so doubtless will be his (forthcoming) highly detailed chronological study of Spinoza's life and circle with its very extensive discussion of the primary sources. I am grateful too to the much-lamented Michiel Wielema (1959–2018) another indefatigable archive researcher who came up with valuable finds. Without the labours and invaluable research contributions of these scholars it would not have been possible to provide anything like the factual ground-plan and extensive documentary basis that underpins this present biography.

On a more personal level, my most important debts are to my wife, Annette Munt, who devoted much time to help me edit and refine the text of this biography and to the two scholars, Richard Popkin (1923–2005) and Wim Klever, who were my chief debating partners on the topic of Spinoza and Spinozism at an earlier stage, in the late 1980s and through the 1990s when I began researching on Spinoza. Additionally, through her many years of research in the archives and libraries of Italy, her publications and learned suggestions and comments, Pina Totaro whose work I much admire and with whom I have sporadically been in contact over the years, has greatly strengthened several aspects of what follows, and not least what might be termed the "Italian dimension." A good deal is owed too for valuable information and comments to Sonja Lavaert, Mogens Laerke, Victor Tiribás, Winfried Schröder, Odette Vlessing, and Eric Jorink. Finally, to all these names I must add those of Ed Curley, Dan Garber, Maxime Rovere, Yosef Kaplan, Antony Mckenna, and Yitzak Melamed with whom I have enormously enjoyed lively debates about Spinoza and the world of late seventeenth-century clandestine philosophy over many years and to all of whom I again feel a vast debt of gratitude.

As regards the growing documentary basis, in addition to what is noted above it is important to mention the greatly expanded two-volume edition of the collection of historical documents relating to the life, activities and friends of Spinoza, published in Germany in 2006 under the title *Die Lebensgeschichte Spinozas* edited by the eminent Spinoza scholar, Manfred Walther, at Hanover. This indispensable two-volume compilation is a landmark reworking and expansion of the work of Jakob Freudenthal whose contribution is explained further in the conclusion to this volume. Because all previous accounts of Spinoza's life were based on limited, unsatisfactory, and often poorly edited sources, Freudenthal's work represented a major shift. In conceiving and carrying out what Richard Popkin terms "a fundamental nineteenth-century study," Freudenthal achieved something unique, the fruits of which have proved of lasting value.

Finally, it remains only to thank in every way the Institute for Advanced Study, Princeton, to whose ever stimulating community, the scene of many a "Spinoza discussion," I have been fortunate to belong now for a quarter of a century. I am especially grateful to Alexis May for her ever reliable support especially with organizing the illustrations and to Marcia Tucker and the Institute librarians who have helped organize our Library's special Spinoza collection and have made our Institute's library such a wonderfully stimulating place to research, ponder, and to rethink one's views.

These are the persons and resources who have chiefly enriched the raw material and documentary base, and helped shape the ground-plan for a biography that I have slowly been assembling since my intensive discussions in 1995 in Los Angeles, with Dick Popkin, with whom I first broached the feasibility of embarking on such a venture as this volume has since slowly evolved into. It has taken nearly three decades to put the plan into effect and all of those named above have left their mark in numerous ways on the final outcome.

Contents

List of Illustrations   xv
List of Tables   xxi

PART I. SETTING THE SCENE

1. Introduction   3
2. Unparalleled Challenge   21
   2.i Philosophy that Survived by a Thread   21
   2.ii Banning Spinoza's Books and Ideas   24
   2.iii Spinoza and Europe's Late Seventeenth-Century Intellectual Crisis   33

PART II. THE YOUNG SPINOZA

3. Youthful Rebel   49
   3.i Caution and Audacity   49
   3.ii Heretical Opinions   65
   3.iii Expulsion from the Synagogue   71
4. A Secret Legacy from Portugal   79
   4.i Crypto-Judaism and Religious Subversion   79
   4.ii Vidigueira   82
   4.iii Spinoza's Mother's Family   88
   4.iv Absolutism Enthroned   92
   4.v Exiles Fleeing Portugal   96
   4.vi Revolutionary Subversion by Means of Philosophy   100
5. Childhood and Family Tradition   111
   5.i From *Brit Milah* to *Bar Mitzvah* (1632–1645)   111
   5.ii Spinoza's Forebears, the Mechanics of Community Leadership   118
   5.iii The Sephardic Cemetery at Ouderkerk   128
   5.iv The Spinozas of Amsterdam and Rotterdam   132
6. Schooldays   148
   6.i *Ets Haim*   148
   6.ii Uriel da Costa   159
   6.iii World Events Viewed from School   162
   6.iv Last Years of Schooling   170
   6.v Family Tensions   181

7. Honour and Wealth ... 189
    7.i Son of a Merchant ... 189
    7.ii The First Anglo-Dutch War (1652–1654) ... 196
    7.iii Spinoza Becomes Head of the Family ... 202
    7.iv Collapse of the Family Fortune ... 212
    7.v Renouncing his Inheritance ... 220

8. Teaching Skills: Van den Enden, Latin, and the Theatre (1655–1661) ... 229
    8.i Disciple of a Schoolmaster ... 229
    8.ii A Career in the Church Abandoned ... 236
    8.iii Spinoza Embraces Cartesianism ... 243
    8.iv Learning from the Roman Playwrights Terence and Seneca ... 252
    8.v A New Form of Pedagogy ... 256

9. Collegiants, Millenarians, and Quakers: The Mid- and Late 1650s ... 261

10. "Monstrous Heresies": Beyond Bible and Religious Studies ... 289
    10.i First Writings ... 289
    10.ii The La Peyrère Episode ... 293
    10.iii Dr Juan (Daniel) de Prado (1612–1670) ... 303
    10.iv Denounced to the Inquisition ... 309
    10.v Eternal Things and their Unchangeable Laws ... 319

PART III. REFORMER AND SUBVERTER OF DESCARTES

11. Forming a Study Group ... 327
    11.i The Birth of a Philosophical System (1659–1661) ... 327
    11.ii Translation, the Key to Making Philosophy Effective ... 338
    11.iii Bridging the Gulf between Collegiants and Freethinkers ... 342
    11.iv An Abhorred Clique ... 344

12. Rijnsburg Years (1661–1663) ... 352
    12.i The Move to Rijnsburg ... 352
    12.ii Meeting Oldenburg ... 363
    12.iii Steno and Anatomical Dissection ... 368
    12.iv Debating Cartesianism with the Leiden Cartesians ... 380

13. Spinoza and the Scientific Revolution ... 385
    13.i Challenging Bacon and Boyle ... 385
    13.ii Spinoza and Experimental Science ... 391
    13.iii Mathematics and Scientific Truth ... 402

14. "Reforming" Descartes' Principles ... 409

15. Writing the *Ethics* ... 439

16. Voorburg (1663–1664)	456
16.i The Setting	456
16.ii Spinoza and Huygens	461
16.iii A Local Dispute	468
16.iv *De Jure Ecclesiasticorum*	480
17. Spinoza and the Second Anglo-Dutch War (1664–1667)	487
17.i Rivalry with England	487
17.ii Plague and the Outbreak of War	494
18. Invasion, Slump, and Comets (1665–1666)	507
18.i The Greatest Curse of Mankind	507
18.ii Are Comets Fearful Omens?	515
18.iii Descartes' Laws of Motion	528
19. Spinoza, Meyer, and the 1666 *Philosophia* Controversy	535
19.i A Bitter Controversy	535
19.ii The Revolt of Johannes and Adriaan Koerbagh	543
19.iii The *Philosophia* and the Reformed Church	547
19.iv The Utrecht *Collegie der Sçavanten*	551
20. From the Jaws of Defeat (1666–1667)	563
20.i Faltering Dialogue with the Royal Society	563
20.ii The Sabbatian Frenzy (1665–1667)	567
20.iii Science and Miracles	577
20.iv The Sway of Kings	583

PART IV. DARKENING HORIZONS

21. The Tragedy of the Brothers Koerbagh (1668–1669)	599
22. *Nil Volentibus Arduum*: Spinoza and the Arts	624
23. Twilight of the "True Freedom"	648
23.i Last Years in Voorburg	648
23.ii The Move to The Hague	651
23.iii Ideological Conflict	665
23.iv Democratic Republicanism	673
24. Revolution in Bible Criticism	684
24.i The Dutch Background	684
24.ii Ezra the Scribe	691
24.iii The Masoretic Age	702
24.iv Spinoza's Critique of Meyer	708
25. Spinoza Subverts Hobbes	720
25.i Hobbes, Spinoza, and the Gospels	720
25.ii Hobbes and Spinoza on "Freedom"	726
25.iii Happiness and the "Highest Good"	735
25.iv From the "Highest Good" to the "General Will"	741

26. Spinoza Completes his Philosophical System   748
    26.i Emancipating the Individual   748
    26.ii Popular Sovereignty and the "General Will"   760

27. Publishing the *Theological-Political Treatise*   770
    27.i First Steps to Suppress the *TTP*   770
    27.ii A Text Left Unchallenged   784
    27.iii Spinoza's Clandestine Subversion of Religion 791
    27.iv Steno Responds   799

28. Intensifying Reaction (Early 1670s)   804
    28.i How Does One Refute the *TTP*?   804
    28.ii Collegiant Uproar and the *TTP*   814
    28.iii Encounter with Van Velthuysen   823
    28.iv Remonstrants (Arminians) against the *TTP*   830

29. Spinoza's Libertine "French Circle"   835
    29.i *Libertinage* in the 1660s   835
    29.ii Spinoza Confides: The First Phase   842
    29.iii Spinoza's Reformism: The Later Phases   846

PART V. LAST YEARS

30. Disaster Year (1672)   861
    30.i Slump and Collapse   861
    30.ii Salvaging the Republic   875
    30.iii The Fullana Affair   887
    30.iv Monarchy Lambasted   892

31. Denying the Supernatural   898

32. Entering (or Not Entering) Princely Court Culture (1672–1673)   913
    32.i Contemplating Emigrating   913
    32.ii The Offer of a University Chair at Heidelberg 919
    32.iii The Court of Hanover   925

33. Creeping Diffusion   935
    33.i The *TTP*'s Clandestine Editions   935
    33.ii Spinoza "Invades" England   944
    33.iii The Suppressed Dutch Version of the *TTP*   954

34. Mysterious Trip to Utrecht (July–August 1673)   963
    34.i The Utrecht *Collegie der Sçavanten*   963
    34.ii Portraying "Spinozism" in 1673   982
    34.iii Across the French Lines   987
    34.iv Chaotic Aftermath   997

35. Expanding the Spinozist "Sect"	1003
35.i "Vile, Godforsaken Atheists"	1003
35.ii "Spinozism" Far from Being a Vague Category	1014
35.iii A Sect Bred in the Universities and Professions	1018
35.iv A Disciple Rescued: Van Balen	1026
35.v The Expanding Sect of the 1680s and 1690s	1034
36. Amsterdam Revisited (1673–1675)	1039
36.i The Orangist-Calvinist Reaction Intensifies	1039
36.ii Summer Weeks in Amsterdam	1048
36.iii Failed Attempt to Publish the *Ethics*	1057
36.iv What is True in Christianity?	1064
37. Hebrew in Spinoza's Later Life	1074
37.i Studying Hebrew Grammar	1074
37.ii Reconstructing Biblical Hebrew	1079
37.iii Old Testament, New Testament: Jews and Christians	1085
38. Encounter with Leibniz (1676)	1092
38.i Leibniz and Spinoza	1092
38.ii Discussing Spinoza in Paris	1095
38.iii Leibniz Visits Holland	1107
38.iv Leibniz's Dual Approach to Spinozism	1111
39. Fighting Back	1119
39.i The English Reception	1119
39.ii Spinoza "Invades" France (1676–1680)	1131
40. Last Days, Death, and Funeral (1677)	1143
40.i Reclusive but Contested Last Days	1143
40.ii Funeral at the Nieuwe Kerk (New Church)	1156
41. A Tumultuous Aftermath	1164
41.i The Battle of the *Ethics* (1677)	1164
41.ii Spinoza's Circle after 1677	1183
41.iii Spinoza and the Glorious Revolution	1188
41.iv The Emergence of the "Dutch" Spinoza	1194
42. Conclusion	1205
Bibliography	1223
Index	1283

List of Illustrations

4.1	Spinoza family tree.	84
4.2	Dom António, *Prior of Crato "king of Portugal"* (1531–95), engraving. © The Trustees of the British Museum.	94
4.3	*Antonio Pérez* (*c.*1540–1611), portrait, oil on panel. Reproduction courtesy of Album/Alamy Stock Photo.	102
4.4	*Philip II* (1527–98) in 1565, oil on canvas. © Photographic Archive Museo Nacional del Prado.	104
5.1	*Map of the Amsterdam Vlooienburg quarter* (1625) by B. F. Van Berckenrode. Reproduction courtesy of Rijksmuseum, Amsterdam.	116
5.2	*Barge conveying mourners to the Sephardic cemetery at Ouderkerk*, by Romeyn de Hooghe, paper etching. Reproduction courtesy of Rijksmuseum, Amsterdam.	130
5.3	*The Amsterdam Sephardic Synagogue the young Spinoza attended*, by Jan Veenhuysen. Leiden University Library shelf mark COLLBN P 317 N 290.	143
6.1	*Rabbi Isaac Aboab da Fonseca* (1605–93), in 1681. © Courtesy of the John Carter Brown Library, Brown University, Providence, RI.	153
6.2	*Menasseh Ben Israel* portrait etching by Rembrandt. © Jewish Museum London.	163
6.3	*Joseph Solomon Delmedigo* (1591–1655), portrait engraving by W. Delff after a painting by C. Duyster of 1628. Reproduction courtesy of The Picture ArtCollection/Alamy Stock Photo.	174
7.1	*The Amsterdam Exchange in 1612* by Claes Jansz Visscher. Reproduction courtesy of Amsterdam City Archives.	191
8.1	*The Athenaeum Illustre at Amsterdam in 1650*, oil on panel. Reproduction courtesy of Teylers Museum Haarlem, the Netherlands.	246
10.1	Isaac de La Peyrère. *Praeadamitae, Sive, Exercitatio Super Versibus Duodecimo, Decimotertio, & Decimoquarto, Capitis Quinti Epistolae D. Pauli Ad Romanos: Quibus Inducuntur Primi Homines Ante Adamum Conditi* [Amsterdam: Louis and Daniel Elzevier], 1655. IAS Spinoza Research Collection.	295
11.1	*Theodor Kerckring* (1638–93), *c.*1670, by Jürgen Ovens, oil on canvas. Reproduction courtesy of bpk Bildagentur/Art Resource, NY/photo: Elke Walford.	348

xvi LIST OF ILLUSTRATIONS

12.1 The house in which Spinoza lodged in Rijnsburg (1661–3). By courtesy of the Leiden City Archives. 355

12.2 *Ruins of the Rijnsburg Abbey*, c.1640–1645, by Aelbert Cuyp, DM/995/804, oil on panel, 48.9 × 73.3 cm. Dordrecht Museum, on loan from the Royal Cabinet of Paintings Mauritshuis, The Hague 1995. 357

12.3 *Henry Oldenburg* (1619–77), by Jan van Cleve, oil on canvas, 1668. © The Royal Society. 363

12.4 *Nicholas Steno* (1666–77) by Justus Sustermans. By courtesy of Uffizi Gallery, Florence, Italy. 371

13.1 *Robert Boyle* (1627–91) by Johann Kerseboom, oil on canvas. The Royal Society. 392

14.1 *René Descartes* (1596–1650) by Jan Lievens, chalk on paper, 24.1 × 20.6 cm. Groninger Museum, loan from Municipality of Groningen, donation Hofstede de Groot, photo: Marten de Leeuw. 413

14.2 Spinoza, *Renati Des Cartes Principiorum philosophiae Pars I, & II, More Geometrico Demonstratae*. Spinoza; 1. Amstelodami: apud Johannem Riewerts, in vico vulgò dicto, de Dirk van Assen-steeg, sub signo Martyrologii, 1663. IAS Spinoza Research Collection. 423

14.3 *Florentius Schuyl* (1619–69) by Frans van Mieris the Elder, 1666. Reproduction courtesy of Mauritshuis, The Hague. 425

16.1 View of the village of Voorburg, showing the length of Kerkstraat, by Iven Besoet (1720–69). Reproduction courtesy of Artokoloro / Alamy Stock Photo. 459

16.2 The waterfront at Voorburg. Reproduction courtesy of the Rijksmuseum, Amsterdam. 459

16.3 Huygens' residence "Hofwyck", in Voorburg. Drawing by Christiaan Huygens (1629–95), Codices Hugeniani Online. HUG 14, ff. 05r. Brill Primary Sources Online through Leiden University Libraries. 462

16.4 *Gisbertus Voetius* (1589–1676), after portrait by Nicolas Maes, late seventeenth century. Fine Arts Museums of San Francisco. 473

17.1 *King Charles II* (1630–85), oil on canvas, c.1660–5. By courtesy of National Portrait Gallery, London. 489

18.1 *Christiaan Huygens* after unknown artist, line engraving, early to mid-eighteenth century. NPG D30754 © National Portrait Gallery, London. 511

18.2 *Bernhard von Galen, Bishop of Münster (1606–78), on horseback* by Wolfgang Heimbach, oil on canvas. Stichting Westerwolds Monumentenfonds. 514

18.3 *Johannes Hudde (1628–1704), burgomaster of Amsterdam, 1686.*
By courtesy of Rijksmuseum, Amsterdam. 523

19.1 Lodewijk Meyer, *Philosophia S.Scripturae Interpres*. Eleutheropoli:
s.n., 1666. IAS Spinoza Research Collection. 536

20.1 *Sir Robert Holmes sets fire to the Dutch merchant fleet off Terschelling,
19 August 1666*, drawing by Willem van de Velde. Reproduction
courtesy of Rijksmuseum, Amsterdam. 583

21.1 Adriaan Koerbagh, *Een bloemhof van allerley lieflijkheyd sonder
verdriet*, T'Amsterdam: Gedrukt voor den schrijver, 1668. IAS
Spinoza Research Collection. 603

23.1 *Daily activities along the Paviljoensgracht with the St. Jacobskerk
in the distance*. The Hague. Reproduction courtesy of ART
Collection/Alamy Stock Photo. 653

23.2 *View of the Heilige Geesthof at The Hague*, paper etching after
drawing by Gerrit van Giessen. Reproduction courtesy of Rijksmuseum,
Amsterdam. 655

25.1 *Portrait of Thomas Hobbes (1588–1679)* from Le Boë Sylvius,
Totius Medicinae Idea Nova. IAS Spinoza Research Collection. 721

27.1 [Spinoza], *Tractatus theologico-politicus*. Hamburgi [i.e. Amsterdam]
Apud Henricum Künraht [i.e. Jan Rieuwertsz], 1670. IAS Spinoza
Research Collection. 774

28.1 *Lambert van Velthuysen (1622–85) by Jan van Wijckersloot, 1665.*
Inv. no. 2260, Collectie Centraal Museum, Utrecht/© aankoop 1898. 824

28.2 *Philippus van Limborch (1633–1712) at the age of 78*, engraving.
Reproduction courtesy of Rijksmuseum, Amsterdam. 831

29.1 *Charles de Saint Denis de Saint-Évremond (1613–1703)*, portrait
from Pierre Desmaizeaux, *Oeuvres Meslées de Mr. de Saint-Evremond:
Publiées Sur Les Manuscrits de l'auteur*. Seconde ed. Revue, Corrigée
& Augmentée de la vie de l'auteur. A Londres Chez Jacob Tonson, 1709. 836

29.2 [Spinoza], *Reflexions curieuses d'un esprit des-interressé sur Les
Matieres les plus Importantes au Salut, tant Public que Particulier*
(at 'Cologne' [i.e. Amsterdam], 1678). IAS Spinoza Research Collection. 854

29.3 [Spinoza], *La clef du santuaire* [sic]. A Leyde [i.e. Amsterdam]:
Chez Pierre Warnaer [i.e. Jan Rieuwertsz], 1678. IAS Spinoza
Research Collection. 855

29.4 [Spinoza], *Traitté des cérémonies superstitieuses des Juifs tant Anciens
que Modernes*. Amsterdam, 1678. IAS Spinoza Research Collection. 856

30.1 *Louis XIV of France (1638–1715), in 1670* by Claude Lefèbvre.
Reproduction courtesy of incamerastock/Alamy Stock Photo. 862

30.2 J.B., *Sleutel Ontsluytende de Boecke-kas van de Witte Bibliotheeck*.
In 's Graven-Hage: By Nil Volentibus Arduum, 1672. IAS Spinoza
Research Collection. 873

33.1 [Jean-Baptiste Stouppe], *La religion des Hollandois: Representée en plusieurs lettres écrites par un officier de l'armée du roy, à un pasteur & professeur en theologie de Berne.* A Cologne: Chez Pierre Marteau, 1673. IAS Spinoza Research Collection.   936

33.2 [Spinoza], *Tractatus Theologico-Politicus.* Hamburgi Apud Henricum Künrath [sic], 1670 [i.e. 1677 or 1678] see Table 33.1. IAS Spinoza Research Collection.   939

33.3 *Franciscus de Le Boë Sylvius, Totius Medicinae Idea Nova Seu Francisci de Le Boe Sylvii. Medici Inter Batavos Celeberrimi Opera Omnia.* Amstelodami: Apud Carolum Gratiani [i.e. Jan Rieuwertsz], 1673. IAS Spinoza Research Collection.   942

33.4 [Spinoza], *Danielis Heinsii: Operum Historicorum Collectio.* Editio 2. Lugd. Batav ["Leiden" i.e. Amsterdam]: Apud Isaacum Herculis, 1673. IAS Spinoza Research Collection.   943

33.5 [Spinoza], *Tractatus Theologico-Politicus: Cui Adjunctus Est Philosophia S.Scripturae Interpres. Ab Authore Longe Emendator.* [Amsterdam], 1674. IAS Spinoza Research Collection.   949

33.6 [Spinoza], *De Rechtzinnige Theologant, of Godgeleerde Staatkundige Verhandelinge.* Te Hamburg [i.e. Amsterdam], by Henricus Koenraad, 1693. IAS Spinoza Research Collection.   960

34.1 *Johannes Baptista van Neercassel* (1623–1686) with episcopal attributes, oil on canvas. By courtesy of Museum Catharijneconvent, Utrecht.   966

34.2 *Johannes Georgius Graevius* (1632–1703) by unknown artist. Reproduction courtesy of University of Amsterdam.   974

35.1 *Dr Cornelis Bontekoe* (1647–85), engraving. Reproduction courtesy of Rijksmuseum, Amsterdam.   1019

36.1 *View of the new Amsterdam Portuguese Jewish Synagogue (on the left) inaugurated in 1675*, engraving by Adolf van der Laan, c.1710, call no. A41.1.21.1. Reproduction courtesy of the Library of the Jewish Theological Seminary.   1054

36.2 *Christophorus Wittichius* (Christoph Wittich) (1625–87). © Fitzwilliam Museum, Cambridge.   1061

36.3 *Abraham Heidanus* (1597–1678), engraving after Jan André Lievens. Reproduction courtesy of The Picture Art Collection/Alamy Stock Photo.   1062

40.1 *The New Church on the Spui (The Hague), in 1668* by C. Elandts. By courtesy of Collection of The Hague Municipal Archive, the Netherlands.   1157

41.1 [Benedictus de Spinoza]. *B.d.S. Opera Posthuma.* [Amsterdam], 1677. IAS Spinoza Research Collection.   1180

41.2 *Spinoza.* Reproduction courtesy of BTEU/RKMLGE/Alamy Stock Photo.   1182

41.3 *Pierre Bayle* (1647–1706), *c.*1675, by Louis Elle le Jeune, oil on canvas.
Photo: Gérard Blot, © RMN-Grand Palais/Art Resource, New York. 1195

42.1 Johannes Colerus, *Das Leben des Bened. von Spinoza*. Spinoza
Frankfurt und Leipzig: s.n., 1733. IAS Spinoza Research Collection. 1210

List of Tables

7.1	The VOC share price on the Amsterdam Exchange 1648–59	200
7.2	The *imposta* and *finta* payments (in guilders) to the Amsterdam Portuguese Jewish community by the head of the Spinoza family 1641–58	208
12.1	Students and research assistants at Leiden whom Spinoza knew or who figured in his life-story	379
29.1	The false titles of the clandestine French *TTP*	853
33.1	Early clandestine editions of the quarto Latin *TTP*	940
33.2	Octavo variants of the *TTP* (Amsterdam, 1673–4)	941
33.3	The Dutch versions of the *TTP*	961

PART I
SETTING THE SCENE

1
Introduction

If one could measure the stature of a thinker by how many refutations of his work appeared in the three decades following his death, it would be a shrewd bet that Spinoza would win the prize.[1] No other thinker or writer of early modern times attracted so much hostility and recrimination. Although a few other front-rank miscreants of the world ran him close for being universally reviled and vilified in his own time, Philip II of Spain and Hobbes for example, no other personage of his era came even close to being so decried, denounced and condemned in weighty texts of exhaustive length, over so long a span of time, in Latin, Dutch, French, English, German, Spanish, Portuguese, Hebrew, and other languages. A curious reception indeed for someone who preached continually against prejudice, envy, and hatred and showed no desire whatever to gain coveted positions, honours, property, wealth, or power.

Born in Amsterdam, in November 1632, Spinoza lived a relatively short life, dying nine months short of his forty-fifth birthday, in February 1677. For an ever curious, inquiring scholar of his aspirations and standing, he travelled remarkably little. Always anxious not to waste time, Spinoza was not one for frequent leisurely chats, jollification, or, as far as one can tell, for romance. He mostly eschewed quarrels, rarely sought publicity, and in the end had to abandon his efforts to get his masterpiece of pure philosophy, *The Ethics* (1677), published during his lifetime. He spent so much of his time buried in the solitary obscurity of his study, reportedly often working at night and sleeping during the day, that those who knew him best during his maturity went for months on end without seeing him at all. One might expect such a seemingly uneventful life would conduce to a nice, short biography. However, this is far from being the case.

There are many reasons why a comprehensive, detailed biography of Spinoza is desirable. It is not simply because he figures among the dozen or so foremost Western philosophers since classical times or was prominent in the general history of intellectual culture, political thought, and Bible criticism as well as philosophy properly speaking, though those reasons alone suffice to justify any aspiring biographer devoting years of research to the task. A more detailed picture, made possible by the extensive and impressive new research of recent decades, is needed also for broader historical reasons. For despite the unparalleled hostility Spinoza's

---

[1] Pitassi, "Un manuscrit genevois," 180.

philosophy provoked in his own time, there was also from the first fervent and highly influential enthusiasm for his views albeit until the 1780s exclusively in furtively secret, clandestine circles. Despite the high-pitched overwhelmingly negative reaction which only subsided to a more subdued level, noted a leading observer and critic of the early Enlightenment era, Jean le Clerc (1657–1736), from around 1725, certain strands of Spinoza's philosophy powerfully promoting a wide range of key modern values diffused steadily if slowly and with difficulty, contributing in highly original fashion to laying the groundwork of present-day liberal democratic modernity. Chief among these key features of his thought were his stress on individual autonomy, separation of the moral sphere from organized religion, unrestricted religious toleration, full freedom of thought and expression, press freedom, and a conception of government's responsibilities to society uncompromisingly insisting on the inherent superiority of the democratic republic over other forms of state, whether monarchy, aristocracy, oligarchic republic, or theocracy.

A comprehensive account of Spinoza's life also contributes to a broader understanding of early modern Europe, a clearer perception of how it was that despite the tide of fierce hostility surrounding his every move, he nevertheless mustered a remarkable amount of hidden, clandestine support. Measured in terms of what established philosophers in universities and academies then and later recognized as major new contributions to philosophy, Descartes, Locke, and Leibniz were undoubtedly the three most important philosophers of early modern times down to the high Enlightenment era, far outstripping Spinoza. Measured in terms of lasting long-term subversive impact on the foundations of early modern thought, religion, and political theory, it was undoubtedly Spinoza, far outstripping all of these, who exerted the greatest impact. This occurred first in Holland, then England, Germany, and France, and finally other lands, to such an extent that Spinoza must be considered the first founder of a major secular philosophical sect since classical times, since the rise of Stoicism, Neoplatonism, and Epicureanism, in a way that Machiavelli, Hobbes, and Locke ultimately could never rival, a movement that consciously set out to reform and, in effect, remake, that is to say revolutionize humanity and our world, helping drive the tendency historians now term "Radical Enlightenment."

Although, owing to the implications, many Enlightenment scholars today remain reluctant to admit the fact, a vast amount of evidence proves incontrovertibly that Spinoza was among the most important figures shaping not just the early Enlightenment, but the entire Western Enlightenment down to the nineteenth century. He was not just a major influence on, but a decades-long central obsession of, Leibniz, Bayle, Le Clerc, Toland, Diderot, Voltaire, Lessing, Mendelssohn, Kant, Goethe, Herder, Fichte, Schelling, and many a lesser figure. But this unique role and status was due not just to his innate philosophical talents but, to a great extent, to his life story and activities combining and distilling in highly original fashion a uniquely broad convergence (and clashing) of religious traditions, heretical sects, rival political cultures, languages, and scientific and philosophical approaches reflecting the fact that seventeenth-century Amsterdam and the whole urban core of Holland was at that time strikingly and challengingly more religiously, culturally, and linguistically diverse than Paris, Rome, Venice, London, Berlin, or Madrid, or indeed anywhere else on earth.

No doubt a modern Englishman, Frenchman, or German would immediately assume that the Spanish Jewish Baroque poet and chronicler, Miguel Levi de Barrios (1635–1701), was absurdly exaggerating when remarking, in 1684, that not only was Europe in the seventeenth century the most dominant part of the world, but that Europe's commercially most resplendent emporium, the "famous city of Amsterdam," was also Europe's greatest marvel in terms of cultural diversity eclipsing all the rest as the "Babel and Athens of different languages," publishing, art, cultivation of the "new philosophy" (Cartesianism), and new kinds of humanist study.[2] This truth is also hard for modern historians to grasp. But during the seventeenth century, Paris, London, Berlin, Venice, Madrid, and all the era's other great capitals were all religiously, linguistically, and culturally less pluriform, less multicultural, and less global than Amsterdam. On top of that, given that Descartes and Bayle as well as Spinoza spent most of their intellectually creative lives in Holland, the Netherlands until 1700 was also unquestionably the world's then philosophical centre.

The daunting task of writing a comprehensive, detailed biography of a man for whom philosophical striving was everything becomes more daunting still when we consider how limited were Spinoza's correspondence and circle of long-term personal contacts. If other great philosophers of the age were eager for extensive networking, Spinoza was not. He practically never seems to have initiated a correspondence with someone he did not know. Leibniz, a titan of the pan-European "republic of letters," may have been altogether exceptional, leaving well over 20,000 letters. But Locke left around 3,650 and Bayle's letters, note the editors of the now complete published Bayle correspondence, total around 1,740.[3] Even Descartes, who left far fewer, only around 800 letters, bequeathed approximately nine times as many as Spinoza from whom we have a mere forty-eight letters with another forty addressed to him, totalling just eighty-eight in all.[4]

Yet, within the limitations imposed by a short life, poor health (at any rate by his early forties), and static existence, Spinoza led a quite extraordinary life. From a certain stage, deteriorating health and a gradually encroaching, at the time incurable, lung disease increasingly impeded his activities. Yet, despite his restricted circumstances and studied reclusiveness, his life can hardly be called

---

[2] Den Boer, *Literatura sefardí*, 13. [3] Bayle, *Correspondance* xiv, 1.
[4] Steenbakkers, "Spinoza's Correspondentie," 7–8; Steenbakkers, "Spinoza's Life," 13; Spinoza, *Collected Works* (ed. Curley) i, 162.

uneventful. Whatever else a biographer says about him, Spinoza's life was no quiet, leisurely stroll to the grave past rows of scholarly volumes. Rather it provoked an unprecedented international uproar. That Spinoza's philosophy constitutes a re-evaluation of all values was abundantly obvious to contemporaries as it is to us today. In his *Ethics* Spinoza analyses the working of the human passions and, thrusting aside all religious or theological underpinning for our moral order, lays down the principle that what "we call good, or evil, is what is useful or harmful to preserving our being in the sense of what increases or diminishes our power of acting," a principle determined strictly by "reason" that in Spinoza is both individual *and* collective, bearing on how one leads one's own life and on society as a whole. This principle, which he declares man's sole true moral basis, was no recipe for personal or group selfishness. Rather, as he presents it, it stands in constant tension with, almost outright opposition to, our instinctive nature and personal impulses, feelings and judgements about what we desire, or do not desire. For these are, for the most part, not based on rational calculation but impulse and "appetite," or rather whatever we individually momentarily imagine will bring us "happiness" or "sadness," which much of time, according to Spinoza, is barely considered, highly imaginative, or seriously deluded. Man is irreversibly part of nature and cannot act otherwise than in accordance with his nature but doing so in the best and wisest way is an arduous, often painful, learning process in which everyone needs all the help educators, more experienced family, neighbours, and others, and good laws, as well as willingness to learn, can proffer.

Spinoza defines "good" as "what we certainly know to be useful to us," and "bad" as what we surely perceive prevents us from acquiring some "good." "Virtue" Spinoza defines in a way that at first seems rather strange. But we soon come to see that he uses the term logically within his framework, presenting it as man's "very essence" in the sense of being man's power to bring about things, good rather than bad, in accordance with his specific nature. But although his ethical schema is based on a metaphysical relativity of "good" and "bad," his moral doctrine clearly produces naturalistic social and political certainties and absolutes within the human context. His principles contradicted all existing religions and codes of conduct. What in effect Spinoza presented to the world was what the Dutch Calvinist preacher, the younger Frans Burman (1671–1719), denounced as a general overturning of all then accepted "grounds of truth and certainty, denying there is any God distinct from Nature and abolishing all natural obligation to obey His commandments and true morality."[5] Spinoza's morality amounted to a new outlook on life, a new concept of what human happiness is, and undeniably stood in every way opposed to every Christian principle, belief, and tradition as taught

---

[5] Burmannus, *'t Hoogste goed*, 3–4; Israel, *Radical Enlightenment*, 420.

by the churches (albeit not to Christianity as reinterpreted by him), as well as all revealed religion of whatever kind, every hierarchical social order, all custom, tradition, and received morality. For any theologian, political leader, editor, or teacher of his time it was wholly impossible to openly endorse his views, and even being suspected of adopting them in a concealed, esoteric, and partial fashion carried serious risk.

Spinoza was a philosopher who set out to reform philosophy, religion, politics, and society's understanding of human happiness. It was, and is, natural enough to pour scorn on such a project. Spinoza was a "fanatic" a leading French savant and convener of scientists in Paris, Melchisédec Thévenot (c.1620–92) sarcastically remarked in 1674, "qui veut réformer le monde [who wants to reform the world]," an impossible, even insane ambition.[6] But the most staggering fact about Spinoza's life is that, against all the odds, gradually, unseen and clandestinely, he eventually partly succeeded. Although the real furore Spinoza universally provoked began only in 1670, during the last six or seven years of his life, more locally Spinoza met with fierce opposition on all sides from a much earlier stage. Such was its cogency that, behind the scenes, his philosophy attracted from the outset, gaining ground with each passing decade, a small fringe of intellectually inclined types ready to risk being shunned to embrace his philosophy in tiny clandestine groups. For the immense army of opposing academics, theologians, statesmen, law-makers, magistrates, schoolmasters, and pastors of his own country and neighbouring lands sworn to crush his system and coterie, his movement proved, both in his own day and for two or three centuries after, exasperatingly difficult to attack, persecute, and crush, partly due to its furtive way of organizing and diffusing its ideas and partly because Spinoza's system of ideas was so rigorously and deftly worked out that it proved highly resistant to being rebutted on purely rational and evidential grounds.

Spinoza by no means fits in the same category as Descartes, Hobbes, Locke, Leibniz, Bayle, or Rousseau. These were all towering thinkers; but all of these lost their direct relevance to modern life within a few decades, or at any rate half a century, after their deaths, subsequently remaining meaningful mostly to scholars and those interested in the history and development of Western thought. But this is not the case with Spinoza. Spinoza's relevance not only persisted but in much of the world has tended to increase and is today in many countries greater than ever, most strikingly in Latin America, North America, and the Far East. By no means all scholars today rejoice in this fact. But even those most unsympathetic to this only recently fully emerging historical reality—Spinoza's long veiled but unparalleled centrality and historical impact during the Enlightenment era—find it impossible, much to their exasperation, to deny the facts. "Of all

---

[6] RLC MS Thott 1266/part iv. Thévenot to Graevius, Paris, 28 Dec. 1674.

seventeenth-century philosophers," notes Frederick Beiser, a leading expert on the history of eighteenth- and nineteenth-century German thought, in 1999, "Spinoza has come closest to the mentality of the modern age."[7] By the late eighteenth and the nineteenth century, Spinoza's status as a unique re-evaluator of all values began to assume a positive, and for some, such as Goethe, Heine, Shelley, and George Eliot, even heroic glow. It did also, at least during his middle period, for that other great modern re-evaluator of all values and prophet of "modernity"— Friedrich Nietzsche (1844–1900). Nietzsche, while diverging from Spinoza in several significant ways, to an extent also avowedly echoed his predecessor.[8]

Among the salient features of this debate about Spinoza's historical and current role is disagreement about his political thought, one of the most important dimensions of his philosophy. Until Spinoza's time there had never been any prominent thinker in the West or East who prioritized the democratic republic over all other forms of state. "Doubts have been expressed as to whether Spinoza was really a democrat," observed the eminent Dutch historian E. H. Kossmann, in 1960, "but the text of his work gives no reason for doubt." Whatever other philosophers ancient, medieval, or early modern concluded about reality and politics, Spinoza's "intellectual convictions led him," as Kossmann put it, to conclude that "democracy was the original and, so long as it was designed properly, the best form of government."[9] (Spinoza was all too aware that it is prone *not* to be designed properly.) Many scholars oppose Kossmann's view. For many, it is extremely difficult to concede that the first powerful and influential expression of modern democratic thought in no way derived from or found inspiration in, the Anglo-American world. Again, a fact extremely exasperating for many scholars (who until a few decades ago, preferred to omit Spinoza from the canon of major modern political thinkers entirely), but established in recent decades as undeniable historical reality.

Considerable distaste arises too from Spinoza's obvious scorn for whatever is commonly and popularly accepted. Spinoza was not the kind of revolutionary who sought to stir up the common people and provoke violent dissension or mass revolt. For the opinions of "the multitude," for the accepted view of things, not just of ordinary people but nearly all people at every level including kings, princes, statesmen, churchmen, academics, preachers, and aristocrats, Spinoza showed astoundingly scant deference or respect. But while inclined to think practically all humans in his own time lacked a realistic understanding of the universe they inhabited, he solemnly vowed to regard humanity's collective ignorance and proneness to superstition, as he viewed it, as a universal natural blindness, a reality humanity cannot easily escape, a formidable burden afflicting everyone collectively rather than something merely deserving contempt.

[7] Beiser, "Homesick Hidalgo," 4.   [8] Garrett, "Spinoza's Ethical Theory," 308.
[9] Kossmann, *Political Thought*, 75–6.

Even Machiavelli and Hobbes, then, massive though their impact was, could not rival the sheer scope or intensity of blanket negative reaction that Spinoza incurred. In the Netherlands, exclaimed the Franeker professor and preacher Johannes Regius (1656–1738), in 1713, the world of godlessness, atheism, and impiety was dominated intellectually not by Machiavelli, nor Hobbes or Bayle, despite the impact of these thinkers, but specifically the figure of Spinoza.[10] The same could be said for early Enlightenment France and Germany, and even, startlingly, once one gets past the early 1680s, for England, the major European land where Spinoza's modern reputation has always counted for least. Certainly, by Spinoza's time, Machiavelli had long been regarded throughout Europe as a highly impious and immoral influence, but one could hardly cite him as an outright, systematic denier of Revelation or the divine status and character of Scripture. Hobbes, no less than Spinoza, was everywhere deemed an "atheist" and often seen as no less dangerous, malevolent, and anti-Scripturalist than Spinoza. Among those who had made it their business to "disparage the Holy Scriptures, and revealed religion," commented Richard Kidder (1633–1703), bishop of Bath and Wells, in 1694, "three writers have denied Moses wrote the Pentateuch: Hobbes, in his *Leviathan*, the author of the *Praeadamitae* [La Peyrère] and Spinoza."[11] Neither Hobbes nor anyone else, however, so comprehensively subverted confidence and belief that the Scriptures are divine revelation and are the true foundation of mankind's moral code or did so by employing such a rigorous system of Bible exegesis and historical argument. No one else went so far in severing theology from philosophy, wholly secularizing ethics, rejecting the very possibility of miracles and revelation and denying *supernaturalia* of every kind, all credence in spirits, demons, devils, angels, ghosts, magic, alchemy, divinely inspired prophecy, and sorcery.

Furthermore, some of the greatest minds of post-1700 modern humanity including Lessing, Herder, Goethe, Shelley, George Eliot, Heine, Nietzsche, Freud, and Einstein considered Spinoza's philosophy the most inspiring guide in their personal lives. For them, this was sometimes less a question of persuasive argument than Spinoza's rare ability to uplift, enlighten, and refine the most inquiring and poetic leanings, assisting individuals place their own existence on a higher, more meaningful level. If Freud had a notoriously low opinion of philosophy and philosophers in general, "I readily admit my dependence on Spinoza's doctrine," he wrote: "throughout my long life I sustained an extraordinarily high regard for the person as well as the thought achievement [*Denkleistung*] of the great philosopher Spinoza."[12] Einstein, we know, read Spinoza's greatest work, the *Ethics*, several times, commencing well before securing his first paid job, at the age of twenty-three, at the patent office in Bern,

---

[10] Regius, *Beginselen*, 359–68.   [11] Kidder, *Commentary on the Five Books* i, preface.
[12] Yovel, *Spinoza and Other Heretics*, x; Whitebook, *Freud*, 93, 397–8.

Switzerland, in 1902: "I think [Spinoza's] *Ethics*," he wrote to his cousin Else, his future wife, thirteen years later, in September 1915, "will have a permanent effect on me."[13] Einstein's life-long devotion to strict determinism, universal causality, and the unity of the universe in its determined causality, including in the sub-atomic sphere of particles and their supposedly uncertain movements, closely chimed at a fundamental level with a philosophy which insists, as Spinoza expresses it in the *Ethics, Part One*, "that in nature there is nothing contingent, but all things are determined from the necessity of the divine nature to exist and to act in a certain way."[14] In particular, Einstein's insistence on the universal character and unity, the *Einheitlichkeit*, of the universe fitted with Spinoza's determinism, universalism, and general approach, something alien to all medieval philosophy, even Maimonides who, in other respects evinces significant affinities with parts of Spinoza's system. Einstein's drive to establish the principles of the universe driven by a pervasive *Verallgemeinerungsbedürfenis*, or need to universalize, remained an overarching constant throughout his life-long striving to renew the basis of modern physics. Throughout his triumphant years developing relativity theory and subsequent unsuccessful final years of his scientific efforts at the Institute for Advanced Study, Einstein endeavoured to uncover, prove, and explain the oneness of the laws of physics at all levels in the shape of his "unified field theory."[15]

The drive to generalize and unify our vision of reality infused not only Einstein's scientific efforts but also his social ideals and view of politics which rested on deep, emotional aversion to all forms of fascism and chauvinistic nationalism. Characteristically, he insisted on calling himself a "European" rather than a "German." Equally, the drive to unify shaped his distinctive view of religion and the relationship of science to religion. Is not the essence of what is best in all the great religions better than any one religion? Is it not better to view Moses, Jesus, and Buddha as equally valid prophets than to insist on one? Like Spinoza, Einstein was convinced there is such a thing as "true religion," but that this true religion has little to do with what most people understand by "religion."[16] Consisting of an ethical core, basically justice and charity, it is infused with a sense of wonder and awe at the unimaginable grandeur and unity of the universe.

When anxiety first arose among the public, in 1929, as to whether or not the man acknowledged as the world's greatest scientist of the age might be an "atheist," Rabbi Herbert S. Goldstein famously sent Einstein an urgent telegram: "Do you believe in God? Stop. Answer paid, fifty words. Stop." Often sparing with words, Einstein needed only thirty for his reply: "I believe in Spinoza's God, who

---

[13] Holton, "Einstein's Third Paradise," 33.   [14] Spinoza, *Ethics* I, Prop. 29.
[15] Jammer, *Einstein and Religion*, 45–7; Holton, "Einstein's Third Paradise," 29–30.
[16] Carlisle, *Spinoza's Religion*, 142–4; Carlisle's is the outstanding book-length discussion of Spinoza's "true religion."

reveals Himself in the law-governed harmony of the world, not in a God who concerns Himself with the fate and doings of mankind."[17] "We followers of Spinoza," he added, in a private letter, a few months later, "see our God in the wonderful order and lawfulness of all that exists and in its *Beseeltheit* [inspired animation], as it reveals itself in man and animal."[18] Einstein believed not only that this "cosmic religious feeling" of awe was the strongest and noblest motive driving scientific research in modern times but also that humanity generally is slowly but gradually moving towards what he envisaged as this new higher conception of religion. As mankind's awe before the unity and coherence of the universe grows together with the impulse to renew human society on the basis of justice and charity, it would give birth to a new universal "true religion" stripped of all superstition, dogma, intolerance, hatred, and bigotry that will ultimately replace all the scriptures, priests, rabbis, gurus, cardinals, and mullahs of the world with the collected and integrated findings of philosophers and scientists.

Spinoza's family settled in Amsterdam having emerged from a clandestine crypto-Judaism in the Iberian peninsula locked in constant and irresolvable combat with Spanish and Portuguese royal absolutism, the Catholic Church, and especially the Inquisition, the ultimate symbol of oppression, persecution, theological narrowness, and extreme dogmatic intolerance in Spinoza's day, the constant ominous shadow over his own forebears in Portugal. The Inquisition was a powerful institution that for well over three centuries imprisoned, tortured, and executed literally thousands of martyrs. This dark Iberian context was a crucial factor in Spinoza's background, early life, and formation and likewise an essential dimension for understanding his thought generally. The contrast between Spinoza's Ibero-Jewish background and the Dutch social context in which he lived fed his passionate yet cautious involvement in the political scene of his day, his tenacious defence of certain encouraging features of his immediate milieu. No matter how wretched and oppressive the circumstances of men living under brutal and relentless tyranny, a much better human context is conceivable and achievable. He remained acutely aware throughout his life that he and those around him were less at risk in their activities and persons in the Dutch Republic than anywhere else at the time. Publishing their views may have been forbidden, teaching them to students impermissible, openly debating their views with others inadvisable. Yet, despite these barriers, he and his circle enjoyed "the rare happiness of living in a republic where every person's liberty to judge for himself is respected, everyone is permitted to worship God according to his own mind, and nothing is thought dearer or sweeter than freedom."[19] This passage is undoubtedly tinged with sarcasm. But while he is here criticizing the limitations and incompleteness of seventeenth-century Dutch freedom, he was nevertheless also

---

[17] Jammer, *Einstein and Religion*, 48–50; Holton, "Einstein's Third Paradise," 32.
[18] Quoted in Jammer, *Einstein and Religion*, 51.   [19] Spinoza, *Theological-Political Treatise*, 6.

expressing a deeply felt positive emotion. Indeed, Spinoza never ceased to place a high value on the Dutch Republic during its Golden Age. However imperfect, it offered a greater degree of religious liberty and freedom of conscience and thought than any other society at the time, including Britain prior to the Glorious Revolution of 1688. Indeed, the England of Cromwell and Charles II figured among the specific targets of his political criticism, even if substantially less so than Philip II's Spain and Louis XIV's France.

There is an important sense in which the Dutch Republic was, as one historian called it, the first "modern society" and this is doubtless why its greatest thinker was, in Beiser's sense, the "first modern philosopher." But while he valued it, Spinoza remained acutely aware of the limitations of Dutch freedom in his day, of its precariousness and instability, the constant threat to the religious liberty and political freedom he enjoyed there, emanating from what he considered the oppressive role of the clergy and angry resentment of the monarchically-inclined Orangist political faction among the Dutch public and regents. But most basic of all as a threat to liberty and personal fulfilment, he maintains, was the ignorance, intolerance, theological dogmatism, the uncomprehending notions and all-encompassing "superstition" of the great mass of society (kings, princes, aristocrats, and academics included).

Spinoza's distinctive interpretation of what human "superstition" is was directly linked to his own family's long and complex encounter with the Inquisition. To Spinoza's mind "superstition" and false belief form the most powerful, pervasive, and dangerous force in human life, in politics, religion, and education, and are by no means the outcome merely of ignorance. Rather, as with the Spanish and Portuguese Inquisition, its most obnoxious fruit, "superstition" for Spinoza is credulity forged into politically empowered oppressive dogma, laws, and institutionalized practice. He envisaged mankind's greatest foe as a product of our inability to understand the nature of things powered by universal desperation laced with our unending expectation that a good life can after all be salvaged from the wretchedness and misery engulfing most of humanity, albeit without most men having the slightest idea how. For Spinoza believes that it is by manipulating humanity's rudderless fear and hope that the cunningly self-seeking are able to sway the masses into applauding and embracing not just the crassest notions but also despotic, exploitative control, forging their own servitude. In Spinoza's theologico-politico-philosophical system, much the most formidable pillar of despotism defined as government by elite groups and their vested interests opposing the "common good" and the interest of the majority, the basis of all systems preying on the majority in the interest of the few, whether headed by several tyrants or a single despot, is always the artful exploiting and building on the universal foundation of credulity and "superstition." Ignorance, misinformation, and superstition rule humanity.

The myriad rulers, religious heads, and oligarchs whose power, glory, and wealth are built on "superstition" have a problem, though, in that "superstition" left to itself tends to be unstable. The vast mass of the world's wretched, fearful, and desperate, as Spinoza understood things, can readily be made to embrace nonsense and believe total lies, as has been shown time and again. That part is easy. But because men are wretched without understanding why, they tend to rush headlong from one hoped-for cure for their distress to the next. Consequently, contends Spinoza, to stabilize the control, profits, and advantages "superstition" affords masters, despots, and exploiters, great energy and resources are invested in formulating and buttressing particular forms of superstition to solidify and render them durable by introducing impressive ceremonies and elaborating an intricate, fabricated theology lessening the need for direct coercive force. By developing special castes of priests and theologians to further elaborate religious dogma and adorning their teaching with grandiose art and architecture, music, rituals and processions, "holy" dogmas can be made stable, alluring, impressive, and durable.[20] What any given religious teacher or theologian believes or does not believe about God and His commandments makes little difference in Spinoza's schema: coercively imposed religious authority designed to keep the "common people" in thrall to particular beliefs and doctrines, penalizing, segregating, or executing those who dissent, is by definition devoid of truth value and can never rise above "pagan superstition" because its social purpose is to promote hateful "servitude."[21]

Christianity is not of itself something negative in Spinoza's eyes. True Christianity, he insisted, is a religion of "love, joy, peace, moderation and good will to all men" and thus immensely valuable. Unfortunately, organized Christianity's most striking feature in his day, in Spinoza's view, was largely the opposite, consisting chiefly of the "extraordinary animosity" of the different confessions endlessly battling each other and fiercely suppressing dissenters, Orthodox against Catholic, Catholic against Protestant, Calvinist versus Lutheran, Trinitarian against Anti-Trinitarian, confessions "giving daily expression to the bitterest mutual hatred." Each revealed religion claims to be the true one. But the only difference a careful observer can discern between Catholics, Protestants, Muslims, and Jews, suggests Spinoza, is the distinctive dress and customs, and particular places of worship they attend, "otherwise their lives are identical in each case."[22] The reason for this "deplorable situation," this sea of hatred and implacable and unending war of creed against creed, according to Spinoza, is quite simple: Christianity, after Christ's death and immediately after the Apostles, was perverted from its proper course into "superstition" and ecclesiastical hierarchies enabling theologians, irrespective of which creed they

---

[20] Spinoza, *Theological-Political Treatise*, 3. [21] Spinoza, *Theological-Political Treatise*, 7.
[22] Spinoza, *Theological-Political Treatise*, 7.

professed, to hold sway over the common people, while giving birth to the warring ancient churches of the Near East, Africa, and Europe. The Church Fathers, held Spinoza, proved avid chiefly to control, polemicize, secure their own church's "lucrative positions," and be "considered great dignitaries."[23] In Spinoza's thought," true religion" and the actuality of our world's churches are two completely different things usually in outright opposition to each other.

Morality and "true religion," then, including true "Christianity," were understood by Spinoza as something entirely separate from what churchmen and most people call "religion," though he himself, like Einstein later, was perfectly willing to acknowledge a core of "true religion" in every faith to the extent that it does actually promote the higher moral values. "True religion," he argues, boils down to an ethical core. Few have ever expressly agreed with Spinoza's estimate of the value of his ethical and political ideas to humanity at large. However, those who have include some of the most creative and exceptional. The English novelist George Eliot, on reading Spinoza in the early 1840s, was immediately captivated by his recipe for enabling men to escape the "shackles of superstition." She set to work to translate two of Spinoza's major works from Latin into English, a large part of the *Tractatus Theologico-Politicus* of 1670 over a prolonged period (1843–9) and then the *Ethics*, in 1854–6.

George Eliot adopted Spinoza as her particular philosophical moral guide, but eventually felt frustrated by the difficulty of effectively rendering Spinoza's core ideas meaningfully to a wide audience. From her first full-scale novel, *Adam Bede* (1859), onwards, she set out to transcend what she saw as the restricted usefulness of straightforward translation with fictional dramatizing. In her first novel, her main character, Adam, like *Silas Marner* (1861) in her third, remains trapped in a whirl of damaging emotions and false notions only mitigated as he painstakingly learns to understand, evaluate, and take responsibility for the true nature of his emotional difficulties and personal predicament. In her late novel, *Daniel Deronda* (1876) Eliot illustrates how the life of a person (Gwendolen) devoted to pure selfishness eventually shrivels but can ultimately be elevated and reinvigorated by a more experienced person who has learnt to find happiness in helping others lift themselves from misery. For both Spinoza and Eliot, correcting our ideas is not just a philosophical procedure helping the individual clarify her or his thoughts, but the means to redeem individuals individually and collectively and reform society and institutions. The remedy afforded by true liberating understanding, in Spinoza and Eliot, is indispensable both for individuals and the well-being of groups and society as a whole, and the basis for the fundamental principles of the state.[24] In *Middlemarch*, with admirable skill, Eliot conveys a sense of how every person's "life impinges on many others," how the individual's life is entwined with

---

[23] Spinoza, *Theological-Political Treatise*, 7–8.
[24] Atkins, "George Eliot and Spinoza," 2, 7–9; Deegan, "George Eliot," 1–4.

that of the community, and how every community's established prejudices and false judgements threaten the well-being of, and pose a challenge of responsibility to, every individual.[25]

Lack of religious affiliation, observes Beiser, and his variegated and rich cultural background "makes Spinoza the perfect symbol of the modern alienated intellectual, the prime example of the alienated thinker who was at home everywhere and nowhere. Is it any wonder that the Dutch, Portuguese, Spanish, Christians, and Jews all claim him? It is a tribute to Spinoza – and part of the fascination of the man – that all are both right and wrong."[26] Writing a comprehensive biography of Spinoza therefore presents an unusual set of challenges. In the first place a whole catalogue of dramatically different religious and philosophical traditions converged and to a degree fused in Spinoza and in his life's project in highly exceptional fashion.[27] In Spinoza, medieval Islamic-Jewish philosophy, early modern Marrano clandestine intellectual and religious subversion, Cartesianism, Spanish scholasticism, Jesuit pedagogy, the experimental philosophy of Bacon and Boyle, Radical Reformation Christian Socinianism and irenicism, and early modern Neo-Epicurean *libertinage érudit* were all powerfully merged.

Besides this unusual medley of influences it is essential to convey some sense of how and why certain features of his thought but not others proved uncommonly inspirational to some of the world's most exalted minds. Fortunately, Spinoza's own powerful sense of purpose in life, rigorous writing style and conciseness, make it relatively easy to impart awareness of the impressive coherence interconnecting all his major and minor texts, linking his life-story to his philosophy and interventions in Dutch politics and religion, and also how the different religious and other traditions converging in his life related to his attitudes, activities, and legacy. To convey an initial glimpse of Spinoza's ultimate legacy one need only point to his greatest philosophical work, the *Ethics*. A person can be "free" as an individual in the most vital respects, he contends here, even under a tyrannical, oppressive regime. Equally, in a democracy a person can easily live a thoroughly wretched, miserable, and unworthy life effectively as "a slave" of others or of one's own emotions. But the optimal context for advancing individual "reason" and virtue alongside and to some extent together with collective freedom and well-being, the context most conducive to both, constitutes what he was the first great thinker to project as the "democratic republic."

The centrality of the political dimension in Spinoza's general philosophy and ethics is indeed a key feature of his thought. Because happiness and pleasure form the foundations of the "good" relative to other things, and pain and sorrow the "bad," Spinoza's system has, as a direct consequence, that "whatever is conducive

---

[25] Levine, "Determinism and Responsibility," 351; Gatens, *Spinoza's Hard Path*, 48.
[26] Beiser, "Homesick Hidalgo," 4.
[27] Mason, *God of Spinoza*, 15; Nadler, "The Jewish Spinoza," 510; Walther, *Spinoza Studien* ii, 227.

to man's social organization, or causes men to live in harmony, is advantageous, while those things that introduce discord into the state are bad" (*Ethics*, Part IV, Proposition 40).[28] Hence, it is owing as much to its effects on oneself, as on others, insists Spinoza, that "hatred can never be good" (*Ethics*, Part IV, Proposition 45). Defining "hatred" as "hatred towards men," Spinoza holds that all hatred foments desire to destroy, subjugate, or humiliate those we loathe while every emotion allied to hatred, like envy, anger, contempt, and thirst for revenge, is debasing and "bad" in relation to reason and man's own individual being. Equally, where the rule of law prevails "in a state unjust," that is nearly all societies, the oppression, resentment, and negative consequences generated simultaneously fill he who hates with base emotion while harming those who are hated. Correcting men's thinking and improving our forms of government matters greatly, therefore, to everyone without exception from the wisest to the most ignorant. For, as things stand, not only do people commonly believe things that are completely untrue but passionately commit themselves to false ideas in organized blocs, often in fanatical fashion, causing immense damage to their immediate milieu, themselves, and everyone else.

In the work of combating universal ignorance and superstition, and seeking to build a better society, all peoples and nations, in Spinoza's view, are equal. It was a fundamental axiom of his thought that mankind is universally identical in its basic nature, and universally blinkered in much the same way, even while particular societies and qualities of life remain sharply differentiated, depending on the type and quality of political constitutions, institutions, and laws prevailing.[29] Thus, for example the "Jews today have absolutely nothing that they can assign to themselves but not to other peoples."[30] War, fanaticism, intolerance, and misplaced dogmatism are the central curses and obstructions in everyone's life, as in that of Spinoza's own life and experience. Removing false notions and prejudices from people's minds not only helps in making individual lives happier, more satisfactory, and more their own responsibility but assists also in reducing strife, war and quarrels and promoting social harmony.

In Spinoza's philosophy, the same freedom and better life acquired for the individual by ridding one's mind of false or, as Spinoza termed them, "inadequate" ideas, our striving toward the "blessedness [*zaligheid*]" that is the highest state that humans can attain, is also the recipe for achieving a better and more satisfactory form of society and politics. "Whatever conduces to the universal fellowship of men," goes one of Spinoza's more renowned maxims (*Ethics* IV, Prop. 40), "that is to say, whatever causes men to live in harmony with one another, is profitable and, on the contrary, whatever brings discord is evil." In her (for long unpublished)

---

[28] Spinoza, *Collected Works* (ed. Curley) i, 570 (translation from the Latin modified by myself).
[29] Spinoza, *Theological-Political Treatise*, 45–6, 48, 56; Kossmann, *Political Thought*, 79.
[30] Spinoza, *Theological-Political Treatise*, 55.

manuscript translation, George Eliot especially prized this dimension of Spinoza, rendering this maxim: "Those things which cherish human society, or which cause men to live together in concern, are useful; and, on the contrary, those things are evil which occasion discord in the community."[31]

Men can agree and dwell in harmony, Spinoza teaches in Part V of his *Ethics*, only insofar as they restrain their individual passions and organize their community under the guidance of "reason." Unfortunately, men rarely do so as most concern themselves only with their own personal advantage, causing strife and collisions at every turn. Nevertheless, crucially for the fate of mankind, it is also true that it is "when each man most seeks his own advantage for himself, that men are most useful to one another." This, of course, is the essence of trade, and providing commercial and other services, which had long been the sphere of activity of Spinoza's forebears not just in Portugal but from the 1590s also in France and the Spanish Netherlands as well as North Africa. It was equally the essence of political negotiation and even arguably theology and academic life as well as of the vast web of behind-the-scenes dialogue and negotiation between the warring Lutherans, Calvinists, Anglicans, Catholics, Mennonites, Quakers, fringe Christian Millenarians, and Jews, confessions all especially numerous in the Holland of his day. But at the same time, this usefulness of all to everyone is the principal reason why Spinoza judges the democratic republic, seeking the optimal set of conditions for each person to develop their own individual lives as they wish, to be inherently superior to every other form of regime.[32] This insight of Spinoza's, that all theology, religious debate, and politics, like commerce and family relations, is about power seeking, manipulation, jockeying for position and advantage, provides the rationale behind his distinctive doctrine that the force of reason, however imperfect, is always a collective as much as individual phenomenon and one not necessarily, or even usually, understood by those who directly experience and benefit from this collective reason. Every particular desire or emotion can be either good or bad depending on circumstances except for one solitary major exception: by Part IV, Proposition 61 of the *Ethics*, "a desire that arises from reason cannot be excessive."[33] Never was there a more unbending rationalist.

If mankind's religious status ever reaches the stage where "the piety or impiety of each person's faith should be judged by their works alone," everyone will then understand, as they miserably failed to do for the most part when he lived, that the unique result, wherever everyone is truly free "to obey God in a spirit of sincerity and freedom," is that "only justice and charity [are] esteemed by everyone."[34] Throughout his most productive years as a thinker and writer Spinoza was widely denounced as an "atheist," and enemy of public and private morality, a great

---

[31] Atkins, "George Eliot and Spinoza," 83; Gatens, *Spinoza's Hard Path*, 49–53.
[32] Spinoza, *Collected Works* (ed. Curley) i, 563.
[33] Spinoza, *Collected Works* (ed. Curley) i, 581.   [34] Spinoza, *Theological-Political Treatise*, 10.

corrupter of mankind, charges he angrily rejected. Spinoza himself always insisted, as he reiterates at both the beginning and close of his *Tractatus Theologico-Politicus* that he wrote in all sincerity taking "great pains to ensure above all that everything I write entirely accords with the laws of my country, with piety, and with morality."[35] He did not accept that he was an "atheist," indeed angrily disavowed any such designation. But among the foremost consequences of his underlying approach to philosophy, religion, ethics, science, and political thought is his concluding that there is no such thing as divinely-sanctioned or justified "religious authority." Coercive regulation of belief on the basis of dogma or church decree is always "superstition" from whatever source it derives and whatever it preaches. Only civil government and its laws possess the right to rule over men and even these only outside the sphere of individual conscience, thought, and belief. For Spinoza, no religious authority exists or ever could exist.

No aspect of Spinoza's *Tractatus Theologico-Politicus* of 1670 (henceforth the *TTP*), his second most important work, matters more than his insistence that he had written it for the benefit of all, to combat what he considered mistaken ideas and false theological notions prevalent in the society in which he lived, and especially to fight "superstition" and denial of freedom of thought. However, he then importantly qualifies this pronouncement by adding that he had not written it for direct consumption by "the multitude" or the great majority of readers, since he considers it impossible to challenge the prevailing "superstition" and ignorance shaping the world in which men live head on. Rather, his highly subversive treatise should be read, he recommended, only by that small band of "philosophical readers" capable of thinking independently, rationally, and critically. Broadly speaking, the same goals and provisos characterize his most important work, the *Ethics*. For the kind of philosopher he aspired to be, and turn others into, great caution was requisite—even in the relatively free Dutch Republic of the Golden Age. Both wholly uneducated minds, he explains, and those possessing some education but conventionally shaped and devoid of real philosophical and critical apparatus, are not just powerfully driven and torn by fear and hope, but inherently dangerous to any vocal dissident. For "most people are quite ready to believe anything," as he puts it on the first page of the *TTP*, and in their ignorance all too ready to assault and crush whoever opposes their cherished prejudices.[36]

Yet how can one possibly "reform the world," one might object, if like medieval Islamic thinkers, Maimonides, and Spinoza, or Toland, Voltaire, d'Holbach, and Condorcet later, one believes "the ignorant" do in fact overwhelmingly outnumber "the wise," if the great majority of mankind possess no intellectual grasp of the human condition or morality and politics at all, and when, as Spinoza says, "every man judges what is good according to his own way of thinking"?[37] Here his vision

---

[35] Spinoza, *Theological-Political Treatise*, 12.
[36] Spinoza, *Theological-Political Treatise*, 5.
[37] Spinoza, *Ethics* IV, Prop. 70.

diverges markedly from that of the great medieval Jewish thinker Maimonides, who adhered to a similar (originally Platonic) dichotomy dividing all mankind into the philosophically-inclined versus the ignorant multitude comprising everyone else.[38] Spinoza's answer is that wherever an increasingly free interplay of views and interests is permitted, each individual's needs within society will collectively spur and steer society, guided by the balancing and offsetting of conflicting interests, in the right direction. True though it is that men are continually a great nuisance to each other, and the greatest cause of mankind's distress and disasters, yet, paradoxically, "from the society of our fellow men," we nevertheless derive "many more advantages than disadvantages."[39] On this ground he believed, "reason" can advance if and wherever freedom of thought, debate, and to publish prevail—a colossal "if" he ceaselessly reiterates.

It is indeed a striking feature of Spinoza's philosophy, and indication of its intensely political character, that it remains unnecessary for most, or even more than a handful, to perceive the truth intellectually. To live in accord with reason understanding the basic principles of morality, science, and politics is reserved for very few. But all can benefit from the advance of "reason" because the pressure of social needs and fear of insecurity automatically creates a framework of social tendencies, a context of laws and customs, enshrining to a greater or lesser degree (depending on the character and quality of the state) morality's authentic principles. Any law, Spinoza maintained (whether or not altogether convincingly), no matter how vigorously enforced must become discredited and progressively weakened where its negative consequences for the whole are manifest, and its inherent morality brought into doubt, helped by the few possessing wisdom pronouncing it damaging, divisive, irrational, and absurd. Even if only the freest, most rational individuals, understand religion, politics, and morality and can exhort the need to negate damaging common notions of doctrine, revelation, miracles, martyrdom, heroism, magic and faith fomenting strife and fanaticism, and that damage society, the whole body exudes an inherent but fragile automatic tendency and impulse to move in the right direction wherever this is not blocked by organized, doctrinally-sanctioned error, myth, and tyranny mobilizing "superstition" to forcibly underpin oppression. The understanding of the wise and free can provide the needed intellectual steering mechanism, justifying and reinforcing the operations of law and custom, and guiding society as a whole to better things, as long as public affairs of every kind remain open to free discussion and unrestricted rational criticism with respect to their social and moral consequences.

The political arena and the falsely "religious" and theologically tainted ethical sphere, for Spinoza, interact on every level and affect, usually adversely, the quality

---

[38] Pines, "Spinoza's *Tractatus Theologico-Politicus*," 499–500; Fraenkel, *Philosophical Religions*, 181–92.
[39] Spinoza, *Collected Works* (ed. Curley) i, 564.

of life and happiness of the individual, even the most rational, in fundamental ways. This is because, Spinoza explains in the Part IV of his principal work of philosophy, "a man who is guided by reason is more free in a state where he lives according to a common decision, than in solitude where he obeys only himself."[40] The free individual's own freedom and virtue, in other words, are enhanced where he aligns with what Spinoza terms "the common advantage" working both for others and himself. From the argument of Part IV of the *Ethics* we see clearly that throughout Spinoza's system the political is always directly linked to the ethical—so that nothing is worse in studying Spinoza's philosophy than the (unfortunately) common practice of detaching and considering the *Ethics* separately from the *TTP* and the unfinished *Tractatus Politicus* [*TP*]. For just as the collective in Spinoza always stands in indirect and complex relation to the individual, collective reason seeking the "common advantage" is a force for the advancement and benefit of society no less in Part IV and Part V of the *Ethics* than in Spinoza's strictly political writings.

This "common advantage" benefits everyone, the aware free man no less than the vast majority, the "superstitious," scantily educated humans unable, according to Spinoza, to grasp the reality of things, those who live by passions and emotion spiced by misguided religious notions, rather than by reason. Still, even where "reason" registers some gains, the ignorance of the vast majority always represents a continuing threat to the well-being of society as a whole and to everyone in it. Spinoza's philosophy and moral teaching, then, as presented in the *Ethics,* are in no way inconsistent, or out of balance (as is sometimes suggested), with Spinoza's democratic republican political theory or life-long unrelenting attack on the sway and pretensions of ecclesiastics whether Catholic, Protestant, Muslim, or Jewish, all of whose pretensions, such was his ambition, he resolutely set out to demolish utterly in the interest of truth, science, and society.

---

[40] Spinoza, *Ethics* IV, Prop. 73.

2
Unparalleled Challenge

2.i Philosophy that Survived by a Thread

Spinoza's death represents a unique landmark in intellectual history. Paradoxically, it was his physical death in The Hague, on 21 February 1677, that opened the door, as far as the late 1670s and 1680s were concerned, to his initial massive European reception and recognition as one of the leading, or rather most challenging, thinkers of the age. From the moment he passed away, he stood beyond the reach of the authorities secular and ecclesiastical, and could no longer be threatened, silenced, arrested, or imprisoned.

Nevertheless, for some months immediately following his death, in fact for most of 1677, the bulk of Spinoza's surviving philosophical writings remained unprinted as well as unpublished, precariously surviving in just a very few manuscript copies. For ten months after breathing his last, Spinoza's philosophical legacy remained not just generally unknown but highly vulnerable and exposed to the threat of immediate extinction. From a post-1677 perspective, the ten months following his death were an ominously silent lull before the storm. For behind the scenes, unknown to him, and witnessed by very few, amidst the seeming silencing of his philosophy since his earlier failed attempt to publish the *Ethics* in 1675, there unfolded between February and December 1677 a tense aftermath which actually marks the riskiest, most dramatic, and decisive narrow escape of his entire life's work and legacy.

It took ten months of arduous work in strict secrecy to collect, copy, edit, translate, and prepare for publication the substantial body of material, including the *Ethics*, that the editors bundled together as the "*Opera Posthuma*." At the time, practically no one beyond a handful of international observers in the know—Leibniz, Tschirnhaus, and Steno prominent among them—knew of the efforts in progress to edit and publish his posthumous works. During that time agents acting for the Dutch Reformed Church (Calvinist), the papal authorities, and others, including a rabbi, strove to locate those manuscripts and organize their destruction. This meant that most of his clandestine project remained at risk of obliteration for the whole of that time. Only by the narrowest margin did most of Spinoza's legacy survive at all. The *Opera Posthuma* comprising the first edition of the *Ethics*, his thus far unpublished second political tract, the *Tractatus Politicus*, correspondence and several lesser tracts suddenly appeared at the end of 1677. Had they been able to locate the still unpublished main body of his work in time, the ecclesiastical and secular authorities would have suppressed it quite conceivably forever. Looking back from the 1690s, the Lutheran preacher Johannes Colerus (1647–1707), author of the first published and most reliable contemporary biography of Spinoza, published in 1705, fully appreciated just how slim the margin was by which mankind had failed "to be rescued," as he envisaged it, from the most subversive body of ideas yet to afflict Christendom. Colerus later rented the same lodgings where Spinoza had lived for a time in The Hague and also got to know his last landlord, Hendrik van der Spijck (d. 1715). From him Colerus gathered first-hand information about Spinoza's final months and death, enabling him to demonstrate by what an amazingly fine thread Spinoza's main philosophical legacy survived to see the light of day and "from whose sheath [Spinoza's publisher and editors] this cursed arrow [the *Opera Posthuma*] was shot into the world."[1]

Had the authorities managed to intercept his manuscripts in time, most of Spinoza's philosophical work might well have vanished forever. Admittedly, several manuscript copies of the *Ethics* existed before publication so there was a chance one at least might survive from early modern times even if publication had been successfully aborted in 1677. But only one solitary pre-1677 manuscript copy is known to have survived until today. Besides *The Ethics*, the *Tractatus Politicus*, his last work, left unfinished at the time of his demise, also existed in just one or two manuscripts, as did his early, unfinished *Treatise on the Emendation of the Understanding*. The margin by which most his legacy survived was indeed exceedingly slim. In the end, despite coming close, the concerted efforts to trace and halt the clandestine publication of Spinoza's works failed. The *Opera Posthuma*'s furtive editing and printing in Amsterdam was completed and, in December 1677, the hazardous further process of secretive distribution commenced. But from then on, it was the recently deceased thinker, advocate of everything most opposed to the officially and religiously sanctioned prevailing order in early modern Western thought, who held the initiative in the rapidly escalating continent-wide war of ideas and values he so powerfully unleashed.

The *Opera Posthuma* came out in two different versions, Latin and Dutch, both bearing the publication date "1677" without mentioning any place of publication or publisher on the title-page, and copies first became available to readers either at the end December 1677 or, more probably, in January 1678.[2] If Spinoza had already provoked uproar earlier, in 1670, by publishing his *Tractatus Theologico-Politicus*, the full scope of his philosophical enterprise and political and social reformism only became evident with the appearance of the *Opera Posthuma*. In 1678, it became immediately clear, moreover, and for some this was a particularly disturbing aspect of the revolution in ideas Spinoza engineered, that his

---

[1] Colerus' biography in Freudenthal/Walther, *Lebensgeschichte* i, 140–1.
[2] Van de Ven, *Printing Spinoza*, 377–8.

posthumous intervention would not be confined to the rarefied sphere of academic Latin-readers but was already breaking through to the wider world of vernacular language—first in Dutch, a language then widely read in northern Germany and Scandinavia as well as in the Low Countries, followed that same year by the *TTP*'s appearance in French and, in 1689, also in English. Still, organized repression of Spinoza's works was not without a measure of success. From the moment diffusion began, the *Opera Posthuma* was banned in his native Holland as well as in France, Italy, the German states, and the Spanish world, and by the papacy, and other than the 1677 Dutch edition, the *Ethics* remained untranslated into any modern European language until 1744 when it appeared (still clandestinely) in German.

Not since the Reformation had anything quite like Spinoza's forbidden, furtive, often masked impact—universal and deeply unsettling—occurred in early modern times. No greater error is to be found in the traditional historiography of philosophy and political thought than the curiously stubborn myth prevalent through the twentieth century that there is no need to discuss Spinoza's impact in his own time because his reputation was "very soon eclipsed" and because his work was "generally neglected until the end of the eighteenth century," so that, effectively, during his own time and the Enlightenment he had no impact.[3] No historical notion could be more absurdly unhistorical—or more instructive of the dangers of letting judgements rest on previous scholarship, and what has often been repeated by numerous scholars in the past without directly consulting the historical context and documentary evidence.

Far from being little noticed, all the top minds of the era began frantically wrestling with the Spinoza phenomenon almost immediately after his death and continued doing so for decades afterwards; indeed in a few cases this process began already in the 1660s, arising from interaction with Spinoza personally or via letter. Robert Boyle encountered Spinoza's scientific ideas already well before 1670, while the greatest Scandinavian scientist of the era, Nicholas Steno (1638–86) ceaselessly battled Spinoza's system from the mid-1660s onwards. Leibniz, fascinated but deeply troubled by the *TTP*, was already linking the *TTP* to the Dutch thinker's wider philosophical system expounded in *The Ethics* which he had glimpsed in manuscript by the mid-1670s and, for the rest of his life, wrestled with Spinoza's system continually both within himself and in discussion with others including his princely employer. John Locke acquired his copy of the *TTP* in 1672 and made notes from it over the next two or three years, appropriating as his own Spinoza's remark that the ancient Israelites were ignorant of natural causes and attributed all occurrences directly to divine intervention;[4] while Hobbes read Spinoza before the latter died and famously reportedly admitted that

---

[3] Hampshire, *Spinoza*, 234; Mason, *God of Spinoza*, 247–8; Scruton, *Spinoza*, 110–11.
[4] Nuovo, "Locke's Proof," 57–8.

the younger thinker had "outthrown him a bar's length," as one said of someone who has outdone you, "for he [Hobbes] durst not write so boldly." By the mid-1670s such leading French minds as Pierre-Daniel Huet, Bishop Bossuet, and Richard Simon were likewise deeply embattled with Spinoza while Pierre Bayle perused the *TTP* both in Latin and French during 1678–9 and, clearly perceiving the unparalleled challenge it presented, not least to himself, during 1679 made haste to obtain copies also of the *Opera Posthuma* and Spinoza's 1663 book on Descartes to examine the full range of his work.

Spinoza's canny publisher, Jan Rieuwertsz (1617–87), initially avoided distribution of the *Opera Posthuma* in Amsterdam, as he had earlier, in 1670, with the *TTP*, following a carefully planned underground book distribution strategy. On 28 January 1678, the local Hague Reformed Church council were the first body to officially sound the alarm on receiving reports that Spinoza's *Opera Posthuma* had appeared "both in Latin and Dutch [duyts]." The gathering was horrified and delegated one of its principal pastors, Dominee Amya, who took a special interest in countering Spinoza's already much resented ideas, to represent the consistory at the next gathering of the Reformed Church's South Holland Synod and petition the provincial high court of Holland to ensure "distribution of [Spinoza's] books be stopped as far as possible."[5] Advised by local magistrates, Amya and his colleagues appealed to the full sitting provincial high court, the Hof van Holland, where "several frightful passages from the said book of Spinoza were read out aloud." This did the trick: the Hof, the highest judicial authority in the land, had "all copies of the said book," states the South Holland Synod's record of the proceedings, "seized from all the bookshops of The Hague that very day."[6]

2.ii Banning Spinoza's Books and Ideas

On February 4, 1678, the Leiden Reformed consistory likewise expressed profound shock at the appearance of the anonymous *Opera Posthuma B.d.S.*, these ominous initials standing, some members of that gathering too already knew, for the notorious "Benedictus de Spinoza." One of Leiden's leading Calvinist ministers, Petrus van Staveren (1632–83), had by then already examined and selected extracts from the text. To ensure the assembly grasped the full gravity of the situation, Van Staveren's extracts were read aloud to the assembled ministers and elders. "It is a book," admonished Van Staveren using uniquely solemn language, "which perhaps since the beginning of the world until the present day has

---

[5] GA The Hague, Hervormde Gemeente 203/4, fo. 131. res. 28 Jan. 1678.
[6] *Acta der particuliere Synoden van Zuid-Holland* v, 236; Israel, "Banning of Spinoza's Works," 12.

no equal [...] in godlessness and that endeavours to do away with all religion and set atheism [*atheisterij*] upon the throne."[7]

Everything possible, the consistory agreed, must be done to suppress "such unheard of abominations" and sent Van Staveren and another minister to the Leiden burgomasters to urge the immediate banning of that "damaging and poisonous book" from the bookstores as well as to "seek a general prohibition of *Opera Posthuma* by decree of the States of Holland."[8] But the challenge did not lie simply in Spinoza's books. Leiden's consistory also exhorted its members to strive "so far as we can to halt" the spread of Spinoza's opinions to other individuals through discussion and group meetings. Van Staveren and his delegation read out their sensational extracts from Spinoza's work to the burgomasters, on 11 February, reporting back to the consistory that the burgomasters and city council had then at once seized all the stocks of Spinoza's works in Leiden.[9] Another notably vigilant theologian who reacted swiftly was the famed Remonstrant preacher Philippus Van Limborch (1633–1712), the greatest Arminian theologian of the era, at Amsterdam. After closely studying the *Opera Posthuma*, he warned his fellow Remonstrant minister at Rotterdam, Christiaan Hartsoeker, on 28 February 1678, that it confirmed his view of Spinoza as an "atheist" who talked constantly of God to mask his atheism.[10]

Official reaction at Amsterdam followed only some weeks after the initial impact in The Hague, Leiden, and elsewhere. Local crack-downs were one thing, but the consistories and synods, as well as The Hague and Leiden magistracies, felt that a more general state prohibition was essential given the *Opera Posthuma*'s uniquely menacing character. A joint delegation from the South and North Holland Synods met with Gaspar Fagel (1634–88), general secretary or "Pensionary" of the Republic's most powerful body, the States of Holland, to present a file full of extracts which the synods had jointly prepared for his attention proving Spinoza's *Opera Posthuma* are full of exceptionally "atrocious errors which tend to the utter dishonoring of God, damage to the Church and leading astray of unaware people." Fagel and the States promptly recognized what was at stake—the threat the "blasphemous and atheistic propositions," as the Pensionary of Leiden called them, found in "*Opus Posthumus* B.d.S. [sic]" represented and especially the risk of Spinoza contaminating readers and leading astray "wavering persons [onvaste menschen]" unsteady in their faith. With the Pensionary of Leiden, Pieter Burgersdijk (1623–91) one of the main movers, a

---

[7] GA Leiden, Acta Kerkeraad vi, res. 4 Feb. 1678; Israel, "Banning of Spinoza's Works," 11–12; Van Bunge, "Spinoza's atheïsme," 90.
[8] GA Leiden, Acta Kerkeraad vi, res. 11 Feb. 1678; Freudenthal, *Lebensgeschichte Spinozas in Quellenschriften*, 174–5.
[9] GA Leiden Kerkenraad vi, res. 11 Feb. 1678; Israel, *Radical Enlightenment*, 291.
[10] Simonutti, "Vindiciae Miraculorum," 613–14.

States of Holland commission swiftly drew up the desired prohibition.[11] It is noteworthy that in their high-level confidential political discussions, both preachers and Holland's principal regents together powerfully decried and lambasted the "blasphemous book of Spinoza" as they called it. Yet, they took great care not to mention Spinoza's name in public. Rather, it remained steadfast church and state policy down to the 1690s, as it had been since the *TTP*'s appearance in 1670, that that particular dreaded name, notorious among the secular and ecclesiastical authorities alike, and everything about the man except his sinister initials B.d.S. should remain screened off from public notice as far as possible to minimize drawing attention to Spinoza the person, thinker, and author. For some time, suppress the books, stay silent about the man, was the presiding rule.

Carefully avoiding specifying the condemned author's name, the comprehensive ban published by the States of Holland, on 25 June 1678, was almost unique in Dutch book history for the level of detail Holland's principal regents felt it necessary to enter into when explaining why they were issuing so unusual and sweeping a measure. A certain book, announced the States of Holland, entitled *B. d.S. Opera Posthuma*, had appeared containing "very many blasphemous and atheistic propositions by which not only the simple reader may be misled from the only and true path to blessedness," but which also seriously impugn the doctrine of the Incarnation and Resurrection of Christ and "other very essential articles of the general Christian Faith [het algemeene christelijcke geloof]," rejecting the "authority of the miracles by which God Almighty wished to show his omnipotence and divine power to reinforce the Christian faith," and dismissing belief in miracles as sheer ignorance, urging the reader to suspend all belief in them. Because the author defends all these "heterodox and godless propositions," expounding lots of "arguments that directly conflict with the explicit text of the Holy Scriptures, and against the teaching of blessedness," the States expressly prohibited the printing, selling, and dissemination of the said book "with the greatest indignation," pronouncing it "profane, atheistic and blasphemous," so that the text in both its Latin version and Dutch translation was now everywhere forbidden under pain of severe penalties, the States having resolved to "use every way and means to suppress it and remove every opportunity for ordinary folk [eenvoudige ingezetenen] to be seduced by reading such godless propositions."[12]

The published decree of the States cites "B.d.S" but omits mentioning Spinoza by name, even though confidentially, in the high-level discussions of the provincial States, the work was freely referred to as being by "Spinoza."[13] Equally, in the

---

[11] ARH NHK, Oud Synodaal Archief, Acta Enkhuizen, p. 3. res. 3 Aug. 1678; RNH Acta Noord-Holland Synod 6, 1 Aug. 1678, Enkhuizen, Licentieus boekdrukken.
[12] *Groot Placaet-Boeck* iii, 525–6. Placaet, 25 June 1678; Weekhout, *Boekencensuur*, 106.
[13] *Res. Staten van Holland*, 17 March and 25 June 1678.

South Holland Synod's debate about the *Opera Posthuma* at Leiden, in July 1678, the meeting heard how the intervention spearheaded by Dominee Amya of The Hague against this now prohibited book had been concerted, leading to the decree drawn up on Fagel's initiative, and further that the *Opera Posthuma* were, "in the light of all consideration by Spinoza [na alle bedencken, van Spinoza]." Among themselves, the Dutch Reformed synods from now on freely identified the condemned book's author as "Spinoza."[14] But this again would remain confidential churchmen's information not destined for the public for a considerable time afterwards, it remaining high priority in Holland and neighbouring lands, even if impossible to rigidly observe, to prevent people generally finding out about "Spinoza."

The Dutch Reformed Church's North Holland Synod discussed the "*Opus Posthumus* B.d.S." and the States of Holland's ban at its gathering at Enkhuizen, on 3 August 1678. There too, were read out the extracts with which the joint *deputati* of the North and South Holland synods had persuaded Fagel "to work for the forbidding and suppression of such horrible errors [gruweliijcke dwalingen] that can lead to such utter dishonour of God, harm to the Church, and leading astray of wavering persons," and that had secured prompt passage of the prohibition of "that said blasphemous book of Spinoza."[15] But the menace had by now spread beyond the confines of Holland. The Reformed Synod of the neighbouring province of Utrecht discussed B.D.S. *Opera Posthuma* in September, together with a report on the provincial ban and seizures from Holland's bookshops.[16] The Utrecht burgomasters and *vroedschap* [city council] then issued their edict on 24 October 1678, explaining that the renewed and rephrased measure was needed "to prevent all confusion, dissension and perplexity."[17] Differently than in Holland, Utrecht's edict conflated the twin Socinian and Spinozist threats, forbidding all booksellers, printers, and book buyers to print, obtain from outside the province, distribute or sell, under threat of heavy financial penalty, "any Socinian or Arian books, these being blasphemous and wholly pernicious, and especially not the *Bibliotheca Fratrum Polonorum*, the *Leviathan* of Hobbes, the *Philosophia S.*

---

[14] *Acta der particuliere synoden van Zuid-Holland* v, 236; Weekhout, *Boekencensuur*, 106.
[15] ARH NHK Oud Synodaal Archief 184, Acta 1678, Hoorn, 3 Aug. 1678, p. 3.
[16] RA Utrecht, Acta Synodi Provincialis Trajecti 4, Acta 1678 (10 to 19 Sept. 1678), session 5, art. 23. In Utrecht, the provincial Reformed synod aimed to merge their proposed measures against the *Opera Posthuma* with a broad provincial ban highlighting a shortlist of the most pernicious books presently vitiating their province, listing besides Spinoza's *Opera Posthuma*, the anonymous *Philosophia S. Scripturae Interpres* [Philosophy the Interpreter of Scripture], Spinoza's *Tractatus Theologico-Politicus* of 1670, Hobbes' *Leviathan*, and the Anti-Trinitarian Socinian collection, the *Bibliotheca Fratrum Polonorum*. Delay in the provincial States, though, caused frustration in the Synod, resulting in their decision, since "such books are mostly sold in the city," to settle for now for an edict of suppression, imposing a heavy financial penalty or corporal punishment for all those who print or sell such books "from the city alone."
[17] GA Utrecht MS 121 vroedschapsresoluties (1674–9), fos. 194v and 199, res. 23 Sept. and 24 Oct. 1678; Bamberger, "Early Editions," 26–7.

Scripturae Interpres, the *Tractatus Theologico-Politicus* 'of Spinosa' and *B.d.S. Opera Posthuma* and similar material in whatever language it may be."[18]

Printers defying this Utrecht decree of 24 October 1678 against so-called "Socinian" books were to be banned from printing and fined 3,000 guilders, for many the equivalent of ten years' salary. Selling copies incurred a 1,000 guilder fine for the first offense and, for the second, banishment from the city. All printers and booksellers were also required to appear in person before the city magistrates within three days of the decree date to surrender all "printed or manuscript copies of such books [...] to be suppressed, kept or destroyed" by the city government as they judged fit. Any book dealer suspected of concealing copies was to be summoned to declare on oath before the magistrates that he had no copies concealed on pain of a one hundred guilder fine for the first refusal and being permanently banned from selling books in Utrecht for the second. The Utrecht provincial Synod of the Reformed Church gratefully thanked the burgomasters for these measures at its 1679 gathering, while reminding the city magistracy of the need to stringently enforce repression of these books.[19]

Spinoza's impact after death was not just greater than modern scholars mostly acknowledge, but in subversive effect uniquely far-reaching. Nevertheless, the efforts at repression certainly had a broad effect. Spinoza's books could not be used in teaching, nor cited in academic works except in the most negative possible terms, nor advertised or freely distributed. Selling the book exclusively "under the counter" entailed considerable risk for the bookseller. If, from the 1670s, polemical debates about Spinoza's ideas on religion and politics, as distinct from his philosophical system, worryingly escalated, the combined censorship efforts of the synods and secular authorities did at least prevent the *Tractatus Theologico-Politicus*, Spinoza's main work of Bible criticism, appearing in German and in English until 1689 and, at any rate until 1693, in Dutch. After Spinoza's death, the *Opera Posthuma* did circulate clandestinely in Dutch (from 1678), but being a work of pure philosophy it was difficult for most readers. Meanwhile, all clandestine editions lacked Spinoza's name and the true place of publication and, apart from a brief outline in the anonymous preface to the *Opera Posthuma* (by Jarig Jelles) offered only the scantiest details about the mysterious author and his background. The profile of the man responsible for these uniquely outrageous, or, depending on your viewpoint, courageous, ideas remained a virtual blank for everyone beyond a handful of intimates and friends.

Preachers and officials in the last quarter of the seventeenth century could comfortably assume their prohibition effort was at least hugely restricting

---

[18] RA Utrecht, Acta Synodi Provincialis Trajecti 4, Acta 1679, session 4, art. 30; Vande Water, *Groot- Placaat-Boek* [...] *Utrecht* iii, 432; Freudenthal/Walther, *Lebensgeschichte* i, 392–3; Israel, "Banning of Spinoza's Works," 13.

[19] RA Utrecht, Prov. Kerkgeschiedenis iv, Acta Synodi 1679, session 4, art. 30; Vande Water, *Groot Placaatboek* [...] *Utrecht* iii, 432–3; Steenbakkers, "Mort de Spinoza," 736.

awareness of those of Spinoza's ideas most directly damaging to belief and church doctrine while keeping the identity of Spinoza the man, and all knowledge of him, effectively out of the limelight. In the first few years of its published existence, the *TTP* remained largely confined to Latin-reading academics, theologians, medical men, and lawyers, although that safeguard was soon disturbingly breached. While practically all pre-1677 refutations discussing the *TTP* in the Netherlands, as in Germany, kept unwaveringly to Latin, one major exception stood out, that of the Dordrecht regent, Willem van Blijenbergh (1632–96), *The Truth of the Christian Religion and the Authority of Holy Scripture* (1674), which appeared in the vernacular. Van Blijenbergh deliberately dragged discussion of the *TTP* into Dutch by quoting long passages from Spinoza verbatim. Even so, despite knowing Spinoza personally and having discussed his philosophy with him, he did keep to the prevailing rule that opponents should not mention the banned author's name and should say nothing whatever about him as a person. Labeling the *TTP* merely "a certain blasphemous book," Van Blijenbergh too adhered to what proved a temporarily effective defensive strategy—powerfully assault the contemptibly unchristian ideas while carefully hiding Spinoza's identity, whereabouts and everything about his life, legacy, and circle.

Spinoza's ideas had to be powerfully rebutted but at the same time the public needed to be kept from knowing who he was and learning anything about the supposedly profoundly malevolent author being suppressed. Van Blijenbergh felt driven to publish his rebuttal in Dutch by the crying need, as he saw it, not just to warn the public against the ideas of an unnamed personage bolder and more insolent, he declares, even than the pagan poet Juvenal, and the last pagan emperor, Julian, and viler than Machiavelli, but also the need, as he saw it, to shield Cartesianism and Cartesians like himself from all responsibility for this unmentioned culprit's concepts. To protect Descartes and the Cartesians from all association with the dangerous new influence seemed to him such an overriding priority that, ill-advisedly in the eyes of many, he was willing to pay the price of quoting sizeable chunks of Spinoza word for word in the vernacular.[20] In the innumerable published attacks on his books and key ideas, the continuing rule for years after Spinoza's death, was that Spinoza's name should remain unmentioned and that his ideas should be refuted only in a language and terminology most people could not understand.

By January 1678, Spinoza's philosophical system had been salvaged from extinction and permanently affixed by his designing Amsterdam allies to his subversive critique of religion, politics, society, and the Bible. From December 1677, the perceived menace of Spinoza rapidly escalated, and, gradually, during the course of the 1680s, "Spinoza" as such, rather than just one or another of his

---

[20] Saldenus, *Otia theologica*, 25; Servaas van Rooijen, *Inventaire*, 658; Van Bunge, *From Stevin to Spinoza*, 115; Israel, "Early Dutch and German Reaction," 77, 89.

writings incipiently began to emerge as an actual *persona* and target of his opponents, though usually in distorted, exaggerated, or mythical terms. Van Blijenbergh also contributed to this further transition, publishing a second book against Spinoza, his *Refutation of the* Ethica *or Moral Science of Benedictus de Spinosa* [*Wederlegging van de Ethica of Zede-kunst van Benedictus van Spinosa*] (Dordrecht, 1682), a 354-page work on Spinoza's views about substance, modes, God, and the human soul, again quoting verbatim numerous key propositions, doctrines, and quotations in Dutch, connecting the *TTP* to the *Opera Posthuma*, and now, changing course, citing "Spinoza" as the personage responsible for the unheard of furore surrounding his books. To ordinary readers Van Blijenbergh explained that Spinoza seeks to deprive man of his free will and deprive God of all understanding and will, thereby overthrowing all religion and theology and replacing these, directly contrary to Descartes, exclusively with science-based philosophy.[21] Realization that the unprecedented commotion caused by the *TTP* and *Opera Posthuma* stemmed from an identifiable personage called "Spinoza," however, became only vaguely and marginally discernible for most contemporaries from the early 1680s. Inhibition against discussing Spinoza the man continued albeit slowly losing its effect through the 1680s but only came to be jettisoned entirely in the 1690s, due especially to publication of the first lengthy article on Spinoza, that in French by Pierre Bayle, which was in fact the longest article in his entire *Dictionnaire*, of 1697.

Van Blijenbergh denounced Spinoza for damaging society by separating ethics and morality from organized religion, reducing the latter to the status of pure fabrication, and trying to project, unconvincingly in his view, a purely humanistic moral order for mankind, tied to mathematical science, establishing an ethics purely "philosophical and natural." Spinoza denied what nearly everyone believed, including all the other great philosophers of the age, namely that Christianity far more effectively teaches men truth as well as morality and virtue than can any purely naturalistic system.[22] Instead of dividing all reality, like Descartes and Locke, into two separate, unconnected spheres—mathematical science unlocking physical reality on the one hand, faith and religious authority explaining and governing everything crucial that stands above nature and above reason, on the other—Spinoza overturned the existing order by representing all reality as governed by one single set of rules, the mathematical-scientific, while abolishing the supernatural, everything "above reason," and with this all religious authority (as well as the basis of Locke's philosophy).

Because Spinoza's philosophy was judged to have deeply disturbing consequences for religion and society, the Reformed Church consistories deemed it insufficient just to ban Spinoza's books. Already during the 1670s, Spinoza's ideas

---

[21] Blijenbergh, *Wederlegging van de Ethica*, 128, 216.
[22] Blijenbergh, *Wederlegging van de Ethica*, 352–4.

had unmistakably become the intellectual profile of a new clandestine philosophical sect and the Reformed synods in addition to banning his books recognized the necessity of stopping people discussing and teaching his ideas at clandestine meetings by forbidding discussion of Spinoza in homes and workplaces. In July 1681, a certain Anthony van Dalen (not the famous Anthonie van Dale of Haarlem), the son of a family of middle-ranking officials employed in The Hague, appeared before the local Reformed consistory complaining about an embarrassing scene in the Kloosterkerk, a church in the center of The Hague, where he was refused the Eucharist for reportedly spreading "godless opinions"; this, he protested, affected his reputation and career. Under Reformed Church procedure it was against proper form to refuse admission to the Lord's Supper (Eucharist) without such exclusion being first formally resolved on beforehand by the local consistory, so Van Dalen had grounds to complain; but the gathering was hardly impressed by that as he had been overheard uttering blasphemous and unacceptable statements by half a dozen witnesses, including a Reformed church-warden entrusted with visiting the sick, who had engaged in several angry exchanges with him. The matter was investigated and the plaintiff summoned to appear. When he did so, in October, he was interrogated about his "praising Spinoza and his views very much," and telling others that "everything that is in Nature, is God."

Evidence gathered by his local minister plainly revealed the consequences of Van Dalen's reading and idealizing Spinoza in terms of local behaviour and attitudes, and the implications for early modern belief, theology, and the cultural primacy of churchmen.[23] One witness confirmed Van Dalen had several times engaged in discussion with him in the nearby village of Voorburg where some still remembered Spinoza (who lived there during much of the 1660s). Van Dalen went about spreading godless views, being a person who "prized the books of Spynoosa very highly for having expressed the matter in dispute [that God is Nature and Nature is God] so clearly that few were unable to grasp it."[24] Not only did this person, insisted another witness, a widow who knew him, deny the Holy Trinity and Christ's divinity, but to her infinite disgust even denied the Redeemer was conceived by the Holy Ghost rather than by sexual intercourse. Van Dalen also denied "creation of the world from nothing" and would acknowledge the existence of neither angels nor devils, she complained, and even maintained that heathens worshipping "the true God, that is Nature," are "closer to blessedness than Christians," and that "philosophical conviction [philosophisch geloof]" is the highest form of conviction.[25] Among locals, understandably, Van Dalen's talk provoked furious outrage.

---

[23] GA The Hague, Hervormde Gemeente, Kerkenraad iv, 178–9, res. 11 Oct. 1681; Wielema, "Onbekende aanhanger," 25, 34, 37, 39.
[24] Quoted in Wielema, "Onbekende aanhanger," 40.
[25] GA The Hague, Hervormde Gemeente, Kerkenraad iv, 179. res. 11 Oct. 1681 and p. 180, res. 7 Nov. 1681; Wielema, "Onbekende aanhanger," 27, 39–40.

Van Dalen reportedly also claimed to know a preacher with a position nearby secretly holding similar views (almost certainly a reference to the philosopher Petrus van Balen (1643–92) who had been interrogated by The Hague consistory a few months before). As the accused refused to make any statement or confess anything whatever to the consistory, the local Reformed classis censured Van Dalen and banned him indefinitely from the sacraments and participation in the Lord's Supper. He later moved to Amsterdam where, in October 1689, there were renewed complaints, recorded by the Reformed consistory there, that Van Dalen was still holding meetings and trying to instil his "atrocious opinions" into others.[26]

Spinoza's legacy was a double one of ideas and an underground movement of forbidden discussion and both proved exasperatingly difficult to eradicate. From publication of the *TTP* in 1670, Spinoza's books dominated what may be termed the early radical Enlightenment sector of the banned sections of the Dutch book world. Of the other prohibited sectors, Socinian books, politically offensive works, and erotic items, the first especially loomed larger than the radical Enlightenment category in terms of numbers of titles and copies in forbidden circulation. But within the Enlightenment category of unacceptable publications, Spinoza towered over every other radical writer, even all the others—Van den Enden, the Brothers Koerbagh, Lodewijk Meyer, Abraham Cuffeler, Petrus Van Balen, and Hadrian Beverland—combined, indeed even with Hobbes' *Leviathan* thrown in too. Although his books were published furtively, without his name appearing on their title-pages or in their contents, Spinoza gradually became known as author of the most widely selling, penetrating and challenging set of texts within the radical sub-section circulating under the counter. Besides the *TTP* and *Opera Posthuma*, the anonymously published *Philosophia S.Scripturae Interpres* [Philosophy the Interpreter of Holy Scripture] (probably by Spinoza's friend, Lodewijk Meyer) and another fiercely anti-ecclesiastical anonymous text, *De Jure Ecclesiasticorum* (1665) whose author has never been identified, were also often wrongly attributed to "Spinosa."

Undeniably, among the banned under-the counter radical books circulating in the Republic during the last third of the seventeenth century, those either by or wrongly attributed to "Spinoza" formed by far the most preponderant category as is proved by the printed auction catalogues of those booksellers appending separate sections headed "Libri prohibiti [Prohibited books]" to their book auction lists. It may sound contradictory that "prohibited books" could be advertised in book auction catalogues, but while the authorities could seize banned books from printers and bookshops, it was legally impossible to sequestrate works from private libraries. Some *libri prohibiti* belonged to men of high rank. Constantijn

---

[26] Wielema, "Onbekende aanhanger," 32–3.

Huygens, for instance, William III's secretary, had the *TTP*, *Opera Posthuma*, and Meyer's *Philosophia* in his private collection.[27] Moreover, copies of both the largest subcategory, Socinian books, and, from 1678, Spinoza's banned works, could reputably be possessed for purposes of refutation by theologians and other academics and, consequently, book auctions from the 1670s down to 1700 featuring "libri prohibiti" nearly always took place in the university town of Leiden. Some catalogues state that this portion of the auction was restricted to specialist buyers only and would be conducted separately, afterwards, in a private room. Still, these auction catalogues represented an obvious path to subtly advertise early radical Enlightenment authors and titles among a wider public.[28]

2.iii Spinoza and Europe's Late Seventeenth-Century Intellectual Crisis

Meanwhile, having begun in the Netherlands, a comparable but much larger drama surrounding Spinoza was unfolding abroad to begin with principally in Germany and then England. Already before Spinoza's death in February 1677, Boyle, Oldenburg, Henry More, Ralph Cudworth, and several others had been privately wrestling with Spinoza for years, but in their various ways they likewise sought to restrict awareness of Spinoza among the public. The problem was that what was seen as the enormity of Spinoza's blasphemies caused shocked outcries that could not everywhere be stifled. Thus, the English Anglican clergyman Lancelot Addison (father of Joseph Addison) in his *The Present State of the Jews* (1675), having read between the lines of the *TTP*, declared Spinoza as bad as Vanini, a shameless naturalist equating God with nature. This was later noted by Bayle in his journal *Nouvelles de la république des lettres*, in June 1684, where Bayle also discusses ambivalently the view of The Hague preacher Willem Saldenus (1627–94), in his *Otia theologica* that the best way to fight Spinoza is not to answer his arguments but rather keep as silent as possible and avoid Van Blijenbergh's highly unfortunate practice of quoting him in the vernacular.[29]

In England public alarm was sounded with special urgency by one of the most influential Puritan preachers of the Restoration era, Richard Baxter (1615–91), a Shropshire-born philosophical theologian, among the few leading English intellectual figures of the day who did not study at Oxford or Cambridge. With Baxter's intervention, in the mid-1670s, commenced the wider Spinoza drama in the English-speaking world. A giant of Puritan piety and culture with a lasting

---

[27] Pettegree and Der Weduwen, *Bookshop of the World*, 326.
[28] Der Weduwen, "Sold in a Closed Room," 11–12, 16–18; Pettegree and Der Weduwen, *Bookshop of the World*, 13, 325–7, 330–2.
[29] De Vet, "Spinoza en Spinozisme," 8.

legacy in the American colonies as well as Britain, Baxter headed a group of preachers, the Baxterites, among whom John Howe, William Bates, and Roger Morrice were prominent, seeking reconciliation between Presbyterians and the Church of England, urging "comprehension" to overcome the splits within English Protestantism and a tolerant softening of Calvinist theology. Baxterites placed a particular stress on "reason" and the uses of "philosophy." Miracles, insisted Baxter, have not happened since biblical times and do not happen today. He detested what to him was the superstitious, fervent preoccupation with present-day miracle-working rife among Catholics and Quakers. In unique fashion, he felt bound, early on, to reveal to his countrymen the immanent and appalling challenge Spinoza's writings confronted Christianity with and the spiritual crisis they were unleashing.

One of England's pre-eminent preachers, during the Civil War a principal minister in Cromwell's New Model Army, Baxter knew of the *TTP* and was shocked by it apparently as early as 1673. He then intervened with several texts, notably his *Catholick Theologie* of 1675–6, and the opening chapter of the *Second part of the Nonconformists Plea for Peace* (April 1680), a well-known call for reconciliation among the warring English church factions in the making for some years before 1680, with its important section entitled "The Principles of Spinoza and such Bruitists against Government and Morality" (c.1676). In his *Catholick Theologie*, Baxter allots Spinoza a prominent but still secondary role as history's number two most pernicious philosophical "necessitarian" after Hobbes—the "doctrine of necessitation," an obscure figment from ancient times, having now been elevated into a current threat by "Hobbes and Benedictus Spinosa's owning it"[30] (before long English commentators too would dispense with mentioning Spinoza's first name). Like most English commentators, Baxter exaggerated the affinities between Hobbes and Spinoza.

Although Baxter had no formal university training, he undoubtedly figured among the most acute philosophical observers at the time, and, like Spinoza, had a robust suspicion of conventional academic pretensions to expertise and insight. "I have met lately with University-men," he observed in the early 1680s, "that cry'd up Cartesius as if they had been quite above Aristotle and Plato, and when I tried them, I found that they knew not what Aristotle and Plato said (nor what Cartesius neither)."[31] If his prose was not always elegant, Baxter was a vigorous religious reformer offering insights broader and deeper than those of virtually any other pre-1680 English commentator on Spinoza, pointing out early on key features that others signally missed. From around 1675 onwards, he laid greater stress than the rest on Spinoza's links with Descartes, and, like Howe and the

---

[30] Baxter, *Catholic Theologie*, 108, 114, 118; Boucher, *Spinoza in English*, 23; Sytsma, *Richard Baxter*, 261.
[31] Sytsma, *Richard Baxter*, 9, 11.

Natural Law theorist and future bishop Richard Cumberland (1632–1718), on the Epicurean tendency in both Hobbes' and Spinoza's ethical thought. Historically especially significant is Baxter's early recognition that Spinoza was broader, more radical and more dangerous, and in some respects worryingly more alluring, than Hobbes.[32] Where other English commentators steadfastly but misleadingly portrayed Spinoza as a "disciple" of Hobbes, Baxter, realizing Spinoza was displacing Hobbes from first place, even in England, first represents them as equals, in 1675 and then reverses the order of priority making Spinoza more important even than Hobbes. This, he accurately grasped, was because the new "Epicurean deism," as his fellow leading Puritan moderate John Howe (1630–1705) termed it, was politically more active and socially reformist than the "old Epicureanism" and also because Spinoza's thought is more directly opposed to the monarchical English constitution, hence politically more subversive of monarchy and "mixed government" (i.e. by king and Parliament together), than that of Hobbes.

Most commentators focused on Spinoza's denial of miracles and rejection of the Mosaic authorship of the Pentateuch; only a few looked further. Admittedly, Howe became equally fixated, from 1678, on Part I of *The Ethics*; but Baxter ties Spinoza's subversion of revealed religion not just to his philosophical system but, unusually, also to his political thought. A former Cromwell chaplain and Cromwell admirer committed to a qualified version of the Calvinist doctrine of predestination and divinely revealed morality though he was, Baxter drew conclusions from reading Spinoza that he found useful for his own political agenda and war on "superstitious" religion. Since the English Restoration, in 1660, he along with Bates figured among the foremost peacemakers of the realm striving to end the long and bitter conflict between Nonconformists and the Anglican Church and find some viable path to peaceful coexistence (with a common focus on struggle against Jesuits and Quakers) and unity around a core of Christian belief. Driven by such concerns, he made a point of stressing the loyalty of Nonconformists to Charles II and the crown and to the post-1660 English monarchical constitution.[33]

Politics, Baxter saw, was assuredly one reason why Spinoza was displacing Hobbes as chief inspiration of the English "deists" whom, like most other observers, he thoroughly detested. In the later 1670s, it was still unusual in England to rank Spinoza as head of all the "Bruitists" (i.e. Epicurus together with "Hobbes, Spinosa, Pompinatius, Vaninus, etc."), placing him at the top of the list of miscreant thinkers menacing England's monarchical and Christian stability and glory. But this Baxter undertook to do. If any reader "will think we have tediously digressed against this Apostate Jew," by reversing the familiar order in this way,

---

[32] Sytsma, *Richard Baxter*, 234, 236–9.
[33] Sytsma, *Richard Baxter*, 241–2; for Baxter's views on the true "unity" of Christianity see his *The Quakers Catechism* of April 1655.

"the reason is," he explains, "because the pernicious book [the *TTP*] having most subtilly assaulted the text of the Old Testament, is greedily sought," by the newly emerged deist underground, "and cryed up (with Hobbes his equal) in this unhappy time."[34] But Hobbes soon ceased to be his equal in Baxter's eyes.

If Spinoza has much to say about tyranny, Baxter, Bates, and Howe well knew what tyranny was. Baxter himself was dragged into court and imprisoned several times under the Restoration. Later, under James II, in 1685–6, he would be incarcerated for seventeen months for "seditious libel" and insulting bishops. Not one to underestimate what England's Nonconformists were up against, in 1676 he began writing a key political tract pleading for exclusion and persecution of England's Puritans to cease. Urging toleration for Presbyterians, and peace between the main churches of Restoration England, he made cautious use of lengthy reflections on "the principles" of Spinoza albeit carefully omitting all mention of the latter's more comprehensive toleration argument itself. Not everything in Spinoza is totally reprehensible, he explains, but even what is valuable must be handled with extreme care. "Baxterites" were all for toleration but the toleration they demanded was a limited one furnished with certain very clear exceptions and firm proscription of views not to be tolerated under any circumstance (Spinoza's philosophy included). Where God, for Baxter, "is the absolute universal rector of all mankind," it is Spinoza rather than Hobbes who inspires those who think "God is no governour, nor hath no laws (but mens), nor justice, nor mercy" holding that "all religious worship and exercise of godliness is but the determination of rulers for the publick peace, and is wholly within their power and at their will," so that there exists no religious authority. Hobbes fell considerably short of that.

A monstrous common feature "in the doctrine of the Sadducees, Spinoza, Hobbes and their bruitist followers," for Baxter, was that they all "set up individual self-interest as a man's chiefest end and object of rational love and desire, and own no good, but that which relatively is good to me, that is either my personal life and pleasure as the end." But if that is the essence of "Epicurean deism" and what Bruitists stood for, it was Spinoza's conception of "natural law," not that of Hobbes, that defines this clash of fundamental concepts in Baxter's *Church-History* (1681).[35] It is Spinoza's political thought, here contrary to Hobbes, that bars unqualified transfer of each individual's power to the prince. Thus, Spinoza directly threatens princely authority and power. No one could possibly tie to Hobbes the domestic English subversive republican tendency disrupting Britain since the 1640s and now reviving in the last quarter of the century, rife especially in radical deism. Hobbes' view of democracy and the informal power of "the

---

[34] Baxter, "Principles of Spinosa," paras. 3 and 4; Colie, "Spinoza in England," 190–1; Van de Ven, *Printing Spinoza*, 282.
[35] Baxter, *Church-History*, "The Preface," 1; Sytsma, *Richard Baxter*, 239, 261.

multitude" as threatening the stability of the state, was simply not useful to republican deists.[36] Spinoza's system, on the other hand, perfectly fitted Baxter's argument that the entire "bruitist" tendency in English culture menaced Restoration monarchy and England's constitution no less than it threatened faith and preachers: "thus, if Princes will ever set up Epicurisme, Atheisme and Infidelity, they shall set up Rebellion with it," an argument against England's budding deist movement cogent only when subordinating, as Baxter does, Hobbes to Spinoza as leader of the "Bruitist" tendency.[37]

If Spinoza was democratic republican where Hobbes was an absolutist monarchist placing ecclesiastical affairs firmly under the crown, Spinoza was more threatening than Hobbes also in another way. Baxter, Howe, and Bates extolled the virtues of toleration up to a point while underlining the fatal effects of tolerating those who reject Christ's divinity, miracles, and the Resurrection "in whyche consist our whole salvation." How to combine toleration with strict intolerance of all rejection of core Christian doctrine was their special dilemma. For everyone wanting more toleration in England and America while simultaneously opposing full toleration, Spinoza was tactically crucial, posing the real challenge where Hobbes does not.

Like their great Anglican adversary, the future bishop Edward Stillingfleet (1635–99), Baxterites were keen irenicists seeking to end strife among Protestants, but strictly on the basis of "moderate" irenicism rejecting all tendencies incompatible with core Christian teaching. Like Stillingfleet, a leader of the Latitudinarians, the equivalent tendency within Anglicanism, Baxterites demanded a clear and inviolable red line permanently separating desirable, justified toleration from undesirable, unacceptable toleration. Baxter and Stillingfleet agreed that "bare talking for or against toleration without distinguishing the tolerable from the intolerable" is neither edifying nor helpful. To both "he that will tolerate all is bad, and he that will tolerate none that differith, is mad." Both had to confront, at one extreme, what Baxter called the "dogmatical word-warriors," strict Calvinists, High Church Anglicans, and other intolerant factions fomenting splits among the churches; these they had to tolerate. At the opposite extreme stood Hobbes' and Spinoza's execrable "bad religion word-warriors" whose views needed to be strictly forbidden.[38] Agreeing that because "wasp nests should be destroyed," as Baxter put it, it does not follow that "ergo bee-hives should be destroyed," Baxter and Stillingfleet concurred too that their list of "the bad" "Separatists" to be proscribed, should include Catholics and Quakers, as well as "Antipaedeobaptists [Anabaptists]" and especially those Baxter calls "deists" whose "universal toleration" was a wholly despicable "Trojan Horse."

---

[36] Hoekstra, "Lion in the House," 192–4, 201–2, 206–8; Field, *Potentia*, 147–8.
[37] Baxter, "Principles of Spinosa," para. 4; Colie, "Spinoza in England," 191.
[38] Baxter, *Catholick Theologie*, title-page; Cooper, *John Owen, Richard Baxter*, 66.

In fact, Baxter believed even more passionately than Stillingfleet in God's "detestation of those that withdraw from the unity of his church." The difficulty was that the future bishop and the Puritan, once allies and now foes, violently disagreed as to what "unity" consisted in and what "peace" was, on where and how to draw the indispensable red line.[39] Who were the real "Separatists"? After Stillingfleet became Dean of St Paul's, in 1678, Latitudinarians and Baxterites openly clashed over this in the London parishes. A thoroughgoing "latitude man" Dean Stillingfleet may have been, but his unacceptable fringe included the Nonconformists with their insistence on separating themselves from the Church of England and maintaining their own congregations and services. By contrast, Baxterites located "the unity" of God's church not in any institutional arrangement but in core Christian doctrine, including the Trinity and infant baptism, and greatly resented Anglican claims that Puritans were "plotters, or cherishing principles of rebellion." Bitterly denouncing Stillingfleet's "desire of our silencing and not being tolerated," Baxter pronounced it absurd to denounce Nonconformists for separatism while making no effort to condemn and excommunicate "prophane swearers, cursers, drunkards, fornicators, haters of serious piety, Hobbists, infidels, atheists, Sadducees etc." swarming around the Anglican Church's fringes, the morass of immorality Puritans refused to tolerate, their strictures marking the true red line.[40]

Puritans since 1660, averred Baxter, had become wholly submissive to monarchical absolutism and Charles II's authority, and had no desire to plot or challenge monarchy. Spinoza by contrast (but not Hobbes) champions "democracy" and "universal toleration," a toleration fundamentally different, he insists, from that of Puritan moderates and Anglican Latitudinarians—an unrestricted freedom of thought Anglicans and Puritans agree is far worse than even intolerance. Since "Atheists" like Spinoza undermine not just morality and religion but monarchy and proper toleration too, those "greedily" crying up the views of Epicureans like Spinoza and Hobbes are decidedly "more worthy to be banished five miles from all cities and corporations than ourselves." Puritans should be tolerated; Spinozists and other "bruitists" (along with Quakers and Jesuits) should not. It is indeed remarkable that a leading Puritan publicist, writing in 1679, just two years after Spinoza's death, in the short preface explaining the intentions of his *Church-History* should highlight "Spinosa," insisting on his overriding importance for Britain and her colonies as well as generally, while doing so without even mentioning the miscreant's full name. Adding "Benedictus" was already superfluous in England by 1679, so quickly had the resonance of Spinoza's surname and

---

[39] Baxter, *The Quakers Catechism*, 2–3; Lamont, *Richard Baxter*, 20.
[40] Baxter, *Catholick Theologie*, 114, 118; Baxter, *Richard Baxter's Answer to Dr. Edward Stillingfleet's Charge*, 21, 58, 84; Shaw, *Miracles*, 136–7.

the code "B.d.S." spread on all sides despite the untiring efforts internationally to prevent this.

If Stillingfleet publicly pronounced on Spinoza chiefly in the late 1690s during his polemical exchanges with Locke, contending that Locke's "thinking matter," his notion that matter can be endowed with the power of thought is theologically dangerous and borders on Spinozism, clearly, like Baxter, he had been grappling with the challenge of Spinoza's Bible criticism and the *Ethics* for much longer, in fact since the 1670s, albeit in his case silently. Stillingfleet's personal library, preserved today in Dublin, features not only the *TTP* (1670), the *Opera Posthuma* (1677), and Spinoza's book on Descartes (1663) but several key texts relating to Spinoza's life and work, including his friend Meyer's *Philosophia* (1666) and Lambert van Velthuysen's *On natural religion, or against the* Tractatus Theologico-Politicus *and* Posthumous Works *of* Spinoza (Rotterdam, 1680). No doubt Stillingfleet spotted early on that the Spinoza had perfected what to him was a particularly obnoxious subversive technique. When quoting Spinoza's precise wording at one point in his late 1690s unfinished draft intended to rework and update his *Origenes sacrae* (1662) presenting what he saw as the "rational grounds of the Christian faith," Stillingfleet perceptively responds to a remark of Spinoza by objecting: "this one would think were spoken like a true Christian philosopher: but [Spinoza's] way is to use our expressions and to couch his own meaning under very plausible terms."[41]

Strikingly, Baxter, besides opening up the public debate over Spinoza more than others, avoided the harsher terms of scorn and condemnation contemporaries normally heaped on Spinoza's books. While already highlighting what he saw as Spinoza's now unique significance as a threat by the mid-1670s, he betrays an unmistakable hint of sympathy for certain aspects of his radicalism. However much he abhorred his "atheism," anti-Scripturalism, ethics, democratic republicanism, and full toleration, unlike the towering irenicist champion of the established church, Stillingfleet, Baxter was no less convinced than Spinoza that "superstition" and claims of present-day miracle-working remained a continuing defect afflicting everyone,[42] more pernicious even than the "dogmatical word-warriours." Over the centuries, he agreed further, churches and churchmen had indeed, just as Spinoza maintains, systematically falsified all history and especially church history, exploiting superstition, fanaticism, unreasoning fervour and ignorance to grab not just episcopal authority and undue wealth but political influence to which churchmen are in no way entitled. Baxter too favoured applying rigorous historical criticism to set the record straight and enable "princes and magistrates to see what hath corrupted and disturbed the churches in former times and what cause they have to keep the secular power from the clergy's

---

[41] Quoted in Hutton, "Edward Stillingfleet and Spinoza," 270.   [42] Shaw, *Miracles*, 61, 109.

hands." Here Baxter stood much closer to Spinoza than to Stillingfleet. In fact, a potent dose of unremittingly critical history, held Baxter, was exactly what was required to prove to "the ignorant, vulgar and unlearned zealous sort of Christians," that is practically everybody bar the Puritans, how lamentable "want of knowledge of church history" over the centuries has hopelessly misled and mired mankind in "many erreurs."[43] This was exactly Spinoza's view.

While abominating "the principles of Spinosa and such Bruitists against government and morality,"[44] and Spinoza's godless necessitarianism as distinct from the now undeniably narrower, lesser threats posed by Hobbes, Epicurus, Vanini, Gassendi, and Descartes, our Puritan divine also sensed something, however hard to admit it to himself, magnificently true buried deep in the heightened danger to Christianity, truth, and humanity Spinoza represented. During 1679, while writing his "Principles of Spinoza," and his *Church-History*, Baxter studied also the *Opera Posthuma* which enabled him to show readers that all components of Spinoza's system—the necessitarianism, political thought, un-Hobbesian natural law theory, metaphysics, ethics, and Bible criticism—fit together as a single uniquely menacing edifice and, no matter how much one loathes that whole, it is something magnificent. Grudgingly, he felt obliged to appreciate Spinoza's conception of Christian universalism. Nor could he deny that he too venerated such an ideal transcending all inter-confessional doctrinal polemics and schism to focus on the most essential core. Tellingly, he answered Stillingfleet's charge that the Puritans were "separatists," in 1680, by asking: "is our consent with the Universal Church [of Christ], or your singularity from it, liker to schism and separation?"[45]

Accordingly, Baxter the implacable foe of Quakers, "Separatists," Ranters, Jesuits, and bishops, found it hard not to acknowledge the uplifting significance of Spinoza's doctrine of "Christian" universalism detached from particular churches and from power-hungry ecclesiastics, his scorn for all theological schism and faction. "Spinoza," he notes, "taketh the knowledge of our union with universal nature (which he calleth God) to be man's perfection and his chief good, in comparison of which sensual pleasure, riches and honour are but troubles further than they are a meanes thereto." "That the churches of Christ are dolefully tempted and distracted by divisions, no man will deny that knoweth them."[46] A twinge of admiration showed through especially where he adds: "And if he [Spinoza] had better known God, as Creator and Governor and end of the material universe which he took to be God and had joined holy uniting joyful love to the universe [...] to God himself" and to this added belief in the

---

[43] Baxter, *Church-History*, "The Preface," 3–4; Marshall, *John Locke, Toleration*, 110, 113, 296, 303, 448.
[44] Baxter, "Principles of Spinosa," title-page; Sytsma, *Richard Baxter*, 261.
[45] Prince, *Shortest Way with Defoe*, 105; Colie, "Spinoza in England," 190.
[46] Baxter, *Church-History*, "The Preface"; Cooper, *John Owen, Richard Baxter*, 66.

"perpetuity of an immortal state, he had been happily in the right, which missing he became a seducer of himself and others," a truly remarkable insight from a Puritan.

Meanwhile, in France, awareness of the novelty, breadth, and gravity of the threat Spinoza represented among the intellectual elite began, as in England and Germany, in the early 1670s but gained momentum noticeably more slowly than in Holland, Germany, or Britain, partly due to the war of 1672–8 between France and the Dutch Republic and partly to the strictness of the French royal censorship. What trickle of awareness existed in the Paris of the mid-1670s emanated from the presence of Dutchmen and Germans informed about recent developments elsewhere, especially Leibniz, Huygens, and Tschirnhaus.

For some years, France remained slower to react to Spinoza than England, Germany, or the Republic. But this changed suddenly at the end of the war. In August 1678, the head of the Catholic Church in the Dutch Republic, the Vicar Apostolic Johannes Neercassel received word from the Abbé de Pontchâteau (1634–90), one of the Jansenist reformers in Paris best connected with French ministers and with the curia in Rome. Suddenly, Pontchâteau felt deeply alarmed by the challenge of Spinoza in a way he had not been even a few weeks earlier. Neercassel had dispatched a copy of the *Opera Posthuma* to Arnauld, the presiding Jansenist in Paris, the previous May and now "M. Arnauld has read the book of Spinosa," explained Pontchâteau, and says "it is one of the most malicious books in the world. He has shown it to [Bishop Bossuet] so that he should use his standing at court to prevent its dissemination in France."[47] Devoted to rendering Jansenism acceptable to Louis XIV and the Pope, this court ecclesiastic was only too ready to join the phalanx of the highly placed sworn to intensify repression of heresy and impiety.

The ensuing systematic suppression of Spinoza's works in France presented a formidable obstacle to the early spread of his ideas there. In October 1682, the learned Abbé Jean Gallois (1632–1707), a member of the Académie française in high standing at court, wrote, from Paris, to Christian Huygens, then in The Hague, about the extreme difficulty of learning anything at all about Spinoza in France. Five years before, in September 1677, Leibniz had written to his friend Gallois, from Germany, reporting Spinoza's death and Steno's arrival in Hanover, and inquiring, after describing Spinoza's philosophy as a mix of the strange and the penetrating, whether Gallois knew Steno's open letter to Spinoza, published in Florence in 1675.[48] For years Gallois had been hearing from abroad about this "Spinoza." A figure known internationally as a leading French *érudit*, by 1682,

---

[47] Pontchâteau to Neercassel, Paris, 5 Aug. 1678 in Neveu, *Sebastien Joseph du Cambout de Pontchâteau*, 447–8; there has been some confusion among scholars as to whether this letter refers to the *TTP* or *Opera Posthuma*, but see Spruit and Totaro, *Vatican Manuscript*, 22; Orcibal, "Jansénistes face à Spinoza," 85.

[48] Laerke, *Leibniz lecteur*, 107n6.

Gallois felt exasperated that circumstances obliged him to remain wholly ignorant of this universally menacing miscreant's books and philosophy. Unfortunately, he complained to Huygens, it was practically impossible to obtain copies of the *Opera Posthuma* or the *TTP* in Paris, as also of Richard Simon's recently published and banned work. Gallois requested Huygens as a particular favour to send him copies of both main works of Spinoza from Holland. "I shall try to send them as soon as I can," replied the renowned physicist, promising to try to smuggle them in via the Dutch ambassador to Paris or one of his entourage "for you know the prohibitions and careful searches being made at the frontiers regarding books, extending even to ransacking travelers' bags."[49] The ploy succeeded; Gallois received his copies.

Bayle too, around two years after settling in Holland, in 1681, complained of these searches for forbidden books at the French frontier, remarking that the hindrances were even worse if one tried to send prohibited Dutch texts to France by the sea-route because "no-one here wants to let them be brought onto their vessels through fear of seeing them confiscated together with all their cargoes."[50] Concerted efforts to stem Spinozism's dissemination continued. Yet, within a staggeringly short time, well under a decade, Spinoza moved from being almost completely unknown to being central on the French cultural scene, his role transformed beyond all recognition. The change amounted virtually to an intellectual revolution.

The speed and extent of this shift starting in 1678, was due less to publication of the *Opera Posthuma*, however, than the simultaneous, no less surreptitious and illegal, but outside France, soon decidedly fashionable 1678 French translation of the *TTP*. Neither the *Histoire critique du Vieux Testament* (1678) of Richard Simon which was quickly suppressed, on Bossuet's initiative, because it seemed to underwrite some of Spinoza's conclusions, despite its effort to rebut Spinoza's Bible criticism and bolster church authority by downplaying the status of Scriptural authority so as to reinforce papal and ecclesiastical authority instead, nor Huet's keenly expected *Demonstratio Evangelica* (1679) nor Bossuet's powerful declamations, served to stem the rising tide of libertinage and irreligion gaining momentum in France among the aristocracy and literary elite powerfully aided by Spinoza's sudden "invasion."

If Spinoza's penetration of Britain from the 1670s was, in the long run, more subversive than that of Hobbes earlier, at least in terms of cultural diffusion and formative effect on deism and the early Enlightenment, a still more potent factor shaping the broad historical phenomenon of Spinoza's unparalleled, astounding impact on the Western Enlightenment was the appearance, at the close of the Franco-Dutch War of 1672–8, of Spinoza's *TTP* in a highly competent

---

[49] Huygens to Gallois, The Hague, 19 Nov. 1682 in Huygens, *Oeuvres complètes* viii, 400–2; Vernière, *Spinoza et la pensée française*, 118–19.
[50] Bayle to Jacob Bayle, Rotterdam, 12 Apr. 1683 in Bayle, *Correspondance* iii, 333.

French version soon widely disseminated across Western Europe. This remarkable development, beginning in 1677–8, and its cultural and social consequences, could almost be deemed a kind of retaliatory Dutch invasion of France, a poetic vengeance for Louis XIV's invasion of the Republic, in 1672, an invasion of France more effective than the republican conspiracy which brought Spinoza's old Latin master, Franciscus van den Enden to the gallows, at the Bastille in 1674. Spinoza's retaliatory counter-invasion was an incursion no one had expected and that caused a much profounder, longer-lasting shock than Van den Enden's 1674 anti-monarchical conspiracy in Normandy.

If neither the excellent quality of the French translation of the *TTP* nor its Dutch publisher's success in disseminating the book widely[51] signifies much philosophically or affects how we construe Spinoza today, this pocket-sized duodecimo edition, easy to peruse in carriages and coffee-shops, and carry about unnoticed, exerted a massive impact on European culture and society in the immediate aftermath of Spinoza's death, between 1678 and the early eighteenth century, especially on higher culture and society outside scholarly circles, more so probably than any other edition presenting Spinoza's ideas. The fact that the translator rendering this book into elegant French happened to be a keen adherent of Spinoza, able to render his views accurately and effectively, but at the same time was a prominent anti-Louis XIV propagandist, helps to explain the stunning scale of Spinoza's generally explosive post-1678 French impact and his sudden posthumous assault on French absolutism.[52]

The 1678 French version of the *TTP*, then, became the principal channel by which Spinoza's thought penetrated beyond the restricted world of academe and Latin-reading theologians and philosophers to become a major resource, a *machine de guerre*, of Europe's aristocratic libertines, freethinkers, and boldly independent high society readers of whatever stripe, causing a shift of decisive cultural importance. However, this impact, if far-reaching, was far from being evenly balanced: it was definitely not Spinoza's democratic republicanism that attracted the libertine, freethinking constituency, nor indeed Spinoza's ethical counsel and guidance regarding how to live a good life. What drew a broad new following, massively pervading the early Enlightenment and colouring the diffusion of the underground Radical Enlightenment, was the attack on "superstition" and "priestcraft," Spinoza's comprehensive rejection of religious authority.[53]

Not many copies needed to seep through, experience proved, to generate a swiftly widening impact. "Spinoza," confirmed the Oratorian priest Michel Le Vassor (1648?–1718), in his major work *De la véritable religion* (Paris, 1688), had indeed now effectively displaced Vanini and Hobbes who had both by then receded into the background in France. Spinoza was now the uncontested prime

---

[51] Totaro, "Introduzione," p. xl, n57. [52] Francès, "Un gazetier français," 415–16, 419.
[53] Israel, *Radical Enlightenment*, 295–320; Lavaert, *Vrijheid, gelijkheid, veelheid*, 278–81.

"héros des athées [hero of the atheists]" even if one who on finding himself at death's door, as the sudden fad for speculating about Spinoza's death-bed scene had it, through fear of betraying "his principles did not dare endure the presence of a church minister." There were now in France, unfortunately, a "great number of persons who make profession of following the opinions of "Spinosa" and "have studied his principles."[54] In the escalating war between Christianity and libertine unbelief, admonished Le Vassor, everything depends on crushing the grave and growing threat posed to French society by Spinoza whom he dubbed "the greatest atheist ever known [le plus grand athée que l'on ait jamais vű]."[55]

Le Vassor did not think much of Spinoza's philosophical system; but it was Spinoza's Bible criticism, not his metaphysics, that shook France so powerfully in the late 1670s, the miscreant's chief ally being the irresistible fascination of his denial of miracles and the divine inspiration of Holy Writ to impious minds. Part of the danger was the obvious attraction Spinoza's critical methodology exerted also on certain allegedly misguided ecclesiastics, like Richard Simon, professing to be fighting the menace by investigating further the exegetical issues La Peyrère, Hobbes, and Spinoza had raised. The way to defeat Spinoza and rescue the innumerable unsteady minds sucked into his orbit was by more effectively reconciling religion and science, faith and reason than had been done thus far, showing the world the reality of the Creator God by demonstrating what deep down everyone already knows: that the laws and workings of nature cannot be the mere "effect of change or of a blind nature [l'effet du hazard ni d'une nature aveugle]," while insisting more than ever on the unquestionable overriding authority of Jesus Christ and church tradition.[56]

By 1680, Arnauld, Bossuet, Simon, Huet, Justel, Le Vassor, Gallois, Lamy, Bayle, Malebranche, Fénelon, all of France's principal intellectual lights identified Spinoza and his ideas as a vast intellectual challenge confronting France, something qualitatively very different from anything seen previously. Virtually all leading expert contemporary opinion in France, as in Holland, Germany, and Rome, judged that Spinoza, despite certain common affinities, delivers a quite different message from Hobbes, one that from the perspective of late seventeenth-century governments, universities, and churches, and not least philosophers, as one commentator expressed the point in Latin, in 1707, was incontestably "deterior, et magis impius [worse and more impious]," and hence a graver challenge.[57]

At the same time French intellectual strategies for countering Spinoza failed to gather momentum. Countering Spinoza was indeed now high priority the

---

[54] Le Vassor, *De la véritable religion*, 4.
[55] *Histoire des Ouvrages des Savants* vi (March–August 1689), 82; Clair, "Spinoza à travers les journaux," 208; Israel, *Radical Enlightenment*, 450.
[56] Le Vassor, *De La Véritable religion*, 10–14; Vernière, *Spinoza et la pensée française*, 156–7; Clair, "Spinoza à travers les journaux," 215–16.
[57] Spruit and Totaro, *Vatican Manuscript*, 73.

quarrelsome but well-connected Benedictine, Dom François Lamy (1636–1711), a leading expert on Cartesianism and someone much resenting the Sorbonne's anti-Cartesians, concurred with Bossuet, Arnauld, Simon, and Le Vassor. By the mid-1680s Lamy had produced an extended refutation which he presented to Malebranche, Bossuet, and others for their support and endorsement but which they hesitated to endorse and he long hesitated to publish. Like all the leading lights, he was outraged by Spinoza's philosophy and counted it the chief intellectual challenge facing France. But it was no use simply rebutting Spinoza's "errors," he agreed, "because his power did not at all consist in the arguments with which he supports each error," bur rather in the connections with which he "closely binds his errors together with a few principles that seem incontestable."[58] No refutation of Spinoza could prove effective unless it attacks the devious but artful interconnectedness of his system as a whole. Unlike Le Vassor but like Bossuet and Baxter, Lamy also accounted Spinozism a political danger. It was not just his Bible criticism but also its links to Spinoza's philosophy and political thought, Lamy believed, that were attracting eager followers. However one ranked Spinoza's "principles," by the early 1680s, measured as a threat to the French church and state, Spinoza's challenge incontestably, he thought, eclipsed every other since Calvin's time.

If the appeal to impertinent, fashionable types of the French translation of the *TTP* was a problem, Lamy chiefly wrestled with what he considered ultimately the principal threat, the *Opera Posthuma*.[59] But refutations of Spinoza's basic ideas that were inadequate struck him, much as they struck Leibniz and Justel, as far worse than not replying at all. After starting his *Le nouvel athéisme renversé, ou Refutation du sistême de Spinosa* [The new Atheism overthrown, or Refutation of the System of Spinoza], in 1683, and having taken four years to complete his draft, Lamy hesitated to publish it and, after consulting widely between 1683 and 1687 still held back, vacillating owing to the difficulty of the enterprise but also due to receiving contradictory advice, some colleagues urging publication in Latin for a scholarly audience, others, mindful of the *TTP* seeping through in French, recommending something accessible, in the vernacular. Each strategy involved disadvantages. Finally, he decided against Latin which would be like "throwing pearls to the pigs" [the doctors of the Sorbonne]. To perfect his targeting and maximize his clout he went over and over his text, spending in all thirteen years refining and polishing, only finally publishing it, in 1696.[60]

Holding back so long was a grave disadvantage, admitted Lamy, but this foe reducing God to the status of a "machine" or at best an "animal" was formidable

---

[58] Lamy to Jean Mabillon, 23 Oct. 1689 in Zaccone Sina, *Corrispondenza di François Lamy*, 62–3.
[59] Vernière, *Spinoza et la pensée française*, 242–5; Kors, *Naturalism and Unbelief*, 86–91.
[60] Lamy, *Le nouvel athéisme renversé*, avertissement 1; Lamy, *Corrispondenza*, pp. xlvi, 67n, 370–1; Albiac, *Sinagoga vacía*, 214–17.

and difficult to combat effectively, and getting his refutation right made such long delay unavoidable. Such massive delay was particularly regrettable, he agreed with other observers, because "the number of Spinoza's *sectateurs* was continuing to grow by the day;" Spinoza's "errors," it was now clear, were turning "the minds of many young people,"[61] and this despite all the effort expended over the years on demolishing Spinoza's system "in the Netherlands as in France, Britain and Germany." In fact, this unparalleled menace was still growing in 1707, commented the Leipzig Lutheran theologian, Gottlob Friedrich Jenichen (1680–1735), despite the fact that Spinoza had now been comprehensively "refuted" "by Bredenburg, Van Blijenbergh, Van Mansfelt, Van Velthuysen, Van Til, Wittichius, Jaquelot, Jens, [Henry] More, De la Motte, Musaeus, Rappolt, Huet, Le Vassor, Lamy, Yvon, Poiret, Bayle and others."[62] This seemed a formidable list to set against society's sobering predicament, and yet Jenichen still managed to omit from his stunning list a no less hefty proportion of major refutations specifically targeting Spinoza written since the 1670s including Steno, Baxter, Howe, Wilson, Batelier, Kuyper, Simon, Le Clerc, Orobio de Castro, Clarke, Anne Conway and Jacob Thomasius. By the beginning of the eighteenth century, the pan-European controversy over Spinoza was colossal but seemed to be doing little to counter his creeping penetration.

---

[61] Lamy, *Le nouvel athéisme renversé*, avertissement, 4–5; Hutton, "Edward Stillingfleet and Spinoza," 262–3, 274; Kors, *Naturalism and Unbelief*, 86, 88–90.

[62] Jenichen, *Historia Spinozismi Leehofiani*, 329; Immanuel Weber, in 1696, lists the principal refutations of Spinoza as those of "Henry More, Mansveld, Velthuysen, Blijenbergh, Pierre Poiret, Abbadie, Wittichius, and Pierre Yvon," see Weber, *Beurtheilung*, 140–1.

PART II
THE YOUNG SPINOZA

3
Youthful Rebel

3.i Caution and Audacity

Spinoza's life was one of resolute audacity tempered by his personal motto: "caute [caution]." His life-story was one of rebellion, apostasy, and proposed reforms culminated in the 1670s and continuing until his dying day. Hence a key question is when did his extraordinary career as declared adversary of practically everything commonly thought and believed commence? One might suppose this project of what France's then leading science impresario, Thévenot, called this "fanatic" would-be reformer of men's errors, commenced with his dramatic expulsion from the Jewish community for defying rabbinic authority, in July 1656. But even a cursory glance at the circumstances of that event, shows that cannot have really marked the commencement of his life of studied, planned revolt.

Born on 24 November 1632 in Amsterdam, and, as far as we know, given a normal Sephardic Jewish upbringing, celebrating his *bar mitzvah* in November 1645, the young Spinoza presumably continued studying in the community's school, in the usual fashion, under the supervision of the Amsterdam Sephardic community's rabbis, at any rate until his fourteenth or fifteenth year, until around 1646 or 1647. This means that as a teenager he was primarily familiar with texts in Spanish and Hebrew, and with everyday conversation in Portuguese. His formal education within the Sephardic congregation would not have ceased until 1645 at the earliest. Later reports that the young Spinoza studied to become a rabbi which would have entailed graduating to the higher classes of the community school, seemingly have no basis in fact as the names of these students were recorded and his does not figure on the lists. Over the next several years, from around 1644–5, while obliged, no doubt, to work part of his time in his father's far-ranging business, he obviously continued pursuing knowledge but now as a freelance, independent-minded, inquiring youth, reading and studying on his own, something he was accustomed to do throughout the rest of his life. From contemporary testimony, we know that he attended evening gatherings and adult education discussion classes, a component central to the Amsterdam Sephardic community culture at the time, being a community composed largely of newcomers to formal Judaism (and the Low Countries) arriving from Iberian lands. Debate in these evening gatherings centred on issues of Torah and rabbinic law presided over by the rabbis who were also the community's head teachers. All the earliest sources for Spinoza's life, including comments of his own, agree that his chosen initial sphere of study over many years was the Hebrew language, Bible, and rabbinic law.

Since all four Sephardic rabbis he encountered at the community school *Ets Haim* [Tree of Life] and at evening discussion meetings such as in the *yeshivah* (community college) "Keter Torah," founded by Rabbi Saul Levi Mortera (*c.*1596–1660), in the early 1640s,[1] spent most of their working lives within the Amsterdam community, these personages had the greatest impact on Spinoza's education, reading, and intellectual formation throughout his childhood and early teenage years. He would have been personally fairly familiar with all four, except perhaps Rabbi Isaac Aboab da Fonseca (1605–93) who left Amsterdam in 1641 when Spinoza was nine, to head the first Jewish community in the New World, the congregation *Zur Israel* [Rock of Israel], in Pernambuco, chief town of the then Dutch colony of northern Brazil. But even Aboab da Fonseca returned to Amsterdam, resuming his former role, following the collapse of the Dutch colony in Brazil, in 1654, so Spinoza possibly knew him fairly well too.[2]

Of the three rabbis most familiar to him, David Pardo (*c.*1591–1657), second in seniority, was less involved in teaching and community affairs than the other two and is almost never mentioned in connection with Spinoza's life, though his son Josiah Pardo, much later played an interesting role in the lives of Spinoza's sister, Rebecca, and his nephews, after they emigrated to the Caribbean. The remaining two rabbis were the stern senior figure, Levi Mortera, whose sermons to the congregation have in considerable part survived, and the famed Menasseh ben Israel (1604–57), known to history for his role in the re-admission of the Jews to England in the mid-1650s, just before Spinoza's expulsion from the community. Mortera had many contacts with Spinoza's father ever since the latter joined the community in the early 1620s and was well-known to all members of the Spinoza family. Menasseh, whose Portuguese name was Manoel Dias Soeiro, was a many-sided figure, an eloquent orator with some distinctly mystical and messianic leanings which clashed with Moreira's more legalist, dogmatic, and rigid attitudes.

Besides being a rabbi, Menasseh was the first major Jewish printer and publisher of Hebrew books in north-west Europe and it was he who freed Dutch Jewry from its early dependence on comparatively expensive ritual, legal, and other Hebrew-language books imported from Venice and Basle. Menasseh was also fond of illustrations, and presumably used these in his teaching; by the time Spinoza reached the higher grades at his community school, Menasseh had been familiar with Rembrandt over many years. Rembrandt is thought to have first consulted Menasseh about to how to inscribe the Hebrew letters and spell the

[1] Révah, *Spinoza et Juan de Prado*, 27; Méchoulan, "Regard sur la pensée juive," 56.
[2] Salomon, "La vraie excommunication," 192n38.

Aramaic words, in connection with the "writing on the wall" in his famous painting of Belshazzar's Feast (1635). Rembrandt's well-known portrait of Menasseh was etched in 1636 when Spinoza was four; he was a grown man by 1655 when Rembrandt provided four engravings for Menasseh's book *Piedra gloriosa* (1655) about Nebuchadnesar, one of which dramatically depicts a resolute little David intrepidly confronting a towering, gigantic Goliath.[3]

Among Menasseh's most memorable public moments was the address he delivered in the synagogue on the occasion of the famous visit of Queen Henrietta Maria of England (1609–69), accompanied by the Prince of Orange, Frederik Hendrik (Stadholder: 1625–47), the Dutch head of state, on the eve of the English Civil War, on 22 May 1642, when Spinoza was ten. The entire Sephardic community must have been electrified by this occasion since nothing like it had occurred previously in the community's history. If an event of this magnitude was previously unheard of among the Amsterdam Sephardim, lesser visits by touring foreign notables, by this date, were becoming increasingly fashionable, and the community's *parnasim* (elders) and principal merchants were becoming aware of the advantage to themselves of impressing and encouraging the curiosity of prominent visitors. As in Venice and Hamburg, the elite of the Amsterdam Sephardic congregation, unlike noblemen of the day, and the wealthiest Christian merchants, needed to avoid attracting hostile attention through outward display of opulence in lifestyle and attire which led to their seeking other outlets for their wealth. The Amsterdam Sephardic elite, dispensing (until later in the century at least) with palatial exteriors for their houses, fine carriages, town gardens, splendid outfits and the like, compensated via a distinctive inward-oriented opulence, conspicuous inside their homes and within the synagogue.

Menasseh was chosen by the *parnasim* to deliver the main address on that, for the synagogue, splendid occasion, doubtless due to his eloquence and his being better known to the world outside Judaism than the austere, inward-looking Mortera.[4] Spinoza may well have admired Menasseh's enterprising, outgoing attitude and ability to engage with all kinds. In any case, the respect Menasseh gained among the fringe Protestant groups in Amsterdam for his obvious interest in inter-communal discussions and willingness to debate with Christians on whatever issue of Scripture, is likely to have appealed to Spinoza who, given his subsequent attitudes, may well have become, well before his father died in 1654, likewise involved in such outgoing discussion. The choice of Menasseh for such an honour, in 1642, may have further stoked the already smouldering tension between Menasseh and Mortera but undoubtedly enhanced this great moment for the community. With the English queen looking on, Menasseh seized the opportunity to extol the great achievements of the Dutch Revolt against Spain,

---

[3] Schwartz, *Rembrandt, his Life*, 175–6, 305; Nadler, *Spinoza: A Life*, 89.
[4] Nadler, *Menasseh ben Israel*, 109–10; Nadler, *Spinoza: A Life*, 64, 87.

comparing the feats of Frederik Hendrik's older brother and predecessor as Stadholder, Prince Maurits (Stadholder: 1585–1625), to those of Judas Maccabeus (d. *c*.160 BCE), the greatest of the Maccabees in the struggle of the Jews against the oppression of the Seleucids while paying fulsome compliments also to the formidable Frederik Hendrik. "We no longer consider Castile or Portugal our fatherland," he intoned, "but Holland. We do not think of the Spanish or Portuguese kings as our lords, but the States of Holland together with you [the Dutch Stadholder]."[5]

The Ets Haim community school where Spinoza studied was without doubt among the best, and best furnished, in the Jewish world at that time, possessing a library and collection of manuscripts founded in 1616 which is today the oldest major Jewish library still intact surviving anywhere in the world. The young Spinoza had abundant scope for engrossing himself in study in Spanish, Portuguese, and Hebrew. It is certain, moreover, that until late 1655 when he was twenty-three, a year and a half after his father's passing away, he remained a regular member of the synagogue, participating in community life, after his father's death in March 1654, paying his dues as head of his household and showing no outward sign of rebelling against or defying the community, or rabbinic authority in any fashion serious enough to be reported by the rabbis or community elders who were constantly disciplining community members for misconduct of whatever sort. This is a fundamental point. Because so much of the concrete evidence about Spinoza's life dates from after his departure from Amsterdam, in 1661, by which time he was nearly thirty, it is all too easy to forget that Spinoza spent well over half his earthly life unremarkably, attending synagogue regularly, reciting prayers in Hebrew and appearing to all the world an observant Jew.

As a youth, Spinoza grew familiar with Menasseh's best-known book, his *El Conciliador* (3 vols., 1632–51), the first part of which appeared in the year Spinoza was born, 1632, but to which extensive follow-up sections were added over many years. This remained for many decades, and not only within the Jewish community, a famous guide devoted to reconciling and harmonizing seeming discrepancies and difficulties in the Old Testament text, an issue that remained a life-long preoccupation of Spinoza. But as Spinoza approached maturity, Menasseh's beguilingly smooth, systematic resolution of all difficulties in the Hebrew he came to view more as a sleight of hand than genuine, satisfactory exegesis. Spinoza later made cutting allusions to Menasseh's *Conciliador* in Chapter X of his main work of Bible criticism, the *Tractatus Theologico-Politicus* (1670), after restating his central conclusion that all the evidence proves "Scripture is sacred only in so far as we understand through it the [essential] things signified there, but

---

[5] Quoted in Nadler, *Menasseh ben Israel*, 110.

not as regards the words, language and forms of discourse in which those things are expressed." What studying the Scriptural text actually proves, concludes Spinoza, to the intense indignation of most, is that "all books expounding and teaching the highest things are, no matter what language they are written in, or by whom, equally sacred, that is the Scriptures are no more holy or sacred than any other book of moral instruction." Spinoza then adds, a few passages further on, "as for considering it devout to adapt some passages of Scripture to fit others [for which Menasseh was renowned], this is nothing but a ridiculous notion of piety. For [these conciliators] alter clear passages to fit obscure ones, and correct others to fit mistaken ones, using corrupt sections to pervert sound passages. However, I would not wish to label them blasphemous, since they have no intention to speak evil, and to err is indeed human."[6]

Saul Levi Mortera and Menasseh ben Israel, then, were the two scholars looming largest in Spinoza's early intellectual formation. Of these, Mortera was decidedly the senior of the two and had a much higher salary than the other, at 600 guilders yearly. Ever since the union of Amsterdam's early seventeenth-century three house synagogues into one united congregation, in 1639, with Levi Mortera appointed the congregation's chief rabbi, Menasseh found himself in a subordinate position which he clearly resented.

These two, though long-term colleagues, were far from being on amicable terms, and feuded bitterly from at least the early 1640s onwards,[7] and still did in 1653–4 when Spinoza emerged as head of the Espinoza family firm. The two disagreed over many issues of Torah interpretation, not least Levi Mortera's fierce anti-Christian polemical stance. Menasseh preferred to present himself not as a public enemy of Christianity but rather a bridging figure known for promoting friendly Jewish–Christian dialogue, a role more appreciated among the Amsterdam Christian dissenting congregations, especially the Collegiants with whom he regularly held discussions, than among his own community. Mortera's and Menasseh's wrangling reached such a pitch, that the community's governing board, the *Mahamad*, or council of elders, on several occasions officially intervened to restrain their bickering. Recording their deliberations about the Mortera–Menasseh quarrelling in the book of the community elders' resolutions, the *parnasim* were continually anxious to prevent their clashes and unflattering allusions to each other in their sermons from becoming a source of open discord and communal disturbance. Above all the *Mahamad* strove to prevent their feuding becoming a major public scandal within the Jewish world.

The community elders several times took disciplinary measures, culminating in early 1654, just as Spinoza became the head of his family household following his

---

[6] Spinoza, *Theological-Political Treatise*, 151–2; Salomon, "Introdução," lxxiv; Proietti, "Spinoza et le 'Conciliador'," 49, 51–4.
[7] Salomon, "Introdução," xcii; Nadler, *Menasseh ben Israel*, 108–9.

father's death when they issued stern admonitions (in Portuguese) ordering the rabbis to desist from discussing disputed issues before the community under pain of dismissal from their posts.[8] As his father had long been a prominent figure in the Amsterdam community, Spinoza knew both rabbis fairly well personally, as well as from their teaching and sermons. This whole business was very much his first lesson, outside his own family, in the play of power, strategy, and emotion lurking behind religious doctrinal disputes preoccupying rival religious leaders, and the politically and socially divisive consequences of such rifts. During the years of his childhood and youth, moreover, his native city brimmed with rival warring churches and sects along with loudly self-promoting religious fringe movements to a greater degree than any other major city in all Europe. The chief feature of institutionalized religion, a youth growing up in Amsterdam in Spinoza's day might all too readily conclude, is bitter rivalry, division, ceaseless wrangling, and hatred.

With regard to outward conduct as a synagogue-goer, Spinoza remained, as far as most members of the congregation could tell, a faithful, loyal member of the community until late in 1655. The abrupt lapsing of his synagogue dues that autumn, considered in detail further on, points to a decisive break in his life at that point resulting, to all outward appearances, from a very sudden open rupture with the community.[9] It is important, though, to be wary of assuming this abrupt change of direction reflected the recent impact on him of a particular individual, as has been argued by several experts on Spinoza's life, most notably I. S. Révah,[10] here following the lead of Gebhardt and Dujovne, and also José Faur. These eminent scholars all assumed some fundamental change in Spinoza's outlook at this relatively late juncture, the autumn of 1655, to explain this sudden outward rupture and what followed, attributing the change in Spinoza's supposedly hitherto conventional, regular Jewish life to the arrival and disruptive influence of a dissident Portuguese crypto-Jew fleeing Spain, the physician Dr Juan (alias Daniel) de Prado (1612–72), with whom the young Spinoza associated during the mid- and later 1650s. During his earlier career in Spain, De Prado had been a committed crypto-Jew but later evolved into an anti-rabbinic "deist." Disagreeing with this explanation, other scholars have conjectured that the supposed sudden break was due rather to Spinoza's coming under the influence of the locally notorious, reputedly atheist but outwardly Catholic schoolmaster, Franciscus van den Enden (1602–74), with whom Spinoza also associated at that time, a thesis already aired by several writers on Spinoza in his own time and in the eighteenth century.[11]

---

[8] Salomon, "Introdução," xcii; Nadler, *Menasseh ben Israel*, 161–3.

[9] Vlessing, "Excommunication of Baruch Spinoza" (1997), 15.

[10] Révah, "Aux origines de la rupture," 367–8; Révah, *Spinoza et Juan de Prado*, 27; Méchoulan, "Herem à Amsterdam," 126, 129; Kaplan, *From Christianity to Judaism*, 131.

[11] Diez, *Benedikt von Spinoza*, 5; Israel, "Popularizing Radical Ideas," 283.

In the summer of 1656, Spinoza and De Prado were both investigated and severely disciplined by the rabbis and *parnasim*. Both were threatened with the community ban [*herem*] by the elders, at the prompting of the rabbis, in particular Mortera.[12] De Prado, though, despite being formally reprimanded first and provisionally banned shortly before the decree condemning and expelling Spinoza (in July 1656), was not definitively expelled from the community by *parnasim* and rabbis until some months after Spinoza. Repenting and submitting to communal authority, De Prado was made to mount the *theba*, the rostrum, or reading platform at the centre of the synagogue, and read out a text of submission expressing profound contrition for "having had bad opinions and shown little zeal in the service of God."[13]

Gebhardt, Dujovne, and Révah all believed the much older, more experienced Sephardic dissident and deist with an impressive academic background, who had held clandestine discussions about religion for decades in Andalusia while growing increasingly critical of Judaism as well as Christianity, was the decisive spur and instigator behind Spinoza's much noticed sudden rebellion against rabbinic authority during late 1655 and 1656. But assigning decisive significance to De Prado's arrival on the scene means assuming an abrupt change in Spinoza's ideas and goals well over half way through his life just months, or at most a year before his own expulsion from the community. This hardly seems plausible in the light of what we know of his character, in no way given to dramatic shifts or sudden impulse but rather inclined to cool detachment and bold thinking usually but not always cautiously masked.

During the weeks preceding the *Mahamad*'s resolution on whether to expel Spinoza and what kind of *herem* to impose, they collected testimony substantiating the allegations then circulating of Spinoza's "bad opinions" and his openly violating the Mosaic Law. Although in his case these testimonies are unfortunately now lost, such sworn testimony was undoubtedly collected by the rabbis and *parnasim* at the time, just as occurred in the cases of Uriel da Costa and De Prado where much of this material does survive, providing some indication of how the proceedings would have gone. By late 1655 De Prado was proving defiant and difficult in the *yeshivah* and among the community's youth, being reported for subverting students with his sceptical notions and disparaging the existing Hebrew text (of which De Prado himself knew almost nothing). In particular, he reportedly held that the Old Testament Hebrew as it stands is confused and hopelessly defective, while insisting on the need for Latin erudition to keep abreast of the latest Bible criticism (points that sound suspiciously like borrowings from Spinoza).

---

[12] Kaplan, "Intellectual Ferment," 306–7.
[13] Dujovne, *Spinoza* i, 92, for a Spanish translation; for the Portuguese text see appendix 1 in Révah, *Spinoza et Juan de Prado*, 57.

"On a Monday evening, before the class started while he was talking to me," reported a student called Jacob Monsanto (among those testifying against De Prado, early in 1658, following Spinoza's expulsion) to Rabbi Mortera, De Prado asked, among other things: "what reason do we have to believe in Moses' Law any more than the teachings of other sects? If one lends greater credit to Moses than Mahomet, there must be a justifying reason, otherwise all is just a chimaera." De Prado also expressed scepticism about whether there is any divine reward or punishment in the hereafter, claiming the "world had not been created but had always existed in the same way," a view we know from the 1658 Inquisition testimony he and Spinoza at that time happened to share.[14] Since De Prado knew practically no Hebrew, one must ask whence De Prado derived his notion that the Hebrew text of the Torah is a bundle of man-made confusion? Since it seems Spinoza too by this point claimed the Old Testament text is corrupted, there is no one likelier than Spinoza to have inserted into the older man's mind during their discussions the idea that the Mosaic Five Books have not come down to us in remotely pure form.

De Prado was never shy about (secretly) propagating his deistic and anti-Scriptural ideas to others, either in Spain earlier or, during 1655–6, in Amsterdam. In a passage of the *Epístola invectiva*, a polemical text written against De Prado later by the Amsterdam Sephardic physician and polemicist Isaac Orobio de Castro (1617–87), the latter refers to a young Jewish student in Amsterdam reportedly decisively misled by De Prado's deistic ideas who went on to suffer unfortunate consequences. A learned man but largely ignorant of formal Judaism whom Orobio had known over many years when he too lived as a crypto-Jew defying the Inquisition in Spain, De Prado, he recorded, deserved firm disciplining not least "because one [of those studying with him] with *grandísimo escandalo* [the greatest scandal] among our nation arrived at his extreme ruin due to this [deistic] tendency, and [De Prado also] infected others who, outside Judaism, had given heed to him and his stupid sophistries."[15] Understandably, several scholars jumped to the conclusion that the young student Orobio refers to here was Spinoza. But in retrospect this inference has come to seem rather doubtful. During 1655–6, De Prado and Spinoza were not the only ones fomenting rebellion against the rabbis in Amsterdam, and De Prado, we know, did win over to his dissident views several other students and newcomers to formal Judaism. Orobio's remark probably refers to some beginner studying Judaism, quite likely that most fascinating dissident, Daniel Ribera, a former Christian monk of non-Jewish extraction, a Catalan who had acted treasonably against the Spanish crown

---

[14] Révah, *Spinoza et Juan de Prado*, 27–8; Yovel, *Spinoza and Other Heretics*, 72; Muchnik, *Une Vie Marrane*, 429–31, 466.

[15] Gebhardt, "Juan de Prado," 279; Dujovne, *Spinoza* i, 96; although the reasoning here is not fully convincing and (eventually) Révah came to reject this interpretation, as Kaplan has, see Kaplan, *From Christianity to Judaism*, 151.

in support of the Portuguese secession of 1640 and lived many years in Brazil; Ribera later converted to Judaism and joined the Amsterdam community where, alongside De Prado, he became an adjunct teacher of Latin and other lay subjects before, in 1655, embracing De Prado's "deism" and rejecting immortality of the soul.[16]

The thesis that Spinoza was lured from Jewish orthodoxy by De Prado becomes still more unlikely when we consider Spinoza's sole surviving autobiographical passage at the start of his first extant text, his treatise on the *Emendation of the Intellect* composed in Amsterdam shortly after his expulsion. Thanks to Mignini's and Van den Ven's research, Spinoza, it is now accepted, composed this, his earliest surviving work, the *Tractatus de Intellectus Emdendatione* [*TIE*] (probably including the relevant remarkable autobiographical passage), no later than 1659, and probably several years earlier.[17] At considerable length and with striking eloquence Spinoza here dwells on the protracted, very arduous inner struggle that prepared the way for his launching out on his philosophical quest, emphasizing that his inner doubts and uncertainty about how to direct his future life dragged on over a prolonged period of time. This autobiographical passage at the start of the *TEI* which, if we accept Van de Ven's revised chronology, may well date from 1656 or early 1657,[18] accords with all the early accounts of Spinoza's life which means Spinoza's modern biographer should set aside all suggestion of any sudden break. While Spinoza's more dramatic second stage of revolt certainly commenced only in late 1655, a vital earlier stage of rebellion against rabbinic authority (as I myself have long argued),[19] though not yet against outward Jewish observance and regular synagogue attendance, commenced long before, probably even before leaving school as a fourteen- or fifteen-year-old.

"After experience had taught me that all things that regularly occur in everyday life are empty and futile," Spinoza recalls in this passage, echoing Seneca's sentiments in his *Letters to Lucilius*, about the difficulty of a philosopher's life, "and I realized that all things which were the cause or object of my fear had nothing which is intrinsically good or bad in them, except insofar as the mind is moved by them, I decided at last to try to discover whether there is anything that is the true good, discernible as such in itself and by which alone the mind is affected when everything else is stripped away."[20] Later in life, Spinoza expressly

---

[16] Kaplan, *From Christianity to Judaism*, 282; Muchnik, *Une Vie Marrane*, 418, 432–42.
[17] Mignini, "Nuovi contribute per la datazione," 515–25; Israel, "Philosophy, Commerce," 125–6; see also Nadler, *Spinoza: A Life*, 207n64.
[18] Mignini, Steenbakkers and Van de Ven all agree that the TEI was a work of the late 1650s begun perhaps as early as 1656, see Steenbakkers, "Spinoza's Life," 28–9.
[19] First proposed in lectures at UCLA in Los Angeles in 1995, and in debate with Richard Popkin (1923–2005); the argument first appeared in my 2002 essay on Spinoza's expulsion from the Amsterdam community, see, Israel, "Philosophy, Commerce."
[20] Spinoza, *Opera* ii, 5; Spinoza, *Collected Works* (ed. Curley) i, 7; De Dijn, *Spinoza: The Way*, 181–9; Klever, *Spinoza Classicus*, 22; Nadler, *Think Least of Death*, 8–9.

acknowledged that when young, and understanding things only in a more partial and fragmentary way, he had been too ready to reject contemptuously that part of himself drawn to honours and wealth and "not in keeping with a philosophical attitude of mind," the things that formerly seemed "to me *vana, inordinata, absurda* [vain, disordered and absurd]."[21] For his early resolve to pursue the "highest good" disregarding all else proved far easier to embrace as an ideal than accomplish in reality. This most decisive resolution of his career Spinoza then confesses cost him much painstaking effort that reached resolution only after a prolonged period of vacillation and doubt.

"I say 'decided at length' because, it seemed inadvisable initially, to want to discard something certain for something uncertain." He

> could see, of course, the advantages acquired through honour and wealth [of the kind his father had built up] from which I would be excluding myself should I devote myself seriously to something different and new and saw that if the highest happiness does lie in those things, I should then have to do without them. But if it does not, and I devoted myself to them, then again I would fail to attain the highest happiness. So I used to ponder whether it might be possible to achieve my new way of life, or at least certainty about it, without changing the outward order and form of my everyday existence. Often I attempted to do so but always in vain.[22]

Clearly, Spinoza's "highest good" in the 1650s was very much a personal exploration and not yet his quest for the "common good" of the later 1660s which was as much a political and social as individual preoccupation. Originally, his restless quest was essentially for individual personal salvation. The undoubted echoing of the Stoic philosopher Seneca here is often taken as grounds for dismissing this lengthy, unusually personal-sounding passage as something purely rhetorical, something essentially marginal to Spinoza's biography, being reminiscent of Augustine's *Confessions* and Descartes' *Meditations* encased in Cicero and Seneca.[23] But that is hardly plausible. Accepting the thesis that this passage amounts to nothing more than autobiographically irrelevant Seneca-style rhetoric, as tend to do those defending the Révah (and Popkin) thesis of a sudden change in Spinoza's outlook only shortly before the 1656 drama, means directly contradicting Spinoza's claim that "often I attempted to do so

---

[21] Spinoza, *Opera* iv, 166; Spinoza, *Correspondance* (ed. Rovere), 202; Moreau, *Spinoza, L'expérience*, 219.

[22] Spinoza, *Opera* ii, 5; Spinoza, *Collected Works* (ed. Curley), i, 7; Israel, "Philosophy, Commerce," 126; Jaquet, *Spinoza à l'oeuvre*, 70.

[23] Israel "Philosophy, Commerce," 125–9; Carlisle, *Spinoza's Religion*, 22; for the argument against viewing the passage as autobiographical which I reject as unconvincing, see Moreau, *Spinoza, L'expérience*, 45–50, 136–50.

[break away from the established pattern of my life] but always in vain," a conclusion which scarcely seems justified. No matter how captivated Spinoza was, in the late 1650s, with Latin studies, and drawn to Seneca especially—and his taste for Seneca does represent a notable feature of his biography—rhetorical effect directly contrary to the actual facts remained always completely alien to Spinoza's deeply earnest nature. What he actually says, moreover, correlates far better with other facts than the alternative: Spinoza's undeniable competence as a sophisticated philosopher by 1657–9 at the latest, hardly fits with the supposition that his break-away and philosophical odyssey commenced only in 1655–6. The only convincing conclusion is that his rebellion began long before 1655.

Spinoza's unwavering goal was to get at the truth of things, seeking the truth not least about himself. Giving up the enviable status his father enjoyed in the community did indeed entail surrendering a great deal, at any rate prior to 1655. Spinoza's father had been ailing and bed-ridden for some time before he died and needed a lot of assistance during the early 1650s. Spinoza's older brother, Isaac, meanwhile, had died in 1649, leaving Spinoza, now the oldest son, clearly earmarked for the role of head of the family. There was no one else in line to take charge other than a younger brother, Gabriel. Furthermore, Spinoza's older brother, Isaac, died at a point where the family firm stood at the peak of its prosperity, so there was certainly much at stake. Spinoza himself and all around him must have assumed he would take over the running of the business and responsibility for family affairs, just as he in fact did, when his father passed away in 1654. From 1649 onwards, with a sick father, ailing stepmother, sisters, infant nephews, and a younger brother to take care of, the young man Spinoza had numerous practical challenges and complexities to face.

Overseeing a wide-ranging business and affluent household alongside pursuing serious study existed as a theoretical option for several years before and after his father's death, but only as long as the family firm of which he was formally head during the years 1654–6 remained viable permitting him to follow his father as a successful merchant and prestigious member of the community. As a prominent heir of what the eighteenth-century chronicler of the community, Franco Mendes, called "huma boa familha portugueza [a good Portuguese family]," while business and family functioned reasonably smoothly, Spinoza could not easily forsake the responsibilities or the challenge.[24] This is why this autobiographical passage about forgoing or not forgoing "wealth and honour," far from being something to dismiss as irrelevant literary rhetoric,[25] as some do, actually holds vital clues relating to the period down to when Spinoza reached his twentieth year, in 1652, after which the family situation rapidly deteriorated.

---

[24] Franco Mendes, *Memorias*, 60.
[25] Schnepf, "Enlightened Radicals," 97; also Popkin in conversation with me.

Following his initial inner struggle (which must roughly correspond to the period 1649–54), the young savant, already picturing himself as a philosopher earnestly committed to the pursuit of truth, became convinced of the insuperable difficulties he faced while persevering with the life for which inheritance, family, background and community, and his older brother's death, prepared him. Experience eventually proved that he could not effectively reconcile his existing lifestyle with what he had come to see as his personal quest. Keeping up an outward charade of loyalty to rabbinic authority, colluding with practices, notions, and beliefs which by this time, several years prior to his expulsion from the synagogue and the Sephardic community he inwardly rejected, Spinoza ran into insuperable barriers in the mid-1650s generated by his firm's bankruptcy and the attendant nagging debts and burdensome complexities and demands on his time and energy. Freedom to study texts and explore the topics he wished to involve himself with, discussing without hindrance his intellectual concerns, now increasingly collided with the increasingly onerous reality of his dramatically transformed family and community situation.

After a time, reports Spinoza in the same passage, his resolve to lead a double existence, a life of wealth, honour, family, and community alongside private pursuit of truth in his personal sense, came to appear misconceived and futile. "What occurs in life, that is what men, to judge from their activities, esteem the highest good," continues Spinoza, "can be classified under three headings – riches, status and pleasure. But the mind is so distracted by these that it cannot in the end ponder any other good."[26] After years of soul-searching prevarication, Spinoza finally made up his mind that opting for the lonely path of intrepid inquirer after truth means abandoning the conventional path of status and wealth, that is renouncing a good inherently limited and uncertain, "for one uncertain not by its nature but only with regard to achieving it."[27] Yet, still he hesitated. Even after resolving his inner struggle intellectually, he still encountered great difficulty in acting on his desire for a decisive transformation in lifestyle. For taking such a leap in practice, it is not enough, he records, simply to recognize the quest for enlightenment and insight to be the path to the highest good and set this theoretically over desire for honour, status, wealth, and power along with family responsibilities. Exit still remains elusive; a dramatic extra push may be necessary.

In the opening pages of *On the Emendation*, Spinoza recalls that, even after becoming convinced that pursuit of truth is a better way of life than seeking status and money, "I still could not, on that account, put aside all greed, desire for sensual pleasure and love of esteem."[28] This cannot refer to any later point than

---

[26] Spinoza, *Opera* ii, 6; Spinoza, *Collected Works* (ed. Curley) i, 8; Nadler, *Think Least of Death*, 9.
[27] Spinoza, *Opera* ii, 6; Israel, "Philosophy, Commerce," 127.
[28] Spinoza, *Collected Works* (ed. Curley) i, 10; Hampshire, *Spinoza*, 24–5; Nadler, *Spinoza: A Life*, 101–2.

1653–4 since, during 1655, Spinoza's convoluted predicament began to resolve itself. Spinoza's remarks here need to be set alongside the picture that emerges from the archival deeds and *finta* payments which reveal a rapid collapse in the family's financial and commercial standing between 1654 and 1656. The convergence in time of these two decisive developments, resolution of his personal predicament and collapse of the family fortune, solidly anchored in documentary evidence are of obvious relevance to each other. Together, they signify that the Spinoza of the early 1650s, finding it difficult to abandon the allure of money and social standing, faced a painful dilemma troubling him over a substantial period of time but by 1655–6, he could finally take the plunge, indeed to an extent was pushed to, as the family firm collapsed. Spinoza emerged suddenly in open defiance of rabbinic authority precisely when wealth and "honour" had wholly withered away in any case. It was in 1655–6, with the allure of status and wealth finally closed off due to external circumstances, that his bitter clash with the synagogue furiously erupted leading to individual withdrawal and then formal ejection from the community.

Since it is impossible that even the most brilliant student, after an unremarkable childhood and lengthy period of religious conformity, could suddenly become a strikingly adept philosophical mind familiar with the Latin terminology of philosophy by 1658 so as to already conspicuously put in the shade De Prado, someone who had been reading Latin in Spanish universities for many years, as we know was the case from testimony against both men submitted to the Madrid Inquisition in 1658 (discussed further on), he had certainly been engaged on his solitary quest for quite some years by then. Spinoza also proved himself a more unbending adversary of the rabbinic, or as he, like Uriel da Costa before him, called it "Pharisaic," religious and intellectual culture boxing him in than did De Prado. All this forms an insuperable body of objection to the argument that Spinoza rebelled late and suddenly and was able to master Latin and become a highly proficient expounder of Cartesianism "in just a couple of years," as Popkin expressed it, after his excommunication.[29]

De Prado and Spinoza did become friends and allies, in 1655, but, as Yosef Kaplan convincingly argues, without either figure profoundly influencing or shaping the other. In fact, if there was anything of a teacher–student element in their friendship it is far more likely to be the other way around from what Révah hypothesized, with Spinoza instructing De Prado in the intricacies of the Hebrew Old Testament and rabbinic argument. They became allies in dissent, in 1655, but this was mainly due to the prior efforts of each separately. The two men fortified and broadened in each other a ready store of doubts and inclination to challenge rabbinic authority.[30] "Already since his childhood he vacillated in his Jewish

---

[29] Popkin, *Spinoza*, 20; Yovel, *Spinoza and Other Heretics*, 79.
[30] Kaplan, *From Christianity to Judaism*, 132; Nadler, *Spinoza: A Life*, 172–3.

belief," records David Franco Mendes (1713–92), the chief chronicler of the community in the mid-eighteenth century, recalling the congregation's then long established view, while "he always had a propensity for study and learning languages."[31] Bayle, Colerus, Basnage, and other later sources affirm much the same and this should become the accepted view.

Late seventeenth- and eighteenth-century sources should not, of course, be used as if they are solidly reliable evidence about anything relating to Spinoza's early life. But neither should such evidence be wholly discarded as there is good reason to suppose these sources, Jewish and non-Jewish, reflect inherited collective traditions within and without the Amsterdam Sephardic community. Where carefully checked, both streams deserve being assigned at least some qualified pertinence to Spinoza's early life. All considered, the community's own accepted account of Spinoza's early course, and that of the non-Jewish scholars surveying his life later, correspond better with the few major primary sources at our disposal bearing on Spinoza's early life, above all the highly significant autobiographical passage at the start of the *TEI*, than do the views of those modern scholars depicting a Spinoza supposedly observant and deferential to Jewish tradition and the congregation until well into his twenties followed by sudden conversion to a defiant and rebellious stance, due supposedly to encountering some powerful personality holding entirely exceptional views.

Another early source supporting the conclusion that Spinoza's inner estrangement from religious authority and outer rebellion against Jewish orthodoxy represent two completely different stages in his biography, dates from 1677. This was Jarig Jelles' preface to the *Opera Posthuma* where Spinoza's Collegiant friend who may well have known him prior to the rupture with the synagogue in 1656 (though there is no proof of this), and certainly knew him during much of his subsequent life, emphasizes that Spinoza had for many years been immersed in Hebrew and rabbinic studies before his expulsion from the congregation, being "driven by a burning desire to find the truth." His inner rebellion intensified because he failed to obtain satisfaction from his teachers or from what he read, so that he "decided to try himself to see what he could achieve." Only much later, though still before 1655, recalls Jelles, did the young scholar hit upon the writings of Descartes (very likely first in Dutch or French rather than Latin), texts which proved of great help to him in his efforts. There seems little reason to doubt then that from an early point in his life Spinoza began a quiet, inquiring inward rebellion against what his teachers taught, while studying the Torah and the medieval Jewish commentators, and then later, but still prior to 1655, striking out into broader fields, studying Latin, discovering aspects of philosophy and learning about Descartes.[32]

---

[31] Franco Mendes, *Memorias*, 60.
[32] Jelles, "Voorreeden," 1–2; Akkerman, *Studies*, 216–17; Akkerman and Hubbeling, "Preface to Spinoza's Posthumous Works," 110–11.

All this tallies also with other precious late seventeenth-century sources, such as Bayle, Van Til, Halma, and Colerus who all maintain that Spinoza devoted himself from early on to the study of religious matters—"l'étude de la théologie," as Bayle put it—"in which he devoted himself thoroughly for many years before he went wholly over to philosophy."[33] Bayle, fifteen years Spinoza's junior, the third great philosopher to grace the Dutch Golden Age (after Descartes and Spinoza), and the world's greatest sceptic regarding what most people think and believe, was the very opposite to a sceptic when it came to historical inquiry and fact. He demonstrated this incontrovertibly in the 1680s and 1690s when researching and ascertaining a range of historical topics that interested him, including Spinoza's life and legacy. Bayle went to exceptional lengths, consulting everyone he could think of to obtain the most accurate knowledge available including interviewing the son of Spinoza's publisher, the younger Jan Rieuwertsz (c.1651–1723), who had the same name as his father, and had known Spinoza as a boy as well as later, and had assisted his father in clandestinely publishing and selling Spinoza's works.[34]

A decidedly suspect later source but still worth mentioning is *La Vie de Spinosa* usually thought to date from soon after Spinoza's death but which may date from as late as 1700 or shortly after, a text usually ascribed to the exiled French journalist, Jean-Maximilien Lucas (1647–97). If he was indeed the author, as was claimed in the early eighteenth century, Lucas probably knew Spinoza personally during the latter's last years. *La Vie* affirms that Spinoza "was not yet fifteen [hence in 1646] when he began formulating difficulties that the most learned among the Jews found difficulty in resolving," causing his teachers considerable embarrassment but with whose replies Spinoza, at that early stage (around 1646–8), feigned to be satisfied. This early testimony correlates too well with the other evidence to be wholly ignored in this connection.[35] Spinoza's inner—as distinct from his outer—rebellion against the rabbis commenced much earlier than the open break, possibly a decade earlier, and no later than the late 1640s.

Among the "languages" Spinoza assiduously studied, Hebrew undoubtedly predominated in the early stages. Destined to be a foundation of his Bible criticism, it was a language Spinoza—a personality of unswerving continuity— would carry on studying for the rest of his life and about which he would later draft an unfinished grammatical compendium. Before long, Latin too became a major strand in his self-development, but there is every reason to conjecture that it was his early immersion in Hebrew passages of Scripture as a boy that first planted the seeds of his cautious questioning and incipient youthful rebellion. Hence,

---

[33] Halma, *Het Leven*, 5; Bayle, *Écrits sur Spinoza*, 21; Mignini, "Dottrina spinoziana," 53–4.
[34] Lomba, "Pierre Bayle, Spinoza's Reader," 224; Van Bunge, "Spinoza's Life," 214.
[35] [Lucas], *La Vie*, 12; Salomon, "Introdução," xcvii–xcviii.

there is no reason to be surprised that on leaving the synagogue, in late 1655 or early 1656, Spinoza was already sufficiently accomplished in discussion of Scriptural text problems that he could write a now lost full-length treatise, his *Apologia*, in Spanish, the usual language of intellectual debate within the Sephardic community, justifying his wide-ranging disagreement with the rabbis.

Van Til, Bayle, and Halma all agree that this *Apologia* was written but never published. Nevertheless, notes Halma, a not insignificant Dutch source and nowhere more relevant than here, "it is known that many things in it came out later by being absorbed into his *Tractatus Theologico-Politicus* published at Amsterdam in the year 1670, [...] that damaging and abominable book in which [Spinoza] undermines religion and secretly sowed the seeds of atheism that were then seen openly raised to their full height in his *Opera Posthuma*."[36] Several modern scholars have cast doubt on whether this *Apologia* ever really existed. But the argument against is decidedly weak compared with the argument *for* its existence which is attested by a range of diverse and completely unconnected contemporary sources including the pro-toleration Coccejan theologian, Salomon van Til (1643–1713), who styles it Spinoza's "Apology for his apostasy from Judaism, against the Old Testament."[37] According to Van Til, a scholar deeply shocked by Spinoza's denial of Scripture's divine status and who, in 1678, using at least one account of an interview with Spinoza that is no longer extant, wrote that:

> this opponent of religion [Spinoza] was the first to dare to overthrow the authority of the books of the Old and New Testament, and try to show the world how these writings had been repeatedly altered and transformed through human diligence and how it had been possible to elevate them to their reputation for godliness. Objections of this kind he collected in a Spanish treatise against the Old Testament under the title "A Defense of my Departure from Judaism"; but on the advice of friends he suppressed this text and undertook to introduce these ideas somewhat more skillfully and less vehemently in another work, published in 1670, under the title *Tractatus Theologico-Politicus*.[38]

Those scholars throwing doubt on the existence of the *Apologia* reject the claims of Bayle and Halma asserting the existence of this text written against the rabbis and the fact it was never published,[39] contending that Bayle and Halma may

---

[36] Halma, *Het Leven*, 7–8; Mignini, "Données et problèmes," 12; Curley, "Spinoza's Lost Defense," 9–12.
[37] Til, *Voor-hof der heydenen*, 5–6; Bento, "Spinoza and the Hebrew State," 238.
[38] Til, *Voor-hof der heydenen*, 6; Curley, "Spinoza's Lost Defense," 9–10; Steenbakkers, "Spinoza's Life," 52n69; contrary to Curley's translation, I do not think the Dutch word "spaarzamer" here can mean "briefly."
[39] Bayle, *Écrits sur Spinoza*, 22; Halma, *Het Leven*, 7.

simply have followed Van Til, and that this entire notion is probably a myth since "all reference to Spinoza's presumed *Apology* (e.g. Pierre Bayle in the *Dictionnaire*) take their cue from Van Til, writing in 1694."[40] But in fact, the story has come down to us via several different channels, as shown by the testimony of the younger Jan Rieuwertsz, son and heir of Spinoza's publisher and likewise an Amsterdam bookseller. Someone who knew Spinoza personally in early life, he is known to have still been selling Spinoza's books clandestinely in the 1690s. According to Rieuwertsz, his father, Spinoza's regular publisher, had long kept this particular manuscript, "a big work" against the rabbis written in Spanish, in his own possession.[41] This evidence is quite independent of Van Til.

Furthermore, a poet belonging to the Amsterdam Sephardic community, Daniel Levi de Barrios (c.1625–1701), who was also an early chronicler of the community, refers to the 1656 manuscript in a remarkable passage written considerably earlier than Van Til's statement. Levi de Barrios confirms the *Apologia*'s existence in Spanish, having either heard about its contents or seen it himself, calling it a formidable piece of work.[42] Admittedly, Levi de Barrios did not formally join the Sephardic community in Amsterdam until the 1670s. But during the 1660s he lived as a (crypto-Jewish) Spanish officer and man of letters in Antwerp and there knew De Prado who, after his expulsion from the Portuguese Jewish community of Amsterdam and short-lived alliance with Spinoza, dwelt in Antwerp from 1658 until his death in 1670 and contributed several pieces to De Barrios' poetry collection *Flor de Apolo*, published (in Brussels) in 1665.[43] Some of the information De Barrios garnered about the young Spinoza of 1655–6 probably derived directly from De Prado.[44] Over the years De Barrios collected all kinds of information about the Amsterdam community, in both the Spanish Netherlands and Holland which he visited regularly, almost certainly without ever reading Van Til's statement of 1682, not that there is any reason to cast doubt on Van Til's reportage of the *Apologia*. Spinoza's lost Spanish text undoubtedly existed and prefigured the *TTP*. We do not know for sure whether Spinoza ever actually submitted his manuscript response to the rabbis, in 1656; but if De Prado and other members of the community read it, presumably the rabbis did too.

3.ii Heretical Opinions

The Mortera–Menasseh rift was certainly one source of drama and instability in the Amsterdam Sephardic community during the early and mid-1650s, but there

---

[40] Steenbakkers, "The Text of Spinoza's *Tractatus*," 31.
[41] Freudenthal/Walther, *Lebensgeschichte* i, 85; Van Eeghen, *Amsterdamse boekhandel* iv, 65.
[42] Rothkamm, *Institutio Oratoria*, 510–11; Israel, "Philosophy, Commerce," 129.
[43] Faur, *Shadow of History*, 150–1; Albiac, *Sinagoga vacía*, 367–8.
[44] Gebhardt, "Juan de Prado," 281–2, 285; Faur, *Shadow of History*, 151.

was another seizing attention no less disruptive and disturbing at that time. This was the feud between the congregation and an acquaintance of Spinoza's father, Lopo Ramirez (alias David Curiel), a wealthy and prominent member of the community, and his brother-in-law, Manoel Dias Henriques, over guardianship of their niece, Rebecca Naar, whose father had died in 1641 leaving her a massive legacy under the supervision of the Amsterdam city Orphans' Chamber. What started as a feud between Rebecca's mother and the girl's male guardians over alleged accounting misdemeanours on their part, from 1651 escalated with Lopo and his brother-in-law coming under the community ban or *herem* for defying the *parnasim* on various counts, in particular Lopo's refusal, after his wife's death, to marry a niece, Sarah Curiel, whom he had allegedly gotten with child after promising marriage. Not just a leading merchant, Lopo was also a diplomatic agent performing services for the Spanish court and the authorities in Brussels, the capital of the then Spanish Netherlands (i.e. modern Belgium). His efforts to mobilize the Amsterdam magistrates to force the lifting of the *herem* and secure his and his brother-in-law's unconditional re-admittance to the synagogue, produced such outrage within the community that it provoked a serious riot at the synagogue on 29 April 1651.[45]

To evade the fury of the congregation without yielding ground, Lopo first attended the Ashkenazic synagogue instead of the Portuguese, and then, in 1653, moved to Antwerp while remaining observant and strictly keeping to the Jewish sabbath. The physical commotion subsided, but the legal and communal furore continued, culminating in the summer of 1656, at exactly the same time as Spinoza's excommunication. Lopo and his relative contended that the marriage of Rebecca's parents had never been registered in accord with a Dutch judicial regulation of 1580, that she was therefore legally illegitimate and that her sizeable legacy, amounting to 116,000 guilders deposited with the Orphans' Chamber rightfully belonged to her father's two sisters—who just happened to be Lopo's and Manoel's wives. So vast were the legal and social implications of the furore over Rebecca's alleged illegitimacy, guardianship, and disputed legacy that the States of Holland as well as the Amsterdam courts found themselves being dragged in. It was a classic illustrative lesson in the collision that can occur between religious authority and the civil law of the land, at that moment a topic of particular interest to the young Spinoza, as we shall see.

Eventually, the city government confirmed the validity in Amsterdam of all Sephardic marriages contracted according to Jewish law and ruled against Ramirez. In terms of its legal, financial, and political implications for the community, the Lopo Ramirez affair greatly eclipsed in significance the then considerably lesser business of Spinoza's quarrel with the rabbis. Spinoza was

---

[45] Swetschinski, *Reluctant Cosmopolitans*, 239–40; Hagoort, "Persons of a Restless Disposition," 160–1.

nevertheless placed under a far more stringent and severe *herem* than was imposed on the—from a communal and social perspective—far more important, more disruptive rebel, Lopo Ramirez. However, there was a logical, very important reason why a minor *herem* was imposed on Ramirez and an altogether more severe form of *herem* on the perceived lesser rebel: Spinoza's case unquestionably mattered far less to the community legally, socially, and financially, but Spinoza's defiance of Jewish law and rabbinic authority was altogether more fundamental and explicit as regards challenging religious authority.[46]

Scholars today sometimes allege that we do not know why Spinoza was expelled from the Jewish community. But this is entirely misleading. In fact, we know exactly why Spinoza was expelled with a certainty scarcely leaving room for doubt. The uniquely severe wording of the *herem* used in his case could result only from outright defiance of rabbinic authority and teaching and cannot possibly have another explanation. Levi De Barrios, writing five years after Spinoza's death, confirms in his *Triumpho del govierno popular* of 1682, that Spinoza was banned on account "of his bad opinions [por sus malas opiñones]," in response to which he produced "a book which looks like a golden chalice [hizo un libro que al parecer es vaso de oro]" but was "filled with poison liquor." More specifically, Spinoza objected that "the Jews have no obligation to observe the Mosaic Law because they no longer have a state [los Judíos no tienen obligación de observer la Ley Mosaica en quanto no tienen imperio]."[47] This particular assertion is significant, since precisely this argument later figured as a central doctrine of the *TTP*. Having a purely political origin, Spinoza reportedly argued, the Mosaic Law no longer applies to modern Jews. During his pre-Cartesian phase, Spinoza evidently already possessed a system of Bible criticism and revisionism of Jewish teaching conflicting with the essentials of what the rabbis taught, something he could hardly have arrived at owing to De Prado's influence since the latter was no expert in this area and knew no Hebrew or Aramaic.

Further confirmation is provided by a mystical book, the *Certeza del Camino*, by the Spanish Jewish messianist Abraham Israel Pereyra (d. 1699), a rich merchant from Madrid who had gained his fortune in Spain.[48] Arriving in the late 1640s in Amsterdam as a New Christian fleeing the Inquisition, Pereyra later recalled both the gravity of the episode in the community, in 1655–6, and sense of peril to religion and communal unity to which the Spinoza affair contributed. Knowing little about Judaism but eager to learn, Pereyra, like Ramirez, knew lots about Spain, the Inquisition, finance and the international scene of the day and

---

[46] Hagoort, "Persons of a Restless Disposition," 169–70; Israel, "Philosophy, Commerce," 136–8; Nadler, "The Jewish Spinoza," 492.
[47] Levi de Barrios, *Triumpho del Govierno Popular*, 85; Kaplan, *From Judaism to Christianity*, 265; Israel, "Philosophy, Commerce," 129.
[48] AGS Estado 2070. Brun to G. de la Torre, Cambrai, 27 Aug. 1649; Israel, *Diasporas*, 234, 238, 392–3, 517.

lamented the troubles that would surely ensue in the Sephardic community should "we depart from the doctrine and statutes that Moses our Rabbi received in Sinai." His book, published amidst the Sabbataean frenzy of the Jewish year 5426 [1666], denounces the "diabolical" outlook of those in the community propagating the view of "Machiavelli and others who deny the deity even as a first principle," as if it were what everyone should follow, impiety being their aim "as ours is to defend the truth." One might readily question whether Pereyra is referring here to Spinoza. But like other Dutch Sephardic writers of the late seventeenth century, he could not resist punning on the Spanish meaning of the names of the two leading Jewish heretics in 1655–6, "Espinosa" and "Prado." In his book, he represents the rebels "deny[ing] the deity even as a first principle" as a treacherous terrain of thistles and thorns [*espinas*], amidst a green pasture [*prado*] seething with poisonous snakes.[49] A similar pun recurs in the fourth part of Orobio's *Epístola invectiva*, certainly again alluding to Spinoza, at a time when Spinoza's *Apologia* was likely still in the community's possession, referring to how De Prado and other heretics concoct objections from seemingly difficult or thorny passages [*espinosos*] in the Hebrew Scriptures.[50]

Levi de Barrios too was fond of this enduring pun, and in a striking verse concerning the events of 1655–6, published in 1683 but penned earlier,[51] records that Spinoza's previously highly appreciative teacher, "the very wise Rabbi Saul Levi Mortera," had, earlier, in the communal evening class, the *yeshivah* "Keter Torah" for youths well advanced in Hebrew studies,[52] fought an epic battle defending religion with his intellect, wisdom, and pen, "contra el ateismo [against atheism]." The two arch-heretics of Amsterdam Sephardic Jewry pitted against him, De Barrios recalls, were "thorns [Espinos] that in meadows [Prados] of impiety" "seek to glow with the fire that consumes them. That flame is the zeal of Mortera who burns among the brambles of religion so as not go out [*Espinos son los que en Prados de impiedad, dessean luzir con el fuego que los consume; y llama es el zelo de Mortera que arde en la çarça de la religion por no apagarse*]."[53] To ensure that even the inattentive reader would not miss his allusion, De Barrios even underlines the words *Espinos* and *Prados*. Again, he could hardly have ventured to make such a statement had it not tallied with the collective Sephardic memory in Amsterdam. De Barrios supplies no date for these public

---

[49] Pereyra, *Certeza del camino*, 81; Méchoulan, "Regard sur la pensée juive," 59–60; Kasher and Biderman, "Why was Spinoza Excommunicated?," 114–15.
[50] Dujovne, *Spinoza* i, 99; Muchnik, *Une Vie Marrane*, 494–5.
[51] Freudenthal/Walther, *Lebensgeschichte* i, 269; Saperstein, *Exile in Amsterdam*, 9.
[52] Salomon, "Introdução," xii; Kaplan, *From Christianity to Judaism*, 128, 265, 426; Nadler, *Spinoza: A Life*, 104–5.
[53] Levi de Barrios, *Triumpho del Govierno Popular* section "corona de la ley," p. 2; Dujovne, *Spinoza* i, 96; Gebhardt, "Juan de Prado," 281–2; Révah, *Spinoza et Juan de Prado*, 22, 27; Vaz Dias and Van der Tak, "Spinoza Merchant," 155; Yovel, *Spinoza and Other Heretics*, 89–93; Bento, "Spinoza and the Hebrew State," 240.

clashes between Mortera and Spinoza in the *yeshivah* "Keter Torah," but the presence here, alongside Spinoza, of De Prado who only arrived in Holland from abroad, that year, means the poet must be referring either to 1655 or to early 1656. That Spinoza did indeed confront and challenge Mortera in a defiant manner is fully consistent with the rest of our evidence.

The roots of Spinoza's argument about Scripture in his mature work, moreover, are shown by his own testimony to originate in his early life prior to 1656. In the *TTP*, when discussing the disjointed character of Old Testament statements about history and chronology, the mature Spinoza says he sees no coherent historical sequence, only a disorderly heap of text illogically thrown together, "despite a long search. I say nothing here that I have not been long pondering deeply, and despite my having been steeped in the common beliefs about the Bible from childhood on, I have not been able to resist my conclusion."[54] Among his most deeply-held objections to observance and rabbinic authority was indeed his claim that God's "election" of the Jews is just an ancient "superstition," a figment of the collective Jewish imagination assuredly useful politically for the ancient Hebrew republic and its citizens but which affords no justification for Jews remaining legally separate from other peoples in the post-exilic era when no longer dwelling within the borders of their own republic. Indeed, no particular people, held Spinoza, can be specially elected by the true God, that is the Order of Nature, for privileges above any other, any more than a particular individual can be predestined for particular happiness above others. Spinoza's answer to anti-Semitism and "hatred" of the Jews, in his time as ubiquitous as in ours, was that they should abandon their religious and social self-separation and amalgamate with the rest albeit without necessarily converting to Christianity—unless, as he famously suggests, they can reassert themselves and recreate their own state.[55]

It follows that Spinoza's early studies and anti-rabbinic inferences were connected with his eventual, much later expulsion from the community but only indirectly and were not the immediate cause of the public scandal that blew up dramatically in 1655–6. The synagogue, its lay governors and the rabbis, though strict in demanding decorum and exacting outward conformity to religious authority and observance within their community, took scant interest in the personal views of congregants as such. Rather, in their obsession with "conserving" the unity, integrity, and respectable profile of the community, the board of elders and rabbis, far from emulating the Inquisition in seeking to discipline the individual's inner thought-world, lent over backwards to coax the inwardly recalcitrant to outwardly conform, as no one knew better than De Prado, De Barrios, and Pereyra. What finally counted for the synagogue governing board

---

[54] Spinoza, *Theological-Political Treatise*, 136; Nadler, *Spinoza: A Life*, 134.
[55] Touber, *Spinoza and Biblical Philology*, 55–6; Bento, "Spinoza and the Hebrew State," 245–7; Jaquet, *Spinoza à l'oeuvre*, 72.

was outward form only. Neither belief nor inner personal doubts had much direct bearing on communal self-censorship and discipline.

Consequently, a blow-up of the proportions of 1656 would have been entirely impossible on the basis of Spinoza simply following his own private philosophical inclinations. Such a scandal could occur exclusively in the wake of public, open defiance and refusal to observe the religious law and absolutely *not* on any other basis. Admittedly, Mortera personally, unlike the governing board of elders [*Mahamad*] or Menasseh, did nurture something like an inquisitorial attitude and zealously investigated and repressed those he deemed "heretics." "When it happens that among [our Jews] there is some heretic," he wrote four years after Spinoza's banishment, in 1660, in his major Portuguese text, *O Tratatdo da Verdade da lei de Moises* [Treatise of the Truth of the Law of Moses], doubtless recalling Spinoza along with Uriel da Costa, De Prado, and Ribera, "they eject him and with that the evil ceases"; such persons neither prosper nor build a following within the community, but rather "by divine permission and providence, the foam and scum is removed from this people which remains always pure and united in its Law and religion."[56] This happens now, held Mortera, just as in ancient times: thus, the Sadducees challenged rabbinic authority rejecting key rabbinic doctrines, yet, happily, divine providence, without using force or the Inquisition's brutal methods, entirely erased them from the scene.[57] Spinoza's view of the Sadducees was far more positive.

Where Christians, from the moment their Gospel was born have been continually divided into factions, always quarrelling and fighting each other, argued the uncompromising Mortera, the people of Israel had always been one and unified under the Law of Moses. To gather information about the views of suspected "heretics," he was accustomed to recruit students to spy on them. Apparently, Spinoza was among those kept under surveillance in 1655–6. But even where he thus took the initiative, Mortera could accomplish little by way of effectively persecuting those he deemed "heretics" without clear evidence that the suspect individual was actively striving to subvert others and defy the community.[58]

The Amsterdam Sephardic community, Yosef Kaplan has demonstrated, undoubtedly widened its use of the *herem* during the seventeenth century, employing this measure both more frequently and more broadly than Jewish communities in earlier times. So doing, the *Mahamad* created a broader, more versatile tool of social control, censorship, and discipline.[59] During the weeks preceding Spinoza's formal expulsion from the community, in 1656, the *Mahamad* was particularly anxious to curb travel by congregants to "lands of idolatry" where members of the Sephardic community would need to conduct themselves like "Christians," conceal all Jewish observance and seemingly pray

[56] Mortera, *Tratado da Verdade*, 123–5; Salomon, "Introdução," civ.
[57] Mortera, *Tratado da Verdade*, 123, 347.   [58] Quoted in Salomon, "Introdução," ciii–cv.
[59] Kaplan, "Religion, Politics," 5–7.

like Christians, while lacking access to Jewish texts and kosher food. Another offense expressly forbidden by the *Mahamad* during the weeks immediately preceding the furore over Spinoza, was refusal to accept ritual honours and offices during synagogue services such as opening the ark and reading the weekly Torah portion. The regular, ordinary *herem* was almost casually employed to discipline young men's behaviour in the streets, and punish financial misconduct and marital transgression. For the *parnasim* were not just the governing body of a religious community but directors of a judicially autonomous community. In 1662, Philip van Limborch, the renowned Remonstrant preacher long familiar with Amsterdam and future close friend of Locke, among the leading Dutch advocates of toleration and freedom of expression, urged the Amsterdam city government to intervene to limit the Sephardic community's judicial privileges and autonomy because such authority creates a sphere of outward conformity of belief and behaviour, suppressing religious debate and restricting open dissent.[60] Harbouring unacceptable ideas could be grounds for action by the community but only when expressed openly in discussion with others, after repeated reprimands and admonitions for such dissent to cease were ignored.

In the seventeenth and eighteenth centuries, the *herem* was frequently used in Amsterdam and often a comparatively minor affair. During these two centuries it was resorted to over a hundred times. However, this has relatively little relevance to Spinoza's case because normally the *herem* was a briefly worded reprimand leading, soon afterwards, to congregants mounting the *theba* in the centre of the synagogue from where the Torah scrolls were read out, to express public contrition and repent. During the months prior to the Spinoza affair such ceremonial apologies, often for "visiting lands of idolatry," occurred several times almost as a routine matter.[61] Reflecting its comparative unimportance, the *herem* was always readily rescindable after appropriate signs of contrition by the offender, payment of small penalties, and formal reaffirming of the "authority of the Torah, the communal leadership, and entire congregation," though given his peculiar temperament, such submission doubtless presented a particular psychological and intellectual barrier discouraging Spinoza from ever contemplating such a step.[62]

3.iii Expulsion from the Synagogue

In any case, very different was the altogether exceptional, extra-length form of *herem* imposed on Spinoza and De Prado. Much more elaborate wording was employed in these cases, following a specially transcribed formula Mortera had

---

[60] Kaplan, *Judíos nuevos*, 40.
[61] GAA PJG 334, fos. 357, 381, 406, 408; Tiribás, "Mobility, Clandestine Literature," 1066.
[62] Kaplan, "Religion, Politics," 7; Kaplan, *Judíos nuevos*, 39–40; Popkin, "Spinoza's Excommunication," 265.

received from Venice following the condemnation of Uriel da Costa, in 1618.[63] This format, being a far more solemn decree, had a very different tone and character from the familiar ban. In Spinoza's case, the text was worded with an unparalleled vehemence including resounding curses absent even from the ban imposed on De Prado.[64] Hence, it is not at all the case, as some scholars maintain, that we have no real idea why Spinoza was excommunicated from the community and do not know the reasons for the *herem* pronounced against him.[65] His expulsion cannot have had anything to do with his embracing Cartesianism, as has been suggested, or harbouring unorthodox views about the Torah,[66] or any sort of ordinary jurisdictional clash. Nor, given its wholly exceptional features, can the special *herem* imposed on Spinoza have been related to the usual run of offences, or provoked by anything of a private nature. It could result only from open, deliberate rebellion, stubbornly and defiantly continued, against rabbinic and synagogue authority with no other explanation being to the slightest degree feasible. The first line of the *herem* indicates that the current public scandal had been in progress only since "ha dias [a short time]." Recorded in a clear manuscript hand in the *Mahamad*'s records, or *Haskamoth*, the main text of the ban on Spinoza, as declaimed before the congregation, reads:

> The *Senhores* of the *Mahamad* make known to you all that, having for some time had reports of the bad opinions and deeds of Baruch de Espinoza, they tried in different ways and with promises to get him to change his bad ways, but not being able to change him – rather the contrary – they received every day more notices of the horrendous heresies he was practicing and taught, and abominable deeds he was practicing. Having many trustworthy testimonies of this, these points were written down and attested in the presence of the said Espinoza, [errors] of which, however, he remained convinced. All of which being examined in the presence of the *senhores hahamim* [rabbis], [the *Mahamad*] deliberated their [the rabbis'] opinion that the said Espinoza should be banned and set apart from the nation of Israel, as they now proscribe and condemn him with the following *Herem*: with the sentence of the angels and of the holy ones we ban, set apart, curse and damn Baruch de Espinoza with the consent of God (may he be blessed) and that of all of this holy congregation in accord with these holy scrolls and the 613 precepts written in them, and with the *Herem* with which Joshua banned Jericho, the curse with which Elijah cursed the young men, and all the

---

[63] Salomon, "Introdução," xlix; Salomon, "La vraie excommunication," 188.

[64] GAA PJG 334, fo. 408: "Nota do herem"; Salomon, "La vraie excommunication," 181–9; Méchoulan, "*Herem* à Amsterdam," 128; Wesselius, "Spinoza's Excommunication," 46; Kasher and Biderman, "Why was Spinoza Excommunicated?," 100–1; Kaplan, "Religion, Politics," 6.

[65] Popkin, *Spinoza*, 27–30; Van de Ven, "Spinoza's Life and Time," 10.

[66] Kasher and Biderman, "Why was Spinoza Excommunicated?," 131–2, 140–1; see also Wesselius, "Spinoza's Excommunication," 57.

curses written in the Law. May he [Spinoza] be cursed by day and cursed by night, cursed when he lays down and cursed when he gets up, cursed when he goes out and cursed when he returns. Adonai will not wish to pardon him; rather, from now on, the fury and anger of Our Lord [Adonai] will fume against him and he will come under all the curses written in the book of this Law. And God will erase his name from under the heavens, and Adonai will set him apart on account of his wickedness from all the tribes of Israel, with all the curses of the firmament written in the book of this Law. And all you loyal to Adonai your God, all of you alive today, be admonished that no one shall converse with him face to face, or in writing, nor do him any favor, nor be with him under the same roof, nor approach closer to him than four cubits [six feet], nor read any paper prepared or written by him [nem leer papel algun feito ou escritto pelle].[67]

Usually with the *herem*, in Amsterdam and Western Sephardic communities generally, the resolution to expel was resolved in the first place by the community's lay governing body, the *Mahamad*, and not the rabbis—or any particular rabbi,[68] be it Mortera or another. Yet, in this case the consultative involvement of the rabbinate is expressly emphasized, as is the exceptional stubbornness manifested by Spinoza, in his refusing to be "convinced" by their contrary arguments. As Révah pointed out long ago, the unparalleled vehemence of the *herem* imposed on Spinoza can only mean the "escandalo [scandal]" he caused with his utterances against the Law of Moses and rabbinic authority stood out as something wholly exceptional, surpassing even De Prado's offense in communicating deistic ideas to others of the congregation. The text of the ban clearly states, in a manner that conventional forms of the *herem* do not, that Spinoza was being expelled for both "malas opinoes [bad opinions]" and evil actions, and hence not opinions alone.[69]

Yet, even after this, the synagogue authorities, rather than insist on permanent ostracization, would much have preferred to conciliate this son of a former *parnas* [community elder] and keep Spinoza within the community provided he agreed to keep his views to himself. This important aspect of the affair is confirmed, over a century later, by the eighteenth-century chronicler of the community, Franco Mendes, doubtless contemplating the original text of the ban on Spinoza, buried in the *Haskamoth*, the official community records, but also having, as he did, community oral tradition at his disposal. He also consulted published sources such as Colerus and Basnage, but may, in addition, have seen community written

---

[67] GAA PJG 334, fo. 408. "Nota do herem que se publicou da Theba em 6 de Ab, contra Baruch Espinoza"; Gans, *Memorboek*, 91; Méchoulan, "Herem à Amsterdam," 126; Kaplan, "Religion, Politics," 6.
[68] Kaplan, *Judíos nuevos*, 39–46; Oravetz Albert, "Rabbi and the Rebels," 173–6, 181.
[69] Franco Mendes, *Memorias*, 61; Révah, *Spinoza et Juan de Prado*, 30; Révah, "Aux origines de la rupture," 369; Méchoulan, "Herem à Amsterdam," 128; Nadler, *Spinoza: A Life*, 127–9; Nadler, *Spinoza's Heresy*, 13–14.

sources no longer available today. Spinoza's "perversity," he records, "reached the point of giving the greatest scandal in the sight of the nation by abominably sowing [blas semando] his ideas about everything relating to tradition, and even violating the sabbath and festivals; for these reasons, he was several times admonished by the rabbis and *parnasim* of the community."[70] When all else failed, only then was he expelled.

There is every reason to accept that this was indeed the case. One can scarcely doubt these efforts by the *Mahamad*, including attempts to buy him off, were aimed, rather than to suppress his views as such, at getting him to keep his opinions to himself without influencing others and not openly defy the requirements of observance and ritual,[71] just as the *parnasim* had obviously been seeking to arrange for months before issuing the *herem*, and as early accounts of his life and the text of the ban itself indicate. The community attempted "different ways" to persuade him to cease his public defiance and offered "promises to get him to change his bad ways," that is reform his objectionable conduct, and to prevent him expressing unacceptable views, but had not been "able to change him – rather the contrary." In short, in July 1656, with the community preferring reconciliation if attainable, public scandal caused by open rejection of the Law effectively forced the initially reluctant *parnasim* to banish him. Hence, it is logical to conclude that it was Spinoza who took the initiative in refusing to compromise and in withdrawing, and finally provoking this dramatic rupture. As we shall see, Spinoza's and De Prado's own explanation for their expulsion, recorded in the Spanish Inquisition evidence of 1658, was that they had indeed been claiming the Mosaic Law is no longer binding or applicable and that, accordingly, the Talmud, Jewish observance, and rabbinic authority lack validity. They appear to have made a point of assuring fellow Iberians resident in or visiting Amsterdam during the years immediately following their expulsion from the congregation that this was what lay behind what had occurred.

The rabbi who intoned the *herem*, apparently Aboab, was a cultivated figure, widely read in philosophical and secular as well as Jewish religious literature, and a Kabbalist. If the full procedure traditionally prescribed for the *herem* of the severe variety were followed in this instance, the reading out of the curses (with Spinoza himself probably absent) was accompanied by the blowing of the *shofar* [sheep's horn] amidst an array of (black?) candles. Absent for over a decade, officiating in the Sephardic community of Recife between 1642 and the fall of Dutch Brazil, in 1654, Aboab had only recently rejoined the Amsterdam rabbinate, since September 1654, officiating in place of Menasseh who was absent through late 1655 and all 1656 in connection with his efforts to persuade Cromwell to readmit

---

[70] Franco Mendes, *Memorias*, 61; Méchoulan, "*Herem* à Amsterdam," 126–7.
[71] Freudenthal/Walther, *Lebensgeschichte* i, 86; Popkin, "Spinoza's Excommunication," 267.

the Jews to England.[72] Aboab's perspective on Spinoza was presumably limited just to the last two years, though he may have remembered him as a boy. Unlike Mortera, Aboab was also unconnected, as far as is known, with Spinoza's father and the Spinoza family of his grandfather's generation.[73] No doubt it was Mortera, though, as several later reports indicate, who spearheaded the prior investigation while Aboab went along with the proceedings possibly less zealously. Equally, it was Mortera, affirm later sources, who initiated investigation into De Prado's teaching, ideas, and influence on the community's older students.[74] Owing to long ties with the Spinoza family, Mortera may well have chosen not to officiate in this instance.

A key source bearing on these issues are the notes of the future professor Gottlieb Stolle (1673–1744), a Silesian jurist from Liegnitz who, in 1703–4, accompanying a young nobleman called Hallmann and the latter's cousin, visited Amsterdam on an educational tour, or what in Germany was called a *Bildungsreise*. A pupil of the famous Halle luminary Christian Thomasius (1655–1728), Stolle later taught at Jena figuring among the best-known university teachers of Early Enlightenment Germany. Setting out in April 1703, the three travellers spent an entire year on their study trip, encompassing much of Lower Germany before proceeding by way of Bremen and Emden to Groningen, Franeker, Amsterdam, Haarlem, Leiden, The Hague, Rotterdam, and Utrecht. While in Holland, Stolle and Hallmann had it prominently on their agenda, at the request of Thomasius, to glean all the information they could about Spinoza from everyone traceable who had actually known him. Like Leibniz, Bayle, and Colerus, Thomasius was keen to discover everything he could about Spinoza the thinker, the writer, and the man.

Stolle and Hallmann conducted interviews in various Dutch towns and universities with whoever they could trace who had known Spinoza personally. What they gleaned about the drama of 1656 was again, that it was Spinoza's declaring the Pentateuch a "human" book rather than divine revelation and rejecting the continued applicability of the Law of Moses to modern-day Jews, that formed the crux of the grounds for the *herem* and Spinoza's expulsion from the community. Fortunately for modern researchers, both Stolle and Hallmann took extensive diary notes of their many conversations with savants and others about a range of topics, including these precious reminiscences of Spinoza. These notes were then left forgotten, unpublished, locked away in the university library of what was then Breslau (now Wrocław), the capital of Silesia, forgotten until long after.[75]

When finally rediscovered, Stolle's and Hallmann's material proved a valuable fund of information about various aspects of later Golden Age Dutch learning and

---

[72] Salomon, "La vraie excommunication," 187.
[73] GAA PJG 334, fo. 373. Res. Mahamad 29 Elul 5414.
[74] Swetschinski, *Reluctant Cosmopolitans*, 266, 271, 273; Muchnik, *Une Vie Marrane*, 425, 429.
[75] Freudenthal/Walther, *Lebensgeschichte* ii, 51–4.

academic life. In Haarlem, the visitors met the eminent Mennonite physician and scholar Anthonie Van Dale (1638–1708), whose notorious book denying the ancient Greek and Roman oracles had ceased functioning with the coming of Christ, demonstrated that the oracles' suppression resulted not from any miraculous process arising from Christ's coming, but, nearly four centuries later, in the time of Theodosius the Great and other Christian emperors of the late fourth and the fifth century, owing to imperial suppression of the pagan temples. On 18 July 1703, Stolle visited the famous Cartesian mathematician and philosopher Burchard De Volder in Leiden who, like others, assured him that Bayle did not understand Spinoza's thought correctly.

In Amsterdam, one of their meetings, in a tavern called "Zum Bremer Hauptmann," was with an old man who had entertained unconventional views on theology "from his youth onwards having known paradoxical people" and "had also known Spinoza well." This person likewise confirmed Spinoza was banished for maintaining that the Books of Moses were a "human book" not written by Moses. Afterwards, Spinoza lacked means of upkeep, he added, but conducted himself "very circumspectly" and associated with Mennonites who gave him money and lent support because they considered "it untrue that Spinoza adhered to such outlandish and evil views [as others accused him of]. There were some who became very friendly with him [doubtless an allusion to Spinoza's friends, Jelles, Balling, and De Vries]; and because they met regularly with him in a particular place and there freely discussed religious and philosophical matters together, they were led astray by him into his particular viewpoints."[76]

In The Hague, Stolle visited the Huguenot preacher Jacques Bernard (1658–1718) and the journalist Basnage de Beauval. "Spinoza does not have many adherents here," Bernard assured him, any longer "but did have a whole crowd in Overijssel, among them not just many savants but even some preachers," an obvious allusion to the Spinozist minister Frederik van Leenhof (1647–1715).[77] In Rotterdam, the group conferred, on 6 August 1703, with Bayle who opened by praising Thomasius and complaining that Dutch booksellers were too slack in presenting his works to the public but soon turned to the issue of Spinoza, while proving distinctly defensive regarding De Volder's accusation. He too, though, readily conceded that Spinoza had lived his last years in The Hague very soberly, having no use for luxury and display. He had not received financial support from many "Maecenaten but had received an annual pension from a Mennonite and although he had sometimes been asked for his opinion about matters of state, in which he was very astute [*scharfsichtig*], yet had not drawn any money from that." Informing Bayle of the various "Spinoza" interviews he had managed to arrange in Holland, Stolle expressed his bafflement that several interlocutors presented

---

[76] Guhrauer, "Beiträge," 485; Freudenthal/Walther, *Lebensgeschichte* i, 83.
[77] Guhrauer, "Beiträge," 510.

Spinoza as someone letting his views be clearly known, whereas others held that he deviously concealed them: Bayle sensibly suggested that perhaps both assessments were correct in accord with the different phases of Spinoza's life.[78]

The evidence of Stolle and Hallmann supports the conclusion that, after long concealing his subversive views, Spinoza in 1655 deliberately provoked his clash with rabbinic authority, creating a full-scale "scandal" within the community especially by denying the Torah was sacred and of divine origin. At a certain point he began infiltrating into discussions heresies he had obviously developed in his mind long before the open break. Since the *herem* against Spinoza expressly states that henceforth no member of the community should speak with him, or read anything that he wrote, it may well be that in addition to what Franco Mendes terms Spinoza's "contumacia e obstinacão [contumacy and stubbornness]," a prime factor in escalating the communal "perturbations" and triggering the *herem* was that Spinoza, like De Prado, "had some *partidarios* [supporters]," though today there is scant concrete evidence of that.[79]

Due possibly to conflicting advice from a panel of rabbis famed for their disagreements, during the summer of 1656, some of the *parnasim* may have hesitated, or still hoped Spinoza would back down and compromise. Such a supposition would explain the curious fact that the decree of expulsion itself is dated 27 July but the actual ceremony, according to the community's chronicler, Franco Mendes, at which the *herem* was read out by Rabbi Aboab, the so-called *shamta* (ceremony of anathema or excommunication), and the ritual blowing of the *shofar* putting into effect and publicly proclaiming Spinoza's expulsion from the synagogue, cutting off all contact, occurred only on 22 Elul 5416, that is 11 September 1656, more than six weeks later.[80] It seems probable therefore that Spinoza was actually effectively ousted from Jewish orthodoxy and all contact with practising Jews and Jewish life not on 27 July 1656, the date found in most modern accounts of his life, that is 6 Av—three days before *Tisha b'Av* [Ninth of Av] the annual fast day commemorating the great disasters of Jewish history headed by the destruction of Solomon's Temple by the Babylonians, and the destruction of the Second Temple by the Romans—but rather some six weeks later, in the early autumn of 1656, in accordance with the precedent set in Venice, in 1618, allowing the banished violator an interval, supposedly one month, to consider and duly repent before the *herem* takes effect.[81] Still, the 6th of Av, 27 July 1656, was the date the judgement of the *parnasim* and rabbis was reached and recorded, and the clock set ticking, the date affixed to the recorded *herem* itself, and this, by a strange

---

[78] Guhrauer, "Beiträge," 511; Freudenthal/Walther, *Lebensgeschichte* i, 88.
[79] Franco Mendes, *Memorias*, 61.
[80] Franco Mendes, *Memorias*, 61; Freudenthal/Walther, *Lebensgeschichte* ii, 137; Kasher and Biderman, "Why was Spinoza Excommunicated?," 101–2.
[81] Kasher and Biderman, "Why was Spinoza Excommunicated?," 98, 100–1; Wesselius, "Spinoza's Excommunication," 47.

twist of fate, we shall see further on, coincided with a week in which important developments unconnected with this unfolded in the world of Dutch academic philosophy.

As usual with instances of *herem*, then, the community seemingly waited, even hesitated, hoping for signs of contrition and repentance from the miscreant promising to mend his ways. Presumably, it was either shortly before the July date or during this interval down to 11 September 1656 that Spinoza penned his first major text, the lost *Apologia* in Spanish, justifying his rejecting the rabbinic view of the Torah as sacred divine revelation. What is certain is that between July and September 1656, and indeed both before and after the latter date, very differently from Da Costa, De Prado, and most others, Spinoza made no effort whatever to seek reconciliation with the community, offered no regrets, contrition, or attempt at reconciliation.

Such conduct meant facing up to a whole range of harsh consequences. For the psychological effect of total ostracization from the community in which one was brought up and schooled, especially when raised in a language milieu different from that of the surrounding society, and the abruptness of being ousted, was in most cases huge, exerting a severely wrenching effect on the ousted personage as the tragic stories of Uriel da Costa and De Prado abundantly illustrate.[82] Da Costa was just as convinced as Spinoza that the Pharisees of their day (i.e. the rabbis) sought to enslave their congregations intellectually and socially but still tried to secure rehabilitation at great cost in terms of personal stress and humiliation. De Prado too keenly resented the rabbis' imposing a little "Inquisition" in Amsterdam, but nevertheless felt so deeply unsettled by his expulsion that he repeatedly attempted to get his *herem* lifted, and succeeded initially, after accepting terms of capitulation that involved mounting the *theba* in synagogue and humiliatingly offering public contrition before the congregation for the great "escandalo" he had caused.

Yet, where Uriel da Costa and De Prado both clung to the congregation and were in some sense ultimately defeated by the rabbis and their rigid vision of what Judaism is, and compelled to bow down, Spinoza from the very outset of his struggle with rabbinic authority seems to have been resolved to avoid any such submission, humiliation, and repentance by simply separating himself completely from Judaism and the milieu in which he had grown up. Spinoza "himself did very often own [in later years]," as the English version of Colerus' biography puts it, "that he was excommunicated by them, and declared, that from that time he broke all friendship and correspondence with them." "Some Jews of Amsterdam who knew Spinoza very well," adds Colerus here, "have also confirmed to me the truth of that fact."[83]

[82] Albiac, *Sinagoga vacía*, 243–5, 250, 343; Den Boer, *Literatura sefardí*, 79, 97, 119.
[83] Colerus, *Life of Benedict de Spinoza*, 11.

4
A Secret Legacy from Portugal

4.i Crypto-Judaism and Religious Subversion

It would be a gross oversimplification to interpret Spinoza's life and thought as essentially shaped by his family's "Marrano" (Iberian crypto-Jewish New Christian) background in Portugal. Nevertheless, his family's "Marrano" background *was* a powerful formative factor in his upbringing and the dramatic changes in his life in the 1650s, a key strand in the circumstances grounding Spinoza's unique outlook and philosophy. As with many Portuguese "New Christians" [*cristãos novos*] or Marranos (or *conversos*), the sect of former Jews forcibly converted to Catholicism by the Portuguese king in 1497, as the sixteenth century wore on, religious loyalties among the successive generations of Spinoza's forebears, grandparents and parents grew more complex, fragmented, and diverse.[1]

Like most forcibly converted Portuguese Jews, the Spinoza clan almost certainly originated in Spain and fled across the Spanish border to avoid forced baptism, reaching Portugal in 1492, the year Ferdinand and Isabella ordered the expulsion of those Spanish Jews refusing to convert to Christianity. Former Portuguese "New Christians" returning to normative Judaism in seventeenth-century Holland, Italy, England, and elsewhere where Judaism was tolerated, often discarded or partly discarded their enforced "Christian" names, adopting instead a Jewish or "synagogue" first and (often but not always) second, name—except for purposes of international trade where retention of the royally imposed "Christian name" was more usual. Where families still conserved knowledge of their pre-1492 Jewish names, they often dropped altogether their post-1492 Spanish or Portuguese surname, reverting to their authentic medieval Iberian Jewish surname, as may have been the case with Spinoza's maternal grandmother, Maria Nunes, in Holland afterwards called Miriam Senior. By contrast, Spinoza's paternal grandfather, "Pedro Rodrigues de Espinosa," son of a Lisbon merchant baptized in Portugal, when free of oppression, in later life adopted the synagogue name "Isaac de Espinoza" retaining the same appellation as in Portugal.

Accordingly, the name "Espinosa" or "Espinoza" may well have been the family's surname prior to their expulsion from Spain. Sephardic surnames among Portuguese Jewish migrants in early modern Europe, North Africa, and

---

[1] Borges Coelho, "Orígenes," 132.

the Near East frequently derived from medieval Spanish place names, and such centuries-old family surnames, certainly in some cases, persisted afterwards in seventeenth-century Holland. Assuming Spinoza's surname is indeed a toponym in this sense, the family may have originated in either Espinosa de los Monteros,[2] a village north of Burgos, close to Santander and the Spanish north coast, or Espinosa de Cerrato, near Palencia also in northern Castile but south of Burgos. Alternatively, if not a genuine toponym reaching back to the Middle Ages, the family's pre-1492 Spanish Jewish surname by the seventeenth century had simply been lost to the mists of time.

It was the Jews of Portugal specifically, a crucial point to note, rather than those of Spain who generated the main body of hidden crypto-Judaism, Iberian intellectual culture's remarkably contorted but prime early modern subversive seedbed. Spain's Jews in 1492, having to choose conversion or expulsion, faced the choice of either opting to remain Jews which meant emigrating, or else keeping their homes, possessions, and vocations at the price of compulsory Christianization. After 1492, converts remaining in Spain, despite having been baptized against their will (and, after baptism, forbidden to leave), remained much less active in the long term as *judaizantes* [crypto-Judaizers] than those in Portugal, a striking difference partly due to the much better prospects for successfully integrating into Spanish than into Portuguese society in the first half of the sixteenth century. By contrast, nearly all the roughly 40,000 Jews who migrated from Spain either overland, or by sea, to Portugal in expectation of avoiding forced baptism, in 1492, just five years later, in 1497, were forcibly converted nonetheless (with the small number of Jews living in Portugal previously), this time, though, without any option of refusing baptism (again) and departing. These migrants, having already rejected Christianity at the cost of abandoning homes and possessions in Spain, tended to be doubly resentful and estranged, experiencing royal-ecclesiastical pressure to convert to an unwelcome faith twice within five years and finding now far fewer possibilities for successful integration than their former co-religionists remaining in Spain. Compelled to submit to elaborate outward veneration of a faith many or most inwardly abjured, this group, including the Espinoza family, often submitted only sullenly while secretly adhering to their old faith. In most of Spain (apart from Mallorca) crypto-Judaism sustained itself much less intensively and extensively as an underground sect.

In Spain, the "large number of Jews" who converted, as Spinoza himself later expressed the point in his *TTP*, "were granted the privileges of native Spaniards and deemed worthy of all positions of dignity."[3] Initially, only sporadic discrimination due to ethnic origin hindered admission to Spain's professions, public office, and religious orders whereas in Portugal, after 1497, due to the great size of

---

[2] Dujovne, *Spinoza* i, 52.
[3] Spinoza, *Theological-Political Treatise*, 55; Borges Coelho, "Orígenes," 119.

the influx relative to the smaller size of native Portuguese society, legal exclusion and marginalization of "New Christians" took effect at once. Marginalized socially by royal decree, in Portugal the new converts were excluded *en bloc* from offices and honours and kept segregated from mainstream society thereby remaining readily identifiable as a separate and despised social caste. This marked divergence between Spain's "New Christians" and those of Portugal was encouraged by the Spanish crown under Ferdinand and Isabella who tenaciously resisted the bifurcation of society many Spaniards called for, refusing systematic legal segregation and debarment. Opposing for now the growing demand for "purity of blood" statutes excluding "New Christians" of Jewish or Muslim descent from public office, noble status, and the military orders, the Spanish crown kept the gates open for over half a century. Eventually, statutes debarring New Christians were systematically adopted also in Spain, but only in the later sixteenth century and, by then, Spain's converts had largely disappeared as a separate social group, having become absorbed (except again in Mallorca), so that enforcing these statutes principally affected new arrivals and recent immigrants.

After 1580, when the union of the crowns of Spain and Portugal opened the way to easier cross-border migration, the situation changed again becoming more complex. Many of Portugal's resolute crypto-Jews migrated back to, or through Spain, but henceforth remained socially a largely cordoned off separate new caste also there, being now commonly called the "Portuguese" or "Portuguese New Christians," even though these families had mostly originated before 1492 in Spain. Furthermore, although these returnees soon again became Spanish rather than Portuguese-speaking, until late in the eighteenth century they were still invariably classified by their neighbours, by royal authorities and the Inquisition, whether living in Spain, Spanish America, or elsewhere outside Portugal, as "Portuguese." Underground locally nurtured crypto-Judaism outside Portugal after 1580, including in mainland Spain and Spanish America, was thus largely confined to networks of these so-called "Portuguese" families stemming from Portugal.

Spinoza's claim in his *TTP* that former Jews accepting Christianity in Spain disappeared as an identifiable separate group, owing to a more open royal policy than in Portugal, becoming indistinguishable from other Spaniards "so that in a short time there were no remnants of them left and no memory of them," as he expresses it, is doubtless something of an exaggeration.[4] Prejudice against "New Christians" as a despised, suspect separate caste equally typified Portuguese *and* Spanish society at the end of the fifteenth and through the sixteenth century, not least in Espinosa de los Monteros where various ugly incidents occurred.[5]

---

[4] Spinoza, *Theological-Political Treatise*, 55; Salomon, *Portrait of a New Christian*, 171; Bodian, *Dying in the Law of Moses*, 20; Saperstein, *Exile in Amsterdam*, 477n68.

[5] Amador de la Rios, *Historia social*, 589.

Nevertheless, *limpieza de sangre* [cleanliness of blood] laws proclaiming those of "New Christian blood" unworthy of position and honour became widespread in Spain only during the late sixteenth century and, as a consequence, after 1580, practically all resolute Iberian crypto-Jews wherever they were encountered, including in Spain and Spanish America as well as the rest of Europe and the New World, predominantly descended, as the Inquisition's archives abundantly confirm, from families forcibly converted in Portugal, in 1497. This also applies to the great majority of former New Christians returning to normative Judaism, whether Spanish- or Portuguese-speaking, in seventeenth-century Venice, Hamburg, and Holland.

This tortuous outcome is clearly reflected in Spinoza's account of the striking phenomenon of Jewish survival as a people and religion through the millennia. In his view there was nothing whatever miraculous, sacred, or divinely ordained about Jewish survival; it merely reflects segregation, coercion, and discrimination. Judaism was perpetuated, he maintains, by preserving distinct religious rites and restricting marriage to their own group, resulting in social segregation driven by the resentment of those around them rigorously segregating them as a sect but operating as the vital factor in their survival. Jews eventually integrate socially where such discrimination lapses, and remain separate where it persists.

4.ii Vidigueira

Spinoza's paternal grandfather, known earlier under his Portuguese name as Pedro Rodrigues [or Roiz] Espinoza, but in Holland as Isaac de Espinoza, was born in Lisbon around 1559, according to an Inquisition report of 1612 concerning escaped Judaizing heretics. In adult life, his parents Fernando d'Espinoza and Mor Álvares, had lived mainly in the small, inland southern Alentejo town of Vidigueira where her family had dwelt probably since the end of the fifteenth century. A minor rural township near Évora, in 1527 boasting some 1,500 inhabitants, Vidigueira was situated in the heart of a wine-producing region, the seigneurial rights over which the crown had assigned as a reward, in perpetuity, to the great navigator Vasco da Gama (1469–1524) and his heirs, the counts of Vidigueira. Several of Spinoza's forebears were employees in the service of the counts, including a grandfather of Mor Álvares called Manoel Álvares, a collector of rents for the counts, his brother, and a cousin, Francisco Álvares Falcão, who was an *administrador* of the count's lands. Spinoza's sixteenth-century paternal forebears also owned at least two vineyards locally. Mor's father, hence Isaac's grandfather and Spinoza's great-great-grandfather, named Gabriel Álvares, born and raised in Vidigueira, was another local tax-collector.[6] Besides employment in

---

[6] Vaz Dias and Van der Tak, "Spinoza Merchant," 136, 138; Révah, *Des Marranes à Spinoza*, 169; Salomon, "Introdução," xcvi.

the service of the counts and other administrative functions, Gabriel was secretary of the town orphanage.

Sephardic Jews had long been accustomed to name first sons after the paternal grandfather and second sons after the maternal. Thus, Spinoza's older brother was named "Isaac" after their paternal grandfather, Pedro (see Figure 4.1). Spinoza's father, Michael d'Espinoza, likewise had an older brother and he was named Fernando d'Espinoza after their paternal grandfather, the husband of the younger Mor Álvares. First daughters were named after the paternal grandmother, and second daughters after the maternal, so Spinoza's older sister, Miriam (his father's second daughter), was named after their maternal grandmother, Miriam Senior (alias Maria Nunes). Spinoza himself, as Michael's second son, was named "Baruch" after the spouse of his maternal grandmother, that is Miriam's husband, Baruch Senior (Henrique Garces). Equally, the older Isaac's mother, Spinoza's great-grandmother, Mor Álvares, was named after an older Mor Álvares who was the wife of her grandfather, Manoel.[7] Spinoza's father, Michael d'Espinoza, being a younger son of Isaac [alias Pedro Rodrigues] Espinoza, received his Portuguese baptismal name—"Gabriel Álvares d'Espinoza"—not from Isaac's grandfather but a different "Gabriel," probably the father of Isaac de Espinoza's wife.

Vidigueira's main church, Santa Casa da Misericórdia, among the oldest surviving churches in Portugal, still today dominates the town centre standing close to the town's main square and the "Street of the Merchants" where, or near where, parts of the Spinoza family lived. It was just one of several local churches, chapels, and shrines where, generation after generation, the Spinoza family were long habituated to regularly appear, kneel, cross themselves, and display outwardly to all onlookers their staged veneration of Christ, and familiarity with the array of Catholic saints, endlessly emulating the prayer and pious practices of Catholic Christians. One can hardly doubt that Spinoza's subdued but noticeable life-long aversion to the Catholic faith and its practices was closely connected to this longstanding repressive scenario and age-old scene of family humiliation. Since inculcating loyalty to the Law of Moses, marking the Jewish sabbath, fasting on Yom Kippur and other typical crypto-Jewish practices needed to be kept strictly secret, it was far too dangerous to tell children that what the Church taught is untruth and idolatry until, we see from the pattern recurring in the Portuguese Inquisition archives, reaching the age of fourteen or fifteen. As children they were thus brought up believing in a faith that they were then persuaded by parents, older siblings, and other relatives is entirely false, but only on reaching an age when they could be made to grasp fully how perilous it would be for them and their families should they let slip any sign of inner rejection of the enforced faith. Crypto-Jewish allegiance in the sixteenth-century Portuguese context

---

[7] Borges Coelho, *Inquisição de Évora*, 494; Borges Coelho, "Orígenes," 125; Vaz Dias and Van der Tak, "Spinoza Merchant," 136, 138.

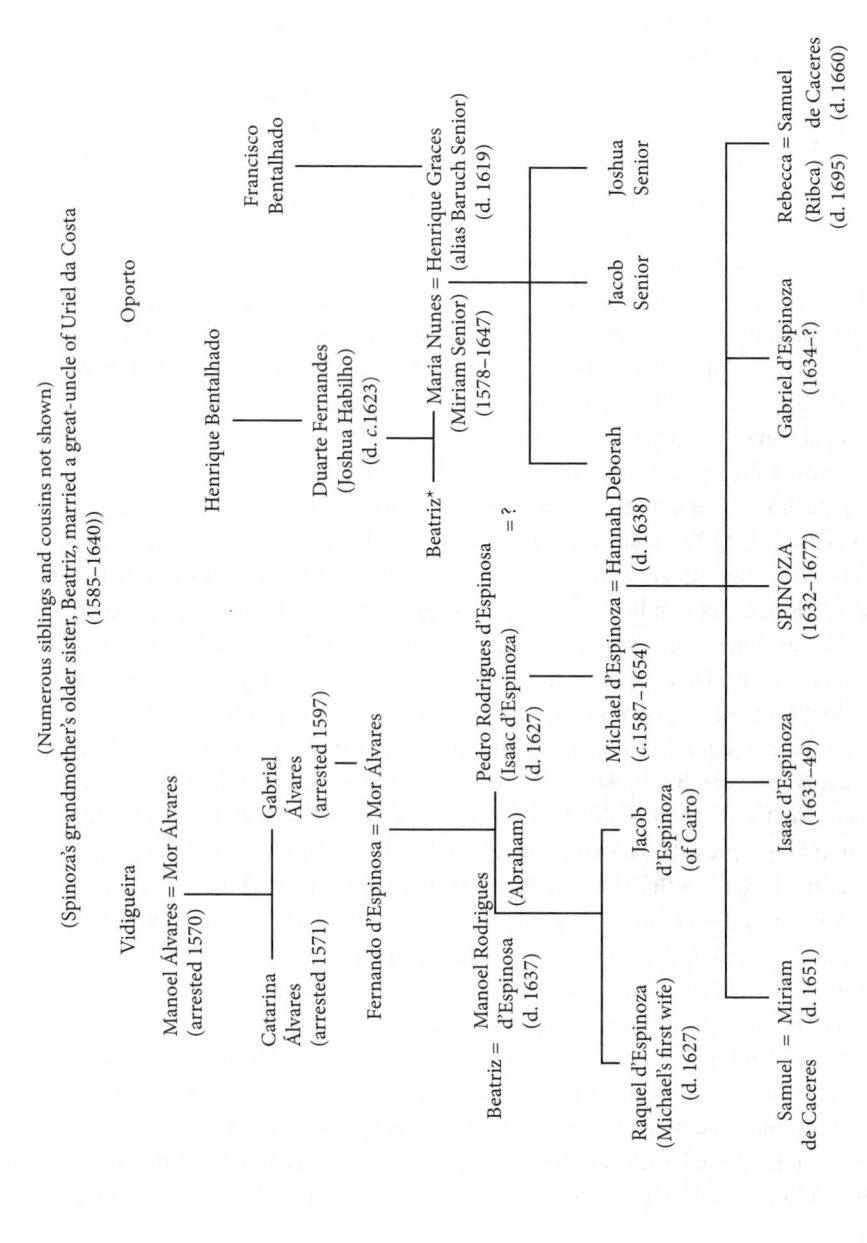

Figure 4.1 Spinoza family tree.

became a matter of family as well as religious loyalty but always carried with it an immense baggage of fear, psychological tension, and stress, and for some conflicted loyalties.[8]

Crypto-Judaism in sixteenth- and seventeenth-century Iberia was basically an affair of family secrets, guarded revelations, and hidden networks. A notorious "scandal" played a key part in the post-1497 history of the Vidigueira locality, involving a dense local network of underground religious subversion uncovered by the authorities at Beja—another small township about twenty-six kilometres south of Vidigueira where part of the Álvares family dwelt. In 1570–2, this fraught, long-remembered furore gripped the whole Évora region, affecting the Spinoza family's entire subsequent history. It revolved around a clandestine seditious network flourishing there in the late 1560s that drew the Évora Inquisition tribunal into protracted investigations. The affair remained a topic of local gossip and legend for generations, involving not only *cristãos novos* but also "Old Christians" of non-Jewish descent who entered into the conspiracy persuaded by neighbours of Jewish descent that core Christian doctrine is assuredly fabrication by theologians devoid of genuine links with the Old Testament. Shockingly for many, several Old Christians were drawn into the Judaizers' underground meetings, rites, and rituals and this collective rejection of Church doctrine as "false" teaching. Its lynchpin was a university graduate, the Licenciado Luis Vaz da Costa, who reportedly convened secret meetings in his study surrounded by old books where he assured his following that the Church was just a usurping tyrant propagating lies. Using phrases of Hebrew as well as Latin, he taught that the Law of Moses was the true law under which they must organize their lives.[9]

So widespread was this "conjura de Beja [conspiracy of Beja]," that during 1570–2, it landed no less than fifty-five male and female prisoners in the Évora Inquisition dungeons, adding a further layer of feverish suspicion to the already tense culture of religious fervour gripping the area, seething with prejudice, hatred, and theological bigotry.[10] The *conjura*, the Inquisition evidence establishes, was not just about secretly conserving Jewish practices and rituals in and around Vidigueira and Beja, but involved secret active proselytizing, to win over the vacillating, extending subversive networks teaching that the Catholic Church is tyranny and worship of Christ pure "superstition." Uncovered during 1570, half a century before Spinoza's birth, this notorious "conspiracy of Beja" fatally entangled a considerable number of Spinoza's ancestors variously seized in Beja, Vidigueira, and Évora. On 3 July 1571, Mor Álvares' grandfather, the tailor Manoel Álvares, was seized along with several other relatives, including a sister

---

[8] ANTT Inquisao de Lisboa 7192, "Proceso de Duarte Nunes da Costa," citing the files relating to his sisters and brother-in-law, fos. 11, 13, 15–16.
[9] Saraiva, *Inquisição e Cristãos-Novos*, 132.
[10] Borges Coelho, *Inquisição de Évora*, 356–62; Borges Coelho, "Orígenes," 127.

of Mor's father, Catarina, detained in Évora along with her husband,[11] the *administrador* of the conde's estates, Álvares Falcão. Two other imprisoned relatives, brothers living in Beja, Luis and Tomás Álvares Barzelai, previously "reconciled" after prolonged imprisonment and torture were burnt at the stake for "Judaizing" in the grand Évora auto-da-fé of 1572.[12] Other family members were repeatedly subjected to torture, before being "reconciled" and paraded in humiliation before Évora's populace in autos-da-fé.[13] But on orders of Portugal's Inquisitor General, a stubborn hard-core refusing, even under torture, to confess or betray other family members were transferred to dungeons in Lisbon, and tortured there before appearing in the still grander auto-da-fé staged in Lisbon on 31 January 1574.

Because of the nature of Portuguese crypto-Judaism as a family phenomenon, any single Inquisition arrest for "Judaizing" tended to swiftly envelop entire families. In a fresh round of arrests ravaging the family towards the end of Philip II's reign, in August 1597, Isaac's maternal grandfather, Gabriel Álvares, was arrested at the age of sixty-three and imprisoned for suspected Judaizing together with two of his sons and several other relatives, also tortured and stripped of their possessions.[14] His elder son, Manoel Álvares (named after his grandfather), was imprisoned for years before eventually appearing in the auto-da-fé "celebrated" at Évora on 10 June 1602.[15] Among those seized in 1597 were Gabriel's two sisters, Mor Álvares (named after her grandmother) and Isabel Álvares and her two daughters who were likewise tortured and stripped of their possessions. Baptized in Vidigueira, Isabel and her daughters were found to be secretly observing the Friday night advent of the Jewish Sabbath, cleaning beforehand and then lighting candles, keeping the Yom Kippur fast, and disrespecting (working at home on) the, to them, inauthentic Christian day of rest, Sunday.[16] Gabriel's daughter, Mor Álvares, was denounced too, though fortunately for her, she had already escaped Portugal.[17] Altogether, so many of Spinoza's forebears in Portugal were seized, tortured, imprisoned, had their possessions confiscated and were paraded in autos-da-fé in Évora, Lisbon, and Coimbra, that it is impossible to estimate the number, but it certainly exceeds twenty, with several burnt at the stake. At the same time, contemporary Inquisition records of the 1580s and 1590s show that many on both sides of his family surreptitiously left the country.

Spinoza's father, Michael d'Espinoza (*c*.1587–1654), was born and baptized as "Gabriel Álvares Espinosa" in Vidigueira.[18] According to one Amsterdam notarial

---

[11] Borges Coelho, *Inquisição de Évora*, 494–5; Borges Coelho, "Orígenes," 127; Salomon, "Introdução," xcvi.
[12] Borges Coelho, *Inquisição de Évora*, 182. [13] Borges Coelho, "Orígenes," 127–8.
[14] Vaz Dias and Van der Tak, "Spinoza Merchant," 136, 138; Révah, *Des Marranes à Spinoza*, 169; Salomon, "Introdução," xcvi.
[15] Salomon, "Introdução," xcvi; Israel, "Spain's Empire, 'superstitio'," 86.
[16] Borges Coelho, "Orígenes," 129.
[17] Borges Coelho, "Orígenes," 125, 128; Salomon, "Introdução," xcv.
[18] GAA NA 1502, p. 100. deed, 9 Dec. 1642 (J.V.Oli).

deed, of December 1642, he was then "about fifty years old," placing his birth date after 1590, but according to at least three other notarial deeds (of 1627, 1633, and 1634) he was more probably born in 1587 or 1588.[19] Later, in Holland, he used his Portuguese name "Gabriel Álvares Espinosa" in his overseas business dealings,[20] but locally was principally known as "Michael [Miguel]." While still a young boy, at around eight or nine in 1597, he left Portugal for good together with his father, Pedro Rodrigues d'Espinoza [Isaac], and other relatives, emigrating to Nantes, a family flight that occurred well before the so-called "general pardon" of New Christians of 1605.[21] Michael was old enough, though, later to recount to his children details of Vidigueira's viticultural agrarian environs and their family's secretive, fraught life there, including the tragic story of the *conjura de Beja*.

At Nantes, the Spinoza family, dwelling ostensibly as New Christians, belonged to the international "Marrano" diaspora, a far-flung network constituting one of the most dispersed and yet socially cohesive religious and cultural groupings of the early modern Atlantic world. Rather like the Portuguese New Christian community at Rouen, with which Michael later had trade connections, "at Nantes, the Portuguese were divided in the late sixteenth century," as one authority explains, into two factions, "between judaizers and Catholics." According to a prisoner of the Lisbon Inquisition, the merchant Manoel Botelho originally from Beja, who spent three years in Nantes (1602–5) before the 1605 "Pardon General" but afterwards ill-advisedly returned to Lisbon and was arrested in 1609, for Judaizing since 1605, the internal religious feuding and "grandes differencias" between the Portuguese "Christianizers" and "Judaizers" at the start of the new century were an unending battle carried on in Nantes practically every day.[22] Imprisoned for years in the Lisbon Inquisition dungeons resisting the charge that he was a heretic apostate from the holy Catholic Church, testifying repeatedly through 1609–10 and again in March 1611, Botelho claimed to be one of those repudiated by the Nantes Judaizers as "a pagan and idolater" worshipping the false Messiah Christ and the Holy Trinity. Among the principal "Judaizers" stubbornly rejecting Christianity whilst pretending to live outwardly as Christians whom Botelho reported to the Lisbon Inquisition, in 1611, were Michael's father, Pedro Rodrigues d'Espinoza, and still more prominently, Michael's uncle, who was the family's major merchant in Nantes, his father's brother, Manoel Rodrigues d'Espinoza [Abraham d'Espinoza], whom Botelho confirmed in his Inquisition confessions, were the sons of Fernando d'Espinoza.[23] Manoel [alias Abraham], we

---

[19] Freudenthal/Walther, *Lebensgeschichte* i, 210–11; Michael was born in Vidigueira according to his marriage vows on the occasion of his third marriage, in 1641; see ibid., 191; Borges Coelho, "Orígenes," 126.

[20] Borges Coelho, "Orígenes," 126.

[21] Révah, *Des Marranes à Spinoza*, 170; Salomon, "Introdução," xcv.

[22] ANTT Inquisition Archives TSO-IL-28-318 "Proceso de Manoel Botelho" fos. 28, 65; I am grateful to Jeroen van de Ven and Ton Tielen for bringing this Inquisition *proceso* to my attention.

[23] ANTT Inquisition Archives TSO-IL-28-318 "Proceso de Manoel Botelho" fo. 64v.

know, had been residing in Nantes with his wife Beatriz (who died there in childbirth), since around 1591 or 1592, hence approximately five or six years before his brother, Pedro, and his nephews arrived.[24]

The Nantes Portuguese New Christian community remained tiny throughout the next half century or so, rarely rising above ten or a dozen families. Nevertheless, it was a significant transit point for New Christians migrating elsewhere. Over a hundred Portuguese New Christian families, including that of Manoel and Beatriz Rodrigues d'Espinoza, received naturalization papers at Nantes between 1575 and 1600.[25] Few stayed long, being resented as intrusive business competitors seeking to establish seeds of Judaism in a town where, reportedly, the name of "Jew" was detested. Their right to settle and do business there long remained contested, especially by that thriving port's old-established merchant community. However, Manoel, Pedro, and their fellow Judaizers possessed valuable connections with the Atlantic sugar trade, with Portugal, Brazil, and the Azores, that native French merchants lacked, so that Henri IV down to 1610, and, later, Richelieu, showed little inclination to support the persistent efforts of locals to have the Portuguese New Christian intruders expelled, as would certainly have occurred had the Catholic League, with Spanish help, triumphed over Henri, during the long-lasting French Wars of Religion (1562–98).

Observing the role of economic rivalry in the complaints against them, Louis XIV's famous minister, Colbert, later remarked that "commercial jealousy will always move [local Catholic] merchants to be of the opinion that the Jews should be expelled; but it is necessary to look beyond these reactions based on particular interest to judge sanely whether the commerce they conduct through the correspondence they have with all parts of the world with those of their sect, is of such a character as is advantageous to the state."[26] Colbert had little doubt that it was. But Louis XIV, as he grew more ambitious in building his ascendancy across Europe, learnt, like Philip II before him, that denying Protestants and Jews toleration and unbendingly imposing Catholic uniformity, powerfully reduces scope, by pulling church and state tighter together, for individual judgement and criticism, thereby bolstering—far more than Colbert's policy—royal dominance and glory.

4.iii Spinoza's Mother's Family

Spinoza's mother, Hannah Deborah, for her part, descended on both her father's and mother's side from a leading Oporto commercial family, the Bentalhados, several of whom, in the sixteenth and early seventeenth century, were suspected

---

[24] Bruyn Kops, *A Spirited Exchange*, 282.   [25] Mathorez, "Notes sur l'histoire," 324.
[26] Brunschvicg, *Juifs de Nantes*, 14; Révah, *Des Marranes à Spinoza*, 64–6.

crypto-Jews cast into Inquisition dungeons and repeatedly interrogated and tortured. Others, though, to all appearances opted for sincere commitment to the Catholic faith, or found themselves painfully caught somewhere in between. If such Sephardic former New Christian writers as De Prado, Orobio, and Levi de Barrios felt a lifelong sensitivity to the trauma of persecution and repression to which the Church and Iberia's monarchs had subjected them and their forebears, it is no accident that repression rooted in what Spinoza terms "superstition" and "hatred" emerges among the most prominent themes of his political and general philosophy. In his mature writing, a particular point where Spinoza's ideas strikingly converge with his family history is his remarkable commentary on religious martyrdom.[27] Among source material relating to his life and thought, the exchange of letters about this topic, in 1675, with his alienated former disciple, Albert Burgh (c.1648–1708), who, in 1673, repudiated Spinoza's teaching and embraced Catholicism in Italy, is among the few instances when our studiedly cool and cautious philosopher noticeably loses his temper. Religious persecution, especially church-inflicted martyrdom, remained a red flag to him, a deeply emotional and unsettling topic.

Spinoza's maternal grandmother, Miriam Senior, earlier called Maria Nunes (1578–1647), born in Ponte de Lima, in northern Portugal, whom Spinoza knew well in his youth, had an older sister, Beatriz Nunes, married to an Oporto lawyer, Paulo Brandão, who on his father's side, was a great-uncle of the notorious and tragic Uriel da Costa (c.1585–1640).[28] Uriel's great-aunt by marriage, Beatriz, was thus also Spinoza's great-aunt, and her daughter, Paula, married another relative of Maria Nunes.[29] Spinoza thus had several family ties to the man who was Amsterdam Sephardic Jewry's most infamous heretic during his own youth. Baptized under the name "Gabriel da Costa," Uriel studied canon law at Coimbra University from 1600 to 1608, albeit with interruptions while experiencing growing personal difficulties. In his autobiographical record, *Exemplar humanae vitae* (not published until 1687), Uriel mentions that his father, Bento da Costa Brandão who died in Oporto, in 1608, was a faithful Christian, and Uriel himself claimed to have still been a fervent Christian bent on an ecclesiastical career on becoming a university student at Coimbra. But certain doctrines—that one is absolved from sins only by confessing to a priest and the notion of eternal damnation—began troubling him. By 1605, overcome with doubt, he began researching into the early sources of the Christian faith. The more he researched

---

[27] Bodian, *Dying in the Law of Moses*, 250n38; Yovel, *Spinoza and Other Heretics*, 187–8.
[28] Révah, *Des Marranes à Spinoza*, 122–3, 125, 146; Schwarz, *Uriel da Costa*, 86.
[29] Uriel had an older brother called Jacome (Abraham) da Costa (1580–1646) who married a cousin of Miriam and Beatriz, a certain Genebra Nunes, and a brother, Joseph da Costa (d. 1664), who settled in Amsterdam and became prominent in the Sephardic community and the sugar trade with Brazil. From both his brothers Uriel would, in his last years in Amsterdam, remain bitterly estranged. Osier, *D'Uriel da Costa à Spinoza*, 143, 160 n40, 163n50; Borges Coelho, *Inquisição de Évora*, 482.

Christianity's origins the more sceptical he grew. His mother, Branca Dinis, after marriage Branca da Costa, to whom he remained extremely close, came from a family where crypto-Judaism remained alive, and is known from Inquisition sources to have willingly followed her son, after her husband's death, in reverting to crypto-Judaism which he did around 1609.[30] When the Inquisition began making inquiries, in 1614, Branca fled Portugal together with Uriel and his wife, and her three other sons, spending her remaining years as a Jewess, now called "Sarah da Costa," first in Hamburg with Uriel and then Amsterdam where she died and was buried according to Jewish rites, in October 1628.[31]

Spinoza was only eight when, in April 1640, his deeply troubled relative, Uriel da Costa—having convinced himself the rabbis had perverted original authentic Judaism no less than the Church Fathers had misrepresented and falsified the teaching of the Jew Jesus and, since 1623, in open rebellion against the rabbis no less than the churches—ended his life by suicide. As a child, it may be that Spinoza was kept unaware of his family's connections with the notorious Da Costa. But, as a teenager, given how Uriel was then publicly reviled by Jews and Christians alike and the open conflict that arose between Da Costa and his brothers, Abraham and Joseph, who dwelt near the Spinozas in Amsterdam, the likelihood is that relatives, especially his grandmother, Miriam (alias Maria Nunes), who lived nearby until Spinoza was fifteen, and her sons, *did* explain to her grandson his own family ties to the fraught and tormented Uriel as well as the intricacies of an affair now well-known to his school-fellows that was a public as much as family scandal.[32]

If the Da Costa's family's deep religious rift was a striking phenomenon with a continuing resonance, the split within Spinoza's mother's family, the Bentalhado clan of Oporto, if less sensational, was equally profound and far-reaching. Two brothers, sons of a physician of the Bentalhado family, and second cousins of Spinoza's grandmother Miriam, hence uncles of Hanna Deborah, Spinoza's mother, entered the Jesuit order (among the few Iberian orders that did not then debar New Christians as formal policy). Both achieved considerable contemporary stature in Spain, the elder, Father Manuel López (1525–1603), rising to become Jesuit provincial of Toledo from 1568 to 1573;[33] the younger attaining notoriety as a theorist of a somewhat parallel kind to his philosophical great-nephew in Holland later. This remarkable personage, Enrique Henríquez (1536–1608), entering the Jesuit order, in Portugal, at sixteen in 1552, eventually became a famous professor at Córdoba, and later Salamanca, teaching moral

---

[30] Révah, *Des Marranes à Spinoza*, 138, 157, 160, 163, 165, 167; Yovel, *Spinoza and Other Heretics*, 45; Schwarz, *Uriel da Costa*, 14–17.

[31] Révah, *Des Marranes à Spinoza*, 125, 136–9, 162; Albiac, *Sinagoga vacía*, 278, 280; Salomon and Sassoon, "Introduction," in Da Costa, *Examination of Pharisaic Traditions*, 19.

[32] Révah, *Des Marranes à Spinoza*, 122–3; Osier, *D'Uriel da Costa à Spinoza*, 82; Koen, "Duarte Fernandes, Koopman," 178–9.

[33] Maryks, *Jesuit Order as a Synagogue*, 118–19, 127.

philosophy and political theory, and figuring among the teachers of the later much more renowned Jesuit theorist, Francisco Suárez. When Henríquez entered the order, the Jesuits still adhered to their original policy of ignoring "purity of blood" statutes, remaining open to *conversos* and encouraging New Christians throwing in their lot with Christianity to regard the order with particular favour.

A third brother, João Lopes, settled in the Azores, becoming a proprietor of some substance on the island of São Miguel, in 1568–70, where he organized accommodation for the first Jesuits in the Azores and the first endowment for the Jesuit college, at Ponta Delgada.[34] Things went less smoothly, though, from the 1580s, as the Spanish Jesuits descended into a bitter internal battle between their *converso* component and their *converso*-phobic majority anxious to eradicate what were now deemed their founding figures' embarrassingly disreputable and debasing Jewish origins. In the contentious, charged atmosphere of the late sixteenth century, the *converso* background of their first Superior General, Ignatius Loyola (1491–1556) and *converso* second Superior General, Diego Laínez (1512–65) became, for many, a deeply shameful reality needing to be scrupulously veiled. Henríquez emerged as a rebel at a moment when the battle within the Jesuit movement over whether or not to debar baptized Christians of Jewish or Muslim descent from entering the order reached its climax at the fifth General Congregation of the Jesuits, in 1593, when exclusion of everyone not of Old Christian birth, though still bitterly contested, was finally implemented.

At this point, the first part of Henríquez's best known work, the *Theologia Moralis Summa*, a detailed summation of church law and procedures, published in two parts at Salamanca in 1591 and 1593, stirred controversy by assigning, as critics saw it, insufficient weight to ecclesiastical authority in Christian society. Few copies of his *Theologia Moralis* survived in Iberian lands, the book being suppressed by decree of August 1591 and again in 1603. But it eventually achieved some impact abroad, after being reprinted in republican Venice, in 1597 and 1600, and again, in 1613, at "Maguncia" [Mainz] as *Summae theologiae moralis libri quindecim*. Clashing with his order when ordered to delete passages colleagues disapproved of, and antagonized by the General Congregation's *converso*-phobic policy, Henríquez rejected their strictures and, in 1593, broke with the Jesuits, joining the Dominicans instead.[35] Soon, though, he discovered that the Dominicans were even more bigoted against *conversos* than Jesuits and broke in turn with them, negotiating his reversion to the Jesuits. Henríquez's collision with authority then intensified further when his second main work, *De Pontificis Romani clave*, appeared at Salamanca in 1593. Again, Henríquez was censured for evincing insufficient zeal for papal and ecclesiastical sway over civil society and giving secular authority too much power over ecclesiastics. Following papal

---

[34] Borges Coelho, *Inquisição de Évora*, 499–500.
[35] Maryks, *Jesuit Order as a Synagogue*, 65–6, 148–9.

protests, nearly all copies of this text were gathered up and burnt by the papal nuncio in Madrid, on 7 August 1603, so that today this text is exceedingly rare. In disgrace, Henríquez died at Tivoli, in Italy, in 1608, with a considerable question mark hanging over his head. Even if Spinoza never learnt anything about his Jesuit great-uncles in Spain, it is not hard to discern elements of affinity between him and them arising from the longstanding family spiritual dilemma, the deeply tortured religious context of the century-old Portuguese New Christian spiritual and intellectual inheritance.

4.iv Absolutism Enthroned

Portuguese crypto-Judaism was a deeply entrenched underground network of clandestine religious subversion obstreperously resistant to religious intimidation, persecution, and surveillance, with special relevance to the later emergence of Spinozism as an underground intellectual movement resolutely subversive of all accepted religious belief and core Christian doctrine. But from the 1580s onwards there was also a further layer of parallelism in what became their common political oppositional tendency as Portuguese crypto-Judaism acquired in addition a layer of underground political activism.

In the year 1580, taking advantage of Portugal's succession crisis, Philip II of Spain sent in an army to conquer Portugal, making himself also "king of Portugal" against the wishes of many, perhaps most, of the country's inhabitants. Acquiring Portugal, observed one of Philip's advisers, would be a major strategic gain for Spain, a crucial step to securing Spain's world mastery, and the "principal, most effective, and decisive instrument and remedy for reducing the Netherlands" to Habsburg and Catholic obedience, that is to the power of the Spanish crown and papal authority.[36] Fittingly, given the invasion's repressive intent, it was commanded by the same champion of Castilian imperialism, Don Fernando Álvarez de Toledo, Duke of Alva (1507–82), who between 1567 and 1573 had subjected the Low Countries to a reign of terror to crush rebellion and heresy there. Alva's repression in Holland was not quickly forgotten; and neither was his subsequent crack-down in Portugal: quite the contrary, it was all vividly remembered in Spinoza's time. In Spinoza's mind, Alva's tyranny was a prime historical example of "superstition" and hate, fuelling persecution and subjecting, as he expresses it in his angry reply to Albert Burgh, in 1675, innumerable Calvinists, Lutherans, Mennonites, and other religious dissidents "to all manner of torments."[37]

After crushing the Portuguese resistance, in 1580, Spain's monarch drastically curtailed Portugal's historic liberties and privileges as he had those of the Dutch in

---

[36] Israel, "King Philip II," 138; Israel, "Spain's Empire, 'superstitio'," 88.
[37] Spinoza, *Opera* iv, 318; Spinoza, *Collected Works* (ed. Curley) ii, 474.

1567–73, and would later crush those of Aragon in 1591–2.[38] By 1580, Philip II had become the world's foremost standard-bearer of the kind of coercive religious uniformity then most useful for buttressing overweening royal absolutism. Philip attended the auto-da-fé of 1 April 1581 in Lisbon in person to demonstrate the close pact between Church and triumphant crown in suppressing all religious dissent. Even though during the sixty-year span of Portugal's forced union with Spain (1580–1640) frequent quarrels between ecclesiastics and royal representatives erupted over seating arrangements and points of precedence between royal officials and ecclesiastics, the essential concept of the auto-da-fé, as staging the full splendour of monarchical and ecclesiastical power hand in hand, jointly projecting monarch, nobility, and Church leading the masses chanting their unwavering support, in crushing all heresy, was powerfully reinforced. These immense grand gatherings magnificently celebrated unremitting collective denunciation and coercion of whoever defies church doctrine and authority especially the residue of detested, vilified Judaism.[39]

An ominous consequence of the 1580 changes in Portugal for the "New Christians" of Jewish descent, including the Álvares and Espinozas of Vidigueira, was a substantial further strengthening of the Portuguese Inquisition's powers. Oppression of New Christians, already severe, reached new peaks of intensity in the 1580s and 1590s. But in the face of Portugal's subjection and increased persecution, neither New Christians remaining in Portugal, nor those dispersing to other lands, remained religiously or politically inert. They felt drawn, understandably, to supporting the international coalition opposing Philip—the Dutch, the English crown, and the Huguenots in which the English queen, Elizabeth I, was a major participant. Portuguese resistance to Spanish occupation crystallized around the figure of Dom António (1531–95), the so-called "Prior of Crato," strengthening ties between his movement and the crypto-Jewish segment among Portuguese New Christians in exile as well as in Portugal, that soon became conspicuous. In a sense, Portuguese crypto-Judaism always had a political aspect because of its secretive organizational character and inherent opposition to royal policies. But the Dom António episode lent this tendency added impetus.

During the 1580s and 1590s, many Portuguese, in Portugal and in exile, including members of Spinoza's family, actively opposed Philip's rule. Marranos, whether remaining in Portugal or fleeing abroad during the 1590s, had abundant cause to back Philip II's foes, namely the Huguenot leader, the future King Henri IV of France (reigned: 1589–1610) who during the 1580s and 1590s was at war with both the French Catholic League and Philip, in alliance with Elizabeth I of England, and Prince William of Orange, leader of the Dutch Revolt against Spain (until Philip contrived to get him assassinated in 1584). Portuguese

[38] Valladares, *Conquista de Lisboa*, 63–4, 105–7; Duerloo, *Dynasty and Piety*, 24.
[39] López-Salazar Codes, *Inquisición y política*, 243, 246–8, 256–7.

Figure 4.2 Dom António, *Prior of Crato "king of Portugal"* (1531–95), engraving. © The Trustees of the British Museum.

cristãos novos, for obvious reasons, had even more grounds than other Portuguese to support Dom António as leader of the local resistance to Philip's post-1580 mastery of Portugal and its extensive empire.

Dom António (Figure 4.2), an illegitimate descendant of King Manoel I of Portugal (reigned: 1495–1521), had long been in rivalry with Philip as pretender to the Portuguese throne.[40] Before Alva conquered the country, in 1580, Dom António was accepted by many or most Portuguese as rightful heir to their crown, despite much of the nobility and high clergy, and the regent, Cardinal Dom Henrique, ally of the Inquisition and noted enemy of the New Christians, supporting Philip's claims. Crowned king at Santarém, on 23 June 1580, amid great popular fervour stiffened by profound unwillingness to fall under Castilian domination, Dom António's regime lasted only two months. After losing the Battle of Alcántara (25 August 1580) on the outskirts of Lisbon to the Castilians,[41] he managed to escape to France. There he eventually mustered a sizeable force of 58 vessels and some 6,000 men, mostly Huguenots fitted out in the port of Nantes, with which he sailed to the Azores, islands divided over the succession dispute,

---

[40] Deed of Jan Fransz. Bruyningh, Amsterdam, 16 Dec. 1596 in *SR* 1 (1967), 111–12; Hermann, "An Undesired King," 140; Israel, *Revolutionary Jews*, 37–43.

[41] Faria, "D. Antonio 1er, Prieur," 1–2; Bouza Álvarez, "De las alteraciones de Beja," 110.

with São Miguel and Santa Maria acclaiming Philip while Terceira and the rest recognized Dom António.[42] Enthusiastically received on Terceira, Dom António actually reigned there as "king of Portugal" from July to November 1582. His fleet was defeated, though, by a Spanish armada off São Miguel, in late July 1582, after which Terceira was overrun by Spanish troops in the summer of 1583 and repression ensued.[43] However, Dom António, herald of Portuguese opposition to Philip II throughout the Atlantic world, with a handful of followers escaped yet again, back to France.

Dom António's mother, Violante Gomes, was of Jewish descent, and in Portugal he seems to have had many connections with other Portuguese New Christians.[44] The English envoy, Edward Wotton, sent by Elizabeth I to Lisbon in 1579, informed Francis Walsingham, head of the English secret service and someone with a keen interest in Portuguese affairs, that Dom António had numerous bastard children by New Christian women.[45] During his subsequent long years of exile in France and England, Dom António's relations with Portuguese New Christians outside Portugal were, of necessity, close as they were the only Portuguese at hand with substantial financial resources and a strong motive to back him. The Marrano diaspora's fervent support for Dom António's cause, or *antonianismo*, was soon noticeable across Western Europe, obvious not least to Philip himself and frequently commented on by his diplomats. Reports of the late 1580s from Venice confirmed that Dom António sought alliances not just with the embattled (still Protestant) French monarch, Henri IV, and the Dutch, but also with the Ottoman Turks. In Venice, "cada dia se descubren nuevos judíos que vienen de Portugal [every day new Jews are discovered coming from Portugal]" commented the Spanish ambassador there, in July 1590, "and all of them are extremely passionate for Dom António of Portugal, so it seems this plague of rebellion comes with Judaism [y todos ellos son apasionadíssimos por don António de Portugal que parezce que viene esta plaga de rebellion con la judería]."[46]

Judaism and political subversion had indeed become linked in an international and far-reaching *antonianismo* pregnant with implications for the future. Its New Christian adherents expected, having been given assurances that this would follow, that Dom António's triumph would mean emasculation of the Inquisition. The same Spanish envoy returned to the subject a few weeks later, adding that both those Portuguese openly reverting to Judaism living in the ghetto

---

[42] Martin and Parker, *Spanish Armada*, 94; Valladares, *Conquista de Lisboa*, 168; Duerloo, *Dynasty and Piety*, 25; López-Salazar Codes, *Inquisición y política*, 49.
[43] Faria, "D. Antonio 1er, Prieur," 2; Gómez-Centurión Jiménez, *Felipe II, La Empresa*, 181; Valladares, *Conquista de Lisboa*, 42, 58, 147–52; Israel, "King Philip II," 140–2.
[44] Faria, "D. Antonio 1er, Prieur," 2; Hermann, "An Undesired King," 141; Israel, "Spain's Empire, 'superstitio'," 88–9.
[45] Van de Kamp, *Emanuel van Portugal*, 44–5.
[46] Quoted in Ruspio, "La presenza portoghese," 78.

at Venice, as well as those outside the ghetto living outwardly as "Christians," fervently supported Dom António's conspiracy and were working for him as spies, patrons, and helpers of those in his service.[47] Venice was one focus of concerted Portuguese Jewish and New Christian opposition to the Spanish monarchy, but Nantes and its vicinity, where members of the Spinoza family settled, remained especially pivotal to Dom António's tenuous but vital communications with Portugal and the Azores with special relevance to the Portuguese Atlantic anti-Habsburg conspiracy. In 1584, Dom António for a time resided in the castle of Sarzeau, close to Nantes, and during 1585 for some months in Nantes itself, continually harassed and threatened by agents and supporters of Philip and the Catholic League. Striving to revive his flagging cause, he sent out and received messengers and issued letters of marque for fees (and a cut of the proceeds) licensing French and English privateers to raid shipping belonging to Philip's subjects. Nearly trapped several times by the anti-Protestant, pro-Spanish French Leaguers, Dom António fled France, via La Rochelle, for England in August 1585. He later returned and died in Paris, at the age of sixty-one, in August 1595, ending what his Portuguese adherents considered his fifteen-year "reign" (1580–95).

Disaffection in Portugal and among the Portuguese Atlantic diaspora undoubtedly exerted a material effect on the course of the great events that shook the world in the 1580s and 1590s and with Dom António's death showed little sign of flagging. Walsingham's papers show that Elizabeth counted on a stream of intelligence flowing from Lisbon and Oporto supplied by Dom António's supporters, including detailed reports on the ships, troops, and massive preparations for the great Armada against England of 1588.[48] After the Armada's defeat, Walsingham, working with Dom António's entourage, persuaded Elizabeth to send a smaller counter-armada to strike at Spain, using some of the English veterans stationed in the Netherlands, a venture with which the States, guided by Oldenbarnevelt, readily cooperated. The reason Portugal was selected as the 1589 expedition's target was that Dom António's supporters had tirelessly implanted in allied minds the idea that the mere sight of an Anglo-Dutch fleet would cause the Portuguese masses to rise in revolt,[49] though in the event not much of a rising materialized and the Anglo-Dutch force was easily repulsed from the gates of Lisbon.

4.v Exiles Fleeing Portugal

Clandestine subversion as practised by the Portuguese New Christians of Nantes, though less furtive and secretive than under Inquisition surveillance in Portugal,

---

[47] Ruspio, "La presenza portoghese," 79.
[48] Parker, *Grand Strategy of Philip II*, 215; Duerloo, *Dynasty and Piety*, 27.
[49] Den Tex, *Oldenbarnevelt* ii, 16, 18; Bouza Álvarez, "De las alteraciones de Beja," 98.

was simultaneously religious, commercial (constantly evading Spanish royal trade policies and monopolies), and political. According to a Portuguese visitor to Nantes where he met Manoel (Abraham) and Pedro Rodrigues d'Espinoza (Isaac) around 1610, and later reported on them to the Inquisition, they conducted themselves in Nantes, as far as he could tell, as "good Christians."[50] Yet they were resolute concealed subversives and by no means only in a religious sense. During the 1580s and 1590s, many Portuguese, Old Christians and New Christians alike, deeply resented Philip's acquisition of the Portuguese crown, and after Dom António's demise many Portuguese exiles in France continued lending support to his sons, and to Henri IV, as their protector and ally.[51] Dom António had two recognized sons and heirs, Emmanuel and Cristóvão (beside others unrecognized), born in Tangiers where Dom António had resided during the late 1560s and early 1570s. The elder, Emmanuel, inherited his claim to the Portuguese throne while the younger, Cristóvão, devoted his life to his father's cause. Hence, Dom António's demise did not mean the end of *antonianismo* as a subversive movement any more than of Portuguese New Christian clandestine plotting to combat the Spanish crown and Inquisition and rescue relatives trapped under unrelenting oppression in Portugal and its colonies.

In claiming the Portuguese throne (supported by the Dutch States-General and by William the Silent's successor as Stadholder, Prince Maurits), Dom António—whose heart was embalmed and encased in a casket preserved in a friary chapel in Paris—was succeeded by "Dom Emmanuel of Portugal" (*c*.1588–1636) who at an early age married a daughter of William the Silent, Countess Emilia of Nassau (d. 1629), who converted to Catholicism to fit her new Portuguese courtly role. This "royal" pair, supposedly continuing the "true" line of the Portuguese succession (which lived on until the twentieth century), resided at the castle of Wychen, near Nijmegen, in Gelderland.[52] Most Portuguese nobility and clergy, meanwhile, supported Philip's regime, so that the continuing disaffection in Portugal evinced a popular rather than elite character and found expression only by clandestine means. After the failure of the 1589 expedition, anti-Habsburg opposition within Portugal grew more sporadic than earlier but still persisted.

Among signs of continuing support for *antonianismo* after the fiasco of 1589, were a flood of anti-Philip II posters that swept Beja and Vidigueira, in 1593, all swiftly seized by worried authorities still vividly recalling the *conjura* of 1570, and a further wave of excitement in Évora, Beja, and Vidigueira, in 1596, during the tense weeks of the second Anglo-Dutch expedition along the Iberian coast, now

---

[50] Borges Coelho, "Orígenes," 126.
[51] Deed of Jan Fransz. Bruyningh, Amsterdam, 16 Dec. 1596 in *SR* 1 (1967), 111–12; Bouza Álvarez, "De las alteraciones de Beja," 110, 114–16.
[52] Faria, "D. Antonio 1er, Prieur," 5, 7–8; Israel, "Maurits en de wording van de buitenlandse politiek," 71.

with Dom Cristóvão on board.[53] Since Dom António's failure in 1589, English commanders showed less enthusiasm for landings in Portugal and chose Cadiz as their main target.[54] After successfully attacking and sacking the port in June 1596, the commanders decided Cadiz could not be held and, on July 4, burnt the city to the ground. Soon afterwards the fleet appeared off the Portuguese coast where it also sacked Faro, in the Algarve, but captured relatively little booty apart from wine casks and stocks of books.

The French Wars of Religion dragged on until 1598, ensuring continuation of the contest between Spain and Henri IV of France, and the feuding at Nantes and Rouen between Catholic pro-Spanish and crypto-Jewish pro-Protestant Portuguese factions quarrelling over religion and politics. Among the earliest surviving Amsterdam notarial deeds relating to the Nantes Portuguese crypto-Jews' links with Holland is a power of attorney assigned by a leading Amsterdam Portuguese merchant, Manoel Rodrigues Vega, to Manoel Rodrigues [alias Abraham] d'Espinoza of Nantes, that is Isaac de Espinoza's brother and head of that part of the Spinoza family that preceded Spinoza's grandfather to Nantes. This power of attorney concerned a valuable cargo of textiles en route from Amsterdam to Viana do Castelo in Portugal, consisting of Haarlem linens, baize cloth, buffalo hides and more belonging to eight merchants residing in Amsterdam, Antwerp, Lisbon, and Oporto. This cargo had been seized from the ship *De Hoop*, a few weeks after the sack of Cadiz, in 1596, by Spanish troops based at the coastal town of Lorient, some 170 kilometres north-west of Nantes, along the southern Brittany coast, at the mouth of the River Le Blavet. The power of attorney, dated 16 December 1596, authorizes Spinoza's great-uncle, Manoel Rodrigues d'Espinoza, to appear before royal officials on their behalf and initiate proceedings to reclaim the seized textiles.[55] The Spanish troops involved belonged to a force Philip had sent to Brittany, in 1590, to assist the French Catholic League in their fight to thwart the Protestant contender to the French throne, Henri IV, and his toleration policy. These Spanish troops in Brittany were part of a sustained effort to prevent a *de facto* religious toleration in France and a broad Catholic–Protestant compromise under the French crown as the basis for ending the French civil war and ultimately shifting the balance of power in Europe against the Habsburgs. Should Philip and the League fail to stop him, Henri IV would secure effective toleration not just for the Huguenots but also the Judaizing Portuguese exiles settled in the ports of western and northern France.

To block Henri IV's efforts to secure full control over the region and block the path of Dom António (and after 1595 his successor), these Spanish troops

---

[53] Bouza Álvarez, "De la alteraciones de Beja," 106, 110, 114, 116.
[54] Hammer, "New Light on the Cadiz Expedition," 182–4.
[55] SR 1/ii, deed 10, Amsterdam, 16 Dec. 1596; Mathorez, "Notes sur l'histoire," 324–6; Vaz Dias and Van de Tak, *Spinoza Mercator*, 5–6.

remained on the Breton coast until the end of the Spanish–French conflict when they were withdrawn under the Peace of Vervins (1598). Besides fighting Huguenots, they were there to stiffen Catholic League support which was as strong in Nantes as was animosity toward Marrano migrants arriving from Portugal.[56] Choosing Abraham d'Espinoza as the local Portuguese leader to represent the then principal Sephardic merchant in Holland (who had moved to Amsterdam from Nantes)[57] and his associates in retrieving cargo seized by Spanish troops in Brittany, proves that beside being known in Holland as a staunch crypto-Jew, the head of the Spinoza family in Nantes was well-known there too to be a reliable political opponent of the Spanish presence and Catholic League's religious and political aims. He was regarded as experienced in legal and political dealings with local authorities and in a position to conduct formal legal proceedings, as authorized by the deed, with local "governors, colonels, captains and other persons in the service of His Majesty [i.e. Henri IV]."[58]

After Dom António's death, the small Nantes Portuguese community remained deeply split between pro-League "Christian" Portuguese *conversos* and pro-Huguenot Judaizers until the early 1620s when the confessional war within finally lapsed due to the permanent departure of the crypto-Jewish group, including the Spinoza clan, from Nantes. Spinoza's family transferred from western France to Holland during the Twelve Years Truce between the Dutch Republic and the Iberian peninsula (1609–21), a period of more direct and much increased trade between Amsterdam and the Iberian peninsula, and therefore heightened opportunities for the Spinoza family's overseas trading activities. The Nantes crypto-Jewish congregation gradually withered after 1609, the remaining remnant of Nantes Portuguese opting for a Catholic future.[59]

The examples of Spain and Portugal clearly stood at the heart of Spinoza's central thesis that "superstition" and ignorance can only be combated by introducing more freedom of thought and less authoritarian political structures, especially as "ignorance which is the source of all wickedness," as he expressed the point later, rests on belief in miracles and faith based on "superstition." "But I doubt very much," he added, writing to Oldenburg towards the end of his life, "whether kings will ever permit application of the remedy to this evil."[60] This did not mean that mankind was unalterably eternally burdened with monarchy, oppression, and religious coercion but rather, held Spinoza, that nothing can be hoped for from kings and the existing status quo which, in turn, destined all efforts

---

[56] Bruyn Kops, *A Spirited Exchange*, 277–9.   [57] Roitman, *The Same but Different?*, 41, 84n, 88.
[58] Vaz Dias and Van de Tak, *Spinoza Mercator*, 6; Israel, *Revolutionary Jews*, 45; by contrast Bruyn Kops interprets the episode as meaning Manoel had good official contacts with the Spanish authorities, Kops, *A Spirited Exchange*, 282.
[59] Révah, "Les Marranes," 66; Israel, *Diasporas*, 256–7.
[60] Spinoza, *Opera* iv, 308; Spinoza, *Collected Works* (ed. Curley) ii, 333.

to achieve better things to prolonged, resolute unfaltering subversion against overwhelming odds, a status quo presided over by churches and kings.

4.vi Revolutionary Subversion by Means of Philosophy

Spinoza's life-long hostile view of kings and monarchy was assuredly shaped in part by his perspective on his family's history and views about the successive struggles of the various parts of the Spanish global empire to break free of the tyranny that Philip II extended and intensified. Although the Portuguese risings against Philip in 1580 and 1589 failed, and the rising against Philip in the Azores collapsed in 1582, the Portuguese did eventually secure their independence from Spain after a long struggle that resumed in 1640. Spinoza's mother and father both belonged to families that had resisted the tyranny of Church and crown in Portugal and France for decades, both religiously and politically, and were directly affected by the Spanish intervention in the French Wars of Religion down to 1598. But Spinoza's life-long intellectual involvement with the complex scenario of international struggle against the despotic hegemony of Philip II went further than that. Indeed, opposition to Philip and resistance to his tyranny, culminating in armed revolt, is a topic of considerable prominence in Spinoza's political thought, ingrained in his cultural background and that of the Portuguese Jewish social group among which he lived for the first nearly two-thirds of his life.

Spinoza was never an optimist regarding the prospects for a fully successful revolution toppling ruthless oppression, but he did think that carefully planned revolutionary subversion could achieve solid, lasting results. As Spain under Philip represented the epitome of royal absolutism in his eyes, chief seat of tyranny, the Inquisition, intolerance and "martyrdom," Philip's empire stood at the heart of his thesis that tyranny and oppression can be successfully overcome but only by undermining the hegemony of "superstition" and ignorance first. The general outlook was unpromising, even dismal; but where attitudes rooted in superstition are effectively undermined by clandestine intellectual enlightening, tyranny and repression will erode and eventually totter and collapse, for these cannot flourish without their chief pillar—credulity and ignorance. As freedom of thought and expression, toleration and more representative, responsible political structures gain ground, these, he contends, can eventually triumph for the benefit of all. On Spinoza's premises, "to reform the world," as Thévenot sneeringly described his aims, in April 1675, is indeed a daunting task apt to be continually thwarted, but ultimately not an impossible dream.

If Spinoza commenced his rebellion in Hebrew studies and Bible criticism fighting rabbinic authority, his mature philosophy constitutes a highly sophisticated generalized assault on "superstition," miracles, theology and ecclesiastical authority allied to tyranny and especially monarchy. Spinoza came to view "superstition" and religious authority as his principal general targets because these seemed to him the chief foundation supporting thrones as well as churches and scholastic systems of philosophy and theology—to his mind forming an immense religious, political, educational, and ethical barrier to human happiness which it is in everyone's interest to demolish but only the merest handful recognize as their primary foe. To appreciate Spinoza's life and legacy it is essential to realize the vastness of the mental and social barriers he saw as obstructing and blighting human life and happiness much as his own family history comprised a saga of fighting oppression, the Inquisition, theology, rigid scholasticism, absolute monarchy, false myths of martyrdom (obscuring the real martyrs), and the might of Spain in her imperial glory.

Of course, absolute rulers whose power rests on "*superstitio*" and popular credulity would try to suppress all efforts to demystify society and dispel "ignorance" and fanaticism, using the coercive force at their disposal. No one, Spinoza came to believe, will conquer the formidable structures of authority and superstition simply by stirring up popular anger and inciting mass insurrection. Summoning the populace to rise in arms, as Dom António's allies and supporters did, and as the Aragonese rebels did in 1591, he judged self-defeating, an inevitable recipe for failure and redoubled repression because the people, through no fault of their own, possess no grasp of the reality of things. He did not want "the common people" to read his work, he declares at the end of the preface to his *TTP*, "and make a nuisance of themselves by interpreting it perversely, as they do with everything." However, Spinoza's "vulgus" [common people] should not be understood as a socio-economic bloc, the poor and ill-educated, but rather, as in Maimonides and Elijah Delmedigo, as everyone unable or unwilling to distinguish truth from falsehood, all who are addicted to *superstitio*, that is the non-philosophers, the vast majority of every class including not least kings, ecclesiastics, scholastics, and noblemen.

Spinoza sought to undermine the existing order by capturing the intellectually most aware outside the academic and ecclesiastical establishment, that is everyone, rich or poor, able and willing to think critically and independently, and through them eventually the rest of society. Spinoza thus envisaged his political "revolution" as a veiled process of infiltration like that practised by the Portuguese crypto-Jews among his forebears, only now a secularized penetration geared to undermine "superstition" and credulity and disarm theology and religious leaders as the path to defeating tyranny itself while eschewing mass insurrection and violence on the failed model of the defeated uprisings of Portugal, the Azores, and Aragon. The revolution he sought to foster was one hardly anybody would notice most of the time until tyranny's foundations were sufficiently corroded as to approach immanent collapse. To avoid being promptly crushed, the crucial early phases of subverting the monarchical-ecclesiastical complex must remain under cover, concealed from view like the crypto-Jewish networks in Portugal and, after 1580, in Spain and Spanish America. Once the world's theologians and false prophets find themselves effectively confronted and discredited by this silent intellectual undermining, the tyrants presiding over human servitude bolstered by *superstitio* will have less and less chance of successfully perpetuating their universally damaging sway.

All three major revolts against Philip II—the Dutch, Portuguese, and Aragonese—became deeply embedded in Spinoza's outlook and political thought, much as they were actually entangled in the convoluted reality of the late sixteenth and early seventeenth century. Recognizing this raises the question of Antonio Pérez (1540–1611) (Figure 4.3), who was undoubtedly one of Spinoza's favourite authors and especially relevant in this context. A royal official with exceptionally wide practical knowledge and experience, Pérez had been Philip II's secretary of state for some twelve years (1566–78), in succession to his father, Gonzalo Pérez. Spinoza rarely comments on a particular rebellion. But studying Pérez prompted him to rework several of the latter's conclusions about the dilemmas of anti-monarchical subversive, revolutionary politics as exemplified by the case of Aragon in 1591–2. Both writers believed a valid theory of politics must be based on reason, nature, and understanding the mechanics of self-interest: "que ninguno fue tan amigo de su vecino," as Pérez pithily expresses it, "que no lo sea de sí más

Figure 4.3 *Antonio Pérez* (c.1540–1611), portrait, oil on panel. Reproduction courtesy of Album/Alamy Stock Photo.

[that no one loves his neighbour so much that he does not love himself more]."[61] Spinoza's last work, his *Tractatus Politicus*, includes a substantial passage praising the medieval Aragonese for establishing a form of monarchy rich in constitutional checks and legal constraints so resistant to monarchy's undesirable traits and royal pretension as to represent the closest thing to an ideal monarchy Spinoza could envisage—namely, one totally emasculated.[62] So well did this kingdom function that the Aragonese "continued for an incredible length of time unharmed, the king's loyalty towards his subjects being as great as theirs towards him," though, tellingly, here Spinoza modifies Pérez's account slightly by placing greater stress than does Pérez on the role of large councils in fixing and safeguarding society's liberties.[63] The situation changed, though, when Ferdinand of Aragon married Isabella of Castile, thereby becoming effective ruler of both kingdoms: "for the liberty enjoyed by the Aragonese began to displease the Castilians, who therefore ceased not to urge Ferdinand to abolish these rights." Using Pérez's account,[64] Spinoza praises Ferdinand for wisely resisting such pressure. "Accordingly, the Aragonese retained their liberties from the time of Ferdinand, though no longer by right [of their own power] but by favour of their too powerful kings, until the reign of Philip II who oppressed them with better luck, but no less cruelty, than he did the United Provinces."[65]

Pérez's political career and reflections offered a unique framework enabling Spinoza to weave together the Dutch and Aragonese revolts with the Portuguese resistance into a broad perspective, viewing the world as a perpetual fight between royal-ecclesiastical tyranny and the good of society. The Dutch Revolt confronted the court in Madrid with the challenge of how the empire's different realms, with their disparate local laws, traditions, and attitudes could be integrated under the centralizing policies and religious uniformity demanded by the crown. Two rival factions evolved at court in Madrid: a hardline Castilian, imperialist view tied to militant religious intolerance championed by Alva, and a more conciliatory wing opposing the hardliners, more sympathetic to local particularist tendencies, headed by Ruy Gomez, prince of Eboli, and later Pérez. The factions' rivalry was a power struggle but also a clash of principle between the Alva faction's Castilian outlook and their opponents' preferring conciliation to outright subjugation and advocating retention of elements of the Dutch, Flemish, Aragonese, and Portuguese constitutions.[66] Initially modest, Pérez gained a uniquely influential

---

[61] Domínguez, "Presencia de Antonio Pérez," 169; Blanco Mayor, "Quevedo y Spinoza," 195.
[62] Balibar, *Spinoza et la politique*, 87–8; Domínguez, "Presencia de Antonio Pérez," 174–5.
[63] Méchoulan, "Spinoza lecteur," 296–300; Prokhovnik, *Spinoza and Republicanism*, 185.
[64] Domínguez, "Presencia de Antonio Pérez," 174–5.
[65] Spinoza, *Tractatus Politicus*, 364–5; Domínguez, "Presencia de Antonio Pérez," 175; Gascón Pérez, *Aragón en la monarquía* ii, 42.
[66] Elliott, *Revolt of the Catalans*, 19.

position as Philip's secretary, advising the king increasingly forthrightly, until finally he overstepped the mark.[67]

Pérez's fall from grace, in 1579, coincided with a broad shift in Philip II's policies from a more cautious, inward-looking to a grandiose Atlantic imperialism soon to exert an immense impact on Portugal and the Portuguese New Christians.[68] Secretly arrested, Pérez suffered imprisonment in Madrid for eleven years (1579–90) until finally, helped by friends, he escaped to the Aragonese capital, Zaragoza, where, being Aragonese himself, he claimed asylum under that kingdom's historic privileges and liberties [*fueros*]. When Philip (Figure 4.4) tried to circumvent Aragon's *fueros*, in May 1591, and re-arrest him via the Inquisition, the sole institution in Aragon not subject to stringent limitations, the fugitive was set free by a rioting mob yelling "viva la Libertad!" A second Inquisition attempt to seize Pérez, in September 1591, provoked a full-scale uprising in Zaragoza which definitively freed him, enabling him to escape to France and then England, and ally with Henri IV, Elizabeth, and Dom António. Given that in his political writings later Spinoza usually prefers generalities to particular political contexts, it is striking that he repeatedly returns to the topic of Philip II's reign, and not least

Figure 4.4 *Philip II* (1527–98) in 1565, oil on canvas. © Photographic Archive Museo Nacional del Prado.

---

[67] Kamen, *Philip of Spain*, 212–13.
[68] Gómez-Centurión Jiménez, *Felipe II, La Empresa*, 179; Valladares, *Conquista de Lisboa*, 72–3.

to the successful Dutch Revolt and the sadly unsuccessful 1591–2 Aragonese rebellion. Philip mobilized a Castilian army with which he crushed the insurrection and entered Zaragoza in November 1591. In the ensuing crackdown, several dissident nobles were executed.[69] An intimidated Cortes of the realm, convened at Tarazona, in June 1592, duly submitted to stringent curtailment of Aragon's constitution and laws designed to permanently tighten the king's grip.

Meanwhile, Spinoza's Dutch Revolt was assuredly no rebellion in the ordinary sense. What was best about it was that the States of Holland and the other provincial assemblies that abjured Philip "rescued" the Dutch from monarchical despotism. In characterizing the Dutch Revolt against Philip II, in Chapter XVIII of the *TTP*, Spinoza deliberately repeats the then fairly conventional claim that the States of Holland "did not, to our knowledge, ever have kings but only Counts, to whom the right of government was never transferred." Willing to justify armed rebellion in a cautious way wherever it does ultimately ameliorate conditions for society, he deliberately lauds the "Dutch Revolt" without endorsing the element of popular rebellion that helped drive it. Spinoza carries his warning against popular involvement, and the inadvisability of popular armed resistance to rulers, to the extent of denying the Dutch Revolt was strictly speaking a "rebellion." The States of Holland had "always reserved to themselves authority to remind [the medieval counts of Holland] of their duty, retaining the power to defend their authority and the citizens' liberty, and rescue themselves from them should they become tyrants, and generally keep a check on them, so that they could do nothing without the permission and approval of the States."[70]

From 1572, Spanish tyranny was indeed effectively checked in the northern Netherlands—by a massive revolt against royal authority lasting decades (1566–1609), a revolt revealing the positive side of the "multitude" when wisely led, as it was by Oldenbarnevelt.[71] Oppressive, grasping tyrannies like those of Philip II, Louis XIV, and Charles II, inferred Spinoza, are not invulnerable and can be weakened by the assaults of a thinker like himself. Philosophy can fight oppression by planting in men's minds realization that the true cause of their being wretched, of being victims of contempt for their well-being, lies in their own ignorance and credulity. The difference between citizenship and being a subject, an important distinction in Spinoza, is that between being a member of society obeying laws benefiting the whole and an individual coerced into obedience for the royal, aristocratic, and ecclesiastical advantage of those tyrannizing over society for their own benefit.[72] Ultimately, the difference between despotism and the free republic boils down to the level of awareness of those in society, being the

---

[69] Kamen, *Philip of Spain*, 290–1.
[70] Spinoza, *Theological-Political Treatise*, 237; Israel, "Spain's Empire, 'superstitio'," 81–2.
[71] Spinoza, *Theological-Political Treatise*, 236–7; Moreau, "A-t-on raison de se révolter?," 29–30.
[72] Bove, "Avènement de la citoyenneté," 57, 67; Lavaert, "Renversement de Spinoza," 40–1.

difference between the ignorant having their way and the ignorant being taught, guided, and where necessary, prodded, by those promoting the "common good." The more the latter is facilitated, the more organized intellectual subversion will lead to republican, democratic, and tolerant structures.

Pérez got to know his new ally, Dom António, personally, in the summer of 1593, when both stayed at Windsor engrossed in deliberations with Elizabeth's (and Walsingham's) Portuguese Marrano physician-in-chief, Ruy López (c.1517–94), a personage renowned for his medical skills, diets, and arcane concoctions but so entangled in international intrigue and court faction that he aroused the jealousy of key courtiers including the Earl of Essex who was infuriated by his disclosing that he had venereal disease. Accused of playing a double game, López was tried as a "traitor," and executed in London in June 1594 before a jubilant crowd shouting "hang the Jew."[73] Until his own death, in Paris, in 1611, Pérez remained the foremost international publicist denouncing Philip's oppressive absolutism. His trademark trenchant style denouncing the favour of princes as "false, feeble, deadly, the shadow of death itself," greatly appealed to Spinoza: "for as Antonio Pérez excellently observes," remarks Spinoza in his *Tractatus Politicus*, "an absolute dominion is to the prince very dangerous, to the subjects very hateful, and opposed to the institutes of God and man alike, as innumerable instances show [nam (ut Ant. Perezius optime notat) imperio absolute uti principi admodum periculosum, subditis admodum odiosum, et instutis tam divinis quam humanis adversum, ut innumera ostendunt exempla]."[74] Spinoza here only slightly alters Pérez's wording: "el uso del poder absolute es muy peligroso a los reyes, muy odioso a los vasallos, muy ofensivo a Dios y a la naturaleza, como lo muestran mil ejemplos [the exercise of absolute power is very dangerous for kings, very hateful to their subjects, and very much opposed to God and nature as a thousand examples show"].[75] The borrowing is unmistakable.[76] Pérez's views about Spain and politics generally Spinoza cites with obvious relish and, for him, rare concurrence regarding both principle and specific judgements such as their common admiration for the moderation of "Ferdinand the Catholic."[77]

No one who has read history, observes Spinoza in his last major text, the *Tractatus Politicus*, can fail to know that the "good faith of counsellors [of kings] has generally turned to their ruin; and so, for their own safety they need to be cunning and not faithful."[78] Here again he is directly alluding to Pérez's *Las obras y relaciones del Ant. Pérez secretario de estado, que fue del rey de España,*

---

[73] Van de Kamp, *Emanuel van Portugal*, 86–8.
[74] Spinoza, *Tractatus Politicus*, 346–7; Van de Kamp, *Emanuel van Portugal*, 86–7.
[75] Antonio Pérez, *Relaciones y cartas* i, 208; Domínguez, "Presencia de Antonio Pérez," 172.
[76] Domínguez, "Presencia de Antonio Pérez," 168.
[77] Boyden, "'Fortune Has Stripped You'," 30, 33; Domínguez, "Presencia de Antonio Pérez," 175.
[78] Spinoza, *Tractatus Politicus*, 334.

Don Phelippe II deste nombre [The Works and Descriptions of Antonio Pérez, former secretary of state of Don Philip II, king of Spain] (Geneva, 1644), a text of over a thousand pages infused with the hard-headed realism and naturalism characteristic of this author. Unrelenting in denouncing Philip's tyranny, this book was one of only two specifically political works in Spanish remaining on Spinoza's shelves and inventoried in Spinoza's personal library after his death (listed as no. 96 in Offenberg's reconstruction).[79]

Spinoza's highlighting Pérez perhaps also helps explain his astounding claim, in the *Tractatus Politicus*, made at a time when the Republic was menaced anew, this time by the tyranny of Louis XIV, that his own political thought possessed "practical" significance for everyone whereas virtually all other political theories do not. The importance Spinoza assigns to his political theory and subversive campaign against "divine right" monarchy follows from a deep conviction that his political philosophy was anchored in the experience of exceptionally percipient leaders, Pérez prominent among them, but also some of his own ancestors, experience of direct practical use for the betterment of humanity. In places, in his later work, Spinoza uses phrases that are remarkably dismissive of the entire existing tradition of political thought, presumably including even Machiavelli and Hobbes, the entire corpus consisting, he suggests, of "either obvious fantasies, or schemes that could only have been put into effect in Utopia," whereas his political thought, by contrast, does provide applicable guidance that *is* the fruit of experience.[80] If virtually all previous theorists merely concocted "chimaera," airy theories unrealizable outside utopia,[81] Spinoza aimed to reform the world by placing political theory on an unrelentingly "realistic" level genuinely promising tangible change for the better.[82]

It is a remarkable irony that one of the world's first expounders of modern democratic republicanism should cite virtually word for word key maxims of the very man who long served as adviser to the religiously unbending despotic monarch who further strengthened the Inquisition in Portugal and whom Spinoza himself identifies as the world's chief symbol of monarchical oppression, unconstitutionality, and tyranny. Spinoza prizes Pérez too for demonstrating the uselessness of unplanned, spontaneous popular uprisings based on popular resentment and anger. If Spinoza's conclusion that royal absolutism is

---

[79] Offenberg, "Spinoza's Library," 320; Blanco Echauri, "Espinosa y el pensamiento político," 179; Domínguez, "Presencia de Antonio Pérez," 165; until relatively recently scholars wrongly supposed the "Antonio Pérez" referred to here was the "other Antonio Perez." Thus, R. H. M. Elwes who produced the 1883 translation into English of Spinoza's political works, the standard translation for over a century (following the Dutch Spinoza editor, Vloten), confuses the "Antonio Pérez" Spinoza cites with "a publicist, and professor of law in the University of Louvain in the first part of the seventeenth century," author of a certain *Ius publicum* (1657); see the footnote in Elwes' translation of the *Tractatus*, 334.
[80] Spinoza, *Tractatus Politicus*, 33.   [81] Curley, "Kissinger, Spinoza and Genghis Khan," 329.
[82] Curley, "Kissinger, Spinoza and Genghis Khan," 315.

undermined only by weakening "superstition" and "ignorance" and the common people cannot be emancipated directly by popular rebellion but only circuitously by being freed from "superstition" and credulity first is correct, then the only effective politics benefiting society is fomenting a republican, demystifying ideology clandestinely directed at changing the thinking of present and future officeholders, professionals, and scholars, infiltrating society neither from above nor from below but, as Spinoza always preferred throughout his life, unremittingly sideways via subversive discussion, universities, and intellectual groups.

It is entirely natural for monarchies and their usual practice, explains Spinoza, in both the *TTP* and the *Tractatus Politicus*, to deceive and foment strife and war, as well as oppress their subjects and limit the scope of individual liberty and men's pursuit of happiness. The great virtue of democratic republics, by contrast, is their fostering freedom of judgement and discussion and promoting peace. More natural than monarchy, the democratic republic cannot indeed survive without free and open expression of differing views. Since Spinoza's revolutionary call, though democratic and unyielding, was never an appeal to the common people, the *vulgus*, in the sense of the credulous and ignorant multitude of all classes, but a summons to those sufficiently philosophical and geared to reality to grasp the basic mechanisms of society, politics, and religion, Spinoza considered university towns and political capitals the most promising seedbed for the kind of revolutionary subversion he had in mind. These were the places where one was likeliest to find those willing to gather in covert groups and collude, like his forebears, in extending veiled networks but now based on reason and science rather than clandestine religion opposing what most people believe. Such a strategy, in his eyes the only way *superstitio* and divine right monarchy can be combated and toppled, is also in Spinoza's thought-world the exclusive path to eradicating the clergy's grip on conscience and opinion, and by which the Inquisition could be fought and eradicated, and victimization of dissidents of whatever stripe ended. He saw it as the sole means too by which the Jews could be rescued from the segregation in which they were imprisoned and integrated on equal terms into the main corpus of society.

Spinoza did not deny the Dutch Revolt against Spain was a great, elevating revolution but steadfastly differentiated between armed popular rebellion leading to the unrestrained violence powered by ordinary discontent that is generally just useless effort and waste of lives, like the Portuguese risings of 1580 and 1589, and Aragonese revolt of 1591, and well-directed rationalizing, democratizing initiatives infiltrating the constitutional process, creating new constitutional realities, and, where useful, reviving old ones. Rather than extol armed rebellion in the usual sense, Spinoza presents the Dutch Revolt as an instance of the States rescuing the people from monarchical despotism and then presiding wisely over the emergence of the most affluent, freest society of his time. Spinoza's Dutch Revolt was a salvage operation by representatives acting just in time to prevent tyranny consolidating. The right of sovereignty had been "always vested in the Dutch States and was the principle the last Count of Holland [i.e. Philip] strove to usurp. Hence it is by no means true that the [Dutch] rebelled against him when they recovered their original power which they had by then almost lost."[83] The curious, not particularly original, way he describes the Dutch Revolt, justifying the rebel republic as a real gain in political and social circumstances while denying the efficacy of popular, unstructured armed revolt against longstanding monarchy, exonerates one particular successful anti-monarchical revolt while simultaneously adhering to his usual anti-insurrectionist stance. The emancipating agent was undoubtedly the representative assembly, the people's representatives and political leaders.

Spinoza's remarks on Roman history further illustrate his distinctive blend of antipathy to unfocused armed resistance with the need for planned, structured, meaningful resistance to tyranny and oppression resulting in lasting improved constitutional arrangements, something he thinks the English dismally failed to accomplish during their revolution of the 1640s.

The liberty and toleration attainable by the democratic republic, argues Spinoza, greatly assist in checking and driving back intolerance and "superstition" while republican public order and peace clearly favours the progress of knowledge and the arts and sciences, as well as general security and freedom of expression, proving that democratic republics are inherently superior to theocracies, oligarchies, and monarchies, all other forms of state, and not least superior to aristocratic republics like Venice and Genoa (which Spinoza sharply criticizes). In fact promoting reason, knowledge, and understanding is the exclusive and sole path to improving ourselves and everything else, whether in the political sphere or any other, because everything follows from sufficient and necessary causes according to Spinoza's system so that understanding the causes of why things are as they are is the only way to alter circumstances (and ourselves) and change things for the better. Raising the level of understanding, in short, is the exclusive means to produce a politics more conducive to human happiness both collectively and on an individual basis.

Hence, it is always advisable for all human societies to exert themselves to transcend the degrading, dismal patterns of existence under kings, autocrats, aristocrats, oligarchs, and priests and rise to a more elevated intellectual level, with the ultimate goal being to devise and consolidate democratic republics. Accordingly, the *TTP*, and Spinoza's last work, the *Tractatus Politicus*, very far from being insurrection-friendly though they are, are nevertheless profoundly revolutionary in a more basic sense.[84] Spinoza was an activist believing revolutionary sedition in certain circumstances and places where an established tradition

---

[83] Spinoza, *Theological-Political Treatise*, 235–7.
[84] Spinoza, *Collected Works* (ed. Curley) i, 490–1; Rovere, *Spinoza. Méthodes pour exister*, 36–40.

of constricting monarchy exists, as in Aragon and Holland, can surreptitiously develop in such a way as to achieve lastingly beneficial results. For the "multitude," that is most people at all social levels, is inevitably unpromising revolutionary material being unable to grasp the truths which philosophy, politics, and "true religion" teach that are essential to improving men's lives. So irrational and unpredictable is the "multitude," in fact, that, as far as possible, it should be excluded from shaping the revolutionary scenario Spinoza proposes. Subversive in every respect, Spinoza's political thought is nevertheless the very opposite of rabble-rousing, multitude-lauding, or insurrection-friendly.[85] The supreme lesson the Dutch Republic taught humankind in his age was the inherent superiority of republics to monarchy and freedom of conscience to church tyranny, and the enduring reality of the deep-seated hopes of men for improvement.

Spinoza's antipathy to monarchy and religious authority, and preference for republican forms, was chiefly a product of the Dutch politics of his own lifetime but was undoubtedly also shaped in some degree by his inherited ideological perspective reaching back to the sixteenth century. It was no accident that the poetry of the *converso* poet João (Moshe) Pinto Delgado (1580–1653) figured among the small number of *converso* works kept in Spinoza's personal library, since Pinto Delgado and his family were prominent among Rouen's Judaizing Portuguese *conversos* in the early seventeenth century and played a political-religious subversive role comparable to that of the Spinozas in Nantes.[86] Pinto Delgado's Spanish poems appeared at Rouen, in 1627, dedicated to Cardinal Richelieu, the new chief enemy of the Spanish crown. Later, the poet transferred to Amsterdam, serving during 1636–40 as one of the *parnasim* (governadores) of the Amsterdam Sephardic school around the time Spinoza commenced his schooling, when his father, Michael, was a *parnas* [governing elder] of the community. Very likely Spinoza knew him. As I. S. Revah and Miriam Bodian point out, Pinto Delgado's poetry contains striking lines reflecting the *conversos'* fusing of political with religious subversion memorably capturing the polar opposition between Spanish and Jewish allegiance by drawing a deliberate contrast with a famous line of a sonnet dedicated to Philip II by another Spanish poet celebrating "una Monarca, un Imperio y una Espada [one monarch, one empire and one sword]." Pinto Delgado's countervailing lines answer that for those genuinely seeking piety and truth there exists only "un Dios, un pueblo, una Ley [one God, one people, one Law]."[87]

---

[85] Begley, "Support and Distrust" (forthcoming).
[86] Bloom, *Economic Activities*, 103; Kaplan, *From Christianity to Judaism*, 308.
[87] Bodian, "Some Ideological Implications," 209.

5
Childhood and Family Tradition

5.i From *Brit Milah* to *Bar Mitzvah* (1632–1645)

Spinoza is usually thought of as someone living banished and essentially outside the Jewish community. But he did not exit the enclosed world of Jewish observance and orthodoxy until September 1656, at nearly twenty-three, over half way through his life, leaving behind not just a religious but a family inheritance of great complexity and formative power rooted in a Portuguese-Spanish speaking cultural environment steeped in tradition which, until then, was also his.

Born on 24 November 1632, Spinoza, following Jewish custom, would have been circumcised a week and a day later, on 1 December, amidst, as usual on such occasions, a cheerful gathering of family and friends, with much singing and chanting. At eight days old, Spinoza received the synagogue name "Baruch," meaning "Blessed." Until excommunicated, in 1656, the Amsterdam Portuguese synagogue's archives invariably referred to its new congregant as "Baruch d'Espinoza (or Despinosa)" whereas in everyday life, and, later, in business dealings, again until 1656, Spinoza, in the usual manner of his community, was generally known by his Portuguese name, "Bento." No document survives in which, in later life, Spinoza himself ever used the name "Baruch."[1]

The ancient ceremony of *brit milah* [circumcision], followed by a family feast, doubtless took place with his parents, Michael and Hannah Deborah, his great-uncle, Abraham d'Espinoza (d. 1637), and grandmother, Miriam Senior (alias Maria Nunes), centre stage, older siblings, aunts, uncles, and cousins milling around. Besides the circumciser [*mohel*], the longstanding family friend and ally of Abraham in community affairs, Rabbi Saul Levi Mortera, was likely also present, being known to have attended Spinoza's older brother, Isaac's, circumcision twenty-one months earlier, in February 1631.[2] In the prayers recited during the ceremony, an honoured and prominent place is always assigned to the two grandfathers, paternal and maternal, if still living, but in this case they presided only symbolically through the intoning of their names. For, unlike Abraham, neither survived to witness the day. Among the gathering those old enough to appreciate precedence and rank would have acknowledged Abraham as the pre-eminent male family member present, and Spinoza's grandmother, Miriam, among the women.

---

[1] Nadler, *Spinoza: A Life*, 50–1; Steenbakkers, "Spinoza's Life," 19.
[2] Saperstein, *Exile in Amsterdam*, 9n.

Michael's father, Isaac [Pedro Rodrigues] d'Espinoza, Spinoza's paternal grandfather, had died in 1627. After living as a "New Christian" in Portugal, he lived outside Jewish orthodoxy also at Nantes, a background not unusual among Western Sephardic Jews of this period. He died, though, living as a Jew in a port with close maritime links to Nantes, namely Rotterdam,[3] from where his coffin was brought for Jewish burial in the community cemetery close to Amsterdam. Given that Spinoza's older brother was named "Isaac" after this paternal grandfather, Sephardic tradition stipulated that, as his parents' second son, Spinoza should be named after his maternal grandfather. Accordingly, Spinoza was named "Baruch" after Hannah Deborah's father, "Henrique Garces" who, in the synagogue, synagogue records, and memorial prayers was always referred to as "Baruch Senior (or Senhor)" (d. 1619), an appellation received because others of his family returning to normative Judaism had reclaimed, or adopted, the medieval Jewish surname "Senior," just as other former New Christians, including relatives, took other longstanding medieval Spanish Jewish surnames like "Aboab," "Abrabanel," and "Habilho," sometimes from genuine continuity, having secretly conserved memory of their former names since 1492 through the subsequent centuries of repression.[4]

"Baruch Senior," alias Henrique Garces, as he was usually called, son of Francisco Bentalhado and Violante Gomes of Oporto, had left Portugal still unmarried. In Northern Europe, he lived most of his adult life not as an observant Jew but still ostensibly as a New Christian, though residing now chiefly in the Spanish Netherlands, at Antwerp. There, one encountered no active persecution of Jewish tradition and practices as in Iberia; but open practice of Judaism and parading one's different identity, as in Amsterdam and Rotterdam, was not permitted. Provided he kept his beliefs (whatever they were) to himself and private practices discreetly under cover, Garces was unlikely to be interfered with in Holland or the Spanish Netherlands. Still, as a Portuguese New Christian residing in the Catholic southern Netherlands, Henrique was expected to attend Catholic mass whilst there and conduct himself outwardly as a practising Catholic. Listed as belonging to the "Portuguese nation" of Antwerp, in January 1611, Spinoza's maternal grandfather figured among seventy-five male household heads participating in the annual election of the Antwerp "consuls" of the officially staunchly Catholic and anti-Protestant, as well as anti-Jewish merchant guild of Antwerp's so-called "Portuguese nation."[5]

When Garces, son of Francisco Bentalhado, married a Bentalhado relative, probably a niece, Maria Nunes (after her marriage Miriam Senior), Spinoza's maternal grandmother (see Figure 4.1)—such "avunculate marriage" then being

---

[3] Bruyn Kops, *A Spirited Exchange*, 283.   [4] Borges Coelho, *Inquisição de Évora*, 498–9.
[5] Révah, "Pour l'histoire des Marranes," 143; Koen, "Amsterdam Notarial Deeds," *SR* ii (1968), 113n46.

frequent in Western Sephardic communities—their wedding was celebrated in synagogue, in Amsterdam, on 17 June 1605. When, shortly before their wedding, Henrique registered his intention to marry Maria, or Miriam as she was called in Holland, in Amsterdam, accompanied by his future bride's parents, namely his own uncle, Duarte Fernandes (Joshua Habilho or Gabilho; 1541–1623), and the latter's wife, Isabel Nunes, Garces was in the process of becoming Duarte's son-in-law as well as his nephew—assuredly no small matter.[6] For Henrique's prominent and domineering uncle and father-in-law, the wealthy merchant, Duarte Fernandes (d. c.1623), Spinoza's maternal great-grandfather, was decidedly a presence to reckon with.

Son of Henrique Bentalhado of Oporto, Duarte Fernandes, after living and trading in early life in Lisbon and Ponte de Lima, fled Portugal during the 1590s.[7] After a period in Venice, he became and for many years remained among the two or three foremost Jewish merchants in Holland, noted especially as an importer of sugar from Portugal and supplier of Baltic grain to northern Portuguese ports such as Viana, Aveiro, and Oporto though he dealt also in jewels. Sugar then rated among the main motors of Amsterdam's commercial expansion, a sector where Portuguese Jewish merchants played the leading role owing to family ties with Portugal and also Brazil, then the world's principal supplier of sugar.[8] In 1605, Duarte had not been in Holland long.[9] The earliest recorded sign of his presence dates from August 1602. Prominent in commerce during the early years of the Amsterdam Sephardic community's formation, he emerged as an energetic community leader and zealous builder of normative Jewish community life.

Marrying Duarte's daughter, Maria Nunes, Spinoza's grandmother, involved Henrique Garces increasingly with Sephardic Jewish life and business, his frequent travel back and forth between Amsterdam and Antwerp serving as a conduit between the Sephardim of the former and ostensibly Catholic Portuguese of the latter. He conducted business dealings especially on Duarte's behalf. Passing back and forth between the Jewish and Catholic milieus of Amsterdam and Antwerp, while residing for lengthy periods in the south, Henrique presumably took his wife, known in Antwerp as Maria Nunes Garces but in Holland as "Miriam," and their sons, Jacob and Joshua Senior, and daughter, Spinoza's future mother, Hannah Deborah,[10] much of the time along with him. This made it impossible for either Henrique or Maria Nunes to show vigorous commitment to Judaism outwardly—at least while in the Spanish Netherlands. There, adhering to Jewish practices even privately in the home, and consuming only *kosher* food, was neither easy nor prudent.

---

[6] Kaplan, "On the Burial of Spinoza's Grandfather," 28.
[7] Borges Coelho, "Los orígines," 130; Borges Coelho, *Inquisição de Évora*, 499.
[8] Israel, "Spain and the Dutch Sephardim," 5; Schreuder, *Amsterdam's Sephardic Merchants*, 24–7, 53, 61–4.
[9] Koen, "Duarte Fernandes, Koopman," 78.
[10] Révah, "Pour l'histoire des Nouveaux-Chrétiens," 294; Borges Coelho, "Los orígines," 129.

Spinoza's maternal grandparents thus formed a living bridge between two deeply antagonistic religious and cultural worlds which, in Henrique's case, seems to have been reflected in a certain detachment, even coolness, towards formal Judaism. Henrique played no active part in promoting Jewish life and institutions in the manner of his father-in-law. Indeed, vacillating in religious matters as well as in domicile and possibly political allegiance too, he entered into no formal connection with any of the eventually three synagogues of early seventeenth-century Amsterdam. He attended, or at least visited synagogue whilst in Amsterdam but, being uncircumcised, was not permitted to participate in services, wear the ritual prayer shawl (*tallit*) or put on *tefillin* (phylacteries).[11] On the other hand, his family's residing much of the time in Antwerp as ostensible Catholics undoubtedly suited aspects of Duarte's own wide-ranging business and diplomatic activities.

There was nothing particularly unusual about Henrique's bridging role in the often conscience-torn world of the Portuguese *cristãos novos* or New Christians. Henrique's brother, Paulo (Abraham) Garces, another nephew of Duarte's, was apparently even more divided between Christianity and Judaism. Born and baptized in Lisbon, on arriving in Amsterdam with his mother when aged six, Paulo was circumcised, and raised as a practising Jew in Duarte's household. At the age of twelve, speaking Dutch as well as Iberian languages, Duarte assigned him to the service of Don Samuel Pallache (c.1550–1616), the Jewish diplomatic agent of the Moroccan sultan in the United Provinces who normally employed Spanish as his diplomatic and business mainstay but, in Holland, needed helpers familiar with Dutch as well as Spanish to translate. Paulo later accompanied Samuel to Morocco, visiting the picturesque, fortified base at Mogador [Essaouira] as well as Agadir and Safi, ports with which Amsterdam's Portuguese Jewish merchants had frequent commercial and cultural contacts. While assisting Duarte's far-ranging business dealings, Paulo later also visited Hamburg and London. But in April 1620, repudiating Judaism and apparently his family—albeit conceivably at Duarte's direction—Paulo suddenly appeared before the Holy Office tribunal in Lisbon, eager to confess, repudiate Judaism, and beseech reconciliation with Christ.[12] Duarte, we should note, also had other relatives living in Lisbon as apparently pious Catholics, operating as business correspondents. One among them, Gaspar Lopes Enriques, recorded as residing in Lisbon in 1612 and 1615, was yet another of Duarte's numerous (at least seven) sons.[13]

In Amsterdam, meanwhile, the number of Sephardi Jews expanded from around 350 in 1610, to around 1,000 by 1630 and nearing double that figure by

---

[11] Roth, "Strange Case of Hector Mendes Bravo," 241.
[12] García-Arenal and Wiegers, *Un hombre en tres mundos*, 112–14; García-Arenal, "Conexiones," 181; Kaplan, "On the Burial of Spinoza's Grandfather," 31.
[13] Koen, "Duarte Fernandes, Koopman," 179, 181.

1650 as Spinoza approached adulthood, representing over 2 per cent of Amsterdam's population, though contemporary estimates sometimes place the number considerably higher.[14] When Spinoza was an infant, Amsterdam's Jewish population was still smaller than Venice's where the ghetto in 1612 reportedly enclosed around about 1,500 inhabitants. The visibly freer, less legally restricted congregation in the north was then still also less prestigious and authoritative in the wider Western Sephardic world but rapidly catching up with Venice in institutional and commercial standing and rabbinic status.[15] On the other hand, compared to Venice and all the rest of Italy, let alone Iberia or Germany, restrictions and oppressive pressure to convert was much less severe in Amsterdam and the Netherlands generally, resulting in dramatically lower rates of formal conversion to Christianity.

The Spinoza family dwelt in a particular segment of Amsterdam, a rectangular man-made artificial island on the south side of the River Amstel, known as "the Vlooienburg," in probably the same house they still occupied in the early 1650s (Figure 5.1). It was situated on a canal called the Houtgracht (filled in in 1882 and now part of the Waterlooplein), along the bottom long edge of the Vlooienburg, facing away from the river, a district no great distance from the city's main harbour area,[16] and easily reached from anchored ships in the port by means of the ubiquitous canal boats. The Spinoza residence was the fifth house along the Houtgracht canal, at the left end. Mostly owned by Sephardic householders in the seventeenth century, among the Houtgracht's row of houses were two adjoining, the "Moyses" and the "Aaron," later acquired (the first in 1682) by the Catholic "hidden church" dedicated to Saint Anthony of Padua, situated behind them. Much later, after restrictions on Catholic church-building in the Netherlands were lifted in the early nineteenth century, the seventeenth-century houses, including that where Spinoza's family once lived, were demolished to make way for the tall, grandiose Catholic church and its outbuildings standing there today erected between 1837 and 1841. Ironically, the Catholic Church, which the Spinoza family and their neighbours had resisted in mind and deed over generations, in the end triumphed over their neighbourhood, topographically at least, a success only marginally marred by the new edifice remaining commonly known as the "Moses and Aaron Church" instead of "Saint Anthony of Padua."

The name "Vlooienburg," recalled the locality's former proneness to flooding by the nearby River Amstel. First reclaimed in the 1590s, the district was built up

---

[14] Nusteling, "Jews in the Republic," 48, 59–60; Nusteling, *Welvaart en werkgelegenheid*, 24–5; Fuks-Mansfeld estimates 586 men in 1621, and by then a much higher total of 2,300 souls, an estimate agreeing with that of the Spanish *arbitrista*, Francisco Retama; Fuks-Mansfeld, *Sefardim in Amsterdam*, 67.

[15] Roth, "Strange Case of Hector Mendes Bravo," 231.

[16] Vaz Dias, *Spinoza Merchant*, 128; Freudenthal/Walther, *Lebensgeschichte* i, 213–14; Bloom, *Economic Activities*, 64–5; Hell, "A Walk," 55, 58.

Figure 5.1 *Map of the Amsterdam Vlooienburg quarter* (1625) by B. F. Van Berckenrode. Reproduction courtesy of Rijksmuseum, Amsterdam.

into a dry, rectangular embankment or artificial island on the eastern edge of the old medieval city, as part of Amsterdam's so-called "Tweede Uitleg" [Second Outlay] or urban expansion. Following the Revolt against Spain and years of hard struggle, Amsterdam along with the Dutch maritime economy generally, expanded spectacularly, starting in 1585, the year of the fall of Antwerp to the Spaniards and consequent heavy immigration from there. In fact, during the half century immediately preceding Spinoza's birth, Amsterdam experienced the fastest population growth, and expansion of its remarkable ethnic, cultural, and religious diversity, in its entire history. Demographic historians estimate around 30,000 inhabitants in 1585, over 50,000 by 1600, 105,000 at the time of the first population count, in 1622, reaching around 120,000 by 1635 and 160,000 by 1650 placing the Sephardic community at just over 2 per cent of the total.[17]

During the early seventeenth century, nearly all of Amsterdam's Sephardic immigrants dwelt in, or close by, the (Joden-) Breestraat and Vlooienburg though

---

[17] Abrahamse, *Grote Uitleg*, 34; Nusteling, *Welvaart and werkgelegenheid*, 234–5; Israel, *Dutch Republic*, 621.

the locality was not cordoned off and nothing like as separate from the rest of the city as the Venetian, Roman, and Frankfurt ghettos. Nor were Jews out in the streets dressed differently from others. No walls or formal restrictions segregated the Jewish district, and many Christians, Rembrandt among them, lived in the immediate neighbourhood. In the houses behind Spinoza's lived a number of Catholics, and Catholic religious services were regularly held close by. The Vlooienburg, near where the Amsterdam Opera stands today, was enclosed on one side by the Breestraat, the main street where Rembrandt purchased a large house in 1639 and lived until he went bankrupt in 1656, a year or so after Spinoza's own bankruptcy. As the city's population burgeoned, the district rapidly transitioned from what, in the 1590s, had been a zone of warehouses, timber stores, and workshops into an essentially residential district.[18] Backing on to the River Amstel, on the three other flanks ran three canals, the Verwersgracht (now Zwanenburg), the Leprozengracht [Lepers' Canal] and, furthest from the river, the Houtgracht [Timber Canal] where the Spinozas lived. Along the same canal, and close by, stood the synagogue which the family attended, the Bet Ya'acov, or Bet Jacob ["house of Jacob"], one of three small Sephardic synagogues in Amsterdam at the time.

When Spinoza was approaching the age of four, Amsterdam was struck by one of the most severe of the five major plague epidemics to afflict the city during the Golden Age, that of 1636 (the last and other most severe outbreak occurred in 1664). As in 1602, 1624, 1655, and 1664, in 1636 Amsterdam was gravely affected, losing some 10 per cent of its population. Very likely, the epidemic stemmed from the fighting and expansion of armies around the borders of the young Republic at the height of the Thirty Years War. The outbreak affected virtually the entire United Provinces, border areas not least. Yet, notwithstanding Amsterdam's poor air quality, crowding, and often poor sanitary conditions, in 1635–6 many outlying Dutch villages were no less badly, or even worse, stricken by the epidemic.[19] Frequency of contact with foreigners in large maritime centres like Amsterdam and Rotterdam, it has been suggested, may have brought relatively higher levels of immunity to locals than was the case elsewhere. Breadth of international contact in family backgrounds may also have helped shield particular social and ethnic groups. At any rate, in 1656, Rabbi Mortera, musing on the latest plague epidemic in Amsterdam, that of 1655 which caused slightly fewer deaths in the city than the 1635–6 outbreak, invoking the Lord's singular blessings and interventions on behalf of His Chosen People, convinced himself that despite nearly a thousand persons per week dying of plague in Amsterdam over several months, in 1655 as in

---

[18] Fuks-Mansfeld, *Sefardim in Amsterdam*, 87–8; Abrahamse, *Grote Uitleg*, 194, 255–6.
[19] Curtis, "Was Plague an Exclusively Urban Phenomenon?," 150, 157, 166; Alter, "Plague and the Amsterdam Annuitant," 38; Israel, *Dutch Republic*, 625; Prak and Hesselink, "Stad en gevestigden," 107–8.

1636, the city's Jews, owing to divine intervention on their particular behalf escaped almost completely unscathed.[20]

5.ii Spinoza's Forebears, the Mechanics of Community Leadership

Once safely past infancy, Spinoza very likely heard much about distant foreign parts and secret religious subversion, ambivalence in beliefs, complex and shadowy conversions, moves from Christianity to Judaism and vice versa, real and ostensible, along with exotic tales about Morocco, a country with which his father, Michael, as well as his grandfather, great-grandfather and other relatives possessed longstanding trade and family links. Presumably, he will also have heard something of the furtive crisscrossing between Holland and the Spanish Netherlands which the grandfather after whom he was named, and his grandmother frequently undertook. Spinoza, plainly, was far from being the first of his family in Holland to draw the conclusion that strict adherence to Torah, Talmud, and Jewish tradition was not worth the cost in terms of segregation from mainstream society and broad areas of activity and opportunity. At any rate, Spinoza's mother's relatives stood out more than most, for wide experience in bridging lands and religions, and for religious subversion,[21] boasting an even more remarkable past than Spinoza's father's ancestry. For besides Iberia and North Africa, Hannah Deborah's family left their mark in the murky world of early seventeenth-century political negotiation and conspiracy in the Low Countries.

In January 1605, Duarte and two other newly arrived Portuguese Jewish traders, backed by a letter from Prince Emmanuel of Portugal, heir and successor to the pretender to the Portuguese throne, Dom António, had petitioned the States General for a letter of endorsement and protection (during a time of war with Spain) authorizing them to trade freely with Portugal, Spain, and North Africa. When the States General hesitated to grant their petition (having earlier placed restrictions on trade with Spain and Portugal), Emmanuel wrote for a second time on behalf of his ally Duarte, and his associates, leading to lengthy deliberation in Amsterdam and Rotterdam, followed by the States General definitively rejecting their petition, on 18 July 1605.[22] Duarte stayed put, nevertheless, and abundantly flourished.

Philip III of Spain (reigned: 1598–1621) and his advisers worried that the upstart Republic would become not just alluring to hardened crypto-Jewish religious refugees fleeing the Iberian peninsula but a magnet, economic and social,

---

[20] Mortera, *Tratado da Verdade*, 77; Hagoort, *Beth Haim in Ouderkerk*, 54; Saperstein, *Exile in Amsterdam*, 104.
[21] Révah, *Des Marranes à Spinoza*, 170.   [22] Van de Kamp, *Emanuel van Portugal*, 215–16.

pulling in wavering Iberian New Christians from all sides. Spain's global primacy seemed directly threatened by the emerging Dutch and Dutch Sephardic transatlantic network linking Iberia with Brazil, the Caribbean, and Spanish America as well as western France, attracting migrating New Christians and reinforcing crypto-Judaism along with Dutch influence (and perhaps also Portuguese recalcitrance) in all those regions, while simultaneously draining off from the Habsburg southern Netherlands to Holland the thriving Portuguese New Christian community based in Antwerp.[23]

Among other steps, taking advantage of the resumption of traffic between the northern and southern Netherlands during the Twelve Years Truce between Spain and the Republic (1609–21), Spanish officials in Brussels intervened surreptitiously in Holland, behind the scenes, encouraging the Jews' theological opponents, the Calvinist ministers, to vociferously protest to the Amsterdam city government against Jews being allowed to practise their religion openly. Initially, Amsterdam's Sephardic refugees could practise their religion only in the privacy of their homes. Until the truce, they did not yet enjoy anything remotely like official or full toleration. Duarte played a notable part in helping transform the situation. When, in 1612, Spanish ministers in Brussels learnt that the community of escaped "heretics" fleeing the true Church had reached agreement with some builders for construction of what eventually became Amsterdam's Neveh Shalom Portuguese synagogue, they became apprehensive about seeing the first purpose-built, formal synagogue in "rebel" territory become an open challenge to the Spanish crown's unrelenting suppression of crypto-Judaism throughout the Iberian Atlantic world. Given how rapidly Dutch commerce and shipping were expanding during the Twelve Years Truce, Spanish ministers regarded a new synagogue as an unwelcome further spur to the (now temporarily permitted) burgeoning Dutch trade with Spain and Portugal, and also their (still officially forbidden by the Spanish crown) trade with the Iberian New World colonies. To the Spanish way of thinking (and that of many others), it was outrageous beyond comprehension, the pinnacle of perversity, that a city ruled by "heretic" regents should forbid Catholic practice while formally permitting Judaism.

Strict Calvinists also considered it an unforgivable affront to Christian values to permit open practice of Judaism. It was as "Christian" magistrates that the Amsterdam burgomasters were petitioned to prevent Judaizing Portuguese newcomers and refugees openly returning to Judaism.[24] The marqués de Guadaleste, Philip III's minister at the court of Albert and Isabella in Brussels, reported to Madrid, in July 1612, that he was trying "by secret means" to intervene behind the scenes to stop Amsterdam's "Portuguese" establishing a formal Jewish

---

[23] Koen, "Duarte Fernandes, Koopman," 185.
[24] Zwarts, *Eerste rabbijnen*, 65–71, 116; Israel, *Diasporas*, 196–7.

congregation and halt their proceeding with the synagogue construction project as planned under a contract drawn up with the builders, in January 1612.[25] The Dutch Reformed Church council of Amsterdam, an influential body in the city, seemed to Guadaleste to offer the best path to intervening effectively to thwart the Jews; and however bizarre the thought of Spanish officials colluding with Calvinist ministers, following the Reformed Church's protests, the Amsterdam city government did indeed vote, on 8 May 1612, to forbid Amsterdam's first public synagogue. Construction was ordered to cease immediately.

Duarte, a longstanding activist in community affairs and founder of the first Sephardic congregation in Amsterdam, was among the leaders who negotiated the building contract.[26] Duarte's plans were briefly thwarted by this behind-the-scenes Spanish-Calvinist collaborative venture, but not for long: he and his associates had their own contacts in city government keen to promote religious toleration and encourage the flourishing Sephardic community's trade with its unparalleled network of family and group ties in Brazil, the Caribbean, and the entire Ibero-American Atlantic world. Just months later, with a nod and a wink, and assurances Duarte's and his group's synagogue services would be conducted in a discreet and quiet manner, the interrupted construction of the new synagogue was tacitly permitted to resume.[27]

Before long, Jews enjoyed an exceptional degree of toleration in Amsterdam compared to their situation elsewhere at the time. Besides not needing to separate themselves in any particular district, they were not required, as in Rome, Venice, and Frankfurt, to wear distinguishing marks on their clothing marking out Jewish status for all to shun and disdain. Still, this did not mean there were no restrictions constraining the nascent congregation. In 1615, to avoid all "scandal" and annoyance, the States General asked the pensionaries of Amsterdam and Rotterdam, Adriaan Pauw and Hugo de Groot [Grotius], respectively, to formulate appropriate rules to regulate Jewish worship in Holland. Although many of Grotius' restrictive recommendations were ignored, the toleration the community subsequently enjoyed always featured definite limits. The Amsterdam city government locally formalized toleration of Jews and Judaism in 1616, as did the States of Holland, more broadly, in 1619, conceding full freedom of worship in their province, and freedom for Jews to reside, trade, and practise their religion wherever city governments admitted them, as at Amsterdam and Rotterdam. But they were still denied permission to settle in most Dutch towns, the great majority of which, including Leiden, Haarlem, Delft, Dordrecht, and Utrecht, continued barring Jews from settling. In addition, Jews were strictly forbidden to

---

[25] AGS Estado 627, consulta Consejo de Estado, Madrid, 7 July 1612.
[26] Koen, "Duarte Fernandes, Koopman," 178.
[27] Zwarts, *Eerste rabbijnen*, 65–71; Fuks-Mansfeld, *Sefardim in Amsterdam*, 52–3; Swetschinski, *Reluctant Cosmopolitans*, 175.

convert any Christian to Judaism, declare or print anything against Christianity, or contract mixed marriages or have sexual relations with Christians, in the latter case supposedly even prostitutes, under penalty of heavy fines.[28]

Much the most restrictive persisting barrier, however, was that Jews, as in nearly all of Christian Europe, remained firmly debarred from virtually all craft, retail, and professional guilds (as remained the case until the late eighteenth century). Excluded from retailing, the crafts and professions, Jews had scant alternative but to stick, as nearly everywhere in Christendom, to trade, finance, and a few newly arisen or imported particular crafts, deemed Jewish specialities, such as diamond-cutting and polishing. Excluded from the butchers' guild, even the supply of *kosher* meat depended on Jewish ritual slaughterers working as paid employees of Christian butchers. Excluded also from the city bakers' guild, both the Sephardic and Ashkenazic communities had to rely on the dozen or so German Lutheran bakers on the Vlooienburg to prepare their bread including all the Passover *matzah* and other special baked items for holidays. Like the butchers' shops supplying *kosher* meat, these bakers operated under the supervision of the *parnasim* to ensure they complied with Jewish dietary laws.[29]

As with other leading Dutch Sephardic enterprises of the day, Duarte built an international and transatlantic network relying chiefly on far-flung family ties, especially his numerous sons and other close relatives including Henrique Garces, in Antwerp. From Amsterdam, Duarte plied his extensive and wide-ranging business with Oporto, Lisbon, Antwerp, Venice, and Hamburg, and also Tangiers and Saleh, in Morocco. Maintaining a vast web of contacts outside the Republic, he forged an unseen, secret empire that was simultaneously commercial, religious, diplomatic, and political.[30] In nurturing his behind-the-scenes religious-commercial-diplomatic empire, Duarte viewed the Spanish presence in the southern Netherlands and the wider world less as an outright foe than a clumsy giant requiring canny handling.

It typified Guadaleste's wider predicament during the Twelve Years Truce—the interval between the first part of the Eighty Years War (1568–1609) between Spain and the Dutch and the protracted second phase (1621–48)—that the Spanish crown under Philip III, in its undercover dealings in Holland, found it expedient simultaneously to thwart and yet encourage Duarte's wide-ranging activity. Building on this, Duarte made himself both a carefully masked nuisance and valued contact and source of information for the courts of Habsburg Brussels and Madrid especially with regard to overseas commercial and North African policy. While sparing no effort to nurture Jewish life in Holland, strengthen Judaism, and encourage more New Christians to leave Iberian lands and revert to normative

---

[28] Gans, *Memorboek*, 28; Fuks-Mansfeld, *Sefardim in Amsterdam*, 54–7.
[29] Swetschinski, *Reluctant Cosmopolitans*, 20–1, 48, 177; Hell, "A Walk," 59.
[30] Swetschinski, *Reluctant Cosmopolitans*, 108.

Judaism, as well as promoting Dutch involvement in Morocco—projects directly contrary to Spanish objectives—Duarte was also a well-known supporter of the Truce and confidant of those key figures in the States of Holland who, like Philip III and his ministers (wishing to disengage from Northern Europe), were aiming to renew the Truce due to expire in 1621.

Though seeking to maximize Dutch and especially his own commercial penetration of Iberian markets, forging links directly contrary to the Spanish Habsburg interest, Duarte seemed useful to ministers in both Brussels and Madrid for strengthening Dutch-Spanish diplomatic and political ties and also for advancing Spanish goals in North Africa. Duarte Fernandes was indeed a formidable personage, Guadaleste explained to Philip III's ministers in Madrid, "inteligente y prudente" and definitely a man of integrity "though a Jew." The word "integrity" here makes one wonder whether for an experienced diplomat, Philip's chief minister in Brussels was not being a trifle naïve. Certainly, the envoy of the sultan of southern Morocco, the Jewish diplomat-trader, Samuel Pallache, with whom Duarte collaborated closely from the moment this curious Moroccan first arrived in Holland, was much involved in complex dealings with Madrid; but he was also a master of dissimulation. He too worked in convoluted fashion both for and against the Spanish interest. Of course, we must bear in mind that prominent Sephardic Jews at this time, and some Portuguese New Christians in Antwerp, not unnaturally, felt entirely justified in taking the Spanish crown for a ride whenever opportunity offered.[31]

Son of a rabbi descended from an eminent family once prominent in Córdoba prior to 1492, Pallache, when in Holland collaborated chiefly with Duarte, their alliance commencing not in 1596, as Levi de Barrios states, but twelve years later, in 1608, when the two were present in Amsterdam together at synagogue services. A native of Fez, and among the most intriguing personalities of the age, Pallache's comparatively sophisticated knowledge of Hebrew and Judaism, and of Jewish tradition in North Africa and the Mediterranean, greatly surpassed that of most Portuguese immigrants to the Low Countries. His role and advice in the early stages of community formation in Amsterdam were widely appreciated.[32] Both Duarte Fernandes and Pallache figured among the founders of Amsterdam's second Sephardic congregation, the Neveh Shalom synagogue. Both dealt in diamonds, rubies, and other jewels.

Meanwhile, Antwerp where Spinoza's grandfather, Henrique, Duarte's nephew and son-in-law, mostly resided as a main agent of the family's burgeoning business empire, was a particular worry for the Spanish crown, being a major centre of communications and commerce between Holland and Iberia, and seat of the main Portuguese New Christian community in Northern Europe. In late 1609,

[31] Gans, *Memorboek*, 34.   [32] Gans, *Memorboek*, 35.

a nephew of Pallache, offering secret information and claiming to want to convert to Christianity but having been prevented by his father and uncle, secured an interview with Guadaleste, in Brussels, and submitted before local magistrates damaging accusations against several Jews, in particular Duarte and Henrique, for helping organize the current Moroccan anti-Spanish diplomatic effort in Holland. In July 1610, a lengthy lawsuit began in Brussels which in the end fizzled out inconclusively either because the judicial authorities were ordered by Guadaleste to desist, or else because they despaired of the ever thicker fog into which their inquiries led them. Henrique Garces was guilty, according to testimony officials gleaned from "Isaac Pallache, Jew of Fez"—a son of Samuel Pallache's brother, Joseph—not just of secret dealings at Spain's expense with Samuel in Holland, but of working for the Moroccan sultan directly "against the true Catholic Church and Spain." Among his lesser offences, Garces, a "Christian" baptized in Oporto, allegedly syphoned off rubies and other jewels entrusted to him by Samuel and this witness's father, Joseph Pallache, selling them for himself in Antwerp. Other witnesses confirmed Henrique was a dubious type collaborating with Samuel Pallache and Duarte Fernandes who had accompanied Samuel to The Hague, in 1610, in connection with the latter's diplomatic activities for the Moroccan sultan.[33] The inconclusive proceedings in Brussels, however, also yielded conflicting testimony from other Antwerp Portuguese businessmen affirming Henrique's trustworthiness and Isaac Pallache's untrustworthiness and the latter's betrayal of his father and uncle.

Isaac Pallache submitted charges too against Duarte's key contact in Brussels, the future intermediary in the top secret negotiations several years later between Oldenbarnevelt and Philip III's ministers in Madrid, namely the shadowy Fray Martín del Espíritu Santo whom, Isaac alleged, had slandered him. Isaac claimed to have letters in his possession proving Fray Martín who had lived and prayed, supposedly venerating Christ, for thirty years in the monastery of the Misericordia, in Lisbon, was conspiring with Duarte, perfidiously betraying Church and king "and is now a declared Jew who openly shows himself to be one in Amsterdam, and God only knows" for what he and the others do pray.[34] Among the most bizarre of the many curious Portuguese New Christian personages of the early seventeenth century, Fray Martín was a Carmelite mendicant from Mértola, in southern Portugal's Alentejo region, near the Spanish frontier where his brother, Bernardino de Bondía, was secretary of the orphanage. Though a friar who had resided for a time in Rome, Fray Martín was indeed also a secret Judaizer and during the years 1603–7, apparently played a leading role in organizing emigration from Portugal and resettlement of Portuguese New Christian

---

[33] Kaplan, "On the Burial of Spinoza's Grandfather," 29–31; García-Arenal and Wiegers, *Entre el Islam y Occidente*, 90–3; Samuel, *At the End of the Earth*, 128, 157–9.
[34] García-Arenal and Wiegers, *Entre el Islam y Occidente*, 97.

refugees in France, especially Rouen, where many of the immigrant families came from Mértola.[35] For a time, he also enjoyed the confidence of the formerly Protestant but now Catholic French king, Henri IV, until he betrayed, or apparently betrayed, that monarch in May 1607 by secretly contacting the secretary of the Spanish embassy in Paris and (seemingly) switching sides, entering the Spanish king's service. Fray Martín then shifted his base of operations to the Spanish Netherlands, where he now enjoyed the favour of the regent, the Archduke Albert, bringing many Rouen Portuguese with him to Antwerp. At some point subsequently, he entered into the pervasive underground network operated by Duarte and Henrique.[36]

Henrique had sent letters to Samuel Pallache, in Holland, the Brussels magistrates discovered further, addressing him under the pseudonym "Manuel Diaz," that included passages inserted in secret cipher, a suspicious circumstance for which Henrique, when interrogated, refused to offer any explanation. Under questioning, he did admit that, on being tipped off that their house would be searched, his wife had removed all his account books and that Duarte had supplied him rubies to sell in Antwerp. He admitted too that his wife, Maria Nunes Garces (Spinoza's grandmother), was born and raised in Lisbon and baptized a Catholic before being brought as a child by her parents to Venice where her family reverted to Judaism and dwelt in the ghetto. Subsequently, she was raised as a Jewess but, thankfully, was now again (a seemingly) forthright Catholic lady. This supposedly vacillating lady, Spinoza's much-travelled grandmother who later dwelt with her sons, Jacob and Joshua, close by his home, almost certainly figured among Spinoza's chief sources of information about his family history and Portuguese (and Venetian and Antwerp) background.

The most important behind-the-scenes negotiation Henrique participated in, partly on behalf of the Spanish monarch, was acting as Fray Martín del Espíritu Santo's interpreter and assistant when the latter served as chief go-between in the secret negotiations between Philip III and Oldenbarnevelt during 1611–12. Duarte, like the rest of the Sephardic leadership in Holland, was fervently committed to ending the long drawn out struggle between Spain and the Dutch not least for commercial reasons. This secret effort, eventually abortive, to convert the Twelve Years Truce between Spain and the Dutch into a formal full peace, would have meant Spain acknowledging finally the independence of the Dutch Republic from the Spanish crown.[37] Duarte and his circle, prizing his firmly tolerationist stance, staunchly supported Oldenbarnevelt and his policies in the face of growing Calvinist opposition. When Philip III's peace strategy finally collapsed, following Oldenbarnevelt's overthrow by Prince Maurits, in 1618, and the war clouds

---

[35] Révah, "Premier établissement," 542–3.   [36] Révah, "Premier établissement," 551–2.
[37] AGS Estado 2294, Mancicidor to Philip III, Brussels, 31 Dec. 1611; Israel, *Dutch Republic and the Hispanic World*, 16–17; Thomas, "Jerónimo Gracián de la Madre de Dios," 310.

gathered anew, Duarte gave up on the Low Countries and transferred to Hamburg which then had the second most important Sephardic Jewish community in Northern Europe, so as to sustain his Iberian links also after expiry of the Truce, in 1621.[38]

The Spanish crown's other main involvement with Duarte stemmed from its efforts to advance Spain's strategic position in North Africa. Collaboration between Duarte Fernandes and Samuel Pallache grew especially close after the latter returned as envoy of Sultan Mulay Zaydan (ruler of southern Morocco in the period 1603–27), for a second stay in Holland, charged, as Menasseh ben Israel recalls in his *Hope of Israel*, with conferring with the States General. At that time, Morocco was torn by civil war and suffering mounting Spanish incursion, culminating in Spanish occupation of Larache [El Araish] in 1610 and La Mámora [al-Ma'mura] in 1614 (occupied by Spain during the years 1614–81). Philip III's strategy on the Barbary Coast was to try to consolidate a string of northern Moroccan fortified ports enabling Spain to control the large stretch of African coast facing both flanks of the Iberian peninsula, an incursion advanced in collusion with the embattled sultan of northern Morocco, Mulay Zaydan's brother and bitter rival, Mulay-al-Sheikh, a committed ally, or rather pawn, of Spain.[39]

Mulay-al-Sheikh's abject pact with Spain rendered Mulay Zaydan fiercely anti-Spanish and eager to secure friendly relations, diplomatic support, and also arms and munitions from the United Provinces (and England). At The Hague, Samuel Pallache negotiated a treaty of commerce and friendship between the court of Marrakesh and the Dutch Republic that was concluded in December 1610.[40] Samuel and Duarte, however, began playing what eventually became a highly convoluted treble game supplying secret information to probably both warring Moroccan courts from The Hague while supplying Madrid with information from Holland and Morocco. Their consistent objective throughout was to forge their own informal empire of trade, influence, and Judaism, spanning the worlds of Islam, Protestantism, and Catholicism, and the sea-lanes from Morocco to Holland and Hamburg. In 1615, Duarte seems to have been instrumental in assisting Guadaleste lure Pallache, while officially still serving the court of Marrakesh, into secretly re-entering Spanish service, thenceforth venturing on a still more intricate game of duplicity towards Madrid and the Moroccan courts.

A driving force in the wider Sephardic community and principal founder of the Neveh Shalom synagogue, in 1612, among Duarte's other notable benefactions was his paying for the printing, in Amsterdam that year, for use in Holland and Hamburg, of the standard Spanish-language prayer-book, or *Siddur*, earlier

---

[38] Koen, "Duarte Fernandes, Koopman," 183; Swetschinski, *Reluctant Cosmopolitans*, 112.
[39] Israel, *Diasporas*, 155–7, 160; Israel, *Dutch Republic and the Hispanic World*, 12–13; García-Arenal and Wiegers, *Entre el Islam y Occidente*, 52; Waite, *Jews and Muslims*, 119.
[40] García-Arenal and Wiegers, *Entre el Islam y Occidente*, 87–9; García-Arenal, "Conexiones," 174.

adopted by the so-called *Ponentini* (Western Sephardic Jews) of Venice.[41] This was the prayer-book Spinoza would have used throughout his childhood and early life when attending services in the synagogue. Duarte was also one of the synagogue leaders who arranged the joint purchase by both the then existing congregations Bet Ya'acov and Neveh Shalom, in 1614, of the grounds at Ouderkerk that became Amsterdam Sephardic Jewry's principal cemetery. Given his family's experience of persecution by the Inquisition, it is unsurprising that Duarte, whose synagogue name was "Joshua Habilho," felt a deep commitment to reconstituting Iberian Judaism in Northern Europe and antagonism towards Catholicism (albeit not the Spanish crown). His long-lived merchant brother, Manoel Bentalhado of Oporto who died in the Inquisition dungeons of Coimbra, resisted obdurately in his crypto-Judaism despite bouts of torture, until the age of eighty-eight, something extraordinary at the time. His remains were ceremonially burnt before the massed crowds of faithful at the Coimbra auto-da-fé of 15 September 1602.

As Philip III's efforts to expand Spain's strategic position in the Maghreb unfolded, and the Spanish fleets based in Gibraltar and Cadiz were reinforced, Guadaleste reported in August 1615 to Madrid that Duarte Fernandes was "una persona de gran opinion a quien escuchaban los Estados [a person of high standing to whom the States General listen]." That his great-grandfather had had the ear of Oldenbarnevelt and leading regents was something Spinoza undoubtedly knew. In November 1615, Duarte and Samuel signed a secret pact with the Spanish crown comprising twelve clauses, the substance of which was that Pallache would receive 200 *ducados* monthly in return for passing "useful" information to Brussels, via Duarte, about the diplomatic contacts of France, England, and the Dutch with the two rival Moroccan courts (and the Turks) and everything affecting Spanish interests in the Maghreb.[42] Samuel died in January 1616, but his relatives continued his far-flung activities together with Duarte. In April 1616, Samuel's nephew, Moseh Pallache, accompanied by Duarte and the latter's son, Bento Enriques, participated in a high-level strategic discussion, in Brussels, with Guadaleste and Spain's most distinguished military commander, Spinola, concerning Morocco's warring factions, ports, corsairs, and the *Morisco* and Jewish communities. Philip and his chief adviser, the duke of Lerma, were contemplating annexation of the main Moroccan corsair base at Saleh, then virtually an independent republic, and knew Jewish and Moroccan aid could help advance this scheme. For sufficient payment, suggested Moseh, the assistance of the Jews of Saleh and Fedala could help bring Spain's plan to fruition. Guadaleste

---

[41] Swetschinski, *Reluctant Cosmopolitans*, 172; Salomon, *Portrait of a New Christian*, 149; Israel, *Diasporas*, 93.

[42] AGS Estado 2302: Duarte Fernandes, "Memoria de las cosas tratados y asentados con Samuel Pallache."

approved; but Spinola, less inclined to take Duarte's inexperienced protégé seriously, refused to agree.[43]

Between 1609 and 1618, Duarte travelled regularly to Brussels where, together with Henrique, he mixed politics with business and both with his complex, wide-ranging family affairs—and religion. By 1616, he had so angered the bishop of Antwerp with his unstinting efforts to persuade Antwerp Portuguese New Christians to forsake Catholicism and opt for secret Judaism in the southern Netherlands or, better still, public Judaism in Holland, that Duarte had seriously compromised his standing in Antwerp.[44] Several highly-placed ecclesiastics complained at this time about certain meddling persons prompting Judaizing relatives and friends in Antwerp to infiltrate Jewish books by sea into the Spanish-speaking world as a means to circumvent the Inquisition.[45] In November 1616, Duarte obtained a missive from the States General for the regent Archduke Albert in Brussels, requesting that he be allowed to resume his stays in Antwerp despite the bishop's demanding his expulsion.[46] To ministers in Madrid, Duarte complained early in 1617, reminding them that he had been communicating directly with Madrid since 1615 and had sent Philip III's ministers reliable *relaciones* containing advice about long-distance and colonial trade.[47]

Undoubtedly, his unusual, complex family history, and the activities of Duarte Fernandes, Abraham d'Espinoza, and his grandfather, Henrique Garces, were a factor in what would otherwise seem an improbable, even incomprehensible, tendency for Spinoza to assume, in his political writings, that he possessed some special awareness of the hidden mechanics of social and political power, access to the inner practicalities and secrets that other political theorists lacked. Knowing the "Baruch" after whom he was named and, still more, Duarte, together with the latter's seven sons and other family members, were deeply immersed in conspiracy and secret international dealings which they mingled with commerce, family affairs, and religious allegiance was assuredly an element in his believing he possessed unique insight, some exceptional ability to penetrate the behind-the-scenes hidden workings of influence and power which would otherwise seem bizarre, pretentious, and inexplicable.

---

[43] AGS Estado 2301: "Memoria de lo que yo Mosseh Pallache dijo en Bruselas a Duarte Fernandes"; Israel, "Spain and the Dutch Sephardim," 14; García-Arenal and Wiegers, *Entre el Islam y Occidente*, 140.
[44] AGS Estado 2302: Duarte Fernandes, "Memoria de las cosas tratados y asentados con Samuel Pallache"; Garcia-Arenal and Wiegers, *Entre el Islam y Occidente*, 121.
[45] Thomas, "Jerónimo Gracián de la Madre de Dios," 311.
[46] *Resolutiën der Staten-Generaal* new series 11 (1613–16) (The Hague, 1984), 727.
[47] AGS Estado 2302: Duarte Fernandes, "Memoria de las cosas tratados y asentados con Samuel Pallache."

5.iii The Sephardic Cemetery at Ouderkerk

Henrique Garces alias Baruch Senior found himself spending more time in Holland than in Antwerp from around 1616. In January 1617, he definitively transferred his family from Antwerp to Amsterdam. Not long afterwards, he applied to the Amsterdam *parnasim* for permission to be buried, after death, in the Ouderkerk Sephardic cemetery, a clear signal of at least residual Jewish allegiance. Yet, despite this, on settling in Amsterdam, he apparently showed little interest in participating in prayer services, joining neither the Bet Ya'acov nor Neveh Shalom synagogue. This was expressly recorded in the cemetery register. Henrique apparently adhered to his own personal selective crypto-Judaism avoiding the great bulk of ritual Jewish observance, an interesting point in relation to Spinoza's own later disinclination to formally become a Christian. Especially striking, besides refraining from regular synagogue attendance and outward observance, Spinoza's maternal grandfather, it was recorded, remained uncircumcised for the entire remainder of his life.[48]

This fact is noteworthy (though not particularly unusual among former Portuguese New Christian refugees in Northern Europe at the time), because, since biblical times, being uncircumcised figured among the sternest reproaches known to the ancient Israelites and post-exilic Jews. Among seventeenth-century Amsterdam Sephardim, it was a severe, standing reproach and blotch on one's reputation requiring a good deal of defiant distancing and estrangement to withstand. When he died and was buried at Ouderkerk on 13 March 1619, a remarkable entry was made in the communal burial register, the *Livro de Bet Haim* [The Book of the House of Life]—a register commencing in 1614 kept by successive community administrators in Sephardic Portuguese dotted with Hebrew terms—with the words "was buried Baruk Senior, by his other name Henrique Garces whom they circumcised after his death" and he was laid to rest next to the uncircumcised twelve-year-old "son of Lobato" buried the previous November.[49] In other words, having refused circumcision while he lived, Henrique's corpse was circumcised by the community after death, prior to burial and the prayers recited over his grave.

Henrique's "circumcision" after death was a decidedly odd and, for the Spinoza family, perhaps embarrassing occurrence. One might dismiss it, like the story of the political philosopher Enrique Henríquez, the Jesuit turned Dominican who then became a Jesuit for the second time, as a tale too remote from Spinoza's own life to possess much relevance to his biography. Yet, as Yosef Kaplan rightly

---

[48] *Livro de Bet Haim*, 26, 31; Salomon, "Saul Levi Mortera," xcvii; Borges Coelho, *Inquisição de Évora*, 499.
[49] *Livro de Bet Haim*, 93, 103, 135; García-Arenal, "Conexiones," 179; Kaplan, "Religion, Politics," 13; Kaplan, "This Thing Alone will Preserve," 238.

argues, even if he was not shown his grandfather's final resting place as a boy—albeit even that seems unlikely given that Henrique's widow, Miriam (alias Maria Nunes), Spinoza's grandmother and her sons, his uncles of the "Senior" clan, lived close by on the Vlooienburg—this bizarre episode must have long remained a nagging issue in the mind of the adolescent and then young man Spinoza. That he was still unaware of this story as an adolescent seems highly improbable since the long-remembered "uncircumcision" of his grandfather was humiliatingly commemorated and marked out for all to see by his final resting place's peculiar location in relation to the rest of the cemetery and the graves of Spinoza's other deceased relatives. For his grandfather's grave was located outside the bounds of the cemetery proper separated from the graves of his honoured forebears, at a fringe reserved for uncircumcised marginal types not fully belonging to the community.

When attending the burial of his prematurely deceased older brother, Isaac, who died at eighteen, in 1649, when he himself was nearing seventeen, Spinoza had doubtless already been numerous times to Ouderkerk. Known to Amsterdam's Portuguese Jews as 'Oukerqua', this cemetery which his great-grandfather had helped the community acquire, was situated in the village of Ouderkerk aan de Amstel (not to be confused with Ouderkerk aan de Ijssel), five miles south of central Amsterdam, at some two hours' walk from Spinoza's home. For family funerals in Spinoza's day, the main burial party, the men wearing dark coloured cloaks and attired in large hats, customarily accompanied the coffin from Amsterdam's Jewish quarter in horse-drawn river barges along the River Amstel which ran virtually due south from the city centre (Figure 5.2). Every time the teenager Spinoza and his relatives gathered for funerals in Ouderkerk, whether conveyed by *trekschuit* [river barge], or walking, he must have wondered why the grandfather after whom he was named languished under the lasting insult of banishment from the honoured inner precinct occupied by his other prominent deceased relatives to the outer fringe.[50]

Each time Spinoza walked through the cemetery grounds he doubtless noted that his grandfather's gravestone lay beside the remains of "pessoas indignas" [unworthy persons] meaning "uncircumcised" New Christians, illegitimate not fully converted children of gentile women by Sephardic fathers, and Jewish mulattos from Brazil.[51] Still, ignoring dishonour to ensure burial beside a husband or wife scorned by community dignitaries, and buried beyond the fence, could still be the preferred choice of a living loved one. "Unworthy" or not, at the particular request of Spinoza's grandmother, Miriam Senior, and her son Joshua, submitted to the board of the now united single Sephardic community Talmud Torah, in

---

[50] Gans, *Memorboek*, 126; Hagoort, *Beth Haim in Ouderkerk*, 11, 13.
[51] *Livro de Bet Haim*, 107, 135; Kaplan, "On the Burial of Spinoza's Grandfather," 35; Kaplan, "This Thing Alone will Preserve," 237.

Figure 5.2 *Barge conveying mourners to the Sephardic cemetery at Ouderkerk*, by Romeyn de Hooghe, paper etching. Reproduction courtesy of Rijksmuseum, Amsterdam.

March 1640, the *parnasim* gave permission for her, on her death, to be interred beside her posthumously circumcised husband, hence together with him, beyond the fence. Although the *parnasim* consented at the time, recording their doing so verbally, being unwilling to do so formally in writing,[52] when she died, in November 1647, around the time of Spinoza's fifteenth birthday, his grandmother's plea for burial beside her husband was nevertheless set aside.

Miriam was laid to rest in row 27, grave no. 24 in a ceremony at which her son-in-law, Spinoza's father, Michael d'Espinoza, promised the largest donation (twenty-four guilders), and her sons, Joshua and David each half that sum. Most probably, the ignoring of her wish, as Spinoza doubtless knew, was due to the preference of his father, Michael, now very much the family head, not to further besmirch the family's reputation in any way. Spinoza and his brother Isaac were doubtless also present and this entire proceeding must have struck the teenage brothers (and Joshua and David) as decidedly peculiar: instead of being laid to rest beside their grandfather, according to her long-stated wish, which was simply

---

[52] GA Amsterdam Hagoort ed. *Livro de Bet Haim* [...] *Talmud-Tora*, 23 res. 29 March 1640.

pushed aside, Miriam's remains, presumably following the preference of Michael and other family members and the *Mahamad*, were interred far away, in a quite different location, beside other relatives.[53]

As a teenager, Spinoza doubtless "inquired into the reasons," as Yosef Kaplan puts it, "why the older Baruch was buried beyond the fence, far from the other members of the family." At some point, he would have discovered the facts of his grandfather's posthumous circumcision and grandmother's thwarted wish. Even if the affront to their memory elicited no strong feelings of indignation, a fifteen-year-old was bound to frown at the congregation's refusal to honour his grandmother's final wish (if that was what happened), or alternatively, that his grandmother at her end, was pressured into changing her mind, perhaps by his Senior uncles, or his father, Michael, and for that reason did not lie beside his grandfather. When writing up "his criticism of Judaism," after cutting himself off from the community following his excommunication in 1656, suggests Kaplan, Spinoza "also found a way of expressing his contempt for the ceremony of circumcision which the elders of the community had posthumously and humiliatingly imposed on his grandfather."[54]

In any case, Spinoza's aversion to orthodox Jewish ritual observances as revealed in the *TTP*, and unenthusiastic view of circumcision, very likely did originate in his teenage years. In the *TTP*, strikingly, Spinoza cites Paul, as he calls him (always omitting the term "Saint"), his favourite biblical personality, with warm approval for affirming (Paul 2:25–6): "if the circumcised break the law, their circumcision will become uncircumcision and if, on the other hand, the uncircumcised obey the command of the law, their uncircumcision is regarded as circumcision."[55] Spinoza, moreover, identifies circumcision as the factor that explains more than any other how and why Jews survived as a people over so many centuries scattered among the nations while remaining for millennia wholly separate, and consequently hated by all other nations. "I think the sign of circumcision has possessed such great importance as almost to persuade me that this thing alone will preserve their nation forever, and indeed, were it not for the fact that the principles of their religion weaken their courage, I would believe unreservedly that at some time, given an opportunity, since all things are changeable, [the Jews] might re-establish their state, and God," Spinoza in the *TTP* adds, with a sarcastic flourish, "will choose them again."[56]

Still, Spinoza saw nothing positive or beneficial in the fact that it is the "resentment of the gentiles to a large extent that preserves them." Whatever their observances, Jews are no different from other peoples, any more than the

---

[53] GA Amsterdam Hagoort ed. *Livro de Bet Haim* [...] *Talmud-Tora*, 176; Kaplan, "On the Burial of Spinoza's Grandfather," 35.
[54] Kaplan, "On the Burial of Spinoza's Grandfather," 36–7; Kaplan, "This Thing Alone will Preserve," 238, 242; Bento, "Spinoza and the Hebrew State," 261–3.
[55] Spinoza, *Theological-Political Treatise*, 52–3.   [56] Spinoza, *Theological-Political Treatise*, 55.

Chinese with their pigtails with whom, in this passage, Spinoza memorably compares them. Moreover, awareness of the grandfather who, like other relatives, chose to live beyond the confines of Judaism, suggests Kaplan, must consciously or unconsciously have played into his own decision, later in life, to live beyond the fences of Judaism.[57] Awareness of the circumstances of his grandfather's and grandmother's burials must have added in some fashion to his later insistence on the universal equivalence of all men morally and irrelevance of observing religious ceremonies, symbols, and practices for defining or determining a person's moral and "true religious" standing.

5.iv The Spinozas of Amsterdam and Rotterdam

In business affairs Spinoza's paternal grandfather, Isaac d'Espinoza alias Pedro Rodrigues d'Espinoza was, like Henrique Garces and his great-uncle, Abraham (alias Manoel Rodrigues) d'Espinoza, known usually by his Portuguese name. Both Isaac and his brother Abraham departed Nantes during the latter part of the Twelve Years' Truce. Having lived most of their lives in Portugal and then France where open practice of Judaism was forbidden, Pedro [Isaac], like his brother, Manoel [Abraham], thus spent a far greater proportion of his life frequenting Catholic places of worship than attending synagogue. Still, it was not inappropriate that they both ended their lives as practising Jews and received honoured Jewish burials at Ouderkerk. For despite outwardly living, like all New Christians in France's western ports at the time, like Catholics, they undoubtedly did so insincerely, carefully conserving the family's tenacious tradition of secret Judaizing.[58]

That the Spinoza family's crypto-Judaism at Nantes remained steadfast and was well-known among the nascent Sephardic synagogues at Holland at that time is fully confirmed by the fact that, in 1615, the heads of the Amsterdam Portuguese Jewish marriage dowry, or "Dotar" society, appointed Abraham d'Espinoza, or Manoel Rodrigues d'Espinoza as he was known there, as their society's representative at Nantes. A key charitable institution of Amsterdam's (and generally Northern Europe's) Sephardim, the Dotar was responsible for overseeing, arranging, and endowing marriages of "orphan and poor girls" of the "Portuguese and Spanish [Jewish] nation" throughout the coastal zone of Europe from Saint-Jean-de-Luz on the Franco-Spanish border to Danzig. Only recently established, on the initiative of Rabbi Joseph Pardo, in February 1615, the Amsterdam *Santa Companhia de Dotar Orphas e Donzellas* [Holy Society for Providing Dowries for Orphan Girls and Young Women], was modelled, like much else in the

---

[57] Kaplan, "On the Burial of Spinoza's Grandfather," 37–9; Bento, "Spinoza and the Hebrew State," 263.
[58] GA Amsterdam NA 391, fo. 195.

Amsterdam community at the time, on its Venetian counterpart, the *Hebra Kedossa de cazar orfans* [Holy society to marry orphans] established in 1613. A major reason for these societies' existence was the need to redress the adverse gender balance in the Venetian, Amsterdam, and Hamburg communities caused by the fact that most early fugitives arriving from the Peninsula were male.

The function of these institutions was to locate and draw into practising Judaism poor, dowry-less Portuguese New Christian girls "of good conduct and manners, chaste and honourable, without any taint of vileness," especially in lands where open practice of Judaism was forbidden. Secretly contacted, they were offered dowries if willing to marry in synagogue with either would-be, or actually, professing Jews and reconstitute their lives as Jewesses in Venice, Amsterdam, Hamburg, Rotterdam, or wherever formal Judaism was permitted. In terms of prior commitment, all that was required of maidens the society contacted, and agreed to assist, was readiness to repudiate the explicitly Christian avowals so relentlessly drilled into them where they grew up and "confess the unity of the Lord of the world," and the "truth of His Most Sacred Law."[59] Directed by merchants, the Dotar thus provided financial assistance stretching over vast distances, arranging marriages across international borders usually in Portugal, Spain and France, but also in Brazil.

The Amsterdam Dotar was unique in the Sephardic world for its transatlantic reach, with its three associated New Christian agents residing (as secret Jews) in Pernambuco (Recife), from where the merchants organizing the Amsterdam Dotar imported most of the sugar forming the principal segment of their transatlantic business during this early formative period. First among the fifteen merchants listed as founders of the Amsterdam society, and first of those financing it, was "Joshua Habilho," that is, Duarte Fernandes.[60] The very first meeting of Amsterdam's Dotar society, a unique line of communication strengthening established networks linking organized Sephardic Jewry in lands where Judaism was tolerated with lands where practising Judaism was forbidden, took place on 14 February 1615 in Duarte's house.[61] One of its first three directors, Duarte was influential in selecting the organization's appointed agents resident along the European coastline, extending from Saint-Jean-de-Luz to Danzig, covering the society's European remit.[62]

In October 1615, the newly established Dotar appointed seven locally resident correspondents or agents in the main European ports outside the Iberian peninsula with which the Amsterdam Sephardim traded, residing respectively at

---

[59] Révah, "Premier règlement imprimé," 652; Swetschinski, *Reluctant Cosmopolitans*, 87, 100, 178–81.
[60] Fuks-Mansfeld, *Sefardim in Amsterdam*, 60–1; Koen, "Duarte Fernandes, Koopman," 179–80; Israel, *Diasporas*, 81, 206; Levie Bernfeld, *Poverty and Welfare*, 29.
[61] Révah, "Premier règlement imprimé," 659.
[62] Révah, "Premier règlement imprimé," 658, 668, 691; Israel, *Diasporas*, 81, 93, 95, 161, 196, 604.

Saint-Jean-de-Luz, Bordeaux, Paris, Nantes, Rouen, Antwerp, and Hamburg. Rouen played a notable part in Duarte's commercial empire as chief source of the linens figuring prominently among the goods he regularly shipped to Portugal and its empire in exchange for the sugar and other goods he imported. Abraham d'Espinoza's election to membership of the Amsterdam dowry society as its principal Nantes representative reflects both his status as leader of the Nantes Portuguese community, and reputation in the eyes of Duarte and his associates as an actively proselytizing committed crypto-Judaizer among the Nantes Portuguese, someone consistent in opposing Christianity and Spain, a reputation enhanced by the Espinoza family's long involvement with crypto-Jewish subversion in Portugal. It signifies also that, in 1615, Abraham was viewed by the Dutch Sephardic community with confidence based on a longstanding prior reputation for dependability in financial dealings and religious matters.[63]

Abraham d'Espinoza did not, though, remain the Dotar society's representative in Nantes for long. By June 1616, he himself had transferred to Amsterdam well before his brother, Isaac, who remained in Nantes for several more years, seemingly as his brother's correspondent and agent there. Abraham then joined the Amsterdam Dotar society now as a regular member, paying a subscription of twenty guilders (a month's salary for a skilled artisan) while his brother, Pedro Rodrigues (alias Isaac Israel) d'Espinoza became his successor as the society's agent at Nantes.[64] It remains unknown why precisely either Abraham, and afterwards Isaac, transferred from Nantes to Holland but some interesting detail about the family's settling in Amsterdam is preserved in the surviving burial register of the Bet Ya'acov congregation which the Spinoza family, like most of the newcomers in those years, joined. Although Isaac too had transferred to Amsterdam by February 1620 when he witnessed a notarial deed there, he evidently chose not to stay, for he died, it is recorded, in Rotterdam, from where his body was transported to Ouderkerk and interred, on 9 April 1627, six weeks after the burial of his niece who died in childbirth, his brother Abraham's daughter, Rachel d'Espinoza, first wife of his son Michael, Spinoza's father.[65]

After an earlier visit to Amsterdam, on his way back overland to Nantes, in around 1614, Abraham d'Espinoza had met up in a tavern, at Orléans, with the future rabbi Saul Levi Mortera.[66] Between 1612 and 1616, Mortera too lived in France, serving as private religious adviser to the Sephardic court physician (and personal physician to Marie de Medici), Elija Montalto (1567–1616), a former Marrano converted to Judaism in Venice, who used his court position in France to actively encourage Portuguese New Christians resident in France to repudiate

---

[63] Israel, *Diasporas*, 81–2; Bruyn Kops, *A Spirited Exchange*, 280–1, 283.
[64] Révah, "Premier règlement imprimé," 660–1; Roth, "Strange Case of Hector Mendes Bravo," 236.
[65] SR XVI/ii (1982), 197–8; *Livro de Bet Haim*, 70, 117, 139; Frampton, *Spinoza and the Rise*, 124–5.
[66] Nadler, *Menasseh ben Israel*, 23; Salomon, "Haham Saul Levi Morteira en de Portugese Nieuw-Christenen," 133.

Christian belief towards which he evinced a quite exceptional antagonism in several clandestine polemical tracts (in manuscript) which he penned on this subject. Mortera, though not himself Portuguese or Spanish (he came from Venice), was married to a Portuguese woman and spoke and wrote Portuguese fluently.[67] In that tavern, over their fare, these two devoted propagators of secret Judaism meeting in the heart of France, a kingdom from which all Jews were officially prohibited from living since the final decree of expulsion of 1394, doubtless discussed especially the peculiar predicament of the crypto-Jews resident in France at the time. When Montalto died, in 1616, the twenty-year-old Mortera accompanied his corpse to Amsterdam for burial at Ouderkerk, and then stayed on there. From that point on commenced Mortera's rabbinic career proper, ministering to the Bet Ya'acov congregation. Abraham, for his part, settled in Amsterdam around the same time.[68]

On arriving at Amsterdam, Abraham must have brought a relatively large fortune with him. For "Abraham Espinoza of Nantes," as the undisputed head of the family in Holland was known in synagogue, paid a substantial communal tax, or *finta*, to the Bet Ya'acov congregation, fixed in the first year, 1616, the *Livro de Bet Haim* records, at twenty guilders,[69] which is considerably more than was paid by most newcomers joining the community, including, not long afterwards, his brother, Isaac. At that time, heads of households were usually assessed for the *finta* at just one, two, six, or ten guilders. His high *finta* rating proves Abraham was much wealthier than most newcomers as well as more prominent as a known Judaizer in France. Duarte Nunes da Costa (Jacob Curiel) (1587–1664), among the foremost Sephardic traders in all Europe, later a key leader of the Hamburg community, who, in March 1622, purchased a large mansion on Amsterdam's (Joden-) Breestraat for 5,900 guilders, an extremely large sum at the time, on joining the same Beth Ya'acov synagogue, in late 1621, paid twenty-six guilders in *finta*, not vastly more than Abraham.[70] A surviving Amsterdam notarial deed of December 1624 reveals that among his other assets, Abraham then owned three sixteenths (the rest of which was owned by two other "Portuguese merchants") of a Dutch vessel called *De Margriete* chartered to sail to Faro, in southern Portugal and spend seven weeks there loading entirely with figs for the Amsterdam market. Since figs later figured among the main items in which the Spinoza firm dealt in the 1640s and 1650s, it seems also from other evidence that the family had a long tradition of trading in dried figs.[71]

Despite knowing little Hebrew and little of formal Judaism, Abraham quickly became a prominent as well as conscientious member of Bet Ya'acov synagogue,

---

[67] *Livro de Bet Haim*, 34–7; Salomon, "Vraie excommunication," 182.
[68] *Livro de Bet Haim*, 25–6; Fuks-Mansfeld, *Sefardim in Amsterdam*, 47; Bento, "Spinoza and the Hebrew State," 243.
[69] *Livro de Bet Haim*, 144.   [70] Israel, "Duarte Nunes da Costa (Jacob Curiel)," 19.
[71] SR 29/2 (1995) p. 228. Deed no. 3264, 18 Dec. 1624.

the first of the original three Amsterdam synagogues to be founded, it is thought, around 1600–2.[72] In regular contact with the community's then young assistant rabbi, Mortera, Abraham served as *administrador* of the congregation's burial society during 1619–21, a period when his name was often listed together with Mortera's in the congregation's records.[73] Both Bet Ya'acov, and the second congregation, Neveh Shalom, formed between 1608 and 1610, where Duarte Fernandes was a leader, based their governance, ceremonies, and prayer practices on the Venetian Sephardic model with lay elders, or *parnasim*, forming the *Mahamad* as the community governing board was called. The last of the three communities, Beth Yisrael, was formed in 1619 following an epic quarrel erupting in July 1618 that tore the Bet Ya'acov congregation in two, a conflict that began over a rabbinic decision to reject a recently appointed new communal *shohet* [ritual slaughterer] as insufficiently versed in the rules and rituals of preparing *kosher* meat.

This suspect *shohet* had been appointed by David Farar (1573–1624) (alias Francisco Lopes Henriques), a remarkable *parnas* and one of the first university-trained physicians among the Amsterdam Sephardim. Though widely respected, Farar was frowned upon by some community members for being "interested only in philosophy" and his relatively relaxed attitude to Jewish observance and tradition, as well as disdain for the Kabbalah [Jewish mysticism].[74] Farar was too lax regarding ritual matters, complained his critics, and in interpreting *Aggadic Midrashim*, the supplementary body of laws not directly drawn from the biblical text (unlike the *Halachic Midrashim*) but from rabbinic inferences from the text and from commentaries of Rashi and other medieval exegetes.[75] Farar was opposed by a hardline traditionalist, rabbinic faction led by Joseph Pardo (1561–1619) seeking to compel those less strict in observance than themselves to submit to stronger rabbinic authority. Originally from Salonika, Pardo had long exerted a formative influence on the institutions and practices of the Amsterdam Sephardic community, much as his grandson, Rabbi Josiah Pardo, would do later in the Caribbean.

When Farar protested before the congregation against the ban on the *shohet*, Pardo placed him under a rabbinic ban, the *herem*. In the ensuing furore, the anti-Farar traditionalist faction initially held the upper hand, despite rabbinic opinion in Venice being divided, with the famous Rabbi Yehudah Arieh da Modena who admired Farar's learning and constructive role in building the Amsterdam community, ruling that Pardo had overstepped the mark. Backed by the Salonika rabbinate and the congregation's richest member, Baruch Osorio, the anti-Farar

---

[72] Pieterse, *Daniel Levi de Barrios als geschiedschrijver*, 62.
[73] *Livro de Bet Haim*, 35–9; Hagoort, *Beth Haim in Ouderkerk*, 30.
[74] Silva Rosa, *Geschiedenis*, 15–16; Fuks-Mansfeld, *Sefardim in Amsterdam*, 61–2; Swetschinski, *Reluctant Cosmopolitans*, 173.
[75] Kaplan, "Jews in the Republic," 119; Kaplan, *Judíos nuevos en Amsterdam*, 24–5, 48n5.

faction secured a legal distraint on the synagogue building and its contents, thereby (temporarily) gaining physical possession of the premises and its ritual objects, records, and books.[76] During this raucous rift within Bet Ya'acov, Farar's chief allies were his friend, Rabbi Mortera and another of that year's *parnasim*, "Abraham Espinosa of Nantes."[77] This pro-Farar faction, with Abraham among its leaders, formed what became the residual rump of Bet Ya'acov.

On 19 July 1619, a leader of the opposed faction, now treasurer of what became the break-away stricter synagogue, Beth Yisrael, went to see Abraham, presenting religious legal rulings (*denim*) signed by seventeen Salonika rabbis, directing the community to settle the rift by rabbinic authority and divide the synagogue's ritual objects, furniture, and library equally between the two now separate congregations. Pardo's break-away traditionalist group welcomed the Salonika rabbinic judgement, insisting there was no need to introduce any non-Jewish jurisdiction into the dispute. Rejecting their insistence on purely rabbinic arbitration, Abraham answered that the affair had been submitted to the city magistrates to arbitrate and both sides must abide by what they decided.[78] The magistrates appointed three arbiters and, eventually, in August 1619, passed judgement recognizing the larger faction, with Abraham still a *parnas*, as rightful possessors of the Bet Ya'acov premises with sole possession of the building, ritual objects, Torah scrolls, pews, records, and library. Soon afterwards, Mortera who had been briefly jailed, probably for too vociferously disputing some aspect of the magistrates' proceedings, was bailed out by Abraham and now succeeded Pardo as the Bet Ya'acov's permanent rabbi.[79]

One principle Spinoza and his great-uncle, Abraham, the most prominent member of their family in Amsterdam Sephardic communal life, apparently shared, was the conviction that it is not religious authority but the civil law of the land that should arbitrate major disputes affecting community affairs, just as in relation to the rest of society, a point Spinoza firmly adhered to already while belonging to the congregation, as we shall see, as well as, more broadly and philosophically, after his expulsion. From 1618, the now three Amsterdam Portuguese synagogues remained for the next two decades organizationally separate, each with its own *Mahamad*, albeit sharing the same school and cemetery, until, finally, after long negotiations, the three synagogues succeeded in uniting as one large congregation governed by a single *Mahamad* of six *parnasim*, in 1639.

Abraham d'Espinoza lived and conducted his business activities on the Amsterdam Houtgracht. His household included a son, Jacob, and daughter, Rachel, who would be Spinoza's father's first wife until her death in 1627. In the

---

[76] D'Ancona, "Komst der Marranen," 229; Fuks-Mansfeld, *Sefardim in Amsterdam*, 61–3, 65; Swetschinski, *Reluctant Cosmopolitans*, 172–3.
[77] Salomon, "Vraie excommunication," 183; Saperstein, *Exile in Amsterdam*, 6–7, 134.
[78] D'Ancona, "Komst der Marranen," 235; Fuks-Mansfeld, *Sefardim in Amsterdam*, 63, 65.
[79] Nadler, *Spinoza: A Life*, 36; Saperstein, *Exile in Amsterdam*, 166–8.

early years after the furore of 1618–19, Abraham remained a prominent communal figure, his reputation unencumbered by a presumably embarrassing minor episode in December 1620 when he and his maidservant, Toboda, who had apparently accompanied the family from Nantes, were briefly jailed by the magistrates allegedly for violating the ban on sexual relations between Jews and Christians.[80] From April 1621 to April 1622, corresponding to a half each of the Hebrew years 5381 and 5382 (hence from the autumn of 1621 to autumn 1622), Abraham again served all three congregations as *administrador* of the Ouderkerk Sephardic cemetery board, so that during that year the burial records and accompanying tax lists of the community were again compiled by him.[81] Throughout the second half of the 1620s he was almost continually a member of the *Senhores Quinze*, the joint committee of fifteen representing all three congregations convening irregularly whenever some exceptional question or difficulty arose affecting all three of Amsterdam's Portuguese Jewish synagogues.[82]

Spinoza's father, Michael, recorded in the Evora Inquisition records of "escaped heretics" marked for immediate arrest upon capture, as "Gabriel (Miguel) Alvares d'Espinosa,"[83] was simultaneously Abraham's nephew and, from the early 1620s until early 1627, his son-in-law. Such close family intermarriage, repeated generation upon generation, was typical of the Western Sephardim at this time, a phenomenon motivated partly by the need, in Iberian lands, to preserve secrecy within the family for reasons of self-preservation in an extremely hostile milieu. Later, in the Dutch context, it was driven chiefly by reliance on family ties to underpin durable long-distance commercial networks as well as the desire to keep fortunes intact within the family. At the time, there was little understanding of how biologically disadvantageous for individual health and well-being this long entrenched, Talmudically endorsed practice was. The frailty of many family members and the constant precariousness of Spinoza's own health was doubtless due in no small part to these biologically highly unconducive traditional marriage practices.

The cemetery Abraham assumed responsibility for in 1619–22 was at that time accommodating around fifty burials per year.[84] Beside recently deceased Sephardim, Ouderkerk included also graves of a few Ashkenazic Jews, the small Ashkenazic community of Amsterdam possessing no cemetery of their own until 1642. Ouderkerk featured the gravestones also of several individuals whose remains had been transported over impressive distances from countries where practising Judaism was forbidden, like Elija Montalto, the renowned personal physician to Marie de Medici who died in 1616, at Tours, or from elsewhere in the

---

[80] Vaz Dias and Van der Tak, *Spinoza Merchant and Autodidact*, 124; Bruyn Kops, *A Spirited Exchange*, 283.
[81] *Livro de Bet Haim*, 37, 41; Dujovne, *Spinoza* i, 53; Nadler, *Spinoza: A Life*, 35.
[82] Vaz Dias and Van der Tak, *Spinoza Merchant and Autodidact*, 120.
[83] Salomon, "Introdução," p. xcvi.   [84] Hagoort, *Beth Haim in Ouderkerk*, 41.

United Provinces, as with Samuel Pallache who, as both Menasseh and the poet-chronicler Levi de Barrios record, "died at The Hague in [January] 1616."[85] Pallache's funeral was a remarkable Ouderkerk occasion, notes Menasseh, because that "most eminent Prince Maurice [of Nassau] and the nobles attended his funeral," that is accompanied the funeral procession to Ouderkerk as far as the cemetery gates, the term "nobles" here meaning, the States General's resolutions indicate, members of the *Raad van State* [council of state] and some other States deputies.[86] Iberian New Christians from wherever they came were eligible for interment at Ouderkerk "provided the men had been circumcised prior to burial."[87]

Under Abraham's watch during 1619–22, there were no celebrity funerals like those of Pallache or Montalto at the "Joode Kerkhof" [Jew Churchyard], as the locals called Ouderkerk, but on 1 May 1621 there was an impressive gathering for the burial of a certain Eliau Abenatar, a throng including Mortera, Farar, and the heads of the prominent Curiel [Nunes da Costa] family. Among other funerals that year supervised by Abraham, from April 1621 to April 1622, was that of a "child from the house of Isaac d'Espinoza," on 28 October 1621, hence an infant nephew. Compared to Abraham, judging from the voluntary *promesas* [contributions to the community at burials] donated on that occasion, his brother Isaac was altogether a lesser figure with far more limited means.[88] Subsequently, at Ouderkerk, on 7 January 1625, records the *Livro de Bet Haim*, was "buried Sara Espinosa, sister of Abraham Espinosa of Nantes" though she was equally the sister of the unmentioned and seemingly considerably less important Isaac.[89] Together with their mother, she had fled Portugal early in life, to Nantes, at the same time as Abraham. The next generation, though, would witness preponderant status within the family strikingly transferred from Abraham's line to that of Isaac.

During the Hebrew year 5386, hence from the autumn of 1625 to the autumn of 1626, Abraham was again elected a *parnas* of the Bet Ya'acov,[90] which had much the largest congregation of the three Amsterdam synagogues and that drawing most non-Jewish visitors and sightseers. The stature of *parnas* reflected real status and authority within the then still joint Sephardic-Ashkenazic Jewish community which, by this time, had reached fairly sizeable dimensions and was a significant factor in the rise of Dutch primacy in global commerce. As *parnas* Abraham regularly figured among the small circle overseeing the congregation's internal affairs, communal and religious, including schooling, poor relief, the supply of

---

[85] Menasseh ben Israel, *Mikveh Israel*, 104; Hagoort, *Beth Haim in Ouderkerk*, 22, 28.
[86] *Resolutiën der Staten-Generaal* new series 11 (1613–16) (The Hague, 1984), 578; García-Arenal and Wiegers, *Entre el Islam y Occidente*, 13–14.
[87] Kaplan, "This Thing Alone will Preserve," 237.
[88] *Livro de Bet Haim*, 99; Vaz Dias and Van der Tak, *Spinoza Mercator*, 4.
[89] *Livro de Bet Haim*, 112, 137; Borges Coelho, "Los orígines," 126.
[90] *Livro de Bet Haim* states 5386, Nadler states 5385; see *Livro de Bet Haim* 59; Nadler, *Spinoza: A Life*, 35.

kosher meat, punishing misconduct, paying the rabbi and teachers, maintaining the synagogue and cemetery and fixing the regular contributions, the *finta* lists, of the congregation as well as representing the community in dealings with the city government and States of Holland.

On 1 December 1625, though, Abraham, unwell and "extremely pale," signed an authorization before a local notary assigning full powers of attorney to his chief assistant, his son-in-law, Michael de Espinoza (d. 1654), known in business under his Portuguese name, "Gabriel Alvares d'Espinosa," empowering Michael, among other things, to pay in and withdraw from Abraham's personal bank account at the famous Amsterdam Wisselbank (Exchange bank) adjoining the city hall, in Dam Square, the heart of Amsterdam. This arrangement was witnessed by Rabbi Mortera, confirming his continuing close personal association with the family and its affairs. Michael was now also the chosen executor of Abraham's will, wealth, and legacy.[91] Through the later 1620s, Abraham apparently recovered sufficiently to resume some overseeing activity, and Michael continued collaborating closely.

In October 1626, an Enkhuizen vessel, *Den Gulden Harinck*, returning from Saleh to Amsterdam, was seized by the English and brought into Plymouth. Practically the entire cargo on board belonged to Amsterdam Sephardic merchants. A dozen or so businesses were affected, including that of "Abraham and Michiel de Espinoza." Together with the others they settled on an authorized proxy to act for them in seeking to retrieve the seized goods. In trade with Morocco, significantly, the Spinozas—like David Curiel (alias Lopo Ramirez) and Joseph Cohen (alias Jeronimo Henriques), a major supplier of gunpowder to the corsairs whose brothers Yehudah Cohen and (later at least) Benjamin Cohen resided in Saleh—regularly employed their Hebrew rather than the Portuguese names they invariably used in trading with France, Portugal, Brazil, Spain, and Hamburg.[92] Employing their Hebrew names in Muslim lands was presumably a way of emphasizing that they were not Christians, Hebrew names being apparently more palatable in Muslim North Africa than Iberian Christian ones. The Portuguese Sephardic community at Saleh a few years later included a certain "Isaac Espinoza," though it is not clear what, if any, his relationship to the family in Holland was.[93] If Spinoza's own business contacts in Saleh or elsewhere in Morocco were ever cited during the last years of his father's life, or after his death, Spinoza too, as Michael's son and heir, would have been referred to as "Baruch," and not "Bento."

Michael's first marriage to his uncle Abraham's daughter, Rachel (Raquel) probably took place in early 1622, assuming the "abortive grandson" of

---

[91] Vaz Dias and Van der Tak, *Spinoza Mercator*, 9–10; Vaz Dias and Van der Tak, "Spinoza Merchant," 120; Frampton, *Spinoza and the Rise*, 124; Bruyn Kops, *A Spirited Exchange*, 283.
[92] GA Amsterdam NA 632, fo. 227. Deed, 9 Nov. 1626; Israel, *Diasporas*, 298.
[93] De Castries, *Sources inédites* iv, 241; Israel, *Diasporas*, 301.

"Abraham d'Espinoza" buried at Ouderkerk, on 29 December 1622, was her child. Theirs was the kind of marriage between cousins common at the time among Portuguese Jews, and it certainly brought Michael significant resources in the shape of Rachel's dowry, such as were not available from his own father. The marriage probably shows Abraham already viewed Michael rather than his own son, Jacob, as his principal partner. The shift in the balance within the family in the 1620s is reflected also in the fact that Michael, more than any other family member aside from Abraham, began figuring prominently in the Bet Ya'acov synagogue records and *Livro de Bet Haim* burial register, confirming Michael d'Espinoza was indeed Abraham's effective successor and heir, as well as Isaac's. Why Michael assumed this role rather than Abraham's own son, Jacob, who scarcely figures by comparison, remains unclear but, presumably, Jacob was either less competent or too frequently abroad, or both.

On 3 December 1623, records the *Livro de Bet Haim*, (another) "still-born son of Michael d'Espinosa was buried." Five months later, on 29 April 1624, after a further miscarriage, the register records the burial of "a premature infant of the wife of Michael dEspinosa," a child not yet named.[94] Infant mortality at the time was high, representing at Ouderkerk between 30 and 40 percent of all burials.[95] This must have been a dismal time for Rachel and Michael, and Rachel's father too, alleviated momentarily perhaps by Michael's being chosen, half a year later, in October 1624, by Bet Ya'acov's rabbi, Mortera, as *chatan bereshit* [bridegroom of the Beginning (of the Torah)], for the *Simchat Torah* festival, the joyful occasion concluding the annual cycle of readings from the Torah and commencement of the next annual cycle, the *chatan bereshit* being the ceremonial reciter of the "blessing over the [new] beginning."[96] The cloud of gloom surrounding Michael's immediate family, however, soon returned. After just five years of married life, on Sunday 21 February 1627, or 5 Adar of the year 5387 of the Jewish calendar, records the green linen-wrapped parchment-bound *Livro de Bet Haim*, "is buried Rachel Espinoza."[97]

Rabbi Mortera attended her funeral offering one of the customary *promesas*, reflecting Michael's, as well as his uncle's, stature among the congregation's inner elite and proximity to Mortera personally.[98] Also at Rachel's funeral, a substantial *promesa* of ten guilders, half a month's salary for a well-paid working man, was made by Abraham's son, Jacob, now presumably already an international trader in his own right but often abroad. When Isaac d'Espinoza, Michael's father, and Spinoza's paternal grandfather, passed away barely seven weeks later, his body was transported from Rotterdam, to Ouderkerk and interred,

---

[94] *Livro de Bet Haim*, 107.   [95] Hagoort, *Beth Haim in Ouderkerk*, 41.
[96] Saperstein, *Exile in Amsterdam*, 9n18; Van de Ven, *Documenting Spinoza*, ch. 1.
[97] *Livro de Bet Haim*, 65, 68, 70, 139; Vaz Dias and Van der Tak, *Spinoza Mercator*, 4.
[98] *Livro de Bet Haim*, 65, 68, 70, 139.

on 9 April 1627, in "row 9, number 20," just two spaces from his niece and daughter-in-law's resting place.[99] At his brother's funeral, Abraham promised ten guilders to the community chest.

The interval between Rachel's death and Michael embarking on his second marriage, with Hannah Deborah, may have been under a year.[100] Now about thirty-nine, Michael was doubtless anxious to establish a family and procure a competent male heir. It is unclear after whom Hannah Deborah was named but she may have been called after a certain "Deborah Senior," buried at Ouderkerk on 5 November 1625,[101] who would then have been her paternal grandmother, the mother of Henrique Garces. No record survives giving the exact date of the marriage of Michael and Hannah Deborah, but it must have occurred somewhere between late 1627 and early 1629,[102] because their eldest child, Miriam, on registering her forthcoming marriage to the future rabbi, Samuel de Caceres, in June 1650, declared her age as twenty-one indicating her birth in or around 1629. A sermon delivered by Mortera in February 1631, marking the birth and circumcision "of the son of the honourable Michael d'Espinosa," shows that Spinoza's elder brother, Isaac, arrived not much more than a year later.

Abraham d'Espinoza again served as a *parnas* of Bet Ya'acov in 1629–30. But after 1630, it was Michael who succeeded him as most prominent and honoured family member within the Sephardic community and business world. Michael had first been assessed for the *finta*—the bi-annual contribution to the community costs and charities of each head of household above a certain level of means—in the Hebrew year 5383 (1622–3). He was assessed to pay ten guilders.[103] This self-imposed communal tax was paid each year at *Pesach* [Passover] and *Rosh Hashanah* [the New Year Festival], at a rate fixed by the community treasurer, or *gabay*, on the basis of assessed assets and wealth. A *finta* of ten guilders in 1622 indicates a trader of some substance but modest, middling status. Both his resources and prospects would initially have been considerably less than those of Abraham's son, his cousin Jacob, with whom he would later quarrel. Chosen for lower functions within the community for several years, Michael rose to be *parnas* of the Bet Ya'acov alongside a distant relative, Abraham da Costa, a brother of Uriel da Costa, in the Hebrew year 5398 (1637–8), reflecting his rising status.[104] His first surviving son, born a year and nine months before Spinoza, in February 1631, was named, following custom, "Isaac" after Michael's father.[105] As long as he lived, this elder son enjoyed precedence among the family's younger generation ritually and legally over the second son, namely Baruch (Bento) d'Espinoza.

---

[99] *Livro de Bet Haim*, 66; Vaz Dias and Van der Tak, *Spinoza Mercator*, 4.
[100] Dujovne, *Spinoza* i, 54; Walther, "Spinoza in seiner Welt," 74.
[101] *Livro de Bet Haim*, 115, 138.   [102] Van de Ven, *Documenting Spinoza*, ch. 1.
[103] *Livro de Bet Haim* 49, 52.
[104] Vaz Dias and Van der Tak, "Spinoza Merchant," 130–1; Nadler, *Spinoza: A Life*, 46–7.
[105] Saperstein, *Exile in Amsterdam*, 9n; Van de Ven, *Documenting Spinoza*, ch. 1.

Michael d'Espinoza and Uriel da Costa's brother, Abraham, were both members of the joint committee of the three congregations, the *Senhores Quinze*, when the negotiations leading to the merging of the three original synagogues into a single united Amsterdam Sephardic community, named "Talmud Torah," concluded in 1639. Spinoza's father was thus one of those who drew up the united community's statutes, in July 1639, including, rather ironically considering he was father of a philosopher who would argue more forcefully than any other of early modern times for unrestricted freedom to publish, as article thirty-seven, the regulation that "no Jew may have printed in this city, or outside of it, any books in 'Ladino' [i.e. Spanish or Portuguese], or Hebrew, without the express permission of the Mahamad."[106] At this point, the three congregations' resources, educational facilities, archives, treasuries, books, ritual object collections, and committees were merged, and the largest building of the three, the Beth Yisrael synagogue, became the synagogue of the now united congregation, remaining so until 1675 (Figure 5.3).

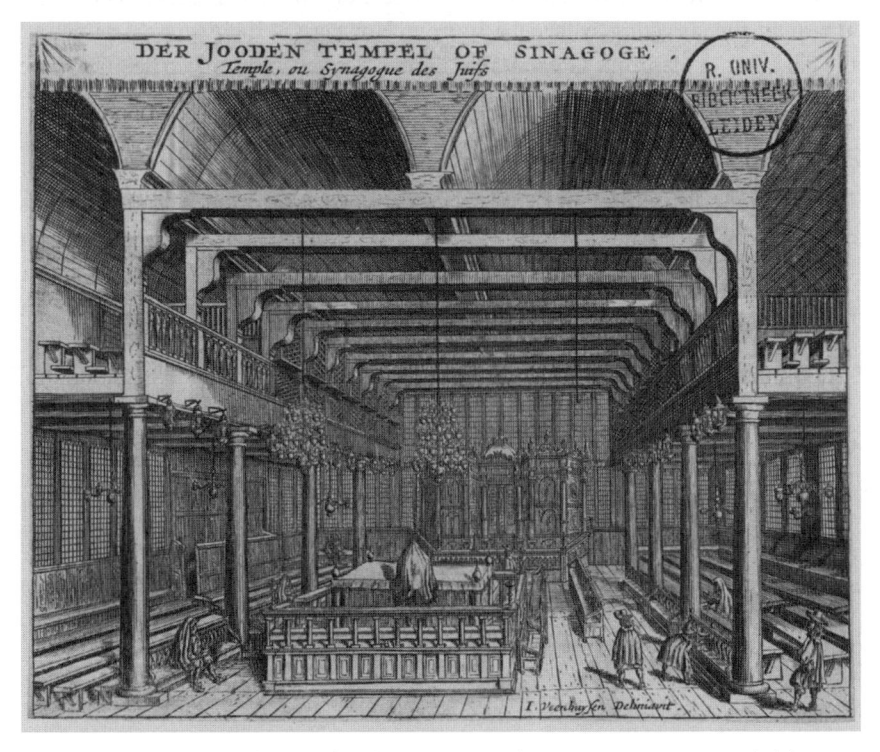

Figure 5.3 *The Amsterdam Sephardic Synagogue the young Spinoza attended*, by Jan Veenhuysen. Leiden University Library shelf mark COLLBN P 317 N 290.

---

[106] GA Amsterdam PA 334, 19, fo. 25; Kerkhof, "Préstamos," 416; Kerkhof, *Portugees en het Spaans*, 99.

A still higher honour accrued when "Michael despinosa" was elected to serve among the *parnasim* of the united congregation Talmud Torah for the Hebrew year 5410 (1649–50), the year marking the high point of the Spinoza family's prestige and success among the Amsterdam Portuguese Jewish community.[107] The 1640s marked also the high point for Da Costa's two brothers, Joseph da Costa serving on the *Mahamad* twice, in 1639–40 and 1648–9 and Abraham in the Hebrew year 5406 (1645–6).[108] When Michael completed his last term as *parnas* in 1650, Spinoza was nearing his eighteenth birthday, and, more importantly from a ritual and family standpoint, had now replaced his deceased older brother as principal heir to his father and to the family business. The gates stood wide open, or so it appeared, for him to follow in his father's footsteps as one of the community's pre-eminent figures, solidly among its social, commercial, and governing elite. Wealth, family tradition, and status were arrayed invitingly before him.

Hannah Deborah, meanwhile, so far as we can tell, remained very much in the background. Neither her full maiden name nor any other details about her appear in the surviving synagogue sources. Nowhere is she expressly named as the daughter of Henrique Garces (alias Baruch Senior) and Miriam Senior. There is no doubt, though, that she was Spinoza's mother and was the daughter of Miriam Senior and Henrique Garces, as later relatives' genealogical records provide full confirmation that Hannah Deborah was indeed, as the manuscript *Livro e nota de ydades* of Ishac Aboab records, Henrique's and Miriam's daughter and the "wife of Micael Espinoza."[109] Besides their daughter, Hannah Deborah, Henrique and Miriam had three sons, Jacob, Joshua (named after her grandfather, Duarte), and David Senior. Additional evidence of Hannah Deborah's family background derives indirectly from the burial register where it notes that at the funeral of Miriam Senior, in November 1647, which Spinoza, now fifteen, doubtless also attended, her sons David and Joshua Senior stood at the head of the funeral party together with Michael d'Espinoza. On that occasion, as we have noted, Michael registered the largest single *promesa*, exactly consonant with his being Miriam's affluent and successful son-in-law.[110] Definitive evidence that she was indeed Spinoza's mother is her simple gravestone which still survives at Ouderkerk to this day, inscribed "Grave of Senhora Hanah Deborah d'Espinosa, wife of D. Mikael Despinoza, that God took to Himself on 28 Hesvan 5399 [5 November 1638]."

---

[107] GA Amsterdam PA 334/1393, "Registro dos parnasim," p. 5; Nadler, *Spinoza: A Life*, 93.
[108] GA Amsterdam PA 334/1393, "Registro dos parnasim," pp. 3–5.
[109] Aboab, "Livro e Nota," 294; Révah, *Des Marranes à Spinoza*, 170.
[110] GA Amsterdam Hagoort ed. *Livro de Bet Haim [...] Talmud-Tora*, 176; Freudenthal/Walther, *Lebensgeschichte* ii, 90; Koen, "Duarte Fernandes, Koopman," 179; Kaplan, "On the Burial of Spinoza's Grandfather," 27, 35–6; Borges Coelho, *Inquisição de Évora*, 501.

Hannah Deborah and Michael eventually had a total of five children together, their first daughter, Miriam, named after her grandmother, the two elder sons, Isaac and Baruch, another daughter, Rebecca [Ribca], and their third and youngest son, Abraham (Gabriel), named after his great-uncle, Abraham. By his first marriage, Michael seems to have already had a daughter named after his own mother who died soon after birth. Alternatively, Michael's mother, Isaac d'Espinoza's wife (whose name is unknown) may have been called Miriam too. The marriage of Spinoza's parents lasted barely more than ten years. On 8 September 1638, a notary visiting the Spinoza household on the Vlooienburg, requesting acceptance of a bill of exchange at the demand of a certain Simon Barkman with whom Michael had dealings, found both Michael and Hannah Deborah separately confined to their sickbeds. "The wife of the said Miguel [Michael] d'Espinoza lying ill," he recorded, "on another bed, in the same room," explained "that due to the illness that has befallen my husband, the bill of exchange will not be accepted."[111]

Spinoza had to witness his mother's terminal illness over many weeks, with his father lying sick at the same time. Hannah Deborah died on 5 November 1638 and was interred at Ouderkerk that same day, at a time when Spinoza, still aged under six, was old enough to remember her, and the occasion of her funeral for the rest of his life, a traumatic experience after the numerous other recent deaths in the family occurring just around the time he was about to start school.[112] An irreplaceable loss at that tender age, Hannah Deborah, one can hardly doubt, lived on in his memory and unconsciously as a missing presence that always signified a great deal to him.[113] Her demise left his father a widower with five young children on his hands, the oldest only nine. From the age of six until nine Spinoza would have been chiefly raised by his grandmother, Miriam, helped by Michael's housemaid. Only after a three-year interval, did the now well-established, affluent widower "Michael de Espinose of Vidigueira," marry his third bride, Esther (alias Guiomar de Solis), apparently yet another relative.[114]

There is no reason to suppose the now nine-year-old Spinoza especially enjoyed the banqueting and family jubilation surrounding Michael's third wedding. Esther, moreover, was not a product of his familiar surroundings but a Portuguese New Christian newcomer, only recently arrived, "born," according to one source, "in London where she was baptized," Jewish life and religious practice at that time being still forbidden in England as in France.[115] Consequently, Esther lacked knowledge of formal Judaism, and possessed no knowledge of Holland and none of the Dutch language, but did speak

---

[111] Vaz Diaz and Van der Tak, "Spinoza Merchant," 188; Nadler, *Spinoza: A Life*, 55.
[112] Freudenthal/Walther, *Lebensgeschichte* i, 191.
[113] Dujovne, *Spinoza* i, 54, 56; Vaz Dias and Van der Tak, *Spinoza Merchant and Autodidact*, 113.
[114] Vaz Dias and Van der Tak, *Spinoza Mercator*, 21.
[115] Nadler, Tielen, and Tiribás, "Two New Documents," 811.

Portuguese. Of necessity, Portuguese remained, more than ever, the sole language of the household, intensifying the separateness of his immediate family in the surrounding Amsterdam context. Spinoza's stepmother can hardly have been of much help to Spinoza in contending with the usual schoolboy anxieties during his first years at school. The urgent need for better Jewish social and cultural assimilation into the wider society around them would remain a constant theme of Spinoza's thought.

We have no way of knowing how far the emotional void in his life left by losing his mother before his sixth birthday was filled by his stepmother and his grandmother, Miriam Senior, who lived close by and for another nine years after her daughter's death. We can be certain, though, that as a teenager Spinoza was able to reconstruct a good deal of his mother's life and personality, and her extraordinary family history, providing food for thought of religious, historical, and political scope of a decidedly uncommon kind, chiefly from his grandmother, for whom the young Bento was the prime surviving link with her own dead husband, Baruch Senior. His uncles and cousins who lived nearby doubtless had much to tell him also about his grandfather, his great-grandfather, Duarte Fernandes, Fray Martín del Spiritu Santo, and the drama of the Dutch–Spanish conflict.

Abraham's only son, Jacob, another key source for the schoolboy Spinoza, returned after a long spell in the Near East in or around 1637 when Spinoza was five. On 22 December 1637, only five months after Michael himself became a member of the Dotar society, Jacob, described as Miguel's cousin, was elected at the request of "Miguel [i.e. Michael] despinoza" to the Dotar "in place of his father Abraham despinoza of Nantes."[116] Returning to Amsterdam before Hannah Deborah's death, Jacob stayed on in the city for several years. The months of his mother's last illness, decline, and death were thus also for Spinoza a rare opportunity to learn from a first-hand source, a long absent close relative, in a way that others could not, about the Holy Land and Muslim countries.[117]

The Holy Land and Morocco can hardly have failed to figure prominently in family dinner table conversation during Spinoza's boyhood. No doubt connected with these discussions, in 1638, Michael served a spell as *parnas* of the community's Terra Santa [Holy Land] society and donated a substantial 150 guilders to that society's remittance chest to assist the upkeep of the Sephardic communities of Jerusalem, Tiberias, Safed, and Hebron.[118] On 14 January 1639, Jacob appeared before Michael's regular notary, Jan Volckertsz Oli, who was familiar with both Portuguese and Spanish but seemed a touch confused by Near Eastern geography, for the legal deed he drew up refers to "Jacob Espinosa resident at Grand Cairo in

---

[116] Vaz Dias and Van der Tak, *Spinoza Mercator*, 16; Kerkhof, "Préstamos," 425–6; Frampton, *Spinoza and the Rise*, 124, 126.
[117] Van de Ven, *Documenting Spinoza*, ch. 2.
[118] Vaz Dias and Van der Tak, *Spinoza Merchant and Autodidact*, 133.

Palestine [sic] and presently here, son and legal heir of the deceased Manoel Rodrigues Espinosa alias Abraham Espinosa, his father."[119] After many years in Morocco, Egypt, and Palestine, Jacob's return from afar, and the stories he told, must have injected an exciting element into the life of a boy with an exceptionally far-ranging mind, eager to escape from constricting familiar perspectives.

[119] Vaz Dias, "Spinoza Merchant and Autodidact," 133–6.

6
Schooldays

6.i *Ets Haim*

During 1635-6 and again in 1642–3, Spinoza's father served on the governing board of the Amsterdam Sephardic community's school system, or *Academia y Yeshiba Ets Haim* [Tree of Life Academy and Religious College], also called the Talmud Torah school, often referred to in the plural as "the schools." The *Yeshiba* proper were the levels of higher education.[1] As a school governor, Michael was well acquainted with the teachers, administrative details, and book provision, responsibilities that inevitably involved him and, tangentially, his three sons even more than before with rabbis Mortera, Aboab, and Menasseh and the synagogue *hazan*, or communal cantor who were all required to spend much of their time in the school.[2]

The earliest known surviving documentary reference to "Baruch Espinoza" dates from the Jewish year 5397 (1636-7) when Spinoza was around four and a half. His name is entered in a complex double-column list of supporting members of the communal *Ets Haim* society, the charitable body raising funds for the school, accompanied by the entry "son of Michael espinosa" which was later crossed out. This means Spinoza was listed among the society's members making contributions and supporting provision of schooling free of charge to avoid the boys from poorer families being kept out or forced to curtail their education early to assist their family's bread-winning.[3] On the assumption the community's boys would need a thorough education for their future vocations and to support their families, as well as fulfil their religious obligations, communal policy was to provide schooling on an equal basis for rich and poor, free of charge for all the boys.[4] It is not known exactly when Spinoza himself first entered the beginners' class formally studying the Hebrew alphabet and elementary Hebrew reading, but first level pupils often formally began learning to read only from around seven. For the Jewish school year 5398 (1637–8), the now five-year-old "Baruch" is again

---

[1] Nadler, *Spinoza: A Life*, 45, 70; Sclar, "A Communal Tree," 46; Van de Ven, *Documenting Spinoza*, ch. 3.
[2] Vaz Dias and Van de Tak, *Spinoza Mercator*, 14–15; Baumgarten, "Quelques possibles sources," 130–1.
[3] Vaz Dias and Van der Tak, *Spinoza Merchant and Autodidact*, 147; Nadler, *Spinoza: A Life*, 70; Nadler, Tielen, and Tiribás, "Two New Documents," 804.
[4] Rosenberg, "Op welke school," 58; Vaz Dias and Van der Tak, "Spinoza Merchant," 151.

listed under the *Ets Haim* membership with his brothers, Ishac (Isaac) and Abraham (Gabriel) Espinoza, as contributing to the school's support, this time spelt "Baruch Espinosa" but again, following his expulsion from the community, in 1656, tellingly crossed through, reflecting the post-*herem* deletion of all record of his membership and contributions.[5]

Amsterdam's *Ets Haim* or Talmud Torah school, founded around 1616, was shared and paid for by the three congregations together. Since 1620, the school occupied an originally rented house adjoining Bet Ya'acov, right on the Houtgracht, hence just doors from Spinoza's own home.[6] Walking to school, for Spinoza, took barely two minutes, and for years the school building enlarged with an adjoining house acquired to add space for classrooms, in 1639, must have been something of a second home. Assuming he began his schooling at six or seven, as many boys did, and not earlier, Spinoza would have commenced Hebrew studies, and studying the daily prayer-book, or *siddur*, only after his mother's death.[7]

The Talmud Torah school's board of governors, or school *parnasim*, directed education strategy, appointed the staff, paid the teachers' salaries, scheduled the classes, and obtained the necessary writing materials, books, and, for older boys, prayer shawls and *tefillin* [phylacteries]. The more advanced teachers at the fourth and fifth levels having no wider synagogue functions were each paid thirty-two and a half guilders monthly or 390 guilders yearly, slightly more than a well-paid artisan, hence a respectable salary for a teacher at that time. (Salaries of the Reformed preachers of Friesland who enjoyed considerably higher status than mere teachers stood at 400 guilders, increasing to 450 only as late as 1699.)[8]

In Amsterdam, the Sephardim placed exceptional emphasis on ensuring unusually broad schooling, education combining religious and some secular studies. Being sons of merchants and brokers, and their assistants and middlemen, engaged in overseas trade, insurance, brokerage, and all manner of multi-language transactions, for their future vocations the boys needed to be not just adequately literate and numerate in the usual sense but familiar with using documents and accounts in several languages. As the community's families were often entirely new to formal Judaism and the Hebrew language, schooling was also, for many, the principal route back to effective family renewal of Jewish observance, to forging meaningful links with the Hebrew Scriptures, rabbinic tradition, and the Law, as well as preparing for life in a busy commercial metropolis. These requirements persuaded the Amsterdam Sephardic community to allocate greater

---

[5] Freudenthal/Walther, *Lebensgeschichte* i, 215; Pieterse, *Daniel Levi de Barrios als geschiedschrijver*, 97; Kaplan, "Jews in the Republic," 118; Saperstein, *Exile in Amsterdam*, 105–6.

[6] Swetschinski, "Vestiging," 92; Swetschinski, *Reluctant Cosmopolitans*, 182; Sclar, "A Communal Tree," 46.

[7] Licata, "Nature de la langue," 48.

[8] RA Groningen, Archief van de Provinciale Synode van Stad en Lande vol. 4, report on the June 1699 Frisian synodal gathering, res. 2 May 1700.

resources and care to formal education than was usual in the Jewish world at the time. Thanks to the Venetian and other Italian Jewish Renaissance models that Pardo, Mortera, and Menasseh emulated and built on, the Amsterdam Talmud Torah school swiftly achieved a high standard coming to be admired throughout Europe as the unmatched model of Jewish schooling scarcely equalled for high standards elsewhere, albeit the emphasis was still heavily on Hebrew and religious studies with secular studies tacked on as marginal extras rather than the core.[9]

The earliest description of the school dates from 1648, when Spinoza was sixteen and had probably recently left, an account written by Rabbi Shabtai Sheftel Horowitz (1592–1660) who, after travelling from Frankfurt to Poland, continued on to Holland. Shabtai attached the account to his appendix to a famous book, *Shnei Luhot ha-Brit* [Two Tablets of the Covenant], by his father, Isaiah Halevi Horowitz (c.1555–1630) of Frankfurt and later Prague. During his last years, in the 1620s, his father was a rabbi in Jerusalem and was buried in the Holy Land, at Tiberias. Shabtai visited Amsterdam specifically to publish his father's book. "With great emotion and pleasure I remember," he recalls,

> how I travelled from Frankfurt to Posen and then by sea to Amsterdam where I met some important people, including Jewish scholars. There I visited their schools, each school independent [the Sephardim and Ashkenazim being organizationally separate communities by that time]. There I observed that the small children learn the entire Torah [Pentateuch] and later [in the higher classes] the rest of the Old Testament and eventually the whole Mishna and when they are big [i.e. reach thirteen] commence learning the Talmud together with the commentaries of Rashi and the *Tosafot* [medieval commentaries on the Talmud], so that as they grow older they can better bring learning into their daily lives.

"With tears I ask myself," asks Shabtai, "why these methods are not applied in our land [Germany and Austria]: Oh may this tradition spread over the entire Jewish world!"[10] There was little prospect of that, though, since *Ets Haim*'s high standard of teaching, well-qualified teachers, exceptional range of books and facilities could not easily be replicated elsewhere without comparable resources.[11] When Spinoza commenced schooling, the *Ets Haim* school library still listed only 167 books, rising to 210 books by 1642 when Spinoza was ten; by 1680, when the library's

---

[9] Swetschinski, *Reluctant Cosmopolitans*, 210–11; Kaplan, "Joden in de Republiek," 153.
[10] Quoted in Rosenberg, "Op welke school," 55–6; Albiac, *Sinagoga vacía*, 113.
[11] Rosenberg, "Op welke school," 60; Vaz Dias and Van der Tak, "Spinoza Merchant," 150; Gans, *Memorboek*, 107; Swetschinski, *Reluctant Cosmopolitans*, 210–11; Walther, "Spinoza in seiner Welt," 75.

contents, open to the students during school hours, were first described, it figured among the largest collections of printed and manuscript Judaica in existence.[12]

Most non-Hebrew books used in the higher grades, and found in the school library, as with the Sephardic communities of Livorno and Venice, were in Spanish rather than Portuguese, Dutch, or other languages. Next to religious knowledge and instilling Hebrew grammar, the Sephardic schools relied on Spanish translations of the Torah in the early stages of schooling, and depended, throughout, on fluency in reading, speaking, and understanding Spanish. There is little sign, though, that formal schooling, aside from using Jewish religious texts in Spanish, or renderings from Hebrew texts, placed much emphasis on teaching the boys to speak and write either Spanish or Portuguese correctly, or included any Spanish or Portuguese literature.[13] Sermons and announcements in synagogue, on the other hand, were in Portuguese, so the boys did not only imbibe Portuguese at home or in the street. Since all the schoolboys regularly attended synagogue services and the weekly sermons delivered in Portuguese, many by Mortera, these formed a crucial element of the congregation's educational system and religious and intellectual culture. While the designation "Portuguese" to describe the Amsterdam Sephardic community always included a Spanish dimension, prior to a mid-century large influx from Spain beginning in the late 1640s, hardly any members of the community had actually been raised in Spain and spoke a pure contemporary Spanish.[14]

Meanwhile, by the 1640s the community's "Portuguese" already betrayed signs of degrading into a local communal dialect or lingua franca. As written by Saul Levi Mortera (who was not raised in Portugal), it was clear and serviceable but often unidiomatic, ungrammatical, and featured numerous imported Dutch, Spanish, and Italian terms and Hebraisms. The considerable difference in status between the Portuguese and Spanish languages was accentuated further by the fact that Amsterdam, Antwerp, and Brussels were all major centres for publishing classic Spanish literature and historical works, but not Portuguese literature. By the time he reached adulthood, Spinoza probably regarded the household language in which he was raised as a mere fringe dialect and corruption of a living language. In this connection, it is striking, but unsurprising, that the inventory of the small library Spinoza left behind him at his death, shows a significant proportion of Spinoza's home reading material late in life comprised books in Spanish, including poetry, but that he possessed nothing whatever in Portuguese which for him was clearly just a spoken vernacular, not a living intellectual or literary language like Spanish, Hebrew, or Latin.[15]

---

[12] Rosenberg, "Op welke school," 57–8; Albiac, *Sinagoga vacía*, 114; Sclar, "A Communal Tree," 47.
[13] Kerkhof, *Portugees en het Spaans*, 126–7, 165.
[14] Kerkhof, *Portugees en het Spaans*, 61, 163–6.   [15] Rothkam, *Institutio Oratoria*, 318, 321.

From 1639, when the community's school system was reorganized and expanded, there were seven grades or classes known as *escuelas* attended—in theory, but with exceptions—from the age of seven to fourteen.[16] Spinoza, having no mother and with his father extremely busy, was very likely an exception in starting school early. In 1639–40, there were already seven main teachers, one for each level, the teacher of the initiating class being Mordechai de Crasto who continued teaching it until 1649 (later, in 1666, he apparently became a leading local Millenarian enthusiast hailing Sabbatai Zevi as the long-awaited Messiah).[17] The second grade was taught by the synagogue-paid cantor, or *hazan*, Joseph Coen Faro (d. 1681), among the most familiar faces and voices around the synagogue who by 1639 was receiving 250 guilders per year for the teaching segment of his work; under him, the boys began more systematic study of the Mosaic Five Books while closely studying each weekly portion of the Law.[18] The synagogue cantors, or *hazanim*, were usually also placed in charge of the library and issuing textbooks. Beyond basic literacy and numeracy, noted Rabbi Shabtai Sheftel, in 1648, most teaching at Spinoza's school was geared to studying and learning to translate the Mosaic Five Books "from beginning to end," followed by examining the rest of the biblical books. In the third grade, taught by a certain Jacob Gomes, the boys explored the section for the week at greater depth, helped by Rashi's universally renowned commentary.[19] Examining the Prophetic Books and Chronicles began at level four. From 1639, at several levels, Haham Isaac Aboab da Fonseca (1605–93) (Figure 6.1), particularly bolstered teaching of Hebrew grammar and, to an extent, all grammar, his personal library holding more books in Latin (over a hundred) than in all other languages apart from Hebrew combined.[20] From Aboab, still in Amsterdam until 1642, Spinoza would certainly not have gathered the impression that Latin studies were at all contrary to Jewish learning. Talmud entered in the more senior grades. But how far studying Talmud really entered the picture, for the older boys, remains unclear. All the boys gained some entry into the Talmud but, as Nadler remarks, there is little sign that Talmud study left a particularly deep imprint on the young Spinoza. Later, in the *TTP* he refers six times to the Talmud but always for the sole purpose of underlining contradictions and discordances that he thinks stemmed from haphazard selection and reworking from a wider range of once extant texts of those Old Testament books the Pharisees eventually pronounced "sacred" Scripture.[21]

---

[16] Pieterse, *Daniel Levi de Barrios als geschiedschrijver*, 98; Vaz Dias and Van der Tak, "Spinoza Merchant," 150–3; Levie Bernfeld, *Poverty and Welfare*, 99, 348; Gans, *Memorboek*, 107; Nadler, *Spinoza: A Life*, 71.

[17] Pieterse, *Daniel Levi de Barrios als geschiedschrijver*, 98–9, 102, 160; Rosenberg, "Op welke school," 63.

[18] Pieterse, *Daniel Levi de Barrios als geschiedschrijver*, 160.

[19] Pieterse, *Daniel Levi de Barrios als geschiedschrijver*, 160.

[20] Den Boer, *Literatura sefardí*, 108.

[21] Spinoza, *Theological-Political Treatise*, 39, 140, 141, 147, 150 154; Nadler, *Spinoza: A Life*, 108.

Figure 6.1 *Rabbi Isaac Aboab da Fonseca* (1605–93), in 1681. © Courtesy of the John Carter Brown Library, Brown University, Providence, RI.

In the fifth grade, the boys were taught by Selomo ben Joseph about whom nothing is known except that in 1651 his eighteen-year-old daughter, born in Amsterdam, married the brother of a former crypto-Jew burnt to death by the Lisbon Inquisition.[22] "Martyrs," like the brother of Spinoza's fifth grade teacher's son-in-law, were specially venerated by the Sephardic community and hearing their stories was a prime collective experience for the pupils. Several dramatic episodes were highlighted. When Spinoza was seventeen, in January 1648, for example, electrifying news reached Amsterdam announcing the gruesome end, on 15 December 1647, in Lisbon, of one of the most renowned Sephardic martyrs of the mid-seventeenth century. The news created an unusual stir in Amsterdam because this son of Portuguese New Christian parents from Bragança, Isaac de Castro Tartas (c.1623–47), who, for a time, had lived in southern France, had for a year or two himself been a pupil at the community school Spinoza attended,

---

[22] Pieterse, *Daniel Levi de Barrios als geschiedschrijver*, 98, 116; Rosenberg, "Op welke school," 63.

before emigrating, at the age of eighteen, in 1642, to Dutch Brazil with the group of Jewish settlers led by Rabbi Aboab.[23] After a brief period participating in military duties at Paraíba, in northern Brazil, the young man moved on to Bahia in the Portuguese zone, apparently planning to teach Judaism to New Christians living under the Portuguese crown and church. Denounced to the bishop of Bahia by persons who had seen him entering synagogues in the Dutch zone, in Paraíba and Recife, he was arrested, in December 1644, at episcopal demand, transported to Lisbon and transferred to the Inquisition. Despite unremitting efforts, from March 1645, over many months to force renunciation of his apostasy, he remained unmovable.

When nothing more could be done, the Inquisitors having meticulously checked, as they were required to, that he had indeed been baptized as an infant in Portugal (which he denied)—baptism being for them the essential precondition for rightly subjecting him to imprisonment, torture, and loss of possessions—he was duly condemned to excommunication, confiscation of all belongings, and "relaxation" to the secular arm, their euphemism for being burnt at the stake. Paraded before the faithful at the auto-da-fé of 15 December 1647, before the royal palace in Lisbon, a backdrop of combined mass religious zeal and royal splendour, the crowds witnessed his refusing to kneel before the cross and hence declining the offered "mercy" of being garrotted first before being consigned to the flames. Accordingly, he was burnt alive. Expiring amidst the flames the twenty-four-year-old reportedly exclaimed "Shama Israel...Adonai echad [Hear oh Israel...the Lord is One!]." "Jamais l'on n'a vue une telle resolution et constance [Never has one seen such resolution and constancy]," commented the French envoy who was present.[24]

Many Sephardic community members could remember De Castro Tartas personally, or knew his parents and brothers who remained in Amsterdam and the impression made on the community by the reports from Lisbon was profound. Menasseh and Levi Mortera, the latter reportedly delivering a public eulogy on the Sabbath following arrival of news of their pupil's demise at the stake, were among those keen to keep his memory alive.[25] He was "a learned young man, versed in Greek and Latin," recalls Menasseh in his *Hope of Israel*, "whom I knew and spoke with."[26] It was not in fact unusual for a youngster "in the [Sephardic] schools" to acquire Latin and Greek as well as Hebrew, a point relevant also to Spinoza's case. Rudiments of Latin, the main language of Spinoza's future intellectual endeavour,

---

[23] Fuks-Mansfeld, *Sefardim in Amsterdam*, 64, 73; Kaplan, *From Christianity to Judaism*, 111; Feitler, *Inquisition, juifs et nouveaux-chretiens*, 181.
[24] Menasseh ben Israel, *Mikveh Israel*, 100; Wiznitzer, "Isaac de Castro," 70; Israel, *Conflicts of Empires*, 162.
[25] Mortera, *Tratado da Verdade*, pp. lxxxii, 1193; Saperstein, *Exile in Amsterdam*, 144, 218–19, 425.
[26] Menasseh ben Israel, *Mikveh Israel*, 99–100; Wiznitzer, "Isaac de Castro," 71, 74; Feitler, *Inquisition, juifs et nouveaux-chrétiens au Brésil*, 150.

and on which Spinoza subsequently built for the rest of his life, a language then indispensable to future physicians, was readily available in the school to at least some students.

The sixth and seventh levels formed the *yeshivah* where it was the rabbis who taught. There one studied Torah and Talmud more intensively, Rashi's commentaries and now also Maimonides in some depth. It was at this point, soon after his *bar mitzvah*, or slightly later, that Spinoza first studied the medieval philosopher and exegete Moses Maimonides (1138–1204) who lived his early life in Córdoba but mature years chiefly in Morocco and Egypt. Having absorbed elements from both Ibn Sina (Avicenna) (*c.*980–1037) and Ibn Rushd (Averroes) (1126–98), Maimonides represented a fusion of Islamic and Jewish thought, and fusion of Aristotelian philosophy with Jewish tradition, that would remain a lasting presence in Spinoza's mind, and in his Bible criticism and general system, usually without Spinoza mentioning him. Whenever Spinoza does cite Maimonides explicitly, as in the *TTP*, he does so in a hostile manner, criticizing his Aristotelian principles and his allegedly not applying reason rigorously enough—as, for example, when disagreeing with Maimonides' account of the Noahide laws. For both Maimonides and Spinoza, the Seven Laws that the Torah affirms God delivered to Noah prohibiting idolatry, blasphemy, murder, adultery, theft, eating limbs torn from living animals, and refusing to live under the rule of law, are binding on, and unite, all humanity representing a minimal universal creed, perpetually valid for all mankind. The mature Spinoza, though, insisting that anyone unfamiliar with Scripture who nevertheless has "healthy opinions and follows a true manner of living, is completely blessed and really has the Spirit of Christ in him," that is reaches the highest level of human existence, complains that "the Jews think exactly the opposite" maintaining that "true opinions and a true manner of living" do not suffice to bring someone "to blessedness if men embrace these laws only by the natural light [ex solo lumine naturali] of reason and not as laws revealed prophetically to Moses," a perverse view, according to Spinoza, which Maimonides "dares to affirm openly."[27]

Yet, despite his disapproving remarks, on balance, Spinoza's affinities with, or amended borrowings from, Maimonides, specialists point out, are at least as profound and important, and arguably more so, than his criticism.[28] Both thinkers share a biting contempt for anthropomorphic representations of God as susceptible to love or hate and for supposed shifts in the divine attitude towards groups or individuals. Both see the "intellectual love of God" as man's *summum bonum*, the path to a life of perfection and blessedness, to "true religion" which is a

---

[27] Spinoza, *Opera* iv, 79; Frankel, "Spinoza's Rejection of Maimonideism," 84–5; Kraemer, *Maimonides*, 352–3; see also Curley's note in Spinoza, *Collected Works* (ed. Curley) ii, 151n14.

[28] On this complicated point, see Harvey, "Portrait of Spinoza," 169–70; Kraemer, *Maimonides*, 331, 374–5; Levy, *Baruch or Benedict?*, 20; Frankel, "Spinoza's Rejection of Maimonideism," 85–6; Green, "A Portrait," 92–3, 97; Chalier, *Spinoza lecteur*, 7–20.

combination of intellectual love of God, Spinoza's famed *amor Dei intellectualis* (echoing Maimonides' philosophical love of God) with "piety," that is practising "justice and charity." For both, the biblical prophets give expression to strands of moral truth via their exceptional power of imagination. Maimonides certainly did not go as far as identifying God with nature; for Maimonides God is incorporeal and transcends the physical world. Matter he sees as purely passive and inert. But he significantly diminishes the dualism of God and nature with his Aristotelian stress on God constituting the "pure form" giving shape and meaning to everything in the physical world, making God and the world in some sense identical at least in the realm of form and thought.[29]

It was during his teenage years at school that Spinoza first encountered also other medieval Jewish thinkers who would figure in his subsequent life, notably the Navarrese exegete, grammarian, poet, physician, astronomer, astrologer and philosopher of Neoplatonic tinge, Abraham Ibn Ezra (*c*.1092–*c*.1167) who also lived many years in Córdoba (like Averroes), and left his mark on Spinoza's Bible criticism. Though rebelling less against traditional Judaism than his son (who converted to Islam), Ibn Ezra was a bold innovator, critical of all existing traditions of Bible exegesis, including that of the Karaites, and as hostile to straightforward uncritical readings of Scripture as to allegorical and esoteric readings. Spinoza describes him as a "man of independent mind and no slight learning, and the first of those I have read to take note of this prejudice [the assumption that Moses wrote the Pentateuch]."[30]

Another medieval figure important in Spinoza's education was the Provençal thinker, Gersonides (or Levi ben Gershom) (1288–1344), active in the region of Avignon and Perpignan. Like Maimonides and Ibn Ezra, Gersonides proved a formative influence edging in directions Spinoza would follow later, in fact going further than any other major medieval Jewish thinker in exalting the role of philosophy, closely identifying mathematics with the operations of reason, and holding that religion and the Torah itself are best explained under the sovereignty of reason. With his scepticism about miracles and "minimalist" view of the process of divine creation, Gersonides was considered something of a heretic and freethinker, and, like Averroes and Maimonides, held that the philosopher possesses special knowledge and understanding above and in important respects also at odds with what most people think, more elevated knowledge that it is his duty to selectively diffuse in society for the benefit of all. Rarely given to praising other thinkers, Spinoza, in later life, cites Gersonides in the notes he appended to the *TTP*, when disagreeing with his chronology of the Forty Years the Israelites spent

---

[29] Harvey, "Spinoza and Maimonides," 41–2; Fraenkel, "Maimonides' God," 170–1; Nadler, "The Jewish Spinoza," 497.
[30] Spinoza, *Collected Works* (ed. Curley) i, 193; Rudavsky, "Science of Scripture," 65–6, 76; Lazarus-Yafeh, *Intertwined Worlds*, 74.

in the desert; "this rabbi," he remarks, was "otherwise an extremely learned man [virum alias eruditissimum]."[31]

When Spinoza attended the school, Rabbi Mortera regularly taught only in the highest grade, at *yeshivah* level, hence was not formally one of Spinoza's teachers. Even so, as a pupil, Spinoza must have encountered all three Amsterdam rabbis, and the community's *hazan* Faro, frequently at school, synagogue, and at the cemetery, indeed occasionally too at his home. Mortera, having been in early life closely associated with the vehement anti-Christian polemicist Eliahu Montalto, liked to focus attention on the community's martyr-dotted history of secret struggle against Church and Inquisition and their forebears' ceaseless struggle against Christianity and Christianizers among their own ranks and families, a continuing struggle fought for centuries underground in Portugal, Spain, and all their colonies. His emphatic stance lent the Sephardic culture of early seventeenth-century Amsterdam a considerably more combative, polemical resonance than was usual in other Jewish communities, even if this was kept largely veiled from outsiders.

If Menasseh's more conciliatory attitude towards Christianity became more widely known outside the community than the views of Mortera and the other rabbis, it was the latter's approach that presided internally. Despite Menasseh's efforts to soften and offset it, vehement, deeply emotional anti-Christian polemicizing that had to be strictly curtained off from the outside world remained a fundamental feature of the Amsterdam school and family culture Spinoza imbibed early on. After his estrangement from the community, he rejected this tradition in part, valuing especially Christianity's moral core, but he also continued it in part, especially as regards Christology and Christian theology. The community's uniquely large collection of anti-Christian texts was preserved exclusively in manuscript, and purposely kept strictly cordoned off from outsiders. Only much later, in the early eighteenth century, would word seep out among Europe's freethinkers and deists, like Anthony Collins in England, that a unique store of manuscripts exceptionally critical of Christianity, with nothing comparable conserved elsewhere, were kept in the Sephardic synagogue in Amsterdam causing these to become a rich source for non-Jewish radical subversives. For the good of the community, the boys were strongly discouraged from discussing religion with Christians in the streets, marketplaces, and anywhere else; but this did not alter the reality that Christian theology and belief was heavily targeted at Spinoza's school, as also, if subtly, in Spinoza's mature thought and writing.[32]

Discipline was strict and teaching hours long. A rare contemporary record states that the classes commenced "when the clock strikes eight" and the boys

---

[31] Spinoza, *Oeuvres* (ed. Moreau) iii, 670–1; Levy, *Baruch or Benedict?*, 18–19, 31, 61–2; Nadler, "Spinoza as a Jewish Philosopher," 67–8.

[32] Popkin, *Spinoza*, 10–13; Israel, *Revolutionary Jews*, 102–8.

studied until eleven whereupon everyone left for three hours, to go home for their meals, while rabbis and teachers attended to other duties. Students then returned to school, resuming at two and continuing until five in the evening, or in winter, when daylight was shorter, until the hour fixed for evening service in the synagogue. During the year 1642–3, when Spinoza was ten, around half way through his schooling, his father, previously a school governor in 1635–6, again served on the board of governors [*parnasim*] responsible for the school.[33] With a six-hour day, six days a week routine continuing for seven at a minimum and probably eight or nine years in Spinoza's case, the basic education he and his brothers, Isaac and Gabriel, received would have been unusually thorough by the standards of the orthodox Jewish world of the day, and for that matter the rest of the world. Unavoidably, as long as his schooling continued, Spinoza spent much of his life in and around the synagogue, participating in services, reciting Hebrew prayers and with his brothers sitting through countless sermons in Portuguese.

Spinoza received a thorough education; but it is striking, given that the names of those studying at the highest *yeshivah* levels were recorded, that his name is missing from these lists of older students. Later reports that Spinoza studied to become a rabbi seem to be purely mythical. Numerous gifted pupils left school after completing seven levels, usually a year or so after reaching *bar mitzvah* age, especially where fathers preferred not to do without their assistance in their business activities or work. Indeed, wealthy Sephardic family heads like Michael d'Espinoza, unlike Polish Jews of that age and later, were rarely, if ever, eager to see their sons train as religious scholars or rabbis, preferring them to follow them into their business, the path to conserving family wealth and gaining more honours and status in the community (as *parnasim*). Furthermore, Michael's business was highly complex with a wide geographical reach, and he constantly required assistance with translating and dealing with non-Sephardic business contacts, customers and notaries, needing more help than others due to his very limited Dutch (Portuguese and French being throughout his main business languages).

While there is insufficient evidence for this to be more than conjecture, it seems likely Spinoza was indeed withdrawn from school, at his father's insistence, not just earlier than some other boys he knew but contrary to his own intensely studious inclinations.[34] The compulsive drive that already as a teenager alienated him from the usual concerns of others and in later life impelled him obsessively to avoid everything that could conceivably disturb his unremitting impulse to study and think, his ceaseless anxiety not to lose precious time from studying, thinking, and writing, a feature all his early biographers emphasize, may well have taken root early on as a form of youthful sullenness and resentment at having to leave

[33] Vaz Dias, *Spinoza Merchant*, 131.
[34] Rosenberg, "Op welke school," 60–1; Nadler, *Spinoza: A Life*, 92–3, 103; Salomon, "La vraie excommunication," 192n40.

school earlier than he wished. In any case, Spinoza's departure from formal schooling, after between seven and nine years of study, probably occurred around 1646 or 1647 when he was fourteen or fifteen.[35]

6.ii Uriel da Costa

Throughout his boyhood, Spinoza must have communicated with his father and stepmother virtually entirely in Portuguese, their household language. Doubtless there was much the teenage Spinoza learnt about his family's past in Portugal, France, and Holland, and the political dramas of the 1640s can only have stimulated his curiosity about Iberia and the family past. At school, Spinoza learnt about martyrs, and at home about those in his own family history, but also about reprehensible dissidents and rebels against the community. Although Spinoza was himself distantly related to Uriel da Costa by several marriages between members of the D'Espinoza family and Da Costa's, back in Portugal, his father may possibly have said as little as possible about the colossal scandal surrounding their relative that rocked the community when Spinoza was young. Yet, later on, in his schooling, and on approaching adulthood, Spinoza must have heard plenty of talk about Uriel da Costa (1585–1640). Mortera was a central figure in the Da Costa scandal, and no one knew better than he the details and tragic consequences for Uriel himself, or was more preoccupied with the challenges of irreligion and heretical defiance in the community which the Da Costa affair brought to everyone's attention.[36]

Da Costa's rebellion against Judaism commenced while living in Hamburg some years after his rejection of Christianity. Troubled by what seemed to him glaring inconsistencies between what is commanded in the Torah and the obligations required by the Oral Law of Jewish tradition, he openly clashed with rabbinic authority and the community elders. He could not see what rabbinic Jewish orthodoxy and observance had to do with the ancient Israelite religion profiled in the Bible. He wrote up his objections and sent them to the Sephardic congregation of Venice who asked Venice's foremost scholar of the day, Leone Modena (1571–1648) to arbitrate. Condemning Uriel for his critique, Modena directed the Hamburg Sephardic community to place him under communal ban unless he recanted. Refusing, he was duly ostracized in both Hamburg and Venice, in the latter case in a highly exceptional ceremony organized in late 1618, in the "Ponentine synagogue." The text of this *herem* shows Uriel was condemned *in absentia* for rejecting rabbinic tradition and the Oral Law including circumcision

---

[35] Licata, "Nature de la langue," 48; Kerkhof, *Portugees en het Spaans*, 50.
[36] Salomon, "La vraie excommunication," 184, 188, 196–7; Saperstein, *Exile in Amsterdam*, 23, 185, 209.

in a more direct, explicit, and defiant manner than anyone previously: "he asserted that the *denim* [laws] by which Israel was and is governed were all invented by ambitious and malicious men" after biblical times.[37]

Despite the *herem*, Uriel remained in Hamburg until February 1623, trading with Portugal and Brazil under his Portuguese name "Adam Romez." He also reworked his highly provocative critique of the Jewish Oral Law and the "Pharisaic" priestly (rabbinic) temperament into a treatise including denial of the immortality of the soul which a zealous opponent at Hamburg, Dr Samuel da Silva (1570–1631), in his defence of the soul's immortality, afterwards published in part, in 1623, at Amsterdam (without Da Costa's knowledge). Under rabbinic ban at Hamburg and Venice, in 1623 da Costa transferred to Amsterdam where he attempted to join that community. For his "arrogance," "wickedness," and "wrong opinions," he soon came under severe pressure there too. In May 1623, delegates from the boards of elders of the three then still separate Amsterdam congregations, the *Senhores Quinze*, met with the rabbis to decide whether Uriel could be admitted or not. Summoned before the *Senhores* and rabbis, "mild and gentle persuasion was applied to bring him back to the truth." But finding that "through pure obstinacy and arrogance he persists in his wickedness and wrong opinions," the *Senhores Quinze* duly confirmed that the Venetian *herem* applied also in Amsterdam.[38]

Da Costa, having brought his text with him, retaliated for the *herem* by publishing, early in 1624, his full critique of Pharisaic Judaism in favour of a purer biblical Hebrew religion under the title *Exame das Tradições Phariseas* [Examination of the Pharisaic Traditions]. Shortly afterwards, he himself relates in his autobiographical *Exemplar humanae vitae* [Example of a Human Life], the *Senhores Quinze* turned to the Amsterdam magistracy charging him with publishing a book denying "immortality of the soul" with a view to "subverting not only the Jewish but also the Christian religion." Briefly arrested, he was released a week later on bail paid by his brothers, Mordecai (Miguel) and Joseph (João) Da Costa and then banished from Amsterdam. The magistrates condemned the entire stock of his book to be publicly burnt, an event apparently presided over jointly by the city magistracy and the Sephardic elders.[39] Only two copies are known to have survived this virtual obliteration—one in the hands of the Spanish Inquisition, later lost, the other unrecognized, gathering dust in the Royal Library of Copenhagen, until it was rediscovered in 1990, when Da Costa's long-lost book was finally retrieved and republished.

---

[37] Salomon and Sassoon, "Introduction," in Da Costa, *Examination*, 10; Proietti, *Uriel da Costa*, 27–8; Muchnik *Une Vie Marrane*, 395.

[38] Da Costa, *Examination*, 15; Muchnik, *Une Vie Marrane*, 99–101; Salomon and Sassoon, "Introduction," in Da Costa, *Examination*, 15; Nadler, *Spinoza's Heresy*, 171; Schwarz, *Uriel da Costa*, 54.

[39] Salomon and Sassoon, "Introduction," in Da Costa, *Examination*, 17–18; Albiac, *Sinagoga vacía*, 254, 261, 266, 298–9.

Da Costa never knew that his fiercely suppressed book did in the end survive. Although they allude to his views occasionally, neither Menasseh nor Mortera ever directly mention him in their published works (or surviving sermons), any more than did Spinoza later, nor would they have wanted echoes of the clashes surrounding Da Costa's or Spinoza's rebellions to resound among the schoolboys and wider congregation, preferring to avoid drawing attention to their defiance and wishing to safeguard the reputations of the Da Costa and Spinoza families.[40] After around four years living in Utrecht, outside of Jewish society, Uriel returned to Amsterdam where, by the late 1630s, he was living near the main synagogue. Spinoza must have known him at least by sight even if, at first, he had no idea who he was. Then, in 1639, when Spinoza, now seven, and just starting school, terms were agreed by the now united synagogue under which Da Costa could recant and be readmitted. Accepting the conditions he had refused seven years before, he now submitted to mounting the *theba* in the centre of the synagogue and reading out before the congregation a formal declaration of recantation. There also he bent to receive the *malqut*, or symbolic thirty-nine lashes. Lacking the power to inflict actual physical penalties, the Jewish community had to make do with this symbolic ritual, an outward show of formalized contrition requiring the miscreant also to prostrate himself at the foot of the *theba* stairs for worshippers present to step over,[41] an elaborately staged performance doubtless causing a great stir and leaving a profound impression on the schoolboys.

Humiliated, dejected, still observing some Jewish rites, including fasting on the Day of Atonement but fixing that holy day's date differently from the rabbis, and estranged from his brothers—who (like Spinoza's siblings later), apparently observed the ban against him which his mother, Branca da Costa, long an active Judaizer in Portugal, did not[42]—Da Costa died in April 1640 when Spinoza was nearing eight, reportedly committing suicide by shooting himself with a pistol at his lodgings. Then and later, Spinoza and his fellow pupils must have heard varying versions of his life-story. The scandal was long remembered in the community as were reports of Da Costa's heretical views even though, seemingly, his principal book, the *Examination*, was destroyed and his autobiography, the *Exemplar*, lay unpublished until 1687. His defiance of rabbinic authority was sensational but also tragic, serving as a stern admonition for many. How far, if at all, Da Costa's dismal end entered Spinoza's thoughts prior to and during his open defiance, in 1655–6 and later, we can only guess.[43] Nowhere in what survives from his pen does he mention him.

---

[40] Saperstein, *Exile in Amsterdam*, 208–10; Nadler, *Spinoza: A Life*, 98–9, 105.
[41] Salomon and Sassoon, "Introduction," in Da Costa, *Examination*, 20–2; Kaplan, "Social Functions of the 'Herem'," 131–2.
[42] Salomon and Sassoon, "Introduction," in Da Costa, *Examination*, 18; Yovel, *Spinoza and Other Heretics*, 45; Nadler, *Spinoza: A Life*, 81.
[43] Osier, *D'Uriel da Costa à Spinoza*, 77–8, 82.

The Sephardic community records reveal that the *Mahamad*, the community governing board, and consequently the rabbis too, took little interest in members' own personal philosophical ideas and reading, doctrinal disagreement, or intellectual differences when expressed at home or even in small group discussion more broadly. Private deviance of that sort was never among the reasons for issuing bans against heterodox or disobedient members of the congregation. Typically, where serious disagreements occurred, as for example, with the quarrel between Mortera and Menasseh, the *parnasim* also made little attempt to adjudicate regarding the questions at issue. The elders' primary concern throughout was to safeguard the community's standing, unity, and dignity, shielding it from hostile external recrimination, preventing the open spread of what were deemed irreligious ideas, and to prevent factions forming and unseemly bickering. Private doubts, eagerness to learn Latin, studying Cartesianism, quietly developing heterodox views about the Mosaic Law or immortality of the soul were, in themselves, of scant concern to the *parnasim*, most of whom were affluent merchants with little knowledge of Hebrew or rabbinics, and little interest in what particular individuals believed or thought. What they were avid to crack down on was openly defiant, disrespectful behaviour of a kind apt to cause uproar, scandal, or division among the congregation or lead students or others to openly contradict the rabbis.

6.iii World Events Viewed from School

When Spinoza started school around the time of the merger of the three communities, in 1639, Menasseh, third in rank among the rabbis, was still in the background of the community's educational establishment, with no regular role in the school. This changed, though, when his then friend but later rival, Rabbi Aboab, took up his position at Recife, in Brazil, in 1642. Menasseh was appointed to replace him receiving a substantial raise in salary.[44] On 22 May 1642 (Hebrew year 5402), he then gained further prominence with the occasion of the unprecedented visit of England's French-born queen, Henrietta Maria, an event which aroused great excitement among the pupils and the entire congregation. Having expressed her desire to see the Amsterdam Portuguese synagogue, the queen arrived accompanied by her daughter, the Princess Mary, the Stadholder Frederik Hendrik, Frederik Hendrik's sixteen-year-old son and heir, Prince Willem II, the future Stadholder (1647–50), and a train of magnificently attired nobles.[45] Never before had the synagogue, or probably any early modern

---

[44] Pieterse, *Daniel Levi de Barrios als geschiedschrijver*, 168; Nadler, *Menasseh ben Israel*, 95–6, 106.
[45] Menasseh ben Israel, *Gratulação*, 4; Franco Mendes, *Memorias*, 51–2; Offenberg "Jacob Jehuda Leon," 105–6; Gans, *Memorboek*, 47; Nadler, *Spinoza: A Life*, 86.

synagogue, been visited by royalty or personages of princely status and such an event would occur only very rarely later.

It was the third day of their tour of Amsterdam[46] when the synagogue received this glittering royal party escorted by cavalry, heralds, and trumpeters, headed by the queen consort of the "king of Britain, France and Ireland," as Menasseh ben Israel (Figure 6.2) pompously styled her in his celebratory oration to mark the occasion. As the Maccabees freed the Holy Land from the oppression of the Seleucids, founding the Hasmonaean dynasty in 175–164 BC, so the House of Orange freed the Dutch by leading the revolt "against the very cruel tyrannies of Spain." Menasseh especially thanked the Stadholder and States of Holland for

Figure 6.2 *Menasseh Ben Israel* portrait etching by Rembrandt. © Jewish Museum London.

[46] Dapper, *Historische Beschryving*, 246–7.

dealing with the modern descendants of the Hasmonaean Jews very differently from the rulers of Spain, Portugal, and most of Europe, in a spirit of justice and toleration.[47] During their visit, probably connected with efforts, at the start of England's Civil War, to raise desperately needed funds for her embattled husband, Charles I, the royal visitors inspected the synagogue and also, probably in adjoining rooms there, rather than at his house where he normally displayed it, Leon Templo's model of the Temple of Solomon along with ritual objects and other exhibits. They also paused to stand under an ornate bridal canopy.[48] Henrietta Maria was hoping, no doubt, amidst the bowing, courtesies, and rhetoric, to meet some wealthy financiers ready to offer loans to warring monarchs on the security of the piles of royal jewels she had brought with her from England. Menasseh pointedly emphasized in his oration the Jews' unshakeable loyalty to the rulers under whose governance they dwelt, a prominent theme also later, in his "humble" address *To His Highness The Lord Protector of the Commonwealth of England, Scotland and Ireland* (1655), Oliver Cromwell, the man who led the forces that overthrew Charles I.

Since ancient times the Jews had (supposedly) remained uncommonly loyal to all those who govern the societies among which they live, a point integral to the argument Menasseh laid before Cromwell, in 1655, when urging readmittance of the Jewish people to England. In their Sabbath-day prayers, prior to a prayer for their own people, and following the custom of Jews everywhere in their local vernacular or in Hebrew, Amsterdam Sephardim recited in Portuguese the so called "Hanoten gebed." In this prayer the congregation supplicate "He that giveth salvation unto kings and dominion unto Lords, He that delivered his servant David from the sword of the enemy, He that made a way in the sea, to bless and keep, preserve and rescue, exalt and magnify, and lift up higher and higher . . . ," at which point was intoned the name of the relevant king, prince, or other presiding figure. "The King of Kings defend [this ruler] in his mercy, make him joyful, and free him from all dangers and distresse." Jews ceaselessly upheld the "never broken custome" of reciting prayers for the well-being of those ruling over them "wheresoever they are, on the Sabbath-Day, or other solemne feasts."[49] Never had the Jews been disloyal to the kings of Spain and Portugal until Ferdinand and Isabella released them from their age-old loyalty, in 1492, by expelling the community's forebears in the cruellest, most oppressive fashion.[50] Their community spoke Portuguese and Spanish, observed Menasseh in his address but now abjured altogether, he assured the royal visitors and congregation, and forever, the

---

[47] Menasseh ben Israel, *Gratulação*, 4–5; Nadler, *Menasseh ben Israel*, 108–10.
[48] Fuks-Mansfeld, *Sefardim in Amsterdam*, 109; Kerkhof, *Portugees en het Spaans*, 109.
[49] Menasseh ben Israel, *To His Highnesse the Lord Protector*, 13; Kerkhof, *Portugees en het Spaans*, 30–1.
[50] Menasseh ben Israel, *To His Highnesse the Lord Protector*, 14; Fuks-Mansfeld, *Sefardim in Amsterdam*, 120.

monarchs of Spain and Portugal, recognizing only the sovereignty of the United Provinces' States General, a lesson regularly hammered home in the community school. Such prayers for the well-being of the States General, States of Holland, city government of Amsterdam, and the Stadholder, Spinoza and his schoolfellows heard continually resounding in the synagogue in Amsterdam of the early 1640s.

Officially, the community had long ago repudiated their former allegiance to the crowns of Spain and Portugal. But in the early 1640s, following the rebellion of December 1640, under the duke of Braganza, initiating the prolonged struggle over Portuguese secession from Spain, there was intense sympathy and support among the Western Sephardim for the new post-1640 Portugal in its fight against Spain. In January 1641, the Portuguese rebel leader, recently proclaimed Portugal's King João IV (reigned: 1640–56), threw open Portugal's ports to the Dutch and, for the first time since Spain's trade embargoes were reimposed, in 1621, Dutch vessels were welcomed legally into Portugal's harbours and the Azores. Enthusiasm for Portugal's secession from Spain, fuelled by promise of closer relations between Portugal and the Republic and easier access to Brazil, Madeira, and the Azores, caused something of the old messianic excitement of the movements of Dom Sebastian and Dom António to resurface. During 1640–4, the euphoria infusing the Amsterdam Portuguese trade was reflected in a surge in Sephardic accounts at the Amsterdam Wisselbank, up from 89 in 1640 to 126, or 8 per cent of the total by 1646.[51] Extravagant hopes, equally, infused the synagogues of Recife and Olinda, in Brazil, where Sephardic numbers reached their peak, at around 1,450, in 1644, and expectation rose, fanned at the time in Holland and Portugal, that João IV would move to curtail the Inquisition's sway in metropolitan Portugal and its American, African, and Asian colonies. In the event, however, despite the echoes of *antonianismo*, and despite much of the Portuguese Inquisition establishment remaining loyal to Philip IV rather than supporting the rebel "king," nothing of the kind transpired; the new ruler simply could not afford to risk antagonizing society and the Portuguese clergy by easing the stifling repressiveness and intolerance of faith and piety.[52]

At school and at home, the young Spinoza inevitably heard much excited talk about the Portuguese secession, Brazil, and the Inquisition. Well before 1640, certain Portuguese Inquisitors loyal to the Spanish crown had warned Madrid that it might be best for them to expel the entire New Christian community from Portugal, despite their being baptized even though many would inevitably revert to Judaism, because these despicable people were not just an ineradicable religious plague ceaselessly eroding Christian faith underground but also a serious political threat to the stability and integrity of the Spanish empire, as *antonianismo*

---

[51] Van Dillen, "Vreemdelingen," 14; Israel, "Economic Contribution," 510, 516, 519–20.
[52] López-Salazar Codes, *Inquisición y política*, 86, 357.

abundantly proved.[53] During the early 1640s, excitement over the Portuguese rebellion reached the furthest corners of the Sephardic world. By 1642, Portuguese New Christians arrested by the Inquisition as far away as Mexico, were avowing mystical expectations of swift deliverance by a divinely salvaged, regenerated independent Portugal.[54] Prominent members of the Amsterdam community, Jeronimo Nunes da Costa especially, and the latter's father, now "Agent of the Crown of Portugal," at Hamburg, materially assisted the Portuguese secession by arranging shipments of naval stores and weaponry to Portugal. Even Menasseh was swept up in the enthusiasm when dedicating the second part of his *Conciliador*, in 1641, to the "benign king João IV back [in possession of] his natural and hereditary realm until now unjustly possessed by another," expecting, now Dutch-Portuguese hostilities had ended, there "will follow the hoped for peace which to me, a Portuguese with a Batavian heart, will be highly welcome."[55]

Ardent expectation was at its height, in 1643, when the renowned Jesuit missionary and visionary, Father Antonio Vieira (1608–97), highly esteemed by the recently enthroned João IV, persuaded Portugal's new monarch that Sephardic resources could and should be tapped to support Portugal's fiercely contested secession (the struggle for which remained in the balance throughout the 1640s and 1650s) just as in the 1580s and 1590s Portugal's exiled Jews had aided Dom António. Fending off Spain's mounting counter-attacks had already emptied the Lisbon treasury and would require vast sums in the future. Sephardic loyalty to their old homeland could be won by means of a firm, lasting alliance between Portugal's Jews in exile and the new, reborn Portuguese crown, a pact made, for now, from necessity, for essentially political and financial reasons, but ultimately intended to erase their stubborn Judaism finally and bind those still in Portugal, Brazil, and Portuguese India [Goa] finally and irrevocably to Christ.[56] As part of his grand messianic vision to reunite Jews and Christians, Brazil with Portugal, and finally elevate the entire world, Vieira visited Amsterdam and held discussions with the Sephardic leadership in 1646, and again in 1647 and 1648, while vigorously urging the Portuguese monarch, in 1643 and over the next years, to curb the Inquisition's power. Portugal should secure from the Pope a general amnesty for the New Christians (like that of 1605), proclaiming forgiveness for all past religious offences alike for those within and outside Portugal.[57] João IV carefully considered this but in the end did not dare take so bold a step.

---

[53] López-Salazar Codes, *Inquisición y política*, 72; Bouza Álvarez, "De las alteraciones de Beja," 110, 115–16.
[54] Israel, *Race, Class and Politics in Colonial Mexico*, 129.
[55] Menasseh ben Israel, *Segunda Parte del Conciliador*, "epistola dedicatoria"; Silvério Lima, "Prophetic Hopes," 373.
[56] Vieira, *Obras Escolhidas* iv, 11, 52–4; Saraiva, "António Vieira, Menasseh ben Israel," 35; Israel, *Conflicts of Empires*, 154; Silvério Lima, "Prophetic Hopes," 369–71.
[57] Vieira, *Obras Escolhidas* iv, 42–4, 48–9; Lúcio de Azevedo, *História dos Cristãos Novos portugueses*, 238; Silvério Lima, "Prophetic Hopes," 374–5.

Vieira, fired by his chiliastic dream for Portugal to lead mankind's redemption, sideline the Inquisition, and emancipate humanity from oppression, was as remarkable a Millenarian as any to be found among the Amsterdam Collegiants. Spinoza must have observed him on occasion since he visited the synagogue and toured the Amsterdam Jewish quarter multiple times, and especially liked listening to the sermons of Menasseh and Mortera (apparently he preferred the latter), holding intense discussions with both. With Menasseh his deliberations especially focused on their common Millenarian expectations. Themes from their discussions are likely reflected in Menasseh's own Millenarian vision in his *The Hope of Israel* (1650).[58] Vieira's brand of Lusocentric Millenarianism certainly appealed to some and mattered to the whole community, being propagated by someone known to be close to the restored throne, virtually an informal diplomatic representative of the new king. In Holland, Vieira's immediate objective, with the help of the Portuguese crown's official "Agent" in the United Provinces, Jeronimo Nunes da Costa, was to persuade Sephardim and Dutch leadership alike (partly by bribing members of the States General, several of whom were bought in this way), that despite the growing differences over Brazil (still divided between the Dutch and Portuguese), reconciliation and peacemaking were preferable to war and that the new king would offer a hefty ransom for the Dutch zone, perhaps even guarantee Dutch possession of a reduced rump, the captaincy-general of Pernambuco (Recife), in exchange for the Dutch returning the rest to Portugal.[59]

Vieira's Millenarian vision was certainly far-reaching: he envisioned Portugal as redeemer of the world with a mission to reconcile and reunite Jews and Christians, free Brazil's Amerindians and all the New World from oppression and slavery, and finally prepare mankind for general redemption. The greatest Portuguese champion of the Brazilian Indians of the age, as of the New Christians and Jews, Vieira was heartened that some Amsterdam Jews too felt they were on the threshold of general redemption and would soon, as Menasseh expressed it, in 1655, see "the MESSIA come and restore our nation." The difficult part, in Vieira's estimation, was to persuade them that this would actually be the Messiah's Second Coming as Christ had already come, and they must now all convert to Christianity.

Vieira's later missions to Holland, in 1646 and 1648, sought to revive this pre-1645 pro-Portuguese enthusiasm, following the tumultuous and disastrous events of 1645 when the pro-Portuguese mood in Amsterdam was suddenly and completely upended due to the Portuguese planters in Dutch Brazil rebelling against the Dutch West India Company [WIC] and devastating most of the colony's sugar

---

[58] Saraiva, "Antonio Vieira, Menasseh ben Israel," 47; Van den Besselaar, *Antonio Vieira en Holland*, 23; Nadler, *Menasseh ben Israel*, 138–9.
[59] Israel, *Conflicts of Empires*, 154–6; Alden, "Some Reflections," 9.

plantation economy. News of the Portuguese planters' burning the plantations and wrecking Dutch Brazil's economy (around the time of Spinoza's *bar mitzvah*, in 1645), and the revolt being backed by the Portuguese crown, triggered a violent backlash against Portugal and João IV's policies in the United Provinces, not least among the Dutch Sephardic community. The collapse of Dutch northern Brazil over the next six or seven years, and accompanying sharp contraction of Sephardic trade with Portugal and Brazil, while the military struggle between the West India Company's troops and the Portuguese for possession of the hinterland of Recife dragged on, caused increasingly embittered and strained relations.

Great indignation against Portugal flared up at Amsterdam, the Portuguese envoy at The Hague, Sousa Coutinho, reported in the late summer of 1645 to his superior in Paris, the Conde de Vidigueira, a descendant of the same counts who had employed successive generations of the Spinoza family in Vidigueira, "and the Jews would like to condemn me to be stoned which would be very easy to accomplish here."[60] Feeling ran so high in the synagogue that the Amsterdam burgomasters ordered the *parnasim* to make announcements in the synagogue to restrain their community's indignation. Complying on 13 September 1645 (22 Elul 5405), two months before Spinoza's *bar mitzvah*, the *Mahamad*, on the same day as issuing a regulation forbidding anyone to exit the synagogue during sermons and readings of the Torah, forbade community members to utter public insults, or pronounce "unruly words against the ambassador of Portugal."[61] Spinoza and his school friends doubtless particularly relished the curses and insults, but could hardly avoid being intrigued by this furore that seethed for the rest of the 1640s. They must all have heard a good deal about the transatlantic drama and been attentive to the sharp reversal in their parents' attitudes and loyalties, from fervently pro-Portuguese until 1645 to bitterly anti-Portuguese, just as Spinoza was preparing his Hebrew portion to recite in synagogue during his *bar mitzvah*.

Some Amsterdam Jews, the Portuguese ambassador reported to Lisbon, openly called for a powerful Dutch naval counter-offensive to subject Portugal to a good thrashing.[62] To further stoke Dutch sentiment against Portugal, Sousa Coutinho reported in July 1647, Amsterdam's Sephardim were deliberately spreading misinformation about non-existent Castilian victories over Portuguese arms and imagined risings in the Portuguese countryside against João IV, and falsely alleging seizure of Dutch ships and their being commandeered to fight the Dutch in Brazil.[63] Even Jeronimo Nunes da Costa was deliberately spreading fake news regarding Portugal's prospects. Despite their disappointment at the

---

[60] *Correspondência diplomática de Francisco de Sousa Coutinho* i, 308.
[61] GA Amsterdam APJ 19 (Hascamoth), 281. res. Mahamad 22 Elul 2405; Israel, *Conflicts of Empires*, 158.
[62] *Correspondência diplomática de Francisco de Sousa Coutinho* iii, 314.
[63] *Correspondência diplomática de Francisco de Sousa Coutinho* ii, 237.

failure of the fleet sent to Brazilian waters under Admiral Witte de With to halt the crumbling of Dutch Brazil, in December 1647, the Jews kept up their publicity campaign against Portugal and the Portuguese efforts in Brazil through the late 1640s and early 1650s, and also made adjustments to their trade networks. Spinoza's father, working with his brother-in-law, Manoel de Tovar, for example, unable to send the same quantities of Canary Island wines to Brazil as before 1645, joined with other Amsterdam Sephardic merchants in re-routing most of their Canary Islands' wine exports to the English market instead, one of the commercial-political shifts in commercial strategy which Spinoza and his brother, Isaac, were now old enough to learn about and discuss among themselves.[64]

The drift of large numbers of Sephardic settlers from Dutch Brazil back to Holland to escape the fighting and disruption added a new economic burden and caused waves of bitter dispute within Amsterdam Portuguese Jewry, as well as the Dutch provincial assemblies, over how to respond. The States of Zeeland urged vigorous armed action by land and sea to support the WIC; the States of Holland, or at least most of its voting towns, preferred less drastic counter-measures. While Jeronimo and his father, caught in a painful predicament, half-heartedly continued supporting Portugal, roughly in step with Vieira who quietly endorsed the insurrection in Dutch Brazil, most Amsterdam Sephardim and merchants, after 1645 lent strong emotional support to Zeeland, the WIC, and those advocating forceful action against Portugal.

On the practical side, Vieira, when he returned, tried to purchase more naval munitions and fast, light, up-to-date war frigates, but due to Dutch opposition, apparently only managed to secure one, the others needed being procured with the help of Jeronimo's father, Duarte, in Hamburg. More central to Vieira's post-1645 theologico-political Millenarian project was securing Portuguese Jewish (and New Christian) funds and support for a new joint-stock company that was established in Lisbon, in 1649, known as the *Companhia do comercio para o Brasil* [Company of Commerce for Brazil]. This was needed to concentrate Portugal's trade with Brazil in heavily armed fleets able to fend off both Spanish attacks and the forays of Dutch, mainly Zeeland, privateers (in whose ventures some Amsterdam Sephardic merchants invested) who at this stage were capturing large quantities of Portuguese shipping in the Atlantic and directly threatening Portugal's maritime links with the Azores and the New World. The politically daring feature of the *Companhia* as originally set up was that all funds invested in the joint-stock company would, as Vieira urged, remain exempt from confiscation by the Inquisition. João IV issued orders for the exemption to take effect. But following protests in Lisbon, and appeals to the Pope who supported Vieira's

---

[64] Worsley, *The Advocate*, 7; Woolf, "Foreign Trade," 44; Israel, *Conflicts of Empires*, 309–10; Israel, *Diasporas*, 272, 275.

critics, Portugal's Inquisitors contrived to block implementation of this bitterly resented nod to the *cristãos novos*.[65]

Even without this concession, though, the *Companhia* played a substantial role in restoring Brazil's slave and sugar economy and ensuring Portugal's long-term dominance in Brazil. But its success represented a further menace to what remained of Dutch Brazil—a deeply divisive challenge to the Amsterdam Jewish merchant elite at a time when Michael d'Espinoza was among the serving *parnasim*. Despite the fiercely anti-Portuguese mood in the community during the later 1640s, since 1645, the Amsterdam *parnasim*, hoping for some compromise solution in Brazil, still retained a strong interest in negotiating with the Portuguese crown through Vieira.[66] Very likely, as a previous *parnas*, closely familiar with Sephardic Jewry's links with Portugal, Michael was among the community leaders conferring with Vieira confidentially, in 1646, about his plans for Brazil, the Jews, and the Inquisition's future. As a *parnas* in 1649–50, Michael became directly involved in the discussions surrounding the *Companhia* and Vieira's projects as well as in the community's pressuring the States to step up Dutch efforts to salvage Dutch Brazil, and the Sephardic synagogues of Recife, Olinda, and Paraíba, and doubtless discussed the absorbing drama and its political, military, naval, commercial, and religious complexities with his sons.

Vieira's Millenarianism had, all along, brought deep frowns to the brows of the Inquisition. Inquisitors appreciated that his grand schemes might well help secure Portuguese independence, the empire, and Portugal's grip on Brazil, strengthen João IV, thwart Spain, be a great relief to Amerindians, and bring the New Christians closer to Christianity. But that was all nothing to them compared with Inquisition sway over society and power to confiscate Judaizers' possessions. Any outcome that eroded religious policing, repression, and hence religious authority they rejected out of hand. Despite continued royal favour and the support of local Jesuits, Vieira came under investigation by the Coimbra Inquisition tribunal which eventually succeeded, in 1665–7, in sufficiently compromising him for propositions favouring Judaism and limiting ecclesiastical privilege,[67] to get him placed under severe restrictions that practically silenced him. Obliged to leave Portugal, Vieira spent his last years in isolation at Rome.

6.iv Last Years of Schooling

The rest of the 1640s were a frantically busy time for Menasseh, a zealous servant of his community as rabbi, teacher, head of the city's main Hebrew printing press,

---

[65] López-Salazar Codes, *Inquisición y política*, 87–8.
[66] Vieira, *Obras Escolhidas* i, 100–5; Israel, *Conflicts of Empires*, 162–6; Alden, "Some Reflections," 10.
[67] Muhana, "António Vieira: A Jesuit Missionary."

and independent scholar. His principal burden were the "six [hours] in the school" and "one and a half in the public academy and the private one of the senhores Pereyra."[68] Besides his teaching load, he spent two hours per day in the synagogue conducting prayers and teaching, and then, from eleven to twelve, making visits and "giving audiences to all who require me for their affairs." Menasseh was indeed a remarkable figure in the Amsterdam community when Spinoza was in his middle and higher grades at school, and when approaching his twenties. Spinoza certainly saw plenty of him, especially in the early 1640s when the pupils, more than any other segment of the congregation, daily witnessed Menasseh at work. Some were impressed too by his unusually open and inquiring attitude towards the Christian world outside.

When the boys approached the two highest grades, which the community called the *yesiba* [*yeshivah*], the pupils would have been thirteen and fourteen, with knowledge of Torah and Hebrew reaching a fairly sophisticated level. They were now being introduced to the legal arguments of Maimonides, Joseph Caro, and other great codifiers of rabbinic Law as well as medieval Sephardic Hebrew poetry. Among the Hebrew and Spanish-language texts post-*bar mitzvah* adolescents were urged to read as accompanying and follow-up material, were Yehuda Halevi's *Cuzary*, the *Nomologia or Discursos Legales* (1629) of Rabbi Immanuel Aboab stressing the corrupt, defective character of the Greek and Latin renderings of the Scriptures Christians rely on to buttress Christianity's alleged muddling of Scripture, Menasseh's *Conciliador* (1632), and Leon Templo's description of Solomon's Temple, *Retrato del Templo de Selomoh* (1642).[69]

This last must have been of special interest to all students at the synagogue school. Born probably in Spain or Portugal, Jacob Yehudah Leon Templo (1603–c.1675) arrived in Holland as an infant and spent much of his life in Zeeland. Moving to Amsterdam around 1642, soon after his famed book on Solomon's Temple appeared at Middelburg, in Spanish and Dutch, he may have been among Spinoza's teachers during his final year or two at school. Living round the corner from the Spinozas, on the Vlooienburg, this auxiliary rabbi kept a veritable Jewish museum in his house, familiar to the boys of the synagogue school, displaying fine ritual objects as well as his famed model of King Solomon's Temple that Templo himself had painstakingly constructed over many years, supported by the Collegiant leader, Adam Boreel, and by Menasseh.[70] Leon Templo's published account of Solomon's Temple based on details recounted in the Bible, and in Josephus, proved immensely popular in both Spanish and Dutch, and from 1643 in its French version, and included a detailed

---

[68] Nadler, *Menasseh ben Israel*, 107; Van der Wall, *Mystieke Chiliast*, 163.
[69] Swetschinski, *Reluctant Cosmopolitans*, 211–12; Yerushalmi, *From Spanish Court*, 356n14, 424–5, 427.
[70] Offenberg, "Jacob Jehuda Leon," 99, 104; Quatrini, *Adam Boreel*, 69.

description of the large model that he had made. Originally, Leon Templo dedicated his book to the States of Zeeland, in 1641; but not to be outdone, the States of Holland, in April 1643, awarded him fifty guilders, in recognition of the fascination his book and model aroused in the Republic.[71] A copy of his booklet was presented to Princess Mary and the future Stadholder William II by Leon Templo himself during their visit to the Portuguese synagogue. The text appeared also in Hebrew (in 1650) and eventually Latin and German (in 1665).[72] The model went on permanent display, with a small fee charged for entry, further enhancing the attraction of the synagogue premises and of Leon Templo's house museum to fashionable visitors through the 1640s, and later. In 1661, the synagogue elders noted that numerous non-Jews regularly visited the synagogue premises and its surroundings in particular to inspect the model. Doubtless, it greatly impressed the schoolboys with Solomon's splendour.[73] A topic familiar to him from his schooldays onwards, Solomon would remain a prominent theme in Spinoza's thinking about the Old Testament and ancient Israelites during his maturity.

Another longstanding preoccupation anchored in Spinoza's mind early on was a theme promoted among the congregation and its schoolboys especially by Mortera, later taken up in his poetic chronicle by Levi de Barrios—the notion of the ancient Hebrew republic as a uniquely valuable exemplum in human political history. Although Mortera, unlike Spinoza later, says nothing about democracy in his account of the ancient Hebrew republic, he does emphasize that it belonged to the whole people, that God was its only sovereign, and that it uniquely delivered prosperity to all, adding that both the original Hebrew republic and the post-Babylonian revived republic based their admirably evenly spread prosperity on farming the land in which all participated, and not on long-distance "maritime trade" confined to a few, thus avoiding becoming a society like the Jewish people of their day, divided between a few wealthy and many poor.[74] Spinoza's treatment of the Hebrew republic later, in his *TTP*, focuses on the fact that it was no theocracy governed by priests, or form of state controlled by any elite or group, but a republic directed in accord with what the people believed was divinely revealed law, a democracy in the sense that no individual or group monopolized political power and everyone belonging to the whole was equally responsible for upholding, as well as benefiting from, its laws. This strand of Spinoza's mature thought was hence at least incipiently rooted in the Sephardic congregation of Amsterdam and its school, his community's ideal that the divine law alone was sovereign in the Hebrew republic, a point much emphasized by Mortera in his

---

[71] *Resolutien van de Heeren Staten van Holland* 1643, res. 27 April 1643; Offenberg, "Jacob Jehuda Leon," 99–100; Gans, *Memorboek*, 37, 40.
[72] Offenberg, "Jacob Jehuda Leon," 110–11.
[73] GA Amsterdam PJG 19, p. 493, res. 13 Av 5421; Offenberg, "Jacob Jehuda Leon," 105–6; Hell, "A Walk," 69.
[74] Mortera, *Tratado da Verdade*, 201.

Tratado da Verdade da lei de Moises (1659) and afterwards celebrated in Spanish verse, in the early 1680s, by Levi de Barrios.[75]

It is not clear how far the boys were formally instructed in Dutch, geography, cosmography, general history, or mathematics but they must have gained at least some guidance in all these fields. Girls, insofar as they became literate, like Spinoza's younger sister Rebecca, were left to study at home, strictly secluded from the boys in the synagogue and its premises. One wonders if the boys also studied selected mathematical and scientific passages from Yoseph Shlomo Delmedigo's *Sefer Elim*, one of the few mathematical books in Hebrew then available in print, which Menasseh published, in 1629. Although Spinoza was born three years after the furore that blew up around Delmedigo and his ideas, this affair too can be seen retrospectively to have resounded significantly in Spinoza's early life and education. Evidently, Spinoza developed and retained a particular interest in Delmedigo—in later life he kept two of Delmedigo's works in his small personal library, the *Sefer Elim* and the *Ta'alumoth Hokhmah*.[76]

Yoseph Shlomo [Joseph Solomon] Delmedigo (1591–1655) (Figure 6.3), known in Hebrew as "Yashar" or "Yosef mi-Qandiy'ah [Joseph of Candia]" and in Amsterdam Latin as "Joseph del Medico Cretensis [of Crete]," came from Candia, a Venetian stronghold in Crete. A descendant of an earlier Jewish philosopher Elija Delmedigo (or Elijah mi-Qandia (c.1458–1493), Yoseph Shlomo studied medicine, partly under Montalto, and at Padua, in 1609–10, also astronomy under Galileo himself. When younger, he travelled across the Near East from Cairo to Constantinople and, afterwards, to Poland, and also to Vilna in Lithuania where he served as physician to Prince Radziwill, in the years 1621–4. At the Lithuanian Karaite centre of Troki, he had memorable encounters with Karaite scholars.[77] Later, Delmedigo lived briefly in Hamburg and then, from 1625 to 1629, in Amsterdam. In 1626, he was provisionally engaged as rabbi of the Beth Yisrael congregation at an annual salary of 500 guilders and briefly did take up the position in Amsterdam, but the arrangement did not continue after 1626 due to what followed.

Despite obvious efforts to conceal or shade his more radical views among the community leadership, by 1626 Delmedigo was under a degree of suspicion which increased markedly shortly afterwards.[78] Spinoza's later interest in Delmedigo is especially significant in the light of Delmedigo's life-long complaint that Jews were falling behind others in study of the sciences and mathematics, that their religion

---

[75] Mortera, *Tratado da Verdade*, 185–201; Kaplan, "Mortera's Democratic Hebrew Republic," 10–13.
[76] Van Sluis and Musschenga, *Boeken van Spinoza*, 41–2; Adler, "Joseph Solomon Delmedigo," 145–6; Adler, "Epistemological Categories," 207–8; Krop, "Spinoza's Library," 28.
[77] Révah, *Spinoza et Juan de Prado*, 17; D'Ancona, "Delmedigo, Menasseh ben Israel," 110–11, 123; Ben-Zaken, *Cross-Cultural Scientific Exchanges*, 79.
[78] Pieterse, *Daniel Levi de Barrios als geschiedschrijver*, 64, 153–4; Pozzi, "Libro misterioso," 697; Kaplan, *Judíos nuevos*, 151; Adler, "Epistemological Categories," 206.

Figure 6.3 *Joseph Solomon Delmedigo* (1591–1655), portrait engraving by W. Delff after a painting by C. Duyster of 1628. Reproduction courtesy of The Picture ArtCollection/Alamy Stock Photo.

and general outlook needed reforming and rationalizing, and that the Karaites were one useful guide by which Jews could reassess and rework strict rabbinism and observance into a broader universalism. It has even been proposed, and is certainly an intriguing suggestion, if perhaps stretching the point, that the "Venetian circle calling for a Jewish radical enlightenment" (Montalto, Delmedigo, and, as regards church teaching, to an extent Mortera) was one root of the later "Radical Enlightenment promoted by Spinoza."[79]

In any case, Delmedigo was a larger than life character whom Michael d'Espinoza knew personally. In fact, in June 1629, Michael intervened to help him out financially at a critical moment in Yoseph Shlomo's life shortly before he left the Netherlands. Like Uriel da Costa, he was someone about whom Spinoza and his brothers must have heard much from other community members, and at school, as well as their father. Although cautious, unlike Da Costa, and reluctant to defy religious authority or say anything openly contradicting what all men had believed for millennia, and inclined to muffle his more radical thoughts behind

---

[79] Ben-Zaken, *Cross-Cultural Scientific Exchanges*, 103; Fraenkel, "Spinoza's Philosophy of Religion," 379.

clouds of wordiness, he too was a decidedly subversive figure in early modern Jewish culture. In Bible criticism, he particularly admired Ibn Ezra who had also debated with Karaites and introduced new scientific terms into Hebrew,[80] praising him for his rationalizing scientific approach, much as Spinoza would later.[81] More broadly, Delmedigo was a thoroughgoing naturalist, prizing astronomy and close observation, the first such pioneer on a comprehensive basis in the Jewish world, and one who broadly followed Hasdai Crescas in arguing for perpetual creationism and rejecting simple creationism in the sense of creation at a particular moment in time; he also stressed the need to keep theology and philosophy separate and, while admiring Maimonides, like his earlier relative, Elija Delmedigo, criticized him for mingling the two, insisting on separating philosophy from theology, again tendencies Spinoza later shared with him.[82] Like Averroes and Maimonides, and indeed Spinoza later, full access to the truth—understanding the world philosophically—both Delmedigos considered something reserved for the "select few."

While in Constantinople, Delmedigo had closely observed the spectacular, unusually bright comet that blazed across the night sky from November 1618 to January 1619 arousing great anxiety throughout Europe and the Ottoman lands as well as stimulating debate. Watching one night, early in 1619, amidst a large crowd that became "terrified of the great novelty," viewing it as "a sign and precursor of a [terrible] forthcoming event," Delmedigo assured one and all that comets are purely natural phenomena rather than supernatural omens of any kind.[83] Convinced by Galileo's teaching and its relevance to philosophy, he inserted an account of heliocentric astronomy into the mathematical sections of his *Sefer Elim*, presenting it as a reply to questions from a Karaite scholar of Troki.

Delmedigo's views on astronomy, and way of problematizing "creation from nothing," and creation in time, in the style of Gersonides and Crescas, were forward-looking without doubt but provoked a considerable controversy within the Amsterdam Sephardic community, as did rumours that his views on immortality of the soul were unsound. At one point in his main text, Delmedigo appreciatively repeats Galileo's witticism (attributed to an ecclesiastic) that the "Holy Ghost may teach us how to get to Heaven, but certainly does not teach how the heavens go." By the time Delmedigo's unorthodox ideas began arousing concern within the Amsterdam Sephardic community, in 1629, still well before Galileo's trial and condemnation by the Inquisition and papacy, in 1633, the Copernican system was becoming highly controversial in wider Dutch society, as well as throughout the rest of Europe, a breath-taking innovation rejected not

---

[80] Stroumsa, *Andalus and Sefarad*, 75, 164n12; Adler, "Epistemological Categories," 206–7.
[81] Cohen, *Spinoza en de geneeskunde*, 39–40; Nadler, *Book Forged in Hell*, 108–11.
[82] Langermann, "Proclus Revenant," 376; Fraenkel, "Reconsidering the Case," 222; Fraenkel, *Philosophical Religions*, 206–7, 212, 255, 258.
[83] Ben-Zaken, *Cross-Cultural Scientific Exchanges*, 79–81.

only by the Catholic Church but also by most Protestants, Orthodox, Muslims, and Jews.[84]

Menasseh ben Israel "was my close friend and persuaded me to publish the questions" of the learned Karaite of Troki, recorded Delmedigo, in 1630.[85] Intrigued as always by new ideas, Menasseh was in the midst of seeing Delmedigo's book through the press when, on 13 May 1629, only four days before the recorded, and probably connected, meeting between Michael d'Espinoza and Delmedigo about payment of a letter of exchange from Hamburg, the young rabbi was summoned before the *Senhores Quinze* (including Spinoza's grandfather, Abraham) and told he must submit the already partially printed work to a committee of inquiry headed by Rabbi Abraham Cohen Herrera (*c*.1570–*c*.1635).[86] The investigating committee included a scholar charged with translating Delmedigo's Hebrew into Portuguese. Hoping to circumvent opposition to his publishing project, Menasseh had by this time already obtained a favourable ruling from a panel of four Venetian rabbis, including Simone Luzzatto, Delmedigo's teacher, and Leone da Modena who, as something of a reformer himself, was less anti-Karaite than most rabbis.[87] But Menasseh had revealed only part of Delmedigo's text to them. Annoyed by this attempt to circumvent the Amsterdam *Senhores* by reaching out to the Venetian rabbis, his colleagues reprimanded Menasseh, and refused to permit publication of any of Delmedigo's scientific work without further exacting scrutiny, forcing him to suspend printing.

Examined by this special commission consisting of five rabbis chaired by Cohen Herrera, including Aboab and Menasseh who openly disagreed and six *parnasim* from the three congregations, the inquiry reached their decision on 2 September 1629, signed by them all, obliging Menasseh to delete everything "contrary to the honour of God, his holy Law, and to good customs," meaning making extensive cuts as directed.[88] By then Delmedigo had already left Holland, in May 1629, to avoid the inquiry and likely humiliation, provided with the cash Michael d'Espinoza paid out to him. Delmedigo had acknowledged payment in full of 696 guilders, well over a year's salary for him, remitted by Antonio de Azevedo, in Hamburg, through the good offices of "Miguel d'espinosa as merchant and inhabitant of this city."[89] The episode led to Delmedigo's *Sefer Elim* appearing in a form usable for teaching purposes but with sections deleted and bad feeling

---

[84] Adler, "Joseph Solomon Delmedigo," 142; Levy, *Baruch or Benedict?*, 25.
[85] D'Ancona, "Delmedigo, Menasseh ben Israel," 124; Pozzi, "Libro misterioso," 697.
[86] D'Ancona, "Delmedigo, Menasseh ben Israel," 149–50; Swetschinski, *Reluctant Cosmopolitans*, 263; Den Boer, *Literatura sefardí*, 84.
[87] Ben-Zaken, *Cross-Cultural Scientific Exchanges*, 96–8.
[88] D'Ancona, "Delmedigo, Menasseh ben Israel," 150–1; Pozzi, "Libro misterioso," 698; Gans, *Memorboek*, 44–5; Swetschinski, *Reluctant Cosmopolitans*, 151, 262–5; Nadler, *Menasseh ben Israel*, 54–7.
[89] GA Amsterdam NA 398B, fo. 397. Deed Nicolaas Jacobsz, 17 May 1629.

lingering between Aboab and Menasseh. Twenty-seven years later, in 1656, it would be Rabbi Aboab who headed the synagogue commission sitting in judgement on Spinoza.

Making his way to Hanau and then nearby Frankfurt, Delmedigo took with him the manuscript of his second book entitled *Abscondita Sapientiae* [Ta'ahmoth Hochma] which he clandestinely published, at Hanau, it is thought, in 1629 or 1630, with the false place-name "Basel" on the title-page, of which there was later a copy in Spinoza's library (albeit with its title-page missing).[90] After decades of further wandering, the now universally discredited Delmedigo reportedly died in Prague, in October 1655, sunk in poverty, feeling his life had been ruined by rabbinic narrowness and bigotry.[91]

Long before his rupture with the synagogue, in 1656, the adolescent Spinoza obviously knew a good deal about rabbinic censorship, the risks of challenging embedded "prejudices" and steep costs of defying religious authority. From their orthodox perspective, though, the *parnasim* and Cohen Herrera had cause for suspicion and for suppressing Delmedigo's more daring thoughts. For it was not just Karaite mathematics and astronomy that Delmedigo admired while in Cairo, in 1616–17, and again, after passing through the Holy Land, in 1618–19, in Constantinople, and later at Troki. Despite his guarded language, Delmedigo was intensely critical of the restricted character of contemporary rabbinic culture, deploring how Jewish printing, through being supervised by rabbis and their censorship, had become a tool for stifling instead of encouraging science and discussion, a point Menasseh emphatically agreed with. Delmedigo respected the Karaites in no small part for their loyalty to what was authentically ancient in Judaism and opposing what he too deemed rabbinic Judaism's excessive preoccupation with observance and strict community discipline.[92]

A product of the Italian Renaissance and Galilean science, Delmedigo was nevertheless also something of a mystic. He may have deemed comets purely natural phenomena, and questioned "creation from nothing" and in time, but he believed in a Hermetic-Kabbalistic secret tradition of knowledge, supposedly reaching back to Moses, which included heliocentric cosmology, a clandestine legacy supposedly truly Hebraic, ancient, and authentic but obscured by rabbinic obscurantism. His sojourns in Ottoman lands and Lithuania were part of what Delmedigo envisaged as his grand mission to retrieve this lost ancient tradition by gathering all the ancient manuscripts he could locate. A true bibliomaniac, Delmedigo gathered a vast collection which he somehow managed to transport around with him, though he seemingly lost his books during his last destitute

---

[90] Pozzi, "Libro misterioso," 706–8; Van Sluis and Musschenga, *Boeken van Spinoza*, 41.
[91] Adler, "Mortality of the Soul," 34–5.
[92] Cohen, *Spinoza en de geneeskunde*, 38–9; Kaplan, *Judíos nuevos*, 152; Ben-Zaken, *Cross-Cultural Scientific Exchanges*, 78, 80, 85, 103.

years towards the close of his life.[93] His refined Kabbalism included, though, a masked critique, hardly to the taste of Cohen Herrera or Aboab, of Kabbalah as usually conceived.[94]

The mature Spinoza may have scoffed at Delmedigo's Hermetic-Kabbalistic mysticism, but undoubtedly sympathized, whenever he first discovered it, with Delmedigo's insistence on a strict separation between philosophy and theology, and aversion to rabbinic neglect of science and his dislike of rabbinic obsession with observance of religious law to the exclusion of nearly all else. But if drawn to all this, the mature Spinoza would have been still more interested in the key Marrano question which was also the central issue for Uriel da Costa, both Delmedigos, and, before them, Gersonides: how does one effectively undermine restrictive and oppressive religious authority clandestinely and surreptitiously enough to avoid bringing the roof down on one's head. Whether Delmedigo's work was actually an early pathway to Galilean principles and astronomy during Spinoza's youth, or just an eventual signpost and point of reference, at a later stage, Delmedigo's books and collision with the synagogue certainly possessed lasting relevance to and exerted a formative effect on Spinoza's life.

In philosophy, Delmedigo was no great trailblazer but here and there did produce exceptional insights that sometimes converged with strands of Spinoza's later mature philosophy, most notably his anti-Aristotelian identification of will and intellect and claim that there are no simple observations or affirmations that do not involve intellectual judgement regarding their veracity. Particularly relevant to Spinoza's later development, it has been noted, was Delmedigo's distinctive approach to epistemology combining reason and trained experience in observation. Delmedigo, whom Galileo had permitted to look through his telescope at the heavens, insisted that a few people know things through training in observation techniques that most people do not know and argued not just for freedom to philosophize but that tradition and what most people believe presents a serious obstacle to propagating truth, and hence to human well-being and education. The words of the Torah, he suggested, are no guide to scientific truth. Especially characteristic of both Delmedigo and Spinoza was the anti-Cartesian concept, fully developed later in Spinoza's *Ethics*, Part II, Proposition 49, that the human mind cannot perceive an idea, proposition, or equation clearly without also either simultaneously assenting to or rejecting that proposition via one's will and absorbing its truth or falsity into one's own thinking. Thus our minds respond differently to two and two makes four, two and two makes five, fish exist and so do unicorns. This means that will and mind are not, after all, distinct, from which followed Spinoza's principle that "the will

---

[93] Cohen, *Spinoza en de geneeskunde*, 39–40; Ben-Zaken, *Cross-Cultural Scientific Exchanges*, 85–8, 90, 93.

[94] Pozzi, "Libro misterioso," 703–4; Swetschinski, *Reluctant Cosmopolitans*, 263.

and the intellect are one and the same," the functioning of the mind, a key plank of his philosophical doctrine.[95]

Relevant too is Delmedigo's ordering of three categories of knowledge. Similar fusing of perception, will, and intellect in categorizing different kinds of knowledge would later become a key ingredient of Spinoza's early and then mature theory of mind, epistemology, and science as set out in his *Ethics*. So would separating empirical knowledge as the first category from what was Delmedigo's and Spinoza's shared second category, namely complex propositions or conclusions based on empirically gathered information inferred by reason, culminating in the third order—insight based on cumulative life experience, having gathered many such conclusions, sometimes termed "intuition."[96] Delmedigo's and Spinoza's convergence regarding the first order of knowledge is perhaps the most striking meeting point and most counter to tradition: every straightforward empirical observation in science, even collecting raw data, can never be separated in our minds from judgement about its accuracy and meaning.

As a boy, Spinoza undoubtedly had a highly developed intellect and at a certain point that intellect began accumulating nagging doubts as to how the world was being viewed and understood by those around him. Among early biographies of Spinoza's life, Lucas' account may well be largely hagiographic, or even mythical, but it contains observations, based perhaps on grains of recollection of others, relevant as supporting evidence for how to envisage and schematize Spinoza's education in its evolving stages. Lucas describes a preliminary phase when the boy initially became puzzled by discrepancies between what Mortera and others taught and what he himself found in Scripture. Spinoza's development after his boyhood education down to his expulsion from the community Lucas plausibly divides into three distinct later phases. From about fifteen, hence around 1647, he reports, Spinoza took to posing difficulties that the most learned of the Jews found hard to resolve. As he was past *bar mitzvah* age, this was probably in the evening classes, or adult *academias*, rather than at the school. Noticing his sceptical queries were often unwelcome, the youth at this point learnt to adopt a deliberately low profile to avoid angry clashes.[97]

Early doubts were followed by a further stage of inner rebellion and growing internal tensions, as Spinoza gradually isolated himself from other community members. Having been "steeped in the common beliefs about the Bible from childhood on," Spinoza recalls in the *TTP*, it was only after engaging in "a long search," spurred by what looked like fundamental lack of knowledge in the Prophets, that he arrived at firm conclusions about what he came to see as

---

[95] Spinoza, *Collected Works* (ed. Curley) i, 484–5; Adler, "Joseph Solomon Delmedigo,"147; Swetschinski, *Reluctant Cosmopolitans*, 264; Jaquet, "From Parallelism to Equality," 6–7.
[96] Adler, "J. S. Delmedigo as Teacher," 180–1; Adler, "Epistemological Categories," 210–12.
[97] [Lucas], *La Vie*, 12–13, 16.

the Old Testament's disjointed and corrupt character, and lack of intellectual coherence.[98] These burgeoning internal doubts and tensions then led to a dramatic third phase—open rupture with Mortera, the *parnasim*, and the congregation—commencing in late 1655 when Menasseh was away in England. "From that moment he broke entirely with them and that was the cause of his excommunication [dès lors il rompit entièrement avec eux, et ce fut la cause de son excommunication]."[99] If effective separation normally followed imposition of the *herem*, in Spinoza's case there is good reason to conjecture that it preceded it.

Basic education ended at fourteen. But many pupils stayed in the higher classes, at least for a time; so, even while known not to have continued through the highest classes, there is no way of knowing when exactly Spinoza finished formal schooling. Those few studying for the rabbinate continued studying in the *yesiba* for long periods, well into early adulthood, sometimes until the age of twenty or even twenty-two, as with Samuel de Caceres, son of Daniel de Caceres (alias Miguel Gómez), who was twenty-two when he became Spinoza's brother-in-law on marrying his sister, Miriam, in June 1650.[100] This placed De Caceres, viewed as a scholar, emphatically above Spinoza in the communal hierarchy. The names of the highest-grade students were carefully recorded. But whereas his rabbinic brother-in-law, Samuel, is listed amongst the highest grade for 1651, Spinoza's name is not. Besides being his brother-in-law, Samuel, simultaneously, was yet another distant relative of Spinoza's grandmother, Maria Nunes.[101]

Not continuing at school into the uppermost levels means that, unlike De Caceres, Spinoza may never have been taught formally by Mortera, though he certainly saw much of him and encountered him in discussion in the evening *academias*.[102] The academically serious *yeshivah* "Keter Torah," founded by its director or *ros*, Mortera, in 1643, and endowed by a wealthy merchant, not only studied and discussed Torah every day supposedly for two hours after work, guided by rabbinic authority, but also staged "disputes" chaired by Mortera in which rabbinic students were evidently the stars and Spinoza's brother-in-law Samuel especially honoured as an outstanding disputant.[103] Thus the story that Spinoza was Levi Mortera's favourite and most studious and perspicacious "disciple," recounted by Lucas and later by other early biographers,[104] is partly mythical but, given Mortera's links with his family, may possess a kernel of truth. Meanwhile, the description fits Spinoza's studious brother-in-law admirably. In July 1648, Samuel, "son of Daniel de Casseres," who was to become intertwined with Spinoza's life in several ways, and obviously *was* an outstanding

[98] Spinoza, *Theological-Political Treatise*, 136; Nadler, *Spinoza: A Life*, 134.
[99] [Lucas], *La Vie*, 18–24; Saperstein, *Exile in Amsterdam*, 9.   [100] Aboab, *Livro e Nota*, 294.
[101] Freudenthal/Walther, *Lebensgeschichte* i, 197; Nadler, *Spinoza: A Life*, 98.
[102] Vaz Dias and Van der Tak, "Spinoza Merchant," 154.
[103] Pieterse, *Levi de Barrios als geschiedschrijver*, 106–7; Baumgarten, "Quelques possibles sources," 131.
[104] [Lucas], *La Vie*, 14–18; Saperstein, *Exile in Amsterdam*, 10.

yeshivah student, was engaged by the synagogue *parnasim* as a *sopher*, that is, official religious scribe entrusted with translating incoming letters in Hebrew into "Ladino" or the Amsterdam Sephardic version of Portuguese (peppered with Hebraisms and Dutch terms) and entering into the community records whatever needed inscribing in Hebrew; for this work, the *Mahamad* allocated an annual salary of 200 guilders. According to Levi de Barrios, he also sometimes stood in as assistant synagogue cantor.[105] Although not a fellow student of his rabbinic brother-in-law in the school's uppermost levels, Spinoza presumably often debated with him privately, at home, as well as together with Mortera, Menasseh, and Isaac Aboab in the evening *academias*.

6.v Family Tensions

There is no sign of real division within the Spinoza family down to the late 1630s. But after the death of Spinoza's mother, splits and divisiveness seemingly marred the family's sense of solidarity. At first, relations between Spinoza's father and the brother of his deceased first wife, Rachel, namely Abraham d'Espinoza's son, Jacob, after the latter's return from the Near East, appeared cordial. But in late 1638, just weeks after Spinoza's mother died, there commenced a dispute which must have been distressing for the then six-year-old Spinoza and his siblings between their newly-welcomed back, exotic uncle and their father. The two men appeared before Michael's regular notary, Jan Volckertsz Oli, on 14 January 1639, to wind up what remained of the former partnership between Abraham and Michael for trade with Saleh, the main corsair base on the Barbary Coast where the Sephardic Jews, especially newly arrived Portuguese Jews with family ties in Amsterdam, were the chief suppliers of naval stores, munitions, and arms, the largest proportion of these being shipped by sea from the Netherlands. At Saleh, the States General's support for their Jewish citizens in the North Africa trade underpinned Dutch trade pre-eminence over rival commercial powers such as England.[106] At this point, Michael bought out what remained of Jacob's inherited share in the Spinoza Saleh trade, for just 220 guilders, the equivalent of a year's salary for a lowly working man, securing all the remaining assets and goods jointly traded in by him and Jacob's father, with Morocco, and pulling payments and debts still owed for goods delivered, henceforth into his own sole possession.[107]

The quarrel commenced during the next two weeks over either the transfer of assets or some other aspect of Michael's partnership with Abraham. Less than a fortnight later, the two were back before Michael's notary, with Jacob again

---

[105] Pieterse, *Daniel Levi de Barrios als geschiedschrijver*, 58–9, 102, 151; Kerkhof, "Préstamos," 416.
[106] Israel, *Diasporas*, 293–301, 304–9; Waite, *Jews and Muslims*, 196.
[107] Vaz Dias and Van de Tak, *Spinoza Mercator*, 17; Nadler, *Spinoza: A Life*, 40–1.

described as temporarily in Amsterdam and normally living in "Grandcajro jn Palestina," agreeing to avoid a formal lawsuit and legal costs and submit their rival claims to communal arbitration which both swore to abide by. The arbitrators were three "honourable men" of the community: Joseph Cohen, a leading figure in the Barbary trade and someone familiar with both Abraham and Michael, a Matthias Aboab, and Doctor Jacob Bueno (d. 1661), a physician active in organizing the community's poor relief, trained at Salamanca and a relative of the Ephraim Bueno whose portrait—hanging today in the New York Metropolitan Museum—Rembrandt painted in 1647.[108] Jacob Bueno, one of two prominent community figures to whom Menasseh dedicated his *Thesouro dos denim* [Treasury of the Laws] (1647) for communal use, may have been the Spinoza family's regular physician. Although it remains unclear exactly what the dispute was about, it certainly concerned Abraham's legacy and the North Africa trade and, for the next two months Michael and Jacob laid their rival "questions, differences and pretensions" regarding Abraham d'Espinoza's estate with relevant documents before these three arbitrators, conferring with them until a final settlement was drawn up by the same notary, on 21 March 1639.[109]

Under this settlement which both accepted, Michael, who had obviously been understating Abraham's assets in some fashion, agreed to pay Jacob a further 640 guilders, in exchange for which Jacob abandoned all outstanding credits, sums owed, and subsequent returns to Michael and his heirs forever. The dispute almost certainly means Michael had been deliberately ungenerous and grasping towards his cousin, Spinoza's uncle, raising the possibility that the fraught tensions within the Spinoza family in Amsterdam during Spinoza's boyhood and adolescence— which were not limited to the dispute between Michael and Jacob—stemmed from Michael being mean-minded and grasping also in other respects. It must have raised eyebrows within the wider family that at the funeral of his first wife, Jacob's sister, Rachel, in 1627, Michael donated to the synagogue as his *promesa* in her memory the staggeringly slender sum of one guilder (suggesting their marriage was not a close one),[110] and certainly there were other occasions when Michael stood accused of stinginess in financial dealings as with the complaints against him, lodged in 1652 by a Dutch skipper and the owners of the ship he captained, concerning the insulting treatment he and his crew received from Michael's agents in Rouen and Le Havre.[111]

Meanwhile, Spinoza obviously spent much of his time buried in books. Whether or not he was fond of his stepmother, Esther, Michael's third wife, it was she who raised him from before his ninth birthday onwards. Michael's third

---

[108] Cohen, *Spinoza en het geneeskunde*, 46; Hes, *Jewish Physicians*, 90.
[109] Vaz Dias and Van der Tak, *Spinoza Mercator*, 20; Freudenthal/Walther, *Lebensgeschichte* i, 224–6; Frampton, *Spinoza and the Rise*, 126–7.
[110] *Livro de Bet Haim*, 65.   [111] Freudenthal/Walther, *Lebensgeschichte* i, 234–6.

marriage, however, remained childless, as had his first marriage, so there was no occasion for Spinoza, his older brother Isaac, or younger brother Gabriel (born in the mid-1630s), nor older sister Miriam, or younger sister Ribca (Rebecca), born last of the five, to feel the usual jealousy and rivalry of half-siblings for subsequent offspring of their father and stepmother. Nor did they suffer at all from their father's legacy being divided via their stepmother's will between two otherwise largely unconnected families: for when she died, Spinoza's stepmother simply left all her possessions, without restriction, to Michael.

Yet, there is reason to believe Spinoza's own mother's legacy, from her dowry, to her children was not registered and respected as it should have been either in or after 1638, but rather, as Spinoza claimed later, in his dealing with the civic law courts in 1655–6, that his father had simply absorbed Hannah Deborah's dowry and possessions improperly into his trading capital, without leaving any safeguard for her children. This may have been a ground of a longstanding grudge harboured by Spinoza against his father. While losing one's mother early on must, from the outset, have manifold effects on a young boy, in Spinoza's case there were particular features of his mother's life and family, and her loss, he could not have appreciated until approaching adulthood, and that may have subsequently deepened his sense of loss and grievance. For Michael's marriage to Hannah Deborah presumably brought Spinoza's father greater wealth, in the shape of her dowry, than he himself possessed previously, a likelihood that poses a question of some significance in Spinoza's life-story.

Spinoza's unremitting bookishness, cultivating his Hebrew and learning more about Jewish religious tradition would not have been too much of a problem initially, around the time of his *bar mitzvah*, in November 1645 and subsequently, even assuming Spinoza was already earmarked for a life of business. Van de Ven suggests that he may well have started work in the family firm soon after his *bar mitzvah* as early as 1645 or 1646; Nadler thinks it more likely he attended first level of the *yeshivah* and remained a full-time student until 1648.[112] In any case, his older brother, Isaac, was then his father's obvious successor as head of the family firm and participant in synagogue affairs, so even if Spinoza did cease formal schooling as early as 1646, or soon after, between the ages of fourteen and seventeen, his father's business as yet had no very pressing need of him. To an extent, he remained free to follow his own course as he liked. But when Isaac died, on 24 September 1649 [18 Tishrei 5410] (according to his gravestone), at eighteen, the situation changed completely. Spinoza, now nearing seventeen, must suddenly have come under intense pressure, being now himself prospective "cabeza de casa," as the community records term the head of each household. At this point, he was assuredly badgered into setting his books aside and spending his days

---

[112] Van de Ven, *Documenting Spinoza*, ch. 3.

supporting his father's far-ranging business dealings, translating documents, interpreting, and in transactions with non-Jewish retailers, grocers, skippers, and the like. For it is certain, as we have seen, that Michael, having grown up in France, possessed only very poor spoken Dutch and needed practically everything said or written in Dutch translated and explained to him.[113]

In June 1650, Samuel de Caceres and Spinoza's sister Miriam celebrated their wedding, with Spinoza doubtless present alongside his father and the rest of the family, and with Mortera and Menasseh (who were both close to the bridegroom) also present. Michael's appearance at the time was described by a Portuguese youth who, after reverting to Judaism in Amsterdam, and having second thoughts, had recently reverted to Catholicism in Portugal and provided the Lisbon Inquisition with details concerning several prominent "Judaizing heretics" baptized at birth as Catholics he had encountered while living in the home of Jeronimo Nunes da Costa (Moseh Curiel). Michael d'Espinoza he styled a baptized "merchant born in this city [Lisbon] short in stature, fat, with a white face and forty-five years of age,"[114] referring presumably to when he first met him, around 1639, a rough estimate that in fact considerably underestimated his age.

De Caceres, with no parents alive, worked, we have seen, for the *parnasim* and rabbis as a *sopher* skilled in Hebrew calligraphy, drawing up marriage contracts, copying sermons and documents, composing letters in Hebrew to be sent abroad, and translating Hebrew terms and records. He also looked after the community's collection of books and manuscripts,[115] and for a small additional salary, stood in as assistant rabbi to Menasseh. On marrying into the Spinoza family, aged twenty-two, he was still studying, having opted for a full rabbinic career. Being the publicly designated scholar of the family, there was scant likelihood that he would be of any help to Michael in his business dealings, or serve to deflect any of the pressure Spinoza now came under. Rather, as the family's recognized scholar Samuel was bound to intensify that pressure. Over time, Samuel proved a true disciple of the Amsterdam rabbis and instrument of their authority.[116] As husband of Michael's eldest daughter, and as the family's rabbinic scholar, De Caceres was entitled to rights of precedence within the family in the sphere of learning and as their religious authority, especially regarding interpretation of disputed points, while doubly ensuring that all practicalities and business affairs were firmly shunted onto Spinoza.

In 1651, Miriam d'Espinoza and Samuel de Caceres, the newly married couple, had a son whom they named Daniel after Samuel's Portuguese grandfather. Miriam, however, died at the age of twenty-one during, or soon after her child's

---

[113] Van der Tak, "Spinoza's Payments," 194–5.
[114] Révah, *Des Marranes à Spinoza*, 176–7; Nadler, Tielen, and Tiribás, "Two New Documents," 811.
[115] Pieterse, *Levi de Barrios als geschiedschrijver*, 151; Saperstein, *Exile in Amsterdam*, 10.
[116] Pieterse, *Levi de Barrios als geschiedschrijver*, 58–9, 102, 151.

birth, according to her gravestone on 6 September 1651 [20 Elul 5411], a mere fifteen months after their wedding.[117] In accord with accepted Jewish practice in such instances, Samuel then married Miriam's (and Spinoza's) younger sister, Ribca [Rebecca], by whom Spinoza's rabbinical (double) brother-in-law afterwards had three other children: Hanna, named after Ribca's and Spinoza's mother; Michael named after their father; and Benjamin. This made De Caceres more firmly than ever titular religious and intellectual head of the family.

One wonders whether around 1650 there was already some sort of rivalry, including doctrinal disagreements about how to interpret Torah passages and Jewish Law between Spinoza and his newly acquired brother-in-law, the rising star of the *yeshivah*. There certainly must have been later due to the great scandal Spinoza provoked in 1655–6. Intriguingly, and surely significantly, when Mortera died, four years after Spinoza's excommunication, Samuel, who was considered an excellent sermonizer, delivered the main eulogy at his funeral at Ouderkerk, on 4 February 1660, employing a familiar metaphor designating Mortera a chastising "fire" consuming heresy. Samuel answered his own rhetorical question on that occasion, "when does fire break out" to consume heresy, by replying "when thorns [espinos] are found nearby."[118] The use of "thorns" as a way of alluding to Spinoza without naming him to Sephardic audiences, in conformity with the *herem*, was destined to recur in striking fashion again and again.

When Samuel himself then died, later in 1660, not long after his sermon at Mortera's funeral, Rebecca found herself left to raise four children on her own.[119] Whatever she thought of her now disgraced and ousted brother and his abilities as a businessman, and his relations with her father and husband, she can hardly have been pleased by his failure, a few years before, to salvage the family firm during 1654–5, after Michael's death. By the time of Spinoza's excommunication there was not much "honour and wealth" for any of the family members to enjoy. Spinoza's youngest nephew, Benjamin de Caceres, like his uncle Gabriel, Spinoza's younger brother, and Rebecca herself eventually migrated to the Caribbean. Benjamin was among the Sephardic Jews afterwards expelled from Martinique by Louis XIV, in 1684–5, following which he, like Rebecca, settled on Curaçao.[120] After his death, what remained of Spinoza's family all eventually migrated across the Atlantic to the Caribbean.

To satisfy his thirst for knowledge and escape from the pressures at home and around the synagogue, after finishing his formal schooling, the young Spinoza of the years 1649–55 needed an alternative route other than the communal *yeshivah* and there were in fact other openings for discussion and higher study available in

---

[117] Freudenthal/Walther, *Lebensgeschichte* i, 198.
[118] Emmanuel, *Precious Stones*, 19; Saperstein, *Exile in Amsterdam*, 9–10; Gullan-Whur, *Life of Spinoza*, 48.
[119] Vaz Dias and Van der Tak, *Spinoza Mercator*, 22; Nadler, *Spinoza: A Life*, 98–9.
[120] Emmanuel, "Juifs de la Martinique," 515–16.

Amsterdam. Not the least of these was the city-maintained Athenaeum Illustre, a higher education institution inaugurated—despite the efforts of Leiden University via the States of Holland to prevent it—with a lecture by the great scholar Gerardus Vossius (1577–1649), in January 1632, nine months before Spinoza's birth. Because the college was "Remonstrant" in origin without allegiance to the Reformed Church, it was not authorized to confer academic degrees. It served as a kind of high-level preparatory school for those planning to enrol at university and was thus valued as a training ground for budding young scholars from non-Reformed backgrounds entering the world of higher studies. Linked to the Remonstrant community, the Athenaeum exuded a discreetly oppositional attitude to the public Church which would have suited Spinoza well enough.

No record of the students was kept in the seventeenth century, and practically nothing is known about its students, so there is no way of knowing to what extent Spinoza did attend lectures there, if at all. But it seems likely that he did, even probable, given that it was situated close to where he lived; and while this supposition is pure conjecture it is strengthened by the fact that Menasseh organized much of his bridging effort to generate Jewish dialogue with Christian non-Calvinists, especially Remonstrants and Collegiants, in large part through debates at the Athenaeum.[121] Lectures there were in Latin, a language Spinoza was probably already studying before his brother's death, in 1649. Menasseh had long had contacts at the Athenaeum and was especially friendly with Vossius and his elder son (who did translation work from Hebrew into Latin for Menasseh but died young from smallpox), which suggests intellectually adventurous Sephardic youths may have been drawn to the advantages of studying there, especially when interested in ancient history, philology, philosophy, mathematics, and natural science. Later in life, Spinoza and Vossius' younger son, Isaac, knew each other and were virtually neighbours in Voorburg for some years.

Due to its generally anti-Calvinist and anti-Aristotelian attitude, the Athenaeum had from early on been teaching Galileo's heliocentric astronomy, of which Vossius was a bold defender. The school's first professor of mathematics and astronomy, Martinus Hortensius (1607–39), was bolder still and an admirer of Descartes. In fact, Hortensius made the Amsterdam of the 1630s the northern focus of European discussion of Galileo's thesis and methodology.[122] After Vossius' death, in 1647, the teacher at the Athenaeum most likely to seize Spinoza's attention was Alexander de Bie (1623–90) who began teaching there in 1653, lecturing, unusually, but usefully for those just getting started in Latin, in Dutch as well as Latin. Though reluctant fully to embrace Copernican astronomy, and ambivalent on the subject of comets, De Bie was an enthusiast for physics demonstrations and experiments, and highly regarded by the Republic's leading

---

[121] Israel, *Dutch Republic*, 474, 483; Nadler, *Menasseh ben Israel*, 83–9.
[122] Vermij, *Calvinist Copernicans*, 32, 40, 112, 126–7; Van Miert, *Humanism*, 57–8, 247, 250–3.

scientist, Christian Huygens. De Bie also taught philosophy and linked philosophy to mathematics and physics. To cap his appeal, from Spinoza's perspective, De Bie was a specialist in "oriental [i.e. Near Eastern] languages," especially Hebrew and Arabic.[123]

Admittedly, Remonstrant (and Cartesian) influence at the Athenaeum Illustre of Amsterdam waned somewhat in the 1650s, and the general tone grew more conservative and Calvinist. But there was still much to interest a budding young philosopher like Spinoza. If in the early 1650s, the Athenaeum's philosophy courses were not especially hostile to Aristotelianism or hospitable to Cartesianism, its teaching schedule was characterized, unlike the situation later, after 1664, by an unusually heavy stress on coupling physics with philosophy.[124] With its daily lectures (De Bie's regularly beginning reportedly at eight in the morning), the Athenaeum Illustre of the 1650s provided a unique window on the world of seventeenth-century humanistic learning coupled with up-to-date mathematics and physics including optics and geography. De Bie, moreover, developed a particular interest in optics and the anatomy and workings of the human eye, a subject to which Spinoza became strongly attracted at some point in the 1650s as he pursued his studies.

By the early 1650s, in any case, friction between Spinoza and his brother-in-law was unavoidable and tension between him and his father and sisters hard to avoid. For these reasons, despite lack of direct supporting evidence apart from the details revealed about Spinoza's mother's legacy by the court case in 1655 (to be discussed further on), it is important to ponder seriously—diverging here from Nadler who considers the claim "most unlikely"—the remarkable statement of the Kiel University professor Sebastian Kortholt (1675–1760), about this, admittedly made late in the day, in 1700, but based on a conversation (of around 1697) with Spinoza's former landlord and landlady, the Van der Spijcks, and hence derived from first-hand evidence. Kortholt, moreover, spoke also with others he met in Holland who had known Spinoza personally. "According to their testimony," asserts Kortholt, already "as a boy [Spinoza] awakened in his father hatred for him because, though destined to be a merchant, he dedicated himself wholly to studying."[125] Arguably, this conclusion eminently fits the facts as we have them. Michael d'Espinoza in the late 1640s was a strong personality who had secured wealth, respect, and status but now faced a major problem: alienated from his nephew Jacob, following the demise of his eldest son, Isaac, and his daughter's marriage to a scholarly rabbinic student—he urgently needed full-time assistance from competent relatives with his complex business and legal transactions and,

---

[123] Van Miert, *Humanism*, 214, 255–6, 291; Vermij, *Calvinist Copernicans*, 125–6, 182, 185.
[124] Van Miert, *Humanism*, 222–4, 332; Strazzoni, *Burchard de Volder*, 14–15.
[125] Kortholt, "Preface," 74–5; Nadler, *Spinoza: A Life*, 70; Kortholt's view was echoed later by Diez in his notable biography of Spinoza of 1783, Diez, *Benedikt von Spinoza*, 4–5.

consequently, must have looked chiefly to his highly intelligent second son, Bento, for vigorous undivided full-time support. Taking all facts into consideration, including Spinoza's later sense of grievance through never receiving his mother's legacy allotted to him and his siblings but diverted by his father into the general pool of the family business,[126] this thesis of Kortholt's seems far from "unlikely."

---

[126] Vlessing, "Excommunication" (2002), 146; Van de Ven, "Spinoza's Life and Time," 11.

7

Honour and Wealth

7.i Son of a Merchant

From September (Tishrei) of the Hebrew year 5410 (1649) to September 1650, "Michael de spinose," as he appears in the register of community's *parnasim*, served as *parnas* of the, since 1639, united community of the three former congregations. To be a *parnas*, that is "elder" or *sustentador* as De Barrios terms it in Spanish, of the united Sephardic congregation now amounting to some 2,000 persons, placed Michael firmly among the community's governing elite. Merged after negotiation between the three communities' fifteen elders under forty-two articles of unification, signed by all the community's "cabezas de familia [heads of family]," including Michael, the new synagogue bore the name Talmud Torah.[1] At the peak of his commercial success, Spinoza's father was now, from every standpoint, an honoured leading figure among that stratum, and there is no reason to suppose the intellectually precocious Latin-studying Spinoza was unappreciative of the high status and affluence his father had obtained for his family. No one could then know that in the not too distant future this elevated status would rapidly melt away.

Menasseh dedicated the Spanish version of his *The Hope of Israel*, entitled *Mikveh Israel. Esto es, Esperança de Israel*, published in the Jewish year 5410 [1650], to the seven "very noble, very wise and very eminent" *parnasim* in office that year, the third in his list being "Michael Espinoza." Calling himself a "theologo y philosopho Hebreo" [Jewish theologian and philosopher], and sharing something of Vieira's euphoric fervour, his aim in writing *Mikveh Israel*, Menasseh explains in the dedication, was to reveal that "this hope that sustains us, that of the advent of the Messiah, is an expectation of happiness to come," recent developments in the Americas in his view proving this hope was soon to be fulfilled.[2] Spinoza kept a copy of this text, which for him probably carried some lingering baggage of youthful memories and nostalgia, in his personal library down to his death.[3] The English version, published the following year, was dedicated to England's Parliament.

---

[1] GA Amsterdam PA 334/1323 "Registro dos parnasim," 5; Pieterse, *Levi de Barrios als geschiedschrijver*, 71–2, 165–6.
[2] Menasseh ben Israel, *Mikveh Israel*, 61–2.
[3] Servaas van Rooijen, *Inventaire*, 684; Offenberg, "Spinoza's Library," 320; Proietti, "Spinoza et le 'Conciliador'," 50.

During the last year Michael served as *parnas* of the united community, 1649–50, he lost his eldest son, Isaac, his principal helper, heir, and support. Nothing is known as to the cause of his untimely death. At that moment, Spinoza had no option but to take Isaac's vacant place as Michael's designated principal heir and future "head of the household" and family firm with its convoluted web of connections in France, Portugal, Spain, Morocco, Brazil, and the Canaries and close ties with rabbis and community governance. Pressure to push his books aside mounted. While still intensely conscious that all things commonly valued by mankind in life are "vana et futilia" [vain and futile], pondering his personal dilemma and its implications for his adult life, he continued turning over and over in his mind, as he did continuously in the years before breaking with the community, "the advantages acquired through honour and wealth from which I would be excluding myself if I sought to devote myself seriously to something different and new." In the autobiographical passage at the outset of *On the Emendation of the Understanding*, he is clearly referring to the "advantages" arising from the substantial prestige, wealth, and status accruing over decades, reaching back to Abraham d'Espinoza and Duarte Fernandes, that he himself, following in his father's tracks, was directly heir to. Accordingly, he continued debating within himself, Spinoza explains, whether it might be possible to pursue his urgent quest for truth and the scholarly life "without changing the outward order and form of my everyday existence which I often sought to do but *frustra* [in vain]."[4] Given this prolonged irresolution, his inability during the early and mid-1650s to resolve his basic life course dilemma, the timing of his final break with the community, in late 1655, was arguably more a consequence of the drastic change in family circumstances soon to occur, suddenly forcing him to accept that honour and wealth were lost in any case, than any unprompted final resolution of his long inner wrestling with his basic predicament.

The late 1640s were a time of rapid growth in the Amsterdam Sephardic community's size and resources due chiefly to the sudden expansion of Dutch trade with Southern Europe at the close of the Eighty Years War (1568–1648), especially from 1647 when Spain's embargoes were finally lifted, the Dunkirk Flemish privateering campaign against Dutch shipping ended, and the ensuing sudden lowering of marine freight and insurance rates markedly boosted Dutch competitiveness vis-à-vis their competitors, all coinciding with a massive fresh influx of New Christians fleeing Spain. The total of registered Sephardic accounts at the Amsterdam Exchange Bank, a key indicator of the shifting dynamics of Sephardic economic status, we have seen, shot up mirroring the jump in the community's fortunes. After resumption of the war with Spain, in 1621 (following the Twelve Years Truce), the number of Sephardic accounts fell from 114, in 1620,

---

[4] Spinoza, *Opera* ii, 5; Israel, "Philosophy, Commerce," 126.

to just 76, or 5 per cent of the total by 1625, and still languished well short of the level attained in 1620, in the early 1640s; but from the mid-1640s to 1651, around the time of the Spinoza firm's peak year, the total far outstripped earlier levels, reaching an impressive 197, or 10.5 per cent of the 1,875 registered accountholders.[5]

During the late 1640s, and through the 1650s, Amsterdam's Jewish community was bolstered also by an influx of Ashkenazic refugees from Eastern Europe due to the Chmielnicki massacres in the Ukraine and Poland. By 1650 the total Jewish population in the city reached approximately 2,500, with around 1,600 to 2,000 of these Sephardim.[6] By the time Spinoza assumed direction of the "Espinoza" family firm in early 1654, or, more likely, given his father's sickness, in part already earlier, the Jews had become a prominent, even highly conspicuous element in the city's day-to-day business life. "The Burse or Exchange" (Figure 7.1), reported John Ray, an English traveller, in 1663, was a place where "merchants of all nations resort [...] but of all Strangers, the Jews are the most numerous, who

Figure 7.1 *The Amsterdam Exchange in 1612* by Claes Jansz Visscher. Reproduction courtesy of Amsterdam City Archives.

---

[5] Van Dillen, "Vreemdelingen"; Israel, *Dutch Republic and the Hispanic World*, 336–47; Israel, *Empires and Entrepots*, 422; Israel, *Conflicts of Empires*, 307–16.
[6] Nusteling, "Jews in the Republic," 58–9.

fill one walk." In Amsterdam, a city which "allowed the free and open exercise of their religious worship," they live "together in one quarter of the city, and [...] are in better condition and richer than in most places where they are tolerated. They are for the most part of a dark or tawny complexion and have black hair,"[7] a physical profile, contemporaries confirm, fitting Spinoza exactly.

The boom in Western Sephardic commerce produced a spectacular trebling of the Amsterdam Portuguese community's revenue from its *imposta* tax on members' commerce between 1640 and 1650, commencing with the recovery of trade with Portugal following Portugal's secession which removed Spain's embargo on that trade-route in 1640, and received its biggest boost from the final peace between Spain and the Dutch, signed at Munster, in Westphalia, on 30 January 1648, ratified by the States General on 5 June, an event celebrated throughout most of the United Provinces (but resisted by Zeeland and Leiden).[8] Three months later, in October, the cornerstone was laid for the new Amsterdam town hall, planned to be the most magnificent in Northern Europe, a resplendent symbol of peace and prosperity under the city's burgomasters and regents.[9] From 1647, with restoration of direct seaborne trade links with Spain and removal of the main risks to passage through the Straits to and from the Mediterranean, Amsterdam Sephardic commerce with the Iberian world and Mediterranean burgeoned so splendidly that Spain's first resident envoy in Holland, the Burgundian nobleman Antoine Brun (1599–1654), after arriving at The Hague in 1649, found himself spending much of his time wrangling with the Amsterdam city government over Spain's mounting concerns regarding the expanding role and penetration of Holland's Sephardic Jews.

One difficulty was that nothing whatever was expressly stated about the Jews in the Dutch–Spanish peace treaty's terms which, the States General insisted, covered all their subjects, native born or immigrant, ensuring Dutch Jews the right to conduct commerce freely in Spain's (European) ports. Dutch Jews could now conduct trade with merchants in Spain legally and directly, accepted the Spanish crown, but remained forbidden, under the expulsion of 1492, to set foot in the country. Nor in the case of those baptized were they exempt from confiscation of property ensuing from religious offences committed in Iberia before (or after) their exit, leaving their goods and cargoes at risk of confiscation by the Inquisition. Jews trading with Spain from Holland had to remain physically outside Spain, negotiating through middlemen, "factors" either Protestant or Catholic, while the former New Christians among them that had fled Iberia had to continue plying their overseas trade using their accustomed web of pseudonyms and aliases about

---

[7] Ray, *Observations topographical*, 41; Kaplan, "Amsterdam's Jewry," 265–7.
[8] Israel, *Dutch Primacy*, 197–213; Israel, *Empires and Entrepots*, 204–12; for the *imposta* figures, see Vlessing "Portuguese-Jewish Merchant Community," 228, 230.
[9] Dapper, *Historische Beschryving*, 328, 331–2.

which every Amsterdam Sephardic businessman in the 1650s, Spinoza included, possessed detailed knowledge.[10]

During the years Spinoza was a merchant, Dutch Sephardic merchants' attention remained firmly focused on metropolitan Portugal, Spain, and the Mediterranean. After Brun formally presented to the States General in The Hague Philip IV's refusal to permit Jews to enter or reside on Spanish territory (including the Spanish Netherlands and Spain's possessions in Italy), the States sent several delegates to remonstrate. The king's response Holland's regents declared a contravention of the peace treaty the terms of which covered *all* the Republic's resident citizens. The pensionary (town secretary) of Amsterdam spoke vigorously "in favour of the said Jews," reported Brun to Madrid, "saying Christendom owed them much for having been loyal guardians of the Sacred Scriptures, that to think of doing away with all that nation was against the will of God who announced through his Prophets that the remnants of that people would one day convert [to Christianity] at the end of time," that the Amsterdam, Rotterdam, and other city governments received them, dealt with them as their own subjects, and got on well with them, and that the Pope himself who is head of the Catholics and the Holy Roman Emperor admit them to their lands.[11] Every sovereign knows what is best for his own subjects, retorted Brun: the practices of one land differ from those of another "due to different considerations that apply to each in particular." Philip afterwards retreated marginally, permitting Dutch Jews forced to put into Spanish ports by storms or mishaps off the coasts of Spain, Naples, and Sicily to land, retrieve assets, and leave undisturbed, provided they had never been "baptized Christians or my subjects."[12]

Expansion of Dutch overseas commerce during the late 1640s, meanwhile, provoked bitter jealousy in England where London merchants found themselves largely ousted from their 1621–47 ascendancy over maritime trade with Southern Europe, much as they had already lost their primacy since 1640 over the Portugal trade. If Amsterdam Jews bitterly resented the 1645 Portuguese planters' revolt in Dutch Brazil, and the support the revolt received from the Portuguese crown, deeming this a breach of the 1641 Dutch–Portuguese treaty,[13] the losses there amounted to considerably less than the gains accruing from the boom following the lifting of Spain's remaining embargoes, in 1647, and the fully reopened Dutch–Portuguese trade in Europe. Fighting for independence from Spain and desperate to avoid full-scale war with the Republic, the Portuguese crown remained careful, despite the escalating conflict in Brazil, not to obstruct Dutch trade with

---

[10] Israel, *Dutch Republic and the Hispanic World*, 423–5; Kaplan, "Amsterdam, the Forbidden Lands," 53; Herrero Sánchez, *Acercamiento hispano-neerlandés*, 136.
[11] AGS Libros de La Haya 32, fos. 118–19. Brun to Philip IV, The Hague, 30 Sept. 1650.
[12] AGS Libros de La Haya 32, fo. 185. Philip IV to Brun, Madrid, 2 Dec. 1650; Israel, *Dutch Republic and the Hispanic World*, 424–6; Herrero Sánchez, *Acercamiento hispano-neerlandés*, 102, 136.
[13] *Correspondência diplomática de Francisco de Sousa Coutinho* i, 308.

metropolitan Portugal. In fact, the Portuguese ambassador in The Hague showed considerable nervousness about Amsterdam's obviously formidable leverage with the States, and consequently also about the leverage local Sephardim enjoyed with the Amsterdam city government.[14]

Michael d'Espinoza's rapid enrichment and success as a merchant during the 1640s, signing commercial transactions in a firm and confident hand "Michael despinoza," reflects the growing confidence of the Amsterdam Sephardic merchant community generally at the time. His surviving freight contracts reveal a continued focus on Portugal, the Canaries, and also Morocco, the one Old World country with which the Amsterdam Sephardim significantly expanded their trade during the years of the Spanish trade embargoes, mostly avoiding direct connections with mainland Spain. From Portugal, Michael imported chiefly sugar, olive oil, figs, and almonds. A month after the celebrations marking the Peace of Munster, in July 1648, Michael de Espinoza freighted a vessel to ship cargo to Faro in the Algarve, and then, at Vila Nova, on the Atlantic side, take on an entire shipload of the best figs for the Amsterdam market.[15]

However, the evidence of Michael d'Espinoza's account in the Amsterdam Exchange Bank from 1641 to 1651, from when Spinoza was nine until he was nineteen, proves the Spinoza firm was not just exporting to and importing from Portugal, the Canaries, and Morocco by sea, but also involved in indirect dealings in Spain. Altogether, during the year 1651–2 alone, the Amsterdam Exchange Bank records show, Michael conducted transactions with at least thirty-seven different businessmen, of whom twenty-six, or around two-thirds, were Sephardim.[16] While importing wine, Brazil sugar, and illicitly transported American products, including silver from the Spanish Indies, via the Canaries, Michael collaborated also with other prominent Amsterdam Sephardic merchants such as Juan and Elias de Paz, Lopo Ramirez, Abraham and Isaac Pereyra (alias Francisco and Antonio da Gurre also Gerardo and Carlos van Naarden) plying a swelling undercover trade with key Portuguese New Christian merchants in Madrid and Seville and with Fernando Álvarez and Antonio Correa de Mesquita (alias Hendrik and Roberto Van der Sterre) who imported wool from central Castile via Bilbao and Santander. Michael thus engaged in a range of commercial and financial operations involving Spanish and Mediterranean goods besides products specific to Portugal and Brazil,[17] sometimes collaborating with little-known merchants of the Sephardic community like a certain Isaac Montalto with whom, in August 1642, he jointly freighted a vessel to sail with goods to

---

[14] *Correspondência diplomática de Francisco de Sousa Coutinho* ii 313–14 and iii, 101, 380.
[15] GA Amsterdam NA 1531, fo. 45. Deed, 30 July 1648; Israel, *Dutch Republic and the Hispanic World*, 374.
[16] Bruyn Kops, *A Spirited Exchange*, 284.
[17] Vaz Dias and Van der Tak, "Spinoza Merchant," 146–7; Israel, "Spain and the Dutch Sephardim," 58–9.

Tetuán in Morocco from where it was instructed to load with cargo including West African gold and Spanish American silver, and proceed on to Livorno.[18]

The Canaries, even more than Madeira and the Azores, had served since the early days of the Brazil sugar trade as a prime stopover point en route from Western Europe to Brazil. Canarian winegrowers chiefly cultivated the Malvasia grape, the same type used to produce sherry wines in the Jerez region of Andalusia and the sweet, syrupy Málaga wine fashionable in the seventeenth century, Andalusian wines well adapted, like those of Madeira, to long-distance transportation to the Portuguese and Spanish Indies. The Canaries mattered greatly owing to the convenience of their geographical position in the Atlantic, the suitability of their harbours, and because Canary wines sold splendidly in Brazil.[19] They proved popular also in England.[20] By 1642, Spinoza's father was already shipping "Spaensche wijnen," that is either Canariote or Málaga wines, to Dutch Brazil.[21] But the Spanish embargoes had an effect even in the Canaries and their lifting in 1647 rendered Dutch participation in the Canaries traffic easier than before.[22]

Michael was not then entering a new traffic when, in November 1648, at the Amsterdam offices of the notary Volckertsz Oli, together with Manuel and Affonso de Tovar—relatives of his wife, Esther, Spinoza's stepmother—who maintained regular dealings with the islands, he signed documents freighting a Dutch vessel to sail with cargo on behalf of all three to the Canaries.[23] Much of the wine and French linens Amsterdam Sephardic merchants shipped to Brazil via the Canaries was afterwards sent on to Buenos Aires, Tucumán, and Potosí, in the heart of the Spanish Indies. In November 1651, Spinoza's father chartered and loaded a ship called the *Eendracht* to sail for Tenerife and anchor there for seven weeks; it was instructed to load with a mixed cargo, officially registering its return load as consisting of local products, doubtless mainly Canariote wine, but presumably including unregistered silver and valuables received from the New World.[24]

While the Spinoza family prospered between 1640 and 1651, like much of the rest of Amsterdam Sephardic community, at the same time the community's poor relief burden rose steeply due to the rise in numbers of destitute Portuguese New Christians arriving from the Iberian peninsula either direct or via France or Italy, and the added burden of refugees from devastated Dutch Brazil, many of whom returned to Holland in distress right through the decade 1645-54, during which the Dutch position in northern Brazil steadily crumbled. Mortera accounted it yet

---

[18] GA Amsterdam NA 1527, p. 128, deed, 25 Aug. 1642 (J. V. Oli).
[19] Israel, *Diasporas*, 269-70.   [20] Israel, *Diasporas*, 278; Strum, *Sugar Trade*, 250, 301, 307.
[21] GA Amsterdam NA 1502 (J. V. Oli), fo. 100, deed, 9 Dec. 1642.
[22] Israel, *Diasporas*, 275; Herrero Sánchez, *Acercamiento hispano-neerlandés*, 135; Strum, *Sugar Trade*, 289, 315; Santana Pérez, "Holandeses y la utilización," 336.
[23] GA Amsterdam NA 1532, fo. 135. Deed, 7 Nov. 1648 (J. V. Oli); Israel, *Diasporas*, 275.
[24] Israel, "Further Data," 16; Israel, *Diasporas*, 279; Santana Pérez, "Holandeses y la utilización," 340-1.

another miracle performed by the Lord on behalf of his people, the Jews, when the last batches of those stranded in Brazil arrived back safely in Holland;[25] but the added burden of poor relief, expanded schooling, and other costs, was formidable. Also urgently requiring charitable assistance was the influx of Ashkenazic refugees from the Chmielnicki massacres in the Ukraine. The community's main source of revenue were its compulsory communal taxes, the *imposta*, a tax levied mainly on overseas trade reflecting the vicissitudes of the country's maritime economy, and the *finta* tax on registered assessed wealth above a certain level. The *finta* on assessed wealth could remain relatively low, imposing no great burden, as long as the *imposta* remained buoyant; but when the *imposta* slumped due to overseas commerce being cut back, as happened suddenly prior to the onset of the First Anglo-Dutch War (1652–4), sharply reversing the previous twelve years of expansion, the *finta* had to rise swiftly and substantially to compensate.[26]

7.ii The First Anglo-Dutch War (1652–1654)

Anglo-Dutch relations plummeted from the late 1640s, well before the outbreak of war, principally for commercial reasons. England's bitter resentment over its stark loss of overseas trade to the Dutch with their larger stock of shipping, lower freight rates, and better ties to Iberian and Ibero-American markets, resulted, from 1650 onwards, in English privateers and Parliamentary naval vessels seizing Dutch merchant vessels on the high seas on a variety of pretexts. These ranged from (well-grounded) accusations that Dutch vessels were carrying munitions of war and other supplies to English royalists in Barbados and elsewhere, to shipping goods for Portuguese subjects at a time of deteriorating relations between Cromwellian England and the Portuguese crown which remained allied with England's royal house. During 1651, no less than 140 Dutch ships were forcibly intercepted by the English in the North Sea, Channel, Irish Sea, Atlantic and Caribbean and brought into English ports. The States General's protests at this English bludgeoning and "tyranny" on the high seas had scant effect.

In the summer of 1651, Michael d'Espinoza was expecting a cargo of Canaries products, perhaps also including illicitly transferred American silver, on the *De Prins*, "which vessel, during its voyage from the Canaries to these lands was taken by the English and brought to England."[27] Under deeds drawn up on 20 July 1651, Michael empowered his London agent, Antonio Fernández Carvajal (Abraham Israel Carvajal), who had imported Canary wines into England since the early

---

[25] Mortera, *Tratado Da Verdade*, 28.
[26] Swetschinski, *Reluctant Cosmopolitans*, 113, 197–8; Levie Bernfeld, "Financing Poor Relief," 72; Vlessing, "Portuguese-Jewish Merchant Community," 228.
[27] GAA NA 964 unpaginated, deed, 27 Nov. 1651 (B. Baddel).

1640s and with whom he had been dealing at least since 1644, to act for him in reclaiming that lost cargo.[28] Fernández Carvajal, a former New Christian cryptoJew active in the Canaries, now in London, was among the chief founders of England's first post-Expulsion synagogue, the Sephardic "Creechurch Synagogue," established in December 1656 a year after the famous Whitehall Conference of December 1655 summoned by Cromwell to debate Menasseh's petition for Jewish resettlement in England.

Besides the cargo lost on *De Prins*, Michael engaged Fernández Carvajal to try to reclaim either the goods or value also of two other consignments captured by the English before war was declared. One consisted of 2,821 *alqueires*, or over 30,000 litres, of Portuguese olive oil loaded in barrels and "pipes" likewise seized on the high seas en route to Holland and brought to London by Parliamentary naval vessels. Under Michael's authorization sent to London, "the said oils truly belong to him alone as real property without anyone under the crown of Portugal, or enemy of the Republic of England, having any part or portion in any way [estant que les dites huiles luy appartiennent en vraye, seule et réelle proprieté sans que personne sous la couronne du Roy de Portugal, ou ennemies de la République d'Angleterre, en aye aucune part ni portion en quelque manière]."[29] The second consignment "forty one pipes, four quarteux and twenty barrels of olive oil marked 'M.D.' [Michel Despinosa]," loaded at Aveiro on the *Fortuin*, in January 1651, had likewise been seized on its return voyage to Holland.[30]

Another thirty Dutch vessels were seized by the English in January 1652 alone.[31] During February and March 1652, the situation deteriorated so fast that the Dutch admiralty colleges imposed a halt on all shipping leaving port, detaining many ships already loaded with cargo despite reminders to the States General that the herring fleet desperately needed Portuguese salt imports. The general standstill caused a tide of protests from merchants, "many complaining of the great damage they are suffering from this."[32] In May 1652 occurred the first major clash between the two navies in the Channel. The Dutch sent yet another embassy to London in a final attempt to avoid all-out war but this, reportedly, was received with such arrogance and contempt as to provoke a strong backlash in Holland, leaving no alternative but for the two republics to fight it out in stunningly destructive sea battles in which most advantages lay with England. The total of Dutch ships lost to the English during the war contemporary reports estimate at between 1,000 and 1,700, the Amsterdam burgomasters placing the losses at around 1,200 vessels. Among the greatest man-made catastrophes in Dutch history, the largest single

---

[28] Woolf, "Foreign Trade," 44; Israel, *Diasporas*, 272, 274, 282, 288.
[29] GAA NA 967, p. 302, deed signed by Michael d'Espinoza, Amsterdam, 20 July 1651; see also Israel, "Philosophy, Commerce," 133–4.
[30] GAA NA 967, p. 302, deed, 20 July 1651.
[31] ARH SG 5899/I Dutch ambassadors to Parliament, London, 19 Jan. 1652.
[32] ARH SG 5548/i. Amsterdam Admiralty College to States General, 19 March 1652.

calamity to the Dutch trade entrepôt during its Golden Age,[33] it caused the Spinoza family a substantial share of losses.

One paralyzed sector, until recently among the most booming, was trade with the Canaries. By the early 1650s, the burgeoning Dutch traffic with Tenerife and La Palma was regarded by the Council of State in Madrid as among the most troubling loopholes in their imperial monopoly system regulating the trade of the Indies. Spain and France being still at war until 1659, the Canaries served for over a decade as a main conduit for prohibited French products, especially Normandy linens and sailcloth exported via Rouen, illicitly shipped by the Dutch, to enter mainland Spain, Spanish America, and Brazil, and for unregistered Spanish American silver, to the anger of Spanish authorities, seeping out via the Canaries to Holland, France (and Livorno). In February 1652, Spain's envoy in The Hague, Brun, formally protested at this flagrant breaching of Spanish trade regulations in the Canaries, particularly highlighting the role of Amsterdam Jews collaborating with Rouen *conversos*, committing "significant frauds and violating the terms of the Spanish-Dutch Peace to the great prejudice of His [Spanish] Majesty, sending ships laden with merchandise to the Indies without calling in Spain [first] to register the goods or paying any customs duties." To this end, they send ships, complained Brun, "direct to the Canary Islands where, under pretext of loading local products and wines they register only the said products [mentioning no illicitly shipped Indies goods], defrauding his Majesty of his revenue from all the other merchandise. At this moment, there are three vessels loaded with Rouen linens at Texel," destined for the Canaries awaiting favourable winds. The illicit goods being transferred in this instance were the property of Portuguese New Christian merchants based at Rouen working in particular with a certain "Pereyra" and his brother (Abraham and Isaac Pereyra alias Francisco and Antonio da Gurre, in Amsterdam), who had sent another brother to reside in the Canaries, and through this organization the Jews illicitly imported goods via different Canary Island ports. Several ports were being used in the Canaries, noted Brun, to conceal the scale of the traffic, two vessels at Texel being readied for Tenerife, the third along with another, at Middelburg, for La Palma (Santa Cruz de la Palma), the chief port of Gran Canaria.[34]

Before the outbreak of war in 1652, a newly introduced improved system of regulation eased the Spanish crown's problem temporarily. The Dutch, "except for some Jews who usually were those who committed the biggest frauds,"[35] seemed willing to accept the requirement of witnessed certificates issued by Spain's consul in Amsterdam confirming no illicit French or English goods figured amidst

---

[33] Aitzema, *Historie* vii, 768, 872, 900; Berchet, *Cromwell e la repubblica*, 73; Israel, *Dutch Primacy*, 210.

[34] ARH SG 704 Brun to States General, The Hague, 1 Feb. 1652; Israel, "Further Data," 14–15; Israel, *Diasporas*, 275–6; Santana Pérez, "Holandeses y la utilización," 340.

[35] AGS Estado Legajo 2091 (1657) res. Consejo de Estado, Madrid, 22 March 1657.

cargoes exported from there.[36] But mounting resistance to such checks meant the local military *capitán general* of the Canaries, Alonso Dávila, could less and less enforce it. Accused of engaging massively in fraud himself, the unpopular, despotic Dávila railed against the influx of Dutch Jews into this lucrative sphere and it was perhaps on his initiative that the Canaries Inquisition spy, or "familiar," Captain Salvador Alonso de Alvarado, visited Amsterdam several times during the 1650s.[37] When the Anglo-Dutch War ended, in 1654, the States simply refused to order the admiralty colleges to continue helping prevent export of banned French (and now also, during 1654–60, English) products to the Spanish world. Prohibition of any manufactures entering Spain and its empire on Dutch vessels the States declared "contrary to the treaty of Peace and liberty of commerce."[38]

The English were even angrier at Dutch primacy in the Canaries than the Spanish authorities. The shift in dominance of the Canaries commerce since the late 1640s was so conspicuous it counted among the reasons for England's going to war—first with the Dutch, and afterwards with Spain. Benjamin Worsley's indignant tract, *The Advocate* (1652), complained that "at Spain, Canaries, Zante, with several other places in the Streights" where the Dutch "formerly rarely laded hither [i.e. to England] one ship of goods; they now lately laded hither more than wee."[39] England made strenuous efforts to regain what was lost in the Canaries by force and intimidation, culminating, on 20 April 1657, in an attack by an English fleet under Robert Blake on Tenerife itself. Dávila had brought ashore much of the valuable cargo on board the returning Indies fleet, then anchored under the castle guns, but failed to save most of the ships from destruction.

One segment of the Dutch global trade system that remained less heavily stricken than the rest during the First Anglo-Dutch War, was the East Indies trade. VOC [Dutch East India Company] shares on the Amsterdam Exchange proved at this time an indicator less sensitive to the Dutch trading system's general ups and downs than it became later, due to the Dutch still enjoying a wide margin of naval and commercial superiority in the East Indies. Rising through the successful decade of the 1640s, reaching a level of 539 per cent of face value by April 1648, VOC shares stood at 532 in December 1651, then slumped during the war to around 400 per cent, not too severe a plunge considering the harsh conditions gripping the rest of the Amsterdam Exchange during 1654–6 (Table 7.1).

Outside the well protected sphere of the East Indies trade, the rest suffered severely. Naval defeat and English privateering depressed Dutch European trade, fisheries, and industries from the outset. The paralyzing slump adversely affected

---

[36] AGS Estado Legajo 2091 (1657). Alonso Dávila to Philip IV, Tenerife, 15 Nov. 1656.
[37] AGS Libros de la Haya 50, 19, 61, 64, 262, 369; Wolf, *Jews in the Canary Islands*, 159–76.
[38] AGS Estado Legajo 2091 (1657). Gamarra to Philip IV, The Hague, 19 Oct. 1657.
[39] Worsley, *The Advocate*, 7; Israel, *Dutch Primacy*, 204.

Table 7.1 The VOC share price on the Amsterdam Exchange 1648–59

July	1644	400	March	1653	434
April	1648	539	March	1654	400
May	1649	528	April	1654	450
Feb.	1650	537	July	1656	358/360
Dec.	1650	525	Sept.	1657	340
March	1651	530	Dec.	1657	365
Aug.	1651	530	July	1658	400
Dec.	1651	532	May	1659	348
Sept.	1652	438	Jan.	1663	445

Sources: Lister, *Life and Administration* iii, 300, 316, 318–19, 382, 387; Israel, *Dutch Primacy*, 255; Petram, *World's First Stock Exchange*, 75, 81–3, 199–200.

virtually every sphere of activity—seaborne trade, shipping, fish and grocery markets in all Dutch towns, the art market, and also the universities. "The situation of our province," wrote the Groningen professor, Maresius, to a friend, on 30 May 1652, "and sad condition of our fatherland oppresses me."[40] Despite Dutch victory in the naval battle off Livorno, in March 1653, and subsequent shutting of the English out of the Mediterranean, and comparable success, especially after Denmark–Norway entered the struggle on the Dutch side, in February 1653, shutting England temporarily also out of the Baltic, the overall impact on Dutch commerce, shipping, and industry was catastrophic.[41] Normal seaborne trade was almost completely paralyzed. Thousands of unused ships, tens of thousands of seamen desperate for work and pay, businessmen stunned by steep losses, and a rich domestic consumer market attuned to absorbing products from all over and processing them for re-export abroad, were now suddenly dislocated, starved of work, sales, and supplies. Yet, it was impossible for the internally highly dynamic, integrated Dutch domestic economy and financial system simply to cease functioning all at once.

To keep overseas trade going, some large, escorted convoys were organized by the admiralty colleges. On 16 July 1652, Michael d'Espinoza, together with another prominent merchant, Francisco Lopes d'Azevedo (Abraham Farar), appeared before Volckertsz Oli with the skipper of the *St Pieter*, an Enkhuizen galliot, a species of vessel equipped with both sails and oars suitable for hugging coasts closely and evading privateers in becalmed coastal water. Michael and his partner in this venture freighted the vessel to sail either in convoy with other ships from Texel, or alone, to the port of Vila Nova in the Algarve, and there stay for weeks until October, until able to load with figs of the most recent crop and almonds, unless the fig harvest failed, in which case the skipper should load sugar and olive oil instead. Once loaded, the *St Pieter* was to return, keeping to the

---

[40] Van Berkel, *Universiteit van het noorden*, 188.   [41] Israel, *Dutch Primacy*, 207–10.

shallows and coasts, with all speed.⁴² Long a family speciality, Michael d'Espinoza imported figs especially from Vila Nova.

During the war, Michael was not especially keen on the Dutch admiralty colleges' protective naval convoy system. Besides inevitable delays in setting out, the great drawback lay in being one of a crowd, dallying for weeks in port in Portugal, waiting for return convoys to organize which meant that on returning, whatever goods the merchant imported, having been in short supply for months, suddenly became abundant, thereby drastically narrowing profit margins. From the profitability angle, risking going it alone seemed the better option. On 1 August 1652, in the midst of the war, Michael and a trading partner, using the pseudonym "Frederic Felix," freighted another Enkhuizen galliot suited to fast movement hugging coasts, the *Oranjeboom*, to sail to Faro in the Algarve, unload there and reload two-thirds of its cargo space with the new harvest's figs, and one third with almonds, returning with all speed, without waiting for convoy, offering an extra gratuity for the skipper "if he is back first in the city here with the new figs."⁴³ Being back first meant considerable extra profit for the merchant. No doubt Michael discussed the risks and ins and outs of his wartime trade strategy with Spinoza and Gabriel, and perhaps Rebecca and Samuel. During the early 1650s, the young Spinoza must have been something of an expert on figs, almonds, olive oil, Canary wines, French linens, and Brazil sugar as well as clandestine trade practices and false aliases.

But however Dutch merchants played it, staying in port or venturing out, using convoys or not, the war spelt high risk and rocketing marine insurance rates. Either one paid heavily for marine insurance or one took the entire risk onto one's own shoulders. Even if the foe captured practically nothing, extra costs and losses from their much reduced but riskier traffic were inevitably heavy. The Spinoza family's eventual financial collapse stemmed in part from loss of business as much as actual losses of cargoes at sea which, in turn, often also meant more than just loss of the cargo itself, due to prior outlay on the exported goods still needing to be paid for. Thus, in the summer of 1651 the Dutch vessel *The Nightingale* sailed to Normandy to take on French linens, consigned by Michael's correspondent, Antonio Rodrigues de Morais, in Rouen, from where the Spinoza family firm, like Jeronimo Nunes da Costa, regularly obtained French linens for shipping to Portugal, Brazil, and the Canaries. At Lisbon, the vessel unloaded and reloaded with Brazil sugar, including ten chests, loaded by Simon Fernandes Dias for "Michael de Espinoza," in Amsterdam, but as much or more for Rodrigues de Morais, in Rouen. Sailing back, before reaching Le Havre, the vessel was seized in the Channel by *The George*, and taken to London. The result was that Michael lost his sugar but also assumed an additional debt to Rodrigues de Morais for his

---

[42] GA Amsterdam NA 1536, pp. 11–13. Deed, 16 July 1652 (J. V. Oli).
[43] GA Amsterdam NA 1536, pp. 16–17. Deed 1 Aug. 1652 (J. V. Oli).

linens. Occurring as it did before the formal outbreak of war, Michael joined a consortium of Amsterdam merchants, headed by Jeronimo (who also dealt regularly with Rodrigues de Morais),[44] in petitioning England's High Court of the Admiralty, in August 1651, probably unsuccessfully, for restitution.[45]

7.iii Spinoza Becomes Head of the Family

All cargoes seized during the war itself, from July 1652 down to April 1654 were in any case irrecoverable. The overall setback was immense. The war was certainly the prime reason for Spinoza's swift business collapse, though not all the losses suffered by him and his family at this point were due to pillaging by the English. In June 1652, the Amsterdam vessel 't Vat [The Cask], having evaded danger on its outward voyage to the Algarve, for figs and other fruit, was violently pillaged in full view of the port of Faro by Moroccan corsairs. The States General, in May 1653, wrote to the ruler of Saleh on behalf of the principal "bevrachter" (trader freighting the vessel), identified as "Michael d'Espinosa merchant of Amsterdam."[46] In September 1654, with Spinoza himself now heading the business, the Dutch consul at Saleh reported back also on an earlier interception, the plundering of *De Witte Valck* by Barbary corsairs three years before, on 30 September 1651, off Cape St Vincent, en route to the Algarve for figs and almonds; the corsairs, the consul confirmed, had released the crew but seized "diverse merchandise belonging to Michael Spinoza, Jewish merchant of Amsterdam, and among those who freighted the vessel," confirming 3,000 guilders of losses to Spinoza's business from this blow alone, enough to pay a Reformed preacher's salary for six to seven years.[47]

That scholars and businessmen are two separate breeds can hardly have been more painfully engraved on the young Spinoza's consciousness than when a curious incident occurred in the synagogue around the time of his twentieth birthday. War with England had begun, but the family's affluence and prominence to all appearances remained intact for now. On 24 November 1652, a group of distinguished scholars visited the Portuguese synagogue headed by two figures who were later to play notable roles in Spinoza's own life, Isaac Vossius (1618–89), son of Gerardus Vossius, the Athenaeum Illustre school's first rector, later a notorious freethinker as well prominent philologist and Bible critic, and the French ecclesiastic and future tutor of the Dauphin, Pierre Daniel Huet (1630–1721). The two were returning from Stockholm after a year-long study

---

[44] Israel, "An Amsterdam Jewish Merchant," 32–3.
[45] PRO London, HCA 30/495 petition of "Nicholas Joris" [i.e. Jeronimo Nunes da Costa), 14 Aug. 1651.
[46] De Castries, *Sources Inédites de l'histoire du Maroc* ser. 1, vol. v, 348–50.
[47] De Castries, *Sources Inédites de l'histoire du Maroc* ser. 1, vol. v, 311–13 and vol. vi, 99.

tour scouring libraries to examine early manuscripts and Hebraica. Destined to be one of the foremost ancient history and Bible savants of the seventeenth-century, Huet would also become one of the foremost adversaries of Spinoza's Bible research and criticism.

Vossius and Huet were escorted to the Houtgracht and the synagogue, by Menasseh. The two spent weeks in and around the synagogue premises, meeting the scholars, "conferring and discussing" and each stimulating the questions and erudition of the other. For unlike most Catholic churchmen, Huet was an indefatigable enthusiast for Hebrew and Hebrew studies as the path to better comprehending Scripture; indeed, he would later claim to "have read the Hebrew text twenty times." Son of a Huguenot convert to Catholicism, Huet was also less hostile to Protestantism than most Catholic ecclesiastics but one who, nevertheless, remained fiercely hostile to Jews and Judaism. To Menasseh personally, though, he showed no hostility, but rather, greatly valued his "long and frequent conferences with him on matters of religion" judging him "a very good man of gentle spirit, agreeable, rational, and free of the many Jewish superstitions and empty dreams of the Kabbala." Expert in Bible studies and Hebrew, Huet deemed post-biblical Jewish rabbinic scholarship infuriatingly obtuse. He deemed it crucial to Christianity's complete fulfilment to compel the obstinate Jews to acknowledge finally the meaning of their own sacred writings.[48]

Everyone in the community witnessed the group's learned, leisurely, highly animated tours around the synagogue and its outbuildings, and their weeks-long debate with the community's principal scholars (no doubt prominently including De Caceres but excluding Spinoza). Even those not directly participating must have glimpsed something of the proceedings. On one occasion, Huet and Vossius, likewise an eager orientalist much in contact with Menasseh, were escorted by the rabbi to the very front of the synagogue while a service was in progress. "Paying great attention to the ceremonies," Huet later recalled accidentally stepping on a corner of the Torah ark, causing a stir among the congregation interpreting this as "some intended gesture of disrespect to their religion" until Menasseh redeemed the situation by gently drawing the erudite future bishop's attention to his foot, securing his "modest and submissive promptness" in altering his stance and restoring calm.[49] After Amsterdam, Huet proceeded to Leiden to examine the Hebraica there, and then to Rotterdam to render homage to the statue of Erasmus, later also one of Spinoza's heroes.

Following prolonged ill health, Michael d'Espinoza died on Saturday 28 March 1654, towards the close of the war that ruined his business. This was a year and

---

[48] Huet, *Huetiana, ou Pensées diverses*, preface p. xvii; Tolmer, *Pierre-Daniel Huet*, 141; Lennon, *Plain Truth*, 2; Shelford, *Transforming the Republic of Letters*, 28; Nadler, *Rembrandt's Jews*, 109.

[49] Huet, *Huetiana, ou Pensées diverses*, 226–7; Nadler, *Menasseh ben Israel*, 156–7; Shelford, *Transforming the Republic of Letters*, 36.

five months after the death of his third wife, Esther, Spinoza's stepmother, on 24 October 1652.[50] Esther, naming Michael her sole and "universal heir" in her will, had been too weak to sign it herself, a fact attested by two reputable witnesses.[51] Already in charge of the business, in practice, for some time, Spinoza, still short of his twenty-second birthday, was now officially *yahid*, head of the family and responsible for his younger brother, Gabriel, and the firm, though not for his two sisters—Miriam, the eldest having died in childbirth, and the younger, Rebecca, being married to her rabbinic candidate husband, De Caceres. Michael's last illness meant a rapid, unavoidably burgeoning profile for Spinoza in the general religious and cultural life of the community. His father's death meant Spinoza now had to preside over numerous family and synagogue rituals as well as the family's business and tax affairs, while at the same time intellectually and ritually perennially deferring to De Caceres.

Leading the prayers at the Ouderkerk cemetery could not commence the day Michael died, as under Jewish law, preparing graves, transporting coffins, and burial itself are impermissible on the sabbath except exceptionally with special rabbinic exemption (as during the coronavirus pandemic at the Bucharest Jewish cemetery in March 2020).[52] Immediately after his father's funeral, Spinoza also had to organize and lead the special after-death Jewish rituals of mourning. On the death of a parent, the grieving offspring and their spouses and closest kin gather in the home and sit "shiva [Hebrew for seven]," that is sit together in the family home for seven days reciting memorial prayers and remembering and discussing the deceased and his or her virtues, on each day of which friends and others, presumably in this case including Mortera and Menasseh, drop by and join in the more formal prayer sessions. Given how many deaths there had been in recent years in the family, this must have been a memorably solemn and sorrowful week.

Organizing his father's funeral, after the sabbath, it presumably likewise fell to Spinoza to select the spot and the exceptionally, not to say stunningly, simple tombstone marking his father's grave, still in place at the Ouderkerk cemetery today, offering a striking contrast to those of other *parnasim* and worthies. For graves of former *parnasim* and prominent merchants were often handsomely adorned with elaborately carved emblems reflecting the deceased's high standing. John Evelyn (1620–1706), the famed gardener and diarist, then still a student, while in Holland, in August 1641, described visiting

---

[50] There has long been some confusion as to whether Spinoza's stepmother died in October 1652 or October 1653, the wrong date being given in Vaz Dias and Van der Tak, *Spinoza Merchant and Autodidact*, 182–4; Nadler, *Spinoza: A Life*, 99; Gullan-Whur, *Life of Spinoza*, 52; for the correct date, see Dujovne, *Spinoza* i, 86; Vlessing, "Excommunication" (1997), 19; Vlessing, "Excommunication" (2002), 144; Freudenthal/Walther, *Lebensgeschichte* i, 192.

[51] Vaz Dias and Van der Tak, "Spinoza Merchant and Autodidact," 183–4; Vlessing, "Excommunication" (2002), 144; Freudenthal/Walther, *Lebensgeschichte* i, 192.

[52] Freudenthal/Walther, *Lebensgeschichte* i, 200–1.

a place (without the Towne) called Over Kerk, where they [the Jews] had a spacious field assign'd them for their dead, which was full of sepulchers, and Hebrew Inscriptions, some of them very stately, of cost. In one of these Monuments, looking through a narrow crevise, where the stones were disjointed I perceived divers bookes to lye, about a corps for it seems when any learned Rabby dies [they] bury some of his Bookes with him, as I afterwards learned: of these, by the helpe of a stick that I had in my hand, I raked out divers leaves which were all written in Hebrew characters but much impair'd with age and lying.[53]

It was roughly around this time, between 1650 and 1655, that the famed landscape painter Jacob van Ruisdael (1628–82), highlighting the grandeur of several of the tombs, executed two drawings, and afterwards his two memorable paintings of the Ouderkerk cemetery. Many elaborate tombstones surrounding Spinoza's father's grave paraded Hebrew inscriptions, or, if in Portuguese or Spanish, flowery, flattering expressions stressing the deceased's venerable dignity and position. Michael's tombstone, by contrast, merely states: "G[rave] of the blessed Michael Despinoza who died on 10 Nissan of the Year 5414." Such simplicity might have been due to family funds being scarce, or aversion to the usual flowery adornments and conventional pieties; but it may also reflect something rather different—lack of closeness between Spinoza and his father.[54] It is striking too, that Spinoza's father's grave was placed at some distance (forty-seven paces) from that of his mother, Hannah Deborah (rather ironically with both Menasseh ben Israel and Saul Levi Mortera being subsequently buried between the two).

From early 1654, the family business was run by Spinoza and his younger brother, their firm henceforth legally registered in the Amsterdam notarial and other records as that of "Bento e Gabriel d'Espinosa."[55] Since Spinoza's father had suffered poor health for some years before his death, Spinoza had to step up his involvement in his father's affairs, overseas trade connections, and the problems arising from his dealings abroad, with these encroaching more and more on his daily routine well before Michael's demise, obliging him to spend much time in notaries' offices, at the Amsterdam Exchange Bank, in and around the Bourse rather than in bookshops, the town library and other tranquil locations forming his natural habitat. These increased tensions between his private inner philosophical odyssey and public profile in the business district and synagogue inevitably

---

[53] Kaplan, "Amsterdam's Jewry," 283; Hagoort, *Beth Haim in Ouderkerk*, 48, 56.
[54] Vega, *Beth Haim van Ouderkerk*, 31; Yovel, *Spinoza and Other Heretics*, 55; Rotthier, *Naakte perenboom*, 54; Nadler, *Rembrandt's Jews*, 190–1.
[55] Vaz Dias and Van der Tak, "Spinoza Merchant and Autodidact," 184–5.

meant that combining status with his intellectual quest was growing harder and harder to manage.

Like other Dutch merchants at the time, Spinoza's father had had to drastically cut back on regular overseas activity from 1651, rendering every voyage and cargo still ventured cause for stress and worry. Enough ventures ended badly to inflict lasting damage on the family's finances. Part of the problem was the growing debt to their Rouen correspondents for linens received, which explains why the heaviest debts encumbering Spinoza's capital, and blighting his and his brother's business prospects in 1654–6, were to two prominent Portuguese New Christian merchants living in Rouen, Antonio Rodrigues de Morais and Duarte Rodrigues Lamego, a relative of Jeronimo Nunes da Costa.[56]

Disintegration of the family business during 1654–5, clearly, was not primarily due to Spinoza's own failure to focus adequately on business (though possibly this was a contributing factor) but rather loss of cargoes and other setbacks due to the Anglo-Dutch conflict and deep slump, an extreme instance of the wider trend afflicting the Amsterdam community during the early and mid-1650s. Still, at the point Spinoza took over the firm it was not yet evident that the family's capital, assets, and import-export business had sunk beyond hope of recovery. Although Spinoza could not fail to realize by early 1654 that the family firm was in grave difficulties, the full seriousness of the situation only became evident sometime later.[57] For the remainder of 1654 and early 1655, he fought hard to stave off bankruptcy and save his firm's and family's honour and standing. However, by mid-1655, he and his siblings had to accept they were effectively bankrupt, and that what was left of his parents' legacy amounted only to substantial debts and formidable legal entanglements.[58] This phase of his life—the evaporation of the family's wealth and standing and effective end of his business, as well as involvement with the synagogue—coincided with a renewed spurt of confidence in his native city following the end of the war and completion of the city's magnificent new town hall (putting those of Antwerp and London in the shade) and the ceremonies of inauguration on 29 July 1655, with parades, fanfares, and militia displays in Dam Square in front of the town hall. Whatever the gloom among Spinoza's relatives, the general mood by the summer of 1655 was rapidly recovering.

Spinoza's financial collapse after succeeding his deceased father as *yahid* (the family's head and principal paying member) was reflected in his compulsory communal payments of *imposta* and *finta* during the last year of his synagogue membership, the Jewish year 5416 (1655–6). In the structure of the Sephardic

---

[56] Vaz Dias and Van der Tak, "Spinoza Merchant," 163; Vlessing, "Excommunication" (1997), 23; Israel, "Philosophy, Commerce," 165; Nadler, *Spinoza: A Life*, 139.
[57] Levie Bernfeld, "De Financiering," 440.
[58] Vlessing, "Twee bijzondere klanten," 155–6, 160; Israel, "Philosophy, Commerce," 135, 139.

community's revenues and finances, these two taxes, *imposta* and *finta*, had long been the financial pillars funding the synagogue and its institutions, the rabbis' and assistant teachers' salaries, maintenance of the synagogue buildings, and upkeep of the community school and library, as well as administration of the Ouderkerk cemetery, *kosher* meat sale supervision, and, most pressing of all, during hard times, poor relief for those on the congregation's registered "poor list."[59] Each spring, at the close of the financial year, before the sabbath preceding Passover, the community treasurer (*gabay*) needed to provide an account of the departing *Mahamad*'s financial management over the preceding year showing there had been no mismanagement or overspending beyond listed income.[60]

Community revenues thus served a wide variety of purposes. The *imposta* had long been used also to assist New Christian families moving from lands where formal practice of Judaism was forbidden to integrate into Jewish life, as with the Spinozas' move from Nantes to Amsterdam. Funds were regularly remitted each year also to the Holy Land to support the Sephardic religious communities of Jerusalem, Safed, Tiberias, and Hebron and redeem captives from the Barbary corsairs. There were also sometimes heavy extra commitments linked to unforeseen events. In 1626, letters from Jerusalem had reached the *Senhores Quinze*, including Spinoza's grandfather, Abraham, describing the oppressive rule of the Ottoman governor, Muhammed ibn Farouk, who, since 1623, had inflicted great hardship on the nearly 3,000 Jews dwelling there, an affront to the "whole people of Israel" that moved the joint board to vote a subsidy of 2,400 guilders on top of their regular annual remittance to the Holy Land.[61]

During 1654–5 "Baruch dEspinoza," the synagogue records show, continued his payments to the community, but his *imposta* payments fell much more steeply than those of the community as a whole. The overall level fell from their peak in 1650 by between a third and a half in the difficult years 1650–3 before recovering the lost ground during 1654–6, just when Spinoza's business was collapsing. In fact, by agreement with the community treasurer and elders, Spinoza's *imposta* assessment was drastically reduced and eventually written off at zero. His *finta* payment was reduced to five guilders. If we then consider the first year in which his younger brother, Gabriel (Abraham) d'Espinoza, assumed the running of the business following Spinoza's expulsion from the community, the year 5417 (1656–7), the Spinoza *imposta* and *finta* dues were now both assessed by the *gabay* acting for the community at zero, confirming that the financial ruin of the firm Michael had built up over thirty years was now complete (Table 7.2).[62]

---

[59] GA Amsterdam PJG 13 "Libros dos termos de ymposta da nação," founding articles.
[60] Swetschinski, *Reluctant Cosmopolitans*, 196–7.
[61] GA Amsterdam PJG 13 "Libros dos termos de ymposta da nação," fo. 19v.
[62] Van der Tak, "Spinoza's Payments,"190–2; Israel, "Philosophy, Commerce," 139.

Table 7.2 The *imposta* and *finta* payments (in guilders) to the Amsterdam Portuguese Jewish community by the head of the Spinoza family 1641–58

Year	Head of the family	Imposta	Finta
5394 (1633–4)	Michael d'Espinoza	18.2	?
5398 (1637–8)	Michael d'Espinoza	55.13	?
5399 (1638–9)	Michael d'Espinoza	33-8	12-10
5400 (1639–40)	Michael d'Espinoza	30-12	12-10
5401 (1640–1)	Michael d'Espinoza	103-12	12-10
5402 (1641–2)	Michael d'Espinoza	39.6	12-10
5403 (1642–3)	Michael d'Espinoza	31.14	12-10
5404 (1643–4)	Michael d'Espinoza	48-10	12.10
5405 (1644–5)	Michael d'Espinoza	42-8	12.10
5407 (1646–7)	Michael d'Espinoza	?	12.10
5408 (1647–8)	Michael d'Espinoza	14-10	12.5
5409 (1648–9)	Michael d'Espinoza	41-1	12.5
5410 (1649–50)	Michael d'Espinoza	75-7	12.5
5411 (1650–1)	Michael d'Espinoza	35	12.5
5412 (1651–2)	Michael d'Espinoza	62-9	12.5
5413 (1652–3)	Michael d'Espinoza	26-13	12.5
5414 (1653–4)	Baruch de Spinoza	17.7	12.5
5415 (1654–5)	Baruch de Spinoza	22	10
5416 (1655–6)	Baruch de Spinoza	0	5
5417 (1656–7)	Abraham (Gabriel) de Spinoza	0	0
5418 (1657–8)	Abraham (Gabriel) de Spinoza	0	0
5419 (1658–9)	Abraham (Gabriel) de Spinoza	0	0
5420 (1659–60)	Abraham (Gabriel) de Spinoza	0	0

Sources: GAA 334 inv. no. 173, pp. 17–268 and 174, pp. 18–41; Van der Tak, "Spinoza's Payments," 190–1; Révah, "Aux origines de la rupture," 367; Israel, "Philosophy, Commerce," 139; Nadler, *Spinoza: A Life*, 119–20; Van de Ven, *Documenting Spinoza*. I am indebted to Odette Vlessing, former staff member at the Amsterdam city archives, and Jeroen van de Ven, for their help in assembling this table.

Admittedly, with many or most families losing ground until early 1654, the general downturn meant that *imposta* and *finta* payments of the entire community dropped appreciably between 1651 and 1654. Such was the distress of some previously affluent families that there were also other cases where both the *finta* and the *imposta* assessments fell drastically. But the general contraction of the community's overall wealth percentage-wise was not nearly as steep as that of the Spinoza family in particular. There was also vigorous resistance to such reductions owing to the rising burden of communal expenses, indeed great urgency to bolster the community's overall income from *imposta* and the *finta* at this difficult time as far as possible. Reductions were obtainable only where, as with the Spinozas, demonstrable severe reverses in family circumstances were unquestionably evident.

Simultaneously, there occurred a sharp rise also, the Sephardic community's poor relief registers show, in the proportion of impoverished families being supported. Without counting those helped to emigrate to Livorno, the Caribbean, and elsewhere, the number of families on the communal poor list nearly doubled between 1640 and 1655 from under a hundred, to 180, with those temporarily supported bringing the total much higher.[63] Meanwhile, despite growing numbers of regular paying members of the Sephardic community during the late 1640s and in 1650, by which date there were 308 *finta*-paying families, actual returns from *imposta* fell precipitately in the years 1651–5. It is incorrect, therefore, to claim, as one scholar has, that the "yields of the Jewish communal taxes, the *imposta*," were at their zenith at the point Spinoza was expelled and that the commercial prosperity of the community was assured.[64] That was not at all the case. In fact, the overall outlook for the community's finances immediately before, during, and after the fierce and bitter war with England remained deeply worrying until the recovery of the late 1650s. Along with temporary heavy reduction in the *imposta* and increased social pressures, recession meant the level of *finta* had to be raised to fund the synagogue and its poor relief services while at the same time enabling the community treasurers to grant reductions in payments to some families.[65]

On 3 Tamuz 5414 (18 June 1654), shortly after Spinoza became household and family business head, in view of the "many and very urgent necessities growing worse every day both as regards those [impoverished] persons living here, as well as others recently arrived from different parts," and the rising burden of communal expenditure on salaries, institutions, and charities, the *Mahamad* voted an emergency supplementary *imposta* to cover the shortfall. Relieving the distress of the poor and the Sephardic refugees from Brazil, "our duty to lighten the distress of our poor brethren," affirmed "in many places in our Holy Law," the elders reminded themselves and the community, was an unavoidable obligation. To service the levy, the *Mahamad* at this point listed 125 heads of affluent (or seemingly still affluent) communal households, roughly the upper half of the *imposta*-paying families, including themselves, to pay this extra amount, with "Baruch Despinosa," as his name is spelt here, in June 1654, being placed fifty-first on the list. Spinoza's name was then afterwards crossed off this notable roll of prominence, uprightness, and honour, following his expulsion from the community in 1656. But although his name was crossed out in accordance with the *herem*, the scribe made no effort to render his deleted name illegible.[66] Massive new pressure on the congregation and its finances during one of the most critical phases in Dutch Sephardic Jewry's history explains why, during the 1650s specifically, much of the elders' energy, and especially that of Menasseh, went into promoting schemes to spur emigration of Sephardic and Ashkenazic poor

---

[63] Levie Bernfeld, "Financing Relief," 66.
[64] This is the view of Odette Vlessing, in Vlessing, "Excommunication" (2002), 142.
[65] Levie Bernfeld, "Financing Relief," 76–7, 100; Levie Bernfeld, "De Financiering," 431.
[66] GA Amsterdam PJG 334, invent. no. 19, fos. 366–7, res. 3 Tamuz 5414; Levie Bernfeld, "De Financiering," 428; Nadler, Tielen, and Tiribás, "Two New Documents," 806–8.

overseas to whatever new spheres of settlement abroad were at hand, in particular Livorno, New Amsterdam (New York), and the Caribbean—especially Barbados, Curaçao and Martinique, and (from 1654) England.

Alongside regular compulsory communal tax payments, fascinating details survive in the community records regarding Spinoza's *promesas*, that is notes submitted during synagogue prayers promising sums towards communal charities, like the *Bikur Holim* society for care of the sick, or support of needy, stricken Sephardic congregations abroad, including the Holy Land, and refugees from Brazil. Such "promises" of donations were especially made on occasions when a congregant was honoured by being called up in synagogue on the sabbath, or a religious festival, to read from the weekly Torah portion, or perform other ceremonial roles, like opening the doors of the ark during synagogue services. In 1654–5, following his father's death, Spinoza's recorded payment of *promesas* was still quite high at 55 guilders which means Spinoza attended synagogue regularly, especially to recite the *Kaddish* prayer for the dead that Jewish tradition requires the eldest son to continue reciting after the initial seven days of mourning, in the presence of a *minyan* (ten adult Jewish males) and gave generously to charity.

Whatever Spinoza's thoughts about death, decimated families, and his problematic future course, the *promesa* evidence proves he continued conforming to synagogue convention and practice, dutifully performing his filial duty in accord with tradition, and paying his synagogue dues well into 1655, a pattern persisting uninterruptedly until mid-1655 after which his *promesa* payments (as well as compulsory dues) tailed off dramatically, the last small voluntary *promesa* Spinoza made in synagogue dating from March 1656.[67] Thus, until late 1655, arguably even as late as March 1656, there was still no sign of rupture in Bento de Espinoza's dutiful compliance with his synagogue responsibilities and community posture.[68]

Spinoza seems then to have attended synagogue fairly regularly until reaching the age of twenty-three and then ceased doing so. Switching from the 1654–5 phase of public conformity to the community's rules and procedures to the late 1655 and early 1656 phase of open and public withdrawal is best explained by an increasingly tense relationship with the synagogue immediately prior to the open rupture, presumably largely due to Spinoza realizing he could only free himself from a future life trapped in drudgery by means of such a rupture. It became clear to him that if he did not rebel, his future was one of ceaseless, grinding effort to repay hefty debts and resolve endless legal entanglements, toiling in the shadow of his for the moment intellectually more eminent rabbinical brother-in-law. The sole feasible exit was to circumvent the community's authority and power to determine the status of his debts, responsibilities, and obligations by resorting to

---

[67] Van der Tak, "Spinoza's Payments," 190–1; Vlessing, "Excommunication" (1997), 16.
[68] Vlessing suggests March 1656 rather than late 1655, see Vlessing, "Excommunication" (1997), 16.

the Dutch civil courts which alone offered hope of escape from the burgeoning maze of debt and legal procedures. Equally, though, rabbinic and *Mahamad* objections to bypassing the *parnasim* to seek legal redress cannot have been the primary reason for the uniquely severe *herem* eventually imposed. Legal proceedings and business failure were just the starting point of the tortuous drama that now ensued.

Michael's last known business dealings, dating from October and December 1653, were transacted at the offices of his regular notary, Benedict Baddel (1594–1658). Besides seeking to recover sums owed to him by other Amsterdam traders, including the widow of the deceased Claude Surmonde,[69] the striking feature of his last business transactions was his accepting a letter of exchange remitted from Madrid, dated 28 January 1653, drawn on Juan Álvarez of Antwerp that involved paying out a very large sum on behalf of the Spanish king "for different purposes of his royal service," on demand of the Spanish Ambassador at The Hague, Antoine Brun, payable before the end of November 1653. That Michael was still instrumental in large-scale dealings in the last October of his life, paying out big sums under his signature "Michael despinoza," shows that in late 1653, with Bento probably already heavily involved in business activity, there was as yet no problem with their business profile or credit status.[70] Baddel, a French-speaking member of the Walloon church whose office was nearby on the Rokin, remained Michael's preferred notary until the end of his life, owing to his finding it easier to arrange his affairs in French than Dutch. (Interestingly, there is a notarial reference of August 1652, to a legal notice for Michael written in Dutch "translated by his daughter [Rebecca]" who, clearly, could read, write, and also translate, presumably into Portuguese.) After his father's death, Spinoza too continued some dealings with Baddel.

Michael's last business dealings do, though, reflect the catalogue of setbacks he had recently suffered. Two other December 1653 transactions handled by Baddel involved legal protests by Michael regarding refusals to pay sums due to him authorized by letters of exchange. One payment was rejected, presumably because Michael had fallen short in some way, by a key Sephardic partnership trading with Spain, that of Fernando Álvarez and Antonio Correa de Mesquita (alias Hendrik and Robert Van der Sterre [in Spain "Bandersterre"]).[71] The second refusal of payment to the dying Michael was by "Francisco and Antonio da Gurre," trading aliases used in their transactions with Spain by Isaac and Abraham Israel Pereyra, leading Amsterdam Sephardic merchants trading with Madrid, Seville, and the Canaries, a firm not advisable to get into dispute with. In 1656, Abraham Israel

---

[69] Van de Ven, *Documenting Spinoza*, ch. 3.
[70] GA Amsterdam Notarial Archives, MS 5075/971C, pp. 1229–30, 1258–9, 1376–7; I am extremely grateful to Jeroen van de Ven and Rik Wassenaar for drawing my attention to these documents.
[71] Van de Ven, *Documenting Spinoza*, ch. 3; Israel, "Spain and the Dutch Sephardim, 59; Caro Baroja, *Los Judíos* ii, 148.

Pereyra (d. 1699), would be one of the eight-member *Mahamad* that imposed the *herem* on Spinoza and one may wonder what the twenty-one-year-old Spinoza thought of this outstanding Marrano figure, soon regarded as a model of Sephardic piety by some, whose New Christian name in Spain had been "Thomas Rodriguez Pereyra."

According to Spanish royal court records, Pereyra fled Madrid for Amsterdam with his family, in 1646, absconding with a large sum of cash belonging to the crown.[72] He settled in Amsterdam, joining his brother, Isaac, who had preceded him there. In later life, Thomas (Abraham) proved a harsh critic of Marranos lingering in the Iberian world as "New Christians" and of synagogue members in Holland lax in their religious duties.[73] From the late 1640s onwards, he was a leading figure in the community and its governance despite knowing no Hebrew and just starting to learn about Judaism, a deficiency he compensated for by donating handsomely to charities and building prestige in the synagogue, partly perhaps to justify and sanctify, so to speak, his coup against the Spanish royal treasury. He joined in supporting the *yeshivah* his brother had founded in 1644, later called that of the "Brothers Pereyra" of which Menasseh was principal. In 1656, Pereyra helped establish the *yeshivah* Tora Hora in Amsterdam and, in 1659, the *yeshivah* Hesed le-Avraham, in Hebron.[74] He later would become a fervent follower of Sabbatai Zevi, leader of the greatest messianic upheaval in the Jewish world of the early modern era. Until then, he vigorously endorsed the community's judicial autonomy. For him it "was the *Mahamad* that stands above everyone else and must make their legal rulings consistent with the opinion of the Torah," and decide everything "according to the opinion" of the rabbis.[75] More highly educated and learned newcomers, meanwhile, lacking his stacks of cash, like Spinoza's newly arrived comrade, in 1655, the physician Juan De Prado, found themselves ranked lower in status than they thought their academic background and professional standing deserved.[76]

7.iv Collapse of the Family Fortune

For Spinoza, fully realizing how much his father's recent setbacks and failures blighted his and his family's prospects took time. But already early in 1654, the

---

[72] AGS Estado 2070. Brun to Geronimo de la Torre, Cambrai, 27 Aug. 1649; Levi de Barrios, *Relación*, 279, 288; Israel, "Spain and the Dutch Sephardim," 44, 58; Israel, *Empires and Entrepots*, 398.

[73] Albiac, *Sinagoga vacía*, 121–37; Kaplan, *Judíos Nuevos*, 37, 49n12; Muchnik, *Une Vie Marrane*, 273–4, 275–6, 278, 495.

[74] Israel, *Empires and Entrepots*, 406–7; Nadler, *Rembrandt's Jews*, 201; Nadler, *Menasseh ben Israel*, 108–9.

[75] Van de Ven, *Documenting Spinoza*, ch. 4; see also Kaplan, "Between Religion and Ethnicity," 200, 2003.

[76] Swetschinski, *Reluctant Cosmopolitans*, 276; Israel, *Diasporas*, 233–8.

disordered state of Michael's affairs must have meant a decidedly dispiriting start. Only gradually did the full extent of his father's debts, and how much was owed to him by traders abroad and locally, become clear, not to mention how convoluted were Michael's often obscure dealings in Portugal, France, Morocco, and Spain. Spinoza struggled on for over two years striving to sort out the mess together with his younger brother, trying to maintain his household in appropriate style as well as retain their parents' housemaid, as the relevant records show.[77] Spinoza endeavoured to uphold their standing as reputable merchants and his family's status in the synagogue, with consistently fulfilling (until late 1655) his synagogue duties and responsibilities while at the same time clinging, as far as he could, to his studies.[78]

The drastic reduction of Spinoza's *finta* assessment, eventually down to nothing by 1655, and the lessening of his *imposta* by over half, at a time of heightened pressure on the community budget and raised communal exactions, not only reflects the Spinoza household's reduced financial circumstances but also meant a lowering of status, heralding the collapse of Spinoza's business prospects, and that of Gabriel and the rest of the family dependent on the brothers, a collective family setback formally broadcast via the synagogue to the community and wider Sephardic diaspora. It spelt depletion of the family's "reputation" and credit-worthiness as well as of its capital. Although there was nothing uncommon about such precipitate downgrading at a time when many Dutch ships and cargoes were lost, their sudden loss of ease and standing was bound to be a humbling experience.

Above all, Spinoza needed to sort out the chaotic state of his father's finances and debts, as other family members and family friends no doubt encouraged him to do. In fact, he settled a considerable number of his father's outstanding debts during the year following his death, making substantial payments in November and December 1654, for example, to Juan de Paz (1,189 guilders), the later famous financier Antonio Lopes Suasso (1,149 guilders) who would be a *parnas* of the synagogue at the time of Spinoza's *herem* in 1656, and the younger Bento Osorio (1,167 guilders). But he settled these debts only step by step as he managed to retrieve other amounts owed to his father, sums paid into his account, for example by Isaac Furtado (1,134 guilders), Guillaume Bellin, David Senhor, and also the famous firm of Bartholotti.[79] Bellin was presumably Guillaume Bellin de la Garde, originally from Saint-Malo, an Amsterdam-based specialist in the contraband trade between France and Spain whilst the two countries remained at war until

---

[77] Vaz Dias and Van der Tak, "Spinoza Merchant," 158.
[78] Révah, "Aux origines de la rupture," 367; Yovel, *Spinoza and Other Heretics*, 7; Nadler, *Spinoza: A Life*, 117–19; Vlessing, "Excommunication" (1997), 18–20.
[79] Vlessing, "Twee bijzondere klanten," 156, 160.

1659, a leading pioneer of the Dutch contraband trade also with Spanish Upper Peru (Potosí) via Buenos Aires which was just commencing in the mid-1650s.[80]

On assuming control of his father's account at the Amsterdam Exchange Bank, in March 1654, Spinoza then already saw evidence of mounting difficulties ahead. A recently discovered notarial deed from the Amsterdam city archives, dated 1 April 1654, thus just four days after Michael's demise (when they should have been wholly absorbed in their ritual mourning period, the *shiva*), records Spinoza and his brother Gabriel meeting together in the heart of Amsterdam, on the Dam, at the office of the notary Joost van den Ven (1610–66) (who also extensively used French in his business) with the prominent merchant and *parnas* Jeronimo Nunes da Costa (Moseh Curiel) (1620–97), whom they knew well and who seems to have been appointed by the *Mahamad* as a kind of family adviser, to help sort out the difficulties left at Michael's death. This meeting was to protest two letters of exchange drawn on Michael from two non-Jewish Rouen merchants, Jacques de Baie and Samuel Bonnidio, connected with the Portugal trade, the first for 426 Portuguese *escudos*, the second for 1,000 *escudos*.[81]

A man of high standing, raised in Hamburg where his father, Duarte Nunes da Costa (1585–1664), was a leader of the Sephardic community, Jeronimo had resided in Amsterdam since 1642 and, in 1645, been named official Agent of the Portuguese crown in the United Provinces by King João IV. Though still relatively young, he already figured among the most experienced, wealthiest Sephardic merchants of the age, with knowledge of olive oil, figs, almonds, and sugar importing from Brazil via Portugal, the Canaries, and the Azores second to none.[82] Another reason for his acting as a kind of honest broker in this instance were his years of collaboration with Rodrigues de Morais and the Rodrigues Lamego family, the wealthiest of the Rouen Portuguese merchant dynasties into which his aunt, his father's sister, Sarah, had married and to which Michael d'Espinoza was especially heavily indebted.[83]

The *Mahamad* was perfectly aware at the time of Michael's death that the Spinoza brothers were still minors under Dutch law, and that in such instances, even though it was not yet clear that Michael's business was effectively bankrupt, serious problems relating to inheritance, debts, and creditors could arise. Now a prominent man of business in his own right, Spinoza needed to withdraw from the risky, volatile network of overseas ventures in which his father had engaged and transfer whatever he could of the family's diminished resources into investments and savings promising some continuity, security, and stability. One sign that this was indeed his business strategy is the apparent complete absence of any fresh

---

[80] Freeman, *Silver River*, chap. 4, cue 20.
[81] Van de Ven, *Documenting Spinoza*; I am grateful, once again, to Jeroen van de Ven for his kindness in sharing his knowledge of this deed with me well before publication of his volume.
[82] Israel, "An Amsterdam Jewish Merchant," 21–2.
[83] Israel, "An Amsterdam Jewish Merchant," 23, 32.

freight-contract business initiative during the two years he was an active merchant. The legal documents relating Spinoza's activities in the 1654–6 period surviving in the Amsterdam notarial records seem all to pertain to unsettled debts, protested letters of exchange, and matters of inheritance.

Retrieving money owed to his father proved arduous work. One amount owing known to have been successfully recovered was the 876 Portuguese *cruzados* owed by a Lisbon merchant, Guillermo de Belhem, presumably for goods delivered earlier in Portugal, drawn on someone living in Hoorn. In November 1655, Spinoza, in his own name and that of his brother, Gabriel (Abraham), signed the bill of exchange over to another Amsterdam Sephardic Jew, Joseph Francis, a financier, insurer, and dealer in bills of exchange, being paid the sum owed in full (with deduction of the usual fee for servicing international bills of exchange).[84] Another asset Spinoza sought to recover, a sum of 500 guilders, more than enough to keep a family for a year, was owed to him by a young jeweller, Antonio Alvares, who had arrived in Amsterdam from Paris some years before. It was money originally owed, since November 1654, to another Sephardic jeweller, Manuel Duarte, who had endorsed a bill of exchange for the 500 guilders to "Bento despinosa"; suggesting it was connected with the jewellery trade, perhaps payment for silver used for setting jewels, or else gems from Brazil or the Caribbean. Whatever the payment was for, Duarte and another young jeweller, Manuel Levy, had several times gone to Alvares to collect the cash for Spinoza. On 4 May 1655, Duarte and Levy testified before a notary, on Spinoza's behalf, that they had repeatedly seen Alvares "to request payment after the said bill of exchange had become due," but always been fobbed off with fresh promises to pay up which had failed to materialize. On 7 May 1655, two members of staff of the Amsterdam *schout* [chief sheriff] appeared before the notary, Adriaan Lock, testifying on behalf of "Bento despinosa, merchant here" that, at the latter's request, they had kept a certain Antonio Alvares in detention since the end of April, in a room at a local inn, *De Vier Hollanders*, under constraint by the city authorities until he paid up. Alvares had then asked Spinoza to come to the inn so that they could reach agreement. On his appearing, though, Alvares punched Spinoza on the head with his fist without the latter uttering a word, or doing anything in response. Restrained by the sheriff's men, Alvares calmed down, a settlement was agreed and signed, and Spinoza left with one of the sheriff's men to collect money to pay the inn-keeper for Alvares's food and the costs of his arrest and detention, it being understood Antonio would repay this too to Spinoza. But when Spinoza returned, a brother of Antonio, Gabriel Álvares (who ironically bore the same Portuguese name as Spinoza's father), "was standing in front of the inn," testified the sheriff's men, "and struck the plaintiff [Spinoza] on the head with his fist without any

---

[84] Vaz Dias and Van der Tak, "Spinoza Merchant," 162; Bloom, *Economic Activities*, 165, 196.

cause," knocking off his hat, after which Gabriel gathered it up and "threw it in the gutter," stamping on his hat so as to ruin it. Spinoza, added the official, made no gesture or move to retaliate whatsoever.[85]

Cool, calm and slow to anger, the twenty-three-year-old Spinoza undoubtedly was. He liked to think himself a realist, and more adept than others in everyday affairs, an attitude confirmed by several remarks he made later, like his observation at one point that the true philosopher is not less but rather more worldly than the common merchant, not least in realizing that true *laetitia*, or happiness, cannot lie in single-minded pursuit of profit. This he substantiated by retelling the tale of the ancient philosopher Thales of Miletus (*c.*625–547 BC). His hero, Thales, tired of friends chiding him for his poverty, decided to show his poverty was from choice, not necessity, and that he knew well enough how to amass what he deemed unworthy of his efforts. Having perceived, from natural signs, that a bumper olive harvest lay ahead,[86] Thales hired all the olive presses in Greece before they were needed; then, with the olives being harvested and the presses needed, rented out at high prices what he had hired cheaply, amassing huge wealth in a year "which he then dispensed," adds Spinoza, "with a generosity equal to the shrewdness with which he had acquired it."[87]

Among the more curious transactions before notaries Spinoza conducted during his brief career as a merchant, was his appearance together with a certain "Isaac (Jacques) da Costa," probably a son of Abraham or Joseph, and hence nephew of Uriel and a distant relative of Spinoza's, in May 1655, to verify the complex identity and dual aliases of the merchant Elias de Paz, one of his father's creditors. Rendering this instance of collusion with business concealment the more remarkable was that Spinoza and Da Costa appeared together with the Amsterdam notary clerk, Manuel Lavello who (unknown to them) was surreptitiously acting as informer secretly cataloguing Amsterdam Sephardic merchants' aliases on behalf of the Spanish ambassador in The Hague who was eager to uncover the concealed names of key Sephardic merchants engaging in illicit commercial dealings with the Iberian world. Asked to attend by Elias de Paz, one of the more prominent figures subverting the Spanish trade system and regulations whom they clearly knew well, Spinoza and Isaac da Costa confirmed that he used two different trade aliases in his business dealings and that Elias de Paz, "Simão Barbosa Homem," and "Simão de Dias Nunes" were all one and the same Portuguese Jewish merchant. Elias was apparently a son of Juan de Paz who had used these aliases in dealings with key New Christian financiers in Madrid, such as the unfortunate Fernando Montezinos arrested by the Inquisition with all

---

[85] Vaz Dias and Van der Tak, "Spinoza Merchant," 159–60; Walther, "Spinoza in seiner Welt," 76.
[86] Israel, "Philosophy, Commerce," 133–4.
[87] Spinoza to Jelles, The Hague, 17 Feb. 1671, in Spinoza, *Collected Works* (ed. Curley) ii, 391–2; Lavaert, *Vrijheid, gelijkheid, veelheid*, 192; LeBuffe, "Why Spinoza Tells People to Try," 144.

his considerable wealth confiscated, the year before, in 1654.[88] Spinoza, whose knowledge of clandestine practices in commerce and law evidently preceded his gaining expertise and innovating in clandestine intellectual subversion, signed his testimony "Bento despinoza."[89]

Although Spinoza, during his time as a merchant, apparently arranged hardly any freight contracts for overseas trade, effectively discontinuing his father's importing from Portugal, Morocco, and the Canaries, he clearly spent many hours in notaries' offices and at the Bourse, discussing complex scenarios and studying documents in various languages connected with his father's overseas dealings and especially debts and sums owed to him. Inevitably, he learnt much about the intricacies of overseas trade at the time, with Spain, Portugal, the Canaries, Brazil, England, and Morocco cropping up in conversation and frequently on his mind. Several of his debt conferences were certainly with Baddel who, as it happens, in February 1655, also took a statement from the Collegiant Jarig Jelles, then thirty-five years old and dealing wholesale in groceries, including Mediterranean fruits, about purchases of casks of raisins from another Sephardic merchant.[90] A future close friend, the young Bento may well then have known him already.

Both Jelles and Spinoza were yearning to be done with keeping accounts, settling debts and commerce generally, and turn to the study of religion and philosophy. Since 1655, Jelles inhabited a house and shop, called "The Hope on the Water," located in the Karnemelksteeg [Buttermilk Alley], in the oldest part of the city, near the harbour, no great distance from Spinoza's house, where he sold groceries and imported consumables, purchased in some cases from Sephardic importers. Perhaps he also bought figs and olive oil from the Spinozas, and that is how the two first became acquainted. Spinoza also visited the offices of Volckertsz Oli (d. 1681) with whom his father had dealt frequently and whose services were regularly used in the mid-1650s also by Jeronimo Nunes da Costa, while others of Spinoza's notarial business transactions during 1654–6 took place at the premises of Adriaan Lock (1624–80), a native Amsterdammer whose office was in the Warmoesstraat, one of Amsterdam's oldest streets close to the harbour, not far from Jelles' shop.[91]

If some sums owed to the firm were retrieved and, during 1655, trade generally recovered from the Anglo-Dutch War, it was no longer the case by late 1655 that trade and community service still offered Spinoza any realistic prospect of the status and wealth which, earlier in life, he had been so reluctant to relinquish. It was now clear all round that Michael d'Espinoza's estate was encumbered with a

---

[88] Israel, *Empires and Entrepots*, 404, 415; Bloom, *Economic Activities*, 11–12, 175–6.
[89] Vaz Dias and Van der Tak, "Spinoza Merchant,"161; Borges Coelho, *Inquisição de Évora*, 491; Swetschinski, *Reluctant Cosmopolitans*, 77; Israel, *Diasporas*, 238.
[90] Van der Tak, "Jellesz' Life and Business," 11, 15; Spruit, "Cristianesimo ragionevole," 525–6.
[91] Bosma, *Repertorium*, 7, 32, 85; Israel, "An Amsterdam Jewish Merchant," 26–7.

disastrous basket of debts and that Bento faced not just bankruptcy but vast entanglement in costly and onerous legal proceedings—hardly encouragement for Spinoza's planned life of contemplation and uninterrupted study. After a further short spell lasting into the autumn in which Spinoza was close to being financially ruined but still persevering as a contributing member of the *kahal* [congregation], there followed the period of under a year, spanning from late 1655 or early 1656, until his expulsion, announced in July and effective from September 1656 when he figured as an openly lapsed figure making no attempt to conform to his synagogue obligations.

While during the Jewish year 5415 (1654–5), Spinoza paid 22 guilders in *imposta* and 10 in *finta* reflecting the firm's diminution in turnover and business status compared with a few years before, during the following year 5416 (1655–6) no *imposta* was demanded and his *finta* payment was halved, showing the community accepted that the firm's activity and resources had plummeted disastrously. Further reductions in *imposta* and *finta* to zero the following year, and years, signalled that the community treasurer and *Mahamad* now acknowledged the Spinoza family firm had hit rock bottom and was bankrupt. Strikingly, during 1655–6 Spinoza paid his now much reduced *imposta* tax during the first half only, a significant development in his life, of itself. This unusual circumstance, paying the *imposta* tax for the first half of the year but not the second, means that by late 1655 Spinoza had in effect ceased active trading.[92] From the same point, October 1655, or perhaps slightly later, Spinoza also ceased attending synagogue regularly.[93]

That the firm of "Bento and Gabriel de Spinoza," unlike Dutch Sephardic Jewish trade generally, failed to recover in the aftermath of the Anglo-Dutch conflict, or indeed after his expulsion from the community, is shown by the fact that subsequently *imposta* and *finta* payments by Gabriel remained at zero throughout the late 1650s. Both the firm's collapse and Spinoza's estrangement from formal Judaism occurred, therefore, precisely during the brief period he himself was actively running the family firm. Direct and concise in all his dealings but also shrewd, it is hardly plausible that all was conformity and harmony inwardly in Spinoza's mental world as well as outwardly until shortly before his expulsion from the community. The only plausible inference is that his rebellion against rabbinic authority remained masked, purely internal, until mid-1655, and then became openly defiant once there was no longer any point, as he viewed matters, in veiling his true self and thoughts for the sake of family and status.

This explanation also best fits with the account of the mid-eighteenth-century Amsterdam Sephardic chronicler, David Franco Mendes (1713–92), among the three most prominent neo-Hebrew poets of his age, and someone who in the

---

[92] Vlessing, "Excommunication" (2002), 144.   [93] Van der Tak, "Spinoza's Payments," 192.

1760s went to considerable lengths to investigate his community's traditions. In the Jewish year 5416 (1656), states Franco Mendes, the Amsterdam community suffered "grandes perturbaçoims com o atheo Baruch Espinosa [great perturbations with the atheist Baruch Spinoza]."[94] This may not mean Spinoza was as yet necessarily an "atheist" in any meaningful modern sense, but does confirm that his expulsion was the open, bitter, and scandalous culmination of a process subsequently long remembered, as affirmed by the community's earlier chronicler, De Barrios, and that at its core lay Spinoza's now outright rejection of Jewish religious authority. If Spinoza's initial rebellion was private and imperceptible, from late 1655 his rebellion was outward, public and defiant, a dramatic contrast between two very different phases reflected likewise in Pierre Bayle's account of Spinoza's life, first published in 1697. For Bayle records that Spinoza "alienated himself, nevertheless, only little by little from the synagogue and would perhaps have continued longer to remain on tactful terms with them [s'aliena, néanmoins que peu à peu de leur synagogue; et peut-être aurait-il gardé plus longtemps quelques mésures avec eux]," were it not that on coming out of the theatre one day, he was attacked by a fanatical Jew with a knife who wounded him only slightly but whom he believed sought to kill him. Whatever this alarming assault was about, assuming it really happened, what matters, beyond Spinoza's escaping unscathed, is not the tale of the knife attack, or other altercations about money or religion, but rather that Spinoza's life course at this point experienced a decisive and sudden transition. After a long spell of acting the honoured merchant, regularly taking his place in synagogue, and reciting *kaddish* for recently deceased relatives, he switched from masked inner rebellion coupled with outward conformity to outward defiance breaking openly with the congregation.

Doubtless one element in the drama of 1655–6 was Spinoza's growing weary of an interminably frustrating religious, financial, and legal predicament, trapping him in activity and high-stress confrontations in which, at bottom, he had little interest. Not only must he have seethed with impatience to be rid of the phantom of now vanished allurements that once held him back, but the stress seemingly was now really tormenting him. In the *Emendation*, Spinoza confesses to reaching a point where he felt he had to make a drastic decision to change his life course "for I saw that I was in the greatest danger, and had to seek a remedy with all my strength however uncertain it might be – like a man suffering from a fatal illness who, foreseeing certain death unless he employs a remedy, is forced to seek it, however uncertain, with all his strength."[95] It was a moment of near despair highly conducive to drastic action. What formerly had been restraining attachments, his father's wealth and status, and his family responsibilities, were now excruciating entanglements, an intolerable quagmire of clashes with businessmen and the

---

[94] Franco Mendes, *Memorias*, 60–1.
[95] Spinoza, *Collected Works* (ed. Curley) i, 9; Sangiacomo, *Spinoza on Reason*, 17.

synagogue. What seemed a manageable predicament when first settling debts and sorting out problems arising from his father's estate, in 1654, by late 1655 had turned into a nightmarish maze blocking his chosen path and a growing problem for the community itself, as the debts and other difficulties relating to Michael's legacy clearly impacted also on other estates entangled with Michael's affairs and other members of the congregation, beside leaders of the Rouen Portuguese New Christian colony.

7.v Renouncing his Inheritance

One aspect of Spinoza's open challenge to congregational authority was disagreement concerning the binding character of the Torah and the Mosaic Law, the status of rabbinic rulings, discord not so very different from the clashes engulfing Uriel da Costa and Delmedigo earlier. Realizing that "honour" and "wealth" would not be his in any case set in motion the practical drama of whose law and whose jurisdiction would govern the liquidation of his father's business and consequences of his business collapse. This became closely linked to his wider collision with rabbinic authority and the *parnasim*. On 16 March 1656, just under two years since his father's death, and half a year prior to his expulsion from the synagogue, Spinoza, stepping outside the community's jurisdiction, obtained legal release from the encumbrances relating to his father's estate from the Amsterdam board of civic Orphan-Masters under the purview of the city magistracy. These proceedings took place, doubtless in Spinoza's presence, in the *weeskamer*, or Orphans' Chamber, of the new city hall. The manoeuvre was appropriate under Dutch law because Spinoza, not yet twenty-four, was still legally a minor (until twenty-five) according to the *weeskamer*. As Spinoza's contemporary, the chronicler Olfert Dapper (1636–89), states in his famous *Historical Description of the City of Amsterdam* (1663), "all fatherless and motherless children are called orphans and minors until they are twenty-five years old and also remain until then under guardianship."[96] Spinoza had Dutch law on his side and could show, in addition, that when signing deeds accepting his father's legacy and assuming responsibility as head of the family firm, including the debts, in March 1654, he had not sufficiently understood how damaging his father's indebtedness and business failures actually were to himself and his siblings.

On 16 March 1656, the Amsterdam *Heeren Weesmeesteren* [Orphan-Masters] appointed a certain Louis Craeijers known to them as a reliable, responsible personage familiar with both commerce and the laws of inheritance and debt "as legal guardian of Bento d'Espinosa, son of Michael d'Espinosa born of Anna

---

[96] Dapper, *Historische Beschryving*, 489; Vlessing, "Twee bijzondere klanten," 157; Van de Ven, *Documenting Spinoza*, ch. 3.

d'Espinosa." Craeijers' specific role was "to represent, promote and account for the rights of Bento d'Espinosa and, further, regulate and administer his possessions to their best allowable use, and profit, which guardianship and administration was accepted by the said Louis Craeijers" who thereupon "promised to acquit himself of this duty properly."[97] This marked a considerable breakthrough for Spinoza but also a widening of his clash with community and family, for it meant he was circumventing the community's jurisdiction, and there was no reference in the procedure to his brother, Gabriel, his business partner hitherto, which suggests, as Gabriel afterwards remained in business on his own, that he refused any part in this transaction and that henceforth Spinoza and his brother went their separate ways.[98]

Further confirmation that this important development did indeed represent an abrupt change of direction and strategy on Spinoza's part, with notable implications for several aspects of his biography, lies in a second document, arguably among the most important we possess relating to Spinoza's early life. This was a court judgement connected with Craeijers' guardianship and Spinoza's appeal to the Orphan-Masters board, dated just a week later, 23 March 1656, by the provincial high court of Holland, the *Hooge Raad* in The Hague,[99] confirming an earlier provisional decision of the Amsterdam Orphan-Masters. Louis Craeijers, the *Hooge Raad* judgement records, on being appointed Spinoza's legal guardian, had "reverently" brought to their attention "that to the same Bento de Spinosa a considerable amount [een important capitael] is due from the estate left by his mother, chargeable to the above-mentioned Michael de Spinosa without [Bento] having received any benefit [*contentement*] from it during his father's life." Although the said Bento de Spinosa should have been a *gepriviligieerde crediteur* [privileged creditor], *preferabel*—having preference to others *jure legalis hypothecate* [hypothetically under law]—he ill-advisedly, and "misled by the rashness of his youth," had taken "it upon himself to pay a few debts of the said estate so that afterwards he could more easily – if this could be done with modest expense – conduct himself as heir to his said father. But because it now appears the said inheritance is encumbered with many arrears to the extent that the said inheritance would be extremely damaging to the said Bento de Spinosa," he had now resolved that "it is best to abstain from it in all respects so as to avoid being pursued by the creditors."[100] It was an effective release and exit strategy under law, but it closed the door for ever on his business career

---

[97] Freudenthal/Walther, *Lebensgeschichte* i, 257–8; Vaz Dias and Van der Tak, "Spinoza Merchant," 162–3; Vlessing, "Excommunication" (2002), 145; Schuyt, *Spinoza*, 24.
[98] Gullan-Whur, *Life of Spinoza*, 61–2; Israel, "Philosophy, Commerce," 135–36.
[99] On the Hof van Holland, see Israel, *Dutch Republic*, 38, 63, 129, 855.
[100] Freudenthal/Walther, *Lebensgeschichte* i, 258–9; Vlessing, "Twee bijzondere klanten," 158; Van de Ven, *Documenting Spinoza*, ch. 4.

and permanently ruptured relations with the community, his family, and his father's creditors.

Spinoza, accordingly, was permitted in March 1656 to renounce his father's inheritance retrospectively, as of March 1654, along with all debts connected therewith, the provincial high court directing the Amsterdam magistrates to act according to their decision. Spinoza's father, it was now legally recognized, had withheld from him what he should have received from his mother's legacy. Craeijers also obtained the high court's assent to two further submissions on Bento's behalf: he had petitioned "their Lordships to concede a mandate" by which the "said Bento de Spinosa could, if necessary, be discharged from any act committed as heir that he might in any way have committed regarding his said father's inheritance"; secondly, concerning his deceased mother's assets, that Spinoza receive preference "above all other creditors and in particular above Duarte Rodrigues Lamego, Antonio Rodrigues de Morais and the curators of the estate of Pedro Henriques with regard to the goods of the said Michael de Spinosa."[101] (Part of Michael d'Espinoza's indebtedness arose from his being one of the "curators" of the estate of Pedro Henriques.) Thus, with this *mandement van relief* [order for relief], the *Hooge Raad* released Spinoza from his crushing burden in all respects, placing him legally in the right and removing an immense burden and stress from his shoulders but at the cost of permanently blighting his reputation as a merchant and ruining the family firm.

Just two months after Spinoza was brought under the protection of the Amsterdam Orphans' Chamber, shielded from repayment demands from the linen exporters of Rouen and his other creditors, the great artist Rembrandt van Rijn (1606–69) resorted to the same legal mechanism hoping to save his splendid house, not far from Spinoza's, from the hands of his creditors, by transferring ownership to his son, Titus, then fifteen. Through extravagance and ill-advised spending during his years of affluence, Rembrandt, by 1656, found himself as encumbered and indebted as the sober Spinoza and in immediate danger of losing everything to his own baying pack of creditors. As a minor, Titus came likewise under the protection of the Amsterdam Orphans' Chamber. Drawing up its inventory of Rembrandt's assets, to ascertain the facts of his bankruptcy, on 25 July, the Orphans' Chamber completed its inventory the next day, on 26 July, just one day before the drawing up of the *herem* expelling Spinoza from his community.

There may well also be a significant direct link between the two convoluted family dramas. For at the end of July, the city government, very likely spurred by complaints from Sephardic merchants affected by the Orphans' Chamber decision in the Spinoza case, accepted that, however anxious to regulate situations in which

---

[101] Freudenthal/Walther, *Lebensgeschichte* i, 259; Vaz Dias and Van der Tak, "Spinoza Merchant," 163–4.

"good families can be ruined unexpectedly," they must also shield merchants owed large sums by bankrupt correspondents. The city authorities began devising an in-between stance to safeguard creditors in part while affording reduced but still substantial protection to legal minors.[102] Fortunately for Spinoza, he slipped through just in time to dodge the new ruling, but unfortunately for Rembrandt, he was just too late. Although his house was legally separated from the rest of his estate and placed under Titus' ownership, on 17 May 1656, at a later stage, in April 1658, when the city courts placed Titus under the Orphans' Chamber, which assigned him the same Louis Craeijers as his guardian, the change in the law meant that the house had to be sold off nevertheless. This was because auctioning off Rembrandts' pictures and other assets produced sums falling far short of what was needed to cover his debts, though Titus still received some protection being left under obligation to pay only part of Rembrandt's remaining debt load.[103]

Spinoza's fortunate sudden release from massive encumbrance was a lesson he never forgot, an outcome that transformed his situation and life prospects in the most fundamental fashion. His long-term friend, Jarig Jelles (1620–83), in his brief survey of Spinoza's life in his preface to the *Opera Posthuma*, describes Spinoza at this early stage of his career as "detaching himself from all the worldly troubles and anxieties [wereltsche beslommeringen en bekommernissen] that generally hinder the quest for the truth."[104] Besides Spinoza's subsequent lifelong principle that Jews living outside their own state should live under the law of the land where they dwell and not under their own separate communal religious law, there was another principle at stake here, more central to Spinoza's later system of social ethics, namely that everyone should base their life on the need to "conserve their being." Men and women should learn to "conserve their being" by maximizing their just and charitable capacity to sustain their life and activity at the best and freest level they can, and as they themselves wish to do.

Seeking to preserve one's being in Spinoza's sense means eschewing far more than just passive humility, austerity, and submissiveness. Spinoza was far from turning the other cheek when refusing to punch back at the Alvares brothers. Although Spinoza approaches close to traditional Christian ethics when recommending that we repress desires based on hatred and dedicate ourselves to those based on love, his ethics, like Nietzsche's later, was profoundly unchristian in its sweeping rejection of humility beyond a realistic appraisal of one's own worth and all penitent austerity and unthinking, uncritical submissiveness to authority. To him this mattered as much as rejecting desires based on false premises, pursuit of money and socially esteemed honour and all quest for outward status rather than

---

[102] Vlessing, "Excommunication" (1997), 27; Van de Ven, *Documenting Spinoza*, ch. 3; Schwartz, *Rembrandt*, 193.
[103] Vlessing, "Excommunication" (1997), 28; Nadler, *Rembrandt's Jews*, 36.
[104] Jelles, "Voorreeden," 1–2; Freudenthal/Walther, *Lebensgeschichte* i, 2–3.

being true to one's own deeper impulses and longings. For Spinoza, "greed, ambition and lust really are species of madness, even if they are not counted among the diseases." Neither profit nor monkish abstinence, nor battlefield glory, nor loyalty to lords and monarchs, nor any religious cause, are ideals worth anyone's time, much less devoting their lives to, or worse, sacrificing their lives for; personal this-worldly fulfilment is what essentially matters.[105]

By securing his own emancipation, in early 1656, Spinoza unavoidably affronted a whole phalanx of rabbis, relatives, and former associates of his father. He must have known what to expect from his refusing the continued mediation of the Jewish community in resolving his business problems and entrusting the outcome wholly to the Dutch legal apparatus. For his case was not the only one provoking a mighty communal uproar at the time. There was another still in progress which had begun years earlier, in 1641, over the huge legacy, including 116,000 guilders deposited with the Orphans' Chamber, left to the infant heiress Rebecca (Ribca) Naar of which Lopo Ramirez (David Curiel), an uncle of Jeronimo Nunes da Costa and prominent member of the community, had long been trying to dispossess the infant by appealing to the city magistrates. Lopo's goal was to divert Rebecca's inheritance in favour of his own wife, her aunt, and a sister-in-law, by questioning the girl's legitimacy and challenging other aspects of the legacy. The furore over his circumvention of the community's authority to alter the terms of a major inheritance via the city magistrates was still dragging on when the Spinoza and Rembrandt cases were settled. In turning to the city magistrates Spinoza obviously knew that, in the view of the *Mahamad* and the rabbis, issues of marriage status, guardianship of minors, and inheritance within the community lay exclusively in their domain, so that his strategy would inevitably provoke a rupture fatal to his general as well as financial standing and relations with the synagogue.[106]

Nor could Spinoza be at all sure, when embarking on his new course, that matters would be settled as quickly as actually occurred. The Lopo Ramirez saga was only finally settled by the Hof van Holland, on 30 September 1656, after Spinoza's expulsion from the community.[107] Financially and legally, for the Sephardic community the Lopo furore remained, down to 1656, much the more serious of the two cases. The sums of money involved were far larger, and the legal implications much wider, given Lopo's calling into question communal jurisdiction over Sephardic marriages and deciding the legitimacy or illegitimacy of their offspring. Here too, the two cases may have been connected behind the scenes. Lopo certainly, and Michael d'Espinoza seemingly, during late 1653 and 1654,

---

[105] Spinoza, *Collected Works* (ed. Curley) i, 557, 571; LeBuffe, "Why Spinoza Tells People to Try," 120–1, 131–3; Schnepf, "Enlightened Radicals," 97–8.
[106] Fuks, "Rechtsstrijd onder Amsterdamse Sefardim, 175–9; Israel, *Conflicts of Empires*, 209–10; Kaplan, "Amsterdam, the Forbidden Lands," 38–9; Van de Ven, *Documenting Spinoza*, ch. 4.
[107] Fuks, "Rechtsstrijd onder Amsterdamse Sefardim," 183–4; Israel, *Conflicts of Empires*, 216.

were among a small band of Sephardic merchants involved in a scheme to secure permission from Brussels, through mediation of Antoine Brun, for an inconspicuous orthodox Jewish house synagogue to be located in the Antwerp suburb of Borgerhout,[108] by offering more loans and support to the governor-general of the Spanish Netherlands.

These deliberations, involving even the Archbishop of Mechelen [Malines], had, by December 1653, proceeded quite far. Leopold Wilhelm, the Austrian Habsburg governor of the Spanish Netherlands during 1647–56, being also commander of the Spanish monarchy's principal *plaza de armas* [place d'armes] and the army of Flanders (which, as late as the summer of 1657, still comprised over 60,000 troops fighting France), was desperately strapped for cash. Lopo, as a veteran supplier of munitions of war, as well as financial loans, to the southern Netherlands, was well-placed to assist Spain's war effort against France and it was probably he who had recruited Michael d'Espinoza to join in this effort. In April 1654, following the intervention of the papal nuncio in Spain (who, in February, had been alerted by the papal nuncio in Brussels), condemning these secret talks to establish "a synagogue at a place called Borgerhout, near Antwerp," the governor was asked to explain himself to the royal council in Madrid. A group of Amsterdam Sephardim requesting this permission, he explained, were offering a very substantial financial subsidy which the Spanish troops in Flanders desperately needed. After further discussion about this matter in the Council of State in Madrid, on 16 June 1654, Philip IV wrote to Leopold Wilhelm, expressly forbidding the forming of any kind of Jewish congregation in the southern Netherlands.[109]

The *Mahamad*, it has been suggested, unofficially supported this project despite their being at odds with Lopo. Certainly, it was a project Michael d'Espinoza, in view of his financial dealings during late 1653 with Brun and also Vincente Richard, secretary of the Spanish embassy at The Hague, and links with Lopo, must have known a good deal about. No doubt Spinoza too was aware of this meandering affair. In any case, jurisdictionally, the synagogue elders found themselves challenged by Ramirez vastly more than by Spinoza, and yet Lopo, despite the greater gravity of his worldly offence, came only under a minor ban, the so-called *niduy*, a measure short of even the conventional *herem*, let alone a *herem* of the unique severity imposed on Spinoza.[110] Legally and financially, the Lopo Ramirez case greatly outweighed Spinoza's in significance; it was exclusively

---

[108] AGR Brussels SEG 257, fo. 133. Leopold Wilhem to Philip IV, Brusssels, 17 April 1654; Ouverleaux, "Notes et documents," 29–41; Israel, *Conflicts of Empires*, 211–12; Muchnik, *Une Vie Marrane*, 324–35.

[109] AGS Estado 2185, consultas de estado res. 7 Feb. 1654; Israel, *Conflicts of Empires*, 211–16; Israel, "Menasseh ben Israel and the Dutch Sephardic Colonization Movement," 152; Herrero Sánchez, *Acercamiento hispano-neerlandés*, 137–9.

[110] Fuks, "Rechtsstrijd onder Amsterdamse Sefardim," 179–80; Israel, *Conflicts of Empires*, 210–11.

with respect to defying religious authority that the Spinoza case wholly eclipsed the Ramirez affair.

The glaring contrast in severity of the respective bans is crucially important. For what was at stake in the Ramirez episode was purely jurisdictional, financial, and political, whereas the Spinoza challenge involved far more. There was no doubting Lopo's strict adherence to Jewish observance even while living in exile in Antwerp from 1653 to 1660 with special permission from the governor-general. He organized synagogue services in his home regularly and scrupulously deferred to rabbinic authority in the purely religious sphere, remaining punctilious in these respects.[111] The *Mahamad* in fact always observed a distinction between religious law, religious loyalty and integrity, and rules and regulations pertaining to what they called "buen gobierno [good government]," like their regulation that deceased converted black and mulatto Jews, mostly former servants, should be buried in a separate section at Ouderkerk, or the *Mahamad*'s rules discriminating against Ashkenazic Jews, like that adopted in 1639, declaring that no one should give charity to Ashkenazic beggars at the doors of the synagogue. These latter rules had no particular status in religious law.[112] Lopo did not question rabbinic authority or the synagogue's religious jurisdiction; he transgressed only with respect to "gobierno." Where Spinoza never made any attempt afterwards to repent and apologize, or try to persuade the community to lift the *herem*, Lopo eventually sought compromise. In the summer of 1666, ten years after Spinoza's expulsion, Lopo was finally reconciled with the Amsterdam community after offering contrition and 1,000 guilders toward the synagogue poor chest, proposals accepted by the *Mahamad* in consideration of Ramirez's long absence "and the present needs of the poor."[113] When he died that October, Lopo was accordingly buried at Ouderkerk without hindrance or discrimination.

Spinoza's venturing outside the community's jurisdiction was a major affront, an added reason for the furious hostility with which the community elders now regarded him. But however decisive for the timing of the rupture between Spinoza and the community, and formative for his future path in life, it is wrong to assume, as some scholars have, that Spinoza's legal manoeuvres to evade his father's debts and obligations were *the* or even *a* principal cause of the resounding drama of his permanent expulsion from the community less than four months later, in July 1656. What the *Mahamad* deemed disrespect to its authority by flouting its jurisdiction in financial and inheritance matters could be grounds for a *herem*, but a *herem* couched like that proclaimed against Spinoza with its unparalleled length, vehemence, and stress on his "malas opines" and "monstrous heresies,"

---

[111] Kaplan, "Amsterdam, the Forbidden Lands," 48; Israel, *Conflicts of Empires*, 200–1, 210, 214; Muchnik, *Un Vie Marrane*, 226.
[112] Kaplan, *Judíos Nuevos*, 67, 72–3, 85–6, 95.
[113] GA Amsterdam, PJG 19, p. 562, res. Mahamad, 15 Sivan 5426.

cannot possibly have been due to a jurisdictional clash. The jurisdictional dimensions of the case before the *parnasim* paled by comparison with Spinoza's defiance of religious authority, his revolt against the Mosaic Law and Jewish observance.

Usually, the *herem* was meant as a short-term disciplinary, temporary occurrence. Between 1622 and 1683 thirty-six men are listed in the Portuguese Sephardic community records as having been excommunicated for disobedience, two for a single day (one of whom was Menasseh, in 1640, when Spinoza was only eight). Only in four of these thirty-six cases of *herem*, including that of Spinoza and the second *herem* imposed on Juan de Prado, was the decree of banishment never subsequently rescinded. For the period after 1639, there are only two examples other than that of Spinoza, and neither was worded with the severity of that imposed on Spinoza. Nearly all other instances where a *herem* was resorted to resulted in banishment under relatively mildly worded decrees for a few days, a week, twenty days (nine instances) or, in a handful of cases, more than a year. The wording of Spinoza's *herem* was altogether unique in its gravity and emphasis on a whole range of stubbornly persisted in offences.[114]

Uriel da Costa, Spinoza, and De Prado constitute a separate and very restricted category of communal expulsions, "for giving public and open expression to their critical opinions concerning traditional established Judaism,"[115] with the *herem* decreed against Spinoza, uniquely, being even severer in tone and wording than that imposed on De Prado.[116] Accordingly, interpreting Spinoza's expulsion from the community, the fiercest, most vehement Sephardic communal condemnation of the entire Dutch Golden Age, as resulting from anything less than full-scale religious as well as jurisdictional defiance makes no sense, a conclusion strengthened by the affirmations of Bayle and Halma that Spinoza's collaboration with the then not yet notorious schoolmaster Van den Enden stretched back some time before his open rupture with the synagogue.[117]

Still, if neither the arrival of De Prado in Amsterdam, in 1655, nor his links with Van den Enden, nor the earlier arrival, in the spring of 1655, of the French heretic of possible Marrano descent, Isaac La Peyrère whose sensational book, *Praeadamitae*, caused a stir in Holland during these months, was the main catalyst spurring Spinoza's shift from inner rebellion to open defiance in 1655–6, there is no reason to doubt that all these arrivals and the controversies arising in their wake were contributory factors in Spinoza's shift to open revolt. If in late July 1656 Spinoza was expelled definitively from the community while De Prado was merely reprimanded for defiance of rabbinic authority and urged to repent and reform,[118] this can only further confirm that Spinoza's rebellion at this point was considered

---

[114] Kaplan, "Social Functions of the *Herem*," 127–9.
[115] Kaplan, "Social Functions of the *Herem*," 137; Israel, "Philosophy, Commerce."
[116] Kaplan, "Social Functions of the *Herem*," 140n80.
[117] Bayle, *Écrits sur Spinoza*, 22; Halma, *Het Leven*, 6–7⸮
[118] Muchnik, *Une Vie Marrane*, 412–13.

more reprehensible than that of his new-found ally, and something unparalleled in Dutch Jewish history.

With nothing remaining to him from his father's fortune, Spinoza, from 1655 onwards, needed to find some other way to support himself. This he did at an extremely modest level by occasional teaching and, after learning the technique of lens-polishing, selling high-quality lenses for microscopes and telescopes which, reportedly, one or more of his friends (possibly Jelles, the only one of his early friends definitely known to have had a strong interest in optics), helped him sell. From this point onwards, he earned his livelihood in a manner yielding enough for him to subsist on while guaranteeing complete independence and freedom to study and contemplate as much and whenever he chose.[119] His awareness of the benefits of *libertas philosophandi* later pervaded Spinoza's "Letter 21," of 28 January 1665, to Willem van Blijenbergh, written from near Schiedam where Spinoza had taken refuge from the plague. "Even if I found that the fruit which I have so far gathered via the natural intellect were false," Spinoza here memorably attests, "it would still render me my happiness, since I delight in it and seek to pass my life, not in sorrow and sighing, but in peace, joy and cheerfulness and by so doing I ascend a grade higher."[120]

---

[119] Rovere, "Avoir commerce," 2–3.   [120] Spinoza, *Collected Works* (ed. Curley) i, 376.

8

Teaching Skills

Van den Enden, Latin, and the Theatre (1655–1661)

8.i Disciple of a Schoolmaster

In 1656, under the *herem* if not some months before, as seems more likely, Spinoza moved out of his parents' house and found lodgings elsewhere. "As soon as [Spinoza] had left the Jews," recalled the Amsterdam bookseller, Jan Rieuwertsz the Younger, son of Spinoza's publisher, who counted himself fortunate to have known Spinoza personally in his youth, "he took to teaching children to earn his bread."[1] This solid evidence the younger Rieuwertsz provided in discussion with the visiting German scholar Gottlieb Stolle, in 1703. Spinoza's teaching career in Amsterdam, closely linked to that of a former art dealer turned schoolmaster, Franciscus van den Enden, proved brief but lastingly formative.

Van den Enden, "taught with good success and a great reputation," affirms the 1706 English version of Colerus' biography, "so that the richest merchants of [Amsterdam] entrusted him with the instruction of their children until they discovered he was teaching his students something else besides Latin. For it was eventually found out that he sowed the seeds of atheism in the minds of those young boys."[2] Van den Enden was indeed a remarkable personality and striking presence in Spinoza's life. Surveying the scene, in 1694, the Reformed minister Salomon van Til (1643–1713), deplored how "the evil" of early modern atheism had spread in sixteenth- and seventeenth-century Europe, noting that it began in Italy, spread next to France and finally to Holland. The Devil, he added, "the Prince of Darkness, found a great tool for diffusing this evil in an Amsterdam schoolmaster who, in this turbulent city, sought to use every opportunity to spread his view that Nature is the only God, and who later, in France, entangled in internal intrigue, ended his life on the gallows." But a younger disciple of Van den Enden then took up his sinister cause, building on his foundation to "give that view a fine appearance." This was "Benedictus de Spinoza, an apostate Jew who, to begin with, pretended to be an admirer and expounder of the Cartesian

---

[1] Guhrauer, "Beiträge," 488.
[2] Colerus, *Life of Benedict de Spinoza*, 3–4; Freudenthal/Walther, *Lebensgeschichte* ii, 19–20.

philosophy."[3] Himself an adherent of Cartesianism and Cocceianism, Van Til clearly thought Spinoza followed Van den Enden as regards his "atheism" and lack of reverence for Holy Scripture.[4] In recent decades, there has been a continuing debate among scholars as to how extensive the influence on Spinoza of this exceptional, against-the-grain schoolmaster really was.

During his early phase of inner rebellion against rabbinic authority, until 1655, and later more open defiance (1655-6), Spinoza's intellectual quest was by no means confined to discussion just with members of the Sephardic community. Even if one is unpersuaded by Colerus' and Lucas' testimonies claiming the period before the 1656 *herem* was a time of decreasing contact with the Jewish community and growing connection with "Christians" outside, there is no denying that Spinoza met and conversed with non-Jewish business associates and contacts at the Amsterdam Bourse, and elsewhere. Spinoza was well aware, years before his expulsion that, however skilled in Hebrew and Bible exegesis, he could not develop his intellectual skills, or compare theological traditions and notions, his principal concern early on in his intellectual career, without acquiring better Latin and some Greek. "He himself sufficiently understood how much these learned languages were necessary for his purpose," records Lucas, "but faced the difficulty of finding opportunity to immerse himself in them. As [Spinoza] pondered this incessantly and spoke about it at every meeting, a successful teacher of Latin and Greek, Van den Enden, offered him assistance, tuition and lodging in his house, without requiring any other recompense than help in teaching his pupils when he was capable of it, for part of his time."[5]

Franciscus van den Enden (1602-74) was later remembered as charming in conversation, free-spending, luxury-loving, and generous. Money mattered less to Van den Enden, reports suggest, than a refined life of learning and high culture, with an emphasis on rhetorical effect, didactic theatre, and imparting to the young his views about life and its pleasures drawn from experience, the classics, and the arts.[6] Although Spinoza himself never mentions him anywhere in his surviving writings and letters, numerous seventeenth-century sources confirm Van den Enden's role in setting Spinoza on his life's path. The old man, whom Stolle met in the Amsterdam tavern "Zum Bremer Hauptmann," who had known Spinoza personally, claimed Van den Enden originally encountered Spinoza in an Amsterdam Collegiant discussion circle which, as we shall see, may indeed be

---

[3] Til, *Voor-hof der heydenen*, 5.
[4] Til, *Voor-hof der heydenen*, 5; Van der Wall, "The *Tractatus* [...] and Dutch Calvinism," 216; Mangold, "Salomon van Til," 342, 347, 357.
[5] [Lucas], *La Vie*, 24.
[6] [Lucas], *La Vie*, 24; Van den Enden, *Philedonius, 1657*, ed. Proietti, 81-2; Du Cauzé de Nazelle, *Mémoires*, 94, 97, 10, although there are doubts about the authenticity of its attributed authorship, the description of Van den Enden as such in the latter text appears to be genuine, Du Cauzé de Nazelle, *Mémoires*, 94, 97, 107.

the case.⁷ Alternatively, he may have met him in connection with the Catholic house-churches near Spinoza's home since Van den Enden's family regularly participated in their services.

Joining forces with Van den Enden, Lucas represents as part of Spinoza's mounting open defiance of the Sephardic congregation immediately preceding his expulsion when "Mortera, irritated by the disdain his disciple evinced toward him and the Law," switched from his earlier solicitous, friendly attitude to one of hostility and the "pleasure base minds find in vengeance."⁸ When exactly Van den Enden and Spinoza began their didactic collaboration remains unknown, but taking all the testimony together, it seems safe to assume they joined forces prior to the 1656 *herem*, their collaboration strengthened by a common love of languages and background of clashes with religious authority. Van den Enden spoke Spanish and French fluently and possessed inside knowledge of the workings of the Spanish regime in Brussels, assuredly further points of attraction for Spinoza.

Short in stature, Van den Enden reportedly possessed an exceptional gift for explaining difficult topics clearly and incisively.⁹ Given the few direct sources about Spinoza's early intellectual development, the number and variety of reports citing Van den Enden leave little room for doubt that he significantly influenced the young Spinoza in more ways than one, not just raising his Latin to a sophisticated level but leaving a considerable mark on his ideas about teaching and awareness of classical literature. In 1677, the head of the Catholic Church in the Republic, the Vicar Apostolic Jan Neercassel, reporting six months after Spinoza's death to the papal nuncio in Brussels, Lorenzo Casoni, and the Inquisition in Rome, described Van den Enden as "Spinosae magister" [Spinoza's teacher], and the recently deceased philosopher his "disciple Spinoza [ejus discipulus Spinosa]," styling Van den Enden "a bad Christian, or rather deserter from religion [malus Christianus, vel potius Christianis religionis desertor]" who, while still living outwardly as a Catholic, exerted a malign influence on his pupils.¹⁰

With several members of the Sephardic community trained in the academic Latin of the era, and readily at hand, including De Prado after his arrival in mid-1655, and the latter's ally, the teacher Daniel Ribera, the young Spinoza seemingly commenced his Latin studies within the Sephardic community well before the *herem*. But several sources concur that Spinoza first encountered the later notorious ex-Jesuit prior to his expulsion from the community, and Van den Enden seems to have been the chief influence on the young Spinoza's Latin studies and

---

⁷ Guhrauer, "Beiträge," 485.   ⁸ [Lucas], *La Vie*, 24.
⁹ Du Cauzé de Nazelle, *Mémoires*, 97–8.
¹⁰ Neercassel to Casoni, 9 Sept. 1678 in Orcibal, "Jansénistes face à Spinoza," 464–5; Totaro, "Documenti," 105.

familiarity with Roman rhetoric, literature, history, and the theatre from quite early on. Spinoza eventually attained a high level of Latinity (if not quite up to the expert level of Van den Enden, his later friends, Lodewijk Meyer, and Johannes Bouwmeester, or, for that matter, Descartes) and undeniably showed a life-long keen interest in aspects of Roman literature, especially drama and history. On the other hand, there is little sign Van den Enden played any real part in Spinoza's eventual switch from religious studies to pure philosophy, or in guiding his steps, in the late 1650s, towards Cartesianism and scientific work.

Although his parents were weavers,[11] Van den Enden was highly educated, having attended an Augustinian school in his native Antwerp with a view to an ecclesiastical career. His older brother, Johannes, was a Jesuit and army confessor attached to units of the Spanish forces stationed in the southern Netherlands. Having studied with the Jesuits, Franciscus became a Jesuit novice at Mechelen, in 1619, and aspired to join the Jesuit Order, like his brother. But despite passing his exams, his career with the Jesuits was suddenly cut short, in 1621, for unstated reasons, a later report attributing this to his having seduced "a young lady."[12] His training having equipped him to teach Latin, between 1624 and 1628, he practised that vocation as a lay teacher, in the Jesuit colleges of Mechelen, Oudenaarde, Aalst, Winoxberge, and Cassel. In 1629, though, he interrupted his already substantial teaching career, returning to Louvain (Leuven) to resume studying theology with the Jesuits. But on completing the four-year training to enter the Jesuit Order, shortly before graduating, in 1633, following consultation between the Jesuit provincial head in the southern Netherlands and the Superior General of the Jesuit order in Rome, he was again denied entry.

This eventually notorious schoolmaster's anonymous biographer, supposedly the French nobleman Du Causé de Nazelle, records that Van den Enden was inordinately fond of women and, in 1633, was caught in an adulterous relationship with the wife of a military officer.[13] He was then definitively expelled from the Jesuit Order for his "errors" which some have taken to signify his already being immersed in unorthodox thinking. Yet, there is scant sign of religious unorthodoxy or even hint of interest in philosophy in the Van den Enden of the 1630s (in 1633 Descartes had published nothing yet), or indeed at any point down to the late 1650s. The closest modern research has got to pinpointing Van den Enden's turn to "atheism" with any certainty is to the years between 1657 and 1661.[14] The intervention of Rome and Van den Enden's exclusion from the Jesuit Order seems to have been due rather to suspicion of his being a "dangerous" influence in another sense, less for intellectual or moral reasons than his clearly documented

---

[11] Meininger and Suchtelen, *Liever met wercken*, 8.
[12] Cauzé de Nazelle, *Mémoires*, 98; Meininger and Suchtelen, *Liever met wercken*, 9.
[13] Maury, "Conspiration républicaine," 379; Meininger and Suchtelen, *Liever met wercken*, 11.
[14] Mertens, *Van den Enden en Spinoza*, 36; Mertens, "Spinoza's Amsterdamse vriendenkring," 71; Lavaert, *Vrijheid, gelijkheid, veelheid*, 142.

ties with a Spanish religious fraternity vigorously patronized by the Spanish governors-general of Flanders through the 1630s and 1640s, known as the *Congregación de los Esclavos del Dulce Nombre de Maria* [Congregation of the Slaves of the Sweet Name of Maria], an elite body founded in 1626 by the Augustinian Bartolomé de los Ríos y Alarcón (1580–1652). Shunned by the Jesuits, the *Congregación* evolved into an international network sworn to bolster Spanish absolutism and Spain's interests in Northern Europe and was well-connected with the court at Brussels, becoming after 1650 an openly anti-Jesuit, if not yet quite pro-Jansenist, body.[15]

During the 1630s and 1640s, rather than becoming a radical dissident, Van den Enden seems to have remained firm in his pro-Spanish Catholic allegiance. From 1620 to 1647, his mentor, Ríos y Alarcón, served as a close adviser of the Archduchess Isabella, Philip IV's representative in Brussels, and then of the next regent, the Cardinal-Infante Ferdinand (1609–41), Philip IV of Spain's younger brother, governor of the Spanish Netherlands from 1635 to 1641. More warrior than churchman, the Cardinal-Infante succeeded in holding the line in what, for Spain, was now a two-front war against the Republic and France. On arriving in Brussels, following his shared victory, together with the Austrians over the Swedes at Nördlingen (1634), Ferdinand initially figured in the Catholic world as a great military hero. His governorship of Flanders was soon marred, though, by a terrifying episode known as the "sack of Tienen" which Spinoza vividly evokes in his 1675 exchange with Albert Burgh, as Leibniz later noted when evaluating Spinoza's reply to Burgh, in 1677, in notes for his then Catholic employer, Duke Johann Friedrich of Brunswick-Lüneburg.[16]

In 1635, with the Thirty Years War raging and now merging with the Eighty Years War, Spanish forces in the Low Countries failed in their defensive moves to thwart a Dutch invasion force under Stadholder Frederik Hendrik advancing to link arms with an invading French army under the marshal of Châtillon (a nephew of Frederik Hendrik).[17] Joining Châtillon in central Brabant, Frederik Hendrik, commanding a combined force of 60,000 men, laid siege, in May, to Tienen (Tirlemont). Ferdinand blamed his failure to prevent the Dutch and French joining forces on subordinates; the papal nuncio blamed it on the Cardinal-Infante going hunting whilst prayers for the operation's success were being recited in the churches. Tienen resisted only briefly. When the town fell it was brutally sacked by the combined Franco-Dutch army, its officers losing control of their men who reportedly killed dozens and committed numerous rapes, something virtually unheard of in the Low Countries struggle since 1621,

---

[15] Proietti, "Vita e opere," 21, 27–8, 31; Klever, "Inleiding," 16; Rovere, "Honors and Theater," 811.
[16] Spinoza, *Collected Works* (ed. Curley) ii, 475; Leibniz to Duke Johann Friedrich, undated (early 1677?) in Leibniz, *Sämtliche Schriften und Briefe* 1st ser. ii, 8; Laerke, *Leibniz lecteur*, 106–7.
[17] Israel, *Dutch Republic and the Hispanic World*, 252.

the Protestant Huguenots, Dutch and Swiss among them savagely pillaging and wrecking the town's churches and chapels.[18]

But by a stroke of poetic justice, these very atrocities permanently wrecked the invaders' own cause among the outraged Belgian populace. Shocking acts of sacrilege, destruction of sacred images, and desecration of chapels aroused such revulsion south of the great rivers as to leave the Spanish crown in the Low Countries vindicated, elevated, and, paradoxically, morally strengthened, a fact that powerfully impressed itself on Spinoza's thoughts.[19] What particularly stood out among the acts of sacrilegious vandalism perpetrated by the Protestant soldiery long remembered by locals, was their desecrating "the hosts," the unleavened wafers used for sacred mass in the town's churches, throwing them on the ground and feeding them to their horses to eat, a detail Spinoza mentions specifically in his letter to Burgh.[20] Two years after the event, in 1637, Ríos y Alarcón published his *Phoenix Thenensis* dedicated to the Cardinal-Infante, a collection of sermons, reminiscences, and poems celebrating Tienen's recovery after the horrific onslaught and the restoration of images of the Holy Virgin. This pious compilation included a three-page poem by Van den Enden, then living in his native Antwerp, exalting the "cult of the Virgin and reverence for the esteemed Father [Ríos y Alarcón], his patron."

Abominating the atrocities, Van den Enden's poem styled Calvinism an infernal plague and compares the women's weeping after the sack of Tienen with the laments of Hecuba after the sack of Troy.[21] Throughout his career he relished rhetorical parallels linking classical literature to modern life, later something of a feature of Spinoza's political writings too. Celebration of the restored holy images smashed by Franco-Dutch-Swiss sacrilege subsequently focused on what became post-1635 Tienen's most celebrated cult, that of "Our Lady of the Remedies." But while exalting the "Holy Virgin Mary, most assured remedy for all evil and safeguard for all that is good," Van den Enden's poem chiefly lambasts Protestantism: "heresy, armed with torches shows what hatred is capable of; in Tienen, lies buried the old Tienen: may Piety note that, O You who will dwell in the city, with words that remain forever in your hearts: this singular destruction was needed to prove what heresy hides behind its alluring face, and spreads venomously when afforded the opportunity."[22] Three years old when Tienen was sacked, Spinoza doubtless learnt the details twenty years or so later, in the 1650s, from Van den Enden at the latter's school or home.

[18] *Correspondance de Richard Pauli Struvius*, 65; Blanco Mayor, "Quevedo y Spinoza," 194.
[19] Spinoza, *Collected Works* (ed. Curley) ii, 474-8; Orcibal, "Jansénistes face à Spinoza," 59; Israel, *Dutch Republic and the Hispanic World*, 252; Vermeir, *Staat van oorlog*, 117–18.
[20] Spinoza, *Correspondance* (ed. Rovere), 372; Blanco Mayor, "Quevedo y Spinoza," 195.
[21] Proietti, "Vita e opere," 37; Van den Enden, *Philedonius, 1657*, ed. Proietti, 31–4.
[22] See Karel D'Huyvetters' online article "O Thenae! Some Remarks on the Sack of the Flemish City of Tienen," p. 3 and appendix; Van den Enden, *Philedonius, 1657*, ed. Proietti, 36–8.

Neither heresy's perverseness nor the wonders of the Blessed Virgin, though, were quite the lesson Van den Enden or Spinoza drew from the episode. Spinoza invokes the Tienen atrocities when answering Burgh, to mock the latter's conversion which he describes as devoting oneself to a "divine justice that allows the Devil to deceive men with impunity, but does not permit men, haplessly deceived and ensnared by the Devil, to go unpunished." How can one call that divine justice? Moreover, nothing could be more absurdly contrived than belief in the Catholic host and holy wafer: "such absurdities might be tolerated if you worshipped a God infinite and eternal, but not one which Châtillon, in a town the Dutch call Tienen, fed to his horses without being punished [by divine providence]."[23]

In 1641, Ríos y Alarcón published at Antwerp a further literary monument to his "Maria the Virgin of Remedies" cult, further theologico-political propaganda exalting Spanish absolutism anchored in faith. A magnificently illustrated folio appeared, entitled *Hierarchia mariana* in which Erasmus Quellinus certainly, and Rubens very likely, had a hand, celebrating the Cardinal-Infante's latest triumph— the Battle of Kallo of June 1638.[24] On the left bank of the Schelde River, a complex of defensive forts just below Antwerp, Kallo was the scene of a night-long battle in which the Cardinal-Infante's troops, suffering only light losses, repulsed a three-pronged surprise attack, capturing or sinking sixty to seventy troop barges and overwhelming the Dutch invaders. In this sole sizeable, pitched battle between Spain and the Dutch during the second part of the Eighty Years War (i.e. since 1621), the protracted twenty-seven-year struggle otherwise mainly comprising blockades and sieges, hundreds of Dutch troops were killed and some 2,500 prisoners captured, including two colonels and numerous sailors along with eighty-one river craft and dozens of heavy guns. It was the "greatest victory Your Majesty's arms have had," the Cardinal-Infante assured Philip IV, "since the Low Countries war began." It blighted Dutch hopes of soon capturing Antwerp and incorporating the entire Lower Scheldt estuary within the Republic.[25] Van den Enden, styled "a physician of Antwerp," contributed an elaborate Latin poem, twenty-eight pages long, to the celebratory volume.

Celebration of the Cardinal-Infante's "stupendous triumph" culminated in a solemn procession into Kallo, on 8 September 1638, headed by Father Ríos y Alarcón, a spectacle accompanied by artillery salutes from the surrounding forts and some two hundred boats thronging the river close by. Watched by large crowds, the procession reinstalled the repaired image of the Holy Virgin desecrated by the Dutch; a *Te Deum* followed. Spain's triumph was a double one,

---

[23] Spinoza, *Collected Works* (ed. Curley) ii, 474. Spinoza to Burgh, The Hague, end of 1675 or early 1676.
[24] On this battle, see Israel, *Dutch Republic and the Hispanic World*, 259.
[25] ARB SEG 219, fos. 254v–255v; *Resolutien van de Heeren Staten van Holland*, 1638, 100. Res. 30 June 1638; Vermeir, *Staat van oorlog*, 146.

proclaims Van den Enden's poem, exalting the Spanish king's younger brother and the restored Virgin Mary,[26] citing a "sacred painting" commissioned by Ríos y Alarcón in Antwerp, the "mother and nurse of all painting," to propagandize the entire Eighty Years War in art as an epochal world-transforming struggle between holy faith and loathsome heresy. Applauding the assassination of William of Orange, in Delft, in 1584, Van den Enden's poem was a consummate pious eulogy of absolutism, persecution of heresy, and church sanctioned political assassination.[27]

8.ii A Career in the Church Abandoned

Since nothing in Van den Enden's thought and writing foreshadows Spinoza's own emergence as a radical Cartesian, scientist, or Bible critic, and he apparently penned nothing of a radical character before the early 1660s, aside from elevating his Latin, this leaves two main respects in which the pre-1660 Van den Enden undoubtedly contributed to shaping Spinoza's distinctive outlook. These were his particular style of teaching and their common deep affection for the Roman classics including Seneca and ancient Stoicism. Spinoza both appreciated and criticized ancient Stoicism and, in those key areas where he already by 1658 diverged from mainstream Cartesianism such as his determinism, one substance doctrine, and equation of God and Nature, Spinoza's emerging stance does seem in certain respects like a fusion of Cartesianism with ancient Stoicism.[28] Contemporaries often exaggerated this seeming link to Stoicism. "No egg more resembles another than does Spinoza's system that of the Stoics," averred one Dutch scholar in 1690, restating here not just the view of Bayle but also that of Van Til, Jacques Bernard, Leibniz, Buddeus and many another.[29]

One modern scholar has gone so far as to claim that the "central doctrines and the connections between them" in Spinoza's *Ethics* "constitute [...] a reworking of Stoicism."[30] This is assuredly overstating the case. Apart from anything else, Spinoza always rejected the teleological conception of divine providence central to Stoicism and has a rather different and narrower conception of virtue.[31] Still, the young Spinoza was familiar with strands of ancient Stoicism, in particular Seneca, and some affinities *are* striking. Glazemaker's translation of Seneca's *Moral Letters*

---

[26] Proietti, "Vita e opere," 40–7.
[27] Proietti, "Vita e opere," 27, 48; Van den Enden, *Philedonius, 1657*, ed. Proietti, 36, 40–8.
[28] Long, "Stoicism in the Philosophical Tradition," 369–78; Miller, *Spinoza and the Stoics*, 21–3.
[29] Hassel, "Voorreden," pp. iii–iv; Til, *Voor-hof der heydenen*, 257; Bayle, *Écrits sur Spinoza*, 70–1; Israel, *Enlightenment Contested*, 458.
[30] James, "Spinoza the Stoic," 291; Long, "Stoicism in the Philosophical Tradition," 369–70; Miller, *Spinoza and the Stoics*, 2, 8–9, 207.
[31] Kisner, *Spinoza on Human Freedom*, 81; Garrett, *Nature and Necessity*, 493.

to *Lucilius* published in two volumes, in 1654 and 1671,[32] was among the astoundingly few works in Dutch found in Spinoza's personal library at the time of his death. Although Colerus, Van Til, Goeree, and other sources, like Steno, identify Van den Enden as the chief source of the "atheistic" tendency which to them was the prime feature of Spinoza's thought, it seems probable that, while introducing Spinoza to the world of classical humanism, the Dutch art scene, the Roman historians and tragedians, and elevating his Latin to a proficient level, as regards identifying God with Nature, Van den Enden at most did no more than chime in with an anti-Scripturalism and denial of divine providence and immortality of the soul, by the late 1650s already firmly anchored in Spinoza's outlook, as the Inquisition evidence of 1658, discussed further on, confirms.

Definitively expelled from the Jesuit Order aged thirty-one, Van den Enden abandoned his pursuit of a church-orientated career around 1640. He then joined his younger brother Martinus collaborating in his art publishing business, based in Antwerp, where Franciscus married, in 1642, and his two eldest children were born. His next four children, though, two dying in infancy, arrived after he and his wife moved to Amsterdam in 1644 or 1645, a transfer northwards due not to expulsion from the Spanish Netherlands for religious deviancy or freethinking, as some have conjectured but, rather, as Frank Mertens has shown, linked to his activity as an art dealer. At Amsterdam during the 1640s, to all appearance, he remained a loyal Catholic forming ties with the city's local Catholic "hidden churches," in particular the Dominicuskerk, among the largest Catholic congregations in the old centre of Amsterdam, where several of his children were baptized.[33]

Van den Enden's presence in Holland may have had a behind-the-scenes political dimension but, at this stage in his career, it can hardly have been radical in character. Diplomatic involvement is implied by lines of a celebratory poem written about him later by a pupil of his, Antonides van der Goes (1647–84), who became a prominent Rotterdam physician and, from the 1660s, noted poet and playwright. During the Dutch–Spanish peace negotiations, at Munster (1643–8), Van den Enden played some shadowy part, records Van der Goes, in assisting or advising the Spanish delegation headed by the Conde de Peñaranda.[34] "Spain on your advice alone concluded the peace,"[35] affirms Van der Goes' verse, while Van den Enden's first biographer, Du Cauzé de Nazelle, adds, still more vaguely, that in these years he travelled across much of Europe, "everywhere giving rise to great admiration of his knowledge."[36] Probably, he acted as a translator and informant reporting on contacts (which we know he had) with members of the Amsterdam

---

[32] Van Sluis and Musschenga, *Boeken van Spinoza*, 62–3; Esteves do Couto, *Marvelous Travels*, 42.
[33] Proietti, "Vita e opere," 60–1, 69; Mertens, *Van den Enden en Spinoza*, 27–8.
[34] Meininger and Suchtelen, *Liever met wercken*, 12–13.   [35] Proietti, "Vita e opere," 50.
[36] Meininger and Suchtelen, *Liever met wercken*, 16.

city government, hence an agent of some sort working to encourage the gradual but contested shift of Dutch sentiment in favour of settling with Spain. Whereas until late 1644, Madrid and Brussels vested their hopes in secret contacts with The Hague, seeking to win over the Prince of Orange and detach him from his French alliance with handsome offers, in December 1644 Spanish ministers, realizing Frederik Hendrik was "deceiving those who are there on the part of His Majesty, diverting them with ceremonious and polite words to gain time and dispose of matters to his advantage," changed tactics switching to courting the anti-Orangist peace faction in Holland, especially Amsterdam's regents.[37]

These negotiations marked a crucial transition for both the southern and northern Netherlands, virtually guaranteeing the two parts of the Low Countries would long remain essentially separate religiously and politically. Overcommitted and financially desperately overstretched, now fighting four simultaneous wars—against the Dutch, French, Portuguese, and Spain's insurgent realm of Catalonia—Spain was much the more eager of the two sides to settle quickly. The difficulty was that the seven Dutch provinces were split, with Zeeland and Friesland especially supporting Frederick Henrik and his son and successor Willem II (Stadholder: 1647–50), in seeking to prolong the war, allied to France to exploit Spain's new vulnerability and overrun more of Flanders and more Spanish colonies overseas. But the Stadholder's plans meant continued heavy spending on a large military and naval apparatus while Holland, and Amsterdam in particular, tired of heavy taxation and obstacles to commerce, favoured peace.

When Spinoza first met him, possibly as early as the late 1640s, Van den Enden had no discernible interest in, or connection with Cartesians or scientists, and no particular involvement with philosophy. He had not yet become remotely the democratic republican he became later. He was though, like Antonio Pérez, someone with exceptional knowledge of political propaganda, secret diplomacy and court intrigue, as well as the power-seeking of Jesuits and other religious orders, which must have added to the reasons why Spinoza, in later years, liked to think destiny had afforded him rare insight into the mechanics of power and politics behind the scenes that other political theorists lacked. When the Dutch–Spanish peace treaty of 1648 was finally ratified and celebrated, with unprecedented festivities in Amsterdam, Spinoza was sixteen. After moving to Amsterdam, Van den Enden continued earning his living through art dealing in conjunction with his brother at Antwerp, Martinus van den Enden (1605–73?), a successful publisher of prints from paintings by (and after) Rubens and Van Dyck, most notably marketing a historic, today immensely valuable album of eighty portraits known as the *Iconographie*, produced by Van Dyck and his studio, a renowned collection subsequently published in many editions.

---

[37] AGS Estado 2063, *consulta* of the Junta de Estado, 4 Jan. 1645; Israel, *Dutch Republic and the Hispanic World*, 352–7.

The resulting assemblage of prints "after Van Dyck" was arranged in three principal series: first, princes and military commanders, next statesmen, advisers to princes, thinkers and philosophers, among them Lipsius, Puteanus, De Peiresc, and Constantijn Huygens, and third, noted artists and collectors, the last being much the largest section. It was a veritable landmark in art history.[38] Although the idea itself originated with Van Dyck or Rubens, the decision to expand Van Dyck's original collection of portrait prints into a major business venture was Martinus'. Profiting from Rubens' recognition of the commercial possibilities of reproducing an ambitiously large series of prints of painted portraits, Martinus retained control of the copperplates and publishing the *Iconographie* down to the mid-1640s.[39] Around 1647, or earlier, Franciscus acquired a shop with the name "In de Konstwinckel" [In the Art-Shop], in the Nes, a narrow alleyway in the centre of Amsterdam. This amply furnished shop, rented from the regents of the Amsterdam leper house, became his art and bookstore, and family home, a residence where Van den Enden evidently attracted numerous artists, trainee artists, and scholars as well as, presumably, the young Spinoza.[40]

One room was rented out during 1648–9 to a gifted but sickly pupil of Rembrandt, Leendert van Beyeren (1620–49), whose wealthy lumber merchant father was also an art collector.[41] When his father died, around 1638, Van Beyeren had inherited a considerable collection, much of which he now loaned to Van den Enden's lively establishment. When Van Beyeren also died aged only twenty-nine, in the autumn of 1649, while still lodging there, a notarial inventory of his possessions, dated 10 October 1649, describes his walls as covered with sketches and paintings including a large "Ecce Homo" and a "Tobias," prints from the *Iconographie*, and prints of works by Rembrandt, Dürer, and Lucas van Leyden. Van den Enden himself organized the sale of Van Beyeren's belongings but kept the *Ecce Homo* on his dining room wall. When visiting the house during the time he frequented Van den Enden's milieu, and rubbing shoulders with at least one or two of Rembrandt's students, Spinoza had every opportunity to compare the work of great Antwerp artists with that of their Dutch counterparts on view at Van den Enden's and acquire some sense of the overall Low Countries art scene.

Van den Enden's publishing, book- and map-selling, and art dealing enterprise survived only for a few years, though, collapsing, like Spinoza's business, during the slump of the First Anglo-Dutch War (1652–4). As recorded by the Amsterdam bankruptcy court, dated 12 September 1652, "Franchoijs van Eijde" found his affairs in such difficulties that "he presently has no means to repay his debts to his common creditors promptly." He sought to enter with them into a reasonable agreement for a revised schedule of repayment. Portraits of Prince William and

---

[38] Brown, *Drawings of Anthony van Dyck*, 190–1.
[39] Brown, *Drawings of Anthony van Dyck*, 190–3; Mertens, *Van den Enden en Spinoza*, 11.
[40] Mertens, "Where Thou Dwellest," 56.   [41] Schwartz, *Rembrandt*, 127, 195.

the Princess Royal, this 1652 inventory records, were hanging on Van den Enden's walls, together with pious Catholic religious pictures.[42] The bankruptcy terms involved closure and sale of his shop and a repayment schedule spanning seven years.[43] The inventory lists unsold paintings, copies, and prints displayed all over the house and a cellar containing a printing press and "certain quantity of unbound books and prints," doubtless many imported from Antwerp. His remaining stock included 130 books ready for sale (unfortunately with no titles given).

Until 1650, Franciscus, though hugely interested in politics, showed no discernible inclination for political theory as such, or republicanism. But in 1650 occurred the clash between Stadholder William II and Amsterdam for control of the Republic, culminating in the Stadholder's siege and occupation of the city, the second of the three great internal political crises to rock the Dutch Republic during the Golden Age—the other two being Oldenbarnevelt's downfall (1618) and the "Disaster Year" (1672). The 1650 episode left an indelible imprint on Amsterdammers. Revulsion against William II and the abortive Orangist attempt to subdue their city by force boosted interest in the domestic political scene and republican ideas. By 1654, when the war with England ended, Van den Enden and Spinoza both had abundant reason to regard Orangists as a threat to the Republic, and Cromwell's "commonwealth" as a menacing bogus republic.

A possible first sign of the eventual radical shift in Van den Enden's own politics is the sole text definitely known to have been published by him, carrying the logo "Franciscus vanden Enden, in den Nes" as publisher, namely, the *Short Justification [...] of the Freedoms, Rights, Privileges and worthy Usages of the province of Holland* (1587), originally written in the time of Leicester's government in the Netherlands, in 1585-7. This attack on Leicester's regime as "tyranny" Van den Enden published in 1650, precisely when the Prince of Orange attempted to use force against Amsterdam to coerce change in the power balance in the Republic and entrench his own princely authority. The text was oppositional, undoubtedly, but also entirely traditional in its reasoning.[44] Slim evidence, but it might signal Van den Enden's longstanding involvement in politics now shifting from attachment to absolutism, religious uniformity and deference to Spain to appreciation of the United Provinces' republican tradition and religious freedom.

In any case, it is incorrect to claim that "no bookshop in Amsterdam was more likely to attract freethinkers than Franciscus van den Enden's."[45] On the contrary, while clearly a gathering point for art lovers and artists, there is no sign that it was a meeting-point for freethinkers. Another unresolved question is what role, if any, Van den Enden's expertise in medicine played in his career, or whether Van den

---

[42] Mertens, *Van den Enden en Spinoza*, 23-7; Meininger and Suchtelen, *Liever met wercken*, 20-1.
[43] Meininger and Suchtelen, *Liever met wercken*, 22-4; Proietti, "Vita e opere," 68-9.
[44] Mertens, *Van den Enden en Spinoza*, 30-1.   [45] Gullan-Whur, *Life of Spinoza*, 58.

Enden ever practised medicine. He was regularly described as a physician with a medical degree, from the 1630s onwards, and presumably this is why Bayle, in his long article on Spinoza in his *Dictionnaire historique* (1697), claims Spinoza studied "the Latin language under a physician who taught that subject in Amsterdam," adding, citing Jelles in a footnote, that from an early stage in his intellectual career Spinoza studied "theology" meaning religious studies, and only subsequently "devoted himself entirely to the study of philosophy."[46]

Bankrupted by the First Anglo-Dutch War, to support his family Van den Enden reverted to school-teaching. He opened his soon highly successful school on the Singel, the canal marking the boundary edge of medieval Amsterdam but now at the heart of the seventeenth-century city, just a short walk from Spinoza's house. Opening in 1652 or the next year, assisted by his two daughters, now in their teens—who had themselves received what, at the time, for girls, was an exceptionally thorough classical education—Van den Enden's Latin school on the Singel quickly won renown, proving attractive especially to wealthy parents pertaining to churches other than the Reformed and hence reluctant to entrust their sons to the official civic Latin School where sternly Calvinist attitudes prevailed. The school's reputation remained intact for some time, records Colerus, a Lutheran pastor in Amsterdam from 1679 until he moved to The Hague in 1693,[47] "until it began to be noticed that he was instilling into his pupils something more than Latin, namely the first seeds and principles of godlessness."[48] This, he claimed, is "a matter of fact which I could prove if there were any need to, by the testimony of several honest gentlemen, still living, some of whom have been elders of the Lutheran Church at Amsterdam. Every day those good men may bless the memory of their parents for taking steps, in good time, to remove them from the school of so pernicious and impious a master."[49]

Even if Van den Enden was already then an unbeliever subverting young minds under the cover of outward Catholic conformity, which hardly seems likely given that his school long enjoyed a high reputation, it would not necessarily follow that his "atheism" exerted any great impact on Spinoza, as so many commentators later assumed. Even were Van den Enden already a freethinker in the mid-1650s, their encounter may have merely reinforced, exactly as with De Prado, a long-germinating tendency in Spinoza to a profound scepticism about revealed religion. It is perfectly plausible that what most impressed Spinoza, apart from Van den Enden's literary skills and mastery of the classics, was not any freethinking leanings but simply the astounding mix of confessions represented in his school which was highly unusual and its lack of attachment to any particular confession.

---

[46] Bayle, *Écrits sur Spinoza*, 21.   [47] Blasé, *Johannes Colerus*, 13–14, 73, 128–9.
[48] Colerus, *Korte, dog waaragtige levens-beschrijving*, 100; Klever, "Inleiding," 20; Rothkamm, *Institutio Oratoria*, 133–4.
[49] Halma, *Het Leven*, 5; Colerus, *Life of Benedict de Spinoza*, 4.

Although sons of Calvinists also attended, Van den Enden's school brought its few staff, including the young Spinoza, into daily contact with a unique array of sons of dissenting Arminians, strict Mennonites, liberal Mennonites, Collegiants, and sons of leading members of the Lutheran congregation, notes Colerus, and Catholics besides.[50]

Through the 1650s, Van den Enden's intellectual interests remained predominantly literary, humanist, and classical while also linked to art, diplomacy, and the rhetoric of statesmanship without extending to anything philosophical or to political theory. Evidently Spinoza's association with Van den Enden predated not only Spinoza's turn to philosophy and science but also Van den Enden's turn to republican political theory. Though their acquaintance probably reached back before 1653, Spinoza's commitment to spend his days studying with Van den Enden and earn his bread helping manage the school clearly occurred in late 1655 or early 1656. But Van den Enden, the evidence shows, only immersed himself seriously in political theory, emerging as a fervent democratic republican, from 1661 when invited to write his text about the condition of the Dutch colony of New Netherland. It is therefore possible, even probable, that Van den Enden had not yet arrived at his later radical stance prior to or during the time he and Spinoza collaborated closely in the mid- and later 1650s.[51]

Their close collaboration cannot have begun after Spinoza's expulsion from the synagogue, in 1656, not just because our best sources affirm an earlier date, but also because of Spinoza's ability, by 1658 at the latest, to follow philosophy courses given in Latin at Leiden, and then already noted skill in philosophy as testified before the Madrid Inquisition. His philosophical dexterity had by 1658 already rendered him locally renowned in Amsterdam, making any notion of a post-1656 commencement inconceivable. A pre-1652 beginning to their association seems far likelier, as running an art shop did not of itself preclude Van den Enden from privately coaching pupils in Latin. The Monnikhoff and Colerus biographies, when recounting the start of Spinoza's Latin studies, mention a certain "German student" as his first Latin mentor before he turned to Van den Enden for more expert guidance. According to J. Monnikhoff (1707–87), who may have had independent sources, Spinoza received his first Latin lessons at his parental home, after which his parents sent him to learn Latin with the "famous master of medicine and languages, François van den Enden who not only made him wholly competent in this language but also (however outside the knowledge of his parents) instilled such thoughts in him, that afterwards became the foundation of his particular teaching."[52]

This suggests it was indeed Spinoza's father who, in the late 1640s, first arranged his Latin lessons, which might seem puzzling given that at that time

---

[50] Colerus, *Korte, dog waaragtige levens-beschrijving*, 100; Rothkamm, *Institutio Oratoria*, 133–4.
[51] Lavaert, "Prelude," 69.   [52] Monnikhoff, "Beschrijving van Spinoza's leven," 201–2.

there were few career possibilities open to Jews of a kind requiring knowledge of Latin (and academic study) other than that of physician. But if Spinoza did indeed begin studying Latin before his older brother, Isaac, died in 1649, when, as a second son, he could have sought a career outside commerce, he may briefly have been destined for a medical career, in which case Van den Enden with his expertise and medical degree was a perfect choice.[53] Assuming Monnikhoff did possess information different from that available to Bayle and Colerus (a point that remains disputed), his report supports the view that Spinoza was taught by Van den Enden much earlier than is sometimes claimed.

After moving out of the Jewish district and away from his family home, in 1656, but still living in Amsterdam (with stays in Leiden) and needing to support himself while learning the craft of grinding lenses and constructing microscopes and telescopes, Spinoza doubtless depended for a time on the teaching job available to him at Van den Enden's school. Here, he certainly learnt novel methods of teaching and rhetoric as well as the classics. For the teaching methods prevailing there sharply diverged from those of the city's Calvinist Reformed schools and also other schools of traditional confessional format.[54] Indeed, working at the school as an assistant teacher in the mid-1650s may well have been the aspect of his encounter with Van den Enden with the greatest impact on Spinoza's subsequent life, not least through his lasting association with several younger pupils who later played a role in his life, including Albert Coenraadszn Burgh (1650–1708) whom Spinoza reprimanded when citing the atrocities of Tienen, in 1675. The son of an Amsterdam burgomaster who acknowledged having once been "a disciple" of Spinoza, after school Burgh studied at Leiden and eventually converted to Catholicism in Italy. Spinoza also stayed in touch with the later renowned Amsterdam anatomist and chemist Theodore Kerckring (1638–1693). Another pupil at Van den Enden's school likely to have been taught partly by Spinoza was the poet Pieter Rixtel (1643–73) who later distinguished himself in the literary and theatre life of Haarlem.

8.iii Spinoza Embraces Cartesianism

Whatever his father intended, Spinoza's own basic purpose in perfecting his Latin with Van den Enden's help was not to pursue a career in medicine but his chosen path in Bible criticism and religious studies. "Having learn'd the Latin tongue well," as the 1706 English rendering of Colerus put it, Spinoza applied himself to the study of Divinity for some years. "In the meantime, his wit and judgment increased every day: so that finding himself more disposed to enquire into natural

---

[53] Monnikhoff, "Beschrijving van Spinoza's leven," 201; Colerus, *Das Leben*, 10.
[54] Mertens, "Van den Enden and Religion," 64; Rothkamm, *Institutio Oratoria*, 134.

causes, [eventually] he gave over Divinity, and betook himself altogether to the study of natural philosophy."[55] Supported also by other key sources, including the recollections of Steno, this order of studies seems reasonably certain and means Spinoza's progress in philosophy was largely independent of Van den Enden and intellectually separate from his teaching and absorbing Latin and Roman literature, important in his life though these elements were.

There is nothing surprising about Spinoza's acquiring a budding interest in Cartesianism, in the mid-1650s, but there is some question as to who or what prompted him to reach the impressively high level of expertise in Cartesianism linked to mathematics and optics that we know he had achieved by the late 1650s. Since this was clearly not Van den Enden or his school, we should consider the testimony of the Danish anatomist, geologist, and churchman Niels Stensen, or Steno as he was usually known, a close associate and friend of Spinoza during the period 1660–3. According to his testimony to the Congregation of the Faith in Rome, in September 1677, a few months after Spinoza's death, Spinoza's rejection of the idea of a benign creator of the world and of divine providence stemmed from two distinct and quite separate factors in his early development: interaction with Van den Enden on the one hand,[56] and, secondly, immersion, owing to other influences, in the philosophy of Descartes, in optics and in science generally.[57] This way of expressing the point deserves close attention: Steno regarded Van den Enden and Cartesianism as two essentially distinct albeit partly simultaneous influences on Spinoza.

In April 1660, having arrived in Holland from Denmark shortly before, Steno lodged for some months as a student in the house of the prominent local physician, Gerardus Blasius (1627–82), since 1659 "city physician" of Amsterdam and, from 1660, first professor of medicine at the Amsterdam Athenaeum. A central figure in medical and science research circles in Amsterdam, Blasius later founded the so-called Collegium Privatum Amstelodamense, a research society flourishing in the years 1664–73, conducting group research much in the spirit of the Florentine Academia di Cimento and the London Royal Society.[58] But already earlier there were gatherings and science demonstrations at the Athenaeum itself. While lodging in Blasius' house, Steno did much of the research on the salivary glands (in front of both ears) and the route saliva takes from the main salivary parotid gland into the mouth, afterwards known as the "ductus Stenoniensis [Steno's duct]," or "ductus parotideus [parotid duct]," the first of a series of anatomical discoveries made during his years in Holland that would establish his enduring fame. However, Blasius' attempt to steal, for himself, the credit for this discovery made in his own

---

[55] Colerus, *Life of Benedict de Spinoza*, 7. [56] Totaro, "Documenti," 97.
[57] Totaro, "Documenti," 97.
[58] Jorink, "Modus Politicus Vivendi," 16–19, 35; Mertens, *Van den Enden en Spinoza*, 52–3; Van Vugt, "Structure and Dynamics," 102.

home laboratory, provoked a quarrel over precedence that dragged on for years.[59] Steno then transferred from Amsterdam to Leiden.

While "studying at the University of Leiden, in Holland, fifteen and sixteen years before," Steno testified before the Roman Inquisitors, in 1677, he had "occasion to converse familiarly with the said Spinoza who was born a Jew, but by profession is without religion" and who was preoccupied with "two dogmas [i.e. Van den Enden's teaching and Cartesianism] which at that time I knew only confusedly." This passage is usually taken to mean that Steno first encountered Spinoza at some point in the year or two after matriculating at Leiden, on 16 July 1660. But Steno does not say that; he states only that he and Spinoza began "talking familiarly" in Leiden.[60] Given Steno's medical research under Blasius, that the latter was a close friend of Johannes Koerbagh, and that Steno probably also knew the Brothers Koerbagh at this time,[61] and that during 1660, a year when both Steno and Spinoza were in Amsterdam, many anatomical dissections and physics and chemistry disputations and demonstrations took place at the Athenaeum, it seems quite likely that Spinoza and Steno first met during those Athenaeum classes and discussions.

Since Spinoza was still based mainly in Amsterdam and by now immersed in optics and science generally, he presumably participated, like the later famous naturalist and microscopist Jan Swammerdam (1637–80), in scientific gatherings and experiments in some local context, and very likely in the surge of scientific activity and debate at the Athenaeum (Figure 8.1). Spinoza, we must bear in mind already formulated what would develop into his basic rule governing scientific experiments by around 1658. "Before we equip ourselves for knowledge of singular things," he writes in his *Emendation of the Intellect*, and study those "aids" that help us "know how to use our senses, and undertake, according to secure laws, and in order, the experiments that enable us to understand the thing we are investigating," it is necessary first to "acquire a sufficient knowledge of eternal things and their infallible laws, and the nature of our senses."[62] People whose heads are stuffed with imaginary notions, prejudices and wrong thinking cannot observe, assess, or study anything scientifically.

Steno was clearly won over to his own transformed scientific outlook in two successive stages—first to observational science, dissection, and demonstration while initially resisting the fast encroaching, stirring new zeal of the Cartesians for the "certainty of philosophy." Experimental science was then gaining a firm hold in England and Holland alike. By contrast, the Cartesianism arousing enthusiasm for science-based philosophy among the young intellectuals Steno encountered in 1660, was almost entirely confined to the Dutch academic sphere. His own

---

[59] Lindeboom, "Short Biography," 5; Totaro, "Documenti," 104–5.
[60] Steno, "Libri prohibiti," 68; Scherz, *Niels Stensen*, 32–3, 149.
[61] Jorink, "Modus Politicus Vivendi," 20–1.   [62] Spinoza, *Collected Works* (ed. Curley) i, 42.

Figure 8.1 *The Athenaeum Illustre at Amsterdam in 1650*, oil on panel. Reproduction courtesy of Teylers Museum Haarlem, the Netherlands.

conversion to Cartesianism was clearly subsequent to his plunging into observational-experimental science. Whether his Cartesian phase began whilst he was still at the Amsterdam Athenaeum, or the following year in Leiden, this twenty-two-year-old Dane himself attests that he too was caught up for a time in this fervour for philosophy closely tied to science and mathematics, especially the epistemological "certainty" the Cartesians gloried in. By September 1661, writing to his professor, Bartholin, in Copenhagen, Steno announced that Cartesianism had now almost completely conquered his initial reservations. For a time, from 1661, he assured Leibniz years later, he even considered Descartes' philosophy "infallible."[63]

It is hard for us today to fully grasp the immense impact Cartesianism had on young thinkers ardent for science, like Spinoza and Steno. It was not just a question of adopting a particular philosophical framework and terminology but marked a revolutionary shift in thinking from a scholastic world in which things exist as names in formal categories to one grappling with the precise functioning of actual things in terms of measurement, observation and motion, steeping oneself in experimental science, a shift then encouraged by the findings and views of many of the Dutch universities' leading scientists. When he first got to

[63] Cohen, *Spinoza en de geneeskunde*, 62; Totaro, "Niels Stensen (1638–1686)," 150; Scherz, "Biography of Nicolaus Steno," 64–67; Israel, *Dutch Republic*, 585–7.

know him in the early 1660s, Steno reported later, in 1677, Spinoza had given up Talmudic and rabbinic studies with which he had occupied himself for some years, impelled by two distinct factors—the intervention of a "certain Van Enden suspected of atheism" and, secondly, "reading the philosophy of Descartes."[64] Spinoza's conversion to Descartes' "new philosophy" clearly considerably preceded his own.

The Cartesians certainly viewed their philosophy as a revolution in science, medicine, and culture generally. Thanks especially to Steno, but also Blasius and others, by 1661, Spinoza already had a more realistic, sophisticated notion of anatomy, muscles, glands, the nervous system, the human brain and mind than Descartes himself had possessed.[65] Sternly warning against the pitfalls of mere terms and categories, and insisting on the indispensability of researching reality through investigation, measurement, observation, dissection, and experiment were among the most constant features of Spinoza's philosophical effort for the rest of his life, whether in optics, attending dissections and experiments, Bible criticism or assessing sermons or composing philosophical and political treatises.

Given that Cartesianism was Spinoza's intellectual second stage as a serious thinker, Spinoza's initial conversion doubtless began in mid-1650s Amsterdam, in part at the elder Jan Rieuwertsz's bookshop, a location destined to play a pivotal role in his life, and in conversation with the likes of Rieuwertsz's chief translator of Descartes from French, Jan Hendriksz Glazemaker (*c.*1619–82). However, taking the process further, as for all budding scholars at the time, depended in part on getting his Latin up to a sufficient level but also on opportunities for attending lectures and demonstrations, probably like Steno afterwards at the Athenaeum first and then Leiden, a sequence tightly linked to his immersing himself in the world of lens-grinding, microscopes and optics, of experiments, and more generally, mathematics.

Given that Spinoza's earliest surviving writings, the *Treatise on the Emendation of the Intellect* and *Korte Verhandeling* date from the late 1650s, and many characteristic features of Spinoza's thought are present already there, we know the basics of Spinoza's own distinctive philosophical system were already emerging by 1658.[66] Much of what Steno witnessed in Spinoza in 1661—his preoccupation with philosophy, zeal for certainty, and what he perceived as Cartesianism's tight links to science and mathematics—we see from the *Emendation* and the Madrid Inquisition reports, had already formed in Spinoza's mind several years earlier. There is therefore no avoiding the conclusion that the early formative steps in Spinoza's philosophical career began in the early and mid-1650s and are

---

[64] Steno, "Libri prohibiti," 33; Totaro, "Ho certi amici," 31; Totaro, "The Young Spinoza and the Vatican Manuscript," 320.
[65] Cohen, *Spinoza en de geneeskunde*, 63.
[66] Van Bunge, "Spinoza's filosofische achtergronden," 105; Israel, "Philosophy, Commerce," 129–30.

relatively unconnected with his encounter with Van den Enden. By 1660, Van den Enden was a veteran teacher and, there is no reason to doubt, a seasoned freethinker "suspected of atheism" as Steno put it, and perhaps had been since prior to meeting Spinoza. But as the leading expert on Van den Enden, Frank Mertens stresses, he showed no particular interest in Cartesianism while in the later 1650s, the second stage of Spinoza's philosophical career, it *was* unquestionably Cartesianism linked to microscopes and optics that provided Spinoza's principal entry path into the sphere of philosophy and science.

Most likely, Spinoza first embraced Cartesianism, optics, and geometry in Rieuwertsz's bookshop when encountering the growing array of translations of Descartes' works from Latin and French into Dutch recently published by Rieuwertsz and that enabled Rieuwertsz and Glazemaker to turn the shop into a unique showcase and repository of the revolutionary new philosophical system open to a wider public than just the Latin-reading academic fraternity. It was effectively the sole such showcase of popularized Cartesianism in the world prior to 1660, though this does not alter the fact that Spinoza cannot have developed advanced skills in these areas, as he indisputably had by 1658, without sitting in on lectures and demonstrations at the Athenaeum and in Leiden, and without at least some connection with leading Cartesian minds geared towards optics. Someone or something prodded Spinoza to embrace Cartesianism and experimental science whilst he still lived in Amsterdam, lodging with Van den Enden, and, in looking beyond Glazemaker and Rieuwertsz, we are, unfortunately, reduced to pure conjecture. Nowhere else in Europe did Descartes' philosophy arouse so much heated debate, enthusiasm, and also efforts to revise some of his basic concepts as in the Dutch Republic in the 1650s. If the Dutch Cartesian controversy in the late 1650s spurred Spinoza's interest and intellectual development, the same is equally true of Spinoza's most important friends of the 1660s, including Jelles, Lodewijk Meyer, Bouwmeester, and Adriaan Koerbagh. All these figures, along with numerous professors and other students, became immersed in exploring how exactly Descartes' revolution in philosophy impacts on the fields of ethics, medicine, natural philosophy, anatomy, and not least theology.[67]

Since most of Spinoza's non-Jewish friends of the pre-1658 period were Collegiants with limited interest in Cartesianism, optics, and mathematics, likely candidates for having stimulated and helped initiate the shift in Spinoza's focus well prior to 1658, apart from Glazemaker and Rieuwertsz, seem very few. But there is one figure who stands out as a star of Cartesian theorizing specifically in Amsterdam, in the late 1650s—the future regent and burgomaster, Johannes Hudde (1628–1704). Spinoza and Hudde are known to have worked together on problems in optics at a later stage, and, since mathematics became one of

[67] Van Ruler, "Spinoza in Leiden," 40.

Spinoza's specialities at this time, it seems relevant also that Hudde figured among the editors of the mathematical works of Frans van Schooten (1615–60), Descartes' principal ally teaching at Leiden during the 1640s, who at the same time, until his death, in 1660, was the Republic's leading mathematician doing more than anyone else to tie Cartesianism closely to geometry. Hudde contributed three papers to the collection entitled *Excercitationes Mathematicae* (Leiden, 1657), a copy of which Spinoza kept in his personal library. Hudde also contributed to Van Schooten's 1659 edition of Descartes' *Geometria*.[68] Besides being a pupil and editor of Van Schooten and eager Cartesian more prominent than any other in Amsterdam in the late 1650s, at that juncture Hudde was also a leading figure in microscope research.

After several years of study at Leiden, Hudde by 1656–7 had emerged as preeminent in all the relevant fields in Amsterdam and, besides, was an activist, a polished theologico-political polemicist intervening with anonymous pamphlets in current debates scorning, for example, the strict Calvinist preachers' opposition to Copernican astronomy. A man of science and Cartesian reason, Hudde was convinced widening freedom to philosophize would be a public benefit. For the rest of his long and distinguished career in Amsterdam, he strove to use science to promote civic improvements and his influence to fend off the theologians' demands for more intolerance and restrictions on freedom of thought.[69] As a possible alternative to Hudde one might consider the leading professor in philosophy, mathematics, and science teaching at the Amsterdam Athenaeum, Alexander de Bie (1623–90), a friend of Huygens, who began lecturing there in 1653 and who drew enthusiastic students to the Athenaeum.[70] However, De Bie was an eclectic in philosophy unlikely to impart zeal for Cartesianism while Hudde was the only luminary already advanced in a highly sophisticated Cartesianism by the late 1650s who is regularly mentioned later in connection with Spinoza.

By 1657, Hudde had formed his alliance with the Cartesian republican regent, Lambert van Velthuysen, at Utrecht, and other prominent pupils of Van Schooten, to a limited extent including the Pensionary of Holland, Johan de Witt. As regents, these men had their political disagreements; but throughout his ascendancy in Dutch politics, De Witt recognized Hudde as the second most brilliant mathematician in the Republic after Huygens. In effect, there emerged a high society regent network constituting a behind-the-scenes front of progressive, pro-Copernican, pro-Cartesian regents interested in intervening in public debates with a view to eroding the grip of Calvinist theology. No one understood better

---

[68] Van Sluis and Musschenga, *Boeken van Spinoza*, 39; Thijssen-Schoute, *Nederlands Cartesianisme*, 79–80.
[69] Van Bunge, *From Stevin to Spinoza*, 55, 57, 61, 67, 93; Vermij, *Calvinist Copernicans*, 157, 194, 289–90, 292; Jorink, "Outside God," 89–90.
[70] Van Miert, *Humanism*, 73–5, 99, 292, 390; Scherz, "Biography of Nicolaus Steno," 64.

than Hudde the need to disseminate Cartesianism and heliocentrism without challenging the public church head-on, to operate inconspicuously, withholding their own names and profiles while intervening forcefully on a rhetorical level by publishing anonymous pamphlets.[71]

The sole contemporary source mentioning Hudde in connection with Spinoza's early turn to Cartesianism is a note by the prominent Danish savant and anatomist from western Jutland, Ole Borch (Olaus Borrichius) (1629–90), since 1660 professor of botany, chemistry, and philology at Copenhagen, one of Steno's teachers and among the best Scandinavian Latinists of the age. In the entry for September 1661, in Borch's *Itinerarium*, recording his travel experiences abroad during 1660–5, he records that while touring in the Leiden area, close to Rijnsburg, he learnt from a German physician living nearby that residing locally was a certain "Spinoza, ex-Jew turned Christian and now almost an atheist who so excells in Cartesian philosophy that in many points he surpasses Descartes himself with his distinct and cogent concepts." "However," Borch then added, as an exponent of Cartesianism "many prefer by far Hudde of Amsterdam who contributed the little treatise on furcation [i.e. forklike structures] to the recent edition of Descartes's works on geometry."[72] Borch's noting that local learned opinion envisaged two alternative versions of Cartesianism diverging in certain respects may imply both a gulf and a dialogue between Spinoza and Hudde that was already known to some, and in progress for some time. As later evidence shows, Hudde and Spinoza continued to interact in friendly fashion on both the philosophical and mathematical levels, especially as regards optics, while fundamentally disagreeing about the metaphysical and religious implications of Cartesianism.[73] The divide Borch pointed to in 1661 would later cement into a lasting rift between the Cartesio-Spinozism of key figures of the *cercle Spinoziste*, such as Meyer and Glazemaker, and the mainstream majority bloc of the Republic's academic Cartesians anxious to avoid all appearance of challenging the theologians and the Reformed Church.

Three letters from Spinoza to Hudde survive, though from various evidence the existence of at least another six is postulated.[74] Their collaboration is documented also by a letter addressed to Huygens by a Dutch hydraulics engineer working for the French, posted from Dunkirk, in 1676, where he recalls first hearing about Huygens' admirable feats in science eleven years before, hence in 1665, when in Amsterdam attending "many wonderful meetings and conversations in the

---

[71] Vermij, *Calvinist Copernicans*, 290–3, 314–15; Jorink, "Outside God," 96.
[72] Freudenthal/Walther, *Lebensgeschichte* i, 276 (doc. 80); Scherz, "Biography of Nicolaus Steno," 91–2; Van de Ven, *Documenting Spinoza*, see the chronology.
[73] Borch, *Itinerarium* i, 228; Klever, "Spinoza and Van den Enden," 315; Van de Ven, "Spinoza's Life and Time," 14–15; on the dichotomy of Dutch Cartesianism versus 1660s Cartesio-Spinozism, see also Van Bunge, "Spinoza's filosofische achtergronden," 106.
[74] Steenbakkers, "Spinoza's Correspondentie," 16.

company of Johannes Hudde, Benedictus de Spinoza and [Burchard] de Volder [later] professor at the University of Leiden."[75] Burchard de Volder (1643–1709), another future friend of Spinoza, was also first drawn to Cartesianism and experiments at the Amsterdam Athenaeum. Spinoza's three surviving letters to Hudde (none survive from Hudde to Spinoza) all date from 1666 and all suggest the core of their disagreement lay in the Cartesian division of reality into two basic substances, extension and mind, which Hudde embraces and Spinoza rejects and, beyond that, whether God is equivalent to all that there is, or whether God and Nature are entirely separate.

While disagreeing with Spinoza, Hudde is clearly interested in his views. Respecting the social distance between them, Spinoza addresses the eminent regent with a certain reserve, but his letters indicate too that there was nothing new about their interaction which seems more likely to date from Spinoza's time in Amsterdam than subsequent years. The letters clearly reveal that by the mid-1660s Spinoza felt he now has the edge over Hudde in pure philosophy; there he is the mentor. At the same time, while displaying his own not inconsiderable expertise in the mathematics of light rays and preoccupation with optics, he readily acknowledges Hudde's pre-eminence in those fields. A future Amsterdam burgomaster, Hudde was a prominent man, and because it was a priority of the *Opera Posthuma*'s editors, after Spinoza's death, to conceal all trace of links between Spinoza and important figures who would not wish to be associated with him in the public mind, the three letters, in Dutch, as originally published in the seventeenth century, all appeared with Hudde's name purposely deleted, the first being styled "B.d.S. to..." and the other two "B.d.S. to the same."[76]

Still, even if we accept that rather than Van den Enden, others such as Hudde, Glazemaker, and De Bie, enthusiasts steeped in optics and mathematics, prompted and spurred Spinoza's plunging into Cartesianism, mathematics, and optics, including microscope-making, in the mid- and late 1650s Van den Enden undoubtedly eventually emerged among the most notorious and prominent of the group that evolved later into the *cercle Spinoziste*, and played a leading role in Spinoza's encounter with Stoicism and other ancient philosophy, and especially in encouraging his blanket repudiation of religious authority and perhaps in tying this rejection to democratic republicanism, the defining characteristic of the nascent Radical Enlightenment.[77]

---

[75] Huygens, *Oeuvres complètes* viii, 3–4; Klever, "Burchardus de Volder," 193, 234; Israel, *Radical Enlightenment*, 247–8; Mertens, *Van den Enden en Spinoza*, 64.
[76] Spinoza, *Nagelate Schriften*, 572–80.
[77] Israel, *Radical Enlightenment*, 169, 176, 259; Israel, *Enlightenment that Failed*, 14–15, 56–7, 71, 164, 937.

8.iv Learning from the Roman Playwrights Terence and Seneca

Among the innovative aspects of Van den Enden's teaching particularly relevant to Spinoza's further development was a didactic method that proved highly successful with the parents and public as well as his students—his practice of getting his pupils to stage plays in Latin. Using Ancient Roman plays in the original language had long been a technique of Renaissance era teachers but was not, or was no longer, the norm in the Republic. The first recorded performance staged by Van den Enden and his students, a representation of the "destruction of Troy" based on Virgil, took place in February 1654 during celebrations surrounding the marriage of an Amsterdam burgomaster's daughter, Cornelia van Vlooswijck. In 1657, Van den Enden's school, then at the peak of its success, received permission to stage two plays of Terence at the Amsterdam civic theatre and the drama *Philedonius* written by Van den Enden himself. The highpoint of Van den Enden's didactic career and impact on Amsterdam's cultural life was his students' performances at the main Amsterdam civic theatre, or [*Stads*]*schouwburg*, of Terence's *Andria*, on 16 and 17 January 1657, his *Eunuchus*, on 21 and 22 May 1658, and the *Trojan Women* [Troades] of Seneca, on 28 and 29 May 1658.[78]

The plays of Terence, or Publius Terentius Afer (*c.*185–*c.*159 BC), a writer of North African Berber extraction brought to Rome originally as a slave, but, due to exceptional gifts, given a solid Latin and Greek education by his owner and eventually freed, and those of the Stoic philosopher Lucius Annaeus Seneca (d. AD 65), were particularly prized for teaching purposes. The moral lessons and maxims of Terence and Seneca, Spinoza certainly never forgot. He appears indeed to have taken part in these performances, or else helped prepare pupils to perform them, because philological analysis of the *TTP* and his other works reflects his being steeped in Terence and Seneca, no doubt as a consequence of his years as Van den Enden's protégé. *Eunuchus*, in particular, a play abounding in subversive humorous comment on human error and delusion, by a slave, seems to have appealed to Spinoza.[79] The relevant hints in Spinoza's mature prose were first noted in a philological study of Spinoza's writing undertaken in the years 1900–15 by Jan Hendrik Leopold (1865–1925), among the foremost Dutch poets since Vondel and an accomplished classicist much preoccupied with Stoic and Epicurean influences in Dutch culture.[80] His study was continued later by Omero Proietti and Foppe Akkerman. Unattributed quotes and phrases borrowed from Terence, they showed, pervade Spinoza's writing, proving that phrases

---

[78] Bordoli, *Etica, Arte, Scienza*, 103.
[79] Meininger and Suchtelen, *Liever met wercken*, 26; Proietti, "Vita e opere," 76; Rothkamm, *Institutio Oratoria*, 130, 134–5, 370.
[80] Akkerman, *Studies*, 3; Klever, *Spinoza Classicus*, 31.

derived from Terence lingered in Spinoza's recollection almost word for word, for the rest of his life.

Given that no direct confirmation of Spinoza's links to Van den Enden are found in his writings, repeated use of phrases from Terence's and Seneca's plays constitutes the most concrete evidence of creative interaction with Van den Enden beyond mere study of Latin grammar.[81] Spinoza was doubtless recalling his experience with these plays a short time later when composing his first surviving text, *Treatise of the Emendation of the Intellect* (c.1658–9) where he discusses how our minds think in terms of singularities reducing pluralities and groups to categories. "If someone has read only one comedy, he will retain it best so long as he does not read several others of that kind, for then it will flourish in isolation in the imagination." But after reading several of the same kind, they form a category in our minds and "we imagine them all together and they are easily confused."[82]

A building not surviving today, the Schouwburg, Amsterdam's civic playhouse, standing on one of the city's main canals (Keizergracht 384), was designed by Jacob van Campen (1596–1657), a disciple of Palladio and main founder of the restrained classicizing style typical of the Dutch Golden Age culminating in his famed Mauritshuis, in The Hague. Originally scheduled to be inaugurated with the play *Gijsbrecht van Amstel*, by Vondel, the day after Christmas, in December 1637, the Schouwburg had been temporarily stopped from proceeding by the Reformed Church council [*kerkeraad*] of Amsterdam, opposing all theatre and stage performance in principle, its intervention sparking a debate in the city government which, however, in January 1638 led to the *kerkeraad* being overruled. The theatre nevertheless remained a standing provocation to strict Calvinists while Van den Enden whose school was yet another irritant in their eyes, caused further annoyance by having the female parts in the plays he directed performed not by male actors dressed as women, as was customary in Northern Europe at the time, but by girl students, emulating the prevailing practice on the Italian and Spanish stage since the late sixteenth century. (Actresses playing female parts first appeared on the English stage only after the Restoration, in the early 1660s.)

Although Seneca too remained a living force in Spinoza's mind, most echoes from his time at Van den Enden's school derive from Terence's plays, especially *Andrea* and the *Eunuchus*, Terence's Latin being clearly the favourite source of rhetorical inspiration for Spinoza while composing the *TTP*, the *Ethics*, and the unfinished *Tractatus Politicus*. Indeed, it is likely that Spinoza actually acted the principal role, the wise slave Parmeno, in *Eunuchus*, on stage, since the largest

---

[81] Mertens, *Van den Enden en Spinoza*, 35; Haitsma Mulier, "Spinoza en Tacitus," 69; Klever, *Spinoza Classicus*, 31–2; Akkerman, "Taal en tekst," 17–18.
[82] Spinoza, *Collected Works* (ed. Curley) i, 36.

number of Terence-borrowings in his later writing derive from that particular role.[83] Both his plays and Terence himself clearly afforded the Roman world an unforgettable demonstration of the power of education to emancipate and elevate the enslaved that left an indelible mark on Spinoza. Leopold and Proietti also argued that Spinoza must have kept up his reading of Terence's Latin during his later years, from the late 1660s onwards.

Seneca, the other Roman playwright whose plays Van den Enden principally used as teaching tools, was an author whose tragedies (in the Basle edition of 1541), still figured in Spinoza's library at the time of his death. Proietti notes that Spinoza's earliest work, the *Tractatus de Intellectus Emendatione* with its key autobiographical passages, echoes several phrases from Seneca's *Letters to Lucilius*. In Spinoza's mature works, borrowings from Seneca occur less often than those from Terence, but include wording encapsulating one of Spinoza's most characteristic political maxims, notably his use of Seneca's dictum from *The Trojan Women* "violenta imperia nemo continuit diu, moderata durant [violent regimes never survive for long whereas moderate regimes do last]," a (questionable) maxim echoed twice in the *TTP*, first in chapter five where Spinoza writes: "however human nature does not allow itself to be absolutely compelled, and as the tragedian Seneca says, no one has maintained a violent regime for long; it is moderate regimes that endure,"[84] and in chapter sixteen where Spinoza repeats: "for no one has maintained a violent government for long, as Seneca says."[85] *Trojan Women* is a tragedy about atrocities, sacrilege, and who was responsible, during the devastation of Troy following the eventual fall of the city to Agamemnon and his army.

Van den Enden's own neo-Latin play, *Philedonius*, was performed by his students at the end of 1656 and on 13 and 27 January 1657. It was afterwards published in Amsterdam, in 1657, with a poetic preface by the great Dutch poet Joost van den Vondel (1587–1679). In the recent scholarly literature about Spinoza, scholars disagree concerning this curious play. Marc Bedjai and Wim Klever claim it seeks, under a mask, to promote a radical philosophical message and even expresses something approaching proto-Spinozism; against this, Proietti, Mertens, and others hold that the play and its chief figure, Philedonius, led by painful experience to contemplate *aeterna* [eternal things], repudiating the love of finite and ephemeral things that had preoccupied his youth, is entirely traditional and unexceptional in content whether from a Christian or Senecan Stoic perspective. Proietti even suggests it reveals a crypto-Jesuit Catholicizing tendency. Certainly, it provides no obvious sign that Van den Enden had yet abandoned the faith that fired him in earlier years. There may, though, be a hint of

---

[83] Meininger and Suchtelen, *Liever met wercken*, 29; Rothkamm, *Institutio Oratoria*, 370, 502.
[84] Spinoza, *Theological-Political Treatise*, 73; Klever, *Spinoza Classicus*, 20.
[85] Spinoza, *Theological-Political Treatise*, 200; Totaro (ed.) Spinoza, *Trattato*, 566, 660.

the change in Van den Enden's outlook and thinking, insinuated in the Vondel poem introducing the published version of *Philedonius*, in 1657.[86]

A vigorous advocate of toleration and connoisseur of Latin, Vondel, the son of Mennonite parents who lived in the proximity of Van den Enden's school, had shocked his enthusiastic following years before, around 1641, by converting to Catholicism. Vondel knew Van den Enden and his school and remained over many years sympathetic towards him until his defection from Catholic belief became (more) evident. He almost certainly also knew or at least occasionally encountered Spinoza. The name "Philedonius" itself, implies the Vondel poem prefacing the text, might be a pun on the name of Philodemus of Gadana (*c*.110–40 BC), an Epicurean philosopher whose house and library of scrolls lay buried beneath the volcanic eruption that flowed from Mount Vesuvius and submerged Pompei and Herculaneum in AD 79, but some of whose epigrams and poems with an erotic slant were known to Latin scholars in Van den Enden's day, preserved in a Byzantine anthology, the *Anthologia Graeca*.[87] If the relevant passage in Vondel is indeed an insinuating dig at Van den Enden for deserting his Catholic allegiance, Vondel's poem contains the only known possible contemporary allusion, prior to 1660, that Van den Enden was, by 1657, already cultivating a clandestine circle of "atheists" in Amsterdam.

In his poem, Vondel calls Van den Enden's play "Lusthart" [Friend of Lust] rather than lending its title a more elevated Epicurean designation as Van den Enden obviously intended, such as "Friend of Well-Being." Intended to flatter Burgomaster Cornelis van Vlooswijk (1601–87), the prominent father of one of the boy actors, who figured, with his wife, among Vondel's chief patrons, the poem hails their son, Nicolaes, as a budding statesman benefiting from teaching which on one level appears to handsomely compliment Van den Enden and his school, his ardour for art and use of the theatre:

> ...Wisdom speaks
> In church, school and theater: and here lacks,
> Neither tongue, nor speech. She can also work silently,
> In man's heart, and preach by mute signs;
> Because letter, paint, and print indicate her sense,
> And depict her aims for intellect and eye.
> She threatens and invites by punishment and reward,
> In painting or live tableau vivant.

But while the poem flatters the Van Vlooswijks and puns on their name with its reference to "flower" [flor], it can be read as insinuatingly ambiguous with respect

---

[86] Mertens, *Van den Enden en Spinoza*, 36–7.   [87] Korsten, *Dutch Republican Baroque*, 157.

to Van den Enden and the school. In particular, the following passage referring to "smothering snakes" seems to imply there was also evil at work in the school that needed countering by the Van Vlooswijks and the city government. It may be significant in this regard that no further reference to any connection between Vondel and Van den Enden is found dating from after 1657.[88]

> Of good and evil, each to its disparate nature,
> Which straightens those that are wandering, giving new birth,
> Likewise your youth should unfold, like a flower,
> And use life's spring for the welfare of the citizens.
> One who can smother snakes so easily,
> Will outgrow the school, and become a worthy statesman.

Stung by Van den Enden's success at the civic theatre, the Amsterdam Reformed consistory stepped up its opposition. Two weeks before the first performance of Terence's *Andria*, a play about a convoluted love relationship, in January 1657, the Amsterdam Reformed Church council learnt that a "certain Van den Enden, popish schoolmaster here," was preparing to stage a Terence comedy at the Schouwburg performed by his pupils including children of Reformed Church members. "As much as possible should be done," the consistory resolved, "to prevent this," starting with having the Reformed parents spoken to and told "many reasons why they should not allow their children to participate." Due to this intervention, all participants in subsequent performances were offspring of Catholic or non-Reformed Protestant families. But that was not the end of the matter. Unrelenting in their efforts, the *kerkeraad* eventually succeeded in getting the civic theatre permanently denied to Van den Enden, so that after 1658 no more public performances by his pupils occurred. This was the first of many a clash with local Reformed Church councils that Spinoza would experience during his life.[89]

8.v A New Form of Pedagogy

Philedonius reveals no obvious sign of a subversive attitude toward religion or traditional moral standards, as is hardly surprising in a play advertising Van den Enden's and his school's merits before the public. Moreover, the surviving reports affirming Van den Enden had a secret "atheist" philosophy nowhere specifically refer to the period before 1660, just as nothing prior to that date suggests Van den Enden was yet a democratic republican. In striking contrast, a plethora of reports

---

[88] Korsten, *Dutch Republican Baroque*, 157–9; Mertens, *Van den Enden en Spinoza*, 39.
[89] Proietti, "Vita e opere," 77; Klever, "Inleiding," 26–7.

relating to the early 1660s style him an "atheist" with a secret philosophy, but by then a small circle of clandestine devotees of irreligious philosophy had gathered in Amsterdam and were circulating clandestine manuscripts among themselves. All considered, it seems Van den Enden while assuredly Spinoza's mentor in classical studies, rhetoric, and studying the statesmanship and diplomacy of the recent past, was not his mentor in anti-Scripturalism, Cartesianism, or his philosophical conception of God.[90] Where Van den Enden definitely preceded Spinoza, during the early 1660s, was in affixing their post-1660 common rejection of religious authority to democratic republicanism. In addition, he seems also to have strongly influenced Spinoza's views on pedagogic technique, opposing prevailing patterns of education and redefining what is most beneficial for society in the educational sphere.

During the years between writing *Philedonius* in 1656 and around 1660 when Van den Enden began edging toward irreligion and, except for outward formalities, confessional indifference, it is not unlikely that it was actually the young Spinoza, now increasingly devoting himself to philosophy, especially Cartesianism, who was prodding Van den Enden in new directions intellectually, rather than vice versa, in the way Spinoza's previous biographers assumed. It remains certain in any case that the two men interacted in creative fashion and reinforced distinctive and significant tendencies in each other. Van den Enden was already breaking with his Catholic heritage and the Catholic Church to a degree when he established his school, because schools of Catholic complexion in Amsterdam approved by Catholic priests did not teach children belonging to other confessions. The most striking feature of his didactic method, standing in stark contrast to all other schools in the United Provinces, was simply that his school was not attached to, nor endorsed by, any confession whatsoever. It accepted boys from all backgrounds, Reformed, Catholic, Lutheran, Collegiant. Not being subject to any particular religious authority, his school's deconfessionalizing tendency reflected Van den Enden's growing antipathy to confessional and ethnic distinctions. Children, according to his educational doctrine, should be treated as a group all equal in importance, much as he later regarded *evengelijkheid*, equality of status, as the key principle in political theory. Where children are too young to grasp the purpose of the Republic's laws intellectually they should be imbued with respect for rules based on equality and freedom via ceremonies and their school's veneration of them. Characteristic too was Van den Enden's stress on the need to rigorously improve body and mind together via theatre, sports, and group discussion.[91]

---

[90] Mertens, "Van den Enden and Religion," 62–5; Klever, "Spinoza and Van den Enden," 318–19; Klever, *The Sphinx*, 167; see also Rovere, "Présentation," 202.
[91] Van den Enden, *Vrije Politijke Stellingen*, 146–7, 149, 151.

Especially distinctive was his emphasis on the best education being a shared learning experience, involving the teacher as much as the children, group activity seeking to increase and elevate the shared knowledge of the group, doubtless one reason why he valued theatre so highly as a teaching tool. Van den Enden opposed the use of prizes or any tendency toward segregating, grading, and creating a hierarchy in the classroom, a stance which apparently became something of a shared principle with Spinoza. In the *Ethics*, Spinoza seems more inclined than Van den Enden to view "hate and envy" as something unavoidable to which men are "naturally inclined"; but he entirely agreed with his former teacher that, unfortunately, "education itself adds to natural inclination. For parents generally spur their children on to virtue only by the incentive of honour and envy," a wrong approach counterproductive from society's point of view.[92] Equally unusual, not to say bizarre, was Van den Enden's emphatic bias against doctoral and professorial titles, his resisting the assumption that society should classify particular individuals as belonging to special grades of learning, ranking them higher in society than others. He goes so far as to call academic titles "the notorious ruin of all proper knowledge and precious equality-based freedom." No teacher should be licensed to dictate so-called "truths" simply on the basis of his authority; the right to teach should rest purely on ability to demonstrate the grounds and reasons for things evidently, cogently, and convincingly.[93]

One should despise qualified special holders of knowledge in particular areas, held Van den Enden, who "in the manner of present-day theologians, jurists and physicians invoke for proof someone else's say so, or text," thus expounding what is merely the authority of someone else.[94] Though a teacher of Latin first and foremost, paradoxically, Van den Enden thought Latin should generally be replaced by the vernacular for most higher education purposes so as to render education inclusive rather than an area reserved for elites. In contrast to universal practice in the universities, teaching should be in the vernacular "so that all and everyone of the citizens can freely hear and obtain access to it."[95] He recommended also that the local vernacular should be everywhere supplemented by teaching boys and girls a second modern language, an internationally agreed modern language capable of replacing Latin as the new universal language (suggesting French for this role) linking nations and peoples. During the 1660s, Van den Enden and Spinoza shared something of a common anti-university bias. Van den Enden proposed reforming and merging secondary education with higher education by establishing locally authorized "communicatijve collegien"

---

[92] Spinoza, *Ethics* III, Prop. 55; Rovere, "Honors and Theater," 815.
[93] Van den Enden, *Vrije Politijke Stellingen*, 152–3; Van den Enden, *Free Political Propositions*, 145–6.
[94] Van den Enden, *Vrije Politijke Stellingen*, 153; Van den Enden, *Free Political Propositions*, 146.
[95] Van den Enden, *Vrije Politijke Stellingen*, 195; Van den Enden, *Free Political Propositions*, 147.

[community colleges] based on the educational methods he favoured.[96] Unlike Hobbes who was eager to bring higher education under the crown rather than leave extensive influence in the hands of the Anglican Church, Van den Enden and Spinoza proposed local academies free of both political and ecclesiastical direction.[97]

Van den Enden's political writings all date from the early and mid-1660s, and were essentially a response, largely positive, to the democratic republicanism of the Brothers De La Court. "At the end of the year 1661," he writes in the preface to his *Vrije Politieke Stellingen* [Free Political Propositions] (1665), "I had not yet the slightest idea ever to publish or bring to light even the least jotting about political matters until, quite unexpectedly," the opportunity arose to present a text on behalf of a group of prospective colonists on the question of New Netherland (today the states of New York, New Jersey, and Delaware). In writing political theoretical texts of a radical character, combining democratic republicanism and his plea for basic equality with rejection of religious authority (the combination chiefly characterizing the Radical Enlightenment), Van den Enden did undeniably precede Spinoza; but in considerable measure he built and followed on from the De La Courts, and began doing so only after Spinoza left Amsterdam.[98]

Writing his first text, *On the Emendation of the Intellect*, begun probably as early as 1656 or 1657, hence soon after breaking with the synagogue, when teaching at Van den Enden's school and beginning to philosophize, Spinoza believed he finally perceived what the "highest good" is. It is "knowledge of the union the mind has with the whole of nature [cognitionem unionis quam mens cum tota Natura habet]."[99] An important part of "achieving the highest human perfection" is grasping that one needs to form groups or societies "enabling as many as possible to attain [such union] as easily and also as surely as possible," that is introduce a new kind of adult education, and also establish the right *doctrina*, philosophy and method, "for educating children."[100] During the years he was embarking on his career in philosophy, Spinoza was first and foremost a teacher, and the experience in teaching he acquired in Van den Enden's establishment reflected what was in multiple respects assuredly the most innovative pedagogy to be found in Amsterdam.[101] Spinoza remained in his native city, the sphere of his early intellectual efforts, until his move to Rijnsburg in early 1661.

Dating from around the time Spinoza departed, there is a highly significant reference to his activities in Amsterdam in Ole Borch's diary, or *Itinerarium*, dated

---

[96] Van den Enden, *Vrije Politijke Stellingen*, 154–6; Van den Enden, *Free Political Propositions*, 146–7; Rovere, "Honors and Theater"; Laerke, *Spinoza and the Freedom*, 157–8.
[97] Laerke, *Spinoza and the Freedom*, 164–5.
[98] Van den Enden, *Vrije Politijke Stellingen*, 125; Weststeijn, *Commercial Republicanism*, 57; Lavaert, *Vrijheid, gelijkheid, veelheid*, 111–12, 116.
[99] Spinoza, *Oeuvres* i, *Premiers écrits*, 70.   [100] Spinoza, *Oeuvres* i, *Premiers écrits*, 72–3.
[101] Rovere, "Honors and Theater"; Laerke, *Spinoza and the Freedom*, 156–7.

17 May 1661, a note stating that a certain Scandinavian colleague, Höjerus, had assured him that besides the rest of the astounding medley of sects in Amsterdam, there are also here some "atheists," mostly "Cartesians, among them an impudent Jew." This is almost certainly a reference to Spinoza and the circle around Van den Enden.[102] Later, adverse rumours about Van den Enden's character and teaching would intensify, but there is no real sign that he got into serious trouble with the city authorities at any point during the 1660s. The successful schoolmaster continued teaching in Amsterdam, undisturbed as far as we know, for years to come, his school in Amsterdam still seemingly functioning as late as 1670. He did not move to Paris until after the marriage of his daughter, Clara Maria, with his former pupil, Spinoza's friend Theodore Kerckring, in February 1671. After transferring to Paris, later that year, Van den Enden opened his new school there.

Neither is there any sign in the surviving sources that Van den Enden was actually made to close the school in Amsterdam by the city government due to adverse talk or unacceptable teaching, just a good deal of subsequent speculation about this.[103] Nor is there is any indication in the sources of further contact between Van den Enden and Spinoza after the budding philosopher left Amsterdam in 1661, albeit that does not necessarily mean there was none. Although Spinoza acquired Latin relatively late and during his school years missed that long, immensely thorough grounding that afforded Descartes and Hobbes their wide vocabulary and confident flourish in writing the language, and while Spinoza's Latin prose in later life always needed some editing and grammatical correction, he did attain an effective command of the language, a good feel for classical Roman rhetoric, and a rare precision, concision, and clarity of expression in writing Latin which compares favourably with that of other philosophers of the age.[104] This was largely thanks to Van den Enden at a crucially formative phase in his life.

---

[102] Borch, *Itinerarium* i, 128; Klever, "A New Source," 215; Rovere, *Le Clan Spinoza*, 241–2; Secrétan, "Qu'est-ce qu'être libertin," 33.
[103] Mertens, *Van den Enden en Spinoza*, 4–5; Meininger and Van Suchtelen, *Liever met wercken*, 63, 70–1.
[104] Akkerman, "Taal en tekst," 4, 11–12, 22; Rothkamm, *Institutio Oratoria*, 338–40.

9

Collegiants, Millenarians, and Quakers

The Mid- and Late 1650s

All early sources for Spinoza's life confirm that after expulsion from the Sephardic community, in July (or September) 1656, he spent the next five years or so in the metropolis, then the most thriving mercantile centre and religiously mixed and fragmented city in Europe. The foremost lesson seventeenth-century Amsterdam taught the young Spinoza was the need to contemplate seriously and assess the astounding range of religious division, dispute, and variety characterizing Holland's largest city and especially the seething plethora of fringe religious sects with their distinctively, at times breathtakingly high ideals for mankind. These ideals were impressive, even supremely lofty, albeit the practice often considerably less so. All considered, there was much to learn from so arresting a spectrum of deeply earnest disagreement found especially at the fringes— Collegiants divided into Spiritualists and Rationalists, Socinians, rival streams of Mennonites, Arminians, Moravian Brethren, and Quakers—all deeply divided but also all sharing a passionate, sweeping rejection of every mainstream European church whether Catholic, Lutheran, Calvinist, Eastern Orthodox, or, deemed a church in this context, Jewish. Among the fringe adherents, some were Amsterdammers, some refugees from abroad, and others migrants expelled from elsewhere in the Republic. For an imposing scenario of religious dissidence, a veritable mountain of rejection of what most people believe, nowhere else in the Western world could even remotely rival it.

For an opposition-minded, studious, and independent-minded teenager raised in the Amsterdam of the mid-seventeenth century with Spinoza's background, nothing could be more straightforward than to start by assuming the world's dominant churches plus the synagogue along with the vast majority everywhere have nothing but the most absurdly false and credulous notions to offer—after all, many hundreds of exceptionally pious and eloquent neighbours, often much more serious and resolute in their personal piety than regular, mainstream churchgoers, thought exactly the same. Fringe religious groups, refusing life under a paid clergy and organized religious authority on principle, seemed distinctly more appealing to an outcast from his own religious community given their passionate earnestness, minority status, oppositional character, intensity of their willingness to discuss with others their search for truth, and above all, their being obviously far more knowledgeable about religion than the vast majority of society obediently heeding priests, salaried pastors, and rabbis. What firmly bound all the anti-church fringe groups together was their common belief that mainstream churchmen have nothing uplifting to teach, that all the main churches teach unsupported fabrication, and that our world finds itself in a perfectly deplorable state (partly due to intolerance and oppressive superstition imposed by the main churches in alliance with monarchs), and, what is more, that the entire scene urgently needed thoroughgoing reform and systematic elevation to a higher level.

The impact of Amsterdam as the Western world's number one haven of persecuted refugee sects on anyone living there in the 1650s, especially someone with an avid intellect and powerful imagination at odds with any given particular religious community, was inevitably far-reaching. Since denying the Holy Trinity, divinity of Christ and Resurrection were all officially illegal and subject to penalties in Holland by decree of 19 September 1653, and throughout the United Provinces, the large Socinian (Anti-Trinitarian) component among the fringe movements could congregate only in a few places in the Netherlands— principally Amsterdam, Rotterdam, and Rijnsburg—and had to lead if not a semi-underground existence then one distinctly muffled as far as broadcasting their views to the wider society was concerned.

Early biographies of Spinoza and sources relating to his life are unanimous too in recording that his overriding intellectual passion during the period immediately prior to the *herem*, and perhaps briefly afterwards, remained Bible criticism and religion. Spinoza, remarks his Collegiant friend, Jarig Jelles, in his preface to the *Opera Posthuma*, "from his childhood on, busied himself with studying, and for many years in his youth, was chiefly concerned with religious studies."[1] Only later did his "burning desire" for knowledge of the truth render philosophy his prime interest. There is no watertight proof confirming this sequence of stages in his development but it certainly makes better sense, and better fits the sources, than any other supposition.

Exactly when Spinoza first encountered his later close Collegiant friends, Jarig Jelles (c.1620–83), Pieter Balling (d. 1664), Simon Joosten de Vries (c.1633–67), and his Millenarian (or chiliastic) Collegiant go-between associate, Petrus Serrarius (1600–69), someone with whom he stayed in contact over many years, remains unknown. But Spinoza presumably knew all or most of these remarkable personages at an early stage, well before 1660.[2] Perhaps most crucial of all these close allies was the veteran bookseller Jan Rieuwertsz the Elder (c.1616–87) whose home and bookshop was a gathering point of Socinian meetings or "conventicles" as well as lovers of dissident books, that is books containing what a Catholic ecclesiastic later styled everything "bizarre and impious" contrived by

---

[1] Jelles, "Voorreeden," 1; Rovere, *Spinoza par ses amis*, 30.
[2] Mertens, "Spinoza's Amsterdamse vriendenkring," 70–1; Manusov-Verhage, "Jan Rieuwertsz, marchand," 238, 241–2; Waite, "The Drama," 120–1; Steenbakkers, "Spinoza's Life," 25–6.

"petulant and arrogant minds." His shop stocked the finest array of Descartes' works in the vernacular as well as Latin then to be found anywhere. But he was also one of the main clandestine publishers of Collegiant pamphlets, illicit pamphlets being one of the main channels by which Collegiants projected their universalism and irenicism to the outside world. If no one in Holland did more to spur diffusion of Descartes' thought than this enterprising publisher, no one else did more to publicize Collegiant rejection of the commonly accepted notions of what Christianity is and how it needs to be fundamentally reformed to become at all authentic.[3]

A member of the Amsterdam booksellers' guild since 1640, locally famed for his skills in clandestine diffusion of banned Socinian ideas denying the Holy Trinity, Christ's divinity, Original Sin and more, Rieuwertsz's bookshop "in't Martelaarsboek" (in the Martyrs' Book), was located near the homes of De Vries and Jelles in the long, narrow street now called the Dirk van Hasseltssteeg, then the Dirk van Assensteeg, running off the Nieuwezijds Voorburgwal, situated nearer the Nieuwendijk end.[4] It was a meeting place where "many Socinian persons go now and then to listen to lectures together," reported a Reformed pastor to the Amsterdam Reformed Church council, on 29 November 1657, "though no one can ascertain or discover whether any Socinian prayer gathering was held there. Every day Jan Knol disseminates his poison there."[5] That the ambience of Rieuwertsz's bookshop was informally intensely Socinian, the Reformed Church council knew for certain. Due to its suffused, whispered collective denial of Christ's divinity and the Trinity, Rieuwertsz's house, observes a pamphlet of 1655, was nicknamed "the School of Mockers."[6]

Jan Knol (d. 1672) was a prominent Amsterdam Collegiant preacher, resolutely Anti-Trinitarian and averse to all conventional theology, eloquent and sharp-tongued, with a taste for pamphlet polemics and satirical humour—and greatly resented by the city's Reformed pastors. He was an important supplementary influence on the *cercle Spinoziste* as it evolved at the end of the 1650s; later the Koerbagh brothers were among those attending Socinian gatherings at his home.[7] It was Knol who translated into Dutch the Polish Brethren's Socinian "Rakow Catechism" which appeared in 1659, published in Amsterdam but with its title-page falsely stating "Rakow" as place of publication.[8] In 1669, Knol's defiance of

---

[3] Manusov-Verhage, "Jan Rieuwertsz, marchand," 246–7; Van der Deijl, "Dutch Translation," 209n6; Quatrini, *Adam Boreel*, 78, 388.
[4] Van Eeghen, *Amsterdamse Boekhandel* iv, 63–4; Pettegree and Der Weduwen, *Bookshop of the World*, 331, 333.
[5] Meinsma, *Spinoza et son cercle*, 154, 156; Visser, "Kritisch commentaar," 289; Esteves do Couto, *Marvelous Travels*, 33; Quatrini, *Adam Boreel*, 174–5.
[6] Meinsma, *Spinoza et son cercle*, 159; Fix, *Prophecy and Reason*, 146, 211.
[7] Kühler, *Het Socinianisme*, 186–7; Fix, *Prophecy and Reason*, 146–7.
[8] Van Bunge, *Johannes Bredenburg*, 12–13; Visser, "Kritisch commentaar," 343n59 and 349n206; Israel, *Dutch Republic*, 913.

the world's principal churches reached a peak when he famously stated that "Christ never said he was the true God; if he had said that then the Jews were right to kill him."[9] Bigoted fury overflowed at this report, but despite an angry official inquiry by the city government, pressured by the Reformed consistory, Knol eluded serious consequences through lack of witnesses willing to testify against him.

Spinoza presumably first encountered at least some of his anti-church Collegiant allies in Rieuwertsz's bookshop, especially in the mid-1650s, in the period of his open, growing alienation from the Portuguese Jewish community. It would otherwise be hard to fathom how he could have formed such a close and lasting connection with so extensive a group largely confined to Amsterdam, when he himself, from early 1661 onwards, dwelt a considerable distance away. Jelles, Balling, Knol, and Rieuwertsz also had a regular association with Rijnsburg where Spinoza lived in 1661–3, a village with which Collegiants had special ties; but they had no connection with the academic circles he frequented in and around Leiden, or with his subsequent milieu in Voorburg or The Hague and its environs where he would spend the last stages of his life. So his life-long friendship with these personages must almost certainly have originated well before 1660.

Assuming what Rieuwertsz junior told Stolle and Hallmann during their study trip in 1703, about Spinoza earning his living immediately after leaving the Jews mainly by teaching children is correct,[10] Spinoza's regular involvement in teaching probably only lasted two or three years; in late 1658, at any rate, two Spanish witnesses who had got to know Spinoza in Amsterdam testified before the Madrid Inquisition that "Spinoza" was a young man with "no occupation."[11] By the late 1650s, evidently, he was entirely independent and self-employed, replacing his earnings from regular teaching by occasional tuition and selling lenses for microscopes and telescopes that he painstakingly ground himself. His independent lifestyle had the advantage of enabling him to work irregularly just part of the day, for limited periods when it suited, and was hence more readily combined with study, meditation, and lengthy group discussion than school teaching. Occasional tuition still provided part of his meagre income through the late 1650s and into his Rijnsburg years (1661–3).

The Amsterdam of 1656, and Rieuwertsz's house most of all, were a shop window offering to the ousted young Spinoza what to him must have seemed an appealing general truth. Cut off from mainstream Jewish life as well as the Amsterdam Exchange, the entire mercantile sphere, from late 1656, Spinoza found himself left largely adrift and alone in Europe's most tolerant city. He

---

[9] Visser, "Kritisch commentaar," 289.
[10] Freudenthal/Walther, *Lebensgeschichte* i, 86 and ii, 56; Mertens, "Spinoza's Amsterdamse vriendenkring," 71.
[11] Révah, *Spinoza et Juan de Prado*, 11.

rubbed shoulders, unavoidably, with a host of divergent sects. After clashing with the rabbis, leading to an ousting of unparalleled vehemence, Spinoza may already, by this point, have been edging towards his later famous doctrine—among the most distinctive features of his thought—that "true religion" does not lie in any group's doctrines or rites but in "justice and charity." Experience taught him, Spinoza observed later, towards the end of his life, that "in every church there are very many honourable men who worship God with justice and charity, for we have known many such among the Lutherans, the Reformed Church, the Mennonites and the Enthusiasts [i.e. Spiritualists and Quakers]."[12] Catholics alone he omitted from his list, the church towards which he came closest to bearing a permanent grudge as to any particular group, due to Catholicism's unrivalled international sway and what to him was its surpassing tyranny over the individual and fondness for reinforcing political oppression.

Among the "very honourable men" encountered everywhere in his new context, worshipping God with "justice and charity," was a figure newly arrived in Amsterdam who established there the headquarters of his sect, the Moravian Brethren, in August 1656, the sixty-four-year-old renowned "pansophist" Jan Amos Comenius (or Komensky) (1592–1670), the world's first major advocate of universal education in the vernacular as the unique path to humanity's moral elevation to a higher level. A religious teacher with only a few of his former Czech following still around him, Comenius spent the rest of his life in the city on the Amstel regularly attending Collegiant meetings. Head of the Bohemian and Moravian Brethren, Comenius led a marginal sect that had survived intense persecution in the Czech lands underground. Destined for a distinguished record on both sides of the Atlantic and eventually the Indian subcontinent and Africa too, the Moravians' founder, Jan Hus (1372–1415), had been burnt at the stake for heresy in 1415. Increasingly scattered, especially after the Protestant defeat at the Battle of the White Mountain, near Prague, in 1620, the Moravians had been persecuted throughout the Austrian Habsburg Empire and more recently Poland where many had sought refuge.

Fiercely repressed in Poland, Comenius with a few loyal followers settled finally in Amsterdam, in 1656, becoming friendly, among other Collegiants, with the passionate Millenarian Spiritualist, Serrarius.[13] A doughty fighter for toleration and critic of Calvinists (besides Catholics, Eastern Orthodox, and Lutherans), Comenius soon clashed, like his new friend, Serrarius, with the radical Socinians and also with Descartes' followers whose philosophical approach he also opposed.[14] Since the 1630s, Comenius had been accused of leaning towards "Pelagianism, Socinianism and fusing the divine with the human" by the Moravian Brethren's

---

[12] Spinoza to Albert Burgh [Dec. 1675], in Spinoza, *Collected Works* (ed. Curley) ii, 474.
[13] Rood, *Comenius*, 19; Woldring, *Jan Amos Comenius*, 117.
[14] Woldring, *Jan Amos Comenius*, 174–5; Israel, *Enlightenment that Failed*, 117–21.

conservative members and, to keep his group together, needed to preserve, residually at least, something of the old theology upholding the (in Amsterdam) bitterly contested Trinity against outright Anti-Trinitarians.

Comenius' great project was his quest for pansophia unifying all knowledge—empirical knowledge about the world around us fused with Holy Scripture and the true essence of Revelation—an "omniscientia" merging philosophy, science, and theology into a single unified system common to all men. But after personally witnessing the onset of the English Civil War in 1641–2, devastating religious war in Germany and Bohemia-Moravia, and religious oppression in Poland, he adjusted his approach to a redemptive "panorthosia," combining the quest to systematize all knowledge with his plan to unify mankind by comprehensively reforming society, law, education, and politics via his Christian conception of universal education.[15] Convinced that precious moral good exists in all Europe's warring creeds and factions but, equally, that society must eliminate, after sifting the best out of its staggering welter of creeds, the negative effects generated by prevailing wrong confessional belief, he tirelessly met with others, discussed and pondered.

Moravians, like other Protestants, reviled the alleged abuses of Catholicism, urging that religion be taught solely in the vernacular, not Latin, but went further than most "Radical Reformation" fringe groups, in insisting true religion is pious conduct not belief in theological doctrines, emphasizing the purely pastoral role of religious leaders, and abjuring use of theology to forge rigid confessional alliances with rulers. The Collegiant movement, from the outset, was Comenius' natural meeting place and intellectual forum. But while Comenius approved Socinian-Unitarian exalting of "reason" as the supreme criterion inspiring their "critical, anti-church, antidogmatism" throughout his career and, like the Polish Brethren who began arriving in Amsterdam and Rotterdam in some numbers in 1660, exalted education as the path to a better society, he also believed Christianity's future lay in shaping an undogmatic, enlightened faith with the Trinity as a spiritual symbol and inspiration at its core. This mystical strand infused his conception of the world's unity and oneness, the oneness of all knowledge, his idea that theology, science, and philosophy inevitably form a single entity, and that men must learn to grasp the essence of things, not lose themselves in the vastness of detail and diversity.[16]

Nothing could be more uplifting than Comenius' pansophist social and educational goals. The trouble was that while insisting on quiet, tolerant debate in the main, when it came to the one, solitary theological cornerstone he insisted on—the Trinity which the more liberal Collegiant spirits around him rejected—he flew into rages that seriously compromised his high ideals. The classic instance was his

---

[15] Čisek, "From Pansophia to Panorthosia," 212, 223–34, 226.
[16] Kuchlbauer, *Johannes Amos Comenius' anti-sozianistische Schriften*, 70–5.

battle with Daniel Zwicker (1612–78), a refugee apostate from Lutheranism repudiated by his family (his father and brother were Lutheran ministers) and hounded from Danzig, who settled in Amsterdam, in 1657, immediately forming an alliance with Comenius. In late 1658, Zwicker profited from his new-found freedom in Amsterdam to publish anonymously his *Irenicum Irenicorum*, one of the strongest pleas for universal peace and toleration of the era, reconstructing early Christian teaching prior to the ecumenical Council of Nicaea (AD 325) to show how all the main churches had conspired in the fourth century AD to forge a gigantic web of fabricated theology, an edifice of religious fraud and superstition with the Holy Trinity at its core, dating from three centuries after the crucifixion without any genuine ties to the New Testament or authentic early Christianity let alone the Old Testament. None of Spinoza's Collegiant friends objected to anything there, or Zwicker's striving to be a "conciliator of all contemporary Christians." But Comenius, despite saying nothing when shown the text before publication, and being in full agreement with Zwicker that everything in our world requires thorough reform because the institutionalized "Christendom" of modern times is based on "ignorance," pride, condemnation of others, desire for temporal power and possessions, and contempt for truth, exploded in righteous fury.

Zwicker's insisting "I am neither a Lutheran, nor Calvinist, nor Remonstrant, nor Greek [Orthodox], nor papist, nor Mennonite, nor member of whatever sect of today," presented no difficulty for Comenius. Apart from resenting Zwicker's rather arrogant tone and manic zeal, the sole sticking point was the Trinity. There is not, Zwicker concurred with the Socinians, a word about the Trinity in the Gospels, and firmly denying Christ's divinity is the sole way to restore Christian integrity. It was here that Comenius fiercely dissented. Not that Zwicker, in reconstructing the history of early Christianity and attempting to wrest it from the churches, was entirely at one with mainstream Socinian tradition either. Socinians usually eschewed historical research, preferring to rely on deductive "reason" aided by the Holy Ghost. Consequently, Zwicker felt disinclined to label himself a "Socinian,"[17] and to an extent stood alone against Comenius and those supposedly insisting on "reason" but avoiding the historical approach he favoured.

Forgetting they shared a common irenicist platform uniting all the Radical Reformation fringe groups, the initial friendship between Comenius and Zwicker erupted into bitterness and ferocious public dispute. So infuriated was Comenius by Zwicker's subordinating Scripture to historical research and reason, that he publicly denounced him in the most vehement terms, in early 1660, publishing a rebuttal of his plans for peace and unity among Christians entitled *De Irenico Irenicorum Admonitio*. He went so far as to denounce his erstwhile comrade to the Amsterdam Reformed consistory for illegal Anti-Trinitarianism.[18] That even the

---

[17] Bietenholz, *Daniel Zwicker*, 61; Mulsow, "The 'New Socinians'," 49, 52.
[18] Bietenholz, *Daniel Zwicker*, 48, 84–8; Kolakowski, *Chrétiens sans église*, 226–7.

most universalist, irenicist creeds lapse into unbridled hatred and fury the moment the Trinity and Christ's divinity are broached was a lesson not lost on Spinoza. He could hardly help imbibing a great deal from Amsterdam's unprecedented array of fringe creeds and relating these experiences to his own family's long and painful saga of persecution at the hands of the most oppressive, persecuting religious authority found anywhere, Iberia's Inquisition. Spinoza fully shared the dissidents' contempt for pervasive church authority via salaried clergy claiming exclusive knowledge of religious truth, insisting on rigid congregational discipline and selective charitable assistance to the poor based on confessional allegiance.

Avowed Anti-Trinitarians, Spinoza and his Collegiant friends undoubtedly felt more at home among the ultra-tolerant, loosely organized, irenicist-rationalist sects rejecting the principle of moral and social direction by specially trained clergy than among any other of the numerous lesser churches such as the Remonstrants, varieties of strict Mennonites, and the Greek and Armenian Orthodox, which all stood fast to religious authority, deference to the pulpit, and dogmatic theology. Besides Scripture readings, hymns and psalm-singing, and elaborate adult baptisms Collegiant prayer gatherings chiefly featured talks and discussions.[19] The Collegiant leader most emphatic in insisting Christ never authorized any particular church, group, or doctrine to represent his teaching, nor endorsed any Christology, often speaking at Collegiant meetings, was Galenus Abrahamsz de Haan (1622–1706). Among their most eloquent spokesmen, no one was more committed to erasing confessional differences and splits,[20] but his irenicist efforts only further deepened the rifts splintering the Mennonites, causing rupture especially with the "Old Mennonites," a confessional stream intent on restoring the authority of congregation, elders, and dogma.

Originally from Harlingen, in Friesland, born around 1620 and a bachelor all his life, Spinoza's close friend Jarig Jelles served, from 1653, as a deacon in the liberal Mennonite congregation of Galenus, a group reportedly much drawn to Rieuwertsz's bookstore and closely allied with other Collegiants. A respected member of the "Galenist" community in Amsterdam throughout his days, he was described as a "merchant," who, rather than running a grocery shop, engaged seemingly in wholesale distribution of groceries and spices to retailers delivering not only to various towns in the Netherlands, including Franeker, in Friesland, but at least on one occasion, as far away as Riga, in the Baltic. Very likely, he had had business links with Spinoza and perhaps also others of his family prior to 1656.[21] Notarial deeds of 1655–6 confirm Jelles was then still running this business, and

---

[19] Rues, *Tegenwoordige staet*, 315–16; Fix, *Prophecy and Reason*, 51–2.
[20] Meihuizen, *Galenus Abrahamsz*, 103–8; Van der Wall, *Mystieke Chiliast*, 202, 234–5; Israel, *Dutch Republic*, 672; Tosel, "Figure du Christ," 141–2; Waite, "The Drama," 118–20, 132.
[21] Jelles, *Belydenisse*, "Na-Reden" (by Rieuwertsz?), 230; Van der Tak, "Jellesz' Life and Business," 15–16; Mertens, "Where Thou Dwellest," 17–19, 22, 37–8.

among other groceries, stocked dried fruit bought from Portuguese Jewish traders, including raisins from Malaga, in one instance supplied by Simon Rodrigues Nunes who, like the Spinozas, also imported figs from Villanova, in Portugal.[22] An affluent wholesale dealer, Jelles supported various pious and charitable causes including, at least late in life, two orphanages, one attached to his ally Galenus' church, linked to the Collegiant community. His liberal faction stalwartly opposed the strict Mennonites, rejecting the idea of any church being governed by elders laying down authority and spiritual guidance for individual members.[23]

At some point before or around 1660, Jelles too underwent a spiritual crisis and abandoned his life of (direct) trading and amassing money, to devote his days to the search for "truth" and wisdom "with which he occupied himself for thirty years" with impeccable consistency and indifference to attacks on him as an apostate abandoning orthodox Christian belief. Rather than selling his business, he seems to have continued to draw on its proceeds while his former assistant ran it, living off what he had gained, and entered into a world of discussion and study among the Collegiants, observed Bayle later,[24] where, from early on, unlike Serrarius and Comenius, he figured among the zealous "Cartesians" and firm Anti-Trinitarians.[25] His Christian fervour resolutely subordinated belief and faith to "reason," "true reason" in Jelles' eyes being "the spirit of Christ"; everything not firmly grounded on "reason," especially in the Old Testament which he heavily subordinates to the New, but in the New also, he firmly discarded.

Despite lacking higher education and Latin, Jelles was an outstanding example, notes Bayle, of a type apt to reinforce Spinoza's, Van den Enden's and the Koerbaghs' deep conviction that those lacking university degrees are not thereby debarred from insight, engaging with philosophy, and the search for truth, and that what they lack constitutes no barrier to reaching the highest level of discernment with a success many academics and ecclesiastics well-endowed with Latin and university degrees regularly fail to attain owing to "superstition." That a person ignorant of Latin need not belong to what Spinoza termed the "multitude" whereas most of those possessing Latin and university degrees do, became a point fundamental to his outlook. Though dependent on whatever texts he could procure in Dutch,[26] Jelles was a life-long avid reader, devoting himself to pursuit of "knowledge of the truth" while living a life of piety, calm, and quiet. Purchasing many of his books and translations from his fellow Collegiant, Rieuwertsz, he

---

[22] Vaz Dias and Van de Tak, *Spinoza Mercator*, 26; Freudenthal/Walther, *Lebensgeschichte* ii, 4; Bloom, *Economic Activities*, 79; Mertens, "Where Though Dwellest," 39–41.
[23] Van der Tak, "Jellesz' Life and Business," 20; Fix, *Prophecy and Reason*, 207.
[24] Bayle, *Correspondance* vi, 318–19.
[25] Jelles, *Belydenisse*, "Na-Reden" (by Rieuwertsz?), 230; Siebrand, *Spinoza and the Netherlanders*, 37–44; Akkerman and Hubbeling, "Preface to Spinoza's Posthumous Works," 158.
[26] Jelles, *Belydenisse*, "Na-Reden" (by Rieuwertsz?), 230–2; Klever, *Mannen rond Spinoza*, 132.

constantly urged him to commission the translation of relevant texts available so far only in Latin, Greek, and Semitic languages.

Jelles long remained a force urging fusion of what he judged the true essence of Christianity, its moral teaching, with philosophy in the vernacular to extend his circle's conception of general enlightenment, the key feature of the *cercle Spinoziste* from the early 1660s onwards. Also crucial to Spinoza's life-story, and the close bond between Spinoza and his Collegiant friends, was their radically Anti-Trinitarian naturalist conception of Christ, an approach fully embraced by Jelles who negated all the theological doctrines and mysteries of the main churches—the Trinity, Resurrection, Redemption, church sacraments, Ascension, Original Sin, and especially the "divinity of Christ." For Jelles, restoring God's unity and oneness meant reducing Christ to just a specially inspired, elevated man, an inspired Jew who became a supreme moral leader, but one lacking all supernatural status or quality, making him the "Son of God," as Spinoza later concurred, only in the metaphorical sense of reaching "eternal wisdom" and God's awareness of himself.[27]

By contrast, Serrarius fostered a quite different perspective: for him, the "Holy Ghost" *is* the sole true guide to understanding Scripture.[28] A Netherlander of Walloon origin who happened to be London-born, and who studied at Christ Church College, Oxford, from 1617 to 1619,[29] Serrarius knew English well and, until his death in 1669, would serve as principal conduit linking Oldenburg and Amsterdam and, as part of his role as intermediary in Anglo-Dutch scholarly correspondence, also linking Spinoza with England.[30] Originally, Serrarius had intended to become a preacher of the Walloon Calvinist Church and for a time had been a Reformed Church preacher at Veere, in Zeeland. But at the age of twenty-eight he had undergone a personal spiritual crisis that led him to resign from his pulpit and break entirely with conventional Protestantism which he now dismissed as mere "Christianity in name."[31] Throughout his subsequent career he spared no effort, much like his friends Boreel and Spinoza, to debunk the main churches. True Christianity, he maintained, is something very different from what nearly all "Christians" believe it is.

Among the Collegiant movement's founders in Amsterdam and a key ally of Galenus and Comenius, Serrarius and the fervently pious Adam Boreel (1602–65) also played a unique role in cultivating friendly relations between Collegiants and Jews. Serrarius and Boreel both enthused over Leon Templo's model of the

---

[27] Jelles, *Belydenisse*, 44–6; Meinsma, *Spinoza et son cercle*, 153–4, 174n33; Kolakowski, *Chrétiens sans église*, 217–25; Manusov-Verhage, "Jan Rieuwertsz, marchand," 248–50; Spruit, "Introduzione," xlv–l.
[28] Van der Wall, *Mystieke Chiliast*, 476–8; Huenemann, *Spinoza's Radical Theology*, 13–14.
[29] Van der Wall, "Petrus Serrarius and Menasseh ben Israel," 168–9.
[30] Hutton, "Henry Oldenburg," 109; Van der Wall, *Mystieke Chiliast*, 262, 264–5.
[31] Van der Wall, *Mystieke Chiliast*, 41–5.

Temple of Solomon which long remained of special interest to Christian Millenarians and Messianists.[32] Boreel headed a distinct stream within the Amsterdam Collegiant movement, the Boreelists, a semi-Socinian group avid for Hebrew studies and contact with Menasseh. The Boreelists were as emphatic as Serrarius and (the post-1644) Comenius on the need for Christianity's fundamental reform but seemingly unconcerned about the Millennium, preferring Christianity's return to its pre-Nicaean authenticity shorn of confessionalizing obsessions, freed from millennia of false theology and fabricated church power, and released from confessional loyalty to powerful organizations equipped with approved teachers. Boreelists too opposed every main Protestant church and, still more vehemently, Catholicism and Greek-Russian Orthodoxy.[33]

Boreel, having, like Serrarius, spent much time in England, had ties to many fringe theologians there, and, like Serrarius and Comenius, exalted a chiliastic universalism aimed at reuniting all Christian creeds and merging Christianity with Judaism. During the mid-1640s, Boreel worked with Leon Templo and the Scots Calvinist minister John Dury (1596–1680) on a key joint Christian–Jewish project: a new edition of the Mishnah, published in 1646 in Amsterdam by Menasseh's son, Joseph, in two versions—Latin and Hebrew—the latter complete with vowel points. By making the Mishnah—the first post-biblical collection of rabbinic literature, dating from the early third century AD, supposedly reconstituting the Oral Law of the Second Temple Pharisees—more widely accessible to less scholarly Jews, Dury and Boreel hoped to forge a vehicle for bringing Jews and Christians closer together and ultimately to facilitate conversion of the Jews.[34]

This drive to reunite under a new consensus was the root of Serrarius' friendship with Boreel and Comenius and doubtless also Spinoza.[35] A familiar figure among the Sephardic community as well as the Collegiants, Serrarius was known to the Jews as the "good Christian friend who lives here in Amsterdam in friendship with the rabbis," or at any rate with Menasseh who, like Serrarius, believed in the imminence of the messianic Fifth Kingdom supposedly predicted in the Book of Daniel. These ties, strengthened by meetings at his home, mattered greatly to Serrarius, the Jews having a central role in his Millennial scheme—his belief that the Second Coming would entail the Jews' mass conversion and their glorious restoration to the Holy Land which would, in turn, trigger a general transformative process lifting the entire world into the Millennial Age, the thousand-year temporal paradise inaugurated by Christ's imminent return in which all things would be dramatically transformed for the better. Universal

---

[32] Colie, *Light and Enlightenment*, 26–7; Waite, *Jews and Muslims*, 180; Offenberg, "Jacob Jehuda Leon," 101.

[33] Iliffe, "Jesus Nazarenus Legislator," 379–81; Nadler, *Menasseh ben Israel*, 135–6.

[34] Van der Wall, "Amsterdam Millenarian Petrus Serrarius," 78–9; Nadler, *Menasseh ben Israel*, 135–6; Quatrini, *Adam Boreel*, 61–6.

[35] Fix, *Prophecy and Reason*, 73–4; Quatrini, *Adam Boreel*, 300, 384–5.

yearning to overcome the misery and wretchedness of this world, Amsterdam's Collegiant and liberal Mennonite chiliasts around Serrarius funnelled, much like Boreel, Zwicker, and Comenius, into their cherished prospect of a transformed and glorious future for all soon to dawn.[36] The Quakers, yet another newly arrived group in Amsterdam, equally promised pending immediate redemption, but by yet another divergent spiritual route, insisting that nothing needs to be awaited, the Light is already here, firmly planted within us, only most do not yet know it.

Menasseh saw much of Serrarius and Boreel prior to his departure to England, on his mission to persuade Cromwell to readmit the Jews to England, in September 1655, and engaged in a series of private theological debates with them on the subject of the Messiah, no easy topic for a Jew and Christian to agree on. Going far beyond other Christians in this respect, Serrarius and Boreel were passionately devoted to their project of converting the Jews to belief in Christ. But despite this, Menasseh evinced patience and persistence in continuing these debates, remaining genuinely friendly with both men who stood out, going well beyond most other Millenarian conversionists in their insistence on the need for "love and respect" for the ancient Jewish people. Another of their favourite projects, from 1649 until the late 1650s, was their scheme to produce and publish a New Testament in a convincing Hebrew akin to that of the Old Testament and the Mishnah, but in the end they had to abandon their efforts due to the difficulty of finding appropriate, genuine-sounding Hebrew terms and expressions. Zealous to convert the Jews, Serrarius merged that burning aspiration with encouraging them to dream of their future return to their ancient homeland, restoration of the Temple in Jerusalem, and resumption of Levitical rituals.[37] Most contemporaries were horrified. Knowing Serrarius, Boreel, Leon Templo, and Menasseh shared a common project in part, one disgusted Calvinist theologian, Samuel Maresius (1599–1673), at Groningen, labelled the mystical Spiritualist Serrarius a *semi-Judaeus* despite his firmly supporting (unlike many other Collegiants) the doctrine of the Trinity.[38]

Maresius, later one of Spinoza's fiercest opponents, was a Calvinist professor known for polemical zeal and insisting true faith is about basic theological commitment and belief. A prolific writer renowned for the wide range of his attacks on Millenarians, Socinians, Arminians, Catholics, Mennonites, Lutherans, and Jews, few escaped Maresius' scathing Calvinist intolerance. Yet, though most Collegiants met only with contempt from him, so impressive was Comenius' rhetoric that when he lectured in Groningen even Maresius admitted to being moved by his stirring summons to universal peace. He and Comenius became

---

[36] Van der Wall, *Mystieke Chiliast*, 203–6; Kolakowski, *Chrétiens sans église*, 179–80, 208, 651.

[37] Nadler, *Menasseh ben Israel*, 137, 183, 187; Van der Wall, *Mystieke Chiliast*, 167–9, 172, 175; Van der Wall, "Amsterdam Millenarian Petrus Serrarius," 73, 75–9; Popkin, "Some Aspects," 6, 11–12.

[38] Van der Wall, "Petrus Serrarius and Menasseh ben Israel," 166–7; Fix, *Prophecy and Reason*, 57, 198.

friends, albeit only briefly. Maresius soon reverted to furiously condemning the universalism, anti-ecclesiasticism, and irenicism of Comenius no less than that of Serrarius, Boreel, and Galenus.[39]

Rabbi Mortera, meanwhile, rejected Menasseh's outgoing, amicable approach to Jewish–Christian dialogue. Nevertheless, he too singularly departed from the typical early modern rabbinic attitude to Christianity, understandable under the circumstances, that of staying as quiet, neutral, polite, and unengaged as possible. Mortera's strategy, despite the restrictions on free expression under the Republic's blasphemy laws, was quite the opposite at any rate in conversation, sermons (not in Dutch), and his (unpublished) Portuguese texts. Engaged, fervent, and aggressively anti-Christian, strongly influenced in this respect by the redoubtable Montalto,[40] Mortera made a speciality of privately admonishing selected Christians, particularly religiously dithering New Christians whom he sought to sway, of the falsity of Christianity. But he wholeheartedly agreed with the Collegiant Anti-Trinitarians that mainstream Christians, even of the most erudite sort, were pitiably ignorant about "that man" (Jesus Christ), his life, times, and language, and about Christianity's true origins and what he considered the Nicaean Council's outrageous fabrications, and regarded this as clear proof that we live, alas, in the maddest of worlds. Socinians, to him, were another matter. They too he considered ignorant about the real Jesus; but at least they grasped that he was a man and not God and that the Church Fathers and the main churches, through ignorance of Hebrew and the sources, and their fabricated rigmarole about redemption, were guilty of hopelessly perverting their own religion and flock.[41]

All Spinoza scholars agree the evidence points to Spinoza experiencing encounters with Amsterdam's religious fringe groups, especially Collegiants, from even before his separation from the Jewish community.[42] These contacts surely intensified after July 1656, even though, as Colerus observes, Spinoza never joined any of the fringe congregations with which he interacted.[43] Doubtless Spinoza's contacts among the fringe groups remained varied as was the case with Rieuwertsz, Jelles, Balling, Serrarius, and the other individuals he became friendly with. If Serrarius played a unique role in relations between Sephardim and Collegiants, and later served as a key link between Spinoza, his friends in Amsterdam, and London, Serrarius was equally a bridge between Collegiants and Quakers,[44] in part because he knew English better than most others. His connection with the newly arrived Quakers, like that with Comenius' Moravians

---

[39] Woldring, *Jan Amos Comenius*, 155, 117, 176–7; Quatrini, *Adam Boreel*, 53, 80.
[40] Weisz, "Remembering Eliahu," 4–5; Salomon, "Introdução," xl.
[41] Mortera, *Tratado da Verdade*, 149, 335–7, 491.
[42] Dujovne, *Spinoza* i, 116, 124–5; Popkin, *Spinoza*, 40.
[43] Dujovne, *Spinoza* i, 117; Mignini, "Dottrina spinoziana," 54; Quatrini, *Adam Boreel*, 5–6.
[44] Meihuizen, *Galenus Abrahamsz*, 59–60; Van Bunge, *Johannes Bredenburg*, 18–21.

arose from his passionate irenicism and his viewing himself as a "servant of God's universal church," the life-long foe of all the major religious confessions, religious divides, and separate church traditions. As for Serrarius and the Collegiant Millenarians, so for the Quakers too Christ's Second Coming was imminent.[45]

For these reasons, it makes sense to take Richard Popkin's thesis (and that of several Quaker historians) more seriously than most Spinoza scholars do, namely that Spinoza is the Jew referred to, in 1657, by William Ames (d. 1662), a former Baptist minister who spoke Dutch and at this time—later they fell out—was a close ally of the Collegiants. Ames was a persecuted figure who had converted to Quakerism in Dublin and arrived in Amsterdam in the spring of 1656, leading the fledgling group of Quaker refugees then seeking refuge in Holland.[46] In 1656-7, banished from the Jewish community, Spinoza was very much feeling his way. The Quakers, a conspicuous group of newcomers, the first of whom had only begun arriving in 1655, sought a safe haven in Amsterdam much like the Moravians and, from 1660, the Polish Brethren but, from the outset, confidently, even stridently, propagated in the Netherlands their novel and, for many, disturbing teaching, provoking resistance, anger, and irritation in many quarters.[47]

"There is," Ames reported back, on 17 April 1657, to the lady of Swarthmoor Hall, Margaret Fell (1614–1702), the woman later known as the "mother of Quakerism,"[48]

> a Jew at Amsterdam that by the Jews is cast out (as he himself and others sayeth) because he owneth no other teacher but the Light and he sent for me and I spoke toe him and he was pretty tender and doth owne all that is spoken [of him], and he sayde to read of Moses and the Prophets without [the Light] was nothing to him except he came to know it within: and so the name of Christ it is like he doth owne. I gave order that one of the du[t]ch copyes of thy book should be given to him and he sent me word that he would come toe our meeting but in the meantime I was imprison'd.[49]

It has been objected that there were other Jews in Amsterdam, placed under the ban of the community in the mid-1650s, and supposedly a Jew called "Wilhelmus"

---

[45] Van Cauter, "Another Dialogue," 125.

[46] Kannegieter, *Geschiedenis van de vroegere Quakergemeenschap*, 12; Van Slee, *Rijnsburger Collegianten*, 388; Popkin, *Third Force*, 125.

[47] Van der Wall, *Mystieke Chiliast*, 214–16; Burnet, "Quaker Missionaries," 1–3; Quatrini, *Adam Boreel*, 179.

[48] Accepting the date Popkin and Mignini give; see Popkin, "Introduction," 1; Mignini, "Données et problèmes," 13, 20; however, Hunter specifies 17 April 1656, remarking that it is "of great significance" that this meeting "took place more than three months before the excommunication," see Hunter, *Radical Protestantism in Spinoza's Thought*, 34.

[49] Popkin, "Introduction," 1, 3; Popkin, *Spinoza*, 32; Katz, "Quakers and Jews," 204; Kannegieter, *Geschiedenis van de vroegere Quakergemeenschap*, 328–9; Van Cauter, "Another Dialogue," 131; Bernet, "Quaker Missionaries," 4.

who reportedly joined the Amsterdam Quakers at this time. But except for Dr Juan de Prado who was anxious to rejoin the Sephardic community and not definitely expelled until 1658, hence subsequent to this letter, and in any case knew little Hebrew or Dutch, none were definitively cast out in the sense that they remained permanently outside the community's bounds without prospect of return, like this personage. Apart from Spinoza, there is no known indication of any other Jew in Amsterdam "cast out" by the Jews who was Dutch, interested in Bible criticism, and who possessed similar exceptional skill with languages. Admittedly, the "Jew" who translated Fell's tracts into Hebrew simply renders Fell's English quotations from the Old Testament into Hebrew without the scrupulous care Spinoza later took to ferret out the original true meaning of the Hebrew.[50] But there is no reason why the Jew in question should have taken Fell's bizarre plans and exhortations with any particular seriousness. He would have been intrigued, even amused, rather than convinced by her message. So while the inference that this translator assisting the Quakers in Amsterdam was indeed Spinoza is not certain, it remains by far the most plausible explanation of Ames' letter and his mentioning this particular Jew's guarded interest in following up his discussion with Ames and learning more about the Quakers and their ideas. Hence, it seems justified to at least provisionally follow Popkin in inferring the personage referred to here was indeed Spinoza. Popkin became the most insistent, committed scholar building on what is actually a longstanding thesis among Quaker historians, reaching back long before Popkin, that the young Spinoza was interested in Quaker irenicism and pleas for religious freedom.[51]

To fully appreciate the implications of this, one should note that during the 1650s the Quakers were considerably bolder in their Anti-Trinitarianism and hostility to established churches and forms of ecclesiastical dominance than they became later, when coming under growing pressure to soften their former "enthusiastic Anti-Trinitarianism" and rejection of traditional Christology. Fell, in her yearning to sway "you all, who are out of the Light," moreover, was among the most obdurate in resisting the constraints on religious freedom instituted by Cromwell, and then tightened by Charles II and the 1660 English Restoration. Her husband, a Lancashire magistrate and member of Parliament, was so averse to Cromwell's authoritarianism that he resigned his seat in Parliament, and Margaret herself was so adamant in opposing Charles II's restrictions on religious freedom that she was sent to prison, in 1664; one of at least 11,000 Quakers imprisoned in England during the Restoration, she remained incarcerated until 1668.[52]

---

[50] Cassuto, *Spinoza hébraïssant*, 138–40.
[51] Mignini, "Données et problèmes," 12–13; Van Cauter, "Another Dialogue," 122, 131; Rediehs, "Candlestick Mysteries," 154.
[52] Harris, *Restoration*, 76–7, 302–3; Marshall, *John Locke*, 105–6.

Quaker radicalism peaked in the 1650s and early 1660s tending to moderate noticeably from the late 1660s and through the 1670s, a trend that became still more marked when the Quakers grew anxious to secure toleration from crown and Parliament in the wake of the Glorious Revolution of 1688 under the terms of England's Toleration Act of 1689. In the 1650s, the situation was very different: for denying what everyone else apart from Socinians believed, Quakers were actively persecuted by the English Commonwealth under Cromwell, in accordance with the Blasphemy Law of 1650 outlawing Anti-Trinitarian views and statements, and found themselves under heavy pressure also in their new foothold, Holland. When Spinoza encountered Quakerism, this group were unyielding in repudiating traditional Christology, demanding individual freedom of conscience, and refusing communal supervision, features that can only have made the Quakers, including the harassed and persecuted Ames, as appealing to Spinoza (initially) as to those anti-clerical Collegiants who were averse to Trinitarian dogma.[53]

Doubtless what especially appealed to Spinoza was the deep conviction of all the refugee fringe groups, Quakers along with Boreelists, Moravians, Polish Brethren, Galenist Mennonites, and Spiritualist Collegiants, that the vast majority of Christendom, like the Jews and the vast majority of humanity, had thus far got everything hopelessly muddled owing to ignorance and superstition and sadly lapsed into what Balling termed a "sea of confusion."[54] Like the Collegiants, Boreel, and Spinoza, Quakers believed the world's so-called "Christians" were missing the point, as blind to "the Light" as heathens and Jews. Another feature of Quakerism commonly regarded with consternation and horror by Protestant England and mainstream Protestants in Holland alike, but attractive to Spinoza, was their downplaying the actual text of Scripture as in some measure derivative, secondary, and corrupt, and their highly individualistic approach to interpreting Scripture, though he was doubtless less taken with their "Light within," the true "spirit of Christ" as one's guide, instead of relying on philosophical reason. For Quakers, no less than Spinoza, doctrines and dogmas laid down centuries after Christ by fabricating, power-grabbing theologians and churchmen counted for no more than the rules of observance imposed by rabbis.[55] To begin with, there seemed as little for Spinoza to object to intellectually in the Quaker creed as in that of his Millenarian Spiritualist friends. A striking feature of Spinoza's angry repudiation of Catholicism as something negative and oppressive, in his 1675 letter to Albert Burgh, was his identifying just and charitable behaviour, wherever we find it, not just as the chief criterion of "true religion" but the *only* genuine sign of allegiance to Scripture's teaching and being infused with the "spirit of Christ."[56]

---

[53] Manning, "Accusations of Blasphemy," 28–9, 32–3; Hutton, *Benjamin Furly*, 36–9, 103–5.
[54] Kolakowski, *Chretiens sans église*, 211; Klever, *Mannen rond Spinoza*, 18.
[55] Van Cauter, "Another Dialogue," 125–6.
[56] Spinoza to Albert Burgh [Dec. 1675], in Spinoza, *Collected Works* (ed. Curley) ii, 474; Gullan-Whur, *Life of Spinoza*, 83; Licata, "The Law Inscribed," 205.

Anti-Trinitarian Collegiants, like Jelles, Balling, Knol, Zwicker, Galenus, and Rieuwertsz, certainly placed greater stress on the primacy of reason than the mystically inclined Quakers, Boreelists, or Serrarius' chiliastic Spiritualists. Quakers construed the "Light within" as a spiritualist inspiration, and Balling who at least in this respect came quite close to them in appealing to the "inner light," may have deliberately steered ambiguously between the two positions.[57] An attractive aspect of the Quaker conception of the "Light within" for Spinoza, as for Balling and Jelles, was that it largely erases both the theological and historical significance of Christ. In one respect, indeed, the Quakers may have seemed an improvement on the position of the Millenarian Spiritualists: for the Quaker, Christ, the "inward redeemer," has always, since the creation of the world been "the Light." No future Coming, particular miracles, or past resurrection possessed much significance in the Quaker scheme of things, and especially not Jesus' supposedly founding a church. These notions Quakers replaced with the living, individually felt "spirit of Christ" which they equated with the "Light within." The height of blasphemy in the eyes of most Protestants at this time, such belief was likely to appeal to Spinoza even if here he stood closer to his Collegiant friends Jelles, Balling, and De Vries. Jelles, though never willing to compromise the integrity of the Scriptural text to the extent Spinoza was, broadly agreed that the truth of religion and the truth yielded by reason and philosophy must be identical, and that the "true fruits of the Holy Spirit" as Spinoza later expressed it in his letter to Burgh, are "justice and loving-kindness," the only certain sign of the "true universal faith."[58]

The Quaker leaders in Amsterdam during 1656–8, in the aftermath of Spinoza's exit from the Sephardic community, were Ames who, while in Amsterdam, lodged in Serrarius' house at least for a time, William Caton (1636–65), a relative of Fell's, John Stubbs (c.1618–75), Humble Thatcher, and John Higgins, all of whom Spinoza would have encountered in the company of Serrarius, Balling, Rieuwertsz, Knol, and other Collegiants at this time.[59] Many Amsterdam Collegiants and Spiritualists, and Galenus too, attended the early Quaker meetings in the city, in the same spirit that Quakers, once their Dutch was up to it, visited the synagogue, held meetings with Sephardic Jews, and entered into lively discussions with them. Altogether less pleased with the new arrivals was the Amsterdam Reformed Church council which lodged several complaints against the emerging Quaker community, commencing in October 1656, culminating on 14 April 1657, when Ames and Humble Thatcher were arraigned before the city magistrates for

---

[57] Kolakowski, *Chretiens sans église*, 210–11; Bordoli, *Ragione e scrittura*, 265; Van Cauter, "Another Dialogue," 129–30.
[58] Spinoza, *Collected Works* (ed. Curley) ii, 474; Akkerman and Hubbeling, "Preface to Spinoza's Posthumous Works," 157.
[59] Van der Wall, *Mystieke Chiliast*, 214; Popkin, *Third Force*, 124–9; Meihuizen, *Galenus Abrahamsz*, 58–60; Iliffe, "Jesus Nazarenus Legislator," 382; Bernet, "Quaker Missionaries," 1–3.

holding "meetings at which a teaching was taught that is unheard of and altogether in contradiction to the Holy Writ leading to perturbation of the general peace which in a well ordered city should not be permitted." Annoyed by the Quakers' refusing to remove their hats in their presence, the magistrates gave Ames and Thatcher forty-eight hours to pack up and leave. The two departed, very unwillingly, and Ames was soon back.[60]

Assuming he was indeed the Jew in question, Spinoza would have been brought into contact with Ames either by Serrarius—Serrarius being one of Ames' principal Dutch contacts, though there is no proof Spinoza and Serrarius yet knew each other[61]—or else by Jelles, Balling, or another Collegiant friend. The text Ames entrusted to the "Jew" was a Dutch translation of Margaret Fell's Letter to Menasseh, *Aen Menasseh Ben Israel*, which Ames, no doubt following Serrarius' advice in part, had had rendered into Dutch before his arrest.[62] Thus, the courteous Jew Ames encountered and who agreed to translate the grand "Lady of Swarthmoor" into Hebrew, was almost certainly Spinoza. Fell aptly entitled the first of her pamphlets rendered into Hebrew, addressed to Menasseh (then in England negotiating the possible return of the Jews into that realm): *For Menasseh-Ben Israel, the Call of the Jews out of Babylon, which is good tidings to the meek, liberty to the captives, and of opening of the prison doors* (London, 1656).[63] No one cared more about "opening the prison doors" than Spinoza and his Collegiant friends. Indeed, nothing else in Spinoza's biography is as certain as his categorical embracing, from early on, of tolerance, reason, and a true ethics sifted from religious authority as the key to opening "the prison doors," the sole exit from man's wretchedness and sole remedy for curing humanity's supreme malaise—the unremitting, debasing hatred of each other that men, through their monumental ignorance, fanaticism, and superstition, invest with every ounce of their being.

Amsterdam's Quakers went all out to convert the Jews, assailing them as vigorously as Serrarius and the Boreelists. After some months, Caton became quite hopeful, reporting to Fell that her presentiment about them might soon become reality "for I believe there is a sparke in many of their bosomes which in the processe of time may kindle to a burning flame."[64] The Jew the Quakers had engaged duly translated the Dutch version of her text into Hebrew, which was then printed expressly for a Jewish audience. Caton distributed copies among the Jews "at their Synagogue, some to the rabbyes, and some to the Doctors," he reported to Fell, on 26 June 1657, "and I cannot understand that they have

---

[60] Kannegieter, *Geschiedenis van de vroegere Quakergemeenschap*, 13–15, 32; Burnet, "Quaker Missionaries," 3.
[61] Van der Wall, *Mystieke Chiliast*, 217–18.
[62] Popkin, "Introduction," 6; Waite, *Jews and Muslims*, 191–3.
[63] Popkin, "Introduction," 4; Waite, *Jews and Muslims*, 191.
[64] Burnet, "Quaker Missionaries," 4; Van der Wall, *Mystieke Chiliast*, 217.

anything against it, but only they apprehend that the author doth judge that the Messias is come already and they looke for him yet."[65]

In the autumn of 1657, Fell contacted Caton also about translating a second text, entitled *A Loving Salutation to the Seed of Abraham*, "among the Jewes, where ever they are scattered up and down the face of the Earth: and to the seed of Abraham among all people upon the face of the Earth, which are all out of the way: wandring up and down from mountain to hill, seeking rest and finding none." She summoned the world's Jews to turn "your minds to within, where the light shines in the heart."[66] "I have bene with a Jew," reported Caton to Fell, on 15 November 1657, and "shown him thy books. I have asked him what language would be fittest for them, he told me Portugees or Hebrew; for if it were in Hebrew they might understand it at Jerusalem or in almost any other place of the world. And he hath undertaken to translate it for us, he being expert in several languages."[67] The Friends had money aplenty for translating and printing their brochures in Amsterdam, but intolerance and resistance to their teaching from most Dutch religious leaders they encountered, including the rabbis, proved disheartening at times. From 1657, when Caton and Thatcher were arrested in Middelburg for interrupting church services and soon after forced to spend several weeks in a Rotterdam madhouse, things steadily grew more difficult for the movement in the Republic.[68] In October 1657, Caton styled Amsterdam "this barren place where I am sometimes perplexed but not in despaire."

In March 1658, by which time outright conflict had erupted between the Amsterdam Quaker leadership and the Collegiant Spiritualists and Millenarians, Caton dispatched another letter to Fell reporting on the translation of her second text being rendered into Hebrew, the *Salutation*. "As touching thy booke (titulated *A Loving Salutation*) I have gotten it once translated into Dutch, because the Jew that is to translate it into Hebrew, could not translate it out of English. He hath it now, and is translating it, like he hath done the other, which Samuel Fisher and John Stubbs have taken along with them; the Jew that translates it, remains very friendly in his way."[69] Once translated, Caton had Fell's second tract too printed and distributed at the synagogue. The "very friendly in his way" can be taken to mean that Spinoza was courteous, inquiring and intrigued, but not in the habit of falling over himself to imbibe their message and somewhat inclined to keep his distance.

---

[65] Popkin, "Introduction," 6; Popkin, *Third Force*, 126.
[66] Fell, *A Loving Salutation*, 22, 24, 26.
[67] Popkin, "Introduction," 6, citing Caton to Fell, 18 Nov. 1657 Caton Mss. (Quaker Archives, Haverford College) fo. 38 bis; Gullan-Whur, *Life of Spinoza*, 81.
[68] Kannegieter, *Geschiedenis van de vroegere Quakergemeenschap*, 19; Bernet, "Quaker Missionaries," 4.
[69] Popkin, "Introduction," 7; Waite, *Jews and Muslims*, 193.

The mention of Fisher and Stubbs refers to the mission on which these two Quaker leaders embarked, after setting out from England and spending some time in Amsterdam, stopping off at a string of synagogues across Europe, as they made their way to Constantinople with the aim of converting to Quakerism first the Jews, then the Pope (a major Quaker objective), and, finally, the Ottoman Sultan. Samuel Fisher (1605–81), an Oxford graduate converted to Quakerism by Stubbs and Cotton, in 1654, was the only one of their leadership with a university training and academic expertise in Bible exegesis. During his weeks in Amsterdam before setting out for Germany, reported Caton, Fisher, presumably relying on interpreters, valiantly strove to advance the Quaker cause "in the synagogue in Amsterdam and among [the Jews] at Rotterdam; they were pretty moderate towards him: (I meane they did not abuse him) but assented to much of that which he spoke; he had some discourse with two or three of their Doctors in private at Amsterdam; and they seemed to owne in words the substance of that which he declared; but they were in bondage as people of other forms are."[70] Apparently, Fisher and Caton were in the habit also of visiting Jewish houses and arguing there for hours, urging the Jews to embrace Quakerism.

The eternal Word of God, contended Fisher, cannot be derived directly from man-made writings describing historical events. Just as Protestants from the outset had profoundly muddled their renderings of Scripture, the Jews had sadly mistaken for the Word what they found written in the Torah which had originally lacked vowel signs, and this alone had fostered all manner of errors and ambiguities. Scripture's importance, Fisher insisted, lay in its general moral principles, not particular passages or details—a point Spinoza too later emphasized. God's Word existed prior to Moses, held the Quakers, prior to being written down, and lives on today within us, not in faulty, tortuously derived transcripts of ancient texts: God's "word stayes forever," as one Quaker missionary expressed it, "beyond the Holy Bible."[71] The Hebrew Bible is undoubtedly corrupted, Fisher assured the Jews everywhere where he stopped en route, in Germany, as he had in Amsterdam and Rotterdam, loudly deploring "the idolatry of the Torah" they practised. However offensive to most Jews and Christians, here was discourse apt to win Spinoza's concurrence. But while Fisher questioned the Mosaic authorship of the Pentateuch, and insisted extensive corruption of Scripture had occurred, his role as innovator in Bible criticism has been somewhat exaggerated by some scholars.[72]

Readily joining in their gatherings, Serrarius and his circle were initially as enthusiastic about the Quakers as the Reformed Church councils of Amsterdam, Rotterdam, and Middelburg were hostile. The eventual clash between Collegiant

---

[70] Popkin, "Introduction," 7–8; Popkin, *Spinoza*, 41–2; Katz, "Quakers and Jews," 201.

[71] Popkin, "Introduction," 9–10; Frampton, *Spinoza and the Rise*, 217–22; Van Miert, *Emancipation of Biblical Philology*, 238; Burnet, "Quaker Missionaries," 9.

[72] Popkin, *Third Force*, 355–7; Malcolm, "Hobbes, Ezra, and the Bible," 429–30.

Spiritualists and Amsterdam Quakers erupted rather suddenly, in late 1657 and continued until Ames' death in 1662, to a large extent becoming a feud between Ames and Serrarius (and also Higgins versus Boreel), a quarrel first at Collegiant gatherings, at Serrarius' house, and then in pamphlets. Trouble began the moment it was realized that, for the Quakers, human history is already "fulfilled," theirs was a "realized eschatology" not one of eschatological expectation as with Serrarius and Boreel, so that, as Quakers saw things, Christ's kingdom is already here, at any rate for those who feel the "spirit of Christ" within them and are inspired by it.[73] While hard-core rationalist Collegiants, like Jelles and Balling, whom the Quakers accused of placing excessive stress on "reason" in interpreting the words of Scripture, harboured serious reservations too, it was the Spiritualist Collegiants, Serrarius and Boreel, fired by chiliast expectation who took the lead in denouncing the Quakers, adding them to their lengthening list of foes of "true Christianity," though it was not until the summer of 1660 that the final break occurred. To Collegiants, the Quakers seemed to be trying to carve some exclusive entry to divine revelation for themselves, envisaging their own group as Christ's exclusive tool for redeeming the world.[74]

A culminating showdown occurred on 24 August 1660, at the home of Serrarius, while Spinoza was still in Amsterdam. The drawing up of retaliatory texts and items of disagreement, afterwards published in a swirl of clashing pamphlets, several by Rieuwertsz, led to what was virtually a sustained formal public disputation. We have no way of knowing whether Spinoza was present that day or not, but many of his friends certainly were, and at the very least he must have heard about it afterwards. In angry scenes, Ames and Higgins confronted Serrarius, Galenus, and Boreel (who also knew English well). The "Light, presence and power of God," Ames and Higgins insisted, is already fully known, but only to those within the Quaker movement; its being exclusive to Quakers meant that all those outside their movement lack "the Light" and hence are without "the spirit of Christ." While everyone had agreed all along that main churches, Orthodox, Catholics, and Protestants alike, had got everything confused, and no clergy or dogmas are justified, Quakers fiercely repudiated Serrarius' and Galenus' claim that Christ left no instructions about the forming of a true Christian community and the Collegiant notion that anyone truly cultivating the "spirit of Christ" is just as justified as another. Once they grasped its universalist, anti-sectarian character, the Quakers angrily opposed what in French has been termed the "anti-confessionalisme radical" of Galenus and his liberal Mennonite supporters including Balling and Jelles, and the Collegiant movement generally.[75]

---

[73] Van der Wall, *Mystieke Chiliast*, 218–21; Huenemann, *Spinoza's Radical Theology*, 5, 14; Birch, *Jesus*, 63.
[74] Iliffe, "Jesus Nazarenus Legislator," 381–2; Rediehs, "Candlestick Mysteries," 156, 158–9.
[75] Van der Wall, *Mystieke Chiliast*, 221–3; Fix, *Prophecy and Reason*, 196–7; Kolakowski, *Chrétiens sans église*, 202–8; Quatrini, *Adam Boreel*, 180; Rovere, "Shaping the Freedom," 104–5, 108, 112.

Convinced that future great effort and worldly projects were required, Serrarius and Boreel felt frustrated and, in their fight with Ames, adopted an angry and bitter tone. The "Fifth Kingdom," insisted the Quakers, is a spiritual realm already here, leaving no need for Jews to be rescued from their dispersal, or for any external event; all that is required for mankind's release from universal misery and degradation is for all to turn their "minds to the Light" within, whereby, joining with the Quakers, all will come to know "the one teacher, by which the Lord teaches his people, Jew and gentile, Barbarian, Scythian, Bond and Free."[76] All peoples stand in need of being gathered in "not by external happenings but this eternal Light of the Lord." For the Quakers it was superfluous, deplorable distraction to concern oneself with future political events, as did Christian and Jewish Millenarians like Serrarius, Boreel, and Menasseh yearning for and striving to bring about the fulfilment of history, the coming of the thousand-year Kingdom.[77]

Collegiants, less appalled by Quaker rejection of pending millennial redemption than Serrarius and Boreel, chiefly objected to the mystical wayward uses to which Quakers often put "the Light," their blank refusal to equate "the Light" with philosophical reason. Some "rationalists" close especially to Galenus, joined in Serrarius' campaign, the leading figure among this "rationalist" faction of Rijnsburgers rejecting Quaker notions of "the Light" being Pieter Balling (d. 1664) who, by 1662–3, we see from their correspondence, figured among Spinoza's closest friends and allies and was the translator of his book on Cartesian philosophy into Dutch. There is no proof Spinoza and Balling who spoke Spanish fluently and had been an agent for Amsterdam and Haarlem merchants in Spain as a young man before earning his living as a trader, were already friends, or knew each other, in 1657–8, though scholars agree this seems probable, given that after 1661 Spinoza lived away from Amsterdam and Balling stayed in Amsterdam, dealing with importers bringing in goods from Iberian lands, including all varieties of dried fruits, raisins, figs, almonds and the like that the Spinozas had dealt in.[78] But whether already friends before 1660 or not, there is no doubt that Balling's important tract, *Het Licht op den Kandelaer* [The Light on the Candlestick] (1662), sometimes called the first "Spinozist publication," was in part a rationalizing text intended as a gentle rebuttal and correction of Ames' conception of "the Light," but rebutting in the most unpolemical, conciliatory terms stressing the value of dialogue, interaction, and patience towards those who disagree.[79]

---

[76] Fell, *A Loving Salutation*, 32; Fix, *Prophecy and Reason*, 198–9.
[77] Van der Wall, *Mystieke Chiliast*, 219–21; Waite, *Jews and Muslims*, 191–3; Quatrini, *Adam Boreel*, 181–3.
[78] Meinsma, *Spinoza et son cercle*, 153; Spinoza, *Collected Works* (ed. Curley) i, 351; Israel, *Radical Enlightenment*, 170n60.
[79] Simonutti, "English Guests," 36–7; Siebrand, *Spinoza and the Netherlanders*, 24–5; Hunter, *Radical Protestantism in Spinoza's Thought*, 42–4; Rovere, "Shaping the Freedom," 123, 128.

The ultra-tolerant Balling, a Collegiant infinitely committed to continuing dialogue, playing a reconciling role as a bridge between Spiritualists and Quakers, and between both those factions and Cartesian philosophy,[80] focused as insistently as the Quakers on the "Light within" as the exclusive guide to truth. But he remained a thoroughgoing rationalist in his approach to truth. Every individual, he insisted, disregarding all existing churches, churchmen, tradition and theology, must ground their understanding on the "light of truth" within themselves. However, this, Balling argued, introducing a definition from Descartes, is no inspiration of the spirit but "a principle certain and infallible," the rod of reason clashing with the inner Light spiritualism of both Quakers and Serrarius' Collegiant stream. Balling strove to convert Quaker and Spiritualist "Light within" into the "light of truth, the true light that enlightens every person who comes into the world," gathered via Cartesian philosophical reason.[81] This "infallible" aid yields "clear and distinct knowledge of truth in the intellect of every person by which he is so entirely convinced as to the nature and essence of things that it becomes impossible to doubt it [daar aan te konnen twijffelen]."[82] This "clear and distinct" knowledge supersedes all other guides being "the first principle of religion," and guide to moral conduct, the judge of good and evil.[83]

As the rift between Collegiants and Quakers widened, yet another major split opened up in the later 1650s, this time between the Spiritualist and rationalist currents within the Collegiant movement, or between "philosophical" and "anti-philosophical" Collegiants, with Cartesianism becoming a seriously divisive factor. Comenius had been in direct contact with Descartes himself, in the late 1630s and early 1640s, their encounter resulting in disagreement initially revolving around Descartes' separation of philosophy from theology, and the physical world from the world of the spirit. His pansophism was superior to Cartesianism, held Comenius, because it brings together the sacred *and* profane sciences. During their one (four-hour) face-to-face discussion, arranged by Heidanus, Heereboord, and another professor, in 1642, at the castle of Endegeest, near Leiden, Comenius and Descartes had debated whether reason and knowledge can be envisaged as purely abstract in the Cartesian sense.[84] Comenius the pansophist believed the visual and the sensual in all its aspects are fundamental to knowledge and integral to reason itself. Rather than Descartes' pure abstract reason, he developed a conception of reason rooted in a dialectic of rationality working with sense-experience infusing all our perceptions, inferences, and conclusions.

---

[80] Van der Wall, *Mystieke Chiliast*, 227; Fix, *Prophecy and Reason*, 154; Rediehs, "Candlestick Mysteries," 166–7.
[81] [Balling] *Het Licht*, 4; Fix, *Prophecy and Reason*, 200–3; Israel, *Radical Enlightenment*, 343–4; Klever, *Mannen rond Spinoza*, 18–21.
[82] [Balling] *Het Licht*, 4; Popkin, *Third Force*, 132–3; Rediehs, "Candlestick Mysteries," 158–9.
[83] Siebrand, *Spinoza and the Netherlanders*, 26; Laerke, *Spinoza and the Freedom*, 37, 43, 176.
[84] Thijssen-Schoute, *Nederlands Cartesianisme*, 615–21; Van der Wall, *Mystieke Chiliast*, 474.

For Comenius, using illustrations, pictures of all kinds and diagrams is basic to educational technique for both smaller and older children.

In envisaging the human mind as a dual mechanism processing our responses to everything in terms of reason dialectically interacting with sense-experience, Comenius found himself clashing with Descartes and Bacon, as also with another great philosopher whose strict empiricist stance, postdating Spinoza's death, evolved in the 1680s, namely John Locke (1632–1704). Locke envisages the mind as an empty slate, a *tabula rasa* [blank slate] receiving sense impressions via experience from which all our ideas and notions, valid and invalid, are subsequently derived by rightly applying or, where mistaken, insufficiently applying, our reason. For Comenius, by contrast, sense-experience and inference proceed together and remain always inseparable which meant colliding with Baconian and, later, Lockean empiricism as well as Cartesianism, these all being anchored in a strict dualism of mind and body, sharply separating thought processes from feelings and sensual impulses. Here Comenius stood closer to what would become Spinoza's approach.[85]

Due in part to the religious background of the Moravian Brethren, and especially Comenius' unprecedented emphasis on education rather than belief or doctrine as the chief instrument for elevating society, and the need to bring peace to humanity ending persecution, fanaticism, and intolerance as well as war, Comenius was a true precursor of the Radical Enlightenment. Redefining religion, much like Spinoza, as pious conduct, not belief, rejecting professionally trained priesthoods and rendering education universal, Comenius edged toward the stance of Unitarian democrats of the eighteenth century, like Richard Price and Joseph Priestley during their mature years, striving to combine a rationalized, de-theologized Christianity with one-substance philosophy and universalism in morality. Comenius agreed with Quakers and Collegiants (and Spinoza) that without some revolutionary overturning of the ignorance and oppression imposed by society, monarchy, and ecclesiastics, the persecution, exile, and Wars of Religion tearing Europe asunder, and marginalization of minority communities like the Moravians, Polish Brethren, and Quakers, would never cease. Differently, though, from the Quakers and Serrarius' chiliasts, Comenius envisaged a revolution in human outlook as one of "enlightenment," with important affinities to that budding in Spinoza's mind: only by rescuing men from the ignorance and superstition buttressing oppressive governments and theologically based religious authority, can they enter the realm of universal justice and charity presided over by a universal "college" of enlighteners designed to adjudicate and direct human harmony and peace.

---

[85] Floss, "Problem of Comenius' Sensualism," 103–5; Čisek, "From Pansophia to Panorthosia," 205.

Spinoza, then, was not as unique as one might suppose in his life-long ambition to fundamentally reform our world by transforming humanity morally and educationally. In their different ways, Comenius, Galenus, Serrarius, Boreel, Fell, Fisher, Jelles, Rieuwertsz, Balling, the Koerbaghs and Van den Enden, along with Spinoza, were all revolutionaries seeking to emancipate and morally transform our world. They all plotted the overthrow of the status quo of their time built on Catholicism, Protestantism, kings, ecclesiastics, theology, laws restricting free expression, church and state directed universities, and aristocracy. Their sects were all dedicated to universal, thoroughgoing change and reform but remained divided over the issue of "reason."

By 1659, Comenius' worries and frustration about Cartesianism's impact had grown still more pronounced. That Descartes posthumously captured a large part of the philosophical establishment in the Dutch Republic and won over some theologians too, no one could deny; that the young Spinoza was equally impressed with Descartes' feat, and perhaps a little jealous too, is plainly evident. After long lingering on the fringes of philosophy and the sciences, Descartes' philosophical approach was by the late 1650s powerfully invading philosophy, medicine, and science, at any rate in the Netherlands, but also causing turmoil and rebellion on every side, rather like, Comenius suggested, the young revolutionary fisherman, Masaniello, leading the 1647 Neapolitan revolt against the Spanish crown.[86] During the 1660s, Comenius and Serrarius collaborated as allies in concerting their anti-Cartesian campaign among the sects. If Descartes took scant interest in Comenius' utopian pansophism, Comenius constantly pondered Descartes' philosophy. He did not find Descartes remotely as clear and distinct as others professed to. In 1645, he assured his friend, the Polish astronomer Johannes Hevelius, that he did not wish to speak in unfriendly fashion about anyone, but "I search [vainly] for Descartes in Descartes [Cartesium in Cartesio desidero]."[87]

On multiple levels, the Collegiants of the late 1650s faced a deep internal crisis, the factors impelling Cartesian philosophy to prominence in the feuding between the vying fringe streams soon evolving into the biggest split of all. Some, with Serrarius and Frans Kuyper (1629–91) prominent among them, reacted with growing hostility to the trend equating the "inner Light" with reason. Embracing Cartesianism and championing "reason," claiming, like Balling, Jelles, De Vries, and Rieuwertsz, that Cartesianism does not compromise Christian truth, collided with both Quaker "inner Light" and Collegiant Spiritualist enthusiasm. Anti-philosophical Collegiants, like Serrarius and Kuyper, exalted the integrity and primacy of Scripture over all else, viewing "rationalist" reconciliation of philosophy and theology brokered by Cartesianism and "philosophical" Collegiants as just another godless contrivance distracting men from "the Word," maligning Holy

---

[86] Rood, *Comenius*, 144–5.   [87] Rood, *Comenius*, 141–2; Popkin, *Third Force*, 91, 108–9.

Scripture's integrity, another false "enthusiasm" to be discarded with the errors of the strict Mennonites, Remonstrants, and Quakers, along with the main churches and Judaism.[88]

Until 1661, Spinoza personally witnessed the fragmenting quarrels within the anti-confessionalist, anti-church sects only in Amsterdam. But on moving to Rijnsburg, the third main centre of the Collegiants, in 1661, he gained a wider, more national perspective on the divisive, seething Collegiant scenario and its proliferating rifts. In the late 1650s and early 1660s, Rotterdam echoed Amsterdam as a scene of recurrent quarrels and splits among the anti-church fringe groups.[89] With its resident English community, Rotterdam, the second main Collegiant centre, was also the second main focus (with Utrecht the third) of Quaker efforts in the Netherlands, the house of the famous bibliophile merchant Benjamin Furly (1636–1714), "De Lantaarn," becoming a key meeting place in the 1660s. Serious contention in Rotterdam began in 1657, when a liberal splinter group of Rotterdam Mennonites insisted on holding their discussion "college" with prayers together with local Remonstrants and independent Collegiants. Led by Jacob Ostens (1630–78), an Anti-Trinitarian rationalist and tolerationist surgeon, those seeking to dilute Mennonite discipline and dogma by advocating Amsterdam-style "colleges," and meeting with Remonstrants, provoked bitter strife especially among the Mennonites. Ostens, nicknamed by foes the "Galenus of the Rotte[n]-town," became yet another of Spinoza's circle of close personal Collegiant friends. Ostens and his Socinian rationalist irenicism looked admirable to some, including Spinoza, but there was no denying that he nonetheless permanently split Rotterdam's Mennonites and alienated most Remonstrants, his radicalism provoking endless strife.[90]

For the young Spinoza of 1656–61, rubbing shoulders with Collegiants and Quakers was a passing phase, but a significantly formative one in which he found himself immersed in a uniquely uplifting and idealistic but endlessly divisive and furious theological-philosophical whirlpool, an ultimately irresolvable triangular battle of Scripturalists versus rationalists versus "inner Light" enthusiasts. Spinoza no doubt observed the scene with detachment and a touch of scorn, much as every Collegiant, Quaker, and Moravian disdained the established churches and university-trained theologians and Bible scholars, a legacy he shared with Balling, Jelles, Comenius, Galenus, Knol, Ostens, Rieuwertsz, and the rest of those who, like him, exalted "reason." Encountering the Quakers in 1657–8, and then Serrarius' Spiritualists remained a large part of his and their common intellectual and cultural heritage. Together with other "rationalists" among the Collegiants, Spinoza shared

---

[88] Van Slee, *Rijnsburger Collegianten*, 391–2; Israel, *Radical Enlightenment*, 347–8; Huenemann, *Spinoza's Radical Theology*, 13–14; Salatowsky, "Socinian Headaches," 168.

[89] Burnet, "Quaker Missionaries," 1–3, 5; Simonutti, "English Guests," 35–6.

[90] Van Bunge, *Johannes Bredenburg*, 33–8; Meinsma, *Spinoza et son cercle*, 286, 397; Van Slee, *Rijnsburger Collegianten*, 108–12, 303.

an escalating scepticism and detachment, viewing the anti-philosophism, anger, and passionate zeal of all the "Spiritualist," "Inner Light," and "Scripture alone" "enthusiast" warring groups with a mix of sympathy and disdain.

As Spinoza and his ally De Prado explained to other Iberians with whom they conversed during these years, Spinoza and De Prado busied themselves inquiring and "studying which was the best [religious] law."[91] It is highly unlikely that Spinoza ever seriously considered converting Jews to any church, but assisting the Quakers in diffusing their subversive ideas and revolutionary zeal to the Sephardic community, especially the principle of individual inspiration in interpreting Scripture superseding tradition, was likely to have appealed to him at least briefly. His encounter with the Quakers was short-lived, but arguably something of their approach survived in his view of the "spirit of Christ" as wholly detached from history, dogma, and churches, a sphere where both the actual historical figure and the divine supernatural Christ of theology dissolve leaving only the supreme moral example. The enthralling spectacle of inter-Collegiant and Quaker controversy and dispute, of Spiritualists and rationalists at war over how to interpret Scripture and Quaker efforts to overturn the entire accepted structure of Christian practice, assumptions, and belief, was basic to Spinoza's future life and thought also in another way: it can only have spurred his preoccupation with asking what then is the true methodology enabling men to reach a correct understanding of Scripture?

The Collegiant quarrels and wrangling of these years undoubtedly intensified Spinoza's awareness of how religious zeal blights harmony, cooperation between groups, tolerance and debate, the politically disastrous character of religious strife and the great difficulty of overcoming such rifts besides the unending problem of religion's relationship to philosophy and science. Where is the "true good" if not somewhere above and beyond the seething mass of warring creeds and theologies? Without doubt, for Spinoza, the fundamental lesson was that none of these fringe churches, whether the Quakers, Moravians, liberal Mennonites, or Spiritualist Millenarians, though all are indeed closer to the truth than the main churches, can possibly be the true "universal church" as Koerbagh expresses the point in his *Bloemhof* of 1668, all being too riven with quarrels and "hatred" for that to be at all conceivable. Even all the churches classed together cannot be considered the veritable "Catholic" or "universal church," notes Koerbagh, unless they can somehow reconcile themselves to each other in love and harmony and discard their perennial wrangling.[92]

Above all, the seething plethora of religious division confronted Spinoza and those he recruited to his way of thinking with the challenge of finding the way out of Balling's universal "sea of confusion," a viable exit from bitter entanglements in which even the most upright of Collegiants—Serrarius, Boreel, Comenius,

---

[91] Révah, *Spinoza et Juan de Prado*, 67.
[92] Koerbagh, *Bloemhof*, 125–6, 270; Quatrini, *Adam Boreel*, 383–6.

Zwicker, Ostens, and Knol—seemed inextricably caught up. Rejecting trained and salaried clergy, and allowing everyone who feels inspired to stand and deliver his opinion is a fine ideal. But as no one can say more than he knows, how can that be useful, asked Koerbagh in 1668, if true knowledge of God and the Bible remains elusive? If uncovering the true good is alluring to Jews, Protestants, Catholics, pagans, Muslims, and deists alike, and none are morally superior to the rest, then for Spinoza the precious path could not lie in religious studies. True knowledge of God and salvation for Spinoza, as for the Brothers Koerbagh, came to seem obtainable only via the path of philosophy and science.

10
"Monstrous Heresies"
Beyond Bible and Religious Studies

10.i First Writings

While still based in Amsterdam, during the formative six years 1655–61, Spinoza forged most of his lasting friendships and many of the connections that shaped his future intellectual development. During that period he also composed his two early works, his *Treatise on the Emendation of the Intellect*, written at some point in the late 1650s perhaps as early as 1657–8 which remained unfinished and appeared only as part of the *Opera Posthuma*, after his death in 1677, and his more mature (but long unpublished) *Korte Verhandeling van God, de mensch en deszelfs welstand* [Short Treatise on God, Man, and His Well-Being] dating from roughly 1659–60.

Scholars in the past tended to view the *Korte Verhandeling* as Spinoza's first surviving text and the *Emendation* as a later work, a kind of introduction to the *Ethics*. But since the 1980s, the arguments in favour of classifying the *Emendation* as Spinoza's first surviving text and definitely a product of the later 1650s, have come to be generally accepted. The *Emendation* undoubtedly reflects an earlier stage in Spinoza's development where the concept of Nature is already central but the distinction between *natura naturans* or the self-creating force of nature, and *natura naturata* or the passive, existing state of nature, a distinction characteristic of the *Korte Verhandeling* and the *Ethics*, as yet remains absent. Reflecting Spinoza's outlook of the later 1650s, the *Emendation* offers a window onto Spinoza's early philosophical approach rather than being an introduction to the *Ethics*, as long supposed. This new revised chronology has clear implications for how we view Spinoza's transition from his expulsion year, 1656, into the recognizable philosopher of 1658–60.[1]

In the *Emendation*, Spinoza's embryonic philosophy introduces the idea that governs the whole of his life's work, that if one is to successfully forsake constricting conventional attitudes such as seeking wealth, honours, and ordinary pleasures to ascend towards higher levels of human perfection, powerful remedies and guidance are requisite. True knowledge in accord with the eternal laws of

---

[1] Mignini, "Données et problèmes," 15–16, 20; Spinoza, *Collected Works* (ed. Curley) i, 4.

nature must be sought "together with other individuals if possible," shared effort reflecting the unison of the individual mind with the totality of nature which is the final objective, making it "part of my happiness to take pains that many others may understand, as I understand, so that their intellect and desire accord entirely with my intellect and desire." The "highest human good" Spinoza envisages as an individual but simultaneously collective quest for a better life necessitating a shared innovating philosophy rooted in group discussion, providing untrammelled freedom of expression and all the prerequisites facilitating a life of health, virtue, and joy, including a new approach to educating children and much effort to work out "the whole of medicine." Spinoza's emphasis is on radically changing lives by "healing the intellect" to uproot and "banish error as far as possible," directing "all sciences toward one end and goal namely that we should achieve, as we have said, the highest human perfection." Fighting error and false thinking here becomes humanity's overriding need, lending Spinoza's early project, no less than his later vision, an astoundingly ambitious scope. Besides organized religion and the sway of priesthoods, he aimed from the outset to unseat all existing structures of authority and practice in education, the sciences, medicine, and, ultimately, politics too. "So anything in the sciences which does nothing to advance us toward our goal [of collective improvement in this world] must be rejected as useless, in a word, all our activities and thoughts should be directed to this end."[2]

In the late 1650s, Spinoza was busily drawing up sweeping plans to "reform the world," expressing himself in a simple, straightforward, not always particularly confident Latin. In part, Spinoza's life's project can be seen as a renewal of the reformism inherent in Descartes' outlook and Cartesianism itself. By deviously "building on the principles of Descartes," complained one hostile commentator, in 1696, expanding on Bayle's account of Spinoza's life, "he spread his ruinous seed by mouth and by pen, and brought some pupils and adherents to support his godlessness."[3] Steeping himself in Cartesianism was certainly central to Spinoza's development as a thinker during the mid- and later 1650s. Significantly, he studied Descartes in Dutch first and then Latin but not in French, a language almost totally absent from his personal library.[4] His breaking with the Amsterdam Portuguese Jewish community, furthermore, coincided with a dramatic moment in the philosophical and medical spheres especially in the Dutch universities, rendering Cartesianism a pivotal public, political, and cultural battleground, forming the backcloth to his early writings.

For years the Reformed classes and synods had bombarded the secular authorities in the United Provinces with demands for more stringent religious policing. They sought stricter measures against Catholics, Socinians,

---

[2] Spinoza, *Collected Works* (ed. Curley) i, 10–11.   [3] Halma, *Het Leven*, 2–3.
[4] Van Sluis and Musschenga, *Boeken van Spinoza*, 30–2, 36–8, 47; Moreau, *Spinoza et le spinozisme*, 40.

Remonstrants, Mennonites, Jews, Quakers, sabbath breakers, theatregoers, dance schools, prostitutes, and more. In September 1653 and again in March 1656, the States acceded to the synods' demands as regards rigorously banning the printing, importing, and distributing of "Socinian books," that is texts denying the Trinity and Christ's divinity and miraculous resurrection.[5] Additional measures sought to repress the practice and teaching of Catholicism. But to the Calvinist devout committed to what historians have called the "Further Reformation," the measures taken thus far seemed frustratingly inadequate. The North and South Holland synods jointly complained to the States, on 31 July 1656, that existing curbs on sabbath violation, swearing, taking God's name in vain, staging plays, holding dances, and running dance schools, as well as illicit religious gatherings, and "licentious books" remained all not just insufficient but deplorably inadequate. Yet hitherto the synods had not appended philosophy and science to the growing list of spheres where harmful deviation from Christian propriety required stronger intervention of religious and public authority to police together.

It was specifically during the 1650s that the conservative phalanx within the Reformed synods began seriously resisting Galilean astronomy and what the Calvinist theologian Melchior Leydekker (1642–1721) later termed the encroaching "empire of the philosophers [het rijk der philosophen]," an intellectual domain derived from Cartesianism but creeping beyond Cartesianism, menacing European society's millennia-old Christian *kerkelijke Republijk* [church republic] and what most considered society's proper subordination to faith, ecclesiastical sanction, and scholasticism. Besides tougher measures to curb unbelief, undesirable dress, homosexuality and immodest or sexually alluring conduct, and "licentious," irreligious, and theologically undesirable publishing, tighter rules were needed to check also philosophy's trespassing inappropriately onto theology's domain.[6] The moves afoot in the synods, however, alarmed the Leiden academic senate, provoking a political-philosophical clash that culminated just twelve days before the advent of the *herem* on Spinoza, when the university curators brought the issue of philosophy to the floor of the States of Holland. The curators and Leiden burgomasters asked the States to adjudicate following efforts of The Hague Reformed classis to rally the South Holland Reformed synod behind their demand for the States to ensure "the integrity and power of the Holy Scriptures be not further violated" by philosophy professors. The Reformed preachers did not seek to curtail "liberty to philosophize," the synods assured the universities and provincial States, but did insist on effective measures to wall off harmful

---

[5] *Resolutien van de Heeren Staten van Holland* vol. 1656. Res. 3 and 4 March 1656; Israel, *Dutch Republic*, 911–12.

[6] Leydekker, *Historische en theologische redeneringe*, "Voor-reden," 2; Israel, "Philosophy, Deism," 174–5.

philosophical principles from the sphere of theology so that "God's church be not soured and the devout further saddened."

The very day after the *herem* against Spinoza was signed, the States debated the Leiden theology faculty's response, drafted by three leading theology professors— Johannes Cocceius (1603–69), Abraham Heidanus (1597–1678), and Johannes Hoornbeek (1617–66)—setting out their proposed compromise with the synods.[7] After further negotiation the philosophy furore of 1656 was settled for the interim with what proved a temporary solution formulated in the States' resolution of 30 September 1656. While the affairs of God and His Word are manifest by every path, declared the States, "still these are much more quickly, easily, surely and safely understood out of God's Word itself than through, and from, natural reason [als door en uyt natuyrlicke reden]." Wherever human reason seemingly contradicts Holy Scripture, philosophers shall not undertake "to explain Scripture in accordance with their principles," and theology and philosophy must remain strictly separate (the theologians' most essential demand), each with "its own fixed frame and limits," leaving philosophy permanently confined in scope, never permitted to intrude on the theological domain, on Scripture exegesis or church primacy over society, morality, and education. Philosophers must abstain henceforth from intruding on core theological ground lest theology be compromised by "freedom to philosophize."[8]

Holland's presiding figure, the States' chief secretary or "Pensionary," Johan de Witt (Pensionary of Holland, 1653–72), drafted the requisite decree consulting with the two most liberal Leiden theology professors, Cocceius and Heidanus. All of Holland's voting towns approved this measure forbidding philosophers to interpret Holy Scripture "according to their principles" except for staunchly Orangist and strictly Calvinist Leiden which, at odds with the University, sided with those demanding tougher measures against "Cartesianism." To strict Calvinist opponents of Cartesianism, De Witt's view that the only urgent issue was for the States to "prevent abuse of freedom to philosophize to the detriment of true theology and Holy Scripture" seemed insufficient.[9] Even so, the constraints imposed sufficed to create a potentially destabilizing rift by inviting secularizing philosophy to take root, as it were, outside the universities and insinuate itself into society, culture, and politics along paths from which academic philosophy itself remained strictly barred. Over the next four decades, Dutch theologians increasingly deplored the phenomenon of spreading non-theological, non-academic secularized "philosophy" as a subversive underground secretly, and at times not so secretly, challenging and undermining Christian belief and ecclesiastical sway outside the universities.

---

[7] *Resolutien van de Heeren Staten van Holland* vol. 1656, pp. 163, 173. Res. 24 and 28 July 1656.

[8] *Resolutien van de Heeren Staten van Holland* vol. 1656, p. 241. Res. 30 Sept. 1656; Israel, *Dutch Republic*, 894, 916.

[9] ARH SH 2647, fo. 324. De Witt to Leiden burgomasters, undated [August] 1656; Israel, *Dutch Republic*, 89.

The point where the concerns of the rabbis and *Mahamad* governing the Sephardic community met and tallied with those of the Reformed synods in 1655–6, was in their worries about a subversive philosophical movement clearly and indubitably present and alive at that juncture among the Portuguese Jewish community in Amsterdam which seemed no less corrosive of religious authority, if not more so, than anything troubling the synods. It was not simply that the Sephardic community had no desire to be blamed by the Calvinist-Orangist bloc for harbouring radically irreligious and dissident voices. The evidence was abundantly clear that rabbinic authority, the *Mahamad* and orthodoxy itself were menaced by a subversive intellectual current rife among their own ranks.

10.ii The La Peyrère Episode

In the past, scholars were often divided between those following Gebhardt and Révah who viewed the tradition of Iberian Marrano freethinkers rebelling against rabbinic authority as the primary impulse shaping Spinoza's immediate post-1655 rebellion, and initial emergence as an unremittingly subversive thinker, and those following Klever, Van Bunge, Steenbakkers, and other Dutch experts viewing the mix of Dutch rationalist Collegiants and freethinkers, and especially those who became Spinoza's friends and allies, the *cercle Spinoziste*, as the primary formative stimulus and context. Both sides present cogent arguments regarding the disputed origins of Spinoza's revolutionary impulse towards universal reform—was it Jewish or Dutch? However, it seems that Spinoza's unique capacity to fuse widely divergent cultural streams into a single synthesizing approach, his ability to bridge gulfs and provide a meeting point for both Iberian and Northern European traditions, clearly reflects the exceptional cultural visage of Golden Age Amsterdam itself, a setting shaping his outlook with its incomparably wide spectrum of distinct cultural streams. These converging currents he managed to concoct into a formidably coherent recipe combining dissident Marrano "deism" and strands of medieval Jewish thought together with Collegiant anti-theology and academic Cartesianism later all topped with some Hobbes and not least Spinoza's own emerging critique of the "Scientific Revolution" in progress around him, pointing out the limitations of the pure "experimental method" in science.

Since Spinoza's banishment from the synagogue was the outcome of a long and complex process of inner rebellion against Jewish tradition and orthodoxy reaching back to a much earlier stage in his life, seeking to identify a decisive "corrupter" whom Spinoza encountered only in 1655–6 seems definitely misplaced, whether this "corrupter" is envisaged as Van den Enden,[10] any other

---

[10] Klever, *Spinoza Classicus*, 12, 314–15.

of his Dutch friends, the Marrano freethinker De Prado, or the maverick Isaac La Peyrère.[11] Growing up in the midst of an exceptionally religiously diverse Amsterdam, a city and context in which none of the three principal suggested "corrupters," Van den Enden, De Prado, and La Peyrère, grew up, Spinoza was arguably far better conditioned and equipped than any of these to negotiate and absorb an exceptional range of heterodox views, enabling him, from early on, to venture well beyond all of these figures, first in comparative religious studies and Bible hermeneutics, and later in the 1650s, general philosophy.

Given the vast range of dissident views circulating, the Sephardic elders and rabbis had little choice but to confine their religious policing merely to what actually shocked or caused strife among the congregation.[12] If Spinoza's "official break with Judaism" cannot be attributed to any particular outsider leading him astray, neither can any one set of influences be said to lie behind Spinoza's open rupture with the community in 1655–6. Rather, as Nadler rightly states, and the Inquisition evidence recording Spinoza's views dating from 1658 confirms, Spinoza was ejected from the synagogue for defiantly and openly challenging rabbinic Judaism, and openly rejecting the validity of the Law, though Nadler too perhaps slightly overstates the role of Spinoza's (undoubted) denial of "immortality of the soul" in his expulsion. In Amsterdam, no one cared greatly whether Uriel da Costa denied the soul's immortality or not until his denial was published. Spinoza, De Prado, and others in their Spanish and Portuguese-speaking group did reject "immortality of the soul" in 1655–6, as was confirmed by Fray Tomás de Solano, one of the informers testifying to the Madrid Inquisition about Spinoza and De Prado (based on conversations held in 1658), but since the *parnasim* and rabbis were not "censorious about individual beliefs and views as such provided members did not openly preach heresy," what alone preoccupied the Jewish elders was curbing "escandalo [scandal]," among the commonest terms used in the *Haskamoth*, or official records of the synagogue governing board in its discipline proceedings of the 1650s and 1660s. Their unwavering aim was to suppress outward defiance and stop "bad opinions" being imparted to other congregants, in particular students, as well as the outside world.

Spinoza's open rupture with the synagogue coincided with the public scandal over La Peyrère's widely condemned book *Praeadamitae* [Men before Adam] published in the summer of 1655 (Figure 10.1). Popkin closely associates La Peyrère's scandalous book which he claims "Spinoza used extensively," and which "probably" influenced Spinoza (and De Prado) profoundly, with the onset of Spinoza's rebellion.[13] Isaac La Peyrère (1596–1676), secretary of the Prince of Condé, had brought his work of Bible exegesis from France to

---

[11] On this search for the original "corrupter," see Nadler, *Spinoza: A Life*, 138–47.
[12] Kasher and Biderman, "Why was Spinoza Excommunicated?" 116–17.
[13] Popkin, *Spinoza*, 20–1, 30, 42, 59.

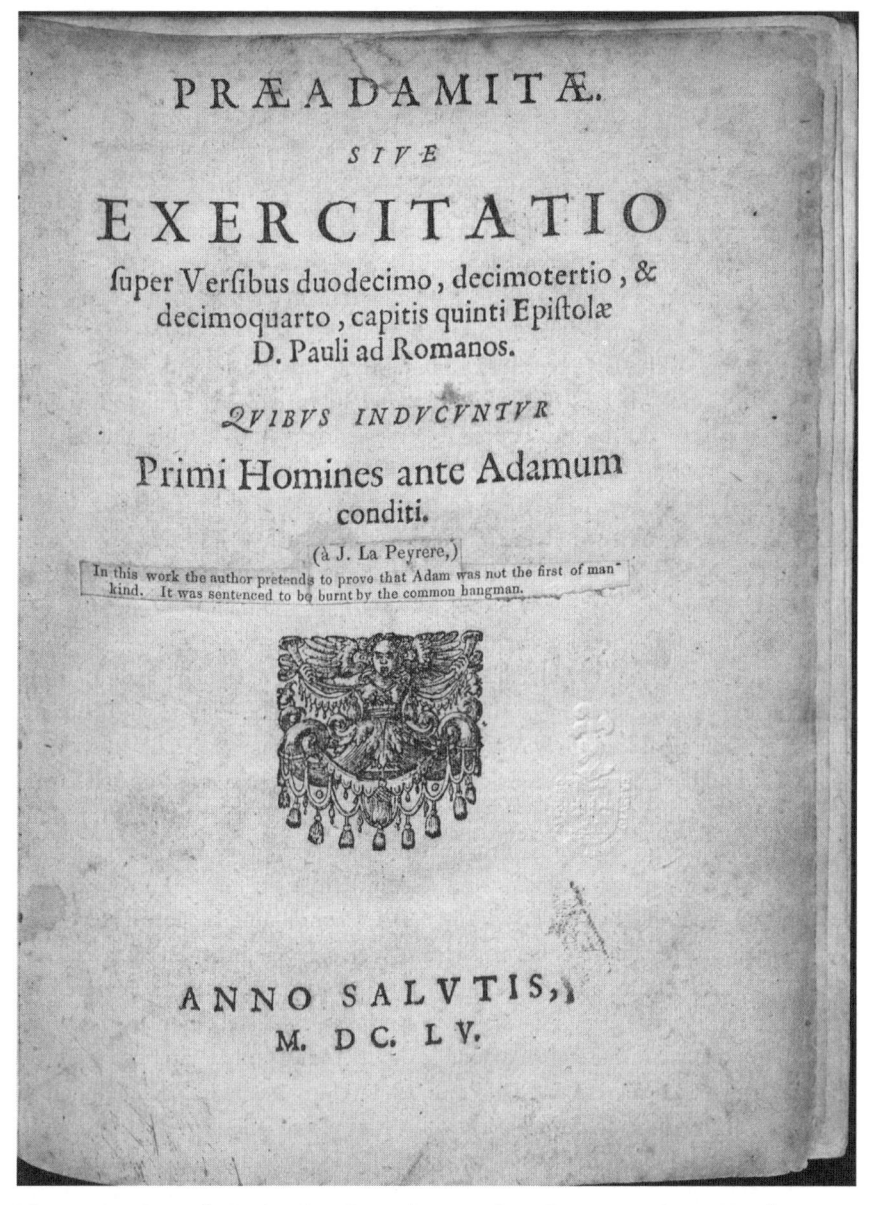

Figure 10.1 Isaac de La Peyrère. *Praeadamitae, Sive, Exercitatio Super Versibus Duodecimo, Decimotertio, & Decimoquarto, Capitis Quinti Epistolae D. Pauli Ad Romanos: Quibus Inducuntur Primi Homines Ante Adamum Conditi* [Amsterdam: Louis and Daniel Elzevier], 1655. IAS Spinoza Research Collection.

Amsterdam, early in 1655. Despite prompt efforts to suppress it, five editions appeared that year, three in Amsterdam, one in Basel, and another in an unknown location.[14] An English version appeared in 1656. Undoubtedly, La Peyrère's publication provoked a tremendous uproar locally and internationally that continued for four or five years, rousing Gijsbertus Voetius (1589–1676), doyen of the strict Calvinist theologians and the Utrecht Theology Faculty to a strong public condemnation leading to the banning of the *Praeadamitae* by the Hof of Holland, on 16 November 1655, and a week later by the States General. At the time, no one seriously interested in Bible criticism could long remain unaware of its claims that there were men on earth before Adam, that Adam was the "primus et pater" [first and forefather] of the Jews but not of humanity,[15] that Moses did not write the Pentateuch,[16] and, what caused greatest indignation, that the biblical text had become corrupted during the course of time and presents a highly unreliable account of the chronology of mankind's existence since the Creation. Further controversial points were La Peyrère's claims that the Flood happened only in the Holy Land, not over the whole earth,[17] that wonders such as God making the sun stand still in the sky to help Joshua were not miracles but natural events,[18] and that solid evidence proves the world is much older than the biblical account states, Chinese history, for example, reaching back 10,000 years.[19]

"Certainly, La Peyrère's biblical criticism," it has been argued, "had a strong effect on the next generation of Bible scholars, especially Spinoza and Richard Simon."[20] After all, it is entirely reasonable to suppose that a "rebel like the young Spinoza would have been intensely curious about this controversy," and the same applies to De Prado and his ally, Daniel de Ribera. Fiercely resented by Protestant preachers, La Peyrère's highly provocative book is known to have been in Spinoza's personal library at his death,[21] albeit there is no way of knowing when he acquired it or whether it played any part in formulating his lost *Apologia* of 1656. There is no evidence either to support the contention that Spinoza's ally in 1655-9, Juan de Prado, adopted some of the "heretical views of La Peyrère," or that the controversy "played a role in triggering a small rebellion in the synagogue." In particular, there are no good grounds for assuming "Spinoza went on from critique of La Peyrère and De Prado to develop a really full-fledged biblical criticism," or that he shared the basically theological and "messianist" approach of La Peyrère to the Bible initially but "by 1658–59 had given up such a venture."[22] It

---

[14] Jaumann, "Einleitung," pp. lxxviii, lxxix, lxxxv.
[15] La Peyrère, *Praeadamitae* i, 393–5, 433; Jorink, "Horrible and Blasphemous," 429–30.
[16] La Peyrère, *Praeadamitae* i, 393.   [17] La Peyrère, *Praeadamitae* ii, 606–15.
[18] La Peyrère, *Praeadamitae* ii, 586–7.
[19] La Peyrère, *Praeadamitae* i, 459–67, 478–81 and ii, 671–3, 929–31.
[20] Popkin, *Isaac La Peyrère*, 72; Nellen and Steenbakkers, "Biblical Philology," 42–3.
[21] Popkin, *Spinoza*, 20; Van der Wall, *Mystieke Chiliast*, 172; Servaas van Rooijen, *Inventaire*, 660; his copy was published in Amsterdam by Elsevier, Van Sluis and Musschenga, *Boeken van Spinoza*, 40.
[22] Popkin, *Isaac La Peyrère*, 86; Popkin, "Spinoza and La Peyrère," 190–1.

seems far likelier that Spinoza took careful note of, but also remained rather detached (as later reflected in the *TTP*) from the various attempted refutations of La Peyrère's book including those of Voetius and Maresius, as well as the feigned refutation by Isaac Vossius, *De Vera Aetate Mundi* [On the True Age of the World], of 1659, an even more subversive work than La Peyrère's. (Vossius, a more formidable scholar than La Peyrère, contended that the false chronology given in the standard Old Testament Hebrew text can be corrected by relying on the Greek Septuagint, prepared by Greek-speaking Jews in Alexandria between the third and second centuries BC, a version he considered an earlier, more authentic and reliable redaction of the Old Testament than the final Masoretic version of the Hebrew.) In any case, in 1655–6 Spinoza found himself surrounded by a whirl of rival philological claims and "messianist" pretensions and all manner of clashing and sensational theories about Scripture.

While La Peyrère had been discussing his pre-Adamite theory for many years prior to 1655 with key scholars, including Grotius and the internationally renowned philologist and Bible critic Claude Saumaise,[23] his theories were little known outside restricted circles until publication of his immediately notorious book. However, Spinoza and De Prado were rebelling against the Jewish Oral Law, the Mishnah, and rabbinic authority in the first place and it is unlikely La Peyrère can have been of much relevance here especially since this curious Frenchman knew no Hebrew (or Greek). On balance, given that Spinoza was strongly disinclined to be anyone's disciple, was widely read, and never mentions La Peyrère anywhere in his extant writings, it seems more probable that he never belonged in any concrete sense to the sect of "pre-Adamites," an intellectual group regularly denounced by theologians in the late seventeenth century, or was even "a partial disciple" of La Peyrère.[24]

What Dutch and other contemporaries called the "pre-Adamite sect in Amsterdam" certainly existed at least in the eyes of some, and De Prado and Spinoza, active as they were in Amsterdam, no doubt encountered and interacted with La Peyrère's perspective just as they did with a swirl of other competing trends.[25] In this sense, references in Dutch sources, in the mid- and late 1650s, to the "Pre-Adamite sect" at Amsterdam as, for example, in Samuel Maresius' refutation of La Peyrère, do refer to an actual group, including the small circle of Bible sceptics among the Sephardim, led by Spinoza, De Prado, and Ribera, and a few like-minded non-Jews meeting at Rieuwertsz's bookshop.[26] But this sort of

---

[23] Nellen and Steenbakkers, "Biblical Philology," 42–3; Jorink, "Horrible and Blasphemous," 434–45.
[24] Popkin, "Spinoza and La Peyrère," 191; ten years later, modified to "very partial disciple" in Popkin, *Isaac La Peyrère*.
[25] Kaplan, *From Christianity to Judaism*, 132–3; Muchnik, *Une Vie Marrane*, 412.
[26] Popkin, *History of Scepticism*, 220; Muchnik, *Une Vie Marrane*, 411–12, 475–6; Van Miert, *Emancipation of Biblical Philology*, 207, 211.

labelling by Maresius and others probably only signifies that the group shared certain themes rather than were actually, in a more concrete sense, disciples of La Peyrère. Still, it is hard to imagine that the uproar engulfing La Peyrère concerning topics of fundamental import to Spinoza and De Prado, as well as Menasseh and Mortera, did not seize their attention.[27] Along with the rest of the Republic's clergymen, Amsterdam rabbis, including Menasseh who knew and approved of La Peyrère's first book, *Du Rappel des Juifs* (1643),[28] and knew something of La Peyrère's claims about the Pentateuch before publication of the *Praeadamitae*, were certainly alarmed. When the book appeared, Menasseh began writing a refutation that in the event never appeared and is now lost.[29] Spinoza and De Prado may have enjoyed debating various contentions of this nominal "Calvinist" from Bordeaux, seemingly of Marrano origin, a strikingly philosemitic thinker and Bible interpreter passionately committed to ending finally the millennia-old rift between Jews and Christians (not least in France).

In any case, La Peyrère stayed in Holland only over the winter of 1654–5 and part of 1655, apparently meeting hardly anyone while arranging publication of his *Praeadamitae*, and there is no way of knowing if, while in Amsterdam, he ever met Spinoza or De Prado. It is pure conjecture to suppose either took any particular interest in the noisy controversy surrounding La Peyrère, or that Spinoza acquired his personal copy of the book at this time. Spinoza and De Prado were undoubtedly familiar with La Peyrère's key doctrines in the late 1650s and shared some of them, but equally clearly rejected others such as his messianic schema. Regarding themes they shared, like the corrupt status of the biblical text, the problem is to know how far La Peyrère's arguments added to or changed positions they held already before, during, or after 1655.[30] The same applies to Hobbes who also questions the status of the Bible as a holy text of impeccable integrity and universal account of man's history, though there is little sign at this stage that Hobbes could have been an influence on Spinoza's budding Bible criticism.[31] The "pre-Adamite sect" seems to have been more of a rhetorical label, a way of targeting a disparate array of dissidents than a genuinely identifiable stream.

Hoping for a positive reception, La Peyrère came to Holland to publish his unsettling theories because the Republic at that time was more tolerant than anywhere else. But his contending that the Old Testament's chronology is seriously awry, he must quickly have been warned, wildly overstepped the bounds of what Dutch society would tolerate. La Peyrère fled the country even before the book appeared. Once published, his text unleashed a veritable storm of condemnation for advancing "false, damaging and provocative teachings conflicting with

---

[27] Kaplan, "Intellectual Ferment," 308; Popkin, *Isaac La Peyrère*, 84, 87.
[28] Popkin, *Isaac La Peyrère*, 99–103.   [29] Van der Wall, *Mystieke Chiliast*, 685n73.
[30] Nadler, *Spinoza: A Life*, 116, 158, 322; Muchnik, *Une Vie Marrane*, 475–8.
[31] Malcolm, "Hobbes, Ezra, and the Bible," 392; Popkin, *Spinoza*, 20, 67.

God's Word." Assailed, Popkin notes, especially by orthodox Calvinists, the latter did not forgo the opportunity to link La Peyrère's "heresies" to the alleged depredations of Cartesian philosophy, even though La Peyrère makes no reference to Descartes.[32] In November 1655, the States of Holland and those of Utrecht, prompted by the university theology faculties, formally prohibited the work, ordering seizure of all copies from the bookshops.[33]

An argument of La Peyrère's that gained some traction in the mid-1650s was that the history of the world, as the Chinese chronicles confirm, stretches back into the past much further than the Old Testament affirms. The great antiquity of Chinese history is something Spinoza himself never mentions but De Prado does and probably did borrow from La Peyrère since he too reportedly specified that Chinese history was 10,000 years old.[34] The notion was taken up also by several other members of the group of radical intellectuals around Spinoza in the late 1650s, notably the Cartesian publicist, Jan Hendriksz Glazemaker, whose translation work and prefaces show him deliberately stressing Chinese civilization's great antiquity to prove the unreliability of biblical chronology.[35]

But the crucial point is that the small "rebellious group" within the Jewish community in 1655–8 had a wide range of sceptical tradition deeply rooted in their Marrano background to draw on. To an extent, De Prado and others of his circle were consciously following in the footsteps of Uriel da Costa, recollection of whom among the Sephardic community remained a vivid one.[36] But their outlook fed also on an older scepticism generated by a long history of finding oneself inwardly and outwardly buffeted between Judaism and Christianity. Many of Spinoza's forebears had been crypto-Jews, but by no means all; some had been committed Catholics, others, like his maternal grandfather after whom he was named "Baruch," spent their lives drifting between Christianity and Judaism. Resulting from the repressive force of the Inquisition and majority uniformity behind Catholic doctrine, seventeenth-century Spain and Portugal in fact nurtured one of the most highly developed underground secret intellectual countercultures of early modern Western Europe clandestinely devoted to repudiating Church teaching and doctrine and resisting a commonly prevailing status quo forcibly imposed by secular and ecclesiastical authorities.

This resentful masked Iberian tradition of freethinking, prevalent principally but far from exclusively among New Christians of Jewish descent, was a highly distinctive tradition of underground rebellion fed partly by medieval and Renaissance era clandestine traditions of thought. Men like De Prado and other dissident Iberians raised and educated within the Iberian peninsula kept alive

---

[32] Van Miert, *Emancipation of Biblical Philology*, 208.
[33] *Resolutien van de Heeren Staten van Holland* 1655, p. 390. Res. 24 Nov. and 27 Nov. 1655; Popkin, *Isaac La Peyrère*, 14, 181n56; Van Miert, *Emancipation of Biblical Philology*, 210.
[34] Albiac, *Sinagoga vacía*, 587; Muchnik, *Une Vie Marrane*, 412, 476.
[35] Esteves do Couto, *Marvelous Travels*, 95–7.   [36] Proietti, *Uriel da Costa*, 66–9.

crypto-Averroist and crypto-Epicurean currents which consolidated among New Christian university students in Coimbra, Salamanca, Alcalá, Seville, and Córdoba and subsequently penetrated Amsterdam Sephardic Jewry. Gripped by constant fear of exposure to the Inquisition and its numerous spies, this hidden counter-culture's unrelenting denial of Christ and Christian belief readily fused with Renaissance revival of ancient pagan and medieval clandestine philosophical traditions, and revolt against rabbinic Judaism. But unlike his ally, De Prado, who was a direct product of this Iberian underground, Spinoza is best viewed as a more complex phenomenon, a heady blend of seething Iberian cultural rebellion combined with strands of medieval Jewish philosophy, Dutch Collegiant critique of mainstream Christianity, and contemporary Dutch Cartesianism.

If, as Jacob Klatzkin famously argued in his Hebrew-language biography of Spinoza, in 1923, Spinoza's feel (and love) for the Hebrew language, including the Hebrew of medieval Jewish philosophy, always remained in some sense more basic to his thought processes and grasp of concepts than his formal conceptualizing in Latin, it is truer still, as has been observed, that in terms of literary sophistication and feel for the subtleties of expression and rhetoric, Spinoza always remained more at home in Spanish (and in conversation Portuguese) than Latin or any other language.[37] Unsurprisingly, the specifically Iberian free-thinking underground fed by strains of dissident crypto-Judaism received sustenance also from a hidden Iberian non-Jewish rebellion against oppressive religious policing and, consequently, additionally featured a small but formidable smattering of Iberians of non-Jewish origin. This debunking proselytizing tendency, as witnessed by the 1560s Conjura de Beja, with its admixture of Old Christian de-Christianizing dissidents, proved impossible to eradicate from Iberian "New Christian" society and, equally, from the Sephardic diaspora overseas. Among Judaizing exiles from Spain and Portugal present in Amsterdam and denounced to the Lisbon Inquisition, in 1617, by the famed renegade New Christian, Hector Mendes Bravo, for example, were Manoel Martins, an "Old Christian" who "had been in the service of the bishop of the Algarve" working for the Inquisition but who afterwards rejected Christianity and embraced Judaism, a second suspect "Old Christian," Manoel Cardoso, who married a New Christian woman, and, thirdly, the son of a stubborn Judaizer burnt by the Inquisition, a "brother of Diogo Gomez Duarte" who, says Mendes Bravo, studied typography in Lisbon before migrating to Amsterdam and was known as an "Epicurean or atheist who does not believe in any religion."[38]

---

[37] Akkerman, *Studies*, 25, 46, 49; Blanco Mayor, "Quevedo y Spinoza," 191; Rothkamm, *Institutio Oratoria*, 321.
[38] Roth, "Strange Case of Hector Mendez Bravo," 237; Révah, *Spinoza et Juan de Prado*, 14, 16; Proietti, *Uriel da Costa*, 68; Israel, *Diasporas*, 81–4, 88, 90.

Spinoza's rebellion prior to his expulsion in 1656 was thus much less intrinsically unusual or culturally alien to Iberian cultural history than one might suppose; what was dramatically different about Spinoza's Spanish culture was his weaving the elements of this Iberian cultural underground together into a highly sophisticated new system of thought incorporating also elements of Cartesianism and Collegiant critique of mainstream Protestant Christianity. As has been rightly remarked, at the very heart of Spinoza's enterprise stood his ambition to break down what he saw as the divisive faith-built (false) religious constructs dividing mankind theologically, politically, and philosophically, and replace these with a new unifying and harmonizing structure accommodating a scientific, social, and intellectual togetherness of all minds.[39] The essential impulse here, aligning with De Prado but sharply contrasting with La Peyrère and Hobbes, was to eradicate theology altogether from the veritable social and educational as well as the political and philosophical basic frame of humanity.

In evaluating the unique distinctiveness of Spinoza's early outlook, it is therefore essential to set alongside the contributions of Van den Enden, De Prado, and La Peyrère, and alongside the lessons learned from his Dutch Collegiant friends, the strands Spinoza imbibed from medieval and Renaissance Jewish thought especially from Ibn Ezra, Gersonides, Maimonides, Crescas, and Yoseph Shlomo Delmedigo. Bracketing all these together as the Ibero-Dutch welter from which Spinoza emerged affords a better and more accurate interpretation than focusing on any single figure.

Spinoza's two earliest surviving texts, the *Emendation* and the *Korte Verhandeling*, in fact manifest a number of common features set to reappear in more developed and systematic form in his mature philosophy, that seem to relate less to recently experienced Cartesian influences than to older traditions of philosophy imbibed in his school and post-school days. This applies not least to his epistemology—his ordering of human knowledge into three or, counting his rejected category, four categories, a feature of both the *Emendation* and the *Korte Verhandeling* as well as, later, of the *Ethics*. Spinoza's first class of "knowledge" is that of "report," accepted authority and what others tell you, the lowest rung of purported information which possesses no positive value in terms of knowledge status, being inherently unreliable. Only Spinoza's remaining three categories represent valid knowledge and possess positive value epistemologically. These stand in a hierarchical but also interactive, cumulative relationship to each other.

The lowest rung of genuine, positive knowledge, is what we learn from direct experience, observation, and collected data. Where observation and recording are accurate, this is always valid knowledge but so fragmentary that of itself it does not teach us much and is unlikely to be interpreted correctly unless there is adequate

---

[39] Brykman, *Judéité de Spinoza*, 12.

rational grounding in the mind. The next rung up is reasoning on the basis of correctly recorded and experienced observation where we combine facts together and correctly infer meaningful conclusions; this offers more useful, valuable knowledge, a framework of broadly correct inferences from data. Finally, the third rung in the order of the epistemologically valid categories, and the most elusive, evolves as the mind builds up its store of correct information, on the one hand, and correct inferences, on the other, that is when the intellect becomes steeped in the first and second kinds of true knowledge; this highest rung then permits leaps to truth via intuitive inference driven by the cumulative force of observation and reasoning, hence knowledge, already acquired making possible perspectives of a wide-ranging, overarching kind.[40]

Two more fundamental pre-Cartesian elements consistently prominent in Spinoza's thinking are his determinism or necessitarianism and his identification of God and Nature. The reference Spinoza makes to the medieval Catalan Jewish philosopher, Rabbi Hasdai Crescas (c.1340–c.1410), the most systematic determinist in medieval Spanish Jewish thought, as well as a noted religious and educational reformer, at the close of his letter on the infinite to his friend Lodewijk Meyer, dating from April 1663, is significant here.[41] It suggests that rejection of free will and insistence that everything that happens, including all our thoughts, is determined by the order of Nature and linked in an infinite series, did indeed precede his encounter with Cartesianism (as well as Van den Enden, De Prado, and La Peyrère) being actually rooted in philosophic traditions he studied well before 1655.

This is not to imply that Spinoza's most noteworthy divergence from Cartesianism, his denial of freedom of the will, which is also anti-Aristotelian and anti-Platonic, was simply borrowed unmodified from Crescas and his followers. Neither men nor anything else in the universe act from freedom of will according to Crescas but are determined in an infinite progression; but for Crescas it remains true that God, as the incorporeal cause of everything, does possess freedom of choice. Spinoza's God, or order of Nature, by contrast, lacks this divine volition and choice at the heart of everything, which was later Leibniz's chief objection to his system.[42] Elimination of free will, human *and* divine, remained central to Spinoza's philosophy throughout, including, by the mid-1670s, his political theory.[43] There are grounds, though, for thinking that Spinoza's God, being fully integrated with matter into the universe, resulted in part at least from examining Hasdai Crescas' critique of Maimonides and of Aristotelianism in his *Or Hashem* [The Light of the Lord] (1410), a book

---

[40] Spinoza, *Collected Works* (ed. Curley) i, 12, 55, 98–9, 138–9.
[41] Spinoza, *Collected Works* (ed. Curley) i, 205; Harvey, *Physics and Metaphysics*, 143–4, 156–7.
[42] Harvey, "Hasdai Crescas's Critique," 6–7; Levy, *Baruch or Benedict?*, 20, 26–7, 31; Manekin, "Spinoza and the Determinist Tradition," 36–7, 56; Green, "A Portrait," 88–9.
[43] Jaquet, "L'Actualité du *Traité Politique*," 18–19.

Spinoza read in Hebrew, and especially from pondering Crescas' rejection of the medieval Aristotelian notion that matter is finite, passive, and divisible and from his averring that, if God creates and infuses the form of everything intellectually, His divine being pervades all things.[44]

Spinoza's thought-world arguably reflects an overarching intellectual universalism without the expulsion of 1656 constituting any real break in his intellectual evolution, a system anchored in rejection of religious authority (both before and after 1656) and a Bible criticism inseparable from the vigorous Dutch intellectual context of his time but equally from the truncated and tortured past of his family's centuries-old Iberian heritage. This approach diverges from many earlier interpretations of Spinoza's life and involves subordinating Van den Enden, La Peyrère, and De Prado to firmly lesser roles, viewing them as significant influences and allies certainly but not mentors or major spurs to his development.

10.iii Dr Juan (Daniel) de Prado (1612–1670)

Spinoza undoubtedly broke more dramatically and completely, as well as abruptly, with organized Judaism, Jewish orthodoxy and the rabbis than either Da Costa or De Prado. The very completeness of the public break enabled him to continue and more fully profit from a subsequent, more tranquil phase largely free (for the rest of the 1650s and early 1660s) of the continuing stress, harassment, and violent polemics the other two found themselves embroiled in for years afterwards. Spinoza's post-*herem* experience, consequently, far better suited an intrepid philosopher searching for an unimpeded path to explore contemporary philosophy and the world of science, one more conducive to the swift progress he actually achieved, than the paths of Da Costa and De Prado. Unlike them, his *herem* was not the start of a long saga of conflict with the community and trauma but, quite the reverse, emancipation of the self from a deeply stressful and constricting predicament, separation from formal Judaism but not from the Iberian clandestine tradition of rejection of all received structures of thought.

Da Costa and De Prado came to view Judaism and Christianity as conjoined or similar insofar as both sanction coercive sway over belief and conduct and support a higher education edifice of scholastic philosophy devised, they thought, to bind ropes around "reason" and subordinate philosophy to theology.[45] Hence, among key features of Da Costa's and De Prado's rebellions, later adopted by the mature Spinoza, was their unwavering quest for an overarching criterion by which to

---

[44] Harvey, *Physics and Metaphysics*, 4; Fraenkel, "Hasdai Crescas on God," 89–90, 96, 98, 100–5.
[45] Salomon and Sassoon, "Introduction," in Da Costa, *Examination*, 39–41; Kaplan, "Karaites," 203–5; Muchnik, *Une Vie Marrane*, 388–9, 435, 473–4, 497; Ben-Zaken, *Cross-Cultural Scientific Exchanges*, 97–8.

measure doctrinal and Scriptural truth content, a methodology derived in part from quasi-Karaite scepticism stressing the primacy of the original text (rather than later interpretation), rigorous text criticism, and critical resort to strands of ancient philosophy that Spinoza would later bring to a much more elevated philosophical level. Drawing on the late medieval Iberian clandestine tradition tinged with Averroism, Da Costa and De Prado, along with others, devised a particular brand of anti-theological "true philosophy," as Da Costa calls it, as their primary weapon for combating religious authority.

Although such scepticism did, via Ibn Ezra and Delmedigo, have genuine roots in dialogue with Karaites, in Da Costa's and De Prado's writings one finds little that explicitly ties their rejection of the Mishna and Jewish Oral Law to Karaism, the medieval Jewish religious movement originating in the eighth century flourishing in parts of the Near East and in Lithuania insisting that the written Torah is the sole ground of Jewish religious law and that the Talmud and Oral Law are non-binding. Nevertheless, during the 1630s and 1640s, it became usual among the rabbis and religious leadership, when alluding to Da Costa-style heterodoxy, to label it "Karaism." This was more of a rabbinic term for the undercurrent of scepticism with which they were contending than a genuine derivation from Karaite contexts, but it tightened the link between the two. Unable to resolve his own doubts about Scripture and submit to orthodoxy, the renegade Mendes Bravo mentioned above was among those admonished by the rabbis to cease being a "Karaite."[46]

Early in life, when studying at Alcalá de Henares, in 1635–6, De Prado was close friends with Orobio de Castro, his future chief opponent in the Netherlands,[47] both being of Portuguese origin born in the Bragança region but raised in Andalusia, and at that time committed to a shared crypto-Judaism. When De Prado left Alcalá to complete his medical studies elsewhere, Orobio recalled in the 1660s, his friendship with him was interrupted for several years. A forced confession to the Inquisition by De Prado's brother-in-law, a Portuguese crypto-Jew tortured by the Inquisition in 1654, reveals that Orobio had been converted to secret Judaism by De Prado, in 1638–9, and confirms that De Prado's secret "Judaism," like Da Costa's, was an academic construct derived from secret study during his years at university.[48] Orobio too developed into a fervent Latin-reading crypto-Jew furtively researching ancient and medieval anti-Christian thought. In the early 1640s, however, De Prado while in Andalusia, edged away from clandestine Judaism, repudiating all religious authority and embraced a deism proclaiming an irreligious universalism he would later share with Spinoza. When Orobio and De Prado reconnected, in 1643, when Spinoza was still only eleven,

---

[46] Kaplan, "Karaites," 206–8; Israel, *Diasporas*, 84.
[47] Révah, *Des Marranes à Spinoza*, 257; Muchnik, "Orobio contra Prado," 31.
[48] Muchnik, *Une Vie Marrane*, 120–1, 136–7, 145–6; Yovel, *Spinoza and Other Heretics*, 58–9.

Orobio found to his amazement that his once ardently crypto-Jewish comrade now rejected crypto-Judaism as well as Christianity.[49] An Iberian exponent of crypto-deism who contributed to De Prado's "conversion" was another Portuguese Marrano who had studied at Alcalá whom Orobio knew (and had no high opinion of), a rebel against Christianity and Judaism alike named Juan Pinheiro [or Piñero], a physician later living in Seville where he died around 1662. Pinheiro also "converted" other Marrano university graduates in Andalusia to "deism."[50]

No man's spiritual status, held De Prado, can depend on what faith he professes and what religious tradition he avows allegiance to; all equally can achieve salvation in the "law that they observe whether Jews, Moors, or Christians." Judaism, Christianity, and Islam, much as Spinoza argued later, are all essentially human, political constructs, none being genuinely derived from divine revelation, or based on Scripture, and all being equal in their merely human and partial validity.[51] De Prado and Orobio subsequently remained caught up in clandestine debate in Andalusia, dispute that intensified over the years, but still to an extent remained joined in underground intellectual conspiracy against all conventional and officially approved belief systems, preserving something of their former friendship. Throughout the 1640s and early 1650s, while still in Spain, De Prado, though now a deist, by no means cut his ties with crypto-Judaism: rather, he continued manifesting a strong sense of group solidarity, participating in secret family observances and rituals and sharing fellow Judaizers' thoughts and dangers. He and the crypto-Jews, including Orobio, were still comrades together secretly combating religious oppression and the detested brutal tyranny of the Church and its ecclesiastics.[52]

This hardened, resilient crypto-Jewish intellectual culture of sixteenth- and seventeenth-century Spain and Portugal was indeed one of the greatest subversive impulses of the early modern Western world (on both sides of the Atlantic). After studying at Osuna and Alcalá de Henares, Orobio taught for a time at the University of Seville (1641–3) and then set up as a practising physician first in Seville, then other Andalusian towns, including San Lúcar de Barrameda and finally Cadiz. Arrested for "Judaizing" in 1654, he spent two years in Seville's Inquisition dungeons before appearing in an *auto de fe* there, in June 1656, a month before Spinoza's expulsion from the synagogue.[53] Publicly "reconciled" to the Church, as the expression went, after release Orobio stayed several more years

---

[49] Muchnik, "Orobio contra Prado," 35.
[50] See especially Muchnik, *Une Vie Marrane*, 342, 344, 347–8, 351; see also Gebhardt, "Juan de Prado," 285–90; Kaplan, *From Christianity to Judaism*, 126; Révah, *Des Marranes à Spinoza*, 279.
[51] Kaplan, *From Judaism to Christianity*, 126; Yovel, *Spinoza and Other Heretics*, 61–5; Muchnik, "Orobio contra Prado," 35.
[52] Albiac, *Sinagoga vacía*, 354–6; Muchnik, *Une Vie Marrane*, 137, 145–6, 349.
[53] Révah, *Spinoza et Juan de Prado*, 14.

in Seville before migrating, in early 1660, to Bayonne where a sizeable Portuguese crypto-Jewish community flourished and he had relatives. Godfather at a baptism there, on 24 June 1660, he still then signed under his "Christian" name as "Balthasar Alvares de Orobio."[54] Later, he transferred to Toulouse to teach at the university there, and finally Amsterdam where, in late 1662, he reverted to normative Judaism and set up once more as a high society physician. He soon discovered that De Prado had preceded him, seven years before, and become Spinoza's ally in defying rabbinic authority.

If Orobio de Castro's Hebrew, Talmudic and rabbinic knowledge were sparse, his stature as a scholar with expertise in medicine and philosophy rooted in the Spanish universities and fervent crypto-Jewish leanings reaching back to his youth were impressive. He was a life-long foe of Christian doctrine but not of Iberian scholasticism, and after reverting to formal Judaism in Amsterdam, Orobio deployed old-style Aristotelianism in upholding orthodoxy in defence of the rabbis and as a weapon against both De Prado's "deism" and, later, the underground "Spinozism" that was Spinoza's legacy to the Jewish as well as the Christian world. More than any other Jewish writer of the era, Orobio strove, through the 1660s, 1670s, and 1680s, in the tradition of Mortera's mentor, Elias Montalto (1567–1616), to reconcile Judaism with philosophical reason while attacking Christianity's foundations and assailing the waywardness of hesitant New Christians and deists. Defending rabbinic authority, he employed arguments adapted to the multi-layered Marrano cultural context which led to his writings eventually becoming absorbed into a paradoxical post-1700 legend created by Radical Enlightenment underground freethinkers, his posthumous eighteenth-century legacy turning him into a fictional "Orobio de Castro" at war with Christianity *and* all other religious institutions and authority.[55]

Underground subversive intellectual tendencies seethed more in early seventeenth-century Spain and Portugal than anywhere else in Europe. Frequenting Spain's universities in the 1630s, De Prado, Orobio, and other university-trained "New Christians" prided themselves on their secretly piecing together scraps of buried Jewish knowledge recorded in Latin, garnered from university libraries, and building their collective subterranean rejection of Christianity, silently constructing a crypto-Judaism differing vastly from mainstream Jewish tradition by focusing on subverting Christian doctrine far more obsessively and vehemently than Jewish orthodoxy ever ventured to do. Repudiating the Gospels, Church Fathers, and university theologians in every conceivable respect, these veteran crypto-apostates had decades of experience secretly debating with New Christians more inclined to submit to ecclesiastical authority.[56] In certain respects, highly literate crypto-Jews,

---

[54] Nahon, *Métropoles et périphéries sefarades*, 107.
[55] Kaplan, *From Christianity to Judaism*, 466–7; Israel, *Revolutionary Jews*, 111–23.
[56] Yovel, *Spinoza and Other Heretics*, 57–9.

mostly university trained physicians, like De Prado, Orobio, and Pinheiro were reviving intellectual traditions tinged with crypto-Averroism reaching back centuries before the 1492 expulsion from Spain. Fourteenth- and fifteenth-century rabbis sometimes denounced this resurgent "Sadducean" tendency as a subterranean rationalism feeding on Maimonides' and Gersonides' legacies. Culminating in Da Costa and then Spinoza, this clandestine tradition denied immortality of the soul, and reward and punishment in the hereafter, elevating natural laws above religious authority and the commandments of the Torah.[57]

This conspiratorial, philosophically inclined concealed group ideology, forged by decades of silent underground struggle and oppositional group culture, De Prado brought with him from Iberia in mid-1655, just as Spinoza was sinking deeper into financial difficulty while simultaneously struggling to free himself from the burdensome, entangling legacy of his father. In Amsterdam, De Prado immediately joined the Sephardic congregation while at the same time being accepted by the city *collegium medicum* as a practising physician. A synagogue member, but knowing little Hebrew and relatively little of orthodox Judaism, he at once joined forces with the rebellious young Spinoza. Spinoza, De Prado, and later De Prado's other main ally in Amsterdam, Daniel de Ribera (c.1616–94), another fierce rebel against Christianity but only half-hearted Jewish proselyte, an Old Christian of Catalan background whose original name was José Carreras y Coligo, formed an active coterie nourishing and further shaping the "deistic" proclivities each found in the other. They launched a joint challenge to rabbinic authority, clashing, remarks Levi de Barrios, especially with Mortera in the *yeshivah* Keter Torah.[58]

A Catalan of non-Jewish origin and priest trained at Salamanca University, Ribera sympathized (as did not a few Catalans) with the 1640 Portuguese revolt against the Spanish monarchy. After moving to Lisbon, he was sent by the new Portuguese king, in 1645, to Bahia, in Brazil where, partly due to contacts with Jews in the Dutch zone, he scandalized pious opinion by expressing doubts about the Trinity and papal pretensions. Arrested, he was sent back to Lisbon where the Inquisition incarcerated and tortured him for a year before banishing him from Portuguese territory forever. The ship conveying him to France, however, was captured by the English. In London, Ribera first converted to Protestantism, before moving to Amsterdam where, after sizing up the scene, he had himself circumcised, and joined the Sephardic community, and was appointed an auxiliary teacher in Latin and Spanish at the schools, in February 1657.[59] Allying with

---

[57] Kaplan, "Foi et scepticisme," 31–3, 38–40; Proietti, *Uriel da Costa*, 102–3; Muchnik, *Une Vie Marrane*, 364–73; Muchnik, "Orobio contra Prado," 31.

[58] Levi de Barrios, *Triumpho del govierno popular*, section "La Corona de la ley," p. 2; Révah, *Des Marranes à Spinoza*, 224–5; Kaplan, *From Christianity to Judaism*, 128–33; Préposiet, *Spinoza*, 50.

[59] Levie Bernfeld, *Poverty and Welfare*, 350n201.

De Prado and Spinoza, and unable to refrain from making irreverent remarks about Moses and the Scriptures, he too soon clashed with the rabbis.

De Prado, meanwhile, more hesitant in defying the community openly than Spinoza or Ribera, remained for tactical reasons more willing to mouth conciliatory pronouncements to placate the rabbis.[60] In this respect, he adhered to the outwardly submissive Marrano tradition more closely than the young Spinoza. Humbly recanting after his first public collision with the rabbis, his expressions of contrition and promises to reform were initially accepted. Renewed trouble then led to the *herem* pronounced on De Prado, on 14 February 1657 which, though less vehement than that clapped on Spinoza seven months before, was nevertheless also an unusually extended text, recounting how "Dr Daniel de Prado" had relapsed into former faults after solemnly promising publicly to repent and reform, and was found by "the *senhores* of the *mahamad* to have fallen again into his bad and false opinions contrary to our Holy Law and with these to have led astray some young students."[61] Hoping to have the *herem* rescinded, De Prado then asked the Hamburg Sephardic *Mahamad* to intercede on his behalf, but they rejected his request, on 22 May 1657.[62] Definitive expulsion ensued, though, only in February 1658, a year and a half after Spinoza's expulsion, when the rabbis and *parnasim* placed him under the major *herem* for persevering "in his evil and false opinions contrary to our holy Law, and due to his views being instrumental in disaffecting a number of young students."[63]

"Daniel de Prado" as he was called in synagogue, was not definitively expelled by the *Mahamad* until 1658, when it became obvious that his 1656 and 1657 retractions were insincere and that he had again, witnesses attested, lured "different persons," especially "young students," into his subversive views. Consulting with the rabbis, the *Mahamad* unanimously resolved that the "said Daniel de Prado be put under *herem* [...] and set apart from the nation," banned for causing a "great scandal." When De Prado's son, David, tried to get the *herem* lifted, later in 1658, and again in June 1659, forwarding a text written by his father urging the irregularity of the procedures against him and blaming Rabbi Mortera's spite and meanness, the rabbis remained adamant: inquiring into De Prado's teaching methods and subversive remarks to pupils convinced them that he adhered still to underground Averroist notions that there is no divine providence, that the world was not created but exists eternally, that the Mosaic Law lacks divine foundation and presents a confused chronology, and that the soul dies with the body.[64]

---

[60] Révah, *Spinoza et Juan de Prado*, 27–30.
[61] Révah, *Spinoza et Juan de Prado*, 28; Nadler, *Spinoza's Heresy*, 14–15.
[62] Révah, *Spinoza et Juan de Prado*, 30; Méchoulan, "Herem à Amsterdam," 125–6.
[63] Kaplan, *From Christianity to Judaism*, 135.
[64] Kaplan, *From Christianity to Judaism*, 142–3; Nadler, *Spinoza's Heresy*, 173–4, 190n34; Muchnik, *Une Vie Marrane*, 444–7.

As De Prado again pleaded his readiness to repent and reform, a renewed thorough investigation of all that had transpired ensued. Eventually, the *Mahamad* offered De Prado the community's help to emigrate to another Jewish community abroad but refused to lift the *herem* unless he agreed to leave the Republic. With Mortera and Aboab present, the *parnasim* finally resolved that De Prado could not be permitted to rejoin the congregation, and that his name be removed from the community's poor list.[65] This left the ostracized De Prado in the same isolation as his comrade, Spinoza, but still in Amsterdam hoping to get the ban lifted, and despite the *herem*, still passing his time with a few of the more independent-minded members of the Sephardic community.

Joining forces with De Prado and Ribera prior to his ejection from the synagogue, rather than marking any significant change in Spinoza's thinking, chiefly matters for signalling his emergence as a controversialist and publicly engaged philosophical voice involved in a local affray. Popkin was right to remark that "it may well be that it was the way Spinoza presented the ideas [in 1656] rather than the ideas themselves that brought about such a strong reaction."[66] De Prado and Ribera undoubtedly widened Spinoza's awareness in some respects, expanding his knowledge of Spain, Portugal, and Brazil, and of crypto-Judaism, while confirming Iberian universities were still steeped in what Spinoza doubtless reckoned a hopelessly backward Aristotelianism, but can have contributed little to his engaging with the "new philosophy" or alienation from traditional Judaism, as such. Spinoza's plunging into the world of Cartesian philosophy and science, and his exacting Bible criticism, in other words, were not rooted in contacts with De Prado and Ribera, albeit his image in the community was for a time powerfully shaped by close association with them.

For several years, from 1655 to 1658, Spinoza went about Amsterdam together with De Prado getting into all manner of discussions with other Iberians, much as he did outside the community when debating with Collegiants (and Quakers) in Dutch. At times, De Prado and Spinoza performed a kind of philosophical-theological double-act debating in lively fashion with Sephardic Jews but also with other Iberians and Ibero-Americans, invariably conducting their joint performance in Spanish as De Prado did not speak Dutch or Portuguese.

10.iv Denounced to the Inquisition

Although the July 1656 rabbinic ban required Jews to cut off all contact with the trebly cursed outcast, during the crucially formative next five years of Spinoza's life (1656–61), he spent much time debating with not only Collegiants, Quakers,

---

[65] Révah, *Spinoza et Juan de Prado*, 29; Levie Bernfeld, *Poverty and Welfare*, 99.
[66] Popkin, *Spinoza*, 34; Den Boer, *Literatura sefardí*, 301n32.

and non-Iberian freethinkers but clearly also with De Prado and the circle of Sephardic freethinkers and heretics, besides other fringe Iberians, Catholic and Jewish. By 1658, two years after his expulsion, we know from the testimony of a Spanish friar and a Spanish army officer, both stranded in Holland for some months, who regularly conversed with him and De Prado in Amsterdam, that Spinoza already seemed more impressive philosophizing in group discussion than his much older ally, despite De Prado's long academic scholastic training in Spain. The two visiting Spaniards, on finally returning to Madrid, in 1659, lost no time in informing the Inquisition authorities about Spinoza and De Prado. The key documents summarizing the friar's and officer's sworn testimony before the Inquisition authorities, discovered in the 1950s in the Madrid archives by I. S. Révah, are dated 8 August 1659.[67] On that day the friar appeared before Inquisitor Doctor D. Gabriel de la Calle y Heredía, at the Madrid Inquisition tribunal offices, to report several "heretics" he had encountered in Amsterdam, De Prado and Spinoza among them.[68]

Fray Tomás Solano y Robles, an Augustinian friar from New Granada in South America, had been captured by the English while at sea, near the Canaries, in May 1658, on a ship en route to Spain, and brought to London. Released after two months' imprisonment, he crossed to Amsterdam from where, he claimed, he planned to proceed directly either to Rome or Spain but, for whatever reason, lingered instead in Amsterdam supposedly unable to obtain passage, from August 1658 until March 1659, when finally he sailed for Cadiz. During those seven or eight months he stayed in the house of a German Catholic from Cologne, a certain "Yambrune [Jan Brun]," whose house had a clandestine chapel where he jointly officiated during that time with an Irish Franciscan in daily reciting mass.[69] Besides ministering to Catholics, Solano received medical treatment from and debated with the Jewish physician, Dr Miguel (Abraham Israel) Reynoso from Seville, a baptized Catholic apostate now turned Jew,[70] and regularly conversed also with other Spanish and Portuguese Judaizers including one, Gonzalo Suárez, fleeing the Inquisition in Mexico. Reynoso had at some point already been reported to the Augustinian monastery on Tenerife for being as "good [a] Jew" in Amsterdam "as he had been a good Christian in Spain."[71]

After arriving in Amsterdam, in 1646, with his medical doctorate from Coimbra, Dr Reynoso enjoyed high academic and social status and had been brought onto the Sephardic community's governing board, in 1654.[72] Besides the two physicians, Reynoso and De Prado, who both did much to bolster medical

---

[67] Further on these documents, see Révah, *Des Marranes à Spinoza*, 197–200, 211, 232, 241; see also Popkin, "Spinoza's Excommunication," 266.
[68] Révah, *Spinoza et Juan de Prado*, 32; Muchnik, *Une Vie Marrane*, 412.
[69] Solano y Robles, *Deposición*, 61; Albiac, *Sinagoga vacía*, 152, 155.
[70] Pieterse, *Daniel Levi de Barrios als geschiedschrijver*, 126.
[71] Beinart, "Jews in the Canary Islands," 63. [72] Muchnik, "Orobio contra Prado," 34.

expertise among the Sephardic community, Solano met also other members of the Sephardic congregation, among them an "Old Christian" actor, well known in Seville in the 1640s, Lorenzo Escudero, who had provoked great scandal in that city by fleeing and converting to Judaism in Holland, and, also from Seville, a confectioner named Samuel Pacheco, who earned his living preparing "chocolate and tobacco." Solano met these personalities at the lodgings of a certain Don Joseph Guerra, an "Old Christian" merchant from the Canaries in Amsterdam seeking remedies for his leprosy whose house Solano frequented because Don Joseph, going blind from his illness, needed support.[73] On Tenerife, leprosy had a long history but was not considered infectious (though it was); understandably, the sickness often caused acute depression.

Becoming friendly with Guerra, Solano in effect joined a whole group of Iberians regularly gathering at his home to keep Guerra company and cheer him in his own language. Nothing was said in Solano's testimony about Guerra's trading activities, but both he and his brother, Fulano, were later reported to Madrid by the Spanish ambassador at The Hague for dealing in contraband traffic between Holland and the Canaries, and via the Canaries between Amsterdam and Spanish America, suggesting Don Joseph may have already long been familiar to Spinoza and other Sephardic merchants involved in the Canaries trade, possibly including Spinoza's father.[74] Intermediaries were crucial to that trade, as Sephardic Jews could not safely set foot in the Canaries where the Inquisition was highly active. On 1 June 1659, two months before Spinoza was reported to the Madrid Inquisition, an auto-da-fé was celebrated before the cathedral church, Santa Ana de las Palmas, seat of the diocese of the Canaries, at Las Palmas on Gran Canaria, a public event in which several Judaizing apostates were condemned, in person or effigy, before huge crowds in the plaza.[75]

For handling their Canaries trade, Amsterdam Sephardic merchants needed a mix of New and local Old Christians, local middlemen, like Guerra, being indispensable to the flow of Canariote wine across the Atlantic, and to England, and illicit extraction of silver from the Spanish Indies, and sugar from Brazil. Don Joseph gladly welcomed Spinoza, De Prado, and the latter's son, David de Prado, into his Amsterdam lodgings, along with Dr Reynoso who was probably treating Guerra for his sickness. Being ignorant of Dutch and eager for sophisticated Spanish-speaking company, Reynoso too liked frequenting Guerra's house. Before fleeing Seville around 1646, Reynoso had known both De Prado and Orobio, in Andalusia, yet another reason why they now all convened together for discussions at Guerra's place, with Solano, Pacheco, and Spinoza. Though in less

---

[73] Révah, *Spinoza et Juan de Prado*, 33–4; Muchnik, *Une Vie Marrane*, 320.
[74] AGS Estado leg. 2198 (1661) Gamarra to Philip IV, The Hague, 14 June 1661.
[75] Millares Torres, *Historia de la Inquisición en las Islas Canarias* iii, 38; Israel, *Diasporas*, 274.

danger than his Jewish friends, when afterwards returning to the Canaries, Guerra proved still to be very much in awe of the Inquisition. In March 1662, like Solano earlier, Don Joseph likewise felt obliged to testify before the Inquisition among others denouncing De Prado and his son.[76]

The worthy friar had discussed religion with all of these personalities, he explained to the Inquisitors, to discover more about Amsterdam Jews, being filled with zeal to persuade them, or so he assured the Inquisition, "to abandon the Law of Moses" and revert to Christ, but without success. These gatherings, mixing the serious with the convivial at Don Joseph's lodgings, Pacheco doubtless enlivened with samples of his confectionery art. It was at this time that Amsterdam emerged as the centre of the European chocolate trade and preparation of new methods of flavouring confectioneries with chocolate. In earlier times, cacao was consumed as drinking chocolate (modern refined hard chocolate for eating only arrived in the nineteenth century), but thickened chocolate was now being used on cakes and confectioneries. According to two reports of 1657 from the Spanish consul, Jacques Richard, to the Spanish minister, Esteban de Gamarra, in Brussels, this "Pacheco" was the person who first mixed Central American vanilla with chocolate, in Northern Europe, and was considered Holland's most innovative and outstanding *chocolatier*.[77]

Reynoso and Pacheco attended synagogue morning and evening on the Jewish sabbath but remained in contact not only with Christian Iberians but, in violation of the *herem*, with freethinkers ejected from the synagogue. One crucial point Spinoza undoubtedly took to heart from conversing in this milieu was that opposition-minded intellectuals with university doctorates, like De Prado, Reynoso, and Ribera, forging like Da Costa before them an underground network permanently at odds with Church and all Christian theology, constituted a far more formidable adversary of religious authority and all theological claims, existing education, and scholastic philosophy, than any group of scholars conventionally educated in mainstream Christianity or Judaism. From their long years of concealment, furtive dedication to clandestine research and debate, and thorough familiarity with Christian doctrine and Latin erudition, they had learnt how to subvert with lasting impact. Knowing the scene and the risks intimately, they exploited their university careers not just to secure medical or other degrees but to extend their subversive clandestine religious-philosophical intellectual culture, demonstrating how a sustained, secretly proselytizing intellectual avant-garde can combat and within their closed, private sphere, crushingly defeat even the world's cruellest, most despotic belief system.

The main theme of Solano's submission to the Madrid Inquisition was his testimony against Lorenzo Escudero, a personage reputedly of Morisco descent

---

[76] Muchnik, *Une Vie Marrane*, 172–3, 321.
[77] AGR SEG Correspondance de Jacques Richard, Richard to Gamarra, 22 Feb. and 19 Dec. 1657.

who despite the worthy friar's efforts stubbornly refused to return to the Church. Circumcised, assuming the name "Abraham Gera Peregrino," Escudero remained within Judaism.[78] Solano also remonstrated at length, he told the Inquisitors, with Dr De Prado "who had studied at Alcalá," and a certain "fellow, Espinosa whom he understands is a native of one of the Dutch cities."[79] These two had formerly "adhered to the Law of Moses and the synagogue but been expelled and separated themselves from it due to their becoming atheists." They told him themselves they were circumcised and used to keep the Law of the Jews but later changed their view "because it seemed to them that the said Law was not the true one, that souls die with the body, and that there is no God except philosophically." Solano's Inquisition submission includes the only surviving statement that Spinoza studied at Leiden University, presumably in the period 1657-8, reporting that Spinoza "had studied at Leiden" and "hera buen filósofo [was a good philosopher]," offering stiff opposition, presumably, to the friar's pious admonitions.

Solano said nothing comparable about De Prado who, if he had discovered the "new philosophy" at all as yet, must certainly have been less proficient in Cartesianism than Spinoza, for at that time Cartesianism remained very much a Dutch phenomenon not yet penetrating deeply even in France, let alone other European lands.[80] Converting others to construing the world in entirely new terms, through debate, his submission suggests, was already central to the budding young philosopher's agenda. De Prado and Spinoza openly admitted to no longer believing in the Law of Moses, testified Fray Tomás, and it was due to this and their contending that men's souls die with the body (a key doctrine of Da Costa), and that there is no God except "philosophically," that they were ejected from the synagogue.[81] De Prado he estimated at about thirty years old (he was actually around fifty), "tall, slender with a big nose and brown skin."[82] "Spinoza is in body a small man with a handsome face but pale, with black hair, black eyes, is twenty-four years old, has no occupation and is of the Jewish nation," meaning a Jew born outside the Iberian world and not a baptized Marrano like De Prado. Unlike De Prado, Reynoso, Ribera, and Escudero, all baptized and circumcised, Spinoza remained unbaptized and hence, not being a relapsed Christian like the others, was exempt from Inquisition jurisdiction.

The next day, 9 August 1659, it was the turn of Captain Miguel Pérez de Maltranilla to testify. An infantry captain of the army of Flanders who had spent some time in The Hague, this officer had stayed in Amsterdam, in the

---

[78] Solano y Robles, *Deposición*, 61; Wilke, "Clandestine Classics," 64.
[79] Révah, *Spinoza et Juan de Prado*, 32; Albiac, *Sinagoga vacía*, 157.
[80] Freudenthal/Walther, *Lebensgeschichte* i, 272 and ii, 145; Klever, "Spinoza's Life and Works," 22; Totaro, "L'Enigme du nom," 172; Préposiet, *Spinoza*, 48.
[81] Révah, *Des Marranes à Spinoza*, 198; Mignini, "Données et problèmes," 9; Van Bunge, *Baruch of Benedictus?*, 7.
[82] See appendix II of Révah, *Spinoza et Juan de Prado*, 61-5; Muchnik, *Une Vie Marrane*, 413-14; Nadler, *Book Forged in Hell*, 10-11; Fraenkel, "Spinoza's Philosophy of Religion," 378-9.

same house as Solano, between November 1658 and January 1659, and likewise been greatly scandalized by the renegade Escudero and the other reprehensible apostates abounding in Amsterdam. He too had often talked with and listened to Spinoza and the physician De Prado. On one occasion the captain had accompanied Friar Tomás to the Portuguese synagogue, like other visiting non-Jewish Iberians during the 1650s,[83] to witness for himself the unbelievable disgrace of a city where Catholicism has status lower than Judaism, and to see whether any Jews could be shown "their errors" and retrieved for Christ.

To the testimony of the friar, Pérez de Maltranilla added some interesting additional details. The fifty-year-old De Prado, testified Pérez de Maltranilla at the Inquisition hearing in Madrid, on 9 August 1659, was tall with a thin face, black hair and beard and had long lived in Córdoba for which he expressed much nostalgia. Reynoso was short, sixty years old with a large beard; Pacheco, the chocolate-maker, was forty-four, tall and dark with a black beard. Where "the fellow Spinoza" came from, Pérez de Maltranilla did not know, having met him only at the house of Don Joseph Guerra. Regarding Spinoza's Iberian ties, he knew only that Spinoza mentioned never having been to Spain "but having a desire to see it."[84] Spinoza was "a well-built young man, slim with long black hair, a small moustache of the same colour, a handsome face; he is twenty-three years old." Many years later, in 1700, Leibniz, who spent several days in his company, in 1676, remarked that Spinoza leading a philosopher's life "tranquil and private," indeed had an "olive complexion and something Hispanic about his face [avait un teint olivâtre, et quelque chose d'Espagnol dans son visage]."[85]

During his months in Amsterdam, from November 1658 to January 1659, Pérez de Maltranilla acknowledged being frequently present when the group gathered at Don Joseph's house where he heard Dr Reynoso and Pacheco affirm "they were Jews and professed their Law" and refused to eat anything cooked in pork fat, whereas "Dr Prado and this fellow Spinosa," he heard "relate many times how they had been Jews and professed their Law," but had "separated themselves from it because it was not good, but was false, and that, due to that, they had been excommunicated and were studying to discover what was the best [religious] law so that they could adhere to it, though it seemed to him that they did not profess any."[86] Professedly searching for truth and the "best religion," De Prado and Spinoza also mentioned, the captain added, regretting their expulsion from the synagogue due to their losing the financial support of the community, though this presumably applied exclusively to De Prado.

---

[83] Beinart, "Jews in the Canary Islands," 64.
[84] Pérez de Maltranilla, "Déposition," 68; Révah, *Spinoza et Juan de Prado*, 33.
[85] Freudenthal/Walther, *Lebensgeschichte* i, 332.
[86] Pérez de Maltranilla, "Déposition," 67; Albiac, *Sinagoga vacía*, 159.

Why exactly De Prado's financial situation should have been precarious during his stay in Amsterdam remains something of a puzzle considering that he was registered with the city *collegium medicum* and was practising medicine in the city. Presumably, being unable to speak Dutch, and dependent on mostly Jewish, Spanish, and Portuguese-speaking patients, these mostly ceased consulting him after the first *herem*. This would explain why he regularly received poor relief from the community from December 1656 until definitively expelled from the community, that is until April 1658, when this support ceased,[87] and also why he was more reluctant than Spinoza to cut ties with the congregation, though in the circumstances of 1658, it is not impossible that financial woes were troubling Spinoza too. Stories circulated later, reports Halma, that the synagogue authorities had offered him support, a yearly pension if he would abide by the community's religious laws and regulations.[88] Spinoza and De Prado regretted losing contact with other Jews, Solano too informed the Inquisitors, but were content to remain "in the error of atheism," convinced "there is no God except philosophically and that souls die with the body and hence they have no need of faith."[89]

Pérez de Maltranilla expressed particular disgust at the irreverent tone of discussion at Don Joseph's lodgings, and how these several personages meeting there discussed books, ideas, and religion. Particularly vile, declared Pérez de Maltranilla, was a book "composed" in "Castilian verse, praising the death of an obstinate Jew burnt by the Córdoba Inquisition for denying Christ which De Prado had had printed in Amsterdam and which, as he watched, was distributed in the house of the said D. Joseph Guerra." Learning what the book contained, he, of course, or so he assured the Inquisitors, "did not wish to read it, but rather threw his copy away."[90] The book the officer described was the *Elogios, que zelosos dedicaron a la Felice Memoria de Abraham Nuñez Bernal*, extolling the martyrdom of Manuel (alias Abraham) Nuñez Bernal (c.1612–55), head of a family of Portuguese crypto-Jews in Ecija, in Andalusia, burnt at the stake at the Córdoba *auto de fe* of 3 May 1655. This book of poetry and prose extracts was printed in 1656 by the Amsterdam printer David de Castro Tartas (1630–98), brother of the Isaac de Castro Tartas burnt at the stake in Lisbon, in December 1647 whom Spinoza probably also knew.

Each apostate burnt at the stake Reynoso and the others referred to "as a martyr," something Maltranilla found deeply abhorrent.[91] The volume also celebrates other "martyrs" of the Córdoba *auto de fe*, especially Isaac de Almeida Bernal, a nephew of Nuñez Bernal, "burnt alive sanctifying the name of the

---

[87] Muchnik, *Une Vie Marrane*, 310–12, 314–15, 415; Kaplan, *From Christianity to Judaism*, 135n78; Levie Bernfeld, *Poverty and Welfare*, 437n79.
[88] Halma, *Het Leven*, 6.
[89] Solano y Robles, *Deposición*, 64; Révah, *Spinoza et Juan de Prado*, 33.
[90] Pérez de Maltranilla, "Déposition," 68; Muchnik, *Une Vie Marrane*, 321.
[91] Pérez de Maltranilla, "Déposition," 67–8; Tiribás, "Mobility, Clandestine Literature," 1051.

Creator," aged twenty-two, after five years of imprisonment, torture, and pressure to recant commencing when he was only seventeen. Pérez de Maltranilla could not remember the name of the despicable principal Christ denier burnt in Córdoba, but vividly recalled that it was De Prado who had edited this volume, and proudly exhibited the book to everyone present. "This Dr Prado was the one who composed [this] book with different poems in Spanish praising the obstinate Jew [Nuñez Bernal] burnt by the Inquisition of Córdoba [...] whom the Jews call a martyr."[92]

In Amsterdam, De Prado had gathered a literary circle around him, and he and his fellow contributors, including David de Castro Tartas who was eager to extol the memory of his brother's heroic death at the hands of the Church, had produced this collection of poems and prose extracts by no less than twenty-two contributors to celebrate the true, that is the crypto-Jewish "martyrs" and devastatingly lambast and disparage autos-da-fé and the Inquisition.[93] An impressive volume in which the Inquisition is unsparingly vilified, the *Elogios* begins by echoing the Latin motto surrounding the emblem on the triumphal standard of the Inquisition raised before the crowds of faithful at autos-da-fé—"Rise up O Lord! And judge your cause [Esurge Domine et judica causam tuam]"—to draw attention to the Inquisitors' crassness and ignorance by correcting their mistranslation of the Hebrew, which should read rather "Rise up, O Lord! And fight your battles."[94]

A collective work, De Prado's *Elogios* included, besides poems by De Prado, Ribera, and the brothers of Nuñez Bernal, contributions by several personages who had dwelt "as Jews" in Dutch Brazil but been forced to leave, in 1654, for Amsterdam, as impoverished refugees.[95] In late 1654 or 1655, they had all joined in expressing their detestation of this faith that burns men to death at the stake to enforce what, to them, were absurd, repugnant dogmas and beliefs. Copies of the *Elogios* reached as far as Livorno, in Tuscany, taken there by another brother of Nuñez Bernal and by several of the contributing poets. Given its content, the *Elogios* was a book the Inquisition in Italy, no less than in Spain, Portugal, and Brazil was anxious to suppress. However, De Prado's book also contravened Jewish orthodoxy as defined by Mortera and the Sephardic community governing boards by exalting secret adherents of Judaism staying in "lands of idolatry" where they had to pose outwardly as Christians instead of escaping to lands where Judaism was permitted and they could observe the Law. Religious heroes were being

---

[92] Révah, *Spinoza et Juan de Prado*, 33, 67–8.
[93] Roth, "Abraham Nuñez Bernal," 38, 43; Muchnik, *Une Vie Marrane*, 174, 218, 316; Den Boer, *Literatura sefardí*, 301.
[94] Den Boer, *Literatura Sefardí*, 99, 137; Den Boer, "Le 'Contre-Discours'," 55; Tiribás, "Mobility, Clandestine Literature," 1066.
[95] Roth, "Abraham Nuñez Bernal," 43; Den Boer, "Amsterdam as 'Locus'," 94; Den Boer, "Le 'Contre-Discours'," 50; Tiribás, "Mobility, Clandestine Literature," 1050–1.

created by De Prado, Ribera, and their literary coterie out of men entirely ignorant of Hebrew, Torah, and the rabbinic rules of observance, dreaming up an underground imagined "Judaism" according to their own ideas rather than proceeding under rabbinic guidance.

Besides feeling challenged by clandestine Marrano reimagining of "Judaism" largely lacking rabbinic direction, the rabbis and *parnasim* of Hamburg and Livorno as well as Amsterdam felt troubled by another strain lurking amidst the literary group around De Prado—its leaning, in part at least, towards Sadduceeism and Karaism, posing the question whether true "Judaism" is a modern Pharisaic orthodoxy of observance and rules supervised by rabbis, or a body of tradition retrieved by Marranos reaching back to biblical times, a cultural and intellectual inheritance flexible, tolerant, and with a philosophical tincture, offering a wide spread of choices and preferences to the individual. Here the rabbis rightly detected the militant deism of De Prado and Ribera lurking behind the veil of Marrano crypto-Judaism. The *Elogios*, accordingly, was banned by the synagogue as well as the Inquisition.

Ribera, the apostate priest, actually contributed more to the *Elogios* than any other poet.[96] The last of the group to arrive in Amsterdam, being first mentioned in March 1656, he too wholeheartedly rejected Catholicism but was hardly a Jew either. After joining the community, a considerable list of accusations against him were brought before the *Mahamad* and rabbis, including reports that he ridiculed the "Law of Moses," did not observe the dietary laws, and denied divine providence. Suffering pain from his circumcision, he was accused also of abjuring revelation and the immortality of the soul. Worse still, he allegedly confided to his Sephardic students that Moses was as much a liar, impostor and "grande feiticeiro [great magician]" as Christ and Muhammed, and that "what Moses said was as much a lie as what Muhammed and Christ said."[97] The clandestine legend of the "Three Impostors" (Moses, Christ, and Muhammed) was very much rife in the seventeenth-century underground Iberian subversive tradition, and evidently nowhere more so than among disillusioned former crypto-Jews Ribera associated with.

In 1655, two distinct strands had merged in De Prado's literary circle and in producing the *Elogios*, deists and committed Judaizers, who, despite his efforts to unite them in discussion, subsequently increasingly disagreed and under pressure of the *Mahamad*'s investigations, began attacking each other. Among those accusing Ribera was another contributor to the *Elogios*, Jacob (Manoel) de Pina, an exile from Brazil and friend of De Prado, soon to leave Amsterdam for Livorno, who, in August 1656, had his own book of poetry, the *Chanças del ingenio*, banned

---

[96] Roth, "Abraham Nuñez Bernal," 44; Albiac, *Sinagoga vacía*, 608–22; Tiribás, "Mobility, Clandestine Literature," 1064.
[97] Kaplan, *From Christianity to Judaism*, 142–3; Tiribás, "Mobility, Clandestine Literature," 1082n130; Albiac, *Sinagoga vacía*, 350–1, 597–602.

by the *Mahamad*, for alleged erotic content.[98] Between late 1656, after Spinoza's expulsion, and late 1657, most contributors to the *Elogios* feeling distinctly unwelcome in Amsterdam, chose to emigrate from Amsterdam in different directions, the Judaizers mainly to Livorno. Ribera, the last of the poetic dissident group in Amsterdam apart from De Prado, was still cited in the community registers, in September 1657. By 1658, though, he was back in London where he immediately converted to Protestantism for the second time. Finally, after spending many years living as an Anglican, he departed for Spain and reverted to his religious starting point, re-embracing Catholicism.[99] In 1659, De Prado, finally abandoning hope of gaining readmittance to the Amsterdam Sephardic community, left too and settled in Antwerp.

For Spinoza, the debate over the *Elogios* was a unique opportunity to learn more about the crypto-Jewish and Marrano networks in Andalusia and Brazil, about tensions within Judaism and the effects of rabbinic censorship on Jewish life, and also about how wide-ranging subversive clandestine alliances function and their pitfalls. A further aspect of special interest to Spinoza, as well as others in the community, was the military role of several Brazilian Sephardic exiles belonging to the literary group contributing poems and texts, notably Captain Diogo (alias Moíses Cohen) Peixoto and a lesser officer, Jacob Cohen Henriques, who had both served in the local Dutch West Indian Company militia garrisoning Paraíba before the 1645 revolt and, from 1645, in defending the Dutch zone of Brazil from the Portuguese. In the early 1640s, as Menasseh ben Israel proudly recalled, Isaac de Castro Tartas too had been one of the Jewish militia at Paraíba and, "being under military command, was obliged to defend his post, as do our people in that land where owing to their fidelity, they are entrusted with the most important positions. But who would even imagine that?"[100]

This new, previously long unheard of spectacle of Jews assuming military roles while simultaneously promoting Judaism, was a much-discussed topic in Jewish Amsterdam in the mid- and late 1650s. Peixoto, who had led a small crypto-Jewish group of fighters on the very northern edge of Dutch Brazil, his house serving as the synagogue at Paraíba until the 1645 Catholic revolt against the Dutch drove them back to Recife,[101] provided an early premonition of the possible eventual renewal of a military dimension to Jewish life, something not seen since Roman times. No doubt the spectacle helped pose in Spinoza's mind a question he would raise later in the *TTP*: would the Jews ever overcome the submissiveness and passivity of their present existence and recover their ancient military prowess?

---

[98] Swetschinski, *Reluctant Cosmopolitans*, 243; Den Boer, *Literatura sefardí*, 84.
[99] Yovel, *Spinoza and Other Heretics*, 60–1; Tiribás, "Mobility, Clandestine Literature," 1064, 1073, 1075; for most of these details about Ribera's life I am indebted to Victor Couto Tiribás.
[100] Menasseh ben Israel, *Mikveh Israel*, 100; Wiznitzer, "Isaac de Castro," 71; Feitler, *Inquisition, juifs et nouveaux-chrétiens*, 152, 177.
[101] Feitler, *Inquisition, juifs et nouveaux-chrétiens*, 151–3.

Spinoza, the Inquisition records prove, was regularly in the company of De Prado, and in regular contact with other Iberian Jews at any rate down to 1659, as indeed he continued to be in later life, the Sephardic cultural world remaining part of the everyday texture of Spinoza's existence. Meanwhile, these Iberian involvements in no way compromise the evidence proving Spinoza was, at the same time, in close contact with non-Jewish Collegiants, Quakers, and freethinkers. Rather, overall the evidence proves the young Spinoza remained intellectually simultaneously engaged with different language, cultural, and religious (and irreligious) circles and that it was precisely his aptitude for adjusting to, and absorbing, very different milieus, the entire Amsterdam dissident scenario, that enabled him to become the philosopher he was. Given De Prado was a writer and poet but not necessarily a formidable thinker, Solano's testimony that Spinoza was already accomplished in "philosophy" by 1658 hardly suggests he was Spinoza's intellectual mentor. Rather, it strengthens the case for assuming the reverse.

While all our early sources record that Spinoza shifted from Bible and religious studies to "philosophy," apparently before 1656, it is Monnikhoff who most emphasizes this as a key feature of Spinoza's biography. Claiming Cartesianism first deprived Spinoza of his earlier respect for the teaching "and falsely named religion of his ancestors in which he had been brought up," Spinoza began appearing infrequently in their synagogue, giving rise to the presumption among them that he was now finally detaching himself from their "sect and assembly," something they strove to prevent, records Monnikhoff (following Bayle, Halma, and Colerus), by offering an annual pension of a thousand guilders if he would remain among them and attend synagogue regularly.[102] Since 1,000 guilders was considerably more than the annual salary of the community's principal rabbi, such a sum seems exceedingly unlikely, but given the strenuous efforts made to keep De Prado and other defectors loyal within the synagogue, the *Mahamad*, perhaps at Jeronimo's suggestion, may well have offered Spinoza and his surviving brother financial aid to ease their family's predicament in exchange for outward submission to their authority. If so, it seems plausible that his brother and sister, Gabriel and Rebecca, would have been in favour of such an arrangement and that Spinoza, by refusing, was also breaking with them.

10.v Eternal Things and their Unchangeable Laws

From 1660 down to the mid-1680s, De Prado's old comrade, Dr Orobio de Castro, the latter's surviving manuscripts show, pressed on with his offensive against unbelief and opponents of rabbinic authority, focusing chiefly on his escalating

---

[102] Monnikhoff, "Beschrijving van Spinoza's leven," 203–4; Colerus, *Korte, dog waaragtige levensbeschrijving*, 104; Bayle, *Écrits sur Spinoza*, 22.

personal dispute with his former friend, De Prado, now living, from 1659, in Antwerp. Their continuing dispute vastly overshadowed, in his mind, the battle against Spinoza and Spinozism or the *theologi politici* as he occasionally referred to Spinoza's adherents. This was not because Orobio thought De Prado the foremost opposition figure, or a more formidable adversary than Spinoza, but because, for a time, he considered the alluring De Prado's arguments a more immediate threat to the community. Orobio's manuscript polemical writings against De Prado, commencing with his *Tratado contra la impiedad de los deistas, que niegan la Sacra Escriptura* [Treatise against the Impiety of the Deists, who deny the Sacred Scripture], date from the years 1663–4. It was then that Orobio introduced in writing his generic distinction between two main psychological categories, as he saw it, of former New Christians arriving in Venice, Hamburg, and Amsterdam, finding themselves at last free of the repression and danger that had for so long overshadowed their lives in the Peninsula.

Most of this influx from Iberia, observes Orobio, evinced an unassuming attitude, admitting their ignorance of Hebrew and Jewish law, humbly deferring to "those who, being raised in Judaism and learned in the Law, are in a position to explain it." "Since they do not suffer the horrible disease of pride," these men are easily healed "from the sickness of ignorance." Others, though, particularly those who studied at Iberian universities and were trained in secular learning, medicine, and philosophy, though "as ignorant of the Law of God as the others," arrive "full of vanity, pride and arrogance, convinced they are very wise." These cannot be cured of their sickness of mind but become a menace to everyone: "they think they will lose credit as erudite men if they agree to learn from those who are educated in the sacred Law; consequently, they feign great science by contradicting whatever they do not understand."[103] It was not De Prado alone but rather De Prado and his circle, including Ribera and probably Spinoza too, that Orobio is attacking in his *Epistola invectiva* of late 1663. At one point, he speaks of "those who full of contrariness, pride, haughtiness, persuaded they are very learned in all fields, make themselves out to be ingenious, discerning and knowledgeable, employing sophistical arguments with no basis. The worst of it is that they secure a reputation among some who, due either to their youth or naturally perverse characters, presume to be discerning and although they understand nothing of what the foolish philosopher says against the Law of God, still they pretend to understand him."[104] Both Gebhardt and Révah inferred, surely rightly, that Orobio is here not addressing the errant De Prado but rather a "philosopher" tending to "atheism," a thinker distinct from Jewish heretics such as the modern Sadducees and Karaites,

---

[103] Kaplan, "Intellectual Ferment," 291; Yerushalmi, *From Spanish Court*, 45, 325; Albiac, *Sinagoga vacía*, 92–3; Bodian, *Dying in the Law of Moses*, 180.
[104] Albiac, *Sinagoga vacía*, 93; Swetschinski, *Reluctant Cosmopolitans*, 261; Muchnik, "Orobio contra Prado," 48.

that is from "heretics" who accept the essence of Judaism and the divinity of the Torah while rejecting the Talmud and rabbinic authority.[105]

It is tempting to infer that Orobio here is not just assailing a group repudiating the Law and its observance presented as a broad threat to the community but referring too to Spinoza. Kaplan casts doubt as to whether this supposition is correct, and whether Orobio can have known anything about Spinoza when he first arrived. But it is unlikely that Orobio went to considerable lengths to uncover the tracks of his old ally De Prado, now turned adversary and rival, gathering details about his recent activities and arguments without discovering his connection with Spinoza whose ideas at this point to an extent overlapped with De Prado's.[106] Orobio's *Epistola invectiva*, in any case, skirts around what surely must have been a fundamental factor in the communal conflict, the main barrier learned Marrano newcomers encountered on arriving in Amsterdam or any centre where normative Judaism was permitted. Having for many years braved the most adverse circumstances as autonomous scholars in Spain, each nurturing his own private reconstruction of "Judaism" from Latin texts and, like Da Costa, constructing in the mind an image to fit their own notions of what "Judaism" was and should be, it must have been hard, indeed near impossible, suddenly to discard their long-practised individual freedom to judge and to submit tamely to the rigid rules and dogmatic rulings of rabbis and orthodox Jewish tradition. What Orobio deemed haughty pretension in these banished persons rebuffed by rabbis clearly impressed some young people so that the rebellion perpetrated by the likes of Da Costa, De Prado, and Spinoza served to broaden the wider cultural and social predicament experienced by Western Sephardic communities consisting mostly of former Marranos. Theirs was a challenge often referred to as a revived "Karaism" or "Sadduceeism" rooted in their personal difficulties in accepting the binding character of rabbinic authority, of prayer and ritual obligation, the requirements of sabbath and *kosher* observance, the world of Mishnah and *halakhah*.[107]

The rebels formed a dissident culture of Jewish modernity that Orobio simply rejected. He embraced *halakhah*, the rules of observance and Jewish religious law in a way many of his kind did not. He rejected their deism and philosophical atheism claiming man is naturally limited so that his reason, essential though it is, is insufficient without divine revelation to know the will of God.[108] The whole "miserable setback" caused by those unwilling to defer to rabbis, claimed Orobio,

---

[105] Révah, *Spinoza et Juan de Prado*, 39; Muchnik, *Une Vie Marrane*, 405; Yovel, *Spinoza and Other Heretics*, 52–3.
[106] Révah, *Spinoza et Juan de Prado*, 38–9; Kaplan, *From Christianity to Judaism*, 150–2.
[107] Kaplan, "Intellectual Ferment," 291–6; Muchnik, "Orobio contra Prado," 45.
[108] Révah, *Spinoza et Juan de Prado*, 22; Méchoulan, *Hispanidad y Judaísmo*, 64; Yovel, *Spinoza and Other Heretics*, 51–2; Berti, *Anticristianesimo e libertà*, 48–9; Maia Neto, "Struggle against Unbelief," 433.

had its origin in the ignorance of a physician "whose pride did not permit him to grasp the divine antidote provided by the teaching of our ancient and modern sages and learned men." Here he is certainly referring to De Prado. However, under his influence, another of these "sophists grew very arrogant, his arrogance growing in equal measure with his incredulity," this personage causing "great scandal to our nation, descended by this path into the bottomless pit carrying also others, themselves outside of Judaism, to believe in him and his foolish sophisms," a reference almost certainly, though Kaplan disputes this, to Spinoza.[109]

Spinoza not only eventually established a following, or philosophical sect, as observers of his life and activity later became aware, but undoubtedly intended, at least from 1655 onwards, in defiance of religious authority, to establish precisely such a sect devoted to pursuit of truth philosophically, harnessing discussion groups, education, medicine, and all the human sciences useful for such a collective endeavour toward the *summa humana perfectionis* [highest human perfection], as he himself expresses it, in the *Emendation* at around this time, and to "form a society that is to be desired permitting as many as possible to enter as easily and surely as possible."[110] This powerful social dimension added to Spinoza's rigorous secularism and rationalism already by 1655 constituted a revolutionary collective effort, a new programme best explicable as the outcome of quarrels with rabbis and the profound impact of Jewish freethinking, readily combined with Spinoza's conclusions from observing the welter of vying Christian sects making seventeenth-century Amsterdam what it was.

Driven by its own Iberian historical background, the crisis within the Amsterdam Sephardic community was, ultimately, also part of a wider spiritual crisis of the era. Virtually all of society, the Voetian preacher Melchior Leydekker (1642–1721) pointed out, including the Jews, had for many centuries unreservedly committed themselves heart and soul to believing in *supernaturalia*, wonders, Satan, demons, magic and witchcraft as well as divine revelation, immortality of the soul, and providential signs. Over the millennia belief ruled humanity unchallenged. With nearly all of society wholeheartedly trusting in what churches and churchmen taught through the ages, in the past there had thankfully been scant risk of society and culture ceasing to be fundamentally church-based, shepherding the great majority well clear of secular philosophy, heathendom, and wickedness into a life governed by a comprehensively theological view of the world. Christians had always been secure in their faith. But in his day, unfortunately, there were deeply disturbing signs of a new and grievous malaise—an underground sect driving what today we would term the intellectual secularization of society, a malaise, Leydekker notes, that was far from being solely a Christian phenomenon.

---

[109] Dujovne, *Spinoza* i, 92; Révah, *Spinoza et Juan de Prado*, 22; Muchnik, *Une Vie Marrane*, 452; Kaplan, *From Christianity to Judaism*, 151.
[110] Spinoza, *Premiers Écrits*, in *Oeuvres* i, 72–3.

Indeed, Dutch Jews were especially prone, he remarked in the midst of the 1692–3 "Bekker controversy" over the reality of diabolical powers and witchcraft, to abandon unquestioning belief in the miraculous and in *supernaturalia* on which all religion relies. This drift away from faith was profoundly disturbing for all believers. Even Menasseh ben Israel, he added, had confessed in discussion with Voetius, the hardline Calvinist preacher known as the "Calvinist pope" of Utrecht, that he honestly "did not know whether devils exist!"

If people cease believing in miracles, revelations, and the supernatural, lamented Leydekker, then churches lose their authority and their power. Reprehensibly, the Jews of Holland were abandoning faith more extensively and more dramatically than anyone else, becoming the witting and unwitting allies of godless *philosophen* busily dismantling unquestioning trust in the reality of the supernatural: "de hedendaagsche Joden zijn mede in haar geheel Sadduceen [the modern-day Jews are in their entirety Sadducees]," allies or potential allies of a philosophical rationalism blighting all religious authority, acceptance of the supernatural, and belief in demons.[111]

To prevent their, to Spinoza and De Prado, precious, underground revolutionary consciousness being swiftly crushed by the everywhere, for the moment, more powerful superstition-based ideologies, this new way of thinking needed initially to be disseminated, they thought, during a prolonged gestation phase clandestinely, via informal networks diffusing ideas forbidden by kings and priests and operating below the surface, horizontally and unseen. As Marrano experience sufficiently proved, this is the only effective way to challenge overwhelming tyranny built on political and religious authority collaborating together.

If Spinoza viewed orthodox Judaism and messianic expectation for the future with deep scepticism, he shared with the other great Sephardic rebels and the Marrano diaspora at large, the same set of long-term political and intellectual foes, starting with the Inquisition to which his own toleration theory has aptly been termed "the antithesis."[112] For there was no combating the power of the Inquisition without looking well beyond it, given the Inquisition, whether in Iberia or in the sixteenth-century Low Countries, was only able to imprison, persecute, and torture at will due to men's superstitious credulity and veneration for kings, popes, and churchmen. It was not Christianity that rendered mainstream churches and Inquisitors powerful, as he saw it, but ignorance and credulity allied to monarchy. If Philip was more vigorous in bolstering the Inquisition and extending religious repression than his predecessors, this was because Philip sought world mastery and, to achieve this, geared his rule to "superstition" more than any predecessor. If he exploited every resource at hand, including assassination of his opponents, to further his absolutist goals, he justified his actions by proclaiming

[111] Leydekker, *Historische en theologische redeneringe*, "Voor-reden," 2.
[112] Yovel, *Spinoza and Other Heretics*, 34.

his repressive tyranny a war of "true faith" against heresy, a crusade Spinoza's entire family reviled to the depths of their being.

Spinoza and his post-1656 comrades, De Prado and Dr Reynoso, abhorred too what to them was the blinkered scholasticism and Aristotelianism of Spain and Portugal's universities—Salamanca, Alcalá de Henares, Córdoba, Seville, Évora and Coimbra—essential props to the repressive faith they strove to combat, a scholasticism with which Da Costa, De Prado, and Reynoso possessed deep familiarity. Academic learning shaped all the professions and in Portugal and Spain never wavered in its age-old pact with church and theology, and with imperious persecuting monarchy. Against the old scholasticism, the young Spinoza first embraced the new "scholasticism" of the mid-seventeenth-century Dutch universities, the burgeoning academic Cartesianism of the day, but, before long, was actively subverting the "new scholasticism" too.

PART III
REFORMER AND SUBVERTER OF DESCARTES

11
Forming a Study Group

11.i The Birth of a Philosophical System (1659–1661)

When the aspiring young Spinoza of the late 1650s switched his attention from Bible studies and dispute with the rabbis to Cartesian philosophy, he was embarking on the most decisive and formative phase of his life. But this was no retreat from an engaged activist subversion of religious authority into the quieter realm of pure philosophizing far from the public gaze, but an amalgamation of philosophy with activist critique of religious authority that effectively continued his campaign of 1655–6 welding the two strands into a subversive political as well as anti-church strategy.

Well-equipped with Hebrew and now also Latin, by 1658 Spinoza was, if not physically vigorous, an increasingly confident, twenty-seven-year-old philosopher well past his initial phase of preparing himself to become a teacher of others. This is clear from his *Emendation* and from how advanced by 1662 his chief philosophical work, the *Ethics*, then already was. Though younger than several others of the dissident study group with which he became associated locally, and while, initially, Van den Enden was the best-known member, there is good reason to suppose Spinoza was either already its leader or else rapidly becoming so. Such was his penetration and incisive grasp, by the time he left his native city for good, in 1661, now aged twenty-nine, his leadership of the group, as several contemporaries reported, was acknowledged by all.

Whether this study group, flourishing in the late 1650s, ceased meeting for a time when Spinoza left Amsterdam, as Akkerman suggested in 1980,[1] is unclear, but if it did, the interval before it resumed, in 1662, must have been a short one. Among the study circle's stalwarts figured the Collegiant Simon Joosten de Vries (c.1633–67) whose surviving letter to Spinoza, dated Amsterdam 24 February 1663, attests to the existence and format of the circle at a slightly later stage. De Vries, writing in Latin (he was a competent Latinist),[2] complains about not seeing enough of Spinoza and opens with the words: "for some time now I have been anxious to visit you, but the weather and long winter have prevented me."[3] Fortunately, the original manuscript version was eventually found, because the truncated edited version published after Spinoza's death, in the *Opera Posthuma*

---

[1] Akkerman, *Studies*, 98–9; Steenbakkers, "Spinoza's Life," 25–6.
[2] Spinoza, *Correspondance* (ed. Rovere), 79.   [3] Spinoza, *Collected Works* (ed. Curley) i, 190.

and *Nagelate Schriften* of 1677 (the only versions available in early modern times) wholly omit the crucial passage describing the Amsterdam discussion group and its manner of proceeding. In 1677, the editors deemed it advisable to withhold from the wider world everything relating to the group's identities, preferring not to reveal even that such a study group ever existed or functioned as the original collective launchpad of Spinoza's clandestine movement.[4]

De Vries' letter confirms that the group only began gathering regularly in a formal way or, perhaps, reconvening with a specific focus on Spinoza's texts sometime after Spinoza himself had left Amsterdam. "As for our group," wrote de Vries, "it proceeds as follows: one of us, with each one taking his turn, reads out, explains according to his own conception and then proves everything, following the sequence and order of your propositions. Then, if it happens that one cannot satisfy the other, we have thought it worthwhile to make a note of it and write to you so that, if possible, it may be made clearer to us. In this way, under your guidance, we shall be able to defend the truth against those who are religious and Christian only in a superstitious manner, and stand against the attacks of the whole world!"[5] Scholars in the past have been fascinated by the study group as a small, private philosophical forum digesting the main lines of Spinoza's thought already in 1662–3, during the period he was composing a great part of his most important work, the *Ethics*, but rarely sufficiently stress his followers' self-awareness as a furtive opposition group conscious that their basic assumptions were so challenging and unacceptable to most that they needed to stand "against the attacks of the entire world"—arguably the more important point.

An admirer and loyal friend of Spinoza, De Vries, a distant relative of Jelles, played a long-term, supportive role in Spinoza's life, particularly in later years when the philosopher became increasingly sick and less able to support himself by grinding lenses and making microscopes. Mentioning the term "propositions" and this letter's timing show De Vries is referring here to the group's discussion of "De Deo," Part I of the *Ethics*, which was probably extant in draft by the time Spinoza left Amsterdam, in 1661, and certainly ready for discussion by 1662, in a Dutch version prepared by the Collegiant Pieter Balling.[6]

Replying from Rijnsburg to De Vries' letter soon after, in March 1663, Spinoza addresses his adherent slightly oddly, if this was actually his wording, as "the learned young man Simon de Vries," though he was only a year or two younger than himself. He is equally unhappy, Spinoza says, that so much time had passed since their last meeting, but finds satisfaction in that "my nightly studies are of use to you and our friends. For in this way, while you are far from me, I who am

---

[4] Spinoza, *Nagelate Schriften*, 514; Spinoza, *Collected Works* (ed. Curley) i, 190n56.
[5] Spinoza, *Collected Works* (ed. Curley) i, 190; Spinoza, *Briefwisseling*, 105; Spinoza, *Correspondance* (ed. Rovere), 80.
[6] Steenbakkers, "Nederlandse vertalingen," 10.

absent speak to you all." Here is a rare instance of Spinoza mentioning his life-long, later notorious habit of working long hours at night. Eager to portray Spinoza as a withdrawn anti-social recluse, the Kiel professor Sebastian Kortholt would later depict Spinoza as toiling over "his dark writings by lamplight from the tenth evening hour until the third," while the world slept, mostly abstaining "from human contact during the daytime." Unlike Colerus who rejected Spinoza's views but admired his person, and Bayle who claimed to reject his views while admiring his personality, the Kortholts, father and son, abhorred both his views and his personality which they sought to project in a negative light. A recluse at times, Spinoza was nothing like as remote at other times. John Toland would later follow Bayle in professing to reject Spinoza's views (while not doing so), and portraying Spinoza as "a great and good man in many respects."[7]

"Your 'collegium'," that is the Amsterdam study circle discussing his texts, Spinoza describes as "wisely instituted."[8] The difficulty De Vries asked Spinoza to help the group resolve concerned the nature of "definitions" and arose because "you do not distinguish between different kinds of definition," and because, while tending to Borelli's view that a definition must be essential, known and true, they were vacillating between that and several other definitions of "definition."[9] The question seemed crucial because the synthetic approach underpinning their "geometric manner" of demonstration for working out essential truths, an approach Meyer and Spinoza were keen to place at the heart of their philosophizing, relies for its efficacy on firm and unquestionable definitions. "For definitions," as Meyer expressed the point in his preface to Spinoza's *Principles* of Descartes' philosophy, in 1663, "are nothing but the clearest explanations of the words and terms by which the things to be discussed are designated," and "since a certain and firm knowledge of anything unknown can only be derived from things known certainly beforehand, these things must be laid down at the start, as a stable foundation on which to build the whole edifice of human knowledge."[10] Without reliable definitions, there cannot be any reliable "geometric order" delivering fresh synthetic insights and truths.

The most essential "distinction" among types of definition, answers Spinoza, is between actual things and concepts. "For instance, if someone asks for a description of the Temple of Solomon, I should provide an exact description of the Temple as it was." But if what is required is a provisional definition of something conceivable but not actual, like a temple one might wish to build and is planning, then the definition would be looser, broader, more flexible in character. "So a definition either explains a thing as it is in itself beyond the intellect, and then it

---

[7] Freudenthal/Walther, *Lebensgeschichte* i, 74–5; Van Bunge, "Spinoza's Life," 216, 219; Israel, *Enlightenment that Failed*, 149–56.
[8] Spinoza, *Collected Works* (ed. Curley) i, 193; Van de Ven, *Documenting Spinoza*, ch. 5.
[9] Spinoza, *Collected Works* (ed. Curley) i, 191–2.   [10] Garrett, "Virtues of Geometry," 22.

should be exact" or else "something we conceptualize or can conceptualize" when what matters is only that it can be conceived.[11] Spinoza sent De Vries a second letter from Rijnsburg, soon afterwards, later in March, providing the last definite evidence of the existence of the study group, answering a (now lost) further letter from De Vries with queries from the group concerning the opening propositions of the *Ethics*, further proving the *Ethics* was now under close scrutiny by the Amsterdam circle. By 1663, even though approximately half of the *Ethics* was now complete in draft, Spinoza as yet seemingly had no clear idea as to the eventual scope of his principal work or how long it would take to finish.[12]

What the group particularly focused on earlier on, down to 1661, we learn from other evidence, was Spinoza's second text, the *Korte Verhandeling* or "Short Treatise on God, Man, and his Well-Being," written originally in Latin, in or shortly before 1659, though, perhaps after a further stay in Leiden, revised or touched up in 1662,[13] a text that has survived only in a Dutch version thought today to have been translated from Latin by Balling. Long unpublished and soon forgotten, this text survived buried in oblivion until rediscovered in the 1850s; it was published for the first time by J. van Vloten, in 1862. When writing the *Korte Verhandeling* in and around 1659, Spinoza's basic divide between "religion" and "philosophy" was clearly less emphatic and rigid than it became during the 1660s.[14] His earlier ambition seems to have been less to segregate religion from philosophy than surreptitiously to fuse the two employing theological terms to mask key secularizing categories. It better fitted with his pro-Collegiant strategy and connections to postulate something like a quintessential pure theology underlying the warring confessions, a true Christian core, which is ultimately identical to true philosophy and that unifies religion and philosophy. In pursuing this strategy, he deploys familiar Calvinist terms like "providence" and "predestination" in seemingly innocuous but actually carefully devised ways. Thus, Chapter VI of his *Korte Verhandeling* holds that "if something has no cause for its existence, it is impossible for it to exist, as something that is contingent has no cause," while whatever has a "determinate and certain cause of its existence [...] must necessarily exist." This chapter Spinoza entitles "Of God's Predestination."[15]

Still revising passages in late 1661, Spinoza long remained gripped by doubt as to whether it would be wise for him to publish this early and short but openly subversive package of thought. Undoubtedly, the general outlook in the Dutch Republic as regards freedom to publish, and freedom of theological, philosophical, and political debate, had greatly improved since Oldenbarnevelt's day. Such

---

[11] Spinoza, *Opera* iv, 42; Spinoza, *Correspondance* (ed. Rovere), 84.
[12] Mignini, "Données et problèmes," 11, 20; Akkerman, *Studies*, 99; Totaro, "The Young Spinoza and the Vatican Manuscript," 330.
[13] Mignini, "'Introduction au *Court Traité*," 164; Mignini, "Données et problèmes," 14–15, 20; Steenbakkers suggests 1661–2, in Steenbakkers, "Spinoza's Life."
[14] Leo, "Spinoza's Calvin," 146–7.   [15] Leo, "Spinoza's Calvin," 149–54.

freedoms as the Republic had come to embody contrasted starkly with conditions in France, Germany, Britain, and the Spanish Netherlands, let alone Italy, Spain, or Portugal; but even in Holland such liberty remained fragile and its outer limits unclear. In 1661, he "did not as yet have any definite plans for its publication," he explained to his new friend, in London, Henry Oldenburg who had recently visited him in Rijnsburg, being worried "that the theologians of our time may take offence, and, with their customary hatred, assail me who holds violent quarrels in horror. But I shall take account of your advice in this matter." Spinoza would have liked to publish his treatise, but after prolonged hesitation, deemed it wiser to hold back.

"So that you are aware of the contents of this work of mine," Spinoza explained to Oldenburg, "which could more than a little offend the haranguing agitators [i.e. preachers and Orangists], I explain that many attributes attributed to God by them and by all whom I know of, I regard as pertaining to created things. Conversely, other things that they, because of their prejudices, consider created things, I consider attributes of God that they have wrongly understood. Also, I do not separate God from Nature in the way all those known to me have done [et etiam, quod Deum a natura non ita separem ut omnes, quorum apud me est notitia, fecerunt]. That is why I await your advice. For I regard you as a most loyal friend whose good faith cannot be doubted."[16] In the *Korte Verhandeling* his argument is indeed that "Nature consists of infinite attributes of which each is perfect in its kind. This agrees perfectly with the definition one gives of God."[17] Already in 1659, well before composing his major works, the equivalence of God and Nature was deeply embedded in Spinoza's consciousness and that of his entire circle.

The *Korte Verhandeling* as it survives today commences with a brief but stunning preface by an unknown member of the circle that reads:

> Previously written in Latin by B.D.S. for the benefit of his pupils who wished to devote themselves to the practice of ethics and true philosophy, it is now translated into the Low German [i.e. Dutch] tongue for the use of lovers of truth and virtue, so that those who boast so much on this subject, pressing their rubbish and dirtiness on simple people as if it were ambergris, may eventually have their mouths shut for them and stop vilifying others since, as yet, they have no understanding of God, themselves, or how to take into consideration everyone's well-being; and that the sick in mind [that is virtually the whole world] might be cured with the spirit of gentleness and toleration, after the example of the Lord Christ, our best teacher.[18]

---

[16] Spinoza *Opera* iv, 36; for the English translation see Spinoza, *Collected Works* (ed. Curley) i, 188; see also Spinoza *Correspondance* (ed. Rovere), 75–6.
[17] Spinoza, *Collected Works* (ed. Curley) i, 68.
[18] Spinoza, *Korte Geschriften*, 244–5; Secrétan, "Qu'est-ce qu'être libertin," 36.

This is assuredly not how Spinoza himself would have expressed the text's purpose, but is valuable testimony displaying the fervent polemical streak in the circle's group *esprit*, its sense of being pitted against nearly all existing opinion, and preoccupation with the example of Christ. Still Spinoza made no move to publish the *Korte Verhandeling*. Around 1659–60, his basic approach was still to seek the supreme good philosophically for those willing to join him in his quest but not yet to actively oppose the existing status quo. The early 1660s may well be a period of transition in terms of a shift from a quasi-Epicurean guarded passivism to a more engaged activist programme of subversion, but at the point that he penned the *Korte Verhandeling* the practical advice Spinoza offered earlier in the *Emendation*, about how to steer through daily life without colliding with the powers that be, still seemingly held good. His followers should converse with all others outside their circle, he urges them, in the earlier text, around 1657–8, "ad captum vulgi," as ordinary folk understand things, and not as the group does, "for we gain a considerable advantage if we concede as much to their understanding as we can, and in this way they will give a favourable hearing to the truth." Meanwhile, the group should enjoy ordinary pleasures so far as does not interfere with their health and seek money and honours only so far as serves to sustain life and health comfortably, generally conforming to "those customs of the community that do not conflict with our aims." At this stage, actively seeking to improve society more broadly was not yet on Spinoza's agenda.[19]

Remarkably, this alliance of rationalist Collegiants and radical Cartesians were able to come together around their common rejection of the main churches and all attempts to restrict and censor discussion of religion and the Bible. In this connection, it is worth noting that the first major public controversy the group was caught up in was provoked by the *Philosophia S.Scripturae Interpres* [Philosophy the Interpreter of Holy Scripture] (1666), a book finished well before 1666 which, its anonymous author says, he had long hesitated to publish knowing it would a provoke a furious reaction from the theologians. Not wanting to earn their "bitter hatred" and be dragged into an ugly contest, the author, probably Meyer, after discussion with some of the others, eventually agreed to publish it only for the sake of the public good. In developing his Bible criticism, he explains, he had had an expert guide, "an eminent person well skilled in these matters [the alterations and manipulations of the biblical text, both Hebrew and Greek]," it being "the longstanding opinion of this same person, who is considerably experienced in every aspect of this subject and its literature [i.e. Spinoza]," that both "the Old and the New Testament are full of disputed, obscure and false as well as variant readings and interpolations."[20]

---

[19] Spinoza, *Collected Works* (ed. Curley) i, 12; LeBuffe, *Spinoza on Reason*, 142–3; Sangiacomo, *Spinoza on Reason*, 27–30.

[20] [Meyer], *Philosophy as the Interpreter*, 231–2.

Although the Spinoza of the late 1650s, writing the *Emendation* and the *Korte Verhandeling* is not yet applying his full-blown geometric order [ordo geometricus] to his method of presentation, he makes clear that geometric concepts—quantity, planes, distance, space, motion, perspective, weight, and construction in terms of what holds or fails to hold edifices together—are the key to distinguishing truth from what he calls the "false and fictitious ideas" dominating commonplace thinking. Basic here is his view that extension (body) and thought (mind) are not different substances but different attributes of the same substance. In several places, notably the appendices to the *Korte Verhandeling* Spinoza includes brief sections set out in "geometric manner" and when answering Oldenburg's first letter, in September 1661, expressly affirms, when discussing the question of substance and the relationship of extension to thought, and of the one substance to God, that "I can think of no better way of demonstrating these things clearly and briefly," for his correspondent's benefit, "than prove them in the geometric manner."[21]

Another notable feature of the *Korte Verhandeling*'s short preface quoted above is its unifying Spinoza's original effort, religious studies, with his second phase, immersion in Cartesian philosophy. Above all, it reflects Spinoza's way of merging the two distinct currents among his friends of the late 1650s, Collegiants and freethinkers, by providing a fresh perspective on human life that is fundamentally secular-scientific, rejecting the supernatural, but tying this rational philosophy to the Anti-Trinitarian Christian morality of his Collegiant friends (one of whom, probably Balling or Jelles, wrote the above introductory passage). Spinoza's reluctance to publish and carefully devised intellectual strategy together formed a tactic designed to fend off accusations of "atheism" and moral nihilism opponents were already levelling against him, while delivering unseen, subtle blows safe from retaliation.

It was the *Korte Verhandeling* in its Dutch rather than Latin version, then that was intensively studied and discussed by the group. This too is significant. Spinoza's written legacy survives today largely in Latin, but his original emergence as a philosopher occurred in an extramural, non-academic context, an Amsterdam discussion forum chiefly attuned to the everyday vernacular. Several of his group lacked academic training in Latin, though they all probably knew some Latin. Aside from De Vries, Balling who is mentioned at the end of De Vries' letter, Meyer, Van den Enden, and Jelles, it is unclear who the circle's other members were; but several sources provide some indication of its general character and the relevant names. The younger Rieuwertsz later listed Spinoza's main discussion partners during his last Amsterdam years (i.e. 1656–61), as he recalled them, in this order: "Glasemaker, Van Enden, Rieuwertsz [i.e. his father], Balling,

---

[21] Spinoza, *Collected Works* (ed. Curley) i, 166.

Jare Gillids [i.e. Jarig Jelles], and a physician, M. Ludovicus Meijer."[22] By 1663, there is reason to assume the group included also Johannes Bouwmeester, and Adriaan and Johannes Koerbagh.[23]

Another valuable source is the diary of the visiting Danish savant Ole [Olaus] Borch (1626–90). After travelling to Holland overland via Bremen and Lingen, Borch, before proceeding to Leiden where he spent most of the rest of 1661, stayed for several weeks in Amsterdam, from December 1660 to January 1661. Following his initial tour of Amsterdam's churches, stock exchange, and main gathering places, in December 1660,[24] he met the Collegiant Serrarius and inspected the Portuguese synagogue. Most of the rest of his two-year Dutch study sojourn, Borch spent in libraries and gathering information about the various intellectual circles in the great commercial metropolis, Amsterdam, and in Leiden, from a variety of contacts, including Steno. In Amsterdam, he showed keen interest also in the unparalleled variety and complexity of the city's religious sects, taking careful note, not least, of the Collegiants and Jews. Revisiting the Portuguese synagogue, on 29 July 1661, together with the Amsterdam Collegiant Adam Boreel, he inspected also the famous model of the "Temple of Solomon" and house museum of Rabbi Judah Leon Templo.[25] In July and August 1661, he held several long discussions with the Millenarian spiritualist and Collegiant Serrarius, who afterwards became the main intermediary between Spinoza and the London scientific scene in the years 1661–5.[26] Among the renowned scholars he interviewed in Holland were Le Boë Sylvius, Gronovius, Blasius, Vossius, Vorstius, Cocceius, Rumphius, and Comenius.[27] In some cases, Borch had more than one long interview with each. Taking detailed notes of his discussions, he aimed to build a comprehensive picture of the Dutch scholarly and scientific scene.

First hearing about the "Cartesian atheists" in Amsterdam, in May 1661, the topic of the Amsterdam freethinking circle cropped up several times more in his later discussions. On 3 April 1662, when in Amsterdam, he was visited by a certain Johannes Alexander from whom Borch learnt more about several of the city's dissident groups, about William Ames, Quaker meetings, the conventicle of "the Brunisti," about "Anabaptists of various kinds" and also that "there are atheists here, especially Cartesians like Van den Enden, Glazemaker, etc. who certainly also indoctrinate others."[28] This passage citing Van den Enden and Glazemaker continues: "they do not declare themselves to be atheists. They speak continually

---

[22] Meinsma, *Spinoza et son cercle*, 514; Esteves do Couto, *Marvelous Travels*, 109.
[23] Knol, "Waarom hield Spinoza," 3; Nadler, *Spinoza: A Life*, 238; Krop, *Spinoza, een paradoxale icoon*, 79; Spruit, "Introduzione," p. xiv; Mignini, "Inleiding," 229; Van Bunge, *Spinoza Past and Present*, 196–7, 201; Gullan-Whur, *Life of Spinoza*, 53–4.
[24] Borch, *Itinerarium* i, 6.
[25] Offenberg, "Jacob Jehuda Leon," 102–5; Klever, "Spinoza and Van den Enden," 313.
[26] Borch, *Itinerarium* i, 187, 222.   [27] Woldring, *Jan Amos Comenius*, 156.
[28] Borch, *Itinerarium* ii, 92; Klever, *Mannen rond Spinoza*, 133; Scherz, "Biography of Nicolaus Steno," 91.

about God but by God mean nothing other than the whole universe [sed per Deum nil aliud intelligere quam totum hoc universum] as was shown by a certain recently and deviously written Dutch text with the author's name suppressed." This valuable evidence referring to a manuscript circulating formulating, or setting out, the "atheism" of this circle but lacking the author's name, was almost certainly Spinoza's *Korte Verhandeling* doing the rounds in manuscript and providing an overall sketch of his monist philosophy, the philosophical product of his last years in Amsterdam.[29]

Completed in or around 1659, the *Korte Verhandeling*, the key early exposition of Spinoza's thought, survives today only in two slightly different manuscript Dutch variants, based on a copy made by the eighteenth-century physician J. Monnikhoff (1707–87).[30] Intended exclusively for circulation among close friends and allies, it seems the whole group, and not just Spinoza individually, viewed it as a summary of their ideology, a polemical weapon for assailing what the vast majority believe and most preachers teach. Spinoza here spells out for the first time his doctrine that God and Nature are identical, that "outside God there is nothing," that he is both agent and the one acted upon.[31] God, Spinoza maintains, does not will, govern, intervene in, or communicate with humans outside of nature and the framework of its unalterable laws, so that revelation, miracles, and prophets are all delusions. God is neither benevolent nor malevolent, just the totality of eternal reality.[32] "Divine providence" he redefines as the unalterable order of nature, his "particular providence" signifying each particular thing's striving to subsist and perfect itself.

"Good" and "evil" Spinoza here projects as values not innate in nature, or divinely proclaimed, but strictly relative to man and his needs. Thus, by the late 1650s, Spinoza already held that "good and evil do not exist in nature,"[33] but instead are evaluations relative to where in nature we find ourselves, judgements elevating us toward human perfection: "therefore, whatever helps us to attain that perfection, we shall call good, and whatever hinders our attaining it, or does not assist it, we shall call evil."[34] However, at some point during the late 1660s, after reading Hobbes and while progressing with the *Ethics*, Spinoza significantly changes his mind about good and evil in one respect: in the *Korte Verhandeling* man first makes judgements about what is good or bad and then seeks whatever we decide is good. In 1665 by which time he had written most of the *Ethics* in its

---

[29] Borch, *Itinerarium* ii, 92; Klever, "Spinoza and Van den Enden," 319–22; Korsten, *Dutch Republican Baroque*, 311–12; Scherz, "Biography," 91; Mignini, "Introduction au *Tractatus*," 32; Mignini, "Introduction au *Court Traité*," 166, 172–3.
[30] Mignini, "Introduction au *Court Traité*," 161.
[31] Spinoza, *Collected Works* (ed. Curley) i, 68, 72.
[32] Spinoza, *Collected Works* (ed. Curley) i, 84; Mignini, "Dottrina spinoziana," 56–7; Moreau, *Spinoza, L'expérience*, 219.
[33] Spinoza, *Short Treatise*, 91; Mignini, "Introduction au *Court Traité*," 177.
[34] Spinoza, *Short Treatise*, 103; Matheron, *Individu et communauté*, 226–7.

original form, Spinoza still kept to what has been termed his "intellectualist position that it is knowledge that determines desire and not the contrary." In later years, though, when revising his *Ethics*, Spinoza reversed his position on this point: "it is clear that we neither strive for, nor will, neither want nor desire, anything because we judge it to be good; on the contrary, we judge something to be good because we strive for, will it, want it, and desire it [*Ethics* III, Prop. 9]."[35]

Whatever particular individuals may judge to be their "good" and "bad," the authentic model of the "true good," whatever enhances the perfection of any man or woman in terms of their happiness, understanding, and fulfilment is a criterion Spinoza defines in relation to the collectivity, to society, as much as the individual.[36] Hence, while "bonus et malus" [good and bad] remain always relative values with no ontological existence in themselves, there nevertheless exists an objective "good" viewed as a purely human individual *and* collective perspective not just valuable but indispensable to individual striving to preserve one's being when properly set in the context of the common well-being of society. Linking Spinoza's early writings, the *Emendation* and the *Korte Verhandeling* with the *Ethics* and his political theory, this fundamental alignment of the individual *and* collective is more basic to Spinoza's thought than modern academic philosophers usually allow.[37] For not only are the highest happiness [summa felicitas], and the "true good" closely connected but both are tied to the *salus populi*, the "common good" that is the highest goal of society and politics.

In the *Korte Verhandeling* Spinoza likewise first introduces, indeed makes his fullest use of, his famous distinction between *natura naturans* and *natura naturata* meaning God (or the laws of nature) determining all created things, a coupling often associated with Spinoza but actually Averroist and medieval scholastic in origin that seemingly held rather less significance for him later than at this early stage. Spinoza indicates his awareness that Thomists first introduced these terms into Western thought.[38] "The Thomists have also understood God by this phrase, but their *natura naturans* was a being, as they call it, beyond all substances," whereas, for Spinoza, *natura naturans* is God and the sole existing substance.[39] His adopting the twin terms, active and passive, despite only marginally figuring in the *Ethics*, has been aptly called, a "hostile takeover," as these inherited categories would subsequently never revert to their medieval sense.[40]

When the two German scholars Stolle and Hallmann visited Rieuwertsz's family bookshop in Amsterdam, in late June 1703, seeking more facts about Spinoza's life, they were astounded, Stolle records, to be shown a manuscript

---

[35] Spinoza, *Collected Works* (ed. Curley) i, 500; Sangiacomo, "Adam's Sin," 18–19.
[36] Spinoza, *Collected Works* (ed. Curley) i, 500; Scribano, "Connaissance du bien," 59–60, 62.
[37] Bartuschat, "Theory of the Good," 235–44; Scribano, "Connaissance du bien," 60, 72.
[38] Spinoza, *Collected Works* (ed. Curley) i, 90–2; Steenbakkers, "Vijandige overname," 36–8, 43.
[39] Spinoza, *Opera* i, 47; Steenbakkers, "Vijandige overname," 43.
[40] Steenbakkers, "Vijandige overname," 46; Levitin, *Ancient Wisdom*, 399.

"transcribed in Spinoza's own hand" that Rieuwertsz's father had kept, which they supposed was an early draft of the *Ethics* "as Spinoza originally composed it," though organized and "set out in chapters quite differently from the eventually published version with its more difficult format *methodo mathematico*."[41] In 1677, Spinoza's editors all agreed that the *Ethics* "was much better worked out than was this manuscript," but the younger Rieuwertsz also "acknowledged that it contained several things not found in the printed version." He pointed "especially to a chapter on the Devil, of which nothing is found in the published *Ethics*," citing Chapter XXI of the *Korte Verhandeling* answering the question "whether the Devil exists?" Actually, in the later published version, this chapter on the Devil stands as Chapter XXV, so either Stolle made a slip in transcribing his comments or else was shown a different draft than that surviving today. Since, for Spinoza, no essence contrary to the divine essence can exist, observes Stolle, he "seemed to deny the Devil's existence."[42] This chapter, one of the *Korte Verhandeling*'s shortest, occupying under a page, does indeed reject outright, in a way Hobbes did not—but Adriaan Koerbagh, later in the 1660s, did—the Devil's existence and the existence also of all other demons. Since neither the "Devil" nor lesser devils have any element uniting them with or deriving from the existence of God (or Nature), as all existing things must, "they cannot possibly exist."[43]

"Since there is no necessity to postulate devils," argues Spinoza, "why should we postulate them? For we have no need, as others have, to suppose devils to find the cause of hate, envy, anger and such passions. We have come to know them sufficiently without the aid of such fictions."[44] In the early 1690s, merely venturing close to publicly denying demonic existence dragged Balthasar Bekker (1634–98) and others into a much fiercer imbroglio and rumpus over this question than ever arose in Spinoza's day. But nowhere else in his oeuvre does Spinoza directly or openly deny the Devil's existence in the emphatic manner he does here, so that his posthumous works, the *Opera Posthuma*, lack this particular dimension. Only in this private manuscript, the *Korte Verhandeling*, and hence exclusively among his small discussion circle does Spinoza's teaching categorically reject the Devil's existence and that of all demons.

During 1659-62, the *Korte Verhandeling*'s function was to serve as an exploratory work for discussion among his following in Amsterdam, without him or his group directly assailing the prevailing public church's teaching, or any opposed doctrine. But by 1661 his early letters to Oldenburg reveal, Spinoza was pondering whether to make the *Korte Verhandeling* available to a wider audience and, for a time, seriously considered publishing it, but vacillated until eventually deciding

---

[41] Freudenthal/Walther, *Lebensgeschichte* i, 91–2.
[42] Freudenthal/Walther, *Lebensgeschichte* i, 91–2; Spinoza, *Collected Works* (ed. Curley) i, 46; Mignini, "Inleiding," 227; Van de Ven, *Documenting Spinoza*, ch. 5.
[43] Spinoza, *Short Treatise*, 145.   [44] Spinoza, *Collected Works* (ed. Curley) i, 145.

caution was indeed the better policy.[45] In the end he left the text incomplete and unrevised, perhaps also growing dissatisfied with his formulation of some points, apparently losing interest as he became immersed in writing the *Ethics*.[46]

11.ii Translation, the Key to Making Philosophy Effective

When weighing Borch's remarks, Spinoza scholars mostly focus on the mention of Van den Enden. Although there was potential conflict between him and the Collegiants, and after a time Van den Enden did in fact seriously antagonize Collegiant opinion, until around 1660 he regularly participated in Collegiant meetings and was seemingly tolerated by them. Still, as regards Cartesianism and also the evolution of the Spinoza study circle, Borch's mention of Glazemaker is arguably more significant, especially in the light of details Stolle later recorded for posterity, after conversing with Rieuwertsz junior. Just when Spinoza was first finding his feet, in 1656–7, after leaving the synagogue, the indefatigable Jan Hendriksz Glazemaker (1620–82), collaborating closely with the elder Rieuwertsz, was zealously rendering the bulk of Descartes' sizeable oeuvre into Dutch. Glazemaker was indeed among the most remarkable of those playing a formative part in Spinoza's life.

A born Amsterdammer from a Frisian Mennonite family, living on the picturesque Brouwersgracht in central Amsterdam, married since 1651 to a daughter of a prominent Frisian Mennonite surveyor and mathematics teacher,[47] Glazemaker's first occupation, before becoming a professional translator in the mid-1650s, was as a glass grinder (hence his surname). Despite having a brother-in-law who was a leader of the conservative "Flemish Mennonite" wing, Glazemaker's sectarian background framing his early life and personal friendships evidently ceased shaping his personal outlook (aside from his life-long antipathy to Calvinists and Catholics) from around the time he became friendly with Spinoza.

The very first translations of Descartes into the vernacular, in the Netherlands, began appearing only in 1656 and these early translations were all the work of this one enthusiast and collaborator with Rieuwertsz, as were many later ones. Glazemaker was a serious, indefatigable ideologue. As a translator, he rarely bothered with polishing or embellishing his prose, and of the prodigious quantity of material he translated for publication during his post-1655 career little was literary in character. Rather, it was always Glazemaker's unswerving purpose, in alliance with Rieuwertsz, to make a great quantity of precious knowledge

---

[45] Mignini, "Inleiding," 227–8; Van de Ven, *Documenting Spinoza*, ch. 5.
[46] Knol, "Waarom hield Spinoza," 4–5.
[47] Thijssen-Schoute, *Nederlands Cartesianisme*, 87–9, 650.

available to the ordinary reading public possessing no Latin or French, especially philosophy, science, and mathematics together with reliable information about distant parts of the world. He aimed to produce a lot fast but accurately, clearly and straightforwardly, always using current Dutch terms without importing into his prose unfamiliar terminology from Latin, Greek, or other tongues, to help readers imbibe important new perspectives with relative ease.[48] His, and his group's, aim was to transform the world by enlightening their brethren.

Glazemaker achieved fame by diffusing Cartesianism among the public in an accurate, easily accessible style winning local renown that lasted over half a century.[49] During the crucial late 1650s, he stood out as the sole major translator of Descartes' works into Dutch and among the principal early volumes he and Rieuwertsz brought out was Descartes' *Proeven der wysbegeerte* (Amsterdam, 1659), a collection of Descartes' papers on astronomy, anatomy, animals, and measurement, together with his *Letter to Voetius* rejecting that Calvinist fundamentalist's fierce criticism that perfectly illustrates Glazemaker's role as propagator of a popular Cartesianism lending particular emphasis to mathematical precision and repudiating Calvinist intolerance. Significantly, a copy of the *Proeven* figured among the books in Spinoza's personal library when he died, among the very few in Dutch that he possessed.[50]

Glazemaker may well have been the first to spur Spinoza's interest in Cartesianism during their early conversations at Rieuwertsz's bookshop, though that is pure conjecture. He was not in a position to mentor Spinoza to a highly sophisticated level in philosophy and science, but during the 1655–8 period was uniquely placed (as Van den Enden was not) to help stimulate Spinoza's early interest in Cartesian philosophy and steer him toward mathematics and lens grinding. Several reports of the 1660s indicate also that Glazemaker was no longer a Collegiant or Socinian in any meaningful sense but now an "atheist," at least in seventeenth-century terms. In his case, this charge was solidly grounded. Research on his travel translations shows Glazemaker was a classic representative of the early "Radical Enlightenment" in its strict definition—that is a publicist tying rejection of religious authority to democratic republicanism while seeking to disabuse the ordinary public of their trust in old beliefs, authorities, and hierarchies, or what he calls delusions, ignorance, and "superstition." He clearly reflects the ease with which a consistent thinker could shift from Socinian and Collegiant perspectives to a strictly secular Radical Enlightenment stance.

Indications of Glazemaker's new outlook appear in his 1666 rendering of Marco Polo's travels where, in the wake of La Peyrère and Isaac Vossius, he

---

[48] Akkerman, *Studies*, 102–3; Akkerman, "Taal en tekst," 10; Esteves do Couto, *Marvelous Travels*, 44, 59.
[49] Duijkerius, *Vervolg van 't leven*, 195; Akkerman, "Jan Hendrikszoon Glazemaker," 333.
[50] Van Sluis and Musschenga, *Boeken van Spinoza*, 31–2; Meinsma, *Spinoza et son cercle*, 264; Verbeek, *Descartes and the Dutch*, 128n113.

shows avid interest in China and eagerness to demolish biblical chronology as well as insistence on "reason" as the key to understanding the world. Removing what he considered impurities from the French version (rendered from the original Italian) he was translating from, he shows not just eagerness to delete all references to Christ being divine and to the Trinity, as one might expect from a Socinian, but an undisguised *anti-Christianisme* that stretches considerably further. Not satisfied with removing all reference to saints, the Virgin Mary, the holy cross and relics, he erased from his version the original text's references to *supernaturalia* of whatever kind, including angels, devils, miraculous events, all reference to religion as a divinely given guide and to revelation. In his translation, unlike the original text, no one is ever converted from one faith to another supernaturally or in a spiritually meaningful way. With astounding boldness, Glazemaker even claims in his preface to the reader that "because the zeal of our first Christians largely destroyed the ancient sciences, not much is left that can be utilized by us, and what survives of [the ancients'] theology, history, law studies, medicine and philosophy fell into such contempt, and these sciences became all so decayed, that even in the case of principal ancient authors who were not taken from us, we cannot properly understand, let alone emulate, their marvelous and pre-eminent wisdom."[51] Christianity's role he apparently viewed as essentially destructive.

Since the early Christians did not assist the progress of humanity and human knowledge, according to Glazemaker, but rather massively set it back, it is pertinent to ask whether he still remained in any meaningful sense within the Collegiant fold at the time of Spinoza's exit from the synagogue or whether he was already reputed to be a "Cartesian atheist." In 1657 and again in 1658, he and Rieuwertsz published the first Dutch translation of the Koran (rendered from Du Ryer's 1647 French version) with some supplementary material about the life of Muhammed and early Islamic history. This, it has been suggested, reflects the greater tolerance and relative unconcern for Muslim rejection of Christ's divinity characteristic of Mennonites and Anabaptists generally, a feature seemingly fitting with Socinian views.[52] But while Glazemaker does represent Islam as a false religion and illusory, claiming the Koran derives largely from the rabbinic Talmud, he discards the usual antagonistic attitude typical of earlier Anabaptist authors and Du Ryer, and altogether breaks with Christian tradition, including the Mennonite approach, by attempting to expound Islamic teaching in a serious fashion without any slanderous comment. He offered an objective historical account of an important religious phenomenon in a way that lacked real precedent, one more early glimmering perhaps of the early Radical

---

[51] Esteves do Couto, *Marvelous Travels*, 90–6; Klever, "Jan Hendrickz Glasemaker," 28–30.
[52] Waite, "Menno and Muhammed," 1015; Hamilton, "Quran in Early Modern Europe," 138.

Enlightenment tendency.[53] Glazemaker's version was subsequently reprinted numerous times down to the 1730s.

The United Provinces of the 1650s and 1660s, far from being a wholly safe haven for freedom of thought and belief, was no secure anchorage for seriously subversive ideas such as those of Glazemaker and Spinoza, ideas which may have fallen short of outright radical secularism but certainly entailed erasure of all confessional differences, pronouncing all religions equivalent in truth value and viewing all generally accepted theological doctrines, Christian, rabbinic, and Islamic, as essentially forgeries. The Republic was also far from immune to external pressure, even if home-grown citizens were less immediately at risk in this respect than refugees from neighbouring powerful kingdoms like those of England and France whose rulers constantly badgered the Dutch authorities to cut back their Republic's freedoms. The English ambassador, Sir George Downing, succeeded, with a touch of kidnap and strong-armed tactics wherever legal corridors proved obstructive, in getting several prominent English regicide refugees seized and abducted from Delft, in March 1662, and dispatched back to England where they were promptly tried and executed for treason.[54]

The furious theologico-political controversies that were such a basic feature of his era were not just an object of personal distaste and aversion for Spinoza: in his eyes they were a symptom of malaise in society, of basic instability and lack of much needed safeguards for freedom of expression. At the close of Part II of the *Ethics*, he shows how closely he viewed his general philosophy as being tied to his social and political agenda. His philosophy, he says, is useful for "improving social life in that it teaches us not to hate, nor scorn nor mock anyone, nor feel anger or jealousy toward anyone. In addition, it teaches each to be satisfied with what he possesses, and help his neighbour not from womanish pity, nor faction loyalty, nor superstition, but solely, as I shall show in the Fourth Part [of the *Ethics*], by the force of reason as the times and situation of society require." His philosophy was designed to contribute to "society in general," or "welfare of the commonwealth," in that "it teaches how citizens are to be governed and led by reason, not so that they should be turned into slaves, but that they may freely conduct themselves in the best way," or as George Eliot translates Spinoza's expression, "but as freely doing those things that are best."[55]

---

[53] Hamilton, "Quran in Early Modern Europe," 134; Esteves do Couto, *Marvelous Travels*, 84–90; Waite, "Menno and Muhammed," 1013–15; Waite, *Jews and Muslims*, 98; Den Hollander, "Qur'an in the Low Countries," 225–6.
[54] Namely Okey, Corbet, and Barkstead, see Lister, *Letters and Papers*, 151.
[55] Spinoza, *Ethica* in Spinoza, *Oeuvres* iv, 238–9; Eliot, *Spinoza's* Ethics, 159.

11.iii Bridging the Gulf between Collegiants and Freethinkers

Wary of preachers and the authorities, and anxious to avoid antagonizing the Cartesian faction, Spinoza also had another reason for proceeding in as inconspicuous and inoffensive manner as he could—his need for a bridge between philosophy and the search for the "true Christianity" of his Collegiant allies and friends whose support remained essential to him. Arguably, the most striking feature of the "true religion" Spinoza formulated and taught in the early 1660s is the use of his doctrine of God, and what he considered the veritable Christian message, to fuse two in some respects mutually hostile strands incipiently attracted to his teaching—that of individualist freethinkers of largely secularizing bent, like Glazemaker, Van den Enden, Bouwmeester, and Meyer, and that of the larger group of Collegiant background and devotion with which he had been connected possibly longer, Jelles, Balling, Rieuwertsz, and De Vries. Among Spinoza's friends, the "rationalist" Collegiants were those most likely to act as human bridges between the worlds of dissident fringe Christian religious culture and Cartesianism, between Christ the teacher of men and zeal for freethinking philosophy.

The forbidden, clandestine character of his teaching certainly affected Spinoza's general strategy and everyday relationships with others. The only student definitely known to have been tutored by Spinoza in Rijnsburg was the son of an Amsterdam grocer, a certain "Johannes Casearius (Caescoper)" (1642–77), whom Spinoza may have known earlier, possibly at Van den Enden's school, who enrolled as a twenty-year-old theology student at Leiden, in May 1661.[56] Over the winter of 1662–3, he lodged in the same house as Spinoza, in Rijnsburg. De Vries, in his letter of February 1663, expressed jealousy of this student because he could lunch, dine, and, when out walking, discuss all manner of topics with his mentor. To this, Spinoza answered that he should not be envious as "there is no one who is more obnoxious to me, and toward whom I am more on my guard, than him. Therefore, I would admonish you, and all who I know, not to share my insights with him until he has reached a more mature age. He is still too childish and too unbalanced and more concerned with novelty than truth."[57]

This tension between Spinoza and his paying pupil was doubtless theological at least in part. After transferring his studies, for a time, to Utrecht, Casearius passed his examinations to become a Reformed Church preacher, in October 1665. Sometime later, he entered the service of the VOC and, in January 1668, set sail en route to Cochin, in southern India, to serve as a preacher in the Dutch Malabar coast enclaves. There, besides preaching, he supplied the Latin text for the famous botanical project, the *Hortus Indicus Malabaricus* (1678) initiated by the governor,

---

[56] Spinoza, *Correspondance* (ed. Rovere), 79n2; Spinoza, *Briefwisseling*, 449.
[57] Spinoza, *Briefwisseling*, 109; Gullan-Whur, *Life of Spinoza*, 143; Mertens, "All in the Family," 55.

Hendrik Adriaan van Rede tot Drakenstein (1636-91), providing the Latin captions to that illustrious volume's illustrations. Whether or not Casearius ever had occasion to mention Spinoza and his ideas in southern India, from there, in any case, he was never to return. Four months after Spinoza's demise, in June 1677, Casearius died in India of a tropical fever.[58]

Both before and after 1656, clandestinity was clearly fundamental to Spinoza's general approach. Veiling his ideas from those not part of his network, both near and far, remained vital both to his lifestyle and strategy as a general reformer of religion, philosophy, society, and ethics. Partly caution, his strategy stemmed also from aversion to clashes and quarrels, and expending precious time and energy on public controversies such as raged all around in the Holland of the 1660s, as more broadly in Europe, an ingrained feature of his personality, accentuated no doubt by his emotionally painful confrontation with the synagogue in 1655-6. After 1656, avoiding intellectual battles remained a deeply embedded character trait until his dying day. He several times confided to friends in later years that he did not think it worth answering published attacks on his philosophy, sometimes using wording that sounds aloof and arrogant but that arose chiefly from deep conviction that vast mental energy and time gets wasted on noisy, vehement disputes that seize wide attention but serve no real purpose, disagreements that, like most theological controversies of his time, generally keep both sides equally remote from the truth. "Most controversies," he says in Part II of the *Ethics*, "arise from this, that men do not correctly explain their own mind, or else interpret the view of the other man badly. For in reality when men most vehemently contradict one another, they either think the same thing, or are thinking of different things, so that what they consider errors or absurdities in the other are not." Vanity and vying for position in society only renders the world's vast and useless morass of contention worse.[59]

If men cannot freely disseminate the true philosophy through argument and public controversy, because laws, churches, and authorities will not permit it, then one must proceed behind the scenes, surreptitiously. For it remains imperative to diffuse the true philosophy. Why does it matter to infiltrate true knowledge beyond one's own small group of disciples more broadly in society, in a way that both the Epicureans and Averroists strongly counselled against, given that most people do not wish to learn? Why should a clandestine group like his infiltrate and challenge the stubbornly ignorant and prejudiced multitude? Had not the Epicureans already recognized in ancient times that to devote oneself, and risk everything, battling to enlighten men who, guided by faith and what is generally believed, abominate the truth is a total waste of time and lives? The

---

[58] Spinoza, *Briefwisseling*, 449; Freudenthal/Walther, *Lebensgeschichte* ii, 22; Meijer, "De Ioanne Caesario," 236-7; Mertens, "All in the Family," 56.
[59] Spinoza, *Ethica* in *Oeuvres* iv, 226-9; Carlisle, *Spinoza's Religion*, 86-7.

ancient (and early modern) Epicurean alternative was to foster a non-combative secret counter-culture content to cultivate its own garden concealed from the rest. This is insufficient, explains Spinoza, at the close of Part II of the *Ethics*, because knowledge of the truth opens the door to much that is useful for the lives of all men and for society. The true philosophy "besides ensuring us complete peace of mind, also teaches us in what our greatest happiness, or blessedness, consists [in quo nostra summa felicitas sive beatitudo consistit], assuredly exclusively in the knowledge of God which induces us to conduct ourselves in accordance only with what love and piety recommend." From this both the individual and society as a whole benefit and we "clearly understand how far those stray from the truth who, in exchange for their virtue and most elevated actions, as if in exchange for the greatest servitude, expect to be honoured by God with the greatest rewards as if virtue itself, and serving God, were not happiness itself and the greatest freedom."[60]

11.iv An Abhorred Clique

If Spinoza's study group considered their gatherings precious and high-minded, their public reputation in Amsterdam could hardly have been worse. During the very weeks when Borch jotted down disparaging comments about the Amsterdam "atheist" circle, he expressed immense admiration for something in his view vastly more elevated and precious—the achievements of Giuseppe Borri. In April 1662, four days after meeting Johannes Alexander, Borch visited the spacious mansion of this remarkable Italian researcher, alchemist, and mystic. If Spinoza and his group were contemptible, here was someone the most erudite professors like himself could extol wholeheartedly. While his study group furtively admired Spinoza's metaphysics and ethics, Giuseppe Francesco Borri (1627–95) was apparently the most discussed, admired, and inspiring intellectual figure in Amsterdam at the time Spinoza was writing his *Ethics*. Where Spinoza the "atheist Jew" was loved by few and reviled by most, Borri had all Amsterdam at his feet, being constantly lauded by the city's elites and visiting savants. His lofty insight was what those in the know urged everyone to revere. In 1660, there was scarcely any savant in all Europe, let alone Amsterdam, for whom scientists and scholars, the likes of Borch and Spinoza's friend, Kerckring, expressed greater awe and veneration, a truly consummate Baroque era irony.

Son of a renowned Milan physician educated by Jesuits in Rome, Borri's career was enviably successful until he came to grief in the 1670s when belatedly exposed as one of the century's greatest tricksters and impostors. Handsome, persuasive,

---

[60] Spinoza, *Ethica* in *Oeuvres* iv, 236–7.

polite and agreeable, while living in Rome, early in his career, during a visit to the church of Santa Maria Maggiore, he experienced a mystical revelation in which St Michael presented him with a "sacred sword," enabling him to found a religious sect and recruit a considerable following, including some lower clergy, to which he imparted amazing "prophecies." He exhorted his followers to submit to strict vows of poverty and devotion which reportedly involved entrusting their savings to him for safekeeping. "Heretical" aspects of his teaching, however, soon drew the attention of the Inquisition, even though his extending the immaculate conception of Christ also to Mary herself, on whose semi-divine status, he insisted, logically made it necessary to believe also in *her* "immaculate conception," which did in fact later become a core Catholic doctrine confirmed by the papal bull *Ineffabilis Deus* in 1854. Fleeing Rome, Borri renewed his cult in Milan until there too the Inquisition grew suspicious and he fled to Switzerland, and then Protestant Strasbourg, where, briefly, he shone with his impressive "miracle cures" but soon had to abscond again due to the failure of certain of his "cures."

Amsterdam, though, proved ideal. Borri quickly spellbound the public with the wondrous and miraculous. No one there seemed to care that, in Rome, he had been condemned for heresy to be burnt at the stake, and was actually burnt "in effigy," on 3 January 1661, on the Campo de' Fiori where, in February 1600, the papacy burnt to death the great Renaissance philosopher, cosmologist, and occultist Giordano Bruno.[61] Wealthy visitors of standing were always welcome in elite circles in Amsterdam and Borri's glowing reputation, grounded now more on "science" than faith, a winning mix of "miracle cures" and alchemical displays, was soon reflected in his magnificent lifestyle. Where the loathed Spinoza lived modestly, Borri boasted a huge mansion attended by six footmen, with stables and a handsome coach, all partly funded by a 100,000 guilder loan from a former senior East India Company official. In April 1661, the city burgomasters conferred honorary citizenship upon him.

Struck by Dutch scholars' obsession with Descartes, Borri countered that Descartes had derived his basic ideas from Renaissance Italian thinkers, Cardano especially. What chiefly impressed Borch and Kerckring were Borri's experiments on the eyes of dogs and geese where in fact he was a not insignificant innovator, proving able to separate and extract the "three humours"—the aqueous, vitreous, and lens, the watery gel-like substances on the eye's surface—and demonstrate that these are inessential to eyesight itself which recovers when these are extracted. Kerckring and Borch were both fascinated by Borri's eye dissections, though the admiring Kerckring felt offended by Borri's reluctance to confide details of his clinical procedures obliging him painstakingly to pick his own way over the same arduous ground before succeeding with similar eye dissections.

[61] Koch and Koch, "Borri the Prophet," 161–3.

In Borch's eyes Borri was also a high authority on the intellectual life of Amsterdam. When Borch visited him, Borri assured him that the insidious Amsterdam schoolmaster, Van den Enden, instead of impressing audiences with the wonderful and the holy, combining faith and science like a true savant, vilely dared "negare omnia quae in sacris habetur [deny everything that is in the Scriptures]," repudiating everything sacred, revealing himself to be an outright atheist, "his religion being nothing other than pure reason [nullam esse aliam quam sanuam rationem]." Still more contemptible, Van den Enden "did not accept that Christ is God." Borch recorded these remarks about Van den Enden in early 1662, some months after first learning about the clandestine Amsterdam "atheist" society and hearing that, currently, the chief vehicle of opposition to miracles and the miraculous in Amsterdam, the staunchest resistance to the supernatural and to demons was the surreptitiously circulating manuscript, later called the *Korte Verhandeling*.[62]

Apart from Spinoza's surviving correspondence, Borch's diary remains our best source on the Amsterdam "circle" of the early 1660s even though, it must be admitted, he himself took scant interest in Spinoza or his scorned Amsterdam following as a behind-the-scenes intellectual phenomenon challenging received ideas. A "scientist" of his time, Borch felt far more drawn to fervent mystics and Millenarians like Comenius, Serrarius, and Borri than to sceptics and freethinkers. Spinoza's following entered his purview merely as a contemptible counter-narrative to the gloriously uplifting story of Borri and the wondrous unity of faith and science. Unlike his pupil, Steno, neither did Borch pay much attention to Cartesianism. He had no wish to enter into contact with Cartesian circles, let alone freethinkers, and made scant effort to gather additional facts about Spinoza or Van den Enden. His admiration was wholly reserved for those "proving" that "science" does confirm the supernatural, those wholeheartedly patronizing "scientific occultism." It was Borri's revolution, not Spinoza's, that gripped him and most respectable opinion, a fact that helps explain the contempt, almost hatred, for prevailing opinion, the sense of being a hounded few utterly at odds with virtually all the rest so powerfully infusing the preamble, cited above, appended by Spinoza's friends to their circulating version of the *Korte Verhandeling*.

Shortly after Borch's visit to Borri's mansion, Alexander dropped by and, touching on various topics, resumed his commentary about Van den Enden, observing that the controversial ex-Jesuit's way of circulating clandestine manuscripts setting out a secret philosophy among a circle of friends somewhat resembled the technique of Adam Boreel, the ally of Comenius, Serrarius, and Rabbi Leon Templo. Given that Van den Enden and Spinoza were familiar with Boreel from Collegiant meetings, where few were more prominent than this

---

[62] Borch, *Itinerarium* ii, 94; Klever, "Spinoza and Van den Enden," 318; Mignini, "Introduction au *Court Traité*," 166.

fervent religious reformer strongly committed, like Serrarius, to reconciling Christians and Jews, Alexander's comparison of Van den Enden and Boreel seems striking. The similarity he saw, explained Alexander, was limited, though, to their debating and discussion methods and did not extend to content. Where Boreel strove to reinforce Christian belief in his way, Van den Enden used discussion groups for the opposite purpose. This was why, he added, Van den Enden was now no longer permitted "to dispute," that is participate, in Collegiant meetings, having in the last debate uttered remarks savouring of "atheism."[63] Most significant here is that Van den Enden's exclusion from Collegiant circles occurred at a relatively late stage. Clearly, prior to 1662, he did debate regularly with Collegiants, a fact suggesting that his attitude to religion might have recently shifted due to interaction with Spinoza.

After hearing Borri profile Van den Enden as "an atheist who denies sacred things," and that Christ "was divine,"[64] Borch heard more about the Amsterdam "atheist" study circle in further conversations, soon afterwards, including from Theodor Kerckring (1638-93), then fast becoming a noted anatomist and medical man whom Borch visited on 25 April 1662. Borch was eager to make Kerckring's acquaintance due to the close proximity of their research interests. Before long Borch and Kerckring would become firm friends. In his school years, around 1656 to 1659, Kerckring had been a pupil of Van den Enden and also Spinoza. Six years younger than Spinoza, he had enrolled when eighteen as a medical student at Leiden, on 12 May 1659,[65] and there, during the early 1660s, under the famous Franciscus de le Boë Sylvius (1614-72), acquired the sophisticated skills in dissection and human anatomy that secured his later reputation. After graduating, Kerckring practised as a physician in Amsterdam until 1675, living in a house on the Keizersgracht, the second most impressive of the recently developed canals in the city, on a part of the canal, Borch notes in his diary, just behind the city's "Westerkerk" [West Church].[66]

A portrait of Kerckring survives today in the Hamburg Kunsthalle, made around 1660 by Jürgen Ovens (1623-78), a Lutheran German Frisian portrait painter, living in Amsterdam, who depicts him as a handsome, affluent, foppishly dressed young man, seated before his books and a globe signifying ardour for science, decidedly more the sort to consort with the freethinking likes of Bouwmeester and Meyer than with Collegiants (Figure 11.1). An eager researcher in anatomy, chemistry, and alchemy, relying heavily on microscopes, he soon emerged in these fields among the most renowned specialists of the age. "I too have an excellent microscope," he mentions with some pride in his principal anatomical work, the *Spicilegium anatomicum* (Amsterdam, 1670), "made by that

---

[63] Borch, *Itinerarium* ii, 94–5; Klever, "Spinoza and Van den Enden," 318–19.
[64] Mertens, "Van den Enden and Religion," 65.   [65] Jorink, "Modus Politicus Vivendi," 25.
[66] Borch, *Itinerarium* i, 29; Jorink, "Modus Politicus Vivendi," 25.

Figure 11.1 *Theodor Kerckring* (1638–93), c.1670, by Jürgen Ovens, oil on canvas. Reproduction courtesy of bpk Bildagentur/Art Resource, NY/photo: Elke Walford.

noble mathematician and philosopher Benedictus Spinoza, through which the lymph vessels, where they enter their conglobate glands, appear to split into various firmaments and where their extensions come out they seem to unite again as one."[67] He remained in contact with Spinoza and Van den Enden and was personally familiar with Van den Enden's family.[68] Spinoza kept several of Kerckring's publications in his personal library, and he and Kerckring were still in contact during the early 1670s, as Stolle learnt when, in 1704, he was shown one of Spinoza's letters to Jelles that has not survived, dated 17 April 1673, where Spinoza, inquiring about a point of anatomy, also sends his best wishes to Kerckring.[69]

Though he knew and respected Van den Enden and Spinoza, Kerckring does not appear to have been one of the "atheist" circle as such. His enthusiasm was for up-to-date observational science, including Borri's eye experiments, and notwithstanding Borri's reluctance to confide in him, he continued admiring especially his

[67] Kerckring, *Spicilegium anatomicum*, 178.   [68] Kardel and Maquet, *Nicolaus Steno*, 91.
[69] Spinoza, *Briefwisseling*, 307; Spinoza, *Correspondance* (ed. Rovere), 287.

stripping the watery surface layers of the eye and demystifying the "three humours." He himself made several minor discoveries in human and animal anatomy. Spinoza he esteemed for his conversation, science, skill as a mathematician, and microscopes rather than his philosophy. Still, unlike Borri and Borch, he had no interest in denigrating the Amsterdam study circle or Van den Enden. On the contrary, in 1671, he would marry Van den Enden's daughter, Clara Maria, the young lady reported by Colerus (and others since) to have been the object of Spinoza's amorous attentions prior to his leaving Amsterdam. Kerckring was able to marry her only after converting to Catholicism to make the marriage possible. In his *Spicilegium anatomicum*, he writes only positively about his former teacher and future father-in-law, expressing gratitude for his instilling into him his passion for science and learning and "introducing me to the liberal arts and philosophy."[70]

Borch also heard more about Van den Enden shortly afterwards when conversing with a local pharmacist who knew about the Amsterdam philosophy group. This prompted Borch to add some qualifying words in his diary, very likely resulting too from his talks with Kerckring. The circle around Van den Enden, wrote Borch, now amending his previous remarks, do "believe in God and are not really atheists since they believe in God albeit in another manner than has been accepted up to now – they conceive God to be the nature of things, the best of what is in nature almost the quintessence of all virtue and perfection; the more they acquire both of these with enthusiasm, the closer they are to God [quam quo optatius obtinerent eo se esse Deo viciniores]."[71] With further discussion and guided by Kerckring, Borch had now gained a more accurate perspective on the group. Nevertheless, though Van den Enden was clearly still regarded as *a*, or perhaps by some *the*, leading member of the discussion circle, there is no evidence, Frank Mertens points out, that it was Van den Enden who inspired Spinoza's equating God with Nature and no real evidence that he took much interest in philosophical issues at all.

During the early 1660s, with Van den Enden still apparently the best known of the group in Amsterdam, it was nevertheless Spinoza, not Van den Enden, Glazemaker, or any of the others, who provided the study group's textual and intellectual backbone. "It remains only for me to say," Spinoza concludes his *Korte Verhandeling* by admonishing "the friends for whom I write this," that they should not be overly astonished by the novelty and unfamiliarity of the ideas presented here, "for it is well-known to you that a thing does not cease to be the truth because it is not accepted by many." At the same time, the group being all

---

[70] Kerckrinck, *Spicilegium Anatomicum*, 199; Nadler, *Spinoza: A Life*, 126.
[71] Borch, *Itinerarium* ii, 102; Mertens, "Van den Enden and Religion," 65; "nempe Deus esse naturam rerum et optimum quodque in natura, atque quasi quintam essentiam omnium et optimum virtutem et perfectionem, quam quo optatius optinerent eo se esse Deo viciniores."

too "aware of the character of the century in which we live, I request you urgently to take care about spreading these points to others. I do not say you should keep them altogether to yourselves, but only that if you ever begin to communicate them to someone, you should have no other goal and no other motive than the *heijl* [welfare, good] of your fellow man, and do so only after very clearly ascertaining that your reward for your work will not be betrayed."[72]

Yet, however much they admired Spinoza and his intellect, it would be misleading to suggest the Amsterdam study group of 1658–63 uniformly comprised "Spinozists" in any exact sense. There are good reasons, we shall see, for classifying the Brothers Koerbagh as "Spinozists" in the full sense of the term, but this is less true of some others. Jelles admired and felt personally loyal to Spinoza, and was at pains to demonstrate that his friend's philosophy is compatible with Christianity. Strands of his thought entailed systematic exclusion of the supernatural while his reducing Christ to the status of a moral teacher shows strong affinities with Spinoza's stance and a strong secularizing tendency. Still, the affinities had their limits and Jelles continued to radiate a Christian fervour and veneration for Scripture diverging markedly from Spinoza.[73] Meyer lacked Jelles' pious Collegiant allegiance, but seems in some respects to have hovered mid-way between Cartesianism and Spinozism, albeit overall closer to the latter.

The study group was a secretive, marginal phenomenon in the cultural life of Amsterdam of the early 1660s. Yet, quite a few prominent persons knew about the circle and the main lines of its teaching, and discussed them with others, usually but not always highly negatively. But the group was also the testing ground of Spinoza's philosophy pursuing his social-cultural strategy by working to extend his subversive challenge to the general status quo. For this reason, it is important to consider the significance of Spinoza's early group strategy in relation to both his life as a whole and the radical break in the cultural life of his time that his intellectual development represents. With regard to society, his philosophical approach in the late 1650s and early 1660s with its furtive, masked activism represented a dramatic rupture with both the Epicureanism and neo-Averroism of the past.

Where Averroes insisted truth cannot conflict with truth, that philosophers and non-philosophers understand religion and philosophy very differently, and that the two spheres should not mingle, leaving the multitude permanently confined to their simplistic, superficial understanding of the world, relegating genuine appreciation of truth wholly to the "select few," late medieval "Christian Averroists" in Europe resorted to the notion of "double truth" to extricate themselves from any risk of delegitimizing the faith of the multitude. Where Maimonides amended

---

[72] Curley's translation does not fully convey the meaning here, see Spinoza, *Korte Verhandeling*, trans. Koops, 200–1; Spinoza, *Korte Geschriften*, 383; Spinoza *Collected Works* (ed. Curley) i, 149–50; Meijer, "De Ioanne Caesario," 233; Mignini, "Inleiding," 228–33; Bordoli, *Etica, Arte, Scienza*, 99.

[73] Van Bunge, *Spinoza Past and Present*, 51, 197; Spruit, "Introduzione," xiv–xv, xlv–xlvi, xlix.

Averroes by arguing that philosophical truth fundamentally pervades the words of Torah and biblical prophecy, and that the people should be taught selected key parts of philosophical truth but philosophical truth dressed in easily grasped parables and poetic terms for their benefit, that is that philosophical truth and science should be broadcast among the multitude via Scriptural "interpretation," but that ultimately philosophy and religion comprise the same fundamental truth, Elijah Delmedigo, from whom Spinoza borrowed much of his appreciation of the Averroist riddle, criticizes and reprimands Maimonides for mixing Scripture and philosophy. He reverted to a more strictly Averroist stance, while claiming the barriers between the world of the "multitude" and that of the "select few" can be slowly shifted by the progress of science.

Spinoza's approach of the early 1660s, though, more drastically reworks the Averroist conundrum, introducing a new element. While agreeing that truth cannot contradict truth, and with Elijah Delmedigo that Maimonides erred in contending that biblical prophecy mirrors the truths established by philosophy in poetic easily understood terms, he rejects Averroes', Maimonides', and Delmedigo's concurrence in holding that revealed religious truth constitutes the essential foundation to which all of society must adhere, reversing the hierarchy so that philosophy and science are now the primary basis of truth to which all else must conform. This did not mean, though, that those parts of philosophy, especially moral philosophy, most essential to non-philosophers are not embedded at least in approximate terms in large parts of Scripture. For Spinoza, philosophy and science now reigned supreme while, for him too, nothing can be true in philosophy that is not also evidently true in religion, with religion remaining, for the multitude, in some sense a substitute for philosophy.[74]

Fusing the New and Old Testaments together (for philosophical purposes), but also pointing out that the Koran and other Scriptures should be included here, Spinoza concedes that a residue of truth is found in Scripture (in fact in all Scriptures) dressed up in parables that remain of vital importance to the many given that the multitude can never penetrate beyond this residue. But at the same time Spinoza held that by group cultivation of philosophy, science, and biblical criticism it is possible to radically alter the balance between the "select few" and the multitude, intellectually and politically, and in this way change the basic dynamics of the Averroist conundrum. By means of clandestine networking and group formation, the "select few, the sages," can gradually encroach and gain the initiative and even perhaps eventually capture control of law-making (much as Maimonides hoped to do), achieving moral and political leadership by subordinating Scripture to reason, reforming religion no less than philosophy and wresting control of "true religion" from churchmen.

[74] Fraenkel, "Could Spinoza Have Presented," 3, 6, 14; Fraenkel, *Philosophical Religions*, 255–6.

12
Rijnsburg Years (1661–1663)

12.i The Move to Rijnsburg

Before moving to Rijnsburg, in 1661, Spinoza spent a period away from the city proper, seeking quiet on the rural edge of Amsterdam, lodging in a house "on the road to Ouderkerk," the village lying a few miles due south where the Sephardic cemetery and graves of his parents and grandparents were located. There, "far from his friends and associates," he quietly pursued his studies and developed his philosophical system while, for his upkeep, cutting and grinding lenses for microscopes which his friends then collected and sold for him. Concentrating his thoughts, "he reportedly lived there in very sober fashion."[1]

Borch's earliest mention of Cartesian "atheists" in Amsterdam, of May 1661, dates from when Spinoza had probably already been residing on the city's outskirts for some time. Though still only twenty-nine, and despite having, as yet, published nothing whatever, Spinoza, now engrossed in writing his *Ethics*, was becoming known locally as a philosopher. Then, in the summer of 1661, he definitively left his native city "so as to be less disturbed in his reflections by his regular friends," explains Jelles, in his *Voorreeden* [Preface] to the *Opera Posthuma*, establishing himself "far from those who knew him, first in Rijnsburg, and afterwards in Voorburg." "Although he separated himself, so to speak, from all the world," adds Jelles, "due to his learning and great insight, he was known to very many persons as is evident from his correspondence."[2]

It is unclear exactly when or from where Spinoza moved to Rijnsburg—whether from the environs of Amsterdam, or Leiden—but certain that he afterwards left Rijnsburg for Voorburg in April 1663. The most reliable dating presently available, refined by Mignini, Steenbakkers, and Van de Ven, has Spinoza living in Rijnsburg for nearly two years, from May or June 1661 until late April 1663.[3] Spinoza had already been residing in rented rooms in this village (in Latin called Rhenoburg), close to Leiden, for several weeks when, in July 1661, he received his—for them both significant and memorable—visit from the prominent Anglo-German savant Henry Oldenburg (1619–77), a key figure in the international

---

[1] Colerus, *Korte, dog waaragtige levens-beschrijving*, 120; Monnikhoff, "Beschrijving van Spinoza's leven," 204.
[2] Jelles, "Voorreeden," 2.
[3] Mignini, "Données et problèmes," 10; Van de Ven, *Documenting Spinoza*, ch. 5.

republic of letters with innumerable scholarly and scientific contacts all across north-western Europe. Spinoza was then still a newcomer in Rijnsburg, enjoying the quiet of a village remote from the activity and noise of Amsterdam, conducive to his "investigation into the truth."[4] Possibly, his eventual lung ailment was sufficiently troubling him already for purer air also to have been a factor. To escape the bad air and mists of Amsterdam then perceptibly aggravating the ailments of those not in particularly good health, seventeenth-century medical men like his friends, Bouwmeester, Meyer, Kerckring, Adriaan Koerbagh and others, regularly urged those with respiratory ailments, much as did, in December 1660, Oldenburg his close friend, the Collegiant leader and Hebraist, Adam Boreel, to flee the city centres with their stagnant canals and accumulations of waste and trash of all kinds, generating a ceaseless stink.[5] Commenting on the general health of the Dutch, in his *Observations*, published in 1673, Sir William Temple observed that the Republic's inhabitants "are generally not so long liv'd, as in better Airs; and begin to decay early, both men and women, especially at Amsterdam; for, at The Hague (which is their best Air) I have known two considerable men, a good deal above seventy, and one of them in very good sense and health: but this is not so usual as it is in England, and in Spain." Gout and scurvy were especially prevalent and "all hot and dry summers bring some [diseases] that are infectious among them, especially into Amsterdam and Leyden: these are usually fevers, that lye most in the head, and either kill suddenly, or languish long before they recover."[6] As Lucas notes, Spinoza later "preferred The Hague to Amsterdam because the air there is healthier."[7] Rijnsburg's outskirts, like the road to Ouderkerk earlier, offered fresher, cleaner air besides a place of "solitude" for undisturbed contemplation.

Leaving the great metropolis of many sects for his country retreat at Rijnsburg, Spinoza undoubtedly encountered much that was new. Moving to a village where he was religiously, culturally, socially, and intellectually largely isolated, even his way of writing his own name reflects detachment. On exiting the synagogue, he had discarded his boyhood and early adult business name "Bento" together with his pre-1656 Amsterdam synagogue name, "Baruch." Henceforth, when offering his first name, he styled himself "Benedictus," though there is little sign that he was fond of, or became used to, this slightly pompous designation either. Rather, when signing, his usage noticeably vacillated. Although Lodewijk Meyer (1629–81) was among the friends with whom, at this juncture, he was collaborating closely, someone in whom he evidently felt complete confidence, a meeting of minds and not just about Descartes, the (relatively few) letters surviving in

---

[4] Jelles, "Voorreeden," 1.
[5] Iliffe, "Jesus Nazarenus Legislator," 381–2; a speculative point well put in Rovere, *Le Clan Spinoza*, 242.
[6] Temple, *Observations*, 113.   [7] [Lucas], *La Vie*, 34.

holograph from these years from Spinoza to Meyer reveal that even to him he generally signed "B. de Spinoza," or alternatively "B. d'Spinoza." Writing to Jelles he signed "B.d.S";[8] writing to Bouwmeester, and also to Hudde, he signed "Bened. de Spinoza." Only to Henry Oldenburg did he sign off fully as "Benedictus Spinoza." Curiously, instability in signing his name assumed a slightly different pattern later.[9] In his last years, he reverted to rendering his signature in more Iberian fashion. If he addressed Van Velthuysen, in the autumn of 1675, as "B. de Spinoza," his holographs to Leibniz, in November 1671, sign off as "B. despinoza," and to Graevius, in December 1673, as "Benedictus despinoza."[10]

At Rijnsburg, Spinoza stayed in contact with his Amsterdam "regular friends" by post and personal visits. As before, these divided into two groups, secularizing freethinkers devoted to theatre and the arts (Bouwmeester, Meyer, Glazemaker, and Van den Enden) and the rationalist radical extremity of the Collegiant and Socinian movement (Balling, Jelles, De Vries, and Johannes Koerbagh) who, though no less emphatic about toleration, denying Christ's divinity and scorning theologians, were more insistent than Spinoza on the centrality of Christ and Christian piety. Home to one of the foremost Collegiant communities in the Republic, Rijnsburg was also largely free of the pressures for religious uniformity usual in small Dutch towns. Within walking distance of the University of Leiden, the village had its advantages but can hardly have been ideal for Spinoza's purposes, since he stayed only a relatively short time, less than two years, before moving on to the busier, noisier environs of Voorburg and The Hague.

The house where Spinoza now found lodgings, only recently built, apparently between 1656 and 1660, belonged to a Collegiant surgeon, Herman Dircksz Homan. Providing extra detail not found in Colerus, Monnikhoff adds that the "house in which [Spinoza] lived in this village stands on its western edge (toward the sea), south of the Vliet between the wagon-way and the footpath to the [neighbouring village of] Katwijk aan den Rijn, on the east side of the lane [today named Spinozalaan]," then called the Katwijkerlaantje [or little Katwijk lane]. Today it remains a quiet, distinctly rural spot. The house where Spinoza rented rooms is still "recognizable by the inscribed stone on the front gable where is carved the fifteenth and last verse of the 'May morning sunrise,' a poem found in the third volume of verse by pastor-poet D[irk] R[afaelsz]. Camphuysen." Dating from 1660, hence the year before Spinoza's arrival, the lines on the stone plaque read: "Oh! If all men would be wise, And would be good as well, The Earth would be a Paradise, Now it is mostly a Hell."[11] If it was sheer coincidence that Spinoza

---

[8] Freudenthal, *Lebensgeschichte*, 223; Spruit, "Introduzione," p. xv.
[9] Spinoza, *Collected Works* (ed. Curley) i, 188, 206, 216, and ii, 22, 39, 42; Spinoza, *Briefwisseling*, 129, 145, 236, 254; Totaro, "L'Énigme du nom," 174.
[10] Spinoza, *Briefwisseling*, 297, 308, 390; Totaro, "L'Énigme du nom," 175.
[11] Freudenthal/Walther, *Lebensgeschichte* i, 172–3; Van Vloten, *Benedictus de Spinoza*, 25; Van Suchtelen, "The Spinoza Houses," 475; Schuyt, *Spinoza*, 25.

Figure 12.1 The house in which Spinoza lodged in Rijnsburg (1661–3). By courtesy of the Leiden City Archives.

found rooms in a house adorned with this telling verse on its façade, it was splendidly fitting (Figure 12.1). Yet, it seems somehow unlikely that it was pure coincidence. For the short-lived Dirk Rafaelsz Camphuysen (1586–1627), who had once stayed in Rijnsburg for a time, was the first Collegiant to argue with great emphasis that, besides requiring full freedom of expression, all Christian believers are equal in authority and that paid clergy with their directives and sermons are the prime abuse and failing of the Christian churches generally.[12]

One of the Collegiant movement's founders, descended on his mother's side from a Mennonite family persecuted in earlier generations, Camphuysen was a poet, artist, and preacher much admired by Remonstrants, Mennonites, and Collegiants. He was among the pastors who suffered dismissal from his pulpit for Arminian sympathies during the nationwide purge of Remonstrants (adherents of Arminius) following their condemnation by the Calvinist majority of the Reformed synods during the fierce Orangist-Calvinist political struggle culminating in the epoch-making, and by Collegiants and Remonstrants as well as Spinoza deeply resented, overthrow of Oldenbarnevelt and his supporters, in 1618–19. Camphuysen had fled into exile, in East Friesland where this noteworthy poet-theologian had set up as a publisher, in Norden, and apparently had some connection with the Rieuwertsz family. Rieuwertsz's father later migrated to Amsterdam from that locality. Not only Camphuysen's poems, but also his

---

[12] Kolakowski, *Chrétiens sans église*, 90, 92; Quatrini, *Adam Boreel*, 229–30.

hymns, rhymed psalm translations, and poems set to music, were greatly cherished among the Collegiants whose movement had established itself in Rijnsburg in the 1620s, seeking refuge from the Reformed Church's continuing theological-political onslaught.[13]

Camphuysen was especially a hero to Rieuwertsz who published his theological works with a preface by himself precisely at this time (1661), and again in 1672, as did the younger Jan Rieuwertsz, his son, in 1699. Rieuwertsz the elder admired Camphuysen's undaunted defiance not just of persecution and intolerance but all organized churches and churchmen, contempt for theological strife between churches and the very idea there exists a cast-iron confession or creed believers must embrace. By the late nineteenth century, the house was in a distinctly dilapidated state. But Monnikhoff's description enabled Dr Willem Meijer (1842–1926), first secretary of the present-day Vereniging Het Spinozahuis [Spinoza House Society], the museum and seminar centre occupying and conserving the house since 1897, to identify it and uncover more details of the house's history. A neat, dignified cottage on the village edge, it stood beside fields, approximately an hour-and-a-half's walk, some four miles from Leiden University, with a similar distance to the sea on the other side.[14] Spinoza's new milieu was thus linked to a fiercely independent religious fringe culture that, in Amsterdam, had already for years been meaningful and attractive to him. The village having been the Collegiants' first base, the entire movement were often still referred to as "the Rijnsburgers."

Rijnsburg's connection with Rieuwertsz, Jelles, Balling, and other friends, allies, and old acquaintances was seemingly one attraction; but important too, undoubtedly, was the independent judicial status Rijnsburg enjoyed. During the Middle Ages the vicinity was ruled by an abbess, head of the famous Abdij [Abbey] of Rijnsburg, a Benedictine nunnery founded in 1133, around the picturesque remains of which the village still centres, a church where several of Holland's medieval counts lay buried. Until the Revolt against Spain, a haven for unmarried noble ladies obliged or willing to live as nuns, the abbey was laid waste by the rebels, in 1574, causing the nuns to depart for good. In Spinoza's day, the site was a crumbling ruin commanding the tranquil vicinity, depicted among other artists by Aelbert Cuyp in a landscape of around 1642, hanging today in the Dordrecht Museum. Spinoza, dwelling close by, would have contemplated the ruins almost every time he ventured out (Figure 12.2).

The last "abbess" died in 1620, leaving the jurisdiction under the direct legal and political control of the Holland *ridderschap* [nobility] which remained a significant, usually moderating voice in the province's main governing body, the

---

[13] Rues, *Tegenwoordige staet*, 315–16; Van Slee, *Rijnsburger Collegianten*, 66–71; Kolakowski, *Chrétiens sans église*, 120–1, 132n32; Manusov-Verhage, "Jan Rieuwertsz, marchand," 247–8.

[14] Van Miert, *Emancipation of Biblical Philology*, xvii.

Figure 12.2 *Ruins of the Rijnsburg Abbey*, c.1640–1645, by Aelbert Cuyp, DM/995/ 804, oil on panel, 48.9 × 73.3 cm. Dordrecht Museum, on loan from the Royal Cabinet of Paintings Mauritshuis, The Hague 1995.

States of Holland, commanding one vote out of nineteen. Hence, despite the disappearance of the abbess, the village still remained a noble *heerlijkheid*, manor or seignory, placing it usefully, from Spinoza's perspective, outside the jurisdiction of the neighbouring strongly Orangist-Calvinist city of Leiden or any locality directly under civic supervision—a reassuring protective wall for the Collegiants gathering there, as also now for Spinoza, a juridical shield against the generally far-reaching ire of local Reformed preachers and church councils. Due to its early role in the development of the Collegiant movement and the regular gatherings held there attended by Collegiants from all over the Netherlands that would have been scarcely possible anywhere else, Rijnsburg always remained in some sense the Collegiant movement's spiritual home. These gatherings took place twice-yearly, at Pentecost and on the last Sunday of August each year, bringing large crowds to the village, congregating around two main buildings, one the equivalent of their prayer, discussion, and hymn-singing hall, the other, the "groote huis," their large hostel for visitors.[15]

Nearby Leiden, meanwhile, was considerably more than just a university town, being a great hive of activity of all kinds and "next to Amsterdam the greatest city

---

[15] Rues, *Tegenwoordige staet*, 311, 316; Van der Tak and Brunschvicg, *Spinoza*, 24; Fix, *Prophecy and Reason*, 39–40, 46, 125.

in Holland and well built," as the English traveller John Ray describes, in 1663, "well walled and trenched about, encompassed with pleasant walks of lime trees." The Republic's second largest city, Leiden then boasted some 60,000 inhabitants, numerous canals featuring 120 bridges, and approximately 13,000 mostly small houses, many belonging to textile weavers descended from Flemish artisan families forced to migrate northwards during the Spanish reconquest of Flanders in the early 1580s. In outlook, Leiden's textile workers were traditionally strongly Calvinist and Orangist, a backbone of Calvinist rigour.[16] Leiden's city government, since Oldenbarnevelt's overthrow a bastion of domineering Calvinism and Orangism, often clashed in the States of Holland with the Amsterdam regents and with De Witt's Dordrecht.

An Amsterdammer attuned to the deep religious, linguistic, and cultural divisions in Dutch society, Spinoza was more familiar than most Europeans of the time, even indeed most Dutchmen, with the numerous fringe subsidiary religious communities the Protestant world had engendered over the last century and a half. Through day-to-day contact from early on, he had witnessed the successive waves of immigrants, Moravians, Quakers, Jews from Eastern Europe as well as Iberia, and, most recently, Polish Socinians and the influx of English royalist exiles streaming in since the English Civil War (1642–51). Before leaving Amsterdam, in 1661, Spinoza must also have noticed a very different new wave of English immigration—ousted Parliamentarians, Puritans, and republicans expelled by, or refusing compromise with, the revived Stuart monarchy, now restored to power since 1660. "It is not to be credited," complained England's ambassador, Sir George Downing, from The Hague, in June 1661, around the time of Spinoza's move to Rijnsburg, "what numbers of disaffected persons come dayly out of England into this country." Noticeable everywhere, Rotterdam was especially a magnet for this fresh influx: "they have settled at Rotterdam an Independent, Anabaptist, and Quakers Church," reported Downing, "and doe hire the best houses and have great bills of exchange come over from England to them."[17]

Less regularly involved in group discussion than in earlier years, Spinoza gave little thought to personal comfort or ease. Rather, reports Jelles, he devoted all his time and effort single-mindedly to his three key concerns—Cartesian philosophy, religious studies (especially Bible criticism), and optical science. Renting two rooms from his new landlord in what, for the surgeon who owned it, was essentially a summer out-of-town second house, one room Spinoza used for living in, the other for cutting and grinding lenses with the round metal "dishes" he considered "safer and better" than the cutting machines more often used for this work, by the Huygens' Brothers for example. In this second room too, he constructed and stored his microscopes and telescopes.[18] Besides thinking,

[16] Ray, *Observations topographical*, 31, 36.   [17] Lister, *Letters and Papers*, 151.
[18] Klever, "Insignis opticus"; Van Delft, *Antoni van Leeuwenhoek*, 89.

reading, receiving visits, and grinding lenses, Spinoza had one other regular focus—the university, its scholars, libraries, grounds, and philosophy lectures, which involved undertaking long walks to Leiden.

Borch, while attending lectures and inspecting the collections in Leiden, that September, made two notable entries in his travel diary regarding Rijnsburg's unusual new inhabitant, the first after encountering a certain "D. Langermann," one of two brothers, either Christian or Johannes, then studying at the university, sons of a prominent Hamburg businessman specializing in spices, coffee, and the like. Meeting on 9 September 1661, first they discussed the sciences, especially geology; but Langermann, a connoisseur of local cafés and café gossip, before long moved on to the new beverages—tea, coffee, and chocolate—then growing popular in Holland and London but then less well known in Scandinavia and Germany. Finally, they drifted on to the subject of Spinoza. In nearby Rijnsburg, related Langermann, "there is an ex Jew turned Christian, but now almost an atheist, who does not respect the Old Testament and considers the New Testament, the Koran and the Fables of Aesop to be all of equal value [qui Vet. Test. nil curat, Nov. et Alcoranum et fab. Aesopi pari aestimat pondere], a person who otherwise lives in a sincere and irreproachable manner occupying himself with making lenses and microscopes [et conficiendis perspicillis et microscopiis occupari]."[19] This is actually the first mention of Spinoza's relatively recently acquired expertise in grinding lenses and constructing optical instruments, reportage decades earlier than the testimony of Kerckring, Colerus, and Monnikhoff.[20] It was by no means, though, the first mention of what is sometimes termed Spinoza's "critical theory," his radical text criticism viewing the myths and religious traditions of mankind as all being on the same level in terms of spiritual status, his regarding all texts reflecting human belief and imagining to be equally open to rational "deconstruction."[21]

It was a key doctrine already basic to Spinoza's system when settling in Rijnsburg that all revealed religions whether Judaism, Christianity, or Islam, as interpreted by clergymen are equally misguided in their traditional and public guises, the only meaningful differences dividing these religions being hatred of each other, a perennial "hatred deriving from mere report." Religious strife, for Spinoza, arises from self-serving, superficial, and biased accounts of one faith by another "as we observe," he stresses, "in the hate Turks feel against Jews and Christians, Jews against the Turks and Christians, and Christians for Jews and Turks, etc." "The ignorant," that is everyone in society comprising "the multitude" or "the vulgus," deserve our "compassion rather than contempt or hatred. For how ignorant most of those [Turks, Jews, and Christians] are of one another's religions

---

[19] Borch, *Itinerarium* i, 214; Freudenthal/Walther, *Lebensgeschichte* i, 276 and ii, 146; Klever, "Spinoza and Van den Enden," 315; Totaro, "Documenti," 108.
[20] Totaro, "Documenti," 108; Steenbakkers, "Spinoza's Life," 26–7.
[21] Norris, *Spinoza and the Origins*, 28, 30, 92.

and customs!"[22] A favourite theme of Glazemaker, this topic presumably figured prominently in Spinoza's conversations with him. All the great religions Spinoza deemed equally ignorant of each other and, worse, equally ignorant of the truth.

By 1661, Spinoza's locating the Scriptures on the same level as Aesop's Fables and the Koran had apparently seeped into local Leiden folklore and academic hearsay. Langermann and Borch were not the only commentators of these years to record Spinoza flabbergasting conversation partners with such comparisons. The later renowned German jurist, Samuel Pufendorf (1632–94), who enrolled in Leiden in the spring of 1660, and years later would bitterly condemn Spinoza's demolition of natural law theory in the second (1684) edition of his famous *De Jure naturae et gentium* [the Law of Nature and the Nations] (1672),[23] likewise recounts this, to contemporaries, lurid tale evidently doing the rounds in the environs when Pufendorf, Borch, De Volder, and others attending the lectures of Heidanus, De Raey, Heereboord, and Gronovius first got to hear of Spinoza. During this formative period for these young scholars, Pufendorf later reminisced, in a letter of June 1688, to one of Germany's leading early Enlightenment scholars, Christian Thomasius (1655–1728), he had happened to encounter Spinoza personally.

Though not the first occasion Pufendorf expressed hostility to Spinoza and his doctrines, this letter of 1688, curiously mixing Latin and German, is notably personal. Recalling that over a quarter of a century earlier, when studying at Leiden in 1660–1, he had entered into conversation with the young Spinoza, he found him audacious and brash, a "leichtfertiger Vogel [frivolous bird]," and "deorum hominumque irrisor [mocker of gods and men]." Spinoza even had the effrontery, he heard then, to have his copies of the New Testament and the Koran bound together! Spinoza's lack of formal academic training and deference for scholarly authority made him appear outrageously pretentious to the likes of Pufendorf who always denied that there was anything profound in Spinoza and, apparently, made no effort to read Spinoza's chief work, the *Ethics*, when it appeared, or even most of the *TTP*.[24] Still, in 1688 he concurred with Thomasius that scholars must devote whatever time and effort was required to destroy this outrageous Sophist ["dass man ihn funditus destruire"], because somewhat to Pufendorf's amazement, since 1661 Spinoza, for all his absurdity, turned out to be a formidable threat to faith, authority, and the hierarchical social order he, Pufendorf, strove so unremittingly to uphold.

Later in September 1661, Borch and a companion set out from Leiden on a local tour, round the Rhine estuary villages towards the sea, taking in also Rijnsburg

---

[22] Spinoza, *Short Treatise*, 101.
[23] Freudenthal/Walther, *Lebensgeschichte* i, 277; Curley, "Samuel Pufendorf (1632–1694) as a Critic," 94–6; Steinberg, *Spinoza's Political Psychology*, 52.
[24] Freudenthal/Walther, *Lebensgeschichte* i, 277 and ii, 146–7; Curley, "Samuel Pufendorf (1632–1694) as a Critic," 95–6.

where they fell into conversation with another German acquaintance whom he and his companion met near Katwijk-aan-Zee. A medical doctor, this "Menelaus" recounted various titbits of scholarly news relating to oriental studies at Leiden before moving on to the now locally notorious "ex Jew turned Christian and now almost an atheist living in Rijnsburg who excels in Cartesian philosophy to such an extent that in many points he surpasses Descartes himself with his distinct and compelling concepts [in philosophia Cartesiana excellere, imo ipsum in multis superare Cartesium distinctis et probabilibus conceptibus]."[25] A butt of gossip in and around Leiden, Spinoza was clearly gaining a local reputation for scandalous views about the Bible and Koran, but also for exceptional skill in debating Descartes' philosophical legacy and expertise with lenses and microscopes.

In 1661, when Oldenburg, Borch, Pufendorf, Huygens, and Steno first heard of and encountered him, Spinoza's philosophy amounted already, and arguably more so than later, to a new type of quasi-religious creed designed to unite the confessions and teach how best to live and achieve happiness, guided by propositions Spinoza had "no doubt will seem rather shocking to some people." "Because man is part of the whole of Nature, depends on it and is governed by it," Spinoza taught his followers, "he can do nothing of himself, toward his salvation and well-being" but must remain part of an eternal and immutable order emanating unalterably from "God or Nature" with the result that "the true love of one's fellow man which this knowledge gives us, disposes us so that we never hate him, or are angry with him, but instead are inclined to help and bring him to a better condition." Because true knowledge serves here to further the "common good," such knowledge "frees us from sadness, despair, envy, fright and other evil passions" which Spinoza calls the authentic "real Hell," since according to him, no supernatural Hell exists or ever could exist. "True religion and our eternal salvation and happiness," which is the same as "true Christianity," derive therefore from studying the laws of Nature and seeking our well-being together, in sympathy with others, in seeking out, grasping and elevating ourselves on the basis of those laws.[26] This remained his essential credo, also later, when completing the last pages of his *Ethics*.

When Spinoza plunged into studying Descartes' philosophy, observed the Cartesian physician Cornelis Bontekoe, it was just beginning to penetrate the "navel of the old School Philosophy." Having saturated himself in Descartes' thought, Spinoza began freely philosophizing by introducing extraneous elements learned earlier when immersing himself in mathematics and Hebrew studies, two subjects, suggested Bontekoe, liable to affect the mind adversely, unsettling one's reason and make one stupid.[27] As the fundamentals of "Cartesianism rest on

---

[25] Freudenthal/Walther, *Lebensgeschichte* i, 276; Klever, "Spinoza and Van den Enden," 315; Scherz, "Biography of Nicolaus Steno," 91–2; Van de Ven, *Documenting Spinoza*, chronology.
[26] Spinoza, *Short Treatise*, 127–9.   [27] Israel, *Dutch Republic*, 895.

mathematical reason, it was easy for Spinoza to grasp part of it." (For the same reason, Bontekoe can hardly have been serious in his remark about mathematics.) Equally, as a geometry teacher it was easy for Spinoza to take on "young disciples" who came to him from the university where at that time the true philosophy (i.e. Cartesianism) "still suffered under the cross," being attacked and persecuted. These students, recounts Bontekoe, "often came to visit him in Rijnsburg [dikwils op Reinsburg kwamen besoeken]," so it was easy for Spinoza after a certain point to "formulate a part of [Descartes'] *Physica* in geometric order in textual form and publish it, a book that is still to be found and by many all too well known."[28]

It would be relevant to know if the future Cartesian philosopher Arnold Geulincx (1624–69), formerly a professor at Louvain (Leuven) but dismissed from his chair in 1658, who studied at Leiden from that year until 1662 also figured among Spinoza's contacts at this time. There is no proof that he did; but given the obvious affinities between their respective views on ethics, and that Geulincx became one of the most influential of the Leiden Cartesians, it seems likely this was the case. A native of Antwerp, brought up a Catholic, after being dismissed in disgrace for unknown reasons (most likely alleged sexual misconduct), after teaching at Louvain for twelve years, on settling in the north he converted to Calvinism and from 1662 taught philosophy at Leiden being appointed a full professor there in 1665, before dying in the plague epidemic of 1669, leaving his main work, *The Ethics*, still unpublished. The book was then edited and in 1675 published by his controversial, loud-mouthed former student, Dr Bontekoe, subsequently one of Spinoza's noisiest (apparent) local opponents.

Bontekoe's testimony about the background to Spinoza's first published work, his exposition of Descartes' philosophy, of 1663, emanating from someone who himself was a student at Leiden in the years 1665–7,[29] asserts something barely hinted at elsewhere, namely that students from the university gravitated to Spinoza while he lived in Rijnsburg, to consult with him and take lessons in geometry and Cartesianism and that it was in this connection that Spinoza wrote his *Principia Philosophiae Cartesianae* of 1663.[30] While historians have mostly stressed Rijnsburg's Collegiant associations, concurring with Jelles in interpreting Spinoza's move there from Amsterdam as motivated by desire for the quiet of the countryside, Bontekoe's comments add to the evidence that Spinoza's move, in the summer of 1661, was driven as much by desire for proximity to the university and the stormy Cartesian controversies in progress there, that the young philosopher deliberately positioned himself near the epicentre of the philosophical agitation gripping the Netherlands to experience the Cartesian controversies at first hand.

---

[28] Bontekoe, *Brief aan Jan Fredrik Swetsertje*, 21.
[29] Thijssen-Schoute, *Nederlands Cartesianisme*, 280; Otterspeer, *Groepsportret* [...] *de Leidse Universiteit, 1673–1775*, 58.
[30] Meijer, "De Ioanne Caseario," 232–3; Nadler, *Spinoza: A Life*, 180–1.

12.ii Meeting Oldenburg

When Spinoza got to know Oldenburg, in 1661, he thus already possessed both a developed philosophy solidly established in essentials and a bizarre standing at Leiden and its environs, a peculiar mix of good and bad reputation as a philosopher and outright denier of all conventional notions and common beliefs. Although not yet thirty years of age, to some he was already recognizably a towering moral guide teaching a new-fangled "true religion."

Oldenburg (Figure 12.3) was a Bremen-born German theologian, diplomat, and science reporter who, since the 1640s, had spent most of his life in England, and for years been close to one of England's leading scientists, Robert Boyle. Among the founders of the, in 1660, recently established Royal Society in London, Oldenburg became the Society's first secretary, making him, the year after his trip to Holland, a central figure in the scholarly and scientific world of the time. Since the mid-1650s, he was also a close friend of Boreel and took a particular interest in his schemes to use Hebrew studies and improved relations with Jews as a means to ultimately convert them to belief in Christ. Returning to London shortly after an encounter that proved profoundly meaningful for them both, Oldenburg penned

Figure 12.3 *Henry Oldenburg* (1619–77), by Jan van Cleve, oil on canvas, 1668. © The Royal Society.

the first of his surviving letters to Spinoza, dated 26 August 1661, assuring his new friend that their recent discussions focusing on the philosophies of Descartes and Bacon "in your *secessu* [solitude or retreat] in Rijnsburg" had meant much to him. He urged that they remain in touch by letter and fulsomely complimented Spinoza for combining "knowledge of important things with humanity and elegant manners [morum elegantia]." The connection with England, through Oldenburg, would be of lasting importance in Spinoza's life.

Oldenburg had toured Holland for approximately a month, from early July to early August 1661, carefully surveying the Dutch scholarly and scientific scene. En route from Bremen, where he had been visiting family, he travelled in leisurely fashion to Amsterdam where he met various savants and religious enthusiasts, including Boreel and Serrarius. Serrarius' and Boreel's repudiation of all organized churches with clergy and pulpit remained a topic of abiding interest to Spinoza, and also to Oldenburg who nurtured a strong interest in Millenarian schemes as well as the future conversion of the Jews. Indeed, finding out what had gone wrong with Spinoza's apostasy from Judaism and subsequent failure to embrace Christianity was one element in Oldenburg's curiosity about him and was doubtless encouraged by Boreel who had particular ties with Rijnsburg.[31] Serrarius probably already knew Spinoza in Amsterdam, in the late 1650s if not earlier, meeting him in Rieuwertsz's bookstore or at a Collegiant or Quaker meeting, and Oldenburg very likely first heard word of Spinoza while in the company of Serrarius and Boreel, though the suggestion that Oldenburg might find it worth his while making a detour to Rijnsburg to meet Spinoza whilst en route to The Hague, could equally well have originated in Leiden with his cousin Cocceius, or else Steno. In fact, prior to visiting Rijnsburg Oldenburg probably heard about Spinoza in Amsterdam *and* Leiden.

Despite his own Calvinist background in Bremen, Oldenburg evinced considerably less interest in the intricacies of inter-Calvinist polemics of the kind Cocceius was endlessly caught up in than the lofty Neoplatonist speculations of Henry More and in spiritualists and Millenarians like his Amsterdam friends Boreel and Serrarius. Broad-minded and perennially eager to learn more about conflicting viewpoints in his three chosen fields—natural history, theology, and philosophy—Oldenburg was in contact with a great variety of savants, including Hobbes. A man of science *and* faith, he was unshakeably convinced of the close convergence of religion and science, something at that time far more usual than Spinoza's approach. Like Boyle, Serrarius, Steno, Borch, and Swammerdam, Oldenburg believed without question that the best scientific research, the true scientific spirit, ties science intimately and uninterruptedly to religious truth.

---

[31] Van der Wall, *Mystieke Chiliast*, 264–5; Hutton, "Henry Oldenburg," 107–9, 115–16.

Actually, for Oldenburg natural history and philosophy were fairly recent enthusiasms embarked on only at a middle point in his career. He had first become acquainted with the Dutch scholarly world in the 1640s when studying briefly at Utrecht, but then his chief concern was with divinity. During the early and mid-1650s, he chiefly devoted himself to tutoring sons of wealthy English gentlemen. Only during 1655–7, at around thirty-six, after a stay in Oxford and his life-changing early encounters with the famed naturalist and chemist Robert Boyle, did he acquire his subsequently inexhaustible zeal for the "experimental philosophy," scientific innovation, and the principles of Bacon. During the late 1650s, Oldenburg spent much time in France, travelling as far as the world-renowned school of medicine at Montpellier to which he reacted rather negatively, observing that the "physicians of Montpellier are excessively devoted to Galen; they obstruct the whole field of medicine. Only one or two among them pursue the spagyric art and these few excite the hatred and loathing of the rest."[32] At Paris, Oldenburg made lasting contacts among the scientific fraternity, notably with Steno's and Swammerdam's later patron, the legendary scientist, traveller, orientalist, and diplomat Melchisédec Thévenot (c.1620–92), whom a Parisian colleague designated "one of our best and most curiosity-driven philosophers," someone who long figured among the foremost French commentators on the science of the age. A copy of Thevenot's *Voyages* [Travels] in three volumes figured among the most expensive books in Oldenburg's personal library.[33]

England, Oldenburg's experiences in France and Germany convinced him, was indisputably ahead of the rest in the scientific field especially due to the happy collaboration of Boyle, and England's other leading experimentalists, with a band of supportive, keenly interested aristocrats. Prominent among the latter was William, 2nd Viscount Brouncker (1620–84), an Oxford-educated Anglo-Irish nobleman with a taste for mathematics and interest in medicine (also a renowned gambler and chess player), the Royal Society's first president. Baconian "experimental" science made England, Oldenburg was convinced, the key to real scientific progress, holding (accurately enough until Colbert, Louis XIV's new chief minister, persuaded the king to establish the Paris Académie des Sciences, in 1666), that the powerful and specifically English formula—Bacon's legacy in combination with aristocratic and court support—was conspicuously missing in France, Germany, and the Netherlands alike.

After a stay in Leiden where his cousin, Cocceius, figured among the most renowned Reformed theology professors of the age,[34] Oldenburg toured Utrecht after arriving there on 29 July, then The Hague, from where he departed on 3 August, and finally Rotterdam, before embarking for England.[35] Practically last on his list of scholarly visits in Holland was his interview in The Hague with the

---

[32] Avramov, "Apprenticeship," 195.   [33] BL MS. Add. 4255, fo. 237.
[34] Oldenburg, *Correspondence* i, 415–16.   [35] Van de Ven, "Spinoza's Life and Time," 83.

eminent astronomer and physicist Christiaan Huygens (1629–95), whom he had met earlier that year in London. Between March and May 1661, Huygens had stayed for over a month conducting experiments in London and conferring with Boyle and other prominent figures in the world of English science and culture, including Christopher Wren, and Oldenburg. Oldenburg arrived in The Hague, Huygens afterwards reported in a letter to Sir Robert Moray (1609–73), another of the leading figures of the Royal Society, at the end of July.

During the evening of Oldenburg's visit to his house, in early August, Huygens proudly showed him the moon through his then uniquely powerful telescope.[36] Though the exact timing is unclear, Oldenburg had dropped by at Spinoza's lodgings in Rijnsburg while staying at Leiden, probably in mid to late July, ten days or so before renewing his acquaintance with Huygens. Spinoza's reputation as a philosopher introducing breath-taking novelties, relentless in correcting the slips and errors of others, and sceptical about all belief but hostile to philosophical scepticism directed at the power of reason,[37] was now spreading and had caught Oldenburg's attention. Seemingly, for all his considerable caution about publicizing his ideas, the young Spinoza was, as he had long been since the early 1650s, a vigorous and provocative debater. The most surprising feature for contemporaries was that this reputed "atheist" reportedly lived an otherwise upright, irreproachable life, quietly occupied with preparing lenses for both telescopes and microscopes. When visiting Leiden earlier, Huygens informed Moray, presumably partly referring to Spinoza, Oldenburg "spoke with some philosophers whom I know so far only by name."[38] Still, given his pre-eminence in European science at the time, Huygens, unsurprisingly, would always remain a considerably more important Dutch contact for Boyle, Moray, and Oldenburg than Spinoza.

During their conversation, at Rijnsburg, in July 1661, Oldenburg discussed the latest scientific developments, especially stressing, he recalled afterwards when writing to Spinoza, the decisive innovativeness and epoch-making importance of Boyle and the London "college of philosophers of which I spoke to you," doubtless mentioning also Huygens' productive recent stay in London. Spinoza, for his part, described experiments he himself had participated in or witnessed in Amsterdam and Leiden, and showed his guest his experiment room with his lens-cutting equipment, lenses and microscopes indicating his own familiarity with the world of scientific investigation gradually acquired in recent years. "It is largely due to this era," observe historians identifying the central features of the seventeenth-century scientific revolution and its role as a pivotal new chapter in Western thought, "that we owe the ethos of modern science – empirical, cumulative and deeply quantitative in its methods, iconoclastic in its view of previous

---

[36] Oldenburg, *Correspondence* i, 413; Kuyper, *Dutch Classicist Architecture*, 166.
[37] Spinoza, *Short Treatise*, 112.
[38] Huygens to Moray, The Hague, 1 Aug. 1661 in Huygens, *Oeuvres complètes* vi, p. iii.

intellectual traditions, and assertive of its ability not just to understand nature, but also control it. Perhaps most fundamental, however, was the adoption at this time of a new world-view, involving a complete change in the way in which nature was conceived."[39] The leading natural philosophers of the seventeenth century overthrew the hitherto prevailing Aristotelian and Galenic notions which typically depicted nature as a wise and benevolent being that did nothing in vain.

By this broad measure, Bacon, Descartes, Boyle, Oldenburg, Steno, Swammerdam, Huygens, Hudde, Kerckring, De Volder, Thévenot, and Spinoza were all solidly men of the scientific revolution believing experiment and mathematics had established new criteria of precision and truth and that all pre-Baconian natural philosophy was now defunct. All agreed as to the unique value of experiment both for testing theoretical explanations and discovering new facts and consequences. Exact data and experiment combined with careful scrutiny of the results were the path by which dramatic new truths would be discovered. And yet a vast philosophical and scientific gulf separated the English strict empiricism of Bacon and Boyle from the more sweeping, philosophically ambitious fusing of wide-ranging empiricism with the *esprit de système* of the Continental Cartesians including that incorrigibly dissident critic of Descartes, the intellectually highly ambitious young Spinoza.

Science was Oldenburg's passion and surveying every aspect of it his special domain. Yet, like Boyle and at the time also Steno, Borch, and Swammerdam, and like most scientists of the Enlightenment era generally, but unlike Spinoza (and Huygens), Oldenburg also believed the true scientific spirit fully harmonizes with the Holy Spirit and with revealed religion. For Spinoza, and this was what made him a significant Enlightenment philosopher of science, "nothing happens in nature which can be attributed to anything wrong in it, for nature is always the same and its virtue and power of acting are everywhere one and the same thing, that is, the laws and rules of nature according to which all things happen, and things change from one form to another, are always and everywhere the same." So the way to understand anything, including men's emotions and how they affect our lives and politics, "must also remain the same, that is, through the universal laws and rules of nature. That is why the emotions of hate, anger, jealousy etc., considered in themselves, happen through the same necessity and virtue of nature as do all other particular things."[40] Spinoza held his approach to mean that the interactions of our emotions and their intensity are to be understood as effects within our bodies explicable in terms of "lines, planes and bodies" by which our power of acting is increased, decreased, or left unchanged. Emotions like hatred and anger weaken us by detracting from our power to act rationally and

---

[39] Davis and Hunter, "Introduction" to Boyle, *A Free Enquiry*, p. ix.
[40] Spinoza, *Ethica*, in Spinoza, *Oeuvres* iv, 242-3.

do good and therefore need to be better understood and more responsibly navigated by us all.[41]

Another key tenet then already basic to Spinoza's system was that "each and every particular thing that comes to exist becomes such through motion and rest," a doctrine grounding his argument that all of reality, all body and soul, is governed by the same comprehensive set of interacting physical laws governing all motion and rest.[42] This accounts for the subtle tension infusing the Oldenburg–Spinoza encounter from the outset, albeit one Oldenburg, with his well-honed tact and diplomatic talent, prevented from becoming a barrier between them until a much later stage (the early 1670s). Noting Spinoza's modest circumstances and lack of equipment and resources, Oldenburg must at once have concluded he had more to offer philosophically than to the exciting new world of empirical science, but grasped too that the two spheres were differently connected in Spinoza's mind than in Boyle's and his own, and felt intrigued by Spinoza's criticism.

Many times during his life Spinoza would be accused of being an "atheist" spreading an "atheistic" philosophy, a charge that always angered and troubled him. He invariably rejected the accusation outright. Yet, in rejecting the charge, instead of veiling or qualifying his claim that there is no knowing God who can change the immutable laws of Nature that govern all reality, guide the course of events, or perform miracles, or who rewards or punishes men, he invariably reacted, strikingly, by treating the accusation as a moral slur, wrongly implying he was purveying immorality. When, for example, the Utrecht Cartesian Van Velthuysen accused him of being an "atheist," in 1671, Spinoza rebuked him for being indifferent to "what manner of life I pursue"; saying that had he known "he would not so readily have been convinced that I teach atheism, as atheists are usually inordinately fond of honours and riches, which I have always despised as is known to all who are acquainted with me."[43] Though entirely typical of Spinoza and his attitudes, it is a strange reply to the charge of not believing in the Christian God.

12.iii Steno and Anatomical Dissection

It was shortly before, or after, Spinoza settled in at Rijnsburg too that Spinoza and Steno became friends, as the latter recalled a decade later in his 1675 open letter denouncing the dangerously spreading "contagion" that Spinoza's philosophy had come to represent.[44] Enrolling at Leiden University on 27 July 1660, Niels Stensen

---

[41] Spinoza, *Ethica*, in Spinoza, *Oeuvres* iv, 242; Nadler, *Think Least of Death*, 82–3.
[42] Spinoza, *Short Treatise*, 95.
[43] Spinoza, *Collected Works* (ed. Curley) ii, 386; Spinoza to Ostens, undated but 1671; Blom, "Lambert van Velthuysen," 203.
[44] Steno, "Libri prohibiti," 33; Totaro, "Ho certi amici," 27, 31; Van Vugt, "Structure and Dynamics," 102.

(1638–86) or Nicolas Steno as he was usually called outside Scandinavia, lodged in rooms rented from the mother of the physician Gerard Blasius "on the Rapenburg," Leiden's main canal, close to the anatomical theatre and the botanical gardens. At the time, Kerckring was lodging close by. The Blasius house in Leiden known as "The Half Moon" was also where Borch stayed whilst in Leiden.[45] "Here are no colleges for students to live in, as in our universities," observed Ray when visiting Leiden, in 1663, excepting two hostels "for the maintenance only of poor scholars, but the students live in private lodgings in the town, where they can best provide for themselves." Neither were "scholastical habits as gowns or caps worn by any of the students, but they walk up and down, come to the Schools, and perform their exercises in cloaks. The professors when they read lectures or preside at disputations wear gowns." Especially bizarre for those familiar with Oxford and Cambridge was the astounding absence even of deferential raising of caps: in Leiden, there was simply no "capping professors or university-officers in the public Schools."[46]

Blasius often moved between Amsterdam and Leiden and is known to have been friendly with Johannes and Adriaan Koerbagh, and others of Spinoza's circle. Among Steno's closest associates at Leiden in and after 1660 was his fellow anatomist Kerckring who had enrolled as a medical student in March 1659,[47] and with whom he long remained friendly in later life, and another soon eminent researcher, perhaps the greatest Dutch comparative anatomist of the Golden Age, Jan Swammerdam (1637–80), or as Steno Latinized his name, that "most ingenious youth and zealot for anatomical dissections, Mr Squamerdamius," who arrived in December 1661 and with whom Steno would also remain close.[48] Raised in Amsterdam, Swammerdam spent two years studying medicine in Leiden (1661–3) where he got to know several of Spinoza's friends and almost certainly Spinoza too. Son of an Amsterdam pharmacist who resisted his father's desire that he become a Calvinist minister, Swammerdam spent his Leiden years studying hard and often discussing dissection with Borch, Steno, and Kerckring. Unusually for a student, noted Borch, Swammerdam already possessed a microscope of his own. All deep into dissection and what was to be discovered from it, Steno, Kerckring, and Swammerdam were often present during dissections, as in January 1661 was Borch, and, on occasion, Spinoza too.[49]

One of the three outstanding Dutch Golden Age naturalists alongside Huygens and Van Leeuwenhoek, Swammerdam, like his comrade Steno, was deeply religious but, unlike Steno, never identified with any particular church. He acquired exceptional skills during the early 1660s dissecting dogs and other animals, but

---

[45] Totaro, "Documenti," 104; Jorink, "Modus Politicus Vivendi," 19.
[46] Ray, *Observations topographical*, 35–6.   [47] Scherz, "Biography of Nicolaus Steno," 91.
[48] Lindeboom, "Short Biography," 4; Scherz, *Niels Stensen*, 34; Schierbeek, *Jan Swammerdam*, 41.
[49] Scherz, *Niels Stensen*, 35; Jorink, "Outside God," 87–9.

later came to focus especially on study of insects, his life-long passion. When back in Amsterdam during the mid-1660s, now refusing a career as a physician, provoking further quarrels with his father, Swammerdam pursued no conventional career at all. Rather, he devoted his time and effort entirely to collecting and studying insects and microscope research, initially participating in the Collegium Privatum under Blasius until, in 1666, a row over precedence erupted between these two, just as earlier between Steno and Blasius, when the latter tried to pass off as his own one of Swammerdam's finds.[50] A fervent protagonist of physico-theology, putting him on an entirely different track from Spinoza, Swammerdam discerned God's designing hand in even the tiniest details of nature, such as the embryonic existence of the bodies of butterflies in the caterpillars from which they emerge.

By the mid-1670s, however, Swammerdam's deeply pious, mystical leanings had become a disruptive factor for his science. Plunged in spiritual crisis, gripped by religious fervour, he was drawn into the ultra-austere movement of Antoinette Bourignon (1616–80), a charismatic fanatically devout woman who fled Mons, in 1662, after a scandal arising from the harsh regime imposed at her girls' orphanage leading to the death of one of her girls. Proclaiming the imminence of the end of days and the Last Judgement, Bourignon summoned Swammerdam to forsake all for prayer and burn his scientific work, much of which he did in fact burn, including his treatise on the silkworm while other texts he abandoned unfinished. During 1673–5, this scientist of ardent faith with a decidedly independent view of life, dwelt in abstemious seclusion among Bourignon's ascetic commune at Husum, a North Sea port in the extreme north of Germany.[51] He was destined to die even younger than Spinoza, leaving this world at only forty-three.

Steno spent in all three and a half years studying and researching in Leiden, and attending the lectures of renowned professors, especially of the Huguenot physician, chemist, and anatomist, Franciscus de le Boë Sylvius (1614–72), a dominant personality and soon the highest-paid Leiden professor. A staunch adherent of Harvey's theory of circulation of the blood, Le Boë Sylvius urged students to undertake original scientific research by practising dissection. Prior to his appointment at Leiden, in 1658, as a well-known physician in Amsterdam, he already figured among the most fervent Cartesians of the day. Spinoza very likely too attended his lectures at Leiden in the late 1650s and early 1660s and discussed his approach with Steno and other friends. Cartesian in philosophy, a leader of the Cartesian movement in the northern Netherlands, expert in demonstrating bodily processes, Le Boë Sylvius was a founder of the so-called iatrochemical school of medicine, a clique building their medical theories on the hypothesis that all animal and human life, correctly functioning or malfunctioning, healthy or diseased, is

---

[50] Lindeboom, "Jan Swammerdam," 113, 117; Jorink, "Modus Politicus Vivendi," 35.
[51] RL Copenhagen MS Thott 1261/4 Petrus Francius to Graevius, Amsterdam, 2 Feb. 1674.

governed by chemical reactions, especially of alkalis, depending on whether these are in correct balance with, or harmfully clashing with, acids. This notion was central to their synthesizing theory of animal and all physical human life supposedly operating in strict accord with the general laws of physics and chemistry. The Dutch iatrochemical school would later become a principal target of Boyle's chemistry investigations and stern strictures in his *Reflections upon the Hypothesis of Alcali and Acidum* (1675). It may well also have been Le Boë Sylvius that Spinoza had in mind when referring, in his *Korte Verhandeling*, to how misleading scientific theories can stem from experience, false inference being typical of physicians who "when they have found a certain remedy to be good in some cases, usually regard it as something infallible."[52]

Steno (Figure 12.4) swiftly emerged as a leading anatomist and researcher in animal dissection specializing in the brain, muscles, and later also the heart, of both animals and humans. At this stage, reading widely in learned literature, "he felt a very high regard for the philosophy of Descartes and everybody who was praised for his understanding of Descartes," very likely the initial basis for his

Figure 12.4 *Nicholas Steno (1666–77)* by Justus Sustermans. By courtesy of Uffizi Gallery, Florence, Italy.

---

[52] Spinoza, *Short Treatise*, 101–2.

friendship with Spinoza. Researching the heart, in the autumn of 1662, seeking to "compare the structure of the heart to that of the muscles," it remained the case, he recalled later, that "I considered the system of Mr Descartes to be infallible." Subsequent research on rabbits' leg muscles and other muscles, however, planted growing doubts about Descartes' approach in his mind: "the first muscle I tested revealed to me the essential basis of the structure of the muscle which so far nobody had known and which [I inferred] demolished the whole system of Mr Descartes." But that could not displace Cartesianism as a powerfully overarching, everywhere intrusive, if not wholly dominant force at the time, in Leiden, and more generally in Dutch intellectual life. The problem with Cartesianism, Steno afterwards contended, was that Descartes "forgetting his method" and neglecting the quest for certainty above all, took to presupposing things to be true and certain which "he has not established on reasonable grounds."[53]

Spinoza too sat in on science demonstrations and attended the Leiden dissecting theatre at this time, so, if they had not been introduced already earlier in Amsterdam, by Kerckring or another who knew Spinoza previously, Steno and Spinoza may first have met there.[54] The lecture rooms, *hortus botanicus*, and the anatomy theatre, all certainly familiar to Spinoza, were over an hour's walking distance from his Rijnsburg lodgings, not too far for a young man to undertake fairly regularly.[55] At one stage, records Steno, Spinoza "came to me every day to watch the dissecting of the brain that I was engaged in with different sorts of animals [when trying] to locate the seat of the start of motions, and the terminal of the [body's] sensations."[56] All the young researchers conferred together. Yet, though they conversed a lot, and Spinoza carefully observed Steno's anatomical findings, including his reversing of the controversial self-taught anatomist Lodewijk De Bils' mistaken theory of the lymph flow in relation to blood circulation, as Ruysch afterwards confirmed, Steno, for his part, acquired at that time only a very fragmentary notion of Spinoza's own philosophical system. What was clear to him, as it was to others, though, including Swammerdam, was that in religious matters Spinoza remained very much an independent mind. Swammerdam would later prove scarcely less impatient than Spinoza with Steno's post-1667 unrelenting identification of Christian truth with one particular church and confession (the Catholic).[57] But for all their differences, Swammerdam, during his later deep crisis of 1673–5, was tormented by similar nagging doubts as Steno and experienced a comparable vigorous emotional reaction against science, though in his case this proved only temporary.

---

[53] Scherz, *Niels Stensen*, 42–3; Totaro, "Documenti," 107; Kardel and Maquet, *Nicolaus Steno*, 88–90, 94.
[54] Totaro, "Documenti," 107; Kardel and Maquet, *Nicolaus Steno*, 92n.
[55] Rotthier, *Naakte perenboom*, 60.
[56] Totaro, "Documenti," 100; Kardel and Maquet, *Nicolaus Steno*, 91–2.
[57] Jorink, "Outside God," 85–7.

When attending lectures or disputations not held in the anatomical theatre, Spinoza assembled with the students in one of a handful of small lecture rooms in the principal "Academia" building, known also as the "Schools." This brick building, still standing today, was described, in 1663, as "three stories high, containing two rooms on a floor. The lower two are the Divinity and Physick Schools. The middle the Law and Philosophy Schools." Since the mid-1650s Spinoza had doubtless heard all, or most, of Leiden's then academic celebrities lecture and preside—Le Boë Sylvius, Cocceius, Golius, Gronovius, De Raey, Bornius, Heidanus, Van Horne, the professor of anatomy and surgery, and finally Leiden's mathematical genius Frans Van Schooten. During the early 1660s, Steno, Kerckring, Meyer, the Koerbaghs, De Volder, Swammerdam, and Spinoza, must certainly have all frequently gathered, discussed, and debated in and around the confined space of the university lecture halls, anatomy theatre, and the academic "physic garden," or *hortus botanicus* where the medicinal plants were grown. These gardens, behind the main university building, among the pleasantest spots adjoining, were "a square of less than an acre of ground," notes Ray, or "not so big as a fourth part of ours at Oxford," but "well stored with plants, of which there have been at sundry times several catalogues printed."[58]

In the renowned Leiden University anatomy theatre, one of the first established in Europe north of the Alps, founded in 1594, where Steno, Kerckring, and Swammerdam conducted dissections, one encountered not just apparatus and instruments for dissection but an "innumerable company of skeletons of all manner of creatures." One found there "alsoe severall mummies; old heathenish reliques and idols; many sorts of minerals," besides "skins of beasts, parts of exotic animals and other rarities," including, by 1663, an armadillo and some elephant skulls.[59] The full natural history collection, much of it kept in the store-rooms during term, was brought out on display in the summer when there were no lectures and fewer students. As it attracted also foreign visitors, a catalogue of the collection appeared in English some years later, in 1678, item one on the list being the head of an elephant, number two the "head of an elk," three a rhinoceros skin and horn, five a crocodile, six the "four feet of an elephant." Besides such exotic items and the skeletons of cows, wolves, baboons, and an ape, there was also an ethnographic collection including three ancient Egyptian idols and some Chinese antiquities besides a "pair of Muscovian breeches and coate," "a Muscovian monk's hood," Lapland breeches, and a pair of skis "on which the Norwegians, Laplanders, and Finlanders ride over high snowy mountains."[60]

But however exciting at first, anatomical dissection after a while came to seem decidedly less than satisfying to Steno who, like Swammerdam, Boyle, and

---

[58] Ray, *Observations topographical*, 35–6.
[59] Ray, *Observations topographical*, 36; Hoftijzer, "*A Study Tour* into the Low Countries," 94.
[60] *A Catalogue of all the Cheifest* [sic] *Rarities*, 1–3.

Oldenburg, was essentially a zealot for science fused with religious faith.[61] He felt frustrated that empirical science, his own scientific findings, always seemed inconclusive, animal and human organs turning out to be endlessly connected to other parts and organs, and exploration to become ever more intricate and complex without ever allowing clear or complete conclusions to emerge. Steno's innermost conviction garnered from pursuit of science turned out to be the very reverse of Spinoza's credo, that "the more we come to understand natural things," as the latter expresses it in the *TTP*, "the greater and more perfect the knowledge of God we acquire," so that: "the more we learn about natural things, the more perfectly we know the essence of God (which is the cause of all things) and thus all our knowledge, that is our highest good, not only depends on a knowledge of God, but consists in it altogether." Consequently, Spinoza concludes, "that man is necessarily most perfect and most participates in the highest happiness who most loves and most enjoys above all other things, the intellectual knowledge of God, who is the most perfect being."[62]

Disillusioned with Cartesianism and, over the winter of 1662–3, already feeling thwarted with the results produced in Leiden's anatomy theatre, Steno experienced his first but far from last spiritual crisis. Craving for religious fulfilment began jarring at a deep level with the unbending rationalism of Cartesianism and disorientating lack of spiritual upliftment afforded by his empirical research—and, as he saw it, doubtless also his friend Spinoza's ideas.[63] Descartes' fixed and immutable laws of nature and geometric way of reasoning, and Spinoza's too, concluded Steno, render miracles and the supernatural problematic or impossible, thereby dismally failing to meet the ultimate test of truth by bringing the reality of Christian doctrine, the centrality of Christ and the miraculous, to the fore.[64]

Steno focused chiefly on anatomy and specifically muscles, the respiratory system, blood circulation, the heart, brain, and philosophical and theological problems besetting the Cartesian doctrine of mind–body duality. While continually pondering Descartes' methods and ideas, and the medical Cartesianism of Le Boë Sylvius, Steno's pioneering anatomical investigations at Leiden, during 1662–3, filled him with doubts especially regarding Descartes' notions of the relation between mind and body. A particular difficulty was Descartes' hypothesis about the pineal gland, the hypothetical gland he postulated as the crucial link connecting body and mind in humans. Looking back from the perspective of 1680, on his own tortuous path drifting away from science towards faith and eventual conversion from Lutheranism to Catholicism, in 1667, reports Steno, in his *Defensio epistolae de propria conversione* (1680), eventually he felt pushed to

---

[61] Kermit, "Oneness in Niels Stensen's Life," 24–6.
[62] Spinoza, *Theological-Political Treatise*, 59; Nadler, "Spinoza's Theory of Divine Providence," 13, 29.
[63] Scherz, *Niels Stensen*, 43–4; Totaro, "Documenti," 103–4.
[64] Jorink, "Modus Politicus Vivendi," 37–8.

abandon research and scientific reason altogether and opt for faith, the two for him being henceforth in unresolvable conflict. The more his 1660s anatomical researches progressed, the more doubtful he became as to whether anything Descartes taught about the motions of the heart, circulation of blood, mind–body relationship, and muscle movement fits the empirical evidence. "Hence I arrived at two conclusions: firstly, if those who in the judgment of many are considered divinely brilliant [like Descartes] erect theses so remote from truth in relation to such a clear and easy matter where we can appeal to direct experience [i.e. dissection and anatomy], who can guarantee they deserve more credence when proposing dogmas about God and the soul where one cannot carry out any such investigation?"[65]

Steno stayed in Leiden until late 1664 returning to Copenhagen in March 1665. Recalling his Leiden research years later, in the early 1670s, he insisted on the "extremely strong argument that occurred to me [at that time] for dampening the arrogance of the human mind, namely, that researchers, despite their efforts and speculations over many hundreds of years, have discovered nothing about the true causes of animal movement and its nature." Furthermore, "all those who have proposed their own explanation in these matters with great authority have provided us with nothing but false dogmas instead of proofs." Daily he thanked God "for having at last made manifest the mistakes of all those who went astray."[66] Steno thanked the Lord too for keeping him safe from a particular lurking menace. "While studying in the University of Leiden," he recalled years later, in his submission to the Inquisition authorities in Rome, in 1677, "I had occasion to talk familiarly with the said Spinoza who was Jewish by birth, but by profession without any religion." As he and Swammerdam viewed the unsettling outcome, others were less fortunate than themselves in escaping Spinoza's insidious snares.[67]

Steno severely criticized Descartes for neglecting his own method, for failing to experiment rigorously "which was the first instrument of the discovery of my mistakes." Yet, what is the point, at the end of the day, in persevering with observational scientific research? Experimental science certainly reveals the errors and confusion of others, but also reveals the inconclusiveness and ultimate pointlessness of pure scholarship and research. Science without miracles and religion to Steno is not reality and hence not true science. If one accepts Spinoza's schema, scientific knowledge forms the basis of a happy and fulfilled human life blessed with understanding of man, the world and reality generally. But according to Steno, scientific research "would have led me away from striving for religion."[68] What scientific research can never do, he contended later, like

---

[65] Scherz, "Biography of Nicolaus Steno," 96; Jorink, "Modus Politicus Vivendi," 37.
[66] Totaro, "Niels Stensen (1638–1686)," 153–4.
[67] Steno, "Libri prohibiti," 33; Totaro, "Ho certi amici," 33.
[68] Scherz, *Niels Stensen*, 45; Scherz, "Biography of Nicolaus Steno," 94–5.

Swammerdam, but unlike Oldenburg and Boyle, is reveal the ultimate truth of things and of our reality which is to say it must always remain something essentially marginal.

This was directly opposite to Spinoza's conclusion. In the last few pages of the *Ethics* Spinoza speaks of God and the soul and puts the finishing touches to his theory of knowledge as a human resource that our minds acquire in four basic ways, dividing human knowledge into four different categories. The first category, what one is told or is passed on by tradition, is scientifically worthless and mostly inaccurate. The second, the result of sense-experience, does represent genuine first-hand knowledge but is so complex, fragmentary, tied to particular perspectives, and hard to decipher correctly, that, if one goes no further, one still construes everything wrongly. It is the third and fourth avenues of knowledge that lift men to a higher level, enabling us to surmount our sea of confusion. The third order of knowledge involves processing sense-experience via correct reasoning to reach rational inferences about the reliable data collected. The fourth, called by Spinoza "intuition," is what occurs among a few after accumulating a substantial mass of correct inferences of the third kind (or as he calls it elsewhere, jettisoning the first category completely) the "second" kind. Knowledge of the "third kind" in Spinoza's sense, his *scientia intuitiva*, combines the insights reached after building a mass of correct inferences drawn from data to reveal the underlying structures of reality. Even if grasped only by very few, held Spinoza, rejecting a knowing God who rewards and punishes, and the immortality of the soul, is therefore not speculation or "dogma" but fundamental truth.[69]

After completing their undergraduate studies, Steno and Swammerdam spent around two years together in Paris, residing at the mansion, or private Paris science academy, of Thévenot, the renowned French patron of science and learning. Thévenot presided over weekly meetings of the leading group of natural scientists active in Paris during the 1660s, and in 1664–5, Steno and Swammerdam both delivered long-remembered formal discourses, most notably Steno's famously crushing rebuttal of Descartes' views on the mind–body relationship which, four years later, was published by Thévenot, in 1669.[70] These 1664–5 gatherings chaired by Thévenot must almost certainly have been the moment when Spinoza was first noted and talked about in Paris. Thévenot would remain a significant figure in the lives of Steno, Swammerdam, and, more indirectly, Spinoza, forming a particularly close friendship with Swammerdam that would last over many years down to the latter's death, in 1680.[71] No naturalist of the age devoted to international science networking, as well as nurturing science

---

[69] Spinoza, *Collected Works* (ed. Curley) i, 612–17.
[70] Swammerdam, *Letters to Thévenot*, 8–10; Totaro, "Niels Stensen (1638–1686)," 153; Kermit, "Oneness in Niels Stensen's Life," 24; Jorink, *Boeck der natuere*, 230–1.
[71] Lindeboom, "Jan Swammerdam," 115, 119; Jorink, "Modus Politicus Vivendi," 35; Jorink, "Outside God," 91.

research in his own country, had a more detailed, frequently refreshed familiarity with Holland and Dutch learning and science than Thévenot, not even Oldenburg. A passionate bibliophile much preoccupied with Hebrew studies and other oriental languages as well as travel and science, Thévenot's personal library would later contain Spinoza's Hebrew grammar separately bound as well as his *Opera Posthuma*, Steno's works, many volumes recounting travels to distant lands, and Menasseh's *Conciliador*.[72]

Of all the leading intellectual lights of Paris, Thévenot was the very first, very likely reaching back as far as the mid-1660s, and continuing right through the 1670s, to take note of the staggering extent and implications of Spinoza's ambitious course and follow the progress of his life project. Not long after the departure of the two young Protestant naturalists, Thévenot's academy was brought under the patronage of the French monarch and, in December 1666, renamed the Académie Royale des Sciences, marking the formal institutionalization in France of science as an organized effort governed by a strict set of procedures for how experiments should be objectively observed, recorded, and moderated by the scientific community as a body, and priority disputes adjudicated, a key landmark in the emancipation of modern science from alchemy, idiosyncrasy, and private musings.[73]

That nature is God's "second Bible" open for all, more powerful than anything for convincing non-believers of God's omnipotence, no one believed more fervently than Swammerdam. Back in Amsterdam, he laboured for years analysing muscles, eye structures, and insects, at times working with the artist Otto Marseus van Schrieck (c.1613–78) who specialized in representing toads, fungi, snakes, and insects, and kept a garden plot housing lizards and snakes. But by the late 1660s, Swammerdam was becoming more and more withdrawn and, by 1673, was close to concluding, like Steno, that science simply does not bring one closer to the truth, to God, Christ and the soul's immortality, hence where he wished to be. His religious crisis and abandonment of science was a grave disappointment to Thévenot and Oldenburg, though, differently from Steno, Swammerdam's for a time exclusive focus on introspection, prayer, and religious duties proved temporary. Reverting to scientific research eventually, after 1675, he recovered some stability, becoming a frequent visitor to meetings of the Cartesian group, the *Sçavanten*, at Utrecht.[74] But only from around 1678, in the last two years or so of his life, did he steady sufficiently to get (most of) his chief work written. When he died, in February 1680, from malaria caught while collecting insects from pools and bogs on Amsterdam's outskirts, his magnum opus, the *Bibliae naturae*, was

---

[72] *Bibliotheca Thevenotiana, sive Catalogus impressorum et manuscriptorum librorum Bibliothecae viri clarissmi D. [...] Thevenot* (Paris, 1694), pp. ii, 3, 103.
[73] Jorink, *Boeck der natuere*, 230–1, 245–57; Wootton, *Invention of Science*, 96, 357.
[74] Lindeboom, "Jan Swammerdam," 117–18; Jorink, "Outside God," 98–101.

still in a fragmentary, unfinished state. Swammerdam bequeathed his unpublished papers to his life-long ally, Thévenot; but the latter, seeing their unfinished state, simply left his papers in a drawer unedited and forgotten.[75] Only much later, in 1737, thanks to the renowned Herman Boerhaave was his principal work finally edited and published.

The life trajectories of Steno and Swammerdam would seem to prove the contrary to Spinoza's core ethical contention that happiness or well-being stems from the intellectual understanding of nature. Yet, Spinoza's outlook (like Koerbagh's), though utterly different from Steno's, was in some ways ultimately not so very remote from Swammerdam's: God is the source of all that happens in Nature and determines Nature's unalterable laws governing all that occurs; pure empirical research is not the origin of true understanding but rather helps guide us there, a refining tool enabling us to connect the main lines, uncover the basic structures.[76] In the early 1660s, Spinoza showed eager interest in the dissections and findings of his friends engaged in anatomical research, as he did in the mathematical problems bequeathed by Van Schooten (which he discussed with De Volder), and heartily joined with Steno and Kerckring, as with Huygens later, in their ongoing inquiries. Above all, Spinoza had no intention of repeating Descartes' greatest mistake—allowing his speculations to become largely detached from empirical science. Overhasty extrapolation and unsupported system-building, Spinoza could not agree more, lead to many a fundamental error (from which Le Boë Sylvius was not exempt) and which scientific experiment alone can conclusively dispel. Philosophy without constant immersion in the latest empirical science is a waste of time.

Burchardus de Volder (1643–1709), also from Amsterdam, an ardent Cartesian of Mennonite background and another of Spinoza's friends, likewise studied at Leiden under Le Boë Sylvius, for three years until July 1664.[77] At that time the number of students studying in the arts and medical faculties was tiny by modern standards and, meeting constantly for lectures and discussions, all the students studying there at any given time undoubtedly knew each other quite well. It is therefore worth presenting a table with a list of those studying at Leiden who in one way or another played a part in Spinoza's life and legacy and whose names crop up also elsewhere in this volume (Table 12.1).

Steno before long came to reject his friend Spinoza's suppositions in every respect. What he later saw as the atheistic dimension of Spinoza's thought, and what he regarded as Spinoza's deliberate distortion of Descartes' system, should chiefly be attributed, he afterwards concluded, to two principal factors:

---

[75] Jorink, "Modus Politicus Vivendi," 36; Jorink, "Outside God," 105–6.
[76] Jorink, "Outside God," 94–5; Wielema, "Adriaan Koerbagh," 65.
[77] Klever, "Spinoza and Van den Enden," 313; Klever, *Mannen rond Spinoza*, 20; Jorink, "Modus Politicus Vivendi," 25; Strazzoni, *Burchard de Volder*, 18.

Table 12.1 Students and research assistants at Leiden whom Spinoza knew or who figured in his life-story

Student	Faculty	Years	Student	Faculty	Years
Abraham van Berkel	theology/medicine	1654–69	Adriaan Koerbagh	medicine/law	1656–62
Albert Burgh	?	1668–73	Johannes Koerbagh	theology	1656–62
Cornelis Bontekoe	medicine	1665–7	Lodewijk Meyer	phil./medicine	1654–60
Oleus Borch	medicine	1661–2	Bernard Nieuwentijt	medicine	1675
Johannes Bouwmeester	medicine	1651–8	Frederik Ruysch	medicine	1658–64
Johannes Casearius	phil./theology	1659–63	Georg Hermann Schuller	medicine	1671–2
Peter van Gent	theology/medicine	1663–9?	Nicolas Steno	medicine	1661–4
Arnold Geulincx	phil./medicine	1658–62	Jan Swammerdam	medicine	1661–3; 1666–7
Reynier de Graaf	medicine	1658–62	Solomon van Til	theology	1664–6
Johannes Hudde	law/maths	1654–63	Ehrenfried von Tschirnhaus	law	1668–72
Theodor Kerckring	medicine	1659–60?	Jacob Vallan	phil./medicine	1652–8
			Burchardus de Volder	medicine	1661–4

Sources: DDPhil; Jorink, "Modus Politicus Vivendi," 15, 20, 24–8; Mertens, "All in the Family," 53, 57–8; Mertens, "Where Thou Dwellest," 31–2; Van Ruler, "Spinoza in Leiden," 31, 35; Thijssen-Schoute, *Nederlands Cartesianisme*, 280–1, 359.

"interaction with a certain Van den Enden suspected of atheism" and his unfortunate enveloping himself excessively in the philosophy of Descartes. Van den Enden doubtless came up in Spinoza's discussions with Kerckring, as well as Steno at times. These two primary impulses in Spinoza's development in the early 1660s, Van den Enden and the Cartesian system, were also the factors, suggested Steno, when submitting information about Spinoza to the Roman Inquisition in 1671, that explain why Spinoza interrupted his earlier preoccupation with religious studies and critique of *Rabbinismo*, and wholeheartedly turned instead to natural philosophy, to following research into natural phenomena seeking to appraise the sphere of experiment and scientific observation.[78]

Steno being among Spinoza's principal associates of the early 1660s, his testimony is the earliest and clearest we possess pointing to Van den Enden's substantial role in his intellectual development as well as his life-transforming switch from primary concentration on religion and Bible criticism to science, the world of experiment, mathematics, and philosophy. Since Spinoza's embrace of science, and closely following empirical research in science, is so fundamental to his biography and undoubtedly preceded Spinoza's leaving Amsterdam and getting to know Steno, this vital shift must therefore also have been closely linked to his embrace of optics and skills in preparing lenses for microscopes and telescopes which he acquired, it would seem, immediately or very soon after his exit from the Sephardic community.

Subsequently, it figured among Steno's core tenets, he assured Rome's Inquisitors, in 1671, that experiments provide no answers to the principal questions that challenge us. His denunciation of false claims to scientific reliability, he clearly believed, applied to Spinoza every bit as much as Descartes and indeed every philosophical inquirer into truth attempting to separate science and philosophy from theology. Descartes and Spinoza both placed rational constructions over Christian commitment, seeking to tie reason to observation and empirical science.[79] Mixing with Leiden students in the early 1660s, Steno soon found himself uncomfortably associating also "with people of a very free understanding" who believed they were "completing" or 'perfecting" Descartes' philosophy.

12.iv Debating Cartesianism with the Leiden Cartesians

By 1667, after discarding the Lutheranism in which he had been raised, having converted to Catholicism, Steno came to view the study group around Spinoza as not just a dangerous clique of erring ex-Cartesians, but to envisage their philosophizing, researches, and inferences from scientific research as the very

---

[78] Steno, "Libri prohibiti," 33; Totaro, "The Young Spinoza and the Vatican Manuscript," 320.
[79] Steno, "Libri prohibiti," 34–5; Totaro, "Ho certi amici," 33, 36n6.

"Antichrist" itself. This still left open, though, the question whether Spinoza was merely revealing the true character of Cartesianism, whether "the principles of Spinoza are hidden in the Cartesian philosophy," as the Franeker philosophy professor Johannes Regius (1656–1738), an unbending Aristotelian *scholasticus* hostile to Cartesianism, later contended, or whether Spinoza and his following deviously twisted and reworked Cartesianism into a new system that was far more insidious.[80] Experience since the 1660s, Regius was convinced, proved "that all who openly became Spinozists, had first been Cartesians, as had Spinoza himself." Because "the Cartesians" remained a powerful presence in all the Dutch universities with a large stake in denying the truth of this while their conservative academic opponents had an equal stake in insisting that it was true, this unresolved clash of views over whether Spinozism does or does not directly emanate from Cartesianism dragged on interminably in the Republic from the early 1660s for over half a century.[81]

Pondering its enormous impact in the 1650s and 1660s in the northern Netherlands, and incipiently in France, Steno came to consider Cartesianism a major threat to Christianity as well as intellectual challenge given that Descartes' reputation and that of his followers stood so high in Holland and beyond. If Descartes had proceeded on false presuppositions, starting from a basis of doubting, "many people throw themselves into still more serious error rendering the whole of Christianity so powerless, assuming they do not reject it entirely, that hardly anything remains in them other than echo and empty shadows." In short, the circle of persons Steno knew in the early 1660s, in and around Leiden, seeking to reform Cartesianism—Spinoza, Meyer, and the Koerbaghs—with their quest for "the so-called completion of the Cartesian philosophy, but in reality its destruction," embraced a philosophy disastrously merging body and spirit together, a philosophy all-encompassing, monistic and materialistic, exalting empirical science which he now repudiated, as finally became obvious "in Spinoza and his followers. Forgetting their own hypotheses, they extolled the said method as a demonstration" and "with Descartes" refused to admit that they do not know how mind and body unite, and how movement relates to substance.[82] With their ruinous philosophical abstractions and hypotheses erasing divine reward and punishment in the hereafter, these impostors, Spinoza and his following, rendered "theology, the practical and the speculative, a mixture of a thousand absurdities." By allowing only one single substance, they turn God into an aggregate of all material things and thereby endow man with their despicable freedom and separation from theology and church discipline, encouraging

---

[80] Regius, *Beginselen der beschouwende filozofy*, voorrede.
[81] Regius, *Beginselen der beschouwende filozofy*, 92; Goudriaan, *Reformed Orthodoxy*, 2–25, 57–8n116.
[82] Scherz, "Biography of Nicolaus Steno," 94–5.

"enjoyment of all delights of sins as the use of praying as well as of punishments and reward after death are cancelled." Cartesianism produces Spinozism, and Spinozism stifles Christian faith encouraging resort to a life of pleasure in this world.[83]

Among those Steno later targeted in this way was Spinoza's lively, many faceted friend, Johannes Bouwmeester (1634–80), who had enrolled at Leiden much earlier than the others, in March 1651, and after more than six years there, graduated in medicine in May 1657, after which he travelled in southern France and Italy.[84] Already then Bouwmeester was familiar with his later close colleague, Meyer, and with Adriaan Koerbagh having family ties with the Brothers Koerbagh who were nephews of Jacob Vallan, an uncle of Bouwmeester by marriage. Later, after marrying Maria Oortmans, a daughter of Petronella de La Court, he also had ties to her cousins, the political theorists Johan and Pieter de La Court.[85] Unfortunately, relatively little is known about the friendship of Spinoza and Bouwmeester. Only one of Spinoza's surviving letters (Letter 37), printed in both the *Opera Posthuma* and the *Nagelate Schriften* as "B.d.S. to J.B." dating from June 1666 is definitely known to have been addressed to Bouwmeester while the other (Letter 28 of June 1665) usually assumed to be addressed to him in modern editions of Spinoza's correspondence, is an attribution resting on weak evidence. Still, a variety of sources proves for certain that the friendship between Spinoza and Bouwmeester mattered greatly, over many years, to them both. References in other correspondence, Van de Ven has shown, proves there once existed a series of other letters between Spinoza and Bouwmeester.[86]

Visiting Leiden University in the late 1650s and beginning of the 1660s, and dwelling in Rijnsburg in the years 1661–3, Spinoza acquired friends, an increasingly sophisticated command of Descartes' philosophy, and also valuable insight into the intricate play of philosophical, theological, and political factions in the university and among the students. Becoming familiar with the ceaseless tension between science research data and correctly drawing theoretical conclusions, he discovered that Descartes had faced increasing opposition to his mechanistic conception of the world during his last years in Holland, and that it was the Voetian strict Calvinist theologians who were concerting and orchestrating the gathering opposition to Cartesian ideas at Leiden as well as Utrecht and other universities. By the late 1650s every sign pointed to a tremendous conflict brewing in the universities, consistories, and cultural life more broadly over the innovating

---

[83] Scherz, "Biography of Nicolaus Steno," 95.
[84] Klever, "Hoe men wijs wordt," 341; Steenbakkers, *Spinoza's Ethica*, 16–17; Mertens, "All in the Family," 49.
[85] Meinsma, *Spinoza et son cercle*, 213n86; Mertens, "All in the Family," 49; Mertens, "Spinoza's Amsterdamse vriendenkring," 80n2.
[86] Steenbakkers, "Spinoza's Correspondentie," 13, 16; Van de Ven, *Printing Spinoza*, 62.

principles highlighted by leading Cartesians that were widely deemed to conflict with religious truth, theology, and piety.

When Descartes left Holland and migrated to Sweden, in August 1649, his life in the Netherlands was being rendered increasingly confrontational by Voetius and his allies. He gloomily predicted that the latter would eventually secure the general condemnation of his system by the university senates, mobilize opinion against him in the consistories, and, finally, with academic backing and that of the consistories, pressure the regents into muzzling him and suppressing his books.[87] In fact, the 1650s Cartesian controversy at Leiden developed into a complex stalemate with the city regents, and those of the States of Holland more generally, remaining divided and adopting an indecisive, ambiguous stance. There was simply no agreement as to whether teaching Cartesian philosophy was permissible or not. At the point Rembrandt painted his famous painting of Aristotle contemplating the bust of Homer (1653), Aristotle was assuredly no more than half-toppled.

The theological aspect of the struggle heavily influenced how the controversy affected the universities and was discussed in the local Reformed church councils. The wrangling spread to several nearby German universities, especially Herborn, where Spinoza's later German Calvinist friend Christopher Wittichius or Wittich (1625–87) taught in 1651–2, and Duisburg where he taught in 1652–5.[88] Wittichius became especially controversial while teaching at the "high school" at Nijmegen from 1655 to 1671. Due to his insisting on the inaccuracy of Scripture on astronomical matters, Wittichius came to be firmly associated by Cartesians and anti-Cartesians alike with the principle that Scripture offers not literal truth but truth adjusted to the uneducated understanding of ordinary folk.[89] This, the Cartesian claim that proved most divisive, also provided the chief link between Cartesianism and the Coccejan tendency in Dutch Reformed theology, namely the thesis that Scriptural accounts of natural events should be interpreted not literally but figuratively, and that when duly adjusted to allow for rhetorical usage, linguistic habits, and historical context, one discovers there is really no conflict between Scripture and Descartes' principles, even with respect to the Copernican thesis that the earth revolves around the sun which Cartesians embraced and religious conservatives such as the Voetians rejected and denounced. Those professors coming to the fore as promoters of Cartesianism in the 1650s, such as Wittichius and Abraham Heidanus (1597–1678), a close ally of Coccejus, also angered Calvinist hardliners by publicizing their Cartesian ideas in the vernacular. Coccejus, head of the pro-Cartesian faction among the theologians, openly began

---

[87] Descartes, *Correspondance* iv, 323–4; Israel, *Dutch Republic*, 587; Gaukroger, *Descartes*, 361, 386–7.
[88] Aalderink, "Christopher Wittich," 130.
[89] Du Bois, *Schadelickheyt*, 11–12, 15, 31; Van Bunge, *From Stevin to Spinoza*, 51–2; Vermij, *Calvinist Copernicans*, 252–9.

espousing Cartesianism in the 1650s and claiming Scripture passages that Voetians deemed incompatible with Cartesianism should not be read literally. Although the Cartesians had some allies in town governments, like Hudde and the Utrecht regent, Lambert van Velthuysen (1622–85), by the mid-1650s they began to feel seriously threatened by the mounting reaction in the Reformed consistories.

Van Velthuysen, for his part, caused widespread offence with a pamphlet entitled "Proof that neither the doctrine of the sun standing still and the earth moving round it, nor the principles of the philosophy of Renatus Descartes, are in conflict with God's Word" (1655), reissued under a slightly altered title in 1656, an open challenge to Voetians, directed especially against a conservative Leiden Reformed minister, Jacob Du Bois (d. 1661) with an interest in astronomical topics. Aggrieved by Van Velthuysen's strictures at his expense and shocked that "nearly all the students who study philosophy at Leiden are Cartesians," and that Cartesianism was rapidly infiltrating at Utrecht and Groningen as well, Du Bois accused Van Velthuysen of not being satisfied with spreading Cartesianism among the students in Latin but of also being "the first attempting also to render the common man Cartesian."[90]

Anxious to prevent the conflict deepening further as it spread beyond the universities spilling over also into Friesland and Groningen, De Witt, in 1656, we have seen, persuaded the Leiden curators to agree to the negotiated compromise cemented by an edict of the States of October 1656. Under that decree and a further arrangement in 1658, philosophy became academically more clearly separated and autonomous from theology, supposedly leaving freedom to philosophize guaranteed, but in exchange, left all interpretation of Scripture and discussion of theological issues out of bounds to philosophers, a sphere reserved for theologians alone where the public Church's views presided uncontested and unchallenged.[91] But the compromise proved unsustainable. The truce lasted down to Spinoza's Rijnsburg years but remained always vulnerable, tense, and precarious.

[90] Du Bois, *Schadelickheyt*, 3; Goudriaan, *Reformed Orthodoxy*, 129–30.
[91] Israel, *Dutch Republic*, 894–5.

13

Spinoza and the Scientific Revolution

13.i Challenging Bacon and Boyle

The chief line of inquiry for the young philosopher Spinoza in the late 1650s and still on arriving in Rijnsburg, in 1661, was grappling with the principles and implications of Descartes' system. This meant thinking also a good deal about the scientific and medical issues of the day, direct engagement with scientific activity and challenges that would remain an integral part of Spinoza's efforts right through the 1660s though this aspect tended to wane after 1670 and his book collection, as it stood at the end of his life, strongly suggests that involvement with science never quite rivalled his involvement with Bible studies as an intellectual passion.[1] Throughout the 1660s, Spinoza remained uninterruptedly a close observer of the science scene and participant in science experiments so that Jelles, one of those encouraging him to experiment, certainly included science experiments when remarking in his preface [Voorreden] to the *Opera Posthuma*, that Spinoza "spent most of his time researching into the nature of things, and in placing what he discovered in order, so as to be able to share it with others, and spent very little time in relaxing or refreshing the spirit."[2] Such discussion and "research into the nature of things" clearly entailed both experimenting himself and vesting much time in following the experimental work of leading experts in a variety of fields.

As part of his effort to reform the Cartesian philosophy in all respects, he immersed himself in mathematics and astronomy and, through his friendships with Steno, Kerckring, Hudde and others especially kept himself abreast of the latest research in optics, anatomy, and human and animal dissection. In his opening missive to Spinoza, dated 26 August 1661, Oldenburg asks his "Cartesian" friend to go deeper and in more detail into two main points discussed during their lengthy meeting: first, how exactly does Spinoza establish a "true distinction between Extension and Thought"; and, second, "what defects do you detect in the philosophy of Descartes and Bacon, and how in your view can these be removed and replaced by more solid views."[3] The wording here perfectly illustrates Oldenburg's courteous style of offering respect and coaxing out further

---

[1] Gabbey, "Spinoza's Natural Science," 149; Gabbey, "Spinoza on Natural Science" (2022), 193.
[2] Jelles, "Voorreden," 2; Gabbey, "Spinoza on Natural Science" (2022), 194–5.
[3] Oldenburg to Spinoza, London, 16/26 Aug. 1661 in Spinoza, *Collected Works* (ed. Curley) i, 163–4; Spinoza, *Opera* iv, 7; Spinoza, *Correspondance* (ed. Rovere), 47–8.

information and expression of views, encouraging correspondents to feel part of what to him, as to Thévenot, was a multi-sided collective international scientific-religious-philosophical dialogue. The philosophy of Francis Bacon (1561–1626), a much-admired figure at the time, nephew of Queen Elizabeth's chief minister, Burghley, and someone who himself became Lord Chancellor of England, in 1618, was a significant but controversial force also in Dutch philosophical circles, as Oldenburg was aware, albeit to a lesser degree than in England. Among leading Leiden professors, Adriaan Heereboord (1614–61), entangled in battles over Cartesianism in the 1640s and 1650s, had especially urged students to read Bacon, recommending his system as of enduring relevance, second only to that of Descartes.[4] Boyle's *Certain Physiological Essays* (1661) were now in the press and Oldenburg closes by promising to send Spinoza a copy of the Latin version via an intermediary as soon as it was available. (The Latin version was delayed, however, until 1665.)

Replying in September 1661, Spinoza assures Oldenburg, in his earliest surviving letter, of the pleasure their friendship and unfolding debate, including about Bacon, gave him "albeit I do not think this will be a means of binding you closer to me unless I have your kind indulgence." He fully realized the wide gap between his and Oldenburg's assessments of Bacon's relevance as well as between his and Oldenburg's respective religious views.[5] His own premises about God conceived as First Cause, and substance, he explains, differed substantially from those of Descartes, but also from Bacon's, both of whom, as regards philosophy and religion, in his view, "had gone far astray from true knowledge." This must have astounded, even shocked, Oldenburg. After briefly outlining his definitions of God, extension and motion and why he thought there can be only one substance encompassing the totality of everything, Spinoza reluctantly passed on to what he considered Descartes' and Bacon's shortcomings but only to oblige Oldenburg, he remarked, since "it is not my custom to expose the errors of others."[6]

Someone with Spinoza's eagerness to keep up-to-date with recent science might well have been expected to scorn Bacon's geocentrism, rejection of Copernicus and heliocentrism,[7] and suspensive eclecticism, or persistent disinclination to choose between alternative and rival explanatory models.[8] Still, one wonders if Spinoza fully grasped how far Bacon was lionized by members of the London Royal Society as their founding father and chief inspiration, second in importance only to England's monarch himself. In Wenceslaus Hollar's engraving of a design

---

[4] Thijssen-Schoute, *Nederlands Cartesianisme*, 98; Otterspeer, *Groepsportret* [...] *de Leidse Universiteit, 1673–1775*, 393; Gaukroger, *Descartes*, 466n13.

[5] Spinoza, *Collected Works* (ed. Curley) i, 167.

[6] Spinoza, *Collected Works* (ed. Curley) i, 167; Rothkamm, *Institutio Oratoria*, 372.

[7] Gaukroger, *Francis Bacon*, 17, 26; Jorink, *Boeck der natuere*, 312; Wootton, *Invention of Science*, 83–5, 107.

[8] Gaukroger, *Francis Bacon*, 28.

by John Evelyn used by its first historian, Thomas Sprat, as the frontispiece to the Royal Society's first official history, published in 1667, Bacon is represented in the foreground flanking King Charles on one side with the society's first president, Brouncker, on the other.[9] In recent philosophy and science no one stood as high in prestige.

Someone of Spinoza's temperament was in any case unlikely to feel drawn to Bacon's view of knowledge, experimentation, and fact-gathering as a quest for power and dominion over the world, or elitist view of science as a carefully organized and regulated pursuit best conducted under the supervision of rulers and courtiers. Spinoza's epistemology from its beginnings in the treatise on the *Emendation of the Understanding* to its fullest exposition in the *Ethics* does indeed envisage knowledge acquisition as a means to empowerment but less over nature than over our own thoughts, relationship to nature, and state of mind. In principle, Spinoza's empowerment through gaining knowledge is essential to the happiness of everyone but deferential towards nature.[10] For Bacon, who lived in great style at his country retreat near St Albans, receiving many high-born visitors, the details and findings of scientific research were less a topic for general reasoning and discussion than an elevated, exclusive sphere, shrouded in secrecy, a special preserve of court and aristocracy,[11] where knowledge progresses less from "arcane learning to public knowledge," as some scholars claim, than from the private arcane to a shared collective aristocratic sphere of carefully guarded group arcana lodged at the heart of statecraft.[12] For someone of Spinoza's temperament this represented both a limitation on individual freedom to think and experiment and on the public need for access to knowledge.

The more specific critique of Bacon which Spinoza offered Oldenburg related mainly to Bacon's epistemology. Descartes and Bacon he brackets together as regards what he termed "their third error," the unfortunate fact, after confusing First Cause and substance, that "they have never grasped the true cause of error." Spinoza agreed with Descartes, Bacon, and Boyle that thus far in history human reason and science had proved astoundingly error-prone and doubtless sympathized with Bacon's innovative stress on error as being as much the result of internal wrong inference from facts as seizing on incorrect perceptions. But he did not agree with Bacon and Boyle that any of this was due to "the Fall," or that the true exit from human error is by adhering to carefully recorded experimental observations reached under strict conditions while keeping these findings separate from wider reasoning, firmly segregated from what Oldenburg's colleague, Robert Hooke, first curator of experiments at the Royal Society, called the "dangers in the

---

[9] Shapin and Schaffer, *Leviathan and the Air-Pump*, 33; Gaukroger, *Francis Bacon*, 2.
[10] Renz, "Spinoza's Epistemology," 146.
[11] Aubrey, *Brief Lives*, 36; Jütte, *Age of Secrecy*, 240; Malcolm, *Aspects of Hobbes*, 319–20; Harrison, *Territories of Science and Religion*, 138–9.
[12] Gaukroger, *Francis Bacon*, 6–9.

process of human reason."[13] How can one observe and collect facts prior to evaluating those data, if like Joshua watching the sun stand still, one lacks all critical awareness of one's own prior assumptions when gathering them? How can a strictly cause and effect-based outlook on the world arise from simply conducting experiments? Oldenburg must have been taken aback by Spinoza's full-frontal dismissal of Descartes and Bacon together on all basic premises concerning God, cause, and substance. Spinoza's almost contemptuous evaluation of Bacon meant spurning, apart from its fact-gathering and zeal for experiments, the entire methodological and ideological basis of England's Royal Society. No wonder, when afterwards reporting his exchanges with Spinoza to Boyle, Oldenburg characterized him as a bizarre and eccentric being.[14]

Despite beginning by saying he would not expand on Bacon's epistemological errors since "he speaks very confusedly on this subject, and simply makes assertions while proving hardly anything," Spinoza launched into a scathing critique. Oldenburg's jaw must have dropped at Spinoza's objecting to Bacon's discussion of intellect and error, presumably referring to his *Novum Organon* (1620): "in the first place, [Bacon] takes for granted that the human intellect, quite apart from the fallibility of the senses, is by its very nature liable to error, and configures everything after its own nature rather than after the analogy of our universe, so that it is like a mirror presenting an irregular surface to the rays it receives, mixing its own nature with the nature of real things, and so forth." Spinoza rounds here on a key feature of Bacon, his belief that the human intellect, aside from fallacies to which our senses are prone to lead us, errs inevitably by its essential nature as well as our upbringing and education, so that it cannot reflect accurately by reasoning but "imagines" everything it encounters according to its own nature: "omnique fingit ex anologia suae naturae."[15]

The origins of human error, held Bacon, Boyle, and Hooke, lie not just in the complexity of what lies outside our minds but in our very thought processes, reasoning itself, having deep roots in human nature and our innate inclinations and backgrounds so that amending our misconceptions is not simply a question of locating mistakes in our reasoning, as in Descartes or Spinoza, but of recognizing and limiting the consequences of the inherent error proneness of human reason itself. On these grounds, the new culture of experimental science Bacon founded and inspired demanded purging the mind of its prior assumptions and suppositions, and exclusive reliance on observed and recorded objective tests that do not assume greater regularity and uniformity in nature than is demonstrated and do

---

[13] Harrison, *Territories of Science and Religion*, 88; Aalderink, *Philosophy, Scientific Knowledge*, 22.
[14] Spinoza, *Collected Works* (ed. Curley) i, 167; Brenner-Golomb, *Importance of Spinoza*, 77–8, 110–11; Gullan-Whur, *Life of Spinoza*, 115–16.
[15] Spinoza, *Collected Works* (ed. Curley) i, 167–8; Spinoza, *Briefwisseling*, 75–6; Mignini, "Fictio/ Verziering," 48–9.

not rely to any meaningful extent on intellect.[16] This was where Bacon's, Boyle's, and Hooke's emphatic, uncompromising (but narrow) empiricism held sway, prioritizing observation of facts and making these the primary tool for reaching conclusions about nature while restricting inference to a minimum and reason to a subsidiary role.[17]

Spinoza had no objection to Bacon's rule that natural history should be the basis of philosophy but rightly perceived that, for Bacon, the human intellect distils and abstracts, following its own vagaries in a way that distorts the reality of nature. What he rejects is Bacon's "crooked mirror" interposing what, to him, was an unacceptably wide wedge between experimental science and rational philosophizing. Spinoza would never accept that rigorous, mathematically precise reasoning based on correct premises or findings can lead to wrong conclusions whereas for Bacon mathematics is not a reflection of nature's operations, or key to unlocking nature's laws and secrets. Its usefulness for science in Bacon's system remained in fact extremely limited. Oldenburg for his part remained solidly Baconian, as he showed with his second letter to Spinoza, of September 1661, insisting that "our conceptions of the mind" are highly uncertain since "our mind conceives many things that do not exist and is most prolific in multiplying and augmenting things once conceived" with the consequence that it is hard to see how one can infer the existence of God just from a conception that we have of Him. Against this, Spinoza insists the human mind and will are determinate parts of a being that is itself part of nature, or in union with nature, maintaining that both our adequate and inadequate ideas hence inescapably follow the same unalterable laws as the rest of reality, so that men can in fact learn to sift adequate ideas reflecting reality accurately from inadequate ideas that also reflect reality but inaccurately, albeit, he explains in his *Emendation*, exclusively where one learns how to strictly infer one true idea from another, conquering prejudices and the effects of the imagination driving inadequate thinking by developing one's capacity for making accurate distinctions based on true ideas. Our immense range of inadequate ideas that need casting aside are of three types, the false, fictional, and doubtful, but all are rooted in the human imagination and hence are in union with nature.[18]

The clash with Bacon was less a question of empiricism versus rationalism than of two different and rival kinds of empiricism, one standing alone so to speak, the other tightly bracketed with mathematical reason, Spinoza's being more tied to prior conclusions, hypotheses, and subsequent inference than Bacon's. An obvious strength of Spinoza's text criticism and critical theory, for example, is precisely its unparalleled rigorous empiricism. But by no means should one

---

[16] Gaukroger, *Francis Bacon*, 25–27; Aalderink, *Philosophy, Scientific Knowledge*, 22, 25–6.
[17] Brenner-Golomb, *Importance of Spinoza*, 76–8; Gaukroger, *Failures of Philosophy*, 136.
[18] Spinoza, *Collected Works* (ed. Curley) i, 21; Sangiacomo, *Spinoza on Reason*, 15, 23, 32, 47–9.

suppose from this that it was basically a "bottoms-up, inductive approach – more British-looking than Continental," or maintain that "Spinoza wants to start not with general presuppositions, whether theological or philosophical dogma, but with particulars and facts – with history – and then work his way up to broader generalizations," and then contrast Spinoza's approach with that of the Cartesians, including Lodewijk Meyer, aligning it with that of the "other great propagator of a new philosophy and patron of the new sciences, Sir Francis Bacon, whose works Spinoza knew in detail."[19] Rather, Spinoza systematically opposed the Baconian conception of empiricism, using arguments that would form the basis of his critique of Boyle. Had Spinoza really been an admirer of Bacon and Royal Society methods, and had his approach to hermeneutics really resembled the "contours of Bacon's thought," the result would certainly have been refusal to envisage history as an exclusively natural process in favour of a largely literalist approach to the Scriptures such as Bacon, Boyle, and their followers, Oldenburg among them, actually adhered to. In Bacon's discussion of Bible hermeneutics, in his *De Augmentis Scientiarum*, the Bible is the one text that should never be approached in a purely naturalistic fashion, as if just any human text. "Divine inspiration" is indispensable for interpreting Scripture, held Bacon, who for this reason made no effort to develop a naturalistic explanation of religion. Furthermore, for Bacon, wherever doubts arise as to how to understand a particular Bible passage, the public church must be final arbiter, a principle entirely alien to Spinoza.

Rejecting Bacon's notion of scientific procedure that one should gather the data and examine the facts free from prior philosophical assumptions about the workings of reality, Spinoza insists rather on an empiricism gathering data and the facts as comprehensively as possible within the frame of a presiding metaphysical system, unfolding and not yet fully worked out but grounded on the principle that one cannot accurately observe and interpret discoveries without a system of natural cause and effect in mind.

Thus, far from refusing to start "with general presuppositions" in the manner of Baconians, Spinoza's empiricism and text criticism is always firmly anchored in his metaphysics where his distinctive approaches to history and natural history merge, a reality shaped exclusively by natural forces without the intervention of any supernatural agency, a framework well beyond the scope of empirical demonstration. Thus, his philosophical system and strictly empirical text criticism and science remain inseparable, rooted in one-substance doctrine, conflating body and soul and eliminating the supernatural, so that unlike Bacon, Boyle, and the Royal Society's devotees, Spinoza pushed scientific thinking to levels and across boundaries where Lockean empiricism could not follow. Within Spinoza's framework,

---

[19] Preus, *Spinoza*, 161–4; Verbeek, *Spinoza's Theologico-Political Treatise*, 101; Van Cauter, "Spinoza on History," 14–15, 45, 48.

all parts and particular things pertaining to reality whether physical or mental are reduced to the level of the empirical, the world of the spirit and belief no less than physical objects whereas for Bacon, Boyle, Locke, and Newton much of reality is correctly interpreted only via prior presumption of Christian truth, supernatural agency, and "the Fall," and hence much of their reality remained "above reason" and beyond experiment, science, and the empirical.

Boyle, whose Bible criticism powerfully influenced the shaping of Locke's own biblical hermeneutics and "above reason" doctrine, stood much closer here to Bacon than did Spinoza.[20] Excluding all prior assumption of supernatural agency was not only Spinoza's greatest innovation and strength as a text critic, and social and text theorist, but also the chief feature of his general system and approach to experiment and the one that most clearly set him apart from (and against) the predominant tendency, the Baconian and then Lockean-Newtonian tradition, in British thought. Whatever the virtues of Bacon's empiricism, Spinoza was certainly right to think Baconian methodology is open to challenge by its failure to tie science together with general philosophy in the traditional sense—man's search for happiness, the best way to live, and the best way to understand reality overall.[21]

Observation of itself is of little use, contends Spinoza, rejecting Bacon's (and Oldenburg's) narrower empiricism and their separation of science from philosophy (and theology) without an exacting, rigorously correct reasoning deriving inferences from it. To this extent, and in his suspicion of pure experiment without any philosophical principles underpinning it, Spinoza was far more Cartesian than Baconian.[22] But, for Spinoza, both Descartes and Bacon err in defending "freedom of the will" and, as a result, compound human error by positing supposedly free volitions. To Spinoza, this meant embracing nonsense not just about human motivation and conduct but also about inference and deduction. Both Descartes and Bacon, held Spinoza, land themselves in insoluble difficulties concerning the will, by making this a mental construct wholly detached from any unified human body-mind entity, an approach that can only produce endless muddle.

13.ii Spinoza and Experimental Science

Spinoza's emphasis on the unity of experimental research in science with general philosophy has led to a degree of confusion regarding his approach to close observation, data collection, and mathematical measurement in modern science that needs clearing up, and there is no better way to explain and illustrate his stance than by considering his view of Boyle's efforts which Oldenburg

---

[20] Lupoli, "Boyle's Influence," 38–42; Russo, "Thread of Discourse," 137.
[21] Gaukroger, *Failures of Philosophy*, 14; Harrison, *Territories of Science and Religion*, 88–91.
[22] Van Ruler, *Crisis of Causality*, 226–34; Brenner-Golomb, *Importance of Spinoza*, 77.

repeatedly encouraged Spinoza to re-examine, evaluate, and comment on but whose judgements he then found deeply puzzling.

The son of an Anglo-Irish aristocrat, Robert Boyle (1627–91), the first Earl of Cork, highly conscious of his social standing, is described by his biographer, John Aubrey, as "very tall (about six foot high) and straight, very temperate and virtuous and frugal," despite being a bachelor enjoying a huge annual income deriving mostly from estates in Ireland (Figure 13.1). Eschewing sensual pleasures and all luxury (not unlike Spinoza), he was converted to "experimental" science as a young adult in the late 1640s and established his first laboratory on an estate he inherited in Dorset. A nobleman of unusually stern moral and religious conviction, speaking Latin with exceptional fluency, the moral and religious implications of scientific endeavour were for Boyle a matter of immense urgency. While embarking on his career in scientific experiment which he believed useful not just as a study in itself but, in Baconian fashion, generally for influencing the affairs of this world, including medicine, and for better religious insight, he intensified his life-long engagement (like Thévenot) with studying classical languages, Hebrew, Syriac, and Arabic. He strove to digest the results of the best and

Figure 13.1 *Robert Boyle* (1627–91) by Johann Kerseboom, oil on canvas. The Royal Society.

most up-to-date endeavour in the study of ancient religions as well as Bible criticism. Using his fortune to pursue his scientific-religious goals, "at his own cost and charges," as Aubrey expresses it, "he got translated and printed the New Testament in Arabic, to send into the Mahometan countries."[23]

In his late twenties, in around 1655, this truly outstanding scientist and scholar moved to Oxford soon becoming the prime rising star among the Oxford group of natural philosophers around Robert Hooke and Christopher Wren (1632–1723), a circle serving as the forerunner of the Royal Society. Oxford henceforth remained his base, but during the early 1660s, from its inaugural meeting, on 28 November 1660, he regularly attended Royal Society meetings in London, relying on his indefatigable protégé, Oldenburg, as his permanent London scientific agent, record-keeper, correspondent, and newsgatherer from the Continent. In Britain and Europe more generally, no one better epitomized the new Baconian cult of careful, cumulative empirical research, precise measurement and group witnessing of results, as the pillar of the new "natural philosophy" and for defining its relation to Bible studies and revealed religion. It was obvious from the start that Spinoza was not the kind of thinker or commentator on science the pious and aristocratic Boyle would wish to develop any serious interaction with.

In his second letter to Spinoza, Oldenburg raises the question of the validity of our conception of God's existence, asking how Spinoza could possibly be "certain that body is not limited by thought, nor thought by body? For it is still a matter of controversy as to what thought is, whether it is a corporeal motion or a spiritual activity quite distinct from what is corporeal." Oldenburg could not see how the second axiom Spinoza expounds in his letter "that there exists in nature nothing but substance and accidents" could be considered convincing since time and place, according to most thinkers, belonged to neither category. As for Spinoza's third axiom that "things having different attributes have nothing in common," this was so far from evident to Oldenburg that "the entire universe seems rather to prove the contrary. All things known to us both differ from one another in some respects and agree in other respects." Finally, Oldenburg discerned nothing but difficulty in Spinoza's fourth axiom, that "things which have nothing in common with one another cannot be the cause one of the other."

Politely apologizing for his "befogged intellect," Oldenburg pointed out that God has nothing formally in common with created things; "yet we almost all hold him to be their cause." In fact, Oldenburg confesses to being "overwhelmed with doubt" about the entire sequence of Spinoza's propositions, and beseeches Spinoza "by the friendship on which we have embarked, to deal with me frankly and confidently." He closes by summarizing once again the basic Baconian principles of his, Boyle's, and their Society's "mechanical philosophy." "In our

---

[23] Aubrey, *Brief Lives*, 54–5; Wootton, *Invention of Science*, 460.

Philosophical Society," he reminds Spinoza, "we are engaged in making experiments and observations as energetically as our abilities allow" while composing a detailed record of these scientific efforts, "convinced that the forms and qualities of things can best be explained by the principles of mechanics, that all nature's effects are produced by motion, figure, texture, and their various combinations, and that there is no need to have recourse to inexplicable forms and occult qualities, the refuge of ignorance [to explain them]."[24] Both sides in this encounter rejected scholasticism and the legacy of the past. The difficulty was that neither Oldenburg nor Boyle took the view, as Spinoza clearly did, that since all the processes of bodies, including our own bodies, result exclusively from the fixed laws of motion and rest, so the perceptions of the mind or soul are likewise equally rooted in the actions, that is motion and rest, of bodies and the universe.[25]

Boyle felt a life-long powerful antipathy to all Epicurean and Hobbesian materialist and atheistic trends, albeit when assailing those he rejects in print he nearly always avoided specifying which adversaries he is targeting.[26] Although it emerges from Oldenburg's correspondence that Boyle periodically discussed Spinoza's comments on his work with him, Boyle never mentions Spinoza in his surviving letters and writings, despite receiving, over the years, numerous reports about him from others besides Oldenburg. Every past resurgence of what he regarded as essentially a form of ancient pagan Greek philosophy, Boyle judged a looming menace to society, morality, and the Christian faith. "Even in these times," deplores Boyle, in *A Free Enquiry into the Vulgarly received Notion of Nature* (1686), a book written partly in the 1660s but only completed in the mid-1680s, with a preface written nearly five years after Spinoza's death, in what is almost certainly an allusion to the rise of the Spinozist sect in Holland, "there is lately sprung up a sect of men, as well professing Christianity as pretending to philosophy, who (if I be not misinformed of their doctrine), do very much symbolize with the ancient heathens, and talk much indeed of God, but mean such a one as is not really distinct from the animated and intelligent universe, but is on that account very differing from the true God that we Christians believe and worship. And though I find the leaders of this sect to be looked upon by some more witty than knowing men as the discoverers of unheard-of mysteries in physics and natural theology, yet their hypothesis does not at all appear to me to be new." The wording of the last sentence confirms that he is not referring to the surge of neo-Epicureanism of the kind precious to the likes of the freethinking diplomat William Temple, a current that generally showed little interest in the new science. Whether this is an allusion to Spinoza and his circle or not, we may be sure Boyle viewed Spinoza and every aspect of his philosophy with unremitting distaste while not directly saying so in print.

---

[24] Spinoza, *Collected Works* (ed. Curley) i, 169–70.   [25] Spinoza, *Short Treatise*, 133–4.
[26] Davis and Hunter, 'Introduction' to Boyle, *A Free Enquiry*, p. xvi.

Answering Oldenburg's second letter, in late September or October 1661, with a hint of impatience, Spinoza apologizes for keeping his missive to a minimum "for want of time." He was preparing "to go to Amsterdam," he explains, to spend a week or two there. "From a philosopher," he answers somewhat testily, "one may expect that he knows the difference between fiction and a clear and distinct conception, and knows also the validity of this axiom, that every [adequate] definition, or clear and distinct idea, is true."[27] Nothing could be more un-Baconian. The effect was again to highlight the deep divide separating the Baconian from the Cartesian approach. Spinoza concludes by reminding Oldenburg that contrary to his view that "God has nothing formally in common with created things," he maintains "the exact opposite," namely that God is not outside or distinguishable from the reality of all that is. To this, Oldenburg replied promptly, though also briefly, from London, on 21 October 1661, enclosing a copy of the Latin version of Boyle's *Certain Physiological Essays*, as previously promised, and asking Spinoza to let him know, in due course, his judgement of Boyle's efforts. As regards Spinoza's clarification of his own views, Oldenburg thanked him for throwing additional light on their discussion but confesses that he has not yet managed "to dispel all the darkness which I believe will happily occur when you will distinctly and clearly explain your views on the true and primary origin of things. For as long as it is not clear to me by what cause and in what way things began to be, and by what connection they depend on the first cause, if there is such a thing, then everything that I hear and I read seems to fall apart."[28]

Oldenburg's request that Spinoza comment on Boyle's treatise on niter (or nitre, the mineral form of potassium nitrate) started an exchange about this compound and its composition that lasted nearly two years. When Spinoza replied, more than two months later, probably in December 1661 or at the start of 1662—and certainly not as late as April 1662, as stated in most editions of Spinoza's *Letters*[29]—he devotes the bulk of his long missive to discussing Boyle's experiments, assigning only a few sparse lines to answering Oldenburg's plea for further light on "how things began to be, and by what connection they depend on the first cause."[30] With evident unease and impatience, Spinoza professes to be unable to "see that I have omitted anything." It was in this letter that he informs Oldenburg of his *Korte Verhandeling* and candidly describes the gravity of the worrying personal predicament in which his views on God and Nature had landed him in the Dutch Republic. Evasive on the wider issue, Spinoza displays a keen, detailed interest in Boyle's experiments. While sympathetic to Boyle's eagerness to demonstrate the mechanistic character of chemical processes, and demolish

---

[27] Spinoza, *Briefwisseling*, 81; Spinoza, *Correspondance* (ed. Rovere), 57.
[28] Spinoza, *Opera* iv, 15; Spinoza, *Collected Works* (ed. Curley) i, 172.
[29] Spinoza, *Correspondance* (ed. Rovere), 76; the wrong dating is found in Spinoza, *Collected Works* (ed. Curley) i, 188; Spinoza, *Briefwisseling*, 101.
[30] Spinoza, *Collected Works* (ed. Curley) i, 188.

Aristotelian qualities along with some (though for Boyle not all) traditions of alchemy with their occult qualities, such experiments, he insists, must be rigorously scrutinized and checked. Overall, he comes across as remarkably sceptical about many of Boyle's specific findings.

Spinoza felt perfectly competent to subject Boyle's observations in chemistry to experimental checks and questioning himself, employing his own very modest resources. This letter which ends with the earliest surviving example of Spinoza's original signature appended to a Latin text, signed "Benedictus Spinoza," includes a lengthy discourse on Boyle's experiments with saltpetre, the colourless to white mineral crystals found in encrustations in caves and desert regions, a mineral readily soluble and available in quantity at the time throughout Europe and the Ottoman Empire and of great political and strategic importance, being the essential raw material used in manufacturing gunpowder. His detailed analysis shows Spinoza had not only witnessed experiments in Amsterdam and Leiden but was practised in and equipped for performing small scientific experiments himself. The saltpetre trade, it is worth noting, formed a mainstay of the Dutch commerce with Saleh, a major strand of his father's business activity, and Jews had long been regarded as specialists in boiling and preparing saltpetre for the armies and fleets of the Mediterranean world, especially in the Ottoman sultan's domains.[31]

By examining the constituent parts of saltpetre and then reconstituting saltpetre after having separated its constituent parts, Boyle believed he had proved saltpetre "is a heterogeneous thing, consisting of motionless and volatile parts," as Spinoza expressed it, its behaviour showing its nature as a compound "is quite different from the nature of its component parts, although it arises from nothing other than a mixture of those parts." Unpersuaded by this conclusion, Spinoza suggests a further experiment to put the matter to the test—an experiment that would demonstrate whether or not liquefied nitrate essence of saltpetre lacks the properties of the compound saltpetre and cannot be crystallized without the help of the salts [potassium carbonate] that constitute the saltpetre compound. Boyle's conclusions looked to Spinoza insufficiently mathematical, quantitative, and anchored in motion and rest. Boyle weighed and measured; but what he had observed leading to his view that nitre's essence is entirely different in behaviour from saltpetre, due to the transformative qualities of the compound, in Spinoza's view "does nothing to confirm his conclusion." At the very least one must check whether the quantity of salts remaining in the crucible after burning off the nitre essence is always "constant from the same quantity of saltpetre, and varies in proportion to the quantity of saltpetre"; for without this quantitative check Boyle cannot prove nitre essence possesses fundamentally different properties, indeed

---

[31] Jütte, *Age of Secrecy*, 987–8.

almost opposite qualities, to the saltpetre compound. The explosive motion of the particles of saltpetre, holds Spinoza, is actually present in the essence of nitre too but there is defused and deadened in varying degrees according to the amount and type of salts present in the essence.[32] Spinoza remained firmly opposed to Boyle's idea that chemical admixtures as such, rather than different circumstances of heat and cold and the effect of blocking agents, cause chemicals to change their fundamental nature. Many particles of the spirit of nitre, argues Spinoza against Boyle's conclusion, if they do not disappear in smoke when extracted, are blocked by inert agents, forced to "lose the motion they possessed, and stop in their course, in the same way as a cannonball when it hits sand or mud."[33]

To disprove Boyle's thesis that it was effectively the chemical mix, the compound character of the saltpetre, a combining of static and moving particles, that creates the highly volatile mix constituting saltpetre, Spinoza repeatedly melted some saltpetre in a crucible until the latter became white-hot and then lighted it with a live coal, collecting the resulting smoke in a cold glass flask until the flask became moistened within, and then moistened it more by breathing on it, and finally by putting it outside the house to dry in the cold air of the garden behind his Rijnsburg lodgings. The result was that small but unmistakable saltpetre icicles appeared "here and there in the flask," proving the spirit of nitre's volatility and disproving Boyle's thesis, or so Spinoza believed. Since the experiment's heating procedure was apparently conducted inside, one wonders whether Spinoza's landlord was at all aware of experimental activities in his house involving heating items up to dangerously white-hot temperatures prior to carrying the results into the garden. One wonders too whether he performed these experiments entirely on his own or with others present, and whether anyone ever complained about the fire risk.

To prove the particles revealed by his experiment and collected in the flask were not particles of the compound, as Boyle maintained, but of concentrated pure nitrate without any salts, Spinoza next performed a second experiment causing the smoke to rise through a tube over a foot long "as though through a chimney, so that the heavier particles adhered to the tube, and I collected only the more volatile particles as they passed through the narrower aperture" at the top. Thereupon, exactly the same separation and forming of pure nitrate icicles occurred as before. Spinoza then performed a third experiment with his crucibles and tubes from which he concluded that the stable parts of saltpetre automatically separate from the volatile when melting, and that it is the flame that drives them upwards separately from one another. With this, he claimed to have proved that when the fixed parts are separated by a crackling noise, the particles adhering to the flask

---

[32] Spinoza, *Briefwisseling*, 85–6; Spinoza, *Collected Works* (ed. Curley) i, 173–6; Moreau, *Spinoza, L'expérience*, 269–76.
[33] Spinoza, *Opera* iv, 19; Spinoza, *Collected Works* (ed. Curley) i, 175; Duffy, "The Difference," 128.

and coalescing into small icicles consist only of the volatile particles, and that these consist of pure nitre. Here, therefore, was the inherently volatile component of saltpetre, a finding entirely contrary to Boyle's.

Spinoza performed also a further experiment, using lighted coals, a damp paper bag, and sand, to demonstrate that under some conditions nitrate particles become inflammable and under others resistant to burning so that, once again, he had "proved" that it is not at all, as Boyle incorrectly deduced, the compound that creates the explosive mix. "If I had time for further experimentation," he stated abruptly, after describing this experiment, "I might have added other demonstrations which would perhaps make the matter entirely clear. But as I am very much occupied with other matters, you will forgive me if I put this off for some other time and proceed to other comments."[34] At this point, during 1662, Spinoza had left aside both the *Korte Verhandeling* and his unfinished earlier text, *On the Emendation of the Intellect*.[35] Now a mature, confident philosopher, Spinoza was deep into setting out the early parts of what would later be his *Ethics*, the sections on God and the world, the ideas that so baffled Oldenburg. Yet, science experiments were and would continue to be an integral part of the ambitious schema he was developing.

Boyle deflected Spinoza's criticism, rather dismissively, by pointing out that the conditions required for formal experiments of the kind he was engaged in, in a proper laboratory, are both rigorous and exclusive, something specialized and altogether aloof from what one finds in everyday situations.[36] Spinoza, though, did not desist from his sceptical evaluation of Boyle's results, despite the latter's obvious displeasure, judging them questionable, insufficiently mathematical and quantitative, and too apt to separate chemical reactions from the normal motions of physics. Spinoza was broadly disinclined to accept that chemical admixtures intrinsically, rather than under different circumstances of heat and cold and attended by different effects of blocking agents of varying composition, do actually cause chemicals to change their fundamental nature and behaviour. Opposing Boyle's insistence on the specialized character of Baconian science culture, its aloofness sealing it off from everyday discussion and debate, and from meaningful scrutiny outside the laboratory, Spinoza repeatedly states that he finds Boyle's experiments excessively elaborate, often a laborious way of demonstrating things philosophy can more easily demonstrate without such elaborate preparations and high level seclusion. In Spinoza's opinion, Boyle's elaborate empiricism mostly yielded conclusions either demonstrably incorrect or else perfectly obvious in any case.

Alongside his tubes, flasks, and crucibles, Spinoza's main science instrument was the microscope and he expressly states his interest in using it to examine

---

[34] Spinoza, *Collected Works* (ed. Curley) i, 178.
[35] Mignini, "Données et problèmes," 19–20.
[36] Macherey, "Spinoza lecteur et critique," 747.

particles not visible to the naked eye. What then was Spinoza's view of experimental science and its relationship to mathematics and philosophical truth? In recent years, an attempt has been made to claim Spinoza's mind was foreign to the true spirit of the Scientific Revolution. In history of science circles, following especially the claims of Eric Schliesser, the notion has caught on that Spinoza is far removed from positively recommending experimental science and urging the precise and systematic measurement of real processes in order to advance our knowledge of nature. Rather, he supposedly held a view of science that was remote from a modern scientific view.[37] Yet Spinoza was nothing if not an eager empiricist in science and one who refused to permit non-scientific arguments, that is argument not derived from natural causes, into explanations of any phenomenon, including discussion of miracles and demons. In important respects this rendered him more, rather than less, stringently "scientific" and experiment-orientated than Bacon, Oldenburg, and Boyle.

According to Spinoza, it is not rigorous reasoning that is at fault, but the limitations of our senses, and how readily our senses deceive us, that feed human error causing the philosophical and general scientific usefulness of experimental results to be often marred and usually limited. Here, in fact, he stood rather close to Steno's view. Certainly, it is incorrect to assert that while Newton later agreed "with Spinoza that measured quantities, like the velocity of a body relative to some reference, depend on our senses," Newton, the ultimate measure of a true scientific attitude, appreciated, where Spinoza did not, that beside "sensible measures of quantities, there are also real quantities that can be deduced from their sensible measures,"[38] implying Spinoza is sceptical about whether experiments do yield genuinely reliable knowledge, as distinct from what appears true to our senses. Spinoza does not deny the fundamental truth of our perceptions when corroborated by mathematically measured observation and geometrically precise inference from these results, but merely insists on how limited is the perspective provided by our senses, even when observing things correctly, and how fallible mere observation is in isolation, on its own, when insufficiently buttressed by rigorous evaluation checking data and context.[39]

A famous example he gives to illustrate what he means is his "worm's eye view" thesis elaborated in a later letter to Oldenburg, of November 1665. If a small worm-like creature swimming in human blood possessed the same sight and reason that we do, it would naturally think reality consists of swimming in a highly complex fluid, with admixtures of other bodily fluids while constantly bumping into entities, particles or corpuscles, and so forth. Our rational

---

[37] Schliesser, "Spinoza and the Philosophy of Science," 155–89 and in particular 157n8; Schliesser, "Newton and Spinoza," 455.
[38] Quotation from Peterman, "Newton and Spinoza," 6.
[39] Moreau, *Spinoza, L'expérience*, 272–4; Chaui, *Nervura do real*, 610–12.

human-sighted worm would not be able to measure the frequency and impact of such collisions even using careful observation and experimental science. Nor would there be anything wrong with the worm's specific conclusions or the universal outlook it assembles from its results, only the outcome would be severely limited in relation to the entirety of the universe owing to the worm perceiving each entity it bumps into as an individual whole instead of seeing it is an interactive part of an infinitely vaster and more complex whole.[40] Man's predicament is essentially the same.

Alongside positive gains, held Spinoza, much muddle and confusion results from compiling exact measurements of planetary trajectories, comets, chemical reactions and many other things scientists were studying in his time, not least in Boyle's laboratory. But the muddle he deplores results not from the experiments, or empirical procedure per se, and still less the mathematics used to measure the changes and motions observed, producing the detailed measurements. Error stemmed, in his view, from the way scientists like Boyle and Kepler, the later mentioned by him in connection with comets, couch their findings and measurements, their drawing conclusions supposedly from the data, in a wrong-headed erroneous fashion, thereby generating only more confusion. Wrong conclusions usually result from scientists lacking the intellectual rigour and consistency to extrapolate meaningfully from the specific to the more general. Unlike Boyle and the Royal Society, Spinoza (like Descartes) believed experiments on their own cannot do much, even when offering correct results (which is frequently not the case), without careful correlation within a correctly conceived wider conceptual frame, one consistent with mathematical principles and logic and providing a coherent overview of reality which, to his mind, is precisely where Kepler, Bacon, and Boyle, and to an extent Descartes and the Dutch Cartesians, fell down: they combined observed results with notions of God and the universe, actual recorded data with residual alchemical and Aristotelian and, in Kepler's case, Platonic mystical notions, that to Spinoza's mind are fundamentally incorrect. Boyle trusted in the transmutation of chemical elements by chemical processes altering the basic characteristics of the element, thinking actually much closer to traditional alchemy than Spinoza's contrary view. Spinoza died a decade before Newton made his great scientific breakthrough, but no doubt would have regarded his mixing mathematical science with passionate commitment to theology, and attributing gravity to divine Providence, a breach of proper scientific method no less striking than Boyle's.[41]

Spinoza had nothing against Boyle's zeal for demonstrating experimentally that "all tangible qualities depend solely on motion, shape and other mechanical states"

---

[40] Spinoza, *Briefwisseling*, 231; Shapin and Schaffer, *Leviathan and the Air-Pump*, 253.
[41] Spinoza, *Collected Works* (ed. Curley) ii, 22; Schliesser, "Spinoza and the Philosophy of Science," 157–8, 177; Wootton, *Invention of Science*, 533.

rather than scholastic inherent qualities, albeit he believed Bacon and Descartes had already made this fully evident in any case. There are no grounds for supposing Spinoza shared Hobbes' rather more emphatic and comprehensive "anti-experimentalism."[42] Rather, Spinoza's chief objection to Boyle's chemistry is his claim that Boyle had been insufficiently thorough in exploring all ramifications of his experiments, in short had not experimented enough.[43] Furthermore, Boyle, he believed, retained too much respect for residual scholastic and Aristotelian notions that, since Descartes, should be deemed wholly redundant and discarded. On occasion, this led Boyle to devise superfluous experiments such as his demonstrating that heat results from motion. Since heat must be the "outcome of purely mechanistic movements, is not the same conclusion equally clear from the fact that two pieces of wood, however cold they are, when rubbed against each other, produce a flame simply due to that motion?" Stinking matter stinks more when stirred or heated up. Likewise, the fact that sound results from motions of different bodies, and measurably different states, is readily proved by familiar actions like boiling some water.[44]

Spinoza could not quite grasp why Boyle insisted on investing so much time and effort in demonstrating that the Aristotelian "puerile and frivolous doctrine of substantial forms and qualities rests on a weak foundation,"[45] since to his mind, nothing could be more obvious anyhow. Where Boyle was more evidently justified in their controversy was in stressing the difference between formal and informal experiment. Spinoza perhaps fell short in failing to acknowledge the validity of Boyle's insistence on essential formal requirements for experimental science such as observation by others, accurate reportage on the scene, and capacity for replication.[46] Nevertheless, while in Amsterdam and at Leiden, Spinoza had keenly participated in such formal, group experimental culture and, arguably, was as much a product of the Scientific Revolution as Descartes, Boyle, or Newton. He diverged from what later came to be the quintessentially empiricist "scientific" attitude geared to painstaking observation and experiment chiefly by demanding the research scientist's zeal be buttressed by philosophical insight, critical scrutiny, rigorous inference, directness and a coherent framework of reference.[47]

The English scientist's readiness to observe and record in terms of mere apparent and tactile qualities like colour, smell, flammability, roughness and smoothness sensible to the eye and touch indicated to Spinoza that Boyle was

---

[42] Shapin and Schaffer, *Leviathan and the Air-Pump*, 139; Gabbey, "Spinoza's Natural Science," 171; Wootton, *Invention of Science*, 289.
[43] Macherey, "Spinoza lecteur et critique," 742–3,749; Moreau, *Spinoza, L'expérience*, 269, 272, 274, 277; Duffy, "The Difference," 131.
[44] Spinoza, *Collected Works* (ed. Curley) i, 179; Spinoza, *Correspondance* (ed. Rovere), 68.
[45] Gullan-Whur, *Life of Sp[inoza*, 117; Gabbey, "Spinoza's Natural Science," 179.
[46] Macherey, "Spinoza lecteur et critique," 746–7; Duffy, "The Difference," 130–1; Wootton, *Invention of Science*, 349–55.
[47] Spinoza, *Opera* iv, 24–8; Spinoza, *Collected Works* (ed. Curley) i, 178–81.

still in part thinking in terms of scholastic "qualities." Boyle insisted he was interested in facts, not interpretation, arising from chemistry experiments; but it lay at the core of Spinoza's objection that accurate observation and recording require conceptual preconditions and sound premises. To Spinoza's mind, Boyle's approach betrayed a lack of objective precision in terms of observed movements and measurable change in the shape, velocity, connection, separation and direction of particles and clusters, hence an un-geometric, inadequate observational philosophy. Every mathematical proposition implies an infinite sequence of logically connected inferences; though harder to isolate and profile, so does every fact.

In the long run, Spinoza's long drawn-out indirect encounter with Boyle can hardly be said to have gone well. Spinoza had no interest in explaining reality in terms of the sensible, tactile observable qualities but only in terms of unalterable laws of movement and rest, concepts "fixa et aeterna [fixed and eternal]."[48] Neither scientist had a clear concept of chemical elements, and of the difference between elements and compounds: that would arrive only in the next century with the work of the great French chemist, Lavoisier.[49] At one point Spinoza reprimands Boyle for suggesting "chemical experiments" can demonstrate the infinite divisibility of matter. The doctrine itself is undeniable philosophically but we know it for certain only by philosophical demonstration, and through calculating. For it is by reason and mathematical calculation that we divide bodies to infinity, and hence also the forces required to move them, something "we can never confirm by experiments." Elsewhere, Spinoza criticizes Boyle's resort to experiment to demonstrate that motions of matter occur which are wholly invisible to us. "Without this experiment and without going to any trouble," retorts Spinoza, "the thing is sufficiently evident from the fact that in winter our breath, which is obviously observed to be in motion, nevertheless cannot be seen to be so in summer, or in a heated room."[50]

13.iii Mathematics and Scientific Truth

At times, Spinoza was almost caustically critical of Boyle's assumptions and methods. He insists on the basic distinction between "notions deriving from popular usage," a highly disparaging label in his eyes, "or which explain Nature not as it is in itself but as it relates to the human senses" and concepts that "are pure and which explicate Nature as it is in itself."[51] The difference lay in the latter

---

[48] Macherey, "Spinoza lecteur et critique," 761–3; Ramond, *Qualité et quantité*, 174–5.
[49] Gabbey, "Spinoza's Natural Science," 179–80; Duffy, "The Difference," 123, 127.
[50] Spinoza, *Collected Works* (ed. Curley) i, 185.
[51] Spinoza, *Collected Works* (ed. Curley) i, 181–5; Moreau, *Spinoza, L'expérience*, 273–4.

being strictly mathematical and, at least in principle, measurable like the laws of motion and rest. Ordinary notions relating to the senses like visible and invisible, tangible or intangible, hot and cold, and solid and fluid, being all relative to our senses should never be reckoned "concepts of the highest generality" or what we would call scientific categories. When criticizing Boyle's analysis of fluids and fluidity, Spinoza reaffirms his view that, in principle, motion of fluids and vapours is "obvious to those who give sufficient attention to those concepts that explain Nature as it is in itself, not as it relates to the human senses." He makes clear, though, that he does not reject Boyle's empiricism in such instances as useless. "On the contrary, if such natural history were done in the case of each different fluid with the greatest possible accuracy and faithfulness, I would consider this, as would all philosophers, very useful and desirable, even absolutely necessary, for understanding their distinguishing features."[52] But each entry should confirm a wider pattern, remaining a detail in a vast descriptive catalogue.

The contention that Spinoza's "comprehensive proscription on abstraction makes it very difficult to see how Spinoza can allow that mathematical science furnishes knowledge of nature in any way and indeed he does not" will doubtless continue to be warmly greeted by opponents of the Radical Enlightenment thesis, but, like most of their reasoning, this supposed objection scarcely makes sense.[53] Assuredly, when writing to his friend Lodewijk Meyer, in April 1663, Spinoza affirmed that it can be "clearly seen that measure, time and number are nothing other than ways of thinking, or rather ways of imagining. It is therefore not surprising that all who have attempted to understand the workings of nature by such concepts which furthermore have been badly understood, have so wondrously tied themselves up that finally they could not extricate themselves except by wrecking everything and admitting the most absurd absurdities."[54] Since mathematical relationships when applied to reality are just "aids to the imagination," they are abstractions yielding only a fragment of the truth since "there are many things that can in no way be apprehended by the imagination but only the intellect, such as substance, eternity, and other things." The former being abstractions from the truth are true only up to a point. And indeed, certain key features of Spinoza's world view, aspects of truth he deems characteristic of and inherent in everything—his rigid universal determinism, the interconnectedness of all things, and the principle, much beloved by Einstein, that the "ordo et connexio idearum idem est, ac ordo et connexio rerum" [the order and connection of ideas is the same as the order and connection of things],[55] guaranteeing the accuracy of

---

[52] Spinoza, *Opera* iv, 34; Spinoza, *Correspondance* (ed. Rovere), 73–4; Peterman, "Spinoza on the 'Principles of Natural Things'," 42.
[53] Gabbey, "Spinoza on Natural Science," 213–14, 222; Peterman, "Newton and Spinoza," 6.
[54] Spinoza, *Opera* iv, 57; Spinoza, *Collected Works* (ed. Curley) i, 203.
[55] Jammer, *Einstein and Religion*, 52; Schliesser, "Spinoza and the Philosophy of Science," 173.

mathematical recording of natural processes—could never be confirmed or refuted by any experiment.

Using mathematical mental constructs [*entia rationis*], argues Spinoza, we are being logical, rational, and correct in our deductions up to a point, but when using "such aids to the imagination" we are also abstracting the processes we study from their background and context in substance and modality, by which they flow from eternity; and without perceiving how they so derive we can never form an exact conception of them.[56] This means correct deductions from mathematical data differ from wrong deductions only in a relative sense: the former are more adequate, and mathematically more coherent, than the latter,[57] but to be useful must in addition rest on "a sufficient knowledge of the eternal things and their infallible laws," and "the nature of our senses." For otherwise we cannot properly use our senses to guide us in organizing experiments, to check, test, and question research results rightly, or weigh, evaluate, and infer in accord with proper method and rules from each new result so as to determine whether it is "true or false." Above all, we cannot determine the circumstances of singular things within the right framework of eternal realities and unchangeable laws.[58] It is not then through experiment and research data alone but by examining conclusions inferred from facts, and probing them in relation to earlier definitions and conclusions that truth is sifted from false notions.

The key is to grasp the method by which "to distinguish a true idea from all other perceptions" and to exclude from our reasoning all those other suppositions readily adopted but thoroughly unreliable and in this way "restrain the mind from confusing false, fictitious and doubtful ideas with true ones." But it is a key few ever acquire. Unlocking truth in other words, presupposes prior knowledge of the "form of truth and knowledge of the intellect and its properties and powers"; and before launching into investigating "singular things," and undertaking experiments, holds Spinoza in the *Emendation*, sweeping aside the Baconian approach, two indispensable steps must precede everything else if serious pursuit of the truth is to result. In effect, Spinoza wholly rejected Boyle's and Oldenburg's commitment to the "argument from design," their seeking the cause of things, like Kepler and later Newton, in assumed divine purpose, their conviction that God must at the outset have impressed "determinate motions on the parts of matter" and guides them "as he thought requisite for the primordial constitution of things," as Boyle expressed it, "and that ever since, [does] by his ordinary and general concourse maintain those powers which he gave the parts of matter to transmit their motion thus and thus to one another."[59]

---

[56] Spinoza, *Briefwisseling*, 125; Spinoza, *Collected Works* (ed. Curley) i, 203–4.
[57] Spinoza, *Opera* iv, 58; Spinoza, *Briefwisseling*, 99; Spinoza, *Correspondance* (ed. Rovere), 73–4.
[58] Spinoza, *Collected Works* (ed. Curley) i, 42.   [59] Boyle, *A Free Enquiry*, 25.

One can hardly have expected Oldenburg, and still less Boyle, to be receptive to Spinoza's critique, and still less to Spinoza's jarring lack of deference and characteristically incisive remarks. Oldenburg duly passed on Spinoza's lengthy commentaries to Boyle who, for a time, probably did intend to respond directly. "The author himself joins with me in thanking you most warmly for the thoughts you have shared with us," Oldenburg writes, in the same letter in which he informs Spinoza that the "college of philosophers" about which they had talked when Oldenburg visited Rijnsburg, "has now, by our King's grace, been converted into a Royal Society and presented with the public charter whereby it is granted special privileges; and there is a very good prospect that it will be endowed with the necessary funds,"[60] a charter granted on 15 July 1662. The joint response to his criticism finally reached Spinoza, soon after this, probably in late July 1662, quite some time after he had dispatched his long and detailed commentary on Boyle's nitre experiments to England. Boyle "would have indicated [his thanks] more quickly," explained Oldenburg, "had he not entertained the hope that he might soon be relieved of the quantity of business with which he is burdened so that he could have sent you his reply along with his thanks at the same time. However, so far he finds himself disappointed of this hope, being so pressed by both public and private business that at present he can do no more than convey his gratitude to you, and is compelled to defer to another time his opinion on your comments."[61] Needless to say, that occasion of more time and opportunity never came. Jealous of his privacy and, as usual, keeping nearly everyone at a distance, Boyle was too busy, and insufficiently interested, to respond to Spinoza directly.

The Boyle–Spinoza encounter always remained essentially indirect, though it seems Boyle, while apologizing for the delay indirectly, originally did intend to respond—at any rate via Oldenburg, and then, after a time, simply let the matter drop. It has been claimed that "Spinoza and Boyle seem never to have exchanged letters directly,"[62] but Van de Ven's detailed reconstruction of Spinoza's correspondence suggests the probable existence of a brief, direct correspondence, a mere single exchange of letters (now lost) each to the other, dating from July 1663, shortly after Spinoza's departure from Rijnsburg. Probably, there was no other direct interaction between Boyle and Spinoza either earlier or subsequently.

Saying nothing further about Boyle, Oldenburg devoted most of his relatively short letter of July 1662 to offering advice, for which Spinoza had asked, regarding his own work. Oldenburg urges him not to deprive

> scholars of the learned fruits of your acute understanding both in philosophy and theology but let these be published whatever the growling of the pseudo-theologians. Your Republic is very free, in it one can philosophize most freely

---

[60] Spinoza, *Collected Works* (ed. Curley) i, 189–90; Wootton, *Invention of Science*, 37.
[61] Spinoza, *Collected Works* (ed. Curley) i, 189.   [62] Colie, "Spinoza in England," 194.

[liberrima est Republica vestra, liberime in ea philosophandum]: your own prudence will suggest to you that you must present your concepts and views as modestly as you can. Leave the rest to Fate. Go ahead, then, excellent sir, putting all fear of offending the wretched little men of our time aside; long enough, have we appeased ignorance and nonsense! Let us spread the sails of true knowledge and let us search more deeply than ever before into Nature's mysteries. In your country, your meditations can be printed, I think, with impunity and there is no need to fear that they will give offense to the wise.[63]

Wisely, Spinoza was far from persuaded of the accuracy of that.

When Oldenburg next wrote, on 3 April 1663, he apologized at length "for my long silence," assuring Spinoza that the recent illness "of the very noble Boyle" had prevented him "from replying to your observations" on saltpetre at an earlier date while the pressures of his own duties had prevented him from writing. "I am resolved, with Heaven's help," exclaimed Oldenburg, "to do everything to make sure that henceforth our epistolary exchange shall in future not be interrupted for so long."[64] Thanking him again, for commenting on his experiments, Boyle conveyed his basic response to Spinoza through Oldenburg. This was that he had not tried to conduct a complete analysis of saltpetre and its characteristics but merely prove the "common doctrine of substantial forms and qualities accepted in the schools rests on a weak foundation, and that what they call the specific differences of things can be reduced to the magnitude, motion, rest and position of the parts," something Spinoza had insisted all along was already sufficiently obvious in any case. Boyle left him in no doubt that he considered Spinoza's theories about the relationship of nitrate essence to saltpetre compound to be "without proof," and views on the inflammability of saltpetre and non-inflammability of nitrate essence and the rest, to be "merely unproved speculations."[65] In the same letter, pledging friendship and loyalty, Oldenburg again urges Spinoza to publish "that little work [the *Korte Verhandeling*] of such great importance, in which you treat of the origin of things and their dependence on a first cause, and also [his other treatise] on the emendation of our intellect."[66]

Still at Rijnsburg in late April 1663, Spinoza answered Oldenburg only some months later, in July, from Voorburg, near The Hague.[67] After leaving Rijnsburg, he had spent the several intervening weeks in Amsterdam, seeing his treatise on Descartes' philosophy through the press. One reason Spinoza made his debut in the public world of scholarship with his *Renati Des Cartes Principiorum philosophiae Pars I & II*, an overall account of Descartes' thought, he explained to

---

[63] Spinoza, *Opera* iv, 37–8; Spinoza, *Collected Works* (ed. Curley) i, 189–90.
[64] Oldenburg to Spinoza, London, 3 April 1663 in Spinoza, *Collected Works* (ed. Curley) i, 197.
[65] Spinoza, *Collected Works* (ed. Curley) i, 197–8, 216–17.
[66] Spinoza, *Collected Works* (ed. Curley) i, 199–200.   [67] Spinoza, *Briefwisseling*, 128–9.

Oldenburg, was his hope, presumably with the likes of Hudde and Van Velthuysen in mind, that "there will be some men holding high positions in my country who will want to see the rest of what I wrote, and which I acknowledge as my own, and so will take care that I can make them available to the common judgment without risk of danger. Should this come about I have no doubt that I shall publish some things immediately; if not, I shall keep silent rather than thrust my opinions on men against my country's wishes and make them furious with me."[68]

"I am also extremely grateful to the most learned Mr Boyle," he assures Oldenburg, on 27 July 1663, "for being so good as to reply to my notes, even if he does so in passing and as if occupied with something else [quamvis obiter et quasi aliud agendo]." "My observations are not of such importance," grants Spinoza, "that that very erudite gentleman should spend time in answering them that he could otherwise devote to higher thoughts."[69] There then follow four to five pages reaffirming his previous claims regarding saltpetre, inflammability and non-inflammability, vigorously rebutting Boyle's counterclaim that the "commonplace and doubtful experiments" adduced by Spinoza "where we do not know what is contributed by nature and what by other factors" were altogether less relevant than his own, "where the contributing factors are clearly established." Replying almost by return of post, just a few days later, on 31 July 1663, Oldenburg asks Spinoza to send his Descartes book to London as soon as it appeared, via the ever available and amenable Serrarius. "For the rest, allow me to say that I am by no means content with your continued withholding of the writings which you acknowledge as your own, especially in a Republic so free that, there, you are permitted to think what you please and to say what you think [tam libera, ut sentire ibi, quae velis, et quae sentias dicere liceat]. I wish you would break through those barriers, especially since you can conceal your name and thus place yourself beyond all risk of danger."[70]

Shortly afterwards, Oldenburg sent Spinoza two more letters, in August 1663, again touching on his differences with Boyle, reporting "an excellent experiment [...] which greatly distresses those who affirm a vacuum, but very much pleases those who deny it [like Descartes, the Cartesians, and Spinoza]."[71] He relates too another detailed conversation with Boyle about Spinoza's observations, but now proposes, doubtless at Boyle's suggestion, future disengagement between them as regards experiments, of the desirability henceforth of a division of labour separating their respective efforts, since Spinoza and Boyle were "both in agreement on the main point," meaning the inadequacy of all past science and their common devotion to a mechanical conception of science but yet, seemingly, operating on

---

[68] Spinoza, *Collected Works* (ed. Curley) i, 207–8.
[69] Spinoza, *Opera* iv, 64; Spinoza, *Collected Works* (ed. Curley) i, 208.
[70] Spinoza, *Opera* iv, 70. [71] Spinoza, *Collected Works* (ed. Curley) i, 214.

different levels. Eventually, Boyle and Spinoza could unify their respective efforts "in striving to cultivate a genuine and solidly based philosophy. May I urge you especially, with your keen mathematical mind, to continue to establish basic principles, just as I ceaselessly try to coax my noble friend Boyle to confirm and elucidate them by experiments and observations repeatedly and accurately made."

Oldenburg pronounced it the role of "our native philosophers in our kingdom," to experiment while "you in your own land will actively do your part, whatever growling or accusations may come from the crowd of philosophers or theologians."[72] In London, Spinoza was assuredly being judged and was now tactfully being told, that he was an outsider irrelevant to the progress of true science.

---

[72] Spinoza, *Opera* iv, 74–5; Spinoza, *Collected Works* (ed. Curley) i, 218.

14
"Reforming" Descartes' Principles

Not long after Spinoza's move from Rijnsburg to Voorburg, in early August 1663, his friend Simon de Vries arrived at his new lodgings with a packet from Amsterdam, sent by Lodewijk Meyer, containing the printed proofs of Spinoza's pending first published book, his *Renati Des Cartes Principiorum philosophiae Pars I & II*. This was his exposition of Descartes' philosophy, setting out the basic principles of Descartes' system, especially as expounded in the latter's *Principia philosophiae* [Principles of Philosophy], the work Descartes began in 1641 and published in 1644, presenting his natural philosophy as a coherent whole based on his metaphysical claims. Spinoza had reworked these into a new rigorous and concise format, with a simple eloquence that would soon impress readers.

Descartes, Spinoza explains, calls "all things into doubt, not as a skeptic who has no other end than doubting, but to free his mind from prejudices so that finally he might discover the firm and unshakable foundations of the sciences." Everywhere, Spinoza insists on mathematical reasoning as the basis of science and all reliable knowledge, and the need to recognize this as the most vital key to understanding our world, reflecting the central concern of Descartes' book which chiefly seeks to interpret our universe as a whole in terms of motion, rest, force, and action.[1] With Part One, Proposition 14, Spinoza entirely endorses Descartes' un-Baconian contention that, since God is no deceiver, our thoughts about reality must be true wherever we find that "we must necessarily assent" to a proposition expressed and perceived "clearly and distinctly."[2]

At times even more Cartesian than Descartes, Spinoza proclaims the inability of our unaided senses to understand much about the hardness, softness, or significance of the varying textures of different sorts of matter, a point central to his critique of Boyle.[3] What mathematical reason, or what we term science, can explain objectively is motion, impact, mechanical connection, variation resulting from force, proportion, pressure, timing and spatial relationships. Much of Spinoza's text is in fact devoted to discussing the laws of motion and rest and those aspects of variation in the composition of matter depending on motion and rest, hence on the mathematical reasoning he deems applicable to all reality,

---

[1] Spinoza, *Collected Works* (ed. Curley) i, 231; Gaukroger, *Descartes*, 363, 364–77.
[2] Spinoza, *Collected Works* (ed. Curley) i, 256.
[3] Spinoza, *Collected Works* (ed. Curley) i, 265, 267.

including the new aspects of anatomy revealed by dissection where amenable to clear explanation.

Spinoza's book commences with a preface by Meyer: "The author," Meyer explains, "entrusted to my care the whole business of printing and publishing it, since he lives in the country far from the city, and could not be present" while his book was being prepared for the press.[4] At hand in Amsterdam, Meyer therefore stood in for the author, at his request, as regards editing and finalizing the text, and also writing the book's preface where he forcefully introduces the idea that the "best and surest method of seeking and teaching the truth in the sciences is that of the mathematicians who demonstrate their conclusions from definitions, postulates and axioms." This accounts for the book's subject matter: for "the brightest star of our age," holds Meyer, namely Descartes, was the first to seriously build on this foundation, applying mathematical reason to demonstrate what is true being his foremost philosophical principle.[5] Meyer had "often wished," he mentions, that someone skilled in formulating philosophical arguments in both the "Analytic and the Synthetic manner," that is in analysing propositions by bringing out what is contained in them besides formulating propositions that introduce new knowledge or claims, would undertake to set out Descartes' system in the synthetic (or geometric) order familiar to mathematicians, building up certain new knowledge step by step. He himself had tried to undertake this task, he adds, but found himself unequal to it. He had hence been delighted to learn that Spinoza had laid out part of Descartes' *Principia* in the synthetic manner, in geometric order, for one of his students.

"More than anyone else," Steven Nadler rightly affirms, Meyer "was responsible for bringing Spinoza's writings to publication, both while Spinoza lived and after his death with the posthumous publication of his works."[6] If not perhaps *the* chief organizer, Meyer was certainly among the prime orchestrators of "Spinozism" as a body of text and a philosophical underground movement. Through the spring of 1663, conferring closely with Meyer, and perhaps mainly at his entreaty, Spinoza rapidly reworked and expanded his account, based on the already extant shorter exposition, expounding the principles of Descartes' system in clear, systematic fashion for the benefit of the general public. Since he was preparing the book at the urging of friends, reports Meyer, and wrote the book in a hurry, feeling under pressure to get on with "more important business in which he was involved" (presumably his work on the *Ethics*), circumstances "allowed him only two weeks in which to complete this work"[7]—a detail Spinoza wished the public to know so that not too much attention should be paid to slips or terms or expressions that

---

[4] Meyer, "Preface," 227; Klever, "Spinoza's Life and Works," 29; Barebone and Rice, "Introduction," xiii, xxviii.
[5] Meyer, "Preface," 224–5. [6] Nadler, *Spinoza: A Life*, 202; Nadler, *Book Forged in Hell*, 120–1.
[7] Meyer, "Preface," 228.

seemed obscure. (Spinoza did not actually complete the task but instead published it with most of its third part still lacking.)

From this, one might readily extrapolate that the book was just a minor venture, a rushed outline of Descartes' system that Spinoza had not previously planned to publish. But this was hardly the case. Spinoza had been obsessively immersed in Descartes, discussing and pondering his system uninterruptedly probably at least since the mid-1650s. Moreover, at this time he was supplementing his modest income from selling optical instruments by coaching students from nearby Leiden specifically in Cartesianism. Also, like everyone in Holland seriously engaging with Descartes' system, he was immersed in the great flurry of debate among the Leiden and Utrecht philosophy professors about how to interpret and how (and indeed whether) to teach Descartes' principles.[8] Far from being a mere textbook or off the cuff exposition dashed off on the side for students and beginners, the book actually reveals considerable complexity, steering subtly, even deviously, between expounding Descartes' principles and reformulating, revising and surreptitiously overturning them;[9] as Bontekoe and other later commentators stressed, it was a foray of crucial significance in Spinoza's development not just as a "reformer" of Cartesianism specifically but as a "reformer" of philosophy, religion, political thought, and our world more generally.

Publishing the book in Latin first and then translating and publishing the book in Dutch, given Meyer's longstanding commitment to rendering important philosophical and scientific findings into the vernacular, was doubtless planned from the outset. Spinoza's ostensible purpose was to present himself as a stalwart of the Cartesian fraternity and subscriber to characteristic Cartesian positions, the general reform of the sciences especially. He closely follows Descartes in the book's early sections, showing that whatever else one doubts one cannot doubt one's own doubting so that no one can avoid concluding: "I doubt, I think, therefore I am [dubito, cogito, ergo sum]." Seizing on this truth, Descartes had simultaneously, Spinoza assures readers, uncovered also the foundation of all the sciences, the measure and rule of all truth: "whatever is perceived as clearly and distinctly as that from clear unquestionable evidence is true."[10] From this foundation follows the unchallengeable next step, namely that all forms of our thinking, whenever we perceive, affirm, deny, sense, imagine, will, or do not will, something, are likewise real substantive processes wholly exempt from those things that can be called into doubt. Since mathematical reason proves we make mistakes continually by accepting or refusing things we assume, imagine, fear, trust in, and so forth, Descartes grasped that we derive most of our notions wrongly through not arriving at them by philosophical method and allowing our minds to be filled

---

[8] Garber, "Spinoza's Cartesian Dualism," 132.
[9] Nadler, *Spinoza: A Life*, 244–5; Santinelli, "À partir de *Spinoza in Italia*," 32.
[10] Spinoza, *Collected Works* (ed. Curley) i, 233.

with "prejudices." But whenever the philosopher, or anyone else, assents only to what is deduced clearly and distinctly from an unchallengeable first foundation, following the method thus established, always rigorously excluding every report, assumption, belief, and association, no one can doubt the truth of any step in the procedure as long as the inference is cogently inferred from the geometrically unassailable steps taken before. It soon emerges, though, Descartes explains, that beyond our existence we can be totally certain of nothing whatever, even the reality of our bodies, without a conception of God guaranteeing that he is no deceiver.

All outcomes of our thinking that we cannot doubt, Descartes proves, form a unity, a unifying substance which he calls mind. But just as "we clearly perceive the mind, or thinking substance," without our bodies, undeniably our senses perceive our bodies clearly without mind. According with how divine power has organized reality as it appears to us, the "mind can exist without the body and the body can exist without the mind." Since whatever exists does so by the power of whatever preserves the existence of all existing things, Descartes deduces that this preserving, moving, and creating power, namely God, exists necessarily, is eternal, and is one; and, furthermore, is the most perfect being which means "God is supremely truthful and not a deceiver" (Proposition 13), confirming that truth is absolute, real, and accessible to us. Hence, "whatever we perceive clearly and distinctly is true" (Proposition 14), and everyone possesses the faculty of recognizing and distinguishing between what is true and false.

In his *Descartes' Principles*, Spinoza is particularly insistent on the importance of mathematics to philosophy as well as natural science. Descartes (Figure 14.1) was the first thinker to go beyond Copernicus, Kepler, and Galileo, in conceiving the entire physical universe, the whole of physical reality, to be governed by a single, overarching and cohering set of fixed natural laws that are everywhere, always applicable, and mathematical in character, a principle never previously upheld, not even by Galileo, and one to which Spinoza would always strongly adhere. This was the solidest (and most un-Baconian) link between Descartes and Spinoza. Descartes was also the first to claim all philosophical, or for that matter any other doctrines must be proved with "clear and distinct" propositions and arguments possessing the same precision as mathematics, or as Spinoza expresses it in his *Principles*, Descartes, having proved God exists, created the world and is no deceiver, could conclude that "mathematical truths, or all things that seem to him most evident, cannot be at all suspect."[11] This escape from, indeed abolition of, scepticism, or "liberatio ab omnibus dubiis [liberation from all doubts]," applies, though, only where propositions are couched with the same precision as mathematical propositions "clearly and distinctly," for error creeps in wherever

---

[11] Spinoza, *Opera* i, 145; Spinoza, *Principles*, 11.

Figure 14.1 *René Descartes* (1596–1650) by Jan Lievens, chalk on paper, 24.1 × 20.6 cm. Groninger Museum, loan from Municipality of Groningen, donation Hofstede de Groot, photo: Marten de Leeuw.

rigorous precision is lacking. Mathematical precision, for Spinoza, had been enthroned as the perennial measure and model for philosophy as for science.

Since only what we perceive clearly and distinctly is certain, everything else people think or believe is either automatically wrong or pervasively error-prone. Consequently, whenever our faculties of willing and assuming are prevented from intruding beyond what is correctly understood by clear and distinct steps of the intellect, insofar that is as we prevent ourselves willing or assuming anything beyond what we correctly understand, we shall unerringly live, think, trust, and believe purely in accord with what is true. A life based on reason is the only life in accord with the reality of the universe and what is true, and philosophical reason the only reliable path to living one's life on the basis of truth.

Most people imagine there are all sorts of causes for the joy, misery, and other bodily sensations they experience, located beyond physical existence, such as God, angels, spells, magic, or demons. But whenever we propose a cause beyond physical existence for our pleasure, pain, fear, or actions "we immediately destroy the clear and distinct concept that we have."[12] So keeping to the path of truth

---

[12] Spinoza, *Collected Works* (ed. Curley) i, 261.

guided by our perceptions means we must "admit nothing but what we have perceived clearly and distinctly," which in practice compels us to acknowledge that "extended substance is the only cause of our sensations." According to Descartes, everything consists, reason demonstrates, of one or other of just two substances—thought [mind] and extension [physical existence]—except for God who stands above substance, or is a third substance. Spinoza seemingly follows Descartes in asserting that the only supremely perfect being "God is incorporeal" (Part I, Prop. 16), pointing to the divisibility of extended substance as an imperfection incompatible with the perfection of God, Descartes' ground for claiming that extension is not an aspect or attribute of God.[13] It is striking that Spinoza does so here. Because this was undoubtedly one key point where, as he himself explained to Oldenburg, in April 1662, and to others, his own view directly contradicted that of Descartes. As has long been noted, "Spinoza was the only seventeenth-century thinker who attributed a body to God, explicitly and unequivocally." It is wrong, though, to suppose that "it took him some time to reach this conclusion," or that, earlier, part of him agreed with Descartes.[14] Rather, from the outset, in the late 1650s, the *Korte Verhandeling* shows, Spinoza adhered consistently to his divergent view. In April 1662, he assured Oldenburg, writing to him from Rijnsburg, "I do not separate God from Nature as everyone known to me has done."[15]

In the second part of his book, Spinoza follows Descartes in defining extension, claiming that it involves a contradiction to think that a vacuum can exist (Part II, Prop. 3). Likewise, Spinoza sets out the fundamental rules that follow from Descartes' analysis of extended substance, the most crucial being (Part II, Prop. 6) that "matter is indefinitely extended and the matter of the heavens is one and the same as that of earth"; that God still preserves "the same quantity of motion and rest which he first imparted to matter" (Part II, Prop. 13); and that "each thing, insofar as it is simple, undivided and considered in itself alone, always perseveres in the same state as far as it can" (Part II, Prop. 14), so that each and every body in motion "tends of itself to continue to move in a straight line, not in one which is curved," including everything that moves in a circle, as for example a stone in a sling. This means (by Part II, Prop.17) that everything in circular orbit strives to move in a straight line away from the centre of that circle, and that whenever a body is forced to diverge from its previous track "that variation will always be the least that there can be."[16] Finally, it emerges that all extended substance follows the same set of universal, eternal laws of motion and rest to which there is (as Descartes should, at least, have argued) no possible observable

---

[13] Spinoza, *Collected Works* (ed. Curley) i, 260; Schmaltz, "Spinoza and Descartes," 70, 73.
[14] Funkenstein, *Theology and the Scientific Imagination*, 81.
[15] Spinoza to Oldenburg, Rijnsburg, April 1662 in Spinoza, *Collected Works* (ed. Curley) i, 188; Buyse, "Le 'Démasquement'," 18–19.
[16] Spinoza, *Collected Works* (ed. Curley) i, 280–94; Garber, *Descartes' Metaphysical Physics*, 285.

exception, confirming once again that geometrical argument demonstrating proportion, spatial relations, motion and impetus is the only path to true knowledge of natural things.

One obvious way that Spinoza is here reforming Descartes and Cartesianism is by expounding his principles using the "geometric method" as his main tool of presentation and argument. Throughout his career as a philosopher from the late 1650s until his death, the *ordo geometricus* remained Spinoza's preferred method of ordering and presenting his philosophy. He clearly thinks the "geometric" style is the aptest way to expound also the essentials of Descartes' philosophy. But Descartes himself had not thought so which is why Meyer was so anxious that Spinoza should "render in the Synthetic order what Descartes wrote in the Analytic." Although intensely interested in geometry too, like his adherents in Leiden and Amsterdam, and while occasionally dabbling in using geometric style, generally speaking Descartes had avoided it as it seemed to have no direct application to metaphysical problems and hence many particular issues he sought to research, including how body and mind connect (though he never really got far with this point). Such topics, it seemed to him, require an analytical approach—start with the problem, dissect it into its parts and analyse these to find the causes.[17]

Because extension and mind are fundamentally different substances for Descartes, it was far less evident to him than to Meyer and Spinoza that a mathematical way of reasoning must provide the key to an overall exposition of truth in its entirety. From the very outset, in the 1650s, in his optics and study of experiments, and in his Bible criticism, Spinoza too showed himself a practised hand at analysing perplexing or curious phenomena and seeking their natural causes. Of course, to an extent the analytical and geometric-synthetic approaches were complementary in Spinoza's thought as in Descartes, Hobbes, and Leibniz. But, unlike the others, Spinoza assigns priority to the geometric method alone when expounding his philosophy (and that of Descartes), because to him the same general principles governing bodies, motion, and rest apply to and explain everything without exception which means that an overall framework of consistency, revealing the whole of reality to be governed by the same set of rules, is essential to conveying the unity and rational interconnectedness of everything.

Analysis was always basic to Spinoza's general method, to his Bible criticism, political thought, and to his experiments, but not to his method of presenting his philosophy which from the outset down to his last work remained rooted in the geometric style of exposition. The basic reason why analysis and synthesis on a geometric basis are not complementary for Spinoza, in contrast to the others, when it came to presenting his (and Descartes') philosophy, is that pure

---

[17] Meyer, "Preface," 227; Kambouchner, "Spinoza and Descartes," 57–8; Della Rocca, *Spinoza*, 9; Garrett, "Virtues of Geometry," 20, 26.

analysis tends to reinforce as well as conceal or leave untouched adjoining and surrounding fallacious and fictitious assumptions, notions, and inferences whereas the chief task of philosophy, for Spinoza, Meyer, and their entire group, was to eradicate the wrong thinking they deemed universally prevalent (including in Bacon and Descartes). The only safeguard against analysis of problems leading to retention of incorrect assumptions—such as Descartes' doctrine that there are two basic substances—is an unbreakable chain of undeniable inference from clear and certain definitions, hence an overarching geometric method used systematically. Thus, while analysis is indispensable to extending our knowledge piecemeal, it is *ordo geometricus* alone that enables one to sum up, link the parts together and present the wider picture. Although *ordo geometricus* was universally in fashion among the Dutch Cartesians of the 1650s and 1660s, including Van Schooten, Hudde, and Christiaan Huygens, three of the leading figures making Holland briefly the centre of the Europe's mathematical world in the mid-seventeenth century, Spinoza alone extends the new three-dimensional geometric outlook with its lines, surfaces, planes, motions, and proportions to everything including discussion of God, good and evil, and the human passions.

To an extent, Spinoza's expounding and reforming of Descartes' principles was direct and straightforward. But there was another dimension to the undertaking far less direct and open. On the surface Spinoza embraces Descartes' account of the reality accessible to humans and even adopts here his substance dualism affirming two independent, self-constituting elements—mind and body. Even if briefly and tersely, in contrast to the *Korte Verhandeling* and the intriguing appendix or supplement that follows his *Principles*, the *Cogitata Metaphysica*, Spinoza here seemingly agrees that mind and body are "really distinct" and even classifies both as *substantiae* [substances] distinct from each other as he had also earlier, in his letter to Meyer on the infinite, sent from Rijnsburg dated 20 April 1663. Admittedly, under Cartesian influence, in the late 1650s and early 1660s, mind and body do appear more separate for Spinoza than would be the case in his mature thought later. Even so, in the *Korte Verhandeling*, Spinoza affirms without hesitation that there exists only one substance or entity entirely causally independent of all other entities and that human minds and bodies are just separate "modes," or specific configurations, of the only two "attributes," or aspects of substance, accessible to humans, namely mind and extension. Furthermore, although his attributes here seem to be self-standing and to correspond to what others call "substances,"[18] he qualifies this by adding that the perfections of extended reality cannot be denied to God, since bodily existence can be denied

---

[18] Spinoza, *Opera* i, 169; Spinoza, *Collected Works* (ed. Curley) i, 253; Knol, "Waarom hield Spinoza," 9; Garber, "Spinoza's Cartesian Dualism," 121, 123, 126.

only where this involves imperfection. Thus, Spinoza concurs with while subtly unifying, widening, and deepening the scope of Cartesian truth and certainty.[19]

During the editing process and finalizing the proofs, Spinoza and Meyer collaborated closely. Writing from Voorburg, on 26 July 1663, replying to Meyer's query as to whether he had correctly edited the propositions in a particular section (which he had), Spinoza responds also to his worry about his reference to the "personality" of Christ where, originally, Spinoza wrote "I do not know what the theologians mean by the word 'personality'." That the "son of God is the father himself follows very clearly," answers Spinoza, from his axiom that "two things that converge in agreement with a third thing agree with each other. But this matter is of no importance whatever to me, so if you think this [form of words] can offend some theologians, then do as seems best to you." While, like most of Spinoza's friends, Meyer too denied Christ's divinity, for reasons of prudence he deleted Spinoza's original expression, substituting vaguer wording only faintly implying that Jesus cannot be the "Son of God": "it is quite false that God can communicate his eternity to creatures." Since the "Son of God" cannot be a living creature that is born, dies, or is resurrected, he must be "rather, like the father, eternal." For the first time Spinoza implicitly committed to the printed page what has been aptly termed his "anti-theological Christology."[20]

As Spinoza says nothing about his Descartes book in his letter of April 1663, or earlier, the claim in Meyer's preface that Spinoza was urged to take up the task, and dashed the book off hurriedly, may well be true on one level and yet also something of a rhetorical flourish, even perhaps deliberately misleading, in line with Spinoza's desire to avoid too obviously appearing to subvert aspects of the collective Cartesian project. Apparently, undertaking the task, writing it up and preparing it for publication did indeed all take place in a very short space between May and late July 1663. However, expounding and criticizing Descartes had been Spinoza's chief focus for six or seven years by this point, and latterly Spinoza had become used to systematizing his thoughts "géometriquement," as Lucas puts it, often adding geometrical diagrams to illustrate his points. With the book extant in proof, almost ready for the press, by late July Spinoza requested several last-minute alterations to Meyer's preface and an eleven-line insertion to his own text, to be added on page 75, all of which the printer inserted at the last moment in a noticeably different and smaller type.

In complying with the urging of friends to expand the short exposition of Descartes' principles he had originally prepared for teaching, Spinoza expanded it, as he himself explained, writing to Oldenburg, into a fuller coverage of the

---

[19] Spinoza, *Collected Works* (ed. Curley) i, 254; Moreau, *Spinoza, L'expérience*, 98–9; Verbeek, *Spinoza's Theologico-Political Treatise*, 162–3.

[20] Spinoza, *Briefwisseling*, 128–9, 456; Spinoza, *Collected Works* (ed. Curley) i, 206, 337; Tosel, "Figure du Christ," 129, 131; Chaui, *Nervura do real*, 408–10; Nadler, *Spinoza: A Life*, 242.

topic hastily.[21] While agreeing to undertake the task, Spinoza had asked Meyer to help polish his Latin style and add the accompanying preface especially to explain why, with Spinoza supposedly adhering closely to Descartes' principles, some arguments modify or depart from Descartes' positions. Spinoza's "scruples," Meyer's preface firmly asserts, "forbade him to depart in the slightest degree from Descartes' views or dictate anything not corresponding with, or contrary to, his doctrines."[22] However, the author aimed to demonstrate key conclusions drawn from Descartes' principles, affirms Meyer, "insofar as these are found in his writings, *or are such as ought to be deduced validly* [my emphasis] from the foundations [Descartes] laid." Here was a clear hint that Spinoza strictly adhered to expounding Descartes' principles as Descartes should have expounded them rather than as he had, albeit no one should suppose that Spinoza here was "teaching either his own opinions or only those of which he approves."[23]

The entire undertaking was distinctly odd in that, further on, following these remarks, Meyer makes it perfectly plain that while Spinoza departs from Descartes' reasoning only to render his principles clearer to the reader, and more consistent with each other, nevertheless, although Spinoza thinks some of Descartes' "principles" are true, "there are many he rejects as false and concerning which he holds a quite different opinion."[24] In short, no real attempt is made to conceal Spinoza's wide divergence from strict Cartesianism or pretend that his Descartes' *Principles* is a straightforward exposition of Cartesianism as Descartes expounded it. Insisting that he diverged fundamentally from Descartes was indeed something Spinoza himself regularly emphasized when communicating with Meyer and the Amsterdam discussion group, and also when writing to Oldenburg, in July 1663.[25] In terms of his own intellectual evolution, it was obvious even before he left Amsterdam that Spinoza believed he had on many levels advanced considerably beyond Descartes.

The chief errors of both Descartes and Bacon, Spinoza had assured Oldenburg in September 1661, are "first and foremost that they have strayed so far from knowledge of the first cause and origin of all things; second, that they do not know the true nature of the human mind; third, that they never grasped the true cause of error."[26] Clarifying all of these is so essential that only persons "lacking any education or desire for knowledge will fail to see how necessary true knowledge of these three things is." Moreover, Spinoza points out in the same letter, to its no doubt astounded recipient, Descartes separates human will from the intellect and envisages it as free in a way that he, Spinoza, wholly rejects. Meyer underlines this

[21] Spinoza, *Collected Works* (ed. Curley) i, 229, 227.
[22] Spinoza, *Collected Works* (ed. Curley) i, 167; Verbeek, *Spinoza's Theologico-Political Treatise*, 154.
[23] Spinoza, *Collected Works* (ed. Curley) i, 229, 228–9; Klever, "Spinoza's Life and Works," 30.
[24] Spinoza, *Collected Works* (ed. Curley) i, 229; Thijssen-Schoute, *Nederlands Cartesianisme*, 389.
[25] Spinoza, *Collected Works* (ed. Curley) i, 207; Schmaltz, "Spinoza on Eternity," 209.
[26] Spinoza, *Opera* iv, 8; Spinoza, *Collected Works* (ed. Curley) i, 167.

particular divergence in his preface, pointing out that Spinoza, contrary to Descartes, thinks "the will is not distinct from the intellect." Neither are the passions which sway our wills separate from our intellects, the passions being, for Spinoza, in essence inadequate ideas controlling our actions.[27] Undeniably, the strategy Spinoza and Meyer resort to is a distinctly curious, even bizarre one for an ambitious young philosopher and his admirers to adopt but also subtle, devious, and effective. During his final months at Rijnsburg, Spinoza was aligning cautiously with, but simultaneously less obviously distancing himself from, the Dutch Cartesians.

Without too blatantly subverting Descartes' teaching in the early sections of this little more than eighty page text (without counting the supplement, the *Cogitata Metaphysica*), Spinoza develops a conception of God as universal, perfect, and the cause of all creation and sustaining creation, in a way that hints at, or does not preclude, his underlying identification of God with everything that is. He insists on the unity of God and his power, will and intellect being all one. Because the God he delineates is constant, eternal, and never changes his decrees, Spinoza's God is undeniably a free cause but cannot be said to have a free will that can alter the direction of anything previously determined. Spinoza is hence also stricter (and more un-Baconian) than Descartes in never straying from mathematic reason as "this unshakable foundation of ours" for certain knowledge. Mathematics becomes, for the first time, the absolute basis of all science and sound knowledge without theology being allowed access at any point. Spinoza slips in asides that follow from this rule that obviously clash with Descartes' principles such as that it is "impossible for one to think that something may come from nothing."[28]

In the book's concluding sections, the fundamental divergence between Spinoza and the Cartesians becomes more obvious. For Spinoza, God is the universal cause of all motion without any exception, whereas in Descartes God is the substantive, generalized universal cause of motion in inanimate things and perhaps animals but not humans or spirits. Here God might be the ultimate cause in a more occasional "modal" sense but supposedly always leaves space for freedom of the will. "Because motion has God alone as its cause," held Spinoza, "it never has any power to exist of itself, but is, as it were, created by God at every moment."[29] Consequently, where Descartes emphatically upholds the reality of miracles, maintaining that God intervenes to alter the normal order of nature for his own reasons "and to show his power to men," Spinoza directly contradicts him, objecting that such interventions cannot be known or allowed for in any way by philosophy which must be kept perennially separate from theology, for Spinoza an

---

[27] Meyer, "Preface," 230; Barebone and Rice, "Introduction," xviii; Sangiacomo, *Spinoza on Reason*, 35.
[28] Spinoza, *Collected Works* (ed. Curley) i, 243, 261; Schliesser, "Newton and Spinoza," 439.
[29] Spinoza, *Collected Works* (ed. Curley) i, 277; Garber, *Descartes' Metaphysical Physics*, 275–9.

absolute divide that figures much less rigorously in Descartes.[30] Equally, the existence of angels, he adds, in the *Cogitata Metaphysica*, cannot be known by us.

Meyer's generalization both true and yet misleading, sanctioned by his friend, that the author nowhere contradicts Descartes' core principles plainly means in reality that Spinoza nowhere contradicts conclusions Descartes *should* have drawn from his principles. Not contradicting Descartes holds good, Meyer maintains, even in the book's substantial forty-six page supplementary section, the *Cogitata*, where Spinoza launches into a bolder foray into metaphysics. On one level, this supplement's purpose is to confirm Spinoza's joining with the Cartesians in opposing the more traditional positions of the Western world's Neo-Aristotelians about time, eternity, existence, qualities, and essence. It repeatedly asserts that their "substantial forms and real accidents" are "clearly absurd,"[31] and that the philosophers of the past erred by judging "the things from the words, not the words from the things." At the same time, he reaffirms, or appears to reaffirm, key Cartesian positions such as that substance divides into two basic kinds, "extension and thought." Unrelenting Cartesian stress on the distinctness of "extension and thought" is indeed a fundamental feature of all Spinoza's early philosophizing.

However, while holding ostensibly to Descartes' substance dualism and approximating to several of his views about matter, claiming "God is the principal cause of motion" (Part II, Prop. 12) rather than the only cause, Spinoza is notably wary and elusive, in fact skips the point when it comes to Descartes' central principle that matter is inert and motion wholly external to matter, a difference that would later evolve into a key distinction between Cartesianism and Spinozism and a key element in Spinoza's doctrine that God is a free cause but does not possess freedom of will, and this is clearly hinted at already here.[32] Moreover, while paying lip service to mind being a separate mode, a thinking dimension created by God *ex nihilo* [from nothing], Spinoza scarcely supports the Cartesian view that mind is a separate substance and, in the *Cogitata* one after another, systematically erodes and deliberately undermines this and other core doctrines insisted on by Descartes himself and his chief academic expositors such as Professor Adriaan Heereboord (1614–61), a mainstay of the Leiden philosophical fraternity whose private classes and lectures Spinoza himself had almost certainly attended a few years earlier, prior to leaving Amsterdam.[33]

"For it is one thing to inquire into the nature of things," runs Spinoza's typically robust anti-scholastic empiricism in the *Cogitata*, "and another into the modes by

---

[30] Spinoza, *Collected Works* (ed. Curley) i, 276–7, 340–1; Garber, *Descartes' Metaphysical Physics*, 300–5; Israel, "Spinoza as an Expounder," 50; Buyse, "Le 'Démasquement'," 32–3.
[31] Spinoza, *Collected Works* (ed. Curley) i, 316.
[32] Spinoza, *Collected Works* (ed. Curley) i, 266–7, 276; Gaukroger, *Descartes*, 377; Schmaltz, "Spinoza and Descartes," 71–2, 76; Buyse, "Le 'Démasquement'," 19.
[33] Steenbakkers, "Vijandige overname," 50n44; Schmaltz, "Spinoza on Eternity," 209.

which things are perceived by us."³⁴ Here, he directly hints at and even sketches out for the first time in print several of his most characteristic philosophical positions. Although he states outright that "God is the cause of all things, and that he acts from absolute freedom of the will," he hardly means by *ex absoluta libertate voluntatis* what Descartes means by "freedom of the will." For while Spinoza's God is certainly a free cause and "nothing happens except by divine power alone," everything that occurs happens necessarily. God is immutable; in God thought and extension are one; and since in God there is no inconsistency or change, "he must have decreed from eternity that he would produce those things he now produces; and since nothing is more necessary in its existence than what God has decreed should exist, it follows that a necessity of existing has been in all created things from eternity."³⁵

Interestingly, Spinoza here expressly precludes the stance Leibniz would later adopt to escape Spinozist necessity: "nor can we say that those things are contingent because God could have decreed otherwise," since the very concept of eternity "means nothing could have happened either before or afterwards." Although, some scholars claim Spinoza, in his early work, wobbles somewhat between an Aristotelian conception of "eternity" as duration without end or beginning, and a Platonic conception remote from all time and duration, here Spinoza clearly insists, as he expresses it later, that "in eternity there is no when, nor before, nor after [in aeterno non detur quando, nec ante, nec post]," nor any relationship with time, from which "it follows that God never existed before those decrees, nor could exist without them [Deum ante sua decreta non fuisse, nec sine ipsis esse posse]."³⁶

When "ordinary people" find "no stronger proof of God's providence and rule than that based on ignorance of causes," or what they call "miracles," contends Spinoza, they reveal that they have "no knowledge whatever of the nature of God's will and have attributed to him a human will."³⁷ This universal error of anthropomorphism he considers the prime cause of human "superstition." God neither loves, nor hates, nor becomes angry with anyone or anything and never diverges from his necessary laws of motion and rest. Spinoza here asserts too the relativity of the moral concepts of "good" and "bad," a relativity central to his unpublished writing, the *Korte Verhandeling* earlier, but now for the first time affirmed in print. He anchors this stance, moreover, in a way that directly contradicts Descartes' corresponding standpoint: "nothing is said to be either good or bad considered alone, but only in respect to another thing to which it is advantageous in acquiring

---

³⁴ Spinoza, *Collected Works* (ed. Curley) i, 302; Steenbakkers, "Vijandige overname," 43.
³⁵ Spinoza, *Opera* i, 238, 243; Spinoza, *Collected Works* (ed. Curley) i, 304, 309.
³⁶ Spinoza, *Opera* ii, 75; Spinoza, *Collected Works* (ed. Curley) i, 309, 316–17; Chaui, *Nervura do real*, 422, 428, 432, 434; Steenbakkers, "Vijandige overname," 39.
³⁷ Spinoza, *Collected Works* (ed. Curley) i, 326.

what it loves, or the contrary."[38] Even God, it turns out, cannot be said to be "good" in the absolute sense proclaimed by theologians, as God is not relative to anything else. Here, indeed, one finds the ground plan of Spinoza's deployment of "natura naturans" and "natura naturata."[39] Sin and intrinsic good and evil are conceptually wholly extinguished.

After checking and finalizing the manuscript "which you sent me through our friend De Vries," Spinoza wrote, to Meyer, Rieuwertsz, and the others involved in producing the book in Amsterdam, on 3 August 1663, informing them that "I now return it to you through him." Actually, it was not De Vries who brought the package back to Amsterdam, for though "our friend De Vries promised to take it with him," Spinoza adds in a postscript, as "he does not know when he is returning, I am sending it by someone else."[40] In Rieuwertsz's bookshop "in 't Martelaars-Boek" [in the Martyr's Book] in the "Dirk van Assensteegh," today the "Dirk van Hasseltssteeg," a small alley running off the Nieuwezijds Voorburgwal, one of central Amsterdam's main streets, in the heart of the city, not far from the city hall, burgomasters' offices and city government, the bookshop where much of consequence in Spinoza's life had already occurred and would occur later, this, the only book ever to appear under his own name during Spinoza's lifetime, was prepared for publication. So fast did publishers and printers set to work that the Latin version appeared already later that August (Figure 14.2).[41]

Spinoza was distinctly nervous, his early August reply to Meyer shows, about the pending publication, owing doubtless to his not altogether straightforward, in fact academically decidedly subversive strategy and goal, and his already distinctly dubious reputation. Worried about his substantial departures from Descartes' demonstrations and intentions, he asked Meyer to introduce several last minute alterations while again insisting on the text's essentially didactic purpose, "point out at the same time, either there [page 4] or wherever you please, that I composed [the First Part] in two weeks. Thus, forewarned, no one will suppose what I present is so clear that it could not have been expounded more clearly and not be put off by a mere word or two which, here and there, they may find obscure." He also urges Meyer to state more forcefully that "I have demonstrated many things in a different way from how Descartes demonstrated them, not to correct Descartes but only to preserve my order of exposition and not increase the number of axioms and, for the same reason," he adds, "have needed to prove many things Descartes leaves

---

[38] Spinoza, *Collected Works* (ed. Curley) i, 313–15; Israel, "Spinoza as an Expounder," 42; Douglas, *Spinoza and Dutch Cartesianism*, 86; Nadler, *Think Least of Death*, 16–17, 30.
[39] Spinoza, *Collected Works* (ed. Curley) i, 314–15; Steenbakkers, "Vijandige overname," 43; Douglas, *Spinoza and Dutch Cartesianism*, 71–2.
[40] Spinoza, *Collected Works* (ed. Curley) i, 216, Spinoza to Meyer, Voorburg, 3 Aug. 1663.
[41] Van Eeghen, *Amsterdamse boekhandel* iv, 63; Van de Ven, *Documenting Spinoza*, ch. 6.

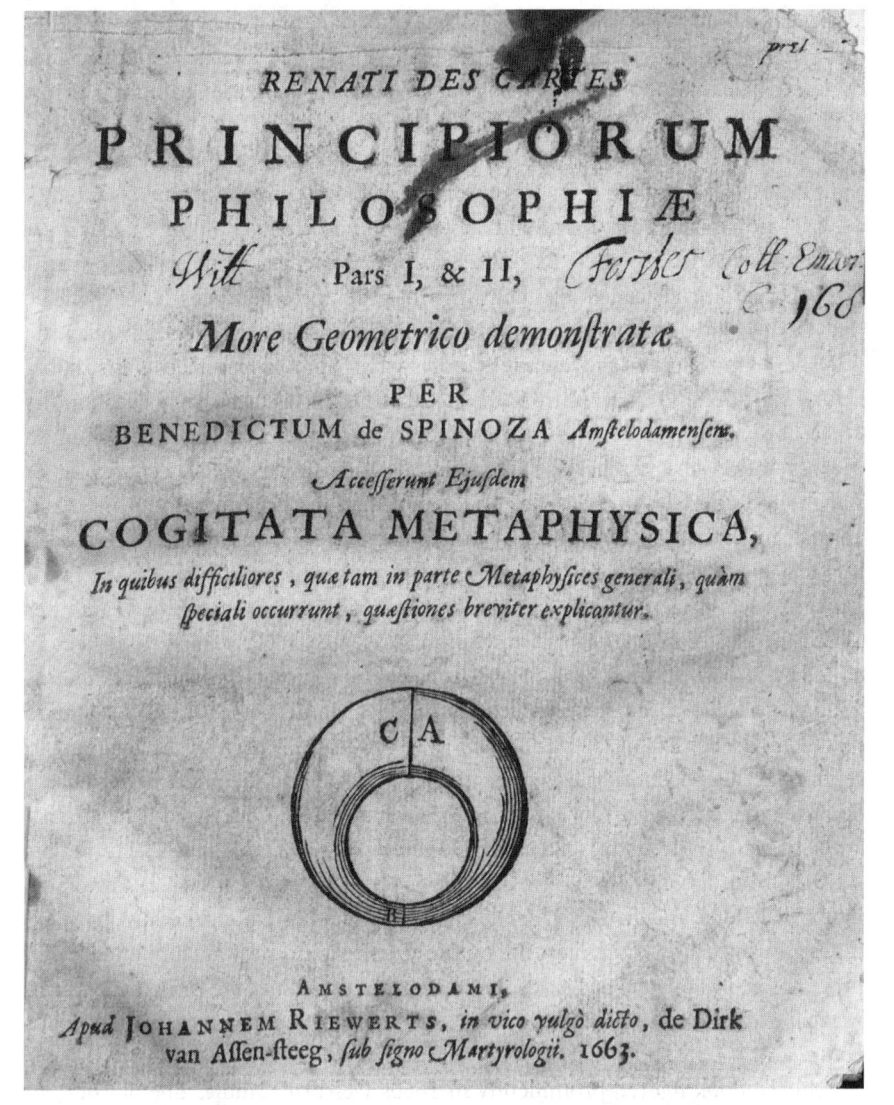

Figure 14.2 Spinoza, *Renati Des Cartes Principiorum philosophiae Pars I, & II, More Geometrico Demonstratae.* Spinoza; 1. Amstelodami: apud Johannem Riewerts, in vico vulgò dicto, de Dirk van Assen-steeg, sub signo Martyrologii, 1663. IAS Spinoza Research Collection.

devoid of any proof, besides other things Descartes omitted."[42] It is thus quite wrong to construe the book as just an exposition of Descartes' arguments and conclusions.

---

[42] Spinoza, *Collected Works* (ed. Curley) i, 229.

Finally, Spinoza asks Meyer to "omit at the end what you wrote against that petty man [*illum homunculum*], and delete it entirely." This refers to one or other declared public opponent of the young "atheist" and the group of fringe "Cartesians" around him, presumably teaching at one of the Republic's higher education institutions. Although various candidates have been proposed, perhaps the likeliest, as Klever argues, was the remarkable Florentius Schuyl (1619–69), a well-known medical man and botanist since 1640 holding a chair at 's-Hertogenbosch, in Dutch Brabant. Son of a preacher, Schuyl was an ardent Cartesian of official academic establishment stamp and stout defender of the view that Cartesianism admirably supports the Christian faith.[43] Forgotten today, he was a key figure in Dutch Descartes studies when Spinoza penned his first book. Schuyl's prominence derived from the fact that Descartes when, at his peak in the 1630s, preparing *De l'Homme*, one of his principal books, examined human corpses and visited butcher shops in several Dutch towns to inspect corpses of slaughtered animals, studying the brains and nervous systems of both men and animals to further his investigation of the linkage of body and mind. But, worried this text could offend the theologians and provoke the authorities, in the event Descartes left it to one side. The book only finally appeared twelve years after Descartes' death, in a crucial Latin edition in August 1662, published at Leiden, edited by Schuyl, entitled *Renatus Descartes de Homine, Figuris et latinate donatus a Florentio Schuylio*, a copy of which Spinoza kept in his personal library.[44] Steno read Schuyl's edition of *De Homine*, in May 1662, and it played a pivotal part in reinforcing his rejection of Descartes' theory of mind and the brain, as very likely Spinoza's rejection of it too; probably, Spinoza and Steno discussed it together.[45] Two splendid portraits of Schuyl survive today, one in The Hague's Mauritshuis showing him in confidant, not to say domineering, pose (Figure 14.3). A notable figure at Leiden and in Dutch intellectual (and medical) life generally by 1662, especially regarding discussion of the mind and brain, he was appointed a full professor of philosophy at Leiden, in 1664, and, in 1667, to the principal chair in medicine making him director also of Leiden's botanical garden (*hortus botanicus*).

Schuyl's book figured prominently in 1660s Descartes studies due not only to the intrinsic importance of Descartes' theory of the mind and brain but also to Schuyl's forty page preface "Ad Lectorem," stressing the crucial role in contemporary philosophy of Descartes' discussion of the mind–body relationship, highlighting his ontological dualism fundamentally separating body and mind, and underlining the fundamental divide between men and animals, and between men

---

[43] Sassen, *Wijsgerig onderwijs*, 28–33; Thijssen-Schoute, *Nederlands Cartesianisme*, 301–2, 389; Klever, "Qui était l'homunculus," 24–7; Barebone and Rice, "Introduction," xx; Van de Ven, *Printing Spinoza*, 33.
[44] Van Sluis and Musschenga, *Boeken van Spinoza*, 38.
[45] Grigoropolou, "Steno's Critique of Descartes," 121.

Figure 14.3 *Florentius Schuyl* (1619–69) by Frans van Mieris the Elder, 1666. Reproduction courtesy of Mauritshuis, The Hague.

and the rest of nature, precisely the basic Cartesian grounding Spinoza was busy undermining. For Descartes and Schuyl, animals lack the immaterial souls (minds) rendering men a unique God-designed species possessing reason, judgement and speech, purposely endowed by God with souls immaterial and immortal.[46] Even if Klever's conjecture (rejected by Van de Ven) proves incorrect, and the demeaning reference *illum homunculum* is to someone else, Schuyl's preface certainly must have grated on Meyer and Spinoza less by proclaiming the decisive truth value of Descartes' breakthrough, the unassailable cogency of Descartes' reasoning separating the human body and soul, and its perfect accord with church teaching, than by his pointedly attacking certain despicable, unworthy persons trying to tarnish the glory of Descartes' achievement.

According to Schuyl, certain disreputable persons in Holland were attempting to banish "truth from its throne, putting shadows in its place" by injecting perplexing difficulties, useless questions, and sly qualifications designed to hurl mankind disastrously back into the morass of "atheism," that heap of useless philosophizing of "Zoroaster, Pythagoras, Anaxagoras, Plato, Pliny, Plutarch and

---

[46] Schuyl, "Ad Lectorem," pp. A2v and A4; Van Ruler, *Arnold Geulincx's* Ethics, pp. xi–xxii.

Lipsius" from which even the great Aristotle proved unable to extricate it.[47] Who the despicable types fouling the venerable truth of Descartes' principles were, Schuyl preferred not to say outright, but, by 1662, this was clear enough to scholars in and around Leiden. To add insult to injury, intentionally or unintentionally (the former seeming more likely), the Latin phrase Schuyl employs when depicting these reprobates hindering solid Christian good sense—"obscuris, intricatis et spinosis argutiis"—utilizing the Latin word "spinosus" meaning "prickly" or like "piercing thorns," plainly resorts to the same pun on Spinoza's surname that his Sephardic opponents regularly employed.[48]

Whether to jibe back or not jibe at *illum homunculum* mattered to Spinoza because he did not wish to find himself from the outset at war with the established academic Cartesian fraternity, or be perceived as undermining their project. His aim was to proceed with exemplary caution. Spinoza wanted Meyer's cutting reference to the relevant professor deleted because, for now, he wanted all polemics meticulously avoided. "I should like everyone to be able readily to accept that this publication is meant for the benefit of all men, and that in publishing it," he and his friends were "motivated solely by a wish to spread the truth, and hence that you [i.e. his friends, were...] chiefly concerned to make this little book welcome to all, that you are inviting men in a spirit of goodwill to take up study of the true philosophy, and that your aim is the good of all. This everyone will readily believe when it is observed that no one is attacked and nothing advanced that may be offensive to any person."[49] Should however the scholar in question "or some other display his malevolent mind" afterwards, Meyer would then be free to denigrate "his life and practices" and would find himself doing so with applause. (Having lost his mother and two brothers in the plague of 1635–6, Schuyl himself died of the plague, in 1669.)

Following Spinoza's directions to the letter, Meyer explained that the author "had been forced to demonstrate quite a number of things that Descartes asserted without any demonstration, and add others that he completely omitted." To this, Meyer added the puzzling, not to say self-contradictory, claim that no one should suppose Spinoza is teaching here "his own opinions, or only those he approves of"; for while judging some of Descartes' doctrines to be true, he explained, Spinoza rejects others as false and "admits that he has added some views of his own."[50] The book appeared late in August with its various figures and diagrams presumably drawn by Spinoza himself (he evidently had a taste for drawing visual representations of his ideas), together with his lengthy appendix, the *Cogitata Metaphysica*, which is separately stated to have as its "author Benedictus de

---

[47] Schuyl, "Ad Lectorem," p. A3v; Kors, *Naturalism and Unbelief*, 110.
[48] Schuyl, "Ad Lectorem," p. A2; Spinoza, *Correspondance* (ed. Rovere), 119.
[49] Spinoza, *Opera* iv, 72–3; Spinoza, *Correspondance* (ed. Rovere), 119.
[50] Meyer, "Preface," 229; Israel, "Spinoza as an Expounder," 42.

Spinoza Amstelodamensi [of Amsterdam]." Heading Meyer's curious prologue appears a ten-line eulogistic poem, "Ad librum," warmly extolling the book and stressing Descartes' debt to Spinoza and also the author's future debt to himself, meaning Spinoza's duty to present his own philosophy for the world's benefit. The poem is signed I.B.*M.D.*, the last two initials in the original edition being in a slightly different font, these initials standing, scholars agree, for "Iohannes Bouwmeester M.D. [Medicinae Doctor]."[51]

The Dutch version of Spinoza's work, in places slightly bolder in emphasis and expanded (by about a page and a half, or forty-eight sentences, of new material), under the title *Beginselen van de cartesiaansche wijsbegeerte*, appeared well over a year later, Van de Ven estimates, in early December 1664, with a title page announcing Rieuwertsz as publisher and the translation from Latin to be by "P.B." (almost certainly Pieter Balling). The printer was Herman Aelsz, in Amsterdam, the same who was afterwards sentenced, in June 1668, to a 630 guilder fine for printing the allegedly blasphemous *Bloemhof van allerley Lieflijkheyd* of the Brothers Koerbagh, Spinoza's allies in challenging the existing order of thought and belief.[52] Significantly, one of Spinoza's most central and challenging doctrines, that "the common people find no stronger proof of God's providence and rule than that based on their ignorance of causes," is an additional paragraph present only in this 1664 Dutch version where Spinoza adds also: "it is laughable for the philosophers whenever ignorant of the causes of things to seek refuge in God's pleasure." The absence of this provocative addition in the original Latin raises the question whether this and other small addenda in the Dutch version originated with Spinoza himself (as seems likely), their omission from the Latin version reflecting his earlier anxiety to deflect initial suspicion and ire as much as possible, or with Balling, Bouwmeester, or Meyer. Jelles who was later reported to have paid for the publication was as a rule distinctly averse to polemics and conflict.[53]

Spinoza's *Descartes' Principles* played an important part in his emergence as an intellectual force on the contemporary Dutch scene and internationally. Locke read the book soon after it appeared, he mentions in a notebook he began in 1664, leaving a note to himself to read more of this author's work.[54] The first time Leibniz ever mentions Spinoza in a surviving letter was in April 1669, when, agreeing with his mentor, Jacob Thomasius, that "the disciple [Clauberg] is clearer than the master [Descartes]," he remarks that none of the principal interpreters of Descartes whom he lists as "Clauberg, De Raey, Spinoza, Clerselier, Heereboord,

---

[51] Spinoza, *Opera* i, 134; Steenbakkers and Bordoli, "Lodewijk Meijer's Tribute," 241–3; Van de Ven, *Printing Spinoza*, 31, 306.
[52] Van de Ven, *Printing Spinoza*, 60–5; Steenbakkers, "Nederlandse vertalingen," 8; Spruit, "Cristianesimo ragionevole," 525n3.
[53] Mertens, "Where Thou Dwellest," 25–6, 40.
[54] Klibansky and Gough, "Introduction," p. xxxi, n9.

Tobias Andriae, and Henricus Regius," provide anything but "paraphrases" of Descartes' main ideas, suggesting that either he had not studied Spinoza's book closely or was going merely by hearsay without having yet examined the book himself.[55]

Spinoza's commitment to the project and willingness to invest time in it, in any case, seems to have been limited. As published in August 1663, the book is clearly signposted as unfinished, with Part III constituting just a small fragment of four pages, purporting or at least intending to "set out" the workings of nature on the basis of the principles expounded in the first two parts, encompassing "everything that is observed in the whole of nature" mathematically conceived and expressed, the most universal principles of natural things, and "those things that follow from them." This third part was meant to provide a universal natural history to help us "understand the nature of plants and of man," "how they gradually come to be and are generated from seeds," and "how the stars, earth and finally all those things that we find in this visible world could have arisen," including comets. It presumably implied some theory of natural self-creation, a proto-evolutionary theory, but what Spinoza actually offers, starkly brief and flimsy, scarcely goes beyond claiming that everything we see in the heavens is made of the same matter as everything on earth, and that matter on earth, as in space, consists of minute particles (or atoms) wrought into different arrangements shaping the infinite variety of things.[56]

Spinoza was never to develop a theory of atoms or discuss these questions in any detail. In his preface, Meyer points out that the book is unfinished, expressing the hope, shared doubtless by all the group, that Spinoza would eventually bring out "a new edition to follow this hurried one, to expand which we shall also try to persuade him to complete Part III, concerning the visible world in its entirety." Finishing the project would require also "some propositions concerning the nature and property of fluids" in Part II "and I shall do my best to persuade the author to do this at the same time."[57] Meyer and the group hoped to see a complete philosophy of natural science. But their attempts to persuade Spinoza to expand this text with more scientific matter were unsuccessful, not because he failed to see that such an overview of universal natural history was an essential goal for him, but because he did not yet feel ready to undertake it and, perhaps more relevant, was gripped by the impulse to get on with his main work, the *Ethics*, now reaching its middle and even perhaps later sections. During the fifteen-month interval between publication of the Latin text, in August 1663, and the Dutch version, Spinoza added nothing substantial to his *Descartes'*

---

[55] Leibniz to J. Thomasius 20/30 April 1669 in Leibniz, *Sämtliche Schriften und Briefe* 2nd ser., i, 15; Laerke, *Leibniz lecteur*, 76–7.
[56] Spinoza, *Collected Works* (ed. Curley) i, 294–8; Van de Ven, *Printing Spinoza*, 62.
[57] Meyer, "Preface," 228; Manzini, "When Was Spinoza," 198–9.

Principles beyond a few clarifications and remarks, opting simply to leave his incipient Part III standing as a bare fragment.

"I have not thought about the work on Descartes," admitted Spinoza to Van Blijenbergh, writing from Schiedam in January 1665, "nor given any further attention to it since it appeared in Dutch, the reason for which would take too long to tell."[58] No doubt he felt he had too much still to learn about the laws of motion, fluids, atoms, astronomy and a great deal else to be able write more at this stage. What can be said about Spinoza's theory of creation and evolution, as summarized in the *Principles* and the *Cogitata*, is that everything that exists follows the same set of rules, that "creation is an activity in which no causes concur except the efficient ones," so that a "created thing is that which presupposes nothing except God in order to exist," and that God's or Nature's "activity remains the same in creating the world as in preserving it." Spinoza's creation and evolution, unlike those of Descartes, thus form a single uninterrupted continuum. Very likely, Spinoza was now simply unwilling to set aside what to him was the true philosophy to go through the motions of restating what he saw as Descartes' errors.[59]

Spinoza's correspondence with the pious Calvinist Willem van Blijenbergh (1632–96), a prosperous Dordrecht grain merchant, cousin and close friend of the artist Samuel van Hoogstraten (1627–78), commenced shortly after the *Beginselen* appeared in late 1664. An amateur philosopher and poetry lover who by preference read philosophy books in Dutch, Van Blijenbergh initiated their half year (December 1664–June 1665) correspondence on 12 December 1664, referring specifically to the translated version. His first letter arrived two weeks after Spinoza took up temporary lodgings on the "Long Orchard" farm, near Schiedam when seeking refuge from the plague outbreak raging at the time: "I have now had the honour of reading through, frequently and attentively, your recently published treatise," began Van Blijenbergh, and found it very "solid."[60] The two got off to a good start. A regent member of the city government in close touch with literary and artistic circles in and around Dordrecht, but also with the Reformed consistory, Van Blijenbergh was a noted intellectual presence locally, and at first sight exactly the kind of philosophically inclined regent Spinoza hoped to draw to his side.

In his first missive, Van Blijenbergh evinces the sort of amateur zeal for philosophy, in enthusiastic support of Cartesianism so prevalent in the United Provinces at the time. A passionate Cartesian, he felt drawn to those Cartesians, in particular Abraham Heidanus (1597–1678), aiming to harmonize Cartesianism

---

[58] Spinoza, *Collected Works* (ed. Curley) i, 382; Van de Ven, *Documenting Spinoza*, ch. 6.
[59] Spinoza, *Collected Works* (ed. Curley) i, 334–5; Manzini, "When Was Spinoza," 200–1.
[60] Spinoza, *Collected Works* (ed. Curley) i, 354–7; Van Dalen, "Willem Laurensz. van Blijenbergh," 347, 349.

with Reformed theology. It soon emerged, though, that Van Blijenbergh was not one to show flexibility on theological issues. During the latter part of his six-month correspondence with Spinoza, from April or May 1665, he was at the same time writing a tract defending Heidanus, his favourite Cartesian hero, and also the hard-line Utrecht Calvinist preacher, Cornelis Gentman (1617–96), against an unnamed Mennonite (in fact, Spinoza's friend, Jacob Ostens) accused by Van Blijenbergh of being a barely disguised Socinian.[61]

Fascinated but also puzzled by Spinoza's exposition of Descartes, Van Blijenbergh's priority was to harmonize Cartesianism with Christian truth or, as he put it, "reason" with Holy Scripture which at this point,[62] in his struggle against "ruinous heresy" and the "contagious sickness and cancer" of *Socinisterij*, meant ensuring nothing seeped through uncontested that does not fully harmonize with Reformed Christology, the Trinity and Original Sin, revolving around the belief that Christ the Son sacrificed himself for all men to redeem their sins, was miraculously resurrected and is the sole path to redemption. "Eternal punishment of the godless" and belief that Christ, being divine and not a man, could not sin, mattered immensely to Van Blijenbergh. Socinian suggestion that God does not foresee or know evil human acts beforehand, that humans possess free will, he agreed with Heidanus, would unacceptably compromise divine omniscience and omnipotence.[63] Here, Spinoza diverged widely from Heidanus *and* the Socinians.

What motivated Van Blijenbergh to undertake this epistolary debate was eagerness to elicit a "fuller statement of [Spinoza's] own view." A central problem in his mind, his text against Socinianism reveals, was how to reconcile God's omniscience and omnipotence with the existence of evil in the human mind and will; either God knows about and causes that evil, he rightly saw, in which case he is responsible for it, or does not, in which case he lacks foreknowledge of events to come.[64] To him this was a troubling predicament. By the time he penned his second reply to Van Blijenbergh, dated Schiedam, 28 January 1665, Spinoza had realized, from the latter's follow-up missive, of 16 January, "that I was quite mistaken" in thinking he and his correspondent were in accord, now seeing "that we disagree not only about the things ultimately derived from first principles, but also about the first principles themselves."[65] Their initial jointly avowed shared Cartesianism thus immediately fell apart under scrutiny.

As Spinoza could not openly admit to not considering God omniscient or in possession of foreknowledge, he answered evasively that, indeed, nothing can happen contrary to God's will, and that Adam's sin, and indeed all sin, should

---

[61] Blijenbergh, *Sociniaensche Ziel*, 7; Van Dalen, "Willem Laurensz Van Blijenbergh," 364.
[62] See Blijenbergh to Spinoza, Dordrecht, 16 Jan. 1665 in Spinoza, *Collected Works* (ed. Curley) i, 361.
[63] Blijenbergh, *Sociniaensche Ziel*, preface and pp. 11–12; Van Bunge, "Tragic Idealist," 269–70.
[64] Spinoza, *Collected Works* (ed. Curley) i, 355–6; Blijenbergh, *Sociniaensche Ziel*, 11–16, 28–9; Sangiacomo, "Adam's Sin," 4.
[65] Spinoza, *Collected Works* (ed. Curley) i, 375; Laerke, *Spinoza and the Freedom*, 64.

be deemed lack of "perfection" rather than positive evil, adding that Scripture discourses in parables and ways comprehensible to the common people and not in precise terms. The difficulty here was that Spinoza appeared to hold that God is not just the creator and cause of everything which Calvinists could readily accept, but that God is directly responsible for men's shortcomings and wrongdoing.[66] Perturbed by the notion that wrongdoing is simply a lesser good, or absence of perfection, rather than positive evil, Van Blijenbergh responded three weeks later with a fifteen-page letter again lauding Spinoza's penetrating insight and admitting to using several of his arguments in his own thinking and writing, but expressing bafflement at Meyer's remark "in the Preface," that "you have a completely different view of God and the soul, and particularly of the soul's will," from Descartes. Equally disturbing, from Spinoza's letter he inferred that however penetrating his mind "you do not assign that infallible character and divine truth to Holy Scripture that I believe to be there."[67]

This particularly long letter, dated Dordrecht, 16 January 1665, the first where Van Blijenbergh's full name appears in the *Opera Posthuma* (in the earlier exchange he appears simply as W.v.B.) reveals profound dissatisfaction with Spinoza's schema whereby "the godless" are merely less "perfect" than the pious and equally doing God's bidding, or at least acting as God made them. "Indeed, does it not seem to be a contradiction in God that he should give us an order to restrain our will within the limits of our understanding, and yet not give us so much essence, or perfection that we can accomplish that?"[68] If "nothing happens against God's will," if evil, according to Spinoza, is just lack or loss of a better state of mind and body, Spinoza's argument seemed to him to signify that godless unbelievers obey God no less than do believers, men being as dependent on God as plants and stones. Why then restrain our will within the limits of understanding? "From what has been said, it seems impossible that evil, or being deprived of a better state, for God, should be a negation."[69] This deprives us of prayer and aspiration towards God. If God has no knowledge of evil, why would he punish evil? Provided I can escape the judge, why should I not commit all kinds of wrongdoing for self-enrichment? What kind of moral system makes fear of punishment the sole restraint on those moved chiefly by the passions with which God has endowed them? Scripture alone shows the path out of the moral maze. It was a powerful moral challenge. Instead of winning Van Blijenbergh over, Spinoza had utterly shocked him.

Less than two weeks later, on 28 January, Spinoza answered with one of his longest surviving letters, seven pages long, mostly cogently to the point, insisting

---

[66] Spinoza, *Briefwisseling*, 154; Spinoza, *Collected Works* (ed. Curley) i, 355; Van Bunge, "Tragic Idealist," 270–1.
[67] Spinoza, *Correspondance* (ed. Rovere), 153; Spinoza, *Collected Works* (ed. Curley) i, 371.
[68] Spinoza, *Nagelate Schriften*, 539; Spinoza, *Briefwisseling*, 170.
[69] Spinoza, *Briefwisseling*, 171.

that one "who abstains from knavery only from the dread of punishment (I hope that this is not you) does not in any way act from love and does not at all esteem virtue,"[70] but at the same time, somewhat impatiently expresses frustration and annoyance. Still paying lip service to his correspondent's love of truth, he regrets their being much further apart than he had anticipated. No demonstration in philosophical terms, however cogent, "has weight with you," he complains, far from altogether fairly, "unless it agrees with the explanation which you, or theologians known to you, attribute to sacred Scripture." For this reason, "I can hardly believe we can instruct one another with our letters." For his part, there were many places where he did not understand Scripture's meaning but was so convinced by demonstrations of reason that even should he prove to be wrong "they would still make me happy, since I enjoy them and seek to pass my life, not in sorrow and sighing, but in peace, joy and cheerfulness," words his later critic Nieuwentijt highlighted to demonstrate that Spinoza was an impostor, not a genuine seeker after truth.[71]

To this, Van Blijenbergh answered loftily, on 19 February, in a letter sent on, from Schiedam, after Spinoza had returned to Voorburg, that he too, having "expected an amicable and instructive exchange," regretted finding instead that Spinoza's second letter "does not sound very friendly." Even so, he felt compelled to persist in urging him to explain himself more clearly, rightly remarking that Spinoza does not "assign the soul the freedom Descartes ascribes to it," and inquiring: "if our soul does not have that freedom, is our action not God's action and is our will not God's will?"[72] Replying in mid-March a trifle testily, Spinoza denied giving "the slightest reason for offence." But however tiresome, Van Blijenbergh was deeply earnest and by no means missing the point. At his own suggestion, he soon afterwards paid Spinoza a visit in Voorburg, in late March, a springtime face-to-face conference which he wished could have lasted longer, he remarked later, that left him no clearer than before. "How shall I be able to distinguish," he complains, quite justifiably, "when reading your *Principles* and *Cogitata Metaphysica* what is given as Descartes' opinion from what is stated as your own?"[73]

In his published attack on the *TTP*, a decade later, in 1674, a copy of which Spinoza kept in his personal library,[74] Van Blijenbergh, besides condemning the Koerbaghs' *Bloemhof* (1668) for "vomiting forth utter godlessness, atheism and subversion of the Christian religion in the most blasphemous manner," vividly recalls his person-to-person discussion with Spinoza, of March 1665, about God's omniscience. Once while speaking about this with "the gentleman [Spinoza]" he

---

[70] Spinoza, *Collected Works* (ed. Curley) i, 380.
[71] Nieuwentijt, *Regt Gebruik der Werelt Beschouwingen*, 6.
[72] Spinoza, *Collected Works* (ed. Curley) i, 386.
[73] Spinoza, *Collected Works* (ed. Curley) i, 391.
[74] Van Sluis and Musschenga, *Boeken van Spinoza*, 36–7.

believed to be the *TTP*'s author, though he did not know this for certain, the latter answered: "since religion is so obscure and dubious, why should not the government of the republic secure the same effect, the community's obedience, using stiff punishments, as is achieved by that deceptive means of religion?" From this "one can very easily perceive the opinion of this man, and those like him, concerning the role of religion" and its status. As for Spinoza's "design" to introduce a "political religion" into society, he concludes: "had I not found in our writer the marks of a fine intellect, at this point I would have been persuaded that he was raving mad."[75]

With his *Descartes' Principles* Spinoza gained a place for himself in the front rank of European expositors of Cartesian thought, and attracted widespread attention, but also stoked puzzlement and suspicion. His book figured among the most authoritative commentaries on Cartesian philosophy through the 1660s, yet in the very text where he professes to expound Descartes' system for students and academics, held Van Blijenbergh, and later Bontekoe, Van Til and others, Spinoza, in subtle but fundamental ways, perverts Descartes' meaning and basic principles: "the composition of that work is done against the express meaning of Descartes [de samenstel van dat werk is gemaakt tegens d'expresse meining van Descartes]," Bontekoe rightly affirmed after Spinoza's death. Likewise, when tutoring students, adds Van Til, he attracted them "under pretence of being an admirer and expounder of the Cartesian philosophy and then, behind this facade, subtly began undermining some of its principles."[76] Always subversive, Spinoza's real aim in employing the geometric method here, held Bontekoe, was

> to mix his diabolical concepts with those of Descartes and coax Cartesians to accept them the more easily, so that they, believing him a true Cartesian, often acknowledge these as authentic Cartesian ideas when they are not, being concepts which actually besmirch that philosophy, obscure and destroy it and often without anyone noticing, overthrow it. One sees all this from the work's foul preface, and from the *Cogitata Metaphysica* appended to it. In the Preface [by Meyer], Spinoza has the effrontery to claim that in that book he had had to deal with things according to Descartes' opinion, but has insight into still higher *principia* whereby he can provide other and better explanations of things than can Descartes.[77]

Curiously, modern scholars agree that Spinoza departs substantially from Descartes' intentions, especially in the last part, the *Cogitata Metaphysica*, but generally *not* that we here encounter a deliberate strategy of subterfuge, as Van

---

[75] Blijenbergh, *Waerheit van de Christeliycken Godts-dienst*, 386, 433; Klever, "Spinoza Interviewed," 319; Spinoza, *Correspondance* (ed. Rovere), 397; Van Heertum, "A Not So Harmless Drudge," 404.
[76] Van Til, Voor-hof, *Voor-hof der heydenen*, 5.
[77] Bontekoe, *Brief aan Jan Fredrik Swetsertje*, 22.

Blijenbergh, Bontekoe, Van Til, and other contemporaries maintained, sabotage designed to further Spinoza's own philosophical, political, and anti-Christian agenda covertly. In fact, the *Cogitata* has been relatively understudied by Spinoza experts.[78] While there is indeed "a good deal of (mainly implicit) criticism" in this text, it still remains usual to assert that this stems from failure sufficiently to "submerge his own thought and allow his subject to speak for himself" rather than from Spinoza's own schemes and ambitions.[79] This has reinforced the tendency, based on what Spinoza himself says, writing to Oldenburg, in July 1663, to regard the book as something unplanned which his Amsterdam friends, especially Meyer, persuaded him to undertake, and altogether marginal to his own plans, "basically a text book in the Cartesian philosophy," as it has been put.[80] Some modern commentators even wrongly claim Spinoza is genuinely defending and restating Descartes while ironing out some inconsistencies.[81]

The Oldenburg correspondence, however, proves conclusively that Spinoza not only rejected all Descartes' main premises and considered his own standpoint more compelling but, at the same time, remained fearful of presenting his objections to Descartes too directly. When advising Oldenburg that he had composed the book to instruct "a certain young man [Johannes Casearius (1642–77)] to whom I did not want to teach my opinions openly,"[82] he virtually admits that the text's purpose was to instil his own ideas covertly, masked as Cartesian ideas. Had Spinoza referred to his exposition of Descartes as his own brainchild, this would have been tantamount to confessing that he was deliberately undermining Descartes' system in an underhanded fashion and doing so as a preparatory step, hoping to clear the way for his *Ethics*, the first three parts of which were complete by the summer of 1665 but which, though much more important to himself and his friends, he long hesitated to publish.

Among the earliest and most important appraisals of Spinoza's intellectual development, we have seen, is that in Nicolas Steno's famous undated "open letter" to Spinoza, composed some time before November 1671.[83] This was quite a few years before Steno saw the prepublication manuscript version of the *Ethics*, in 1676. In 1671, Steno refused to accept that the "entire philosophy of Descartes, however diligently examined and reformed by you," can explain "in a demonstrative way even this single phenomenon, how the impact of matter on matter is perceived by a soul united to the matter." Once a Cartesian intensively

---

[78] Van Ruler, "Spinoza in Leiden," 39; Israel, "Spinoza as an Expounder," 41.
[79] Curley, *Behind the Geometrical Method*, 4; Curley, "Spinoza—as an expositor of Descartes," 133–4.
[80] Nadler, *Spinoza: A Life*, 197, 204–5; Israel, "Spinoza as an Expounder," 41; Popkin, *Spinoza*, 49–50; see also Meijer, "De Ioanne Caesario," 234.
[81] Coppens, "Descartes, Spinoza en het Nederlands cartesianisme," 10.
[82] Spinoza, *Collected Works* (ed. Curley) i, 207; Thijssen-Schoute, *Nederlands Cartesianisme*, 390.
[83] Klever, "Steno's Statements," 303–4; Totaro, "Niels Stensen (1638–1686)," 147; Totaro, "Documenti," 105.

discussing Cartesianism with Spinoza, but also a scientist increasingly critical of Cartesianism during his Leiden years (1661–4), by 1671 Steno had long repudiated Cartesianism. Knowing Spinoza's objective had by no means been just to iron out errors and "reform" Descartes' philosophy in some marginal sense, Steno correctly grasped that Spinoza's unstated, surreptitious scheme was wholly to eliminate the supernatural and altogether abolish the separate standing of mind and "soul" as a separate substance.[84]

A key strand of what Steno, like Van Blijenbergh and others, rightly conceived as Spinoza's overturning of Descartes' philosophy, a strand directly contradicting Descartes' stance (and Christian doctrine), was his outright rejection of freedom of the will. Admittedly, in several passages the *Cogitata* seems to uphold Descartes,' Heereboord's, and Heidanus' doctrine of freedom of the will. But no sooner does Spinoza state that "freedom of the human will" is preserved by the will of God than he adds that no "man can will or do anything but what God has decreed from eternity that he should will and do. How this can happen and human freedom still be preserved," he adds elusively, "is beyond our grasp."[85] Free will and acting from necessity inexplicably merge, and the same seems to be true of God himself who, Spinoza says, "acts from absolute freedom of the will," yet at the same time, we have seen, the laws of nature are eternal, fixed and constant (implying nature itself is eternal and not created), laws that emanate from God in whom "necessity of essence is not distinguished from necessity of existence [essentiae necessitas non distinguitur a necessitate existentiae]."[86] To Steno as to Van Blijenbergh, Bontekoe, and Van Til, it seemed plain the Spinoza of the early 1660s was designedly undermining rather than seeking to reform and perfect Descartes' philosophy.

Still more important, though, stressed Steno, in 1680, three years after Spinoza's death, while residing in Leibniz's proximity at Hanover, this surreptitious design was the work not just of Spinoza but also of Meyer and the entire group around him. In 1680, Steno refers to the *Spinozistas* as a clique who by then had become "many" but already then, at that time, in 1663–4, formed a formidable cell. If in the early 1660s those joining Spinoza in subverting Descartes' system were far fewer than later, he himself had known several of these individuals quite well and could attest to the deviousness of their long-term design.[87] A deliberate mix of Descartes' philosophy with a partly concealed subversive revision of Descartes' thought, a group strategy devised by Meyer, Balling, Rieuwertsz, and

---

[84] Klever, "Steno's Statements," 304–5; Koistinen, "On Steno's Letter," 12–14; Israel, "Spinoza as an Expounder," 45.
[85] Spinoza, *Collected Works* (ed. Curley) i, 309–10, 344–5; Schmaltz, "Spinoza on Eternity," 209.
[86] Spinoza, *Collected Works* (ed. Curley) i, 304, 307, 309; Douglas, *Spinoza and Dutch Cartesianism*, 84–5.
[87] Totaro, "Niels Stensen (1638–1686)," 157; Van Bunge, "Spinoza's filosofische achtergronden," 103–5.

Bouwmeester as well as Spinoza, their undoubted goal was to combine demolishing Aristotelian scholasticism insofar as it survived in the universities with profiting from Cartesianism's recent advances in the Dutch universities to rework Descartes' system sufficiently inconspicuously to carry at least some of the latter's impressively substantial and growing following with them.

Another insightful judgement about Spinoza's aims in 1663 was made in the mid-eighteenth century by the prominent German theologian, Wolffian Pietist and bibliographer, Siegmund Jacob Baumgarten (1706–57), who averred, lecturing at Halle in 1754–5 that:[88]

> In the *De Principiis Cartesianae*, Spinoza gave the appearance of merely wanting to rework Descartes' theories more accurately and astutely [than had Descartes], but there already laid the ground for asserting his own fallacies which specifically consisted in seeing all things as only formations and parts of one basic essence or one substance, so that God, as Spinoza contends, is the most integrated thing in the whole world, in that all other things are actual parts of the same.[89]

The 1664 Dutch edition publicized the distinctly provocative and for many contemporary readers disturbing notion that any scholar asserting that the "things whose causes are unknown to them have happened solely by God's pleasure and from his absolute decree" is offering the public nothing but crass obfuscation. The confusion surrounding God's will arises from men's attributing something like the human will to God when actually "God's will is clearest to us when we conceive things clearly and distinctly." The sort of philosophical evasion and circumvention of the truth characteristic of Descartes and the Cartesians (and not least Schuyl), in Spinoza's estimation, was the "sole foundation of credulousness [i.e. superstition] and perhaps also of much knavish trickery," a prod at the Leiden academic establishment as much as the general public.[90]

The most arresting innovation in Spinoza's first published book was, as he expresses it in his incisive Latin, that "the whole of Nature" is "one being" [unum ens] and hence the whole of Nature, the entirety of reality, is governed by the same interacting set of natural laws, or as he puts it by God's "decree concerning *natura naturata*."[91] Nothing occurs, there are no causes of anything, other than those belonging to the single set of immutable "efficient causes" that constitute Nature.

---

[88] Santinelli, "À partir de *Spinoza in Italia*," 32–3; Garber, *Descartes' Metaphysical Physics*, 280–2.
[89] "Er hat darin den Schein geben wollen, dass er nur des Cartesii Lehrbegriff genauer verknüpfen und scharfsinniger einrichten wolle; worin aber schon der Grund geleget worden, seine eigenthümlichen Irrthümer zu behaupten, dass er alle Dinge für blosse Bildungen und Theilungen des einigen Grundwesens oder der einigen Substanz angesehen, so dass Gott, der vom Spinoza behauptet wird, das allerzusammengesetzte Ding in der ganzen Welt ist, indem alle andere Dinge eigentlich Theil desselben ausmachen," Baumgarten, *Geschichte der Religionsparthyen* (1754), 38; Israel, "Spinoza as an Expounder," 44–5.
[90] Spinoza, *Opera* i, 260–1; Spinoza, *Korte Geschriften*, 175.   [91] Spinoza, *Opera* i, 264.

God's will, in other words, is "immutable," just as Descartes claims in his *Principia* which, in turn, requires us to admit (in a more consistent way than did Descartes) that God "can do nothing against his own decrees, that being something impossible through being incompatible with God's perfection";[92] hence there can be no difference between Creation and the ordinary course of Nature: "God's way of acting is the same in creating the world as in preserving it."[93] Finally, closely tied to these teachings and no less disconcerting to Van Blijenbergh, Steno, and many another, is the connected doctrine that "Sacred Scripture must teach the same things" as natural reason teaches. "For true statements do not contradict truth [nam veritas veritati non repugnant]," holds Spinoza in the ninth chapter of the supplementary *Cogitata*, "nor can Scripture teach the silly things [nugas] ordinary folk suppose it does." For wherever we encounter anything "contrary to the natural light, we can refute it with that same freedom with which we reject the Koran and the Talmud."[94] Like the rest of his revisions, this project for reforming our understanding of Scripture, Spinoza and his following believed, needs to be undertaken, as Spinoza expresses it, "for the good of all."

It was not long before these sweeping claims landed not just Spinoza but his entire circle in collision with Schuyl, Van Blijenbergh, Heidanus, and the entire Dutch Reformed Cartesian establishment academic, theological, and official. During the later 1660s, this was not, as yet, a public rift. Enough of Descartes remained in the *Beginselen* for the work to represent a major problem and liability not just for the Cartesian fraternity in the Dutch and German Calvinist universities, but also for the large public of non-Latin reading Dutch laymen drawn to Cartesianism as a philosophy harmonizing with science, medicine, and religion. Spinoza, in effect subverts Cartesianism from two different angles simultaneously, undermining it philosophically while subtly casting it in an impious and religiously suspect light in theologians' eyes, adding fuel to the fire of the Cartesian controversies as a culture war within the universities, Reformed consistories, and ranks of the dissident churches.

Unsurprisingly, academics felt a decided reluctance during the next six years, until publication of the *TTP*, to publicize, debate, or contest Spinoza's philosophical approach to Descartes openly. Better to sweep it under the carpet, without making it a point of contention. To that extent Spinoza's strategy proved clever and effective. Only behind the scenes did Spinoza's boldly reforming, irreligious revisions published at this juncture provoke an incipient negative response among some Cartesians as well as among the anti-Cartesian academic fraternity. Cartesian anxiety to guard and publicly shield Cartesianism's reputation led to avoidance of any open clash over Spinoza's exposition throughout the rest of the

---

[92] Spinoza, *Opera* i, 266; Garber, *Descartes' Metaphysical Physics*, 284–5.
[93] Spinoza, *Opera* i, 269; Spinoza, *Collected Works* (ed. Curley) i, 335.
[94] Spinoza, *Opera* i, 265; Spinoza, *Collected Works* (ed. Curley) i, 331; Bordoli, *Ragione e scrittura*, 207.

1660s, leaving the door ajar, so to speak, in such fashion that Spinoza can be said to have won the opening round in his assault on the religious and intellectual status quo by default, leaving him and his following strengthened and empowered to carry the process further. The privately controversial status of Spinoza's account of Cartesianism remained for now a quiet, for most unnoticed hidden disruptive force buried amidst the wider Dutch intellectual, cultural, and medical drama of the 1660s.[95]

[95] Israel, "Spinoza as an Expounder," 53; Douglas, *Spinoza and Dutch Cartesianism*, 89.

15
Writing the *Ethics*

With the *Korte Verhandeling* circulating among his following by 1660–1, and the Descartes book costing little time, Spinoza spent most of his stay at Rijnsburg and the early part of his Voorburg period drafting the main body of his *Ethics*. The *Ethics* clearly represents a more developed and mature stage in his thinking than the *Korte Verhandeling*, and one much more systematically worked out in "geometric order," so it is not surprising that eventually he simply discarded the shorter work, leaving it in an unfinished state rather than trying to thoroughly rework its categories and terminology. In 1677, the earlier, less mature text was simply set aside by the editors of Spinoza's *Opera Posthuma*.

De Vries' letter and Spinoza's reply of February 1663 show that by the winter of 1662–3 a draft of much of Part I of the *Ethics* was already circulating among the group of friends and being intensively discussed.[1] Part I of the (eventually) five parts constituting the *Ethics*, entitled *De Deo* [About God], it seems clear, was written during 1662.[2] By 1665, we know, Spinoza was well into Part III and perhaps near to having a complete draft of the *Ethics*. In terms of setting out his philosophy as a comprehensive system and organizing it as a body of text, the *Ethics* is thus essentially a product of the years 1661–5,[3] though its basic themes and connections, it is important to remember, were already largely formed in his mind by 1659–60. What Spinoza was essentially doing during 1661–5 was formulating and working out more precisely implications and insights arrived at late in the 1650s. After 1665, the process slowed dramatically; it took another twelve years, until late 1677, before the *Ethics* appeared in print; but throughout that lengthy period the first two-thirds or so of the work, though later afterwards here and there revised and further refined, nonetheless stood largely complete and, in terms of Spinoza's daily work routine, left largely standing on one side.

The most striking feature of Spinoza's philosophy is its extraordinarily high degree of internal cohesion and unity, a cohesion following directly from the metaphysical propositions set out and justified in *Ethics* Part I. Holding that if things have nothing in common with each other one cannot be the cause of the

---

[1] Knol, "Waarom hield Spinoza," 20, 26; Steenbakkers, "Textual History," 28.
[2] Mignini, "Données et problèmes," 20; Steenbakkers, "Textual History," 27–8; Della Rocca, *Spinoza*, 25.
[3] Moreau and Steenbakkers, "Introduction" to Spinoza, *Oeuvres* iv, *Ethica*, 15–16.

other, Spinoza defines "substance," one of his key concepts, as something existing entirely within itself independently from everything else, that is possessing "zelfstandigheid" (standing by itself). A substance does not therefore depend on or require the existence of anything else to be formed or to exist. Since a substance cannot be produced or created by anything else and by definition is the only cause of itself, while everything we see, know or can conceive of being is undeniably directly connected causally, there *can* be only one substance in the universe. This one substance Spinoza calls "God or Nature." According to his *Ethics* Part I, Proposition 14, "except God, no substance can be or be conceived."[4] When acknowledging that most people, including most philosophers, envisage the totality of what is very differently, Spinoza explains men's predominant tendency to misunderstand and misconstrue everything as caused by men's natural failure to distinguish between intellect and imagination.

"Products of the Imagination," including the bizarre images pervading us when dreaming and that we remember when we awake, Spinoza wrote, in July 1664, to his friend Balling, with whom he was then discussing the essentials of his system and the difficulties of translating it into Dutch, always "arise from the disposition either of the body or the mind."[5] Imagination, in effect, distorts our understanding in accordance with our constitution. When we postulate a number—one, six, or ten—abstractly, we understand that it is a unity, a sum; but habitually, it is easier and more natural for our minds to imagine "ten" as ten separate things. Equally, men like to imagine creation from nothing, he points out in *Ethics* Part I, or creation of one thing by something that has nothing whatever in common with it, just as we can imagine things disappearing without trace. But all such imagined creation or disappearance, he emphasizes, even more than in the *Korte Verhandeling*, is always just a fable, something logically impossible.[6] Instead of "creating," Spinoza always speaks of "God or Nature" generating or bringing forth (from something else). Those basing their views on "imagination" rather than "intellect," that is practically everyone in the world, Spinoza repeatedly refers to in the *Ethics* as the great bulk of humanity, the uncomprehending mass, "my opponents," meaning the academically appointed university philosophers and theologians along with the illiterate and uneducated.

What Spinoza's proof of God's existence and unity means is that God is absolutely the first cause and that by Proposition 17 "God acts from the laws of his nature alone, and is compelled by no one," and consequently God is the only completely free agent not caused by anything; everything else being dependent on

---

[4] Spinoza, *Collected Works* (ed. Curley) i, 420.
[5] Spinoza to Balling, Voorburg, 20 July 1664, in Spinoza, *Briefwisseling*, 150; Spinoza, *Collected Works* (ed. Curley) i, 353; Steenbakkers, *Spinoza's* Ethica, 1, 3.
[6] Spinoza, *Collected Works* (ed. Curley) i, 421, 445–6; Knol, "Waarom hield Spinoza," 9–10.

this one substance. Since "freedom" in Spinoza's *Ethics* signifies not lack of constraint, but possessing "power," God is also the only omnipotent being. It is from God's infinite power and nature alone that all things flow which means that nothing can exist outside God, signifying that there is no Devil, no demons, no magic, no heaven or hell, no afterlife and no divine authority interpreted by men separate from nature, only the unchanging, unalterable laws of nature, that is God's omnipotence which "has been actual from eternity and will remain the same actuality to eternity,"[7] beyond which nothing exists and nothing is exempt. Only those who do grasp that "God's intellect, will and power are one and the same," are in a position to understand "true religion" which is essentially pursuit of the moral and social good of men, some fragments of which, fortunately, are patchily present in (albeit much of the time are also damagingly absent from) every earthly church and religious stream, whether Christianity, Judaism, Islam, or another, equally and without distinction. A further consequence of Spinoza's proof of God's existence is that nothing exists that is more sacred than other things and no one exists who is closer to God than anyone else, rendering all religious ceremonies and sacraments without exception total human fictions, sometimes useful in a limited way, but frequently not. One readily sees how and why Spinoza's position looked "atheistic" and "blasphemous" according to the notions of early modern times (and the nineteenth century), but was not at all "atheistic" according to Spinoza himself and his followers.

Because "God is the immanent, not the transitive, cause of all things," according to Proposition 18, and nothing possesses an independent existence outside God, there is no such thing as either evil or sorcery, wrongdoing in human terms being as much the consequence of God as the purest piety. Philosophers rejecting this conclusion, he says, claim "God does all things for the sake of the good," locating a great deal outside of God which does not depend on God, thereby delimiting his infinite presence and power, creating imaginative schemas installing limits on God's power, intellect, and will. This, the usual approach when envisaging a benevolent God, Spinoza rejects as an "absurdity" not worth discussing.[8] God is neither benevolent nor malevolent. God's attributes are eternal and immutable, "all things which follow from the absolute nature of any of God's attributes (Proposition 21) have always had to exist and be infinite"; so something determined to produce a given effect "has necessarily been determined in this way by God, and one which has not been determined by God cannot determine itself to produce an effect (Proposition 26)." Consequently, nothing occurs contrary to the fixed laws of nature and there have never been or could be any miracles or revelation. Nothing can contrive not to follow the eternal laws of nature which means by Proposition 29, "that in nature there is nothing contingent, but all things

---

[7] Spinoza, *Collected Works* (ed. Curley) i, 425–6.
[8] Spinoza, *Collected Works* (ed. Curley) i, 439.

have been determined from the necessity of the divine nature to exist and produce an effect in a certain way."

A further consequence is that there can be no "creation" in the sense of giving specific existence to defined formal essences such as mankind, or indeed anything else not resulting from pure natural cause and effect shaping things through the passage of time. There can be no such thing as an essence remaining when an essential feature characterizing that thing is removed.[9] In the *Korte Verhandeling*, Spinoza calls God's eternal decree his "providence" and employs also several other terms taken from Christian theology, such as "son of God" and "predestination" reflecting the Collegiant milieu within which his system originally arose. In the *Ethics*, by contrast, he dispenses with all such terms, including "creation," reflecting a conscious de-Christianizing of his terminology and way of expressing himself following his departure from Amsterdam.[10] *Natura naturans*, Spinoza maintains, is the "eternal and unchanging essence" of things, God's immutable power and attributes, the unchanging set of laws governing the totality of nature, whereas *natura naturata* designates "whatever follows from the necessity of God's nature," the outcome, the existing reality before us. An important philosophical principle ensuing from this is that any actual human or other intellect always comprehends God's attributes and effects rightly or wrongly, "and nothing else." Since only one substance exists, everything men and animals think, will, and imagine, corresponds somehow to what is real and, rather than being right or wrong, is really, in Spinoza's terms, either adequate or inadequate. Since nothing exists or can be conceived without God, whatever comes into the mind in some sense must exist also in nature.

Consequently, "the will, like the intellect is only a certain mode of thinking" shaped by our assumptions, impressions, desires and so forth, so that, by Proposition 32, "the will cannot be called a free cause, but only a necessary one." This means everything humans do, all politics and culture, and religion too, "are related to God's nature just as motion and rest are and as are absolutely all natural things." Since there can be no fundamental gap between human nature and nature itself, what men do is determined exclusively by nature as a whole, and our history is simply part of natural history. Everything and everyone is subject to the same single set of rules. Because all things necessarily follow from God's nature and have been determined from the necessity of God's nature to exist and produce an effect in a certain way for all eternity, nothing is contingent and everything follows or is the outcome of the same fixed laws and forces which means the exclusive path to truth is that of mathematically based science—scholarly research, observation, investigation, experiment, measurement, exploration,

---

[9] Spinoza, *Opera* ii, 84; Rovere, *Spinoza. Méthodes pour exister*, 24–5.
[10] Knol, "Waarom hield Spinoza," 10–12.

dissection, and comparison. There is no other truth and no one can possibly understand anything other than by study and research of nature.

Our inadequate way of understanding reality, including our own reality, is therefore itself an aspect of nature. Because we rely so much on our eyes for seeing, teeth for chewing, plants and animals for food, men found it impossible to believe all these "things had made themselves" but naturally assumed, knowing they had found these things and "not provided them for themselves," that, just as they themselves make and devise things, some "ruler or rulers of nature endowed with human freedom" has been far-sighted enough to prepare all these things for them, including their food, taking care to provide everything necessary specifically for their benefit and use. "Hence, men maintained that the gods direct all things for their benefit in order to bind men to them and be held by men in the highest honour." But because different groups have thought up different ways of worshipping God or the gods and "like to think that God cherishes them more than the rest," their prejudices evolved into established "superstition" (i.e. via church authority) and struck deep roots in men's minds. Spinoza is especially concerned to reject all aspects of theological thinking that envisage mankind as a privileged segment of nature, all notion that the gods, and later God, purposely designed nature and its plants and animals for our particular use in order to feed and sustain men. Hence, an important general consequence of Spinoza's identifying God with nature is the removal of all conscious intent or purpose from God's creative power, his sweeping denial of all divine teleology, one of the most distinctive features of his philosophy.

Unwillingness to identify any basic difference between men and other creatures stands among the points where Spinoza's philosophy most conspicuously goes against the general trend of early modern philosophy and perhaps all earlier philosophy. In particular, he refrains from asserting the essential superiority of humans over animals on the basis of intelligence or their supposedly being a specific, distinct essence defined by possessing reason. Men are simply part of nature like every animal and, at bottom (contra Descartes), there is nothing fundamentally different about the mind–body relationship in men than in animals, an outcome enabling him to easily skirt the irresolvable difficulties Descartes became entangled in when arguing that animals do possess perception, memory, imagination, and experience of passions, like humans, as well as muscles, hearts, and capacity for movement but, lacking souls (minds), are nevertheless unable to consider what they see, form judgements or reach decisions according to rational argument. Thus dogs and horses, like humans, experience fear, hope, and pleasure, and can be taught to perform certain actions when humans give a signal, but do all this, holds Descartes, without giving their feelings or actions any thought. For Spinoza, by contrast, humans possess no thinking ability, or soul, that is above and beyond the rest of nature. Spinoza, though, it must be said, is not particularly informative on the subject of animal life. For someone interested in dissection and spending much time staring through microscopes, he noted down remarkably little about live bodies in general, animals and humans in relation to animal life.[11]

One particular consequence men suffer when opting for teleological thinking is that theologians and philosophers need to explain the storms, earthquakes, diseases, floods, and other disasters that afflict societies as expressions of divine intent, hence of divine dissatisfaction and anger, offering explanations made plausible only by specifying alleged wrongs by erring humans against the divine being or beings thereby constantly reinforcing men's superstitious notions of sin, transgression, heresy, idolatry, blasphemy, sacrilege, and wrongful worship. Directed by churchmen and other religious leaders, men prefer to extend and entrench their ignorance in this manner, rather than deepen their science, and cultivate truth and true virtue. For theologians, much of what happens still seems hard to fathom or incomprehensible. "So they considered it certain that the judgments of the gods far surpass man's grasp," a basic superstition which alone would cause the truth to remain hidden from the human race for all eternity "if mathematics which is concerned not with goals, but only with realities and properties of figures, had not shown men another rule and measurement of truth."[12] "Common prejudices," the usual way of thinking, thus represents a perennial obstacle to mankind, hindering everyone whether men realize this or not.

Ascertaining the true causes of things leads to comprehension but is also the sole means to acquire capacity to reform and improve things. Consequently, it often happens that "if, like a learned person, one investigates the true causes of miracles, and endeavours to understand natural things and not wonder at them like a fool, one is constantly looked on and denounced as an impious heretic by those whom the people venerate as interpreters of nature and the gods."[13] One of Spinoza's most salient conclusions follows: for priests and other clergy "know that if ignorance goes, then stupid wonder, the sole means they possess of explaining and justifying their authority, is also removed." Interestingly, the Dutch version here, changes all the Latin singulars into the plural, setting "heretics" who investigate and are learned against the "fools" believing what churchmen tell them. Meanwhile, different sects and groups employ human imagination differently, conjuring up divergent "authorities," so it is little wonder that innumerable controversies arise which prove totally insoluble, so that they "finally give rise to skepticism."[14] On the other hand, where we set aside imagination and resort exclusively to intellect as in mathematics, clear reasoning yields incontestable conclusions with everyone who understands agreeing on the result, and the logical

---

[11] Gaukroger, *Descartes*, 392; Jaquet, *Spinoza à l'oeuvre*, 36–9.

[12] Spinoza, *Opera* ii, 79; Spinoza, *Nagelate Schriften*, 40.

[13] Spinoza, *Opera* ii, 81–2; Spinoza, *Nagelate Schriften*, 42; Rovere, *Spinoza. Méthodes pour exister*, 36–7.

[14] Spinoza, *Collected Works* (ed. Curley) i, 445.

steps leading to it, and hence also on the means to understand, improve, and correct our world.

In the *Ethics* Part II Spinoza moves on to those attributes of God that are accessible to us, namely thought and extension. If bodies of whatever sort are simply modes of the attribute "extension," particular minds of whatever sort are just modes of "thought." Moreover, the two attributes, though separate in how we envisage them, remain always the same entity under two different aspects. A key principle here is bodies and thoughts are features or results of different attributes or aspects of God but relate to the same entities. Spinoza follows Descartes in insisting that each attribute of a substance must be conceived through itself, but is stricter than Descartes in refusing any causal relationship of any sort between thought and extension, yielding one of the most renowned Spinozist maxims (Part II, Prop. 7): "the order and connection of ideas is the same as the order and connection of things [ordo et connexio idearum idem est, ac ordo et connexio rerum]." Thus, a circle existing in nature and the idea of that circle which is in God, "are one and the same thing."[15]

So God does not decree things to function in one way, and then another, as in Descartes; they are as they are from all eternity and could never have been otherwise. Bodies move, now more quickly, now more slowly, or are at rest. Any entity moving or at rest "must be determined to motion or rest by another body, also determined to motion or rest by another, and then again by another, and so on to infinity." So bodies are singular things that nevertheless all share a great deal, as our bodies are affected by innumerable things in different ways and we affect the things around us in innumerable ways. Whether we consider natural phenomena as physical objects, or think of them as concepts, one and the same order and connection of causes always follows one from another, Spinoza illustrating this principle with the example of humans. If human minds can do more than many other minds, and some human minds can do more than other human minds, this stems, holds Spinoza, from the structure of our and other bodies. "All bodies either move or are at rest," so all bodies are distinguished from each other by virtue of motion and rest, speed and slowness, and not by any inherent, absolute difference. Therefore, the superior awareness of some minds to others must arise in some way from certain bodies possessing a wider range of options, being more pliable or adaptable to different conditions, better suited to a greater variety of activities, more able to react to threats and challenges, and more capable of noticing and doing multiple things at once, than others.

Thus, by Part II, Proposition 14 "the human mind is capable of perceiving a great many things, and is the more capable the more its body can be disposed in a great many ways." Equally, notions we develop instinctively about external bodies

---

[15] Spinoza, *Opera* ii, 89; Della Rocca, *Spinoza*, 43; Steinberg, "Knowledge," 149.

tell more about the condition of our own bodies than the nature of the external bodies. Thus, connections we make between images and ideas, our memories, always relate to our experiences and how we have been affected by things. Thus, a soldier, finding traces of a horse in the sand, thinks immediately of the horseman, and hence warfare, whereas a farmer, perceiving the same hoof marks, thinks of horses pulling ploughs, fields and cultivation. Everyone is accustomed to connect images of things in one way or another, passing from one thought to another, in the context of their situation and activity. This approach renders Spinoza's notion of the relationship between perceptions and ideas more complex than is found in either Descartes or Hobbes. For Descartes, perceptions are either correct or incorrect as approximations to actual things which, when correct, directly correspond to our ideas of essences, whether men, angels, horses or whatever, an approach encouraging a bias towards accepting that ideas long assumed and generally approved, like the existence of angels, are objectively true. For Spinoza all ideas are more or less adequate but stem from mental constructs or concepts about things only related to perceptions indirectly, a view closer to Hobbes' approach in regarding ideas as always derivative from mental constructs and only indirectly connected to sensual impressions. The difference between Hobbes and Spinoza lies in the former chiefly emphasizing sense perception as the source of our ideas and Spinoza especially stressing the operations of the mind and imagination in constructing ideas.[16]

Since no ideas or imaginings can be absolutely false, it follows, by Part II, Proposition 36, that our "inadequate and confused ideas," that is the great bulk of our thoughts, "follow with the same necessity as adequate or clear and distinct ideas." Whatever ideas follow in the mind logically from ideas that are adequate in the mind correspond to reality as do all other ideas to a lesser degree. It is at this point that Spinoza reaffirms and refines his late 1650s epistemology, reviewing again his three different types or degrees of knowledge, based respectively on imagination, reason, and "intuition," in a way similar to his approach in the now abandoned *Korte Verhandeling* but slightly adjusting the schema and using different terms. Everyone begins with "knowledge of the first kind" consisting of impressions and thoughts garnered from random experience, things recollected, or reported, by others and our seeing or imagining new things.[17] The "second kind of knowledge" is that ordered by reason [*ratio*], what we learn from using reason to process our impressions, random facts, and what people tell us, putting this immense mass in order by gathering things into meaningful groups and categories, confirming generalizations and creating universals based on itemizing properties of things such as when we speak of dogs, horses, or reptiles. This is the

---

[16] Renz, "Spinoza's Epistemology," 149–50.
[17] Steinberg, "Knowledge," 150–1; LeBuffe, "Anatomy of the Passions," 191; Rovere, *Spinoza. Méthodes pour exister*, 75.

sphere of adequate ideas based on correct appraisal of the characteristics and causes of things.[18]

The third kind of knowledge which Spinoza earlier called clear and distinct knowledge he now labels "intuitive knowledge [scientia intuitiva]." After acquiring a large share of knowledge of the first and second kinds, processing that knowledge by using an adequate idea of the overarching forms and processes characterizing thought and extension, we can extend our reasoning by skipping logical steps to reach hitherto unseen conclusions that logically follow from what we knew before. Thus knowing two is double the amount of one, if someone asks what is the equivalent ratio relating to three, we deduce intuitively that six is the equivalent ratio without traversing all the steps involved, and we are now acquiring knowledge of the third kind. This "third order" of knowledge, the Koerbagh Brothers, with whom, along with Meyer, Balling, De Vries, and Jelles, Spinoza discussed the basics of his system while working it out in the early to mid-1660s, either did not hear about, or were unconvinced by. For in the Koerbagh Brothers' principal philosophical text, *A Light Shining in Dark Places* (1668) where overall they shadow Spinoza's system remarkably closely, they keep here to just his first two orders of knowledge, impression-gathering and processing impressions via *ratio*.[19] Modern philosophers and commentators too have generally concurred that Spinoza's "knowledge of the third kind" stands among the more questionable, elusive, and problematic components of his system.[20]

Both knowledge of the second and third kind, we apprehend from Spinoza's schema, involve adequately assembling and classifying data and knowledge of causes and then inferring further knowledge from these firm foundations, with the result that the conclusions arrived at must, by definition, necessarily also be true. "A true idea," holds Spinoza (Part I, Axiom 6) "must agree with its object." Hence, all errors and mistakes stem from our perceiving and interpreting causes and facts wrongly from impressions, reports, images, beliefs, and theology, constantly confusing and mangling our knowledge of the first kind. Whenever an idea proves unassailable from whatever angle examined by adequate thinking, we know it must necessarily be true. Since consistency and logical coherence always connect and join adequate ideas, Spinoza feels confident in affirming that "as the light makes both itself and the darkness plain, so truth is the standard of both itself and of what is false."[21]

---

[18] Knol, "Waarom hield Spinoza," 20, 26; Steenbakkers, "Textual History," 33; Nadler, *Think Least of Death*, 42–3; LeBuffe, *Spinoza on Reason*, 65.

[19] Laurens, *De Rede: bron van geluk*, 56–7.

[20] Steenbakkers, *Spinoza's Ethica*, 163–4; Steinberg, "Knowledge,"154–5; James, *Spinoza on Learning*, 186–9.

[21] Spinoza, *Collected Works* (ed. Curley) i, 478–9; Garrett, "Representation, Misrepresentation," 190–2.

No matter how stubbornly a person may cling to some false notion, and how difficult it may be to get that person to doubt it, argues Spinoza, it is incorrect to claim that person is convinced or certain of his or her fervent conviction. For certainty is not absence of doubt but a positive affirmation based on reasoning without any admixture of report, imagination, belief, or supposition. Images of things, doctrines we have heard about or been taught, things we vividly imagine, may leave no doubt whatever in someone's mind, but no one reasoning adequately can, for one moment, consider such "certainty" evident, proven, or rational. Among notions Spinoza classifies as obvious products of our distorting *imaginatio* rather than reason is the idea of contingency. For reason clearly shows that outcomes always follow necessarily from processes that are unalterable in nature. Another prevailing fiction that needs discarding, he contends, here departing dramatically from Descartes, is free will. Descartes could never overcome the problems surrounding his claim that men make free choices while God is the ultimate cause of everything. Rather, he simply states that it is beyond our comprehension how these two things are compatible and leaves it at that. Spinoza, seeking resolution and consistency at every point, temperamentally unwilling to leave anything as a declared unsolved difficulty or contradiction, remained unmoved by the difficulties that Van Blijenbergh and others pointed to, arising from his tenet that everything one does is determined by causes within and outside oneself, but yet that person is to a greater or lesser extent free depending on how far he or she can restrain his or her passions. Since one cannot will or not will something without envisaging its effects and consequences, and without affirming or denying it, and as we cannot will anything that we cannot sense, perceive, or imagine, Spinoza persisted in holding that "will and the intellect are one and the same," a point consistent with his approach and satisfyingly combining mind and body but often baffling all the same.[22]

Accepting that all things follow from God's eternal decree, that is from the unchangeable laws of nature, nevertheless lays the basis for our moral life, giving us peace of mind and teaching us that our greatest happiness or blessedness lies in knowledge of truth alone and doing only those things that, reason shows, love and morality advise. "From this we clearly understand how far those stray from the true estimation of virtue, who expect to be rewarded by God with the greatest rewards for their virtue and best actions." Accepting that all things follow from God's eternal decree teaches us to hate no one, mock no one, be angry at no one and be helpful to our neighbour not from "unmanly compassion, partiality, or superstition but from the guidance of reason." Finally, adds Spinoza, his distinctive moral "doctrine also contributes to no small extent, to the common good of

---

[22] Spinoza, *Collected Works* (ed. Curley) i, 485; Carlisle, *Spinoza's Religion*, 83.

society insofar as it teaches how citizens are to be governed and led, not so that they may be slaves, but that they may freely do the things that are best."[23]

Rejecting the idea that the human will is free and that a human is an independent dominion within a dominion, in Part III of his *Ethics* Spinoza compliments the moral philosophers of antiquity for giving much admirable advice on the right way of living while maintaining that so far no one has "determined the nature and powers of the affects" or emotions and what the mind can do to moderate our emotions and their adverse effects. Descartes' effort to do this he dismisses as a clear failure. Since the rules and laws of nature according to which all things happen are always the same, the first point to grasp is that the correct way to understand the nature of anything, of whatever kind, including the play of emotions, is likewise always the same in accord with the laws of nature. Hence, the uglier affects, whether hate, anger, envy or whatever, follow from the same necessity and force of nature as all other singular things: they have causes and properties that can be understood, and by understanding and better evaluating them, usefully modified.

Since body and mind are parallel dimensions of the same thing, conceived now under the attribute of thought, now under the attribute of extension, "the body cannot determine the mind to thinking, and the mind cannot determine the body to motion, or to rest." Consequently, the order or connection of things is one whether nature is conceived under this attribute or that. Hence the order and connection of the emotions and actions of the body is by nature always one with the turns and passions of the mind. Since only knowledge and understanding correcting one's ideas can moderate and restrain one's impulses and appetites, and as knowledge and understanding among men is in short supply, it is hardly surprising that men have nothing less under their control, "as experience teaches all too plainly," than their tongues and nowhere prove more helpless than in seeking to moderate their appetites. As "the infant believes he freely wants milk, the angry child that he wants vengeance, the timid person that he wants flight," and the chatterbox supposes he or she wishes to talk from a free disposition of mind when really he or she cannot control his impulse to speak, we imagine that we freely want those things that we want badly when it is obvious to the careful observer that in fact we are anything but free in doing so.

Experience proves, as indeed does reason, that it is ignorance of the causes driving their behaviour that causes men to imagine that they are free in willing this or that, so it is clear that the accompanying decisions of the mind leading to satisfying those impulses are in reality nothing but the appetites themselves and vary from person to person as the disposition of each body varies. As the decision of the mind and determination of the body by nature work together, "or rather are

---

[23] Spinoza, *Collected Works* (ed. Curley) i, 490–1.

one and the same thing," recollection, association, and assumptions about things in the mind lie behind the emotions driving the impulses and actions of our minds and bodies. But if we set to work to regulate and reorganize our recollections, associations, and assumptions by learning and experiencing better and drawing more rational conclusions from our experience, our impulses of mind and hence our bodily actions will automatically be modified by what we have learnt, hence improved by the force of reason.

But before we can appreciate the significance of this, one must first secure a firm grasp of the laws of nature governing our most basic instincts and impulses. By the famous sixth Proposition of Part III, "each thing, as far as it can by its own power, strives to persevere in its being [unaquaeque res, quantum in se est, in suo esse perseverare conatur]."[24] With his law of *conatus* [striving], Spinoza daringly innovates, giving much greater attention to the concept in the *Ethics* than in the *Korte Verhandeling*, or the Descartes book, seeing it as applying always and equally to humans, whether a human's mind is crammed with inadequate ideas, as is usual, in which case it plays a significant role in shaping our errors and misrepresentations of things or, alternatively, whether one aims to live in accordance with reason. Earlier, Hobbes constructed a theory of *conatus* basic to his physics denoting the impetus of any physical body in movement which he also applies innovatively to his theory of human motivation and desire. But Hobbes' *conatus* is essentially the play of particular desires, motives, or aversions to things viewed as internal movements or reactions stemming from the heart and brain against the incursion of some pressure, stimulus, or challenge from outside our bodies. Hobbes did not develop a theory of *conatus* as the evolving generalized tendency in any given body to respond in its own compound distinctive way, perceiving, deliberating, learning from experience, and eventually regulating its own responses to external stimuli.[25]

Variation in our striving according to individual personality, following Spinoza's conception of *conatus*, is wide-ranging, a complex simultaneously physical and mental phenomenon with much longer-term characteristics and a wider scope than that of Hobbes which is restricted essentially to external stimuli arousing our greed or fear at particular moments, operating on a much simpler level, being just the will to acquire greater power, on the one hand, and preserve ourselves and stay alive, on the other.[26] Under Spinoza's schema, increasing our power means moving towards greater perfection which entails using our reason to regulate the passions. Every mind nurtures both inadequate ideas and true ones

---

[24] Spinoza, *Opera* ii, 146.
[25] Jesseph, "Hobbes on 'Conatus'," 79–81; LeBuffe, "Anatomy of the Passions," 200; LeBuffe, "Spinoza and Hobbes," 83–4.
[26] Matheron, *Individu et communauté*, 87–9; Jesseph, "Hobbes on 'Conatus'," 85; Koistinen, "Spinoza on Action," 182–4.

but with the balance constantly changing within each individual as well as between individuals and among groups. Where our *conatus* or striving is considered only in the mind it is called "will," but when expressed by mind and body together, is termed "appetite." Appetite characterizes the very essence of man from whose nature necessarily follow those things that promote his preservation. Desire Spinoza defines as appetite together with consciousness of this appetite in the mind. From this, Spinoza concludes, reversing his earlier tenet in the *Korte Verhandeling*, that "we neither strive for, nor will, nor want, nor desire anything because we judge it to be good; on the contrary we esteem something to be good because we seek it, will it, want it, and desire it."[27]

The changes to which the mind is subject divide into two classes: those enabling us to pass to a higher perfection and those causing retreat to a lower perfection. Since men strive, like all things, to persevere in their being, Spinoza equates human striving for higher perfection with striving to increase our power of acting. Broadly, the joyful passions enable the mind to pass to a greater perfection, hence to more freedom and power of acting, while sadness in its various forms lowers us to greater imperfection and being less free. The emotion of joy affecting mind and body together Spinoza calls pleasure or cheerfulness; emotions of sadness affecting both he calls "pain or melancholy." Together, joy, melancholy, and desire constitute Spinoza's three primary "affects" from which all other emotions arise as variants. By Part III, Proposition 12, "the mind as far as it can, strives to imagine those things that increase or aid the body's power of acting."[28] As long as the mind imagines those things that increase or assist our body's power of acting, the body improves its capacity to increase its power of acting which (by Part III, Prop. 11) means also that the mind's power of thinking is enhanced and assisted. By contrast (by Part III, Prop. 13), "when our mind imagines those things that diminish or restrain the body's power of acting, it strives, as far as it can, to recollect things that negate their existence." In this case, the power of both mind and body is lessened until the mind can imagine something else that counters or cancels the restraining thought, so the mind will strive as far as it can to imagine this contrary thing. From this, argues Spinoza, we can grasp better what love and hate are. "Love is nothing but joy with the accompanying idea of an external cause, and hate nothing but sadness with the accompanying idea of an external cause." Hence, he who loves necessarily strives to have present and keep the thing he loves while he who hates strives to remove or destroy whatever he hates.

From this, Spinoza identifies also what are hope and fear, confidence and despair, satisfaction and remorse. Hope is nothing but an inconstant expectation

---

[27] Spinoza, *Collected Works* (ed. Curley) i, 500; Garrett, "Representation, Misrepresentation," 198–200.
[28] Spinoza, *Collected Works* (ed. Curley) i, 502; Della Rocca, *Spinoza*, 155–8.

of joy arising from the image of a future or past thing whose outcome we doubt; fear is an unstable form of sadness caused by the image of a looming threat or setback. But where the element of doubt common to both hope and fear is removed, the first turns into confidence and the second into despair. Pride Spinoza construes as the joy stemming from thinking more highly of oneself than is justified, scorn from thinking less highly of another than is just. It is natural for us (by Part III, Prop. 28) to "seek whatever we imagine will bring joy, and avert or destroy what we suppose contrary to it, or that will lead to sadness." From this we see why it is natural for men to be envious and glad of others' failings, and saddened by others' virtues, given that everyone is affected by joy, and a still greater joy the more his own actions express perfection and the more he imagines he finds in himself something he does not associate with others. But if someone fears his own actions are weaker than the performance of others, he will be saddened and strive to lay this sadness aside either by wrongly underestimating his equal's actions or by magnifying his own as much as he can. Man's natural inclination to hatred and envy, unfortunately, is then often aggravated by wrongly conceived education. For parents mistakenly spur their children on by holding up the incentive of honour and stirring envy.[29]

While the origin and basic drives in human nature are natural and common to all men, the specific balance of imagining and knowledge, the particular range of experience, hope, and despair in each individual creates different patterns of appetite that vary vastly from individual to individual. There is no small difference, for example, between the brief satisfaction a drunkard experiences and the more stable and lasting satisfaction that a philosopher obtains. While everyone's state of mind and levels of joy or sadness stem from the same quest for perfection and the joy that accompanies it, actual outcomes vary enormously. Since much depends on whether the sadness that diminishes and hinders a person, or, alternatively, the joy which empowers and activates a person, prevails on a more or less constant manner, learning to think more realistically about ethics and learning to conduct oneself morally can, at any stage, exert an immensely powerful positive effect on every person's life.

The ultimate model, Spinoza's ideal, is the "free man" who lives under the guidance of reason as far as possible for any human, and therefore hates and envies, and is melancholy, as little as is possible. Spinoza's "free man," by understanding his own feelings and interactions with others, possesses freedom in the sense of maximum scope for successful outcomes and solutions. At the other extreme, lack of ability to moderate and restrain the affects, Spinoza, moving on to *Ethics* Part IV, labels "bondage." For anyone who is under the control not of himself but of *fortuna*, that is chance or luck, is ensnared by its grip so that, often,

---

[29] Spinoza, *Collected Works* (ed. Curley) i, 525–56.

even if he or she recognizes the course which is best, such an individual is still compelled to submit to what damages him or her. "Bondage" strikes him as a far more appropriate term for what is systemically harmful in human life by depriving us of possibilities for good outcomes and improvement, than terms like "bad" or "evil," for these, like the category "good," fail to relate to anything that actually exists in nature, being simply imaginative ways of thinking, notions formed by comparing one thing to another and realizing that one thing is relatively better for us, or for society, than another. Still these terms are useful to ethical thinking as long as we remember they are purely relative and relate to nothing intrinsic in God or Nature. For one and the same thing can be good, bad, or indifferent entirely depending on the context and its relation to human well-being. Music, for example is good for one who is melancholy, bad for one who is in mourning, and neither good nor bad for the deaf. By "good" Spinoza means "what we certainly know to be useful to us," and by "evil" whatever we know impedes our taking advantage of some good.

Being determined by our nature and the circumstances around us in all our states of mind and actions, a human emotion cannot, by Part IV, Proposition 7, be restrained or removed except by an affect contrary to it and stronger than the emotion to be restrained, that is by a corporeal cause or change affecting the body with a joyful feeling opposite to and stronger than the adverse emotion. Scope for improving ourselves grows the more we understand the causes of the behaviour and things around us. There are many reasons why most people are moved more by opinion than by "true reason" and why ignorance and superstition consistently dominate in human society. Nevertheless, reason remains of immense value, actual or potential, for everyone. "Since reason demands nothing contrary to nature, it demands that everyone love himself, seek what is genuinely useful to him [as defined by reason], desire that really leads to greater perfection, and that everyone should seek to preserve his own being as far as he can." As virtue is nothing other than acting from the laws of one's own being and striving to preserve one's being as best one can, the "foundation of virtue is this very striving to preserve one's own being while happiness consists in being able to preserve one's being." As there is nothing preferable to it, or more useful to us, we ought to desire virtue for its own sake. "Those who kill themselves are weak-minded and completely conquered by external causes contrary to their nature. Virtue is human power itself which is defined by man's essence alone [virtus est ipsa humana potentia, quae sola hominis essentia definitur]."[30]

It is "by the laws of his own nature that everyone necessarily desires, or is repelled by, what he considers to be good or bad," Spinoza next argues (Part IV, Prop. 19), since our knowledge of good and bad stems from our experience of joy

---

[30] Spinoza, *Opera* ii, 223–4.

and sadness. From this it follows also (Part IV, Prop. 20) that "the more each strives to obtain what is useful to him [as defined by reason], that is preserve his being, the more he is endowed with virtue; and, on the contrary, the more each neglects to seek what is useful to him, that is to his being, the more he is powerless."[31] Pity, he dismisses as something negative for the person guided by reason. Likewise, "humility is not a virtue, since it does not arise from reason [humilitas virtus non est, sive ex ratione non oritur]."[32] Repentance too he dismisses as stemming not from reason but rather emotions heightening feelings of wretchedness. Self-esteem by contrast is a "joy that is really the highest thing we can hope for." Both excessive pride and excessive despondency compound "very great ignorance of oneself," both indicating "very great weakness of mind." Our weaknesses are therefore destructive of the individual and the community. "In as far as men are torn by affects that are passions, they are apt to oppose and be contrary to one another." Yet, however formidable our weaknesses, it remains true that "men still find from experience that by helping each other they can provide themselves much more easily with the things that they need, and that only by joining forces can they avoid the dangers that threaten on all sides." Reason is thus the exclusive route both to individual and to collective improvement.[33]

Politics and human organization, consequently, are highly dependent on the application of reason which is their foundation, and if reason is consistently beyond the reach of most people, it can, nevertheless, be instituted and broadened for the benefit of all via laws, politics, and human organization. "Insofar as men live under the guidance of reason," by *Ethics* IV, Proposition 35, "to that extent do they always necessarily agree [Quatenus homines ex ductu rationis vivunt, eatenus tantum natura semper necessario conveniunt]." Individuals rarely live under the guidance of reason. Our lives are so constituted that men are usually envious of and burdensome to each other. Yet, it unalterably follows (by Part IV, Prop. 36) that "the greatest good of those who seek virtue is common to all, and can be enjoyed by all equally," and (by Part IV, Prop. 37) "the good which everyone who seeks virtue wants for himself, he desires also for other men, and this desire is greater as his knowledge of God is greater." For insofar as men "live according to the guidance of reason, they are most useful to other men; hence, under the guidance of reason, we necessarily strive to bring it about that men live according to the guidance of reason."

Because the guidance of reason teaches a great many things that help improve human life, Spinoza can wrap up his ethical system (by Part IV, Prop. 61) by declaring that unlike every other kind of desire, "a desire that arises from reason

---

[31] Spinoza, *Ethics* (ed. Akkerman and Steenbakkers), in *Oeuvres* iii, 368–9.
[32] Spinoza, *Opera* ii, 149.
[33] Spinoza, *Opera* ii, 232; Steenbakkers, "Textual History," 34; Rovere, *Spinoza. Méthodes pour exister*, 40–1.

cannot be excessive." It should be more frequently asserted by philosophers and historians than it is, that Spinoza's deployment of "reason" [*ratio*] in grounding his ethics, critique of religion, and political theory, in his *Ethics* and the *Tractatus Theologico-Politicus*, are inseparably tied together at every point and this conjunction is the very key to correctly understanding his overall system.[34]

---

[34] LeBuffe, *Spinoza on Reason*, 2, 160–1; James, *Spinoza on Learning*, 39–40, 174–9.

16
Voorburg (1663–1664)

16.i The Setting

It remains unknown why Spinoza chose to leave Rijnsburg shortly after 20 April 1663, several months prior to his Descartes book appearing, and move to Voorburg, close to The Hague, the locality that remained his neighbourhood and social milieu for the rest of his life. Given Voorburg's proximity to The Hague, the reason can hardly have been need for additional tranquillity, as Lucas suggests, a more peaceful repose than Rijnsburg offered,[1] nor health reasons and a choice for life close to the sea, being now no nearer the shore than before. Whatever his reasoning, this probably included desire for proximity to a major centre of communication and to the fascinating theatre of the Republic's political power.

Settling in at Voorburg in the summer of 1663, Spinoza soon began to feel even more uncomfortably exposed to public disapproval, and precariously wedged in opposition to the prevailing edifices of religious authority, local government, and established academe than before. Contrary to Oldenburg's urging, he clearly preferred to err on the side of caution rather than risk publishing a text like the *Korte Verhandeling* bound to enrage the theologians, synods, universities, city magistrates, and ultimately the States of Holland. Intellectually, meanwhile, he was hovering on the edge of estrangement from the Republic's powerful Cartesian faction while colliding to a degree with the more narrowly empiricist scientific culture of Bacon, Boyle, Steno, and Oldenburg whose methods and assumptions in experimental science he endorsed in part but whose underlying theological premises and implacably non-committal, eclectic, and tentative attitude to what he called sound principles he felt at odds with. While "caute" remained his firm maxim and discretion his preferred route, Spinoza was not one to contemplate abandoning his far-reaching schemes of subversion; rather he steadily expanded his commitment to clandestine undermining of the prevailing status quo while reassuring his band of loyal sympathizers, the "friends for whom I write this," as he expresses it at the close of the *Korte Verhandeling*, that they must not

---

[1] [Lucas], *La Vie*, 32; Mignini, "Données et problèmes," 10; Gulan-Whur, *Life of Spinoza*, 154; Van Boheemen and Bosscher, "Daniel Harmensz Tijdeman," 45.

feel surprise to find "my opponents," in fact virtually the entire world, ranged against them.[2]

Oldenburg solemnly vowed not to let their correspondence drop. But drop it he did from the late summer of 1663 down to April 1665, the interruption this time lasting over a year and half,[3] a period of furious activity in London in experimental science, publishing and almost every cultural sphere, as well as mounting confidence in England's future as the dominant sea power and colonizing empire. During the early 1660s Charles II succeeded in combining a new political and religious stability with startling changes in style and fashion, to all appearances reversing completely the austere Calvinism of the pre-1660 Puritan regime. For England's newly restored aristocratic intellectual elite and wits it was a heady time, not least for literature, theatre, and refined pleasure. In 1662–3, this new confidence and brilliance briefly infused also cultural relations between England and Holland, a quiet, scintillating interlude soon disastrously shattered. On 3 February 1664, shortly before Anglo-Dutch relations again began to sour, Samuel Pepys, running into "[John] Dryden the poet (I knew at Cambridge)" and all the fashionable talkers of the town, "stopped at the great Coffee-house" in Covent Garden, the favourite locality of Christiaan Huygens when in London, to enjoy some "very witty and pleasant discourse."[4]

In neither country was this lighter interlude to last, not that Spinoza showed any sign of easing up at any stage. His undeviating goal was to establish a following devoted to pursuing the truth philosophically, in disregard of religious authority, seeking human well-being and man's true ethical path among a like-minded coterie planning reform in education, medicine, the arts, and all the human sciences, everything supportive of a collective drive to the highest human perfection.[5] But before pushing forward the subsidiary sciences, the first priority, he and his group insisted, was for men to learn to distinguish between truth and falsehood, reality and illusion, the essential first step on the road to improvement and happiness being the purging and purifying of the human understanding enabling men to grasp things correctly. Since learning to sift truth from what humans, relying on wondrous reports, received tradition, false authority, magic and superstition generally believe, everything that deludes and misleads them, requires men first to learn how to understand things at first hand from their real essence alone, and since even the most sophisticated and highly educated are usually diverted from such inquiry by their passions and prejudices, even this first step requires immense effort. Such colossal foes are ignorance and credulity that even the essential preliminaries are only rarely taken. Among the restricted circles where

---

[2] Spinoza, *Short Treatise*, 150.
[3] Spinoza, *Collected Works* (ed. Curley) i, 218, 393; Keesing, "Frères Huygens," 111.
[4] Quoted in Winn, *John Dryden and His World*, 130–1.
[5] Spinoza, *Collected Works* (ed. Curley) i, 11.

improvement of the understanding does occur, each avowed searcher after truth and the highest good must focus with all seriousness on their collective goal, earn just enough "to sustain life and health" and enjoy ordinary pleasures only to the extent needed to sustain our well-being while "conforming to those customs of the community that do not conflict with our aim."[6]

In late April 1663, all packed up, Spinoza's books, microscopes, lens-cutting instruments, everything he possessed including his few pieces of furniture, were ferried, doubtless by barge—the usual method of moving bulky items at the time in Holland—past Leiden, via the waterways to his new locale in Voorburg. That done, he spent the next several weeks, perhaps a month or more, in Amsterdam, conferring with the friends, especially Meyer and Rieuwertsz, then seeing his first book, Descartes' *Principles of Philosophy* through the press.[7] Once back from Amsterdam, Spinoza settled in at Voorburg in early July. During his first two or three weeks in "this village where I am now living," as he put it writing to Oldenburg, he felt positively besieged by friends coming to visit him from elsewhere: "I have hardly been my own master because of the friends who have been kind enough to visit me."[8]

Located south-east of The Hague, Voorburg was then a suburban village, on the Vliet, the main waterway linking The Hague with the nearby city of Delft. The latter, in 1660, was a city with around 25,000 population, hence approximately the same size as The Hague, but only half that of slightly further away Leiden.[9] Spinoza's lodgings, records Monnikhoff accurately, were located in the Kerklaan [Church Lane], or Grote Laen [Main Lane] today the Kerkstraat [Church Street] (Figure 16.1), leading from the village Reformed church down to the waterfront (Figure 16.2), still today retaining something of its seventeenth-century character, located just over half an hour's walk from The Hague city centre, a location ensuring Spinoza was henceforth, for the rest of his life, closely tied to the cosmopolitan, stimulating cultural and social milieu of The Hague.[10]

The house, at Kerkstraat 39, was located alongside the small harbour for river barges, the Kerckhavensloot [the Church harbour sloot] known to locals as "Het Watertje" [The Little Water], a small harbour connected by a narrow waterway forming the southern lower section of the Kerklaan providing direct easy access to the nearby main waterway, the Vliet, lying south-east of the Kerklaan and hence easy transit by passenger barge to Delft, one way, and to Leiden and Amsterdam, the other. Towards the end of Spinoza's Voorburg period, in March 1668, his landlord, the decorative house painter Daniel Harmensz Tijdeman (or Tydeman, d. 1677)

---

[6] Spinoza, *Collected Works* (ed. Curley) i, 19–21.
[7] Spinoza, *Collected Works* (ed. Curley) i, 207; Van de Ven, "Spinoza's Life and Time," 17.
[8] Spinoza, *Collected Works* (ed. Curley) i, 207.
[9] [Lucas], *La Vie*, 30; Verhoeven, *De derde stad van Holland* i, 377.
[10] Van der Leer, "Een speurtocht," 55; Van Boheemen and Bosscher, "Daniel Harmensz Tijdeman," 45.

VOORBURG (1663–1664) 459

Figure 16.1 View of the village of Voorburg, showing the length of Kerkstraat, by Iven Besoet (1720–69). Reproduction courtesy of Artokoloro / Alamy Stock Photo.

Figure 16.2 The waterfront at Voorburg. Reproduction courtesy of the Rijksmuseum, Amsterdam.

purchased a second house, again near the church, on the south side of the nearby Herenstraat, the second of the two streets of Old Voorburg and then perhaps, as today, busier than the Kerklaan. Very likely Spinoza moved with Tijdeman round the corner to the Herenstraat, but he may have stayed in the first house, Kerkstraat 39, the quieter location.[11] Either way, Spinoza lodged in the pleasant mix of quiet and liveliness that was Voorburg altogether for six to seven years and there composed much of the *Ethics* and all of his second most important work, the *Tractatus Theologico-Politicus*.

Much greater ease of communication by passenger barge in all directions was undoubtedly one key factor determining Spinoza's new choice of residence.[12] Both of Tijdeman's houses occupied fairly lively spots adjoining the Voorburg market and shops close to the barge traffic along the Vliet linking The Hague with Leiden, Amsterdam, and Delft. Rather than seeking complete tranquillity, Spinoza seems rather to have had his fill of the less accessible rural quiet of Rijnsburg's outskirts and wanted something still comparatively quiet but yet livelier and easier to reach for friends and visitors, close by a harbour for the so-called *trekschuiten*, the barges providing regular passenger services to Delft, Leiden, and Amsterdam. A busy thoroughfare once called the Fossa Corbulensis, the Vliet was a historic canal originally dug, in 47 AD, on the orders of the Roman general Gnaeus Domitius Corbulo (*c*.7–67 AD), a brother-in-law of Caligula who, when based at Cologne as governor of Roman "Germania Inferior," planned to connect the Lower Rhine at Leiden with the mouth of the River Maas (Meuse). Once a Roman camp styled "Forum Hadriani," Voorburg in the 1660s was in fact considerably less tranquil than Spinoza's previous more rural, outlying neighbourhood in Rijnsburg.

Proximity to the sea served Spinoza's hopes for better health in fresher, purer air but essential too to furthering his plans and ambitious reform project, undoubtedly, was easier communication with The Hague, Amsterdam, Leiden, and Delft. In addition, his new choice may have reflected other priorities. Whether proximity to the Huygens' country retreat played a part in his choice of location remains unknown, but before long deliberations with the Brothers Huygens about optics and mechanics, and chemical experiments became of no small importance to him and, to an extent, to them, and it was pertinent that his lodgings were within easy reach, a leisurely few minutes' walk from the Huygens Brothers' imposing out-of-town mansion and gardens, named Hofwijck, a residence that has been called "an architectural revolution that went according to plan." In Spinoza's new setting, Hofwijck was a perennial familiar landmark, coming into view whenever he strolled around the locality. Elegant and comfortable, with

---

[11] Schuyt, *Spinoza*, 26; Van de Ven, "Spinoza's Life and Time," 16; Van de Leer and Boers, *Huygens and Hofwijck*, 93; so designated in the so-called "verpondingsregisters," the house is listed as no. 50.

[12] Van der Leer, "Een speurtocht," 78.

splendid gardens, designed by the older Constantijn Huygens (1596–1687) together with the artist and architect Jacob van Campen (1596–1657), and overseen during construction by another renowned artist, Pieter Post, Hofwijck stood beside the Vliet on three sides surrounded by water and woods yet also close to the two-street village centre.[13]

On first settling in Voorburg, in 1663–4, Spinoza had not yet suspended, much less abandoned, his effort to provide an overarching reformed "Cartesian" natural history which would, among much else, reduce all qualities including colours and texture to mechanical movements of light and matter, ordering a great range of phenomena under the laws of mathematical physics. Very likely, it was during this period, as part of the ambitious undertaking still very much in his mind during 1663–4, while preparing for the projected new edition of his book on Descartes' *Principles* that Meyer had in mind, and the Dutch translation, that Spinoza composed his famous lost treatise rejecting all "superstitious" explanations of rainbows. Jelles, Lucas, Kortholt, and Colerus all attest to the existence of Spinoza's "Treatise on the Rainbow," and its circulation among his loyal circle.[14] Subsequently, due either to strong criticism of his argument (by Huygens?) or remaining himself dissatisfied with it, he pushed it unfinished to one side. Eventually, it was either inadvertently lost permanently or, in his last days, he himself committed it to the flames as Jelles and Colerus suggest,[15] though in June 1703, the younger Rieuwertsz assured Stolle that "Spinoza did not burn the treatise on the Rainbow though it was not found among his manuscripts after his death, so it must still be somewhere hidden in the hands of a friend."[16] Spinoza, in any case, aimed to show that all natural phenomena to which men attribute supernatural characteristics are really effects of natural processes. Thus, in Genesis 9:13 where "God informs Noah that he will put a rainbow in the clouds, this action of God's is assuredly no other than refraction and reflection affecting the sun's rays seen through drops of water."[17]

16.ii Spinoza and Huygens

No fine residence could be found anywhere at the time more purely *more geometrico* than Hofwijck—a large cube with pyramidal roof containing an impressive array of books, art, and scientific (and musical) instruments (Figure 16.3). Its severe geometry was offset by its impressive collection of

---

[13] Klever, "Spinoza en Huygens," 14–15; Jorink, *Boeck der natuere*, 30–2.
[14] Jelles, "Voorreden," 4; Klever, "Insignis opticus," 62.
[15] Van de Ven, "Spinoza's Life and Time," 18; Steenbakkers, "Spinoza's Life," 34; Gullan-Whur, *Life of Spinoza*, 118, 302.
[16] Guhrauer, "Beiträge," 489; Freudenthal/Walther, *Lebensgeschichte* i, 86.
[17] Spinoza, *Theological-Political Treatise*, 89.

Figure 16.3 Huygens' residence "Hofwyck", in Voorburg. Drawing by Christiaan Huygens (1629–95), Codices Hugeniani Online. HUG 14, ff. 05r. Brill Primary Sources Online through Leiden University Libraries.

paintings assembled by the brothers' still living, elderly father, Constantijn, who in earlier life had been secretary to two stadholders and gained fame throughout the United Provinces as a poet, musicologist, and the most noted art connoisseur of the age. According to the great historian Huizinga, "this highly talented, though not truly great, man was one of the purest representatives of Dutch culture in his day."[18] Among much else, the older Constantijn took a keen interest in optics. Descartes had presented him with portions of his *Dioptrique*, in 1634 and conferred with him about optics along with other topics later of great interest to his sons, and also to Spinoza.[19]

When Spinoza arrived in Voorburg, Hofwijck was inhabited by the elder Constantijn and, intermittently, his three sons—Constantijn junior (1628–97), Christiaan, the middle brother, and the youngest, Lodewijk Huygens (1631–99). Inaugurated in 1642, their residence and gardens quintessentially expressed classicist simplicity, geometry's sway over all reality, learned science experiments and the centrality of painting in Dutch cultural life, along with the alluring promise of

[18] Huizinga, *Dutch Civilization*, 63.
[19] Van der Leer and Boers, *Huygens and Hofwijck*, 37–8; Van de Ven, *Documenting Spinoza*, ch. 7.

delving beyond one's immediate surroundings.[20] As early as 1654, Christiaan Huygens had begun grinding lenses together with his older brother who did much of the practical work (linking him, in some respects, more closely to Spinoza's world), hoping especially to construct new and better telescopes for their astronomical research. Spinoza came to know the younger Constantijn at least as well, and perhaps better than Christiaan the famed scientist.

When Spinoza first got to know Christiaan, most probably in the autumn of 1664, and presumably presented the brothers with a copy of his Descartes book (Christiaan had a copy in his library when he died), the splendid residence housed an impressive quantity of optical, astronomical, and other scientific apparatus. Commencing in 1654 with a twelve-foot telescope with which, in March 1655, Christiaan caused a sensation by discovering "Titan," Saturn's largest icy moon (now known as Saturn VI), the two elder brothers, taking the Copernican system of astronomy for granted, advanced rapidly on both the practical and theoretical side. From 1656, when they constructed their soon renowned 23-foot telescope, Christian registered several further striking discoveries. In 1659, two years before showing his devices to Oldenburg, and four years before Spinoza's arrival, Christiaan won international fame with his *Systema Saturnium* revealing his discovery of the ring around Saturn, the "thin, flat ring, nowhere touching, and inclined to the ecliptic" surrounding the planet. Before long, he had also revealed the permanent markings on Mars' surface and demonstrated that it took Titan sixteen days to circle Saturn.

Combining nature, gardens, art and elegance with learning and science, Hofwijck during the 1660s was as intense a focus of science, art, and cultured conversation as one could find in the Netherlands or anywhere in the Western world at the time. Christiaan was well on the way to recognition as the foremost scientist of the day in Holland, or anywhere, prior to Newton's arrival on the scene in the 1680s—while Constantijn, his talented and astute brother, friendly with ambassadors and statesmen, was destined, from 1672, to become secretary to the new Stadholder, William III. However, Christiaan Huygens "that eminent and justly famous virtuoso," as Boyle called him, writing to Oldenburg, in October 1663,[21] was away yet again, in Paris and London, from April 1663 until May 1664, so this outstanding figure devoted to optics, astronomy, and basic physics, can hardly have conversed much with Spinoza in Voorburg before mid-1664. Nor is there definite evidence that they did meet personally prior to the autumn of that year. But during late 1664 and early 1665, Christiaan spent most of his time at Hofwijck due to the latest plague outbreak and whilst there was acutely conscious of how few persons in the vicinity, or anywhere in The Hague area, apart from his talented older brother, were at hand with whom he could discuss his scientific

---

[20] Kuyper, *Classicist*, 154; Rotthier, *Naakte perenboom*, 75–7.
[21] Oldenburg, *Correspondence* ii, 123.

work. In this respect Spinoza was assuredly a welcome arrival.[22] A later letter to Oldenburg confirms that Spinoza and Huygens discussed Descartes' laws of motion "at Mr Huygens' place" at some point in or around October 1664.

Galileo had been the first to try to establish the laws of motion of hard bodies. Descartes, in his *Principia mathematica* (1644), pushed the project further, using his deductive theoretical method, not experiments, and providing a theological underpinning for fixed physical laws by stressing God's immutability. Since "God is the principal cause of motion," as Spinoza formulates his argument, and (by the *Principles* Part II, Prop. 15) "every body in motion tends of itself to continue in a straight line, not one which is curved," "every body moving in a circle, it follows, as for example a stone in a sling," is continually determined to fly off at a tangent. Since, according to Descartes, God has ordained all things from eternity, and any "variation in anything proceeds from a stronger force," while (by Part II, Prop. 6) "matter is indefinitely extended and the matter of the heavens is one and the same as that of the earth," everything permanently rotating in the heavens must be forced from their natural straight lines and tangents by a superior force explaining the trajectories of heavenly bodies.[23] Descartes proposed six immutable rules covering the laws of all physical movement resulting from hard body impact. But Christiaan, examining Descartes' laws of motion mathematically, began finding them problematic as early as the 1650s and set about attempting to reformulate them.[24]

Very likely, Spinoza was on occasion a trifle irritated by Huygens' seigneurial condescension, fondness for his wider family circle and its high status, and his tendency to express confident, sweeping rejection of Descartes' innovations wholesale as he did, for instance, when later communicating with Bayle.[25] Never diffident before even the most accomplished in thought or science, Spinoza proved far from deferential in the face of Huygens' stunning virtuosity in every field of physics and astronomy. Rather, he judged him overambitious and tended to question Huygens' proposed revisions of Descartes' laws of motion, doubting even whether Huygens would ever produce his promised treatise on the laws of motion. In the summer or early autumn of 1665, Spinoza was again deep in discussion with Christiaan at his residence about various topics, but with Descartes' laws of motion remaining their prime topic of debate and disagreement. "I think you are waiting for it in vain," remarks Spinoza in surviving fragments of a letter to Oldenburg of around 1 October 1665, expressing doubt as to whether Huygens' projected treatise on the laws of motion would ever

---

[22] Hobbes, *Correspondence* ii, 842; Keesing, "Frères Huygens," 111–12; Steenbkkers, "Spinoza's Life," 32; Van der Leer and Boers, *Huygens and Hofwijck*, 94; Van de Leer, "Een speurtocht," 79–80.
[23] Spinoza, *Collected Works* (ed. Curley) i, 261, 266, 269, 276–8.
[24] Gaukroger, *Descartes*, 371–7, 412; Bertoloni Meli, "Axiomatic Tradition," 29, 33.
[25] Gaukroger, *Descartes*, 421n37; Bertoloni Meli, "Axiomatic Tradition," 33; Gullan-Whur, *Life of Spinoza*, 171–2.

appear. "It is some time now since he began boasting of having discovered and shown by calculation rules of motion and laws of nature very different from those Descartes announced, claiming Descartes's rules and laws are almost all wrong. However, thus far he has provided no proof of this."[26] The "some time since" here probably means 1662 or 1663 as Huygens' manuscript *De motu corporum ex percussione* is known to have circulated in London that latter year.

"I know that he told me, about a year ago [hence around October 1664]," Spinoza declares, at the end of this fragment reporting his latest discussions with Huygens, "that everything he had discovered by calculation concerning motion was afterwards confirmed in England by experiment. But I find that hard to believe, moreover, with respect to Descartes' sixth law of motion, I judge that [Huygens] and Descartes are both entirely mistaken."[27] Descartes' sixth rule, according to Spinoza's formulation, holds that "if a body A at rest is precisely equal to Body B that is moving towards it, A will partly be pushed by it and partly drive B back in the opposite direction" in such proportion that one quarter of the moving body's velocity transfers to the pushed effect and three-quarters to the rebounding effect in the direction from which the colliding body comes.[28] Such questions remained a lively topic in Voorburg, London, and Paris over the next year. Spinoza's overly bold criticism of Holland's foremost scientist, not least on this point, he may well have regretted when, soon afterwards, he was contradicted by Oldenburg's reporting experiments in London confirming the accuracy of Huygens' reformulation. Nevertheless, Huygens left his text revising Descartes' laws of motion to one side and it was not actually published until after Huygens' death, by his pupil, Spinoza's friend, Burchardus De Volder. Spinoza was right then that the treatise would not appear in print in their lifetime; but it did exist in provisional form, with its claims confirmed in good part by experiments in London, and this treatise did eventually appear in 1703.[29]

The contrast between Hofwijck's stateliness, and the splendour of its art holdings, and Spinoza's modest lodgings and lifestyle could hardly have been more striking. Though chiefly interested in astronomy, optics, and other aspects of physics, the brothers exhibited an elegant aristocratic curiosity also in a great many other things, not unlike their many-faceted father. Besides optics, and science more generally, there were several other points were Spinoza and the Huygens brothers connected. Spinoza's landlord, Daniel Tijdeman, was one of the roughly 300 painters active in The Hague area during the seventeenth century's third quarter and, according to Monnikhoff, it was he "who probably gave

[26] Spinoza, *Collected Works* (ed. Curley) ii, 13; Klever, "Spinoza en Huygens," 19–20.
[27] Spinoza, *Collected Works* (ed. Curley) ii, 14; Spinoza, *Correspondance* (ed. Rovere), 200–1.
[28] Spinoza, *Opera* i, 218; Spinoza, *Collected Works* (ed. Curley) i, 288; Keesing, "Frères Huygens," 116–17.
[29] Gaukroger, *Descartes' System*, 121–5; Klever, "Spinoza en Huygens," 20; Bertoloni Meli, "Axiomatic Tradition," 34–5.

[Spinoza] his first introduction and knowledge of the art of drawing," though according to Colerus, Spinoza's love of drawing and the art of portraiture commenced earlier, in Amsterdam, after leaving the Jewish community but before leaving the city centre.[30]

Spinoza studied drawing, reports Colerus who, like Sebastian Kortholt before him, was shown some of Spinoza's drawings by Van der Spijck, after acquiring what he needed to know of the craft of lens-grinding: having "perfected himself in that art," as the 1706 English translation of Colerus expresses it, "he apply'd himself to drawing which he learned of himself, and could draw a head very well with ink, or with a coal." "I have in my hands," recounts Colerus, "a whole book of such draughts, amongst which there are some heads of several considerable persons, who were known to him, or had occasion to visit him."[31] Whenever he first began drawing portraits in addition to his physics diagrams, it was a pastime likely to be stimulated by Tijdeman but also the Huygens brothers, Christiaan and Constantijn, who like their father were both intensely interested in sketching from life. However Spinoza acquired his skill in portraiture, the Huygens brothers acquired theirs when young, both taking lessons as youths, at a drawing club in The Hague drawing models, a polite pastime but also part of their education.[32]

Keenly interested too in architecture, antiquities, and Italian art of which he saw much during his journey through France and Italy in 1649–50,[33] for decades the younger Constantijn continued practising drawing, experimenting with different kinds of crayons, pencils, and inks,[34] even after becoming the Prince of Orange's secretary, in 1672, and having less leisure for art. Many of his sketches—unlike Spinoza's (none of which, as far as is known, have survived)—remain with us still today, often landscapes, though his last known drawing was a self-portrait of 1685. When William III, now king of England as well as Stadholder, asked him, in 1691, whether he had finally abandoned his drawing, Constantijn confirmed that he had.[35] When Spinoza interacted regularly with both brothers, communicating with Christiaan (who was frequently away in Paris) probably less than with Constantijn, the latter was at the peak of his enthusiasm for telescopes, microscopes, optics and also art, including study of unusual perspectives. In June 1665, Constantijn drew two wide perspectives of The Hague from the tower of the St Jacobskerk, the city's principal and tallest church.[36] Beyond optical and physics diagrams, Spinoza's interest, as far as we know, remained confined to portraits, a favourite activity also of Constantijn's. Among portraits included in the sketch

---

[30] Freudenthal/Walther, *Lebensgeschichte* i, 172–3; Spinoza, *Briefwisseling*, 33, 56, 58, 163; Buijsen, *Haagse Schilders*, 29.
[31] Colerus, *Life of Benedict de Spinoza*, 34; Kortholt, "Preface," 178.
[32] Huizinga, *Dutch Civilization*, 76; Buijsen, *Haagse Schilders*, 43.
[33] Heijbroek, *Met Huygens op reis*, 27–8.   [34] Heijbroek, *Met Huygens op reis*, 30–1.
[35] Heijbroek, *Met Huygens op reis*, 35.   [36] Heijbroek, *Met Huygens op reis*, 53–5.

book of Spinoza's that Colerus later inspected was a striking depiction of a figure dressed as the rebel fisherman Masaniello (1620–47), leader of the 1647 Neapolitan popular revolt against the Spanish viceroy of Naples, a rising against the Spanish crown following imposition of heavy additional taxes on the Neapolitan populace to help pay for Spain's efforts to subjugate Portugal and Catalonia, a picture that was actually, Colerus was assured, a self-portrait by Spinoza of himself depicted as the rebel leader.[37]

During the quarter century 1650–75, artistic activity, no less than experimental science, reached their zenith at The Hague and its environs. Since The Hague lacked a seaport and views with ships, maritime painting was the one obvious gap among the art genres practised there. Given Spinoza's interest in portraits, it is perhaps worth mentioning that compared with the Dutch Golden Age's other flourishing art centres, The Hague, though a place where landscape, still-life, history painting, and genre painting all also flourished, especially nurtured portraiture owing to the proximity of the Prince's household and the States General, and constant swirl of ambassadors and other leading men found there.[38] Prior to Spinoza's arrival, the most admired and influential artist's studio in The Hague, in terms of followers and sales, was that of the renowned landscape artist Jan van Goyen (1596–1656). Spinoza's landlord, Tijdeman, was at the opposite extreme by this measure, an obscure figure, mainly employed in decorative painting, none of whose work, if any survives, being known as his today. Dwelling in the vicinity for at least nine years, married since 1654 to his wife called Margaretha, and a member of the local Voorburg militia, Tijdeman was later involved in some sort of brawl or incident in 1675, in which he lost an eye.[39]

Christiaan and Constantijn already knew Spinoza by reputation and possibly personally when he arrived and began his settled life in Voorburg, in July 1663. If science and drawing were shared enthusiasms, and all three took the truth of the Copernican system in astronomy for granted (unlike most of the society in which they lived), there was nevertheless also much besides their more elevated social status and political involvements that served to distance the brothers from Spinoza. The figure of Masaniello may have ranked high amongst Spinoza's heroes dedicated to unseating kings, courts, and tyranny, but Spinoza's incipient anti-monarchism was a preoccupation the Huygens brothers emphatically did not share. Admittedly, where their father was punctilious in his religious duties, Christiaan, by the standards of the time, was, like Spinoza, strikingly irreligious and indifferent to confessional differences. However, unlike Spinoza, Christiaan disliked discussing theological topics and while adhering in his own mind to a

---

[37] Colerus, *Vie de Spinosa*, 59–60; Totaro, "Masaniello, la Hollande," 19, 30.
[38] Buijsen, *Haagse Schilders*, 32.   [39] Buijsen, *Haagse Schilders*, 351.

vague deism, for the rest preferred simply going along with family tradition and good form.[40]

Even so, Spinoza and the Huygens brothers undoubtedly concurred, when the great comets controversy of 1664–5 commenced, that they had to watch their step when declaring, along with the mainstream Cartesian fraternity, that heavenly movements follow only a fixed set of immutable laws, that no natural phenomena possess supernatural significance, and that Scripture provides no basis for believing that unusual heavenly movements portend ominous events, as the Voetians, the strict Calvinists, in particular tended to insist.[41] Voetius, their venerated chief theologian, who took the lead in the Netherlands in rejecting Copernican astronomy, repeatedly affirmed that comets, as the New Testament records, are *portenta in coelo* [portents in the sky], heralding God's wrath and calamities or drastic changes on earth.[42] Spinoza and the Huygens brothers shared a common rejection of the supernatural in astronomical matters and joint insistence on the unalterable mechanical regularity of nature (albeit without either Spinoza or Huygens making any public announcement of the former).

Spinoza was at this time at the very height of his involvement with the Dutch world of science and, alongside his being a leading commentator on Cartesianism, it was in the sphere of science debates that he too was best known. Recalling "the year 1665 when I went to live in Amsterdam," Pieter Baert, later a professor of hydrography at Dunkirk, writing to Huygens eleven years later, in February 1676, described his being present there (at the Athenaeum?) "during many wonderful meetings," that is gatherings for lectures including physics demonstrations, "where, I heard your eminence [i.e. Christiaan Huygens] spoken highly of in the arts of natural philosophy and mathematics, especially by Mr. Johannes Hudde, Benedictus de Spinoza and Dr. De Volder [later] professor of natural philosophy at the University of Leiden."[43]

16.iii A Local Dispute

Beside a possible common interest in portraiture, Tijdeman and Spinoza appear to have been local allies also in a very different way. Two years after Spinoza's arrival there erupted a furore of a kind frequently occurring in Dutch local politics at the time, a revolt by elements of the local Reformed Church community against the sway of the established strict Calvinist clique reflected in a deep split in the local *kerkeraad* [Calvinist church council]. It was a fierce quarrel reflecting local social

---

[40] Keesing, "Frères Huygens," 114.
[41] Gaukroger, *Descartes' System*, 15–16, 67; Jorink, *Reading the Book of Nature*, 150, 163–5.
[42] Van Ruler, *Crisis of Causality*, 11–20; Jorink, *Reading the Book of Nature*, 150–4.
[43] Huygens, *Oeuvres complètes* xviii, 34; quoted in Strazzoni, *Burchard de Volder*, 123.

tensions. Since the Twelve Years Truce and the conflict of 1618–19 leading to Oldenbarnevelt's downfall, it had been a constant provincial and civic government concern to safeguard society's fragile unity and stability by defending the public church's doctrinal cohesion without allowing it to become too dominant and intolerant. The *via media* the regents aimed for proved no easy goal. Though a concern shared by both the country's vying political factions, the States party faction of De Witt and the Orangist regent faction allied to the Calvinist orthodox, they proceeded with decidedly different emphases, rarely finding stable compromises.

If the stricter Reformed Church clergy had little choice but to heed their political backers' admonitions of restraint, they invariably pushed harder than their regent allies. As the exclusive public church of the Republic's Seven Provinces, the Reformed Church's consistories and preachers were closely tied to the functioning of the state at every level, especially financially since the Church possessed little property or resources of its own. "The Calvinists," observed Temple accurately, in 1673, "make the body of the people, and are possessed of all the publick churches in the dominions of the state, as well as of the only ministers or pastors, who are maintained by the publick; but these have neither lands nor tithes, nor any authorized contributions from the people, but certain salaries from the state, upon whom they wholly depend." For this reason, churchmen of the orthodox Calvinist party could never set themselves in outright opposition to the States General or the States of Holland, but continually strove to pressure the state towards more theologically-orientated, less tolerant policies, incessantly nudging towards goals the consistories demanded, especially less freedom of thought and more restrictions on conduct. Hence, while bound to the state, financially and politically, the pastors, Temple notes, were "often very bold in taxing and preaching publickly against the vices, and sometimes the innocent entertainments, of persons most considerable in the government, as well as of the vulgar"; and were "in general, throughout the country, passionate friends of the interests of the House of Orange; and, during the intermission of that authority, found ways of expressing their affections to the person and fortunes of this prince, without offending the state, as it was then constituted."[44]

The rival ideological blocs permeating Dutch life and society at the time did not of course resemble modern political parties but, rather, were patronage networks, informal groupings either more or less inclined towards the Stadholder and Calvinist orthodoxy, as well as purveying different views about the character of the union and Generality, and about piety and social discipline. Doubtless this was one reason Spinoza liked hearing reports of sermons, as Colerus records, and, on occasion, attended church himself.[45] It was a society that could cope with the

---

[44] Temple, *Observations*, 125. [45] Colerus, *Vie de Spinosa*, 72.

resulting culture wars and ever present tension in theology stemming from the struggle in the universities between Voetians and the Cocceians (or strict and liberal Calvinist factions) up to a point. The leading theologian among the liberal Calvinist faction, Johannes Cocceius (1603–69), who happened to be Oldenburg's cousin, strove over many years to avoid being drawn into too direct a clash with Voetius. Basically, Temple felt, Dutch toleration usefully mitigated religious fury: "it is hardly to be imagined, how all the violence and sharpness, which accompanies the differences of religion in other countrys, seems to be appeased or softened here, by the general freedom which all men enjoy, either by allowance or connivance; nor, how faction and ambition are thereby disabled to colour their interested and seditious designs with the pretences of religion, which has cost the Christian world so much blood for these last hundred and fifty years."[46]

It impressed Temple that

> in this Commonwealth, no man having any reason to complain of oppression of conscience; and no man having hopes, by advancing his religion, to form a party, or break in upon the state, the differences [of confession] make none in affections, and little in conversation, where it serves but for entertainment and variety. They argue without interest or anger; they differ without enmity or scorn and they agree without confederacy. Men live together, like citizens of the world, associated by the common ties of humanity, and by the bonds of peace, under the impartial protection of indifferent laws, with equal encouragement of all art and industry, and equal freedom of speculation and enquiry.[47]

That was a vision of the union of the United Provinces at its best, but during the last years of the De Witt era proved a standard of toleration difficult to sustain.

While both theologico-political blocs patronized and protected the public church, they clashed relentlessly over how much influence to accord its ministers in local affairs, education, culture, social life, and administering charity, and how much toleration to grant the Republic's other main churches, Mennonite, Remonstrant, Lutheran, and Catholic, and to dissident sects like the Collegiants and Quakers. Thus, the rival Voetian and Cocceian factions within the theological fraternity presiding over the Dutch Reformed Church quarrelled ceaselessly over such topics as tolerance of others, sabbath observance, theatre, dance halls, Copernican astronomy, and the issue of Cartesianism. Most of the South Holland Synod agreed with the strict Calvinists that Cocceius' theology unacceptably dilutes the pure Word of God and legitimizes ungodly work and pleasure on the sabbath in contravention of the Fourth Commandment. Despite the Republic's greater affluence and evident advantages when compared with the

---

[46] Temple, *Observations*, 125–6; Haley, *English Diplomat*, 307.
[47] Temple, *Observations*, 126–7.

surrounding monarchies, England, France, and Spain, beneath the surface, Temple soon realized, the United Provinces of the mid-1660s were in difficulty due to the rift within society and the public church: "this strong disease, that had been so long working in the very bowels of the state,"[48] now a growing menace, was an endemic, underlying instability, a "distracted estate of a domestique sedition or discontent, which, like ill humours in a body, make any small wound dangerous, and a great one mortal," internal strife driven by theology that would powerfully contribute to bringing about the terrifying near collapse of the Republic in 1672.

During the 1660s, the universities were one sector where the traditional grip of the strict Calvinists looked especially vulnerable. A notable recent gain for the anti-Voetians, via the Utrecht city council, was the appointment in 1662 of Frans Burman (1628–79), a zealous Coccejan of German background, to a chair in theology at Utrecht as a means of bolstering "moderation" in the university and checking Voetius, the leading figure since the early 1640s proclaiming the great danger lurking in Cartesian notions of nature and causation, and in the Cartesian tendency to separate theology from philosophy. Burman, a protégé of the foremost liberal Reformed theologian on the Coccejan-Cartesian side, Heidanus, whose widowed daughter he later married, did not fail to confront Voetianism at every turn. His *De moralitate sabbati* (1665) became one of the most controversial and disputed mid-seventeenth-century Coccejan publications on Sabbath observance, prompting a hail of rebuttals from strict Calvinist opponents. Eventually, the States of Utrecht, following Holland's example, simply forbade further publications on this overly divisive topic and all further dispute about the question among university professors.[49]

Raging around Spinoza during his most crucially creative years was thus a theological conflict deeply embedded in the Republic's rival political factions. The Dordrecht regent and political writer, Johan de Wit (1618–76), a cousin not to be confused with the Pensionary of Holland, Johan de Witt, a personage even more hostile to Voetians than the Pensionary, authored a massive three-volume work on public prayers, titled *Public Gebedt* (Amsterdam, 1663–4), that figured centrally in the tumultuous controversies of the day, this so-called "Public Prayers" controversy of the mid-1660s quickly becoming a key battleground. This affray followed from the efforts of Pensionary De Witt and his allies in the province of Holland to alter the symbolic significance and change the order of public prayers for civil authorities recited in Reformed Church services. The quarrel marked the culmination of years of wrangling in all Seven Provinces over the order and content of the "public prayers." In 1654, the Stadholder of Friesland, Groningen,

---

[48] Temple, *Observations*, 163–4.
[49] Visser, *Geschiedenis van den sabbatstrijd*, 121, 159, 180; Van Ruler, *Crisis of Causality*, 303–19; Israel, *Dutch Republic*, 665–6.

and Drenthe, William Frederick of Nassau (1613-1664), guardian as well as both brother-in-law and cousin of the boy prince, William II, seeking to tighten links between Orangists and the strict Calvinist faction in the public church, had pushed a resolution through the States of Friesland, obliging Friesland's Reformed preachers to always place first in the order of public prayers that for the well-being of the Prince of Orange.[50] In Holland, the established order placed the prayer for the States General first which, according to Pensionary De Witt, undesirably misled uneducated, unsophisticated folk into thinking the States General rather than the States of Holland were "the undisputed sovereign and, next to God, only supreme authority in this province." To correct popular notions, De Witt and his allies, facing vociferous resistance from the consistories and some town councils as well as Friesland, decreed that the prayer for the States of Holland must come first in order, that for the States General second, and for the city government or local authority under which one lived third, with no public prayer at all for the Prince of Orange.[51] This new formulary was sent to all the town councils of Holland, including Delft which was responsible for its implementation in Voorburg, in March 1663, with instructions to require the consistories to ensure implementation and uniform practice.

That the public church had long encouraged "serious discrepancies in prayers for the supreme and secondary authorities," a charge frequently echoed by Mennonites, Collegiants, and other dissenters, or tried to foment "among the people" the misconception that the States General was the supreme authority in Holland, many preachers and consistories indignantly denied.[52] Society's malaise, held the Voetians, was chiefly caused by De Witt's "True Freedom" and the regents oppressing the Reformed Church consistories, depriving them of "their freedom" to appoint "upright preachers." Who were the "upright preachers"? Holland's apologists for toleration and freedom of thought had no doubts as to their identity. Nor were they restrained in the language they used to describe them. In an anonymous propaganda pamphlet, the *Schotschen Duyvel* [The Scots Devil] (1663), De Witt's cousin, De Wit, characterized the strict Calvinist leadership—"Voetius, Teellink, Smout, Essenius, Lodenstein, Gentman and Ryssenius"—as "all rebellious, frustrated, overweening, impudent and shameless slanderers of persons high and low." The *Schotschen Duyvel* lumped Voetians together with the Old Mennonites and strict Lutherans as all of a piece, all against "freedom" and "moderation." "That is what you call freedom," protested De Wit, expressing sentiments close to Spinoza's heart, "the freedom to enslave everybody."[53] The Leiden political writer and economist Pieter de La Court went so far

---

[50] Van den End, *Guiljelmus Saldenus*, 177; Janssen, *Princely Power*, 163, 168.
[51] Israel, *Dutch Republic*, 761-4; Stern, *Orangism*, 97.
[52] GA Leiden, Acta kerkeraad v, res. 13 April 1663.
[53] [De Wit], *Den Schotsen Duyvel*, 63, 68-9; Rowen, *John de Witt*, 14.

as to claim Voetians were not at all genuinely devout people but "godless men, much worse than atheists" perverting the Reformation and true sense of Scripture with their ruthless pursuit of power.[54] It was in this overheated atmosphere, in 1665, amidst intensification and politicization of the conflict between Voetius (Figure 16.4) and Cocceius, that Spinoza suspended work on the later sections of his *Ethics*, to apply himself urgently to the escalating interaction between politics and theology.

Among the final propositions of Part IV of the *Ethics* are several that should be read as direct commentary on the threatening scenario confronting our philosopher. Thus the last but one proposition in *Ethics* IV reads: "superstition [i.e. Calvinism and some other Christian theology], though, seems to affirm that the good is what brings sadness and, against this, what brings joy is bad. But as we have already said no one, unless envious, delights in my *impotentia* and misfortune. For the more joy we feel the more we pass to a greater perfection, and hence participate more in the divine nature; nor can joy that is driven by the true

Figure 16.4 *Gisbertus Voetius* (1589–1676), after portrait by Nicolas Maes, late seventeenth century. Fine Arts Museums of San Francisco.

---

[54] De La Court, "Brieven," 131.

reasoning of our advantage ever be bad."[55] This may be profound philosophy but was also a direct reaction to Voetian theology and intervention in the current politics of the Republic.

The States party-faction favoured the Cocceian side in the cultural-theological wars gripping the country because Cocceians, like the De Witt faction among the regents, strove to soften the edge of confessional strife and prevent dogmatic orthodoxy dominating the public church and, through it, society, lifestyle, education, and general culture. Spinoza suspended work on his main philosophical project, *The Ethics*, in the summer of 1665, he explained to Oldenburg, in his undated letter of around late September 1665, because the internal crisis increasingly gripping the Republic was seriously affecting his own personal situation, life, and local reputation; and it is not hard to see what he meant. Turning to write the *TTP*, Spinoza spelt out for Oldenburg three principal reasons for his sudden dramatic change of tactics, intellectual focus, and daily routine: firstly, the "prejudices of the theologians; for I know these are the main obstacles which prevent men from giving their minds to philosophy"; second, the unpleasant atmosphere he increasingly encountered in Voorburg, the "opinion of me held by the common people who constantly accuse me of atheism; I am driven to avert this accusation too as far as I can." The common people's hostility was perceived by Spinoza, by this stage, as something seriously affecting his and his group's immediate prospects, though, at this point in his career, before publication of any major controversial work, he must have meant principally the attitude of local churchgoers in Voorburg, how he was looked at in the street, plus hostile sentiment among the Leiden academic fraternity, and the impact this exerted on his everyday life and prospects. His third objective was the urgent need to defend and "vindicate freedom to philosophize and to say what we think," because "here it is in every way besieged by the excessive authority and egotism of preachers."[56]

A continuing major focus was the ceaseless struggle over appointments to Reformed Church preachers' positions in the towns and villages of Holland. The immediate context of Spinoza's involvement was just such a battle in the church consistory and city government of Delft under whose jurisdiction Voorburg lay.[57] The republican faction held that *Hollandse vrijheid* [Dutch freedom] required the preachers' authority to be more tightly restricted, "for where the preachers have too much authority," as one pamphlet expressed it in 1663, "there things generally do not go well as is evident from the situation in Scotland and other places."[58] Scotland regularly served as prime exemplum among the Dutch of how things go wrong when Calvinist preachers and bigotry gain too much sway. To this,

---

[55] Spinoza, *Opera* i, 275–6; Spinoza, *Collected Works* (ed. Curley) i, 593.
[56] Spinoza, *Collected Works* (ed. Curley) ii, 14–15; Klever, "Spinoza's Life and Works," 36; Fraenkel, "Spinoza's Philosophy of Religion," 381–2.
[57] Bleyswijck, *Beschryvinge der Stadt Delft*, 58; Verhoeven, *De derde stad van Holland* i, 341.
[58] Van der Hoeven, *Hollandse Vrijheid verdedigt*, 37.

Voetians replied that the political campaign against the well-intentioned and true teachers had now gone so far that the authority of pulpit and chancel was disastrously reduced causing the general corruption of religion and true piety. Instead of genuine Calvinist "reformation," in Holland religion was now "wretchedly deformed" by Arminian-minded excessively tolerant regents, and worse, gnawed by the curse of *Socinianerye* [Socinianism] and *Atheisterye* [atheism] creeping into the consistories and city councils.[59] The Holland regents, the orthodox complained, deliberately selected Cocceians rather than "upright" candidates for the "best places" as preachers in the towns. It was even rumoured that De Witt and his accomplices pursued a secret policy under which "in all the big towns no Voetian preachers should be admitted" to preaching positions by the city councils, a policy allegedly motivating not a few contemptible theological turncoats to "change their mantels and begin reading more of Descartes than the Bible."[60] Occasionally attending at church sermons, as Spinoza did, must have been intended as a way of assessing the moral quality of the Reformed preachers' teaching, observing the flow and temper of local affairs and testing the political water.

In 1665, following the retirement of Voorburg's local village *dominee*, Dr Jakobus van Oosterwijck (1597–1674), the post of Reformed preacher in the village became vacant. It was a position of great influence in local Voorburg life, as the village Reformed preacher also supervised the orphanage and decided who among the poor and needy received charity, whether in money or bread, and who did not. In Voorburg, the local Reformed church literally dominated the vicinity in which Spinoza dwelt. As regards poor relief and other areas of social welfare, Oosterwijck had long been prominent also in Delft itself. In the protracted tussle that flared over his successor, the two rival factions, Voetian and Cocceian, were backed by very different elements in the village. The majority bloc, the orthodox faction, endorsed by a considerable list of backers calling themselves the "principal inhabitants of Voorburg,"[61] supported the nomination of Dominee Eduardus Westerneyn (1632–74) who, after a protracted struggle, eventually secured the post and would remain Voorburg's Reformed preacher for four years (1665–9) before moving on to Leiden. The opposition, the more liberal wing, in which Spinoza's landlord, Tijdeman, was prominent, was headed by two dissident members of the consistory, Cornelis Rottenveel and Hendrik van Galen, supporting a young candidate [proponent] from Zeeland named Van der Wiele. After a long weeding out procedure, beginning with sixteen names under consideration, Westerneyn and Van der Wiele were the last candidates on the shortlist.[62]

---

[59] *Genees-Middelen voor Hollandts-Qualen* (1672) (Kn. 10,376), 5–6.
[60] *Appendix Van 't Catalogus van de Boecken*, 4–5.
[61] Freudenthal/Walther, *Lebensgeschichte* i, 279.
[62] Freudenthal/Walther, *Lebensgeschichte* ii, 147–8; Van Vloten, *Benedictus de Spinoza*, 51; Steenbakkers, "Beyond the Legends," 12; Steenbakkers, "Spinoza's Life," 31.

In Voorburg, the Calvinist orthodox were not just more rigid in theology than their opponents but also apparently cultivated a narrower, more parochial view of local society tinged with class prejudice. They expressly "disavowed and disdained" Tijdeman's faction as an idle, peripheral clique of troublemakers, living off charity and alms, partly wage-earning servants, mostly persons of "little or no wealth or property."[63] It would be a wretched church council, they contended, that regulated itself by the judgement of such types.[64] Moreover, their opponents, the consistory complained to the Delft city government, were unworthy also in other respects, many being outsiders [vreemdelingen] "or people coming to live here from elsewhere" rather than propertied solid old Voorburg stock. The majority bloc of the Delft Reformed consistory, for its part, found it hard to believe Tijdeman and his allies had any proper authorization for their stinging submission to the Delft burgomasters protesting about the local Reformed consistory's procedures. Their submission opposing the orthodox, submitted the previous winter, preceding Westerneyn's nomination, was in fact bitterly resented. The Delft city government itself was divided but, until 1672, broadly supported De Witt's policy, opposing the Orangist–Voetian alliance striving to reduce toleration, strengthen church policing of society, and secure the stadholderate for William III. However, as in most larger Holland towns, at Delft the situation was complicated by strong local popular support for Calvinist orthodoxy among the lower, less educated, strata encouraging the Reformed Church council to regularly denounce the laxity of the curbs on the Catholic minority which, in Delft, was substantial, a minority rightly perceived to be growing as a proportion, amounting by the 1660s to over a quarter of the population.

Delft's hardliners were led by Johannes Goethals (1611–73), a fanatical Voetian, advocate of more stringent sabbath observance and tougher anti-Catholic measures, and an ardent Orangist.[65] During 1666, the Delft Reformed Church council's meetings, when not chaired by the consistory's senior figure, the poet-preacher Volkerus van Oosterwijck (1602–75), were mostly chaired by Goethals closely supported by Thaddeus de Lantman [also de Landman] (1622–81), another fervent Voetian and Orangist (and ally of Saldenus) and a personage who would play a prominent role in Spinoza's life.[66] The heads of the Voorburg orthodox faction, explaining the "truth and circumstances" of the Voorburg dispute to the Delft burgomasters, rejected outright the Tijdeman faction's allegations. Protesting that their opponents' submission denouncing the strict Calvinists' machinations was fraudulent, introducing false arguments inspired by extraneous influence, the Voorburg orthodox urged the burgomasters to consider that "the

---

[63] Van Vloten, *Benedictus de Spinoza*, 260–1; Freudenthal/Walther, *Lebensgeschichte* i, 280.

[64] Van Vloten, *Benedictus de Spinoza*, 261; Freudenthal/Walther, *Lebensgeschichte* i, 279.

[65] Verhoeven, *De derde stad van Holland* i, 406; Israel, *Dutch Republic*, 606, 801, 805; Stern, *Orangism*, 4.

[66] Delft Stadsarchief 445 (Kerkeraad) vol. 6, fos. 302, 305v, 309.

aforementioned Daniel Tijdeman has lodging with him, in the rented out part of his household, an A[msterdammer?] ... Spinoza, born of Jewish parents, but now, so it is said, an atheist or someone who mocks all religions, and in any case a harmful presence in this republic [schadelijck instrument in deze republijcque], as many learned men and preachers, among them Dominee De Lantman and those who know [Spinoza], can attest."

The majority faction of the Voorburg *kerkeraad* presumed that it was in fact Spinoza who actually composed the text of the protest, which is far from certain though not improbable. What is certain is that Spinoza was being deliberately targeted by local Reformed preachers as an "atheist" and unwelcome local presence.[67] The "many learned men" were presumably chiefly Leiden professors and local preachers with De Lantman cited as knowing most about Spinoza and possessing damaging information that could be employed against him which, given the accustomed role of the Reformed preachers in surveying and regulating the conduct and thinking of their localities, implies De Lantman was now already collecting hearsay and testimony potentially usable against Spinoza locally should complaints about his conduct and utterances come up for formal deliberation by the local church council, as subsequently happened multiple times, in the 1670s, at The Hague. Not long after transferring to Voorburg, Spinoza, then, not only felt himself to be but actually was caught up in an escalating affray with local theologians, directly clashing with the anti-Cartesian as well as some of the Republic's academic Cartesian fraternity, while growing locally notorious for disdaining the beliefs and notions of "ordinary people." Many comments in Spinoza's *Tractatus Theologico-Politicus*, the major new initiative on which he embarked at this time, constitute a general plea relevant to all societies but, at the same time, are direct interventions in the protracted quarrel of 1665-6 at Voorburg and Delft.

De Lantman was well-known in Delft as well as Voorburg and The Hague, and a militant voice among the orthodox Calvinist preachers of the entire South Holland region. A preacher at Delft for eight years (1656-63), he assumed his new role and pulpit in The Hague, in June 1663, after considerable vacillation, his move being much discussed at the time with De Lantman himself feeling torn

---

[67] "Nota. Dat den voorsz. Daniel Tijdeman in sijn gehuijrde huijsinge||heeft bij hem inwoonen een A...||Spinosa van joodsche ouders gebooren, sijnde nu||(soo geseijt wert) een atheist off ^{die} met alle||Religiën spot, ende immers een schadelijck instrument in deze republijcque, soo veele geleerde mannen ende||predicanten onder andere dom^e. Lantman ende andere ||die hem kennen, connen getuijgen, die de Requeste, aende||heeren Burgem^{ren} gepresenteert (soo die van de kercken||raet presumeren) geschreven heeft" ("Lijste van de Naemen der heeren Ingelanden ende principale inwoonders tot Voorburch, ende Lidmaten der gereformeerde gemeijnte Jesu Christi aldaer... noch oock niet genegen sijn tot den persoon van Vander Wiele Zeeus proponent..."), see Freudenthal/Walther, *Lebensgeschichte* i, 280-1; Van Vloten, *Benedictus de Spinoza*, 51, 260-1; Meinsma, *Spinoza et son cercle*, 284; Rotthier, *Naakte perenboom*, 79-80, 246; Van de Ven, *Printing Spinoza*, 96; Van Boheemen and Bosscher, "Daniel Harmensz Tijdeman," 49-51.

between staying and accepting the call [beroeping] to The Hague.[68] A bulwark of Voetianism and Orangism, there was apparently considerable reluctance among his Delft congregation and the Delft consistory[69] to see him go. A crucial factor in deciding to accept when The Hague burgomasters and Hof van Holland approved his new appointment, in June 1663, was what De Lantman called the "weakness and indisposition of some of the preachers there," in The Hague.[70] Calvinist stringency and policies at The Hague needed beefing up with a strong, vocal personality. Claiming to set aside his own personal preference in moving to The Hague, De Lantman projected his move as holy obligation enabling him to contribute more to the "spread of God's *eer* [honour] and greater strengthening of his Church," meaning his forceful personality, Calvinist fervour, and aversion to Remonstrants, Socinians, and Spinoza, would wield more political clout in The Hague, especially the Stadholder's court, than he could exert in Delft.[71] His successor in Delft was Saldenus who moved there from Enkhuizen.

When Spinoza arrived in Voorburg, De Lantman was still in Delft, and hence prominent also in church affairs at Voorburg, but in the process of transferring to his new preaching post in The Hague.[72] By 1665, De Lantman at The Hague was fully fulfilling his mission, like Goethals almost openly challenging the authority of the De Witt regime not least by criticizing its conduct of the newly commenced war with England and publicly denouncing the alliance with Catholic France. On one memorable occasion, insinuating that religion would be far better served by having the Prince of Orange at the helm than De Witt, De Lantman publicly expressed unmistakable fury at the alleged laxity of the De Witt regime to his congregation in The Hague with a sermon citing the Book of Hosea II on the subject of "Israel punished and restored."[73]

According to their information, the Voetian–Orangist bloc of the Voorburg Reformed consistory admonished the Delft burgomasters, it was not Tijdeman himself but actually this undesirable and pernicious "instrument," Spinoza, "or so those of the church council assume," who had written up the fiercely contested "*Requeste* presented to burgomasters."[74] This intruder from outside, a presumptuous apostate Jew daring to interfere in Voorburg local church politics intriguing against the strict Calvinist faction, was the real author of the resented ideological challenge. Thus, Spinoza started work on the *TTP*, one can scarcely doubt, in a wary mood connected with the local Voorburg battle, deeply antagonistic towards

---

[68] Delft Stadsarchief 445 (Kerkeraad) vol. 6, fos. 273 and 274. Resoluties of the kerkeraad 18 June and 25 June 1663; De Bie, Lindeboom, and Itterzon, *Biografisch Woordenboek* v, 575.
[69] Delft Stadsarchief 445 (Kerkeraad) vol. 6, fo. 273. Res. 18 June 1663.
[70] Delft Stadsarchief 445 (Kerkeraad) vol. 6, fos. 275, 275v. Res. Kerkeraad, 27 June 1663.
[71] Delft Stadsarchief 445 (Kerkeraad) vol. 6, fos. 276v–277. Res. Kerkeraad, 2 July 1663; see also Gullan-Whur, *Life of Spinoza*, 166, 260.
[72] Delft Stadsarchief 445 (Kerkeraad) vol. 6, fos. 275–7. Res. 27 and 29 June 1663.
[73] De Bie, Lindeboom, and Itterzon, *Biografisch Woordenboek* v, 575.
[74] Freudenthal/Walther, *Lebensgeschichte* i, 280; Steenbakkers, "Beyond the Legends," 13.

the local strict Calvinist faction not just as a religious current but as a social group and educational force. Spinoza doubtless had Westerneyn's backers, the Voorburg Reformed community's rich men and property owners in mind when depicting those social elements professing Voetian piety and demanding stricter censorship as "greedy, fawning people who have no moral character – their greatest comfort is to think about the money they have in the bank and to fill their fat stomachs," types Spinoza graphically contrasts with "those whom a good upbringing and moral integrity and virtue have rendered freer."[75]

In June 1666, after many months of wrangling and indecision, the Delft burgomasters finally approved Westerneyn's appointment as Voorburg's *predikant*, leaving the Tijdeman faction defeated.[76] Thus, when Spinoza suspended work on his *Ethics* he was feeling the advance of the Reformed preachers and their excessive authority to be a growing menace both in the Republic generally and also in his particular locality. "If, finally, we remember that everybody's loyalty to the state, like their faith in God, can only be known from their works," affirms Spinoza, in the *TTP*, "that is, from their charity toward their neighbour, it will not be doubted that the best state accords everyone the same liberty to philosophize as we showed that faith likewise allows."[77] He was now in head-on collision with the faction passionately denying this. For Spinoza, no religious authority has any right to censure views, books, or discussion.

If at a deeper level, the *TTP* was intended to revolutionize Bible criticism and reconsider the whole question of church governance and toleration in relation to political thought generally, it is nevertheless in considerable part also a topical, polemical political intervention. Because the intellectual strategy Spinoza adopts in the *TTP* involved deep immersion in Bible hermeneutics and biblical history, his interrupting the philosophical project constituting the core of his life's work at this juncture involved not just a sudden change of perspective and subject matter but also a degree of reframing his overall project into a more activist, combative enterprise as well as one now precariously balancing continued intellectual focus on reforming Descartes and natural science, and especially detaching the latter from religious assumptions, alongside revived commitment to fields of study in which he had specialized earlier in life. If Meyer's less complex Bible criticism, published in 1666, remained for some time the main focus of attention, Spinoza's subtler, deeper approach to Bible criticism in the *TTP*, although not published until 1670, already at this time involved him in re-immersing himself in Hebrew studies, Ibn Ezra, Maimonides, Gersonides, and both Delmedigos whose discussions of the Old Testament all became notable aides and themes for the *TTP*, along with Josephus' historical works and the New Testament.

---

[75] Spinoza, *Theological-Political Treatise*, 254.
[76] Delft Stadsarchief 1/98, fo. 267, burgomasters' resolution, 7 May and 12 June 1666.
[77] Spinoza, *Theological-Political Treatise*, 254.

16.iv De Jure Ecclesiasticorum

The bitter clash between Spinoza and the Voorburg Reformed Church leadership commencing in 1664 or 1665, would only intensify in subsequent years spurred by later events. Meanwhile, a few voices began to be heard that adopted a more radical stance than the mainstream of De Witt's supporters. Chief among these was the explosive publication *De Jure Ecclesiasticorum* [On the Right of Ecclesiastics] by a learned, highly competent foe of the Voetians, a text published at Amsterdam, in 1665, without giving any name of author or publisher. Fictitiously attributed to "Lucius Antistius Constans," its full title designated *De Jure Ecclesiasticorum* a book "in which is taught what authority is attributed to ecclesiastics by divine and human law [*quo docetur, quodcunque divini humanique iuris ecclesiasticis tribuitur*]." Alarmed, this vigorously argued text explains, by the fraudulent misuse of religion to seize an unjustified authority and power over society, it aimed its blows relentlessly at the Reformed Church establishment and the entire Voetian–Orangist ideological bloc, raising quite a storm at the time. It was cited by several church councils in their routine complaints to local town governments during the late 1660s, at 's-Hertogenbosch, Deventer, and elsewhere as among the worst instances of what the church councils called "licentious book printing" of the sort that should be banned.[78] For the rest of Spinoza's lifetime, it figured among the four most condemned and decried books in the Dutch Republic, one of the "four musketeers" of the unholy department of the "bookshop of the world" along with Hobbes' *Leviathan*, the *Philosophia S.Scripturae Interpres*, and Spinoza's *Tractatus Theologico-Politicus*, one of the four titles singled out for special condemnation, in 1674, by the States General itself in a way other books were not.

In fact, *De Jure Ecclesiasticorum* turned out to be the foremost seventeenth-century text accusing clergymen everywhere, those of all the main churches as distinct from the fringe sects, of abuse of power by claiming divine sanction for an authority that never existed, that Christ never authorized, and that finds no legitimacy in Scripture. All human inequality of status, authority, and privilege, insists *De Jure*, including all ecclesiastical authority and establishment, is decreed and maintained exclusively by human, not by sacred authority or divine decree.[79] It claimed, as the early eighteenth-century Anglo-Irish polemicist, William Carroll, rendered fragments of it into English, that all institutionalized "inequality betwixt man and man, in the civil society, is descended or deriv'd from the vice-gods," that is human lieutenants speaking for the gods. Everyone's rights in the state of nature continue in more orderly fashion after the formation of the state,

---

[78] Weekhout, *Boekencensuur*, 287, 344; Lavaert, *Vrijheid, gelijkheid, veelheid*, 73–5; Lavaert, "Lieutenants," 152.

[79] [Constans], *De Jure Ecclesiasticorum*, 38, 154–5; Lavaert, "Lieutenants," 150, 154, 157–60.

argues this radical text, and "there cannot be two independent powers in the same society"; this being one of the essential points of radical republican political thought as expounded by Spinoza, Van den Enden, and Johan and Pieter de La Court.[80] In the *statu civili*, civil society, the basic equality prevailing among men in the state of nature persists but now in a more orderly, structured way than before.[81] Since *De Jure* claims all political, legal, and religious power without exception derives from the sovereignty of the whole people acting as a collectivity, political power begins, but also remains, democratic in all legitimate operations as well as in origin. There are no special privileges, or order of society, nor any religious authority or divine authorization of *ius circa sacra* that natural reason or the law of Nature stipulates as grounded by the decree of God in human society, and no inherent rights for clergy any more than for nobles, no independent authority that "can rightly and truly be ascribed to the clergy."[82]

Outraged Orangists and Voetians sought to affix blame for what, to them, was an unprecedented affront and challenge. Church power over society and everyday life was being outrageously challenged. One obvious suspect in 1665 was Pieter de La Court at Leiden. Both Brothers De La Court—Johan had died in 1660— proclaimed the democratic republic to be, of all forms of government, the "naturlijkste, redelijkste, vreedzaamste en voordeligste voor de ingezetenen [most natural, rational, peaceful and most advantageous for the inhabitants]," in their repeatedly republished book *Consideratien van staat*, a copy of which, in a 1661 version, Spinoza had among his personal library.[83] But the democratic republicanism of *De Jure* and the De La Courts was at the same time a rejection also of De Witt's ideology of the "True Freedom." For the mainstream republicanism of the governing De Witt faction, while abjuring the hereditary principle and vigorously proclaiming religious toleration and freedom of expression, together with individual liberty more broadly, imposed strict limits regarding participation in politics and the character of political power. De Witt's republicanism did profess to depart from the Venetian-Genoese model of aristocratic republicanism especially in holding to De Witt's principle that in "a free republic no one has any right by birth to the high dignities" and offices of the state.[84] But while in De Wittian theory the hereditary principle plays no part in a well constituted republic, in practice the supposedly non-hereditary, non-noble representatives postulated by De Witt and his circle turned out to be just a small privileged circle of affluent

---

[80] [Constans], *De Jure Ecclesiasticorum*, 38; Carroll, *Spinoza Reviv'd*, 8–9; Lavaert, "Lieutenants," 155, 159.

[81] [Constans], *De Jure Ecclesiasticorum*, 131, 139, 154.

[82] "Omnem inaequalitatem ecclesiasticorum non minus aut aliter, quam caetorum civium a solis prodiis procedure: nec ullum illorum et horum discrimen esse," [Constans], *De Jure Ecclesiasticorum*, 52; Carroll, *Spinoza Reviv'd*, 9.

[83] V.H. [De La Court], *Consideratien en Exempelen*, 292; Van Sluis and Musschenga, *Boeken van Spinoza*, 57.

[84] [De Witt], *Deductie ofte declaratie* (1654), 121, 180; Weststeijn, *Radicale Republiek*, 37–9.

urban regents, an informal oligarchy wholly monopolizing political power. De Witt acknowledged the hereditary principle to be a menace in a "free state," as the history of the Visconti at Milan and the Medici at Florence abundantly illustrated, and agreed that all high officeholders should be chosen by the representatives of the cities and countryside, but in his system these representatives turned out to be exceedingly few. The regent body supporting De Witt was a narrow, exclusive, undemocratic clique, verging on being a hereditary elite, defending valuable freedoms with a power base evidently too narrow to provide stability and durability in the Republic.

De Jure hence propagates a more radical form of Dutch republicanism than De Witt and his allies stood for. Democratic republicanism's superiority, held Johan de La Court, the more daring of the two brothers, was doubly proven by the fact that in all other forms of government *salus populi*, the welfare of the people, is just a mask [dekmantel] for self-interest. Only in the democratic republic is *salus populi* genuinely the supreme law, the highest injunction. Given that each person seeks his own welfare, and commits his energy and effort to that, it follows necessarily that the voices of all gathered together, and decisions made by majority vote, reflecting the majority's will, embrace "het beste van 't gemeen [the welfare of the whole]."[85] With officeholders and magistrates chosen yearly, by majority vote, these officeholders, despite privately favouring their own personal interest like everyone else, find themselves constrained, by the form of the state and its laws, to serve their fellow citizens "with all care and courtesy." Consequently, the "democratic or popular form of government" will not impose unnecessary wars and taxation on the people as monarchies and aristocratic republics regularly do (and England's mixed constitution did more than most).[86]

The democratic state, held Johan de La Court, is, among the different forms of government "absolutelijk de beste [absolutely the best]."[87] But all forms of state have their particular weaknesses and imperfections, and here the democratic republic is no exception. The entire structure of democratic theory the brothers created revolves around the notion that in a properly ordered society the "laws must be so drawn up that all the citizens, by reason of their own advantage and to avoid disadvantage, respect the general well-being."[88] Yet their own Hobbesian social psychology taught that individual drives and passions as a rule prove stronger than an individual's rational judgement.[89] They themselves laid such stress on how monarchs and aristocrats deceive and betray the common people, aided by preachers, that (like Van den Enden and Spinoza subsequently) they became caught in a seeming contradiction not easy to resolve. Among the very

---

[85] V.H. [De La Court], *Consideratien en Exempelen*, 253.
[86] V.H. [De La Court], *Consideratien en Exempelen*, 254–5, 282.
[87] V.H. [De La Court], *Consideratien en Exempelen*, 282.
[88] De La Court, *Politike Discoursen* i, 95.   [89] De La Court, *Politike Discoursen* i, 105.

first political theorists in the modern Western world to proclaim the democratic republic indisputably the best form of government for everyone (except thwarted elites), at the same time the De La Courts stressed that the common people, misled by prejudice, "appearances" and their passions, are also the principal threat to that very same well-being. For the De La Courts, as for Spinoza afterwards, the political world is a dangerous arena where the "common good" faces three great challenges that it must somehow navigate and overcome—monarchy, aristocracy, and what they call "het dumme graauw" [the stupid mob].

How exactly, given Spinoza's key principle that "reason" is the soul and foundation of the democratic republic, is locating sovereignty in the people to be reconciled with the people's ignorance and superstition? The De La Courts supposed that improving and expanding education would help: as men are naturally curious and eager to learn the truth, the causes of superstition's sway and the prevailing general ignorance about reality and how things occur, including most men's inability to understand the essential mechanics of politics and religion, can be revealed and shown to all. Since defeating the three great menaces, monarchy, aristocracy, and popular ignorance, is essential for rescuing the common will of those who remain ignorant and deceived, the aims, claims, and activities of the clergy, like the machinations of royal propaganda, must be vigorously combated and discredited.[90] The overriding characteristic of all the Dutch radical circle's collective endeavour was tying comprehensive elimination of religious authority in education, moral philosophy, social theory, and politics to this thoroughly un-Hobbesian democratic tendency, based on the principle of individual equality and the quest for happiness and personal and collective advantage.[91]

De Jure was a decisive ideological blast at a crucial point in the Republic's fraught politics, presenting a theory of *ius circa sacra*, the institutional relationship of state to religious authority, revealing a high degree of overlap with Chapter XIX of the *TTP*.[92] Leibniz was among those who long wondered about the authorship of *De Jure Ecclesiasticorum*, at one point wrongly classifying it as the work of "Jacobus Koerbagh" [i.e. Adriaan Koerbagh] who, he notes, was condemned for writing "impious books" and died in prison. Many contemporaries, noted both Bayle and Leibniz towards the end of their lives, believed one only had to compare the two texts, *De Jure* and the *TTP*, to appreciate their common "style and principles" and to suppose that the *De Jure Ecclesiasticorum* (1665) was also from the pen of Spinoza.[93] "But I have reason to doubt this," added Leibniz: "the initial letters LAC lead me to believe that the author of the book was [Pieter]

---

[90] V.H. [De La Court], *Consideratien en Exempelen*, 259.
[91] Klever, *Mannen rond Spinoza*, 11, 31–3, 61–2, 245–6; Krop, *Spinoza, een paradoxale icoon*, 94–102; Van Bunge, *Spinoza Past and Present*, 60–4, 195–8.
[92] Moreau, *Spinoza. État*, 66–7; Lavaert, "Lieutenants," 155, 157, 160.
[93] Bayle, *Écrits sur Spinoza*, 23, 54–5; Lavaert, "Lieutenants," 151.

de La Court, or Van den Hof, famous for works on *The Interest of Holland*, *Political Equipoise*, and numerous others that he published (some under the signature V.D.H.) assailing the power of the Stadholder of Holland; for the memory of Prince William II's attempt on the city of Amsterdam was still quite fresh." Memory of William II was relevant, Leibniz explains, because most Reformed churchmen in the Netherlands took the side of William III, son and heir of William II, "suspecting M. De Witt and what was called the Loevestein faction of favouring the Arminians, the Cartesians, and other sects they feared still more, while endeavouring to rouse the populace against them, and not without success as the aftermath proved."[94]

Pieter de La Court lauded *De Jure* as an excellent book, but judging from what he says about it, it seems that he did not write it himself. Suspicion fell also on Meyer, the attribution proposed by Colerus, claiming information from those who knew that the book was indeed by "L.M.," though this suggestion too was rejected by the great mid-eighteenth-century German bibliographer Siegmund Baumgarten who, seeing no other plausible alternative, assigns it to Pieter de La Court, as does Lucas.[95] But for many, or most, Spinoza remained the chief suspect. This "abominable and godless defamatory text," as Colerus called it, "was attributed by many to Spinoza," and this long remained a stubbornly repeated attribution or misattribution, it being listed among Spinoza's works, for example, in Bayle's *Dictionnaire*, and such standard eighteenth-century histories of thought as Giambattista Capasso's *Historiae Philosophiae Synopsis* (Naples, 1728). But when asked whether he indeed penned that historically important, highly explosive piece, Spinoza always strenuously denied writing it, as Lucas, Leibniz, and Colerus—who reports having obtained assurance of this from several sources—all affirm. The text features Latin expressions not found in Spinoza's works and, according to Lucas, Spinoza assured his "best friends that he was not the author of this book."[96] Who the fictitious "Lucius Antistius Constans" was remains still today an unsolved puzzle. Still, it is difficult to believe that Spinoza was not in some way implicated in its genesis and production. If Spinoza was not involved in writing *De Jure*, whoever did write it was certainly thinking along closely parallel lines.

If some early eighteenth-century authorities discounted Bayle's attribution of *De Jure* to Spinoza owing to its divergent Latin style, its referring to God as "Deus optimus maximus," for example, an expression Spinoza never uses, the probable explanation of the mystery is that while one of his Latinist friends, presumably Meyer or Bouwmeester, actually penned *De Jure*, it was essentially a collaborative

---

[94] Leibniz, *Theodicy*, 350; Laerke, *Leibniz lecteur*, 369.
[95] Baumgarten, *Nachrichten* iii, 26–7; [Lucas], *La Vie*, 60; Freudenthal/Walther, *Lebensgeschichte* i, 132; Capasso, *Historiae Philosophiae Synopsis*, 396.
[96] [Lucas], *La Vie*, 60; Israel, *Enlightenment that Failed*, 53–6, 58–9, 64–5; Laerke, *Spinoza and the Freedom*, 221–3.

effort written with more than a little encouragement and input from Spinoza. *De Jure*'s content closely matches Spinoza's characteristic views on ecclesiastical rights, the non-existence of religious authority apart from that of the state, and the character of specifically democratic republicanism more broadly. Accordingly, it still today seems probable that this highly divisive classic Radical Enlightenment (i.e. combining rejection of religious authority with democratic republicanism) text *was* a product of Spinoza's circle and an example of its collective activism proving rather effective.

In early eighteenth-century England, William Carroll and his mentor, George Hickes (1642–1715), a former High Anglican Dean of Worcester compelled to resign, in 1690, for refusing to recognize William III's enthronement,[97] while also mistakenly assuming *De Jure* was directly Spinoza's work, rightly identified *De Jure*'s political theory and rejection of all religious authority as both quintessentially Spinozist and as the basis of Matthew Tindal's much resented text, *The Rights of the Christian Church Asserted* (1706), which provoked a great storm in England by reaffirming the Spinozist thesis that all pretended ecclesiastical and church authority and rights are pure fiction without any legitimation in Scripture.[98] Baumgarten concurred with Bayle, Carroll, and Hickes' conclusion that comparing parallel passages proves *De Jure* is indeed the primary source from which Tindal derives his central arguments. In a sermon preached in London, in October 1708, Robert Moss, Dean of Ely, designated the anonymous author of *The Rights* which provoked one of the greatest public controversies of early eighteenth-century England, "a more disingenuous caviller perhaps, and more scurrilous scoffer, than ever was Julian the Apostate."[99]

Combining rejection of religious authority with democratic republicanism was a revolutionary new coupling in human history, a combination of principles chiefly inspired by the peculiarities of the political crisis gripping the Dutch Republic at the time but powerfully drawing on Machiavelli, Descartes, and Hobbes, authors thoroughly familiar to all five of the likeliest candidates as chief author—Meyer, De La Court, Spinoza, Koerbagh, and Bouwmeester. It was thus a crucial step in the inception of the Radical Enlightenment conceived as a crucial stream of the Enlightenment as a whole. The timing of *De Jure*'s publication also plainly links it to the furore over appointments to the Reformed pulpit in which Spinoza was involved in 1664–5, a time when Spinoza and Meyer were collaborating particularly closely. It is fair for the modern historian to conclude, therefore, that if "L.M." was indeed the book's principal author, as Colerus argues, it was very likely discussed and revised as a group venture or project, and hence best

---

[97] Champion, *Pillars of Priestcraft*, 179–80; Brown, "Theological Politics," 195; Brown, "Locke as Secret 'Spinozist'," 217.

[98] Brown, "Locke as Secret 'Spinozist'," 232n79; Krop, "Secularism of Spinoza," 96–7; Israel, "Intellectual Origins," 14; Bordoli, "Monopoly," 126; Lavaert, "Lieutenants," 151.

[99] Moss, *A Sermon Preach'd at the Parish Church of St Laurence-Jewry, London*, 8.

regarded as produced by the whole circle of allies and friends, including Bouwmeester, Spinoza, and Koerbagh.[100]

Neither *De Jure* nor the clashes of 1664–5 were soon forgotten. De Lantman would shortly become notorious throughout Holland for overstepping the mark with his furious preaching against the "Perpetual Edict," De Witt's attempted permanent suppression of the stadholderate, of 5 August 1667, marking the culmination of the States party's efforts to permanently emancipate Holland from the stadholderate and consolidate the "True Freedom." The Perpetual Edict sought to separate the captaincy-general of the armed forces in the Seven Provinces—a command that remained essential—from the stadholderate, defined by its political powers and legislative functions so as to entirely abolish the latter in the province of Holland. De Witt's position at that time was still strong enough to push the measure through the provincial States. Deliberating on 2 August of that year, the Orangist Leiden city government noted that while several others of Holland's eighteen voting towns, including Enkhuizen, Alkmaar, Edam, and Schoonhoven, were also opposed in principle, Leiden alone stood resolute in doing everything possible to support Orangist dynastic principle against De Witt's views.[101]

So vitriolic was De Lantman, prime foe of Spinoza in Voorburg and The Hague, in denouncing the *Perpetual Edict* from the pulpit that he was specially reprimanded for his conduct by the States of Holland. Worse was to follow, perfectly vindicating Spinoza's case. During the rioting in the Holland towns accompanying De Witt's downfall and the Orangist take-over of power during the summer of 1672, the list of Calvinist preachers who stood out as most notoriously and scandalously inciting popular unrest and spurring mobs to riot against the republican regime, stirring the people into a rage and making the coup possible, contemporary witnesses testified, were Goethals at Delft, Jacobus Borstius (1612–78), a master at swaying the ill-informed in Rotterdam, and, at The Hague, Simon Simonides (1629–75), preacher at the Klooster Church in the town centre and, irrepressible in this regard, the fiery Thaddeus De Lantman.[102]

---

[100] Leeuwenburgh, *Het Noodloot*, 120; Lavaert, *Vrijheid, gelijkheid, veelheid*, 74.
[101] GA Leiden Sec. Arch. 453, res. Vroedschap, 2 Aug. 1667.
[102] Roorda, *Partij en factie*, 107n4; Stern, *Orangism*, 137–8.

17

Spinoza and the Second Anglo-Dutch War (1664–1667)

17.i Rivalry with England

By the mid-1660s Spinoza had already forged for himself and his circle of confidants and allies in Holland a fully fledged philosophical approach and outlook obnoxious to many and perplexing to Dutch Cartesians and to Oldenburg. But if Spinoza found himself particularly opposed by several locally well-known preachers, headed by De Lantman, few yet were in a position to fully grasp how his approach and group were spreading the seeds of an entire ideology of clandestine subversion of prevailing structures of authority, in religion and theology, but also science, philosophy, and, via *De Jure Ecclesiasticorum* and Spinoza's mid-1660s shift of focus, accepted political theory—a vast but still partly masked project.

By now, Spinoza had a considerable body of text in store, including most of his *Ethics*, but still had not published anything beyond his cautious subversion of Descartes' core principles. What especially clouded the horizon in 1664 was the onset, for the second time in twelve years, of war with England. During the Second Anglo-Dutch War (1664–7), beginning unofficially in 1664, and officially on 4 March 1665, communication between Holland and England, along with Dutch overseas trade links generally, again became tenuous. Through this troubled period, Spinoza confronted the menace of war together with the onset of plague, while remaining, as before, highly conscious of the risks for himself and his group arising from his activity, locally and more broadly, in challenging religious authority, ordinary thinking, and "superstition." Spinoza's connection with Oldenburg, and, through him, indirectly with the Royal Society, having briefly resumed after lapsing for a second time, was disrupted again, this time by an interval of over two years.

At the peak of his creativity as a philosopher but avoiding any move towards open confrontation with the forces of the status quo, guided by his maxim "caute," Spinoza felt intensely engaged with everything transpiring around him but also daunted, he confided to Oldenburg, by the formidable barriers and difficulties obstructing his philosophical project. These were now further complicated by the wartime obstacles severely affecting the whole of society around him. War clouds already gathered over the winter of 1663–4, as Britain and the Dutch Republic drifted inexorably into the long and bitter prelude preceding formal commencement of the Second Anglo-Dutch War. Escalating trade rivalry fomented a tense situation in which the British crown was increasingly attracted to employing aggressive force to tilt the global maritime, commercial, and colonial balance finally in England's favour and secure unchallenged supremacy over the "British Ocean," as some called the North Sea, ousting the Dutch from their increasingly beleaguered trade primacy. Especially bitter was the maritime powers' colonial rivalry, not least a quarrel concerning the Malabar coast of southern India, with the English East India Company indignant that the Dutch "doe absolutely claime to themselves the whole pepper trade att Cocheene and parts adjacent."[1]

Some had been agitating for a more aggressive approach to the Dutch for some time. Reporting to London in September 1663, Sir George Downing bitterly denounced

> this trick of the Hollanders to declare warre with the natives in the East Indies and upon the Coast of Africa, with whom his Majestie's subjects have any trade, and then thereupon to forbid them all trade with them, and to continue the warre till they have brought those natives to an agreement with them, to sell them all their commodities, and then to keep the English from trading, upon the accompt that the natives have agreed with them, to sell all to them; - this trick, I say, hath not only bin the ruine of numbers of his Majesty's subjects, but beaten them out of many mighty trades, and will certainly in conclusion utterly overthrow the English East Indian, and African Companies, if nothing be applied for remedie but words.[2]

Furious anger and resentment welled up. "Wee cannot but highly resent these unfriendly proceedings," declared Charles II (Figure 17.1), in October 1663, vowing he and his inner circle of royal advisers and ministers fully intended to "procure satisfaction."[3] Nor was it just colonial trade but rather the entire commercial scenario that aroused anger in London. The poet Dryden caught the prevailing mood with his verse admonition that "Trade, like Blood should circularly flow" but unjustly and unaccountably "Stopp'd in their [i.e. Dutch] Channels, found its Freedom lost: Thither the wealth of the World did go, And seem'd but shipwreck'd on so base a Coast."[4] But those chiefly responsible for instigating the escalating maritime struggle in London were a court faction of five, called "the cabal," Charles' most intimate advisers, the leading figure in foreign affairs being

---

[1] Downing to Clarendon, The Hague, 29 July 1664 and Downing to Clarendon, The Hague, 9 Aug. 1664, in Lister, *Letters and Papers*, 336; Israel, *Dutch Primacy*, 248–51.
[2] Downing to Clarendon, The Hague, 18 Sept. 1663, in Lister, *Letters and Papers*, 249.
[3] Charles II to Downing, 30 Oct. 1663 in Lister, *Letters and Papers*, 257–8.
[4] Van der Welle, *Dryden and Holland*, 29–31.

Figure 17.1 *King Charles II* (1630–85), oil on canvas, c.1660–5. By courtesy of National Portrait Gallery, London.

Charles' secretary of state, Henry Bennett, First Earl of Arlington (1618–85), a veteran cavalier, royalist, and proponent of expansionist policies. Among the king's most trusted servants cultivating influence close to the throne, and most involved in supplying his numerous mistresses, Arlington was fiercely monarchical, anti-republican and, though not as fiercely anti-Dutch as Downing for that reason (despite his beautiful Dutch wife), did indeed deem the Republic a "base" coast ready for a good thrashing. Eager for colonial expansion and a resolute foe of religious toleration much inclined to oppress Nonconformists at home, king, Church, and aristocracy were Arlington's and his friends' unwavering priorities.

The initial focus was West Africa where, in January and February 1664, a force of eleven vessels under Sir Robert Holmes (1622–92) seized two Dutch forts at Goeree and then moved down to the Gold Coast (today Ghana) where Holmes occupied several more Dutch enclaves in April.[5] By the 1660s, diplomats, merchants, and financiers following movements of Dutch East and West India Company shares on the Amsterdam Exchange as a measuring rod of the

---
[5] Klooster, *The Dutch Moment*, 101–2.

Republic's prospects and of merchant sentiment, watched jubilantly or nervously, depending on allegiance, as the VOC share price slipped from a high of 498 per cent of founding value, in early 1664, to 481 in late March 1664, 443 by August, and 407 by 20 January 1665.[6] With war declared, VOC shares dived more precipitately, though less steeply than WIC shares, through the spring, to 336 in April, 322 by June, and 318 by July1665, reflecting a full-scale Dutch recession and the onset of numerous bankruptcies.[7]

The Dutch had no desire whatever for all-out war; but neither could they simply knuckle under: "as long as ever," complained Downing from The Hague, at the end of April, "De Witt sees a possibility of sailing between Scylla and Charybdis – a breach on the one hand, and giving satisfaction on the other – he will eternally shuffle and cut capers with me."[8] But the "alarms increase so every day from England," that attempting to "saile between Scylla and Charybdis" also intensified Dutch internal strife, spreading dismay "which also still keeps down the East Indie actions [shares]."[9] Very different was the mood across the Channel, where the satisfaction widely felt for every additional blow England dealt the Dutch only fuelled the thirst for settling accounts, with the nobility sharing the court's contempt for the supposedly "base" bourgeois types running the Republic and the Republic's general ethos. The Dutch were resented in England, scorned for their "impertinence," mercantile culture and lack of a true aristocratic elite and courtly style, lack of deference for superiors, refusal to exalt royalty, and lack of martial spirit or, what Dryden called their "crouching at home" while "cruel when abroad" in Africa, the Caribbean, and the Indies.

To not a few Amsterdam Sephardic traders encountering difficulties at home, it began to seem attractive to transfer to the Caribbean. Encroaching wartime slump was the probable reason for the firm of "Bento y Gabriel de Espinoza" finally winding up and disappearing at this point from the Amsterdam notarial records. Spinoza's brother, Gabriel, emigrated to the West Indies, during 1664, the first of Spinoza's close relatives to do so.[10] One wonders whether Spinoza saw his brother one last time in Voorburg or Amsterdam before his departure. Dutch Sephardic migration was certainly yet another cause for English indignation, England's Caribbean merchants, in May 1665, complaining that Lord Willoughby, Charles II's governor of Barbados during 1650–2, had unfortunately "countenanced the Jews [in the English colonies] who have become very numerous and engrossed the greatest part of the trade of the island, to the great discouragement of English merchants, their dealings being principally with those of their own tribe in

---

[6] *Hollandsche Mercurius* 1663, 93; Lister, *Letters and Papers*, 300; Israel, *Dutch Primacy*, 255.
[7] Lister, *Letters and Papers*, 382, 387; Petram, *World's First Stock Exchange*, 200–1.
[8] Downing to Clarendon, 18 April 1664, in Lister, *Letters and Papers*, 306.
[9] Downing to Clarendon, 22 April 1664, in Lister, *Letters and Papers*, 307.
[10] Vaz Dias and Van der Tak, "Spinoza Merchant," 185–7; Nadler, *Spinoza: A Life*, 101.

Holland."[11] At first, Jews were especially drawn to Barbados, the prime sugar producer among the Caribbean islands, a location from where they developed regular contact with London, New Amsterdam (New York), and Newport, Rhode Island, but especially Amsterdam. Such migration benefited the Sephardic diaspora easing their economic predicament in Holland. But their expanding presence in the Caribbean provoked only complaints to London. In March 1664, Charles II further enlarged the scope of the Navigation Acts, decreeing that "ships outward bound for his Majesty's Plantations must alsoe go from England," a measure, reported Downing, which "doth very much trouble them here; for that it breakes all the Jewes correspondency att Barbadoes and elsewhere, and hinders them the sale of vast quantities of the manufactures of the country [i.e. from Holland to the Caribbean]." But it took time for measures suppressing this "correspondency" to bite and only gradually was Barbados rendered less alluring to Sephardim seeking respite from the slump in Holland.[12] Around seven years later, in 1671, Gabriel d'Espinoza moved on, possibly via London, to Jamaica.[13] But in Jamaica too suspicion was rife that Caribbean Sephardic Jews sympathized more with Holland than with England. Until the end of the Second Anglo-Dutch War, there was persistent talk of the Jews' treacherously preferring the Dutch, and accusations they were disclosing movements of English ships and men to the enemy.

If Charles II welcomed every "design for rooting the Dutch out of the West Indies," so did many others. By the end of August 1664, there was excited talk everywhere in Jamaica and generally in the taverns around the English Caribbean heightening the alluring prospect of England seizing "New Amsterdam" and the rest of New Netherlands (New York, New Jersey, and Delaware), a prospect widely discussed since May 1664. In an interview with De Witt in mid-May, Downing reported from The Hague, "he told me they had a great allarme about a new business, viz., that the English should be now about sending to take New Netherland. I replyed that I knew of no such country but only in the mapps; that, indeed, if their people were to be believed, all the world were New Netherland, but that when that business shall be looked into, it will be found that the English had the pattern of first possession of those partes."[14]

New Netherland was duly attacked and seized in early September 1664, with scant resistance at New Amsterdam, but a stiff fight in Delaware. With a courtly flourish "New Amsterdam" was renamed "New York," after the king's brother, the

---

[11] Sainsbury, *Calendar of State Papers: America and West Indies* (1661–8), 296; Kayserling, "Jews in Jamaica," 710–11; Schreuder, *Amsterdam's Sephardic Merchants*, 192.

[12] Sainsbury, *Calendar of State Papers: America and West Indies* (1661–8), 528–30; Zahedieh, "Second Anglo-Dutch War in the Caribbean," 190–1.

[13] Kayserling, "Jews in Jamaica," 710.

[14] Downing to Clarendon, The Hague, 6 May 1664 in Lister, *Letters and Papers*, 320; Harlow, *History of Barbados*.

Duke of York.[15] British monarchy was splendidly prevailing over "base" republican notions and England's forceful acquisition of territories powerfully vindicated amidst what by now was a transatlantic war fever. In February 1665, the governor of Jamaica reported to London that all the pirates and rovers of Jamaica were eagerly "plotting how to take [the Dutch island of] Curaçao, and are applying for [royal] commissions."[16] A naval force, out from Jamaica, consisting mainly of buccaneer volunteers led the Caribbean sweep, capturing St Eustatius and Saba from the Dutch, in July 1665, and soon also Tobago (New Walcheren) and western Guyana.[17] Triumphant bludgeoning under his British majesty's royal banner and direction was indeed transforming the world map and global trade.

With the Dutch ejected from New Netherland and much of the West Indies, the focus soon shifted back to West Africa and rivalry for slaves and gold. "We have received very considerable news from Guiny," Oldenburg excitedly advised Boyle, on 29 September 1664; "it is that Major Holmes [Sir Robert Holmes (c.1622–92)] and some other ships sent thither to reinforce him, have not only taken four well-laden Dutch ships in those parts, but also Cape Corso [today in Ghana]," and were set to attack the "only remaining considerable place of the Dutch there, which is Castell della Mina [Elmina]; unto which enterprise they are said to have the readiness of 30,000 natives, who are affirmed to hate the griping genius and severe government of the Dutch." "This I look upon as the foundation, of an implacable warre: and what can be the next, but that the Dutch will make it their whole business in the East Indies to expel the English thence? For which purpose, tis strongly surmised, that they have already dispacht orders over land thither, to put such a work in execution, seeing they find England disposed (so they say) to ruine them everywhere."[18]

In fact, De Ruyter and his fleet of thirteen warships were ordered out from Cadiz not to the East Indies but West Africa, news of which caused Dutch West India Company shares to rebound wildly, after plunging disastrously for months on the Amsterdam Exchange, but "which may be worth little if our nation prevayll on that coast," remarked one of Downing's informants hopefully.[19] To add to the deepening crisis severely afflicting Dutch morale and their economy by mid-1664 was the new plague outbreak commencing in Holland in late 1663 and culminating in 1664, this being the penultimate plague epidemic in the province (the last occurring in 1666). By the summer of 1664 this same triple crisis of war, plague, and slump was also seriously ravaging Holland's universities and thriving art scene. Before long, though, the conflict began affecting England's shipping,

---

[15] Klooster, *The Dutch Moment*, 98–9.
[16] Sainsbury, *Calendar of State Papers: America and West Indies* (1661–8), 280.
[17] Israel, *Dutch Primacy*, 274; Klooster, *The Dutch Moment*, 104–5; see also Zahedieh, "Second Anglo-Dutch War in the Caribbean," 198–9 who, however, provides the wrong dates for the operation.
[18] Oldenburg, *Correspondence* ii, 239–41. Oldenburg to Boyle, London, 29 Sept. 1664.
[19] BL Add 22926, fo. 48, unsigned informer to Downing, 13 Sept. 1664.

economy, and morale too, exerting a paralyzing effect on Oldenburg, the Royal Society, and intellectual and scientific endeavour also in London.

A time of political, financial, and scholarly turmoil for the Dutch and English, the years 1664–7 were also a moment of feverish speculation among the many Millenarians of the age, like Boreel and Serrarius, and especially among the Jewish people. In Western and Near Eastern Sephardic life, these years were a phase of vast additional upheaval both spiritual and messianic. The paralysis of seaborne trade throughout Northern Europe and the Mediterranean caused by the Anglo-Dutch conflict not only confined shipping to port on all Europe's coasts, and generated a general slump in international commerce, but lent added impetus first in the Near East and soon everywhere to the extraordinary upsurge of messianic excitement surrounding the figure of Sabbatai Zevi (1626–76), the rabbi of Smyrna considered by many the long-awaited "messiah." In fact, by 1665, Sabbatai stood at the centre of the greatest upsurge of messianic fervour in early modern Jewish history—an impassioned longing for release from oppressive, confining ghettoization, or, in Spinoza's terms, a clutching at delusory hopes driven by anxiety and fear.

Scientists, scholars, and philosophers comprising the Anglo-Dutch segment of the international "republic of letters," where genuinely sharing their lofty ideals across borders, sank into deep dismay. In the fraught circumstances of 1664–5, the scientific fraternity bitterly lamented the ruinously disruptive consequences of war and surging of bellicose national sentiment, urging the preferability of peace and stability for human well-being, society, and all the arts and sciences and a resolving of international disputes with a calm, compassionate approach. Yet, beneath the high-sounding veneer surged, not least in the Oldenburg–Boyle correspondence of these years, a bellicose pride in the naval and military feats of one's own side and deep animus against one's country's foes. Much the same could be said of the other side too, including the loftily philosophical Spinoza. If his view of the great drama proved cooler and less emotional, lacking the fervent expectation of vast changes engineered by divine providence infusing the zeal of many, he too felt emotionally deeply involved.

As hostilities commenced, Oldenburg and Spinoza solemnly vowed friendship for each other and revulsion for hatred, conquest, and war as the unending foes of all science and philosophy. Yet, each remained fiercely loyal to his own side and values, albeit with a difference between their parallel feelings of intense commitment, of which Oldenburg, like the English diplomat most familiar with the Dutch scene and The Hague, Sir William Temple, was profoundly aware. Deep loyalty to the Republic, basic to any biographical study of Spinoza was, after all, loyalty to a broad toleration and republicanism, a set of new social, political, and religious principles, while England at this time remained an aspiring absolutist monarchy bent on curbing religious toleration and bolstering and exalting the grip of court, aristocracy, and state church over society and culture generally while furthering colonial expansion by brute, undisguised force of arms. Under the political and cultural dominance of a proud, disdainful courtly clique and royal mystique, Oldenburg, Boyle, Dryden, Pepys, and many another evinced a fawning subservience hard for today's modern reader to sympathize with. The royal court in London aimed to crush and humiliate the Republic, at that time religiously the most tolerant European land, boasting freedoms uniquely permitting broad scope for inquiry, philosophizing, and criticizing religion, laws, and government, as Oldenburg, Boyle, and Temple knew perfectly well. Stifling the Republic as a beacon of political and religious freedom and independence, and turning it into a mechanism of their power, was as basic to Charles II's and Arlington's goals as extinguishing Dutch commercial and colonial primacy.

17.ii Plague and the Outbreak of War

There was one affliction besetting the Dutch during 1664, though, that Oldenburg, Boyle, and their friends did not exult to see advancing—the plague. Commencing in May 1663, by early autumn the outbreak at Amsterdam, noted Pieter de La Court, was growing steadily worse.[20] By November 1663, word of the outbreak had reached Hobbes in the library at Hardwick Hall, seat (or a seat) of the Earl of Devonshire, in Derbyshire.[21] By early 1664, the position was worse. "There dyed this last weeke," noted Downing in March 1664, "of all diseases at Amsterdam 223 which is 17 more than the week before. It is hoped that this weeke there will not be so many"; but in ensuing weeks the figures inexorably rose.[22] In Amsterdam, reported Downing to London, in early May 1664, "there are dead this weeke to the number of 338; and if the plague thus increase within, and a warre with his Majesty without, there will be little need," he added, "of that vast new towne they are making there."[23] In late May, Downing advised Lord Clarendon, "there dyed last weeke at Amsterdam 362, so that your Lordship may see the plague increaseth there every week much."[24] Simon Joosten's brother Frans and the latter's wife were among those who died in Amsterdam and were buried in the first week of June. In all, during 1663–4 some 30,000 of the city's 200,000 population perished, the great majority from the plague, burials in Amsterdam totalling 24,148 in 1664 as against an already high annual total of 9,752 in 1663.[25]

---

[20] De La Court, "Brieven," 124–5, and 129. La Court to J. Van der Voort, Leiden, 5 Sept. 1663 and to Van der Voort, Leiden, 24 Sept. 1663.
[21] Hobbes, *Correspondence* ii, 576–7.   [22] Lister, *Letters and Papers*, 300, 304, 305, 308.
[23] Downing to Clarendon, The Hague, 6 May 1664 in Lister, *Letters and Papers*, 319.
[24] Downing to Clarendon, undated (late May) in Lister, *Letters and Papers*, 323.
[25] Nusteling, *Welvaart and werkgelegenheid*, 243; Prak and Hesselink, "Stad en gevestigden," 107–8, 112; Mertens, "Where Thou Dwellest," 48.

Largely confined to Amsterdam initially, the plague's serious impact in the Leiden area and The Hague began in the summer of 1664, becoming a lively topic, records Pepys, in the London coffee-houses. "There dyed this last week at Amsterdam 739," reported Downing in early August, and now "the plague is scattered generally over the whole country, even to little dorps and villages; and it is got to Antwerp and Brussels, so that they will not suffer any ships or vessels of Holland or Zeeland to come to Antwerp."[26] Another of the epidemic's victims that summer was a son of Pieter Balling, about whose loss Spinoza wrote the sole surviving letter (translated into Latin) between him and this versatile Amsterdam Mennonite Collegiant who had translated much of his work and, by the summer of 1664, had already finished rendering the *Ethics*' first two parts into Dutch.[27] Balling evidently visited Spinoza several times in both Rijnsburg and Voorburg, carrying letters to and from Amsterdam and discussing his renderings of Spinoza's texts. Spinoza may well have known him since the days he himself was involved in commerce, in the mid-1650s, meeting him perhaps on the Amsterdam Exchange. A highly accomplished translator, according to the younger Rieuwertsz and "very experienced in the Greek and Latin languages," Spinoza clearly respected Balling's judgement and good sense, addressing him in this letter, dated 20 July 1664, as "learned and most sagacious."

It is not known in what language Spinoza wrote to Balling, but it seems likely, as Hubbeling and Akkerman suggest, that he wrote in Spanish with which Balling was very familiar. Spinoza's July letter was dated nearly a month after Balling had informed him of his loss and grief. The news filled him, responded Spinoza, "with great sadness and solicitude for you," albeit his sadness was "much diminished when I reflect on the wisdom and fortitude that enable you to scorn the blows of destiny, or what are considered such, at the very time when they are assailing you with their strongest weapons. Nevertheless, my concern for you grows every day and hence I beg and entreat you by our friendship to take the trouble to write to me at length."[28] Given the plague raging in Amsterdam, Spinoza's disinclination to come in person would have been understood. Regarding Balling's belief that he had received a prior omen of his son's demise, Spinoza expressed forceful scepticism. When his son was still well, Balling believed he had had a supernatural premonition, hearing warning groans like those his son "uttered when he was ill." Such groans, urged Spinoza, he heard only in his imagination. "None of the effects of the imagination due to corporeal causes can ever be omens of things to come, because their causes do not involve any future things." Yet, the imagination is highly worthy of regard since "we find, it follows in the wake of the intellect in all

---

[26] Downing to Clarendon, The Hague, 9 Aug. 1664 in Lister, *Letters and Papers*, 333; *Calendar of State Papers... Venice*, vol. 34, p. 35.
[27] Meinsma, *Spinoza et son cercle*, 153; Akkerman says "June 1665," Akkerman, "Taal en tekst," 7.
[28] Spinoza to Balling, Voorburg, 20 July 1664 in Spinoza, *Opera* iv, 76; Spinoza, *Correspondance* (ed. Rovere), 123; Spinoza, *Briefwisseling*, 149.

things, linking together and interconnecting its images and words just as the intellect does its demonstrations, so that there is almost nothing we can understand without the imagination instantly forming an image." This explains, he affirms, the linkages of art and literature with truth and our deeper feelings and intimations.[29]

Imagination, for Spinoza, is a purely natural phenomenon, ruling out all premonitions, revelations, and supernatural interventions, but with a complex, vital relationship with our intellect and understanding. In a certain naturalistic sense, therefore, the "effects of the imagination or images which have their origin in the constitution of the mind can be omens of some future event"; this being so "because the mind *can* have a confused perception beforehand of something that is to come." Whatever Balling thought of that, by early September, the epidemic was gaining fresh momentum: "there are this week dead at Leyden," reported Downing to Clarendon, "250 odd, and at Amsterdam 1041."[30] Friends, colleagues, and would-be visitors now all kept their distance, as did the Dordrecht regent, Van Blijenbergh, who, in his first letter to Spinoza, mentions that it was "the epidemic" that had led him to initiate their debate about Descartes' philosophy by letter rather than coming to visit him in Voorburg.[31] Week by week the despair and gloom deepened. Having lost his son, Balling himself died from the plague on 20 December 1664, soon after publication of his Dutch version of Spinoza's book on Descartes' *Principles*. When Spinoza completed the third part of the *Ethics*, in the spring or summer of 1665, spurred no doubt by the plague, he at once began searching for a replacement for Balling to prepare an authorized version in the vernacular and help ensure the work's survival.[32]

Anglo-Dutch relations, meanwhile, descended from bad to worse. To Downing, De Witt complained that Charles II had seized New Netherland and Cape Corso "by force, without so much as saying a word to us." "His Majesty," replied Downing, "did not looke upon himself as obliged to give them any account of what he did in relation thereunto, for that he did not looke upon them as at all interested therein, no more than he should thinke himself obliged to let them know his mind, or to have their consent, in case he should thinke fit to proceede against any Dutch that live in the Fenns in England, or in any other part of his dominions, of which he always understood that land they call New Netherland to be a part."[33]

Westminster's haughtiness remained unrelenting, but there was now unmistakably a note of unease too due to Dutch success in winning moral support from

---

[29] Spinoza to Balling, Voorburg, 20 July 1664, Spinoza, *Collected Works* (ed. Curley) i, 352–3; Gatens and Lloyd, *Collective Imaginings*, 19–22; James, *Spinoza on Learning*, 61, 72.
[30] Lister, *Letters and Papers*, 339.   [31] Spinoza, *Collected Works* (ed. Curley) i, 355.
[32] Akkerman, *Studies*, 99, 106–7, 146; Fix, *Prophecy and Reason*, 200; Mertens, "Where Thou Dwellest," 45.
[33] Downing to Clarendon, The Hague, 4 Nov. 1664 in Lister, *Letters and Papers*, 350.

France, Denmark, and other quarters. By late November, Downing was distinctly worried by Dutch efforts to secure Louis XIV's backing and other diplomatic efforts abroad. "The Dutch use much of the Foxe in asserting their cause against the English," remarked Oldenburg who, like those around him, evinced a powerful bias against the rival nation despite his own Calvinist background. Indeed, the Royal Society's secretary seemed fully to share in the prevailing sense of England's innate right to assert her supremacy. Why were so many foreigners less sympathetic to England than to Holland? It seemed inexplicable. The Dutch "beare the world in hand," gaining sympathy, he complained to Boyle, in November 1664, by promising "they will submit all to the arbitration of any prince, or state; and they insinuate into the body of our merchants, that it is only to raise a particular Royall Company" that the royal court was making so much effort in Africa, the Caribbean, and elsewhere.[34]

The States General strove assiduously to avert all-out war. Yet these people "doubt not but to be able," complained Downing, "in case matters are not composed, to drive the English quite out of the East Indies; and they also make no question, but that all will be settled in Guiny, and those other parts, to their hearts desire, by De Ruyter."[35] Before long, news reached London that De Ruyter's fleet had indeed appeared off West Africa and swiftly recaptured the lost forts. For good measure, the Dutch seized the castle at Cormantine too, a main English base in the region. "Among the merchants" at the London commercial exchange, noted Pepys in his diary, on 22 December 1664, the "news of our being beaten to dirt at Guinny, by De Ruyter with his fleete," seemed to point to "the utter ruine of our Royall Company, and reproach and shame to the whole nation, as well as justification to them in their doing wrong to no man as to his private [property], only taking whatever is found to belong to the [Royall] Company, and nothing else."[36] Such restraint served only to inflame opinion still more against Dutch insolence. Charles' court readily took advantage of the feelings of outrage.

There is no knowing for sure if Spinoza penned the opening of *Ethics* Part IV around this time or later, but those lines perfectly express Spinoza's acute sense of how, when jealousy, envy, and resentment capture men's thinking, they cause great damage to themselves. "Human inability to moderate and restrain the passions I call servitude. For a man subject to the passions is not under his own rule but that of *fortuna* [fate], and so much under its power that he is often compelled, however much he sees the things that are best for himself, nevertheless to pursue the worse goals."[37] At court, in London, there were still confident hopes of securing a "firm league" between the crowns of England and Denmark-Norway,

---

[34] Oldenburg to Boyle, London, 5 Nov. 1664 in Oldenburg, *Correspondence* ii, 292.
[35] Downing to Clarendon, The Hague, 25 Nov. 1664 OS in Lister, *Letters and Papers*, 352.
[36] Pepys, *Diary*, 22 Dec. 1664.
[37] Spinoza, *Opera* ii, 205; Spinoza, *Collected Works* (ed. Curley) i, 543.

an arrangement vital for England retaining unobstructed access to the Baltic and the flow of masts and other essential naval stores from Scandinavia. During October and November 1664, Sir Gilbert Talbot, England's envoy at Copenhagen, assured the Danish court that the Dutch "designe to monopolize all trade to the exclusion of all other princes which was in effect to drive at the sole power by sea in as much as it is impossible for any prince long to maintain navigation without commerce and trade by sea."

Reportedly, the Danish king too resented "the exorbitant growth of the Hollanders at sea by possessing themselves of all trade," and gave every indication of supporting English plans to bring "the Hollanders upon their knees." The snag was that Denmark-Norway could only assist in thrashing the Dutch if a Dutch–Swedish alliance was prevented, which meant England must send a fleet to reinforce Denmark which had but few warships available. Since "all their Norway mariners are run into the Hollanders' service for want of employment at home," Denmark would also need English subsidies to pay Norwegian and Danish sailors recalled from Dutch service, money that would be well spent, urged Talbot, for should the Danish king "command them back, the States [General] would not be able to put their fleet to sea."[38]

"The plague is now decreasing, God be blessed, at Amsterdam," Oldenburg informed Boyle, in November 1664, "and the number of the dead is diminished from 1050 to 800 a weeke." But if the worst seemed over at Amsterdam, by late 1664 the plague was still spreading further south, north, and east, at Flushing, Enkhuizen, and Zutphen, as at Leiden and Delft, causing the first deaths from the epidemic in Voorburg in September, and persisting at a low level through 1665–6 whilst the war at sea was at its height. To reduce the risk to himself, Spinoza, like many others moving temporarily from the environs of big cities to the countryside, took refuge on a farm called the "De Langen Bogert," belonging to Alewijn Gijsen (c.1627–83), the Mennonite brother-in-law of his Collegiant friend, Simon Joosten de Vries (who had a one sixth share in the property), Gijsen being the husband of De Vries' sister, Trijntje. On this farm, located outside Schiedam, in a rural district or *ambacht* called Oud-Mathenesse, Spinoza stayed from late December 1664 until mid-February 1665, apparently two or three weeks longer than originally planned in early January.[39] While there, he probably met also others of the local Collegiant community prominent in the Rotterdam-Schiedam area, including perhaps the leading regent and herald of toleration, Adriaen Paets, and also Jacob Ostens who would play a role in Spinoza's life in the early 1670s

---

[38] PRO SP 75/17 (Denmark-Norway), fos. 190–191v. Talbot to Bennett, Copenhagen, 11 Oct. 1664.
[39] Spinoza, *Briefwisseling*, 163; Schuyt, *Spinoza*, 26; Van Boheemen and Bosscher, "Daniel Harmensz Tijdeman," 46; Mertens, "Where Thou Dwellest," 47, 49n171; Van de Ven, *Documenting Spinoza*, ch. 6.

while Spinoza undoubtedly strengthened his ties with Simon Joosten de Vries' family.[40]

The 1663-5 plague epidemic was only marginally less severe than the earlier plague epidemics of 1624-5 and 1635-6. All three major seventeenth-century Dutch plague contagions, the figures show, were remarkable in that despite the generally poor air and sanitary conditions in the largest cities, death rates in small towns and many villages were not significantly lower. As usual, the poor proved more vulnerable than the affluent. But there appears also to have been a tendency for large population centres exposed to frequent contacts with foreigners, like Amsterdam and Rotterdam, to again enjoy better immunity to the virus in proportion to population overall than small outlying rural communities.[41] Still, an isolated farm such as Spinoza chose no doubt offered greater protection than either big towns or secluded villages.

When Oldenburg wrote to Spinoza, in late April 1665, shortly after Charles II had formally declared war, in March, the conflict was in its opening stages.[42] But already then over two hundred Dutch prizes had been seized at sea and brought into English ports, and most Dutch footholds in the New World had been overrun. Most of Europe's diplomats and informed onlookers agreed with Downing that, given the royal battle fleet's size, the firepower superiority of England's "great ships," and her much larger population, England must surely repeat her earlier success and again defeat her rival as in 1652-4. It was probable, commented the Swedish resident in The Hague, that England would swiftly overpower the Republic and soon be "maitresse des mers [mistress of the seas]," reducing the Dutch to a firmly subordinate role.[43] Along with the plague's ravages, financial and psychological pressure steadily mounted. To man their outgoing fleet in April 1665, the Dutch East India Company had to offer seamen a staggeringly high 16 to 18 guilders per month to lure them to sign on.[44] Yet, few in Holland felt disposed to submit to the mounting pressure. The robustness of Dutch popular resolve to defend their Republic was noted by the French envoy in January 1665: "the people are very aroused and accord for this war whatever is asked of them [les peuples sont fort animez, et accordent pour cette guerre tout ce qu'on leur demande]."[45]

In their correspondence of these years, Oldenburg and Spinoza equally strove to maintain an impeccably lofty, high-sounding attitude towards the other, guarding against letting slip any sign of emotional commitment to their own side, or resentment at the perceived arrogance and pretensions of the other. But, hardly

---

[40] Van der Tang, "Spinoza en Schiedam," 176-8; Van Bunge, "Tragic Idealist," 268; Wielema, *Filosofen aan de Maas*, 39.
[41] Curtis, "Was Plague an Exclusively Urban Phenomenon?," 143, 145, 159-60.
[42] Rommelse, *Second Anglo-Dutch War*, 121.   [43] Israel, *Dutch Primacy*, 270.
[44] Downing to Clarendon, The Hague, 14 April 1665 in Lister, *Letters and Papers*, 375.
[45] D'Estrades, *Lettres* iii, 17.

surprisingly, neither fully succeeded. "Mr Boyle and I often talk about you," Oldenburg assured Spinoza, in his letter dated London, 28 April 1665, "your learning and your profound reflections." From a recent letter from their mutual friend, Serrarius, he was delighted to hear that Spinoza was alive, thriving, "and that you remember your Oldenburg." Expressing profound regret "that I have been deprived for so many months of that very pleasant correspondence that I used to have with you," he apologized for being overburdened with official business and personal difficulties but assured him "my great fondness for you and my firm friendship will always remain steadfast and unshakable over the years." He and Boyle eagerly desired "to see the fruits of your talent brought to birth and entrusted to the warm embrace of the learned, and are confident that you will not disappoint us in this." By this point Boyle's study of saltpetre, solidity and fluidity had appeared in Latin as well as English, "and there lacks only opportunity for sending you copies."[46] Boyle had recently produced also a treatise on colours, and another about temperature, and discussed a recent invention of the Florentine Accademia di Cimento with which he was then busily experimenting—thermometers. "Nothing but this inauspicious war [nullum nisi bellum hoc infaustum]," averred Oldenburg, "prevents my sending you these books" along with a copy of the *Micrographia* of Robert Hooke (1635–1703), a treatise of microscopic observations in which many things are discussed boldly and philosophically that he knew would keenly interest Spinoza too. Despite the misfortune of the present conflict, hopefully "our booksellers will find a way of sending copies of all these to your country."[47]

Oldenburg's April letter, answered Spinoza in late May 1665, had been delivered from London "doubtless by Mr Serrarius" to "an Amsterdam bookseller," presumably Rieuwertsz, who then gave it to "a friend of mine" who brought it himself to Voorburg. Encouraged at finding "you are as kindly disposed to me as ever," Spinoza for his part asked often "after you and your state of health from Mr. Serrarius and from Christian Huygens Z.D." (lord of Zuilechem, the Z.D. indicating the Gelderland village of which he was titular lord), "who also told me he knows you." Spinoza was conversing quite frequently at this point with Huygens and evidently saw Serrarius every now and again, a figure even more obsessed at this juncture with the messianic upheaval gripping the Jewish Near East than with the Anglo-Dutch conflict raging all around. From Huygens, Spinoza had heard that "the most erudite Mr Boyle" was well and thriving, and had now published his treatise on colours, a book Huygens could lend him in English had "I been skilled in the English language." Glad Boyle's text was now available in Latin, Spinoza had learnt nothing yet about the invention of the thermometer, though Huygens had mentioned the latest developments in

---

[46] Spinoza, *Opera* iv, 158.
[47] Spinoza, *Opera* iv, 158; Spinoza, *Collected Works* (ed. Curley) i, 393.

microscopes and the new lenses devised in Rome by Giuseppe Compani (1635–1715), enabling the great Giovanni Domenico Cassini (1625–1712), professor of astronomy at Bologna since 1650, to make his latest observations. Spinoza was keenly interested in these "certain telescopes devised in Italy with which they could observe eclipses of Jupiter caused by the intervening of its satellites and also the shadow on Saturn made by its ring" that Descartes had taken to be planets, news making him still more astonished at how rash and hasty Descartes had been with his mistaken conjectures about Saturn's ring, mistakes which Spinoza and Huygens had discussed.[48]

If England was widely expected to win the war, international sympathy obstinately tended to the Dutch side, Europeans blaming England for the general disruption causing English merchants resident in Iberian and Italian ports bitterly to "complaine" of foreigners' bias against them, and what Charles' envoy in Madrid called "the Spaniards' partiality towards the Dutch."[49] Dutch ships filled the bays of Cadiz and Málaga while the Dutch and Spanish were suspected of colluding together to plot the ousting of the English from Tangiers (which England occupied during the years 1661–84). The general attitude in Spain and Morocco was such as "makes our people in those parts cast out many a longing eye for a lusty squadron from home."[50] Before long, it was not just war and interruption of commerce that were discouraging merchants and disrupting science on the English side. With the New Year, the bubonic plague epidemic took hold in London too. It appeared to recede during the spring, but reappeared from late April with the coming of warmer weather, when, too late, realizing the plague was already gaining impetus, the London Corporation introduced drastic quarantine measures. "Great fears of sickness here," noted Pepys, on 30 April 1665, "it is being said that two or three houses are already shut up. God preserve us all."[51] By midsummer 1665, the "interrupting of the correspondence with Holland," disrupting interchange between England and the Continent, Oldenburg informed Boyle, was increasingly hampering the Royal Society's overseas contacts.[52]

During the summer months of 1665, the main Dutch fleet was inexplicably slow to emerge and go into action. "I hear many things concerning English affairs," remarked Spinoza writing to Bouwmeester, in Amsterdam, in early June, impatient to hear better war news, "but nothing certain. The people do not stop suspecting everything bad, and no one can think of any reason why the fleet does not set sail. And indeed the situation seems to remain precarious. I am fearful that our side want to be too wise and provident. But in due course the outcome

---

[48] Spinoza, *Opera* iv, 159; Spinoza, *Correspondance* (ed. Rovere), 188–9; Vermij, *Calvinist Copernicans*, 148–51.
[49] PRO SP 94/49, fo. 43. Fanshaw to Arlington, Madrid, 19/29 July 1665.
[50] PRO SP 94/49, fo. 22. Fanshaw to Arlington, Madrid, 5/15 July 1665; PRO SP 94/49, fo. 47. Wescombe to Fanshaw, Cadiz, 19 July 1665.
[51] Israel, *Dutch Republic*, 625.   [52] Oldenburg, *Correspondence* ii, 459.

will finally show what they really have in mind and what their design is – may the gods prosper it. What our friends there [in Amsterdam] think and what they know for certain," added Spinoza, referring to Bouwmeester's considerable circle which included the Brothers Koerbagh, "I very much desire to hear."[53] Something dramatic must occur soon. "All possible industry is used in getting ready their fleet," Downing reported to London a few days later: "De Witt scarce sleeps night or day."[54]

Dutch hopes of a prompt and successful naval offensive against the English were by no means fulfilled. Assuredly, it was an improved, unprecedentedly large battle fleet that was got ready. But De Witt, constantly prodding the admiralty colleges and intimately involved in the preparations, faced chronic difficulties of logistics, discipline, and manning. Where the English could resort to the royal press-gang, forcibly kidnapping men to serve the crown, a resource unjust but reliable and efficient, such practices were impermissible under the "base" republican laws that neighbouring monarchs and aristocracies found so contemptible, forcing the States General to rely on volunteers and hired foreign seamen, Scandinavian and German especially, the States of Holland authorizing the admiralty colleges to virtually double naval seamen's pay, at immense cost to the state and populace. Yet, still, the volunteers forthcoming were too few.[55] Since the First Anglo-Dutch war of 1652–4, the likelihood of heavy casualties and horrific wounds, with frequent amputations of limbs, had become too familiar to make even eighteen or twenty guilders monthly seem an entirely attractive offer.

Furthermore, the Dutch fleet suffered from the same ideological split and political quagmire as afflicted the Republic as a whole, with several admirals insisting the Prince of Orange must now be named formally commander of the navy.[56] When the Republic's battle fleet, 103 ships carrying 21,613 men and 4,869 guns, finally emerged and engaged the enemy, it was heavily defeated with the loss of seventeen warships off Lowestoft, on 13 June, by the English fleet commanded by the future James II. Though fought well out to sea, Lowestoft being 143 miles north-east of London, so loud was the thundering of the guns that everyone in London reportedly flocked to the riverside and parks to listen. The distant thundering was distinctly audible simultaneously at The Hague, situated at a like distance across the waves. Dutch morale collapsed in the midst of battle when Admiral Obdam's flagship, the *Eendracht* (84 guns; 500 men), received a broadside and its powder store blew up, killing the admiral and all but five of his men and causing the rest of the fleet to disperse in panic and disarray.[57]

---

[53] Spinoza, *Opera* iv, 163; Spinoza, *Briefwisseling*, 219–20.
[54] Downing to Clarendon, The Hague, 23 June 1665 in Lister, *Letters and Papers*, 388.
[55] Israel, *Dutch Primacy*, 275; Rommelse, *Second Anglo-Dutch War*, 128.
[56] Rowen, *John de Witt*, 590; Israel, *Dutch Republic*, 767.
[57] Jones, *Anglo-Dutch Wars*, 158–9; Bruijn, *Dutch Navy*, 86; Israel, *Dutch Primacy*, 274.

"The great ships are the ships that do the business," Pepys, secretary to the royal admiralty, noted with satisfaction shortly afterwards, "they quite deadening the enemy."[58]

Their defeat might easily have spelt the Dutch fleet's complete destruction had Oldenburg's superior, Lord Henry Brouncker (c.1627–88), president of the Royal Society and a frequent companion of Pepys, whose knowledge of ship design and mathematics brought him aboard as the duke's "gentleman of the bedchamber," not confused or countermanded key orders. Nevertheless, in London, there was immense joy at the news of this triumph. Pepys, his "heart full of joy," lit a celebratory "great bonfire" at his gate, and distributed coins among the local boys,[59] as well as exclaimed in his diary: "a greater victory never known in the world. They are all fled; some 43 got into the Texell and others elsewhere, and we in pursuit of the rest."[60] In Amsterdam, VOC shares on the stock exchange sank to 322, among the lowest points of the war, where the price languished until August, two months later, when the arrival of news of the safe homecoming of the returning VOC fleet from the East Indies lifted them back to 395.[61]

Bolstering the confidence of the London court war faction for many months, Lowestoft further strengthened the growing perception across Europe that England was indeed fundamentally reshaping the global balance of power and, with it, world trade, finance, maritime power, and colonial sway. The Dutch were practically on their knees, reported Downing to London jubilantly, on 23 June 1665, the latest letters from Amsterdam showing "that at this time, nothing [...is done there] in pointe of trade; nor any money to be had upon any termes."[62] But from July onward, the mood on both sides of the Channel noticeably shifted, partly due to the "Great Plague" now tightening its grip on London. As the pestilence raged, the royal court fled the city along with most of the aristocracy, officials, physicians, and wealthy merchants. In July, Thévenot and the Parisian science circle sent word expressing their horror at the news of the plague's depredations and concern for his friend Oldenburg's safety.[63] "But, Lord!," noted Pepys, in August, "how sad a sight it is to see the streets empty of people, and very few upon the [Ex]change! [...] and about us two shops in three, if not more, generally shut up."[64]

"Thus this month ends with great sadness upon the publick," he recorded a fortnight later, "through the greatness of the plague everywhere through the kingdom almost. Every day sadder and sadder news of its increase."[65] Retreating first to Salisbury for the summer, in September the court set up with reviving pomp and a bigger entourage in Oxford, attended by most of the Royal Society, leaving the Society's activities in London suspended and Oldenburg virtually alone

[58] Pepys, *Diary* i, 589.
[59] Tomalin, *Samuel Pepys*, 181; Coats and Lemmers, "Dutch and English Dockyards," 157, 162.
[60] Pepys, *Diary* i, 585.   [61] Israel, *Dutch Primacy*, 255; Israel, *Dutch Republic*, 769.
[62] Lister, *Letters and Papers*, 382; Petram, *World's First Stock Exchange*, 201.
[63] Hobbes, *Correspondence* ii, 854.   [64] Pepys, *Diary* i, 616.   [65] Pepys, *Diary* i, 622.

as their beleaguered sentinel in the capital. Along with London's high society physicians, most Anglican and other clergymen, as also the newly arrived Rabbi Jacob Sasportas, also hurriedly departed, leaving the capital's abandoned "company of parish clerks" compiling the report entitled *London's Dreadful Visitation*, forlornly beseeching their superiors that "neither the physicians of our souls or bodies may hereafter in such great numbers forsake us."[66]

The confidence and momentum gained at Lowestoft dissipated slowly during the summer, particularly after the English fleet failed to capture the richest prize at hand, the returning Dutch East India fleet after its long and gruelling voyage back to home waters. To evade interception on the last lap, the VOC fleet, as expected, circumvented the top of Scotland together with a returning Mediterranean convoy that had joined it off Spain. The combined fleet then sought safety in western Norway, under the Danish crown, in the fortified harbour at Bergen. Believing he had already defeated this plan by secret diplomacy, Charles II assumed the Danish monarch had issued orders, as promised, for his commanders to switch sides and help seize the rich returns from the Indies, causing colossal loss to the Dutch and helping replenish Charles' fast emptying coffers. However, at court in Copenhagen turmoil reigned, producing a sudden reversal of policy: instead of joining the attackers, Bergen's garrison kept to Denmark's longstanding Dutch alliance. To the amazement of the English commanders, the Danish "blockhead who is so much in debt to the Hollander, having now a treasure more by much than all his crown was worth," as Pepys furiously expressed it, that "would forever have beggared the Hollander," did not after all break with the Dutch and seize "the greatest treasure into his hands that ever was together in the world."[67] Instead, the cornered Dutch fleet was ushered in under Bergen's forts and guns which, loaned to the Dutch, were then turned on the English, with the Danes soon incomprehensibly joining in. Months of court intrigue designed to finally devastate Dutch morale turned instead into humiliating repulse.[68] By 11 August, to the chagrin of London's merchants, VOC shares on the Amsterdam Exchange, with most of the East Indies fleet secure, soared back to their early June level of 395 "and as they say are yet rising."[69]

"We were considerably foiled at Bergen," complained Oldenburg to Boyle, in late August, yet it was "not without a great losse to the Dutch," our fleet "having as we say, sunk three of their ships, and destroyed above 1,000 men," and sure to capture more, the word being that the two fleets were "like to engage again very shortly."[70] With the Dutch backed by Denmark-Norway as well as France, a brave

---

[66] Tomalin, *Samuel Pepys*, 167–8, 255; Lyons, *The Royal Society*, 63.   [67] Pepys, *Diary* i, 631.
[68] Jones, *Anglo-Dutch Wars*, 16–64.
[69] BL MS Add 22926, "News from The Hague," 11 Aug. 1665; *Hollandsche Mercurius 1665*, 109; Lister, *Letters and Papers*, 382, 387.
[70] Oldenburg, *Correspondence* ii, 481. Oldenburg to Boyle, 24 Aug. 1665; Jones, *Anglo-Dutch Wars*, 163–4.

face had to be put on the situation in London. "With France, to aid the Dutch, the Danes unite," sneered Dryden, the poet overseeing the London literary scene at the time, in his anti-Dutch propaganda epic *Annus Mirabilis* (1667), "France as their tyrant, Denmark as their slave. But when with one three nations join the fight, They silently confess that one [i.e. England] more brave."[71] Shreds of satisfaction could be gleaned from that.

"Every day we expect news of a second naval battle, unless perhaps your fleet has return'd into port again," Oldenburg replied to Spinoza in late September, answering his letter of 4 September, now sadly lost. Oldenburg's reply shows Spinoza had again commented on Boyle's experiments while also offering remarks about the senseless savagery and destructiveness of the conflict at sea. Besides the plague which spread havoc enough, agreed Oldenburg, "we have this dreadful war which brings with it nothing but an Iliad of misfortunes and almost banishes all civilized behavior from the world." However, he could not resist pointing out, repeating a refrain then common in England and incorporated into Dryden's epic poem, that the "courage with which, as you [Spinoza] suggest, your men go into battle," was not heroic or admirable but rather "of a bestial kind, rather than human. For everyone sees that if men followed the dictates of reason, they would not tear one another to pieces as they do."[72] Like Boyle and Dryden, Oldenburg remained convinced England's "valour" was of a more elevated kind than that of the Dutch.

Eager to curb hatred and vengeance, Spinoza, in the months before breaking off his work on the latter sections of the *Ethics* was clearly far less concerned with martial valour than with another human quality. Between February 1663 and June 1665, Spinoza had completed Part I "On God," Part II "On the Nature and Origin of the Mind," and a good part of Part III of the *Ethics*, on the emotions, reaching at least as far as Proposition 20 with its resonance sadly relevant to the present situation: "He who imagines that what he hates is destroyed will rejoice."[73] But if envy, jealousy, and resentment cause so much strife internal and external to society, what has the opposite effect and overcomes aggression, war and division? Far from extolling glory and valour, or their opposite, humility and withdrawal from worldly affairs, Spinoza's central claim at this juncture was his contention that "men who are governed by reason, that is those who, from the guidance of reason, seek their own advantage, seek nothing for themselves that they do not desire also for other men. Accordingly, they are just, loyal and honest."[74] From June 1665, for the next four years Spinoza chiefly focused his thoughts on men's delusions about conflict, society, and monarchy, and, equally, their delusions

---

[71] Quoted in Van der Welle, *Dryden and Holland*, 29.
[72] Spinoza, *Collected Works* (ed. Curley) ii, 11; Van der Welle, *Dryden and Holland*, 31.
[73] Akkerman, *Studies*, 99; Parkinson, "Introduction," 8.
[74] Spinoza, *Opera* ii, 223; Spinoza, *Oeuvres* iv: *Ethica*, 368–9; Spinoza, *Collected Works* (ed. Curley) i, 556.

about "miracles" and divine intervention contrary to the laws of nature, and, not least, the pervasiveness and pernicious nature and effects of hatred.

Now was not the time, Spinoza realized, as the dramatic summer of 1665 unfolded, for calm contemplation of the sort required for completing the latter sections of his *Ethics*, his chief contribution to philosophy. He had now worked out the entirety of his ethical system, but a certain amount remained to be done rounding off the concluding sections of his chief work. Yet, for now, there was no denying that his attention was firmly fixed on the war, and, equally, on the conflict within the conflict—the Orangists striving to weaken De Witt and engineer an early peace to benefit the Prince of Orange combined with the Reformed Church's campaign for a powerful "Further Reformation" in alliance with the English crown. With messianic expectations also surging on all sides, Spinoza took the momentous decision, as he explained to Oldenburg, to set his *Ethics* aside for now and concentrate instead on what would be his major political intervention and his lasting foray into the fraught sphere of what most people believe.

Writing to Bouwmeester (if Bouwmeester was indeed the recipient, and not Meyer or another of his Latinist physician friends), from Voorburg, in June 1665, Spinoza confirmed that he was about to send the finished sections of the "third part" of his *Ethics*, now that Balling had died, to this particular physician "if you wish to be its translator"; otherwise he would send it to Simon Joosten de Vries who would gladly undertake the task. This early Dutch rendering was definitely not meant for general consumption—and not destined to be the later complete translation, prepared afterwards by Glazemaker and eventually published, in 1677. It was intended rather for private discussion of Spinoza's philosophical system among his circle in Amsterdam. At this point, Spinoza seems to have envisaged the *Ethics* as nearly finished and be assuming it would consist of just these three parts, not the five parts it ultimately comprised.[75] Hence, early in the war, Spinoza supposed he had virtually completed his main life's work, even though the final sections would now inevitably drag on longer than he had expected hitherto. For now, philosophy focusing on moral theory and the individual needed to move to the back burner awaiting calmer times. In late 1665, Spinoza's compelling need, understandably, was to switch his focus to the mechanics of society, religion, war, and politics.[76]

---

[75] Spinoza, *Collected Works* (ed. Curley) i, 396–7; Spinoza, *Correspondance* (ed. Rovere) 194n1.
[76] Steenbakkers, "The Text," 29; Parkinson, "Introduction," 8–9.

18
Invasion, Slump, and Comets (1665–1666)

18.i The Greatest Curse of Mankind

"I see that you are not so much philosophizing, as theologizing, if one may use that term, for you are setting down your thoughts on angels, prophecy and miracles," replied a surprised Oldenburg, in late September 1665, a trifle sceptically, to Spinoza's summer missive announcing the *Ethics* being put on hold for now and his turning to write the *TTP*. "But perhaps you are doing this philosophically. However that may be, I am sure the work will be worthy of you and something I shall very much want to read." Boyle joined him in warmly thanking Spinoza for his detailed comments on the nitre experiments. Unfortunately, "at this dangerous time," the Royal Society, explained Oldenburg, had had to suspend its public meetings and experiments, though some of its Fellows "have not forgotten that they are such" and were continuing their research privately. Oldenburg, meanwhile, wished to know more of Spinoza's progress. "Since these difficult times are a bar to freedom of communication, I do at least urge you," he continued, "not to be reluctant to explain in your next letter your plan and object in this [new] writing of yours."[1]

Spinoza, responding in early October, again invoked the dreadful consequences of the second Anglo-Dutch conflict, and set out, for Oldenburg's benefit and Boyle's, his precise reasons at this juncture for suspending work on the *Ethics* and explained his immediate objectives. A missive of exceptional importance for structuring Spinoza's biography, this letter survives only in two incomplete, undated, but lengthy fragments, judged by scholars to date from around 1 October 1665, reflecting a deep sense of the relentless force and futility of the now already long raging struggle and the dire political consequences for society and the stable coexistence of religious loyalties such massive international conflicts entail.[2] These passages outlining the reasons for his interrupting his chief project, *The Ethics*, at this crucial juncture, with war raging around and domestic politics overheated, survive only because Oldenburg afterwards quoted them verbatim writing to Boyle and to another principal figure of the Royal Society,

---

[1] Spinoza, *Collected Works* (ed. Curley) ii, 11; Spinoza, *Correspondance* (ed. Rovere), 197.
[2] Spinoza, *Collected Works* (ed. Curley) ii, 12–15; Spinoza, *Briefwisseling*, 224–5.

the Scottish royalist and long-time opponent of Cromwell, Sir Robert Moray (*c*.1608–73). One of Charles II's privy councillors, a man of far-reaching influence, like Brouncker, a frequent companion of Pepys, and an enthusiast for chemistry, Moray figured among the Royal Society's founding heads. A nobleman who had sought refuge in the Low Countries when plotting against Cromwell and working for the monarchy's restoration in the late 1650s, Moray abhorred republican ideas and "the Dutch way," and had no interest whatever in Spinoza whom he referred to, when answering Oldenburg, as "your Hollander." Oldenburg who thought of Spinoza more as a "Spaniard," replied that although Spinoza lived in Holland, he was assuredly "no Hollander."

Delighted that England's "philosophers," meaning Boyle and the Royal Society, were well and had not forgotten their responsibility to the republic of letters, Spinoza here assured his Royal Society friends that he looked forward to receiving further reports of Boyle's and the Society's experiments once the fury of the war abated sufficiently for regular correspondence to resume, or as he vividly puts it, "when the warriors are sated with blood and resting so as to renew their strength somewhat." The outlook remained dire but also arresting in its destructive pointlessness. "If that famous scoffer [Democritus] were alive today, he would surely be dying of laughter. For my part, these convulsions move me neither to laughter nor tears, but rather to philosophizing and closer observation of human nature. For I do not think it right to laugh at nature, and far less to deplore it, reflecting that men, like all else, are only a part of nature, and that I do not know how each part harmonizes with the entirety of nature – which I perceive therefore only partly and in a fragmentary way." Earlier in life, he himself had viewed things more disconnectedly, he admitted, "and not in keeping with our philosophical attitude of mind; such features of nature then appeared to me vain, disordered and absurd." Now, viewing matters more comprehensively, he realized that all the parts must be studied together to enable us to derive a more accurate grasp of the picture overall. "Now I let everyone go his own way; and truly, for those who wish it, let them die for what seems good to them, provided I may live for the truth."[3]

Rejecting martial valour no less than Christian humility and pity, Spinoza's idea of a "free person [homo liber]," a concept he fully introduced seemingly only at this relatively late stage, is someone who sufficiently broadly emancipates him or herself from destructive forms of emotional "bondage" to be "free" of all the common misconceptions.[4] By Proposition 69 of Part IV of the *Ethics* (composed later), he held that "the virtue of a free man is seen to be as great in avoiding dangers as overcoming them." In the following lines, Spinoza explains that by "dangers" he meant everything that imperils or detracts from the individual's life and those around him or her, such as pain, discord, and hatred. As it is natural for

---

[3] Spinoza, *Collected Works* (ed. Curley) ii, 14; Lloyd, "Spinoza and the Idea," 13.
[4] Nadler, *Think Least of Death*, 47; James, *Spinoza on Learning*, 44–9.

man and necessary to his being to feel both fear and daring, Spinoza here offers a classic instance of how, from his philosophical standpoint, a philosopher-scientist's purely naturalistic method of viewing human morality yields a universally valid perspective not in the sense that all men or most will ever adopt it, or any faith ever sanction it, but universal in a purely conceptual sense once immortality of the soul is jettisoned, so that, even if no one but a Spinozist embraces his approach, it still remains more rational and beneficial and hence according to philosophical reason superior, as a formulation of how men should conduct themselves before danger than any creed or set of values not devised on the basis of reason. Minimizing the superstition and credulousness to which our anxieties and fears give rise within us, the arduous path to rationality is the one and only path to individual freedom.

Whatever codes, creeds, or traditions ruling castes exhort their following to adopt, whether exalting courage, glory or martyrdom, or eternal salvation via austerity, submission to authority, and meekness, all codes proclaimed by kings, commanders, prophets, priests, forefathers, tradition, churches or the "gods" themselves, however much these actually rule our world are all nevertheless, in the eyes of Spinoza's hypothetical earnest seeker after truth, unalterably inferior and deluded. The only system of values persuasive to the rational mind is also the optimal solution for the individual and for society when based on a realistic appraisal of how, amidst any given danger, the rational person best balances caution against bravado, self-sacrifice and impetuous leaps involving unwise, unnecessary risk. In every individual, daring or meekness coexist in varying proportions. Both are inherent, necessary drives in humans. What Spinoza calls "virtue" or fortitude is therefore the strength of mind, or inner impulse guided by reason, needed to sensibly balance and counterpoise what everyone possesses in greater or lesser degree—anxiety and apprehension alongside potentially reckless daring and impetuosity.

Is it better, for oneself and those around you, to confront the enemy or flee? A simple calculus shows what balance or combination of courage and fear best aids humans in confronting risk and minimizing danger, transcending all established moral codes aiming to exalt supposed ideal ethical qualities lodged by some in bravado, by others in self-abasement. "Therefore," asserts Spinoza, in his corollary to this proposition, "for a free man timely retreat is as much a mark of courage as fighting; that is the free man chooses flight by the same courage or spiritedness that he chooses battle."[5] Scorning heroic codes and stirring legends, Spinoza anchors his argument in his previous Proposition but one, number sixty-seven of the *Ethics* Part IV, his famous maxim that "a free man thinks of death least of all things, and his wisdom is a meditation on life, not death."[6] Yet, because

---

[5] Spinoza, *Ethics* IV, Prop. 69, corollary; Spinoza, *Opera* ii, 262.
[6] Spinoza, *Ethics*, IV, Prop. 67; Klever, *Ethicom*, 599–600.

reason does not guide most men, it is always kings, prophets, and priests, no matter how little they know or care, and despite their lacking genuine authority to proclaim the "true" basis of morality, whose guidance and approval the multitude seeks at immense cost to itself and society generally.

According to Spinoza's definition, a "free man" lives according to the dictates of reason, that is primarily seeks the "good," which in his ethics is an objective absolute, not a relative value, a summons "to act, to live, to preserve one's own being in accordance with the principle of seeking one's own advantage." From this, it follows that by instinctively seeking one's own conservation and benefit, and doing so rationally, one avoids unnecessary risks and "thinks of death least of all things," firmly rejecting the alluring delusion of eternal life and shutting out from one's mind how dying heroically or, alternatively, piously, might enhance one's posthumous image and reputation. All dangled promise of how one can enhance one's spiritual status and standing in the eyes of others via more extrovert or reclusive conduct, adopting a bolder or humbler approach, or piously seeking salvation of one's soul, is wasted effort.[7]

Like Mandeville's, Helvetius', d'Holbach's, and Bentham's moral calculus later, but unlike that of Shaftesbury, Spinoza's denies absolutely the existence of any essential "good" or "evil" outside society's and the individual's worldly well-being, existing either in nature or some imaginary promised higher realm. Spinoza's ethics, in short, is "relativistic" metaphysically but an "absolute" socially and politically, presenting the democratic republic as the only format devoted to the common good by virtue of its particular moral system and the values embedded in its fabric of laws. If the First Anglo-Dutch War finally tipped Spinoza into discarding his earlier lifestyle as a respected merchant and congregant, triggering his first life-changing philosophical turn, the fury and disruption of the Second Anglo-Dutch conflict directly contributed to his shelving the *Ethics* for the time being, helping fix his new focus on politics, how to secure social stability and theology's role in society.

Spinoza's crucial but only partially surviving letter of October 1665 evidently commented extensively on Huygens' recent experiments at Voorburg, reaffirming his view that Huygens (Figure 18.1), who was indeed strikingly ambitious in his aspirations and had been since childhood, was overly self-promoting and tended to claim unwarranted success for his findings. Huygens, in the late autumn of 1665 preoccupied with his planned move to Paris where he had been assigned precedence in Louis XIV's new academy of sciences, for his part certainly reciprocated Spinoza's critical gaze. Not unlike Boyle and others, Huygens was beginning to feel impatient with Spinoza's "Cartesian" obsession with fitting everything into an all-embracing theory instead of keeping an open mind about broader questions while

---

[7] Spinoza, *Ethics* IV, Prop. 40; Nadler, *Think Least of Death*, 179–81.

Figure 18.1 *Christiaan Huygens* after unknown artist, line engraving, early to mid-eighteenth century. NPG D30754 © National Portrait Gallery, London.

following the meanderings of the new scientific empiricism that staked all on experiment and research.[8] Spinoza's early October letter arrived at a moment of some nervousness at court and in the Royal Society regarding French intentions, the potential scope of the Franco-Dutch alliance, and Huygens' customary secretiveness. Lord Arlington had recently received warnings from Paris that France's aspiring young monarch, Louis XIV, secretly designed not just "to destroy the whole English trade [to France], that neither our cloth nor any of our manufactures shall have vent, which must needs ruine the merchant," but, with Huygens' help, was scheming too to outstrip England (and ultimately Holland) likewise in the sciences.[9] Huygens' move to Paris in the spring of 1666 could readily be construed as, and was, part of a suspected Franco-Dutch scientific conspiracy, paralleling Dutch efforts at sea and tentacles in Denmark-Norway, to thwart England's promised glorious primacy.

"Colbert intends to sett up a society lyke ours," Moray warned Oldenburg, "and make Huygens director of the designe." The Royal Society worried especially about the potentially ominous significance of Huygens' discoveries for fixing

[8] Keesing, "Frères Huygens," 116–18.   [9] Lister, *Letters and Papers*, 409.

longitude and "applying the motion of pendulums to clocks and watches" as a "means found out of bringing the measures of time, to an exact regulation."[10] In London, the Royal Society was directly involved in the war effort, in particular by examining the uses of Huygens' pendulum clocks for fixing longitude at sea, a key desideratum. Several English naval commanders had agreed to take Royal Society apparatus and experimental pendulums on board and report back on their performance, further enhancing Huygens' importance in English eyes. But Huygens remained secretive, owed England no allegiance, and had now eluded the Society.

As part of its strategy, it remained a priority for the Royal Society, at this juncture, not to break outright with Huygens, or indeed Dutch savants more generally. Congratulating him on his prominent new position in Paris, in May 1666, Oldenburg expressed his hope (in French), that "in time, all nations, however little civilized, will join hands as dear colleagues, and make a union of their intellectual and material forces to banish ignorance and inaugurate the reign of the true and useful philosophy [la vraye et utile philosophie]."[11] It was hardly in this spirit, though, that Louis XIV reigned for a record seventy-two years (1643–1715), making known early on that he intended his reign to be pre-eminently "glorious" not only in conquest and military exploits but also, surpassing all the rest, in the arts and sciences. The newly founded Académie Royale des Sciences began meeting in Colbert's library, in June 1666, with six or seven mathematicians and physicists present and Descartes' laws of motion, recent eclipses of the sun, and Boyle's experiments among their initial chief topics for research and debate.[12]

Useful information was a key part of what Oldenburg sought from his wartime exchanges with Dutch correspondents, for no other channels of information with the Netherlands were open and the king had expressly permitted the Society "to maintain the traffick of sciences, when all other commerce is intercepted,"[13] rendering Oldenburg's wartime correspondence with Spinoza part of a uniquely slim thread. Whatever he gleaned from Holland, Oldenburg at once shared with his superiors, including anything relevant gathered from Spinoza whom, when corresponding with the Society's leading figures, he prudently called "a certain odd philosopher (whom you [i.e. Boyle] know better than He [Moray], it being Signor Spinoza) [who] hath very lately written to me concerning Mr Huygens, his transmigration into France, his penduls, and his progress in dioptricks, etc." Addressing Boyle, after first discussing his recent exchange with Spinoza with Moray, in October 1665, Oldenburg refers to Spinoza tellingly not as a major

---

[10] Sprat, *History of the Royal Society*, 127; Vermij, *Calvinist Copernicans*, 191.
[11] Oldenburg, *Correspondence* iii, 129–30. Oldenburg to Huygens, London, 15 May 1666.
[12] *Histoire de l'Académie Royale des Sciences*, vol. 1 (1666–86), 2, 7–9, 43, 79, 160.
[13] Sprat, *History of the Royal Society*, 127–8; Lyons, *The Royal Society*, 65.

intellectual voice worthy of respect but as Boyle, Moray, Brouncker, and his superiors viewed him—as a decidedly bizarre, ultimately insignificant curiosity. This reflected the Royal Society's broader perspective which, as its historian Thomas Sprat remarks, consisted less of professional scholars than "gentlemen, free and unconfin'd," who were "equal observers without dependence."[14] In their eyes, and Boyle's and also Oldenburg's, Huygens always mattered considerably more than Spinoza and that was more than ever the case in 1665. Recalling the London trials with colliding balls he had witnessed at Huygens' Covent Garden lodgings years before, experiments organized to test Huygens' theory of motion carried out in the presence of Lord Brouncker, Moray confirmed that the tests bore out Huygens' predictions and calculations in the "business of motion." It was "concluded by all that [Huygens'] solution did agree with the experiments that had been made." "Of this you may assure your friend [Spinoza]," meaning that Spinoza erred here and that Huygens was "sure to have the better of Descartes in those things that have been determined by experiments."[15] Descartes' laws of motion should be set aside and, for the most part, so should Spinoza.

For Boyle, Moray, Huygens, and Oldenburg, the Anglo-Dutch struggle, with its hints of a French threat in the background, was scientific, cultural, and philosophical as well as naval, colonial, and commercial. The Royal Society gentlemen disdained the Republic, its usurped commerce and standing and had its vigorous academic and scientific Cartesianism firmly in their sights. The Royal Society, notes its first historian Sprat, rejoiced that "the English genius is not so airy and discursive, as that of some of our neighbours, but that we generally love to have reason set out in plain undeceiving expressions, as much as they to have it deliver'd with colour and beauty."[16]

Oldenburg and Moray were especially heartened by what for Charles II's court and Englishmen generally was the stirring news of the intervention of the bellicose, militaristic prince-bishop of Münster, Christoph Bernhard von Galen (1606–78), and his opting to stand shoulder to shoulder with England (Figure 18.2). This vehemently anti-Dutch champion of Catholic Counter-Reformation, ruling the large ecclesiastical principality of Münster, seized the opportunity offered by the war to invade from the east, crossing the Ijssel in force in late September 1665. No one cared more for princely authority and faith as a means to exalt princely glory, or more aspired to suppress the scorned liberties of the Republic. Within days, invading Munsterite troops penetrated through the

---

[14] Moray to Oldenburg, 27 Nov. 1665 in Oldenburg, *Correspondence* ii, 625; Sprat, *History of the Royal Society*, 67.
[15] Oldenburg, *Correspondence* ii, 561–2. Moray to Oldenburg, Oxford, 10 Oct. 1665; Hutton, "Henry Oldenburg," 106.
[16] Sprat, *History of the Royal Society*, 40.

Figure 18.2 *Bernhard von Galen, Bishop of Münster (1606–78), on horseback* by Wolfgang Heimbach, oil on canvas. Stichting Westerwolds Monumentenfonds.

United Provinces' eastern defences. Moray exulted at the "declaration hee sent to the States [General, in The Hague] which talks a gallant strain."[17]

The prince-bishop, suddenly a great hero in London, "was a soldier in his youth," explains Sir William Temple, and "seems in his naturals rather made for the sword than the cross: he has a mortal hatred of the Dutch for their supporting his city of Munster against him," referring to the civic rebellion at Münster that Von Galen crushed in 1661, and for their opposing "his bridling those citizens by a very strong citadel he is building there."[18] As the diplomat who negotiated the treaty between the prince-bishop and Whitehall, and best knew the corridors of power at The Hague, none was better placed to appraise the fast moving chessboard than this thoroughgoing Epicurean and most discerning of Anglo-Irish gentlemen. Abasing the people, exalting the Church and crushing the "Dutch way" for the sake of religion and princely sway formed the very core of the prince-bishop's ideology and the basis of his military pact with Charles.

---

[17] Oldenburg, *Correspondence* ii, 540; Rowen, *John de Witt*, 603–4.
[18] Temple, *Letters written by Sir William Temple, Bart.*, i, 5.

18.ii Are Comets Fearful Omens?

No one was more keenly aware than Spinoza that monarchical tyranny allied to contempt for the toleration and republican system of the Dutch now imperiously dominated the European scene, laying toleration, freedom of expression, and republican thinking under siege both literally and figuratively to the United Provinces' seaward and landward sides. Invading with 20,000 troops, partly financed by London, in September 1665, the martial prince-bishop quickly overran large slices of eastern Overijssel and Gelderland and then Drenthe, directly threatening also Groningen and Friesland, spreading terror throughout the land. Aiming for the Ems estuary where a bridgehead could be established enabling a projected English expeditionary force to land, the Munsterite invasion swept towards Groningen where the university abruptly closed and the students vanished.[19] A swingeing blow to Dutch prospects, this invasion from the east greatly cheered sentiment for a time on the English side of the Channel. Besides posing a grave strategic threat, the Munsterite invasion spread the plague to areas previously less affected along with extensive pillage and destruction, causing the flight of substantial numbers of refugees straggling along the roads from Overijssel southwards and westwards into Holland. Several, including a refugee schoolmaster, reached Voorburg where they were put up in the village and received charity.[20]

Dutch efforts over the next weeks, hampered by bad weather, did little to fend off the now double threat to the Republic and its people. A missive from Amsterdam that Oldenburg received around this time, now lost, probably from Serrarius, describing the collapse of Dutch morale, greatly boosted his spirits. Word from Holland, he assured Boyle, "does not only acknowledge their late great losse, but laments withal, that they see, that all the power they can make, and all the policy they can use, availes them nothing, divine providence appearing so adverse to them." Many were now excitedly invoking divine providence in England, rejoicing that the Dutch feel "extremely defeated in their expectations, the soberest of them" realizing the proximity of the abject defeat facing them now Charles' alliance with the Munsterites was bearing such rich fruit. "The Dutch fleet have their rendez-vous at Goeree," Oldenburg reported, in late September, "where De Witt is said to be, and to bragg still of a resolution to come out once more abroad before winter, and to find out the English. If he doth, I am apt to think, he comes out to seek, what he hath no great mind to find."[21] "Seeing the seapower of

---

[19] Rowen, *John De Witt*, 604; Rommelse, *Second Anglo-Dutch War*, 145, 147; Van Berkel, *Universiteit van het noorden*, 215.
[20] GA The Hague, Archief Hervormde Gemeente Voorburg 15 'Reeckeninge en bewys van Jacob van Leeuwen, diacon der gemeente, fos. 34v–35, 39 and vol. 393, fos. 41–4.
[21] Oldenburg, *Correspondence* ii, 527.

England" the Dutch were expected finally to buckle under, especially "now the Bishop of Munster is also actually upon their skirts, and finds as yet no considerable resistance," and because, assuredly "France will prove a broken reed to them." Oldenburg envisaged a suitably triumphant peace soon to emerge yielding colonies and commercial advantages that would finally secure England's unquestioned dominance under her then still admired and lauded king: certainly, all looked much rosier than during the past summer for England's maritime, colonial, and scientific hegemony.[22]

The prime scientific issues of late 1665 remained the plague, pendulums, comets, and the reality of heavenly omens. At first, during the eight-month interruption in the Royal Society's meetings, work on editing the Society's *Transactions* continued in Oxford; but, by early 1666, further progress with the Society's reports, Oldenburg informed Boyle, was becoming "very doubtfull, because of the plague keeping still on foot, and discouraging all sorts of people from settling to business."[23] "Our Society will not readily resume its meetings," he informed Huygens, in January 1666, "before the Court returns to Whitehall." But if meetings and the *Transactions* were suspended, the wider scientific debate about pendulum clocks, ship design and velocity, astronomy and the universe actually intensified at this juncture spurred by the war and, equally, by the comets of December 1664 and March 1665, astronomical events that seized the attention of scientists and scholars everywhere.

The great comet controversy of 1664–5 was simultaneously scientific, popular, and theological. The scientific quest notably intensified. In fact, the comets of 1664–5 initiated the first genuinely intercontinental, global debate involving science and its significance known to history. Astronomers all over Europe, including Huygens, Boyle's protégé Robert Hooke (1635–1703), the renowned Italians, Giovanni Borelli (1608–79) at Pisa, and Gian Domenico Cassini (1625–1712) in Rome, as well as Hevelius at Danzig and astronomers in Paris, furiously debated the amazing comet sighted in late December 1664 almost simultaneously in Florence, Rome, Paris, The Hague, Danzig, Russia, and London, and for several days thereafter, while, at the same moment, New Englanders heard with astonishment that the phenomenon arousing immense wonder in Boston was likewise observed in "Virginia, Jamaica, St Martha, Cartagena and Barbados." But at the same time, theologians and the general public remained resolute in construing the comets as deeply ominous signs predicting actual events relating to the war and plague epidemic. Most of the public discussion, in fact, did not focus at all on the science and mathematical-astronomical dimensions of the controversy; what seized the public's attention was the theology, astrology, and classical authors' accounts of comets, especially

---

[22] Oldenburg to Boyle, London, 28 Sept. 1665 in Oldenburg, *Correspondence* ii, 533.
[23] Oldenburg to Boyle, London, 16 Jan. 1666 in Oldenburg, *Correspondence* iii, 16–17.

the meaning of comets as divine admonitions of events about to occur.[24] It was the first comet observed in Europe with such clarity and brightness since 1618, when "there appeared a great comet," as the New England Puritan astronomer and pastor, Samuel Danforth (1626–74) explained, portending great evil soon to befall mankind, for, accordingly, that "same year there brake forth the Bloody Wars in Germany."[25]

The second blazing comet was widely observed and tracked in March, April, and May 1665. Danforth was among many observers in America who believed, like many in Europe, that the new sightings were of the same comet seen the previous December and that, like earlier comets, this fresh ominous omen did "precede, if not portend great calamities."[26] Spinoza, during part of April 1665 was in Amsterdam (a city now mercifully recovered from the plague),[27] discussing the process of completing and translating his *Ethics* as well as plague and war with his friends, and no doubt also preoccupied with comets. Together the two sets of sightings generated a vast debate that lingered for years. Were these sightings of one and the same comet, and what did they in fact portend? Within the Dutch Reformed Church, comets at this juncture further widened the longstanding quarrel between defenders of the supernatural and the rationalizers, Voetians insisting the phenomena were indeed supernatural omens directly linked to the war and plague while many Cocceio-Cartesians, with the Utrecht *Collegie der Sçavanten*, the scholarly clique that included Burman, Graevius, and Van Velthuysen well to the fore, denying they were necessarily portents and seeking to narrow the scope of the supernatural.[28] Spinozists alone, though, ruled out in principle all possibility of miraculous heavenly omens and movements of any kind whatsoever.

Spinoza had several times of late discussed with Huygens recent advances in the field of astronomy, he informed Oldenburg, in the spring of 1665, including (Cassini's) recent observations of Jupiter's satellites and rotations, and the particulars of the new Italian telescopes. Given the timing, Huygens and Spinoza no doubt discussed comets too and, given a later remark of Spinoza about Kepler, in November that year, it seems Huygens and Spinoza not only agreed regarding the overall purely natural and mechanical character of the universe but also, regarding Huygens' continuing uncertainty, in contrast to Borelli and Cassini, as to whether they were dealing with two separate comets or just one. But few anywhere, beyond a handful of astronomers, other scientists, and sophisticated courtiers, yet embraced a comprehensively mechanical view of the universe in the manner of Descartes, Huygens, Hudde, and Spinoza.

---

[24] Jorink, *Boeck der natuere*, 158–60; Van Miert, *Humanism*, 259–61.
[25] [Danforth], *Astronomical Description*, 13; Boschiero, "Giovanni Borelli," 11; Jorink, *Reading the Book of Nature*, 149–50.
[26] [Danforth], *Astronomical Description*, 14.
[27] Spinoza, *Collected Works* (ed. Curley) i, 394–5.   [28] Jorink, *Boeck der natuere*, 165–7.

What Calvinists in Britain, Puritan ministers in New England, and Dutch Reformed preachers of Voetian stripe alike insisted on was that comets, whatever they predict, *are*, men must acknowledge, supernatural phenomena. They are unquestionably divine omens, because none can deny that the "Holy Scriptures, which are the authentic and unerring canon of truth," as Danforth expresses it, "teach us to look at Comets as portentous and signal of great and notable changes."[29] When the "philosopher of Rotterdam," Pierre Bayle, recalled the comets debate of 1664–5, in his famous treatise on comets first published five years after Spinoza's death, in 1682, he noted with evident satisfaction that nothing more vividly illustrates the crassness of superstition and astrology and the dangers attending what most people think than this episode. Both the plague and the Second Anglo-Dutch War, after all, massive scourges though they were, actually ceased soon afterwards.[30] Always sceptical about what most people believe, Bayle made great play of the fact that comets were usually considered omens of evil, but, whenever it suited, this crass belief was not infrequently ridiculously reversed to make comets predict forthcoming favourable events.[31]

Cartesianism, Bayle also observed, certainly played a helpful role in damping down some of this firestorm of superstition and the risks to society it poses. Most notably, on 18 January 1665, Spinoza's contemporary and later discussion partner, Johannes Graevius (1632–1703), a leading professor of classics and rhetoric at Utrecht, and enthusiast for Cartesian philosophy, in close touch with Thévenot in Paris, delivered a highly controversial public lecture on comets fiercely "demolishing the common opinion about these" as signs of pending disaster. Prevailing notions he denounced as ancient pagan superstition lodged still in general ignorance now mercifully crumbling before the advance of Cartesian philosophy. His scathing *Oratio* provoked a long remembered commotion at Utrecht and, reprinted later, in 1681, was a key source for Balthasar Bekker.[32] But even before 1665 and Graevius' *Oratio*, De Bie's students at the Amsterdam Athenaeum had been urged to deny comets are omens foretelling calamities. In this connection, a 1662 disputation between De Bie, who took a special interest in comets, heavenly movements, and meteorology, and the young Nicolas Witsen (1641–1717), a future Amsterdam burgomaster was particularly memorable, and one to which his uncle, Johannes Hudde, apparently contributed.[33]

Reviled for espousing Copernican astronomy and claiming the earth moves around the sun, the Utrecht Cartesians were now additionally accused of representing all celestial motions, comets included, as purely natural phenomena

---

[29] [Danforth], *Astronomical Description*, 12; Nord, "Teleology and News," 25, 28.
[30] Bayle, *Pensées diverses* i, 104–5.
[31] Bayle, *Pensées diverses*, 108–11; Chaui, *Nervura do real*, 291–3.
[32] Jorink, *Boeck der natuere*, 156–64; Van Miert, *Humanism*, 259, 262, 274; Knuttel, *Balthasar Bekker*, 150.
[33] Jorink, *Boeck der natuere*, 155–6; Van Miert, *Humanism*, 262–3, 272.

explained and driven by Descartes' vortices.[34] Cartesians opposed the theological and popular view, albeit some, including Graevius, showed little interest in the mathematics or Descartes' vortex theory as such. Equally, there were non-Cartesians, among them Spinoza and the Huygens Brothers, who did grapple seriously for months with the science. Prominent among the latter, also striving to combat the prevailing "superstition" with hard scientific evidence, was the idiosyncratic Isaac Vossius at Voorburg whom Huygens looked down on despite his possessing a powerful telescope but Graevius admired and to whom he sent a copy of his *Oratio*.[35]

Those claiming comets are supernatural portents faced the baffling difficulty that the outcome, supposed to be calamitous, seemed not always dire while some maintained, ridiculously according to Bayle, that comets actually precede and announce beneficial happenings. "Tis true," avers Danforth, rather weakly, that "some Comets have been thought to presage good to the world, as that in the days before Augustus, before the birth of Christ [...and] another before the death of Nero: Another before the reformation of Wycliffe; Another before the reformation of Luther; but most commonly they are observed to precede, if not portend, great calamities."[36] Comets, including those of 1664–5, were indeed often construed more as divine admonitions than portents: "this Blazing Star," Danforth warned New Englanders, "being in conjunction with diverse other awful providences and tokens of wrath, calls upon us to awake out of security, and to bring forth fruits meet for repentance"; through such signs "God calls upon New-England to awake and repent."[37] The omens were indeed regularly construed as urgent summonses to increased contrition, churchgoing, and repentance.

In Italy, opinion was no less deeply divided over how to explain these perplexing heavenly phenomena. The "smallness of its parallax," or arc of movement in the heavens, observers inferred, meant these phenomena were in fact very distant; for it was understood, notes Danforth, that "the lower and nearer any planet is to earth, it hath the greater parallax."[38] Leading astronomers realized this discovery finally disposed of the old Aristotelian idea, prevalent in the Middle Ages, that comets are sublunary phenomena closer to the earth than the Moon, though many contemporaries still denied that comets are actually very distant and superlunary. Few as yet could accept that cometary theory offers additional evidence against geocentrism and wholly vindicates Copernicanism. Even Borelli (who believed there were two separate comets in 1664–5), while broadly embracing the Copernican-Galilean system and granting comets are superlunary as well as embracing, unlike most Italian astronomers of the age, Descartes' idea that

---

[34] Benthem, *Holländischer Kirch-und Schulen-Staat* ii, 57–8; Thijssen-Schoute, *Nederlands Cartesianisme*, 444–6; Vermij, *Calvinist Copernicans*, 323–36; Jorink, *Boeck der natuere*, 167.
[35] Jorink, *Boeck der natuere*, 169.   [36] [Danforth], *Astronomical Description*, 14.
[37] [Danforth], *Astronomical Description*, 15; Nord, "Teleology and News," 16.
[38] [Danforth], *Astronomical Description*, 1–2.

celestial motions generate centrifugal forces, an idea nowhere found in Copernicus, Kepler, or Galileo, still refused to absorb all observed planetary and comet motions into a single comprehensive heliocentric system relying exclusively on mechanical causes open to mathematical description throughout.[39]

Cassini's recent observations of the "eclipses of Jupiter caused by the interposition of satellites" and of "a shadow on Saturn made as it were as if by a ring" caused Spinoza "to wonder not a little at Descartes' rashness in claiming the reason why the planets next to Saturn (for he thought its projections were planets, perhaps because he never saw them touch Saturn) do not move was because Saturn does not rotate on its own axis. This hardly accords with his own principles, though he could very easily have explained the projections from his own principles, had he not been under a false preconception."[40] There could be no better illustration of Spinoza's philosophy of science: data collection and observation are the key to new advances, fresh results urgently need to be documented and publicized; but explaining them adequately means integrating them into a viable, overarching, consistently applied framework of principles constantly further refined, which Spinoza, like many astronomers of the 1660s, did not believe Kepler or Descartes ever came close to doing.[41]

Among the international astronomical fraternity debating the 1664–5 comets was a prominent citizen and councillor of Danzig, Johann Hevelius (1611–87), from a wealthy brewing family and head of the Danzig brewers' guild. Leiden-educated, "that distinguished astronomer of Danzig," as Oldenburg calls him, had established his own private observatory on the roofs of three adjacent houses his family owned in that Polish port city, an observatory which, however, later tragically burned down in 1679. A disciple of Kepler, he installed there what at the time was among the longest, most powerful telescopes in existence,[42] adding to his prominence among the chief experts on lunar topography and comets. In a letter of around 20 September 1665, curiously sent to his friend (incorrectly addressed "at the house of Mr Daniel, painter, in Adam and Eve, on the Baggyne Street," in The Hague), Oldenburg informed Spinoza that Hevelius had recently sent him copies of his *Prodromus Cometicus* (1665) "in which he gives a full description of the first of the two recent comets" and mentions his planning a second treatise "concerning the second comet also, and to submit it too to the judgment of the learned."[43]

Drawing Spinoza into discussing astronomy, comets, and Huygens, Oldenburg's next sentence inquires as to Spinoza's view of Huygens' pendulums,

---

[39] Boschiero, "Giovanni Borelli," 17, 22.
[40] Spinoza, *Briefwisseling*, 214–15; Spinoza, *Correspondance* (ed. Rovere), 188–9.
[41] Brenner-Golomb, *Importance of Spinoza*, 388, 392–3.
[42] Wootton, *Invention of Science*, 87.
[43] Spinoza, *Collected Works* (ed. Curley) ii, 12. Oldenburg to Spinoza, undated; Spinoza, *Briefwisseling*, 223.

especially those "said to show the measure of time so exactly that they can serve to find the longitude at sea?" As part of their war effort, the Royal Society sought to exploit the usefulness of the new pendulum clocks, several of which had been sent to West Africa the previous year with Holmes and his fleet to test their applicability, but so far with mixed results. Hence, Oldenburg's inquiry, given the contending navies were both struggling with the unresolved problem of fixing ships' longitude positions at sea with greater exactitude, was a decidedly leading question. Claiming to have used Huygens' "pendulum watches" successfully off West Africa, on his return Holmes reported favourably on their use to the Royal Society. But the instruments were not yet yielding satisfactory results, as Huygens admitted, and trials to improve longitude fixing techniques were continuing on both sides of the Channel, in London notably through the efforts of Hooke. Where, however, prior to the war, during 1662–4, Huygens had fully collaborated with the Royal Society in its sea-trials of his maritime pendulum clocks corresponding with the Society, via Moray,[44] in 1664, he broke off contact.

In the relevant surviving fragment Spinoza replies: "you would like to know how in this country Huygens' pendulum clocks are thought of. I cannot answer you with much certainty," he states evasively, but "do know the instrument maker who has a patent assigning him exclusive rights to make them, has completely suspended this work for now, because he cannot sell them. I do not know if this is due to the disruption of trade or because he offers them at too dear a price; he fixes the price at 300 guilders each." With the wages of Dutch navy seamen inflated by wartime exigencies to around 20 guilders monthly at this time, the instrument maker's price represented the equivalent of fifteen months of a highly paid mariner's pay. In any case, for the remainder of the war, neither side contrived to fix longitude reliably.

"I have not yet heard," remarks Spinoza at the close of this surviving fragment, "that any Cartesian does explain the phenomena of the recent comets on Descartes' hypothesis, and I doubt whether these can be thus adequately explained."[45] Spinoza refers here to Descartes' theory of the *vortex*, or vortices, in part adapted from Kepler except that, unlike Kepler, Descartes does not claim his "whirlwinds of light matter" driving planets' orbiting around the sun are generated by the Sun or that the Sun is hence the ultimate cause of planetary orbits.[46] Both Kepler's and Descartes' vortices were hard to reconcile with any convincing cometary theory conforming with the data being gathered from observation, and much more and better data were being gathered. By June 1666, Spinoza was working with Hudde on constructing an extra-large new telescope

---

[44] Van der Welle, *Dryden and Holland*, 40; Bennett et al., "Huygens' Clocks," 563; Tomalin, *Samuel Pepys*, 255; Hutton, "Henry Oldenburg," 109.
[45] Spinoza, *Briefwisseling*, 224, 226; Giancotti Boscherini, *Lexicon Spinozanum* i, 188.
[46] Applebaum, "Keplerian Astronomy after Kepler," 478; Jorink, *Boeck der natuere*, 153–4, 157.

and arranging for new grinding plates to be made for him, for polishing lenses. It was of both practical and theoretical concern to him to be clearer about the best way to process lenses for telescopes and microscopes. Spinoza's engagement with astronomy, clearly, was at its height at this time.

Since Galileo, there had been much experimenting with combining the effects of concave (bulging inwards) and convex (bulging outwards) lenses. But "I cannot see what we gain," Spinoza concluded from experience, "by grinding convex-concave lenses [quid vitris convexo-concavis tornandis profiamus]," or as the Dutch version in the 1677 *Opera Posthuma* puts it, "bulging out and bulging in lenses," that is preparing one outward curved lens thin and curving inwards [bollige en holle] in the middle.

Most early telescopes, including Galileo's, featured two lenses: the first closest to the eyes was concave, curving inwards on both sides and thin at the centre, while the second, towards the end of the tube, was convex bulging outwards both ways, hence thicker at the centre.[47] As usual, Spinoza disagreed with all prevailing assumptions and practice. "For, on the contrary," he urged Hudde, "if I have done my calculations correctly, combined convex and flat glasses [bollige en platte]," that is lenses curved outwards around the rim but flat at the centre, causing light rays to converge at a point, "will definitely be more useful." Spinoza supports his claim by referring to Hudde's earlier small treatise *Specilla circularia* (1656) and with several mathematical equations. From their correspondence, it emerges that Spinoza was studying a copy of Hudde's *Specilla circularia* on "curved lenses" for both microscopes and telescopes [tam microscopia quam telescopia] while discussing broader scientific and mathematical issues—as well as metaphysical questions about God—with Hudde (Figure 18.3), a veteran Cartesian who had taken part with Van Velthuysen in the fiery Dutch pamphlet war of 1655–6 between Cartesians and Calvinist conservatives over the Copernican system. "Still," Spinoza concludes, "as I have no doubt that you [Hudde] have long since considered these points, and made more rigorous calculations about them, and have reached a decision about this, so I seek your opinion and advice regarding it."[48]

After laying aside his *Ethics* to focus on the *TTP*, in the summer of 1665, Spinoza still combined his philosophical work and writing with lens-polishing, constructing microscopes and telescopes, and questions of optics. It was during the first year or two following his move to Paris that most of Huygens' surviving remarks about his and his brother's interaction with Spinoza were recorded, comments revealing a curious mix of respect and upper-class disdain. While referring to the Amsterdam regent mathematician-astronomer, Hudde, as

[47] Snyder, *Eye of the Beholder*, 64.
[48] Spinoza, *Opera* iv, 186; Spinoza, *Collected Works* (ed. Curley) ii, 31; Van de Ven, "Spinoza's Life and Time," 22; Schliesser, "Spinoza and the Philosophy of Science," 158.

Figure 18.3 *Johannes Hudde* (1628–1704), burgomaster of Amsterdam, 1686. By courtesy of Rijksmuseum, Amsterdam.

"Monsieur," when writing to his brother, Christiaan refers to the philosopher as plain "Spinoza." In September 1667, Huygens wrote asking his brother "what size of aperture Spinoza and Monsieur Hudde determine" is needed for a forty-foot "great telescope" and then offers his own estimate. Evidently, he considered his brother, and Hudde and Spinoza, as the three pre-eminent authorities on astronomical instrument construction in The Netherlands. "According to my calculation," averred Huygens, "[the aperture size] should be five *pouces*," that is around five inches.[49]

There was no doubting the exceptional quality of Spinoza's small lenses for microscopes. "I still remember the ones the Jew of Voorburg inserted in his microscopes," Huygens remarked, in October 1667, "which had an admirable polish although this did not extend over the whole lens."[50] The following month Christiaan referred again to the "admirable" quality of the microscope lenses of the "Jew of Voorburg." Writing to his brother (in French), over a year after the above exchange between Hudde and Spinoza, Huygens, always a curious mix of scientific secrecy and openness, again cites Hudde and Spinoza as the leading

---

[49] Huygens, *Oeuvres complètes* vi, 151; Keesing, "Frères Huygens," 113; Vermij, "Bijdrage," 28–9.
[50] Huygens, *Oeuvres complètes* vi, 155; Van der Leer and Boers, *Huygens and Hofwijck*, 94.

Dutch experts aside from himself and his brother on lenses for both microscopes and telescopes, but regarding one aspect also remarks "that the sieur Spinoza, as far as I can see, has so far scarcely penetrated this topic, and you are hardly charitable to leave him thus in error," presumably meaning that his brother, Constantijn, rivalling Spinoza and Hudde and much occupied with preparing lenses for microscopes and telescopes, should have told Spinoza that Christiaan had advanced further than he had in revising the theoretical dimension.[51]

Constantijn made some attempt to set Spinoza right regarding the laws of refraction but apparently met with resistance as Spinoza continued with his own attempts to formulate a mathematical theory of refraction. A month later, in November 1667, Christiaan again strikingly refers to the "très excellents" microscope lenses prepared by "the Jew of Voorburg," when complimenting his brother on his concentrated labours on telescopes and microscopes, adding that the "Jew of Voorburg" had used his instruments to finish small lenses that were "wholly excellent, I do not know why you do not do the same. If he continues to work also with large lenses, I would be grateful if you would let me know how well he succeeds."[52] As for their disagreement over telescope aperture sizes, Christiaan, in December 1667, pronounced this more a question of "experience" than "theory," suggesting that, rather than argue on a theoretical basis, they should just "leave our Jew to his apertures" and let experience refute him. Huygens clearly doubted whether Spinoza could justify his divergent claims.[53] That same month, Christiaan repeated that "we must leave our Jew to his apertures, and experience must refute him better than theory can, for determining apertures in microscopes and telescopes indeed has its first foundation in experience."[54] Let me know, inquires Christiaan of his brother a week later, "where you are at in *microscopie* and whether you have learnt anything of what our Israelite is doing."[55] If the specifications "of the Israelite are not good for three and six foot telescopes," Christiaan wrote to his brother, in April 1668, "he is still far from succeeding with the big apertures he had concerted together with Monsieur Hudde."[56]

"It is true that experience confirms," conceded Christiaan in May 1668, "what Spinoza says about small *objectifs* for microscopes representing objects more distinctly than big ones with proportionately large apertures," when multiplying the size of minute objects by twenty or thirty times, "and no doubt the reason for this can be found, although neither the sieur Spinosa nor I know what it is as yet." Still, he and his brother had made progress with their manner of preparing convex

---

[51] Christiaan to Constantijn Huygens, Paris, 9 Sept. 1667 in Huygens, *Oeuvres complètes* vi, 148, 151.
[52] Christiaan to Constantijn Huygens, Paris, 4 Nov. 1667 in Huygens, *Oeuvres complètes* vi, 158.
[53] Huygens, *Oeuvres complètes* vi, 164; Keesing, "Frères Huygens," 114.
[54] Christiaan to Constantijn Huygens, Paris, 2 Dec. 1667 in Huygens, *Oeuvres complètes* vi, 164; Klever, "Insignis opticus," 47, 50.
[55] Christiaan to Constantijn Huygens, Paris, 9 Dec. 1667 in Huygens, *Oeuvres complètes* vi, 168.
[56] Christiaan to Constantijn Huygens, Paris, 6 April 1668 in Huygens, *Oeuvres complètes* vi, 205.

lenses, as had Huygens' with his theorizing, and Christiaan seemed anxious that Constantijn should mention as little as possible about his latest findings "to the Israelite, lest through him, Hudde or others should penetrate into this speculation which has also other utilities."[57] Clearly, there was a pronounced element of rivalry between the Brothers Huygens and Hudde, as well as with Spinoza, in the fast-unfolding field of optics.

Steeped in Cartesianism as a youth and profoundly influenced by Descartes' ideas, Huygens, far more than Descartes' old ally, Van Schooten, or Hudde, but like Spinoza, also viewed himself as the reformer and corrector of Descartes whose laws of motion, light, and much else he deemed (much to Van Schooten's dismay earlier) profoundly defective.[58] Since Huygens and Spinoza both considered themselves in a sweeping sense reformers of Descartes and Cartesianism, including in astronomy and optical science, Voorburg during 1666–7 became the focus of an undeclared, sustained, historically significant intellectual and scientific rivalry over the complex business of correcting Descartes' scientific legacy. Between Huygens and Spinoza there was disagreement both theoretical and practical regarding the laws of refraction and optics, lens sizes and shapes, and instrument apertures.

As it happens, the greatest practitioner of microscopy of the seventeenth century, Anthony van Leeuwenhoek (1632–1723), the discoverer of bacteria, sperm cells, and blood cells, was born in the same year as Spinoza (and Vermeer) and greatly advanced the science of microscopy, constructing over 500 microscopes, residing like Vermeer in Delft, only about four miles distant from Voorburg.[59] Like Hudde, Huygens, Spinoza, and most of the Dutch naturalists, Van Leeuwenhoek too preferred the single-lens microscope to the compound microscopes with extendable tubes widely in use in Europe at the time, because single lenses caused less distortion to the resulting image.[60] But where Spinoza, Hudde, and the Brothers Huygens were all renowned in the microscopy field by the mid-1660s, Van Leeuwenhoek was just beginning to learn the lens-grinding art and registered notable discoveries only in the following decade, after Spinoza ceased being active in the field, sending his first report to the London Royal Society in 1673.

To Spinoza's October missive Oldenburg responded immediately, on 12 October 1665, with Boyle joining him, he remarks, "in sending cordial greetings." Boyle and Oldenburg wished to know, apparently responding to Spinoza's comments about comets and Descartes' vortices, how his philosophizing was progressing. "Above all if you have any light to cast on the difficult question of how

---

[57] Christiaan to Constantijn Huygens, Paris, 11 May 1668 in Huygens, *Oeuvres complètes* vi, 213–15; Klever, "Insignis opticus," 51.
[58] Vermij, *Calvinist Copernicans*, 149. [59] Snyder, *Eye of the Beholder*, 112.
[60] Snyder, *Eye of the Beholder*, 206.

each part of Nature accords with the whole, and the manner of its coherence with other parts [quomodo unaquaeque pars naturae cum suo toto conveniat, et que ratione cum reliquis cohaereat], please do us the favour of letting us know your views." Oldenburg reminds him that when discussing Huygens' treatise on motion, a topic of considerable interest in London, Spinoza had claimed Descartes' rules of motion were nearly all wrong, though not having Spinoza's book on Descartes' philosophy at hand, Oldenburg could not remember whether "you point that error out there, or whether you followed Descartes closely so as to gratify others."[61]

Either way, Spinoza, he knew, professed to have penetrated beyond Descartes in key respects, holding "that many of those matters which Descartes himself claimed surpass human comprehension – indeed, even more sublime and subtle topics – can in fact be plainly understood by men and clearly explained," as indeed Meyer's preface to Spinoza's Descartes book asserts. Yet again, Oldenburg implored Spinoza to publish the results of his philosophizing and entrust these to the "world of philosophers to cherish and to foster [...] Why do you hesitate my friend, what do you fear? Make the attempt, go ahead, complete this task of such high importance, and you will see the entire company of genuine philosophers supporting you."[62] Spinoza, wisely, still held back.

"I had lately meanwhile," Hevelius' thoughts and data about the comets, reported Oldenburg, but these clashed with those of Adrien Auzout (d. 1691), in Paris who was arguing for very different trajectories. A leading French astronomer, Auzout was among the founders of the Paris astronomical *Observatoire*, a new body, formally established in 1667, that the Académie des Sciences in Paris had pressed for during 1664–5 in the wake of the excitement over comets. The 1664–5 comets, Auzout was convinced, followed parabolic (elliptical) orbits, that is followed long oval trajectories which Hevelius denied, contending they moved in curves with the concave side towards the sun, a disagreement now being examined by the Royal Society. When settled, Oldenburg promised to communicate the Society's judgement to Spinoza. "This much I can already assert, that all astronomers – or at any rate those known to me – are of the opinion that there were not one but two comets, and I have not yet met anyone who has tried to explain these phenomena according to the Cartesian hypothesis." More convinced of the Copernican thesis than Auzout, Hevelius had, however, made observational errors. All told, it proved impossible to untangle the difficulties until much later, further proof doubtless in Spinoza's eyes of the misleading potential of incomplete, possibly faulty observational data.

Finally, Oldenburg asks Spinoza to let him know what was being reported "in your country about a peace treaty [between the Dutch and England] and about the

---

[61] Spinoza, *Opera* iv, 167–8; Spinoza, *Collected Works* (ed. Curley) i, 15–17.
[62] Spinoza, *Collected Works* (ed. Curley) ii, 16–17.

progress of the Bishop of Munster. I believe the whole of Europe will be involved in war next summer, and everything seems to be tending toward a strange transformation. As for us, let us serve the supreme Deity with a pure mind, and cultivate a philosophy that is true, sound and profitable."[63] Replying from Voorburg on 20 November 1665, Spinoza sent one of his longest surviving missives to Oldenburg much of which is a philosophical excursion explaining that he assigns neither beauty nor ugliness, order nor disorder, to Nature conceived as a whole.[64] By the "coherence" of the different aspects and parts of Nature "I mean simply this: that the laws or nature of one part adapts itself to the laws or nature of another part in such a manner that there is the least possible opposition between them. On the question of the whole and its parts, I consider things as parts of a whole to the extent that they are in the closest possible harmony." Insofar as entities are different from one another "to that extent each one forms in our minds a separate idea, and hence is considered a whole, not a part." But this is an artificial abstraction on our part, since wholes in reality are always parts of some larger entity until we reach the infinity of the universe. All individual things without exception are both parts and wholes. But insofar as we conceive individual things separately, each stands as a separate whole and is not contemplated by us as part of the larger whole which it actually is.[65]

It is here also that Spinoza advances his famous example of the worm's eye view and explained in the same letter "why I think that the human body is a part of nature," and also that

> as far as the human mind is concerned, I think it is a part of nature too. For I maintain that there is also in nature an infinite power of thinking, which insofar as it is infinite, contains within itself objectively the whole of nature, and whose thoughts proceed in the same way as does nature, its object. Next, I maintain that the human mind is this same power, not insofar as it is infinite and reflects the whole of nature, but insofar as it is infinite and reflects only the human body. For this reason I maintain that the human mind is a part of a certain infinite intellect.[66]

Readily comprehensible in retrospect, Spinoza's notion can have made little sense to his contemporaries pondering the outer boundaries of physical reality— space, time, and energy. In Newtonian terms these were all distinct entities, separate absolutes. But viewed from the perspective of Einstein's revision of Newtonian science later, the picture looks very different: what to Newton were

---

[63] Spinoza, *Briefwisseling*, 228–9. [64] Spinoza, *Briefwisseling*, 230.
[65] Spinoza, *Collected Works* (ed. Curley) ii, 18–19; Spinoza, *Briefwisseling*, 231–3.
[66] Spinoza, *Correspondance* (ed. Rovere); Spinoza, *Collected Works* (ed. Curley) ii, 20 (reworked by myself).

absolute entities, each governed by its own rules, in fact blend and interact as one system in ways difficult for our minds to comprehend, so that Newton's concepts, though intuitively easier to grasp than Spinoza's conceptualization were, arguably, further from the truth as Einstein refashioned physical reality in the twentieth century.[67] Here again we encounter the tension between Spinoza's project with its universalism and sense of the totality and unity of everything, precisely the characteristics that later so appealed to Einstein in Spinoza's philosophy, and the strictly empirical approach of the Royal Society based on experiment and measurable data.

For Spinoza, as for Descartes, the laws of Nature must form a single coherent whole as regards principles of interaction and mechanics, in which all the different laws of science consistently conform to one another. "I had lately another letter from Signor Spinoza," Oldenburg recounted, in late November, to Boyle in Oxford, "who is very much your servant, and who entertains me with a discourse of his, concerning the agreement and coherence of the parts of the World with the whole, which is not unphilosophicall, in my opinion, though it would perhaps be tedious to you, to have a letter filled with it [Spinoza's ruminations]; and this makes me forebeare to send it to you." Accustomed to finding that broaching Spinoza's all-encompassing approach, or aspects of it, with Boyle met invariably with a lukewarm, not to say largely unsympathetic reaction, Oldenburg, perceiving that Spinoza was not being taken seriously in Oxford, henceforth merely sent Boyle copies of some of Spinoza's letters.[68]

18.iii Descartes' Laws of Motion

Among other points in his letter, Spinoza corrects Oldenburg's recollection that he had ever claimed "the Cartesian rules of motion are nearly all wrong; if I remember rightly," he answered, "I said that Mr Huygens thinks so, while I did not assert any of the rules were wrong except the sixth." This was Descartes' law stating that any given body at rest and exactly equal in size to another body impacting against it, is in part pushed forward by the colliding body and in part caused to rebound such that one quarter of the velocity of the moving body transfers to the pushed effect and three-quarters to the rebounding effect in the direction from which the colliding body came. About this law, Spinoza recalled writing that he "thought that Mr. Huygens too was in error at which point I asked you to tell me about the experiment which you have conducted in your Royal Society concerning this hypothesis; but I gather you are not permitted

---

[67] Brenner-Golomb, *Importance of Spinoza*, 227.
[68] Oldenburg to Boyle, London, 21 Nov. 1665 in Oldenburg, *Correspondence* ii, 615.

to do so, as you have made no reply concerning this matter."⁶⁹ When Oldenburg passed this on to Boyle, the latter responded like Moray, expressing scepticism about Spinoza's criticism of Huygens: "I am much obliged to your Spanish philosopher for the favourable opinion he is pleased to have of mee, and beg you to returne to him my humble thanks for his civilitys to mee. But as to what he says of Monsr. Huygenius I doubt he is therein a little too severe and perhaps the more so because he, I mean your Spanyard [Spinoza] has appeared so publicly a professed Cartesian, though I am glad to find that he dissents from Descartes, about one of the rules of motion, as I doe about more than one."⁷⁰ While Boyle evidently regarded Spinoza as more tied to a Cartesian frame in scientific matters than he actually was, Huygens and Boyle were right to doubt Descartes' laws of impact and motion overall, despite their continuing topicality in the mid-1660s and importance over several decades in stimulating new scientific thought and research.

Boyle expressed thanks for Spinoza's remarks about his recent publications. Not the least aspect of Anglo-Dutch rivalry troubling Boyle and Oldenburg was the likelihood the Dutch, with their ascendancy over the international book trade, might profit from the state of war between the two nations to capture a still larger, more commanding slice of sales of English science publications, including Boyle's reports of his experiments and other material from Royal Society *Transactions*, in continental Europe than they possessed already.⁷¹ For decades, English publishers and booksellers had resented how the continental market for scholarly books in Latin was dominated by Dutch publishers obtruding even into Britain itself. At Oxford, roughly a quarter of all scholarly literature on sale in the bookshops was imported from the United Provinces.⁷² "The same Spinoza," Oldenburg assured Boyle, "expresses a very great respect for you and presents you his most humble service, and is displeased [as Boyle was], that the Dutch stationers, will, in spight of our teeth, sell off one of their owne Latin impressions of your *History of Colours*, before the [Latin] translation, made here, can be sent thither."⁷³

Contrasting with Oldenburg's (not wholly concealed) hopes for Dutch setbacks, Munsterite advances, and an early peace in England's favour, Spinoza wrote to Oldenburg of the Munsterite offensive in an indignant, scornful manner. "The Bishop of Munster, after mounting an ill-advised invasion into Frisia, like Aesop's goat into the well, has met with no success. Indeed, unless the winter begins very early, he will not be able to withdraw from Frisia without heavy losses." The Dutch, explained Spinoza with evident satisfaction, had adeptly flooded extensive areas as part of an elaborate circumventing defensive operation thwarting the

---

⁶⁹ Spinoza, *Collected Works* (ed. Curley) ii, 20.
⁷⁰ Boyle to Oldenburg, (Oxford?), 14 Oct. 1665 in Oldenburg, *Correspondence* ii, 569.
⁷¹ Pettegree and Der Weduwen, *Bookshop of the World*, 349.
⁷² Pettegree and Der Weduwen, *Bookshop of the World*, 274–5.
⁷³ Boyle to Oldenburg, (Oxford?), 14 Oct. 1665 in Oldenburg, *Correspondence* ii, 569.

prince-bishop's attempts at further advances. His invasion of the eastern Netherlands causing hopes to soar in England, Spinoza dismissed as dismally wrong-headed, a reckless project from which Von Galen would extricate himself only with difficulty and at such cost that the foolhardy bellicose prince must have been lured into it by some cunningly treacherous adviser. Spinoza's highly negative estimate of the prince-bishop's chances proved correct only a short time later, when the Munsterite advance was halted and turned into retreat. The prince-bishop commenced his disorderly withdrawal from Dutch territory around two weeks after Spinoza predicted his humiliation.[74]

Regarding an imminent peace, there was much rumour-mongering, confirmed Spinoza, partly explained by the dispatch of a Dutch envoy to France for preliminary negotiations with England to be held there and partly by the fact that "those of Overijssel who strive with all their strength to bring in the Prince of Orange, more in order, as many think, to obstruct the Hollanders than for their own interest, imagined they had hit on a scheme that would secure peace." Like De Witt and the "True Freedom" faction, Spinoza despised this Orangist inspired attempt by the Overijssel nobles and regents to get the young Prince nominated to head a peace-seeking mission to negotiate a peace beneficial to England (and to the Prince and his supporters), at the expense of Dutch commerce and colonies. Overijssel would willingly meet English demands, Spinoza rightly feared, if these altered the balance of power within the Republic against Holland, which was why Overijssel was pressing in the States General "to send the said Prince to England as a mediator." He discerned little likelihood, though, that the Orangists would successfully outflank De Witt and the States of Holland by demanding restoration of the stadholderate in the midst of the war. For "in present circumstances the Hollanders are not thinking of peace, even in their dreams, unless things should come to such a pass that they should have to buy peace with their money."[75]

This was an accurate enough assessment. Two crucial factors enabled the Republic to survive the setbacks of 1665 undefeated—the impressive resolve of the populace of Holland's cities to withstand the pressure and press on with the war to defend what they had, and the Republic's commanding a greater stock of funds than Charles II or any rival. By late 1665, an increasingly frustrated Charles II was fast running short of cash while the Dutch were not. Still, Orangist and Reformed efforts to undermine De Witt remained a grave menace.[76] Strict Calvinists and Orangists aspiring to elevate the Prince and finally overthrow the "True Freedom" made strenuous efforts throughout the Republic to mobilize the common people against the States of Holland. Holland was being disloyal to the House of Orange and to religion, proclaimed Spinoza's most vocal public

---

[74] Spinoza, *Collected Works* (ed. Curley) ii, 21; Rowen, *John de Witt*, 606; Israel, *Dutch Republic*, 770.
[75] Spinoza, *Opera* iv, 175; Rowen, *John de Witt*, 666, 669; Stern, *Orangism*, 110.
[76] Israel, *Dutch Republic*, 771.

enemy, Thaddeus De Lantman, from the pulpit even at this critical juncture condemning De Witt's (temporary) alignment with Catholic France. So reprehensible did De Witt's supporters consider De Lantman's conduct that the States of Holland formally reprimanded him, ordered him to steer clear of politics in his sermons, and announced suspension of his preacher's salary until he undertook to comply which he stubbornly refused to do.[77]

As for "peace with the English," it appeared to Spinoza, there was no hope for the time being. "For the last week or two, there has been no new development worth mentioning." For now, the war would simply continue. Uncertainty prevailed too regarding the situation in Germany, especially the objectives of the Swedish army operating there, a force intended to join the Munsterites, some supposed, in invading the Republic. Other observers, though, claimed the Swedes were heading towards Louis XIV's great garrison at Metz. These, though, remarks Spinoza, "were all simply guesses."

Dating his letter, Voorburg, 20 November 1665, Spinoza was still wondering whether the two comets were in fact one. "I should like to know," he asks in his postscript, "whether the conviction that there were two comets is held by all astronomers on account of their trajectories, or because they want to conserve Kepler's hypothesis."[78] Experimental science generates advances of itself without the help of philosophy. But it remains problematic, especially when conducted in isolation from philosophizing, by preventing the curious or concerned individual acquiring any overall view of the world system as a general perspective or insight into the universal format of reality. Experimental science is all very well, and the best route to furthering scientific knowledge, but, as Spinoza saw it, mid-seventeenth-century experience, not least the contested reception of Kepler's findings and the Copernican approach, and uncertainty surrounding the data about the comets,[79] proved experimental science on its own is less decisive in linking science to general culture and religion, and hence changing the world, than when combined with an overarching philosophy equipped to usher science into humankind's everyday thoughts and challenge and transform the prevailing world view in educated minds and conversation and the universities.

England's wartime literary champion, Dryden, was as eloquent an illustration of Spinoza's strictures as one could find. The medieval Aristotelian world view Dryden poetically dismissed as "The Longest Tyranny that ever sway'd / Was that Wherein our Ancestors betray'd / Their Free-Born Reason to the Stagirite / And made his Torch their universal light."[80] This was fitting, given Dryden's recent

---

[77] See Aitzema, *Historie* v, 504; Aitzema, "Brieven," 152; *Sleutel Ontsluytende de Boecke-kas*, 6; *Resolutien van de Heeren Staten van Holland* 1665, res. 7 Nov., 5 Dec. 1665; Rowen, *John de Witt*, 435.
[78] Spinoza, *Opera* iv, 175; Spinoza, *Briefwisseling*, 234–5.
[79] Applebaum, "Keplerian Astronomy after Kepler," 458–9; Schliesser, "Spinoza and the Philosophy of Science," 177.
[80] Quoted in Van der Welle, *Dryden and Holland*, 35.

election to membership of the Royal Society and moral support for it and for experimental science. Experimental science splendidly helped demolish the Aristotelian world view and excise it from people's minds. Yet, for all that, Dryden remained a superstitious astrologer of the kind Bayle ridiculed, harbouring suspicion of "reason" as man's guide, while also powerfully reflecting the perplexity and confusion regarding comets and comet theory at the time. Comets his epic poem *Anno Mirabilis* (1667), depicting the Second Anglo-Dutch struggle, represents as supernaturally foretelling calamities, and yet, just as often, also favourable events. However one approached the issue, contends the poet, the incontrovertible point is the vast supernatural significance of comets. That divine providence shaped the course of the Second Anglo-Dutch War was readily proven. None could deny that the comets of 1664–5 prognosticated England's resounding triumph over the Dutch. Comets could thus as readily betoken happy as catastrophic events, as the comet (in fact supernova) of May 1630, announcing King Charles II's glorious birth, amply demonstrated.[81]

This preponderant view of the age that comets are indeed awesome signs of supernatural significance betokening divine intent good and bad, Bayle would not only later deride in his *Pensées diverses* of 1682 but did so specifically in relation to the Anglo-Dutch struggle. Looking back, the comets of 1664–5 seemed to him to augur neither resounding success nor failure for either side. After a long, bitter, and bloody struggle, the English "found themselves exactly where they were before the war, and the Dutch so little weakened that Dutch affluence flourished after the war more than was desirable for their tranquility," so that after six or seven years of expanded confidence and prosperity they fell into the terrible trap of their "disaster year" of 1672; and if someone "tells me that prosperity is sometimes the most terrible chastisement God can inflict on men, I answer that adversity is sometimes the greatest gift He can bestow."[82]

As enthusiastic as any for careful observation and empirical science, Spinoza was distinctive in insisting that empirical science on its own is insufficient and can even hinder rationalization of men's world view, as happened after Galileo's disastrous confrontation in 1633, in Italy, with a repressive papacy and Inquisition. For Galileo and Kepler, as for Boyle and Newton later, revealed religion and science must ultimately conjoin and confirm the unity of scientific truth with revelation, nature being conceived as the executor of the orders of the Great Architect.[83] This principle was foundationally entrenched at the inauguration of the Royal Society when its founders assured the Church of England that churchmen had nothing to fear from growing court and aristocratic promotion of science. The universe adheres to its eternal state of order, stability, and harmony, few doubted, exclusively owing to a miraculous creation and continuing divine

---

[81] Van der Welle, *Dryden and Holland*, 18, 26.   [82] Bayle, *Pensées diverses* i, 108–9.
[83] Redondi, "Spinoza, Critic of Galileo," 117–18.

intervention of a providential kind featuring particular no less than general miracles. If there were differences between Protestant and post-Tridentine Catholic Bible hermeneutics, and some Protestants were distinctly more willing than others to discard what to Cartesians were mistaken notions about the motions of the Sun, Moon, and Earth found in Scripture, claiming this was due to Scripture's need to adapt revelation to the ignorance and credulity of the common people of the time, ultimately these varying traditions converged in seeing the entire heavenly scheme as divinely intended and ordered.

Submitting to ecclesiastical sensibilities and pressure, Galileo had had to step back further than Kepler in respecting the literal meaning of Joshua and the miracle of the Sun and Moon standing still prior to finishing his battle at Gibeon, and discreetly veil his heliocentric astronomical system. But Kepler too acknowledged the story as a genuine miracle albeit he held that God stopped the Earth, not the Sun, performing a miracle which appeared to Joshua and his army to make the Sun stop in its course.[84] While Spinoza cites neither Galileo nor Kepler by name, it is clear to whom he is referring when remarking, in chapter II of the *TTP*, that among the divergent ways of construing the story of Joshua and the Sun standing still, there is that of those who could philosophize more accurately than most (having imbibed more contemporary science) and who "recognize that the earth moves around the Sun and that the Sun is at rest, or does not move around the Earth" but for all that "make great efforts to derive" a crassly false reading "from that passage even though it is obvious that it will not permit such a reading. I am really astonished at them."[85]

Spinoza resumes his critique of Galileo, Kepler, Boyle, Auzout, and the other chief men of science (aside from Huygens) in chapter XV of the *TTP*, "assuredly, I am utterly amazed that men should want to subject reason, the greatest gift and the divine light, to ancient words which may well have been adulterated with malicious intent. I am amazed that it should not be considered a crime to speak disparagingly of the mind, the true text of God's thought, and proclaim it corrupt, blind and depraved, while deeming it the highest offence to think such things of the mere letter and image of God's word. They consider it pious not to trust their reason and their own judgment and impious to have doubts concerning the reliability of those who have handed down the sacred books to us. This is plain stupidity, not piety."[86] In Spinoza's view, a preponderant problem in contemporary science was that Galileo, Kepler, Boyle, and the rest made spectacular new discoveries about the motions of the Earth, planets, stars, and comets, but instead of integrating their findings into a consistent framework built on principles

---

[84] Redondi, "Spinoza, Critic of Galileo," 114; Brenner-Golomb, *Importance of Spinoza*, 388.
[85] Spinoza, *Theological-Political Treatise*, 34; James, *Spinoza on Philosophy*, 52–3, 56–7, 64; and wrongly explaining this, Schliesser, "Spinoza and the Philosophy of Science," 156–7, 166.
[86] Spinoza, *Theological-Political Treatise*, 188.

buttressing their own research, tried to adapt their findings to notions of a knowing Creator God performing miracles general and particular while twisting Scripture to mean something absurdly different from what the text actually says, thereby forging a false overall framework depriving men of much of the benefit of their own discoveries. The uniqueness of mathematics as a model for all the sciences and for philosophy, in Spinoza's mind is precisely that it is a study anchored in an inexorable logic and experience extending our knowledge by rigorous inference.[87]

With controversy raging over whether or not the new comets were supernatural "signs from heaven," and Cartesians, like Graevius, Van Velthuysen, and Wolzogen, interpreting them as purely natural phenomena without moral significance in opposition to the more popular Voetian conviction, the ensuing clashes often degenerated into bad-tempered personal encounters, like that between the Utrecht theologian Van Mansvelt and a preacher named Colvius. The Utrecht *Collegie der Sçavanten*, figuring Burman, Van Velthuysen, Wolzogen, Graevius, and Van Mansvelt, found itself at the forefront of the escalating culture wars over the meaning of science and the place of the supernatural in daily life, a contest in which Reformed theologians and preachers siding with the Cartesians tended to be Cocceians, albeit even Cocceius, while struggling to sort things out, had himself rejected the idea that the Earth revolves around the sun, until as late as 1660.[88] Voetius, for his part, was perfectly correct in holding that nearly all theologians and philosophers down to the 1660s firmly rejected Copernicanism defined as heliocentrism. But the very strength of the Voetian reaction against Copernicanism and Cartesianism made the links between these two firmer than they would otherwise have been.[89]

In this contest, the increasingly besieged Utrecht *sçavanten* were potentially, at least to an extent, Spinoza's natural allies. Yet, other factors, especially Spinoza's increasingly leprous reputation for irreligion and mocking Reformed preachers, at the same time rendered it wholly impossible for them to ally with him openly. This left Spinoza and his group riskily exposed as isolated outliers at the very fringe of a massive cultural and intellectual furore, a consuming fire that could all too readily engulf them.

---

[87] Brenner-Golomb, *Importance of Spinoza*, 392.
[88] Thijssen-Schoute, *Nederlands Cartesianisme*, 446; Fix, "Comets," 162–3; Vermij, *Calvinist Copernicans*, 110–11.
[89] Van Ruler, *Crisis of Causality*, 18n26; Vermij, *Calvinist Copernicans*, 323.

19

Spinoza, Meyer, and the 1666 *Philosophia* Controversy

19.i A Bitter Controversy

The last years of the "True Freedom" in the United Provinces witnessed a "recrudescence of ideological warfare" closely linked to the fraught political context, a deepening theologico-political and philosophical public quarrel fought throughout the country in the provincial assemblies, town councils, consistories and pamphlets, extending even to passenger barges and inns.

The Second Anglo-Dutch War enabled Orangism to surge up with renewed vigour, helped by the Republic's inability to extricate itself from conflict with England, and by the young Prince of Orange, William III, being, by 1666, only two years from attaining his majority (at eighteen, late in 1668). However adroit De Witt's expedients, increasingly divisive feuding over how the aspiring young prince should be incorporated into the Republic's fraught power structure became unavoidable.[1] Renewed sparring around the House of Orange at the same time inevitably merged with a no less fierce resurgence of old quarrels over toleration, sabbath observance, and social discipline, generating a feverish intellectual atmosphere and flurry of polemical publications. Leading figures of the Dutch Reformed synods and Orangist regents supporting the public church seized the opportunity to escalate alarm and indignation at the advances of Cartesianism, Socinianism, irreverent Bible criticism, suspected atheism, and freethinking.

Spinoza's *Ethics* and *TTP* both analyse how and why divisive factions form in societies, how fervent and protracted but ultimately pointless internal struggles come to be conceived as all-important intellectual and moral rifts, and how such controversies emotionally trap numerous individuals infusing their conscious lives with ill-informed but highly divisive, damaging and unhelpful attitudes. One of the most furious intellectual controversies of the age commenced in the early summer of 1666 when Rieuwertsz, Spinoza's publisher, anonymously brought out the 115-page *Philosophia S.Scripturae Interpres* [Philosophy the Interpreter of Holy Scripture], which its author, an eager member of the *cercle Spinoziste*, probably Meyer, admits to having long hesitated to publish for fear of

---

[1] Rowen, *John De Witt*, 666–84, 781–94; Israel, *Dutch Republic*, 791–4.

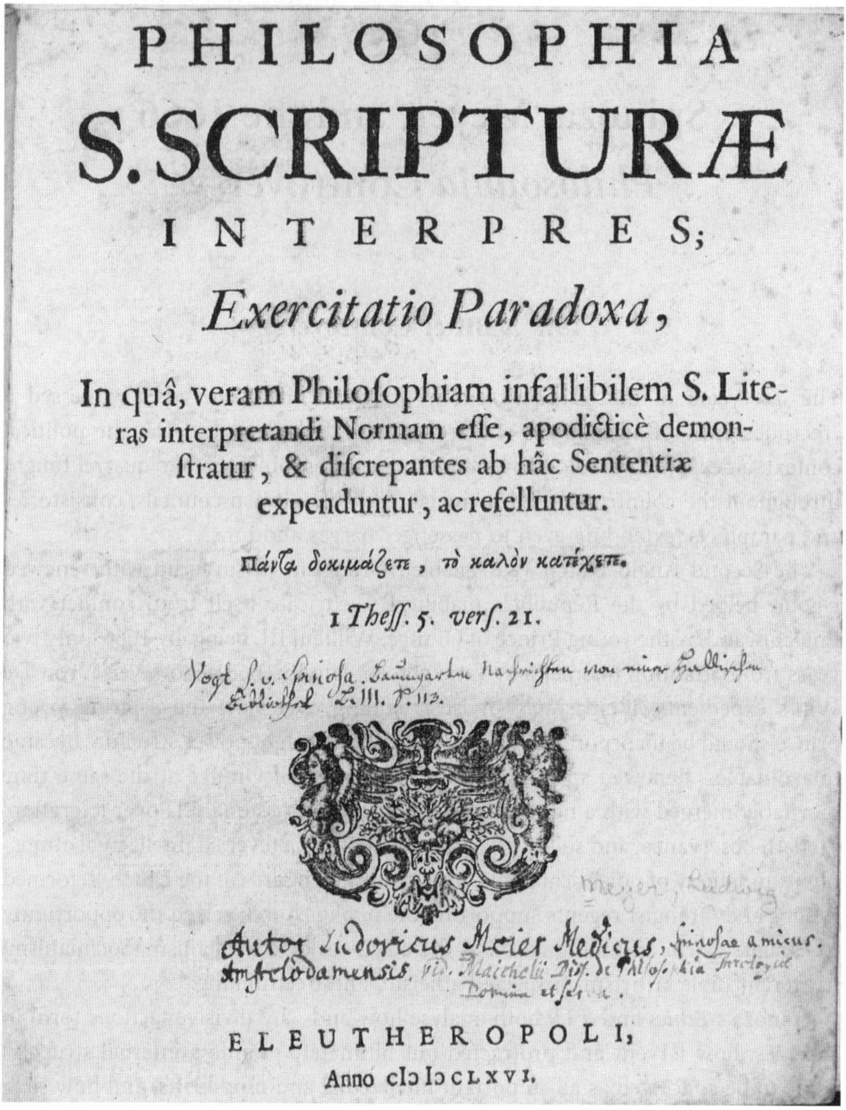

Figure 19.1 Lodewijk Meyer, *Philosophia S.Scripturae Interpres*. Eleutheropoli: s.n., 1666. IAS Spinoza Research Collection.

the outcry it would provoke. Its title-page cites no author or publisher and gives its place of publication as "Eleutheropoli" [at Freedom City] (Figure 19.1). Its appearance followed shortly after a distinctly stressed Spinoza switched from working on the *Ethics* to more direct confrontation with the preachers and prevailing opinion by embarking on his *TTP*. A letter Spinoza wrote at this point to his close friend, Bouwmeester, on 10 June 1666, thanking him for his many recent kindnesses, mentions his feeling so "hampered by different entanglements and worries that only after much effort have I been able to free myself from them."[2] He was presumably referring to the escalating ideological conflict in general but also specifically the local battle in Voorburg over Westerneyn's appointment, only finally settled in favour of the Calvinist orthodox on 12 June 1666, and not least the furore over the *Philosophia*.

The *Philosophia* proved dynamite, the outcry provoked posing an immediate challenge, and perhaps threat, to Spinoza's circle as a group. The affair did not directly implicate Spinoza, but indirectly it involved Spinoza in several ways. Frustratingly for the consistories and universities, no one at all could be identified as the author, while the exceptional uproar arising from its making philosophy the "rule and guideline by which Holy Scripture must be studied and evaluated," as a Remonstrant critic put it,[3] drew an unremitting spotlight onto Spinoza and his group as prime suspected source of the blatantly anti-Scripturalist conspiracy it revealed. The unprecedented outcry left the whole *cercle Spinoziste* in an even more exposed, fraught position than earlier, rendered still more precarious the following year when the significantly expanded 137-page Dutch-language version followed up the original text, stoking additional outrage.[4] Again published clandestinely by Rieuwertsz, the Dutch version exemplified the group's drive for popular enlightenment, a campaign dear to the hearts of Meyer, Bouwmeester, and Adriaan and Johannes Koerbagh especially, conveying in the vernacular the most challenging new philosophical, scholarly, and scientific ideas, and providing further proof that whoever the principal author or authors were, the book undeniably reflected the goals of conspiring radical Cartesians, most likely Spinoza's "atheistic" movement.

Only much later, certainly by the 1680s, as Bayle reports in a letter of 1686,[5] was the *Philosophia* widely identified as the work "of a certain physician of Amsterdam" assumed (as still today) to be Lodewijk Meyer which, if correct, makes the *Philosophia* much his most provocative text, though the only evidence that it is (principally) his, rather than another of the group's freethinking physicians, or indeed several members of the group working together, derives from later reports, notably of Bayle, Benthem, Colerus, Rieuwertsz the Younger, and Leibniz.[6] Not that their striking agreement regarding his authorship should be set aside. In his *Theodicy* (1710), Leibniz is quite clear that it was "Lodewijk Meyer, a physician of Amsterdam," who anonymously published *Philosophia Scripturae*

---

[2] Spinoza, *Opera Posthuma*, 527; Spinoza, *Nagelate Schriften*, 580; Spinoza, *Correspondance* (ed. Rovere), 227; Spinoza, *Collected Works* (ed. Curley) ii, 32.
[3] Molinaeus, *Betoverde Werelt van D. Balthazar Bekker*, 16.
[4] Rice and Pastijn, "Introduction," 5; Akkerman, "Tractatus," 233–4.
[5] Bayle, *Correspondance* vi, 318–19.
[6] *Lettres sur la vie* [...] *de Wolzogue*, 4; Guhrauer, "Beiträge," 488; Nellen and Steenbakkers, "Biblical Philology," 49n107.

Interpres. Leibniz knew of the closeness of Meyer's collaboration with Spinoza and other allies at first hand having met Meyer during his visit to Holland, and he remained throughout noticeably more confident than most contemporaries that he did know who the author was, though in recent decades scholars have tended to agree that Bouwmeester and perhaps the Koerbaghs were substantially involved in composing the *Philosophia* too.[7]

Even assuming that the original Latin version did issue primarily from Meyer's pen, his closest friend, Bouwmeester, almost certainly contributed, and being a better Dutch stylist as well as accomplished Latinist, may well have had a hand too in the Dutch rendering, though according to what Stolle heard from the younger Rieuwertsz, the main translator was actually Glazemaker.[8] Vigorously suppressed by city and provincial authorities, the translation seems never to have been subsequently republished. The Latin version, however, exerted some impact internationally and reappeared in 1674, in a smaller octavo version, frequently bound together with Spinoza's *TTP*, a version seemingly imported in some quantity into England and Germany. By coupling the two texts, this 1674 edition reinforced the enduring impression abroad that Spinoza had authored both works. Johannes Musaeus (1613–81), for example, a Lutheran theologian at Jena who fiercely denounced the TTP in his *Tractatus Theologico-Politicus [...] Examinatus* (1674), emphasized what to him seemed parallels and like paradoxes linking the two texts, and in later editions of his book cites "Spinoza" as the author of the *TTP* and the *Philosophia*.[9]

Publishing the *Philosophia* anonymously was an inevitable precaution on Rieuwertsz's part; he was taking a considerable risk in any case. But its anonymity posed an enduring problem for the book's countless opponents and detractors, as well as Meyer and his allies, as speculation as to who the culprit was inevitably rebounded on those with whom he associated and even everyone vigorously championing Descartes in the Dutch context whenever, as with Van Velthuysen, they had antagonized Voetian preachers by seeking to free public debate from theological shackles. Whoever this "rationalistischer anti-Scriptuarius" was, as one German commentator styled the perpetrator of this universally vilified book, his work precipitated a commotion of uncommon significance in seventeenth-century theological debate, exposing deep divisions in Dutch culture and reverberating strongly in Protestant Germany and the Baltic.

The book infuriated but also threw into disarray a host of professional theologians and academics by claiming to be "following in Descartes' footsteps," presenting Descartes as the "first who after so many ages brought hidden truth to

---

[7] Leibniz, *Theodicy*, 82; Laerke, *Leibniz lecteur*, 281.

[8] In 2001, I mistakenly assumed Meyer translated the *Philosophia* into Dutch himself, see Israel, *Radical Enlightenment*, 200; but Stolle's notes indicate that Glazemaker was the main translator, see Freudenthal/Walther, *Lebensgeschichte* i, 94.

[9] Musaeus, *Tractatus [...] examinatus*, 1.

light out of the hideous gloom of dense darkness, renewing philosophy from its very foundations"—here echoing perhaps Lucretius' hailing of Epicurus. Not only did the *Philosophia* boldly jettison all traditional Catholic and Protestant Bible criticism in defiant fashion, but directly linked Descartes to this enterprise,[10] rendering the book impossible to ignore or else simply suppress. Outrageous though it seemed, it had to be powerfully countered, as Voetius' successor as leading spokesman of the strict Calvinist wing, Petrus van Mastricht (1630–1706), later acknowledged.[11] Perfectly aware of the boldness of their venture, the author (or authors) claimed to be bestowing a great benefit on society by putting a stop to the endless damaging theological disputes dividing Christendom and trapping men in a wretched state of doubt and confusion. It is essential to heal theology's rifts even though the remedy meant the entire overthrow of traditional theology in an even more sweeping sense than the group's Collegiant Socinian friends were urging.

Scripture, contends the anonymous author, is generally "obscure and doubtful," so that there is no way to interpret the Holy Books reliably other than by using reason and science, hence "philosophy," as one's principal tool. While on one level he is here reworking the old Averroist conundrum that religion is merely the common people's substitute for philosophy, quite unlike medieval philosophical subversives he announces outright to the public that all of Scripture is totally meaningless without the interpretive assistance of philosophy, a direct and radical departure from Averroist tradition in all its manifestations, whether Islamic, the late medieval Christian "double truth" approach, or the legacy of Maimonides, Gersonides, and Delmedigo. One great difficulty mercifully removed to everyone's benefit by this groundbreaking approach, claims the author, is the age-old pitfall of the Trinity. Theologians endlessly dispute the meaning of the Trinity, the "alderheylighste Drie-eenheydt [the most holy Trinity]," some considering it "a mystery, others a monstrous, heaped up farrago of all absurdities [quae apud quosdam theologos mysterium audit, apud alios monstrum omnium absurditatum farragine refertum]."[12] Theologically, says the author, the Trinity must forever remain irretrievably irresolvable and bitterly contested and thus will permanently damage all society. Is this church doctrine found in Scripture? So obscure is Scripture, the reader is told, that it is impossible say whether that doctrine is there or not. How then can the quandary be resolved? Thankfully, philosophy proves with all certainty that "one is not three," "that one and the same identical thing cannot be resurrected, that the world is eternal, and that a virgin cannot produce a child." In this way, philosophy rescues us from an eternal trap

---

[10] Meyer, *Philosophy as the Interpreter*, 24, 28.
[11] Mastricht, *Novitatum Cartesianarum Gangraena*, 104–48; Leydekker, *Verder Vervolg*, 6–7; Israel, *Radical Enlightenment*, 200; Kato, "Petrus van Mastricht," 135–6.
[12] [Meyer] *Philosophie d'Uytleghster*, 47; Bayle, *Correspondance* vi, 320.

by proving what the *Philosophia* is careful not to state too directly (as that would blatantly violate the laws forbidding denial of this dogma), namely that the Trinity is nonsense.[13] Those insisting that the doctrine of the Trinity is absurd were, of course, Meyer, Bouwmeester, and their Collegiant friends.[14]

The claims of theologians, if authoritative for most people being supposedly anchored in Scripture, are not really, readers needed to learn, anchored in Scripture at all, hence these are not just "obscure" but devoid of all validity wherever departing from sound philosophical premises. Thus, where theologians claim the Book of Genesis proves God created the universe from nothing, the relevant biblical passages being in fact unclear, cannot be made to unambiguously say the world was created by the Almighty from nothing. Theologically and among the people, the resulting impasse is thus again irresolvable and gravely damaging; happily, philosophy at once again rescues mankind from irresolvable difficulty, by proving "nothing comes from nothing." As "nothing can be made from nothing," philosophy proves there never was a Creation of the sort narrated in Scripture.[15] The correct reading of Genesis therefore is that God shaped the cosmos out of pre-existing matter. In effect, the indispensable tool for resolving all Scripture's obscurity, is what the *Philosophia* calls "true and certain knowledge of things" which it firmly equates with "Cartesianism."[16]

Yet, rhetorically at least, the *Philosophia* could hardly be accused of stepping beyond the bounds of Wittichius' principle, seconded by Van Velthuysen, that an "accurate and philosophical knowledge of natural things is not to be gathered from Scripture [cognitionem accuratam et philosophicam rerum naturalium ex sacris literis havriri non posse]."[17] Exploiting the well-known principle of leading Cartesians (now beginning to feel distinctly queasy), that "no conclusions of true philosophy are contrary to theology [Nullae verae philosophiae dogmata theologicis esse contraria]," the *Philosophia* cheerfully subsumes theology wholly into philosophy, subordinating the former to the latter in a manner no Averroist or Maimonidean could condone,[18] diverging here from Spinoza and the Koerbaghs seemingly as regards one sole point—pronouncing Scripture indeed the infallible word of God,[19] a rhetorical tactic which no one can have believed sincere, since no point of traditional Christian theology is left in any way intact. Far from adhering to the Averroist and Maimonidean principle that neither the truths demonstrated

---

[13] [Meyer], *Philosophie d'Uytleghster*, 70–1; Wilson, *Scriptures Genuine Interpreter*, 147–9; Curley, "Notes," 78; Lagrée, "Louis Meyer," 39–40; Bordoli, *Ragione e scrittura*, 155.

[14] [Meyer], *Philosophie d'Uytleghster*, 56–7; Wilson, *Scriptures Genuine Interpreter*, 126–9; Lagrée, "Louis Meyer," 39.

[15] [Meyer], *Philosophie d'Uytleghster*, 59; Andala, *Cartesius verus*, 10.

[16] [Meyer], *Philosophie d'Uytleghster*, 37, 52–3, 126.

[17] Wittichius, *Consensus veritatis*, 15; Velthuysen, *Bewys*, "Voor-Reden"; Kato, "Petrus van Mastricht," 134.

[18] Fraenkel, "Reconsidering the Case," 218, 235; Fraenkel, *Philosophical Religions*, 169.

[19] [Meyer], *Philosophie d'Uytleghster*, 57; Laerke, *Leibniz lecteur*, 284–5.

by philosophy nor the parables and poetic images religion utilizes to interpret them should ever be divulged to the public, the *Philosophia* urges that philosophical truth be thoroughly divulged to everyone as soon as possible.

Given mankind's perennial inability to interpret Scripture correctly, after millennia of ceaseless hatred and wrangling, all men should rejoice in Cartesian philosophy coming to our aid, finally bringing closure to the strife, instability, and slaughter perpetrated everywhere by religious conflict, culminating in the horrors of the Thirty Years War.[20] New Testament passages like Paul's Letter to the Corinthians where philosophy and philosophers appear to be slighted by Jesus and the Apostles, and which theologians invoke to extol theology's primacy, are easily explained away, holds the *Philosophia*, citing Clement of Alexandria's stricture that Scripture condemns not Greek philosophers who were truly wise but only "those who appear wise to themselves."[21] It is not "true philosophy" that Paul condemns, explains Meyer, only the thoroughly unhelpful irrational fantasies of Platonists, Epicureans, Aristotelians, Stoics, and Sophists.[22]

Divisions in society are healed by establishing a reliable correlation between true philosophy and "correct" theology setting out the truths which require careful sifting from the trash of what generally passes for "theology" and its false truths: "and thus we say that everything true or false in theology is true or false also in the true philosophy, and, conversely, everything true or false in true philosophy is likewise true or false in theology; and whatever in the one is true, can never be false in the other" but both fully converge albeit with philosophy always remaining the measure, precisely the principle Spinoza taught his study group in his early writings.[23] Meyer and Bouwmeester had clearly taken to heart what Spinoza says in the appendix to his Descartes book, the *Cogitata Metaphysica*: "it is sufficient for us to demonstrate those things clearly" which we can grasp most definitely by natural reason "to know that Sacred Scripture must also teach the same things."[24]

At first glance, the *Philosophia*'s claim that Scripture states infallible divine truth but is obscure, and Spinoza's pronouncing Scripture humanly crafted, corrupt, and often devoid of the truth except in the moral sphere, appear very different. But both equally insist that Scripture is not concerned with representing the truth. The sacred books are "obscure" and difficult, holds the *Philosophia*, because the Bible seeks to assist man's salvation with narratives and stories that everyone can follow, showing men the path, enhancing our moral consciousness especially when resorting to philosophy for the real meaning. Scripture cannot put

---

[20] Moreau, "Principes," 120; Nellen and Steenbakkers, "Biblical Philology," 50.
[21] [Meyer], *Philosophie d'Uytleghster*, 60.
[22] [Meyer], *Philosophie d'Uytleghster*, 68; [Meyer], *Philosophia*, 56-7; Klever, *Mannen rond Spinoza*, 74.
[23] [Meyer] *Philosophie d'Uytleghster*, 69; Preus, *Spinoza*, 56, 60, 65.
[24] Spinoza, *Collected Works* (ed. Curley) i, 331; Fraenkel, "Could Spinoza Have Presented," 3.

"the truth in our minds or render it clearer or more distinct or confirm it; but, as we have said before, its function is to provide occasion and material for thought, making us think about things about which we would perhaps never otherwise have reflected." Only when understanding Scripture's goal is to elevate men to the "highest blessedness" do we grasp how the Bible conduces to men's "good beyond all else, except not as regards teaching the truth." It is as a moral prop, providing crutches for the unknowing, unphilosophical multitude, that the Bible's utility "is greatest, far surpassing the utility of other books."[25]

Unfortunately, no evidence has survived of discussion about the book among the *cercle Spinoziste* either before or after publication aside from several remarks in the *Philosophia* itself pointing to such discussions. Among these is a curious reference, obviously indebted to Spinoza rather than Bouwmeester or any other of the study group, in connection with Meyer's question: "how can one know what is said in Scripture literally, what figuratively and what allegorically? How can one know what sense is false" given that this infallible text contains so many discrepancies, contradictions, and obscure statements? In a fairly long adjoining passage, Meyer castigates an unnamed commentator who answers this question by saying: "When Scripture in a given passage delivers a clear and definite teaching, that is dogmatizes," it should be interpreted "strictly and literally" and where it speaks incidentally and more haphazardly appearing to contradict such teachings, it should be construed figuratively and in agreement with what it appears to contradict. This is clearly parallel to the passage in Spinoza's *TTP* where Spinoza criticizes Judah al-Fakhar, a Jewish physician of early thirteenth-century Toledo who fiercely opposed Maimonides' Aristotelian rationalism for holding precisely this view, an insight Meyer assuredly borrowed from Spinoza himself rather than any other member of the *cercle*.[26]

The *Philosophia*'s preparation doubtless occurred primarily in Amsterdam with Spinoza himself more than marginally involved,[27] especially regarding passages where Hebrew expertise was requisite, and his views on Bible hermeneutics were most respected. In 1666, Meyer and the others participating in the *Philosophia*'s composition and the furious controversy that followed, still conceived of Spinoza's project as essentially the perfection and completion of the great reform project of Descartes. Very likely the few differences between Meyer and Spinoza in the sphere of Bible criticism—and eventually also concerning Descartes—were aired among them tentatively in private. For these strands of disagreement were afterwards set out in print, albeit without mentioning any names, in the *TTP*, on which Spinoza was already working when the *Philosophia* appeared. In the *TTP* the

---

[25] [Meyer], *Philosophy as the Interpreter*, 239.
[26] Spinoza, *Theological-Political Treatise*, 187–90; [Meyer], *Philosophy as the Interpreter*, 170–1; Fraenkel, "Could Spinoza Have Presented," 45.
[27] Fraenkel, "Could Spinoza Have Presented," 41, 45; Lavaert, *Vrijheid, glelijkheid, veelheid*, 142.

Philosophia is alluded to extensively, if obliquely, albeit without drawing much attention to these relatively minor disagreements. The divergences between Meyer and Spinoza must have been discussed behind the scenes already well before 1665–6.[28]

19.ii The Revolt of Johannes and Adriaan Koerbagh

The furore over the *Philosophia* formed a key part of the immediate background to Spinoza's *TTP* and also of a second powerful offensive campaign on the part of the *cercle Spinoziste*—the astoundingly bold attack on common belief mounted by the Brothers Koerbagh. By the mid-1660s there was an entire circle of allies and disciples associated with Spinoza on various levels, committed to the proposition that philosophical reason should displace theology and what men believe and that a new subversive intellectual activism was requisite to sap the common's people's trust in theology, churchmen, and revealed religion to expand the sphere of reason and philosophy for the benefit of all, in particular by dampening down the ideological conflict threatening the Republic's political, social, and ideological stability.

The circle envisaged Spinoza as having in some sense completed Descartes' achievement (and that of Hobbes) in philosophy and mathematical reasoning, and penetrated beyond, especially by replacing theology with a more convincing philosophical conception of God and his creation. Just before or just after the *Philosophia* appeared, both Brothers Koerbagh were cited by the Amsterdam Reformed consistory, in June 1666, for exerting an unacceptably malign influence locally, in Amsterdam by spreading their views among local folk—and in Adriaan's case also for cohabiting with a girl out of wedlock and fathering an illegitimate child—accusations linked to reports of their denying Christ's divinity in discussion with others linked to a formal complaint about a recent Collegiant gathering at which Socinian views, in violation of the law, had been openly proclaimed.[29]

A preacher expert in combating Socinians and Socinianism, Petrus Leupenius (1607–70), was duly dispatched to the Koerbaghs' home, on the Amsterdam Singel, to investigate on behalf of the consistory, and during July 1666, Johannes, a long-term theology student who spent ten years studying at Utrecht, Leiden, and Groningen, was interrogated about five key points of doctrine. Since Johannes was a "proponent" (candidate), for the Dutch Reformed ministry, the "inquisitorial" investigation at this stage focused far more on him than his physician brother, Adriaan. Asked his views about Christ's divinity and

---

[28] Steenbakkers, "Spinoza in the History," 320; Lavaert, *Vrijheid, glelijkheid, veelheid*, 82, 170, 178.
[29] GA Amsterdam MS 376/ll Acta Kerkeraad, res. 10 June 1666; Leeuwenburgh, *Het Noodlot*, 136–7.

about heaven, he answered that the doctrine of the Trinity is neither found in Scripture nor can be "demonstrated through clear and distinct reasoning," so that veneration of the man Jesus as if he is divine is sheer "superstition."[30] The notions of "heaven" and "hell" as taught by the churches Johannes also rejected outright, these terms referring in his view merely to states of mind in this world, blessed or wretched—which was precisely Spinoza's standpoint.[31] Asked about his views on the status of Scripture, Koerbagh answered that the biblical books were composed by God-fearing men at different times to the best of their abilities. When asked what that meant, he refused to elaborate.

Disturbed by these answers, later that same July the Amsterdam Reformed consistory assigned a second preacher, Dr Langelius, to interview Johannes. What did Koerbagh mean by calling God an "eenich weesen" [single being]. As God is infinite, replied Johannes, here displaying evident familiarity with Spinoza's unpublished manuscripts, there cannot be any being or anything apart from God, so that "all created things are not beings but modifications or modes of being, limited or extended by rest and motion."[32] Asked to explain his views on Creation, Koerbagh responded that "nothing was created out of nothing and cannot be so created," and every true concept of God shows that He is identical to His Creation, replies that left Langelius and his colleagues perplexed and appalled. On being rebuked for such blasphemous sentiments, Langelius afterwards reported, the young man suddenly grew contrite and submissive, (seemingly) acquiescing when assured God is distinct from His Creation and did "create the universe from nothing." Finally, he ostensibly "admitted" after all, that the Reformed Church's doctrine is the truth and that assuredly "Deus esse triunum [God is three in one]."[33]

By 1666, Johannes' views closely paralleled those of Spinoza and the entire *cercle*, but when all this was reported to the consistory verbatim, nothing specifying such a connection was recorded in the minutes. From Johannes' choice of words, it is clear, though, that he had embraced, or been converted to, a creed drawing its central arguments and way of reasoning from Spinoza and not from Hobbes, even though reading Hobbes did play some part (how much remains disputed) in his and his brother's "conversion" to clandestine philosophical reason as the key to totally reforming society.[34] In 1660 (with Spinoza still in the city),

---

[30] GA Amsterdam MS 376/ll. Johannes Koerbagh, "Korte doch Oprechte Antwoord," p. 235; see also, Koerbagh, *A Light Shining*, 83–97, 230–1; Van Heertum, "Reading the Career of Johannes Koerbagh," 3, 10, 36.

[31] GA Amsterdam MS 376/ll. Johannes Koerbagh, "Korte doch Oprechte Antwoord," p. 235; Meinsma, *Spinoza et son cercle*, 341; Meinsma was the first modern author to point out Johannes' important role.

[32] GA Amsterdam MS 376/ll, p. 236, "Naerder Onderhandelingen," 27 July 1666; Weekhout, *Boekencensuur*, 103; Van Bunge, "Introduction," 18; Klever, *Een nieuwe Spinoza*, 54–5.

[33] GA Amsterdam MS 376/ll, p. 236, "Naerder Onderhandelingen," 27 July 1666; Wielema, *March of the Libertines*, 85–6; Leeuwenburgh, *Het Noodlot*, 139; Van Bunge, *From Stevin to Spinoza*, 103.

[34] Weekhout, *Boekencensuur*, 103; Lavaert, "An Excellent Mathematician," 261, 271.

Johannes passed his candidate's examination before the Reformed classis of Amsterdam, enrolling as a trainee candidate to become a preacher of the public church which involved signing the required formula of confession committing to the official creed of the Reformed Church.

Johannes' familiarity with Spinoza and his ideas may date from the 1657–8 period in Leiden, from the end of the 1650s in Amsterdam, or perhaps more likely from a slightly later stage, after returning to Leiden to continue his studies, in 1662. According to two later radical writers, Hadrian Beverland and Willem Goeree, both brothers originally imbibed their "atheistic" ideas from Van den Enden's circle in Amsterdam, in the early 1660s, and other evidence supports this.[35] On departing Leiden for Groningen, in September 1659, Johannes had studied under the prominent Huguenot theologian Samuel Maresius (Desmarets) (1599–1673) while Adriaan pursued his medical studies in Leiden where his closest friends were Meyer, Bouwmeester, Van Berkel, and his cousin, another physician, Jacob Vallan (1637–1720). Vallan, Stolle learnt many years later from the younger Rieuwertsz, was another "sonderbahrer Freund" [special friend] of Spinoza.[36]

It was probably during the years 1661–3 when Spinoza lived in Rijnsburg and was frequenting Leiden, then, that Adriaan had the opportunity to confer with Spinoza several times, discussion he would later admit to when interrogated about this, in 1668.[37] Johannes' conversion to a Spinozist outlook most likely occurred after he returned from Groningen to complete his theological studies at Leiden, hence also from around 1662–3,[38] a juncture when Adriaan had contacts in addition, he later admitted, with Van den Enden. Given that Maresius was a strict Calvinist and prolific polemicist against Socinians and Arminians as well as Catholics, and that Johannes' Groningen dissertation was prepared under Maresius' direction, appearing in 1663, it seems unlikely there can have been anything seriously suspect about Johannes' person or reputation much before his return from Groningen.[39] In any case, together with his older brother to whom he remained very close, Johannes was drawn into the circle around Meyer and Bouwmeester, both of whom—later reports stress the primacy here of Bouwmeester—reinforced Spinoza's philosophy in the brothers' company prior to all of them, except Spinoza, returning to Amsterdam in the mid-1660s.

Johannes thus probably converted to his militantly anti-Christian new philosophical outlook around 1663, a relatively short time before the *Philosophia*'s

---

[35] Beverland, *De Peccato originali*, 110; Goeree, *Kerklyke en Weereldlyke*, 665; Wielema, "Adriaan Koerbagh," 571; Laurens, *De rede: bron van geluk*, 26.
[36] Mertens, "Spinoza's Amsterdamse vriendenkring," 73–4.
[37] Jongeneelen, "Philosophie politique," 252; Hubbeling, "Zur frühen Spinozarezeption," 153.
[38] Israel, *Radical Enlightenment*, 186.
[39] Van Heertum, "Reading the Career of Johannes Koerbagh," 1, 12, 34.

appearance in 1666.[40] After 1666, Johannes did not desist from instilling his "blasphemous" ideas into the minds of others and was summoned twice more to face further interrogation, in January 1668.[41] Though essentially an anti-Christian text, the two brothers' aborted book, *A Light Shining in Dark Places* (1668), also showed they were vigorously pro-Socinian in the sense of maintaining that that particular current alone among the churches was free from impure and deceitful theological fabrications not found in Scripture such as belief in Christ's divinity: "only the Socinians are completely purified" of the principal fallacies corrupting all the main churches "so that this sect may rightly be called restored or purified religion."[42] Still, the brothers were definitely post-Socinian in their conceptions of God and Creation and in their naturalism. The public controversy over the *Philosophia* thus coloured the immediate background to the Koerbagh Brothers' bold project no less than Spinoza's.

Meyer (or the joint authors of the *Philosophia*) were thus the first of the circle to provoke a major public controversy but did so as close allies tightly linked ideologically to both Spinoza and the Koerbaghs. But while all these four sought to dissolve theology entirely into philosophy, their respective approaches to Bible hermeneutics as well as Descartes' doctrine of the will did diverge in some interesting secondary respects. They all conceived the Bible to be a purely human text in which there is no sacred, miraculous, or divine intervention, and all were convinced that only philosophy and natural science teach men what is true. But they applied the principle of reason to Scriptural studies in different ways. In 1670, the *TTP* resumed the unresolved debate between them in a masked fashion, without explicit reference to either Meyer's book, or the 1666 controversy. Where Spinoza offers an elaborate theory of what revealed religion and Scriptural prophecy is, and how and why the Israelite authors of the Old Testament construed the world as they did, consolidating his new science of contextual Bible criticism based on the distinction between the "true meaning" of passages and expression, and "truth" as the reality of things, without expecting to find philosophical truth in Scriptural language and notions, the *Philosophia* shows little interest in reconstructing the "true meaning" of Scripture, or in historical context, and little grasp of the many philological issues Spinoza raises, despite Meyer being an acknowledged expert in terminology and theory of grammar. In this respect the Koerbaghs stood closer to Spinoza, taking a more serious interest than Meyer in etymology and the precise meaning of key Hebrew terms. Although for Spinoza, the Koerbaghs, and the *Philosophia* alike, the Bible is not a guide to universal or general reality but a means of prodding ignorant and superstitious folk to obey moral injunctions, and for Spinoza and the brothers Scripture does

---

[40] GA Amsterdam MS 376/ii, p. 353. Acta Kerkeraad, res. 5 Jan. 1668.
[41] GA Amsterdam MS 376/ii, pp. 361, 364–5. Acta Kerkeraad res. 19 and 26 June 1668.
[42] Koerbagh, *Een Ligt*, 322–3; Lavaert, "An Excellent Mathematician," 265.

exhibit an inner core of vaguely perceived truth that needs aligning to the reality of things as shown by Spinoza, the *Philosophia* differs in asserting that Scripture *is* "divine revelation" and that its assertions ultimately possess a more precise philosophical meaning via careful "Cartesian" parsing.[43]

Still, insisting on Scripture's obscurity, Meyer speaks much like the other three of approximations to "truth" and highly inaccurate and obscure but helpfully picturesque allegories useful and relevant only in some very vague, remote, and indirect sense when properly aligned with philosophical truth. "From this it follows most evidently," holds the *Philosophia*, "that all expositions of Scripture opposed to truth are also opposed to its true meaning and are therefore false, unauthentic, spurious and should be banished far from the mind of God."[44] Following the *TTP*'s appearance, in 1670, discerning readers, like Van Velthuysen, quickly realized, as have several modern scholars, that without saying so explicitly, Spinoza is resuming the 1666 debate over the *Philosophia* while skirting around the furore surrounding it, with a carefully veiled critique rejecting only that element of Meyer's position that was rhetorical imposture, namely his contention that Scripture *is* divine revelation and *is* "infallible."[45] Here, the Koerbaghs tended to follow Spinoza rather than Meyer.

19.iii The *Philosophia* and the Reformed Church

Spinoza, the Koerbaghs, Bouwmeester, Van Berkel, and the rest, as well as Meyer, were all deeply immersed in the controversy over the *Philosophia* and sought to learn appropriate lessons from the noisy affray and its ramifications. On 24 July 1666, while Johannes Koerbagh was under interrogation in Amsterdam, the local Haarlem church council, debating the problem of "licentious books," identified the *Philosophia* as the most pernicious volume then on sale and being discussed in their city. Extracts were read out by the council's *visitadores librorum* and a resolution taken to urgently alert all the Reformed consistories and Holland city councils to the abominable "godlessness and blasphemy" of that book and bring it before the next gathering of the North Holland synod.[46] At Leiden, the book was formally condemned by Wittichius and Cocceius in the name of the theology faculty. Friesland's theologians appealed to the States of Friesland's standing committee which took immediate steps under a decree dated 10 November 1666, to suppress the *Philosophia* in their province, including Franeker University, as a

---

[43] Walther, "Biblische Hermeneutik" (1995), 274–5; Lagrée, "Sens et vérité," 84–7; Touber, *Spinoza and Biblical Philology*, 38–9.
[44] Meyer, *Philosophy as the Interpreter*, 93–4.
[45] Laerke, *Leibniz lecteur*, 282; Lavaert, *Vrijheid, gelijkheid, veelheid*, 179, 202.
[46] GA Haarlem, Reformed Classis Haarlem vii, Acta classis res. 24 July 1666.

blasphemous plunging of the "sacred Word of God into doubt," threatening booksellers who stocked and sold it with heavy fines.[47]

At Utrecht, the Reformed consistory petitioned the city burgomasters to halt sales of the book in their province "as the States of Friesland have done in such praiseworthy fashion."[48] The States of Utrecht promptly followed Friesland's "praiseworthy example," instructing the magistracies in their province to seize all copies they could find and, "since the book violates the placards of the States General and this province against all Socinian and similar writings," prevent the book's sale, the Utrecht city burgomasters endorsing the province-wide ban on 31 December 1666.[49] Also at Utrecht, an official investigation was launched to try to unmask who the anonymous author of this abominable text was. The chief suspect, initially, was the Voetians' local bugbear, the regent Lambert van Velthuysen (1622–85), a champion of the Cartesian cause much reviled by the Calvinist orthodox, a prominent figure keenly interested in all disputes involving Reformed preachers. Van Velthuysen was soon cleared, though, leaving suspicion to focus elsewhere, including on Spinoza; but to the exasperation of the synods all efforts to uncover the perpetrator of this uniquely challenging book proved fruitless.

Because the *Philosophia*'s arguments were fiercely attacked and labelled "Cartesian" by a whole phalanx of Voetian academic authorities—Koelman, Essenius, Nethenus, and Vogelsang[50]—this furore proved a major factor in further inflaming the quarrel between Cartesians and anti-Cartesians within the Reformed Church and in the Dutch universities and Lower Rhine Reformed universities (Duisburg and Herborn). Meanwhile, the controversy further stoked also other deeply rooted inter-church quarrels long in progress, generating an across-the-board uproar over the place of "reason" in theology and Bible criticism, the true principles of Bible hermeneutics, the status of philosophy and which groups in which churches were chiefly responsible for philosophy's escalating intrusion.

Magistrates and synods alike regularly tarred the *Philosophia* as illustrative of "Socinian" subversion of Christianity and the main churches. Yet, some of the fiercest reaction, it soon emerged, stemmed precisely from among the Socinian segment of the Collegiant community where Spinoza, Meyer, Rieuwertsz, and the Koerbaghs had numerous friends and acquaintances. Where the *Philosophia* treats the public church with unremitting hostility, using philosophical arguments that "stormed and devastated" its "fortresses" like a conquering army,[51] it shows far more respect for the unchurched anti-Trinitarian fringe. Yet, while summoning the

---

[47] Knuttel, *Verboden boeken*, 117; Meyer, *Philosophy as the Interpreter*, appendix 4.
[48] GA Utrecht Acta Kerkeraad viii, res. 24 Dec. and 31 Dec. 1666.
[49] GA Utrecht Acta Kerkeraad viii, res. 14 January, 4 February, and 18 March 1667.
[50] Israel, *Radical Enlightenment*, 202–8; Goudriaan, *Reformed Orthodoxy*, 50.
[51] [Meyer], *Philosophie d'Uytleghster*, 113.

Collegiants to join the philosophers as allies and fight together against their common foes, the Calvinists, Catholics, and Lutherans, the *Philosophia* also carefully distinguishes its philosophical stance from Socinian theology, indeed berates the Socinians for their unwillingness to interpret Scripture altogether in accord with "reason." Whenever they encounter difficulties of biblical interpretation, complains the *Philosophia*, instead of turning to philosophy to remove all difficulty, Socinians invoke the Holy Ghost to assist and enlighten them with the result that they too continually slide into a mire of confusion and theological strife (as was undeniable) entirely of their own making.

There is no such thing as divine inspiration or "inner light," holds the *Philosophia*, distinct from the "natural light of reason" that can assist Collegiants or Christians of whatever stripe in investigating Scripture, though, as some contemporaries noted, the *Philosophia* (unlike Spinoza) does not claim Scripture is a purely human document or claim that it is not divine revelation. What Socinians and such Remonstrants who truly venerate Episcopius' principles of toleration should do, urges the *Philosophia*, is follow its call and proclaim philosophy the sole, exclusive, and "infallible measure" of Scripture.[52] Collegiants had been battling for years to preserve their own unity in the face of internal wrangling over the Trinity, possessing few means to circumvent the mounting quarrels within their own ranks between their rationalizing, avowedly Socinian wing, and the more conservative tendency retaining the Trinity and traditional Christology in some fashion. With Collegiant Trinitarians angrily rejecting the *Philosophia*'s summons and Socinians regarding it more sympathetically but with reservations, the furore could only further exacerbate the Collegiants' internal divisions as well as embitter further relations between Collegiants and Mennonites, Collegiants and Remonstrants, and Collegiants and the Reformed Church.

Among the *Philosophia*'s prime opponents was Jan Pietersz Beelthouwer (*c.*1603–*c.*1669), a former member of the Reformed congregation of Enkhuizen where, in the 1640s he had earned his bread as a *ziekentrooster* [visitor to the sick]. Expelled from Enkhuizen at the Reformed consistory's demand owing to his Socinian views, in February 1656, Beelthouwer had sought refuge in Amsterdam, his great passion being to convert Jews, deists, Epicureans and others to Christianity by proving the Old Testament truly announces the coming of Christ as the Messiah. Acquiring some Hebrew, besides Latin and Greek, he had already, on earlier visits, entered into discussions with Menasseh, Leon Templo, and other Jews as well as Spinoza. By 1661, his writings indicate, he had learnt to admire Spinoza's philosophical views, and what he assumed were Spinoza's as yet still generally unknown hermeneutical principles. While railing against Meyer,

---

[52] [Meyer], *Philosophie d'Uytleghster*, 119–26; *Lettres sur la vie* [...] *de Wolzogue*, 43–5; Klever, *Mannen rond Spinoza*, 78.

three years before the *TTP*'s publication, in 1667, he not only praises Spinoza while condemning the anonymous author, supposing them to be at odds with each other, but, remarkably, ranges Spinoza against the claim that biblical prophecies are unclear and ambiguous. He denounced especially the contention that the divine spirit does not guide us in rightly interpreting Scripture. That Beelthouwer thought it helpful in his widely read Dutch text to invoke Spinoza with whom, he tells us, he had had discussions, when arguing that the Old Testament Prophetic Books had remained largely uncorrupted and are God's word, proves how discreetly and respectfully Spinoza had proceeded in the mid and late 1650s when acquiring his reputation in Collegiant circles as an expert in Bible exegesis.[53]

Serrarius, another leading Collegiant Trinitarian anti-Socinian who knew the anonymous author (or authors) and certainly connected the *Philosophia* to the radical Cartesian group around Spinoza, Van den Enden, Meyer, and the Koerbaghs, being one of those most connected with Spinoza over the years, also intervened in the controversy. A stalwart Millenarian, like his friend, the great Czech Millenarian Comenius, whose own brief refutation of the *Philosophia* is appended to Serrarius' text, Serrarius felt profoundly disconcerted by this book which, he nevertheless acknowledged, no less than Leibniz later, to be of profound significance.[54] Besides Comenius, he communicated his dismay to colleagues elsewhere in Europe with whom he was in regular contact, notably the anti-Cartesian Millenarian John Dury (1596–1680), a Leiden-educated Scottish Presbyterian and close friend, based in Switzerland at Basel, and Johann Heinrich Heidegger (1633–98), a leading Hebraist and Bible exegete at Zurich who became the chief Swiss commentator on the alarmingly dangerous new "philosophical" sect arising in the Netherlands.

Seeking to combat not just the *Philosophia* but the entire effort to enthrone philosophy in place of divine inspiration and the Holy Ghost, Serrarius dresses his admonitions in resounding biblical and Millenarian imagery, affirming the limitations of the new Cartesian philosophy and especially the radical dissenters espousing it, and the wrongheadedness of their challenge to the truths of revealed religion. Serrarius, like Comenius, grants Descartes' excellence in mathematics and physics, and even metaphysics, but rejects all notion that his purely mechanistic conception of the world and the physical laws of nature are the key to deciphering all truth physical and spiritual. To his mind, the *Philosophia* was far from successful in unravelling the perplexing passages of Scripture whose author is God.[55] Whatever Meyer, Van den Enden, Spinoza, and their radical Cartesian coterie maintained, Scripture's true meaning is grasped only via the "inner light"

---

[53] Beelthouwer, *Antwoordt*, 21–3, 127; Van Bunge, *Johannes Bredenburg*, 185; Bordoli, *Ragione e scrittura*, 246–56; Israel, *Radical Enlightenment*, 204.
[54] Van der Wall, *Mystieke Chiliast*, 468–72; Bordoli, *Ragione e scrittura*, 265.
[55] Serrarius, *Responsio*, 14; Van der Wall, *Mystieke Chiliast*, 475; Rice and Pastijn, "Introduction," 12–13.

aided by the "Holy Ghost." To infuse philosophy with divine wisdom and fail to separate "natural light from the divine light, what is innate in man from what is received from God," amounts to idolatry, he admonished: for whoever chooses that path in effect places philosophy above Christ, and than that nothing is more wicked and blasphemous.[56]

Commenting on the anonymity of the author, and clandestine character of the radical Cartesian sect generally, Serrarius compared their reformed Cartesianism to the adulterous woman in Proverbs 7 who dares not reveal herself in broad daylight (construing the latter as the blessed age of the early church). Only now, as dusk falls, in our corrupt era preceding the Second Coming and the age of justice, does philosophy venture out superficially alluring, like the harlot she is, tempting men to perdition. For who does not love philosophy, the love of wisdom, when kept within her proper sphere? But when she ventures forth beyond her proper bounds no whore is more brazen than philosophy. She had seduced the writer of the *Philosophia* who runs after her like an ox to the slaughterhouse. Has she not lured him from the family of the Lamb of God (like Van den Enden) to bow down before the new Golden Calf of reason?[57]

19.iv The Utrecht *Collegie der Sçavanten*

The uproar intensified further, Leibniz later noted, with the publication, in November 1667, of the 274-page systematic refutation of the *Philosophia* by the liberal Calvinist theologian, Louis Wolzogen (1633–90), professor of theology at Utrecht since 1662, and someone who had known Descartes in person as a twenty-year-old. This work, *De Scripturarum Interprete*, a copy of which was listed in Spinoza's library after his death, later reappeared also in English and became pivotal to the entire controversy, as both Leibniz and Bayle later observed, by further widening the split in Reformed ranks.[58] Belonging to the Cartesian group of academics at Utrecht led by Van Velthuysen, Mansvelt, Graevius, and Frans Burman, Wolzogen enjoyed a position of influence among the anti-Orangist faction of the Utrecht city government and had much to lose should he fall victim to censure by the Calvinist orthodox.

Though of Austrian Protestant origin, Wolzogen had acquired excellent French studying at Saumur and Geneva, and long been a preacher to the French-speaking Walloon churches at Groningen, then Middelburg and, since 1664, at Utrecht where he doubled as a university theologian. Quite apart from his Cartesian and

---

[56] Fix, *Prophecy and Reason*, 173; Bordoli, *Ragione e scrittura*, 265; Israel, *Radical Enlightenment*, 204–5.
[57] Serrarius, *Responsio*, 55; Van der Wall, *Mystieke Chiliast*, 475–83.
[58] Israel, *Radical Enlightenment*, 205–8; on Spinoza's copy, see Offenberg, "Spinoza's Library," 321.

Cocceian views, strict Calvinists disapproved of him due to what they considered his inappropriately elegant lifestyle, especially his much remarked on powdered wig and liking for card games, features hardly befitting the Calvinist austerity expected of professors.[59] His abiding interest in libertine, heterodox, and Spinozist thought became conspicuous only later when his personal library was auctioned off after his death, its contents including Spinoza's *Opera Posthuma*, La Peyrère's *Praeadamitae* and works of De La Court, Beverland, Bekker, Van Dale, and Aubert de Versé.[60]

Wolzogen, complained his critics, was insufficiently robust in rejecting the *Philosophia*'s arguments. Rumoured to know who the "physician of Amsterdam" responsible for the *Philosophia* was, and be familiar with him, Wolzogen was additionally censured for refusing to disclose his identity. Opponents within the Reformed Church avidly seized on this as a stick with which to beat this too independent-minded churchman accused of subtly colluding with what Leibniz termed "un hérétique libertin." "Herr Vogelsang, Herr van der Waeyen, and some other anti-Cocceians also assailed his book amidst much acrimony," added Leibniz, "though the accused [i.e. Wolzogen] won his case in a synod,"[61] that is, in the end was not formally condemned by his own church. Reinerus Vogelsang (1610–79), a theology professor at 's-Hergtogenbosch (Sylva ducensis) whose refutation of the *Philosophia*, entitled *Contra libellum, cui titulus, Philosophia S. Scripturae Interpres*, appeared at Utrecht in 1669, furiously decried the anonymous author's trespassing beyond Descartes' own firm red line, violating the Cartesians' rule that Cartesian principles should never encroach on *Verbum Dei* [the word of God].[62] It was entirely contrary to authentic Cartesian principles to apply rational criteria, as the *Philosophia* does, to the sphere of the divine, spiritual and supernatural. Vogelsang and others were certainly justified in holding that the *Philosophia*'s anonymous author, by applying Descartes' notion of "clear and distinct ideas," that is mathematically precise reasoning, to matters of doctrine and faith, revealed himself to be a thoroughly deviant Cartesian as well as a religious heretic, propagating what Maresius termed "immoderate Cartesianism."[63]

Wolzogen was bitterly attacked for his less than wholehearted condemnation of the *Philosophia* also by the austere purist Jean de Labadie (1610–74), a former Jesuit who had defected from Catholicism, in 1650, joining the strict Calvinists and who now lambasted Wolzogen's widely read retort to the *Philosophia*. Denouncing "the book of Herr von Wolzogen," as perfectly pernicious, observes Leibniz, De Labadie claimed it reflected the compromises and abuses infiltrating and corrupting the Reformed Church itself which now, however, declined to

---

[59] Thijssen-Schoute, *Nederlands Cartesianisme*, 444–7; Kolakowski, *Chrétiens sans église*, 750.
[60] [Wolzogen], *Catalogus*, 11–12, 19–20, 30.
[61] *Lettres sur la vie [...] de Wolzogue*, 45; Leibniz, *Theodicy*, 82–3.
[62] Rice and Pastijn, "Introduction," 15; Bayle, *Correspondance* vi, 320.
[63] Rice and Pastijn, "Introduction," 11; Laerke, *Leibniz lecteur*, 284.

condemn him, a synodal judgement he refused to accept. Accusing the Reformed of retreating before heresy, not least by refusing to condemn Wolzogen outright, he now defected from the public church to found his own austere sect fusing Reformed Pietism with Jansenism. The Voetian faction of the Reformed having earlier eagerly endorsed De Labadie now, in 1669, furiously repudiated him as did the Utrecht city government.[64]

The widening furore over the *Philosophia* was bound to render Spinoza's own fraught relationship with the Cartesians, and the Utrecht *Collegie der Sçavanten* specifically, more precarious than it was already ever since publication of his book on Descartes, in 1663. The local academic Cartesian clique at Utrecht, however staunchly opposed to the hard-core strict Calvinists who besides being also strongly entrenched within the University, commanded much broader Calvinist support outside, needed to tread carefully. Burman, leading the way in coupling Cocceian theology with a Cartesian approach to natural knowledge, had pulled them into a seemingly endless two-front war with the Voetians that was both theological and philosophical. Attempting to reconcile Scripture with Galileo's proofs that the Earth revolves around the sun, Burman (who later himself came to be suspected by some of "Spinozist" tendencies), argued that Scripture often employs phrases borrowed from popular usage "when speaking about natural things," and where, seemingly, "Scripture speaks against the Earth revolving around the Sun," it uses "common language which is not appropriate for expressing the precise truth of things."[65] Precisely this was the view of Wittichius too. The difficulty was that this embarrassingly resembled what the *Philosophia* also contended, even if Meyer and Spinoza applied the principle more broadly.

Burman, Van Velthuysen, and their group rejected Voetian claims that validating Copernicus and Galileo is contrary to Scripture. Where Voetians subordinated everything to a strict reading of Scripture, Cocceius, Burman, Wittichius, Graevius, and their following deployed an elaborate philology opening the door to Cartesian reconciliation with theology by distancing theology in some degree from natural knowledge. The clash between the Voetian hardcore Calvinists and Utrecht Cartesio-Cocceians had already noticeably intensified since January 1665 following Graevius' oration and then pamphlet *De Cometis* [Concerning Comets], written "against the ordinary person's opinion that comets announce disasters." Born in the electorate of Saxony at Naumburg (where Nietzsche later came from), and trained in classical philology at Leiden, Graevius had converted from Lutheranism to Calvinism to qualify to teach in the Reformed universities and, after several years at Duisburg and Deventer, been appointed, in 1662, to the chair of rhetoric at Utrecht. Although principally a classical philologist and editor

---

[64] Van den End, *Guiljelmus Saldenus*, 189.
[65] Burman, *Synopsis theologiae*, 296–7; Vermij, *Calvinist Copernicans*, 324–5; Gootjes, "Collegie der Sçavanten," 181.

of Greek and Roman texts, Graevius was a zealous Cartesian and proponent of the international "republic of letters" viewed as embracing all learning and the sciences as a unity.

Wolzogen too belonged to Burman's and Graevius' lively discussion circle, the *Collegie der Sçavanten*, and certainly already knew about Spinoza since at least 1663.[66] Facing difficulties enough already, Wolzogen, Van Velthuysen, Burman, and Graevius needed to tread carefully and remained anxious to bolster the middle ground between Calvinist subjection of philosophy to theology, that is Voetius' subordinating fallible human reason to the infallibility of Scriptural authority, at one extreme, and the *Philosophia*'s wholly subordinating theology to philosophy, at the other. Rejecting the one claim Voetius made in common with the Spiritualist Collegiants—that the "Holy Ghost is the highest, absolute, infallible judge and interpreter of Scripture"[67]—the *Collegie der Sçavanten* defended their middle path by striking what they considered a reasonable, genuinely Cartesian balance between reason and religious authority, between philosophy and theology. Wolzogen's *De Scripturarum Interprete*, appearing with approbations from the university curators and Utrecht city government, sought to establish a clear dividing line between legitimate use of reason in Bible criticism from what most readers deemed the illicit subordination of Holy Writ perpetrated by the *Philosophia*.[68] Above all, Wolzogen aimed to rescue Cartesio-Cocceian exegetical methods and his group's attack on "superstition" from a potentially disastrous linkage in the public mind with an underground group and book which Voetians strove to associate not just with blasphemy and godlessness but also with Cartesianism, Cocceianism, anti-Orangist political conspiracy, and the *Collegie*. Should the *Philosophia*'s arguments triumph, acknowledges Wolzogen, then all religious authority and theology collapses.[69] Theology's reign would be over and churchmen and theologians reduced to marginality. Therefore, the solution he and his colleagues recommended was much the best path forward.

The problem was that his stance supposedly demonstrating a wide gulf between the respective positions of the *Philosophia* and his Cartesio-Cocceian allies landed him in a morass of difficulties. He and his allies held that reason must decide which rational interpretation applies to non-rational Scriptural statements, except where a non-rational meaning is expressly proclaimed. Wolzogen made a point of denouncing Socinianism, as all professors teaching in Dutch and Lower Rhine universities and gymnasia were required to do; but Socinians, he held, were right to condemn any Bible interpretation that conflicts with reason; moreover, the Socinian stance accorded considerably less with the *Philosophia*'s godless stance

---

[66] Bordoli, *Ragione e scrittura*, 289.   [67] Quoted in Goudriaan, *Reformed Orthodoxy*, 51–2, 62.
[68] Wolzogen, *De Scripturarum interprete*, 221–6; Bayle, *Dictionnaire* iii, 2582; Strazzoni, *Burchard de Volder*, 128.
[69] Wolzogen, *De Scripturarum interprete*, 225–6; Touber, *Spinoza and Biblical Philology*, 95, 99.

than its anonymous author claimed.[70] "Reason" cannot conflict with God's Word as revealed in Scripture, he agreed with the *Philosophia*, and is essential for construing Scriptural passages correctly.[71] Thus, while rhetorically repudiating the *Philosophia* and defending theology, he nonetheless appeared to align with the *Philosophia* (and Socinianism) in key respects, agreeing that philosophical truth cannot be contrary to theological truth and that philosophical truths are as certain as theological tenets.[72]

Reason and philosophy must as a rule prevail in Bible exegesis and theology, contends Wolzogen; but this rule he subjects to two crucial inviolable provisos: first, in theology, one must only admit as pertinent propositions "natural truths" demonstrated by philosophy and science beyond all question, and secondly, converging here with Wiszowaty (and the later teaching of Locke), everyone must exclude from truth identical in philosophy and theology the core "mysteries" of the Christian faith which, by definition, are above (but not contrary to) reason.[73] Our knowledge of Christ, the certainty of Christ's divinity, is not part of the rest of what we know. While the *Philosophia* and also many Socinians violate these fundamental limits, and are therefore greatly at fault, Socinians nevertheless err less reprehensibly than the *Philosophia* because a wide gulf remains between advocating unremitting subordination of Scripture to philosophy like the *Philosophia* and eschewing, as Socinians do, interpretations conflicting with reason while otherwise manifesting sincere reverence for Christ, the Holy Ghost, and the biblical text.[74] By blaming Socinians less than the *Philosophia*, and denouncing the *Philosophia* less harshly than most theologians believed he should, Wolzogen provoked a hail of criticism, some of it suggesting he must be in secret league with the Socinians *and* with the authors of the *Philosophia*.[75] Many agreed with the judgement of hostile theologians at Deventer published by Wolzogen's adversaries at Middelburg, in 1669, accusing him of barely masked Socinian leanings and sympathies.[76]

With Wolzogen attacked from all sides for placing "reason" on a par with spiritual authority, not least within his own Walloon (French-speaking Reformed) Church, the latter's synod suffered a severe rift at its meetings, in 1668 and 1669, over whether he should be formally condemned or not. The rift was inflamed in particular by the then still strict Calvinist faction leader and ally of Voetius, De

---

[70] *Lettres sur la vie* [...] *de Wolzogue*, 44–5.
[71] Mastricht, *Novitatum Cartesianarum Gangraena*, 56, 61, 75; Ryssenius, *Oude rechtsinnige waerheyt*, 13, 20.
[72] [Meyer], *Philosophia*, 57; Israel, *Radical Enlightenment*, 206; Goudriaan, *Reformed Orthodoxy*, 53, 59.
[73] Thijssen-Schoute, *Nederlands Cartesianisme*, 448; Bordoli, *Ragione e scrittura*, 304–6; Touber, *Spinoza and Biblical Philology*, 216–17.
[74] Wolzogen, *De Scripturarum interprete*, 221, 225–6.
[75] Leydekker, *Verder Vervolg*, 9; Van Bunge, *Johannes Bredenburg*, 108.
[76] *Ordeel van eenige theologanten tot Deventer*, 10–11, 24.

Labadie, who found the Calvinist Walloon Church in Holland altogether too accommodating for his taste. In a frenzy of theological ire, the ex-Jesuit charged Wolzogen verbally and in print with Pelagianism, demi-Pelagianism, Socinianism, Arminianism, Papism, profanity and despicable blasphemy.[77] Wolzogen retaliated, charging De Labadie with schismatic tendencies and behaving in a manner "injurieuse et atroce."[78] Cocceius, Wittichius, Burman, and others rallied to Wolzogen's side while, in Friesland, the young Balthasar Bekker wrote from Franeker, in March 1669, responding to Wolzogen's pleas for support, saying he had read his treatise twice and unreservedly supported his views. "God will aid you in the future," wrote Bekker, "in persevering with as much courage and steadfastness as you have hitherto."[79]

Wolzogen did persevere and eventually, aided by De Labadie's obstreperousness, won through after a fashion with support from allies realizing that they, and the Cartesian cause generally, would be disastrously placed should Wolzogen undergo formal censure and rejection by the synods and universities. He was supported too by the anti-Voetian Utrecht city government anxious to avoid open schism and unrest in their city. The Voetians failed to get him condemned; there was no formal censure. De Labadie defected and the Utrecht city government made clear to the consistory there that they wanted this ultra-conservative Labadist sect, separating itself from the public church, permanently ejected from Utrecht.[80] In 1670, Wolzogen left Utrecht to become pastor of the Walloon church in Amsterdam and the furore subsided.

Nevertheless, there was no denying the clandestine Amsterdam group's *Philosophia* represented a fundamental challenge of a revolutionary kind, urging nothing less than the total dissolution of theology into "philosophy." It paraded an entire new set of criteria and system of authority by which the entire moral order, indeed all human affairs, should be weighed and judged, affixing to the term "theologian" a highly pejorative meaning—someone swayed by irrational belief, someone biased, dogmatic, superstitious, and deceitful, precisely as in Spinoza's correspondence, the Koerbaghs' texts, and the radical tract *De Jure Ecclesiasticorum* of 1665 which, by some, was attributed to Meyer.[81] The Dutch edition of the *Philosophia* discloses slightly more information than the Latin text about the revolutionary "new system of philosophy" buttressing its arguments, mentioning that its approach, introduced by Descartes, had been extended, improved, and broadened "by others wishing to follow in his footsteps and bring into the light the issues of God, the rational soul, man's highest happiness,

---

[77] *Réponse à la prétendue conviction*, 7; Israel, *Radical Enlightenment*, 205–8.
[78] *Réponse à la prétendue conviction*, 9.   [79] *Lettres sur la vie [...] de Wolzogue*, 132–7.
[80] Van Lieburg, *Nadere Reformatie in Utrecht*, 122; Israel, *Radical Enlightenment*, 207–8.
[81] Moreau, *Spinoza, L'expérience*, 349n3.

and other such things."[82] To the likes of Serrarius, Beelthouwer, Comenius, Wolzogen, Burman, Van Velthuysen, Graevius, Wittichius, and doubtless De Lantman too, it was now crystal clear who was at the heart of it all, to whom the *Philosophia* was alluding—namely, Meyer, Bouwmeester, Van den Enden, the Brothers Koerbagh, and Spinoza.[83]

Nor were they the only ones. If most readers missed or were baffled by the allusion to these "others," by this time the most alert readers in the main Dutch cities were not. Among the latter, was Johannes Koerbagh's teacher at Groningen, the Huguenot professor Samuel Maresius (Des Marets) who in the late 1660s made a speciality of investigating and assailing the chiliasm of Serrarius, Comenius and De Labadie, and the liberal Cocceianism of Wolzogen and the Utrecht Sçavanten. Now he began investigating in addition this new and more radical clandestine freethinking current. There was an obvious need to identify who these miscreants, "these others," were.[84] At Groningen, where great alarm was provoked by the *Philosophia*, a faction of Reformed theologians led by Maresius that in the past had been ceaselessly at odds with Voetius, from this point on accepted that "the Cartesians" posed so great a menace to the public church's unity and stability, that old quarrels with Calvinists more rigid and austere than themselves needed now to be set aside. Shocked by the *Philosophia*, Maresius during 1667 staged several disputations among his students refuting it. As he edged closer to the Voetians, he cut back his own previously relatively favourable stance towards Cartesianism and Copernican astronomy.[85] By 1669, Maresius' horror at the stunning conclusions of the *Philosophia* had brought him and his following into public alliance with the Voetian bloc against the Cartesians and he was using his influence also to intensify the campaign now afoot against Cartesianism in Switzerland. By the time, in 1670, his main critique of the *Philosophia*, *De Abusu Philosophiae Cartesianae* [Concerning the Abuse of the Cartesian Philosophy], was ready for the press, Spinoza's *TTP* had appeared too so that, at the last moment, Maresius was able to make revisions widening his target so as to bring the *TTP* too within his sights.

Lambasting Heidanus and Wittichius, as well as Wolzogen, Burman, Van Mansvelt, and the Utrecht *Collegie der Sçavanten*, Maresius roundly blamed the Cartesians for the tempest unsettling theological studies in the Calvinist world reaching as far as the Huguenot communities of France and Germany. The Swiss he lauded for erecting sturdier barriers against Cartesianism than had the Dutch. By wholly subordinating theology and Scripture to philosophy, the *Philosophia*'s author, he pointed out, had gone much further towards undermining theology

---

[82] [Meyer], *Philosophie d'Uytleghster*, 136; Beelthouwer, *Antwoordt*, 10–13; Moreau, "Louis Meyer," 74.
[83] Thijssen-Schoute, "Lodewijk Meyer," 15–16; Van Bunge, *Johannes Bredenburg*, 108–9.
[84] Woldring, *Jan Amos Comenius*, 176–7.
[85] Vermij, *Calvinist Copernicans*, 320–2; Krop, *Spinoza, een paradoxale icoon*, 158–60.

and churchmen than had Descartes and the Cartesians. The two threats should be classified separately, he granted, and henceforth he labelled the authors of the *Philosophia* and their following *pseudo-Cartesiani*.[86] But the fact that *pseudo-Cartesiani* were undeniably much worse than Cartesians did not mean that genuine Cartesians should be let off the hook regarding the continuing colossal damage being wrought. Condemning *pseudo-Cartesiani* as delinquents perverting their master's system was insufficient because Descartes' system itself, he now took to arguing, harbours deep within itself insidious seeds, the source of the contagion eroding church supremacy, theology, and Holy Scripture's hegemony, a fact plainly evident from the deeply disturbing corrosive effect of the writings of Burman, Wittichius, and Wolzogen on ordinary folk's belief in angels, demons, and the Devil.[87]

Replying to the challenge from Groningen, Wittichius and Van Mansvelt issued a pamphlet under the pseudonym "Petrus van Andlo" deriding Maresius for his rapprochement with his old foe, Voetius, arguing that the respectable Cartesianism taught in the Dutch academies *was* the sole effective antidote to the "atheist" threat, the only way to shore up Holy Writ's authority and the Reformed Church, including popular belief in angels and devils.[88] Steeped in the furore over the *Philosophia* as the contents of his personal library shows,[89] Maresius responded with his 67-page *Vindiciae*, a counterblast repeating that he was not repudiating Cartesianism as such, but chiefly denouncing abuse of Cartesian principles in theology and Bible criticism. He had been making specific inquiries, Maresius reveals, about the intellectual background of the *Philosophia* and its links with the *Tractatus Theologico-Politicus* which had now superseded it as the number one challenge to Christian belief and authority. The *TTP*, Maresius had now discovered, was the work of "Spinoza, ex-Jew, blasphemer and formal atheist" whose abominable views, whatever "Van Andlo" claims, "derived from Descartes' principles and represent as dire a threat to the Christian faith as has ever been known."[90] Spinoza's godlessness, held Maresius, far surpasses even that of the *Philosophia* and, though spiced with Machiavelli and Hobbes, undeniably stems chiefly from Descartes.[91]

"Afterwards, in Holland," Leibniz later summed up, "people spoke of 'rational' and 'non-rational'" theologians, a faction distinction often mentioned by M. Bayle who finally declared himself against the former. But there is no indication that the precise rules have yet been defined which the rival parties accept or reject regarding use of reason in the interpretation of Holy Scripture."[92] This judgement, which Leibniz still adhered to towards the end of his life, he originally reached, his

---

[86] Maresius, *De Abusu*, 77; Douglas, *Spinoza and Dutch Cartesianism*, 56, 62.
[87] Maresius, *De Abusu*, 62–3, 77; Thijssen-Schoute, *Nederlands Cartesianisme*, 481.
[88] Jöcher, *Allgemeines Gelehrten Lexicon* ii, 378–9; Nauta, *Samuel Maresius*, 363–4.
[89] Israel, *Radical Enlightenment*, 211.   [90] Maresius, *Vindiciae Dissertationis suae*, 4.
[91] Maresius, *Vindiciae Dissertationis suae*, 7.   [92] Leibniz, *Theodicy*, 83.

notes reveal, while sketching his reservations about the *Philosophia*, in a text entitled *Commentatiuncula de judice controversiarum*, penned when residing at Mainz, in 1669–71.[93] A slightly earlier text of Leibniz, entitled *Nova methodus* (1667), also discusses the controversy unleashed by the *Philosophia*, touching on the distinction between the true sense of a text and the truth of a proposition, somewhat in the manner of Spinoza three years later,[94] though Leibniz never questioned Scripture's divine status as such, only the meaning and authenticity of particular passages, here steering closer to the *Philosophia* than Spinoza. Like Bayle later, Leibniz pondered long and hard regarding Spinoza, Meyer, the Koerbaghs, and the "rationalists." Critical of Meyer, Leibniz, in 1671, was nevertheless in part attracted to Spinoza's approach while always anxious not to violate the limits of what is allowable according to the Lutheran Church.

Revulsion against the growing assault on piety, tradition, and religion made manifest by the *Philosophia*'s challenge to theology and the churches prompted some notable defections from Cartesianism. For empiricist anti-Cartesians like Boyle, Locke, and Newton, though, there was never any great difficulty in defending the "reconcilableness of reason and religion." By imposing tight limits on what reason, guided by experience and experiment, can show, thoroughgoing empiricism offers greater flexibility and scope than Cartesianism with respect to revelations, miracles, alchemy, and the supernatural generally. What has not been and cannot be tested by experience need not fit any rational or philosophical framework; so English-style empiricists could later claim to have redeemed mankind from the sway of theories like those of Descartes and Spinoza, and to be more reliably safeguarding core Christian theology. In their eyes, "the Atheists' philosophical objections" were not nearly so "considerable" as some esteemed them, "so a Christian is not obliged to make his faith of a deity a mere postulation, since besides philosophical arguments, he may allege sufficient historical proofs, the miracles that were wrought by Christ and his followers, being undeniable proofs of the Christian religion, and that God must be the author of them." However, what was required for the strict honest empiricist scientist to effectively counter dangerous "Cartesian" and Spinozist tendencies with faith and solid Biblicism were Boyle's supposedly unimpeachable "historical proofs." If these failed to suffice one could still fall back on a strictly Baconian stance but this, as Hobbes objected, still left Boyle and his experimentalists dangerously prone to adhere to all manner of occult, superstitious, and dubious belief. Socinian tradition sought at least, like Locke later, to guard against the peril Boyle leaves everyone exposed to by insisting on the distinction between "above reason" restricted to the deepest Christian mysteries and whatever is "contrary to reason."[95]

---

[93] Laerke, *Leibniz lecteur*, 302–3. [94] Laerke, *Leibniz lecteur*, 308–9.
[95] Boyle, *Theological Works* i, 375–6; Boyle, *Early Essays*, xxxvi, 153; Israel, *Enlightenment that Failed*, 112–16; Nuovo, *John Locke*, 37, 233–4.

Theology in Meyer, the Koerbaghs, and Spinoza, is not just subordinated to philosophy but wholly stripped of independent standing and validity.[96] In the *Philosophia*, there exists only one order of truth, because there is only one order of nature, and that order is revealed and defined by philosophical reason alone, a position identical to Spinoza's as Meyer himself acknowledges in his preface to Spinoza's book on Descartes where he remarks that the reader must not think that Spinoza agrees with Descartes when the latter states that "this or that surpasses human understanding": for Spinoza "judges that all those things and even many others more sublime and subtle," that Descartes says are above reason "can not only be conceived clearly and distinctly but also explained very satisfactorily," provided the human intellect is guided in its search for truth and knowledge of things along a different path from that which Descartes opens up. The stance of Spinoza, the Koerbaghs, and Meyer indeed differs dramatically from that of Wittichius and Wolzogen, as well as of Boyle and Locke, but diverges from Wittichius only in carrying Cartesian principles of exegesis to their ultimate conclusion, eliminating all "mysteries" *supra rationem* [above reason] which Wittichius, like Descartes, and Van Limborch, Le Clerc, and Locke later, tried to fence around.[97] Wolzogen was right that the *Philosophia*'s author develops a Bible exegesis that is "wholly original and that no one maintained before him," doing so not by giving reason the right to interpret Scripture "comme les Sociniens" but by assigning that authority without qualification to systematic philosophy, justifying this reversal of ultimate authority by citing the nature of text criticism, correct Bible hermeneutics, and "the nature of God himself."[98]

Much was at stake because the social and educational functions and authority of the churches depended on their exclusive right to interpret Scripture's meaning and define the requirements of faith. Here, the *Philosophia*'s argument produced much the same explosive impact as the hard-hitting *De Jure Ecclesiasticorum*.[99] The latter holds that all spiritual and worldly authority and the property appropriated by ecclesiastics is usurped "unjustly and in an impious manner," as only the secular power can legitimately exercise public authority. Although hardly anyone publicly pointed to the connection between the *Philosophia* and *De Jure*, in 1666,[100] the likelihood that both texts are by Meyer is strengthened by their common focus on curbing and weakening the churches' sway over the public and over common thinking as much as possible, a goal fully shared by the Koerbaghs

---

[96] Walther, "Biblische Hermeneutik" (1995), 240.
[97] Meyer, "Preface" to Spinoza, *Principles of Cartesian Philosophy*, 6; Moreau, *Spinoza, L'expérience*, 545–6; Bordoli, *Ragione e scrittura*, 116–17; 147; Jaquet, *Spinoza à l'oeuvre*, 148.
[98] *Lettres sur la vie* [...] *de Wolzogue*, 45.
[99] Bordoli, *Ragione e scrittura*, 5, 29–34; Malcolm, *Aspects of Hobbes*, 46.
[100] Colerus, *La Vie de B. de Spinosa*, 97; Basnage, *Histoire des Juifs* ix, 1038; Wolf, *Bibliotheca Hebraea* i, 241.

and which, Spinoza assured Oldenburg, moved him too to set pure philosophy aside for now and turn to write the *Tractatus Theologico-Politicus*.[101]

The gap between Meyer and Spinoza is thus primarily rhetorical. Meyer employs rhetorical imposture; Spinoza does not. Dispensing with Meyer's rhetoric of philosophy being "the interpreter" of Scripture and Scripture truly being divine revelation but too obscure to be self-explanatory, Spinoza in the *TTP* contends that only those unable to grasp the difference between theology and philosophy, including practically all the academic combatants involved, dispute over which prevails over the other. Where the *Philosophia* insists theology is reducible to philosophy, Spinoza asserts—complying with the States of Holland edict of 1656—the complete separation of theology and philosophy: "neither is theology dependent on reason, nor reason on theology." Few discerning contemporaries failed to appreciate that the difference here was purely rhetorical, a mere tactical ploy, and that behind the rhetoric, even if the later text delves deeper and is more sophisticated, the two approaches substantially converge in subordinating all theology and all church authority unreservedly to philosophy's sway.[102]

The Platonist Henry More (1614–87), veteran fellow of Christ's College, Cambridge, had had his difficulties with Cartesianism ever since corresponding with Descartes himself in the late 1640s. Since then, he had maintained that "this mechanical way would not hold in all phaenomena"; but only later did it strike him that Cartesianism, for which he publicly expressed admiration as a young don, was actually proving extremely dangerous, so that his earlier mild reservations would be of no help if he did not, following publication of the *TTP*, now that he perceived the true situation more clearly, stand and vigorously renounce Cartesianism publicly. Eventually, the disturbing news from Holland aroused in him an unshakeable resolve to vigorously join the international drive to push Cartesianism "quite out of credit."[103]

Philosophy was gradually gaining momentum in society, avers the *Philosophia* with satisfaction on the last page; and "although [true] philosophy is still confined to a very small and narrow circle and this cannot yet contribute much" to uncovering the truth for all, "there is a quite reasonable hope that in these times, when its chief [modern] founder and propagator, René Descartes, first lit a torch for the world of letters and showed the way by his example, that the boundaries of philosophy will be extended far and wide by those who tread in his footsteps."[104] The *Philosophia* ends with a remarkable prognostication announcing the forthcoming publication of new principles about God, truth, and man's

---

[101] [Meyer], *Philosophie d'Uytleghster*, 52–3, 126; Beelthouwer, *Antwoordt*, 11–13; Moreau, "Principes," 120; Steenbakkers, "Johannes Braun," 199–200; Israel, *Radical Enlightenment*, 202–9.

[102] Spinoza, *Tractatus Theologico-Politicus*, 228–36; Bordoli, *Ragione e scrittura*, 221–3; however, some modern commentators take Spinoza at face value here, Thijssen-Schoute, "Lodewijk Meyer," 16; Preus, *Spinoza*, 74, 135.

[103] Boyle, *Correspondence* iv, 231.   [104] [Meyer], *Philosophy as the Interpreter*, 240–1.

supreme beatitude. "On the subject of God, the rational soul, man's highest felicity and other subjects that concern the attainment of eternal life, there will be published works of authority in interpreting Scripture and these will prepare the way, making it even and straight, whereby the Church of Christ, hitherto divided and torn by continual dissension, may smoothly unite and come together in friendship and love."[105]

Here, the *Philosophia* is announcing the pending publication of the *TTP* and afterwards Spinoza's general philosophy bursting in on the general scene. This memorable passage, formerly thought to refer to the *Korte Verhandeling*, has in recent years been viewed by scholars as a direct pointer, as it surely is, to the *Ethics* together with the *TTP*, the two works together comprising the far-reaching ideology of their sect then being excitedly discussed in Amsterdam among the very circles that produced the *Philosophia* and the even more alarming texts of the Brothers Koerbagh.

In setting aside the *Ethics* for the time being and turning to the *TTP*, Spinoza was thus not just defending his own corner but leading, steering, and reinforcing his group, proclaiming his solidarity with the authors of the *Philosophia*, the Koerbaghs, and the entire clandestine sect holding that church authority needed dismantling thoroughly and that "our salvation or happiness," as the Brothers Koerbagh expressed their common goal, "our greatest good, consists specifically in the knowledge of and communion with God [i.e. nature] whereby we shall secure the greatest satisfaction of mind in all things."[106]

---

[105] [Meyer], *Philosophy as the Interpreter*, 241; Fraenkel, "Could Spinoza Have Presented," 36.
[106] Koerbagh, *A Light Shining*, 336–7.

20
From the Jaws of Defeat (1666–1667)

20.i Faltering Dialogue with the Royal Society

"The experimental philosophers are very scrupulous" in research, experimenting, and gathering findings, affirmed Thomas Sprat (1635–1713), chronicler of the Royal Society, a prominent Anglican ecclesiastic and author of the *History of the Royal Society of London* (1667). But by no means, he declared, did this erode their basically theological view of the world. With humanity now "after the time when Christianity began to spread into the farthest nations, and when the power of working wonders had ceas'd," they could not "suddenly conclude all extraordinary events to be the immediate Finger of God."[1] Nevertheless, it ranked high among the Royal Society's aims to demonstrate that its scientists have, by their efforts, "taken off the unjust scandal from natural knowledge, that it is the enemy to divinity."[2]

Reinforcing theology's primacy was indeed among the Royal Society's stated principal goals. By contrast, a rationalized world view equal to combating "superstition," credulity, and religious strife in the way Spinoza's circle proposed, overthrowing theology's primacy in science, politics, social theory, education, and law and replacing it with a sweeping new political and moral theory exclusively grounded on reason and mathematically based science, required something dramatically different from, and beyond, the Royal Society's pure experimental approach. In the eyes of Spinoza, Meyer, the Koerbaghs, and Bouwmeester it was specifically the mathematical reasoning of their "reformed" Cartesianism, not the Royal Society's experimental "philosophy," as it was termed in the 1660s, that was driving the real revolution in thought, replacing theology with science and criticism in society. While avidly following experimental science, Spinoza never doubted that the Baconian experimental creed of Boyle, Sprat, and Oldenburg represented a far more timid, restricted motor of change than the philosophical engine his group were preparing.

There were grounds enough for such a view. It was only from the 1640s to the 1660s in fact, due to the breakthrough of Cartesianism, that sizeable segments of literate society for the first time in the world's history shifted to a coherently heliocentric, Copernican, and mechanistic view of the universe, achieving the

---

[1] Sprat, *History of the Royal Society*, 11, 82; Van der Welle, *Dryden and Holland*, 17.
[2] Sprat, *History of the Royal Society*, 132.

revolution in culture and society that Copernicus and Galileo failed to achieve, a crucial mid-century change but fundamentally divisive as was particularly evident in the Netherlands where the entire Voetian Reformed bloc, and a great many others, ploughed on for decades beyond 1650 vehemently opposing heliocentrism, the new comet science, and the new Bible criticism, carrying much of the populace with them while ensuring a deep rift running through the whole of contemporary culture and society.[3] In the Republic, this ideological divide in scholarly and intellectual life gripped all the universities and colleges, creating ceaselessly warring phalanxes of competing theologians attached to the public church, rival teams of academics of all kinds publicly battling it out for and against a rationalizing, heliocentric and mathematically oriented world view. The friction between science and theology would persist all across Europe beyond 1700 and through the next century. As regards secularizing human knowledge and the frame of the "Scientific Revolution," this left the European mind for a time divided into four camps or seedbeds of what became the Western Enlightenment—Aristotelians wholly rejecting such reform, Baconians going a quarter of the way, moderates going half-way (Cartesians), and radicals going the full course (Spinozists).

Entering the fray by composing the *TTP* meant deferring publication of his principal work of philosophy, the *Ethics*, for the foreseeable future, a change of strategy on Spinoza's part that could be (and by Oldenburg was) construed as retreat, even defeat. Changing tactics, Spinoza now had to explain to his followers, interested foreign observers, and, even perhaps himself, why he was shelving his main project and plunging into a bitter two-front war (against Voetians and Cartesio-Cocceians). Besides battling the hardcore Calvinists, he now had to face a fierce backlash from at least some "Cartesians," the group he had long hoped to win over to his side. The war he was waging was assuredly not that his Dutch compatriots were fighting against England. However inexorably the war of guns and ships gripped the attention of most, of Oldenburg, Boyle, and all around him, to Spinoza it seemed a futile, tragic waste of lives, energy, and resources without rhyme or reason that would not occur were society, politics, and men's thinking more rationally ordered. Even so, there was a solid connection between their war and his. His war of reason against "superstition," a vastly more important conflict for all humanity to his mind, not least for the battling seamen on either side, was in no small part a passionate protest against the war of guns and killing.

Earlier seemingly an almost certain triumph for England's king, by the winter of 1665–6, the outcome of the maritime struggle seemed to be growing increasingly hard to predict. Indications that things might turn out better for the Republic than originally expected were becoming more numerous. For one thing, the success of

---

[3] Vermij, *Calvinist Copernicans*, 157, 182; Wootton, *Invention of Science*, 19–20, 33, 40–1, 48–9, 107.

the Munsterite invasion seemed suddenly very much in question. Conflicting reports starting in October 1665 were for weeks simultaneously greatly reassuring to the English court and the Royal Society and deeply disconcerting: "we are very much afraid here," admitted a suddenly worried Oldenburg to Moray, at the end of October, reversing his own optimism of a few weeks earlier, "that those Munsterian forces that went into Groninguerland, are in great danger to be drowned there." A week later, Oldenburg relayed a "letter from Amsterdam [probably Serrarius] which saith, that the Bishop is broken into Friesland, but that 5 or 6,000 of his men are shut up in Windschoot by piercing the dykes round about, which, as the letter adds, makes his condition very dangerous, unlesse he force those passages, which they strengthen from day to day."[4] Oldenburg should take heart, replied Moray on 3 November, the Bishop of Munster had assured his resident "here," meaning Oxford, that his men had retaken a key strategic point near Winschoten threatening to cut him off and "that he hath furnished all the places hee hath taken well with all provisions and posted himself so strongly that all the forces in the Low Countries will not dislodge him."[5] In fact, the Munsterites, though welcomed by many Catholics, were both outmanoeuvred and increasingly drenched in disdainful propaganda. But it was not until December that the Munsterite sweep across Drenthe and Groningen could be seen to be not just disappointingly receding but facing total fiasco, leaving not a few at Charles II's court—still in Oxford due to the pestilence in London—expressing furious frustration.

The winter of 1665–6 offered some respite, bringing a temporary halt to the clashes at sea but also increased difficulties of communication. In November 1665, writing to Oldenburg, Spinoza regretted that the continuing bad weather prevented his venturing into The Hague which meant, among other things, delaying his letter by a week. Due to winter-time interruptions in communication, he complained, he seldom received his mail "at the proper time" and often, "one or two weeks elapse before I receive it." Such is the "disadvantage of living in a village." Even so, Oldenburg was able to answer less than three weeks later, in December. Regrettably, "as yet," agreed Oldenburg "there appears no hope of peace between England and the Netherlands." Boyle's "very kind greetings" he forwarded yet again while expressing hope that with the plague receding "our Royal Society will soon return to London and resume its weekly meetings" (as they did in March). He promised to send word "of whatever of its proceedings is worth knowing," especially experiments putting to the test or, as he and the Royal Society supposed, confirming Huygens' analysis and revisions of Descartes' laws of motion, a topic on which he and Boyle, Moray and the others had been in

---

[4] Oldenburg to Boyle, London, 31 Oct. 1665 in Oldenburg, *Correspondence* ii, 586.
[5] Moray to Oldenburg, Oxford, 3 Nov. 1665 in Oldenburg, *Correspondence* ii, 590–1.

disagreement with Spinoza for some time, albeit without doubting he too had something to contribute.[6]

During the spring of 1666, the picture changed dramatically. Von Galen was forced to accept that his drive for faith and princely glory had been humiliatingly thwarted. The beaten prince-bishop knew who to blame for his humiliation. "This winter has passed with much noise made by the Bishop of Munster," recounts Temple; his "chief complaints have been want of those sumes of money stipulated by his Majesty to be furnished him both before and after his taking the field." Indignant at what he saw as Charles' failure to provide the promised subsidies, or shield him from the French, Von Galen now left Charles in the lurch, negotiating a separate peace with The Hague, despite Temple being dispatched to Munster, in March 1666, with instructions to offer money and troops afresh. Temple arrived in Munster, on 22 April, to find the prince-bishop had already signed his separate peace.[7] This was shrugged off in England as merely the baseness to be expected from a German Catholic prince-bishop. "Let Munsters Prelate ever be accurst," exclaims Dryden's decidedly premature poetic celebration of England's "triumph" in the war, "in who we seek the German Faith in vain: Alas, that he should teach the English first, That Fraud and Avarice in the Church could reign!"[8] Charles and his envoys abroad assumed an unruffled stance. "This would cause no alteration in the King my master," his Paris envoy assured the Dutch peace negotiators there, in April, when they suggested the balance had shifted.

The Dutch should never have "conceived" England's monarch to be "stronger for the Bishop of Munster joyning with him; nor did he conceive himself to be at all the weaker for the Bishop of Munster breaking his faith, and abandoning him; nor did he feare [the Dutch] any whit the more for the King of Denmarcks joyning with them, or the Elector of Brandenburg, or those other German princes doing the like, or the King of France either." Dutchmen might be "happy" with France half-heartedly backing them in name (many courtiers knew of Louis XIV's intense personal antipathy to the Republic and republicanism), "but my Master had the right on his" side and would "certainly not alter his mind upon those considerations."[9] The war dragged pitilessly on.

Spinoza was obviously not providing London with any useful war news or scientific news, indeed was providing no useful news at all. Until December 1665, in Oldenburg's mind Spinoza remained essentially just a notable commentator on Descartes and his philosophy, especially as regards Cartesianism's relation to science, in particular the laws of motion and the question of comets: "I wish you

---

[6] Spinoza, *Collected Works* (ed. Curley) ii, 22–3; Lyons, *The Royal Society*, 63.
[7] Temple to Sir John Temple, Brussels, 10 May 1666 in Temple, *Letters written by Sir William Temple, Bart.* i, 52; *Calendar of State Papers: Venetian* 34, pp. 292, 294; Haley, *English Diplomat*, 57; Rowen, *John de Witt*, 606, 608–9.
[8] Dryden, *Annus Mirabilis*, verse 37; Van der Welle, *Dryden and Holland*, 29.
[9] Hollis to Arlington, Paris, 28 April 1666 in Lister, *Letters and Papers*, 434.

would undertake the task of making clear to me wherein you consider both Descartes and Huygens went wrong with respect to the laws of motion," he again urged Spinoza. In any case, he would not, Oldenburg reiterated, let the turmoil of war disrupt their correspondence again. Shortly before his writing this Moray had written to him that "[Robert] Hooke will satisfy your Hollander [Spinoza] that would know if wee think the new [spectacle] two comets. I do, for one."[10] Accordingly, in his December letter to Spinoza, Oldenburg signed off with the words: "I shall shortly let you have news, God willing, as to what our philosophers think about the recent comets." He never did. This last exchange between them, of late 1665, was followed by an immensely long gap of practically ten years, until June 1675, when the long interrupted contact between the two finally resumed.[11]

20.ii The Sabbatian Frenzy (1665–1667)

"At every hour we hear the rumour," Oldenburg mentions in this December 1665 missive to Spinoza, without saying Serrarius was his source, but knowing more information was likely to be available in Holland than England, "concerning the return of the Israelites who for over two thousand years have been dispersed, to their homeland. Few here believe it, but many want it. Do let your friend know what you hear and think about this matter."[12] "As for my view," confided Oldenburg, "I cannot put any faith in this news as long as it is not reported from the city of Constantinople which is most involved in this business, by men worthy of being believed. I want to know what the Amsterdam Jews have heard about this, and how they are affected by such an announcement, which, if true, will surely bring about the final overturning of all things in the world."[13]

Writing to Boyle soon afterwards, at the start of 1666 [New Style], Oldenburg reiterated how the "deadnes of trade and correspondency" was distressingly affecting his entire interaction and scientific communication with the Continent.[14] The stalling of routine business almost everywhere throughout coastal Europe and the Near East seemed, however, only to enhance the appeal and fascination of the mystical and extraordinary. Oldenburg's attention, as with many in England and Holland at this time, and Serrarius and Boreel most of all, was powerfully gripped by the most grandiose chiliastic schemes. Much of this

---

[10] Moray to Oldenburg, 27 Nov. 1665 in Oldenburg, *Correspondence* ii, 625.
[11] Oldenburg to Spinoza, London, 8 Dec. 1665 in Spinoza, *Collected Works* (ed. Curley) ii, 22–4; Hutton, "Henry Oldenburg," 108–10; Van de Ven, "Spinoza's Life and Time," 22; Steenbakkers, "Spinoza's Correspondentie," 12n8.
[12] Spinoza, *Opera* iv, 178; Spinoza, *Briefwisseling*, 239, 476; Scholem, *Sabbatai Sevi*, 545.
[13] Spinoza, *Opera* iv, 178; Spinoza, *Briefwisseling*, 239–40; Popkin, *Spinoza*, 46–7.
[14] Oldenburg to Boyle, London, 30 Dec. 1665 in Oldenburg, *Correspondence* ii, 652.

Millenarian fervour of 1665–6, convulsion religious and political that was also economic in that the Anglo-Dutch conflict continued to paralyze a great part of the maritime trade of the Mediterranean area and the Caribbean, freezing the usual channels of trade and finance, focused on the growing ferment among the Jews of Europe and the Near East. Excited reports of this spiritual upheaval and promised redemption, the movement of Sabbatai Zevi (1626–76) with its ecstatic jettisoning of age-old religious restrictions and observances, had filtered through, by mid-1665, creating a considerable stir in Holland, Germany, Eastern Europe, and England alike. Serrarius, avid for every scrap of news from the Near East, and the messianic movement among the Jews, was intoxicated with the topic relaying whatever he heard to England.[15]

What made the business vital to Oldenburg, Boyle, Serrarius, Boreel, and many another, was the possibility, amounting in some to unshakeable belief, that Sabbatai Zevi was indeed the forerunner, or precursor of the Christ about to come again, teaching the Jews about the Messiah and how they had misunderstood their own history and their future. For Serrarius and Boreel it was the key to final Christian–Jewish reconciliation and reunification and the redemption of our entire world. What was at hand was a universal divinely forged resolution of all conflict. Sharing their excitement, one English Puritan explained that what so stupendously enthused him in 1666 was not the prospect of Sabbatai Zevi as the Messiah of the Jews ("God forbid!"), but the start of "the grand revolution, the redemption of the whole Israel of God," and final subsuming of Judaism into Christianity.[16]

"The Holland letters," reported Oldenburg, in January 1666, to the Anglo-Irish lord, Baron William Brereton, a member of Parliament and the Royal Society, "continue their stories of the Jewes, and now tell us, that they have appointed their Rendezvous at Jerusalem by the first of Aprill, and that the Jewes of Amsterdam, as well as in other places, doe resigne their houses, resolved to repair to Palestina with the first conveniency. It may be," he continued reflecting on the almost total paralysis of Europe's maritime trade due to the raging conflict, that "they will doe so for want of trade in Holland."[17] Many chose to emigrate, but midway through the maritime war, it was difficult to find passage. Neutral trading cities in the Baltic, Iberia, and along the coasts of Italy too were gripped by the general paralysis of shipping and commerce so that even the most dramatic news from afar percolated through only slowly. In March, passing on news from Amsterdam, Oldenburg sent Boyle reports originating with the French envoy in Constantinople. Like most of the French merchant community in Ottoman lands, initially this diplomat had scoffed at talk of the "le Roy des Juifs [i.e.

---

[15] Scholem, *Sabbatai Sevi*, 470, 521, 524, 545; Dweck, *Dissident Rabbi*, 89–91.
[16] Van der Wall, *Mystieke Chiliast*, 444; Van der Wall, "Amsterdam Millenarian," 88–91, 94n56.
[17] Oldenburg to Brereton, London, 16 Jan. 1666 in Oldenburg, *Correspondence* iii, 18.

Sabbatai Zevi]," but now had changed his mind. "Now Christians as well as Jews write from Constantinople," signalling "confirmation of the reports concerning [...] the Israelites and the great hopes, the Jewes entertain of recovering their land very shortly."[18]

If the Jews were right about the (Second) Coming, reunification of all Christians, Jews, and Muslims under Christ's banner was imminent and Ottoman lands stood at the heart of it all.[19] At the end of his life, Boreel figured among those most uplifted by Near Eastern developments, though he died in June 1665, just as the excitement was stirring and he and his circle, communicating with Boyle through Oldenburg, were preparing for the press a "translation of the Old Testament into the Turkish language" arranged in Holland, which they and Boyle—who likewise felt tremendous enthusiasm—planned to publish in England. Also keenly looked forward to by Oldenburg and Boyle was another last text of Boreel, a culminating effort, described as "concerning J.C. Legislator and the Discourse of Reasonableness of the Laws of Christ," dating (incorrectly) the Gospels to the time of Christ's life and death, "proving" the Gospels were really composed by the Apostles and companions of Christ in whose names they were written and that all the miracles and prophecies contained therein were true. Both Oldenburg and Boyle (who paid) willingly arranged the expensive copying, costing five or six pounds, of an extra manuscript of this text earmarked for the Society. Beside finally "proving" that Christianity's precepts *are*, while the laws of the Chinese, pagans, Jews, and Muslims are not, the laws of God, Boreel included a scathing dismissal of the Quakers and other "Enthusiastae" along with clear "proofs" that essential truth cannot be known via Cartesianism.[20]

Boyle and Oldenburg viewed Boreel as among the world's chief contenders for Christianity against the impostors, sceptics, deists, atheists, Jews, and other non-Christians. Yet, Boreel and Spinoza, though worlds apart on the surface, converged remarkably closely in one crucial respect: for both visionaries the ceremonies and theology of all the main churches (including the synagogue) are fake and fundamentally invalid, while Spinoza too accepted, rhetorically at least, notably in the fourth chapter of the *TTP* where he presents his account of Jesus Christ's significance, that "Christ" (he never uses the name "Jesus") is indeed the "mouthpiece of God" who spoke to men more clearly than any other prophet, someone "not sent to teach the Jews alone but the whole of humanity," and that even if (as Spinoza discreetly but plainly hinted) he performed no miracles, was not the Son of God, nor born of a virgin, nor resurrected, his mind as projected in

---

[18] Oldenburg to Boyle, London, 6 March 1666 in Oldenburg, *Correspondence* iii, 49.
[19] Popkin, *Spinoza*, 40, 63; Popkin, *Third Force*, 140, 231–2, 362–3; Van der Wall, "Amsterdam Millenarian," 90–1; Waite, *Jews and Muslims*, 194, 213–24.
[20] Iliffe, "Jesus Nazarenus Legislator," 383–9, 393–4.

the Gospels commands a universal reach and remains the purest, best way to teach ordinary people the truth concerning God, ethics, and obedience to the law.[21]

One truly fascinating aspect of the unprecedented expectation during 1665–6 of a universal miraculous cure for all ills, is that the Millenarians' dreams were in fundamental ways not so very different from Spinoza's and his clique's vision, certainly less remote than one might initially suppose—except that Spinoza based his project to "reform the world," as Thévenot later scornfully called it, on philosophical reason triumphing in its eternal combat with ignorance, credulity, and "superstition" whereas for Serrarius, Boreel, Boyle, Oldenburg, and most opinion, the point rather was to trust in miracles and divine intervention, not philosophy. It would be of great interest to know how Spinoza felt about Sabbatai and his messianism and how he responded to Oldenburg's query; but alas his reply, if there was one, is lost.

Spinoza doubtless thought long and hard about the astounding mix of emotion, despair, and hope, the wild excitement engulfing the Jews of Amsterdam, Hamburg and all Europe, North Africa and the Near East while composing his culminating assault on "superstition," mass delusion, and existing structures of theology and religious authority. Not only did many Jews in Holland as elsewhere greet the Messiah's coming with delirious exaltation, but many now ceased their routine religious obligations and, as Oldenburg reported, began selling their houses and uprooting themselves, actively planning the long peregrination back to Palestine.[22] Either side of the Channel many long remained engrossed in the drama: "the Jews seem to promote their enterprise with vigour in Arabia and Palestina," Oldenburg assured Boyle, in March, "two or three dozen prophets that are said to be amongst them, doing good service to the pretended king, who is said," as Christian Millenarians construed Sabbatai's significance, "not to assume the dignity and office of the Messiah, but to lead to him."[23] The Second Coming *was* indeed imminent!

Among those reporting to London on Mediterranean developments at this point was the English resident in Florence, much in favour at the Tuscan court, Sir John Finch (1626–82), anatomist, physician and before long close colleague of Steno, recently arrived in Italy where he settled semi-permanently. In February 1666, Finch, a participant in the meetings of the Florentine Accademia regularly in touch with Oldenburg, reported on the Sabbatai Zevi ferment in Ottoman lands directly to Lord Arlington describing also the general situation in Tuscany. Stressing the now total absence for over nine months of Dutch ships from Tuscany's main port of Livorno, he noted that the near paralysis of shipping

---

[21] Spinoza, *Theological-Political Treatise*, 63–4; Strauss, *Spinoza's Critique of Religion*, 118–19; Iliffe, "Jesus Nazarenus Legislator," 396.

[22] Van der Wall, *Mystieke Chiliast*, 404–5; Popkin, *Spinoza*, 47.

[23] Oldenburg to Boyle, London, 13 March 1666 in Oldenburg, *Correspondence* iii, 59.

and trade was greatly distressing locals and the Jews. The situation was distinctly promising from England's standpoint except that the Italians generally, like the Spaniards, evinced what struck Finch as outrageous lack of gratitude towards King Charles and his subjects for freeing them from humiliating dependence on the Dutch trading system. Happily, Florentines would now find themselves depending more on England's monarch than the Dutch, a colossal gain for all; yet that was not how they felt. This "strange partiality of the city of Florence for the Dutch (a city whose poor live by the consumption of their manufactures in England, and whose rich are rendered so from the same cause)," seemed quite unaccountable, though three months later he again acknowledged that "scarcity of shipping rendreth this place [Livorno] much lessen'd in trade; in six months time here have not been three Dutch ships."[24]

Distressingly, in Tuscany, even properly "solemnizing" English victories before the public, as the English court required, proved exasperatingly difficult. Despite his labours to shift local opinion against the Dutch, he was encountering bitter "jealousy of His Majesty's growing power at sea." Meanwhile, "many families of Jews have come to Livorno from Rome, Verona, and Germany [...] to embarque to find their Messiah," though many also were now turning back. At Venice too by the late spring of 1666, uprooted Jews were abandoning their efforts to reach Jerusalem, finding no shipping to take them to Palestine, despite there being no trade for them to return to.[25]

Meanwhile, the court of the Ottoman Sultan increasingly frowned on the vast turmoil the upheaval was creating throughout the Mediterranean, Europe, and the Near East. For a time, Ottoman displeasure and absence of shipping seemed only to further stoke the fervour of Jewish and Christian Millenarianism. But in September 1666, seeking finally to put a stop to it, the Sultan confronted Sabbatai with the choice of converting to Islam or being beheaded. Yet even his choosing the former and (at least outwardly) converting to Islam and changing his name officially to "Mehmed Pasha," failed fully to quench the zeal. Compelling Sabbatai Zevi to convert, court officials at Constantinople correctly calculated, would damp down the frenzy; but their remedy worked neither quickly nor completely.

The prolonged commotion caused a profound split in the Amsterdam Jewish community, as likewise in Hamburg, with growing numbers of Sephardim, even more than Ashkenazim, angrily opposing the euphoria, but with supporters and opponents of Sabbatai increasingly raging against and even seeking to intimidate the other side. Among other things, this resulted in ironic jibes circulating in the synagogue, and among the Sephardic dealers and merchants at the Exchange, invoking the communal bans imposed on Uriel da Costa, De Prado, and Spinoza.

---

[24] PRO SP 98/6. Finch to Arlington, Livorno, 12/22 February 1666.
[25] PRO SP 98/6. Finch to Arlington, Livorno, Finch to Arlington, 19/29 May 1666.

A Spanish-language satire circulated among the Sephardic traders at the Exchange, in early May 1666, ridiculing the Sabbatian faction. It was condemned by a furious *Mahamad* on 3 May 1666, with an edict requiring anyone knowing anything about its authorship to appear within twenty-four hours to expose the culprits. Deriding the Sabbatai zealots' threat to impose a sweeping *herem* on "the unbelievers," that is those rejecting Sabbatai, this biting satire pretended to condemn those prominent members of the community publicly denying Sabbatai's messiahship, naming several of the most sceptical merchants opposing the frenzy, such as Antonio Lopes Suasso, a member of the *Mahamad* that year. Some Sephardic opponents of the Sabbatian movement were clearly equating the excitement with foolishness, ignorance, and lack of understanding. But part of the satire was its parodying the sensational curses earlier heaped by the congregation on (the unnamed) Uriel da Costa and Spinoza under the severest form of *herem*, reciting the curses the community was considering imposing on the anti-Sabbatai opposition, Hebrew curses only ever actually pronounced previously in Amsterdam against Spinoza.[26]

Whether or not Spinoza heard anything of the Amsterdam *herem* affray of 1666 with its echoes of his own *herem* of ten years before, or replied to Oldenburg, or knew of his brother's activities, since 1664, in the Caribbean, he certainly knew the Sephardic community was deeply split, that some of those once close to him, like Pereyra, had become Sabbatian enthusiasts fixated on the Near East while trying to emigrate eastwards whereas others, like his brother, had fled the slump in the opposite direction, investing their hopes rather in the Caribbean, while a great many were caught up still in the unsettling turmoil over whether Sabbatai Zevi was the Messiah come at last or not.[27] Spinoza's view was indubitably sought by other friends besides Oldenburg and his response passed by members of his circle to others; and we do possess the response of another prominent figure among the underground philosophical fraternity which undoubtedly closely corresponded to Spinoza's own assessment. Nowadays, commented Adriaan Koerbagh, retelling the Sabbatai Zevi story a year later, in *A Light Shining in Dark Places* (1668), the Jews "are still awaiting such a king or prince (Messiah) who will release them from the dispersion and subjection in which they now find themselves, and lead them back to the land they once occupied." Restoring the Jews to their own land and state, the Brothers Koerbagh pronounced by no means impossible, given the transience of states and empires. No one knew for sure whether this would ever happen or not; but if the Jews "imagine that they will return to [the Holy Land] by some frantic feats and superstitious performances that they call 'miracles,' [we] say to them that they will never effect their return there by that means, but rather, from now on, all those taking that path may soon very well fare in the same

---

[26] Wilke, "'Messie mystique' et la Bourse," 198–201; Dweck, *Dissident Rabbi*, 129–30.
[27] Scholem, *Sabbatai Sevi*, 529; Israel, *Diasporas*, 397–404.

manner as poor Sabatha Zebi [i.e. be imprisoned and forced to submit to Islam]."[28]

That Spinoza too thought, and probably told his friends, that the Jews, though no chosen people, might one day be gathered in again from their dispersion and recover their homeland, emerges from his brief discussion about this in the *TTP*. After remarking that the "sign of circumcision has such great importance as almost to persuade me that this thing alone will preserve their nation forever," Spinoza adds: "and in fact, were it not that the principles of their religion weaken their courage, I would believe unreservedly that at some time, given an opportunity, since all things are changeable, [the Jews] might re-establish their state, and God will choose them again."[29] Spinoza's view, with its sarcastic remark about God choosing "the Jews again," was certainly a judgement on the seething turmoil of 1665–7 into which Sabbatianism plunged the entire Jewish world. Like his Koerbagh disciples, he pronounced such a final outcome feasible, but was unshakeably convinced that no such eventuality could ever occur via a miraculous process.[30]

News of Sabbatai's apostasy was not definitely confirmed in Europe until December 1666, and some rabbis in Ottoman lands refused in any case to abandon faith in Sabbatai's messianic status.[31] Serrarius too, Spinoza doubtless gathered, remained unflinching in his mystical "philo-Jewish chiliasm" like some other fringe Protestants, and while most Jews now hastily retracted their brief allegiance, a segment mesmerized by Sabbatai's meteoric rise and supposed miraculous feats, shared an unconquerable faith in pending final redemption through him. As the news of Sabbatai's apostasy, disbelieved by many at first, gradually sank in, Serrarius remained at one with the hard core of stubborn believers among the Jews in Holland and elsewhere denying they had been deceived or that Sabbatai had truly converted (Sabbatai himself intimated to followers that he had not). To true zealots, Sabbatai's apostasy was just a temporary dip in the fulfilment of messianic prophecy preceding the triumphant return to the Holy Land of the "king of the Jews."

Serrarius still envisioned a universal process bringing about the union of all true (i.e. unchurched) Christians and Jews into one single uplifted spiritual body, and strove to pull other Millenarian enthusiasts and mystics, notably Comenius and John Dury along with him. The Scots former Calvinist educated in Holland who happened to be a nephew of Boyle by marriage, had dedicated himself, like Comenius, to reuniting all Protestant sects and was a great enthusiast for alchemy. He too longed for Judaism's reunification with Christianity.[32] Amazingly,

---

[28] Koerbagh, *A Light Shining*, 194–5.
[29] Spinoza, *Theological-Political Treatise*, 55; Scholem, *Sabbatai Sevi*, 543–4.
[30] Spinoza, *Theological-Political Treatise*, 55–6.   [31] Scholem, *Sabbatai Sevi*, 536–7, 753–4.
[32] Van der Wall, "Amsterdam Millenarian," 86, 91; Van der Wall, *Mystieke Chiliast*, 462–3.

continuing through 1667, Serrarius battled on to secure wider acknowledgement of Sabbatai as a momentous divine intervention proclaiming the imminence of the Second Coming. "As for the Jews," Serrarius assured Oldenburg as late as July 1667, "their hope revives more and more. Those of Venice sent an expres to Adrianopolis [Edirne]" having received trustworthy information from someone who interviewed Sabbatai Zevi in person and found him "not turned Turk, but a Jew as ever in the same hope and expectation as before. Yea, from Smyrna by way of Marseilles we have it, that at Constantinople the Jews return to their fasting and praying as before and so doe some here [i.e. at Amsterdam] likewise. It appears both in regard of Christians and of Jews, that God's works ever were a riddle to flesh and bloud, and a stumbling-block to worldly minds. Therefore, we need to look to our-selves, lesse we be surprised and drawn away amongst those, that would not have Christ to reign." Many persons allow Christ "a kingdom in Heaven," Serrarius gloomily admonished the misguided around him, "but not on Earth. This, they conceive, is, and will remain, their fashion but quite other was the expectation of the saints at all times, since they saw the iniquity prevailing here; and therefore they prepared themselves for another day in which Justice shall prevaile. So I pray God we may do likewise."[33]

This far-reaching spiritual upheaval throughout much of Europe and the Near East, conspicuous especially in the Jewish world with a great many Jews believing fervently that the Hebrew commonwealth of biblical times was about to be restored with the coming of the Messiah, Spinoza doubtless dismissed as dreamy delusion, wishful thinking to offset the cruel realities of their situation. But what factors do actually dissolve and restore republics? And how does a republic like that of the Dutch, or the ancient Hebrews, successfully withstand the might of far stronger empires? Given the context, it was surely no accident (even assuming that parts of this material had been penned by Spinoza long before) that the longest, most detailed segment of historical analysis in the *TTP* is a lengthy discussion of the strengths and weaknesses of the ancient Hebrew Republic, both the first Hebrew republic down to the Babylonian captivity, and the second from Ezra down to the destruction of Jerusalem by the Emperor Vespasian in AD 70.

Superstition Spinoza identifies as one reason for the ancient Hebrew Republic's resilience and endurance. But he also identifies several, to his mind, more positive features, clearly being impressed by the Hebrew state's reliance on its own citizen soldiers and eschewing of foreign mercenaries, and adherence to the principle that the land be divided equally among the citizens so that all citizens should have a vested interest in the republic and its survival. Ancient Israelites, consequently, were healthily disinclined to fight wars for the sake of attacking and dispossessing others while yet remaining strongly motivated to defend their own land and chief

---

[33] Serrarius to Oldenburg, Amsterdam, 5 July 1667 in Oldenburg, *Correspondence* iii, 446–7; Popkin, *Spinoza*, 47–8.

strongholds when threatened, especially their national and religious centre, Jerusalem.³⁴ To his mind there was a topical lesson there.

The ancient Hebrew state's eventual dismal fate also offered to citizens of other republics a useful warning of the dangers of looking to strong leaders (like Saul or the Prince of Orange) to solve their problems for them and save them from menacing challenges. His discussion here also reflects the admiration he felt for the Roman historian Tacitus (*c.* AD 56–*c.*120) whom Spinoza cites several times, often without explicitly mentioning his name (taking for granted his readers' familiarity with his texts), and whose *Annals* present politics as a continual fluctuating drama. Admiring Tacitus' pithy political maxims and skilful presentation of the "theatre" of political power was commonplace in Spinoza's day, and Spinoza possessed two different copies of Tacitus' complete writings in his personal library, including the famous edition by the great humanist Justus Lipsius (1547–1607).³⁵ But Tacitus' terse, biting Latin style, hatred of tyrants, and underlying republican antipathy to emperors and the corrupted Roman senate that wallowed in the most abject appeals to emperors "from the time of Augustus and Tiberius onwards,"³⁶ held a special attraction for Spinoza, as earlier for Machiavelli. During this tense, critical period, he was evidently immersing himself in the texts of both Tacitus and Machiavelli.³⁷

Adopting a republican reading of Tacitus meant rejecting the prevailing "monarchist" approach promoted by most early modern Tacitus scholars, not least Lipsius who, like Bodin and later also Hobbes, was convinced monarchy is the best form of state, and the shift from republic to monarchy a step up for Rome, one of the many points where Spinoza's political thought clashes with Hobbes' approach.³⁸ Clearly familiar with the early modern "monarchist" Tacitist literature, including a work on the "secrets" of statecraft by an obscure Altdorf professor, Arnold Clapmarius (1574–1634), a copy of which Spinoza kept in his personal library, he firmly rejects the view that a great advantage of monarchy is its greater ease of secrecy in complex, delicate statecraft. Spinoza directly attacked this standpoint later in his *Tractatus Politicus*, turning the very words of Tacitus that Clapmarius quotes against the latter, insisting that "it is far better for the honest policies of a state to be open to its enemies than for the guilty secrets of tyrants to be kept hidden from the citizens. For those who are able to shroud in

---

³⁴ Spinoza, *Theological-Political Treatise*, 220–4; James, *Spinoza on Philosophy*, 280–7.
³⁵ Van Sluis and Musschenga, *Boeken van Spinoza*, 18, 83; Bastiani, "Spinoza against Political Tacitism," 1043.
³⁶ Tacitus, *Annals*, 37; Mellor, *Tacitus*, 9.
³⁷ Haitsma Mulier, "Spinoza en Tacitus," 68; Klever, *Spinoza Classicus*, 134–5; Akkerman, "Taal en tekst," 22.
³⁸ Israel, *Dutch Republic*, 566–7; Mellor, *Tacitus*, 144; Bastiani, "Spinoza against Political Tacitism," 1046; Hoekstra, "Lion in the House," 195.

secrecy their dealings in affairs of state [as Charles II, Louis XIV, and Von Galen invariably did] have the state entirely in their hands."[39]

Here, once again, we encounter one of the principal features of what one might call the unity and continuity of Spinoza's life and legacy. Spinoza was strikingly more subversive of existing systems of thought, political science, structures of authority, and religious traditions than any other early modern thinker, including Machiavelli and Hobbes. Yet, at the same time, one discerns a deep-rooted unifying drive in his philosophy to reconstitute all that is best and most valuable in the world's systems of thought and faith to help assemble a new unifying whole, not just rendering the Old Testament and New equal in both message and standing, as he characteristically does, and furthering "true religion" based on recognition of the reality of things, but together with his Collegiant friends, seeking basic reform of "Christianity" as well as of Cartesianism, moral theory, Bible criticism, and, he hoped, optics. His was a reconstitution of all the religious traditions and philosophical systems, and simultaneously a quest for unity of thought and action.

Just as Sadducees for Spinoza are preferable to Pharisees as representatives of Judaism, and ancient Israelites to rabbis, both positive and negative elements abound in all religious traditions, and there exists no more urgent task for the philosopher than gathering and integrating all the best ingredients together. If "true religion" and correct use of reason converge in truth, "true religion" and reason equally converge in guidance for life and conduct, in promoting love instead of hate, the "common good" in place of division and strife.[40] Just as Spinoza's own circle can be said to have been formed by two groups, Christian Collegiants *and* godless freethinkers, so he sought to contrive a viable means to fuse his naturalism ruling out everything supernatural with the deeply pious religious motivation of his Collegiant allies, while tracing a path too for reuniting Christianity with a Judaism purged of superstition, impurities, and Pharisaic narrowness.

Spinoza, the Koerbaghs, and his other friends remained keen observers of the euphoria and were entirely at one with their Millenarian friends, and the deceased Boreel, about the "iniquity prevailing here," and the need to strive with all our being for the coming of another day when "justice shall prevail." A revolution of life and thought in this world was indispensable, held Spinozists no less than Serrarius' Millenarians and Sabbatians, a more just world is needed, and that great revolution was coming. But left untouched by such eruptions of spiritual fervour, Spinoza believed he could see the path to redemption more clearly than the Millenarians. Rejecting Jewish Sabbatianism and his friend Serrarius' chiliastic aspirations, and detaching political allegiance and respect for the law from

---

[39] Spinoza, *Political Treatise*, 91; Gebhardt, "Spinoza gegen Clapmarius," 347.
[40] Strauss, *Spinoza's Critique of Religion*, 117, 119, 247; Carlisle, *Spinoza's Religion*, 4, 143–4.

religious belief, stood at the heart of his reform programme. Spinoza saw no reason why Jews converting to Islam, like Sabbatai, or for that matter any Turk honouring God by practising justice and love towards one's neighbour, should be supposed to possess less of the "spirit of Christ" than himself or anyone else.[41]

If the special observances and ceremonies of the Jews were obsolete in Spinoza's view, "Christian ceremonies, such as baptism, the Lord's supper, feast days, public prayers, and any others that always have been common to all Christendom" he equally discards as no longer relevant even if they had been instituted by Christ and the Apostles which, he remarks "is until now not sufficiently evident to me." For these were only instituted as "external signs" of the universal church several centuries later and not as things that contribute anything to "blessedness or have anything sacred in them." Indeed, it clearly follows from the "principles of the New Testament," held Spinoza, that all those living "under a government where the Christian religion is forbidden," not just the martyrs suffering under the emperors, from Nero to Diocletian, but all "obliged to do without [churchgoing and sacraments] will yet be able to live a good life notwithstanding."[42]

Since no sacraments, churchgoing, or communal Christian practices proclaimed by churches can correctly be said to have been established by Christ and the Apostles, and none are requisite anyway for living a worthy, upright life, the Dutch empire so disdained by the English acted quite rightly, held Spinoza, in forbidding each and every communal Christian practice where this was contrary to local laws as "in the empire of Japan where the Christian religion is forbidden and the Dutch who live there must abstain from all external worship by command of the East India Company." Spinoza discerned nothing whatever reprehensible in what remained a source of profound embarrassment to most, and a frequent sneer at Dutch expense in English and other anti-Dutch sentiment at the time.[43] Spinoza, in effect, dissolves the differences between Christians, Jews, and Muslims much like, but more comprehensively, than Boreel and Serrarius.

20.iii Science and Miracles

"Let princes and states make warre and shed blood; let us cultivate virtue and philosophy, and study to do good to mankind: *non sileant amplius leges nec Musas inter arma; sed vocales sint quam maximo in maximo strepitu bellorum* [war silences neither laws nor muses; rather these are best heard above the din of battle],"[44] was the stirring vow upon which Spinoza and Oldenburg had solemnly

---

[41] Spinoza, *Theological-Political Treatise*, 207; Leezenberg, "How Comparative," 28.
[42] Spinoza, *Oeuvres* iii, 224; Spinoza, *Theological-Political Treatise*, 75.
[43] Spinoza, *Theological-Political Treatise*, 75–6, 207; Israel, *Dutch Primacy*, 171–2.
[44] Oldenburg to Boyle, London, 24 March 1666 in Oldenburg, *Correspondence* iii, 69.

joined hands, in 1661, and were still together sworn to uphold. Theirs was a stirring message but one that turned out to be difficult to promote in practice. Recovering from the plague, it was not until February 1666 that England's Royal Society could reassemble at Gresham College and, on the 21st of that month, gather for its first post-pestilence officially recorded London meeting, an event that lifted Oldenburg's spirits, reviving his old sturdy scientific idealism.[45]

Spinoza's former fellow Cartesian reformer and devotee of science, Steno, meanwhile, during his first year in Florence compiled a treatise, based on his latest research, on muscle theory. In the mid-1660s, he was still an avid researcher. In October 1666, he famously dissected the head of an unusually large white shark caught in a large sling off Livorno, dragged ashore and beaten to death on the beach. Based chiefly at Pisa and Florence during his scientifically productive early period in Italy, Steno served also as chief font in Italy of information about the state of science and the intellectual ferment in Northern Europe, the Netherlands especially, advising his new colleagues at the famous Florentine Academy, the Accademia del Cimento (1657–67), a group devoted to promoting science and scholarship headed by Giovanni Alfonso Borelli (1608–79), a physiologist and astronomer zealous for building on Galileo's legacy, then the Accademia's leading voice. Steno still agreed with Descartes about one thing—his sense of the new science and philosophy ushering in a revolutionary transformation in the life of man. Introducing his muscle treatise, Steno lamented the hundreds of useless volumes on medicine and pharmacy heaped up over the centuries, all based on ignorance and superstition, leaving the sick and injured of his day still being dragged through "a thousand torments" owing to man's ignorance of basic anatomy, physics, and medicine. Thanks to the new science—observation, measurement, and correct theorizing based on geometry and mathematics, as Galileo initiated and Descartes developed, together with dissection (not least his own)—medicine was finally on track to become transformed utterly and to vastly benefit mankind. "And why should we not assign to muscles what astronomers assign to the sky, what geographers to the earth, and, to take an example from microcosm, what writers on optics grant the eyes?"

Borelli, likewise an enthusiast for muscle theory and applying mathematics to science, at this point shared with Steno his belief that, by showing how mathematical reason governs science, it was Galileo specifically who had initiated this fundamental revolutionizing of our modern world. Steno couched his treatise on muscle theory in "geometric" style, venerating Galileo's legacy as was *de rigueur* at the Accademia at the time. Thinking geometrically and mathematically, he still agreed with Spinoza, is the sole correct, meaningful way to explore science, medicine, and all physical reality. Fond of the Accademia which to him, as to

---

[45] Oldenburg, *Correspondence* iii, p. xxiii.

Finch, seemed perfectly to express the ethos of group research in science, Steno particularly admired its combining science with religious devotion. Like Spinoza, he viewed the pure empiricist approach of the English, eschewing broad theorizing, as too narrow. But while they agreed there, Steno believed Spinoza's very different reform programme was utterly misconceived. While consolidating his position at the forefront of anatomical and fossil studies in Italy from his new base, Steno explained to his Florentine colleagues what to him were the failings of Cartesianism, including its radical "atheistic" offshoot, namely Spinoza and his circle.[46]

However, all was not tranquillity in Florentine science either. Steno's irascible Neapolitan colleague, Borelli, who had known Galileo personally in early life, tended to resent how northerners, the *Oltramontani*, were increasingly usurping the lead, elbowing Italians aside in what should remain Galileo's transformed world of science. He neither appreciated Steno's sudden pre-eminence nor considered him the embodiment of "modesty and good manners" that others at the Grand Duke's court took him to be. Before long, Borelli departed in a huff. After his departure, in March 1667, the Florentine Accademia swiftly fell apart, largely disappearing from the active science research scene. Steno lingered for the duration of the war, still immersed in scientific research but henceforth also plunging into the intensified spiritual endeavour soon to bring about his conversion to Catholicism, unqualified revolt against Cartesianism and all philosophy and, finally, his total abandonment of science.[47]

At Livorno, on 24 June 1666, witnessing the intense fervour of the Corpus Christi procession, Steno felt overwhelmed by intense religious emotion. His experiences in Holland had filled him with incipient revulsion against freethinking, irreligion, and lack of faith, but now Steno was seized with a powerfully heightened militant commitment to the miraculous and divine providence that transformed his life and career. During 1667, his scientific colleagues found Steno devoting more and more time to prayer and studying theology and ecclesiastical history, leading in November 1667 to his formally forsaking the Lutheran "heresy" and converting to the Church of Rome. On abjuring the Protestant "heresy," Steno, it was reported to the Pope, appeared repeatedly before the Father Inquisitor, Hieronymus Baroni da Lugo between 4 and 7 November, submitting a detailed report on the abominable religious mayhem prevailing in the United Provinces. Dutch fragmentation of sects, admonished Steno, must arouse the revulsion of every pious person. After "carefully studying all the sects" in the Republic, Steno "found them all to be vanity and poison." Only Catholicism offers

---

[46] Scherz, "Biography of Nicolaus Steno," 159–62; Scherz, *Niels Stensen*, 164–72; Wootton, *Invention of Science*, 96, 300, 347.
[47] Scherz, "Biography of Nicolaus Steno," 161; Totaro, "Niels Stensen (1638-1686)," 153–4; Van Vugt, "Structure and Dynamics," 196.

true solace and redemption, a better world and better life for all, a truth Steno vowed to broadcast to all his former friends in Holland, Germany, and Scandinavia. He embraced Catholicism ardently, Spinoza afterwards learnt,[48] but as yet did not wholly abandon science. For a time, he shifted from anatomy to geology and the earth's structure, becoming a principal founder of this exciting new science.[49] Only from the early 1670s, abandoning all hope of bettering the world through science in favour of an exclusively spiritual approach, did he launch his active campaign to counter Cartesian reformism (and Spinoza) and to help render Italy less welcoming to Protestants, science, and to new ideas.[50]

Whatever Spinoza thought of Steno's conversion, and Serrarius' fervour, this was not the happiest of times for him personally. "Various concerns and troubles," about which he provides no details, kept Spinoza "so occupied" during the first half of 1666 that these difficulties caused him, he admitted, to lag considerably behind with both correspondence and his activities more generally, presumably referring to experiments and his work on microscope lenses as well as composing the *TTP*. Summer lightened Spinoza's mood but also spelled resumption of the action at sea.

In the bloody and ferocious Four Days' Battle, fought near the Thames Estuary, in mid-June 1666, both sides boasted success despite heavy losses.[51] Victory celebrations were held in London and many other places, though those in the know, like Secretary Pepys for example, realized that despite the celebrations and pretence of victory "I do find great reason to think that we are beaten in every respect, and that we are the losers."[52] In Brussels, total confusion about the outcome was made worse by the English resident, Temple, and his Dutch counterpart arranging rival firework displays and bonfires proclaiming their conflicting claims to victory.[53] In Paris, where the English were prevented from mounting a rival display, the Dutch envoy supplemented his bonfires and fireworks with a huge banquet for invitees backed by trumpets, music, and free wine for passers-by.[54] At Leiden, the University curators lit up fifteen *pektonnen* (pitch barrels) before the principal Akademie building.[55] In Amsterdam, revellers lit so many bonfires the whole city looked aflame with one of the burning pitch barrels curiously capped by an effigy of Charles II in the shape of a dog with a crown.

Scholars today concur that the Dutch won the battle—but only by a slender margin. The English lost around ten of their eighty ships sunk, burnt, or captured, a noted symbolic element being the burning of *The Royal Prince*, and some 1,000

---

[48] Spinoza, *Collected Works* (ed. Curley) ii, 473; Totaro, "Niels Stensen (1638–1686)," 157.
[49] Scherz, *Niels Stensen*, 67–70; Scherz, "Biography of Nicolaus Steno," 200.
[50] Scherz, *Niels Stensen*, 71–2; Totaro, "Documenti," 98; Van Vugt, "Structure and Dynamics," 102.
[51] Bruijn, *Dutch Navy*, 87; Rommelse, *Second Anglo-Dutch War*, 160; Hattendorf, "Competing Navies," 107–8.
[52] Pepys, *Diary* ii, 45. [53] Haley, *English Diplomat*, 93–4.
[54] Rommelse, *Second Anglo-Dutch War*, 160; Haley, *English Diplomat*, 93.
[55] P. de La Court to J. Van der Voort, Meerborg, 21 June 1666 in La Court, "Brieven," 160–1.

men killed, around 1,450 wounded, and another 1,800 captured and brought to Dutch soil.[56] Morale plummeted for a time. In July, Pepys was much embarrassed by a large crowd of women invading the admiralty yard "coming to get money for their husbands and friends that are prisoners in Holland," and were "clamouring and swearing and cursing us [the admiralty staff]."[57] The initial "great dejectedness" in London nevertheless lifted later in the summer, helped by court propaganda and the rapid receding of the plague. Dryden, in his triumphal *Annus Mirabilis*, adhering to the early misleading reports of the Four Days' Battle as an outright victory, and omitting all mention of mismanagement, poor strategy, inept performance, and royal failure to pay England's seamen, continued presenting the war as unreservedly a glowing national triumph.[58] The young Louis XIV, having formally declared war on the Republic's side, in January 1666, made clear he was intervening only marginally for his own advantage, being content to watch Dutch sea-power substantially pruned back by a former ally who had deserted him and needed a lesson. Louis seriously intervened only to help rebuff the Munsterites, but even this limited support obliged the English court to worry continually about the French battle fleet's location and intentions.[59]

The English and Dutch populations continued to receive sharply varying accounts of what was happening. Amidst the fast days, thanksgiving, and ringing of church bells, preachers on both sides of the Channel reassuringly discerned the hand of divine providence powerfully working for their side. Despite paying dearly for their marginal victory, losing four vessels sunk, and with many more damaged, 1,550 men killed, including three admirals, and 1,300 wounded, the Dutch afterwards circulated highly inflated reports which, besides greatly offending English ears, De Witt believed with seriously damaging consequences. De Ruyter, supposedly, gained a decisive victory, with some reports, relates Pieter de La Court in a letter of 21 June, estimating English losses at "little less than forty ships" and 8,000 men dead, wounded, or captured. Reality was being grotesquely distorted and falsely propagated by a public seemingly much preferring delusion to the truth.

The Koerbaghs who in 1668 publicized Spinoza's views more boldly than had any others of his circle, ridiculed this outpouring of pious thanksgiving on their side in their *A Light Shining in Dark Places* (1668), deriding especially popular belief in angels miraculously intervening as active forces, preferring one side to the other in the great naval battles. In this "battle between the Dutch and English, in which the Hollanders proved victorious and bravely chased the former so as to crush them completely (as they deserved from us)," the Dutch nevertheless failed

---

[56] Rommelse, *Second Anglo-Dutch War*, 158–9; Hainsworth and Churches, *Anglo-Dutch Naval Wars*, 147–8.
[57] Pepys, *Diary* ii, 64.   [58] Winn, *John Dryden and His World*, 170.
[59] Hattendorf, "Competing Navies," 108.

to finish the job because "a dense fog appeared," suddenly making it impossible to find the enemy, which was obviously due, or so most contended, to God's direct intervention. For "during the pursuit, God, taking pity on the English, sent an angel into the Dutch fleet which, for a while, struck all the Hollanders together, from largest to smallest, with blindness, so that they could not pursue their English foes who in the meantime, helped by mist, happily sailed away." Was that fog, demanded the Koerbaghs sarcastically, not a miraculous event?[60] This was all utter stupidity. This "good angel for which the English should thank God mightily, by which they were saved" was just a dark fog that descended "preventing the Hollanders from seeing far" and causing them to fear running aground nearby or becoming scattered, and hence obliged them to halt their pursuit and turn back. "I count as miracles," affirmed the Koerbaghs, "all natural workings – for they are infinite – whereby God helps one side or the other," making it "unnecessary to contrive supernatural or unnatural happenings, or describe some things so inexactly and absurdly, that one resorts to such adornments."[61] Rather, "all of natural science must proceed with as much certainty as mathematics." Hence, "they seem to me to go against the whole of natural science and all philosophy who affirm that miracles are possible and can be worked by God."[62]

"Miracles," "angels," and "devils" the Koerbaghs, Meyer, Van den Enden, and Spinoza viewed very differently from Steno, Boreel, Serrarius, Oldenburg, or Boyle. Already, well before publication of Spinoza's *TTP*, a fundamental point for them was that supernatural events are metaphysically impossible, a contradiction in terms. No true miracles have ever occurred. The ancient Israelites, affirms Spinoza in the *TTP*, introduced the tradition of citing "miracles" to convince pagans believing in visible gods that a more powerful, unseen divine providence was on their side and "that all of nature was directed by the governance of the God they adored solely for their own benefit. So attracted have people always been to this idea that to this day they have not ceased inventing miracles to substantiate the belief that they are dearer to God than others and the ultimate reason for God's creation and continual governance of all things."[63]

The next mighty naval clash, the Two Days' Battle, or "St James Day Fight," was fought on 4 and 5 August 1666 off North Foreland, east of the Thames estuary. This time, none could doubt England's triumph. Humiliating defeat and a shambolic retreat caused a bitter quarrel between the two leading Dutch admirals, De Ruyter and the younger Tromp, the first allied to De Witt, the latter a fervent Orangist, further exacerbating tensions between the Republic's political factions while considerably troubling the admiralty colleges and fleet. An additional shock

---

[60] Koerbagh, *A Light Shining*, 414–15; Jones, *Anglo-Dutch Wars*, 27, 170–1; Hainsworth and Churches, *Anglo-Dutch Naval Wars*, 147.
[61] Koerbagh, *A Light Shining*, 414–17; Laurens, *De rede: bron van geluk*, 40.
[62] Koerbagh, *A Light Shining*, 482–5; Laurens, *De rede: bron van geluk*, 47–51.
[63] Spinoza, *Theological-Political Treatise*, 82; Wielema, "Two Faces," 66–7.

was the subsequent penetration by Holmes' squadron through the "sea-gate" to the inner side of the island of Terschelling where, huddling for safety, was anchored a fleet of over 150 loaded Dutch merchantmen. Using salvoes and fire ships, Holmes succeeded in setting virtually the entire convoy alight and destroying it.[64] In London, the guns of the Tower were fired in salute, and there were "bonfires also in the street for this late good successe."[65]

20.iv The Sway of Kings

Eager to exploit Dutch dejection at this setback and "Holmes' Bonfire" (Figure 20.1), Lord Arlington, increasingly directing Charles' foreign policy, asked Temple to write "some small paper" to "awaken the good patriots in Holland" to their true interest—their need finally to submit to England. Temple duly published, in French, his *Lettre d'un Marchand de Londres* (1666) purporting to be a missive from a London merchant to an Amsterdam merchant friend, urging the Dutch to use more honesty towards their own people and halt the gush of delusion falsely suggesting they were holding their own, and acknowledge the great extent of their defeats and hopelessness of their position. Warning of the

Figure 20.1 *Sir Robert Holmes sets fire to the Dutch merchant fleet off Terschelling, 19 August 1666*, drawing by Willem van de Velde. Reproduction courtesy of Rijksmuseum, Amsterdam.

---

[64] Jones, *Anglo-Dutch Wars*, 25, 44, 172; Rommelse, *Second Anglo-Dutch War*, 162–3.
[65] Pepys, *Diary* ii, 81.

danger of relying on a duplicitous ally, like Louis XIV (ironically, the option Charles and Arlington would before long follow to their own grief), France's monarch, the Dutch were admonished, sought only to annex Flanders and reduce the Republic to dependence on his unscrupulous self, whereas they could assuredly trust in Charles' unblemished uprightness and England's solid integrity.[66] Stressing French duplicity and his own distress at the destruction of shipping and Dutch misfortune, Temple admitted to having long reflected on the causes of the present conflict and its remedies. Such deadlock stemmed from the Dutch either naively overrating their French alliance or else misinterpreting English intentions, wrongly assuming either that the French "will be able to make you our masters, or that we want to make you our slaves."[67]

With severe slump gripping their ports, even small fishing harbours, and redundancy the great mass of seamen,[68] prospects looked dire indeed for the Dutch. But the picture changed suddenly with the flames and fumes of the "Great Fire of London" which raged uncontrollably for five days (2–7 September 1666), so that "a consuming pestilence" was followed by "a more consuming fire," as Dryden put it, the flames destroying around 13,200 houses and 87 parish churches as well as St Paul's Cathedral, gutting roughly three-quarters of "London, Empress of the Northern Clime." "Scarce recover'd" from the plague, records Sprat, "we receiv'd a second and deeper wound which cannot be equal'd in all history, if either we consider the obscurity of its beginning, the irresistible violence of its progress, the horror of its appearance, or the wideness of the ruin it made, in one of the most renown'd cities of the world."[69] It was a terrifying experience. Installing himself and his wife in the admiralty offices, Pepys dug a pit in the admiralty garden, to save his impressive store of wine and "parmesan cheese," the garden where he wandered after dark to "see how horribly the sky looks, all on fire in the night, [...] enough to put us out of our wits; and, indeed, it was extremely dreadful for it looks just as if it was at us and the whole heaven on fire."[70]

Such catastrophe, it went without saying, must be someone's fault. Churchmen of the era universally agreed that disasters mean someone was being divinely punished for something, but not on who was being punished for what. In Holland, there was much talk of divine retribution, especially for "Holmes' Bonfire." But in England, few thought anything of the kind, although some disgruntled Puritans ascribed the calamity to God's wrath due to sin and "uncharitableness." A more appealing explanation for most was that the catastrophe was due to Catholic conspiracy and foreign, probably French, treachery. Several foreigners were set upon by mobs.[71] It was especially hard for the Anglican establishment to explain

---

[66] [Temple] *Lettre d'un Marchand de Londres*, 3–4; Kishlansky, *Monarchy Transformed*, 244, 248.
[67] [Temple] *Lettre d'un Marchand de Londres*, 8; Haley, *English Diplomat*, 96.
[68] GA Delft 1e Afdeling 13/5, 52. Res. Vroedschap, 21 July 1666.
[69] Sprat, *History of the Royal Society*, 120.   [70] Pepys, *Diary* ii, 93.
[71] Harris, *Restoration*, 79–80, 150–1; Rommelse, *Second Anglo-Dutch War*, 164–5.

why divine providence should wreak such punishment on England. Obviously, the divinity was not helping the Dutch and only irredeemable Puritans claimed "the Fire" was retribution for laxity and lewdness prevailing at court, in Whitehall. Divine intervention works on different levels, some noted, and thankfully *had* positively intervened to guard the king, royal court, and their surroundings at Westminster, steering the raging flames away from the high end. The conflagration had menaced but did not reach the royal quarters. It devastated only the city's poorer and middling areas, grounds surely for at least some modicum of thanksgiving. Those taking the brunt of the losses, London's non-aristocratic citizenry, should submit with "humility to the judgments of Heaven."

The Dutch, meanwhile, "hearing we are all on fire in London, resolved immediately to come out again," a distraught Oldenburg alerted Boyle, "and are now at Margat-rode [Margate]. Our fleet, upon the hearing thereof, will quickly come to them with this wind, and then there may be another fight, if they stand it." But the Great Fire greatly hampered naval operations, particularly financially: from now on "the great stress will be," as Oldenburg expressed it, "how to raise money for carrying on the warre, and to rebuild the citty, at the same time."[72] Besides the navy, the catastrophe disrupted much else in the nation's culture and activities. The warehouses, stocks of books and shops of the London stationers, publishers and book dealers, many located around St Paul's, were wiped out, totally decimating the book trade and many collections, making it impossible to publish anything further for the time being.[73] As for "rebuilding of the citty," opinion in ruling circles, Oldenburg explained, on 2 October, is

> still very perplext, there appearing three parties in the House of Commons about it. Some are for quite a new model, according to Dr Wren's draught; some for the old, yet to build with bricks; others, for a middle way, by building a key and enlarging some streets, but keeping the old fortifications and vaults. I heare this very day there is a meeting of his Majestie's Councill and others of the nobility, with the leading men of the citty, to confere about this great work and to try whether they can bring it to some issue, before the people that inhabited London, doe scatter into other parts.[74]

The most worrying aspect, it emerged, apart from the blow to morale, was scarcity of funds. As the months passed, it became increasingly obvious that the States General's treasury could better withstand the colossal strain than could Charles II. But it was also becoming harder to outgun and board the Dutch warships due to their shipyards producing larger vessels with more guns and

---

[72] Oldenburg to Boyle, London, 2 October 1666 in Oldenburg, *Correspondence* iii, 238.
[73] Oldenburg to Boyle, London, 16 October 1666 in Oldenburg, *Correspondence* iii, 244.
[74] Oldenburg to Boyle, London, 2 October 1666 in Oldenburg, *Correspondence* iii, 238.

higher decks and gun placements. By late 1666, "on high-raised decks," as Dryden pithily expressed it "the haughty Belgians ride."[75] Still, the chief reason for the months of humiliating English defeat and frustration that now ensued was shortage of funds causing lack of supplies and pay for the fleet. Dockyard workers were protesting, seamen growing more vociferous in complaining about not being paid, rope-makers and other suppliers frequently refusing to deliver essential munitions for the fleet.

Lack of funds for the navy was exacerbated by the relative failure, in comparison with the 1652–4 conflict, of the "privateering war" against Dutch merchant shipping in European waters. Where during the First Anglo-Dutch War immense damage was inflicted on the foe bringing in enviable proceeds, at the expense of Dutch merchants—including the Spinoza brothers and their father, the bottom being knocked out of the firm of "Bento y Gabriel Despinoza" along with many another—the second conflict yielded comparatively little. From March 1665, with Dutch merchantmen forbidden to venture out, the Republic's (especially Zeeland's) privateers together with the French were now capturing more English vessels than vice versa, a major factor in diminishing enthusiasm for the conflict.[76] This left Charles all the more dependent on Parliament which was anything but eager to be forthcoming. Demanding money with which to prosecute the war, Charles reluctantly had to admit to the skeleton Parliament meeting that month (at Oxford instead of Westminster), that the conflict was indeed proving "more chargeable [than] I could imagine it would have been" and agreed to submit to a parliamentary committee, in which Brereton was prominent, to investigate the navy's expenses, use of funds and accounts.[77]

The king's prestige and that of the monarchy was conspicuously losing some shine. "Our Parliament has not yet concluded anything about the way of raising the 1,800 pounds [allocated in principle]," complained an exasperated Oldenburg later that autumn, "nor is the modell yet agreed upon by which the city is to be rebuilded." Before long, shortage of cash and naval stores forced the laying up of many of the crown's principal warships. By the autumn of 1666 there was neither money to keep the fleet at sea nor to prepare it, over the winter of 1666–7, for action in the spring, leaving the kingdom crouching almost entirely on the defensive.[78] On visiting the London Exchange, in early April 1667, Pepys heard "mighty cries for peace, and that otherwise we shall be undone," and "yet," he added, "I do suspect the badness of the peace we shall make."[79]

Little happened over the winter months, or in the spring. Finally, in June 1667, after a brief foray into the Thames estuary, De Ruyter, following De Witt's secret

---

[75] Dryden, *Anno Mirabilis*, stanza 79; Van der Welle, *Dryden and Holland*, 31.
[76] Bruijn, *Dutch Navy*, 87; Israel, *Dutch Primacy*, 278; Rommelse, *Second Anglo-Dutch War*, 172–3.
[77] Quoted in Rommelse, *Second Anglo-Dutch War*, 149; Hattendorf, "Competing Navies," 109.
[78] Oldenburg, *Correspondence* iii, 274; Rommelse, *Second Anglo-Dutch War*, 175.
[79] Pepys, *Diary* ii, 214.

plan, pulled off his famous "raid on the River Medway" (19–24 June), when the Dutch, breaking the chain across the river, penetrated to Chatham and Gillingham, bombarded the fortifications with cannon fire, burned or captured three "first rates" and another ten warships, and seized and towed away the flagship of the English fleet, the *Royal Charles*, a stupendous humiliation that caused deep ructions at court and profound shock to Oldenburg personally. "It is a sad sight," recorded Pepys in his diary, "to see so many good ships sunk there in the river, while we would be thought to be masters of the sea."[80] "The good news of the Dutch being beaten off at Harwich," on 2 July, raised spirits slightly. "Our fleet attempted Harwich-Castle but were beaten off with the losse of some 60 men," reported Serrarius to Oldenburg, on 5 July 1667, in a letter also reporting the, to him, more important news from Venice and Edirne of stubbornly reviving hardcore Sabbatian hopes.[81] But repelling the Dutch from the only major safe anchorage on England's east coast between the Thames and the River Humber indeed hardly compensated for the Medway disaster or now near hopeless logistics, the freezing of bank loans, fury of the seamen's wives, and prostrate condition of the navy.

The conflict dragged on; but now hopes of peace began surging too. Peace negotiations, notwithstanding continuance of Anglo-Dutch hostilities through the summer, were at last advancing "at great passes," as was hardly surprising. However, from May 1667, the entire picture, and not just in north-western Europe, was suddenly dramatically transformed by Louis XIV's unexpected, unprovoked assault on the Spanish [southern] Netherlands. Carefully timed, French forces invaded the southern Netherlands, in May, at a moment when the Spanish army of Flanders was much reduced, and the Anglo-Dutch conflict still unresolved. This creeping, slow invasion besieging fortified towns was a turn of events extremely disturbing to both England and the Republic but, in the long run, far more menacing and costly to the Dutch, as Bayle later pointed out, a reality which perhaps finally explained the meaning, he suggested jocularly, of the 1664–5 comets and continuing debate about what those alleged omens signified.[82]

"While we are thus at odds," averred Serrarius in early July, two weeks after the Medway episode, with Louis XIV touring Flanders in person to inspect his conquests, "the French go on and have now gotten alsoe Douay and are to attack Bruxel next."[83] One immediate consequence was that, despite the weakening of English resolve to continue the war, the Dutch, much to King Charles' relief,

---

[80] Pepys, *Diary* ii, 269.
[81] Serrarius to Oldenburg, Amsterdam, 5 July 1667 in Oldenburg, *Correspondence* iii, 446–7; Haley, *English Diplomat*, 130–3; Harris, *Restoration*, 71–4.
[82] Bayle, *Pensées diverses* i, 108; Haley, *English Diplomat*, 121–4; Sonnino, *Louis XIV and the Origins*, 9–18.
[83] Serrarius to Oldenburg, Amsterdam, 5 July 1667 in Oldenburg, *Correspondence* iii, 446–7; Haley, *English Diplomat*, 129; Herrero Sánchez, *Acercamiento hispano-neerlandés*, 168.

shelved their hopes (as they would not otherwise have done) of swift gains and recuperation of lost colonies. French gains thus aided a deeply thwarted monarch fearful of further humiliation by the Republic and accelerated the Anglo-Dutch peace negotiations but, ultimately, also cleared the path for the Anglo-French monarchical collusion behind the scenes, resulting five year later in De Witt's overthrow and the Republic's near collapse. The Anglo-Dutch conflict ended for now with the initial signing of the main articles of the Peace of Breda, on 31 July 1667, though that was not quite the end, as disputes over unresolved details lingered and the Dutch declined to stand down their fleet until the treaty was ratified. Pepys, visiting the London Exchange as the news began circulating, found the business world "not at all glad of it, but rather the worse, they looking upon it as a peace made only to preserve the king for a time in his lusts and ease, and to sacrifice trade and his kingdoms only to his own pleasures: so that the hearts of merchants are quite down."[84]

Serrarius, Bouwmeester, Rieuwertsz, and others kept Spinoza informed of what was being reported in Amsterdam about developments in England, the southern Netherlands, and the Near East, and doubtless alerted him too to the unfortunate mishap that befell Oldenburg. During the war's final stages, unsurprisingly, besides infighting among the courtly schemers responsible for England's disaster and the king's dalliances, harsh words and recrimination redounded at every lower level. Aware Parliament would investigate the shambles engulfing the navy, Pepys, being secretary of the admiralty, frantically concealed, as best he could, money he had corruptly syphoned off which, if much less than what Brouncker pilfered, was still substantial. If Brereton accused Pepys of corruption in the king's presence, Pepys, on 29 August 1667, described Brouncker as "a pestilential rogue, an atheist that would have sold his king and country for 6d almost." Oldenburg, for his part, caused offence by incautiously writing to someone "some words of complaint, of neglect and security on our side," afterwards admitting his "rashnes and folly" in venturing indiscreet "expressions" about the royal court's shortcomings.[85] If Charles was mostly indifferent to accusations of pilfering the public purse provided aristocrats served him loyally in other respects, there was much the high-born, like Brouncker, could get away with that underlings, Oldenburg now discovered, could not. Arrested, he was "committed" to the Tower of London and incarcerated for around a month "for dangerous desseins and practices" and found himself forced to "beg His Majestie's pardon [...] upon my knees." His indiscretion he attributed to profound distress at seeing "things goe no better for England, than they did," to believing there "were oversights and omissions somewhere which might prove prejudiciall to the honour of the king and the prosperity of the nation." He could not reconcile himself to the defeat, and

---

[84] Pepys, *Diary* ii, 298.
[85] McKie, "Arrest and Imprisonment," 35; Tomalin, *Samuel Pepys*, 190–3.

mismanagement of the war and the country's finances. Above all, he "felt heartily affected to see such insolence acted against England by a people, that but 80 years agoe, with folded hands implored the compassion and assistance of England [against Spain], and are in great part obliged to England for their present prosperity."[86]

Humbly submitting his petition from his cell to the king, on 5 August, he styled himself "Henry Oldenburg of Bremen" pleading for royal clemency, having written "severall rash and censorious expressions, for which he now stands committed to your Majesty's Tower."[87] To Arlington personally, Oldenburg confessed to allowing "those inconsiderate and foolish words" to slip out, protesting they arose not from treacherous design but purely "from affection," and the "great discomposure of mind I was in, to see the affairs of England not succeed so well, as I wished, and to find the honour and safety of his Majesty and his kingdoms endangered (such was my impertinent presumption to think) by the invasion of an insolent enemy." All his acquaintances knew "my love, concern and zeale for the king's and the kingdom's interest and prosperity," and "my hearty affection for the king and whole nation being resolved by God's assistance, to spend myself and my small abilities in their service." For someone once known, during the Cromwell era, for republican sympathies, Oldenburg showed scant sympathy, at any point, for the Dutch Republic's plight.

Kept in the Tower, obliged to pay for his own upkeep, until late August, Oldenburg was deeply shaken. It was not an experience that encouraged him, once out, to renew former contacts with anyone in Holland which perhaps explains his failure to resume correspondence with Spinoza at the end of the war. Incarceration in the Tower, he admitted afterwards, did "much prejudice me; many persons, unacquainted with me, and hearing me to be a stranger, being apt to derive a suspicion upon me. Not a few came to the Tower, merely to enquire after my crime, and to see the warrant; in which, when they found that it was for dangerous designs and practices, they spread it over London, and made others have no good opinion of me." When released, Oldenburg felt "so stifled by the prison-air," he wrote to Boyle on 3 September 1667, "that as soon as I had my enlargement from the Tower, I widen'd it, and took it from London into the country, to fann myself for some days in the good air of Crayford in Kent." "I shall live, fully to satisfy his Majesty and all honest Englishmen of my integrity, and of my real zeal," he assured Boyle, and "spend the remainder of my life in doing faithfull service to the nation to the very utmost of my abilities. I have learned, during this commitment, to know my reall friends."[88] Perhaps Boyle helped

---

[86] Oldenburg (via the hand of the Bishop of Exeter) to Arlington, The Tower, 15 July 1667 in McKie, "Arrest and Imprisonment," 33.
[87] McKie, "Arrest and Imprisonment," 38–9; Hutton, "Henry Oldenburg," 107.
[88] Oldenburg to Boyle, 12 Sept. 1667 in McKie, "Arrest and Imprisonment," 40.

accelerate his release. In any case, Oldenburg's confinement helps explain the cutting off of his main lines of contact with Holland. His correspondence with Spinoza was not his only foreign correspondence broken off at this point, though his interaction with Spinoza was interrupted for much longer than most others of significance.[89]

With the peace treaty signed, Pepys found most Londoners "pleased with their being at ease, and safe of a peace, that they may know no more charge or hazard of an ill-managed war: but nobody speaking of the peace with any content or pleasure, but are silent in it, as if of a thing they are ashamed of; no, not at court, much less in the city."[90] Dutch commerce meanwhile surged back strongly, as did the arts and sciences. Foreign tourists began arriving in considerable numbers, many eager to glimpse the waterways and fortifications that trapped the Munsterites and the war fleet that, to the amazement of most, against the odds defeated the English. One eminent foreign visitor to The Hague that autumn was Cosimo III de' Medici (1642–1723), eldest son of Tuscany's Grand Duke, soon to reign himself as Grand Duke (1670–1723). Fascinated by military engineering and the sciences, Cosimo eagerly inspected the Dutch fortifications, arsenals and battle fleet, spending much of the winter of 1667–8 in The Hague, now suddenly a heightened focus of cultural and diplomatic life.[91] Still deep into optics and telescope and microscope lens curvatures, as well as Bible criticism and political theory, Spinoza pressed on with writing the *TTP*. Whatever the shortcomings of the Dutch regents as a class, the likes of De Witt, Van Velthuysen, and Hudde struck Spinoza as an incomparably more responsible governing body than the courtiers of the monarchs running affairs in London and Paris.

Despite the insistent propaganda trumpeting Charles II's uprightness, integrity, and resolve, the prevailing myth to which (whatever their private doubts) Oldenburg, Boyle, Dryden, and Temple all abjectly lent their pens, the disasters and human cost of the Second Anglo-Dutch War unquestionably stemmed chiefly from royal arrogance, duplicity and scheming, from grasping royal and aristocratic ambition, as did Louis' aggression against the Spanish Netherlands. Many suffered on all sides and, according to the budding republican consciousness reflected most powerfully in the mid and late 1660s by the De La Court Brothers, Van den Enden, and Spinoza, this was wholly the fault of monarchy as an institutional structure and principle and its aptness for privileging greed, lust, and arrogance above the common good.

Prior to the war, Spinoza had felt a strong sense of being the chief initiator of an underground intellectual project to topple the oppressive theological and metaphysical structures of the day from beneath and a keen awareness of the risks and

---

[89] Meinsma, *Spinoza et son cercle*, 326–7; Hutton, "Henry Oldenburg," 108–9.
[90] Pepys, *Diary* ii, 322.   [91] Wagenaar, *Toscaanse Prins*, 18–20.

difficulties such a grand design entailed. But only while composing his *TTP*, spurred by the Anglo-Dutch conflict and the mounting risk from Louis XIV, obvious from May 1667, did he begin applying the laws of nature, as he understood them, more specifically to the political sphere and absorbing in a systematic way the fiercely anti-monarchical arguments of the De La Courts and Van den Enden. While composing his *TTP*, he showed himself a writer much less willing than Temple, Oldenburg, Huygens, or Boyle, to "let princes and states make warre and shed blood," as Dryden expressed it, as if it were their God-given right, sanctioned by scientific and philosophical quiescence, to wreak devastation. In England and France, these monarchs enjoyed the acquiescence and willing collusion of the intellectual elite as they mostly had in the past. But for the many onlookers either side of the Channel disgusted by the spectacle, the question of why men willingly sacrifice their own lives and die in the service, and for the sake of, such base, intriguing, ignorant, and deceitful enthroned personages, why men think it glorious to devote their lives and efforts to further exalt such ridiculously upstart royal pretensions to glory, became henceforth a central, guiding theme.

"Reason" was Spinoza's weapon against superstition and theological oppression as it was also for Huygens, Hudde, and Van Velthuysen. But from the mid-1660s, Spinoza's "reason" became in addition a key tool for teaching society how to avoid being continually lied to by the ambitious, calculating courtiers staffing princely courts, evade being misled to their own infinite cost and dragged into meaningless devastating conflict contrived to serve the greed of others. "It is not," contends Spinoza, in the final chapter of the *TTP*, "the purpose of the state to turn people from rational beings into beasts or automata, but rather to allow their minds and bodies to develop in their own way in security and enjoy the free use of reason, rather than participate in conflicts based on hatred, anger and deceit or in malicious disputes with each other. Therefore the true purpose of the state is in fact freedom."[92] But no such freedom as he envisaged could flourish under kings and aristocrats, or under the baseness of princely courts like that of Münster.

Spinoza's philosophy of freedom both individual and collective refused to defer to anything like the extent then considered *de rigueur*, to kings, church authority, or the principle of hereditary nobility. This "freedom" from the clutches of ruling elites was the chief goal of politics, according to Spinoza, and there was absolutely no way that such emancipation could ever be the acknowledged purpose or chief principle of the princely state as structured around the courts of Louis XIV, Charles II, or the bellicose, citizen-scorning prince-bishop Von Galen, or for that matter Cosimo. Nor could his political thought be diffused in any society of his time without society first thoroughly discrediting accepted notions about kings, royal courts, aristocracy, princes, and politics.

---

[92] Spinoza, *Theological-Political Treatise*, 252.

The highly unedifying scene of Anglo-Dutch conflict before his eyes, and French royal presumption and expansionism, left Spinoza in no doubt that the "chief feature of a democratic state is that its excellence is valued much more highly in peace than in war."[93] Armed conflict may sometimes be hard to avoid, but it is also hugely destructive and contrary to the essential goals for which men in general come together in the first place to form society and organize their state. "War ought to be waged," urged Spinoza in his last treatise, the *Tractatus Politicus*, begun in 1675, "only for the sake of peace, so that when it is finished, the weapons may be set aside." Hence, when cities are "captured by the right of war, and the enemy subdued, the peace terms must be set up in such a way that the captured cities need not be protected by a garrison. Either grant the enemy the right to buy back the cities for a price, once the peace treaty has been accepted, or [if that course creates a permanent threat to the border region] destroy the cities completely and resettle the inhabitants elsewhere."[94] Non-expansionism in this sense he considered a golden rule of politics, an essential lesson for all of humanity, but one impossible to propagate under the sway of kings and nobles.

Citizens, contends Spinoza, have a permanent investment in, and interest in preserving and guarding peace in a way that kings, princes, mercenaries, and nobles, unfortunately do not. For structural reasons, monarchies like that of Charles II were much likelier to initiate and wage war than republics, especially democratic republics. If Charles' court was chiefly responsible for the colossal damage of the Second Anglo-Dutch War, that was not just owing to Charles' own personal shortcomings but equally the fault of his court and those around him, as was true likewise of Louis XIV, Von Galen, and their courtiers: because those "men who have too much leisure often spend their time contemplating wicked actions. It is because of the nobility especially that kings are prone to wage war. For a king surrounded by nobles, there is more security in war than in peace."[95] This was the heartfelt creed of a philosopher whose personal experience, since 1651, had taught him to detest war and view its true authors, the likes of Arlington and Downing, as abject scoundrels—an accurate enough assessment.[96] Meanwhile, like Machiavelli, Spinoza, impressed no doubt by De Ruyter and his men, indicated his dislike also for "mercenaries," arguing that states should rely for defence exclusively on their own citizens.

Spinoza's conviction that a republic like the United Provinces, and indeed republics generally, are structurally inclined to embrace peace as far as possible, and that all wars troubling the Low Countries since 1566 were essentially caused by the ambitions of the monarchs of Spain, England, and France, especially Philip II, Charles II, and Louis XIV, together with their respective nobilities and

---

[93] Spinoza, *Political Treatise* (ed. Curley), 547.
[94] Spinoza, *Political Treatise* (ed. Curley), 542.
[95] Spinoza, *Political Treatise* (ed. Curley), 554.
[96] Kishlansky, *Monarchy Transformed*, 244–50.

princeling allies, now became a fundamental plank of his political and general vision, a general law of history. "If we attempt to calculate the periods in which the Israelites were allowed to enjoy complete peace" in their history, Spinoza concludes in the eighteenth chapter of his *TTP*, "we shall find a significantly vast difference" between the period without kings and those when they were under kings. In the time "before kings, they often passed forty and even, on one occasion (you may hardly believe this), eighty years in harmony without foreign or internal wars." But no sooner had kings acquired control of the state, than the reasons governing policymaking were no longer, as before, peace and liberty "but rather pursuit of glory, and we read that all the kings fought wars except only Solomon whose virtue, that is wisdom, flourished better in peace than war." Negative in its effects on the ancient Hebrew Republic, monarchy and lust for power displace and extinguish pursuit of the common good in every human society. Criticism of the state was therefore unnecessary in the period before King Saul, there being then no need "to counsel the people." "But once monarchy was chosen by the ancient Hebrews, there was always a large number of prophets" including unfortunately "false prophets," both being symptoms of the defects of monarchy, because there was always thenceforth far more in society and politics to complain of that was gravely wrong than there had been before the advent of kings.[97]

What Spinoza chiefly appreciated in biblical Hebrew prophecy was its being predominantly directed against reprobate kings. Rather than being persons divinely inspired, biblical prophets, in Spinoza's eyes, were private men of exceptional imagination bringing complaints and special grave warnings of importance to human well-being, delivering admonitions to society and the state from outside the councils of power. In his mind there existed an obvious parallel between their ceaseless predicament, facing an often hostile people unwilling to listen, and the predicament he and his allies faced in striving to help rescue De Witt's "True Freedom" and the very real blessings of the Republic from the pervasive errors of popular thinking, that is "superstition," Orangism, churchmen, and bigotry colluding with grasping, ignorant royal neighbours.

Spinoza valued some features of the Old Testament prophets, but did not think much of their general approach and strategy. Rather, to his mind, they went about reforming society and the state in entirely the wrong way. "By means of the liberty which they usurped to admonish, scold and rebuke," the prophets "had more success in antagonizing than reforming the people." They usually did more harm than good destabilizing the state by too directly censoring the sovereign, so that "religion lost more than it gained due to such license, besides the fact that serious civil wars arose because the prophets took so much authority for themselves." The correct procedure for fundamental reformers outraged by kings and genuinely

---

[97] Spinoza, *Theological-Political Treatise*, 233.

seeking improvement is to not to antagonize, but instead persuade and subtly transform the true sovereign, the people, by gently behind the scenes deploying the quietly pervasive power of reason.[98]

By the summer of 1667, most people in Holland and England alike longed for peace. But peace alone, leaving all else unchanged, remained absurdly insufficient in Spinoza's eyes. Many spoke of Dutch prosperity being at risk, but few made mention of "freedom," press liberty, and "liberty to philosophize" which figured among Spinoza's prime concerns. One who did yearn for peace and to fortify this yearning within an elevating universal moral and religious framework was Comenius who, seeking to advance his message that peace matters more than all else and that moral ills, lust for gain, self-seeking and thirst for colonies had caused this atrocious war, came in person, in July 1667, to Breda where the peace talks were taking place, to lecture the delegates of both sides and present them with copies of his book, *Angelus Pacis* [The Angel of Peace]. The duty of governments, for Comenius, is to establish as durable a peace as men can devise, a goal requiring universal education, teaching upright values and a more just world order based on lawful government and "freedom."[99]

Spinoza could wholeheartedly agree with that. But to him Comenius' approach hardly seemed realistic. Peace alone is by far insufficient when kings, nobles, and churchmen hold sway and when the people, steeped in ignorance and superstition, abjectly follow them. What he saw as the utopian schemes of Serrarius, Boreel, and Comenius for a just world were to him as irrelevant in the highly perilous political and diplomatic climate confronting the Dutch in the late 1660s as the scolding of the Israelite prophets in ancient Jerusalem. What society needed was assuredly peace, but peace anchored in stability, security, and greater inner unity, involving practical understanding of the mechanics of politics and shoring up the pillars of republican freedom from within; what Holland's neighbours needed was to learn how destructive of the general interest their glorious grasping kings, courts, and ecclesiastics actually were.

The entire European scenario was transformed by Louis XIV's invasion of the Spanish southern Netherlands. Temple, in the summer of 1667, still based in Brussels, pronounced it a venture greatly encouraged by the distraction of England and the Dutch, caused by their inconclusive conflict and mutual suspicion. "De Witt is resolved that their fleet shall not give over action till the very ratifications of the treaty are exchanged: in which he certainly pursues his interest that the war may end with so much the more honour abroad [for the Dutch], and heart at home."[100] But there was a high price to pay for his (partial) victory since during

---

[98] Spinoza, *Theological-Political Treatise*, 232.
[99] Woldring, *Pansofie van Comenius*, 118–19; Woldring, *Jan Amos Comenius*, 160–1; Ranalli, "Unity of Brethren," 27.
[100] Temple to Lord Arlington, Brussels, 19 July 1667 in Temple, *Letters written by Sir William Temple, Bart.* i, 110–11; Haley, *English Diplomat*, 100–1.

this interim the Dutch could exert no pressure to restrain the French. Frustratingly, the business of finalizing the Breda peace process between England and the Republic dragged on well into the autumn, while the French advances crept further and further. By October 1667, the far-seeing Temple judged the situation ruinous for Flanders, ominous for England, and menacing above all, as time would surely tell, for the United Provinces.

"For if the French shall carry Flanders, as they very well may in another campaign by the weakness and disorders of the government here (Brussels), the Dutch are sensible that they must fall to be a maritime province to France upon the best terms they can."[101] England and the Republic, as well as Spain, predicted Temple, must urgently "take such measures as are wise and necessary in such a conjuncture, which is perhaps the most important, that has been in a great while in Christendom, and may have consequences that none alive will see the end of."[102] The summer and autumn of 1667 was indeed a fateful turning point in Western history and political philosophy.

[101] Temple, *Letters written by Sir William Temple, Bart.* i, 127; Haley, *English Diplomat*, 155, 167, 186, 248.
[102] Temple, *Letters written by Sir William Temple, Bart.* i, 128.

PART IV
DARKENING HORIZONS

21
The Tragedy of the Brothers Koerbagh (1668–1669)

The tragedy of the Brothers Koerbagh was, in a way, that of early modern society more broadly. The Dutch Republic was probably the first modern society to escape majority illiteracy and yet it continued to guard its university-trained professions behind a façade of Latin, deriving its technical terms from a language unfamiliar to most and loaded with mysterious meanings. Owing to Calvinist stress on the need to immerse the individual man and woman in Scripture, literacy levels in Holland stood considerably higher at this time than in Britain, Germany, France, or Italy. Yet, medicine, the law, theology, and the workings of government, along with all higher education, remained fenced off from the majority by a language and terminology meaningless to most. An increasingly literate, book- and pamphlet-laden sphere of public criticism and cultural context, the Dutch Republic lifted society out of some of the darkness shrouding illiterate societies, greatly expanding demand for translations of works of science, philosophy, theology, history, and the classics into the vernacular, but yet without lessening the divide between university-trained elites and a popular literacy shaping mass attitudes permeated by religious doctrine but devoid of insight into the workings of the professions, government, medicine, law, theology, and science. The result was an intensifying clash between rising literacy and entrenched non-comprehension of how modern specialized knowledge functions, strife between specialization and entrenched ignorance, fast engulfing new areas and issues.

When discussing the destructive schism between Remonstrants and Counter-Remonstrants in Dutch society during 1617–19, in his *TTP*, Spinoza obviously had in mind not only the early seventeenth-century victims of Calvinist bigotry and condemnation such as Arminius, Episcopius, and Grotius but also the targets of Voetian indignation in his own time—the Koerbaghs, Meyer, and other recent victims of Reformed theological ire such as Wolzogen, Jan Knol, Wiszowaty, and the remarkable Abraham van Berkel (1639–86).[1] Van Berkel, a classic "perennial student" who had studied theology and then medicine at Leiden for fifteen years, was a staunch republican and friend of Pieter de La Court, fascinated by the lure of redirecting Hobbes' *Leviathan* (which he translated into Dutch and provided with

---

[1] Spinoza, *Theological-Political Treatise*, 257–8.

a preface) for anti-monarchical purposes. A close ally of the Koerbaghs, after studying theology in Leiden from the age of fifteen, beginning in 1654, and planning a career in the Reformed Church, Van Berkel switched to medicine in 1662 and, finally, in 1669, to classics.[2] In 1665, he anonymously published his translation of Sir Thomas Browne's *Religio Medici* enriched with footnotes revealing a marked libertine tendency and fascination with the figure of notorious Italian freethinker, Vanini, burnt at the stake at Toulouse in 1619.

In 1667, the same year the *Philosophia* furore peaked, Van Berkel published at Amsterdam his soon contentious Dutch version of Hobbes' *Leviathan* which helped reinforce the *cercle Spinoziste*'s conception of sovereignty as unitary, all-embracing, and indivisible, requiring subordination of all church power. Concealing his identity on the title-page as A.T.A.B., and deliberately undermining Hobbes' pro-monarchical intent, Van Berkel supplemented the *Leviathan* with additional subversive twists not intended by Hobbes, especially in the footnotes. Whether it was the hail of ecclesiastical condemnation greeting this publication, or an earlier clash with the law, in Delft, over unpaid debts, that forced him to flee, during the late 1660s the Koerbaghs' passionate enlightener translator friend sought refuge hiding in the autonomous (lordly) jurisdiction of Culemborg, near Utrecht.[3] From an early stage, Van Berkel took a keen interest in the history of unbelief and rejection of Christianity (and monarchy) and was unquestionably an early representative of the Radical Enlightenment; however, unlike his friends the Brothers Koerbagh, there is no sign in his editions that he took any particular interest in Spinoza or his philosophy.

When contemplating current victims of theological repression, Spinoza doubtless had in mind above all his friend Adriaan Koerbagh (1632–69) and the latter's younger brother, Johannes (1634–72), sons of a successful ceramics manufacturer who had died young, in 1644, bequeathing sufficient affluence for them to devote their lives to study and pursuit of truth. Enrolling in the Utrecht philosophy faculty in 1653, the brothers witnessed there at close quarters the escalating clashes over Cartesian philosophy. Lifelong close allies, in 1656 the brothers transferred to Leiden where they joined Meyer, Bouwmeester, Vallan, and Van Berkel, all fellow Leiden students at the time.[4] Apart from Johannes, all were then studying medicine, Meyer during 1654–60, Bouwmeester in 1651–8, and Vallan in 1652–8, and attending the same classes and events as Adriaan; all were drawn too to the philosophy courses.

Classic perennial students, Adriaan studied nine years in all, switching from medicine to law, while Johannes kept to theology and philosophy for ten years,

---

[2] Wielema, "Abraham van Berkel's Translations," 206; Weststeijn, *Radicale Republiek*, 62; Leeuwenburgh, *Het Noodlot*, 117.

[3] Meinsma, *Spinoza et son cercle*, 231, 242; Geldersblom, "The Publisher," 162–4; Wielema, "Abraham van Berkel's Translations," 207; Lavaert, *Vrijheid, gelijkheid, veelheid*, 145–8.

[4] Vandenbossche, "Adriaan en Jan Koerbagh," 167; Weststeijn, *Radicale Republiek*, 236.

getting to know most leading Dutch academics of the day personally and spending lengthy periods at Franeker and Groningen as well as Utrecht, but longest at Leiden. An *album amicorum* [book of friends], comprising extracts, poems, and signatures, compiled to celebrate the conclusion of Johannes' studies at Leiden, features the signatures of fifty-four well-wishers, a large proportion being his teachers, Abraham Heidanus, Adriaan Heereboord, Franciscus de le Boë Sylvius, Jacobus Golius, Gijsbertus Voetius, Samuel Maresius, Johann Friedrich Gronovius, and not least Johannes Cocceius several of whose works Johannes Koerbagh possessed in his personal library and to whom probably he owed his interest in Hebrew. The rest of the well-wishers, apart from a smattering of Collegiant universalists including Comenius, mostly comprised his friends of the emerging radical fringe, notably Meyer, Bouwmeester, and Vallan, with all of whom Johannes clearly became friendly during the early 1660s if not the late 1650s.[5]

A cousin of the Koerbaghs and medical student at Leiden since 1652, Jacob Vallan (1637–1720), later a "special friend" of Spinoza according to the younger Rieuwertsz, graduated in medicine, in 1658, with a dissertation on angina. On 27 January 1664, Vallan and his mother, Maritje, a sister of the Koerbaghs' mother, Trijntje Adriaensdr,[6] both attended as witnesses the baptism of a daughter of Vallan's sister, Lucia, and her husband, the prominent Amsterdam publisher and bookseller, Johannes van Ravensteyn (1618–81).[7] Vallan's house in Amsterdam stood near that of the Koerbaghs who lived no great distance from Rieuwertsz's house which, in turn, was close to those of Jelles and Meyer. Vallan practised as a physician in Amsterdam until 1669, then became town physician of Leiden and, in February 1675, professor of practical medicine at the University, taking over from his and the Koerbaghs' former teacher, Le Boë Sylvius, much of the practical surgical instruction for medical students. Friendly with Meyer in the late 1650s and 1660s, Vallan had family ties too with Bouwmeester whose house in Amsterdam was likewise within easy walking distance of those of Rieuwertsz, Jelles, and Meyer as well as the Koerbaghs. According to one recent theory, during 1662 and 1663, not only Meyer and Bouwmeester but also Adriaan and Johannes joined the reading club formed by Balling, Jelles, and De Vries that met, certainly for some of their meetings, in the bookseller Rieuwertsz's premises.[8] When around 1667, Jelles moved to another part of central Amsterdam, he rented a house from the Brothers Koerbagh, becoming effectively their tenant as well as neighbour.[9] By the mid-1660s, both brothers were now ardent zealots for Van den Enden's, Meyer's, Van Berkel's, and Bouwmeester's exciting new ideology of popular

---

[5] Van Heertum, "Reading the Career of Johannes Koerbagh," 13–14; see Bijlage 2 in Leeuwenburgh, *Het Noodlot*, 229–30; Mertens, "Johannes Koerbagh's Lost *Album*," 80–1, 83.
[6] Leeuwenburgh, *Het Noodlot*, 116, 130.   [7] Leeuwenburgh, *Het Noodlot*, 116.
[8] Leeuwenburgh, *Het Noodlot*, 154.
[9] Mertens, "All in the Family," 60n30; Mertens, "Where Thou Dwellest," 29.

enlightenment conveying Spinoza's core ideas, and were based back in their native city.

The Koerbaghs knew their Hobbes. But, in their Bible criticism and philosophical views it is important to stress that they were *not* disciples of Hobbes, as is often claimed, but emphatically disciples of Spinoza. Their philosophical approach was based on conceiving substance as existing independently and without causal connection with anything else, this one substance being "God from which all subsidiary or dependent beings derive."[10] Therefore, they held, there is no such thing as "metaphysics," only natural science as nothing can exist above or outside of nature; equally, there are no such things as miracles, magic, or demons.[11] Their concept of substance they derived either directly from conversing with Spinoza, or else perusing the *Korte Verhandeling*, or both. Further, their "dictionary" listing and explaining foreign terms long since or recently adopted into Dutch, *Een Bloemhof van allerley lieflijkheyd sonder verdriet* [A Garden of All Kinds of Loveliness without Sorrow] (1668) (Figure 21.1), ascribes the Pentateuch's entire authorship to Ezra "as the wisest and most learned people hold," denying Moses wrote any of the Five Books, hence, like Spinoza, adopting a more radical position than Hobbes according to whom Moses "wrote all that which he is there said to have written."[12] Also un-Hobbesian was their comprehensive programme for reforming society by assisting the common man in the street to understand key terms in theology, law, social status, and science thereby fundamentally transforming people's relationship to religion, the law, society, and education.

In fact, the *Bloemhof* emanates a strongly un-Hobbesian antipathy to the entire established mystique of nobility (as well as royalty). He who is "non-noble" they tellingly define not as someone of non-noble lineage but one who, even if of royal descent, is "ignorant and uncomprehending"; whereas, on the contrary "noble is he who is wise and learned even if the offspring of the poorest beggar."[13] What is definitely un-Spinozistic, especially in Adriaan's approach, is the overtly, no holds barred manner in which he advances his reform programme. Thus, under the heading "Reformed religion," in their *Bloemhof*, one reads that the term "Reformed," referring to the Reformed "or wrongly termed Calvinist" faith, should rightly designate a restored, purified religion. Since the (Calvinist) Reformed Church is only "slightly changed from the Roman Catholic," it is not at all a religion based on "wisdom, truth and reason," for such a religion would not require the power of the "sword, flames and the gallows" to be upheld "like all the other religions of the world known to me."[14] As for "heresy," the false religions of

[10] Koerbagh, *Bloemhof*, 275, 381, 444, 609, 632–3; Laurens, *De rede: bron van geluk*, 30–1.
[11] Koerbagh, *Bloemhof*, 444–7; Montag, "That Hebrew Word," 132.
[12] Hobbes, *Leviathan* iii, 592–3; Koerbagh, *Bloemhof*, 292, 325–6; Klever, *Mannen rond Spinoza*, 103; Lavaert, *Vrijheid, gelijkheid, veelheid*, 150; Laurens, *De rede: bron van geluk*, 22–4, 28.
[13] Koerbagh, *Bloemhof*, 346; Van Bunge, *Spinoza Past and Present*, 62–3.
[14] Koerbagh, *Bloemhof*, 327–38, 337–9; Laurens, *De rede: bron van geluk*, 19.

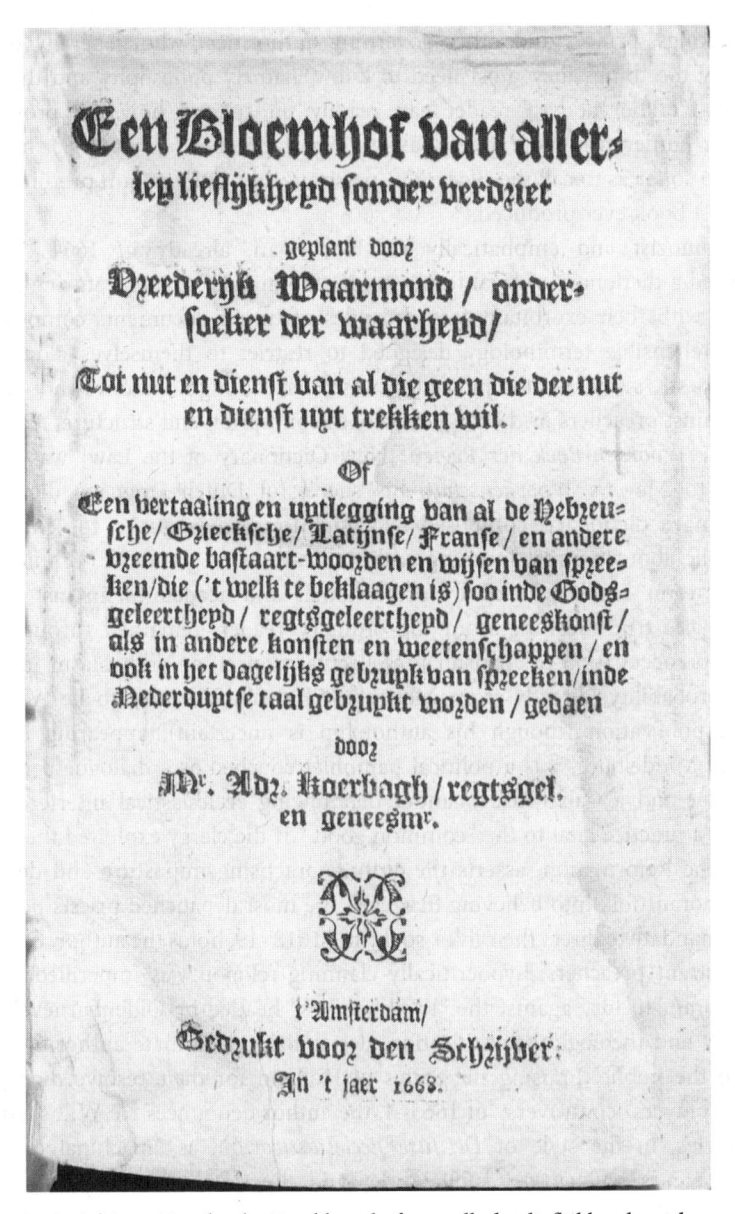

Figure 21.1 Adriaan Koerbagh, *Een bloemhof van allerley lieflijkheyd sonder verdriet*, T'Amsterdam: Gedrukt voor den schrijver, 1668. IAS Spinoza Research Collection.

the world require that bogus notion because "each faith seeks to conserve its incomprehensible articles of belief with ignorance and force." The abuse of power and control over people's lives that churchmen everywhere thirst for and usurp, contends Adriaan, succeeds only due to the "ignorance and lack of learning of rulers, kings, princes and other governing authorities" who generally despise precisely the things they most need to know, namely philosophy and the "true religion."[15] The modern reader can readily understand how the prominent German Lutheran bibliographer Valentin Ernst Löscher (1673-1749), in 1714, could go so far as to call the *Bloemhof* "pessimus, hic, qui unquam prodiit, liber," the worst book ever produced.[16]

A Spinozist and emphatically no Hobbesian, already in 1664 Adriaan published a dictionary of legal terms, under the initials "A.K.," featuring jibes at lawyers with their exorbitant fees and piles of turgid documents composed in incomprehensible terminology designed to restrict to themselves alone their quasi-priestly sway over the judicial process; here, though, there was not yet any sally against preachers or theology.[17] In both conception and structure, Adriaan's *'t Nieuw Woorden-Boek der Regten* [New Dictionary of the Law] was closely related to Meyer's *Woordenschat*, his successful Dutch language dictionary. Producing a dictionary, composed in straightforward language, to "enlighten" the public about the real meaning and implications of grandiose technical and generic terms regularly used by professionals and academics, in his view to obscure the true meaning from the ordinary reader, remained throughout a central preoccupation of Adriaan's intellectual project, an enthusiasm imbibed, in all probability, directly from Meyer.[18] What scholars take to be Adriaan's second publication (though his authorship is uncertain), appearing later in 1664, at Middelburg, was a political pamphlet couched as a dialogue between a Zeelander and a Calvinist Hollander denouncing ecclesiastical interference in politics, a practice fatal to the "common good." If the clergy exploited the people before the Reformation, asserts the author, practising imposture and deceit to trick ignorant folk into believing that even the most debauched priests possess a divine mandate to direct their lives, so during 1618-19, holds the author, Counter-Remonstrant preachers, hypocritically claiming religion was imperilled, stirred the ignorant to fury against the "loyal patriots" headed by Oldenbarnevelt with calumny and theological mystification, destabilizing legitimate authority at vast cost to the public. Praising the States of Holland for their resolve during the "public prayers" controversy of 1663-4, the author denounces De Witt's Voetian adversaries, in the style of *De Jure Ecclesiasticorum*, as "machinateurs" and "perturbateurs" subverting public order and the state to advance their own standing and sway.[19]

---

[15] Koerbagh, *Bloemhof*, 367-8; Krop, *Spinoza, een paradoxale icoon*, 99-102.
[16] Van Heertum, "A Not So Harmless Drudge," 415.
[17] Vandenbossche, "Adriaan en Jan Koerbagh," 168; Weekhout, *Boekencensuur*, 132.
[18] Leeuwenburgh, *Het Noodlot*, 123-5; Laurens, *De Rede: bron van geluk*, 12.
[19] [Koerbagh], *'t Samen-spraeck*, preface pp. i-iii and pp. 2, 31, 34-5; Jongeneelen, "Unknown Pamphlet," 405-6; Wielema, "Two Faces," 60; Fukuoka, *Sovereign and the Prophets*, 137.

As there is no evidence of the Brothers Koerbagh evincing radical tendencies before 1663, their radicalization may have just begun then,[20] spurred by the "public prayers" controversy. In any case, back in Amsterdam, both brothers were certainly full-fledged members of the radical fringe in both a political and theological sense by 1665. In the early summer of that year, shortly after returning from a trip to Amsterdam where Spinoza had missed finding his friend at home, when leaving, Spinoza wrote a letter usually assumed to be to Bouwmeester, complaining that his friend had not lately visited him in Voorburg, as expected, or written to him for some time to discuss, among other things, his medical problems. Several scholars have noted that this letter to an unnamed physician friend might equally well have been addressed to Meyer, Vallan, or Van Berkel rather than Bouwmeester, or indeed Adriaan Koerbagh. If addressed to Koerbagh, it would be the sole surviving fragment of a correspondence, or so Meinsma conjectured, afterwards completely hidden away or destroyed by Spinoza and his following for reasons of self-protection.[21]

Spinoza and this unnamed physician, the letter indicates, were on friendly terms and the physician was advising Spinoza about his recurrent fever, seemingly the form of the malaria then endemic at Amsterdam that he had had before but which surged back during his latest visit to his native city. As a soothing medication, his correspondent was recommending Spinoza to try "conserve of red roses," a syrup or conserve of pounded sugared roses apparently. As several scholars point out, this was a favourite remedy of Adriaan's, given that he devotes an entire, relatively long separate article to this recondite topic in his *Bloemhof*, albeit that article says nothing about its medical properties and it is also possible that this article in the *Bloemhof* on "conserve of red roses" was in fact one of Bouwmeester's extensive contributions to the volume.[22] "I expect some of the conserve of red roses which you promised," writes Spinoza, "though I have now for a long time felt better" than when he last visited the physician at home (in Amsterdam).

This letter of 1665 was omitted by the editors from the *Opera Posthuma*, in 1677, on the curious ground of "being of no value." Yet, while it probably has no connection with the lung sickness that eventually took Spinoza's life, it does indicate a notable phase of Spinoza's medical history, his suffering from the same or a like form of recurrent Amsterdam malarial fever as ended Swammerdam's life in 1680. It was an illness intermittently hindering Spinoza's work in the mid-1660s, feverish attacks causing him, on occasion, to "open a vein" seeking relief, though the last opening of a vein, in Voorburg, after returning from Amsterdam in late May 1665, he reports, hardly seemed to help. He did, though,

---

[20] Van Heertum, "Reading the Career of Johannes Koerbagh," 1, 12, 34, 37.
[21] Meinsma, *Spinoza et son cercle*, 295–7, 315n62; Leeuwenburgh, *Het Noodlot*, 117–19.
[22] Koerbagh, *Bloemhof*, 183; Meinsma, *Spinoza et son cercle*, 315 n62; Bordoli, *Etica, Arte, Scienza*, 74; Leeuwenburgh, *Het Noodlot*, 117; Bloksma, "Spinoza, a Miraculously Healthy Philosopher," 37–8; I thank Cis van Hertum for her comments on this point.

since leaving Amsterdam and returning to Voorburg eventually feel considerably better, "because of the change of air, I think. But I have suffered two or three times from tertian fever [tertiana]. By good mode of life [bona diaeta] finally I have driven it out and put it on the most evil cross [i.e. sent it to hell]. Where it has gone to I do not know, but I shall take care that it does not return."[23] Healthy lifestyle with good air and plenty of walking was undoubtedly a key preoccupation of Spinoza's. The relative mildness of this attack of fever and his having suffered malarial attacks several times previously suggests a certain level of immunity had built up. Since infectious mosquitoes returned each year in seventeenth-century Amsterdam only in August, this fresh feverish attack probably resulted from dormant febrile parasites, or hibernating hypnozoites, lodged in the liver. Quite possibly, Spinoza, as many had, first suffered from malarial fever in Amsterdam as a child.[24]

The letter also reveals Spinoza had long been urging this physician friend "to apply yourself with real energy to serious work, and prevail on yourself to devote the better part of your life to the cultivation of your intellect and your soul. Now, I say, while there is yet time, and before you complain that time, and indeed you, have slipped by." This could hardly pertain to Meyer but does perhaps fit Bouwmeester who, despite his energy and domineering manner, causing him to acquire the nickname "Dr Dick alias bully, or Nero the bogeyman,"[25] hardly implying lack of confidence, does in fact seem to have been strangely loath to commit himself to writing anything under his own name. Spinoza suspects this particular medical friend of suffering from feelings of inferiority. If Meyer in the poem he wrote to celebrate his friend, Bouwmeester's birthday, in November 1673, abundantly praises his intellectual ability, wide knowledge and ability to inspire others, he also rebukes him for his reluctance to write and lack of confidence intellectually.[26] Spinoza too believes his friend is talented intellectually and "practically certain you have rather less confidence in your abilities than is right, but afraid that you may inquire into, or propose something, unworthy of a man of learning," a phrase that may well apply to Bouwmeester rather than Adriaan Koerbagh.

Writing to Bouwmeester later, in June 1666, Spinoza answers his query about how to advance "in thinking about the most excellent things" without distraction and being side-tracked. There is no freedom of the will, reaffirms Spinoza, but "we can make certain and untiring progress in the study of things of the highest importance," can "direct and interconnect our clear and distinct perceptions," but only by the "true method" involving "constant meditation and a most

---

[23] Spinoza to Bouwmeester (?), undated, in Spinoza, *Opera* iv, 162–3; Spinoza, *Correspondance* (ed. Rovere), 193n1; Spinoza, *Briefwisseling*, 219; Spinoza, *Collected Works* (ed. Curley) i, 396.
[24] Bloksma, "Spinoza, a Miraculously Healthy Philosopher," 34–5.
[25] [Boeckelman], *Onschult of Zamenspraak*, 4, 27; Bordoli, *Etica, Arte, Scienza*, 159.
[26] Steenbakkers and Bordoli, "Lodewijk Meijer's Tribute," 248–9, 252.

steadfast mind and purpose, to acquire which one must establish a fixed way and manner of life and have a definite aim in view."[27] If Bouwmeester never did find a long-term project of his own, he nonetheless powerfully contributed to the ideas and achievements of both Meyer and the Koerbaghs. A hostile pamphlet, the *Koeckoecx-Zangh* (1678), by a medical rival, designates Bouwmeester, rather than Meyer, as the one who "writes books claiming philosophy and natural reason are the Interpreter of God's Word," who concocted the anonymous *Philosophia S. Scripturae Interpres* (usually attributed to Meyer). If you are curious about the "atheism" of the "big-faced Johannes Bouwmeester," mockingly advises this pamphlet, ask Johannes Ravensteyn (Vallan's brother-in-law) about "those lessons [Bouwmeester] gave to his brother-in-law, Koerbagh."[28]

After discussing his illness, in the letter of June 1665, Spinoza informs his unnamed medical correspondent that his principal philosophical work, the *Ethics*, is now well advanced, and "regarding the third part [...], I shall soon be sending some of it to you, should you wish to be its translator, or to our friend [Simon Joosten] De Vries." Although earlier not intending to send any of the text until it was complete, Spinoza had now changed his mind because the project was taking longer "than expected, I don't want to keep you waiting too long. I shall send it up to about the eightieth proposition." Thus not only did the recipient, whether Bouwmeester, Koerbagh, or conceivably Vallan or Van Berkel, have previous access to Spinoza's early writings along with De Vries, but this personage too was in line at this point as a reader and possible translator of the *Ethics*. As the final version of the *Ethics*, first published in 1677, had only fifty-nine propositions in Part III and seventy in Part IV, it seems Spinoza had now completed the first three out of the present five parts by early 1665 and at least a good chunk of Part IV too, with presumably a larger proportion of Part IV and perhaps the start of Part V ready by the summer when he switched to writing the *TTP*.[29]

Soon afterwards, the Brothers Koerbagh were cited in the minutes of the Amsterdam Reformed consistory of 10 June 1666, Johannes for spreading "godless views" and Adriaan for disorderly lifestyle,[30] leading to the summonses described earlier, including Johannes' encounter with Petrus Leupenius, a pastor with experience of investigating Socinian gatherings for the church council.[31] Demanding Koerbagh explain himself in writing regarding five key theological points, Leupenius received from Johannes, later that summer of 1666, a text headed "Jan Keurbach's Short but Upright Reply to Five Questions put to Him

---

[27] Spinoza, *Collected Works* (ed. Curley) ii, 32–3.
[28] *De Koeckoecx-Zangh*, 8, 10; [Boeckelman], *Onschult of Zamenspraak*, 28; Bordoli, "Account," 176–7.
[29] Spinoza, *Correspondance* (ed. Rovere) 194; notes to Spinoza, *Briefwisseling*, 468–69; Spinoza, *Collected Works* (ed. Curley) i, 396.
[30] GA Amsterdam MS 376/11, p. 225. Acta Kerkeraad, res. 10 June 1666.
[31] Meinsma, *Spinoza et son cercle*, 115; Evenhuis, *Ook dat was Amsterdam* ii, 236; Van Bunge, "Introduction," 17.

by Petrus Leupenius, minister of the Word of God in this city," that was afterwards examined by the consistory and copied verbatim into its minutes. Having earlier shown no particular radical tendencies when becoming a candidate for the Reformed Church pulpit, by the mid-1660s Johannes had been fully converted to Anti-Trinitarianism and a steadfast Spinozist viewpoint. Whether it was Johannes or his older brother who initiated their embracing Spinoza's core concepts remains unclear, as is the question whether they gained access to Spinoza's early unpublished philosophical manuscripts, like Jelles, De Vries, and others of Spinoza's circle, though, given what followed, this seems probable.[32] In any case, by 1666 both Koerbaghs, working together, belonged unequivocally to Spinoza's Amsterdam circle of disciples.[33]

To Leupenius' first question, "what do you understand by the concept God?" Johannes replied, God is "the only, eternal, unending, omnipotent, omniscient and ubiquitous independent, unchanging and supreme being." On the question of the Holy Trinity, the most essential point for Leupenius, he answered that he could not find the term *Drieenigheid* [Trinity], or any equivalent, in Scripture and hence concluded no such doctrine can rightly be derived from Scripture; nor can the idea that there "should be three distinct divine personae in the single being of God [in het eenvoudige weesen Godts] be demonstrated from clear and distinct reasoning."[34] Venerating Jesus, the man, as if he were divine, is hence sheer "superstition." Regarding resurrection of the dead, again no "clear and distinct idea" about it can be derived from Scripture. Asked about heaven and hell, he replied that the notion of "Heaven" in Scripture means the blessed state of the chosen, while "Hell" denotes the wretched state of those who are not blessed, a doctrine spelt out afterwards in the two brothers' last and most radical book, *Een Ligt schijnende in Duystere Plaatsen om te verligten de voornaamste saaken der God geleertheyd en Gods Dienst* [A Light Shining in Dark Places to Illuminate the Main Questions of Theology and Religion] (1668).[35]

Interrogation resumed on 5 August 1666 before the full consistory who were deeply shocked, the young ex-proponent Johannes was told, by his "blasphemous" views and grave offence against society in propagating such malevolent opinions among "ordinary and common folk."[36] More interviews over the next weeks resulted in stern admonitions not to express his intolerable views about Christ and Scripture again and warnings that if he defied the consistory by communicating his views to others, he would be hauled before the city magistrates and

---

[32] Roodenburg, *Onder censuur*, 201; Wielema, "Two Faces," 58; Laurens, *De rede: bron van geluk*, 21–42.

[33] Van Bunge, "Introduction," 28; Mertens, "Johannes Koerbagh's Lost *Album*," 84–5.

[34] Johannes Koerbagh, "Korte doch Oprechten Antwoord," GA Amsterdam MS 376/11, p. 235; Meinsma, *Spinoza et son cercle*, 340–1; Weekhout, *Boekencensuur*, 103.

[35] Johannes Koerbagh, "Korte doch Oprechten Antwoord," GA Amsterdam MS 3766/11, p. 235; Klever, *Mannen rond Spinoza*, 103–4; Montag, "That Hebrew Word," 132.

[36] GA Amsterdam MS 376/11, p. 234. Res. Acta Kerkeraad, 5 Aug. 1666.

severely punished. Both brothers became more cautious for a time, but beneath the surface these clashes only hardened their disgust with religious authority. The following summer, in June 1667, the consistory heard that Johannes was "once again beginning to speak of the Holy Scriptures and catechism in a very blasphemous manner."[37] Two preachers were sent to rebuke him afresh. He denied disparaging church doctrine and again undertook not to do so. But six months later, two young theology students sent to spy out a recent Collegiant meeting on the Amsterdam Rokin, reported seeing him seated with the principal speakers and, when addressing the gathering, declaring their meetings legitimate despite many of those present affirming that Christ is not the "true God" but "just an eminent teacher or prophet."[38]

Still technically a candidate for the Reformed ministry, Johannes was summoned yet again, in January 1668, but this time, far from being contrite, flew into a rage berating the consistory "not like a doctor of theology [...] but like a raving or possessed person."[39] Ordered outside until he calmed down, on reappearing he was asked whether attending illegal Collegiant gatherings and denigrating the Reformed confession was compatible with his accepting and signing the Reformed creed five years before. "He acted as he thought then, he answered, when he knew no better, but was wiser now." Questioned again about Christ's divinity, the encounter lapsed into a total impasse. He refused to answer "even if he were to be torn to pieces."[40] Appearing twice more before the consistory that January, Johannes remained recalcitrant.[41] At a further interrogation, on 1 March 1668, after first refusing "in rude terms" to discuss his views, Johannes reaffirmed that the Trinity, three persons in one being, is a doctrine found nowhere in Scripture but only in church teaching, that nothing can be made from nothing, and that his "concept that there is only one infinite spirit that is one infinite body, divided into different *modifications* comprising both Creator and all created things was by no means so strange." Whether or not anyone else in the room realized it, Johannes' adherence to Spinoza's thought and terminology on the main issues relating to God, Nature, and the Creation was again being confirmed directly from his own mouth.[42]

At Amsterdam, attention switched that February to the *Bloemhof*, a book usually treated today as written by Adriaan alone, but probably the work of

---

[37] GA Amsterdam MS 376/11, pp. 303, 307. Acta Kerkeraad res. 9 and 23 June 1667.
[38] GA Amsterdam MS 376/11, p. 351. Acta Kerkeraad res. 29 Dec. 1667; Van Bunge, "Introduction," 18.
[39] GA Amsterdam MS 376/11, p. 353. Acta Kerkeraad res. 5 Jan. 1668; Meinsma, *Spinoza et son cercle*, 355-7.
[40] GA Amsterdam MS 376/11, p. 353. Acta Kerkeraad res. 5 Jan. 1668; Van Bunge, "Introduction," 20.
[41] GA Amsterdam MS 376/11, pp. 361, 364-5. Acta Kerkeraad res. 19 and 26 June 1668.
[42] GA Amsterdam MS Kerkeraad 11, p. 374 res. 1 March 1668; Israel, *Radical Enlightenment*, 186-9; Secrétan, "Qu'est-ce qu'être libertin," 37.

both brothers with others of the circle, Bouwmeester in particular. In the consistory's view, it brimmed with blasphemous remarks "about God, the Creation, our Saviour Jesus Christ, Son of God, and the divine and perfect Word of the Lord,"[43] calling the Church's teaching pure fabrication and deceit. Set out as a typical dictionary, with affinities to Meyer's dictionary, it classifies the Holy Trinity as simply a "versiering" [adornment] without justification in Scripture, obfuscation devised by churchmen to extend theology's sway and that of the clergy over society.[44] In the *Bloemhof*, a relatively small number of entries on theology, observes Leibniz in his *New Essays*, provoked an exceptional degree of indignation.[45] There is doubtless truth in the later rumours that the input of the "devilish Dr Dick," as some of his foes called Bouwmeester, was pervasive. But as much as the ideas, what especially riled contemporaries was the aggressive, insolent tone, and the Brothers' insisting theologians have no special knowledge of divine matters that any thinking individual does not possess and are systematically deceiving the people, the *Bloemhof*'s entry on the "Reformed Church" claiming the name is a misnomer because the Calvinist church is rooted in bigotry and oppression, not "wisdom, truth and reason."[46]

Rejecting all the main churches, the *Bloemhof* denies the existence of angels, Satan, and everything supernatural, terming the common usage of these terms "a great abuse of the theologians."[47] Abjuring the Trinity outright, the book was blatantly illicit under the 1653 decree and subject to instant suppression by civic and provincial authorities. Profoundly "Spinozistic," several articles such as "essentie," "metaphysica," and "substantie," unambiguously affirm there is only one "nature" and that nothing outside it can exist;[48] that this one entirely self-contained Being is God, with everything else stemming from that one self-contained Being.[49] This central doctrine of Spinoza, the Koerbaghs were thus publishing at a time when all of Spinoza's own writings spelling out this doctrine remained unpublished and, what is more, nearly a decade before the publication of Spinoza's *Opera Posthuma*.

The true meaning of the biblical term "angel," given its Greek root, the Koerbaghs took to be simply a "messenger"; here, following Hobbes' *Leviathan*, but where Hobbes does not ultimately deny the existence, in the New Testament, of supernatural apparitions called angels, the Koerbaghs, following Spinoza's

---

[43] GA Amsterdam MS 376/11 p. 372. Acta Kerkeraad, res. 23 Feb. 1668.
[44] Koerbagh, *Bloemhof*, 498–9, 632–3; Leeuwenburgh, *Het Noodlot*, 125–6; Lavaert, "Entre clandestinité," 45.
[45] Leibniz, *New Essays*, 277; Laerke, *Leibniz lecteur*, 93n6; Van de Ven, *Documenting Spinoza*, ch. 7.
[46] Koerbagh, *Bloemhof*, 327–8; Koerbagh, *A Light Shining*, 51–3; Fukuoka, *Sovereign and the Prophets*, 208–11.
[47] Koerbagh, *Bloemhof*, 268, 670; Wielema, "Two Faces," 59; Lavaert, "An Excellent Mathematician," 262; Lavaert, "Entre clandestinité," 37–8.
[48] Koerbagh, *Bloemhof*, 444; Klever, *Mannen rond Spinoza*, 89.
[49] Koerbagh, *Bloemhof*, 275; Van Bunge, "Introduction," 73–4.

teaching—but preceding publication of his views—emphatically do.[50] Magic, sorcery, and spells are all dismissed as absurdities without basis in reality. The Greek term "heresy," so fundamental for the main churches, they classify as another abusive fabrication since the word "heretic" really only means a "follower" choosing his sect. Aiming to demystify all key foreign words absorbed into the vernacular, the term "Bible," holds the *Bloemhof*, "is a bastard Greek word signifying just a book, no matter which, whether Renard the Fox or Till Eulenspiegel."[51] What a pity we do not have more "heretics," cultivating "reason from which the truth stems," for then there would be less division and hatred in the world "as the truth is one and simple." "I lament that churchmen say it is a great abuse or sin to render all such Greek, Hebrew and other terms in general usage into plain, clear Dutch," to be generally understood, lest the "common man, as they fear, should grow wise."[52]

It would be hard to find a more open, direct attack on Christianity as generally defined, on all the churches, church tradition, practice and doctrine, not just mainstream but even of the most rationally Socinian Anti-Trinitarian variety. "Redemption" is construed as meaning rescuing a person or persons from this-worldly need, distress, and unfreedom, especially ignorance, by instructing him, her, or them, in wisdom and helping those thus "redeemed" to attain the "highest happiness" and eternal blessedness, "so that this form of redemption is the greatest redemption that can be conceived." As for Jesus, "a carpenter, the son of Maria, and supposed son, or so it was claimed, of Joseph the carpenter," he was indeed a redeemer among the Jews "because he taught the people and sought to bring them to wisdom and knowledge by which awareness of the highest good is reached." But the notion that by letting his blood flow, his suffering and death, he atoned for and absolved us of our sins, totally lacks basis in Scripture and is flat contrary to the truth. Who the real father of this worldly redeemer was, remains unknown and, "hence, ignorant people claimed he was God, God from eternity and the Son of God from eternity and that in worldly time he was born of a virgin without a man coming to her: but these tenets have no basis in Scripture and are contrary to the truth."[53] Later, in *Een Ligt*, one reads that Jesus "insofar as he was a teacher who brought some people from ignorance to knowledge, thus far was he also a saviour"; and insofar as he "guides us toward knowledge, so far can he be said [...] to be our saviour, and we his saved, but not in any further sense."[54]

---

[50] Koerbagh, *Bloemhof*, 303, 670; Koerbagh, *A Light Shining*, 404–5, 410–11, 460–73; Hobbes, *Leviathan*, 266–70; Osier, "L'Herméneutique," 332; Vinciguerra, *Spinoza et le signe*, 289–90.
[51] Koerbagh, *Bloemhof*, 95; Jorink, *Reading the Book of Nature*, 91.
[52] Koerbagh, *Bloemhof*, 293; Lavaert, *Vrijheid, gelijkheid, veelheid*, 152–3.
[53] Koerbagh, *Bloemhof*, 276–7, 664; Nadler, *Book Forged in Hell*, 42; Van Heertum, "Reading the Career of Johannes Koerbagh," 2–3.
[54] Koerbagh, *A Light Shining*, 153; Van Bunge, *Spinoza Past and Present*, 198.

Flagrantly illegal, all this was highly offensive even to many Collegiants, let alone regular Protestants, Catholics, and Orthodox. The Collegiant poet Joachim Oudaen (1628–92) would later, in 1687, include Koerbagh among his list of the world's worst "kinderen van duysternis [children of darkness]," the others being Vanini, La Peyrère, Meyer, Spinoza, and Hobbes.[55] The Amsterdam Reformed consistory and district classis promptly dispatched delegates to the city hall to read out selected passages of the *Bloemhof* to the burgomasters who, duly appalled, in March 1668, ordered the entire stock seized from the bookshops.[56] This was swiftly done, or so they claimed, but some copies had already seeped out and today surviving copies of the *Bloemhof* are not especially rare, over seventy being known to exist. Six months later, Rieuwertsz was among five Amsterdam booksellers arraigned by the city *schout* [sheriff] for selling Koerbagh's "blasphemous" book.[57] At Utrecht too, the book was condemned by church council and burgomasters as "blasphemous" and confiscated from the bookshops; in late April 1668, it was likewise condemned by the synod of Overijssel meeting at Deventer.[58]

Legal proceedings regarding this "scriptum pessimum, blasphemum, atheisticum" commenced almost at once. Although some copies carry the pseudonym "Goedaart Onderwys [Well-meaning Education]" on the title-page, the author, unwisely setting alongside his other pseudonym "Vreederijk Waarmond [Peaceful Mouth of Truth]" out of misplaced bravado, instead, self-identifies himself on the title-pages of most copies (roughly sixty of the surviving seventy), as "Adriaan Koerbagh, lawyer and doctor."[59] Informed by the magistrates' chief officer, the city *schout*, that he faced trial and must on no account leave the city, Adriaan defied the order and fled. Assuming the pseudonym "Pieter Wilte," he went undercover in Culemborg together with his comrade, Van Berkel, already hiding there, bringing with him the manuscript of his last and most radical work denouncing theological repression, *Een Ligt schijnende in Duystere Plaatsen*, which begins by identifying God or Jehovah with everything in existence, the one being that is "the being and essence of all things." "All that one sees, hears and feels," proclaim the Koerbaghs, "is nothing but a mode of being dependent on this being."[60]

With Adriaan in hiding, Johannes was again summoned before the consistory where, on 1 March 1668, he flew into another of his rages, denouncing the consistory and dismissing the Trinity as a *contradictio in terminis*, a fanciful "poem" contrived by theologians (much as *Een Ligt* pronounces the Trinity "not

---

[55] Israel, *Radical Enlightenment*, 367; Siebrand, *Spinoza and the Netherlanders*, 60n, 148.
[56] GA Amsterdam MS 376/11, pp. 377, 379. Acta Kerkeraad res. 8 and 15 March 1668.
[57] Van Eeghen, *Amsterdamse boekhandel* iv, 88; Van Heertum, "A Not So Harmless Drudge," 395, 397.
[58] GA Utrecht MS Acta Kerkeraad viii, res. 13, 20 and 27 April 1668; Weekhout, *Boekencensuur*, 288.
[59] Koerbagh, *Bloemhof*, title-page; Van Heertum, "A Not So Harmless Drudge," 396; Van Bunge, "Introduction," 29–30.
[60] Koerbagh, *A Light Shining*, 57–9; Laurens, *De rede: bron van geluk*, 21–3.

so much above, as rather contrary to reason," a senseless mystery nowhere found in Scripture).[61] Asked whether he had collaborated with his brother in writing the *Bloemhof*, he admitted "having corrected some passages when it was in the press, as well as to seeing nothing wrong with its contents."[62] Even their ever bold relative, Pieter de La Court, felt the *Bloemhof* threw all caution to the winds with its reckless blasphemies.[63]

In their next book which they planned to publish as soon as possible, *Een Ligt*, the brothers again put forward a clearly Spinozistic conception of God and creation, holding that "there cannot be more than one independent substance [datter niet meer als een selfsstandigheyd kan zijn] on which everything depends," while true salvation is simply human happiness in this world with reason and knowledge the sole path to this "blessedness," the goal of all sound human aspiration.[64] In thus seeking to present Spinoza's vision of reality and religion to the public, the brothers, highly significantly, were substantially preceding Spinoza himself, or rather in some sense acting as his mouthpiece, by forthrightly proclaiming such views in print in the *Bloemhof* and proposing to follow this up rapidly with *Een Ligt*. Everything in Scripture not in accord with "reason" they pronounced useless and vain. "It is better to know than to believe" as nothing should be accepted as true unless clearly grasped, since everything true in philosophy is true equally in theology, and there is nothing true theologically that is not true philosophically, and there can be no separation between the two, precisely Meyer's point and, though expressed differently in the *TTP*, also Spinoza's.[65] Good and Bad in the brothers' schema is not a divinely ordained moral system and has no connection with church doctrine, but is rather a relative standard measuring what is good or bad for the individual and his neighbour.[66] "Heaven" in their system means being united with God through knowledge. All core Christian dogmas are expressly rejected and the "greatest salvation" is declared to consist "in bringing one or many (the more, the greater the saviour) out of ignorance to knowledge, wisdom and understanding, by which the soul attains life, that is immortality and knowledge of God."[67] This was hardcore firmly un-Hobbesian Spinozism, its basic principles and terms being not just Spinoza's but fervently "Spinozistic."

---

[61] Koerbagh, *A Light Shining*, 93–7; Weber, *Beurtheilung der Atheisterey*, 129; Israel, *Radical Enlightenment*, 190.
[62] GA Amsterdam MS 376/11, pp. 374, 377. Acta Kerkeraad res. 1 and 8 March 1668; Koerbagh, *A Light Shining*, 74–5; Meinsma, *Spinoza et son cercle*, 359.
[63] Weststeijn, *Radicale Republiek*, 236; Lavaert, *Vrijheid, gelijkheid, veelheid*, 163–5.
[64] Koerbagh, *A Light Shining*, 68–9, 82–3, 116–21; Meinsma, *Spinoza et son cercle*, 332–3; Wielema, "Two Faces," 62–3; Wielema, "Adriaan Koerbagh," 571.
[65] Koerbagh, *A Light Shining*, 96–101; Van Bunge, "Introduction," 23; Nellen and Steenbakkers, "Biblical Philology," 55.
[66] Koerbagh, *A Light Shining*, 206–11; Van Bunge, "Introduction," 25.
[67] Koerbagh, *A Light Shining*, 142–3; Lavaert, *Vrijheid, gelijkheid, veelheid*, 159–61.

Kings and princes have historically practically always neglected the very study most necessary for responsible rule, namely "true" or real theology—that is worldly wisdom (i.e. philosophy). By manipulating the ignorance of kings, churchmen have long arrogated to themselves a sway to which they are not entitled. Here the brothers were at one with *De Jure Ecclesiasticorum*, their friends Van Berkel, Meyer, Van den Enden, Bouwmeester, and the De La Courts as well as Spinoza. Eager to rescue men from the stifling mental prisons theology and despotic regimes impose on mankind, emancipating humanity from superstition, seeking to lead men towards individual and collective happiness, the Brothers Koerbagh outdid Spinoza in their audacity, or, as they doubtless saw it, stood in for him, taking the flak, in projecting his explosive categories into the public sphere.[68] Aligning closely with his views at all points, they stressed even more than Spinoza himself that "they who are deeply ignorant are certainly very miserable; those are deeply unhappy who possess no understanding enabling them to judge between what is an impossibility, a contradiction and lie, from what is a possibility or the truth." Accordingly, salvation consists exclusively in rescuing those steeped in ignorance, prejudice, fictions and lies, and guiding them "to knowledge by education and reason to the truth."[69] Christ was "our savior, certainly," but only insofar as he taught the people and brought them to knowledge, understanding, and wisdom; faith plays no part whatever in what Christ taught and nor could his suffering and dying expiate anybody's sins or "bestow any happiness on us."[70]

"One should not accept anything as true and certain but what is understood and clearly grasped, as clearly as one perceives that the whole is greater than its parts and that all parts of a whole together constitute the whole." Everything not clearly understood in precise geometric terms should be rejected, so that for a sound, well-constituted society it is necessary to dissolve belief entirely in knowledge and geometrically expounded philosophy.[71] Frequently reiterating that knowledge is worth infinitely more than faith, Koerbagh's books, it has been justly observed, "are certainly far more outspokenly anti-Christian than anything Spinoza ever dared write."[72] Where the *Bloemhof* states that Jesus was not God but merely a remarkable individual conceived normally, albeit illegitimately, 1,167 years ago without our knowing who his father was,[73] *Een Ligt* adds that the Jews are surely entirely justified in not recognizing Jesus as the "son of

---

[68] Wielema, "Two Faces," 59.
[69] Koerbagh, *A Light Shining*, 116–17; Van Bunge, *Spinoza Past and Present*, 197–8.
[70] Koerbagh, *A Light Shining*, 130–5, 142–5; Klever, *Mannen rond Spinoza*, 97–8.
[71] Koerbagh, *A Light Shining*, 99–101; Wielema, "Two Faces," 59, 66–8; Laurens, *De rede: bron van geluk*, 48–57.
[72] Wielema, "Adriaan Koerbagh," 571; Laurens, *De rede: bron van geluk*, 45–6, 51; Lavaert, "An Excellent Mathematician," 256, 264; Secrétan, "Qu'est-ce qu'être libertin," 41.
[73] Koerbagh, *Bloemhof*, 354, 664; Meinsma, *Spinoza et son cercle*, 366.

God," since Jesus, contrary to what the churches say, is nowhere foretold in the Hebrew Bible.[74]

Despite the Koerbaghs' anti-theological thrust, it remains true that the Spinozistic sect emerging in the 1660s arose essentially from blending Socinian Anti-Trinitarian theology and rationalism with Spinozist philosophy and therefore cannot be deemed altogether secular in its origin and early formation.[75] A residual Christian echo perhaps pervades Johannes' and Adriaan's idea that he who seeks to instruct the multitude will likely suffer, and become a martyr, in the face of popular ignorance, bigotry, and fury. Exactly this was their own fate, a perspective grounding and encouraging Adriaan's apparent willingness to expose himself to great loss and suffering for the good of all,[76] though when afterwards imprisoned, Adriaan reportedly felt much aggrieved that he alone suffered the consequences of his books while shielding others complicit in his project, the most audacious ingredients being actually contributed by Bouwmeester.[77]

If for Jelles and Balling especially, searching for a genuinely "Christian" creed remained a key component of their joint crusade against churchmen, Johannes showed by his continued participation in Collegiant gatherings that the moral tradition and underground sect he helped foment and to which he nailed his colours retained some characteristics of a religious sect. Still, like Meyer, Johannes was critical of even the most rationalistic tendency among the Socinian Collegiants. Socinians reject Christ's divinity and all theology connected with such belief, and, for them too, Jesus is just a man; but, unlike the Koerbaghs, they deliberately played down his illegitimate birth and the fact he is nowhere foretold in the Old Testament. They invoke Christ as specially elevated, claiming divine inspiration confirms a unique status in him, a point Spinoza too seemingly acknowledges, and hence that Christ should be adored and, in some sense, prayed to. Here, despite still regarding Socinians as close allies and styling Socinianism the only "truly reformed" church, the Koerbaghs signally departed from even the most radical Socinian Collegiants.[78] Furthermore, since Socinians deny Jesus' divinity and the Trinity, their quasi-adoration of Christ leaves them open to the charge that their reverence amounts to a species of idolatry: "for to worship a man," as some Collegiants verged on doing, asserts *Een Ligt*, "is idolatry."[79] Like Meyer earlier and Bayle later, to the Koerbaghs even the most "rationalistic" Socinians remain backward, inconsistent theologians rather than scholars

---

[74] Koerbagh, *A Light Shining*, 192–5.
[75] Wielema, "Two Faces," 64–5; Salatowsky, "Socinian Headaches," 181–3.
[76] Van Heertum, "Reading the Career of Johannes Koerbagh," 3–4.
[77] [Boeckelman], *Onschult of Zamenspraak*, 28; Bordoli, "Account," 176; Leeuwenburgh, *Het Noodlot*, 207.
[78] Israel, "Meyer, Koerbagh," 200; Lavaert, "An Excellent Mathematician," 270.
[79] Israel, "Meyer, Koerbagh," 203; Salatowsky, "Socinian Headaches," 192–3.

thinking forthrightly and philosophically. Socinians are they "who do not yet in everything entirely use reason."[80]

Operating incognito under the alias "Pieter Wilte," by late spring Adriaan was collaborating with Van Berkel to get *Een Ligt*, their last and boldest book, printed. However, in late April 1668, Amsterdam's magistrates and clergy discovered that Adriaan was in Culemborg "disseminating his filthy opinions also there."[81] Avoiding the printer of the *Bloemhof*, in Amsterdam, Herman Aeltz, now under close surveillance, *Een Ligt* had been entrusted to a certain Johannes van Eede, in Utrecht. Disaster struck when appalled by the "strange opinions" he found in the book, Van Eede, having printed as far as page 176, refused to continue. Doubtless virtually any printer would have been shocked to find on the very first page that the Christian clergy "preach hate instead of love," that most, "especially those who are the most powerful and have most followers or supporters, do the reverse of the Saviour's bidding in both words and deeds," and that churchmen were responsible for the Wars of Religion.[82] With Van Eede antagonized, Johannes was summoned to Utrecht to help to get him to resume printing, Van Berkel and Johannes assuring him the book would not be marketed without official approval. When he refused, Johannes reportedly exclaimed: "what do you want to print if you do not wish to print the truth? A heap of almanacs and books full of lies?"[83]

Van Eede not only refused to return the manuscript but revealed that it was no longer in his possession. Revealing the affair to the authorities without informing the Koerbaghs, he had passed the manuscript to the local magistracy in Utrecht (who then promptly passed it on to their colleagues in Amsterdam). Learning of this, Johannes and Van Berkel proceeded to Culemborg to alert Adriaan and provide money of which he was running short. There were thus many reasons for the judicial and Reformed Church authorities of Utrecht and Amsterdam to suspect Johannes of being a, even perhaps *the*, principal culprit. After all, it was he who had been the principal suspect hitherto, who was steering the book through the press in Utrecht, and who had studied theology and knew some Hebrew, a prime tool of *Een Ligt*.

Hobbes, it is worth noting, met with no general denunciation until the 1660s. Even then, though under some pressure, he was by no means in hiding, being protected by the favour of the third Earl of Devonshire, and discreetly by the king.[84] Ostracized to a degree, and excluded from the Royal Society, he was forbidden to reprint his *Leviathan* and under threat from a parliamentary commission charged with gathering information on such books "as tend to Atheisme,

---

[80] Koerbagh, *A Light Shining*, 271; Wielema, "Adriaan Koerbagh," 68–9; Israel, "Meyer, Koerbagh," 205.
[81] GA Amsterdam MS Acta Kerkeraad 11, p. 383, res. 19 April and 26 April 1668.
[82] Koerbagh, *A Light Shining*, 46–7; Krop, *Spinoza, een paradoxale icoon*, 96–8.
[83] Meinsma, *Spinoza et son cercle*, 361–2; Leeuwenburgh, *Het Noodlot*, 192.
[84] Malcolm, "Summary Biography," 21, 24.

Blasphemy or Prophanenesse, or against the Essence or Attributes of God," and in particular the "booke of Mr Hobbs called the *Leviathan*."[85] Still, Hobbes never ventured anywhere near as far as the Koerbaghs (or Spinoza) and especially not the "blasphemous" statements about Christ and Christianity in *Een Ligt*. On returning from Utrecht and Culemborg, Johannes was arrested on 10 May while crossing Dam Square in the city centre after walking, by unfortunate coincidence, smack into the Amsterdam *schout* Cornelis Witsen (1605-69), a prominent but stern figure much involved ten years earlier in the proceedings surrounding Rembrandt's bankruptcy. Witsen detained him on the spot.

The Amsterdam magistrates lost little time in conferring with the Reformed consistory about the seized manuscript and printed sections of *Een Ligt*. Meeting on 17 May, the consistory heard that "Doctor Johannes Koerbagh" had been imprisoned pending trial in connection with the printing of the blasphemous *Een Ligt schijnende in Duystere Plaatsen*, from which selected passages, communicated to them by the magistrates, were read out, causing a "great wrenching of the soul" among the assembly. The next day a Reformed church delegation delivered their account of Johannes' reprehensible record at the town hall. Following a series of tense confrontations over the years with Johannes, the preachers had no difficulty in discerning parallels between his views, as previously expressed to them, and the contents of *Een Ligt*. Johannes had expounded to them several of what were in fact key doctrines of *Een Ligt*, such as insisting that the world could not have been created *ex nihilo* and declaring, using Spinozistic terminology, that there is "only one infinite Spirit and one infinite Body distinguished solely in their respective modifications." Furthermore, in places the book relied on skills in Hebrew which Johannes possessed but Adriaan did not. With all this reported to the burgomasters, Johannes was remanded pending further investigation.[86]

Summoned for trial, in Amsterdam, under threat of banishment for life and confiscation of all his possessions, Adriaan, meanwhile, at dire risk in Culemborg, had fled to a fresh hiding place.[87] In June, Witsen asked the consistory for copies of their records concerning Johannes, especially "his opinions."[88] During the ten weeks during which he remained behind bars, Johannes' allies in Collegiant circles and among the radical fringe doubtless discussed the distressing news among themselves. Friends and acquaintances knew what was afoot, but not the wider public. Thus far, only one reply to the *Bloemhof* had been readied for the press, by the same Mennonite Socinian, Jan Pietersz Beelthouwer (*c*.1603-*c*.1669), who had earlier published a rebuttal of the *Philosophia*. Nervous about publishing a second sally against radical ideas denying the validity of theology without the magistrates'

---

[85] Curley, "I durst not write," 507; Malcolm, "Summary Biography," 23-4.
[86] GA Amsterdam, Acta Kerkeraad 11, p. 385, res. 17 May 1668; Van Bunge, "Introduction," 30-1.
[87] Meinsma, *Spinoza et son cercle*, 363; Leeuwenburgh, *Het Noodlot*, 194.
[88] GA Amsterdam, Acta Kerkeraad 11, p. 387. res. 3 June 1668.

concurrence, Beelthouwer asked permission but, in July, was told by Hans Bontemantel and others in the city government that he should not publish his refutation because it would encourage badly inclined readers to want to read the *Bloemhof*, a book so appalling that in any case it entirely refutes itself.[89]

As word circulated that the Amsterdam burgomasters, magistrates, and consistory were seeking out Adriaan's whereabouts, a financial reward for his capture was posted in The Hague, Leiden, Utrecht, and Amsterdam. On 6 July 1668, an anonymous letter reached the Amsterdam town hall offering details of Koerbagh's whereabouts in return for payment. Authorized to offer between one thousand and fifteen hundred guilders, a very substantial sum, several years' salary for an artisan, Witsen, while in Utrecht, received a second message from the anonymous informant who, moved by his deep faith and respect for religion, was anxious to disclose the whereabouts of the accused, but because this person was a trusted friend he could only do so for a larger sum. If he received at a tavern at Everdingen, between Culemborg and Vianen, run by a landlady called "Joppie," an officially sealed guarantee from the burgomasters that 3,000 guilders would be paid to him by 13 July, he would supply all the information required including about the missing "learned Dr Van Berkel," likewise complicit in composing prohibited books, and someone who held many conversations with Koerbagh in Culemborg. Unwilling to pay more or officially seal a communication to an anonymous person, the burgomasters adhered to their original offer of 1,500 guilders.

The "friend" accepted the money and duly provided the details. Seized on 18 July, in his new hiding place, in Leiden, along with all the papers found in his rooms, Adriaan was brought under guard to Amsterdam and incarcerated in the famous early seventeenth-century clock tower and high security goal, the Jan Rodenpoortstoren, one of the city's most imposing sights. The next day, the Koerbaghs' house was ransacked for additional evidence.[90] Now thirty-five years old, Adriaan was tried in late July by a panel of regents including Hudde and Hans Bontemantel. On a table before the magistrates lay his seized letters, copies of the *Bloemhof*, and the half-printed *Een Ligt*. With Van Eede and others testifying against him, his trial lasted several days with a guilty verdict a foregone conclusion. Adriaan made no attempt to deny his authorship, but did deny that he had collaborated with others. Aware of Van Berkel's role and that Johannes had "long been suspected by the consistory," the magistrates wished to uncover the extent of their complicity and find out who else was involved. Was Johannes a co-author or perhaps "even the principal author of the two books?"[91]

---

[89] Meinsma, *Spinoza et son cercle*, 363–4; Van der Wall, *Mystieke Chiliast*, 470.
[90] GA Amsterdam MS Arch 5059/39/9. Aantekeningen Bontemantel, pp. 413–14, 459, 19 July 1668.
[91] GA Amsterdam MS Arch 5059/39/9. Aantekeningen Bontemantel, p. 414.

Adriaan never refers to Spinoza by name in his writings any more than Spinoza's surviving correspondence ever mentions Koerbagh. It was obvious, though, by 1668, that these texts claiming "there exists only one substance that is, Being, or all in all,"[92] and that the common beliefs of the people and churches are nonsensical, stemmed from a broader conspiracy than just Adriaan himself. Aware they were dealing with a group movement and effort, the judges gathered additional information from various sources, including Beelthouwer. Some steps in the interrogations were almost certainly attempts to implicate Spinoza in the "blasphemies" surrounding Christ's divinity, the publicizing of which was the principal crime of which Adriaan was accused. There was nothing haphazard, therefore, about the judges' dragging Spinoza's name into their questioning and deliberations. Under Dutch law it was not illegal to define God as the totality of everything, but repudiating the Trinity, Christ's divinity, that Christ died to expiate men's sins, and the sacred status of Scripture, as well as claiming Christ's coming is not foretold in the Old Testament, were all serious offences. So too was the *Bloemhof*'s claiming Old Testament prophecies about the peoples of the world eventually following the Messiah better fit Muhammed than Christ and that it remains unknown who Jesus' father was.[93]

He was the sole author of the *Bloemhof* and *Een Ligt*, insisted Adriaan, having composed the latter mostly in Amsterdam but finished it in Utrecht and at Culemborg. Asked about his brother's, Van Berkel's, and Spinoza's roles, he replied that Johannes "had never helped with it, while Spinoza too possessed no knowledge of it [ende dat Spinose daer ook geen kennisse van heeft gehadt]."[94] Asked if "Dr Berkel had not helped, he again answered no." Told that it seemed unlikely that he wrote these books entirely alone, he admitted perhaps consulting others now and again when he had particular questions.[95] Bontemantel, who probably knew both brothers from their student days, noted that Koerbagh, under questioning, though sullenly submissive, stuck stubbornly to his claim that he alone was responsible. His brother had corrected details here and there but not anything "offensive." As for his core argument, he had not "spoken about the matter" with Johannes or with Spinoza,[96] though he did admit having several times conferred personally with Spinoza, confirming from whence his overall philosophical approach derived, while stalwartly shielding Spinoza from any involvement in denying the Trinity or composing his books. Protecting his brother and Spinoza clearly mattered to Adriaan. Still, he did now frankly

---

[92] Koerbagh, *A Light Shining*, 80–3; Nadler, *Book Forged in Hell*, 43.
[93] Koerbagh, *Bloemhof*, 354, 664; Freudenthal/Walther, *Lebensgeschichte* i, 285; Koerbagh, *Een Ligt*, 173–85.
[94] GA Amsterdam MS Arch 5059/39/9. Aantekeningen Bontemantel, pp. 460–1, 26 July 1668; Meinsma, *Spinoza et son cercle*, 366.
[95] GA Amsterdam MS 5061/318 Confessie-Boeck, fo. 115, 21 July 1668; Freudenthal/Walther, *Lebensgeschichte* i, 285–6; Van de Ven, *Documenting Spinoza*, ch. 7.
[96] Meinsma, *Spinoza et son cercle*, 366; Leeuwenburgh, *Het Noodlot*, 199.

admit his personal link and conversations with Spinoza that our other evidence merely implies.[97]

Both brothers acknowledged living in their mother's house, in Amsterdam, and taking their meals together. But they had separate studies and kept their activities, they insisted, highly implausibly, strictly separate. Asked whether he knew Hebrew, Adriaan answered negatively. Asked if he knew the meaning of a Hebrew term he had used, later construed from the archival record to be *Shevuoth*, the Jewish early summer festival celebrating the wheat harvest in the Holy Land, but more likely *Shekhinah*, a metaphysical term meaning God's dwelling or presence,[98] he explained that he looked up words he needed to research in Buxtorf's dictionary (several of Buxtorf's Hebrew lexicons were in Johannes' library). The most he would concede was occasionally asking Johannes about the roots and meaning of particular Hebrew terms. Otherwise both brothers admitted only that Johannes had corrected an uncontroversial section or two. Asked whether he considered the *Bloemhof* "blasphemous," he refused to answer.

When his turn came to appear before the judges, after ten weeks' imprisonment, on 21 and 26 July, Johannes stuck to the same story. His brother wrote Dutch better than he did and had not involved him in composing his books. He had never read either work and did not know what was in them.[99] Understandably incredulous that the two dwelt in the same house without ever discussing the content of Adriaan's two books, the judges asked why then Johannes had involved himself with the Utrecht printer of *Een Ligt*. While shielding himself, Johannes proved as scrupulous as his brother in also protecting Spinoza, Bouwmeester, and Van Berkel. Both brothers refusing to admit anything further, their answers were afterwards read out to them. The prosecuting magistrate, Witsen, demanded harsher sentencing for both than was finally settled on—thirty years' imprisonment for Adriaan, with confiscation of all belongings, public condemnation via a ceremony in front of the city hall with the prisoner placed on a scaffold, his offences read out, right thumb to be cut off and tongue pierced with a red-hot iron. After long deliberation, the magistrates decided against any such spectacle or proclamation before the public.

The judges' and preachers' chief priority was to ensure the public learned as little as possible about the Koerbaghs and their books. All proceedings would remain behind closed doors. For Adriaan, they opted for ten years' imprisonment, followed by ten years' banishment from the city upon release, with a 4,000 guilder fine, and a further 2,000 guilder penalty to cover the costs of the proceedings and

---

[97] Vandenbossche, "Adriaan en Jan Koerbagh," 172; Wielema, "Two Faces," 58; Klever, *Mannen rond Spinoza*, 90; Leeuwenburgh, *Het Noodlot*, 198; Touber, *Spinoza and Biblical Philology*, 37.

[98] Meinsma, *Spinoza et son cercle*, 365–6; Montag, "That Hebrew Word," 133–4; Van Heertum, "Reading the Career of Johannes Koerbagh," 5.

[99] GA Amsterdam MS 5061/318 Confessie-Boeck, fos. 117–117v, 21 July 1668 and pp. 119–21, 26 July 1668.

his imprisonment.[100] The Amsterdam printer of the *Bloemhof*, the Catholic Herman Aeltsz (1621–96), employed by Rieuwertsz, in 1663, to print the Dutch version of Spinoza's Descartes book, also a witness, was fined 630 guilders, two years of a working man's salary, for his part in the group conspiracy.[101] But as to whether Johannes should be imprisoned too, albeit for a shorter term, have to pay a fine and costs, and be subjected to flogging behind closed walls, the judges could not agree. The *schout* proposed twelve years behind bars and a hefty fine for Johannes who had, after all, confessed to denying the Trinity and Resurrection of Christ, and could be presumed to have helped write the books. But as no proof of involvement in *Een Ligt* had emerged, Bontemantel "could not see on what grounds banishment could be justified, much less several years imprisonment and confinement."[102] Imprisoning or banishing a prisoner who had already spent ten weeks in prison and admitted no complicity or crime, would give him personally a bad conscience, Bontemantel recorded in his notes, since in "our country" the law did not investigate or punish opinions concerning religion but only attendance at banned meetings and proven involvement in forbidden publications. This argument of Bontemantel helps explain why Johannes got off relatively lightly and Spinoza escaped unscathed. Finally, the regents accepted that Adriaan alone should be imprisoned.

Their judgements were not announced publicly in the usual manner. The entire business remained behind closed doors, the magistrates being anxious especially to avoid drawing attention to the suppressed books and the brothers' ideas.[103] Nevertheless, word about the case spread informally. The leading Remonstrant preacher in Amsterdam since 1667, and foremost expounder of Arminianism of the entire second half of the seventeenth century, Locke's future friend, Philippus van Limborch, professor of theology at the Remonstrant seminary and among the best informed observers of the Amsterdam scene of the day, was horrified by Koerbagh's view of "the Creation" and clear about the connection between the Koerbaghs and Spinoza, as well as Koerbagh's participation in Spinoza's circle. He described him as belonging to "that herd" [grex] as he called the *cercle Spinoziste*, writing to Van Velthuysen in September 1671, a point he reaffirmed a decade later, writing to Le Clerc, in 1681, where again he calls Koerbagh "quidam ex ejus sequacibus [a certain one of Spinoza's adherents]."[104] Koerbagh's books, this great champion of Arminian (i.e. moderate Enlightenment) toleration excluding pagans, Catholics, and some others opposing the fundamentals of Christian belief

---

[100] GA Amsterdam MS Arch 5059/39/9. Aantekeningen Bontemantel, pp. 463, 466, 26 July 1668; Lindeboom, *Stiefkinderen*, 347.
[101] Van Eeghen, *Amsterdamse boekhandel* iii, 14; Jagersma and Dijkstra, "Uncovering Spinoza's Printers," 290–1.
[102] GA Amsterdam MS Arch 5059/39/9. Aantekeningen Bontemantel, pp. 469–71, 26 July 1668.
[103] Meinsma, *Spinoza et son cercle*, 368.
[104] Meinsma, *Spinoza et son cercle*, 519; Simonutti, *Arminianesimo*, 83–4.

from being tolerated, assured his longstanding contact, Henry More, in March 1669, were not just "impious and blasphemous," but bound God to act according to the laws of nature and under necessity, despicably denying miracles, Christ, and divine providence. Such views, Van Limborch did not doubt, fully deserved the fines inflicted on Koerbagh and his ten years' imprisonment.[105]

Locked up in the Willige Rasphuis, on the Amsterdam harbour front, Adriaan was initially reported to be in a state of fury, avid to convince all and sundry of the truth of his "ruinous" views. But after a few months he grew silent and contrite. In December 1668, the Reformed consistory sent a city preacher to visit him and, should God provide means to free him from "the snares of Satan," retrieve his soul.[106] Koerbagh now evinced great contrition for his blasphemous books, this preacher reported, "wishing he had never written them."[107] The consistory agreed to send a preacher again at a later stage, but that opportunity never came. Koerbagh died in his cell, in the Willige Rasphuis, in October 1669, a year after receiving his sentence, apparently without changing his views, and was buried in Amsterdam on the 15th of that month. Hearing he had not repented before any churchman, local opinion remained broadly unsympathetic. Rumours circulated afterwards to the effect that his burial was overshadowed by satanic forces in the form of a black hen (a later version says a flock of black ravens). According to Van Limborch writing to Henry More, in December 1669, and a reader who inserted a manuscript note about this into his copy of the *Bloemhof*, as well as later, by Goeree, in 1705, a black hen "jumped on Koerbagh's coffin and could not be chased away however hard by-standers tried."[108] Superstition proved victorious over the Koerbaghs after all.

Adriaan's tragic end must have exerted a deeply sobering, intimidating effect on the *cercle Spinoziste*, as was doubtless the primary lesson intended by the Amsterdam magistracy. Johannes, dejected but stubborn, remained under the Amsterdam consistory's surveillance and was again reported several times subsequently for attending Collegiant gatherings. On 11 January 1671, at a gathering of 400 people at the Collegiant meeting place on the Rokin, he figured among the speakers, recorded the church council, yet again referring to Jesus Christ our Saviour, in blasphemous fashion, "speaking against his eternal divinity."[109] But Johannes was careful never (again) to express Spinozistic views in writing. The traumatic effect of his brother's fate also seems to have suppressed his thirst for subversive books, judging by the contents of his library of over 700 books publicly auctioned, shortly after his own demise, in September 1672, at a bookseller's on the Singel, in Amsterdam, in early 1673. For between 1668 and his death he

---

[105] Colie, *Light and Enlightenment*, 43; Simonutti, "Vindiciae Miraculorum," 628; Van Heertum, "A Not So Harmless Drudge," 408.
[106] GA Amsterdam MS Acta Kerkeraad 376/xii, fo.10, res. 13 Dec. 1668.
[107] GA Amsterdam MS Acta Kerkeraad 376/xii, fo. 59, res. 10 Oct. 1669.
[108] Van Heertum, "A Not So Harmless Drudge," 410.   [109] Leeuwenburgh, *Het Noodlot*, 209.

purchased strikingly fewer and less bold works than before.[110] After 1669, Van Berkel, retreating into a shell, likewise ceased all expression of his former anti-Orangist, republican, and freethinking outlook, his personal library demonstrating a comparable loss of interest in new books of the bolder sort.[111]

Spinoza's life was short, but he outlived both Brothers Koerbagh despite their being younger than him, especially through his writings. Doubtless as shocked and horrified by Adriaan's fate as Johannes and the rest of his circle, Spinoza must have asked himself periodically whether it was worth pressing on, whether he should simply lie low, shelve the *TTP* and leave it unpublished. Equally, though, given his unremitting resolve, the episode must have spurred him on to devise some less reckless way than Adriaan had used to assail the theologians. The question in his mind was how to hit back at the world's churchmen less directly and blasphemously but ultimately more lastingly and devastatingly than his followers.

---

[110] Van Heertum, "Reading the Career of Johannes Koerbagh," 17.
[111] Wielema, "Abraham van Berkel's Translations," 222–3; Van der Deijl, "A New Language," 173–4, 178–9.

22

Nil Volentibus Arduum

Spinoza and the Arts

For Spinoza and his allies, seemingly the only viable way forward, from 1668, was to contrive less direct confrontations with authorities, secular and ecclesiastical, a more cautious advance via underground propagation and closed gatherings. Several of Spinoza's friends and disciples were attracted to the idea of an indirect approach to reforming society via a literary and arts society, or *kunstgenootschap*. A month after Adriaan Koerbagh's demise, at the tavern *Stil Malta*, not far from the Koerbagh residence in Amsterdam, Meyer, Bouwmeester, and other reform-minded personages convened to formally establish a new drama, poetry, and intellectual society which they named *Nil Volentibus Arduum* [Nothing is Hard for the Eager] (henceforth, abbreviated as NIL), designed to effect change in the public outlook by spurring constructive critical thinking using the arts. The society's choice of name undoubtedly reflects the circle's rejection of Stoic (and Averroist) resignation and abstention; they stood for vigorous activism in the sense of energetic critique of society and its institutions and commitment to reform.[1]

Holding its inaugural meeting with nine local citizens attending, on 26 November 1669, the society was a body with its own constitution and rules endorsed by the city government that took itself and its meetings very seriously. Membership was by invitation only while invited guests could attend only under strict conditions. During its early years whilst Spinoza still lived, the group's originally eleven members met weekly on Tuesday evenings from five to eight in the tavern *Stil Malta* on the Amsterdam Singel. Meetings were conducted in an egalitarian spirit but with fixed rules, the chairman's and secretary's roles frequently revolving among the membership. Smoking, gaming, and other distractions were forbidden, with small pecuniary fines exacted for late arrival and other infringements of procedure.[2] At least forty meetings during the years 1669–71 focused on discussing theatre theory; much of the group's remaining time at meetings was devoted to reading aloud translations and poems.

---

[1] Van Suchtelen, "Nil Volentibus Arduum," 393; Bordoli, "Art, public et république," 40–1.
[2] Dongelmans, *Nil Volentibus Arduum*, 29; Holzhey, *"Als gy maar scherp wordt,"* 120; Steenbakkers and Bordoli, "Lodewijk Meijer's Tribute," 244–5.

Although scholars have studied the society, it has rarely been asked how far this Amsterdam "collegie" [society] converged with Spinoza in his reforming goals and actually exerted a significant impact on the theatre world and the Republic's arts scene as regards promoting ideals of responsible governance, civic virtue, and critical evaluation of what best assists society and the individual. Philosophy's goal, Spinoza fervently believed, not unlike Marx later, is not just to understand the world but transform it for the better. Spinoza's own revolutionary strategy recommended transforming our world neither by inciting the masses to revolt nor entrusting far-reaching reform to some mighty "enlightened despot," like Frederick or Catherine the Great, in whom Voltaire and the young Diderot later vested their hopes. His strategy operated neither from below nor from the top, but furtively sideways, like the crypto-Jewish and crypto-deist underground coteries of early modern Iberia, secretively but effectively disseminating "the truth" against the main body of a ferociously oppressive superstitious world, albeit exclusively among small, confined numbers of the highly literate. It worked by forming small elite groups of committed adherents sharing their precious store of clandestine knowledge and scheming how to spread the message inconspicuously behind the scenes.

As to the message Spinoza and "his sect" (as it already began to be called by the early 1670s) sought to spread, no one summed it up better than Spinoza himself in the opening pages of his *Theological-Political Treatise* (1670). Due to our emotional make-up and difficulties in distinguishing truth from falsity, most men are ready to believe anything, so that vast falsehoods can easily dominate society's entire political, social, and religious sphere ensuring our world is largely ruled by "superstition," delusion, and misinformation. Living under a blanket of managed credulity inflicts immense damage on everyone since society is readily enslaved by "superstition" and made to function in ways contrary to the well-being and interest of the great majority. However, ever since progress in mathematics and science (that is since Galileo) taught philosophers to see more clearly what truth is, and how better to distinguish between truth and untruth, enforcing schemas of faith that mislead everyone has become more difficult. Philosophy, defined as fighting "superstition" and curbing individual passions and delusions, consequently, began to progress, especially via the insights of Machiavelli, Descartes, and Hobbes. For the theatre and the arts, the conclusion followed that literary and aesthetic values can be yet another way to mislead men but are not, in reality, intrinsically separate from pursuit of truth and cognitive science, but rather another path to the truth that can be employed, not to dazzle, enchant, pull the wool over men's eyes, or bemuse, but to enlighten.[3]

---

[3] Norris, *Spinoza and the Origins*, 259–60; Rovere, "Spinoza au théâtre," 84–5.

Still, despite incipient inroads into tyranny and oppression, ignorance and "inadequate ideas" according to Spinozists continue to prevail everywhere ensuring individual inability to make the most of our lives.[4] The point of disseminating subversive philosophical ideas then, is to assist men and women live richer, more fulfilling lives by emancipating them from their misconceptions, that is by enlightening them sufficiently to free them from the control of tyrants, exploiters, and theologians. Acquiring adequate ideas philosophically is arduous work, though, and Spinoza recognizes that few are capable of it. Fortunately, there are other, more broadly appealing, ways to strengthen humanity's disposition, enabling men and women to learn to see through imposture, spot "superstition," and adopt a beneficial plan of life. Men can learn to enjoy and cultivate the beautiful, rare, and fascinating in life in ways that enhance and elevate human disposition for joyful living, strengthening our thinking and bringing us closer to perfection while lessening the melancholy and despondency that weaken and remove us further from adequate ideas. Here, the arts along with humour, laughter, good food and drink, beautiful plants and fine gardens, all contribute. By pleasurably impressing, entertaining, teaching and fascinating, the arts bring people together in appreciating good things and laughing together. Nurturing the arts helps each individual nurture his or her disposition for joyful living and grow stronger by moving closer to evaluating men and their actions correctly.[5]

Accordingly, semi-veiled societies and discussion groups like his Amsterdam study circle and the NIL assumed special importance in Spinoza's plans and hopes as an activist and cautiously optimistic—Schopenhauer thought absurdly over-optimistic—philosopher. For Spinoza, no individual can lead a fulfilling life without glimpsing the "reality of things" and conducting him- or herself on the basis, as one scholar expressed it, of a "correct grasp of the abilities and weaknesses of human beings, together with a true understanding of the world they inhabit."[6] Accordingly, the arts as vehicles for our enjoyment and joyful disposition are, or should be, more than just amusement or distraction but an aid towards spreading adequate ideas, an effective plan of life, or *ars vivendi*, potentially accessible to all, enabling even the illiterate and totally unschooled to cultivate their minds, temperaments, and capacity for life. Justified self-esteem, for example, by Proposition 52 of Part IV of the *Ethics* is one path by which anyone can attain feelings of joy and strengthen their temperament; and for those unable to bolster their individual confidence through "reason," the path still remains open via skilled decorative work, impressive acting, culinary skills, or sportsmanship. Spinoza's philosophy of the arts, therefore, leaned heavily against viewing the

---

[4] Israel, *Enlightenment that Failed*, 69–70, 85, 89–92, 104, 197, 413, 598, 856–7, 924.
[5] Spinoza, *Ethica*, in *Oeuvres* iv, 398–9; Uhlmann and Gatens, "Spinoza on Art," 430–1, 433, 435; Rovere, "Spinoza au théâtre," 89.
[6] James, "Freedom, Slavery and the Passions," 223, 433.

arts as mere distraction and empty show.[7] Although Spinoza claims cheerfulness is always good, the quality of good cheer matters greatly. It does not help us, for example, to disdain or ridicule others. "Between derision and laughter," he writes in the *Ethics*, "I see a huge difference [inter irrisionem et risum magnam agnosco differentiam]"; wholesome laughter resides far from the glee low minds derive from mocking jibes and jeering at others.[8]

Nil Volentibus Arduum arose in the Dutch theatre world, but was not a theatre society as such, narrowly focused on reading, selecting, and producing plays. Rather, it was an opposition forum for debating theatre theory and practice and discussing issues of language and the arts in relation to the theatre. In fact, the NIL was conceived, and to an extent functioned, as an agent for the general reform of the arts and seemingly succeeded in exerting a noticeable effect, steering things in a certain direction over several decades. *Nil Volentibus Arduum* was formed following a phase of prolonged disagreement among the Amsterdam Schouwburg [theatre] directors and later became the target of several acrimonious attacks in print aiming to vilify it in the eyes of the public. No doubt the furious quarrel erupting in and around the Schouwburg in 1668-9, leading to the society's founding, was in the first place a clash of personalities. Especially, Meyer and the lawyer, playwright, and poet Andries Pels (1631–81), another of the society's leading lights later depicted by their opponents as a godless type,[9] had been feuding with several other Schouwburg directors. Meyer himself had been a director since 1665, but resigned in protest, in 1669, before the NIL was set up, dissatisfied with the kind of plays being chosen and the manner of selecting them.[10] This dispute was about whether the directors' responsibility was to provide what the Amsterdam public wanted, catering to existing taste, which allegedly meant providing sensation, exoticism, and splendid costumes but not meaningful plots while maximizing ticket sales (the proceeds from which partly went to help fund the city's Calvinist charitable institutions), or whether the theatre's responsibility was to promote worthwhile themes and topics, dramas morally and educationally uplifting.[11]

At the same time, the NIL, and Meyer especially, were great enthusiasts for Corneille, Racine, and French contemporary classicist dramas which were intellectually refined and provided emotionally intricate plots while, by contrast, most 1660s Amsterdam theatre directors preferred Spanish plays which were more easily turned into vehicles for display, costume, over-the-top rhetoric, and sensationalism.[12] This does not mean the NIL rejected all Spanish theatre or uncritically

---

[7] Spinoza, *Ethica*, in *Oeuvres* iv, 404–4; Uhlmann and Gatens, "Spinoza on Art," 433.
[8] Spinoza, *Ethica*, in *Oeuvres* iv, 398–9.
[9] *De Koeckoecx-Zangh*, 11; Dongelmans, *Nil Volentibus Arduum*, 3–4.
[10] Holzhey, "*Als gy maar scherp wordt,*" 84–5; Leo, "Nil Volentibus Arduum," 131.
[11] Van Hardeveld, "Lodewijk Meijer," 71–3, 102–3; Rovere, "Spinoza au théâtre," 88.
[12] Jautze, Álvarez Francés, and Blom, "Spaans Theater," 35; Smith, "Politics of Tragedy," 223–34.

preferred French culture as such. They disliked the heroizing and eulogizing of monarchy, the tendency to foment adoration of kings characterizing Corneille's plays. Bouwmeester in particular urged that plays staged in the Republic should help elevate the political notions and responses of the audience and not appeal to the base adoration characteristic of the mob at its worst.[13] Nor did they spurn the plays of Lope de Vega (1562–1635) who (more than any Dutch dramatist) was much the most frequently produced dramatist on the Amsterdam stage at the time.[14] While staying in Madrid in 1671, Spinoza's friend Jacob Vallan, who was close also to Meyer and Bouwmeester, and related to the Koerbaghs, was asked by Meyer to buy up all the copies of Spanish dramas he could lay hands on for the society's use.[15] After he was appointed professor of practical medicine and anatomy at Leiden, in February 1675, Vallan still actively participated in the NIL.

Among the society's principal aims was to emulate the Académie Française by purifying and reforming the vernacular, standardizing use of imported foreign and scientific terms, clarifying rules of grammar and generally elevating the Dutch language so as to assume its place as one of culture and refinement comparable with French and Spanish, a mission Meyer especially espoused.[16] Through indifference to literature and the arts, he and Bouwmeester complained, and failure to emulate French efforts to elevate their language, "we make our language contemptible not only among other peoples but, even among our own countrymen, so disapproved of that most people, including the most eminent, are ashamed to be more practiced in using their mother tongue than the French language."[17] In his famous dictionary explaining and refocusing meanings of imported foreign *kunstwoorden*, that is technical terms especially of Latin, Greek, and French origin, beside older, disused Dutch words and "bastard words," by which he meant words of foreign provenance *vernederlandst* [Dutchified] in spelling and pronunciation,[18] a dictionary appearing in 1669 in its fifth, and greatly expanded 946-page edition as *L. Meijers Woordenschat* [L. Meijer's Dictionary], Meyer rebukes professional scholars for hindering the public's acquisition of vast amounts of useful knowledge by burying everything in abstruse terminology and pedantic Latin devised to monopolize entire fields of knowledge for themselves.[19] Intelligent persons would make far more rapid progress in philosophy, to their own and everyone's benefit, he contends, if not spending years unprofitably wrestling with Latin.[20]

---

[13] Cornelis, "Reassessment," 166, 171; Leo, "Nil Volentibus Arduum," 139.
[14] Jautze, Álvarez Francés, and Blom, "Spaans Theater," 16.
[15] Dongelmans, *Nil Volentibus Arduum*, 65; Van Hardeveld, "Lodewijk Meijer," 40–1.
[16] Van Hardeveld, "Lodewijk Meijer," 65; Israel, "Spinoza, Radical Enlightenment and the General Reform," 390–1.
[17] Harmsen, *Onderwijs in de Toneel-poëzy*, 16.
[18] Van Hardeveld, "Lodewijk Meijer," 158, 415.
[19] Van Hardeveld, "Lodewijk Meijer," 7, 170, 194, 412; Israel, *Radical Enlightenment*, 198.
[20] Thijssen-Schoute, "Lodewijk Meyer," 25.

The NIL's membership consisted predominantly of writers proficient in Latin, university-trained physicians and jurists of a high cultural level. For them, the stage should appeal to popular taste but at the same time fulfil an additional, more elevated function. Doubtless it was due to their professional background that the group sought sophisticated recreation for those of their kind while simultaneously improving themselves.[21] But while seeking high-level forms of recreation that broaden the public's outlook might be dismissed as a typically elitist preference of city physicians and jurists wanting what best suited their own recreational needs, a key principle of the NIL's formal agenda was that intellectually robust and meaningful theatre need not be unappealing to the less educated and less informed. Well-judged plays with meaningful content can even be *more* appealing to the less literate, they contended, than the far-fetched, absurd, and spectacular material the current directors judged requisite for maximizing receipts; furthermore it was by dexterous use of the arts that conventional minds can best be "purged" of prejudices and false assumptions.[22] The NIL's chief maxim was that the theatre's purpose and "voornaamste nut [principal usefulness]" is to elevate the public morally and teach it to learn pleasurably.[23] Prodding audiences towards a more thoughtful, critical, independent, and appraising attitude to what they witness on stage meant cutting back on the visual, sensational, and purely spectacular and whatever conforms to commonplace, popular assumptions and credulous ways of thinking.[24]

Although Spinoza was not present in Amsterdam most of the time, and there is no evidence that he attended any of its meetings, a striking point of convergence between Spinoza and the NIL was their common preoccupation with the problem of "wonder" [bewondering] and its effects on the individual and society in general. "Wonder" for Spinoza is less an emotion or "affect" than an undesirable state of awe in which men suspend all judgement and reasoning, a natural response to the unfamiliar and surprising but also one readily exploited by demagogues, priests, quacks, magicians, and tyrants who deliberately ransack all available arts, myths, and mysteries to awe the multitude with their superior proximity to the higher powers and the fictions that supposedly govern our reality. Thus, the world of ancient temples, cults, and idolatry together constituted an immense age-old "theatre" designed to fill men with amazement and wonder, daunting them with the stunning splendour of everything highlighted, artfully rendering onlookers subservient to those instilling that wonder.[25]

---

[21] Holzhey, "Als gy maar scherp wordt," 106–7.
[22] [Meyer], *Philosophia*, 42; Holzhey, "Als gy maar scherp wordt," 102–3, 106–7; Leo, "Nil Volentibus Arduum," 132, 134–5, 144.
[23] Kronenburg, *Kunstgenootschap Nil Volentibus Arduum*, 53–5; Sangiacomo, *Spinoza on Reason*, 222.
[24] Holzhey, "Als gy maar scherp wordt," 102; Kooijmans, *Frederik Ruysch*, 104; Rovere, "Spinoza au théâtre," 89.
[25] Rosenthal, "Miracles, Wonder," 236–9; Leo, "Nil Volentibus Arduum," 125–6, 132, 135.

Awe and wonder in the real world, as in the civic theatre, serve essentially exploitative, demeaning purposes, but can conceivably be redirected to stimulate reason, discernment, and good judgement, elevating the spectator to a higher level instead. Religion itself, Spinoza maintains in the Preface to the *TTP*, was originally unsteady in fulfilling what he saw as its original social function, namely to persuade people "to adore their kings as gods," but became a firmer, steadier instrument of social control the more it was reinforced with glittering ceremonies, pomp, and splendour to excite awe.[26] Among the chief problems societies face, held Spinoza, is that "there are many men who take the outrageous liberty of trying to appropriate the greater part of [religious] authority and utilize religion to win the allegiance of the common people (who are still in the thrall of pagan superstition) with the aim of bringing us all back into servitude again."[27] Unfortunately for everyone, admonishes Spinoza, "churches became theatres where people went to hear ecclesiastical orators rather than to learn from teachers."[28] In this way, churches that stage grand gatherings become the allies of demagogues, fraudsters, and tyrants.

Much of the drama theory expounded at the NIL's meetings, presented in the form of individual papers prepared beforehand and revised after discussion, was gathered and edited by Meyer and Bouwmeester.[29] Redacted in 1670, and discussed by the group on 16 December 1670, this collective compilation was intended for publication but never appeared in the seventeenth century.[30] The text survived in manuscript in the Leiden University Library, appearing in print only in 1765, nearly a century later, under the title *Nauwkeurig Onderwijs in de Toneel Poëzij*, its title-page adorned with a telling vignette by the artist Gérard de Lairesse. Its forceful introduction, by Bouwmeester, declares "ignorance" the chief foe of the arts and sciences and chief motor of persecution, especially stressing what the NIL considered the theatre's prime moral function, its duty to convey human motives and thoughts through words in a "clear and distinct" manner, accurately and constructively. A key requirement was to render theatre didactic so as to avoid the wonder-inspiring, obscure, mysterious terms which allegedly theologians and academics thrive on, presenting stage plays in a responsible way, discouraging angry, unconsidered, or undesirable reactions and impulses among audiences.[31]

An interesting case in point, with an obvious bearing on Spinoza's biography, was a drama by a local playwright and poet, Thomas Asselijn (*c*.1620–1701) about

---

[26] Spinoza, *Theological-Political Treatise*, 5; Rosenthal, "Miracles, Wonder," 241.
[27] Spinoza, *Theological-Political Treatise*, 6–7.   [28] Spinoza, *Theological-Political Treatise*, 7.
[29] Harmsen, *Onderwijs in de Toneel-poëzy*, 489–90.
[30] Harmsen, *Onderwijs in de Toneel-poëzy*, 2, 11; Steenbakkers, *Spinoza's* Ethica, 104; Sangiacomo, "Dichters en Profeten," 99.
[31] Van Suchtelen, "Nil Volentibus Arduum," 394; Van Hardeveld, "Lodewijk Meijer," 71; Israel, "Spinoza, Radical Enlightenment and the General Reform," 391.

Masaniello (1620–47), the fisherman who led the Neapolitan anti-Spanish revolt of 1647. First performed in Amsterdam, in 1650, the play was published and performed several times in 1668, and again in 1669, 1671, and 1675. The play was fiercely criticized by the NIL, especially Pels, a member particularly insistent on the theatre's edifying role and duty to eschew the trivial. With Asselijn allied to the anti-NIL theatre faction, personalities were again a factor. But the NIL judged the play a misuse of the stage by putting wrong political notions and responses into people's heads. Since Spinoza reportedly sketched himself dressed like Masaniello, very likely at around this time and possibly in response to the play, he may perhaps have taken more than a passing interest. Projecting a simplistic, negative view of popular discontent, the drama broke convention by bringing a rioting mob on stage,[32] arousing repugnance for mob violence, plundering, and how, after a few days, the fisherman turned revolutionary leader, Masaniello, becomes a megalomaniac "king," an outright tyrant, before being assassinated by nobles. The NIL did not object to the play's citing "rights of the people," or its principle that "zoo bloeyt en staaat, daar 't regt der volkeren werdt gehandhaft [thus the state flourishes where the rights of the people are maintained]." What the NIL disliked was the play's highlighting the bloodshed and unruliness rather than the causes of the people's failure and the rights at stake, sensationalizing the incitement of the mob over a mere tax increase, and conveying what the NIL judged the wrong message for an audience insufficiently attuned to the veritable purposes of government.[33]

Assuming that 1668-9 was the moment when Spinoza pondered the Masaniello story, he would then have been in the midst of writing the *TTP* and have classified Masaniello as a classic instance of justified popular dissatisfaction betrayed by false hope, illustrating the uselessness of armed rebellion where "reason" and "virtue" provide no guiding principles and there exists no understanding of how to construct a democratic republic. Spinoza consistently scorned revolution that is just angry, violent bluster and achieves nothing more than replacing one "king" with another.[34] The NIL, like Spinoza, was democratic in the sense of desiring government (and the arts) to be for the welfare and by the consent of the people, but also firmly anti-insurrectionary and anti-populist.

Philosophy, especially Cartesian philosophy supplemented by Spinoza, were certainly one strand in the NIL's programme of general reform of the arts, much as the several physicians among their number envisaged Cartesianism as crucial for reforming medicine, anatomy, and science. Meyer and Bouwmeester were intensely interested in the implications of the "new philosophy" for general

---

[32] Drees, "Revolt of Masaniello," 207; Bordoli, "Art, public et république," 44–6.
[33] Drees, "Revolt of Masaniello," 208–11; Van Suchtelen, "Nil Volentibus Arduum," 399, 403; Totaro, "Massaniello, la Hollande," 26, 29; Bordoli, "Art, public et république," 44–5.
[34] Spinoza, *Theological-Political Treatise*, 235; Totaro, "Massaniello, la Hollande," 31–2.

culture, and in promoting new philosophical ideas in the vernacular. At the society's meeting on 29 December 1671, it was recorded that Bouwmeester agreed to "translate a certain Arabic book from the Latin."[35] This was *Het leeven van Hai Ebn Yokdhan* [The Life of Hai Ebn Yokdhan], his planned Dutch version of the 1671 Latin rendering by the Oxford Arabist Edward Pococke (1604–91), a philosophical novel by the medieval Andalusian philosopher Ibn Tufayl (*c.*1100–85), vividly describing the arduous efforts of an individual in total isolation to arrive at a rational view of the world. It tells too of the inevitable collision between reason and what most people think, rendering organized religion superfluous to the rational individual's search for God as existence and the nature of true virtue.[36] Published by Rieuwertsz in 1672, *Hai Ebn Yokdhan* was deliberately reworked for the public by the NIL to suggest the extreme difficulty of reaching an adequate grasp of the "reality of things" on one's own and reveal the power of participation with others in the work of identifying "true religion" with the truths of philosophy.[37]

The printed attacks on the NIL of the late 1670s pointed especially to its reputed association with irreligion and moral and social subversion. Two of its leaders, Meyer and Bouwmeester, the public were warned, were close associates of Spinoza and belonged to a circle of freethinkers associated with Van den Enden and the godless Koerbagh who, imprisoned for blasphemy, died in his cell in Amsterdam, in October 1669. One such attack, the *De Koeckoecx-zangh van de Nacht Uylen* [The Cuckoo-Song of the Night Owl], of 1677, the year of Spinoza's death, sarcastically styled the society a "trash of dishonest people" responsible for the "priceless dictionary" of "Doctor Koerbagh," for discovering "Philosophy is the Interpreter of Scripture" [of Lodewijk Meyer], and approving the "*Theologische Politike Redenkaveling* [Theological Political Reason-Trimming]," that is Spinoza's *TTP*.[38] *De Koeckoecx-zangh* was part of a bitter pamphlet war linked to a controversy over obstetrical practice and medical care that erupted that year between two rival Amsterdam medical factions with the gynaecologist Andries Boeckelman (d. 1679) seeking to reform the Amsterdam surgeon's guild, in alliance with the famous anatomist Professor Frederik Ruysch (1638–1731), but in conflict with the city's more traditional-minded surgeons and the physician Bonaventura van Dortmund (1633–1710).[39]

This feud overflowed into the theatre world because the reformers' principal foes included a master-surgeon, Jan Coenerding (1632-1705), prominent in the

---

[35] Dongelmans, *Nil Volentibus Arduum*, 78–9, 93; Van Hardeveld, "Lodewijk Meijer," 39.

[36] Bordoli, *Etica, Arte, Scienza*, 112–13; Israel, *Enlightenment Contested*, 628–9.

[37] Thijssen-Schoute, *Nederlands Cartesianisme*, 414–17; Bloch, *Avicenna and the Aristotelian Left*, 36–7; Holzhey, "Als gy maar scherp wordt," 90.

[38] *De Koeckoecx-Zangh*, 8; [Boeckelman], *Onschult of Zamenspraak*, 4; Bordoli, *Etica, Arte, Scienza*, 158.

[39] Thijssen-Schoute, *Nederlands Cartesianisme*, 366–7, 419; Kooijmans, *Frederik Ruysch*, 91–3, 96–101. I am grateful to Jeroen van de Ven for his suggesting that I add these details.

surgeon's guild, who was also a director of the Amsterdam Schouwburg from which he apparently syphoned off receipts, and because Meyer was helping Boeckelman, it later emerged, write his pamphlets.[40] Both the *Koeckoecx-zangh* and another tract stemming from the Boeckelman affray, a year later, claimed Bouwmeester had collaborated with Koerbagh in composing his unchristian blasphemous texts.[41] In this second text, Bouwmeester is styled the devilish freethinker "Dr Dick alias Bullebak [bully]" and "Nero de Bulleman due to the good service he provides girls and women of the neighbourhood." As for Dr Meyer, the *Koeckoecx-zangh* styles him "a greater atheist than Vanini who was burnt in France for his atheism."[42]

In the *Koeckoecx-zangh* several rhetorical voices join in, one complaining that *Nil Volentibus Arduum* "would be tolerated by no Turkish regime" as it "seeks to tear fear of God out of men's hearts and with one sweep eradicate subjects' binding obedience to their lawful government."[43] The NIL's opponents expressly associated the group with Spinoza, with Koerbagh's ideas, the devious schemes of Bouwmeester, and political subversion, as well as attempting fundamentally to reform the theatre and surgeon's guild.

An anonymous third pamphlet attacking the NIL published around 1677 or 1678, this time in French, the *Sentiments d'un Voyageur sur plusieurs Libelles de ce temps*, preserved today in the Amsterdam University Library, feigns to believe there were actually two different societies called *Nil Volentibus Arduum*, or at least two contrasting faces on one body—one public, praiseworthy, and devoted to theatre and language studies seeking to improve the moral tone of society and purify the vernacular and its use, the other furtive, concealed behind this respectable façade, comprising "plusieurs esprits bizarres, prophanes, athées, pour ne dire diaboliques [several bizarre, profane and atheistic, not to say diabolical minds]," holding secret meetings in Amsterdam at which the "Holy Trinity is mocked, Scripture treated like a fictional tale, and they plot to scale the heavens and remove God from his throne."[44]

Driven by curiosity, this fictional traveller scours the Amsterdam bookshops and discovers that this clandestine "malevolent and impious" conspiracy was designed to poison men's minds and, for this purpose, "published a number of books of which I was shown several, including a certain *Tractatus Theologico-Politicus* and the *Philosophia S.Scripturae Interpres*." Appalled by their horrifying contents, this imaginary visitor begs the magistrates to strive harder to suppress

---

[40] Kooijmans, *Frederik Ruysch*, 103–5; Israel, "Spinoza, Radical Enlightenment and the General Reform," 388.
[41] [Boeckelman], *Onschult of Zamenspraak*, 4, 27–8; Leeuwenburgh, *Het Noodlot*, 207.
[42] *De Koeckoecx-Zangh*, 8; Bordoli, "Account," 175–6; Kooijmans, *Frederik Ruysch*, 104; Israel, "Spinoza, Radical Enlightenment and the General Reform," 387–8, 404.
[43] *De Koeckoecx-Zangh*, 8; Bordoli, *Etica, Arte, Scienza*, 158–9; Nadler, *Spinoza: A Life*, 242.
[44] Text reproduced in Bordoli, "Account," 177–9; Bordoli, *Etica, Arte, Scienza*, 160–1, 243–6.

this venomous "collegie" and lock its members up "so that they do not poison others with their contagions but [are left to] wallow in their own filth until, suffocating, they acknowledge the untruth of their paradoxes."[45]

That the NIL was broadly averse to Calvinist orthodoxy was natural enough since Voetians believed all theatre was profane and that the Amsterdam theatre should be closed. That the NIL was popularly suspected not only of evincing political bias against monarchy but also against Calvinist stringency and Orangism and to favour De Witt's "True Freedom" emerges from telling details in several of the anti-De Witt propaganda tracts published around the time of the *coup d'état* that overthrew De Witt in 1672. Thus, the pamphlet *Sleutel, Ontsluytende de Boecke-kas van de Witte Bibliotheek* [Key Unlocking the Book-Case of the De Witt Library] (The Hague, 1672) denouncing De Witt for allowing "Arminians" to creep back into the city governments and oppress the "House of Orange," published probably in August 1672, lists as item number 26 among De Witt's supposedly pernicious book collection a copy of the "Perpetual Edict," and as number 33 the "*Tractatus-Theologico-Politicus* by the apostate Jew Spinoza, brought out from Hell in which, in an unheard of atheistic manner, [is taught] that God's Word must be explained and understood by Philosophy, brought out with the knowledge of Mr Jan [de Witt]," and supposedly published "in The Hague" by "Nil Volentibus Arduum."[46]

There is no reason to suppose Spinoza lacked appreciation for Bouwmeester's multifaceted lifestyle and preoccupation with spreading in the vernacular what both conceived as true wisdom. As a young man, Bouwmeester, reports the *De Koeckoecx-zangh* sarcastically, had brought back many "fine things" from Italy, presumably art works and books along with atheistic ideas; also, he possessed "all the secret writings of Dr Van den Enden who died in France high in the air," a reference to the now notorious schoolmaster hanged for conspiracy against Louis XIV, in 1674.[47] As his activity with the NIL illustrates, this many-sided art-loving personage was preoccupied with how men entwined in the complex whirl of big city life in a place like Amsterdam can nevertheless structure their lives positively and adopt a method by which to keep to the path of self-improvement and seek insight into the "highest things." Spinoza too had long struggled with the wide gap between the many demands of a busy career in Amsterdam and searching for an uplifting philosophical lifestyle useful to society.[48] At the end of the June 1665 letter, Spinoza admonishes the recipient, whether Bouwmeester, Koerbagh, or another of his physician friends, not so much of the need for "uninterrupted

---

[45] Bordoli, "Account," 178; Bordoli, "Art, public et république," 36.

[46] *Sleutel, Ontsluytende de Boecke-kas*, title-page and p. 15.

[47] *De Koeckoecx-Zangh*, 5, 8, 10; Bordoli, "Account," 176-7; Van Suchtelen, "Nil Volentibus Arduum," 393.

[48] Spinoza, *Nagelate Schriften*, 58-82; Spinoza, *Collected Works* (ed. Curley) ii, 32-3; Klever, "Hoe men wijs wordt," 342.

meditation" as the usual English translation renders it, but rather, as the Dutch indicates, "steady reflection" about life and about one's own, stable resolve to steer through the busy welter of everyday experience with a robust, fixed sense of purpose. Besides diffusing atheistic notions and teaching Koerbagh his godless ideas, *De Koeckoecx-zangh* charges Bouwmeester with being also a chief instigator of [Meyer's] idea that "philosophy or natural reason *is* the interpreter of God's Holy Word," and still more remarkably with having "forged with Spinoza and others the *Theological Political Reason-trimming* [i.e. the *TTP*] prohibited by the States General [smelt met Spinoza en anderen de *Theologische Politische Redenkaveling*, die van de H.H. Staten [General] verboden is]."[49]

Bouwmeester had his finger in many pies, but Spinoza and Bouwmeester, like Meyer and the Brothers Koerbagh, firmly shared the view that the highest wisdom is open to all, including those without Latin, is not exclusively confined to those with scholarly training and higher learning, and needs to be made more readily accessible to all. Since the core of practical, applied philosophy, in their eyes, is ethics, how to guide individual life to higher and happier levels, the non-scholarly, non-Latin reading individual, male or female, is just as much in need of, and deserving of, true philosophy as anyone else. Hence, Meyer's applied ethical theory: if "I" seek what is "good," useful, and helpful to me and benefit from the help of others, then I must in turn support my neighbours' efforts to secure what is "good" for them. Theatre and poetry, for the NIL, was hence chiefly a learning forum providing a window on human actions helping us to discern motives and the results of our actions in relation to others, enabling people to refine their judgements about themselves and others.[50] Moral improvement in Spinoza's philosophy results from individual effort together with group effort in society and the political sphere, and is basically a combination or fusion of the two.[51]

Yet, despite their undoubted commitment to the subversive ideas embodied in the writings of Koerbagh and Van den Enden, and close ties with Spinoza, it is important not to overstate Meyer's and Bouwmeester's philosophical indebtedness to Spinoza specifically.[52] In their by this time longstanding *cercle Spinoziste*, of which Spinoza was in some degree a product as well as a leader, Meyer, Bouwmeester, and Vallan were exceptionally erudite and wide-ranging, and the latter two were also well-travelled men who willingly lent assistance to Spinoza and took an eager interest in his philosophy along with Cartesianism, but to them philosophy chiefly mattered for its relevance to their general programme of reforming the arts, purifying the vernacular, and elevating the public morally

---

[49] *De Koeckoecx-Zangh*, 10; Bordoli, "Account," 176.
[50] Harmsen, *Onderwijs in de Toneel-poëzy*, 31; Sangiacomo, "Dichters en Profeten," 100.
[51] Here, I disagree with the analysis of Sangiacomo who views Meyer's ethical theory as an in-between position, mediating between Descartes and Spinoza, see Sangiacomo, "Dichters en Profeten," 103–6.
[52] Thijssen-Schoute, *Nederlands Cartesianisme*, 357; Van Hardeveld, "Lodewijk Meijer," 51.

and politically. In certain cases, their emphases were different, Meyer viewing "wonder," for example, at least on the stage, less altogether negatively than Spinoza. In Meyer's and especially Bouwmeester's case, like Beverland's later, cultural and ethical emancipation included an emphasis on the erotic. Spinoza should not be thought of as the exclusive influence shaping their intellectual and broader cultural lives and strategies. Rather it was the group as a whole that chiefly counted, with language, theatre, and the arts their primary forum.

Spinoza and the NIL converged in key respects, and both had good reason to envisage cultivation and advancement of the values they shared and the kind of philosophy they deemed useful for ameliorating society, science, and the arts, as best propagated behind the scenes and by indirect means. One segment of Spinoza's philosophy particularly relevant to the NIL's programme for the arts was his theory of the "affects" or emotions, how each individual constitutes an arena of conflicting emotions, as do blocs of humanity likewise.[53] Here Spinoza seemed distinctly more useful than Descartes. Spinoza's uniquely detailed discussion of the "affects" as not just an individual but also social phenomenon not only allows the arts a primary role in reforming society and raising the general level, but suggests there might be ways in which the stage matches philosophy itself as a value-projecting, elevating force. Especially the great mass of complacent minds unwilling to consider, reconsider, or change their views, championing crass notions without questioning their validity, is most prone to having their insensitive, unreceptive complacency ruptured by the arts.[54] The differences between Descartes' and Spinoza's theories of the "affects" impacted on the group's preoccupation with representation of situations and individuals, and especially their interest in emotion producing either ill-considered or well-considered actions and outcomes on stage. This assisted too with connecting theatre theory to a wider, general reform of the arts, raising the question of the NIL's not inconsiderable role in later Dutch Golden Age art history.

Spinoza's monism and stress on immanence means the individual mind is no separate dominion or sphere unto itself but a constantly interactive cumulative individuality grounded in the body and shaped by coping with life and engaging with others.[55] There are no human interactions that are not also interactions simultaneously of minds and bodies with both bodily concerns and mind impulses finding visual expression, however subtle, that can be rightly or wrongly reported and interpreted by others. A constant preoccupation of the NIL's reforming the stage was representation of emotion, behaviour, and social types in a realistic, logical, coherent manner. To raise society's moral level in a meaningful fashion,

---

[53] Moreau, *Spinoza, L'expérience*, 383–5, 398.

[54] Uhlmann and Gatens, "Spinoza on Art," 435; Israel, "Spinoza, Radical Enlightenment and the General Reform," 390.

[55] Further on the relevance of this component to the arts, see Gatens, "Benedict Spinoza and George Eliot," 9.

instructing and enlightening audiences while simultaneously imparting pleasure, human conduct and responses needed to be depicted in a "realistic," or what the group considered philosophically accurate, coherent manner.[56] This meant ditching Descartes' doctrine of the passions, as expounded in Les Passions de l'Âme (1649), published in Dutch by Rieuwertsz, in 1656, in a translation by Glazemaker who fulfilled a support role for the NIL as well as for Rieuwertsz. Even though the Ethics remained unpublished, Spinoza's account of the emotions seeking to improve on Descartes was certainly long familiar to, and much admired by, Meyer, Bouwmeester, Vallan, and Glazemaker and infused their thought on drama theory.[57]

Meyer's theory of the emotions, scholars point out, significantly diverges from Descartes who envisages the passions as deriving from bodily changes causing movements in the soul, an entity quite separate from bodies, empowering the mind to make judgements about those emotions. By contrast, Meyer's approach is closer to Spinoza's monistic schema, presenting joy, sadness, and desire as all primary and simultaneous mind–body impulses, feelings coloured by our minds having long before prejudged what is "good' and "bad" in our eyes, basic impulses from which the more complex gradations of gratitude, regret, nostalgia, and other subsidiary emotions all stem. Basic impulses, for Spinoza, are direct, necessary reactions, bodily states amenable to being steered in a more or less positive direction depending on judgement and the calibre of our ethical striving.[58] Representing these processes on stage, and especially ability and inability to master the passions' negative consequences in ways people could grasp and benefit from, was a prime concern of the NIL, a group preoccupation not learnt or borrowed from any one figure but rather a shared collective approach evolving over many years.

That Meyer's theory of the emotions approximates to Spinoza's framework and conception of *conatus* is reflected in his maxim: "true virtue is nothing other than the constant will ceaselessly to pursue one's real advantage," a principle hardly derivable from anywhere other than the (strikingly un-Stoic) relevant passages of the *Ethics*, such as *Ethics* IV, Proposition 24: "Acting absolutely from virtue is nothing else in us but acting, living, and preserving one's life (these three signifying the same thing) by the guidance of reason, from the foundation of seeking what is useful to oneself"[59] [Ex virtute absolute agere nihil aliud in nobis est, quam ex ductu rationis agere, vivere, suum esse conservare (haec tria idem significant),

---

[56] Kronenburg, *Kunstgenootschap Nil Volentibus Arduum*, 54–5; Van Hardeveld, "Lodewijk Meijer," 74.
[57] Holzhey, "Als gy maar scherp wordt," 69–70; Spies, "Lodewijk Meijer en de hartstochten," 39, 41–3, 48.
[58] Bordoli, *Etica, Arte, Scienza*, 129, 132; Harmsen, *Onderwijs in de Toneel-poëzy*, 361, 365–6, 368–9; Thijssen-Schoute, "Lodewijk Meyer," 3; Thijssen-Schoute, *Nederlands Cartesianisme*, 426–7; Steenbakkers, *Spinoza's Ethica*, 105, 112–13; Spies, "Lodewijk Meijer en de hartstochten," 43, 45.
[59] Spinoza, *Collected Works* (ed. Curley) i, 558.

idque ex fundamento proprium utile quaerendi]."[60] The two closely converge also in that Spinoza and Meyer both judge "wonder [admiration]" not a "passion" or emotion, as in Descartes, but a confused, ambivalent mental reaction to the unusual or what amazes us, so that, whether in real life or on stage, wonder and amazement are more likely to trap individuals and societies in harmful assumptions than prod us towards a more elevated perspective.[61]

Living well, held Spinoza (and the NIL), is primarily a social activity deeply alien to the lives of hermits and monks, recluses dwelling far from others, mockers of human existence despising human pastimes, and Stoics disdaining all other human goods apart from their narrower notion of "virtue." In the NIL's scheme of things, humility, abstemiousness, withdrawal, and pious austerity are all negative qualities. Mockery Spinoza rates among the basest forms of pleasure-seeking. Rather "it is the part of a wise man, I say, to restore and refresh himself with moderate and pleasant food and drink, and also pleasant smells, with the beauty of vigorous plants, with decoration, music, games that exercise the body, theatre and all else of this sort which we all can enjoy without causing harm to another. For the human body is formed of many different parts of diverse nature," holds the *Ethics*, "which constantly require new and varied nourishment, so that the whole body may be generally apt for all the things that follow from its nature and, likewise, that the mind too may be capable of understanding many things at the same time." "Such a style of life accords best both with our principles and the common practice."[62]

A further point where Spinoza and his friends of the NIL converged was in rating laughter and joking as pure joy while stipulating "a great difference between mockery" which Spinoza considers harmful "and laughter." Laughter and joy, if not excessive, are good in themselves (Proposition 41). "Nothing forbids our pleasure except a grim and sad superstition. For why is it more proper to relieve our hunger and thirst than to rid ourselves of melancholy?" There is no god "nor anyone else," holds Spinoza, "unless he is envious, who takes pleasure in my lack of power and my misfortune, nor does he conceive as virtue our tears, sighs, fear and other things of that kind that are signs of *impotentia* [powerlessness] of the mind. Suffering and imploring divinities for mercy bring us no closer to God. Rather, the greater the joy we are affected with, the higher the perfection to which we ascend, that is the more we participate in the divine nature."[63] George Eliot, in her translation, renders this: "the more pleasure we feel the more progress do we make towards perfection, i.e. the more do we necessarily partake of the divine

---

[60] Spinoza, *Opera* ii, 226; Bordoli, *Etica, Arte, Scienza*, 135–7.
[61] Steenbakkers, *Spinoza's Ethica*, 120–2; Leo, "Nil Volentibus Arduum," 141–4.
[62] Spinoza, *Ethica*, in *Oeuvres* iv, 398–9; Spinoza, *Collected Works* (ed. Curley) i, 572.
[63] Spinoza, *Ethica*, in *Oeuvres* iv, 397–9; Spinoza, *Collected Works* (ed. Curley) i, 571–2.

nature. Hence to use things and as far as possible enjoy them (not indeed to satiety, for this is not enjoyment) is the part of a wise man."[64]

"This rule of life is the best and to be commended in every way," affirms Spinoza, but it was one requiring an important shift of philosophy away from theology, because Descartes only partially reformed philosophy without satisfactorily linking the respective spheres of body and mind. Mind and body, contended Meyer, like Spinoza, are one and require nurturing together under the unalterable "general laws" of nature which Cartesianism first introduced into modern thought (Galileo had no notion of the universe being wholly governed in its routine working by overarching "general laws"). These principles, for Meyer, Bouwmeester, and the Koerbaghs are essential components of human reality as well as reality generally. Still, despite their emphasis on reinvigorating body and soul through varying experiences and activities, including with others in groups, Spinoza himself, records Jelles in his preface, focused his entire life's effort on putting everything he had discovered "into order." So great was his "burning desire to uncover the truth" that, while mixing protracted withdrawal with bouts of clandestine group activism, he himself spent "very little time on relaxation and refreshing the soul," entirely contrary to how he thought people in general should live.[65]

As minds and physical reality are closely integrated for Spinoza, Meyer, and Bouwmeester, grammar is a product of the human mind but simultaneously a mirror of physical reality so that all languages, inferred Meyer, necessarily follow a single basic universal grammatical logic. On this ground, Meyer became a researcher obsessed with the quest for the thus far undiscovered hidden general laws governing language and grammar, and hence to an extent also Bible criticism, theatre, and the arts. His grand project was to produce a general Dutch "grammatica" and alongside it a grammar of grammars, his *Algemeene Spraakkunst*, or *Grammatica generalis*, setting out the rules of human language universally to reflect the group's single unified human reality in all its diversity, an ambitious project that gradually emerged in draft but ultimately remained unrealized.[66] A draft of the first part of his general grammar Meyer apparently submitted to the NIL in February 1677, just days before Spinoza's unexpected demise, and not inconceivably it was Spinoza's death, and the sudden urgent need to convene with Rieuwertsz, Bouwmeester, and Jelles to prepare Spinoza's *Opera Posthuma* and its Dutch version for publication, an overridingly urgent but arduous and complex team project, that interrupted and eventually permanently diverted Meyer from his and the society's grammatical venture during and after 1677.[67]

---

[64] Spinoza, *Ethics* in George Eliot's rendering, 260.
[65] Jelles, "Voorreden," 3; Deleuze, *Spinoza: Practical Philosophy*, 21–3.
[66] Dongelmans, *Nil Volentibus Arduum*, 111, 113–14, 126, 145; Israel, "Spinoza, Radical Enlightenment and the General Reform," 394–5; Israel, "Popularizing Radical Ideas," 287.
[67] Dongelmans, *Nil Volentibus Arduum*, 167, resolution of 2 Feb. 1677.

If not all the NIL's ambitious schemes came to fruition, the group nevertheless succeeded in exerting an impact over several decades, arguably down to the mid-eighteenth century. As regards facets of their programme that were uncontroversial and not in themselves subversive, the city government's more progressive-minded regents took an interest and proffered support, viewing their theatre and literary theories as useful especially for improving educational methods in Amsterdam's schools,[68] and raising standards at the Schouwburg. At the same time, several regents, especially perhaps Hudde, Bontemantel, and Koenraad van Beuningen, felt some forbearance for the NIL's more daring schemes. One discerns a certain parallel with their encouraging the working partnership of Rieuwertsz and Glazemaker, the foremost mechanism for diffusing Cartesianism in the vernacular in the United Provinces during the 1650s and 1660s, as well as perhaps clandestine diffusion of Spinoza's works. Much as Rieuwertsz's bookshop attracted a predominantly Socinian clientele generating an unmistakeably subversive resonance which the city's Reformed Church council loudly condemned without their objections preventing Rieuwertsz becoming official printer to the city government, so the society gained a heightened role in the Schouwburg when the theatre reopened its doors, in 1678, following prolonged closure due to the war of 1672–8 with France. At that point Meyer and Bouwmeester were appointed "regents" of the Schouwburg just when they had completed the more clandestine task of preparing Spinoza's *Opera Posthuma* for the press, suggesting *Nil Volentibus Arduum* must have enjoyed some discreet behind the scenes support within the city government.

It was through preoccupation with portraying emotion realistically, with theory of the "affects" (*affectus* in Meyer's dictionary defined as meaning emotion or preference), and the relation of emotions to occurrences in human life and the wider human reality, that the NIL's reform programme primarily connected with the concerns of contemporary Dutch writers on art. Rather remarkably, the home of the prominent Amsterdam artist Gérard de Lairesse (1640–1711) became the main venue for the NIL's meetings from 1676 onwards.[69] "In future the gathering shall be held," state the society's *notulen* [minutes] of 5 May 1676, "in the house of Monsieur Lares," on the Nieuwmarkt; the candles, beer, and other necessaries for its meetings would be provided by Pels and another member.[70] On 29 September 1676, the regular meeting had to be cancelled due to the death of De Lairesse's mother.[71] By 1676, De Lairesse who had a close association in particular with Pels (who shared his and Arnold Houbraken's criticism of Rembrandt), had won a glowing reputation among the Dutch elites and become affluent. He produced a

[68] Kronenburg, *Het kunstgenootschap Nil Volentibus Arduum*, 78.
[69] Roy, *Gérard de Lairesse*, 48–9; Cornelis, "Reassessment," 172.
[70] Dongelmans, *Nil Volentibus Arduum*, 149–50.
[71] Dongelmans, *Nil Volentibus Arduum*, 156.

series of illustrations for the published versions of Pels' plays as well as renowned stage sets and backdrops for the Schouwburg, subsequently carefully preserved until destroyed by the fire that burned the theatre down in 1772.[72]

Raised in Liège as a Catholic, De Lairesse had since 1666 become an apostate from Catholicism and member of the Walloon Church. The significance of being the artist most directly linked to the NIL lies in his being more sweepingly critical of Dutch Golden Age painting than any other seventeenth-century writer on art, more insistent on the need for a general reform of painting in line at least partly with the views of the NIL.[73] De Lairesse, like his friends of the NIL, believed there were many recently discovered things that remained "hidden from our ancestors," and from this "we may believe that our successors will be more knowledgeable than we are; as the arts and sciences are much improved in recent times, so we may hope for their further advancement in the present age."[74] He fully embraced the NIL's goal of raising society's cultural knowledge and diffusing new knowledge widely. Well known for scorning lowlife scenes, he disdained the mere mechanical imitation of nature and genre, including the still life and preoccupation with portraits that figured so prominently in Dutch art at the time.[75] He became a noteworthy art theorist especially after being forced to give up painting due to going blind, in 1689. Throughout his mature career, in his paintings and etchings, and recommendations to other artists, De Lairesse aimed to escape the fleeting present moment, transcend the ordinary, and represent what is most real in the sense of lasting and significant in life which he sought to achieve by combining classicizing beauty with "realistic" depiction of gesture, feeling, and response.

Where still lifes, landscapes, portraits, and lowlife scenes restrict the artist to simply replicating what we see around us, the great advantage of a classicizing style, held De Lairesse, is that the artist can represent in an eloquent, convincing manner everything that matters, how we respond to dramatic, tragic, or extreme situations, and can make myths, symbols, fables, and moral dilemmas "real" for onlookers. Genre scenes can provide some scope for elevating effects as Frans van Mieris (1635-81) proves, he notes, with his refined, elevated art, but, generally, depicting the ancient world allows greater scope and freedom.[76] Despising the commonplace and the "everyday," De Lairesse compared the proper effects of paintings on viewers with theatrical performances (as understood by the NIL).[77] They should aim to instruct and elevate while giving pleasure, teaching virtue through beauty by moving the viewer to beneficial responses and emotions.[78]

---

[72] Roy, *Gérard de Lairesse*, 49; Israel, "Spinoza, Radical Enlightenment and the General Reform," 396-7.
[73] De Vries, "Changing Face of Realism," 222, 224; Weststeijn, *Visible World*, 36.
[74] Kemmer, "In Search of Classical Form," 99-100; Israel, "Spinoza, Radical Enlightenment and the General Reform," 395-6, 402.
[75] De Lairesse, *'t Groot Schilder-Boek* i, 178; Arasse, *Vermeer*, 17.
[76] De Lairesse, *'t Groot Schilder-Boek* i, 172.   [77] De Vries, *Gerard de Lairesse*, 82.
[78] Kemmer, "In Search of Classical Form," 92-4, 113.

For De Lairesse, as for Pels, Meyer, and Bouwmeester in their drama theory, what is real differs significantly from what immediately meets the eye, requiring penetrating discernment and depiction with care and decorum, classicizing elegance uncovering true naturalness in an authentic manner.[79]

Among seventeenth-century writers on art whose ideas attracted De Lairesse's attention was another figure with more unambiguously radical tendencies who also shared many views of the NIL. This was the Middelburg antiquarian, publisher, and art critic Willem Goeree (1635–1711), who in an early publication, his *Inleydinge tot de Al-ghemeene Teycken-Konst* [Introduction to the Art of Drawing] (Middelburg, 1668), published the year before the NIL was founded, expressed his hope for a more enlightened age when "amateurs of learning" would be sufficiently numerous and eager in each city to gather for regular meetings as a *college* or literary society blending the arts together with scholarship in the vernacular, and reforming the former in the light of the latter.[80] Training artists must not be just a matter of learning to draw from life, the mere technical skills needed for accurately reproducing details of what lies around us, but of also acquiring and diffusing historical understanding, deeper discernment through scholarly conviviality, sociability, and debate. Like Meyer, Bouwmeester, and his own son, Jan Goeree (1670–1731), born in Middelburg, apparently a pupil of De Lairesse and among the leading engravers and book illustrators of the early eighteenth century,[81] Goeree loved congenial literary get-togethers, poetry, and art. Among his son Jan Goeree's more notable book prints was an elaborate depiction of Solomon's Temple, signed "J. Goeree del. et fecit," devised as the frontispiece to the now rather rare Amsterdam edition of Frederik Van Leenhof's intensely Spinozistic book *'t Leven van Salomon en zyn bewys der Ydelheden* (1700) [The Life of Solomon and his Proof of the Vanities], where Van Leenhof, following Spinoza, depicts Solomon's wisdom as uniquely valuable but a wholly natural phenomenon without any supernatural or miraculous component.[82] Like De Lairesse, Goeree read widely, expressing controversial and oppositional views on numerous sensitive topics and stood out as an eager amateur expert on classical antiquity, classicism, and ancient history with a fondness akin to that of Meyer and Bouwmeester, for a distinctively lay style of vernacular, extramural non-academic erudition.

Appreciating the relevance to artists of Descartes' and Spinoza's theories of the passions,[83] Goeree was something of a living link between the founding generation of the *cercle Spinoziste* of the 1650s and 1660s and the art world of the late seventeenth and early eighteenth century. He knew, and had dined "more than

---

[79] De Vries, *Gerard de Lairesse*, 91–3.
[80] Mijnhardt, *Tot heil van't menschdom*, 82; Taylor, *Dutch Flower Painting*, 79, 88–9.
[81] Roy, *Gérard de Lairesse*, 148n332.
[82] Frederik van Leenhof, *'t Leven van Salomon en zyn bewys der Ydelheden* (Amsterdam, 1702).
[83] Weststeijn, *Visible World*, 173.

once," he reports, with Franciscus van den Enden, Spinoza's Latin master who had for a time likewise been active as an art dealer. While perhaps too young to have known Van den Enden when he ran his art shop in the Nes, common ties to the art world certainly shaped Goeree's connection with him later. Goeree must have spent periods in The Hague and Amsterdam well before moving to Amsterdam permanently, having got to know Van den Enden "very well," at some point before the notorious ex-Jesuit left for Paris, in 1671.[84] If Meyer and Bouwmeester strove to formulate general laws governing drama and the arts, theirs was an ambition they shared with De Lairesse, Goeree, and certainly at least one or two other contemporary art critics. For Goeree and De Lairesse, no less than Meyer and Bouwmeester, good art relates a story imparting pleasure *and* instruction, founded on the unalterable laws of nature, a logical system of rules to be followed with near mathematical precision.[85] Over the decades, Goeree developed and refined his distinctive outlook blending religious heterodoxy with art and architectural theory, an outlook acquired by no means solely through books but also through cultivating the company of other freethinkers. Besides knowing Van den Enden personally, he became acquainted with numerous notable personalities in various cities. In The Hague—where he also knew Christian Huygens—he enjoyed long discussions, he informs us, with Isaac Vossius "whose courtesy and friendliness I cannot sufficiently praise."[86] In 1677, three years after Van den Enden's execution in Paris, Goeree permanently transferred to Amsterdam his book- and printshop and famed collection of architectural models which, he tells us, he hoped would be seen and appreciated by others "tot nut van 't gemeene best" [for the advantage of the common good], a favourite expression of his.

Goeree was a key art theorist of the later Dutch Golden Age whose ideas about art were of central concern to De Lairesse, and whose radical intellectual stance and familiarity with the freethinking circle around Van den Enden are certain. Over the years Goeree increasingly earned the reputation of being a writer of suspiciously radical (and probably Spinozist) views. He was seemingly the suspect purveyor of heterodox opinions denounced by David Van Hassel, in his preface to the Dutch-language version of Christopher Wittichius' *Anti-Spinoza*, published in 1695. According to Van Hassel, no egg resembles another as much as Spinoza's philosophy resembled that of the Stoics which this modern impostor had rehashed and disgracefully served up as his own, but without his shameless plagiarism at all deterring his insidious following, men such as the dubious personage in question (i.e. Goeree), exerting a deplorable influence throughout society.[87] Goeree was later specified by name as a rebel against church authority at gatherings of the

---

[84] Bedjaï, "Libertins et politiques," 32; Klever, "Inleiding," 17–19; Nadler, *Spinoza: A Life*, 78–9.
[85] De Vries, *Gerard de Lairesse*, 85, 104, 109–10.
[86] Goeree, *Voor-Bereidselen Tot de Bybelsche Wysheid* i, 105.
[87] Hassel, "Voorreden," to Witichius, *Ondersoek*, pp. i–ix.

North and South Holland synods, in 1703, and again at the North Holland synod convening at Alkmaar, in August 1704, for expressing Bekkerite views in his account of early Israelite history, his *Mosaize historie der Hebreeuwse Kerke* [Mosesistic History of the Hebrew Church] (1700), a work illustrated with prints by Jan Luiken (1649–1712), that caused a stir also for its bold criticism of how the Reformed Church had proceeded in the Balthasar Bekker affair.[88] Holding that one cannot at all understand the Bible without a detailed knowledge of ancient Jewish antiquities and history, and generally ancient Near Eastern, especially Egyptian history,[89] Goeree defended Bekker's stance on witchcraft, Satanism, and demonism and style of Scriptural exegesis.[90] Sorcery and magic, he repeatedly states, insisting on the fraudulent powerlessness of the Egyptian magicians recounted in the Pentateuch, do not in reality exist.[91]

Given their quantity and sometimes expensive format, his books evidently sold fairly well despite being only sparsely cited in the scholarly literature of his time (and later). His learned vernacular texts, observed the Spinozistic novel *Philopater* (1697) cuttingly, proved useful not just to the general public but also to supposedly learned preachers needing material for their sermons.[92] Goeree did not hesitate to accuse professional theologians of betraying a seriously inadequate knowledge of Hebrew—a language he vigorously championed and claimed to have devoted a lifetime of study to. Like Koerbagh, Meyer, and the NIL, he accused the churchmen of his day of arrogantly claiming a wholly bogus authority on the basis of qualifications they actually lacked, manifesting profound ignorance of ancient history, Jewish and Gentile, and antiquities.[93] His supreme offence in the eyes of Reformed ministers was his scornful rejection, like Meyer, Bouwmeester, and all their set, of the idea that theology and Bible study, and religious truth generally, constitute a fenced off professional precinct, the speciality of trained theologians, "a land which they have appropriated on their own authority to exercise their authority there, imposing an absolute domination and sovereign dictatorship."[94]

Superstition including belief in demons and sorcery Goeree ranks among the worst curses afflicting humanity, manipulative priesthoods having regularly exploited popular credulity, demonology, and idolatry to enhance their power and exact obedience.[95] In his views on miracles, magic, and the Devil, moreover, Goeree goes noticeably beyond Bekker, invoking the Devil seemingly more in the spirit of the Koerbaghs than his Frisian hero as essentially just human desire, a

---

[88] Haarlem, Noord Hollands Archief, Provinciaal Kerkbestuur van Noord-Holland van de Nederlands –Hervormde Kerk, MS. Acta North Holland Synod, inv. nr. 8, acta Edam 31 July/9 Aug. 1703 and acta Alkmaar July/Aug. 1704.
[89] Leemans, "De weg naar de hel," 259.
[90] Goeree, *Mosaize Historie* ii, fol. v; Goeree, *Kerklyke en Weereldlyke*, 678–81.
[91] Goeree, *Mosaize Historie* ii, fols. 1v–2r and iii, 126–7, 137–9.
[92] [Duikerius], *Het Leven van Philopater*, 119.   [93] Goeree, *Mosaize Historie* ii, fols. 8r–9r.
[94] Goeree, *Mosaize Historie* ii, fol. 9r; Leemans, "De weg naar de hel," 264.
[95] Goeree, *Mosaize Historie* i, 23 and ii, 685–8; Israel, "Popularizing Radical Ideas," 282.

force at war "with reason and goodness" in the human soul, that cannot be driven out of any human being except with the end of a person's life.[96] Explaining all supposedly demonic and magical phenomena narrated in Scripture in naturalistic terms, Goeree regularly dismisses "possession" by devils as recounted in the New Testament as merely incidences of mental illness, fits, and madness.[97] Following Van Dale, he dismisses the *Sibylline Books* as fraudulent, in no way prophesying the coming of Christ.[98] Pagan oracles, he notes, ridiculing Bishop Huet's efforts to vindicate the Church Fathers here, continued to flourish "for around 400 years after Christ's birth" and did not cease through any supernatural agency, much less the coming of Christ, being suppressed only due to state decrees issued against pagan divination and soothsaying by the Emperor Theodosius and his sons, Arcadius and Honorius.[99]

"Why," asks Goeree, like that other dissident artist theorist Arnold Houbraken, "did the Saviour not vigorously combat and contradict all these gross errors?"[100] Regrettably, Christ and the Apostles made no effort to counter the superstitious beliefs of the people of their time especially regarding demonology. Indeed, Christ himself "sometimes used phrases accepting the teaching of demons and power of possession." Linked to his Anti-Trinitarianism, this remark implies a stance coloured by Spinoza's idea that Christ and his Apostles, by using phrases expressing the credulous beliefs of the common people, were concerned only to teach the people "obedience" to the moral code, remaining unconcerned with enlightening men more broadly, or propagating "truth."[101]

In their respective art theories, Goeree, De Lairesse, and also Arnold Houbraken (1660–1719) were at one in multiple respects especially their conviction that training artists should not be just a matter of learning to draw from life, and other technical skills, but chiefly of acquiring and diffusing historical and scientific understanding, while participating in a group culture of teaching and instruction enlivened by conviviality, sociability, and debate—precisely the culture promoted by the NIL. Goeree designated accurate drawing "de Baer-moeder, en voedster aller consten en wetenschappen [the womb and wetnurse of all arts and sciences]."[102] A recurrent theme of Goeree's writing is that men should strive not just for themselves but more especially for *'t gemeene best*, for "the common good" or "the utility of one's neighbour, and above all that the public good should be cherished at heart above everything else."[103]

---

[96] Goeree, *Mosaize Historie* ii, 649–50, 687–93.
[97] Goeree, *Mosaize Historie* i, 22 and ii, 688; Leemans, "De weg naar de hel," 261–2, 269.
[98] Goeree, *Mosaize Historie* ii, 667; Israel, *Enlightenment Contested*, 429.
[99] Goeree, *Mosaize Historie* ii, 662–5; Israel, *Radical Enlightenment*, 363–4, 428.
[100] Goeree, *Mosaize Historie* ii, 688, 702; [Houbraken], *Philalethes Brieven* i, 119–20, 125, 128–30.
[101] Goeree, "Preface" to Petrus Cunaeus, *République des Hebreux* (Amsterdam, 1705), i, p. 9.
[102] Goeree, *Inleydinge Tot de Al-ghemeene Teycken-Konst*, fol. 4v; Knolle, "Een goede kunstwerkplaats," 187.
[103] Goeree, "Preface" to Cunaeus, *République des Hebreux* ii: fol.1r; Israel, "Popularizing Radical Ideas," 275–6.

If Spinoza contends that the free and rational person strives most of all "to conceive things as they are in themselves and remove impediments to true knowledge, such as hatred, anger, envy, scorn, pride, and other passions of similar kind,"[104] as Eliot translates his words, De Lairesse, Goeree, and Houbraken venerated art that captures dramatic and emotional reality accurately and meaningfully by emphasizing "posture [*houding*]," truthful reflection of movement, positioning and response expressing the reality of the situation, demanding an art eschewing the false, magical, sensational, and irrational. Among the lessons Houbraken diffused—and a key to his notion of good judgement in artistic matters—was that the artist should strive always "om waarheden te verthoonen [to convey truths]." De Lairesse, in his religious painting, strove not for historical accuracy but naturalness in the sense of avoiding angels, haloes, demons, holy ghosts, etc. while representing Jesus, Mary, John the Baptist and others who were actual persons in thoroughly human fashion. Where Rembrandt depicts the snake in his "Adam and Eve" as an unworldly monster, De Lairesse presents an actual snake with its head metamorphosed into the head of a real woman,[105] implying the "Fall" was merely a succumbing to sexual temptation, later a favourite theme of Beverland's. De Lairesse, Goeree, Houbraken, and Van Hoogstraten were all unyielding foes of superstition, ignorance, and belief in the magical and miraculous, and, discreetly, also theology. Wherever the artist fails to represent men truthfully in the NIL's sense, he falls short and reprehensibly helps perpetuate "false ideas."[106]

Since only a dozen or so authors active in the Netherlands between 1600 and 1750 wrote at all "extensively" on the history, trends, and leading figures of Dutch Golden Age art, those critics advancing a conception of general reform in art reflecting the criteria of the NIL, combining art criticism with radical ties and tendencies, in fact constituted a not inconsiderable proportion of the total of those writing on art.[107] As a group, the reforming art critics and stage theorists together consciously aimed at a general reformation of all the arts, tying the visual arts closely to the theatre, offering a plan for renewal with roots firmly in the reforming activities and attitudes of Spinoza's circle of intimate friends and allies, both the *cercle Spinoziste* and the drama society set up in Amsterdam, in 1669.

The fundamental purpose of the *res publica*, insists Spinoza in the *Theological-Political Treatise*, "is not to dominate or control people by fear or subject them to the authority of another. On the contrary, its aim is to free everyone from fear so that they may live in security as far as possible, that is, may retain to the highest

---

[104] George Eliot's rendering of Spinoza, *Ethics*, 278; Spinoza, *Collected Works* (ed. Curley) i, 587.
[105] Cornelis, "Reassessment," 173.
[106] [Houbraken], *Philalethes Brieven*, 3–4; Alpers, *Rembrandt's Enterprise*, 24, 38, 95; Gerson, *Rembrandt's Paintings*, 48; Van de Wetering, *Rembrandt*, 150, 169, 175, 179, 255, 282, 353.
[107] Slive, *Rembrandt and his Critics*, 177.

possible degree their natural right to live and act without harm to themselves or others."[108] Spinoza did not think this can be achieved by inciting the masses against the authorities or via the intervention of some Messiah or Saviour. But he and his following did discern a possible if highly uncertain, arduous, path to their common goal: to help people discard false and hate-engendering beliefs and credulous dread via a process of "enlightenment" as it later came to be called, a cultural and social "reformation," their preferred word, advanced by various means especially theatre and the arts.

As things stood in 1670, very few, in Spinoza's estimation, possessed the ability to distinguish truth from falsity; but one's capacity can be vastly expanded and extended through a well-honed campaign of systematic adult re-education. One might say that the NIL found an after-echo in George Eliot's notion that after studying Spinoza's words and becoming inspired by them, there comes a need to shut his books and devise some way to amplify his message for a larger segment of society through fiction writing and the arts. Through literature, painting, and the stage everyone can gain traction from melancholy to joyful thoughts, from a slavish to a freer disposition, from incomprehension to glimpsing the truth of things.[109]

---

[108] Spinoza, *Theological-Political Treatise*, 252; James, "Freedom, Slavery and the Passions," 228.
[109] Carlisle, "Introduction," to Eliot, *Spinoza's* Ethics, 7; Uhlmann and Gatens, "Spinoza on Art," 434–5.

23
Twilight of the "True Freedom"

23.i Last Years in Voorburg

In the late 1660s Spinoza focused his energies on grasping the, for him, now overwhelmingly relevant political and religious realities of the moment. To philosophize in peaceful surroundings, he had earlier selected Rijnsburg and then Voorburg which offered better proximity to postal services, bookshops, barge traffic, and pharmacies, and readier contact with other microscopists, as well as his Amsterdam support team, and publisher. Switching focus to the spheres of government, diplomacy, and military affairs along with science and scholarship, and avid for the latest news, in the late 1660s he adopted the approach of a natural philosopher finding in the environs of The Hague a front seat from which to observe political developments which, due to the Republic's relative openness, were more readily watched by the public and scrutinized by the keen observer (far too much so in the view of many regents), than in any other major power hub of the age. Being close to The Hague, and from 1670, in The Hague's town centre, enabled Spinoza to analyse the play of actors, information, and decision-making with as much proximity as in other lands was confined to the adept courtier or royal adviser.

Each of Spinoza's several moves affected his manner of life in some measure, but none seems to have altered his unwavering adherence to a lifestyle so sober it astounded all who knew him. It is "unbelievable how modestly and sparingly," relates Colerus, the most reliable of his early biographers, "he lived, not forced to by extreme poverty, for money enough would have been offered to him, but from inborn sobriety and feeling he possessed enough, and his not wishing to be known as someone living at the expense of others." Among bills, receipts, and notes of payment kept after his death, which he examined when shown them by Van der Spijck early in the next century, Colerus found graphic indications of this extreme sobriety. "In one whole month I find just two half pints of wine on his account, and although [Spinoza] was often invited to dine with others, yet he preferred to eat his own bread than the delicacies of others."[1] Simon Joosten de Vries, Colerus records, once offered him 2,000 guilders to enable him to live in greater style which Spinoza reportedly refused in the presence of his landlord.

---

[1] Colerus in Freudenthal/Walther, *Lebensgeschichte* i, 122–3.

Shortly before his death, De Vries again sought to arrange an annual pension for Spinoza, proposing the sum of 500 guilders yearly which Spinoza declined. According to Colerus, Spinoza finally agreed to 300 guilders per annum, though a recently discovered notarial deed, signed by De Vries at his home on the Singel in Amsterdam, the evening before he died, on 16 September 1667, adding a codicil to his will, specifies that he actually left to "Benedictus de Spinosa living in Voorburgh" 250 guilders yearly for as long as he lived, this he then received presumably from Trijntje's husband Alewijn Gijsen (who lived until 1683) with whom Spinoza had stayed on the farm near Schiedam over the winter of 1664–5.[2]

As Spinoza pushed on with the *TTP* through late 1667, everyone in Holland was eagerly debating the amazing events of the late summer, culminating in the Medway Raid and peace talks with England, in a mood partly of joyful relief after prolonged stress, anxiety, and gloom, but euphoria shot through, since May, with mounting alarm due to the French advances in the Spanish Netherlands. As squabbling over the final terms with England dragged on, Louis XIV flagrantly exploited the opportunity afforded by Anglo-Dutch absorption in their global maritime-colonial rivalry to annex more key border areas of the southern Netherlands and establish a commanding strategic superiority for France in Western Europe. For the Dutch, this posed an immediate future threat greater than even the bitter resentment of England. With Spain now gravely weakened, France's neighbours all risked becoming perilously marginalized. "The general belief here of the most intelligent," reported Temple from Brussels, in late May 1667, "is that France has had the skill or good luck" to lull to sleep "both us and the Hollander in this great conjuncture" and, by adroit moves obstructing an early peace between England and the Dutch, "amuse us both in a slow treaty till they have made so great an impression in these countreys, as will give neither of us the liberty to take those measures upon this affair, to which either of our interests might lead us." Rather than prolonging the Breda peace negotiations, wrangling over issues like the East India island of Polaroon, England, in Temple's judgement, should throw her weight into the scales to stop Louis becoming sole arbiter of the Low Countries and master of Europe: "they say that by delaying our treaty for the point of Polaroon, [England] is losing a dinner for mustard," and that every day longer the peace was deferred diminished the scope for effective collaboration to thwart Louis. "In short," Temple summed up, "all prepare for a warm summer."[3]

When the major fortress city of Lille fell to the French, in late September, panic gripped the central regions of Flanders, including Louvain, the Spanish Netherlands' most renowned centre of learning, and the English Catholic nunnery

---

[2] Colerus in Freudenthal/Walther, *Lebensgeschichte* i, 126–7; Van der Tang, "Spinoza en Schiedam," 182; I am grateful to Van de Ven and Rik Wassenaar for making the information about this notable manuscript find available to me.

[3] Temple to Lord Holles, Brussels, 29 May 1667 in Temple, *Letters written by Sir William Temple, Bart.* i, 108.

there, founded in 1609. "The Reverend Mother hath sent to desire me to recommend them to your Lordship's favour," Temple alerted Henry Jermyn, Earl of St Albans (1605–84), a keen gambler well-connected at the French court and chief architect of the subsequent secret Anglo-French collusion against the Dutch, a major voice in the redesigning of London, earning this foppish courtier the sobriquet "Father of the West End." The reverend mother requested that he intervene to protect them. "Our poor nuns at Louvain have more faith than most," urged Temple, resorting to the sardonic humour fashionable at Charles' court, "in case the scholars and learned there should not find arguments enough to defend their town against the French, who I can assure your Lordship, will not lose much by the bargain as far as I see, of that nunnery, nuns and all; for it seems by their faces, as well as their buildings, to be an ancient foundation, and gone much to decay."[4]

If the Republic failed to provide sufficient freedom of expression for Spinoza to publish his philosophical and other ideas openly, he nevertheless greatly appreciated the precious freedoms it did afford, for these greatly surpassed what was on offer elsewhere at the time. Enjoying "the fruits of this liberty" meant not just freedom to choose one's religion (or lack of it) but a broad personal freedom of movement, judgement, speech and to criticize. "With its great growth" Amsterdam is now "the admiration of all nations. In this flourishing Republic, this superb city, people of every sect and nation live together in the greatest harmony [...] and no sect is so hugely resented by others that its members (provided they harm no one and give each man his due and live honestly) are not defended by the public authority under the protection of the magistracy."[5] Yet, those freedoms, Spinoza well knew, had been direly threatened by the 1617–19 schism between Remonstrants and Counter-Remonstrants that toppled that great founding statesman, Johan van Oldenbarnevelt (1547–1619), a struggle fired by religious bigotry that now in his time was powerfully flaring up again. However harmful division rooted in doctrinal strife is, it is difficult to avoid, especially as such schisms arise, according to Spinoza, not "from intense passion for truth (which is the fount and origin of amity and gentleness), but great lust for power. It is thus plainer than the noonday sun that the real schismatics are those who condemn other men's books and subversively instigate the insolent mob against their authors, rather than the authors themselves who for the most part write only for the learned and consider reason alone their ally."[6] The true agitators disrupting society and impeding his own efforts and all those with novel or daring ideas to offer hence "are those striving to do away with freedom of judgment in a free

---

[4] Temple to Lord St Albans, Brussels, 13 May 1667 in Temple, *Letters written by Sir William Temple, Bart.* i, 93.
[5] Spinoza, *Theological-Political Treatise*, 257; Krop, "Spinoza en Amsterdam," 16–17.
[6] Spinoza, *Theological-Political Treatise*, 258.

republic – a freedom which cannot be suppressed."[7] Not totally "suppressed" perhaps, but De Witt's "True Freedom" would soon dishearteningly shrivel in the public sphere, publishing, and the universities.

It was obvious enough to observers that Dutch toleration was a delicate bloom. Once peace was finally concluded, Temple, accompanying his sister who had "a very strong fancy to a journey into Holland, to see a country she had heard so much of," travelled incognito from Brussels across Holland to gain a feel for the country's intensifying simultaneously internal and external predicament. Temple was disappointed with aspects of what he saw, including the latest architecture: when contemplating the new Amsterdam city hall, he repeated Bernini's witticism on seeing the Louvre—"una granpiccola cosa [a big little thing]." "The chief pleasure I had in my journey was, to observe the strong freedom that all men took in boats and inns, and all other common places, of talking openly whatever they thought upon all the publick affairs, both of their own state and their neighbours: And this I had the advantage of finding more by being incognito, and think it the greatest piece of the Liberty that country so much values: the government being otherwise as severe, and the taxes as hard, as among any of their neighbours."[8] Precious too, noted Temple, was that the magistrates were indeed remarkably objective in dealing with individuals whatever their background, sect, or social status, maintaining a rule of law "so much different from the style of most other places."[9]

23.ii The Move to The Hague

Spinoza remained in Voorburg until some point between September 1669 and early 1670.[10] During his last months in Voorburg, now close to completing the *TTP*, he was still, as he had been for years, intensely interested in the challenge of reforming Descartes' laws of motion. As his letter with its three diagrams to Jelles, of 5 September 1669, his last surviving missive from Voorburg, demonstrates, he was still then devising ingenious science experiments with tubes, dishes, and the like, including water containers and wooden apparatus with blocked and unblocked channels permitting water to flow at different rates, trying to measure how far pressure of different amounts of stationary water, and pressure and velocity of different quantities of flowing water, change under altered conditions.[11]

---

[7] Spinoza, *Theological-Political Treatise*, 258.
[8] Temple to Sir John Temple, Brussels, 10 Oct. 1667 in Temple, *Letters written by Sir William Temple, Bart.* i, 120–1.
[9] Temple to Sir John Trevor, The Hague, 24 Jan. 1670 in Temple, *Letters written by Sir William Temple, Bart.* ii, 164.
[10] Van de Ven, "Spinoza's Life and Time," 26; Monnikhoff, "Beschrijving van Spinoza's leven," 205; Kingma, "Spinoza in zijn Haagse periode," 15.
[11] Spinoza, *Collected Works* (ed. Curley) ii, 40–2.

After living in Voorburg for roughly five years, Spinoza moved to the centre of The Hague during the winter of 1669–70, because various friends of his "of standing" in the town, notes Monnikhoff, including army officers, wanted to visit him more easily. This was shortly before, or just after, publication of the *TTP*. There, renting a room from a widowed landlady, the widow Van Velden, on the Stille Veerkade, he lived for roughly a year, or a little under, apparently working and sleeping in the same second-floor (presumably fairly spacious) room at the back of the house which his biographer, the Lutheran preacher Colerus himself occupied a quarter of a century later. Spinoza's lodgings on the Stille Veerkade Colerus significantly describes as "his laboratorium or workplace where he slept and worked," a point Monnikhoff later repeated. Working and sleeping in the same large room would certainly have heightened further Spinoza's unfortunate inhaling of the glass dust (crystalline silica) that had for some time been exerting a toxic effect on his lungs.[12]

After a year or so on the Stille Verkade, in around November 1670, either finding those lodgings too expensive or for some other reason, Spinoza moved for the last time, a short distance, round the corner, to the house of the young and only recently married Lutheran "meester-schilder" [master painter], Hendrik Van der Spijck (d. 1715) on the Paviljoensgracht, now number 72. At Van der Spijck's residence, lodging for eighty guilders yearly while providing his own food and drink, he would remain until his death less than six years later. Spinoza's work and bedrooms were again located one floor up, this time apparently at the front. The fact that he once again chose rooms on the second floor suggests that, at this juncture, there was nothing yet too conspicuously worrying about his health or agility.[13] His new landlord, explains Monnikhoff, had two different occupations, as a decorative (not art) painter and a "solliciteur militair"—that is officially registered arranger of ad hoc cash loans to officers commanding army units, especially to provide early advances on their men's (far from regularly assigned) pay from the States General.[14] Army officers coming and going would be a regular feature of Spinoza's last years.

"This village [The Hague] is reckoned the largest (and is questionless the pleasantest) in Europe," observed the usually rather dismissive William Nicolson, in 1678. "The streets are pav'd with brick as at Rotterdam. The Language that is spoke here," he records (Nicolson studied Anglo-Saxon and Old Germanic languages), "is the most corrupted (though most fashionable) in

---

[12] Colerus' account in Freudenthal/Walther, *Lebensgeschichte* i, 120; Monnikhoff, "Beschrijving van Spinoza's leven," 205–6; Bloksma, "Spinoza, A Miraculously Healthy Philosopher," 25–6.

[13] Van Suchtelen, "The Spinoza Houses," 477; Bloksma, "Spinoza, A Miraculously Healthy Philosopher," 23, 25; Van de Ven, "Spinoza's Life and Time," 24; Van de Ven, *Documenting Spinoza*, ch. 7.

[14] Monnikhoff, "Beschrijving van Spinoza's leven," 206; Freudenthal/Walther, *Lebensgeschichte* i, 174; Gullan-Whur, *Life of Spinoza*, 237.

Holland: which must needs arise from the dayly confluence of ambassadours, and their numerous attendants, from all countreys in Europe."[15] The house where Spinoza boarded stood on the today filled-in Paviljoensgracht, then an actual canal, situated on the town's south-eastern side, a few minutes' walk from both The Hague's two principal churches, the St Jacob's or Groote Kerk and the Nieuwe Kerk [New Church], and no great distance from the assembly halls of both the States General and States of Holland (Figure 23.1). From Spinoza's modest lodgings it was not far either to the Huygens' imposing town house beside the Binnenhof, the area of government buildings.

Spinoza's rooms were located in the artisan, less stately section of town, though it was just a short walk from there to the more fashionable central and northern districts where most ambassadors' residences, Huygens' town house, and, beyond that, the House of Orange's Noordeinde palace were situated.[16] Going the

Figure 23.1 *Daily activities along the Paviljoensgracht with the St. Jacobskerk in the distance.* The Hague. Reproduction courtesy of ART Collection/Alamy Stock Photo.

---

[15] Nicolson, "Iter Hollandicum," 88.
[16] Kingma, "Spinoza in zijn Haagse periode," 15; Neuman, "Aller steden pronkjuweel," 20.

opposite way, in Spinoza's time, brought one to open countryside and wide rural views with windmills just beyond the town's eastern rim. If longer walks were desired, Delft was not far, nor were the sand dunes close to the shore just west of The Hague, while to the north lay one of the pleasantest walks in the environs, the "Haaghse Bos" which Nicolson rated "the largest and pleasantest wood in Holland." "Tis observable that the greatest part of those many thousands of trees which grow in this wood, are oaks: of which kind you shall scarce meet with any more in all Holland."[17] North-westwards from the built-up area crossing the sand dunes, one encountered a recently finished "straight paved lane" to the coastal fishing village of Scheveningen, or "Sheeveling" as the English called it, and the bracing North Sea shore.

What most struck foreign visitors about The Hague when Spinoza dwelt there was its openness and fresh air, its village-like character despite its open, sprawling extent, contrasting with the more densely populated, unhealthier nearby cities of Delft, Leiden, Dordrecht, and Rotterdam. In 1674, The Hague's total population, according to an official estimate, stood at 27,000 (less than half Leiden's but roughly three times that of Oxford), an increase of around 10,000 since the 1620s.[18] In 1675, the Cartesio-Cocceian Hebraist and Walloon Church pastor, Johannes Braun (Jean Brun) estimated The Hague's population at 30,000 inhabiting 6,000 houses, with around one fifth of the total, around 6,000, being Catholic. With few sectarians and Jews present, a larger proportion than was usual in other Dutch cities adhered to the Reformed Church.[19] If Reformed preachers were even more dominant here than elsewhere, the town militia were more raucously pro-Orangist and anti-De Witt in sympathy than elsewhere, though Spinoza was doubtless more inclined to chat with scholars, booksellers, and apothecaries.[20] The Hague boasted at least a dozen apothecaries that a person suffering a serious long-term lung ailment could consult about medicinal ointments and syrups. In 1706, by which time the town's population was only slightly larger than in 1670, the town boasted nineteen apothecaries and druggists forming their own guild (*apothekersgilde*).

The house where Spinoza lodged in his last six years was part of a row near The Hague's southern rim constructed in the 1640s on land purchased in 1641 by the renowned painter Jan van Goyen (1596–1656) who had settled there permanently in 1631. A quarter of a century old, the house had only recently been acquired by the Van der Spijcks. Van Goyen had had remarkably few pupils apart from his future son-in-law, the still more renowned artist, Jan Steen (1626–79), his assistant, who arrived from Leiden around the time he married Van Goyen's oldest daughter, Margriet, in 1649. His income from painting Van Goyen had

---

[17] Nicolson, "Iter Hollandicum," 88–9. [18] Oldewelt, "Bevolking van 's Gravenhage," 114–17.
[19] Braun [Brun], *Véritable religion*, 168.
[20] Van Gelder, "Schutterij en Magistraat in 1672," 58.

supplemented by investing in local real estate. But during the First Anglo-Dutch War, he too suffered financial ruin, moving, after being forced to sell off his art collection, into a smaller house shortly before his death, in 1656. Van der Spijck's father purchased the residence from Steen's father in 1669. Before moving to the nearby Bierkade, Steen lived either in the same house as Spinoza afterwards, or close by. Opposite Spinoza's lodgings, across the canal, stood the homes for impoverished old widows built around a courtyard founded in 1616, called the Heilige Geesthofje [Holy Ghost court] (Figure 23.2). Spinoza would have frequently walked past or through the courtyard with its *juttepeer* tree, a specifically Dutch kind of small, juicy pear, later famous as the oldest known fruit-bearing example of the species surviving until recent times.

A rear entrance to Van der Spijck's house fed onto a back passage leading to the Bierkade or Beer Wharf, the adjoining canal round the next corner, along which much of The Hague's beer arrived from Delft. Here too Spinoza must have frequently strolled and observed much of interest. A constant hive of activity, this stretch of canal was where Van Goyen himself in his later years, and several pupils, including Steen, worked, bought, and sold, albeit Steen departed, in 1654,

Figure 23.2 *View of the Heilige Geesthof at The Hague*, paper etching after drawing by Gerrit van Giessen. Reproduction courtesy of Rijksmuseum, Amsterdam.

to set up a brewery in nearby Delft (which soon failed), after which he moved to Leiden. Another hugely talented artist working nearby was the unfortunate Paulus Potter (1625–54) who, after producing a hundred splendid paintings, mostly of animals, died of tuberculosis at only twenty-nine. In 1670, selling pictures and art supplies in the vicinity continued in lively fashion. Around 600 artists worked in The Hague during the seventeenth century, around half the total, some 300 artists, during the century's third quarter (1650–75).[21] Quantitatively, artistic activity was close to its peak when Spinoza arrived but soon tailed off sharply, due to the "disaster year" of 1672.

Whereas scenes of Dutch domestic life, the "genre scenes" so prized today—and at the time by the ordinary burgher—were in relatively scant demand in this fashionable, international milieu, the portrait, the sphere in which Spinoza himself exhibited some skill, was most generally in demand.[22] The most eminent portraitist dwelling nearby was Adriaen Hanneman (1604–71) who remained active until his death and, like other leading Hague portraitists, had a decidedly international clientele.[23] The greatest artist painting in The Hague for most of the time Spinoza resided there, though, was Caspar Netscher (1635–84), who had learnt his highly refined art as a pupil and assistant of Gerhard ter Borch, in Deventer, in the later 1650s, but then worked in The Hague from 1662 until the end of his life. Though earlier active chiefly as a genre painter, from around 1670, Netscher too focused on portraits rather than genre and history painting, his former specialities. At The Hague, experience taught, portraits exuding refined elegance were what sold best. His magnificent portrait of Christiaan Huygens of 1671, hangs today in The Hague's Historical Museum.

Spinoza's fascination with portraits focused less on fine finish, elegance, or any aspect of their material make-up, than the artist's ability to capture the objective reality behind the image presented. Consider, he says, in his Descartes book, a portrait of a prince. If we "attend only to the materials, we shall find between it and other portraits no inequality that would oblige us to search for different causes [...], but if we consider rather the image as an image [of someone, or something] we must immediately search for a *causam primam* [first cause] matching in form and in standing what the image contains by representation." In this, the real, objective truth driving our appreciation of the portrait, lies a mix of the passive reality of the model, and the active cause, power, and skill of the artist, a mix producing images adequate and inadequate.[24]

Spinoza was a talked about, familiar presence among the leading lights of intellectual and scientific life in The Hague—a milieu at its peak in the late

---

[21] Buijsen, *Haagse Schilders*, 29–30.   [22] Buijsen, *Haagse Schilders*, 219.
[23] Buijsen, *Haagse Schilders*, 31–3, 155.
[24] Spinoza, *Opera* (ed. Gebhardt) i, 157; Spinoza, *Collected Works* (ed. Curley) i, 245; Ramond, *Qualité et quantité*, 32–3.

1660s when Temple, Vossius, and Saint-Évremond too resided there. Relatively expensive for rents and living costs compared with more outlying Voorburg or Rijnsburg, there was little point in moving to The Hague centre if one lacked interest in current politics and the town's international milieu and clientele. In 1670, it was as true as in 1697 that The Hague was the "only town in all the Provinces," as the wealthy London banker and Tory politician, Sir Francis Child, expressed it, "for people of fashion, pleasure and gallantry."[25] There is no definite proof Spinoza and Temple knew each other, but certain that during his last years the philosopher invested part of his remaining time conversing among the thriving medley of sophisticates, officers, collectors, scientists, and internationally renowned "esprits," as the French called them, the famous minds and wits congregating in The Hague.

Spinoza cultivated high-level contacts not for personal gain or position, nor for pleasure or fashion, but unlike most others, for insight, to learn their views, engaging with leading minds about philosophy, science, mathematics, politics, and war news. In this way, Spinoza amassed detailed knowledge of what was afoot in such varied fields as military affairs, local and national politics, mathematics, optics, and astronomy. When Leibniz, writing from Frankfurt, sent his first letter to Spinoza, in February 1671, bringing to Spinoza's attention his own efforts in optics and his essay entitled *A Note on Advanced Optics*, enclosing two copies, the other for Hudde, he could justly affirm that he "was unlikely to find a better critic in this field of study," than Spinoza, adding that "I hear that the highly accomplished Hudde too is eminent in this field, and is doubtless well known to you. So if you can also obtain his judgment and approval for me, you will add greatly to your kindness." Spinoza replied a month later, saying he found Leibniz's account of his efforts with apertures and lenses insufficiently clear, being unable to fathom what he meant by claiming his procedure made it possible to gather light rays so that "the apertures of the glasses can be of any size without impairing distinctness of vision," and requesting further details. Hudde, meanwhile, answered via Spinoza that "he does not have time at present, to examine" Leibniz's essay, but "hopes to be free to do so in a week or two."[26]

Already then, Leibniz was wrestling with the implications of accepting that the laws of nature are geometrically necessary, trying to find a way to reconcile this with divine wisdom, foresight, and governance of the universe. Impressed by recent advances in thinking about the "laws of nature," he also felt profoundly challenged. He spent his life seeking to circumvent the unalterableness of what he called "the subordinate laws of nature," including gravity, so as to restore convincing philosophical-scientific grounds for divine free will, providence, and "miracles." Optics played a pivotal role because he believed his new principle of

---

[25] Van Strien, *British Travellers*, 72–3.   [26] Spinoza, *Collected Works* (ed. Curley) ii, 393–5.

the movement of light, that "light travels from the radiating point to the point illuminated by the easiest of all paths," was a precious clue as to how he could reconcile efficient causes, the immediate causes of light movements, reflections, and refraction, with "final causes" in that God must have decreed those laws of nature, as the efficient causes best serving His desire for the wisest and best overall order of things, thereby merging efficient causes with final causes.[27] Here already emerging was the incipient rift between Spinoza and Leibniz: for the final cause defined as the ultimate purpose for which something occurs excluded from discussion of the laws of nature by Descartes, is abolished outright by Spinoza. Only from the mid-1670s, scholars agree, did Leibniz seriously begin struggling with the implications of Spinoza's rejection of final causes in nature. But in optics, Leibniz seems in incipient fashion already to have been striving to reconcile efficient and final causes to circumvent prioritizing the laws of nature.[28]

The 1650s and 1660s in the Dutch cultural world and science were key decades for diffusion of Cartesianism and propagating Copernican-Galilean astronomy. But stiff resistance persisted, especially in theologically strict Calvinist circles, and there were also notable other anti-Cartesian voices, including a prominent freethinker chiselling at traditional notions, Isaac Vossius (1618–89), among Holland's best-known maverick intellects of the age. Vossius knew Steno and Swammerdam well from frequenting their company, together with Thévenot, in Paris, in 1664–5, and Huygens from long before. Earlier, he had debated intensively with Menasseh ben Israel and La Peyrère. Son of the renowned humanist Gerardus Vossius, he had travelled widely, especially in England, Scandinavia, and France. On arriving in Stockholm, in 1648, to assist Queen Christina in transforming Stockholm into an intellectual centre, and enriching her library, he had clashed personally with Descartes during the latter's final months. Descartes had arrived at the Swedish court towards the end of 1649 full of expectation, only to be discouraged, in the weeks prior to his catching the pneumonia, in February 1650, from which he died, because Vossius' personality and lessons in Greek and ancient history proved more to the Queen's taste than did he himself and his philosophy.[29]

For a time, during the 1660s, Vossius lived just round the corner from Spinoza's lodgings in the Kerkstraat, in Voorburg, so the two must have seen a good deal of each other and probably Spinoza had at least some access to his remarkable collection of books, manuscripts, and curiosities.[30] Vossius' library, among The Hague's largest, was visited in January 1668 by the Tuscan Prince Cosimo III, during his unofficial incognito visit accompanied by his entourage of noblemen.[31] As Grand Duke (from 1670), Cosimo would become known for his Catholic piety, strict implementing of Inquisition decrees against banned books and ideas, and

---

[27] Garber, *Leibniz*, 256–9. [28] Garber, *Leibniz*, 226–7, 230–2.
[29] Gaukroger, *Descartes*, 415; Jorink, "In the Twilight Zone," 136–7.
[30] Van de Leer, "Een speurtocht," 56. [31] Wagenaar, *Toscaanse Prins*, 107, 195.

repressive regulation of the University of Pisa, and already at this time expressed hostility to Cartesianism, including, reportedly, Spinoza's book on Descartes. One wonders, though, whether the report circulating later that Spinoza, on requesting an interview, was told the prince preferred not to meet "such a man," having heard about his irreligious views, can really be true. For Lorenzo Magalotti (1637–1712), disciple of Galileo, former secretary of the Florentine science academy, and expert on comets, who knew Steno well, and was accompanying and guiding the future Grand Duke on this occasion, later reported that Cosimo did confer with Spinoza during his several months at The Hague.[32]

Isaac Vossius loved recounting anecdotes about Descartes and his followers to whoever would listen, and doubtless this figured prominently in his discussions with Spinoza. "A butterfly whom no one can hope to pin to a single spot on the map of the Republic of Letters," he lived mostly at The Hague between 1664 and 1670, but in 1670 moved to London where he had earlier, in 1664, been elected a Royal Society fellow.[33] By the time Spinoza and Vossius met (or renewed their acquaintanceship), Vossius had been quite successful, much to Huygens' chagrin, in making himself the talk of the scientific fraternity via a whole series of much discussed publications. One enthusiasm common to all three celebrities was certainly optics, Vossius being yet another practised researcher in the field and collector of microscopes and optical instruments. Possessing a telescope nearly thirty feet long, he had been obsessively discussing scientific theories with Huygens and Hudde at The Hague and Voorburg since the late 1650s, albeit Huygens dismissed him as a bungling amateur with "absurd" ideas about refraction, exasperatingly impervious to "better instruction."[34] It is not known when exactly Spinoza ceased actively crafting lenses and microscopes. But this is likely to have been around or shortly after moving to The Hague's centre. He thus ceased active involvement in the field just before his exact contemporary, Antonie van Leeuwenhoek (1632–1723), an artisan dwelling in nearby Delft, revolutionized microscope-making, from around 1673, through intricately grinding lentil-shaped or either-side double bulging lenses to achieve much stronger magnification than previously attainable.[35]

Another obvious topic of conversation between Spinoza and Vossius was Bible studies where Vossius too doubted the authenticity of the Mosaic Five Books and questioned biblical chronology regarding which he figured among the most controversial authors of the era. Vossius' *De Vera aetate mundi* [On the True Age of the World] (1659) challenged all accepted early Bible chronology reaching

---

[32] Casini, *Introduzione all' illuminismo* i, 232; Totaro, "Niels Stensen (1638–1686)," 161; Israel, *Radical Enlightenment*, 44.
[33] Grafton, "Isaac Vossius," 74; Van Delft, *Antoni van Leeuwenhoek*, 45–6.
[34] Dijksterhuis, "View from the Mountaintop," 176; Jorink, "In the Twilight Zone," 131–2.
[35] Van Berkel, "Intellectuals against Leeuwenhoek," 188–9; Jorink, *Boeck der natuere*, 250; Van de Ven, *Documenting Spinoza*, ch. 7.

back to Creation but also La Perèyre's thesis that humanity was many millennia older than the Hebrew Bible affirms. Persuaded by the Jesuit missionary Martino Martini (1614–61) whose *Sinicae historicae decas primo* (Munich, 1658) showed the impossibility of reconciling ancient Chinese annals with the Vulgate's chronology of the Creation and Flood, Vossius proposed a more modest adjustment to accepted Christian estimates for the date of the Creation at around 4000 BC (Scaliger's date for the Creation was 3,950 BC; curiously, the ancient Maya fixed Creation at around 3,114 BC). Endorsing Chinese claims regarding the great antiquity of their records,[36] Vossius contended that the Jewish Septuagint, the pre-Christian mid-third century BC original Greek translation of the Hebrew Scriptures, a text widely used by Hellenized and Romanized Jews in the age of Jesus, rendering the cosmos 1,200 to 1,500 years older than the Old Testament Hebrew text, placing the Creation at 5,550 BC, was based on older, less corrupted Hebrew versions than the later Hebrew text adopted by the churches. The Septuagint's chronology, he argued, better fits reality as shown by the Chinese records than the latterly accepted Hebrew version and is thus the most authentic, reliable version available. From this, he concluded that only about one and a half thousand years needed adding to the traditionally accepted chronology for the Creation, Flood, and writing of the Mosaic Books.[37]

Spinoza had no difficulty with Vossius' thesis that accepted Bible chronology is totally wrong, or his contention that the Chinese "preserve in their monuments and annals, a continuous history of 4,500 years," and therefore "possess writers even more ancient than Moses,"[38] and indeed may have borrowed from Vossius his idea that the Chinese preserved themselves as a distinctive civilization "for many thousands of years, so that they far surpass all [other] nations in antiquity."[39] The existing Hebrew text, Spinoza agreed too, is corrupt in many places. What he rejected was the notion that serious corruption occurred only after the advent of the Septuagint, Vossius' argument that it was rabbinic tradition, steeped in blind superstition, that gave rise to later text corruption from which the Septuagint remains largely free, thereby subordinating the Masoretic text to the Septuagint in terms of authenticity.[40] Rather than assigning the Septuagint pristine status and priority, Spinoza dismissed it as a late and irrelevant offshoot, as, with regard to early history, he dismissed all renderings from the Hebrew as irrelevant, including the Vulgate and the official Dutch 'States' Bible. So fixated was Spinoza on the original text to the exclusion of the Septuagint and the third variant, the Samaritan Bible, that he cites the Septuagint only once in the

---

[36] Popkin, *Isaac La Peyrère*, 81; Nellen and Steenbakkers, "Biblical Philology," 44; Jorink, *Boeck der natuere*, 108–9.
[37] Wauters, "Libertinage érudit," 45–7; Jorink, *Boeck der natuere*, 110.
[38] Wauters, "Libertinage érudit," 47; Boyle, "China and the Radical Enlightenment Context," 3.
[39] Spinoza, *Theological-Political Treatise*, 55–6.
[40] Grafton, "Isaac Vossius," 43–4, 67, 71, 77–8.

entire *TTP* where he claims that comparison of the Septuagint with the Hebrew proves the Greek version was "revised after the second restoration of Jerusalem by Judas Maccabeus" in 164 BC and hence long postdated the existing Hebrew text. Scholars today date the Septuagint broadly to around 250 BC, so Spinoza was not far off the mark and did have grounds for side-lining the Vossius thesis.[41]

Still, Vossius and Spinoza concurred on some aspects of Bible criticism, and both were wholly at odds with the accepted views of their day. Over the centuries ancient texts undergo extensive disfiguring, they agreed, due to faulty copying, mistakes in rendering punctuation, vowels, signs, and so forth, and to this rule Scripture was no exception. Vossius too rates human reason far above Scripture while, according to his young ally Hadrianus Beverland, likening the great clashes of theology of the day, such as that between Voetians and Cocceians, to ludicrously irrelevant battles of mice and frogs.[42] Critical reason must preside over every text no matter how hallowed it may be. Both Vossius and Spinoza agreed too, following La Peyrère, in denying the universal character of the Flood, both seeing the Flood as an essentially local event in world history leaving many civilizations and peoples untouched.[43]

It was not only in the Septuagint, it has to be said, that Spinoza showed little interest, but Greek and Greek studies of whatever sort. Indeed, a striking feature of his life and library is that unlike many or most prominent scholars and thinkers of previous generations since the Renaissance, Spinoza showed relatively little interest even in the philosophy of the Greeks, his attitude to Plato and Aristotle remaining remarkably dismissive and to Stoics and Epicureans distant and noncommittal.[44] Vossius, meanwhile, was far more drawn to controversy and heated debate than Spinoza, regularly engaging in quarrels with scholars, scientists, and theologians of all stripes. Like Temple, Saint-Évremond, and other late seventeenth-century neo-Epicureans, but unlike Spinoza, Vossius showed little serious interest in post-Galilean contemporary experimental science or in mathematics' role in renewing science and philosophy which, presumably, led Spinoza to view Vossius' bold scientific theories with much the same detached amusement and disdain as Huygens. His friend, Saint-Évremond rated Vossius' astounding erudition more highly than most but also thought him lacking in polish, a roughhewn character knowing nearly all Europe's languages while unable to speak any of them properly or elegantly. Moreover, if Vossius too refused to believe in divine revelation or Scripture's sanctity and considered most men's opinions, especially belief in spirits, devils, and angels, superstitious nonsense,[45] what especially amazed Saint-Évremond and many others was Vossius' stunning credulity in

---

[41] Spinoza, *Theological-Political Treatise*, 268; Touber, *Spinoza and Biblical Philology*, 4, 63.
[42] De Smet and Elias, "Isaac Vossius," 149.   [43] Wauters, "*Libertinage érudit*," 47, 50n24.
[44] Moreau, *Spinoza et le spinozisme*, 44.
[45] Wauters, "*Libertinage érudit*," 49; Boyle, "China and the Radical Enlightenment Context," 5, 11.

other respects, his extraordinary willingness to credit outlandish notions. According to one eighteenth-century report, Charles II jested that Vossius would believe anything provided it is not in the Bible. Saint-Évremond sighed over his "credulité imbecille," for everything "extraordinary, fabulous, and not remotely believable."[46]

Vossius' erudition, though, undoubtedly exerted some impact on the early Western Enlightenment especially by stressing the universal significance of Chinese learning, traditions, and political culture, esteem which Temple with his Epicurean Sinophilia and Saint-Évremond enthusiastically shared.[47] Chinese society, insists Vossius, in his *Variarum observationum liber* (London, 1685), is not just the oldest but most praiseworthy segment of "civilized humanity if one measures human achievement in terms of peace, stability and cultivation of the arts and sciences."[48] For him, the Chinese were the only people who succeeded in realizing the Platonic philosopher-king ideal so that "for many thousands of years, almost only philosophers or people loving philosophy have ruled there."[49] The first Westerner to affirm Chinese philosophy's and medicine's general superiority, as well as Chinese civilization's unmatched antiquity, his was a stance Temple eagerly shared. Temple was later scorned by Bishop Gilbert Burnet as someone who believed "things were always as they were from all eternity" considering religion "fit only for the mob. He was a great admirer of the sect of Confucius in China, who were atheists themselves but left religion to the rabble. He was a corrupter of all that came near him. And he delivered himself up wholly to study, ease and pleasure."[50]

Spinoza's sole recorded encounter with Vossius concerned the alchemical experiments of a local high society physician, alchemist and purveyor of mystery cures, Johannes Fridericus Helvetius (1630–1709), whose real name was Johann Friedrich Schweitzer (Swetzer), a fierce foe of Cartesianism and ally of strict Calvinist theologians, renowned for supposedly knowing how to transmute base metals into gold. Writing to Jelles, in March 1667, Spinoza mentions "with regard to the Helvetius affair," having "spoken about it with Mr Vossius who (not to recount in a letter all that passed between us) laughed heartily about this, and showed surprise that I should ask him about such a silly thing." One wonders, on this occasion, whose leg was being pulled by whom. Leibniz too, when in Holland in 1676, showed considerable curiosity about Helvetius' alchemical feats.[51] Spinoza, in any case, fascinated by experiments, showed remarkable tenacity in

---

[46] Desmaizeaux *Vie de Messire* [...] *de Saint-Evremond* i, 215; Meinsma, *Spinoza et son cercle*, 345n24; Wauters, "Libertinage érudit," 38.
[47] Israel, *Enlightenment Contested*, 640–3; Boyle, "China and the Radical Enlightenment Context," 1–5.
[48] Vossius, *Variarum observationum liber*, 56–7, 77; De Smet and Elias, "Isaac Vossius," 156, 162–4.
[49] Boyle, "China and the Radical Enlightenment Context," 5.
[50] Quoted in Boyle, "China and the Radical Enlightenment Context," 2–3.
[51] Spinoza, *Collected Works* (ed. Curley) ii, 37; Malcolm, "Leibniz, Oldenburg and Spinoza," 231.

investigating Helvetius' method in this instance, going to the trouble of visiting a silversmith, Brechtvelt, who examined his gold and spoke "about it quite differently from Vossius," saying it "expanded and became much heavier with the weight of the silver he introduced into the crucible to effect the separation," being convinced "the gold that transmuted his silver into gold contained something unusual," as did others present at the experiment. "Then, I went to Helvetius himself, who showed me the gold and crucible with its interior still covered with a film of gold, and told me he had thrown into the molten lead [by way of extraneous ingredients] scarcely more than a quarter of a grain of barley or mustard-seed." Studiedly non-committal, Spinoza simply commented "that was all I have been able to learn about this matter."[52]

Spinoza and Helvetius seem to have been on reasonably friendly speaking terms, although no personality was fiercer and more polemical than the latter in The Hague's raging ideological strife. His vitriolic diatribes against Cartesianism, Cocceianism, and, before long, Spinozism, as well as Cartesian medical reformism, made him a focal point of the philosophical and theological polemics of the day. Not only is Cartesianism the seedbed of Spinozism, held Helvetius in the late 1670s, but Christian physicians, as well as scholars, are duty-bound to fight both streams of thought.[53] Christian piety, held Helvetius, cannot be reconciled with the philosophical reason Cartesians apply to religious, moral, and social as well as scientific issues. By refusing to admit what is irreconcilable with philosophical reason,[54] Cartesianism, he contended, wrecks all belief in the Immaculate Conception, Incarnation, Holy Ghost, Trinity, and the Resurrection, and destroys credence in everything supernatural, magical, and miraculous—including Creation, resurrection of the dead, Satan, Heaven, Hell and the glorious secrets of alchemy which he himself displayed to one and all.[55] Such a catastrophic shift wrecks theology's pre-eminence over mankind, producing chaos in religion, morality, scholarship, politics, and society itself. He accused his chief Cartesian medical foe at The Hague, Dr Cornelis Bontekoe, and every thoroughgoing Cartesian, of admitting to not believing in angels and refusing in Scripture "everything that conflicts with reason."[56]

In medicine, Helvetius reviled Cartesian proclivity to explain every ailment, every change in a person's physical condition, in terms of natural reason and natural causes alone. The Cartesian principle that all Nature's workings, including the motions of the sun, moon and planets, result from physical movements caused by other movements, one bringing about the next in a necessary but infinite sequence, reduces all bodily states, and conditions of illness and health, including

---

[52] Spinoza, *Collected Works* (ed. Curley) ii, 37.
[53] Helvetius, *Adams oud Graft, Opgevult*, 79; Thijssen-Schoute, *Nederlands Cartesanisme*, 292–3.
[54] Helvetius, *Adams oud Graft, Opgevult*, 40–1, 99, 216.
[55] Helvetius, *Adams oud Graft, Opgevult*, 104–7, 116; Helvetius, *Davids Slinger-steen*, 112, 194–5.
[56] Helvetius, *Adams oud Graft, Opgevult*, 81–2, 125, 253.

each individual life's duration, to purely natural conditions explicable in mechanistic terms. The likes of Bontekoe (and Spinoza) leave no room for providence, or supernatural agency, much less Galenist humours.[57] Even plague epidemics, protested Helvetius, are classed by Cartesians, heedless of divine providence and punishment of the wicked, as part of the ordinary course of nature.[58] The height of impiety, this "Bontekoeist position" merges or confuses soul with "thought," closely linking the latter with body.[59]

Vossius and Helvetius were symptoms of the rift destabilizing Dutch science, medicine, and society before Spinoza's eyes. The strongly ideological, polemical streak in large parts of Spinoza's *TTP*, especially his assault on the ecclesiastical sphere, religious authority, and priestly power, the *TTP*'s most prominent single theme, stems directly from the intensifying theologico-political crisis gripping every aspect of life and culture in the Republic. Resident nearby in The Hague, the young Prince of Orange, William III, was now nearing his majority and De Witt found himself faced by the thorny challenge of incorporating this aspiring Prince into the Republic's power structure in a conspicuous and placating, yet also as marginal a fashion as feasible, a tactic the intelligent and ambitious young Prince and his relatives would inevitably resist. De Witt's strategy pivoted on the States of Holland's "Perpetual Edict [Eeuwig Edict]" of August 1667, passed at the close of the Anglo-Dutch War, abolishing the stadholderate in Holland "forever" and separating permanently the captaincy-general of the armed forces from the stadholderate while also stipulating that the young Prince, now approaching eighteen, could not become the Republic's captain-general until reaching the age of twenty-three. This was the foundation propping up the "True Freedom" during the last phase of De Witt's ascendancy, legislation that consequently became the focal point of the Republic's internal power struggle over the next five years.[60]

Dissension over the Perpetual Edict and renewed tussle over the stadholderate, proceeded hand in hand, much as in previous great political crises, with a powerful resurgence of the old controversies over the Reformed Church's place in the fabric of the Republic, and that of religious minorities, individual freedom, religious toleration, and freedom of expression. Publicists and ideologues supporting the values De Witt represented, eager to defend the "True Freedom," like Spinoza, Pieter de La Court, and Van den Enden, were acutely conscious of the precariousness of those freedoms, and the formidable opposition to consolidating them that the resurgent Orangist-Voetian tide represented.[61] La Court's *Aanwysing der heilsame politike Gronden* (1669), a reworking and reassertion of his democratic republican theory, was banned by the States of Holland, in May

---

[57] Bontekoe, *Drie Verhandelingen*, 7; Vermij, *Calvinist Copernicans*, 188–9, 213.
[58] Helvetius, *Davids Slinger-steen*, 255.   [59] Helvetius, *Adams oud Graft, Opgevult*, 254–5.
[60] Israel, *Dutch Republic*, 791–4.
[61] Israel, *Dutch Republic*, 785–94; James, *Spinoza on Philosophy*, 290–4; Mertens, "Van den Enden and Religion," 76.

1669, chiefly at the demand of the South Holland synod, for its sallies at the expense of the public church and demanding the "free practice of all religions and sects."[62] But that highly controversial work also greatly antagonized Orangists as well as the devout by dismissing the stadholderate as an obsolete remnant of the medieval past irrelevant to the true functioning of the States of Holland. La Court's rejection of the stadholderate as a threat to public well-being abounds in cutting remarks linking Orangism to the militant Calvinist faction's bigotry and intolerance. From 1667, Orangism grew stronger as a populist political-theological ideology challenging the De Witt regime, gaining new strength from improving relations with England and from the Republic's deteriorating strategic predicament, its being trapped between Louis XIV and Charles II.

23.iii Ideological Conflict

To discredit the Reformed Church's Voetian wing, La Court highlighted the antagonism between William the Silent and the Calvinists during the Revolt against Spain, reminding readers that the Calvinists had aligned with Leicester, a despotic representative of a foreign monarch, against their own Stadholder, William.[63] Toleration, insisted La Court, is essential to a trading republic, an asset boosting urban population and activity.[64] A plethora of other books and pamphlets similarly gave expression to republican antagonism to the surge of Orangism and Calvinist intolerance. But much the most devastating counterblast to religious authority, the stadholderate and intolerance, and their intruding on republican values, was Spinoza's *TTP*, a masterpiece of democratic republican polemical political intervention enmeshed in philosophy, combining Bible criticism with political theory and rejection of all forms of ecclesiastical autonomy within the state, Jewish and Christian.

Spinoza's intervention was also deeply personal. He felt passionately that the intolerance encountered in his daily life at Voorburg and then The Hague, though elaborately dressed in theological terminology, really boiled down to ambition, greed, prejudice, and lust for power. In his view (and that of La Court, Temple, Saint-Évremond, and Vossius) all church governance and theology possesses this character. His own high moral evaluation of free expression and tolerance, he knew, originated in his personal experience of the freedoms, disparateness, and commercial character of Amsterdam, which he eulogized as a symbol for the world, where "people of every sect and nation live together in the greatest harmony. Before transacting a loan to someone, they just want to know whether he is rich or poor and whether he is known to behave with good faith or

---

[62] Van Rees, *Verhandeling*, 786; Japikse, *Johan de Witt*, 278–9; Weststeijn, *Radicale Republiek*, 234.
[63] La Court, *Aanwysing*, 399–400.   [64] La Court, *Aanwysing*, 60, 65–6, 382, 398.

deceitfully." Religion and sect play no part in arranging dealings involving trust since religion has nothing to do with any person's moral standing and there is no sect that does not live under the protection of the city magistracy.[65] A person's worth and professed faith, in Spinoza's vision, are really quite separate, setting morality apart from confessional identity, a lesson inherent in his own background.

Spinoza passionately defended De Witt and his "True Freedom" but also believed too many compromises had been made from the Dutch Revolt against Spain onwards, limiting toleration, free expression, and the Republic's free exercise of its sovereignty. Restrictions on thought and freedom of conscience and the impulse to tighten those restrictions are ubiquitous in human society. Decrees "laying down what everyone must believe and forbidding anything from being said or written against this or that dogma, were often introduced to appease, or rather surrender to, the fury of those who cannot tolerate free minds, and who, with their stern authority easily convert the zeal of the volatile common people into rage and turn this against whoever they please."[66] Spinoza was speaking from experience. The crux of the challenge facing Spinoza, like La Court, was how to defend and fortify a far-reaching comprehensive, freedom of thought and expression in a republic beset by deep rifts sharply polarizing public opinion. Unlike La Court, Spinoza makes little attempt to assail Orangism as a political construct head-on. His goal politically is to accord to everyone the right "to think and judge for himself" while insisting this does not license men to act in anger and hatred or undermine the laws and institutions of the state. "Thus no one can act against the sovereign's decisions without prejudicing its authority, but they can think and judge and consequently also speak without restriction, provided they merely speak or teach by way of reason alone, not by trickery or in anger or from hatred, or with the intention of introducing some alteration in the state on their own initiative."[67] Hence, arguing that "a law should be repealed by giving sound reasons for doing so" is perfectly legitimate, provided the petitioner does nothing contrary to the law while it remains in force. "If, on the other hand, [opponents] use the freedom to accuse the magistrate of wrongdoing and render him odious to the common people or make a seditious attempt to abolish the law," against the magistrate's will, as Orangists strove to erase the "Perpetual Edict" barring the stadholderate, then they are "nothing more than agitators and rebels."[68]

Spinoza's aim was to devise a theological-political stance benefiting all societies while at the same time intervening directly in the Republic's specific circumstances. Every point in the *TTP* is directly linked to the furore surrounding De Witt, William III, Voetians, and Orangists, exactly as the *Tractatus Politicus* is

---

[65] Spinoza, *Theological-Political Treatise*, 257; Rovere, "Avoir commerce."
[66] Spinoza, *Theological-Political Treatise*, 256.   [67] Spinoza, *Theological-Political Treatise*, 252.
[68] Spinoza, *Theological-Political Treatise*, 253.

to the mid-1670s, but, equally, argues in terms of theoretical abstraction, seeking to establish general principles of universal validity. Spinoza's two political treatises, though abstract and generalized in the main, are nevertheless, as Herman Cohen recognized long ago, passionately engaged polemical interventions in the society of his time.[69] The daringly subversive contemporary relevance and applicability of what he has to say, Spinoza typically masks behind cautious generalities, treating the contemporary Dutch predicament as exemplary of the political problems of the wider world, past and present; and, in so doing, arguably achieved one of the most crucial steps in the development of modern political theory, helping found the tradition of modern democratic republicanism. It was activist political and social reformism, coolly generalized and theoretical on the surface, but driven by the force of his philosophical principles and a passionate moral commitment bursting out at brief but revealing moments in his political texts and correspondence.

Attacked throughout the *TTP* is what Spinoza considers the illicit, oppressive character of the authority churchmen of all types usurp for themselves over society, the republic, its education system and its laws. As with *De Jure Ecclesiasticorum* and La Court's treatises, for Spinoza "religion has the power of law only by decree of those who exercise the right of government so that God has no special kingdom among men except through those who exercise sovereignty. I also wish to demonstrate that religious worship and pious conduct must be accommodated to the peace and interests of the state and consequently be determined by the sovereign authorities alone."[70] Institutionalized religious authority independent of and in tension with the sovereign is always illicit and always a threat to society. There is no such thing as a reserved sphere of authority for churchmen, no such thing as a revelation, theology, or ecclesiastical sphere supreme over the law. The problem was that "very many people vigorously deny that this right [of *ius circa sacra*, i.e. jurisdiction over sacred matters] belongs to the sovereign authorities, and refuse to recognize them as interpreters of divine law. From this, they arrogate to themselves license to accuse and condemn sovereigns and excommunicate them from the church, as Ambrose long ago excommunicated the emperor Theodosius." What such religious leaders "are in effect doing is dividing the sovereign power and attempting to devise a path to power for themselves."[71]

"No one can rightly obey God," contends Spinoza's *TTP*, "if they do not adapt pious observance to the public interest to which everyone is bound, and do not, as a consequence, obey all the decrees of the sovereign power," including everything

---

[69] Cohen, *Spinoza, On State and Religion*, 1–3.
[70] Spinoza, *Theological-Political Treatise*, 238; Lavaert, *Vrijheid, gelijkheid, veelheid*, 183.
[71] Spinoza, *Theological-Political Treatise*, 238–9, 259.

relating to religion.[72] He refused to "waste time on the arguments of my opponents striving to separate sacred law from civil law by maintaining that only the latter belongs to the sovereign authorities while the former belongs to the universal church,"[73] a sentiment aimed at the Perpetual Edict's opponents, Orangists and Voetians seeking to undermine the States' authority. Spinoza rarely uses the sarcastic tongue in cheek evasiveness later typical of deist anti-Christian discourse in the next century, but on particularly sensitive topics occasionally does. No one should reply to his argument, he adds, that the "disciples of Christ" were "indubitably private" men and yet righteously took it upon themselves to preach a religion at variance with the Roman Empire's laws. Such political subversion by men of faith, argued Spinoza, is never authorized by faith in Christ, because Christ and his disciples are a uniquely holy instance, an exception no one may emulate "unless he too has the power to work miracles," obvious sarcasm on Spinoza's part as, in his view, no one, Christ included, ever possessed or could possess such power.[74]

Citing the humiliation of the medieval German emperors by popes, Spinoza deplores the Pope's bringing "all the kings under his control until finally he ascended to the very pinnacle of supreme power."[75] Religious authority separate from that of the state is a gigantic menace to all societies, being the most potent political instrument for opposing the sovereignty of the state: "what no monarch could achieve by fire and the sword, churchmen could accomplish by the sole power of the pen. From this instance alone one readily appreciates the strength and power of this right [over religious affairs] and how vital it is for sovereigns to keep this authority for themselves alone."[76] Unfortunately, there has always been fierce controversy over division of power in Christian states, adds Spinoza, "whereas, so far as I know the Hebrews never had any doubts about this."[77]

In the *TTP*'s nineteenth chapter, Spinoza offers an account of "the beginnings of the Christian religion" to prove the wholly exceptional character of what he presents as a uniquely problematic context. As it was "not kings who originally taught the Christian religion, but rather private individuals acting against the will of those exercising political power, whose subjects they were," when political authority first adopted Christianity "churchmen had to instruct the emperors in the religion they themselves had devised." In Constantine's time this was unavoidable, all Christians agree, but also a wholly unique, otherwise inadmissible case necessitating that private persons be the interpreters of Christianity in just that single, unrepeatable context. This power that ecclesiastics possessed only in

[72] Spinoza, *Theological-Political Treatise*, 243; James, *Spinoza on Philosophy*, 255–8.
[73] Spinoza, *Theological-Political Treatise*, 244; Fukuoka, *Sovereign and the Prophets*, 155–7.
[74] Spinoza, *Theological-Political Treatise*, 244–5.
[75] Spinoza, *Theological-Political Treatise*, 246; James, *Spinoza on Philosophy*, 155, 297.
[76] Spinoza, *Theological-Political Treatise*, 246; Nadler, *Book Forged in Hell*, 203.
[77] Spinoza, *Theological-Political Treatise*, 247.

Constantine's time indisputably remains the sole exception because Christianity's veracity is proven to mankind exclusively and only by Christ's "miracles." Entirely otherwise, affirms Spinoza, was the situation in the ancient Hebrew Republic because their religion began at the same time as their state and Moses held supreme power and taught the people and selected the pastors. It was his quasi-royal authority that "had most influence with the people," and afterwards it was effectively the Hebrew kings who "exercised authority in sacred matters."[78]

Ancient Israelite kings exercised an authority less complete than that of Moses, nevertheless "almost the whole organization of the sacred ministry and the selection of ministers depended on their decree." Thus, King David "designed the structure of the Temple" and decreed how the Levites should perform their duties.[79] Towards the prophets whom he sees as wrongly interfering more than rightly criticizing, Spinoza adopts a mostly dismissive, negative attitude. Where Maimonides places the prophets on a par with the greatest philosophers, Spinoza's prophets were exceptional only through possessing greater powers of imagination than other men. One should not look to them for instruction because "those most powerful in imagination are less expert at merely understanding things; men with trained and powerful intellects possess a more modest power of imagination and keep it under better control, reigning it in, so to speak, and not confusing it with understanding." Consequently, "those who look in the books of the prophets for wisdom and knowledge of natural and spiritual things are completely on the wrong track."[80]

All this needs to be said, despite "the outcry from credulous people who detest none more than those who cultivate real knowledge and true life. Distressingly, it has now come to the point that people who freely admit that they do not possess the idea of God [i.e. those who understand no science or philosophy] knowing him only through created things whose causes they are ignorant of, do not hesitate to accuse philosophers of atheism," the very accusation under which Spinoza himself laboured.[81] As prophetic knowledge is "inferior to natural knowledge" and cannot provide clarity about anything except basic moral issues, what the prophets teach remains decidedly limited in scope. Since it is imagination that inspires prophecy, moreover, "God granted some prophets a far greater gift of prophecy than others." Hence, the prophets "really were ignorant" and inevitably "held contradictory views." Since knowledge about natural and spiritual matters is by no means to be obtained from them and yet, "the Bible's authority depends

---

[78] Spinoza, *Theological-Political Treatise*, 244–5; James, *Spinoza on Philosophy*, 296.
[79] Spinoza, *Theological-Political Treatise*, 247–9; Proietti, *La Città Divisa*, 81.
[80] Spinoza, *Theological-Political Treatise*, 27; Rosenthal, "Miracles, Wonder," 240–1; Nadler, *Book Forged in Hell*, 62–72.
[81] Spinoza, *Theological-Political Treatise*, 27; James, *Spinoza on Philosophy*, 106.

upon that of the prophets," biblical teaching can have no application outside the moral sphere.[82]

After the ancient Hebrew Republic, the era of the Old Testament kings starting with King Saul (reigned: *c.*1037–1010 BC) was undoubtedly a time of political decay and Spinoza concedes that the prophets arose, often at the start of a new reign, to proclaim the shortcomings of these kings and expose their fondness for extraneous gods and luxurious foreign influences. But their interference and intended reformism, according to Spinoza, accomplished hardly any good. They introduced no improvements. "Even if they deposed a tyrant, the causes of tyranny still remained, and so all they achieved was to bring in a new tyrant at the expense of much citizens' blood. Consequently, there was no end to strife and civil war, and the reasons why the divine law was violated remained always the same; these reasons could be removed only by overthrowing the [monarchical] state entirely."[83] But the prophets offered no path to understanding how society could escape the ills of monarchy and recover the solidity of the ancient Hebrew Republic.

By contrast, Christian states, despite Christianity's undoubted superior legitimacy to every other faith which Spinoza (ostensibly) affirms, experienced from the outset a nagging defect. Behind the scenes as much as in public, ecclesiastics more insidiously menace men's basic freedoms even than oppressive kings. Spinoza could freely condemn the main churches for power-seeking and intolerance as long as he heaped his severest strictures for contriving dogmas as levers of power on the ancient Pharisees and those sharing the Pharisaic temperament. But when stressing "how dangerous it is to refer purely philosophical questions to divine law, and make laws about opinions which men can or do dispute," alluding to the States of Holland's decrees of 1653 and 1656 outlawing Socinian views and publications, and Anti-Trinitarian conventicles he was on trickier ground. It was under this edict that Meyer's *Philosophia* and many other works, including, later, the *TTP*, were suppressed.[84]

Kings and ecclesiastics are both, for Spinoza, perennial foes to society's well-being. Yet, the greatest threat, he maintains, arises from the common people in their ignorance, anger, and bigotry whenever misled by agitators, false prophets, and scheming demagogues. Here again, Spinoza employs the term "common people" not in the usual sense to denote the ordinary, poor, and lacking in status, but in his special philosophical sense shared by his circle, reminiscent of the medieval Averroists and Maimonides. Adriaan Koerbagh assures readers in the *Bloemhof* that everybody is "ignoble," whatever their lineage, if they are ignorant

---

[82] Spinoza, *Theological-Political Treatise*, 191; Rosenthal, "Miracles, Wonder," 238–9; Fukuoka, *Sovereign and the Prophets*, 190–2.
[83] Spinoza, *Theological-Political Treatise*, 229.
[84] Israel, *Dutch Republic*, 708, 910–12, 915; James, *Spinoza on Philosophy*, 143, 209, 215, 293.

and lack knowledge of the reality of things, and inserts a special footnote about this in his *A Light Shining in Dark Places* (1668): "I take ordinary people here to mean not lowly people poor in money and status but rather common people in [terms of] knowledge, judgment and use of learning whether they are noblemen or ignoble, rich or poor." If the common people defined in this way, possessed more knowledge, judgement, and use of learning, and "somewhat less prejudice and trust in what most people think, they would soon realize they are being misled."[85]

Where theology rules, holds Spinoza, "the common people's anger tends to prevail. Pilate knew that Christ was innocent but ordered him to be crucified to appease the fury of the Pharisees. To deprive those richer than themselves [their theological and priestly opponents] of their offices, the Pharisees aimed to stir up controversies about religion and accuse the Sadducees of impiety. Following the Pharisees' example, all the worst hypocrites everywhere are driven by the same frenzy (which they call zeal for God's law), to persecute men of outstanding probity and known virtue [like Oldenbarnevelt], resented by the common people for precisely these qualities, by publicly reviling their opinions and inflaming the anger of the barbarous majority against them." Subversive ambition of this kind hiding "under the cloak of religion" is difficult to check where sovereign authorities err by permitting a cult of which they themselves are not the heads.[86] Where the people are thus stirred up, magistrates have "very little influence with the common people; rather the authority of the theologians, to whose authority they think even kings must submit, acquires overwhelming weight."[87] Experience "teaches us these things with new examples every day."

Spinoza's strategy for combating what he viewed as the impediments to human well-being was in important respects shaped by Holland's epic struggle to free herself from the global empire forged by the Habsburg Emperor, Charles V (king of Spain: 1516–55), culminating under Philip II (reigned: 1555–98). That epic struggle continued through the era of Oldenbarnevelt and Grotius, and the stadholderate of Frederik Hendrik (1625–47), and in a way, persisted even into his own time, since the toleration, freedom of thought and expression, and other liberties fought for from 1566 onwards, held democratic republican critics of the De Wittian "True Freedom," such as Van den Enden, the De La Courts, the Koerbaghs, and Spinoza, were still not fully or safely secured. One obvious menace to the "True Freedom" was the institution of the stadholderate vested in the House of Orange, an institution suspended in the province of Holland since 1650, but which many or most wanted restored. Spinoza, though, judged it a harmful monarchical anomaly and obsolete vestige from the past contradicting the basic

---

[85] Koerbagh, *Bloemhof*, 346; Koerbagh, *A Light Shining*, 78–9; Klever, *Mannen rond Spinoza*, 99; Lavaert, "An Excellent Mathematician," 255.
[86] Spinoza, *Theological-Political Treatise*, 234; Proietti, *La Città Divisa*, 185–8.
[87] Spinoza, *Theological-Political Treatise*, 234.

principles of the state that ought never to have been retained, that never should have outlasted the early stages of the Dutch Revolt.[88] Opposition to the "True Freedom" was led by the House of Orange and the Reformed clergy, but it was nevertheless still popular ignorance and bigotry that provided their main support and hence, it seemed to radical critics, the muscle behind their hegemony.

While the United Provinces accorded religious minorities an unprecedented level of toleration, and individuals exceptional personal liberty and freedom of expression, freedoms Spinoza immensely cherished and relied on, the ruling oligarchy's support among the public was far too narrow to reliably guarantee the Republic's long-term stability and survival. Oldenburg, like Sir William Temple and many foreigners at the time, likewise appreciated the toleration and freedom of expression offered by the United Provinces, but what foreign observers did not always fully appreciate was how menacingly these enviable freedoms were challenged, how inherently precarious they were and in need of constant defending and cultivating to flourish. Spinoza, by contrast, was acutely conscious of the Republic's inherent instability. During the years 1667-72, the embattled Johan de Witt (1625-72), leader of the republican-minded oligarchy controlling the Republic in the years 1650-72, faced a steadily worsening predicament, aggravated by the growing ideological and church-political deadlock in which the Republic seemed trapped.

For some, the Republic's internal instability had been all too evident since its founding. Allied to the strict Calvinist Counter-Remonstrants, Maurits of Nassau (Stadholder: 1585-1625) had demonstrated the vulnerability of the Arminian, Grotian, and republican "Loevestein" legacy to his Orangist alliance of princely house with Calvinist orthodoxy, in the years 1617-19, by engineering the overthrow of Oldenbarnevelt, the statesman who contributed more than any other, after William the Silent himself, to shaping the Republic's institutions. Oldenbarnevelt's downfall and execution was a profound setback, in Spinoza's view, that could never have occurred without a background of fierce theological strife. "When the controversy about religion began to agitate office-holders and the Dutch provincial assemblies earlier this century, it led after a time to a complete split." It was at this point that Spinoza remarks that such rifts "do not arise from an intense passion for truth," the fount and origin of amity and gentleness, "but from a great lust for power."[89] This was clear "for if men had not nurtured hopes of aligning the law and government on their side, and triumphing over their opponents with the common people's applause, securing

---

[88] Spinoza, *Tractatus Politicus* in *Oeuvres* v, 126; Verbeek, "Spinoza on Aristocratic and Democratic Government," 72; Moreau, "A-t-on raison de se révolter?," 28.
[89] Spinoza, *Theological-Political Treatise*, 257-8.

high positions for themselves, they would never have fought one another so unrestrainedly; and such fanaticism never would have swayed their minds."[90]

A second near fatal collision had occurred in 1650 as Spinoza neared maturity. Stadholder William II (in office: 1647–50), intent on seizing power, clashing with Amsterdam and again allied to the strict Calvinists, dragged the Republic to the verge of civil war. Fortunately for the United Provinces' freedoms and stability, armed conflict was averted by that overweening prince's conveniently timed death from smallpox later that year. But the relative calm of the ensuing period in the later 1660s gave way to renewed ideological warfare. The impending political crisis of 1672, soon to convulse the Republic and also engulf Spinoza and his followers, was the third deeply threatening *revolutio* of the Dutch Golden Age.

Spinoza, like the Brothers La Court and the Koerbaghs, regarded the events of 1617–19 and 1650 as salutary lessons for all, but also as episodes sowing deep division, unleashing harmful passion, and producing decrees designed to halt theological dispute which "actually had quite the opposite effect, stirring men up rather than disciplining them while enabling some to consider themselves authorized by such decrees to arrogate boundless illicit sway to themselves."[91] If the "True Freedom's" adversaries viewed the two earlier episodes of severe upheaval in 1618 and 1650 as ones in which ungodly "Arminian" dissidents received their just deserts for betraying church and prince, the republican-minded of Spinoza's time viewed the coup of 1618–19 and attempted coup of 1650 as abominable oppression and injustice, painful lessons that had lost none of their relevance in their day. To discerning observers, the 1617–19 struggle between Remonstrants and Counter-Remonstrants provided an alarming precedent to the resumed friction of the late 1660s and fall of the De Witt regime in 1672.

23.iv Democratic Republicanism

Putting philosophy to practical use subversively and, by so doing, raising the level of human happiness generally was Spinoza's unyielding aim. Nowhere does the conventional myth of Spinoza, the reclusive, isolated thinker, clash more with the reality of his life than in the extraordinary boast, at the start of his *Tractatus Politicus*, echoing Machiavelli, that virtually all previous writers on politics, presumably including Machiavelli and Hobbes, "conceive men, in effect, not as they are, but as they would like them to be and that is why, mostly, they have composed satire in the guise of ethics and have never conceived a politics which could be put to any practical use, but instead notions applicable only in Utopia or

---

[90] Spinoza, *Theological-Political Treatise*, 256; Steinberg and Viljanen, *Spinoza*, 41.
[91] Spinoza, *Theological-Political Treatise*, 258; Koerbagh, *A Light Shining*, 250–9.

the Golden Age of the poets where there would be no need for them."[92] Conceiving men as they are, explains the *Ethics*, means dispensing with reviling or scoffing at human failings and learning to study "human actions and appetites just as if I were considering lines, planes or bodies."[93]

Not only are "the multitude" of whatever social category, from kings downwards, as distinct from discerning individuals belonging to the subversive underground, blind to how men find themselves ceaselessly oppressed and taken advantage of politically and religiously, held Spinoza, but with regard to constructive application of knowledge, the results of study, science, and philosophizing, the competence of past philosophers, theorists, and academics is thus very much in question too. One might think the most relevant books about politics were written not by theorists or philosophers but rather statesmen. However, neither the men of theory nor the politicians and statesmen had really examined the different forms of state systematically as Spinoza proposed to do.

> So when I applied my mind to politics, I did not intend to do anything new or unheard of, but only deduce the things relevant to this science with the same freedom of mind we are accustomed to use when inquiring into mathematical topics, taking care not to laugh at human actions, or lament or detest them, but rather to understand them, considering the human emotions – love, hate, anger, envy, glory-seeking, compassion, and all the other movements of the heart, not as vices of human nature, but as properties pertaining to that nature, just as warmth, cold, tempests, thunder and other phenomena of this sort pertain to the nature of air which, however inconvenient, are nevertheless necessary and have particular causes by which we try to understand their nature.[94]

Spinoza proposed to elevate political theory to an altogether more "realistic" level, yielding tangible improvement, by creating a new social science based on precise observation of human conduct and practices to replace existing political theory. His was an incisive "realism" that has always attracted a few: if Bolívar figures prominently among them, Henry Kissinger too remarked, in an interview, of December 1972, that Spinoza and Kant were the two thinkers who "influenced me most."[95]

The three greatest, most intractable ills burdening and degrading mankind, according to Spinoza—tyranny, religious authority, and ignorance—at first sight appear to be distinct curses afflicting humanity, only remotely connected. Closer

---

[92] Spinoza, *Collected Works* (ed. Curley) ii, 503.
[93] Spinoza, *Collected Works* (ed. Curley) i, 491–2; Hirschman, *Passions and the Interests*, 13–14; Lloyd, *Part of Nature*, 77.
[94] Spinoza, *Tractatus Politicus* in *Oeuvres* v, 88–91; Spinoza, *Collected Works* (ed. Curley) ii, 503–5; Lavaert, *Vrijheid, gelijkheid, veelheid*, 244–5.
[95] Curley, "Kissinger, Spinoza and Genghis Khan," 315, 329.

investigation, though, reveals their actually being highly interdependent, mutually buttressing each other. Consequently, all three must be tackled together and, though impossible to overcome entirely, checked and pruned back in everyone's interest by means of a carefully devised social and political strategy. Here, Spinoza emerges as an original, profoundly revolutionary figure. Monarchy, the dominant political European form in his time, including its stunted offshoot, the Dutch stadholderate, Spinoza classifies as highly undesirable, a pernicious ideology and defective institutional form, fundamentally detrimental to human well-being, the factor chiefly responsible for the wars of the age and the wretchedness wars bring. The major conflicts of the time—the Eighty Years War (1566–1648), the Thirty Years War that devastated Germany (1618–48), and the Franco-Spanish War (1635–59)—all stemmed principally from royal and princely ambition tied to ecclesiastical and theological structures supporting absolutist pretensions and power.

The ultimate antidote to oppression and persecution in Spinoza's eyes is, of course, his own philosophy, or something like it, leading to the ousting of kings, princes, and "small councils," and ending ecclesiastical supervision. But absolute rulers, their power depending principally on "superstition," would surely use every means in their power to forestall the demystification of society leading to their own disempowerment. "But truly, whether kings will ever concede the bringing forward of a remedy for this evil, I doubt very much [Verum an huic malo remedium adhibere reges unquam concedent, valde dubito]."[96] "It may indeed be the highest secret of monarchical government," affirms Spinoza in the preface the *TTP*, "and utterly essential to it, to keep men deceived, disguising the fear that controls them with the specious name of religion, so they will fight for their servitude as if fighting for their own safety, and not think it humiliating but supremely glorious, to spill their blood and give their lives for the glorification of a single man."[97] No great optimist regarding the chances of elevating humanity by conquering ignorance and eradicating kings and autocrats along with aristocracy and religious authority, Spinoza saw no chance at all of achieving a better world without doing so.

But if monarchy is intrinsically damaging to human well-being, of humanity's three great adversaries, tyranny, religious authority, and ignorance, it is the last that Spinoza judges the most damaging to the common good, and fatal to the democratic republic, because ignorance is what chiefly feeds the credulity and incomprehension underpinning the despotism and religious authority chaining humanity down. Lessening human wretchedness and improving society is hence directly linked to fighting ignorance. This idea, fundamental to Spinoza's system, that all human society whatever its distinctive social and religious history,

---

[96] Spinoza, *Opera* iv, 308; Spinoza, *Briefwisseling*, 400.
[97] Spinoza, *Tractatus Theologico-Politicus*, 6; Moreau, *Spinoza et le spinozisme*, 89.

basically consists (contrary to what nearly everybody assumes) of two primary groups—those comprehending basic philosophical truths, the sages, and the majority tied to *appetitus* and superstition—signally marks Spinoza off in his political and social thought from Machiavelli, Hobbes, and other early modern political thinkers and stands among the basic concepts he shares, or borrowed, from the medieval thinker Maimonides, who exerted, we have seen, a substantial influence on Spinoza's ethical and social thought as well as Bible exegesis, despite Maimonides evincing far more confidence in philosophers' capacity to directly guide society towards greater rationality than Spinoza.

This divergence between Spinozist and Maimonidean classification helps explain why Spinoza's approach required an indirect and subversive enlightening strategy. Though convinced worthwhile change, via revolutionary transformation of the monarchical state into a democratizing republic, is conceivable and attainable, this can occur only with great difficulty, as the Dutch Republic's emergence demonstrated, and is never directly achievable by the masses since what most people believe, commonplace thinking, rests on ignorance and "superstition," the chief pillars upholding the pretensions of those preying on the majority. Hence, only via clandestine groups of the more informed who do understand the "reality of things," can enlightened networks erode the credulity on which monarchy and religious authority rest, and can those qualified to frame beneficial constitutions, laws, and civil religions gain sufficient leverage to coax the multitude into acquiescing in laws and institutions beneficial to everyone, enabling society to edge, however arduously, towards a rational outcome democratic by serving the "common good."[98]

By deftly combating religious "superstition" in this way, disempowering popular prejudice and tyranny conjoined, toleration can be established, freedom of expression extended, oppression checked, peace strengthened, science and the arts promoted, and useless wars and vainglorious self-sacrifice for entirely worthless, meaningless causes minimized. Such gains are achievable wherever the stultifying "glory" of kings and blind religious faith are sufficiently eroded by Spinoza's vanguard of intellectual subversive groups as to become seriously discredited. Toleration, republics, and democracy, proclaims Spinoza's hidden creed, benefit men, whereas monarchs, ecclesiastics, and ordinary people's beliefs, Christian, Jewish, and Islamic, do not. Since royal tyranny and absolutism can only be undermined by weakening "superstition" and "ignorance," and the common people cannot be emancipated from "superstition" directly, the sole applicable and practicable revolutionary strategy and politics available for bettering human society is to foster republican, demystifying ideology clandestinely.

---

[98] Harvey, "Portrait of Spinoza," 168–9; Frankel, "Spinoza's Rejection of Maimonideism," 88–91.

Spinoza's political conundrum, how to extricate society from tyranny and oppression, is thus tied to an ethical conundrum involving the inevitably of clandestinity and deception if men are to progress. In a letter to Jelles of February 1671, Spinoza cites an ancient Greek adage recorded by Erasmus, attributing it (possibly wrongly) to Thales of Miletus (c.620–c.548 BC), the first of the great Greek thinkers, envisaging him as the one who first placed philosophy, and with it all human thought on the right path. The adage serves to illustrate Spinoza's doctrine that the most fundamental gap between human types is that between "the wise" and the multitude, a point directly linked not just to individual pursuit of happiness but also to religion, politics, and the collective fate of everyone. "Thales" showed "that it is not by necessity, but voluntarily, that the wise possess no wealth." Moreover, "all things," said "Thales," "are common among friends; the wise are friends of the gods"; and since all things belong to the gods, there is a sense in which "all things belong to the wise." Spinoza echoed these ancient observations to show "how much better and more excellent" were such thoughts than those of a certain despicable author who had authored a text entitled *Homo Politicus, or the Political Man* which "some time ago one of my friends sent me," and he had heard much about, that promoted pursuit of wealth and honours as the principal goals of life which Spinoza lambasts as "the most harmful book men can devise."[99]

Homo Politicus, or "the Political Man" was a text written, or rather patched together, by a somewhat disreputable German professor at Geneva, Philipp Andreas Oldenburger (1617–78), tracked down in a notable study by Mogens Laerke. *Homo Politicus* profiles the social and political types caring for nothing except their own advancement and using every deceitful means to achieve it, an exercise Spinoza felt so outraged by that he told Jelles he was thinking of writing a short book to refute it.[100] The author recommends that "you should not be true to anyone except when it is to your advantage, otherwise placing the highest value on deceiving, promising without performing, lying, false oaths, and much else." It is a passage of Spinoza's surviving correspondence replete with moral revulsion, highly revealing about the philosopher, illustrative of Spinoza's general attitude to the individual, society, politics and the pursuit of happiness, the importance of friendship and working together in groups and likewise the question of what really counts as "deceit," which may entail also a remarkable hidden irony. It remains unclear which of the several editions of *Homo Politicus* Spinoza read and so abhorred in 1671 (there are considerable divergences among the versions issued in the 1660s), and it is uncertain whether the version Spinoza decried included a

---

[99] Spinoza, *Collected Works* (ed. Curley) ii, 390–1; Laerke, "*Homo Politicus*: Spinoza, Oldenburger," 157–8.
[100] Spinoza, *Collected Works* (ed. Curley) ii, 391; Laerke, "*Homo Politicus*: Spinoza, Oldenburger," 137.

striking passage found in several but not all editions, borrowed from the essayist Jean-Louis Guez de Balzac (1597-1654) about crypto-Jewish friars in Iberia in the time of Philip III bearing uncanny resemblances to figures in his own family history.

In this remarkable passage Guez de Balzac recalls hearing from a prominent ecclesiastic in southern France, the Dominican Nicolas Coeffetau (1574-1623), that in Iberia existed certain monasteries where the friars outwardly preached Christian doctrine by day, exhorting one and all to follow Christ, while in their hearts nurturing only secret Judaism and, unknown to their congregants, utterly repudiating Christ. In the eyes of Coeffetau and Guez de Balzac nothing could be viler or more perverse, whereas for Spinoza mouthing superstitious platitudes pleasing to the authorities as a means of saving oneself from the Inquisition, countering the ignorant, and teaching values helpful to society is positive conduct. To Spinoza, like his Jesuit great uncle Enrique Henriquez, and even more relevantly here, Fray Martín del Espiritu Santo, the crypto-Jew involved with his great grandfather, Duarte Fernandes and his grandfather, Henrique Garces, in the secret peace negotiations between Spain and the Dutch, in The Hague, in 1611-12, decades of concealing crypto-Judaism in the Lisbon monastery of La Misericordia, seeking whatever is best by side-stepping, or pretending to go along with the errors of common belief, constituted the very essence of a truly moral effective politics, resonant, however extensive the concealment, not of deceit and infidelity but of "true religion."[101] For Spinoza, discerning the difference between insidious, damaging deception and constructive stratagems useful for undermining tyranny and oppression and coaxing the unruly and superstitious *vulgus* in the right direction, amounts to a fundamental rule of politics.

The usual things men pursue are not worth living for. What is worth living for and benefits everyone, wisdom, the path to "reason" and hence happiness, is generally ignored. However, close-knit groups of the wise can perhaps devise ways to shift the balance meaningfully for everyone, and for the benefit of all, by "deceiving" those who tyrannize over others and think in base, commonplace terms reflecting the values of the multitude. Meanwhile, while attempting to initiate positive reforms circuitously, by forming behind-the-scenes networks working for the benefit of all, the wise are forever at loggerheads with the base-minded, the latter compounding humanity's age-old wretchedness using perverse notions justifying oppression and persecution and nurturing prejudices altogether harmful to the individual and society collectively. An activist of a special kind, profoundly wary of "the multitude," the exclusive way forward for Spinoza was his brand of hidden activism secretly forging more contexts like that of De Wittian Holland by systematically undermining monarchy, clergy, and aristocracy and

---

[101] Laerke, *Spinoza and the Freedom*, 105-7; see Guez de Balzac, *Apologie contre le Docteur de Louvain*, 289; Laerke, "*Homo Politicus*: Spinoza, Oldenburger," 150.

advancing "reason" through underground debate eventually generating freedom of expression and all the advantages of the democratic republic.

But the path was strewn with obstacles. Spinoza's ideal republic, a goal attainable in principle by every human society, he thought, would extend and fortify what was attractive in De Witt's "True Freedom" by providing wider representation and securing broader support. A positive *"revolutio,"* for Spinoza, meant enhancing and elevating society's general well-being by comprehensively replacing the ills of monarchy and religious authority with a republic dedicated to the "common good" rather than that of the few, based on the representative principle, something few in England in the 1650s had understood.[102] Rigorous constraints on kings, princes, ecclesiastics, and all would-be tyrants, need to be instituted and firmly held in place by large councils, laws, and constitutional arrangements proceeding in the name of all of society—legislatures and large councils remaining throughout Spinoza's political ideal for stabilizing the "common good."

In the *TTP* Spinoza ties together what he saw as the failure of the English Commonwealth of the 1650s to the war Cromwell instigated against the Dutch. Spinoza attributes that aggression, the First Anglo-Dutch War, to the deliberate misleading of the English people by a power-hungry, autocratic statesman (Cromwell) acting as a virtual "king," needing to distract attention at home from the unedifying realities of his domestic policies, the lack of consultation and debate and repression of Parliament as well as of his opponents at home. For political purposes, Cromwell, in Spinoza's view, needed to disguise the fact that despite executing their king, Charles I, in January 1649, the English had failed to remove the specific disadvantages of monarchy and despotism and failed to establish a genuine republic. War with the Dutch, Spinoza believed, served to distract a people lacking understanding of what a genuine republican revolution is and how to achieve it, preventing their recognizing Cromwell's tyranny for what it was. The English, thinks Spinoza, paid a high price in bloodshed and turmoil, enduring a long civil war but in the end merely exchanged Charles I for Cromwell, in effect just a "king" under another name.[103]

Spinoza's observations on Roman history further illustrate his distinctive preference for purposeful planned rejection of autocracy, monarchy, and oppression over unfocused violent resistance. Although, unlike Hobbes and Saint-Évremond, he shared Machiavelli's deep fascination for the ancient Roman Republic and preference for it over the Roman imperial system that succeeded it, he did not share Machiavelli's reverence for that republic. For him, Rome was no surpassing

---

[102] Spinoza, *Theological-Political Treatise*, 236; Israel, *Enlightenment that Failed*, 71–2; Moreau, "A-t-on raison de se révolter?," 18; Cristofolini, "Peuple et multitude," 54.
[103] Spinoza, *Theological-Political Treatise*, 236.

model, but rather yet another example of failure from which to learn. "Admittedly, the Roman people [under their Republic] could far more easily rid themselves of a tyrant and change their form of government [than could the English], the right to choose the king and his successor being in the hands of the people [...] Indeed, of the six kings they had in earlier times, they slaughtered three." But when, finally, the Romans tired of kings altogether "all they achieved thereby was to choose many tyrants [i.e. the Roman senate], instead of one, and these kept them in ceaseless strife, and foreign and civil wars, until finally the form of state once again became monarchical [with Augustus and the establishment of the empire] except only, as in the English case, for the change of name."[104] Spinoza's—and broadly the Radical Enlightenment's—rejection of oligarchic republics, governed like that of ancient Rome by nobility or any other kind of elite, the predominant form of republic, the "aristocratic republic" of his day, was as fundamental to his political theory as aversion to monarchy and deserves greater emphasis than it usually receives.

Hence, the Romans too, despite the advantage of their republican origins, ultimately failed to extricate themselves from the ruinous maze of despotic tyranny everywhere ensnaring mankind. Casting off tyranny stiffened by religious authority is never an easy or simple process. If the ancient Romans and seventeenth-century English dismally failed to escape monarchical and aristocratic despotism and achieve the democratic republic, Spinoza's other prime illustration of the difficulties involved in moving towards republican stability, the Hebrew Republic of Old Testament times, did actually edge closer to the goal, at least fleetingly, by adopting the principle of "theocracy," which, in Spinoza, as earlier in Maimonides and before him Philo, does not mean rule by clerics or priests but rather the sovereignty of "God." Having escaped bondage in Egypt under the pharaohs, the Israelites created what in Spinoza's view, differently from Hobbes, was an imagined sovereignty which, though based on "inadequate ideas," had the advantage, in practice, of requiring everyone to share equally in a venerated non-human sovereignty offering real possibilities of stability and a successful democratic republic.[105]

Among humanity's chief concerns, essential for edging towards the "common good," held Spinoza, is learning how to avoid despotism and war, something impossible in his schema without lessening veneration for false prophets, idols, and gods. If Philip's absolutism and the Inquisition were great scourges that uprooted his own family's existence in Portugal, appreciating how deeply "theologico-political" subversion aimed against majority attitudes but seeking to

---

[104] Spinoza, *Theological-Political Treatise*, 236; Matheron, *Christ et le salut*, 50; Mosbah, "Ultimi Barbarorum," 323.
[105] Spinoza, *Theological-Political Treatise*, 213–14; Verbeek, *Spinoza's Theologico-Political Treatise*, 125–31; Novak, "Spinoza and the Doctrine," 89–90; Proietti, *La Città Divisa*, 51–6.

benefit the majority's condition and circumstances was ingrained in Spinoza's consciousness, family traditions, and the social group among which he grew up, helps clarify why his chief targets, the structures of authority he sought to undermine, were so broadly conceived, being religious, political, and philosophical all at the same time. Much as Philip II's Spain was the headquarters of absolutist monarchy, Inquisition persecution, intolerance and Aristotelian scholasticism bundled together, making Iberia under Philip seem its veritable opposite, the Dutch Republic stood out as the world's chief repository of liberty of expression and individual freedom, as the socio-political antithesis of the new royal absolutism generally. Louis XIV never quite rivalled Philip in Spinoza's scheme of royal tyrants but likewise served as a symbol of grasping monarchy marring human well-being and society—as did, Spinoza's correspondence with Oldenburg reveals, a third champion of monarchical sway and its consequences, Charles II of England.

Living in the centre of The Hague around 1670, the epicentre of the struggle for the soul of the Republic, any religious and philosophical critic opposing the Calvinist preachers was bound to become emotionally caught up in the spiralling political turmoil, and fear the mounting threat to free expression and toleration. Even well before 1672, it was quite impossible to live in the vicinity of The Hague, possessing Spinoza's outlook, and not focus on the intensifying drama, the menacing political and intellectual malaise obviously rooted in the Republic's very form and structure. For all its achievements and enviable features, De Witt's Republic remained deeply fraught, subject to rifts and faction-fighting among its rival power elites with its public church and universities, army, navy, and legislative bodies all hopelessly divided. Opposition to De Witt's regent regime was further bolstered by the grudging resentment of the more rural fringe provinces, Friesland, Zeeland, and Overijssel especially, towards the longstanding political, financial, and cultural dominance of the most urbanized, populous, and affluent province, Holland. Regents supporting De Witt and opposing the Orangists and strict Calvinist party saw themselves regularly denounced in tracts and pamphlets as the despicable "Loevesteynsche factie [Loevestein faction]," a scornful epithet alluding to the name of the fourteenth-century fortress where Grotius had been imprisoned in 1619–21.

If it is altogether natural for monarchies, contends Spinoza, in both the *Tractatus Theologico-Politicus* and the *Tractatus Politicus*, to deceive their subjects, foment strife and war, and oppress individual liberty and men's pursuit of happiness, democratic republican values, very differently, favour international and religious peace and the pursuit of individual and collective "virtue." Since there is nothing preferable to virtue, or more useful to us, taught Spinoza's ethical theory, given that "virtue is nothing but acting from the laws of one's own nature," and since "reason" demands nothing contrary to nature, it requires that "everyone love himself, seek his own advantage, what is really useful to him, and desire what will really lead men to greater perfection, and finally, that everyone should strive to preserve his own being as far as he can." Thus, "we ought to want virtue for its own sake."[106] Accordingly, only that form of government should be supported by citizens that aims at the "common good," the *salus populi* in Spinoza's sense but not that of Hobbes, maximizing prospects for the general attainment of "virtue," reason and peace. This is all the more essential in that the individual liberty and toleration natural to the republic also promote progress of knowledge and the sciences and thus society's striving to counter division based on "superstition." The greatest advantage offered by democratic republics is their safeguarding freedom of judgement and discussion. This is so vital in fact that the democratic republic cannot survive without permitting free expression of differing views.

The current Dutch political crisis at the start of the 1670s, like the earlier conflict between Remonstrants and Counter-Remonstrants in 1617–19, illustrated the Republic's inherent fragility all too clearly. Against it, Orangists offered a more authoritarian, less republican, more theologically-tinted model; and, unfortunately for De Witt supporters, it was their opponents who increasingly held the upper hand in terms of popular and church backing. But why exactly, in the Dutch context of 1670, did republican values attract insufficient popular sympathy and backing for De Witt's "True Freedom" to maintain political stability and a stable toleration? How could its support base be broadened?[107] Both sides in the ongoing contest were fuelled by ambition and quest for power. But where Orangists drew on Calvinist doctrine, preachers, and the common people's faith for political and ideological backing, the republican faction, despite minimizing the hereditary principle in allocation of offices and power, and stronger commitment to freedom of thought, conscience, and the press, were clearly unable to sufficiently convince the wider public of the value of these principles. Hence the lasting significance of Spinoza's revolutionary strategy, his design—which was equally that of the De La Courts, Van den Enden, and the Koerbaghs—to weaken religious authority while surreptitiously broadening participation and support for the republic by substituting democratic in place of oligarchic republicanism.

This was the nub of Spinoza's problem in politics. In Spinoza's view, the "True Freedom," as De Witt called his republican ideology, was gravely menaced by popular support for the princely house and religious intolerance. Gaining momentum from a series of major public controversies, large segments of the populace raged against the entrenched regent oligarchy, the republican tendency, dissident and fringe groups, minorities, and the country's unparalleled freedoms and toleration. The gravity of this theological-cultural divide in society pitting two irreconcilable blocs—Orangists versus De Witt's republican "True Freedom"—

---

[106] Spinoza, *Ethica* in *Oeuvres* iv, 366–9.
[107] Feuer, *Spinoza and the Rise of Liberalism*, 150–3; Saar, *Immanenz der Macht*, 53.

against each other, and the profound instability and dangers it entailed, arose chiefly, many recognized, from lack of a sufficiently broad base supporting the republican values of the "True Freedom." As Spinoza explains in his *Tractatus Politicus*, "those who in fact held the sovereignty [in Holland] were far too few to be able to govern the people and repel powerful opponents. Hence, the latter could plot against them with impunity and finally managed to topple them." The oligarchic republic's collapse, in 1672, in Spinoza's view, resulted "not from wasting time in useless deliberations," as admirers of kings and princes contended, "but from the Republic's defective constitution and the fewness of its legislators."[108] Yet, even with its serious structural weaknesses—especially this fatal fewness of those participating in consultation and the exercise of power and its dismally inadequate support base—such a narrow consultative republic as the Dutch Republic of 1670 was, insisted Spinoza, still inherently far superior to monarchy and to aristocratic republics ruled by small ennobled oligarchies, usually with a single presiding city controlling a substantial surrounding territory, as at Venice, Genoa, and the Swiss cantons of Zurich, Geneva, and Berne.

Since it is impossible, according to Spinoza, to combat tyranny and subservience rendering mankind generally wretched via mass insurrection or inciting the people to defect, the best chance of successfully conquering ignorance and achieving a beneficial *revolutio* is found wherever the drive to combat "ignorance" is aided by a favourable historical background and institutional context as was the case, in particular, in the sixteenth-century Low Countries. Under the right conditions and with the best principles and values being surreptitiously propagated, those leading the way in Spinoza's sense, those following the dictates of reason and understanding the nature of "virtue" will institute superior practices and forms of consultative decision-making in the interest of all. Since "it follows that men who are governed by reason, that is those who, from the guidance of reason, seek their own advantage, want nothing for themselves that they do not want for other men, they are just, honest and honourable." The individual can hope "for nothing more helpful to conserving his being than that all men should so agree in all things, that the minds and bodies of all would compose, as it were, one mind and body, that all should strive together as far as they can, to conserve their being, and that all should seek, together for themselves, at the same time, the common advantage of all."[109] With this Spinoza became the first of the modern "general will" theorists.

---

[108] Spinoza, *Tractatus Politicus* in Oeuvres v, 126.   [109] Spinoza, *Ethica* in Oeuvres iv, 368.

24

Revolution in Bible Criticism

24.i The Dutch Background

Towards the end of the 1660s Spinoza's attention focused chiefly on politics, for the first time, and equally on the roots of religious authority and faith, the most powerful of political factors, which the society of his time located in the Bible. It was impossible, in his context, to revolutionize political theory in the way he sought to do without revolutionizing Bible criticism too and this he simultaneously set out to do. Spinoza transformed Bible criticism by insisting on the need to approach Scripture with the new philological tools and textual competence of the kind introduced by humanist interpreters since Erasmus like Scaliger, Cappel, the elder Vossius, Grotius, and Saumaise, but also on the basis of fundamentally new principles: by studying the Bible, indeed all revelations and scriptures, free of every prejudgement about their meaning and significance, critically examining each chain of tradition and authority, whether Jewish, Christian, or Muslim, with wary detachment and cautious distrust. There is no denying that, like Boreel, Vossius, and later Sandius he was predisposed to assume, very differently from the scholars named above, that religious authority, rather than being at all legitimate, had systematically falsified the picture.

It was the humanist tradition itself, some modern scholars contend, culminating in Scaliger and Grotius, rather than any philosophical transition rooted in Descartes, Hobbes, and Spinoza, that constitutes the real revolution that transformed the Scriptures into texts with their own complex human history while fundamentally questioning the accepted chronology of biblical history.[1] But this is to confuse two very different conceptions of, and approaches to text "historicity." The humanist revolution in exegesis, the Erasmian drive to examine the earliest surviving manuscripts and versions to establish a reliably authentic text stripped of accretions and impurities, certainly revealed that the Scriptures exist in different versions with troubling variations originating at different times, in Hebrew, Samaritan, Syriac, Greek, Latin, and Ethiopic, and that the status and authenticity of some biblical books is questionable. It also rendered modern translations of

---

[1] See Levitin, "From Sacred History to the History of Religion"; Van Miert, *Emancipation of Biblical Philology*, preface pp. xxi–xxiii; Touber, *Spinoza and Biblical Philology*, 6–9, 34–5; Jorink, "Horrible and Blasphemous," 430–1, 446–7.

Scripture like the King James Bible or the Dutch "States Bible" in important respects secondary and highly problematic. Some late humanist scholars also began asking wider historiographical questions such as about the relationship of ancient Judaism to ancient Egypt. Do the Mosaic ordinances reveal a connection with ancient Greek religion and philosophy? Yet, humanists worked without questioning the basic exegetical assumptions on which the main churches' foundational doctrines rested, accepting the sacred character of at least an uncorrupted Scriptural core without doubting Mosaic authorship of the Pentateuch, the miracles recounted, or that the New Testament is an authentic continuation and fulfilment of the Old with Christ's redeeming role foretold in the Old Testament. On the whole, they assigned a stable meaning to key *supernaturalia* like God's "voice," Torah, soul, angel, demon, and "son of God."

Whatever the philological difficulties at the fringes, the variety of Bibles Christians used were deemed uncorrupted at the core and in their essence. This was not the private view of the freethinking Bible critic Isaac Vossius, but even he, in his *De Vera Aetate Mundi* (1659), pretends that it is. This is very different from Spinoza's view that the biblical texts prized in his day are so remote from the original *sententia* [meaning] of Scripture as to be highly misleading fabrications. Where the emphasis of Renaissance and seventeenth-century European Bible hermeneutics was on resolving or marginalizing inconsistencies and contradictions, even when the result was to expose more inconsistencies, Spinoza's emphasis, uniquely, fell on proving inconsistency, contradiction, and superstition to be the essential core, the essence, not the margins of Scripture.

The revolution Spinoza (but decidedly not La Peyrère or Hobbes) introduced sought to demonstrate something very different from the seventeenth-century Dutch humanists—the complex historicity, fragmented character, and instability of the Bible's essential content, the profound ignorance of scientific reality found there, and the impossibility of grasping Scripture's true meaning without applying a strict scholarly method based on mathematical reason. Distinguishing between Spinozist exegesis and high-level mid-seventeenth-century Dutch Christian Hebraism matters greatly. For Spinoza chiefly revolutionized Bible criticism via a remarkable additional breakthrough in hermeneutics, his method of how, without prior assumptions or prejudgements, to read and understand the Bible or any text by heeding the distinction, never previously asserted so unrelentingly, between the intended or "true" meaning of the original passage and "truth of fact"—the reality of things as the philosopher understands when applying Cartesian mathematical principles, or as we would say scientific reasoning. Discerning what the original author intended to say, entails uncovering not just a text's linguistic and manuscript history but the historical and motivational context of beliefs and structures of thought shaping key terms and phrases, demonstrating the gulf between an ancient text's true sense and truth of fact, between *verus sensus* and *veritas rei*.

Spinoza's was thus a more strictly scientific approach than any other attempted in the seventeenth century even by the most famous Bible scholar, Richard Simon (1638–1712).[2] "Lest we should confuse the true sense [*verus sensus*] with the truth of the thing [*veritas rei*]" or the "truth of things [veritas rerum]," the former should be sought "only in the use of language, or reasoning acknowledging no other basis than Scripture itself."[3] Spinoza's denial that theology has any relevance whatever to Scripture was altogether unique. Such a project meant transcending far beyond the scope of humanist hermeneutics and the exegetical traditions established by Erasmus, Scaliger, Cappel, Saumaise, the elder Vossius, and Grotius. Certainly, Spinoza's revolution in Bible hermeneutics was not a break with the past stemming from nowhere. The importance and European impact of the Dutch "emancipation of Biblical philology" prior to Spinoza *is* often underestimated by modern scholars. But one should avoid too the opposite error of seeking to "severely qualify" Spinoza's originality by claiming "the types of arguments Spinoza wields in the TTP essentially continue an uninterrupted tradition of humanist philological criticism originating in Valla, Erasmus, and the Polyglot Bibles, of the sixteenth century and the advance of Hebrew scholarship, through Scaliger and his Leiden school of philologists [...] and on into the wider context of Dutch society."[4] That is highly misleading. Since "truth of fact" for Spinoza meant conformity to the immutable laws of nature conceived as a single set of principles governing the totality of reality by a fixed and immutable system of natural laws interacting and mutually complementary, formulated with mathematical precision, a conception of reality totally detached from the miraculous, supernatural, and wondrous, his approach was inconceivable before Descartes introduced the notion of a single set of laws governing all of physical but not mental or spiritual reality, a perspective not available even to Galileo, let alone Erasmus, Scaliger, Cappel, or Grotius. For Renaissance scholars trained to the highest standards of humanist exegesis there was little awareness of a total divide between the natural and supernatural, belief and reality, between biblical "superstition" and factual truth, hence no path to demolishing the Bible's unique status as divine revelation.

At the heart of Grotius' revolution in Bible hermeneutics and legacy to the rationalist, philosophizing Collegiants and Remonstrant theologians like Van Limborch and Le Clerc, was a multilingual exegetical approach seeking to erase the many discrepancies and corrupted passages in the biblical text as it has descended to us while proceeding on the assumption that Scripture is indeed

---

[2] Israel, "Introduction" to Spinoza, *Theological-Political Treatise*, pp. x–xvii; Rudavsky, "Science of Scripture," 77–8.
[3] Spinoza, *Opera* iii, 101; Walther, "Biblische Hermeneutik" (1992), 642–3, 650–1; Preus, *Spinoza*, 160–1; Spruit, "Introduzione," pp. xl–xli.
[4] Van Miert, *Emancipation of Biblical Philology*, p. xxiii; Jorink, "Horrible and Blasphemous," 431, 446–7.

divine revelation infused with God's justice, universal truth, and the Christian message and hence that this core of truth is key to resolving every problem and discrepancy. Pondering the two different versions of the divine delivery of the Decalogue, for example, Grotius faced the discrepancy between Exodus 20, where the Ten Commandments are proclaimed directly by God, and Deuteronomy 5, where it is Moses who transmits the Decalogue, presenting it to "all Israel." If for Hobbes, this divergence posed no problem, providing a link connecting divine revelation to his prioritizing of kingship, implying law is brought to the people by monarchs,[5] Grotius viewed the two accounts of the commandments' arrival as a worrying disparity requiring resolution. He ascribed it to Moses operating from memory and omitting something important in one case while in both instances unfailingly preserving the divine revelation's core.[6] As more generally with biblical discrepancies, Grotius viewed the problem as a natural consequence of legitimate transmission, the authentic text (he did not think all the biblical books were authentic) corrupting marginally via subsequent replication but fraying always at the edge, preserving intact the essential integrity and divine origin of text and doctrine. This differs markedly from Spinoza's conception of the age-old process of the Scriptures' chaotic evolution across the centuries resulting in extensive loss, confusion, and multiple phases of later redacting.

Undoubtedly, the special character of the Dutch Golden Age cultural milieu itself, and vigour of the rationalizing Erasmian-Grotian tradition, was a powerful factor in Spinoza's exegesis. The innovative techniques developed in Dutch universities down to the 1650s, brought the latest philological approaches to new levels of sophistication penetrating beyond what was achieved elsewhere in Europe down the late seventeenth century. Grotius' *Annotationes* or notes on the Old and New Testaments, commencing around 1619 underwent a remarkably long gestation, being published only towards the end of his life, in 1645, and certainly formed an indispensable part of this background. Richard Simon later rightly remarked, in August 1703, that in the *TTP* Spinoza "followed the opinion of Grotius" in maintaining that many books of the Bible were not divinely inspired,[7] while the foremost Enlightenment era German "anti-Scripturalist" rejecting Scripture's divine inspiration, Hermann Samuel Reimarus (1694–1768), cites Grotius more frequently than Spinoza in his anonymous *Apologia*, to underpin his anti-Christian arguments.

Far more expert in Greek and early Christian Latin than Spinoza, Grotius was the greatest, most innovative Bible critic and philologist since Joseph Justus Scaliger (1540–1609), and one distinctly more inclined than predecessors to use

---

[5] Hobbes, *Leviathan* iii, 812–16, 886; Fukuoka, *Sovereign and the Prophets*, 74, 78–9.
[6] Van Miert, *Emancipation of Biblical Philology*, 144; Touber, *Spinoza and Biblical Philology*, 100.
[7] "Spinosa a suivi le sentiment de Grotius…"; quoted in Van Miert, *Emancipation of Biblical Philology*, 168.

historical contextualization to explain key biblical passages. Grotius, held Reimarus, foreshadowed the early eighteenth-century English deist (more plausibly atheist) Anthony Collins (1676–1729), in explaining Scripture in a rigorously critical manner, except that Grotius simultaneously strove to defend Christianity's essentials and reconcile the Old and New Testaments. That his efforts to salvage the New Testament's integrity and sanctity produced some "utterly strange" arguments he failed to see. First Grotius compromises the New Testament with his advanced techniques, objected Reimarus, then tries to repair the holes with unconvincing, at times ridiculous, explanations.[8]

Grotius's Bible hermeneutics, like that of Bacon and Hobbes, was built on entrenched assumptions, theologico-political priorities differing fundamentally from Spinoza's.[9] Like Hobbes later, Grotius undoubtedly viewed Scripture as a documentary corpus written at different times rather than a single cohesive divinely given revelation.[10] But his governing distinction between essential and non-essential passages for issues of faith sought to fortify faith around core unifying theological concepts, striving to transcend the Catholic–Protestant and the Arminian versus Counter-Remonstrant divides by clarifying the quintessential core of irrefutably authentic, universally agreed doctrine, an irenic, deeply Christian ideal permeating his entire approach. If Grotius' semi-naturalism looked corrosive to Lutheran and Calvinist commentators, this was because he radically reduces, without marginalizing, the miraculous, the role of the supernatural in matters of faith. Dismissing many supernatural explanations, the aspect that most attracted Collins and Reimarus to his exegesis later, Grotius held that most of what is true in the Bible and religion is natural and rational without any wondrous component intervening. Thus, the eighteenth-century Lutheran Hebraist and Bible critic Ernst Friedrich Neubauer (1705–48), writing in 1736, viewed the German deist assault on Christian Bible interpretation in his time as rooted in seventeenth-century Dutch inclination to marginalize and reject the miraculous, broadly stemming, he notes, from Grotius and, following him, the renowned late seventeenth-century text critic Jean Le Clerc (1657–1736).[11]

Grotius' undermining of Lutheran and Calvinist *philologia sacra*, of established Protestant theology, and his campaign to salvage core Christian belief was so far-reaching and problematic that it is hardly surprising Calvinist theologians suspected his tract *De Satisfactione Christi* (1617, a text Spinoza kept in his personal library), intended to rebut the Counter-Remonstrant charge that he was unorthodox and veered towards Socinianism, was just a sham, his hidden true goal being to reinforce Socinian subversion of Christianity.[12] Yet, in fact Grotius valiantly

---

[8] Reimarus, *Apologie oder Schutzschrift* i, 61; Israel, *Democratic Enlightenment*, 202–3.
[9] Israel, "Grotius and the Rise," 19–31.
[10] Malcolm, "Hobbes, Ezra, and the Bible," 423–4; Israel, "How Did Spinoza Declare War?," 200–6.
[11] See Neubauer's notes to Rambach, *Collegium historiae ecclesiasticae Veteris Testamenti*.
[12] Blom, "Grotius and Socinianism," 131; Touber, *Spinoza and Biblical Philology*, 47.

accommodated the consequences of claiming the churches' traditional Christology is devoid of biblical foundation while fighting to authenticate the Bible's integrity and veracity by uncovering what he envisaged as the underlying rationality of its account, and of the Prophets,[13] an approach foreshadowing the later efforts of Boyle, Locke, Van Limborch, and Le Clerc.[14]

Not the least difficulty Grotius' hermeneutics entangled him in was that of "God's justice." Rejecting all voluntarism, all suggestion that God is an absolute master without reference to an external standard of right and wrong, Grotius unifies God's presiding role with the inherently universal and natural character of justice by presenting God as a "rector" or "princeps" overseeing the moral community. When God punishes he enforces not his own will as such but the community's, thereby upholding the moral order men naturally embrace, leaving nothing arbitrary in his judgements as would a "dominus absolutus." Yet, while his God is not subject to the law like a human judge but the ultimate supervisor and guardian of that law, his universal natural law still erects a system, justice itself, rational and natural, situated in some sense above God's will and, therefore, beyond divine providence.[15] Grotius could never fully extricate himself from the dense thickets his own innovations enveloped him in.

Spinoza focuses on the Old Testament rather than the New partly for reasons of prudence, but also because, unlike Hobbes, he lacked expertise in Greek, though he did study some Greek for comparative purposes. His sophisticated grasp of Hebrew since his teenage years prompted "some of his friends," records Jelles in his Preface to the *Opera Posthuma*, in 1677, to ask him to write the Hebrew Grammar which was left incomplete at his death. "They well knew that he had been initiated in the study of Hebrew from a very young age and, for many years, been assiduously occupied with it, steeped in its special character and exceedingly expert in it."[16] Among his books, Spinoza possessed several specialized works on Hebrew grammar and also comparative grammar, studies on Spanish, Latin, and Old German as well as Greek and Hebrew. Indeed, one finds no more subversive feature of his transformation of Bible criticism than his insistence that without analysing the grammar, and using grammar to reconstruct the complex language "history" of biblical terms and concepts, including the New Testament's Semitic language pre-history, there is scant chance of understanding the Bible correctly.

Scriptural accounts, of course, abound in wonders, or, as Spinoza construes it, narratives of unusual happenings in nature adjusted to the superstitious understanding of those who constructed these accounts. Hence, discerning the "true meaning of the text" can follow only from analysis of Scripture itself and

---

[13] Fukuoka, *Sovereign and the Prophets*, 193, 204–5.
[14] Kühler, *Het Socinianisme*, 86; Schmidt-Biggemann, "Edifying versus Rational Hermeneutics," 62; Van Miert, *Emancipation of Biblical Philology*, 164–8.
[15] Kühler, *Het Socinianisme*, 82–3; Blom, "Grotius and Socinianism," 122, 124, 132–4, 145–6.
[16] Spinoza [B.d.S.] *Opera Posthuma*, 688; Spinoza, *Abregé de grammaire hébraique*, 33.

everything wondrous must be examined on the basis of the original language, choice of words and expressions, "just as knowledge of nature must be sought from nature itself."[17] Without uncovering ancient Israelite language, culture, and customs, held Spinoza, we may be sure, nothing at all can be correctly grasped. The New Testament having been composed by Jews thinking in Aramaic and Hebrew, expressing themselves in Hebraizing terms in writings subsequently completely lost, held Spinoza, and only much later rendered by third parties into Greek, and subsequently other languages of which Christ and the Apostles had no knowledge, means the obstacles hindering comprehension of the Bible generally are redoubled in the case of the New Testament. Because "they Hebrewize, however [hebraisant tamen]," all efforts to establish even approximately realistic explanations of Gospel meanings without grounding one's analysis in the original expressions, terminology, history, ancient politics, and religious culture, which is impossible without finding the original Hebrew texts, are essentially useless. This renders all papal councils, Protestant councils, Orthodox councils, or any Christian councils based on the Greek and other translations fundamentally inauthentic, and their laying down doctrines like the Trinity, Ascension, Resurrection, and Redemption through the Church's teaching, all devoid of any valid basis in Scripture, essentially just fabrications from extraneous languages and concepts. The entire corpus of theology the warring churches fight over is thereby reduced to one vast invalid edifice grounded in elaborately constructed false readings.[18]

Nor is it just one cultural and historical context that grounds the meaning of biblical phrases and expressions. The Bible, argues Spinoza, does not speak with remotely a single human or divinely inspired voice but with voices of different writers at different times with distinct personalities and perspectives under conditions often profoundly changed from those prevailing in the age of the earliest fragments. Pentateuch, Old Testament prophecies, historical accounts of the kings, and the different Gospels all arose under dramatically altered conditions; and besides changing contexts one must allow for each prophetic or Apostolic voice's individual style, whether elegant, rough-hewn, angry or patient, concise or prolix. In Spinoza, unlike Maimonides, there is no starting assumption that the biblical prophet was a man eminent in wisdom and political astuteness, let alone one chosen by God. Above all, the complex evolution of language usage, of Hebrew itself, ranging from that of the ancient Israelites to the Apostles' Aramaic Semitic vernacular, inspires Spinoza's systematic reduction of all wondrous and impressive expressions to mere linguistic devices, peculiarities of idiom rather than profound mysteries requiring theological explanation.[19]

---

[17] Spinoza, *Theological-Political Treatise*, 99.
[18] Israel, "Introduction," pp. x–xiii; Totaro, "Le *Compendium*," 66–7.
[19] Montag, *Bodies, Masses, Power*, 10–12; Totaro, "Le *Compendium*," 68–70.

24.ii Ezra the Scribe

Pivotal to Spinoza's (and the Koerbaghs') approach, and Leibniz's alarmed reaction on first reading the *TTP* in 1671, is the pre-eminence Spinoza assigns to Ezra the Scribe whose dates scholars today usually place around 480–440 BC, half a millennium or so after the era of David and Solomon (located by most scholars in the tenth century BC), and several centuries more since Moses and the Exodus from Egypt.[20] The biblical figure Ezra, Spinoza claims, "not only applied himself zealously to seeking out the law of God but also to elaborate it."[21] Deuteronomy should be considered the first book Ezra "wrote" partly because "it contains the laws of the country which was what the people most needs," but also "because this book is not connected by any link with what comes before in the way the others are." Deuteronomy being by Ezra "scriptum, adornatum & explicatum [written, adorned and explained]," there is no way of knowing how substantial the original Mosaic element that it conserves really is. "If we had the book of the Law of Moses itself, I do not doubt we would find great discrepancy [magnam discrepantiam] between it and what survives from Ezra both in the words and order and reasons for the ordinances."[22]

Presenting Ezra as the real author of the Pentateuch was probably no new theme in Spinoza's thinking in the late 1660s. Van Til records his having seen an unpublished letter where Spinoza is described as a teacher at pains to inculcate the Ezra thesis into his followers.[23] Late seventeenth-century commentators broadly recognized three prime perpetrators of this subversive revisionist theme—La Peyrère, Hobbes, and Spinoza. But there was a fourth notable exponent, the Koerbaghs, who, being largely muzzled, remained unknown to most European readers. In 1692, the Voetius disciple Jacobus Koelman (1632–95), a schismatic conservative Calvinist preacher bitterly resentful of the Republic's tolerant policies, claimed the "Cartesian atheist Spinosa built his rejection of the authority of Moses books on the arguments of La Peyrère," a point suggested also by Popkin and some other modern scholars.[24] However, it is probably impossible today to sort out the true order of precedence with respect to this innovation. The processes of interaction and transmission among La Peyrère, Hobbes, the Koerbaghs, and Spinoza are far from straightforward and can now no longer be precisely reconstructed (if they ever could be), since we do not know how far La Peyrère's ideas figured in Spinoza's 1656 "Apology," and it remains unclear

---

[20] Goldenbaum, "Die *Commentatiuncula*," Beilage; Grafton, "Spinoza's Hermeneutics," 195; Lavaert, "Entre clandestinité," 38–9.
[21] Spinoza, *Opera* iii, 127.
[22] Spinoza, *Opera* iii, 128; Strauss, *Spinoza's Critique of Religion*, 265.
[23] Van Til, *Voor-hof der heydenen*, 172–3, 196; Abbadie, *Traité de la vérité* i, 284–5, 315–16; Malcolm, "Hobbes, Ezra, and the Bible," 388–9.
[24] Koelman, *Het Vergift*, 276; Mori, *Athéisme et dissimulation*, 186, 204.

whether Hobbes or La Peyrère reintroduced the Ezran argument first, and how far the Koerbaghs and Spinoza were indebted to them for their reliance on it. Even if Spinoza was prompted in part by La Peyrère and Hobbes, it would be quite erroneous to suppose Spinoza simply reiterates what they say: rather, his strikingly more sweeping radicalism is plainly far closer here to that of his loyal followers, the Koerbaghs.[25] The Koerbaghs' contribution to propagating the Ezra thesis was not only published two years before Spinoza's, in 1668, but was certainly familiar to some besides Spinoza and his circle, since the *Bloemhof* was not all that rare.

What chiefly matters, though, is that Spinoza and the Brothers Koerbagh, by effectively denying that Moses wrote any of the Five Books, or at least claiming nearly all of the Old Testament was written by Ezra, were substantially more systematic advocates of the Ezra thesis than La Peyrère or Hobbes. According to the *Bloemhof*, notes one German writer who did mention it as a key source for the "Ezra thesis," in 1696, "it was Ezra who wrote the Jewish books, not Moses and the Prophets."[26] This is not to ignore the importance of Hobbes who, in his *Leviathan* (1651), states "that the whole Scripture of the Old Testament was set forth (in the form we have it) after the return of the Jews from their captivity in Babylon," and that if the Apocrypha is any guide here, "the Scripture was set forth in the form we have it in by Ezra, as may appear by that which he himself saith in the second book."[27] "For as the books of the Old Testament," he adds, "are derived to us from no higher time than that of Ezra, who by the direction of God's spirit retrieved them when they were lost, those of the New Testament, of which the copies were not many, nor could easily be on one private man's hand, cannot be derived from a higher time than that wherein the governors of the church collected, approved, and recommended [them] to us as the writings of those apostles and disciples under whose names they go [hence, several centuries later]." Hobbes' treatment of the Ezran thesis is clear and unquestionably extremely important too but really just a brief sketch of the thesis rather than application in detail in the style of Spinoza. Also, it relies partly on Ezra book 2, a late, unreliable text, post-AD 70 in origin, which Spinoza dismisses as nothing but ridiculous "legends inserted by some trifler."[28]

In any case, it was no recent innovation, in Hobbes' and Spinoza's time, to claim most of the Old Testament was redacted in the fifth century BC from older surviving fragments we no longer possess, half a millennium or more after Solomon's Temple arose and a millennium or so after Moses, and that the editor

---

[25] Malcolm, "Hobbes, Ezra, and the Bible," 386; Nadler, *Book Forged in Hell*, 39–40; Lavaert, *Vrijheid, gelijkheid, veelheid*, 150–1.
[26] Koerbagh, *Bloemhof*, 96, 325–36; Weber, *Beurtheilung der Atheisterey*, 128–9; Malcolm, "Hobbes, Ezra, and the Bible," 387–98.
[27] Hobbes, *Leviathan* iii, 598–600.
[28] Hobbes, *Leviathan* iii, 600; Malcolm, "Hobbes, Ezra, and the Bible," 390–8; Touber, *Spinoza and Biblical Philology*, 68–9; Israel, "How Did Spinoza Declare War?," 201–2; Curley, "Spinoza's Contribution," 363–4.

who preserved, collected, and redacted the Hebrew Bible we possess today, was Ezra the Scribe, albeit in the Christian world this objection had been largely submerged for many centuries. If Spinoza, rather than La Peyrère or Hobbes, was the first modern exegete to revive and expound the thesis at length and in detail, the claim that Ezra was the principal figure in redacting and canonizing the Jews' biblical "twenty-four books," was originally a Hellenistic, anti-Christian trope expounded by Porphyry (AD 234?–305?) and other pagan polemicists.[29] It was the sudden post-1650 renewal of an ancient standpoint that caused a scholarly upheaval bound to weaken confidence in the Mosaic integrity of the Pentateuch and authenticity of the Prophetic books. Reintroduction of the Ezra theory fell as a scholarly bombshell in the 1650s and 1660s, resulting in its being subsequently propagated widely by both freethinkers and Christian apologists, Catholic and Protestant, wrestling with this deeply troubling new reality.

Furthermore, even if seemingly something shockingly novel in the Christian world, the theory as such had long been entrenched in the Islamic world and had been familiar early on among Iberian Jewry, even if it did not survive as a continuous underground tradition (as it probably did). Since it became commonly accepted among Muslims that the biblical text, unlike the Koran, despite authentic elements, is severely corrupted, one must remember that several medieval Muslim scholars, most notably the Andalusian jurist, historian and poet Abu Muhammed ibn Hazm (994–1064) of Córdoba, claim the Hebrew Bible is for the most part forgery and fabrication and chiefly the work of "Azra al-Warraq," that is "Ezra the Scribe." Son of an official at the court of the last Caliph of Córdoba, from a family of Christian background, imprisoned several times during the civil wars following the collapse of the caliphate, in 1031 AD, and appalled by the internecine rivalries and faction-fighting wrecking the caliphate, Ibn Hazm was deeply cynical about human nature and motivation. Well versed in biblical Hebrew, Ibn Hazm was the first Muslim scholar to subject the Bible to close critical scrutiny.[30] Over many years seated among the arcades of the great mosque of Córdoba polemicizing against Jews, Christians, Shi'ites, Samaritans, and Zoroastrians, parading his pessimistic vision of human politics and society, Ibn Hazm dismissed Judaism as a fragmented tradition based on a tortuous edifice concocted by Ezra and his priestly clique.

Although Ibn Hazm never met any Samaritans, he was keenly interested in them as a surviving divergent Jewish sect, classifying them as one of the five sects into which he divides the Jews of his day—Rabbanites, Karaites, Saduqiyya [Sadducees], Samaritans, and 'Isawiyya [followers of Isa al-Isbahani]. Knowing the Samaritans view their own (slightly different) version of the Pentateuch as the

---

[29] According to the Masoretic text (Pentateuch—5 books; Prophetic writings—8 books; post-Prophetic writings [Kesuvim]—11 books); Lazarus-Yafeh, *Intertwined Worlds*, 68–74.
[30] Lazarus-Yafeh, *Intertwined Worlds*, 26; Roth, "Forgery and Abrogation," 204.

authentic version, truer than the Rabbanite text, he notes their ambivalent, often hostile, attitude towards "the cursed Ezra," whom Ibn Hazm construed as chief falsifier of the post-Pentateuchal main body of the Bible.[31]

Ibn Hazm's attack echoed later in efforts to refute his Ezra thesis in the works of medieval Spanish Jewish writers, such as Abraham Ibn Daud (c.1110–1180) of Córdoba and Toledo, Maimonides, and the Catalan rabbi Solomon ibn Adret (1235–1310).[32] Ibn Daud, writing in Toledo, in 1168, counters Ibn Hazm's Ezra thesis by pointing out that the Jews venerate the same biblical text everywhere from India to Spain, proving the text's incorruptibility. If Ezra had fabricated, how could he have secured universal Jewish agreement "to follow his covenant"? The Christians hate Jews just as much as do the Muslims, adds Ibn Adret, but never adopted anything of the Ezra thesis, proof, he thought, of its implausibility.[33] Whether Spinoza gleaned something of the thesis from medieval Hebrew sources or the clandestine subversive Spanish intellectual world that produced the "deism" of De Prado or more directly from contemporary reports from Morocco, or the same hints in earlier sources that enabled Ibn Hazm to construct his Ezra thesis, there is really no compelling reason why his version should be regarded as particularly indebted to La Peyrère or to Hobbes.

On the Muslim side, Ibn Hazm's thesis was further elaborated in the twelfth century by one of the foremost Sephardic writers who embraced Islam and then polemicized against the Jews, Samuwal al-Maghribi (c.1126–1175 AD), so-called because his father had been a Moroccan rabbi, from Fez, who settled in Baghdad where Samuwal spent much of his life. A famed mathematician and astronomer, al-Maghribi augmented Ibn Hazm's Ezra thesis notably by exploring the motivation behind Ezra's role and its historical consequences, attributing to Ibn Ezra the sidelining of the Davidic dynasty during the Second Temple period and subsequent pre-eminence of the priests (Levites) of the House of Aaron.[34]

In fact, several early Christian writers also assign Ezra a pivotal role in restoring the Scriptures,[35] notably the Palestinian Eusebius (c.260–340 AD), bishop of Caesarea around 314 AD, so that there is perhaps no real need to cite a Muslim background to the mid-seventeenth-century Ezra thesis, even if Islam lent it a more sceptical and hostile gloss. "When Nebuchadnezzar took the [Jewish] people into captivity," records Eusebius, the Scriptures were destroyed, but then, seventy years later, when "the Jews returned to their own country, in the reign if Artaxerxes, king of Persia, [the Lord] inspired Ezra the Priest of the tribe of Levi to re-create all the utterances of the old Prophets and restore to the people

---

[31] Roth, "Forgery and Abrogation," 205; Lazarus-Yafeh, *Intertwined Worlds*, 60–1.
[32] Roth, "Forgery and Abrogation," 207–9, 217–18, 222–4, 236; Whittingham, "Ezra as the Corrupter," 253–7; Kraemer, *Maimonides*, 17.
[33] Roth, "Forgery and Abrogation," 208, 224.
[34] Lazarus-Yafeh, *Intertwined Worlds*, 68–71, 74, 99.
[35] Whittingham, "Ezra as the Corrupter," 258.

the Law given by Moses."[36] However, the foremost classical source for this topic remained Porphyry of Tyre, an older contemporary of Eusebius, raised in Semitic lands amidst Semitic languages prior to the last great persecution of Christians unleashed by Diocletian (303-313 AD) before Constantine proclaimed Christianity the Roman Empire's official religion. A distinguished Neoplatonist philosopher, trained in Athens and Rome, and disciple of Plotinus, Porphyry wrote his *Adversus Christianos* [Against the Christians] while residing in Sicily during the late 260s and early 270s and was rated by Eusebius among the foremost unbelievers opposing the Jewish Scriptures. "Nothing that Moses wrote has been preserved," contends Porphyry, "for all his writings are said to have been burnt with the Temple." In itself, this contained nothing irreconcilable with Eusebius' account, but from it Porphyry draws drastically different consequences: all those writings "written under [Moses'] name afterwards were really composed inaccurately one thousand, one hundred and eighty years after his death by Ezra and his followers."[37] Porphyry, retorted an indignant Eusebius, tries to "slander the sacred scriptures" by suggesting the words of Moses had been subverted by later interpreters.[38]

The Koerbaghs' *Een Ligt* initially seems more tentative than the *Bloemhof* on the Ezra question, affirming that "it is not really known who the authors of the Hebrew scriptures were, one can only guess. Some scholars think a certain Ezra copied them from several other Jewish writings and put them together, but I have no idea what the truth is." But then further on, decrying the Jews' superstitious disposition, he exclaims: "what reason will you give that one should believe Ezra who wrote your books as is commonly believed, more than those of heathen writers? I see nothing, I tell you, that you can state with certainty."[39]

The roots of the Ezra thesis then were various. Nevertheless, late seventeenth-century theologians such as Abbadie, Huet, Le Pin, Van Til, Witsius, and Heidegger never doubted that Spinoza specifically, and not Hobbes or anyone else, stood above the rest as the primary, principal, most dangerous, most culpable contemporary advocate of the Ezran theory. Wherever the goal was to combat the Ezra thesis in later years as, for example, in 1684, in the treatise on the truth of Christianity by the renowned Huguenot divine Jacques Abbadie (1654-1727), Spinoza stands as the only modern author the defender of Christianity needs to discuss and refute.[40] The rest could safely be left unmentioned. Spinoza diverges most from La Peyrère's and Hobbes' brief sketches in the uniquely broad scope he

---

[36] Eusebius, *History of the Church*, 212-13.
[37] Eusebius, *History of the Church*, 258; Porphyry, *Against the Christians*, 41; Whittingham, "Ezra as the Corrupter," 259.
[38] Porphyry, *Against the Christians*, 43n20; Eusebius, *History of the Church*, 258-9; Lazarus-Yafeh, *Intertwined Worlds*, 45, 63.
[39] Koerbagh, *A Light Shining*, 290-1, 399; Lavaert, "Entre clandestinité," 38-9.
[40] Abbadie, *Traité de la vérité* i, 284-5, 315-16, 318-20.

lends the Ezra thesis, attributing not only most of the Mosaic Books and their laws but also the bulk of Joshua, Judges, Ruth, Samuel, and Kings (but not the Book of Ezra) to Ezra the Scribe.[41] He also holds that editing the material gathered and stored by Ezra was not completed by him so that much of the Old Testament remained unsorted and fragmented at the time of its canonization.

Among Spinoza's main aims in developing his Ezra thesis was to establish (rather questionably) that during the half century or so of the Babylonian captivity, and then under the Persian kings, the ancient Israelites "completely abandoned the Law of Moses, and let the ordinances of their country fall into oblivion as obviously superfluous," and "began to mingle with the other nations, as is abundantly clear from Ezra and Nehemiah."[42] Another key argument of Spinoza's is that the "thematic structure and organization of the histories also prove" there was throughout only one main "chronicler who had set himself a particular goal." The chronicler's design was to prove the Israelites fared well or ill, in the era prior to their deciding to be ruled by a monarch, and later, from Saul onwards, under their kings, according to whether or not they respected or abandoned the laws that Moses had proclaimed. "All these books therefore collude to one end: to teach the sayings and edicts of Moses and illustrate them by the outcome of events."[43]

That Ezra was the principal Old Testament writer for Spinoza was less important in itself than arguing that "three things taken together, namely unity of theme in all these books, their interconnectedness, and their being derivative works [quod sint Apocrypha] written many centuries after the event, make us conclude, as we said above, that they were all composed by a single historian." Though he is reasonably sure this was Ezra whom, he says, he will consider to be their author until someone demonstrates a more certain candidate, he admits he cannot prove this conclusively and that the main point is that they were all assembled by the same scribe after the Babylonian captivity.[44] To reinforce his Ezra thesis, Spinoza revives the esoteric message of what the medieval Jewish scholar Abraham Ibn Ezra (1093–1187 AD) called the "Secret of the Twelve" [mysterium duodecim], noting that Ibn Ezra is the earliest source he had found expressing views comparable to his own on the Pentateuch's authorship. This secret, though, he explains, was so sensitive and subversive that his medieval predecessor dared not state it outright. Instead, he "indicated the matter with obscure words," claiming Moses spoke to all Israel, saying, "if you understand the riddle of the twelve...then you will know the truth."[45]

---

[41] Hamilton, *Apocryphal Apocalypse*, 228, 245; Frampton, *Spinoza and the Rise*, 228–9; Rudavsky, "Science of Scripture," 76–7; Nadler, *Spinoza's Heresy*, 26.
[42] Spinoza, *Theological-Political Treatise*, 71.   [43] Spinoza, *Theological-Political Treatise*, 127.
[44] Spinoza, *Theological-Political Treatise*, 127; Harvey, "Spinoza on Ibn Ezra's 'Secret of the Twelve'," 42; Montag, *Bodies, Masses, Power*, 16; Grafton, "Spinoza's Hermeneutics," 189, 191.
[45] Spinoza, *Opera* iii, 118; Harvey, "Spinoza on Ibn Ezra's 'Secret of the Twelve'," 42–3; Totaro, "More on Spinoza," 37–40.

Though open to interpretation in different ways, Spinoza explains the "secret of the twelve" as alluding to the "whole Book of Moses" being inscribed on the space of "just one altar consisting," rabbinic commentary records, "of just twelve stones... from which it follows the Book of Moses was vastly shorter than [our] Pentateuch."[46] While Spinoza somewhat misrepresents Ibn Ezra, turning him into a scholar almost wholly circumventing Moses' original authentic Pentateuch, stretching the truth here seems intended to enlist Ibn Ezra as a path-breaking early exponent of Spinoza's rule that etymology and grammar, scholarly research and reason have primacy over tradition, authority, and faith.[47] By contrast, for his conclusions, Hobbes relies on the Vulgate, the Septuagint, and the King James version of the Bible in English, sources all very late, hopelessly corrupted and inadmissible according to Spinoza. Viewing his own approach as following on from Ibn Ezra, rather than Hobbes, Hebrew philological research, he argues, not sceptical guesswork based on late, remote, derivative, secondary texts must be our exclusive guide.

The young Leibniz of 1671 found Spinoza's Ezra thesis intensely alarming, but in marginal notes on his personal copy of the *TTP*, preserved today in Mainz, jotted down a striking counter-argument later echoed by Abbadie: "When opposing those who attack the canon of the Old Testament of Sacred Scripture using Ezra [ab Esdra], this argument appears very strong: not all the Hebrews returned to Jerusalem from the Babylonian Captivity, a great part of them certainly remained" scattered over the Babylonian and Persian empires. How could Ezra, without huge resistance and dissension, possibly have introduced an altered or rewritten version of Scripture into a text tradition reaching back much earlier? Surely, he could not.[48]

While Ezra collected surviving fragments and narratives by different authors, contended Spinoza, he failed to integrate the material fully and complete his project: "he made no final version of the narratives contained in them," sometimes just adding narratives, "copying them out as they were," passing them on "to posterity without examining them properly or setting them in due order. I cannot conjecture the reasons (except perhaps an early death) that prevented him from completing his task in every respect." From his failure to properly redact the edited version, arose, besides many discrepancies, passages of almost word for word repetition in different parts of Scripture, errors of chronology and illogical breaks in the narrative. Biblical chronology consequently remains an irresolvable tangle. Solomon is stated, in Kings, to have built the First Temple 480 years after the Exodus from Egypt, but if we add up the periods in which the Jews are stated to

---

[46] Spinoza, *Opera* iii, 119; Abbadie, *Traité de la vérité* i, 284–5; Harvey, "Spinoza on Ibn Ezra's 'Secret of the Twelve'," 48–51.
[47] Totaro, "More on Spinoza," 42–3; Cassuto, *Spinoza hébraïssant*, 146.
[48] "Leibniz' Marginalien" in Goldenbaum, "Die *Commentatiuncula*," Beilage, 105; Abbadie, *Traité de la vérité* i, 318–19; Grafton, "Spinoza's Hermeneutics," 195.

have been under Moses' rule, and then the Judges, the total is 580 years even without counting the time when Samuel was Judge and other intervals missing from the count.[49] The record of Saul's reign, as the Jewish historian Flavius Josephus (Joseph ben Matthias) (37–100 AD) pointed out long before, in his historical work, the *Antiquities* (93–94 AD), somehow became mutilated in the surviving Hebrew text, obscuring the fact that Saul "reigned for eighteen years while Samuel was still alive, and for another two [actually rather more] after his death" and muddles its account of the Philistine invasion of Israelite territory.[50]

For demonstrating Scripture's inconsistencies and discrepancies, Josephus emerges as one of Spinoza's essential sources. Despite providing the fullest surviving account of first-century Palestine and one depicting early Christianity as marginal to the life of the country at the time of the Great Jewish Revolt of 66–74 AD, with little prominence among the rival sects of the day, Josephus was frowned on by rabbinic tradition due to his defecting to the Romans which, however, was no blot on him in Spinoza's eyes. At least twenty-four Latin Josephus editions had appeared in Europe between 1470 and 1540; in his personal library, Spinoza possessed a Latin edition of the *Antiquitates* and *De Bello Judaico* bound together, published at Basel by Johann Froben, in 1540.[51] Spinoza uses Josephus partly, as here, as a historical source, for clarifying points of fact, but also as a commentator sifting truth from myth using a distinctly sceptical approach to what he reads in the ancient Scriptures. Thus, Josephus advises everyone to make up their own minds about the biblical miracles which should be accounted for in whatever way seems right to the reader without attributing to them any doctrinal significance.[52] Ambivalent towards Pharisees and the elite priestly caste from which he himself descended, and, by extension, rabbinic tradition, Josephus was especially prized by Spinoza for his account of the disastrous great Jewish revolt against Rome, a prime instance of the folly of turning to Millenarian revolutionary leaders promising vast rewards and the transformation of everything for the better who proceed by stirring up the ill-informed masses. In Josephus' eyes, the masses were as superstitious and unreliable as in Spinoza's.[53] Spinoza respected Josephus too as a statesman seeking compromise between Judaism and the Graeco-Roman cultural world, acknowledging the self-destructive futility of rebelling against Roman rule while blaming the Pharisees chiefly (and the Romans less) for the ensuing catastrophe and the Second Temple's destruction.[54]

---

[49] Spinoza, *Theological-Political Treatise*, 133–4; James, *Spinoza on Philosophy*, 168–9; Curley, "Spinoza's Contribution," 369.
[50] Spinoza, *Theological-Political Treatise*, 135; Proietti, *La Città Divisa*, 151–4; Totaro, "Note," 617n51.
[51] Proietti, *La Città Divisa*, 35–7; Totaro, "Note," 537n86, 584n102; Klever, *Spinoza Classicus*, 254.
[52] Spinoza, *Theological-Political Treatise*, 96; Proietti, *La Città Divisa*, 229; Klever, *Spinoza Classicus*, 255–6.
[53] Attridge, "Josephus," 195–6, 198–200, 210; Feldman, "Josephus' Portrait of Ezra," 200–1.
[54] Attridge, "Josephus," 196; Feldman, "Josephus' Portrait of Ezra," 202–4.

Spinoza is not in fact as antagonistic to Jews as a people and Judaism's ancient traditions and historical legacy as some modern writers suggest. Rather, he clearly nurtured marked preferences among the rival Jewish sects of first-century Palestine, with the Pharisees coming decidedly low down on his list. Not unlike Josephus, he viewed the Great Revolt of 66–74 AD more as a kind of cultural civil war among Jews than specifically a Jewish war against Rome, a bias doubtless coloured by his own personal experiences earlier in life. His was a view of Jewishness essentially hostile to rabbis, priestly castes, and all suggestion the Jews were a divinely chosen people of higher spiritual status than others. Among his chief conclusions is his idea that the Jews are not a "chosen" people in any spiritual or eternal sense but simply one people among many, their biblical "election" signifying merely the effectiveness of their laws when they formed an independent republic which they achieved for only a relatively short period from Moses until the anointing of Saul as their king, in the eleventh century BC, and then, again, under the Persian kings, in the age of Ezra whose loyalty to Persia Josephus stresses.[55]

Another key point for Spinoza, where Josephus again lent support, was that classical era Judaism was actually a whole array of warring sects, of which the Sadducees were the wisest and least superstitious. Judaism as we know it, holds Spinoza, rests on a canon non-existent before the Maccabean era. "The books we now possess were selected, in preference to many others, by the Second Temple Pharisees who also set out the forms for prayers, and these have been accepted purely owing to their decisions."[56] This important supplement to Spinoza's Ezra thesis pivots on one of the allegedly most crucial but poorly recorded episodes in Jewish history, the so-called "Great Assembly [Knesset ha-Godolah]," held in Maccabean times to put in order and institutionalize Jewish observance and the Law that Jewish tradition attributes to Ezra and his followers. The Pharisees, as Spinoza describes them, are more ignorant and untrustworthy, and stem from a less educated background than the Pharisees Josephus actually portrays.[57] Scripture's true message, holds Spinoza, was usurped and twisted into an instrument of control by Pharisees believing in resurrection of the dead, which the Sadducees, sensibly in Josephus' (and Spinoza's) view, rejected. Phariseeism was then perverted into a still worse current by the Zealot revolutionaries of the AD 60s.[58] By denigrating doctrines introduced by the Pharisees, Spinoza felt he was not disparaging the authentic, true Hebrew tradition.

---

[55] Spinoza, *Theological-Political Treatise*, 48; Feldman, "Josephus' Portrait of Ezra," 197–200; Raphael, *Jew among Romans*, xxii–xxiii; Nadler, *Spinoza's Heresy*, 37–9; Steinberg, *Spinoza's Political Psychology*, 101–2.
[56] Spinoza, *Theological-Political Treatise*, 153.
[57] Gafni, "Historical Background," 24; Attridge, "Josephus," 186, 195.
[58] Spinoza, *Theological-Political Treatise*, 153–4; Raphael, *Jew among Romans*, 29–30, 143.

Pharisaic Judaism, explains Spinoza, derives from what in Jewish tradition is called the "Great Synagogue" or "synagoga quae dicitur magna,"[59] a Great Assembly supposedly convened by Ezra and his companions to recover the holy texts, but actually an assembly, proposes Spinoza, in the thirty pages of *Adnotationes* [notes] added during his last years, to clarify the *TTP*'s arguments, that "did not convene until after the conquest of [the Near East] by the Macedonians," hence after Alexander the Great. "The opinion of Maimonides, Rabbi Abraham ben David and others that the presidents of this council were Ezra, Daniel, Nehemiah, Haggai, Zechariah and so on, is a ridiculous fiction, resting on no other foundation than rabbinical tradition which claims the Persian empire lasted a mere thirty-four years." Spinoza here affirms more forcefully a correction earlier introduced by the Mantuan Jewish scholar Azzariah de' Rossi (c.1511–78), that the ancient or first Persian empire actually spanned two to three centuries (roughly 550 to 330 BC). This blatant rabbinic twisting of history the Christians later adopted. "This is the only way they can argue the decrees of this Great Synagogue or Synod composed solely of Pharisees were accepted by the Prophets who received them from other Prophets and so on reaching back to Moses who received them from God Himself and handed them on to posterity by word of mouth not in writing."[60]

Maimonides' Bible exegesis Spinoza both expressly rejects and tacitly borrows from and interacts with, not infrequently reworking or simply reversing Maimonides' position. While agreeing with Maimonides that biblical prophecy was a purely natural phenomenon, Spinoza rejects Maimonides' claim that behind Scripture's literal meaning, Moses and the Prophets obscurely reveal profound philosophical truths which philosophers alone are equipped to unravel. Dismissing Maimonides' thesis that the literal meaning is not the real meaning which remains concealed, as "absurd," Spinoza insists the literal meaning *is* the real meaning and that the Prophets had no special access to profound truths. Maimonides' view he considers both wrong and harmful in its political implications because it fortifies belief that Scripture is the repository of divine truth and hence ultimate source of law, bolstering those holding that morality, law, and education must be based on Scripture and hence on what Spinoza saw as the usurped, fabricated authority of rabbis and churchmen over society.[61]

"The Pharisees [i.e. rabbis] may persist in believing these things [about the early restitution of an authentic biblical text] with their usual obstinacy," holds Spinoza, relying largely on Josephus, but experts on the struggle between the Pharisees and Sadducees know this Great Synagogue was an all-Pharisee affair designed to

---

[59] Spinoza, *Opera* iii, 269–61.
[60] Spinoza, *Theological-Political Treatise*, 269–70; Proietti, *La Città Divisa*, 190; Grafton, "Spinoza's Hermeneutics," 191, 193–4.
[61] Nadler, *Book Forged in Hell*, 62–6; Chalier, *Spinoza lecteur*, 7–8; Frankel, "Spinoza's Rejection of Maimonideism," 86–7, 91–2.

consolidate their control over the emerging religion. "It is certain, moreover, that no prophet participated in this assembly and that the Pharisees' decrees which they call 'traditions' received their authority only from the Council."[62] Actually, there were no sects among the Hebrews, holds Spinoza towards the end of the *TTP*, "until after the priests usurped control during the second state [i.e. Second Temple era] acquiring the authority to issue decrees and manage the business of the state and make their authority eternal, and, finally, wanted to be called kings."[63] To further their quest for power, the Pharisees fomented superstition and the "true sense of and interpretation of the Laws was perverted." Using whatever would bring the common people to their side, they "twisted Scripture, to accommodate their base morality," as attested, Spinoza claims, by Malachi.

Already earlier, Uriel da Costa, in his *Examination* cited Josephus as holding that the Pharisees exploited the false notion of immortality of the soul to rally "the masses around them."[64] Meanwhile, avers Spinoza, the "wiser people affirmed that no laws should be kept unless they were in writing." This was the essence of the historic rift between Sadducees and Pharisees. According to the former, all other decrees which the Pharisees termed "traditions of the fathers, should by no means be observed [minime custodienda esse]." However, that was while the Hasmonaean Jewish republic remained extant.[65] Where no Jewish state exists, concludes Spinoza, neither the Oral nor the Written Law is genuinely binding on Jews.

Spinoza considers Ezra's intervention decisive for the shaping of the Hebrew Scriptures as we have them, while seeing Ezra's redaction as unfinished and itself proving highly unstable and precarious during the next several centuries until Maccabean times due to the severity of Hellenistic oppression after the rule of Alexander the Great. Although Josephus does not actually claim Ezra largely wrote the Pentateuch as we have it and begrudges the Samaritans' blaming mainstream Judaism, and especially Ezra, for corrupting the Mosaic text as they separately and to a limited extent differently preserved it, Spinoza construes Josephus as supporting his extended Ezra thesis. Only two or three copies, he believed, of Ezra's redaction survived.[66] "Anyone who wonders by what mischance there was such a dearth of copies after Ezra should simply read the first chapter of Maccabees or Josephus' *Antiquities*, 12.7. It seems something of a miracle they could preserve even these few copies through such prolonged and powerful persecution."[67] The chief difference, then, between Spinoza and La Peyrère and Hobbes as Bible critics and advocates of the Ezran thesis, is the much greater level of detail into which Spinoza delves when demonstrating what he saw as the

---

[62] Spinoza, *Theological-Political Treatise*, 270.
[63] Spinoza, *Opera* iii, 222; Klever, *Spinoza Classicus*, 262.   [64] Da Costa, *Examination*, 345–6.
[65] Spinoza, *Opera* iii, 223.
[66] Feldman, "Josephus' Portrait of Ezra," 210; Touber, *Spinoza and Biblical Philology*, 69.
[67] Spinoza, *Theological-Political Treatise*, 142; James, *Spinoza on Philosophy*, 171.

complex evolution of the biblical text, his setting out what amounts to a whole historiography of the biblical text, in effect introducing a substantially different approach from that of La Peyrère and Hobbes.

The Hebrew Scriptures' evolution from Moses' time down to the First Temple's destruction proved long, haphazard, and uncertain, with the Babylonian captivity, the next stage in Scripture's evolution, causing much loss and confusion. But much additional text restitution, finding of forgotten texts, and redacting occurred, he argues, also after Ezra. The four books of Ezra and Nehemiah were "not written by either Ezra or Nehemiah" but rather "these books were written long after Judas Maccabeus restored worship in the Second Temple," a century before Rome conquered the Hasmonean kingdom and "we assert, were written by one and the same author, though I cannot even guess who he was."[68] Re-dedication of the Temple by Judas Maccabeus, in 164 BC which the Jewish festival of Hannukah celebrates, thus occurred roughly three and a half centuries after the re-dedication in 516 BC, following the Babylonian captivity, hence over halfway through the so-called Second Temple era (516 BC–AD. 70). Spinoza thought this explains why these particular books are so full of errors of chronology, genealogy, and incorrect family names.[69]

If Ezra's redaction and the Hellenistic era represent two different evolving phases of Bible text redaction, culminating in the instability caused by the persecution prior to the revolt of Judas Maccabeus (167–164 BC), Spinoza viewed the Hasmonaean era itself as yet a further phase of turmoil affecting the biblical text caused by the escalating conflict between Pharisees and other Jewish sects, especially Sadducees, resulting in profound discord and wrangling about books and texts. "Our conclusion is evident: no canon of sacred books ever existed before the time of the Maccabees. The books we now possess were selected, in preference to many others, by the Second Temple Pharisees who also set out the forms of prayers, and these have been accepted purely as a consequence of their decisions."[70]

24.iii The Masoretic Age

But the Maccabees were not the end of the Old Testament's long, severely interrupted and bumpy evolution. Added difficulties hampering accurate grasp of biblical passages stem from the subsequent convoluted history of Hebrew writing, spelling, and grammatical analysis during the early Christian centuries

---

[68] Spinoza, *Theological-Political Treatise*, 148–9.
[69] Spinoza, *Theological-Political Treatise*, 149–50; Strauss, *Spinoza's Critique of Religion*, 267; Grafton, "Spinoza's Hermeneutics," 191.
[70] Spinoza, *Theological-Political Treatise*, 153, 268–70; Matheron, *Christ et le salut*, 59; Feldman, "Josephus' Portrait of Ezra," 191.

and the fact that time has "rendered many words obsolete and antiquated." Nouns shifted in meaning, many passages being very divergently interpreted from Talmudic times (AD 70–500) onwards. Nor were even Talmudic times the end of the shifting story. Concentrated in the Galilean town of Tiberias, scribes conserving and copying these variant readings during the last phase of transition, that of the Masoretes, continued redacting the Scriptures from the sixth to the tenth century AD until the time when rabbinic authority finally endorsed the resulting body of text as canonical. Only in the last phases were vowel points and punctuation inserted, as Meyer too emphasizes. Meanwhile, many variants passed down thus far were subsequently deleted or revised after the tenth century to resolve finally areas of doubt and disagreement still lingering since Talmudic times.

Highlighting the vowel points as a post-Talmudic amendment was nothing new in the seventeenth century. The Renaissance era Jewish scholar Elias Levita (1469–1549), based in Rome and Venice, made an issue of this long before when debating with Christian scholars. Taken up by the Huguenot scholar Louis Cappel (1585–1658), Levita's claim about the late advent of vowels and punctuation was fiercely opposed by other Christian Hebraists like the Buxtorfs. For Spinoza, the vowels' late arrival was just one among many factors explaining Scripture's proneness to discrepancy, unreliability, and obscurity. Besides other gaps, "the Masoretes," holds Spinoza, also signalled "twenty-eight places where a vacant space is left in the middle of a paragraph," as for example in Genesis 4:8 where Scripture states "And Cain said to Abel his brother... and it came to pass, while they were in the field," and so on.[71] Emphasizing the instability of the Hebrew text through Hellenistic, Roman, Talmudic, and Masoretic times in this way became an important boundary marker separating the Dutch post-Erasmian Bible hermeneutics forged by Scaliger, Grotius, and their seventeenth-century followers from Spinozist Bible criticism.

Scaliger judged the Masoretic text more reliable than the Septuagint (very differently from Spinoza's friend in The Hague, Isaac Vossius), and did not use the latter as an instrument for throwing doubt on the integrity of the Hebrew text, and neither did the leading exegetes who followed him, Drusius, Grotius, and Daniel Heinsius.[72] Vossius, feigning to repudiate La Peyrère, did powerfully intervene, in 1659, with his *De Vera Aetate Mundi*, claiming the insurmountable difficulties of biblical chronology flagged by La Peyrère largely disappear if instead of the severely corrupted Masoretic Hebrew text one substitutes the more reliable Greek of the Septuagint, thereby adding nearly 40 per cent, another 1,440 years to

---

[71] Spinoza, *Theological-Political Treatise*, 137–43.
[72] Van Miert, *Emancipation of Biblical Philology*, 44, 83, 116–17, 144, 149, 202; Touber, *Spinoza and Biblical Philology*, 50.

the age of the world, to the highly defective chronology in the Hebrew.[73] One ironic, paradoxical result of Vossius' and especially Spinoza's findings demonstrating corruption of the Hebrew version during the Masoretic age was that both their approaches, different though they were, proved more directly damaging to Protestantism than to Catholicism. Catholic scholars could partially deflect their critique by bending Spinoza's and Vossius' objections to support their Church's contention that Protestant *Sola Scriptura* constitutes an inadequate basis for Christian belief. Church authority, Church Fathers, and the papacy, conserving the true Christian tradition, and not Scripture, must ultimately decide and preside.[74]

Spinoza had five copies of the Bible in his personal library, two in Hebrew, two in Latin, one in Spanish and nothing in Greek, reflecting his basic orientation.[75] He also possessed Immanuel Tremellius' 1569 Syriac (Aramaic) translation of the New Testament printed in Hebrew characters which he used to elaborate his foundational principle that the Gospels "were written in the Hebrew language [qui Hebraea lingua scripta fuerunt]," and are to be comprehended exclusively on that basis and not as churchmen construe them.[76] His distinction between the true sense of the text and the "truth of things" was closely linked to his insistence that the minds of the biblical narratives' authors seethed with supernatural happenings and miracles. By rigorously analysing not just the wording but nuances, obscurities, and shifts in use of Hebrew terms and expressions, he demonstrated, conclusively in his view, that ignorance of the laws of nature and superstition pervade the successive religious cultures dominating the different eras in which the Bible took shape, proliferating successive styles of appealing to the miraculous, wonders, and divinely inspired prophecy.

Moses was the greatest of the Prophets, Spinoza acknowledges, but, like all prophets, prophesied not through divine revelation but solely "imagination." Unlike some modern Bible critics, Spinoza did not question Moses' historicity. But locked into the primitive beliefs of his time, Spinoza's Moses expressed a more limited notion of God's creative power, providential capacity, and ability to foresee the future and men's actions than did later religious outlooks.[77] Like all religious leaders, he explained the world in terms that would reinforce his followers' faith, using imagined, scientifically and philosophically false notions that then changed over time because different prophets and then scribes and priests all viewed events and occurrences according to their own era's striving to

---

[73] Jorink, "Horrible and Blasphemous," 442–4.

[74] Totaro, "Le *Compendium*," 88–9; Moreau, *Spinoza, L'expérience*, 351–2; Preus, *Spinoza*, 142–3.

[75] Nadler, *Book Forged in Hell*, 104; Van Sluis and Musschenga, *Boeken van Spinoza*, 16, 21, 24, 27, 29.

[76] Spinoza, *Theological-Political Treatise*, 154; Totaro, "Introduzione," p. xxxvi; Totaro, "Le *Compendium*," 68.

[77] Spinoza, *Theological-Political Treatise*, 36–7; Van Bunge, *Spinoza Past and Present*, 72–4.

fathom the processes of nature and society.[78] It is the Bible's historicity as well as the evolution and grammar of its language and expressions that Spinoza for the first time converts into a principal tool for unlocking its meaning. Refusing to consider anything other than the historically conditioned "intended meaning," noted Leibniz early in 1677, around the time of Spinoza's death, is "le fondement" of the *TTP*.[79] Spinoza was surely right to claim the "true" meaning of biblical texts and "truth of fact" had in fact been continually conflated and "confused" down to his own day.

If we ask how these two things, truth and true textual meaning, came to be so emphatically separated in his mind, the answer lies principally in his and his following's collective resolve to exclude the supernatural from all interpretation of the Bible, and do this in a more systematic manner than ever previously attempted. When explaining the need not to confuse the veritable sense of the text with the truth of things, and how the first must be coaxed from the language usage together with "reasoning acknowledging no other basis than Scripture itself," Spinoza offers a largely original as well as witheringly effective exegetical historical-critical apparatus for Bible interpretation, predicated on the Bible's historicity and non-sacred status. Despite what is often claimed, this does not in fact approximate to Hobbes' position. For Spinoza, study of religion and generally what in German are called the *Sozial- und Geisteswissenschaften* in principle differ not at all methodologically from the other sciences, leaving no church and no monarch entitled to authorize or seek to legitimize any particular version.

"I say that the method of interpreting Scripture scarcely differs from that of interpreting nature, but rather absolutely agrees with it [Dico methodum interpretandi Scripturam haud differre a methodo interpetandi naturam, sed cum ea prorsus convenire]."[80] The right method of interpreting nature, for Spinoza, consists in constructing a natural history from which we can derive definitions of natural things that can be treated as reasonably objective data. To meaningfully interpret Scripture, we must assemble all the facts surrounding its history that we can and deduce the Bible writers' thinking by valid inferences from "history," inferring from established facts and principles.[81] Relying on mathematical reasoning anchored in historical research, signifies that Spinoza's compendium of

---

[78] Spinoza, *Opera* iii, 101; Walther, "Biblische Hermeneutik" (1992), 642, 650–1; Preus, *Spinoza*, 160–1.
[79] Leibniz to Duke Johann Friedrich (undated, early 1677) in Leibniz, *Sämtliche Schriften und Briefe* 1st ser. ii, 9.
[80] Spinoza, *Opera* iii, 98; Lagrée, "Thème des deux livres," 9–10, 36–7; Klever, *Mannen rond Spinoza*, 79–80; Preus, *Spinoza*, 157–8, 164–6, 168, 175.
[81] Walther, "Biblische Hermeneutik" (1992), 636; Goldenbaum, "Philosophische Methodendiskussion," 153–5; Montag, *Bodies, Masses, Power*, 6–7; Goetschel, *Spinoza's Modernity*, 61–4.

Hebrew grammar, far from being an extraneous item detached from his philosophical system, needs to be considered a basic component integral to it.[82]

To assume beforehand that the Prophets knew things we would otherwise not know, or were aware of what we have discovered since, as was usual in his time, Spinoza considers wholly illegitimate. The evidence obliges the scholar to conclude that both Joshua and the author of the biblical narrative recounting his history, really believed, like Isaiah, that the sun revolves around the earth. In his day, commentators either ignored this or twisted the text to say something different from what it clearly says, or explained difficulties away without conceding Joshua's (and Isaiah's) ignorance of astronomy.[83] For Spinoza, in sharp contrast to Maimonides, biblical Prophets, though splendidly endowed with imagination, were profoundly ignorant about everything except basic morality, so that what is worthy of respect in modern times boils down exclusively to their "piety."[84]

To grasp a complex text's multi-layered historicity one must bear in mind that language is used differently in different periods and differently also by the learned and unlearned, so that while it is the former who propagate and preserve texts, it is not they who principally fix the meaning and nuances of words or how they are employed. According to Spinoza's rules of criticism, it is insufficient to know the language in which a text is composed, and be familiar with its characteristic idioms, usages, and grammar. One must first determine the meaning of a text as precisely and literally as possible but then also learn to view this *sensus literalis* as a fragment of a wider complex of beliefs and ideas, a self-defining and contained, if rarely coherent, system of beliefs about our world which, in turn, to be rationally understood, requires philosophical interpretation in terms of nature and natural forces. It was an idea requiring a prior theory of culture and religion, of motivation and human striving, such as embodied since the mid-1660s in Spinoza's not yet completed *Ethics*. A religion, for Spinoza, is a belief system built on imagined transcendental realities answering to men's deepest psychological and emotional desires and needs, a natural phenomenon in that, he argues in the appendix to Part I of the *Ethics*, human emotions are so structured as to prompt us to attribute anthropomorphic, teleological explanations to natural phenomena and all occurrences we fail to comprehend and, hence, trust in the existence of a transcendental order on high beyond our imagination.[85]

Even though scribes may alter the meaning of passages by intention or error, or construe them differently from how they were understood earlier, no one can change how words and phrases are used in conversation and are understood in a

---

[82] Totaro, "Introduzione," 4–7; Totaro," Le *Compendium*," 67; Touber, *Spinoza and Biblical Philology*, 48.
[83] Spinoza, *Theological-Political Treatise*, 33–4; Israel, "How Did Spinoza Declare War?' 202–3.
[84] Spinoza, *Theological-Political Treatise*, 35; Preus, *Spinoza*, 173–4.
[85] Spinoza, *Collected Works* i, 439–46, 123; Preus, *Spinoza*, 169–71, 196–7.

particular society at a particular time. By correlating everything relevant to a given usage within its historical context, a solid hermeneutics can approximate to establishing the correct reading of a text which then, in turn, helps the scholar unmask the style of manipulation, the form of theological imposture, dogmatic distortion, or illicit extrapolation forged by the theologically minded using dogma to shepherd populations. It is a method enabling one to expose what is spuriously introduced by religious authority, and locate past shifts in doctrine and the chief instances of falsification.[86] In short, Spinoza's "universal rule for explaining Scripture" is one that assigns no meaning to Scripture that analysis of the text does not lay before us in the clearest fashion.[87] Understanding a text is hence not a matter of discerning what is "true" in it or authoritative, as with Grotius, Hobbes, and Meyer, but a strictly historical-critical as well as linguistic exercise rooted in a purely naturalistic philosophical standpoint.

What was quintessentially modern and revolutionary in Spinoza's text criticism but also chiefly sets it at odds with the text criticism of our contemporary Postmodernism, is his stress on the Bible's historicity. The "historical" here which is also the characteristic "modern" sense would be conceptually impossible without wholly eliminating supernatural agency from the historical process something still unthinkable for most early modern thinkers and writers. When studying natural phenomena of whatever sort, affirms the *TTP*'s seventh chapter, we must first uncover those features that are most universal, such as the laws governing motion and rest, laws that are eternally true, and then descend by stages from the most general to the more specific.[88] When studying texts, including Scripture, Spinoza urges a like procedure, identifying what is most general and fundamental in the narrative first. "What is most universally declared in Scripture (whether by prophets, scribes, or Christ) is that God exists, is one, and omnipotent, that he alone should be venerated and cares for all, favouring above others those who venerate him and love their neighbour as themselves, etc. [quod Deus unicus et omnipotens existit, qui solus est adorandus, et qui omnes curat, eosque supra omnes diligit, qui ipsum adorant, et proximum tanquam semet ipsos amant etc.]"[89] While such universals are historically determined poetic concepts, inexact and vague, and it is impossible to infer from the Bible "what God is" or how he "provides for all things," nevertheless such universals amount to more than fictitious or arbitrary intended meanings, being inadequate but still meaningful approximations to the "truth of things." The correct opposition in human ideas, held Spinoza, is not between the rational and irrational but between the more and less rational.

[86] Monnikhoff, "Beschrijving van Spinoza's leven," 213; Klever, *Mannen rond Spinoza*, 61–4; Steenbakkers, *Spinoza's Ethica*, 17–21.
[87] Preus, *Spinoza*, 160–1; Van Rooden, "Spinoza's Bijbeluitleg," 126–7.
[88] Spinoza, *Tractatus Theologico-Politicus*, 33–4; Rudavsky, "Science of Scripture, 73–4.
[89] Spinoza, *Opera* iii, 102; Walther, "Biblische Hermeneutik" (1992), 657.

Spinoza's *TTP* has been called "the most important seventeenth-century work to advance the study of the Bible and religion generally" with an enduring importance within Western civilization as the work which "disarmed the religious interpreters who would enforce conformity."[90] But while all scholars today acknowledge Spinoza as an important innovator, few show how and why he pushed this study to a level dramatically beyond anything envisaged by Hobbes, let alone Locke or Newton. Spinoza transformed Bible criticism through insisting on the need to approach the subject free of all prejudgements about its meaning, free from every chain of tradition and authority whether Jewish, Catholic, Protestant, or Muslim, never wavering from the distinction between the intended or "true" meaning and "truth of fact," and proving how damagingly society has confused the imagined true sense with the truth of things. To his mind, a genuinely coherent historical-critical method of exegesis cannot at any point be reconciled with the received opinions of believers, or the theology of any church.[91]

24.iv Spinoza's Critique of Meyer

While Meyer's impact in Britain and France was never great, in Germany he was remembered as the first more or less openly "rationalistischer Anti-Scriptuarius" [rationalist anti-Biblicist], the man whose *Philosophia* revealed in highly disconcerting ways the new philosophy's capacity for harnessing Scripture, provoking an unprecedented outcry. Yet, there is a well-established tradition in Protestant critical theology claiming there was nothing particularly modern or significant in the Bible hermeneutics of Spinoza's friend Lodewijk Meyer (1621–89). Meyer himself, though, was convinced his Bible criticism was a revolution in the field bound to provoke a titanic eruption of fury from "the theologians." This was the reason that he had long hesitated to publish his text, being unwilling to incur the "bitter hatred" to be expected from theologians.[92] Meyer's challenge to conventional Protestant thought about the Bible is also often labelled essentially "Socinian," albeit with a Cartesian tinge, and left at that.[93] But in the late seventeenth century, Bible critics recognized that Meyer's criticism is neither truly Socinian nor Cartesian in character but rather both innovative and subversive. The staunchly anti-Socinian English divine John Wilson, writing in 1676, when abominating the *Philosophia* rightly noted also that it goes further than any Socinian would in invalidating Scripture. The controversial pastor Louis

---

[90] Goetschel, *Spinoza's Modernity*, 53–4, 56–7; Preus, *Spinoza*, p. x.
[91] Spinoza, *Opera* iii, 101; Walther, "Biblische Hermeneutik" (1992), 642–3, 650–1; Walther, "Spinoza's Critique," 110–11; Preus, *Spinoza*, 160–1.
[92] [Meyer], *Philosophy as the Interpreter*, 226–7.
[93] Thijssen-Schoute, *Nederlands Cartesianisme*, 397–8; Scholder, *Birth*, 135; Parker, "Spinoza, Locke," 173.

Wolzogen likewise emphasized the need to differentiate Meyer's critique from that of the Socinians.[94]

Yet, there was certainly also a perceptible gap in exegetical approach to Scripture between Spinoza and Meyer, and this requires careful defining. If in 1666, Meyer's *Philosophia* was scarcely less controversial than the *TTP* in 1670, at any rate in the Netherlands and Germany, the ensuing controversy reveals also that Meyer's "Cartesian" approach yielded notions about Scripture that were less than quintessentially "modern," and in some respects remote from Spinoza's. With his strong sense of mission to enlighten the public by steering key intellectual debate into the vernacular, and awareness of the indignation provoked by denial that church tradition and training afford any access to truth that others lack, Meyer remained among Spinoza's chief collaborators.[95]

Meyer, Wolzogen, and other participants in the 1666-7 public controversy over interpretation of Scripture are sometimes held to have moved in a thought-world so different from Spinoza's that the *TTP* without mentioning him by name is tacitly combating Meyer's exegetical ideas, as well as his theological foes. Modern scholars remain somewhat divided over whether Meyer's Bible criticism marks a radical break diverging fundamentally from Spinoza's, or did not mark a revolutionary break but rather illustrates the enduring grip of older assumptions, or thirdly, despite superficial differences, was actually closely aligned with Spinoza's approach. This third scholarly camp argue that, despite differences in style and terminology, Spinoza and Meyer broadly converge differing only in aspects of methodology.[96] There is also an interesting fourth view combining elements of the first and third interpretations. According to this view, when Meyer wrote the *Philosophia* during the early 1660s and discussed it with his friends, Spinoza broadly agreed with him, seeing Scripture, when correctly "interpreted" as a repository of basic truth that converges with truths demonstrated by philosophy, but that during the later 1660s, as Spinoza composed his *TTP*, a wide gap opened up between their respective positions due to Spinoza temporarily shifting his stance. According to this theory, Spinoza was caught between two different tendencies or models he was ultimately unable to reconcile, on the one hand viewing religion as "a replacement" for philosophy, providing the basis for the best life available to non-philosophers because the multitude is "unable to understand higher things," as he expresses it, writing to Van Blijenbergh, while yet, on the other hand, denying religion's claims to present the truth so as to defend freedom to philosophize, with the latter becoming Spinoza's main thrust in the *TTP*.[97]

---

[94] *Lettres sur la Vie* [...] *de Wolzogue*, 44; Wilson, *Scriptures Genuine Interpreter*, 17, 30.

[95] Preus, "A Hidden Opponent," 367-8; Preus, *Spinoza*, 14, 34-67, 100-1, 159-61, 165.

[96] Represented most extensively by Lagrée, Moreau, Iofrida, Curley, and Preus; see Lagrée, "Sens et verité," 83-9; Moreau, "Principes," 120-1; Curley, "Notes," 77-9.

[97] Fraenkel is the main exponent of this view, see Fraenkel, "Could Spinoza Have Presented," 2-3, 24, 26-7; Fraenkel, "Reconsidering the Case," 230-2; Fraenkel, *Philosophical Religions*, 280-1.

Here, though, it is argued that Spinoza, as Bible critic, presided over a group project, and neither temporarily, nor in the longer term, did there exist any wide gap between Spinoza and Meyer. Contrary to the fourth approach, Spinoza was not caught between two different models, and although he certainly displayed greater subtlety and depth than Meyer as a Bible exegete, broadly he aligned closely with him. Indeed, the essential unity of their common quest needs reaffirming.[98] Neither of them adopted a Socinian stance. Despite internecine divisions, all Dutch, German, and Polish Socinianism recognized the Bible as the sacred Word of God, and hence clear in principle, possessing a holy status quite distinct from other texts. Certainly, there are textual difficulties requiring explication via use of reason. But the *recta ratio* Socinianism invokes to elucidate Scriptural meaning works by using parallels, comparing textual contexts, and appealing to practical common sense, seeking to explain Scripture solely from Scripture without involving any external criterion or aid other than the *Sanctus Spiritus* [Holy Ghost]. Thus, only in a limited way did Socinian "reason" diverge from orthodox Lutheran and Calvinist insistence on *Scriptura sui ipsius interpres* [Scripture the interpreter of itself].[99] By contrast, Meyer asserts the biblical text's overall "obscurity" and thus the need for an external arbiter, and that this pervasive obscurity can never be dispelled other than by the "true philosophy," meaning via reason alone, *media philosophica* without recourse to the Holy Ghost. The "Belgick Exercitator," complains the English Puritan Bible commentator John Wilson, in his *The Scripture's Genuine Interpreter* (1678), "rises higher in denying the Scriptures perspicuity than any that I have ever met with."[100]

Meyer expressly rebukes his Socinian friends for inconsistency in first claiming it is for "reason alone" to resolve Scripture's difficulties and then stipulating that "reason" alone does not suffice to rescue us from them, rendering the aid of the Holy Ghost indispensable too.[101] Appalled by Meyer's frequent reiteration of Scripture's all-enveloping "obscurity," Serrarius counters by insisting one must distinguish between the written and the "living" Word. All Socinians reject the doctrine of strict Calvinist theologians, like Voetius and Petrus van Mastricht, that human reason is inherently corrupted by Original Sin, but hold also that reason can never displace the Holy Ghost from primacy in interpreting Scripture.[102] For Meyer and Spinoza, by contrast, human reason alone elucidates Scripture's meaning. Meyer's significance lies in his categorical denial that traditional theology, or

---

[98] In particular, Wim Klever and Roberto Bordoli; see Klever, *Mannen rond Spinoza*, 61–85; Klever, *Definitie*, 220, 225–6; Bordoli, *Ragione e scrittura*, 101, 116–17.

[99] Thijssen-Scoute, *Nederlands Cartesianisme*, 396–7; Scholder, *Birth*, 36–7; Hardeveld, *Lodewijk Meijer*, 54.

[100] Touber, *Spinoza and Biblical Philology*, 39; Wilson, *Scriptures Genuine Interpreter*, 178; Meschonnic, *Spinoza*, 182.

[101] Thijssen-Schoute, *Nederlands Cartesianisme*, 398; Israel, *Radical Enlightenment*, 204.

[102] Serrarius, *Responsio*, 13–15; Van der Wall, *Mystieke Chiliast*, 478–9; Van Burg, "Petrus van Mastricht," 57.

any theology or divine inspiration apart from philosophy can meaningfully interpret Scripture. Hence, the 1666 furore should be considered the first great early enlightenment public controversy as well as the first of the major "Spinozist" controversies.

The question of Spinoza's relation to Meyer's Bible hermeneutics matters not just for Spinoza's own biography and his personal relationship to Meyer, but also because it raises the broader question of whether or not the *cercle Spinoziste*'s new text criticism did constitute a group revolt against Europe's humanist legacy, was a philosophical strategy invading the sphere of text erudition from without, stemming from the clash of philosophy and theology, or whether, as some scholars claim, the late seventeenth-century new *critique* arose rather from the humanist tradition and ultimately had little to do with philosophy, Cartesian, Spinozist or other, emerging independently, from gradual improvement in humanist text scholarship itself which Spinoza then idiosyncratically borrowed. If Spinoza's philosophy and the new Bible criticism were essentially separate with Spinozism exerting scant influence and Socinianism rather more while Cartesianism preserved the spiritual dimension intact, one is free to argue that little pressure emanated from the new philosophy to fundamentally recast the rules of text criticism. Such a conclusion would rule out any great "revolution" in erudition in the late seventeenth century and reinforce the notion that pre-1600 humanism remained a, or even *the*, prime shaping force in forging "modernity."[103]

Those discerning basic disparity between Meyer's Cartesian "rationalist" and Spinoza's basically "historical" exegesis,[104] make three specific claims: first, being a "daring partisan of Cartesian philosophy" Meyer precludes any proper grasp of the historical dimension even if it did not deter his violating Descartes' own strict directives regarding "separation between philosophy and theology" (thereby undermining true Cartesianism).[105] Second, the *Philosophia* is held to retain obvious traditional elements. While claiming to be "a super-rationalist in his approach to biblical interpretation," Meyer nevertheless "retained a magical view of the Bible," allegedly not unlike Balling, Jelles, and other Collegiant Socinians. Thirdly, while professing to be a "trenchant critic of some of orthodoxy's dearest first principles," he allegedly accepted "uncritically some of its characteristic dogmas," paradoxically embracing as axiomatic scriptural infallibility and even the Holy Trinity.[106] But all this is hardly convincing. Meyer's "scriptural infallibility" is clearly just a deliberately feigned tool of demolition

---

[103] Walther, "Biblische Hermeneutik" (1995), 227–31; Verbeek, *Spinoza's Theologico-Political Treatise*, 99–109; Van Miert, *Emancipation of Biblical Philology*, 232; Touber, *Spinoza and Biblical Philology*, 8–9.
[104] Preus, "A Hidden Opponent," 67–8; Preus, *Spinoza*, 14, 34–67, 100–1, 159–61, 165.
[105] Preus, *Spinoza*, 14, 39–40, 55, 57, 75, 154; Iofrida, "Linguaggio e verità," 26–7.
[106] Preus, *Spinoza*, 34, 57–9.

and his Holy Trinity pure unadulterated imposture. At bottom, Meyer and Spinoza adhere to a basically identical stance throughout.

Pivotal here is whether or not Meyer follows Spinoza in claiming the truth of Scripture "must be sought from Scripture alone, just as knowledge of nature must be sought from nature," whether or not for Meyer too, the "true meaning" of biblical passages diverges from the "truth of things."[107] It is sometimes denied that Meyer does follow Spinoza here and at least one recent scholar even refuses to accept that Meyer held that "Scripture is full of contradictions, discrepancies and imperfections," claiming this designation "fits Spinoza, not Meyer."[108] But to defend this view one must show that Meyer, who was adept in elusive writing, meant his introductory rhetoric sincerely and really strove to "demonstrate how Scripture's divine truths might be recovered through a philosophical method," an interpretation flying in the face not only of Meyer's own subsequent statements, implying a wide gap between the "truth of things" and the "true meaning," but how his book was understood by contemporaries, albeit Wolzogen does accept his claim that Scripture is divine revelation and, on this ground, denies that Meyer can be classified with those (like Spinoza and the Koerbaghs) interpreting the Bible as a purely human text like any other.[109]

Theological disputes, insists Meyer, are legion and revolve invariably around conflicting interpretations of Scripture so that the essential problem for Christians is "to build the Palace of the most holy theology not on sand but stone."[110] Although theological disputes and religious leaders' incessant quarrels, rivalries, and clashes are ubiquitous and damaging, theologians' infighting will never cease as long as their conflicting interpretations of Scripture remain a fenced off arena specially reserved for them and remain the tools of rival spheres of influence. The fact that much of Holy Scripture is impenetrably obscure and diversely interpreted in no way deters theologians from presenting "Holy Scripture, God's infallible Word, as their holy mainstay, and fetching from there many passages with which to ground their interpretations and opinions."[111] Thus, the question what is the right method of interpreting Scripture is a question crucially relevant to everyone. Highlighting what is at stake, showing how decisive text interpretation is for theology which Meyer insinuatingly styles "the Princess of the sciences [de Princes der wetenschappen]," he powerfully contributes to the philosophical-critical revolution he helps promote by continually stressing the overriding centrality of irresolvable dispute over Bible interpretation. The great "paradox" Meyer professes to solve is that despite being the "infallible" Word of God, the bright

---

[107] Spinoza, *Tractatus Theologico-Politicus*, ch. VII; *Lettres sur la Vie* [...] *de Wolzogue*, 43; Preus, *Spinoza*, 177; Thijssen-Schoute, *Nederlands Cartesianisme*, 399–400.
[108] Preus, *Spinoza*, 38n.   [109] Lagrée, "Louis Meyer," 35–8; Israel, *Radical Enlightenment*, 202.
[110] [Meyer], *Philosophie d'Uytleghster*, Voorreden, p. vii; Curley, "Notes," 77–8.
[111] [Meyer], *Philosophie d'Uytleghster*, p. vii; Van der Wall, *Mystieke Chiliast*, 479; Bordoli, *Ragione e scrittura*, 106.

light at the beginning and end of all theology, "Scripture is obscure and ambiguous [Scripturum esse obscurum et ambiguam]" throughout, in both Testaments or, as he puts it in the sometimes more revealing Dutch version (which he prepared himself, often slightly altering the emphasis of his original Latin), "in many places obscure and doubtful [in veel plaatsen duyster en twijfelachtigh]."[112] Endless theological strife dominates our world, holds Meyer, because Scripture is "the infallible Word of God" yet so obscure and doubtful that theological doctrines are eternally bound to be contested owing to their supposedly divine but actually questionable grounding in Scripture. No core Christian doctrine of any kind, whether the Bible's infallibility, the Trinity, Original Sin, or Christ's divinity, can be clearly derived from Scripture, leaving the entire edifice of church doctrine standing on sand, not solid ground. Why is the Bible so full of obscurity? The essential reason, explains Meyer, echoing Spinoza, is that the New Testament employs many Hebraisms and Hebrew turns of phrase which mostly do not signify what people think they mean, a point he shares also with the Koerbaghs, especially as Hebrew and Greek terms like "Amen," Messiah, sabbath, angel, bible, and many others are inaccurately or falsely derived from the Hebrew and converted into "bastard" terms powerfully distorting their original significations,[113] and also, Meyer adds, again following Spinoza, because Old Testament Hebrew originally lacked vowel points which likewise renders the familiar rendering of many phrases dubious.[114] Additional obscurity arises because New Testament Greek originally lacked punctuation and accents which were added, often in questionable fashion, much later.[115] The result is a boundless sea of uncertainty and dubious translation in the States Bible and all other current Bibles, eternally irresolvable except via philosophy.

This sea of obscurity all Bible interpreters must traverse to elucidate the intended true meanings. This is possible, holds Meyer, because the true sense of Scripture forms a coherent whole as is "evident from the fact Holy Scripture has God himself for its author who used such scribes as He led by the hand along the path of truth and by whom, in writing it, the spirit of truth was present and in whom not even the shadow of falseness or deceit can be present." God being its author, Scripture, like truth itself, cannot be otherwise than a divinely guaranteed and coherent whole. "Hence, it is entirely certain that everything written in it, is nothing but the purest truth and intention" and has a sacrosanct wholly "exceptional" status, even though the text is so obscure that no theological explanation can ever be secure and whatever philosophy demonstrates as indubitably true,

---

[112] [Meyer], *Philosophie d'Uytleghster*, 37–8; [Meyer], *Philosophia S.Scripturae Interpres*, 31; Meyer, *Philosophy as the Interpreter*, 25, 89; Juffermans, *Drie perspectiven*, 305; Walther, "Biblische Hermeneutik" (1995), 274–5; Lagrée, "Sens et vérité," 84–7.
[113] [Meyer], *Philosophy as the Interpreter*, 80–1.
[114] [Meyer], *Philosophy as the Interpreter*, 78–81.
[115] [Meyer], *Philosophy as the Interpreter*, 82.

being a pronouncement of God, must incontestably be the true signification of whatever biblical passage relates to it. "From all this, it follows very clearly that all interpretations of Scripture which conflict with the truth likewise conflict with the true meaning of Scripture, and consequently are false, incorrect and invalid and must be excluded from the divine meaning." "The sense of Scripture is twofold," as Wilson paraphrases Meyer's argument, "either sensus simpliciter dictus, or verus," so that "the sense of the Scripture is either the sense of the words which they themselves offer or the true meaning of the author in those words. These, says he, are seldom the same but different, yea opposite."[116] Whatever the literal sense of a passage of Scripture, in other words, or whatever theology construes it as meaning, that literal or theological sense is invariably false when and wherever it conflicts with what philosophy teaches, which indeed, as outraged contemporaries objected, is a strange foundation on which to base Scripture's infallibility and sacred status. It is a stance in essence identical to Spinoza's.

Conceding divine authorship of the Bible, as Meyer does, ostensibly acknowledges Scripture's infallibility placing it in a totally different category from all other texts, hence superficially follows the Socinians rather than Spinoza, but this applies only to such interpretations of biblical passages as conform to the dictates of natural philosophy. Beyond this, neither Scripture's "infallibility," nor its special status, possesses significance. Nothing is true except what accords with what is demonstrated by science and philosophy. Consequently, the most striking seeming disparity between Meyer and Spinoza turns out to be more apparent than real. For Spinoza, Scripture must be treated, for purposes of analysis and interpretation, as no different from any other text. For Meyer, supposedly, Scripture has a totally unique status being divinely authored, a claim necessary to his ironic imposture that "Cartesian" philosophy is the "infallible" and only true interpreter of the Bible. But the underlying reality for Meyer and Spinoza, namely that it is always philosophy alone, and never ever theology or church tradition, that unlocks the Bible's true meaning, remains identical.

If God is "the fountain and origin of all truth," then God, avers Meyer, must also be "the founder and guardian of all true philosophy or wisdom," a point already stressed by Wittichius. Anyone interpreting Scripture is thus free to insist on the absolute, unvarying convergence of "true philosophy" with the "true" meaning of Scripture, since truth, as Wittichius and Wolzogen emphasized, cannot contradict truth. Meyer thus feels as free as Spinoza to infer, wherever sound philosophical reasoning clashes with a Scriptural passage's apparent meaning, that the latter is a false reading. Like Spinoza, Meyer stresses the Bible's habit of misleadingly employing anthropomorphic language when describing

---

[116] [Meyer], *Philosophia*, 47; Meyer, *Philosophy as the Interpreter*, 113–16; Wilson, *Scriptures Genuine Interpreter*, 124–5, 197–8; Klever, *Mannen rond Spinoza*, 73.

God's attributes and actions as, for instance, when God "sees" or "hears," "loves" or "is angry."[117]

A further benefit of his exegetical method, holds Meyer, is that we can now unravel the age-old controversy over the sacrament of Holy Communion. From the earliest beginnings of their faith, Christians construed the words "hoc est corpus meum" in conflicting ways, stoking up hatred, division, and strife: Catholics say the bread is truly Christ's body, alleging transubstantiation; Lutherans say the bread is momentarily united with Christ's body and speak of consubstantiation; the Reformed consider the bread just a symbol of Christ's body. All revile and antagonize each other. Theologically, these conflicting views are equivalent in status, each deriving equally from Scripture's words; yet they are irreconcilable. Except for one, the rest must be wrong. For from the laws of nature, it follows that one body cannot be in more than one place at a time, and two different bodies cannot simultaneously occupy the same space. Since nothing derived from Scripture can be true where conflicting with clear and distinct reason, the Calvinist doctrine, it follows, is the sole correct one, and the Catholic and Lutheran doctrines are superstitious absurdities, as Calvinists, also disclosing other contradictions in Catholic and Lutheran theology, rightly contend.[118] Here again, the real point, contemporaries readily understood, was not to endorse Calvin but subject theology entirely to philosophy.

Despite wide differences in style of argument and terminology, the underlying convergence extends also to another dimension of Meyer's case that Scripture is "infallible." Just as, in Spinoza, wrong ideas always in some measure correspond to truth and are merely "inadequate," and less rational than better ones, for Meyer, no matter how impenetrable the Bible's literal meaning generally is, it always corresponds in some abstruse fashion to reality. Here, and in the subtitle of Meyer's book "In which true philosophy is shown to be the infallible norm of interpreting Scripture [in qua, veram philosophiam infallibilem S.Literas interpretandi normam esse]," Meyer is really only adapting Wittichius' revolutionary (Cartesian) maxim that "human knowledge is dual, the vulgar and the accurate, or the common and philosophical [cognitio humana duplex, vulgaris et accurata, sive communis et philosophica]." There exist two different but parallel orders or forms of knowledge that widely diverge but are inseparably connected, ordinary thinking being merely a highly inaccurate, muddled version of what is true.[119]

In rhetoric at least, Meyer binds himself closer to Cartesianism and Cartesians than does Spinoza. Yet, there is no great gulf between Wittichius' professedly Cartesian methods of Bible exegesis and Spinoza's principle that Scripture speaks

---

[117] Spinoza, *Theological-Political Treatise*, 64–5, 241; Meyer, *Philosophy as the Interpreter*, 72, 93, 105, 113–15.

[118] [Meyer], *Philosophy as the Interpreter*, 117–18; Lagrée, "Sens et vérité," 84.

[119] [Meyer], *Philosophie d'Uytleghster*, 69; Preus, *Spinoza*, 56, 60, 65; Israel, *Radical Enlightenment*, 201.

"according to the erroneous opinions of ordinary folk [secundum erroneam vulgi opinionem]," or the *Exercitator*'s contending "philosophy to be the infallible interpreter of Scripture [philosophiam infallibilem esse Scripturae Interpretem]." In Van Mastricht, unsurprisingly, the *Exercitator Paradoxus* is consequently used as a stick with which to flay Wittichius, Van Velthuysen, Burman, and Wolzogen whom he accuses of leading the common people, indeed all society, with their *cognitio humana duplex* down the path to perdition by undermining popular belief in demons, angels, and other spirits besides divine Providence and divine inspiration of Scripture. Teaching the world that "clear and distinct ideas" are the "unica omnis veritatis norma [the only criterion of all truth]," in the end, avers Van Mastricht, leads directly to the *Exercitator Paradoxus* (Meyer) decimating all theology.[120]

Meyer's guiding hermeneutic principle "that between philosophical and theological truth there can be absolutely no conflict [inter veritatem philosophicam et theologicam nullam omnino pugnam esse posse]" removes all contradiction between the theologians' Scripture and "true philosophy."[121] Meyer's essential point, like Spinoza's, is that Scripture's true meaning can never be determined by mainstream Protestant *Sola Scriptura*, Catholic Church authority, or Collegiant principle as propounded by Serrarius and Beelthouwer, prioritizing inspiration via the Holy Ghost. Religious authority Meyer thereby demolishes just as thoroughly as Spinoza. When stressing that "no doctrines of true philosophy are contrary to those of theology [nulla verae philosophiae dogmata theologicis esse contraria],"[122] Meyer is not assigning some special "magical" status to Scripture or distancing himself from Spinoza, but rather following Spinoza as his guide in dissolving all theology into "geometrically" argued philosophy. This underlying parallelism between Spinoza and Meyer (and the Koerbaghs) is reflected in the fact that Meyer here and there alludes directly to Spinoza (without naming him) as his guide in Bible criticism.[123] From recognizing that philosophical and theological truth are identical, mankind derives great benefit rendering superfluous and eventually ending the interminable strife of theologians which has everywhere engendered schism, strife, and repression.[124]

Meyer's *Philosophia*, in short, interposes if not exactly the same gulf between "true meanings" and the "truth of things" as in Spinoza, then an effective approximation. Admittedly, Meyer's Bible exegesis produces an at first glance strikingly different construing of the Prophets. Where, for Spinoza, unlike

---

[120] Mastricht, *Novitatum Cartesianarum Gangraena*, 403–9; Kato, "Petrus van Mastricht," 129, 134–6.
[121] [Meyer], *Philosophy as the Interpreter*, 136–41.
[122] [Meyer], *Philosophia*, 57; Van der Wall, *Mystieke Chiliast*, 478, 483–7.
[123] [Meyer], *Philosophy as the Interpreter*, 231–2.
[124] Moreau, "Principes," 120; Lagrée, "Sens et verité," 84; Lagrée, "Louis Meyer," 32–3; Bordoli, *Ragione e scrittura*, 89, 104.

Maimonides, biblical prophecy arises from exceptional imagination and has no particular relation to truth understood philosophically, but rather brims with contradiction, in Meyer prophetic utterance does emanate from divine inspiration and is a kind of encoded, poetic truth, seemingly drawing Meyer closer to Maimonides than Spinoza. Bible Prophets, holds Meyer, are "God's messengers [Gods gesandten]," but the difference here, once again, is purely rhetorical. For Meyer, Maimonides, and Spinoza, whatever the role of imagination and "inspiration," prophecy remains remote approximation to philosophical truth; all three agree that prophecy ceased after biblical times and can be understood from Scripture alone; all three empty prophecy of everything miraculous, and all three maintain that the Prophets offer supposedly revealed doctrine while its real meaning remains perpetually "obscure."[125]

Were it really true that Meyer's method does not break with but rather reinforces Scriptural "exceptionalism," the massive public controversy surrounding the *Philosophia* would become inexplicable since the main charge fuelling the outcry was that the author deviously reduces Scripture to the level of any other text. Although Meyer does state that "truths and true meanings are everywhere coupled with an indissoluble link [veritates et veros sensus indissolubili nexu ubique copulari]," this in fact again aligns, as the reaction demonstrates, closely with Spinoza's stance because Meyer's claim here applies no more or less to Scripture than to other texts. His principal thesis is not that the Bible is wholly exceptional with unique truth value but rather that the "text (and God behind it) cannot teach anything that is opposed to reason." This is a "core idea of Meyer's rationalist hermeneutic," but does not mean he aligns here with Maimonides, or that "directly contrary" to Meyer's "claim, Spinoza will urge a historical analysis of the context, which alone can reveal any author's intention and meaning."[126]

"The books of the Old and New Testament," holds Meyer, "are the infallible Word of almighty God." But both the terms "infallible" and "almighty," here exude a particular "philosophical" resonance. He means "infallibility of Scripture," Meyer explains, "following in the footsteps of Descartes," in striving to reach the first foundation of truth by first rejecting everything doubtful or uncertain. In theology, one can disagree about or doubt everything except one thing—Scripture's infallibility. "For if one also wished to do away with this, one would jump beyond theology's limits and need to be convinced with arguments drawn from elsewhere, rather than theological arguments." By exalting Scripture's "infallibility," Meyer's clear purpose is to drag theology into the dock and keep it there, making deliberately subversive use of the universal Protestant (and Socinian) principle that Scripture grounds all theological truth. It was a tactic all the more

---

[125] Preus, *Spinoza*, 173–4, 196; Chalier, *Spinoza lecteur*, 135–9, 141–2.
[126] [Meyer], *Philosophy as the Interpreter*, 238; Moreau, "Principes," 124; Curley, "Notes," 79, 81; Preus, *Spinoza*, 54.

effective in that the Cartesians—few if any of whom considered the anonymous author of the *Philosophia* a genuine "Cartesian"—constantly stressed that philosophical truth and "truth of Scripture *are* equivalent," that true (i.e. Cartesian) philosophy is just as infallible as Scripture, placing philosophy and Scripture in perfect unison.

Mimicking Cartesian rhetoric helped Meyer underline the Bible's imperfections and obscurities. Far from being inconsistent, this enables him to insinuate without directly affirming the absurdity, as he and his friends saw it, of theological polemics and what society generally believes. Meyer's "infallibility" of Scripture, what he calls the unquestioned "foundation of all theology [grondvest van alle theologie]," is meant to revolutionize the foundations of scholarly and moral authority and demonstrate, in conjunction with Spinoza, the spuriousness of theological claims. Just as the jurist can do nothing without first stipulating the text of the law, "so also the entirety of theology is built on God's Word, and hence nothing must be brought before the theologian, or accepted from him, except what is drawn from there." Such elaborate imposture, breathing aversion to theologians just as fierce as that of the Koerbaghs and Spinoza, was inherent in the Radical Enlightenment from its very commencement in the 1650s down to the early nineteenth century.

Admittedly, the general convergence between Spinoza and Meyer's argument that "philosophy" is the "infallible rule" by which to interpret Scripture involves an element of divergence too. In the *TTP*, Spinoza without mentioning Meyer anywhere by name, is undoubtedly commenting on and nuancing the work of his friend. Where Spinoza distinguishes between use of reason to reconstruct biblical meaning from reasoning to evaluate the truth value of biblical meanings, seeing these as two quite distinct philosophical investigations, Meyer often merges these and even pronounces them identical. In Scripture uniquely, asserts Meyer, the true sense of the text (*sensus verus*) always corresponds to what is true (*veritas*) since God is omniscient and does not lie.[127] For Meyer, consequently, beyond countless minor discrepancies due to scribal error over the centuries, there are many apparent major obscurities and contradictions in meaning between biblical passages, but, in theory at least, no real ones, whereas for Spinoza seeming contradictions like the impossible chronology 1 Kings 6 offers, and the proportions 1 Kings 7 gives for the building of the Temple of Solomon 480 years after the Exodus from Egypt, reflect the imperfect and confused character of the entire biblical text.[128] This nuance distinguishes the text criticism of Meyer and Spinoza but not the philosophical premises underpinning their respective exegetical systems. Theology, both agree, is no independent source of truth. Only philosophy teaches what is true. Both consider the Bible a purely human and secular text,

---

[127] Meyer, *Philosophy as the Interpreter*, 96–8.
[128] Spinoza, *Theological-Political Treatise*, 34–5, 133.

meaningful judgements about which are made exclusively by those thinking philosophically.

The main difference is more one of depth of understanding than basic premises. Spinoza's elaborate theory of what religion is, and how and why religion construes the world as it does, forges a new science of contextual Bible criticism, analysing usage and intended meanings, and extrapolating from context, using reason as an analytical tool without trying, or pretending, to uncover philosophical truth embedded in Scriptural expressions. Meyer, by contrast, is less concerned with showing what religion is than demonstrating how Scripture's allegories and doubtful passages can be aligned with philosophical truth. Where the Bible, for Meyer, is a rhetorical storehouse the claims of which can be shown, however obscurely, to correspond to philosophical truth, Spinoza offers a much profounder demonstration that Scripture is not in any meaningful sense a guide to reality, though one can extract from it rudiments of moral philosophy; like Meyer, he still accepts that thinking theologically, being steeped in Scripture, where carefully policed and shepherded, can be a useful start to approaching truth philosophically. Both equally ascribe to religion regulated by the state a useful contributory role in upholding the rudiments of morality and discipline among an ignorant and ill-informed majority.[129]

Bracketing Meyer together with Spinoza in a category opposing Collegiants and Socinians as well as major churches and mainstream Cartesians also explains Rieuwertsz's decision, in 1674, to reissue the *Philosophia* bound together with the *Tractatus Theologico-Politicus* and why contemporaries outside the Netherlands often assumed the two books were from the same pen. Spinoza and Meyer equally hoped "the boundaries of philosophy will be extended far and wide by those who will tread in [Descartes'] footsteps," ensuring the new philosophy, the only "torch for the world of letters," enables men to reach the "highest felicity" possible.[130] While it is an exaggeration to claim, as Klever did, that Meyer's "book [...] is completely in line with the theories developed in Spinoza's book," the divergences, though not insignificant, are far less fundamental than some contend, having mainly to do with the complexities of Spinoza's historico-critical method of text analysis which Meyer, despite his long-cultivated expertise in language studies, grammar, and text criticism mostly fails to adopt.

---

[129] Meyer, *Philosophy as the Interpreter*, 238–9; Wolzogen, *De Scripturarum Interprete*, 274; Strauss, *Spinoza's Critique of Religion*, 170; Moreau, "Principes," 125–6.

[130] Meyer, *Philosophy as the Interpreter*, 240.

25
Spinoza Subverts Hobbes

25.i Hobbes, Spinoza, and the Gospels

The general principles guiding Spinoza's text criticism paralleled those he applies to the study of nature generally, so that, at least in Spinoza's terms, Bible criticism is conceived as simultaneously "scientific" and "historical" in a fundamental new sense diverging from the approaches of Grotius and Hobbes as well as Bacon, Locke, and Newton. Meanwhile, Hobbes' political thought had powerfully penetrated the Dutch republican milieu, during the 1660s, exerting a considerable impact clearly evident in the work of the De La Courts, the Koerbaghs, Lambert van Velthuysen (1622–85), and Spinoza. However, in responding to Hobbes, key passages of the *TTP*, the *Tractatus Politicus*, and the *Ethics* reveal a wide gulf between Spinoza and Hobbes.

Starting in the mid-1660s, and unfolding down to his last years, Spinoza's preoccupation with Hobbes was an important and lasting aspect of his biography as well as the wider Dutch intellectual scene, not least because their two names came to be regularly bracketed together from the 1670s onwards (more to Hobbes' reputational disadvantage, it must be said, than to Spinoza's), with many contemporaries and much recent scholarship presenting them, somewhat misleadingly, as closely linked in supposedly unleashing comparably pernicious and outrageous viewpoints on the European scene.

Following its first Dutch edition, in 1647, at a time when Hobbes' name was much less under hostile scrutiny than later, Hobbes' *De Cive* [On the Citizen] (1642) was a well-known text in the Republic, and, during the 1650s, the Utrecht regent, Van Velthuysen, emerged as a leading promotor of Hobbes' influence. From early on, Hobbes (Figure 25.1) was a powerful voice in Dutch intellectual life, and Spinoza possessed a copy of *De Cive* in his private library.[1] However, Hobbes' chief impact on Spinoza ensued later, in the wake of the Dutch version of the *Leviathan* translated by a close ally of the Koerbaghs and Spinoza, the anti-Orangist, anti-monarchical Abraham van Berkel (1639–86). Published in 1667, the translation's early reception exactly coincided with the years when Spinoza was composing the *TTP*.

---

[1] Weststeijn, *Commercial Republicanism*, 148–9; Field, *Potentia*, 150.

Figure 25.1 *Portrait of Thomas Hobbes* (1588–1679) from Le Boë Sylvius, *Totius Medicinae Idea Nova*. IAS Spinoza Research Collection.

Though Hobbes and Spinoza continually came to be bracketed together in hostile fashion by contemporaries, careful comparison not only complicates the comparison but reveals a wide gap across a range of issues to the extent that Hobbes and Spinoza can be said really to represent a battle of opposites more than an allied pair. If theologians were increasingly unhappy with how Hobbes (and La Peyrère) dealt with theological matters, Hobbes never rejects revelation or denies divine providence outright even when insisting revelation only possesses the force of law when the sovereign declares it to be revelation. Neither does Hobbes deny the possibility of miracles, or that salvation lies in faith in Jesus Christ.[2] Even when at his most provocative and idiosyncratic, Hobbes is generally more ambiguous than Spinoza and, especially before 1670, hostility towards him was more sporadic. For Hobbes everything concerning God remains the sphere of religious authority as endorsed by the sovereign, that is the state church. Spinoza flatly rejects such positions and certainly endorsed Van Berkel's deliberate twisting of Hobbes' meaning in his rendering of the *Leviathan* when negating Hobbes' assertion that the sovereign, through the state church, is entitled to suppress

---

[2] Hobbes, *Leviathan* iii, 682–8; Fukuoka, *Sovereign and the Prophets*, 73–5.

scientific or philosophical views even when these are true: "for disobedience may lawfully be punished in them, that against the laws teach even true philosophy."[3]

Hobbes' entire construct of sovereignty endorsing unrestricted imposition of state church doctrine is indeed fundamentally anathema to Spinoza for whom Christ was neither resurrected nor a saviour. If churches and churchmen know nothing about God, in Spinoza's view kings are even more damagingly ignorant and misinformed: God is accessible to mankind exclusively via reason. Nor could Hobbes support his original and distinctive readings of Scripture by referring to the Hebrew, for Spinoza the exclusive key to unlocking Scripture's meaning. If Spinoza "disarmed the religious interpreters who would enforce conformity,"[4] nothing remotely equivalent could be said of Hobbes.

Hobbes' name became infamous long before Spinoza's and, undoubtedly, after 1670 Hobbes was frequently considered the senior partner, and by no means only in Britain. Late seventeenth-century commentators regularly attribute what was widely envisaged as growth in infidelity and disbelief to the joint impact of "Hobbes and Spinoza," invariably in that order. But as the realities of Europe's spiritual crisis increasingly made themselves felt from the 1680s onwards, there were solid reasons why this conventional order of names came to be seen by some as in need of reversal. The kind of new-style English freethinker now infiltrating society, as described by the Anglican clergyman Matthias Earbery, in 1697, perceives Hobbes, England's chief founder of subversive deism, as indispensable to every budding deist, "indeed a very pretty fellow, and not easily scared with religious bugbears." However, the author of the *TTP* "deserves rather to be esteemed his [i.e. Hobbes'] tutor than his scholar, he has such a knack of exposing all the defects of those books you call the Scriptures, with that strength of reason and solidity of judgment that apparently shews it to be the work of the Incomparable Spinosa." If Hobbes opened the door, according to Earbery's allegorical account of deism, it is Spinoza, not Hobbes, who "turned" this archetypal immature freethinker "into a perfect Deist," the rebellious dissident who with unprecedented effrontery "threw away his Bible, and set up this book [the *TTP*] in the room of it."[5]

For Grotius, Bacon, Locke, and Newton, and—rhetorically at least—also Hobbes, the Bible remains divinely inspired, so that the supernatural, and what is "above reason," remain unquestionably real and ultimately preside, ensuring difficulty and theological ambiguity on such fundamental topics as revelation, divine providence, Christology, and the Trinity. Here again one encounters Spinoza's commitment to science in a comprehensively modern sense radically

---

[3] Hobbes, *Leviathan* iii, 1102; Fukuoka, *Sovereign and the Prophets*, 131–5; Parker, "Reception," 291–2.

[4] Goetschel, *Spinoza's Modernity*, 53–4, 56–7; Preus, *Spinoza and the Irrelevance*, p. x; Laerke, *Spinoza*, 72, 172; Rosenthal, "Spinoza's 'Republican Idea'," 403–4.

[5] Earbery, *Deism Examin'd and Confuted*, 3–4, 7.

different from that of most contemporaries. It is a fundamental principle with Spinoza that natural processes are shaped exclusively by physical motion, mechanistic cause and effect, with the consequence that *a priori* there can never be any miraculous episode or element in history or the present, no wonders of any kind in the past or at any time, no oracles nor any human spokesman interpreting the supernatural for the rest of society, a stance contrasting strikingly not just with that of Descartes, Boyle, Newton, and Locke, but Hobbes too, all mind and human beliefs being systematically incorporated into an indivisible, all-encompassing natural process.

Hobbes does not deny but rather expressly affirms that God "sent into the world his son Jesus Christ, to redeem mankind from their sins and bring them into his everlasting kingdom, to be saved for evermore."[6] Whereas Hobbes invokes Jesus Christ as "the Messiah" and, albeit with some equivocation, salvages the Trinity, Spinoza never refers to "Christ" as "Jesus," never calls him "the Son," never the "Messiah," and never "the redeemer." Where Hobbes' Jesus performs miracles, and is in part a prophet and part God himself, Spinoza's Christ is not God, nor a prophet, nor performs miracles since "everything narrated in Scripture actually happened naturally."[7] Spinoza not only rejects the Trinity, Christ's divinity, and the Resurrection privately, telling Oldenburg later that he simply did not comprehend what these doctrines mean, but in print never classifies the biblical figure "Jesus" as a sacred or special being. "Christ" *is* clearly central in Spinoza's framework and does teach men "the way of salvation," but remains an inter-faith pedagogue devoid of all theological significance representing an eternal principle of Nature, "the wisdom of God," and "the wisdom that is above human wisdom."[8] Spinoza's "Christ was sent not to teach the Jews alone but all of humanity," and hence "taught only universal truths," "the universal law alone," but since, in his philosophy, no one can "be sent," the phrase is clearly a metaphor for his natural appearance as a teacher. "Christ taught" truth, Spinoza several times reminds readers, but introduced no rules, laws, or ceremonies, and definitely no "sacred law" separate from the civil law as Spinoza says "my opponents" claim; what Christ the teacher disseminated was primarily "moral doctrine" available to all everywhere and at any time, teaching it to all without reference to faith, rituals, and ceremonies, and without authorizing texts, baptism, Christological doctrine, churches or churchmen.[9]

Spinoza's treatment of the New Testament, if much briefer, is assuredly no less startling than his treatment of the Old. If Christ's Apostles possess high spiritual

---

[6] Hobbes, *Leviathan* iii, 760–73; Osier, "L'Herméneutique," 338–9, 343–4; Lasker, "Reflections," 62–3.
[7] Spinoza, *Theological-Political Treatise*, 90; Osier, "L'Herméneutique," 341; Fukuoka, *Sovereign and the Prophets*, 255.
[8] Spinoza, *Theological-Political Treatise*, 19; Carlisle, *Spinoza's Religion*, 109–11, 180–1.
[9] Spinoza, *Theological-Political Treatise*, 64, 70, 103; Hubbeling, *Spinoza*, 102–3.

status according to Hobbes, as do the Gospels named after them, reaching back to Christ's time, for Spinoza the Apostles' sole positive significance is that they followed Christ in propagating his worldly teaching, albeit each, he explains, taught wisdom in his own way, just as all teachers have their individual styles "even in the mathematical science whose truths are indubitable." Consequently, many things are asserted in the Gospels, he contends, "which from the point of view of religion we are now able to dispense with."[10] Furthermore, Spinoza's "Apostles" evinced as many, or more, reprehensibly negative as positive effects. Given the legal and general context in which he wrote, and the Koerbaghs' experiences, here Spinoza needed to show exemplary caution. Yet, while the "spirit of Christ" receives high status, the same can hardly be said for the Apostles and Gospels. Up to a point, Spinoza acknowledges the Apostles as "prophets" but since in the *TTP* (chapter II) prophets lack knowledge of natural things and "rarely" receive direct inspiration from God, basing their admonitions on "imagination," not knowledge, their prophetic role could not, of itself, secure them any great importance. The relevant issue for Spinoza is whether the Apostles composed "their Epistles" as private individuals or rather as learned teachers [doctores]. The latter was the case, he determines, so that, when conveying Christ's teaching, it was "as teachers, not prophets, that the Apostles preached." When Paul proclaims a "command from God, he does not mean an instruction or command God revealed to him but simply the teachings Christ dispensed to his disciples on the mountain."[11]

"Since the Apostles' Epistles, one must conclude, were composed by light of natural reason alone" without any divine inspiration, the Gospels inevitably reveal basic disagreements arising from "contention between the Apostles [ex contentione Apostolorum]" and the task each had "to teach and admonish as each of them judged best." Not only does Scripture prove "each of the Apostles chose his own particular way," but the Apostles were always "in the same position as other teachers, for teachers have their own individual styles of teaching." Hence, when teaching Christ's moral lessons, the vital strand of his teaching, the Apostles all taught the same thing, albeit geared to the understanding of the uninformed, but whenever they ranged out to more philosophical matters, "they completely disagreed about the foundations" of religion, as one would expect. Thus, Paul claims redemption comes from faith alone "and that no one is justified by works," while "James in his Gospel teaches that a person is justified by works and not by faith alone." Disagreement over the basics prevailed throughout from Christ's death onwards, holds Spinoza, so that "many disputes and schisms have arisen because different Apostles constructed religion on different foundations."[12] If there is a

---

[10] Spinoza, *Theological-Political Treatise*, 161, 169; Osier, "L'Herméneutique," 338.
[11] Spinoza, *Oeuvres* iii, 410–13; Spinoza, *Theological-Political Treatise*, 155–6.
[12] Spinoza, *Oeuvres* iii, 424–6; Lagrée, *Spinoza et le débat*, 208.

uniquely precious and authentic Christian ethics, no genuinely Christian theology ever existed or could exist.

For Spinoza, the Gospels' fundamental incoherence stems also from the fact that the New Testament books originated long after Christ's death at different times and were composed by different individuals.[13] The Gospels, Koerbagh had already stressed, were "only written down long after [Christ] died," and reveal "contradictions" in their accounts of Jesus' genealogy; and while "it is firmly believed the Greek Scriptures were written by those whose names stand at the beginning of the books," which the Koerbaghs and Spinoza denied, "some believe Matthew wrote his book in Hebrew." The Koerbaghs say nothing about the other three Evangelists' original language,[14] but for Spinoza all the Gospels are incomprehensible without Hebrew expertise because their authors were "Hebrews" and, while propagated in other languages, their sayings "are full of Hebrew idioms."[15] Fundamental reform of Christianity is urgently needed, Spinoza agrees with the Koerbaghs (or more likely they with him), as "disputes and schisms have ceaselessly disturbed the church ever since Apostolic times, and will surely never cease to trouble it, until religion is finally separated from philosophical theories and reduced to the extremely few, very simple dogmas Christ taught to his own."[16]

"Christ" figures in Spinoza's thought exclusively as a universal non-sacred moral teacher. What remains unclear is whether he ever identifies his "Christ," the pedagogue with the actual historical figure, Jesus. Because Spinoza always calls him just "Christ," he seems to imply, discreetly, that the historical personage described in the New Testament is not the Christ, or that there is no particular correlation between the two. Spinoza's Christ is a transcendent image, supreme teacher, the "very mouth of God," and ultimate symbol of earthly wisdom and reason and supreme moral example to men, the Jesus of Socinian tradition, that is the best human conceivable, reworked into an extreme rationalist. Like the Koerbaghs, Spinoza views him as a human who "truly has within him the spirit of Christ," that is not a person believing doctrines, performing rituals, invoking commandments or reciting prayers, but one with "salutary opinions and a true conception of living, and truly happy," belonging to no faith or religion other than Spinoza's "true religion." Christ indisputably occupies a "unique place [...] in Spinoza's thinking"; but his Christ is a unremittingly subversive construct unconnected with the churches' Jesus.[17]

If Hobbes takes "faith in Christ" more seriously than Spinoza, Spinoza takes the Scriptural text itself, including the New Testament, more seriously than Hobbes,

---

[13] Spinoza, *Theological-Political Treatise*, 168–9.
[14] Koerbagh, *A Light Shining*, 167, 289–91; Fukuoka, *Sovereign and the Prophets*, 211.
[15] Spinoza, *Theological-Political Treatise*, 100.
[16] Spinoza, *Theological-Political Treatise*, 161; Nadler, *Book Forged in Hell*, 173–5.
[17] Lagrée, *Spinoza et le débat*, 26, 77, 91; Israel, "Introduction" to Spinoza, *Theological-Political Treatise*, pp. xvii–xx; Hunter, *Radical Protestantism in Spinoza's Thought*, 56.

not just as a historical and cultural record, and product of a complex textual genealogy, though that is crucial, but also, where the text is rightly understood and its manner of accommodating the ignorant notions of the common people of biblical times allowed for, a precious source of human wisdom, of "true religion" in the sense of laying out the path to justice, charity and uprightness, and the good of society. Hobbes' "true religion" based on Jesus Christ by contrast, is very different. "The points of doctrine concerning the kingdom of God," held Hobbes, "have so great an influence on the kingdom of man, as not to be determined but by them that under God have the sovereign power."[18] "True Religion," for Hobbes, is whichever set of doctrines and style of belief and confession the sovereign, king, or commonwealth proclaims the sovereign ruler's will, hence remains firmly tied to his sovereignty-orientated, monarchist political theory.[19] For Spinoza, by contrast, denying the ruler true sovereignty and any role in determining "true religion," Scripture's meaning is of paramount significance. Nor, from his universal, democratic, and anti-monarchical perspective, can true sovereignty have any connection with any ruler's will.

This divide, moreover, operates to ensure another—their glaringly contrasting understanding of the meaning of "superstition." For Hobbes, the difference between "true religion" and "superstition" is that one is "publicly allowed" and the other is not, while religious belief is what one believes oneself and "superstition" what those of other persuasions believe.[20] Since Hobbes' "true religion" is the choice of the sovereign ruler and those supporting the sovereign, religious leaders justifiably devise rules and laws to extend the sovereign's sway and control.[21] For Spinoza, the difference between "superstition" and "true religion" is that the latter is based on justice and charity while superstition is based on ignorance, error, and fabricated doctrine as exemplified by the teaching of all the main faiths, Anglican, Catholic, Lutheran, Calvinist, Jewish, and Muslim and, universally, by the generally intolerant religious policies of kings. The church Spinoza deemed closest to "true religion" was that of the rationalist Collegiants of his friends, Jelles, Balling, and Rieuwertsz which, due to its Anti-Trinitarianism and rejection of traditional Christology remained clandestine and illegal.

25.ii Hobbes and Spinoza on "Freedom"

A no less yawning rift between Hobbes and Spinoza lodges in their vying conceptions of freedom. Because Hobbes' "true religion" is what the sovereign

---

[18] Hobbes, *Leviathan* iii, 708; Lagrée, *Spinoza et le débat*, 11, 138, 205, 235.
[19] Hobbes, *Leviathan* ii, 446–8 and iii, 780–4; Hunter, *Radical Protestantism in Spinoza's Thought*, 86.
[20] Hobbes, *Leviathan* ii, 86 and 272–3; Preus, *Spinoza and the Irrelevance*, 171–2; Israel, "How Does Spinoza's 'Democracy' Differ?," 236–7.
[21] Hobbes, *Leviathan* ii, 164–8; Fukuoka, *Sovereign and the Prophets*, 170.

decrees, Spinoza felt something approaching antipathy to Hobbes' political theory on several levels. Among the most vital points of Spinoza's approach is that a subject's acting in obedience to the sovereign is compatible with human freedom only when the "*salus* of the whole people, not that of the ruler, is the supreme law." Someone venerating and loyally following the king or autocrat simply because he is king or effective ruler, thirsting for royal favour or glory, is not a free man but a slave. In Spinoza's philosophy only acting in accord with "reason" makes men free, whereas for Hobbes it is absence of personal constraints on the individual that defines "freedom." Accordingly, for Hobbes a glory-seeking warrior, alcoholic, or crony of Charles II is acting freely in abandoning himself or herself to lust, thirst for war, or excessive alcohol, whereas for Spinoza one is never acting freely when indulging in passions harmful to oneself or others.[22] Unrestrained venting of brute appetite is, rather, the epitome of "bondage." In a note at the close of the *TTP*, Spinoza remarks, presumably because he considers wars always damaging to society as a whole, and usually provoked by kings, that "contrary to what Hobbes says, reason recommends peace without reservation," adding that while in discussion and writing the free man should promote only what "reason" advises, he should never act divisively or be conspiratorial but always strictly obey the law.[23] "Contrary to what Hobbes says" should be regarded as among the regular, indispensable keys to Spinoza's entire biography.

Another striking divide between the two great dissident figures concerns the history of the Scriptures. For Spinoza as for Hobbes, there remain shreds of Deuteronomy and other fragments of the Pentateuch genuinely deriving from Moses' teaching. But this remnant counts for less in Spinoza than Hobbes where the residual core is strongly affirmed and associated with the sovereign (a feature again subverted by the republican-minded Van Berkel in translation).[24] Where Hobbes deems this precious Mosaic core a fundamental pillar of the state and social stability, Spinoza empties it of both sacred status and truth content, deeming it as jumbled and incoherent as any other biblical fragment—and in its view of God still more depleted. Whatever its sense, this remnant, though thoroughly worthy of scholarly inquiry, remains as devoid of "truth" as any other segment, and devoid too of continuing political or theological significance, leaving Spinoza remote from Bacon and Locke, but scarcely less so from Hobbes.[25]

For contemporaries, Hobbes and Spinoza polarized most strikingly on the question of miracles. For Hobbes, there are miracles men must venerate. For Spinoza there are not. Where for Spinoza there is no such thing as a miracle and never has been, Hobbes makes no such sweeping claim. Assuredly, Hobbes too

---

[22] Kisner, *Spinoza on Human Freedom*, 52–6; Garrett, *Nature and Necessity*, 488–90.
[23] Spinoza, *Theological-Political Treatise*, 201, 271–2; Garrett, "'Promising' Ideas," 195; Laerke, *Spinoza and the Freedom*, 242–3.
[24] James, *Spinoza on Philosophy*, 167; Fukuoka, *Sovereign and the Prophets*, 84, 131–5.
[25] Spinoza, *Theological-Political Treatise*, 63, 128–9; Hobbes, *Leviathan* iii, 592–3; Parker, "Spinoza, Locke," 177.

frowns on "this aptitude of mankind to give too hasty beleefe to pretended Miracles," and, like many Protestant writers at the time, scoffs at numerous miracles proclaimed by Catholics, but nowhere does he deny the reality of biblical miracles as such, or that these "signified the Admirable works of God, and therefore they are also called Wonders." Even if, privately, one might doubt a particular miracle, as regards any miracle proclaimed by the sovereign, he insists, one's "private reason must submit to the public" in politics, education, and the law, a highly un-Spinozistic proviso sincerely meant or not.[26]

The difference was highlighted by the Cambridge don Thomas Browne (c.1654–1741), fellow of St John's College, in an anti-Spinoza booklet published in several editions rebuking the "deist" Charles Blount for designedly bracketing Hobbes and Spinoza close together on the question of miracles. "Spinoza indeed is the great patron of this assertion," asserts Browne, "viz., That there is no such thing as a miracle, if we take the word to signifie a work above or beside nature." Hobbes, on the other hand, Browne points out, flatly contradicting Blount, was "point blank of a contrary mind." All that is required to clear Hobbes of suspicion of propagating the same view as Spinoza is to examine what he wrote on the subject "and we shall soon find that he admits and supposes miracles" in that "very sense, wherein he is produced" in Charles Blount's *Miracles, No Violations of the Laws of Nature* (London, 1683) "to deny them."[27] Browne was entirely right: Spinoza expressly rules out miracles; Hobbes asserts them.

Hobbes, furthermore, glides over the supernatural encountered in biblical stories preferring not to analyse Scripture's *supernaturalia* in a detailed, systematic manner, marginalizing the supernatural rather than making it a focus of attention while insisting the essential drift, not the detail, of Scripture "giveth the true light."[28] If no zealous "defender of revealed religion" or the authenticity of biblical prophecy, neither does he attempt to reconstruct the beliefs and thought processes at work or convey the outlook and religious culture of those who produced the texts. Also, Hobbes offers no theory of biblical prophecy. All told, held Leo Strauss, in 1930, "Hobbes is much less interested than is Spinoza in a specific Bible science."[29] Toland, who with his elaborate exegetical style aimed at systematically dislodging traditional belief, accordingly adopted a specifically "Spinozist hermeneutical methodology," and *not* a Hobbesian one.[30]

Spinoza's Bible hermeneutics, like his epistemology generally, is empirical on every level, seeking to focus squarely on the facts, the reality of the text, critically inferring meaning only from linguistic evidence. Yet, at the same time, it relies on essentially *a priori* philosophical demonstration much like Spinoza's "knowledge

---

[26] Hobbes, *Leviathan* iii, 692–6; James, *Spinoza on Learning*, 90.   [27] Browne, *Miracles*, 3–4.
[28] Walther, "Biblische Hermeneutik" (1992), 636–7, 654; Malcolm, *Aspects of Hobbes*, 536.
[29] Strauss, *Spinoza's Critique of Religion*, 104; Popkin, "Spinoza and Bible Criticism," 389, 395–6, 399; James, *Spinoza on Learning*, 91.
[30] Lucci, *Scripture and Deism*, 104–7; Hudson, *Enlightenment and Modernity*, 132–3.

of the second kind" in the *Ethics*, the entire procedure being underpinned by his prior claim that the Bible text abounds in stories, parables, examples of limited knowledge, and myths constituting an impressionistic, incomplete, and defective grasp of reality rooted in purely human imagination, assumptions and interpretation of things, a general inference rooted in empirical, first and second order findings following Spinoza's declared scientific method.[31] Although biblical universals are historically determined and hence poetic concepts, inexact, limited, and vague, and it remains impossible to infer from the biblical text "what God is" or how he "provides for all things," nevertheless such universals are not arbitrary significations but meaningful albeit inadequate approximations to the "truth of things."

Given Hobbes' assigning ultimate authority over the public church and the public interpretation and status of Scripture to the monarch, and supports government censorship to suppress dissent, subjecting "private" reason to public requirement, his approach is remote from Spinoza's additionally in showing far less concern for freedom of thought and expression, and for freeing contemporary states, institutions, and laws from the grip of publicly endorsed (establishment) theology and theologians. In striking contrast to Spinoza (and Blount and Toland), Hobbes seeks neither to emancipate men from "priestcraft" nor from oppressive censorship. The latter required more actively countering the "superstition" of the multitude, the veneration felt by most for religious authority, symbols, and doctrine. Bible study, for Spinoza, is hence indissolubly linked to secularization of society, emancipation and the quest for personal freedom in a way that for Hobbes it is not. Early in the *TTP*, Spinoza affirms the "natural right" of the individual person. This extends as far as one's desire and power extend, and "no one is obliged by the right of nature to live according to the views of another: rather, each is the defender of his own liberty."[32] Believing in miracles and "wonders," for Spinoza, but not Hobbes, constitutes an ever-present threat to state, society, *and* individual pursuit of happiness. Spinoza inaugurates a process of elucidation and enlightenment intended to free both individuals and society in the sense of erasing theology from men's outlook, an enterprise which Hobbes simply has no part in.[33]

Both historically and in recent studies in history of political thought there lingers a long-entrenched tradition of viewing Spinoza's political thought as essentially marginal and largely derivative from Hobbes, of insisting on Spinoza being a "disciple" of Hobbes. Although this view has been objected to at least since

---

[31] This is meant in part as a criticism of Schliesser's account of Spinoza's theory of knowledge and approach to science, see Schliesser, "Angels and Philosophers," 509–11, 514 and to Schliesser, "Spinoza and the Philosophy of Science."

[32] Spinoza, *Theological-Political Treatise*, 10–11; Verbeek, *Spinoza's Theologico-Political Treatise*, 47; Fukuoka, *Sovereign and the Prophets*, 350–5.

[33] Nadler, *Spinoza's Heresy*, 34–6; Rosenthal, "Miracles, Wonder," 231, 245.

Ignac Einhorn's *Spinozas Staatslehre* (1851), the idea of Spinoza's Hobbesian derivativeness and marginality is so deeply entrenched in the accepted canon of history of political thought that it remains even today still a major stumbling block, resulting in Spinoza's striking continuing marginalization from textbooks on the history of political theory and the reading public's awareness. The basic error lies in assuming that because Spinoza, like the De La Courts and Van Velthuysen, took a keen interest in Hobbes, that he was following in his footsteps in some fundamental way when what Spinoza was actually doing was devoting considerable effort to systematically overturning Hobbes, much as he subverts Bacon, Boyle, and Descartes. For Hobbes' approach, Spinoza substitutes a contrary conception reflected in Bible criticism, and their diverging views on the relationship of philosophy to theology, scholarship and science, and especially in their political and social thought.

This is not to deny, of course, that Hobbes was "a major influence" on radical thinking and the early Enlightenment generally.[34] But given Hobbes' pervasive monarchism, subordination of religion to the sovereign, and relative lack of concern for toleration and freedom of thought, it is plainly absurd to claim Hobbes precedes or parallels Spinoza in the emergence of the "Radical Enlightenment." If the radical Enlightenment is to be assigned the centrality it needs to receive in any historically accurate and meaningful discussion of the Enlightenment, then the contrasts between Hobbes and Spinoza must be acknowledged more fully and plainly. If one closely compares the two on religious authority, censorship, *supernaturalia*, demonology, miracles, revelation, Scripture's integrity and Christianity's beginnings, there simply are no convincing grounds for bracketing Hobbes and Spinoza together and the same applies to the essentials of "general will," natural law, contract, and democratic republican political theory.

Where Hobbes has a "negative" conception of liberty as freedom from constraints, Spinoza proposes a "positive" conception, offering a freedom lodged in activity, striving, discussion and collaborating. Because Hobbes' liberty requires only protection and internal security, shielding men as far as possible from internecine strife, hatred and conflict, from the fear and insecurity attending such internecine strife, Hobbes' political orientation tends towards strong monarchy, a powerful executive and unimpeded state power, with sovereignty firmly detached from and above society (and the churches). For this reason, Hobbes, or at least Hobbes unamended by the De La Courts, Van Berkel, the Koerbaghs, and Van den Enden, was not, and never could be, an integral part of the Radical Enlightenment. Spinoza's political model is dramatically different, not just due to the historical circumstance that Spinoza lived in the Dutch Republic at the height

---

[34] Malcom, *Aspects of Hobbes*, 536; Springborg, "Enlightenment of Thomas Hobbes," 528.

of the "True Freedom," but because his "ex solo Libertatis amore [from love of liberty alone]" embraces a freedom that is personal and alert to oneself but always joined to a universal project linking us all with each other, rooted in rigorous self-criticism and criticism of others but also cooperation and assisting each other. The path to human happiness involves pursuing an active, conscious "love of liberty" fending off vices, indolence, and bad passions, and focusing one's critical-analytical intellect on the virtues personal and collective. It is a part-Stoic, part-Epicurean conception of the moral self, and of philosophy as such, inseparably tied to freedom of expression and debate, and freedom of political judgement, locating sovereignty in society itself instead of above it. Spinoza lodges sovereignty in the "common good" of society, retaining and transferring as much as possible of the individual and group freedoms of the "state of nature" to his ideal democratic republic. Here, Spinoza stands closer to Rousseau than to Hobbes;[35] however, in postulating a hard, lonely path to personal liberty, and a still more arduous path to collective "freedom," Spinoza stands as distant from Rousseau as from Hobbes.

Suggesting Spinoza was ever basically a follower or disciple of any other thinker, even fleetingly, is in any case difficult to reconcile with the general thrust of his biography and attitudes. Any such claim would require much incisive supporting argument because so many different intellectual traditions converge in his thinking and because of his highly independent and confident temperament. Surveying his life and general outlook reveals Spinoza's attitude to the whole gallery of humanity's great thinkers from Plato and Aristotle onwards down to Descartes to be always stunningly dismissive, making the very notion of his being anyone's follower or disciple in any real sense highly problematic even before investigating more closely. It is hence unsurprising that a close reading of Spinoza's political and social theory confirms that while he does indeed regularly employ Hobbes as a source, using his key ideas, like those of Machiavelli and Grotius, as starting points for his own positions, his conscious aim in his political thought is to overturn Hobbes' framework. He consistently reworks it into something quite alien to what Hobbes intended both in practical consequences and intellectual implications.

Long familiar with *De Cive* (1642), it is possible that Spinoza was familiar with little or nothing else by Hobbes until as late as 1667. Much of Hobbes' oeuvre, including the *Leviathan* (1651) may well have remained unknown to him until after the Second Anglo-Dutch War ended. But whether or not that is the case, most of Hobbes' writings suddenly became readily available in the Dutch context at the very time Spinoza was in the midst of composing his *TTP*. A key edition, Hobbes' *Opera philosophica* appeared in Latin at Amsterdam in 1668, containing

---

[35] Vernière, *Spinoza et la pensée française*, 485.

a wide range of his work—*De Corpore* (1655), the *Dialogus physicus* (1661), *Problemata physica*, and *De Homine* (1658). Also that year, in 1668, at Amsterdam, appeared the Latin edition of the *Leviathan*, specially prepared by Hobbes himself, mostly during 1667, a masterpiece which, we have seen, was preceded by the (resolutely republicanizing) Dutch translation, published at Amsterdam, in 1667.[36]

Spinoza consciously wrote with an eye to his relationship to Hobbes, and we know that others, in particular Jelles, questioned him by letter and in person about how his political theory relates to that of Hobbes. While Hobbes' impact on Spinoza was considerable, as with the De La Courts, Koerbaghs, and the entire *cercle Spinoziste*, it is much less obvious that the short-lived Johan de la Court (1622–60), who was the very first to lay the foundations of the Dutch democratic republican tradition, in the 1650s, really owed much to Hobbes. Rather than being some sort of offshoot or variant of Hobbes (as many modern scholars like to suggest), it seems the general thrust of Dutch democratic republicanism began independently. Spinoza's objective was never at any point to underwrite or reinforce Hobbes' theories, and least of all his support for absolute monarchy. But like the De La Courts, Van den Enden, and Van Berkel, he reworked Hobbes with the conscious goal of incorporating elements of his thought into his and their prior democratic republican framework opposing all royalism and absolutism, as also Orangism. In short, Spinoza's application of political and moral theory to social questions, and approach to toleration, censorship, ecclesiastical rights, privilege, law and religious authority, indeed every main strand of his social and political thought, drew him to an approach opposing, rather than endorsing salient features of Hobbes' thought.[37]

A striking example of what initially looks like proximity to Hobbes in Spinoza's approach, rooted in their common thoroughgoing naturalism, are their respective theories of "good" and "bad," and "just" and "unjust." But on closer scrutiny here too they turn out, as in practically every case, to fundamentally diverge in a manner that has broad implications for the contrasting orientations of their respective systems of ethics and social thought, as well as their rival political philosophies. The "Lawes of Nature are Immutable and eternall," holds Hobbes, and what men consider "good" and "bad" has no other basis in natural law, or religion, than subjective evaluation, depending on whatever seems desirable, and therefore "good," or repugnant, and hence bad, to the individual, a view undoubtedly shocking to most readers at the time, but with which Spinoza agrees thus far. In both the *TTP* and *Ethics* Spinoza further aligns closely with and probably borrows from Hobbes in accepting that we seek what we think is "good" because

---

[36] Malcolm, *Editorial Introduction*, 273–86.
[37] Weststeijn, *Commercial Republicanism*, 150–1; Hoekstra, "Lion in the House," 195, 201, 216–17; Israel, "How Does Spinoza's 'Democracy' Differ?," 233–4.

we desire it, shifting here from his earlier view in the *Korte Verhandeling*. It is an invariable universal law of human nature, concurs Spinoza, that no one fails to pursue whatever he thinks good unless hoping for a greater good, or fearing greater harm, nor chooses to suffer any evil except to avoid a greater one, or while hoping for a greater good. We seek what we deem "good" because our *conatus* impels us towards it, and "between two good things, every individual will choose that which he thinks the greater good, and of two bad things that which seems to him less bad."[38] But, from here on, Hobbes and Spinoza diverge fundamentally. For "seems" is the operative word here, insists Spinoza, given that individual judgement usually misjudges.[39]

For both Hobbes and Spinoza there exists also a sense in which the collective good and the collective bad emerges and rises above the subjective evaluations of individuals. For both thinkers this collective "good" has a higher status than the particular desires of individuals. For Hobbes, the chief example of this absolute and collective good, is peace which conduces to everyone's security and life while the supreme example of the collective "bad," is war. Hobbes' collective good, furthermore, under the rubric "peace" encompasses more than just safety from organized violence: "all men agree on this, that Peace is Good, and therefore also the way, or means of Peace, which [...] are Justice, Gratitude, Modesty, Equity, Mercy and the rest of the Lawes of Nature [Iustitia, Gratitudo, Modestia, Aequitas, et caeterae Leges naturae], are good, that is to say Morall Vertues, and their contrary, Vices, Evill."[40] Yet, in Hobbes' moral philosophy "whatsoever is the object of any man's appetite or desire, that is it which he for his part calleth good," so that conflicting individual aims and wishes still dominate the social sphere and, aside from peace and security, exercising justice, and cultivating personal virtues, there exists nothing like a lasting, wider collective good, nothing like a permanent "summum bonum [highest good]" that the sovereign state can pursue for its citizens and institutionalize in law, or that can be enforced in any way on the ruler and permanently merged with the practice of sovereignty.[41]

In this respect, Hobbes' and Spinoza's paths diverge widely. For Hobbes' minimalist approach to the collective good rooted in nature's unalterable laws is, in turn, closely linked to Hobbes' monarchism and *de facto* indirect support for whatever coercive ecclesiastical authority and church censorship a particular sovereign chooses to impose on his subjects. Given the centrality of security and order, in Hobbes' schema, "the people rules in all governments," including monarchies, though he admits its sounds strange to maintain, as he does, "that in a monarchy, the subjects are the multitude, and (however it may seem a

---

[38] Scribano, "Connaissance du bien," 71–2; LeBuffe, *From Bondage to Freedom*, 100–1.
[39] Spinoza, *Theological-Political Treatise*, 198.
[40] Hobbes, *Leviathan* ii, 242–3; Hobbes, *De Homine*, 47–53; Field, *Potentia*, 16, 67, 246–7.
[41] Garrett, *Nature and Necessity*, 510; Garrett, "'Promising' Ideas," 199–200; LeBuffe, *From Bondage to Freedom*, 200–3, 207–8.

paradox) the king is the people," since it is his will and power that upholds the unified common good. Subversive thinking against kings, suggests Hobbes, frequently occurs owing to poverty and misery so that "all the poor commonly lay the blame on the evil government, excusing their own sloth and luxury; as if their private goods forsooth were wasted by public exactions."[42]

It is thus central to Hobbes' philosophy that the minds of the poor should be subject to direction from above. Hobbes was just as convinced as Spinoza that "potent men digest hardly anything that setteth up a power to bridle their affections; and learned men, any thing that discovereth their errours, and thereby lesseneth their authority; whereas the common people's minds, unlesse they be tainted with dependence on the potent, or scribbled over with the opinions of their doctors, are like clean paper, fit to receive whatsoever by publique authority shall be imprinted in them." Here Hobbes and Spinoza share a common starting point. But where Hobbes believes the elite trained at Oxford and Cambridge as administrators and clergy should be so fashioned by the princely sovereign as to "instruct the people in the essential rights (which are the naturall and fundamentall lawes) of sovereignty," Spinoza deems it vital that neither prince nor church should control education. For Hobbes, it is not only the sovereign ruler's duty to fill his subjects' minds with political and religious views buttressing his sovereignty, "but his benefit also, and security, against the danger that may arrive to himself in his natural person, from rebellion."[43] By contrast, Spinoza was deeply averse to instilling authoritarian political and religious ideas defending the rule of monarchs into anybody's mind. Opposed to imprinting on the "clean paper" of people's minds, he demands rather free and open debate and free and open teaching at all levels as the optimal path to elevating the general level of "reason" in society. Regarding the poor, Spinoza is the antithesis of Hobbes.

Hobbes' stance here is not just different from that of the De La Courts, Van den Enden, and Spinoza but involves a wholly opposed conception of society, freedom, and society's relationship to the political sphere. "Things which are of assistance to the common society of men," explains Spinoza in the *Ethics*, defining his "highest good," or cause "men to live together harmoniously, are useful; those, on the other hand, are evil which bring discord to the state."[44] Discord and internal strife being something all too prevalent in both Hobbes' England and Spinoza's Holland of the 1650s, 1660s, and 1670s, this already poses the question: what causes internal rift and dissension and how is it best minimized? But in Spinoza, unlike Hobbes, the scope of what is "useful" socially and politically corresponds to what "reason" recommends, building a slow, gradual, and halting universal liberation from

---

[42] Hobbes, *De Cive*, 250–1; Hoekstra, "Lion in the House," 216; Fukuoka, *Sovereign and the Prophets*, 84–91.
[43] Hobbes, *Leviathan* ii, 524; Balibar, *Spinoza et la politique*, 84–5.
[44] Spinoza, *Collected Works* (ed. Curley) i, 546, 550, 564–5.

"human servitude" rooted in everyone's primitive emotions, strengthening as we rise from autocracy and priestcraft and begin to glimpse the "highest good," or *summum bonum* which in Spinoza is a combination of individual and collective enhancement of individual and collective capacity secured by "reason" and pursuit of virtue, a programme central to his schema and broadly absent from Hobbes.[45]

25.iii Happiness and the "Highest Good"

Striving for happiness, Spinoza believes, though an individual quest on one level, is ultimately inseparable from the social and political milieu, hence inevitably a collective quest too. For Spinoza, rescuing men from the "discord" all too frequently tearing society apart, is not a function of embracing strong leaders, or forging robust monarchies which can only lead to formalized servitude, nor creating a dominant nobility like that of the Roman Republic, but a collective upwards ascent to the sovereignty of "reason." The more ignorance, hatred, and the emotions prevail, the more we descend into "discord." Where men live under the rule of emotion and the passions, they remain enslaved to the passions and subject to unending strife. Division decreases, conversely, as reason gains ground "and therefore men, in proportion as they live under the guidance of reason," as George Eliot renders Spinoza's Proposition 35 of Part IV of *The Ethics*, "will necessarily be in accord with one another."[46]

The gulf between Hobbes and Spinoza in political, legal, and social theory begins, then, with Spinoza's collective "good" extending over and encompassing far more ground than that of Hobbes who confines his collective sphere to minimizing danger and maximizing security combined with a more traditional conception of natural law defining just and unjust in a manner compatible with the idea of a divine legislator. Where Hobbes' "natural law" stays in line with that of Grotius and Pufendorf envisaging a set of divinely given and sanctioned precepts, Spinoza's common good demolishes that tradition by removing all connection with divine will and command.[47] Meanwhile, Spinoza's *summum bonum* is also a far more active force in promoting human well-being and liberty. While Spinoza too stresses the indispensability of peace and security, he considers these only part of the core collective good driving government based on the *salus* of the whole people, a Spinozistic notion entrenching religious toleration together with freedom to publish and, especially vital to him, protecting freethinking, unpopular individuals, and minorities of all sorts. Everyone, whether they realize

---

[45] Garrett, *Nature and Necessity*, 511; Israel, "How Does Spinoza's 'Democracy' Differ?" 236.
[46] Spinoza, *Ethics* IV, Prop. 35; Spinoza, *Ethics* (trans. George Eliot), 249.
[47] Steinberg, *Spinoza's Political Psychology*, 52–3, 62; James, *Spinoza on Learning*, 104–5.

it or not, needs shielding from despots, priests, and aristocrats and also from the crowd, the uninformed multitude or unsympathetic majority, so that tackling prejudice and superstition, bridling theology and the clergy, become key objectives of Spinoza's liberation process.

In confronting the ignorant and bigoted majority, a much more urgent and important preoccupation of Spinoza than for Hobbes, his schema again sharply diverges not just by replacing kings, the hereditary principle, and bishops with government by "large councils" that are representative of opinion in society but by offering through the democratic republic an enriching, emancipating perspective, widening opportunity for personal happiness for all, something, however, which necessarily also requires a militant, strongly coercive aspect to rein in bullies and demagogues which, for Spinoza, includes curbing false prophets, crowd-pulling preachers, dynasts and would-be usurpers, all the potential tyrants. No matter how concealed and buried it may be, the true aim of society "and every state," argues the *TTP*, is not just to enable men to live securely (as in Hobbes), but rather freely and "satisfyingly" avoiding strife and providing scope for every individual to develop his or her potential to the utmost.[48]

When moving from the state of nature into society, men do in a formal sense, Spinoza agrees, transfer their "natural right" to the sovereign; but then, severely qualifies this, preserving as much of that "natural right" as possible also under the state, albeit now in an institutionalized, controlled way supervised by the sovereign. Spinoza's social contract is therefore a minimized less meaningful divide than that of Hobbes whose social contract is the lynchpin of his whole political theory. Where for Hobbes creating the state means departing from nature, rendering life in the state of nature and life under the state as different as day and night, for Spinoza the state is just part of nature from which there is no exit. Spinoza replicates nothing like the finality and wide scope of the transfer of control envisaged by Hobbes, his construct not really being a social contract at all. Indeed, it vanishes completely in his later political text, the *Tractatus Politicus*.[49] A citizen's "natural right," it turns out, is never actually transferred or alienated at the inauguration of human society, or as Spinoza expresses the point, the "transfer of each person's natural right" to the sovereign power "in many respects [...] will always remain merely theoretical."[50]

Definitively transferred by Hobbes, "natural right" of the individual in Spinoza is merely collectivized and institutionalized to become society's guiding principle.[51] Spinoza's profound reworking of Hobbes' logic, here, pivots on the idea that those enslaved to their individual passions and appetites are not free and that the "only

---

[48] Spinoza, *Theological-Political Treatise*, 47, 200–1; Brykman, *Judéité de Spinoza*, 78, 84–5, 98–103.

[49] Matheron, *Individu et communauté*, 287–354; Montag, *Bodies, Masses, Power*, 91–2; Lagrée, *Spinoza et le débat*, 181; James, *Spinoza on Learning*, 111.

[50] Spinoza, *Theological-Political Treatise*, 208.

[51] Spinoza, *Theological-Political Treatise*, 208–10; Lavaert, *Vrijheid, gelijkheid, veelheid*, 228–9.

free person is one who lives with his entire mind guided solely by reason."[52] Hence, the great majority incapable of following the dictates of reason of their own volition can still do so, in essentials, in Spinoza's scheme by obeying the collective sovereignty of the socially responsible and representative democratic republic passing laws for the benefit of "all the people." It is in this sense that the ignorant and bigoted, no matter how unbridled and misconceived their superstition, prejudices, fanaticism, and hatred of others, are still in practice free, that is "forced to be free," in the democratic republic, for no one is a slave "who does by command of the sovereign what is useful for the community and consequently for himself."[53] Even the most furious raging bully imaginable when arrested and locked up is thereby rendered more free.

Rather than Hobbes' theoretical "social contract" elevating society in one fell swoop from the state of nature's brutal miseries to achieve greater safety for all, Spinoza predicates no clear break between the "state of nature," for him really more a fiction than an actual stage in man's development, and what comes after. The early phases of human development he conceives rather as a searching for effective group responses to natural difficulties eventually attaining the level of "civil society."[54] The Old Testament Hebrews offer the classic instance of a group binding themselves in alliance with God to observe His laws, and, for Spinoza, such alliances, instituting "religion" among the people as their first set of laws, is a natural step for all human groups. Fleeing as a body of escaped slaves, the ancient Hebrews formed their republic using a legal framework understood by them as founding a "religion" but via this "religion" created an imagined sovereignty of all the group, recognized by all, by which they had saved themselves.

Spinoza contends that "freedom," the true goal of every human society as he means the term, and therefore every state, if virtually never attained in practice under kings or priests, cannot flourish either under aristocratic republics like early modern Venice and Genoa, a point heavily stressed too by the De La Courts. While for Spinoza democracy is always preferable to monarchy, aristocratic republics, and priestly theocracy, Hobbes, viewing monarchy as better representing "the people" than any assembly or council, "strongly rejected the idea that there was more liberty in a democratic regime than under a monarchy." Deemed closer to nature than other political forms, for Spinoza democracy "approaches most closely to the freedom nature bestows on every person."[55] For "in a democracy no one transfers their natural right to another in such a way that they are not thereafter consulted but rather to the majority of the whole society of which they

---

[52] Spinoza, *Theological-Political Treatise*, 201; Lavaert, *Vrijheid, gelijkheid, veelheid*, 228.
[53] Spinoza, *Theological-Political Treatise*, 201; Saar, *Immanenz der Macht*, 36–7.
[54] Jaquet, *Spinoza à l'oeuvre*, 82–7; Field, *Potentia*, 152–6.
[55] Malcolm, *Editorial Introduction*, 23.

are part. In this way all remain equal as they had been previously in the state of nature."[56]

In *De Cive*, Hobbes holds that there can be no such thing as "mixed monarchy," contrary to what many in England liked to suppose, or any compound of monarchy, aristocracy, and democracy. As well as superior to aristocracy and democracy, monarchy is always ultimately absolute.[57] No wonder when circulating an early draft of this text privately, Hobbes found the following points "most bitterly excepted against: that I made the civil powers too large; but this by ecclesiastical persons. That I had utterly taken away liberty of conscience; but this by sectaries. That I had set princes above the civil laws; but this by lawyers."[58] Yet, Hobbes' insistence on monarchy's superiority is even more pronounced in *Leviathan* than in *De Cive*, reflecting a hardening of his view that monarchical sovereignty is inherently absolute even where, as in England, customary arrangements long assigned representative functions to Parliament, since in his schema, no sovereign can ever permanently alienate his own role as sole true representative of the people.[59] In Spinoza, the reverse is true; no individual ruler can be a genuine representative.[60]

In a pivotal chapter of the *Leviathan*, chapter XXX, Hobbes expressly warns his compatriots against looking enviously at the prosperity and well-being of the neighbouring Dutch Republic. The people must be "taught" that "they ought not to be in love with any forme of Government they see in their neighbour Nations, more than with their own, nor (whatsoever present prosperity they behold in Nations that are otherwise governed than they) to desire change." For, the "prosperity of a People ruled by an Aristocraticall, or Democraticall assembly," held Hobbes, "cometh not from Aristocracy, nor from Democracy, but from the obedience and concord of the Subjects: nor do the people flourish in a Monarchy, because one man has the right to rule them, but because they obey him."[61] Nowhere is the basic divergence between Hobbes and Spinoza clearer than in Spinoza's idea that in a properly organized republic the sovereign is society itself, society as a whole wherever based on "reason" and promoting harmony and self-fulfilment among its citizens, leaving each to exercise the natural right to conserve himself as best he can. When obeying the laws, it is everyone's wish, and everyone's right, to advance their own personal quest for happiness, so when the republic defends that interest and right as it should, men are not, in reality, transferring their own "natural right" to anyone but conserving it in a new and improved format. Asking what are the essential differences between Spinoza's

---

[56] Spinoza, *Theological-Political Treatise*, 202; Saar, *Immanenz der Macht*, 38; James, *Spinoza on Learning*, 129.
[57] Hobbes, *De Cive*, 191, 194; Field, *Potentia*, 5.   [58] Hobbes, *De Cive*, 105.
[59] Malcolm, *Editorial Introduction*, 20–2, 25–6.
[60] Here James and Verbeek are arguably mistaken, see James, *Spinoza on Learning*, 132.
[61] Hobbes, *Leviathan* ii 524–5; Malcolm, *Editorial Introduction*, 23–4.

political theory and that of Hobbes, Jelles received the reply from his friend that Hobbes removes the "natural right" under the state whereas he, Spinoza, preserves it intact and unimpaired. That captures the point precisely.[62]

"Human society," it turns out, despite formal transfer of each individual's right to society, "can therefore be formed without any alienation of natural right, and the contract can be preserved in its entirety with complete fidelity, only if every person transfers all the power they possess to society, and society alone retains the supreme natural right over all things, i.e., the supreme power, which all must obey, either of their own free will or through fear of punishment. The right of such a society is called democracy." "Democracy," Spinoza then goes on to say, "is properly defined as a united gathering of people who collectively have the sovereign right to do all that [this pooled, collective right] has the power to do." Here, especially, it makes sense for Spinoza to claim that where Hobbes cancels the natural right of the citizens, he, Spinoza, preserves it in its entirety.[63]

Spinoza's solution to the problem of how best to organize human society and politics stemmed in part from his own experience, his lifelong rebellion against religious authority as intrusive, usurping despotic power reaching back to the 1650s. But his personal war on bigotry and ecclesiastical repression, though commencing with his revolt against rabbinic sway and the *parnasim*, had its roots in his family's sixteenth-century history, rebellion against Philip II and Spain's Inquisition, against absolutism and global empire, an impulse translating, in Spinoza's case, into fierce opposition to the quest for personal domination whether of Cromwell, Charles II of England, the prince-bishop of Munster, or Louis XIV. Hence, the "foundation and purpose" of Spinoza's democratic republic far transcended the need "to avoid the follies of appetite and, as much as possible, constrain men within the limits of reason, so that they may dwell in peace and harmony."[64] Since it is "reason," not any form of personal sovereignty, let alone religious authority or majority opinion, that defines his *summum bonum*, Spinoza assumes the highest good is something most people will be permanently unable to comprehend and few leaders will pursue in practice. Indeed, to begin with, no one at all will grasp it and, working for it, will always be an uphill task because "all men are born completely ignorant of everything," he notes, "and before they can learn the true rationale of living and can acquire the habit of virtue, a good part of life has elapsed even if they have been well brought up, while in the meantime they must live and conserve themselves so far as they can, by the sole impulse of appetite."[65]

---

[62] Spinoza to Jelles, The Hague, 2 June 1674 in Spinoza, *Collected Works* (ed. Curley) ii, 406; Garrett, "'Promising' Ideas," 196; Steinberg, *Spinoza's Political Psychology*, 49; Saar, "Immanence," 10n12, 12.
[63] Spinoza, *Theological-Political Treatise*, 200.   [64] Spinoza, *Theological-Political Treatise*, 201.
[65] Spinoza, *Theological-Political Treatise*, 196; Israel, "How Does Spinoza's 'Democracy' Differ?" 230, 239.

Spinoza's anti-Hobbesian schema also means that the more society and government do encapsulate and promote the advance of "reason," the more people will comprehend the advantages and goals of the democratic republic, grasp the meaning of virtue, and learn to lead fulfilling and happier as well as longer lives. Spinoza's perspective can be viewed as a more refined version of Van den Enden's idea, likewise opposing Hobbes' conception of men as naturally each other's enemies, always greedy and apt to pillage. Already, in 1665, in Van den Enden, the bad passions in men originate in princely rule and gain free rein from oppressive, tyrannical government whereas, wherever the state is a well-ordered and administered republic, men become friends to each other and dwell in harmony.[66]

The distance between Spinoza (aligned with Van den Enden, the De La Courts, Van Berkel and the Koerbaghs) and Hobbes becomes starkly evident where their divergent conceptions of the best kind of state and the "highest good" result in Hobbes defending the existing monarchical, aristocratic, and ecclesiastical order as against the efforts of the *cercle Spinoziste* systematically to undermine it. Meanwhile, Spinoza also aspires to reform the individual as well as the collectivity. Another notable aspect, we have seen, of self-emancipation through reason, for Spinoza, aiding individuals in their quest for happiness by promoting "reason," is liberating men from enslavement to the tyranny of money where money is used not for purchasing essentials but a tool to control others. Emancipation from preoccupation with making money, he considers a step towards both personal happiness and collective harmony. Hobbes, by contrast, since he does not reject the generally established order or attempt to ground the wider conception of freedom that Spinoza champions, but seeks rather to reinforce the principle of monarchy, aims to weaken protest and resistance by the poor and discontented.

The moral order underpinning Spinoza's republic clearly possesses a double role, encouraging and constraining: for while promoting everyone's individual liberty and happiness, its institutions need simultaneously to ensure society's bigoted elements, no matter how numerous, prejudiced, and ignorant, are compelled by rational laws to respect the freedom of others, for otherwise no individual's liberty can be secure. It is in this sense, paradoxically, that they are "forced to be free." This two-way enriching and constraining drives the legal apparatus of Spinoza's "common good," a more refined version of Van den Enden's earlier idea of the "algemeene accorderende interest [general agreeing interest]" first spelled out in a published text in his *Vrije Politieke Stellingen* [Free Political Propositions] (1665). This shift away from and against Hobbes represents a major (if unrecognized) step in the history of modern political thought, Spinoza being the true founder of the secular "general will" as Diderot, d'Holbach, Rousseau, and Condorcet later renamed this Spinozist concept in the 1750s.

---

[66] Van den Enden, *Vrije Politijke Stellingen*, 140–1; Lavaert, *Vrijheid, gelijkheid, veelheid*, 131.

Hobbes and Spinoza both conceive of sovereignty as unitary and indivisible,[67] but the former vests it essentially in an individual ruler whose sovereignty is over, rather than identical with, society's well-being and the social order, the latter lodges it in the collective well-being so that sovereignty essentially remains within society viewed as a whole, and not in any individual, which is why sovereignty only correctly functions and is rightly conceived and legislated for in a democratic republic.[68] Spinoza's was a revolutionary recipe democratic in form expressly opposed to the principles of monarchy and aristocracy and geared to minimizing religious authority and maximization of individual freedom.[69]

Discussing the difference between "slavery" and political liberty in chapter XVI of the *TTP*, Spinoza contends that humans live in freedom only "in a state and government where the *salus* of the whole people, not that of the sovereign, is the supreme law."[70] Both "salus" here, and "supreme law [summa lex]," signify the common "well-being," "prosperity," and vigour, or better, the "common good."[71] The gulf between Hobbes and Spinoza here clearly reveals itself in their contrasting use of the term *salus* which Hobbes employs early in his pivotal chapter XXX of *Leviathan* when explaining what he means by calling the sovereign monarch rather than any assembly or parliament the true "representative" of the people. "By salus of the people I understand not just preserving the life of the citizen, but also the contentments of life by which every man lawfully shall acquire for himself without danger to the commonwealth or to himself [In Salute autem Populi comprehendo non solum Civium vitam sed etiam Commoda vitae, quae Cives singuli, sine Civitatis damno vel periculo sibi juste acquisita tenuerint]."[72] For Hobbes, the *salus* of the people does therefore enhance personal well-being beyond mere safety, but remains always purely individual freedom, not the freedoms of society, individual freedom devoid of any collective will of the people linked to freedom of thought and discussion, freedom to criticize laws and authority, or right to be represented in assemblies and cultivate whatever religious or irreligious orientation one wishes.

25.iv From the "Highest Good" to the "General Will"

In Spinoza's *Ethics* and his political treatises, which are more closely aligned throughout than is often suggested, individual quest to perfect one's intellect is the path to "summum nostrum bonum [our highest good]." Because most people,

---

[67] Malcolm, *Editorial Introduction*, 25–6, 29; Fukuoka, *Sovereign and the Prophets*, 166–70.
[68] Israel, "Introduction," xxix–xxx; Spinoza, *Theological-Political Treatise*, 199–200.
[69] Spinoza, *Theological-Political Treatise*, 200; Spinoza, *Collected Works* (ed. Curley) ii, 287.
[70] Spinoza, *Theological-Political Treatise*, 201; Spinoza, *Opera* iii, 194–5; Michael Silverthorne and I here translated "salus" as safety; but on reflection this now seems mistaken.
[71] Brykman, *Judéité de Spinoza*, 80, 97; James, "Freedom, Slavery and the Passions," 229; Goudriaan, *Reformed Orthodoxy*, 302.
[72] Hobbes, *Leviathan* ii, 521.

including most elites, fail to understand or respect the highest good, preferring their own private interest instead, it remains always best for the state to be governed by a group executive with powers of decision diffused as widely, that is into as many hands as possible. Hence, democracy is inherently superior to aristocracy while in aristocratic republics, like the Dutch Republic, the republic improves the more the ruling oligarchy is broadened, power shared, and decision-making depends on presenting arguments, consultation, and discussion. For the more public affairs are discussed, the more individual self-interest is curbed and the better the "common good" served. Promoting "general will" defined by reason, as forged by Spinoza and inherited later by Diderot, d'Holbach, Condorcet, Volney, and Destutt de Tracy, who all call it *volonté générale*, employing the term with a vehemently anti-Rousseauist twist, requires freedom of thought, expression and to publish, and raising the general intellectual level.

The contrast between Hobbes' royalism and Spinoza's republicanism is often cited. But what is frequently missed is Spinoza's evaluating every form of government not just differently from Hobbes but in a deliberately anti-Hobbesian fashion. Within the category of republicanism, Spinoza crucially gives preference, in a way deeply characteristic of his approach, to the democratic republic over the aristocratic republic, weighing the two forms against each other being a characteristic feature of Dutch republicanism from Johan and Pieter de La Court, Van den Enden, and Van Berkel, onwards, a dimension broadly lacking from English "classical" republicanism until the age of Thomas Paine and Richard Price. Dispersing power, spreading consultation, debate, and participation more broadly remains always vital to the functioning of Spinoza's sovereignty because only such consultative spread can guarantee the curbing of private interest and that the "common good is consulted [ut communi bono consulatur]."[73] "Hence, wherever a few decide everything out of their inclination," as Spinoza expresses it in chapter IX of the *Tractatus Politicus*, both "liberty [libertas] and the common good [communeque bonum] are lost."[74]

Accordingly, the *Tractatus Politicus* argues that "small councils must be prevented from gaining power at the expense of great councils," as had unfortunately occurred with damaging consequences in the early modern republics of Venice and Geneva. Thus, it is entirely wrong to assert that while "Spinoza prefers both democracy and aristocracy to monarchy, [...] it is not at all clear what his preference is between democracy and aristocracy."[75] In both the *TTP* and *TP*, Spinoza invariably expresses not just preference for, but the inherent superiority

---

[73] Spinoza, *Opera* iii, 329; Spinoza, *Collected Works* (ed. Curley) ii, 569; Giancotti Boscherini, *Lexicon Spinozanum* i, 116.

[74] Spinoza, *Opera* iii, 352; Spinoza, *Collected Works* (ed. Curley) ii, 594; Giancotti Boscherini, *Lexicon Spinozanum* i, 116.

[75] Melamed, "Charitable Interpretations," 271–2; Field, *Potentia*, 151n.

of democracy as against both monarchy *and* aristocracy, a stance fundamental to his conception of the "common good."[76]

Hobbes and Spinoza do at least converge, one might object, in rejecting religious authority as an entity separate from political sovereignty. Both refuse to accept that any priesthood or clergy possesses an independent authority distinct from the political sovereign. But their manner of rejecting independent religious authority, and the consequences they draw, turn out, once again, to be markedly different. Hobbes makes no effort to restrict the sway of England's ecclesiastical hierarchy over behaviour, opinion, or education, his intervention here amounting only to insisting on subordinating the clerical arm to the political sovereign, a point vital for him, and his denying the Scriptures are "made Laws by the Universall Church."[77] In Spinoza, there *is* no universal church, and all churchmen are always equally subordinate to the political sovereign. His concern is to minimize as far as possible the power of any church to impose theological concepts or restrict toleration, censure ideas, or in other ways obstruct freedom of thought, discussion and to criticize, which in Hobbes are barely concerns at all. Furthermore, in Spinoza this curbing of ecclesiastical authority applies to the public church authorized by the sovereign most of all.

Conceding to everyone liberty of saying what one thinks may not only be accorded without damaging the "peace of the republic," affirms the last page of the *TTP*, but "such freedom is essential to it." Limiting or removing freedom of expression, on the other hand, Spinoza deems wholly destructive of the "republicae salus," the well-being of the republic.[78] Issuing decrees about doctrinal issues on the part of the sovereign state is likewise "completely useless." His subordinating religion, piety, and religious leaders together with the opinions and prejudices of most people to the rule of reason and the "peace and interests of the state," Spinoza, at the start of chapter XIX, terms adjusting religion to the "peace and utility of the republic [republicae paci et utilitati accommodari]."[79]

Hobbes and Spinoza nurtured opposed notions too about what they both term "theocracy." For Hobbes, "theocracy" is basically a means of forging a robust and stable autocracy where there exists no tradition of hereditary monarchical legitimacy. Thus, for example, the ancient Israelites by transferring their "natural right" directly to God, and accepting the sovereignty of God, actually transferred executive and legislative power to Abraham and then to Moses who, for Hobbes was the paradigmatic "Erastian" ruler, using control over the priesthood as the prime instrument of his power. Although Moses did not compile the Five Books

---

[76] Vernière, *Spinoza et la pensée française*, 485; Israel, "Introduction," xxx; Lavaert, *Vrijheid, gelijkheid, veelheid*, 237–8; Steinberg, *Spinoza's Political Psychology*, 164–5.

[77] Hobbes, *Leviathan* iii, 606–7; Israel, "Introduction," xvii–xviii; Field, *Potentia*, 131, 152.

[78] Spinoza, *Theological-Political Treatise*, 258–9; Spinoza, *Opera* iii, 247; Giancotti Boscherini, *Lexicon Spinozanum* i, 114–15 and ii, 974.

[79] Spinoza, *Opera* iii, 229; Spinoza, *Theological-Political Treatise*, 238.

commonly attributed to him "entirely," according to Hobbes, "and in the form we have them; yet he wrote all that which he is there said to have written, as for example the volume of the Law which is contained, as it seemeth, in the 11 of *Deuteronomie*, and the following chapters to the 27,"[80] a view in part designed to elevate Moses into the sole repository of sovereignty in the ancient Israelite state that he forged. However extensive the power and influence of priests in a Hobbesian theocracy, the priests, Moses' Levites, are still a "ministry" and not the sovereign.[81] Hobbes greatly prefers the Anglican system of bishops to Calvinist government of the church by presbyteries, precisely because the latter intrude more on political sovereignty than the former while bishops are more readily controlled by the crown than presbyteries.[82]

Spinoza, by contrast, views the principle of government by God, the notion of divine sovereignty, differently and decidedly positively, viewing it as a bar to autocracy and ecclesiastical influence. Because enshrining the divine Law as the ancient Israelites had, transfers men's natural right "to God," and as God did not actually rule them, the ancient Israelite republic, in his eyes, became a state based on principles supposedly decreed by God creating a sovereignty more closely related to the "common good" of the democratic republic than to either monarchy or priestly rule. Led by Moses, the escaped slaves envisaged their pact with the power above as a fundamental law decreed by their imagined providential God. Crucially, "the Hebrews did not transfer their right to another person but rather all gave up their right equally, as in a democracy."[83] "The Hebrews," explains Spinoza, surrendered their right equally, "crying out with one voice: 'We will do whatever God shall say'," making no mention of an intermediary. "It follows that they all remained perfectly equal as a result of this agreement. The right to consult God, receive laws, and interpret them remained equal for all, and all equally without exception retained the whole administration of the state."[84] It was not long though, before this pristine Hebrew republic, as Spinoza envisages it, was corrupted by the fears and ignorance of the Hebrews. Abolishing the "first covenant," they transferred their right to consult God and interpret His edicts to Moses, turning Moses into the "sole maker and interpreter of the divine laws." This meant also transferring to Moses the right to consult God and interpret His decrees, and then to whoever Moses chose as his successor.[85]

Envisaging God as the judge who punishes offences against His Law Spinoza identifies as the earliest stage of civil society, the beginning of reason's effort to

---

[80] Hobbes, *Leviathan* iii, 592, 666, 668–72; Nadler, *Book Forged in Hell*, 116.
[81] Hobbes, *De Cive*, 314–20, 324–7; Hobbes, *Leviathan* iii, 816–17, 976–7; Cooper, "Reevaluating Spinoza's Legacy," 477.
[82] Malcolm, *Editorial Introduction*, 34–6, 40; Fukuoka, *Sovereign and the Prophets*, 167–70.
[83] Saar, *Immanenz der Macht*, 334–7; Cooper, "Reevaluating Spinoza's Legacy," 475–8; Kaplan, "Morteira's Democratic Hebrew Republic," 15–16.
[84] Spinoza, *Theological-Political Treatise*, 214; Cooper, "Reevaluating Spinoza's legacy," 477–8.
[85] Spinoza, *Theological-Political Treatise*, 215; Sangiacomo, *Spinoza on Reason*, 97–9.

combat the force of appetite and the passions.[86] Everyone enslaved to appetite and the passions, whatever their social status, remains a "slave" imprisoned in the "state of nature."[87] Before long, though, despite the historical importance of their forging the first recorded sovereignty based on "general will," rather than a political frame imposed by monarchical tyranny and priests, the ancient Hebrews wretchedly failed. Despite participating in ceremonial occasions like the Passover festival serving as political and social reminders, a reinforcing commemoration of the people's emancipation from slavery to a higher level, the ancient Hebrews proved no more successful in the difficult task of instituting the common will as the true and lasting frame for sovereignty than the Romans or the English later. For the democratic republic, the proper and principal goal of all men, is a treasure hard to secure and harder still to retain.

In fact, in Spinoza's eyes the Hebrews pioneered humanity's sad regression from the right path by transferring sovereignty first to Moses, as God's interpreter, then to Aaron and the Levites, and finally Joshua. As long as their initial democratic framework, the "laws of the people [populi]," survived, these remained uncorrupted. But no sooner did the Hebrews place themselves under kings, than war and strife were endemic and everything rapidly deteriorated.[88] Spinoza's account of the ancient Hebrews, it has been objected, seems to have "little consistency": his "conclusions [...] can be read as a defense sometimes of royal, sometimes of popular democratic and (theocratic) republican government."[89] But actually Spinoza never defends or inclines towards royal government, or monarchy, and never justifies priestly rule. Nor is there any contradiction in holding that at some stages priests and theologians introduced "superstition" while at other stages kings did. Every individual or group working in their own interest against the *salus populi* in Spinoza, employs "superstition" to manipulate and cheat the multitude. Only democratic republican government working for promotion of the "common good" proves resistant to individual and group self-interest.

Not only is Spinoza's view of original theocracy different and more benign than that of Hobbes, it is used also to illustrate further the dangers surrounding all attempts to stabilize and conserve the democratic republic and prevent degeneration into autocracy and priestcraft, as well as the indispensability of "enlightenment" combating what most people believe, for the successful formation of the democratic republic.[90] The democratic republic is superior to monarchy *and* aristocratic republics in the *TTP* partly because there "all men remain equal as

---

[86] Spinoza, *Theological-Political Treatise*, 201–2; Jaquet, *Spinoza à l'oeuvre*, 90.
[87] Spinoza, *Theological-Political Treatise*, 201.
[88] Spinoza, *Theological-Political Treatise*, 233–4; Balibar, *Spinoza et la politique*, 60; Cristofolini, "Peuple et multitude," 51.
[89] Verbeek, *Spinoza's Theologico-Political Treatise*, 125, 135.
[90] Cooper, "Reevaluating Spinoza's legacy," 478–80.

they had been previously in the state of nature,"[91] partly because it affords more liberty to all than monarchy or aristocracy, but especially because it best promotes the "common good." "Spinoza's main motivation" for opting for democracy, it is sometimes argued, stems from a somewhat "naïve form of realpolitik" supposing "a large group of people with a vast variety of conflicting desires is unlikely to agree on extremely irrational policies."[92] But that is only one reason Spinoza proposes as to why big councils work better than small ones, and why in political matters the democratizing principle is the right path to amelioration. The reasoning offered in the *Tractatus Politicus* for democracy's superiority is less emphatic than in the *TTP* but nevertheless perfectly clear: private vested interest preying on the majority is more easily veiled in small than big councils while the clashing of individual wills, motives, and desires in large councils gives collective reason more scope for resolving disagreement, rooting out deception, shaping the outcome and promoting the "common good."

However much at odds this may sound with the conventional canon of Western political thought, Spinoza was hence more comprehensively committed to fighting monarchy, aristocracy, superstition, and populism, and thus, from the perspective of the Radical Enlightenment, considerably more useful in political theory than Hobbes, Locke, Rousseau, or Kant, more effective in battling mankind's greatest curses, the three great plagues that Spinoza's projected *revolutio* seeks to conquer—tyranny, religious repression, and popular thinking anchored in ignorance. Rousseau, on the other hand, by rejecting representative democracy and dispensing with safeguards for dissenting minorities and freedom of expression, was less likely to appeal to spokesmen of any religious or other kind of minority anxious to secure equal civic rights and freedom of expression. For Rousseau's system presents grave risks to the individual and to minorities, a lesson painfully revealed by the horrors of fervently *Rousseauiste* Counter-Enlightenment *Robespierrisme* in the French Revolution.[93]

For all these reasons, the *TTP* was profoundly subversive of Hobbes' political, religious, and social philosophy as it was of everything else characterizing the structures of authority of the age, Scripture most of all. Hobbes and Spinoza were both great thinkers. Both had an immense impact on their times. To the question may not Hobbes "have been the more far-reachingly and deeply influential of the two?" nearly all political theorists and historians today would still answer in the affirmative.[94] Preference among scholars for seeing Hobbes as the primary figure remains vigorous, and Antoine Lilti has shown that even French scholars express outrage whenever the long dominant (but misleading) tradition of stressing the

---

[91] Spinoza, *Theological-Political Treatise*, 202.
[92] Melamed, "Charitable Interpretations," 271; Israel, *Revolutionary Jews*, 55–6, 65–6, 73–4.
[93] Steenbakkers, "Beyond the Legends," 23.
[94] Malcolm, *Aspects of Hobbes*, 537; Springborg, "Enlightenment of Thomas Hobbes," 528.

basically English origins of the Enlightenment's early phases and Hobbes' primary role in the rise of deism is questioned. But for those acknowledging the force of the distinction between radical and mainstream Enlightenment, it is impossible to find cogent grounds for claiming the Western world's first major democratic republican thinker, the philosopher who went furthest in developing Bible criticism, eliminating religious authority, and promoting the happiness and fulfilment of the individual in society and under government, counted for less in shaping the radical tendency than the rigid monarchist who barely stirred to defend toleration and freedom of thought, and turned the individual into a mere subject with scant scope for freedom of expression.

Where Hobbes summons the English to be firm Anglicans, Spinoza does not seek to make his contemporaries Jews, Protestants, Catholics, or Muslims.[95] Regarding moral status and "true religion" all are equal in his eyes. In these respects, the Bible criticism of Blount, Toland, and Collins tends to follow Spinoza, far more directly and obviously than Hobbes or Locke. Hobbes and Spinoza both aimed to dampen strife and dispute and promote peace in society. But Hobbes did not finally emancipate interpretation of Scripture from ecclesiastical authority, remove the supernatural, or complete the transition from regarding Scripture as sacred literature to rendering it a purely human, non-divine creation. Rather, like Bacon, Hobbes entrusts its public status, deciding which purported biblical texts are canonical, specifying what is and is not binding, and its general explication, to the Church of England and, via that church, ultimately the hereditary sovereign.[96]

Unlike Spinoza or the Koerbaghs, Van Berkel, Van den Enden, and Meyer, Hobbes did not seek to use reason, as it has been aptly put, to "set mankind free from ignorance, superstition and blind submission to the political as well as the ecclesiastical power."[97] In these respects, Spinoza, for whom there is no such thing as a biblical canon, religious authority or the sovereign's sway over "true religion," was fundamentally an Enlightenment founder in a way that Hobbes simply was not.

---

[95] Mason, *God of Spinoza*, 136–7.
[96] Osier, "L'Herméneutique," 336–7; Malcolm, "Hobbes, Ezra, and the Bible," 425–7; Lucci, *Scripture and Deism*, 42–3, 109.
[97] Vinciguerra, *Spinoza et le signe*, 250–3; Lucci, *Scripture and Deism*, 43.

26
Spinoza Completes his Philosophical System

26.i Emancipating the Individual

Despite having interrupted his writing of the *Ethics* in 1665 and leaving his principal work of philosophy aside, unfinished, down to the early or mid-1670s, it was decidedly in the late 1660s, as he worked out the concluding political chapters of the *TTP* that Spinoza completed the basic framework of his overall system, integrating his political thought and philosophy of religion together with his epistemology, metaphysics, and his ethics. It is therefore worth pausing at this point in his biography to review his project as a whole especially to consider how and why all the parts fitted closely together as they clearly did, in his own mind, by the late 1660s. The complex relationship between his tying all the key ingredients together in one highly integrated bundle and the specific personal and historical circumstances shaping his life at this culminating moment in his philosophical career will then become somewhat clearer.

Originating in an attempt to reform Descartes' system, Spinoza's philosophy radically diverged from the essentials of Cartesian dualism, absorbing important strands of medieval Jewish philosophy, ancient Stoicism, Roman historiography, the science culture of his time, and Hobbes. Without doubt, the unprecedented degree to which Spinoza eliminated supernatural powers and beings, and all possibility of miracles and separation of body and soul, proved extremely shocking to the religious sensibilities of his age. Accordingly, during the Early Enlightenment he was everywhere regularly termed, as the Welsh writer Jenkin Philipps put it, "atheorum princeps" or "prince [or chief] of atheists."[1]

Yet, Spinoza's approach to reality and human life also enabled him to offer an inspiring moral and social philosophy rejecting social hierarchy and all forms of priestly religious authority that attracted a small but tenacious underground following of friends, allies, and adherents. Combining a vision of individual self-improvement with how political forms and society can be coaxed to optimal effectiveness for benefiting the lives of all, Spinoza forged a lasting basis for

---

[1] Israel, *Enlightenment Contested*, 178–80, 184, 186.

oppositional attitudes towards oppressive structures governing social, religious, and political institutions, law, lifestyle, and education.

Spinoza asked why exactly a great many people lead unnecessarily unfulfilled, miserable and wretched lives. His *Ethics* argues that individuals usually fail to gain insight into the nature of the universe and their position in it and identifies their inadequate understanding of themselves, their emotions, and their surroundings as the reason for their being readily misled and entangled in self-defeating notions. He viewed men's inadequate thinking as a form of bondage, the chief defect negatively affecting the quality of people's lives, hampering personal happiness and driving subservience to priests and aristocrats, and willing or unwilling, sometimes even ardent, submission to tyrants. Without men realizing it, their own limited grasp of reality keeps them trapped in this mix of internal and external bondage. Accordingly, Spinoza commences Part IV of his *Ethics* by redefining human "slavery" as individual lack of power to guide, moderate, and restrain one's emotions. Individual freedom, by contrast, is the fruitful outcome of learning to use one's reason to control one's own passions while successfully resisting exploitative and invasive pressures arising from the desires and schemes of others. "So long as we are not torn by emotions contrary to our nature," he maintains in the *Ethics*' final part, "we have the power of ordering and connecting the inclinations of the body according to the order of the intellect [Quamdiu affectibus, qui nostrae naturae sunt contrarii, non conflictamur, tamdiu potestatem habemus ordinandi, et concatenandi Corporis affectiones secundum ordinem ad intellectum]."[2]

It may seem strange that men can experience emotions "that are contrary to our nature [qui nostrae naturae sunt contrarii]," but much as in Hobbes, Spinoza's primitive state of man encourages strife, subjection, and stark hierarchies, offering nothing at all welcoming or appealing.[3] Unlike the natural state of Hobbes, though, Spinoza's original natural state is not just unsafe and highly imperfect, both individually and collectively, but remains fundamental to our being, shaping our emotional make-up, and impossible to fully discard while also, however, allowing for the possibility of emerging from the cage of our initial, instinctive impulses, for slowly improving and refining our basic nature. Here, there is no Hobbesian "social contract" suddenly lifting whole societies from the state of nature to a fundamentally new level in one fell swoop, nor any reason to want to switch back to a happy natural state lost amidst the maze of modern artificiality by stripping away corrupt layers obscuring man's original supposedly pure nature, as with Rousseau. Even men's optimal level of self-fashioning or "state of blessedness," as Spinoza labels it, inescapably remains tied to the "state of nature," so that everyone starts out in utter ignorance and renews man's perpetual climb

---

[2] Spinoza, *Ethics* V, Prop. X; Spinoza, *Opera* ii, 287; Spinoza, *Collected Works* (ed. Curley) i, 601.
[3] Hoekstra, "Lion in the House," 206–9; Field, *Potentia*, 168–74.

towards a better individual life and better society, an unending and ceaselessly tortuous process with "knowledge of natural things" the only path forward for individuals and society.

Having one's mind dominated by inadequate ideas without any countervailing remedy in Spinoza is the prime well of misery, deprivation, and the blighting of individual and collective life. Unlike other would-be reformers of our world like Comenius, Serrarius, Boreel, Steno, or Baxter, Spinoza does not view contemporary man as possessing the option of wholesale transformation or conversion into a fundamentally different kind of moral being via religiously attained self-renewal, whether by submitting to a particular church as Steno exhorted, or embracing Boreel's (or Baxter's) unchurched Christian "universalism." In Spinoza's reform project, uniquely, men's collective fate depends on the success, or otherwise, of the most rational in society persuading the rest to introduce reason-based, democratic republican laws and institutions, legal and political frameworks buttressing the "common good" in which everyone, including those unwilling or unable to discard their prejudices and fixations (who are then "forced to be free") live freer, less conflictual, more fulfilling lives. Individual true freedom is attained only via pursuit of "virtue," or what in places Spinoza terms "love of freedom alone" which aims to know the virtues and their causes, filling one's mind with the happiness deriving from true knowledge and learning to apply that knowledge. The final goal of the best life, Spinoza's *Ethics* teaches, the absorbing of "true religion" and piety into the philosophically-minded individual, means occupying the mind with the virtues of justice and charity, and the happiness these bring when cherished for their own sake. But the path for the individual is not a feasible path for society. The overriding problem remains that most men cannot see the best path. Nevertheless, Spinoza believes collective general elevation of humanity is still attainable via the collective impact of the rational self-elevation of the few who do understand.[4] Through introducing beneficial forms, education and laws, the unknowing multitude and the "select few" become tightly bonded and interdependent.

The person on the right path is one "who strives to moderate his emotions and appetites" and does so "from the love of Liberty alone [ex solo Libertatis amore]." *Libertas* is indubitably a key ethical as well as political term in Spinoza, and it is here especially that the concerns of the *Ethics* and the *Tractatus Theologico-Politicus* of 1670, as well as his last text, the unfinished *Tractatus Politicus*, most strikingly converge. In the *TTP* and the *Ethics* our knowledge of nature's laws, and hence of God, and adjusting ourselves and our society to them, constitute the *summum bonum*, the highest good, and are the "highest felicity and happiness of

---

[4] Tatián, *Spinoza, filosofía terrena*, 10; Mosbah, "Ultimi Barbarorum," 320; LeBuffe, *From Bondage to Freedom*, 18–21.

man, his final end and the aim of all his actions."[5] Pursuing truth, and adjusting our lives to the truth, is a ceaseless struggle but also rewarding work: conquering our endless false notions and restraining our cruder instincts and impulses is the key to individual success in leading a free and happy life and, equally, to our improved collective fate.

The links between Spinoza's *Ethics* and his political and social philosophy remain extremely close throughout, a point often insufficiently stressed in modern philosophy teaching. Embracing Spinoza's premises about individual striving for knowledge and self-improvement renders it impossible to circumvent the political problem of how to organize and structure a secular moral order and arena of free expression, hostile to every form of political and legal support for theological rulings and dogmas which Spinoza deems false values and misconceptions. His philosophical system necessitates a political and legal reform agenda designed to erect a robust and durable legal framework for attaining the optimal level of self-fulfilment and "freedom," or what he calls the "well-being of the people," and repel threats to that political construct. Society's "common good," the "salus populi" [salvation of the people], or salus multitudinis [salvation of the multitude], as he sometimes terms it,[6] is conceived as the grounding that nurtures and maintains the freedoms, restraints, and laws needed for fostering maximum independence of individual critical judgement and growing group consensus, or rational self-development for all.

For Spinoza, a vast divide separates those who are "free" in his sense and the "multitude," the bulk of mankind. To an extent a much-noticed article by Yitzchak Melamed on "Charitable Interpretations" in philosophy rightly stresses that Spinoza harbours a distinctly low opinion of the masses. In one sense, he does. However, in Spinoza's schema it is not the masses conceived as an economic or class category that is at issue but something very different. Like the conventional court political culture of his age, Spinoza envisaged the multitude more in educational and ethical terms than as a socio-economic stratum. But where Tacitus, Lipsius, and the monarchist Tacitists of his time viewed the *multitudo* or *vulgus* as equivalent to the common people and the uneducated, Spinoza characteristically reinterprets the original Tacitean quotes and expressions to project the *vulgus* rather as those who are ignorant, everyone that is possessing neither "iudicium aut veritas [judgement nor sincerity]," as Tacitus puts it.

Spinoza concurs with Tacitus (and Hobbes) that the *vulgus* are the chief source of instability and trouble in the republic, the dissatisfied, superstitious, inherently unreasonable element, always demanding something new. He quotes and wholeheartedly agrees with Tacitus' dictum that "in vulgo nihil modicum, terrere, ni

---

[5] Spinoza, *Theological-Political Treatise*, 59–60; Giancotti Boscherini, *Lexicon Spinozanum* i, 115.
[6] Giancotti Boscherini, *Lexicon Spinozanum* ii, 973–5.

paveant [in the *vulgus* there is no moderation, they terrify unless cowed]."[7] But he typically does so subverting such familiar contemporary Tacitists as Justus Lipsius, who regularly equated the *vulgus* with the common people, while also contradicting Hobbes (as well as slightly modifying Tacitus himself). For the reader soon discovers that this ever-present peril to the political stability of society, the overpowering perennial menace of the *vulgus*, embraces everyone whose mind is ruled by ignorance, superstition, and the passions, the direst segment of the "whole world against us" actually being our world's kings, ecclesiastics, aristocracy, and the bulk of its academics. The sages, or the wise, on the other hand, holding the line for humanity against the *vulgus*, are the few (as in Maimonides and Delmedigo before him), found indiscriminately scattered among the rich, middling, and poor.

Spinoza then is by no means discriminating against, or looking down on, the poor and uneducated but rather scorning in particular "those who confine to the common people the faults inherent in all mankind."[8] Much as Spinoza cites the New Testament to undermine Christianity, and the Old to sap rabbinic Judaism, he reworks Tacitus to undermine the early modern era's prevailing Tacitean-Lipsian and Hobbesian monarchical political culture.[9] Spinoza's *vulgus* are simply the great majority of humans in their conventional state, that is men thinking in the usual inadequate manner whatever class of the population they belong to, encompassing everyone pursuing power for self-seeking purposes, who amass money to control others, oppress rather than aid others and, by making no effort to seek the truth, sadly miss the reality of things. Since the "credulous and untrustworthy" powerful and rich are usually as much or more of a menace to society than the illiterate, they are consequently more blameworthy than the credulous poor. Conversely, the poorest and lowliest, where thinking rationally, are in principle just as capable of thinking philosophically and escaping "bondage" as anyone else. Abominating rulers like Philip II of Spain, Louis XIV of France, and Charles II of England, Spinoza's overall approach demotes monarchs and their courtiers, along with princes, ecclesiastics, academics, and the wealthy elites to the ranks of the lowest and worst of the "multitude," meaning those thinking harmfully, in inadequate terms.

Distinctly unimpressed by the aristocracies and super-rich of his day, Spinoza sharply distinguishes between money-making for procuring necessities and amassing money as financial-commercial capital for self-aggrandizement, as an instrument of power, social control, and pride. Scorning use of money as a path to luxury and tool of dominance and control was basic to his general philosophy of

---

[7] Tacitus, *Annals*, 47; Spinoza, *Political Treatise*, 90; Bastiani, "Spinoza against Political Tacitism," 1053–4.
[8] Spinoza, *Political Treatise*, 90; LeBuffe, *Spinoza on Reason*, 170, 200n13.
[9] Mellor, *Tacitus*, 81–2, 91, 94; Bastiani, "Spinoza against Political Tacitism," 1044–6, 1054.

life and wider critique of conventional thinking—the everyday notions and prejudices vitiating "happiness," obscuring the true goal of human life, an attitude fed doubtless by his own personal exit from affluence and ease following his family business collapse and break with the synagogue.[10]

Yet, working in groups, collaboration, and therefore trade, remain essential to raising the level of human existence. Without exchanging the goods they produce for other items they need, individuals can hardly provide for their needs on their own, states the appendix to *Ethics* IV. "Money has provided a convenient means of acquiring all these items which is why thinking about money usually occupies the minds of the multitude more than anything else. For they can hardly conceive any species of joy without the accompanying idea of money as its cause." Those who "seek money," though, like big merchants and financiers, accumulating wealth not from "need, nor for necessities" like the poor and modestly comfortable, "but because they have acquired the arts of money-making and pride themselves on it very much," are locked in a vice vitiating individual pursuit of happiness in many respects.[11] Here his own father was likely among those he had in mind.

Accepting Spinoza's premises, the path to wisdom is potentially open to everyone. In a society like seventeenth-century Holland where practically everyone was taught to read, it was more a matter of individual choice whether one devoted oneself to the quest for truth and pursuit of understanding or not than in more traditional societies where literacy was and is sharply curtailed. Admittedly, in Spinoza's system too religion's outward forms are still needed because the "masses should be taught primarily to be obedient," but claiming that, for Spinoza, "insofar as knowledge may impede obedience, it should not be taught to the masses" is incorrect, indeed entirely contradicts his basic position.[12] For it can "not be doubted," contends Spinoza, "that the best state accords to everyone the same liberty to philosophize as we showed that faith likewise allows."[13] At the heart of Spinoza's democratic impulse is his conviction that everyone, equally, possesses the right to freedom of thought and expression, to examine philosophically, criticize others and explore doctrines, no matter how much Catholic, Calvinist, Lutheran, Anglican, Muslim, and Jewish religious teachers demand that they should conform and not question. Here we find the basic ground why, both the *TTP* and in his last text, the *TP*, Spinoza repeatedly manifests an unyielding preference for democracy as against both monarchy and

---

[10] Tosel, *Spinoza, ou l'autre (in)finitude*, 149–51; Casarino, "Marx before Spinoza," 195; Israel, *Revolutionary Jews*, 48–50.
[11] Spinoza, *Opera* ii, 274; Spinoza, *Collected Works* (ed. Curley) i, 593; Schnepf, "Enlightened Radicals," 97–8.
[12] Melamed, "Charitable Interpretations," 271.
[13] Spinoza, *Theological-Political Treatise*, 254; Fraenkel, *Philosophical Religions*, 256.

aristocracy, an anti-Hobbesian bias already inherent in his formulation of the "common good."[14]

When Spinoza states in the *TTP* that "the true purpose of the state is in fact freedom," he clearly means a "freedom" that includes security, stability, and absence of internecine strife; but at the same time, unlike Hobbes, he places great stress on the need to secure equal freedom for all citizens to seek their happiness under the laws, develop their minds and bodies, and especially "use their reason freely." Establishing the best form of state is itself the most crucial means, in Spinoza, for creating the conditions enabling individuals to pursue knowledge, overcome inadequate thinking, and move towards the supreme good, a line of argument constituting the vital link between the *Ethics* and the political treatises.[15] "*Sapere aude* [dare to know]," it has been objected, "the (somewhat pompous) slogan of Kantian Enlightenment is not the advice Spinoza would offer the masses."[16] But this hardly reflects the reality of Spinoza's system where the more citizens seek the truth, the better and the more stable the democratic republic becomes. Mankind's great problem is that most men impelled by prejudice and their passions are incapable of following the path of "reason" so that what progress humanity achieves depends on instituting principles, laws, moral norms, and structures of authority the nature of which is correctly grasped by just a few.

The democratic republic needs to be sufficiently robust to withstand the ceaseless disruptive pressure of the "multitude" whose inadequate notions constantly menace the democratic freedoms, and hence the basic functioning and purpose of the state.[17] So even when Spinoza's democratic republic achieves temporary success, it always stands uncomfortably close to mankind's unenviable original state, hence to disaster and wretchedness for everybody, especially as the truth or falsity of men's ideas, asserts the *Ethics*, has little bearing on the emotional force with which men desire others to think as they do, and orchestrate group hatred to attack those they oppose. Furthermore, while men when encountering others disagreeing with their opinion, do often tend to pause in their love or hatred for someone or something to reconsider, and tend to hesitate even if usually only momentarily when hearing contrary views, wherever and whenever free discussion is curbed, and men are efficiently policed into groups loving or hating the same things as themselves, everyone loses because organized ignorance is then greatly bolstered and fortified.[18]

---

[14] Vernière, *Spinoza et la pensée française*, 485; Israel, "Introduction" to Spinoza, *Theological-Political Treatise*, viii–xxxiv, here p. xxx.
[15] Spinoza, *Theological-Political Treatise*, 252; James, "Freedom, Slavery and the Passions," 228; Sangiacomo, *Spinoza on Reason*, 97–9.
[16] Melamed, "Charitable Interpretations," 271.
[17] Moreau, *Spinoza. État*, 46–7; Gatens, *Spinoza's Hard Path*, 26–7.
[18] Spinoza, *Ethics* III, Prop. 31; Matheron, *Individu et communauté*, 166–71; Moreau, *Spinoza. État*, 49–50.

An emotion is bad or harmful, affirms Spinoza, "insofar as it prevents the mind from being able to think" (*Ethics* IV, Prop. 26 and Prop. 27). Here, the best known English translation is slightly too abbreviated. Spinoza's Latin reads: "affectus eatenus tantum malus, seu noxius est, quatenus mens ab eo impeditur, quominus possit cogitare," that is an emotion is bad or harmful only insofar as the mind is "impeded by it, in how much less it can think."[19] The idea that unbridled emotion clouds the mind and hampers human reason is basic to Spinoza's ethical approach. This close connection between controlling passions, understanding things correctly, and human happiness, Spinoza reaffirms when explaining *Ethics* V, Proposition 15: "he who understands himself and his affects clearly rejoices [qui se, suosque affectus clare, et distincte intellegit, laetatur], and this joy is accompanied by the idea of God. Hence, he who loves God by the same reasoning does so the more, the more he understands himself and his emotions."[20] Of course, God being Nature neither loves nor hates, and cannot reward or punish, or in any way reward or return the love men feel for Him—indeed God makes no response to humans loving Him, so that he who loves God does not expect God should love or reward him in return, or favour him above others.

"Libertas" is fundamental, but given Spinoza's necessitarianism, his denying freedom of the will is also a deeply paradoxical element.[21] Freedom's most vital function is where, as with "libertas philosophica or libertas philosophandi," it advances within the individual by removing barriers to critical thinking and discussion like uncontrolled emotion, superstition, or holding bigoted or dogmatic views, and equally in society by removing barriers erected by despotic governments or intolerant churches seeking to block criticism, freedom of expression, and propagation of adequate thinking.[22] Here, in encouraging our collective transition to greater rationality, the ethical, intellectual, and political are intricately bound together. Hence, Spinoza's *libertas philosophandi* is also closely tied to enlarging the freedom men enjoy when cultivating and expanding their understanding together in groups, through schooling children, adult education, public debate, informal discussion, art and the theatre, all these being potential collaborative reservoirs and channels, urges Spinoza, contributing to stable and lasting human happiness.[23] For joyful living, one must cultivate one's understanding and appreciation of the arts, plants, fine food and drink (in moderation), and above all seek positive, instructive encounters with others.

---

[19] Spinoza, *Ethics* V, Prop. 9; Spinoza, *Collected Works* (ed. Curley) i, 601.
[20] Spinoza, *Collected Works* (ed. Curley) i, 603–4; Giancotti Boscherini, *Lexicon Spinozanum* ii, 650–1.
[21] Levine, "Determinism and Responsibility," 349; Gatens, *Spinoza's Hard Path*, 45.
[22] Giancotti Boscherini, *Lexicon Spinozanum* ii, 650.
[23] James, *Spinoza on Learning*, 79, 124, 126–7; LeBuffe, *Spinoza on Reason*, 168–9; Laerke, *Spinoza and the Freedom*, 147–9.

Basic to Spinozism, in contrast to Stoicism and Christianity, is Spinoza's contention that the will, or mind, cannot directly master, curb, or redirect emotions or prejudices. Will and intellect being one, men and women can engineer alterations in the interplay of will and emotion within themselves only by more rationally and effectively mobilizing or unleashing one impulse against another. To balance one's desires and emotions rationally and successfully, intricate introspection is required leading to readiness to examine and confront false beliefs, superstitions, obsessions, prejudice, awe, delusions, damaging habits like monkish reclusiveness, and teachings driving the hatred feeding bigotry, contempt, discrimination, and demands for doctrinal purity that debase, hinder, and inflict suffering on individuals and societies. In this way, knowledge powering the bridling of destructive passions in favour of positive ones becomes the prime instrument of human freedom.[24] For Spinoza, as with Nietzsche (in his middle period), it is knowledge alone that makes possible "our de-deification of Nature" driving what became the Enlightenment's push to "naturalize" humanity,[25] enabling us better to come to terms with reality, our reality and ourselves.

"Wherever, for example, God's nature is known to us," as Spinoza expounds his subtle "compatibilist" argument, the reality of God's existence follows just as necessarily from our nature "as it flows from the nature of a triangle that its three angles are equal to two right angles"; and yet, we are never so free, argues Spinoza, as when we knowingly affirm its truth. "Because this necessity is really nothing other than God's decree, as I have already clearly shown in my Appendix [i.e. the *Cogitata Metaphysica*], we may understand after a fashion by what arrangement we do something freely, that is are the cause of our doing it notwithstanding we do it necessarily and from God's decree."[26] By contrast, indulging lust for money or pleasure, according to Spinoza, is not an expression of "freedom" but yielding to the bondage of our passions. Understanding and accommodating, rather than denying and resisting, what is necessary and true constitutes Spinoza's "libertas." Accordingly, wanting to live under a restrictive order, demanding theocracy, monarchy, or an aristocratic republic, thereby enslaving oneself and others, or swearing undying allegiance to a false creed, no matter how passionately one believes in it can never be a "free" choice for anybody, no matter how great one's fervour for faith, priests or tyrants, or government propaganda cultivating baseless lies contrary to reason. Ignorance and credulity condemn every such believer to "unfreedom." Only free philosophizing and pursuit of truth, via free expression, choosing life in a democratic

---

[24] Hardt, *Gilles Deleuze*, 54; Uhlmann and Gatens, "Spinoza on Art," 430, 436.
[25] Schacht, "Nietzsche's *Gay Science*," 76.
[26] Spinoza, *Opera* iv, 130; Spinoza, *Briefwisseling*, 190; Spinoza, *Collected Works* (ed. Curley) i, 378–9.

republic and eschewing meaningless theological wrangling secures human "freedom" in Spinoza's sense.

Spinoza explicitly rejects Descartes' freedom of the mind contending that "our liberty lies not in a kind of contingency, nor in knowing whether something is good or bad, but in our way of affirming or denying real things; the less indifferently we affirm or deny, the more we are free."[27] Reconciling freedom with necessity in this fashion, Spinoza proclaims his guiding principle. As developed in the *TTP* and subsequently, his approach signifies that the truly "free," those living according to reason, do not require the republic's freedoms and laws to help them dwell as free citizens; those who do need them are the ignorant, superstitious, and base-minded "multitude," courtiers and ecclesiastics especially. It is the ignorant and misinformed, the great majority, who require the full force and coercive power of the democratic republic to shepherd them in the right direction. Central to Spinoza's schema is his notion of coercing the majority into living in accordance with "freedom" by preventing their intimidating and harming others with their lust for power and wealth, misinformation, false pretensions, bigotry and excesses. When classifying members of society in ethical terms, Spinoza's system acknowledges four distinct levels or types of citizen. First comes the free man acting in accordance with society's laws on the basis of reason alone, the optimal benchmark, with no one consistently attaining this level. Second, is the pious person obeying on grounds of religious teaching. Citizens sullenly complying solely from fear of punishment comprise the third class, while those unable to bridle their unruly passions who regularly break the law undergoing punishment, furtive exile, or concealment in consequence, form the lowest, most degraded category.[28]

As the "true purpose of laws is normally evident only to a few," holds Spinoza and "most men are almost incapable of grasping what is rational, and hardly live by reason at all, legislators, to constrain all men equally, wisely contrived another goal, very different from the one that necessarily follows from the nature of laws: they promise those obeying the laws things the common people most desire, and threaten those violating them with what they most fear. In this way they have tried to restrain the common people like a horse with a bridle, so far as they could."[29] Part of this "bridle" is the public or "civil religion," ceremonies adopted by the state, which Spinoza views (like Rousseau who became acquainted with his writings under Diderot's influence in the late 1740s)[30] as a purely political device.

---

[27] Spinoza, *Opera* iv, 127; Spinoza, *Collected Works* (ed. Curley) i, 376.
[28] Israel, *Democratic Enlightenment*, 636–7, 725–6; Fraenkel, "Spinoza's Philosophy of Religion," 389; Kisner, *Spinoza on Human Freedom*, 177–8.
[29] Spinoza, *Theological-Political Treatise*, 58; Spinoza, *Collected Works* (ed. Curley) ii, 127; Fraenkel, "Spinoza's Philosophy of Religion," 387–8.
[30] Villaverde, "Rousseau, lecteur de Spinoza," 118.

"Piety" is useful to society, hence organized religion's doctrines and ceremonies, though untrue, are in part useful too.

Rejecting humility, repentance, and pity, arguing we should be benevolent towards others on the basis of reason and justice, not pity, are typical *exempla* of Spinoza's applied moral mechanics, a moral relativity pivoting, as Nietzsche recognized, seeing this as a point where his own uncompromising naturalism converges with Spinoza's, on wholly eliminating the concept of unmitigated or innate "evil."[31] The elementary principle of Spinoza's morality, that "evil" does not exist while "cheerfulness" [hilaritas] cannot be excessive and is always "good," recalled in the minds of the theologians of his time the impiety of ancient heretical sects like the Pelagians whose rejection of Original Sin was universally condemned. Unlike Hobbes, Spinoza proposed a naturalist doctrine of good and bad, a relativity existing prior to the forming of states that seemed shamelessly "evil" to most readers by suggesting the supreme "Christian" virtue of humility is inherently bad and that extra-marital intercourse, homosexuality, and love of wine—and even very occasionally assassination—are variously good or bad depending on circumstances, while melancholy, self-denying abstinence, and self-abasement are always intrinsically "bad" (*Ethics* IV, Prop. 42).[32]

If a man becomes more conscious of his limitations by contemplating something more powerful than himself, holds Spinoza, this is not "humility" but a rational process of appraising one's capabilities more accurately in the light of reality—thereby enhancing one's subsequent capacity and effectiveness. Humility is reckoning oneself inherently weak, inferior or base in deference to others under a collective supposedly supernaturally imposed code of values and commandments. Christian humility is therefore classified by Spinoza as inherently "bad" for humans, being a passive, deferential emotion depressing the individual in his or her own estimation, and that of others, and eroding confidence in oneself without enhancing anyone's capabilities and effectiveness. Hence, it encourages misplaced deference and self-abasement.[33] Since the essence of "virtue is to preserve one's own being under the guidance of reason," a person ignorant or deluded about himself, like one vowing to remain meek, or striving for monkish seclusion and abstinence, is by Spinoza's definition devoid of virtue; and because he or she acts least of all from "virtue," that person becomes "the most impotent in spirit."[34] Equally, for Spinoza repentance "is not a virtue" even if useful in certain contexts. For a person following the dictates of reason, or trying to, it is absurd to repent in the religious sense since heightened awareness of the need to avoid what is "bad"

---

[31] Kisner, *Spinoza on Human Freedom*, 135, 212; Look, "Becoming," 327.
[32] Spinoza, *Ethics* IV, Prop. 24 and Prop. 56; Moreau, *Spinoza. État*, 60–1.
[33] Spinoza, *Ethics* IV, Prop. 56; Matheron, *Individu et communauté*, 160–1.
[34] Spinoza, *Ethics* IV, Prop. 24 and Prop. 56.

in the action in question is most effective where resolved on without any self-demeaning process.

Self-esteem, or as Spinoza calls it, *acquiescientia in se ipso* [contentment in oneself], by contrast, provided it does not inflate into arrogance, unjustified bravado, or false, exaggerated notions of one's worth, talent, and abilities, engenders a reflective joy and satisfaction and hence is life-enhancing and "good." This strand of pride and self-congratulation in Spinoza and his following his former Danish friend turned adversary, Steno, especially abhorred. Where humility focuses excessively on one's failings and inadequacy, on self-reproach for failure to satisfy requirements imposed by others, and is damaging by constraining one's striving, "self-esteem" focused on what one does well in one's own terms, can be either good or bad depending on whether it supports or hinders effort and striving for excellence.[35] "Self-esteem," whatever churchmen say, is in itself an inherent virtue, albeit a "good" requiring careful cultivation and vigilance lest it swells into "pride" rooted in exaggerated notions of one's worth. At its worst—whether based on individual presumption or dynastic or aristocratic pretension—exaggerated self-esteem nurtures false, distorted ideas of one's status and rank damaging to oneself and others, thwarting constructive cooperation.

Since most people do not live under the guidance of reason, conventional false "virtues" like humility, repentance, self-abasement, and pity are, however, provisionally useful contrivances, concedes Spinoza, even indispensable to wise legislators constructing a polity based on the greatest good for all equally. Since most of humanity rages and intimidates when not fearful [terret vulgus, nisi metuat], the only way to instil sufficient awe to buttress the "common good" effectively is to proclaim what seems impressive, wondrous, and true to the ignorant and credulous mind. "So it is not surprising that those prophets who showed regard for the good of the whole community, and not just the few, have zealously advocated humility, repentance and reverence."[36] Despite his hostility to churches and clergy, Spinoza judged revealed religion's moral influence on society and individual lifestyle, in the case of most individuals, potentially positive at least in part. Even if the more unruly types enslaved to passions and irrational emotion are immune to such pressures, those embracing the false dictates and virtues of revealed religion, the ordinary pious, despite their failure to understand, "can in the end far more readily be shepherded than the rest" to "follow reason's guidance, that is become free persons and enjoy the life of the blessed [multo facilius, quam alii, duci possunt, ut tandem ex ductu rationis vivant, hoc est, ut liberi sint, et beatorum vita fruantur]."[37]

---

[35] Curley, *Behind the Geometrical Method*, 127; Laerke, *Spinoza and the Freedom*, 102–4.
[36] Spinoza, *Opera* ii, 250; Matheron, *Individu et communauté*, 435.   [37] Spinoza, *Opera* ii, 250.

26.ii Popular Sovereignty and the "General Will"

"General will" has rarely been identified as one of the truly innovative strands of Spinoza's thought. Yet it is among the keys to his entire system and many features of his biography. The central problem of politics as Spinoza identifies it, in both the *TTP* and his later *Tractatus Politicus* (1675–6), two treatises composed in sharply differing contexts but essentially unified in message, is that "good citizens" are few so that most people, notwithstanding the social class to which they belong, rich or poor, are chiefly motivated by selfish pleasures, self-interest, and short-sighted impulses and emotions rooted in ignorance, credulity, and fanaticism, a conclusion Spinoza applies, we have seen, to kings, courtiers, ecclesiastics, and academics as much as, if not more than, any other group. Consequently, the multitude, kings included, possess little understanding of what the "common interest" is and no respect for the *salus populi* which they ignore. The multitude's moods and preferences, moreover, constantly swing unpredictably. Since most men are not guided by "reason," neither their loyalty to the republic nor obedience to the law can be relied on. Hence, what Spinoza saw as society's supreme predicament which he would later spell out in Chapter 6 of the *Tractatus Politicus*: "the commonwealth is always in greater danger from its citizens than from its [external] enemies; for 'rari quippe boni' [for the good ones, assuredly, are rare]."[38]

Society only possesses a stable common will and genuinely democratic character, securing liberty and equal right to pursuit of happiness for all where its laws and institutions are organized, and remain fixed, on the basis of "reason" enabling the "common good," or general will, to govern legislative decisions and laws. Because making the people sovereign, enabling society as a whole to rule as the veritable sovereign, is something most people cannot comprehend, the power of a free people becomes genuinely sovereign, that is able to constrain all to live in harmony and freedom, when and only when reason presides. But given universal human nature, a functioning democratic republic is always an exacting challenge, impossible without elevated guidance establishing appropriate laws which might originate in the inspired leadership of a Moses, but to be durable and solidly established require collective ceremonies, such as the Jewish Passover, commemorating what is best in the people's history. Both the overall reality and the values best suited to human well-being can only be projected by philosophers.[39]

Lacking such a framework, the ancient Hebrew Republic degenerated into monarchy which, besides wars and other pitfalls, exposed their body politic to growing clerical sway with proliferating splits, sects, reforming prophets and false

---

[38] Spinoza, *Tractatus Politicus* in *Oeuvres* v, 142–3.
[39] Spinoza, *Theological-Political Treatise*, 210–11; Spinoza, *Political Treatise*, 66; Balibar, *Spinoza et le politique*, 46; Cristofolini, "Peuple et multitude," 58.

prophets more and more destabilizing society.[40] Another lesson the Hebrew Republic's degeneration and debasement offers, for Spinoza, is that theology rears its head when sovereignty is transferred from "God" or the whole people to the high priests and when the "common good" is forgotten. Once priests and theology preside, society is in for unending rifts and feuding. "There were no sects in [the ancient Hebrew] religion," insists Spinoza, "until the high priests secured authority to issue decrees and manage the business of government in the second Commonwealth," that is the Hasmonaean Jewish republic (c.165 to 63 BC). These men "usurped control of the state and finally even wanted to be called kings, so their authority could be made permanent." The levers of government once seized, the priests continually strove to expand their power "by promulgating fresh edicts about belief, ceremonies and everything else, and attempting to lend such rulings as much authority as the Laws of Moses had." Thus, the true object of the laws was lost and "religion degenerated into fatal superstition," with much consequent harm to society.[41]

Societies deteriorate and unravel in this fashion because thirst for power leads to exhorting the multitude and pulling in the common people behind theologians and priests. Proliferation of rulings and ceremonies generates illicit sway and growing scope for dispute and commotion with the result that priestly power-seeking increasingly divides society into bitterly warring religious factions.[42] The rift in the Hasmonaean Jewish republic Spinoza especially highlights is that between Pharisees and Sadducees the latter being those he deems the "wiser sort." To strip those wealthier and more elevated than themselves of their offices, the "Pharisees aimed to stir up controversies about religion accusing the Sadducees of impiety. Emulating the Pharisees, the worst hypocrites everywhere, stirring the same frenzy (which they call zeal for God's law), persecute men of outstanding probity and known virtue, resented by the common people for precisely these qualities, by reviling their opinions, and inflaming the barbarous majority's anger against them." This is the chief threat to all societies and everyone's interest but not one easily checked "as it hides itself under the cloak of religion."[43] Crucial here is the fundamental distinction in Spinoza's system between "multitude" as "barbarous majority" enslaved to their passions and "the people" whose "common good" is ultimately at stake and who can embrace the "common good" and their own freedom, eschewing the unreasoning fury of the "multitude," only by being shown the way, guided by laws fixed by "reason." In Spinoza's political theory, the "people" is an abstraction, the good of which is the ultimate goal of everyone insofar as they possess understanding; the "multitude,"

---

[40] Spinoza, *Theological-Political Treatise*, 232–5; Novak, "Spinoza and the Doctrine," 93–4; Cooper, "Reevaluating Spinoza's Legacy," 479–81.
[41] Spinoza, *Theological-Political Treatise*, 231–2.
[42] Spinoza, *Theological-Political Treatise*, 232.
[43] Spinoza, *Theological-Political Treatise*, 233; Cristofolini, "Peuple et multitude," 46.

by contrast, often virtually its opposite, is an abstraction too but one always menacing, encompassing everyone lacking understanding who remains enslaved to credulity, prejudice, and their passions.

Teaching the dictates of reason therefore counts among the chief goals of education and politics. As Spinoza puts it in the *Ethics* (Part IV, Prop. 37), "the good which everyone who seeks virtue wants for himself, he desires also for other men, and this desire is greater the more he acquires knowledge of God [Bonum quod unusquisque qui sectatur virtutem, sibi appetit, reliquis hominibus etiam cupiet, et eo magis quo majorem Dei habuerit cognitionem]."[44] For this reason, swearing by the "common good," will buttress men's taking of oaths in court and in council more effectively than any theological construct because those asked to swear before magistrates or representative bodies "will be much more careful to avoid perjury if commanded to swear by their country's well-being and liberty, and by its supreme Council, than when asked to swear by God. Vowing by God introduces a private good the nature of which each evaluates himself; but when pledging the *libertas* and well-being of one's country, one swears by the common good of all [per commune omnium bonum]," the meaning of which one does not decide because it equates with the common sense of justice. If such a one "perjures himself," adds Spinoza, "he thereby declares himself the enemy of his country."[45]

When ensuring the "common good is attended to [ut communi bono consulatur]," what chiefly matters is distributing power and responsibility broadly.[46] As most individuals ignore "summum nostrum bonum" in their personal thinking, preferring their own advantage at the expense of everyone else, open debate and democratic assemblies are always inherently more advantageous for society, and for pursuing the "common good," than theocracy, aristocracy, or monarchy. Openness of public debate is a cumulative advantage so that in oligarchic republics like Spinoza's own native United Provinces, or the early modern Swiss canton republics, such as Zurich, Berne, and Geneva, the broader the oligarchy, the more representation and power is spread and decision-making requires discussion, the harder it is to veil self-seeking and corrupt pilfering from the public coffers and the better the common good is served. Small secretive councils always constitute a threat to republics and must be prevented from gaining influence and power "at the expense of great councils" as happened, with lamentable consequences, at Venice, Genoa, Berne, Zurich, and Geneva. "Hence, when a few decide everything out of their own inclination," as Spinoza expresses the point in the *Tractatus Politicus*, "liberty and the common good [communeque bonum] are lost."[47] In this

---

[44] Spinoza, *Ethica*, in *Oeuvres* iv, 386–7.
[45] Spinoza, *Collected Works* (ed. Curley) ii, 588; Giancotti Boscherini, *Lexicon Spinozanum* i, 116.
[46] Spinoza, *Opera* iii, 329; Spinoza, *Collected Works* (ed. Curley) ii, 569; Giancotti Boscherini, *Lexicon Spinozanum* i, 116; Tosel, "Théorie de la pratique," 197–8.
[47] Spinoza, *Opera* iii, 352; Spinoza, *Collected Works* (ed. Curley) ii, 594; Giancotti Boscherini, *Lexicon Spinozanum* i, 116; Begley, "Spinoza, Before and After," 568, 578n73.

way, the claim that perfecting our individual and collective intellect is the true path to advancing "summum nostrum bonum [our highest good]" equally infuses the *TP*, *TTP*, and the *Ethics*.

The notion that the great majority must be compelled to be free, that "whoever refuses to obey the general will shall be constrained to do so by the entire body: which means nothing other than that he shall be forced to be free," is sometimes scorned by modern commentators as a ridiculous paradox in political thought more associated with Rousseau than the true originator of this idea, Spinoza.[48] But it is basic to Spinoza's freedom that it is constituted less by limits placed on state power than by use of state power to impose limits on human selfishness and unconcern for others.[49] The sources, moreover, firmly indicate that Rousseau derives his *volonté générale*, like much else, via Diderot, from Spinoza. The principle of "General Will" actually makes less sense in the context of Rousseau's society where ordinary men and women, the world's "simple souls," are naturally good and men have far less need to learn anything from books or be guided by reason to acquire "virtue" than in Spinoza where the ignorant, far from naturally finding the right path themselves to a free, virtuous, and stable life, must be shepherded by the state inculcating a dogma-free rational civil religion.[50] And while state coercive power alone cannot "free the mind from theological prejudices [mentem a praejudiciis theologicis liberare]," it can in Spinoza's judgement effectively curb the immense harm would-be charismatic "leaders," prophets, Pharisees, mullahs, preachers, inquisitors, and theologians universally inflict on mankind.

Restraining the passions in the name of the "highest good," or "general will," is of overriding importance for the happiness of the great majority gripped by "superstition," and the fears and hopes on which it thrives, because "superstition," explains Spinoza in the preface to the *TTP*, remains a constant looming danger to everyone including the rare rational being. Superstition being, for most, what justifies and legitimizes tyranny, oppression, civil strife, external war, sorcery, persecution, scapegoating, witch-hunts, inquisitions, and general intolerance,[51] the democratic republic must, according to Spinoza, possess a sternly coercive function operating in parallel with its positive, enriching, and emancipating functions. Good laws and institutions are the fruit of reason, but are also simultaneously the chief bridle on the uncomprehending, self-seeking, and those eager

---

[48] Vernière, *Spinoza et la pensée française*, 484; McShea, *Political Philosophy of Spinoza*, 64; Tosel, "Théorie de la pratique," 199.

[49] Villaverde, "Rousseau, lecteur de Spinoza," 87–8; Peña, "República, libertad," 164–5; Israel, *Enlightenment that Failed*, 87–8, 291–5; Laerke, *Spinoza and the Freedom*, 137–40.

[50] Rousseau, *Social Contract*, 53; Villaverde, *Rousseau y el pensamiento*, 226; Israel, *Enlightenment that Failed*, 88, 291, 915.

[51] Spinoza, *Theological-Political Treatise*, 5.

to intimidate others. Nothing emerges more plainly from the *TTP* than that the aim of society "and every state" is not just to enable men to live securely, as in Hobbes, but also "satisfyingly," providing scope for every individual to develop his or her potential to the utmost.[52] The "foundation and purpose" of Spinoza's democratic republic is "to avoid the follies of appetite and as much as possible bring men within the limits of reason, so that they may dwell in peace and harmony." Thus, Spinoza's democratic republic inevitably possesses a double aspect: while beckoning all to elevate themselves, through knowledge, to follow the moral and political guidelines laid down by reason, promoting individual liberty, emotional stability, and happiness, the moral order underpinning its institutions must simultaneously constrain the ignorant, those that have to be "forced to be free."

These two impulses, rationalizing and constraining, together form Spinoza's "common good," though he is not the inventor of the basic concept itself which is essentially the "algemeene accorderende interest" spelled out in Dutch republican circles in the early 1660s not least by his older associate and Latin teacher Franciscus Van den Enden in his *Vrije Politieke Stellingen* (1665), a key text of Dutch seventeenth-century theoretical republicanism, and fundamental to a political thought tradition published in Dutch so crucially important historically and yet so generally ignored in the teaching of Western political thought. The most anti-Hobbesian and anti-Lockean element of all the anti-Hobbesian and anti-Lockean strands in Spinozism, this was the concept that later became the general interest, or "general will" as Diderot and d'Holbach (but not Rousseau) adopted it, in the 1750s. General interest as used in the main "general will" tradition means what best conduces to society's collective and to individual pursuit of worldly happiness, when the common best is defined by reason and directed by popular sovereignty, the collective power of all in society where their individual interests are treated as equal and theology is wholly set aside. This was far distant from Rousseau's position which he purposely detached and distanced from "reason."

Spinoza, followed by Diderot, d'Holbach, Condorcet, Volney, and Destutt de Tracy later, vests sovereignty not in any person, dynasty, institution, or assembly, and still less in the expressed wishes of ordinary people, but in the rationally determined "common good" of society as a whole. As a consequence, Spinoza envisages society's "common good" rooted in individual equality of freedom of expression and right to happiness as a conceptual unity and, where necessary, a coercive force. Walter Eckstein already in the 1940s, pointed to the affinities between the political ideas of Spinoza and Rousseau and "even almost literal coincidences in the expression of those ideas which can hardly be considered accidental." The same point was made by Paul Vernière and, later, Maria José

---

[52] Spinoza, *Theological-Political Treatise*, 47, 200–1.

Villaverde.[53] But this overlap is only partial. Spinoza buttresses his moral and political construct of the "common good" via a commonly shared civil or public "religion" devoid of theological dogma not as the directly expressed will of the people but rather, quite unlike Rousseau, as defined and determined exclusively by philosophical-scientific reason, prioritizing justice, equity, and charity, and giving these organizational form enshrined in laws and rights, a common good nearly always opposed to that of the ruler, or ruling elite, *and* the expressed will of the majority.[54] "No one can doubt," contends Spinoza,

> how much more beneficial it is for men to live according to laws and the certain dictates of reason which, as I have said, aim at nothing but men's true interests. Besides there is no one who does not wish to live in security and as far as possible without fear; but this is very unlikely to prevail as long as everyone is allowed to do whatever they want and reason is assigned no more right than hatred and anger. For there is no one who does not live pervaded by anxiety whilst surrounded by hostility, hatred, anger, and deceit, and does not strive to avoid these as far as they can. If we also reflect that without mutual help, and cultivation of reason, human beings necessarily live in great misery, as shown in Chapter Five [of the *TTP*], we shall realize very clearly that it was necessary for people to combine together to live in security and prosperity. Hence, they had to ensure they would collectively have the right to all things that each individual had from nature and that this right would no longer be determined by the force and appetite of each individual but by the power and will of all together. Men would, however, have had no hope of achieving this had they confined themselves only to the promptings of desire – for, by the laws of desire, everyone is drawn in different directions. Thus, they had to make a firm decision, and reached agreement, to decide everything by the sole dictate of reason (which no one dares to contradict openly for fear of appearing perfectly mindless). They had to curb their appetites so far as their desires suggested anything to anyone they did not want done to themselves. Finally, they were obliged to defend the right of others as their own.[55]

In this way, Spinoza conceives the "common good" to be a natural phenomenon which always actually exists in the background and finds expression as a man-made moral and political construct even though, usually, despite its roots in human nature, it fails to be promoted by government and society to the extent and in the manner it should. Among the most crucial elements of this "common

---

[53] Eckstein, "Rousseau and Spinoza," 270; Vernière, *Spinoza et la pensée française*, 482–3, 486; Villaverde, "Rousseau, lecteur de Spinoza."
[54] James, "Freedom, Slavery and the Passions," 229.
[55] Spinoza, *Theological-Political Treatise*, 197–8.

good" is that "war should be waged only for the sake of peace." One critic, denying Spinoza sought to minimize the curse of war, claims Spinoza lacked a sense of universal justice and in the *Tractatus Politicus* (Chapter 6, section 35 and Chapter 9, section 1) even favours "genocide" and whole cities being "completely destroyed." But from the relevant passages it plainly emerges that Spinoza does not mean that inhabitants of recalcitrant border cities should be liquidated together with their cities and surrounding fortifications but only that these inhabitants be moved elsewhere. Here, the 1677 Dutch translation of the *TP* rightly clarifies for us that it was specifically the walls and turrets of obstreperous cities likely to become hostile strongholds, not their inhabitants, that Spinoza wanted destroyed.[56]

In his essay "Spinoza and the General Will," published in 2015, David Lay Williams remarks on the surprising fact that "Spinoza is never cited as part of the general will tradition." His remark is not entirely accurate as several scholars, contrary to the conventional view, have argued that Spinoza was the chief initiator of Europe's secular "general will" tradition.[57] What *is* true in Williams' comment is that historians of political thought in general, and especially in the Anglo-American tradition, have long ignored this vital step in the origins of Western democratic "modernity" seen as a corpus of thought and theory redefining the "common good" as realistically attainable only through the democratic republic. Like some others, Williams also wrongly suggests Spinoza's "general will" concept was essentially a deviation from what he calls "the dominant Platonic version." But by the mid and later eighteenth century what dominates in European political thought has no trace of the Platonic but, rather, is the purely secular and materialist "general will" expounded by Diderot, d'Holbach, Helvétius, Condorcet, Destutt, and Volney; and this "dominant" Radical Enlightenment "general will" theoretical tradition always is—even in the pre-1756 Rousseau—unbendingly anti-Platonic and essentially materialist in tone and approach. For what should be recognized as the dominant Spinozist "general will" tradition (in contrast to the, by 1670, wholly marginal Platonic tradition), theology needs marginalizing as far as possible, being the prime obstacle to the "common good," and what is called "civil religion" should function exclusively in the service of "collective reason," universal moral values, society and the state. This was always the main intellectual tradition of "general will" down to the early nineteenth century from which Rousseau, from 1756, dramatically deviated.[58]

Rejecting Eckstein's thesis that Rousseau's direct borrowing from Spinoza is plain and evident, Williams wrongly claims there is "insufficient evidence for a

---

[56] Melamed, "Charitable Interpretations," 271–2; Spinoza, *Collected Works* (ed. Curley) ii, 593n10.
[57] In particular, Walter Eckstein, Paul Vernière, Maria José Villaverde, and myself; see Williams, "Spinoza and the General Will."
[58] Israel, *Enlightenment that Failed*, 290–306.

claim this strong," and that "to be sure, the general will does not dominate Spinoza's political thought as Rousseau's would dominate his." He admits, though, that "examination of Spinoza's work reveals [the general will] to play a significant role."[59] In fact, in Spinoza's political theory, the "general will" *is* as dominant and central as in Rousseau, and in important respects more so, as was recognized in 1987 by Villaverde.[60] Inaccurate though it is, Williams' account does at least recognize that the *TTP* is in essential ways a depiction of the confessional and political strains threatening to tear the Dutch Republic apart during its Golden Age, and to Spinoza's horror, did tear De Witt and the "True Freedom" apart in 1672.[61]

Spinoza, one might object, unlike Diderot, d'Holbach, and Rousseau, offers no one specific term for the "general will." But close examination of the wording leaves no doubt as to the equivalence of Spinoza's concept to Diderot's, d'Holbach's and Condorcet's Radical Enlightenment deployment of the term. Spinoza's "common good" never equates to majority views about society and cannot do so. Through the force of just laws it lays down guiding rules by which the ignorant and superstitious who find nothing in the "highest good that they can touch or eat," are nevertheless compelled to respect and defer to the "common good," thereby enhancing their own as well as everyone else's freedom. In deploying this key concept Spinoza uses slightly different wording in different places but it is clear throughout that his "highest good" always designates the supreme good of society when the interests of all are treated equally. "One is living in freedom," whether one realizes it or not, holds Spinoza when defining the difference between political "slavery" and political liberty in the *TTP*, "in a state and government where the *salus* of the whole people, not that of the supreme ruler, is the highest law [ubi salus totius populi, non imperantis, summa lex est]."[62] The "salus" here clearly designates the well-being or welfare of society, that is the "common good."[63] It is true that Spinoza nowhere deploys a specially coined, fixed term for the concept. Efforts to strip men of freedom of expression, he explains, is deeply destructive of the well-being of the republic. The expression used here is once again "Republicae salus."[64] But when Spinoza elaborates on the need to subordinate religious worship and pious conduct to the "peace and interests of the state" on opening chapter XIX, he speaks rather of adjusting things to "the peace and utility of the republic [reipublicae paci et utilitati accommodari.]"[65]

---

[59] Williams, "Spinoza and the General Will," 115.
[60] Villaverde, *Rousseau y el pensamiento*, 226; Tatián, *Spinoza, filosofía terrena*, 12–17.
[61] Williams, "Spinoza and the General Will," 131.
[62] Spinoza, *Theological-Political Treatise*, 201; Spinoza, *Opera* iii, 194–5.
[63] James, "Freedom, Slavery and the Passions," 229.
[64] Spinoza, *Theological-Political Treatise*, 258–9; Spinoza, *Opera* iii, 247; Giancotti Boscherini, *Lexicon Spinozanum* i, 114–15 and ii, 974.
[65] Spinoza, *Opera* iii, 229; Spinoza, *Theological-Political Treatise*, 238.

Spinoza's "general will," then is profoundly anti-Hobbesian and anti-Rousseauist and provides the root of the radical democratic republican political thought tradition grounded in Spinozism. A doctrine Rousseau initially embraced, following Diderot, he later significantly diverged from it, forging his own outlying version of "general will." The essential difference is that the mature Rousseau's *volonté générale* is based not on reason, as in Spinoza and Diderot, or d'Holbach, Condorcet, Volney, and Destutt de Tracy, but on common sentiment, the instinct and feelings of the people, something totally distinct from and opposed to Spinoza's approach. "To act under the instruction of reason," as Spinoza expresses it in the *Ethics*, frees the individual from the slavery of the emotions and hence benefits the individual and benefits society collectively at the same time. Spinoza's "general interest" aims to establish a particular kind of state, that which best supports individual pursuit of worldly happiness for all, based on a common good directed by popular sovereignty subjecting all law, education, theology, ecclesiastical authority, and Revelation to its sovereign supremacy. The collective power of the citizens where each individual's interest is treated as equal and social elites and churches are stripped of all sway over society is the true sovereign in Spinoza's thought. Nothing could be more fundamentally at odds with Hobbes on the one side and Rousseau on the other.

Finally, one must consider the place of "universal and equal rights" in Spinoza's, Hobbes', and Rousseau's divergent conceptions of the political order. If Hobbes, with his Leviathan state, strong monarchical tendency, and lack of safeguards against intrusive ecclesiastical authority and censorship, is hardly an inspiration for a post-metaphysical modern seeking escape from monarchical absolutism and religious authority, Rousseau, rejecting representative democracy and lacking safeguards for dissenting minorities is no adequate inspiration either, as the vicious brutality of ideological politics during the French Revolution illustrate. Rousseau leaves minorities and dissenting voices perilously exposed.

Meanwhile, it is important to remember that Spinoza was *not* the "source, origin or originator" of this combining of the "common good" with the democratic republic and rejection of religious authority. The roots rather lay in the wider radical tendency and thrust of republicanism in the later Dutch Golden Age. The profound ideological divisions and instability of the Dutch Republic led to a much more clearly articulated clash of basic republican theories, of aristocratic republicanism versus democratic republicanism, than did any Italian, Swiss, British, or indeed American republican discourse prior to the late eighteenth century. Equally, it was the Dutch Republic's maintaining a wider religious toleration than then found in any other neighbouring society, its permitting greater freedom of expression and to publish than other European lands (including Britain until after the Glorious Revolution of 1688), as well as more freedom of movement and an unavoidable coexistence of many groups together in the same cities, that moulded the Dutch Republic into the first broadly urbanized "modern" Western society.[66]

Within this uniquely fraught social and political scenario, it was of course not Spinoza individually but the entire *cercle Spinoziste* that engineered this crucial intellectual shift so vital and central in Western history. The fact that Spinoza stands out as the sole great thinker among the group, and that the rest are today all but forgotten should not give rise to an underestimation of the role of the circle around him. Spinoza did formulate some of the key points more incisively and enduringly than the others, and was the first to incorporate their collective approach into an overarching philosophical system, but he was not the first to formulate several of the key points, nor the most emphatic and forceful in doing so. When Van den Enden's concept, expounded originally in the mid-1660s, was publicized on insurgent posters prepared for posting up in the rebel areas of Normandy by the conspirators plotting the 1674 republican conspiracy against Louis XIV, the now elderly Van den Enden rendered the idea into everyday French, describing the rebel aim in resisting Louis XIV to be to advance "le bien commun et général."[67] Nothing is harder, as the Hebrews, Romans, Aragonese, and English all discovered, than creating a stable collective sovereignty representing the purely secular "bien commun et général" as understood by the De La Courts, Van den Enden, the Koerbaghs, and Van Berkel no less than Spinoza, the common good guaranteeing basic freedoms for all, on an equal basis, with all religions and doctrines equally subordinated to society, justice, and the state.

Spinoza was clearly preceded by the Brothers De La Court, Van den Enden, and Adriaan Koerbagh, both in articulating democratic republicanism's superiority over aristocratic (or oligarchic) republicanism and the urgent need to eliminate all religious authority. More important still, he was preceded by these in firmly joining these two key components together. But this still leaves Spinoza, both philosophically and as a political theorist, the foremost of the group who laid the Radical Enlightenment's theoretical foundations. For today, this fundamental coupling of democratic republicanism with rejection of religious authority is firmly anchored—despite some arguably distinctly weak efforts to argue against it—in the recent historical literature as the overarching, prime defining feature of the Radical Enlightenment.[68]

---

[66] Israel, *Dutch Republic*, 1–5.
[67] Maury, "Conspiration républicaine," 398; Rothkrug, *Opposition to Louis XIV*, 165.
[68] Further on this point, see Israel, "'Radical Enlightenment': A Game-Changing Concept," 37–9.

27
Publishing the *Theological-Political Treatise*

27.i First Steps to Suppress the *TTP*

Spinoza laid aside his *Ethics* incomplete, in 1665, as the Second Anglo-Dutch War erupted, convinced he could not safely publish his principal work, much less obtain a reasonable hearing, under existing circumstances. Propagating his philosophical system in the mid-1660s thus became linked to devising ways to circumvent on one side a state-supported church mostly backing the Orangist faction, and, on the other, a besieged De Wittian regime continually being pressured into making concessions to the Reformed synods. Leaving the *Ethics* unfinished, and instead turning to write the *Tractatus Theologico-Politicus*, Spinoza felt driven to intervene in his own special fashion in the contest between the rival Calvinist-Orangist and Cartesio-Cocceian blocs gripping the universities, city governments, and provincial assemblies, joining the fight against the "prejudices of the theologians," as he put it writing to Oldenburg.[1] Hoping to help shore up the "True Freedom" and the edifice of Dutch toleration and freedom of expression, among other objectives he was searching for ways to circumvent the censorship apparatus of church and state and secure his own freedom of expression.

Even to those unaware of Spinoza's circle and who the author was, it was obvious that the *TTP* combined an immediate political and polemical purpose with long-term reformist objectives including dissemination of elements of a far-reaching theologico-political philosophy. Like the Koerbaghs, Meyer, Bouwmeester and his other allies, Spinoza resented how the Scriptures were commonly used, especially by Voetius and his allies, and by particular local adversaries in and around The Hague, like De Lantman, to tighten congregational discipline, enhance preachers' power, and as a political tool, to extend their clutches over public affairs, education, and culture (including theatre, entertainment, and the arts). Seventeenth-century theologians, like religious leaders today, regularly produced Bible quotations to reinforce their authority and demonstrate the need to enforce their judgements on morals, education, politics, and social

---

[1] Spinoza, *Collected Works* (ed. Curley) ii, 14–15; Totaro, "Religion catholique," 97.

issues of all kinds, ranging from enforcing stricter sabbath observance to denouncing circuses, dance halls, and the stage.

The restrictions hampering many besides himself were rooted above all, held Spinoza, in credulity and "superstition." Superstition, as he saw it, empowered theologians to fence off and fortify religious doctrine and Bible interpretation, making this their particular domain, creating an enclosed sphere confined to those specially trained in their state-endorsed "theology" dominating all intellectual and cultural spheres, a spurious pseudo-science, enabling churchmen to mislead the common people by exploiting their ignorance to usurp illicit authority, power, and status for themselves. In considerable part, Van Velthuysen, Burman, Wittichius, Heidanus, Graevius and the others locked in battle with the Voetian-Orangist bloc agreed with this assessment. By 1670, they too were fiercely decrying the unjustified pretensions of theologians. But they denounced "superstition" and the Reformed Church's overbearing influence without denying the core teaching of Scripture, Christ, and Christianity itself or the Church's sway over religious doctrine as such.

Vehement quarrels pervading all church history since Christianity's first origins, Spinoza agreed with Meyer and the Koerbaghs, had everywhere caused endless, unnecessary and socially damaging strife. To extricate society from the ceaseless quarrelling and bitterness of seventeenth-century Europe's rival confessions and theological traditions, and free men's minds from prejudice and blind acceptance of human fictions as God's teaching, scholars must uncover the true method of interpreting Scripture, the means whereby society can extricate itself from this "deplorable situation." Revealing Scripture's authentic meaning, Spinoza further agreed with Meyer, requires scholars to "make a fresh examination of Scripture with a free and unprejudiced mind, and assert nothing about it, and accept nothing as its teaching, which does not very clearly derive from it. With this goal in mind," avers Spinoza, "I devised a method for interpreting the sacred volumes."[2]

The Bible, Spinoza several times affirms in the *TTP*, was not written for the learned but for men of all conditions. For readers in his day "the difficulty of comprehending the Bible lies exclusively in the language and not the sublimity of its content."[3] Theologians, though, sought to convince others that the content was impenetrable to all but those learned in theology, requiring highly specialized knowledge that supposedly churchmen alone possess, a strategy pursued by uncovering "in Scripture mysteries too profound to be explained in any human terms and, on this ground, imported into religion so many philosophical issues the Church now resembles a university and religion a field of erudition or, rather, ceaseless erudite controversy," yet devoid of genuine erudition. "If you inquire

---

[2] Spinoza, *Theological-Political Treatise*, 9.   [3] Spinoza, *Theological-Political Treatise*, 172.

what mysteries they detect hidden in Scripture, you will uncover nothing but the fabrications of Aristotle or Plato or some like (obscure) philosopher that mostly could be more readily dreamt up by a layman than deduced from Scripture, even by the most consummate scholar."[4]

Theological debate, in short, had long been enmeshed in the speculations "Aristotelicorum et Platonicorum [of Aristotelians and Platonists]" like medicine, astronomy, and philosophy itself, shackled to promote dominance and control instead of search for truth. Not that dragging complex philosophical issues into interpreting Scripture in any way heightened regard for philosophers: rather, complained Spinoza, churchmen usurped primacy over philosophers to dominate them as they dominated everyone else. "So I apply myself," Spinoza explained to Oldenburg, "to exposing such prejudices and removing them from the minds of sensible people." A particular problem for him personally was the "opinion of me held by the common people," locals "who constantly accuse me of atheism," a charge stirred by hostile preachers in his environs: "I am driven to avert this accusation too, as far as I can."

Publishing the *TTP*, he hoped, would help clear the path to publishing his *Ethics* and promote the wider drive for "freedom to philosophize and to say what we think." Here, Spinoza was directly contradicting the fond assumption of Oldenburg, Thomasius, and other foreign contemporaries that the Republic was then much the freest, most tolerant of societies. Nothing so clearly vindicated Spinoza's more realistic appraisal than the tragic circumstances of Adriaan Koerbagh's death; the finishing touches were put to the *TTP* just after Koerbagh's demise in prison.

Not only Spinoza and his publisher but the printer too was taking a grave risk by producing and distributing the *TTP* which was bound to provoke uproar and be suppressed by the authorities. Due to Herman Aeltsz's role in printing Spinoza's Descartes book, and involvement in the *Bloemhof* affair, neither he, nor presumably Rieuwertsz, wanted him involved in this new subversive venture. Rieuwertsz was accustomed to employing different Amsterdam printers, and in this instance the printer's identity was only recently discovered by closely examining the typography of the book's ornamental capitals.[5] The obscure but efficient printer engaged, Israel Abrahamsz de Paull (1632–80), had his shop in the Tuinstraat, in the Jordaan, a less reputable part of Amsterdam where he subsequently continued through the 1670s, thereby playing a crucial role in the entire process, printing also the later clandestine editions of the *TTP* which closely shadow the original version in appearance.

---

[4] Spinoza, *Theological-Political Treatise*, 173; Totaro, "Religion catholique," 98.
[5] Jagersma and Dijkstra, "Uncovering Spinoza's Printers," 291, 293–4; Leeuwenburgh, *Het Noodlot*, 178, 197.

Judging from the earliest reactions to the *TTP*, dating from April and May 1670, the first Latin quarto edition was ready for release around the end of 1669, or start of 1670, a few months after Koerbagh's demise. This fresh anonymous challenge to the authorities commenced its surreptitious distribution early in 1670, by March at the latest. The tacit connection with the Koerbaghs must have been plainly evident to many at the time. Spinoza was certainly referring in part to the profound shock Koerbagh's trial and early death represented for him and his followers in his ironic Tacitean interjection in his preface: "we are fortunate to enjoy the rare happiness of living in a republic where every person's liberty to judge for himself is respected, everyone permitted to worship God according to his own mind, and nothing is thought dearer or sweeter than freedom."[6] Spinoza's Latin was now noticeably more confident than it had been a few years earlier; but the rhetorical purpose of his incisive echoing of classical rhetoric here, emulating Van den Enden, was more powerfully to persuade.[7] Spinoza's core thesis in this passage was that this freedom, in which some in the United Provinces took great pride, "may not only be permitted without danger to piety and the stability of the republic but cannot be refused without destroying the peace of the republic and piety itself." Regarding toleration and freedom of thought, the United Provinces might be an improvement on lands of the Inquisition like Portugal, Spain and Italy, and most of Europe, including France, Germany and Restoration England, but that did not alter the grim truth that the "True Freedom" stood in dire peril, hanging in the balance with increasingly formidable internal forces aiming to replace precious liberty, individual and collective, with prejudice, bigotry, and ecclesiastical control.

The first quarto edition of the *Tractatus Theologico-Politicus*, of 1670 (Figure 27.1), despite some ninety typographical errors of mostly minor significance, turned out to be the most faithful to Spinoza's manuscript of the entire series of anonymous and clandestine Latin editions that one after the other seeped out surreptitiously through the 1670s. In this and every subsequent edition, down to the late eighteenth century, the title-page deliberately omits the names, indeed any detail at all about the author, publisher, or printer, offering a wholly fictitious publisher's name, "Künrath," a fictitious place of publication, "Hamburg," and no designation at all for the author. Nowhere in the text is there any detail about the author. Most copies appeared in quarto size but with a small proportion in larger luxury format. As an added precaution, Rieuwertsz commenced his furtive distribution in locations well away from Amsterdam.[8]

On the level of sheer indignation and alarm, ecclesiastical and civil, reaction was immediate. But, strangely, in complete contrast to the earlier furious reactions to La Peyrère, in 1655, and to the *Philosophia* in 1666–7, replies countering the

---

[6] Spinoza, *Theological-Political Treatise*, 6; Balibar, *Spinoza et la politique*, 33–4.
[7] Akkerman, "Taal en tekst," 14–15.   [8] Van de Ven, *Printing Spinoza*, 8, 120–2.

Figure 27.1 [Spinoza], *Tractatus theologico-politicus*. Hamburgi [i.e. Amsterdam] Apud Henricum Künraht [i.e. Jan Rieuwertsz], 1670. IAS Spinoza Research Collection.

TTP's arguments with reasoned, cogent refutations, perplexingly, failed to appear month after month following its appearance, and soon year after year. Where there was an immediate rush to extinguish the "flame" of La Peyrère's *Praeadamitae* fifteen years before, and stem the *Philosophia* uproar in 1666, during 1670, 1671, and 1672 whole armies of theologians at home and abroad failed to come up with anything concrete or scathing in reply to the *TTP*. For the book's furious detractors this was massively frustrating especially since this was bound to imply in some way that Spinoza's attack was simply too formidable, complex, and subtle for its innumerable opponents to deal with. Despite the book's unparalleled challenge to core belief and the unprecedented indignation it provoked, putting together a solid rejoinder to its arguments proved exceedingly difficult and impossible to do swiftly. If expressing furious outrage was universal, countering and discrediting the book effectively, it was soon clear, would be no easy task. Where the *Philosophia* was met by an abrupt, powerful counter-offensive in print, full-length, incisive replies to the *TTP* were scarcely anywhere in evidence for years after its appearance. Due to their obvious shortcomings and inadequacies, the scant replies that did appear only further heightened the unprecedented alarm and anxiety the *TTP* generated. In fact, so tortuously dragged out was the scholarly reaction, that by the time Spinoza, in his sole surviving letter to Leibniz, in the autumn of 1671, privately acknowledged being the author of this vast challenge, Leibniz too, since obtaining his copy in late 1670 or early 1671, had, like innumerable others, been grappling with the *TTP* for months without finding any relief for the deep alarm he felt at the paltry trickle provided by those attempting to answer Spinoza in print. Leibniz long continued wrestling within himself for convincing counter-arguments to the *TTP*, and a later lost (or suppressed) letter of his to Spinoza, of around 1672, is known to have presented his private attempt to refute some aspects.[9]

If there were no meaningful refutations of the Koerbaghs' books either, these had been quickly and effectively suppressed, a challenge nipped in the bud, with no subsequent editions appearing, so the threat there rapidly receded, going largely unnoticed. By contrast, the *TTP*'s first printing was backed by subsequent clandestine editions subversively appearing over the next decade while the furore surrounding the book's claims and arguments from the outset remained conspicuously at the forefront of the Dutch synods' and consistories' ceaseless protests, causing the *TTP*'s impact in terms of complaint, controversy, and copies circulating to grow steadily along with the exasperation this stoked. The whole business was marked not just by bitter controversy but by appalled perplexity and, untypically for the era a practically universal holding back. The non-appearance of systematic, large-scale substantial refutations soon itself became a major factor in what for many was an unmitigated disaster.

This historically highly significant double response to the *TTP*—immediate, furious condemnation, drawing unusually wide attention on all sides, alongside staggering delay in terms of cogent, argued reaction, continued for over three years after the *TTP*'s first appearance. Spinoza, in effect, resumed the Koerbaghs' offensive against generally accepted "truth" and core belief less directly and pugnaciously than they had, but, highly disconcertingly for the secular and

---

[9] Friedmann, *Leibniz et Spinoza*, 66; Goldenbaum, "Die *Commentatiuncula*," 80–1; Otto, *Studien*, 18–19; Laerke, *Leibniz lecteur*, 94–7.

ecclesiastical authorities, with far more penetrating and lasting success. Carefully avoiding mentioning anything directly contrary to the Trinity, Christ's divinity, his dubious parentage or role as redeemer, or anything resembling ancient and medieval Jewish claims that the Old Testament does not foretell Christ's coming, Spinoza devised a more circular route to the same conclusions. Using an insinuating means to defeat the system in a manner infinitely galling to opinion at the time, he accomplished the same feat the Koerbaghs had attempted, only more adroitly and less recklessly.

The unfamiliar mix of official, ecclesiastical, and public anger alongside stunning failure to answer the anonymous miscreant's arguments lent a peculiarly anguished quality to the protracted international controversy surrounding the *TTP*'s early reception. The authorities' inability to identify author, publisher, or printer only further fuelled the huge furore suffusing the early reaction, a cultural phenomenon revealing much about the academic, theological, and political world of the late seventeenth century. "It is no exaggeration to say," as one scholar describes the book's impact on Leibniz, one of the greatest minds of the era, that the initially sluggish but eventually massive Dutch, German, French, English, Scandinavian, Italian, and wider European response to the *TTP* during the two decades following its publication was "le grand évènement intellectual [the great intellectual event]" of the age, with innumerable readers sharing Leibniz's awareness of the extreme seriousness of the challenge, his alarm, fascination, and restless impatience to see the book effectively overthrown.[10] This unique combination fundamentally shaped the prolonged furore over the *TTP* in a way that really has no parallel in early modern intellectual history, stretching far beyond anything seen in response to Hobbes.

Leibniz initially viewed the *TTP*'s author as simply a disciple of Hobbes in political thought and in his irreligion. Little by little, repelled but also fascinated by the sheer boldness of the Bible criticism, Leibniz garnered from his wide-ranging network of correspondents shreds of evidence about the *TTP* and the entire clandestine movement surrounding this work which intrigued as much as disturbed him. Already earlier, in 1667, he had read the *Philosophia S.Scripturae Interpres* (1666) with its subversive application of Cartesian principles to Bible criticism provoking a huge furore in the Netherlands.[11] Learning from Graevius, in April 1671, that the *TTP*'s author "is said to be a Jew named Spinoza," in April 1672, he heard indirectly, via a scholar corresponding with the prominent Leiden medical professor, Theodore Craanen (1633–88), that *De Jure Ecclesiasticorum*, another outrageous Dutch clandestine text about which he was seeking information, was being attributed to Van Velthuysen. As word trickled through to

---

[10] Vernière, *Spinoza et la pensée française*, 100; Laerke, "G. W. Leibniz's Two Readings," 106.
[11] Laerke, *Leibniz lecteur*, 280–1; Laerke, "G. W. Leibniz's Two Readings," 116; Antognazza, *Leibniz on the Trinity*, 50–1.

Germany that the *TTP*'s author was "Spinoza" some readily assumed that it was Spinoza who had authored the *Philosophia* too. By 1671, rumour was also circulating in Germany that the now increasingly notorious Spinoza had penned other works too of like or worse content that had not yet appeared.[12]

The consternation the *TTP* aroused was further intensified by the failure of the uproar to serve as a unifying mechanism among the vying scholarly and religious factions rallying their best experts in Bible criticism and philosophy to demolish the book. To Petrus van Mastricht (1630–1706), a pre-eminent Calvinist adversary of Socinians, Remonstrants, Cocceians, and Cartesians, at the time professor at Duisburg and later Voetius' successor at Utrecht, the book marked the culmination of the great catastrophe he believed Cartesianism precipitated by insidiously freeing philosophy from its millennia-old "handmaiden" status, subject to theology. Theology's age-old primacy over all other disciplines, acknowledged even by Descartes, had been replaced by an initially timid autonomy which, however, from 1670, with the appearance of the *TTP*, menacingly loomed into a would-be autonomous force ominously seeking to conquer or usurp hegemony over all theology, Bible studies, and church–state relations along with all other studies.[13]

Compared to the *Philosophia* furore, the battle of the *TTP* was characterized above all by its much wider, deeper international impact and, despite its astounding initial slowness to escalate intellectually, far greater eventual intensity, duration, and consequences. In the older secondary literature about Spinoza it is routinely affirmed that owing to the Dutch Republic's exceptional degree of toleration and freedom of expression the outcry failed to produce any repressive pressure whatever for four years, until 1674, several authors even claiming the angry response merely "led to efforts to suppress it" that were then thwarted by De Witt. Such longstanding assumptions are historically highly inaccurate. The anonymous text was never anywhere regarded with sufferance and a tolerant eye by the secular authorities any more than by ecclesiastical authority either before or after the passing of the edict of the provincial High Court of Holland, the Hof, in The Hague, of 19 July 1674, expressly banning the *TTP* along with Hobbes' *Leviathan*, the *Philosophia*, and the most targeted Socinian work then circulating, the *Bibliotheca Fratrum Polonorum*. The North and South Holland synods breathed a sigh of relief that the States of Holland were now more "strongly forbidding" these four particular pernicious "soul-destroying books full of horrors [zielverderffelycke boeken, vol van gruellen],"[14] as the North Holland synod styled them, but there was never a moment when any of them were freely on sale or

---

[12] Leibniz, *Sämtliche Schriften* 2nd ser. *Philosophischer Briefwechsel* i, 200. Walter to Leibniz, Leiden, 13 April 1672; Israel, *Radical Enlightenment*, 504–5.
[13] Goudriaan, *Reformed Orthodoxy*, 57–9; Rester, "Petrus van Mastricht," 96; Kato, "Petrus van Mastricht," 135–6.
[14] RNH Acta Noord-Holland Synod 6, Alkmaar, 7 Aug. 1674, "licentious boekdrukken."

when there was not a sustained official effort to suppress the production, distribution, and vending of Spinoza's bombshell.

The true dimensions of the social, cultural, and political response to the *TTP* only became clear to historians in the 1990s following scholarly research in the unpublished records of the city governments and the Reformed Church synods and consistories. In reality, this research showed, suppressing the book in accord with existing legislation, especially the law of 1653 against Socinian books, topped the agenda from the start, existing legislation of the States fully sufficing for the authorities to eradicate the book from the bookshops, penalize those selling it, and severely punish author, publisher, and printer if these could be discovered, caught, and indicted. Even though, given the institutional structure of the Republic, these efforts were inevitably rather localized and uncoordinated, they were sufficiently orchestrated and effective to ensure that for the rest of his life Spinoza had to stick to the furtive practices of a clandestine author, much as he had since his earliest writings in the late 1650s, fighting an interminable war of attrition with a censorship system vowing to obliterate his *libertas philosophandi*.

When eventually the *TTP* and *Philosophia* were publicly banned by name, by exceptional decree of the Hof van Holland, in 1674, they were still then banned as "Sociniaensche Boecken," making abundantly clear that these works had never been permitted at any time, nor could they ever be used in colleges or cited favourably in public debate, though copies could be reserved for study by suitably qualified churchmen for purposes of refutation.[15] Like erotic and politically sensitive books, "Socinian books" constituted a defined legal and bibliographic category permanently prohibited, infringing the ban on which could at any time entail serious consequences for authors, printers, publishers, and booksellers. Following the Koerbagh affair, there were repeated raids on bookshops in Amsterdam and other towns in search of Koerbagh's *Bloemhof* and other forbidden "Socinian" books. In April 1669, one bookshop owner at Leiden from whose premises "some Socinian books" were seized, was allowed to retrieve them from the town hall under sworn avowal "to sell them only to [approved] preachers."[16]

When the Utrecht publisher of Koerbagh's *Een Ligt* took fright, in 1668, handing the manuscript over to the authorities, he was responding, therefore, to a particular set of legal constraints. The searches were far from fully effective. Indeed, some dissenting member(s) of the Amsterdam city government seems to have warned bookshop owners and publishers "in secret" prior to the 1669–70 searches, enabling them to hide their stocks beforehand.[17] Plainly, substantial numbers of copies escaped seizure. But Amsterdam still went through the motions of applying the law and booksellers still needed to hide their stocks of forbidden

---

[15] Israel, *Dutch Republic*, 911–13; Israel, *Radical Enlightenment*, 275–8.
[16] GA Leiden, Secretarie Archief 191, res. Burgomasters, 5 April 1669.
[17] Van Gelder, *Getemperde vrijheid*, 165.

books away from their main premises keeping the trade strictly "under the counter." Such books always remained wholly shut out from respectability, higher education, and being discussed in any other than wholly negative terms, not just for years but for well over a century. Anyone defying the public church and other main churches through complicity in publishing or selling what were deemed explicitly anti-Christian texts incurred considerable risk.

From 1653 onwards, the Republic thus possessed a set of general rules, especially stringent anti-Socinian ordinances, applying to all publications touching on theological, philosophical, moral, political, and erotic topics. These were aimed not just against the Anti-Trinitarianism and virtual Anti-Trinitarianism of Collegiants like Zwicker, Stegmann, Wiszowaty, Knol, Crellius, Rieuwertsz, Jelles, and Balling, but also against all wider use of "reason" to erode belief in core Christian "mysteries," construe Christianity as just a moral code, or negate church authority by attacking core theological dogma. Holland's anti-Socinian decree of 19 September 1653, reissued and reformulated in December 1654, laid down rigorous censorship guidelines, promptly replicated by the States of Utrecht and Zeeland, and soon the States General, the federal body, for the entire United Provinces including the Generality Lands (northern Brabant and Drenthe). The term "Socinian" in effect became a blanket judicial designation anchored in statute, covering any attack on core Christian belief and any doctrine questioning Christ the Redeemer whether strictly Socinian in character or not. Suppression of the *Philosophia* of 1666 and the Koerbagh publications for "blasphemy" proceeded exclusively under this existing anti-Socinian legislation. Socinians, declared the outraged Van Mastricht, do not acknowledge the sacrifice made by Christ to redeem the sins of believers, claiming "we are justified not by faith in Christ but observance of the commands of Christ," turning doctrine, sacraments, and grace into mere moral precepts, holding "faith that saves consists in nothing other than observing the commands of Christ."[18] If people accept their teaching, churchmen and church ceremonies lose all sway over society.

Energetic efforts to suppress the *TTP* began in the spring of 1670, as emerges from the archives recording local prohibition procedures in Utrecht, Leiden, Haarlem, and elsewhere. The Utrecht Reformed consistory, registering great alarm that "a certain profane and blasphemous book has appeared entitled *Tractatus Theologico-Politicus*," urged the city burgomasters to step in as early as 8 April 1670, with Professor Frans Burman (1628–78), according to his son, many years later, having by then already read the *TTP* and expressed deep indignation. Burman was the first reader outside Spinoza's circle known to have reacted to the published *TTP*, and apparently first also to have learnt that Spinoza was its author.[19] Three days later, on 11 April 1670, the Utrecht burgomasters

---

[18] Quoted in Rester, "Petrus van Mastricht," 101.
[19] Steenbakkers, "The Text," 30; Van de Ven, *Printing Spinoza*, 96–7.

ordered the book's seizure from the city bookshops.[20] After discussing the matter further with the full city council, they proposed suppression also on a wider, provincial basis, as was reported to the Utrecht provincial Reformed synod, in September that year, after the question of Hobbes' *Leviathan* and Spinoza's *TTP* was deliberated in the States of Utrecht.[21] At the Utrecht provincial synod's meeting the following year, in September 1671, the synodal minutes noted that the *Bibliotheca Fratrum Polonorum* was not being sold in this province, and little action as yet had been taken regarding [Van Berkel's rendering of] Hobbes, but, thankfully, the *Tractatus Theologico-Politicus* had been "seized [opgehaelt] by the magistrates," meaning all copies of Spinoza's book located had been removed from the bookshops of the province and city.[22]

The Leiden Reformed consistory, expressing great indignation, discussed the *TTP* at its meeting on 9 May 1670. Three pastors were dispatched to the burgomasters to "demonstrate" the treatise's blasphemous "contents and enormities or rather obscenities [vuijligheden], reading out bits and demanding the book's seizure and suppression."[23] Needing little persuading, the burgomasters resolved on 16 May 1670 that "a certain treatise entitled *Theologico Politicq* with its godless passages should be seized by the *schout* [sheriff]," a resolution recorded in the burgomasters' record book [*Notulenboek*] as well as the consistory proceedings.[24] That same day, the consistory thanked the burgomasters for so promptly directing the city's *schout* to seize all copies from their city's bookshops.[25] At Haarlem, the consistory, meeting on 27 May 1670, denounced the *TTP* as that "scandalous book," the worst of the "licentious" books presently targeted,[26] urging members to show maximum vigilance in combating it, as did the district classis, on 10 June, where the *TTP* was condemned for its "blasphemous and unchristian maxims."[27]

Due to Rieuwertsz's clandestine distribution strategy, Amsterdam followed only three months after Utrecht, on 30 June, when the Reformed consistory cited the "harmful" book called *Tractatus Theologico-Politicus* as the single

---

[20] GA Utrecht Kerkeraad 9, res. 8 April 1670 and res. 11 April 1670; I first drew attention to this at the Rotterdam conference in 1993, see Israel, "Banning of Spinoza's Works," 9; Freudenthal/Walther, *Lebensgeschichte* i, 287 and ii, 150–1; Gootjes, "First Orchestrated Attack," 25, 31.

[21] RA Utrecht, Provinciale Kerkvergadering III, Acta Synodi Provincialis Ultrajectinae, Sept. 1670, sessio 6, article 4; Israel, "Banning of Spinoza's Works," 9.

[22] RA Utrecht, Provinciale Kerkvergadering III, Acta Synodi Provincialis Ultrajectinae, September 1671, sessio 6, article 30; Bamberger, "Early Editions," 31; Israel, "Banning of Spinoza's Works," 9.

[23] GA Leiden Acta Kerkeraad V, res. 9 May 1670, article 4; Israel, "Banning of Spinoza's Works, 8; this document, first found by myself, in 1993, was then reported to the editors of the two-volume documents collection, the *Lebensgeschichte*, who included it in their compilation, in 2006, see Freudenthal/Walther, *Lebensgeschichte* i, 288 and ii, 156.

[24] GA Leiden Secretarie Arch. 191, p. 60 res. Leiden burgomasters, 16 May 1670; Israel, "Banning of Spinoza's Works," 9; Freudenthal/Walther, *Lebensgeschichte* i, 288.

[25] GA Leiden Acta Kerkeraad V, res. 16 May 1670, article 2; Freudenthal/Walther, *Lebensgeschichte* i, 289.

[26] GA Haarlem, Acta Kerkeraad ix, res. 27 May 1670; Israel, "Banning of Spinoza's Works," 10.

[27] RA North Holland, Geref. Kerk, Acta classis Haarlem vii, res. 10 June 1670.

worst current instance of "licentious book printing,"[28] a message communicated to the neighbouring classes of Edam and Alkmaar, as well as the North Holland synod, during July.[29] Drives to suppress the book ensued on all sides, especially in Leiden and Haarlem which were stricter in such matters than Amsterdam. At The Hague, on 7 July 1670, the church council echoed the district classis in demanding the South Holland synod act against a malicious recent book, the *TTP*, and a second work Reformed ministers wanted suppressed, Van Velthuysen's *Tractaet van de afgodery en superstitie* [Treatise of Idolatry and Superstition] (1669), which at Utrecht, during 1670, thus simultaneously with the *TTP*, also caused great indignation by questioning church censorship and the role of the synods and consistories in society and intellectual life.[30]

The South Holland synod, gathering at Schiedam, in July 1670, condemned the *TTP* along the same lines as the North Holland synod where the Amsterdam deputies read out extracts from that "damaging" book soon afterwards, on 4 August. While protesting to the secular authorities about the longstanding problem of "licentious printing and sale of all kinds of foul and blasphemous books," the South Holland synod cited only one title by name, the "scandalous book entitled *Tractatus Theologico-Politicus*" from which extracts were read out aloud to the meeting and which, the gathering concurred, was a "work as foul and blasphemous as any that are known of or that the world has ever seen, and about which the Synod must complain to the utmost."[31] Preachers participating in these synodal gatherings were directed, on returning to their respective towns, to remind the town magistracies that such literature was strictly banned under the law and must be seized from the bookshops "especially that foul and utterly blasphemous book the *Tractatus Theologico-Politicus*."[32]

The North and South Holland Reformed Church synods also together took steps to persuade the States of Holland at its next gathering at The Hague to issue a more formal province-wide ban "on this and all other blasphemous books." Holland's local classes and church councils were urged to present and read extracts to their town magistrates and ply the burgomasters beforehand with lengthy quotes from the *TTP* when demanding town deputies delegated to the pending gathering of the States receive written instructions urging action. The synods' *deputati* even read out to the assembled legislature the batch of extracts from the *TTP* compiled by the preachers at Amsterdam. The States of Holland then provisionally debated issuing such a decree during their sessions of March

---

[28] GA Amsterdam, Acta Kerkeraad 12, p. 110, res. 30 June 1670.
[29] RA North Holland, Geref. Kerk, Acta classis Alkmaar, fo. 168, res. 22 July 1670; RA North Holland, Geref. Kerk, Acta classis Edam, res. 28 July 1670; Freudenthal/Walther, *Lebensgeschichte* i, 289–90.
[30] Kingma, "Spinoza en zijn Haagse periode," 17; Velthuysen, *Vierde Apologie*, 5–7.
[31] *Acta der particuliere Synoden van Zuid-Holland* iv, 531; Kingma, "Spinoza in zijn Haagse periode," 17; Van Bunge, "Spinoza's atheïsme," 89.
[32] ARH NHK Oud Synodaal Archief 183, p. 3 acta, 5 Aug. 1670 (classis Amsterdam).

and September 1670.³³ The point of this would be to give the campaign of suppression added impetus and vigour. Probably no other learned work has ever become remotely as familiar to an entire political elite and the whole membership of a major legislative body as the *TTP* did within nine months of its appearance, in 1670. During 1670, Holland's regent class not only knew about but read and joined in examining at least those extracts from the *TTP* judged the most outrageous.

Acting together, the two Holland synods' deputies also brought their formal submission or *remonstrantie* to the province's Raadpensionaris, De Witt, and discussed the Amsterdam classis extracts from the *TTP* with him personally, urging him to present their admonition to the States and help secure passage of the projected province-wide ban.³⁴ Clearly, De Witt too was perusing the *TTP* at least by late 1670. The synods' joint submission to the States, likewise featuring extracts from the *TTP* assembled by the "Brothers from Amsterdam," was afterwards sent by the States to its standing committee for further consideration, recorded the North Holland synod gathering, when again considering "the damaging book called the *Tractatus Theologico-Politicus*" the following year at Hoorn. The States then requested the Hof, the provincial high court, by resolution of 16 March 1671, to examine the question further and advise accordingly.³⁵ The synods jointly succeeded in getting their campaign against the *TTP* tabled for further discussion by the States, noted the prominent Amsterdam regent, Hans Bontemantel, in his diary on 25 September, their petition for a special placard banning the book being presented by the president of the Hof. But for whatever reason, nothing further transpired that autumn at The Hague, in the States or the Hof, very likely because De Witt dragged his feet, and over the winter the matter then stalled. The Synod of Groningen, meanwhile, reviewing the reports, on 5 May 1671, alerted all preachers in their province about the "*Tractatus Theologicus* [sic], an abominable book, on liberty to philosophize."³⁶ During 1671 and 1672 province-wide suppression of the *TTP* in Groningen and Friesland followed, apparently on the model of Utrecht.³⁷

De Witt evidently promised the Holland synods to take care of the matter, but when the *deputati* came to review the issue with him later, during the crisis of early 1672, inquiring what progress had been made, Holland's beleaguered Pensionary,

---

[33] ARH NHK Oud Synodaal Archief 183, p. 16, acta, 5 Aug. 1670 (classis Amsterdam); *Acta der particuliere Synoden van Zuid-Holland* iv, 531; RNH Acta Noord-Holland Synod 5 (RNH Inventaris 380) Acta Hoorn 4 Aug 1671, art. 7 "Licentieus boekdrukken."

[34] ARH NHK Oud Synodaal Archief 183, pp. 9–10, art. 7 acta 4 Aug. 1671 (Hoorn).

[35] ARH NHK Oud Synodaal Archief 183, pp. 46–7, art. 40, acta 4 Aug. 1671 (Hoorn); RHN Acta Noord-Holland Synod, Hoorn, 4 Aug. 1671, art. 40.

[36] RA Groningen, Archief van de Provinciale Synode van Stad en Lande, 3 (Acta 1657–81), res. 5 May 1671, point 9.

[37] RA Groningen, Archief van de Provinciale Synode van Stad en Lande 3, Acta Groningen, 28 April 1673, "observata in Synodo Frisico."

hardly surprisingly, had to admit that that he had forgotten all about it amidst the onset of war and prevailing mayhem. That Holland's Pensionary had other things on his mind amidst the French invasion than the *TTP* was then reported back to the North Holland synod, just two weeks before De Witt's assassination, at its meeting from 2 to 6 August 1672, at Enkhuizen.[38]

As far as forming a commission to suppress the worst "Socinian" books more effectively was concerned, and formally banning the *TTP* by name on a provincial basis, the synods found themselves, amidst the turmoil of invasion, thrust back to square one. Exasperated, they re-submitted their *remonstrantie*, raising the issue yet again with the States delegates of "Leiden, Amsterdam, Gouda, Rotterdam, Alkmaar and Hoorn," some of which, caught up in the wider political crisis, showed no particular urgency in this matter, leaving the synods to wait in vain for a response. Still more dispiriting for those demanding more energetic action, the synods' *deputati* advised the North Holland synod, meeting at Edam in August 1673, after conferring with their most helpful allies, Leiden's delegates to the States, that "in this conjuncture of the times, being burdened with many other cares, still nothing has ensued [in the States]," but the States would attend to the matter in due course. The classes were all urged to keep up the pressure.[39]

Amidst the greatest crisis the Republic faced during the seventeenth century, the States of Holland were otherwise preoccupied than with controversial books. Nevertheless, in their judgement of 16 April 1671, the Hof van Holland confirmed judicially that Hobbes' *Leviathan*, the *Philosophia*, and the *TTP* "directly" violated the 19 September 1653 placard forbidding publication of "Socinian books," and under its terms must be suppressed by all the magistracies.[40] And indeed, the counter-offensive, backed by the universities, conducted by the judicial and ecclesiastical authorities against publishing and distributing the *TTP* during the years 1670–4 continued fairly rigorously throughout.[41] Furthermore, all authorities, from De Witt down to local level, knew perfectly well, while avoiding mentioning his name in published proceedings, that the abominable author they were reading, complaining about, and repeatedly denouncing was "Spinoza," as the authorities bluntly referred to him in their proceedings. The Utrecht text critic and professor of classics and rhetoric, Johann Georg Graevius (1632–1703), in his letter to Leibniz of 12 April 1671, described the *TTP* as a work "following the Hobbesian path but going much further," known to have been written by the Jew Spinoza "who was recently excommunicated due to his monstrous opinions."[42] A "*liber pestilentissimus* [most pestilential book]," reducing "natural law" simply

---

[38] ARH NHK Oud Synodaal Archief 184, p. 6, art. 4, acta 2 Aug. 1672 (Enkhuizen).
[39] ARH NHK Oud Synodaal Archief 184, p. 9 art 7, and p. 32 art. 39, acta 8 Aug. 1673 (Edam); RNH Acta Noord-Holland Synod, Edam, 8 Aug. 1673, "Licentieus boekdrukken."
[40] Israel, "Banning of Spinoza's Works," 10.
[41] Israel, "Banning of Spinoza's Works," 4–10; Israel, "Early Dutch and German Reaction," 78–80.
[42] Leibniz, *Sämtliche Schriften* 1st ser., i, 142. Graevius to Leibniz, Utrecht, 22 April 1671.

to the nature of things, and opening the window wide to "atheism," it had been "proscriptus ab Ordinibus [banned by the States]."[43]

Graevius knew very well what he was saying, even if what exactly he meant by "the States" remains unclear, as he may have been referring to the States General, the States of Holland, or just the "States" of his own province, Utrecht. The *TTP*, in any case, was causing a tremendous stir.[44] Leibniz may briefly have wondered whether the reports identifying "Spinoza" as the author were reliable, but could doubt no longer on receiving a reply to his first letter to Spinoza, in October 1671. Here, Spinoza virtually admits to having written the *TTP*.[45] "If the *Tractatus Theologico-Politicus* has not yet come into your hands," adds the postscript in his letter replying to the "most learned and most noble Leibniz," of November 1671, "I shall send you a copy unless that would be inconvenient."[46]

By then, Spinoza was, clearly, not just stoical about being mentioned as the author, but cheerfully distributing copies himself to further his subversive effort, as he continued doing in subsequent years.[47] As far as is known, there was never any official move to summon or interrogate, much less instigate his arrest, by any judicial body, presumably because hearsay evidence on its own was considered insufficient grounds for such an inquiry, especially as it remained unclear whether Spinoza had actually broken the letter of the law by denying Christ's divinity or the Trinity. Legally, only expressly denying Christ's divinity and the Trinity could automatically incriminate an author. What Holland's Reformed synods did accomplish was to ensure that year after year through the 1670s, all the deputies from the local church councils and classes were instructed to remain particularly vigilant in looking out for the four worst books, including the *TTP*, those texts "which creep forward like a cancer," continually urging their local councils to ensure the States of Holland and the Hof kept up their efforts to suppress them and other such damaging books.[48]

27.ii A Text Left Unchallenged

Frans Burman, professor of theology at Utrecht since 1662, gave the *TTP* a first reading in early April 1670, then studied it more closely, his diary records, during

---

[43] Freudenthal, *Lebensgeschichte* (1899), 193; Meinsma, *Spinoza et son cercle*, 398; Nadler, *Book Forged in Hell*, 221.
[44] Laerke, *Leibniz lecteur*, 95; Nadler, *Spinoza: A Life*, 351; Laerke, *Spinoza and the Freedom*, 195.
[45] Laerke, "G. W. Leibniz's Two Readings," 104–5; Nadler, *Book Forged in Hell*, 220, 264n19; Israel, "Early Dutch and German Reaction," 79–80.
[46] Spinoza, *Collected Works* (ed. Curley) ii, 395. Spinoza to Leibniz, The Hague, 9 Nov. 1671.
[47] Spinoza, *Opera* iv, 234; Laerke, "G. W. Leibniz's Two Readings," 105.
[48] RNH Acta Noord-Holland 6, Amsterdam, 27 July 1676, "Licentieus boekdrukken."

May.[49] Realizing the unprecedented challenge it represented, and conferring with Graevius, Van Velthuysen, and other allies, at Utrecht, in June, Burman appealed to the Republic's then probably most accomplished Hebraist, Jacobus Alting (1618-79), at Groningen, to intervene. Alting must accept his responsibility, urged Burman, given his special philological skills, to undertake the urgent task of countering Spinoza. The Bible expert perhaps best qualified in the United Provinces to take up cudgels against the *TTP*, Alting was a true *scriptuarius*, a label Voetius and Maresius scornfully applied to experts in Coccacian Bible exegesis, and every Reformed scholar rejecting their fundamentalist approach to the, to them, sacrosanct official "States Bible."

During 1668-70, Alting, to whom the leaders of the Cartesian-Coccacian academic faction briefly looked to rebut Spinoza compellingly but without yielding ground to Voetius, Van Mastricht, and the Calvinist hard core, had recently clashed bitterly over issues of "scripturalism" with Samuel Maresius (Des Marets) (1599-1673). Invoking the Old Testament Hebrew text as the sole truly sacred version, Alting rejected Voetius' and Maresius' fundamentalist rigidity regarding the States Bible. Nevertheless, he felt disinclined to plunge into this new affray, daunted by the difficulties and his own perplexity regarding Bible chronology. When appealed to again, in September, he again declined to reply to the *TTP*, though not, he explained, due to underestimating the gravity of the challenge. Later, in March 1671, he agreed to assist a younger philologist, his former pupil, Anthony Perizonius (1626-72), now professor of theology at the Deventer Illustre School, in the task of refuting the *TTP* and defending the Bible against the charge of being "corrupted," a task over which, noted Perizonius, many scholars were now "sweating."

Writing from Utrecht, on 27 April 1671, Graevius duly informed Leibniz about Perizonius' efforts. But though an accomplished Hebraist, Perizonius inconveniently proved also a highly divisive figure, at loggerheads in Overijssel with local Orangist and Voetian preachers eager to recast prayers for the state in the public churches in the order they preferred. His opponents detested him as an excessively bold "Scripturian" assigning primacy to interpreting Hebrew passages instead of rigidly following church doctrine. In any case, after months of "sweating" over Spinoza's exasperating "Ezra thesis," Perizonius died, in October 1672, without completing his draft.[50] His son, Jacobus Perizonius (1651-1715), later also a renowned classical philologist, offered to complete and publish his father's rebuttal but was dissuaded by Graevius who judged the text too overtly anti-Voetian and preoccupied with discussing Hebrew, more apt to divide than unify opinion

---

[49] Steenbakkers, "The Text," 30; Gootjes, "First Orchestrated Attack," 23, 31; Touber, *Spinoza and Biblical Philology*, 79.

[50] Touber, "Biblical Philology," 329-34, 338-41, 346; Thijssen-Schoute, *Nederlands Cartesianisme*, 40, 447, 461-2; Goldenbaum, "Zwischen Bewunderung und Ensetzen," 4n4; Van de Ven, *Documenting Spinoza*, ch. 9.

in what was now an international furore where any refutation less than compelling and unifying as well as condemnatory must prove counterproductive.[51] Discussing the *TTP* intensively, the Utrecht's literary and philosophical club, the *Collegie der Sçavanten* was striving, in the interest of bolstering the Cartesian bloc as a whole, to effectively seize the initiative in the campaign to refute the *TTP*.

Observers aware of the radical fringe around Spinoza viewed the *TTP* as an attack not just on theologians, synods, and magistracies, and retaliation for the brutal crushing of the Koerbaghs, but also an immediate threat to Cartesians and Cocceians. Finding Alting unwilling and the younger Perizonius inadequate, they now vested their hopes in Regnerus van Mansvelt (1639–1671), professor of logic and metaphysics at Utrecht and regular member of the Utrecht *Collegie der Sçavanten* alongside Graevius, Burman, and Van Velthuysen. Writing again to Leibniz a week after informing him that it was "Spinoza" who wrote the *TTP*, Graevius reported that it was now Van Mansvelt who was shouldering chief responsibility from the Cocceian-Cartesian side for penning a comprehensive refutation of that "horrible book." Meanwhile, even before Burman's urgent appeal to Alting, in July 1670, the Utrecht Cartesians fixed their gaze also on another pupil of Alting's to assist in an auxiliary, subsidiary way, by striking fast and fiercely to herald the way, so to speak, for Van Mansvelt's longer, deeper, and more thorough refutation.

Still, it was not until early 1671, already well over a year after the *TTP*'s anonymous appearance, that any published reply to the *TTP* of any sort appeared in The Netherlands, and even then it was not actually composed in the Republic but in a neighbouring locale in Germany. The person chosen to herald their offensive while the public and scholarly world awaited Van Mansvelt's refutation, was the young, twenty-four-year-old pastor Johannes Melchior (1646–89), a great admirer of Burman who had studied at Groningen under Maresius and Alting, and at Leiden under Cocceius. Though now preacher in the Rhineland village of Frechen, near Cologne, Melchior knew the Dutch cultural scene and, later, as professor of theology at Duisburg and then Herborn, would figure among the foremost Reformed theologians of the German Lower Rhine area. In May 1670, when happening to be in Utrecht for his marriage to a sister of the professor of mathematics there, Hugo Ruysch (d. 1690), he discussed strategy and the urgency of rebutting the *TTP* with Graevius and others of the *Collegie der Sçavanten*.[52]

Initially, writing from the Rhineland on 1 July 1670, Melchior responded to Graevius' request that he assist his allies by offering to refute the *TTP* as part of a large book he was already working on.[53] He had now examined the *TTP* and agreed the anonymous author combined great subtlety of intellect and systematic

---

[51] Gootjes, "First Orchestrated Attack," 36–7; Gootjes, "Tussen Vriendschap en vijandschap," 23; Touber, *Spinoza and Biblical Philology*, 79–82, 85–6, 189.
[52] Gootjes, "First Orchestrated Attack," 31.   [53] Gootjes, "Le Réseau cartésien," 50–1.

research with boundless impiety. His initial offer was not accepted. What was needed, rather, Graevius hurriedly replied, was something short, sharp, and readily publishable since as yet nothing at all had appeared denouncing the *TTP*. Later that summer, on 11 September 1670, Melchior duly dispatched from Cologne a short draft tract which he enclosed for review by Graevius, Burman, and Van Velthuysen. "What you most celebrated sir exhorted me to do," wrote Melchior, "namely rip apart the anonymous author of the impious discourses [of the *TTP*], I have undertaken in the form of a letter to an old friend."[54] In this way, while awaiting Van Mansvelt's (and Van Velthuysen's) extended refutations, the Utrecht Cartesians ushered Melchior in as their precursor, announcing to the public that the Cartesians were as indignant as any at the *TTP* and also prompter and more effective than all the rest in taking up furious cudgels to fight it.

Despite dying prematurely at forty-three, Melchior proved remarkably prolific, churning out a formidable list of Latin works of which his *TTP* rebuttal, the *Epistola ad amicum, continens censuram libri cui titulus Tractatus Theologico-Politicus*, was among the earliest. Despite the Cartesians adopting Melchior's tract merely as a provisional salvo rather than substantive counterblast, preparing the ground for Van Mansvelt's and Van Velthuysen's more extended efforts, a further lengthy delay nevertheless embarrassingly ensued after Melchior finished his tract, in September 1670, presumably due to the need for extensive revisions, before this first published response to the *TTP* within the Republic actually appeared.

From his own and others' inquiries, Melchior, by July 1670, was fairly certain Spinoza was the *TTP*'s author,[55] and, after a fashion, he would soon become the first opponent to publicly expose him as such. Remarkably, though, Melchior identified him, colluding here with the Utrecht *Collegie der Sçavanten*, only in approximate fashion, partly as reinsurance, in case the reports that Spinoza was the culprit were wrong, but seemingly mainly due to the Cartesians' worries about repudiating and demolishing a well-known leading expounder of Cartesianism. Accordingly, each time Melchior's tract cites Spinoza, his name is deliberately distorted so as to render it unrecognizable by most of the public while clearly identifiable by those in the know.[56] Still more bizarre, after further discussion, this curious evasion, purposely misspelling Spinoza's name, was endorsed by his Utrecht colleagues who nevertheless altered Melchior's original suggestion for the spelling. The problem for them was less whether Spinoza was really the author than how to profit from resoundingly denouncing him without drawing unwelcome attention to his being one of Cartesianism's chief expositors. Melchior first raised this delicate point with Graevius, in September 1670. Based "on your

---

[54] Gootjes, "Le Réseau cartésien," 53–4; quoted in Latin and English in Gootjes, "First Orchestrated Attack," 32.
[55] De Vet, "Letter of a Watchman," 38; Gootjes, "Le Réseau cartésien," 52.
[56] [Melchior], *Epistola ad amicum*, 4–6; De Vet, "Letter of a Watchman," 36–7; Israel, "Early Dutch and German Reaction," 77–8.

conjecture [i.e. that Spinoza was the culprit]," "I called the author Zinospam, for I wanted expressly to name Spinoza" but yet do so without too precisely identifying him.[57] In 1670–1, with the wider public at home and abroad still broadly unaware who Spinoza was, it did indeed seem sensible to deliberately distort his name in this way just in case the conjecture was wrong and especially to divert attention away from Spinoza personally while ensuring the Cartesians could not afterwards be accused of showing any partiality towards him. After carefully considering the matter, the Utrecht *Collegie der Sçavanten* agreed to adjust "Zinospa" to "Xinospa."

Published by Burman's regular publisher at Utrecht, but owing to delays, only in April 1671, Melchior's tract appeared without Melchior's name on the title-page, solely under his initials "J.M.V.D.M.," his sponsors, Graevius and Burman, being concerned about his youth (being still only twenty-four) and lack of status. Melchior nevertheless proved quite perspicacious. Behind Xinospa's Bible criticism, he explained, lurks an entire clandestine philosophy presenting a comprehensively godless conception of the universe and human life, excluding all supernatural agency, theology, and ecclesiastical authority. Largely eschewing the issue of Cartesianism,[58] as his Cartesian sponsors directed, he found fault with Spinoza's Hebrew philology, his presenting biblical prophecy as the outcome of purely human "imagination" rather than revelation, and construing biblical utterances as couched in imaginative terms adjusted to the uninformed understanding of the common people. For the loathsome Xinospa the will of God "is nothing other than the power of nature [non aliam esse quam naturae potentiam]." Where Cartesians proclaim the reality of the miraculous, Xinospa's *sophismata* negate God's commandments, deny all religious authority, subvert church direction of society, and mislead the "people into supposing everything needed for human salvation can be provided by natural reason and intellect alone."[59] Such false hypotheses, claiming Scripture is not the word of God, destroy rather than stabilize the foundations of religion and the republic.[60] The tract reappeared in a second edition under a different title in 1672.

The Utrecht *sçavanten* were a wide-ranging but closely knit circle that included several members of the Utrecht city government. "They had for several years been meeting together every week," noted Graevius later, in April 1674, "to discuss a range of studies in which I expounded for these powerful magistrates some satires of Juvenal, Suetonius, and Grotius' *De Iure belli et pacis*; in anatomy, we studied the principal parts of the body like the heart, eye, ears, spleen and others, guided here by De Bruyn, an excellent, experienced master of dissection; we also read and

[57] Quoted in Latin and English in Gootjes, "First Orchestrated Attack," 32–3.
[58] Krop, *Spinoza, een paradoxale icoon*, 150.
[59] [Melchior], *Epistola ad amicum*, 4–6, 33, 46–7; De Vet, "Letter of a Watchman," 38; Nadler, *Book Forged in Hell*, 221; Touber, *Spinoza and Biblical Philology*, 87–92.
[60] [Melchior], *Epistola ad amicum*, 33, 46–7; Israel, "Early Dutch and German Reaction," 77–8.

debated new books as they appeared, whether on the causes of natural things, or about other fields of study."[61] This *Collegie der Sçavanten*, by opponents accused of seeking "to root out the true godly and pious lovers of the Church and Prince [of Orange],"[62] stood at the forefront of the then Dutch intellectual scene not least in the fields of philosophy, science, and political theory, and it was Van Mansvelt, fresh from feuding with Maresius, who was their primary champion billed to crush the *TTP*.

Unlike Melchior, Van Mansvelt was a well-known figure of considerable standing. Such was the general alarm provoked by the *TTP*, that despite having various projects in hand, he had agreed, Graevius informed Leibniz, to lay aside, for now, all other pressing controversies. Cartesianism firmly dominated in the Dutch universities, Graevius assured Leibniz, with Aristotelianism wholly "prostrate"; but the *TTP* represented a major threat to Cartesianism and academic stability, as well as the entire existing order in religion and society. Hard at work refuting that "infamous and horrible book," Van Mansvelt used arguments at least partly reflecting their group discussions of the *TTP* chaired by Van Velthuysen.[63] However, unexpectedly, on 29 May 1671, soon after Graevius informed Leibniz of his friend's undertaking the task, with his refutation still incomplete, Van Mansvelt too suddenly died. Delivering the main oration at his funeral, Graevius assured those attending that the (unnamed) author of the *TTP* sought to destroy Scripture's authority and demolish every proper notion of God. His appalling book was an attack on Cartesianism, moreover, no less than religion. Where Van Mansvelt and true Cartesians defended "liberty to philosophize" lawfully, abiding by the States' regulations,[64] this author blatantly violated the States' decree of 1656 by ostensibly separating philosophy and theology while in reality not doing so.

Thankfully, Van Mansvelt had completed large sections of his rebuttal before dying, but his draft needed considerable further attention before being brought to the press. Graevius and his colleagues were still working on it a year later, in May 1672, when Louis XIV's invasion forced further delay. Distressingly for many, it remained unpublished right through 1672–3. Impatient though the *sçavanten* were for Van Mansvelt's *Adversus anonymum Theologico-politicum*, their principal reply to Spinoza, to preponderate in Dutch reaction to the *TTP*, the need to strengthen it as much as possible unfortunately delayed its posthumous appearance until 1674.

---

[61] Quoted in Latin and English in Gootjes, "First Orchestrated Attack," 27–8.
[62] Pamphlet quoted in Thijssen-Schoute, *Nederlands Cartesianisme*, 445.
[63] Leibniz, *Sämtliche Schriften* 1st ser. i, 142 and 148; Bouveresse, *Spinoza et Leibniz*, 221; Israel, *Radical Enlightenment*, 503; Israel, "Early Dutch and German Reaction," 79; Gootjes, "Tussen Vriendschap en vijandschap," 22.
[64] Van Bunge, "Early Dutch Reception," 228; Krop, *Spinoza, een paradoxale icoon*, 163–72.

The stunning, much commented on, extreme paucity of published response to the *TTP* throughout 1670–3 hence resulted partly from a series of accidents but especially from fear of refuting the *TTP* with insufficient force. The various mishaps hampering the crushing retribution so many longed to see could not, however, prevent the notion spreading that the Republic's best minds were indeed "sweating" to produce an adequate answer. In addition, by 1673, the Dutch Cartesians also had to face the damaging calumny propagated by French wartime propaganda denigrating the Republic as a land of scandalous freedom where every brand of religion and form of licence was permitted. With half of the Republic under foreign occupation, Jean-Baptiste Stouppe's *La Religion des Hollandois*, published in May 1673, assured all Europe that the entire corpus of Dutch theologians and university professors, the Cartesians included, had proved totally incapable of producing a single full-length refutation during three entire years since the *TTP*'s appearance. Spinoza's "sectateurs [followers]," explained Stouppe, dared "not show themselves openly, because his book overthrows absolutely the foundations of all religions and has been condemned by public decree of the States and it is forbidden to sell it. But that has not stopped it from being publicly sold";[65] and despite being officially forbidden, the irresponsible Dutch, charged Stouppe, were doing practically nothing to counter the arguments of the most shocking, damaging, and pernicious book of the age.

"Among all the theologians that are in the country," as the Dutch version of Stouppe's book expressed the point, "not one has dared to write against this author [Spinoza] who shows great understanding and knowledge of the Hebrew language and all the ceremonies of the Jewish religion and their customs as well as philosophy. Since the theologians cannot say the book is not worthy that someone should go to the trouble to refute it, people will not be able to resist remarking, given that [the theologians] remain silent, that they are unwilling to face up to the challenge." The Dutch scandalously permit this pernicious book to go unanswered, concluded Stouppe slyly, either because they "agree with the views of that author, or possess neither the confidence nor ability to tackle him."[66]

Appearing five years after the *TTP*, the principal reply to Stouppe's propaganda onslaught, Jean Brun's *La Véritable religion des Hollandois* (1675), itself long delayed by the war, vigorously defended Dutch society against the charge of excessive religious freedom, a point of shame rather than pride for many contemporaries, and sought to discredit Stouppe's remarks about the failure of the Dutch to answer the *TTP*. But this part of Brun's reply to Stouppe was conspicuously weak: it did little more than reaffirm what Stouppe had said. "Monsieurs les États," the provincial States, had "tried to stifle it from its birth, have condemned it

---

[65] Stouppe, *Religion des Hollandois*, 66; Stouppe, *De God-Dienst Der Hollanders*, 25–6.
[66] Stouppe, *De God-Dienst Der Hollanders*, 26.

and forbidden its sale by public decree," but down to 1674, the *TTP* unfortunately met with no substantial intellectual response from the Dutch.[67]

27.iii Spinoza's Clandestine Subversion of Religion

Being known among the wider reading public in the Netherlands and Germany thus far exclusively as a leading exponent of Cartesian philosophy, efforts to expose "Spinoza as the author of the *TTP*," and target him specifically as the source of the blasphemies troubling society, were bound to be divisive and potentially a major vulnerability of the "Cartesians." Unlike the *Philosophia* controversy where the mystery of the anonymous author's identity remained unresolved (as still today, though it is generally assumed Meyer was the principal author), in the case of the *TTP* it was widely reported within weeks around The Netherlands, and with a considerable degree of certainty, who the despicable "anonymus" was. The Utrecht Cartesians knew before most others, Graevius and his group, we have seen, already in April 1670. At Groningen, their chief adversary, Samuel Maresius, announced, in July 1670, that his inquiries proved this most atrocious of texts to be from the pen of "Spinoza, ex-Jew, blasphemer and formal atheist."[68]

Very differently from the Cartesians, Maresius at once took to highlighting Spinoza's authorship of the *TTP* in the context of the continuing scholarly uproar over Cartesianism gripping all the Dutch universities, to demonstrate at the expense particularly of his principal polemical opponent, Van Mansvelt, now endorsed by his Utrecht colleagues as Cartesianism's chief adversary of the *TTP*, that "it is clearer than the noonday sun" that Spinoza's horrendous views and Bible criticism derive directly from basic Cartesian principles.[69] For the Dutch universities, this was inevitably a deeply disturbing development, as it was also for the German Calvinist universities, Duisburg, Herborn, and Heidelberg.

A fundamental threat to religion, the *TTP* was henceforth regarded too as a particular threat also to the Cartesian faction. By late 1670, it was obvious the *TTP* was becoming a pretext for intensifying the Voetian campaign to counter Descartes' philosophical and scientific legacy. It illustrated even "far more" than the *Philosophia*, held Maresius, what he called Cartesian "use and misuse of reason in theology and faith."[70] "Abuse of Cartesian philosophy," Maresius and the Voetians insisted, stemmed from Cartesianism's reliance on reason leading to their subverting the fundamental tenets of Reformed theology, indeed all genuine

---

[67] Braun [Brun], *Véritable religion* i, 159–60.
[68] Maresius, *Vindiciae Dissertationis suae*, 4; Israel, "Early Dutch and German Reaction," 77.
[69] Maresius, *Vindiciae Dissertationis suae*, 4; Van Bunge, "Early Dutch Reception," 228–9; Israel, "Early Dutch and German Reaction," 77–8.
[70] Van Berkel, *Universiteit van het noorden*, 167.

Christian faith, by decimating credence in miracles, angels, and other *supernaturalia*. A Huguenot trained in Paris and Geneva, and among the Republic's most pugnacious theologians, Maresius' turn against the "Cartesians" in 1670 attracted widespread attention as it looked like a dramatic volte-face. Ever since arriving in Groningen, in 1643, Maresius had quarrelled bitterly with Voetius and his following and aligned cautiously with pro-Cartesian and Coccejan elements. Although already shifting from a pro- to an anti-Cartesian stance since the *Philosophia* controversy in 1666, only in 1670 did he emerge in open opposition to "abuse of Cartesianism," proclaiming Cartesianism the primary source of Spinozism.[71]

Having known Descartes personally and admired him, he still had "many friends" among the Cartesians, claimed the Maresius of the early 1670s.[72] He would always adhere unfailingly to his distinction, now gaining vital importance, between *genuini Cartesiani* [genuine Cartesians], and *pseudo-Cartesiani* like the author of the *Philosophia* and Spinoza.[73] However, he now realized that Reformed theology in the Netherlands had sunk during the late 1660s into a desperately "sad condition" owing to the advances of Cartesianism as well as of pseudo-Cartesianism, Socinianism, and Cocceianism to all of which Maresius now proved as hostile as Voetius while profiling Spinoza less as a unique phenomenon than an extreme manifestation of a far broader malaise gripping religion in the Republic and vitiating the Dutch universities. Dropping his former hostility to Voetians, Maresius now pointedly joined with them in attributing the "atheist Spinoza's atrocious" views and Bible hermeneutics to the *indifferentismus* and *libertinismus* spiced with some Hobbes and Machiavelli broadly generated by Cartesian premises.[74]

Van Mansvelt and his former pupil, Wittichius, rapidly became the chief targets attacked by Maresius for propagating the Cartesio-Coccejan "sickness" so harmful to theology and church control of society stemming from Cartesianism's allegedly profoundly problematic aspects.[75] Prior to taking up cudgels against Spinoza, Van Mansvelt had, during 1670, responded to Maresius' recent publications with several hard-hitting pamphlets. Acknowledging "Spinoza" was the author of the *TTP*,[76] Van Mansvelt agreed too that a secure method for distinguishing genuine Cartesians from pseudo-Cartesians was now required and even agreed that the surest proof of genuine Cartesian adherence was professed belief in the existence

---

[71] Thijssen-Schoute, *Nederlands Cartesianisme*, 481; Krop, *Spinoza, een pardoxale icoon*, 158–9.

[72] Maresius, *Vindiciae Dissertationis suae*, 3.

[73] Maresius, *Vindiciae Dissertationis suae*, 10, 17; [Van Mansvelt], *Animadversiones Ad Vindiciae Dissertationis*, 19; Gaukroger, *Descartes*, 360; Van Berkel, *Universiteit van het noorden*, 174–5.

[74] Maresius, *Clypeus orthodoxiae*, 10; De Vet, "Letter of a Watchman," 38; Goudriaan, *Reformed Orthodoxy*, 110.

[75] Goudriaan, *Reformed Orthodoxy*, 8, 58, 110; Krop, *Spinoza, een paradoxale icoon*, 159.

[76] [Van Mansvelt], *Animadversiones Ad Vindiciae Dissertationis*, 7, 19; [Van Mansvelt], *Specimen confutationis dissertationis*, 5, 9–17.

of angels and demons. He rejected, though, Maresius' charge that Cartesianism itself insidiously opens the door to atheism and the ideas of Vanini, and ultimately Spinoza. The infallible test Maresius himself recommended for distinguishing between *genuini Cartesiani* and the *pseudo-Cartesiani* Van Mansvelt urged him to take more seriously. For genuine Cartesians do unreservedly assert the existence of the supernatural leaving only *pseudo-Cartesiani* denying the existence of supernatural spirits and demons. Ridiculing Maresius' reconciliation with Voetius after their many years of wrangling, and rebuffing his "calumny" against the Cartesians, Van Mansvelt, before he died, presented the gulf between real and *pseudo-Cartesiani* as actually much deeper and more crucial than Maresius was suggesting. Genuine Cartesians unreservedly embraced Christian truth, Christology, immortality of the soul, divine creation, angels and demons; Cartesians, experience showed, were the sturdiest, most reliable and active adversaries, furthermore, of the vile unbelievers embracing Spinoza and the *Philosophia*.[77]

Braving the jeers at his first combating and now allying with Voetius, Maresius claimed to have consistently led the same unremitting crusade "against Socinians, Catholics, Praeadamites, universalists, visionaries and fanatics" in France and the Netherlands alike, throughout his career. His new alliance with Voetius represented no threat to the standing and careers in the universities of *genuini Cartesiani* provided they sincerely combined Cartesianism with orthodox Reformed theology on the key points. Descartes, after all, Maresius reminded readers, defended core Christian doctrine including immortality of the soul, denial of which was the first step towards atheism. If Descartes too embraced serious errors like endorsing the Copernican thesis (Maresius, like the Voetians staunchly opposed those arguing the earth circles the sun),[78] he always distinguished between body and soul, and never interpreted Scripture in the light of philosophy which did not, in any case, need "interpreting" since, contrary to the *Philosophia* (and Spinoza), its true meaning is nowhere difficult to discern.[79]

Maresius professed to be the "friend" of Descartes and the Cartesians still, as he was of Plato and Aristotle too, but his greatest commitment was always to Christ which meant combating the "pseudo-Cartesiani" and "abuse of Cartesian philosophy in matters relating to theology and faith."[80] A scourge of Remonstrants, Mennonites, Socinians, and Catholics as well as libertines during the entire thirty years he held his chair in theology at Groningen (1642–73), possessing a collection of 2,567 books rated among the foremost theological collections of that province,

---

[77] [Van Mansvelt], *Animadversiones Ad Vindiciae Dissertationis*, 14, 19, 67; Maresius, *Clypeus orthodoxiae*, 4.
[78] Maresius, *Clypeus orthodoxiae*, 52–3; De Mowbray, "Libertas philosophandi," 45.
[79] Maresius, *Clypeus orthodoxiae*, 53, 62, 75; Preus, *Spinoza*, 85–6.
[80] Maresius, *Vindiciae Dissertationis suae*, 3, 5–7, 9, 64; De Mowbray, "Libertas philosophandi," 45–6; Goudriaan, *Reformed Orthodoxy*, 8.

Maresius made it his business to thoroughly investigate the persons behind grave threats to theology's ascendancy over society. In July 1670, having denounced the *Philosophia* for four years, for "abuse" of Cartesian principles, his *Vindiciae Dissertationis suae* still offered no clue as to who wrote that text but confidently specifies Spinoza as author of the *TTP*.[81] In fact, by July 1670, there was no doubt whatever who wrote the *TTP* and Spinoza was hardly trying conceal the fact; and yet Graevius and the *sçavanten* still continued publicly denouncing the *TTP* without publicly citing Spinoza, preferring to damp down the growing hue and cry against Spinoza personally as far as they could.

By early 1670, Spinoza had clearly now displaced the Koerbaghs, the *Philosophia*'s author, and Hobbes as supreme foe of the churches and of Scripture's sacred status. By the summer of 1670, though obvious enough in the Netherlands and in Germany, there was still no sign of this yet being realized in England, Italy, or France. Spinoza, now possibly The Hague's single most notorious inhabitant, had become the prime marker fencing off respectable academic philosophy and science from the murky underground world of illicit anti-theological radical thought.[82] Yet, for this very reason, Spinoza's swift emergence as reputedly the most abominable of all thinkers, and most fatal to Christian truth and authority, the Cartesio-Cocceians persisted in keeping up what was now essentially a bogus public "anonymity" surrounding the anonymous *TTP*, upholding the frayed mask publicly concealing its author. They were defending themselves by continuing with this pretence.

Thus, when it finally appeared (anonymously) in 1674, Van Mansvelt's rebuttal, notes Colerus,[83] resoundingly condemned the *TTP* as a uniquely abominable book deserving to be "ad aeternas damnandum tenebras [damned to the eternal shadows]," but yet did so saying nothing at all about Spinoza the man and not even naming him even though Van Mansvelt had been perfectly aware who the author was for over three years. Instead, he merely claimed never to have set eyes on the anonymous author and to abominate his "absurd doctrines." Despite its decidedly belated appearance, in 1674 the work was still entitled, as Van Mansvelt originally intended, *Adversus anonymum Theologico-Politicus*, clear evidence the Dutch Cartesians were deeply concerned lest any focusing of attention on a well-known expounder of Descartes could all too readily backfire on them. A fervent Cartesian, Van Mansvelt was particularly at pains to uphold the fundamental distinction between body and spirit characteristic of Descartes' work and highlight the advantages of the Cartesian two-substance approach for blocking the *TTP*, atheism, and all naturalism.

---

[81] Huisman, "Bibliothecae instructissimae," 323; Touber, *Spinoza and Biblical Philology*, 78–9.
[82] Lagrée, *Spinoza et le débat*, 114–15; Israel, "Early Dutch and German Reaction," 86–7.
[83] Colerus, *La Vie de B. de Spinoza*, 58.

In Germany, meanwhile, Spinoza's emerging international profile was noticeably less centred on his role in local Dutch disputes. How precisely to draw the dividing line between *genuini Cartesiani* and *pseudo-Cartesiani* was scarcely of interest in Germany's predominantly Lutheran and Catholic universities. German reaction began at the largest Lutheran university, Leipzig, probably owing to distribution of copies commencing there, that spring, at the Leipzig Book Fair, the country's largest. Leibniz's mentor, the university's professor of moral philosophy, Jakob Thomasius (1622–84), already denounced the *TTP* on 8 May 1670 in an oration, later published as *Adversus anonymum de libertate philosophandi*, assailing especially the *TTP*'s notion of "freedom to philosophize."[84] In September 1670, Leibniz wrote to his mentor, from Frankfurt, designating the *TTP* an "intolerably licentious book on liberty to philosophize" which Thomasius, Leibniz did not doubt, had soundly thrashed as deserved.[85] More copies were presumably distributed at the Frankfurt Book Fair, an equally dominant event in the German book trade, in September.[86]

An anti-Cartesian eclectic, figuring among the more prominent figures in German academe, Thomasius enjoyed high status as Europe's first real exponent of history of philosophy. Now he became also the first scholar anywhere in Europe to publicly rebut the *TTP*, his refutation preceding Melchior's, the first appearing in The Netherlands, by many months. Delivered originally as a lecture, at Leipzig, on 8 May 1670, only a month after the first references to Spinoza's book in Utrecht, in August 1670, Thomasius published a fuller version under the title *Programma adversus anonymum de libertate philosophandi*. So while Thomasius' initial sally of May 1670 was actually the first refutation appearing in print, it was then not yet an attack on Spinoza personally and his philosophy. Until the summer of 1670, news of Spinoza being the *TTP*'s author had not yet penetrated the German universities; in August, Thomasius still portrayed the *TTP* as anonymous, referring to the author only as "that abominable monster shunning the light."[87] It was on republishing his text, two years later, that Thomasius added his footnote, based on information received probably late in 1670, explaining that although the anonymous author "nowhere utters his name; I learned afterwards that this impious text's author was Benedict Spinoza, a blasphemous ex-Jew and formal atheist," profiling him (apparently repeating information sent by Leibniz) as "a Jew cast out of the synagogue [aposynagogos] on account of his monstrous opinions [ob opinionum monstra]."[88]

---

[84] Otto, *Studien*, 15; Israel, "Early Dutch and German Reaction," 83; Van de Ven, "Spinoza's Life and Time," 25; as Begley showed, in 2018, I myself, like most Spinoza specialists, was mistaken in supposing that knowledge of who the author was circulated in Germany as early as May 1670.
[85] Leibniz, *Sämtliche Schriften* 2nd ser. *Philosophischer Briefwechsel* i, 66; Laerke, *Leibniz lecteur*, 94.
[86] Otto, *Studien*,19; Pettegree and Der Weduwen, *Bookshop of the World*, 267–8.
[87] Bamberger, "Early Editions," 13n30; Walther, *Spinoza Studien* iii, 179; Zenker, *Denkfreiheit*, 101.
[88] Lavaert, *Vrijheid, gelijkheid, veelheid*, 185; Begley, "Naturalism," 2–3.

The *TTP*'s advocacy of full "freedom of thought and speech," Thomasius identified as its most pernicious feature, such a principle being "pestilential" for both society and religion.[89] Where Melchior says little about the political dimension, Thomasius focused on what, to him, were the ruinous consequences political and social of the *TTP*'s closing chapters, the argument that "in a free republic everyone is permitted to think whatever he wishes, and say whatever he thinks." The "anonymus" might think such a thing beneficial, but nothing, he insisted, could be more damaging to a Christian society. Thomasius endorsed authoritarian Lutheran princely rule and rigorous censorship of books and thought to reinforce the existing political and religious order. He pointed out the considerable and deeply menacing significance of Spinoza's tying freedom of thought to undermining monarchy and aristocracy which before long would prove the defining feature of the nascent Radical Enlightenment. Thomasius indeed recognized in a way few others did at the time how fundamental this linkage is in Spinoza's approach. Freedom of expression and the ties between the *anonymus*' toleration and his democratic republic would harm any society, held Thomasius, but was especially corrosive of monarchy and aristocracy, Europe's dominant forms of state and social organization. Monarchy and aristocracy, he insisted, are the only correct and religiously endorsed forms for society, and would be so eroded by freedom of expression as inevitably to drift towards democracy. The "anonymus," admonishes Thomasius, does not admit outright that his secret purpose is to undermine monarchy and aristocracy, but he hints at this plainly enough.[90] Politically, Thomasius was far more perspicacious than Melchior or any other early critic of Spinoza.

In a Christian society under princes it would be catastrophic if some became convinced they should be free to think and say whatever they want. The *TTP*'s consequences for religion, society, and morality Thomasius linked partly to the proto-deism of Herbert of Cherbury but, in its political dimension, especially to Hobbes. What society requires, in his view, was cohesion, unity of doctrine, and academies under a monarchically backed single church confession coexisting only with such philosophy as defers without question to theology, his own preference being for Aristotelianism. Amsterdam, the toleration model presented by the *TTP* for all the world to emulate may be a place where "the sects, as I hear, do all enjoy peace with other men."[91] But peace among men, between confessions and sects, is worthless, indeed ruinous, where men are not at peace with God, the only harmony that truly matters. Thomasius' public condemnation of May 1670 was arguably among the most crucial attacks on Spinoza during his life, even if

---

[89] Freudenthal/Walther, *Lebensgeschichte* i, 151; Laerke, *Leibniz lecteur*, 182, 187, 278–9.
[90] Begley, "Naturalism," 6–8; Walther, "Machina civilis," 187–90; Israel, "Early Dutch and German Reaction," 81.
[91] Spinoza, *Theological-Political Treatise*, 250, 259; Walther, *Spinoza Studien* iii, 185; and quoting Thomasius, Begley, "Naturalism," 15–16.

Spinoza himself never saw it, because Thomasius, almost uniquely, connects the *TTP*'s freedom to philosophize—extending philosophy to all truth, covering every doctrine and institution—and the book's hostility to theology to its vigorous advocacy of democratic republicanism. For Thomasius, democratic republicanism meant the collapse of all religious authority and all subordination to princely government.

Thomasius' Leipzig colleague, the Lutheran theologian and Latin poet Friedrich Rappolt (1615–76), "a man of the greatest wisdom and learning," followed him in publicly assailing the *TTP* in his inaugural lecture as full professor of theology, on 1 June 1670, an onslaught likewise being prepared since early May. Rappolt too condemns the *TTP* as a deeply pernicious text, but, differently from Thomasius, hardly touches on the political and social dimension, focusing instead on the theological aspects. Shocked especially by the book's allocating the right to interpret Scripture to every individual whose conscience is free and independent, eliminating all ecclesiastical authority, he was incensed by its reduction of Christianity, the true "cult of God," to simply justice and charity, "cultum Dei in sola Justitia et charitate consistere." Our world stands on faith, doctrine, sacraments, belief in the miraculous and the supernatural. The venom of what the "anonymus" calls "true religion" completely abolishes miracles, revelation, theology, and church primacy in culture, education, and society, and over church affairs.[92] A month later Rappolt assailed the *TTP* again in a more substantial polemic, his *Oratio contra Naturalistas* pronouncing the *TTP* the most virulent and harmful manifestation of *Naturalismus* thus far to have penetrated Germany. An ancient current originating in ancient Greece, brute naturalism had been recently revived by the English naturalist Herbert of Cherbury. But this new outpouring was far more menacing, being a soul-destroying, devastating *Naturalismus* anchored in a philosophy trampling on all accepted belief. For Rappolt, not the New Philosophy, nor any philosophy, but only faith, Revelation, and authorized religious guidance, provide a path to truth or can bring men to salvation.[93] Like Thomasius, Rappolt attacked the *TTP* in 1670 without as yet mentioning Spinoza or dragging his name into the fray.[94]

Next, another ally, Johann Konrad Dürr (1625–77), on 30 June 1670, in an address at Altdorf, the Lutheran university of the Imperial Free City of Nuremberg, likewise denounced the *TTP*'s plea for *libertas philosophandi*. With Altdorf University already battling Socinian influence in the sixteenth century, and home to a tradition of combating Socinianism, Dürr especially highlighted

---

[92] Rappolt, *Opera theologica*, 2162–3; Walther, "Machina civilis," 190; Israel, *Radical Enlightenment*, 623.
[93] Rappolt, *Oratio contra naturalistas* in Rappolt, *Opera theologica*, 1390–1, 1404–5; Friedmann, *Leibniz et Spinoza*, 62; Otto, *Studien*, 16, 26–7.
[94] Bamberger, "Early Editions," 30; Israel, "Early Dutch and German Reaction," 83; Nadler, *Book Forged in Hell*, 220–1.

the, to him, frightful parallels between the *TTP*'s anonymous author and that much reviled renegade from the Lutheran Church, Daniel Zwicker.[95] Like Thomasius and Rappolt, Dürr presumably learnt the *TTP*'s author's name only later in 1670, when the initial reports that Spinoza was the "abominable monster" in question reached Heidelberg and then quickly spread to other German universities.

Usually anonymous works of highly notorious reputation, like *De Jure Ecclesiasticorum*, Meyer's *Philosophia*, or the notorious Spinozistic sequel to the novel *Philopater* (1697), remained anonymous at the time and for decades afterwards, submerged in doubt, mystery and obscurity for generations as regards authorship and circumstances of the book's production. By contrast, the TTP's seeming public "anonymity," buttressed by the Cartesians' manifesting their reluctance to provoke a hue and cry against him personally, helped preserve Spinoza's supposed "anonymity" for a considerable time and was decidedly a curious and paradoxical outcome especially as, in this case, not a single other author was anywhere mentioned as a possible alternative candidate, a striking contrast with the *Philosophia* furore.

From the summer of 1670, Spinoza and his hidden following found themselves embroiled in a three-cornered conflict that would continue without interruption for many years. The Utrecht *Collegie der Sçavanten* felt trapped between the pressing need to disassociate their Cartesian fringe from Spinoza and atheism and to shield themselves from accusations that Cartesianism conduces to Spinozism, and the charge of not combating Spinoza and abuse of Cartesianism forcefully enough. This afforded Maresius, Voetius, Van Mastricht, and the Dutch and German anti-Cartesian fraternity ample scope to exploit the undeniable links between Spinoza and Cartesianism. What better evidence than the *TTP* for indicting Cartesianism as ultimately fatally corrosive of the Christian mysteries and belief in the supernatural? The Cartesian menace's worst manifestations, they claimed, were undoubtedly the *Philosophia* and Spinoza. But the campaign to smear Cartesianism itself with the tar of Spinoza's godless philosophy and Bible criticism before long spurred the Cartesians, in turn, to escalate their attacks first on the *TTP* and, by the mid-1670s, to assail Spinoza and Spinozism directly in an increasingly frantic attempt to counter accusations that Cartesianism is inherently prone to produce the devastating consequences manifested by the *TTP*. No one described the Cartesians' predicament more accurately or scornfully than Spinoza himself, when writing to Oldenburg, in September 1675: "the stupid Cartesians, because they are thought to be on my side," try to remove the suspicion under which they languish "by ceaselessly denouncing my opinions and my writings, as they continue to do."[96]

---

[95] Zenker, *Denkfreiheit*, 107–9, 111.   [96] Spinoza, *Collected Works* (ed. Curley) ii, 459.

As divisions deepened, Maresius, having formed a behind-the-scenes pact with his former foe, Voetius, to enable them to unite against the common threat of radical Cartesianism, from July 1670 came under pressure to publicly rebut Van Mansvelt's counter-charge that after decades of wrangling with hardline Calvinists he was now unaccountably jettisoning his previously relatively tolerant stance. He was not opting for narrowness and bigotry, he angrily retorted, or entering into an unprincipled "conspiracy" with Voetius simply to crush the Cartesians.[97] Nor was he abandoning Groningen's long-established neutrality regarding Cartesian philosophy by intervening in the decades-old war between Aristotelianism and Cartesianism ruinously spreading further dissension and confusion in the universities. Nevertheless, his *De abusu philosophiae Cartesianae* (Groningen, 1670), proved beyond doubt that his anti-Cartesianism and anti-Copernicanism had both now hardened and become closely linked. By violating the bounds set by the States of Holland and other provinces to defend core theology, Christian truth, and the States Bible's integrity, *pseudo-Cartesiani* were following the lead of an "atheist Jew" who had undoubtedly originally begun by embracing Descartes' principles and insidiously perverted them. *Pseudo-Cartesiani* also violate Christian truth with their astronomy, held Maresius, by supporting the Copernican thesis that the earth revolves around the sun whereas Descartes here had remained irreproachably cautious. This further development in contemporary philosophy, stemming from Descartes and Hobbes, Maresius pronounced a social catastrophe encouraging a general upsurge in the Netherlands of "Indifferentismus" and "Libertinismus."[98]

27.iv Steno Responds

In this way, a striking consequence of Spinoza's *TTP* in 1670 was to broaden and intensify in society and academic life the controversies surrounding Cartesians, Hebrew-oriented philologists and Copernicans alike. In the Netherlands, many blamed Cartesianism for the catastrophe of the *TTP*, but abroad there were also many who followed Stouppe in blaming the Republic itself and its "True Freedom" for the *TTP*'s "anti-Scripturalism" and assault on core Christianity. Prominent here was Nicolas Steno who, since 1668, had been undertaking a leisurely northern European tour on behalf of the Roman Church. He arrived back in Holland after six years of absence, in around December 1669, coinciding with the second edition of his classic work on the structure of muscles,

---

[97] Maresius, *Clypeus orthodoxiae*, 4; De Mowbray, *Libertas philosophandi*, 45–6; Krop, *Spinoza, een paradoxale icoon*, 159; Van Berkel, *Universiteit van het noorden*, 796n21.
[98] Maresius, *Vindiciae Dissertationis suae*, 4, 51–4; Maresius, *Clypeus orthodoxiae*, preface and pp. 10, 62–3, 68–9; Vermij, *Calvinist Copernicans*, 320–2.

Elementorum myologiae Specimen, seu Musculi descriptio geometrica (1667), published at Amsterdam in 1669, a copy of which soon arrived in Oldenburg's personal library.[99] Steno was hence present in Holland just prior to the *TTP* storm breaking and immediately after it broke. He had by now abandoned all involvement in new scientific research and, though not yet as rigid as later, considerably aggravated with his tireless theological pestering those former friends he now met again, especially Swammerdam who had not yet entered into his religious crisis or become disillusioned with Cartesianism.[100]

On 30 December 1669, Steno visited the famed Tacitus and Seneca expert, Johann Friedrich Gronovius (1611–71), in Leiden. Staying for several months more, through early 1670, he remained mostly in Amsterdam, spending much time conferring with his old comrades Swammerdam and that supreme French *curieux* and news gatherer of the republic of letters, Thévenot, doubtless both providing Steno with more up-to-date information about Spinoza than he could glean from most others. Though likewise increasingly drawn away from science to faith, Swammerdam leaned theologically in a quite different direction from his Danish friend.[101] Thévenot afterwards stayed in contact with both men, as well as with Graevius, De Volder, and other luminaries, during the final years of Spinoza's life remaining one of the main channels by which news of Dutch intellectual battles and scientific developments, including Spinoza and his remarkable circle seeking to reform the world, percolated through to Paris.[102]

In 1670, Steno took decidedly more interest in investigating the condition of Dutch Catholicism and reasons for Dutch society's predominant aversion to Catholicism, than in renewing old friendships. Seemingly, he neglected to contact Le Boë Sylvius and other former scientific mentors and colleagues.[103] Changed priorities made him unwilling to spend much time with most of those he had readily consorted with just a few years earlier. Christianity universally, he felt, was direly under siege with the most menacing developments emanating from the Netherlands. On 30 April 1670, by which time the *TTP* was being read and reacted to on all sides in the Republic, and especially Utrecht, he wrote to Graevius from Amsterdam, passing on warm greetings from Thévenot and Swammerdam but apologizing, claiming illness, for not coming to visit him or attend meetings of the Utrecht *Collegie der Sçavanten*.[104] Apparently, he deliberately avoided seeing the Cartesians or his old friend, Spinoza. Nonetheless, whilst in Holland and subsequently, Steno continued pondering a good deal about Spinoza and his circle and closely monitoring reaction to the *TTP*.

---

[99] BL MS Add. 4255, fo. 238, Oldenburg, "Catalogue of My Books taken A 1670 Octob. 3."
[100] Swammerdam, *Letters to Thévenot*, 57, 59, 84; Jorink, "Modus Politicus Vivendi," 37.
[101] Kardel and Maquet, *Nicolaus Steno*, 252.
[102] Swammerdam, *Letters to Thévenot*, 8–9, 15, 18; Strazzoni, *Burchard de Volder*, 68–74.
[103] Kardel and Maquet, *Nicolaus Steno*, 248–50.   [104] Gootjes, "First Orchestrated Attack," 28.

Departing in the early summer of 1670, Steno travelled via Utrecht (without stopping to see Graevius or other former friends) overland to Florence, arriving back a month later. Ensconced once more in Tuscany, he took up his pen and, from July 1670, produced a series of religious apologetic writings, one of which, later entitled the *Nicolai Stenonis ad novae philosophiae reformatorem de vera philosophia epistola* [A Letter of Nicolas Steno to the Reformer of the New Philosophy about the True Philosophy], completed in late 1670 or early in 1671, figures among the most memorable letters ever addressed to Spinoza during his lifetime.[105] Whether Spinoza actually received it then, or later, remains unknown. However, this Latin missive was eventually published at Florence, without naming its target, as an open letter "to the Reformer of the New Philosophy," in September 1675, and did certainly come to Spinoza's attention during the last year or two of his life, since Leibniz recorded, shortly after Spinoza's death, while indicating that he too disagreed with Spinoza about many things, that "due to the great difference between their views, Spinoza was not particularly affected by the exhortation of Mr Stensen [i.e. Steno]. Actually, Mr Stensen it seems to me, assumes far too much to convince a man who believed so little."[106]

Steno opens this key missive by remarking that although there is no author's name affixed to the *TTP*, he has heard from others in Holland recently that "you" (i.e. Spinoza) are its author and that, in addition, he had his "own reasons for believing the book is indeed composed by you." Regrettably, "while public peace is what you seek, you are creating complete chaos and while aiming to free yourself from all danger, you expose yourself quite unnecessarily to the gravest danger." The peril, he insisted, was all too real for both Spinoza's body and soul, as well as society generally, and

> since I see shrouded in such darkness a man who was once my good friend, and even now, I hope, not unfriendly toward me (for I am persuaded that the memory of our former close relationship still preserves a mutual love), and since I remember how I too was once entangled, if not exactly in the same errors, yet in misconceptions of a most serious kind, all the more does the gravity of the peril from which I escaped make manifest God's mercy toward me, and the more I am moved by compassion, to pray also for you, for the same heavenly grace accorded to me, albeit not through my own deserving it but solely through Christ's goodness.

Christ, or at least the Christ of the Catholic Church was the overriding issue. For despite the great gulf that had come between them, Steno remained convinced

---

[105] Scherz, *Niels Stensen*, 247; Scherz, "Biography of Nicolaus Steno," 264–71.
[106] Freudenthal/Walther, *Lebensgeschichte* ii, 176–7; Totaro, "Niels Stensen (1638–1686)," 155; Laerke, "G. W. Leibniz's Two Readings," 110; Laerke, *Leibniz lecteur*, 107–8.

Spinoza was a man ready to listen to cogent argument, that your "love of peace and truth which I once perceived in you is not yet extinguished by your darkness, giving me some hope that you will listen [...] and attend to this explanation of what our Church [...] promises to all and provides for those willing to come to her."[107]

> I know what objections you raise to miracles, nor do we put our trust solely in miracles; but when we see the result of a miracle to be the perfect conversion of a soul from vice to virtue, we rightly ascribe this to the author of virtues. For I consider it the greatest of all miracles, that those who have spent thirty, or forty years or more in full gratification of their desires should, in a moment of time, turn from all wickedness to become the most holy examples of virtue, as I have seen with my own eyes and embraced with my own hands as they often moved me and others to tears of joy.

There was no way Spinoza could deny this. From a later conversation between Leibniz and Steno (who first met in November 1677), it seems Steno was referring here to a Maltese knight, Buonacorsi, who while revelling in a brothel, was so affected on hearing of the near martyrdom of the Jesuit Father, Francesco Giuseppe Bressani (1612–72), an able mathematician from Rome, captured and tortured by the Iroquois, in Canada, dying afterwards injured and sick in Florence, that he at once abandoned his life of pleasure to become a priest himself. Nor could Spinoza deny the Catholic Church's universal moral achievement, "especially as your sentiments concerning the Pope at Rome are much milder than those of our other adversaries and [unlike Calvinists] you admit the necessity of good works." To test this, Spinoza should carefully examine "our own writings, as your own doctrines on the power of prejudice will readily persuade you to do." Since "you are guided by true love of virtue," Spinoza would assuredly do so.[108] He must also reassess his own philosophy rigorously. "You concern yourself with matter in motion as if the moving cause were absent or non-existent. [...] Scrutinize, I pray, all those demonstrations of yours and show me just one explaining how the thinking thing and extended thing are united, how the moving principle unites with the body that is moved."

Fiercely criticizing Descartes, Steno hoped to sway Spinoza, partly using what he saw as the inconclusive evidence of science, just as he hoped to win over Swammerdam and many another. His argument centred around his inability to see how a man's soul "which is spiritual, can perceive the change of movement in a corporeal object," or how animals, which may have no soul, "can have perception of that movement occurring in the nerves." It all remained a total mystery, he

---

[107] Spinoza, *Collected Works* (ed. Curley) ii, 451–2; Scherz, "Biography of Nicolaus Steno," 265–6.
[108] Spinoza, *Collected Works* (ed. Curley) ii, 455–6.

wrote, explaining his worries regarding science, philosophy, and religion to his fellow anatomist, the Florentine luminary Marcello Malpighi (1628–94), on 24 November 1671, not long after penning his long letter to Spinoza. Spinoza could no more explain the sensation of pleasure or pain than the emotions of love and hatred. Above all, it seemed quite impossible that philosophy and science could ever explain such things. Rather, it "seems to me to be such a wonderful action of the omnipotent Creator that I cannot wonder enough at it."[109] Hence, that "demonstrative certainty [certitudo demonstrativa] of yours," as he put it in his published letter to Spinoza, is confined within the narrowest bounds. The "entire philosophy of Descartes, however diligently examined and reformed by you, cannot explain to me in demonstrative form even this single phenomenon of how the impact of matter on matter is perceived by a soul united to matter. And as regards matter, I ask what knowledge you provide apart from a mathematical assessment of quantity regarding figures not yet proven to consist of any kind of particles, except hypothetically?" Since so much about the structure of bodies was not understood, including what enables minds to perceive corporeal objects, Steno felt convinced that to "invent new principles explaining the nature of God, the soul, and the body," as Spinoza had, "is just the same as inventing fictitious principles."[110]

More perhaps than anyone else outside of Spinoza's immediate circle, Steno grasped how the *TTP* is embedded in a wider vision of science and complete system of philosophy "reforming" Descartes; but in a unique way, with his uncompromising "radical experimentalism" he also felt especially equipped, both scientifically and theologically, for the challenge of defeating his system. Should Spinoza require further persuading, concludes Steno, he would gladly undertake "the task of showing you how your doctrine is inferior to ours, sometimes through contradiction, sometimes through its uncertainty." Should he humbly succeed in persuading Spinoza to convert and "offer to God, as the first fruits of your repentance, a refutation of your errors," this would be an immense treasure for society and the general good. Where "your first writings have turned aside a thousand minds from true knowledge of God, your repudiating them finally, endorsed by your own example, may bring back, led by you as by a second Saint Augustine, another thousand to God. This grace, I pray for with all my heart. Farewell."[111]

---

[109] Quoted in Scherz, "Biography of Nicolaus Steno," 271.
[110] Spinoza, *Collected Works* (ed. Curley) ii, 455–6; Scherz, "Biography of Nicolaus Steno," 267; Totaro, "Steno in Italy," 281.
[111] Spinoza, *Collected Works* (ed. Curley) ii, 458; Totaro, "Niels Stensen," 154; Gullan-Whur, *Life of Spinoza*, 274–5.

28
Intensifying Reaction (Early 1670s)

28.i How Does One Refute the *TTP*?

If Spinoza's goal in interrupting his work on the *Ethics* to compose his *TTP* was really to clear away the obstacles to presenting his philosophy to the public and avert accusations of being an "atheist," his scheme could not have failed more miserably.[1] If the real motivation, perhaps partly unconscious, was to offer an exceedingly provocative, not easily countered challenge to all accepted norms and structures of authority while further deepening the country's existing ideological and religious tensions, then it succeeded spectacularly.

The early swift impact of the *TTP* among the large, widely dispersed academic fraternity in Protestant Germany, at Jena, Halle, Leipzig, and Altdorf was broadly one of stunned horror. In contrast to Britain, Germany's leading intellectual figures already knew about Spinoza prior to publication of the *TTP*, but at first did not associate the anonymous *TTP* with the Spinoza who authored the book on Descartes' principles. Studying the *TTP* since the autumn of 1670, a whole year before he obtained his own personal copy via his usual bookseller in Frankfurt, in October 1671, the twenty-four-year-old Leibniz made extensive marginal notes in brown ink first in the Archbishop of Mainz's copy, preserved today at Erfurt alongside some notes of his employer who dubbed the *TTP* "audacissimus et licentiosissimus [extremely audacious and licentious]."[2] Writing to Thomasius, in October 1670, after seeing his teacher's recently published rebuttal of the *TTP*, Leibniz styled it "an intolerably licentious book [liber intolerabiliter licentiosus]" sprouting from Hobbes, a philosopher he admired in some respects and loathed in others.[3] Leibniz's initial judgement, that the *TTP* represented an extreme Hobbesianism, would colour his view of Spinoza until the end of his long life.[4]

Writing to Graevius, the same month that Van Mansvelt died, in May 1671, Leibniz passed further judgement on the *TTP* which he still did not yet identify as by Spinoza (although he already knew about him), greatly regretting that "a man with so much erudition seems to have sunk so low." The critique the author "launches against the Holy Books has its foundations in the *Leviathan* of Hobbes

---

[1] Van Bunge, "Spinoza's atheïsme," 102, 106.
[2] Notes discovered by Ursula Goldenbaum in 1994, see Otto, *Studien*, 16–17; Laerke, "À la recherche," 387; Van de Ven, *Printing Spinoza*, 111–12.
[3] Goldenbaum, "Der historische Ansatz," 89–90. [4] Laerke, *Leibniz lecteur*, 181–4, 280.

but, as is not difficult to prove, is often defective. Such writings tend to undermine the Christian religion whose edifice has been consolidated by the precious blood, sweat and prodigious sacrifices of the martyrs. If only the [defenders of religion] can persuade someone equal to the anonymous author in erudition but surpassing him in respect for Christianity to refute his many paralogisms and abuse of oriental [i.e. Hebrew and Aramaic] philology."[5]

On further studying the *TTP*, in 1671, Leibniz reaffirmed that it was indeed a formidable book by a highly intelligent dissident, comprehensively denying everything the churches teach and what practically everyone believes. After discovering its author's identity, Leibniz still remained noticeably reticent about mentioning Spinoza's name when citing the *TTP* in correspondence with other scholars and especially as regards his contacts with him. At once fascinated and troubled by the *TTP*'s unrelenting naturalism, Leibniz underlined the passage in his own copy claiming the true method of interpreting Scripture is "the same as the true method of studying nature."[6] But, as Leibniz grasped from the outset, merely finding the *TTP*'s content repellent was hardly the point. The question was how effectively to answer its troubling arguments in print. Given the *TTP*'s formidable character, there was no point in responding hastily, before marshalling sufficiently strong arguments as he judged Thomasius unfortunately had done.

Effective counterarguments built on a thorough command of Bible and Hebrew studies sufficient to defeat Spinoza's expertise were required; but precisely that was the problem. As nothing of the sort had been forthcoming during the early or mid-1670s, anxiety over the astounding lack of adequate replies only grew. Complaints on this score continued from the early 1670s to the late 1690s. The "author of this book," as the English clergyman, Matthias Earbery expressed it, looking back towards the close of the century, "was very well versed (pardon so favourable an expression) in the writings of Moses and the Prophets, understood the original language and had made a diligent search, to find all the weak places, wherein he might assault and ruine the impregnable fortress of reveal'd religion. Mr Hobbs had another way of trifling with those books of Scripture, and wresting some particular places to his odd opinions: But this Author begins at the very root and foundation, by taking away all divine authority, from Prophecy, Miracles, or Inspiration," and reduced all the most sacred figures "to be no other than Mad-men, or Impostors."[7] Earbery was far from being the only observer recognizing a wide gulf between the premises and methodology of Hobbes and the more systematic "anti-Scripturalism" of the author so many preferred not to name.

---

[5] Leibniz to Graevius, Frankfurt, 5 May 1671, in Leibniz, *Sämtliche Schriften* 1st ser. vol. 2, p. 148; Laerke, *Leibniz lecteur*, 95–8, 214, 861; Nadler, *Spinoza: A Life*, 350; Stewart, *Courtier and the Heretic*, 110.
[6] Goldenbaum, "Die *Commentatiuncula*," 69, 84–5.
[7] Earbery, *Deism Examin'd and Confuted*, 3, 5.

Mounting dismay at the glaring inadequacy of the initial attacks on the *TTP*, expressed not least by Leibniz, became an additional reason for the distressingly long delay in producing larger-scale refutations of the *TTP*, as did the *TTP*'s unexpected ability to attract attention beyond academic circles in a way La Peyrère, the *Philosophia*, and Koerbagh's books had not. Any clergyman must, like himself, feel enormous repugnance, avowed Earbery, when explaining why he was offering the public *An Answer to a book intitled Tractatus Theologico-Politicus*,[8] soon more commonly known under its second edition's changed title, *Deism Examin'd and Confuted* (London, 1697), nearly three decades after the book's original appearance, taking up cudgels against "a book, which if it had its due deserts, ought to be confined to silence and darkness for ever." He felt compelled to write so long after the *TTP*'s appearance due to the sheer lack and inadequacy of previous efforts and the fact that "most who have wrote upon this subject have either done it in such a philosophical manner, as is not easily intelligible to the vulgar, or have proceeded against [Spinoza], and his party, by such philosophical arguments, as tho the very learned" were the only audience. That would hardly do. Earlier demolition efforts had appealed to specialist *érudits* when the real battle, it was becoming clear, needed to be fought in society more broadly. As the *TTP* uproar escalated in Britain (from the mid-1670s) and France (from the late 1670s) as well as Germany, Spinoza's notoriety was beginning to surge on all sides. By the 1690s, the old strategy of keeping quiet about the author and confining the controversy to Latin-language publications had become seriously inadequate, for "whilst the argument is only toss'd too and fro amongst learned men," the real peril arises "when such Deistical principles begin to be popular, and seize upon the minds of those, who though they want reason" still make up the bulk of society.[9]

Spinoza, some modern scholars assert, did not write for "the masses." One key *TTP* passage reads in translation: "I know how deeply rooted in the mind are the prejudices embraced under the guise of piety; I know too that the masses [*vulgus*] can no more be freed from their superstitions than from their fears." Current English translations usually continue: "finally, I know the masses are unchanging in their obstinacy, that they are not guided by reason, and that their praise and blame are at the mercy of impulse. Therefore, I do not invite the common people to read this work, nor all those who are victims of the same emotional attitudes. Indeed, I would prefer that they disregard this book completely rather than make a nuisance of themselves by misinterpreting it after their wont."[10] But arguably this and like renderings into English misrepresent its meaning. For Spinoza here is assuredly not expressing reluctance to present his book before a wider public. The Latin *vulgus*, repeated several times, though conventionally rendered as "the

---

[8] Boucher, *Spinoza in English*, 65–6.   [9] Earbery, *Deism Examin'd and Confuted*, preface p. 3.
[10] Spinoza, *Theological-Political Treatise* (trans. Shirley), 56; Nadler, *Book Forged in Hell*, 25.

masses," in this instance requires a different translation. As Spinoza himself states in the preceding passage, the book was written for "philosophical" readers in the sense of anyone able and willing to listen to arguments and capable of putting reason before theology. Such a reader could be any discerning mind open to cogent argument.

Indeed, Spinoza's admonition here cannot be meant to confine the book to professionals, academics, and theologians, categories he did not respect and to which many of his own following did not belong. Neither can he have intended to exclude the ordinary individual and general public. Rather, as always in his writing, and among his circle, not least the Koerbaghs, his "vulgus," or "multitudo," means commonplace minds in the sense of those unable to free their thinking from superstition and bigotry, those guided by common assumptions rather than reason. Spinoza's "vulgus" carries a particular meaning that from the outset characterized the Radical Enlightenment, insisting that the humble lay person lacking status and money who reads and thinks rationally is not part of the "ignoble" mass, as Koerbagh expresses it. A correct rendering of the above passage should follow rather from Spinoza's (and Koerbagh's) earlier admonition that their appeal was meant for those able to think philosophically and listen to reason. "As for the others, I am not particularly eager to recommend this treatise to them, for I have no grounds to expect that it will please them in any way." The passage should then continue:

> I know how obstinately prejudices that our sensibility has embraced in the form of piety stick in the mind. I know that it is as impossible to rid the *vulgus* [i.e. ordinary-thinking people] of superstition as to rid them of fear. I know the constancy of the *vulgus* is obstinacy, and that in approving or finding fault they are not governed by reason but swayed by impulse. I do not therefore invite the *vulgus*, and those struggling with the same feelings as they, to read these things. I would prefer them to ignore the book altogether than make a nuisance of themselves by interpreting it perversely, as they do everything, and while doing no good to themselves harming others who would philosophize more freely were they able to overcome the barrier of believing reason should be subordinate to theology.[11]

In Amsterdam, especially at Collegiant gatherings, Spinoza had encountered many humble, unpretentious readers flatly rejecting the teaching of the main churches and searching for the truth while perfectly willing to listen, debate, and consider different views in amiable fashion. There were reasonable, unpretentious, attentive, and friendly listeners with open minds in every land, and

---

[11] Spinoza, *Theological-Political Treatise*, 12.

Earbery, in 1697, put his finger on an increasingly crucial component of the drama—the growing numbers of non-specialist lay persons becoming detached from men's age-old subordination to theology, church, and clergy and hence susceptible to Spinoza's arguments. If most contemporaries agreed society was and must remain church-subordinate, and commentators like Thomasius and Earbery viewed the predicament of the *TTP* as arising primarily from weakening church control over belief and thinking, slippage of commonplace belief was undeniably increasing. In England, the conservative-minded of the 1690s and early 1700s often attributed this widely acknowledged intellectual and religious cultural shift, a key factor in the early Enlightenment, to the fall of the late Stuart monarchy of Charles II and James II, and growing impact of the "Dutch way," ensuing from the Glorious Revolution of 1688. Things had gravely lapsed, concurred many, "since too much liberty has relax'd the reine both of civil and ecclesiastical power." Many agreed the *TTP* "ought rather to be punished by the judge, than refuted by the divine," with severe penalties, but prevailing post-1688 conditions entrenching the "Dutch way" in Britain rendered it impossible to stamp Spinozism under using the old intolerant methods of suppression and the law.[12] During the phases of the *TTP*'s late seventeenth-century reception, old-style Stuart repression in Britain ground to a halt, blocked by the complexity of the intellectual challenge at hand and disruptive effects of the era's great political changes.

Crushing the *TTP* intellectually seemed an urgent matter everywhere. Leibniz found himself pondering from early on, who, if anyone, in Germany did possess sufficient erudition to refute it forcefully enough to shield the public from such looming peril. Though widely praised for his writings against the Socinians, in this case he himself lacked, he knew, the relevant philological skills in Hebrew, though he by no means supposed this exempted him from joining the battle to defeat the *TTP*, at least by fulfilling an auxiliary role, collective effort being essential for resolving the furore the book provoked and to minimize its impact on philosophy, politics, and society. Writing to other learned men, Leibniz roundly denounced the *TTP* as he felt bound to do. Still, having been taught by the eclectic Thomasius to open his mind to all philosophical influences choosing whatever is most cogent, he also felt obliged to scour the *TTP* to sift what was admissible from what was inadmissible. Like his mentor, he had sworn to select the best from whatever quarter and "forge a synthesis of the major philosophical schools while remaining consistent with Lutheran doctrine," a selective, "innovative conservatism," flexibly negotiating and accommodating the latest physics, mathematics, and astronomy, but always in harmony with core theology.[13]

---

[12] Earbery, *Deism Examin'd and Confuted*, 6; Israel, *Enlightenment that Failed*, 51–74.
[13] Mercer, "Leibniz and His Master," 41–2.

Outwardly, when corresponding with others, Leibniz, like everyone else, always fiercely decried the *TTP*. Learning that the *TTP*'s author was Spinoza, hence someone he already knew something about, he could not deny, though, at least to himself, that Spinoza now figured among the foremost modern thinkers, on a par with Bacon and Hobbes.[14] Still, what chiefly mattered was to determine how society could defeat Spinoza, for otherwise, Leibniz understood, his conception of natural right and human freedom would harm Christianity by weakening the Church's evident authority over men. To his mind, the *TTP* was a challenge that urgently needed overcoming by honestly confronting its arguments without resorting to repression.

If Graevius and Burman sought a sufficiently adept champion in the Netherlands, Leibniz, deeply dissatisfied with everything published thus far, engaged in the same exercise in Germany. Addressing a leading Lutheran Bible critic, Gottlieb Spitzel (1639–91) at Augsburg, in March 1672, he was strikingly dismissive of Thomasius' effort. Even more conscious than Burman and Graevius of the need for this champion to be a compelling philosopher, and committed Christian unassailably expert in Hebrew and Bible exegesis, Leibniz pleaded with Spitzel to assume responsibility for exploding the *TTP* whose author, "they say is a Jew," and who, with formidable learning and "much poison" endeavours to undermine Scripture's *antiquitatem, genuinitatem,* and *auctoritatem*. An adequate rebuttal must be philosophically formidable, urged Leibniz, but also the work of a master of Hebrew erudition and related languages "like you or someone like you."[15] Christendom needed such a defender willing to eschew superficial rhetoric and vituperation, circumvent the metaphysical quagmire of Cartesianism and focus unwaveringly on the disturbing real hermeneutical and historical questions raised. Spitzel would competently defend Lutheranism together with the integrity of miracles, angels, and demons. But ignoring Leibniz's flattery, Spitzel excused himself from the task under the pretext, Colerus records, that the "very learned Thomasius and his colleague Rappolt, at Leipzig" had already undertaken it.[16] The *TTP* was abominable, concurred Spitzel, but not for him to answer, albeit in his next publication he did devote several pages to assailing the *TTP* whose "fanatical" author undermines all notion of Revelation, reduces prophecy to "imagination," and acknowledges no miracles or "opera supernaturalia."[17]

Lapsing into universal collective procrastination, the academic world produced nothing like a systematic major refutation. If the disruption wrought in the

---

[14] Goldenbaum, "Der historische Ansatz," 89; Friedmann, *Leibniz et Spinoza,* 66–88.
[15] Leibniz, *Sämtliche Schriften* 1st ser., vol. 1, 193–4. Leibniz to Spitzel, 8 March 1672; Laerke, "À la Recherche," 390; Goldenbaum, "Der historische Ansatz," 94; Laerke, *Leibniz lecteur,* 113–14.
[16] Spitzel to Leibniz, 24 March 1672, in Leibniz, *Sämtliche Schriften* 1st ser., vol. 1, 194–5; Saldenus, *Otia theologica,* 24.
[17] Colerus, *La Vie de B. de Spinoza,* 58; Israel, "Early Dutch and German Reaction," 83.

Netherlands by the French invasion of 1672 compounded the difficulties caused by the protracted delay in meeting Spinoza's challenge, there was no concealing the discomforting truth that Dutch and German Bible exegetes, Reformed, Lutheran, Catholic, and Dissenter alike, felt fury and bitter consternation enough but also profound dismay at being so comprehensively challenged by a non-academic highly expert Hebraist. The difficulty, Leibniz perceived, lay less in Spinoza's expertise in Hebrew philology as such, given there were many Calvinist Christian Hebraists available in the Dutch and German universities and colleges at the time, than the formidable character of his hermeneutical method bolstered by the philosophical system underpinning it. When Van Mansvelt's long and eagerly expected *Adversus anonymum Theologio-politicum* finally appeared, in 1674, it quickly became evident that the deceased Utrecht professor commanded nothing like enough expertise in Bible hermeneutics and Hebrew to meet the challenge. The longest, most detailed refutation thus far, his 364-page text proved decidedly a damp squib, disappointing by being too tied to the specifically Dutch context and the Cartesian predicament, and too focused on the harm the *TTP* was allegedly causing, while insufficiently focusing on Spinoza's Bible criticism and core arguments. Nor was there much sign of Hebrew erudition at work apart from Van Mansvelt's arguing that lack of Hebrew vowels until the Masoretic era together with earlier variant readings, and absence of punctuation, did *not* prevent the biblical text being clearly interpreted in modern times. The *TTP*, argued Van Mansvelt, greatly exaggerates textual difficulties which have largely been overcome thanks to the admirable hermeneutical skills of "Drusius, Buxtorf, Cocceius, Selden, Scaliger etc."[18]

Among the *TTP*'s most harmful aspects, held Van Mansvelt, is its advocacy of unrestricted freedom of thought and expression which among other consequences would permit Socinians and Jews free rein to reject Christ's divinity without anyone preventing them. This "anonymous" author's *libertas philosophandi* differs radically from the "freedom to philosophize" championed by Heidanus, Wittichius, Burman, Van Velthuysen. and other Cartesians, including himself.[19] For Spinoza, the term means freedom to violate precisely those bounds Cartesians responsibly respect, amounting to liberty to trample on the sanctity of Scripture, promoting "errors of every kind, and defend and propagate a profane license." The "political theologian," whoever he is, only feigns to respect the separate status of philosophy and theology as proclaimed by the States of Holland and upheld by Cartesians, the anonymous author's "apparent acquiescence in their separation" being just a cunning sleight of hand. Far from genuinely respecting their separation, what the *TTP*, like the *Philosophia*, actually does is subordinate theology to philosophy to the point that theology loses all autonomy and authority. Where

---

[18] Van Mansvelt, *Adversus anonymum*, 172–3.   [19] Israel, *Dutch Republic*, 892–5.

Cartesians uphold the existing order, the *TTP* "sets out such principles that no sooner would they be admitted than all peace of the republic would necessarily be overthrown."[20]

The Cartesians, moreover, while professing as strict Calvinists to reject the *TTP*'s arguments, seemed more concerned to shield Cartesianism from the charge that the philosophy of the supposedly unknown author stems from and shares basic affinities with Cartesianism than wrestle with his core contentions while nevertheless claiming to be more effective than the Voetians in repulsing the threat. The *TTP*'s toleration, Van Mansvelt agreed, was impermissible in any Christian land. In some instances, notably Amsterdam, the Dutch authorities were indeed being too lax in enforcing the Republic's laws restricting freedom of religion and freedom of expression.[21] But for them the crucial point remained that Cartesians uphold "natural theology" and the separateness of God's being, will, and intellect from nature, whereas the *TTP*'s Bible hermeneutics directly assaults Christian belief in the Holy Trinity, Incarnation, *justificatio per Christum* etc. Worst of all was the *TTP*'s final conclusion: "salutem populi summam esse legem, cui omnes tam humanae quam divinae accommodari debent [the good of the people is the supreme law to which all laws both human and divine should be adapted." This was profoundly erroneous, for the people must seek their salvation above all through faith in Christ, through deference to religion and theology. All human laws should be directed ultimately to that goal to ensure religious observance is promoted and, "finally, that eternal salvation is secured by divine grace through Christ."[22]

Focusing on the general philosophical rather than hermeneutical aspects of Spinoza's argument, Van Mansvelt highlights the *TTP*'s "absurd confusion of God with his creation" by contrasting Descartes' "noble principles" with its godlessness and hideous virtual atheism. Much of the anonymous author's argument, he shows, actually flows from the "absurd mystery" he conjures up by supposing God is not separate from the universe. The *TTP*'s contention that miracles contradict the essence of God's being and providence Van Mansvelt counters by objecting that simply because God acts through natural laws does not mean natural laws characterize all his actions: rather, God is known both through natural laws and His miracles.[23] The *TTP* being in its essence deeply flawed and incontestably unchristian despite its claims to the contrary, it remained a matter of urgency that his work be powerfully suppressed by the authorities.

Van Mansvelt's preoccupation with defending Cartesianism, avoiding the main issues, and focusing on the damage done, unquestionably limited his relevance for

---

[20] Van Mansvelt, *Adversus anonymum*, 4; Israel, "Early Dutch and German Reaction," 82.
[21] Van Mansvelt, *Adversus anonymum*, 4, 362.
[22] Van Mansvelt, *Adversus anonymum*, 166–7, 337; Israel, "Early Dutch and German Reaction," 86–8.
[23] Van Mansvelt, *Adversus anonymum*, 158–62; Van Bunge, "Early Dutch Reception," 238.

Germany and Britain, while keeping Spinoza's identity out of the controversy as far as possible—effective still as far as the wider public was concerned—was becoming decidedly bizarre with respect to the growing band of scholars who knew who Spinoza was. In an earlier text, his 1671 *Animadversiones*, Van Mansvelt had himself remarked that he had never laid eyes on Spinoza and detested his "absurd doctrines";[24] yet, at this late stage, in 1674, the pretence of the *TTP*'s anonymity offered a jolting contrast to Stouppe, Maresius, Thomasius, and others. If his editors stalwartly persisted in boycotting Spinoza's person and name, as well as his wider philosophy, resolved to keep both as inconspicuous as possible, Van Mansvelt and his editors' declaiming "who the author of this *Tractatus* is I neither know, nor want to know," was beginning to assume a forlorn aspect.[25]

Strolling in The Hague, early in May 1674, more than four years after the *TTP* furore began, Spinoza spotted in a bookseller's window the treatise the "professor at Utrecht [Van Mansvelt] wrote against mine that came out after he died," and paused to glance through it. "From the little I read there," he afterwards wrote to Jelles, "I judged it not worth reading through, much less answering. So I left the book to repose there and left its author for what he is, laughing to myself that those who know least are usually the boldest and promptest to write." Booksellers "display their wares in the same manner as other shopkeepers, always presenting the worst merchandise first. They say the Devil is a sly fellow but when it comes to cunning, I think their [the retailers'] slyness far surpasses his."[26] Still, Spinoza cannot have been as entirely disdainful of "the professor" as he sounds here; for at Spinoza's death a copy of Van Mansvelt's treatise lay among his books at his lodgings.[27]

In April 1674, there appeared another substantive (if still relatively short) ninety-six page orthodox Lutheran response by Johannes Musaeus (1613–91), a Jena theologian since the 1640s and known adversary of Socinianism and Catholicism. Actually, most of the more specific argument in this disputation, dedicated to the duke of Brunswick-Lüneburg, was penned by his respondent in the debate, Christian Friedrich Knorr (1646–1704). Knorr and Musaeus jointly expressed their revulsion at this *homo fanaticus*, "by nation a Jew" and "alienated from all religion," aiming to demolish all belief, whose conception of God is purely philosophical. Rejecting Spinoza's "liberty to philosophize," rather, both endorsed Lutheran refusal to tolerate everyone and everything opposing core Christian belief, wanting Anti-Trinitarians and Jews especially repressed. Besides justifying

---

[24] Israel, "Early Dutch and German Reaction," 87; Lavaert, *Vrijheid, gelijkheid, veelheid*, 196.
[25] Van Mansvelt, *Adversus anonymum*, 4; Van Bunge, "Early Dutch Reception," 229, 236.
[26] Spinoza, *Opera* iv, 241; Spinoza, *Briefwisseling*, 310; Spinoza, *Collected Works* (ed. Curley) ii, 407.
[27] Lagrée, *Spinoza et le débat*, 116; Van Sluis and Musschenga, *Boeken van Spinoza*, 48.

ecclesiastical control of books, debate, and morality, they also affirmed, like Thomasius, vigorous support for the German princely and court system.[28]

In addition, Musaeus promoted the thesis, often championed too by Swiss Reformed theologians, that the seeds of the new German atheism so alarming his contemporaries stemmed primarily from a particular rottenness characteristic of the Dutch social and political milieu. Searching for the roots of the atheistic tendency now penetrating Germany, Musaeus had investigated the birthplace and background of the supposedly first self-declared "atheist" in Europe, Matthias Knutzen (1646–?). Copies of Knutzen's openly atheistic 1674 manifesto claiming the Bible is nothing but a "fable full of obscurity and contradictions," and that reason is "another and much better Bible," contending that only "nature is truth," had at this point appeared on the professors' pews in Jena's principal church, causing great consternation. Knutzen originated, Musaeus showed, from a Schleswig coastal village, facing the Netherlands across the North Sea, where some Dutch Anti-Trinitarian Collegiant dissidents had settled; he had grown up there imbibing a deeply pernicious anti-clerical and anti-Lutheran ambience in which the *Philosophia* was read alongside the *TTP*. This pernicious "Dutch" context, in which Cartesianism too was chiefly rooted, was the source of the tide of scepticism and anti-ecclesiasticism now besetting Germany.[29] Knutzen's apostasy Musaeus attributed partly to social resentment but mainly to the nuisance of unauthorized persons examining alleged discrepancies in Scripture for themselves.[30] Knutzen's *Naturalismus* was no isolated phenomenon, held Musaeus, but rather a manifestation of a deeply disturbing new "sect."

Nothing disrupts the peace and stability of society more than freedom of thought and religion, held Musaeus; and with respect to disrupting morality, religion, and the prevailing academic culture, the *TTP*'s author was far worse than any other thinker and had acquired a more dangerous following. A total non-believer regarding the supernatural happenings related in the New Testament and Old alike, he "does not acknowledge any miracles or supernatural events [miracula et opera supernaturalia in Scripturis agnoscit nulla]." Refusing to acknowledge that humanly unalterable physical laws do not bind the hand of God, all the supernatural occurrences in Scripture he reinterprets as just natural events wrongly understood by those witnessing them.[31] With matchless impiety, he denies the divine origin of the New and Old Testament, claiming "Scripture is not the Word of God."[32] Nothing can be learnt about nature or reality from Scripture, he contends, which means Scripture has nothing to teach the wise.

---

[28] Zenker, *Denkfreiheit*, 113–14; Otto, *Studien*, 16, 27.
[29] Musaeus, *Ablehnung*, 1–2; Otto, *Studien*, 77; Schröder, "Einleitung," 18–20; Israel, *Radical Enlightenment*, 630.
[30] Musaeus, *Ablehnung*, 4–5, 11, 15–16; Schröder, "Einleitung," 20; Zenker, *Denkfreiheit*, 236.
[31] Musaeus, *Tractatus...examinatus*, 3, 65–6; Musaeus, *Ablehnung*, 91–3; Laerke, *Leibniz lecteur*, 149.
[32] Musaeus, *Tractatus...examinatus*, 52–3; Israel, "Early Dutch and German Reaction," 90–2.

The sole function of churchmen, proposes the *TTP*'s author, is to impart a few simple moral lessons to the uninformed, rendering all existing episcopal and pulpit authority inauthentic. Prompt and unrelenting repression led by Germany's princes was the correct way to counter the dangerous new sect. Looking back thirty years later, Colerus still rated Musaeus' refutation, despite rarely answering any of Spinoza's more specific points, the most Lutheran and hence best of the replies to the *TTP*.[33]

28.ii Collegiant Uproar and the *TTP*

Collegiants, recorded John Locke later with a touch of admiration, "admit to their communion all Christians and hold it our duty to join in love and charity with those who differ in opinion."[34] But it soon turned out that loving those who disagree is far easier to profess as an ideal than to practise. Tensions had flared among Collegiant ranks already when Spinoza lived amongst them in the mid- and later 1650s, especially the rift between the Spiritualist, Millenarian, and mystical traditions dominating until the 1650s and the "Cartesian" new Collegiant philosophical tendency emerging at that time and associated with Balling, Jelles, and Rieuwertsz. From that point on, the older, mystical "Spiritualist" Collegiant tradition linked above all to Galenus Abrahamsz (1622–1706), Serrarius, and Kuyper, found itself increasingly struggling to withstand the criterion of philosophical-mathematical "reason" applied by the pro-Cartesian faction.[35] Preaching freedom of expression and debate, and comprehensive toleration doubtless constituted an impressive ideal, but came at a high price—exceptional proneness to internal splits.

As the philosophical-rationalist tendency linked to Grotius, Descartes, and Spinoza gained ground within Dutch religious debate, from the 1650s, philosophy increasingly became the factor driving splits among the Collegiants. If the "spiritualist" Petrus Serrarius vigorously defended Christ's divinity, the Trinity, and other "mysteries," there were also many Anti-Trinitarian Collegiants who likewise reacted negatively to the rationalizing philosophical tendency, preferring a more fundamentalist, literal Biblicism in the spirit of Socinus and the Socinian movement prior to Andrzej Wiszowaty (1608–78), a leading Polish Socinian reformer in Amsterdam and first architect of the *supra rationem* (above reason) principle later adopted by Locke.[36] All Socinians, assuredly, identified the "light of reason"

---

[33] Musaeus, *Tractatus... examinatus*, 84, 87–9, 92; Musaeus, *Ablehnung*, 18; Colerus, *La Vie de B. de Spinoza*, 72–5; Hubbeling, *Spinoza*, 101; Walther, *Spinoza Studien* iii, 193–7.
[34] Quoted in Israel, *Radical Enlightenment*, 342.
[35] Van Bunge, "Johannes Bredenburg and the *Korte Verhandeling*," 321.
[36] Van Bunge, "Bibliotheek van Jacob Ostens," 135; Israel, *Enlightenment that Failed*, 112–16.

as man's principal guide in matters of faith and Bible interpretation. But for many, above all Frans Kuyper, this signified nothing more than a hermeneutical method, a means of explaining Scriptural passages consistently from other passages. As with late eighteenth-century English Unitarians, only a minority pushed Socinianism to the point of asserting a consistent, systematic unifying of theology and philosophy, fully merging the light of reason in Bible criticism with the philosophical-scientific explanations of nature's laws, hence the philosophical reason of Descartes and Spinoza.[37] 'Philosophical' Collegiants, therefore, differed fundamentally from both the Anti-Trinitarian (like Kuyper) and pro-Trinitarian (like Serrarius) Collegiants acknowledging Bible narrative, supernatural powers, and miracles more literally, the former a powerful voice in the Collegiant gatherings as later among eighteenth- and nineteenth-century British and American Unitarians.

The theologian, publisher, and writer Frans Kuyper (1629–92) was an ex-Remonstrant preacher who, in 1653, had defected from the Remonstrants after rejecting infant baptism and coming under Socinian and Collegiant influence. He figured among the most energetic of the Amsterdam Collegiant leaders since long before Spinoza's expulsion from the synagogue and certainly knew Spinoza personally. By 1676, he had become the leading Collegiant opponent of "philosophy," science, and especially Cartesianism and Spinozism as influences intruding into religious debate. A fervent Socinian, among the chief editors of the *Bibliotheca Fratrum Polonorum*, after his banishment from the city by the Amsterdam burgomasters for expressing forbidden views, around 1663, he transferred to Rotterdam where he spent the remainder of his life, becoming the Republic's foremost clandestine publisher of Socinian ideas and a leading adversary of the "Cartesian" tendency among the Collegiants as well as of Spinoza. When assailing "philosophy" as a negative influence more generally, Kuyper acknowledged that it was "the atheist Spinoza" above all who "has tried to prove it impossible that there should be any miracles,"[38] but especially targeted Meyer's *Philosophia*, because that text more straightforwardly than the *TTP* proclaims "philosophy" Scripture's "interpreter."[39] Kuyper rejected Christ's divinity and the Trinity no less categorically than Spinoza and Meyer, but insisted "reason," though a subsidiary tool, must remain subordinate to such revealed truths as *are* clearly affirmed as truths in Scripture. Kuyper aimed to convince not just Collegiants and Quakers but the non-academic Dutch reader generally that any untutored mind, if God-fearing and reliant solely on Scripture, easily trounces the Latin-spouting savant in holding to what chiefly matters in life, the truths announced in Scripture being solid beyond question and readily accessible to

---

[37] Bietenholz, *Daniel Zwicker*, 272–7; Sadler, "The Collegiants," 66–7.
[38] Kuyper, *Filosofisch en Historiaal Bewijs*, preface and p. 1; Kuyper, *Bewys dat noch de schepping*, 3.
[39] Kuyper, *Den Philosopherenden Boer*, 15.

common sense. This was the central argument with which he justified rejecting both the Cartesianism and Spinozism of the "rationalists" and the "inner light" Spiritualism of the Quakers in his pamphlet, *Den Philosopherenden Boer* [The Philosophizing Farmer], "dealing with the errors of the present-day Christians, philosophers, Cartesians and Quakers," as its subtitle expresses it, published in two parts, in 1676–7.

While Christendom's great teacher, Socinus, did indeed exalt "reason" as man's principal guide in interpreting Scripture, explains Kuyper, he never intended "reason" to mean intellectualizing, high-level philosophical reason that stumbles when encountering the supernatural but rather the ordinary reasoning of regular men and women, the common sense reason that teaches that without Revelation, faith, and the Holy Ghost man cannot "come to any knowledge of God or religion."[40] "Atheists" following Spinoza, protests Kuyper, tend to be wide-reading presumptuous types who "think no one fit to judge of the truth except themselves. They are usually very inclined to scoff at" and disdain common workmen and peasants, finding no better material for their mockery than popular stories about ghosts and what they consider ridiculous and fanciful tales. But it is ordinary people's simple, earnest belief, pious acceptance of the supernatural, of miracles and spirits, and ordinary common sense that most surely lead to the truth and shame the philosopher, especially the supreme truth of Christ's mission of salvation along with miracles, heaven, hell, angels, devils and exorcism. He who unstintingly embraces the truths of Scripture embraces truth with a fuller, more precise understanding, as well as more upright heart, than Spinoza and his herd.[41]

Kuyper championed the autonomy and supremacy of non-philosophical literal Bible interpretation robustly affirming the reality of supernatural entities, spirits, devils, and satanic as well as benign magical powers, and the necessity for all to believe in such entities as well as in miracles. Kuyper's *Arcana Atheismi* (1676), the foremost Socinian refutation of the *TTP* to appear during Spinoza's lifetime, when reviewed in France, in January 1678, gave occasion for one of the earliest warnings published in France that Spinoza and the *TTP* were indeed helping drive the menace of contemporary "atheism" and "deism" now powerfully invading the French-speaking world.[42] The *Arcana* would also be the spur to the eminent Cambridge don Henry More's decision to reply to the *TTP*, in 1677. Whilst waiting for his copy of Kuyper to be bound, More, shocked by Kuyper's rejection of Christ's divinity, reread the *TTP*, finding "this *Theologico-politicus* such an impious work, that I could not forbeare confuting him whyle I read him," as he put it writing to his friend, Lady Conway. "As for Cuperus [Kuyper] that pretends

---

[40] Kuyper, *Den Philosopherenden Boer*, 28; Fix, *Prophecy and Reason*, 157.
[41] Kuyper, *Filosofisch en Historiaal Bewijs*, preface; Kuyper, *Bewys dat noch de schepping*, 7–8.
[42] Clair, "Spinoza à travers les journaux," 217; Salatowsky, "Socinian Headaches," 168.

to confute him [i.e. Spinoza], truly I do not know that he is better than he whom he pretends to confute."[43]

By the early 1660s, even the more conciliatory Collegiant "rationalists" had been proving a serious obstacle to the Collegiant "Spiritualists" and to Collegiant unity. Mankind, all humanity, the compromising Balling had argued in his *Light on the Candlestick* (1662), finds itself dangerously adrift on a sea of confusion and in desperate need of rescue. All Collegiants could heartily agree that humanity worldwide had been wretchedly misled and wrongly taught by the world's main churches, hence by most of what is supposed to constitute Christendom. Our hopes of salvation therefore lie in uncovering the "light of truth, the true light that enlightens every person who comes into the world." The difficulty, and here Balling deftly fudges the borderline, was how to resolve whether it is the Second Coming and Millennial expectation, the path lit for us by the "inner light" construed as the Holy Ghost and ordinary piety when immersing oneself exclusively in Scripture and what it says, as Serrarius and Kuyper contended, or the "true light" conceived as philosophy and enlightenment.[44] Is the "true light" an emanation of the Holy Ghost, inspiration arising from belief and faith, or Balling's "clear and distinct knowledge of truth in the intellect of every person by which he is so entirely convinced as to the reality of things that for him it becomes impossible to doubt it," delivering a salvation ultimately boiling down to a rationalizing ethical, unbelieving Christianity resembling Spinoza's "spirit of Christ," hence a cult of "justice and charity"? Here was the basic conundrum, and the rift proved irresolvable.

A series of episodes in the 1650s and 1660s had earlier put Collegiant stability and resilience to the test. But the controversy over Meyer's *Philosophia*, in 1666–8, and Serrarius' attack on that book, followed by the impact of the *TTP*, pushed the internal divisions destabilizing the Collegiant movement to a whole new level of crisis. The figure who, more than any other, highlighted the predicament Spinoza plunged the Dutch Collegiant movement into was Johannes Bredenburg (1643–91), a Rotterdam former wine and brandy merchant without university training who, after retiring from business while still under thirty, during the 1672 slump, acquired Latin and considerable learning and joined forces with the "Cartesian" faction of Rieuwertsz and Jelles. Bredenburg's wife was a sister of his friend, the prominent Collegiant poet, dramatist, and ally of Jacob Ostens, Joachim Oudaen.[45] An admirer of the rational, tolerant standpoint of Episcopius and Grotius, the rest of his life Bredenburg devoted to studying philosophy, debating and trying to resolve the fragmenting pressures dividing his community. Above all, he venerated the Collegiant tradition of true toleration and their

---

[43] Quoted in Colie, *Light and Enlightenment*, 74.
[44] Balling, *Het Licht*, 4; Klever, *Mannen rond Spinoza*, 18–21.
[45] Van Bunge, *Johannes Bredenburg*, 46–7.

devotion to reason. It was their great merit but their movement's cross of torment, experience more and more proved, that Collegiants rejected mere authority on principle, banned no one's voice outright and could never accept unreasoned, unexplained condemnation, trusting in honest discussion of opponents' views to uncover the truth. An upright, splendid principle, it would cost Bredenburg and all Collegiants colossal stress.

It became Bredenburg's particular project to reconcile his movement's two warring wings. A version of his principal text, *Treatise on the Origin of the Knowledge of God* [Verhandeling van de oorsprong van de kennisse Gods] was already circulating among his debating circle by 1673, though it was not actually published until 1684. Neither Revelation nor miracles, held Bredenburg, provide firm, unchallengeable certainty about Christianity's truth, or knowledge of God, on their own. Those relying exclusively on belief and faith (like Kuyper and Serrarius) should not be praised but rather rebuked: for such men, like atheists, possess no understanding of God's hand in the processes of nature.[46] Knowledge of truth relying exclusively on faith-based theology is inherently detached, fragmented, and uncertain, and therefore encourages scepticism. If Collegiant toleration reflects their superiority over the world's churches, so equally does their emphasis on reason.

Bredenburg knew his Grotius, Hobbes, and Meyer, but initially it was Descartes who chiefly shaped his thinking.[47] Like Descartes, Bredenburg conceived man as essentially two different substances, a body wholly material and mind wholly immaterial.[48] Philosophy and science are essential for understanding reality but so is Revelation, for, as Descartes proves, the incorporeal part of man cannot be subject to the normal physical laws of nature. Rules governing conduct and belief, what we know is right and wrong, reach us fully and directly only from God. By the early 1670s, already steeped in Collegiant debates and controversies, Bredenburg faced the challenge of showing that his uncompromising embrace of the "new science" and philosophical reason did not of itself inherently tend to slide into supporting Spinozist positions.[49] By 1673, Kuyper in particular had become his implacable opponent taking the lead among the faction opposing the "philosophical" Collegiants in Rotterdam.

In December 1674, Bredenburg published his refutation of the *TTP* under the title the *Enervatio Tractatus Theologico-Politici*, a text directly combating the *TTP* from the rationalist Collegiant standpoint. Originally drafted in Dutch, he then received help in translating it into Latin, being anxious not to infringe the accepted practice thus far that one should avoid discussing Spinoza the man, and his

---

[46] Bredenburg, *Verhandeling*, 8; Fix, *Prophecy and Reason*, 217–18.
[47] Van Bunge, *Johannes Bredenburg*, 98, 115; Wielema, *Filosofen aan de Maas*, 42–3.
[48] Bredenburg, *Verhandeling*, 32–7.
[49] Van Bunge, "Johannes Bredenburg and the *Korte Verhandeling*," 322.

dangerous text in the vernacular. But where other refutations focused exclusively on the *TTP*, Bredenburg's milieu, the Collegiants of Rotterdam, Rijnsburg, and Amsterdam, had by this time undergone a degree of exposure also to Spinoza's philosophical system more broadly due to Spinoza's ideas circulating in the discussion circles around Jelles, Balling, and Rieuwertsz.[50] Bredenburg's importance in Spinoza's life-story and originality lay in his demonstrating that the *TTP* rests on, and is integral to, an entire philosophical system equating God with Nature, presenting an unavoidable challenge to the Collegiant credo. In his *Enervatio*, Bredenburg refers to the distinction between *natura naturans* and *natura naturata* and other wording indicating that he either knew the *Korte Verhandeling* directly or had seen extracts from it. The *TTP*'s author, he explains, holds God to be identical to Nature which has infinite attributes so that all created things, past, present, and future, and all possibilities flow directly from the being of God, and "all possible modifications of the attributes of nature exist necessarily." Anxious to demonstrate that his Collegiant rationalist approach does not lead one to the anonymous author's positions and was the best and most unifying path for the Collegiants to follow, Bredenburg answered that God is *not* identical to Nature, and that the human mind, our soul, is not governed by the unswerving determinism Descartes places only material things under and made subject to natural laws alone, to which the *TTP*'s author disastrously subjects everything.[51]

Due to Bredenburg's connections, earnestness and desire to minimize division among the Collegiants, his *Enervatio* proved one of the most notable refutations of the *TTP*. All those who refuted the *TTP*, Bayle later observed, identified the "seeds of atheism" there, "but no one has elucidated them as adroitly as Jean Bredenburg [mais personne ne les a développées aussi nettement que le sieur Jean Bredenbourg]."[52] This was assuredly Bredenburg's aim in combating the *TTP* which, owing to its "abominations," he was among the first to dub a book "forged in hell." The trouble was that the *Enervatio* itself proved highly problematic in several respects. For one thing, his text was altogether illegal, because, as a Socinian, Bredenburg, like his opponent Kuyper, saw no difficulty in rejecting Christ's divinity, the Trinity, and the Resurrection. But worse was Bredenburg's Collegiant courage in exposing Spinoza's contentions honestly and fully, his explaining why the *TTP* denies Providence, the "power of God to act over and beyond the laws of nature," a denial lodged in its author's "identifying Nature with God himself."[53] Yet, while discussing the philosophy and exegetical methodology behind the *TTP*, Bredenburg seemed unable to produce any particularly compelling arguments showing why Spinoza's approach was wrong. Unsurprisingly, not

---

[50] Kolakowski, *Chrétiens sans église*, 256–7.
[51] Van Bunge, "Johannes Bredenburg and the *Korte Verhandeling*," 323–4.
[52] Bayle, *Écrits sur Spinoza*, 23; Israel, *Radical Enlightenment*, 345–6.
[53] Bredenburg, *Enervatio*, 63–6; Wielema, *Filosofen aan de Maas*, 44; Nadler, *Book Forged in Hell*, 232.

a few Latin-readers, Kuyper foremost among them, suspected his book was a deliberate ploy to propagate Spinozism under the deceitful pretext of refuting it.

The core problem was that Bredenburg, being an earnest Collegiant, simply could not stomach the wider world's eagerness to suppress Spinoza's reasoning without honest, argued consideration. He had avoided discussing the *TTP* in Dutch so that most readers were still kept from learning about it, but his open approach unquestionably helped project Spinoza's arguments, condemned by him but far from fully discredited or neutralized, into at least a limited sphere. If Bredenburg's offensive against Spinoza's rejection of divine providence, miracles, and Revelation, his identifying God with Nature, and determinist view of the human mind and human choices was genuine enough, by bringing the difficulty of overcoming Spinoza on these points more effectively into the light of day than any other Spinoza adversary of the early or mid-1670s, by "sweating" to prove the positions he rejects are wrong, ultimately, his *Enervatio* tended to disseminate rather than refute Spinozism, weaken rather than strengthen the Collegiant counter-offensive, while intensifying his own predicament which was soon that of the entire Collegiant movement.[54]

Wrestling with the implications of Spinoza's Bible criticism and philosophy also divided the Anti-Trinitarian Collegiant bloc of "philosophical" tendency by unavoidably pressing the question of whether limits exist to the primacy of reason in Bible interpretation. Grotius' name Van Mansvelt had purposely omitted from his list of skilful exegetes resolving Scripture's apparent discrepancies, knowing Grotius aggravated rather than remedied the predicament posed by the biblical text's difficulties, especially by affirming the ultimate oneness of reason, natural theology, and revelation.[55] Grotius' commitment to conflating natural and revealed theology linked him to a major strand of Socinian tradition, a faction in the thick of the bitter strife engulfing the Collegiant movement in the 1670s and 1680s.

Divergence between the true meaning of Scripture in the sense of the understanding of those who compiled it and truth of fact, and the need to extrapolate the former before evaluating its relation to the latter, was made basic to the debate surrounding the *TTP* by Spinoza's insistence on something wholly absent from Grotius and Hobbes—his astounding claim that none of the biblical prophets, judges, kings, and Apostles grasped "the reality of things." All were ignorant of basic mathematics, modern science, and philosophy, as well as history, politics, and the working of the passions, leaving them adherents of fundamentally mistaken ideas about the movements of the sun and planets, the nature of kingship, justice and much else. Where Maimonides claims the prophets combine

---

[54] Van Bunge, *Johannes Bredenburg*, 137–8; Wielema, *Filosofen aan de Maas*, 44; Scribano, "Johannes Bredenburg," 67, 73; Smith, "Politics of Tragedy," 246.

[55] Blom, "Grotius and Socinianism," 137.

extraordinary "imagination" with exceptional intellectual power enabling them to unlock hidden dimensions of truth, Spinoza saw biblical prophecy as exceptional imagination alone, devoid of the philosophical insight Maimonides attributes to it,[56] an exegetical principle enabling Spinoza to stake more on analysis of the text where original language versions exist, and on the Hebrew's inherent characteristics and ambiguities, than other contributors to the Dutch seventeenth century's "emancipation of Biblical philology."[57] More than any other representative of what has been termed the new sceptical Bible criticism, whether Grotius, Hobbes, La Peyrère, the Koerbaghs, or Isaac Vossius, Spinoza stresses the Bible's overall textual fragmentary character, disjunctions, chronological errors, and profusion of conceptual and arithmetical mistakes. Scripture, held Spinoza, is highly unreliable evidence written in benighted times remote chronologically from the epochs they recount: "we conclude, therefore, that all the books we have surveyed so far are derivative works [apographa] with the events they recount occurring long before."[58]

Defects owing to text corruption abound everywhere in Scripture, and offering elaborate pretexts to resolve these issues in the manner of Grotius and Menasseh, held Spinoza, only compounds the contradictions and difficulties encountered. Such conciliators "are simply exposing the editors of the Holy Books to ridicule, making it seem these writers do not know how to express themselves or organize what they have to say."[59] "Possibly, some will say that I am wholly undermining Scripture by my manner of proceeding," adds Spinoza, "as it may lead everyone to suspect the Bible is everywhere full of mistakes."[60] But every book authored by humans does contain numerous errors and misconceptions, so why should Scripture be any different? Comprehending the history of human thought and belief through humanity's ancient texts depends, for Spinoza, on combining a particular set of naturalistic philosophical criteria with newly devised rules of text criticism supplementing the philology of the past with systematic elimination of supernatural agency and miracles and great care in reconstructing historical context. These being the same general principles he applies to studying nature, the outcome is that his Bible criticism is "scientific" in a wholly new fashion conceiving all natural processes as shaped by purely mechanistic cause and effect, with mind and human belief inherently part of this natural process. Hence, history, study of religion and generally what in German are called the *Sozial- und Geisteswissenschaften* are in principle no different methodologically from the other sciences: "I say that the method of interpreting Scripture barely differs from that of interpreting nature, but rather absolutely agrees with it [Dico methodum

---

[56] Maimonides, *Guide for the Perplexed*, 225–7, 385; Pines, "Spinoza's *Tractatus Theologico-Politicus*," 499.
[57] Spinoza, *Theological-Political Treatise*, 105–7.
[58] Spinoza, *Theological-Political Treatise*, 126.   [59] Spinoza, *Theological-Political Treatise*, 151.
[60] See, for example, Spinoza, *Theological-Political Treatise*, 153.

interpretandi Scripturam haud differre a methodo interpetandi naturam, sed cum ea prorsus convenire]."⁶¹

If the rift within the Collegiant movement between rationalist and anti-rationalist Collegiants was aggravated and made more complex by the *TTP*, the same is true of the growing split among the "rationalist" Collegiants opposing both Serrarius' Trinitarian Millenarians and Kuyper's anti-rationalist Anti-Trinitarians, and hence widened also the disagreement between "Spinozist" Collegiants like Spinoza's friends Balling, Jelles, Rieuwertsz, Ostens, and later, Jan Bredenburg (1643–91), and the Collegiant strict "Cartesians." Widening both the rift between the "rationalist" Collegiants and Collegiant Bible literalists, and between the radical fringe allied to Spinoza and mainstream "rationalist" Collegiants asserting the separateness on Cartesian lines of body and soul, and matter from the supernatural, the *TTP* heightened divisions throughout the Collegiant body. A passage in Spinoza's sole surviving letter to the Rotterdam Mennonite pastor and physician Jacob Ostens (1630–1708), citing the opinion of his friend, the Utrecht Cartesian, Van Velthuysen, that the *TTP* contradicts Meyer's *Philosophia*, brings this aspect further into view. Writing in February 1671, Spinoza here discusses the long and detailed missive from Van Velthuysen to Ostens concerning the *TTP*, which Ostens, their common friend, visiting from Rotterdam, showed Spinoza and allowed him to copy. Ostens had asked Van Velthuysen for his view of the *TTP* and after some delay, Van Velthuysen sent his remarkable twelve-page missive, dated "Utrecht 24 January 1671" (Old Style, so actually 3 February), maintaining the *TTP*'s "anonymous" author, whatever his "nation and whatever plan of life he follows," while freeing his mind from all prejudices and superstition (of which Velthuysen and Ostens both approved), had grievously lurched to the other extreme "and appears to me to have cast off all religion," surpassing even the deists in rejecting divine providence and reward and punishment in the hereafter.⁶² Ostens felt deeply troubled, but in true Collegiant fashion came to see Spinoza to discuss, listen, and clarify.

A Mennonite surgeon, Ostens was the leading "rationalist" Collegiant in Rotterdam, and another in the thick of the infighting among the dissenter factions in that city.⁶³ Head of the Rotterdam Socinian "rationalist" faction,⁶⁴ learned, uncompromising and pugnacious, and among the most vocal Anti-Trinitarians in Holland, Ostens too was a fervent Cartesian and anti-Orangist keen to restore Christianity to its original authentic character. A powerful ecumenical thrust led him to aspire also, like Comenius, to reunite all Christians on an authentically "Christian" basis which to his mind, like that of Galenus and Balling, meant

---

⁶¹ Goldenbaum, "Philosophische Methodendiskussion," 153–5; Goetschel, *Spinoza's Modernity*, 61–4.
⁶² Spinoza, *Briefwisseling*, 289; Strazzoni, *Burchard de Volder*, 127.
⁶³ Van Bunge, *Johannes Bredenburg*, 33–41; Fix, *Prophecy and Reason*, 44.
⁶⁴ Benthem, *Holländischer Kirch-und Schulen-Staat* i, 902; Van Slee, *Rijnsburger Collegianten*, 382–3.

jettisoning not only Reformed theology but all theologically defined confessions—Catholicism, Lutheranism, Anglicanism, and what to him was the rigmarole of the strict Mennonites. Eager to maximize toleration generally, he sought in the fraught Rotterdam context especially to reconcile Mennonites and Remonstrants.[65] His robust advocacy of toleration and merging of sects, however, provoked bitter dispute within his congregation, the Waterland Mennonites, and a counter-campaign by Holland's conservative Mennonites denouncing him and his principles as "Socinian."[66] Among Rotterdam's warring sects, Ostens' insistent call for love and reconciliation produced only ever fiercer quarrelling and strife. The Mennonites talk much of "love," mocked De Lantman and Saldenus, in 1670, in a jointly written tract denouncing schism, dissent, and defections from God's true church, but in practice foment only hatred.[67] One could see their point.

Closely following the controversy over the *TTP*, Ostens collected in his personal library, along with many other contributions to the furore, copies of Van Mansvelt's *Adversus* (1674), Van Velthuysen's belatedly published critique, and much else. Van Velthuysen's letter rejecting Spinoza's views on prophets, miracles, and the status of Scripture, a troubled Ostens informed Spinoza, formed the core of a pamphlet that he intended to publish, stepping up his attack on the *TTP* on behalf of the strict Cartesians.

28.iii Encounter with Van Velthuysen

Apologizing for delaying many weeks before responding, suggesting Ostens' visit to The Hague to confer with him about the *TTP* controversy occurred probably in the autumn of 1670, Spinoza fiercely rebuffed Van Velthuysen's aspersions. "As Voetius formerly dealt [shoddily] with Descartes," replied Spinoza to Ostens, "so always it is precisely the best that are dragged down by the worst," an angry comment decidedly unfair to the bold but beleaguered Van Velthuysen, as Spinoza subsequently realized.

Lambert van Velthuysen (1622–85) (Figure 28.1), like Ostens and Spinoza, was simultaneously a man of staunch principle and practical affairs striving to make the world a better place. A prominent and courageous figure among the most influential of the anti-Orangist Utrecht regents, having done more than anyone to introduce Hobbes to the Dutch public and steer through the dangerous shoals between religion, philosophy, and civic politics, he had long been at odds with the Reformed consistories whom he accused of overstepping their proper sphere and

---

[65] Van Bunge, "Tragic Idealist," 266–8, 272; Van Bunge, "Rotterdamse collegiant," 65–6.
[66] Van Bunge, "Tragic Idealist," 273–4; Wielema, *Filosofen aan de Maas*, 36, 57.
[67] Van Slee, *Rijnsburger Collegianten*, 108–9, 113; Van den End, *Guiljelmus Saldenus*, 170–1.

Figure 28.1 *Lambert van Velthuysen* (1622–85) by Jan van Wijckersloot, 1665. Inv. no. 2260, Collectie Centraal Museum, Utrecht/© aankoop 1898.

illegitimately subordinating philosophy, science, and astronomy to their sway.[68] What he chiefly objected to in the *TTP* was the author's removing all connection with "truth" in his analysis of the prophets and their admonitions, and claiming Scripture's words reflect the notions of the unlearned and hence are replete with error and untruth. "The author in fact contends that all things are necessarily as they are," and "since they cannot derive that necessity from themselves, must have it from the nature of God, from which they emanate necessarily," thereby contradicting Descartes "whose doctrine he nevertheless wants to appear to accept, that as the natures of all things are different from the nature and essence of God, so their ideas are freely in the divine mind," acknowledging God possesses the freedom and power to direct, re-direct, and alter the nature of things. This the anonymous author of the *TTP* flatly denies, behind his screen wholly opposing Descartes and stripping God of all power to do anything other than He does. "His God is subjected to fate; no room is left for any divine governance or providence."[69]

---

[68] Fukuoka, *Sovereign and the Prophets*, 114–18, 206–7.
[69] Velthuysen to Ostens, Utrecht, 24 Jan. 1671, in Spinoza, *Collected Works* (ed. Curley) ii, 379, 385.

According to the "anonymous," Van Velthuysen further objects, "the man who understands things rightly should devote himself to cultivating virtue not because of God's commandments and laws, or hope of reward, or fear of punishment, but the beauty of virtue itself and the joy men experience in the practice of virtue." "For Holy Scripture, he affirms quite openly and in many places, is not intended to teach the truth or nature of things, but merely uses such expressions as serve its purpose of inclining men to virtue." This also contradicts "the paradoxical theologian" [Meyer] and those agreeing with him "that reason is the interpreter of Scripture." Thus the "political theologian" [Spinoza] repudiates the "paradoxical theologian" [Meyer] "and thoroughly subverts all worship and religion, encouraging atheism by stealth, envisaging such a God as cannot move men to veneration of his divinity since he himself is subject to fate. No scope remains for divine governance and providence; punishment and reward are wholly abolished." So compromised is Holy Scripture's status by this unnamed author's teaching that it follows from it that "the Koran is placed on the same level with the Word of God" leaving no way to prove Muhammed was not a true prophet. For in this author's estimation, it is usual for God, in the case of nations to whom He has not imparted the oracles given to the Jews and Christians, to lead them to virtue, reason, and obedience by other revelations, thereby placing all religions on an equal level as regards truth value and moral status.[70]

Where Van Velthuysen saw contradiction between Spinoza and the *Philosophia*, Spinoza assured Ostens, he was not in fact attacking those agreeing with the *Philosophia*, but rather those opposing its central contention that philosophy is the true interpreter of Scripture, including Maimonides whom he here sets in opposition to the *Philosophia*'s claims. Spinoza could not see why Van Velthuysen should think all who reject reason and philosophy as "the interpreter of Scripture," that is oppose the *Philosophia*, "should be of my opinion, whereas I have always rejected their view no less than that of Maimonides."[71] With this convoluted, often misconstrued argument, Spinoza was apparently assuring a worried Ostens (and Van Velthuysen) that he did not in fact reject Meyer's view but did disagree with Maimonides. That the *Philosophia* was strongly influenced by Spinoza as well as Wittichius and others, especially when discussing Hebrew and Hebrew terms, is hardly surprising as these had been the young Spinoza's particular forte ever since compiling his Spanish *Apologia* against the Synagogue, in 1656. By 1666, his general views on the subject would long have been familiar to Meyer, Bouwmeester, the Koerbaghs, and the rest of his circle.[72]

Where Van Velthuysen saw contradiction here between Spinoza and Meyer, Spinoza claims to have refuted not those who think like the *Philosophia*'s author

[70] Spinoza, *Collected Works* (ed. Curley), ii, 236; Spinoza, *Correspondance* (ed. Rovere), 255–6.
[71] Spinoza, *Briefwisseling*, 286–7, 289; Curley's translation here seems less satisfactory.
[72] Mignini, "Données et problèmes," 12–13, 20; Nadler, *Spinoza: A Life*, 132–3.

(as some scholars today wrongly infer) but rather those rejecting Meyer's argument that philosophy is the measuring-rod of Scripture. Thus, the frequently repeated claim that Maimonides' and Meyer's approaches converge while Spinoza opposes both needs discarding.[73] The correct view is that of the anonymous adversary denouncing the "atheistic" circle in Amsterdam, in 1677, in the pamphlet *Koeckoecx-Zangh van de Nachtuylen van het Collegie Nil Volentibus Arduum*. He brackets Meyer and his fellow physician, Bouwmeester, together with Spinoza, the Koerbaghs, and Van den Enden as a single clique of "honourable people who forged the precious dictionary of Doctor Koerbagh, discovered that philosophy is the Interpreter of Scripture and approved the Theological-Political Reason-Splitting [eerlijke luyden, die het kostelijk woordenschat van Doctor Koerbagh gesmeet hebben, die, dat de Philosophie de Uitlegster zy van de H. Schrifture, uitgevonden, die de Theologische Politike Redenkaveling goet gekeurt hebben]."[74] If Koerbagh's *Bloemhof* needs to be deemed a group effort in some degree, much the same is true of the *Philosophia* and the *TTP*.

The *TTP*'s anonymous author, Van Velthuysen assured Ostens, was no Christian but a universalist, and while he had certainly emptied his mind of superstition, he had then "strayed far beyond that point, renouncing all religion, at any rate not rising above the religion of the deists of whom there are a substantial number everywhere (so deplorable is the morality of our age), especially in France." Certainly, the *anonymus* acknowledges God after a fashion, as maker of the universe, but his God exerts no benevolent or knowing governance over the processes of creation which the "political theologian" calls "wholly necessary," leaving no room for divine precepts and commandments, no room for Christ. God's will being an "invincible necessity" in the *TTP*'s author's eyes, and his decrees immutable, they cannot be influenced by faith, prayer, or sacraments. Nor can there be any divine reward or punishment in this world, or the hereafter, since for him "all things emanate from God by an ineluctable necessity." What the *anonymus* terms "libertas philosophandi" is the right freely to override the legal limits imposed by the States, and ply "errors of every kind, that is defend a profane license, advocating such principles as would, if ever adopted, immediately wreck the internal peace and unity of the republic."[75]

Responding to Ostens' dismayed queries, Spinoza rejected outright Van Velthuysen's charge that he was an "atheist" in the manner he invariably did, that is purely on moral grounds. Where "atheists usually strive immoderately for honour and wealth, I have always scorned such things as all who know me know." An author contending that "God must be recognized as the highest good" and be

---

[73] Lagrée, "Louis Meyer," 41; Klever, *Mannen rond Spinoza*, 80; Juffermans, *Drie perspectiven*, 312; Preus, *Spinoza*, 154, 174; Parker, Spinoza, Locke," 173.
[74] *De Koeckoecx-Zangh*, 8.
[75] Van Mansvelt, *Adversus anonymum*, 4; Lagrée, *Spinoza et le débat*, 124, 126.

"loved as such with a free mind," holding that "the reward of virtue is virtue itself, while the penalty for stupidity and weakness is stupidity itself," cannot have "cast off all religion." But this logically somewhat bizarre objection to the charge of atheism merely proves that Spinoza tendentiously redefines "atheism" as lack of "true religion" defined as justice and charity, doing nothing to deflect accusations that he rejects a benign knowing God who governs the course of things and rewards and punishes men.[76]

Plainly, Spinoza along with members of his circle, the Koerbaghs, Meyer, and Bouwmeester prominent among them, were intent on changing the meaning of the word "atheist" just as they sought to change the meaning of the terms "heretic" and "religion." An "atheist" is certainly correctly defined as a God-denier, agree the Koerbaghs, but if correct understanding is the sole path to true knowledge of God and few possess that true knowledge, while those not knowing God correctly are "atheists," as most of their opponents seem to think, then the "great majority including the theologians are atheists, since the name of God is known by all, his reality but by few. For it is the theologians who teach the people untruth, notably that the world was created from nothing by a knowing God." True theology, by contrast, teaches that nothing can come from nothing and is part of worldly philosophy because in worldly philosophy alone is found "[true] knowledge of God."[77]

Finally, Spinoza rejects also Van Velthuysen's charge that he, as author of the *TTP*, possesses no ground with which to prove Muhammed was not a true prophet. It irked him that Van Velthuysen should accuse him of this, when, like Van Velthuysen, he too considered Muhammed an impostor. "Muhammed was indeed an impostor," affirms Spinoza, "since he completely abrogates that freedom which the universal religion concedes and which I have shown on every ground, by the natural light and by what the prophets revealed, should be wholly conceded." As for Islam as a religion, the case was exactly as with the pagans. Where Muslims worship God on the basis of "justice and charity towards their neighbour, I believe that they have the spirit of Christ and are saved whatever beliefs they may possess based on ignorance and oracles."[78] By adopting this stance, Spinoza was effectively conceding that Van Velthuysen's accusation was correct while also reaffirming his solidarity with the most radical fringe of the Collegiant movement.

The "spirit of Christ [spiritus Christi]," remained Spinoza's regular circumlocution, later used when replying to Albert Burgh, negating not just Christ's divinity, like the Socinians, but also his miracles, resurrection, special access to

---

[76] Spinoza, *Correspondance* (ed. Rovere), 258, 261; Lloyd, "Spinoza and the Idea," 7–8, 12; Laerke, *Spinoza and the Freedom*, 177, 230; Carlisle, *Spinoza's Religion*, 173.

[77] Koerbagh, *Bloemhof*, 78, 135–6.

[78] Spinoza, *Briefwisseling*, 290; Spinoza, *Correspondance* (ed. Rovere), 261–2; Lagrée, "Spinoza et le débat," 80.

the divine, special Scriptural status, status as Redeemer, and even his identification with the biblical Jesus, effectively redefining "Christ" as essentially a symbol of "justice and charity" so that every believing Muslim or Jew possesses exactly the same access to the "spirit of Christ" as the most meticulous churchgoer. If most Christians, like most Muslims and Jews, lack "the spirit of Christ," being plunged in the same depths of meaningless "superstition" insufficiently geared to justice and charity as those they despise, these too find themselves on exactly the same level as most non-Christians.[79]

Theology is assigned a meaningful moral and social role equally by Spinoza and Meyer, but has no part in revealing truth about man, God, and the world, and no claim to authority.[80] For both, it is philosophy (with science) alone, not theology that teaches truth. By claiming, like Meyer, that Scripture is full of obscurity, that biblical prophecy stems from an overactive imagination,[81] that the prophets held contradictory beliefs and prejudices and agree only in their moral ideas, and finally, that biblical expression is "adapted to the understanding and preconceived beliefs of the common people," Spinoza saps theology's foundations, subordinating it to, and effectively merging it with, philosophy no less systematically than Meyer. Both conceive philosophy, unlike Descartes, Van Velthuysen, Burman, and Wittichius, as universal, extending to everything, the apex of the human knowledge pyramid.[82] When concluding his chapter on the separation of theology and philosophy, Spinoza may feign to deplore the "absurdities, disruption and harm resulting from the fact that men have thoroughly confused these two branches, failing to correctly separate the one from the other,"[83] and upholding the separation of spheres enacted by De Witt and the States in 1656, as upheld by Van Velthuysen, but he does not really do so, nor does he oppose Meyer. Rather, there exists for both just one sphere of truth accessed via philosophy alone. Meyer, the Koerbaghs, and Spinoza all seek to end theology's autonomy and deprive it of any role in teaching the path to salvation.

Horrified by the *Philosophia*, and then, four years later, by the *TTP*, theologians, Bible critics, and philosophers alike responded to the first promptly and the second slowly and with immense difficulty, but rightly viewed both as arising from the same challenge, a challenge not just to the Bible, Christianity and tradition, and theology's primacy over philosophy, but the entire Western tradition of exegesis, a looming philosophical and "anti-Scripturalist" but also anti-humanist threat.[84] Both books appeared anonymously and, far from disagreeing, urged a revolutionary new stance generally deemed ruinous religiously, promising "worldly" in place of divine

---

[79] Moreau, Notes to Spinoza, *Oeuvres* iv, 591n258. [80] Yvon, *L'Impieté Convaincue*, 212, 400.
[81] Spinoza, *Tractatus Theologico-Politicus*, 71–2, 233.
[82] Walther, "Spinoza's Critique," 104–5, 111; Moreau, "Louis Meyer," 74–5.
[83] Spinoza, *Tractatus Theologico-Politicus*, 236; Preus, *Spinoza*, 193.
[84] Bamberger, "Early Editions," 13; Van Bunge, *From Stevin to Spinoza*, 115.

salvation and replacing a divinely decreed moral order with a socially geared morality wholly subversive of traditional academic scholarship.[85]

Anti-Cartesians, meanwhile, signally profited from the gains the shattering effect of the *TTP* afforded. The most influential assault on Cartesianism of the 1670s in the Netherlands, Germany, and Scandinavia, the *Novitatum Cartesianarum Gangraena* (1677) of Petrus van Mastricht (1630–1706), written whilst he was still teaching at Duisburg, dedicated to William III and published in Amsterdam in the year of Spinoza's death, reserves some of its fiercest invective for the *Philosophia*.[86] Its chief aim—ironically among Spinoza's objectives advancing from the other side—is to demolish the efforts of Wittichius and his liberal Reformed followers to reconcile philosophy (including Galilean science) with theology via Cartesianism. Like Voetius, Mastricht judges Descartes' entire system, beginning with his procedural principle of "universal doubt," the "primum Cartesianismi fundamentum," or corrosive negation of philosophy's traditional role as handmaiden to theology, foisting the godless, arrogant "magistracy" of philosophy over theology.[87] *Anti-Scripturarii* spearheaded the challenge to religion, society, and true scholarship, but assuredly it was, rather, the men of moderation and compromise, supposedly—Cartesio-Cocceians like Van Velthuysen, Burman, Wittichius, and Wolzogen—Van Mastricht's four particular *bêtes noirs* who were chiefly responsible for the universal catastrophe at hand, by opening the door to the *anti-Scripturarii*. Had not they, like the *Philosophia*'s author, even if less blatantly, proclaimed "reason and philosophy" instead of Holy Writ to be the true divine Revelation?[88]

Still influential among North America's Puritan Calvinists in the following century, Van Mastricht viewed Meyer's *Philosophia* and the writings of Spinoza, "atheus quidem, sed Cartesianus [an atheist certainly, but a Cartesian]," as linked, spearheading a wider philosophical subversion of divinely revealed truth.[89] It was ultimately useless, he held, to single out either Spinoza or the *Exercitator Paradoxus*, as he calls the *Philosophia*'s anonymous author, for special condemnation. There was really no great gulf between Wittichius' and Van Velthuysen's "Cartesian" approach to Bible exegesis and Spinoza's principle that Scripture speaks "according to the erroneous opinions of ordinary folk [secundum erroneam vulgi opinionem]" or the *Exercitator* contending "philosophy is Scripture's infallible interpreter [philosophiam infallibilem esse Scripturae Interpretem]." Spinoza and Meyer are used here as whips to flay Van Velthuysen, Wittichius,

---

[85] Van Mansvelt, *Adversus anonymum Theologico-Politicum*, 3–4; Burmannus, *'t Hoogste goed der Spinozisten*, 12, 47, 49; Preus, *Spinoza*, 105–6.
[86] Scholder, *Birth*, 114, 120–5; Kato, "Petrus van Mastricht," 135.
[87] Mastricht, *Novitatum Cartesianarum Gangraena*, 34; Kato, "Petrus van Mastricht," 131–3.
[88] Mastricht, *Novitatum Cartesianarum Gangraena*, 61; Kato, "Petrus van Mastricht," 134, 136–9.
[89] Mastricht, *Novitatum Cartesianarum Gangraena*, 38, 42–3, 48–9, 70–3; Israel, *Radical Enlightenment*, 214–46.

Burman, and Wolzogen whom Van Mastricht accuses of leading society to perdition by undermining ordinary people's faith in divine Providence and divine inspiration of Scripture and men's credence in demons, angels, and Satan. Teaching the world that "clear and distinct ideas" form the "unica omnis veritatis norma [the only criterion of all truth],"[90] must in the end produce an *Exercitator Paradoxus* demolishing all traditional Bible exegesis and enslaving all theology to philosophy. If Spinoza's overall system was totally unacceptable to practically everyone outside his own following, anti-Cartesians were not altogether wrong in implying that there was also a dash of hypocrisy and perhaps some self-deception enmeshed in the contemporary scholarly reception of Spinoza.

28.iv Remonstrants (Arminians) against the *TTP*

One major reason why Spinoza's early impact has been generally underestimated by historians is because prominent figures deeply preoccupied with his thought, such as Leibniz, Bayle, and perhaps also Locke, felt a pressing need to carefully veil their preoccupation, and their debt. Since no one was more decried and refuted than Spinoza, it was vital for their own standing to make it seem they were not engaged with and indebted to him or his system.[91] If Spinoza had a following directly abetting his efforts, many of those loudly denouncing him, as the rest of the seventeenth century would abundantly attest, were simultaneously borrowing extensively from him without letting on, as many later suspected was the case with Leibniz and Le Clerc and was certainly true of the great French Bible critic Richard Simon (1638–1712), whose protestations that his innovations in *critique* were unconnected with Spinoza were widely disbelieved.[92] Yet, while disavowing Spinoza's influence on himself, Simon was quick to point to how Spinoza's pernicious approach tainted the Bible hermeneutics of his chief Protestant rival, the great Remonstrant theologian, Bible exegete, and expert on text criticism, Jean le Clerc (1657–1736).

If the *TTP* aggravated the splits among Calvinists and Collegiants, the Remonstrants (Arminians) remained less divided but were equally concerned and shaken. Van Limborch (Figure 28.2), the pre-eminent Remonstrant theologian of Amsterdam, took the lead in alerting other Remonstrant preachers to the peril and apparently was the first to alert scholars in England. Just a year younger than Spinoza, having spent the decade 1657–67 preaching at Gouda, he returned to his native city, in 1667, shortly before becoming professor of theology at the Remonstrant college, the Athenaeum. Appalled by the *TTP*, Van Limborch

---

[90] Mastricht, *Novitatum Cartesianarum Gangraena*, 403–90.
[91] Malcolm, "Leibniz, Oldenburg and Spinoza," 226–7, 233–4; Nuovo, *John Locke*, 173–4.
[92] Carpzov, *Historia Critica*, 12, 31; Israel, *Radical Enlightenment*, 450–2.

Figure 28.2 *Philippus van Limborch (1633–1712) at the age of 78*, engraving. Reproduction courtesy of Rijksmuseum, Amsterdam.

substantially helped complete the first published Remonstrant refutation, the *Vindiciae miraculorum, per quae divinae religionis et fidei Christianae veritas olim confirmata fuit, Adversus profanum auctorem Tractatus Theologico-Politici* (Amsterdam, 1673), running to 103 pages, mainly composed by Jacobus Batelier (1593–1672), under whose name the book appeared. Despite appearing three years after the *TTP*, this was nevertheless one of earliest refutations published after Melchior's *Epistola*, from whatever church, in the Netherlands.

A long-serving Remonstrant minister at The Hague, Batelier presumably knew Spinoza personally, at least by sight. Van Limborch corresponded closely with his colleague for months prior to his death, a year or so before his rebuttal appeared. Essentially a vindication of "miracles," this text is sometimes dubbed the "second" Dutch refutation of the *TTP*. In the Netherlands, it certainly attracted more attention than the efforts of Thomasius, Rappolt, or Melchior, not least because Batelier had long been clashing with Voetius and the Reformed Church. Scripture, contended the Remonstrants Batelier and Van Limborch, is indeed absolutely infallible in all core theological matters but frequently somewhat inaccurate when referring to things of a non-religious character, possibly including the question of the sun circling the earth, a stance furiously condemned by Voetius who argued that Batelier's scandalously liberal position meant either the Holy Ghost does not know the truth about physical things or does not want to express it.[93]

Remonstrants counted among the chief advocates of toleration and held that considerable flexibility in Bible interpretation was justified. In March 1668, in a letter to a colleague, Van Limborch expressed support for curtailing the Jewish communities' power to excommunicate dissidents from their midst, citing their treatment of Uriel da Costa, of which he strongly disapproved.[94] But while inevitably clashing with Calvinists and strict Mennonites, Batelier and Van Limborch collided equally with the Collegiants whom they deemed excessively tolerant and grossly in error regarding the Trinity and other core theology. For Remonstrants, unlike Socinian Collegiants, the Trinity, Resurrection, and biblical miracles are sacrosanct Christian doctrine, the uncrossable red line beyond which none shall tread. Condemning the *TTP* for desecrating the "realm of truth," Batelier had much of his refutation ready as early as September 1671, but then hesitated and drew back. In June 1672, much stressed by the upsurge of anti-Remonstrant rhetoric and violence in Holland, following the French invasion, not least at Rotterdam, he died, like Perizonius and Van Mansvelt, before completing his rejoinder to the *TTP*, joining the ranks of those leaving keenly anticipated, unfinished refutations of the TTP for colleagues to complete and steer through the press. Van Limborch duly took charge, and the book finally appeared in 1673, with a second edition in 1674.[95]

Among the most vigilant observers studying the onset of the Spinozist movement, Van Limborch was skilled at detecting signs of penetration in unexpected places. Later, in 1686, he precipitated an ugly quarrel by pointing out in print that Utrecht's leading Coccejan theologian, Burman, when explaining God's omnipotence, regurgitated a passage borrowed straight from Spinoza's *Cogitata Metaphysica* of 1663, including the phrase repeated verbatim that "all things depend absolutely on the decrees of God, so that he is really omnipotent," without acknowledging this.[96] Burman, like innumerable others, was indeed indebted to Spinoza's Bible criticism and theory of religion and extremely anxious not to admit it, as was true also of Van Limborch and the latter's younger colleague, Le Clerc. When Frederik van Leenhof (1647–1715) was publicly exposed as a "Spinozist" in 1703, it came to light that he had been preaching the word of God uncontested for almost a quarter of a century while steeped in every aspect of Spinoza's philosophy. By the time the great German early eighteenth-century critic, Gundling, conceded "that from Spinoza's activity, it cannot be denied something is to be learnt," numerous theologians of the age had found it

---

[93] Vermij, *Calvinist Copernicans*, 163, 249; Goudriaan, *Reformed Orthodoxy*, 126–7, 136–7.
[94] Quoted in Meinsma, *Spinoza et son cercle*, 508–9.
[95] Van Bunge, *From Stevin to Spinoza*, 113, 115; Van Bunge, "Early Dutch Reception," 227, 242; Krop, *Spinoza, een paradoxale icoon*, 151; Nadler, *Book Forged in Hell*, 232.
[96] Barnouw, *Philippus van Limborch*, 29, 83–4, 137; Strazzoni, *Burchard de Volder*, 172.

meaningful to use that source without acknowledging their doing so, and by no means only in the field of Bible hermeneutics. This created an entire layer of accepted insights the source of which was unmentionable. When discussing biblical prophecy in his book on church history, the distinguished Franeker Reformed theologian and Old Testament philologist Campegius Vitringa (1659-1722), for example, a leading expert on Isaiah among the outstanding text scholars of the age, and one who prided himself on offering exegesis based on "freedom from prejudgment and honouring God," had borrowed extensively from Spinoza, demonstrated Gundling, not infrequently almost word for word, without the slightest hint of this to anyone.[97]

"God acts and governs all things from the necessity of his own nature and perfection alone, and his decrees and volitions are eternal truths and always involve necessity." The very hub of his system, this was the first point Spinoza "set out to explain and prove."[98] "God is described as a legislator or prince, and as just, merciful etc.," he contended, only owing to the *vulgus*' lack of understanding and knowledge. The same remoteness from the truth characterized biblical prophecy. The result was not simply a revolution in Bible criticism but a wider revolution of thought producing a "purely secular account of sovereign authority," as it has been put, "one that has no recourse to God as a source of authority," creating a fundamentally new conception of what sovereignty, laws and human (including religious) institutions essentially are, an account diverging not just from prevailing notions but, by denying that God is a lawgiver or judge who rewards and punishes, fundamentally at odds also with the views of Hobbes and Locke. The teachings of the churches are thereby reduced to the status of illicit impositions of power authorized with bogus dogmas and edicts. Ecclesiastical heads build their systems of dogma on contrived constructions, inducing people in a later age to believe those teachings are genuinely based on Scripture. The secularization process at work here hinges on removing all grounds for "imagining" that revelation and divine command are real, and denying either kings or religious authorities are justified in claiming divine sanction for the moral and social order on which their decrees and institutions are grounded. Where Hobbes, like Bacon, elevates the sovereign power to the status of final arbiter of the Scriptural message, acting through its prop, the national church, retaining control of the education of clergy under the sovereign, a point where the two thinkers diverge especially widely, for Spinoza the final arbiter is the "philosophical" individual reader.[99]

Two principal components of the fundamental revolution in text criticism that occurred in the late seventeenth century—rejection of all authorities and asserting

---

[97] [Jahn], *Verzeichnis der Bücher*, 212; De Bruïne, "Theologische faculteit," 279.
[98] Spinoza, *Theological-Political Treatise*, 63–5.
[99] Walther, "Biblische Hermeneutik" (1992), 656; Field, *Potentia*, 76–7, 132–3.

the need to focus philological research on historical and doctrinal contexts for a correct understanding—could be fully embraced without qualification only by Radical Enlightenment thinkers and publicists. For such a methodological revolution entailed wholly discarding, or at least suspending, for purposes of discussion and reasoning, not just the religious authority of Luther, Calvin, and the papacy, but also the Church Fathers and early church councils wholly setting aside ecclesiastical tradition at every level, and the Apostles themselves. Spinozist text criticism was predicated on rejecting all *a priori* authority, something that could only be fully endorsed and adopted by those thinking independently and critically in the manner of Van den Enden, the Koerbaghs, Bouwmeester, and Meyer. Spinoza's summons to study every text, the Bible included, in the same way as one would any aspect of nature, narrowed the criteria of truth to the logic of mathematical proportionality and natural causes and effects. These innovations pervading their exegesis throughout were bound to generate a heightened tension between the natural and supernatural, between authority and data, not just among those they persuaded, or caused to pause and reconsider, but even among their firmest adversaries.

29
Spinoza's Libertine "French Circle"

29.i *Libertinage* in the 1660s

Spinoza's allies, editors, translators, and publishers were mostly of Amsterdam background. But, in addition, he found notable talking partners and allies in The Hague, several of whom were French or French-speaking. The Hague of the late 1660s and 1670s nurtured a clique of cosmopolitan wits who viewed society and religion from no less a rebellious philosophical perspective than Spinoza's Dutch friends but in a markedly different style.[1] In key respects, the predominantly French *libertinage* Spinoza encountered at The Hague especially in the milieu of the famed *bon vivant*, moralist, and fine essayist, Saint-Évremond, constituted a very different cultural and intellectual world from Dutch subversive freethinking of the time and also the "deist" tendency of the 1680s and 1690s emerging in Britain and Ireland. At The Hague in the 1660s, "Epicureans" of the ilk of Saint-Évremond, Sir William Temple, and Isaac Vossius frequented high society gatherings and showed little sign of seeking to attack the existing social and political order. Nor did they project in any way their usually carefully masked inner rejection of the surrounding world's "entire Christian culture."

If a distinctive feature of Spinoza's thought, and "Spinozism" as a sect was its deep sense of engagement and actively subversive character, its wanting to change the world, a chief characteristic of Saint-Évremond's high society circle at The Hague, notes his biographer, Pierre Desmaizeaux (1666–1745), before and after his permanent transfer to the English royal court, in 1670, was its impeccable outward propriety regarding the existing religious order. For Spinoza and his following "all the notions by which ordinary people are accustomed to explain nature [omnes notiones, quibus vulgus solet naturam explicare], result from our "way of imagining without showing the nature of anything." With common thinking constituting the basis of false religion as well as bad education and politics, much of what is generally accepted tends to be not just misleading but damaging to everyone. It matters, therefore, to devise ways to elevate the usual manner of thinking about things, enlightening men, that is, as far as society can.[2]

---

[1] Marburg, *Sir William Temple*, 22; Assoun, "Spinoza, les libertins," 180.
[2] Spinoza, *Oeuvres* iv, 158; Vinciguerra, *Spinoza et le signe*, 284–5; Israel, *Enlightenment that Failed*, 88–91.

Figure 29.1 *Charles de Saint Denis de Saint-Évremond (1613–1703)*, portrait from Pierre Desmaizeaux, *Oeuvres Meslées de Mr. de Saint-Evremond: Publiées Sur Les Manuscrits de l'auteur*. Seconde ed. Revue, Corrigée & Augmentée de la vie de l'auteur. A Londres Chez Jacob Tonson, 1709.

By contrast, the Saint-Évremond circle sought neither to subvert, nor re-educate, nor remake the wider framework.

Charles de Marguetel de Saint-Denis, seigneur de Saint-Évremond (1613–1703) (Figure 29.1), was a Norman nobleman and pupil of Jesuits, nineteen years older than Spinoza, who, like Temple, gained renown as a critic, wit, essayist, and connoisseur of an egotistical aristocratic *épicurisme* pursuing individual happiness in what has aptly been called "une voluptueuse indolence." A veteran officer who fought in several campaigns during the Thirty Years War and the civil war in France (1648–53) known as the Frondes, commencing as a fashionable royalist, he had already spent two or three months in the Bastille for uttering jokes about Cardinal Mazarin at a courtiers' junketing session when he was caught expressing himself disrespectfully about the king's policy with regard to Spain. In 1661, under threat of returning to the Bastille, he went into exile abroad and remained an exile for the rest of his life. Digging deep into ancient and modern literature and erudite in his way, Saint-Évremond assumed the pose of a grave *moraliste* ever watchful to expose whatever he judged superficial, bogus, or pedantic. Never one to defer to tradition, doctrine, or authority simply because it was long-established,[3] he developed a refined, innovative "relativisme historique" characterized by careful, dispassionate comparisons of the starkly different manners, morals, and cultural systems of different ages, lands, and religions.[4]

Most of his subsequent life Saint-Évremond spent in England, at the court of Charles II, in the company of the latter's favourites, with the exception of the years 1665-70 and another short period, early in 1672 when he resided at The Hague and gathered a scintillating circle around him. At The Hague, he greatly enjoyed his discussions with prominent persons including famous savants, "particulièrement MM. [messieurs] Heinsius, Vossius et Spinoza." Very likely it was via Saint-Évremond's correspondence with aristocratic friends that the first reports of Spinoza's widening impact reached France.[5] An Epicurean libertine moralist, in religious matters Saint-Évremond evinced no particular preference for one faith over another. But as most Frenchmen he met in exile were Huguenots, or else foreign Protestants, he was frequently dragged into discussing religion including with Leibniz's amiable Huguenot friend, Henri Justel (1619-93), after the latter fled Paris for London, in 1681, and became royal librarian at Saint James's Palace. Whenever caught up in debating religion or theology, relates his Huguenot biographer, Desmaizeaux, Saint-Évremond resorted to impenetrable inscrutability, insisting religious discussion is not for worldly men of affairs like himself and that Catholicism is the confession best suited to gentlemen unconcerned about theology. As the entry in Sylvain Marechal's *Dictionnaire des Athées anciens et modernes* (1800) observes, Saint-Évremond steadfastly cultivated "le *decorum*."[6] His real view of religion, though, reached well beyond mere indifference, observes Bayle, who counted him among the "virtuous atheists," though this was not immediately recognizable from his writings, becoming discernible only under close scrutiny.[7] Rather than justice and charity, as with Spinoza, "religion" for Saint-Évremond was about how to conduct one's life, a question of culture, lifestyle, and convention not belief.[8]

Much the same could be said of Sir William Temple (1628-99), "as true a son of Epicurus as was Saint-Évremond," and, whilst at The Hague, Saint-Évremond and Temple, as the former remarked when writing to Charles II's secretary of state,

---

[3] Ehrard, *L'Idée de nature*, 544; Bensoussan, "L'*Otium* de l'honnête homme," 387.
[4] Dagen, *L'Histoire de l'esprit humain*, 118.
[5] Cohen, *Séjour de Saint-Évremond*, 1, 78, 87; Hope, *Saint-Évremond and His Friends*, 259; Assoun, "Spinoza, les libertins," 181.
[6] Maréchal, *Dictionnaire des Athées*, 273.
[7] Bayle, *Oeuvres diverses* iii, 414; Mori, "Bayle, Saint-Évremond and Fideism," 324.
[8] Wade, *Intellectual Development of Voltaire*, 123, 580.

Lord Arlington, in July 1668, entertained a warm regard for each other.[9] Isaac Vossius (1618–89), among the foremost freethinkers in the Low Countries in the 1660s was another of Saint-Évremond's close allies during his Dutch years, as also later at court at Windsor and in London, despite differing from him in character and conduct in every way except one. Pedantic and awkward, carrying massive erudition but few social graces, privately Vossius too was anti-Christian but only in a similarly carefully closeted fashion. The sole respect in which he resembled his witty, perfectly mannered French libertine friend, remarks Desmaizeaux, was that whenever questioned about religion, as happened frequently, or pushed to admit the "truth" of Christianity, he immediately closed up, adopting an attitude of strict inscrutability. This fitted with his notorious insistence, preposterous in the eyes of most contemporaries, that regarding "matters of the mind, the arts and sciences, the Chinese were superior to all the Europeans." Vossius was rumoured to believe more in Confucius than in Jesus Christ.[10]

As regards personal lifestyle, Saint-Évremond's path was an easier, more fashionable, entertaining, and comfortable one than Spinoza's and doubtless exerted greater appeal on others. So the question arises how exactly, and when, did groups of libertines and freethinkers in Western Europe graduate from Saint-Évremond's world of sharing jibes about kings and cardinals, repudiating faith in secretive fashion among themselves, to an actively subversive post-Epicurean Radical Enlightenment stance surreptitiously and clandestinely combining rejection of religious authority with the *cercle Spinoziste*'s anti-monarchism, republicanism, and push for fundamental educational reform and reform of the arts? How and why did a closeted *libertinisme* cultivating its alternative morality behind a wall of silent inscrutability about politics and religion, nurturing its *épicurisme* behind the scenes, evolve into an active clandestine movement spreading texts and ideas, becoming a more engaged radical underground, as was first discernible in the early 1670s, designing to mobilize others against the existing social, moral, and political status quo?

Appalled by Louis XIV's invasion of the Dutch Republic in 1672, some Frenchmen felt as outraged by the arrogance of French royal absolutism as did most Dutchmen, a change reflected by the key role of militant republicanism and Spinoza's former Latin master, Franciscus van den Enden (1602–74) in the "Rohan conspiracy," in Normandy, in 1674. News of this remarkable, mostly aristocratic, conspiracy against Europe's most powerful monarch was published in Amsterdam that autumn.[11] Bayle, who was in Rouen at the time, mentions the affair, in December 1674, in a letter to his regular correspondent in Italy, Vincent Minutoli, relating how the conspirators were caught, tried, and then executed at

---

[9] Cohen, *Sejour de Saint-Évremond*, 91.
[10] Desmaizeaux, *Vie de Messire* [...] *de Saint-Evremond*, p. L; Cohen, *Séjour de Saint Évremond*, 44.
[11] Gullan-Whur, *Life of Spinoza*, 267; Smith, "Politics of Tragedy," 248.

the Bastille. So elated was Louis' chief executioner at severing the head of a prince (Rohan) "that he would not deign to profane his hands" by laying them on a mere schoolmaster (Van den Enden), such that, having beheaded three noble conspirators in person, the executioner turned to his subordinates and ordered: "You lot, hang that one there," pointing to the sole non-noble prisoner who was classed as unworthy of beheading, the punishment reserved for high-born traitors. Thus ended the life of the "wretched Van den Enden who is Belgian [i.e. a southern Netherlander] and yet repudiated by both the Dutch and Flemish."[12]

Under mounting persecution, it is scarcely surprising that at least some Huguenots and other refugees fleeing France reacted in thought and deed to Louis' haughty, intolerant, and aggressive monarchism and expansionism by inwardly transitioning to a politically more oppositional outlook and even a republican stance like that so resoundingly proclaimed by Van den Enden and his Norman noble allies in 1672–4. Spinoza's own circle, even aspects of his own outlook, arguably also reflect elements of such a shift to a more engaged strategy at precisely this time. For in the years preceding publication of the *TTP*, Spinoza seems to have been distinctly more guarded and anxious to avoid offending the sensibilities of those he encountered than was the case from 1670, much as he also displayed greater readiness, in the mid-1670s, to directly affront Oldenburg's (and Robert Boyle's) Christian sensibilities than in the 1660s.

During the late 1660s, notes Desmaizeaux, Spinoza held long conversations with Saint-Évremond at The Hague.[13] But with Saint-Évremond, as with the eccentric polymath Vossius, the basic object seems to have been pleasurable, sophisticated conversation for its own sake, refined relaxation, even if attaining real philosophical and ethical relevance. Saint-Évremond and Vossius both took an avid interest in ancient Roman moralists and historians, and it was during his stay at The Hague that Saint-Évremond penned his long essay on the crucial transitions in Roman history from early monarchy to the Republic, and from the Republic to the imperial monarchy of Augustus and Tiberius,[14] a topic in which Spinoza too was keenly interested. Where Hobbes viewed the transition from Roman republic to stable imperial monarchy as a positive development, and Spinoza saw the republic's demise as a dismal setback for liberty,[15] Saint-Évremond, half way in between, holding the virtues, laws, and principles required for sustaining a true republic too exacting for most men, preferred as his political ideal an undemanding moderate monarchy striving for stability by nurturing an amenable milieu such as, in the Roman case, the cautious, calculating emperorship

---

[12] Bayle, *Correspondance* ii, 26–7. Bayle to Minutoli, Rouen, 15 Dec. 1674.
[13] Marburg, *Sir William Temple*, 22.   [14] Darmon, "Le juste et l'utile," 220, 222.
[15] Spinoza, *Oeuvres* iii (ed. Moreau), *Traité théologico-politique*, 534–7, 541–5; Spinoza, *Political Treatise*, 133.

of Augustus (reigned: 27 BC to AD 14) outwardly cherishing the old forms and symbols of republican liberty.[16]

Saint-Évremond regularly frequented, and entertained, all the ambassadors at The Hague providing a perfect conduit for others of his circle, including Vossius and Spinoza, to gain insight and information into the behind-the-scenes world of international politics and high-level cultural and intellectual news. When the Grand Duke Cosimo of Tuscany, supposedly travelling incognito in Holland, spent several weeks in The Hague early in 1668, he certainly did not see much of Spinoza, even assuming the reports that he refused to meet him owing to the latter's godless views are incorrect, but reportedly so enjoyed Saint-Évremond's witty conversation that he asked him to dine with him every evening of his stay.[17]

If Saint-Évremond's ideal was that of the immaculate French-speaking gentleman, not the scholar, the earliest biography of Spinoza, attributed to Jean Maximilien Lucas, relates that, when about town, Spinoza avoided dressing like a scholar or "pedant," indeed never went out without putting on the sort of outfit that generally distinguished "un honnête homme d'un pedant [a gentleman from a pedant]," though Colerus suggests that he paid little attention to his dress and dressed simply and in a bourgeois manner.[18] Saint-Évremond later described Spinoza as "fairly short with a pleasant appearance [avoit la taille médiocre et la physionomie agréeable]" while "his knowledge, modesty and disinterestedness [not being influenced by considerations of personal advantage]" led to his being sought out by "toutes les personnes d'esprit," everyone of intellect and wit at The Hague. But what Saint-Évremond chiefly recalled about Spinoza's manner and conversational style in the late 1660s, records Desmaizeaux, is that no one would gather from his cautious "conversations ordinaires" that he held the views so dramatically revealed to the world later in his *Opera Posthuma* (1678). Rather, concerning the existence of God, Spinoza seemingly accepted the existence of a "being separate from matter [un Être distinct de la matière]" performing miracles who commanded observance of religion so that "justice and charity" be practised and obedience to the political authorities upheld.[19]

To Saint-Évremond, this was also the message of the *TTP*, leaving Desmaizeaux to nuance his view by pointing out that, masked though it is, one does discern when closely examining the *TTP*, Spinoza's total rejection of conventional religion, much as Van Limborch stressed later when writing to Jean Le Clerc, in January 1682.[20] Desmaizeaux then develops an interesting thesis, highly pertinent here, that

---

[16] Darmon, "Le juste et l'utile," 242–3.
[17] Desmaizeaux, *Vie de Messire* [...] *de Saint-Evremond*, xxxiii; Cohen, *Séjour de Saint-Évremond*, 37.
[18] [Lucas], *La Vie*, 42–3; Freudenthal/Walther, *Lebensgeschichte* i, 122–3; Nadler, *Spinoza: A Life*, 306.
[19] Desmaizeaux, *Vie de Messire* [...] *de Saint-Evremond*, xxix; Cohen, *Séjour de Saint-Évremond*, 55; Rothkamm, *Institutio Oratoria*, 257.
[20] See Van Limborch to Le Clerc, Amsterdam, 23 Jan. 1682 in Meinsma, *Spinoza et son cercle*, 526.

Spinoza did not reveal himself all at once. When M. de Saint-Évremond was in Holland, he usually kept up certain precautions in general conversation. But if we must believe M. Stouppe, a few years later he said openly in conversation that God is not a being endowed with intelligence etc. You have doubtless noticed, Monsieur, the same conduct in his books. His *Tractatus Theologico-Politicus* contains the seeds of his atheism, but in a veiled manner; only in his *Opera Posthuma* can one say that he lifted the mask. [Spinoza ne s'est pas découvert tout d'un coup. Il gardoit encore des ménagemens dans la conversation ordinaire lorsque M. de Saint-Évremond étoit en Hollande. Mais, s'il en faut croire M. Stouppe, quelques années après il disoit hautement dans ses discours que Dieu n'est pas un Être doué d'intelligence etc. Vous avez, sans doute, remarqué, Monsieur, la même conduite dans ses ouvrages. Sa *Théologie Politique* contient les sémences de son Athéisme, mais d'une manière envelopée; et ce n'est que dans ses *Oeuvres Posthumes* qu'on peut dire qu'il a levé le masque.]

The "Vous... Monsieur" here is Bayle who, like Voltaire later, was fascinated by Saint-Évremond's personality and especially his religious views, and who requested Desmaizeaux to write his biography of Saint-Évremond.[21] The "Stouppe" he refers to was the same Swiss officer, brother of the governor of Utrecht under French occupation in 1672–3, and Spinoza's host when visiting Utrecht, then still in French hands, in the summer of 1673, who wrote *La Religion des Hollandois*. Outraging the French-speaking Reformed community in the Netherlands, Stouppe's book, accusing the Republic of permitting every kind of scandalous religious dissent while doing practically nothing to counter Spinoza, also prompted claims that he was a rank hypocrite, since, reportedly, he and his officers got on splendidly with Spinoza (whose French apparently was up to this) when the latter dined with them in Utrecht.

Desmaizeaux's hypothesis, echoing that of Salomon Van Til, in 1694,[22] suggests there were actually three stages in the widening projection of Spinoza's views on religion and its relationship to society: first, a masked, guarded phase featuring no active effort to subvert beyond his small, private discussion groups (1650s and 1660s); second, following publication of the *TTP*, and doubtless intensified by the general disruption and turmoil caused by the French invasion of 1672, and the Dutch republicans' deeply felt indignation at the Orangist coup and bolstering of church repression which directly resulted in a more abrasive, actively subversive phase in which he was likelier to unleash what most then considered provocative, blasphemous remarks; and third, following his physical death, in February 1677, the full lifting of the curtain concealing the true scope and content of his activist

---

[21] Desmaizeaux, *Vie de Messire* [...] *de Saint-Evremond*, Avertissement; Wade, *Intellectual Development of Voltaire*, 154, 226; Mori, "Bayle, Saint-Évremond and Fideism."
[22] Van Til, *Voor-hof der heydenen*, 5–7.

engagement, philosophy, democratic republicanism, and anti-church political aims. It is fruitful, perhaps, to consider these three distinct stages unfolding in relation to Spinoza's links with the French-speaking exile community in Holland at the time.

29.ii Spinoza Confides: The First Phase

Besides Saint-Évremond, another more curious source relating to the evolution of Spinoza's activism was the mysterious [Henri] "Morelli," to whom Desmaizeaux refers when listing the three different fictitious titles under which the *TTP* first appeared, in 1678, in French translation. Among the three false title-pages used by the publisher, Rieuwertsz, to disseminate the 1678 French edition, relates Desmaizeaux, the first was *La Clef du Sanctuaire*. "I have these details from Mr Morelli," a close companion of Saint-Évremond's "who was well acquainted" with Saint-Glain, the "person usually taken to have been Spinoza's translator into French."[23] Morelli, reportedly, was familiar with all the French exile libertine circle in The Hague, including Saint-Évremond, and a close friend of Saint-Glain, as well as familiar with and well disposed towards Spinoza.[24]

Morelli's real name, reports Desmaizeaux in a later edition of Bayle's *Oeuvres Diverses*, was "[Enrique] Morales." Born in Cairo, raised in Amsterdam, he was, like Spinoza, of Sephardic origin (and not a "New Christian" as sometimes stated). In early manhood, he toured France and studied medicine in Italy. He may have been, it has been suggested, the foreign physician Bayle cites in a letter to his brother, sent from Sedan, a year after Spinoza's death, dated 23 February 1678, recounting how a certain bizarre foreigner had raised eyebrows at Montauban by freely expressing shocking opinions, in particular uttering "so much good [tant de bien]" about the *Tractatus Theologico-Politicus*.[25] Morelli enjoyed a successful career as a high society physician at The Hague and, later, London, serving as a physician among the fashionable aristocracy, especially the earl of Sandwich, Lord Edward Montagu (1670–1729) and his wife, the famously witty countess of Sandwich, Lady Elizabeth Wilmot (c.1674–1757). Bayle, in 1705, even styled the ex-friar Le Vassor and Morelli as "the two pillars" of conversation at the table of Lord Montagu to whom, in 1705, Desmaizeaux dedicated his biography of Saint-Évremond.[26]

---

[23] Bayle, *Oeuvres diverses* iv, 570–1; Philipson, *Leben Benedikt's von Spinoza*, 110; Vernière, *Spinoza et la pensée française*, 24–6; Bamberger, "Early Editions," 32.
[24] Cohen, *Séjour de Saint-Évremond*, 56, 64; Berti, *Anticristianesimo e libertà*, 104–5; Hope, *Saint-Évremond and His Friends*, 285.
[25] Bayle, *Correspondance* iii, 22, 25n26; Vernière, *Spinoza et la pensée française*, 290; Freudenthal/Walther, *Lebensgeschichte* ii, 43–4.
[26] Bayle, *Correspondance* xiii, 369–70, 370n9.

Designated "mon ami particulier" by Saint-Évremond, Morelli was certainly a hardened "esprit fort" living outwardly as a Catholic, with an avowed passion for the arts, especially music and ancient and modern poetry which formed a particular bond between him and Saint-Évremond who, records Bayle, warmly lauded his outlook and philosophy of life.[27] In 1679, Bayle had a discussion with Morelli in which the latter assured him that "I have known M. Spinoza particularly well [j'ai connu très particulièrement M. Spinosa]," and related more than once that, while at Utrecht, Spinoza *did* meet the Prince of Condé, and that after their discussions the Prince "urged him most insistently to follow him to Paris and join his entourage [lui fit de grands instances pour l'engager de le suivre à Paris, et d'y rester auprès de sa personne]," assuring him that he could count on his protection, board and lodging, and a pension of a thousand *écus*, to which Spinoza supposedly responded by asking His Highness to consider that all his power could not protect him from the bigotry of the court, his name being greatly decried due to the *Traité théologique et politique*, so that there could be no security for him in Paris, nor satisfaction for His Highness, the priests being sworn enemies "of persons who think and write freely about religion [des personnes qui pensent et qui écrivent librement sur la religion]." Spinoza did, though, offer to accompany him to his army camp and, if he could, provide conversational diversion from his wartime responsibilities. The Prince allegedly appreciated his reasoning and thanked him.[28]

Much sought after as a wit and conversationalist until his death, in March 1715,[29] Morelli unquestionably knew Saint-Évremond and Desmaizeaux well; but how well he really knew Spinoza remains in question. His claiming Spinoza told him more than once that he did meet Condé in Utrecht, in 1673, and that the latter urged him to accompany him to Paris, is usually dismissed or cast in doubt by historians today who mostly agree that no such meeting ever took place.[30] Perhaps, Morelli was in the habit of adorning whatever he did know as a means of self-promotion. In any case, he sufficiently impressed Saint-Évremond, Bayle, and Desmaizeaux, for a time at least, to substantially colour their picture of Spinoza and his circle, and, in the late seventeenth century, did pass as one of Spinoza's more notable disciples and a prime authority on his life and achievement. For decades after moving to London from The Hague in the later 1670s, Morelli made a point of claiming inside knowledge of Spinoza's circle.

Morelli was certainly an outstanding wit, as Dryden too attests, and well-known connoisseur of "our poetry" as well as of Virgil. Styling Dr Morelli, his particular friend, Saint-Évremond, rather remarkably, if also frivolously, elevated this Jew,

---

[27] Bayle, *Correspondance* xiii, 370n14; Hope, *Saint-Évremond and His Friends*, 283.
[28] Cohen, *Séjour de Saint-Évremond*, 64; Popkin, *Spinoza*, 107, 111–12; Van de Ven, *Printing Spinoza*, 204.
[29] Bayle, *Correspondance* xiii, 369.
[30] Vernière, *Spinoza et la pensée française*, 22; Van de Ven, "Crastina die loquar," 148.

turned Catholic,[31] to the central persona in a light-hearted poem he composed in 1698 that jokingly, but significantly, underlines the basic difference in philosophical outlook between them [i.e. Saint-Évremond and Morelli] and his all too serious philosopher friend, Spinoza. The poem occurs in a letter from Saint-Évremond to the former famed courtesan Ninon de Lenclos (1620–1705), introducing "my intimate friend Doctor Morelli," who was accompanying the ailing Elizabeth "Countess of Sandwich who is being sent to France for her health."[32] Since abandoning the courtesan life, around 1667, Ninon hosted a celebrated Parisian literary salon dedicated to literature and elegant conversation.

Elizabeth, a famous beauty as well as wit, had married Edward, third earl of Sandwich, in July 1689, when apparently still under sixteen. Her son, heir to the title, died young, and it was actually her grandson, the indolent John Montagu (1718–92), fourth earl of Sandwich, of whom it was reported, after his retiring from royal service, that "seldom has any man held so many offices and accomplished so little" apart from inventing "the sandwich," a contrivance attributed to his eagerness to linger as long as possible at the gaming table. If Lady Sandwich's father was "the wittiest man in England," famed for his high regard for the female mind, recounts Saint-Évremond, "the countess is cleverer still; moreover, she is as generous as she is witty, and her amiability surpasses both her generosity and her wit." "But, I can tell you far more on the topic of the doctor than the patient," jests his letter, asking Ninon also to introduce his friend and physician, Dr Morelli, to "her special and particular friends."[33] Both being religious sceptics doubting the immortality of the soul, Elizabeth and Ninon hit it off and remained good friends down to Ninon's death. In his teasing poem Saint-Évremond extols two famous beauties, Lady Sandwich and his female friend in London, one of Charles II's many mistresses, the promiscuously bisexual Hortense, duchesse de Mazarin (1646–99), known to those less friendly to her as the "Italian whore."

To a degree both these ladies, it seems, followed the spiritual guidance of Saint-Évremond's favourite non-aristocratic freethinker, Morelli, whom he here profiles as a unique spiritual chameleon—"in the Indies a *gymnosophiste*, a mufti in Constantinople, in Jerusalem a *rabbiniste* devoted to Kabbala, je serois ici SPINOSISTE [I would be a Spinozist here], but how can one join that party [the Spinozist sect] when I see two objects of divine beauty so clearly proclaim their celestial origin? If there are still Spinozas, let us not think of how to reply to them [ne songeons point à leur répondre: beau couple, vos rare appas nous suffiront pour les confondre], your lovely figures will suffice to confound them. Audacious spirits, the most hardened incredulity, cannot hold out against your eyes: before

---

[31] Bamberger, "Early Editions," 32n58; Popkin, *Spinoza*, 112.
[32] Hamel, *Famous French Salons*, 145; Popkin, *Spinoza*, 112.
[33] Hamel, *Famous French Salons*, 145–6; Hope, *Saint-Évremond and His Friends*, 283, 285.

you, none can be impious. In your traits, one recognizes the master who made them."[34]

Spinoza, in Saint-Évremond's by turns serious and frivolous eyes, evidently took his philosophical abstractions too seriously. Unwilling to drag theology into debating moral issues, such was Saint-Évremond's stress on style and the niceties of the good life that he remained averse to dragging into conversation not just theology but likewise too much abstruse philosophy and political theory.[35] While courtly libertinism itself was then a familiar enough behavioural phenomenon, especially among French and English aristocracy, this relaxed, rarefied milieu and dimension of The Hague life was undergoing a rapid change when Spinoza resided in Voorburg and then The Hague, in the late 1660s, entering an entire new phase with novel features historians have long been fascinated by, evolving into a more serious, new kind of inquiry-driven, research-based *libertinisme érudit*. Arising in Holland, this transformed *libertinage* was more universalist in approach than pre-1660s *libertinage érudit*, more critical of the existing character of Western society and politics, and more focused on non-European and non-Christian societies, exuding a marked Sinophile tendency, cultivated in particular by Vossius and Temple. It exerted a lasting appeal (not least on Bayle) which continued into the eighteenth century.

Spinoza interacted with the circle around Saint-Évremond at The Hague in the late 1660s but at the same time stood apart from it in attitudes and approach. Both the affinities and differences between these two distinct but in some respects parallel intellectual streams—a flourishing literary epicurean *libertinage érudit* barely encountering Spinoza's furtive, activist Dutch following—seem relevant. Spinoza, like Saint-Évremond, Temple, and Vossius, held that religion originates and functions primarily as a social and political tool. Both Spinoza's system and this new strain of libertinage had their roots in rejection of religious *fundamenta* leading to wider rejection of prevailing structures of morality, thought, and belief, albeit Spinoza's approach owed much to the gravitas of Collegiant Socinian meetings and to medieval Jewish philosophy, neither of which played any part in Saint-Évremond's world. Both Spinoza and his libertine friends at The Hague had good reason to express gratitude for the freedom from monarchical and religious tyranny the United Provinces afforded. Both circles or tendencies seemingly believed the advent of a transformative purely secular ethics serving the common good of society is possible. Differently from older forms of Epicureanism and neo-Epicureanism, Saint-Évremond's strain flourishing at The Hague was incipiently critical of existing society organizationally and politically, guardedly more explicit in rejecting divine revelation and religious authority, and finally,

---

[34] Quoted in Bayle, *Correspondance* xiii, 370–1n14; Vernière, *Spinoza et la pensée française*, 17–18; and in Hope, *Saint-Évremond and His Friends*, 284.

[35] Bensoussan, "L'*Otium* de l'honnête homme," 390–1.

showed more interest than the old libertinism in propagating their views, if not in society broadly then in tightly restricted circles.[36]

The distinguishing points too are striking. There remained a world of difference in terms of dress and style; while Saint-Évremond invested his hopes, like Temple, in the *summum bonum* invoked by Epicurus, Montaigne, Charron, and other great libertines, unlike Vossius or Spinoza, but again like Temple, he took scant interest in natural science and research.[37] Even Vossius took no interest in modern-style mathematically defined science in the way Spinoza did. Conversation, wit, group enlightenment, and enjoyment were the focus of Saint-Évremond's life, and if he wrote scintillatingly, he undoubtedly did so more to entertain his highly placed friends and associates than to impress or instruct, let alone infiltrate, the public. Indeed, Saint-Évremond seemed to many bafflingly reluctant to publish his writings at all, of which hardly any appeared during his lifetime.[38]

29.iii Spinoza's Reformism: The Later Phases

Once the *TTP* appeared, in early 1670, and word got around that Spinoza was its author, the role of "caute!" in Spinoza's life apparently receded. It still mattered greatly not to be caught propagating, or putting his name on anything in print that would generally be deemed blasphemous and could get him hauled, like the Koerbaghs in 1668, before the magistrates. Becoming something of a marked man, attracting local hostility and soon fierce attacks in the press, doubtless further heightened his propensity to reclusiveness, to shutting himself indoors for long periods. But this shift during the last six years or so of his life also created a situation in which there was less reason to restrain expression of his views whenever minor confrontations and serious conversation ensued.

If it is right to discern a new phase in Spinoza's manner and general approach from 1670–2, this may account for an interesting discrepancy in the surviving descriptions of his appearance, demeanour, and conversational style. Saint-Évremond's sketch correlates well enough with what we have from Spinoza's landlord, Van der Spijck, depicting him as of medium height, "courteous and respectful" with a modest manner in conversation.[39] It was easy to see that he "was of Portuguese Jewish descent" with "fairly dark skin, black curled hair and long black eyebrows," and also a "besneden aangezicht [sharply contoured? face]."[40]

---

[36] Wauters, "*Libertinage érudit*," 41. [37] Marburg, *Sir William Temple*, 24.
[38] Desmaizeaux, *Vie de Messire* [...] *de Saint-Evremond*.
[39] The similar-sounding corresponding passage in the biography of Lucas describing Spinoza's person and character is absent from the earliest manuscripts of this text and seems to have been inserted later, by Levier, using phrases based on Colerus, see Berti, "Introduzione" to [Lucas], *La Vie*, xxxix–xl; [Lucas], *La Vie*, 56.
[40] Freudenthal/Walther, *Lebensgeschichte* i, 122–3; Colerus, *Das Leben*, 8: Van Bunge, *Philosopher of Peace*, 25.

But if Saint-Évremond agreed that Spinoza had a handsome face and pleasant manner, by no means everyone did. The Huguenot Leiden theological professor and expert in oriental languages, Étienne Le Moine (1624–89), who encountered Spinoza in the last year or so of his life, when asked to describe him to his fellow native of Caen, Bishop Huet, shortly after Spinoza's death, in July 1677, replied: "he was a man with an unpleasant look about him [c'etait un homme d'un mauvais regard]," promising "only what is base and contemptible," exactly reflecting a "mind" basely formed like his by Judaism, Socinianism, and libertinism. "Had he lived in Constantinople, Peking or Yedo [Tokyo], he would just as gladly have embraced Muhammedanism, *foisme* [Confucianism?] or *amidisme* [Mahayana Buddhism]," as any other creed.[41] (No doubt this feature particularly appealed to Morelli.) Spinoza's "mauvais regard," his "malign look" or expression, suggests that in particular situations, such as when meeting professors like Le Moine, Spinoza no longer felt inclined, as formerly, to conceal his feelings of antagonism. Le Moine's impression fits with Van Limborch's recollection of him at a dinner, in Amsterdam, in 1675, when Spinoza uninhibitedly indicated by frowning and facial expression what he thought of the prayers recited at table and pious demeanour of the others.[42]

That the French-speaking Reformed community in The Hague considered Spinoza an overt threat during the last phase of his life in a way they had not done earlier is proven by formal resolutions taken by the synod of the "Walloon Church" during 1675 and 1676 regarding the danger he was now taken to represent. The Walloon Reformed church in The Hague, and throughout Holland, at this point became as agitated as the Dutch Reformed consistories over the "Spinozist" challenge. In 1675, the "Walloon Synod" convened for its annual gathering in early September, with forty-one delegates, twenty-four *pasteurs*, and seventeen elders present at The Hague, including the famed theologian, Élie Saurin (1639–1703), representing Utrecht. The participant most knowledgeable about The Hague was the local Walloon *pasteur*, Jean Carré (1620–97) who had held that post since 1646.[43] Among the gathering's resolutions was one summoning all the Walloon pastors to join with their Dutch Reformed colleagues to "seek together the most effective means to prevent the said Spinoza from continuing to sow his impiety and atheism [son impiété et son athéisme] in these provinces."[44] To combat "the blasphemies and enormous impieties of Spinoza [blasphèmes et les impietiés énormes de Spinosa]," all the Walloon churches of the Netherlands, "especially of Rotterdam, The Hague, Dordrecht, Utrecht and Breda," were exhorted to gather information with all exactitude and

---

[41] Popkin, "Another Spinoza," 133; Popkin, *Spinoza*, 115.
[42] Van Limborch to Le Clerc, Amsterdam, 23 Jan. 1682 in Meinsma, *Spinoza et son cercle*, 526.
[43] Bayle, *Correspondance* x, 66, 70.
[44] GA The Hague, Waalse Hervormde Gemeente 241/49 "Articles du Synode," Sept. 1675.

try to elicit written testimonies as to whether Spinoza was "indeed the author of the impious book entitled *Tractatus Theologico-Politicus* and is spreading the teachings that are contained in it and how long he has been doing so."[45] Such evidence would be especially requisite for the courts, should the pastors manage to get Spinoza personally indicted. The following year, the Walloon Synod again convened at The Hague with seventeen elders and twenty-three pastors present, Carré for The Hague among them, and again reviewed the issue of Spinoza and the *TTP*, reaffirming that Spinoza's "impietiés enormes" posed a considerable threat and renewing their resolution of the previous year.[46]

Quite apart from Spinoza's writings, apprehension that Spinoza was actively spreading "his teachings" in person through conversation, evinced by several Dutch Reformed consistories during these years, was clearly a mounting worry also within the French-speaking Reformed community. One notable figure converted from the Calvinist faith who became a disciple of Spinoza at this time was the previously mentioned Chevalier Gabriel (or Dominique) de Saint-Glain (c.1620–84)—also rendered as "Saint-Glen" or even "Cienglen"—a shadowy Huguenot journalist originating from Angers (or "Limoges" as Maréchal claims), who lived most of his adult life in the Republic. Of noble background, Saint-Glain briefly served as a Huguenot officer in the States General's army or, as Desmaizeaux puts it, "capitaine au service de Messieurs les États." Settling in The Hague, he married a Frenchwoman, Marie Patoillat, there in June 1669.[47] Registration of the birth of a son shows the family still lived there in 1673.[48] Although, according to one source, it was "en lisant Spinoza," through reading Spinoza, that Saint-Glain underwent his "conversion" to Spinozism, according to Morelli, recounts Desmaizeaux, it was "as soon as he got to know Spinoza," after living in The Hague for a time as a zealous Protestant, that Saint-Glain "became one of his greatest admirers [dès qu'il eût connu Spinoza, il devint un de ses plus grands admirateurs]."[49] Later, Saint-Glain transferred to Amsterdam working as a journalist on the *Gazette d'Amsterdam*.[50]

Morelli knew Saint-Glain well, or so he later claimed.[51] But consorting with the likes of Saint-Glain, if he ever did, would hardly have benefited Saint-Évremond's international reputation. Where Saint-Évremond carefully cultivated his high standing at court in London, and even eventually managed partly to restore his

---

[45] GA The Hague, Waalse Hervormde Gemeente 241/49 "Articles du Synode," Sept. 1675.
[46] GA The Hague, Waalse Hervormde Gemeente 241/49 "Articles du Synode," 9–11 Sept. 1676, art. 7; Kingma, "Spinoza in zijn Haagse periode," 18; Freudenthal, *Lebensgeschichte Spinozas*, 150–2; Vernière, *Spinoza et la pensée française*, 42; Israel, *Radical Enlightenment*, 286.
[47] Meinsma, *Spinoza et son cercle*, 429.   [48] Van Eeghen, *Amsterdamse boekhandel* iii, 63.
[49] Bayle, *Oeuvres Diverses* iv, 570–1n; Maréchal, *Dictionnaire des Athées*, 273.
[50] Meinsma, *Spinoza et son cercle*, 429; Bamberger, "Early Editions," 27; Meininger and van Suchtelen, *Liever met wercken*, 83.
[51] Bayle, *Oeuvres Diverses* iv, 571n; Vernière, *Spinoza et la pensée française*, 24; Berti, *Anticristianesimo e libertà*, 105.

reputation at court, in Paris, Saint-Glain and his wife, Marie, doubtless partly due to their Huguenot background, emanated an implacable hostility to kings, Louis XIV and Charles II especially. In the last year of his life, Saint-Glain published a news journal of anti-monarchical tendency together with his wife, in Amsterdam, the *Nouvelles solides et choisies* which, Bayle reported to his brother Joseph, his widow continued after his death in February 1684.[52] Following representations by royal envoys to the Amsterdam burgomasters, registering the French and English monarchs' grave "displeasure" at the content of certain French-language gazettes published in Amsterdam, Saint-Glain's widow was actually expelled from the city for three years as punishment for voicing vehement republican sentiments.[53]

According to Desmaizeaux's notes to Bayle's correspondence, published in the 1731 The Hague edition of Bayle's *Oeuvres Diverses* (and Maréchal later), it was Saint-Glain, not Jean Maximilien Lucas, the (less likely) alternative candidate who clandestinely translated Spinoza's *TTP* into French, raising a question that remains unresolved still today.[54] As the footnotes appended to the 1719 edition of *La Vie de Monsieur Benoit de Spinosa* express this uncertainty: "with regard to the author of the French translation [of the *TTP*] opinion is divided: some attribute it to the deceased Sr de Saint Glain, author of the *Gazette de Rotterdam*; others maintain that it is the Sr Lucas who became famous due to his *Quintessences*, always full of fresh invectives against Louis XIV. What is certain," adds Desmaizeaux, "is that the latter was a friend and disciple of Mr de Spinosa and the author of this Life."[55] Both men, in effect, were firm disciples of Spinoza.

Jean-Maximilien Lucas (1636?–97), the other possible translator of the *TTP* into French, descended from a prominent Huguenot family of publishers and preachers in Rouen and migrated to Holland around 1667. Like Saint-Glain, he was active as a French-language journalist in the Netherlands and fierce critic of Louis XIV, evidently spending some of his time gathering news in The Hague. Becoming a citizen of Amsterdam in 1670, when twenty-seven, in 1674, he married the then eighteen-year-old Maria Verjannen. So venomous were his sallies against Louis XIV and the French court, that he too found himself in a tense relationship with the Amsterdam regents and, in Paris, was even reported to be a contributory factor in the furious grudge Louis harboured against the Republic, ill-feeling some courtiers counted as an element behind his declaring war in 1672,[56] a point later echoed by Voltaire in his *Siècle de Louis XIV* where he remarks that the "the gazetteer in Holland had been too insolent."[57]

[52] Bayle to his brother, Joseph, Rotterdam, 10 April 1684 in Bayle, *Correspondance* iv, 71, 80n5.
[53] Van Eeghen, *Amsterdamse boekhandel* iii, 62.
[54] Maréchal, *Dictionnaire des Athées*, 273; Gullan-Whur, *Life of Spinoza*, 228–9, 267; Bove, *Vauvenargues ou le séditieux*, 73, 282, 313.
[55] [Lucas], *La Vie*, 36; Freudenthal/Walther, *Lebensgeschichte* ii, 24; Frampton, *Spinoza and the Rise*, 98; Van de Ven, *Printing Spinoza*, 205–6.
[56] Meininger and Van Suchtelen, *Liever met wercken*, 83–5; Berti, *Anticristianesimo e libertà*, 154.
[57] Voltaire, *Siècle de Louis XIV* i, 132; Meininger and van Suchtelen, *Liever met wercken*, 145n15.

Prosecuted and fined several times and finally permanently banished from Amsterdam for his anti-Louis XIV journalism, in the 1680s Lucas spent long periods in Leiden and again at The Hague. He became known later in particular as the "fameux auteur," as Bayle calls him, of the notorious journal *La Quintessence des nouvelles historiques, critiques,* [etc.], initiated in the year of the Glorious Revolution (1688) and published in the form of subversive anti-Louis XIV "lardons," or paper strips, easy to conceal and distribute in clandestine fashion.[58] Bayle loathed his extremely hostile satirizing of Louis XIV's court and, in 1697, designated Lucas someone who, over many years, had published "un si horrible detail de satyres infamantes et grossièrement fabuleuses [such a horrible bundle of infamous and grossly fictitious satires]."[59]

A bitter foe of kings, Lucas was supposedly also the author of the excessively eulogistic text often called the earliest biography of Spinoza. He is designated as such in the preface to the first published version of *La Vie de Monsieur Benoit de Spinosa* which appeared at The Hague, in 1719, though whether Lucas was really the author, and whether this so-called "first biography" really dates from as early a period (shortly after 1678) as is regularly assumed, remains open to question.[60] Grounds for dating this curious account to the period between 1678 and 1688, are two references in the text to the "dernières guerres [the late wars],"[61] the first recounting Condé's presence in Utrecht "au commencement" of the "last wars," the second noting that Spinoza was "not fortunate enough to see the end of the last wars" when the States General recovered the government of their territory previously half lost. Though far from conclusive, this evidence does suggest a date in or shortly after 1678 rather than, as some scholars suggest, after the Nine Years War (1688–97), or even after 1702. Use of the plural here probably reflects the fact that at different stages of the struggle of 1672–78 the Republic fought up to four different adversaries (France, England, Munster, and Cologne), while Louis waged war with the Habsburg Emperor and Spain on the Rhine as well as the Dutch, and each of these conflicts ended at a different time with a separate treaty. A rhetorical eulogy of limited historical value, the "Lucas biography" probably does date from between 1678 and 1688 and is thus probably the "earliest biography" apart from Jelles' preface to the *Opera Posthuma*. If not actually written by Lucas, it was probably penned by Saint-Glain, the alternative candidate.[62]

The French rendering of the *TTP*, meanwhile, was a development of particular historical importance due to its long and profound impact on the contemporary

---

[58] Vernière, *Spinoza et la pensée française*, 24–5; Berti, "Introduzione," xxxiv; Steenbakkers, "Jean-Maximilien Lucas," in *DDPhil* ii, 643–4; this journal, affirm Meininger and Van Suchtelen, began in 1689.

[59] Bayle, *Correspondance* x, 521; Laursen, "Impostors and Liars," 78.

[60] Berti, "Introduzione," xxxv; Lavaert, *Vrijheid, gelijkheid, veelheid*, 256–8.

[61] [Lucas], *La Vie*, 40; Berti, *Anticristianesimo e libertà*, 155; Freudenthal/Walther, *Lebensgeschichte* ii, 11.

[62] [Lucas], *La Vie*, 40, 56, 262n47; Frampton, *Spinoza and the Rise*, 100–3, 106–8; Steenbakers, "Spinoza beyond the Legends," 16–17; Nadler, *Spinoza: A Life*, 50, 52, 69.

scene and the eighteenth century, long remaining the chief vehicle of transmission of Spinoza's ideas into non-academic and non-ecclesiastical circles outside The Netherlands. A rendering of high quality and relatively strict in adhering to the original Latin, albeit consistently lending extra militancy and force to Spinoza's expressions, it was clearly translated by a native French speaker with a competent grasp of Spinoza's doctrines and insights, militantly hostile to both conventional religion and kings; its main failing, apart from a tendency to sharpen Spinoza's attacks on belief and churchmen, being this talented translator's conspicuous ignorance of Hebrew and clumsiness with the Hebrew quotes (seemingly confirming that Spinoza himself did not supervise preparation of this crucial text). Given the less than rigorous attitude to translating at the time, the translator felt free to insert dozens of small variations and amplifications of Spinoza's wording.[63] The French version must have been produced in the Netherlands, beginning perhaps shortly before Spinoza's death, though completed afterwards either in The Hague or in Amsterdam, in collaboration with Rieuwertsz. If begun before Spinoza died, it proceeded with his full knowledge, because at the back are to be found thirty pages of "Remarques" comprising French renderings of all but three of the thirty-three Latin *Adnotationes* to the *TTP* that Spinoza was working on during 1674–5 and which, at the time of his death, survived in his original Latin only in manuscript insertions added to just one or two of the Latin quarto copies.[64] The translation's penetration into France proved swift and efficient, helped no doubt by both Saint-Glain and Lucas being dedicated propagandists specializing in clandestine diffusion of subversive material.

If the translation was begun only after Spinoza's death, then Rieuwertsz, who received Spinoza's surviving papers from The Hague, must have organized the venture in Amsterdam, making the concluding notes available to the translator, or translators, there. For in their original Latin version, these notes remained unpublished until as late as 1802. From 1678, for the rest of the seventeenth century, and throughout the next, Spinoza's *Adnotationes*, while remaining wholly absent from all the Latin versions, were known to scholarship and the wider public exclusively from the French version. However, precisely because these "Remarques" concluding Rieuwertsz's French edition were not present in the published Latin versions, bibliographers and commentators wrongly assumed that, rather than being Spinoza's work which they actually were, they were added by the translator, Saint-Glain or Lucas, on his own initiative.[65]

Spinoza's name is nowhere mentioned in any of the French variants of the *TTP*; nor are those of the translator or publisher. The French *TTP* appeared in two main

---

[63] Vernière, *Spinoza et la pensée française*, 25; Akkerman, "Tractatus," 216; Moreau, "Traduire Spinoza," 226.
[64] Vernière, *Spinoza et la pensée française*, 25–6; Akkerman, "Tractatus," 213, 221; Totaro, "Introduzione," p. xli.
[65] Philipson, *Leben Benedikt's von Spinosa*, 111; Steenbakkers, "The Text," 37.

editions, in apparently eight separate variant printings with the follow up print runs contrived to resemble the first closely, a procedure involving much time-consuming work on replicating as nearly as possible the spacing and each page layout.[66] The variations are found mainly in the title-pages and the font, the text itself being nearly identical in all the variants. Recent bibliographical research has confirmed that all variants fall into two main series, designated X and Y, both series utilizing all three divergent titles but possibly in a different order from that given in Table 29.1. Made to resemble each other closely, the two editions present an intriguing puzzle for bibliophiles, the second being a careful line by line imitation of the first, albeit in the Y series, the type used is slightly larger and "considerably clearer," Bamberger remarks, than in X, and in the case of *La Clef du Santuaire*, the title with most variants, each of the four versions displays a different flowery emblem on the title-page.[67] In rare instances of Y5 Spinoza's portrait was bound in as well.[68] Most copies of the Y series which seemingly came out several years after X, included at least two of the false title-pages which, by contrast, are always used separately in X. A few of the Y series even include all three. Numerous small differences of spacing between the two main editions, X and Y, recorded by recent bibliographical research,[69] are noticeable only when closely comparing the different variants.

Perhaps the two most conspicuous differences in the text between X and Y, are the misprint in the top margin of fo. 9v, where "PREEACE" appears instead of "PREFACE,"[70] and on pages 147–8 where the last line of page 147 in X "mesme; tout cela neantmoins n'eût" moves across to become the top line of the next page in Y. A more general difference is that X's marginal notes are set in noticeably smaller type than the same notes in Y. On page 147 there is a footnote in which "Les Juigs" in X becomes "Les Iuifs" in Y, while the last word in the footnote, "nations," comes only half way across the page in X and at the end, on the right, in Y. "Temple" in X page 475 becomes "temple" with a small "t" in Y.[71] In all the X versions, on page 23, "Iob" is spelled with an "I," in all the Y variants it is spelled "Job." Because Y tends to be more finely bound than X, one can perhaps infer also that the latter was more specifically directed towards an upper class, aristocratic, or bibliophile audience.[72]

---

[66] Brunet, *Manuel du libraire* iii, 368.
[67] Kingma and Offenberg, "Bibliography," figures 13, 16, 17, and 18; Van de Ven, *Printing Spinoza*, 201.
[68] See *The Third Portion of the Beckford Library removed from Hamilton Palace* (London, 1885), no. 2161.
[69] Bamberger, "Early Editions," 32; Kingma and Offenberg, "Bibliography," 16–21; Van de Ven, *Printing Spinoza*, 220–2.
[70] Bamberger, "Early Editions," 32n58.
[71] Kingma and Offenberg, "Bibliography," 16–17; Van de Ven, *Printing Spinoza*, 220–1.
[72] Kingma and Offenberg, "Bibliography," 17n13.

Table 29.1 The false titles of the clandestine French *TTP*

Series	Title
X1	LA CLEF DU SANTUAIRE Par Un sçavant homme de nôtre Siecle. La où est l'Esprit de Dieu, la est la liberté (A LEYDE: Pierre Warnaer, 1678) [NB no accent on "Siecle"; has one accent on "La où," no accent on "la et," and a comma after "Dieu"].
X2	RÉFLEXIONS CURIEUSES d'un esprit des-Interessé sur LES MATIERES les plus importantes au salut, tant Public que Particulier (A Cologne: Claude Emanuel, 1678).
X3	TRAITTÉ Des Ceremonies Superstitieuses DES JUIFS tant Anciens que Modernes (Amsterdam: JACOB SMITH, 1678).
Y1	LA CLEF Du SANTUAIRE Par Un sçavant homme de nôtre Siecle. La ou est l'Esprit de Dieu là est la liberté (A LEYDE: Pierre Warnaer, 1678) [NB no accent on "Siecle"; lower case "u" in "LA CLEF Du"; no accent on "La ou"; no comma after "Dieu"].
Y2	LA CLEF DU SANTUAIRE Par Un sçavant homme de nôtre siecle. Là où est l'esprit de Dieu, là est la liberté (Leiden: Pierre Warnaer, 1678) [NB lower case "s" and no accent on "siecle"; capital "U" in "LA CLEF DU"; two accents in "Là où"; comma after "Dieu"].
Y3	LA CLEF DU SANCTUAIRE, Par Un sçavant homme de notre Siécle. Là où est l'Esprit de Dieu, là est la liberté (A LEYDE: Pierre Warnaer, 1678) [NB "C" in "SANCTUAIRE"; no accent on "notre"; capital "S" and wrong accent in "Siécle"; two accents in "Là où"].
Y4	uses two title-pages: RÉFLEXIONS CURIEUSES d'un Esprit des-Interessé sur LES MATIERES les plus importantes au salut, tant Public que Particulier (Cologne/Amsterdam: Cl. Emanuel/J. Smith, 1678) and TRAITTÉ Des Ceremonies Superstitieuses DES JUIFS tant Anciens que Modernes (Amsterdam: JACOB SMITH, 1678) [NB title identical, but the page emblem and spacing different from in X3].
Y5	[All three false title-pages included] In the IAS copy, the second title is LA CLEF DU SANTUAIRE but is the first in other copies.

Sources: Bamberger, "Early Editions," 27, 31–2; Kingma and Offenberg, "Bibliography," 16–21; completing and often superseding these studies, it should be noted, is Jeroen Van de Ven's comprehensively detailed monograph *Printing Spinoza*, here pp. 200–55.

According to the first published edition of Lucas's *La Vie*, clandestinely produced by Charles Levier at The Hague, in 1719, the X2 version entitled *Réflexions curieuses d'un esprit désinteressé*, of which Voltaire possessed a copy, appeared first, *La Clef du Santuaire* came second, and *Traitté des céremonies superstitieuses des Juifs* third (Figures 29.2–29.4).[73] This last bogus title was the version Bayle read, at Sedan, early in 1679, prior to settling in Holland, when he accounted it "definitely the book most full of impieties I ever read." Since even Bayle failed to realize initially that he was reading the work of "le fameux Spinoza" as he called

---

[73] [Lucas], *La Vie*, 36n; Voltaire, *Questions* vi, 48n.

> # REFLEXIONS
> ## CURIEUSES
> *d'un*
> ## Eſprit des-Interreſſé
> *ſur*
> ## LES MATIERES
> *Les plus Importantes au Salut, tant Public que Particulier.*
>
> A COLOGNE,
> Chez CLAUDE EMANUEL,
> 1678.

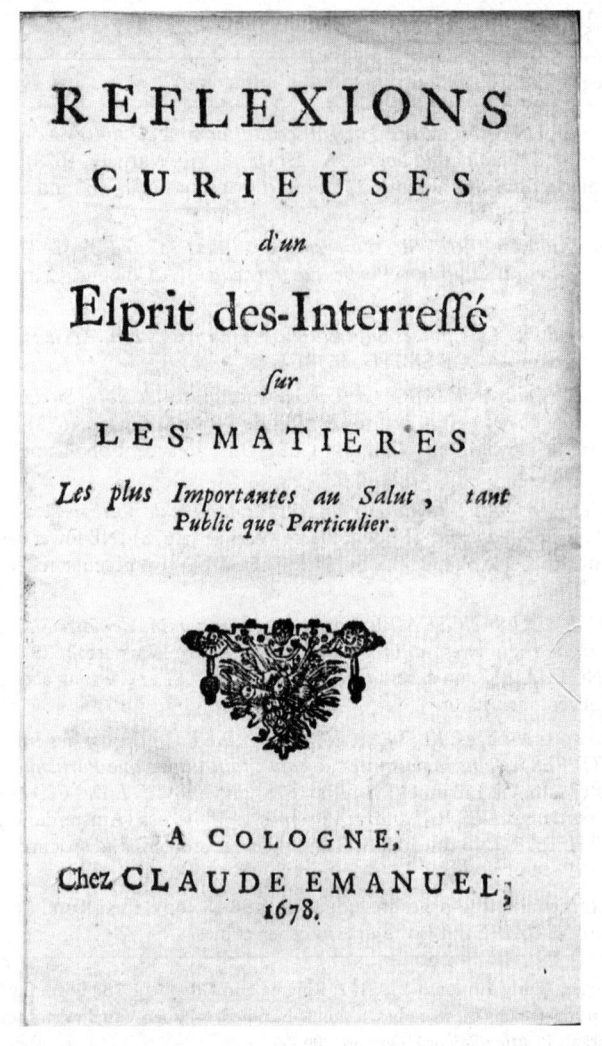

Figure 29.2 [Spinoza], *Reflexions curieuses d'un esprit des-interressé sur Les Matieres les plus Importantes au Salut, tant Public que Particulier* (at 'Cologne' [i.e. Amsterdam], 1678). IAS Spinoza Research Collection.

him already then, most readers must have taken rather longer to make the connection and realize that this impious book was Spinoza's *TTP* in French.[74] However, a note added later by Desmaizeaux to his edition of Bayle's *Oeuvres Diverses* offers a different order of titles that was then adopted as the supposedly correct one throughout the eighteenth century,[75] and inserted later into another print run of Levier's publication of Lucas's biography.

---

[74] Bayle, *Oeuvres diverses* iv, 570.   [75] Philipson, *Leben Benedikt's von Spinosa*, 110.

> LA CLEF
>
> DU
>
> SANTUAIRE
>
> *Par*
>
> Un sçavant homme de nôtre Siecle
>
> *La ou est l'Esprit de Dieu là est la liberté,* 2. Epitre aux Corinthiens Chap. 3. vers. 17.
>
> A LEYDE,
> Chez PIERRE WARNAER,
> M. DC. LXXVIII.

Figure 29.3 [Spinoza], *La clef du santuaire* [sic]. A Leyde [i.e. Amsterdam]: Chez Pierre Warnaer [i.e. Jan Rieuwertsz], 1678. IAS Spinoza Research Collection.

According to Desmaizeaux, Saint-Glain originally called his French translation *La Clef du Santuaire*, the choice of the term "Santuaire" being especially apt as an arcane code already familiar among the clandestine atheistic underground in France, signifying the "sanctuary" of theological-political secrets princes and ecclesiastics employ to hold society in thrall to superstition.[76] "But this title having created quite a stir," its notoriety, it was feared, would endanger distribution and sales, so the title was changed to *Traitté des céremonies superstitieuses des Juifs* and

---

[76] Mori, *Athéisme et dissimulation*, 267–8.

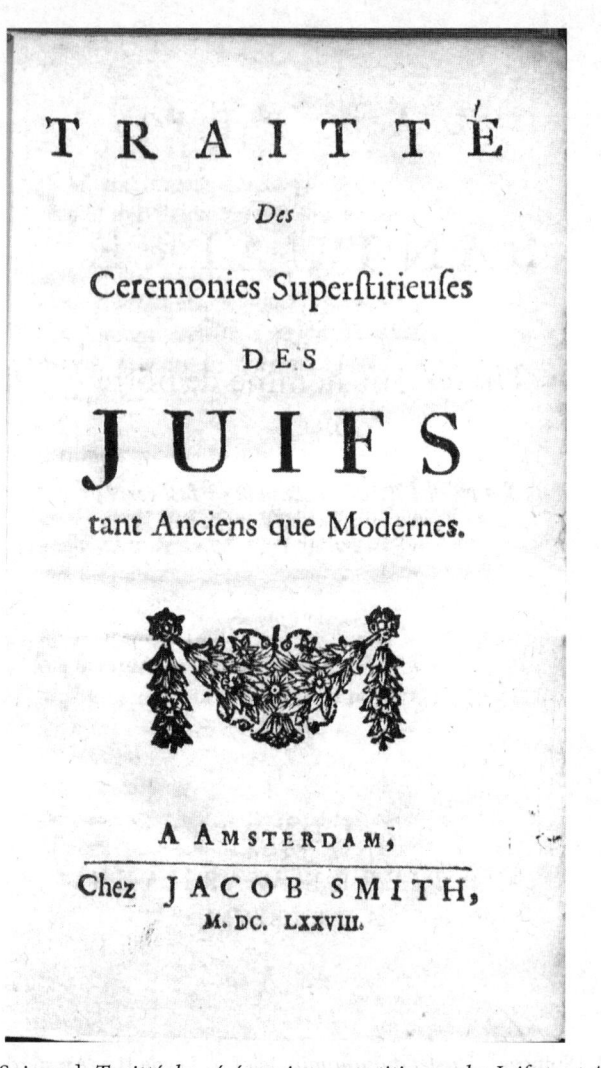

Figure 29.4 [Spinoza], *Traitté des cérémonies superstitieuses des Juifs tant Anciens que Modernes*. Amsterdam, 1678. IAS Spinoza Research Collection.

then, afterwards, "for the same reason," altered again to deflect commotion and unwelcome attention, to *Réflexions curieuses d'un esprit désintéressé*, the third and last title employed. These details, Desmaizeaux says, "he had from Mr Morelli" who "knew le Sr. de St. Glain particularly well [avoit connu particulièrement]."[77] In the early nineteenth century, the renowned French bibliographer, Jacques-Charles Brunet, pronounced *La Clef du Santuaire* the rarest of the three French

---

[77] Bayle, *Oeuvres diverses* iv, 571n, 872; Brunet, *Manuel du libraire* iii, 367–8; Bamberger, "Early Editions," 32n58.

titles; and the Y exemplars containing all three titles the most sought after by bibliophiles.[78]

The French *TTP* exerted a lasting impact on the early Enlightenment. Whether Saint-Glain or Lucas translated it, and whether or not Lucas wrote the "first biography" matters less than the fact that a wholly new French-language subversive strand of *libertinage* was in this way forged in Holland in the late 1670s, fusing Saint-Évremond's high-society *épicurisme* with hardcore Spinozism powerfully rendered into French, to produce a formidably pervasive underground ideology. One might perhaps equally well consider it an adept "takeover" of Saint-Évremond's and Vossius' privately irreligious, literary *libertinage érudit* by Spinoza's "secte [sect]," as Stouppe was the first to call it, rather than a merger. The French *TTP* served as a bridge between two distinct underground traditions, each gaining ground in its own right, creating an expanded "Spinozism" enriched with French-style libertinism feeding the new highly subversive democratic republican irreligious libertinism spreading beneath the surface down to the 1740s, notably in the French clandestine philosophical literature circulating in manuscript and the works of Boulainvilliers and Vauvenargues,[79] before fully maturing in the mid-eighteenth century in the writings of Diderot and d'Holbach. D'Holbach most certainly merged his atheistic materialism with a resolute and powerful democratic crypto-republicanism (albeit this has until recently long remained unacknowledged by modern scholars).[80] French-language "Spinozism," as Voltaire condemned and rejected it, would come to constitute the very bedrock of the Radical Enlightenment.

---

[78] Brunet, *Manuel du libraire* iii, 367.   [79] Bove, *Vauvenargues ou le séditieux*, 31–3, 73–4.
[80] On this point see Israel, *Enlightenment that Failed*, 179–214.

PART V
LAST YEARS

30
Disaster Year (1672)

30.i Slump and Collapse

Since its founding in the 1570s, the Dutch Republic had undergone several grave crises dragging its very existence and legitimacy into question. But none was graver or more unforeseen than the "disaster year [rampjaar]" of 1672. If war with France had seemed likely since February 1672, the English crown's surprise attack on the Dutch, alongside Louis XIV, and the Republic's ensuing near collapse were utterly unexpected. "No clap of thunder in a fair frosty day, could more astonish the world," recalled Sir William Temple later, than England's "declaration of war against Holland in 1672."[1] But far more traumatic for most was the subsequent French invasion and ensuing overthrow of the De Witt regime and collapse of the "True Freedom," later that summer, and its alarming consequences for the Western world's then prime republican model and its freedoms and toleration.

The scale of the mounting threat—strategic, political, and economic—to the Republic, its religious minorities, cultural life, and universities quickly became manifest to all. Spinoza became as immersed as anyone in contemplating this brutally sudden combined assault launched by France and England together, without justification, driven in his view purely by monarchical arrogance, ambition, and greed, and especially preoccupied with the Republic's ensuing political collapse, his involvement being reflected during his last years in devoting much of his remaining time to political and social theory, absorbing and pondering the implications of the disastrous upheaval, and those intricacies of the contemporary political drama he considered not yet adequately covered in the *TTP*.

England commenced her assault by "falling upon their Smyrna fleet, and in consequence of that (however it failed) by a formal declaration, in which we gave reasons for our quarrel, while France contented themselves to give no other for their part in it, than only the glory of that king."[2] Actually, the pretexts Charles II offered were scarcely less flimsy morally and judicially than those of Louis XIV (Figure 30.1) who scarcely bothered to justify his fury against the Dutch for thwarting his annexation of the southern Netherlands in 1667–8 and generally obstructing his pretensions and expansionism. Louis and Charles colluded driven

---

[1] Temple, *Memoirs*,17; Haley, *English Diplomat*, 287; Sonnino, *Louis XIV and the Origins*, 191.
[2] Temple, *Memoirs*, 17; Costerus, *Historisch Verhael*, 141–2; *Histoire de Guillaume III* i, 26.

Figure 30.1 *Louis XIV of France (1638–1715), in 1670* by Claude Lefèbvre. Reproduction courtesy of incamerastock/Alamy Stock Photo.

by overweening royal ambition and contempt for an exasperatingly small republic obstructing their glory.[3] Both loathed the values and pretensions of the recently created upstart mini-state whose style and attitudes, to them sheer insolence, they found intolerable. Deeply uncertain through 1672 and early 1673 whether the Republic would actually survive, Spinoza apparently pondered, in the interests of preserving himself, his philosophical legacy and manuscripts, whether it would be best to uproot and migrate abroad as numerous Dutch writers, artists, and others did at this time, temporarily or permanently. Amidst the gloom of disaster, defeat, and collapse of public morale engulfing Dutch society during these traumatic months, Spinoza felt driven to rethink his democratic republicanism, the characteristics of republics, the character of international power politics, the plausibility

---

[3] Jones, *Anglo-Dutch Wars*, 181–2; Van Malssen, *Louis XIV d'après les pamphlets*, 20; Sonnino, *Louis XIV and the Origins*, 192.

of his favoured "large councils" and notions of citizenship, and his opinions on the bitterly contested role of the Stadholder.

Unprepared for a combined seaborne and land assault on such a scale, and not believing England was "in earnest, till the blow was given, but [thinking] our unkindness and expostulations of late, would end at last either in demands of money, or the Prince of Orange's restitution to the authority of his ancestors," the Dutch found themselves caught totally off guard. Spain, Austria, and the other monarchs "concerned in their safety, could not believe that, after having sav'd Flanders out of the hands of France, we would suffer Holland to fall into the same danger, and my lord Arlington told me at the time that the court of France did not believe it themselves, till the blow was struck in the attack on the Smyrna fleet," that March.[4] Convinced he had more to gain for his throne, if not for his realm, by linking arms with Louis, Charles II likewise affixed royal arrogance to religious intolerance and stunning unconcern for his own country's true interests.

The full gravity of the situation became evident only on 6 April when Louis declared war in alliance with England. Special prayer services for preservation of the state were laid on in all the Republic's main churches, in Utrecht cathedral from 4 May.[5] The prince-bishop of Munster declared war on 18 May, and the Archbishop-Elector of Cologne soon after. The United Provinces faced a full-scale simultaneous attack from the south, west, and east, by France and her German allies on land, and England by sea and land, aimed at stripping the Republic of its standing, trade primacy, wealth, naval power, military capacity, colonies, and independent political clout and decisively shifting Europe's Protestant–Catholic balance in favour of royal absolutism and Catholicism. The Republic of the "True Freedom" with its universally envied trade and wealth was suddenly plunged by brutal monarchical assault into free fall and nowhere else were all dimensions of the Republic's virtual collapse so starkly evident as at The Hague where Spinoza found himself well-placed to observe the frightening general disintegration of morale and astounding mix of despair and fury behind the explosive resurgence of ideological conflict that followed.

A major contributory factor to the speed of the collapse was the "extreme dry season that made rivers fordable where they had never been esteem'd so before."[6] This and a disastrous lack of defensive preparations and alliances enabled the invading French to register "prodigious successes" from the moment they approached the Republic's borders. In early June, Dutch garrisons on the Lower Rhine at Rheinberg, Orsoy, Wesel, and Schenkenschans that had defied Spain for

---

[4] Temple, *Memoirs*, 18. [5] GA Utrecht MS. Acta Kerkeraad 10, res. 4 May 1672.
[6] Temple, *Memoirs*, 19; Rowen, *John de Witt*, 561–2, 829–31, 834.

eighty years, fell to Louis in under a week, leaving the whole Republic aghast and in deep dejection.[7] Crossing the Rhine, south of Arnhem, under the eyes of the monarch, on 12 June, French columns outflanked the entire Dutch defensive system. The States General had no alternative but to abandon their second line of defence, the Ijssel line (and, with it, extensive Dutch territory), and pull their hopelessly disorganized forces back. From De Witt's standpoint, matters were not helped when William III, since February 1672 captain-general of the armed forces, arrested a senior officer, Colonel Jean Barton, marquis de Montbas, appointed by and supportive of the De Witt regime, for abandoning his post. His arrest caused an avalanche of talk of De Wittian treachery and "treason." Taken into custody, Montbas, surrounded by mobs, was almost lynched in Utrecht.[8]

The regent leadership staked everything on holding Holland and Zeeland by means of a tactic that was ruinous for local farmers and peasants—breaking the dykes and flooding the areas providing access from the east while fortifying the "water-line" running from Muiden on the Zuider Zee, in front of Amsterdam, southwards to the great rivers. Everything east of that line was abandoned to the French and to the Munsterites who occupied Deventer and Zwolle later in June. Utrecht offered no resistance to the advancing French who arrived there on 13 June. The city's regents opened their gates, warning the city's Reformed preachers to remain extremely prudent in their conduct and on no account in their sermons incite the people against the occupiers, but, rather, instil "steadfastness of faith, godliness and obedience to the authorities."[9] The only town in the eastern provinces of Gelderland and Overijssel to resist at all was Nijmegen which held out briefly before surrendering on 9 July 1672.

Meanwhile, "the animosities of the parties in Holland," the Republic's ceaseless internal political conflict, noted Temple, "long express'd under their new constitution and De Witt's ministry, began to flame again upon this misfortune of their state. The Prince's friends talk'd loud and boldly, that there was no way to satisfie England, but restoring the Prince, and that the baseness and cowardice of their troops, were the effects of turning out all officers of worth and bravery for their inclinations to the Prince, and mean fellows brought in for no other desert, than their enmity declar'd to the House of Orange." Charles and Louis believed the young prince could readily be turned into a tool of their ambition.

> Upon this, all men expected a sudden change; the States were in disorder and irresolute what to do; the troops were without a general, and, which is worse, without heart; and tho De Ruyter, by admirable conduct kept the infection of

---

[7] Van der Hoeven, *Leeven en Dood* ii, 356; Roorda, *Partij en factie*, 90–4; Rowen, *John de Witt*, 834–6.

[8] *Sleutel Ontsluytende de Boecke-kas*,12; Wicquefort, *Journael of dagelijcksch verhael* i, 5–6; Bruin, *Geheimhouding*, 540.

[9] GA Utrecht Kerkeraad 10, res. 17 and 20 June 1672; Israel, *Dutch Republic*, 798.

these evils out of his fleet, which was our [i.e. England's] part to deal with, yet faction, distrust, sedition and distraction, made such entrances upon the State and the army, when the French troops first invaded them, that of all the towns and fortresses on the German side (held impregnable in all their former wars), not one besides Maastricht made any shew of resistance, and the French became immediately masters of all the inland parts of the Provinces, in as little time as travelers usually employ to see and consider them.[10]

Even without counting the Munsterites and forces of Cologne, the French army of invasion amounted to 118,000 infantry and 12,500 cavalry, initially outnumbering the defending Dutch army (without the civic militias) by four to one. Inferior too to the combined Anglo-French fleet in numbers of warships, the Dutch faced a grim situation also at sea. The decision of De Ruyter and De Witt's brother, Cornelis, the plenipotentiary with the fleet, to cross the North Sea and attack despite the odds, pitting their sixty-two against eighty-two vessels in the allied fleet off the English coast, resulted in one of the decisive battles of the war, the Battle of Solebay, on 6 June 1672, off Southwold, Suffolk, causing heavy losses to both sides. It was no overwhelming victory, but De Ruyter destroyed the English flagship, the *Royal James*, and sufficiently mauled five more of England's "first-rates" to prevent Charles joining the French and Munsterites, thwarting the plan to land troops from the seaward side during the critical summer months. Thanks to the fleet, the drama of general collapse played out from early June without the English being able to directly intervene from their side as planned.

The sudden stark defencelessness of the Republic shocked all Europe. Assailed by land and sea by the continent's two leading monarchies, morale plummeted, commerce and finance were paralyzed, in home waters commercial shipping came to a complete standstill, and the Amsterdam Exchange registered its steepest fall of early modern times. From its peak of 566, in July 1671, as the war clouds gathered, the VOC share price dropped to 406 in February, 370 in March, and 311 in April, before plummeting to 250, in June, its lowest point for the entire Golden Age, albeit recovering slightly though still hovering at a calamitous 290 during July.[11] Academic and cultural life withered. Student enrolments at Groningen (under siege by the Munsterites from late June until 28 August) and doubtless other universities fell to the lowest levels recorded in the century.[12] Public works and building everywhere ceased, including construction of the half-built new Portuguese synagogue of Amsterdam where the Sephardic community drastically cut its annual expenditures, including remittances for Jewish communities in the

---

[10] Temple, *Memoirs*, 19; *Histoire de Guillaume III* i, 27–8.
[11] Israel, *Conflicts of Empires*, 320, 328; Petram, *World's First Stock Exchange*, 161.
[12] Van Berkel, *Universiteit van het noorden*, 220.

866   LAST YEARS

Holy Land.[13] The Amsterdam theatre closed its doors and on recovering, reopening in 1677, failed to regain its old freedom to stage political issues enjoyed under the "True Freedom."[14] That was far from being the only setback impinging directly on Spinoza's circle. The entire publishing industry and world of booksellers was severely stricken along with virtually everything else. The unprecedented slump affected everyone in innumerable ways. The bankruptcy of an Amsterdam paint dealer in April 1673, for example, left him indebted to Rieuwertsz, for books delivered, for sixty-seven guilders but for much more substantial sums to Jelles and Glazemaker.[15]

The art market slumped disastrously and never fully recovered.[16] Vermeer, his art dealing business ruined, suffered financial and emotional collapse.[17] Having previously relied on producing and selling just two or three high quality paintings of his own each year, which, together with his other art dealing, brought in some 600 guilders annually, now, unable to sell his pictures or those by others he had in stock, his wife afterwards testified, and faced by the "very great burden of his children, having nothing of his own," fell into a "decline and decadence" so severe that in a short time he "went from being healthy to being dead." The painter who devoted his art to representing the immanent and after converting without conviction to Catholicism for family reasons, seemingly privately mocked that faith and its pretensions in his last painting *The Allegory of Faith* (1670–2), died in December 1675 amidst the ruin of his art business.[18] The greatest seascape painter of the day, Willem van de Velde (1633–1707), present with the fleet at the great naval battle at Solebay sketching the fighting, unable to continue working in Holland due "to the bad conditions here during these wars," transferred to England later in 1672.[19]

Meetings of the Reformed Church councils, classes, and synods that summer were deeply sombre events. Everywhere one encountered lament and fear. Such a catalogue of calamity could scarcely be anything but divine retribution for heinous sins and wrongdoing, the Reformed Church forcefully reminded everyone, exhorting their congregations that there was much that urgently needed correcting. The "wretched conjuncture" in which "our dear Netherlands" found itself, as the Haarlem Reformed consistory expressed their feelings, on 10 June 1672, issued from the Almighty's anger at the recent rising tide of sin—the people "taking

---

[13] GA Amsterdam PJG 334/19, p. 648; Scholberg, "Miguel de Barrios," 122.
[14] Duits, "De Vryheid, wiens waardy," 123, 126; Bordoli, *Etica, Arte, Scienza*, 106–7.
[15] Van der Tak, "Jellesz' Life and Business," 19.
[16] Israel, *Dutch Primacy*, 293–9; Malcolm, *Editor's Introduction*, 295–7; Bok, *Vraag en aanbod*, 101; Munt, "Impact of the *Rampjaar*," 24–30.
[17] Binstock, *Vermeer's Family Secrets*, 237–8; Hornäk, *Spinoza und Vermeer*, 198; Bok, *Vraag en aanbod*, 101, 123.
[18] Binstock, *Vermeer's Family Secrets*, 224–7, 298, 356; Hornäk, *Spinoza und Vermeer*, 245; Liedtke, *Vermeer and the Delft School*, 168.
[19] Munt, "Impact of the *Rampjaar*," 25; Cordingly, "Introduction," 13.

God's holy name in vain with their swearing, whoring, breaking the Sabbath, less than regular church attendance, profanity, adultery and such like." Calvinist preachers' sermons generally attributed the country's collapse to society's reprehensible sins, but by no means all specifically targeted the De Witt regime in a politically calculating manner, deliberately stoking dissatisfaction and unrest. For example, Willem Saldenus—De Lantman's successor at Delft, in 1664, and from 1677 also in The Hague—discouraged aggressive conduct and attitudes towards the regime despite agreeing with his colleague, De Lantman, Spinoza's old sparring partner, that church authority in the Republic was too weak and society too slow to suppress immorality and *exorbitantien*, shut the theatres, and curtail toleration of Catholics,[20] as well as suppress that "horrible book," the *TTP*, written by the "ex-Jew" and pestilential *novator*, Benedictus Spinoza, and other execrable attacks on Scripture's integrity.[21] Others, however, with De Lantman conspicuous among them, more actively strove to incite popular fury against De Witt and the "True Freedom."[22]

According to Calvinist preachers, a wide spectrum of sins needed addressing and numerous defects correcting. What the flood of anti-De Witt pamphlets of the summer of 1672 demanded were far-ranging political and legal changes restoring what the Calvinists considered proper order in the eyes of God especially by purging the Republic's town halls of seditious elements, the vile horde of Arminians, Barneveldists, Loevesteiners, Socinians, freethinkers, Cartesians, and papists infiltrating officeholding and positions of responsibility. Purging the city governments, together with De Witt's eagerly expected downfall, would open the door, it was hoped, for a general moral and religious "Further Reformation" of the sort vigorously exhorted likewise by the Reformed consistories, classes, and synods.

Among society's key defects highlighted was once again the scandal of "licentious publishing," pernicious books insufficiently suppressed by the secular authorities that the public should not be reading.[23] The four most reprehensible titles on the North Holland synod's list of works not being targeted energetically enough were the "*Bibliotheca Fratrum Polonorum*, the *Leviathan*, the *Philosophia Scriptura Interpres*," and that "outstandingly godless book *Tractatus Theologico-Politicus*."[24] Numerous consistories echoed these sentiments, often repeating word-for-word the North Holland synod's label "outstandingly godless book" when decrying the *TTP*; the classes of Alkmaar, meeting six weeks later, on 19 July, and Edam, meeting on 25 July, besides decrying the same books demanded

---

[20] Van de End, *Guiljelmus Saldenus*, 189–94.
[21] Saldenus, *Otia theologica*, 23–36; Van de End, *Guiljelmus Saldenus*, 190-3.
[22] Roorda, *Partij en factie*, 107; Melles, *Joachim Oudaan*, 87; Munt, "Impact of the *Rampjaar*," 30–1; Smith, "Politics of Tragedy," 227.
[23] GA Haarlem, Acta Kerkeraad 9 (1669–82), res. 27 May and 10 June 1672.
[24] GA Haarlem, Acta Kerkeraad 9 (1669–82), res. 10 June 1672.

more zeal in collecting evidence about how these pernicious texts circulated to discover where and by whom they were being bought and sold.[25] Barraged by petitions for tougher book suppression, in August, the Holland town governments promised to expedite stricter measures but warned the war crisis so burdened their committees at that juncture that it would be difficult to find time and opportunity to deal with such matters.[26]

Within weeks, in June and July 1672, the Republic sank from prosperous and confident stability to stark humiliation and calamity seemingly all but certain to extinguish the United Provinces as a free and independent great power, preserving it only in some territorially truncated and subordinate form. During that exceptionally fraught summer unruly mobs and civic militias raucously took to the streets, intervening in the political process more vigorously than at any other point in the Golden Age. In several cities in the unoccupied zone demonstrators disrupted all sense of normality, violently stoking the ideological warfare between republicans and Orangists, disturbing even normally perfectly tranquil towns, like Enkhuizen and Hoorn. By contrast, The Hague, where agitation seethed over many weeks and De Lantman stood among the foremost figures stirring unrest in the wake of the invasion, became the epicentre of the incitement, rowdiness, and general breakdown of normalcy.[27]

"The King of France march'd as far as Utrecht," records Temple,

> where he fix'd his camp and his court, and from thence began to consider of the ways to possess himself of the rest, which was defended only by their situation, upon some flat lands, that, as they had by infinite labour in canals and digues been either gain'd or preserv'd from inundations, so they were subject to them, upon opening the sluices, whenever the Dutch found no other way of saving their country but by losing it. This, at least, was generally believ'd in the French camp and court; and, as I have heard, was the preservation of the state: for that king unwilling to venture the honour and advantage of such conquests as he had made that summer, upon the hazards of a new sort of war with a merciless element, where neither conduct nor courage were of use, resolv'd to leave the rest to the practices of peace with the States, upon the advantage of the terms he stood in, and the small distance between them; or, if these should not succeed, then he trusted to the frosts of the following winter, which seldom fail in that country, to make all passable and safe for troops and carriages themselves that in summer would be impossible either from the waters, or the depth of the soil.[28]

---

[25] RA Noord-Holland, Haarlem, Geref. Kerk, Classis Alkmaar (1670–78), fo. 206. Acta, 19 July 1672; RA North Holland, Geref. Kerk, Acta Classis Edam, p. 5, res. 25 July 1672.
[26] ARH Ned. Herv. Kerk OSA184, pp. 6, 37. Acta 2–6 Aug. 1672 (Enkhuizen).
[27] De Bie, Lindeboom, and Itterzon, *Biografisch Woordenboek* v, 575.
[28] Temple, *Memoirs*, 19–20.

On 24 June, Louis issued a general decree in the French-occupied areas: liberty of conscience would continue for now along with all existing liberties and privileges, except that Catholics now enjoyed equal footing with the Reformed and could now maintain public churches and conduct religious processions in the open. In late June, the Utrecht Dom, the city's principal Reformed church—an imposing Gothic structure immediately adjoining the main university buildings, dating back to 1254, then (but not after 1674) the largest church in all the northern Netherlands, unique in historical stature, size, and grandeur, and seat of the presiding bishop in the northern Netherlands since the tenth century—once again reverted to being a pre-Reformation cathedral. Those celebrating the change now joyously removed all Protestant symbols, carrying the pews and chairs outside, the best being sold, the rest burnt in the churchyard, while a team of *klopjes*, Catholic "spiritual maidens," washed down the cathedral interior preparatory to Catholic images being reinstalled for the first time since 1580. The Protestant pulpit was removed too and "whipped" outside. Reconsecrated as a Catholic cathedral two weeks after the French entry, on 30 June Old Style (Julian) 1672—under the New Style (Gregorian) calendar, 10 July—the famous Dom was rededicated for Catholic worship with a great display of pomp presided over by Louis' personal confessor, the Cardinal de Bouillon.[29] The public spaces adjoining cathedral and university became for now a "Catholic space" used for processions, outdoor parading of crosses and images and administering of sacraments, and even, for important persons, burials.[30] Utrecht's Catholics who constituted between a quarter and a third of the city's population were jubilant; most of the populace felt bitterly resentful.

Under the surrender terms, Louis agreed to permit most churches and the university to remain for now in Reformed hands. But in every occupied town, the main church and some additional churches were reassigned for Catholic worship.[31] As in 1666, in Overijssel and the parts of Gelderland occupied by the prince-bishop, many Catholics also openly demonstrated support for the invading Munsterites.[32] Jesuit colleges were provisionally set up at Zwolle and Arnhem, and monasteries and friaries at Deventer, Kampen, Harderwijk, and Amersvoort. Louis' carefully selected governor of Utrecht, the Swiss former Protestant general, Pierre Alexandre Stouppe (Stoppa) (1620–1701), now a Catholic convert, worried by the seething religious passion on all sides, was far from insensitive to outraged Protestant sensibilities. To check disorder and interconfessional strife, he issued orders, early in July, that henceforth on Sundays Protestant preachers and

---

[29] Spiertz, *L'Église catholique*, 121.
[30] Wicquefort, *Journael of dagelijcksch verhael* i, 40–1, 69; Van Malssen, *Louis XIV d'après les pamphlets*, 22; Forclaz, "Rather French than Subject," 520–1.
[31] Wicquefort, *Journael of dagelijcksch verhael* i, 104; *Le Conseil d'Extorsion*, 32, 52; Forclaz, "Rather French than Subject," 516.
[32] *Le Conseil d'Extorsion*, 50; Forclaz, "Rather French than Subject," 526.

Catholic priests alike must "admonish their congregations in their sermons to avoid all mockery, ridicule and giving offence."[33] Utrecht's burgomasters besought their citizens not to allow confessional violence to destroy the common peace of the city.

Louis assigned priority for now to restoring order and stability. Unlike towns under Munsterite control, such as Zutphen, Zwolle, Kampen, and Deventer where the prince-bishop ejected Protestant magistrates replacing them with Catholics, in Utrecht sitting Protestant regents were confirmed in office with Van Velthuysen remaining in a presiding role. A leading Cartesian and one of Spinoza's severest critics, Van Velthuysen was the regent who had actually handed the city keys to the French, in June 1672, and subsequently was chief mediator between the city government (*vroedschap*) and the French garrison.[34] In early August, the Utrecht city government drew up five articles revising relations between Protestants and Catholics "for preservation of unity and peace among the city's inhabitants," forbidding Protestants and Catholics to insult each other's religious sensibilities, prohibiting polemical sermons, and changing the board of trustees administering the civic poor relief chest into one of confessional parity consisting of eight Protestants and eight Catholics sworn to uphold confessional parity when administering charity to poor families and the sick and in their administrative decisions.[35] The onerous new taxes the French introduced were also administered by a mixed Protestant–Catholic commission fixing assessments supposedly on the basis of parity. In September, the university auditorium was emptied of military stores and lectures resumed without change to the university administration and leadership.[36]

Collapse of the land defences and retreat to the "water-line" placed over half the Republic's territory under the direct or virtual control of its enemies. Undisguised defeatism reigned in many quarters and many or most were ready to fall at Louis' feet and plead for whatever terms the Republic could salvage. If commerce and shipping were paralyzed, work of many kinds ceased or was interrupted with large stretches of farmland flooded. But amidst the pandemonium there ensued also a huge upsurge in polemical political pamphlets, many carrying sensational accusations originating by word of mouth, detailing scandalous official neglect of duty and "treason." No less than 610 Dutch pamphlets appeared between June and August 1672, a high proportion calling for a thorough purge of "the traitors," the filth of "Loevesteiners, Barneveldists and Arminians" from city governments, those who had opened the town halls, as one tract put it, to "freethinkers,

---

[33] GA Utrecht vroedschapresoluties 1668–79, fo. 200. Res. 5 July 1672.
[34] GA Utrecht vroedschapresoluties 1668–79, fo. 200. Res. 8 July 1672; Wicquefort, *Journael of dagelijcksch verhael* i, 16; Forclaz, "Rather French than Subject," 522.
[35] GA Utrecht vroedschapresoluties 1668–79, fo. 205v. Res. 12 Aug. 1672; Forclaz, "Rather French than Subject," 518–19, 522.
[36] GA Utrecht vroedschapresoluties 1668–79, fo. 209. Res. 16 Sept. 1672.

papists, etc."[37] The people were stirred up further by accusations that De Witt was not only a "tyrannical" autocrat like Cromwell but religiously deeply suspect, possessing a personal library brimming with Socinian, pro-Arminian, and other "impious" literature.[38]

Holland's regents, especially those considered allies of De Witt, were by now in a state of utmost alarm. At Delft, by mid-June, the regents were so on edge and fearful of mass flight that, to set "a good example" and forestall all "disorders and tumult," they forbade any member of the regent body to leave town or send household belongings away without the burgomasters' express consent.[39] Most sitting regents were ready to surrender outright, offering to cede the Generality Lands and pay indemnities to their conquerors, including at least three, Van Velthuysen, Van Nieuwstad, and Hugo Boxel of Gorcum, who afterwards had long, detailed discussions with Spinoza, doubtless about this as well as other controversial matters. Had Louis been less insistent on intimidating the Republic into an even more abject surrender, and Amsterdam less resolute in refusing to submit to the already grovelling terms the rest seemed ready to accept, preferring rather to continue the war, the struggle might well have ended there and then.[40]

Some anti-De Witt pamphlets identified among the worst pestilences and "most active" agitators betraying and ruining Dutch society the "new upcoming philosophers," that is "our Cartesian Brothers, just as formerly it was the Arminian preachers."[41] Especially venomous were a batch of pamphlets accusing De Witt of designing an entire new religious framework for the Republic. These "Arminiaensche staats-luyden [Aminian statesmen]," claimed such Voetian propaganda, over the last twenty years, openly violating the laws, refused to permit the public church to be the sole church flourishing in the Republic but ensured "Jews, Turks, heathens, atheists, Socinians, papists, Arminians, Lutherans, Mennonites, Quakers, Labadists" and others were allowed to flourish and increase, merely for the sake of expanding population and economic growth. With that vile motive, that quick-witted betrayer, De Witt, allegedly no less a theologian than jurist and mathematician, supposedly "brewed all the religions into one, turning them into one religion, the De Witt religion, whose followers will be named the Wittisten." Vilest of all, De Witt and the other hypocrites posing as statesmen had for years ensured that "in all the main cities no Voetian preachers should be appointed because these study the Bible more than Descartes!"[42]

---

[37] *Deductie van den Tegenwoordigen Toestant*, 14; Stern, *Orangism*, 143; Van de Klashorst, "De ware vrijheid," 169; Munt, "Impact of the *Rampjaar*," 12–19, 36.
[38] Roorda, *Partij en factie*, 190–1; Israel, *Dutch Republic*, 798–9.
[39] GA Delft MS. 1e Afdeling 13/5 fo. 81v. Res. Vroedschap 16 June 1672.
[40] Haley, *English Diplomat*, 289; Boxer, "Some Thoughts," 82; Israel, *Dutch Republic*, 800–1.
[41] *Staat-Kundige droom* (1672) (Kn. 10493), p. A3v; *Deductie van den Tegenwoordigen Toestant* (1672) (Kn. 10381), 14.
[42] *Hydra of Monster-Dier*, 13–15; Japikse, "Spinoza en De Witt," 3, 7; Munt, "Impact of the *Rampjaar*," 14.

Among the guiltiest ruling regents from a Voetian perspective was Van Velthuysen at Utrecht. To the Reformed Church council of Utrecht with its strict Calvinist orientation there appeared to be close links between Van Velthuysen's Cartesianism, his exalting toleration, fiercely critical attitude to church authority, and arranging surrender to the French. Since publishing his 1669 Dutch-language treatise on idolatry and superstition Van Velthuysen had been locked in a gruelling feud with the local Reformed consistory over the nature and extent of ecclesiastical jurisdiction, and his refusal to accept that the preachers' authority "is a special ordinance of God and institution of Christ" and that it is indeed from Christ that preachers alone possess the right to preach God's word and administer the sacraments. Where Van Velthuysen held there was no Christian doctrine stipulating that Christ had entrusted the "keys to the kingdom of Heaven" to leaders and heads of churches, the consistory countered that all Reformed preachers insisted that "the keys to the kingdom of Heaven were indeed given to the churches and church principals, and not to civil jurisdiction and the political regents."[43]

Not only was Van Velthuysen too tolerant of Catholics and of sex outside of marriage, and not only did he refuse any firm division between the civil and ecclesiastical spheres, but worse, he had rekindled the conflict of 1618–19 over ultimate control of the church, claiming the magistracy have the right to send commissioners to meetings of the synods and consistories, and influence selection of elders and preachers. In short, viewing church organization and teaching as some sort of extension of civil authority, Van Velthuysen had surreptitiously infiltrated *Arminerye* into the provincial and city government. A particularly foul instance of his turpitude, allegedly, was his attempt to obstruct the ban on Hobbes' *Leviathan* and refusal to accept the church would be afflicted were Hobbes' principles diffused in society.[44]

In 1672, the pamphlets show, religious conservatives still rated Cartesianism, rather than Spinozism, the chief intellectual menace to society. But there were already hints that the balance was shifting and in Reformed eyes Spinozism was well on the way to rivalling Cartesianism as Holland's most pernicious intellectual malaise. By the time Spinoza died, in 1677, Spinozism was clearly displacing Cartesianism in this respect and, by the 1680s, had indisputably secured first place as prime philosophico-theological target of the Calvinist hard core. With the first signs evident in 1672, two or three anti-De Witt pamphlets published that year cite Spinoza as a profound evil deliberately nurtured by De Witt as part of his supposedly betraying all godliness. One pamphlet cites the *TTP* as a hellish book published "with the complicity of Mr. Jan," denouncing De Witt's alleged closeness to the Brothers De La Court and their republican political philosophy.[45]

---

[43] *Tweede Bericht des Kerkenraads van Utrecht*, 7, 12–14.
[44] *Tweede Bericht des Kerkenraads van Utrecht*, 18.
[45] *Appendix Van 't Catalogus van de Boecken* (Knuttel 10437), 4, 7, 8.

SLEUTEL,

Ontsluytende de Boecke-kas van de

WITTE

BIBLIOTHEECK,

Met sijn APPENDIX.

Waer in de duyftere namen der Boecken klaerlijck werden vertoont en bekent gemaeckt.

Door J. B.

BIBLIOTHECARIUS.

In 'sGRAVEN-HAGE,
By NIL VOLENTIBUS ARDUUM. 1672.
Voor Intelligentibus.

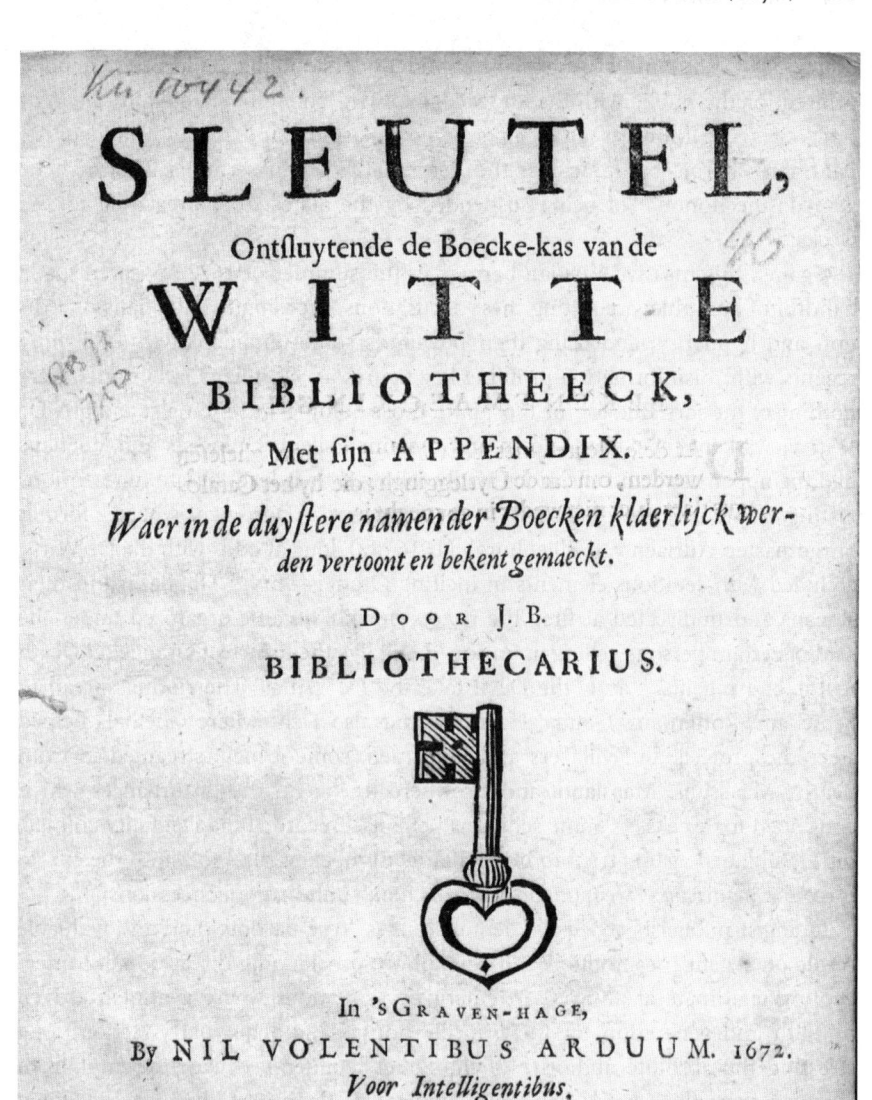

Figure 30.2 J.B., *Sleutel Ontsluytende de Boecke-kas van de Witte Bibliotheeck*. In 's Graven-Hage: By Nil Volentibus Arduum, 1672. IAS Spinoza Research Collection.

Another, the *Sleutel Ontsluytende de Boecke-kas van De Witte Bibliotheeck* [The Key Unlocking the Book-Case of De Witt] by "J.B.," published at The Hague at this juncture (Figure 30.2), included as number 33 in the list of godless books Holland's Pensionary supposedly gloated over (he did actually possess a copy in his library), "the *Tractatus Theologico-Politicus* by the renegade Jew Spinoza, brought out from Hell, in which is shown, in an unheard of atheistic manner, that God's Word must be explained and understood by philosophy, a book printed for the public with the knowledge of Mr. Jan."[46] The same anti-De Witt tract cites the Montbas affair in scurrilous fashion and extols Thaddeus de Lantman's heroic battle against the Perpetual Edict in sermons for which he gained "the honour" of being suspended by the States from preaching for six weeks.[47]

Against this massive Voetian barrage in the summer of 1672 appeared just a handful of pamphlets rebutting these accusations, accusing the Voetians of sedition and hypocrisy, and using their power, as some undoubtedly did, to vilify regents with misinformation profiling key figures as "Socinians" when they were nothing of the sort. But, for the most part, those holding anti-Orangist and pro-De Witt views kept their heads down and remained silent. Orangists and Voetians had the upper hand and the mobs avidly followed their lead. In late June, furious rioting erupted, with women well to the fore, first at Dordrecht where a former burgomaster, Adriaen van Blijenburgh (1616–82), long at odds with the De Witts, colluded with seditious elements in inciting Orangist fury.[48] Haphazard in their slogans and undirected at first, the rioters quickly became organized under the lead of certain persons yelling in unison "Long live the Prince of Orange!," "Death to the bad regents!," and "the Devil take the De Witts!" The rioting spread to Schiedam, Rotterdam, Gouda, Haarlem, and also Delft where Goethals helped steer the protests and villagers and fishermen, some armed, streamed in from nearby Maassluis, Maasland, and elsewhere to join in the disturbances which continued for weeks.[49] "Some seditious persons," recorded the Delft city council, on 11 July, had again "tried to bring a large number of rural folk into the city to force the magistracy, weapons in hand, to make unheard of concessions."[50]

Orangist publicists styled the demonstrators "true patriots" and an invaluable bridle on regent presumption and corruption, proclaiming direct popular intervention legitimate at any rate in emergency situations where genuinely driven by faith and veneration for the princely house. The States party-faction, long stressing the absolute authority of the States, condemned every attempt from below to force the regents' hands. In denouncing the unrest, they regularly cited Middelburg where pressure from the guilds drove the disorder, and Delft, a city allegedly taken over by "fishermen."[51] By late June 1672, many regents were ready to accept that settling for a semi-monarchical state under the Prince's direction was now the only way out of this unprecedented crisis. Crowds besieging the town halls fiercely decried those regents still reluctant finally to set aside the Perpetual

---

[46] *Sleutel Ontsluytende de Boecke-Kas*, 15; Japikse, "Spinoza en de Witt," 11; Nadler, *Book Forged in Hell*, 230–1.
[47] *Sleutel Ontsluytende de Boecke-Kas*, 6, 12.   [48] Rowen, *John de Witt*, 844.
[49] Van der Hoeven, *Leeven en Dood* ii, 396; Israel, *Dutch Republic*, 801.
[50] GA Delft 1e Afdeling 13/5 fo. 86. Res. Vroedschap 11 July 1672; Roorda, *Partij en factij*, 138.
[51] Van der Hoeven, *Hollands aeloude Vryheid* ii, 376.

Edict and yield political as well as military control to William III. It was without doubt the people chanting against "traitors" and religious dissidents who, in July 1672, engineered the coup that restored the Stadholderate.

Following Zeeland's formal recognition of William as Stadholder, on 2 July, a thoroughly cowed States of Holland, shelving De Witt's Perpetual Edict, followed the next day. The coup led to "full restitution of his Highness, now aged twenty-one years, to the office and power of stadholder, with all the powers, and even more, than those exercised by his ancestors,"[52] a disastrous wrong turn in Spinoza's judgement. In his view, broadening, not curbing, decision-making and the representative functions of the *vroedschappen* [city governments] was what was needed, and such fundamental changes should never be driven by popular protest or militia interventions but regularized and institutionalized by legislative deliberation, consciously reducing oligarchy and rendering such bodies more representative in debate and discussion.

Defeated, pro-De Witt regents yielded a shift in power which inevitably meant that the legislatures of the Seven Provinces now lost much of their political authority, and noblemen and military commanders surrounding the Prince would henceforth predominate in military and strategic affairs, and in secret negotiations with foes and other foreign powers. That kings were preferable to republics, being more efficient and orientated for war and secret negotiation, figured among Hobbes' central principles and, with William now Stadholder, a new kind of army and supreme ruling council swiftly emerged. Many available nobles in neighbouring lands were drawn to the new opportunities. From early 1672, a stream of willing anti-absolutist nobles, Huguenot, German, Swiss, and Spanish, a remarkable international medley soliciting and awaiting military commands, flocked to Holland, among them the Catalan crypto-Jewish mathematician, geographer, and military engineer, Lieutenant-Colonel Fullana (c.1623–c.1698) whom Spinoza got to know presumably at this point. Serving in the Spanish army of Flanders during the previous two years, Fullana, like others, now that the Prince commanded the Republic's armed forces, arrived in The Hague offering to help make up the Republic's chronic shortage of experienced officers.

30.ii Salvaging the Republic

Many, perhaps most, Dutchmen regarded De Witt's downfall and the Prince's sudden elevation as a blessing and gratefully acknowledged divine providence at work. Among them was the Prince's grandmother's chaplain, Petrus van Balen (1643–92), who delivered a sermon at this point, in The Hague, proclaiming

---

[52] Temple, *Memoirs*, 23; Israel, *Dutch Republic*, 802–5.

William III God's instrument, the new "David" chosen by the elders "to wage the wars of the Lord for the lawful protection of his country and church."[53] That was exactly also the view of the mobs, though ironically, before long, Van Balen himself converted to "Spinozism," and hence a very different view. Spinoza, even if reduced to silence for the moment, certainly refused to agree. The De Witts' downfall, in his and his followers' eyes, was violently and illicitly engineered by conspirators thirsting to bring Prince and preachers to the helm. As it turned out, despite the Prince's youth and inexperience, the conduct of the war did now undeniably pass into militarily more capable hands than before. But was such a political coup the means to rescue the Republic? Was the gain worth the cost in other respects, especially the long-term implications for the Republic's politics, freedom of expression, and quality of life?

"Choosing a king for the sake of a war as often happens on the pretext that kings wage war much more successfully [than republics]," asserts Spinoza in his last political tract, written after the shift in power, and in open disagreement with Hobbes, "in reality is just stupidity: to desire, so as to be fortunate in war, to be a slave in peace! That is assuming peace can be conceived of in that state where the highest power is transferred, solely due to a war, to one person only, a person who can best show his abilities, and what all gain from power being concentrated in one person, in war. As against this, the democratic state has this special distinction: that its excellence is much better shown in peace than in war."[54] Here, by "democratic" Spinoza means not the sway of the "man in the street" but, as always with the radical thought tradition he helped shape, government for "the people" via large councils representing society's broad interests within a rules-based institutional structure geared to *salus populi*, the common good of the whole, Spinoza's "general will." Despite the setbacks bringing the Prince to the helm, all was not lost: "quia populi salus suprema lex [because the people's welfare is the highest law]," held the *Tractatus Politicus* where Spinoza frequently alludes to the 1672 crisis, "even in a state where a monarchical figurehead is chosen for his abilities in war,"[55] hence even under a powerful leader or figurehead, the *salus populi* or "general will" defined as the people's sovereignty based on "reason" can exert a steadying influence provided there is a "grand council," like the States of Holland representing the towns and cities, where the big cities can defend their influence and autonomy against the prince and his advisers.

A monarchical figure looked to by the populace as their saviour, observes Spinoza, will inevitably seek to break free of the restraints imposed by the States, by favouring and manipulating representatives of the small towns to

---

[53] Broeyer, "William III and the Reformed Church," 109.
[54] Spinoza, *Opera* iii, 309–10; Spinoza, *Tractatus Politicus* in *Oeuvres* v, 166–7; Spinoza, *Political Treatise*, 79.
[55] Spinoza, *Opera* iii, 310; Bove, "Introduction," 92–3; Sharp, *Spinoza and the Politics*, 53, 81, 180.

avoid deferring to the more autonomous views of large cities like Amsterdam where the citizens' interests are broadly represented and one finds more regard for minority churches and sects and their needs. It was predictable that William would seek to build his power base in the smaller towns (exactly as he did), because small towns with a vote in the States, like Schoonhoven, Enkhuizen, Gorcum, Schiedam and Purmerend, experience proved, were less representative of society as a whole than large cities and more readily controlled by princely power and the prince's henchmen. In the changed situation, it was in the big cities, Amsterdam above all, Spinoza afterwards stressed, that republican hopes remained chiefly vested.[56]

The catastrophe of the "Disaster Year," Spinoza did not doubt, was partly due to lapses of judgement and preparedness on the part of De Witt and his colleagues for whom he reserved much of his criticism. But the root of the catastrophe he located less in the deficiencies of any individual than structural defects in the system. Aristocratic republics, like Holland, ruled by multiple cities, are inherently "preferable" to aristocratic republics under single cities, like Venice or Genoa, because in a federative state like that of the Dutch freedom is shared among more of its members: "since regard is paid to the good of others, where one city exerts sole rule, only so far as it suits the ruling city."[57] This rendered the Venetian Republic, in Spinoza's eyes, structurally greatly inferior to the Dutch Republic. But the multiple city Dutch model too exhibited serious vulnerabilities. In an aristocratic or oligarchic republic, like the United Provinces, secretaries and pensionaries (like De Witt), being the most conversant with public business, amass greater influence over large councils than they should, thereby ensuring "the condition of the entire state depends largely on their guidance" which proved "the ruin of the Dutch." Progressive deterioration of the aristocratic republic inevitably follows until its condition becomes "little better than that of a monarchy ruled by a few royal councilors." In the United Provinces, inadequate foundations had created a situation where, once a severe crisis loomed, a few isolated individuals stood at the helm, and those overly prominent "ambitious men" deferred to initially by the legislature as their guides, whether Oldenbarnevelt or De Witt, are then "slaughtered, like sacrificial animals to appease the wrath of those who are enemies to freedom."[58]

A second basic weakness, held Spinoza, was division not just of the population into opposing religious and theological factions, which is inevitable, but also of the ruling patricians into Remonstrants versus Counter-Remonstrants, and, in the 1660s and 1670s, Voetians (Orangists) versus Arminians, Cocceians, and other anti-Orangists, a rift that in principle could be avoided. In a stable aristocratic

---

[56] Israel, *Dutch Republic*, 811; Blom, *Morality and Causality*, 236.
[57] Spinoza, *Political Treatise*, 96, 120, 127; Prokhovnik, *Spinoza and Republicanism*, 112–13.
[58] Spinoza, *Political Treatise*, 117; Blom, *Morality and Causality*, 227, 238.

republic where citizens are free to believe and think whatever they wish and build as many different (modest) churches attended by clergy separate from the public church as they desire, the patrician elite must nevertheless all adhere to the same public church, and that church should possess no churchmen separate from the patricians, trained separate clergy being the most ruinous of practices.[59] If civic religion is needed for guiding society, theological division introduced by churchmen among the governing patriciate is invariably fatal.

The Republic's greatest structural defect paving the way to its downfall in 1672, however, was that the Dutch Revolt of 1572 merely eliminated the power of the "Count of Holland," that is Philip II of Spain, leaving the rest of the state's structure much as before. Rather than a properly constituted representative republic, the United Provinces really resembled a stunted principality without a prince. "To maintain their freedom, the Dutch supposed it sufficed to discard their count, thereby cutting off the head from the body of the state. Schemes to reorganize it in a different form never entered their minds. Leaving all its limbs as they had been previously, Holland remained a county without a count, like a headless body, a form of state without a name. So it is not surprising that most of its subjects have not known where its sovereignty lay." Here was a fundamental thesis of the *Tractatus Politicus*, and the core of Spinoza's analysis of what had gone wrong. The participation base of the United Provinces was simply too confined and narrow for the De Wittian republic to be at all viable.

Consequently, a key contention of Spinoza's last work, though a major theme too of the *TTP*, is that it was not, as most supposed, diffusion of power and extensive consultation but instead the "defective constitution of the state and the fewness of its rulers" that caused the Republic's humiliation and collapse, the narrowness of its support base that encouraged plotting and conspiracies against the patriciate and in the end its complete overthrow. Instead of restoring the stadholderate, the correct remedy for the United Provinces should have been to create a broader, more representative, more democratic republic with the public church drastically reduced.[60] Even though the Dutch approach remained preferable to the Venetian and the Swiss models, its great defect, the year of disaster demonstrated, was essentially identical to that blighting all aristocratic republics— excessively limited participation and representation.[61]

As likewise in the neighbouring monarchies, the ruling elite's shortcomings so evident in 1672 were aggravated, and the fatal theologizing of public life encouraged, held Spinoza, by misconceived governance of higher education and the universities. As things stood, "academies founded at public expense are established not so much to cultivate minds as restrain them," that is, assign theology

---

[59] Spinoza, *Political Treatise*, 118.   [60] Spinoza, *Political Treatise*, 126.
[61] Spinoza, *Political Treatise*, 126; Balibar, *Spinoza et la politique*, 88–9; Prokhovnik, *Spinoza and Republicanism*, 174; Moreau, "A-t-on raison de se révolter?," 27–8.

excessive power not only over society generally but also over the organization and regulation of teaching and fields of study. "But in a free commonwealth, arts and sciences are best fostered when anyone who applies is allowed to teach publicly at his own expense while putting his own reputation at risk." Perhaps Spinoza would himself have liked to lecture to university students. Certainly, he scorned the officially and ecclesiastically endorsed current teaching of philosophy, the sciences, and political and social theory. The best minds should be the teachers, he argued, and these should emerge by an egalitarian process of disputation, student scrutiny, and acclaim.[62]

In any case, restoring the stadholderate by no means ended the Dutch domestic political crisis. Rather, popular protest and rioting against the De Wittian faction (still dominating many town councils), persisted well after William III assumed direction of the Republic's affairs. The propaganda barrage, especially in the form of vitriolic pamphlets, denouncing the "Loevestein" faction as the contagion that brought the Republic to its knees, and the army to humiliation, persisted with unrelenting ferocity in the hope of hastening the ejection of unwanted regents from city governments, and securing a broader transfer of power with the explicit aim of extending the purges also to local government, cultural life, and the academic sphere where the church councils intended to reinforce the hardline Calvinist presence and more effectively curb religious dissent and the "new philosophy."

Since 1648, alleges one pamphlet reviling the heirs of Grotius and Oldenbarnevelt, titled *Remedies for Holland's Ills* [*Genees-Middelen voor Hollants-Qualen*], not only Arminians but Socinians and even Atheism [*Atheisterye*] "crept into the consistories and town halls representing church and state; and in order the better to dispose young men to adopt new opinions, in the universities, so arranged matters as to lead them to adore the seducer Descartes."[63] Owing to the De Witt faction's devious policies, the Republic's universities and consistories alike had suffered deep splits and been extensively infiltrated by pernicious elements. Exploiting the city governments' *ius patronatus* to influence appointments to Reformed Church pulpits, detestable foes of religion had politicized the Reformed Church and rendered it at odds with itself (Voetians versus Cocceians). To advance their insidious schemes, the "Loevestein faction," moreover, had patronized political propaganda like the *Interest van Holland* [of the De La Courts] (to which De Witt himself did indeed contribute) seeking to discredit the Princes of Orange.[64] Not content with infecting Holland, the De Witt faction, by offering opportunities, positions, and jobs, infiltrated their political-religious-philosophical contagion, or

---

[62] Spinoza, *Political Treatise*, 119; Spinoza, *Theological-Political Treatise*, 253.
[63] *Genees-Middelen voor Hollants-Qualen*, 5–6; Rowen, *John de Witt*, 853–5.
[64] *Genees-Middelen voor Hollants-Qualen*, 9; Rowen, *John de Witt*, 391–3.

"freedom" as they perversely called it, also into other provinces, Utrecht especially.[65] This was the political faction, with Van Velthuysen at their head, that arranged Utrecht's speedy capitulation to the French and, on 30 June, even disgracefully ordered the local Reformed Church consistory to cease reciting the established prayers for preservation of the state, imposing a base restriction on the public church![66]

As the unrest mounted, regents publicly associated with De Wittian values found themselves at growing risk of being assaulted not just ideologically but physically in the streets. At Rotterdam, Haarlem, and other towns, several regents' homes were attacked and pillaged. At Rotterdam, six principal regent "traitors" were furiously denounced by the crowds for "plotting" surrender to the French— the most prominent, Pieter de Groot, a brother-in-law of Montbas, and friend of Spinoza's friend Hugo Boxel, being decried as an "atheist" as well as betrayer.[67] The once powerful "Pope of Rotterdam," Willem Van de Aa, like the Schiedam burgomaster, Willem Nieuwpoort, among the chief negotiators of the Act of Exclusion, concerted with Cromwell in 1654, was assaulted and beaten in the street.[68] The ejection of De Witt's allies from the Rotterdam city government was a profound blow to all advocates of toleration there and freedom for fringe sects, Cartesianism, and republicanism throughout the Republic.

The Hague and Delft church councils helped escalate the drive for purges and repression by redoubling their demands for stricter curbs on fringe sects, Catholic prayer meetings, theatre performances, prostitution, and other alleged ungodly excesses.[69] At The Hague where in recent years the local civic militia made no secret of their Orangism, calls for purges of anti-Orangist regents and other undesirables, encouraged by the Prince and his entourage, steadily built up over the summer, generating prolonged further unrest and instability, culminating early in September. As the mayhem in the streets continued week after week at Delft, Leiden, Rotterdam, and The Hague, it was by no means just regents and their homes that were at risk. Any dissenting personage cited in the anti-De Witt propaganda pamphlets, denounced as an opponent of the Prince, antagonist of the Reformed Church, or representative of the new philosophical "opinions," Spinoza included, found themselves exposed. Fearing assault, the Rotterdam Collegiants suspended their gatherings for several weeks, Spinoza's friend Ostens, deeply dejected by his congregation's setbacks, at this point shut himself

---

[65] *Genees-Middelen voor Hollants-Qualen*, 13.
[66] GA Utrecht MS. Kerkeraad 10. Res. 20 June (Old Style) 1672.
[67] Freudenthal/Walther, *Lebensgeschichte* ii, 69n276; Roorda, *Partij en factie*, 107, 162; Israel, *Dutch Republic*, 799; Munt, "Impact of the *Rampjaar*," 10.
[68] Melles, *Joachim Oudaan*, 85; Rowen, *John de Witt*, 850–1.
[69] Van Gelder, "Schutterij en Magistraat in 1672," 58, 65, 68, 71–2; Roodenburg, *Onder censuur*, 292, 337.

away, abandoning his former prominent role among his congregation, apparently meeting his end, a few years later, in 1678, as a drunkard plunged in depression.[70]

As the fury of The Hague's militia units and plebs mounted, along with the hounding of the De Witts during the brothers' last weeks, even the calmest, most phlegmatic of philosophers could hardly avoid feeling anxiety for himself and those associated with him. But while pondering, as he seemingly did, whether to betake himself abroad, Spinoza remained unswerving in his commitment to democratic principles and opposition to the monarchical concept, to emergency measures apt to encourage dictatorship and all preponderance of nobility. Even when society is, for whatever reason, saddled with a quasi-monarchical figure as the Republic was, by August 1672, and as remained the case during Spinoza's last four and a half years and beyond, it still mattered greatly, as no one stressed more than Spinoza, to fence this figure in with institutional safeguards and salvage as much of the legacy of the "True Freedom" within the new framework as possible— which for Spinoza meant the Republic should continue working for the equal benefit of all and not forget that republics are best governed when decisions are broadly reached by representatives voicing the needs and guarding the well-being of all.[71]

The catastrophe itself only convinced Spinoza all the more "that the civil order is naturally established to remove common fear and drive out the common miseries," as the *Tractatus Politicus* puts it, "so what it most seeks to do is what every individual guided by reason would attempt in the state of nature, but there would be unable to do."[72] Man's natural right is far more restricted outside than within society and the state. Minimizing fear by ensuring security and restoring internal order, as well as seeking peace abroad, is the chief function the state fulfils. "What is more, each person, it is certain, can do that much less, and hence possesses less right, the greater his cause for dread, to which we may add that without mutual help men can hardly sustain their lives and cultivate their minds: and thus we conclude the law of nature [*ius naturae*] special to the human race can scarcely be conceived except where men have common rights and at the same time are able to maintain the lands they inhabit, and can cultivate them, defend themselves, and repel all aggression and live according to the common way of thinking of all." This state, "no impartial observer can deny," held Spinoza, "is at its most durable where it possesses just enough military power to guard its possessions without coveting what belongs to others and hence strives by every means to avoid war and preserve peace."[73]

---

[70] Van Bunge, "Jacob Ostens," 273–4; Van Bunge, "Rotterdamse Collegiant," 74–5.
[71] Balibar, *Spinoza et la politique*, 87–8; Kisner, *Spinoza on Human Freedom*, 225, 228.
[72] Spinoza, *Opera* iii, 286; Spinoza, *Political Treatise*, 58–9.
[73] Spinoza, *Political Treatise*, 43; Kisner, *Spinoza on Human Freedom*, 224, 226–7.

A broad spectrum of representatives gathered in a "great council," or legislature, will always fear losing their property and freedom, shun additional taxes for war, and be reluctant to see offspring and relatives obliged to suspend their usual activities to fight for their country. During 1672, Spinoza heard much of the disastrous ill-discipline, indifference, and unreliability of the Republic's hired professional troops, and the greater resolve and reliability of the urban militias. Partly on this ground, he repeatedly expresses hostility to standing forces of professional troops, especially mercenaries recruited abroad, some of whom, at this time, did conduct themselves in a base and cowardly manner.[74] Here following Machiavelli and the De La Courts, he therefore recommends that the Republic dispense with a standing army of paid regular troops and use conscripted citizens, trained in arms as urban militia, serving for short periods without pay. To ensure "citizens are acknowledged by the sovereign before all outsiders and remain in control of their own right as far as civil order or equity permits, it is necessary that the military be composed solely of citizens"; for from the moment the citizens "permit mercenary troops to be brought in, men whose trade is war and find their greatest power amidst discord and sedition," citizens are subjugated, "and the conditions for unending warfare are laid."[75]

Spinoza's perspective here might seem bizarre. Half overrun, the Republic found itself in dire straits militarily, set upon by an alliance of powers wielding overwhelming superior force. No other army in Europe was as mercenary and international as that which William III amassed in 1672–3, forging a military and political culture which Spinoza heartily scorned, but with which, in the end, the Prince did save the Republic. But Spinoza does not claim citizen militias are as efficient at fighting the enemy as paid mercenary troops. "Mercenary troops, accustomed to military discipline inured to cold and hunger," he admits, "generally despise the mass of citizens as their inferiors by far as regards storming cities or fighting pitched battles."[76] His point rather was that there is great advantage to society, and the state is most stable and durable, when its defences suffice to protect its own territory without encouraging aspirations to possess what belongs to others and "for that reason tries by every means to avoid war and keep the peace."[77] Precisely this had been De Witt's goal.

Spinoza's analysis of the military situation made some sense in relation to his republican priorities given that the navy, under De Ruyter, principally relying on native Dutchmen, performed far more reliably and admirably during the disastrous summer of 1672 than the army. Thwarting the English at Solebay, on 6 June 1672, the navy repelled part of the coalition, forcing cancellation for the moment of the planned Anglo-French landing from the west. By contrast, the

---

[74] Spinoza, *Political Treatise*, 91; Cooper, "Statesmen versus Philosophers," 41.
[75] Spinoza, *Opera* iii, 312–13; Cooper, "Statesmen versus Philosophers," 40–1.
[76] Spinoza, *Political Treatise*, 91.   [77] Spinoza, *Opera* iii, 320.

States General's paid mercenary army, largely recruited abroad, failed utterly in the face of the land assault. Moreover, on the front line, ill-discipline among the troops, especially pilfering from local farmers, as Spinoza's military acquaintance, Fullana, emphasized, caused serious problems for officers and real friction between the troops and locals. Soldiery employed by a state, remarked Fullana, should safeguard, not pillage, its inhabitants.[78] Relying on town militias rather than professional troops also struck Spinoza as the way to ensure citizens, rather than soldiers, are esteemed by sovereign authority and that the military sector is subordinated fully to civil society and its needs. Both as regards mercenaries and avoiding foreign wars, Spinoza is here again thinking chiefly about the Dutch case but equally alluding to monarchical France, England, and the German principalities. Among Spinoza's circle, avoiding what they saw as the fatal drawbacks for society of monarchy and quasi-monarchy, as well as narrow oligarchy, remained their overriding political objective throughout.

Proclaimed Stadholder on 4 July, the Prince, impatient to restore stability, calm unrest, and focus on the war, for a time supported the sitting town governments. But as he watched the popular anger and frustration fuelling the demonstrations persist week after week his support waned. Restoring the stadholderate and reorganizing the army, bringing it under firm princely control, was only part of what the "Prince and Fatherland" rioters were demanding. Popular Orangist ideology condemning the "Loevestein faction" as "traitors" ruled the streets. For the militias and civic guilds, saving the Fatherland meant not just fending off the French and restoring the Republic's defences but also purging of the "traitors" undermining princely house and public church and overturning their toleration for religious dissenters. Leaders of the unrest demanded further narrowing of the power structure chiefly to constrict the autonomy of civic government and religious minorities and impose Calvinist values more forcefully on society.[79]

Spinoza's habitual huddling indoors over his desk, at this juncture, was doubtless dictated as much by the prevailing situation as his own inclination. The disturbances climaxed in late August with rioting in several cities, most notably The Hague, culminating in the tragic murder and dismemberment of the Brothers De Witt, on 20 August, the unrest still persisting into early September. The horrific events of 20 August occurred during a brief power vacuum at The Hague, when William was with the army and (perhaps purposely) slow to respond to the States' request to send troops to restore order. The Brothers De Witt were "massacred," remarks Temple, by the "fury of the people at The Hague, and by the fate of ministers that govern by a party or faction, who are usually sacrificed to the first great misfortune abroad that falls in to aggravate or inflame the general

---

[78] Hattendorf, "Competing Navies," 111–12; Kishlansky, *Monarchy Transformed*, 247; Trevor, *Shadow of a Crown*, 62–3; Prud'homme van Reine, *Moordenaars*, 66–7.
[79] Van de Klashorst, "De ware vrijheid," 168–70; Stern, *Orangism*, 100–1, 142–3.

discontents at home." Murdered by the mob in the heart of the Republic's capital, just streets from where Spinoza lodged, the brothers' corpses were "then drag'd about the Town by the fury of the people, and torn in pieces," their clothing ripped to shreds, their mutilated nude corpses hung up by the feet, and their entrails torn out. "Thus ended one of the greatest lifes [Johan de Witt] of any subject in our age, and about the forty-seventh year of his own, after having serv'd or better administer'd, that state as Pensioner of Holland for about eighteen years, with great honour to his country and to himself."[80]

On the night of their deaths there occurred, supposedly, one of the best known episodes of Spinoza's life. Hearing of the murders—or so, according to a nineteenth-century editor, Spinoza told Leibniz during a supper conversation with the latter when he visited The Hague four years later, in November 1676—he was so indignant, that, forgetting his own maxim "caute!," the philosopher rushed to go out to the scene of the atrocity and post up a placard reading "ultimi barbarorum" [worst of barbarians], proclaiming his contempt for the mob's behaviour, but was physically prevented by his worthy landlord, Van der Spijck, who, concerned for house and family as well as his lodger, locked all the doors to keep him securely inside.[81] Possibly true, this appealing story is unfortunately impossible to confirm or deny as the original notes of Leibniz, including his reportedly recounting what transpired that night, subsequently disappeared.

The De Witts' demise was followed by purges of the republican faction from the city governments, often with the local civic militia captains leading the agitation. The purges were especially severe at The Hague, Rotterdam, Delft, and Dordrecht where the Orangist faction headed by De Witt's local chief foe, Adriaen van Blijenburgh, seized control. The main objective of the rioting militias and mobs being the final eradication of the "Loevestein faction" from city government, it was demanded as a fixed rule that no one should henceforth serve on the city councils without formally vowing adherence to the Reformed Church, and that the local Reformed church councils should be no longer constrained by the presence of "political commissioners" sent by the city governments to supervise.[82] Whether it was really "the people" or rather certain "seditious persons" and preachers who incited the rioters to voice these demands, "the people" demanded the purging of "Arminian" and other anti-Orangist and Cartesian-minded regents from positions of influence.

---

[80] Temple, *Memoirs*, 22–3; Haley, *English Diplomat*, 289; Prud'homme van Reine, *Moordenaars*, 123.

[81] Nadler, *Spinoza: A Life*, 356; Laerke, *Leibniz lecteur*, 368; Préposiet, *Spinoza*, 86–7; Prud'homme van Reine, *Moordenaars*, 121.

[82] GA Delft MS, 1e afdeling 13/5, fols. 89–91, 92v. Res. 30 Aug. 1672 and 5 Sept. 1672 and missive to the Prince of Orange dated 2 Sept. 1672 entitled "Consideratien op de requeste ende articulen by eenige Gedeputeerde vande schutterije der stad Delft gepresenteert [...] aan S.Hoogheit."

In the short term, by strengthening city governments' subservience to the Prince, the purges assisted the Republic's recovery. "This Revolution, as it calm'd all at home," Temple explained,

> so it made the first appearance of defending what was left of the country. The state grew united, the army in heart, and foreign princes began to take confidence in the honour and constancy of the young Prince, which they had in a manner wholly lost upon the divisions and misfortunes of the state. The French themselves turn'd all their applications and practices the same way, and made the Prince all the offers that could be of honour and advantages to his person and family, provided he would be contented to depend upon them. The bait they thought could not fail of being swallow'd and about which most artifice was imploy'd, was the proposal of making the Prince sovereign of the Provinces under the protection of England and France.[83]

Yet even though over half of the Republic was now overrun and "what remain'd was under water, and in so eminent danger upon the first frosts of the winter" that the French monarch's handsome offers would have tempted many another, the young Stadholder turned out to be "above it, and his answers always firm, that he never would betray a trust that was given to him, nor ever sell the liberties of his country, that his ancestors had so long defended."[84]

After the purges, the young Stadholder held the States of Holland and Zeeland firmly in his grip, but his internal authority was far from evenly spread. In Spinoza's eyes, despite the changed circumstances, even under a newly powerful Stadholder (or monarch), his maxim that "the people's well-being is the supreme law" still retained some force, even in the face of the mob violence.[85] A key feature of the 1672 Dutch political crisis was that it was the smaller towns of Holland and Zeeland that proved easy prey and quickly became pawns of the Prince, as Spinoza remarks in the *Tractatus Politicus*, while the largest cities, Amsterdam especially where neither Orangists nor Voetians managed to gain much leverage, managed to avoid having their city governments extensively purged. Delft and Leiden also proved resistant to the Stadholder's grip, with the consequence that prospects for Voetians, rosy in 1672, perceptibly weakened as early as 1673-4, just when Spinoza was analysing the outcome of the political drama.[86] This significant rebound of civic feeling and solidarity seized Spinoza's attention: "there is no doubt that the citizens are more powerful, and hence more their own masters, the larger their cities and the better fortified they are. For the safer the place they live in, the more citizens can defend their freedom and the less they have to fear from

---

[83] Temple, *Memoirs*, 24–5.   [84] Temple, *Memoirs*, 25; Haley, *English Diplomat*, 222, 285.
[85] Spinoza, *Collected Works* (ed. Curley) ii, 547.
[86] GA Delft MS, 1e afdeling 13/5, fo. 107. William III to SH, 13 Dec. 1673.

an enemy external or internal." By contrast, towns "needing another's power to preserve them" become pawns of whoever is their protector, hence in the Dutch context pawns of the Stadholder. In an oligarchic republic like the United Provinces, Spinoza also considered it desirable, given each city had to levy an agreed quota of soldiers and pay for them in proportion to size, that their own regents should appoint the colonels and company commanders needed to lead their segment of the army charged with the "common safety of the whole state." Spinoza admired how each major Dutch city retained considerable autonomy, or "freedom" as he calls it, to collect its quota of funds in the way it saw fit.[87] That those raising taxes from the citizenry should also control their section of the military (thereby lessening the overall commander's power), was another of Spinoza's claims about military organization that directly clashed with the new reality, the "Revolution" as Temple calls it, of the De Witts' overthrow and the Prince's assumption of control.

Representatives of small towns, observed Spinoza, "are apt to be specially favoured by the Prince precisely because they are more prone to succumb to his beck and call." "When citizens give their weapons to someone else, and entrust their cities' defences to him, they transfer their right to him unconditionally, and commit it completely to his good faith." If citizens prefer to "remain their own masters and protect their freedom," they must ensure the "military consist only of citizens with no exceptions" and avoid electing any single individual to sole military command, in other words avoid what occurred in 1672. If, as in 1672, "circumstances make it necessary" then "it must be for a year at most." "Reason," Spinoza sums up, assuredly "teaches nothing more clearly than this [ratio autem nihil hoc clarius docet]."[88]

The Prince's assuming military command predictably brought to the fore a horde of Dutch, German, and other foreign nobles, the men William chiefly trusted and relied on for advice, in his diplomacy, secret strategy consultation, and general policymaking, a consequence for statecraft of the 1672 "revolution" that was deeply worrying for those with republican views. In a consultative republic, run by large councils such as Spinoza advocates, state secrets are hard to conceal, but Spinoza considered this a price worth paying.[89] Hostile to monarchy and hereditary aristocracy, neither Spinoza nor any close observer could fail to notice how William's acquiring the stadholderate and combining it with military command brought to the helm of the Republic's affairs figures like the Swedish general, Kurt Christoph von Königsmarck (1634-73) who helped command the "water-line" defences in 1672, and the veteran Prussian field marshal Georg Friedrich, Count von Waldeck (1620-92) who arrived at William's

---

[87] Spinoza, *Political Treatise*, 123.   [88] Spinoza, *Opera* iii, 314–15.
[89] Spinoza, *Political Treatise*, 91.

headquarters at Bodegraven, in September 1672, and figured for the rest of his life among William's closest advisers.[90]

Begrudging the Prince's "preferring of strangers and soldiers of fortune who may solely depend on his favour, and rejecting the Netherlanders," as one informant reporting to London expressed it,[91] by the mid-1670s was a commonplace Dutch complaint. For the good of the commonwealth, and rendering citizens as equal as possible, avers Spinoza in the *Tractatus Politicus*, nobles should be as few as possible. "It is owing to the nobles," he asserts, "that kings are especially prone to wage war. For kings with packs of nobles around them, greater security and calm is derived from war than from peace."[92] This was arguably the social factor behind the aggression of Louis XIV and Charles II and the destructive effects of their policies. Abominating the multitude's ignorance and unruliness, Spinoza judged the nobility no less subject to the baser passions and no less "ignoble" in his sense, and, where numerous, more rather than less of a menace to the commonwealth.

In a stable monarchy where Spinoza's "great council" successfully defends the common welfare, not only the monarch's power but the nobility's too must be minimized in the public interest to as near zero as conceivable. "So that the citizens should be as far as attainable, on terms of equality – in a commonwealth a necessity – none should be considered noblemen except those of royal descent." And since the latter will likely become numerous if permitted to marry and have children, most of the royal family must be prevented from marrying and their children designated as illegitimate.[93]

30.iii The Fullana Affair

The Dutch "water-line" was significantly reinforced during the late summer of 1672, both before and after the De Witts' overthrow. But the officers and engineers chiefly involved in bolstering the Republic's defences soon found themselves transferred from being under local Dutch authorities and city governments and placed instead under foreign nobles only recently arrived on the scene, not always with fortunate results. This is well illustrated by the case of Spinoza's erudite and highly interesting acquaintance, Don Nicolau D'Oliver y Fullana (1623–c.1698), who became entangled in several controversies during late 1672 and early 1673 over defence of the "water-line."

---

[90] Israel, "Dutch Role in the Glorious Revolution," 106; Troost, "William III, Brandenburg," 299, 320.
[91] PRO SP 84/205, fo. 295. "The Commonwealth Party."
[92] Spinoza, *Opera* iii, 316–17; Spinoza, *Political Treatise*, 86; Prokhovnik, *Spinoza and Republicanism*, 208–11.
[93] Spinoza, *Opera* iii, 316; Spinoza, *Political Treatise*, 86–7.

A talented Mallorcan of Sephardic background, Fullana was skilled in cosmography, mathematics, and especially military engineering. An experienced officer already in the 1640s, serving the Spanish crown against the Catalan rebellion of 1640–59, in the 1650s he rose to high rank.[94] Between around 1662 and 1672, he spent much time translating large parts of the later volumes of the Spanish version of the first edition of Jan Blauw's massive ten-volume *Atlas Mayor* (1659–70). Although Spain's power and resources were greatly diminished by this time, the governor-general of the Spanish Netherlands sent what assistance he could from Spanish Flanders to the Dutch, in 1672, and, as part of this effort, Fullana arrived soon after war started, in May, offering his services. Spinoza probably got to know him at The Hague through his landlord, Van der Spijck who, among his activities, was a licensed functionary forwarding loans to officers recruiting men for army units prior to the (often late) arrival of money allocated by the States for their upkeep and wages.[95]

Colonel D'Oliver y Fullana had wide experience in fighting the French and loathed Louis XIV. Assigned initially by the Amsterdam burgomasters to assist with Amsterdam's defences, he depended, being unable to speak or read Dutch, on other Spanish speakers and, while entrusted with rebuilding and strengthening several forts on the "water-line" at Uithoorn protecting Amsterdam's southern flank, recruited at least several other Sephardim into his force.[96] While based near Amsterdam, he joined the Portuguese synagogue in the city, adopting as his Jewish name "Daniel Judah," and found lodgings in the Jewish quarter. Around 1684, he was later styled by his friend, Levi de Barrios, formerly a captain in the army of Flanders, in the latter's verse chronicle celebrating Amsterdam's Sephardic authors, as a Mallorcan "*sargento mayor* in Catalonia and circumcised colonel of infantry who fought the French in Holland" with his Sephardic subordinate "Captain Don Joseph Semah." One wonders whether Spinoza ever asked Fullana, Semah, and de Barrios whether they believed the Jews would one day, in changed circumstances, somehow recover their ancient military prowess.[97]

In an aristocratic republic, like the United Provinces, "company commanders and colonels," holds Spinoza, should "be appointed by the patricians," to syphon power away from the overall commander. This thesis, like other military aspects of his social and political theory, Spinoza had opportunities to discuss during 1672–3 with veteran officers like Fullana, who remained in contact with senior Spanish officers in Brussels and may have influenced the remarks about military matters in

---

[94] Fullana, *Brief geschreven door den Lieutenant Colonel*, 2; Brown, "A Catalan Speaker," 93.
[95] Den Boer, "Amsterdam as 'Locus'," 100–1; Boxer, "Some Thoughts," 83; Petry and Van Suchtelen, "Spinoza and the Military," 367.
[96] Brown, "A Catalan Speaker," 97; Scholberg, "Miguel de Barrios," 145–6; one of his Sephardic soldiers was a fifteen-year-old, impoverished youth from Livorno, named Isaac Lopes de Luna, Levie Bernfeld, *Poverty and Welfare*, 217.
[97] Levi de Barrios, *Relación*, 287; Kaplan, *From Christianity to Judaism*, 226n61; De Boer, "Amsterdam as 'Locus'," 98, 100.

Spinoza's *Tractatus*.[98] Spinoza's concern, clearly, was less with optimal military efficiency than safeguarding the integrity of the republic, that is optimal defensive capacity within an internally secure republican framework. Fullana prized the opportunity to command part of the defences south-east of Amsterdam through the summer and early autumn, but was disappointed, in November 1672, when the Prince's headquarters, without consulting the Amsterdam burgomasters (which Fullana apparently resented), ordered him to transfer to the Bodegraven sector where "experienced officers" were lacking. Fullana now found himself serving under Königsmarck who reportedly communicated with his Mallorcan underling principally in Italian.[99]

"When France lost all hopes of shaking the Prince of Orange's constancy," explains Temple, Louis and the French court "bent all their thoughts upon subduing and ruining the remainder of the country." But having "encamp'd his army near Bodegraven," between Leiden and Woerden, the Prince "made such a stand with a handful of men, as the French could never force."[100] At this point, Fullana commanded a fort close to the Fort Oranje, north-east of Woerden, a vital sector, briefly occupied in September 1672 by a French force under François Henri de Montmorency, duc de Luxembourg (1628–95), the Stouppes and the traitor Montbas (who had escaped from his prison). A month before Fullana's arrival, in early October, 2,800 French troops under Luxembourg and the Brothers Stouppe, sallying forth from occupied Woerden, were repulsed with heavy loss in a fierce night battle around the fort, a success greeted as the first sign, since Solebay, of divine providence again intervening behind Protestantism.[101] In December, though, a month after Fullana's assuming local command, a near disastrous setback occurred. After it became cold enough for the water-line to freeze, Luxembourg crossed the ice in the darkness on 27 December 1672, launching a vigorous night offensive towards the nearby city of Gouda.[102]

Advancing swiftly, the French "made their ravages within two or three leagues of Leyden," records Temple, "with more violences and cruelties than would have been prudent, if they had hop'd to reclaim the Prince or States from the obstinacy of their defense." Had the ice stayed firm, Luxembourg's elite troops once across the water-line would have ravaged the environs of Gouda and Leiden at will and directly threatened The Hague which, unlike the other towns possessed no defensive walls and was especially vulnerable. But "the winter prov'd not favourable to their hopes and designs," recounts Temple, the frosts tempting the French "into marches that prov'd almost fatal to them by a sudden thaw."

---

[98] Spinoza, *Political Treatise*, 123; Scholberg, "Miguel de Barrios," 146.
[99] Fullana, *Brief geschreven door den Lieutenant Colonel*, 1–3; Brown, "A Catalan Speaker," 94, 97.
[100] Temple, *Memoirs*, 26.
[101] Costerus, *Historisch Verhael*, III, 271–8; Troost, "William III, Brandenburg," 86–8; Boxer, "Some Thoughts," 82.
[102] Nimwegen, *The Dutch Army*, 457–8; Van Nierop, *Life of Romeyn de Hooghe*, 103.

Suddenly "frighted [...] into cautions perhaps more than were necessary,"[103] by the prospect of being cut off, the French pulled rapidly back, venting their exasperation by brutally pillaging Bodegraven and Zwammerdam, killing several hundred inhabitants, burning down over a hundred houses and raping many women, some of whose bodies were thrown naked into the freezing water. Seizing on these gruesome atrocities, the artist Romeyn de Hooghe (1645–1708) produced one of his most luridly realistic scenes of the horrors of war, his *Mirror of the French Tyranny committed against the Villages of Holland* (1673), a powerful propaganda print that just weeks later delivered a hefty knock to the reputation of France and its overweening monarch.[104]

The sudden French pullback ought to have resulted in a decisive triumph for the Dutch using their redoubts at Nieuwerbrug and near Bodegraven to trap Luxembourg on his overhasty retreat towards Woerden. With the ice thawing, there was no alternative route back past these forts and Luxembourg's retreat could crucially have been blocked by the force holding the forts under Fullana's superior, the Huguenot Quartermaster, Moïse Pain-et-Vin (c.1620–73). The ensuing fiasco provoked some of the fiercest recrimination of the "Disaster Year." Warned that the retreating French were approaching, on 28 December 1672, Fullana prepared his fort to face attack, several officers afterwards attested, placing everything in readiness to repel the foe. But after making the evening rounds in person to check everything was in order, urging his men to do their duty and fight bravely, orders arrived from Pain-et-Vin to immediately abandon his fort and flee. Pain-et-Vin, in a panic, disastrously ordered an untimely evacuation of his 2,000 men from the very forts scheduled to trap the invaders.[105] Afterwards, another Sephardic Spanish-speaking officer in the Republic's service, Don Joseph Milan, at Fullana's request, confirmed in writing before a notary in The Hague, that Fullana, having put everything in readiness for defence and addressed his men, was greatly upset, between ten and eleven that evening, to receive Pain-et-Vin's absurd command to abandon his fort. On 29 December, Fullana accordingly burnt his supply magazines, bade his men to hurl the fort's canon into the surrounding moat, and marched off.[106]

Such was the gravity of Pain-et-Vin's blunder that the Prince had him court-martialled three weeks later, first by the "War Council," following established military judicial procedure by a mixed committee of regents and commanders. But the court's sentencing him to life-imprisonment failed to satisfy the furious Prince who then controversially overrode established procedure, installing an ad hoc committee chosen by himself to retry the defendant and show it was now he,

---

[103] Temple, *Memoirs*, 27.
[104] Van Malssen, *Louis XIV d'après les pamphlets*, 28–9; Van Nierop, *Life of Romeyn de Hooghe*, 103–7.
[105] Wicquefort, *Journael of dagelijcksch verhael* i, 134; *Histoire de Guillaume III* i, 61.
[106] GA Den Haag, Notarial Archive 461, fo. 210v–11v. 2 Feb. 1673.

not the regents, who decided high matters of state. Bullied by the Prince, this specially arranged court sentenced Pain-et-Vin to death despite objections that Pain-et-Vin's intentions were less culpable than initially reported. This whole affair and Pin-et-Vin's beheading, on 23 January 1673, remained a hot topic at The Hague for weeks.[107]

Fullana was among the officers whose conduct also came under scrutiny. Although it remained unclear for months whether any blame attached to him, and whether he too might be arrested, he was immediately affected financially, receiving none of the overdue salary owed to him for previous months' service, the matter of his arrears of salary dragging on well into 1674.[108] At issue was how Fullana had conducted himself in the face of the enemy. On 1 February, "Benedictus Spinoza" appeared as a witness before the public notary, Johannes Beeckman, in The Hague, together with several senior figures, including Ferdinand Le Fevre, a Huguenot officer serving under Viscount d'Harrey, and the Sephardic Jewish agent of the Danish crown in The Hague, Gabriel Milan (1631–89), a merchant-financier and later notorious governor of the Danish West Indies (1684–6). These two swore on oath to being well acquainted with Lieutenant-Colonel Fullana, presently residing in The Hague, confirming that he had not been arrested, indicted, or disgraced. Spinoza was present partly to translate on behalf of Fullana, presumably at the request of Van der Spijck in his capacity as *solliciteur militair*, but also as a witness to the sworn testimonies, signing the recorded testimony "B. despinoza," just as he had signed another legal document fifteen months earlier.[109]

Milan, like Fullana, had served as an officer in the army of Flanders and, during the late 1660s, prospered as a merchant. Since 1668, he was official "agent general" of the Danish crown, in Amsterdam. Like Baron Manuel (Isaac Nunes) Belmonte, official "resident" of the Spanish crown in Amsterdam, and Jeronimo Nunes da Costa (alias Moses Curiel), agent of the Portuguese crown, Milan was a prominent Sephardic figure spending much time on diplomatic business, negotiating with Dutch officials at The Hague.

It was presumably this unique clique of worldly, prominent, not particularly religiously observant military-diplomatic Jews frequenting The Hague, to whom Kortholt was referring later when he observed, being informed about this by Van der Spijck, that Spinoza "did not always exclude Jews from visiting him at the house."[110] Whilst working on the *Tractatus Politicus*, Spinoza evidently still had some contact with other Jews, especially of this highly untypical variety. One

---

[107] Costerus, *Historisch Verhael*, 330–5; *Histoire de Guillaume III* i, 62.
[108] GA Den Haag, Notarial Archive 461, fo. 337. 17 Jan. 1674; De Bruin, *Geheimhouding*, 573–4; Brown, "A Catalan Speaker," 97.
[109] GA Den Haag, Notarial Archive 461, fo. 209. 1 Feb. 1673 and NA 522, fo. 368; Petry and Van Suchtelen, "Spinoza and the Military," 360; Buijsen, *Haagse Schilders*, 347.
[110] Kortholt, "Preface," 179.

respect in which they were not untypical, though, and that must have gratified Spinoza, was that these men, like the Jews of Amsterdam and the Republic generally, proved strongly and memorably supportive of the Republic against the Republic's foes, strikingly more so than local Catholics, as many observers noted. Two things particularly interested Spinoza—the unaccustomed spectacle of Sephardic Jews of Marrano background demonstrating military experience, wisdom, and skills, and the example of Jews more actively supporting a direly besieged republic than some others in its moment of greatest need.

The notary's office where Spinoza testified in Fullana's favour, like many notaries' offices in The Hague, was located in the buildings around the Binnenhof, the complex housing the States of Holland's assembly hall and also an array of bookshops that Spinoza frequented. This was a spot where one could simultaneously find the latest publications, ponder political theory, and, for someone as keenly interested in political developments as Spinoza, keep a finger on the pulse of political, diplomatic, and military events.[111] The day after Spinoza witnessed on Fullana's behalf, another officer testified for Fullana confirming the veracity of his claims regarding what had transpired at the forts.

30.iv Monarchy Lambasted

By their conduct and actions, Louis and Charles proved themselves contemptible tyrants in Spinoza's eyes. Spinoza's aversion to monarchy (and the stadholderate), like his hostility to preachers, was certainly no less present in the *Tractatus Politicus* than earlier in the *TTP* (contrary to what several scholars have argued), and arguably even more so: "it is slavery then, not peace, that is promoted by transferring all power to one man; for peace, as we already said, consists not in the absence of war but in union or harmony of minds."[112] In Spinoza's view, even the worst monarchy nevertheless remains just a radically debased democracy, and the best possible monarchy a democratic republic moderately degraded by concentration of power in the royal figurehead. Monarchy, to a greater or lesser extent, is always prejudicial to society, much of the harm arising from the fact that kings cannot know, or do much, on their own. One man's power is extremely limited without the assistance of others, so that in any given context monarchical and quasi-monarchical figures (like Louis XIV, Charles II, or William III), simply lack the information needed to decide for themselves what policies to adopt. In reaching decisions, monarchs necessarily rely on subordinates, aides, and advisers, and if these at all resemble Charles' secretary of state, Arlington, and "the cabal," as

---

[111] Petry and Van Suchtelen, "Spinoza and the Military," 362.
[112] Spinoza, *Political Treatise*, 65; Kishlansky, *Monarchy Transformed*, 242–8; Sharp, "Family Quarrels," 104.

they are apt to, the resulting damage negatively affects everyone, even the ruling clique themselves. Hence, monarchy, averred Spinoza, is in "actual practice an aristocracy – not indeed overtly so but a concealed one – and consequently of the worst kind."[113] Nowhere did Spinoza stand further from Hobbes than here. What contemporaries termed royal absolutism Spinoza considers a degraded, corrupt form of aristocracy worse than formal aristocracy.

A basic rule of Spinoza's political science is that the more absolute a monarchy, the more wretched its subjects (and their neighbours); conversely, the only tolerable monarchy is one where the king's power is minimized in every way.[114] What postdates 1672 and is perhaps new in Spinoza's political thought, or at least more emphasized, is his rule, discussed earlier, that a good "commonwealth is always in greater danger from its citizens than its enemies; for good men are but few."[115] Hence, a constitution's rationality should be measured in terms of its capacity to secure a true, harmonious peace internally as well as eschew war externally. The more the republic or constitutional monarchy edges towards broad representation by a large council of representatives, the likelier the common good or *salus populi* is conserved in a stable, orderly fashion, rationally and harmoniously, for the benefit of all. The best kind of monarchy therefore features a "grand council," chosen from among the general populace, focused on the general welfare so that "war is to be made only for the sake of peace, and that with the end of hostilities arms may be laid aside."[116] No decrees whatever should issue from the throne concerning religion, except to suppress creeds deemed subversive of the commonwealth's foundations by the council.[117] In such a monarchy all laws are decreed by the king's "great council," and the "king should not be permitted to contract a foreign marriage," as had Charles I of England when marrying into the French royal house, and Charles II, in May 1662, when forging ties with the Portuguese court by marrying Catherine of Braganza (1638–1705).[118]

To maintain stability, peace, and the citizens' welfare, held Spinoza, very differently from Hobbes or Locke, every state, be it monarchy, aristocratic republic, or democracy, must as far as possible resemble the representative democratic republic grounded on a "great council." For large councils genuinely reflecting a broad range of opinion "will never be disposed in favour of war but always evince much zeal and love for peace."[119] "The people's welfare being the highest law," stable, effective monarchy should not only be guided by a large council of citizens

---

[113] Spinoza, *Political Treatise*, 65–6; Balibar, *Spinoza et la politique*, 87; Matheron, *Individu et communauté*, 405–7; Sharp, "Family Quarrels," 104.
[114] Spinoza, *Political Treatise*, 92–4; Bove, "Introduction," 78–9.
[115] Spinoza, *Political Treatise*, 66; Ramond, "Introduction," 38–41.
[116] Spinoza, *Political Treatise*, 73–4; Giancotti Boscherini, *Lexicon Spinozanum* i, 271.
[117] Spinoza, *Political Treatise*, 75; Sharp, "Family Quarrels," 104–5.
[118] Spinoza, *Political Treatise*, 74; Rosenthal, "What is Real about 'Ideal Constitutions'?," 25.
[119] Spinoza, *Political Treatise*, 80, 82; Ramond, "Introduction," 41–2.

but these representatives must never be chosen for life "but for three, four or five years at most." For if "appointed for life, most citizens would have barely any hope of attaining this office, causing huge inequality among the citizens, incessant murmuring and resentment, and finally sedition –which would not be unwelcome to kings who are eager to dominate," but effectively wrecks the stability of the best kind of monarchy.[120] Genuine breadth of representation benefits society more than anything else.

Perhaps the prime lesson Spinoza drew from the Disaster Year, and chief contrast between the *TTP* and the *Tractatus Politicus*, is his revised estimate of the role of fear, imposture, and emotion in swaying the multitude. Seeing he had earlier underestimated the threat, he now adjusted his conclusions as to how a well-ordered state should steer the multitude towards rationality and the common good. In a severe crisis like 1672 everything plunges into chaos in a moment. "However good its constitution, when the state is gripped by some crisis and everyone, as commonly happens, is seized with a kind of panic so that all pursue a course prompted only by immediate fear with no regard to the future, or the laws; all turn to the man renowned for his victories; they set him free from the laws, extend his command – a very bad precedent – and entrust the entire commonwealth to his good faith which was indeed the cause of the fall of the Roman republic."[121] Hence, the best republic must be so organized that "it is impossible for any single man to attain such a high reputation as to become the focus of all eyes," and although widespread panic must mean disarray and confusion, matters should be arranged so that "no one will be able to evade the laws and appoint someone illegally to a military command without at once evoking the opposition of other candidates." Clearly, Spinoza considered William III's elevation fundamentally illegal (contravening the Perpetual Edict) as well as damaging and unwise. Despite its defects, a multiple-city republic like the United Provinces still offered the best basis for freedom, stability, and durability—with adjustments ensuring a broader basis of participation and support.[122]

The best form of state in Spinoza's thought is that which is rationally governed and best preserves a harmonious peace internally as well as externally. As most men cannot act rationally in the general interest, each preferring his own advantage, wanting to rule rather than be ruled, and driven by "love of glory," the "common good" is best served by whatever political constitution most effectively counters man's emotional instability, irrationality, and ignorance, and preserves domestic harmony and peace abroad. Even the aristocratic republic can be amended to approach the advantages of the properly ordered democratic republic, though in practice this is difficult since patricians as a rule are guided not by zeal

---

[120] Spinoza, *Political Treatise*, 79–80, 82; Prokhovnik, *Spinoza and Republicanism*, 212, 229.
[121] Spinoza, *Political Treatise*, 133; Jaquet, "Longing (Desiderium)," 78–80.
[122] Spinoza, *Political Treatise*, 133–4; Rosenthal, "What is Real about 'Ideal Constitutions'?," 26–8.

for the public good but their wish "to debar the best men from the council and seek as colleagues those subservient to themselves, with the result that conditions in such states are far worse [than in democratic republics] since election to the patriciate depends on the personal choice, unrestricted by law, of a few men."[123]

Informal oligarchy being as damaging as monarchy and formal aristocracy, the well-ordered democratic republic must ensure all adult men are eligible "to vote in the supreme council and serve in offices of state." This then poses the question: "is it by nature or by institution that women are under the power of men [foeminae ex natura an ex instiuto sub potestate virorum sint]? For if this happens merely through institutional practice, then there is no compelling reason for us to exclude women from the government." This point brings the reader to the last surviving page of the *Tractatus*, often called Spinoza's "black page," where he breaks off shortly before his death.[124] Hugely disappointing to the modern reader after all the inspiring insights just preceding it, neither a pointer to modernity nor at all inspiring, this last page reflects what all human history thus far seemed to show. Woman's "weakness," argues Spinoza, is what prevents men and women governing the state together: "wherever in the world men and women are found, we find men ruling and women being ruled and both sexes thus living in harmony." He barely considers the possible objections to this, merely adding: "if women were naturally equals of men and equally endowed with strength of mind and ability – abilities wherein human power and therefore human right consist – then surely so many and such a wide variety of nations would have produced instances where men are ruled by women and are brought up to be inferior in ability. Since one sees such instances nowhere, one may conclude that women do not naturally possess equal right with men and necessarily give way to men."[125] The most that can be said in Spinoza's defence here is that in his age rampant tyrannizing over women was indeed universal.

Spinoza's relentless disparaging of kings, princes, nobles, patricians, oligarchs, and churchmen he himself remarks, "will draw sneers and be laughed at by those supposing the vices common to all mortals are confined only to the plebs, that there is no moderation in the common people who strike terror unless cowed by fear." But however erroneous the thinking of ordinary folk, the fact remains, he insists, that the ideas and decisions of kings, aristocrats, patricians, and ecclesiastics are just as greedy, incorrect, and damaging, and often more so than those of the common people. In Spinoza's political theory, aside from men's automatic dominance over women, no social class or stratum is better qualified than another

---

[123] Spinoza, *Political Treatise*, 136; Lavaert, *Vrijheid, gelijkheid, veelheid*, 236–7; Gatens, "Condition of Human Nature," 50–2, 56.
[124] Gatens, "Condition of Human Nature," 56–60; James, "Politically Mediated Affects," 72–7; Sharp, "Family Quarrels," 109–10.
[125] Spinoza, *Tractatus Politicus* in *Oeuvres* v, 272–3; Gatens, "Condition of Human Nature," 56–60; James, "Politically Mediated Affects," 73–6.

to be rational, and hence better qualified to rule. Imagining "there is no truth or judgment in the common people" was, though, unsurprising in the world in which he lived, given that "important affairs of state are conducted without their knowledge." To seek to "conduct all business without the knowledge of the citizens and then expect them not to misjudge and put a wrong interpretation on everything, is the highest ignorance." Where levels of awareness are raised, where the people learn to suspend judgement on matters inadequately known, and judge matters rightly on the basis of scant information, "they would surely be more fit to rule than be ruled."[126]

Law-abiding citizens are not born as such but rendered worthy by education, laws, and the republic's institutions. "As we have said," concludes Spinoza, paraphrasing Tacitus, "nature is the same in all men [Sed, ututi diximus, natura omnibus eadem est]"; "all become arrogant through domination, all terrorize unless frightened, and everywhere truth is generally trodden under by the hostile or servile especially when despotic power is in the hands of one or a few."[127] Since Spinoza was acutely conscious of the lack of moderation, crassness, and tendency to intimidate abounding among the nobles and ruling elites of the Europe of his day, and saw nothing surprising about elites wrongly assuming that the masses were less capable than themselves, remaining convinced "freedom" and "servility" exclude each other, one may legitimately wonder why did Spinoza, if he was to be consistent, not apply his highly sceptical and innovative, for his time uniquely subversive, de-legitimizing general principle likewise to men's tyrannizing over women.

Although on one level Spinoza appears to be demonstrating how each type of state—monarchy, aristocracy, the one-city republic, the multiple-city republic, and democratic republic—can be optimally reorganized to secure freedom, stability, and security for its inhabitants, in reality in each case the optimal format veers inexorably towards the democratic republic. Spinoza was the first major thinker to advocate the "democratic republic" as absolutely and invariably the best form of government in all circumstances and the first to set out a secular theory of "general will" of the kind that would become, historically, the theoretical backbone of Radical Enlightenment political theory, the main "general will" tradition—that is with Rousseau's *volonté générale* forming a subsidiary, divergent, and arguably less important subcategory. Spinoza in effect was the first political thinker comprehensively to reject aristocracy and monarchy as acceptable let alone preferable alternatives to representative democracy, seeing these as universally invalid, harmful, and disadvantageous to all society and human well-being.

Flatly contrary to Rousseau later, in Spinoza reason alone defines the "general will" which is universally the same. "General will," grounded on "reason," that is

---

[126] Spinoza, *Opera* iii, 319; Kossmann, *Political Thought*, 77.
[127] Spinoza, *Opera* iii, 320; James, "Politically Mediated Affects," 70.

non-particularist, non-Rousseauist "general will" grounds Spinoza's classic concluding principle that "the right of a commonwealth is determined by the power of the multitude as though by that of a single mind. But this union of minds can in no way be conceived unless the republic tends as far as possible to that which sound reason [sana ratio] teaches is for the good of all men."[128] Placing reason on the throne as the basis of society, education, and politics works only where ignorance, credulity, and intolerance are first sufficiently cut back, for men an immensely formidable and difficult task.

---

[128] Spinoza, *Tractatus Politicus* in *Oeuvres* v, 116–17; Bove, "Introduction," 9; Israel, *Democratic Enlightenment*, 633–42.

31
Denying the Supernatural

For the early modern mind the question whether, apart from the Almighty, supernatural things exist, or, as Spinoza and his following maintained, "the imaginings of ordinary men about God and spirits"[1] form a make-believe world of fiction exploited over the millennia by theologians, loomed large. To most it was self-evident, as for virtually all known cultures and peoples in the past, that the supernatural sphere is tangible, impinging, and not just real but among the most powerful realities confronting human beings and pervading their lives. The New Testament fully endorses such belief, reinforcing credence in Satan, angels, the realm of demons, exorcism, and diabolical intrusion into human life. Hence, much was at stake and, as so often, Spinoza here found the entire weight of the past and current thinking (with the partial exception of Hobbes), steadfastly against him. During the seventeenth century's last quarter the issue of the supernatural figured among the foremost of the Reformed Church's concerns in its battle to halt the creeping progress of rationalization, mathematization, secularization, and radical thought.

Philosophical denial of the supernatural as a constant reality is one point where Spinoza (and the Koerbaghs) seemingly do follow in Hobbes' footsteps. Yet, here again crucial differences emerge. From an early stage, probably the late 1650s onwards and certainly by 1660, denying the Devil and demonology was central to Spinoza's philosophical system. Refuting the Devil's existence in the *Korte Verhandeling*, Spinoza abolishes also all demons as "fictions," explaining why neither the Devil nor lesser demons can possibly exist.[2] The Koerbaghs followed Spinoza here, equating angels and devils with "good" and "bad" persons. The word "angel," one reads in the *Bloemhof*, is a mistranslation from the Hebrew for "messenger," misleading the common people into incorrectly believing angels are supernatural spirits. In *Een Ligt*, the brothers likewise flatly deny that angels or demons exist.[3] The word "Devil" for the Koerbaghs is a "bastard" word borrowed from the Greek *diabolos*, signifying in reality someone falsely vilifying or defaming another; its subsequent meaning designating a "bad spirit" being yet another

---

[1] Spinoza, *Theological-Political Treatise*, 26.
[2] Spinoza, *Collected Works* (ed. Curley) i, 57, 145–6; Kortholt, *De Tribus Impostoribus*, 184–5; Knol, "Waarom hield Spinoza," 8.
[3] Koerbagh, *Bloemhof*, 268; Koerbagh, *A Light Shining*, 348–9, 406–11, 416–17, 436–41; Koelman, *Het Vergift*, 510–11.

theologians' fabrication without equivalent in early Dutch.[4] In this way Spinoza's stance laid the basis for a public furore, set to escalate in the late seventeenth century, over whether Satan and demonic forces do or do not exist, entangling Cartesianism in a protracted, furious contest with the Reformed Church later to culminate in the most resounding public intellectual-cultural controversy of the later Dutch Golden Age, the Bekker controversies of the early 1690s.

No Devil exists and there is no demonology, sorcery, or demonic possession, nor satanic influence on individuals, held Spinoza, since "the causes, or better put, what we call sin, preventing us from attaining our perfection, are in ourselves."[5] Beyond our own failings, no other evil forces are at work influencing men. Potentially explosive though Spinoza's stance was, his sweeping rejection of demonic power and Satan's existence remained largely veiled from the outside world, evident to contemporaries, apart from in the *Korte Verhandeling* manuscript slowly gathering dust, solely via conversation and inference from the *Ethics*. Still, even without projecting the point further, from his writing and conversation Spinoza's position was clear enough, as was the identical stance of the Koerbaghs for those who had seen the *Bloemhof*. Before long, Spinozistic denial of the existence of angels and devils became in turn part of the seething controversy dividing the Collegiant movement. Deeply antagonistic towards philosophy, Frans Kuyper led the counter-campaign, intensifying through the 1660s and 1670s, declaring the split between Cartesians and that "philosophy" denying the existence of angels and devils (i.e. Spinoza's and the Koerbaghs') incontrovertible proof that the common man wastes his time by venturing into philosophy. Faith focused on Scripture alone opens the door to truth, solid good sense, and the supernatural, including belief in angels and devils.[6]

Spells, magic, charms, and sorcery, declare the Koerbaghs, are all superstitious non-existing entities; none are real, "the Devil" himself being non-existent. Spinoza and his following thus preceded Bekker by three decades, penetrating in fact well beyond Bekker's later stance, by denying outright the Devil's very existence and that of all supernatural spirits. Intent on reconciling his standpoint with Scripture and church teaching, as everything the Bible affirms must be true, Bekker concurs that Satan does actually exist but cannot influence the minds and doings of men.[7] In his published work, in the 1670s, notably the *TTP* but also by implication the *Ethics* and in his correspondence, Spinoza, like the Koerbaghs, firmly indicates the non-existence of spirits, ghosts, witchcraft, and apparitions of a supernatural character while avoiding drawing attention to or emphasizing his stance,[8] a clear indication of his exercise of "caute." Hobbes, by contrast, does enter further into discussion about this in the *Leviathan*. There is an age-old

---

[4] Koerbagh, *Bloemhof*, 358–9.   [5] Spinoza, *Collected Works* (ed. Curley) i, 146.
[6] Kuyper, *Den Philosopherenden Boer*, 16–18.   [7] Koerbagh, *Bloemhof*, 303, 670.
[8] Spinoza, *Theological-Political Treatise*, xii, 26, 41, 63, 244.

connection between the instinctive errors of ordinary human existence and scholarly error about the world, contends Hobbes. Misconceptions born of dreams and imaginings were the original seedbed of belief in spirits, ghosts, revelations, and demonic possession. He adhered to his denial of incorporeal substances, of the notion of an "unbodily body" to the end of his life, a feature of his thought that caused real unease, even outrage, and a point where his philosophy and that of Spinoza seemingly do converge.[9]

Unqualified elimination of the supernatural, while deeply characteristic of Spinozism is encountered also in other categories of atheists and sceptics, being a necessary but not sufficient qualification for inclusion in the basic category "Radical Enlightenment." Hobbes and Spinoza certainly converge in claiming superstitious belief in demonic power and sorcery harms society and the individual.[10] In the *Leviathan*, wherever Christ appears to cast out demons and evil spirits, he is actually curing lunacy, disease, or some other bodily evil.[11] Hobbes meets objections to this by pointing out that while Christ does speak of spirits "yet he denies not that they be bodies: And where St Paul saies 'we shall rise spirituall bodies,' he acknowledgeth the nature of spirits, but that they are bodily spirits." Moreover, Hobbes wraps his denial of supernatural forces in enough equivocation to support Jesus' and Paul's remarks about spirits (which Spinoza makes no attempt to justify) and does not openly deny the supernatural as a force of divine inspiration in relation to the New Testament as Spinoza does. Above all, Hobbes does not deny or diminish the reality of religious authority which sanctions belief in *supernaturalia*.

Meanwhile, virtually the whole academic body, including the chief practitioners of experimental science, solidly, even militantly, endorsed belief in spirits and ghosts, and to an extent witchcraft. In this respect, Hobbes and Spinoza created a festering, fundamental rift among the leading intellects of the day. Boyle and the Royal Society experimenters unhesitatingly aligned with Cudworth, More, and the theologians on this point against the "Hobbians." The undeniable evidence of "intelligent beings that are not ordinarily visible," Boyle believed, would greatly assist in "the reclaiming" of those he despised as atheists.[12] Equally, Locke's empiricism readily accommodates angels, devils, apparitions, ghosts, and supernatural beings, and Locke who took notes from the *TTP* between 1672 and 1675, unreservedly endorses belief in the truth of all of these.[13] Locke's approach was vastly more approved of than Spinoza's by the bulk of opinion including the progressive elements of Europe's churches throughout the Early Enlightenment. No one could deny, though, that Spinoza's Early Enlightenment marks a more

---

[9] Malcolm, *Editorial Introduction*, 48, 155; MacMillan, "Exorcising Demons," 13–14, 17–18.
[10] Shapin and Schaffer, *Leviathan and the Air-Pump*, 317; MacMillan, "Exorcising Demons," 34–5.
[11] Hobbes, *Leviathan* iii, 1016–24; Malcolm, *Aspects of Hobbes*, 482.
[12] Shapin and Schaffer, *Leviathan and the Air-Pump*, 314–15.
[13] Lucci, *John Locke's Christianity*, 3, 42; Nuovo, "Locke's Proof," 58.

complete, abrupt, definitive break with the past, a bigger stride towards a comprehensively scientific outlook than the positions of Hobbes or Locke.

With regard to "spirits" Hobbes and Spinoza both explicitly raise the question of the philosophical status of ideas confirmed by innumerable sources, the reality of which practically everyone accepts. It was a question Bayle would raise still more forcefully in the 1690s. Is it conceivable that what practically everybody has believed since time immemorial, confirmed and insisted on by churchmen everywhere, and many generations of trained scholars and scientists of every persuasion, could be altogether false, damaging to human life, and without foundation? Could the considered view of the entire theological establishment in all the universities, colleges, and ecclesiastical organizations of Christendom be wholly mistaken? Spinoza and Bayle alone insist they could. So formidable are the bastions of ignorance and credulity that even Christ, emphasizes Spinoza, when striving to raise men to a higher level morally, here simply surrenders to universal ignorance and superstition, making no attempt whatever to counter the general delusion of belief in the supernatural, so universally damaging to human life.

During the early Enlightenment period, as Bayle especially pointed out, the philosophical status and validity of *consensus gentium* [the consensus of peoples] became a crucial battleground, encompassing not least the fight over whether the existence of a knowing God above nature who rewards and punishes is known as an unassailable reality. Even where *consensus omnium* reigns, contended Bayle, where everyone agrees without reservation or question, it remains conceivable that such belief is nonetheless false. Most opinion denied this. Much of Bayle's dispute with the Huguenot theologians known as the *rationaux*, seeking to reconcile theology with science and philosophy by closely allying with Locke and Newton revolved around this point. Bayle quarrelled especially with Jacques Bernard (1658–1718) over whether the "agreement of all peoples" concerning the reality of divine governance and the supernatural is or is not a fundamental verity established beyond question.[14] The fact most people believe something, or even that everyone believes something [*consensus omnium*], retorted Bayle, does not prove such belief is true; rather, the reverse is distinctly likelier given the universal prevalence of superstition. This issue would emerge, three decades after Spinoza's death, as a major split within the early Enlightenment.[15]

In Spinoza's life, detailed evidence of his discussing such issues dates mainly from the autumn of 1674 when he entered into correspondence with a regent in the small, strategically placed fortress town of Gorcum (also spelled Gorinchem) east of Dordrecht, among the bulwarks of the "water-line" defences against the

---

[14] Bayle, *Continuation* ii, 364; Mori, *Bayle philosophe*, 186, 209, 307; Brogi, *Teologia senza verità*, 24, 97–100, 117–19.

[15] [Bernard], *Nouvelles de la République des Lettres* (January–June 1705), 126; Bost, *Pierre Bayle*, 104–6; Israel, *Enlightenment Contested*, 73.

French, on the southern side towards the great rivers. This was Hugo Boxel (1607–80), the well-read pensionary of Gorcum in the years 1660–72 who was also an elder of the local Reformed consistory, steeped in law, theology, and Greek. A keen supporter of De Witt's "True Freedom," and involved in the negotiations with the French in 1672, he was among those purged from office under the Orangist reaction, in 1672.[16] Spinoza and Boxel had already then known each other for some time and doubtless had commiserated together over the blows the Republic had suffered, De Witt's downfall, and the misfortunes felt especially harshly around Gorcum, much of the area around being flooded as part of the water barrier forming the last line of defence against the French.[17] Ruinously for the local economy, Gorcum's environs remained inundated on three sides for fifteen months or more.

"I will say nothing about the war, nothing about rumours, for it is our lot to live in such times," Boxel concludes his first surviving missive to Spinoza, penned originally in Dutch, the language in which they corresponded, correspondence extant today, however, only in Latin translation.[18] Boxel's particular theme during their exchange over several months was the supernatural, apparitions, and especially ghosts. "The great respect in which I have always held you, and still hold you," answered Spinoza, using wording suggesting they had known each other a considerable time, "does not permit me to contradict you, still less to humour you."[19] The two clearly had a history of previous discussion. Boxel's letter had only just reached him the day before, remarks Spinoza in his reply, and was "most welcome because I wanted to have news of you and because it assures me that you have not entirely forgotten me." To Spinoza, Boxel mattered as a friend as well as former leading representative of the anti-Orangist faction and the Cartesian bloc. In a later letter, Boxel refers too to their earlier conversations confirming these had indeed taken place on the water-line, at Gorcum, as well as in The Hague.

Over the decades, Calvinist and later Cartesian influence in Dutch society had left belief in supernatural involvement in everyday life somewhat on the wane. The last woman burnt at the stake (after being strangled) for witchcraft in Holland, Anna Muggen, who admitted making a pact with the Devil and bewitching several individuals, was executed in 1608, ironically enough at Gorcum. Over the next half century both witchcraft accusations and witchcraft trials dwindled, by international standards, to an exceptionally low level in the United Provinces. Nevertheless, both Calvinists and Cartesians evinced a firm resolve to defend

---

[16] Spinoza, *Collected Works* (ed. Curley) ii, 364n21; Coppens, "Spinoza et Boxel," 61–2; Freudenthal/Walther, *Lebensgeschichte* ii, 69; Van de Ven, *Printing Spinoza*, 381.
[17] Blanning, *Pursuit of Glory*, 539.
[18] Boxel to Spinoza, 14 Sept. 1674 in Spinoza, *Collected Works* (ed. Curley) ii, 407–8; Klever, *Een nieuwe Spinoza*, 97.
[19] Spinoza, *Briefwisseling*, 529n50; Klever, *Spinoza Classicus*, 162; Van de Ven, "Spinoza's Life and Time," 27, 32.

the core elements of the realm of the supernatural. In the first of six surviving letters between Spinoza and the Gorcum town pensionary, of 14 September 1674, Boxel inquires flat out as to Spinoza's view of apparitions, spectres, and ghosts. The "ancients believed in their existence," while the "theologians and philosophers of our times still believe in the reality of creatures of this kind, though they do not agree as to the nature of their essence, some claiming they consist of very delicate and fine matter." From their previous discussions, which he found slightly troubling, Boxel inferred that Spinoza was "greatly at variance [with all the rest] on this subject, for I doubt whether you concede their existence. Yet, it cannot escape you that throughout antiquity there recur so many instances and stories about them that it would be difficult indeed to deny them or even call them into doubt."

Although "I still do not know what they are," replied Spinoza, and "no one has ever been able to inform me," he promised to take Boxel's standpoint seriously. However, never having seen an account of supernatural occurrences that appeared at all credible to him, Spinoza asked Boxel to "select from the numerous ghost stories you have read, one or two that are least open to doubt and that most clearly prove the existence of ghosts." "Finally, my dear Sir, before going further into this matter, I beg you to tell me what kind of things these ghosts or spirits are. Are they children, fools or madmen? For what I have heard seems to indicate silly people rather than intelligent beings, or, at best, childish games or the pastime of fools." As regards the innumerable stories featuring ghosts, he ends by suggesting, narrators are encouraged to twist or alter the real facts of occurrences by the absence of witnesses able to contradict them, by their fancies or fears, and perhaps even desire to impress, to raise one's standing among others.[20]

Answering on 21 September 1674, Boxel again invoked their friendship agreeing that "friends may well disagree about indifferent matters without this ever impairing their friendship." Spinoza's impression that everything told about ghost stories suggests one is dealing with deluded folk rather than intelligent beings only confirmed to his mind the old proverb that a "preconceived opinion hinders the search for truth." Admittedly, one often hears of outrageous twisting and manipulation of common beliefs especially regarding supernatural appearances. Magic *is* often deception and the existence of demons that "torment wretched people in this life and the next" often matter for fables rather than reality. "I make no mention of monks and clergymen who report so many apparitions and sightings of souls, spirits and demons, so many stories, or rather fables of spectres that people are bored by them and sick of reading them."[21] Such types "expound these themes merely for their own gain," Boxel readily concurred, "to prove there is a purgatory which, for them, is a mine from which they extract much silver and gold."[22] However, his own belief that ghosts exist stemmed from belief in a Creator

---

[20] Spinoza, *Collected Works* (ed. Curley) ii, 408–9; Spinoza, *Briefwisseling*, 312–13.
[21] Spinoza, *Opera* iv, 248–9.   [22] Spinoza, *Collected Works* (ed. Curley) ii, 411–12.

who would undoubtedly want spirits and apparitions in a universe of beauty and perfection such as He has created. Surely it is "probable the Creator created them as they resemble him more closely than do corporeal creatures." If there can be bodies without souls, as all Cartesians agree, then, equally, "there is a soul without body."

"There are spirits of all kinds," affirmed Boxel, both material and immaterial, visible and invisible "except perhaps of the female sex." This is hardly reasoning, he acknowledges, that will "convince those who perversely believe the world is made by chance," belief in spirits, as he understood it, being anchored in faith in a Creator God and the reality of souls separate from bodies. But belief in ghosts is also hard to deny given the many reports about them abounding down to the present day. As supporting evidence confirming ghosts' existence, Boxel cites besides Plutarch, Suetonius, and the treatise on ghosts and spectres of the Zurich Protestant theologian Ludwig Lavater (1527–86), also Pliny the Younger, Valerius Maximus, Cardano, Melanchthon, and the noted Dutch physician and writer on witchcraft and occultism, Johan Weyer (1515–88), whose books he assumes Spinoza will readily have at hand. Finally, one is allowed to throw in one's own personal experience, or at least indirect experience: a burgomaster of Schiedam, "a learned and wise man, still alive, told me once that sounds of work were heard at night in his mother's brewery" after the workmen had gone home, "exactly as when brewing was in progress during the day which, he swore, occurred several times."[23]

The realm of ghosts, held Boxel, is in fact very different from that of demons, exorcism, and magic. What distinguishes belief in ghosts and phantoms from the superstitions of some clergymen, particularly Catholics, endorsing ridiculous reports of visions and apparitions, were the detailed accounts abounding in Plutarch, Pliny, Suetonius, and Valerius Maximus, which Boxel deemed incontestable evidence confirmed by recent legal and medical scholars who were not churchmen and opposed witchcraft trials and fought superstition, as had Weyer. The thought of gain inspiring many Catholic clergy did not apply here. Closing his letter, Boxel included a passage revealing an interesting aspect of Spinoza's personality, a provocative, teasing side the editors deliberately deleted from the published Latin version of the *Opera Posthuma* but left in the Dutch translation, in the *Nagelate Schriften*. "You remark at the end of your letter that to commend me to God is something you cannot do without laughing [lachen]"; but, "if you still remember that earlier conversation between us," Boxel rebuked him, he had surely given him cause to stop and think. He then quotes a key sentence from Lavater's treatise: "he who dares repudiate what so many concurring witnesses, ancient and modern affirm, seems in my judgment unworthy of being believed in anything, as

---

[23] Spinoza, *Collected Works* (ed. Curley) ii, 411. Spinoza, *Opera* iv, 248; Klever, "Spoken van Hugo Boxel," 55; Coppens, "Spinoza et Boxel," 63, 66.

it is no less a mark of rash effrontery to shamelessly contradict so many historians, ancestors and others of great authority" as to lend unquestioning belief to all who assert that they have seen spirits.[24] Cartesians like Boxel favoured a cautious in-between position in the manner of Weyer. How can the mass of recorded testimony of millennia be entirely rejected?

Spinoza never relied just on the books he had at his own lodgings. But it was far from easy for him to consult particular books not immediately at hand. Delaying until the following month, before replying, Spinoza explained that he had needed to search around, since the heart of Boxel's challenge lay in his classical erudition. He rejoiced that Boxel too felt friends might disagree about such issues without this affecting their friendship and apologized for not writing sooner. The "books you quoted are not at hand, and I have found none but Pliny and Suetonius." Still, Pliny and Suetonius sufficed for present purposes, saving Spinoza the "trouble of consulting the rest, for I am sure they all affirm the same kind of nonsense and love of tales of extraordinary events that astonish men and compel their wonder." Spinoza professed amazement less at the stories themselves than the fact that men of ability and judgement like Pliny, Suetonius (and Boxel) should squander their gifts and misuse their eloquence to persuade readers of such "trifles." The essential question, though, was "whether I who deny spectres and spirits exist am thereby failing to understand those writers who have written on this subject, or whether you, claiming such things do exist, are lending them more credence than they deserve." Boxel's conviction that there are male spirits but not female ones was another aspect Spinoza could not help treating with some levity. This view seemed to him quite unfounded, not to say ridiculous, resembling the "popular imagination conceiving God to be of the masculine rather than feminine gender": "I am surprised those who have seen naked spirits," he added, providing a further glimpse of his derisive sense of humour, "have not cast their eyes upon their genitals; perhaps they were too afraid – or else ignorant of the difference?"[25] He had no wish to resort to ridicule, though, or for Boxel to suppose that he was refusing to be serious.

Spinoza denied outright that he thought "the world was made by chance" rather than by a creator God. It is "certain that chance and necessity are two contrary terms, so plainly he who affirms the world is the necessary consequence of the divine nature is also entirely denying that the world was made by chance, whereas he who believes God could have refrained from creating the world asserts, even if in different terms, that it *was* created by chance, since in that case it arose from an act of will that might not otherwise have occurred."[26] Boxel's contention that "it

---

[24] Spinoza, *Opera* iv, 248–9; Spinoza, *Correspondance* (ed. Rovere.), 298.
[25] Spinoza, *Opera* iv, 250–1; Gullan-Whur, *Life of Spinoza*, 266; Klever, *Een nieuwe Spinoza*, 99; Coppens, "Spinoza et Boxel," 64.
[26] Spinoza, *Opera* iv, 251; Spinoza, *Correspondance* (ed.) Rovere, 300.

pertains to the beauty and perfection of the universe that spirits exist" Spinoza also dismissed outright. Beauty is "not so much a quality of the object one sees as an effect of the object on him who sees it." The loveliest hand still looks unseemly when viewed through a microscope, and other things too appearing beautiful from a distance appear ugly when viewed from close by: "considered in themselves, or in relation to God, things are neither beautiful nor ugly."[27] As for Boxel's other claims, they clashed, Spinoza asserts, not only with his rejection of the supernatural but his doctrine of infinity and divine immanence. Spinoza rejects especially Boxel's notion that "because spirits express God's image more than do other corporeal creatures, it seemed likely that God has created them."

"I frankly confess I do not understand in what way spirits reflect God more than other creatures. This I do know, that between the finite and the infinite there is no proportion so that the difference between God and the greatest and most excellent created thing is no different than between God and the most minimal created thing." Here was the voice of a man used to examining tiny living creatures through microscopes. If he had as "clear an idea of spectres as of a triangle or circle," Spinoza adds, "I would not hesitate to affirm those things have been created by God." But since the idea he had of them corresponded only to that wide category of ridiculous fancies that includes harpies, griffins, hydras and so forth, all fictions created purely by the human imagination, he could not see how they could be anything other than absurdities even if also widely accepted delusions, imaginings just as foreign to God as being from non-being.[28]

Equally unconvincing was Boxel's argument that if a body can exist without a soul, a soul must be able to exist without a body. Can memory, hearing, sight, etc. exist without bodies simply because there are bodies without memory, hearing or sight? "Can a sphere exist without a circle simply because there are circles that are not spheres?" From the great abundance of tales of ghosts and apparitions Spinoza had hoped that Boxel could produce one or two scarcely open to doubt that would go some way to substantiate his standpoint. But the story of the burgomaster and the brewery sounded purely preposterous to him, and all the incidents cited in classical texts he had seen seemed to him as trivial as they were unbelievable. All that was relevant in Suetonius' history of the Caesars (a book not in his own library) was the story that Julius Caesar "laughed at such things and yet was favoured by fortune, according to what Suetonius relates, in chapter 59 of his biography." Everyone pondering the musings and emotions of mortals should laugh at such notions, "whatever Lavater," the archdeacon of the great church of Zurich, who had been one of the most prolific Reformation era Protestant

---

[27] Spinoza, *Collected Works* (ed. Curley) ii, 414–15; Klever, "Spoken van Hugo Boxel," 58.
[28] Spinoza, *Opera* iv, 252–3; Carlisle, *Spinoza's Religion*, 69.

contenders for demonology, "and others fantasizing with him in this matter can adduce to the contrary."[29]

Stung by Spinoza's ridicule, and low opinion of Lavater and Weyer, Boxel replied forcefully reiterating his previous claims. If bodies can exist without memory, so memory can exist without body. As for Spinoza's demand for "demonstrativas probationes" [demonstrable proofs] that there are spirits in the world, he pointed out that in our world there are, outside mathematics, no such "certain proofs as we would wish for." Hence, men must content themselves mainly with probabilities and cogent, convincing conjectures. If arguments by which things are proved were altogether conclusive only fools and the perversely obstinate would ever contradict them. But men cannot be that precise and must content themselves with what is probable.[30] Spinoza's demand for as clear an idea of spirits "as of a triangle" was unreasonable and impossible. "Tell me, I beg you, what idea you have of God, and whether it is as clear to your intellect as a triangle. I know that you have none such, and that, as I have said, we are not so fortunate as to be able to apprehend things through conclusive proofs so that for the most part the probable holds sway in the world." "Spirits are like God," he reiterated, "because he too is spirit." "It is not those defending the existence of spirits who discredit philosophers," concluded Boxel, "but rather those [like Spinoza] denying their existence who do, for all philosophers ancient and modern believe spirits exist."

Ancient authority surely counted and to Boxel and others such evidence seemed more compelling than the rationalizing of a single philosopher. Plutarch attests to such belief in his treatise on the views of the philosophers, "as did all the Stoics, Pythagoreans, Platonists, Peripatetics, Empedocles, Maximus Tyrius, Apuleius and others." Of modern philosophers, there is not one (apart from Spinoza) who altogether denies spirits and spectres.

> Reject, then, the testimonies of what so many wise witnesses had seen and heard, so many philosophers, so many historians, narrating such things. Insist they are all as foolish and deluded as ordinary folk notwithstanding that your answers are unconvincing, some even absurd, and mostly irrelevant to our points of disagreement; nor do you offer any proof to support your opinion. Caesar no more mocked spectres than did Cicero or Cato, but only omens and prognostications and, yet, had he not mocked Spurina, on the day he was destined to die, he would not have received so many wounds from his enemies.[31]

---

[29] Spinoza, *Opera* iv, 254; Spinoza, *Correspondance* (ed. Rovere), 303–4; Klever, *Spinoza Classicus*, 164.
[30] Spinoza, *Opera* iv, 256; Klever, "Spoken van Hugo Boxel," 62–3.
[31] Spinoza, *Opera* iv, 258; Spinoza, *Correspondance* (ed. Rovere), 308–9; Klever, *Spinoza Classicus*, 165.

Boxel's "principia," answered Spinoza, were "longe a mea diversa [far distant from my own]," and he saw little point in prolonging a now clearly stalled discussion.[32] The exchange was becoming decidedly testy, and Spinoza became anxious to bring their now tiresome, sterile disagreement to a close. However useful in the sphere of empirical knowledge and practical experience, Boxel's distinction between probabilities and certain knowledge seemed to him irrelevant to reaching certainty as regards rational inferences from substantiated fact. In everyday life we must stick to what is probable, but in philosophizing we must adhere to what is certain. "A man refusing to eat and drink until obtaining proof that food and drink are good for him would perish of hunger and thirst. But this has no application in philosophizing. Rather, we must take care to admit nothing as true that is merely probable. When one false proposition is allowed, innumerable others follow."[33] This is a clear illustration of Spinoza's distinction between useful empirical knowledge which, as one commentator put it, "is always merely probable, on the one hand, and durable and indubitable theoretical" knowledge, on the other. But this should not be taken to mean Spinoza lacked interest in experiment and empirically gained knowledge or rejected application of measurement and mathematics to understanding nature, as some modern scholars unjustifiably construe his meaning.[34]

To assert, like Boxel, that it is "necessary" and "free" that are opposites, not "necessary" and "contingent" or "fortuitous," Spinoza deemed absurd and opposed to reason: "nobody can deny God freely knows himself and all other things, and yet all are unanimous in granting that God knows himself necessarily. Thus, you fail, I think, to make any distinction between coercion, or force, and necessity." For Spinoza this distinction between necessary self-direction and external coercion remained always of primary significance.[35] Man's will to live, his appetites, and other drives are necessary but do not stem from external coercion. Nothing in Boxel's answers, concludes Spinoza, could alter his view that his conjectures, like the New Testament reports of spirits, demons, and spectres, were altogether as unfounded as his appeal to history of philosophy. "The authority of Plato, Aristotle and Socrates," a now slightly irritated, impatient Spinoza signed off his last surviving letter to Boxel, "carries little weight with me."[36]

He would have been surprised, Spinoza admits in the same letter, had Boxel invoked instead those ancient thinkers for whom he felt greater respect— Epicurus, Democritus, Lucretius "or one of the Atomists or defenders of the atoms," but found it unsurprising he should cite precisely those ancient Greek thinkers "who thought up occult qualities, intentional species, substantial forms

---

[32] Spinoza, *Opera* iv, 262; Nadler, *Spinoza: A Life*, 380.
[33] Spinoza, *Collected Works* (ed. Curley) ii, 421–2.
[34] For this error, see Schliesser, "Spinoza and the Philosophy of Science," 171.
[35] Harris, *Salvation from Despair*, 124; Nadler, *Think Least of Death*, 37.
[36] Spinoza, *Correspondance* (ed. Rovere), 313; Klever, *Spinoza Classicus*, 165.

[qualitates occultas, species intentionales, formas substantiales] and a thousand more such idle notions," these being the very men who contrived also spectres and ghosts giving credence to grandmothers' tales "with a view to disparaging Democritus whose high reputation they so envied they burned all the books he had published amidst so much acclaim."[37] This last alludes to a passage in Diogenes Laertius (AD 180–240), historian of the Greek philosophers, who records that so averse to Democritus's philosophy was Plato that he would like to have burnt it all. Opening a rare window on Spinoza's biases in the field of ancient philosophy and personal likes and dislikes, this passage breathes real antipathy to scholasticism and to Platonism, and high regard for precisely those Greek thinkers, Democritus, Epicurus, and Lucretius, early modern scholars decried and marginalized.

Spinoza's audacity regarding the supernatural culminates in his truly unprecedented approach to the New Testament, his regarding all Christian theological commentary of earlier centuries (he never mentions any post-biblical Christian authorities), and of his own time, on the New Testament as wholly irrelevant to understanding the Gospels. As part of his insistence on approaching the New Testament exclusively on its own terms, disregarding all theology, he relied on the published Syriac (Aramaic) New Testament edited by the Italian Jewish double apostate (first from Judaism to Catholicism and a year later from Catholicism to Protestantism), Immanuel Tremellius (1510–80). For Spinoza, it was axiomatic that while the New Testament survives only in translation (first into Greek), it was originally composed in the language of Jesus and the Apostles (Palestinian Aramaic), or "Hebrew," as he mostly calls it, so that only by examining the Semitic roots can one approach the true meanings of New Testament terms and expressions. Indeed, Spinoza was not entirely certain Tremellius' Syriac version was actually a translation and wondered whether, in part, it could be an older as well as more authentic version preceding the Greek (though it was not).[38]

Spinoza's always strikingly positive view of the New Testament pivots on the distinction he introduces in chapter XI of the *TTP* between prophecy and "teaching," especially the epistolary style Paul develops in his Epistles. Up to a point, Paul of Tarsus, whom he never calls "Saint Paul," emerges as a kind of superhero in Spinoza's eyes, for pushing further the apostolic shift from prophecy (which the Apostles still to an extent engaged), to didactic concerns—explaining, philosophizing, and initiating the transfer of core biblical teaching from Hebrew into Greek. At one point, Spinoza flatly states: "for the Apostles always employ arguments, so that they seem to be engaged in a debate rather than prophesying." Wholly admirable, Christ's Apostles, quite unlike Old Testament prophets summoned to admonish a particular erring nation, "were summoned to preach to

---

[37] Spinoza, *Opera* iv, 261–2; Klever, *Spinoza Classicus*, 65.
[38] Spinoza, *Theological-Political Treatise*, 270; Curley, 'Spinoza's Contribution," 378, 400n48.

everyone without exception and convert all men to religion."[39] Where Old Testament prophets provide "nothing but dogmas and decrees," claiming supernatural inspiration, the Paul Spinoza eulogizes presents his doctrines not as commands but arguments backed by reasoning while continually "submitting them to the judgment of each individual for decision. Thus, Paul regularly engages in debate: in 1 Corinthians 10.15, for example, says 'I speak to you as intelligent men; judge for yourselves what I say'." Especially Paul deserves praise because "the long deductions and arguments of Paul, such as in the Epistle to the Romans, were not written on the basis of supernatural revelation. Rather, the Apostles' modes of discourse and discussion very plainly reveal that they wrote their Epistles not on the basis of divine command and revelation, but simply that of their own natural judgment."[40] Hence, not only can no sacred or ecclesiastical status of any kind be attributed to any Apostle, but it is precisely their disagreeing with each other, their participating in nothing more than common human debate and teaching, the complete absence, as Spinoza sees it, of anything at all genuinely supernatural in the New Testament that makes it valuable.

Never more utterly subversive than when discussing the Gospels, Spinoza urges us to venerate the Apostles and Paul, because they wrote nothing based on divine command or revelation and adhered strictly to teaching, persuasion, and presenting arguments for their campaign to publicize Christ's purely ethical message. Some might claim the Apostles preached religion "by simply telling the story of Christ," which as an historical account "does not come within the scope of reason." Yet, the essence of Christ's life, "like all Christ's teaching," insists Spinoza, "consists primarily of moral doctrine" eminently accessible to everyone by the light of natural reason alone. Hence, it presents no difficulty whatever, quite the contrary, that the Apostles flatly contradict each other about everything beyond pure moral doctrine and disagree entirely about religion's foundations for, fortunately for us all, this proves there is no such thing as a common Christian doctrine outside basic morality. Rather, as "teachers, the Apostles were in the same position as other teachers."[41] Where Paul insists on faith alone and that "no one is justified by works," James, in his Epistle, asserts the reverse, that men are "justified by works and not by faith alone."[42] Basic contradiction in the New Testament is fundamental but also wholesome, proving the impossibility of deriving any meaningful theology or belief from the Gospels; nor, indeed, should the reader expect any. Not only does no such thing as an authentic church legitimately

---

[39] Spinoza, *Theological-Political Treatise*, 158–9; Hunter, *Radical Protestantism in Spinoza's Thought*, 60.
[40] Spinoza, *Theological-Political Treatise*, 156–7; Laerke, *Spinoza and the Freedom*, 63.
[41] Spinoza, *Theological-Political Treatise*, 160–1; Moreau, *Spinoza et le spinozisme*, 98; Curley, "Spinoza's Contribution," 380–1.
[42] Spinoza, *Theological-Political Treatise*, 161, 180; Moreau, *Spinoza et le spinozisme*, 99; Curley, "Spinoza's Contribution," 381–2, 391.

teaching theological doctrine based on the Gospels exist, but no such thing has ever been possible. Rather, "there can be no doubt that many disputes and schisms have arisen because different Apostles constructed religion on different foundations."

In Spinoza's works Paul repeatedly appears as a kind of *alter ego* of Spinoza himself, teaching the true message of Christ (against all the churches). Thus, when Paul teaches that no one is justified by works "but by faith alone" (Romans 3:28), he meant by "faith" not anything supernatural "but nothing other than full mental assent" via sound argument that holds logically. "Finally, [Paul] says no one is blessed unless he has the mind of Christ in him (Romans 8:9) whereby undoubtedly one may understand God's laws as eternal truths."[43] Spinoza's Paul pre-echoes Spinoza again where we read that "Paul acknowledges there is no sin before law is established [Romans 7:7], that is as long as men are considered as living under the government of nature."[44] Yet curiously, at the same time, Spinoza's New Testament *alter ego* occasionally appears also as a virtual arch-villain, the fount of all the strife and dispute splintering and plaguing all the churches ever since. "Disputes and schisms have ceaselessly troubled the church since apostolic times and will surely never cease to trouble it until religion is finally separated from philosophic theories and reduced to the extremely few, very simple dogmas Christ taught to his own."[45] That church history constitutes a unique record of bitter schism and unending theological strife Spinoza deemed undeniable, as was later argued likewise by Orobio de Castro in his disputation with Van Limborch, Le Clerc, and Locke as to whether Jesus was the Messiah predicted in the Old Testament. Orobio, following Spinoza here, likewise held that church history itself proves to every rational person that there is no divinely approved church nor ever could be.

Because Christ battled the "obstinacy and ignorance" of the Pharisees and "exhorts his disciples to the true life," he, and Paul later, felt obliged, Spinoza claims, to systematically use false notions, the ignorant prejudices of the common people, to get their message across so that much of what they reportedly affirmed is unquestionably untrue taken at face value, untruth adjusted to the superstitious notions of the common people for the sake of improving their moral attitudes. "For instance, when Christ challenges the Pharisees (see Matthew 12:26) by asking: 'and if Satan casts out Satan, he is divided against himself; how then will his kingdom stand?' he meant only to sway the Pharisees using their own muddled thinking, not teach that demons exist or that there is any sort of realm of demons." Given its aims, the New Testament, holds Spinoza, necessarily employs untruth

---

[43] Spinoza, *Theological-Political Treatise*, 64; Hunter, *Radical Protestantism in Spinoza's Thought*, 54–5, 61.

[44] Spinoza, *Theological-Political Treatise*, 196; Jaquet, *Spinoza à l'oeuvre*, 90.

[45] Spinoza, *Theological-Political Treatise*, 161; Hunter, *Radical Protestantism in Spinoza's Thought*, 62–4; Laerke, *Spinoza and the Freedom*, 38, 53.

attuned to the superstition of the *vulgus* (including kings, churchmen, and academics).[46]

Nothing is true in Christian teaching, held Spinoza, that supposes the existence of the supernatural. Being an allegorical symbol of universal moral truth, Christ was never resurrected while Paul was a great teacher with admirably solid but also problematic aspects to his teaching. There exists no Satan, nor are there any demons or angels in the New Testament, except insofar as readers misunderstand Christ's teaching. By contrast, Hobbes, while chiefly blaming the ancient Greeks and other pagans for the age-old prevalence of credence in lesser demons and spirits, avoids outright denial of the existence of the Christian "Satan" and the New Testament's angels and demons in the manner of Spinoza, opting for a cautious meandering around the issue.[47] Belief in lesser demons he too suggests is unchristian, nevertheless the discussion of this in the *Leviathan*, highly rhetorical and in part satirical, is hardly an account designed to remove primitive dread which he seems to have thought in some way useful to the political sovereign. Unlike Spinoza, Hobbes remained ultimately ambivalent about Satan, the "kingdom of Satan," and Hell.

"If you are minded to put your trust in such thinkers [as Plato and Aristotle]," asks Spinoza, finally, when ending his exchange with Boxel, ridiculing his fierce anti-Catholicism by way of a parting shot, "what reason have you to deny the miracles of the Holy Virgin and all the saints? These have been reported by so many renowned philosophers, theologians and historians that I could produce a hundred of the latter to barely one [among those denying them]."[48] As no further evidence exists of contact between Spinoza and Boxel, it seems their initially confident mutual trust that friends can agree to disagree about significant things without this disturbing their friendship in the end turned out to be incorrect.

---

[46] Spinoza, *Theological-Political Treatise*, 41; Chalier, *Spinoza lecteur*, 155–6; Bagley, *Philosophy, Theology*, 101–3.
[47] Hobbes, *Leviathan* iii, 265–6; Scott McClure, "Hell and Anxiety," 15, 23–5.
[48] Spinoza, *Collected Works* (ed. Curley) ii, 423–4.

32

Entering (or Not Entering) Princely Court Culture (1672–1673)

32.i Contemplating Emigrating

Over the winter of 1672–3, the lines of the Franco-Swiss-Munsterite occupation of the northern Netherlands and of the Dutch defensive positions facing them, waterways lined with forts, remained for the most part "frozen" in place. Despite French hopes and efforts, there was barely any real movement. Meanwhile, William III consolidated his position within the Republic, gathering more power into his own hands and those of his intimate noble advisers. Yet, the young Prince proved anxious too, so far as was in his power, to dampen the Republic's seething ideological warfare and help restore calm and stability. Cool and astute, William understood the importance of forging more unity and solidarity at such an immensely fraught time in a country so deeply fractured by faction and religion.

Purging regents closely associated with De Witt and the "True Freedom" figured centrally in William III's restructuring of control and power in the Republic over the ensuing three years. By early 1673, he and his underlings had removed 130 out of a total of 460 regents controlling the city governments in the province of Holland alone.[1] Open republican opposition to Orangist dominance was drastically curtailed. But after a while, despite appreciable remaining constraints on his power, the Prince saw compelling reasons to gracefully accept the bounds limiting how far he could take the purges, why it would be unwise, on his part, to push transfer of power and influence beyond the point now reached. For one thing, no more than any other Stadholder could he permanently influence the choice of new regents in Amsterdam, a city as indispensable as ever for all decisions regarding state finances, taxation, and the army and navy. Secondly, even though in some large towns, notably Rotterdam, the Prince did eliminate all obvious opponents, introducing new men and more permanently altering the balance in his favour, elsewhere, as in Delft and Leiden, where Orangist support was traditionally strong,[2] early signs of restlessness at the erosion of the States of Holland's power appeared together with a growing resolve among regents to

---

[1] Israel, *Dutch Republic*, 808.   [2] Israel, *Dutch Republic*, 803–11.

shield their local autonomy and privileges from further incursions by the Prince's creatures who in several cases proved notably more corrupt and intent on building local despotisms than the old guard. The Delft town council, for instance, attempted to restore some of its ousted former regents as early as the autumn of 1673.[3]

Furthermore, the struggle between the Voetian strict Calvinist and the Cocceian-Cartesian liberal tendency within the Dutch Reformed Church and universities could not be resolved, or even provisionally defused, simply by purges and pressure. William quickly grasped that pushing the Voetian agenda harder than he had already was likelier to aggravate than reduce friction. Basing his power on the principle of moderation required compromise with the Cocceians and Cartesians in the church councils and universities, a development encouraged by some of his closest advisers, notably the new Pensionary of Holland, Gaspar Fagel (1634–88), and the Prince's personal secretary, Constantijn Huygens the younger, neither of whom were particularly zealous or committed on the theological front. Another factor, the consistories soon discovered to their displeasure, was that William showed little zeal to expand their local political and economic resources by transferring more surviving local pre-Reformation charitable endowments and bequests to church control. Rather than grant possession of these medieval foundations to church councils as requested, he preferred to control such levers of local affairs himself through his minions. Under the pressure of war, he refused for now even to concede the widely expected substantial rise in pastors' salaries.[4]

Nor was William's disinclination to expand the consistories' and pastors' local influence, assets, and control of real estate merely a question of power-seeking. In outward lifestyle, William appeared austere and distinctly Calvinist, avoiding ostentatious display of luxury and all hint of the flamboyant style of the courts of Louis and Charles, while savouring, perhaps even taking seriously, the people's rejoicing in him as the instrument of God sent to rescue their land from godlessness and the invading French. Privately, though, he remained withdrawn, morose, careful and calculating, and also personally tolerant (doubtless so inclined by his homosexuality), relatively unmoved by thundering from the pulpit. Given the Republic was a land of many churches and sects, pressing beyond the initial purges and following through on the church councils' agenda, he knew, would only inflame rather than calm sentiment, at a time when unity and focus on the war effort were his overriding priorities. Thus, a prominent regent like Adriaen Paets (1631–86), the future patron of Pierre Bayle, a figure much resented by the Reformed consistories as an Arminian and leading advocate of toleration in

---

[3] GA Delft 1e afdeling 13/5, fo. 197. William III to States of Holland, 13 Dec. 1673; GA Delft 1e afdeling 13/5. fo. 111, res. Vroedschap, 30 Dec. 1674.
[4] Broeyer, "William III and the Reformed Church," 110–12.

Rotterdam, was purposely chosen by the Prince, in 1672, to be the States' ambassador in Madrid, signalling that toleration, also for Catholics, would not be substantially cut back.

Yet another factor encouraging the Prince to simultaneously widen his power base while insisting on a more irenic church policy than Voetians desired was the unruly conduct of the Orangist guilds and civic militias during the summer of 1672, which many in court circles and among the regents looked on with undisguised distaste. Middelburg, Zeeland's chief town and an Orangist stronghold, was a place where local elements rather than the Stadholder drove the purges, their ascendancy abundantly exhibiting an intolerant disorderliness he shunned. His immediate underlings' petty local despotisms, William also realized, functioned reliably in a stable way only in small towns around the fringes, and in some cases not even there, and could never buttress a new stability and common purpose at the core of the Dutch state. That the Prince's control in small towns was of limited significance was later reflected in the ascendancy of his favourite, François van Bredehoff (1648–1721), at Hoorn, where packing the town council with loyal Orangists created a locally detested narrower, more corrupt oligarchy than under De Witt. Likewise, the local despotism of Lodewijk Huygens (1631–99), younger brother of Christiaan and Constantijn, William's new *drost*, or chief magistrate, at Gorcum, where ten of the old regents were ejected but the "godlier" new set were blatantly more corrupt and less representative than the old, proved of limited usefulness.[5] Tightly controlled, corrupt local fiefdoms constituted a not inconsiderable portion of the Prince's new power base but could endure only within a context of intricately balanced national unity and compromise with large cities.

None of these underlying mitigating factors guiding the Prince's subsequent governance were obvious yet in 1672–3 and, for the moment, defeat, looming disaster external and internal, deep economic slump, and profound anxiety over the Republic's future ensured the continued drift of intellectuals, artists, artisans, and tradesmen abroad. Over the winter of 1672–3, the unconquered parts of the United Provinces remained in obvious peril due to freezing temperatures and the relative ease afforded for incursions in force across iced-over waterways. Open and without defences, the threat to The Hague was especially obvious. As winter spelt also extreme difficulty in supplying any force attempting to besiege nearby fortified towns, like Leiden, The Hague stood out as a uniquely inviting target for a sudden raid in force—no pretty thought considering how brutally the French had ravaged Bodegraven and Zwammerdam the previous December. If according to Spinoza's philosophy self-preservation mixed with self-assertion were key to

---

[5] De Wit, *Gorcums heren*, 18–21; Israel, *Dutch Republic*, 811.

understanding human nature, including his own, staying put in The Hague over the winter of 1672–3 was a risky choice.

Spinoza cared little about his economic circumstances but, until the spring of 1673, must have dreaded the likely devastation of his immediate surroundings and how that might decimate his plans and possibly his manuscripts and, thereby, also his still unpublished philosophy. Besides dire risk to his immediate vicinity, the Republic's noisy internal clamouring for stepped up repression of Cartesianism and "godlessness" must have hovered in Spinoza's thoughts as he pondered the Republic's grim prospects and his own uncertain future, months during which he received at least one formal invitation to settle abroad. This was from Karl Ludwig, Elector of the Palatinate, offering him a chair in philosophy and mathematics at his university of Heidelberg, the only such formal offer of an academic post Spinoza ever received. With Saint-Évremond and Vossius now safely ensconced in London, and Huygens in Paris, this offer, we know from his own comments later, seemed at least momentarily attractive at that particular juncture when many local artists and intellectuals around him who had not transferred abroad were plunged deep in dejection.

Spinoza was more independent than most, having no family or business to take care of, and no occupation to ply or house containing cherished possessions apart from his manuscripts. Philosophical commitment and compulsion to avoid every regular time-consuming responsibility, including teaching, as far as possible, deprived him of many things that others enjoyed but ensured also a unique degree of personal independence and resilience. That he indeed seriously contemplated emigrating at this time is suggested by his encounter with Lorenzo Magalotti (1637–1712), secretary of the Accademia del Cimento, founded in 1660 in Florence, and the first scientist to describe the "Florentine" closed thermometer or "grand thermomètre de Florence," to measure heat, a device devised by the Accademia del Cimento in 1668.[6] Like his prince, Cosimo III, the penultimate Medici Grand Duke of Tuscany (reigned: 1670–1712), and not unlike Isaac Vossius, Magalotti prided himself on his impressively broad cosmopolitan view of the world, on being a *homo universalis* renowned for love of the arts, literature, the sciences, and travel. Unlike Vossius, he also possessed refined diplomatic skills.

Tall, imposing, descended from a distinguished patrician family, from late 1667 Magalotti spent years as a kind of roving Tuscan envoy, visiting nearly every part of Western Europe, often, as during Cosimo's long stay in Spain and Portugal in 1668–9, as a kind of major-domo to the entourage of the then science and art loving heir to the Tuscan principality. During Cosimo's sojourn in Holland, from December 1667 to February 1668, Magalotti, together with his Parisian friend

---

[6] Strazzoni, *Burchard de Volder*, 524.

Thévenot, accompanied his prince on several visits, including to Swammerdam's collection, in Amsterdam, to inspect his galleries of preserved insects, in particular caterpillars and butterflies.[7] A member of the Royal Society, in London, Magalotti was *the* personage in the Italy of the late 1660s and 1670s, who, second only to Steno, knew most about the Dutch scientific and scholarly scene, and most about Swammerdam, Huygens, Hudde, Isaac Vossius, and Spinoza.

Magalotti's career had commenced in the circle of Galileo and remained powerfully committed throughout to advancing the sciences, from 1660 as secretary of the Florentine Accademia, the circle of distinguished astronomers, anatomists, and medical men meeting regularly in the Palazzo Pitti. Almost the Italian counterpart to Oldenburg, in London, and his friend Thévenot, in Paris, he remained a close friend of Steno too, who, in the late 1660s, dined frequently at his house in Florence. Having presided over Steno's anatomical demonstrations in Tuscany, during 1666, Magalotti, in the later 1660s, also took a close interest in his field research into earth layers and fossils in Tuscany, the Isle of Elba, and elsewhere in north-central Italy. Yet, when back in Holland, accompanying Cosimo, in the summer of 1669, and again in May 1673, Magalotti, while immersed still in the scientific debates of the era, at the same time grew increasingly wary of Dutch Cartesianism, toleration, freethinking, and irreligion, in this regard moving closer to Cosimo and Steno.[8]

Magalotti knew The Hague well, having several times visited for lengthy periods. An admirer of Saint-Évremond, he got to know Isaac Vossius in 1667 before proceeding to Amsterdam that December, to greet Cosimo on the latter's arrival for his first tour of Holland.[9] Over the years he spent much time with Saint-Évremond and Vossius, all avid conversationalists seething with scholarly news and gossip of every kind, and also apparently met Spinoza. Though elaborately courteous, there is no reason to think Magalotti thought especially highly of Spinoza either then or during 1673, though he certainly spent hours in apparently friendly conversation with him in The Hague, in June 1673,[10] and his view of him at that time may have been less negative than later. In any case, in the early 1680s Magalotti sent a letter rebuking an unnamed friend in Protestant lands "beyond the mountains," perhaps in Holland, for expressing admiration "for that ridiculous little man," though he also calls him "the most illustrious and most acclaimed of all that lot [the freethinkers and atheists]," meaning Spinoza.[11] Deeply appreciative of Cosimo's countless visits to churches, monasteries and nunneries, and

---

[7] Swammerdam, *Letters to Thévenot*, 13–14.
[8] Wagenaar, *Toscaanse Prins*, 162; Giancotti Boscherini, "Nota sulla diffusione," 344; Scherz, "Biography of Nicolaus Steno," 197, 201, 204, 207.
[9] Wagenaar, *Toscaanse Prins*, 62; Hope, *Saint-Évremond and His Friends*, 287; Jorink, "In the Twilight Zone," 132.
[10] Magalotti to Graevius, The Hague, 8 June 1673 in RL Copenhagen KB Thott 1263/4 folder "Lorenzo Magalotti"; I am indebted to Albert Goosjes for this reference.
[11] Giancotti Boscherini, "Nota sulla diffusione," 342.

well-publicized gestures of support for the church wherever he went, like his ally, Steno, whose formal conversion to Catholicism, Magalotti wrote from Antwerp, in January 1668, filled him with "infinite joy,"[12] he fervently adhered to the Catholic faith, dreamt of Protestant Europe's reconversion to Catholicism, and became more and more a foe of all freethinking.

The personage Magalotti had met at The Hague, whom he referred to as "primo instruttore e direttore d'ateismo [chief instructor and director of atheism]," continued to trouble his thoughts. On returning to The Hague, arriving from Brussels, in May 1673, Magalotti recalled in this letter to a colleague of the early 1680s, he once again met this here unnamed pre-eminent freethinker, who, now, he records, "considering what could harshly befall him following the great change that occurred in Holland by the beginning of 1673, with the standing and authority of the Calvinist preachers, his fiercest foes, surging to the same extent that the Arminian party lost ground," brazenly requested that he, Magalotti, intercede on his behalf with the Grand Duke. This presumptuous "atheist," related Magalotti, aspired to solve his difficulty by settling with ducal permission in Livorno (where there was a large Sephardic community as well as a tolerated merchant community of Dutch and German Protestants) under Cosimo's protection.[13] Spinoza, presumably, in early 1673 was as yet unaware of the change, then commencing but soon to become more blatant, in the Grand Duke's attitude towards the sciences. For, by 1673, Cosimo was already discarding his early enthusiasm for science and, turning instead, as Leibniz noted years later, towards an eventually intolerant, rigorously anti-scientific religious piety.[14]

Magalotti did not generally seek to dissuade other northern non-Catholics of distinction from visiting and working in Tuscany in the way Steno was beginning to do by 1667, nor was he as ardent as Steno in urging the Grand Duke to support the Inquisition and suppress private freethinking;[15] but courtly discretion led him to discreetly discourage this particularly problematic supplicant by indicating the grave difficulties his transfer to Tuscany would entail. For now Cosimo remained eager to shore up the fast fading scientific and scholarly prestige of his court; he had tried to get Swammerdam to come to settle in Florence and sought to persuade Steno (who had gone back to Denmark in 1672), whom he especially esteemed, to return to Tuscany.[16] But Spinoza, Magalotti knew perfectly well, was not the sort of scientific or philosophical asset Cosimo would wish to acquire. Yet despite his discreetly putting him off, explained Magalotti in his letter, this highly undesirable person persisted, even suggesting that what he was requesting was no big thing. Knowing Cosimo's increasingly negative attitude

---

[12] Scherz, "Biography of Nicolaus Steno," 201; Scherz, *Niels Stensen*, 64, 66; Wagenaar, *Toscaanse Prins*, 162.
[13] Giancotti Boscherini, "Nota sulla diffusione," 342–3.   [14] Totaro, "Steno in Italy," 277, 279.
[15] Totaro, "Steno in Italy," 276–7.   [16] Scherz, *Niels Stensen*, 103.

towards non-Catholics, Magalotti felt amazed at the tenacity of this arch-atheist, amounting, he thought, to bizarre effrontery. Trying again to put him off, he answered the "atheist," "but if the Grand Duke (who I knew was already perfectly aware of this fact) should ask me about your religion, how should I reply?" "Your Honour," suggested Spinoza, "should answer that he says he is a Christian." Magalotti long recalled his disgust at this response: "so far was this fellow a zealous adherent of atheism that not even in the case of such dreaded oppression was he willing explicitly to abjure it." "For that fellow was never a Christian"; rather, "excommunicated from his religion as a declared atheist against his [Jewish] superstition, he was truly an atheist with regard to all religions," but to avoid staying in Holland trapped amidst the dangers there "was willing to call himself a Christian."[17]

32.ii The Offer of a University Chair at Heidelberg

The Elector Palatine, Karl Ludwig (Charles Louis) (1617–80), likewise figured among the most culturally enterprising princes of the era, eager to restore the stability, prosperity, and standing of his court and principality and attract international celebrities. When commencing his rule in 1649, the officially Calvinist Rhenish Palatinate was still plunged in the devastation of the Thirty Years War. The once celebrated Palatine University of Heidelberg, founded in 1386, third oldest of the Holy Roman Empire (after Prague and Vienna), and oldest surviving university in modern Germany, had been pillaged and ruined. The celebrated university library, or Bibliotheca Palatina, the most famous Renaissance era library in all Germany containing some 5,000 printed books and over 3,500 manuscripts, pilfered by Maximilian of Bavaria's forces in 1622, had been presented to the Pope, most of it surviving today in the Bibliotheca Apostolica Vaticana, in Rome. Lutheran early in the Reformation, in line with the local princely court the university had been officially Calvinist since 1563. After re-inaugurating the university, in 1652, amid great festivities lasting nearly a week, Karl Ludwig himself henceforth presided as *rector magnificus*. Over the years, he devoted considerable time and energy to restoring the university to Germany's front rank, often attending public lectures and disputations in person and constantly seeking to attract professors and students.

In 1672, as part of his reforms, the Elector established a new rule in his university: while in the theology faculty all professors must be either Reformed or Lutheran; in the other faculties it was no longer mandatory that only qualified Calvinists and Lutherans were eligible.[18] Having himself studied as a youth at

---

[17] Giancotti Boscherini, "Nota sulla diffusione," 343.
[18] Hautz, *Geschichte der Universität Heidelberg* ii, 179–80, 184–6, 197, 199.

Leiden,[19] Karl Ludwig, unlike Cosimo, was committed to a policy of toleration and maintained an unusually liberal religious stance, partly owing to mercantilist zeal for encouraging trade and nurturing his principality's population and prosperity. Aiming to attract skilled or monied settlers from outside, he did not exclude Jews or fringe Christians like the Schwenkfeldians from those permitted to settle. Heidelberg's Jewish community took root around 1660, as did that of the river port of Mannheim at the confluence of the Rhine and Neckar, a town largely razed to the ground by Catholic troops in 1622, where Karl Ludwig particularly encouraged Jews, Portuguese as well as Ashkenazic, to settle and did attract a small community of the former. Of fifteen Jewish families authorized to settle in Mannheim, in 1660, two were Portuguese.[20]

Karl Ludwig was an older brother of the famed Princess Palatine and Duchess of Hanover, Sophia (1630–1714), one of the most outstanding of seventeenth-century German court ladies. A daughter of the Calvinist princely house of the Palatinate, she was the very first figure of princely status definitely known to have liked Spinoza's post-Cartesian ideas and especially rated the *TTP* highly, albeit the latter not until 1678 when it appeared in French. Friendly with the Hanover court librarian, Leibniz, from 1676, she was later also a patron of John Toland whom she first met in 1701 when he visited Hanover as part of the Anglo-Irish delegation delivering the parliamentary Act of Succession proclaiming Sophia and her offspring heirs to the British thrones. After arriving in Hanover in 1676, Leibniz discussed all manner of things with her, including Spinoza and Steno, figures of considerable interest to her, and about whom, due to her being closely connected with the court at Heidelberg, she doubtless already knew more than a little.

Sophia and Karl Ludwig had been brought up in The Hague, at the court of the then Prince of Orange and Stadholder, Frederik Hendrik, being children of the ill-fated "Winter King," Frederick V of the Palatinate (1596–1632) whose acceptance of the Bohemian crown, in 1618, had, disastrously for himself and his family, triggered the Thirty Years War. With their homeland devastated and their father dying at the early age of thirty-six, Karl Ludwig, their brother Rupert, and Sophia spent their early years in Dutch exile with their future courtly prospects depending on Frederik Hendrik, and the French king. Besides having lived many years in and around The Hague, there were additional reasons for Karl Ludwig's and Sophia's unusually pro-Dutch, tolerant, and in her case decidedly irreverent outlook. Their Scottish-born mother, Elizabeth the "Winter Queen" (1596–1662), was an older sister of Charles I of England, forming the basis for their close connection with the English throne. Sophia, Karl Ludwig, and Rupert, in other words, were James I of England's grandchildren. Both had grown up being more comfortable speaking French and Dutch than in German-speaking milieus. Unlike their brother, Prince

---

[19] Hautz, *Geschichte der Universität Heidelberg* ii, 173.   [20] Israel, *European Jewry*, 123, 139.

Rupert of the Rhine (1619–82) who, in 1644, became commander of the royalist army during the English Civil War, Karl Ludwig was more sympathetic to the parliamentary cause. Witnessing in person the execution of his uncle, Charles I, in London in January 1649, does not seem to have rendered him any warmer towards royal absolutism. There is some reason to believe that Sophia, James I's granddaughter, was not just a religious sceptic but may have shared something of her brother's anti-absolutist attitude. After reading the French translation of Spinoza's preface to the *TTP*, in February 1679, she was decidedly enthusiastic, pronouncing it, writing to her brother on 2 March, "admirable."[21]

Karl Ludwig and Sophia were both somewhat out on a limb also for another reason: besides the usual distaste of Lutherans, Catholics, and Anglicans in Germany and Britain for a Calvinist prince and princess, Calvinist churchmen too regarded Karl Ludwig with considerable reserve due to the notorious scandal of his first marriage and so-called "divorce," in April 1657, which went unrecognized by the churches. After marrying Landgravine Charlotte of Hesse-Kassel (1627–86), in 1650, a princess who loved riding, hunting, and gambling but scorned the intellectual pursuits dear to her husband and sister-in-law, he found himself enmeshed in a notoriously bad-tempered marriage. Charlotte banished Karl Ludwig from her bedroom and their raucous quarrelling reverberated through the court. Yet, she refused to agree to a divorce. Sophia who, prior to her marriage, in 1658, to Ernst Augustus of Hanover, was known as the "Princess Palatine" and resided at court at Heidelberg, considered her sister-in-law stubborn, vain, superficial, and stupid, and ridiculed her tantrums. As the Palatine Reformed Church would not authorize it, an exasperated Karl Ludwig finally, in April 1657, unilaterally proclaimed his "divorce" and married his mistress, a lady-in-waiting.

Sophia, like Karl Ludwig, was thoroughly cosmopolitan and, like their mother, spoke French with fluency and grace, nurturing a special fondness for French literature and culture. A particularly influential presence at court in Heidelberg during the years 1671–8 was that of the aptly named French bibliophile, historian, writer and wit, Urbain Chevreau (1613–1701). A graduate of Poitiers University, erudite and much-travelled, Chevreau had spent the years 1653–5 at the Swedish court in attendance, with Vossius and Pierre-Daniel Huet, to Queen Christina and lengthy periods also in Copenhagen, Venice, and Kassel as well as Hanover where, as chief court wit and intellectual adviser in the late 1660s, he first became friendly with Sophia who arranged his transfer to Heidelberg, in 1670. "I dare say," wrote Chevreau later, referring to Sophia, "France has no finer wit than the present duchess of Hanover, [mais j'ose dire que la France n'a point de plus bel esprit que Madame la duchesse de Hannouvre]."[22] At Heidelberg, Chevreau received the title

---

[21] *Briefwechsel der Herzogin Sophie*, 351.   [22] Chevreau, *Chevraeana*, 90–1.

of court "*conseiller*" and, though trained as a jurist, devoted most of his time to elegant conversation, bibliographical research, and composing numerous plays, two novels, a treatise of moral philosophy, and much of his eight-volume *Histoire du monde* (1686) on which he laboured all told for thirty years.[23] Forgotten today, his anecdotes and high society gossip about famous *érudits* were then much esteemed.

In his memoirs, the *Chevraeana* of 1697, Chevreau, though overstating perhaps his own role in the Elector's choice to fill what, in 1673, Karl Ludwig hoped to make one of Germany's prime professorial chairs, includes some interesting remarks about how Spinoza came to be chosen for the Heidelberg philosophy chair. At Karl Ludwig's court, Chevreau later reminisced, he had numerous talks about books and personalities with the Elector and with the Heidelberg professor of theology Johann Ludwig Fabricius (1632–97), a Reformed pastor from Schaffhausen, Switzerland, trained in Greek and theology who had studied also in Paris. In these conversations, Chevreau recommended various personages for particular posts. On one occasion, "I spoke very favourably [fort avantageusement] of Spinoza, although I then still only knew [the work of] this Jewish Protestant through the first and second parts of his philosophy of M. Descartes." That the freethinking Chevreau, deeply immersed in Bible criticism and problems of biblical chronology, at this point was really unaware of the furore over the *TTP*, however, seems rather unlikely. Since a copy of Spinoza's Descartes book was in the Elector's library, "I read some chapters from it to him" (not needing to translate the Latin but doubtless expanding on some points in French), after which the prince, rather impressed, and encouraged by Chevreau, "decided to call him to his university of Heidelberg to teach philosophy, on condition he did not dogmatize," that is intrude on the theological sphere.[24]

Even supposing that, in December 1672 and January 1673, Chevreau, Karl Ludwig, and Sophia were all unaware of the furore over the *TTP*, which seems improbable, it is certain that Fabricius knew about the *TTP*, and that Spinoza was its author, as early as June 1670, and judged it a dire danger to church and state well before being called upon to write in the Elector's name to The Hague inviting Spinoza to take up the philosophy chair and become his colleague.[25] It seems impossible that he would not have urgently warned the others that Spinoza's standing had radically changed. No longer a useful commentator on Descartes, he was now reputed instead the most dangerous anti-Scripturalist in all Europe, someone decidedly unfitted for their (or any) university. But, possibly, Fabricius felt it would be unwise for him to make any great fuss about this at court.

---

[23] Chevreau, *Chevraeana*, 34–5, 186; Boissière, *Urbain Chevreau*, 27; Freudenthal/Walther, *Lebensgeschichte* ii, 163.
[24] Quoted in Grunwald, *Spinoza in Deutschland*, 289; Vernière, *Spinoza et la pensée française*, 208; Freudenthal/Walther, *Lebensgeschichte* i, 305.
[25] Freudenthal/Walther, *Lebensgeschichte* ii, 166–7.

According to his personal friend and fellow Swiss theologian Johann Heinrich Heidegger (1633-98), who had studied at Heidelberg and later Leiden and followed the Reformed Church's internecine battles in the Netherlands, Fabricius was indeed deeply reluctant to write offering the chair to Spinoza but felt he could not disobey the Elector's direct command.[26] Once he had chosen, Karl Ludwig was evidently rather adamant about his choice. Probably, Chevreau recounted the episode in this manner, focusing specifically on Spinoza's Descartes book, to retrospectively shield the Palatine court's reputation (and his own) from damaging gossip insinuating that Karl Ludwig and Sophia were so drawn to Cartesian innovation and Spinoza's novel Bible hermeneutics (which afterwards certainly appealed to Sophia) that they even ventured to defy prevailing opinion and invite to their court a universally condemned subversive and "atheist" in total defiance of every theological consideration.

Biblical chronology, as it happens, was a prime concern of Chevreau's *Histoire du monde*, published first in Paris, in 1686, then at The Hague in 1687, with more editions following (including an English version in 1701). Drawing on a wealth of sources classical and modern, including Vossius, father and son, Scaliger, and Menasseh ben Israel whom he accounted "one of the most learned men of our century,"[27] Chevreau narrated mankind's history from Creation down to Moses and the ancient Israelite republic, then the Israelite kings, and on to classical times. His approach was to summarize everything scholars had written while indicating the full range of disagreement in neutral tones to avoid offence, devoting over twenty pages to the Assyrian empire and over seventy to the ancient Persian monarchy alone. When estimating the chronological span from the Creation until Christ's birth, he neatly sidestepped the obvious pitfalls by simply listing sixteen different estimates without entering into any dispute. If Rabbi David Gans of Prague (1541-1613) estimated 3,761 years, Rabbi Abraham Zacuto of Salamanca suggested 3,671, Scaliger 3,947, sundry Talmudists 3,784, and so on.[28] Moses' birth he specified at 1598 BC and the Exodus at 1517 BC. The destruction of Jerusalem and the First Temple by Nebuchadnezzar, King of Babylon (reigned: c.605-c.562 BC) he placed at 606 BC, not far out as it happens: modern scholarship fixing that crucial date at 587 or 586 BC.[29] Where the Book of Exodus affirms that the exodus from Egypt occurred 2,666 years after the Creation, Chevreau fixed its date at 2,454 after Creation.[30] Studiously non-controversial, Chevreau's ambiguous neutrality on controversial matters as well as chronology hardly recommended him to Calvinist sentiment.

---

[26] Freudenthal/Walther, *Lebensgeschichte* i, 306-7; Walther, *Spinoza Studien* iii, 186.
[27] Chevreau, *Chevraeana*, 18.   [28] Chevreau, *Histoire du monde* i, 12-13.
[29] Chevreau, *Histoire du monde* i, 61-2, 81; Boissière, *Urbain Chevreau*, 301.
[30] Chevreau, *Histoire du monde* i, 62.

Writing to The Hague, on the Elector's behalf, addressing him as "most distinguished sir," Fabricius invited Spinoza to take up the Palatine chair in philosophy, dating his letter, Heidelberg, 16 February 1673, and signing it as councillor to the Elector for ecclesiastical affairs as well as professor of theology at the University. Spinoza had been "most highly recommended to his Most Serene Highness." "Nowhere," he assured him, "will you find a prince more favourable to men of outstanding intellect, among whom, he judges, you are one."[31] Having studied at Utrecht, Fabricius cannot have been in much doubt as to the effect of bringing even an orthodox Cartesian to Heidelberg, let alone a thinker radically revising Descartes in the subversive style of Spinoza.

Spinoza by no means rejected the offer outright. He pondered the invitation for over a month before replying, apparently considering the location and character of Heidelberg as well as whether the Dutch defences were likely to hold until the spring, that is until the late winter ice thawed and warmer temperatures restored the water barriers rendering further incursions by French and Munsterites unlikely. Perhaps he was in two minds, simply awaiting a clearer picture. Very likely it was at this time, in 1673, when contemplating Karl Ludwig's offer, and curious to read about Heidelberg's environs, that Spinoza acquired his copy of a text published by Johann Sebald Fabricius (1622–97), brother of the theologian Fabricius and also a professor teaching there. This forty-page booklet, kept in Spinoza's small personal library, describes the topography and history of the region including Schloss Eichelsheim, near Mannheim, where Pope John XXIII had been held captive in 1415.[32]

When, eventually, he replied, politely declining the offer, on 30 March 1673, Spinoza could be fairly confident the French would not break through to The Hague that year. "If it had ever been my desire to take up a professorship," he explained, he could have wished only for such a position as the Elector was offering, having long "desired to live under the rule of a prince whose wisdom all admire." That may have been sincerely meant given Karl Ludwig's policies and unusual character. However, after "long consideration of the matter," he had decided to turn the offer down, excusing himself partly by noting that the Elector's promise that, on moving to the Palatinate, he would enjoy the "most extensive freedom to philosophize [philosophandi libertatem habebis amplissimam]," still seemed unclear as to precisely "within what limits his freedom to philosophize must be confined." The other difficulty, "if I am to find time to instruct young students," was that "I must give up my further progress in philosophy." However, it had never been "my intention to teach publicly," and

---

[31] Spinoza, *Collected Works* (ed. Curley) ii, 396.
[32] Van Sluis and Musschenga, *Boeken van Spinoza*, 49; Freudenthal/Walther, *Lebensgeschichte* ii, 69.

so "even though I have weighed the matter for a long time," he had at last resolved to turn the prince's offer down.³³

No doubt Spinoza did indeed ponder long and hard and may have felt that he could hardly devote himself seriously to teaching without "ceasing to advance in philosophy." But chiefly he worried that he could not know exactly within what limits the Elector's promise of "freedom to philosophize" applied, if, as commanded, he was not to "seem to want to disturb the publicly established religion," especially since doctrinal strife, in Spinoza's view, arises not from genuine zeal for religion but clashing emotions and men's propensity to "contradict one another due to which even what is correctly stated usually gets distorted and condemned." He had plentiful experience of malicious academic conduct already while leading a solitary private life: "I would need to fear it much more if I rise to this position of dignity." He was not holding back from hope of better terms or some better opportunity, he emphasized, but exclusively "from love of tranquillity which I believe I can in some measure maintain by abstaining from public lecturing." Even so, he closed by asking Fabricius to "entreat his Most Serene Highness, the Elector, to allow me to deliberate further about this matter." So his refusal at this juncture seems not to have been altogether final.³⁴

32.iii The Court of Hanover

"We wanted to know the reasons for this refusal," records Chevreau in his memoirs, "and from several letters that I afterwards received from The Hague and Amsterdam, I gathered these words 'provided you do not dogmatize'" are "what rendered [Spinoza] apprehensive."³⁵ All considered, it was perhaps for the best that he did not come to the Rhineland, Chevreau added, looking back later, but remained in Holland after all. Fabricius reacted rather differently. Examining the *TTP* again soon after Spinoza's refusal, he confided to Heidegger that he was utterly "horrified" that anyone could think and write so impiously, "so openly blaspheming against the Christian religion itself and Holy Scriptures." Such brazen ungodliness could bring only ruin to church and state. The Dutch governing elite might think differently, but that "such writings should be brought to Germany and diffused among the students, I consider extremely dangerous. I think it far more advisable to suppress [Spinoza's writings] than to refute them."³⁶

---

[33] Spinoza to J. L. Fabricius, The Hague, 30 March 1673, in Spinoza, *Collected Works* (ed. Curley) ii, 397; Laerke, *Spinoza and the Freedom*, 22–3.
[34] Spinoza, *Opera* iv, 236; Spinoza, *Correspondance* (ed. Rovere), 282–3; Zenker, *Denkfreiheit*, 94.
[35] Vernière, *Spinoza et la pensée française*, 209; Freudenthal/Walther, *Lebensgeschichte* i, 305; Steenbakkers, "Spinoza's Life," 37.
[36] Freudenthal/Walther, *Lebensgeschichte* i, 306–7; Walther, *Spinoza Studien* iii, 185.

Not transferring to Heidelberg, it turned out, was indeed wholly for the best. By late March, there were reasonable grounds to assume the Republic's defences would hold. What was still a dire prospect for the Dutch over the winter of 1672–3, steadily improved through the spring and summer, which was far from being the case for the Palatinate. Until 1672, the Elector proved successful in reviving his state, economy, and university and attracting growing student numbers; but from 1673 everything went into reverse, as the Palatinate, especially towns along the Rhine, became again a bitterly contested battlefield between the Empire and France. Caught between the French and the Imperial Habsburg army in an embattled war zone, Heidelberg's students and professors drifted away. On 16 June 1674, the Battle of Sinsheim was fought only fourteen miles from Heidelberg. In July 1674, Imperialist forces converged on Heidelberg while the French commander, Turenne, again crossed the Rhine and ravaged the Palatinate. Further devastation seriously affecting Heidelberg, its environs, and university ensued in 1675–6. Even the most loyal professors eventually fled, Fabricius living as a wandering exile (at least partly in Switzerland) for the rest of his life.[37]

During the mid- and late 1670s, Spinoza's notoriety in Germany steadily grew, and while this of itself guaranteed intensifying hostility of universities and courts towards him, it also meant that for those few noblemen and courtiers harbouring a sceptical view of the confessional polemics and theologians of the day, and with the knowledge and reading to judge for themselves, Spinoza began to assume the dimensions of a heroic martyr figure, the universally banned, despised, and persecuted intellectual hero of the era. One such was certainly the Princess-Duchess Sophia, at Hanover, and through her, and others like her, Spinoza's hidden closet renown, in defiance of the prevailing disapproval, found channels of entry into the intellectual world of princely court culture. Sophia already knew something about the atheistic-republican clandestine circle in Amsterdam and had heard from Karl Ludwig about Van den Enden leaving Amsterdam for Paris before learning of his conspiracy against Louis XIV and his execution, in 1674. Evidently, the plotters of Van den Enden's circle aroused her sympathy. For on hearing about the De Rohan conspiracy in Normandy and hanging of Van den Enden, she expressed keen regret that the latter's republican views had "allowed him to be persuaded by M. de Rohan to enter into an unchristian treason against the king: it is better for these noble spirits always to stick to reasoning, and never to act."[38] Evidently, she regarded Van den Enden, rather than Rohan and his associates as "noble spirits."

Sophia supplemented what she knew of Van den Enden and Spinoza during the last months of the latter's life through her talks with Leibniz whom she first got to know in late 1676. Since his early years as privy councillor to the

---

[37] Hautz, *Geschichte der Universität Heidelberg* ii, 189.
[38] Gullan-Whur, *Life of Spinoza*, 268, 276.

Archbishop-Elector of Mainz (1666–73), Leibniz was a specialist in Protestant–Catholic relations and in reassuring princes in predominantly Protestant regions of Germany of the intellectual solidity of the Christian mysteries, especially Christ's divinity, the Trinity, and transubstantiation, belief shared by mainstream Protestants and Catholics alike, and the rightness of a politics of reconciliation and reunification of Christendom, a healing of divisions via Christianity's core mysteries leading to Catholic–Lutheran reconciliation. But he took a keen interest in all theological perspectives and made a point, when in Paris, of visiting Van den Enden and his school prior to the conspiracy, noting that at that time Van den Enden presented himself publicly as a Catholic of Jansenist leanings, friendly with the great Arnauld.[39] Among those most attracted to Leibniz's theological reconciliationism, from a conservative standpoint, was Duke Johann Friedrich, ruler of Braunschweig-Lüneburg (1625–79), a prince belonging to a Lutheran line who whilst in Italy, in 1651, had converted to Catholicism. Highly unusually, he had done so not from opportunistic calculation of the sort usual at princely courts but sincere personal searching for spiritual truth.

Sophia's brother-in-law and Leibniz's future employer, Johann Friedrich, was the sole principal member of the Hanoverian line to convert to Catholicism and ally with Louis XIV. Accordingly, he took a hostile view not just of ungodly freethinkers but also of toleration and the Dutch Republic. The Dutch he viewed as defying both the Church and the princely absolutism dear to his heart. Famously obese and averse to riding, fencing, and hunting, Johann Friedrich was an exceptionally sedentary ruler—apart from his four trips to Italy during his lifetime for Catholic spiritual refreshment. The rest of his time he devoted to prayer, reading, and discussion. Knowing Leibniz since 1671, Johann Friedrich warmly approved of his writings against the Socinians in defence of the Trinity.[40] No brutal warmonger, bigot, and philistine like the prince-bishop of Munster, he eagerly drew Leibniz to his court near Hanover, as an adviser, appointing him his full-time salaried court librarian in January 1676. At court, Leibniz was expected to take up his new post early that year, that is practically a year before Spinoza's death, but dallied so long in Paris that he arrived many months after his official starting date, with plenty of explaining to do. He had been collecting books for the duke's previously relatively small 3,000 book library, he explained, his visits to London and Holland enabling him to form ties with the Royal Society and leading Dutch scholars and helping create the web of correspondents that would make Hanover a hub of international scholarly interaction and the republic of letters, a focus of high-level scientific, mathematical, and theological debate.

In Paris, promoting the cause dearest to Johann Friedrich's heart, Leibniz had explored prospects for better future Catholic–Protestant relations and assisted the

---

[39] Leibniz, *Theodicy*, 351; Laerke, *Leibniz lecteur*, 361; Bouveresse, *Spinoza et Leibniz*, 222.
[40] Antognazza, *Leibniz on the Trinity*, 11–14, 173n.

Dauphin's tutor, Huet, in the urgent task of combating the greatest intellectual threat to Christianity of the era, namely Spinoza.[41] To impress his new princely employer further, in January 1677 Leibniz named thirty celebrities on his growing list of high-status contacts and correspondents, headed by persons of high rank, boasting two French dukes, Louis XIV's confessor, the Jesuit Father de la Chaise (1624–1709), the heads of the royal library in Paris and Colbert's library, and Monsieur Thévenot, judged by Chevreau the most qualified figure anywhere (along with Gilles Ménage) to be "head of an academy."[42] Leibniz also listed the five most distinguished intellectual and scientific celebrities with whom he had established contact in Holland, namely: Huygens, Hudde, "Spinosa at The Hague," Craanen at Leiden, and "Leeuwenhoek at Delft," a remarkable choice given that most leading French intellects of the day failed to make it onto Leibniz's list.[43] This was just weeks before Spinoza's death. The challenging, dramatic picture Leibniz drew for the prince led the latter too to appreciate the dangerous threat Spinoza and his unprecedented attack on Christianity's core mysteries represented. When Spinoza died, in February 1677, Johann Friedrich was sufficiently aware of Spinoza's intellectual centrality in the world of his time to understand perfectly why Leibniz was so eager to procure from Holland, if he could, manuscript copies of Spinoza's still unpublished writings.[44]

Helpfully for Leibniz (and the Spinoza debate in the Germany of the 1670s), Johann Friedrich was greatly drawn to his new court librarian's personality, ideas, and priorities. Here at his own court was the leading philosopher championing the Holy Trinity against the leading thinker denying Christ's divinity. Leibniz's salary was soon raised and, in the spring of 1677, shortly after Spinoza's death, he was elevated to the status of privy councillor as well as librarian.[45] No prince felt more attracted to schemes to reverse the Reformation and haul Protestant Germany back to the Catholic Church, and it was at the duke's insistence that Steno stayed at the Hanoverian court for two weeks in the late summer of 1674. "During that time," Steno reported to Florence, the duke "invited me three times to his table to discuss religious matters together with some of his courtiers, the first time with the superintendent of all Lutheran preachers of the state."[46]

Leibniz offered Johann Friedrich an alluring prospect, not just plans for reuniting the churches but also, he explains in a letter of the autumn of 1677, solid philosophical proofs of the immortality of the soul and how to "demonstrate in addition the plausibility of our mysteries of the faith and solve all the difficulties

---

[41] Stewart, *Courtier and the Heretic*, 143–4, 149, 188, 205–6.
[42] Bayle, *Correspondance* x, 339n10.
[43] Leibniz to Johann Friedrich, Hanover, Jan. 1677, in Leibniz, *Sämtliche Schriften und Briefe* 1st ser. ii, 17.
[44] Leibniz to Johann Friedrich, Hanover, undated (April or May 1677), in Leibniz, *Sämtliche Schriften und Briefe* 1st ser. ii, 22.
[45] Stewart, *Courtier and the Heretic*, 304. [46] Scherz, "Biography of Nicolaus Steno," 320.

raised by those claiming there are absurdities and contradictions in the Trinity, Incarnation, Eucharist, and resurrection of bodies."[47] Very likely, Leibniz was being less than wholly frank in offering such glowing assurances, but he was a courtier, and his unmatched assistance in proving the truth of "the mysteries" and helping to bring Steno onto the scene were much appreciated. Unlike Fabricius, Cosimo, and Magalotti, Leibniz steadfastly held out for the principle that it is more relevant to rebut intellectual challenges with better arguments than opt for repression, censuring, and prohibition of texts.

Among the collection of manuscript copies and notes taken from Spinoza's correspondence and texts that Leibniz acquired in London (from Oldenburg) and in Holland, during 1676, and brought to Hanover, was a copy of Steno's open letter to Spinoza, published at Florence, in 1675, urging Spinoza to abandon his philosophy and embrace Catholicism. To these he added later a letter from Steno, of 1677, responding to his queries about the evolution of this renowned Catholic convert's views and commitments: "I can tell you," Steno assured Leibniz, "that while in that land of freedom [The Netherlands], I associated with people of a very free understanding. I read all kinds of books and had a very high regard for the philosophy of Descartes and for everybody praised for his understanding of Descartes" (obviously including Spinoza and Meyer). However, his scientific research, especially his dissections, produced findings regarding the structure of the heart that permanently persuaded him that empirical science is "in complete contradiction to everything the greatest and most dangerous philosophers held."[48] This material helped Leibniz convince Hanover's ruler of Steno's stature as a theologian, impressive efforts to promote the Catholic cause, and unmatched efforts to block Spinoza's path.

Guided by Leibniz, the duke petitioned the papal court in Rome to send Steno to Hanover to serve in northern Germany as standard-bearer of the drive for Catholic–Protestant reunification under the auspices of the Catholic Church. Rome assented and Steno arrived at his new headquarters in Hanover as 'Vicar Apostolic' to northern Germany, in November 1677, exactly a year after Leibniz's conversations with Spinoza in The Hague the previous autumn. Steno proceeded to hold earnest discussions with Johann Friedrich, the duke's Lutheran brother, Ernst Augustus, the latter's wife, the Princess-Duchess, Sophia, and their councillor, Leibniz.[49] Steno gladly presided over these Hanover courtly conferences on the menace posed by Cartesianism and by Spinoza; but, with the passing weeks Leibniz came to feel exasperated because the reborn Steno talked only about religion, advancing the Catholic Church, and the threat to religion posed by philosophy. Tiring of the visiting dignitary's continually reiterating his views on

---

[47] Antognazza, *Leibniz on the Trinity*, 4–5, 173n.
[48] Scherz, "Biography of Nicolaus Steno," 94.
[49] Scherz, "Biography of Nicolaus Steno," 3, 117; Laerke, "Leibniz and Steno," 67–8.

these topics, it became clear to him that Steno now altogether rejected science and refused to discuss anatomy, geology, fossils, or any topic Leibniz was keen to learn about.

The year and a quarter between his visit to Spinoza, in November 1676, and publication of the *Opera Posthuma*, in January 1678, was a pivotal moment in Leibniz's life, when he first confronted basic propositions from Spinoza's *Ethics* (in his manuscript notes), and struggled to assess them philosophically and find weaknesses.[50] Free of the constraints inhibiting Huet in France, and Spinoza's early adversaries in England, when conferring with Johann Friedrich, Sophia, and the Hanoverian court, Leibniz did not need to avoid mentioning Spinoza or drawing attention to his work. These were closed circles and he was free to comment on Spinoza however he wished. The last year of Spinoza's life was in fact when Leibniz most intensely wrestled with his philosophy in his own mind, striving to avoid, and help others avoid, "the precipice" which the lure of his philosophy seemingly represented. Conferring with Johann Friedrich, he explained that Spinoza was unlikely to be much impressed with Steno's open letter of 1675 and would simply reply that the church's promise of redemption to penitents turning to faith was appealing "but he had vowed to believe nothing without proof."[51]

While not wholly opposed to prohibition of texts German courts considered menacing to Christian belief, especially Socinian and atheistic texts, Leibniz judged it better, in the case of intellectually highly sophisticated minds like Spinoza, to fight with superior arguments rather than suppression.[52] Nor was he so completely in agreement with Steno's goals and those of his princely employer—or lacking in fascination for Spinoza's arguments—to actively assist in every way in combating Spinoza. Rather, he preferred to remain somewhat reserved in this respect. In his 1677 contacts with Steno, Leibniz took care not to supply details about Meyer and the other editors of Spinoza's texts or reveal anything pertaining to Rieuwertsz's plans to publish Spinoza's *Ethics*, despite knowing perfectly well that Steno called for comprehensive suppression of Spinoza's works and Spinozism. Leibniz kept strictly to himself crucial details about the publication process.[53] Beyond that, he collaborated with Steno and, since he aspired to lead the anti-Cartesian movement in Germany, found his support useful for helping persuade princes, scholars, and not least Sophia, that Descartes' philosophy was ill-grounded, dangerous, and conducive to fomenting "atheism."

---

[50] Laerke, *Leibniz lecteur*, 73, 101; Stewart, *Courtier and the Heretic*, 208, 220–1, 224.
[51] Laerke, *Leibniz lecteur*, 107–8; Laerke, "Leibniz and Steno," 67.
[52] Laerke, *Leibniz lecteur*, 108–11.
[53] Laerke, "Leibniz and Steno," 67–8; Stewart, *Courtier and the Heretic*, 208–9, 218; Bouveresse, *Spinoza et Leibniz*, 229–30.

At Johann Friedrich's court, Leibniz was now the anchor coordinating the international effort linking Paris, Rome, London, Amsterdam, and Hanover, marshalling the intellectual and courtly muscle needed to halt the advance of Cartesianism and oppose Spinoza's underground philosophical sect—albeit without actually doing everything possible to suppress Spinoza's philosophy. In fact, promoting Spinoza's image as a ubiquitous philosophical presence, the most insidious foe of revealed religion and the churches of the age, actually served Leibniz's particular goals better than screening Spinoza's name and person out of the limelight in the manner of Boyle, More, Cudworth, Huet, and the States of Holland. Leibniz was simply not trying to curtail Spinoza's image in the manner of most other prominent intellectual luminaries of the day. Consciously or unconsciously, he behaved almost as if expecting Spinoza's growing notoriety and impact to enhance his own indispensability and admonitions. Accordingly, Leibniz encouraged Sophia and Johann Friedrich not just to concern themselves with Spinoza but also to read and discuss his ideas.

Leibniz explained why Spinoza was potentially a greater threat to the Roman Church than any living Protestant writer, mentioning that he had obtained, from Amsterdam, a manuscript copy of Spinoza's long reply to Albert Burgh with its highly negative assessment of Catholicism and Christian martyrdom.[54] Johann Friedrich asked Leibniz to jot down for him his evaluation of the objections Spinoza put to Burgh, and their weaknesses. The resulting undated note of Leibniz, of early 1677, attaching his observations to the copy of Spinoza's letter, for the duke's attention, still survives. Spinoza's claim that "justice and charity" are the true marks of religion and are found among men of all faiths, Leibniz readily grants, as he does his finding good and wicked men in all churches. "Justice and charity" in themselves, though, are insufficient, Leibniz reassured his princely employer: essential too are the "particular commandments" of God together with Christianity's undeniable mysteries. Spinoza's claim that whatever is believed that is not in accord with reason is "superstition," is definitely false and to be rejected. Hence, Jews and Protestants "are under obligation," he confirmed for his pious employer, "to give reasoned justification for separating themselves from the Roman Church."[55]

But if Johann Friedrich could manage the Latin, leading ladies like his sister-in-law, Sophia, could not. Within weeks of arriving in Hanover, Leibniz was on the friendliest terms with this independent-minded, now forty-six-year old duchess-princess and sophisticated patroness of high culture consuming good books in French at a spectacular rate, who enjoyed dropping insightful remarks around the court designed to promote awareness of the latest intellectual developments.

---

[54] Friedmann, *Leibniz et Spinoza*, 95; Israel, *Radical Enlightenment*, 507.
[55] Leibniz to Johann Friedrich, Hanover, undated, in Leibniz, *Sämtliche Schriften und Briefe* 1st ser. ii, 7–9; Laerke, *Leibniz lecteur*, 106–7.

Moreover, her pre-eminence at the Hanoverian court was about to be enhanced further. Johann Friedrich was a prince that Leibniz respected for his honesty; but more important still was this prince's backing for his own schemes and ambitions. It came as a highly unwelcome shock, therefore, two years after Steno's arrival as "Vicar Apostolic," when Johann Friedrich suddenly passed away, childless, in Augsburg while en route attempting his fifth pilgrimage to Italy's holy sites, in December 1679.

The new ruler, the deceased prince's Lutheran younger brother, Ernst Augustus, was Leibniz's (and Sophia's) exact opposite in lifestyle, being an eager huntsman with no time for reading and conversation with *érudits*. While acknowledging Leibniz's talents, he totally ignored Leibniz's admonition, expressed in writing to Johan Friedrich, shortly before the latter's death, that the enlightened prince is indeed obliged to promote the well-being of society, and therefore should pursue philosophy and higher studies in a broad perspective including history, geography, modern languages, the sciences, and political thought. In Ernst Augustus's eyes all that was far removed from the accoutrements of princely status and dignity.

From 1679, the Princess-Duchess Sophia replaced Johann Friedrich as Leibniz's chief patron and confidante at court. The fast-growing princely library at Hanover remained a point of focus for all the latest learned news from Paris, London, and Holland and developments in the world of philosophy, science, and Bible criticism. But Sophia was no Johann Friedrich and, in some ways, tended to further complicate Leibniz's now less than entirely secure position at court. For one thing, long an enthusiast for Cartesianism, she liked investigating herself wherever she felt Descartes was being insufficiently rigorous. In October 1678, disagreeing with Leibniz, she confided to Karl Ludwig, in Heidelberg, that there is "much in the Christian religion that is contradicted by reason," holding that "we should stick to what our reason shows us, namely that we possess no free will and that everything follows from the chain of cause and effect,"[56] a position actually no more Cartesian than Christian or Leibnizian. Worse still, she mocked Steno's austere piety and tireless efforts to convert her to Catholicism, adding to the reasons why, in the autumn of 1680, he decided to transfer his residence from Hanover to Münster.[57]

In fact, Sophia's own personal piety had itself long been subject to some suspicion. Raised in The Hague during the Thirty Years War, speaking and reading French, Dutch, and German fluently, she so loathed what she regarded as Lutheran bigotry that she was even rumoured at court in Hanover to peruse impious books to relieve her boredom during sermons her courtly responsibilities obliged her to attend. Over time, Leibniz succeeded in steering her away from

---

[56] Bodemann, *Herzogin Sophie*, 81; Israel, *Radical Enlightenment*, 84.
[57] Bodemann, *Herzogin Sophie*, 81–2.

Cartesianism, but it is doubtful if he ever did, from the admiration for Spinoza she privately expressed in the late 1670s, in defiance of the theologians. On 2 March 1679, this granddaughter of King James I of England (and heiress to, though at the time still seemingly remote from, the British thrones) informed her brother she was reading Spinoza's *TTP* in French and found it "admirable." A week later, on 9 March 1679, after reading further, she advised Karl Ludwig that she was still more impressed, adding the extraordinary (and decidedly un-Calvinist) remark that Spinoza's book struck her as "entirely out of the ordinary and altogether according to reason [effectivement bien rare et tout à fait selon la raison]."[58]

In the summer of 1679, Ernst August, on a visit to the Dutch Republic, fell ill with fever and stayed for a time, while recuperating, together with Sophia, under Orobio de Castro's professional care, in the luxurious Amsterdam residence of Spinoza's former associate, the wealthy Sephardic patrician, Jeronimo Nunes da Costa (alias Moseh Curiel) (1620–97), agent of the Crown of Portugal in the United Provinces. Whether or not Jeronimo mentioned having known Spinoza personally as a youth, Sophia continued privately confiding to others her admiration for Spinoza and her collecting details about him.[59] Although no one was aware of it at the time, this was a precarious, indeed crucial moment in the dynastic history of the Hanoverian House and the soon to be united realms of England, Scotland, and Ireland. For Sophia's erudite person was the key link in what later became known in Britain as the "Hanoverian Succession," the ducal couple, Ernst August and Sophia, being the parents of the future King George I of England (1660–1727; reigned: 1715–27), though of course it was not known then that her eldest son, then nineteen, would one day succeed to the British thrones. In fact, Sophia herself missed becoming Queen of England by just a couple of months, dying shortly before the childless Queen Anne, in 1714. Unfortunately, George, Sophia readily acknowledged, was a hopeless ignoramus who studied nothing; it was her younger son, Friedrich August (1661–91), she reported, in 1679, who was, like her, philosophically minded and already thoroughly steeped in Spinoza as well as Descartes.[60] However, her clever son, such was her bitter fate, would die in battle twelve years later, aged only thirty, while the hopeless family fool would eventually reign over Britain and its global empire for a dozen years, founding the modern British royal family.

Sophia's surviving letters to Karl Ludwig reveal that, by 1678–9, her aversion to churchmen was becoming more intense. In the same letter of March 1679, where she observes that the *TTP* is "altogether according to reason," she added a still more stunning remark: if Spinoza had, unfortunately, died, as she had just

---

[58] *Briefwechsel von Herzogin Sophie*, 350–1, 353; Bodemann, 'Herzogin Sophie,' 82–3; Stewart, *Courtier and the Heretic*, 257.
[59] Sophie to Karl Ludwig, Amsterdam, 8 Aug. 1679, in *Briefwechsel der Herzogin Sophie*, 369; Bodemann, 'Herzogin Sophie,' 67.
[60] Bodemann, 'Herzogin Sophie,' 32, 55.

discovered, "then I think the lovers of the faith have, without justification, poisoned him, since the greater part of humanity lives according to lies [je pense, que les amateurs de la foy sans raison l'ont empoisonné, car la plupart du genre human vit du mensonge]."[61] Sophia, for her part, loved truth and found it amazing, considering how many books streamed from the press in her day, that no one had written one praising Spinoza ["qu'on n'en fait pas à sa louange]" or applauding what he has to say about the, for everyone, urgent topic of deception, lies, and popular as well as high-society credulity, superstition, and fanaticism.[62] The clandestine French translation of the *TTP* did much to help generate Europe's incipient Radical Enlightenment particularly in the higher levels of society.

Sophia presumably asked Orobio and Jeronimo for their opinions of Spinoza and his social and political philosophy, and the attitude of the Jewish community towards him, and his now surging underground influence. In any case, during the weeks she and her husband spent in Nunes da Costa's splendid mansion, with its display of rarities, curiosa, exotic imports, and fine books, Spinoza's challenge to the world around her was evidently deeply lodged in her thoughts.

---

[61] *Briefwechsel der Herzogin Sophie*, 350, 353, 368.
[62] Sophie to Karl Ludwig, 9 March 1679, in *Briefwechsel der Herzogin Sophie*, 353; Stewart, *Courtier and the Heretic*, 257.

33
Creeping Diffusion

33.i The *TTP*'s Clandestine Editions

By 1672, it was clear that the Latin version of the *TTP* was having a notable and disturbing impact in the Netherlands and Germany (though not yet in England or France), causing agitation among leading figures at a range of universities including Leipzig, Jena, Duisburg, and Heidelberg as well as Leiden, Utrecht, Franeker, and Groningen. Even if chiefly notorious for undermining revealed religion, the *TTP* was spreading no inconsiderable unease too with its plea for full freedom of expression and to publish and its lack of deference for monarchy, aristocracy, and the oligarchic republic.

By 1672–3, explained the Swiss officer in French employ, Colonel Jean-Baptiste Stouppe (1620–92), writing in Utrecht, Spinoza possessed a "great number of *sectateurs* entirely attached to his views [un grand nombre de sectateurs qui sont entièrement attachez à ses sentiments]," persons who took pains not to reveal themselves openly because their leader's *Tractatus Theologico-Politicus* destroys "absolutely the foundations of all religions." Stouppe's bulky anti-Dutch propaganda pamphlet, *La religion des Hollandois* (Figure 33.1), written prior to Spinoza's visit to Utrecht and published originally in French but afterwards also in Dutch and German,[1] was the very first published account (preceded by Steno in manuscript) ever to report Spinozism's existence as a movement and force in society, an established philosophical creed which, Stouppe affirms, was already strongly rooted and exhibited a notoriously clandestine character.

The revolutionary implications of Spinoza's philosophy, in Stouppe's view, were beyond question. The *TTP* "has for its principal goal to destroy all religions, especially the Jewish and Christian faiths, and instead introduce atheism, libertinage and liberty of all religions [a pour but principal de détruire toutes les religions, et particulièrement la judaïque et la Chrétienne, et introduire l'Athéisme, le libertinage, et la liberté de toutes les religions]."[2] Here then was a clandestine organization seeking a radically secular and tolerant society, with religious authority eradicated from government, law, and institutions, partly derived from a subversive crypto-Jewish tradition that Spinoza had adapted as

---

[1] Stouppe, *De God-Dienst Der Hollanders*.
[2] Stouppe, *Religion des Hollandois*, 65–6; Israel, *Dutch Republic*, 639–40, 921; Nadler, *Spinoza: A Life*, 315; Popkin, *Spinoza*, 109–12; Lavaert, *Vrijheid, gelijkheid, veelheid*, 210–11.

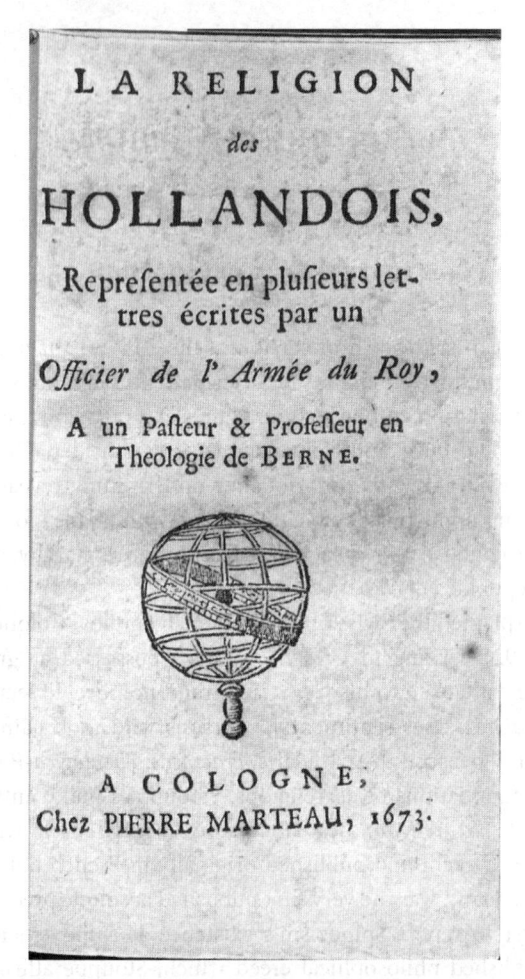

Figure 33.1 [Jean-Baptiste Stouppe], *La religion des Hollandois: Representée en plusieurs lettres écrites par un officier de l'armée du roy, à un pasteur & professeur en theologie de Berne*. A Cologne: Chez Pierre Marteau, 1673. IAS Spinoza Research Collection.

his own. A revolutionary project seeking to substitute democratic republics for monarchy and aristocracy, his movement sought to replace religious authority with free thought and a secularized moral order based on freedom to publish and criticize. Still, Spinoza's objective was never to attack individual personal devotion (where genuine) as such, especially when manifested as "charity and justice," the essence of "true religion" in his eyes, but always to secure social, educational, and political benefits by weakening those authorities, doctrines, and institutions that support and rely on imposed "superstitious" belief-structures.

At the core of Spinoza's "realistic" conception stands his principle that the more the power of kings and autocrats is curbed by constitutional checks and committees and by discrediting the religious sanction tyrants need, the more the clergy's quest to capture politics, moral thought, and education is curtailed, the more society advances and improves. Viable opposition to structures of authority based on ignorance, faith, and tyranny can succeed only by making converts to true "philosophy" and infiltrating hidden sympathizers into the professions and positions of influence. The political revolution Spinoza sought was thus a veiled process of intellectual subversion, drawing supporters from all corners and social strata, aimed at disarming kings, priests, fanatics, *and* the ignorant surreptitiously, inconspicuously, and peacefully. If basic change for the better arising from revolutionary transformation based on reason is achievable, it cannot come about via mass intervention, rioting, or violent insurgency but only by spreading clandestine texts, hidden adherents, and discerning sympathizers horizontally, among the elites, to tilt things in the right direction.

For this to happen, a hidden revolutionary vanguard of highly educated leaders, officeholders, and publicists, freethinkers like Spinoza's friends and allies, must be taught, organized, and motivated first. During the 1660s, when composing his mature works, Spinoza's circle consisted partly of university graduates—physicians, lawyers, and independent gentleman scholars but also partly of non-university trained autodidacts such as Glazemaker, Balling, Rieuwertsz, and Jelles. Advancing by means of clandestine texts seeping through against the wishes of the authorities into society generally as well as in part within the universities, his was an underground movement silently disarming and overcoming mankind's principal foes—monarchy, ignorance, and priestcraft—by discrediting theology, deriding popular credulity, and eventually rupturing the vast theologico-political apparatus locking all humanity, as he viewed matters, into uncomprehending bondage under kings, aristocrats, priests, and corrupt oligarchs. If Spinoza's writings rather than Spinoza himself forged his network of disciples or what Bayle too would later call his "secte" and set out his concrete agenda, his personality and powers of persuasion in conversation played a not inconsiderable part also.

Bayle would later confirm, like Steno, Stouppe, Bontekoe, and others earlier, that Spinoza did indeed succeed in establishing an enduring "sect" by insinuating his subversive influence into society, adding that his adherents included university students, preachers, and professors. Frequently viewed in the late seventeenth and early eighteenth century, as Bayle projected him, as the culminating manifestation of "godlessness" in the world, Spinoza was the thinker who imposed shape and order, summing up and reinforcing two thousand years of monism and rejection of *supernaturalia* in European thought. For Bayle, Spinoza possessed unrivalled status not just as a demolition agent dwarfing Machiavelli, Vanini, and Hobbes but also as the builder of a new system amounting to more than just a theoretical proposition or abstract philosophy. However fallacious a structure, it was an active force affecting men's outlook and lives. As one Dutch observer expressed the point in the mid-eighteenth century, Spinoza assembled a set of phrases, terms, and concepts cleverly linked together so as to make his outlandish system seem less outrageous and more plausible than it actually was to a great many.[3] From this, he went on to exert an unparalleled impact helping shape the attitudes, terminology, and orientation of the entire clandestine atheistic-materialist tendency within the Western world down to the mid-nineteenth century.

The *TTP*'s first edition, or "editio princeps," had a title-page declaring a false place of publication, "Hamburg" (Figure 33.2), and name of publisher, also withholding the author's name, with subsequent editions, from 1672 through the 1670s, all emulating the original title-page and layout. After around 1678–9, fresh editions ceased to appear. Thus, all printed copies of this uniquely subversive book circulating in Latin during the Enlightenment era, until the late eighteenth century, were issued and disseminated clandestinely whilst Spinoza still lived or immediately following his death. All these illicit editions of the 1670s imitated the "editio princeps" (listed here as *TTP* 1) in offering no name of author, obscuring their real place of publication, and concealing the publisher's and printer's names. The first edition seems to have appeared in considerable quantity as copies preserved in special book collections today are far from rare.[4] All these successive clandestine editions of the 1670s bore the same date "1670" except for a few copies of the 1672 edition which do carry the actual date (a printer's error and bibliographical anomaly quickly "corrected" at the printers), after which the rest of that year's edition reverted to the intended ruse that these copies too dated from "1670" while otherwise replicating the same pagination and spelling errors as in the rest of the "1672" edition.[5]

The same publisher, Rieuwertsz, organized the process throughout, bringing out all these follow-up clandestine editions during the Franco-Dutch War (1672–8) and devising the various ploys utilized to make them resemble each other, and in some cases not resemble each other, effectively enough to hide the reality that repeated printings of the same forbidden book followed one after the other. Most differences between editions were very minor except for the deliberate divergences in the cases of *TTP* 4 and 5; for the rest, discrepancies between the various editions and printings are noticeable only when copies are closely compared side by side. Aside from a few more conspicuous discrepancies between editions such as correcting the spelling of the false publisher's name from "Künraht" to "Künrath" in *TTP* 6 and *TTP* 7, for all practical purposes, without making a close comparison, the divergences were largely imperceptible to the general public and the authorities. A few of the more obtrusive discrepancies are listed in Table 33.1. But except for the 1673–4 octavo editions which stand out as

---

[3] Raats, *Korte en grondige betoginge*, 14.   [4] Bamberger, "Early Editions," 15.
[5] Kingma and Offenberg, "Bibliography," 8–9; Van de Ven, "Spinoza's Life and Time," 50.

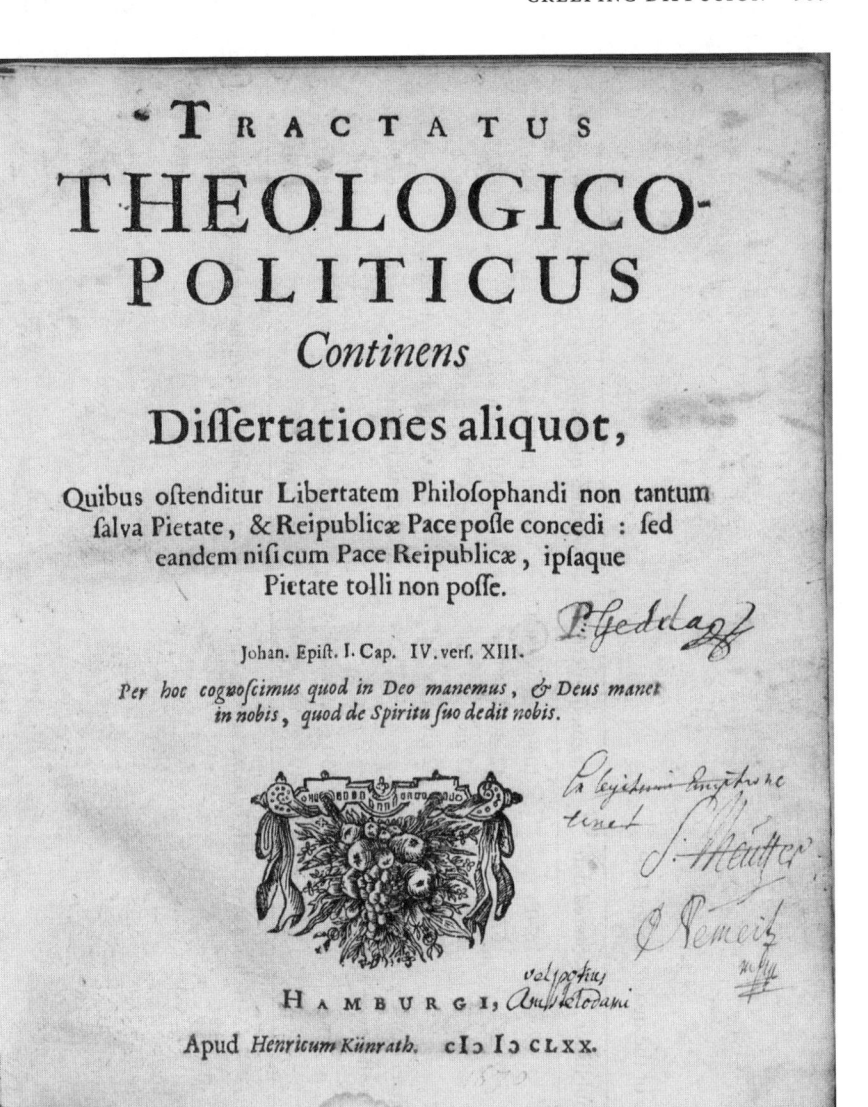

Figure 33.2 [Spinoza], *Tractatus Theologico-Politicus*. Hamburgi Apud Henricum Künrath [sic], 1670 [i.e. 1677 or 1678] see Table 33.1. IAS Spinoza Research Collection.

blatant, defiant outliers, even these differences between editions were unlikely to be noticed by readers or the authorities unless someone actually pointed them out.

For whatever reason, during 1673, as suppression of the *TTP* intensified following the Orangist coup of 1672, Rieuwertsz suspended his bogus repetition of the fictive publisher "Henricus Künraht [sic]" and of "Hamburg," exclusively employed thus far, temporarily switching to what, according to the Table of False Editions compiled by the bibliographer Fritz Bamberger, was (and ever since has

Table 33.1 Early clandestine editions of the quarto Latin *TTP*

Edition	Fictive publisher	Stated date	Pagination errors	Other quirks	Actual date
TTP 1 (Editio Princeps)	Künraht	1670	104 given as "304"	no errata list	1669/70
TTP 2 (quarto)	Künraht	1672	42 given as "24"	cap XVI given as "XIV"	1672
TTP 2a (quarto)	Künraht	1670	42 given as "24"	cap XVI given as "XIV"	1672
TTP 3 (quarto)	Künraht	1670	42 given as "24"	several wrong chapter heads	?
TTP 4 (octavo)	three different false publishers' names			false author's names	1673
TTP 5 (octavo)	bound together with Meyer's book				1674
TTP 6 (quarto)	Künrath	1670	130 given as "830"	Errata as in *TTP* 2	1677?
TTP 7 (quarto)	Künrath	1670	192 given as "92"	no errata list	1678?

Sources: Kingma and Offenberg, "Bibliography," 7–8, 15–16; Bamberger, "Early Editions," 16–33; Van de Ven, *Printing Spinoza*, 76–166; the Abraham Wolf collection at the UCLA Research Library has copies of *TTP* 1, 2, 3, and 4.

Table 33.2 Octavo variants of the *TTP* (Amsterdam, 1673–4)

Edition	Fictive author	Other quirks	Date	Known copies
TTP Octavo 1a	"Heinsius"	–	1673	40
TTP Octavo 1b	"Le Boë Sylvius"	–	1673	5
TTP Octavo 1c	"Henriquez de Villacorta"	–	1673	5
TTP Octavo 2	(no author named)	"English" type used	1674	7
TTP Octavo 3	(no author named)	bound with the Philosophia, altered vignette	1674	83

Sources: Bamberger, "Early Editions," 9–33; Kingma and Offenberg, "Bibliography," 7–8, 15–16; Van de Ven, *Printing Spinoza*, 168–92.

been labelled) "the second edition," a variant carrying three different title-pages (see Table 33.2). All totally fictive, all three were highly provocative, purporting to be learned works by famous scholars with outstanding international reputations.[6] This fresh ploy was obviously meant to be far from quietly inconspicuous in the manner of the earlier and later editions, indeed intended to provoke outrage. Among these today considerably rarer title-pages, the most scandalous at the time presented itself as the *Totius medicinae idea nova seu Francisci de la Boe Sylvii opera omnia* [A New Concept of all Medicine or All the works...] of the famous medical professor, Franciscus de Le Boë Sylvius, who had died shortly before, in November 1672 (Figure 33.3).[7]

This blatant impertinence, as it was perceived, supposedly published by "Carolus Gratiani" at "Amsterdam," was designedly an overt snub to Leiden University but subversive too in a subtler way. For Le Boë Sylvius, Steno's, and Swammerdam's prime mentor, was the chief founder of the Iatrochemical School of Medicine aiming to reconceptualize all life and disease processes in terms of chemical reactions, overturning the whole edifice of traditional academic medicine, a medical reform programme popular with Meyer, Bouwmeester, Adriaan Koerbagh, and the *cercle Spinoziste* as a whole. Thus, the choice of bogus title here could be construed to imply a revamping of the escalating Cartesian revolution in medicine and chemistry, presenting medicine of the mind so to speak, as a fresh stage in the demolition of Europe's immense artifice of Aristotelian and scholastic qualities, substances, categories, and actions conjoined to "fabricated" theology.

---

[6] Bamberger, "Early Editions," 20; Van de Ven, *Printing Spinoza*, 50.
[7] Van de Ven, *Printing Spinoza*, 190–1.

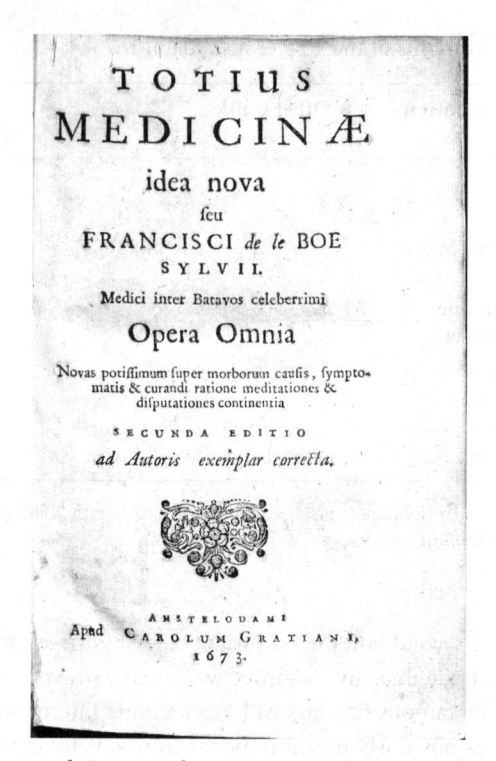

Figure 33.3 *Franciscus de Le Boë Sylvius, Totius Medicinae Idea Nova Seu Francisci de Le Boe Sylvii. Medici Inter Batavos Celeberrimi Opera Omnia.* Amstelodami: Apud Carolum Gratiani [i.e. Jan Rieuwertsz], 1673. IAS Spinoza Research Collection.

Equally condemned as a snub to the university, though again, for the rest, basically just a straightforward reprint of the 1672 *TTP*, was the volume purporting to be a collection of the historical works of Daniel Heinsius (1580–1665), published in "Leiden" by "Isaac Herculis," entitled *Danielis Heinsii, Operum historicorum collectio*.[8] Denounced by the Leiden Reformed Church consistory, on 8 December 1673, this 1673 false edition (Figure 33.4), cloaking an illicit, officially suppressed book under the "names of honest and learned men," provoked particular outrage and protests.[9]

Third and perhaps last of this batch of bogus title-page variants, the solitary one of the three not cited in the Leiden consistory's complaint,[10] purportedly published in Amsterdam by "Jac. Paulli," was the *Opera chirurgica omnia* of the noted Spanish surgeon Franciscus Henriquez de Villacorta (1616–80), an old-style

[8] Van de Ven, *Printing Spinoza*, 185–7.
[9] Kingma and Offenberg, "Bibliography," 11; Bamberger, "Early Editions," 19–20.
[10] Van de Ven, *Printing Spinoza*, 177–9.

DANIELIS HEINSII P.P.

OPERUM

HISTORI-
CORUM

COLLECTIO
Prima.

Editio Secunda, priori editione multo emen-
datior & auctior

accedunt quædam hactenus inedita.

L U G D.   B A T A V.
Apud I S A A C U M   H E R C U L I S.
1 6 7 3.

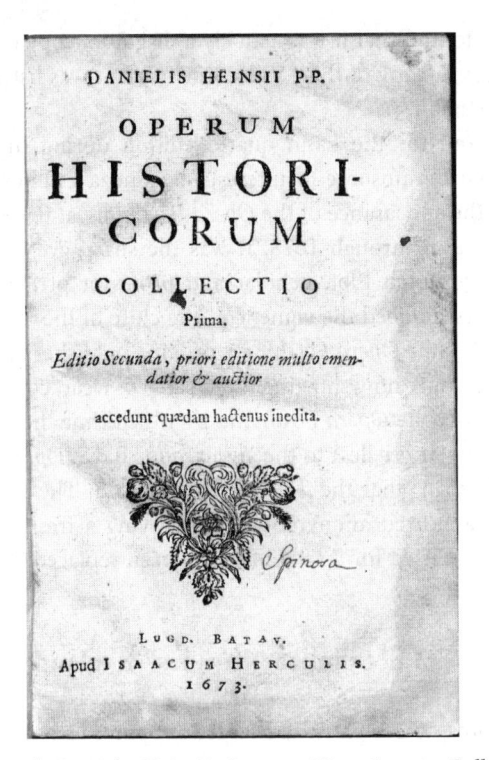

Figure 33.4 [Spinoza], *Danielis Heinsii: Operum Historicorum Collectio*. Editio 2. Lugd. Batav. ["Leiden" i.e. Amsterdam]: Apud Isaacum Herculis, 1673. IAS Spinoza Research Collection.

Galenista medical professor at Alcalá de Henares, then still living, personifying the traditional medicine Le Boë Sylvius and his following aimed to overthrow. This title-page, once considered "far rarer than the other two," though all are fairly rare, was presumably intended as a jibe at the scholasticism still dominating the Spanish universities and perhaps also Spanish royal absolutism given that Henriquez de Villacorta was personal physician to then Spanish King Charles II (reigned: 1665–1700), reportedly a mentally unbalanced monarch known as the "bewitched" and much the least impressive European king ruling during Spinoza's lifetime. Thirty-eight years later, in 1710, the noted German bibliophile and wealthy connoisseur of philosophical book history, Zacharias Conrad von Uffenbach (1683–1734), a few months before acquiring his copy of the Koerbaghs' *Bloemhof*, in 1711, whilst in Groningen, visiting the private museum and special rarities, or *rarissima* of a fellow book-collector whose collection was even larger than his own (15,000 books against 11,000), came across a copy of the "Villacorta" edition among his host's "curiosities," and, on examining it, was much astonished to find that it was actually a disguised copy of the *TTP*.¹¹ In the nineteenth century, a copy of this "Villacorta" variant was listed in the library of Trinity College, Dublin.¹²

Renewed demand for the Latin quarto edition during the years 1677-8 is unsurprising given the upsurge of interest in Spinoza's philosophy and general legacy following the appearance of the *Opera Posthuma* at the end of 1677 and its successful distribution through 1678. It was the sharp eye of the distinguished nineteenth-century Dutch Bible scholar and professor of Syriac, J. P. N. Land (1834-97), who first noticed the vignette at the close of the "Preface" of *TTP* 6 is the same as found in the *Opera Posthuma*, proving publisher and printer were the same in both cases, only now showing more signs of wear, confirming that *TTP* 5 followed shortly after the *Opera Posthuma* by which time the anonymous author of the "Preface" (by Jarig Jelles) to the anonymous B.d.S. *Opera Posthuma* (1677) had confirmed in print that the *TTP* was by Spinoza. The new edition, *TTP* 7, nevertheless still appeared anonymously, employing a fresh vignette indicating that the worn device used for *TTP* 6 had now been replaced.¹³

33.ii Spinoza "Invades" England

Charles II, we know, was a particular target of Spinoza's anti-monarchism, and, unlike most of his countrymen, Spinoza possessed a hidden weapon, his system of political thought, potent enough to hit back with some effect against a monarchical world view he believed responsible for trampling on everything that he held best in society. No specific English reaction to the *TTP* has been recorded definitely dating from 1670, although Henry Oldenburg's surviving "Catalogue of My Books," dated 3 October 1670, at a time when he and Spinoza were not corresponding, does list the *TTP* (without mentioning Spinoza's name). However, this list includes additions inserted later in the early 1670s, so it is not clear that he did acquire his copy in 1670.¹⁴ If he did, Oldenburg kept very quiet about it. Probably the first scholar to deliberately alert leading English academics to the dire menace the *TTP* was taken to represent was Locke's future friend Philippus van Limborch (1633-1712). The greatest Arminian theologian of the later seventeenth century, based at the Amsterdam Athenaeum, Van Limborch knew Rieuwertsz well and all about the Koerbagh affair. Few were better informed about the incipient early 1670s advance of "Spinozism." Collaborating to refute Spinoza

---

¹¹ Huisman, "Bibliothecae Instructissimae," 312-13; Van Heertum, "A Not So Harmless Drudge," 401.
¹² *Catalogus Librorum Impressorum* vii, 574.   ¹³ Bamberger, "Early Editions," 25.
¹⁴ BL Add. MS 4255, fo. 230. Oldenburg, "Catalogue of My Books taken A. 1670, Octob 3."

with fellow Remonstrant ministers in Holland, Van Limborch maintained various contacts in England, and, alarmed by Spinoza's denial of miracles and divine governance of the world, intervened to alert English academe to what was afoot, writing, in January 1671, to Oliver Doiley (1616–63), or D'Oyly as he spelt his name, a senior fellow of King's College Cambridge with whom he had long been in contact and arranging for an Amsterdam bookseller to send him a copy of the TTP.[15] Doiley's copy seems to have been the first to attract attention in Cambridge.

He could not remember having ever read a "more pestilential" book than this "Discursus Theologico-Politicus," Van Limborch assured Doiley, whose author "is believed to be Benedictus Spinoza who, from a Jew, became a Deist if not an atheist [cujus autor creditor Benedictus Spinoza, qui ex judaeo factus est Deista, si non Atheus]." His treatise "ridicules the prophets and apostles" and claims "no miracles ever happened, nor could they happen." Still worse was his discussion of God: in his eyes "there is a necessity to which God is bound, so that he describes God in such a way that he plainly appears to abolish him [datur fatum, cui ipse Deus allegatus est, ita tamen Deum describit, ut eum plane videatur tollere]." "What monstrous things our Batavian land produces!" Dutch toleration was indeed shamefully excessive.[16]

Van Limborch alerted Cambridge to what he regarded as a pressing danger but, at the same time, was anxious that his English colleagues proceed, much as he and his fellow ministers in Holland, in a wary, guarded manner to avoid drawing unnecessary attention to the outrage. It was important that Doiley should show the *Tractatus* only to learned types well practised at sifting good from bad, and that this text, thus far unknown in England, should not fall into undesirable hands or become widely known. Replying in March 1671, Doiley assured Van Limborch that he and his colleagues would handle the business with discretion, indeed were very much on their guard against what was essentially a "Hobbesian" threat. To refute Spinoza's abominations, the *eruditi* of Holland, the land that was the source of this virulent new vein of Hobbesian error, needed to collaborate closely with the English vanguard fighting the Hobbesian menace such as his fellow Cambridge don, Henry More (1614–87) who would gladly join in this continuation of that fight. Doiley hoped More's metaphysical writings, and a pending rebuttal of Hobbes on "natural laws," the *De legibus naturae* (1672) by his ally Richard Cumberland (1631–1718), an Arminian London clergyman who later, in 1691, became Bishop of Peterborough, "may [also] to an extent serve to counteract the

---

[15] According to "The Spinoza Web," De Boer (and following him myself) mistook 23 January for 23 June, see Van Limborch to Oliver Doiley, Amsterdam 23 "June" [in fact January] 1671 in De Boer, "Spinoza en Engeland," 332–3; Colie, "Spinoza in England," 184.
[16] De Boer, "Spinoza en Engeland," 332; Barnouw, *Philippus van Limborch*, 136; Simonutti, "Vindiciae Miraculorum," 614, 625.

poison of that *Theological Treatise* which is full of Hobbesian errors."[17] More and Cumberland too were now brought into the picture.

Henry More read the *TTP* in Cambridge at this early stage, in 1671, and it clearly shocked and had a considerable impact on him. Ever since his early friendly exchange of letters with Descartes in 1648-9, he had had his reservations about Descartes' thoroughgoing "mechanical way," he assured Boyle, then at Christ Church, College, Oxford, convinced the Cartesian approach "would not hold in all phenomena, as I always verily thought." But only now, he explained to Boyle, in December 1671, after reading the *TTP* did he realize that merely entertaining private doubts "would not save us from being accounted among the wits, one of their gang, and a perfect Cartesian as to the hypothesis, and, indeed, no less than an infidel and atheist. And I was informed out of Holland, from a learned hand there [Van Limborch?], that a considerable company of men appeared there [the *cercle spinoziste*], mere scoffers at religion, and atheistical, that professed themselves Cartesians, and that his [i.e. Descartes'] philosophy may naturally have such an influence as this, I can neither deny nor could conceal."

More felt distraught and saw it as potentially a great reproach to himself "to be found of so little judgment, as not to discern how prejudicial Descartes' mechanical pretensions are to belief in God." He was anxious not to be supposed either a fool or a "juggler and deceiver, I not declaring against that philosophy which is the pillar of many of those men's infidelity, and of their atheism, and it is not a week ago, since I saw a letter, that informed me, that Spinoza, a Jew first, after a Cartesian, and now an atheist, is supposed the author of Theologico-Politicus. I suppose you [i.e. Boyle] may have seen the book." More felt the need already then, in December 1671, to take up his pen and assail the *TTP* in particular to "declare my sense of the Cartesian philosophy and vindicate myself from the imputation of so fond a blindnesse, as not to be aware of the danger of that philosophy, if it be credited: and, which is best of all, to put it quite out of credit."[18] Nevertheless, for now, for whatever reason, he did not take up his pen.[19]

Cambridge was certainly the first focal point of Spinoza's challenge in England, being Van Limborch's chief line of contact, though, in December 1671, he also sent a copy of the *TTP* to one of Oxford's leading royalists and Arminians—the notoriously cantankerous and vindictive president of Magdalen College, Thomas Pierce (1622-91), a former Calvinist turned foe of Calvinism appointed head of his college in 1661 (against the wishes of some of the fellows) by the recently

---

[17] De Boer, "Spinoza in Engeland," 333; Simonutti, "Spinoza and the English Thinkers," 192.
[18] More to Boyle, undated but 4 Dec. 1671 in Boyle, *Correspondence* iv, 231; there remains some doubt as to the date of this undated crucial letter; but the alternative date (4 Dec. 1676) assigned elsewhere seems definitely less likely than the 1671 date, see More to Boyle, 4 Dec. 1676 in *Works of the Honourable Robert Boyle* v, 514; Colie, *Light and Enlightenment*, 73-4; Cristofolini, *Cartesiani e sociniani*, 118-19, 126-7.
[19] Colie, *Light and Enlightenment*, 74; Reid, "Henry More and Nicolas Malebranche's Critiques," 765.

restored royal court. Writing to Pierce, Van Limborch repeated his points about Spinoza denying miracles and divine governance of the world.[20] By the winter of 1671-2, several of England's foremost scholars were thus busy examining the *TTP*, among them John Locke, another of the *TTP*'s early English readers, who purchased his copy in March 1672, just before the Third Anglo-Dutch War began. That copy he afterwards sold to the Earl of Shaftesbury, in November 1675, but, at some later point, purchased a second copy to replace it, but now of the 1674 edition.[21] From the early 1670s until the end of his life, in 1704, Locke always took immense care, as any respected reforming thinker then needed to, to avoid being tainted by "Spinosa," and indeed became highly indignant with anyone, such as Bishop Stillingfleet, alleging some affinity between his ideas on matter, imagination, and Scripture, and those of the everywhere boycotted and shunned Dutch thinker.[22]

Cambridge remained the main focus of reaction during the early years of its British diffusion. It was soon a familiar refrain that Spinoza's work is merely Hobbes rehashed even if in some respects definitely worse, a notion that during the early and mid-1670s became so deeply embedded in England as to wholly overshadow Spinoza's role and significance. Indeed, entrenched insistence on Hobbes being the overriding factor, despite Spinoza going further, materially assisted the prevailing strategy of veiling and obscuring Spinoza the person, the author, and the thinker, helping keep his name and ideas out of the limelight and out of the public's consciousness. During 1670-2, there thus began an urgent high-level discussion about the *TTP* and Spinoza in England that remained carefully curtained off from the general public, from students and the book trade, a debate largely confined to the circle of Boyle, More, Oldenburg, Cumberland, and Doiley's Cambridge group, plus a small group in Oxford. Very few copies of the *TTP* circulated on the English side of the Channel before or during the Third Anglo-Dutch War (1672-4), enabling those in the know to confine discussion of the dreaded text for the moment strictly to their own circles.

Yet, if Doiley, More, Oldenburg, Pierce, Locke, and also Boyle (for whom the reality of miracles and of supernatural spirits such as angels and demons were basic scientific axioms) stood warily vigilant against an as yet largely invisible presence which, they realized, nevertheless represented an extremely dire potential challenge, none of them published anything against the *TTP* despite several of them evidently planning to do so. In early 1674, after eighteen months largely cut off from direct communication with neighbours, the besieged remnant of the United Provinces first glimpsed something like a return of normalcy in relations with England. From the late spring, Dutch books again entered England in

---

[20] Simonutti, "Vindiciae Miraculorum," 616, 625.
[21] Parker, "Spinoza, Locke," 166; Harrison and Laslett, *The Library of John Locke*, 238.
[22] Parker, "Spinoza, Locke," 170-1; Hutton, "Science, Philosophy and Atheism," 102-3, 105-6.

quantity, thereby renewing opportunity for infiltrating forbidden works. Distributing an illicit publication as notorious as the *TTP*, though, was no simple matter, raising the question of how far Spinoza simply left Rieuwertsz to devise whatever bookseller's ruses he judged appropriate or was himself party to the finesses of clandestine book distribution.

At this point, Rieuwertsz seized the opportunity to produce a fresh edition of the *TTP* in smaller, cheaper octavo format specifically designed for the British market, with many copies bound together with Meyer's *Philosophia*. For the title-page, he deliberately employed a distinctively "English type" of the sort familiar in England (Figure 33.5). This octavo 1674 edition, made to resemble books published in London, helped by easier communication following the end of the hostilities, explains why the renewed, wider, more vocal and public second stage of the English reaction to the *TTP* occurred specifically in the years 1674–6.[23] Rieuwertsz, whose Amsterdam bookshop functioned almost as Spinoza's personal post office, was a master of bookseller's ploys, but to operate effectively outside the Republic, he needed a behind-the-scenes network, and, as regards England, Spinoza himself clearly participated in the work of illicit book distribution.

As there is scant evidence elsewhere showing how far Spinoza personally collaborated in Rieuwertsz's schemes of diffusion, it is revealing that at this point, just as their long interrupted correspondence resumed, Spinoza requested Oldenburg to take charge of a stock of copies of the illicit *TTP* intended for dispatch to London and arrange distribution there on his behalf. "I shall not decline to receive some copies of the said Treatise," answered Oldenburg distinctly without enthusiasm, on 22 July 1674: "I would ask only this of you, that they be addressed, when the time comes, to a certain Dutch merchant living in London who will make sure that they are passed on to me afterwards. There will be no need to mention that you have sent me books of this sort. Provided they come safely into my possession, I do not doubt that I shall easily arrange to distribute them among my various friends, from here, obtaining a fair price for them."[24] Presumably, he actually did so. Meanwhile, Oldenburg was anxious his name should nowhere appear in connection with the *TTP*.

This was just three days after the provincial high court, the Hof of Holland, issued its 19 July 1674 placard definitively banning the *TTP* throughout Holland, along with Hobbes' *Leviathan*, the *Philosophia*, and the *Bibliotheca Fratrum Polonorum*. The author of the *TTP* is singled out for seeking to "bring minds weak and not well-formed into doubt," undermining the "authority of the Holy Scriptures" and seeking to "overthrow the teaching of the true Christian Reformed

---

[23] Van de Ven, *Printing Spinoza*, 192–9.
[24] Spinoza, *Opera* iv, 273; Spinoza, *Collected Works* (ed. Curley) ii, 435; Spinoza *Correspondance* (ed. Rovere), 326.

TRACTATUS
THEOLOGICO-POLITICUS,

Cui adjunctus est

Philosophia S. Scripturæ

INTERPRES.

Ab Authore longè Emendatior.

Anno Dom. 1674.

Figure 33.5 [Spinoza], *Tractatus Theologico-Politicus: Cui Adjunctus Est Philosophia S.Scripturae Interpres. Ab Authore Longe Emendator.* [Amsterdam], 1674. IAS Spinoza Research Collection.

religion."[25] As many must have noticed, the stated reasons for the special ban applied only in marginal fashion to Hobbes and the *Philosophia*. It was primarily the *Bibliotheca* and the *TTP* that were transmitting unacceptable blasphemies against God and His attributes, denying the Trinity and divinity of Jesus Christ, and his being the true Redeemer, "together with the fundamental chief points of the aforesaid true Christian Religion." The second version of the clandestine octavo edition of the *TTP* with its further variant issued by Rieuwertsz in 1673–4 (see Tables 33.1 and 33.2), the edition bound together with the new issue of Meyer's *Philosophia*, certainly accelerated the *TTP*'s penetration in England as well as riled authorities in the Republic and may possibly have directly helped trigger the Hof van Holland's general ban on Meyer's *Philosophia* and Spinoza's *TTP*. This possibility, that the States' decree was connected with the new octavo edition, is suggested both by its timing and also the decree's wording stating that despite their prohibiting "Socinian and other damaging books," works such as Hobbes' *Leviathan*, the *Bibliotheca Fratrum Polonorum*, the *Philosophia*, and the *Tractatus Theologico-Politicus* were still seeping out and harming the Reformed religion.[26] The Reformed synods in the other provinces welcomed Holland's 1674 "strong placard" against licentious printing, and Friesland, Overijssel, and Utrecht, and probably all the other provinces, afterwards issued similar decrees.[27]

As regular cross-Channel communication resumed, the Spinoza debate revived with it. It was not long before the seriousness of the threat to the existing order posed by Spinoza and his following again came to the fore. To Henry Jenkes (d. 1697), fellow of Gonville and Caius College, and another of Henry More's Cambridge circle, just elected a fellow of the Royal Society, in December 1674, a theologian and Hebraist in contact with him over many years, Van Limborch sent a stunning letter, dated 30 December 1674, expressing satisfaction at the furious outcry against the *TTP* erupting since the recent peace among leading Oxbridge minds and especially Robert Boyle's vigorous condemnation. If Jenkes hoped the God of truth would "illumine [Spinoza's] mind that he see his great error and repent,"[28] word of Boyle's and Oldenburg's disgust and resolve to block the *TTP*, Van Limborch was delighted to report, was now rebounding powerfully in Holland. "I understand that Spinoza, the profane author of the *Tractatus Theologico-Politicus*, heard with amazement and not without some perturbation of mind that his treatise is condemned in England with the unanimous agreement of all." Spinoza reportedly particularly took it ill that the renowned natural

---

[25] *Groot Placaet Boeck* iii, 523–4. Placaet, The Hague, 19 July 1674.
[26] Van Gelder, *Getemperde vrijheid*, 177–8.
[27] RA Gron. APS vol. 3: Provinciale Synode res. Groningen, 4 May 1675 and res. Appingedam, 17 April 1676; RA Utr. PV vol. 3, Sept. 1675, sessio tertia, art. 20.
[28] Colie, *Light and Enlightenment*, 96.

philosopher, Robert Boyle, judged his treatise highly unfavourably, Spinoza having supposedly "especially promised himself the applause of eminent philosophers. We truly congratulate England," concludes Van Limborch, "that she generates and breeds no profane philosophers, but only Christian [ones] for whom we pray all the best from the Father of Lights."[29]

"It does not surprise me," replied Jenkes, in March 1675, that Spinoza "takes it ill," hearing that in England "his book is not valued at all." He too had studied Spinoza's "infamous book with the greatest attention without prejudice or evil will," and could find nothing in it but a despicable design to undermine religion.[30] "In our academy," added Jenkes, meaning either Cambridge or the Royal Society, or perhaps both, Spinoza meets only with overwhelming opposition. Less unforgiving, though, than Pierce, Jenkes could not help wishing this gifted miscreant would experience a redeeming change of heart: Spinoza "used to declare himself a Cartesian scientist, was he but a Christian, or that he never had become the author of the *Theological-Political Treatise*," he would surely remain today an intellect of some standing.[31]

Van Limborch, Jenkes, and Doiley were hopeful the danger was stifled, but this soon proved not to be the case. Another historically important early report is that of Edward Stillingfleet (1635–99), future Bishop of Worcester (from 1689) and renowned bibliophile destined to leave a library of 10,000 volumes at his death, at that time an Anglican vicar in London. He examined the *TTP* during either 1674 or early 1675, and mentions it obliquely in his *A Letter to a Deist*, a text not published until 1677 but completed, Stillingfleet records, in June 1675, hence only half a year after the confident assessments of Van Limborch, Doiley, and Jenkes.[32] "There is a late author, I hear," comments Stillingfleet at the close of his preface to *A Letter*, that "is mightily in vogue among many, who cry up anything on the Atheistical side, though never so weak and trifling." But if, like his sparring partner Baxter, he was deeply worried by the *TTP*'s potential impact, Stillingfleet was equally aware, and thankful, that the wider English public knew little or nothing about Spinoza and, unlike Baxter, he took good care in his printed text to keep to the practice of concealing Spinoza's name and the title of his book, generally aligning with Boyle, More, and Oxbridge in their concerted campaign to avoid drawing attention to Spinoza's ideas. For the present, this highly influential future Arminian Anglican bishop, like Doiley, Jenkes, and Pierce, seemed cautiously confident that Spinoza's thought was being firmly held in check, especially as it was "no difficult task to lay open the false reasonings and inconsistent

---

[29] Van Limborch to Jenkes, Amsterdam, 20 Dec. 1674 in De Boer, "Spinoza in Engeland," 334; Simonutti, "Vindiciae Miraculorum," 626; Simonutti, "Premières reactions anglaises," 130.
[30] De Boer, "Spinoza en Engeland," 335; Simonutti, "Vindiciae Miraculorum," 626.
[31] De Boer, "Spinoza en Engeland," 335; Colie, *Light and Enlightenment*, 96.
[32] Stillingfleet, *A Letter to a Deist*, 135; Simonutti, "Spinoza and the English Thinkers, 193.

hypotheses of [Spinoza's] book which hath been sufficiently done already in that language [i.e. Latin] in which it was written."[33]

Stillingfleet, among the ablest Latitudinarians in England, thus initially worried mainly on a private level. The essential safeguard, Stillingfleet agreed, in 1675, was to restrict the discussion to closed circles and keep Spinoza's name and the *TTP* out of the public's consciousness. So far, the *TTP* had been read only by a few Oxbridge dons and Latin-reading churchmen, "but if for the advancement of irreligion among us, that book be, as it is talked, translated into our tongue, there will not, I hope, want those who will be as ready to defend religion and morality, as others are to decry and despise them."[34] Its appearing in English would indeed transform the situation entirely. From a general cultural and social perspective, shifting from Latin to the vernacular (whether English, Dutch, or another language) was the development those in the know most feared. Keeping Spinoza's name and person out of the discussion, in the shadows, hence remained the rule for the time being, and in these early years it remained de rigueur to refer to the infamous author in question as the "*Theologico-Politicus*" rather than "Spinoza."

Accordingly, by 1675, still nothing had been published in Britain refuting the arguments of the *TTP*. But the pressure was building. Convinced Plato's philosophy "was the most noble and effectual engine to fetch up a man's mind to true virtue and holiness, next to the Bible,"[35] Henry More, among the most formidable and learned polemicists in Britain, and a leader of the anti-Hobbes campaign, found himself repeatedly entreated by allies and friends, Doiley, Jenkes, Van Helmont, and probably Anne Conway, to take up his cudgels against Spinoza as well as against Hobbes. Yet, despite his colleagues' entreaties and his own early resolution to write against Spinoza, More still put off facing the menace publicly, throughout 1674 and 1675 resisting appeals from "highly gifted" persons, as he puts it in the preface to his *Ad V.C. Epistola altera* (1677), owing to the boundless disgust he felt for the *TTP*'s irreligious dismissal of the miraculous and the book's impiety.

For More and Boyle, philosophy and faith stand in closest union. Spinoza's thesis that biblical prophecy is an inner "natural sagacity" grasping God's higher truth prior to argued reasoning, a product of natural human imagination in no instance really delivered by divine intervention or inspired by a God above nature, to More seemed contemptible, even absurd.[36] As for the *TTP*'s sixth chapter denying all possibility of miracles, to More, as Van Limborch, the crux of Spinoza's challenge, God's power, he replied, is certainly in the power of nature, but also separate from and above it, so that, contrary to "Spinozius,"

---

[33] Stillingfleet, *A Letter to a Deist*, preface, last page; Israel, *Radical Enlightenment*, 284.
[34] Stillingfleet, *A Letter to a Deist*, preface, last page.
[35] Quoted in Henry, "A Cambridge Platonist's Materialism," 173.
[36] More, *Ad V.C. Epistola altera*, 567–8; Hengstermann, "God or Space," 168.

unquestionably there can be "true miracles."[37] Only in 1676, when perusing the anti-rationalist Collegiant Kuyper's [Cuperus'] refutation of Spinoza, the *Arcana Atheismi revelata* [The Secrets of Atheism] (1676), whose emphatic Socinian bias struck him as totally unsuitable, did he return to examining Spinoza's anti-Scripturalism and, finally overcoming his repugnance, sat down to the task while waiting for his copy of Kuyper's refutation of the *TTP* to be bound. Spinoza certainly needed combating head-on with a far more crushing and effective rebuttal than Kuyper's.[38] More's contemptuous abhorrence of Spinoza was much the same deep-rooted disgust he felt for the atheistic writings of Pomponazzi, Cardano, Vanini, and Hobbes, all, in his view, contemptible and offering "nothing" substantial. Yet he could not deny that Spinoza was harder to answer than the others: "I found in the author of this treatise [the *TTP*]," he admitted, "a mind a little more complex and astute than in those other authors." Indeed, "I found this Theologicopoliticus such an impious work, that I could not forbear confuting whilst I read him."[39]

Agonized difficulty in reacting in print to the *TTP* was thus no monopoly of Dutch and German scholarship. Despite his wrestling with the *TTP* for years while Spinoza was still alive, it was only in 1679, three years after embarking on the task, that More finally published his fifty-page initial Latin refutation, entitled *Another Letter to V.C.* [Van Helmont] *which contains a brief Refutation of the Theological-Political Treatise*, together with his subsequently written seventy-page refutation of Spinoza's conception of substance. Despite publishing at a point when intensive controversy surrounding the *TTP* had been seething in Cambridge and Oxford rooms for five years, and nine whole years after the *TTP*'s first appearance, More's *Epistola*, astoundingly, apart from those of Baxter and Wilson, was nevertheless the first published discussion of Spinoza's Bible criticism by any English university figure.

John Wilson (dates unknown), another recruit to the chorus so gladdening Van Limborch by pouring vitriol on the *TTP* in England, was a Puritan minister acquainted with Baxter and with the Cambridge scene, who penned his *The Scriptures Genuine Interpreter* after More began his *Epistola* but published it earlier, in 1678. He would never even have thought of taking up his pen to refute the 1674 joint publication of the two anonymous treatises, the *Philosophia* and *TTP* bound together,[40] he explains, "were it not that I understand by the publications of some reverend divines abroad what mischief this author's *Discourse*

---

[37] More, *Ad V.C. Epistola altera*, 573–4; Hengstermann, "God or Space," 161, 177; Shaw, *Miracles*, 77–8.
[38] More, *Ad V.C. Epistola altera*, 565; Colie, *Light and Enlightenment*, 74; Jacob, *Henry More's Refutation*, p. ix; Krop, *Spinoza, een paradoxale icoon*, 47–8.
[39] More, *Ad V.C. Epistola altera*, preface.
[40] A book missing from Boucher's catalogue, *Spinoza in English*, 218; see Israel, *Radical Enlightenment*, 212–14, 745; Levitin, *Ancient Wisdom*, 547.

[i.e. the *TTP*], and some others whose publication it occasioned, have already done in The Netherlands; so I am not without just fears, that those unformed notions and corrupt principles that are, by this means, scattered abroad, may be quickly (if they be not already) propagated amongst ourselves."[41] Despite assigning more pages to the *Philosophia* than the *TTP*, Wilson was definitely more appalled, he relates, by the latter, a truly diabolical text calling "in question the whole truth and consequently the divine authority of the Scripture."

Undoubtedly "the great enemy of mankind" was ultimately responsible for the work of these atheistic "Antiscripturalists." Still, Wilson felt mystified by this deeply insidious writer's motivation. Perplexed by "whose design it is that the author of that Theological-Political Tractat drives," at one point he raises the possibility that it was all, despite the anonymous author's apparent dislike of Catholicism, some devious Jesuitical plot. The author may appear to "intimate his dislike of the Pontifician party; but we know it is consistent enough with the politick principles of men of that way, to speak much more than he hath done, against that very cause that they are studiously projecting, under that cover, to advance."[42] In any case, the anonymous author was obviously part of a gang, and the Devil's and these men's "grand design is utterly to cashier the Scripture as useless and unprofitable" except for promoting a few ethical principles best examined by philosophy, a loathsome notion since "as much as this might be said of the Jews' Talmud and the Turks' Alcoran."[43]

If leading Oxbridge dons were alerted to the threat early on, in 1671, and fully awoke to the seriousness of the challenge in 1674–5, and finally took up cudgels to oppose the threat in the late 1670s, in the event it once again proved easier to announce intentions to write against the *TTP* than actually do so. Much the most successful part of the English anti-Spinoza offensive of the 1670s proved to be keeping Spinoza's name and person a hushed up scandal confined to the intellectual elite, veiled and unseen by the reading public.

33.iii The Suppressed Dutch Version of the *TTP*

The Collegiant movement was undoubtedly one of the main channels by which the creeping diffusion of Spinoza's thought proceeded. But the Collegiant movement was largely confined to Amsterdam, Rotterdam, and Rijnsburg, their Anti-Trinitarian publications were illegal, and it would be quite wrong to suppose that at any point in the last three decades of the seventeenth century the barriers the authorities and churches held in place to prevent Spinoza and Spinozism seeping

---

[41] Wilson, *Scriptures Genuine Interpreter*, preface.
[42] Wilson, *Scriptures Genuine Interpreter*, 245–57.
[43] Wilson, *Scriptures Genuine Interpreter*, 256.

through into society were widely breached. If the octavo Latin version lowered the cost and facilitated the *TTP*'s circulation, for several years refutations and all discussion of the *TTP* remained largely confined to Latin. However, the *cercle Spinoziste* were planning, as early as 1669, to bring the work out also in Dutch translation, a bold step bound to extend its reach dramatically and provoke a still more explosive reaction on all sides.

During late 1669, even before the "editio princeps" appeared, the Dutch translation was being prepared for publication in Amsterdam. Rieuwertsz and Spinoza's most regular and dependable translator, Glazemaker, set to work preparing the Dutch version from a Latin manuscript copy not altogether identical to the not yet ready and released first Latin printed version.[44] Since one of Spinoza's chief reasons for interrupting work on the *Ethics*, in 1665, was to attack church authority and church censorship devastatingly enough to clear his philosophical path, it was logical that the vernacular version, if less important than the Latin from a purely scholarly perspective, should follow promptly. Indeed, publishing it in Dutch was vital to heighten the *TTP*'s impact, expand Spinoza's following, and spread his and the group's philosophy among the people. For those anxious to block Spinoza's penetration of the "public sphere," it was equally vital to ensure Spinoza remained firmly screened out of modern vernacular language debate and publicity. The appearance of the *TTP* in French, in 1678, proved a serious breach in the dykes, but efforts to prevent other vernacular translations of Spinoza's work appearing were for a time successful.

Glazemaker swiftly completed his Dutch version which is known to have been in the publisher's hands by early 1671 at the latest. That it was Glazemaker who translated the text was later mentioned by the clandestine seditious novel, *Philopater*, in 1697, though it appears that another expert Latinist among Spinoza's friends, very likely Bouwmeester, subsequently corrected some passages where it was thought Glazemaker had been insufficiently exact.[45] Indeed, the original Dutch version was not only ready but already in production when, in February 1671, shortly after Van Limborch contacted Doiley, Spinoza made his foremost direct intervention in the *TTP*'s early clandestine diffusion. In his cryptic (almost certainly afterwards heavily doctored) letter dated The Hague, 17 February 1671, addressed to Jelles, Spinoza begins: "Professor N.N. ... [unnamed][46] who recently visited me, among other things mentioned having

---

[44] Akkerman, "*Tractatus*," 224–5; Steenbakkers, "The Text," 36.

[45] [Duijkerius], *Het Leven van Philopater*, 195; Akkerman, "*Tractatus*," 234–5; Akkerman, "Taal en tekst," 10–11; Van de Ven, "Van bittere galle," 109–11.

[46] Spinoza, *Opera Posthuma*, 539; it has been suggested that "N.N." was Craanen, today the consensus is that it was probably Graevius; Spinoza, *Briefwisseling*, 292; Spinoza, *Correspondance* (ed. Rovere), 273n2; Spinoza, *Collected Works* (ed. Curley) ii, 390; Van der Deijl, "Dutch Translation, 211–12.

heard that my *Tractatus Theologico-Politicus* had been translated into Dutch and that someone, he did not know who, has it in mind to print it." In 1677, the editors of the *Opera Posthuma* not only carefully omitted the name of the relevant professor but with their heavily edited version of the letter made it appear that Spinoza himself was in the dark about the matter which can hardly have been the case. "I therefore beg you [Jelles], most earnestly that you be good enough," the later edited text has Spinoza saying, "to find out about this so as, if possible, to prevent its being printed."[47] Spinoza concludes his instruction to Jelles, who obviously had a considerable say in Spinoza's publishing arrangements, by adding that "this is not just my request but also that of many of my good friends, who would not gladly want to see the book forbidden, as will undoubtedly happen if it is published in the Dutch language. I firmly trust that you will do this for my sake and for that of 'de zaak' [the cause]."[48]

The possibility that Spinoza and his "friends" were genuinely unaware that the Dutch version of his *TTP* was in the press is not ruled out by all modern scholars.[49] But it scarcely seems plausible that he and they were really unaware of the arrangements to publish Glazemaker's rendering, as its publication was bound profoundly to affect his and their situation and future life in every way. Nor is it at all likely that Spinoza would not have known that Glazemaker was translating it and who was publishing it. Conceivably, some publisher other than Rieuwertsz was trying to pirate publication of the Dutch version but hardly any manuscript copies of the translation were yet circulating. There was not yet, during the early 1670s, that deliberate circulation of clandestine manuscripts of the Dutch *TTP* in Holland that began at some point in the later 1670s. Another reason why it seems impossible that Spinoza was really in the dark about it, indicating this letter was modified to create a false impression, is because Spinoza takes it for granted that Jelles *does* know who the publisher was and was in a position to halt publication simply by saying that Spinoza had decided against its being published in Dutch for now, as indeed happened. Almost certainly, the wording, as with all the letters published in the *Opera Posthuma*, in 1677–8, referring to Rieuwertsz's and Spinoza's other friends, was carefully redacted after Spinoza's death to conceal the publisher's, editors', and translators' identities and complicity in a wide-ranging and very much still ongoing clandestine project. Tailoring this letter's wording, as it appears in the *Opera Posthuma* and *Nagelate Schriften*, in 1677, was essential not just to mask the clandestine character of what occurred down to February 1671, and the real circumstances of

---

[47] Spinoza, *Nagelate Schriften*, 591; Spinoza, *Briefwisseling*, 292; Spinoza, *Collected Works* (ed. Curley) ii, 390; Weekhout, *Boekencensuur*, 105; Steenbakkers, "The Text," 37.

[48] Spinoza, *Nagelate Schriften*, 591; Akkerman, "*Tractatus*," 232–3.

[49] Van de Ven, "Van bittere galle," 110–11; Van der Deijl, "Dutch Translation," 213; Mertens, "Where Thou Dwellest," 30.

Spinoza's intervention via Jelles, but also to disguise Jelles' and Rieuwertsz's later involvement in publishing the *Opera Posthuma*.[50]

Meanwhile, the *TTP* had from the outset always been officially condemned and suppressed. Had the Dutch version actually appeared in 1671, the ramifications and repercussions for all concerned, given that the author's name was widely suspected, and the translator's and publisher's not too difficult to uncover, might well have been more drastic than anything seen thus far. The likeliest explanation for Spinoza's intervention at this particular point, through Jelles, was that the fury of the academic reaction and the Reformed consistories, over the last year, led Spinoza and his closest allies to realize that it was just too risky for now to go on with their plan. Contrary to the Spinoza circle's original strategy, during 1671 "caute" led to the plans to publish Glazemaker's translation being suspended, leaving what was probably the manuscript copy the printers were using (surviving today in the Royal Library at The Hague), only partly marked up.[51] The downfall of De Witt and the "True Freedom," in 1672, and strengthening of the hardline Calvinist Voetian faction and their repressive capability from 1672, made it seem still less advisable to risk bringing out the Dutch translation during Spinoza's lifetime whilst he was still exposed to danger.

Hopes of spreading Spinoza's thought in the vernacular as a means of reinforcing and expanding his "sect," were thus shelved for the time being. The manuscript copy of Glazemaker's translation, partly marked up by Rieuwertsz's printer was carefully stored away; a second copy remained with Meyer, and a third in the hands of Rieuwertsz that was later inherited by his son. Eventually, additional manuscript copies entered into circulation, albeit at first to a very limited extent. Nevertheless, large chunks of Spinoza's text in Dutch did soon appear, complained The Hague preacher Saldenus in 1684, echoed by Bayle that same year, owing to Van Blijenbergh's at the time much noticed Dutch-language refutation of the *TTP*, published in 1674.[52] Van Blijenbergh broke the rule about confining discussion of the *TTP* to Latin. Hence, especially from 1674, the "Dutch Spinoza" did incipiently penetrate in Spinoza's own lifetime. Though dedicated in September 1674, and brought out soon afterwards, Van Blijenbergh's rebuttal of the *TTP* had actually been ready since 1672, but, like so much else, was delayed by the disruption of the French invasion.

Spinoza's earlier contacts with Van Blijenbergh had long since petered out. By 1670, the two men had become outright adversaries. Yet, it was Van Blijenbergh who, even though proceeding with hostile intent, brought the *TTP*, including its scandalous denial of miracles, firmly within the Dutch vernacular debate despite

---

[50] Van der Deijl, "Dutch Translation," 211; Van Eeghen, *Amsterdamse boekhandel* iii, 41, 162–3.
[51] Akkerman, "*Tractatus*," 229–33; Steenbakkers, "The Text," 36.
[52] Saldenus, *Otia theologica*, 25; [Duijkerius], *Het Leven van Philopater*, 195–6; Van der Deijl, "Dutch Translation," 214–15, 230–1; De Vet, "Spinoza en Spinozisme," 8.

his being far from oblivious to the need, as most contemporaries saw it, to suppress Spinoza rather than discuss his ideas publicly. To an extent, Van Blijenbergh too kept to the practice of veiling Spinoza from the public eye, for he scrupulously avoided mentioning his name and let slip nothing whatever about him as a person. In as far as he went against the consistories, preachers, and university heads placing outright suppression above all other considerations, Van Blijenbergh did so to prove Cartesianism and the Cartesians were not to blame for the disaster. By dedicating his book to the Dordrecht burgomasters, he aimed to convince the Dutch elites that the Cartesians too wholeheartedly backed society's drive to quash Spinoza's ideas, indeed were leading the intellectual counter-offensive to stifle the Spinozist movement. He felt he should exonerate Cartesianism before the public with a modicum of controlled debate of the *TTP* in the vernacular without at any point referring to Spinoza.[53] Van Blijenbergh's claim that he was performing a public service by thus defending Cartesianism in the public sphere was later derided in the *Philopater* novel. His 476-page effort being readily accessible to all and a more extensive discussion of the *TTP* than most of the early Latin-language attacks, undoubtedly helped spread Spinoza's steadily growing presence on the intellectual scene. In fact, by quoting verbatim, Van Blijenbergh did more than almost anyone to entrench the surging war between Cartesianism and Spinozism in the public sphere in the Netherlands.

Conceivably, it was for this reason, as a subtle form of retaliation and parody, that the correspondence section of the *Opera Posthuma* and *Nagelate Schriften* edited by Spinoza's friends after his death allocates more prominence to Van Blijenbergh's somewhat tiresome interaction with Spinoza than any other correspondent apart from Oldenburg. Where Jelles', Glazemaker's and Rieuwertsz's roles in diffusing Spinoza's thought were all fully concealed, Van Blijenbergh's is curiously highlighted.[54] In the first letters of their exchange, the *Nagelate Schriften* identifies Van Blijenbergh merely as W.v.B. of Dordrecht writing to B.d.S., but this changes with their second exchange where the regent discusses the *Cogitata Metaphysica*, with Spinoza's reply being tellingly headed "B.d.S. to W. van Blyenberg."

In 1674, Van Blijenbergh published lengthy quotations from the *TTP* in the vernacular but, curiously, used a different translation from Glazemaker's, an unknown rendering based on Glazemaker's, but diverging from it, that cannot have been Van Blijenbergh's own as he was not competent in Latin.[55] It is not known to whom Glazemaker's copy passed at his death, in 1682. But following Spinoza's death, the number of manuscript copies circulating slowly increased.

---

[53] [Duijkerius], *Het Leven van Philopater*, 169, 171; Van Bunge, *From Stevin to Spinoza*, 115; Israel, "Early Dutch and German Reaction," 89; Van de Ven, *Printing Spinoza*, 312.

[54] Spinoza, *Nagelate Schriften*, 551-2, 559, 564-5, 569, 571.

[55] Krop, *Spinoza, een paradoxale icoon*, 151-2; Van der Deijl, "Dutch Translation," 215; Lavaert, *Vrijheid, gelijkheid, veelheid*, 201.

Philopater, published in 1697, includes a scene where a group of freethinkers cheerfully discuss this question: "I am able to tell you gentlemen," confides Philopater, "that over the years, after a copy was made of [Glazemaker's] original and given, undoubtedly, to a singular good friend [Meyer], and then to another, [eventually] so many copies came into being that the last, when compared to the first, could have won little respect for the translator had it appeared under his name, or at least if it were believed these latter copies were also translated by Glazemaker, so corrupted were they by transcription." Meanwhile, the learned friend [Meyer] kept his copy and "enriched it," adds Philopater, with erudite notes and Latin terms in the margin to help those using the Dutch to gain some notion of the scholarly debate.[56]

A second unsuccessful attempt to publish the *TTP* in Dutch occurred in January 1687, almost a decade after Spinoza's death, spurring the Amsterdam Reformed consistory to one of its more successful censorship efforts of the era. In 1686, the Amsterdam church council learnt of a plan to publish the *TTP* in Dutch on the part of the Amsterdam publisher Jan Claesz ten Hoorn (d. 1714) who had extensively collaborated with Glazemaker and Rieuwertsz in the past, and published many Cartesian works as well as several risqué erotic texts. Someone in Delft sent word that Ten Hoorn had obtained a manuscript of the *TTP* translated into Dutch which he was preparing to print. When consistory *delegati* came to his bookshop to investigate, Jan Claesz denied complicity in anything of the sort until shown letters from Delft proving his complicity. He then confessed to having been preparing the *TTP*'s publication in the vernacular until he realized what a "dangerous" text it was. He had personally then torn up the pages printed thus far and burnt the manuscript from which he was working, thoroughly extinguishing both manuscript and the printed sections. Whatever the truth of that, he was fortunate the book had not yet appeared as otherwise he would certainly have incurred severe penalties. A manuscript copy of the *TTP* surviving today in the Royal Library in The Hague with printers' lines, a corrected version of Glazemaker's rendering, may be the one Ten Hoorn worked from and then claimed to have destroyed.[57]

When the first Dutch-language edition of the *TTP* did finally appear, five years later, in 1693 under the mocking title *The Upright Theologian* [*De Rechtzinnige Theologant*] (Figure 33.6), supposedly published by "Henricus Koenraad," it *was* now Glazemaker's 1669 version that was used.[58] But when a second Dutch version appeared the next year, in 1694, now entitled *Theological-Political Treatise* [*Godgeleerde Staat-kundige Verhandelinge*], the manuscript used was a revised, modified version of Glazemaker's translation prepared long before by another editor,

---

[56] [Duijkerius], *Het Leven van Philopater*, 195; Van de Ven, *Printing Spinoza*, 304–5.
[57] Van der Deijl, "Dutch Translation," 217; Den Hollander, "Qur'an in the Low Countries," 226–7.
[58] [Duijkerius], *Het Leven van Philopater*, 194; Van de Ven, "Van bittere galle," 109.

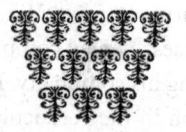

DE
RECHTZINNIGE
THEOLOGANT,
OF
GODGELEERDE
STAATKUNDIGE
VERHANDELINGE.

Uit het Latijn vertaalt.

Te HAMBURG,
By HENRICUS KOENRAAD.
MDCXCIII.

Figure 33.6 [Spinoza], *De Rechtzinnige Theologant, of Godgeleerde Staatkundige Verhandelinge*. Te Hamburg [i.e. Amsterdam], by Henricus Koenraad, 1693. IAS Spinoza Research Collection.

possibly Meyer or Bouwmeester or both, correcting Glazemaker's rendering with changes probably made in 1670–1, when the text was first prepared for publication. This corrected manuscript, later owned in the eighteenth century by Monnikhoff, also survives today in the Royal Library at The Hague and was probably the version of Glazemaker's rendering about to appear in 1671 when

Spinoza intervened to prevent it.[59] Bizarrely, a third Dutch variant edition appeared, also in 1694, this time purportedly at "Bremen" rather than "Hamburg" and employing a different fictitious publisher's name, Hans Jurgen von der Weyl, as well as a third false title *An Upright Theologian or Theological-Political Treatise* [*Een Rechtsinnige Theologant, of Godgeleerde Staatkunde*], and now employing a mysterious, substantially different Dutch translation.[60]

Based on a manuscript newly prepared from one of the late 1670s editions of the *TTP*, rather than the Glazemaker translation, this third Dutch edition presents itself as a competitor to the 1693 edition. Less accurate in several respects, it also lacks the Hebrew wording and phrases Spinoza cites from the Pentateuch found in the 1693 edition recommended by *Philopater*. But precisely because the Hebrew is removed, the 1694 edition claims to be the down-to-earth ordinary man's version, its preface attempting to ridicule the 1693 edition "for its extravagance and affectation," and using Latin terms pedantically inserted in the margins to pinpoint vernacular equivalents of philosophical technical expressions employed in the text. Usefully, these Latin equivalents in the margins lacking from the original Glazemaker rendering, retorted *Philopater*, in 1697, were added later by the same "doctor of medicine and illustrious philosopher," presumably Meyer, who, over the years, kept the manuscript and had long taken a keen interest, like Koerbagh, in helping enlighten the general public by rendering Latin technical terms and other appropriated foreign words unfamiliar to ordinary readers into more readily understood Dutch vernacular equivalents (Table 33.3).[61]

Table 33.3 The Dutch versions of the *TTP*

Date	Title	Published at	Translator
1670	?	(in manuscript only)	Glazemaker
1674	*Waerheyt van de Christelyke Godsdienst*	Leiden	Blijenbergh?
1687	(suppressed during printing)	Amsterdam	?
1693	*De Rechtzinninge Theologant*	"Hamburg"	Glazemaker
1694	*God-geleerde Staat-kundige Verhandelinge*	"Hamburg"	Glazemaker (revised)
1694	*Een Rechtsinnige Theologant, of Godgeleerde Staatkunde*	"Bremen"	?

Sources: Duijkerius, *Het Leven van Philopater*, 194–5; Colerus, *Das Leben*, 60–3; Steenbakkers, "The Text," 35–7; Van de Ven, "Van bittere galle"; Van de Ven, *Printing Spinoza*, 299–355; Van der Deijl, "Dutch Translation," 210–20; Kingma and Offenberg, "Bibliography," 23–5.

---

[59] Akkerman, "*Tractatus*," 235.
[60] Akkerman, "*Tractatus*," 235–6; Steenbakkers, "The Text," 36.
[61] [Duijkerius], *Het Leven van Philopater*, 195; Van der Deijl, "Dutch Translation," 218, 220.

Philopater applauds the published Dutch version of the *TTP* as a great benefit to mankind because copying clandestine manuscripts is laborious and difficult which, unfortunately, means many sensible persons, who could otherwise develop into better philosophers and "become more understanding," had hitherto been prevented from studying it by blinkered and oppressive authorities.[62] The Reformed Church synods could not have disagreed more. The Synod of Gelderland discussed the appearance of a certain "pernicieus tractaet *De Rechtzinnige Theologant*" at its meeting at Zutphen, in August 1694, and resolved to investigate and determine whether "it was, or was not, a translation of the *Tractatus Theologico-Politicus*." When those assigned to investigate concluded that it was, the synod resolved, since the Latin version was "now forbidden everywhere" in the Republic, that each classis of Gelderland take steps to ensure this edition too was strictly suppressed in their locality.[63] When the North Holland synod at its 1695 annual gathering, at Hoorn, discussed the publication under a slightly different title, on 4 August, their visiting "correspondent" from Gelderland reported that his provincial synod had recorded its title as "*De Rechtsinnige Theologant* being a translation of the famous book called *Theologico-Politicus*," hence clearly referring to the 1693 edition.[64] During 1694–5, the synods pieced together that there were now three divergent and differently titled clandestine Dutch versions circulating in print and took steps to ensure all were strictly forbidden.

---

[62] [Duijkerius], *Het Leven van Philopater*, 196.

[63] ARH NHK Oud Synodaal Archief 85, Acta Synod of Gelderland, 15–28 Aug. 1694, art. "Licentieus boekdrucken."

[64] ARH NHK Oud Synodaal Archief 185, Acta Synod North Holland for 1695, Hoorn, 26 July–4 August, p. 7.

34

Mysterious Trip to Utrecht
(July–August 1673)

34.i The Utrecht *Collegie der Sçavanten*

By the summer of 1673, the focus of the Franco-Dutch struggle was already noticeably shifting away from the Dutch heartland. On 18 June, commenced the diplomatic congress at Cologne to formalize the emerging continental alliance headed by the Habsburg emperor and Spanish crown aimed at repelling Louis XIV's expansionism in alliance with the Dutch. Just as this major shift in the strategic situation occurred, Spinoza received a formal request to come to Utrecht from the French commanders there, the Brothers Stouppe, following the intercession of Professor Graevius who seemingly originally projected the visit at a meeting with Johannes Bouwmeester, in Amsterdam, in May or early June.[1] A month before Spinoza set out on his trip, Johann Georg Graevius (1632–1702), the figure who would be his main academic host in Utrecht, received a cheering report, dated 20 June, posted across the lines, from Amsterdam, by the Athenaeum's professor of Greek, confirming that the emerging anti-French alliance was now making its initial moves.[2] Spinoza's trip to, and discussions in Utrecht occurred in late July and August 1673, and to understand the trip's significance in Spinoza's life-story and thought, it is important to consider the fast-changing background.

At the point Spinoza visited Utrecht, the United Provinces' strategic position and prospects had in recent weeks almost miraculously improved. Spain and the Habsburg emperor in Vienna had now recovered sufficiently from their initial disarray in 1672, to concert large-scale joint counter-action. The once formidable Spanish army of Flanders was up from a low point of under 34,000 men, in May 1672, when the French invaded, to 41,000, by March 1673, and by June considerably higher, sufficiently reinforced to actively support the formidable continental anti-Louis XIV coalition now coalescing around the Dutch, Spain, the Emperor, and the Duke of Lorraine, negotiated during the spring on terms now

---

[1] Gootjes, "Spinoza between French Libertines," 4; Gootjes, "Tussen vriendschap en vijandschap," 25–6.
[2] RL Copenhagen MS Thott 1261/4, Petrus Francius to Graevius, Amsterdam, 20 June 1673.

being finalized at Cologne.[3] Crucially, the Imperial army was already in the field, bolstered by Dutch and Spanish subsidies; in July, Louis felt obliged to move much of his invasion force away from the Netherlands, far to the south, considerably reducing the French army of occupation in the Republic, so as to prevent Spanish troops joining the emperor and the latter's allies on the Rhine. When Spinoza set out from The Hague for Utrecht, on 26 July, the combined Austro-Spanish counter-offensive had commenced, the likelihood of the French breaking through the "water-line" had greatly receded, and the prince-bishop of Münster and the Elector of Cologne were close to pulling out of the conflict, further weakening the occupation of the northern Netherlands.

Whilst Spinoza was at Utrecht, in Vienna the Emperor Leopold I (1658–1705) issued his public manifesto of 18 August denouncing Louis' aggression and formally declaring war, cheering the hearts of a great many throughout Europe.[4] France's occupation of the Dutch inland regions was starting to look short-lived and precarious, dampening prospects for Louis' commanders on Dutch soil while emboldening the strategic ambitions of William III and boosting Dutch morale.

Another factor driving the change of mood in the Netherlands and strategic shift preceding Spinoza's foray to Utrecht were De Ruyter's remarkable victories, in June 1673, in the shallows off Zeeland, over the combined fleets of England and France. Not only did this seriously dent England's attack and further paralyze England's commercial shipping and overseas trade, lending an added boost to the Republic's reviving morale, but by July had rendered the war and its exactions so unpopular in England that Charles and the courtiers orchestrating his pro-French, pro-Catholic policy had radically to revise their plans. With the royal treasury empty, Charles' advisers had, reluctantly, to contemplate withdrawing from their huge investment in Louis' aggression without the expected gains. By the summer of 1673, pressure for peace was inexorably building, albeit England's would-be absolutist monarch, still avid for monarchical glory and to break the detested Republic, demanded one last attempt to land troops on the Dutch coast to realize his scheme for joint conquest with the French. Meanwhile, an increasingly confident Stadholder, instead of becoming a useful tool of English and French expansionist, colonial, and Catholic policies, as London and Paris had long assumed, staggered his purported patrons by spurning every offer of terms sufficiently demeaning to the Republic to satisfy the pride of the now seriously out-of-pocket Louis and Charles.

The transformed situation also heightened pressure on William to reassure Europe's other monarchs and the Pope of his willingness to preserve the improved position of Catholics in the Republic and not seriously scale down the toleration

---

[3] Herrero Sánchez, "Monarquia hispánica y el tratado," 103, 109; Herrero Sánchez, *Acercamiento hispano-neerlandés*, 156n337, 195.
[4] BL Add. MS 18289, fos. 154–5; Herrero Sánchez, "Monarquia hispánica y el tratado," 116–17.

reviving Dutch Catholicism now enjoyed. Needing help from the Habsburg powers, Spain and the emperor, the Prince could not avoid giving assurances inspiring confidence internationally that Dutch Catholicism, having surged up strongly in Utrecht and throughout the eastern Netherlands, would not, should Spain and the Emperor help repel the French, be powerfully rolled back by vigorous anti-Catholic pressure internally. Hence, the Prince had urgent reasons to project his defiance of Louis and Charles internationally without pinning it too closely to the Protestant cause or enacting the Calvinist agenda at home with anything like the momentum and rigour his Reformed Church allies expected.

The people of the city and province of Utrecht, local French commanders were well aware, were predominantly Protestant, hostile to the occupiers, and supportive of the Stadholder and the strict Calvinist party. But many local regents, merchants, and professionals, like the Cartesian professors, they also knew, were more inclined to a compromising attitude. The French left the task of actually muzzling the Reformed preachers and sending admonitions to the Utrecht church council to calm their congregants to the burgomasters and city regents who, belonging to the "Louvesteynsche factie [Louvestein faction]," as their opponents contemptuously called them, had been broadly supportive of the De Witt regime until 1672 and had been left in charge when the French occupied the city. The prime foes of Voetius and the Calvinists, in other words, were being propped up by the French and had every reason to fear that William III's triumph would swiftly entail their own humiliation and downfall.[5]

Dutch Catholicism's future, now that Louis and Charles looked increasingly unlikely to overwhelm the stubborn Republic and secure their objectives, was especially a concern of the Catholic Vicar Apostolic in the United Provinces (since 1661), Johannes van Neercassel (1625–86), among the French occupation's closest allies (Figure 34.1). A son of an affluent Gorcum beer-brewer, an Oratorian, trained in philosophy and theology at Louvain, Paris, and Saumur, and speaking eloquent, courtly French, Neercassel had long been a figure prominent in the vigorous behind-the-scenes Catholic revival gaining momentum in the United Provinces since the early 1660s, and remained such down to his death. French and Munsterite conquest of much of the Republic, in June 1672, had greatly exhilarated Neercassel but also presented a tricky dilemma. Should he remain with his flock in Amsterdam or transfer to Utrecht, under Louis' protection? He chose the latter course. From Utrecht, he continued leading the Catholic mission, as Vicar-Apostolic, on both sides of the water-line, overseeing the administering of the holy sacraments throughout the towns and villages of the *Missio Hollandica* which in peacetime involved supervising around 300 semi-secret ambulant secular priests and some 150 regular clergy (monks and friars), camouflaged in lay dress when on

---

[5] Jessurun-ten Dam Ham, *Utrecht in 1672 en 1673*, 119, 133.

Figure 34.1 *Johannes Baptista van Neercassel* (1623–1686) with episcopal attributes, oil on canvas. By courtesy of Museum Catharijneconvent, Utrecht.

the street, but now, in occupied areas, in greatly increased numbers. On his side of the water-line, these were now free to appear in ecclesiastical attire and open alliance with the French and Munsterites.[6]

A Jansenist in theological orientation and staunch ally of "le grand Arnauld," head of the Jansenist movement in Paris and especially of the Sieur de Pontchâteau, an austere and penitent Jansenist influential at court in Paris and Rome,[7] Neercassel had already had several clashes with the Spanish regime in Brussels and with the Jesuits who, in 1672, in the wake of the Franco-Munsterite invasion, established their own *Missio Gallo-Hollandica* with schools at Utrecht, Arnhem, and Zwolle, and with whom his relations steadily deteriorated.[8] He supported Stouppe's propaganda campaign to discredit the Republic and especially vilify Dutch religious toleration internationally, having no difficulty with officially condemning Dutch toleration for despicably accommodating numerous

---

[6] Wicquefort, *Journael of dagelijcksch verhael* i, 44, 198; Rogier, *Geschiedenis* ii, 204.
[7] Vernière, *Spinoza et la pensée française*, 114; Spiertz, "Jansenisme," 153–7; Spiertz, *L'Église catholique*, 90–3.
[8] Spiertz, *L'Église catholique*, 60–2; Kooi, "Paying off the Sheriff," 90–1; Ackermans, "Good Pastors," 268.

sects, while simultaneously pushing for increased toleration for Catholics. The Republic, Neercassel sincerely believed, permitted pernicious heresy and free-thinking to flourish and was fomenting religious chaos. He hoped to witness the final destruction of this "heretic republic" and, in the wake of Louis' and Charles' conquests, see Catholicism triumphant in the northern Netherlands, though, in order to safeguard the system of pastoral support latterly gaining ground in all Seven Provinces and protect Catholicism's recent gains, for the moment he could not avoid pragmatically combining zeal for French royal aspiration with profiting from Dutch toleration on a practical level both in the occupied and the unoccupied Netherlands. Awkwardly for him, from March 1673, with every passing month, the hoped-for final collapse of the Republic seemed increasingly less likely than a pending French withdrawal, increasing his dependence on Dutch toleration.[9]

Two noteworthy features of Neercassel's tactics were his stress on cultivating peaceful, tolerant relations between Catholics and Protestants locally, and amicable contact with the most tolerant Dutch regents. As head of the Republic's Catholics, Neercassel was firmly ensconced for now, with a bevy of priests, in Utrecht cathedral where, with Louis' assent, he enjoyed the title of "Archbishop of Utrecht," though the papacy had not approved his assuming this position. Aligned with the French, Neercassel was eyed with grave suspicion by Brussels, while the papacy steered between the poles, officially acknowledging him throughout the years 1661–86 only as "Vicar Apostolic." The Jesuits, meanwhile, resented Neercassel's grip over the Catholic establishment in the United Provinces and his pro-French, anti-Spanish, anti-Jesuit outlook.[10] Further exacerbating the rift between the pro-French Dutch Catholic faction adulating Louis and the pro-Spanish faction supporting his Jesuit adversaries was an additional factor: as a Jansenist, Neercassel rejected what he regarded as the excessive fervour of popular adoration of images and saints patronized especially by the Jesuits and, in 1673, published at Cologne his severe critique of the ecstatic cult of the "Immaculate Conception of Mary," a cause ardently embraced at the time in Spain and the Spanish Netherlands.[11]

Inevitably, during the time of the occupation, while presiding over the religious affairs of the entire Catholic community either side of the water-line, Neercassel saw much of the Stouppes, his closest allies, whose role in the tentative peace feelers between the French and The Hague possessed special significance for him as the figure presiding over Dutch Catholicism and its future. It was Jean-Baptiste Stouppe, commander of the Swiss mainly Protestant regiment based in Utrecht,

---

[9] Spiertz, *L'Église catholique*, 125; Ackermans, "Good Pastors," 268–70; Totaro, "Congrégation de l'Index," 365.
[10] Rogier, *Geschiedenis* ii, 22–3, 205; Forclaz, "Rather French than Subject," 525.
[11] Rogier, *Geschiedenis* ii, 252; Spiertz, "Jansenisme,"157–8; Kooi, "Paying off the Sheriff," 94–5; Ackermans, "Good Pastors," 266.

moreover, who served as chief publicist orchestrating Louis' and Colbert's wartime propaganda vilifying the United Provinces as a contemptible godless republic permitting a scandalously excessive toleration, and who, during 1673, made a public issue of Spinoza's following, portraying them as a dangerous clandestine sect which the Dutch authorities had conspicuously failed to suppress. It was also Stouppe who, in July, played the chief role in organizing Spinoza's trip from The Hague across the Dutch and then French front lines.

Lieutenant-Colonel Giovanni Battista Stoppa (1623-92), or Jean-Baptiste Stouppe, as the French called him (or Stouppa as the Dutch called him), was a native of the Grisons Romanche district of Switzerland, son of a family from the Lake Como region and a remarkable personage. The writer who first profiled Spinoza's following as a formidable underground "sect" in print, had served as pastor of the French Protestant Walloon church in London's Threadneedle Street during 1652-61, but later quit preaching for soldiering. Throughout the French occupation of 1672-3, this Grisons officer and his older brother, Pierre-Alexandre, were in regular contact with Dutch commanders and officials, and apparently were more respected by them than were Luxembourg and Louis' other commanders. Pierre-Alexandre may have been a former Protestant turned Catholic, but he firmly protested in writing, to Louis personally, records the chronicler Abraham de Wicquefort, about the barbaric atrocities perpetrated by Luxembourg's troops at Bodegraven and Zwammerdam, in December 1672. Unusually honest and above corruption, the elder Stouppe, despite being entrusted with issuing the passports for individuals crossing from the Dutch through French lines into occupied territory, reportedly did not extract bribes from those needing to cross.[12]

Together, the Stouppes remained the principal intermediaries in relations between the French occupiers and the Dutch regents, provincial States, and general populace either side of the water-line. While Pierre-Alexandre had converted, Jean-Baptiste, his brother's chief aide-de-camp, a principal intermediary in the secret peace talks, remained nominally Protestant. During the fifteen months' occupation, he made at least one covert trip to The Hague.[13] A crucial go-between, he mattered especially as prime organizer of contacts between the warring sides, arranging confidential trips to and from The Hague and, as head of French propaganda against the Republic, also sought to hasten the process of peacemaking by disseminating false reports that the Dutch desperately needed to come to terms. Early in 1673, he published his "Advice to the Lords States General of the United Netherlands," a pamphlet in French and Dutch claiming it

---

[12] Wicquefort, *Journael of dagelijcksch verhael* i, 133, 137-8, 145-6, 160.
[13] Jessurun-ten Dam Ham, *Utrecht in 1672 en 1673*, 154-5; Vernière, *Spinoza et la pensée française*, 18-22.

would be "most profitable for them to abandon Spain and establish a good peace with France."[14]

Fluent in Italian, French, German, and English as well as Dutch and Latin, Jean-Baptiste had studied at Padova, Geneva, Strasbourg, and Leiden and possessed erudite qualities virtually no other commander in Louis' army of occupation could claim. By now, he was a veteran intelligence officer. While serving as pastor of the Savoyard refugees in Cromwell's England, at the Walloon Threadneedle Street church, in London, and asked by Cromwell to go to France to report on the condition and mood of the Huguenots, he had gathered more information about Protestant attitudes and loyalties in Switzerland, Italy, and France than practically anyone else. After the 1660 Restoration, Charles II had him expelled from England, in 1661, as a "notorious meddler in matters not of his calling and an intelligencer of the late government."[15]

During the mid-1660s, Jean-Baptiste had spent much of his time translating into French the sermons of the great English Puritan preacher and commentator on society, Richard Baxter, the same who figured among the principal critics of Spinozism in Britain during the 1670s. No one was better suited to conduct secret peace talks with the Dutch, bring Catholic and Protestant representatives together, organize propaganda, or entertain with erudite talk and stories about libertines, conspiracy, and other fascinating undercover goings on across the Europe of 1673 that few others knew as much about. Expert too on libraries and the clandestine book trade, Jean-Baptiste became additionally indispensable to the new commander of the French forces in the Netherlands, Louis de Bourbon, Prince de Condé (1621–86), for procuring hard-to-find, suppressed and exotic books, a service he was still providing for that prince a dozen years later, in the mid-1680s.

When Spinoza arrived in Utrecht, Stouppe's book, *La religion des Hollandois* (1673), was not yet out but stood ready for the press. Authorized for publication, in Paris, on 20 July 1673, a week before Spinoza arrived in Utrecht, it actually appeared, apparently in simultaneous editions at Paris and Holland, in August, either while Spinoza was still in Utrecht or else immediately after he left. It came out anonymously (although Stouppe was soon recognized as the author), with the encouragement, perhaps even under the direction of the French high command. Richard Simon later attributed the commissioning of Stouppe's book to Louis' minister of war, Louvois, who was likewise keen to vilify the Republic internationally to promote French interest and reassure the Swiss Protestants, a major recruitment source for the French army during Louis XIV's reign, that by serving

---

[14] Van Malssen, *Louis XIV d'après les pamphlets*, 25; Patoir, "Polemic Pamphleteering,"18; Forclaz, "Rather French than Subject," 519, 522.

[15] Benítez (ed.), "À Madame...sur les différentes religions," 430; Labrousse, "Jean-Baptiste Stouppe," 60–8; Patoire, "Polemic, Pamphleteering," 14–17; Villani, "Man of Intrigue," 307, 310–11.

in Louis' army of occupation, far from harming the universal Protestant cause, as some Swiss pastors contended, the Swiss would actually be benefiting it.

Where the upright Swiss, according to Stouppe's book, accorded faith and theology proper ascendancy over society, conduct, and thought, Dutch regents "accommodated religion to the Interest of State," as the English translation expresses it, basely subordinating faith to worldly concerns. Where Swiss cantons upheld strict religious uniformity, each in its own manner, and Jews were everywhere forbidden to settle, as befitted every proper Christian land, the Dutch came nowhere near Swiss uprightness but rather allowed all sects to flourish and outrageously permitted Jews "an absolute liberty," a signal disgrace. In fact, the Dutch spent so much time thinking about "growing rich" and accumulating wealth, instead of about piety and Christian truth, that trade had become their chief creed and preoccupation.[16] It would be an absurdity for the Protestant Swiss to feel any sense of solidarity with them.

Much as the Orangist faction used Spinoza's *TTP*, in 1672, as a propaganda instrument to besmirch the De Witt faction, French royal propaganda used the *TTP*, in 1673, as a tool to tar the Republic's reputation and lessen its resolve to fight. Stouppe's remarkable account of Spinoza and his underground movement in *La religion des Hollandois* predates his meeting Spinoza in Utrecht, being already a key feature of his text and pending anti-Dutch propaganda by the early summer of 1673. We know this because a short time before Spinoza left The Hague for Utrecht, Neercassel, who seemingly had a hand in the book's gestation, dispatched a manuscript copy containing the relevant passages about Spinoza and Spinozism to the erudite Piedmontese Cardinal Giovanni Bona (1609-74), a senior Inquisitor in Rome who was closely monitoring Dutch Catholicism's revival and noting its key adversaries.[17] Familiar with Amsterdam, Neercassel knew of Van den Enden and had been friendly with Steno since the early 1660s, and in fact, knew better than most what Spinozism was and may have already encountered Spinoza face to face.[18] Based on information gathered from several well-informed persons, and vetted by Neercassel, Stouppe's description of the Dutch religious scene reflected the knowledge of experienced local observers and was largely accurate and up to date, apart from exaggerating the size of the Catholic presence.

Deprecating Dutch toleration, Jean-Baptiste at the same time gave the impression to his ally, Neercassel, that he himself was vacillating in his Protestant faith. Indeed, according to the Vicar-Apostolic (who was probably being naïve),

---

[16] Stouppe, *Religion des Hollandois*, 95, 106-7, 111, 114-15, 117; Van Malssen, *Louis XIV d'après les pamphlets*, 30-1; Labrousse, "Jean-Baptiste Stouppe," 62-3; Van Gelderen, "Turning Swiss?," 151-3.
[17] Benítez (ed.), "À Madame... sur les différentes religions," 440-1.
[18] Totaro, "Niels Stensen (1638-1686)," 152; Totaro, "Congrégation de l'Index," 364.

Stouppe was now on the verge of converting to Catholicism.[19] Ostensibly pleading the Protestant cause, his book's concealed true aim, the Republic's foremost Catholic ecclesiastic firmly believed, besides crushing the pernicious principle of toleration, was actually to damage Protestantism as much as possible along with the Republic, all with upright godly intent. If Neercassel believed Stouppe really assailed the Republic's image on behalf of Louis, Catholicism, and the Pope, albeit guardedly enough not to endanger Catholics, Stouppe for his part knew of his ally Neercassel's secret missives to Louis of June and September 1672. These, which have been called a "flagrant case of high treason," besought Europe's most powerful monarch, for the sake of faith and the church, not just to assign more buildings and benefices to Catholics in occupied Dutch lands, but finally seize sovereign supremacy over the United Provinces and render permanent the untrammelled public exercise of the Catholic faith while re-imposing Catholic dominance.[20] In February 1673, Neercassel travelled to Paris to confer with Louvois and other officials about fulfilling his great vision for re-Catholicizing the northern Netherlands under the French crown.

Besides Neercassel, information for Stouppe's book was garnered from other notable figures, especially the academy or *Collegie der Sçavanten* including Graevius, Van Velthuysen, and Frans Burman (1628–79), professor of theology at Utrecht and a son-in-law of Heidanus at Leiden, who was among the most active in linking Cartesianism to Coccejan Reformed theology and Coccejan views on church–state relations,[21] and other prominent Cartesians with whom Stouppe often conversed during the occupation. Another who provided detailed information for the book, an intimate friend of Stouppe's in Utrecht, according to the "Walloon" Calvinist pastor Johannes Braun, in his lengthy rebuttal of Stouppe's account, of 1674, was a certain "Pierville or Pierreville," or "Percheville," with whom Stouppe had colluded years before when spying for the "usurper Cromwell" in France. Running a much-frequented coffee-house where irreverent talk flowed over coffee, "chocolade," liqueurs, and the sugary confectioneries this Pierreville had learned to make in England, he was known as the "Koffyman" [Coffee-man] of Utrecht.[22]

As the "Disaster Year" of 1672 metamorphosed into a very different, more international drama by the summer of 1673, Stouppe's role remained, as before, to manage relations between the occupiers and the Dutch political elite and public. As he and Neercassel were already well-informed about Spinoza and his following,

---

[19] Benítez (ed.), "À Madame... sur les différentes religions," 433; Forclaz, "Rather French than Subject," 515, 525.
[20] Frijhoff, "Religious Toleration," 34–5; Spiertz, *L'Église catholique*, 119–21, 160–1; Forclaz, "Rather French than Subject," 524.
[21] Mertens, "All in the Family," 50.
[22] Wicquefort, *Journael of dagelijcksch verhael* i, 14; Benítez (ed.), "À Madame... sur les différentes religions," 440–1; Labrousse, "Jean-Baptiste Stouppe," 60, 62.

his prime motive for organizing and promoting (as well as paying the costs of) his visit to Utrecht was obviously not to learn about Spinoza the man and Spinozism. Though mixed with a dash of intellectual curiosity, his motivation probably sprang, at least in part, from instructions from Louis' minister of war, Louvois, not just to organize propaganda belittling the Republic's international standing but also to encourage, and exploit as far as possible, the anti-Orangist opposition to William III who was now the prime obstacle to Louis and Charles securing their goals in their increasingly costly struggle with the Dutch. As Stouppe informed Louvois with satisfaction, in February 1673, the Utrecht professors with whom he was in close contact, meaning Graevius and Burman, especially the latter who had continuing ties with Leiden, were assuring him (a little optimistically perhaps) that in the province of Holland there were heartening signs "of very great discontent with the Prince of Orange [de très grand mécontentement contre le Prince d'Orange]."[23] A prominent anti-Orangist as well as anti-Calvinist theorist, Spinoza looked like a potentially useful pawn in this complex political dimension of the expanding war.

Utrecht was divided even more bitterly than the rest of the Netherlands between the Dutch warring ideological-theological factions, with much of the Protestant populace believing those regents who had backed the De Witt regime were steeped in *Arminianerije*, *Socinianerije*, and *Cartesianerije* and thus not true Christians at all, but vile betrayers of godliness and true faith scarcely better than the French. Indeed, such was the suppressed anger of plebs and guilds that some Utrecht regents were glad that, for the time being, they *were* being protected by the French. Among the most vulnerable was the physician-regent Van Velthuysen, the regent most closely associated with Cartesianism, anti-Orangism and opposing the Reformed Church's goals. The common interest of the Utrecht *Collegie* and the *cercle Spinoziste* at this point lay in their both facing the threat of a raging plebs fired up religiously and politically by religious authority, both feeling their very survival was threatened by the alliance of Orangism and Calvinism.[24]

Closely connected with Stouppe and leading savants in Paris, Graevius had special reasons to worry about his own position as well as the University, should the French need to withdraw. It was through Graevius, apparently, that Stouppe communicated with Spinoza, in The Hague, contacting him via Bouwmeester, and organized his trip to Utrecht. A letter from Bouwmeester to Graevius of mid-June 1673, preserved today in Copenhagen, confirms that Spinoza's visit had already then been projected for some time, and that the object of his proposed foray across the water-line was to confer with Stouppe, Graevius, and the *Collegie der Sçavanten* (and perhaps also the new commander of the French army in the

---

[23] Stouppe to Louvois, Utrecht, 22 Feb. 1673, in *Receuil de Lettres* i, 295–6; Benítez (ed.), "À Madame... sur les différentes religions," 432; Gootjes, "Spinoza between French Libertines," note 36.
[24] Roorda, "Utrechtse regeringsreglement," 106.

Netherlands), about the present fast-changing state of affairs. The initiative came from key men of learning and philosophy in Utrecht, together with Stouppe; but the letter also reveals that during June, Spinoza, exhibiting his usual caution and wariness, showed no particular eagerness to respond to their urgent request that he come.[25]

An intellectual circle committed to Cartesianism, Cocceianism, and expanding academic freedom by divorcing philosophy and science from theology, the Utrecht *Collegie der Sçavanten* was a small, select, politically and religiously highly vulnerable coterie pitted against the Voetian strict Reformed tendency prevalent among the bulk of the city's Protestant population and local church council. A force in local civic and church politics but precariously placed, it was all too likely to be crushed underfoot, along with the tolerationist faction among the city's regents, as soon as French (and hence Catholic) control of Utrecht lapsed.[26] Although the *Collegie*'s origins reached back to the early 1650s, its role in local academic and intellectual life, growing since Regnerus van Mansvelt (1629–71) became a professor at the University in 1660, and Graevius, in 1661, had only become dominant, much to the indignation of the Utrecht Reformed church council, since the De Witt faction gained ascendancy over the city government in 1662. Since then, the *Collegie*'s impact was reflected in many areas, including broad cultural issues, toleration, university politics, and astronomy. Where Voetius insisted comets were supernatural omens portending evil occurrences, Graevius, though primarily a classicist, in his oration *De Cometis* [About Comets] "against the opinion of the common people," of 1665, countered head-on, presenting the group's Cartesian doctrine that comets are not a supernatural but wholly natural occurrence, caused by vortexes, as the great Descartes had allegedly proven.[27]

But now, tied to Stouppe and Neercassel, the outlook for the Utrecht Cartesians was beginning to look extremely bleak. The predicament of the Utrecht Cartesian professors, and of the anti-Orangist faction in the Netherlands generally, as well as of Neercassel and the Dutch Catholic leadership, were dilemmas the Stouppes understood all too well. Approving Van Velthuysen's antipathy to Voetians, and preference for Cocceians, in *La religion des Hollandois* Stouppe remarks that "they [Voetius and Maresius] assert that he [Cocceius] is an innovator, labelling him a *Scriptuarius*, as if it were a great crime to adhere closely to Scripture and make it the most important of our studies."[28] Graevius (Figure 34.2), a classicist of German background and native of Naumburg in east-central Germany, had taught previously at Duisburg and Deventer. Though immersed in strife between

---

[25] Gootjes, "Spinoza between French Libertines," 4.
[26] Van Bunge, *From Stevin to Spinoza*, 100; Gootjes, "Collegie der Sçavanten," 156–7.
[27] Thijssen-Schoute, *Nederlands Cartesianisme*, 445–6.
[28] Stouppe, *Religion of the Dutch*, 17; Patoir, "Polemic Pamphleteering," 22.

Figure 34.2 *Johannes Georgius Graevius* (1632–1703) by unknown artist. Reproduction courtesy of University of Amsterdam.

Cartesians and anti-Cartesians in the Netherlands, he felt somewhat neutral regarding Dutch politics. Still, he was acutely aware that he was too closely connected to the French for comfort, being an important link with Parisian intellectual circles, several of whose prominent figures, including the duc de Montausier, "governor" of the Dauphin, and Thévenot, had intervened, in 1672, to ensure Graevius and his circle, and Utrecht University generally were properly respected and protected by the Franco-Swiss garrison.[29] Favoured as they were, Graevius was specially exempted, in February 1673, from the general tax the French imposed on the citizens of Utrecht and, later, from having French troops billeted on him.[30]

---

[29] RL Copenhagen MS Thott 1266/4, Thévenot to Graevius, Paris, 15 Dec. 1672; Masson, "Graevius et le duc," 220–1.
[30] Gootjes, "Spinoza between French Libertines," cue 38.

Among the *sçavanten*, Van Velthuysen was perhaps the likeliest potential ally of Spinoza. If no member of the Utrecht city government had been more serviceable to the French than Van Velthuysen as a go-between in communication between the city government and the French command, equally, no one had tried harder, over many years, to secure a broad toleration in the city and defuse tensions between Protestants and Catholics, and between Remonstrants and the Reformed.[31] No one had done more to promote freedom of conscience and religious toleration, or fight "superstition" in the province. No influential figure in Utrecht stood on worse terms with the Reformed synod and, during 1672-3, none worked more closely with the French occupiers. His *Tractaet van de Afgoderye en Superstitie* [Treatise of Idolatry and Superstition] (1669), written with the Koerbagh scandal at its height, attacked not only religious superstition but the principle of religious authority and ecclesiastical regulation of society, especially where used as a repressive or restrictive social and intellectual tool. The local Reformed consistory had first demanded its suppression, in September 1669.[32] Over the next two years, Utrecht's provincial Reformed synod regularly complained about Van Velthuysen, not least when sending missives to the other synods which fully concurred, as the North Holland synod's book inspection commission put it, in July 1671, that Van Velthuysen's was "an extremely damaging book [...] very much in conflict with the holy truth of God's Word, the Heidelberg Confession, and the Dutch Reformed Confession," especially as regards sacraments.[33] But all efforts to get the Utrecht city government to suppress the book as "unjust and damaging" met a brick wall, fuelling yet more controversy.[34]

The Utrecht *kerkeraad* (church council) accused Van Velthuysen of extending toleration in Utrecht beyond all acceptable bounds and peddling "Socinian, Erastian, Papist, and other heterodox opinions,"[35] exhibiting, that is, exactly the proclivities Spinoza most appreciated in him. Voetians particularly abhorred Van Velthuysen's principle that no authentic church jurisdiction exists or can be grounded on the Gospels, and that all church authority derives from the magistracy, a totally false and despicable notion in their eyes. They held that Van Velthuysen's views violated Articles 30 and 31 of the official creed of the public Church, the *Nederlandsche Confessie*. In his 1669 reply, Van Velthuysen, seemingly in broad agreement with *De Jure Ecclesiasticorum*, argues that no Scripture-grounded Christian ecclesiastical authority over matters of conscience ["over de

---

[31] GA Utrecht vroedschapsresoluties 1668-73, fos. 205v, 220. res. 3 Aug. 1672 and 10 Feb. 1673; Fukuoka, *Sovereign and the Prophets*, 206-7.
[32] GA Utrecht vroedschapsresoluties 1668-73, fo. 73, res. 6 Sept. 1669.
[33] RA Noord-Holland, Haarlem, Geref. Kerk, Classis Alkmaar, fos. 185v and 191, res. 22 July 1670 and 28 July 1671; Roorda, "Utrechtse regeringsreglement," 104.
[34] GA Utrecht, vroedschapsresoluties 1668-73, fos. 75, 77, 81, and 88, res. 25 Sept., 11 Oct., 29 Nov., 1669 and 19 Feb. 1670; RA Utrecht, Prov. Kerkgesch. 3, Acta Synodi 13-17 Sept. 1670, sessio 9, art. 2.
[35] Velthuysen, *Apologie voor het Tractaet*, 4, 9; Forclaz, "Rather French than Subject," 521n31.

conscientie"] ever has or could exist, and that there never has been any divinely sanctioned church "authority over consciences."[36] This was simply not something Reformed preachers were prepared to put up with. Despite their disagreements elsewhere, Van Velthuysen was here entirely at one with Spinoza.

Van Velthuysen had long been stoking the fray in Utrecht by influencing university appointments, being instrumental in promoting to their professorial chairs all the prominent Cartesians and known anti-Voetians in Utrecht—Van Mansvelt (in 1660), Graevius (in 1661), and Burman (in 1662).[37] No one was more responsible for forging the now precarious Cartesian hegemony at the University. Utrecht, lamented Maresius, in 1672, once the spearhead of the counter-offensive against Descartes' philosophy, had sadly, during the 1660s, become the very "Acropolis and Capitol of Cartesianism." Even before the French invasion, Utrecht had been seriously obstructing Calvinist efforts to repress the sects and anti-Trinitarians.[38] Maresius' verdict accurately reflected the change at Utrecht in the 1660s but exaggerated Utrecht's role as Leiden, where the medical and philosophy faculties at this time were also dominated by Cartesians, was at least equally important. At Leiden, Abraham Heidanus (1597–1678), a vigorous supporter of Cartesianism and close ally of Coccejus, held court along with Spinoza's friend De Volder, a professor there, from 1670, who would establish the country's first physics laboratory, in 1675, and Christopher Wittichius, teaching from 1671, and at this very time arranging dissertations aimed at persuading unbelieving naturalists that via Cartesianism alone do science and Christianity firmly harmonize together.

At Utrecht and Leiden alike, this formerly growing Cartesian ascendancy was by 1672–3 definitely faltering, indeed had become highly vulnerable, a fragile edifice seemingly bound to collapse in the wake of De Witt's downfall, with Spinoza's theologico-political philosophy a major complicating factor in this escalating cultural and intellectual civil war. There were a great many who were anxious to restore basic harmony to the universities and quieten Leiden and Utrecht to the seemly level of Franeker and Groningen. For those wanting theology's supremacy restored, Groningen University stood as a kind of model, Maresius expressing deep gratitude that his own university had thus far experienced no major rifts. He cherished its success in avoiding the unseemly strife distressing the other Dutch universities, much as he admired that of the Swiss Reformed and German Calvinists in avoiding the rifts of the Dutch Reformed Church. Deploring the strife between Voetians and Cocceians and previously no friend of Voetius, in the past Maresius had not attacked Cartesianism as such and

---

[36] Velthuysen, *Apologie voor het Tractaet*, 10–11.
[37] Gootjes, "Tusssen vriendschap en vijandschap," 21–2.
[38] Douglas, *Spinoza and Dutch Cartesianism*, 20, 23, 30–4, 44; Gootjes, "Collegie der Sçavanten," 173.

had avoided taking sides. But by 1672, he too felt that maintaining Reformed unity in Groningen, and generally in the Republic, required the cutting back of Cartesianism and its being more firmly bridled, as in Switzerland. While still claiming not to oppose "freedom to philosophize" provided philosophy acknowledges theology's general primacy and refrained from intruding on its sphere, by 1672, he was insisting Cartesianism was not only dangerously prone to invade theology's domain but encouraging, as Van Velthuysen's insidious publications abundantly proved, what he and the Voetians considered excessive toleration for fringe Christians, Mennonites, Catholics, and freethinkers.[39]

Utrecht's leading theologian, Voetius, remained a towering presence locally, wielding less influence in the University as a professor than in the city as a preacher where he could at any time rally the less informed ardently believing the sun circles the earth, that comets are ill omens, and Cartesians and Arminians are abominable Christians. While Voetius himself stayed in Utrecht, a prominent young anti-Cartesian philosophy professor, Gerardus de Vries (1648–1705) had, in 1671, resigned his post there and transferred to Leiden, taking many of the firmer Voetian anti-Cartesian students with him, thereby altering the balance in the University in a way that left Utrecht perched more conspicuously than ever as a pro-French haven of Cartesian, anti-Voetian, Cocceian, and pro-Remonstrant sentiment. Resentment against the influence of the *Collegie der Sçavanten* in local university and church affairs as well as civic politics was intensifying amidst a welter of rumour and innuendo. For years the *Collegie der Sçavanten* had held weekly meetings discussing scholarly topics during which the group drank and dined together, some meetings chaired by Burman (who was absent in Leiden during Spinoza's visit), but many chaired, observed Maresius, by Van Velthuysen who, according to him, disgraced the city government not least by revealing himself to be far from altogether hostile to the anonymous *Philosophia S. Scripturae Interpres* and hence "a man evidently unconcerned with the divine will and piety."[40] States party vulnerability at Utrecht then, was political and theological certainly, but also philosophical.

Indeed, the struggle engulfing Utrecht in 1673 was philosophical-theological at root but replete with a whole baggage of wider preoccupations, fears, and anxieties. The "Disaster Year" of 1672 was construed by strict Calvinists as God's punishment for society's sins and inadequacies. Utrecht's prompt surrender had generated a great deal of murmuring, leaving Van Velthuysen's reputation in tatters due to his having led the regent delegation sent to Louis XIV's camp, in June 1672, to negotiate the city's surrender. In the resisting rump of the Republic not under French sway, the inevitable Voetian-Orangist reaction was already plainly underway. Should the French pull back, the same changing of the guard

---

[39] Blom, "Lambert van Velthuysen," 205.
[40] Sassen, *Geschiedenis*, 182–3, 185; Gootjes, "Collegie der Sçavanten," 174.

would surely occur also in Utrecht, only with added ferocity and impetus. Rumour had it that many in the city wished to deal with those regents cooperating with the French like the De Witts had been dealt with at The Hague. At the time of Spinoza's visit, in 1673, nothing could be clearer than that the Utrecht Cartesians, like the Republic's anti-Orangist regent faction, were on the edge of a precipice trapped in increasingly perilous circumstances.[41] Once Utrecht was free of the French, a dangerous surge of popular fury was inevitable, not just against the Cartesians and resurgent Catholicism now ostentatiously prevalent throughout the eastern Netherlands, certainly an acute worry for Neercassel, but also for a whole range of other dissident religious groups. The city populace would surely demand vigorous re-Protestantization of civic policy and a sweeping purge of supporters of De Witt's "True Freedom" from the city government (as indeed happened).

From his later correspondence it seems that Graevius felt he himself and all the Cartesian professors at the University would soon lose their positions.[42] Several of those in the firing line pondered the feasibility of solving their personal predicament by transferring to Paris. Whilst Spinoza was at Utrecht, Thévenot, writing to Graevius from Paris, on 4 August 1673, reported that the duc de Montausier, "governor of the Dauphin," and the Dauphin's tutor or *sous-precepteur*, Huet, desired him to assist with their programme of readings from Roman authors considered suitable for the instruction of Louis XIV's heir.[43] But Thévenot's letter was delayed en route, and when Spinoza arrived it was far from clear what possibilities there were for transferring to France should the situation become critical. Observing Spinoza visiting Utrecht under these fraught circumstances, some contemporaries supposed Spinoza himself must be considering transferring to France under Condé's protection.

On arriving in Utrecht, on 1 May 1673, Condé, a notorious intellectual libertine with whom Stouppe, we know, discussed Spinoza's pending visit, took in the scene evincing his usual intellectual interest but was mainly concerned to uphold Louis' priorities as far as possible and especially prevent any sudden, unseemly collapse of the occupation. Contrary to the mythology swirling around Spinoza at the end of the seventeenth century, Condé's role in Spinoza's visit seems to have been rather minimal. France's most illustrious commander, Condé was received in Utrecht, as the English translation of his biography by the Huguenot Pierre Coste (1668–1747), expresses it, "with all the discharge of canon, and the ringing of bells: Monsieur Stoppa [Stouppe] who was governor there presented him with the keys of the town in a silver basin at his arrival. Having held them for some time in his hands, [Condé] return'd them to him, after which he was

---

[41] Jessurun-ten Dam Ham, *Utrecht in 1672 en 1673*, 128–30.
[42] Gootjes, "Collegie der Sçavanten," 167, 179.
[43] RL Copenhagen MS Thott 1266/4, Thévenot to Graevius, Paris, 4 Aug. 1673.

conducted to the house that had been prepared for him, by the garrison, which was all in arms." Soon afterwards, Condé "lay sick a while, and being oblig'd to keep his chamber several days," and being very much a man of intellect as well as of arms, and a freethinker, as Bayle later stressed, "had the most learned men in Utrecht about him whom he received with all the civilities imaginable."[44]

The six contrived "letters" making up the text of Stouppe's book, supposedly addressed to a Swiss pastor in Berne, identified later as a certain Hommel, are dated from 4 to 19 May 1673, suggesting that Stouppe was composing and reciting to Condé key passages of his account of Dutch religious sects, including what he had to say about Spinoza and Spinozism, whilst in attendance at Condé's bedside during his sickness.[45] Condé apparently remained in the background as regards arranging Spinoza's visit and, in any case, had many more pressing matters to attend to that summer. He went along with Stouppe's and Graevius' proposal, but the Prince had no wish, Stouppe informed the others, for Spinoza to be invited to come to Utrecht "in his [i.e. the Prince's] own name."[46] Condé was undoubtedly interested in Spinoza's basic ideas and subversive impact, but insofar as he participated at all, was probably mainly concerned to discover whatever could be learnt from Spinoza about the mechanics of power at the Stadholder's court, about the Prince's secretary Huygens, the state of the purges and what kind of "Voetian" reaction could be expected in Utrecht once the province reverted to the States General either by negotiated treaty, as proposed, or, as was now increasingly likely, should the French simply be forced to evacuate.

The *Collegie*'s intentions, when requesting Stouppe to summon Spinoza to Utrecht, can hardly have been to confront him with a Cartesian panel challenging his philosophizing and Bible criticism. Their object was to discover more about conditions in The Hague and the unoccupied zone, explore possibilities for a truce between Cartesians and Spinozists, and perhaps negotiate some kind of behind-the-scenes collaboration promoting a revived anti-Orangist, anti-Voetian alliance. Certainly, Van Velthuysen was a potential ally of Spinoza's clique. Cartesians and Spinozists needed to align behind the scenes as well as adjust their public rhetoric somewhat, to improve their chances of surviving the pending Voetian onslaught. The other objective, especially encouraged no doubt by Stouppe and Condé, was to explore ways to form an active behind-the-lines anti-Orangist opposition to William III aimed at prodding him to coming to terms with the French via a compromise satisfactory to them. The latter was no idle pipe dream but hard-nosed practical politics. For it is absolutely certain, as was later reported to the Doge and Senate of Venice, in January 1675, that, as the Stadholder's political grip

---

[44] Coste, *Life of Lewis of Bourbon*, 173; Wicquefort, *Journael of dagelijcksch verhael* i, 190.
[45] Wicquefort, *Journael of dagelijcksch verhael* i, 195, 199; Benítez (ed.), "À Madame...sur les différentes religions," 431, 440–1; Gootjes, "Spinoza between French Libertines," 8n52.
[46] RL Copenhagen MS Thott 1266/4, fo. 4. Stouppe to Graevius, Utrecht, undated.

tightened and the Dutch standing army, now amounting to over 90,000 men, weighed more heavily, with taxation reaching record levels without the Prince giving any proper account to the provincial assemblies of his use of the funds he and his minions appropriated, republican sentiment in the Republic noticeably began to revive.[47]

During June 1673, shortly before his trip, Spinoza was in contact with Stouppe and Graevius.[48] Since contemporary reports indicate that Stouppe came in person *incognito* perhaps several times to The Hague prior to May 1673 as the main go-between in contacts between the French command and the Stadholder's court, possibly Stouppe and Spinoza had already met before the philosopher set out. But the question remains: why did Spinoza want to go? It was hardly in his interest to associate with Stouppe, Condé, or any of the French if he wished to remain in the Republic. Nor is there any evidence suggesting Spinoza's visit was in some way linked to the secret negotiations in which Condé and Stouppe were involved with the Prince, though his visit must have been politically approved and encouraged on the Dutch as well as the French side. For, as we have seen, William III, acting through his secretary, the younger Constantijn Huygens, the official responsible for issuing the Prince's passports to cross over to the French side, had his own reasons for wanting to reassure the Utrecht regents and especially the Catholic community, that he would take steps to restrain the inevitable Calvinist backlash following a French withdrawal.

On 2 July 1673, Neercassel organized a special Catholic service in Utrecht cathedral to celebrate the French capture of Maastricht at the end of June. The Vicar-Apostolic was generally observed by local Catholics (and those scandalized by such conduct), to publicly applaud every French success and lament every Dutch victory.[49] Religion counted for vastly more than citizenship in his eyes and those of many of his flock. But even before Condé's arrival it had by no means been the policy of Luxembourg or the Stouppes to employ intimidation or strong-arm tactics to advance the Catholic cause locally; rather, helped by the fact that much of the garrison were Swiss Protestants, the French command aimed to shield local Protestant sentiment from Catholic pressure, taking care, as at Arnhem and Nijmegen, to antagonize the Reformed population as little as possible. This was even truer once Condé took charge. Still, the Catholic population of Utrecht and Gelderland was substantial, divisions were deep, and the "best part of the Roman Catholics" of the French-occupied territory, as Coste puts it, "so pleased to find themselves under the government of a Catholic king, that their joy cannot be exprest. Being in great hopes that their religion would become the uppermost, they sent delegates to the Prince de Condé to desire him to give them

---

[47] *Calendar of State Papers Venetian* 38 (1673–5), p. 341.
[48] Van de Ven, "Crastina die loquar," 153.
[49] Jessurun-ten Dam Ham, *Utrecht in 1672 en 1673*, 123–4.

those churches the Protestants possessed in the open country." No more wishing to foment religious strife than William III, Condé, however, "answer'd with some railleries that put them clear out of countenance." In case the king "should make himself master of all the country" of the United Provinces, Condé fobbed them off by saying, "they should have as many churches as they pleased." When Spinoza set out for Utrecht, in late July, that no longer looked at all likely.[50]

Still, there was no way to prevent mounting friction in and around Utrecht. The mere sight of Catholicism openly practised, with images and processions in the streets, inevitably stirred resentment, as also at Nijmegen and other occupied towns.[51] As always, some people could barely hide their zest for inter-communal strife. Wicquefort mentions one wine merchant located in the city centre who posted a board over his store bearing the arms of France held aloft by golden angels with "Ludovicus triumphus" painted beneath. All the preachers, Reformed and Catholic, needed muzzling to an extent. There was dissension over the use of particular churches and university buildings, adjusting civic charities to provide equitably for Reformed and the Catholic poor, over opening a Jesuit college (which was not to Neercassel's liking), and bringing in Catholic priests from Flanders. Presumably, friction, or at least confusion, stemmed too from adoption of the Gregorian Calendar by the occupying French and the Catholic Church. Whereas since December 1582, Holland and Zeeland, under pressure from William the Silent but contrary to the rest of Protestant Europe and the other five provinces that afterwards joined the Union of Utrecht, opted for the "new calendar" used in France, the rest with Utrecht had adhered until now to the "Old Style" Julian Calendar. Given the ten-day difference between the two rival calendars, the switch from the Julian to the Gregorian system in Utrecht in 1672–3 offered unbounded scope for muddle and bickering about dates.

By July 1673, little of the once rosy prospect for the Anglo-French alliance still lingered, despite the recent successful siege of the great southern fortress town of Maastricht (15–30 June 1673), in which several new siege techniques of the renowned French military engineer Vauban were used for the first time. Besides Dutch naval victories and, from the Anglo-French perspective deterioration of the international situation, there was the successful reconstitution and expansion of William's field army and, worst of all for the two glory-seeking, grasping kings, fast mounting financial difficulties and the growing presence of the Imperial army on the Rhine. The Spanish governor-general in the southern Netherlands was sending more troops to stiffen the Dutch water-line and, just prior to Spinoza's arrival, Condé received orders to move his camp and many of his troops southwards, into Brabant, to counter the expected pending formal declaration of war by Spain, in alliance with the emperor. As the entire strategic outlook deteriorated for

---

[50] Coste, *Life of Lewis of Bourbon*, 174; Forclaz, "Rather French than Subject," 518–19.
[51] *Le Conseil d'Extorsion*, 49; Jessurun-ten Dam Ham, *Utrecht in 1672 and 1673*, 121, 125–6.

the French, the States General switched in their negotiations with the Stouppes from exploring possibilities for a compromise peace to setting conditions for the soon expected French evacuation and reversion of Utrecht, Overijssel, and Gelderland to Dutch control.[52]

The Hague secret peace talks, consequently, came to nothing. Louis could not bring himself to simply abandon the fruits of his stunning victories of the previous year while the Prince and his advisers, heartened by the changed military situation, were in no mood to offer substantial concessions.[53] Failure of the peace talks, though, did nothing to allay the fears of Utrecht's "Louvesteynsche factie." If Stouppe and Condé showed a marked intellectual as well as political and propaganda curiosity in the emerging underground phenomenon of "Spinozism," the others in Utrecht participating in the deliberations with Spinoza in their city, notably Graevius and Van Velthuysen, were mainly anxious about the general situation facing their university, city, and province.

34.ii Portraying "Spinozism" in 1673

A subsidiary but still significant factor in the calculations of the Stouppes in organizing French war propaganda was the fierce criticism they and other Swiss officers and troops in Louis' armies were being subjected to in their native land by Protestants outraged that fellow Protestants should assist Louis XIV in the, by them, much condemned efforts to crush a fellow Protestant republic. Jean-Baptiste by this time was actually more of a freethinker than a Protestant but still sensitive to admonitions that as an ostensible Calvinist he should be fighting for, not against, the Dutch.[54] In part, he was thus defending himself in his anti-Dutch propaganda claiming the Republic had become ruinous for Christianity generally. Dutch toleration was a pernicious contagion, he argued, menacing all their neighbours by permitting Anti-Trinitarianism to spread barely concealed among Collegiants, Remonstrants, and Mennonites.

According to Stouppe's analysis in *La religion des Hollandois*, the Republic's population, shaped by the insidious poison of Dutch toleration, fell into three roughly equal, warring blocs, being one third Reformed, one third Catholic, and one third *sectaires*—the last an astounding mix of Mennonites, Remonstrants, Lutherans, Jews, Quakers, Socinians, Arians, Brownists, Independents, Boreelists, libertines, and finally *Spinozistes*.[55] Although the Dutch talked of toleration,

---

[52] *Histoire de Guillaume III* i, 62; Jessurun-ten Dam Ham, *Utrecht in 1672 en 1673*, 146.
[53] *Histoire de Guillaume III* i, 80.
[54] Stouppe, *Religion des Hollandois*, 2–3; Benítez (ed.), "À Madame... sur les différentes religions," 433, 436.
[55] Kooi, "Paying off the Sheriff," 90–2, 101; Frijhoff, "Religious Toleration," 33–4, 44; Villani, "A Man of Intrigue," 315.

avarice, he insisted, was their true religion, their toleration being the ungodly mask of regent hypocrisy, indifference, and unrestrained quest for profit. The latter charge was not wholly unfounded since bribes to magistrates and regents, in places like Gouda and Delft, had long played a part in widening toleration for Catholics who, for historical and current political reasons, fell under greater suspicion than the other religious minorities.

Due to far-reaching religious fragmentation, more sects had surfaced in Holland than all the rest of Europe put together. The contrast between Swiss and Dutch Protestantism, argued Stouppe, could hardly be greater. Where the upright Swiss venerated Christ's divinity, devoutly debarring sectarianism and suppressing Anti-Trinitarians, the outrageous Dutch Republic refused to shield core Christian doctrine, so that now large numbers were questioning the "divinité de Jesus-Christ." If this belief so central to Christianity should collapse, with it would lapse the entire structure of theological and church supremacy over morality, society, and education. Where the Canton Geneva piously had "those two heretics [Michael Servetus and Scipio Gentilis]" burnt at the stake for their heinous "errours against the Divinity of Jesus Christ," as befitted the case, the contemptible Dutch refused to "put any Socinians to death, whatever their errours may be."[56] So disastrous an influence were the Arminian Remonstrants that they were practically as bad as the Mennonites in harbouring Socinians and trampling the Holy Trinity under foot. The "land of the States General is not of our [Reformed] religion"; Dutch toleration ravages Christianity.[57]

After surveying the stunning variety of churches constituting the religious madness of the Republic, Stouppe did not think he had adequately covered "all the religions of this country without adding some words about a famous and knowledgeable man [un homme illustre et sçavant] who, according to what I have been told, possesses a large number of followers [sectateurs] entirely attached to his views."[58] Born a Jew, this extraordinary personage is named "Spinoza"—a name later corrected but in the first printing of Stouppe's book arrestingly misspelt "Spinola"—who "has not renounced the religion of the Jews, nor embraced the Christian religion."[59] Strictly speaking, this was true, as the synagogue had expelled Spinoza but he had not formally abjured Judaism or adopted another religion. The "principal goal" of Spinoza's *TTP* "is to destroy all religions and principally the Jewish and Christian faiths, and introduce atheism, libertinage and freedom of all religions." He does not actually assert his atheistic views about the Divinity openly, Stouppe reports, but the *TTP* ceaselessly insinuates this and lets it be discerned. God, holds Spinoza, is not a Being endowed with an infinitely

---

[56] As expressed in the 1681 London edition, quoted in Patoir, "Polemic Pamphleteering," 24–5.
[57] Stouppe, *Religion des Hollandois*, 45, 57, 74; Patoir, "Polemic Pamphleteering," 20, 23.
[58] Stouppe, *De God-Dienst Der Hollanders*, 25; Lavaert, *Vrijheid, gelijkheid, veelheid*, 210.
[59] Stouppe, *Religion des Hollandois*, 91–2; Vernière, *Spinoza et la pensée française*, 19–20.

perfect intelligence as we envisage Him, and is not beneficent, in fact consists of nothing but His power, the power of nature, diffused in all creatures and created things.[60]

Religion, Stouppe explained, Spinoza sees as being devised by humans for the utility of the public, in order to persuade citizens to "live honestly, obey the magistracy and devote themselves to virtue," goals Spinoza supports not because he thinks there is any hope of compensation after death but simply for the excellence of virtue itself and the advantages this brings to the virtuous in this life.[61] To give this remarkable passage lasting impact and ensure its significance was not missed, Bayle later incorporated this entire section verbatim into his article "Spinoza" in his *Dictionnaire* of 1697, making it the account in French that long remained the guiding description of Spinoza's life and work everywhere in Enlightenment Europe.[62] The passage was reproduced also separately in the Dutch translation of Bayle's article by François Halma, at Utrecht, in 1698, under the title "Pierre Bayle, *Het Leven van B. de Spinoza*," the edition of Bayle most frequently owned in the eighteenth-century Republic. Thus, Stouppe's account lingered for many decades encased in the Netherlands as the fixed image of Spinoza and Spinozism.

Like Descartes, Hobbes, and Leibniz, Spinoza believed it possible to improve human life by fundamentally transforming men's outlook and ideas so as to reduce superstition and credulity and restructure society along less divisive lines. However, libertine freethinkers like Stouppe and Condé could not fail to notice that Spinoza pursued this goal much further than any predecessor or other contemporary, nurturing plans for a more totalizing, subversive penetration of society, spreading not just a philosophical system and political theory but also networks of disciples recruited to his programme of hidden communication and clandestine action designed to attack the roots of intolerance, superstition, prejudice, irrational fear, monarchy, aristocracy, ecclesiastical authority, and censorship with a view to forging an overall more secular, tolerant, egalitarian, and stable society less prone to tyranny, inner dissension, intrusive theology, priestly ambition, and rule by dominant vested interests and war.

"Ce Spinola" [this Spinoza], continues the first printing of Stouppe's book, "lives in the country and has been for some time in The Hague, where he is visited

---

[60] Stouppe, *Religion des Hollandois*, 93; [Stouppe], *De God-Dienst Der Hollanders*, 25.

[61] Stouppe, *Religion des Hollandois*, 66, 92–3; Israel, *Radical Enlightenment*, 278; Klever, "Spinoza's Life and Works," 43–4: Krop, *Spinoza, een paradoxale icoon*, 149; Spinoza, asserts Stouppe, "a fait depuis quelques années un livre dont le titre est *Tractatus Theologico-Politicus*, dans lequel il semble d'avoir pour but principal de détruire toutes les religions et particulièrement la judaïque et la Chrétienne et d'introduire l'athéisme, le libertinage et la liberté de toutes les religions. Il soutient, qu'elles ont toutes esté inventées pour l'utilité que le public reçoit, afin que tous les citoyens vivent honnêtement et obéissent à leur magistrat."

[62] Bayle, *Écrits sur Spinoza*, 43–4; on the widespread ownership of *Het Leven van B. de Spinoza*, see Leeuwenburgh, "Meten is weten," 83–5.

by all the *esprits curieux*, and even by young women of standing priding themselves on possessing a clever wit above the usual level of their sex. His followers, his "*sectateurs*, do not dare reveal themselves" openly, because his teaching absolutely subverts, as it is expressed in the 1680 English translation, "the very foundations of all religion, and has been condemn'd by a public edict of the States General [the French says 'par un décret public des États'], and a prohibition put upon the sale of it; yet it is publickly sold. Amongst all the divines, of whom there is a great number in this country, not one has stood up, that has presum'd to write against the opinions which the author advances in the aforesaid treatise."[63] This startling lack of rebuttals of Spinoza's thought Stouppe professed to find all the more stunning in that the author manifests great knowledge of the Hebrew language, ceremonies of the Jewish religion and all Jewish customs, besides philosophy, so that no theologian anywhere could "dare say it does not merit theological pens being taken up to refute" his arguments, especially "given the robustness of learning on which it rests." "If they [Dutch theologians] persist in this silence," he adds, to the understandable outrage of Dutch readers, "one must conclude either that they lack charity in leaving so pernicious a book without any reply, or that they approve of this author's sentiments, or lack the courage and vigour to refute it."[64] Here was disparagement that thrust deeply.

In this manner, news of the new Spinozist "secte," detailed by Stouppe, in 1673, was presented not only to Condé and his officers but in French, Dutch, and German among a wide European reading public. The two early French editions appeared almost simultaneously at Paris and somewhere in the Netherlands under the fictive publisher's imprint "Pierre Marteaux, at Cologne," in August, probably just after Spinoza left Utrecht and returned to The Hague.[65] Because Stouppe's book was rated among the most effective late seventeenth-century "Protestant" appeals against inter-Christian feuding and attacks on the principle of toleration, it was widely read and diffused. Besides German, Stouppe's *Religion des Hollandois* appeared in Dutch again at Amsterdam, in 1674, and in an Italian version, *La Religione degli Olandesi* (Paris, 1674) as well as, eventually, in 1680 and again in 1681, in English.[66]

Stouppe's far-reaching assault on Dutch toleration was eventually answered with a book twice its length, by the Hebraist, Bible critic, favourite pupil of Cocceius, and Cartesian, Johannes Braun [Jean Brun] (1628–1708), then preacher at the Walloon church at Nijmegen, since 1661, and in later life for many years a professor at Groningen. In *La Véritable religion des Hollandois* (1675), dedicated

---

[63] Stouppe, *Religion of the Dutch*, 29; Israel, *Radical Enlightenment*, 278.
[64] Stouppe, *Religion des Hollandois*, 94–5.
[65] Van de Ven, "Crastina die loquar," 150–1; Benítez (ed.), "À Madame...sur les différentes religions," 440.
[66] Vernière, *Spinoza et la pensée française*, 20n1; Benítez (ed.), "À Madame...sur les différentes religions," 441; Patoir, "Polemic Pamphleteering," 3.

to the Prince of Orange and dated 1 December 1674, Braun (or Brun) sought to rebut all of Stouppe's charges. To Stouppe's claim that the Dutch Revolt reveals a "seditious people with no respect for monarchy," he replied that Dutchmen are not at all "seditious" but obedient, loyal, and peace-loving. The charge of avariciousness revealed only Stouppe's blatant hypocrisy, as he himself was renowned for his extravagant lifestyle and, on departing Utrecht in November 1673, left behind piles of unsettled debts. Regarding Socinians, he seemed to have forgotten that the States General strictly forbade their meetings and publications. He had also misleadingly depicted the United Provinces as teeming with Socinians, freethinkers, Boreelists, and Spinozists when in fact, outside Amsterdam, Rotterdam, and Leiden (including Rijnsburg), few such sectarians were found in all the rest of the Republic. In Zeeland there dwelt scarcely any Catholics or sectarians. The Reformed, he points out, were not one third of the population, roughly equal in proportion to the Catholics: there were far more Reformed believers than "papists and sectarians put together."[67] Nor did the Republic permit papists a free hand. Unobtrusive Catholic worship was tolerated in so-called "hidden churches"; but the States' ban on public Catholic practice (outside the French-occupied zone) was everywhere enforced, causing Catholics to continually protest against the restrictions.[68]

As for Dutch efforts to counter Spinoza and Spinozism being staggeringly perfunctory, Braun pointed out that Dutch scholars had been severely hindered by none other than Louis XIV himself whose army, including Stouppe, had invaded and disrupted the Republic. Braun himself had composed a text containing "plusieurs remarques contre ce détestable livre [the *TTP*]," but the French invasion which he experienced first-hand at Nijmegen during 1672–3, caused so much disruption and delay that, eventually, his refutation became superfluous owing to Van Mansvelt's more comprehensive rebuttal appearing in 1674.[69] A future professor of Hebrew,[70] Braun rebuffed too Stouppe's curious claim that Spinoza never renounced "the religion of the Jews." Rather, Spinoza repudiated all Jewish views and renounced "all their observances and ceremonies" and, moreover, observed no dietary restrictions whatever, being accustomed, word had it, even to eat food cooked in (pork fat) lard, "without inquiring whether it is *kosher* or *nefesh*."[71]

The availability of the *TTP* did not reflect dire shortcomings in Dutch society since that truly abominable book circulated equally elsewhere. "I am well aware [this perverse book] has been selling in England, Germany, France and even Switzerland as well as in Holland."[72] There were not even grounds for assuming

---

[67] Braun [Brun], *Véritable religion*, 166; Van Berkel, *Universiteit van het noorden*, 246–7.
[68] Braun [Brun], *Véritable religion*, 171.
[69] Braun [Brun], *Véritable religion*, 163; Steenbakkers, "Johannes Braun," 198–202.
[70] At Groningen, from 1680, see Steenbakkers, "Johannes Braun," 197–8.
[71] Braun [Brun], *Véritable religion*, 158; Vernière, *Spinoza et la pensée française*, 40–2.
[72] Braun [Brun], *Véritable religion*, 159; Vernière, *Spinoza et la pensée française*, 41.

it had been published in the United Provinces since it states "Hamburg" on the title-page.[73] Even assuming the *TTP* was published in the Dutch Republic, the States "sought to suppress that book at birth, condemned it and strictly forbade its sale immediately it appeared in their country, as Stouppe himself admits." Since every true Christian loathes everything Spinoza represents: "it is perhaps for this reason [Calvinist] theologians, Swiss and Dutch, see little real necessity to refute Spinoza, everybody agreeing that the revulsion his teaching universally arouses suffices to refute it of itself and, all the more because there is nothing new in his treatise."[74]

Besides, why should it be a particular Dutch responsibility to repudiate Spinoza and discredit his following? No one disagrees with Stouppe's claim that Spinoza poses a fundamental threat to all Christianity. Therefore, countering him and his movement demands general suppression of Spinoza, Spinozism, Spinozist books and ideas, and his despicable following in all Christendom, and this is the sacred task of Christians everywhere: since they all agree this is necessary, "should not all the Christians there are in the world rush to refute him [tout ce qu'il y a de Chrétiens au monde, ne doivent ils pas accourir pour le refuter]?"[75] It was Stouppe's devious aim, accuses Braun, not just to discredit Dutch society but further disrupt their country by fomenting irreligion and *libertinage*, covertly promoting rather than genuinely seeking to crush atheism and Socinianism.[76] Aside from the fact that Stouppe, encouraged perhaps by Condé, had undeniably assigned Spinoza the person greater prominence than had any other author thus far, whether in Latin or vernacular languages, loudly and deliberately drawing everyone's attention to a phenomenon everyone else sought to curtain off, this ex-preacher officer in French pay had deliberately infiltrated into his book some apparently positive aspects of Spinoza's social and ethical thought. Braun was surely justified in accusing Stouppe (and more discreetly, Condé) of insinuating that Spinoza was far from being altogether reprehensible. Why exactly were the French giving Spinoza a prominent profile directly contrary to the approach of the Dutch and all others? Bishop Gilbert Burnet who knew Stouppe well in the mid-1680s later confirmed that this "man of intrigue but no virtue" was "more a Socinian or deist than either Protestant or Christian."[77]

34.iii Across the French Lines

Whatever intrigues were underway on the part of Stouppe, Graevius, Van Velthuysen, Neercassel, and Condé, since Spinoza travelled little, was temperamentally disinclined

---

[73] Patoir, "Polemic Pamphleteering," 46.   [74] Braun [Brun], *Véritable religion*, 163.
[75] Patoir, "Polemic Pamphleteering," 39.
[76] Benítez (ed.), "À Madame...sur les différentes religions," 428, 442; Steenbakkers, "Johannes Braun," 201.
[77] Villani, "Man of Intrigue," 316, 321.

to seek honours, pensions, or comforts for himself, and hated distractions, one may well wonder why, having initially expressed reluctance to accept Stouppe's invitation to visit Utrecht, he agreed to go at all. Bouwmeester's correspondence with Graevius confirms, as Lucas correctly states, that Spinoza prevaricated for some weeks, agreeing to go only after considerable delay and at the strong urging of Bouwmeester and "his friends."[78]

Such reluctance is hardly surprising given the water-line and war situation separating Utrecht from The Hague, and that the early months of 1673 were a time of continued nervousness and unrest in The Hague.[79] But though perplexing at first sight, if we consider also Spinoza's deep concern with the mechanics of power and fascination with the political and military drama in progress around him, besides his understandable worries about the fate of his "sect" and troubled relationship with the Cartesians, and willingness to support William's behind-the-scenes policy of restraining the Reformed clergy, it is perhaps not so strange that, finally, he wanted to see for himself what was occurring at such a crucial focal point as Utrecht and seize the opportunity to confer with such key personalities as Stouppe, Condé, Graevius, and Van Velthuysen (with whom he had crossed swords in the past but clearly respected), and Luxembourg too, with whom, according to Lucas, he also conversed a good deal. A now deeply worried Van Velthuysen cared passionately about that "very dear liberty" for which the forefathers of the Dutch had fought, and believed this precious legacy was now imperilled less by the French than by Voetians and Orangists.[80] Another prominent personage at Utrecht likely to lose his position, with whom Spinoza conferred amicably at Utrecht, was the longstanding secretary to the city government (from 1662 to 1674), Joachim Nieuwstad (c.1623–96), to whom Spinoza later referred, writing to Van Velthuysen, as "our friend."[81]

If only in some small way, Spinoza must have felt that by his visit he could perhaps contribute to conciliatory outcomes and reassure the most vulnerable. This is suggested also by the fact that Spinoza only eventually set off after clearing his travel plan with "prominent" people in The Hague and securing a safe conduct from the Prince of Orange or some high personage acting in his name.[82] Besides negotiating a veiled truce in the philosophical war between the academic Cartesians and Spinoza, a behind-the-scenes truce soon to take effect, the Utrecht *Collegie der Sçavanten* must have been especially eager, while he stayed amongst them, to discover how Spinoza himself had so adroitly navigated the purges and Voetian backlash unscathed, retaining his calm dignified posture throughout. Spinoza appeared to enjoy the protective esteem of certain

---

[78] Lucas, *La Vie*, 40; Gootjes, "Spinoza between French Libertines," 4–5.
[79] Van Gelder, "Schutterij en Magistraat in 1672," 76, 80.
[80] RL Copenhagen MS Thott 1267. Velthuysen to Graevius, Rotterdam, 11 Feb. 1673.
[81] Spinoza, *Collected Works* (ed. Curley) ii, 460; Meinsma, *Spinoza et son cercle*, 427, 459.
[82] *De Boekzaal van Europe* 1698 (September/October) 297, review of Halma.

"prominent" people in The Hague, as Colerus later expressed it, and now, in the summer of 1673, felt more secure than during his months of deep dismay, in 1672 and early 1673, when he too considered fleeing abroad. How exactly had he contrived this calming outcome in the face of so much adversity, and how could the Utrecht group come under this same unseen protective shield?

Writing to Graevius from Amsterdam, on 29 July, Bouwmeester reported that Spinoza had departed The Hague, heading towards Utrecht, on 26 July, expressing confidence that he must by then already have safely arrived. Presumably, he travelled by passenger barge, via Dordrecht,[83] crossing the water-line passing first through the Dutch defences, showing his Dutch passport, and then crossing the French lines, showing his French passport, and on to Utrecht. Arriving on 28 July, Spinoza stayed slightly over three weeks. The prevailing atmosphere was certainly unlike anything he had witnessed before. Judgements about Utrecht by visiting foreign visitors then varied considerably. Utrecht "is a great town and head of a province," averred the ex-Cambridge fellow and botanist John Ray, visiting a decade earlier, "environed with a thick and high wall and a deep trench"; however, its "streets and buildings [were] far short of the elegancy, beauty and cleanliness of those of Holland, much like the houses and streets of our English towns."[84] "There is little here worth seeing," the later Tory bishop William Nicolson remarked in 1678, "except the pleasant situation of the place, the ruines of a stately cathedrall which was thrown down in the year 1674 by thunder, and their university-library." The latter, noted Nicolson, a connoisseur of scholarly books, "has more printed books though fewer manuscripts (a catalogue of which I transcribed) than that of Leyden."[85] Utrecht's most eye-catching structure, the "Domo or Cathedral church hath a great tall tower, ascended by 460 steps, from [where one] had a fair prospect of the city and the country round about."[86] Spinoza's visit occurred in the very last year the great cathedral stood intact.

Completed in 1382, the famous Dom tower was something Spinoza's gaze must have alighted upon every day of his visit, as it is impossible to walk Utrecht's streets without frequently glimpsing that arresting sight, among the most imposing in the Netherlands. Luxembourg, Condé, the Stouppes, and practically all other visitors to the city who could manage the steps enjoyed the view from the top of the famous tower as well as admired the impressive interior. When Spinoza visited, the cathedral was still firmly in Catholic hands, affording the opportunity, for once in his life, to witness full-dress impressive Catholic masses and listen to a high Catholic ecclesiastic in full regalia (Neercassel) exalting monarchy and condemning the Republic's toleration, multiple heresies, and rebellion against Church and true authority, religious, political, and social. A child of New

---

[83] Gootjes, "Spinoza between French Libertines," 9–10; Van de Ven, "Crastina die loquar," 147–50.
[84] Ray, *Observations topographical*, 44.   [85] Nicolson, "Iter Hollandicum (1678)," 101.
[86] Ray, *Observations topographical*, 44.

Christian *converso* parents whose ancestors had, for generations, been compelled to attend Catholic mass week after week under unrelenting oppression, genuflect with bogus zeal during prayers, and listen to sermons with unfailing outward respect and apparent devotion, always scrupulously careful to betray no sign of their family's secret inner abhorrence, the spectacle presumably elicited in him an array of emotions. It was also a scene that, after the pending French evacuation, no one would witness again—the heart of Utrecht under Catholic religious ascendancy in and around an imposing medieval Gothic structure during the last year the building stood intact.

There was much else besides to arrest Spinoza's attention. The French exacted heavy taxation from the citizenry, but did not intrude Catholics into public offices or interfere with the city government's anti-Orangist regents. The city poor chest for relief of paupers, for now under joint Protestant–Catholic control, provided relief to impoverished Catholics and Remonstrants on an equal basis with the Reformed, an arrangement warming the hearts of those thinking in conciliatory terms.[87] Everyone was avid for war news. The improvement in Dutch fortunes was fast changing the ambience, even though much of importance occurred too far away to be known about as yet. No one knew it then, but Spinoza's arrival coincided with that of Admiral Evertsen's flotilla off New York and the short-lived Dutch reoccupation of New York when, albeit briefly, the town became again "New Amsterdam" in "New Netherland" until, under the peace treaty, it reverted to the English, late in 1674.

Condé left Utrecht on 15 July, nearly a fortnight before Spinoza's arrival, and, as far as is known, never returned. But he may have still been encamped with his troops close by when Stouppe's brother, Pierre-Alexandre, reported in a letter, dated 28 July 1673, that Spinoza, visiting "at the request of my brother," had now arrived. Among other news from The Hague, he informed Condé, Spinoza brought word of the continuing furore over the Viscount de Montbas (d. 1696), the commander who had abandoned key positions, in June 1672, facilitating the French breakthrough the previous summer, and whose betrayal had become a tool of Orangist propagandists against the De Witt faction. Montbas had managed to escape from prison and join the French, and, with the Stouppes, participated in the capture of Woerden in September 1672. Sentenced to death by the Prince's Council of War, the Prince had now had him publicly hanged in effigy at The Hague, on 25 July, just prior to Spinoza's departure.[88]

During his three weeks at Utrecht, Spinoza conversed at length with notable personalities, scholarly, political, and military, even if in the end no opportunity

---

[87] Yasuhira, "Confessional Coexistence," 12–13, 16.
[88] Van de Ven, "Crastina die loquar," 154; Cohen, *Séjour de Saint-Évremond*, 66n; Roorda, *Partij en factie*, 90, 115–16, 145.

arose to meet Condé himself, as Colerus,[89] Lucas, and others reported and most scholars today accept. Bayle, Colerus, Coste, and Lucas all assumed, wrongly, that it was Condé who took the initiative in inviting Spinoza to come to Utrecht. Although Coste's report that Condé "was desirous to see Spinoza" is probably correct and Spinoza seemingly did prolong his stay, very likely awaiting the Prince's return, it still seems that, in the end, their meeting never occurred,[90] though the question of whether they did or did not meet has never been finally settled. Most scholars today discount also the rest of what Coste reports in this connection (rather like Morelli later): that Condé "told him smiling, that if he would follow him into France [as had La Peyrère], he would put him in a way to live in conformity with his theology, that Paris neither wanted [for] fine women, nor pleasures; although he look'd upon him as a deist, and a man who had no religion, he was charm'd with the conversation he had with him."[91]

As Condé may well have encamped fairly close by during late July and early August, one cannot reject this out of hand; and even if one dismisses Morelli and Coste as unreliable here, other sources seem to corroborate their story. Bayle, never a sceptic about historical research, in later years switched from one view to the other, caught between conflicting accounts as additional reports cropped up claiming Condé did in fact hold several conferences with Spinoza either in Utrecht or, more likely, at the Prince's mobile headquarters not far off. The Utrecht editor Halma affirmed, in 1698, here departing from what Bayle originally wrote in his *Dictionnaire* (though Bayle afterwards changed his mind about this), that they did meet.[92] Halma lived in Utrecht, was the University printer from 1674, and was intimately familiar with the cultural life of the city, facts that helped persuade Bayle and others, temporarily, that Halma justly corrected him. Later, Bayle discussed the question with "Mr [Paul] Buissière," who was in Utrecht, in 1672-3, "in his capacity as surgeon at the French army hospital: [Buissière] assured me he saw Spinoza several times enter into the apartments of the Prince de Condé. Thus, there is no room for doubt that the Prince did actually converse with this philosopher." A Huguenot, Buissière left France for Copenhagen, in 1683, but after the Glorious Revolution settled in England, where he became a member of the Royal Society.[93] During the weeks in question, he was Condé's personal apothecary in the occupied Netherlands; he had a brother, Pierre, who knew Bayle since at least 1684 and in the late 1690s sought to correct several of what seemed to him inaccuracies in Bayle's *Dictionnaire*. Later, though, after

---

[89] Colerus, *Waarachtige verrijzenis*, 134.
[90] [Lucas], *La Vie*, 40; Benítez (ed.), "À Madame...sur les différentes religions," 438-9n35; Van de Ven, "Crastina die loquar," 155-6.
[91] Coste, *Life of Lewis of Bourbon*, 173-4.
[92] Halma, *Het Leven*, 11-12; Bayle, *Correspondance* xiii, 423-4n11; Assoun, "Spinoza, les libertins," 202-6.
[93] Freudenthal/Walther, *Lebensgeschichte* i, 72-3, and ii, 43-4; Vernière, *Spinoza et la pensée française*, 22, 293; Bayle, *Correspondance* vii, 7n4, and xi, 358n1; Bayle, *Écrits sur Spinoza*, 165-6.

reading Colerus, Bayle changed his mind again, reverting to his original denial that Spinoza ever met Condé.[94]

Yet, in the light of Halma's and Buissière's assertions, the testimony of the Sephardic physician Henriquez Morales (Morelli), the freethinker later living in London as a nominal Catholic professing to have known Spinoza well in The Hague, cannot simply be ignored. Morelli claimed to have had long discussions with Spinoza about his trip to Utrecht and the Prince's alleged invitation for him to remain in his entourage, under his protection, and accompany him to Paris.[95] Whether or not such conversations with Condé ever took place, the possibility that Spinoza briefly pondered coming under Condé's protection, given his interest the year before in exploring possibilities for a safe haven abroad, remote from the war, in Tuscany or Germany, in itself seems not implausible.[96] In any case, Spinoza lingered longer in Utrecht than was seemingly originally intended, extending opportunity for lengthy discussion with the Stouppes, Graevius, Nieuwstad, and Van Velthuysen among others, while evidently practising his use of his father's second language among the French and Swiss officers.

Put up by Stouppe with all expenses paid, Spinoza, with his southern countenance and courteous manner, no doubt dined with him and other officers in style, as was reported back in The Hague. Braun afterwards accused Stouppe of rank hypocrisy in maligning the Dutch for tolerating Spinoza when he himself hosted and praised him openly during his Utrecht visit, spending much time "fort familièrement avec lui [very familiarly with him]." Presumably, he dined with Stouppe among other places in the mansion where Stouppe resided, belonging to Mme De Borneval, widow of a Utrecht nobleman; Stouppe later extended his best wishes to his "hostess" via a letter to Graevius of July 1674, sent from the French army camp where he found himself eight months after leaving Utrecht.[97] Spinoza joined in a variety of meetings and perhaps attended, in early August, along with many of the French and Swiss officers lodged in the town, a series of comedies put on for their entertainment, by a visiting troupe of Italian "commedianten," much to the disgust of the city's Reformed preachers.

Meanwhile, there was also much talk of Spinoza on the other side of the French lines. On 8 August, the North Holland synod reaffirmed the need for firmer suppression of the *TTP* at its gathering at Edam. The Reformed consistories sought heightened vigilance against that dreaded book in particular, the delegates reported. Key regents, notably the new Pensionary of Holland, Gaspar Fagel (1634–88), a former pensionary of Haarlem and now pillar of Williamite

---

[94] Bayle to editors of *Mémoires de Trevoux*, Rotterdam, April 1706 in Bayle, *Correspondance* xiii, 421, 424n12; Van Eeghen, *Amsterdamse boekhandel* iii, 148–9.
[95] Popkin, *Spinoza*, 111–12; Van de Ven, "Crastina die loquar," 148.
[96] Popkin, *Spinoza*, 109–13.
[97] RL Copenhagen MS Thott 1266, 4, fos. 3–4. Stouppe to Graevius, 1 July 1674 where he calls her "mon illustre hostesse"; Benítez (ed.), "À Madame...sur les différentes religions," 437.

dominance, seemed willing to help step up book suppression, but the Reformed Church authorities also learnt from him, no doubt at William III's expressed wish, that with the war taking up all energy and attention, further measures for repression of books would have to wait.[98] The prominent Collegiant poet Joachim Oudaan (1628–92), who loathed Spinoza as a religious foe "who sought to assume the mask of morality, but came to disturb religion with his *Ethics*," later wrote a verse preface to Adriaan Verwer's 1683 attack on Spinoza and his philosophical sect and legacy, stigmatizing his "great hypocrisy" used to cover "his nudity." Whatever he meant, Oudaan's lines include a bitterly sarcastic reference not just to Spinoza's effort to abolish religion with his philosophy but something heinous he supposedly disclosed while dining with French officers in Utrecht: "one may think of [Spinoza's] virtue and morality as one wishes, the stain can never be washed out from what he boasted at table with the French, that [story] of which Utrecht has knowledge, is better not mentioned here."[99]

What began as a leisurely high-level Utrecht symposium on the present state of affairs, conducted in French and Dutch, became more fraught when news arrived that the English had launched what was to prove Charles II's final effort with France to break the Republic and ensure unchecked royal absolutism and eventual Catholic dominance everywhere, together with English hegemony at Dutch expense throughout the Indies East and West, and along the shores of the Americas and Africa. In June, nearing the Dutch coast, as it repeatedly had, the English fleet this time loomed close to The Hague itself. The last major encounter of the Third Anglo-Dutch War, the Battle of Texel (known to the Dutch as the Battle of Kijkduin), on 21 August 1673 or 11 August Old Style, occurred just after Spinoza's return to The Hague, in the third week of August. But during the intervening two critical weeks a constant state of emergency gripped The Hague. The aim of Charles' last major offensive was to land enough men to secure a bridgehead enabling the readied royal force, the so-called "Blackheath army," to be ferried over, as the Venetian envoy in London reported to the Doge, and landed in the Dutch heartland.[100] If successful, Louis and Charles would finally have triumphed after all and the Republic would lay prostrate under foot.

The intimidatingly massive fleet that crossed the Channel to overawe the Dutch coast, including a French naval contingent, boasted altogether eighty-six warships of sufficient size to mount over forty guns,[101] considerably outstripping De Ruyter's sixty. Carrying a vanguard landing force ready to disembark at Scheveningen, or "Scheveling" as the English called it, "a village by the sea-side

---

[98] ARH NHK OSA 184, Acta 1673, pp. 9, 32. Res. 8 Aug. 1673.
[99] Joachim Oudaan, "Op het werk, 't Mom-aensicht der atheistery afgerukt; of de wederlegginge der Zedekunst, van Benedictus de Spinoza," in Adriaan Verwer, *'t Mom-aensicht der atheistery*, fos. 3v–4v; Meinsma, *Spinoza et son cercle*, 445–6n41; Gootjes, "Spinoza between French Libertines," 11–12.
[100] *Calendar of State Papers Venice*, 59, 71, 85.
[101] Hainsworth and Churches, *Anglo-Dutch Wars*, 186.

a mile from The Hague,"[102] the fleet approached backed by favourable winds with De Ruyter still some distance away. "Then little by little, with the wind favourable," as a panicking Bouwmeester reported from Amsterdam, on 7 August, to Graevius, and via him to Spinoza, "the whole fleet moved toward the shore of The Hague and Scheveningen, with smaller vessels attacking so close they could menace the shore with cannon fire." Fearing bombardment of everything in range (the centre of The Hague was not) and raiding parties landing to pillage and plunder, "many local people were so terrified they began carrying off their valuables in carriages and boats," recounts Bouwmeester, "and, to confess the truth, I too begin to be not a little afraid for the writings and products of his night-time labours kept in Mr Spinoza's lodgings, all that he worked at by lamp-light at night for which I pray for a better fate."[103]

Spinoza's manuscripts, the fruit of his night-time efforts over the years, including the almost completed *Ethics*, his several uncompleted manuscripts and correspondence, were indeed lying unprotected just a mile or so from many hundreds of heavy guns and a landing force thirsting to land, conquer, and pillage. Anxious to help however he could, a thoroughly alarmed Bouwmeester asked Graevius to show his letter to Spinoza and write back immediately, letting him know his reaction and especially his wishes and intentions. Unruffled, Spinoza, who had been in Utrecht at this point for ten or eleven days, showed no particular urgency to return and simply stayed put for more than another week. A second worried letter from Bouwmeester, dated 14 August, arrived from Amsterdam a day or two later, recounting the latest news of the coastal drama, a letter now lost but hardly reassuring, reporting that the two vying fleets hovered, manoeuvring for advantage close to The Hague.

Contemplating Bouwmeester's warnings, Louis' intentions, the English menace, the fate of his manuscripts and predicament of his own philosophy more generally, Spinoza, long feeling trapped between Williamite-Voetian reaction and Cartesian hostility, must have reflected too on the surge of conflicting emotions all around, as he strolled in the famed medieval cloister, the ancient Pandhof garden at the heart of Utrecht, and in and around nearby university buildings and the cathedral. Sunday, 10 August, in Utrecht was declared an obligatory special day of prayer for everyone, with all preachers, Protestant and Catholic, being directed to beseech God to incline Louis XIV's heart towards peace.[104] As the drama unfolded, De Ruyter's skill and superior mobility, besides poor Anglo-French cooperation, in the end successfully prevented the planned landing. De Ruyter's

---

[102] Ray, *Observations topographical*, 30–1.

[103] RL Copenhagen, Ms Thott 1258, Bouwmeester to Graevius, Amsterdam, 7 August 1673 "[...] atque ut verum fatear jam ego etiam nonnihil metuere caepi supellectili litterariae, lucubrationibusque D. Spinosae quas meliori fortunae destinatas precor"; Gootjes, "Spinoza between French Libertines," 10n57.

[104] Wicquefort, *Journael of dagelijcksch verhael* i, 207.

carefully calibrated, continual thrusting forward and back, harassing the English fleet's rear, was later rated by some his finest victory. It was certainly among the most crucial.[105]

As Spinoza witnessed it, Louis XIV's general toleration or "religious peace" proclaimed in Utrecht, in August 1672, was anything but tranquil, giving him a unique opportunity to observe the tension and complexity of a previously unheard of, organized public coexistence of Catholicism and Protestantism. The *Domkerk* or "great church" of St Martin's inevitably stood at the heart of this scene of anguish, excitement, and hand-wringing, set to escalate further in the weeks after Spinoza's departure. He missed by just days the so-called "miracle of Utrecht" or "wonder spektakel" of 19/29 August, when a wall in the choir next to the main altar collapsed revealing a pre-Reformation image of Jesus on the Cross which the Reformation had walled over during the Revolt, plainly announcing, some held, divine providence powerfully intervening on the Catholic side. A poem printed locally summoned all "Duyvelsche ketters [devilish heretics]" to heed this great and undeniable "miracle" and prostrate themselves finally before the true church.[106]

No one could fail to notice innumerable signs of escalating interfaith tension, the emotional stress feeding Catholic defiance and Reformed fury alike.[107] The question of loyalty to the Republic was urgently in the air and the spectacle can hardly have softened Spinoza's personal bias against Catholicism. Many Catholics revered Louis XIV almost as a Messiah come to save the Catholic faith.[108] Nijmegen's Catholics, charged Stouppe's polemical adversary, Braun, preacher to the Walloon congregation there, acclaimed the French in 1672, as they had the Munsterites in 1666, with unrestrained jubilation, displaying "furious rage against the Reformed." In late August and early September, several incidents occurred in Utrecht with bands of Catholic youths harassing churches where Reformed services were in progress and Catholic and Protestant youth gangs clashing with sticks and throwing stones.[109] If Catholics wanted the Republic overthrown, the Jews, notes Braun, through their supportive conduct and public rejection of the French invasion, gained in local Protestant esteem. Where Stouppe deliberately highlighted the uniqueness of Dutch toleration of Jews to vilify and disparage it, rightly claiming all Europe was disgusted that Jews should be treated better than Catholics, Braun reminded readers that Louis too tolerated Jews in Metz and at Bordeaux and pointed to the special services Dutch Jews held in their synagogues

---

[105] Hattendorf, "Competing Navies," 113; Daalder, "Michiel de Ruyter," 278.
[106] Wicquefort, *Journael of dagelijcksch verhael* i, 209–10.
[107] *Le Conseil d'Extorsion*, 52; Israel, *Dutch Republic*, 643; Forclaz, "Rather French than Subject," 518–19.
[108] Braun [Brun], *Véritable religion*, 54–5; Forclaz, "Rather French than Subject," 526–7.
[109] GA Utrecht vroedschap vol. for 1668–73, fos. 234–45, res. 16 Aug. 1673, Kerkeraad 10, res. 1 and 7 Sept. 1673.

throughout the time of the French invasion, reciting special prayers for the salvation of the Republic. He wished, Braun went so far to aver, all native-born Christians had been "aussi bons patriotes [as good patriots]" as the Jews.[110]

Amidst the whirl of hatred, religious tension, and emotion, Spinoza did not forget about philosophy in the more formal sense. Conferring with Graevius, they talked of Descartes the man as well as Cartesianism as a faction in Dutch society, and among some papers Spinoza brought with him to Utrecht and left with Graevius, was a copy of "a letter concerning the death of Descartes," originally sent from Stockholm relating the circumstances of Descartes' demise in Sweden, in February 1650, sent by the physician Johannes van Wullen (1615–50), a copy lent to Spinoza. Six months later, Spinoza, assuming Graevius had "long ago made a copy of it," wrote a brief but notably friendly note "with all affection and fondness," on 14 December 1673, requesting his new Utrecht classicist friend to return the document to him, in The Hague, "as soon as you can," because the owner, whom he refers to "D. us de V." (perhaps De Volder or conceivably Isaac Vossius), had now "several times asked me to return it."[111] If, whilst Spinoza was in Utrecht, Graevius presented him with any copies of his classical editions, none graced the philosopher's library in The Hague at the time of his death, in 1677.

Chiefly, though, Spinoza and Graevius must have discussed their future prospects and that of the new philosophy in the face of the Orangist-Voetian reaction, poised soon to engulf Utrecht too. Dutch Cartesians envisaged Descartes as a kind of Christopher Columbus who discovered the New World of true philosophy, science, medicine, and how to think about reality. Owing to these reprehensible, godless innovations by "Cartesians," complained Voetian preachers, good, pious but unsophisticated folk now sat at home and in taverns arguing over whether the sun does or does not circle the earth, whether, at Joshua's asking, God really made the sun stand still in the sky, and, worse still, whether God really turned Moses' staff into a serpent.[112] This was all highly undesirable. The Dutch philosophical-cultural wars over Cartesianism would continue down to the first quarter of the eighteenth century.

Along with other reprehensible omissions, objected Brun, Stouppe's account signally failed to mention that "excellent man in The Netherlands, a very good theologian as well as major philosopher, namely Monsieur Mansvelt, whilst alive professor at Utrecht" who did impressively stand and combat Spinoza's arguments on a Cartesian basis.[113] However, Van Mansvelt had died before the war,

---

[110] Braun [Brun], *Véritable religion*, 221–5; Van Gelderen, "Turning Swiss?," 151–2.
[111] RL Copenhagen MS Thott 1266, 4, signed "Benedictus despinoza," Spinoza to Graevius, The Hague, 14 Dec. 1673, where the name is given as "D. us de B."; but in Spinoza, *Opera* iv, 238 the name is given as "D. us de V."; and as "Mr. de. V." in Spinoza, *Collected Works* (ed. Curley) ii, 405; Gootjes, "Spinoza between French Libertines," 13n14.
[112] Van Velthuysen, *Bewys*, 1, 4, 25–6; Du Bois, *Schadelijkheyt*, 11–12; Israel, *Dutch Republic*, 892–5.
[113] Braun [Brun], *Véritable religion*, 164.

and his book failed to appear until 1674, after Spinoza's visit to Utrecht. This raises the possibility that Graevius and Burman deliberately avoided mentioning Spinoza's name or person in their edition of Van Mansvelt's text, strictly assailing only the anonymous *TTP*, in part to keep open the possibility of better relations with him. Braun later admitted that Van Mansvelt's book appeared at Amsterdam only many months after Stouppe's book, insisting this delay too was caused by the French. Spinoza would have been "long ago refuted also by numerous others had only Stouppe and his accomplices, by waging this bloody war, not obstructed them."[114]

Certainly, from August 1673, Graevius and Van Velthuysen altered their attitude towards Spinoza. "Scarcely any deist," wrote Van Velthuysen about the *TTP* two years earlier, could have supported the pernicious cause of undermining religion "as maliciously, as skilfully and as cunningly as the author of this dissertation has," making churches, churchmen, and theology all redundant.[115] But now the scenario significantly changed. From 1673, the Utrecht Cartesians' former united offensive against the *Philosophia* and Spinoza shifted towards the back-burner, especially as regards their critique of Spinoza's adamant plea for liberty of expression and to philosophize.

34.iv Chaotic Aftermath

Returning from Utrecht to The Hague, in late August 1673, was probably for Spinoza the most discomforting part of the whole episode. Fed by his evil reputation locally, there was apparently a good deal of ominous murmuring that he was "a spy" and in Utrecht had betrayed state secrets in treasonable correspondence with Condé and the French. Colerus reports that Spinoza's landlord, Van der Spijck, was greatly agitated by the thought that his house might be attacked by a violent mob seeking to drag Spinoza out and put paid to him. He later told Colerus that Spinoza at once reassured him saying: "I am innocent. There are many among the highest placed of the Republic who know exactly why I went to Utrecht and as soon as there is any racket outside your door, I shall go straight out to confront the mob even if they treat me as they did the good Sirs De Witt [Jan de Witt and his brother, Cornelis]. I am an upright *republiquain* and the common best of the Republic is my ideal."[116]

Van Velthuysen, his colleagues and friends, Nieuwstad, Graevius, and the Stouppes, afterwards had plentiful grounds to look back on the summer of

---

[114] Braun [Brun], *Véritable religion*, 164.
[115] Velthuysen to Ostens, Utrecht, 24 Jan. 1671, in Spinoza, *Collected Works* (ed. Curley) ii, 374; Spinoza, *Correspondance* (ed. Rovere), 241–2; Blom, "Lambert van Velthuysen," 204.
[116] Freudenthal/Walther, *Lebensgeschichte* i, 130–1; Steenbakkers, "Spinoza's Life," 39.

1673, and Spinoza's visit, with mixed feelings. Shortly after Spinoza's return, the English maritime offensive finally ended with the removal of the threat by De Ruyter's final victory at Texel. This success was followed by the surrender to the Prince, on 12 September 1673, less than a month after Spinoza's return, of the key French-held fortress of Naarden, among the most important strongholds in the Netherlands, news greeted with undisguised joy by the Protestants of Utrecht confirming which way the wind was blowing.[117] The Republic's survival at last seemed assured, and with it Spinoza's manuscripts rendered safe, at least for now. Yet, one could hardly say the prospects for the *Ethics*, or Spinoza's philosophical legacy more generally, or, for that matter, the *Collegie der Sçavanten* and the Utrecht Cartesians were brightening too.

Outflanked, the French had to evacuate less than three months after Spinoza's visit, beginning in October. During the final weeks of their presence there was much pilfering by French and Swiss soldiers, though the Stouppes, anxious to minimize the lawlessness, reportedly remained well-intentioned to the end, figuring among the very last to leave. The concluding Catholic mass was held in the cathedral on 23 November 1673, or 13 November, as the Reformed community, employing the Julian calendar, recorded this momentous occasion, lamented by some, joyfully acclaimed by others. The last occupying troops departed that same day.[118] Neercassel fled to Antwerp, from where he established contact with the Stadholder's court and, after some months, reassuringly received word that the Prince's firm intention was to preserve the same toleration for Catholics as before 1672, though the Prince specifically withheld his protection from Neercassel personally, due to his treasonous conduct, forcing him to remain in exile until permitted to return and reside in Leiden, in 1679.[119]

Just hours after the French left, States troops (accompanied by Spinoza's old foe, preacher Thaddeus de Lantman) retook the city, amidst a frantic waving of orange flags, scarves, and everything else orange, subjecting it to a five-month second military occupation instrumental in bringing about the institutional and political changes that ensued. Shortly after the last Catholic mass was recited, on the morning of 13/23 November, an angry Protestant crowd emptied the cathedral of the vast array of crosses, images, and altars Neercassel had installed, publicly burning a massive heap of them in the same churchyard where Catholics had burnt the Protestant pews and pulpits sixteen months before. Utrecht cathedral was promptly re-inaugurated for Calvinist worship with a public thanksgiving, presided over by Cornelis Gentman (1616–96), a vehement foe of Cartesians and

---

[117] Wicquefort, *Journael of dagelijcksch verhael* i, 212; Jessurun-ten Dam Ham, *Utrecht in 1672 en 1673*, 148.
[118] Wicquefort, *Journael of dagelijcksch verhael* i, 219, 228–9; Jessurun-ten Dam Ham, *Utrecht in 1672 en 1673*, 159; Yasuhiro, "Confessional Coexistence," 15; Van de Ven, "Crastina die loquar," 149.
[119] Rogier, *Geschiedenis* ii, 209–10; Spiertz, *L'Église catholique*, 125–7; Forclaz, "Rather French than Subject," 529; Totaro, "Congrégation de l'Index," 365.

Cocceians, demanding less toleration and stricter sabbath observance. To celebrate the city's liberation, this special Utrecht thanksgiving was to be repeated annually, from November 1673 onwards, until deep into the eighteenth century.[120] After Gentman's sermon, another triumphalist sermon resounded, preached by Dr De Lantman who offered some searing criticism of the conduct of the Utrecht regents, while yet another sermon celebrating the French evacuation was delivered by the now eighty-four-year-old Voetius himself. Voetius, Gentman, and De Lantman readily lent their authority to popular demands for a thoroughgoing purge of the presiding city regents and their allies, and their prompt replacement with men who "fear the Lord."[121]

Summer storms can be violent, but few were as terrible as the legendary occurrence at Utrecht, as well as The Hague and other Dutch towns on the last day of July and first of August 1674, the year following Spinoza's visit. Sir William Temple was at Bergen-op-Zoom, returning by boat from a diplomatic mission in the Spanish Netherlands when it struck, witnessing it less directly than the populace of The Hague, but on reaching Rotterdam, the morning after the event, found everyone's "mouths full of the mischiefs and accidents that the last night's tempest had occasion'd both among the boats and the houses, by the thunder, lightning, hail or whirlwinds."[122] At The Hague, the following day, he heard reports "from all parts, of such violent effects, as were almost incredible." At Amsterdam, "many trees were torn up by the roots, ships sunk in the harbor, and boats in the channels, houses beaten down, and several people snatch'd from the ground as they walckt the streets, and thrown into the canals."[123] In many places the thunder and lightning were accompanied by "hailstones of prodigious bigness."

"But all was silenc'd by the relations from Utrecht, where the great and ancient cathedral was torn in pieces by the violences of this storm; and the vast pillars of stone, that supported it, were wreath'd like a twisted club, having been so strongly compos'd and cemented, as rather to suffer such a change of figure, than break in pieces as other parts of the fabric did. Hardly any church in the town 'scap'd the violence of this storm, and very few houses," and everyone was awed by the partial collapse of the cathedral where Catholic worship had ended with Reformed worship restored. None doubted that so great a tempest stemmed from wickedness, impiety, and sin, but whose wickedness, and whose sin? The occasion doubtless merely confirmed for Spinoza that the common way of interpreting the world, when imagining destructive things like "storms, of course, earthquakes, diseases etc.," to be due to "the gods being angry because of wrongs done to them

---

[120] GA Utrecht vroedschapsresoluties 2/121, res. 21 Nov. 1729.
[121] GA Utrecht Kerkeraad 10. Res. 13 Nov. 1673; Roorda, "Utrechtse regeringsreglement," 110; Israel, *Dutch Republic*, 664, 673, 791.
[122] Temple, *Memoirs*, 39–40.   [123] Temple, *Memoirs*, 41.

by humans, or faults incurred in their worship," only strengthens the prejudiced in their superstition, as the *Ethics* expresses it, even though their own everyday experience contradicts this.[124]

Conventional religion, held Spinoza, rests chiefly on ignorance and superstition but also thirst for power and man's "insatiable greed." Following the French evacuation, segments of the Reformed community started a concerted agitation, with Gentman's and De Lantman's encouragement, drawing up a petition claiming the "old regents" had badly mismanaged the city's and the province's affairs, neglected the public church, permitting an "excessive" toleration of and compromise with Catholics.[125] The agitation helped lay the basis for William III's successful campaign to transform the provincial institutional structures of Utrecht, Gelderland, and Overijssel during early 1674, and permanently strengthen the Stadholder's political grip in all three of these provinces.[126]

Louis XIV was humiliatingly pushed back. But the ensuing peace talks, Thévenot noted regretfully, writing to Graevius from Paris,[127] stalled yet again while the French remained pinned to a defensive two-front war against the Dutch, Spain and the emperor, and soon found themselves deserted by their English allies. After November 1673, information about conditions in Utrecht percolated through to Paris only via special channels, including Graevius' letters to Thévenot, that became more and more precarious and slow. For months all contact was interrupted between the *Collegie der Sçavanten* and Stouppe who was stationed, during the summer of 1674, with the French forces on the Hainaut border, near Ath. But in July 1674, a letter from Stouppe to Graevius, sent from near Ath, implored him to resume corresponding, promising he could do so without danger as he, though a French commander, wanted only public and scholarly news and "nothing that might be prejudicial to your state." "Feeling deep regret at seeing the desolation of your province, I would feel great joy to learn of its revival." Stouppe especially wanted to hear of the response to *La religion des Hollandois* and whether a recent reply, an anonymous text, vilifying Louis and defending the Dutch, appearing earlier in 1674 but much shorter than Braun's, published in German and "full of insults and invective" against himself and the French soldiery, had appeared yet in French. Braun's rebuttal was published only some months later. Stouppe ends his letter to Graevius expressing regret on learning that the worthy Van Velthuysen had been stripped of his position.[128]

---

[124] Spinoza, *Ethica* in *Oeuvres* iv, 152–3.
[125] Van Kleveren, "Utrecht zonder regeering," 98; De Bie, Lindeboom, and Itterzon, *Biografisch Wordenboek* v, 578; Nauta, "Gisbertus Voetius," 448.
[126] Israel, *Dutch Republic*, 814–18.
[127] RL Copenhagen MS Thott 1266/4. Thévenot to Graevius, Paris, 28 Dec. 1674.
[128] RL Copenhagen MS Thott 1266/4. Stouppe to Graevius, from the French army camp near Ath, 1 July 1674; Patoir, "Polemic Pamphleteering," 30, 55–7.

The States General in The Hague had already decided, prior to the French evacuation, to suspend all the branches of Utrecht's city and provincial government—States, delegated States, Hof, *ridderschap* and city government—pending official investigation, conducted by the Stadholder, into their conduct under occupation.[129] With the States troops arrived a States General commission, headed by Fagel, that immediately disbanded the existing city government, stripping all the sitting regents of their positions temporarily or, as with Van Velthuysen and Nieuwstad, permanently, resulting in a power vacuum that continued until April 1674, when a new, heavily Orangist and Reformed city government was inaugurated. With Utrecht under Dutch military administration during the interim, passionate, vitriolic confessional, ideological, and party-factional strife surged up more stridently than ever.

The "Louvesteynsche factie" were thoroughly purged by William and Fagel from the city government. Important changes to the life of city and province inevitably followed from this, as there was much that Orangists and Voetians had long resented. The advances of the Catholic Church in Utrecht, in 1672–3, were in part reversed, the board of trustees dispensing aid put back exclusively under Reformed control, and the old discriminatory system of administering civic poor relief restored.[130] Poor Catholics and Remonstrants were again, as before 1672, left depending on their own communities for support. Another aspect of the reconfessionalizing reaction of late 1673, was the total extinguishing of the *Collegie der Sçavanten* which at this point permanently ceased its meetings. But despite such changes at the edges, the reality was that William largely refrained from fulfilling Voetian wishes as far as cracking down hard on Catholicism and Arminianism was concerned. Indeed, by the mid-1670s it was clear, as was reported to the Doge and Senate of Venice, that Dutch Catholics since 1672 had overall greatly improved their position in the United Provinces. This was because the Stadholder knew he had only succeeded in thwarting Louis and Charles, and secured the Republic owing to the support of the emperor and Spain, making it highly inadvisable for him to conduct himself as if the Dutch were engaged in a war of religion.[131] But the Stadholder's very inability to crack down on Catholicism meant the Dutch Cartesians and dissident religious sects were now all the more apt to become the scapegoats.[132] Somebody had to be thrown to the lions.

Relations between Spinoza and the Cartesians, accordingly, or at least some of them, now permanently improved. Van Velthuysen and Spinoza clearly felt they now had more in common than before 1673. Where, back in 1671, Spinoza

---

[129] Van Kleveren, "Utrecht zonder regeering," 98, 100–3.
[130] Spiertz, "Jansenisme," 157; Yesuhira, "Confessional Coexistence," 15–16.
[131] *Calendar of State Papers Venetian* 38 (1673–5), p. 342.
[132] Gootjes, "Collegie der Sçavanten," 181–2.

reacted angrily to Van Velthuysen's cutting criticism, complaining of "how perversely he has misinterpreted my meaning – whether from malice or ignorance, I cannot say," from 1673 his attitude changed noticeably.[133] "Whilst Spinoza was alive," attested Van Velthuysen later, "I had many conversations with him" both in Utrecht, in 1673, and afterwards.[134] Spinoza came to recognize him as one of the few commentators who understood the *TTP* and whose judgement he could genuinely respect. The two henceforth conferred closely together. Spinoza's one post-1673 surviving letter to Van Velthuysen, written in 1675, consequently is far friendlier and more respectful than his angry initial response sent indirectly, via his letter to his Rotterdam Collegiant friend, Jacob Ostens, of 1671. To an extent, the two did become allies behind the scenes.

Among letters Graevius received from Paris during the weeks after Spinoza's departure was one from Thévenot, the famed Parisian impresario of science and travel to whom he was close: "what has become of that fanatic who wants to reform the world? [Qu'est devenu de ce fanatique qui veut réformer le monde?]," he inquired, wanting to know the outcome of Spinoza's visit. Thévenot and Graevius entirely agreed that Spinoza stood no chance whatever of "reforming" the world,[135] was overambitious and in this respect indeed a "fanatic," but, for all that, his arguments were such that he had become a permanent factor in both their lives and indeed the intellectual life of all Europe, and one that fascinated them.

---

[133] Spinoza, *Collected Works* (ed. Curley) ii, 460–1; Gootjes, "Tussen vriendschap en vijandschap," 19.
[134] Velthuysen, *Opera omnia* i, p. v; Gootjes, "Tussen vriendschap en vijandschap," 29n26.
[135] RL Copenhagen MS Thott 1266, 4, Thévenot to Graevius, Paris, 19 April 1675.

35
Expanding the Spinozist "Sect"

35.i "Vile, Godforsaken Atheists"

Myths and rumour played a strikingly large part in shaping Spinoza's life and legacy. Although there is no evidence confirming that when Spinoza crossed the "water-line" entering French-occupied territory, in July 1673, he was really entrusted with high-level secret communications from The Hague, in the service of the Republic, as some surmised at the time, or went to meet the commander of Louis XIV's invading French army, Condé, at the latter's request, the trip to Utrecht was nonetheless an expression of engaged and subtle activism. Venturing forth into a danger zone, Spinoza crossed the water-line dividing the French from the remaining Dutch defences, carrying safe conducts from both the French and Dutch sides, and stayed for a time at Utrecht ignoring highly unpleasant rumours rife back at The Hague insinuating that he was engaging in some treasonable activity, conniving with the French.

Spinoza's activism was of a different kind from that of others: he wanted to persuade selected intellectually inquiring individuals to join him in the work of weakening religious authority, reducing persecution, advancing toleration and personal liberty, and fomenting awareness that true citizenship and pursuit of happiness progress only where ecclesiastical direction is cut back and a broader-based republicanism promoted. At Utrecht, Spinoza held long discussions with Stouppe, Graevius, Van Velthuysen, and other republican-minded regents, sounding them out and evaluating the scene while explaining what he hoped could be achieved in the near future by way of blunting the surging Dutch anti-Cartesian reaction and the pretensions of the Calvinist clergy, at a crucial moment prior to the French finally being forced to evacuate the great swathes of the Republic that they had conquered.

But perhaps the most erroneous and distorting of all the myths surrounding Spinoza's life was that which persisted uncritically accepted, generation after generation, becoming a strangely fixed illusion among nineteenth- and twentieth-century academics and political scientists. This was the deeply entrenched notion that "for practical purposes," as one scholar expresses the old trope, "we can disregard [Spinoza's] direct historical influence," because he did not have any, being a "proponent of views which had no real effects in their time."[1]

---

[1] Mason, *God of Spinoza*, 248; for more discussion on this, see Schröder, "Spinozismus in der deutschen Frühaufklärung?"

It would be hard to be more fundamentally mistaken than that. Today, an abundance of evidence shows this deeply rooted, long prevalent and widely accepted mythology, repeated innumerable times, is not just totally wrong but may well have originated in conscious, late seventeenth- and eighteenth-century Enlightenment designs to occlude or erase the clandestine, forbidden anti-religious philosophical underground from men's entire picture of the Early Enlightenment and screen out Spinoza from the record as far as possible as a way of reinforcing the hegemony and promoting the myth of a largely uncontested, universally embraced Lockean-Newtonian "moderate Enlightenment" built on the harmonizing compatibility of science and religion, and of philosophical reason with faith.

The picture that Voltaire later enthusiastically subscribed to of a Western Enlightenment that originated entirely in English ideas and influences, especially English empiricism, inspired by Locke and Newton above all, long exerted a powerful and uncontested allure. But it could remain uncontested only as long as one refrained from consulting the numerous passages in texts of the last quarter of the seventeenth century and opening years of the eighteenth by Steno, Stouppe, Van Velthuysen, Van Blijenbergh, Orobio, Kuyper, Bontekoe, Bekker, Aubert de Versé, Poiret, Bayle, Deurhoff, Leydekker, Halma, Hassel, the *Philopater* novel, Van Til, Limborch, Spandaw, Burman, Bredenburg, Aalstius, Basnage, Roëll, Koelman, Le Clerc, Tuinman, Baxter, More, Simon, Van Leenhof, Earbery, Samuel Clarke, Toland, Collins, Nieuwentijt, and Boulainvilliers, not to mention Leibniz and a mass of German writers, bearing emphatic witness to Spinoza's unprecedented, uniquely pervasive pre-eminence as head of a far-reaching underground movement of crucial international importance. All of these figures emphasize Spinozism's powerfully unsettling international impact in his own time, and the next decades, via a forbidden but widespread clandestine intellectual movement shaped around him and the stunning "effect" of his ideas.[2]

Stouppe's *Religion des Hollandois* (1673) was merely the first of a series of books documenting Spinoza's pervasive intellectual presence first within the Netherlands but soon also outside, a disturbing phenomenon emphatically confirmed by the Vicar Apostolic of the Catholic Church in the United Provinces, Neercassel, in 1678, as we shall see, when writing to the papal envoy in Brussels about the problem of this menacing "sect" based on Spinoza's writings and ideas. For Bernard van Nieuwentijt (1654–1718), among the leading Dutch writers on the relationship of science, mathematics, religion, and philosophy of the early eighteenth century, Spinoza was not simply the number one "atheist" of the age but also the one whose "followers" and "disciples" posed the greatest threat to

---

[2] Israel, *Enlightenment Contested*, 372–3.

higher education and society.[3] On studying Spinoza's arguments, noted Van Velthuysen, not long after Spinoza's death, "many men who are neither wicked nor stupid," abandoned their Christian faith in a providential God presiding over His Creation through accepting Spinoza's views.[4] The Enlightenment that these followers adopted and diffused was very different from that of Locke, Newton, and Voltaire.

Stouppe's dramatic revelation, in 1673, may not have been news in Holland, but certainly was at the time in France, England, Italy, and Switzerland with which he had close connections, and much of the rest of Europe. Thévenot, in Paris, despite being far better informed than most, was greatly surprised, he assured Graevius, in December 1674, that Spinoza "has found adherents in a country like yours where there are lots of wise people," remarking that, here, in France, by contrast, so far no one "had heard talk of this *fanatique* [Spinoza]." The contrast between France and the Netherlands in this regard at this point was indeed striking. With the war dragging on, neither the *TTP* nor Spinoza's ideas more generally registered significant progress in France (unlike Germany), until 1678, when, with the Franco-Dutch war (1672–8) at an end, Spinoza's breakthrough commenced finally also there. Curious about all novelties, and familiar with pre-1670 Holland, Thévenot was uniquely placed as far as French receptivity to Spinoza and his sect were concerned. "You will oblige us very much," he urged Graevius that December, when sending best wishes also from the Stouppe Brothers (though the "one who wrote *La Religion des Hollandois*" was still absent with the troops on the frontier), "if you will write to us about what ensued" with regard to Spinoza and his *sectateurs*. Graevius sent his salutations back to Thévenot and the Stouppes, in France, along with further word about Spinoza.[5]

In terms of published works, Stouppe was the first to present Spinozism as a spreading subversive sect representing a universally dangerous challenge to the accepted ideas of the age. But in terms of communicating a dire warning internationally behind the scenes, he was long preceded by Spinoza's former friend Steno (who indeed, via his friend Neercassel, may have been one source of Stouppe's observations). Despite Spinoza's following being anti-church, hidden and furtive, Steno detected traces of it early on even in Denmark, he found to his consternation, when visiting his homeland, in 1671.[6] Spinozism threatens every aspect of a Christian society, Steno assured the Inquisition authorities in Rome, confidentially, in 1671, and was a sect diffusing widely. He himself, he explained, had only come to recognize this after a certain time. Before renouncing Lutheranism, during his years at Leiden (1661–3), he admitted, he himself had

---

[3] Nieuwentijt, *Regt Gebruik der Werelt Beschouwingen*, 1, 6, 10; Nieuwentijt, *Gronden van Zekerheid*, 244–5.
[4] Velthuysen, *Tractatus de cultu naturali*, dedication.
[5] RL Copenhagen MS Thott 1266/4. Thévenot to Graevius, Paris, 28 Dec. 1674.
[6] Steno, "Libri prohibiti," 35.

been friendly with Spinoza and only slowly come to realize the implications of this atheist's views, perceiving Spinoza's "new philosophy" as a dire "contagion" usurping the role of revealed religion by undermining ordinary men's simple faith, and encouraging a seductive intellectual pride claiming the exclusive path for humans to become free and happy lies in study, philosophizing, and striving through science and philosophy to understand the "nature of things."

Insidiously promoted, Spinozism is socially as well as morally devastating, Steno explained to the Inquisitors, diverting men from faith and devotion to the Church while affording no consolation to the poor, illiterate, ignorant, and wretched, those knowing little or nothing making up the vast bulk of the world's population. Spinoza's philosophy, explained Steno, places trust and hope in science and scholarship instead of Christ and, by so doing, divides humanity into two widely separated categories, the unknowing mass and those with supposedly "adequate ideas" holding that there is only "one substance in the universe infinite and eternal," a clique with an overly high opinion of themselves, indulging, he discovered in Amsterdam and Leiden, in sensual pleasures like sipping wine and smoking tobacco along with their intellectual endeavours. Such self-indulgent conduct Spinoza's followers consider the true path to individual freedom and happiness. Consequently, they attend church only to scoff at sermons among themselves and laugh at the ignorance of the multitude, the great majority whose minds Spinoza's disciples consider full of "inadequate ideas." To Spinozists, "the multitude" whether aristocrats, merchants, or poor men, are "slaves of their appetites," slaves to common (i.e. deluded) thinking, slaves condemned to lifelong misery unless they break free via their master's philosophy. Adherents of this hateful seditious movement, forged from Spinoza's writings, conversation, and activity, trust they can "render the enslaved free" via their path to "reason," though "this is difficult," he and his disciples confess, "and not for all men."[7]

One among those Steno knew Spinoza had converted to his "pagan" sect but whom he himself afterwards succeeded, some years later, in 1673, in retrieving for Christ, in Italy, was the son of a leading Amsterdam regent family, Albert Burgh (c.1650–1708). As a student at Leiden, Burgh had been brought into the Spinozist fold, in the late 1660s, and had greatly admired Spinoza for his penetrating intellect and love of truth, as he himself admits, in his 1675 letter urging his former mentor to abandon his philosophy and seek his redemption instead in religion. At one point, Spinoza recalls in his reply to Burgh, referring to the late 1660s, "when we talked about Steno, in whose footsteps you now follow," and Steno's rejecting Spinoza's views, Burgh had warmly approved Spinoza's counter-arguments. So firmly was he then within Spinoza's orbit that his subsequent conversion to Catholicism was something Spinoza "could hardly believe when

---

[7] Steno, "Libri prohibiti," 34–5; Totaro, "Ho certi amici," 33, 36n6.

others told me about it," until he heard it from Burgh himself. Writing from Florence, in September 1675, Burgh exhorted his former hero, whom he now lambasted as a "wretched little man," "base little earthworm," "food for earthworms puffed up with pride," to forsake his wretched philosophy and acknowledge his quest for truth to be diabolical delusion. In his reply, Spinoza also mentions having discussed Burgh's letter with other close allies and friends, and that it was they who persuaded him to answer Burgh which, initially, he (characteristically) felt disinclined to do.

Burgh's evidence for his new vision of truth was not that of documents, or historical argument, but the common belief and virtue of so many thousands of ordinary people expressing their faith with such certainty, the overwhelming impressiveness of simple piety and faith itself. Like Steno, Burgh too now sought to retrieve Spinoza for Catholicism, entrapped and deceived by the Devil and filled with arrogance though he was. Burgh's chief concern, though, in his long missive was not to convert Spinoza but rather "to call upon you not to persist in corrupting others."[8] Spinoza, besides reminding Burgh that his own ancestors "in the time of the duke of Alva," with great "constancy and freedom of mind, suffered all kinds of torture for the sake of religion," mocked his conversion and his now recognizing the reality of Satan, his "dreaming of a prince, an enemy of God who in spite of God's will to the contrary, leads most men astray and deceives them, good men being rare." Why would an omnipotent God permit the Devil to deceive men with impunity?[9]

And how did Burgh know he had found the best religion? "Have you examined all the religions, ancient and modern, taught here and in the Indies and everywhere throughout the whole world?" When the prominent English thinker Henry More (1614–87) read Spinoza's reply to Burgh's letter, two years later in 1678, he reacted with deep indignation despite his strong prejudice against Catholicism: "so does [Spinoza] insult that youth who has relinquished his philosophical nonsense, not to say atheistic errours, and embraced a Christian faith, though admittedly, by no means sufficiently reformed."[10] At issue here was an early form of Enlightenment clashing head-on with the first glimmerings of counter-Enlightenment. In Steno and Burgh, we find not just the earliest testimony to the impact of Spinoza's sect but also of the anti-intellectual *anti-philosophisme* and admiration of simple pious folk, of those urgently seeking to counter Spinoza without employing arguments drawn from scholarship or science, readily conceding the uselessness of attempting to combat Spinoza and his following with

---

[8] Spinoza, *Collected Works* (ed. Curley) ii, 450, 473; Curley, "Spinoza's Exchange," 11–12; Rogier, *Geschiedenis* ii, 737.
[9] Spinoza, *Briefwisseling*, 410–12; Spinoza, *Collected Works* (ed. Curley) ii, 474–6.
[10] Jacob, *Henry More's Refutation*, pp. xxx–xxxi.

reasoned argument. Burgh spent the rest of his life in Italy, steadfastly adhering to his new creed, dying in Rome, in 1708.

The correct response to Spinoza, held Steno and Burgh, was to combine the ordinary man's uncorrupted religious fervour with the Inquisition's weapons, censorship and repression, the tools for repressing clandestine "philosophy" outright. Backed by the beliefs, needs, and straightforward common sense of the masses, the Inquisition's methods could efficiently block and suppress philosophy rejecting belief in the supernatural, miracles, sacraments, angels, devils and the prince of deception, the Devil. Still, philosophy too, could be marshalled against Spinoza. If Burgh's main point was that the truth of Christ crucified backed by "countless miracles and signs" overrides everything else, it was surely significant too, he taunted Spinoza, that all other philosophers disagreed with his views "except for your disciples."

If, for Steno and Burgh, common belief proves Christ crucified surpasses all else as regards what we know, for them it was equally common belief that proves the reality of "the things wrought by witchcraft and enchantments by mere utterance of certain words, or simply by carrying certain words or signs on some material, or indeed the astonishing phenomena presented by those possessed by demons."[11] Like the anti-intellectualism issuing from Rousseau's pen during the Late Enlightenment era, the culture wars raging in the last years of Spinoza's life appealed, not least through the writings of Kuyper, to the yearning and notions of uneducated "simple souls" with their truer, more genuine grasp of truth than that afforded by "philosophy" and science. The illiterate faith of the God-fearing labouring peasant exalted in such vernacular dialogues as Kuyper's *Den Philosopherenden Boer* [The Philosophizing Peasant] of 1676 had now itself became a force in philosophical debate. A near universal belief swaying such vast masses must, it seemed to many, be a manifest truth. Spinoza's not believing what the great majority believes was, for Burgh as for Henry More, in England, a form of madness.

If one can deny Christ crucified on the basis of Spinoza's arguments, holds Burgh, one might just as well deny the "ancient Romans ever existed, and that the Emperor [sic] Julius Caesar, after he crushed the freedom of the Roman Republic, changed their government into a monarchy."[12] Closing his letter, Burgh exhorts Spinoza, should he require still further overwhelming historical evidence proving him wrong, to consider the reality manifest everywhere that the Jews of their day were utterly downtrodden, as he had seen throughout Italy, and to "weigh also the terrible and unspeakably severe punishment by which the Jews have been forced down to the utmost degree of wretchedness and disaster, because they were the

---

[11] Spinoza, *Collected Works* (ed. Curley) ii, 441–2, 445, 450.
[12] Spinoza, *Collected Works* (ed. Curley) ii, 446.

authors of Christ's crucifixion."[13] What greater proof of the truth could there be than Jewish humiliation and degradation, proof nobody can deny, a truth everyone sees everywhere is true?

Within a quarter of a century the phenomenon Stouppe in 1673 could depict as a bizarre and shameful local peculiarity, a Dutch quirk barely known to the world beyond, had become a ubiquitous international menace. The Zeeland Reformed minister Willem Spandaw, writing in 1700, reviewing the entire history of the world's "godlessness" from the Greek thinkers through the Italian Renaissance to Vanini, concludes: "however no one brought godlessness to a higher peak, placing it on the throne and erecting its banners everywhere, than the cunning Spinoza. France, England – the cadet-school of monstrous opinions – and yes the Netherlands too beside other lands produce a countless horde who adore him as something wondrous. The greatest minds have imbibed his views and, without fear, openly proclaim themselves atheists."[14] By Spandaw's time what was most disturbing about the "harmful propositions of Spinoza," Dutch observers felt, mattering more than any other aspect of his impact, was that his views "concerning religion and politics" were more and more seeping into society and gaining an active following.[15] Loyalty to the House of Orange and religion, consequently, were suffering dreadful setbacks. "That there are now," held one observer, a son of the Utrecht theology professor Burman, "many *Spinozisten*, that is vile, Godforsaken atheists, in our Fatherland, and in some principal cities even meetings held by such pests of the state and all good morals, so that under the mask of discussing philosophy Spinoza's chief principles and atheism are callously inculcated into undisciplined and stupid youth is, as everyone knows, all too true."[16]

What Stouppe in 1673 styled a local challenge eliciting no proper response from the Dutch, a decade later was recognized as a universal challenge requiring an energetic, urgent response from all. The French Socinian Noel Aubert de Versé (1645–1714), living in Amsterdam from 1679 to 1687, when dedicating his best-known book, *L'Impie convaincu*, to the French ambassador at The Hague, the Comte d'Avaux, painted a dramatic picture as early as 1684. Celebrating the count's role in concerting the Peace of Nijmegen (1678) finally ending the Franco-Dutch conflict, Aubert implored him to help conclude also a new and very different kind of war, Europe's spiralling conflict between reason and faith. The ambassador must assist all Christendom fight the atheistic tide now making "furious ravages by means of Spinoza [de furieux ravages par moyen de Spinoza]" and help apply the urgently needed "contrepoison [counter-poison]."[17] Anti-Christianity was being mobilized, he maintained, by a

---

[13] Spinoza, *Collected Works* (ed. Curley) ii, 447.
[14] Spandaw, *Bedekte Spinosist ontdekt*, "Opdragt"; Schröder, "Spinozam tota armenta," 166–9.
[15] Burmannus, *'t Hoogste goede der Spinozisten*, 10, 12.
[16] Burmannus, *'t Hoogste goede der Spinozisten*, 20.
[17] Aubert de Versé, *L'Impie convaincu*, 10; Israel, *Radical Enlightenment*, 353–4.

philosophical system equating God with Nature and erasing all *supernaturalia* from men's consciousness. What was unprecedented, indeed staggering, Aubert pointed out, was that the philosophical intervention of a single, isolated, scorned individual could exert so great an impact on the entire world.

The essence of the intellectual "revolution" wrought by Spinoza was his replacing a world divided into natural and supernatural, a double reality in which philosophy and science were close allies, even subordinate helpmates, of theology with a world constituting a single reality governed by a single set of natural laws with nothing existing beyond those laws. Nature and the supernatural together dually constituting reality was the essence of science as Boyle, Oldenburg, Newton, and Locke understood it. By removing the divide between Creator and Creation, Spinoza forged a single observable reality where everything is governed by a single eternal body of rules accessible only via mathematical reason and measurable motion, a redefining of God and Nature rendering theology and the churches redundant and overthrowing all existing structures of authority religious, political, social, legal, educational, and scholarly.[18] In addition, admonished Steno, Burgh, and Kuyper, it meant abolishing a world where the illiterate and uneducated stand just as close to salvation, via sacraments and the clergy's intercession, as the most avid and erudite scholar, with everything most crucial in life hinging on belief, prayer, and submission. Under Spinoza's schema, having no proper grasp of philosophy means having no proper grasp of anything, no window on truth and salvation, protests Aubert, no path to a meaningful life, no means to rightly organize society, community, and politics. The cursed philosopher in question banishes men from all proximity to blessedness and access to truth.

The resulting spiritual-intellectual crisis inevitably provoked a powerful backlash with consequences already evident in Holland where Spinoza's revolution was patently aggravating the existing culture war surrounding Cartesianism. Admittedly, once the term "Spinozist" gained wide currency, labelling someone a "Spinozist" could readily become little more than an insulting term of abuse. The worthy Frisian Reformed preacher Balthasar Bekker (1634–98), a firm Cartesian but definitely no Spinozist, in the 1680s protested, even before he himself suffered from this prejudice, at how various individuals were being falsely and unjustly classified and condemned "among the ranks of the *Spinosisten*." Such abuse, complained Bekker, like the author of the *Philopater* novel in two parts (1691 and 1697), was demeaning and counterproductive as there was reason enough for alarm without base calumny and name-calling

---

[18] Some have interpreted this "revolution" as the seventeenth-century reversal of a proposed earlier "revolution" in the history of Western philosophy engineered by Philo and those who married Greek philosophy to revelation and theology in the first Christian centuries. For both a good presentation and questioning of this perspective see Fraenkel, "Maimonides' God," 169–70, 203–4; Fraenkel, *Philosophical Religions*, 28, 35–7.

distracting attention from the key issue while further deepening the split between Voetians and Cartesio-Cocceians.[19] Yet, such abuse, like McCarthyite denunciation of Communism in a later age, flourished only because it stemmed from a widely dreaded actual threat.

Spinoza "did not wish to lend his name to a sect," claimed the editors of the *Opera Posthuma*, owing to his supposed natural modesty and his own admonition in Part IV of the *Ethics* that whoever seeks to assist others by providing new insights ought not lend his name to a movement and sect so that all men might advance together towards attainment of the highest good. On this ground, adds Bayle, in his *Dictionnaire*, Spinoza's editors claimed to have indicated Spinoza's authorship on the title-page of the *Opera Posthuma* solely with the soon legendary code "B.d.S." Bayle remained unconvinced. In his view, Spinoza did not lack the ambition to found such a sect, and assuredly he was right.[20] At his end, Spinoza knew he had succeeded in fashioning a substantial, perhaps lasting movement of clandestine subterranean character, relying on furtive methods of communicating, one that had become an established and feared tendency. Yet, despite having long laboured, cautiously, for such an outcome, he cannot possibly have guessed on his deathbed, in 1677, the momentum his movement would soon acquire, in the wake of the *Opera Posthuma* and the 1678 French translation of the *TTP*, immediately following his death.

During the 1670s, opponents could still hope Spinoza's early impact would quickly subside. For a time, it remained a general tactic internationally as far as possible not to draw attention to the names "Spinoza" and "Spinozism," in this respect emulating the Jewish community where these names were officially unmentionable and banned. But by the early 1680s, efforts to screen out Spinoza's name and persona, it was evident, were fast losing their rationale. Even the Jews' own sturdy wall against Spinozism's diffusion in line with the 1656 *herem* outlawing Spinoza's teachings and writings along with his person— rabbinic prohibition forbidding discussion of his legacy and texts, or mentioning his thrice cursed name—functioned meaningfully only whilst Spinoza's impact, books, and adherents remained within certain bounds. It could not work once the barriers were extensively breached, and this was certainly the case by the 1680s, remarked the leading Dutch Jewish physician of the day, Isaac Orobio de Castro (c.1617–87).

On settling in Amsterdam, Orobio, a crypto-Jewish fugitive from Spain, remained for the rest of his life a bulwark of Jewish orthodoxy and ally of the rabbis. Polemicizing against Christian theologians in manuscript and discussion, Orobio fiercely repudiated both Christianity and every heresy within Judaism. Yet, over many years Orobio wrote nothing at all against Spinoza, in conformity with

---

[19] [Duijkerius], *Het Leven van Philopater*, 50; Siebrand, *Spinoza and the Netherlanders*, 73n164.
[20] Bayle, *Écrits sur Spinoza*, 89–90.

the ban. When finally he broke his silence, he felt obliged to explain why he was doing so. Spinoza's philosophy, he had long believed, posed no great threat to society, not because Spinoza's philosophy was not pernicious, unquestionably it was, but because Spinoza's writings appeared to him too abstruse for the unlettered and too fallacious for the learned. But experience now showed that he had misjudged. Contrary to expectation, Spinoza was after all penetrating widely, not just among the Latin-reading public but also well beyond, including among the Sephardic community. Amidst the mounting intellectual and spiritual crisis of the 1680s, it had become undeniable that some ordinary folk *were* being contaminated by Spinoza's "pestilential dogmata," even glorying in them, and that throughout Europe some erudite men were surreptitiously embracing the outcast's "wretched doctrines."[21]

Orobio published his *Certamen Philosophicum* "against the atheist Espinosa," at Amsterdam, in 1684. This was the first Jewish attempt, but also among the earliest general attempts to refute Spinoza's core philosophical, as distinct from his Bible hermeneutical, principles, a fact celebrated in verse by Levi de Barrios.[22] Attacking Spinoza's system using scholastic arguments, Orobio especially targeted Spinoza's views on substance, divine Creation of the universe from nothing, and divine providence or the will of God who, holds Orobio, can will something, or not, as He pleases. By the mid-1680s, other eminent Jews also took to infringing the ban as far as studying Spinoza's writings and privately pondering and discussing his arguments were concerned, as for instance Rabbi David Nunes Torres (1660–1728), at The Hague who, as a young Sephardic scholar fascinated by Holland's mounting late seventeenth-century intellectual crisis, collected for his own personal library copies of the French and Dutch translations as well as the Latin *TTP*, along with the *Opera Posthuma*, *Philopater*, Colerus' biography, and the refutations of Melchior, Bredenburg, Van Blijenbergh, Aubert, and others.[23]

Down to the 1680s, most commentators on the *TTP* and the *Opera Posthuma*, both in and especially outside The Netherlands, persisted in evincing strong, if gradually eroding, inhibitions about mentioning the anonymous author's name, character, reputation, and oeuvre as a whole. Disinclination to attract attention to Spinoza the person, or enhance or inflate his status in any way, persisted in the immediate aftermath of the philosopher's demise, and for a time successfully preserved the wall of international outward silence about his name, life, and person. By the late 1680s and early 1690s, though, even if more notorious than famous, "Spinoza" had emerged among the most talked about names in the Republic. "Who Spinoza was and what heresy he followed," declares the

---

[21] Orobio de Castro, *Certamen Philosophicum*, 389; Israel, *Radical Enlightenment*, 307; Kors, *Naturalism and Unbelief*, 91.
[22] Levi de Barios, *Relación*, 286; Krop, *Spinoza, een paradoxale icoon*, 195–6.
[23] Kaplan, "Spinoza in the Library," 654–9.

Coccejan minister David Hassel, in his introduction to the 1695 Dutch translation of Wittichius' *Anti-Spinoza* (1690), for example, "I do not believe can be unknown to anybody." He left behind, he added, "a no smaller and no less public crowd of followers than the ablest Greek Sophist, adherents who, with their wanton nature and character, driven by the itching of their restless intellects, and thirst for fame, unwaveringly strive to inculcate the ruinous doctrines of their new master into everyone, spreading them far and wide. Furthermore, they succeeded, for within a short time this venom has spread through most of the Christian world and daily grows and creeps further and further."[24]

Critics both in and outside the Netherlands were thus eventually forced to abandon the early common strategy of leaving Spinoza's name and person as far as possible out of the picture. Bayle in particular transformed the scenario for good. His account of Spinoza's career, in his *Dictionnaire historique et critique* (1697), recounts how Spinoza actively sought new circles of friends and allies (without losing old ones) at successive stages of his life, positioning himself where he could most effectively win disciples and infiltrate his subversive ideas into society. His life, career, and disciple-winning activities fascinated and impressed the mature Bayle more perhaps than his philosophy, and this new phenomenon of the 1690s and the opening years of the eighteenth century, focusing on Spinoza's person, coincided with a further surge in diffusion of the *TTP* in the mid-1690s into vernacular languages—French, English, and via several different banned translations, Dutch—a diffusion fuelled by the appearance of the anonymous *Philopater* novels. But Bayle's *Dictionnaire* with its numerous articles locating signs of budding "Spinozism before Spinoza" in ancient thought, and Spinozist tendencies in medieval Islam, Confucianist China, and other exotic contexts, did more than anything else to irrevocably fix Spinoza's person, name, and following in European culture, enduringly establishing his image and standing for the rest of the Enlightenment era. But while Bayle affixed "Spinoza" to many more cultural contexts than had any previous writer, bringing his name and person fully into the limelight (his article on Spinoza was the longest in the entire *Dictionnaire*), as regards the revolutionary impact of Spinoza's ideas and their diffusion, he really did no more than summarize numerous earlier testimonies; essentially Bayle was just summarizing and broadcasting Steno, Stouppe, Orobio, Aubert, Bekker, Bontekoe, and the others profiling "Spinozism" in the 1670s and 1680s.

At no stage during his lifetime did Spinoza exert so huge an impact internationally as in the year following his death, with the publication of his major works, in late 1677, as many contemporaries affirmed. But, even prior to his death, Spinoza had long been a deliberate, calculating subversive, propagating his reformist doctrines gradually, forging what most contemporaries deemed a

---

[24] Hassel, "Voorreden," 1; Israel, *Enlightenment Contested*, 374.

godless, insidious philosophical movement. If Spinoza was "the most impious, most famous and at the same time most subtle atheist Hell has ever vomited onto the earth," declared Aubert de Versé, in 1684, the real challenge now was that philosophical error "every day makes [new] *Spinosistes*." The world had become a battleground between Spinoza and Christ who warns us "to guard ourselves against false teachers and false prophets who come to us in the humble dress of sheep but, underneath, are really ravishing wolves. Such a one was Spinoza who presented his atheism strictly under the appearance and colour of truth, or rather what today passes as such" in many a "Christian" college and university.[25] Not only did Spinoza forge "atheism" into a philosophical system for the first time, as Bayle taught his generation, but he lent it a distinctive vocabulary, set of expressions and terms, conferring on it a currency and plausibility atheism had lacked before.[26]

35.ii "Spinozism" Far from Being a Vague Category

This clandestine intellectual undercurrent creating such a stir in the Republic was variously termed *Spinozismus*, *Spinozisterij*, and even occasionally, as designated at the Synod of Gelderland, at Nijmegen, in August 1712, *Spinosistendom*.[27] As an underground movement and creed, *Spinozismus* was reportedly forged by individuals who either knew the thinker personally or whose lives were significantly affected by key members of his circle.[28] Contrary to what some scholars still today insistently but quite wrongly claim,[29] the term "Spinozism," moreover, was the very opposite of being just a vague term of abuse. Far from being vague and indeterminate, the early Enlightenment term "Spinozist" was rigorous, precise, comprehensive, and profoundly frightening. Besides not distinguishing between God and Nature, and denying the existence of Hell and the reality of all supernatural entities, including spirits, angels, demons, and Christ's resurrection, and mocking the idea of a Satan intervening in human life, four additional specific characteristics of the creed of "Spinoza and his following," held the younger Burman, stood out: firstly, the claim that the moral status of "religion is everywhere the same among all peoples, all having their prophets, so that honest men find no difference in basic values" between Christianity, Judaism, Islam, and for that matter Confucianism and Buddhism.[30] Second, was Spinozism's proclaiming

---

[25] Aubert de Versé, *L'Impie convaincu*, 3–4; Kaplan, "Spinoza in the Library," 659.
[26] Raats, *Korte en Grondige Betoginge*, 14.
[27] ARH NHK Oud Synodaal Archief 86, Synod of Gelderland, Acta Nijmegen Aug. 1712, art. "Liciencieus boekdrukken."
[28] Wielema, *March of the Libertines*, 81.
[29] Here, a whole series of French scholars have grounded themselves in serious error; Israel, *Enlightenment that Failed*, 927–8, 931, 936–7, 939–40.
[30] Burmannus, *'t Hoogste goed der Spinozisten*, 147–9, 244–95; Sluiter, *Overeenstemming*, 42–9.

a universal moral code, or civic religion, focusing on the pursuit of *'t Hoogste Goed* [the highest good], worldly happiness and establishing "peace and love in civil society" via reason alone, divorced from all revelation, faith and religious ceremonies, philosophical "reason" supposedly being man's sole path to salvation.[31] Third, was Spinoza's asserting freedom of judgement and expression, including the right to speak about religion however one likes as "a natural and unalterable right of man," rightly restricted by neither church nor state, a freedom of overriding importance to civil society.[32] The fourth permanent and damaging feature of "Spinozism" invading society was its proclaiming a total break with all past philosophy *and* theology—that is comprehensive dismissal of all philosophy *and* theology prior to Spinoza as fundamentally erroneous.[33]

A more detailed early account of Spinozism's core elements asserting the specific, concrete character of the movement was provided by Bekker in his *Short Account* (Amsterdam, 1683) of general church history since 1666, following on from the standard *Historia ecclesiastica* of Georgius Hornius (1620–70). In, or shortly after 1670, when he was around thirty-six (and Spinoza around thirty-eight), Bekker recounts meeting him in The Hague though he does not say whether he purposely called at Spinoza's lodgings (as subsequently reported by Bekker's detractors), or encountered Spinoza unexpectedly elsewhere. Not yet known for denying the existence of witches, witchcraft, and sorcery, Bekker was already famed for defending Cartesianism in his *De Philosophia Cartesiana* (1668), supporting Wolzogen, and opposing the strict Calvinist faction in the Reformed Church. Where Descartes undertook to reform philosophy in a thoroughly positive way, affirms his *Short Account*, Benedictus Spinoza, "a Portuguese Jew born in Amsterdam," permitted himself so much freedom philosophically that he was banished by his people. In his "first book, on the principles of Descartes, published in 1663, Spinoza still esteemed Descartes' disciples over adherents of other philosophers; but then, anonymously, he published his own very different thoughts in a book on freedom to philosophize, called the *Tractatus Theologico-Politicus*."[34] The authorship of the *TTP* "long remained unknown, or at least in doubt." From Amsterdam, Spinoza moved "to Rijswijk [sic]," Bekker incorrectly adds, "and from there to The Hague where, in conversation with me, he acknowledged that the said book was indeed by him." No one could fault his lifestyle, admitted Bekker: Spinoza lived quietly, earning his living by preparing all kinds of lenses needed for optical science: "I heard testimony from some who knew him and found in his presence no lack of uprightness or courtesy."[35] It was his ideas and following that were the problem.

---

[31] Burmannus, *'t Hoogste goed der Spinozisten*, 10–11, 49, 59–60; Verwer, *'t Mom-aensicht der atheisterey*, 61–3; Sluiter, *Overeenstemming*, 24–9.
[32] Burmannus, *'t Hoogste goed der Spinozisten*, 236–44; Sluiter, *Overeenstemming*, 56–9.
[33] Burmannus, *'t Hoogste goed der Spinozisten*, 4–6.   [34] Bekker, *Kort Begryp*, 39.
[35] Bekker, *Kort Begryp*, 39; Knuttel, *Balthasar Bekker*, 171–3.

Like Burman junior, Aubert de Versé, Bayle, and Leibniz, Bekker perceived nothing vague about the underground movement stemming from Spinoza's efforts. Quite the contrary. Spinozism's six "principal and most particular points," explains Bekker, were: (1) that there is no substance apart from God and that all created things are "modes, that is forms of God's existence;" (2) that the one existing substance has two main properties, extension and thought; (3) that everything depends on an infinite number of causes that follow from one another in an infinite order and in infinite ways; (4) that "nothing and no act is good or evil in itself," notions of good and bad being entities defined by society and its laws; (5) "the Holy Scriptures do not derive originally from God and the holy authors are mistaken in many things"; and (6) "miracles come about by natural causes and can be so explained." By 1683, Bekker had visited London and Paris as well as different parts of the United Provinces, so it is noteworthy that he then adds:

> one must admit that the opinions of Spinoza have spread all too far and too extensively through all parts and types of men and become rooted, including in the homes of the great, and that some of the best intellects are infected with them and that persons of very respectable lifestyle hold them as something divine, and have fallen into godlessness. Hence, the number of those professing religion and religious doctrine only to conform outwardly, from human rather than divine considerations, increases, and if that continues, God help us, what a blow through the heavy fall of such a mass will be given to the frame of God's house.[36]

Philosophy penetrating the common people's consciousness, even if among relatively few, undermining traditional forms of belief, is no longer simply a philosophy, observed several Dutch Reformed spokesmen at the start of the eighteenth century, but a new world outlook, morality, and lifestyle, in effect virtually a quasi-religion. As a would-be usurper of theology's age-old supremacy, "Spinozism" they envisaged as a menacing sect challenging ecclesiastical authority and religion as the presiding force in society. Even in its popular, diffused unsystematic format, insisted the Zwolle Reformed consistory when summarizing Spinoza's system as a current of thought during their inquiry into Frederik van Leenhof's writings in 1704, there was nothing whatever vague about "Spinozism," or *Spinozisterij* as they called it. Rather, it was a highly specific, concrete creed which the consistory handily summarized in seventeen points,[37] the first being that there is only one substance in the universe and that body and mind are one. Second, comes identification of this one substance with "God"; third, this one substance causes "everything that truly exists, so that everything is a manifestation of this one substance"; fourth, God and the totality of nature are hence identical;

---

[36] Bekker, *Kort Begryp*, 39; Koelman, *Het Vergift*, 9; Israel, *Enlightenment Contested*, 373.
[37] GA Zwolle, Acta kerkeraad KA 017/6. Res. Consistory 23 Oct. 1704.

fifth, one interactive, interlinked sequence of causes produces all natural effects, that is all effects, so that nature is autonomous and "an independent cause of itself and through a fixed necessity created and brought forth by itself [een independent oorzaak van zig zelve en door een vaste noodlottigheid van hare zelve gescheept en voortgebragt]," or by what today we might call natural evolution; sixth, "the human soul and body are one and the same thing, so that there are no souls detached from bodies, nor any angel, devil or ghost."

Popular Spinozism's seventh principle, recorded the Zwolle consistory, is that there is no absolute innate "good" and "evil," only what is relatively good and bad in relation to men, and that "sin" and "goodness" are just fabricated terms without reality "devised to hold ordinary ill-informed folk in thrall"; eighth, since everything happens by natural causes alone, men do not stand under the commandments of God as their true Lord and lawgiver; ninth, the theological Fall is nonsense, all men being always equally subject to their passions, so that there is no Original Sin; tenth, man has no free will but is always driven by external causes and, so far as he follows his passions, is a slave ceasing to be so only where he improves and, freeing himself via reason alone, perfects his understanding and, knowing the true order of things, submits to it, "hence making Holy Scripture and Christ's grace wholly unnecessary [waarom de H. Schriftuur neffens Christus' genaade gansch is onnoodig]." Eleventh, the highest good is simply pure understanding of God's eternal order, "conquering one's passions and maintaining oneself in cheerfulness and joy [de overwinning van zijn hersttogten en de behoudenis zijn zelfs met blijdschap en vroolijkheidt]." Twelfth, death in this world ends a person's life and dissolves his being so that there is no resurrection of bodies, or Last Judgement. Thirteenth, neither revealed nor natural religion exist in reality so that secular government alone should oversee all religious belief. Fourteenth, the Holy Scriptures have no more authority than "Plato, Aristotle, Epicurus, Seneca and such like moralists." Fifteenth, there is, though, a universal religion [algemeene godsdienst] which consists in freedom of all views concerning God's revelation and points of belief "apart from love of God and one's neighbour, and espousing grace (without Christ) and venerating justice and obedience to the sovereign and that therewith, whatever one believes, every sort of person is blessed and saved." Sixteenth, blessedness is the innate impulse of our nature to acquiesce in God's eternal order, or the positive working of nature on body and soul, enhancing man's capacity and effectiveness "whereby he graduates to an enduring happiness and the highest good [waardoor hij tot vaste blijdschap en het hoogtste goedt overgaat]." Seventeenth, it is permissible to lie when it is in the interest of conserving oneself to do so.

A further consequence of such principles, complained the younger Burman later, is cultural and social: scorn for the intellectually poorly equipped. This underground culture of the *Spinozisten* disdains all humans apart from themselves as stupid *weetnieten* [ignoramuses], exuding insufferable contempt in particular for churchmen.[38] The "Spinoza" of the early Spinozist sect remained a dynamic social-cultural phenomenon in the Netherlands, and Germany, France and England through roughly the first quarter of the following century. After the 1720s, though, the emerging Radical Enlightenment became less focused on the person and philosophy of Spinoza and, from the 1740s, a new phase began with the lead taken over by Diderot and the core *encyclopédistes*. Among the last admonitions of the early Enlightenment type deploring the specifically "Spinozist" underground was that of Jean Lévesque de Burigny (1692–1785), in his *Histoire de la philosophie payenne* (1724), where he reaffirms that Spinoza had indeed "attiré bien de gens après lui [drawn a lot of people after him]," with which Le Clerc fully concurred in his *Bibliothèque ancienne*.[39] After the 1720s, Spinoza's person and image receded, withdrawing for three or four decades into the background until the 1770s when Voltaire took to re-emphasizing Spinoza's centrality in Enlightenment thought, after which ensued a powerful resurgence of interest in his thought in Germany culminating in the so-called *Pantheismusstreit* of the 1780s revolving around Lessing, Mendelssohn, and Jacobi.

The striking failure of traditional twentieth-century historiography to acknowledge the early impact of Spinoza in a structured, specific way is attributable partly to failure to consult the relevant sources, but certainly also to the clandestine, masked nature of much of his early influence and his following, and thus partly results from the prolonged effort of the intellectual elite in the late seventeenth century prior to Bayle to avoid drawing attention to the detested "sect." In fact, obscuring Spinoza's name, personality and role was widely resorted to, for different reasons, by both opponents and promoters of his thought. The first major propagator of Spinoza's republicanism and view of miracles in England, for example, the so-called "deist" Charles Blount (1654–93), uses Spinoza's thought surreptitiously and subversively, only rarely mentioning Spinoza's name, keeping him apparently out of the picture but in fact entrenching him at its core, to help promote a deist-republican perspective on the English "Glorious" Revolution of 1688–91.[40]

35.iii A Sect Bred in the Universities and Professions

The sources attesting to the early impact of "Spinozism" whether Steno, Stouppe, Kuyper, Orobio, Bekker, Aubert, or Bayle tell us little about Spinoza's personal role in establishing this internationally vigorous early Enlightenment underground offering "true knowledge" of the path to happiness and freedom. In this

---

[38] Burmannus, *'t Hoogste goed der Spinozisten*, 140–3.
[39] Quoted in De Vet, "Spinoza en Spinozisme," 3.
[40] Prince, *Shortest Way with Defoe*, 25–6, 80, 164, 263n98, 204n14, 215.

regard, some additional comment offered in a rare tract of 1680 by the famous "tea-doctor," Dr Cornelis Bontekoe (c.1644–85) (Figure 35.1), renowned for prescribing astounding amounts of tea for practically every ailment, provides some useful additional information. In the existing literature on Spinoza's life, Bontekoe usually goes unmentioned or attracts just an isolated passing reference, even in the revised edition of Meinsma's *Spinoza et son cercle*, the most comprehensive survey of Spinoza's relations with his "circle." Yet, Spinoza, contends Bontekoe providing some detail, played a continually active role in establishing his underground sect, and spreading his subversive ideas in society.

Although he declared himself an outright adversary of the "monster" Spinoza, Bontekoe, by his own admission, often mixed with declared Spinozists and stands out as an intriguing witness to the movement's rise in Spinoza's last years and after his demise.[41] A passionate Cartesian, editor of the works of the Leiden philosopher Arnold Geulincx (1624–69), Bontekoe was a natural rebel, agitator, and

Figure 35.1 *Dr Cornelis Bontekoe* (1647–85), engraving. Reproduction courtesy of Rijksmuseum, Amsterdam.

---

[41] Israel, "Dr Cornelis Bontekoe's Views," 222.

polemicist. An orphan raised in impoverished circumstances, he enrolled at Leiden, in 1665, at the fairly advanced age of twenty-one, or older. Studying without income, he spent several unhappy years "without money and without books."[42] On graduating in medicine, he returned to his native Alkmaar, but his zeal for Cartesianism and medical reform provoked bitter quarrels with local doctors and apothecaries, and in 1670 he returned to Leiden planning to develop his aptitude for philosophy. Teaching private classes, he slowly worked his way from the University's fringes but found himself also increasingly at odds with the academic authorities due to his abrasive style of arguing and agitating for medical reform, stirring student unrest and harassing the anti-Cartesian professor Gerardus de Vries (1648–1705), leading to De Vries' resignation amid vehement protest, in 1674, and his much-publicized return to Utrecht.[43]

Bontekoe was accused of urging students to follow Descartes in systematically doubting everything, despite insisting while teaching, during the years 1674–5, or so he later claimed, "that Descartes never either practised or taught that one should doubt concerning God."[44] Editing Geulincx obliged Bontekoe to examine Spinoza's philosophy closely because elements of Geulincx's thought (and his own) converged, awkwardly, with aspects of Spinoza's system. Two particular difficulties that he and his "closest friend," Heydentrijk Overkamp (1651–94), faced was their claiming that movement is inherent in matter and that Descartes' views on motion and freedom of the will were incorrect. Overkamp rejected Descartes' conception of free will, and adhered to a form of determinism regarding the human will that he attributed also to his friend Bontekoe with whom he often discussed it.[45] In December 1675, the curators ordered Bontekoe to cease "holding all private classes and seminars" and no longer participate "in any lessons, disputations or other academic events."[46] Overkamp had his university dissertation quashed and burnt by the Leiden academic senate,[47] in 1677, for unacceptable propositions and was disciplined again by the academic authorities, in 1680, for insinuating in private classes that Jesus was just a person, his divinity, purity, resurrection after death and mission as the world's saviour being mere fables.[48]

---

[42] Van Ruler, "Spinoza in Leiden," 33–4.
[43] *Dialogue van een Groote Thee en Tobacq-Suyper*, 26–7; Israel, *Radical Enlightenment*, 479; Van Ruler, "Spinoza in Leiden," 34–5.
[44] Bontekoe, *Apologie van den Autheur*, 361–2.
[45] Van Ruler, "Spinoza in Leiden," 34–5; Leemans, *Het Woord is aan de onderkant*, 279; Krop, *Spinoza, een paradoxale icoon*, 115.
[46] *Dialogue van een Groote Thee en Tobacq Suyper*, 27; Thijssen-Schoute, *Nederlands Cartesianisme*, 224, 283.
[47] Bontekoe, *Reden Over de Koortsen*, 44, 47; Israel, "Dr Cornelis Bontekoe's Views," 223–4; Van Ruler, "Spinoza in Leiden," 33–4; Klever, "Clé d'un nom."
[48] Thijssen-Schoute, *Nederlands Cartesianisme*, 286–7; Israel, *Radical Enlightenment*, 310; Ottespeer, *Groepsportret [...] de Leidse Universiteit, 1673–1775*, 97.

In late 1675 or early 1676, Bontekoe moved to The Hague where, as a prominent physician intent on reforming medicine, he encountered Spinoza personally (while avoiding saying so in print) and, for a time, from 1676, frequently visited the old people's home immediately across the *Pavilioensgracht* from Spinoza's lodgings. Bontekoe and Overkamp, meanwhile, also rubbed shoulders with other members of the "Spinozist" sect, including a group in Utrecht. According to the well-known writer on ancient prostitution, the Zeelander Hadrianus Beverland (1650-1715), among the most notorious freethinkers of the age, there was, around 1680, a tavern in Utrecht where Spinoza's close friend, Abraham Johannes Cuffeler (*c*.1637-94) (who moved to Utrecht from The Hague, in 1674) "used to gather along with Overkamp and other atheists."[49] Cuffeler explicitly endorses Overkamp's formulation that "motum esse corpus ipsum extensum et indivisibile [motion is extended and indivisible body itself]" in his *Specimen artis ratiocinandi*, of 1683, a book published supposedly at "Hamburg" by "Henricus Kunraht," unmistakable code causing Cuffeler to be promptly labelled, as the *Nouvelles de la République des Lettres* remarked, "un disciple de Spinoza."[50]

Few doubted this anonymously published book on the art of reason by Cuffeler was "Spinozistic." The North Holland synod meeting at Hoorn, in August 1683, was warned by the Utrecht "correspondent" about this just published book where, under its "specious title, are advocated and defended the harmful principles of Spinoza."[51] The "brothers in Amsterdam" tried to uncover who published it and asked the burgomasters to ban the volume and seize it from the bookshops. But unlike Koerbagh, Cuffeler followed Spinoza also in carefully refraining from making any obviously blasphemous statements, and the burgomasters, after deliberating, took no action.[52] Despite their preachers' efforts in various towns, the North Holland synod, meeting at Enkhuizen in August 1684, lamented, "yet they could not strangle that (devil's) spawn at birth [doch dat gebroedsel in sijn geboorte niet konnen snoren]."[53]

Styling himself "an instrument for suppressing the peripatetic philosophy," Bontekoe's chief difficulty, philosophically, was that while continually eulogizing Descartes, "our great mind" and the "Prince of Philosophers," his actual stance failed to correspond to those of Descartes on several key issues. Agreeing Spinoza's system is fatal "poison," Bontekoe always maintained in his published work that Spinoza's teaching has "nothing in common with [that of] Descartes."[54] Where

---

[49] Siebrand, *Spinoza and the Netherlanders*, 108; Touber, *Spinoza and Biblical Philology*, 164; De Smet, *Hadrianus Beverlandus*, 48.
[50] [Cuffeler], *Specimen artis ratiocinandi* i, 3; Clair, "Spinoza à travers les journaux," 225; Van Ruler, "Spinoza in Leiden," 34.
[51] ARH NHK Oud Synodaal Archief 184, Acta 1683, Hoorn, 5 Aug., pp. 5-6.
[52] Wielema, "Onbekende aanhanger," 33n46; Van Bunge, *Spinoza Past and Present*, 154.
[53] ARH NHK Oud Synodaal Archief 184, Acta (August) 1684, p. 5.
[54] Bontekoe, *Brief aan Jan Fredrik Swetsertje*, 11-12; *DDPhil* i, 130.

Steno and others insisted on "how prejudicial Descartes' mechanical pretensions are to belief in God," Bontekoe maintained the contrary. But while officially "Cartesians," Bontekoe and Overkamp held certain positions that boldly departed from Descartes' teaching, thereby antagonizing genuine Cartesians along with Holland's recalcitrant mass of Galenists, Aristotelians, and Voetians.[55] Scrapping Descartes' *glandula pinealis* thesis and, like Steno and Spinoza years before, ridiculing Descartes' way of connecting body and mind while stressing the mind's "dependence" on the body and functioning of the heart, hence explaining moods and states of mind as determined by bodily states, was bound to strike readers as comparable to the "views of the damned Spinoza [sentimenten van den heylloosen Spinosa]" scandalously conflating body and mind.[56] Since reason is the sole criterion of truth, modifications and "a mass of experiments were requisite," held Bontekoe, before Descartes' system could be fully completed.[57] Both Bontekoe and Overkamp patently shared the Spinozist hope of seeing a wide-ranging programme of social and medical reforms, and weakening superstition and error of every sort.[58]

Bontekoe did his best to play down his divergences from Descartes—his holding that motion is inherent in matter, that extended substance is infinite not finite, mind and body are not separate spheres as Descartes contends, that human actions are all determined,[59] and lastly, his categorical separation of philosophy from theology.[60] But opponents continually highlighted these divergences, calling Bontekoe's discretion his "phariseesche hypocrisie." Menaced by Voetians lumping Cartesians and Spinozists together, strict Cartesians were bound to decry Bontekoe's rejection of key contentions of Descartes. Those Bontekoe styled "rigid" Cartesians retaliated by classing him among the "bastard Cartesians" [Bastart-Cartesianen] undermining true Cartesianism.[61] The only Cartesianism Bontekoe cultivated, suggests one pamphleteer, was that of the godless *Philosophia S. Scripturae Interpres*.[62]

Bontekoe picturesquely compared Cartesianism's rise since the 1640s to the Reformation, for Dutch Protestants the greatest moral, scholarly, and spiritual renewal since early Christian times. With artful malice, the Devil (in which opponents suspected he did not believe), had deliberately brought Spinoza into play, suggested Bontekoe, to wreck mankind's "new reformation" and undermine

---

[55] Bontekoe, *Vervolg van het eerste Deel*, A4, D5v; Bontekoe, *Reden Over de Koortsen*, B2.
[56] Bontekoe, *Tractaat van het excellenste kruyd thee*, 199–200; Israel, "Dr Cornelis Bontekoe's Views," 227.
[57] Bontekoe, *Tractaat van het excellenste kruyd thee*, 199–200.
[58] Overkamp, *Nader Ondersoek*, 96–7, 125, 128–9, 138–9; Thijssen-Schoute, *Nederlands Cartesianisme*, 300–1; Israel, "Dr Cornelis Bontekoe's Views," 223; Van Ruler, "Spinoza in Leiden," 36.
[59] Thijssen-Schoute, *Nederlands Cartesianisme*, 217–18, 310–11; Van Ruler, "Spinoza in Leiden," 34.
[60] Jorink, *Reading the Book of Nature*, 87–8.
[61] Bontekoe, *Vervolg van het eerste Deel*, dedicatie.
[62] *Dialogue van een Groote Thee en Tobacq-Suyper*, 47.

the "good work of the Cartesians, just as at the time of the Reformation [the Devil] brought Ian van Leyden, Knipperdolling, and others [i.e. Anabaptist radicals] into play." Just as Luther, when asked "his view of all that crowd at Münster," understood perfectly and "replied the Devil had brought them into play to render the Reformation suspect to many,"[63] so likewise, Satan brought "Spinoza onto the scene, disguised as a Cartesian, to betray the Cartesians, as the outcome has shown,"[64] a fanciful parallel striking Voetian adversaries as the acme of effrontery.[65] It was far from clear the aggressive, loud-mouthed Bontekoe was genuinely the loyal Cartesian and "Calvinist" he claimed to be—or even minimally a believer in Christianity (and Satan).[66]

Spinoza's person, activities, and books clearly fascinated Bontekoe, as they did Overkamp, Cuffeler, Van Balen, Beverland, Nieuwentijt, Bekker, Aubert, Bayle, and Basnage, something entirely natural in Bontekoe's case, given his conviction that "philosophy is the root of all the sciences" and that wrong philosophical premises were the reason, as he regularly asserted, that medical practice in Holland remained so lamentably backward.[67] Aristotelian scholastics he derided as "our hocus-pocus masters."[68] While publicizing himself as a fervently anti-Spinozist "Cartesian" advancing only "sound philosophy," furthermore, Bontekoe continually extended his familiarity with the underground Spinozist sect, not least in the tavern and café scene at The Hague and Utrecht. He openly admitted frequenting Spinozist gatherings, complaining that whenever someone like himself spends time conversing and arguing with "atheists," getting to know them and becoming familiar with their viewpoints in order to refute them more effectively, dull minds automatically suppose one is a "deceiver and atheist" oneself.[69]

Exploring "Spinozism" was bound to be misconstrued and create further difficulties for someone whose own reputation in orthodox circles was already suspect. But if caution was advisable, Bontekoe's unruly, impulsive temperament was impervious to caution. Warning of the dire threat posed by Spinozism, in the preface to his edition of Geulincx's *Ethics*,[70] in 1675, he denounced Spinoza's teaching as a pure naturalism rejecting everything "that elevates the soul and distinguishes man from the beasts."[71] Yet, opponents did not hesitate to label him too an "atheist." In his *Een Apologie van den Autheur tegens sijne Lasteraars* [Apology of the Author against his Slanderers] (1679), Bontekoe vowed to show the world, should God give time and opportunity, "what sort of atheist I am, when I write refuting that godless work of Spinoza [the *TTP*], and also those of Hobbes

---

[63] Bontekoe, *Brief Aen Johan Frederik Swetzer*, 45, 20.
[64] Bontekoe, *Brief Aen Johan Frederik Swetzer*, 20.
[65] *Dialogue van een Groote Thee en Tobacq Suyper*, 45; Israel, "Dr Cornelis Bontekoe's Views," 229.
[66] Van Ruler, "Calvinisme, cartesianisme, spinosisme," 26.
[67] Bontekoe, *Vervolg van het eerste Deel*, 5v.   [68] Overkamp, *Alle de medicinale* i, 4.
[69] Bontekoe, *Vervolg van het eerste Deel*, 38; Bontekoe, *Brief aan Jan Fredrik Swetsertje*, 13.
[70] *Dialogue van een Groote Thee en Tobacq-Suyper*, 45.
[71] Quoted in van Ruler, "Calvinisme, cartesianisme, spinosisme," 23–4, 28.

and Machiavelli, three of the damnd'est rascals the world has ever seen," and who—"were there not already an Antichrist in Rome—could pass for veritable anti-Christs, embodied devils fighting true religion, true philosophy and true [social] policy."[72] He never enjoyed that time and opportunity, destiny allotting him only a short time to live: in 1685, he severely injured himself falling down stairs, in Berlin, and died aged just thirty-seven.

Bontekoe's career in The Hague, from late 1675 to around 1681, reveals how profoundly Cartesian reform fervour then polarized the medical profession. The sick and dying Spinoza was hardly likely to consult the traditionalist majority medical faction. Ranged against them, in and around The Hague, were Bontekoe and his allies repudiating the old medicine, among them the father of Bernard Mandeville, Dr Michael Mandeville (1639–99), or "Dr Mandeviel," as Bontekoe calls him, a "famous doctor at Rotterdam [...] as experienced in his science as our men at The Hague are determined not to be."[73] Fiercely opposed to blood-letting and purging,[74] Bontekoe refused to accept that his pugnacious tone was excessive. "Is it outspoken that I call 'blind followers of Galen' those who, without doing research, uncritically follow his opinions? Is it outspoken that I call 'murderers and executioners' doctors who, whether from malice and knowingly, or through ignorance, cause the sick to die, or waste away, by prescribing the wrong medicines?"[75] Most of The Hague's physicians, Bontekoe relates, six or seven of them, were "upholders of the old views," with the "old sect" implacably opposed to "me and the truth."[76] This division of The Hague's medical men between conservatives and "Cartesians," further inflamed by Bontekoe's provocative rhetoric, paralleled the larger quarrel raging between the Voetians and Cartesio-Cocceians within the Reformed Church and theology faculties.

A today rare fifty-page polemical open letter by Bontekoe, dated The Hague, 22 July 1680, *A Short Apology for the great Philosopher Renatus Descartes and his Upright Followers* [*Tot een Korte Apologie voor den Grote Philosooph Renatus Descartes en sijne regtsinnige navolgers*], assails in particular his chief local adversary,[77] the militant Voetian alchemist and anti-Cartesian physician, Johann Friedrich Schweitzer (Johan Frederik Swetzer) (1630–1709), usually known— including to Spinoza—as Dr Helvetius. Originally from Anhalt, Helvetius had migrated to the Republic as a student, acquiring his doctorate at Harderwijk, in

---

[72] Israel, "Dr Cornelis Bontekoe's Views," 225.
[73] Bontekoe, *Vervolg van het eerste Deel*, 5v; Bontekoe, *Apologie van den Autheur*, 336.
[74] For Bontekoe's medical reformism, see Munt, "The Impact of Dutch Cartesian Medical Reformers" (PhD thesis, 2004), 59–72; Munt, "Impact of Dutch Medical Authors" (2001), 219, 221–7.
[75] Bontekoe, *Apologie van den Autheur*, 326.
[76] Bontekoe, *Vervolg van het eerste Deel*, dedicatie; Munt, "The Impact of Dutch Cartesian Medical Reformers," 67.
[77] Copy found in the Herzog August Bibliothek at Wolfenbüttel.

1653, with a dissertation on the plague. A "sworn enemy of all reason and understanding,"[78] according to Bontekoe, he long remained the unreformed ardent alchemist seeking ways to make gold whom Spinoza interviewed on this subject in 1667.[79] Shallow, to judge by his pamphlets, and steeped in alchemy, Helvetius nonetheless counted in the ideological strife raging at The Hague, being a well-known controversialist whose diatribes against Cartesianism, Cocceianism, Spinozism, and Bontekoe's medical reformism attracted attention.

In line with the wider Voetian campaign against the Dutch Cartesians in the 1670s, Helvetius' strategy was to lambast Cartesians, including Bontekoe, as abetters and harbingers of Spinozism, Spinoza's thought in his view being an offshoot of that of Descartes. Bontekoe's summoning the world to jettison the old learning, struck Helvetius as the very epitome of Cartesian intellectual arrogance. Helvetius and Bontekoe concurred about just one thing—both seeing Holland as hopelessly torn by philosophico-theologico-scientific cultural wars with wide-ranging implications for the future, leaving the old belief structures crumbling under the weight of Cartesianism which both deemed the prime engine of the intellectual revolution in progress.[80] The "Cartesianism" Bontekoe represented undermines piety, held Helvetius, denouncing his opponent as a dogmatist elevating philosophical reason above all else in human life,[81] for true Christian faith is not a matter of reason but of everything miraculous and wonderful that ordinary Christians believe. Bontekoe's stance merges soul with "thought" and body leaving no difference between his view and Spinozism.[82] Blame for the menace of the "Godforsaken Spinoza and his notorious disciples, the damned Beverland, the apostate P.v.B. and other such types" rests chiefly on the Cartesians.[83] Bontekoe and his friends were "ambassadeurs des antichristendoms Cartesii [ambassadors of Descartes' anti-Christendom]," infamous "Vanninische Bontekoedistens en Spinosistische Beverlandistens, ja een schuim van Aretinische Machiavellistens" [Vanninian Bontekoeists and Spinozist Beverlandists, yes a scum of Aretinian Machiavellians]."[84]

Spinoza's thought, retorted Bontekoe, diverges fundamentally from Cartesianism: "what Cartesian ever said the Books of Moses are fabrications [leugen-schriften], and miracles just natural occurrences?" No Cartesian ever utters such blasphemy, "and you foul slanderer," he challenges Helvetius, "will never offer even a single example." Spinoza's teaching, furthermore, was effectively refuted only by Cartesians, crushed "by Professor Van Mansvelt, and Van

---

[78] Thijssen-Schoute, *Nederlands Cartesianisme*, 292–3.
[79] Spinoza, *Briefwisseling*, 260, 480; Krul, "Haagsche en Amersfoortse krukkendans," 18–20.
[80] Helvetius, *Adams oud Graft, Opgevult*, 79.
[81] Helvetius, *Adams oud Graft, Opgevult*, 40–1, 99, 216, 251.
[82] Helvetius, *Adams oud Graft, Opgevult*, 254–5.
[83] Bontekoe, *Brief Aen Johan Frederik Swetzer*, 19–20.
[84] Helvetius, *Davids Slinger-steen*, 4, 251; Bontekoe, *Brief aan Jan Fredrik Swetsertje*, 13.

Blyenbergh, both well-known Cartesians." Indeed, among the whole body of philosophers or theologians, however much all yell against atheists, "only firm Cartesians enter into combat with that monster." "Yet, despite all this you claim Cartesians are Spinozists even though they, and they alone, I answer, refuted Spinoza."[85] Where Bontekoe and Helvetius did agree was in stressing that a combination of Spinoza's books and his sect of followers congregating in and around The Hague, Leiden, Utrecht, and Amsterdam had resulted in his philosophy rapidly gaining ground.

Since Cartesianism rests on mathematics, held Bontekoe, "it was easy for Spinoza, having grasped part of it," to teach students who often came to visit him in Rijnsburg, just as it was easy for him, as a geometry teacher, to help students from "Leiden University where the true philosophy [i.e. of Descartes] was at that time under the cross [i.e. banned and persecuted precisely as Protestantism had been in the Netherlands before the Reformation], to formulate part of [Descartes'] *Physica* in geometric order in a text and publish it."[86] This book of Spinoza's on Descartes' principles was "still to be found and by many all too well known," because under the mask of teaching Cartesianism Spinoza insidiously introduced his own ideas, and it soon became evident "what these fine principles were" when, in 1670, Spinoza published his *Tractatus Theologico-Politicus* which seeks to overthrow not just the "ware philosophie" [true philosophy] of Descartes but all religion and truth. "And from that time on, [Spinoza] made it his task to sow his perverse seed clandestinely; for which reason he left Rijnsburg for Voorburg, and finally moved to The Hague, thinking that he would find greater scope there for his diabolical *politica* and other atheistic ideas among the frivolous youth and other men of the world who are often much inclined towards such evil, as indeed he succeeded in doing and, still today, one finds his creatures in that place."[87]

This is our earliest source claiming Spinoza moved from Leiden to Voorburg, and then The Hague, purposely to penetrate society more effectively by propagating his philosophy among the cosmopolitan, libertine, courtly, and military personnel encountered there, than he could among a few university students coming to him for tuition. The Hague was where one was likeliest to encounter "Spinozists" due to Spinoza's own recent presence and activity there.

35.iv A Disciple Rescued: Van Balen

Among Spinoza's disciples about whom Bontekoe had detailed knowledge was the future philosopher Petrus van Balen (1643–90), about whose relationship with

---

[85] Bontekoe, *Brief aan Jan Fredrik Swetsertje*, 38.
[86] Bontekoe, *Brief Aen Johan Frederik Swetzer*, 21.
[87] Bontekoe, *Brief Aen Johan Frederik Swetzer*, 23.

Spinoza Bontekoe heard from Van Balen's own mouth, being personally close to him during the mid-1670s, when apparently Bontekoe also received some financial assistance from Van Balen. It typified the shoddy hypocritical character of "this ungrateful Phoenix," claims the anonymous author of the *Dialogue van een Groote Thee en Tobacq-Suyper* [Dialogue of a Great Tea and Tobacco Guzzler] of 1680, a satire targeting The Hague's Cartesian medical reformers, especially Bontekoe, that he should afterwards scorn the very friend who had supported him financially, the "Apostate P.v.B."[88] The latter was notorious at The Hague as the "former *dominee* who, after seemingly rehabilitating himself" following his nervous breakdown in Spain, "went astray for the second time through excessive contact with the seducer [Spinoza]." "So badly" unbalanced was Van Balen by Spinoza's godless views, reports Bontekoe, "that he scandalously abandoned his church duties and parish," and instead of propagating the teaching of Jesus Christ, went about "abandoning God and having gone in the wrong direction," cunningly served "the Devil to the ruination of many a soul" by steering others too in a Spinozist direction.[89]

Bontekoe cites his former friend only as "the Apostate P. van B."; but his alluding to his abandoning his flock leaves little room for doubt that the personage described here is indeed Van Balen, who from 1683 onwards lived and wrote in Rotterdam.[90] Son of a prominent Utrecht family, after graduating in theology at Utrecht, in 1664, Van Balen was assigned to the Dutch embassy in Madrid where discussion with Catholics, especially Jesuits, led to his first spiritual crisis in 1664–5.[91] After renewed theological study at Leiden, guided especially by Cocceius and Abraham Heidanus (the latter attesting to his exceptional ability),[92] he resumed his career as a Reformed preacher, again moving in high circles. In 1670, he was appointed to the prestigious post at The Hague of house preacher to Princess Amalia van Solms, widow of Stadholder Frederik Hendrik. It was probably whilst attached to Amalia's household during 1670–5 that he encountered Spinoza.[93] From 1670, Van Balen delivered sermons regularly at the Palace Noordeinde, at the fashionable end of town (though no great distance from Spinoza's lodgings), including the sermon at Princess Amalia's funeral, in September 1675, which many prominent persons attended, possibly including Spinoza.

Captured by the "seducer" Spinoza, relates Bontekoe, Van Balen also met other "Spinozists" and, after a certain point, went about The Hague surreptitiously expounding Spinoza's philosophy at every opportunity. Palaces being less than

---

[88] *Dialogue van een Groote Thee en Tobacq Suyper*, 34–5.
[89] Bontekoe, *Brief Aen Johan Frederik Swetzer*, 23.
[90] Bontekoe, *Brief Aen Johan Frederik Swetzer*, 20; Van den Hoven, "Inleiding," 14–15.
[91] Van den Hoven, "Inleiding," 14–15; Siebrand, *Spinoza and the Netherlanders*, 68–9.
[92] Van Balen, *De Verbetering der gedachten*, 188.
[93] Van den Hoven, "Inleiding," 13–19; Klever, *Mannen rond Spinoza*, 187–9; Wielema, *Filosofen aan de Maas*, 84.

ideal for nurturing Calvinist austerity, others too were busy at court, in the milieu of the young William III, plying Spinozistic ideas. In November 1681, for example, The Hague's consistory noted that a certain François Langenes, described as a baker in the household of the Prince of Orange, was reportedly "imbued with the opinions of Spinoza and seeking to instill them into others on all sides." The Hague's Reformed consistory sent a leading minister, Amja, and another dominee to interrogate him.[94] When summoned to appear before the consistory, though, Langenes repeatedly failed to appear.[95] In late March 1682, he was recorded as still adhering to and propagating "strange and unhealthy opinions" around The Hague.[96]

Van Balen suffered a second nervous breakdown following Princess Amalia's death, after which he interrupted his preaching career for several years and, abandoning the fashionable world of The Hague, resumed studying, again at Utrecht, seeking spiritual repose and likely participating in the lively Spinozistic circle active there, headed by the lawyer-philosopher Cuffeler whose views on logic exhibit notable parallels with Van Balen's own.[97] Temporarily abandoning theology, Van Balen turned first to medical studies, in 1676, acquiring his Utrecht medical doctorate with a "Cartesian" thesis on the mind–body nexus, albeit not without being required to delete his tenth proposition about which he received a formal rebuke from the presiding theologian, Voetius, in person, for claiming human life functions like animal life and does not depend on the soul, and that even if there were no soul the body would continue automatically in all its functions like animal bodies, a proposition pronounced inadmissible "naturalism."[98] Issues of mind, soul, and melancholy continually preoccupied him, as was reflected afterwards in the medical metaphors abounding in his writings.[99] Searching for a meaningful approach to the mind–body nexus was seemingly rooted in his own personal search for a way out of depression.

Van Balen's brother, Joachim, a lawyer, was yet another of The Hague freethinking coterie preoccupying the local Reformed consistory, being a known friend and supporter of Hadrian Beverland (1650–1715), the young classicist obsessed with the erotic culture of the ancient world who, in the late 1670s, provoked great scandal in Leiden and The Hague with his advanced views on sexual freedom.[100] One probable indication of the friendship between Joachim van Balen and Beverland is a poem composed by "J.v.B, lawyer in The Hague," presumed to be Joachim van Balen, placed above the introduction to

[94] GA The Hague, MS. Hervormde Gemeente 203/4, fos. 182 and 194. Res. 7 Nov. 1681 and 6 Feb. 1782.
[95] Wielema, *March of the Libertines*, 94–5; Klever, *Mannen rond Spinoza*, 189.
[96] GA The Hague, MS. Hervormde Gemeente 203/4, fo. 195. Res. 27 March 1682.
[97] Wielema, *March of the Libertines*, 80, 95; Krop, *Spinoza, een paradoxale icoon*, 95, 115.
[98] Quoted in Klever, *Mannen rond Spinoza*, 188.
[99] Van Balen, *De Vebetering der gedachten*, 54–5, 57–8.
[100] De Smet, *Hadrianus Beverlandus*, 42, 45.

Beverland's irreverent book on Original Sin. Defending Beverland's Spinozistic-erotic vision and approving his campaign to emancipate the human libido as part of the programme to promote human happiness, the poem recounts how Eve first aroused Adam and had sexual intercourse with him, claiming their copulation was the true Original Sin and invokes Hobbes and Spinoza to confirm that the biblical story has no theological significance.[101] Summoned before the local Reformed consistory in this connection, on 7 July 1680, Joachim, "unwilling when questioned to acknowledge whether he wrote that detestable verse prefacing Beverland's book or not," was banned from Holy Communion.[102]

Petrus van Balen, possessing degrees in theology, medicine, and also law, and in need of an income, after considering both medicine and law, reverted once more to preaching. Resuming his role as a Reformed preacher, this time at Breda where some unexplained mishap, early in 1677, shortly after Spinoza's death, caused him to lapse again into depression (conceivably deepened by Spinoza's demise, on 21 February), after which his behaviour for a time became highly erratic.[103] The Prince of Orange's secretary, Spinoza's old friend Constantijn Huygens, who knew Van Balen from his days at the Noordeinde palace, happening then to be in Breda, noted in his diary for 3 March 1677, ten days after Spinoza's death, that Van Balen was afflicted with a severe attack of melancholy.[104] Finding his pastoral duties intolerable, he suddenly abandoned his flock in astounding fashion. Concocting a fanciful story about meeting the Devil disguised as "an old man," he announced from the pulpit that Satan had twice appeared and commanded him to leave his congregation which, regretfully, he must now do. This ridiculous tale, Bontekoe later claimed, confided to him by letter and in conversation, Van Balen himself did not believe in the least.[105]

Absconding from his congregation, Van Balen fled to Ghent in Spanish Flanders where—perhaps with the recent defections from "philosophy" of Steno and Burgh in mind—he publicly announced his conversion to Catholicism (or possibly second conversion given his earlier crisis in Spain). But in his case Catholic worship failed to bring the spiritual solace he craved.[106] Returning greatly agitated to The Hague, he searched for mental and emotional help. Re-embracing Spinozism, he became an object of suspicion in the eyes of The Hague's Reformed consistory, especially Thaddeus de Lantman, Spinoza's old adversary, from around March 1679.[107] Conferring under De Lantman's chairmanship, the

---

[101] De Smet, *Hadrianus Beverlandus*, 42–3; Israel, "Dr Cornelis Bontekoe's Views," 235.
[102] GA The Hague, Hervormde Gemeente Kerkeraad 203/4 (resoluties 1673–1701) p. 155, res. 7 July 1680.
[103] Van den Hoven, "Inleiding," 16.   [104] Van den Hoven, "Inleiding," 16.
[105] GA The Hague, Hervormde Gemeente 203/4, fos. 159–61. Res. Kerkeraad, 4 Oct., 10 Oct., 1 Nov. 1680; Bontekoe, *Brief Aen Johan Frederik Swetzer*, 23; Hollewand, *Banishment of Beverland*, 80.
[106] GA The Hague, Hervormde Gemeente 203/4, fo. 176. Kerkeraad res. 13 Oct. 1681 "Acte van Denunciatie"; Van den Hoven, "Inleiding," 16.
[107] GA The Hague, Hervormde Gemeente, 203/4, res. Kerkeraad, p. 147, res. 31 March 1679.

consistory decided to investigate.[108] When Van Balen sought reconciliation with the Church and re-admittance to Holy Communion, needed for his new chosen career as an advocate before the Hof van Holland, this was refused in September 1679.[109] Van Balen nevertheless briefly worked in The Hague as a colleague of his brother, and of Cuffeler, now a High Court lawyer possessing one of the large residences close to the Prinsengracht canal, who perhaps helped steady and direct him on his new course.[110]

Spinoza, recounts Bontekoe, exerted his pernicious influence not only on the "Apostate P.v.B." but also "in the same way on many persons in our land whom I shall not all name, although I am acquainted with many of them. The Hadrianus Beverland, recently sentenced at Leiden for his godless writings, is also one of that lot, as he has openly shown both by word of mouth and in print."[111] Beverland's erotic philosophy, several modern scholars have noted, is pervaded by "Spinozistic pantheism" and certainly he can be characterized as in some sense a "Spinozist."[112] The most notorious writer on erotic themes of the later Dutch Golden Age, Beverland flaunted radical views closely linked to Spinoza's principle that there is "no other God than the fixed order of nature," though he mostly avoids mentioning Spinoza and at one point asserts that Spinoza "drew from Hobbes the hypothesis that no god should be venerated except for the fixed order of nature and the fatal concatenation of all natural things."[113] Interestingly, Beverland, who was distinctly more interested in the group movement than in Spinoza the person, styles Adriaan Koerbagh "Amstelodamensis ille Thales," the Thales of Amsterdam, implying he was the first real, authentic philosopher of the age endeavouring to demolish theology's doleful sway over individual life and thought, establish independence of judgement, and promote sexual emancipation of the individual.[114] That he himself spent much time in discussion with these "deceivers," "rascals," and "atheists," including Beverland and P.v.B., Bontekoe freely admitted.[115]

Bontekoe's testimony suggests that Beverland was a prominent figure among The Hague Spinozist coterie around and after 1676. He does not say Beverland was led astray by Spinoza in person, as he does with P.v.B., but does claim he was led astray by Spinoza's books, ideas, and disciples. Particularly reminiscent of Spinoza, besides affirming the oneness of body and soul, and oneness of God and Nature, was Beverland's stressing the human individual's lifelong striving to conserve himself—a parallel to Spinoza's *conatus* but with more emphasis on

[108] GA The Hague, Hervormde Gemeente 203/4, fo. 149. Res. 28 April 1679.
[109] GA The Hague, Hervormde Gemeente 203/4, fo. 150. Res. Kerkeraad, 29 Sept. 1679.
[110] Klever, *Mannen rond Spinoza*, 204.   [111] Bontekoe, *Brief Aen Johan Frederik Swetzer*, 24.
[112] De Smet, *Hadrianus Beverlandus*, 122, 129, 147; Van Bunge, *From Stevin to Spinoza*, 158.
[113] Beverland, *De Peccato originali*, 4; Hollewand, *Banishment of Beverland*, 106.
[114] [Beverland], *État de l'homme*, 5–6, 28, 45.
[115] *Dialogue van een Groote Thee en Tobacq-Suyper*, 36; Munt, "The Impact of Dutch Cartesian Medical Reformers," 68–9.

sex. Proximate too was his version of the Ezra thesis which, contrary to Hobbes, but like Koerbagh's and Spinoza's, ascribes virtually the entire Old Testament text to Ezra's post-Babylonian editing.[116] After spending the "Disaster Year" 1672 in Oxford, Beverland passed the years 1673–8 chiefly at Leiden, with stays also in Franeker and at Utrecht where he was friendly with another connoisseur of Spinozism and the erotic, the lawyer Jacob de Goyer.[117] Spending lavishly on books, lady friends, wine and junketing in taverns where Spinozists congregated, as well as on paintings, medals, coins, shells, and other "curiosa," in four years Beverland reportedly exhausted a large legacy he had inherited in 1675.[118] In 1678, forgoing the opportunity of a lucrative career in law, he focused on completing his chief scholarly project, a general encyclopaedia of ancient eroticism entitled *De Prostibulis Veterum* [On the Prostitution of the Ancients].[119]

In the late 1670s, officially studying in Leiden, Beverland spent more of his time in The Hague consorting with an emancipated lady friend, the Juffrouw Liefeld, and writing a second book, *De Peccato originali*, that "atheistic and libidinous work" as the Calvinist preacher Leonard Ryssenius calls it,[120] published according to its title-page (like Meyer's *Philosophia*) at "Eleutheropolis" [i.e. Freedom City]. Partly an exercise in Bible criticism, invoking Hobbes, Spinoza, Koerbagh, La Peyrère, and Van den Enden, it seeks to prove that the dogma of Original Sin taught by all churches (except the Socinians) entirely lacks Scriptural basis, being a pious fraud contrived during Christianity's formative period to mislead the ignorant and superstitious, as it had "over many centuries." Beverland held that "the Pentateuch appears to have been forged centuries after Moses by a soothsayer [Ezra]," as explained (following Hobbes) by "that companion of Koerbagh, and disciple of Van den Enden," Spinoza.[121] A libertine, Hobbesian, and in part Spinozist, particularly regarding his "pantheistic" vision of the world and denial of all disembodied spirits, Beverland, like Koerbagh and Van Balen, reaffirms Spinoza's views about Moses, denying Scripture has reached us in a pure and uncorrupted state.[122]

Curiously, Beverland characterizes Spinoza as "that true descendant of Lucian [genuinum Luciani nepotem, Spinosam]," referring to the ancient Near Eastern satirist Lucian (c.125–after 180 AD), who specialized in ridiculing superstition, belief in the supernatural, and irrational religious observances. This ancient satirist, a second century AD Greek Sophist (of Aramaic-speaking background) who travelled from Antioch to Italy, Gaul, Macedonia, and Greece, and wrote in

---

[116] Beverland, *De Peccato originali*, 110–11, 122–4; Ryssenius, *Justa Detestatio*, 3, 16; Hollewand, *Banishment of Beverland*, 92–103.
[117] De Smet, *Hadrianus Beverlandus*, 22–3.
[118] BL MS Add. 4221 "Biographical anecdotes," fo. 111v; De Smet, *Hadrianus Beverlandus*, 23.
[119] De Smet, "Realm of Venus," 49.   [120] Ryssenius, *Justa Detestatio*, 3.
[121] [Beverland], *État de l'homme*, 57–8, 109–10, 182; Meinsma, *Spinoza et son cercle*, 530.
[122] Beverland, *De Peccato originali*, 110, 122–4; Ryssenius, *Justa Detestatio*, 16; De Smet, *Hadrianus Beverlandus*, 118–19, 127–8; Hollewand, *Banishment of Beverland*, 92–9.

Greek, seems an odd choice for a classical comparison, for Lucian was not, as Klever observes, the source of any of Spinoza's philosophical ideas. But the caustic, mocking strain in Spinoza's conversation flaying pedants, preachers, and long venerated earlier philosophers, Plato and Aristotle especially, did strike some as reminiscent of Lucian's satirical mocking of gods and popular belief. Van den Enden, another mocker, likewise was called a veritable "Lucianist."[123]

Beverland's *De Peccato originali*, a lengthy extract from his main book project, appeared in two separate clandestine editions in 1678 and 1679, the second more polished (of which Bouwmeester had a copy in his library), but this time no longer anonymously.[124] Ill-advisedly, Beverland gave his name on the title-page, provoking a massive furore, his book being crammed with "atrocious obscenities" as the North Holland synod expressed it.[125] Not only the preachers were outraged but also the Republic's leading *érudits* in Greek and Roman studies, most of whom, including Graevius, knew Beverland personally and admired his erudition but were appalled that he should so recklessly assail Scripture and be so devoid of common sense.[126] The Leiden Reformed consistory, ignoring a lengthy script Beverland had sent to justify his views, rejected his defence, denouncing his foul, unchaste, unchristian statements, on 16 June 1679.[127] As a university student offender, Beverland was assigned to the professoriate for retribution.[128] Arrested with the help of his mentor, Graevius, he had to surrender the unpublished manuscript of *De Prostibulis Veterum* to the university authorities (it survives today in the University Library) and was briefly imprisoned,[129] while *De Peccato originali* was banned by the States of Holland, Gelderland, and other authorities. Though released in December 1679,[130] he was heavily fined and permanently banished from Holland and his native Zeeland. After a short stay in Utrecht, he departed in March 1680 for what proved permanent exile in Charles II's England.

Van Balen, meanwhile, having transferred to Rotterdam, found a more stable lifestyle as a philosopher and, in 1683, published his work on logic with a second, expanded edition appearing in 1691, demonstrating "the difference between the old and new style of thought, and superiority of the latter over the former."[131] Law, medicine, theology, and philosophy were all areas requiring fundamental reform, he showed, the practical goal of his *On the Improvement of One's Thoughts* (alluding presumably to Spinoza's *Tractatus de Intellectus Emendatione*) being

---

[123] Klever, *Spinoza Classicus*, 188–92; Meinsma, *Spinoza et son cercle*, 530.
[124] *Catalogus* [...] *librorum* [...] *Bouwmeesteri*, 20.
[125] RNH Acta Noord-Holland Synod 6, Enkhuizen, 1 Aug. 1679, art. 6.
[126] De Smet, "Realm of Venus," 47; Waardt, "Academic Careers and Scholarly Networks," 32–3, 36.
[127] GA Leiden Acta Kerkeraad res. 30 June 1679.
[128] GA Leiden Acta Kerkeraad res. 16 and 23 June 1679.
[129] Waardt, "Academic Careers and Scholarly Networks," 32–3; Vogt, *Catalogvs Historico-criticvs* i, 83–4.
[130] De Smet, *Hadrianus Beverlandus*, 48–9.
[131] Wielema, *Filosofen aan de Maas*, 61, 84–6; Wielema, *March of the Libertines*, 89, 95, 101.

to enable readers to remove inadequate ideas from their minds and improve their quality of life by adjusting their minds to rigorous critical thinking through critically examining their basic premises and beliefs including "mysteries of the faith" using soundly based criteria.[132] This was necessary even in relation to the holiest dogmas given that there exists in Holland not only a public church but an "immense medley of lesser congregations each of which, in accord with its decreed freedom," aims to enlarge its flock, leaving a great many troubled by the conflicting claims they encounter, causing personal inner agony he himself knew only too well. To sift competing religious doctrines, citizens need dependable criteria to judge what is true or false, a sound methodology rooted in the natural sciences.[133] In matters vital to one's salvation, nothing should be accepted without rigorous inquiry, subjecting the vast array of conflicting theological claims to rigorous testing and "understanding the true sense of the words of Holy Scripture."[134]

How exactly our minds should be trained in sound thinking, Van Balen explains more fully in the second part of his treatise, published only after his death when finally out of reach of the magistrates and consistories. A supplement, incorporated into the 1691 edition, expounds his critical method for identifying the true sense of Scripture, in essentials following Spinoza's argument in the *TTP*.[135] When thinking primitively, men believed all natural forces were spirits with bodies like men or animals. The means to rescue oneself from the misery of superstition Van Balen himself had discovered only in halting stages punctuated by bouts of anguish, self-doubt, and remorse encouraged by theologians, an inner struggle won eventually with Spinoza's guidance. Central to his troubles, and those of everyone in similar crisis, was his conception of human awareness being first infantile, then childish, and only finally edging towards clear thinking through sustained effort. Emancipating ourselves from infantile delusion requires philosophy's help, and means learning that the only bodies that exist are tangible, visible ones (even if in many cases visible only with the aid of instruments), and that intangible and invisible bodies do not exist. The immaturity of most people's thinking stems from human proneness to believe in imagined unseen forces in some way higher and more powerful than the bodies we do see. Our wretchedness arises from the superstition fostered by those supposedly possessing special proximity to what deluded followers imagine to be these invisible forces.[136] Disbelief in spirits detached from bodies cures delusion, enabling all to escape their bondage by learning to use their minds with rigour and put their thoughts in proper order.

---

[132] Van Balen, *De Verbetering der gedachten*, 51.
[133] Van Balen, *De Verbetering der gedachten* 51–2; Klever, *Mannen rond Spinoza*, 191; Wielema, *Filosofen aan de Maas*, 86.
[134] Van Balen, *De Verbetering der gedachten*, 52; Israel, "Popularizing Radical Ideas," 288–9.
[135] Van den Hoven, "Petrus van Balen (1643–90)," in *DDPhil* i, 45.
[136] Van Balen, *De Verbetering der gedachten*, 59–60; Klever, *Mannen rond Spinoza*, 193–4.

Van Balen's quest for a purer, reformed logic and Bible criticism, programmes he considered parallel to the progress he believed medical reformers like Bontekoe, Mandeville, and Overkamp were achieving in medicine, helps explain why, for a time, he so trusted Bontekoe. Formerly, "medicine was highly imperfect" and even the best doctors relied only on their own experience of the effects of particular drugs and herbs.[137] Cartesian medicine meant dramatic improvement, or so he believed, due to testing, recording, and investigating, men's thirst for knowledge breaking barriers and revealing the true functions of the bodily organs, especially the movement, circulation, and diverse purposes of the body's fluids. As a result of such discoveries men now possess sound knowledge of what causes ill-health including mental distress and "why these or those things are useful for restoring health."

A general revolution like that (supposedly) transforming medicine was required too, he argued, in the art of pure thinking, or logic, which, however, "has few enthusiasts and even fewer masters" and, consequently, was nowhere near as far advanced as medicine.[138] Van Balen conceived logic as a true *medicina mentis*, or medicine of the mind, this being the reason he chose to write in the vernacular, and not Latin.[139] After recovery from his third breakdown, Van Balen as far as we know, adhered consistently to Spinoza's teaching and experienced no further upsets or changes of heart. Discreetly, he remained Rotterdam's resident active propagator of Spinozist doctrine.

35.v The Expanding Sect of the 1680s and 1690s

Spinozism took root powerfully yet also remained veiled, clandestine, and systematically repressed. Stouppe, in 1673, spoke of Spinoza's followers and "sect" but did not introduce the term "Spinozisme" as such. But within just a few years, well under a decade after Spinoza's death, according to Aubert de Versé's 1684 ringing polemic "against Spinoza," the terms "Spinozistes" and "Spinozisme" became current French as well as Dutch usage.[140] Causing "furious ravages" at The Hague, *Spinozisme*, recounts Aubert became a formidable force primed by the grounding that Cartesianism provided. In Aubert's eyes, directly contrary to Bontekoe, "the principles of Cartesianism" undoubtedly are "the foundations of *le Spinozisme*."[141]

Numerous late seventeenth-century writers note the rapid—and to most contemporaries horrifying—growth of Spinozism as a subversive cultural and

---

[137] Van Balen, *De Verbetering der gedachten*, 54.
[138] Van Balen, *De Verbetering der gedachten*, 54–5, 57.
[139] Van Balen, *De Verbetering der gedachten*, 54–5, 57, 88.
[140] Aubert de Versé, *L'Impie convaincu*, 21, 24, 31, 103–4.
[141] Aubert de Versé, *L'Impie convaincu*, 104; Krop, *Spinoza, een paradoxale icoon*, 181.

anti-theological movement deeply rooted especially in the main cities of the United Provinces but perceptibly spreading in Germany and before long also England and France.[142] In the diaries of Stolle and Hallmann, the first recorded interview in Holland was with the Remonstrant theologian and friend of Locke, Philippus van Limborch (1633–1712), among the best informed observers of Spinozism's emergence as a "sect" at Amsterdam, whom they visited on 19 June 1703.[143] Spinoza and his "sect," Van Limborch explained in conversation with them, did indeed penetrate widely, something tolerated by the Dutch authorities because Spinoza did not establish a "sect" with any discernible organization. Rather, he deliberately refrained from holding organized meetings, confining himself always to conversing informally with friends.[144] Over thirty years earlier, in a letter of September 1671, Van Limborch had commented on the subversive character of Spinoza's "flock" [gregis], recalling a conversation he had had some years before, apparently with Adriaan Koerbagh, which revealed to him that the group had all along identified God with all that exists which, for them, since there is nothing supernatural, meant identifying God with Nature. Reading the TTP had confirmed for Van Limborch his earlier impression, from conversing with Koerbagh in the late 1660s, that Spinoza and his then circle viewed God as identical to "hoc universum" [this universe].[145]

Stolle and Hallmann's 1703–4 quest for material relating to Spinoza's life and his sect resulted in the garnering of the single most varied batch of source material gathered from contemporaries who had known Spinoza personally. Conversation with "paradoxical persons," that is freethinkers, was something Thomasius had urged Stolle not to avoid whilst touring Holland. However, when conversing with such *Spinozisten*, he should do so discreetly, on his guard, patiently eliciting useful information.[146] He should listen more than speak, his mentor advised, restrain his own opinions and draw each "Spinozist" out, gather insight and information so as ultimately to combat them all the better by knowing and mastering their arguments thoroughly. Nor should Stolle refrain from studying Spinoza's texts; rather the contrary, for while one finds there "of course, much that is bad," there is "also much that is good [aber auch manches gute]," so that one needs to be attentive when reading Spinoza and not rush through his writings.[147] The resulting precious material, the Stolle/Hallmann *Beschreibung*, was long forgotten and ignored until rediscovered in the Breslau (now Wrocław) University Library, apparently in 1847, then forgotten again until Freudenthal edited and published most but not

---

[142] Further on this topic, see Israel, *Enlightenment Contested*, 372–6.
[143] Freudenthal/Walther, *Lebensgeschichte* ii, 54–5.
[144] Van Limborch to Le Clerc, Amsterdam, 23 Jan. 1682 in Meinsma, *Spinoza et son cercle*, 526.
[145] Laurens, *De rede: bron van geluk*, 34–5. [146] Freudenthal/Walther, *Lebensgeschichte* ii, 54.
[147] Freudenthal/Walther, *Lebensgeschichte* ii, 54; Klever, "Omtrent Spinoza," 6–7; Zenker, *Denkfreiheit*, 163.

all of the material in 1899, sometimes transcribing incorrectly.[148] The improved, complete version, published by Walther, extends to some fourteen pages, the most valuable parts relating to discussions Stolle and Hallmann held in Amsterdam, in 1703, with the son of Spinoza's publisher, the younger Jan Rieuwertsz (c.1651–1723) then still running his father's bookshop and business.

The younger Rieuwertsz made no effort to conceal his profound admiration of Spinoza, having known the philosopher personally in his youth and heard "marvellous truths" from his lips. Spinoza, he confirmed, did indeed write a long *Apologia* in Spanish against the rabbis, in 1656 or shortly thereafter, a manuscript his father kept in his possession but at some stage had given away, in which Spinoza attacks the Jews—presumably rabbinic authority—"very hard." Writing the *Ethics* had exacted so heavy a toll on Spinoza, he recalled, a vast amount of time and painstaking effort, that in the end he remarked "had he not already completed it, he would never again want to begin [hätte er sie nicht schon fertig, so wollte er nimmermehr anfangen]."[149] Initial editing of the *Opera Posthuma*, he told his visitors, had taken place in The Hague. Rieuwertsz also showed them Spinoza's personal copy of the *TTP* "in which he had added short marginal notes in manuscript," the *Adnotationes* then still known only in French translation.[150]

The younger Rieuwertsz was still seeking to propagate Spinoza's ideas in Dutch society which, in his opinion, would be a solid benefit. He responded to his German visitors' questions, Hallmann's journal records, "gar misstrauisch und heimlich" [suspiciously and secretively], remarking that "much is forbidden in Holland nowadays, as we by no means have the freedom here that we would in England."[151] By 1700, the Glorious Revolution had flipped the old relationship: Holland was no longer freer than England; their pre-1688 roles were reversed. When Stolle asked about *Spinozisten* in contemporary Holland, Rieuwertsz replied evasively that Spinoza had had many admirers in his lifetime, but ten years after his death these were all gone. Now there was practically no one in Holland valuing Spinoza's writings highly, the reason why there were no recent editions of the Descartes book or the *TTP*, and why these, apart from a few copies, were hardly to be found. In Amsterdam, he knew "only one friend who loved Spinoza."[152] But Rieuwertsz had abundant grounds for caution, indeed to fear being exposed by an official search, and needed to avoid giving the impression he was regularly encouraging such readers and selling such material (though we know he was). He did mention, though, that such Spinozist literature as he still

---

[148] Klever, "Omtrent Spinoza," 3, 16; Klever, *The Sphinx*, 123.
[149] Freudenthal/Walther, *Lebensgeschichte* i, 85.
[150] Freudenthal/Walther, *Lebensgeschichte* i, 85.
[151] Manusov-Verhage, "Jan Rieuwertsz, marchand," 88–9.
[152] Freudenthal/Walther, *Lebensgeschichte* i, 86, 89.

stocked he avoided keeping at his printing-house and store; forbidden books he kept hidden in a special place at home.[153]

In the United Provinces of 1700 publishing and distributing Spinoza's *TTP* and *Opera Posthuma* remained prohibited under threat of stringent fines. One could not be punished, under Dutch law, for expressing Spinozistic views in private conversation, like that of Rieuwertsz with Stolle and Hallmann, but under the States' decrees of 1678, which imposed massive fines and lengthy prison sentences for violating the ban, could readily be prosecuted for distributing or reprinting Spinozistic books. Rieuwertsz himself had had several scrapes with the law over this, notably in 1695.[154] He was therefore understandably concerned to give the impression that for a considerable time he had not been selling copies of Spinoza's works. It was regrettable, though, he ventured, that in Holland people did not concern themselves with the "truths" revealed by Spinoza because these could be so useful. Rieuwertsz felt a deeply personal, almost proprietary kinship to Spinoza's legacy, causing Hallmann to remark: "towards Spinoza he shows an uncommon love wishing almost with tears in his eyes that he might still be alive [gegen Spinosam bezeigt Er eine ungemeine Liebe und wünschete fast mit weinenden Augen, dass er noch leben möchte]."[155] The Leiden professor De Volder was another who confirmed the reality of this "sect" to Stolle but did so denying Spinoza was an atheist (arousing suspicion about him in Stolle's mind) and claiming the most zealous Spinoza enthusiasts often misconstrued Spinoza's meaning. In De Volder's view, Spinoza's following should be classified in two camps, those avowing their philosophical allegiance in restricted circles and those remaining solitary and silent.[156] On returning from their trip, Stolle and Hallmann, like Thomasius, took it for granted that there *was* indeed a large Spinozist following in Holland.[157]

Additional testimony as to the formation of underground local Spinozist networks in Dutch cities is found in the history of the Jews by the Huguenot pastor of Rotterdam and friend of Bayle, Jacques Basnage (1653–1723). Published originally in 1713, in a new expanded edition of 1716, Basnage remarks that Spinoza established "a sect that has adopted his principles [une secte qui a adopté ses principes]," but that it was impossible to estimate how large or numerous it was since its adherents were widely dispersed and "are not a formal body or society [qui ne sont ni corps ni societé]." Still, there was no ignoring the reality of Spinoza's following as it was undoubtedly numerous and often included plain workingmen, "c'étoient des artisans."[158] Another observer viewing the situation with alarm was the prominent Reformed theologian Herman Alexander Röell

---

[153] Freudenthal/Walther, *Lebensgeschichte* i, 94.
[154] Gerritsen, "Printing Spinoza," 258.
[155] Freudenthal/Walther, *Lebensgeschichte* i, 90.
[156] Strazzoni, *Burchard de Volder*, 124–5.
[157] Manusov-Verhage, "Jan Rieuwertsz, marchand," 240.
[158] Basnage, *Histoire des Juifs*, ix, 1035.

(1653–1718). He knew the Dutch universities intimately and was sufficiently worried by what he witnessed—reports the eighteenth-century historian of philosophy, Jacob Brucker—to exclaim "would that that execrable name of Spinoza were unheard of in our Netherlands, that one whom whole herds follow as their leader! [utinam inauditum esset in Belgica nostra exsecrabile illud Spinosae nomen, quem tota armenta sequuntur ducem!]"[159]

Likewise in 1716, the erudite German historian of philosophy and teacher of Brucker, the Lutheran savant Christoph August Heumann (1681–1764), based at Göttingen, discussing Bayle's rejection (in note "t" in his long article on Spinoza, in the *Dictionnaire*) of Stouppe's claim, in 1673, that Spinoza's "sectateurs soient en grand nombre," pointedly disagreed. Bayle had his facts wrong or else was deliberately obscuring the truth. If Stouppe exaggerated in saying Spinoza had "un grand nombre de sectateurs, qui sont entièrement attachés à ses sentiments [a great number of adherents who are entirely attached to his views]," Bayle's denial was more misleading. Heumann then repeated the words of Röell: alas "in our Netherlands whole herds follow Spinoza as their leader [Spinosam tota armenta (in Belgica nostra) sequuntur ducem]."

It is indeed a strange paradox, as the largest encyclopaedia of the pre-1750 European Enlightenment, Johann Heinrich Zedler's *Grosses vollständiges Universal-Lexicon* points out, in its long article on Spinoza in the thirty-ninth volume, published in 1744, that Spinoza supposedly disavowed any wish to attach his name to a sect, or organize any such movement, yet an underground sect generated by his disciples came into being and after his death spread everywhere assuming no small proportions.[160]

---

[159] Brucker, *Historia critica philosophiae* iv-2, 697, citing Herman Alexander Roëll, *Dissertatio de religione rationali* (6th edn. Utrecht, 1713), 166; quoted in Schröder, "Spinozam tota armenta in Belgio sequi ducem," 167.

[160] Zedler, *Grosses vollständiges Universal-Lexicon* xxxix, 85.

36

Amsterdam Revisited (1673–1675)

36.i The Orangist-Calvinist Reaction Intensifies

As the Republic's external crisis eased, during the years 1673–4, its internal political and ideological conflict intensified. By 1675 the situation had developed in such a way as to abundantly justify admitting to one's friends a deep sense of unease, as Spinoza did several times that year. For a full-scale cultural war was now in progress. The drive to impose tighter discipline on the universities, as the Haarlem consistory detailed, meeting under the cloud of war and French invasion, on 10 June 1672,[1] and by the North Holland synod at its July gathering that year, had ever since 1672 formed part of a much wider intellectual-religious backlash, or "Further Reformation," intended to cut back toleration, "licentious printing," improper conduct, and dissident thinking.

Restoration of the stadholderate had seemingly cleared the way for major advances for the Reformed Church, but these were unavoidably hampered and delayed by the exigencies of war. The long called for and broadly planned "general programme of [Calvinist] reform,"[2] was virtually pinned to a standstill by the direness of the general situation during 1672–3. After the initial purges of "Loevesteiners" from the city governments and provincial states of Holland and Zeeland, in 1672, there followed a protracted pause and loss of momentum lasting until after the French pull-back, in late 1673. But with the French evacuation of Utrecht, Gelderland, and Overijssel, English defeat at sea and Munsterite withdrawal from the war, growing confidence at all levels enabled the Voetians and church councils to recharge and vent their pent-up frustration into a renewed, powerful and comprehensive Republic-wide drive while redoubling their pressure on the Stadholder.

The Dutch domestic crisis of the mid-1670s was political, religious, and intellectual all at the same time, extending to virtually every aspect of Dutch life. The internal political scene became highly charged especially from April 1674, when the States General formally readmitted to the union the three recently liberated provinces (Utrecht, Gelderland, and Overijssel) after empowering the Stadholder to reform their provincial and civic administrations. Authorized to strengthen his

---

[1] GA Haarlem Acta kerkeraad ix, res. 10 June 1672.
[2] RA North Holland, Geref. Kerk v, Classis Edam, acta 25 July 1672, and Classis Alkmaar, acta 13 and 14 Sept. 1672; Van Lieburg, *Nadere Reformatie in Utrecht*, 146.

own hand by purging those of whom he disapproved from the political scene throughout the three reconstituted provinces, the Prince removed no less than 120 officeholders in the province of Utrecht alone, Van Velthuysen and Nieuwstad among them, a far higher proportion of sitting regents than purged in Holland and Zeeland, in 1672.[3] The Stadholder now possessed a firmer grip on the United Provinces' political apparatus, including the States of Holland, than had any previous Prince of Orange. From late 1673, efforts to curtail toleration involved an intensifying campaign against Catholics, Socinians, liberal Mennonites, and Cartesians.[4] But while the Prince felt obliged to concede considerable ground to his Calvinist allies, he was unable, without prejudicing his alliance with Spain and the emperor, to do much as regards rolling back the Republic's Catholic minority. If Calvinist reaction during the mid-1670s in the end achieved considerably less than the consistories hoped for, their redoubled efforts and pressure did impede or restrain many recent tendencies and developments apart from the revival of Dutch Catholicism, among other initiatives producing fiercer crack-downs on "licentious" book production and renewed offensives against Cartesianism and reform initiatives in the universities.

Besides French evacuation from most of the Republic's territory and Munsterite withdrawal from the war, external pressure eased due to the peace with England, officially ending the Anglo-Dutch War in February 1674 with confirmation that the States General now formally accepted "that the charges and dignities possessed by the Prince of Orange and his ancestors should become hereditary to his children." From early 1674, peace with England greatly improved the Republic's general strategic position and mitigated the economic slump, ending the land and sea blockade previously stifling Dutch commerce, shipping, the publishing industry, and art market. Revival of the economy and all the arts and sciences during 1674–5 was real, but also, whilst the war with France dragged on, far from complete. Rebounding from the lows of 1672–3, the recovery of trade nevertheless remained tepid: in May 1675, the VOC share price hovered between 428 and 443, and in July 1676 still at just 450.[5]

Besides returning New York (captured by the Dutch during the war), and a few other concessions overseas, peace was bought by the Dutch Republic sacrificing what Spinoza, like De Witt, had long judged an essential component of the "True Freedom"—government without a hereditary stadholderate, thereby rendering the Republic less of a republic than it had been. "And thus happily," commented Temple, "ended our part of a war so fateful to the rest of Christendom: the consequences of [which] no man perhaps now alive would see the end of." Temple was not alone in viewing Charles' alliance with Louis as disastrous for all Europe. For Charles and his advisers, however, the situation remained

---

[3] Van der Bijl, "Utrechts weerstand," 139; Israel, *Dutch Republic*, 814–15.
[4] Spiertz, *L'Église catholique*, 127.   [5] Israel, *Conflicts of Empires*, 328.

profoundly unsatisfactory. Circumstances had forced England's monarch to abandon his part, for now, in a joint undertaking with Louis XIV to engineer a truly massive monarchical-aristocratic-ecclesiastical coup forcing one and all into deference to courts, kings, nobles, and churchmen. What was particularly galling for Charles was that Dutch sea-power, the Republic's navy and privateers, had gravely stricken England's seaborne trade during 1672-4, while Louis' hopes of overrunning the Spanish Netherlands (Belgium) to the south of the Republic and dominating all Europe with or without England sharing the spoils, still remained buoyant. Nothing displeased Charles and those around him more than seeing their aspiring absolutism and royal glory humiliatingly cut back while the royal glory of Louis XIV might yet register major gains at the expense of Spain and on the Rhine. If Louis and Charles both felt furious and thwarted, the Anglo-French attack on the Dutch Republic in 1672-4 was viewed by more discerning observers, such as Temple, as a universal setback to be chiefly blamed no doubt on Louis but with no small part of the blame due to the insidious servile advice of five self-seeking fashionable courtiers who had Charles' ear. These were "usually called the cabal, a word unluckily falling out of the five first letters of their names, that is Clifford, Arlington, Buckingham, Ashley and Lauderdale."[6]

Summoned to court, in early 1674, Temple found himself charged with restoring relations with The Hague. "There was no other person," Arlington assured him, "to be thought of for it." In fact, nothing gave Temple greater pleasure than undertaking this task and returning to Holland "where I knew the scene so well." Peacemaking is always good. But the double-edged, fragile new reality imperilled both the Republic's internal politics and the basic European power-balance. An unsteady peace with England was secured, but by delivering a severe blow to what Spinoza, like De Witt earlier, deemed the Republic's very essence and integrity—at the cost of rendering the stadholderate permanent and hereditary and the public church stronger.

With Anglo-Dutch cultural relations restored, along with trade, Oldenburg moved to rebuild his connections with Holland including his old correspondence with Spinoza. Oldenburg, like Boyle, was appalled by the *TTP*, but resolved for now to rein in his dismay and resume correspondence with Spinoza in as undisturbed a fashion as possible. Still, his approach now noticeably differed from what it had been back in the 1660s, his attitude towards Spinoza being now unmistakably more remote, calculated, and suspicious. Spinoza, in a letter of 5 July 1675 (now lost), replied to his friend, that his *Ethics* consisted now of five parts and that he planned, as Oldenburg summarized the matter, in his next letter, dated 25 July, to "put that five-part treatise of yours to the judgment of the public." Worried instead of pleased that Spinoza was about to publish his *Ethics*,

---

[6] Temple, *Memoirs*, 4-6.

Oldenburg, very differently from his warm encouragement of the 1660s, begged him to forgive his pressing stern advice on him, but had to insist that he not compromise in "whatever manner the practice of religious virtue. I insist on this all the more in that our decadent and corrupt age seeks for nothing more avidly than views of a kind that appear to legitimate an avalanche of vices."[7]

In his following letter, of mid-August 1675, Oldenburg thanked Spinoza for the copy of the *TTP* earlier delivered to him personally, mentioning a previous (now lost) letter of his seemingly written over the winter of 1673–4, which had failed to reach Spinoza amidst the turmoil of war, expressing fierce criticism of the *TTP*. Eager to re-establish harmonious relations, Oldenburg now retracted what he calls his overhasty and excessively harsh original judgement of Spinoza's work. This frank admission of his, changing from a largely negative to an outwardly tentatively positive stance, may have partly been due to the intervention of Spinoza's young noble German friend, Ehrenfried Walther von Tschirnhaus (1651–1708), who visited England in May and June 1675, and perhaps also De Volder, earlier also in London, in July and August 1674, both doubtless emphasizing the threat to the "new philosophy" arising from the Orangist and Voetian reaction and seeking Oldenburg's support for Dutch Cartesianism, research, and science.

Entrusting his now close friend Tschirnhaus with a manuscript copy of the *Ethics* which he took with him to England and afterwards to France, Spinoza had made him promise not to show the manuscript to anyone else without his express permission, and not to discuss the details of his philosophy either in London or in Paris where Tschirnhaus was due next. Reporting to Spinoza indirectly via his physician friend, Georg Hermann Schuller (c.1650–79), who then passed the information on to Spinoza, in a letter from Amsterdam of 25 July 1675, together with cordial greetings from Rieuwertsz and another friend, Petrus van Gent (1640–95), yet another Leiden graduate recently converted to Spinozism, Tschirnhaus alerted Spinoza to the unfortunate fact that Boyle and Oldenburg had conceived, as he tactfully put it, "an astounding idea of your person." Thankfully, affirmed Schuller, "Tschirnhaus has not only dispelled that [negative] impression but has also added reasons inducing them to think not just most worthily and favourably again of your person, but also hold the *Tractatus Theologico-Politicus* in high esteem."[8] Of course, Boyle and Oldenburg had not really changed their minds about the *TTP*, or the general implications of Spinoza's philosophy, as they were beginning to perceive them. Earlier, he himself and Tschirnhaus, explained Schuller, had not dared "inform you about all this because of your admonitions," meaning Spinoza's asking his followers not to disclose

---

[7] Oldenburg to Spinoza, London, 8 June and 22 July 1675 in Spinoza, *Collected Works* (ed. Curley) ii, 434–5; Curley, "Homo audax," 283–4.

[8] Schuller to Spinoza, Amsterdam, 25 July 1675 in Spinoza, *Opera* iv, 276; Spinoza, *Collected Works* (ed. Curley) ii, 437; Spinoza, *Correspondance* (ed. Revere), 330–1.

details about him and his work, or discuss his texts and arguments with persons not belonging to his immediate circle.[9] Shrewd as he was in such matters, Spinoza doubtless gave no credence to the optimistic gloss laid on here by Schuller.

His own initial view of the *TTP*, like Boyle's, had been wholly negative and condemnatory, admitted Oldenburg: "at the time, a number of things there seemed to me to verge on being thoroughly detrimental to religion because I was judging them by the measure of the common mass of theologians and the established formulae of confessional creeds which it now seems to me are excessively inspired by confessional factional zeal."[10] Accordingly, he had moderated his view, he explained (without mentioning his conferring with Tschirnhaus and De Volder), after reflecting more closely on the matter and finding in the *TTP* "many things that convince me that you are so far from wanting to damage true religion and sound philosophy that, on the contrary, you seek to establish and commend nothing contrary to the true goal of the Christian religion, and sublimity and excellence of a fertile philosophy." He asked Spinoza to resume corresponding with him regularly and especially to explain his plans, expressing hopes for a successful outcome to his life's project and promising on his sacred oath to divulge nothing Spinoza desired him to keep silent about to anyone.[11] It must have cost Oldenburg considerable effort to write in this vein, professing now to recognize Spinoza's intentions as constructive and benevolent.

Oldenburg bent over backwards to preserve an unusual, intriguing channel of information, but his seemingly accommodating attitude was hardly representative of his or the wider English reaction; and if Boyle knew of it, it was hardly likely to please him. Rather, in England a sudden drastic change for the worse in perceptions of Spinoza was prevalent all round. If Boyle and Spinoza disagreed all along about what science is and signifies for mankind and its future, few other leading lights had taken much notice until recently. But, from 1674, that changed dramatically. In London, Bishop Stillingfleet's shocked reaction in his *Letter to a Deist*, dated 11 June 1675, depicts Spinoza as "mightily in vogue among many" and a prime source of the appalling challenge to faith and revealed religion now welling up in England.[12] During 1675-6, at Christ's College Cambridge, Henry More, and his ally, the College master, Ralph Cudworth (1617-88), colluded in preparing their fierce critique of Spinoza's views pervading parts of the latter's *True Intellectual System of the Universe* (1678).

By early July 1675, the *Ethics* lay finished but unpublished. Spinoza was contemplating the—for him—crucial but dangerous question of how to bring

---

[9] Spinoza, *Opera* iv, 276.
[10] Spinoza, *Opera* iv, 272; here again, I have rendered the sentence rather differently from Curley in Spinoza, *Collected Works* (ed. Curley) ii, 434.
[11] Spinoza, *Opera* iv, 272; Spinoza, *Correspondance* (ed. Rovere), 328, correcting errors of dating and interpretation of earlier editors.
[12] Stillingfleet, *A Letter to a Deist*, preface.

out what must prove a further provocation to a now deeply hostile world of onlookers besieging him on all sides, greatly complicating his increasingly fraught personal situation and reinforcing his own and his expanding but marginalized circle's isolation. Even if published anonymously, as intended, such a work would provoke a public storm of vilification more specifically aimed at him and his followers than the reaction to the *TTP*, and possibly something far worse. At The Hague, rumour circulated that another abominably unchristian work of Spinoza's both existed and would imminently appear. Many were now on their guard against him and his philosophy. The Hague's Reformed Church council, at its gathering on 21 June 1675, entered it into their formal records that "recently, the utterly godless opinions of Spinoza [hoogelijk godvergeten opinien van Spinoza] are beginning both here and elsewhere to creep in more and more." The *kerkeraad* responded by instructing "all preachers to stay very much on the look-out" against his followers and whatever related to Spinoza and his sect, and "also whether any other book by him [following the *TTP*] might be in the press and what other dangers related to this there might be so as to provide a report to this gathering, enabling it to determine what action to take."[13]

By 1675, growing circles of the political as well as academic and ecclesiastical elites perceived Spinoza as a serious and immediate "danger" to society and religion. More than ever, with Koerbagh's fate a constant warning, Spinoza needed to check his impulse to defy and be forthright with his counter-balancing tendency towards "caution." At Leiden, top professors were now fully alerted to this pretentious, all revising, non-academic usurper comprehensively challenging their pronouncements, teaching, and standing. One professor (since 1672), Theodorus Ryckius (1640–90), a specialist on Roman mythology and history, on 14 August 1675 sent a warning to Adriaan van Blijenburgh (1616–82), the Dordrecht Orangist regent and recent burgomaster close to the Stadholder.[14] Formerly prominent on the young Prince's state education committee of guardians in the late 1660s, and one of the States' "deputies in the field" during William III's 1674 campaign, this sworn foe of De Witt's "True Freedom," now among the most influential Williamite regents in The Hague, sat on the States' powerful permanent general standing committee. "There is a rumour among us [in Leiden]," warned Ryckius, "that the author of the *Tractatus Theologico-politicus* is about to bring out a book on God and the mind, a book much more dangerous even than the first. It will be up to you and your people concerned in steering the ship of the Republic," he wrote, summoning the Orangist faction in the upper reaches of government now controlling the States of Holland "to see to it this book is not

---

[13] GA The Hague, Hervormde Gemeente Kerkeraad 203/4, p. 47. Res. 21 June 1675; Freudenthal/Walther, *Lebensgeschichte* i, 320; Kingma, "Spinoza in zijn Haagse periode," 17; Nadler, *Spinoza: A Life*, 335; Israel, *Radical Enlightenment*, 286.

[14] Van der Hoeven, *Leeven en Dood* ii, 17.

published. For it is incredible [incredibile enim est] how much that man who has striven to shatter the principles of our most holy faith, has already damaged the Republic."[15] Spinoza, in 1675, may have been less obviously blasphemous and apt for legal retribution than Koerbagh in 1668, or Beverland in 1678, but key political figures in a position to judge knew perfectly well that his subtler, more cautious, judicially less vulnerable activity was more fundamentally subverting religious authority, ordinary belief, the academic order, and society generally than that of any of his followers.

Another church council resolution at The Hague affirming the urgency of collective vigilance regarding Spinoza followed in early September, with De Lantman presiding.[16] On 16 September 1675, for the second time in ten days, the consistory again considered the dire challenge to the public Church posed by the "opinions of Spinoza" and their spread in society. De Lantman frequently presided at these church council gatherings in The Hague and, being among the preachers most familiar with the Orangist court, was among those most instrumental in Reformed Church council contacts with the Prince.[17] When the Prince's grandmother, Amalia van Solms died, in September 1675, De Lantman headed the consistory's delegation to the Prince to formally express the preachers' commiseration.[18] The resumed Calvinist and Orangist theological-political resurgence following the French withdrawal, from the autumn of 1673, was by early 1675 plainly gaining momentum, with De Lantman, Ryckius, and Van Blijenburgh among the movers, a shift menacing Spinoza's own position and prospects and, more generally, the "new philosophy" in the universities.

The entire bloc of Cartesians in the Republic and the Lower Rhine area now found themselves enveloped in a storm of anxiety over erosion of religious authority, spread of freethinking, and the risks of toleration, experiencing exposure of a new, peculiarly uncomfortable kind. Dutch academic Cartesians reacted by splitting and remaining divided. Some, hoping to ward off the worst of the looming pressure, pushed more loudly than ever to the front of the chorus denouncing Spinoza and his following. Others, though, including Van Velthuysen and Graevius perhaps most obviously, more interested in assisting the revival of republican sentiment now stirring, notably backtracked from outright hostility towards Spinoza and his circle. Following the Orangist purges of 1672–5, these now entered into a behind-the-scenes truce and more positive relationship, building on the foundation laid at Utrecht in 1673. Van Velthuysen, Nieuwstad, De Volder, Graevius, and Wittichius all seem to have

---

[15] Ryckius, *Epistolae ineditae* (1843), 6; I am indebted to Jeroen Van de Ven for this reference.
[16] GA The Hague, Hervormde Gemeente Kerkeraad 203/4, fo. 49.
[17] GA The Hague, Hervormde Gemeente Kerkeraad 203/4, fo. 46. Res. 12 May 1675, fo. 56. Res. and fo. 69. Res. 31 Jan. 1676. Kerkeraad, 16 Sept. 1675.
[18] GA The Hague, Hervormde Gemeente, Kerkeraad 203/4, fos. 52 and 56. Res. 9 and 16 Sept. 1675.

opted for informal behind-the-scenes collaboration with Spinoza against the common menace of Orangism and Calvinist intolerance.

Meanwhile, in their teaching the entire Cartesian faction found themselves obliged during the mid-1670s to draw in their horns and adjust their academic strategies to the new situation by retreating publicly from their bolder philosophical positions and pronouncements of the pre-1672 period. A key figure linking Dutch science and philosophy, Burchardus de Volder (1643–1709), for instance, after becoming a full professor at Leiden, in October 1670, had conducted disputations with titles such as *De Motu Prima* (On the First Movement) (18 April 1671) and *De Unitate Dei* (On the Unity of God) (25 March 1671), closely straddling the border between metaphysics and theology. In the latter case, the *respondens* was the young Bernard Nieuwentijt, then an adventurous youth who later admitted to having at that time been one of those with "Spinozist" leanings himself. By the mid-1670s, though, De Volder and his students were retreating to safer ground, confining themselves to less sensitive topics.[19] If one watched the public sphere alone, it might seem the Cartesian assault on the *TTP*, only slowly, haltingly evolving during 1670–3, now at last evinced real momentum. Respectable academic Cartesians defined "freedom to philosophize," strictly according to what was legitimate under the States of Holland's decree on philosophy of 1656, namely freedom to express their views about whatever does not impinge on Scripture interpretation, revelation, and core Christian doctrine.[20]

But this adjustment in the universities, responding to increased political and ecclesiastical pressure, had the effect of greatly widening the growing gulf between public and private intellectual debate. Following enactment of the 1656 edict, Leiden University's curators had, on 8 January 1657, summoned all three theology professors, Heidanus, Cocceius, and the anti-Cartesian Hoornbeeck, together with the three philosophy professors, De Raey, Heereboord, and Bornius, to sign and swear under formal oath to uphold its provisions. This vow, proclaimed Van Mansvelt's posthumous refutation, in 1674, genuine Cartesians had scrupulously abided by ever since but Spinoza had outrageously violated.[21] In 1656, Leiden Cartesians, including Wittichius, hoping to permanently diminish friction with the Reformed Church synods, had collaborated with the States of Holland's Pensionary De Witt in devising the widest acceptable scope "for philosophy." Genuine Cartesians had all along sought to minimize tensions by separating the "new philosophy" and science from "theology" in university teaching and culture as far as practicable.

But if De Witt's pre-1672 segregation of philosophy from theology had worked by and large, ensuring a comparatively peaceful period down to the late 1660s,

---

[19] Strazzoni, *Burchard de Volder*, 23, 27, 199; Ducheyne, "Curing Pansophia," 275.
[20] Van Mansvelt, *Adversus anonymum*, 3–5.
[21] Ruestow, *Physics at Seventeenth and Eighteenth-Century Leiden*, 47; Israel, *Dutch Republic*, 892–4.

theologians and other increasingly emboldened conservative, anti-Cartesian professors backing the old scholasticism now had the opportunity to resume the offensive. They complained that, whatever the pretence, genuine subordination of philosophy to theology under the 1656 placard had all along been evaded, with a freedom scandalously encouraging Cartesians to overstep the mark with propositions that ultimately lead to Spinoza. In the Voetian-Orangist view, De Witt's placard had been essentially just a dodge cheating true Christians, its function being to quieten things down and maintain a superficial order in the lecture room while insidiously emancipating the "new philosophy," including astronomy and comet theory, from all real subordination to church supervision.

Dissension in the universities sharply intensified from early 1674, not least at Leiden where the quarrel between De Volder and the anti-Cartesian Gerardus de Vries (1648–1705), known as the "hammer of the Cartesians," even provoked fist fights between students. On 3 March 1674, a disturbance broke out on the middle floor of the main Leiden University building during a disputation. Student protest in response to remarks by De Vries caused the latter to storm out of the lecture hall and angrily transfer back to Utrecht where he resumed his anti-Cartesian drive in the philosophy and other faculties. At Leiden, both sides in the furore, Cartesians and anti-Cartesians, complained to the University senate. On 28 June 1674, De Volder and Wittichius together with the Coccejan theologian, Heidanus, were summoned before the new Pensionary of Holland, Gaspar Fagel. Cartesians were not ill-disposed towards the Stadholder, they assured Fagel nor, they tried to convince him, were they a danger to religion.[22] Fagel had his doubts. De Volder had various Royal Society volumes and many texts of Boyle among his books, but besides the latest scientific developments abroad was intensely absorbed, his personal library reveals, also in Machiavelli and republican political theory, possessing all the main texts of the De La Courts including Pieter's banned *Aanwysing* (1669). Radical underground literature too was well represented in his collection of nearly 2,000 volumes which, six months after his death, in 1709, was auctioned off in Leiden, a library including Meyer's *Philosophia* and Spinoza's *Cartesii Principia philosophiae*, the *Opera Posthuma*, and the *TTP*, as well as La Peyrère's *Praeadamitae*, Hobbes' *Leviathan*, Beverland's *De Pecccato originali* (1679), Cuffeler's *Specimen artis ratiocinandi* (1684), and Bouwmeester's Dutch version of *Hai Ibn Yokhdan* (1672).[23]

Open wrangling within the universities during 1674–5 formed part of a much wider phenomenon with serious political and religious as well as academic consequences. Spinoza's response to being put more closely under surveillance was one of barely concealed frustration due to its isolating, restricting impact on him and on his chances of publishing his work. This was the very opposite of what

---

[22] Sassen, *Geschiedenis*, 147; Bamberger, "Early Editions," 29n15; Strazzoni, *Burchard de Volder*, 28.
[23] *Bibliotheca Volderiana*, 3, 5, 7, 41, 45, 87–8, 92.

the *TTP* had been supposed to achieve. If strict Calvinists and Orangists felt the De Wittian fudge violated the proper order of things, Spinoza, maintained Van Mansvelt's editors, whatever he claimed, was violating the law, acting illicitly, in a way academic Cartesians were not. What Spinoza understood by "libertas philosophandi" was plainly seditious: the right to overstep basic theological curbs on philosophical discussion, thereby endangering core Christian doctrine, and this, held the Cartesians publicly, promotes "errors of every kind," amounting to "defending and propagating profane license," to expounding principles "such that no sooner would they be admitted than all peace of the republic would be overthrown."[24] This was precisely Ryckius' point. Anxious the public should not associate academic Cartesians with the wider, more comprehensive toleration that Collegiants, Mennonites, Remonstrants, Catholics, and Spinozists demanded, Reformed Cartesians combined their attack on Spinoza with vigorous defence of the public church and the States' posture under the 1653 (anti-Socinian) and 1656 decrees, rejecting not just Spinoza's full toleration and freedom of expression but often also the less comprehensive but still, according to many, overly relaxed *de facto* toleration prevailing in Amsterdam and Rotterdam in particular.[25]

36.ii Summer Weeks in Amsterdam

Oldenburg's letter of 22 July 1675 reached Spinoza just as he was setting out for Amsterdam, as explained in his subsequent reply, to execute his plan to publish the *Ethics*, or as he expressed it "confide the book about which I wrote to you to the press." But he found nothing reassuring in his trip or his discussions with his friends and allies as regards advancing his philosophy and their common cause. Shortly after Oldenburg penned his July letter, Tschirnhaus' friend, Schuller, also wrote to Spinoza and, doing so from Amsterdam, Spinoza presumably saw his letter first. "Our noble friend Mr Tschirnhaus who is in England and like us, enjoying good health," he reported, had asked him no less than three times to forward, along with his respectful greetings, queries concerning Spinoza's conception of God. In his *Ethics* Part I, Proposition 3, Spinoza writes: "If [two] things have nothing in common with one another, one of them cannot be the cause of the other."[26] To the studious young Silesian aristocrat studying the *Ethics* in manuscript, or at least its early parts, this seemed to mean, since God's intellect differs from human intellect both in essence and existence, and the divine intellect therefore has nothing in common with our intellect, that Spinoza's philosophy signifies that "God's intellect cannot be the cause of our intellect [Dei intellectus

---

[24] Van Mansvelt, *Adversus anonymum*, 4; Strazzoni, *Burchard De Volder*, 128.
[25] Van Mansvelt, *Adversus anonymum*, 4, 362.
[26] Spinoza, *Collected Works* (ed. Curley) i, 410.

non potest esse causa nostri intellectus]."[27] Apparently, Tschirnhaus had not yet fully grasped that for Spinoza all of Nature is comprised in God.

Schuller enclosed also greetings from Rieuwertsz and Van Gent, a close friend of Tschirnhaus since 1669 when both were studying in Leiden, whom Spinoza had got to know at some point in the company of Schuller and Tschirnhaus.[28] As medical students together in the late 1660s, Schuller and Van Gent had been close too, but were now uneasy friends and remained such until shortly after Spinoza's death when they would quarrel violently. For a time, Van Gent kept his own separate private correspondence with Spinoza which, unfortunately, has been entirely lost. One of his letters evidently asks Spinoza to reprimand Schuller for speaking indiscreetly about his doctrines in conversation with a famed Amsterdam alchemist called Vieroort. Schuller actively cultivated the Spinoza circle of friends but appears to have been less serious about Spinozism and philosophy than Tschirnhaus or Van Gent, and, in fact, chiefly a zealot for alchemy. Breaking the rule that members of Spinoza's circle were exhorted to follow, Schuller had confided to Vieroort that there is no Final Judgement in Spinoza's view, no resurrection of bodies, no Devil, no revelations from God in the Bible, and that Jesus was not the son of God but the illegitimate son of Joseph and Mary.[29] Schuller, like Van Gent and Tschirnhaus, was meant to be keeping these points secret.

For some years until 1672, Van Gent too had been a medical student, but for whatever reason, unlike Schuller and Tschirnhaus, failed to achieve a viable career afterwards and remained always desperately short of money. In the years he knew Spinoza, he led an increasingly precarious existence financially and in other respects. He is chiefly relevant to Spinoza's biography for the important role he performed later, in 1677, in helping edit, and, as he himself expressed it, in March 1679, "transcribing the major part of Spinoza's *Opera*," meaning copying out and helping establish the Latin text from the manuscripts, assisting Meyer as principal editor after being brought into the clandestine joint enterprise apparently at the behest of Schuller.[30] Van Gent clearly remained a more serious, devoted disciple and promoter of Spinozism as well as of Tschirnhaus' efforts than the ingratiating, unreliable Schuller. But his sole occupation, apparently, aside from studying, was editing, transcribing, and correcting Latin for publishers, especially Rieuwertsz. Distress and fatigue, he later admitted, drove him to frequent taverns, but he denied Schuller's accusation, during their subsequent quarrel, that he had descended into becoming a hopeless drunkard.[31]

---

[27] Schuller to Spinoza, Amsterdam, 25 July in Spinoza, *Opera* iv, 275.
[28] Van Gent to Schuller, Amsterdam, 23 March 1679 in Klever, "Clé d'un nom," 172, 174; Proietti and Licata, *Il Carteggio*, 22-3, 26.
[29] Proietti and Licata, *Il Carteggio*, 23-4.   [30] Proietti and Licata, *Il Carteggio*, 23, 25.
[31] Spinoza to Schuller, 18 November 1675 in Spinoza, *Opera* iv, 304-6; Proietti and Licata, *Il Carteggio*, 24-5; Van Gent to Schuller, Amsterdam, 23 March 1679 in Klever, "Clé d'un nom," 174-5; Laerke, *Leibniz lecteur*, 363.

Later on, Spinoza received word from Tschirnhaus, via Schuller in Amsterdam, also about the general situation and the situation regarding his philosophy in Paris. The Republic and France being still at war, communication with the French capital for the moment remained less direct than with London, not least as regards smuggling in banned books, though certainly a few copies of the *TTP* did enter France prior to 1678. On arriving in Paris at the end of September or in early October 1675, Tschirnhaus immediately contacted and established a good working relationship with Huygens, as Spinoza (and Oldenburg) had advised, and quickly felt he had won his esteem. Delighted to hear Spinoza still held him in high regard, Huygens reciprocated, expressing his esteem for Spinoza. In Paris, Tschirnhaus claimed to be responding to all queries strictly in accord with Spinoza's instructions, saying little about him personally and nothing about the *Ethics*, telling those he met, Schuller reported, that the only other work he knew of by Spinoza was the treatise on Descartes' principles. His discreet and cautious proceedings, hoped Tschirnhaus, "would not be disagreeable" to his honoured mentor in The Hague.[32]

Pressure for stricter sabbath observance in the Republic, meanwhile, and tighter bans on circuses and "comedies," as well as pressure on Catholics certainly intensified to an extent. During the mid- and late 1670s, De Lantman presided over numerous consistory discussions at The Hague on how to stop "comedies" being performed and generally curb Dutch theatre more stringently.[33] The main Amsterdam theatre for now remained shut. Another aspect of the "Further Reformation" offensive was the mid-1670s renewed drive against Socinian tendencies in the Remonstrant and Mennonite churches. In late 1674, the Leiden consistory studied a report on rumours that Socinian gatherings of "eighteen or twenty, or more persons at one time" were occurring secretly in their city and that, at Remonstrant and Mennonite gatherings, assaults on the "divinity of Christ" and required belief in the "three-in-one God," the inviolable core of all genuine Christian doctrine, were increasing, a tendency for which the Remonstrants bore some responsibility, their theology being based on the works of Episcopius and "Curcellaeus" or Étienne de Courcelles (1586–1659), an Arminian scholar friendly with Descartes and among the initiators in Arminian circles of the drive to reconcile religion with philosophy.[34] In February and March 1675, the Leiden Reformed consistory adopted resolutions severely condemning the "Socinian conventicles" held there and stepping up pressure on the city government to refuse toleration for Remonstrants on account of their less than unstinting opposition to the Socinians.[35]

---

[32] Spinoza, *Opera* iv, 302.
[33] GA The Hague, Hervormde Kerk, kerkeraad 203/4, pp. 87, 90, 127, 130, 141.
[34] GA Leiden Acta kerkeraad, res. 15 Feb. 1675.
[35] GA Leiden Acta kerkeraad, res. 3 March 1675.

Besides stronger measures against Catholicism and Remonstrantism, the Haarlem consistory also demanded measures to check the "creeping in of Socinianism under the disguise of the Mennonites." All local Mennonite preachers, demanded the consistory, should be summoned to the Haarlem town hall, warned to confine their voices strictly within their own confession and within their own church, and be required to forbid the teaching of Galenus and help block further percolation of "atrocious Socinianism."[36] Complaints that the "scandalous and corrupting *Tractatus Theologico-Politicus*" was still being found in bookshops and at book auctions led to pressure for the province-wide crack-down on the *TTP*, the *Philosophia*, and Hobbes' *Leviathan* to be intensified. Although these complaints regularly listed four texts as especially pernicious, it seems clear that the Reformed Church considered the *TTP* to be the worst. Continually denounced,[37] the *TTP* far outstripped Hobbes' *Leviathan* as an object of recrimination, with discussions at the Reformed Church's North and South Holland synods during 1672–4 invariably laying most emphasis on the danger posed by the *TTP* than any other text.

One result of this onslaught during the mid-1670s were efforts to strengthen the censorship mechanism operated by the local Reformed Church classes. Scrutinizing bookshops needed to become more efficient. The classis of Edam, for example, discussing on 12 November 1674 an order passed down by the North Holland synod to strengthen surveillance of local book circulation, agreed to tighten inspection by increasing their *visitores librorum*, or appointed inspectors of books and bookshops, from two to three, and ensuring responsibility for searching out the worst books. This position would no longer be considered honorary, *ad vitam* [for life], but would be henceforth *ambulatoir* with whoever happened to be the oldest *visitor* having to resign at appropriate intervals to be replaced by a younger preacher or elder.[38]

But in the face of increased pressure, the Arminians and Socinians only intensified their efforts and there were also other contrary winds impeding the advance of the Orangist-Calvinist alliance. Some of the shine had been knocked off William's glowing aura as the new "David" and saviour of the Fatherland by his mishandling of the 1675 campaign in the southern Netherlands and failure to capitalize on the massive further diversion of French strength from the Low Countries into which Louis was forced by developments on the Rhine, well to the south. Condé had been withdrawn to reinforce France's posture in Germany, leaving Luxembourg commanding a much reduced force in the Netherlands. By the time Spinoza visited Amsterdam in late July 1675, the Imperialists, aided by

---

[36] GA Haarlem Acta kerkeraad ix, res. 14 June and 30 Aug. 1675.
[37] RNH, classis Haarlem, fo. 206. Acta, 19 July 1672; ARH Ned. Hervormde kerk, Oud Synodaal Archief 184, 37. Acta 1672, art. 38; Acta 1673, p. 32 art. 39.
[38] RNH Hervormde Classis Edam 6, res. 12 Nov. 1674.

Spain, were advancing on a broad front, encircling Trier, and menacing Alsace and Strasbourg. The old marshal Turenne, France's most renowned commander apart from Condé, was killed by an Imperialist cannonball at the Battle of Salzbach, on 27 July, just days after Spinoza arrived in Amsterdam with the manuscript of the *Ethics* in his bags. It was an interesting moment to return to his native city. The theatre remained closed, but everyone was becoming more cheerful. For the first time since 1672, its citizens were savouring the agreeable sensation of feeling safe and free, finally rescued from the dire menace of the invader.

A key factor hampering Orangist-Calvinist consolidation of power and "Further Reformation" reaction was the inexorable cost of the war, maintaining the now huge Dutch army of around 100,000 men which William III had built up around the Republic's defensive lines, an army largely staffed by foreign officers, imposing a crushing fiscal burden at a time when the Republic's trade, stock exchange, and economy had only partially recovered from the catastrophe of 1672.[39] The economy's sluggishness would persist until the war's end, in 1678, visibly impairing the dynamism, affluence, and even appearance of the city. "From the top of one of their watch-towers," noted the future Tory bishop, William Nicolson, in 1678, "we had a good prospect of the city and shipping which was not such an amazing sight as I expected. For (notwithstanding their great Dutch brags of a wood of masts to be seen at this city) I am confident a man may reckon more vessels from the top of the monument at London-bridge then from any watch-tower in Amsterdam."[40]

Dissatisfaction was surfacing over the high taxes and the Prince's "preferring of strangers and soldiers of fortune in the army," as a contemporary English report expressed it, "who may solely depend upon his favour, and rejecting the Netherlanders."[41] As yet, there were only faint signs, though, of the recovery of republican sentiment in the city governments, even at Amsterdam where the city council remained deeply divided between the remaining republican rump under Burgomaster Hendrik Hooft (1617–78) and pragmatists anxious to cooperate with the Prince, under Gillis Valckenier (1623–80), a renowned opportunist and opponent of principled republicans. Valckenier's policy was to prevent recall of those regents purged in 1672 in order to stay in the Stadholder's good books. Consequently, neither the anti-Orangist bloc, nor the anti-war policy, prioritizing peace with France, regained their old preponderance in Spinoza's native city until somewhat later (early 1677).[42] Though a principled republican, Spinoza's best friend in the city government, Hudde, favoured a conciliatory approach, easing

[39] Israel, *Dutch Primacy*, 255; Israel, "Amsterdam Stock Exchange," 848.
[40] Nicolson, "Iter Hollandicum," 100.
[41] PRO SP84/295, report "The Commonwealth Party"; Israel, *Dutch Republic*, 793, 805, 821–3.
[42] Israel, *Dutch Republic*, 828; Troost, *William III*, 132.

rather than acerbating the Voetian-Cocceian rift. Despite the rising groundswell of dissatisfaction, detectable since 1673, stemming from resentment on ideological grounds, the burdens of the long-drawn out war, heavy fiscal pressure, and William's overly princely and courtly style of command, this was not yet translating into a serious republican backlash, and the Prince compensated for whatever checks he suffered by tightening his pact with the Voetian preachers and stirring fundamentalist Calvinist sentiment, precisely the element posing the direst threat to Spinoza's plans, friends, and standing.

It is unclear how many weeks Spinoza spent in Amsterdam. From the last few days of July until probably mid-August1675, he stayed for around three weeks, perhaps longer, at a time when building activity in the city, and also the publishing industry, were noticeably reviving. Since he left in 1661, Amsterdam, apart from numbers of ships in the harbour, had grown strikingly larger and more impressive. Ray's *Observations topographical* published in England during the war, in 1673, but based on observations made in the 1660s, notes that Amsterdam is "the greatest city in all the Low Countries, and one of the richest and best traded empories of the whole world," which Ray and his companion "judged [...] about the bigness of Venice and lesser than one half of London," but with "a great space of ground, wherein they had designed and set out streets, with the intention to make their city for bigness also comparable with the best of Europe, London and Paris not excepted." Between 1663 and 1672, the three most prestigious canals, the Herengracht, Keizersgracht, and Prinsengracht, were all impressively extended with what were now Amsterdam's stateliest residences. By 1671, much of the plan had become fact: "I hear since," added Ray, "that this void ground is filled with rows of stately and beautiful houses."[43]

But everything had come to a halt in 1672 and was only just now reviving. As it happened, Spinoza's stay exactly coincided with the completion and inauguration, in August 1675, amid much pomp and circumstance, of the grand new Portuguese synagogue, now among the city's largest buildings and much the most splendid synagogue in all Europe (Figure 36.1). Suspended throughout 1672-3, work on completing the synagogue had resumed just months prior to the inauguration ceremonies. Whether Spinoza took much notice of the festivities inaugurating the most imposing synagogue seen since ancient times remains unknown, but it was impossible to be altogether oblivious as the solemnities, attracting much attention, continued for eight full days. The festivities were timed to start with the solemn prayers of 2 August 1675, in the Hebrew calendar known as *Tisha b'Av* [9th of Av], a special Fast Day commemorating destruction of the First Temple by the Babylonians in 587 BC, after functioning, according to Josephus, for 470 years, as well as the destruction of the Second Temple inaugurated under Persian rule in

[43] Ray, *Observations topographical*, 40.

Figure 36.1 *View of the new Amsterdam Portuguese Jewish Synagogue (on the left) inaugurated in 1675*, engraving by Adolf van der Laan, c.1710, call no. A41.1.21.1. Reproduction courtesy of the Library of the Jewish Theological Seminary.

515 BC, and later expanded by Herod, obliterated by the Romans six centuries after the First Temple was rebuilt, in AD 70. For added poignancy, the *parnasim* timed the proceedings to mark also the annual commemoration of the decree of expulsion from Spain in 1492. Within a decade of the fiasco of Sabbatianism, the new synagogue's splendour symbolically subsumed and softened even if it could not reverse the destruction of both ancient Temples and the trauma of exodus from Spain, mass forced baptism in Portugal, two centuries of Inquisition repression, and the Sabbatian fiasco.

Whatever Spinoza actually saw of the new synagogue, its environs, and the inauguration ceremonies, there was no way he could avoid hearing accounts of the building's splendid interior and the prolonged festivities witnessed by much of the city. At the very least, he must have seen the great edifice dominating the skyline of the entire neighbourhood where he grew up and conducted business as a young merchant, just a short walk from where his Amsterdam friends lived and worked.[44] Nor can he have failed to reflect on the irony of this grand testimony to the strengthening position of the Jews in Holland, less than a decade after the disastrous messianic frenzy of 1665–6, a movement that had convinced not a few Jews he had known in his younger days that the ingathering of their people was at hand, and that they must all now pack their bags and set off for the Holy Land, abandoning their life in dispersion forever.

---

[44] Nadler, *Spinoza: A Life*, 388.

The inauguration itself was a sumptuous affair intended to impress with pompous display, with the chief donors well to the fore, among them Jeronimo Nunes da Costa (Moses Curiel), the Sephardic "Agent of the Crown of Portugal," and with several burgomasters and regents in attendance, as recorded afterwards in a magnificent engraving by Romeyn de Hooghe. Spinoza's brother, Gabriel, could not participate, having emigrated to the Caribbean in the mid-1660s where, by 1671, he was a naturalized subject of Charles II, living in Jamaica.[45] Nor could Spinoza's brother-in-law, Rabbi Samuel de Caceres, deceased a decade before; but his sister, Rebecca, and nephew, Daniel de Caceres, were surely present. Jeronimo, being involved while serving as a *parnas* in the community's censorship of Spanish and Portuguese-language books, was certainly aware of Spinoza's ideas and the States' ban on his writings. As Agent of the Crown of Portugal, he was frequently in The Hague where, being a prominent figure among the Sephardic community elders, he presumably refused to meet Spinoza, but from time to time must have heard word of the furore provoked by his ideas and his denial of a personal God, miracles, and Revelation.

Spinoza's visit occurred also just days after the death and burial, on 19 July, of his boyhood teacher, Rabbi Judah Leon Templo. Assuredly, Spinoza had not forgotten him. Not only was he familiar as a youth with Leon Templo's Temple model, but his own personal library in The Hague included the *Sefer Tavnit Hekhal* [Book of the Image of the Temple], depicting Solomon's Temple which Leon Templo had dedicated to the Amsterdam community *parnasim* a quarter of a century before, in 1650, when Spinoza was eighteen, listing by name the seven "noble, wise, and most generous *senhores*" in office that year, headed by the *senhor* "Michael D'Espinosa."[46] Solomon, by far Spinoza's favourite Old Testament personality, was "more highly commended in the sacred writing for his prudence and wisdom," the qualities Spinoza admired, "than for his prophecy and piety."[47] If during these weeks Spinoza felt any inclination to visit the graves of his parents and grandparents at Ouderkerk, he would likely have inspected too Leon Templo's gravestone nearby, fittingly inscribed with an image of Solomon's Temple.[48]

Solomon, it is worth recalling, is Spinoza's key biblical exemplum of how humans can best organize their lives and achieve happiness, having "located the fruit of understanding in true life alone and punishment exclusively in lack of it," which "agrees completely," holds Spinoza in the *TTP*, "with our fourth point about the natural divine Law: the same wise man also plainly taught that this

---

[45] Nadler, *Spinoza: A Life*, 101.
[46] Leon Templo, *Sefer Tavnit Hekhal*, dedicação, p.1; Van Sluis and Musschenga, *Boeken van Spinoza*, 40–1.
[47] Spinoza, *Theological-Political Treatise*, 65–6; Moreau, *Spinoza et le Spinozisme*, 96–7.
[48] Offenberg, "Jacob Jehudah Leon," 108.

fountain of life, or the intellect alone, prescribes laws to the wise, as we have so often shown." This revealing (if far from convincing) passage Spinoza concludes by reaffirming that "the wise alone therefore, in Solomon's view, live with a peaceful and stable purpose, unlike impious people whose minds fluctuate between different passions and therefore (as Isaiah 57:20 also says) possess neither peace nor calm."[49]

Solomon and his Temple manifested in Spinoza's mind his notion of authentic ancient Judaism as something inseparably linked to political and legal independence, a defined, undivided entity knowing no theological sects such as Pharisees, Sadducees, and Essenes competing for control and power. Theology and faction-fighting he considered a fatal malaise that spread only later. Equally, the Second Temple's destruction shaped his view of post-Temple Judaism. Following destruction of Solomon's Temple, the Jews "immediately neglected the ceremonies [...] in fact, completely abandoned the Law of Moses and let the ordinances of their country fall into oblivion as obviously superfluous, and began mingling with the other nations as is abundantly clear from Ezra and Nehemiah." This was then reversed under the Second Temple, but "with their state now dissolved, there is no doubt the Jews are no more bound by the Law of Moses than they were before the commencement of their community and state. For while dwelling among other peoples, before the Exodus from Egypt, they possessed no special laws, being bound only by the natural law along with the law of the state in which they were living, so far as it did not conflict with the natural divine law."[50] Modern Judaism, for Spinoza, derives not from the authentic monotheism of ancient Israel and eras of the two Temples but is rather a despotic Pharisaic power-seeking fabrication. "As for the Pharisees retaining the [ceremonies...] after the loss of their state, they did this more in a spirit of opposition to the Christians than to please God." Earlier, "ceremonies served to preserve and maintain the state of the Hebrews," but since the loss of the Second Temple served only to preserve a Pharisaic mirage.[51] Spinoza's preference was for the Sadducees.

After visiting the new synagogue, the English consul, William Carr, commented: "the Jewes, who are very considerable in the trade of this citie have two synagogues, one whereof [the Portuguese] is the largest in Christendom, and as some say in the world, sure I am, it far exceeds those in Rome, Venice and all other places where I have bin."[52] In 1690, another Englishman spoke of "this cathedral" as "one which far exceeds all they have at Rome or Venice."[53] Two focal points inside were, as they remain today, the imposing Ark of the Torah Scrolls and central podium from where the cantor leads the congregation in reciting prayers, and portions of the Torah are read on the sabbath. The ark was carved from imported jacaranda (Brazil) wood, material renowned for its durability and

---

[49] Spinoza, *Theological-Political Treatise*, 66–7.
[50] Spinoza, *Theological-Political Treatise*, 71.
[51] Spinoza, *Theological-Political Treatise*, 71–2.
[52] Carr, *Travellours Guide*, 21, 23.
[53] Northleigh, *Topographical Descriptions*, 60.

splendid shiny veneer, donated by Nunes da Costa.[54] When Holland's foremost painter of church interiors, Emanuel de Witte (1617–92), produced his today oft reproduced rendering of the synagogue's interior, soon after the consecration, he assigned special prominence in the foreground to the visitors' gallery and, in the background, to Jeronimo's splendid ark of Brazil wood.

Very likely it was also during this stay in Amsterdam that Spinoza, out one evening at a dinner with friends and acquaintances, encountered another guest, the Remonstrant theologian and, later, friend of John Locke, Van Limborch, among the leading intellectual lights of Amsterdam, who, when discussing Spinoza later, in his *Theologia Christiana* (1686), focused chiefly on his denial of miracles. Less than half a year younger than Spinoza, he would outlive him by three and half decades. Four years before his main theological work was published, in January 1682, Van Limborch wrote to his ally, Le Clerc, the later adversary of Pierre Bayle, recalling that evening "some years ago" when, unaware Spinoza would be there, he and Spinoza had attended the same supper. He described Spinoza to his younger ally as a dangerous chameleon, a devious man conducting himself in very different ways in different situations, a "Proteus" (in Greek mythology, the god of sea beasts renowned for his ability to change shape) seeking to inculcate harmful notions into imprudent minds without ever openly declaring himself, "masking his poison by revealing his ideas only in mutilated and truncated form."[55]

By no means did he reject all of Spinoza's Bible criticism Van Limborch assured Le Clerc. But in several chapters, "principally that on miracles," this insidious person had been wholly unable to conceal his "atheism." Elsewhere, even more insidiously, he deviously concealed his full meaning and the venomous nature of what he intended to convey about the Bible, religion, and life's true priorities under ambiguous phrases. Unfortunately, this rendered Spinoza's Bible criticism and subversive thought, unlike Koerbagh's, elusive and extremely hard to effectively refute or bring to court. At this dinner, during prayers, he added, Spinoza "showed his irreverent attitude through gestures [presumably rolling up his eyes] by which he seemed to want to convince those of us praying to God of our stupidity."[56] With Le Clerc, and many another, Van Limborch fully agreed that a stronger, more vigorous collective effort by scholars was needed to halt the spread of Spinoza's influence.

36.iii Failed Attempt to Publish the *Ethics*

The chief purpose of Spinoza's stay in Amsterdam, in August 1675, was "to put the book about which I wrote to you," as he afterwards recounted to Oldenburg, "into

---

[54] Franco Mendes, *Memorias*, 76–7; Mendes dos Remedios, *Judeus portugueses em Amsterdam*, 213.
[55] Van Limborch to Le Clerc, Amsterdam, 25 Jan. 1682 printed in Meinsma, *Spinoza et son cercle*, 525.
[56] Van Limborch to Le Clerc, Amsterdam, 23 Jan. 1682 in Meinsma, *Spinoza et son cercle*, 525–7; Israel, *Radical Enlightenment*, 287.

print," concert strategy with Rieuwertsz, and discuss his prospects, and those of his philosophy and followers, with friends and allies, principally Meyer, Bouwmeester, Jelles, and Glazemaker, supplemented now by Tschirnhaus' former student comrades, Schuller and Van Gent, who had both developed close ties with Rieuwertsz. At the same time, Spinoza learnt more of the efforts in progress in Amsterdam and elsewhere to tighten surveillance of publishers and curb opponents of the Reformed Church. After intensive discussion over whether and how to publish the *Ethics*, the collective conclusion was that, for now, it was simply too dangerous to proceed. One wonders whether the circumspect Hudde was among those Spinoza consulted. For the time being, the surveillance under which Spinoza laboured, and the traps set for him, were simply too formidable.

"Since I learnt these things from several men worthy of being relied on," confirming that the theologians "were everywhere conspiring against me," Spinoza explained to Oldenburg in the late summer of 1675, "I decided to postpone the publication I had in hand until I should see how matters would turn out." Before replying to Oldenburg, he had hoped to decide, one way or the other "but the situation seems to get worse by the day so that I do not know what I should do."[57] In the end, he simply left the entire question in the air. Better to accept temporary defeat at the Reformed theologians' hands than risk a more crushing reversal by defying the hard-liners at a moment when they could count on having the ear of the Prince. "While I was working on this" in Amsterdam, Spinoza wrote further to Oldenburg in September, "a rumour circulated that a certain book of mine about God was in the press in which I try to show there is no God [in eo conari ostendere, nullum dari Deum]." This rumour was believed "by many so that certain theologians (perhaps the authors of this rumour), seized the opportunity to go to see the Prince [of Orange] and the [The Hague] city magistrates about me." Moreover, he continued, "the stupid Cartesians, because they are believed to be favourable towards me, try to expunge that suspicion from themselves by constantly declaring their abhorrence of my views and writings." Of the early biographers of Spinoza, Lucas is the most explicit in noting that the Cartesians, precisely because they now felt themselves at risk as originators of the system that formed Spinoza's starting point, reacted against his thought more furiously and resolutely than even the anti-Cartesians—much as the Augustinian Jansenists in France, being accused of affinities with Calvinism, attacked the Calvinists more violently than anyone else. "But the persecution the Cartesians mounted against Monsieur de Spinosa," affirms Lucas, "far from shaking his confidence, only fortified him in his search for the truth."[58]

---

[57] Spinoza, *Opera* iv, 299; Spinoza, *Correspondance* (ed. Rovere), 350; Spinoza, *Collected Works* (ed. Curley) ii, 459; Van Vloten, *Benedictus de Spinoza*, 91.
[58] [Lucas], *La Vie*, 32.

Returning to The Hague in the autumn, Spinoza found the situation far from encouraging. The Hague's *kerkeraad*, meeting on 16 September, heard that the preacher responsible for the Paviljoensgracht district where Spinoza lived had, as directed, made inquiries about their suspect's insidious activities, but "as yet reported no further evidence" of his leading individuals astray, the main thing for which evidence was needed. Usable written testimony of Spinoza's "damaging seduction" of others was still frustratingly lacking, but De Lantman and the other leading figures "judged it necessary that the said preacher must continue by every conceivable means of investigation and all members of the council must assist, so that it can be established as precisely as possible what the position is with regard to the man, his teaching and the propagation of the same."[59] A like admonition requiring heightened vigilance against the "damaging erring spirit [dwaalgeest] Spinoza" was issued by the Leiden Reformed ministry in October.[60] Meanwhile, with his main work of philosophy shelved indefinitely, Spinoza received further news of the Orangist-Voetian backlash in Utrecht from conversations with "our friend Nieustad," that is Joachim Nieuwstad, former secretary of the Utrecht city government since 1662, a fervent Cartesian and specialist in water management physics, who, like Van Velthuysen, had been purged from office in early 1674. Nieuwstad was among those who visited Spinoza in person at The Hague that autumn.[61]

Where Spinoza keenly resented the Cartesians' public campaign against his ideas and adherents, the Cartesians felt increasingly threatened by the mounting Orangist-Voetian reaction and its impact on the universities. Bontekoe and Overkamp were by no means the only young scholars at Leiden severely disciplined for expressing defiantly Cartesian views in a fashion unacceptable to the curators in the mid-1670s. Bernard Nieuwentijt, son of a Reformed preacher, then an ardent young "Cartesian" studying at Leiden, was expelled from the University after two or three years as a twenty-one-year-old trouble-maker at around the same time as Bontekoe (December 1675). In 1682, he would become a physician to the poor in Purmerend. Eventually, becoming affluent and a regent of the small town of Purmerend, north of Amsterdam, after discarding his early Cartesio-Spinozism and inspired now by Boyle, Nieuwentijt plunged into a frenzy of experimentalism and zeal for English empiricism, exalting the "modesty" and learned caution of the Baconian true scholar and scientist. This became the hallmark of the anti-Spinozism of his maturity as he emerged as the leading Dutch physico-theologian theorist and Newtonian of the early eighteenth century.[62]

---

[59] GA The Hague, Hervormde Gemeente Kerkeraad 203/4, fos. 56–7. Res. Kerkeraad, 16 Sept. 1675; Kingma, "Spinoza en zijn Haagse periode," 17.
[60] GA Leiden MS. Kerkeraad 17, fo. 62v. Res. 31 Oct. 1675.
[61] Spinoza to Velthuysen, undated, autumn 1675 in Spinoza, *Collected Works* (ed. Curley) ii, 460.
[62] Ducheyne, "Curing Pansophia," 275–6.

Month by month reports from the university towns showed the Orangist-Voetian reaction in the Netherlands gaining rather than losing momentum. Together with the local Reformed consistory which was ceaselessly urging more action, Leiden University's curators were busy preparing revised articles to regulate philosophy teaching. What was now proposed was an official list of unacceptable arguments and viewpoints prohibited from all university lecturing, discussion, and disputations. The draft list originally compiled by the investigating committee comprised twenty-three forbidden viewpoints; after review, these were reduced to twenty one. Some of those prohibited were genuinely Coccean or Cartesian positions, others (some allegedly taught or debated by De Volder) plainly derived from Meyer's *Philosophia* or else Spinoza, including the ninth, that "Scripture speaks according to the erroneous prejudices of the common people," and tenth, that "the human soul is nothing but the mind with which, when activated, man can live and move." Forbidden outright too was maintaining that "philosophy is the interpreter of Scripture."[63]

After consulting with the South Holland synod and Prince of Orange, the curators published their list of twenty-one prohibited propositions in January 1676, but met with sturdy resistance from the pro-Cartesian and Coccean professors enraged especially by the clear but misleading implication that the Cartesio-Coccean colleagues as a group broadly embraced all or many of these propositions, those of Meyer and Spinoza along with those of Descartes and Cocceius.[64] In the spring of 1676, De Volder, Wittichius (Figure 36.2), and Heidanus (Figure 36.3) jointly published a vehement protest, entitled *Consideratien over eenige saecken onlanghs voorgevallen in de Universiteyt van Leyden* [Considerations on some matters recently arising in the University of Leiden], in which Wittichius handled the theological side, De Volder the philosophical, and Heidanus penned the angry preface—but with Heidanus' name alone appearing on the title-page. Summoned and made to confess to writing the text in defiance of the curators, the now seventy-nine-year-old Heidanus was left to face the consequences alone: on 5 May 1676, he was stripped of his professorship. Disappointingly for Voetians hoping for more removals, De Volder and Wittichius eluded drastic consequences for now, but were left in no doubt they must henceforth keep their heads well down.[65]

The public quarrel over whether the "principles of Spinoza" were, or were not, "hidden in the Cartesian philosophy," as the Franeker professor Johannes Regius

---

[63] Cramer, *Abraham Heidanus*, 102–3; Van der Wall, "The *Tractatus* [...] and Dutch Calvinism," 207–8; Goudriaan, *Reformed Orthodoxy*, 6.
[64] Cramer, *Abraham Heidanus*, 112–14; Strazzoni, *Burchard De Volder*, 132–3.
[65] Cramer, *Abraham Heidanus*, 104–6, 110–11; Van der Wall, "The *Tractatus* [...] and Dutch Calvinism," 208; Sassen, *Geschiedenis*, 162; Strazzoni, *Burchard De Volder*, 28–9; Kato, "Petrus van Mastricht," 129–30.

Figure 36.2 *Christophorus Wittichius* (Christoph Wittich) (1625–87). © Fitzwilliam Museum, Cambridge.

expressed it in 1713,[66] would rage uninterruptedly in the Dutch and German Calvinist universities for decades. Among leading books championing conservative reaction was the *Novitatum Cartesianarum Gangraena* [The Gangrene of Cartesian Novelties] (Amsterdam 1677) by Petrus van Mastricht (1630–1706), Voetius' successor at Utrecht and, like him, a fervent proponent of anti-Copernicanism in the era's scientific disputes. Where Cartesians say the sun stands still and the earth moves round it, the pious embrace Scripture's assurance, contends Van Mastricht, that the earth stays stationary and the sun moves around it. The Church should insist more stringently than it has on the sun circling the earth because erroneous Cartesian thinking readily leads to Spinoza and cannot be tolerated. There is some difference between Cartesianism and Spinozism, Van

---

[66] Regius, *Beginselen der beschouwende filozofy*, "Voorreden."

Figure 36.3 *Abraham Heidanus* (1597–1678), engraving after Jan André Lievens. Reproduction courtesy of The Picture Art Collection/Alamy Stock Photo.

Mastricht's *Gangraena* concedes; but the key point is that Spinoza subordinates theology and Scripture to reason and philosophy as Cartesians also do when rendering "doubt" and "reason" the highest operative principles. Cartesians simply refuse to accept theology's primacy and this no society should tolerate.[67]

Claiming "Scripture speaks of natural things according to the erroneous notions of ordinary people," as Wittichius, Van Velthuysen, De Volder, Burman, and Wolzogen all did, Cartesianism effectively subordinates theology

---

[67] Mastricht, *Novitatum Cartesianarum Gangraena*, 62, 392–5; Kato, "Petrus van Mastricht," 131–3.

to philosophy and Revelation to reason, thereby encouraging the ruinous process, the "gangrene" of Van Mastricht's title, the creeping infiltration by which all Cartesian thought seeks to widen philosophy's autonomy and secularize it, a process that starts by denying philosophy's status as theology's "handmaiden" and ends with vile lording it over the Bible and Christian theology, the universal catastrophe that is Spinozism.[68] Van Velthuysen was one target of Van Mastricht's attack,[69] Wittichius another. Like De Volder, Wittichius had indeed long been violating the supposedly Cartesian principle of strict separation of philosophy from theology and had much to say about Spinoza, not all of it hostile. Undoubtedly, there were elements of misrepresentation in how the curators and Voetian theologians welded Cartesian and Spinozist themes together, but how could one deny that for over twenty years Wittichius had regularly endorsed the notion, as an opponent complained in 1656, that "Holy Scripture speaks of many natural and also sacred things not according to the truth but according to the erroneous notions of ordinary folk."[70] For the rest of his life, Wittichius had to hold back everything he had to say about Spinoza and his philosophy in deference to the 1676 new rules. His eventually well-known book, the *Anti-Spinoza*, which for many was not nearly anti-Spinoza enough, appeared only in 1690, three years after his death.

Where Cartesians claimed Spinoza's thought represents a decisive break from Cartesianism, Van Mastricht's *Gangraena* which appeared just before Spinoza's *Ethics*, repeatedly refers to Spinoza as "Spinosa Cartesianus."[71] Cartesianism *is* distinct from Spinozism, grants Van Mastricht, but also inseparable from the insidious poison underlying both and direly threatening religion, society, and morality. Dedicated to Prince William III, Van Mastricht's book marked the crest of the Reformed anti-Cartesian, anti-Spinozist intellectual reaction and Orangist-Calvinist anti-philosophical alliance, remaining something of a classic in the world of conservative Calvinist orthodoxy long after. For Cartesian professors in the Netherlands and Lower Germany (Van Mastricht was from Cologne), his book remained for decades, down to the nineteenth century, the very face of Calvinist reaction as far even as Princeton and Harvard, becoming a favourite text of the famed New England revivalist minister and academic, Jonathan Edwards (1703–58). Advocates of a pure scientific empiricism remained as convinced as Voetian theologians that hard-core *Spinozisten*, as students, had invariably been *Kartesiaanen* [Cartesians] first.[72] Some of those demanding more separation of

---

[68] Mastricht, *Novitatum Cartesianarum Gangraena*, 56, 61–73, 75, 9; Goudriaan, *Reformed Orthodoxy*, 57–60.
[69] Mastricht, *Novitatum Cartesianarum Gangraena*, 176–96.
[70] Du Bois, *Schadelickheyt van de Cartesiaansche Philosophie*, 11–12, 31; Kato, "Petrus van Mastricht," 134.
[71] "Atheus quidem, sed Cartesianus" see Mastricht, *Novitatum Cartesianarum Gangraena*, 35; Goudriaan, *Reformed Orthodoxy*, 57–8; Van Bunge, *From Stevin to Spinoza*, 121–2.
[72] Regius, *Beginselen der beschouwende filozofy*, 352.

philosophy and theology, and a purely empirical, experimental approach in science without broad theorizing, willingly granted that Spinoza had served one valuable function—explaining Descartes' principles, and hence their dangers, more cogently and clearly than Descartes himself.

Post-1672 efforts at dismantlement of De Witt's "True Freedom" and repression of religious dissent and Cartesianism continued throughout the decade following De Witt's overthrow. The Voetian ecclesiastical establishment oscillated during that time between seeking to suppress Cartesian philosophy in the universities comprehensively and a more targeted, selective approach focusing on the escalating friction between philosophical naturalism and theology. Discussing this at its annual gathering at Leeuwarden, in June 1682, the Synod of Friesland was still debating whether "the Cartesian philosophy should be banned from the University of Franker [de Cartesiaansche Philosophie uyt de Academie van Franeker behoorde gebannen te worden]" altogether; the proper Christian path, one of its preachers claimed, was the desirable model adopted by the "Swiss churches." The more limited Dutch approach held, though, with its central principle: "all philosophical propositions conflicting with holy theology must be banned."[73]

36.iv What is True in Christianity?

Behind the scenes, Spinoza's relationship with the Cartesians, accordingly, was far more fragmented and complex than appeared on the surface. His improved relationship with Van Velthuysen, a victim of the same wave of reaction that affected them all, is reflected in the amicable letter he sent him in the autumn of 1675, addressed to the ex-regent's residence on the Nieuwe Gracht, in the old centre of Utrecht. Spinoza here mentions his preparing *Adnotationes*, supplementary notes, to elucidate key points of the *TTP*, and corrects what Van Velthuysen had heard from Nieuwstad. "I am surprised our friend Nieustad said that I intend writing a refutation of those writings which during recent years have been published against my treatise [the *TTP*], and plan to rebut, among others, your manuscript. To my knowledge, I never had in mind refuting any of my opponents, none seeming to me worthy of a response," a harsh judgement referring to the refutations published thus far, not to Velthuysen's critique in manuscript which he clearly respected. What Spinoza said to Nieuwstad was "that I am resolved to clarify certain somewhat obscure passages in that treatise with some notes, and will attach your manuscript to them, together with my reply, if you agree to this (which is what I requested him to ask you)." But "should you happen to be

---

[73] ARH NHK Oud Synodaal Archief 291 Acta Synod of Friesland, res. Leeuwarden, 13 June, art. 38.

reluctant because some things in my response are stated rather harshly, you have full authority to delete or correct them."[74] "This can be done without any danger to your reputation provided your name is not attached to it." Spinoza was not annoyed with Nieuwstad and had no intention of publishing Van Velthuysen's letter, or his reply, without his full consent, though he hoped he would agree. But to "confess the truth, you would oblige me even much more, if you would put in writing those arguments you believe you can bring against my treatise and append them to your manuscript. This I most earnestly beseech you to do; for there is no one whose arguments I would more gladly consider, knowing you are devoted solely to pursuit of truth and are a man of exceptional sincerity of mind."[75] Since nothing came of this, Van Velthuysen presumably answered no.

It was thus in the autumn of 1675 that Spinoza began compiling the thirty pages of *Adnotationes* found in all modern editions of the *TTP* as an annex, or set of footnotes, but which remained completely absent from all seventeenth-century Latin editions except in two or three exemplars where inserted in manuscript. These thirty-nine *Adnotationes* (or all but three) first appeared, we have noted, after Spinoza's death, in Saint Glain's 1678 clandestinely published French translation. In the original Latin, they survived only in manuscript, in the earliest instances in Spinoza's own hand, inserted into a few copies of the *TTP* printed in the 1670s, such as that preserved today in Haifa and another, at Florence. The original Latin text, comprising around fifteen printed pages, would finally appear in print only in 1802.[76]

Aware since starting the *TTP* in 1665 that it was a potential powder-keg, the altered circumstances of the mid-1670s meant that caution was more essential than ever. Some of his conclusions about the biblical text Spinoza simply could not state in print. The *Adnotationes* clarified a number of points, mostly of detail, but were hardly likely to soften the outcry, much less extricate him from the vast international furore he had provoked. At one point in the *Adnotationes*, Spinoza circumvents a dangerous pitfall by remarking that he would "have preferred to pass over all this in silence for reasons which our difficult times do not allow me to explain," referring to his note about King Jeconiah, the nineteenth "King of Judah" captured and dethroned by Nebuchadnezzar in 598 BC. This was a delicate topic owing to its relevance to Christ's supposed genealogy, the descent that is of Christ's "father," Joseph, as diversely recounted in the Gospels of Matthew and Luke. Tellingly, the word "difficult" here replaces another expression Spinoza used originally, surviving in at least one manuscript copy and crossed through by pen: originally he wrote not "in our difficult times" but in these times of "injustice and

---

[74] Spinoza, *Opera* iv, 300; Spinoza, *Correspondance* (ed. Rovere), 352.
[75] Spinoza, *Collected Works* (ed. Curley) ii, 460–1.
[76] Spinoza, *Opera* iv, 299 and iii, 251–69; Spinoza, *Theological-Political Treatise*, 260; Totaro, "Introduzione," xl; Totaro, "Nota su due manoscritti," 109n6.

reigning superstition [iniuriae et superstitio regnans]."⁷⁷ "Superstition" prevailed here, Spinoza was suggesting, because the Masoretic and Septuagint accounts, as well as Matthew and Luke, perplexingly diverge regarding the details of the generations and names since King David, recounted in the Gospels as Christ's genealogy. Where Matthew assigns twenty-seven generations between David and Joseph, Luke gives forty-two with scant overlap between the respective lists of names. Moreover, besides dramatically contradicting each other, in the light of earlier sources both seem to be bogus, fabricated accounts of Jesus' parentage, something Spinoza understandably preferred not to enlarge on.⁷⁸ Given *superstitio regnans*, it was best simply to provide no explanation at all.

Swayed partly by his Amsterdam circle, Spinoza had for now decided to shelve publication of the *Ethics* indefinitely. The short time remaining to him Spinoza devoted to consolidating his position in other ways and also analysing the political situation. While thanking Oldenburg for his "most friendly warning" not to overstep the mark in his *Ethics*, he made a point of urging him to explain exactly "which dogmata" in the *TTP* "you believe undermine the practice of religious virtue; because those things that seem to me to accord with reason I believe to be extremely useful for virtue." If it was "not too much trouble," Oldenburg should indicate also which *TTP* passages had caused "the most worrying doubts among your learned men [in England]; for I want to clarify this treatise [the *TTP*] with some notes."⁷⁹ The "learned men" in question were Boyle, More, Cudworth, and the other learned scholars expressing fury and shock over the *TTP*.

Replying, on 15 November 1675, Oldenburg's initial response to hearing Spinoza was withholding the *Ethics* indefinitely, was brief, even curt, and seemingly unsympathetic. Acknowledging receipt of Spinoza's letter, recounting that the new "book intended by you for publication is in danger," he moved on to eagerly approving what he assumed was Spinoza's purpose in writing supplementary notes to the *TTP*, "to clarify and soften those passages in the *Tractatus Theologico-Politicus* that have agonized readers." Like Boyle and Spinoza's other critics in England, Oldenburg chiefly worried about those passages that "seem to merge God and Nature into one; how many think that you have confounded the two!" Also, "you seem to many to abolish the authority and validity of miracles by the aid of which alone, almost all Christians are persuaded, the certainty of divine revelation stands." Finally, his English critics say, "you conceal your view of Jesus Christ, Redeemer of the World, and sole Saviour of men, and view of his Incarnation and Atonement," and they desire "you to reveal your thinking about these three topics more plainly." Should Spinoza satisfy "reasonable and

---

⁷⁷ Spinoza, *Theological-Political Treatise*, 268.
⁷⁸ Spinoza, *Theological-Political Treatise*, 268–9; Spinoza, *Collected Works* (ed. Curley) ii, 224–5.
⁷⁹ On the differences in dating this letter, see Spinoza, *Correspondance* (ed. Rovere), 351; Spinoza, *Briefwisseling*, 322; Totaro, "Introduzione," xl–xli.

understanding Christians" on these issues, Oldenburg felt "your affairs," meaning Spinoza's general position, will remain safe.[80] In a postscript Oldenburg asked Spinoza to let him know quickly if his message had reached him.

While still not unfriendly to Spinoza personally, and tactful, by 1675 Oldenburg had clearly sided with those deeming his core theses unacceptable, dangerous, unchristian, and unwelcome. Replying briefly, around 1 December 1675, a trifle testily, Spinoza complained that Oldenburg indicated only the points proving troublesome to English readers whereas he wanted to know also which opinions in the *TTP* Oldenburg regarded as "seeming to undermine the practice of religious virtue." Regarding the three points Oldenburg did raise, "his conception of God and Nature was far removed from what *Neoterikoi* [i.e. the new poetical] Christians are accustomed to defend." Here politely but clearly he rejects Oldenburg's strictures, reaffirming his view that what men today call "Christianity" bears little relation to either true Christianity or truth itself, any more than modern Judaism does to ancient Israelite religion.[81] "For God I maintain is, as one says, the immanent, not the transitive cause of all things. That all is in God and moves in God, is something I affirm, indeed I maintain, together with Paul"—referring here to Paul's address to the Athenians, in Acts 17:22–31, where he states that "in God we live and move and have our being." He agreed too perhaps, "albeit in another way, with all the ancient philosophers and, I venture to say, as far as we can tell from surviving traditions, all the ancient Hebrews, though these have suffered much corruption [from Pharisees and rabbinic tradition]." Those objecting that the *TTP* asserts the "oneness of God and Nature" construing Spinoza as holding that God's being is just a mass of extended matter "are completely wrong."[82]

Regarding miracles, continues this important, exceptionally forthright letter, Spinoza was convinced, "contrary to your view," that "the certainty of divine Revelation" can be based only on "wisdom of doctrine and not at all on miracles – which is to say on ignorance." Having already sufficiently explained this in the *TTP*'s sixth chapter, Spinoza now wished to add only that he judges this distinction between "wisdom of doctrine" and belief in miracles the principal difference between "religion" and "superstition," so that, in his view, the latter "has ignorance, and the former wisdom for its foundation which is the reason, I believe, Christians are not distinguished from the rest by faith, charity, nor the other fruits of the Holy Spirit, but only by mere opinion. Indeed, because they defend

---

[80] Spinoza, *Opera* iv, 304; Spinoza, *Correspondance* (ed. Rovere), 358; Hutton, "Henry Oldenburg," 111; Proietti, *Uriel da Costa*, 20; Curley, "Homo audax," 290–1.
[81] The term "Neoterici" is misleadingly translated as "modern" in nearly all modern translations of Spinoza's letters, including Gebhardt's Spinoza, *Briefwechsel*, 276; but see Spinoza, *Correspondance* (ed. Rovere), 361.
[82] Spinoza, *Collected Works* (ed. Curley) ii, 467.

themselves, as they all do, by citing miracles, that is ignorance, the source of all badness, they convert faith, even if it is true faith, into superstition."

As if Oldenburg and Boyle would not be sufficiently outraged by this, Spinoza discloses his thoughts also on Oldenburg's third point, namely the nature of Jesus Christ: "I say that it is completely unnecessary for salvation to know Jesus Christ according to the flesh. Rather we should take an entirely different view of God's eternal son, namely as God's eternal wisdom as manifested in all things, and especially the human mind, above all that of Christ Jesus. For no one can reach the state of beatitude without this, given that [such philosophical wisdom] alone teaches what is true and what is false, what is good and what is bad." Such wisdom as humans possess is manifested most perfectly through Jesus Christ and exactly this, "as he revealed it to them, was what his disciples preached," so that they could pride themselves above all others in the spirit of Christ.

Finally, "as for what certain churches add to this – that God assumed a human nature [naturam humanam] – I warned expressly that I do not understand what they mean. Indeed, to confess the truth, they seem to me to speak no less absurdly than if someone was to tell me that a circle had assumed the nature of a square," implying that Socinian Collegiants and other Anti-Trinitarians were far less irrational here than mainstream Christians.[83] That Oldenburg and Boyle would be as horrified, or more so, by these remarks as by anything in the *TTP*, was surely obvious to Spinoza. And if this were not enough to permanently estrange Oldenburg, Spinoza adds a comment that reflects his undiminished anxieties about Louis XIV and Charles II. Ignorance is the source of all evil, "but whether kings would ever allow a remedy for this evil I very much doubt," religious "superstition" in his view being the chief prop of Louis' and Charles' bellicose royal absolutism. Oldenburg must assuredly have been taken aback by this response, and if he ever showed the letter to Boyle, the latter would have become even more outraged by Spinoza than he was already. Several manuscript copies of this far from "cautious" and, for most, unforgivable letter were later made, one of which, copied by Schuller, ended up in the hands of Leibniz.[84]

Needless to say, Oldenburg was unhappy with the direction things were taking. Stung by Spinoza's rebuke for excessive brevity and curtness in "his very short letter of November" 1675 (just half a page), into responding promptly, Oldenburg claimed to be making amends this time by explaining himself at unstinting length, though actually this response too was fairly short. What appeared to undermine "religious virtue" to his English critics was the "fatalistic necessity" Spinoza seemingly identifies in all things and human actions. Whatever compels, or brings necessity to bear, objected his critics, excuses, so that "no one will lack ample excuse [for whatever they do] in the sight of God. If we are driven by fate and all

---

[83] Spinoza, *Opera* iv, 309; Spinoza, *Collected Works* (ed. Curley) ii, 468; Colerus, *La Vie de B. de Spinoza*, 67–8; Matheron, *Christ et le salut*, 8; Tosel, "Figure du Christ," 138, 140–1.
[84] Spinoza, *Correspondance* (ed. Rovere), 361.

things unroll by destiny's unrelenting hand following a fixed, inevitable course, they cannot see what place there is for culpability and punishment." With this kind of determinism, argue Spinoza's detractors, the sinews of all law, virtue, and religion, all reward and punishment, are severed. What role is there for blame or punishment if everything follows a fixed and inevitable course?[85]

As for Spinoza's answers on the three questions previously posed, Oldenburg felt his equating belief in miracles with ignorance must be challenged. Surely raising Lazarus from the dead and the resurrection of Jesus "seem to surpass the whole power of created nature and belong only to the divine power?" A crucial red line over which it was impossible for either party to give ground was the resurrection of Jesus, the very foundation of Christianity, as Colerus reminded readers later, the grounding "of our hopes and our consolation," a point where it is as impossible to accept a philosopher's denial as to endorse the objections of a Jew, Muslim, or atheist. Spinoza here seemed to repudiate the essence of Christianity itself. Oldenburg concludes by again requesting that he be more specific about the Son of God: "The whole meaning of the Gospel, in my view, is this: that the only begotten son of God, the *logos* [the Word] who was both God and within God, showed himself in human nature and by his passion and death paid the *antiluptron* [ransom] for us sinners, the price of our redemption."[86]

"At last I see," responded Spinoza later that month with a touch of sarcasm,

> what it is you are urging me not to publish [in my *Adnotationes* and *Ethics*]! But as it is the chief foundation of all the principles in the treatise I intended to publish, I want to explain in a few words in what way I maintain the destined necessity of all things and all actions. For in no way do I subject God to fate [nam Deum nullo modo fato subjicio], but rather conceive that everything follows with inevitable necessity from God's nature in the same way that everyone understands that, from God's own nature, it follows that God understands himself, while yet no one thinks God is compelled by some destiny, but rather that He understands himself entirely freely albeit necessarily. This inevitable necessity of things abolishes neither divine nor human laws. For whether or not the moral teachings themselves receive the form of law, or are legislation from God himself, they are nevertheless divine and salutary, and the good stemming from virtue and love of God will be just as desirable whether we receive it from God as judge, or from the necessity of the divine nature. Nor are the bad things ensuing from evil actions and passions any less fearful because they follow from them necessarily. Thus, whether we do those things that we do necessarily or contingently, we are still led by hope and fear.[87]

---

[85] Spinoza, *Opera* iv, 310; Spinoza, *Collected Works* (ed. Curley) ii, 469; Curley, "Homo audax," 295.
[86] Oldenburg to Spinoza, London, 16 Dec. 1675. Spinoza, *Opera* iv, 310; Spinoza, *Collected Works* (ed. Curley) ii, 469–70; Colerus, *La Vie de B. de Spinoza*, 68.
[87] Spinoza, *Collected Works* (ed. Curley) ii, 470–1; LeBuffe, *Spinoza on Reason*, 175.

"Miracles and ignorance I equate," explains Spinoza, "because those who try to erect the existence of God and religion on miracles seek to reveal something obscure by something more obscure which they are completely ignorant of." After this, Spinoza restates his conception of Jesus. That the Apostles really believed Christ rose again after death and ascended to Heaven, he does not deny; but this belief of theirs he places on the same level as the Israelites' believing God descended from Heaven to Mount Sinai in a column of fire and spoke to them directly. For "these and many other apparitions and revelations of the same sort" were similarly "adjusted to the understanding and opinions of those men to whom God wanted, by these things, to reveal his mind." Hence, nothing occurred for nonbelievers to believe, and "I conclude that Christ's resurrection from the dead was spiritual in reality, something revealed only to the faithful and according to their understanding. Christ was thus endowed with eternity and rose from the dead, but 'the dead' here, as I understand it, is meant only in the sense in which Christ said 'Let the dead bury the dead.'" By his life and death Christ "gave an exceptional example of sanctity, thereby raising his disciples from death to the extent they followed the example of his life and death. Nor is it difficult to explain the entire teaching of the Gospel according to this hypothesis," that is to say that no resurrection and no miracle actually occurred, the theological terms are just poetic metaphors.

The reason Oldenburg, Boyle, and the others suppose the Gospel of John and the Epistle to the Hebrews clash with his own views on Christ and Christianity, suggested Spinoza, lies in their confusing the oriental with European modes of expression. "Do you think that when Scripture says God appeared in a cloud, dwelt in a tabernacle or temple, that God really assumed the character of a cloud, tabernacle or temple?" Obviously not. Consequently, his view that no miracle and no resurrection ever occurred or could occur, Spinoza has no doubt, is the correct view. While John's Gospel is in Greek, it nevertheless clearly Hebraizes, and Hebrew usage here remains decisive. Hence, Jesus by no means rose from the dead, infers Spinoza, and for this reason it is far from surprising that after having "risen," Jesus Christ "showed himself" only to a tiny handful of believers and in no way whatsoever to any doubters, Pharisees, elders or Romans, nor, of course, could he have done so.[88]

In his last but one surviving letter to Spinoza, of mid-January 1676, Oldenburg responded in resigned, patient tones.[89] Spinoza rightly thought he did not wish him to publish his doctrine of "that fatal necessity of all things [...] so that the practice of virtue would not thereby be impeded and rewards and punishments not become worthless." With Spinoza's account of human actions and morality he

---

[88] Spinoza, *Collected Works* (ed. Curley) ii, 471–2; Matheron, *Christ et le salut*, 86–7; Levy, *Baruch or Benedict?*, 163; Curley, "Homo audax," 299–300.

[89] Spinoza, *Opera* iv, 315–16; Totaro, "Le *Compendium*," 66–7.

remained deeply dissatisfied: "for if in all our actions, both moral and natural, we human beings are in God's power just as clay is in the hands of the potter; on what grounds, I ask, can any of us properly be called to account for acting in this or that way when it was quite impossible for him to act otherwise?" Surely, Spinoza's view means everyone can say that being entirely in the power of God, we deserve to be excused for doing everything we do and not acting otherwise.

As for equating belief in miracles with ignorance, "you seem to confine the power of God and knowledge of men, even the most intelligent, within the same bounds," as if God cannot do anything beyond the grasp of men. Since "that history of Christ's passion, death, burial and resurrection seems to be depicted in such natural and vivid colours [historia illa de Christi passione, morte, sepultura, resurrectione vivis adeo coloribus, genuinisque descripta videtur] by the Evangelists, I would dare even appeal to your conscience: do you, provided you are convinced of the truth of the narrative, judge that these things should be believed allegorically rather than literally [allegorice potius quam literaliter esse accipienda]? The circumstances of the event are so clearly described by the Evangelists that they seem thoroughly to convince that their account should be understood literally."[90] Requesting that Spinoza ponder his objections and answer with his customary candour, as a friend, he concludes by passing on Boyle's "kind regards" without mentioning the latter's oft expressed disgust and anger, together with a copy of the catalogue of Boyle's books Oldenburg planned to publish the following year.[91]

Three weeks later, on 7 February 1676, a year before his death, Spinoza replied with a letter surviving only in a copy made several months later by Leibniz, kept today in the Library of Lower Saxony, in Hanover. Someone unable to control his desires and restrain his conduct out of fear of the law is to be excused for his weakness but cannot "enjoy tranquillity of mind and the knowledge and love of God, but of necessity he is lost." Here, yet again, Spinoza asserts the compatibility of determinism with individual freedom in God and man alike that all along, since his earliest days as a philosopher he had insisted on, deriving it partly from medieval Jewish philosophical tradition, in particular Hasdai Crescas in his *Or Adonai* [Light of the Lord] (1410). Whether or not one loves God, expressing this through pursuit of truth, love of virtue, and quest for knowledge, or follows the baser passions and devotes one's life to wrongdoing and vicious living, one is assuredly determined by circumstances internal and external to live that way and to a greater or lesser extent prodded to do so by upbringing, education, and the laws and penal code of one's country. But he who lives in a vicious way following the baser passions alone remains a slave to the passions and is never "free" in Spinoza's sense, whereas he or she who acts well out of love of truth and virtue is

---

[90] Spinoza, *Opera* iv, 325, 328; Matheron, *Christ et le salut*, 84, 86, 88–9.
[91] Oldenburg to Spinoza, London, 14 Jan. 1676 in Spinoza, *Collected Works* (ed. Curley) ii, 478–9.

again determined to act thus but, at the same time, acts freely following his or her passion-curbing inner nature and impulse alone. This "compatibilism" likewise mirrors in some way the freedom of God who acts freely out of the necessity of his own nature.[92]

Spinoza "failed to see how [Oldenburg] could think that by equating belief in miracles with ignorance, I confine God's power and man's knowledge within the same bounds." As for Christ's passion, death and burial, these he accepted literally.[93] The Resurrection alone he construed allegorically [Christi passionem, mortem, et sepulturam tecum literaliter accipio, ejus autem resurrectionem allegorice]; commenting on this later, Leibniz noted that Spinoza expresses himself here ironically.[94] "I do indeed admit," Spinoza had written, "that this is related by the Evangelists with such detail that the Evangelists undoubtedly believed the body of Christ rose again and ascended to heaven to sit at God's right hand, and believed also this miraculous resurrection would have been believed by unbelievers too had they been present when Christ appeared to the disciples. Still, without injury to the teaching of the Gospel, the latter could easily have been deceived, as was clearly the case with other Prophets, examples of which I cited in my last letter. Paul, to whom Christ also 'appeared' later, rejoices in knowing Christ not after the flesh but after the spirit."[95]

Oldenburg had yielded as far as he could but would go no further. "It seems very cruel," he answered, on 11 February 1676, "that God should deliver men up to eternal, or at least dreadful temporary torments for sins which they could in no way have avoided. Moreover, the whole tenor of the world supposes men can refrain from sin, being full of proclamations of rewards and punishments." To deny the possibility of refraining from sin and avoiding punishment is "to say that the human mind operates no less mechanically than the human body." Again, he rejects Spinoza's equating belief in miracles with "ignorance." "Your assertion that Christ's passion, death and burial, is to be believed literally but his resurrection allegorically," he complains in this his last surviving letter to Spinoza, "is not supported by any argument that I can see. In the Gospels, Christ's resurrection seems to be narrated as literally as the rest—and on this article, the Resurrection, stands the entire Christian religion and its truth, and with its removal, the mission of Christ Jesus and his heavenly teaching collapse." That of course was precisely Spinoza's point. "You cannot be unaware how urgently when raised from the dead, Christ laboured to convince his disciples of the truth of the Resurrection properly so called. To seek to turn all this into allegory," urged Oldenburg, "amounts to setting out to negate the entire truth of Gospel history."[96]

---

[92] Harvey, *Physics and Metaphysics*, 144, 150–1, 156; Goetschel, *Spinoza's Modernity*, 50–1.
[93] Spinoza, *Opera* iv, 328–9; Spinoza, *Correspondance* (ed. Rovere), 378–80.
[94] Kortholt, *De Tribus Impostoribus*, 202–3; Curley, "Homo audax," 300, 308.
[95] Spinoza to Oldenburg, The Hague, 7 Feb. 1676 in Spinoza, *Opera* iv, 328.
[96] Oldenburg to Spinoza, 11 Feb. 1676 in Spinoza, *Collected Works* (ed. Curley) ii, 482–3.

How Spinoza replied, if he ever did, we do not know. For this was the last surviving letter that passed between them.[97] Denying the Resurrection outright in print repeatedly and at length was extremely rare in the seventeenth century and highly inadvisable for a living writer wanting to avoid prison. That Spinoza's editors and publisher included Spinoza's words of denial in the *Opera Posthuma*, shortly after his death,[98] may well reflect their use of Spinoza's philosophy to reinforce their own Anti-Trinitarian and Socinian leanings while deflecting responsibility for breaking the law onto a dead man. Something of the unique centrality of Spinoza with regard to denying the truth of Christ's Resurrection, his negating its theological significance by dismissing the occurrence as mythical, emerges vividly from a key text of the era directed against freethinkers, the *De la véritable religion* (1689), of Father Michel Le Vassor (c.1648–1718). This 710-page work, extensively using Huet's arguments, established Le Vassor among the chief combatants of Spinoza's Bible criticism of the 1690s. Le Vassor unreservedly condemns all doubters that "Jesus Christ est incontestablement ressiscité [Jesus Christ was incontestably resurrected]" yet focused his denunciation almost exclusively on Spinoza, to him the world's number one denier of Christ's Resurrection.[99]

Oldenburg's letter of February 1676 to Spinoza marks the close of the surviving correspondence between them. It is likely that Spinoza replied and certain that Oldenburg sent Spinoza at least one more letter eight months later, in October, which he entrusted to the young Leibniz to deliver on reaching Holland. Leibniz, as we shall see, spent quite a lot of time with Spinoza at The Hague in the autumn of 1676 but, for whatever reason, chose not to deliver Oldenburg's letter, perhaps because he was mentioned in it and did not want the dying Spinoza to possess a letter where he himself was named as being in contact with him, especially if containing remarks about Spinoza's Resurrection denial and view of miracles. Oldenburg afterwards angrily protested to Leibniz about his deliberate failure to deliver his missive. But as the evidence stands, nothing more can be said about that mysterious and, for Leibniz troubling, last letter.

---

[97] Steenbakkers, "Spinoza's Correspondentie," 12.
[98] Spinoza, *Opera* iv, 429–30; Spinoza, *Nagelate Schriften*, 512–13: "Voorts, ik versta met u Christus lijden, doot en begraving letterlijk; doch zijn verrijzenis in een geestelijke zin."
[99] Le Vassor, *De la véritable religion*, 25–6, 498–511.

37

Hebrew in Spinoza's Later Life

37.i Studying Hebrew Grammar

Spinoza's letter of June 1665, probably either to Bouwmeester or Adriaan Koerbagh, informing him that he had now completed his *Ethics* (as he then conceived it) as far as what became the start of Part IV, and would soon be sending the finished third part for translation, confirms that the basic format and content of Spinoza's philosophy was largely ready during the first half of the 1660s. This marked the near completion of Spinoza's main philosophical project and culmination of what might be termed the middle phase of his life (1656–65). During his last twelve years Spinoza still sporadically added to, revised, and polished the *Ethics*, rethinking his views on some points, debating queries and objections to what he had accomplished, especially during his last year or two those of Leibniz and Tschirnhaus, but devoted most of his energy and writing to the *TTP* and other concerns.

Some of his remaining time Spinoza gave to conversation and discussion but apparently hardly any more than previously to relaxation. Throughout his adult life, he remained obsessed with life's brevity, seeking out what chiefly matters and marginalizing the rest as far possible, rarely giving time to diversion, entertainment, or teaching, as Spinoza admits in his 1673 reply to Heidelberg, which Jelles cites in his preface to the *Opera Posthuma*, to prove nothing could deflect him from his single-minded focus. "All his writings, sprouted from the same thirst and assiduousness [*zucht en naerstigheid*],"[1] remarks Jelles, to carry out his own project. For this reason, scarcely any of Spinoza's oeuvre was response to polemical attacks, or stemmed from sudden curiosity, or distraction from long-pondered objectives. Contemporary politics was obviously another central preoccupation, fed by disgust with war. At the same time, though, Spinoza appears to have been in some sense turning in on himself intellectually, reviewing his own past, chewing over the *Ethics* and his life-long engagement with Bible criticism and study of Hebrew. Such a conclusion certainly fits the profile of his personal library. Only twenty-seven, or less than one fifth, under 20 per cent of his books, as inventoried in 1677, were texts published and thus acquired by him after 1665, hence during

---

[1] Jelles, "Voorreden" in Spinoza, *Nagelate Schriften*, p. iv.

his last twelve creative years, and none of these suggest any fresh areas of interest or striking out beyond his earlier concerns into fresh spheres.[2]

The treatise later known (though there is no evidence that Spinoza himself ever called it that) as the *Compendium Grammatices Linguae Hebraeae* [Grammatical Compendium of the Hebrew Language], one of Spinoza's main projects during his last years, was his penultimate text, the last before the *Tractatus Politicus*, dating, it is thought, mainly from 1674–5.[3] This was yet another text left unfinished at the time of his death, written at the same time he was compiling his *Adnotationes* to the *TTP*. It was a project, the *Opera Posthuma*'s editors say, he undertook "at the request of some friends who were very keen on the Sacred Language and knew he had been instructed in it from the youngest age, and had assiduously occupied himself with it over many years, profoundly examining its special character and becoming extremely versed in it."[4] "The friends" here were presumably especially Meyer and Bouwmeester who both had a keen interest in grammar and embraced the idea that all languages follow a certain logic of the mind; both devoted years to their quest for a "general grammar" and made it a group priority of their society, *Nil Volentibus Arduum*.

The era from the Renaissance and Reformation until the early eighteenth century was a period when "Christian Hebraism" flourished and a higher status attached to Hebrew studies than in later modern times. Even in the Catholic world, though especially in the Calvinist and Lutheran spheres, Hebrew promoted not least by Luther himself, became a major component of university teaching. Indeed, many Christian experts during this period were convinced Hebrew was the *lingua adamica*—humanity's primal language which God bestowed on all men when bestowing it on Adam. The era of Hebrew's high prestige ended only during the Late Enlightenment when the sacred tongue's cultural status rapidly receded, especially after around 1760.

In his personal library, small as it was, Spinoza possessed various aids to researching the structure and character of Hebrew along with several commentaries and glossaries. If most of Spinoza's books were in Latin, Hebrew was the second largest category with twenty titles as opposed to eighteen in Spanish and thirteen in Dutch (he possessed nothing at all in French, English, or Portuguese).[5] Besides the indispensable 672-page *Sefer ha-Dikduk* [Book of Grammar] of the doyen of Hebrew grammarians, Elia Levita (1468–1549), in a Basle edition of 1543,[6] and Johannes Buxtorf's *Thesaurus* of biblical Hebrew, chief tool of

---

[2] Krop, "Spinoza's Library," 30.
[3] Stracenski, "Spinoza's *Compendium*," 124; Proietti, "Il 'Satyricon'," 266, 268–9; Licata, "Nature de la langue," 53–4; Nadler, "*Aliquid remanet*," 156.
[4] Spinoza, *Compendium* in *Opera Posthuma*, 688; Totaro, "Introduzione," 2; Nadler, "*Aliquid remanet*," 156.
[5] Krop, "Spinoza's Library," 30.
[6] Van Sluis and Musschenga, *Boeken van Spinoza*, 63–4; Licata, "Nature de la langue," 49.

seventeenth-century Christian Hebraists, he possessed the *Arukh* or "storehouse" of definitions, etymologies, and readings of Nathan ben Yehiel of Rome (*c*.1035–1106); the *Sefer Dikduk* [Book of Grammar] of Moses ben Joseph Kimhi (late twelfth century); the 400-page Bible concordance with its glossary arranged in order of the Hebrew roots compiled in 1437–47 by Isaac Nathan ben Kalonymos, published at Basle, in 1580, and the prized *Biblia Hebraica* with commentary published by Rabbi Jacob Lombroso at Venice, in 1639.[7] His shelves featured too the *Clavis Talmudica* of the Leiden professor, Constantijn l'Empereur (1591–1648), one of Europe's chief experts in Semitic languages of the seventeenth century's second quarter.

Levita was right, Spinoza did not doubt, in stressing the corrupted, degraded state of the Hebrew language, its lack of perfection since the Babylonian Exile in the sixth century BC.[8] It is clear from abundant evidence, contends Spinoza that the ancient writers wrote without points, punctuation, and without accents,[9] a view he shared with the "historicist view" of Hebrew reaching back to Louis Cappel (1585–1658), at Saumur. But insufficient attention had been paid, argued Spinoza, to how great a source of ambiguity it is that in biblical times Hebrew lacked vowel signs and punctuation to indicate separate clauses. Vowels are crucial to all language, but in Hebrew remain in some basic sense separate from the forms of words as the ancient Israelites wrote them, so that "among the Hebrews vowels are not letters," but "are called the souls of letters [literarum animae], and letters without vowels are called bodies without souls."[10] Spinoza compares Hebrew letters to the openings of a flute touched by the fingers and the vowels to the resulting sounds. But what actually were these "souls" originally? "While both vowels and punctuation signs had been regularly indicated since a certain juncture with points and accents, these cannot be accepted uncritically having been devised and inserted by scholars of a later era whose authority ought not to weigh with us."[11] Spinoza employs Levita's claims to reinforce his wider argument about post-Talmudic changes to the text and Pharisaic manipulation of its meaning.

Though an accomplished Hebraist analysing the language with a highly original critical-philosophical eye, Spinoza was no great master of Hebrew in the way that Levita or Christian Hebraists such as Buxtorf, Constantijn l'Empereur, or the latter's teacher, Erpenius, had been. His *Compendium* was essentially a didactic work intended to enable enthusiasts for Bible study and grammarians like his *Nil Volentibus Arduum* friends to research the meaning of Scriptural phrases and

---

[7] Van Sluis and Musschenga, *Boeken van Spinoza*, 22, 45.
[8] Baumgarten, "Quelques possibles sources," 153; Licata, "Nature de la langue," 49; Campanini, "*Peculium Abrae* d'Abraham de Balmes," 113.
[9] Spinoza, *Theological-Political Treatise*, 107.
[10] Spinoza, *Opera Posthuma*, 689; Spinoza, *Compendio*, 44; Nadler, "*Aliquid remanet*," 165.
[11] Spinoza, *Theological-Political Treatise*, 107.

passages, by showing how to coax different shades of meaning of terms and phrases and different ways of explaining derivation of complex words from simple roots in a consistent, disciplined manner, following the authentic rules of Hebrew grammar. But much as Spinoza rated himself a daring and radical reformer in philosophy and political theory, we also see from his numerous dismissive remarks in the *Compendium* about previous Hebraists and Hebrew grammarians, Jewish and Christian, that he esteemed himself also a radical reformer, something of a revolutionary, in Hebrew studies too, not least in emphasizing more than any commentator before that Hebrew was an evolving, living language.[12] His judgements about other scholars in the field were often uncompromisingly brusque. One leading Renaissance Hebraist, Abraham de Balmes (c.1440–1523), based in Padua and Venice, he disparages for resisting the basic division of Hebrew vowels into long and short "truly without any reason."[13] His notion of his own standing in Hebrew studies breathes a powerful confidence verging on arrogance.[14]

In fact, his Hebrew grammar Spinoza considered a project no one had ever attempted previously.[15] When introducing what he sees as a new category in Hebrew grammar, the "passive reflexive verb" discussed in chapter XXI of his *Compendium*, he describes this as a form "which seems to be unknown to all the grammarians whom I know," an unawareness he ascribes to a mixture of "ignorance" and scribal errors producing mistaken readings of several passages of Jeremiah and Ezekiel.[16] What was chiefly wrong with the grammarians of the past, he maintained, not least Buxtorf, causing rare usages constantly to be wrongly classified as exceptions or irregularities when they were not, as with passive verbs and actions, was preoccupation with composing grammars of the actual Scriptures as an imagined linguistic unity rather than thinking historically and writing a grammar of the evolving Hebrew language from which the Scriptures sprang, as he sought to do. His notion of biblical Hebrew as a set of incidental snapshots in time recording ancient Israelite Hebrew's long evolutionary process, even if only fragmentarily, was pivotal to Spinoza's conclusions because, as he saw it, much depends on how one understands the ancient Hebrews to have meant their words and phrases in particular periods and how exactly post-Babylonian Captivity editors developed, misunderstood, and mangled earlier suppositions and beliefs.

Hebrew studies' privileged status in Spinoza's lifetime amounted to more than predicating that expert Hebrew was needed for meaningful Bible exegesis and

---

[12] Cassuto, *Spinoza hébraïssant*, 19, 22.
[13] Spinoza, *Compendium* in *Opera Posthuma*, 694; Cassuto, *Spinoza hébraïssant*, 26–7.
[14] Harvey, "Spinoza's Metaphysical Hebraism," 107; Licata, "Nature de la langue," 50–1.
[15] Spinoza, *Compendio*, 141; Harvey, "Spinoza's Metaphysical Hebraism," 107; Licata, "Nature de la langue," 51.
[16] Spinoza, *Compendium* in *Opera Posthuma*, 765, 796–7.

discussion, since the common conviction was that Hebrew was mankind's first language, the primal tongue or *lingua adamica* which in the earliest times all humanity shared until that unity was ruptured by the vast babble of languages issuing from the Tower of Babel. Near Eastern language specialists at leading Protestant universities, with Leiden and Utrecht especially prominent in this respect, recognized the kinship of other Semitic languages like Syriac, Arabic, and Ethiopic to Hebrew but had little sense of languages forming evolving families. They mostly viewed the other Semitic languages, alive and dead, and indeed all others, as in some sense derivatives of the language of Adam, the primeval tongue which they assumed was Hebrew. Medieval Spanish Jewish tradition too, especially the Kabbalistic strain, envisaged Hebrew as the crown of languages, a God-given tongue, enshrining primal wisdom and perfection descending from Abraham, as expressed with rare eloquence in the *Sefer ha-Kuzari* (*c.*1140) by the great poet Judah Halevi (1075–1141) of Toledo, another of the books in Spinoza's possession.

Admittedly, by the early seventeenth century, some leading scholars, with Louis Cappel, Grotius, and Gerardus Vossius well to the fore, were problematizing the traditional picture and introducing a degree of scepticism. As rector of the Amsterdam Athenaeum when Spinoza began his intellectual career, the elder Vossius was probably among the very first pre-eminent Christian scholars Spinoza encountered, if not in person (as seems likely) then by proximity and reputation. Moreover, a copy of Vossius' key work *De Arte grammatica* [On the Art of Grammar] was a crucially relevant item in Spinoza's personal library. While agreeing Hebrew is an extremely ancient idiom, Vossius did not accept that it was the original language of Abraham whom all three great monotheistic faiths acknowledged as their spiritual progenitor. Hebrew, he held, was the language of Canaan before Abraham and his descendants arrived, not that of ancient Mesopotamia whence Abraham came and where Vossius, like archaeologists later, believed sedentary civilization and cities first arose. Ancient Mesopotamian cultures reached back to an earlier point than ancient Egypt or any other human civilization, he contended, and the original language there was an eastern Semitic tongue he called "Assyrian." Abraham needed to learn Canaanite when arriving with his people in Canaan, as they then spoke only "Assyrian" which Vossius considered more or less equivalent to Phoenician. Abraham's son, Isaac, and grandson Jacob, were raised speaking Canaanite, and the earliest Scriptures, claims Vossius, were first written in Canaanite, using the Canaanite-Phoenician square alphabet later known as "Hebrew."[17]

Consequently, Hebrew, held Vossius, is not the primal language, nor Hebrew letters the primal alphabet. The universal language, prior to the Tower of Babel,

---

[17] Klijnsmit, "Gerardus Joannes Vossius on Hebrew," 13–14, 17.

afterwards also Abraham's language, was the eastern Semitic tongue he labelled "Assyrian," or alternatively Chaldean, Aramaic, or Syriac, his hypothetical common language of mankind before the "Confusion of Tongues." From Vossius' reasoning, and Spinoza's elaboration of it, Hebrew, it follows, was never a universal language and not the *lingua adamica*, nor ancestor of the world's existing languages, nor uniquely representative of the human mindset. Vossius left intact and unquestioned, though, the idea that Hebrew is indeed the sacred language, the language of the older Scriptures, and, originally, of all the Scriptures, so that the most fundamental truths for mankind do stem from texts originally written in that language. This is where Spinoza stepped in with his unique intervention in seventeenth-century debate about Hebrew's status. Not only was Hebrew not *the* original, or *the* sacred, language in his eyes, but, in the tattered state it came down to us, sadly had lost much of its early vocabulary, phraseology, and range of expression. Far from being sacred, it is actually more imperfect than most languages while the "meaning of many nouns and verbs occurring in the Bible remains either completely unknown or disputed." Almost all names of "fruits, birds, fish, and very many other words, have perished through the ravages of time."[18]

Unfortunately, too, the ancient Hebrews lost most of their early texts and their original and authentic literary and cultural world, which is indeed no wonder, comments Spinoza, given all the massacres and persecutions they suffered under the Babylonians, Assyrians, and Seleucids. Hence, the ancient Israelites retained only a few fragments of their language and just a few books. Finally, in addition, our knowledge of Hebrew today remains fragmentary because the ancient scribes left no contemporary dictionary, grammar, or work of rhetoric.

37.ii Reconstructing Biblical Hebrew

It was conspicuously only Old Testament Hebrew and the supposed original "Hebrew" versions of the New Testament books, which "though propagated in other languages" Spinoza deemed "full of Hebrew idioms,"[19] that preoccupied his linguistic studies. What Spinoza sought to uncover and reveal to the world was what exactly biblical words and phrases meant to contemporaries dwelling in the ancient Israelite republic, moving from its early to its later phases, and then during the subsequent history of Judaea down to Jesus' time. His small library included Maimonides' *Guide for the Perplexed*, originally composed in Arabic, in its medieval Hebrew version, three Hebrew treatises of Delmedigo bound together

---

[18] Spinoza, *Theological-Political Treatise*, 106.
[19] Spinoza, *Theological-Political Treatise*, 100; Totaro, "Le *Compendium*," 66, 68; Rothkamm, *Institutio Oratoria*, 333; Stracenski, "Spinoza's *Compendium*," 131.

including the *Novelat Hokhmah* [Fallen Fruit of Wisdom] (1631), and several other works in medieval or Renaissance Hebrew, like the commentary on the Torah of Menachem Recanati (1223–90). Yet, nowhere in his *Compendium* or elsewhere does Spinoza show any interest in Talmudic era Hebrew, medieval Hebrew, or Jewish language and culture evolution since Talmudic times. Nor does he show any interest in Aramaic, one of l'Empereur's specialities and pivotal to Vossius' claims. Convinced neither the Old nor New Testament were properly understood in his day, Spinoza's objective throughout was to uncover what Scriptural expressions really signified in ancient Israelite times and hence still signify today from a philosophical, scientifically correct perspective.

The Old Testament term "prophet" provides a good illustration of how Spinoza went about constructing his ancient Hebrew grammar as something distinct from a mere grammar of Scriptural terms, and how and why he thought his language science contributed to a more accurate understanding. Taking for granted that everyday language existed before explanations in terms of supernatural realities or beings, a term like the word prophet, in Hebrew *nabi*, he argues, though always employed in Scripture to mean "prophet," must derive from a root with a more elementary everyday meaning. The first of the *Adnotationes* he compiled to clarify aspects of the *TTP* distinguishes between the biblical term *nabi* and what Spinoza infers must be the original Hebrew meaning that the root of the noun implies— and which modern scholars acknowledge, cognate words in other Semitic languages do in fact indicate. The early meaning, he concludes, was "to announce" or "call out," especially perhaps on behalf of someone else, as Aaron did acting as spokesman for Moses. The term "prophet," Spinoza notes too, derives from a root signifying "to translate," and hence, he deduces, following Rashi, the original Hebrew meaning of the term for prophet was simply "interpreter" or "translator." Here, he praises the famed medieval French rabbi Rashi for his skill in elucidating the term correctly while remarking that Abraham Ibn Ezra, whose "Ezra thesis" he shared and whose Bible criticism he admired, but who disagreed with Rashi about this grammatical derivation, "did not know the Hebrew language so exactly."[20] Unlike Rashi, though, Spinoza's purpose is to prove the utterances of Old Testament prophets, despite their aura of being holy visions, enigmas, and parables, actually contain nothing elevated or divine, their use of language reflecting just everyday expressions of the common people of their time designating commonplace things.[21]

Spinoza fully concurred with the view of Buxtorf and Vossius that the square-letter alphabet that in recent times is called "Hebrew" was not the Hebrew alphabet of Old Testament times (though the early Scriptures were in fact written in an older square-script variant, Paleo-Hebrew script). Still, he was partly right in

---

[20] Spinoza, *Opera* ii, 251; Harvey, "Spinoza's Metaphysical Hebraism," 108.
[21] Totaro, "Le *Compendium*," 73; Goetschel, *Spinoza's Modernity*, 57–8.

deducing, it is not clear on what evidence, but as archaeologists later confirmed, that the classical Hebrew alphabet represents yet another late innovation or imposition, introduced, suggests Spinoza, by Ezra the Scribe. Ezra, he assumes, imported it with him from Mesopotamia, it being "the Syriac [alphabet]," an alphabet "Ezra preferred to the ancient Hebrew letters" which the Pharisees in their sacred writings superstitiously emulated. "Superstitious," as used by Spinoza, invariably means "ignorant." "In truth," he adds, referring the reader to Johannes Buxtorf the elder (1564–1629), "the progenitors [of the Scriptures] more frequently used another alphabet."[22] Buxtorf's biblical scholarship and editing carried weight in the seventeenth century, and while he opposed the notion, taken to new extremes by Spinoza, that major changes were introduced in the post-Babylonian era, he did accept that Old Testament Scripture in the form we have it was indeed redacted by Ezra.[23]

Buxtorf's conservatism denied in particular that the Hebrew vowels were a late imposition, a view slowly gaining ground in the early seventeenth century which, again, Spinoza carried to new extremes. Although the most renowned Renaissance era Jewish grammarian, Elia Levita, based in Padua, Venice, and Rome, had long before already argued, in 1538, that vowel points were adopted into Hebrew script only in the Masoretic era, the fact that Hebrew vowel signs postdate the early Christian era, being of comparatively recent origin, was not yet generally accepted in the Christian world, though from the 1620s this question did become the theme of a prolonged scholarly controversy. Disagreement about vowel points, their precise significance and when they first appeared in Hebrew script, something occurring, modern scholars agree, only long after the early Christian era, during the Masoretic age, between the sixth and tenth century AD, simply dragged on, albeit with several prominent scholars, Vossius included, discreetly inclining towards the latter view.

Another late intrusion into the surviving texts of the ancient Hebrews were the innumerable accents placed over many words which, Spinoza claims, caused only confusion among the Hebraists of his own day. He had been pondering this problem, he says, for many years but had long supposed, like Halevi in his *Kuzari*, that originally these accents served to indicate gestures, changes of facial expression or mood, and the raising and lowering of the voice. Later, though, he recognized that efforts to correlate this with actual examples fail to convince. "Hence," he concludes, "I now believe their introduction came after the Pharisees introduced the custom of reading the Bible in public assemblies every Sabbath so that it should not be read too rapidly as is usually done in the repetition of prayers." "For this reason," he proposed dropping this debate, and except where

---

[22] Spinoza, *Compendium* in *Opera Posthuma*, 691.
[23] Spinoza, *Compendio*, 47n15; Licata, "Nature de la langue," 22.

there are particular grounds to bring the issue up, leave further discussion of their "minutiae to the Pharisees and the no longer relevant Masorites."[24]

During Spinoza's adulthood, Jacob Alting (1618–79), over many years professor of Oriental languages, and later also theology, at Groningen, presided as the leading Hebraist in the Netherlands. Alting strove to defend core Calvinist perspectives employing scholarly Bible exegesis. But he too found himself increasingly entangled in the complications stemming from controversies over Ezra's reform of the Hebrew language and script, difficulties arising especially from his placing uncompromising stress on the need for Christian scholarship to establish the authentic original texts, setting aside later authority. Even the official Dutch Calvinist "States Bible," in his view (to the indignation of Maresius, his colleague and neighbour, living in the same street), cannot be considered as sacred as the original texts in Hebrew. Feeling himself distressingly challenged by the *TTP*, Alting, though zealous in encouraging refutations of Spinoza, was acutely conscious of how "Coccean" preoccupation with emphasizing the centrality of the original Hebrew, rather than standing firm on received ecclesiastical authority and dogma, like the Voetians, potentially exposed him and his followers to charges of opening the door to Spinoza's exegetical-philological challenge, thereby undermining core Calvinism.[25] Alting's plea for a purer, more authentic *theologia scriptuaria* proved dangerously risky. Even so, it still represented a world far removed from Spinoza's radically corrosive critical-historical approach, not least on issues of grammar and punctuation.

After 1670, not surprisingly, mounting opposition to Spinoza's *TTP* caused scholarly opinion to retreat more and more from Cappel's, Grotius', Vossius', and Alting's historicizing approach to Hebrew studies. Hebrew appeared to undermine all confessional theology and therefore should be avoided as a danger zone. After 1670, Alting joined the drift towards strengthening the "Buxtorf" antihistoricist tradition in Hebrew studies, rejecting calls for more focus on Hebrew's historical shifts, changes, and post-Exilic reform. Problems caused by variant readings due to prolonged periods of Babylonian, Hellenistic, Roman, and finally post-Talmudic era precarious conservation, during devastating bouts of upheaval and persecution, and severely restricted numbers of copies of the Scriptures passed down over many centuries, had by the early Middle Ages led to so much difficulty and bafflement over the meaning of some passages, holds Spinoza, that they were simply omitted from the authorized copies redacted in Masoretic times. This further prodded Alting's retreat towards the Calvinist mainstream and insistence on the Hebrew script's integrity, stability, and sacred authenticity immune to subsequent modification. A notable aspect of

---

[24] Spinoza, *Compendium* in *Opera Posthuma*, 697; Zwiep, "Ceci n'est pas une grammaire," 177; here I am departing slightly from other translations, see, for example, Spinoza, *Compendio*, 56.
[25] Touber, *Spinoza and Biblical Philology*, 22, 78–9, 86.

this "Cocceian" retreat was Alting's adamant claim that Hebrew vowels and punctuation are not, after all, some intrusive invention of post-Talmudic rabbis, living in Tiberias long after Christ, but applied "from the very beginning of the language," reaching back to the earliest Hebrew books.[26]

A notably innovative feature of Spinoza's approach, something he claims Jewish and Christian "grammarians did not understand," was his insistence on the exceptional status and centrality in ancient Hebrew grammar of the noun. "For all Hebrew words, except for a few interjections and conjunctions and one or two particles possess the force and properties of nouns." Thus, what in Latin is called an "infinitive in Hebrew is a pure unadulterated noun, so that an infinitive knows nothing about the present, nor past, nor any time whatever." "Because grammarians failed to understand this, they judged many words grammatically irregular which according to usage of the language are entirely regular, and were ignorant of many things one needs to know for a proper grasp of the language and its *eloquentia*." Philosophically, held Spinoza, this grammatical quirk arose from the fact that "people and especially the Hebrews are accustomed to assign human attributes to all things '*like the earth hears, is attentive etc.*,' and perhaps for this reason or another, all names of things are divided into masculines and feminines."[27]

Spinoza utilized all the dimensions of his revisionist approach to Hebrew studies in his drive against contemporary theology and religious authority. No other Bible critic during the second half of the seventeenth century desacralized the Jewish and Christian Scriptures to remotely the same extent, not Hobbes, La Peyrère, Richard Simon, Le Clerc, or anyone else; no other was so insistent that the Hebrew text we possess is not a text handed down by the ancient Israelites but a heavily amended rewriting of remnants by Ezra the Scribe and his followers, then further evolving down to the post-Christian centuries. His motivation driving his preoccupation with Hebrew, stress on Ezra, and composing the *Compendium*, is thus clearly evident. Far from converging with Meyer's aims and the efforts of *Nil Volentibus Arduum* to construct a *grammatica universalis* outlining a universal language serving all human interaction, Spinoza's goal, rather, was to turn the "sacred language" into a desacralizing tool and integral component of his own agenda to deconstruct the entire edifice of religious tradition and theological dogma, built, in his view, on misconstruing words and phrases of Scripture. His approach was designed also to encourage others to deepen and refine their understanding of Scripture by casting off the allegedly vast layers of misinterpretation rabbis and churchman had equally misguidedly heaped on mankind over

---

[26] Klijnsmit, "Gerardus Joannes Vossius on Hebrew," 17, 19; Touber, *Spinoza and Biblical Philology*, 50, 221.
[27] Spinoza, *Compendium* in *Opera Posthuma*, 705; Proietti, "Il 'Satyricon'," 259; Harvey, "Spinoza's Metaphysical Hebraism," 108; González Diéguez, "Spinoza and the Grammar," 487–8.

the millennia.[28] All three great monotheistic religions Spinoza deemed intellectual prisons, each constructed on the basis of texts tortuously derived from a living, spoken language. To him they were three walled-around structures of authorized interpretation, dogma, and observance, devised to organize society, anchor law, and regulate politics while assigning presiding roles to religious leaders. All three sought to promote the power of highly restricted elites at the expense of ordinary men's and women's ability to freely attain individual personal fulfilment.

The lives of all men and women and the well-being of society itself were at stake. But it was certainly not ordinary men and women, in Spinoza's view, who are equipped to challenge the three great strongholds overshadowing human liberty and self-fulfilment. For "our method requires a knowledge of Hebrew; and the common people," being unable to grapple with philosophy generally, "likewise have no time to study that [Hebrew grammar]." Since Spinoza identifies philosophy as the exclusive tool of self-liberation, philosophy operating not just to explain observed natural phenomena and the reality of things around us, ruling out miracles, but also to ferret out the truth about the nature of human well-being and happiness, morality, laws, and politics, the people must be led towards truth and freedom by those few who do understand. Philosophy, as Spinoza sees it, liberates by uncovering the reality of human history. A key aspect, unavoidably, is reconstituting as much of the reality of the spoken language of biblical times as possible to shed light on how appropriation and manipulation of the evolving written text for purposes of enhancing theological and political hegemony, misled generation after generation over the centuries. If Spinoza wanted only "philosophical" readers for his *TTP*, the wider project of freeing humanity from the yoke of false religion he reserves for those who do, or could, grasp the truths he strove to make clearer.[29]

Revealing Scripture's true meaning, in Spinoza's view, involves considering the general historical context and "requires a history of the vicissitudes of all the Biblical books," their derivation, transmission, copying, canonization and so forth, most of which we lack.[30] But besides these more general issues besetting Bible and other text criticism, argues Spinoza, lack of proper study of the Hebrew language in ancient times while it was still a living language and more texts were available, leaves us unaware of large segments of Hebrew grammar which forms yet another serious obstacle to understanding the Scriptures correctly, and this ignorance urgently needs compensating for by researching the ancient language of Scripture as far as this remains possible. Hence, Spinoza attaches great importance to the study of Hebrew grammar as an independent, specialized, self-contained science equipped to partially fill the innumerable gaps and ambiguities in our

---

[28] Totaro, "Le *Compendium*," 65; González Diéguez, "Spinoza and the Grammar," 489.
[29] Spinoza, *Theological-Political Treatise*, 110–11, 117; Nadler, "*Aliquid remanet*," 161.
[30] Spinoza, *Theological-Political Treatise*, 109.

understanding of Scripture and provide tenable explanations, a study in itself of enduring, emancipating value for all.

This route remains precariously open, argues Spinoza, because even though rare texts and their significance are always subject to manipulation, falsification, deletion, forgery, and drastic editing for intrusive purposes, scholars' and theologians' ability to twist the meaning of written texts and fabricate faith cannot extend to altering the sense of words and expressions still in use in a living language. Words in common usage cannot be as arbitrarily altered as can later written texts conserved by individuals and factions at war with others. Studying grammar provides a path to reconstructing how words were derived, compounded, inflected and adopted into idiomatic usages, enabling the language scientist studying a language's grammar to fix the original meanings of terms and expressions with more precision than otherwise possible. The one component of the Bible that has never been corrupted, changed, or manipulated by anyone, argues Spinoza, is the real meaning of words current when the Scriptures were first written whilst Hebrew was still a living, spoken language. "Accordingly, we can easily conceive that the learned could have altered or perverted the sense of a passage in a very rare book which they had under their control, but not the significance of words." While possibilities for corrupting ancient texts abounded at every stage of their later evolution, the scope for changing the meaning of words in the spoken language remained always restricted.[31] The one ancient Israelite tradition surviving today, Spinoza thinks, that has not been corrupted and cannot be corrupted is "the meaning of words in the Hebrew language that we have received from them," making it an urgent matter, therefore, to retrieve these precious authentic meanings by clarifying and extending our knowledge of Hebrew usage and grammar, thereby uncovering truer, more authentic meanings than church and synagogue traditions provide.[32]

37.iii Old Testament, New Testament: Jews and Christians

From an early stage in his life, central to Spinoza's message to those around him, was his claim that the Old Testament Prophets and the New Testament Apostles were not divinely inspired in any conventional sense. Prophets and Apostles, he assured readers, in the *TTP*, did possess "extraordinary powers of imagination but not of understanding," and consequently what God or Nature revealed to them consists exclusively of "some very simple matters." The Bible in both its parts, Old Testament and New, remains a major social and historical reality exerting a vast

---

[31] Spinoza, *Theological-Political Treatise*, 105; Totaro, "Introduzione," 16–17; Stracenski, "Spinoza's Compendium," 135–6.
[32] Spinoza, *Theological-Political Treatise*, 105.

influence requiring a good deal of scholarly attention, including that of the philosopher, to interpret correctly, but possesses practically no inherent spiritual or intellectual significance in terms of ideas, doctrines, findings or insights and is not, and cannot be, the authentic grounding of any religious movement, sect, church, or tradition.[33]

Christian tradition, in Spinoza's view, provides no remotely accurate or reliable understanding of Christ's significance or that of the New Testament. By comparison with other libraries of his time, Spinoza's was staggeringly devoid of Christian theological works, and despite his rhetorical appeals to his audience, and repeated invoking of Saint Paul, he used virtually no Christian studies of any kind when focusing attention on the New Testament.[34] Nevertheless, Spinoza's fascination was by no means just with the Hebrew culture and mental world of the Old Testament. Since biblical Hebrew and its Aramaic derivative was also the exclusive language of Christ and the Apostles, the New Testament too, he insists, can also only be correctly understood via the kind of language reconstruction he proposes. Our world must be seen as one that has been wrongly interpreted and perverted by wrong perceptions of New Testament expressions and terminology throughout even if the real New Testament has not survived for us to study in its original linguistic format, an idea that continued to preoccupy him even in the last stages of his life, a fascination stretching well beyond the confines of Old Testament criticism.

It was in no mildly ironic tone that Spinoza grants, in *TTP* chapter VII on the "Interpretation of Scripture," that ascertaining the true meaning is considerably easier and more certain "for those, if they exist, possessing a solid tradition or a true exegesis inherited from the prophets themselves, such as the Pharisees claim, or those boasting a pope infallible in the interpretation of Scripture, as Roman Catholics profess." Proclaiming, or rather manipulating meaning is easily accomplished by these traditions: their great problem is that it is totally impossible to reconcile their endlessly conflicting interpretations. Many disputes and schisms have disturbed the church ceaselessly ever since Apostolic times that not only have not been but can never be resolved, maintains Spinoza, "and will always disturb [the church] until religion is separated from philosophical theories and reduced to the extremely few, very simple dogmas Christ taught as his own."[35]

But if the Apostles provide no stable platform that any church can rest on, and that no church interprets correctly, Christ's teaching which, Spinoza claims, is effectively only basic moral teaching, *is* firm ground for all provided one is guided exclusively by Hebrew and Aramaic contemporary usage and jettisons all and

---

[33] Spinoza, *Theological-Political Treatise*, 168–72; Totaro, "Religion catholique," 110–11.

[34] Krop, "Spinoza's Library," 34; Tosel, "Figure du Christ," 130, 138.

[35] Spinoza, *Theological-Political Treatise*, 105; Silva Rosa, "That the *Catholica religio* does [not] need," 63–4; Langton, "Modern Jewish Philosophical Approaches," 121.

every doctrinal slant embedded in Greek, Latin, and other late translations, church traditions, and modern vernacular renderings of Old and New Testament narratives and explanations, for these are all fabricated long after these texts were composed without any understanding of, or regard for, original meanings and intention. Church traditions are thus always all entirely inauthentic.[36] Unlike Solomon or Paul, Christ teaches no philosophy (far less any theology). Christ's supreme uniqueness lies in that he alone provides the bridge by which the ignorant can be "saved" in the sense of reaching those moral truths forming the rational basis of what is best in human society and aspiration that most men cannot rationally comprehend due to their ignorance. When concerned with the purely theological (hence irrelevant) implications of his doctrine, each Apostle, being a teacher rather than prophet, discerned something different: thus Paul says salvation comes from faith alone; James says the opposite—that salvation comes from works and not faith alone.[37] Neither doctrine possesses force or significance; for theologizing is wholly absent from Christ's own teaching which proclaims exclusively the simple truths of "true religion."

The most important conclusion Spinoza draws is that the essential message of the Old Testament and the New are exactly the same, and that "true Judaism" and "true Christianity" converge to the point of becoming identical. Spinoza was just as deeply anti-Christian as anti-Jewish when defining these terms in the accepted manner, or as churchmen and the public conventionally did. His presenting his philosophy as rejection of rabbinic Judaism and reaffirmation of Paul's teaching cohered together as a strategy particularly appealing to Collegiants, a strategy useful to all mankind for erasing religious difference including what Spinoza considered the completely futile, endlessly factious wrangling among those Christians closest to Christ, namely the Collegiants themselves.

The chief objective of his grammatical philosophy, a supplementary form of medicine for society, was thus to help retrieve as "full and certain knowledge of the sacred books" as is recoverable. Dismissing rabbinic tradition and papal authority equally, Spinoza concludes that "we can base nothing certain on either of these. The latter [papal authority] was denied by the earliest Christians and the former [Pharisaic doctrine] by the most ancient sects of the Jews."[38] Judaism and Catholicism are thus equally invalid traditions. The biblical chronology the rabbis inherited from the Pharisees, to give one of Spinoza's favourite examples, is altogether "false"; religious dogma had for all practical purposes construed everything in Scripture erroneously. Neither any existing religious authority, Spinoza insists, nor divine inspiration, can make good the damage, nor help explain

---

[36] Cassuto, *Spinoza hébraïssant*, 135–7, 140.
[37] Spinoza, *Theological-Political Treatise*, 160–1; Matheron, *Christ et le salut*, 120, 124–6, 138, 141; Tosel, "Figure du Christ," 146–8; Silva Rosa, "That the *Catholica religio* does [not] need," 63.
[38] Spinoza *Opera* iii, 105; Stracenski, "Spinoza's *Compendium*," 131–2.

anything in Scripture accurately, since, on his premises, only pure scientific reason can explain anything.[39]

It was a remarkable, highly original feature of Spinoza's thought that he viewed the Old and New Testament not as gates to very different worlds but very much as a cultural unity linking together the same linguistic and moral world, jointly comprising the true moral significance of both Jewish and Christian tradition which, though their respective adherents do not realize it, is really one united tradition, a single moral message, however mangled, misunderstood, and betrayed this single inheritance has been by erring generations of rabbis and churchmen. As far as the Bible's moral teaching is concerned, Spinoza's Christ and Paul mark the summit of what went before, not a new start or theology, and certainly not a new era of religious authority. If "true religion," justice, charity, and loving one's neighbour as oneself are the moral legacy of the entire Bible, those elements deemed most specific to Christ's teaching turn out to be embedded in both testaments equally. Christ's teaching, the "spirit of Christ," in Spinoza's Christology is eternal, and available to all through reason, including those who know nothing of the historical Jesus and the Apostles, and have never entered a church or even heard of Christ. As far as their (very residual) valid teaching and cultural heritage is concerned, the two testaments are one,[40] and this common essential core has no connection with any church or theological notions of incarnation, resurrection, or immaculate conception. "Anyone therefore" whether Jew, Christian, Muslim or anything else, "who abounds in the fruits of love, joy, peace, long-suffering, kindness, goodness, faithfulness, gentleness and self-control against whom (as Paul says in his Epistle to the Galatians 5:22) there is no law, he, whether taught by reason alone or by Scripture alone, has truly been taught by God, and is altogether happy."[41]

The specific laws, ceremonies, and observances of the Old Testament, Spinoza argues, applied to the ancient Hebrews alone and only for as long as the ancient Hebrew republic and its successor state, the Maccabean republic, survived. "On the other hand, from Jeremiah it is clear that after destruction of their commonwealth, the Hebrews were not obliged to keep up the ceremonies."[42] When Jeremiah saw that Jerusalem's destruction was "imminent, he prophesied it and said: 'God esteems only those who know and understand that He himself cultivates compassion, good judgment and justice in the world and hence, from now, only those who know this should be esteemed worthy of praise.'" After the Jewish

---

[39] Spinoza, *Theological-Political Treatise*, 106, 112.
[40] Matheron, *Christ et le salut*, 66–7, 69, 72; Tosel, "Figure du Christ," 134–9; Moreau, *Spinoza et le spinozisme*, 97–8; Silva Rosa, "That the *Catholica religio* does [not] need," 60; Birch, *Jesus*, 107; Licata, "The Law Inscribed," 205–6.
[41] Spinoza, *Theological-Political Treatise*, 80; Langton, "Modern Jewish Philosophical Approaches," 118.
[42] Spinoza, *Theological-Political Treatise*, 71.

state's demise, nothing particular was required of the Jews *qua* Jews any longer; they were bound only by the same universal and natural law applying to all men. And the New Testament "fully confirms the same thing, for as we have said, it teaches only moral requirements, for recompense promising the celestial kingdom." The Apostles discarded the ancient Hebrew ceremonies as soon as the Gospel began "to be preached to other nations [each being] subject to the law of a different republic."[43] Thus Paul never converted from Judaism to a new faith, as Christians mistakenly suppose, any more than did Christ or the other Apostles; Paul simply advanced to a more exact grasp of basic religious truth.

The true moral law Scripture teaches, the *religio catolica universalis*, is universal to all and belongs to no one faith or church. If the specific observances of Judaism possess no enduring significance, exactly the same applies to the "Christian ceremonies – baptism, the Lord's Supper, feast-days, public prayers, and any others that have always been common to Christianity. If they were ever instituted by Christ or by the Apostles (which until now is not sufficiently evident to me), they were instituted merely as external signs of a universal church and not anything contributing to blessedness or that have anything sacred in them."[44] If by chance the "Christian ceremonies" really were "instituted by Christ or the Apostles," then they are inconsequential, not "things that enhance human happiness or have any sanctity in them." Yet these inauthentic trivia provoke endless strife between traditions and factions, even though Paul, who was more "philosophically" inclined than the other Apostles, did excellent work in liberating some unphilosophical Jews from "superstition." After the Apostles, furthermore, the early and later churches spread the confusion surrounding the meaning and requirements of the Gospels still further. If the traditions of Pharisees and rabbis are false to the true legacy of the ancient Hebrews, the Christian churches are comparably false to what Spinoza defines as the "spirit of Christ" and the earliest Christians.[45] The final sentence of Spinoza's chapter on the Apostles reads: "truly our age also would be happy if we saw it free from all superstition."[46]

More specific teachings of Christ that are not part of the universal law that reason teaches may perhaps have genuinely been uttered by Christ but lack universal validity, having originated in particular contexts for local reasons, being in this respect no different from teachings of Old Testament prophets operating in the same post-Hebrew commonwealth context. The classic example is Christ's saying "to him who strikes you on your right cheek, turn to him also the other." Such a command is valid only under severe oppression where society is without law and justice: if proclaimed in the time of the Hebrew Republic, Christ

---

[43] Spinoza, *Oeuvres* iii, 216–17; Spinoza, *Opera* iii, 72; Matheron, *Christ et le salut*, 46, 74, 81.
[44] Spinoza, *Oeuvres* iii, 226–7; Spinoza, *Theological-Political Treatise*, 75.
[45] Spinoza, *Theological-Political Treatise*, 104–5; Matheron, *Christ et le salut*, 143; Tosel, "Figure de Christ," 150–3, 157; Totaro, "Religion catholique," 106–7.
[46] Spinoza, *Oeuvres* iii, 426–7; Spinoza, *Theological-Political Treatise*, 162.

"would have destroyed the Law of Moses by this edict." But exactly the same doctrine that Christ taught, when foreseeing Jerusalem's subsequent destruction, "we see Jeremiah also expounded, at the time of the first destruction of the city." The prophets, and Christ along with them, advanced this teaching exclusively where oppression leaves the people otherwise defenceless: "it is nowhere promulgated as a law." Abject submission to impious men "is appropriate only where justice is negated and in times of oppression." Wherever justice is respected, wrongs should be properly and fully redressed.[47]

Offering the other cheek, mistakenly thought of as Christian humility, is thus no universal value, nor a virtue, nor a difference between Jews and Christians. It is not Christ's universal teaching, but relevant only to men languishing under severe oppressors like the Romans in the first-century Holy Land, and never to men living in republics under man-made laws and justice. Thus, the great difference men commonly assume between Jews and Christians has neither religious meaning nor significance in terms of truth or moral force. Morally, however little their adherents grasp this, these two religions (and all the rest) are entirely one, the universal *religio catolica*. Authentic early Judaism, that of the *antiquissimae Judaeorum sectae*, and authentic early Christianity, that of the *antiquissimi Christanorum*, truly converge as one; and only over time did both traditions become progressively corrupted and hence increasingly divided into opposing camps due to ambition and power-seeking fuelled, as always, by ignorance and superstition.

Since Christ's teaching has no relevance to anything dogma-bound Christians teach, his true significance, the "spirit of Christ," is fully embedded everywhere, just as much outside as inside the churches. Here Spinoza mixes deep seriousness with a touch of ironic humour. The historical Jesus certainly existed, but being just a man speaking according to the common people's notions, possessed scant significance in himself. Knowing nothing about Jesus cannot possibly affect anyone's chances of salvation. The teaching and exhortations of churches are irrelevant to everyone's happiness, although, Spinoza adds (no doubt tongue in cheek), once the Pope did "truly conduct himself as the vicar of Christ"—that was when rebuking the medieval Aragonese "for not taking sufficient warning from the example of the Hebrews" about the great danger and disadvantages of instituting a monarchy.[48]

Differently from both schools of Hebrew scholarship prevailing in his day, the historicists following Cappel and anti-historicists following the Buxtorfs, Spinoza held that in the condition in which it survived, after the Babylonian, Assyrian, Hellenistic, and Roman massacres and persecutions of the Jews, Hebrew was more stunted, corrupted, and depleted than other languages. More fragmentary, there is

---

[47] Spinoza, *Theological-Political Treatise*, 105; Matheron, *Christ et le salut*, 95–6, 113.
[48] Spinoza, *Oeuvres* v, *Tractatus Politicus*, 190–1; Matheron, *Christ et le salut*, 68, 95.

also nothing holy or uniquely significant about it, something no other contemporary was prepared to say. In sum, as a Bible critic Spinoza stepped far beyond Grotius, Vossius the Elder, Hobbes, or Isaac Vossius, maintaining that "Scripture would be no less divine even if written in different words or a different language."[49]

Whereas Spinoza felt resentful of the Jews of his time, and bitterly opposed to what he viewed as the fabrications of the Pharisees and rabbis, he felt a strong sense of connection to the ancient Israelites and their republic, and still a deeper connection, for all its fragmentariness and shortcomings, and real love for the Hebrew language. If the general conviction of his age about the status of Hebrew explains why friends wanted to draw on his expertise in Hebrew and discuss interpretation of Hebrew words and phrases with him, this does not explain why, after provoking general uproar with his *TTP*, Spinoza still plied on with his research into Hebrew, pondering the idiosyncrasies of the language, and compiling a Hebrew grammar he believed differed radically in character from all previous Hebrew grammars, Jewish or Christian. In pursuing his goals, he even hoped to usefully retranslate large parts of the Old Testament into Dutch (or Latin?), apparently composing a manuscript draft which he later burnt.

---

[49] Spinoza, *Theological-Political Treatise*, 170; Zwiep, "Ceci n'est pas une grammaire," 164–5.

38

Encounter with Leibniz (1676)

38.i Leibniz and Spinoza

Ambitious and aspiring if as yet largely unknown, during the early 1670s the young German thinker Gottfried Wilhelm Leibniz (1646–1716) resolved to research and evaluate for himself developments in every changing field of thought, science, and knowledge. Aiming to assemble as reliable and up-to-date a picture of the current state of philosophy, religion, and science as possible, he embarked on a vigorous campaign of international networking, writing to Hobbes, Oldenburg, Spinoza, and Comenius among many others. The stir caused first by the *Philosophia* and then the *TTP* convinced him that he needed to investigate the subversive intellectual movement emerging in Holland. He uncovered a whole circle of underground philosophical activity, evolving already for over a decade, that greatly intrigued him.[1]

Everyone involved with the sciences and humanities in Germany at that point realized that *libri damnati* [condemned books] were now more seriously menacing religion, politics, and society than in the past, and that of all subversive writers of the age Spinoza was the most challenging, being broader, deeper, and harder to counter than the rest and more inclined to combine religious subversion with undermining court culture and princely pre-eminence. This uniquely ominous image remained standard for decades: "quid est Benedicti Spinosae libris pestilentius? [what is more pestilential than the books of Benedict Spinoza?]" demanded the great German polymath Daniel Morhof in 1688.[2] What was distinctly unusual among foreign observers of the Dutch philosophical scene was Leibniz's painstaking effort to piece together everything he could glean about Spinoza and his underground intellectual fringe movement. This quest became central to Leibniz's entire intellectual effort because the *TTP* represented a philosophical-exegetical threat to his strategies of defence of the Christian mysteries that went beyond, and seemed more dire, than conventional Socinian claims which he had been much preoccupied with rebutting in his theological writings of the 1660s (showing particular contempt for the arguments of Zwicker). He was resolved to prove that the core Christian mysteries, the Trinity above all, do not conflict with reason.[3] No other outsider matched Leibniz's persistence

---

[1] Lodge, *Leibniz and his Correspondents*, 11; Malcolm, *Aspects of Hobbes*, 529.
[2] Otto, *Studien*, 21.   [3] Antognazza, *Leibniz on the Trinity*, 16, 30–3, 40.

whilst Spinoza still lived, driven by a passionate urgency that was both theological and philosophical, in assembling as exact and detailed a picture of "Spinoza" and the coterie around him as he could.

Towards the end of his life, Leibniz recalled that when he himself was completing his five years of study at Leipzig (1661-6) "Louis [Lodewijk] Meyer, a physician of Amsterdam, anonymously published the book *Philosophia Scripturae Interpres*, by many persons wrongly attributed to Spinoza, his friend; the theologians of Holland bestirred themselves, and their written attacks on this book gave rise to great disputes among them." Leibniz was one of those who found himself corrected some years later when the Leiden professor Theodor Craanen (c.1633-88), writing to him in 1672, explained that the *Philosophia* was not, as many abroad supposed, by Spinoza, but rather by "some Amsterdam physician." Regrettably, agreed Craanen, there still existed no adequate refutation of the *TTP*; but Van Mansvelt at Utrecht was labouring on precisely such a rebuttal; meanwhile, at Groningen, Maresius had entered into bitter dispute with the Cartesians.[4] That furore greatly deepened the divide, notes Leibniz, between Cartesians and anti-Cartesians, that is between those seeking to reconcile theology with philosophy and those refusing to do so, or as some termed this rift, between "rational" and "non-rational" theologians.[5]

Leibniz gathered more information in the autumn of 1675, whilst in Paris, on getting to know Spinoza's young friend and ally, the Silesian nobleman Ehrenfried Walther von Tschirnhaus (1651-1708). Tschirnhaus had first met Spinoza apparently in 1673 or 1674; how he met him remains unclear. The two do not seem to have known each other during Tschirnhaus' early study period in Leiden. Enrolling there, at seventeen, in 1668, the youthful nobleman whose family seat was at Kieslingswalde, twelve miles east of Görlitz, a region then part of the electorate of Saxony (today in Poland), though officially studying law and preparing himself for statesmanship, soon revealed his passion for mathematics and philosophy and immersed himself in Cartesianism which subsequently remained fundamental to his thinking. On recovering from the plague, caught at Leiden, in 1669, Tschirnhaus acquired an avid interest also in medicine and, though never practising as a physician, developed fiercely independent views on that subject too, often disagreeing with professional opinion. Neither during his study period at university (1668-71), nor during the "disaster year" 1672, when he served on the side of the Republic as a volunteer reserve officer for over a year, does he appear to have been in contact with Spinoza.[6]

Tschirnhaus probably first heard about Spinoza as a student, though, and Leiden, by one route or another, probably provided the link by which he first

---

[4] Leibniz, *Sämtliche Schriften und Briefe* 2nd ser. i, 202-4.   [5] Leibniz, *Theodicy*, 82-3.
[6] Wurtz, "Disciple "hérétique," 112; Vermij, "Spinozisme en Hollande," 148-9; Adler, "Education of Ehrenfried," 30-2; Mertens, "Where Thou Dwellest," 33.

made contact with members of Spinoza's circle. His earliest surviving letter to Spinoza, dated 8 October 1674, reached the philosopher from Rieuwertsz's bookshop, sent on by Schuller who had become friendly with his fellow Silesian at Leiden where, after Schuller enrolled as a medical student, in May 1671, the two had lodged for a time in the same house. Though possibly Schuller it could equally well have been Pieter Van Gent who had first introduced Tschirnhaus to Spinoza at some point in 1673 or early 1674.[7] This first surviving letter, focusing on the issue of "free will," suggests Tschirnhaus had received an extract on the topic from Spinoza's unpublished *Ethics*. Introduced to more of Spinoza's unpublished work by the autumn of 1674, Tschirnhaus was in fact the first notable foreign figure known to have seriously examined and questioned Spinoza's philosophical system as distinct from his contributions to Bible criticism, political theory, and Descartes commentary, Leibniz himself still being in the dark about his broader system until the autumn of 1675.[8]

Descartes and Spinoza are both right, avers Tschirnhaus in that first letter, in their apparently opposite conclusions about "free will," each defining his premises differently and consistently; but, ultimately, it is Descartes who is the more right: "you both speak the truth according to your own conception. But if we look to absolute truth, this agrees only with Descartes' view. For in your conception you take as certain that freedom's essence consists in this, that we are not determined by anything." But if the "essence of each thing consists in that without which it cannot be conceived, then freedom can certainly be conceived clearly" despite some element in our actions being always determined by external causes, as there always are causes determining us to proceed in one way rather than another. By no means, though, can "freedom" be clearly conceived if it is accepted that we are compelled in all our actions. Perplexed, like Oldenburg, as to how to combat wrongdoing if our every act is determined, Tschirnhaus asks Spinoza to respond to these difficulties, a request Schuller seconded.

Answering later that month, via Schuller, referring to Tschirnhaus as "your friend," Spinoza remarked that Tschirnhaus' letter was "most welcome to me." In the *Opera Posthuma*, the only edition of Spinoza's correspondence available to readers throughout the Enlightenment era, Rieuwertsz's, Schuller's, and Tschirnhaus' names were all systematically deleted from every letter between them that the editors chose to include, the unnamed Tschirnhaus remaining simply "your friend."[9] Though much distracted by other matters, "not to mention that my health is not especially good," from which we can infer that by this time Spinoza's creeping sickness was seriously interfering with his daily routine, he felt

---

[7] Wurtz, "Disciple "hérétique," 112–13; Vermij, "Spinozisme en Hollande," 149; Laerke, *Leibniz lecteur*, 110n1.
[8] Zaunick, "'Einführung' to Tschirnhaus," 10–11; Laerke, *Leibniz lecteur*, 503.
[9] Spinoza, *Nagelate Schriften*, 635; Van de Ven, *Printing Spinoza*, 359–60.

"zeal for the truth" obliged him to reply as best he could. Regarding the "definition of freedom [Tschirnhaus] says is mine," he answered, "I do not know where he got it from. I maintain that a thing is free if it exists and acts solely from the necessity of its own nature, and compelled if it is determined by something else to exist and produce effects in a fixed and determined way." The human freedom "everyone boasts of possessing consists only in this – that men are conscious of their appetite and ignorant of the causes by which they are determined. So the infant freely believes he wants the milk, the angry boy that he wants vengeance, the timid person flight. The drunkard believes a free decision led to him to utter those things which afterwards, when sober, he wishes he had not said. Likewise, the madman, chatterbox and a great many others believe they act from a free decision of the mind and are not set in motion by impulse." This prejudice being innate in all men, it is hard to release them from it. Indeed, experience teaches that freeing men, or freeing oneself, from the drives is the hardest thing of all so that "often when men are torn by contrary emotions, they see the better course and follow the worse," while still believing themselves free as they want certain things only slightly and others more. Summing up, Spinoza, assures Schuller, "your friend" had wrongly grasped his stance and the issue more generally.

During the autumn of 1674, Spinoza and Tschirnhaus met together at The Hague for a series of intensive philosophical discussions. At that point, Tschirnhaus plunged more deeply into Spinoza's thought as emerges from his next surviving letter to Spinoza, dated 5 January 1675, where he cites the preliminary definitions "added to the Second Part of *The Ethics*" proving Spinoza had shown or lent him at least sections of the manuscript. From Tschirnhaus' question, "when shall we obtain your method of correctly steering reason to acquire knowledge of unknown truths, along with general principles in physics?,"[10] it seems they also discussed *On the Emendation of the Understanding* and that Tschirnhaus hoped to see either a manuscript copy or the published text of that work before long. He posed some extremely challenging questions: "if you have time and opportunity, I humbly ask you for the correct definition of motion and its explanation"; he also asks, boldly rather than "humbly," how, from extension "indivisible and immutable," we can deduce *a priori* that such a great variety of things can arise and exist, and how to explain the difference "between a true idea and an adequate one."

38.ii Discussing Spinoza in Paris

Spinoza answered briefly later that month, and presumably hurriedly, for he says nothing about motion and not much about extension. They met again, probably

---

[10] Spinoza, *Opera* iv, 268; Spinoza, *Nagelate Schriften*, 639; Spinoza, *Collected Works* (ed. Curley) ii, 430–1.

several times in ensuing weeks, and Tschirnhaus clearly won Spinoza's trust and esteem to such an extent that he was allowed to study the manuscript of the *Ethics* at his leisure and discuss it further with Spinoza, during 1675 becoming the first commentator to leave written evidence of having seriously examined and questioned key steps in Spinoza's argument. In May 1675, Tschirnhaus left Holland and travelled to London taking with him the manuscript copy entrusted to him under promise not to show it to anyone else without Spinoza's permission. "Our most noble friend Mr von Tschirnhaus," reported Schuller from Amsterdam, on 25 July 1675, "was still in England," and besides passing on respectful greetings sent his latest searching questions. Tschirnhaus wanted clearer proof than he had seen so far that "we cannot know more attributes of God than thought and extension," and how Spinoza thinks his text proves God's intellect is "the cause of our intellect."[11]

In England, introduced by Oldenburg, Tschirnhaus met Boyle and Newton among others and, from London, sent word of Boyle's and Oldenburg's appalled reaction to the *TTP* and his efforts to mitigate it. Schuller worried that in England Tschirnhaus was dragging Spinoza's name into intensive debates rather more than Spinoza wished him to. From this exchange and Tschirnhaus' next surviving letter to Spinoza, dated London, 12 August 1675, again pressing him to explain more clearly why the human mind cannot "perceive more attributes of God than Extension and Thought," it emerges that Tschirnhaus was busily examining Spinoza's system as well as defending the *TTP* in discussion. In September, he crossed over to France, taking his copy of the *Ethics* with him. The very first person ever seriously to study and also discuss, however guardedly, Spinoza's *Ethics* in Britain, he was likewise the first to do so in France.

In Paris, speaking German and Latin but no French, Tschirnhaus visited Huygens, "as we had advised him to do," Schuller reported back, and established good relations with him. Mentioning that Spinoza "had recommended that he make his acquaintance and that you [Spinoza] value Huygens' person highly, pleased Huygens very much." Huygens "likewise values your person greatly and recently received the *Tractatus Theologico-Politicus* from you," a book that "many people" in Paris, Tschirnhaus had written, had a high opinion of—a decidedly curious comment, true possibly of Huygens but assuredly of few others. Huygens, as impressed with Tschirnhaus' skill in mathematics as Spinoza, recommended him as a suitable tutor (teaching in Latin) for Colbert's son, a charge he accepted for several months. Before long, Tschirnhaus also got to know Leibniz. This "remarkably learned man," he reported back to Schuller and Spinoza, whom he had become good friends with, "is very capable in the various sciences and also

---

[11] Spinoza, *Collected Works* (ed. Curley) ii, 436–7; Zaunick, "'Einführung' to Tschirnhaus," 6; Wurtz, "Tschirnhaus und die Spinozabeschuldigung," 62.

free from the common prejudices of theology," an observation Leibniz himself would not have wished to have spread about then or later.[12]

Whenever meeting persons in Paris who inquired about Spinoza's unpublished writings, claimed Tschirnhaus, he conducted himself as instructed by Spinoza, assuring such interlocutors that apart from the Descartes book and the *TTP*, "he knew of none." However, regarding Leibniz at least, we know he did not stick to this, for Leibniz later noted that "Mr Tschirnhaus has told me many things about Spinoza's book in manuscript [the *Ethics*]." Moreover, the letters Tschirnhaus sent Spinoza from Paris were in part products of discussions with Leibniz about Spinoza's system and very likely formulated partly at Leibniz's prompting.[13] Well versed in physics and metaphysical studies, reported Tschirnhaus, Leibniz thought highly of the *TTP* and "is most worthy of having your writings communicated to him, Sir, if you give your permission." Should Spinoza feel disinclined, he should not worry: Tschirnhaus would continue withholding them "honourably, in accord with the promise he had made. So far he has not made even the least mention of them." It hardly seems, though, that Tschirnhaus was being as discreet as he claimed, and before long would be still less so, after setting out for Rome.[14]

To the request for Leibniz to be shown the *Ethics* in manuscript Spinoza replied, via Schuller, that he was satisfied with Tschirnhaus' discretion regarding Huygens and others but could not agree, for now, to give Tschirnhaus permission to show the manuscript of the *Ethics* that he had with him to this impressively learned person, presently in Paris, called "Leibniz." "I think it imprudent to entrust my writings to him so hastily," explains Spinoza, "I should first like to know what he is doing in France and learn our friend Tschirnhaus's opinion of him after a longer acquaintance and closer knowledge of his character." Meanwhile, Spinoza's greetings should be conveyed to Leibniz as to a "friend of ours," in the most courteous fashion.

During his Paris years (1672–6), still better known at that time as a mathematician than philosopher, and from 1675 close friends with Tschirnhaus, Leibniz thus acquired a conversation partner who knew Spinoza and his circle intimately and had been discussing Spinoza with Oldenburg, Boyle, and others in England shortly before. During the nine months Tschirnhaus stayed in Paris, Leibniz's own interest in Spinoza and his underground network was vigorously renewed, and during their discussions he unquestionably wheedled more about Spinoza, his philosophy and circle from him than Spinoza desired his young protégé to

---

[12] Schuller to Spinoza, Amsterdam, 14 Nov. 1675 in Spinoza, *Collected Works* (ed. Curley) ii, 461.
[13] Schuller to Spinoza, Amsterdam, 14 Nov. 1675 in Spinoza, *Collected Works* (ed. Curley) ii, 461; Laerke, "*De Summa Rerum*," 39–40.
[14] Spinoza, *Collected Works* (ed. Curley) ii, 463.

divulge.[15] Tschirnhaus seemingly did not show Leibniz his copy of the *Ethics* as such but, despite Spinoza's admonitions not to, certainly discussed key themes from it with Leibniz as well as his epistolary exchanges with Spinoza.[16] Leibniz, whilst in Paris, also learnt more about Spinoza and his impact from Huygens, of whom he saw much, as well as details about Spinoza's circle that very few others knew, from Franciscus Van den Enden. Later, in his *Theodicy* (1710), he recalled learning that years earlier, in Amsterdam, Van den Enden's daughter, Clara Maria, had assisted in teaching Spinoza Latin as well as more generally "assisted her father in his teaching."[17]

Van den Enden, "who was also called A. Finibus [or rather Affinius]" Leibniz records, having moved from Amsterdam to Paris, following his daughter's marriage to Kerckring, in 1671, opened a boarding school in the Faubourg Saint Antoine.[18] By the time Leibniz first met him, in March 1672, "this Van den Enden had insinuated himself into M. Arnauld's good graces, and the Jesuits began to be jealous of his reputation" because he was "considered an excellent instructor and told me, when I called upon him there, that he would wager that his audiences would always pay attention to his words." No doubt he was subtly inculcating his republican ideas as well as his subversive notions about religion; for it is clear that in Paris he remained as fervently republican and anti-monarchical as he had been in Holland, in the 1660s, or more so.[19] For this very reason, however, Van den Enden "disappeared, shortly afterwards, being mixed up in the Chevalier de Rohan's conspiracy."[20] Very likely, Leibniz and Spinoza at least touched on Van den Enden and his dramatic end during their discussions in The Hague in the autumn of 1676.

Van den Enden was not just complicit in the conspiracy of the Chevalier Louis de Rohan (1635–74), but as the forty-six page record of his interrogation on 26 and 27 September, and 2 October 1674 by the royal authorities proves, was the Rohan conspiracy's chief political theorist and adviser, intricately involved in the plot to hand over the port of Quillebeuf-sur-Seine, on the Seine estuary in Normandy, to a Spanish force to be shipped there from the Belgian coast. The conspiracy centrally involved the governor of the Spanish Netherlands, in Brussels, the conde de Monterrey, who agreed to send troops, cash, and arms for many additional men, to help halt Louis XIV's expansionism and save both the Republic and the Spanish Netherlands from the French.[21] When the plot was revealed, partly due to Van den Enden's own passionate nature and lack of

---

[15] Kulstad, "Leibniz et Spinoza sur Dieu," 21; Klever, *Een nieuwe Spinoza*, 121; Laerke, *Leibniz lecteur*, 100.
[16] Laerke, *Leibniz lecteur*, 366–7.   [17] Leibniz, *Theodicy*, 351.
[18] Mertens, *Van den Enden en Spinoza*, 23, 63; Lavaert, "Prelude," 66.
[19] Lavaert, "Prelude," 65, 68; Gullan-Whur, *Life of Spinoza*, 275–6.
[20] Leibniz, *Theodicy*, 351; Cauzé de Nazelle, *Mémoires*, 101; Orcibal, "Jansénistes face à Spinoza," 445–56.
[21] Maury, "Conspiration républicaine," 380, 395; Rothkrug, *Opposition to Louis XIV*, 164.

discretion (for Leibniz was not the only one to whom he made boastful remarks), and the principal conspirators were arrested, the leader of the planned uprising, the unruly Chevalier de Rohan, the only aristocrat executed for "treason" in France under Louis XIV, raged against Van den Enden, blaming him for the conspiracy and luring him into leading it.[22] Vilified on all sides, this herald of democratic republican revolution met his end with the other conspirators at the Bastille, on 27 November 1674.

Leibniz also discussed Spinoza with such leading French *érudits* as Arnauld, Justel, Huet, and Thévenot. In his immensely long, self-promoting Latin letter, of late October 1671, to Antoine Arnauld (1612–84), "le grand Arnauld," as he came to be known, among the greatest French theologians and philosophers of the age, prior to his arrival in Paris, Leibniz had already alerted him to the *TTP*, calling it a "horrible book [liber horribilis] on liberty of philosophizing."[23] Arnauld, though, whatever he learnt further about Spinoza and the *TTP* before the close of the Franco-Dutch War, in 1678, clearly preferred not to discuss in print a book he deemed abominable. While worrying how rightly to fix the borderline between theology and philosophy, an issue of great interest to Leibniz, philosophically Arnauld was a leading champion of Cartesianism and of Descartes' separation of philosophy and theology. Spinozism he later came to see as wholly contrary to Cartesianism whereas Leibniz viewed Spinozism as an exaggerated form of Cartesianism, a difference of perspective that long remained a contested point between them. Arnauld and Leibniz evidently respected each other but were never close.

Feeling distinctly more threatened, but also more intrigued than ever, it was Leibniz who prevailed on Tschirnhaus to write to Schuller, in 1675, politely requesting permission for him to see the manuscript of the *Ethics*, and urging him specifically to mention that he held the *TTP* in high esteem. And although Leibniz apparently did not see the *Ethics* in manuscript prior to publication in its entirety, Tschirnhaus did not fully respect Spinoza's wish that he should not "entrust my writings to him so quickly." Rather, Leibniz heard a good deal about the *Ethics*, gathering notes and quotes relating to key features of Spinoza's system from discussion, among other points jotting down that Spinoza held "Deum solum esse substantiam [God alone is substance]," that man is free only insofar as he is not determined by external forces, and that "mentem esse ipsam coporis ideam [the mind is the idea of the body]."[24]

Conjunction of mind and body would also constitute a key element in Tschirnhaus' own thought. Men mostly lack adequate levels of both mental and

---

[22] Maury, "Conspiration républicaine," 778–9, 784; Rothkrug, *Opposition to Louis XIV*, 164–6.
[23] Leibniz, *Sämtliche Schriften und Briefe* 2nd ser. i, 171; Stewart, *Courtier and the Heretic*, 86–7, 111; Laerke, *Leibniz lecteur*, 124, 353.
[24] Beilage ii in Stein, *Leibniz und Spinoza*, 282–3; Goldenbaum, "Zwischen Bewunderung und Entsetzen," 6.

bodily health, he argues in his main book, the *Medicina Mentis* (1687). Accustomed to practising daily exercises and regular enjoyment of athletics, riding, and dancing, the young nobleman stressed the need to cultivate mind and body together, insisting fit and active minds accompany healthy bodies.[25] Although *medicina* was the first word of his title, and Tschirnhaus certainly considered himself a knowledgeable "alternative medical practitioner" or amateur doctor, his book comprises no medicine in the conventional sense. Rather, the *Medicina Mentis* conveys only cures for our thinking, especially the Spinozist idea that we carry within ourselves the rule enabling us to distinguish between what is true and what is false. Thus Spinoza's famous dictum that "as the light makes both itself and the darkness plain, so truth is the standard both of itself and the false, [sane sicut lux seipsam, et tenebras manifestat, sic veritas norma sui, et falsi est]"[26] is repeatedly echoed in Tschirnhaus' remarks objecting to Descartes' seeking out the truth by doubting, since we carry within ourselves the basic rule for distinguishing true from false, a sure method based on mathematical proportion and reasoning.[27]

Constantly busy in Paris though he was, Leibniz found time over the winter of 1675–6 and following months to re-read the *TTP* more exactingly than before, weighing its arguments and transcribing whole pages of excerpts annotated with his comments.[28] Spinoza reveals plainly enough, he observed, that he equates God with the "nature of things," that "God is not a mind but the nature of things [Deum non esse animum, sed esse naturam rerum]."[29] Ever since first encountering the *TTP*, Leibniz saw that to effectively defend the Trinity and core Christian mysteries by reconciling these with the best science and the modern philosophy as he sought to do, a particularly powerful refutation of the *TTP* was indispensable and that this must be the work of an *érudit* capable of matching Spinoza's grasp of Hebrew and exegesis. Briefly, he vested his hopes in the Augsburg Lutheran theologian and Hebrew expert, Gottlieb Spitzel (1639–91) who, however, to Leibniz's chagrin, declined to take up the challenge. In Paris, Leibniz now switched his sights to Pierre-Daniel Huet (1630–1721) as chosen champion to overthrow Spinoza the Bible critic. Isaac Vossius' old companion, partly of Huguenot background, from Normandy, Huet had been an accomplished Hebraist since the late 1640s and was a *habitué* of the Paris Bibliothèque du Roi. Leibniz first met him, in 1673, at the house of the Huguenot scholar and librarian Henri Justel (1619–93), one of the most hospitable local scholars and

---

[25] Tschirnhaus, *Medicina Mentis*, 42, 252–3; Wurtz, "Introduction," 17.
[26] Spinoza, *Opera* ii, 124 (Prop. 43, scholium); Spinoza, *Collected Works* (ed. Curley) i, 479.
[27] Tschirnhaus, *Medicina Mentis*, 99–101; Wurtz, "Théorie de la connaissance," 125–6; Adler, "Education of Ehrenfried," 32–3.
[28] Parkinson, "Leibniz's Paris Writings," 77–9; Kulstad, "Leibniz et Spinoza sur Dieu," 21.
[29] Kulstad, "Leibniz et Spinoza sur Dieu," 21–2.

ENCOUNTER WITH LEIBNIZ (1676)   1101

most knowledgeable about Holland, England, and Germany, possessing one of the best libraries and widest circles of erudite friends in Paris.[30]

Highly placed, close to Bishop Bossuet and the duc de Montausier, former military governor of Utrecht,[31] Huet since 1670 had served as one of the then nine-year-old French Dauphin's court tutors, as teaching assistant tutor [sous-précepteur], under Montausier's and Bossuet's supervision. Member of the Académie Française since 1674, a classicist of "great reputation," editor of the Church Father, Origen (c.185–c.253 AD), Huet was expert on Roman poetry, myth and religion, on early Christianity and the ancient world generally. The young Bayle, having likewise first met Huet at Justel's house, reckoned him "among the most learned men in France" and "Europe."[32] Like Bayle, Leibniz rated him among the most formidable Bible critics of the day, especially admiring his conciliatory approach to confessional disputes and relations between the churches, and his idea that learning should be promoted in friendly fashion across the Catholic–Protestant confessional divide (while all Christians, he thought, together should vigorously scorn and condemn Jewish learning). Huet at that time had not yet embarked on his future campaign against Cartesianism to which earlier he had been sympathetic: but from now on, prodded by Leibniz, he too began viewing Cartesianism as suspect through encouraging a dangerous mingling of philosophy and theology, and as the fount of insidious new forms of scepticism and freethinking. By the 1680s, still fondly remembered by Leibniz, he figured among Europe's fiercest anti-Cartesians.[33]

The young Spinoza may well have laid eyes on Huet in 1652, when the latter toured Amsterdam's Jewish quarter and he and Isaac Vossius visited the synagogue on the Houtgracht accompanied by Menasseh ben Israel. Despite figuring among France's leading Bible scholars and boasting later that he had read the Hebrew Bible through twenty-four times,[34] it is still striking that he was familiar with the *TTP* as early as 1673 when, due to the war, the book was not just unavailable but virtually unheard of in France. Not a single notice had then as yet appeared in the *Journal des Sçavans* or in any French publication warning of the threat to the Church the *TTP* represented, as remained true until around the time of Spinoza's death.[35] One wonders, therefore, how Huet, unlike practically all other leading French scholars, uniquely knew the *TTP* at this early stage.[36] Possibly due to Leibniz, a still likelier explanation, since Huet obtained his copy

---

[30] Huet, *Memoirs* ii, 2; Vernière, *Spinoza et la pensée française*, 106–7.
[31] Shelford, *Transforming the Republic of Letters*, 32–3, 161, 163.
[32] Bayle, *Correspondance* ii, 221–2, 232.
[33] Bayle, *Correspondance* ii, 221, 227n30, 232, 314 and viii, 523; Sassen, *Geschiedenis*, 159, 169; Goldenbaum, "Leibniz as a Lutheran," 184; Lennon, *Plain Truth*, 39–40.
[34] Laerke, "À la Recherche d'un homme égal," 390.
[35] Giancotti Boscherini, "Nota sulla diffusione," 341.
[36] Laerke, "Leibniz on Spinoza's Political Philosophy," 108.

of the *TTP* before the French withdrawal from Utrecht in the autumn of 1673, and seemingly before meeting Leibniz, is that the *TTP* reached Huet via the French commanders in Utrecht through the special book channel Graevius operated during 1672–3 in conjunction with Thévenot in Paris. Although this trickle percolated extremely slowly—Graevius' latest classical edition, the *Lives* of the Roman emperors, dispatched in several copies to Huet, Montausier, and Bossuet in 1672, took many months to reach any of those to whom it was sent[37]—it did precariously function.

Deferring to Huet's expertise on the ancient world, Leibniz not only made a point of discussing Spinoza with him[38] but eagerly encouraged him to take up cudgels and deploy his vast erudition against Spinoza, stressing the urgency and relevance of his demolishing the *TTP* in the great new work of Bible criticism, a major effort of Christian apologetics, the *Demonstratio Evangelica* (1679), Huet had been working on for many years. A work with a very long gestation, reaching back as far as Huet's conferences with Menasseh, in Amsterdam, in 1652, when with deep frustration Huet found himself unable to persuade Menasseh that key passages of the Hebrew Bible do indeed proclaim Christ's coming and the Christian message,[39] the *Demonstratio*'s substantial sections alluding to Spinoza and the *TTP* were added only in the closing stages of the book's genesis. As Leibniz seriously re-engaged with Spinoza's work only in the autumn of 1675, his conferences with Huet about the *TTP* probably commenced around that time.

Confronting Spinoza's arguments afresh, Leibniz frequently discussed the *TTP*'s approach with Huet, Tschirnhaus, and Justel. At a later stage, he examined too and discussed the newly inserted passages concerning Spinoza in Huet's now nearly completed *Demonstratio*, growing familiar with this grandiose effort, like Bossuet and several others, long before it was published.[40] His Bible criticism Huet conceived in the first place as championing the Christian cause against atheists and *libertins*, but also against the Jews' stubborn refusal to acknowledge that the New Testament *is* foretold in, and triumphantly fulfils, the Old. Besides the New Testament's close relation to the Old, he insisted on the internal coherence of the Bible as a whole, and especially its power and authenticity in substantiating Christianity.[41] As regular tutor to the Dauphin from 1670 to 1680, Huet composed much of his *Demonstratio* at Louis' court surrounded by royal splendour, albeit also on occasion at risk of finding his monumental erudition treated irreverently by the bolder court *beaux esprits*.

---

[37] Montausier to Graevius, Saint-Germain, 13 Jan. and 16 May 1673 in Masson, "Graevius et le duc," 224, 226.
[38] Lennon, *Plain Truth*, 1, 4; Laerke, *Leibniz lecteur*, 110, 112, 114–15.
[39] Lennon, *Plain Truth*, 2; Shelford, *Transforming the Republic of Letters*, 36, 153.
[40] Laerke, "À la Recherche d'un homme égal," 391–2.
[41] Laerke, "À la Recherche d'un homme égal," 403–4.

While extolling the excellence and great antiquity of the Hebrew language, Huet remained always fiercely contemptuous of Judaism and Jewish scholarship.[42] It infuriated him that the Jews remained unmovably convinced there is not a single authentic reference to Christ anywhere in the Old Testament genuinely demonstrating linkage between the two testaments, and that the passage on Christ's divinity found in some early manuscripts of Josephus but not in others, they regarded as fraudulent. In Amsterdam, in 1652, Huet found himself locked in disagreement about this alleged "close linkage" with Menasseh "for a long time and in detail"; nothing, though, could get the rabbi to budge.[43] Even more vital than crushing Spinoza, Huet felt the Jews must be made finally to submit to the truth. If other leading Bible scholars, such as Abbadie and Le Clerc, accepted that the disputed passage of Josephus "is suspected by divers learned men to be fraudulently put in by Christians," as Stillingfleet also admitted, in 1675, Huet refused any such concession. To his mind, this crucial passage of Josephus had been vilely excised from the original in some manuscript copies by insidious Jewish editors basely subverting Christian truth.[44]

Leibniz tried to get Huet to be less disdainful towards his opponents, including Spinoza. For Huet felt only contempt for all who resist church teaching, including Isaac Vossius, whom he dismissed as bizarrely deaf to every argument, and Spinoza, whose originality and Hebrew erudition as well as specific arguments he denied. He scorned too the many in the Netherlands who, by this time, reportedly viewed Spinoza as an acute and original mind. Among such deluded observers was one that he himself would become extensively involved with later in the 1670s, the church historian Christoph Sandius (or Sand) (1644–80), who, as the publisher's corrector, corresponded with Huet when helping prepare the 1680 Amsterdam edition of the *Demonstratio* for publication. Sandius, while respectful of his learning and high status, tried to correct Huet on various points. Growing impatient, Huet retorted, in October 1680, that there was impudence and temerity aplenty in Spinoza, but no acuteness, no insight, nor originality. Huet refused to budge from his view that Spinoza was just an impudent hack borrowing "all his arguments from Ibn Ezra, Hobbes' *Leviathan* and from La Peyrère."[45]

Sandius, a graduate of Königsberg University, son of an East Prussian official stripped of his position for Socinian tendencies, had studied in Oxford and London, before settling in Amsterdam in 1668. Well-known to Rieuwertsz and other Collegiants as well as the Polish Socinian exiles in Amsterdam,[46] he earned his living editing and proof-reading but was also involved in the publication of

---

[42] Huet, *Demonstratio evangelica*, 136–7.   [43] Nadler, *Menasseh ben Israel*, 155–6.
[44] Bayle, *Correspondance* vi, 401, 403; Stillingfleet, *A Letter to a Deist*, 13; Le Clerc, *De l'incrédulité*, 88.
[45] Rapetti, *Pierre-Daniel Huet*, 16–17; Dijksterhuis, "View from the Mountaintop," 179.
[46] Kühler, *Het Socinianisme*, 136–7, 216–17; Bietenholz, *Daniel Zwicker*, 1, 37, 46, 48–9; Van Bunge, *Johannes Bredenburg*, 78n136, 274.

many Socinian works and did much to propagate Anti-Trinitarian views in late seventeenth-century Europe, though he seemingly retreated slightly from his father's uncompromising Anti-Trinitarianism to a more nuanced Arian stance. He rejected Christ's divinity but saw some role for the Trinity with Christ having a subordinate human status. A highly erudite critic of traditions of orthodoxy in the early church, and key source of information about Collegiants, Rijnsburg, the Polish Brethren, and Camphuysen, Sandius was also a personal friend of Spinoza and others of his circle.[47] Bouwmeester had in his library most of Sandius' works on ecclesiastical history and theological topics published through the 1670s, while Spinoza kept among his books both the 1669 and 1676 editions of Sandius' important early church history, *Nucleus historiae ecclesiasticae* (Amsterdam, 1669).[48]

No matter how derivative, unoriginal, and contemptible Spinoza was, Huet agreed it was vital to thoroughly crush the *TTP*. For the *TTP*, insists Huet in his *Demonstratio*, removes "the foundations of all true religion, all genuine theology, and the entirety of Christianity." Huet's strategy against Spinoza focused on defending the Pentateuch's Mosaic authorship, for like Bossuet he believed questioning the Mosaic authorship of the Pentateuch means questioning God's authorship of Scripture, given that Moses wrote directly under divine inspiration. In discussion with Leibniz and others, Huet readily acknowledged the urgency of refuting the *TTP*. But he insisted also on the continuing need to do so without drawing the public's attention to Spinoza as its author, and to Spinoza's philosophy and the threat to the church that Spinozism represented—a priority too of the papal authorities in Rome as well as of most of Spinoza's Dutch and English adversaries. Only to those familiar with Huet's code terms was it obvious to readers of the *Demonstratio* that Spinoza headed the list of those introducing impiety and irreligion, using philosophy to undermine theology and the Church's teaching, often by exploiting vulnerabilities opened up by Cartesianism.

Consequently, large sections of the *Demonstratio* focus on Spinoza and the *TTP*, but always in a masked fashion designed to avoid drawing readers' attention to Spinoza the person and his legacy. The *Demonstratio* nowhere mentions Spinoza by name (though Huet did cite "Spinosa" years later in subsequent writings). Instead, in this his major work of Christian apologetics extensively wrestling with Spinoza, he invariably refers to Christianity's number one modern foe as the "philosophus theologico-politicus," the "disputator theologico-politicus," his "adversarius Theologico-Politicus" or else as the "theologico-politicus ratiocinator." Numerous labels were needed because Huet's

---

[47] Kühler, *Het Socinianisme*, 135, 216–17; Bietenholz, *Daniel Zwicker*, 112; Benigni, "Introduzione," xiv–xv.

[48] Servaas van Rooijen, *Inventaire*, 656; Van Sluis and Musschenga, *Boeken van Spinoza*, 34; Laerke, *Leibniz lecteur*, 119.

plagiarist "adversary" unworthy to be mentioned by name, nevertheless protrudes from under Huet's careful camouflage as by far more menacingly insidious than Isaac Vossius, Hobbes, or La Peyrère.[49]

Descartes, Huet was now beginning to think, encouraged by Leibniz, bore much responsibility for the deteriorating situation. Here, he was firmly aligning with royal policy, Louis XIV having issued his first censure against Cartesianism as a directive to the University of Paris in 1671. From 1671, French universities were forbidden to teach students that one must rid oneself of all prejudices and doubt everything before arriving at certain knowledge or that extension, measurement, and dimensions convey the entire knowable reality of bodies.[50] It was among the *Demonstratio*'s aims to clarify the grounds for royal disapproval of Descartes' methodology of doubt, rejecting his rules for ascertaining truth and emphasis on the geometric precision of all soundly grounded reasoning, a campaign Huet pressed home later in his *Censura philosophiae cartesianae* (1689). Descartes erred profoundly in supposing geometry brings men closer to certitude than tradition and age-old textual authority, held Huet, geometry's rules being mere abstraction fomenting endless equations, leaving Cartesianism resting on delusion and unreality.[51] Huet aspired to subvert the "geometrical method" and Cartesian principle of mathematical reason by assigning greater certainty to what, to him, were solid, undeniable historical facts established textually.

Leibniz ended his stay in Paris in 1676, after accepting his new post as librarian at the court of Duke Johann Friedrich of Brunswick-Lüneburg, ruler of the future electorate of Hanover in the years 1665–79. After his departure, Bossuet continued advising Huet, conferring over passages of his text, and was instrumental in securing royal permission for the *Demonstratio*'s publication.[52] Huet envisaged his grand project as a vast offensive to defend the core teaching of all the churches, Catholic and Protestant, by overwhelming "atheistic" irreligious philosophy bundled together with Judaism and the rest of "infidelity" in one vast bloc of irreligion, a campaign partly shaped by Bossuet's and Leibniz's encouragement and input. Leibniz was not wrong to view his high-status friend's assault on the *TTP* as a pivotal development in the war of ideas surrounding the personage the *Demonstratio* left unmentioned with his philosophy now incipiently gripping France as well as Holland, Germany, and England.

The most certain knowledge humans can attain, contends Huet, derives from our ancient sources and texts. Demonstrating his historical and antiquarian method's superiority in uncovering truth shaped his entire undertaking. The

---

[49] Vernière, *Spinoza et la pensée française*, 108, 110–11; Rapetti, *Pierre-Daniel Huet*, 19–20, 37; Laerke, "À la Recherche d'un homme égal," 395–6; Laerke, "G. W. Leibniz's Two Readings," 108.
[50] Bayle, *Correspondance* iv, 90; Schmaltz, *Radical Cartesianism*, 218, 221–2, 244–5.
[51] Tolmer, *Pierre-Daniel Huet*, 437, 543, 539; Schmaltz, *Radical Cartesianism*, 4, 8, 217; Mori, "Ancient Theology," 178–80.
[52] Rapetti, *Pierre-Daniel Huet*, 53.

biblical prophecies' factual reality Huet "proved" by citing ancient sources, showing when and how the events prophets predicted and described occurred, with particular emphasis on Old Testament prophecies triumphantly proclaiming the coming of Christ. By "proving" the prophets really predicted future events which only God could know beforehand, and listing numerous allusions and fulfilments in the Scriptures "proving" direct links between the two testaments, Huet felt he had successfully substantiated the accuracy and divine character of those prophecies.[53] The Pentateuch's Mosaic authorship Huet anchored by relying on the hypothesis (about which Leibniz remained uneasy) that Moses was so towering a prophet as to become a universally pervasive presence everywhere in antiquity, the inspirer of the earliest legal codes, ordinances, and the rites of many ancient peoples. *Prisca theologia* [ancient theology], averred Huet, confirms that truth emanated directly from Moses and diffused in all directions, especially via the ancient Phoenicians acting as intermediaries between the ancient Israelites and the religious and ethical traditions of Mesopotamia, Egypt, and other civilizations, despite these later becoming corrupted by an overlay of polytheistic myth and practices.

When correctly interpreted, the entirety of ancient religious history, held Huet, substantiates the special antiquity and divine status of Moses' writings. In this, Huet was doubtless partly inspired by Josephus one of whose key ideas was that the wisest Greeks, including Pythagoras, Plato, and the Stoics, derived their most substantial ideas, their positive monotheistic conceptions of God and the divine will, from principles Moses taught them. The *TTP*'s "Ezra thesis" Huet blasted with special vigour, assailing it head-on in detail while discussing, one by one, all the Old Testament books.[54] Perusing the near complete text of the *Demonstratio*, shortly before leaving, Leibniz apparently urged Huet to cut some of his flowery rhetoric and make his argument more rigorous.

In his last but one surviving letter to Spinoza, of 2 May 1676, very likely concocted together with Leibniz with whom he had been concerting strategy for months by this point, Tschirnhaus broached the subject of Huet after asking Spinoza how particular bodies with their own motions and shapes fit with the concept of extension in itself, "for in extension, considering the idea absolutely, no such thing occurs." He posed a question too about the concept of "infinity." Finally, very likely also at Leibniz's prompting, he draws Spinoza's attention to Huet, "a man of outstanding learning," writing a major work in part aimed at refuting "your *Theological-Political Treatise*," especially "concerning the truth of human religion," meaning the monotheistic tradition, or *prisca theologia* that

---

[53] Huet, *Demonstratio evangelica*, 38–42, 140; Shelford, *Transforming the Republic of Letters*, 154–5; Laerke, *Leibniz lecteur*, 345.

[54] Huet, *Demonstratio evangelica*, 124–5; Feldman, "Josephus' Portrait of Ezra," 195; Shelford, *Transforming the Republic of Letters*, 35, 157; Mori, "Ancient Theology," 182–3, 185–6; Levitin, *Ancient Wisdom*, 154–5.

Huet, following many Renaissance authors, thought had permeated and guided everything valid in ancient thought, including the philosophy of Plato and Aristotle, and all the ancient civilizations.[55] Interestingly, Tschirnhaus' passage about Huet was later deleted from the Latin version of the *Opera Posthuma*, in 1677, to erase evidence that Spinoza was alerted to Huet by Leibniz, Tschirnhaus (and Sandius) before his work was published, several years before the *Demonstratio* actually appeared. During the crucial months immediately following Spinoza's death, the *Opera Posthuma*'s editors deemed it essential to avoid revealing Spinoza's ties with well-known personages in order to protect their reputations but also to obscure the existence of the *cercle Spinoziste* as the platform and driving force behind the diffusion of Spinozism.[56]

Spinoza was thus alerted beforehand to the drama brewing in Paris around his biblical criticism, if not yet surrounding his name, person, and philosophy. Replying to a (later lost) letter from Tschirnhaus from Paris, on 15 July 1676, seven months before his death, Spinoza inquired in passing whether Huet's treatise against the *TTP* had appeared yet and if so "whether you could send me a copy."[57] Two years after Spinoza's death, in 1679, Sandius assured Huet in a letter that "many authors had previously written" against Spinoza and that Spinoza deliberately chose not to respond to any of them except for one. Spinoza "once said to me," he explained, that although he saw "no necessity to answer any of these [Van Mansvelt, Bredenburg, and Kuyper], you [Huet], however, being a man who far exceeds all these in learning, he did intend to answer."[58]

38.iii Leibniz Visits Holland

Departing for Calais, on 4 October 1676, Leibniz returned to northern Germany in leisurely fashion, laden with masses of books and papers. Breaking his journey in London, he spent several weeks during October conferring with Oldenburg and Boyle about numerous topics including Van Leeuwenhoek's discovery of microscopic creatures or organisms which fascinated Leibniz but which to the Dutch microscopist's frustration elicited scant reaction from England.[59] He discussed too Spinoza's mounting impact in Germany, England, and now incipiently also France, as well as Huet's effort to crush the *TTP* as part of his massive work

---

[55] Spinoza, *Opera* iv, 331; Rapetti, *Pierre-Daniel Huet*, 17–18.
[56] Spinoza, *Nagelate Schriften*, 647; Stewart, *Courtier and the Heretic*, 187–8; Laerke, "À la Recherche d'un homme égal," 393; Van de Ven, *Printing Spinoza*, 360.
[57] Spinoza to Tschirnhaus, 15 July 1676 in Spinoza, *Opera* iv, 335; Spinoza, *Briefwisseling*, 428–9.
[58] Freudenthal/Walther, *Lebensgeschichte* i, 333; *Catalogus* [...] *librorum* [...] *Bouwmeesteri*, 15–16, 20, 22.
[59] Van Delft, *Antoni van Leeuwenhoek*, 110–11.

designed to uproot all infidelity for good. Oldenburg showed Leibniz, and discussed with him, the three deeply shocking letters he had received from Spinoza ten months earlier, in late 1675, denying Christ's divinity and the Trinity, of which Leibniz made copies. Spinoza's views on the Incarnation and Resurrection Leibniz always rejected outright; his approach to miracles he rejected too, albeit in slightly more conciliatory tones.[60] In late October, Leibniz proceeded by boat down the Thames, but, delayed for a week by storms at Sheerness, only crossed the Channel, disembarking at Rotterdam, on 11 November. He arrived in Holland with a lengthy list of contacts and personalities he wished to meet and form ties with, including Van Leeuwenhoek and Hudde whom he rated among the chief experts on the microscope.

Owing to the delay, Leibniz apparently spent less time in Holland than scholars once supposed, just sixteen days as opposed to two months. Much of this time he spent at Amsterdam; but, travelling by *trekschuit* [horse-drawn canal barge] he also visited Haarlem, Delft—where he met Van Leeuwenhoek and inspected his microscopes—and Leiden to tour the university and meet Pieter de La Court and probably Craanen.[61] "I was very much delighted by Leeuwenhoek's observations," he reported to Oldenburg, "and would wish that many other people, in different places, were animated by the same curiosity; it would be a great benefit to natural history."[62] Van Leeuwenhoek had indeed made stunning discoveries since devising new, more powerful microscopes in the early 1670s, and Leibniz undoubtedly admired his unique skill and unprecedented discoveries in the life sciences. His discovery of "tiny animals [bacteria]" in almost everything made a lasting impression on him, as on Tschirnhaus. But due to his lack of academic training, this moody microscopist had an uneasy, marginal relationship with other Dutch researchers. On bad terms with Swammerdam since 1674, in Huygens Leeuwenhoek encountered a scientist who admired his skill but scorned his reasoning abilities. Leibniz too noted the limitations of Leeuwenhoek's non-academic, commercial background, strictly empirical approach (which met with favour from the Royal Society), and lack of erudition in anatomy, languages, and other disciplines. Yet, "I prefer a Van Leeuwenhoek who tells me what he sees," noted Leibniz later, in 1691, "to a Cartesian telling me what he thinks: though it is necessary to join reasoning with observation," a view Spinoza of course shared.[63]

Meeting Meyer and then, in Leiden, Pieter de La Court, doubtless inquiring about the anonymous sensational pamphlet, *De Jure Ecclesiasticorum*, and the

---

[60] Malcolm, "Leibniz, Oldenburg and Spinoza," 235–6; Laerke, *Leibniz lecteur*, 101–2; Laerke, "Leibniz on Spinoza's Political Philosophy," 109; Nadler, *Spinoza: A Life*, 396–7; Ottaviani, "Divine Wisdom," 17, 19.

[61] Malcolm, "Leibniz, Oldenburg and Spinoza," 225; Van de Ven, "Spinoza's Life and Times," 35; Van Delft, *Antoni van Leeuwenhoek*, 204–5.

[62] Quoted in Malcolm, "Leibniz, Oldenburg and Spinoza," 229n14.

[63] Van Berkel, "Intellectuals against Leeuwenhoek," 198; Stewart, *Courtier and the Heretic*, 186, 190–1, 244.

continuing deep political rift dividing the Republic internally, in mid-November 1676 Leibniz finally reached The Hague and made his way to the Paviljoensgracht to confer with Spinoza at his modest lodgings. Plunging into deep philosophical deliberation and examination of propositions from the *Ethics*, they doubtless conversed also about Tschirnhaus, Huygens, Huet, and De La Court, besides Van Leeuwenhoek's microbiology and the political roles of William III and De Witt. Leibniz never said or wrote much about their conversations which the latest research fixes at, or around, the days 18–21 November 1676,[64] thus a mere three months before Spinoza's death. In September 1677, Leibniz confided to the French royal librarian, the Abbé Jean Gallois (1632–1707), editor of the *Journal des Sçavans* and member of the Académie des Sciences, that the climax of his Dutch tour "this winter" last, passing through Holland, was his conversing with Spinoza "several times and at great length [plusieurs fois et fort long temps]."[65]

The story Spinoza supposedly related to Leibniz of what happened to him on the night of the De Witts' murder may perhaps be true. Even though the alleged undated original note in Leibniz's own hand from which the report was taken has disappeared, the account of it by the mid-nineteenth-century French statesman, ambassador, Leibniz scholar and writer on German philosophy, Louis Alexandre Foucher de Careil (1826–91), may nevertheless be reliable. According to Foucher de Careil, Leibniz recorded in his note that Spinoza told him that, on the day of the De Witts' murder, he felt driven to venture out during the night and post up a placard marked "ultimi barbarorum [worst of barbarians]" near the scene of the atrocity. To prevent the outraged philosopher sallying forth and risking being torn to pieces too, and also posing a threat to his house and family, his landlord, Van der Spijck, locked the doors of his house to prevent him leaving.

According to Foucher de Careil, Leibniz reportedly added, in his account of their discussions, that "Spinoza did not clearly see the faults in Descartes' laws of motion and was surprised when I began showing him that they violate the equality of cause and effect."[66] When recalling his Dutch stay later, in his *Theodicy* (1710), Leibniz strikingly reduces the whole episode from a serious philosophical encounter to a mere fleeting social call: "I saw M. de La Court, as well as Spinoza during my return from France, via England and Holland, and heard from them some good anecdotes about the affairs of that time."[67] Even as late as 1710, Leibniz was no more willing than in 1676–7 for it to be generally known that, when young,

---

[64] Van de Ven, "Spinoza's Life and Time," 35; Laerke, *Leibniz lecteur*, 103; several recent sources wrongly state October rather than November, see Gullan-Whur, *Life of Spinoza*, 287–8; see Rovere's notes to Spinoza, *Correspondance*, 451.
[65] Freudenthal/Walther, *Lebensgeschichte* i, 331; Friedmann, *Leibniz et Spinoza*, 79; Laerke, *Leibniz lecteur*, 369–70.
[66] Laerke, *Leibniz lecteur*, 368–9; Stewart, *Courtier and the Heretic*, 197.
[67] Leibniz, *Theodicy*, 351; Malcolm, "Leibniz, Oldenburg and Spinoza," 226–7.

he had taken the most intense interest in the outcast Spinoza, his philosophy and his circle.

Spinoza "has a strange metaphysics full of paradoxes," mused Leibniz half a year after Spinoza's death, "among these, he believes the world and God are just one substance, that God is the substance of all things and that creatures are just modes or accidents. But I noted that some of the supposed demonstrations that he showed me are not correct."[68] This, together with the evidence of Schuller's letters confirms that, whilst at The Hague, Leibniz was shown at least some of Spinoza's demonstrations from the *Ethics* which they then discussed in some detail.[69] Prompted by Spinoza, Leibniz produced a one-page demonstration of the existence of God entitled *Quod Ens perfectissimum existit*, rejecting Descartes' demonstration and Spinoza's. To modern eyes his "proof," which he showed Spinoza, is more bizarre than convincing and Leibniz himself remained only briefly satisfied with it. On the back of his personal copy he reproduced almost word for word three propositions from the first book of the *Ethics* and jotted down notes about two others, seemingly hurriedly, in Spinoza's presence.[70] Though fundamentally disagreeing, Leibniz sufficiently gained Spinoza's trust for their discussions to be harmonious and constructive. Doubtless Leibniz explained also Huet's strategy in attacking the *TTP* and discussed their younger friend, Tschirnhaus, who around this time, in late November 1676, left Paris and set out via Lyon and Turin for Venice, Bologna, Rome, Naples, and Sicily, not returning to his Silesian home until November 1679.

Leibniz and Tschirnhaus alerted Spinoza to Huet's scheme of attack, and likewise relayed word of Spinoza's plan to rebut his *Demonstratio* back to Huet, as did Sandius. Huet heard about this, apparently before Spinoza's death, but felt little concern, he assured Graevius, in May 1679, feeling as before more than equal to Spinoza. When studying the *Ethics*, after receiving his copy of the *Opera Posthuma* half a year later, in September 1679, Huet became more than ever convinced, he assured Sandius in Amsterdam by letter that Spinoza exudes more audacity than understanding and insight.[71]

Sandius, "a man of wide erudition [un homme de grande lecture]," Bayle informed Minutoli, from Sedan in March 1680, had immensely upset the orthodox in Holland, including Huet's friend, Graevius (who also knew Sandius personally), by insisting on the total absence of any basis for the doctrine of the Trinity in the early church, and confirming with much erudition the Spinozist (and Collegiant Socinian) view that the Orthodox, Catholic, and Protestant

---

[68] Leibniz to Gallois, September? 1677 and Leibniz to Placcius, 14 Feb (?) 1678, in Leibniz, *Sämtliche Schriften und Briefe* 2nd ser. i, 379–80 and 394; Bouveresse, *Spinoza et Leibniz*, 223; Laerke, *Leibniz lecteur*, 369–70; Stewart, *Courtier and the Heretic*, 14.
[69] Laerke, *Leibniz lecteur*, 370; Van de Ven, "Spinoza's Life and Time," 35–6.
[70] Laerke, *Leibniz lecteur*, 370, 458–64; Lodge, *Leibniz and his Correspondents*, 92.
[71] Shelford, *Transforming the Republic of Letters*, 155.

doctrine of Christ's divinity is unconnected with the true Christ and a total fabrication throughout.[72] The origin of the correspondence between Huet and Sandius, stemming from the latter's "friendly overtures" to the French *érudit* earlier, at a point when an "Amsterdam edition" of the *Demonstratio* was under consideration, may well have originated, given Sandius' pro-Spinoza sympathies, as some sort of concerted Anti-Trinitarian-Spinozist counter-strategy concocted by members of Rieuwertsz's circle, a rationalist Collegiant design of the sort Rieuwertsz, Jelles, and Meyer might have favoured, to sabotage Huet's anti-Spinozist offensive by slipping in Sandius as a powerful intellectual Trojan horse. For several months, in any case, Huet and Sandius became locked in a tussle about Josephus, an author crucial to Huet and the Socinians and important too to Spinoza. Possessing copies of the *Nucleus historiae ecclesiasticae*, Spinoza himself was doubtless familiar with Sandius' blistering demolition of what both men considered the far-reaching fabrications of the Church Fathers, and of the Orthodox, Catholic, Armenian and other early churches, concerning the original church of Jesus and the Apostles.

According to Sandius, following Zwicker, the Nicaean Council of AD 325, which supposedly authenticated and fixed the basic doctrines of Christianity, was an organized deception contrived to obscure the authentic Anti-Trinitarian and Arian character of pristine early Christianity. In an exchange of letters during the autumn of 1679 (just months before his premature death), Sandius savaged Huet's passionate but weak defence of the *Testimonium Flavianum*, the passage in the early manuscripts of Josephus' *Antiquities* styling Jesus "the Messiah" which some humanist scholars had long suspected was a forgery. It was without doubt a total forgery, Sandius remonstrated—and demonstrated; but nothing Sandius could say could persuade the obstinate Huet of the weakness of his stance. Eventually, Sandius had to give up.[73]

38.iv Leibniz's Dual Approach to Spinozism

Back in Germany, Leibniz took the lead in his tactful, subtly encompassing manner in countering the spread of Spinoza's influence while simultaneously striving to better penetrate and comprehend Spinoza's thought and the activities of his circle of friends. By 1676, prior to the *Opera Posthuma*'s appearance, Leibniz knew more about Spinoza and had read more of his mature philosophy than probably anyone else outside the *cercle Spinoziste*. But he confided this important

---

[72] Bayle, *Correspondance* iii, 223, 224n16 and v, 340; Bietenholz, *Daniel Zwicker*, 106–7, 109; Mulsow, *Enlightenment Underground*, 92–3; Levitin, *Ancient Wisdom*, 487, 497, 499, 504, 526–7.
[73] Shelford, *Transforming the Republic of Letters*, 156–7; Shelford, "Quest for Certainty," 237–8; Mulsow, *Enlightenment Underground*, 187.

aspect of his own life, and Spinoza's, and of his own philosophical development, then and later, to very few, chiefly for reasons of discretion. From his correspondence with Schuller, it is clear that he was constantly anxious to safeguard his reputation, respectability, and standing.

Soon after arriving at Hanover, Leibniz wrote, underlining the importance of Huet's project, to Ferdinand von Fürstenberg (1626–83), prince-bishop of Paderborn (ruled: 1661–83), one of Louis XIV's closest allies among Catholic Germany's princes, and a prince-ecclesiastic renowned for his scholarship, correspondence with other scholars, and lavish spending on cultural and architectural projects. Leibniz, meanwhile, repeatedly urged Huet to finish and publish his *Demonstratio* quickly because "there is in it much erudition and magnificent insights" salvaging the Prophetic books and because it was essential to respond without further delay to the "damage to the canonical authors" inflicted by the *TTP* since 1670.[74]

In March 1678, shortly after the *Opera Posthuma*'s appearance, which Leibniz announced to Justel in early February, Schuller wrote apologizing for the failure to delete Leibniz's name from the Dutch version of one of the published letters despite Leibniz's express instruction, communicated strenuously to Schuller, that the editors must delete everything relating to him. Blaming Rieuwertsz for the unfortunate slip and admitting that the names of Tschirnhaus, De Vries, Jelles, Ostens, and the rest, including himself, had all been entirely deleted, Schuller did not suppose, though, since this isolated failure occurred in a letter about optics and mathematics, that any significant harm was done to Leibniz's reputation.[75] At least one earlier lost letter of Leibniz to Spinoza, dating from March 1672, is recorded as having existed. Indubitably, other letters exchanged between Leibniz and Spinoza existed, now no longer extant, and perhaps also other material linking Leibniz to Spinoza which the editors had at their disposal that *was* carefully deleted from the *Opera Posthuma* and *Nagelate Schriften*, and which Leibniz subsequently made sure never survived for others to see.[76] As for Oldenburg's last letter to Spinoza, this affair forms the most bizarre feature of Leibniz's 1676 tour and heavily veiled long encounter with Spinoza and Spinozism.[77]

When Leibniz was in London conferring with him, in October 1676, Oldenburg, learning Leibniz would be seeing Spinoza later that autumn, entrusted the letter to him. Yet, despite conferring with Spinoza at length and discussing Oldenburg with him, in November, Leibniz failed, or rather chose not, to deliver that letter. Neither did he conserve it among his own papers. One might suppose

---

[74] Leibniz to Ferdinand, December 1676 in Leibniz, *Sämtliche Schriften und Briefe* 1st ser. ii, 239.
[75] Schuller to Leibniz, 19/29 March 1678 in Leibniz, *Sämtliche Schriften und Briefe* 2nd ser. i, 405; Laerke, *Leibniz lecteur*, 99–100; Van de Ven, *Printing Spinoza*, 381.
[76] Laerke, "G. W. Leibniz's Two Readings," 127.
[77] According to Van de Ven's reconstruction of Spinoza's lost correspondence.

he lost it during his passage from England, or some other mishap transpired; but while the letter is lost, its non-delivery is recorded as being deliberate, not due to oversight. Leibniz delivered all the letters Oldenburg entrusted to him to take to Holland, he wrote to Oldenburg from Amsterdam, on 18/28 November 1676, shortly after his several days conferring with Spinoza, except for one—the missive to Spinoza. "Despite my talking to the man to whom you addressed it," he recounted elusively, leaving it to Oldenburg to infer whom he meant, "I had serious reasons [*causas... graves*] for not delivering it, which I can better explain to you in person. Some of his views are not to be rejected," added Leibniz, "but I cannot approve of others, especially since I recognize well enough their source," the term "source" here almost certainly referring to Hobbes.

Oldenburg replied in February 1677, after receiving word of Spinoza's death, sternly reproaching Leibniz for failing to fulfil what he had promised: "I cannot even guess the reason why you did not deliver my letter to Spinoza." The probable explanation for this curious conduct, scholars agree, is that the letter Leibniz brought from London, being one of introduction and recommendation, and given Leibniz's usual flattering and accommodating style of address, probably declared Leibniz's admiration for Spinoza and his achievement, making it a letter Leibniz was "extremely anxious should not be left lying in Spinoza's apartment when he died, to be seen by other scholars or become known in the world of learning."[78] It mattered greatly to Leibniz that his encounter with Spinoza, among the most formative episodes in his own life, should not taint his standing in the world outside. While not wishing the world to know that he was as familiar with Spinoza during the latter's final months, and with his circle, as he in fact was, Leibniz did later confide privately to the Landgrave Ernst of Hesse-Rheinfels, in March 1684, that at The Hague he did indeed confer with Spinoza "at great length" and got to know "some of his followers rather familiarly [quelques'uns de ses sectateurs... assez familièrement]."[79] Presumably, Leibniz conferred with Meyer (in the controversy over whose *Philosophia* he long remained interested), besides Schuller, Van Gent, and perhaps others.[80]

On taking up his post as librarian at the court of Brunswick-Lüneburg, Leibniz sought to persuade his new employer, Duke Johann Friedrich, to permit a considerable expansion in the court librarian's role. Besides duties directly tied to the ducal library, and planning new catalogues, Leibniz aimed to expand his international network of correspondence with Europe's ablest intellects and keep abreast of all the most important new ideas and publications wherever they appeared. In January 1677, a month before Spinoza's death, he boasted to the

---

[78] Malcolm, "Leibniz, Oldenburg and Spinoza," 227, 233–5; Laerke, *Leibniz lecteur*, 102; Van de Ven, "Spinoza's Life and Times," 35.
[79] Leibniz, *Sämtliche Schriften und Briefe* 2nd ser. i, 535; Rommel, *Leibniz und Landgraf Ernst* ii, 535.
[80] Rommel, *Leibniz und Landgraf Ernst* ii, 535; Israel, *Radical Enlightenment*, 506.

duke that in France he now had Arnauld, Gallois, Thévenot and "Mons. Casini director of the king's *observatoire*" among his contacts; "in England, the secretary and several other members of the Royal Society who have for a long time kept up a correspondence with me, besides which it is now four years since I became a member of the Society; and in Holland, I have Monsieur Huygens van Zuylicom, inventor of the pendulum clock whose brother is the Prince of Orange's secretary of state, besides Mons. Hudde, burgomaster of Amsterdam, one of the foremost mathematicians of the century, not to speak of Spinosa at The Hague, Craanen at Leiden, Leeuwenhoek at Delft, and others."[81] Spinoza now figured among the notables of Holland being renowned enough for there to be no need to justify establishing an unremarkable, fittingly non-committal connection with him among a list of others while omitting mention of all the rest of Spinoza's circle whom Leibniz had encountered too besides the democratic republican theorist of Leiden, De La Court.

Leibniz's new employer, Johann Friedrich (1625–79), the somewhat isolated Catholic absolute ruler of a mainly Lutheran principality, who, since converting to Catholicism, in 1651, had devoted all his power and energy to advancing the Catholic cause in every way, had allied, partly on religious grounds, with Louis XIV. With Leibniz he quickly became accustomed to discussing all aspects of Catholicism's prospects in the Europe of the day, including Spinoza's particular views on the Catholic faith and religion generally. During these intense deliberations, some months prior to publication of the *Opera Posthuma* and hence before Leibniz had seen Albert Burgh's letter to Spinoza, Leibniz sent the duke an undated memorandum accompanying a copy he had made of Spinoza's 1675 reply to Burgh. From that reply, Leibniz inferred that Burgh's arguments in favour of the Catholic Church were not particularly strong, while "Spinoza's objections do not satisfy me either." "It is true that justice and charity are the veritable marks of the operation of the Holy Spirit," he assured the prince-duke, but he did "not believe that those upon whom God had bestowed these characteristics" would, on that ground, "disdain the particular commandments of God, the sacraments and ordained ceremonies, or the positive laws divine and human." Nor would they readily "concede to Mr. Spinosa that everything in Catholic practice, ceremonies and doctrine not authorized by reason should pass for superstition, as *superfluum*, as he says, *et consequenter ex sola superstitio institutum*. It is not always for us to judge what is superfluous and what is essential." We do not know all the operations of the universe.[82]

---

[81] Leibniz to Duke Johann Friedrich, January 1677 in Leibniz, *Sämtliche Schriften und Briefe* 1st ser. ii, 15–17.
[82] Leibniz to Duke Johann Friedrich, Hanover, beginning (?) of 1677, in Leibniz, *Sämtliche Schriften und Briefe* 2nd ser. i, 301–2; Goldenbaum, " Spinoza's Parrot," 568.

In the autumn of 1677, Leibniz was much taken up with the arrival at Hanover, from Rome, of a much older friend of Spinoza's, namely Nicolas Steno, now elevated to the status of "bishop" and "Vicar Apostolic" of the Catholic Church in Protestant northern Germany. Steno arrived as a firm ally of Johann Friedrich. Leibniz had by now read Steno's open letter to Spinoza of 1675 and soon pieced together, from conversing with the new arrival, a picture of the young Spinoza of the early 1660s. Like others, including Swammerdam whom Steno had been striving to coax over to Catholicism, he found rather exasperating the reborn Steno's exclusive fixation on theology and church affairs and on how to draw heretics to the true faith, preventing his wanting to discuss any science.[83] Long discussions about Spinoza and his philosophy, and his circle, however, decidedly were on Steno's agenda and there are signs Steno may have helped initiate the shift in Leibniz to the more resolute, emphatic rejection of Spinoza's necessitarianism and conception of God perceptible in late 1677 and 1678 than Leibniz had nurtured a few months before.[84]

All considered, there is little doubt Leibniz was both impressed and shocked, fascinated and antagonized, in almost equal measure by Spinoza in his chosen fields of philosophy and Bible exegesis, but, he asserted in 1683, he did not find Spinoza particularly proficient in mathematics and geometry.[85] Leibniz's mixed negative-positive response pervaded much of the rest of his philosophical career. His attraction to Spinoza, it seems, was strongest in the immediate aftermath of the 1676 encounter, lasting towards the end of the 1670s, followed by a marked shift in the other direction. In Spinoza, he assured his Huguenot friend, Justel, a year after Spinoza's death, he found "a quantity of beautiful thoughts that conform to my own, as some of my friends know who were also friends of Spinoza," an allusion in the first place to Tschirnhaus. But in Spinoza's *Ethics* there are paradoxes "which I find neither true nor plausible."[86] He confessed that he himself had not been entirely consistent in his attitude to Spinoza. Indeed, "I once strayed a little too far in another direction," he later admitted in his *New Essays*, "and began to incline to the Spinozists' view which allows God infinite power only, not granting him either perfection or wisdom, an approach that dismisses the search for final causes explaining everything through brute necessity." Although some of Spinoza's theses were patently wrong, Leibniz admonished Justel, in 1678, still "I consider this book [the *Ethics*] dangerous for those who take the trouble to enter into it."[87]

---

[83] Leibniz, *Sämtliche Schriften und Briefe* 2nd ser. i, 385; Jorink, "Outside God," 102–3.
[84] Laerke, "*De Summa Rerum*," 51–3; Ottaviani, "Divine Wisdom," 17, 24, 35–9.
[85] Leibniz, *Sämtliche Schriften und Briefe* 2nd ser. i, 535.
[86] Leibniz to Justel, 4/14 Feb. 1678 in Leibniz, *Sämtliche Schriften und Briefe* 1st ser. ii, 317; Bouveresse, *Spinoza et Leibniz*, 217; Laerke, *Leibniz lecteur*, 573.
[87] Leibniz, *New Essays*, 73; Bouveresse, *Leibniz et Spinoza*, 219; Israel, *Radical Enlightenment*, 506.

A few days later, writing to Vincent Placcius (1642–99), professor at the Hamburg Gymnasium, Leibniz referred again to Spinoza's *pulchra cogitata* [beautiful thoughts] concisely expressed but inadequately demonstrated, and his "paradoxes." Although the latter's later famous dictionary listing anonymous writings was not published until after his death, Placcius who had also studied at Leipzig in the 1660s, was already a renowned expert on anonymous texts, pseudonyms and false titles, including those of the different versions of the French translation of the *TTP*.[88] As samples of Spinoza's "paradoxes" Leibniz here cites "there is only one substance, assuredly God [non nisi unicam esse substantiam, nempe Deum]"; "creatures are modes or *accidentia* of God [creaturas esse modos seu accidentia Dei]"; "our minds perceive nothing more after this life"; "God lacks understanding and will [Deum intellectu ac voluntate carere]"; "all things happen by unalterable necessity"; "God does not act with intention but by the necessity of nature." Leibniz admits, however, that although Spinoza also inadmissibly denies our future life, he says many excellent things about the emotions.

Even though Spinoza retains the terms "God" and "soul" rhetorically, stressed Leibniz, he entirely abolishes divine providence and immortality of the soul. By 1678, this "God of Spinoza" seemed to Leibniz neither particularly original as a concept, nor far removed from the "God or perfect being of Descartes," which was decidedly not the God most men, including himself, wished to venerate, namely a God "just and wise" doing everything possible for his creatures. For Descartes' God too "has neither will nor understanding" and does not seek the highest good, but is, rather, "something approaching Spinoza's God, being the principle of things, a certain sovereign power, or primitive Nature that puts all into action, that does all that is doable."[89] This view Leibniz repeated several times in the years around 1680: though a great genius to whom the sciences owed much, Descartes had produced a philosophy potentially pernicious and a large flock of followers who should not be admired because Cartesian thought leads directly to the "God of Spinoza" and the "atheists."[90]

Aware though Leibniz was of the wide gulf between Descartes and Spinoza, using "Spinozism" as a weapon to denigrate the more widespread and established Cartesian tendency henceforth remained a fixed feature of his mature thought. Cartesianism, especially as a movement subsequent to Descartes' own writings, Leibniz labelled, like many another, a "*spinozisme caché*,"[91] Above all, Leibniz rejected Spinoza's conception of God: "since God is most wise," insists Leibniz, "he chooses that which is best. We must not think that all things follow from the nature of God without any intervention of his will."[92] This was the crux of his encounter with Spinoza, the essential point where they diverged. That God

---

[88] Leibniz to Justel, 4 Feb. 1678 and Leibniz to Placcius, 14 Feb. in Leibniz, *Sämtliche Schriften und Briefe* 1st ser. ii, 317; and 2nd ser. i, 393, 394.
[89] Leibniz, *Sämtliche Schriften und Briefe* 2nd ser. i, 501.
[90] Leibniz, *Sämtliche Schriften und Briefe* 2nd ser. i, 505–7.   [91] Laerke, *Leibniz lecteur*, 870–2.
[92] Backus, *Leibniz, Protestant Theologian*, 149.

possesses will and intellect and that Scripture is His revelation and divine in character, became the spur to Leibniz's counter-offensive against Spinoza's system over the next decades, a perspective rooted in Leibniz's distinction between metaphysical necessity and a moral necessity whereby God chooses what is best.[93] "God may have his reasons, unknown to us, and I see nothing forbidding the emergence in the world of a kind of society of which He is the head, endowed with certain commandments and positive laws beyond those of justice and charity dictated by natural reason." Indeed, those graced with "justice and charity" are obliged, as far as they can, to discover "if there is something true and solid in these revelations or religions which make so much noise in the world, since these same revelations provide assurance that God does not refuse his grace to those who do what they can on their side." It matters greatly "to know whether there is a higher power endowed with understanding and will who intervenes in our affairs," and this Leibniz with his profoundly Lutheran sensibility was powerfully predisposed to accept.[94]

Leibniz classifies Spinoza as an "atheist" in the sense that his God possesses neither intelligence nor will, nor benevolence, and that there is no divine providence or punishment of wrongs and rewarding of good deeds, and no immortal soul in men except in the decidedly bizarre sense Spinoza professes this doctrine, as an eternal idea of the human essence and its striving for goodness elevated by our striving to be virtuous in our mortal life. Still, while rebuffing Hobbes, Spinoza, and all "atheists" philosophically, princes should not, he urged the Landgrave Ernst of Hesse-Rheinfels, employ the power of the state to punish a godless person solely on account of their individual private opinion, unless they commit acts that are wrongful in themselves as with someone plotting against the state, or committing some lesser crime. Hanover's ruler, Johann Friedrich, had little choice but to be exceptionally tolerant in any case for a seventeenth-century prince, as his own territory was mainly Protestant and precariously lodged between Catholic and Protestant neighbours—and Leibniz approved his tolerant stance.

Atheistic persons like Spinoza should be left to themselves if and whilst they keep their ideas to themselves. But that was the nub of the problem for Leibniz. There was no avoiding the reality of the considerable difficulty, he agreed with the Landgrave, in August 1683, with regard to "atheists like Vanini and Spinosa who strive to win followers [sectateurs]." Here, undeniably, was the real, concrete danger facing princes and there was assuredly room to ponder the issue further, he argued, not particularly helpfully, given the pernicious efforts founders of atheistic sects, like Spinoza, exert in actively spreading the venom of their teaching through society. Arnauld, Leibniz assured the Langrave, called Spinoza "the most

---

[93] Nachtomy, "Infinité de l'être," 122; Backus, *Leibniz, Protestant Theologian*, 162, 164.
[94] Leibniz to Duke Johann Friedrich, in Leibniz, *Sämtliche Schriften und Briefe* 2nd ser. i, 37, 301–2; Goldenbaum, "Leibniz as a Lutheran," 188.

impious and the most dangerous man of this century [le plus impie et le plus dangereux homme de ce siècle]." "Nevertheless, when I consider the natural right that everyone has to say what one thinks is the truth; and that, following the example of Epicurus, such thinkers believe they are greatly obliging the human race by delivering men from their ill-founded superstitions, I dare not decide whether one has the right to proceed against them *aux dernières rigueurs*," with the utmost rigour, that is suppress and execute them.[95] Leibniz had no wish to send the likes of Spinoza to the stake, or at least not accept responsibility for doing so; still, in his eyes, tolerance reaches its limit when it becomes necessary to halt propagation of unacceptable ideas by an underground sect.

In 1676, and to the end of his life Leibniz greatly respected and felt the rigour of Spinoza's system while at the same time finding its conclusions unacceptable, a dire threat to Christianity, something to which general access by readers needed to be forbidden and prevented by the political and ecclesiastical authorities. Even though many of the most characteristic components of Leibniz's philosophy were already in place before he first systematically studied Spinoza's *Ethics* in 1678, from 1678 onwards he viewed his own philosophy as being in some fundamental sense the best and fullest antidote to Spinoza's *Ethics*. In one of his last letters, of December 1714, he says of his system of philosophy, based on monads, that it was "exactly via these monads" that "Spinozism is destroyed [le Spinosisme est détruit]," and that, were there no monads, then Spinoza "would be right." With this Leibniz became the first of a line of modern German philosophers, Hegel, Fichte, and Schelling among them, acknowledging Spinoza as a great thinker presenting a unique and unprecedented challenge, leaving Christianity dangerously exposed: and that were it not for their own particular philosophical contribution (with only Hegelianism following Leibniz in actually defending Christianity), Spinoza would be right.[96]

Spurred no doubt by Descartes' unprecedented success in transforming modern thought and science, Spinoza's plans to reform religion, politics, and the world were breathtakingly ambitious. But Leibniz in turn was scarcely less ambitious and assuredly more bombastic in his private correspondence and conversation in holding his own system up as the one indispensable answer to Spinozism. Where Descartes transformed philosophy and Spinoza aspired to revolutionize the existing order, Leibniz saw himself as the great conciliator poised to restore harmony to the world, reconcile Protestant with Catholic perspectives, modern thought with ancient thought, and princely power, the principle of monarchy, with justice, stability, and proper order. Far-reaching ambition was a shared feature pervading the greatness of each.

---

[95] Leibniz to Langrave Ernst of Hesse-Rheinfels, 4/14 Aug. 1683 in Leibniz, *Sämtliche Schriften und Briefe* 2nd ser., i, 535.
[96] Goldenbaum, "Zwischen Bewunderung und Entsetzen," 6, 27; Goldenbaum, "Spinoza's Parrot," 567–8, 570–1; Nachtomy, "Infinité de l'être," 123.

39

Fighting Back

39.i The English Reception

Through the 1670s and 1680s, leading English intellects such as Boyle, More, Cudworth, Baxter, and Stillingfleet stepped up their concerted campaign to block Spinoza's progress. A key part of their strategy was to detach his arguments from his name and person, targeting the former while masking the latter and preventing either attracting increased attention. Boyle, eager to reinforce belief in miracles, composed several papers in the 1670s and 1680s insisting "almost all mankind agrees in believing in general, that there have been true miracles." The "philosophical difficulties urged against the possibility of the Resurrection," he forcefully reiterates in his *Physico-Theological Considerations about the Possibility of the Resurrection* (1675), "were nothing near so insuperable, as they are by some pretended, and by others granted to be."[1] "The experimental way of philosophizing" via scientific experiment, Baconian *philosophia experimentalis*, contended Boyle, "gives so clear a discovering of the divine excellence apparent in the fabric and conduct of the universe, and the creatures it contains, as may prevent the mind from ascribing such admirable effects to so incompetent and pitiful a cause as blind chance, or the tumultuous jostling of blind particles of senseless matter."[2] "Argument from design" looked infinitely more compelling and more "scientific" than Spinoza's total denial (and Hobbes' much more limited questioning) of Revelation, divine intention, benevolence, final ends, and miracles.

Believing reality, as science reveals it, entirely seconds "acknowledgment and adoration of a most intelligent power and benign author of things," Boyle grew ever angrier at those "prevaricating pretenders to philosophy as little understanding the mysteries of nature, as they believe those of Christianity," the most pernicious of whom, undeniably, were Hobbes and Spinoza.[3] Boyle and his allies could not ignore what was happening, but assuredly could drastically prune back to a minimum the attention society paid Spinoza the thinker and writer. In his *Free Enquiry into the vulgarly received Notion of Nature* (1686), Boyle carefully profiles the phenomenon he is combating without mentioning Spinoza's books or name: "even in these times there is lately sprung up a sect of men as well professing Christianity as pretending to philosophy who (if I be not misinformed

---

[1] Colie, "Spinoza in England," 199–200; Simonutti, "Premières réactions anglaises," 128.
[2] Boyle, *Works of the Honourable Robert Boyle* iv, 65.   [3] Boyle, *Theological Works* ii, 4.

of their doctrine) do very much symbolize with the ancient heathens and talk much indeed of God, but mean such a one as is not really distinct from the animated and intelligent universe, but is on that account very differing from the true God that we Christians believe in and worship."[4]

Silently battling Spinoza in Oxford ever since 1661, hence over many years, from the mid-1670s Boyle did so on a rapidly widening front while still countering him strictly behind the scenes, meticulously omitting all mention of his name and book-titles in his published work. Whilst Spinoza still lived, most others acted likewise, leaving Baxter in this respect an almost uniquely solitary exception. Just one of a crowd in decrying the *TTP* and the *Ethics*, he holds a unique place among early English commentators on Spinoza owing to his regularly calling Spinoza's philosophy that of "Spinoza" and to his highly unusual recognition, early on, that Spinoza's system combines troubling Bible criticism with a democratic republican politics and far-reaching philosophical system posing a different, and arguably greater menace to English society and religion than Hobbes, and one sure to penetrate deeper. He was soon proved right.

Lack of specific public condemnation of the threat during the 1670s, however, before long became a serious nagging difficulty in itself. Not drawing attention to Spinoza initially seemed far more important than publicly combating his arguments, but the apparent outward non-response to the menace rapidly generated intellectual frustration and difficulties. Henry More's first effort against Spinoza, his *Epistola altera* or *Another Letter to V.C.* [Van Helmont], of 1677, resulted, More claimed, from reading the *TTP* through for the first time and feeling a deep need to refute its arguments. But his reply relied on furious, damning rhetoric without engaging in much argument, shortcomings clearly resulting from the continuing emotional block stemming from More's deep abhorrence of what he found there. While answering this "would-be philosopher," he explained, "I constantly had the feeling that I had my nose over a smelling and stinking dung-heap."[5] Reaffirming Mosaic authorship of most of the Pentateuch, like most of the *TTP*'s English antagonists, More rejected Spinoza's (and the Koerbaghs') "Ezra thesis" outright. To Spinoza's claim that little of the Pentateuch is authentically Mosaic in origin, he retorted that Ezra's amendments were minor, mainly consequences of copyists' slips and Hebrew vowels being added only much later. Despite More's vast learning and prestige, some readers felt troubled that his *Epistola altera*, rather than a solid rebuttal with concrete arguments, chiefly merely reiterates over and over that the *TTP* "philosophizes foolishly and thoughtlessly."

Shortly after completing this essay, More encountered the *Opera Posthuma* which convinced him of the need for a second, longer text to combat what he

---

[4] Boyle, *A Free Enquiry*, 47; Colie, "Spinoza in England," 214; Israel, *Radical Enlightenment*, 254.
[5] More, *Ad V.C. Epistola altera*, 574–7.

called "the intolerable petulance and haughty virulence of the completely blind and stupid philosophaster." This he embarked on the following year with his *Demonstrationis duarum propositiarum...Confutatio*, now refuting the *Ethics*. More's two Spinoza refutations, the *Epistola* and the *Confutatio*, appeared for the first time together, in 1679, in his *Opera Omnia*.[6] By 1678, clearly More, like Steno, Van Limborch, Huet, Bossuet, Le Clerc, and Baxter, had fully grasped the fundamental connection of the *TTP* with *The Ethics*.

More's second sally was among the most notable developments in his intellectual career. Spinoza's *Ethics* unravelled, or so he believed, when exposed to his very different, not quite dualistic doctrine of "substance." Like Spinoza and Leibniz, More too viewed himself as a pre-eminent "reformer" of Descartes and Cartesianism; but his starting point on that path differed startlingly from both of theirs. Deeply disturbed by Spinoza's effrontery in mocking all "spirits, visions and miracles," More asserts in his *Confutatio*, as he had many times before, that in nature there exist two separate substances, body and spirit. But where, for Descartes, bodies are extended things while spiritual entities like angels, demons, souls, and God are non-extended, hence do not occupy space, in More's philosophy bodies and spirits alike occupy space. The essential difference in his system is that physical bodies are impenetrable and "discerpible" [i.e. divisible], while spirits are "indiscerpible and penetrable." Crucially, though, only immaterial bodies, or spirits, can initiate movement, pure bodies being inanimate, meaning that, for More, all living things have souls of a kind. For More as for Descartes, then, there exist just two substances with completely different attributes and modes. Spinoza's fusing these into one substance he rejects as total nonsense contrived under the latter's "grand title of geometric order (in order to impress the unlearned and the common people)."[7]

Although the *Confutatio* contains more reasoned argument than the *Epistola*, More's rhetoric in 1678–9 was no less contemptuous than earlier of Spinoza and his philosophy. When criticizing Descartes, More's tone remained always respectful. But when discussing Spinoza, this normally calm and methodical Cambridge don exploded into outraged scorn reflecting the profound intellectual and emotional exasperation he felt. Deeming Spinoza's redefining "immortality of the soul" as completely bogus, he felt his atheistic system "mixes heaven and earth," and that "to the peace and salvation of the universal human species" he all too plainly prefers "his crass, false and absurd philosophy [suamque crassam, falsam absurdamque philosophiam]" seeking to earn himself the reputation of being a talked-about philosopher avid for the "empty glory of quibbling."[8] "Oh you

---

[6] Jacob, *Henry More's Refutation*, p. xi; Reid, "Henry More and Nicolas Malebranche's Critiques," 765; Schliesser, "Newton and Spinoza," 443.
[7] More, *A Brief and Firm Confutation*, 57, 64; More, *Korte en Bondige Wederlegging*, 59.
[8] More, *A Brief and Firm Confutation*, 103, 106; Jacob, *Henry More's Refutation*, p. ix.

philosopher devoid of all shame and intelligence, or rather, Oh you most impudent impostor and hypocrite! [O pudore omni et ingenuitate destitute philosophe, vel potius O impudentissime impostor et Hypocrita!]."[9] But most important of all, More still earnestly hoped Spinoza would not be "talked-about," especially not in English.

Modifying Descartes' dualism by replacing the latter's distinction between body defined as extension and mind (spirit) with his preferred distinction between bodies and spirit, More strove to erect a fully robust dualistic barrier against Spinoza. Where Descartes' matter is inert in itself but with some bodies moving mechanistically without minds or souls, Henry More's bodies are always inert. Being infused by spirit alone makes life, activity, and movement possible. But More's spirits also move without bodies so that More's bodies and pervading spirits both possess extension. Thus, More replaces Descartes' basic duality with a new, less clearly dualist schema, based on the distinction between matter penetrable and unable to penetrate, and spirit penetrating but impenetrable. The supreme spirit, Henry More's God, is a kind of "anima mundi" existing within everything but at the same time above and separate from everything, a Neoplatonist conception of emanation that, like Anne Conway's system, in significant respects approached being a quasi-monism.[10] While Hobbes, perhaps jokingly, reportedly approved of More's "Platonic" approach, it left many contemporaries decidedly uneasy.

More was at loggerheads with a variety of opponents, but "this cunning hypocrite Spinoza [...] secretly deriding all religions and God and Christ however in his writing he prattles of justice, charity, and the spirit of Christ," he detested differently and more intensely than any other opponent except perhaps for the Jesuits and Quakers. His Platonic view of spirit seemed the key to defeating him. Sharing Baxter's loathing of Jesuits, horror of the new non-Scripture-based sects, especially Quakers, and recognition of the great importance of demonstrating the reality of ghosts, visions, and apparitions, More besought his friend Baxter, in 1681, "whether you be satisfyde with the truth of that notion of a spirit" with which he was trouncing Spinoza. Baxter, however, considered More's spirit "liker to corporeity" than to soul, and reliance on penetrability versus indivisibility leaving souls and bodies both possessing extension, unconvincing. What is more he plainly said so, thereby ruining their friendship and provoking a furious quarrel with More during 1682 which persisted subsequently.[11]

More was the antithesis of Spinoza in many respects. Where Spinoza sought to separate philosophy from theology more comprehensively than any other thinker

---

[9] More, *A Brief and Firm Confutation*, 103, 106–9; More, *Korte en Bondige Wederlegging*, 59–61.
[10] Popkin, *Third Force*, 111–12; Henry, "A Cambridge Platonist's Materialism," 181, 184, 186.
[11] Lamont, *Richard Baxter*, 22, 296–7; Reid, "Henry More and Nicolas Malebranche's Critiques," 770, 780.

of the age, no one sought more thoroughly to conflate theology with (Platonic) philosophy than More. Asserting the undeniability of angels, demons, ghosts, and witches, and his principle that matter and motion, "this corporeal world with its motions and revolutions of changes neither existed nor could exist from eternity" but unquestionably was created by a knowing God, More felt outraged not least by Spinoza's correspondence with Van Blijenbergh and Boxel and how he "plainly explodes all stories of ghosts and apparitions" employing the same arguments he uses to dismiss "all miraculous phenomena and removes all trust in them."[12] Spinoza's rejecting innate good and evil and abolishing the innateness of beauty and deformity More found deeply repulsive too, like Spinoza's denial of final causes—as if the placing of our eyes and limbs was not intended by the divine Creator. "Certainly, anyone who does not abhor this is absolutely stupid and of a defective and decayed and, as it were, corroded brain [...] and yet Spinoza prefers to be stupid thus than to acknowledge those final causes in nature, or any substance other than matter."[13]

Henry More boxed himself into a corner. Spirit remained the essential adjunct to his philosophy of "reason"; yet it was far from clear, as Baxter objected, whether his motley of good and bad spirits possessing extension but diffusing in various ways, like light, were or were not separable from the bodies they pervaded. All considered, More's dichotomy of body and spirit seemed more of a quasi-monism than a genuine duality, and his pretended basic distinction resting on penetrability versus impenetrability, lifeless matter versus extended diffusing spirit activating all life and motion, highly problematic. What stood out most was More's fury at Spinoza's disdain for Platonists and Platonism including his appropriation of the Platonic term *natura naturans*. Spinoza was perverting this term into precisely that Cartesian mechanistic materialism he and Cudworth held responsible for the rising tide of "debauchery, skepticism and infidelity" polluting their age. Avid to repel Spinoza using his Platonic concept of the all-pervasive divine agency of supreme good infusing, but at the same standing far above, all created things, More's approach left some suspecting this only rendered his system more susceptible to Spinoza's dismissing Neoplatonist emanation as worthless "speculation."

Christians, held More, are on insuperable ground in defending the Trinity; for "the wisest and most divine of men, I mean the Pythagoreans and Platonists" preciously developed a "doctrine of the Trinity quite like" that of the Christians. Spinoza's pretended theory of the immortality of the soul in Part V of the *Ethics* More debunks as wholly fraudulent because Spinoza thinks the human mind "can imagine nothing, nor can it recollect anything that is past, except whilst the body

---

[12] Jacob, *Henry More's Refutation*, 90; Gabbey, "Disease Incurable," 81–2, 90.
[13] Colie, *Light and Enlightenment*, 74–81; Jacob, *Henry More's Refutation*, 89–90; Schliesser, "Newton and Spinoza," 441.

exists."[14] Even so, embarrassing though it was to admit, More could not deny that Spinoza was right about one thing: "rightly, however, this atheist blames the disappearance of charity and justice from the Christian world; though we profess the Christian doctrine, whose flower and quintessence is justice and charity, we nevertheless hate in turn those whom our religion opposes." To More, it was extremely exasperating that the Christians' undeniable bigotry, divisions, and ceaseless feuding had become "the chief triumph and exultation of the atheists against those who profess the Christian religion." It was a highly unpleasant truth that had to be faced: "nothing confirms an atheist so much" in his atheism "than these barbarities" together with the Catholic doctrine of transubstantiation, "that particular absurdity and contradiction."[15]

Equally prompt to grapple with the *Opera Posthuma* while masking Spinoza's significance was More's loyal ally, Cambridge's eleventh Regius Professor of Hebrew (1645–88), the Master of Christ's College, Ralph Cudworth (1617–88). He too aimed, he discloses in his great work, the *True Intellectual System* (1678), to crush not just the anonymous *TTP* but Spinoza the philosopher while simultaneously remaining careful to avoid engaging with so contemptible a foe in a direct and open fashion. Of course, the best minds, Cudworth concurs, must fight mankind's most pernicious enemies, but for him too, like More and Le Clerc, the important thing was to combat Spinoza without drawing attention to him so as to prevent the public realizing the extent of the challenge he represented. Spinoza's doctrine of God and substance Cudworth judged both indefensible and intolerable. Rather than too much, there is insufficient theology in our world: philosophy *is* unquestionably theology's handmaiden, but so are all other studies: "all virgin and undeflowered arts and sciences are her handmaids."[16] If theology is fully and properly to dominate all thinking as it should and must, then Spinoza must be thoroughly trodden under and core Christian belief remain central in all study. The particular challenge the Cambridge coterie faced in dealing with Spinoza was thus how to beat back his arguments while deflecting readers from recognizing Spinoza's centrality and studying his ideas for themselves.

For the Cambridge Platonists' offensive to succeed, a deft circumvention strategy was necessary, enabling them to crush Spinoza's arguments comprehensively while on the surface appearing not to be discussing Spinoza at all. Accordingly, in his major work Cudworth uses an ancient surrogate, claiming a long forgotten strand of classical philosophy founded by the Greek natural philosopher and third head of the Athens Lyceum after Theophrastus, namely Strato of Lampsacus (BC 339–c.269), who had now suddenly revived and become resurgent so that that which in human life and society should forever remain sunk from view "in perfect silence and oblivion," had ominously re-awoken and again

---

[14] Jacob, *Henry More's Refutation*, 104–5, 108, 114, 117.
[15] Jacob, *Henry More's Refutation*, 106–7. [16] Colie, *Light and Enlightenment*, 47.

become a huge and menacing presence moral, religious, and philosophical: for "Strato's ghost has begun to walk of late."[17] Revived Stratonism welled up, however, "not bare-faced, but under a disguise."

Publicly, Cudworth stood by More holding that the revived Strato's "discourse [is] every way so weak, groundless and inconsiderable, that we could not think it here to deserve a confutation"; it should simply go unmentioned.[18] Privately, though, he was as worried as More, Boyle, Huet, Bossuet, Arnauld, Leibniz, and Le Clerc by this "sagacious" reviver of Stratonism, a thinker, he rightly saw (while keeping this point to himself), who, "discarding Hobbianism," enters the scene as "a kind of Hylozoick Atheist, attributing a kind of life to all matter, [and who] explodes liberty of will, as an impossibility, and contends for universal necessity."[19] Spinoza was the chief "reviver" of Strato's legacy and "Spinozism" his hidden, underground movement that most people needed to be prevented from knowing about. Once the link with Spinoza is established, Cudworth thenceforth focuses unwaveringly on ancient Stratonism, his magnum opus making only one further direct allusion to the great modern malefactor behind the revival of Stratonism where he deplores "that late Theological Politician" who, writing against miracles, claims "a miracle is nothing but a name, which the ignorant vulgar gives, to any *Opus naturae insolitum* [unusual work of nature], unwonted work of Nature, or to what they themselves can assign no cause of," and that were any such thing done "contrary to nature or above it, it would rather weaken than confirm, our belief of the divine existence."[20]

Among others taking up cudgels in the mid-1670s to combat Spinoza head-on alongside Boyle, More, Cudworth, Stillingfleet, Wilson, Conway, and Baxter was John Howe (1630–1705), yet another prominent moderate Puritan minister, a former fellow of Magdalen College, Oxford, and chaplain of Cromwell, in Whitehall, ejected from his curacy at Great Torrington, in Devon, under the 1662 Act of Uniformity. Howe joined with Baxter in helping set the new trend in English intellectual life, being among the first commentators to grasp the real nature of the challenge Spinoza represented, starting, like Baxter and More, in 1676, whilst Spinoza still lived. A declared enemy of Restoration persecution of religious minorities and, like Baxter and Bates, a passionate irenicist in ecclesiastical affairs, Howe summoned England's churches to be reconciled. A widely respected, erudite, eloquent scholar lavishly citing Latin and Greek texts, he was later forced into exile, at Utrecht, during James II's reign (1685–8), but was back in

---

[17] Cudworth, *True Intellectual System* i, preface, p. ix; Mori, *L'ateismo dei moderni*, 74–5, 95–6.
[18] Cudworth, *True Intellectual System* ii, 707; De Vet, "Learned Periodicals," 29–30; Tomasoni, "Il 'sistema'," 651, 658–9.
[19] Cudworth, "On Liberty of the Will," BL Add MS. 4982, fo. 55; De Vet, "Learned Periodicals," 29–30; Parker, "Spinoza, Locke," 168n19; for Levitin's erroneous view of Cudworth's relation to Spinoza, see Levitin, *Ancient Wisdom*, 419–20.
[20] Colie, "Spinoza in England," 187; Popkin, *Third Force*, 339, 344–5; Israel, *Enlightenment Contested*, 445–9.

England from 1687. Howe knew Spinoza's Descartes book, and held More, with whom he was friendly over many years,[21] in high regard. During the 1670s, this imposing Nonconformist preacher, unlike Baxter, also preferred to wrestle with Spinoza only privately. Indeed, he held back even longer than More until a very late stage, not wanting to draw the public's attention to the mounting threat he perceived. He began composing his *Animadversions on Spinosa*, unusually focusing exclusively on the *Ethics* rather than the *TTP*, in 1678 or 1679 shortly after the *Opera Posthuma* appeared; but, for various reasons, this text was then "long delayed" for "many years," appearing finally only in 1702.[22]

"Joining the common cause against Spinoza," at the outset, in the mid-1670s, entirely privately, it was only after painful and prolonged hesitation that Howe eventually decided to come out against Spinoza publicly. Aligning closely with his friend, Henry More, he focused almost entirely on Spinoza's doctrines of substance and God, neither Spinoza's (nor Hobbes') political theory appearing to interest him much. Always anxious to be just and fair, in Spinoza's Descartes book Howe found several good elements; but, unfortunately, "as [Spinoza] grew older, his understanding either became less clear or was more perverted by ill design."[23] Spinoza's mature doctrine of substance in the *Ethics* is so "confutable" that it is easy "to oppose Spinosa to Spinosa. Nor have I ever met with a discourse so equally inconsistent with all principles of reason and religion, and with itself."[24] In fact, Spinoza's philosophy, he agreed with More, is a disgusting heap of nonsense. The problem was that Spinoza's "horrid scheme" and especially "his devotees" were advancing, and for this reason, after vacillating for a quarter of a century, he ventured finally to publish his fifty pages confuting "Spinosa and the rest of his way."

Boyle, More, Howe, Cudworth, Stillingfleet, and most English intellectual giants of the day throughout the 1670s and 1680s remained intent on veiling Spinoza's rise and progress as far as possible. If Baxter set a new trend in British culture as the sole figure expressly drawing the public's attention to the scale of the challenge to Christianity and the breadth of Spinoza's thought whilst Spinoza still lived, Howe joined the fight in 1676, but on a purely private front while long concealing the fact. His *Animadversions on Spinosa*, a section of the second volume of his main work, *The Living Temple*, focuses only on Spinoza's godlessness. "Now this horrid scheme of his," explains Howe, "though he and his followers would cheat the world with names and with a serious show of piety, is as directly levelled against all religion as any the most avowed atheism; for as to

---

[21] Howe, *Animadversions on Spinosa*, 240, 254; Colie, "Spinoza in England," 188–9.
[22] Howe, *Animadversions on Spinosa*, 223; Boucher, *Spinoza in English*, 102.
[23] Howe, *Animadversions on Spinosa*, 254–7; Marshall, *John Locke*, 97, 105.
[24] Howe, *Animadversions on Spinosa*, 253.

religion, it is all one whether we make nothing to be God, or everything; whether we allow of no God to be worshipped, or leave none to worship him."[25]

During the 1670s, England's leading lights confronted the *TTP* and then the *Opera Posthuma* passionately but mostly inwardly. A key intermediary between the Netherlands and England helping stoke this behind-the-curtains furore throughout the decade was the learned mystic Francis Mercurius van Helmont (1614–99), a friend of More and enthusiast for alchemy, Lurianic Kabbalah and also Quakerism who spent much time during 1671–9 at the aristocratic stately home of Old Ragley Hall, near Stratford-upon-Avon, as resident physician of England's greatest female philosopher, the ailing Viscountess Lady Anne Conway (1631–79). A former (private) student, close friend and colleague of More, "who knew everyone who was anyone in the intellectual world," as Hugh Trevor-Roper expressed it,[26] Conway converted to Quakerism in 1677, the same year she wrote her chief work, *The Principles of the Most Ancient and Modern Philosophy*, making her (though this was not known then) the foremost woman thinker of the age and another leading figure among the impressive array privately fiercely engaged with Spinoza's ideas already prior to his death.[27] Conway knew Hebrew besides Greek and Latin and developed a Platonist-Kabbalist metaphysics to which Van Helmont notably contributed, an approach closely resembling in key respects but in others also differing from that of Henry More.[28]

Lady Conway had a problem, though: she could hardly admit that her system, superficially at least, bore several embarrassing resemblances to that of Spinoza which she, no less than the Platonic titans of Cambridge, More and Cudworth, and the Puritan champions, Baxter, Howe, and Wilson, felt driven to rebut. God, she asserts in *The Principles*, maintains and is as one with and, at the same time, the omnipotent creator of, all things. God is "distinct from His creatures" yet "not separated from them, but most strictly and in the highest degree intimately present in them." Like More and Cudworth, Conway was a virtual monist rejecting Descartes' separation of body and spirit into two separate substances, but unlike them also a militant Anti-Trinitarian, indeed more convinced than even Baxter that traditional Christian theology, the divinity of Christ and the Trinity, is indeed pure fabrication wrought by scheming churchmen, a "Stone of Offence to Jews as well as Turks, and other people," a doctrine that certainly "in itself hath no sound reason, nor can be anywhere found in Scripture."[29] Since "spirit and body are originally in their first substance but one and the same thing,"

---

[25] Howe, *Animadversions on Spinosa*, 236; Colie, "Spinoza in England," 189.
[26] Trevor-Roper, *One Hundred Letters*, 73.
[27] Colie, "Spinoza in England," 187; Popkin, *Third Force*, 97, 116–17; Mulsow, *Enlightenment Underground*, 187–8.
[28] Colie, *Light and Enlightenment*, 84–5; Henry, "A Cambridge Platonist's Materialism," 175–7, 181; Popkin, *Third Force*, 112; Gabbey, "Disease Incurable," 79.
[29] Conway, *The Principles*, chapter 1; Colie, "Spinoza in England," 188; Levitin, *Ancient Wisdom*, 487.

she boldly rejected also the entire edifice of previous ancient and modern philosophy, scarcely any of which was anchored in philosophical monism, the doctrine of a single substance which she recognized as the only possible cogent way forward. Hence, in yet another striking affinity between her and Spinoza, she dismisses as entirely worthless all traditional philosophy as well as all conventional Christian theology, "the philosophers (so-called)" having "generally erred and laid an ill foundation in the very beginning." Her sweeping dismissal of practically all past thought was startlingly bold but left her, she acknowledges in her ninth chapter, with the problem of how then to avoid the charge of aligning with the unspeakably despicable Spinoza.

Although she discusses Spinoza only briefly, treating him, rhetorically at least, as a subordinate, adjunct phenomenon, sticking to the useful convention that Hobbes was the principal challenger, in terms of actual argument, since for her monism was the central question, it was unavoidably Spinoza, not Hobbes, with whom she chiefly grappled. Rebutting Hobbes and Spinoza, a pressing issue for her, was also increasingly a pressing issue for society because those preceding her in attempting to rebut Hobbes and Spinoza, whether at home or abroad, had thus far, she insists, made a deplorably bad job of it, employing such "false and feeble Principles" as to leave Hobbes and Spinoza more entrenched than ever. The general run of philosophers, with their failure here had "exposed themselves to contempt and laughter." Despite some disagreements with them, she doggedly stuck to her insistence that her Platonic-Kabbalist monism indebted to Cudworth and especially Henry More who was much venerated by her, "more strongly conduces to the refutation of the Hobbesian and Spinosian philosophy" than anything else.

Lady Conway could not avoid agreeing with Spinoza that the "whole of Creation is still but one substance or entity, neither is there a vacuum in it," but this left her needing effectively to distance herself (and her mentor, More) from "Hobb's philosophy, to which may be added that of Spinosa; for this Spinosa also confounds God and creatures together, and makes but one being of both." She, however, she explains, understands God as one entity together with but, at the same time, separate from and above nature, leaving Him ample scope to knowingly intervene, perform miracles and exercise divine providence. In truth, Hobbes and Spinoza, avers Anne Conway, compounded a godless philosophy "diametrically opposite to the philosophy here delivered by us."[30] Capacity for miracles and revelation constituted the essential difference. But this again was private knowledge only. Written in 1677, Conway's *Principles* too long remained unpublished, only appearing eleven years after her death, in Latin anonymously, at Amsterdam, in 1690, and in English, at London, in 1692.

---

[30] Conway, *The Principles*, chapter 9 (online); Popkin, *Third Force*, 117, 278–9; Shaw, *Miracles*, 77–8.

At the moment Spinoza died from his lung disease, in February 1677, a great deal of time and effort was thus being invested in countering his impact in Britain, and a whole batch of English refutations of Spinoza's thought existed partially written up in manuscript, but, apart from Baxter's texts, absolutely nothing of this long pondered, passionate and complex reaction had yet appeared or would appear for many years. Another notable champion of miracles entering the fray early, to beat down Spinozism, but holding back until late in the day, was Thomas Browne (c.1654–1721) of St John's College, Cambridge, later a noted Nonjuror, not to be confused with the more celebrated Thomas Browne (d. 1682), author of the *Religio Medici*. Before, during, and after the Glorious Revolution (1688–91), St John's College, Cambridge, proved a veritable hive of Anglican Toryism, producing as many Nonjurors (refusing allegiance to William III) as all Oxford's most reactionary colleges lumped together. Having likewise perused the *Opera Posthuma* and the *TTP*,[31] in his tract *Miracles Works Above and Contrary to Nature* (1683), this Thomas Browne sought to do more than just refute Spinoza. For during the early 1680s, it became essential too to counter the deviously anonymous deist, Charles Blount (1654–98), who, without mentioning either of their names, had published in English key texts of Hobbes and Spinoza some months before, making particular use of the sixth chapter of the *TTP* on miracles, without intimating in any way his own subversive intent regarding Christian doctrine, grouping together a batch of materials all denying, or so he claimed, the possibility of miracles.

But this insidious deist conspirator had got his strategy muddled, contended Browne, by insufficiently appreciating, or pretending not to notice, that Hobbes and Spinoza, while engaged in the same godless work, "differ notwithstanding very widely in the way of compassing it, as far as the opposite parts of a contradiction can set them at odds: the one [i.e. Hobbes] asserting that there are works above Nature, the other [Spinoza] denying it: so that the Author of this collection was not very well advised to think they would cotton so well together."[32] No matter what the early seventeenth-century "deist" Herbert of Cherbury and later Hobbes insinuate, their writings promote a deceitful stance altogether less radical than Spinoza's. If one wishes to fight miracle deniers, there is really only one that counts, Browne points out, namely Spinoza, because he alone clearly and straightforwardly maintains, without pretending to believe the opposite, that there never have been any miracles, never will be, and never could be, while supporting this stance with philosophical reasons. Hobbes, entirely differently, admits the truth of "miracles" in principle, even if inclined to throw doubt on particular "miracles." Their two positions, the truth is, contrast fundamentally. What was

---

[31] Browne, *Miracles, Works Above*, 37; Colie, "Spinoza and the Early English Deists," 38.
[32] Browne, *Miracles, Works Above*, 4–5; Colie, "Spinoza and the Early English Deists," 38; Simonutti, "Spinoza and the English Thinkers," 198, 201–2.

worrying here, admonished Browne, was Blount's presenting his texts in English, instead of the original Latin, after going to the trouble of translating Spinoza's whole chapter into English. Blount's imposture entailed cunningly affixing Spinoza's much longer and more cogent text, without mentioning Spinoza's name, being an author the English public thankfully knew nothing about, to much shorter and less significant texts by the infinitely better known and far more talked about figures, Hobbes and Cherbury, now so familiar to the English public. In this way, Blount perniciously ties the more dangerous and radical text on miracles of the unmentioned writer to the less subversive but more notorious familiar authors.

The strategy of Boyle, Cudworth, More, and others, veiling Spinoza's name and person especially from the non-Latin reading Englishman while targeting his arguments, confronted Blount and his allies with the dilemma that most Englishmen in the 1680s still had no idea who Spinoza was, whereas everybody had learnt to abhor the name of Hobbes. In reality, Blount knew perfectly well that Hobbes does not deny the metaphysical reality of miracles, or angels, ghosts, or demons whereas Spinoza emphatically does. It was the English public's horror of Hobbes and unfamiliarity with Spinoza that motivated his tying Spinoza's more menacing argument to Hobbes' notoriety to create this explosive bombshell. Browne recognized that Blount had cleverly absorbed Hobbes' standing into a truly dangerous budding new philosophy both more inspiring and more useful to the emerging deist movement. In 1683, Blount published just one chapter of Spinoza, the first of his texts translated into and published in English.

Whereas the *TTP* appeared clandestinely in French, unsettlingly penetrating French culture from 1678, Spinozism now began invading English-language culture from 1683, but yet still without Spinoza the person being named, profiled, or pointed to.[33] In this respect the strategy followed by Boyle, More, and Cudworth remained effective through the 1680s but paradoxically came to be absorbed into Blount's subversive tactics. For a disadvantage of the prevailing strategy was that the, for most people, obscure as well as anonymous *TTP* often slipped through official fingers where Hobbes' *Leviathan* and other more notorious officially targeted texts did not. Thus, at one of the great English book auctions of the era, in 1686, when the 8,500 books of the Earl of Anglesey, the *Bibliotheca Anglesiana*, were sold off—an occasion at which Isaac Vossius seems to have been present—"a stop was made to the sale of some treasonous and seditious books by public order," preventing the sale of the earl's copy of Hobbes' *Leviathan* while his three copies of the *TTP* (two having belonged to Oldenburg whose library he had purchased at the latter's death) slipped through unnoticed.[34] The absence of

---

[33] Browne, *Miracles, Works Above*, 37; Boucher, *Spinoza in English*, 32, 39; Simonutti, "Spinoza and the English Thinkers," 198–9, 202; Lucci, *John Locke's Christianity*, 21.
[34] Malcolm, "Library of Henry Oldenburg," 10, 30, 50n137.

Spinoza's name from his title-pages, and absence from public notice and discussion, to an extent served as an aid to his clandestine diffusion.

39.ii Spinoza "Invades" France (1676–1680)

From the very outset in 1670, the *TTP* had a highly important and far-reaching impact. Yet it is also true, and a unique as well as equally important historical phenomenon, that its deep impact was from the start rigorously fenced around by authorities, churches, universities, and the main body of the scholarly world, and for this reason was further diffused and deepened gradually, by stages, in an inexorable, unprecedented, and unparalleled fashion. Van Limborch received a letter from Grenoble, in December 1681, from his future close ally, the later renowned Bible critic and Remonstrant theologian Jean Le Clerc (1657–1736), then already edging away from Calvinism to Arminianism, who wished to know whether in Holland Spinoza's work had exerted anything like the stunning impact that suddenly, since 1678, it was now exerting in France. There, he says, it had alienated "many Catholics not only from their confession but also from the Christian religion." Le Clerc would afterwards, in 1683, transfer to Amsterdam as his permanent base and become a staunch ally of Arminianism and Van Limborch. Regrettably, "in our country," answered Van Limborch, that book "has impregnated many minds, alienating them completely from all religion."[35]

By the time of his death, it is quite clear, Spinoza had a formidable international following, particularly in the Netherlands, Germany, and Britain, and by 1678, the year the Franco-Dutch War ended, this was becoming disturbingly true of France too, in the wake of the *TTP* and its diffusion, from that year, in French. In 1685, in his major work *Sentiments de Quelques Théologiens de Hollande sur l'Histoire Critique du Vieux Testament*, Le Clerc followed up Van Limborch's efforts against Spinoza and the *TTP*, in particular by attacking those "unbelievers" who were endeavouring to make the veracity of miracles "uncertain." His principal target was certainly Spinoza, as he later admitted; but Le Clerc at the same time remained loyal to the continuing international effort—Dutch, German, British, Swiss, and French, backed by a great host of Spinoza's opponents—to prevent attention being drawn to Spinoza the thinker and writer among the public and ensuring minimum publicity.[36] There was no way such a strategy could be wholly effective, but with most scholars and publicists adhering to it, it did have a broad and sustained effect across Europe.

---

[35] Meinsma, *Spinoza et son cercle*, 525; Colie, *Light and Enlightenment*, 30–5; Simonutti, *Arminianesimo*, 78, 82–3.
[36] Colie, *Light and Enlightenment*, 110–13; Israel, *Enlightenment Contested*, 35, 76, 203, 386, 766.

In France, initial reaction to the *TTP* was more delayed than elsewhere due to the long war with the Republic and to no small extent also royal censorship. Once the war ended, however, and normal land and sea communication between the Netherlands and France resumed, in 1678, the French response rapidly caught up with the response elsewhere. Reaction to the *TTP* and to B.d.S. *Opera Posthuma* which appeared at the same time as the war ended—but not as yet, reaction to "Spinoza" the writer and person, for there was very little of that for now—was both swift and decidedly unsettling. Considerable effort was invested between 1677 and the 1690s to provide that powerful, decisive rebuttal that practically everyone hoped for, but, as in the Low Countries, Germany, and Britain, despite much intellectual exertion, that crushing reply never actually materialized, generating much heightened exasperation, fury, and worry.

Earlier, after the French withdrew from most of the Republic's territory, in the autumn of 1673, communication between Holland and Paris remained for several years extremely tenuous. "The war is indeed cruel," wrote Montausier, from Paris, to Graevius, in Utrecht, in March 1675, "to strip us of the commerce with your muses," meaning Dutch publishing output.[37] Thévenot writing to Graevius from Paris soon afterwards, recounting his recent stay at Chantilly, in the palace of the Prince de Condé, mentions the excruciatingly delayed over many months but eventual safe arrival of the latest consignment of books sent by Graevius by special courier to himself and Messieurs Montausier and Huet, including accounts of the East Indies, the older Vossius' *De Idolatria*, and recent editions of Tacitus by Gronovius (Amsterdam, 1673), and Ovid by Heinsius.[38] But for practically everyone in France, outside the charmed circles of Thévenot, Condé, the Stouppes, and Huet with their special channels, the *TTP* remained virtually unheard of until after Spinoza's death. Only in November 1677, for example, did Pierre Bayle—an avid reader, exceptionally alert to all new developments in philosophy and theology, at that time teaching at Sedan on France's north-eastern border—for the first time in his wide-ranging correspondence mention the *TTP*, doing so in connection with Kuyper's recent Collegiant refutation.[39]

Once the *TTP*'s French reception started, from 1677–8, it was even faster, wider, and more unsettling than elsewhere, with the vernacular version following immediately on the Latin. A particularly disturbing consequence of the French translation's publication was its obvious appeal to fashionable young people, nobles and courtiers, soon forcing France's debate about the *TTP* into French rather than Latin, despite continuing efforts to keep Spinoza's name, person, and other writings from being brought into the picture. Just as elsewhere, to begin with very few in France clearly connected the *TTP*, and the massive uproar

---

[37] Montausier to Graevius, Saint-Germain, 25 March 1675 in Masson, "Graevius et le duc," 228.
[38] RL Copenhagen MS Thott 1266/4, fos. 3–4. Thévenot to Graevius, Paris, 19 April 1675.
[39] Vernière, *Spinoza et la pensée française*, 108.

surrounding it, with the mysterious philosopher coded as "B.d.S." The suddenly notorious *Tractatus Theologico-Politicus* "has created such a stir," Bayle informed his brother, in November 1677, being a book "where religious matters are treated so *cavalièrement*," that by now his brother too must have heard of it. Although there lingered widespread doubt as to who the author of the *TTP* was, it was actually written "if I am not mistaken by a Spaniard named Spinosa."[40] This officially encouraged cloud of obscurity surrounding Spinoza the person was about to thin, but only slowly.

One consequence of the initial virtual absence of Spinoza's name and image behind the *TTP* was that for a time it was hard for French readers to make the connection between the Latin *TTP* and its French version now circulating under three different, entirely false titles. Three months after Spinoza's death, on 26 May 1679, the young Bayle, now thirty-one, writing to his friend and correspondent, the ex-Protestant minister and scholar, Vincent Minutoli (1639–1709), mentions having just read a book published by "Jacob Smith" at Amsterdam the previous year, entitled *Traitté des cérémonies superstitieuses des juifs, tant anciens que modernes* "which is certainly the work most filled with impious doctrines I have ever read [bien le plus rempli de doctrines impies que j'aie jamais lu]. Never have I seen Holy Scripture treated so cavalierly. The author claims all the Old Testament books, down to but not including the *Chronicles,* are a collection of histories which Ezra compiled from different sources intent on assembling an accurate chronicle of his people's history," but did so gathering texts by different authors agreeing with each other with respect to neither chronology nor sequence of facts, with Ezra hoping to have selected the most probable versions. Ezra's death then intervened before he could redact all his material, leaving a mass of undigested papers without any proper order, so that subsequent editors compiled separate books with names such as 'Exodus', the Book of Joshua and so forth explaining, or so claims the *Traitté*'s author, why one finds scant coherence, concord and accuracy in the Bible's factual narratives and why these cause theologians so many headaches. In its political chapters, the anonymous author asserts that the sovereign is the proper ruler over religious matters in society "which makes me think that the author is the famous Spinosa, who has assembled similar thoughts in his *Tractatus Theologico-Politicus.*"[41] Down to 1680, even Bayle did not realize that the illicit French work suddenly causing uproar in 1678–9, copies of which would be repeatedly seized by royal officers during the 1680s, was actually the *TTP*. Then still a pious Protestant Christian (he changed later),[42] Bayle, in 1678–9, was among those who read the French version of the

---

[40] Bayle to Jacob Bayle, Sedan, 19 Nov. 1677 in Bayle, *Correspondance* ii, 457, 459n19; Israel, "Early Dutch and German Reaction," 75.
[41] Bayle to Minutoli, Sedan, 26 May 1679 in Bayle, *Correspondance* iii, 180–1.
[42] Israel, "Pierre Bayle's Correspondence," 483.

TTP after reading the Latin, initially not realizing that it was simply a French translation of Spinoza's book.

Meanwhile, the first, most widely expected and prestigious French reply to the *TTP* was nearing completion surrounded by fanfares but also, among France's most erudite, with considerable concern. Just four days before Spinoza died, in February 1677, Justel wrote to Leibniz from Paris, alerting him that Huet's magnum opus "on the truth of the Christian religion" was about to go to the press but, unfortunately, despite its author's massive erudition, it was being doubted that it offered "convincing arguments." This was worrying, for besides Julian the Apostate and some others, Huet had to refute the "*Tractatus Theologico-Politicus* of Spinoza" and "reconcile passages which seem to contradict each other"; without that, summed up Justel, "it is useless to attempt an apology of the Christian religion which must be defended strongly or not at all [fortement ou point de tout]."[43] This letter of Justel to Leibniz proved decidedly premature, for though the long-expected book was now finished, for various reasons it was not brought to the press at this point. Huet's *Demonstratio*, while complete, ready for publication, and arousing excited interest in Paris and beyond since well before Spinoza breathed his last, remained held up at the printers from early 1677, as Huet and the royal authorities hesitated to publish this most trumpeted and supposedly crushing French reply to the *TTP* for over two years.[44]

Huet's *Demonstratio evangelica* (1679) was, without doubt, the most hyped-up response to the *TTP* emanating from official circles and the higher reaches of society during its early French reception, vastly outstripping all other refutations in terms of prior publicity, fanfares, and approbation by the exalted. By February 1677, Huet's thunderclap had been generating keen expectation for years. With sincere but premature gratitude, the young, still decidedly pious Calvinist Protestant Bayle informed his correspondent, Minutoli, in August 1677, that Huet's defence of Christianity, he was hearing, was about to appear, was highly innovative and thankfully exceptionally powerful.[45] In Paris, much was being made of Huet's great enterprise, Bayle assured his brother, in September 1677, especially because all previous attempts to demonstrate "the truth of the Christian religion" from historical sources, including Grotius' apologetic work, had failed sufficiently to engage with the full array of sources.[46]

Huet's magnum opus was scheduled internationally to be a major event. When it finally appeared, in 1679, many rushed for what Leibniz, Bayle, and a great many others hoped would prove the eagerly awaited final overthrow of the *TTP*. But besides stoking keen expectation, of which Spinoza was fully aware, it had also, for

---

[43] Justel to Leibniz, Paris, 17 Feb. 1677 in Leibniz, *Sämtliche Schriften und Briefe* 1st ser. ii, 247; Laerke, "Spinoza in France," 508.
[44] Bayle, *Correspondance* ii, 435–6n24.
[45] Bayle to Minutoli, Sedan, 29 August 1677 in Bayle, *Correspondance* ii, 433.
[46] Bayle to Jacob Bayle, Sedan, 19 Sept. 1677 in Bayle, *Correspondance* ii, 440.

years, been arousing worry and doubt. As he lay sick and dying, Spinoza may have gleaned some early indication percolating through from Paris of the soon widespread dismay over whether Huet had in fact effectively refuted him. Particular doubts were being expressed as to whether Huet did convincingly prove the New Testament does follow evidently from the Old, and whether he did demolish the *TTP*'s Ezra thesis, reinforcing Christian notions of the Bible's divine origin.

Bossuet was among the first to congratulate the author. Condé, no doubt recalling his time in Utrecht and what he had learnt about Spinoza there, is known to have consumed Huet's book immediately. (Huet apparently admired Condé's uncommon ability to read widely and get a grip on all the great intellectual controversies of the time.)[47] Republished the following year, at Amsterdam, with Sandius' assistance, the *Demonstratio* appeared down to 1694 in two further editions, one at Leipzig, and another four between 1694 and 1744, the last at Venice.[48] Yet, after the initial spurt, both sales and the book's reception slumped disastrously.

Overall, Huet's vindication of the "truth of the Christian religion" attacked the *TTP* very differently from the new breed of philologically oriented Bible critics like Richard Simon and Le Clerc. Huet's approach, endorsed by Bossuet, proclaimed Scripture's perfection in the most uncompromising tones diverging from Simon's text-oriented research not only in offering sweeping unsupported assertions and diversions but also in avoiding rigorous use of language analysis and philology. Furthermore, where others wrote in French, the *Demonstratio*, Bayle assured his father, in March 1679, manifesting the most prodigious erudition, was composed in the most elegant Latin, keeping the affair out of the hands of the non-erudite. It suffered, however, as a disappointed Bayle along with a great many others had to admit, from Huet's habit of treating what is merely conceivable as if backed by "convincing reasons" and his exasperating reliance on "facts that are scarcely certain," like the "testimony of Josephus in favour of Jesus Christ" and the eclipse of the sun when Jesus was on the Cross, on the day of the Passion. This latter "fact," according to Huet, was recorded not only in Judaea but also among other nations which is hardly credible, Bayle points out, as one finds no mention of this in the Greek and Roman sources.[49] The plain but uncomfortable truth was that this champion of Christianity claiming to be rigorously historical rather than philological, was, for all his erudition, a mediocre, highly unreliable historian.

An obvious reason why the initial worry and dismay the *TTP* caused in France dragged on without any powerful or even satisfactory refutation emerging was that it inevitably took time to realistically assess the *TTP*'s arguments and place these in their proper intellectual context. The entirety of Spinoza's work, not just

---

[47] Huet, *Memoirs* ii, 153. [48] Tolmer, *Pierre-Daniel Huet*, 443–4.
[49] Bayle to his father, Sedan, 1 April 1679 in Bayle, *Correspondance* iii, 154–5, 158n36; Laerke, "Spinoza in France," 508.

the *TTP*, Bayle by 1679 was beginning to realize, formed a system of surpassing impiety. Deeply shocked but also, like Leibniz, greatly intrigued, he evinced a keen interest that rapidly deepened already that year during which, he informed Minutoli, he acquired Spinoza's book on Descartes' philosophy as well as his *Opera Posthuma* "which consists of a large treatise on ethics, some letters and a Hebrew grammar." By the close of 1679, Bayle had studied everything available by Spinoza, though, like Leibniz until 1677, he remained for the moment chiefly preoccupied with his Bible criticism. Also like Leibniz (and More and Conway), by 1679 Bayle felt increasingly exasperated by what seemed to him too the monumental slowness and inadequacy of the entire scholarly world's collective rebuttal thus far of Spinoza's uniquely disturbing "recherches rabbiniques."

With regard to information about Spinoza and his life and work, Antoine Arnauld (1612–94) had a considerable advantage over most of France's other chief luminaries in responding to the menace in that he had heard a good deal about Spinoza before 1678 from several sources including Leibniz, Neercassel, and Van den Enden with whom he had personally conversed, in Paris, during the last two years or so of the latter's life (1672–4).[50] Still, it took until May 1678 for Neercassel to get a copy of the *TTP* to Arnauld. According to his colleague, Pontchâteau, Arnauld read the text promptly and judged it "one of the most wicked books in the world," yet preferred for now to remain silent in public. Arnauld merely passed his copy on to Bossuet to help get the *TTP* prohibited in France.[51] In fact, after initially perusing the *TTP* such was Arnauld's revulsion that he simply refused to read the *Opera Posthuma* at all.[52] But whatever his reluctance, owing to his high standing as one of France's foremost theological commentators and polemicists, and head of the Jansenist movement, over the next months Arnauld, like More in England earlier, found himself besieged by colleagues entreating him to refute the *TTP* and the *Ethics*.

Before long, Arnauld, realizing Spinoza was not just eroding Christian belief but unquestionably was "the most impious and dangerous man of this century [le plus impie et le plus dangereux homme de ce siècle]," felt duty-bound to overcome his repugnance and take up his pen. Recognizing the urgency, later in 1678 he began writing his rebuttal of Spinoza's conception of God and denial of divine providence and the reality of miracles. Unfortunately, though, with his text still in draft, he suddenly had to flee France, in June 1679, due to Louis XIV's growing hostility to the Jansenist tendency. Transferring first to Brussels, taking his refutation of Spinoza with him, but finding himself less welcome on Spanish territory than in Neercassel's orbit, he moved on to Holland, during 1681–4

---

[50] Pontchâteau to Neercassel, Paris, 5 Aug. 1678 in Orcibal, "Jansénistes face à Spinoza," 463.
[51] Arnauld, *Œuvres* x, p. xvi; Orcibal, "Jansénistes face à Spinoza," 450; Vernière, *Spinoza et la pensée française*, 114–15; Totaro, "Congrégation de l'Index," 366.
[52] Arnauld, *Œuvres* x, "Préface historique et critique," pp. xv–xvi.

spending long periods at the *beguinage* at Delft. It was there, in October 1681, that Arnauld somehow managed to misplace and lose a large batch of his papers and books. What he lost without trace in Delft, Neercassel learnt in August 1684, included his long pondered "petit écrit contre Spinosa [little text against Spinoza]"[53]

Arnauld never tried to reconstruct his refutation of Spinoza. In the end, for Arnauld as for Bossuet and Neercassel, answering Spinoza and his books mattered less than suppressing them and preventing people being attracted to his views. After 1681, making no further effort at refutation, Arnauld regularly downplayed his encounter with Spinoza, even going so far as to tell one correspondent, in November 1690, that "I have not read the books of Spinoza," but "know his are very wicked books and that your friend will be quite wrong to read them."[54] After 1684, Arnauld steadfastly stuck to this denial, refusing to discuss Spinoza and his arguments, feeling too repelled by his wickedness and impiety. Instead, from 1683, he plunged into a fiery polemic with Malebranche about the Cartesian legacy, treating Malebranche in part as a more palatable proxy for Spinoza. Condemning rejection of divine providence and all questioning of the possibility of miracles long remained Arnauld's basic stance and played a large role (while omitting all mention of Spinoza and his books) in his protracted feud with Malebranche whom Arnauld, like Leibniz, suspected of nurturing a view of divine omnipotence and providence, distinguishing between God's "general volitions" and "particular volitions" somewhat tainted with Spinozism.[55]

Meanwhile, the most eminent churchman at Louis' court, Jacques-Bénigne Bossuet (1627–1704), though nominally bishop of Condom, ecclesiastical centre of the Armagnac region, residing permanently at court through the 1660s and 1670s, was France's most renowned preacher and upholder of royal absolutism. No one condemned and reviled Spinoza more in his political, philosophical, and biblical exegetical aspects all at the same time. Like Huet, Bayle, Simon, Arnauld, Malebranche, Lamy, Justel, and all of France's then chief intellectual luminaries, once alerted to the menace, in the aftermath of Spinoza's death, Bossuet too had to acknowledge the thorny predicament Spinoza's challenge posed to church and crown. The difficulty was how to counter Spinoza's basic ideas without encouraging a Spinozist breakthrough into the fashionable world of libertine courtiers, unbelievers and malcontent nobles and army officers of the type who colluded with Van den Enden in anti-absolutist conspiratorial activism in Normandy. Energetic suppression of Spinoza's books, Bossuet agreed with Huet and

---

[53] Arnauld, *Œuvres* x, p. xvi; Vernière, *Spinoza et la pensée française*, 116; Rogier, *Geschiedenis* ii, 242–3.
[54] Orcibal, "Jansénistes face à Spinoza," 468; Vernière, *Spinoza et la pensée française*, 115–16; Sleigh, *Leibniz and Arnauld*.
[55] Sleigh, *Leibniz and Arnauld*, 153–64.

Arnauld, should be the first line of defence, and scrupulous avoidance of anything apt to draw attention to Spinoza's name, ideas, and book-titles, the second.

Bossuet, though, also felt challenged in his own personal beliefs, his fury against Spinoza driving him to try to answer some of the core ideas of the incipient *spinozisme* menacing France. He devoted many pages of his most renowned work, his *Discourse on Universal History* (1681), to attacking Spinoza, albeit once again carefully omitting all mention of Spinoza's name and works, and without letting on at all that Spinoza *was* now his and France's principal foe, much as Boyle, More, and Cudworth were doing in England.[56] Like Huet's and Arnauld's, Bossuet's counter-attack was basically rhetorical in character but in his case rooted in a strange mix of unquestioning belief and fideist scepticism. Exalting the power of divine providence that with one stroke, whatever doubters claimed, silenced with Christ's coming all the demons posing as pagan gods servicing the oracles and temples of ancient Greece and Rome,[57] Bossuet powerfully reaffirmed the Mosaic authorship of the Pentateuch (which Simon conserved only in part),[58] the reality of Scriptural prophecies, and the clear, divinely sanctioned linkage of the New Testament with the Old.[59] His universal history "proved" all this by demonstrating the shaping of the successive eras of world history by divine providence, illustrating how history itself confirms not just that the biblical miracles were true "miracles" but that such miracles are central to all human history, the rise and fall of kingdoms and empires being explicable not by political theory but correctly only by the divine plan.

Divine right of kings, argued Bossuet, is indeed decreed by God. Still more crucial, the triumph and glory of the Catholic Church surpasses everything else as a miracle, being the ultimate "miracle des miracles," the fullest sign of God's will.[60] What matters in human life is faith guided by churchmen, all the rest being marginal. Philosophical reason and erudition in particular are contemptibly feeble things, replete with error and uncertainty. For Bossuet, philosophers are just the blind leading the blind. Philosophers and unbelievers might claim "nothing can be created from nothing," but what do philosophers know? It soon became evident, though, that Bossuet's "historical" demonstration of divine providence at work could no more stem the new tide of *libertinage* and irreligion steadily encompassing France than Huet's sweeping mythology of ancient history, Arnauld's zeal, or Simon's philological rigour.

The fact was that there was nothing in Huet, Arnauld, or Bossuet to help soothe Bayle's, Justel's, and Leibniz's deep worries regarding the overall weakness of the

---

[56] Vernière, *Spinoza et la pensée française*, 116–17; Tosel, "Le *Discours*," 97; Israel, *Radical Enlightenment*, 285, 475, 488.
[57] Bossuet, *Discours*, 302, 307–8.
[58] Bossuet, *Discours*, 54–5, 175–84, 237; Tosel, "Le *Discours*," 103–4.
[59] Bossuet, *Discours*, 100, 103; Tosel, "Le *Discours*," 98, 100–1.
[60] Bossuet, *Discours*, 252–57; Israel *Radical Enlightenment*, 475–6.

French and general response to Spinoza's Bible criticism, or the insidious impact, as some saw it, of Bible exegetes assumed to be secretly applying Spinoza's methods without admitting the fact. In France, noted Bayle, the work of Richard Simon (1638–1712) was widely reported to be full of conclusions "hardly favourable to the authenticity and divinity we attribute to the canon of the Scriptures." Bayle was among the many who attributed much of this concomitant "harm" to the *TTP*. Like most leading scholars, in 1679 and the early 1680s, Bayle had not, as yet, actually read Richard Simon's epoch-making *Histoire Critique du Vieux Testament*, a work rigorously suppressed by the French crown on publication, in 1678, but was distinctly unimpressed with the attempt to refute Simon's Bible criticism, published in December 1678, by the Calvinist savant, Ezechiel Spanheim (1629–1710), who, while in England, had managed to examine one of the few surviving copies.[61] Where Bayle was entirely at one with Arnauld was in regarding the *TTP* as so dangerous that "one should not reply at all to this type of book, or, if one does, do so only with maximum force [avec la dernière force]. For there is nothing that has served more to lend impetus to Spinosa's book than the feebleness of some of those who have tried to refute him."[62]

Ordained as a priest in 1670, Richard Simon was a member of the Oratorian order, originally from Dieppe, who increasingly spent his time researching in libraries in Paris. When Leibniz encountered Huet, in Paris in 1673, Simon was already a renowned specialist in Hebrew, oriental books, Bible history, and the Jews. In 1674, there appeared at Paris his French translation of the Venetian rabbi Leone da Modena's *Historia de gli riti Hebraici* (1637), describing Jewish ceremonies and observances, the first Jewish book, it has been noted, addressed to a non-Jewish audience since the days of Josephus and Philo. Reporting from Paris, in March 1675, Bayle encouraged his friend, Minutoli, at Geneva, then contemplating doing something similar, to proceed with his own translation of Leone, and oust that of Simon, as word had it that Simon had added comments lending an anti-Protestant character to his rendering.[63] Realizing, though, that he could hardly match Simon's formidable expertise, Minutoli sensibly drew back.

Simon himself was partly responsible for how closely his own work became linked to the *TTP*, having suggested in his preface that his work was in part a reply to Spinoza. This turned out to be a tragic misstep on his part, due not least to unfortunate timing. Simon's extremely significant scholarly contribution became so entangled with the hostile early French, English, and other reaction to the *TTP* as to long tarnish Simon's own reputation.[64] Simon's Bible criticism powerfully defended the integrity of the Old Testament text against the aspersions of his own

---

[61] Mandelbrote, "Isaac Vossius," 104.
[62] Bayle to Minutoli, Sedan, 1 January 1680 in Bayle, *Correspondance* iii, 204.
[63] Bayle to Minutoli, Paris, 17 March 1675 in Bayle, *Correspondance* ii, 95, 101n28.
[64] Twining, "Richard Simon and the Remaking"; Levitin, *Ancient Wisdom*, 191.

mentor, Jean Morin, and future adversary, Isaac Vossius, with whom, from 1679, he entered into a furious public squabble over the status of the Greek Septuagint, with Vossius claiming the rabbis had vilely corrupted the Hebrew text to de-Christianize it. Despite Richard's claiming to be answering Spinoza in his preface, the indications are that most of his *Histoire Critique* was composed before the *TTP* appeared, and before Simon read it, so that his detailed exegesis was not really a response to, nor significantly shaped by Spinoza. Following in the tradition of Levita, Cappel, and Morin, Simon accepted that the Old Testament canon was indeed fixed after the Babylonian Captivity, chiefly by Ezra, but while acknowledging that this does create some difficulties due to the process of scribal transmission, held that it by no means impugns the core authenticity of the Hebrew text reaching back to Mosaic times. Simon now sought to fend off Spinoza's Ezra thesis with his well-developed philological approach designed to safely accommodate and rescue Scripture's miraculous and sacred status.

Simon far eclipsed Spinoza in sophisticated knowledge of the earliest surviving manuscripts of the Hebrew text, the Samaritan Bible, the Septuagint and much else concerning the history and transmission of the Bible. At the same time, though, he made scant effort to reconstruct the original meanings of Hebrew terms and expressions as Spinoza did, offer a critique of prophecy, question miracles, or critically examine divine providence at work, or to assess the rival ideas and motives of Sadducees and Pharisees and the like.[65] In June 1678, about to be released, the *Histoire Critique*'s misleading and distorted reputation as an unacceptably daring work, moved Bishop Bossuet, no sooner had he set eyes on it, to arrange the seizure of almost the entirety of the first edition of 1,300 copies and order their destruction. Simon's allegedly accepting that the Pentateuch was not written by Moses and extensive utilizing of Protestant interpretations of the Sacred Books (which Bayle initially supposed caused the fury it provoked), led to a decree of the highest royal council, dated 15 June 1678, signed by Colbert, ordering complete suppression of this "rempart de libertinage." To Simon's detriment, the *TTP* became suddenly widely notorious in France as a chief spur to the surging intellectual libertinism and irreligion of the age, just at the wrong moment for him, leaving him besieged, accused by Bossuet, Spanheim, Vossius, and many another of fuelling a general process of Bible subversion in unspoken, devious collusion with Spinoza.

Despite its swift suppression, it seeped out that Simon's book maintains, like the *TTP*, that "all the sacred books were lost in the desolation in which Judaea was plunged under the kings of Babylon," Bayle reported to his brother, "and that it fell to Ezra to make other similar renderings from them." Simon also reportedly rejected the antiquity of the vowel points in the Hebrew text, though there was

---

[65] Twining, "Richard Simon and the Remaking"; Mandelbrote, "Isaac Vossius," 104–6; Levitin, *Ancient Wisdom*, 200n450.

nothing new in that.[66] When Bayle again mentions Simon's books, writing to his brother Jacob, in February 1680, he had still not read the *Histoire Critique* of the Old Testament and knew only that "the book is suppressed in France"; and, from what he had heard, banned due to its daring comments about the Pentateuch's authorship and hence, he thought, "rightly" suppressed.[67] In March 1680, writing to Minutoli, insisting again on the inadequacy of Spanheim's refutation of Simon's "dangerous work," he also cites the polemic, then just beginning, between Simon and Vossius who unambiguously accused his opponent of borrowing Spinoza's arguments.[68] Those assailing his Bible criticism over the next years, Simon soon discovered, would regularly accuse him unfairly of borrowing his main points from Spinoza.[69]

Yet, with Simon suspect and suppressed, Huet unconvincing, Arnauld holding back, and Bossuet pompously irrelevant, the entirety of the published French response to Spinoza, down to the early 1680s, as Bayle and Justel fretted, amounted to practically nothing, effectively just royal and ecclesiastical edicts and repression with the leading French intellectual lights of the day providing little, indeed nothing, in the way of a compelling counter-offensive. Simon's unfortunate experience in 1678 served only to persuade him, and also Jean Le Clerc, to step up their efforts during the late 1670s and 1680s to devise new rules and methods of text criticism especially stressing the need to study historical context and analyse language usage. Both had already begun edging in this direction prior to 1678, but after that date, stung by the *TTP* and the reaction to it, it was crucial to them to press on with refining Bible text criticism without drawing attention to the revolution in Bible exegesis engineered by Spinoza which actually helped spur them on. Avoiding all mention of Spinoza and minimizing his image as much as possible remained central to Le Clerc's intellectual strategy throughout, just as with so many others. Even many years later, he assured the Bishop of Bath and Wells, Richard Kidder (1633–1713), in 1694, while numerous points in his writings about the Bible were specifically arguments directed against Spinoza, with whom he had been wrestling uninterruptedly since the late 1670s, rather than any other opponent, he nevertheless remained as scrupulous as when starting out battling Spinoza in not mentioning his name or books, or saying anything about him. It mattered greatly to defeat him without most people realizing that the insidious Spinoza was Christianity's chief adversary.[70]

Within a year or two of 1677 the entire French intellectual scenario had been dramatically upturned. With Vanini and Hobbes receding into the background,

---

[66] Bayle to his brother Joseph, Sedan, 21 July 1678 in Bayle, *Correspondance* iii, 53, 55n5.
[67] Bayle to his brother Jacob, Sedan, 4 Feb. 1680 in Bayle *Correspondance* iii, 215.
[68] Bayle to Minutoli, Sedan, 24 March 1680 in Bayle, *Correspondance* iii, 223.
[69] Vernière, *Spinoza et la pensée française*, 196–8.
[70] Le Clerc to Richard Kidder, Amsterdam, 5 Nov. 1694 in Le Clerc, *Epistolario* ii, 222–3; Israel, "Early Dutch and German Reaction," 75.

Spinoza had in a muted fashion displaced them at the forefront, becoming, despite all efforts to prevent this happening, the new "héros des athées" as the Oratorian priest, Le Vassor put it. This phenomenon coincided with, and helped stimulate, the marked upswell in deistic thinking in France associated with the 1680s and 1690s. Despite all the efforts of Huet, Bossuet, Arnauld, Malebranche, Simon, and Le Clerc, not only was Spinoza manifestly displacing Hobbes, but by the late 1680s was emerging as "le plus grand athée que l'on ait jamais vu [the greatest atheist ever seen]," as Michel Le Vassor (1648?–1718), put it, and what was worse, attracting a "great number of persons making profession of following the opinions of Spinosa and who have studied his principles."[71] This was despite the fact that those principles are not at all genuinely persuasive, maintained Le Vassor, a for now pro-Jansenist Oratorian priest from Orléans (who afterwards defected repudiating the Catholic Church in 1690 and becoming an Anglican), eager to reconcile Arnauld with Malebranche, in his major work *De la véritable religion* (Paris, 1688).

Assuredly, it was not Spinoza's philosophy, his system as such, but rather his Bible criticism that invaded France so powerfully and suddenly from the late 1670s. What chiefly aided his cause was the attraction of his sweeping denial of miracles, prophecy, and divine providence to impious minds. The right way to block Spinoza and rescue the many deplorably unsteady minds being sucked inexorably into his orbit, held Le Vassor, was to rely not on outright repression but rather on physico-theology to more effectively reconcile religion and science, faith and reason than had yet been done, showing the people the reality of a Creator God in all His true splendour by proving what deep down everyone knows already, that the laws and workings of nature cannot be "the mere effect of chance or blind nature [l'effet du hazard ni d'une nature aveugle]."[72] Perhaps, but the disastrous fact remained, as the *avertissement* introducing *Le nouvel athéisme renversé* of the Benedictine monk François Lamy (1636–1711) deplored in 1696, that, for all that, "the number of Spinoza's *sectaires* continues to grow with each day."[73]

[71] Le Vassor, *De la véritable religion*, 4.   [72] Le Vassor, *De la véritable religion*, 10–14.
[73] Lamy, *Nouvel athéisme renversé*, "Avertissement"; Kors, *Naturalism and Unbelief*, 88.

40
Last Days, Death, and Funeral (1677)

40.i Reclusive but Contested Last Days

Gravely ill for some time, Spinoza's death on 21 February 1677—or 11 February according to the calendar still used in England, Germany, and Scandinavia—was no wholly unexpected occurrence. Yet, despite Colerus' stating that Spinoza had been sick with the *teering* (consumption, or phthisis) for over twenty years "from which he was very thin and obliged to be more than usually modest in his eating and drinking,"[1] there is no real evidence that his fevers of the mid-1660s were connected at all to the consumption from which he suffered in the mid-1670s. Rather, remarks in various letters to and from him suggest that in the late 1660s and early 1670s he remained in reasonably good health.[2] Given that scarcely anyone else was present in the house at the time and he died peacefully, one might think his a quiet, unremarkable demise of little impact. But in fact, as we have seen, his apparently tranquil end marked the commencement of an unprecedented, remarkably convoluted drama—the battle to salvage his principal corpus of writings.

The surviving letters from Spinoza's own hand, dating from the final months of his life, are few and of restricted content, all pertaining to his correspondence with the remarkable young German mathematician, inventor, and philosopher, Tschirnhaus, then still in Paris where he remained until November 1676, before transferring to Italy.[3] At least one notable thinker of the last years of the seventeenth century and opening years of the eighteenth, the Anglo-Irish radical "deist" John Toland (1670–1722), pointed to these last letters as clear evidence for what some (including Toland) contended remained a major weakness in Spinoza's philosophical system. In May 1676, Tschirnhaus, still striving to steer between Descartes and Spinoza, questioned how in Spinoza's system the variety of individual bodies and shapes in the universe can be demonstrated as logically emerging, in principle, from his conception of a single substance.

In response, Spinoza referred to a letter he had sent L.M., that is Lodewijk Meyer (who was clearly familiar with Tschirnhaus), on infinity and the multiplicity of

---

[1] Colerus in Freudenthal/Walther, *Lebensgeschichte* i, 156–7.
[2] Bloksma, "Spinoza, a Miraculously Healthy Philosopher," 38–9, 41–3; Van de Ven, *Documenting Spinoza*.
[3] Zaunick, "Ehrenfried Walther von Tschirnhaus," 7.

things, reaffirming that "from Extension as Descartes conceives it, that is as a mass at rest, it is not just difficult to show the reality of [individual] bodies, as you say, but completely impossible. For matter at rest, insofar as it is in itself, will remain at rest, and will not be set in motion except by a more powerful external cause," providing no scope for change and transition via the effects of movement inherent in matter. "For this reason, I did not hesitate to affirm, earlier, that the Cartesian principles of natural things [rerum naturalium principia Cartesiana] are useless, not to say absurd."[4] His own system, held Spinoza, does however provide this motive, dynamic force. Dissatisfied with this, Tschirnhaus answered that whatever one thinks of Descartes' resorting to the agency of God to explain creation and the formation of individual things, Spinoza had likewise "not shown how this [the reality of individual things] must necessarily follow *a priori* from God's being [ex essentia Dei]" conceived as the order of nature as a whole.[5] Our nobleman mathematician-philosopher could not see how and why, in Spinoza's system, "from an infinite Extension, a variety of bodies can arise [ex ... Extensione infinita corporum varietas exsurgere possit]."[6]

Tschirnhaus, whose name was systematically deleted from both the Latin and Dutch editions of Spinoza's letters prepared the following year—and thus from the only editions available to Toland and his contemporaries—knew Spinoza, unlike Descartes, does not consider God an external agent capable of knowingly creating bodies from matter. He did think, though, that Spinoza was in some way holding back about how he did envisage the creation process, evading the challenge of explaining it in a more open manner. He exhorted his mentor and friend to "assure yourself of this, that whether you indicate something to me candidly or obscure it, my affection toward you will remain unchanged." Spinoza's brief last response, dated 15 July 1676, his final comment to any known correspondent about his system, was that indeed the variety of existing things cannot be explained from extension "alone" but only from the power of an eternal and infinite being, but added nothing more except that "perhaps, if we remain in life, I will settle this with you more clearly later, for until now I have not got any of this in order."[7]

In this last surviving letter to Tschirnhaus, composed less than seven months before his death, Spinoza hints at not having long to live, admits his system is incomplete and that he had not adequately covered the issue of creation. Toland here construes the Latin slightly differently from modern editors so as to read "if I live, perhaps I may some other time deal more plainly with you about these matters," twisting Spinoza's words to imply that he was being evasive whereas

---

[4] Spinoza, *Opera* iv, 332; the reference to L.M. is found only in the Dutch version, see Spinoza, *Nagelate Schriften*, 648.
[5] Spinoza, *Opera* iv, 333; Spinoza, *Nagelate Schriften*, 649.   [6] Spinoza, *Opera* iv, 333.
[7] Spinoza, *Opera* iv, 334; Spinoza, *Nagelate Schriften*, 650; Renz, *Explainability*, 66n.

Spinoza actually says that he "will pursue these matters more clearly with you some other time, if life lasts."[8] In any case, Spinoza never did produce a proto-evolutionary theory, even though the need for one stood out in the eyes of his most earnest followers at the time: how are natural forms and species created by nature, through the force of nature?

In his *Letters to Serena* (1704), Toland seized on this gap to claim that Spinoza, while "not allowing God as first mover" and insisting "motion and rest are the causes of all the diversities among bodies," nevertheless failed to provide either in his *Ethics*, or to "his friend" (unaware this was Tschirnhaus), any account of the origin of motion and its power within matter. Rather overstating Spinoza's "flaw," Toland terms this imperfection all "the more inexcusable because, although his *Ethics* were completed at this time, yet he might change, add, or take away what he would, since the book was not published until after his death."[9] Presenting himself as the thinker who fills the gap, Toland then asserts: "I hold then that motion is essential to matter, that is to say, as inseparable from its nature as impenetrability, or extension, and that it ought to make part of its definition." Yet, while professing to make good a glaring insufficiency in Spinoza, the devious Toland, as some readers remarked at the time, actually does nothing more than just reaffirm Spinoza's (and the Koerbaghs') own basic position.[10]

During his last days Spinoza doubtless did ponder the extent to which he had left significant gaps in his system, what he had achieved and where he had failed, and, as regards the *Ethics* and the unfinished *Tractatus Politicus*, the gloomy truth that thus far he had failed to get the larger part of his corpus of work, including his most important text, the *Ethics*, published. No one was more aware of what remained unaccomplished, of the absence of much of the fabric of the intellectual revolution he had sought to engineer, and the imperfections of his life's work. Years later, when discussing the question of texts missing among Spinoza's known works, on the basis of what he had been able to piece together, Colerus specifies, in addition to the treatise on the rainbow which several of Spinoza's friends in Holland had seen, that Spinoza had also "begun a translation of the Old Testament into Dutch about which he often conferred with persons learned in ancient languages while informing himself about interpretations Christians were accustomed to give to particular passages." The Kiel University professor Sebastian Kortholt, whose short account of Spinoza's life appeared in 1700, too heard about this translation, but says, probably correctly, that it was into Latin, not Dutch.

---

[8] Spinoza, *Nagelate Schriften*, 650; Toland, *Letters to Serena*, 125; Spinoza, *Collected Works* (ed. Curley) ii, 487.
[9] Toland, *Letters to Serena*, 25, 125.
[10] Toland, *Letters to Serena*, 24–5, 120–7; Israel, *Radical Enlightenment*, 612.

Among his last major initiatives, linked to his Hebrew grammar and his Jewish childhood and youth, as much as his maturity, this project to translate the Old Testament in a manner respecting neither rabbis, nor Church Fathers, popes, Luther, nor Calvin, was designed to open society's eyes to the dubious character of the theological doctrines and teachings about revelations, prophecy, and miracles that they fostered and that he deemed fabrications, by showing how peoples have been deceived and misled in schools, universities, and churches for millennia about the actual meaning of key biblical passages. But dissatisfied with what he had done, supposedly at a point "long after completing his rendering of the Five Books, a few days before his death, whilst in his room, he hurled this entire work into the fire."[11]

Always a severe self-critic, Spinoza throughout his life remained conscious of the deep continuity between his revolt against rabbinic authority prior to 1656 and his mature philosophy, political and social thought, and Bible criticism. Relations between Spinoza and the world's believers in revealed religion, Christian, Jewish, and Muslim, could hardly have been worse than they were already, but had Spinoza's Old Testament translation survived it would doubtless have stoked still further what Colerus called the "dispute between we who are Christians and him."[12] Although those commenting on Spinoza's missing texts to Colerus may well have exaggerated how much was lost in this way, there is no reason to doubt that this Old Testament rendering had indeed been a longstanding project that Spinoza was well into when he destroyed it and had discussed it with learned acquaintances and friends over the years.

During his final months, whatever he felt about the now seething public controversy surrounding his name and engulfing his work and ideas, and what to do about his completed but unpublished, and also his unfinished unpublished bundle of work, Spinoza seems not to have overly concerned himself with the indignation and fury he had provoked on every side. The surviving detailed inventory of his books drawn up after his death reveals that, apart from Van Mansvelt's *Adversus anonymum* and Van Blijenbergh's refutation of the *TTP*, Spinoza kept amazingly little of the swelling mass of published polemical and controversial literature surrounding his person and writings. Where the Koerbaghs, Meyer, and Bouwmeester all engaged with the public, seeking to "enlighten" and transform Dutch culture and society, impacting directly those around them, Spinoza, it is sometimes alleged, shutting himself up in his lodgings for weeks on end and sticking to abstruse Latin terminology, by comparison with them stood aloof from the cultural fray of the time, secreting his thoughts and

---

[11] Freudenthal/Walther, *Lebensgeschichte* i, 80–1, 146–7; Colerus, *La Vie de B. de Spinosa*, 68–9; Rothkamm, *Institutio Oratoria*, 316; Totaro, "Le Compendium," 67–8; Steenbakkers, "Spinoza's Life," 54n98.

[12] Colerus, *La Vie de B. de Spinosa*, 65.

himself away. But it seems more accurate to hold that, in the wake of the Koerbagh tragedy, Spinoza too devoted himself to confronting head-on what he, no less than they, conceived as the harmful fabrications and credulity of his time, engaging no less earnestly than his allies the Koerbaghs, Bouwmeester, or Meyer in the campaign to enlighten and change society, but did so on a far broader front than these others, becoming more lastingly effective than they precisely by operating less directly confrontationally and forging his intellectual revolution more philosophically, systematically, and comprehensively.

Another rare exception to Spinoza's otherwise lofty disdain for the furore surrounding him was his reported interest in Huet's pending refutation, news of which Tschirnhaus conveyed to him. Endorsed by French royal authority and a whole bevy of high ecclesiastics, Huet's venture, the book embodying Leibniz's and Bayle's chief expectation of seeing a robust, major refutation of the *TTP*[13] finally shatter Spinoza's credibility, did eventually appear, in 1679, but, as we have seen, met with a lukewarm reception. Leibniz glumly noted that Huet's reception in Paris was unenthusiastic, though he himself, he assured Duke Johann Friedrich, despite reservations about Huet's defence of Moses' authorship of the Pentateuch and attempts to demonstrate Christianity's truth indirectly, via the evidence of pagan religion, was greatly pleased with the result, despite, or so he assured the duke, his employer, Huet's meandering antiquarianism and theological scepticism pouring scorn on all philosophical reasoning, "for I find there great erudition and good arguments regarding the principal thing which is the fulfilment of the [Old Testament] prophecies in Jesus Christ," which Spinoza firmly denied.[14]

In later years, Leibniz still valued Huet as an ally against Cartesianism and its radical offshoots culminating in Spinozism.[15] But, judging from Huet's striking absence from his *Theodicy* of 1710, he seems no longer to have assigned Huet any particular significance in countering Spinoza's Bible exegesis or grounding the "principal thing," the truth of Christianity. Bayle's correspondence, from 1679 onwards, reflects a like disillusionment with Huet's performance.[16] Bayle, at the peak of his creativity in the 1690s, still admired the famed *érudit*, now Bishop of Avranches, in Normandy, for his erudition and polished Latin, and resented the scathing dismissal of his critique of Cartesianism by that "grand Cartésian" De Volder, but no longer rated Huet's efforts against Spinoza highly, especially not his decidedly unconvincing efforts to persuade readers to view ancient mythology as replete with echoes of biblical narratives.[17]

---

[13] Vernière, *Spinoza et la pensée française*, 108, 110–11; Laerke, "À la recherche d'un homme égal"; Laerke, "G. W. Leibniz's Two Readings," 108.

[14] Huet, *Commentarius de rebus ad eum pertinentibus*, 273–314; Rapetti, *Pierre-Daniel Huet*, 41; Laerke, "À la recherché d'un homme égal," 400–10; Laerke, *Leibniz lecteur*, 115.

[15] Laerke, *Leibniz lecteur*, 865–8; Lennon, *Plain Truth*, 8; Shelford, *Transforming the Republic of Letters*, 174.

[16] Israel, "Pierre Bayle's Correspondence," 480, 485–6.

[17] Bayle, *Correspondance* ix, 240–1, 410.

Lying alone much of the time during his last weeks, except for visits of friends and physicians, Spinoza must have mused long and hard about his basic views, moral system, Cartesianism, Boyle's strictly empirical science, his battles with rabbinic Judaism and the Reformed Church, his view of ancient Israelite religion and effort to redefine Christianity, as well as his war on theologians, Orangism, and the entirety of past philosophy, contemplating whether his strategy had been right, what errors he had made, and what he might have accomplished better. On his deathbed, reported Schuller, coughing and fighting for breath, Spinoza doubtless must have worried over the survival of his legacy and especially of his masterpiece, the *Ethics*, now languishing unseen for over a decade, completed but unread, gathering dust, almost wholly inaccessible as well as unpublished. His principal effort, the fruit of years of vigorous philosophical endeavour, of going over the text again and again while adding only relatively little in recent years, remained for now and would perhaps forever be practically unknown to the world outside. He would never know whether his ethical philosophy would ever appear in print, and hence would ever prove useful and inspiring.

There was also the question of his unfinished *Tractatus Politicus* on which he was still working when Leibniz visited in the autumn of 1676. It is noteworthy that towards his end, Spinoza laid aside all other tasks, judging his second political treatise a more useful and urgent goal for his last days than any other of his unfinished projects.[18] The content and object of the treatise, he explains in an undated surviving letter written in the late summer or autumn of 1676, addressing an unnamed friend (probably Jelles), compares the different forms of government, monarchy, aristocracy, and democracy and considers "what is the highest thing that a state can aim at" for the benefit of society? While writing his last surviving lines, Spinoza had his copies of Tacitus close by and repeatedly quoted Tacitus' telling phrases and terse Latin expressions to stress the evils and drawbacks of emperors, kings, and autocrats, restating his fundamental stark dichotomy, the core thesis of his political thought, contrasting the "desert" of a slavish population in bondage under royal, aristocratic, or populist despotism, with the harmonious peace-loving republic based on "general will," free speech, criticism, and discussion.[19]

Towards his end, Spinoza especially devoted his time to considering what makes society harmonious and enables a well-structured republic to function optimally for the benefit of all. Louis XIV, Charles II, and the freshly acquired powers of the Stadholder, William III, evidently dominated much of his thinking during his final months. Central to these reflections was the idea, borrowed from

---

[18] Spinoza to an unnamed friend undated [autumn? 1676] in Spinoza, *Collected Works* (ed. Curley) ii, 488; Spinoza, *Correspondance* (ed. Rovere), 389–90.

[19] Spinoza, *Political Treatise*, 30, 50, 59, 62, 82–3, 92, 94; Stilianou, "Spinoza et l'histoire antique," 133.

Tacitus whom he quotes in this connection, that all men share the same unsteady, readily misled nature, a tendency to domineer when powerful and cringe when intimidated which he contrasts with the prevailing notion among the elites of his own and earlier times that "there is no moderation in the mob, that they terrorize unless they are intimidated," which he here rejects as entirely unreasonable as all men share the same unprepossessing original nature. If the vast edifice of humanity's credulity and ignorance continually menaces everybody's well-being, the secure, fulfilling existence that he and his following recommend for all is menaced no less, and arguably more, by our world's grasping, unreasoning, and ignorant kings, princes, nobles, churchmen, regents, and oligarchs.[20]

It was highly probable, Spinoza had to accept, that his main philosophical contribution would be intercepted, suppressed, and destroyed, as occurred with the Koerbaghs' last book. Had he known that Tschirnhaus would soon lose the precious copy entrusted to him, to the Inquisition of all opponents, he would have felt still more distraught in this regard. Even if the manuscript version of his *Ethics* should escape the likelihood of prompt destruction by the authorities, it still might easily lapse into oblivion, lying in some obscure drawer through fear of the consequences of publishing it, until finally irrecoverable. Were that the final outcome, he would assuredly be remembered almost entirely as just a principal opponent of revelation, religious authority, and Scripture's sacred status.

A week or so before his death, Schuller had either himself been at Spinoza's bedside, in The Hague, or else received word of his fast-deteriorating condition. Five days or so prior to Spinoza's demise, the forewarned Schuller alerted Leibniz, writing from Amsterdam, on 16 February, that "B. de S., I fear, will soon be leaving us, as the phthisis [his consumption or other respiratory sickness] seems to be getting worse each day."[21] But if expected in the near future, Spinoza's expiring on that particular day seems to have come as a complete surprise to the household. Far from being bedbound, that morning the ailing philosopher had been down for a lively talk with his landlord, Van der Spijck and the latter's wife. With no alarming breathing fits or anything untoward disturbing their by no means wholly bedridden tenant, "none of the others living in the house," records Colerus, "had the least notion that his end was so near, and that death would overtake him so suddenly" that Sunday afternoon, when the couple and their several children went off to attend the nearby Lutheran church.

Spinoza had a stoical, imperturbable character [van een stoiquen of ongevoeligen imborst was], Van der Spijck's wife, Ida Margareta Ketteringh, recalled in conversation with Colerus, always showing patient endurance and not complaining about his "wasting disease," or any ailments. So pronounced was this feature of

---
[20] Spinoza, *Political Treatise*, 90–1; Stilianou, "Spinoza et l'histoire antique," 134.
[21] Schuller to Leibniz, Amsterdam, 6/16 Feb. 1677 in Leibniz, *Sämtliche Schriften und Briefe* 2nd ser. i, 303–4; Proietti and Licata, *Il Carteggio*, 53–4.

his personality that "he often chided others," she added, "when they complained or showed themselves cowardly and faint-hearted about their illnesses."[22] Appreciating his orderly lifestyle, Ida Margareta seems to have harboured no objection or complaint about Spinoza of any sort, despite his evil reputation. Colerus gives the impression that she felt a certain reverence for him. She once asked Spinoza, he recounts, whether in his opinion she could be saved "in her religion," to which he answered: "your religion is good, you have no need to search for any other to be blessed provided you devote yourself to a quiet and pious life."[23]

Showing no sign of distress that morning, his landlord and lady were greatly surprised, on their return, to find him dead. With no relatives at hand, it was Van der Spijck who then took charge of the necessary arrangements and funeral costs, and met the outstanding unpaid bills of the apothecary, Johan Schröder, to whom sixteen guilders were owed for medicines, notably for some expensive saffron as well as other powders, and of the barber who shaved and trimmed Spinoza during his last months, an outlay which Van der Spijck recovered afterwards from Rieuwertsz and "the friend in Schiedam."[24]

The doctor "from Amsterdam" in attendance when Spinoza departed this life that Sunday afternoon, fixed the time of his death at 3.00 p.m. on 21 February 1677. This physician Colerus designated, much later, as "L.M.," and has long been presumed to have been Meyer, though the accuracy of this seems debatable since Schuller afterwards informed Leibniz and Tschirnhaus that he himself was present when Spinoza expired. There is no reason, though, why Meyer and Schuller should not have been both in attendance at different times during Spinoza's final days along with one or more local physicians. Bontekoe, the most controversial doctor at The Hague at the time, and the regular physician of the Heilige Geesthofje, the charitable establishment directly across the canal from Spinoza's lodgings, was reportedly present close to the end, as was a certain Sigmund Gottlieb Scholtze who had coffee with Stolle and Hallmann in August 1703 and recounted witnessing Spinoza's "last illness," confirming that Spinoza had died quietly "ex phthisi [from consumption]."[25] The presence of multiple doctors during the now locally well-known philosopher's prolonged final illness over several days and possibly weeks seems entirely plausible, even assuming Schuller alone was present, as he afterwards claimed, during the suffocating acute breathing difficulties of Spinoza's final hours.[26]

---

[22] Colerus, *Das Leben*, 121; Freudenthal/Walther, *Lebensgeschichte* i, 160; Steenbakkers, "Spinoza's Life," 42.
[23] Freudenthal/Walther, *Lebensgeschichte* i, 124.
[24] Freudenthal/Walther, *Lebensgeschichte* i, 160–1; Van der Tang, "Spinoza en Schiedam," 182.
[25] Freudenthal/Walther, *Lebensgeschichte* i, 93; Bloksma, "Spinoza, a Miraculously Healthy Philosopher," 39–40; Van de Ven, *Documenting Spinoza*, ch. 7.
[26] Freudenthal/Walther, *Lebensgeschichte* i, 124–5; Nadler, *Spinoza: A Life*, 407; Steenbakkers, "Spinoza's Life," 42–3.

According to what Schuller wrote to both Leibniz and Tschirnhaus a few days later, reporting Spinoza's death and again mentioning his presence beside his deathbed, Spinoza himself may well have been taken by surprise by his sudden end "because he left us without leaving any testament or last will."[27] One might think this circumstance distinctly odd considering Spinoza had been steadily becoming sicker for some weeks. But if he was still able to go up and down stairs and smoke a pipe near his end, his "wasting away" cannot have appeared too acute. In any case, the only legacy that mattered to him were his remaining manuscripts and their fate. Spinoza doubtless preferred to entrust them to his landlord and to Rieuwertsz by private secret agreement with them rather than reveal his principal concern to any notary. When Spinoza died, according to the subsequent notarized lists, there was nothing of value in his rooms. Whilst attending to the dying man, Schuller confided to Leibniz, some months later, asking him to keep confidential this particular detail which "I whisper in your ear [tibi in aurem]," during those hours "before and after [Spinoza's] death [ante et post ejus obitum]," conducting himself, or so he claimed, "by order of his friends and of Spinoza himself," that he removed for safekeeping whatever was important and valuable in the room, carefully checking through all Spinoza's belongings and papers, including the vital manuscripts stored in the cabinet attached to his writing desk.[28] These, Schuller affirmed, were the only *Spinosiana* found in Spinoza's rooms worthy of note.

Close to or at the moment of Spinoza's death, Schuller does indeed appear to have profited from finding himself alone in the house with the dead philosopher to take charge of at least some of Spinoza's manuscripts, including the original of the *Ethics*, and, if other information provided by Colerus concerning "L.M." applies rather to him, as seems likely, he also helped himself to some gold ducats lying in the room and a knife with a silver handle.[29] When next writing to Leibniz who was always avid for rare books, Schuller coyly hinted that the original manuscript of the *Ethics*, now in the safekeeping "of a friend" (himself, Rieuwertsz, or Van Gent?), might eventually be available for purchase at an appropriate price, by "your prince."[30] A remarkable offer! When he himself died a mere two and half years later, Schuller turned out to be deeply in debt (at least partly due to addiction to alchemy and heavy spending on rare substances for alchemical experiments) and was probably heavily in debt already in February 1677. His initial plan, seemingly, was to raise some urgently needed cash for his own use by selling the

---

[27] Freudenthal/Walther, *Lebensgeschichte* i, 334–5; Schuller to Leibniz, Amsterdam, 16/26 February 1677 in Leibniz, *Sämtliche Schriften und Briefe* 2nd ser. i, 304; Stewart, *Courtier and the Heretic*, 212; Nadler, *Spinoza: A Life*, 406; Steenbakkers, *Spinoza's Ethica*, 58.
[28] Schuller to Leibniz, Amsterdam, 3/13 Nov. 1677 in Leibniz, *Sämtliche Schriften und Briefe* 2nd ser. i, 382; Proietti and Licata, *Il Carteggio*, 55.
[29] Proietti and Licata, *Il Carteggio*, 25, 53–4; Nadler, *Spinoza: A Life*, 406–7.
[30] Schuller to Leibniz, Amsterdam, 2 (?) Oct. 1677 in Leibniz, *Sämtliche Schriften und Briefe* 2nd ser. i, 382; Stein, *Leibniz und Spinoza*, 289; Van de Ven, *Printing Spinoza*, 340.

autograph manuscript which was unlikely to be needed for the publication process once a clearer transcribed copy was in the editors' hands.

Spinoza's philosophical legacy and its fate at his death remained for ten months entirely hidden from the world. If his name had become somewhat notorious in recent years, in the Netherlands and beyond, and many noted the news of his death, very few were in the least concerned with the survival of his philosophical and general intellectual legacy, or even much interested. By far the major point of interest for most contemporaries, virtually the only aspect commanding wide attention, related to his name's lurid association with blasphemy and sacrilege, his now established stature as the most notorious of "atheists." The issue contemporaries were mostly interested in was whether, in his final moments, the chief of "atheists" was (as many confidently reported), or was not, convulsed with sudden overwhelming terror, forced to his knees by divine wrath, and reduced to craven submission and repentance, abjectly beseeching forgiveness before one and all. Reports circulated assuring the public that this was indeed the case, and this was what most contemporaries wished to hear. But at the same time, equally vigorous reports circulated, as Bontekoe, Bayle, Kortholt, Scholtze, and Colerus all attest, asserting the contrary, that this "famous atheist" expired peacefully, in equanimity, without repenting in the least.[31]

In fact, wildly conflicting stories about Spinoza's passing dominated the public image and discussion of Spinoza not just into the next decade but even down to 1700 and beyond.[32] When writing his *Pensées diverses*, in 1682, Bayle, while concurring with Le Vassor that Spinoza was "the greatest atheist that there has ever been [le plus grand athée qui ait jamais été]," added that, according to what he had discovered, Spinoza, realizing his end was near, had asked his landlady to ensure that no church "minister be allowed to enter and find him in that state, the reason being, we have learnt from his friends, that he wished to die without disputes and feared falling into some lapse of mind in which he might utter something that could then be used against his principles." The dying Spinoza was apprehensive "lest it be spread about in the world that on the verge of death, his conscience had been aroused and compelled him to renounce his audacity and repudiate his views," which according to Bayle never happened.[33]

Conflicting stories about Spinoza's end, Halma also remarks, continued circulating for many years, leaving an entire generation dealing with a mass of bafflingly conflicting reports of Spinoza's demise. Readers at the time evinced enormous fascination in deathbed scenes relating to famous men of all kinds, while avidly searching for signs vindicating their own and the surrounding society's religious convictions. Convinced of this question's importance, the

---

[31] Kortholt, "Preface," 179; Colerus, *La Vie de B. de Spinosa*, 82.
[32] Halma, *Het Leven*, "Voorreden," 4–5.
[33] Bayle, *Pensées diverses* ii, 134–5; Israel, *Radical Enlightenment*, 298–9.

honest Colerus decided to investigate this topic so deeply fascinating to his age, and it was precisely because controversy surrounding Spinoza's supposed final humbling before God was so widely disputed that, after arriving in The Hague in 1693, and renting the same rooms Spinoza had rented before moving to his last lodgings, he set out to discover, by painstaking investigation, whatever reliable facts could be gathered about Spinoza's last days. He assigned more attention to this question than any other aspect of Spinoza's life. After researching the matter as thoroughly as he could, Colerus expressed utter amazement at the stupendous amount of myth and nonsense "confirming" this atheist's cringing before Christ and final abject submission, circulating on every side through the quarter of a century since Spinoza's death.[34]

It was part of his fight against universal superstition that one of Bayle's main aims in his *Dictionnaire* (1697) was to focus attention on the demise of famous men, inquiring how far each celebrity's deathbed scene did or did not conform to the convictions avowed by that person in his life and writings. There could be no doubt, he concluded, regarding Spinoza's genuineness and consistency right to the end. To cover himself against accusations of eulogizing the modern age's number one "atheist," Bayle styled Spinoza's deathbed scene a "ridiculous passion" which everyone could see was "mad vanity," but did so without, however, wholly obscuring his admiration for Spinoza's "virtuous" personality. Interestingly, the account given by Bayle of the dying Spinoza in 1682, and again in 1697, defiantly refusing to receive visits in his lodgings by clergymen of any description undeniably predates 1682,[35] and very likely originated with Bontekoe or the latter's detractors.[36] If Meyer and Schuller were both at hand during Spinoza's last days,[37] and by his own admission Schuller went through Spinoza's things, including his manuscripts, even before the philosopher had breathed his last, possibly appropriating more than just a few coins and other valuables, local medical expertise also played some part. According to a rare satirical pamphlet, *Dialogue van een Groote Thee en Tobacq Suyper*, of 1680, the bombastic Bontekoe also claimed to be among the doctors attending Spinoza during his final days.

A key passage reads: "Bontekoe once recounted how he had gone to visit Spinoza as he lay dying and heard from the dying man's mouth that if someone brought him a [Calvinist] preacher or [Catholic] priest to comfort him, [he would take no notice] as he possessed a different comfort." When recounting this story, "Dr Bontekoe" reportedly pretended to mock Spinoza's words, ridiculing his

---

[34] Colerus, *La Vie de B. de Spinosa*, 81–2; Rotthier, *Naakte perenboom*, 196–7.
[35] Bayle, *Écrits sur Spinoza*, 24, 140.
[36] *Dialogue van een Groote Thee en Tobacq-Suyper*, 45; further on the story of Spinoza's refusing to allow any divine of whatever denomination to enter the house, see René-Joseph Tournemine SJ, "Préface," to Fénelon's *Démonstration de l'existence de Dieu* (2nd edn. Paris, 1713), 5–6, 12–13.
[37] *Dialogue van een Groote Thee en Tobacq-Suyper*, 45; Meinsma, *Spinoza et son cercle*, 470, 486–7; Klever, "Spinoza's Life and Works," 50; Nadler, *Spinoza: A Life*, 350.

refusing to "calm himself with the consolations of the common people." In this way, "the [Bonte] cow, to get himself noticed," jeered the satirist, needed "to slander and lie, and vilify Spinosa whom he has never understood, or could understand."[38] Bontekoe had to be cautious when mentioning Spinoza, being himself counted among The Hague's more dubious personalities. Having antagonized most other local doctors, he was himself the target of accusations of atheism and sympathy for Spinoza as well as of hypocritically denouncing him.

Even earlier testimony than that of Bontekoe and Bayle survives concerning Spinoza's deathbed scene. A contemporary at Utrecht who does not name himself but knew the doctor attending at the end, or heard about his experience from someone who did, noted down, in September 1679, that "when [Spinoza's] death approached, he ordered his medications and some necessities to be put beside his bed and told the physician to leave him and lock his door." This entry was found in an unpublished private journal, preserved in the Utrecht archives, composed by someone in Beverland's circle, possibly Beverland himself, or by another young scholar at the University. After secluding himself in this fashion, Spinoza, this diarist adds, survived for three days while his household doctor remained upstairs, on the floor above his head. "And so [Spinoza] died and it is doubtful whether he repented."[39]

What was most troubling about the whole business, complains Colerus, were the numerous accounts even in supposedly learned texts by scholars of standing who should more carefully have checked their sources before disseminating such absurd "fables" and fabrications, recounting Spinoza's falling to his knees and beseeching the Almighty for forgiveness.[40] This showed how readily even the most ridiculous fictions circulate and can be used to mislead. "On this topic I find so many wrong accounts, that I cannot help being amazed that these authors did not do better research, but disseminated their stories merely on the basis of hearsay."[41] A great many claimed, without investigating, that Spinoza underwent severe torments and abjured his "godless" ideas and writings simply because they preferred to believe this; a fact that to Colerus seemed distinctly worrying. Most people, he could not deny, seemingly believe whatever fictions fit their preconceptions rather than search for the truth. Although Colerus' biography appeared first in Dutch, in 1705, it seems likely he originally wrote it in German and that the first edition is a Dutch translation. If this is correct, it is unfortunate that his original wording is lost; for the eighteenth-century German and English editions that appeared, often rather inexact, were all based on the subsequent, less than

---

[38] *Dialogue van een Groote Thee en Tobacq-Suyper,* 45; Israel, "Dr Cornelis Bontekoe's Views," 222–3.
[39] Steenbakkers, "Mort de Spinoza," 735.
[40] Colerus, *La Vie de B. de Spinosa,* 81–2; Colerus, *Das Leben,* 113–14; Van Vloten, *Benedictus de Spinoza,* 117–18; Steenbakkers, Touber, and Van de Ven, "Clandestine Notebook" (online version), 6.
[41] Freudenthal/Walther, *Lebensgeschichte* i, 156–7; Steenbakkers, "Spinoza's Life," 41.

perfect, French translation from the Dutch published in 1706, though the French and later German and English versions did at least correct the wrong date for Spinoza's birth given in the original Dutch account and, inexact and derivative or not, were the editions European readers of the Enlightenment era knew and consulted.[42]

Researching Spinoza's end was the original reason for Colerus writing his biography. "Several times" he interviewed Spinoza's landlord, Van der Spijck and his wife "who are still alive at this time, regarding what they know about this," that is whether Spinoza did take special precautions not to be intruded on by churchmen likely to be bothersome to him, or alternatively, did cry out (which Colerus would perhaps have liked to find verified): "Oh God take pity on me, a miserable sinner!," or was "heard many times sighing and calling out to God." But Van der Spijck and his wife "consistently answered" that they knew nothing whatever that could support any of the "rival claims and for the most part considered these reported circumstances to be false."[43] She never heard Spinoza request, Van der Spijck's wife added, that no churchman be allowed to enter his rooms. Nor could the couple confirm or discount the story that on feeling death approaching, Spinoza swallowed a special juice (the French and German versions of Colerus' biography state "extract of mandragora"—in German, Alraun-Saft), a soporific alkaloid that soothes muscular, joint and other bodily pain, inducing sleep and often hallucinations, then drew his curtains, lost all consciousness and peacefully passed away.[44]

The quarter-century-long controversy over Spinoza's deathbed scene eventually petered out early in the next century, as those insisting Spinoza ended his days distraught and plunged in repentance finally abandoned the battle in the aftermath of Bayle and Colerus, yielding to the researched consensus that Spinoza expired in tranquillity and seclusion without repenting in the least and without any churchman attending. But hostile commentators by no means abandoned their view that such an appallingly sinful person must undergo dreadful retribution for his impiety. The emphasis switched, as in Nieuwentijt's account of Spinoza's end, to reminding readers that God in his wisdom and "freedom does not always punish sins so visibly in this life," but divine punishment assuredly will come and the calm of Spinoza's last days should be considered all staged pretence, his last defiant imposture. The mature Nieuwentijt who in his *Gronden van Zekerheid* (1720) continually addresses himself to Spinoza's "followers" and "disciples," seeking to convince them Spinoza's arguments are as devoid of truth as Aesop's fables, held that not only were Spinoza's principles fundamentally wrong, but, contrary to Bayle, he was also not at all "virtuous." According to

---

[42] Freudenthal/Walther, *Lebensgeschichte* ii, 62; Steenbakkers, "Spinoza's Life," 48n18, 49n38.
[43] Freudenthal/Walther, *Lebensgeschichte* i, 160–1; Steenbakkers, "Spinoza's Life," 42.
[44] Colerus, *La Vie de B. de Spinosa*, 85–6; Colerus, *Das Leben*, 120–1.

Nieuwentijt, falsehood and deliberate imposture pervaded Spinoza's life and philosophy every step of the way, even his final attempt to mislead others with the hideous performance on his deathbed.[45]

40.ii Funeral at the Nieuwe Kerk (New Church)

On the Sunday evening of Spinoza's death, Van der Spijck, having secreted away the crucial contents of his writing desk, made a provisional listing of the deceased Spinoza's belongings, a formal inventory compiled in the presence of two witnesses and recorded by a local notary. Itemized were Spinoza's "seven shirts," "two black hats," two pairs of shoes, blankets, a bedspread, "Turkish" trousers, a cloak and blouse, lens-cutting machine and other lens-cutting and polishing tools, a bookcase, book collection, and some lenses. Apart from the bed, bedclothes, and tools, Spinoza's non-legible belongings consisted of just these few outfits, an oak table, three small tables—two for his tools, and also just one scenic painting and a black-framed portrait (unspecified). Nothing was stated about his papers apart from a key and locked "cassetje" [cabinet or box]. All his belongings were brought into Spinoza's "small room" which was then carefully sealed off, to prevent interference of any kind or further thefts, until an official final inventory could be drawn up.

"The dead body," as the English version of Colerus' biography expresses it, was transferred to his prepared grave in the New Church upon the Spuy (Figure 40.1) four days after Spinoza's demise, on 25 February, "being attended by many illustrious persons and six carriages."[46] It must have been an unusual, even curious occasion. The Nieuwe Kerk [New Church], a recent construction, begun in 1649, planned as a showpiece of the Republic at its height, though with a far more impressive and innovative exterior than its comparatively unimpressive interior, was the second main Reformed church of The Hague, after the town's "Groote Kerk" [Great Church] which dates back to the fourteenth century. The Nieuwe Kerk stands rather grandly not far from where Spinoza lived, a spot he undoubtedly walked past countless times, still today exerting a striking effect,[47] though at the time it must have impressed even more when the building dominated a small island in the River Spui (the nearby water today mostly filled in).

The building broke new ground architecturally, its central plan and cohesive design being modelled in part on the Marekerk in Leiden (1639–49), a highly

---

[45] Nieuwentijt, *Gronden van Zekerheid*, 289–96; Van Bunge, "Spinoza's Life," 223.
[46] Freudenthal/Walther, *Lebensgeschichte* i, 162–3.
[47] Kuyper, *Dutch Classicist Architecture*, 24–7.

Figure 40.1 *The New Church on the Spui (The Hague), in 1668* by C. Elandts. By courtesy of Collection of The Hague Municipal Archive, the Netherlands.

innovative landmark,[48] notably better lit than traditional churches to facilitate perusal of prayer books and bibles.[49] The structure's other noteworthy feature was its bringing the entire congregation close to the pulpit. (With its excellent acoustics, the building now serves, since religious services there ceased in 1969, mainly for concerts.) It was "built," remarks William Montague, author of the *Delights of Holland*, in 1696, "much after the form of the [Sheldonian] theatre in Oxon. [Oxford]," with "no pillars within, so that all the people may see as well as hear the minister,"[50] though Oxford's Sheldonian was actually a later construction, built in 1664-9, to a design by Christopher Wren, marking an equally sharp break from the Gothic style dark interiors of ecclesiastical and university buildings of the past. The Nieuwe Kerk's construction, initiated jointly by the Hof van Holland and city government, completed in 1656, was supervised by two architects, Pieter Noorwits

---

[48] Designed by the Leiden town architect Arent van 'S-Gravesande, brother of the more famous architect Noorwits, another building Spinoza must have seen many times, which helped set a notable fashion for octagonal and other many-sided centrally planned churches. Two other major examples are the Oostkerk in Middelburg (1655-66) and the Noorderkerk in Groningen (1660-4).
[49] Kuyper, *Dutch Classicist Architecture*, 19-21.   [50] Van Strien, *British Travellers*, 130.

(1612–69), and the artist Bartholomeus van Bassen (1590–1652), who, when construction was not yet finished, also painted a splendid townscape with the Nieuwe Kerk as its main subject.

Spinoza's funeral as such was more than modest but hardly a grand affair. Nor, apparently (and perhaps wisely), was any tombstone or plaque prepared. It is not known whether any words were spoken before or after the coffin was lowered into in the vault used for the occasion. Certainly, there was no formal eulogy of the kind renowned university professors then regularly received; and it is hard to envisage what prayers, if any, were recited. The spot where Spinoza was buried lay inside the church, in a vault close to the remains of Johan de Witt. With six other burials in the same vault recorded that same day, Spinoza's corpse was signed in by the official registering burials at the church as arriving and being deposited at 3.00 p.m.[51] Part of the expenses for the occasion were afterwards paid by Schiedam relatives of Spinoza's deceased friend Simon Joosten de Vries, his sister Trijntje and his brother-in-law, Alewijn, who were presumably present among the mourners. The vault was later emptied, in the eighteenth century, when, as with all graves for which leases were not renewed, Spinoza's remains, and those in like circumstance, were disposed of, the more solid parts carted off, the more powdered remnants scattered over the earth of the churchyard.[52]

Visitors today find just a memorial plaque, fittingly placed not in the church itself but outside, in the churchyard. Thus, in a sense Spinoza's earthly remains still grace the spot albeit thinly diffused across the churchyard. "The burial being over, the particular friends or neighbours, according to the custom of the country," recorded Colerus, "were treated to some bottles of wine in the house where the deceased had lodged,"[53] a reception arranged by Van der Spijck. Of those present at the funeral and the gathering afterwards several were doubtless visitors from Amsterdam and nearby Leiden as well as Schiedam. The wine encouraged conversation after the burial and the customary flow of reminiscence about the deceased. Reportedly, many of those present returned later that year, to attend the auction of Spinoza's belongings.

At Amsterdam, Leiden, and The Hague and far beyond, rumours about another book by Spinoza being in existence and about to appear, posing a dire threat to religion, flourished after Spinoza's demise much as they had in the months before. At their 1676 gathering in Middelburg, the "Walloon Synod," the synod of the French-speaking Calvinists in the Netherlands, reiterated their abhorrence of the "blasphemies and impieties of the wretched Spinoza" and the urgency of devising effective remedies "capable of halting and extirpating this known gangrene."[54]

[51] Meinsma, *Spinoza et son cercle*, 484.
[52] Steenbakkers, "Spinoza's Life," 43, 59n172; Van der Tang, "Spinoza en Schiedam," 182.
[53] Colerus, *Life of Benedict de Spinoza*, 89; Van Vloten, *Benedictus de Spinoza*, 119; Nadler, *Spinoza: A Life*, 407.
[54] Quoted in Vernière, *Spinoza et la pensée française*, 42.

Unknown to them, the remarkable international drama over the fate of Spinoza's manuscripts had begun to unfold within hours of his death.

The so-called "first inventory" of the estate of "Benedictus de Spinoza," the provisional initial list compiled by Van der Spijck and two witnesses certifying Spinoza's death on 21 February, recorded nothing whatever relevant to the *Ethics* and his other unpublished writings and correspondence. But by this time the real drama had already commenced: "Spinoza's landlord, Mr Van der Spijck who is still living," Colerus recorded later, "tells me Spinoza arranged for his writing desk containing the manuscripts and letters to be immediately dispatched to Amsterdam upon his death, to the official city publisher, Jan Rieuwertsz, and this [Van der Spijck] at once proceeded to do."[55] This does not quite tally, though, with the report of Spinoza's death that Tschirnhaus, now in Rome whither he had travelled from Paris, via Lyon, Turin, and Venice, received from Schuller, relaying the news of Spinoza's demise not long afterwards. Schuller's letter to Tschirnhaus itself is lost; but according to what Tschirnhaus then reported to Leibniz, some three weeks later, "our friend" in The Hague died in a good state of mind, "with Schuller present, having specified what should happen to his manuscripts" and that he took care of them.[56]

Van der Spijck could not yet settle all of Spinoza's outstanding debts, or organize the auction of his books and tools, because liquidation of his estate could not proceed until local magistrates determined to whom his possessions belonged. In the event, this involved a considerable delay.[57] Nine days after his death and the first inventory, a second inventory of the belongings of the "late Baruch Espinosa," as he was now styled, was ordered by local authorities at the request of "Rebecca Espinosa," Spinoza's widowed younger sister, and his nephew, "Daniel de Caceris."[58] Dissatisfied with what they had been told of the arrangements thus far, Rebecca and Daniel, as Spinoza's closest surviving relatives, were acting here also on behalf of her three children, Hanna, Michael, and Benjamin, born during the late 1650s whilst she was married to the now deceased Rabbi Samuel de Casseres who was also Daniel's father via his first marriage to Spinoza's deceased older sister.[59] Rebecca's daughter, Hanna, named after Spinoza's and Rebecca's mother, had married in Amsterdam, in December 1674, a certain "Isaac de Abraham Idanha," apparently a jeweller.[60] The Hague notary Willem van den Hove (*c*.1650–84) arrived on 2 March 1677 with a legal order to carry out a second, more detailed inventory than the first, and for Van der Spijck to permit

---

[55] Freudenthal/Walther, *Lebensgeschichte* i, 140, 336; Nadler, *Think Least of Death*, 60; Steenbakkers, "Spinoza's Life," 44.
[56] Steenbakkers, *Spinoza's Ethica*, 58; Steenbakkers, "Textual History," 36; Zaunick, "Ehrenfried Walther von Tschirnhaus," 7.
[57] Nadler, *Spinoza: A Life*, 408–9; Steenbakkers, "Spinoza's Life," 44.
[58] Freudenthal/Walther, *Lebensgeschichte* i, 339.   [59] Emmanuel, *Precious Stones*, 194.
[60] Emmanuel, *Precious Stones*, 194; Bloom, *Economic Activities*, 41.

and assist with this. At this point, Spinoza's writing desk and with it the autograph of the *Ethics* appear to have still been in The Hague but not in Spinoza's rooms.

Present at the new listing of Spinoza's belongings, besides Willem Van den Hove (c.1650–84), Van der Spijck, and another witness, was a medical doctor, Abraham Slingerlandt, possibly another of the physicians attending Spinoza earlier, and "Jan Rieuwertsz bookseller at Amsterdam," who presumably had either stayed over since the funeral or else gone back to Amsterdam and then returned. The seals with which Spinoza's rooms had been curtained off were pronounced intact, recorded Van den Hove, when the group entered, and Van der Spijck attested his having drawn up the preliminary list of Spinoza's belongings "to the best of his knowledge without as far as he knew leaving anything unmentioned," which he was ready to affirm "if necessary under oath." Aside from a few added items of clothing, a pair of gloves, a portable chess-set and an "old striped travel bag," the formal legalized second inventory was identical to the first, except this time a detailed list of Spinoza's books was compiled, presumably by Rieuwertsz. Totalling 161 volumes, mostly in Latin, they included a substantial body of Descartes' works, a few in Dutch, among them Descartes' letters translated by Glazemaker, and the political texts of the Brothers De La Court, beside volumes in Hebrew and Spanish, the latter including works of the greatest Spanish writers, Cervantes and Quevedo. Number 161, last on the list, were the works of the Spanish poet Luis de Góngora.[61] Machiavelli's works Spinoza possessed in the original Italian.[62] Significantly, the resulting catalogue included nothing at all in Portuguese, and nothing relating to Portuguese literature or history. Spinoza's books clearly reflected involvement in political theory and Bible criticism as well as contemporary philosophy, and his interest in Roman and Spanish history, but equally a striking lack of interest in classical, medieval, and other pre-Cartesian philosophy and science, and near total absence of Christian theology. A few scientific and mathematical works featured, but fewer than one might expect.

Since the eventual public auction of the belongings of the "Heer Benedictus de Spinosa, born in Amsterdam," as officially inventoried at the time of his death, could not proceed until legal ownership and the issue of costs was settled, the next legal step was to resolve Van der Spijck's dispute with Rebecca and Daniel who were unwilling to foot the bill for funeral costs, medicines, or anything related to Spinoza's end, unless the total outlay proved less than the proceeds from the sale of Spinoza's belongings. Although initially suspicious that something significant was being hidden from them, over the spring and summer months realization that the total of debts would exceed the value of the inheritance gradually took hold. Finally, seven months after Spinoza's death, on 30 September 1677, Rebecca and Daniel appeared before an Amsterdam notary to legalize their decision not to

---

[61] Freudenthal/Walther, *Lebensgeschichte* i, 340–1.
[62] Servaas de Rooijen, *Inventaire*, 629–33; Offenberg, "Spinoza's Library," 309–10.

proceed as "heirs of the said Benedictus de Espinosa, her brother and his uncle respectively" or concern themselves further with his legacy and everything connected with it, and were now "renouncing the said estate and legacy."[63]

Most of what remained of Spinoza's family, including his sister, Rebecca, and nephews, Michael and Benjamin, and probably several others, migrated as a group to the Dutch Caribbean island of Curaçao not long after Spinoza's death, at some point towards the end of the 1670s or early 1680s. Michael, who was named after Spinoza's and Rebecca's father, Michael d'Espinosa, was a *sofer*, chazzan and rabbinic assistant like his father, Samuel, and crossed to the New World to assist Rabbi Josiah Pardo (1626–84), Rabbi Mortera's son-in-law,[64] whom Spinoza must have remembered from his school days, a rabbi who, until 1672, stubbornly continued to believe Sabbatai Zevi was the Messiah and would release the Jews from all oppression and misery, but then, finally abandoning his Sabbatian credo, figured subsequently among the most prominent and important Sephardic religious leaders in the Caribbean.[65] Leaving Amsterdam in 1674, Pardo became the first fully trained rabbi and effective organizer of the educational and charitable institutions of the *Mikvé Israel* community on Curaçao, the premier and model community of the Sephardic Caribbean, based in the island's capital, Willemstad,[66] and, in 1683–4, in his last year, performed a similar function organizing the growing new congregation of Port Royal, in Jamaica.

The global Jewish diaspora, Pardo evidently believed, was part of God's plan so that "Jews everywhere could proclaim the truth of God and his Torah," and by helping organize Jewish community life in the Caribbean, he was contributing to this messianic scheme.[67] As Josiah's assistant, the younger Michael d'Espinoza became a notable figure in the formative early religious history of Curaçao Jewry while Benjamin, who was "communal bridegroom of the Law" on Curaçao in 1685, married a niece of Rabbi Josiah Pardo. The lives of Spinoza's sole surviving sibling, Rebecca, and her eldest son, his nephew, Michael, the *sofer*, who remained unmarried, ended eighteen years after Spinoza's, both of these close relatives dying in the Curaçao Yellow Fever epidemic of 1695.[68]

The Espinoza family's renunciation of Spinoza's legacy simplified matters. But whether notification of this was slow to reach The Hague, or for some other reason, official permission to proceed with the auction was still delayed until mid- or late October when the court in The Hague finally permitted the sale of Spinoza's possessions and books with Van der Spijck named as the person

---

[63] Notarial deed of 30 Sept. 1677 in Freudenthal/Walther, *Lebensgeschichte* i, 371; Vlessing, "Excommunication" (1997), 35; the following year, in 1678, Daniel married Jeudith de David Moreno in Amsterdam, receiving a dowry of 3,600 guilders; but his marriage soon ended in divorce.
[64] Saperstein, *Exile in Amsterdam*, 380, 537.   [65] Gans, *Memorboek*, 96.
[66] Emmanuel, *Precious Stones*, 79, 95; Saperstein, *Exile in Amsterdam*, 8n.
[67] Saperstein, *Exile in Amsterdam*, 337n.
[68] Emmanuel, *Precious Stones*, 195; Nadler, *Spinoza: A Life*, 54.

authorized to collect the proceeds. The public auction was announced two days before the event in the *Amsterdamsche Courant* of 2 November 1677 as due to take place at the house of "Monsr. Hendrick van der Spyck, painter living on the Paviljoensgracht, opposite Dubblet-Street," on the coming Thursday (4 November 1677), starting at nine in the morning when would be offered to the highest bidder "all the belongings left by the deceased Benedictus van Spinoza, including printed books and manuscripts, telescopes and fine microscope lenses, lenses polished and unpolished, and pieces of lens-cutting tools, grinders, and both large and small metal plates, etc. needed for such work."[69] Exactly the same advertisement appeared the same day in the Haarlem paper, the *Opregte Haarlemsche Courant*.[70]

Disposal of Spinoza's belongings, books, and manuscripts and the public auction were clearly orchestrated by Van der Spijck working with Rieuwertsz. Kortholt later noted that several eminent persons attended the auction (a report subsequently retold by Bayle), but, unfortunately, specified only one attendee by name—the enigmatic Dr Bontekoe, who came, he remarks, expressly for the purpose of purchasing Spinoza's library.[71] Bayle here repeats Kortholt's story that "after Spinoza's death, numerous savants, including Bontekoe, attempted to obtain his books." But like Hobbes, "Spinoza hardly aspired to possess a large stock of books and left," he added quite inaccurately, "scarcely forty which savants then acquired at a high price."[72] In fact, the auction included all or nearly all Spinoza's remaining 161 books which together, with the rest of his possessions, fetched some 430 guilders,[73] equivalent at the time to slightly more than a year's salary for a rural preacher or skilled artisan. Nothing is known for certain about the subsequent fate of Spinoza's microscopes and telescopes, but it seems likely an item listed in the 1717 inventory of the princely collection of Duke Friedrich I of Saxe-Gotha-Altenburg (prince: 1675–91), creator of the court theatre at Gotha and the princely *kunstkammer* at Friedenstein, and described as a "tubus" [telescope] with five lenses bound in black-gold leather "made by Spinoza," was acquired originally at this auction and subsequently found its way from The Hague to Gotha.[74]

One wonders how many of those attending the November auction were in the know that behind the scenes a much greater drama was in progress, now almost completed, that mattered far more than the auction. At this point, eight months after the philosopher's death, though it had not yet actually appeared, Spinoza's principal philosophical work, the *Ethics*, which many ecclesiastics of all denominations were avid to locate and stifle before birth, was nearing readiness and shortly to be published together with his surviving other unpublished work. In

---

[69] *Amsterdamsche Courant*, 2 Nov. 1677. [70] Offenberg, "Spinoza's Library," 309.
[71] Kortholt, "Preface," 180; Meinsma, *Spinoza et son cercle*, 486; Steenbakkers, "Spinoza's Life," 45.
[72] Bayle, *Écrits sur Spinoza*, 180; further on this episode, see Meinsma, *Spinoza et son cercle*, 486.
[73] Freudenthal/Walther, *Lebensgeschichte* i, 374. [74] Van de Ven, *Documenting Spinoza*, ch. 7.

fact, by October 1677, several weeks before the auction and unseen by authorities and public alike, Spinoza's *Ethics* and other unpublished writings, or rather those his friends were able to assemble, not only existed newly transcribed, copied, edited, and translated, but were already partly printed and secretly stored away, hidden well out of sight in Amsterdam, and would shortly be ready for release.[75]

Mourned by his circle and friends, Spinoza's passing was hardly regretted by the scientific establishment more generally. His long-time friend across the Channel, Henry Oldenburg, in London, expressed sadness at his death and annoyance with Leibniz for not having delivered the last letter he had addressed to him, but said nothing about Spinoza's legacy or failure to publish his principal work of which he had specific knowledge. Oldenburg's own demise followed just half a year later. His successor as secretary to the Royal Society for three years (1677–80), Nehemiah Grew (1641–1712), was Britain's most distinguished botanist at the time and, employing microscopes, a key investigator of plant physiology. A Cambridge graduate, son of a Midlands Nonconformist minister, Grew also possessed a degree from Leiden, though he does not appear to have spent much time in Holland. He knew about but hardly appreciated Spinoza. Like Boyle, Newton, and Oldenburg, he was a zealous advocate of a *philosophia experimentalis*, conceiving science research and experiment as leading men directly to the God of the Scriptures, with science tightly conjoined to Revelation in every conceivable way. To them, that was the true essence and linkage of science, philosophy, and theology. Much later, in his *Cosmologia sacra* (London, 1701), a work dedicated to the Stadholder-king, William III, Grew again heavily stressed the perfect oneness and reconcilability of science and religion, being moved to demonstrate this anew, he explains, by the need to repel subversive "opinions, especially those of Anti-Scripturalists which have been published of late years, by Spinoza and some others, in Latin, Dutch and English."[76] When it came to challenges to the moderate Enlightenment world view, to questioning its systematically conjoining science with religion and aligning the two, Spinoza was indeed, as much other evidence confirms, now the one and only adversary prominent enough to be worth mentioning.

---

[75] Bayle, *Écrits sur Spinoza*, 180.   [76] Grew, *Cosmologia sacra*, Preface, 1.

41

A Tumultuous Aftermath

41.i The Battle of the *Ethics* (1677)

During his last days, Spinoza entrusted those with him, according to what the younger Rieuwertsz later told Stolle and Hallmann, to arrange the dispatch of his manuscripts, on his death, to his father, the older Rieuwertsz, in Amsterdam. Colerus confirms this, except to say it was Spinoza's landlord, Van der Spijck specifically, who was "instructed" to ensure their dispatch to the older Rieuwertsz. Van der Spijck acted promptly, colluding with Rieuwertsz, without recording anything with any notary, or in writing, organizing the transporting of Spinoza's writing desk and cabinet from The Hague by canal barge to Amsterdam, where the remaining manuscripts were concealed together with what Schuller had already brought over from The Hague. Beyond Spinoza's close circle no one knew anything regarding the non-inventoried items, the all-important *lessenaar* [writing cabinet-desk], correspondence and manuscripts. Rieuwertsz's and Spinoza's other close allies then began sorting, copying, and conferring as to what to publish and how to proceed.[1]

The first obstacle was Spinoza's family. Notified of their inheritance after Spinoza's death, and making inquiries, Rebecca and her stepson-nephew, Daniel, arrived in The Hague in late February or early March submitting an appeal to The Hague town secretary to be assigned charge of the proceedings relating to Spinoza's legacy and the auctioning of his belongings. The funeral itself Rebecca and Daniel presumably boycotted in deference to the 1656 Jewish communal ban, now in force for over twenty years, but to begin with showed eagerness to inherit whatever Spinoza had left of any value, especially after discovering Spinoza had left verbal last instructions requesting that his most precious possessions be dispatched by barge to some confidant or confidants in Amsterdam. They made urgent inquiries as to the whereabouts of Spinoza's cabinet-desk and its undeclared contents. Besides visiting the house where her brother had lodged, and speaking to his landlord, Rebecca and Daniel went down to the quaysides in The Hague to question the bargemen, inquiring especially to whom, in Amsterdam, the desk and some packages were dispatched in so furtive a manner.

Hearing of these inquiries from the barge skippers, Rieuwertsz wrote to Van de Spijck, from Amsterdam, according to Colerus, a month after Spinoza's death, on

---

[1] Freudenthal/Walther, *Lebensgeschichte* i, 94, 140; Van de Ven, *Printing Spinoza*, 337.

25 March, acknowledging safe receipt of the cabinet-desk and manuscripts and alerting him that Spinoza's relatives were trying to locate the crucial items believing the packages might contain valuables. On their inquiring "to whom the desk was sent," the barge skippers in The Hague, as instructed beforehand, had put Spinoza's relatives off the scent by assuring them they kept no record of recipients of the goods they shipped and then reported the episode to Rieuwertsz. "It is best," Rieuwertsz alerted Van der Spijck, that Spinoza's close relatives "should not know" to whom the items were addressed or about their contents. If they discovered in whose hands the items were, they would surely inform others, in order to get possession and might well then be instrumental in getting the manuscripts suppressed under the ban, or at least inform notaries and civic authorities producing the same result.

Initially, in February–March 1677, there was not yet complete agreement among "the friends" about the full dimensions of the publishing project they were undertaking. If it was obvious what Spinoza wanted done regarding the *Ethics*, they knew too that he wanted the *Tractatus Politicus* to be published, as he indicated when writing to an unnamed friend, possibly Jelles, when still hoping to finish this text in a few weeks before being prevented by his deteriorating condition.[2] In this undated letter of the summer of 1676, Spinoza mentions having completed six of the extant eleven chapters (the last just a fragment). He was thus able to add another four chapters over the next weeks while still able to work, principally the sections on aristocracy, which during the autumn of 1676 were almost certainly the last important body of text that he wrote. He was just starting on the crucial last part of the treatise, on democracy, when he became too unwell to continue. But leaving no written instructions or will, it was perhaps less than obvious exactly what Spinoza's intentions were regarding the rest of his surviving unpublished work, most of which lay unfinished, and with respect to translating his work and editing his correspondence.

Spinoza's friends needed to agree on how the team would proceed regarding their division of labour and their overall strategy. Should the *Ethics* appear alone with all haste, leaving the rest, or some of the rest, to appear later, or should everything publishable burst on the scene all at once? Should they publish in Latin only, or bring out some or all of Spinoza's thus far unpublished work in Dutch as well? And how should they deal with those parts of his correspondence of evident philosophical value but dotted with names and remarks the editors had no wish to see made public? If they published the philosophically significant material from the surviving correspondence, what should be included and what excluded?[3] This was not just a question of removing compromising information relating to

---

[2] Spinoza to "a friend," undated (August? 1676) in Spinoza, *Briefwisseling*, 430; Moreau and Steenbakkers, "L'Historique du text," 27.
[3] Akkerman, *Studies*, 67, 77–8; Steenbakkers, *Spinoza's* Ethica, 57, 64–7.

members of their own circle or persons such as Leibniz, Tschirnhaus, De Volder, Graevius, Van Velthuysen, Nieuwstad, and Wittichius connected with Spinoza behind the scenes who would not wish this to be generally known. They were confronted also with the tricky question of how much, if any, personal detail about Spinoza himself to include and, more specifically, how to mould his image and present Spinoza the person to the public. The editorial policy they agreed on clearly reflected a desire to shape Spinoza's image in a particular way, it seeming important, for example, to stress Spinoza's leading a reclusive life of lofty philosophical tranquillity, totally dedicated to the search for truth while concealing or de-emphasizing indications of group activity, activism, collusion, mocking eminent personalities, or seeking to influence young people and recruit followers.[4]

Before reaching agreement on their strategy, the editorial team leaders, Meyer, Bouwmeester, and Jelles, also needed to familiarize themselves with the surviving incomplete texts and jointly evaluate their value. If Jelles lacked the academic training of Meyer and Bouwmeester, he appears to have been backing the Spinoza publication project financially, much as he paid, or at least was later reported to have done so, for the publication of Spinoza's Descartes book in 1663.[5] Possibly none of the lead editors had yet seen the *Tractatus Politicus* or even the *Tractatus de Intellectus Emendatione* [*TIE*, *Tractatus on the Emendation of the Intellect*], as Tschirnhaus, who was particularly eager to peruse that text, first set eyes on it only after Schuller sent him a copy whilst in Rome, in April 1677, and there is no sign of anyone possessing a copy before Schuller went through Spinoza's papers in late February 1677. Conceivably, the editors first read the *Tractatus Politicus* and the *TIE* only in late February and March 1677.[6] Agreement as to when, how, and what to publish clandestinely was reached only after weeks of transcribing, conferring, and perhaps pressuring Schuller.

For some weeks, Schuller seemingly had in his possession the autograph manuscripts of the *Ethics*, and perhaps also the *TIE*, the *Tractatus Politicus*, and some letters. On 29 March 1677, Schuller wrote again to Leibniz, relieved the latter had not yet mentioned the proposed sale of the original manuscript of the *Ethics* to "your prince," for the entire scenario had now changed and Schuller did not want it mentioned to anyone that he had suggested selling and transferring it to Hanover. One should not assume Schuller's shady handling of the autograph he removed from Spinoza's lodgings and initially thought of selling for a substantial sum, could itself obstruct the publication process, as during the spring several fair copies of the original manuscript were made available among the team.[7] Schuller, in any case, fell into line with the maximalist strategy settled on by "the friends," while characteristically boasting to Leibniz that it was he who had brought them

---

[4] Van Bunge, "Spinoza's Life," 215.   [5] Mertens, "Where Thou Dwellest," 26, 34.
[6] Mignini, "Texte du *Tractatus*," 190, 192; Mignini, "Introduction au *Tractatus*," 34.
[7] Steenbakkers, *Spinoza's* Ethica, 55–7.

round to it.[8] After around a month of conferring, agreement on a common plan was reached. The goal was to publish the *Ethics*, unfinished works, and correspondence all together in a single volume. "I give you this information in all confidence," Schuller once again confided to Leibniz (though no one in the Amsterdam circle was more unreliable and indiscreet than him), "not doubting you will keep it hidden from everyone [in his wide international network], even your friends, so that our project will not be opposed."[9]

From late March, the group ploughed on with their daunting, complex undertaking that eventually proved a clandestine triumph for them. The editors opted for the boldest, riskiest, and most ambitious approach—to bring out the *Ethics*, short writings (apart from the *Korte Verhandeling* which was left aside and subsequently forgotten until rediscovered in the mid-nineteenth century), and correspondence together in one large volume, but in separate Latin and Dutch versions released simultaneously. Their decision was to include "everything of any value that we were able to gather together from the papers [Spinoza] left behind, and from copies in the hands of friends and acquaintances," as Jelles puts it in the Preface, and whatever seemed philosophically significant in the correspondence. Possibly something further "by our author" not included *had* survived, but nothing of importance would be found, claimed Jelles, that is not affirmed "many times" in the *Opera Posthuma*, except perhaps "a small essay about the Rainbow which it is known that he wrote," and that, if Spinoza "did not burn it as we believe," may still be found somewhere or other.[10] Commenting on this, years later, the younger Kortholt, utterly disagreeing with Jelles' high regard for Spinoza's philosophy and its reconcilability with Christianity, was equally sure Spinoza had penned a Rainbow treatise he afterwards burnt, but heartily wished he had burnt all the rest of his oeuvre too. Spinoza's philosophy, insists Kortholt, does nothing but obscure God's truth and pervert the testimonies of Scripture: "for thorns never yield figs nor raisins," he added, in mockery of Spinoza's name and former commercial activity together with Jelles' past as a grocer.[11]

A group collaboration requiring swift and furtive copying, redacting and translating of Spinoza's unpublished writings, the team finished the job astonishingly quickly, in just seven or eight months, publishing the posthumous works in one volume, in December 1677. Word circulated later, Bayle remarks (having recently heard this), in March 1686, that the preface was written (in Dutch) by "a certain gentleman of the Mennonite sect named Jarig Jelles, formerly a trader in Amsterdam, who withdrew from business to live off the revenues he had acquired, a man who, however, was hardly erudite; afterwards, it is believed, this preface was

---

[8] Schuller to Leibniz, Amsterdam, 29 March 1677 in Leibniz, *Sämtliche Schriften und Briefe* 2nd ser. i, 304–5; Steenbakkers, Spinoza's *Ethica*, 60.
[9] Meinsma, *Spinoza et son cercle*, 489; Laerke, *Leibniz lecteur*, 570–1; Steenbakkers, "Textual History," 37.
[10] Jelles, "Voorreden," 4.   [11] Kortholt, "Preface," 180–1.

rendered into Latin [...] by Ludovicus Meyer, an Amsterdam physician who died a few years ago, author they say of the paradoxical treatise *Philosophia sacrae Scripturae Interpres* which, not without reason, greatly displeased the theologians."[12] Besides Jelles, Meyer, Rieuwertsz, and Bouwmeester, the remaining active members of the editorial team were Glazemaker, Schuller, and Petrus van Gent, the Leiden-educated young man originally from Nijmegen, familiar at Rieuwertsz's shop at least since 1675 who, working with Jelles, assumed responsibility for much of the transcribing and editing of the Latin.

In the late summer and autumn of 1677, the printers worked secretly from new, carefully checked and revised copies, not Spinoza's originals, so the editing project relied on a good deal of transcribing and here Van Gent's role was especially significant. The agreed plan also required much translation needing to be accomplished quickly but accurately, mainly from Latin into Dutch where Glazemaker, no doubt, highly skilled at this, took the lead, except for some letters and Jelles' preface which had to be rendered from Dutch into Latin. One clear drawback of editing the Latin texts while simultaneously having them translated into Dutch, was that not a few corrections to the punctuation (much of which was missing from the original manuscript) and many errata amended in the revised final Latin transcription never found their way into the *Nagelate Schriften*.[13]

Van Gent, having known Spinoza since his Leiden student days, thus played an unseen and unrecorded but noteworthy role in preserving Spinoza's legacy, which afterwards remained permanently hidden from posterity. In the final edited versions of the *Opera Posthuma* and the *Nagelate Schriften*, all mention of Van Gent as well as Rieuwertsz, Jelles, Schuller, and Tschirnhaus was deleted including, for example, from Schuller's letter of 25 July 1675, from Amsterdam, where Schuller sends Spinoza best wishes from Van Gent as well as Rieuwertsz.[14] The only names deliberately left in the correspondence were either outright opponents of Spinoza, like Van Blijenbergh, Fabricius and Albert Burgh, or else deceased and remote persons, like Balling and Oldenburg. Living for a time in the same house as Schuller, Van Gent, a close friend especially of Tschirnhaus, kept the latter informed about Schuller's various manoeuvres during the months of the editing process.[15] Later, when Tschirnhaus was back in electoral Saxony, during the 1680s Van Gent acted also as postal intermediary between him and De Volder, and between Tschirnhaus and Huygens who, strikingly, addressed the young Van Gent as "doctissimus." When Huygens and Tschirnhaus later quarrelled, in

---

[12] Bayle to Janssen van Almeloveen, Rotterdam, 8 March 1686, in Bayle, *Correspondance* vi, 317–18; Van de Ven, *Printing Spinoza*, 369.

[13] Mignini, "Texte du *Tractatus*," 196, 199–200, 204; Van de Ven, *Printing Spinoza*, 347–8, 360.

[14] Spinoza, *Opera Posthuma*, 590–1; Spinoza, *Nagelate Schriften*, 643; Spinoza, *Collected Works* (ed. Curley) ii, 437.

[15] Akkerman, *Studies*, 45–6; Steenbakkers, *Spinoza's Ethica*, 16; Klever, "Clé d'un nom," 172–5; Proietti and Licata, *Il Carteggio*, 33–5, 40–1.

1687, over what Huygens considered a mathematical error in Tschirnhaus' book, *Medicina Mentis* (1687), Van Gent tried, unsuccessfully, to mediate.[16]

Glazemaker had at his disposal the earlier Dutch renderings of Part I and Part II of *The Ethics* prepared by Balling in 1664–5; but it is still remarkable that he translated the rest into Dutch as fast and accurately as he did.[17] In the days when Balling worked on the text, as far as we know, the book was not yet called the *Ethics*. The earliest recorded instance of Spinoza calling his masterpiece by its eventual name occurs in a letter to Van Blijenbergh of 13 March 1665.[18] But even subsequently, in June 1665, for instance, when suspending work on the now quite advanced text and turning to compose the *TTP*, Spinoza still referred to it, in a letter, as "my *Philosophia*."[19] Whether doubts still lingered about the title in 1677 remains an unanswered issue.[20] There remains some question too as to how the three substantial unfinished works received their titles—Spinoza's last text, the *Tractatus Politicus*, the *Tractatus de Intellectus Emendatione*, and finally the *Hebrew Grammar* which seems to have been tacked on as an afterthought, inserted at the end, after the index had already been printed and given separate pagination from the rest.[21] There is no indication Spinoza ever called the *TIE* or the *Hebrew Grammar* by the names the editors gave them, though he may have done so. Nor is there any instance of the *TIE* being called by the title it eventually received by any of the editors or "friends" before the *Opera Posthuma* appeared.[22]

An especially onerous task for Meyer, Bouwmeester, and Van Gent was checking, editing, polishing, and in places correcting Spinoza's Latin. Collaborating in a group project, the editors agreed to present and interpret the whole mass of Spinoza's writing, including his correspondence, bundled together as a single unified corpus, a supposedly integrated system of thought, of which all his writings formed part, lending expression to this unifying approach by appending a long and detailed *Index Rerum* (to the Latin version only) designed to label and interweave all Spinoza's themes and topics together. Revealingly, they did this in a deliberately combative, slanted, and provocative manner highly illustrative of their group ideology. Thus, under "mind" the Index states "mens et corpus idem sunt [mind and body are the same thing]" and under "justice" and "injustice" that these are non-existent in the "state of nature." "Pharisees" are designated "predecessors of the Roman Church," and Francis Bacon as "Bacon of Verulamium, his philosophical errors noted." The term "atheists" appears with a distinctly Spinozist

---

[16] Klever, "Clé d'un nomme," 170; Vermij, "Spinozisme en Hollande," 156–7; Strazzoni, *Burchard de Volder*, 87.
[17] Akkerman, "Glazemaker, an Early Translator," 26; Akkerman, *Studies*, 127–8.
[18] Spinoza, *Briefwisseling*, 207.   [19] Spinoza, *Briefwisseling*, 219.
[20] Spruit and Totaro, "Introduction," 4.
[21] Spinoza, *Opera Posthuma*, 685, 688–9; Nadler, "Aliquid remanet," 162.
[22] Tschirnhaus to Leibniz, Rome, 10 April 1678 in Leibniz, *Sämtliche Schriften und Briefe* 2nd ser. i, 406; Mignini, "Texte du *Tractatus*," 191.

twist, as persons who "seek honours and wealth [honores et divitias quaerunt]."[23] Among subheadings under Christ, the Index designates Christ's "resurrection" something to be understood only "allegorically," a point repeated further down under "resurrectio Christi," while Christ's nature is "where justice and charity are, there Christ is [ubi Justitia et charitas est, ibi Christus est]."[24]

Spinoza's name was purposely omitted from the title-page. "The name of our author," explains Jelles in his preface, "is given on the title-page of the volume only in the form of his initials," B.d.S. This, he explains, was "for no other reason than that shortly before he died, Spinoza himself expressed the wish that his name not be placed over his *Ethics* which he wanted printed," without however giving any reason for this decision. Spinoza, according to Jelles and his co-editors, "did not want his teaching to be named after him." To explain this, Jelles directs the reader to the appendix of *Ethics* Part IV where Spinoza holds that desire to offer something that is useful "is determined by reason" and linked to "piety" but potentially tied also to "ambition, or the desire by which men, under an imagined false piety, usually stir up discord and sedition." Those truly seeking to help others by good counsel or their actions "so that all may enjoy the highest good," will seek to win "their love and not draw them into admiration; accordingly, a system of thought should not bear [the author's] name, nor give the slightest cause for envy."[25]

Rieuwertsz opted to use the same printers for both the Latin and Dutch versions and, having learnt to trust Israel de Paull's discretion, ruses, and efficiency in producing successive clandestine editions of the *TTP*, turned to him again to typeset and print both language versions.[26] For ten months, Spinoza's philosophical legacy to the world, the result of his lifelong battle against religious oppression and the authorities, and the fate of Rieuwertsz's publishing business, were suspended by a thread in a precarious, highly vulnerable state, in an obscure workshop in a not particularly salubrious part of Amsterdam. If not an open secret, the *Ethics*' existence was nevertheless quite widely known, having been confidentially discussed and cited by those in the know in London, Paris, Hanover, and Rome as well as The Hague and Amsterdam, and was rumoured to exist much more widely. Leibniz in Hanover, Justel and Leibniz's other friends in Paris, including Thévenot, along with Steno and others in Italy, all possessed a fairly accurate notion of what was afoot and of the contents of the pending bombshell, as did Oldenburg, in England, though he died on 5 September 1677, six months after Spinoza, and hence well before the *Opera Posthuma* appeared.

---

[23] Spinoza, *Opera Posthuma*, 658, 678; Rovere, "Présentation," 82, 84, 100–1.
[24] Spinoza, *Opera Posthuma*, 659, 681.
[25] Spinoza, *Opera* ii, 272–3; Spinoza, *Oeuvres* iv, 442–3.
[26] Jagersma and Dijkstra, "Uncovering Spinoza's Printers," 293–5; Van Eeghen, *Amsterdamse boekhandel* iii, 142–3 and v, 381.

As the Reformed Church councils of The Hague and Amsterdam, and the Walloon synod, also had some inkling of what was brewing and were resolved to do all in their power to prevent its publication, maximum wariness and caution on the part of the editorial team was essential. Besides Reformed ministers, others too would soon be drawn into what became a concerted international effort to stifle Spinoza's philosophy at birth. The challenge confronting those avid to quash Spinoza's philosophy was how to locate where the manuscripts were hidden, who had possession of them and what kind of clandestine effort was in progress to publish them. The risks Rieuwertsz and the others were running increased as the weeks passed. By the late summer, a sizeable additional group, including several artisan printers knew of the project which of itself entailed increased risk for all. Had the clues gathered by those aiming to suppress Spinoza's legacy been gathered and acted on in time, curtailing the threat and destroying the venture for good would not have been especially difficult. The very real possibility of permanent destruction of the larger part of Spinoza's legacy can be appreciated from the fact that none of the original manuscripts of the *Ethics* and little of the rest of the material gathered for the production process survived for long subsequently.

Besides the Reformed Church consistories, others too were ready to intervene forcefully if they could find sufficient evidence as to where the repository of evil they hoped to extirpate was located. Especially menacing was the effort initiated by one of Spinoza's principal friends of earlier years, Steno who, having exchanged science for faith and become a priest, now stood high in the Catholic hierarchy. Shortly before leaving for northern Germany, in September 1677, after the papacy appointed him "Vicar-Apostolic to the duke of Brunswick-Lüneburg," and more generally to (Protestant) northern Germany and Denmark, Steno, aware that the Holy Office already knew from others of "the damage done [to religion] by the new philosophy through a certain Spinoza in Holland," submitted a formal written indictment denouncing Spinoza to the papal Inquisition in Rome, dated 4 September 1677. Ironically, this was shortly before Steno moved to Hanover and conducted lengthy discussions with Leibniz who at that pivotal moment, still several months before publication, was among the few who knew more about the *Opera Posthuma*'s current state of progress than Steno and was likewise closely following the fate of Spinoza's legacy, information Leibniz seemingly concealed from Steno. Still more ironically, when Leibniz and Steno first met that September, they disagreed about practically everything except the overriding importance of defending Christianity against the "atheistic" threat posed by Spinoza.

Leibniz doubtless did tell Steno, for this was generally known at the Hanoverian court, that three months before Spinoza's death, in November 1676, he and Spinoza had met in The Hague and conversed "several times and at great length."[27] Taken

---

[27] Leibniz to Jean Gallois, undated Hanover, Sept. 1677 in Leibniz, *Sämtliche Schriften und Briefe* 2nd ser. i, 379; Laerke, *Leibniz lecteur*, 107n, 369.

aback and undoubtedly worried by what he had thus far gathered of Spinoza's ideas and project, Leibniz nevertheless withheld from Steno confidential details about Spinoza's plans that Schuller and Tschirnhaus had confided to him and that might well otherwise have led to the permanent extinction of Spinoza's philosophy. Himself a philosopher and amongst the greatest of all time, Leibniz proved less than enthusiastic about Steno's mission to wholly obliterate Spinoza's legacy due, one supposes, in part to philosophical curiosity and perhaps a touch of the uncertainty to which he later admitted, some corner of his innermost self somehow uneasily suspecting that Spinoza might be right after all. Despite rejecting some of Spinoza's key tenets, Leibniz by no means rejected them all and was privately wrestling within himself over what he had gleaned thus far of Spinoza's system. Hence, he was not among those avid to erase a legacy he had not yet fully studied and pondered.[28] As for Steno, Leibniz considered it unfortunate that he had abandoned science for faith, judging him a great scientist but exasperatingly mediocre theologian.

Steno submitted his indictment of Spinoza in Rome, in September 1677, moved, he explained, by the increasing gravity of the situation and because "the danger of this evil being propagated is so momentous." He urged the Inquisition to spare no effort to uncover who had possession of the manuscript of the *Ethics* and was planning its publication, and take countermeasures to prevent Spinoza's ideas spreading and, no less important, "as far as possible heal those already poisoned thereby."[29] He himself had formerly been friendly with and interacted with Spinoza in Holland during the early 1660s and knew this ex-Jew had subsequently published several books, "some under his own name, others anonymously." The latter, he informed the Inquisition, included the *Tractatus Theologico-Politicus* which provoked a tremendous outcry in Holland and Germany in the early 1670s, and had profoundly shocked him, prompting him to compose a lengthy letter of rebuke which (whether or not he actually sent it to him at the time) he later published, at Florence in 1675, as an open letter. In this published version, though, Steno took scrupulous care to preserve his former friend's anonymity, concealing everything about him, styling his remonstrance a "Letter from Nicholas Steno to the Reformer of the New Philosophy." But now, the situation had changed for the worse and he felt he must identify this pernicious influence to the Inquisition and explain that this subversive interpreter of contemporary science, unnamed in 1675, who was so dire a menace to church and faith was this same malignant reformer of Cartesianism, this "certain Spinoza."[30]

"Although all his printed works show signs of his basic intentions," lately the threat to religion that he posed, Steno assured the Inquisitors, had become more

---

[28] Leibniz, *Theodicy*, 178; Totaro, "Steno in Italy," 281–2.
[29] Steno, "Denunciation of Spinoza's Philosophy," 68; Proietti and Licata, *Il Carteggio*, 400.
[30] Laerke, *Leibniz lecteur*, 107–8; Kardel and Maquet, *Nicolaus Steno*, 251.

serious because in the early stages of his philosophical career Spinoza sought to mask the radical character of his views by mixing "these up with views he did not share, thereby avoiding the risk of making himself too clear, as he did afterwards in certain manuscripts he composed." In his later work, though, Spinoza expressed himself all too clearly especially in the large manuscript in question [*The Ethics*], a venomous new work that Spinoza might have published already, "before his death [in 1675], if some of his confidants had not warned him of the risk to which he would be exposing himself."[31] This information Steno presumably had from Tschirnhaus who remained in close contact with Spinoza down to the latter's death as well as with Leibniz and Schuller. For in Rome, during mid-August 1677, shortly before Steno appealed to the Inquisition to act, Steno and Tschirnhaus met together and discussed religion intensively, just as did Leibniz and Steno soon afterwards. No one ever tried so hard, recalled Tschirnhaus later, to convert him to Catholicism as did Steno that August; Steno strove his utmost to wheedle out of Tschirnhaus also all the useful leads and information regarding Spinoza that he could.[32]

Steno knew of the existence of the *Ethics* long before learning, in August 1677, that Spinoza's principal work in manuscript was now clandestinely being prepared for publication. But until recently, he assured the Inquisition, he had never actually seen this uniquely pernicious text, nor possessed detailed knowledge of its contents. "Until some weeks ago [i.e. in August] when I happened to be here [in Rome]" discussing "religion with a Lutheran foreigner [Tschirnhaus]" whom he left unnamed, he had possessed only the sketchiest notion of the dark menace looming. "After several conversations," this Lutheran, "brought me a manuscript without revealing the identity of its author, begging me however not to show it to others, nor inform them that he [Tschirnhaus] holds similar views." Since his own conversion, Steno had spent much of his time, both in Florence and in Rome, the Grand Duke's librarian, Antonio Magliabecchi, informed the archbishop of Florence, in November 1671, seeking to draw both Protestants and Jews deep into discussion, perfecting his quiet, unyielding knack of gaining the confidence of such persons while passionately imploring them to abandon their beliefs and views and seek salvation in the Catholic faith.[33]

Although Tschirnhaus had been in Rome since late May 1677, it took time for Steno to win his confidence and little by little coax him into finally letting him see the manuscript of the *Ethics*. Once Steno had it in his own hands, he refused to relinquish it until he handed it over to the Inquisition, in late September, over half a year after Spinoza's demise, just weeks before clandestine distribution of the

---

[31] Steno, "Denunciation of Spinoza's Philosophy,"69.
[32] Proietti and Licata, *Il Carteggio*, 399; Scherz, "Biography of Nicolaus Steno," 337; Totaro, "The Young Spinoza and the Vatican Manuscript," 322-3.
[33] Proietti and Licata, *Il Carteggio*, 398-9; Totaro, "Steno in Italy," 274-5, 279.

printed *Opera Posthuma* began. Initially, sticking to his vow, Steno remained discreetly silent, keeping his solemn promise to Tschirnhaus to say nothing about the manuscript, "not imagining," he explained, "the grave evil I would discover when reading the book which I inferred"—and the unnamed Lutheran confessed—"to be by Spinoza." The shock Steno experienced on studying the manuscript arose not from discovering it contained his former friend's philosophy—he knew already that Spinoza's thought subverts faith—but finding how alluring his system was, and the gravity of the intellectual challenge it poses, its insidious implications for belief, tradition, society, morality, theology and church authority everywhere. "I always now carry the manuscript with me so that no one may by chance come into contact with the poison that it contains." Once fully aware, Steno knew his religious duty greatly outweighed his promise to Tschirnhaus. Thus, he made up his mind to "contribute all I can to the glory of God and prevent great harm."

Slightly embarrassed, even so, by his own former closeness to Spinoza and the need to wipe clean this blemish from his past,[34] Steno detailed for the Inquisitors "the main doctrines of this infidel tendency and the way in which further information about similar writings and the persons adhering to it might be gathered." Effective repressive action by the Church was needed not just to quash Spinoza, his books and ideas, but also the dangerous intellectual circle gathering around him that now constituted a well-established underground movement. In fact the major threat was less Spinoza and his books, or any book, than this group movement, or sect. Spinoza had founded an intellectual conspiracy fed by these men's "pretentious overestimation of their intellects and thirst for sensual pleasure," their insistence on the logic of mathematics and science being the sole measure of truth, making their own intellects the measure of everything so that they reject whatever "they cannot form a clear and distinct conception of," an attitude threatening, as Leibniz likewise recognized, everything most people believe and the entire existing educational, legal, and moral order.

Spinoza's adherents taught that "true wisdom consists in enjoying the pleasures of each sense and hence those of the theatre," fine food, and suchlike, as well as "other sensual enjoyments provided these cause no harm to themselves or others. Enjoying life in an intellectual and sensual way, they perceive no need to think of penance, fear God or in other ways sadden the soul." Steno next explained Spinoza's doctrine of "one substance, infinite and eternal," the equivalence of this one substance with God, and resulting from this doctrine, the group's denial of divine providence and freedom of choice in God, along with immortality of the soul and reward and punishment in the hereafter. Proclaiming the necessity of all that happens to be in accord with the laws of mathematics, and their political ideas

---

[34] Totaro, "Steno in Italy," 279; Totaro, "The Young Spinoza and the Vatican Manuscript," 322.

based on the primacy of individual security within civil society and personal happiness, along with general toleration and the need for the civil magistracy to preside over all other institutions and authority, would eradicate all religious authority, thereby destroying church sway over society and the individual.[35] A great deal was direly menaced by Spinoza and his system, the Church and Inquisition most of all.

Rather than returning the manuscript of the *Ethics* to Tschirnhaus as promised, Steno, accordingly, transferred it to the Inquisition. The copy Steno submitted was not a fresh copy, made from Tschirnhaus' manuscript, recent research proving the hand to be that of Van Gent who undoubtedly prepared it for Tschirnhaus in late 1674 or early 1675, before Tschirnhaus left the Netherlands that July. The copy the Inquisition now placed in its files was thus definitely Tschirnhaus' own copy and hence approximately three years older than the first published version of the *Ethics*. The closeness of the manuscript archived in Rome to the published text of 1677 with mostly just a few minor alterations in wording, proves Spinoza added practically nothing to the *Ethics* during the last two years of his life, and that the editors nearly always (with remarkably few exceptions) adhered strictly to Spinoza's wording.[36]

After careful examination, the Inquisition filed Tschirnhaus' manuscript away in its archives, where it was forgotten for centuries, until transferred, in 1922, from the Inquisition archives to the Vatican Library. But instead of being catalogued as the sole known surviving manuscript of the *Ethics*, a status restored to it only in the twenty-first century, this unique manuscript lay buried, obscurely catalogued as a "theological treatise" that "the Bishop Vicar Apostolic Nicolaus Stenonus left with the Congregation of the Holy Office [The Inquisition] on 23 September 1677."[37] Scholarship only finally recovered the manuscript in 2010, hence 333 years after Steno submitted it! In this way, what began as the Inquisition's drive to suppress Spinoza's *Ethics* for good, in the end ironically turned out to be an inadvertent insurance policy safeguarding the existence until today of what might easily have become the sole preserved copy.

The philosophical sect and intellectual reform movement Spinoza established, Steno added, liked to divide mankind into two categories, the great mass who "possess only confused knowledge and are driven by the passions," encompassing the vast majority, "and the other class that possesses adequate knowledge and is no slave of the appetites, but follows reason." This latter furtive underground fraternity were sworn to undertake what a later age would call a mission of "enlightenment," or, as Steno expressed their objective, "pretend that by providing

---

[35] Steno, "Denunciation of Spinoza's Philosophy," 70; Spruit and Totaro, *Vatican Manuscript*, 11–12.

[36] Totaro, "The Young Spinoza and the Vatican Manuscript," 324; Van de Ven, *Printing Spinoza*, 340, 394.

[37] Spruit and Totaro, *Vatican Manuscript*, 26–7; Proietti and Licata, *Il Carteggio*, 64.

mankind with adequate knowledge, they will transform men from slaves into free individuals even though they confess this is difficult and not for everyone – while, in truth," retorted Steno, "it is for no one." Spinoza's disciples, like Tschirnhaus and others whom he knew personally, esteemed themselves highly as devotees of freedom and knowledge, but Steno was far from sharing their lofty view of themselves. "Quite the contrary. Less than three years ago during my travels, I paid a visit to one of them [in Holland] whom I had got to know many years earlier [Meyer?]; I found him smoking a pipe encircled by glasses of wine and beer." Despite being amazed at the change in Steno's ideas since the days he was Spinoza's friend in the early 1660s, this veteran propagator of Spinozist venom remained quite unperturbed, convinced "there exist no virtues more perfect than his own," which Steno dismissed as mere "half-drunken boasting."[38]

Abandoning the science and Cartesian philosophy he had once enthusiastically embraced, and kneeling before Christ, Steno termed "leaving the road to perdition and taking the path of salvation."[39] Given the gravity of the crisis looming, he urged his colleagues at the Vatican to embark on something more systematic than mere outright repression of texts and books. Churchmen must, rather, reach out from Rome, as he strove to do, and whenever a colleague "encounters someone interested in mathematics and Cartesian philosophy who has studied for a time in Holland or England, gain that person's confidence and elicit information from him about these new ideas and those interested in the new philosophical doctrines," so as, in this way, to assemble a broader picture of the looming contagion. For adherents of Spinoza's teaching are always greatly captivated by the world of science. "Followers of this infidelity or apostasy," he explained, by thinking they are reforming existing philosophy, ethics, religion, science, and political thought together, "place all their happiness in the enjoyment of every sense and the delights of the imagination [the arts and the theatre], and to secure this enjoyment aim to learn as many natural and mathematical truths as possible."[40]

To successfully fight Spinoza's burgeoning intellectual underground, Steno urged fellow ecclesiastics and Inquisitors to emulate the recruiting technique of Spinoza's own adherents. For whenever Spinoza's clique encounter persons who "apply themselves to such studies [as mathematics, science, and Cartesianism] they readily approach them, both to learn something new and see whether they can win them over, in the hope their philosophy will attain perfection if more persons apply themselves to it." Steno had closely observed how this abominable sect had grown since the early 1660s and how in recent years "this evil has spread widely and I know the said Spinoza while still alive, actively seeking disciples and converts, frequently received letters from England." Finally, "when pondering

---

[38] Steno, "Denunciation of Spinoza's Philosophy," 11–12, 70–1.
[39] Quoted in Totaro, "Steno in Italy," 279.
[40] Steno, "Denunciation of Spinoza's Philosophy," 11, 69.

remarks of a compatriot when I was last in my own country [Denmark, between 1672 and 1675], a compatriot who had stayed in Holland, I now recognize that the same principles found in the manuscript [of the *Ethics*]" are spreading also there. An intellectual invasion affecting all Europe as far as Scandinavia was underway, though, mercifully, Steno detected no sign of Spinoza's pernicious teaching spreading among Catholics.[41]

Rome's Inquisition heads discussed his submission and, on 18 September, Cardinal Francesco Barberini, head of the Sacred College, alerted the Catholic Vicar-Apostolic in the Netherlands, Neercassel, explaining the danger and directing him to make every effort to discover whatever he could "about a manuscript book of an atheistic character by Spinoza who was a Jew by nation" and whose works were suspected to be "very damaging to the purity of our holy Catholic faith." Neercassel should find out whether there was a new book by Spinoza in the press, or likely to be, and forward copies of Spinoza's already published works, in particular the *TTP*, to Rome.[42] Neercassel, of course, already knew a certain amount about Spinoza and his following. He promptly organized a detective team to try to locate Spinoza's manuscript legacy and identify who was planning to publish his illicit work.

Steno thus played the chief role in mobilizing Rome's efforts to suppress Spinoza's work before publication, launching this initiative in the weeks prior to setting out for Hanover where he stayed from the autumn of 1677 to 1680. Although his campaign to erase Spinoza's main legacy commenced late in the day, it cannot be said to have begun too late.[43] In Amsterdam, the clandestine editors were progressing rapidly. According to Jeroen van de Ven, who has brought research on the publication history of Spinoza's books furthest, the *Opera Posthuma* in their Latin and Dutch versions were ready to go into production and passed by the editors to the printers in Israel de Paull's workshop by late July, thus just prior to Steno's encounter with Tschirnhaus.[44] By early October 1677, printing the *Opera Posthuma*, Schuller reported to Leibniz, was nearing completion. At that point he was expecting distribution to begin within fourteen days and confided this information too to Leibniz who, once again, was urged to keep it strictly to himself since "the theologians" were now making vigorous efforts to prevent publication.[45] Getting all in readiness, though, took longer than expected, partly due to tacking on the Hebrew grammar at the last moment.

---

[41] Steno, "Denunciation of Spinoza's Philosophy," 71–2.
[42] Barberini to Neercassel, Rome, 18 Sept. 1677 in "Letters to and from Neercassel," 330–4; Orcibal, "Jansénistes face à Spinoza," 460; Totaro, "Congrégation de l'Index," 370; Totaro, "Documenti," 97, 100–3; Manusov-Verhage, "Jan Rieuwertsz, marchand," 237–8.
[43] Spruit and Totaro, *Vatican Manuscript*, 7; Totaro, "Congrégation de l'Index," 364.
[44] Van de Ven, *Printing Spinoza*, chs. 1 and 3.
[45] Schuller to Leibniz, Amsterdam, 2 (?) Oct. 1677 in Leibniz, *Sämtliche Schriften und Briefe* 2nd ser. i, 382.

Printing was now completed, Schuller reported in early November, apart from the Index and Hebrew grammar.[46]

To conduct his inquiries, Neercassel employed a churchman thoroughly familiar with Amsterdam and its undercurrents and with many contacts there, an energetic young priest, Martinus de Swaen (1651–1713), later among the leading Catholic clergy in the Republic. De Swaen assembled an impressively ecumenical detective team, including, rather remarkably for a Catholic enterprise, an unnamed rabbi and trainee Remonstrant preacher.[47] Eventually, De Swaen discovered the probable clandestine publisher was the Collegiant bookseller Jan Rieuwertsz, and Neercassel went personally to see him, demanding to know point blank whether he was editing Spinoza's manuscripts. Rieuwertsz lied to his face, denying all knowledge of such a project. Neither among the Christians nor the Jews of Amsterdam, reported Neercassel to Barberini on 25 November 1677, "have I found anyone who had seen this manuscript or knew anything about it." He had uncovered some more facts, though, he added, naively passing on misinformation with which Rieuwertsz had fobbed him off. When Spinoza died "last summer," Neercassel reported back to Rome, he left as "heir to his writings a certain Mennonite or rather Socinian bookseller of Amsterdam. This publisher, named Jan Rieuwertsz, is accustomed to publish whatever is bizarre and impious thought up by impudent and arrogant minds. This bookseller assured me that, among Spinoza's belongings he found no writings apart from some manuscript meditations on the principles of Cartesian philosophy and that [apart from his Descartes book] no other book of Spinoza's has appeared except for the *Tractatus Theologico-Politicus*."[48] Unfortunately, the *TTP* had gained renown, Neercassel explained, owing to Stouppe's book, *La Religion des Hollandois*, attributing to the *TTP*'s author a formidable knowledge of the Hebrew text of the Bible, thereby helping diffuse the poison Spinoza had introduced. Three days later, Neercassel sent the copy of the *TTP* "his eminence Barberini had desired be sent to him" to the papal nuncio in Brussels.

When interrogated by Neercassel, Rieuwertsz hence lied outright. By then, the *Opera Posthuma* was already largely printed and almost ready for surreptitious distribution. But it was a crucial moment, and Neercassel allowed himself to be put off the scent just when outright suppression might still have succeeded. He was consequently responsible for the failure of Steno's and the Inquisition's effort. By late November 1677, with the clandestine edition all but ready for distribution, the efforts to uncover its whereabouts seem to have caused much nervousness, adding to the pressures slowing the publication process down.

---

[46] Steenbakkers, *Spinoza's Ethica*, 6; Van de Ven, *Printing Spinoza*, 370.
[47] Neercassel to De Swaen, Utrecht, 31 Oct. 1677 in Orcibal, "Jansénistes face à Spinoza," 461.
[48] Neercassel to Barberini, Utrecht, 25 Nov. 1677 in Orcibal, "Jansénistes face à Spinoza," 461; Siebrand, *Spinoza and the Netherlanders*, 132–3; Manusov-Verhage, "Jan Rieuwertsz, marchand," 237.

Schuller's October announcement that distribution would begin shortly in the event proved premature by roughly two months. In late December, Schuller informed Leibniz that all was now finally ready and distribution would commence with the New Year.[49] Seemingly, it began just before year's end, in December, since word of the book's appearance already reached the papal nuncio in Brussels, Sebastian Antonio Tamara, on (new style) 3 January 1678,[50] though Schuller only finally dispatched the copy Leibniz was impatiently awaiting in Hanover in late January (Figure 41.1).

Leibniz was among the very first persons outside the Low Countries to receive the *Opera Posthuma* and to react, Schuller having forwarded it from Amsterdam via a Jewish trader heading that way, on 25 January 1678. At the same time, Schuller wrote apologizing for his failure to notice embarrassing details inadvertently left in the published text, in time to prevent their inclusion, meaning Leibniz's first letter to Spinoza, of October 1671, where Leibniz praises Spinoza's "achievements which fame has spread abroad," and his accomplishments in optics. The editors *had* deleted from both the Latin and Dutch versions the heading (restored in modern editions) where Leibniz addresses "Mr Spinoza, celebrated doctor and profound philosopher at Amsterdam," and Spinoza's postscript inviting Leibniz to continue corresponding and offering to send a copy of the *TTP* if it had "not yet reached you," but through oversight, unfortunately, failed to excise Leibniz's signing off as "Gottfridus Leibnitius, doctor in both Laws and councilor of Mainz,"[51] followed by the closing postscript "from B.d.S." to "Gottfr. Leibnits"—no small lapse on Schuller's part.[52]

Leibniz had no wish for it to be known that he had approached, praised, and stayed in contact with a personage now the focus of unprecedented condemnation and vilification everywhere in Lutheran as in Calvinist and Catholic Germany. Removing all reference to himself in the projected volume had stood high on the list of responsibilities entrusted to Schuller. Schuller hoped Leibniz would not be too angry, though, as the offending letter dealt almost entirely with mathematical aspects of optics rather than broader issues.[53] Though doubtless relieved the potentially most damaging mentions of himself in Spinoza's correspondence had been removed, like Schuller's styling Leibniz "free from the common theological prejudices" in his letter of November 1675, and someone who "thinks highly of the *Tractatus Theologico-Politicus*," Schuller's negligence assuredly

---

[49] Schuller to Leibniz, Amsterdam, 31 Dec. 1677 in Stein, *Leibniz und Spinoza*, 291; Steenbakkers, *Spinoza's* Ethica, 6.
[50] Orcibal, "Jansénistes face à Spinoza," 67–8, 80; Steenbakkers, "Textual History," 36; Mignini holds to January 1678 in Mignini, "Introduction au *Tractatus*," 35.
[51] Gottfr. Leibnits to B.d.S., Frankfurt, 5 Oct. 1671 in B.d.S. to Gottfr. Leibnits, undated in *Nagelate Schriften*, 612; Spinoza, *Collected Works* (ed. Curley) ii, 395.
[52] B.d.S. to Gottfr. Leibnits, undated in *Nagelate Schriften*, 613–14.
[53] Schuller to Leibniz, Amsterdam, 6 Feb. 1678 in Stein, *Leibniz und Spinoza*, 291–2; Laerke, *Leibniz lecteur*, 572.

Figure 41.1 [Benedictus de Spinoza]. *B.d.S. Opera* Posthuma. [Amsterdam], 1677. IAS Spinoza Research Collection.

annoyed Leibniz, especially as Schuller's own name, like those of Tschirnhaus and various others, was deleted without any slip in either the *Opera Posthuma* or *Nagelate Schriften* throughout both versions.[54]

---

[54] Stewart's account wrongly assumes this 1675 letter *was* included in the *Opera Posthuma*, Stewart, *Courtier and the Heretic*, 218.

Embarrassed by his failure at the last moment to trap the Socinian publisher, and intercept Spinoza's *Opera Posthuma* when it was still possible to suppress it, Neercassel was far from prompt in reporting what had gone amiss, or even informing the Holy Office of his failure. He did gather more information though. To the secretary of the papal delegation gathering for the international peace conference at Nijmegen, in September 1678, nearly a year after Rome had first instructed him to act, he reported that Spinoza, now a notorious author rejecting belief in reward or punishment in the hereafter, had died at The Hague the previous year from "pthesis" and was "a disciple" of Franciscus Van den Enden, executed for high treason at the Bastille, the ex-Jesuit schoolmaster turned atheist who, since 1674, had become a notorious figure in his own right, especially in France, for plotting against Louis XIV. Soon afterwards, Neercassel sent the papal secretary a copy also of the *Opera Posthuma* for forwarding to Rome together with a letter for Cardinal Barberini explaining that "when I interrogated him about his not yet published works [...] the bookseller whom Spinoza the Jew made heir to his unpublished writings, lied boldly so as not to be prevented from publishing them. In fact, the posthumous works of Spinoza the dissemination of which the discerning solicitude of your Eminence sought to prevent, did actually appear some time ago."[55]

Neercassel's belated account of his failure was read out to the Congregation of the Holy Office, in Rome, on 12 October 1678. Nothing further could be done by the Inquisitors to block propagation of what Neercassel termed Spinoza's "deism" rather than "atheism," except ensure reading Spinoza remained permanently forbidden to all Catholics. The *TTP* already appeared on the papal Index on 16 November 1678. The Inquisition took longer, though, to appraise the *Opera Posthuma*, and only after further investigation of Spinoza's ideas and writings did the Holy Office formally condemn *B.d.S. Opera Posthuma* under a ban published in February 1679, two years after Spinoza's death, further solemnized in March 1679 and renewed in 1690, now expressly including the *Tractatus Politicus* and the *Letters*.[56]

Meanwhile, the *Opera Posthuma* was distributed widely. In around 1680, as a memento of Spinoza, Rieuwertsz arranged the preparation of an engraving from a painted portrait by an unknown artist that one of the friends possessed, making available the resulting printed portrait for binding into copies of the *Opera Posthuma* and the *Nagelate Schriften*, for customers wanting it included (Figure 41.2). This printed portrait provided the correct dates for Spinoza's birth and death and bore a caption assuring readers it was a good likeness of

---

[55] Neercassel to Barberini, 13 Sept. 1678 in Orcibal, "Jansénistes face à Spinoza," 85; Manusov-Verhage, "Jan Rieuwertsz, marchand," 238; Spruit and Totaro, *Vatican Manuscript*, 23.

[56] *Index librorum prohibitorum Benedicti*, 262; Totaro, "Congrégation de l'Index," 361–2; Spruit and Totaro, *Vatican Manuscript*, 23–4; Mori, *L'ateismo dei moderni*, 39.

Figure 41.2 *Spinoza*. Reproduction courtesy of BTEU/RKMLGE/Alamy Stock Photo.

Spinoza but that his writings reflect Spinoza's whole person and mind more accurately still. Rieuwertsz's published engraving then became the standard portrait of Spinoza known throughout the Enlightenment era and subsequently. Around twenty or more copies of the engraved portrait bound into the Latin version survive today bearing the Latin verse eulogy underneath, while another eleven or so, bound into copies of the *Nagelate Schriften*, bear a Dutch version of the eulogizing verse caption on paper slips pasted over the printed Latin caption.[57]

41.ii Spinoza's Circle after 1677

It was thus during the year following Spinoza's death, that his philosophy finally, if elusively, crashed through the barriers onto the European stage. Through their 1677 clandestine efforts, his Amsterdam circle succeeded in at last connecting Spinoza's philosophical system to his subversive critique of religion, politics, and the Bible and broadcasting his overall system to the world in the vernacular as well as Latin. Not the least disturbing feature of the *Opera Posthuma* was its simultaneous appearance in Latin and Dutch, lending fresh impetus to the spread of Spinozism as a transformative world view available to all, helping consolidate the existence of an underground movement observed by the Dutch Reformed synods, as by Steno, with acute unease. A few years later, the dogged Van Blijenbergh further added to their discomfort with his *Refutation of the* Ethica *or Moral Science of Benedictus de Spinoza* [*Wederlegging van de Ethica of Zede-kunst van Benedictus van Spinosa*] (Dordrecht, 1682), a 354-page work focusing on Spinoza's views about substance, modes, God, and the human soul, again quoting verbatim numerous key propositions, doctrines, and quotations from Spinoza in accessible, straightforward Dutch. Van Blijenbergh accused Spinoza of seeking to deprive man of his free will and deprive God of all understanding and will and thereby overthrow all religion and theology and replace these, directly contrary to Descartes, with mathematical science-based philosophy as the exclusive source of truth.[58] As before with the *TTP*, Van Blijenbergh acknowledged the importance of not drawing attention to Spinoza's ideas but identified an even more urgent need, as it seemed to him, to exonerate Descartes and the Cartesians in the eyes of everyone. For him, this need outweighed the obvious danger of further diffusing awareness of Spinoza's philosophy. Spinozism wrecks the existing order by separating ethics and morality from religion, and projecting a purely humanistic moral order for mankind by attempting, unconvincingly in Van Blijenbergh's view, to anchor an ethics solely "philosophical and natural," defying the reality that Christianity teaches men morality and virtue far more effectively.[59]

Spinozism's emergence as a world-shaping force in 1677 was thus the work of Spinoza *and* his circle, not any one individual. Yet, as individuals in their own right, not one of Spinoza's key allies, not even Koerbagh or Tschirnhaus, succeeded at all in becoming significant voices on the international philosophical

---

[57] Steenbakkers, "Spinoza's Life," 49n36; Van de Ven, *Printing Spinoza*, 383–4.
[58] Blijenbergh, *Wederlegging van de Ethica*, 128, 216.
[59] Blijenbergh, *Wederlegging van de Ethica*, 352–4.

stage. Bouwmeester died early, in around his forty-seventh year, in October 1680, notorious locally, but unknown to the wider world, his personal library of 1,112 books, auctioned in April 1681, including two copies of the *TTP*, the *Opera Posthuma*, Spinoza's Descartes book, Meyer's *Philosophia*, and Van Mansvelt's refutation.[60] Meyer too outlived Spinoza by only a few years, dying in Amsterdam, in November 1681, his (or their) authorship of the *Philosophia* remaining generally unknown, while he never completed or published the project for a universal grammar. Jelles pressed on with his "pursuit of truth," as he had for over thirty years, dying at around sixty-three in like obscurity, six years after Spinoza, in 1683. Cuffeler, mentioned in a letter of Van Gent's of 1683 as a "very close friend" of Spinoza, lived on in The Hague until 1694, but his Spinozistic *Specimen artis ratiocinandi* (1684), though noted by Bayle, Howe, and a few others abroad, made little impact. Dying in 1692, Van Balen too remained unknown outside the Republic.

The Reformed, Lutheran, Anglican, and Catholic churches were not alone in their furiously negative reaction. During the 1680s and 1690s, a bitter reaction developed also within the ranks of the Collegiant movement, not only against Spinozism but against "modern" philosophy more generally. Until his death in 1683, Jelles doggedly persisted in arguing for his Socinian Christian perspective on Spinoza's life and philosophy, but the radical rationalist strain he represented had boxed itself into an impossible corner. Only by rejecting rationalizing "new" philosophy altogether, it seemed to some, could the threat of Spinozism be effectively erased. This caused the incipient rift between Socinianism and Radical Enlightenment among the Collegiant movement to widen and exacerbate noticeably in these years, though the Collegiants remained more accommodating to radical ideas than other churches.[61]

Van Gent and Schuller remained close friends for just one more year after Spinoza's demise. From May 1678, these two veteran Spinoza disciples began quarrelling bitterly.[62] Van Gent accused Schuller of thoroughgoing dishonesty; Schuller labelled Van Gent an unreliable drunkard. For his part, Tschirnhaus, doubtless embarrassed by losing his copy of the *Ethics* to Steno, and his unwitting role in the Inquisition's offensive against Spinoza, returned to Holland in 1679, and again in 1682 and 1685, renewing his ties with Amsterdam, his Dutch friends, and personal memories of Spinoza. When Schuller died, in September 1679, and was buried in the Amsterdam Oude Kerk, Van Gent took his place as anchor-man linking Tschirnhaus, when back at his family manor house at Kieslingswalde (today Sławnickowice), in Silesia, with Spinoza's circle in Holland. Their collaboration continued until the mid-1680s. It was Van Gent who took charge of editing

---

[60] I am indebted to Van de Ven for this information, see Van de Ven, *Documenting Spinoza*, ch. 7.
[61] Van Bunge, *Johannes Bredenburg*, 181–215; Fix, *Prophecy and Reason*, 215–31.
[62] Proietti and Licata, *Il Carteggio*, 25; Stewart, *Courtier and the Heretic*, 212–13.

Tschirnhaus' principal work, the *Medicina Mentis*, or "proofs of the upright art of reasoning in which is shown the right way to discover unknown truths," a text published in Amsterdam in Latin and soon, under the title *Geneesmiddel der Ziele*, also in Dutch. It was translated by Ameldonck Block (or Blok, c.1651–1702), an Amsterdam Mennonite silk merchant and member of *Nil Volentibus Arduum*, a competent and erudite translator who was yet another member of the circle of Schuller, Van Gent, and Tschirnhaus, and also a brother-in-law of Simon Joosten's surviving sister, Trijntje Joosten de Vries (c.1631–1701).[63]

On their title-pages, both versions of *Medicina Mentis* are dated 1687, though the Latin actually appeared in 1686. Both versions were published by Jan Rieuwertsz the Younger, but only after prolonged delays and what, to Tschirnhaus, was inexcusable bungling on Van Gent's part. Learned or not, and good Latinist or not, after transcribing Spinoza's Latin texts from his manuscripts, Van Gent failed utterly, not only in his medical career and, subsequently, as a Latin teacher, but even as an editor. Increasingly falling on hard times financially despite receiving some support, it seems, from his friend Jarig Jelles, and in emotional distress, he grew ever more erratic. As his personal difficulties mounted, especially from around 1685, Tschirnhaus took to ignoring Van Gent's repeated pleas to put him up for a time at his Silesian country manor. His former friend, Ameldonck Block, whose impressive book collection, auctioned at the time of his death, included all Spinoza's works in both their Latin and Dutch versions, beside those of Meyer, the Koerbaghs, Cuffeler, Overkamp, the Brothers De La Court, and Sandius, *Philopater* and the refutations of Henry More and many others, unquestionably among the most stunning collections of *Spinozana* of the age,[64] replaced him as principal link with Kieslingswalde. Finally, in 1688, to escape his creditors, Van Gent fled Amsterdam to Vianen, near Utrecht, where he died friendless, bankrupt, and reportedly in despair, in late 1693.[65]

Tschirnhaus too failed in his personal aspirations. If he finally succeeded in causing a minor stir with the work he had been discussing for over a decade with Spinoza, other Dutch friends and Leibniz, his book's publication brought Tschirnhaus neither the recognition for which he hoped, nor much satisfaction. Even though much of his text is mathematical, he and the Amsterdam circle considered it necessary to bring both versions out anonymously, unfortunate though this was, as well as to avoid all direct reference to Spinoza and their circle.[66] Accordingly, *Medicina Mentis* (1687) lavishly praises Descartes, making him centre of attention, leaving Spinoza unmentioned. But although neither title-page carries the author's name, Tschirnhaus, unwilling to remain wholly invisible,

---

[63] Van de Ven, *Printing Spinoza*, 438; Mertens, "Where Thou Dwellest," 35–6.
[64] *Bibliotheca Blockiana sive Catalogus Librorum... Ameldonck Block*; I am grateful to Jeroen van de Ven for drawing this document to my attention.
[65] Proietti and Licata, *Il Carteggio*, 26, 28–30.   [66] Bamberger, "Early Editions," 33n72.

slipped in a dedication initialled E.W.D.T. which proved unwise as, for those with eyes to see, Spinoza was far from really absent from the text.[67] "Virtue," holds Tschirnhaus, is "a person's power, following the laws of sound reason, to sustain his nature and achieve all the true perfections of mind and body"; equally, "virtue" one may define as the "improvement of our nature by following the laws of right reason."[68] The terms "joy" and "happiness" Tschirnhaus employed with striking frequency while making no reference whatever to Christ, Christian doctrine, or church teaching.

Medicina Mentis is one of the first instances of a large work of modern metaphysics and moral philosophy, including analysis of the mind, wholly eschewing all mention of religion, theology, immortality of the soul, and the Bible. It clearly reflects Spinoza's centrality in modern Western thought, yet only cryptically, without citing Spinoza's name, even where directly referring to Spinoza's 1663 text on Descartes' principles which Tschirnhaus cites only as by a "certain author." Elsewhere, he borrows phrases from Spinoza's *Ethics* sometimes almost word for word, paraphrasing Spinoza without acknowledging the derivation,[69] or else obliquely alluding to Spinoza as his model.[70] Inhibited and deeply cautious, Tschirnhaus' book is indeed a classic illustration of why twentieth- and twenty-first century philosophers and historians encounter so much difficulty in grasping the centrality and profound pervasiveness of Spinoza's thought in the late seventeenth and eighteenth century.

Word that it was Tschirnhaus who authored the *Medicina Mentis* percolated through to the German universities nevertheless, bringing him only recrimination and trouble. The "anonymous" author found himself vehemently but not inaccurately assailed for championing *Epikurismus* and, by implication, *Spinozismus*, notably in a journal article of March 1688 by the eminent jurist Christian Thomasius (1636–1711), son of Leibniz's old mentor, Jakob Thomasius, a moderate reformer campaigning for the right to lecture in German instead of Latin who was himself under fire from Lutheran conservatives. For Thomasius, a standard-bearer of toleration and freedom of expression but strictly on a "moderate Enlightenment basis," the inviolable red line, the absolute forbidden limit of acceptable toleration beyond which no one is permitted to tread, is questioning core Christian belief. Spinozism, he contended, can never be tolerated anywhere by any state, society, or church. Here, without mentioning Spinoza's name, Thomasius denounced Tschirnhaus for separating ethics wholly from theology and presenting a methodology geared exclusively to the pursuit of earthly happiness. The resulting negative publicity and insinuation of Spinozist heresy led

---

[67] Tschirnhaus, *Medicina Mentis*, 37; Zaunick, "Ehrenfried Walther von Tschirnhaus," 13, 291; Wurtz, "Introduction," 15–17; Vermij, "Spinozisme en Hollande," 162–4.
[68] Tschirnhaus, *Medicina Mentis*, 101; Wurtz, "Tschirnhaus und die Spinozabeschuldigung," 67–8.
[69] Tschirnhaus, *Medicina mentis* (1687), 52, 96.
[70] Tschirnhaus, *Medicina mentis* (1687), 199; Israel, *Radical Enlightenment*, 638–41.

Tschirnhaus to retaliate with harsh words of his own. But his book did transgress the limits of toleration as understood by Thomasius and the early German moderate Enlightenment. Thomasius' aspersions continued to cast a shadow, even in his relatively remote Silesian vicinity, over the rest of Tschirnhaus' life.[71]

In stark contrast to the Koerbaghs, Meyer, Tschirnhaus, Cuffeler, and Van Balen, Spinoza alone, following his demise, immediately achieved the status of a major presence in the intellectual life of all Europe and did so with astonishing speed. Hardly was he in his grave than he became a widely pervasive presence in numerous contexts in Germany, France, Scandinavia, England, and in tortuous fashion, banished to the depths of the Inquisition archives and whispered about behind closed doors, even Italy. But to begin with, aside from the burning issue of his deathbed scene, Spinoza's growing public presence, pervasive though it was, remained a dark shadow wholly negative in character with scant sign of any interest in his life and personality, or attempt to project a positive image of his person. Spinoza's persona, through the 1680s, stayed almost entirely out of sight, much as in Tschirnhaus' text, an abomination screened out as far as possible from schooling, scholarly and literary journals and higher education, culture and polite conversation. If, down to 1677, there were other famous "atheists" whose notoriety long predated Spinoza's, such as Vanini and in particular Hobbes, who were rivals for his niche, as Bayle remarks, and supplied at least an incipient approach to a deconstructing Bible criticism, from 1677 any such approximate equivalence rapidly receded and ceased to make sense. As Europe's principal international philosophical underground subverting the existing religious, ethical-legal, and political order, from 1677 there was no longer any plausible rival or remotely equivalent presence to Spinoza and "Spinozism."

What by 1677 chiefly marked Spinoza off from Hobbes was the existence of his circle and its movement and the interaction of the religious, social, and political subversive elements associated with his name. What changed soon afterwards was that from the 1690s onwards, the universal threat of Spinoza and "Spinozism" could no longer be kept veiled and unmentioned and was now broadcast, or rather fiercely denounced, on every side. Early eighteenth-century "Spinozism" was unquestionably a concrete reality, observed the astronomer and physicist Johannes Heinrich Müller (1671–1731), in his inaugural address as professor of natural philosophy at the University of Altdorf, near Nuremberg, on 19 June 1714. Its perniciousness, he explained to the assembled students and professors, lay partly in the fact that Spinoza was a more complete and cogent "atheist," more forthright in denying miracles and divine providence than Hobbes or any other. If others questioned miracles too, "Benedictus Spinoza" stood out from all the

---

[71] Wurtz, "Tschirnhaus und die Spinozabeschuldigung," 62–3, 67–8; Mulsow, *Radikale Frühaufklärung* ii, 35; Laerke, *Spinoza and the Freedom*, 45–6, 26n101; Zenker, *Denkfreiheit*, 168–70, 186.

world's other "atheists," including Hobbes, by far, affirmed Müller, exactly as Bayle contends in his *Dictionnaire*, by being more forceful, thorough, and emphatic in denying a knowing, benevolent God who created man and the universe. His "atheism," quite unlike that of Epicurus, Lucretius, Hobbes, and Vanini, powered a much broader, more concerted, activist campaign of reform directed against what Spinoza characterizes as popular ignorance, fanaticism, and superstition. Spinoza deliberately sought to undermine in their entirety Christian theology, religious rulings, and the sway of churchmen, subverting common belief which Hobbes definitely did not. By claiming God and the universe are not distinct, but one and the same, and that nothing happens contrary to the "eternal, fixed and immutable order" of nature, Spinoza broke utterly with the entire existing edifice of accepted belief and authority.[72] Spinoza and Hobbes, consequently, were now on entirely different levels as agents of subversion and reform in Western thought and culture and as long-term influences on the Western Enlightenment, and this was clearly recognized by all leading intellects by the 1690s and the opening of the new century.

41.iii Spinoza and the Glorious Revolution

Hence, only briefly, for the first decade or so after Spinoza's death, did the combined efforts of Protestant, Catholic, and Jewish scholars alike largely curtain off and marginalize Spinoza's significance as a thinker, personality, and writer. Over the medium term, the striking intellectual failure of Boyle's and Henry More's strategy against Spinoza by the 1690s, pointedly illustrates the wider predicament of the intellectual world of the last quarter of the seventeenth century, and how changing historical circumstances utterly thwarted the initial pan-European reaction to Spinoza and Spinozism so resolutely striving to keep the man and his philosophy under wraps.

Boyle's, More's, and Cudworth's efforts to counter while burying the figure and name of Spinoza paralleled the strategies of Huet, Bossuet, and Le Clerc. But in this regard, the 1680s proved a turning point. If a substantial body of texts attests to the centrality of Spinoza's status and arguments in Europe's intellectual life during the decade, Spinoza's name and Bayle's new mythical image of "Spinoza" were still then only just starting to spread among the wider public. Bayle's *Pensées diverses* of 1682, for example, which in the longer run considerably contributed to Spinoza's breakthrough, took time to make its impact felt. Yet, the picture was changing in the 1680s, and few doubted that however urgent a priority, burying the reality of Spinoza the man and thinker was proving formidably difficult. In

---

[72] Müller, *Dissertatio Inavgvralis philosophica de miraculis*, 13–14.

February 1683, Stillingfleet already preached openly in church against "Spinoza" as well as Hobbes,[73] something remarkable given that, to begin with, Spinoza's texts were barely associated with their author at all. But the real collapse of the Boyle-More-Cudworth strategy to screen Spinoza and Spinozism out, ensued, as elsewhere, a little later, in Britain greatly helped by the Glorious Revolution of 1688–9 which opened the gates to a freer press and wider toleration.

Blount and his circle followed up his publication, in 1683, of the English version of Spinoza's chapter on miracles (without Spinoza's name being mentioned) later in the decade by publishing the first complete translation of the *TTP* into any modern language apart from French. Spinoza still went unmentioned. But no one could fail to notice the force of the subversive impetus it reflected. This accurate, expert rendering into English appeared in 1689, in the midst of the turmoil of the Glorious Revolution, entitled *A Treatise partly theological, And partly Political, Containing some few DISCOURSES, To prove that the Liberty of PHILOSOPHIZING (that is Making Use of Natural Reason) may be allow'd without any prejudice to Piety, or to the Peace of any Common-wealth; And that the Loss of Public Peace and Religion it self must necessarily follow, where such a Liberty of Reasoning is taken away.* Nowhere in this publication was Spinoza's name mentioned. Yet, this text (that would later reappear in 1737) proved a landmark in the history of Spinoza's penetration of the English-speaking modern world because, appearing without any official endorsement or approval, with the name and place of the publisher withheld, it paraded a rhetoric that unmistakably linked it to the most radical republican political tendency present in the Revolution as well as to outspoken criticism of the clergy and state church.[74]

Even the identity of the translator who justly claimed to have rendered the book "truly and faithfully (tho' not everywhere word for word)," remains uncertain, though probably it was again the first radical English "deist," Charles Blount.[75] In effect this was one of the clearest early examples of the intimate linkage of democratic republicanism with rejection of religious authority defining the essence of "Spinozism," and the essence equally of the Radical Enlightenment more broadly. No one could possibly mistake this translator's fiery "Spinozist" attitude and passionate fury in hurling this radical democratic republican text, like a bomb, into the turmoil of the Glorious Revolution. The preface, headed "The Translator to the Reader," indeed ranks among the most aggressively antitheological, anti-Tory pro-republican texts of the age: "Religion and government being the subject matter of the book, it is easy to guess what sort of men are likely to decry it; but let those who are angry and find fault with it answer it." Thus, this

---

[73] Parker, "Spinoza, Locke," 170n28.
[74] Colie, "Spinoza and the Early English Deists," 32; Kingma and Offenberg, "Bibliography," 22; Hudson, *English Deists*, 66; Prince, *Shortest Way with Defoe*, 164, 284n104.
[75] Boucher, *Spinoza in English*, 5; Hudson, *Enlightenment and Modernity*, 16; Israel, *Radical Enlightenment*, 605; Van de Ven, *Printing Spinoza*, 293–8.

preface reiterated the truth that seemed so compelling to Leibniz: it is one thing indignantly to decry the *TTP* as Boyle, More, Cudworth, and a host of scholars all did, quite another effectively to refute it. That was the crux. This book by an anonymous author, the anonymous translator assures readers, is one where "the crape gown and the long robe [i.e. academics and lawyers] are both defied to prove there are any tenets in the whole treatise, half so dangerous or destructive to the peace and welfare of human society, as those doctrines and maxims are, which have of late years been broached by time-serving church-men and mercenary lawyers, for which they justly deserve the hatred and contempt of all mankind." This was aimed in particular against those supporting absolutism, Catholicism, and the now tottering Stuart monarchy.

Boyle had long felt deep distress at the splits and quarrels troubling Christendom and the need for a broader toleration albeit within strict limits. This made him sympathetic to the moderate phalanx within the Glorious Revolution and especially an ally of Bishop Gilbert Burnet (1643–1715), the only senior Anglican churchman in whom William III closely confided. When setting up the famous "Boyle Lectures" in London, in 1691, Boyle's goal was to reinforce and fortify the union of religion and science against Christianity's growing host of adversaries, and promote peace between the Christian confessions so as to concert a more formidable collective drive against non-Christians while, at the same time, vigorously maintaining the careful screen he, More, and Cudworth had created, scrupulously shutting out all mention of Spinoza. On setting up his renowned lecture series, Boyle provided, under his will, for a theologian or "preaching minister" to be selected each year to deliver a series of eight sermons "for proving the Christian religion against notorious infidels, viz. Atheists, Deists, Pagans, Jews, and Mohammedans," without "descending to any controversies among Christians," a wholly fresh, rational, tolerant and for many, encouraging post-Revolution approach.[76] The Boyle Lectures embodied the very essence of "moderate Enlightenment."

The first series, later entitled *A Confutation of Atheism* (1692), were delivered by Richard Bentley (1662–1742), among the great classical philologists of the age, an ordained minister and ally of Newton, who had not yet commenced his later notoriously divisive forty-year term as Master of Trinity College, Cambridge (1700–40); the second series, delivered in 1693 by the Bishop of Bath and Wells, Richard Kidder (1633–1703), an opponent of James II and Nonjuring bishops who became a royal chaplain of William III, in 1689, targeted the Jews. But even though Boyle's "Atheists" were always his and Bentley's principal target, and not pagans, Muslims, or Jews, Boyle, even in his founding documents, insisted on not naming his primary foes. Bentley faithfully followed Boyle's strategy in his

---

[76] Bentley, *Confutation of Atheism*, dedication p. xv; Colie, "Spinoza in England," 202–4; Sorkin, *Religious Enlightenment*, 8–9, 29, 60.

Confutation of 1692. The 200 pages of Bentley's text repeatedly remind England's churchmen that they and all of society face the gravest possible current challenge and that "if atheism should be supposed to become universal in this nation (which seems to be designed and endeavoured, though we know the gates of hell shall not be able to prevail), farewell all ties of friendship and all principles of honour, all love for our country and loyalty to our prince; nay farewell all government and society itself [...] all that is laudable or valuable in the world."[77] The present fight was of surpassing urgency for everybody and the Boyle Lectures sought to conquer "our adversaries" in particular by deploying the "argument from design," physico-theology as presented by England's great scientists, especially Boyle and Newton, including the "divine sanction, that hath fixed and determined" the tiniest parcels of life observed through microscopes. Yet, Bentley adhered undeviatingly to Boyle's strategy of dramatizing the threat posed by these fearsome current "adversaries" while simultaneously preventing the public learning who they were, or anything whatever about them. Furiously assailing the arguments of the unnamed, whenever citing authors and texts Bentley mentions only books by ancient Greek and Roman freethinkers, especially Lucretius.[78]

However, vehemently denouncing "our adversaries" in this manner inevitably aroused curiosity as to who these "infidels" were against whom Boyle and Bentley constantly railed. Their principal target were the leaders of the budding deist movement in England, especially Blount who has been termed "the first Englishman to be identified by his contemporaries as a deist"[79] and his allies, including the young Daniel Defoe (1660–1731).[80] Meanwhile, Spinoza's emergence as the ideological mainstay behind this coterie, in place of Hobbes, followed more or less inevitably too from Spinoza's invoking of modern science, more emphatic denial of final causes and divine governance of the world, more geometric, clearer rejection of divine intention, knowledge, and benevolence, and severe critique of monarchy and oligarchy. Spinoza's very reliance on observation and natural science helped stimulate Boyle's and Newton's physico-theological counter-offensive, as likewise that of Swammerdam and Leeuwenhoek. For physico-theology, plainly, was more directly and relevantly deployable for demolishing Spinoza than demolishing Hobbes. The more the discoveries "which are daily made in astronomy and natural philosophy," as Samuel Clarke later expressed the point, "the more clearly is this question [of final causes] continually determined to the shame and confusion of atheists."[81] Science seemingly offered the best means to tackle the looming menace of radical deism.

---

[77] Bentley, *Confutation of Atheism*, 25.
[78] Bentley, *Confutation of Atheism*, 25, 77, 108, 110, 112.
[79] Hudson, *Enlightenment and Modernity*, 60.
[80] Hudson, *Enlightenment and Modernity*, 4, 11, 16, 133; Prince, *Shortest Way with Defoe*, 22–8.
[81] Clarke, *A Demonstration*, 51.

If Hobbes lived much longer than Spinoza, dying in December 1679, long enough perhaps to notice early indications of his ousting from top role in the sphere of intellectual subversion, it was the cultural conditions in Britain at the time that especially favoured the emergence of the deist-republican tendency, the radical Whig strand of the Glorious Revolution. This became still clearer after the Revolution. For the kind of radical deism linked to republican tendencies championed by Blount, Toland, Tindal, Shaftesbury and others, Spinoza was simply altogether more applicable and useful than Hobbes. The English "perfect deist" of the 1690s, as the Kent schoolmaster Matthias Earbery (1658–c.1730) characterizes this newly fashionable subversive type in his *Deism Examin'd and Confuted* (1697), starts deviating from how people should think first by being exposed to Socinian Anti-Trinitarian notions, then strays further by reading Hobbes, but truly goes astray joining the deist tendency only after pushing Hobbes aside for Spinoza. Where Hobbes made a start, edging in undesirable directions, Spinoza assails the "very root and foundation by taking away all divine authority from prophecy, miracles or inspiration" turning all the biblical figures into "either mad-men or impostors."[82]

During his search for a "perfect deism," Earbery's "perfect deist" positively delights in comparing Hobbes with Spinoza. Certainly, the classic English deist of the early Enlightenment still venerates Hobbes, acknowledging him as the forerunner, but he becomes a radical deist only after realizing Spinoza "deserves rather to be esteemed [Hobbes'] tutor than his scholar," because the Dutch thinker's arguments extend further and go deeper.[83] So attached to Spinoza (whom Earbery thought was only pretending to be a "deist") "is the perfect deist," averred Earbery, that "every summer he carried him into the fields with him in his hands, and each winter he wore him in his muff."[84] With Spinoza now prime spur to philosophical incredulity, in Britain no less than on the Continent, the movement generating a "general corruption of manners, contempt of the clergy," and the advancement of irreligious ideas was linked to the new post-classical pro-Dutch republican tendency. Earbery tellingly dubs the new-style deists expressing fashionably irreverent views in the London coffee-shops, like the young Toland, soon a noted leader of the republican wing of the Glorious Revolution, Spinoza's "little disciples of the town"—an apt description considering, as we know today, that Toland was indeed (though this was long denied by scholars) principally indebted for his more controversial standpoints to Spinoza and *not* to Locke.[85]

---

[82] Earbery, *Deism Examin'd and Confuted*, preface p. v; Boucher, *Spinoza in English*, 65; Simonutti, "Spinoza and the English Thinkers," 206; Israel, *Radical Enlightenment*, 608.
[83] Earbery, *Deism Examin'd and Confuted*, 4–5; Hudson, *Enlightenment and Modernity*, 11.
[84] Earbery, *Deism Examin'd and Confuted*, 3; Simonutti, "Spinoza and the English Thinkers," 206–8.
[85] Israel, *Radical Enlightenment*, 608.

Boyle and Bentley were certainly not imagining the seismic shift they deplored. Around 1700, a cultural and religious crisis was stirring in England, explained Nehemiah Grew, Oldenburg's successor as the Royal Society's joint secretary in the years 1677–9, because "not only men of erudition," but, at any rate in London, "the citizens themselves, grown of late more bookish, are very dangerously infected" with "the Anti-Scripturalist contagion increasingly spreading." This was definitely not the fault of science, the Royal Society's new secretary was happy to report, but of a certain class of pernicious writers. Among the leading science researchers of the era, Grew, chief cataloguer and curator of the Royal Society's "museum" in the early 1680s, noted discoverer in plant anatomy, a physiologist convinced there "is a vital substance in nature distinct from a body," strove to advance the "antidoting of this city and kingdom, against a contagion so dismal in itself and the consequences of it." Though he both respected and criticized Van Leeuwenhoek, Grew worked independently, constantly insisting on the "regularity, or Order of Things" in Nature, "tho' we see it not everywhere; yet it is everywhere to be supposed." Furthermore, just as Boyle, Newton, More, Cudworth, Bentley, and Clarke all insisted, this divine order of nature is not only divinely ordained and orchestrated but always at one with the Holy Scriptures. A few inconsistencies and errors may have crept into the text of Scripture here and there, "but the element of corruption in the Biblical text is not very great." Nor are the grounds for doubting Moses' authorship of the Pentateuch.[86]

To Grew, Spinoza's objections were contemptible quibbles. Where the First Book of Samuel affirms the "hand of the Lord" was "against the Philistines all the Days of Samuel," a statement "Spinoza will have to be a contradiction; but without any ground," Grew demonstrates how "All the Days of Samuel" must be taken to refer not to Samuel's life but "his government, that is until Saul was made king," the time when the Israelites were "sorely oppressed" by the Philistines.[87] Where "this same Spinoza will have the Prophets to contradict one another in their doctrine, as well as predictions," science proves the "agreement between the Prophets." True scientists see that science and revealed religion, including the indubitable truth of miracles and the miraculous nature of Christianity's rise, are alike anchored in the firmest evidence: "one great sign of His divine power and Coming was His striking of the Heathen Oracles dumb, as that of Jupiter Hammon [the chief god of Carthage], and those of Apollo." All these oracles, insisted Grew, like Bossuet and Huet were "neglected and forsaken of the people, and of the priests belonging to them, before Trajan's time," and scholarship can offer no surer proof of Christ's coming transforming our world than that.[88] This was impressive rhetoric, but unfortunately erroneous. Grew had failed to keep up

---

[86] Grew, *Cosmologia sacra*, 142–3, 164–5; Lyons, *The Royal Society*, 94–5; Hunter, "Early Problems," 189.
[87] Grew, *Cosmologia sacra*, 179–81.   [88] Grew, *Cosmologia sacra*, 363–4.

with recent historical studies and thus not realized that, in reality, the oracles flourished unabated for well over three centuries after the Resurrection, as Anthonie van Dale demonstrated, in his *De Oraculis Ethnicorum* (1683), thriving uninterruptedly, he proved, until the time of the Emperor Theodosius (AD 379–95).

Science, insisted the Royal Society's second secretary, is the key to true understanding. Moreover, in one respect, he was unusually perceptive: few readers outside the radical deist underground fully appreciated that Spinoza challenges not just Christianity and all revealed religion but also monarchy and its veneration and the existing social order, that the *TTP* and the *TP* firmly couple anti-Scripturalism with radical republicanism. Although there was a deeply-rooted republican tradition in seventeenth- and eighteenth-century England, until the eighteenth century, the English tradition broadly failed to expand on the distinction between aristocratic and democratic republicanism, in this respect strikingly lagging behind Spinoza's republicanism, that of the De La Courts and Van den Enden. However, like Baxter, Grew understood the significance of Spinoza's coupling anti-Scripturalism with the democratic republican tendency. A fervent monarchist (despite his father, a dissenting minister, having been imprisoned for six months, in 1682), Grew rejected Spinoza no less on political grounds than for subverting revealed religion. True science, he claimed, proves monarchy too to be part of the "natural order" and hence also inherent in divine goodness, divine government of the world, and the divine rule for all humanity. Republics are not really republics in the way that they profess to be but "do all of them centre upon that which in effect is the regal: as the United Provinces with their Stadholder, and the Venetians, with their Doge."[89] Radical deism was a religious and political threat combined.

41.iv The Emergence of the "Dutch" Spinoza

International efforts to keep Spinoza the man and the philosopher firmly off stage began to unravel from 1682 with the publication of Bayle's *Pensées diverses sur la comète* which, from a historical and international standpoint, can fairly be said to be among the most crucial events of Spinoza's biography. After Louis XIV closed the Protestant University of Sedan, in July 1681, Bayle (Figure 41.3) moved to Rotterdam where he began collecting information about this mysterious hidden personage who had so interested him since he had discovered him, in 1679, but who was unknown to the world, and meeting persons who had known him personally to glean first-hand biographical information. Bayle's *Pensées diverses* was assuredly one of the most remarkable books of its century and among the

---

[89] Grew, *Cosmologia sacra*, 90–1; Hunter, "Early Problems," 190, 203–4.

Figure 41.3 *Pierre Bayle* (1647–1706), c.1675, by Louis Elle le Jeune, oil on canvas. Photo: Gérard Blot, © RMN-Grand Palais/Art Resource, New York.

works that most forcefully impacted Early Enlightenment thought and study of philosophy. Most of it is not about comets at all but rather the phenomenon of "superstition" and why most people believe things that science shows are untrue, and why this is an abiding problem in human life. A large portion of the book is devoted to reconsidering "atheism" as a moral and philosophical issue. Long sections covering not just dozens but hundreds of pages advanced the novel and subtle but highly subversive idea of the "virtuous atheist," contrasting this new category that Bayle introduced with the immoral majority of mankind, especially the everywhere conspicuous throng of thriving, churchgoing "Christians" who, behind their outward façade, are not really virtuous at all. This undeniable reality posed an enduring moral and philosophical problem everyone should ponder. With this book Bayle single-handedly forged a new moral, theological, and philosophical framework.

By separating virtue and morality from adherence to any religious faith or practice and making Spinoza (but decidedly not Hobbes) the presiding figure of the new category, "the virtuous atheist," who is in some sense superior to the common or ordinary Christian possessing perfect faith but who is ignorant, superstitious, and not particularly virtuous, Bayle introduced "the virtuous atheist" as a category needing to be carefully distinguished from the immoral and debauched "atheist of practice" which Spinoza himself had so fiercely denounced—a crucial early Enlightenment subversive tool. Bayle also promoted rationality and rejection of superstition as the most essential properties of those seeking personal moral elevation. Over time, Bayle's widely read book engineered a considerable change of perspective not least with respect to the person and image of Spinoza. In comparing particular examples of the "virtuous atheist," such as Lucretius, Vanini, and Hobbes, affirming that Spinoza "was the greatest atheist that there has ever been [était le plus gand athée qui ait jamais été],"[90] but at the same time someone infatuated with philosophy, the thinker who weaves atheism into the fundamental principles of philosophy and science, Bayle transformed and noticeably enhanced Spinoza's image in the early Enlightenment world. With one stroke, Bayle hauled Spinoza out of the shadows, turning him into one of the foremost personalities of early modern times, a powerful militant mythical figure pitted against an entire army of theologians, academics, and scientists (including Bayle's particular rival, Le Clerc), straining their utmost to screen him out.

Stunningly, Bayle's foremost philosophical atheist, his chief exponent of *l'athéisme speculatif*, is at the same time a figure of the highest moral stature. By forging this new pervasive myth and engineering a massive breach in tradition, philosophy, and general culture, Bayle hastened the dawning of a new reality, placing Spinoza henceforth on a unique rung as head of a select group, establishing him permanently as a figure of universal significance in human culture with an inevitable impact (whether they realize it or not) on everybody.[91] With the old strategy of screening Spinoza out intellectually shattered, before long (from the 1690s) the image and personality, indeed everything relating to the biography of Spinoza, became, alongside his books and ideas, a focus of intense international attention, fascination, debate, and public dispute.

Subsequently, Bayle ploughed on with his wily and surreptitious "Spinoza" programme, systematically separating moral standing from belief and faith, a campaign culminating in his *Dictionnaire* in 1697, and even after that persisted in gathering more information and documentation between the 1697 and 1702 editions, further expanding his account of Spinoza's life. In Bayle's *Dictionnaire*, the definitive survey text of the West's Early Enlightenment, not only is the article on "Spinoza" the longest and most detailed in the entire work, but Spinoza and "Spinosisme" figure as basic themes also in numerous other articles, resulting in

---

[90] Bayle, *Pensées diverses* ii, 134; Albiac, *Sinagoga vacía*, 15–16; Chaui, *Nervura do real*, 291–7.
[91] Van Bunge, "Spinoza's Life," 218; Préposiet, *Spinoza*, 188–9; Mori, *Bayle philosophe* 190–1, 204–5; Gros, *Dissidences de la philosophie*, 12, 395n28, 421.

the figure of Spinoza presented by this prime early Enlightenment general work of reference becoming universally known and notorious. Through Bayle, Spinoza acquired a contemporary image and publicity powerfully eclipsing in general impact and intellectual significance every other dissident thinker in history, and, at the same time, became a figurehead rendered morally rather alluring as a personality.[92]

At the moment of Spinoza's death, the Dutch universities were as much a battleground on several different levels as ever, and in that setting some of the most revealing discussions and debates about Spinoza's philosophy of the pivotal 1690s took place. Two texts vividly depicting the fraught ambience of the universities at that time, still mired in the Voetian-Coccean controversies, were the anonymous novel *Philopater* (1691) and its sequel (1697). The adept anonymous author of this clandestine two-part foray succeeded in producing a novel that was widely read and, according to Halma, frequently talked about among the Dutch public, young and old, many readers becoming both curious and fascinated.

Both parts of the novel are today thought to be by Johan Duijkerius (1661–1702), although only the second part is pervaded with clearly Spinozistic attitudes and comments. Duijkerius was a candidate for the Reformed ministry licensed to preach who failed to secure a steady preaching post either in the Netherlands or the East Indies. Lacking talent for preaching, he was an adept writer who enjoyed satirizing the quarrels rampant among the theologians of his time, especially those between Voetians and Cocceians which, when eventually the anonymous author's identity emerged, drew down much added indignation on his head. Despite some success in his attempted second career as a schoolmaster and author, a disastrous second marriage and heavy drinking had by 1697 reduced Duijkerius to dire straits, a failed career path reminiscent of that of Van Gent.[93]

Due to the intriguing way it is written and the entertaining guessing game it initiated by depicting prominent academic and other personalities from life without actually naming them (while offering a key to the puzzle with a printed list of relevant names, separately available), *Philopater* and especially its sequel which circulated more furtively than the first part, was enjoyed by all sorts and "honoured with more praise than it deserved." Furthermore, behind the jibes at well-known academics and churchmen, the novel had a serious purpose or, as those denouncing it expressed it, presented material in which "religion and the truth itself were not a little mocked."[94] The second part of *Philopater*, observes Van Limborch, remarking that he could have obtained a copy but chose not to

---

[92] Lomba, "Pierre Bayle, Spinoza's Reader, 224, 232–5; Israel, *Radical Enlightenment*, 333–41; Van Bunge, "Spinoza's Life," 214.
[93] Israel, *Radical Enlightenment*, 315–20; Spaans, "Between the Catechism," 338–40.
[94] Halma, *Het Leven*, "Voorreden," 7.

owing to its repulsive impiety, was a "godless book probably by a Spinozist."[95] One way the sequel reveals its "Spinozist" thrust was by simultaneously supporting, while yet mocking, Balthasar Bekker for his controversial stand against witchcraft: Bekker was unjustly victimized for denying the reality of sorcery, witchcraft, and magic, but, rather ridiculously, held *Philopater*, nevertheless maintained that although the Devil cannot directly influence individual behavior, he *does* nevertheless undeniably exist and does command an empire of evil demons and devilry, because Scripture says so. Spinozists alone, unlike Bekkerites, Philopater made clear, wholly deny the existence of demons, sorcery, magic, and the Devil himself.[96]

Philopater's scandalous sequel, besides differentiating "Spinozistic" doctrines from widely disputed and controversial aspects of Descartes, the Socinians, Bekker and others, challenging scholastic and traditional ways of thinking, afforded a glimpse into the clandestine world of freethinking discussions in university towns and among student groups. Continually denouncing the mixing of theology with philosophy, Duijkerius expounded Spinoza's philosophical system, accessibly and entertainingly, "in the form of a mocking, rollicking get together." His depicting dissident freethinking university students devoted to jollification and junketing seemed scandalously to be praising them for envisaging Spinoza's philosophy as something valuable and in argument impregnable. The book was bitterly denounced for favouring appalling student types believing they alone "are the keepers of the key of this high wisdom," the discerning ones while "all the rest not signing up to their master's views are just idlers erroneously pretending to that honourable title."[97]

Furtively propagating Spinoza's ideas employing satire, the *Spinozisten* in this way gained fresh ground in the minds of some while furthering their efforts to detach theology from philosophy and erode theologians' hegemony over intellectual life and scientific thinking. At Leiden, where the *Philopater* sequel deriding all who rejected Spinoza's thought-world possibly first circulated, the Reformed consistory condemned it on 13 December 1697, calling on the burgomasters to seize the text from the bookshops, as was promptly done.[98] By mid-December, the Rotterdam consistory too were examining this book "of very damaging content." "Various foul and blasphemous extracts" were read out to that gathering on 1 January 1698, though it took until May to prod the Rotterdam burgomasters into seizing the stocks from the bookshops and symbolically burning a copy at the Rotterdam city hall.[99] On 2 January 1698, the Amsterdam consistory likewise

---

[95] Duijkerius, *Het Leven van Philopater*, 11–12, 16; Freudenthal/Walther, *Lebensgeschichte* i, 82; Spaans, "Between the Catechism," 338–9.
[96] Duijkerius, *Het Leven van Philopater*, 152–4.
[97] Halma, *Het Leven*, "Voorreden," 8–9; Spaans, "Between the Catechism," 337–8.
[98] GA Leiden, Acta kerkeraad viii, res. 1 Dec. 1697; Israel, *Radical Enlightenment*, 317.
[99] GA Rotterdam, Acta des kerckenraedts vii, pp. 599–601, 612, res. 18 Dec. 1697, 1 and 8 Jan. 1698, and 13 May 1698.

condemned the "foully blasphemous little book," and brought the evidence of "mocking and denying Holy Scripture" to the burgomasters.[100] They agreed to use all possible means to suppress such evil.[101] Noting the book had already been suppressed in other Holland towns, The Hague's Reformed *kerkeraad* denounced the book on 4 January for its "blasphemous mockery of the Almighty and His Sacred Word and shameless advocacy of the godless views of Spinoza." Again, the worst passages were submitted to the local magistracy.[102]

Later in January, the standing committee [Gedeputeerde] of the States of Friesland likewise banned the book, interestingly offering more specific reasons than their colleagues in Holland: *Philopater* was forbidden to the public for denying the divinity of Christ and Holy Trinity together with "the divine authority of Holy Scripture,"[103] and denying also divine providence and immortality of the soul,[104] for declaring free will a chimaera and Descartes' fundamental duality of body and mind "absurd en frivool."[105] What many commentators also found intolerable was *Philopater*'s devious spreading of Spinoza's doctrine among the non-Latin-reading public, appealing to the common man, pronouncing Glazemaker's only recently published vernacular Dutch version of the *TTP* a great benefit to society. Whereas many persons confined to the lower walks of life but capable of understanding the reality of things were previously excluded from appreciating Spinoza's philosophy, being unable to acquire "more understanding by utilizing knowledge of the Latin language," now the truth, circumventing the barriers of Latin and the academic sphere, was finally made accessible to the discerning non-Latin-reading individual as well.[106]

Philopater also noticeably expanded the debate as to the wider significance of Spinoza's philosophy and over who were the real *Spinozisten* and who were not. Halma was outraged by *Philopater*'s summons to the discerning common man to jettison all conventional theology, repudiate Scriptural authority, and recognize only Spinozists as authentic purveyors of philosophical and theological truth and to learn to itemize those truths more exactly.[107] There was a Spinozistic sect, agreed De Volder in conversation with Stolle and Hallmann, in 1703, but for most it boiled down to just a few maxims. Few people actually read Spinoza's books and fewer still understood them, even among "those who nevertheless want to be considered followers of Spinoza." Although De Volder pronounced Spinoza's absolute determinism and "confusion" of body and mind basic errors, he felt unable to say whether Spinoza was truly "an atheist," given his views on God.

---

[100] GA Amsterdam, Acta kerkeraad xvi, 316. Res. 2, and 9 Jan. 1698.
[101] GA Amsterdam, Acta kerkeraad xvi, 317. Res. 16 Jan. 1698.
[102] GA The Hague, Acta kerkeraad iv, 406. Res. 4 Jan. 1698.
[103] Knuttel, *Verboden boeken*, 123.
[104] Duijkerius, *Het Leven van Philopater*, 156–7, 162–4; Israel, *Radical Enlightenment*, 317.
[105] Duijkerius, *Het Leven van Philopater*, 187; Trinius, *Freydenker-Lexicon*, 35.
[106] Duijkerius, *Het Leven van Philopater*, 196.
[107] Halma, *Aanmerkingen*, 6; *De Boekzaal van Europe* (1698), 294.

What was certain was that "Spinoza was never a Christian, but a Jew." Slightly bemused, Stolle and Hallmann were left suspecting that De Volder himself was a "Spinozist" or at least sympathetic to Spinoza's views.[108]

Why, asks *Philopater*, was the door not opened to all earlier? Why had no Dutch translation of the *TTP* appeared until published clandestinely in Amsterdam for the first time in 1693, even though Glazemaker's translation, the novel explains, had long been available circulating as a clandestine manuscript in several Dutch towns for nearly a quarter of a century? In fact, "so many [manuscript] copies" of the Dutch *TTP* were in existence by the early 1690s, that many, complains *Philopater*, were being copied inaccurately and corrupted. Fortunately, an uncorrupted version kept "by a singular good friend" of the original translator, Glazemaker, namely the eventual publisher, and another copy kept by Spinoza's "learned friend" (probably Meyer), *had* survived, and this was the copy used for the 1693 edition which *Philopater* endorses as the authentic and best version.[109]

After gathering testimony, the Amsterdam Reformed consistory revealed that the publisher of *Philopater*'s second part was the disreputable book dealer Aart Wolsgryn, a "noted Spinozist," previously prosecuted by the city sheriff for selling forbidden Spinozist books,[110] and that the probable author was Duijkerius. The latter, though, resolutely denied having anything to do with the Spinozistic sequel; and since Wolsgryn, while admitting his own offence, denied knowing anything about the sequel's author, in the end Duijkerius, though disgraced by the consistory, was never formally indicted. This was despite several witnesses testifying that, privately, he had acknowledged being the author of the first and second parts.[111] Confusion persisted, as it does still today, as to whether he was, or was not, actually author of both parts.[112] In any case, disgrace and losing his preaching licence drove Duijkerius further into alcoholism and an unruly lifestyle. He died sometime after 1697, plunged, notes Monnikhoff, in poverty and ignominy.[113]

Neither the ecclesiastical nor civic authorities were in a mood for trifling. Tried and sentenced, Wolsgryn was subjected to severe punishment. For violating the ban against publishing "Spinosistische" books denying the Holy Trinity, immortality of the soul, and other essential Christian dogmas,[114] the judges sentenced him on 25 April 1698 to eight years' imprisonment in the same prison where Koerbagh had died twenty-eight years before, followed by twenty years'

---

[108] Freudenthal/Walther, *Lebensgeschichte* ii, 57; Strazzoni, *Burchard de Volder*, 123–4.
[109] Duijkerius, *Het Leven van Philopater*, 195; Van der Deijl, "Dutch Translation," 216–17.
[110] Van Eeghen, *Amsterdamse boekhandel* iv, 49, 65; Wielema, *March of the Libertines*, 89, 92.
[111] ARH NHK Oud Synodaal Archief 185, Acta North Holland Synod, 29 July–9 Aug. 1698 (Alkmaar), p. 12; Roodenburg, *Onder censuur*, 201; Spaans, "Between the Catechism," 337–8.
[112] GA Amsterdam inv. 5061/345. "Confessie-boeck," fos. 227v–28, hearing 7 March 1698; GA Amsterdam, Acta kerkeraad xvii, 6. Res. 10 April 1698; Thijssen-Schoute, *Uit de Republiek*, 180, 197.
[113] KB 128 1 (2) Monnikhoff, "Aanteekeningen," fo. 8.
[114] GA Amsterdam Acta kerkeraad 376/17, p. 9. Res. 15 May 1698; Knuttel, *Verboden boeken*, 103; Roodenburg, *Onder censuur*, 201; Wielema, *March of the Libertines*, 89.

banishment from Amsterdam, and a swingeing 4,000 guilders fine which ruined him financially. This fierce repression of the Spinozistic "blasphemous little book" was duly reported at the warmly approving Gelderland synod, in August 1698, and the Groningen synod, in March 1699.[115] Wolsgryn's punishment and the disgrace of Duijkerius, banned from the Lord's Supper for bad lifestyle, were again discussed at the gathering of Friesland's synod, in June 1699;[116] in April 1700, the Synod of Groningen was still applauding the admirable "zeal" of their Amsterdam colleagues in the *Philopater* affair and the severe punishment of Wolsgryn.[117]

By the 1690s, the Dutch Reformed Church worried not just over the books and ideas of Spinoza, and the fact that he possessed a following, but also the now burgeoning underground hero-worship, the flourishing "mythology" arising around Spinoza's person. The venomous myth of a supposedly "wise and pious Spinosa," charged the preachers, was seeping in, so that more and more people were imbibing this absurdly contrived role model in no way deserving such status, with ruinous consequences for youth, morality, religion, and society.[118] This fresh development was causing all belief in *supernaturalia* to be utterly downtrodden. If only Spinozists deny the existence of the Devil or Hell outright, only Spinozists reject punishment for sin in the hereafter and deny the reality of eternal damnation; only Spinozists "believe in no grace, no Christ, no salvation and indeed no God." Spinozists alone deem religion a wholly social-political phenomenon rather than divinely revealed truth. Only Spinozists reduce Christianity to the level of other religions, deeming all religions of equal status and significance.[119] The spreading Spinoza mythology damaged society, complained one theologian, not least because *Spinozisten* look down on all other men outside their group, indeed on everyone lacking their views, as the "stupidest ignoramuses."[120] In the 1690s, *Spinozisterey* [Spinozism] seemed more than ever a dangerous contagion that needed countering in the most "vigilant and powerful manner."[121]

The "loose and silly youth," especially students, chiefly at fault for embracing Spinozism, became the target of a rival picaresque novel *Kakotegnus* (Amsterdam, 1700), a 230-page parody of *Philopater* penned by a Reformed preacher much applauded in the journals when it appeared. The novel's central figure, Kakotegnus, joins a Leiden student philosophy discussion group and is sadly misled by Spinozist seducers. Initially, the godless concepts he imbibes seem

---

[115] ARH NHK Oud Synodaal Archief 85, Acta Synod of Gelderland, Aug. 1698, art. "Licentieus boekdrukken."
[116] ARH NHK, Oud Synodaal Archief 215, Acta Synod of Friesland, res. Bolswaard, 7 June 1699, art. 14.
[117] RA Groningen, Archief van de Provinciale Synode Stad en Lande 4, Acta Groningen, 21. Res. 2 May 1700.
[118] Burmannus, *'t Hoogste goed der Spinozisten*, 12.
[119] Burmannus, *'t Hoogste goed der Spinozisten*, 147–9.
[120] Burmannus, *'t Hoogste goed der Spinozisten*, 143.
[121] Burmannus, *'t Hoogste goed der Spinozisten*, 23, 25.

attractive. Hardened Spinozists cleverly inculcate intellectual pride into avid young people like him, encouraging them to imagine themselves wiser and more discerning than the great mass of ordinary mortals. The poor youth learns to reject divine revelation, divine providence, and miracles. Later, though, Kakotegnus wrecks his own life with his own perverse ideas, unbelief, and impiety. Victim of Spinozist skulduggery, he succumbs to dire poverty, wretchedly dying a premature ignominious death like those of Van Gent and Duijkerius.[122]

Publishers and booksellers found themselves under an effective ban, but so did the professors. Changed circumstances encouraged what has been called a "paradigm shift" in the 1670s and 1680s, whereby Socinianism which for most of the seventeenth century had been the ultimate affront and betrayal of Christian doctrine in Dutch theological polemics, was now broadly displaced in Dutch society by the still worse contagion of what in the Latin of the era was now regularly termed "Spinozismus," with forms of veiled "Spinozism" causing increasingly frequent and bitter disputes about which professors (with Wittichius and De Volder prime suspects) did, or did not, harbour secretive views conducing to "Spinozism."[123] This change rendered serious discussion of Spinoza's *Ethics* in academic circles more than ever not just problematic but practically impossible. As soon as any leading theologian-philosopher, like Braun, at Groningen, for example, dared state that, despite abominable heresies, one finds also useful and important truths in Spinoza's reasoning, that writer found himself publicly vilified for aiding and abetting the spread of Spinozism, for being a surreptitious accomplice of Spinoza.[124]

A particular difficulty hampering the post-1680s attempts to demonize a now widely targeted, defined and highlighted underground Spinozist sect during the last decade of the seventeenth century was that certain key individuals, for whatever reasons, were suspected by contemporaries of being secret "Spinozists" despite there being no real evidence for this discernible today. It is hard to know, for example, what to make of the testimony Stolle and Hallmann gleaned from the theologian and orientalist of German background, Thomas Crenius (1648–1728), resident in Leiden since 1683, who judged Spinoza excellent in parts of mathematics but understanding nothing of algebra. Crenius pronounced the *Principia Cartesii geometrice demonstrata* Spinoza's best book. In Holland only "paradoxe Bücher" [paradoxical books], he complained, were in demand nowadays: he had recently received a learned, well-written manuscript "against Spinoza" from Hamburg, but could find no publisher for it. Had it been "pro Spinoza," he would soon have found one.[125] The renowned Leiden professor Christopher

---

[122] Roodenpoort, 't Verleidend Levens-Bedrijf van Kakotegnus, 6, 28, 33; Rabus, Twee-Maandelijke Uittreksels (July–Aug. 1701), 686–92; Israel, Radical Enlightenment, 319–20.
[123] Steenbakkers, "Johannes Braun," 205–6; Steenbakkers, "Spinoza's Life," 47n10.
[124] Steenbakkers, "Johannes Braun," 206–7.   [125] Freudenthal/Walther, Lebensgeschichte, i, 87.

Wittichius (1625–87), according to Crenius, was a "great atheist [summus Atheus]," much inclined towards Spinoza's philosophy. Here he concurred (but did not say so) with several notorious remarks in the second *Philopater* novel where it is also claimed that Wittichius, the pre-eminent pro-Cartesian Reformed theologian of the era, despite his famous refutation, the *Anti-Spinoza* (1690), covertly figured among Spinoza's sympathizers and close friends.[126] The latest scholarship on Wittichius, however, finds that he was "certainly no Spinozist" in the way *Philopater* and Crenius assert, despite some real but unstated points of agreement.[127] What is certain is that some leading figures in Dutch intellectual life of the time, like De Volder and Wittichius, knew Spinoza better and viewed him more favourably than was at all advisable to make generally known in public.

For the most part, the Collegiant strand of Spinoza's following tended to wither during the seventeenth century's last quarter, and Spinoza's following increasingly took on a predominantly but perhaps not exclusively secular, intellectually libertine complexion. As the personality of Spinoza the man and thinker began to emerge as a subversive icon, the question arose too as whether he was admired just by clandestine groups or also by many silent, isolated individuals. There were certainly clandestine "Spinozist" groups like that portrayed by Duijkerius, but what was perhaps more important, given that no one could openly propagate Spinozism or advertise or discuss Spinoza's books around 1700, was "that there are many people in Amsterdam who do not recognize each other as sharing the same company," yet, the younger Rieuwertsz thought very probable, "in secret cultivate Spinoza's teachings and consider these to be the best philosophy, even though [like Rieuwertsz, when outside his house] they do not say so."[128]

Had he lived longer, Spinoza, held Rieuwertsz, greatly regretting his early passing, "würde noch viele Wahrheiten entdecket [would have discovered many more truths yet] and would also have opened eyes on many matters."[129] Spinoza had his fervent admirers, but Hallmann wondered whether perhaps the younger Rieuwertsz understood Spinoza in a way that was not "atheistic," a pertinent question since, when reporting (about Spinoza) to Cardinal Barberini, in Rome, years before in September 1677, Neercassel had described the older Rieuwertsz as "quodam Memnonista vel potius Socinano bibliopola urbis Amsterodamensis [a certain Mennonite or rather Socinian bookseller of Amsterdam]."[130] Early on in Spinoza's philosophical career rationalist Collegiants and Mennonites like Jelles, Rieuwertsz, and Pieter Balling had, we have seen, formed the most important group among Spinoza's allies.

---

[126] Freudenthal/Walther, *Lebensgeschichte* i, 87; Duijkerius, *Het Leven van Philopater*, 149–50; Klever, "Omtrent Spinoza," 8; Klever, *Mannen rond Spinoza*, 236; Israel, *Enlightenment Contested*, 317.
[127] Alderink, "Spinoza en Wittichius," 89, 94n61.
[128] Freudenthal/Walther, *Lebensgeschichte* i, 89; Freudenthal, *Lebensgeschichte*, 225.
[129] Freudenthal/Walther, *Lebensgeschichte* i, 89–90.
[130] Manusov-Verhage, "Jan Rieuwertsz, marchand," 237, 241.

While the younger Rieuwertsz did not fully share the intense Socinian Christian outlook of his father,[131] it seems likely that he did envisage authentic admirers of Spinoza as being men trusting, like his father and Jelles, in Spinozism's compatibility with Socinian Christianity, hence with the Christian truth they believed all the main churches betray. If so, this might help explain the younger Rieuwertsz's remark that few remained of the true disciples while yet, at the same time, Spinoza's ideas were doing much good in Dutch society, and could do much more. Support for this interpretation lies too perhaps in the younger Rieuwertsz's particular stress on Spinoza's Bible scholarship and regret that "Spinoza did not understand Greek because otherwise he would have extensively researched on the New Testament and the [false] way it has been translated [by all the churches]," a key tenet of the Socinians.[132]

---

[131] Klever, *The Sphinx*, 125.
[132] Freudenthal/Walther, *Lebensgeschichte* i, 90; on Spinoza and Greek, see Klever, *Spinoza Classicus*, 93.

42

Conclusion

Through the eighteenth and nineteenth centuries down to the twentieth, Spinoza remained relevant to current intellectual debate to an extent, and with a continuing impact, no other seventeenth-century thinker could rival. No leading figure of the post-1750 later Enlightenment, for example, or the nineteenth century, was as engaged with the philosophy of Descartes, Hobbes, Bayle, Locke, or Leibniz, to the degree leading figures such as Lessing, Goethe, Kant, Hegel, Fichte, Schelling, Hegel, Heine, George Eliot, and Nietzsche, remained preoccupied, throughout their creative lives with Spinoza. Such continuing fundamental relevance down to our own time stands out among the most striking features of Spinoza's life and legacy.

No proper appraisal of Spinoza's achievement can be reached without fully considering the spectacularly embattled character of his philosophy, his unceasing efforts to subvert the dominant intellectual, religious, and political structures of his age, and his founding an activist philosophical "sect" that unleashed a fundamental struggle within European culture and ideas and which arguably remains the most important feature of his legacy. It is also true, though, and a central paradox of his life-story, that Spinoza mostly avoided encounters, debates, and networking, and shut himself away for long stretches to refine and further develop his philosophy. Defiant and challenging though he was, for long periods he also remained out of sight and personally reclusive. This aspect was emphasized by a north German official, a correspondent of Leibniz recalling his own visit to Spinoza in The Hague, in 1672, in a letter to Christian Kortholt in April 1681, when he and Spinoza discussed their incompatible views about salvation. He met Spinoza "in his solitude; for he seemed to live for himself only, always alone and as if buried in his study."[1] It was part of Spinoza's style and uniqueness as a philosopher that he grasped that he could challenge and rebel against the society of his time, striving to reform it fundamentally, more effectively by developing his system inconspicuously, in a furtive manner avoiding conflict, than by seeking confrontation. He could not succeed, he grasped, by directly antagonizing and, like the Koerbaghs, openly defying the society around him; his best prospect of succeeding lay in remaining surreptitiously active, promoting his discreet movement behind the scenes while refining his system in discussion with friends.

---

[1] Freudenthal/Walther, *Lebensgeschichte* ii, 48; Steenbakkers, "Spinoza's Life," 46n3.

Although there were many contributors to the rise of the Radical Enlightenment during the half century from 1660, and while it was a set of conditions, social and cultural circumstances—not any individual—that caused the deep rift between the underground radical and the publicly proclaimed moderate mainstream sides of the Enlightenment, Spinoza was unquestionably the most influential, formative figure on the radical side of the equation. While in no way the originator or cause of the fundamental Europe-wide struggle internal to the Enlightenment that ensued, he was the prime framer of the terms and concepts forming the underground opposition to the mainstream Enlightenment through the late seventeenth and throughout the eighteenth century. This fact, soon noted everywhere, not least in England, was eloquently captured by the Baxterite theologian, John Howe, when describing the dilemma facing the Western world's Protestant mainstream at the dawn of the new century in seeking to promote their programme of moderate reform. From the outset, he and the English Protestant mainstream aimed at a carefully defined, limited toleration opposed to full comprehensive toleration that, while upholding "mixed government" (constitutional monarchy), would maintain firm limits on freedom of thought and expression in Britain and Ireland using the blasphemy laws and other means to guard and reinforce core Christianity. From the late seventeenth century, religiously tinted "moderate Enlightenment" in Britain represented a rapidly growing, predominant project, supported by many. "But now, be all this never so plain," warned a worried Howe, in 1702, "it will by some, be thought all false, if they find any man to have contrivance enough to devise some contrary scheme of things, and confidence enough to pretend to prove it, till that proof be detected of weakness and vanity, which must be our further business with Spinoza."[2]

Spinoza's system was totally misconceived, morally wrong, and extremely damaging contended nearly all leading scholars in the decades after his death, not least Howe and the Baxterites; but during the last quarter of the seventeenth century and the early eighteenth, he was also the only plausible candidate for the role of Howe's universal arch-opponent of moderate toleration and enlightened reform, the sole adversary with "contrivance enough" to comprehensively challenge the mainstream. Indeed, even Howe, however menacing and despicable he judged Spinoza's philosophy to be, had to admit that, for all his blasphemous impiety, Spinoza carried it off "with great pomp and boast" and did draw a whole horde of followers after him, emerging uniquely placed, as Bayle and Toland repeatedly stressed, to provide the basic intellectual framework for all radicals rejecting the reconciling "enlightened" principles of the moderate mainstream of the era.

---

[2] Howe, *Animadversions on Spinoza*, 241.

It was Bayle and Toland above all who fixed Spinoza's image during the early Enlightenment as the presiding "athée de système" [system-building atheist], chief "virtuous atheist" and founder of the most subversive of modern philosophical sects, the one employing a wholly new approach ["une méthode toute nouvelle"]. If Spinoza achieved his unique but for the early Enlightenment also predominantly negative status by developing positions ensuring that during his lifetime, and the decades following, he could not be discussed in a positive light anywhere in Christendom but in mainstream culture would continue to be referred to only negatively, Bayle and Toland utilized this circumstance rather cunningly, exploiting the very prejudices consigning Spinoza to darkest notoriety, to problematize and water down objections to his philosophy and, ultimately, in subtle ways ridicule, discredit, and reject them. This Bayle did especially in his *Dictionnaire* (1697), by continually broaching Spinoza in widely divergent contexts causing "Spinoza" to loom over virtually the entire history of human thought since the remotest times and employing his—for many readers deeply baffling—affectation, or imposture, of defending conventional theological claims and conventional judgements using fideistic and sceptical arguments that often seemed painfully inadequate against Spinoza's searing criticism. This in turn figured among the chief reasons for persistent accusations during his lifetime that Bayle himself was a closet "Spinosiste" and atheist (which arguably he was).

Whether or not the mature Bayle was deliberately sabotaging the prevailing view of Spinoza, there is no question that he subtly but effectively ridiculed what most people of his era thought and believed, and that one of his main tools for undermining what most scholars taught, were his frequent forays into history of philosophy and religious sects to advance his "Spinozismus ante Spinozam [Spinozism before Spinoza]" *topos* presenting core Spinozistic positions as something universal and omnipresent pervading a dazzling array of ancient, modern, and oriental contexts. Nor could one mistake his smuggling into the picture an unmistakable dash of admiration by unequivocally placing Spinoza top of his list of the world's "virtuous atheists." Bayle's image of Spinoza as a universal thinker and "virtuous atheist" in the 1680s and 1690s generated a highly potent dissenting trend running flat counter to the predominant effort of the West's intellectual elite to screen out Spinoza the man pushing him into oblivion.

Spinoza's breakthrough to greatness in the 1680s and 1690s, was therefore both astounding and yet strikingly truncated. His was a universal presence in Western thought from the 1670s onwards in several key respects, yet in society generally and the universities he became a major force with shocking, destabilizing impetus largely in a negative, restricted way; the positive features stressed by Bayle being promoted and publicized only underground, in the clandestine, forbidden philosophical literature of the day and bookshops under the counter. On the surface, the impact, confined chiefly to the sphere of critique of religion and Bible hermeneutics, was heavily muffled without his social and political philosophy gaining any respectability. In the decades down to the publications of the mature Christian Wolff (1679–1754), in the 1730s and 1740s, it remained everywhere impermissible to cite Spinoza in teaching, academic debate, and disputations in any positive fashion. One could not recommend his philosophy or suggest his work should be studied or quoted. It remained illegal to publish his philosophy and in most of Europe, including the Netherlands, to advertise or sell his books.

Spinoza nevertheless attained a veiled positive universality almost immediately for a tiny fringe, heirs to his underground network of allies and disciples, envisaging their hero as their supreme guide, as the works of Tschirnhaus, Cuffeler, Van Balen, Van Leenhof, Boulainvilliers, Toland, and Tindal furtively reveal, as did also, more emphatically and defiantly, many unpublished French-language clandestine philosophical manuscripts of the era. Bayle's placing Spinoza first among "virtuous atheists" was taken seriously by exactly this clandestine few, those zealously venerating his memory and cultivating his philosophy in an underhand manner, unseen by most.

Above all it was long forbidden to teach the essential components of Spinoza's philosophy which indeed remained heavily veiled for centuries. At the heart of Spinoza's philosophy was his quest to uncover what makes "life worth living," what defines and explains the good life both individual and collective. In this regard it was slightly unfortunate that the editors of the *Opera Posthuma* changed the original wording in a key phrase of the *Ethics* (Part IV, appendix, point 5), as the surviving Vatican copy of the *Ethics* reveals. For the original wording, partly retained in the Dutch of the *Nagelate Schriften*, was not as it now stands: "No life, then, is *rational* without understanding, and things are good where characterized by understanding while on the contrary, only those things, that prevent us from perfecting our reason and enjoying the rational life, those alone we term evil." The original reading was: "No life, therefore is a *life-giving life* [*vita vitalis;* or *life worth living*] without understanding [nulla igitur vita vitalis est sine intelligentia], and things are good only insofar as they aid men to enjoy the life of the mind, which is defined by knowledge [ut mentis vita fruatur, quae intelligentia definitur] while, on the contrary, only those things hindering man from perfecting his reason and leading a rational life can by us be called bad."[3] Even in the twenty-first century, interpreters of Spinoza, trained in philosophy departments, still often lean too far towards stressing the role of "pure reason" in Spinoza's outlook while ignoring his stress on the quest for the individual and collective good life, the pursuit of happiness, achievable by expanding knowledge with a view to transforming and enhancing the social and political reality around us.

Taking a long view, the protracted, tortuous evolution of Spinoza's image from that of a suppressed presence to an eventually largely positive one reached a

---

[3] Spinoza, *Ethics* Part IV, appendix, point 5, see Spinoza, *Oeuvres* iv, *Ethica*; Spinoza, *Nagelate Schriften*, 252; Spinoza, *Collected Works* (ed. Curley) i, 588–9; Eliot, *Spinoza's* Ethics, 279.

middle stage which proved irreversible, extending from the 1690s to the late eighteenth century, thanks to Bayle and Toland. Spinozism's emergence from the 1690s as a widely recognized subversive tendency throughout Europe forms the backcloth to Samuel Clarke's contention in his *A Demonstration of the Being and Attributes of God* (1705), that Spinoza was indeed now "the most celebrated patron of atheism in our time." Even Bayle's old sparring partner, Le Clerc—abandoning his own earlier refusal to discuss Spinoza, and, by 1713, tacitly acknowledging that his longstanding rival had effectively won this particular battle, eventually switched from his old strategy of never mentioning Spinoza to dubbing Spinoza, "the most famous atheist of our time [le plus fameux athée de notre temps]."[4] One fortunate result of this first historical shift occurring at a relatively early stage, before 1700, was that there lingered still several living contemporary observers with personal memories of Spinoza and his circle able to confide their reminiscences to others. In this way, vivid appraisals, recollections, and evaluations of Spinoza's life were gathered up at the last feasible moment, and then widely publicized by Bayle, the careful, scrupulous Colerus (Figure 42.1), and Sebastian Kortholt.

One such voice more knowledgeable than most about Spinoza the man, Salomon van Til, writing in 1694, provided one of the most accurate and helpful of these late seventeenth-century perceptions of Spinoza's career and achievement:

> Benedictus de Spinoza who to begin with posed as an admirer and the interpreter of the Cartesian philosophy, and behind that mask attracted students to be instructed by him, only gradually brought up grounds to speak against [Descartes]. His skill in mathematics and cutting lenses opened the door enabling him to find access to many prominent persons. Later, showing himself somewhat more openly, this assaulter of belief understood how to sow confusion and attempted to show the world how the Scriptures are of human making, compiled and put together at different times.[5]

Spinoza's explosive intervention in religious studies, in 1670, thus ultimately helped initiate the middle stage of the three basic phases of his posthumous career—wholly curtained off; partial exposure; full emergence—in a way reflecting the three main stages of his actual career during his life. If, during the decades after his death, his philosophy began to be glimpsed by a few as a wide-ranging exceptionally unified system, it emerged only into the half-light and its fraught continuing confinement dragged on subsequently for many decades. Until the late eighteenth century, Spinoza's career's second stage as profiled by Van Til—his

---

[4] Clarke, *A Demonstration*, 20; Israel, *Enlightenment Contested*, 766; Kors, *Naturalism and Unbelief*, 95.
[5] Van Til, *Voor-hof der heydenen*, 5.

Figure 42.1 Johannes Colerus, *Das Leben des Bened. von Spinoza*. Spinoza Frankfurt und Leipzig: s.n., 1733. IAS Spinoza Research Collection.

challenging the idea that the Jewish and Christian Scriptures were divine revelation—entirely dominated Spinoza's now looming but truncated image, the sole aspect of his life that widely pervaded and infiltrated society, ensuring that for most of the Enlightenment era there was still no truly open consideration or discussion of his philosophy, political thought, and authentic legacy.

From the late 1680s onwards, the term "Spinozist" began displacing previous fashions for labelling everything most reprehensible and abominable in society and religion as "Socinian" or "Hobbist." The term "Spinozist" began to be everywhere adopted as a virtual synonym for "atheist," first in the Netherlands, then more widely. As Koelman expressed the point, in 1692, "today among us all atheists are called *Spinosisten*."[6] Evaluating the intellectual climate of his day, in London, in 1709, one of the great language scholars and experts on Russia of the age, Henry William Ludolph (1655–1710), secretary to the Danish embassy in Britain—who earlier, in 1698, had toured the Near East, using his formidable Greek, Hebrew, and other languages to exhort Christians, Jews, and freethinkers

---

[6] Koelman, *Het Vergift*, 487; Mori, *L'ateismo dei moderni*, 57–8.

of every stripe in Jaffa, Jerusalem, and Cairo—assured his brother that "Spinozism has spread itself extremely here [i.e. London] just as much as in Holland [le spinozisme s'est répandu extrêmement ici aussi bien qu'en Hollande]."[7]

Some scholars, unwilling to accept Spinoza's foundational importance for the Radical Enlightenment, claim that such remarks prove very little—only that the term "Spinozist," highly prevalent in the early eighteenth century though it undoubtedly was, seethed merely as a term of abuse, a synonym for "atheist," a term lacking all content. Were this at all true, it would still render Spinoza the focal point of a fundamental question. Why, for a century after his death, should atheists generally suddenly come to be named after the person Spinoza? But the significance of the paradigm shift from "Socinian" and "Hobbist" to "Spinozist" stretches far beyond that. Numerous observations about the growing prevalence of "Spinozism" among freethinkers and the clandestine philosophical underground in Western Europe confirm that the term "Spinozism" in reality carried a formidable baggage and, for contemporaries, signified much more than just "atheism." Even if Spinoza's philosophy could still not be openly discussed and, until the publications of Christian Wolff in the 1730s and 1740s, presented as something universities, scholars, and the public needed to assimilate and digest, for a great many, from the late seventeenth century down to the early nineteenth, the term "Spinozism" indubitably entailed a baggage of considerable complexity and enduring importance combining a range of core radical positions in philosophy, religious studies, and political thought. A "Spinozist," explained Bekker, is someone with a long list of challenging theses, entailing unlimited universal applicability of reason, rejection of all previous philosophy, subversive desire to change men's thinking, and unrelenting hostility to "priestcraft," meaning churches and churchmen (including synagogues and rabbis), among much else. A follower of Spinoza, observed Leibniz succinctly, is a systematic denier of all miracles and the very possibility of the miraculous (thus not a Hobbist), and Revelation as well as divine providence and benevolence. If the term "atheist" could be applied to anyone considered godless, the term "Spinozist" meant an "atheist" denying miracles, revelation, divine providence, the sphere of supernatural, and the validity of religious authority on the basis of an overarching philosophical and political framework. Bekker, Bayle, Clarke, Le Clerc, Toland, Collins, Leibniz, and Wolff all concurred that this was how correctly to represent "Spinozism."

Spinoza's thought in this way acquired an undeniable centrality in the European Early Enlightenment that modern historians and philosophers have mostly been decidedly reluctant to acknowledge (even with respect to Bayle and Toland). But this does not mean Spinoza's life and legacy directly generated, caused, or gave rise to this more radical dimension of the Western

---

[7] Quoted in Bohrmann, *Spinozas Stellung zur Religion*, 76.

Enlightenment. Profound tensions in society combined with recent breakthroughs in science were the essential cause and origin of the Radical Enlightenment, generating accumulating rejection of the social, religious, political, and educational status quo, mounting friction bound to be reflected in subsequent deep rifts in philosophy and social and political theory. The Enlightenment impulse to apply "reason" to resolve society's difficulties resulted in large measure from mounting antipathy to the vast proliferation of sects and factions in the Netherlands, Britain, Ireland, and parts of Germany and endless deadlock of traditional confessional conflict between Catholicism and Protestantism aggravated by the stalemate of the Thirty Years War. Equally, antipathy arose in France, Britain, the Netherlands, and elsewhere to the despotic efforts of rulers such as Louis XIV, Charles II, James II, Spain's monarchs and the German princes to extend and reinforce royal absolutism by minimizing and quashing religious dissent. Late seventeenth-century absolutist efforts to impose religious uniformity often backfired. Thus, Louis XIV's cancellation of the Edict of Nantes, in 1685, caused the flight of many thousands of French Huguenots—and a huge quantity of capital and skills—to Holland, England, Brandenburg, the Rhineland, Ireland, and eventually America, generating a broad social reaction of dismay and resolute opposition. Growing resistance to political tyranny and oppressive religious authority in the minds of the persecuted, generated an inevitable fundamental ideological collision with those promoting enlightened values clashing more and more with those striving to assert faith, church sway, and absolutism more stringently.

Factions and groups demanding toleration, reconciliation of churches, and a loosening of theology's grip over education, morality, and society, were thus the primal motor all across Europe for questioning and reappraising the fundamental principles of society, religion, education and politics. This new tendency so fundamental to shaping modernity was driven also by recent advances in science from Galileo and Descartes through to Huygens, Locke, Leibniz, and Newton. Far from being the work of any one or even several thinkers, the brutal realities and stalled conflicts of the seventeenth century themselves were what effectively generated the motive force and determined the direction of the Western Enlightenment. No aspect of Spinoza's biography is more fundamentally consonant with the basic character of his age than his fierce condemnation of the endless warring, feuding, and "hatred" as he called it, of the everywhere furiously persecuting and intolerant churches, sects, and theologians. For all Christian (and Jewish) reformers and critics of whatever stripe, "reason" came increasingly into play in the 1660s, 1670s, and 1680s, and from then on, remained the prime justification and instrument of reform, the way to resolve and surmount theological rifts and press for more responsible, representative, and conciliatory solutions and government.

The inevitable, unalterable problem with this, from the very outset, was that the basic elements of the "crisis of the European conscience" as it has been dubbed, posed a universal, inescapable predicament for all Western societies, a profound dilemma that all segments of society had to confront. Every particular reform initiative added to and reinforced the same underlying problem. Does applying "reason" to solve society's difficulties mean rationalizing and transforming the entire religious, political, and educational structure of society, or only those parts not subject to religious authority? Does toleration and dampening theological ire mean tolerating all points of view or only those reconcilable ultimately with faith and royal supremacy? Does rationalizing the laws of one's country mean everyone should share the same responsibilities and status under the law, or that noble privilege and separate status, even if adjusted and mitigated, should remain constitutionally, intellectually, and religiously predominant and in large measure beyond critique? What should happen regarding kings, churches, and nobility, the three presiding components of pre-Enlightenment society?

Although some historians still reject the distinction between moderate and radical Enlightenment, this is really just blindness to the inevitable logic of the challenges facing European societies and states at the time. Logically, hardly any in-between positions were available. Either toleration is selective or it is comprehensive; there *is* no in-between position. Either nobility dominates society or it does not. Either religious authority is separate from, and in some respects above, the authority of the sovereign state or it is not. Either education comes under religious authority or it does not. Either kings and in aristocratic republics, nobles, rule society as the undisputed sovereign, as Hobbes insisted they should, or else society as a whole and the "general will" is the sovereign. One or the other but not both must be the guiding principle at any one time. These were always bound to be mutually exclusive conflicting paths allowing few options for nuancing in between. Therefore, it is unhelpful for any scholar to quibble over whether the distinction between moderate and radical Enlightenment is "helpful," meaningful, or valid. Logically, there was never any possibility that Enlightenment bifurcation into two rival streams, moderate and radical, would not be the most fundamental rift within the Enlightenment and would not be the Enlightenment's prime shaping feature from start to finish.

This unavoidable basic rift in Western society, from the late seventeenth century onwards, created an ineradicable connection between Spinoza and the Enlightenment's basic predicament, plainly far more so than in the cases of Hobbes, Locke, Newton, and even Bayle, or any other major thinker of the era, and helps explain why Spinoza remained a living force in Western thought in the nineteenth and twentieth centuries when Descartes, Leibniz, Malebranche, and Locke, as far as current philosophizing was concerned, all became phenomena of the past.

What took longest and proved most difficult to reverse was Spinoza's essentially negative image in mainstream culture. By the 1690s, Spinoza was more notorious than any other "atheist" in history. But even ambiguously and circuitously discussing Spinoza's life and work, as Bayle and Toland specialized in doing, was to invite grave and lasting reproach. Certainly, one could more freely discuss Spinoza in private. In his correspondence Leibniz admits extensive overlap between some of his key ideas and Spinoza's, and that Spinoza played a large part in his own intellectual evolution; but he admitted nothing of the sort, nor could he, in his published writings. Le Clerc and Simon borrowed extensively from Spinoza yet offset this by concealing the fact and invariably harshly denouncing Spinoza. It was Spinoza's following alone that established a resilient tradition refusing all reconciliation of "reason" and faith, rejecting Locke's mantra "supra rationem [above reason]," and the moderates' toleration of some but not of all, while rejecting too the privileged status of churchmen and nobles and repudiating those limiting royal power rather than abolishing it on a democratic republican basis.

If conservative churchmen and reactionary elements were glad to join hands to support the moderate Enlightenment's post-1690 fierce campaign against Spinoza, it was the Lockeans and Newtonians of the early and middle Enlightenment that long remained the backbone of the moderate Enlightenment world view and repression of "Spinozism." If the initial strategy of concealing Spinoza and his identity had collapsed by the 1690s, the prohibition on publishing and positively discussing Spinoza and his philosophy in polite society remained in force for well over a century and was not without considerable long-term effects. If Spinoza's looming negative presence down to the 1720s receded somewhat, in France and Britain at least, in the half century or so that followed, he still remained a major force among the radical underground, hovering everywhere in the background, most notably in the early development of Diderot.

From 1670, for over a century, "Spinozism," concrete, specific, and looming large though it unquestionably did, also remained for the reading public a masked, subterranean force, one that in large part was philosophically silent in its impact, flourishing most obviously in the clandestine philosophical literature. Ira Wade, surveying the French intellectual scene between 1680 and 1750, was basically correct in his judgement, in 1967, that "the greatest single influence exerted upon the writers of this period is that of Spinoza. So great is his influence, in fact, that one is tempted to see in the whole movement a gigantic manifestation of Spinozism triumphant over other forms of thought."[8] But Wade fell seriously short in failing sufficiently to emphasize that this is true only in relation to the "clandestine" oppositional, underground currents of French thought. It was very far from true of official, publicly endorsed philosophy, science, and Bible criticism. Spinozism was the major philosophical inspiration of the underground clandestine philosophical literature, including Diderot's early writings, but remained everywhere rigorously banished from polite society and the universities and,

---

[8] Wade, *Clandestine Organization and Diffusion*, 269; see also Kors, *Naturalism and Unbelief*, 69–99.

outwardly at least, was regularly scorned and disapproved of by Voltaire, Montesquieu, Hume, and the other great moderates.

Voltaire, in his last major venture, the *Questions sur l'Encyclopédie* (1770–2), redoubled his lifelong campaign to counter Spinoza and the wider "Spinozist" challenge, making this one of the central features of his thought and outlook during his last years. A dark symbol of impiety and blasphemy for most, for the radical intellectual wing (Diderot, d'Holbach, and Condorcet) opposed to his own more moderate stance, repeatedly complained the late Voltaire in tones of alarm, Spinoza was the ultimate source of inspiration and a uniquely pre-eminent icon. At a time when Spinoza's books still remained inaccessible and unknown to the vast majority of readers, indeed in most of Europe extremely hard to find, a distorted, in Voltaire's eyes absurdly inflated "Spinoza myth" still ridiculously flourished behind the scenes that, according to him (with some justification), bore no real relation to Spinoza's actual system.

The myth Voltaire assailed as ridiculous was becoming more and more detached from genuine familiarity with Spinoza's actual texts and specific arguments. "What will particularly astonish the crowd of those who cry 'Spinoza, Spinoza'," mocked Voltaire in the fourth volume of his *Questions sur l'Encyclopédie*, "but have never read him," is his proclaiming, in Latin "so as to be understood only by a very small number," that he loves God and derives his ethical principles solidly and directly from that love.[9] Beyond that, held Voltaire, the real Spinoza was impenetrably obscure and in no way deserving of the great renown he enjoyed in the circles cultivating clandestine philosophy. Even Bayle failed utterly to understand Spinoza correctly, urged Voltaire, owing to Spinoza's impenetrable obscurity. "I have always thought, indeed, that Spinoza often did not understand himself and that that is the principal reason why he has not been understood."[10]

Nevertheless, for all his proclaiming Spinoza irrelevant despite his philosophical opponents, the bolder Enlightenment *esprits* insisting otherwise, Voltaire betrayed what he really thought by devoting considerable space during the final phase of his writing, in the 1770s, to the world's unresolved "Spinoza" problem. Indeed, assailing "Spinozism" was the hub of his strategy for countering what he saw as the wrong kind of Enlightenment propagated by Diderot, d'Holbach, Helvétius, the young Condorcet and a host of others. In this indirect fashion, Voltaire too conceded that Spinoza's positive achievement, however much under wraps, was indeed uniquely formidable.

The middle-stage encouraging everyone outside a self-appointed underground intellectual coterie to vilify Spinoza's name while continuing to veil his philosophy, to highlight and abominate "Spinoza" but avoid as far as possible presenting

---

[9] Voltaire, *Questions sur l'Encyclopédie* (1770) iv, 431–3; Israel, *Democratic Enlightenment*, 660–4.
[10] Voltaire, *Questions sur l'Encyclopédie* (1770) iv, 434.

any aspect of his life and work in a positive fashion, proved astoundingly prolonged. But so did the last, post-1780 stage of the tortuous three-stage unveiling of the person "Spinoza" and the reality of his philosophy, replacing the "Spinoza" first wholly suppressed and then, from the 1690s, loudly denounced. The final stage too proved indeed extraordinarily protracted and even, down to today, remains perhaps in some respects incomplete.

It was Lessing, Mendelssohn, and Jacobi above all who engineered the start of the third great shift in perceptions of Spinoza's legacy, especially during the 1780s, provoking the cultural uproar in Germany known as the *Pantheismusstreit* [pantheism struggle] which impacted powerfully on the public consciousness and universities, spilling over into the wider public sphere and bringing Spinoza for the first time into core public debates involving philosophy and scholarship, and for some, and soon many, leading to Spinoza being studied in a now essentially positive, unconcealed fashion. Lessing, Goethe, Herder, Fichte, Schelling, and the young Hegel were the first front-rank European writers to acknowledge Spinoza not in the furtive manner of Bayle, Tindal, Toland, or Diderot but openly, as a major force in Western thought and culture, and at least in some respects a positive one that every serious thinker must study and ponder.

However, this was not the end of the convoluted story of Spinoza's dramatically shifting posthumous reputation and the eventual emergence of his life and legacy into the full light of day. If, from the 1780s down to Nietzsche, Spinoza was central to German thought, nothing of the sort could yet be said of France, Britain, America, or even the Netherlands. Moreover, powerful inhibitions and strictures lingered even in the early nineteenth-century German-speaking world. In the lectures Friedrich Schelling (1775–1854) prepared in the mid-1830s for his students, he publicly admired Spinoza up to a point. It was now useless trying to hide Spinoza's overwhelming centrality, or to deny "the Spinozist system will always remain in a certain sense a model"; still, Schelling felt duty-bound to warn university students against the allure and fatalistic features of Spinoza's philosophy, maintaining that Spinoza's determinism and discussion of the mind do not allocate sufficient scope to "freedom," and that his discussion of God is unsatisfactory. But if another philosopher ever rescues God and "freedom" with another system that does restore these to their full stature but otherwise stands "with just as great contours, with the same simplicity, as a perfect *Gegenbild* [counter-image] of the Spinozist system, this would truly be the highest system conceivable. This is why Spinozism, despite the many attacks on it, and the many supposed refutations, has never really become something truly past, never really been overcome up to now, and no one can hope to progress to the true and complete in philosophy who has not at least once in his life lost himself in the abyss of Spinozism."[11]

---

[11] Schelling, *On the History of Modern Philosophy*, 66.

Spinoza's image had, with huge historical and philosophical implications, been drastically transformed—but thus far in German-speaking Central Europe only, and even there not fully. Discussing Spinoza's Bible criticism continued to be discouraged and his political thought and social reformism remained almost totally ignored, scandalously so, according to the Hungarian-Jewish 1848 revolutionary Ignać Einhorn (or Horn) (1825–75) in his 1851 pioneering study of Spinoza's political ideas.[12] Not until the middle of the nineteenth century, partly due to the growing impact of German Idealism, did France follow Germany in rehabilitating Spinoza and transforming him into a central figure in the history of modern thought, an indispensable philosopher for anyone interested in understanding what matters most. Between 1842 and 1872, the works of Spinoza "translated into French for the first time" by the philosophy professor Émile Saisset (1814–63) appeared in Paris in eventually three volumes in thirty-two separate editions. But this mid-nineteenth-century French effusion placing Spinoza now centre stage was largely the work of Parisian professors and intellectuals like Saisset, the Hegelian moral philosopher Paul Janet (1823–99), and J. F. Nourrison, scholars chiefly seeking to locate Spinoza as a historical landmark, in the manner of Victor Cousin (1792–1867), the dominant influence in shaping university philosophy in nineteenth-century France, especially in relation to Descartes, seventeenth-century "rationalism," and the "French" philosophical tradition. In particular, they aimed to profile Spinoza as an outlying anti-empiricist and antithesis to Descartes, even a religious visionary if not oriental dreamer, whose pantheism supposedly showed how Western reason can yet be yoked, whether meaningfully or threateningly, to a deep non-confessional religious spirituality.[13]

No attention was yet being paid, in Germany or France, to Spinoza's radical political and social reformism, and while some limited interest was shown in his biography, the new French Spinoza studies' main concern was to reveal to the public how the central role of Descartes in Spinoza's development was offset, counterbalanced, even outweighed, by medieval Jewish philosophers, especially Maimonides and Gersonides, a point heavily stressed by Saisset in his long article on "Jewish philosophy," entitled "La Philosophie des Juifs, Maïmonide et Spinoza," in the January 1862 issue of *Revue des Deux Mondes*.

Still, the mid-nineteenth-century French approach opened up important new perspectives. In another long article on Spinoza in the *Revue des Deux Mondes*, of July 1867, Janet asks why, given that Spinoza stands among the most important figures in Western thought, was he a product of Dutch soil and specifically of the late seventeenth century Dutch Republic? It was no use any longer pretending that

---

[12] Israel, *Jewish Revolutionaries*, 437–9.
[13] Moreau, "Traduire Spinoza," 223; Moreau, *Spinoza, L'expérience*, 236–8; Krop, *Spinoza, een paradoxale icoon*, 359.

Spinoza did not possess a unique and fundamental importance in European culture and history. But why was this? The reasons must surely be sought in his biography connecting him to his Dutch background and especially to the difficulties seventeenth-century Europe faced over religious divisions and confessional strife. Attention had to be paid to the fact that late seventeenth-century Holland, unlike France, Germany, Italy, or Britain, opened up a certain "liberty of thought" that rendered organized revolt against religious authority and confessional theology possible and to an extent effective.[14] The in the 1850s discovered *Korte Verhandeling*, observed Janet, transforms our picture by proving Spinoza was not just a producer of ideas and writings but the founder of a "religious" sect, a band of devoted followers rebelling against Christianity as then understood and against all confessional narrowness and existing structures of religious authority, something fundamental, he says, that had until now (1867) not been grasped at all.[15]

Spinoza was indeed one of the "saints of philosophy," agreed Nourrisson, possibly even the foremost such "saint" since Socrates, but unlike the West's other great philosophers was now, recent research into his life showed, proving to have reached down even among the common people and to have established a still extant sect of followers, something, before Hegel at least, no other modern thinker had achieved. Was that not remarkable? Far from Spinoza's following being just a seventeenth-century sect, there was an enduring, slowly growing but increasingly formidable undercurrent so that, in his day, Nourrisson suggested, France was being transformed by Spinoza, its dominant mind-set (among the intellectual class) shifting fundamentally from "Voltairianisme" to "le spinozisme."[16] The extraordinary thing, notes Nourrisson with considerable insight, is that Spinoza, unlike any other great thinker has by turns swung from obscurity and banishment, from being left a "dead dog" as Lessing expressed it, to being celebrated like a demi-god, alternately buried and exalted. There was now a pressing need, anyone seriously contemplating the history of Western thought could only conclude, to investigate this strange, unparalleled phenomenon and finally come to grips with Spinoza's remarkably elusive biography which thus far, stressed Nourrisson, had everywhere been overlooked.[17]

By the 1860s, attitudes to Spinoza in Britain and the United States stood in sharp contrast to those in France and Germany. Yet, even there, one perceived incipient signs of change if only among a far smaller fringe of the intellectual elite and public than in Continental Europe. The Scottish physician and librarian Robert Willis (1799–1878), among the first major medical historians published a translation of the *TTP* in 1862. But its impact was minute. When introducing his

---

[14] Janet, "Spinoza et le spinozisme," 470–2.
[15] Janet, "Spinoza et le spinozisme," 479; Moreau, "Traduire Spinoza," 222.
[16] Nourrisson, *Spinoza et le naturalisme contemporain*, 3, 13.
[17] Nourrisson, *Spinoza et le naturalisme contemporain*, 14–15.

later book, *Benedict de Spinoza: His Life, Correspondence, and Ethics* (London, 1870), Willis complained that "Spinoza may, indeed, be said to be a name among us and nothing more." Aside from "two or three" little-noticed articles, "we have nothing in English calculated to convey a true idea of the life and writings of the man who nevertheless continues, two centuries after his death, to influence the philosophy and religious thought of Europe more powerfully than any individual who has lived since the days of Luther."[18] Willis, who read German and Dutch as well as Latin, French, Italian, and Spanish, was, of course, perfectly correct and greatly struck by this extraordinary anomaly.

Willis' only two significant predecessors—apart from George Eliot—in submitting this resounding complaint, were the famous historian J. A. Froude (1818–94) who, in 1849, provoked public outrage by announcing his defection from conventional Christianity and in July 1855 published a notable article on Spinoza's life in the *Westminster Review*, and George Henry Lewes (1817–78) who, as first editor (in 1865–6) of the influential *The Fortnightly Review*, an English echo of the Parisian *Revue des Deux Mondes*, published a long article, in April 1866, entitled just "Spinoza."[19] By then Froude and Lewes had been studying Spinoza, "hungering for some knowledge of this theological pariah," as Lewes expressed it, since the 1840s. In 1843, Lewes had published an initial exploratory study which he designated "the first attempt to vindicate the great philosopher before the English public," but later admitted that that effort had failed. In 1854, he persuaded his not yet famous partner, George Eliot, to set to work on the first English translation of the *Ethics*, which he himself had earlier started but failed to carry through.[20] It remained effectively unpublished until 2020.

Besides long endeavouring to persuade British opinion that Spinoza mattered which proved no easy task, Lewes was original in stressing the significance of the long autobiographical passage in Spinoza's unfinished early treatise, the *Emendation of the Intellect*, and contending that Spinoza is important for modern readers too as a personality, "one of the most interesting figures in the history of philosophy – a standing lesson of the injustice of mankind to those who are honest in their opinions when the opinions happen to be unpopular" (as indeed was Lewes himself).[21] That autobiographical passage of Spinoza, he insisted, is not idle rhetoric but "serious conviction." Rarely has anyone, he agreed with Nourrisson, undergone such dramatic convolutions in the public sphere, transformed from a devil into a saint, a change which he too attributed chiefly to Lessing and Mendelssohn "whose sincerity and penetration at once discerned in the execrated writings a massive grandeur and serenity which claimed all honour."

[18] Willis, *Benedict de Spinoza*, p. vii.
[19] Carlisle, "Introduction" to Eliot, *Spinoza's Ethics*, 27–31.
[20] Lewes, "Spinoza," 388; Carlisle, "Introduction" to Eliot, *Spinoza's Ethics*, 15, 17, 333.
[21] Lewes, "Spinoza," 388–9; Carlisle, "Introduction" to Eliot, *Spinoza's Ethics*, 18.

Researching and understanding Spinoza the man, uncovering the details of his biography, had by the 1860s finally been recognized as a desideratum of high priority. However, stressed Lewes, if Spinoza is one of the most important personages in the history of Western thought, illuminating his biography will prove no easy task. "Of Benedict himself as a child we know nothing." Of Spinoza's "inward life we know nothing." Study of Spinoza's life, the unfortunate truth was, had barely progressed beyond the point reached by Colerus.[22] Lewes was right. Froude's 1855 article on Spinoza's life and work contributed marginally to making Spinoza better known in the English-speaking world, but, simplistic and hagiographic, it reflected very little of the actual historical context of Spinoza's life.

Nietzsche, meanwhile, contributed appreciably to the nineteenth century's recognition of Spinoza as one of the greatest of philosophers, but without showing any interest in his social and political theories and reformism, or in the "sect" he founded. The modern researcher into Spinoza's life and work who first effectively drew a picture of Spinoza as an ideologically engaged leader of a "sect" involved in a lifelong battle to undermine religious authority, extend toleration, promote freethinking and free discussion, and one beset throughout his life, not only after his death, by active enemies, was probably Johannes van Vloten (1818–83), the pugnacious Dutch ex-professor with a notorious reputation as a fiercely polemical freethinker, especially after resigning his professorship at the Illustrious School of Deventer, in 1867. In his *Benedictus de Spinoza* (1862) which appeared in a second and expanded edition in 1871, Van Vloten felt it his mission to fill in the gaps, correct the distortions inherited from the past and make good what he considered Leibniz's pillaging, ungenerous treatment of Spinoza, Kant's opportunistic, unjustified scorn, and Hegel's failure to grasp Spinoza's true historical significance.

Devoting the latter part of his life to promoting Spinoza's cause, Van Vloten edited crucial editions of his works together with J. P. N. Land (1834–97), lending a fresh spur to Spinoza studies in his own country, and capping his efforts by becoming the driving force behind the public campaign to erect the famous statue of Spinoza inaugurated on the Paviljoensgracht in The Hague, in 1880.[23] More broadly, two centuries after Spinoza's death, Van Vloten partially succeeded, albeit to the furious annoyance of many, in transforming Spinoza into a Dutch national icon.[24] What was original and important about Van Vloten's work regarding Spinoza's life and legacy was mainly his abolishing the myth of Spinoza as an obscure recluse lost in a remote world of metaphysics, replacing this nineteenth-century myth with a more true-to-life picture of an engaged and

---

[22] Lewes, "Spinoza," 389–90, 395, 397.
[23] Van Vloten, *Benedictus de Spinoza*, p. xi; Van Bunge, *Spinoza Past and Present*, 158–9.
[24] Krop, *Spinoza, een paradoxale icoon*, 337.

embattled cultural and social reformer. Beyond that, however, Van Vloten filled hardly any gaps in our picture, only marginally advancing the bleak sketch of Spinoza's life Lewes had provided earlier.

The glaring absence of any reliable and substantive biographical picture remained essentially as stark as before until the path-breaking research of the atheistic freethinker, teacher, and archivist K. O. Meinsma (1865–1929) published in his book *Spinoza en zijn kring* [Spinoza and His Circle] (1896). By using unpublished archival resources for the first time, Meinsma provided a detailed account of the group of disciples and allies around Spinoza and the intellectual context in which he operated. This was followed by the crucial documentary collection published by Jacob Freudenthal (1839–1907).[25] Having spent his early career teaching in Jewish schools and at the Breslau Jewish Theological Seminary (1864–75), it became Freudenthal's special mission to reveal the significance of the Jewish contribution to the history of Western philosophy and while Spinoza could hardly be depicted as an observant Jew or religious being in any conventional sense, he could perhaps plausibly be portrayed as an exceptionally upright, noble-minded personality, the very model of a philosopher as the nineteenth century understood the term, one whose life and thought can be seen as exuding positive ethical significance for all mankind. Later, as professor of philosophy of the University of Breslau (today Wrocław) from 1878, Freudenthal conceived the idea of collecting all traceable official and unofficial contemporary documents throwing light on Spinoza's life, family, and activity, the resulting compilation appearing in 1899.

However, Meinsma was not translated out of Dutch until a French translation appeared in 1983 and there were no revised editions, reprints, or translations of Freudenthal's hard-to-find compilation other than a version appearing in Hebrew at Vilna in 1913. Consequently, for many decades neither foundational resource was particularly easy to consult. The British Library, for example, and many other major libraries, possessed no copy of Freudenthal's volume of documents despite its being the chief resource for would-be biographers of Spinoza and students of his life and activity. The expanded and revised edition of Freudenthal produced by Manfred Walther, in 2006, therefore proved a further outstanding landmark, partly by making many key documents which Freudenthal published for the first and until then only time more accessible, as well as making available a range of precious new documents and commentary.

Spinoza's biography as a substantive field of present-day scholarship and discussion hence stands on the two, until relatively recently rather inaccessible, research foundations of Meinsma and Freudenthal; but much time passed before the grounding these two indispensable bundles of source material could be

---

[25] Freudenthal, *Die Lebensgeschichte Spinozas*.

significantly built on. Despite the notable contributions in the 1920s of Carl Gebhardt, study of Spinoza's life, legacy, and reception only really flowered from the 1960s and especially the 1980s onwards with the work of Révah, Mignini, Klever, Walther, Popkin, Yovel, Nadler, Akkerman, Steenbakkers, Van Bunge, Mertens, Krop, Wielema, Totaro, Laerke, Lavaert, Rovere, Gootjes, and the indefatigable Van de Ven, together forming the present-day international coterie of devoted biographers of Spinoza and his intimate circle—to all of whom this present volume is profoundly indebted.

Bibliography

Abbreviations

AGS	Archivo General de Simancas
ANTT	Arquivo Nacional do Torre de Tombo, Lisbon
ARH	Algemeen Rijksarchief [National Archives], The Hague
ARH OSA	Algemeen Rijksarchief [National Archives], The Hague Hervormde Kerk, Oud Synodaal Archief
BMGN	*Bijdragen en Mededelingen betreffende de Geschiedenis der Nederlanden*
CHRC	*Church History and Religious Culture*
CS	*Cahiers Spinoza*
DDPhil	*Dictionary of Seventeenth and Eighteenth Century Dutch Philosophers* (eds.) Wiep van Bunge et al. (2 vols. Bristol, 2003)
GA Amsterdam	Amsterdam City Archives (Stadsarchief Amsterdam)
GA Delft	Delft City Archives (Stadsarchief Delft)
GA Haarlem	Haarlem City Archives integrated with RNH
GA Leiden	Leiden Regional Archives (Gemeentearchief Leiden)
GA The Hague	City Archives (Haags Gemeentearchief)
GA Utrecht	Utrecht City Archives (Het Utrecht Archief)
GWND	*Geschiedenis van de wijsbegeerte in Nederland. Documentatieblad*
HKB	The Hague, Royal Library
IAS	Institute for Advanced Study, Princeton
IHR	*Intellectual History Review*
JHI	*Journal of the History of Ideas*
JHPh	*Journal of the History of Philosophy*
MeSp	*Mededelingen vanwege Het Spinozahuis* (Voorschoten)
OEMPh	*Oxford Studies in Early Modern Philosophy*
PAJHS	Publications of the American Jewish Historical Society
PRO SP	Public Record Office, London, State Papers
RA Gron. APS	Rijksarchief Groningen, Archief van de Provinciale Synode van Stad en Lande (1595–1815)
RA Noord-Holland	Rijksarchief Noord-Holland, Haarlem
RA Utr. PK	Rijksarchief Utrecht, Provinciale Kerkvergadering
REJ	*Revue des Études Juives*
RL Copenhagen	Royal Library Copenhagen
SR	*Studia Rosenthaliana*
SS	*Studia Spinozana*
TLS	*Times Literary Supplement*
VdV Corr.	Van de Ven, Correspondence reconstruction

Primary Sources

Abbadie, Jacques, *Traité de la vérité de la Religion Chrétienne* (2 vols., Rotterdam, 1684).
Aboab, Ishac, "Livro e Nota de ydades reduzido por my Isahck Aboab," in I. S. Révah (ed.), *Boletim Internacional de Bibliografía Luso-Brasileira* ii (1961), 276–310.
Acta der particuliere Synoden van Zuid-Holland, 1621–1700, (ed.) W. P. C. Knuttel (6 vols., The Hague, 1908–16).
Aitzema, Lieuwe van, *Historie of Verhael van saken van staet en oorlogh in, ende onmtrent de Verenigde Nederlanden* (14 vols., The Hague, 1667–71).
Aitzema, Lieuwe van, "Brieven van Aitzema in het Archief der Brusselse Nuntiatur," (ed.) J. D. M. Cornelissen, *Bijdragen en Mededeelingen van het Historisch Genootschap* 49 (1928), 128–57.
Allinga, Petrus, *Cartesianismi gangraena insanabilis* (Utrecht, 1680).
Amsterdamsche Courant, De (Amsterdam news journal, 1670–8).
Andala, Ruard, *Cartesius verus Spinozismi eversor et physicae experimentalis architectus* (Franeker, 1719).
'Andlo, Petrus ab' [Regnerus van Mansvelt], *Specimen confutationis dissertationis quam Samuel Maresius edidit De Abusu philosophiae Cartesianae* (Leiden, 1670).
'Andlo, Petrus ab' [Regnerus van Mansvelt], *Animadversiones Ad Vindicae Dissertationis quam Samuel Maresius edidit De Abusu Philosophiae Cartesianae* (Leiden, 1671).
Appendix Van 't Catalogus van de Boecken Van Mr. Jan de Wit [...] Bestaende in een partye curieuse en secrete manuscripten (The Hague, 1672) (Kn. 10,437).
Arnauld, Antoine, *Œuvres de Messire Antoine Arnauld* (49 vols., Paris, 1775–81).
Aubert de Versé, Noël, *L'Impie convaincu, ou Dissertation contre Spinoza* (1684), (ed.) F. Benigni (Rome, 2015).
Aubrey, John, *Brief Lives*, (ed.) R. Barber (London, 1975).
[Balling, Pieter], *Het Licht op de kandelaar* (Amsterdam, 1662).
Basnage, Jacques, *Histoire des Juifs depuis Jésus-Christ jusqu'au présent* (new edn., 16 vols., The Hague, 1716).
Baumgarten, Siegmund Jakob, *Nachrichten von einer Hallischen Bibliothek* (8 vols., 1748–51).
Baumgarten, Siegmund Jakob, *Geschichte der Religionspartheyen* (Halle, 1766).
Baxter, Richard, *The Quakers Catechism, or, The Quakers questioned, their questions answered* (London, 1655).
Baxter, Richard, *Catholick Theologie plain, pure, peaceable for the Pacification of the Dogmatical Word-Warriours* (London, 1675).
Baxter, Richard, "The Principles of Spinosa and such Bruitists against Government and Morality," in *The Second Part of the Nonconformists' Plea for Peace* (London, 1680), chapter 1.
Baxter, Richard, *Richard Baxter's Answer to Dr. Edward Stillingfleet's Charge of Separation* (London, 1680).
Baxter, Richard, *Church-History of the Government of Bishops and their Councils Abbreviated* (London, 1681).
Bayle, Pierre, *Dictionnaire historique et critique* (3 vols., Rotterdam, 1702).
Bayle, Pierre, *Continuation des Pensées diverses sur la comète* (2 vols., Rotterdam, 1705).
Bayle, Pierre, *Oeuvres diverses de Mr. Pierre Bayle*, (ed.) Pierre Desmaizeaux (4 vols., The Hague, 1727).
Bayle, Pierre, *Écrits sur Spinoza*, (eds.) Françoise Charles-Daubert and Pierre-François Moreau (Paris, 1983).
Bayle, Pierre, *Pensées diverses sur la comète*, (ed.) A. Prat (Paris, 1994).

Bayle, Pierre, *Correspondance*, (eds.) E. Labousse and Antony McKenna (15 vols., Oxford, 1999–2017).
Beelthouwer, Jan Pietersz, *Antwoordt op het Boeck genaemt, De Philosophie d'Uytleghster* (Amsterdam, 1667).
Bekker, Balthasar, *Kort Begryp der algemeen kerkelijke historien* (1683; new edn., Amsterdam, 1686).
Benítez, Miguel (ed.), "À Madame...sur les différentes religions de Hollande," in G. Canziani and G. Paganini (eds.), *Filosofia e religione nella letteratura clandestina (secoli XVII e XVIII)* (Milan, 1994), 427–68.
Benthem, Heinrich Ludolf, *Holländischer Kirch-und Schulen-Staat* (2 vols., Frankfurt, 1698).
Bentley, Richard, *A Confutation of Atheism* (1692), in R. Bentley, *The Works*, (ed.) A. Dyce (3 vols., London, 1836–8, new edn., 1971) iii, 1–200.
Bernard, Jacques, *Nouvelles de la République des Lettres* (Amsterdam, 1699–1710).
Beverland, Hadrianus, *De Peccato originali* (n.p., 1679).
[Beverland, Hadrianus (Adriaan)], *État de l'homme dans le péché original* (n.p. [Amsterdam?], 1714).
Bibliotheca Blockiana sive Catalogus Librorum...Ameldonck Block (Amsterdam, 1702).
Bibliotheca Thevenotiana, sive Catalogus impressorum et manuscriptorum librorum Bibliothecae viri clarissmi D. [...] *Thévenot* (Paris, 1694).
Bibliotheca Volderiana, seu Catalogus selectissimorum librorum clarissimi expertissimique viri defuncti D. Burcheri De Volder (Leiden, 1709).
Bleyswijck, Dirck van, *Beschryvinge der Stadt Delft* (Delft, 1667).
Blijenbergh, Willem van, *Sociniaensche Ziel onder een Mennonitisch kleedt* (Utrecht, 1666).
Blijenbergh, Willem van, *Wederlegging van de Ethica of Zede-kunst van Benedict de Spinoza* (Dordrecht, 1682).
Blount, Charles, *Miracles, No Violations of the Laws of Nature* (London, 1683).
[Boeckelman, Andries], *De Onschult of Zamenspraak tuschen de Geesten van Imandt en Niemandt* (n.p. [Amsterdam?], 1678).
De Boekzaal van Europe, (ed.) Pieter Rabus (periodical: Rotterdam, 1692–1702).
Bontekoe, Cornelis, *Een Apologie van den Autheur tegens sijne Lasteraars* in C. Bontekoe, *Tractaat van het Excellenste Kruyd Thee* (2nd edn., The Hague, 1679), 321–67.
Bontekoe, Cornelis, *Tractaat van het excellenste kruyd thee* [...] *benevens een Kort Discours op het leven, de siekte, en de dood* (2nd edn., The Hague, 1679).
Bontekoe, Cornelis, *Brief Aen Johan Frederik Swetzer, Gesegt Dr Helvetius, Geschreven en Uytgegeven: Tot een Korte Apologie voor den Grote Philosooph Renatus Descartes en sijne regtsinnige navolgers* (The Hague, 1680).
Bontekoe, Cornelis, *Een Brief aan Jan Frederik Swetsertje, Gesworen Vyand van alle Reden en Verstand, Hoofdlasteraar van de twee groote mannen Coccejus en Descartes* (n.p., n.d. [1681?].
Bontekoe, Cornelis, *Vervolg van het eerste Deel van het Nieuw Gebouw der Chirurgie Of Heel-Konst* (The Hague, 1681).
Bontekoe, Cornelis, *Reden Over de Koortsen; Door welke Aangewesen word, dat de gemene Theorie en Praktijk valsch, schadelijk en moordadig is* (The Hague, 1682).
Bontekoe, Cornelis, *Drie Verhandelingen 1: over de natuur* [...] etc., separately paginated in C. Bontekoe, *Korte Verhandeling van 's menschen leven, gesondheid, siekte en dood* (The Hague, 1684).
Bontekoe, Cornelis, *Een Nieuw Bewys van d'Onvermijdelijke noodsakelijkheyd en groote nuttigheyd van een Algmeene Twyfeling nevens de Reden* (Amsterdam, 1685).

Borch, Ole [Olaus Borrichius], *Itinerarium 1660–1665*, (ed.) H. D. Schepelen (4 vols., Copenhagen, 1983).
Bossuet, Jacques-Bénigne, Bishop, *Discours sur l'histoire universelle*, (ed.) J. Truchet (Paris, 1966).
Boyle, Robert, *The Theological Works of the Honourable Robert Boyle Epitomized* (3 vols., London, 1715).
Boyle, Robert, *The Works of the Honourable Robert Boyle*, (ed.) Thomas Birch (6 vols., London, 1772).
Boyle, Robert, *The Early Essays and Ethics*, (ed.) J. T. Harwood (Carbondale, IL, 1991).
Boyle, Robert, *The Correspondence of Robert Boyle*, (eds.) Michael Hunter, A. Clericizie, and L. M. Principe (6 vols., London, 2001).
Boyle, Robert, *A Free Enquiry into the Vulgarly Received Notion of Nature*, (eds.) Edward B. Davis and Michael Hunter (Cambridge, 2012).
Braun [Brun], Jean, *La Véritable religion des Hollandois* (Amsterdam, 1675).
Bredenburg, Johannes, *Enervatio Tractatus Theologico-Politicus* (Rotterdam, 1675).
Bredenburg, Johannes, *Verhandeling van de oorsprong van de kennisse Gods* (Amsterdam, 1684).
Briefwechsel der Herzogin Sophie von Hannover mit ihrem Bruder, Dem Kurfürsten Karl Ludwig von der Pfalz, (ed.) E. Bodemann (Leipzig, 1885).
Browne, Thomas, *Miracles, Works Above and Contrary to Nature, or, An Answer to a late translation out of Spinoza's Tractatus Theologico-Politicus [...] in a Treatise entitled, Miracles no Violation of the Laws of Nature* (London, 1683).
Brucker, Jacobus, *Historia critica philosophiae* (5 vols., Leipzig 1742–67).
Brunet, Jacques-Charles, *Manuel du libraire et de l'amateur de livres* (3rd edn., 4 vols., Brussels, 1821).
Burman, Frans, *Synopsis theologiae, et speciatim oeconomiae foederum Dei* (Utrecht, 1671).
Burmannus, Franciscus [the younger Frans Burman], *'t Hoogste goed der Spinozisten, vergeleken met den Hemel op Aarden van den heer Fredericus van Leenhof* (Enkhuizen, 1704).
Calendar of State Papers relating to English Affairs in the Archives of Venice, vols. 34 (1664–6) and 38 (1673–5), (ed.) A. B. Hinds (London, 1933–40).
Capasso, Giambattista, *Historiae Philosophiae Synopsis* (Naples, 1728).
Carpzov, Johann Benedict, *Historia Critica Veteris Testamenti oratione inaugurali discussa* (Leipzig, 1684).
Carr, William, *The Travellours Guide and Historians Faithful Companion* (London, 1691).
Carrol, William, *Spinoza Reviv'd, or, A Treatise proving the Book [...] to be the Same as Spinoza's* Rights of the Christian Clergy (London, 1709).
Castries, Henri de (ed.), *Les sources inédites de l'histoire du Maroc* ser. 1 (6 vols., Paris, 1923).
A Catalogue of all the Cheifest [sic] *Rarities in the Publick Theatre and Anatomie-Hall of the University of Leiden* (Leiden, 1678).
Catalogus Librorum Impressorum qui in Bibliotheca Collegii [...] Trinitatis [...] Dublin Adservantur (9 vols., Dublin, 1864–87).
Catalogus variorum & rariorum in quavis facultate et lingua librorum [...] D. Joannis Bouwmeesteri (Amsterdam, 1681).
[Cauzé de Nazelle, Jean-Charles du ?], *Mémoires du temps de Louis XIV*, (ed.) Ernest Daudet (Paris, 1899).
Chevreau, Urbain, *Chevraeana* (Paris, 1697).

Chevreau, Urbain, *Histoire du monde* (2nd edn., 5 vols., The Hague, 1698).
Clarke, Samuel, *A Demonstration of the Being and Attributes of God* (1705), (ed.) E. Vailati (Cambridge, 1998).
Colerus, Johannes, *Korte, dog waarachtige levens-beschrijving van Benedictus de Spinoza, uit autentique stukken en mondeling getuigenis* (Amsterdam, 1705).
Colerus, Johannes, *De waarachtige verrijzenis Jesu Christi uit den dooden* (Amsterdam, 1705).
Colerus, Johannes, *The Life of Benedict de Spinoza* (London, 1706).
Colerus, Johannes, *La Vérité de la Résurrection de Jésus Christ défendu contre B. de Spinoza et ses sectateurs, Avec La Vie de ce fameux philosophe* (The Hague, 1706).
Colerus, Johannes, *La Vie de B. de Spinoza tirée des écrits de ce fameux philosophe* (The Hague, 1706).
Colerus, Johannes, *Das Leben Des Bened. Von Spinoza* (Frankfurt and Leipzig, 1733).
Colerus, Johannes, Dutch version of the biography in Freudenthal/Walther, *Lebensgeschichte* i, (2006), 98–171.
Le Conseil d'Extorsion, ou la volerie des François exercée dans la ville de Nimègue (Amsterdam, 1675).
[Constans, Lucius Antistius], *De Jure Ecclesiasticorum* (Amsterdam, 1665).
Conway, Anne, *The Principles of the most Ancient and Modern Philosophy* (London, 1692).
Correspondance de Richard Pauli Struvius (1634–1642), (ed.) W. Brulez in *Analecta Vaticano-Belgica* 2nd ser. vol. 10 (Brussels-Rome, 1966).
Correspondência diplomática de Francisco de Sousa Coutinho durante a sua embaixada em Holanda (3 vols., Coimbra, 1920).
Coste, Pierre, *The Life of Louis of Bourbon, Late Prince of Condé* (London, 1693).
Costerus, Bernard, *Historisch Verhaal, ofte eene deductie van zaaken, raakende het formeeren van de Republique van Holland ende West-Vriesland [...] Ende het geene dezelve Republique naar het verlopen van een eeuwe in den jaare 1672 is overkomen* (3rd edn., Leiden, 1737).
Cudworth, Ralph, *The True Intellectual System of the Universe* (1678; 2 vols., New York, 1978).
[Cuffeler, A. J.], *Specimen artis ratiocinandi* (3 vols., "Hamburg" [Amsterdam], 1684).
Da Costa, Uriel, *Examination of Pharisaic Traditions*, (ed.) H. P. Salomon and I. S. D. Sassoon (Leiden, 1993).
[Danforth, Samuel], *An Astronomical Description of the Late Comet or Blazing Star* (Cambridge, MA, 1665 and London, 1666).
Dapper, Olfert, *Historische Beschryving der Stadt Amsterdam* (Amsterdam, 1663).
Deductie van den Tegenwoordigen Toestant van dit Nederlandt (n.p., 1672) (Kn. 10,381).
De Lairesse, Gerard, *'t Groot Schilder-Boek* (2 vols., Amsterdam, 1707).
Descartes, René, *Correspondance*, (eds.) Ch. Adam and P. Tannery (12 vols., Paris, 1897–1910).
Desmaizeaux, Pierre, *La Vie de Messire Charles de Saint-Denis, Sieur de Saint-Evremond* in P. Desmaizeaux (ed.), *Oeuvres meslées de Mr. De Saint-Evremond* (London, 1709) i, pp. I–L.
d'Estrades, Godefroy, *Lettres, mémoires et négociations de M. le comte d'Estrades*, (ed.) Prosper Marchand (9 vols., "London" [The Hague], 1743).
Dialogue van een Groote Thee en Tobacq-Suyper, over het wonderlijck hart gevecht voorgevallen in den Haag tusschen [...] Johan Fredericq Swetser, alias doctor Helvetius, en Mennoniste Kees alias Dr. Cornelis Bontekoe (The Hague?, 1680).
Diez, Heinrich Friedrich, *Benedikt von Spinoza nach Leben und Lehren* (Dessau, 1783).

Dryden, John, "Annus Mirabilis. The Year of Wonders 1666. An Historical Poem," in the Project Gutenberg *The Poetical Works of Dryden* (online) vol. 1 (ISO-8859-1).
Du Bois, Jacobus, *Schadelickheyt van de Cartesiaensche philosophie* (Utrecht, 1656).
Duijkerius, Johannes, *Het Leven van Philopater* and *Vervolg van 't leven van Philopater* (1696-7; Amsterdam, 1991).
Earbery, Matthias, *Deism Examin'd and Confuted* (London, 1697).
Eliot, George (trans.), *Spinoza's* Ethics, (ed.) Claire Carlisle (Princeton, 2020).
Fell, Margaret, *A Loving Salutation to the Seed of Abraham among the Jews, wherever they are scattered up and down upon the Face of the Earth*, in R. H. Popkin and M. A. Signer (eds.), *Spinoza's Earliest Publication?* (Assen, 1987), 22-90.
Franco Mendes, David, *Memorias do establecimento e progresso dos judeus portuguezes e espanhoes nesta famosa cidade de Amsterdam* (1769) published in *SR* 9/2 (1975), 1-171.
Freudenthal, J. (ed.), *Die Lebensgeschichte Spinozas in Quellenschriften* (Berlin, 1899).
Freudenthal, J. and Manfred Walther (eds.), *Die Lebensgeschichte Spinozas. Zweite, stark erweiterte und vollständig neu kommentierte Auflage der Ausgabe von Jakob Freudenthal 1899* (2 vols., Stuttgart, 2006).
Fullana, Don Nicolas d'Oliver, *Brief geschreven door den Lieutenant Colonel [...] Fullana* (n.p., 1672).
Genees-Middelen voor Hollants-Qualen vertoonende De quade regeringe der Loevesteinse Facti ("Antwerp," 1672) (Kn. 10,376).
Goeree, Willem, *Inleydinge Tot de Al-ghemeene Teycken-Konst* (Middelburg, 1668).
Goeree, Willem, *Voor-Bereidselen Tot de Bybelsche Wysheid en gebruik der Heilige en Kerkelijke Historien* (2 vols., Amsterdam, 1690).
Goeree, Willem, *Mosaize Historie der Hebreeuwse Kerke* (4 vols., Amsterdam, 1700).
Goeree, Willem, *De Kerklyke en Weereldlyke Historien* (Amsterdam, 1705).
Grew, Nehemiah, *Cosmologia sacra: Or A Discourse of the Universe As it is, the Creature and Kingdom of God* (London, 1701).
Groot Placaet-Boeck vervattende de Placaten...van de...Staten Generael der Vereenighde Nederlanden ende vande...Staten van Hollandt en West-Vrieslandt (9 vols., The Hague, 1658-1796).
Guez de Balzac, Jean-Louis, *Apologie contre le Docteur de Louvain* in J. L. Guez de Balzac, *Socrate Chrétien et autres oeuvres* (Paris, 1661).
Guhrauer, G. E., "Beiträge zur Kenntnis des 17. und 18. Jahrhunderts aus den handschriftlichen Aufzeichnungen Gottlieb Stolles," *Allgemeine Zeitschrift für Geschichte* 7 (1847), 403-511.
Halma, François, *Aanmerkingen op 't Vervolg van* Philopater (Utrecht, 1698).
Halma, François, *Het Leven van B. De Spinoza* (Utrecht, 1698).
Hassel, David, "Voorreden" to Christopher Wittichius, *Ondersoek van de Zede-kunst van Benedictus de Spinoza* (Amsterdam, 1695).
Helvetius, Johan Frederik, *Davids Slinger-steen Geworpen op het Voorhooft van den Goliathistischen Veld-oversten* (The Hague, 1682).
Helvetius, Johan Frederik, *Adams oud Graft, Opgevult met jonge Coccei Cartesiaenschen* (The Hague, 1687).
Histoire de l'Académie Royale des Sciences, vol. 1 (1666-86) (Paris, 1733).
Histoire de Guillaume III Roi de la Grande Bretagne (2 vols., Amsterdam, 1703).
Histoire des ouvrages des savants, (ed.) Henri Basnage de Beauval (journal: 24 vols., Rotterdam, 1687-1709).
Hobbes, Thomas, *Man and Citizen (De Homine and De Cive)*, (ed.) Bernard Gert (Indianapolis, 1991).

Hobbes, Thomas, *The Correspondence of Thomas Hobbes*, (ed.) Noel Malcolm (2 vols., Oxford, 1994).
Hobbes, Thomas, *Leviathan*, (ed.) Noel Malcolm (3 vols., Oxford, 2014).
[Houbraken, Arnold], *Philalethes Brieven. Verzameling van uitgelezene keurstoffen handelende over den godsdienst, natuur-, schilder-, teken-oudheid-, redeneer- en dichtkunst* (2nd edn., Amsterdam, 1713).
Howe, John, *The Living Temple, Part II: Containing Animadversions on Spinosa* in *The Works of John Howe* vol. III (London, 1862), 220-70.
Huet, Pierre Daniel, *Demonstratio evangelica ad serenissimum Delphinum* (Paris, 1679).
Huet, Pierre Daniel, *De Concordia rationis et fidei* (Paris, 1690).
Huet, Pierre-Daniel, *Commentarius de rebus ad eum pertinentibus* (Amsterdam, 1718).
Huet, Pierre Daniel, *Huetiana, ou Pensées diverses de M. Huet, evesque d'Avranches* (Paris, 1722).
Huet, Pierre Daniel, *Memoirs of the Life of Peter Daniel Huet, Bishop of Avranches*, (trans.) J. Aikin (2 vols., London, 1810).
Huygens, Christiaan, *Oeuvres complètes* (12 vols., The Hague, 1888-1910).
Hydra of Monster-Dier... na Hercules is bestreden en overwonnen (Rotterdam, 1672) (Kn. 10,602).
Index librorum prohibitorum Benedicti XIV Pont. Max. jussu recognitus, aque editus (Rome, 1758).
[Jahn, Johann Christian Gottfried], *Verzeichnis der Bücher so gesamlet Johann Christian Gottfried Jahn* (Frankfurt and Leipzig, 1755).
Jelles, Jarig, "Voorreden" to Spinoza, *De Nagelate Schriften van B.D.S.* (Amsterdam, 1677), pp. 1-43 (unpagin.).
Jelles, Jarig, *Belydenisse des algemeenen en christelyken geloofs*, (ed.) L. Spruit (Macerata, 2004).
Jenichen, Gottlob Friedrich, *Historia Spinozismi Leenhofiani* (Leipzig, 1707).
Jöcher, Christian Gottlieb, *Allgemeines Gelehrten-Lexicon* (4 vols., Leipzig, 1750).
Kardel, Troels and P. Maquet (eds.), *Nicolaus Steno: Biography and Original Papers of a 17th Century Scientist* (Berlin, 2013).
Kerckring, Theodore, *Spicilegium Anatomicum* (Amsterdam, 1670).
Kidder, Richard, *A Commentary on the Five Books of Moses* (2 vols., London, 1694).
De Koeckoecx-Zangh van de Nachtuylen van het Collegie Nil Volentibus Arduum, Huylende met eenen naare geest (Zwolle, n.d. [1677]).
Koelman, Jacobus, *Het Vergift van de Cartesiaansche Philosophie grondig ontdeckt* (Amsterdam, 1692).
Koen, M., "Amsterdam Notarial Deeds Pertaining to the Portuguese Jews in Amsterdam, up to 1639," *SR* 2 (1968).
[Koerbagh, Adriaan and Johannes], *'t Samen-spraeck tusschen een gereformeerden Hollander en een Zeeuw* (Middelburg, 1664) (Kn. 8923).
[Koerbagh, Adriaan and Johannes], *Een Bloemhof van allerley lieflijkheid zonder verdriet* (Amsterdam, 1668).
[Koerbagh, Adriaan and Johannes], *A Light Shining in Dark Places* (with original Dutch text), (ed.) M. Wielema (Leiden, 2011).
Kortholt, Christian, *De Tribus Impostoribus* (Kiel, 1680).
Kortholt, Sebastian, "Preface" to Chr. Kortholt, *De Tribus Impostoribus*, French trans. in Bayle, *Écrits sur Spinoza*, 177-81.
Kuyper, Frans, *Arcana Atheismi revelata philophice et paradoxe refutata* (Rotterdam, 1676).
Kuyper, Frans, *Den Philosopherenden Boer* (n.p. [Rotterdam?], 1676).
Kuyper, Frans, *Filosofisch en Historiaal Bewijs dat er Duyvelen zijn* (Rotterdam, 1678).

Kuyper, Frans, *Bewys dat noch de schepping van de natuur, noch de mirakelen die de H. Schift verhaalt, op eenigerhande wijs, teegen de natuurlijke reeden strijdig zijn* (Amsterdam, 1685).
[La Court, Johan and Pieter de], *V.H. Consideratien en Exempelen van Staat, omtrent de fundamenten van allerley regeringe* (Amsterdam, 1660).
La Court, Pieter de, *Politike Discoursen* (2 vols., Amsterdam, 1662).
[La Court, Pieter de], *Aanwysing der heilsame politike Gronden en Maximen van de Republike van Holland en West-Vriesland* (Leiden 1669).
La Court, Pieter de, "Brieven uit de correspondentie van Pieter de la Court," in J. H. Kernkamp (ed.), *Bijdragen en Mededelingen van het Historische genootschap gevestigt te Utrecht* 70 (1956), 82–165.
Lamy, Dom François, *Le nouvel athéisme renversé ou Réfutation du système de Spinoza* (Paris, 1696).
Lamy, Dom François, *La Corrispondenza di François Lamy*, (ed.) M. G. Zaccone Sina (Florence, 2007).
La Peyrère, Isaac, *Praeadamitae—Systema theologicum*, (ed.) H. Jaumann (2 vols., Stuttgart, 2019).
Le Clerc, Jean, *De l'incrédulité où l'on examine les motifs et les raisons générales qui portent les incrédules à rejetter la religion chrétienne* (Amsterdam, 1696).
Le Clerc, Jean, *Epistolario*, (eds.) M. Sina and M. Grazia (4 vols., Florence, 1987–97).
Leibniz, G. W., *Sämtliche Schriften und Briefe*, 1st series, vol. ii (1676–79) and 2nd series vol. i (1663–85) (ed.) E. Hochstetter et al. (Darmstadt, 1926–7).
Leibniz, G. W., *Theodicy: Essays on the Goodness of God, the Freedom of Man, and the Origin of Evil* (La Salle, IL, 1985).
Leibniz, G. W., *New Essays on Human Understanding* (Cambridge, 2012).
Leon Templo, Jacob Judah, *Sefer Tavnit Hekhal* (Amsterdam, 1650) dedicação.
"Letters to and from Neercassel about Spinoza and Rieuwertsz," (ed.) W. N. A. Klever, *SS* 4 (1988), 329–40.
Lettres sur la vie et sur la mort de Monsieur Louis de Wolzogue, pasteur de l'Église Wallone d'Amsterdam (Amsterdam, 1692).
Le Vassor, Michel, *De la véritable religion* (1688; 2nd edn., Paris, 1689).
Levi de Barrios, Daniel (Miguel), *Triumpho del govierno popular, y de la antiguedad holandesa* (Amsterdam, 1683).
Levi de Barrios, Daniel, *Relación de los poetas y escritores españoles de la nación judayca amstelodama* in M. Kayserling, "Une histoire de la littérature juive de Daniel Levi de Barrios," *REJ* 18 (1889), 281–9.
Leydekker, Melchior, *Historische en theologische redeneringe over het onlangs uitgegeve Boek van... Balthasar Bekker* (Utrecht, 1692).
Leydekker, Melchior, *Verder Vervolg van de kerkelyke historie van de Heer Hornius beginnende met het jaar 1687* (Amsterdam, 1696).
Lister, T. H. (ed.), *Letters and Papers* vol. 3, forming the documentary appendix of T. H. Lister, *Life and Administration of Edward, first Earl of Clarendon* (3 vols., London 1837–8).
Livro de Bet Haim do Kahal Kados de Bet Yahcob, (ed.) Wilhelmina Pieterse (Assen, 1970).
[Lucas, Jean Maximilien], *La Vie de Mr Benoit de Spinoza*, in S. Berti (ed.), *Trattato dei tre Impostori* (Turin, 1994), 10–63.
Maimonides, Moses, *The Guide for the Perplexed*, (ed.) M. Friedländer (London, 1928).
Maréchal, Pierre-Sylvain de, *Dictionnaire des Athées anciens et modernes* (1800; new edn., Brussels, 1833).

Maresius, Samuel, *De Abusu Philosophiae Cartesianae* (Groningen, 1670).
Maresius, Samuel, *Vindiciae Dissertationis suae nuperae, De Abusu philosophiae Cartesianae* (Groningen, 1670).
Maresius, Samuel, *Clypeus orthodoxiae, sive Vindiciarum suarum priorum pro sua dissertatione De abusu philosophiae cartesianae* (Groningen, 1671).
Mastricht, Petrus van, *Novitatum Cartesianarum Gangraena* (1677).
Meijer, Lodewijk, *see* Meyer.
[Melchior, Johannes], J.M.V.D.M., *Epistola ad amicum, continens censuram libri cui titulus: Tractatus Theologico-Politicus* (Utrecht, 1671).
Menasseh ben Israel, *Segunda Parte del Conciliador, o de la conveniencia de los lugares de la S. Escritura, que repugnantes entre si parecen* (Amsterdam, 1641).
Menasseh ben Israel, *Gratulação de Menasseh ben Israel, En nome de sua nação, Recitada em Amsterdam aos XXII de Mayo 5402* (1642), (ed.) M. Bensabat Amzalak (Lisbon, 1933), 1–8.
Menasseh ben Israel, *Mikveh Israel. Esto es, Esperança de Israel* (Amsterdam, 5410 [1650], new edn., Madrid 1881).
Menasseh ben Israel, *To His Highnesse the Lord Protector of the Common-wealth of England, Scotland and Ireland: the humble addresses of Menasseh ben Israel* (London, 1655).
Meyer [Meijer], Lodewijk, *Philosophia S.Scripturae Interpres* ("Eleutheropolis" [Amsterdam], 1666).
Meyer [Meijer], Lodewijk, *Philosophy as the Interpreter of Holy Scripture* (1666), (trans.) S. Shirley, notes by L. C. Rice and Fr. Pastijn (Milwaukee, WI, 2005).
Meyer [Meijer], Lodewijk, *De Philosophie d'Uytleghster der H. Schrifture* ("Vrystadt" [Amsterdam], 1667).
Meyer [Meijer], Lodewijk, "Preface" to Spinoza's *Descartes' Principles of Philosophy* in Spinoza, *Collected Works* (ed. Curley) i, 224–30.
Millares Torres, Agustín, *Historia de la Inquisición en las Islas Canarias* (4 vols., Las Palmas, Gran-Canaria, 1874).
Molinaeus, Johannes, *De Betoverde Werelt van D. Balthasar Bekker Onderzogt en Wederlegdt* (Rotterdam, 1692).
Monnikhoff, Johannes, "Beschrijving van Spinoza's leven," *Chronicon Spinozanum* iv (1926), 201–19.
More, Henry, *Ad V.C. Epistola altera, Quae brevem Tractatus Theologico-Politici confutationem complectitur* (London, 1679) in H. More, *Opera Omnia* (3 vols., 1675–9) ii, 563–614.
More, Henry, *Korte en Bondige Wederlegging van het wiskundig Bewijs van B.D. Spinoza met welk hij zijn Atheistise Gronden heeft gepoogd te bekrachtigen* (n.p., 1687).
More, Henry, *A Brief and Firm Confutation of the Demonstration of the Two Propositions in Spinoza which are the Chief Pillars of Atheism*, in Jacob, *Henry More's Refutation* (1991), 55–119.
More, Henry, *Henry More's Refutation of Spinoza*, (ed.) Alexander Jacob (Hildesheim, 1991).
Mortera, Rabbi Saul Levi, *Tratado da Verdade da Lei de Moisés* (Coimbra, 1988).
Moss, Robert, *A Sermon Preach'd at the Parish-Church of St. Laurence-Jewry, London, October 5, 1708* (London, 1708).
Müller, Johann Heinrich, *Dissertatio Inavgvralis philosophica de miraculis* (Altdorf, 1714).
Musaeus, Johannes, *Tractatus Theologico-Politicus, quo auctor quídam anonymus, conatu improbo, demonstratum ivit, libertatem philosophandi examinatus* (Jena, 1674).

Musaeus, Johannes, *Ablehnung der ausgesprengten abscheulichen Verleumdung* (Jena, 1675).
Nadler, Steven, T. Tielen, and V. Tiribás (eds.), "Two New Documents on Spinoza's Biography," *JHPh* 58 (2020), 803–12.
Nicolson, William, "Iter Hollandicum (1678)" in Paul Hoftijzer, "A Study Tour into the Low Countries and the German States. William Nicolson's *Iter Hollandicum* and *Iter Germanicum*, 1678–1679," *Lias* 15 (1988/89), 85–103.
Nieto, David, *De la Divina Providencia* (1704; 2nd edn., London, 1716).
Nietzsche, Friedrich, *Unpublished Letters*, (ed.) K. E. Leidecker (London, 1959).
Nietzsche, Friedrich, *Human, All too Human: A Book for Free Spirits* (1986; new edn., Cambridge, 1996).
Nieuwentijt, Bernard, *Het regt Gebruik der Werelt Beschouwingen* (Amsterdam, 1715).
Nieuwentijt, Bernard, *Gronden van Zekerheid, of de regte Betoogwyse der Wiskundigen* (2nd edn., Amsterdam, 1728).
Northleigh, John, *Topographical Descriptions with historico-political and medico-physical Observations* (London, 1702).
Oldenburg, Henry, *The Correspondence*, (ed.) A. Rupert Hall and Marie Boas Hall (9 vols., Madison, WI, 1965–75).
De Onschult of Zamenspraak tusschen de Geesten van Imandt en Niemandt over de Droevige Pellegrimagie van Lysbet Inatz. van Ravesway (n.p., 1678).
Orcibal, Jean (ed.), "Appendices" to Jean Orcibal, "Les Jansénistes face à Spinoza," in Jacques Le Brun and J. Lesaubrier (eds.), *Études d'Histoire et de Littérature religieuses* (Paris, 1997), 77–86.
Ordeel van eenige theologanten tot Deventer over het boeck Ludovici Wolzogen van den Uyt-Legger der H. Schrifture (Middelburg, 1669) (Kn. 9798).
Orobio de Castro, Isaac, *La Observancia de la Divina Ley de Mosseh*, (ed.) J. Israel Garzón (Barcelona, n.d.).
Orobio de Castro, Isaac, *Certamen Philosophicum, Propugnatae Veritatis Divinae ac Naturalis* (Amsterdam, 1703).
Orobio de Castro, Isaac, *Prevenciones divinas contra la vana idolatría de las gentes*, (ed.) M. Silvera (Florence, 2013).
Ouverleaux, Émile, "Notes et documents sur les juifs de Belgique sous l'ancien régime," published in sections in *REJ* 12 (1883), 8 (1884) and 9 (1884).
Overkamp, Heydentryk, *Nader Ondersoek over het Tweede Deel van de Beginselen der Wysbegeerte van Renatus Descartes* (Amsterdam, 1683).
Overkamp, Heydentryk, *Alle de medicinale, chirurgicale en philosophische werken* (2 vols., Amsterdam, 1694).
Pepys, Samuel, *The Diary and Correspondence of Samuel Pepys, F.R.S. Secretary to the Admiralty of Charles II and James II*, (ed.) J. S. Smith (2 vols., London, 1906, repr. 1910).
Pereyra, Abraham, *La Certeza del camino* (Amsterdam, 5426 [1666]).
Pérez, Antonio, *Relaciones y cartas* (2 vols., Madrid, 1986).
Pérez de Maltranilla, Miguel, "Déposition" in Révah, *Spinoza et le Dr Juan de Prado*, annex 2, pp. 66–9.
Philipson, Moses, *Leben Benedikt's von Spinosa* (Brunswick, 1790).
Porphyry of Tyre (c.232–c.305 AD), *Against the Christians. The Literary Remains*, (ed.) R. J. Hoffman (Oxford, 1994).
Proietti, Omero and Giovanni Licata, *Il Carteggio Van Gent-Tschirnhaus. Storia, cronistoria, contesto dell' editio posthuma spinoziana* (Macerata, 2013).
Raats, Johannes Adrianus, *Korte en grondige betoginge [...] tegen de valsche gronden en stellingen van Spinoza* (The Hague, 1743).

Rabus, Pieter, *Twee-Maandelijke Uyttreksels van alle eerst uytkomende boeken* (periodical: Rotterdam, 1701–4).
Rambach, Johann Jakob, *Collegium historiae ecclesiasticae Veteris Testamentii*, (ed.) E. F. Neubauer (Frankfurt-Leipzig, n.d. [1736]).
Rappolt, Friedrich, *Opera theologica* (Leipzig, 1693).
Ray, John, *Observations topographical, moral and physiological Made in a Journey through part of the Low Countries, Germany, Italy and France* (London, 1673).
Receuil de Lettres, pour servir d'éclaircissement à l'histoire militaire du règne de Louis XIV (4 vols., The Hague, 1740).
Regius, Johannes, *De Beginselen der beschouwende filozofy* (Rotterdam, 1714).
Reimarus, Hermann Samuel, *Apologie oder Schutzschrift für die vernünftigen Verehrer Gottes*, (ed.) G. Alexander (2 vols., Frankfurt, 1972).
Réponse à la pretendue conviction manifeste des calomnies ordinaires levées contre Jean de Labadie [...] En ce qui concerne le livre de Louys de Wolzogue (Utrecht, 1669).
Resolutien van de Heeren Staten van Holland en West-Vriesland (276 vols., The Hague, c.1750–98).
Rommel, Christoph von (ed.), *Leibniz und Landgraf Ernst von Hesse-Rheinfels. Ein ungedruckter Briefwechsel* (2 vols., Frankfurt, 1847).
Roodenport, J., *'t Verleidend Levens-Bedrijf van Kakotegnus* (Amsterdam, 1700).
Rousseau, Jean-Jacques, *The Social Contract and Other Later Political Writings*, (ed.) V. Gourevitch (Cambridge, 1997).
Rues, Simeon Frederik, *Tegenwoordige staet der Doopsgezinden of Mennoniten in de Verenigde Nederlanden Waeragter komt een beright van de Rijnsburgers of Collegianten* (Amsterdam, 1745).
Ryckius, Teodorus et al., *Epistolae ineditae* (The Hague, 1843).
Ryssenius, Leonard, *De oude rechtsinnige waerheyt verdonckert [...] door Des Cartes, Coccejus, Wittich, Burman, Wolzogen [...] etc.* (Middelburg, n.d. [1674]).
Ryssenius, Leonard, *Justa Detestatio sceleratissimi Libelli Adriani Beverlandi... De Peccato Originali* (Gorinchem, 1680).
Sainsbury, W. N., *Calendar of State Papers: Colonial America and West Indies* (1661–8) (London, 1880).
Saldenus, Willem, *Otia theologica* (Amsterdam, 1684).
Schelling, F. W. J., *On the History of Modern Philosophy* (Cambridge, 1994).
Schuyl, Florentius, "Ad Lectorem" (40-page preface) to *Renatus Descartes de homine, figuris et latinitate donatus a Florentio Schuylio* (Leiden, 1662).
Serrarius, Petrus, *Responsio ad Exertitationem paradoxam anonymi cujusdam Cartesianae sectae discipuli* (Amsterdam, 1667).
Sleutel Ontsluytende de Boecke-kas van de Witte Bibliotheeck [by J.B.] (The Hague, 1672) (Kn. 10,442).
Sluiter, Johannes, *Overeenstemming tusschen den heer Fredericus van Leenhof en Spinoza en Philopater vertoont* (Amsterdam, 1704).
Solano y Robles, Fr. Tomas, *Deposición de Fr. Tomás Solano y Robles* (Madrid, 8 August 1659) in Revah, *Spinoza et Juan de Prado*, 61–5.
Spandaw, Willem, *De bedekte Spinosist ontdekt in de persoon van Pontiaan van Hattem* (Goes, 1700).
Spinoza, B. de, *Short Treatise on God, Man and His Well-Being* (c.1659) in Curley (ed.) Spinoza, *Collected Works* i, 59–156.
Spinoza, B. de, *De Nagelate Schriften van B.D.S.* (Amsterdam, 1677).
Spinoza, B. de, [B.d.S.] *Opera Posthuma* (Amsterdam, 1677).

Spinoza, B. de, *Briefwechsel übertragen und mit Einleitung*, (ed.) C. Gebhardt (Leipzig, 1914).
Spinoza, B. de, *Opera*, ed. Carl Gebhardt (5 vols., Heidelberg, 1925, repr. 1987).
Spinoza, B. de, *Tractatus Theologico-Politicus*, (ed.) Carl Gebhardt in Spinoza, *Opera* vol. iv.
Spinoza, B. de, *Korte Geschriften*, (ed.) F. Akkerman et al. (Amsterdam, 1982).
Spinoza, B. de, *The Collected Works of Spinoza*, (ed. and trans.) Edwin Curley (2 vols., Princeton, 1985–2016).
Spinoza, B. de, *Briefwisseling*, (eds.) F. Akkerman, H. G. Hubbeling, and A. G. Westerbrink (Amsterdam, 1992).
Spinoza, B. de, *Principles of Cartesian Philosophy* with *Metaphysical Thoughts*, (trans.) S. Shirley, notes by Steven Barbone and Lee Rice (Indianapolis, 1998).
Spinoza, B. de, *Oeuvres* (bilingual edition, Latin and French), (ed.) Pierre-François Moreau (5 vols., Paris, 1999–2020).
Spinoza, B. de, *Political Treatise*, (trans.) Samuel Shirley, notes by Steven Barbone and Lee Rice (Indianapolis, 2000).
Spinoza, B. de, *Theological-Political Treatise*, (trans. M. Silverthorne), (ed.) Jonathan Israel (Cambridge, 2007).
Spinoza, B. de, *Theological-Political Treatise*, (trans.) Samuel Shirley (1991; 2nd edn., Indianapolis, 1998).
Spinoza, B. de, *Corrrespondance*, (ed.) Maxime Rovere (Paris, 2010).
Spinoza, B. de, *Korte Verhandeling van God, de mens and zijn welstand*, (trans. and ed.) Rikus Koops (n.p., 2012).
Spinoza, B. de, *Abregé de grammaire hébraique*, (ed.) J. Askenazi and J. Askenazi-Gerson (Paris, 2013).
Spinoza, B. de, *Compendio di grammatica della lingua ebraica*, (ed.) with Introduction by Pina Totaro (Florence, 2013).
Sprat, Thomas, *The History of the Royal Society of London for the Improving of Natural Knowledge* (3rd edn., London, 1722).
Spruit, Leen and Pina Totaro (eds.), *The Vatican Manuscript of Spinoza's* Ethica (Leiden, 2011).
Staat-Kundige droom, passende seer wel op diese tijden (Amsterdam, 1672) (Kn. 10,493).
Steno (Stensen), Nicolaus, "Libri prohibiti circa la nuova filosofia dello Spinoza," appendix to Totaro, "Ho certi amici," 33–6.
Steno (Stensen), Nicolaus, "Denunciation of Spinoza's Philosophy to the Holy Office (4 Sept. 1677)," in Spruit and Totaro (eds.), *The Vatican Manuscript of Spinoza's* Ethica, 9–13, and 68–72.
Stillingfleet, Edward, *A Letter to a Deist, in Answer to several Objections* (London, 1677).
Stouppe, J. B., *De Gods-Dienst Der Hollanders, vertoont in verscheide Brieven* (Amsterdam, 1673).
Stouppe, J. B., *La Religion des Hollandois* (Paris, 1673).
Stouppe, Jean-Baptiste, *The Religion of the Dutch* (London, 1681).
Swammerdam, Jan, *The Letters of Jan Swammerdam to Melchisedec Thévenot*, (ed.) G. Lindeboom (Amsterdam, 1975).
Tacitus, Cornelius, *The Annals of Imperial Rome*, (trans.) Michael Grant (Harmondsworth, 1956).
Temple, Sir William, *Lettre d'un Marchand de Londres à son amy à Amsterdam* (London, 1666).
Temple, Sir William, *Memoirs of what passed in Christendom, from the War begun in 1672 to the Peace concluded in 1679* (3rd edn., London, 1693).

Temple, Sir William, *Letters written by Sir William Temple, Bart. and Other Ministers of State, Both at Home and Abroad. Containing an Account of the Most Important Transactions that Pass'd in Christendom from 1665 to 1672*, (ed.) Jonathan Swift (2 vols., London, 1700).
Temple, Sir William, *Observations upon the United Provinces of the Netherlands* (Cambridge, 1932).
Thurloe, John, *A Collection of State Papers* (7 vols., London, 1742).
Toland, John, *Letters to Serena*, (ed.) Ian Leask (Dublin, 2013).
Trinius, Johann Anton, *Freydenker-Lexicon* (Leipzig, 1759).
Tschirnhaus, E. W. von, *Medicina Mentis* (Amsterdam, 1687).
Tschirnhaus, E. W. von, *Medicina Mentis*, German trans. and commentary by Johannes Haussleiter (Leipzig, 1963).
Tweede Bericht des Kerkenraads van Utrecht Aen de Edele Achtb. Vroedtschap tegen De Tweede Apologie van de Heer L. van Velthuysen, wegens sijn Tractaat van Afgodery en Superstitie (Utrecht, 1669).
Van Balen, Petrus, *De Vebetering der gedachten,* (ed.) M. J. van den Hoven (Baarn, 1988).
Van den Enden, Franciscus, *Philedonius, 1657,* (ed.) O. Proietti (Macerata, 2010).
Van den Enden, Franciscus, *Free Political Propositions and Considerations of State* (1665) (ed. and trans.) Wim Klever ("Vrijstad", 2007).
Van den Enden, Franciscus, *Vrije Politijke Stellingen en Consideratien van Staat* (1665; Amsterdam, 1992).
Van der Hoeven, Emanuel, *Hollandse vrijheid verdedigt tegen de usurpatie der stadhouders* (n.p., 1663) (Kn. 8803).
Van der Hoeven, Emmanuel, *Leeven en Dood der doorlugtige gebroeders Cornelis de Witt [...] en Johan de Witt* (Amsterdam, 1705).
Van der Hoeven, Emanuel, *Hollands aeloude Vryheid, buyten het stadhouderschap* (3 vols., Amsterdam, 1706).
Vande Water, Johan, *Groot Placaatboek vervattende alle de placaten [...] der edele Mogende Heeren Staten 's Lands van Utrecht* (3 vols., Utrecht, 1729).
Van Leenhof, Frederik, *'t Leven van Salomon en zyn bewys der Ydelheden* (Amsterdam, 1702).
Van Mansvelt, Regnerus, *Adversus anonymum Theologico-Politicum* (Amsterdam, 1674) (*See also* 'Petrus van Andlo').
Van Ruler, Han, Anthony Uhlmann, and Martin Wilson (eds.), *Arnold Geulincx Ethics* (Leiden, 2006).
Van Til, Salomon, *Het Voor-hof der heydenen, voor alle ongelovigen geopent* (Dordrecht, 1694).
Velthuysen, Lambert van, *Bewys Dat noch de Leere van der Sonne Stilstant en des Aertryx Bewegingh, Noch de gronden vande Philosophie van Renatus Des Cartes strijdig sijn met Godts woort* (Utrecht, 1656).
Velthuysen, Lambert van, *Apologie voor het Tractaet van de Afgoderye en Superstitie* (Utrecht, 1669).
Velthuysen, Lambert van, *Vierde Apologie voor het Tractaet van de Afgoderye en Superstitie* (Utrecht, 1670).
Velthuysen, Lambert van, *Opera Omnia* (2 vols., Rotterdam, 1680).
Velthuysen, Lambert van, *Tractatus de cultu naturali [...] oppositus* Tractatui Theologico-Politico *et* Operi Posthumo B.d.S., in Velthuysen, *Opera Omnia*, vol. 2 (Rotterdam, 1680).
Velthuysen, Lambert van, *Des principes du juste et du convenable. Une apologie du De Cive de Hobbes (1651-1680)* (Caen, 1995).

Verwer, Adriaen, *'t Mom-aensicht der atheisterey afgerukt door een Verhandeling van den aengeborenen stand der menschen* (Amsterdam, 1683).
Vieira, António, *Obras Escolhidas*, (ed.) A. Sergio and H. Cidade (12 vols., Lisbon, 1951–4).
Vogt, Johannes, *Catalogvs Historico-criticvs librorum rariorum* (2 vols., Hamburg, 1747).
Voltaire, François-Marie Arouet de, *Questions sur l'Encyclopédie par des amateurs* (9 vols., n.p., 1770).
Voltaire, François-Marie Arouet de, *Siècle de Louis XIV* (2 vols., Paris, 1858).
Voltaire, François-Marie Arouet de, *Questions sur l'Encyclopédie, par des amateurs* (8 vols., Oxford, 2007–18).
Vossius, Isaac, *Variarum observationum liber* (London, 1685).
Weber, Immanuel, *Beurtheilung der Atheisterey, wie auch derer mehresten deshalben berüchtigsten Schrifften* (Frankfurt-am-Main, 1697).
Wicquefort, Abraham de, *Journael of dagelijcksch verhael van de handel der Franschen in de steden van Utrecht en Woerden sedert hun koomst daer binnen, tot aen hun vertrek* (2 parts, Amsterdam, 1674).
Wilson, John, *The Scriptures Genuine Interpreter asserted; or, A Discourse concerning the right interpretation of Scripture* (London, 1678).
[Wit, Johan de], *Den Schotsen Duyvel, betabbert in den Verresenen Barnevelt* (Utrecht, 1663) (Kn. 8801).
Wit, Johan de, *Public Gebedt* (3 vols., Amsterdam, 1663–4).
Witt, Johan de, *Deductie ofte Declaratie van de Staten van Hollandt ende West-Vrieslandt [...] diendende tot justificatie van 't [...] Acte van Seclusie* (The Hague, 1654).
Wittichius, Christopher [Wittich], *Consensus veritatis in Scriptura divina et infallibile cum veritate philosophica* (2nd edn., Leiden, 1682).
Wittichius, Christopher [Wittich], *Anti-Spinoza* (Amsterdam, 1690).
Wittichius, Christopher [Wittich], *Ondersoek van de Zede-kunst van Benedictus de Spinoza* (Amsterdam, 1695).
Wolf, Johann Christoph, *Bibliotheca Hebraea* (4 vols., Hamburg-Leipzig, 1715–33).
Wolzogen, Ludwig (Louis), *De Scripturarum Interprete* (Utrecht, 1668).
[Wolzogen, Ludwig (Louis)], *Catalogus instructissimae bibliothecae viri D.Ludovici Wolzogen* (Amsterdam, 1691).
Worsley, B., *The Advocate or a Narrative of the State and Constitution of Things between the English and Dutch Nation, in relation to Trade* (London, 1652).
Yvon, Pierre, *L'Impiété convaincue* (Amsterdam, 1681).
Zedler, Johann Heinrich, *Grosses vollständiges Universal-Lexicon* (64 vols., Leipzig-Halle, 1732–50).

Secondary Sources

Aalderink, M., "Spinoza en Wittichius over essentie en existentie," in G. Coppens (ed.), *Spinoza en het Nederlands cartesianisme* (Leuven, 2004), 79–94.
Aalderink, M., *Philosophy, Scientific Knowledge, and Concept Formation in Geulincx and Descartes* (Utrecht, 2009).
Aalderink, M., "Christopher Wittich, Anti-Spinoza (1690)," in Wiep van Bunge, Henri Krop, and Piet Steenbakkers (eds.), *The Bloomsbury Companion to Spinoza* (London: Bloomsbury, 2014), 129–40.
Abrahamse, J. E., *De Grote Uitleg van Amsterdam: stadsontwikkeling in de zeventiende eeuw* (Amsterdam, 2010).

Ackermans, G., "Good Pastors in the 'Missio Hollandica' in the Second Half of the Seventeenth Century," *Nederlands Archief voor Kerkgeschiedenis* 83 (2003), 260–70.
Adler, Jacob, "Epistemological Categories in Delmedigo and Spinoza," *SS* 15 (1999), 205–27.
Adler, Jacob, "J. S. Delmedigo as Teacher of Spinoza: The Case of Noncomplex Propositions," *SS* 16 (2008), 177–83.
Adler, Jacob, "Joseph Solomon Delmedigo, Student of Galileo, Teacher of Spinoza," *IHR* 23 (2013), 141–57.
Adler, Jacob, "Mortality of the Soul from Alexander of Aphrodisias to Spinoza," in Steven Nadler (ed.), *Spinoza and Medieval Jewish Philosophy* (Cambridge, 2014), 13–35.
Adler, Jacob, "The Education of Ehrenfried Walther von Tschirnhaus (1651–1708)," *Journal of Medical Biography* 23 (2015), 27–35.
Akkerman, Fokke, "Studies in the Posthumous Works of Spinoza" (University of Groningen Ph.D. thesis, 1980).
Akkerman, Fokke, "J. H. Glazemaker, an Early Translator of Spinoza," in C. de Deugd (ed.), *Spinoza's Political and Theological Thought* (Amsterdam, 1984), 23–9.
Akkerman, Fokke, "Jan Hendrikszoon Glazemaker (1619/20–82)," in *DDPhil* i, 331–4.
Akkerman, Fokke, "*Tractatus Theologico-Politicus*: texte latin, traductions neerlandaises et Adnotationes," in Fokke Akkerman and Piet Steenbakkers (eds.), *Spinoza to the Letter: Studies in Words, Texts and Books* (Leiden, 2005), 209–36.
Akkerman, Fokke, "Taal en tekst van Spinoza," Vereninging Het Spinozahuis (Voorschoten, 2013).
Akkerman, Fokke and H. G. Hubbeling, "The Preface to Spinoza's Posthumous Works 1677 and its Author Jarig Jelles (c. 1619/20–1683)," *Lias* 6 (1979), 103–73.
Akkerman, Fokke and Piet Steenbakkers (eds.), *Spinoza to the Letter: Studies in Words, Texts and Books* (Leiden, 2005).
Albert, Anne, *Jewish Politics in Spinoza's Amsterdam* (Liverpool, 2022).
Albiac, Gabriel, *La Sinagoga vacía. Un Estudio de la fuentes marranas del Espinosismo* (Madrid, 1987; 3rd edn., 2018).
Alden, Dauril, "Some Reflections on António Vieira: Seventeenth-Century Troubleshooter and Troublemaker," *Luso-Brazilian Review* 40 (2003), 7–16.
Alpers, Svetlana, *Rembrandt's Enterprise: The Studio and the Market* (Chicago, 1988).
Alter, George, "Plague and the Amsterdam Annuitant: A New Look at Life Annuities as a Source for Historical Demography," *Population Studies* 37 (1983), 23–41.
Amador de los Rios, José, *Historia social, política y religiosa de los judios de España y Portugal* (Madrid, 1960).
Andrault, Raphaele, M. Laerke, and Pierre-François Moreau (eds.), *Spinoza/Leibniz. Rencontres, controverses, réceptions* (Paris, 2014).
Antognazza, Maria Rosa, *Leibniz on the Trinity and the Incarnation* (New Haven, CT, 2007).
Applebaum, Wilbur, "Keplerian Astronomy after Kepler: Researches and Problems," *History of Science* 34 (1996), 451–504.
Arasse, Daniel, *Vermeer: Faith in Painting* (Princeton, 1994).
Assoun, Paul-Laurent, "Spinoza, les libertins français et la politique (1665–1725)," *CS* 3 (1980), 171–207.
Atkins, Dorothy, "George Eliot and Spinoza," *Salzburg Studies in English Literature* 78 (1978), 1–18.
Attridge, H. W., "Josephus and His Works," in M. E. Stone (ed.), *Jewish Writings of the Second Temple Period* (Assen, 1984), 185–232.

Aurell, Jaime, "Spinoza's Political Theology in Context: Dutch Democratic Republicanism and Radical Enlightenment," in António Bento and José Maria da Silva Rosa (eds.), *Revisiting Spinoza's Theological-Political Treatise* (Hildesheim, 2013), 13–34.

Avramov, Iordan, "An Apprenticeship in Scientific Communication: The Early Correspondence of Henry Oldenburg (1656–1663)," *Notes and Records of the Royal Society of London* 53 (1999), 187–201.

Backus, Irena, *Leibniz, Protestant Theologian* (Oxford, 2016).

Bagley, Paul J., *Philosophy, Theology and Politics: A Reading of Benedict Spinoza's* Tractatus Theologico-Politicus (Leiden, 2008).

Balibar, Étienne, *Spinoza et la politique* (Paris, 1984; 4th repr., 2019).

Bamberger, Fritz, "The Early Editions of Spinoza's *Tractatus Theologico-Politicus*: A Bibliohistorical Reexamination," *Studies in Bibliography and Booklore* (Hebrew Union College) 5 (1961), 9–33.

Barebone, Steven and Lee Rice, "Introduction" to Spinoza, *Principles of Cartesian Philosophy* (Indianapolis, 1998), xiii–xxx.

Barnouw, Pieter Jacobus, *Philippus van Limborch* (The Hague, 1963).

Bartuschat, Wolfgang, "The Theory of the Good in Part 4 of the *Ethics*," in Michael Hampe, Ursula Renz, and Robert Schnepf (eds.), *Spinoza's* Ethics: *A Collective Commentary* (Leiden, 2011), 233–46.

Bastiani, Marta Libertà de, "Spinoza against Political Taciticism: Reversing the Meaning of Tacitus," *History of European Ideas* 47 (2021) 1043–60.

Baumgarten, Jean, "De quelques possibles sources juives du *Compendium* de Spinoza," in Jean Baumgarten, I. Rosier-Catach, and Pina Totaro (eds.), *Spinoza, philosophe grammairien. Le* Compendium grammatices linguae hebraeae (Paris, 2019), 127–57.

Baumgarten, Jean, I. Rosier-Catach, and Pina Totaro (eds.), *Spinoza, philosophe grammairien. Le* Compendium grammatices linguae hebraeae (Paris, 2019).

Bedjaï, Marc, "Libertins et politiques: le comte de Guiche," *Revue de la Bibliothèque Nationale* 44 (1992), 29–33.

Begley, Bartholomew, "Naturalism and its Political Dangers: Jakob Thomasius against Spinoza's *Theological-Political Treatise*," *The Seventeenth Century* (online journal) (29 August 2018), pp. 1–22.

Begley, Bartholomew, "Spinoza, Before and After the *Rampjaar*," *The European Legacy: Towards New Paradigms* 27 (2022), 563–82.

Beinart, Haim, "The Jews in the Canary Islands: A Re-Evaluation," *Transactions of the Jewish Historical Society of England* 25 (1973/75), 48–86.

Beiser, Frederick, "Homesick Hidalgo: New Attempts to Bring Spinoza to Life," *TLS*, 25 June 1999, 4–5.

Benigni, Fiormichele, "Introduzione" to Noel Aubert de Versé, *L'Impie Convaincu* (Rome, 2015), vii–lxxix.

Bennett, Matthew, Michael Schatz, Heidi Rockwood, and Kurt Wiesenfeld, "Huygens' Clocks," *Proceedings of the Royal Society: Mathematical, Physical and Engineering Sciences* 458 (March 2002), 563–79.

Bensoussan, David, "L'*Otium* de l'honnête homme: Saint-Évremond," in Jean Dagen (ed.), *Entre Épicure et Vauvenargues. Principes et formes de la pensée morale* (Paris, 1999), 383–401.

Bento, António, "Spinoza and the Hebrew State," in António Bento and José Maria da Silva Rosa (eds.), *Revisiting Spinoza's Theological-Political Treatise* (Hildesheim, 2013), 237–63.

Bento, António and José Maria da Silva Rosa (eds.), *Revisiting Spinoza's Theological-Political Treatise* (Hildesheim, 2013).
Ben-Zaken, Avner, *Cross-Cultural Scientific Exchanges in the Eastern Mediterranean, 1560–1660* (Baltimore, MD, 2010).
Berchet, G., *Cromwell e la Repubblica di Venezia* (Venice, 1864).
Berti, Silvia, *Anticristianesimo e libertà. Studi sull'Illuminismo radicale europeo* (Bologna, 2012).
Berti, Silvia, Françoise Charles-Daubert, and R. H. Popkin (eds.), *Heterodoxy, Spinozism and Free Thought in Early Eighteenth-Century Europe* (Dordrecht, 1996).
Bertoloni Meli, Domenico, "The Axiomatic Tradition in Seventeenth-Century Mechanics," in M. Dickson and M. Domski (eds.), *Synthesis and the Growth of Knowledge* (Chicago, 2010), 23–41.
Bianchi, Bernardo, "Marx's Reading of Spinoza: On the Alleged Influence of Spinoza on Marx," *Historical Materialism* 26 (2018), 35–58.
Bietenholz, P. G., *Daniel Zwicker (1612–1678): Peace, Tolerance and God the One and Only* (Florence, 1997).
Billecoq, Alain, *Spinoza et les spectres* (Paris, 1987).
Binstock, B., *Vermeer's Family Secrets: Genius, Discovery and the Unknown Apprentice* (New York, 2009).
Birch, Jonathan, *Jesus in an Age of Enlightenment* (London, 2019).
Blanco Echauri, Jésus, "Espinosa y el pensamiento político del Barroco español," in A. Domínguez (ed.), *Spinoza y España. Actas del Congreso Internacional sobre "Relaciones entre Spinoza y España"* (Murcia, 1994), 79–90.
Blanco Mayor, Carmelo, "Quevedo y Spinoza," in A. Domínguez (ed.), *Spinoza y España. Actas del Congreso Internacional sobre "Relaciones entre Spinoza y España"* (Murcia, 1994), 191–214.
Blanning, Tim, *The Pursuit of Glory: The Five Revolutions that Made Modern Europe, 1648–1815* (London, 2008).
Blasé, J. E. B., *Johannes Colerus en de groote twisten in de Nederlandsche Luthersche Kerk zijner dagen* (Amsterdam, 1920).
Bloch, Ernst, *Avicenna and the Aristotelian Left* (1963; English trans., New York, 2019).
Bloksma, Nanne, "Spinoza, a Miraculously Healthy Philosopher," *MeSp* 113.
Blom, Hans W., "Lambert van Velthuysen et le naturalisme," *CS* 6 (1991), 203–12.
Blom, Hans W., *Morality and Causality in Politics: The Rise of Naturalism in Seventeenth-Century Political Thought* (Utrecht, 1995).
Blom, Hans W., "Grotius and Socinianism," in M. Mulsow and Jan Rohls (eds.), *Socinianism and Arminianism: Antitrinitarians, Calvinists and Cultural Exchange in Seventeenth-Century Europe* (Leiden, 2005).
Bloom, Herbert, *The Economic Activities of the Jews of Amsterdam in the Seventeenth and Eighteenth Centuries* (1937; repr. Port Washington, NY, 1969).
Bodemann, Eduard, "Herzogin Sophie von Hannover," *Historisches Taschenbuch* vi (Leipzig, 1888), 27–86.
Bodian, Miriam, "Some Ideological Implications of Marrano Involvement in the International Arena," in Abraham Haim (ed.), *Society and Community: Proceedings of the Second International Congress for Research of the Sephardi and Oriental Jewish Heritage* (Jerusalem, 1991), 207–17.
Bodian, Miriam, *Dying in the Law of Moses: Crypto-Jewish Martyrdom in the Iberian World* (Bloomington, IN, 2000).

Bohrmann, Georg, *Spinozas Stellung zur Religion* (Giessen, 1914).
Boissière, Gustave, *Urbain Chevreau (1613–1701). Sa vie, ses oeuvres* (Paris, 1909).
Bok, M. J., *Vraag en aanbod op de Nederlandse kunstmarkt, 1580–1700* (Utrecht, 1994).
Bordoli, Roberto, "Account of a Curious Traveller on the Libertijn Milieu of Amsterdam," *SS* 10 (1994), 175–82.
Bordoli, Roberto, *Ragione e scrittura tra Descartes e Spinoza* (Milan, 1997).
Bordoli, Roberto, *Etica, Arte, Scienza tra Descartes e Spinoza. Lodewijk Meyer (1629–1681) e l'associazione Nil Volentibus Arduum* (Milan, 2001).
Bordoli, Roberto, "Wittichius, Christophorus (1625–87)," in *DDPhil* ii, 1083–6.
Bordoli, Roberto, "The Monopoly of Social Affluence: The *Jus circa sacra* around Spinoza," in Sonja Lavaert and Winfried Schröder (eds.), *The Dutch Legacy: Radical Thinkers of the 17th Century and the Enlightenment* (Leiden, 2017), 121–49.
Bordoli, Roberto, "Art, public et république à Amsterdam à l'époque de Spinza," in Pierre-François Moreau and L. Vinciguerra (eds.), *Spinoza et les arts* (Paris, 2020), 35–49.
Borges Coelho, António, *Inquisição de Évora, 1533–1668* (1987; 3rd edn., Alfragide, 2018).
Borges Coelho, António, "Los orígenes de Bento de Espinosa," in Jaime Contreras, Bernardo J. García, and Inacio Pulido (eds.), *Familia Religión y negocio. El Sefardismo en las relaciones entre el mundo ibérico y los Países Bajos en la Edad Moderna* (Madrid, 2002), 113–35.
Boschiero, Luciano, "Giovanni Borelli and the Comets of 1664–65," *Journal of the History of Astronomy* 40 (2009), 11–30.
Bosma, A. I., *Repertorium van notarissen residerende in Amsterdam, 1524–1810* (Amsterdam, 1998).
Bossers, Anton, "Nil Volentibus Arduum: Lodewijk Meyer and Adriaan Koerbagh," in P. A. Tichelaar (ed.), *Opstellen over de Koniklijke Bibliotheek en andere studies* (Hilversum, 1986).
Bost, Hubert, *Pierre Bayle et la religion* (Paris, 1994).
Boucher, W. I., *Spinoza in English: A Bibliography from the Seventeenth Century to the Present* (Leiden, 1991).
Bouveresse, Renée, *Spinoza et Leibniz. L'Idée d'animisme universel* (Paris, 1992).
Bouza Álvarez, Fernando, "De las alteraciones de Beja (1593) a la revuelta Lisboeta Dos Ingleses (1596): Lucha política en el último Portugal del primer Felipe," *Studia Historica: Historia Moderna* (Universidad de Salamanca) 17 (1997), 91–120.
Bove, Laurent, *La Stratégie du* conatus. *Affirmation et résistance chez Spinoza* (Paris, 1996).
Bove, Laurent, "Introduction" and "Notes" to B. de Spinoza, *Traité politique* (Paris, 2002), 9–101.
Bove, Laurent, *Vauvenargues ou le séditieux. Entre Pascal et Spinoza* (Paris, 2010).
Bove, Laurent, "L'Avènement de la citoyenneté politique dans le *Tractatus Politicus*," in Sonja Lavaert and Pierre-François Moreau (eds.), *Spinoza et la politique de la multitude* (Paris, 2021), 57–68.
Boxer, Charles, "Some Thoughts on the Third Anglo-Dutch War," *Transactions of the Royal Historical Society* 19 (1969), 67–94.
Boyden, J. M., "'Fortune Has Stripped You of Your Splendour': Favourites and their Fates in Fifteenth- and Sixteenth-Century Spain," in J. H. Elliott and L. W. B. Brockliss (eds.), *The World of the Favourite* (New Haven, CT, 1999), 26–37.
Boyle, Frank, "China in the Radical Enlightenment Context of the English Battle of the Books," *The Eighteenth Century* 59 (2018), 1–19.
Brenner-Golomb, Nancy, *The Importance of Spinoza for the Modern Philosophy of Science* (Frankfurt, 2010).

Broeyer, Frits, "William III and the Reformed Church of the Netherlands," in David Onnekink and Esther Mijers (eds.), *Redefining William III: The Impact of the King-Stadholder in International Context* (Aldershot, 2007), 109–23.
Brogi, Stefano, *Teologia senza verità: Bayle contro i "rationaux"* (Milan, 1998).
Brown, Christopher, *The Drawings of Anthony van Dyck* (New York, 1991).
Brown, K., "A Catalan Speaker at Esnoga: Nicolau d'Oliver i Fullana," in Shlomo Berger, M. Brocko, and Irene Zwiep (eds.), *Zutot-Sephardica* (2003), 87–97.
Brown, Stuart, "Theological Politics and the Reception of Spinoza in the Early English Enlightenment," *SS* 9 (1993), 181–200.
Brown, Stuart, "Locke as Secret 'Spinozist': The Perspective of William Carroll," in W. van Bunge and W. Klever (eds.), *Disguised and Overt Spinozism around 1700* (Leiden, 1996), 213–34.
Bruijn, Jaap R., *The Dutch Navy of the Seventeenth and Eighteenth Centuries* (Columbia, SC, 1993).
Bruin, G. de, *Geheimhouding en verraad. De geheimhouding van staatszaken ten tijde van de Republiek (1600–1750)* (The Hague, 1991).
Brunschvicg, Leon, *Les Juifs de Nantes et du pays nantais* (Nantes, 1890).
Bruyn Kops, Henriette de, *A Spirited Exchange: The Wine and Brandy Trade between France and the Dutch Republic in its Atlantic Framework, 1600–1650* (Leiden, 2007).
Brykman, Geneviève, *La Judéité de Spinoza* (Paris, 1972).
Buijsen, Edwin, *Haagse Schilders in de Gouden Eeuw. Het Hoogsteder Lexicon van alle schilders werkzaam in Den Haag 1600–1700* (The Hague-Zwolle, 1998).
Burnet, Claus, "Quaker Missionaries in Holland and North Germany in the Late Seventeenth Century," *Quaker History* 95 (2006), 1–18.
Buyse, Filip A., "Le 'Démasquement' de Descartes par Spinoza dans les *Principia Philosophiae Cartesianae*," *Theoria* (Paris) 2 (2012), 15–43.
Campanini, Silverio, "Le *Peculium Abrae* d'Abraham de Balmes et la question des sources du *Compendium*," in Jean Baumgarten, I. Rosier-Catach, and Pina Totaro (eds.), *Spinoza, philosophe grammairien. Le* Compendium grammatices linguae hebraeae (Paris, 2019), 105–26.
Carlisle, Clare, *Spinoza's Religion: A New Reading of the* Ethics (Princeton, 2021).
Caro Baroja, Julio, *Los judíos en la España moderna y contemporánea* (3 vols., 2nd edn., Madrid, 1978).
Carvalho, Joaquim de, "Orobio de Castro e o espinosismo," *Memorias da Academia das Ciencias de Lisboa. Clase de Letras* 2 (1936), 183–252.
Casarino, Cesare, "Marx before Spinoza: Notes before an Investigation," in D. Vardoulakis (ed.), *Spinoza Now* (Minneapolis, 2011), 179–234.
Casino, Paolo, *Introduzione all'Illuminismo 1. Scienza, miscredenza e politica* (Rome-Bari, 1980).
Cassuto, Philippe, *Spinoza hébraïssant. L'hébreu dans le "Tractatus theologico-politicus" et le "Compendium grammatices linguae hebraeae"* (Paris-Louvain, 1999).
Chalier, Catherine, *Spinoza lecteur de Maïmonide. La question theologico-politique* (Paris, 2006).
Champion, Justin, *The Pillars of Priestcraft Shaken* (Cambridge, 1992).
Chaui, Marilena, *A nervura do real. Imanencia e libertade em Espinosa* (São Paulo, 2006).
Čisek, Jan, "From Pansophia to Panorthosia: The Evolution of Comenius's Pansophic Conception," *Erudition and the Republic of Letters* 4 (2019), 199–227.
Clair, Pierre, "Spinoza à travers les journaux en langue française à la fin du XVIIe siècle," *CS* 2 (1978), 207–39.

Coats, Ann and Alana Lemmers, "Dutch and English Dockyards and Coastal Defence, 1652–89," in D. Ormrod and Gijs Rommelse (eds.), *War, Trade, and the State: Anglo-Dutch Conflict, 1652–89* (Woodbridge, 2020), 137–78.

Cohen, Gustave, *Le séjour de Saint-Évremond en Holland et l'entrée de Spinoza dans le champ de la pensée française* (Paris, 1926).

Cohen, Hermann, *Spinoza on State and Religion, Judaism and Christianity*, (trans.) R. S. Schine (1915; English edn., Jerusalem, 2014).

Cohen, Mozes Herman, *Spinoza en de geneeskunde* (Amsterdam, 1920).

Colie, R. L., "Spinoza and the Early English Deists," *JHI* 20 (1949), 23–46.

Colie, R. L., *Light and Enlightenment* (Cambridge, 1957).

Colie, R. L., "Spinoza in England, 1665–1730," *Proceedings of the American Philosophical Society* 107 (1963), 183–219.

Cooper, Julie, "Reevaluating Spinoza's Legacy for Jewish Political Thought," *The Journal of Politics* 79 (2017), 473–84.

Cooper, Julie, "Statesmen versus Philosophers," in Yitzhak Melamed and H. Sharp (eds.), *Spinoza's Political Treatise: A Critical Guide* (Cambridge, 2018), 29–46.

Cooper, Tim, *John Owen, Richard Baxter and the Formation of Nonconformity* (Abingdon, 2017).

Coppens, Gunther, "Descartes, Spinoza en het Nederlands cartesianisme," in G. Coppens (ed.), *Spinoza en het Nederlands Cartesianisme* (Leuven, 2004), 7–14.

Coppens, Gunther, "Spinoza et Boxel. Une histoire de fantômes," *Revue de métaphysique et de morale* 1 (2004), 59–74.

Cordingly, David, "Introduction," in *The Art of the Van de Veldes* (London, 1982), 11–20.

Cornelis, Bart, "A Reassessment of Houbraken's *Groote Schouwburgh*," *Simiolus. Netherlands Quarterly for the History of Art* 23 (1995), 167–80.

Cramer, J. A., *Abraham Heidanus en zijn cartesianisme* (Utrecht, 1889).

Cristofolini, Paolo (ed.), *L'hérésie spinoziste. Actes du colloque international de Cortona* (Amsterdam, 1995).

Cristofolini, Paolo, "Peuple et multitude dans le lexique politique de Spinoza," in Chantal Jaquet, P. Sévérac, and A Suhamy (eds.), *La Multitude libre. Nouvelles lectures du Traité Politique* (Paris, 2008), 45–58.

Curley, Edwin, *Behind the Geometrical Method* (Princeton, 1988).

Curley, Edwin, "Homo audax: Leibniz, Oldenburg, and the *Theological-Political Treatise*," *Studia Leibnitiana* 27 (1991), 277–312.

Curley, Edwin, "'I durst not write so boldly,' or How to Read Hobbes' *Theological-Political Treatise*," in *Hobbes e Spinoza. Scienza e politica: atti del Convegno internazionale, Urbino 14–17 ottobre 1988* (Urbino, 1992), 497–513.

Curley, Edwin, "Notes on a Neglected Masterpiece: Spinoza and the Science of Hermeneutics," in Graeme Hunter (ed.), *Spinoza: The Enduring Questions* (Toronto, 1994), 64–99.

Curley, Edwin, "Samuel Pufendorf (1632–1694) as a Critic of Spinoza," in Paolo Cristofolini (ed.), *L'hérésie spinoziste. Actes du colloque international de Cortona* (Amsterdam, 1995), 89–96.

Curley, Edwin, "Kissinger, Spinoza and Genghis Khan," in Don Garrett (ed.), *The Cambridge Companion to Spinoza* (Cambridge, 1996), 315–42.

Curley, Edwin, "Spinoza—as an Expositor of Descartes," in Genevieve Lloyd (ed.), *Spinoza: Critical Assessments*, vol. 1 (London, 2001), 133–9.

Curley, Edwin, "Spinoza's Exchange with Albert Burgh," in Y. Y. Melamed and M. A. Rosenthal (eds.), *Spinoza's Theological-Political Treatise: A Critical Guide* (Cambridge, 2010), 11–28.

Curley, Edwin, "Spinoza's Lost Defense," in Yitzhak Melamed (ed.), *The Young Spinoza: A Metaphysician in the Making* (Oxford, 2015), 9–32.
Curley, Edwin, "Spinoza's Contribution to Biblical Scholarship," in Don Garrett (ed.), *The Cambridge Companion to Spinoza* (2nd edn., Cambridge, 2022), 354–404.
Curtis, Daniel, "Was Plague an Exclusively Urban Phenomenon? Plague Mortality in the Seventeenth-Century Netherlands," *Journal of Interdisciplinary History* 47 (2016), 139–70.
Daalder, Remmelt, "Michiel de Ruyter: A Multi-Purpose Hero," in D. Ormrod and G. Rommelse (eds.), *War, Trade and the State: Anglo-Dutch Conflict (1652–89)* (Woodbridge, 2020), 273–92.
Dagen, Jean, *L'Histoire de l'esprit humain dans la pensée française de Fontenelle à Condorcet* (Paris, 1977).
D'Ancona, J., "Delmedigo, Menasseh ben Israel and Spinoza," *Bijdragen en Mededelingen van de Genootschap voor de Joodsche Wetenschap in Nederland* 5 (1940), 105–52.
D'Ancona, J., "Komst der Marranen in Noord-Nederland: de portugeesche gemeente te Amsterdam tot de vereeniging (1639)," in H. Brugmans and A. Frank (eds.), *Geschiedenis van de Joden in Nederland* 1 (Amsterdam, 1940), 229–46.
Darmon, Jean-Charles, "Le juste et l'utile à l'épreuve de l'histoire: Saint-Évremond," in Gianni Paganini and E. Tortarolo (eds.), *Der Garten und die Moderne. Epikureische Moral und Politik vom Humanismus bis zur Aufklärung* (Stuttgart, 2004), 215–44.
Davis, Edward B. and Michael Hunter, "Introduction" to Robert Boyle, *A Free Enquiry into the Vulgarly Received Notion of Nature* (Cambridge, 2012).
De Bie, J. P., J. Lindeboom, and G. van Itterzon (eds.), *Biografisch Woordenboek van Protestantsche Godgeleerden in Nederland* (5 vols., The Hague, 1943).
De Boer, T. J., "Spinoza en Engeland," *Tijdschrift voor Wijsbegeerte* 10 (1916), 331–6.
De Bruine, J. C., "De Theologische Faculteit van de Franeker academie in de achttiende eeuw," in G. Th. Jensma and F. Westra (eds.), *Universiteit te Franeker, 1585–1811* (Leeuwarden, 1985), 275–85.
De Dijn, Herman, *Spinoza: The Way to Wisdom* (West Lafayette, IN, 1996).
Deegan, Thomas, "George Eliot, George Henry Lewes and Spinoza's *Tractatus Theologico-Politicus*," *George Eliot-George Henry Lewes Studies* 22/23 (Sept. 1993), 1–16.
Deleuze, Gilles, *Spinoza: Practical Philosophy*, (trans.) R. Hurley (San Francisco, 1988).
Deleuze, Gilles, *Expressionism in Philosophy: Spinoza* (New York, 1992).
Della Rocca, Michael, *Spinoza* (New York-Abingdon, 2008).
Della Rocca, Michael (ed.), *The Oxford Handbook of Spinoza* (Oxford, 2018).
De Mowbray, Malcolm, "Libertas philosophandi. Wijsbegeerte in Groningen rond 1650," in Henri Krop, J. A. van Ruler, and A. J. Vanderjagt (eds.), *Zeer kundige professoren. Beoefening van de filosofie in Groningen van 1614 tot 1996* (Hilversum, 1997), 33–46.
Del Olmo, Ismael, "Against Scarecrows and Half-Baked Christians: Thomas Hobbes on Spiritual Possession and (Civil) Exorcism," *Hobbes Studies* 31 (2018), 127–46.
Del Olmo, Ismael, "'Such Fictitious Evil Spirits': Adriaan Koerbagh's Rejection of Biblical Demons and Demonic Possession in *A Light Shining in Dark Places* (1668)," *Religions* 10 no. 280 (2019), pp. 1–15.
Den Boer, Harm, *La Literatura sefardí de Amsterdam* (Alcalá de Henares, 1995).
Den Boer, Harm, "Le 'Contre-Discours' des Nouveaux Juifs. Esprit et polémique dans la littérature des juifs sépharades d'Amsterdam," in E. Benbassa (ed.), *Les Sépharades en littérature* (Paris, 2005), 47–65.
Den Boer, Harm, "Amsterdam as 'Locus' of Iberian Printing in the Seventeenth and Eighteenth Centuries," in Y. Kaplan (ed.), *The Dutch Intersection: The Jews and the Netherlands in Modern History* (Leiden, 2008), 87–110.

Den Hollander, August, "The Qur'an in the Low Countries: Early Printed Dutch and French Translations," *Quaerendo* 45 (2015), 209–39.

Den Tex, Jan, *Oldenbarnevelt* (5 vols. Haarlem, 1962–72).

Den Uyl, Douglas J., *God, Man and Well-Being: Spinoza's Modern Humanism* (New York, 2008).

Der Weduwen, Arthur, "Sold in a Closed Room: Auctioning *Libri Prohibiti* in the Dutch Golden Age, 1670–1720," in Arthur der Weduwen, Andrew Pettegree, and Graeme Kemp (eds.), *Book Trade Catalogues in Early Modern Europe* (Leiden, 2021), 319–60.

De Smet, Rudolf, "Realm of Venus: Hadriani Barlandi [H. Beverland] *De Prostibulis Veterum*," *Quaerando* 17 (1987), 45–58.

De Smet, Rudolf, *Hadrianus Beverlandus (1650–1716)* (Brussels, 1988).

De Smet, R. and W. Elias, "Isaac Vossius," in H. Dethier (ed.), *Woordenboek van Belgische en Nederlandse vrijdenkers* (Brussels, 1979), 149–83.

Deursen, A. Th. van, *De Geschiedenis van Nederland, 1555–1702. De last van veel geluk* (Amsterdam, 2004).

De Vet, J. J. V. M., "Learned Periodicals from the Dutch Republic and the Early Debate on Spinoza in England," in C. W. Schoneveld (ed.), *Miscellanea Anglo-Belgica* (Leiden, 1987), 27–39.

De Vet, J. J. V. M., "Letter of a Watchman on Zion's Walls: The First Reaction of Johannes Melchior to the *Tractatus Theologico-Politicus*," in Paolo Cristofolini (ed.), *L'hérésie spinoziste. Actes du colloque international de Cortona* (Amsterdam, 1995), 36–48.

De Vet, J. J. V. M., "Spinoza en Spinozisme en enkele 'Journaux de Hollande'," *MeSp* 83 (2002).

De Vries, Lyckle, "The Changing Face of Realism," in David Freedberg and Jan de Vries (eds.), *Art in History, History in Art: Studies in Seventeenth-Century Dutch Culture*. Getty Center Publication (Santa Monica, CA, 1987).

De Vries, Lyckle, *Gerard de Lairesse: An Artist between Stage and Studio* (Amsterdam, 1998).

De Wit, H. P., *Gorcums heren. Regentenpolitiek* (Gorcum, 1981).

Dijksterhuis, Fokko Jan, "A View from the Mountaintop: The Development of Isaac Vossius' Optics, 1658–1666," in Eric Jorink and Dirk van Miert (eds.), *Isaac Vossius (1618–1689): Between Science and Scholarship* (Leiden, 2012), 157–87.

Domínguez, Atilano, "Presencia de Antonio Pérez en Spinoza," in A. Domínguez (ed.), *Spinoza y España. Actas del Congreso Internacional sobre "Relaciones entre Spinoza y España"* (Murcia, 1994), 165–78.

Dongelmans, B. P. M., *Nil Volentibus Arduum. Documenten en bronnen* (Utrecht, 1982).

Douglas, Alexander, *Spinoza and Dutch Cartesianism* (Oxford, 2015).

Drees, Marijke Meijer, "The Revolt of Masaniello on Stage, an International Perspective," in Theo Hermans and Reinier Salverda (eds.), *From Revolt to Riches: Culture and History of the Low Countries, 1500–1700* (London, 2017), 207–13.

Ducheyne, Steffen, "Curing Pansophia through Eruditum Nescire: Bernard Nieuwentijt's (1654–1718) Epistemology of Modesty," *Hopos: The Journal of the International Society for the History of Science* 7 (2017), 277–301.

Duerloo, Luc, *Dynasty and Piety: Archduke Albert (1598–1621) and Habsburg Political Culture in the Age of Religious Wars* (Farnham, 2012).

Duffy, Simon, "The Difference between Science and Philosophy: The Spinoza-Boyle Controversy Revisited," *Paragraph: A Journal of Modern Critical Theory* 29 (2006), 115–38.

Duits, H., "De Vryheid, wiens waardy geen mensch te recht bevat," in E. O. G. Haitsma Mulier and W. R. E. Velema (eds.), *Vrijheid. Een geschiedenis van de vijftiende tot de twintigste eeuw* (Amsterdam, 1999), 99–131.

Dujovne, León, *Spinoza, su vida, su época, su obra, su influencia* (4 vols., Buenos Aires, 1941).

Dweck, Yaacob, *Dissident Rabbi: The Life of Jacob Sasportas* (Princeton, 2019).

Eckstein, Walter, "Rousseau and Spinoza: Their Political Theories and Their Conceptions of Ethical Freedom," *JHI* 5 (1944), 259–91.

Ehrard, Jean, *L'Idée de nature en France dans la première moitié du XVIIIe siècle* (Geneva, 1981).

Elliott, J. H., *The Revolt of the Catalans (1598–1640)* (Cambridge, 1963).

Emmanuel, I. S., *Precious Stones of the Jews of Curaçao* (New York, 1957).

Emmanuel, I. S., "Les Juifs de la Martinique et leurs coreligonnaires d'Amsterdam au XVIIe siècle," *REJ* 123 (1964), 511–16.

Emmanuel, I. S. and S. A. Emmanuel, *History of the Jews of the Netherlands Antilles* (2 vols., Cincinnati, 1970).

Esteves do Couto, Patricia R., *The Marvelous Travels of Fernando Mendez Pinto* (Lisbon, 2012).

Evenhuis, R. B., *Ook dat was Amsterdam. De Kerk der hervorming in de gouden eeuw* (2 vols., Amsterdam, 1967).

Faria, A. de, "D. Antonio 1er, Prieur de Crato, XVIIe Roi de Portugal. Exile, mort et inhumé à Paris le 26 août 1595," *Congrès des sociétés pour l'histoire de Paris* (Paris, 1913), 1–8.

Faur, José, *In the Shadow of History: Jews and Conversos at the Dawn of Modernity* (Albany, NY, 1992).

Feitler, Bruno, *Inquisition, juifs et nouveaux-chretiens au Brésil* (Louvain, 2003).

Feldman, L. H., "Josephus' Portrait of Ezra," *Vetus Testamentum* 43 (1993), 190–214.

Feuer, Lewis Samuel, *Spinoza and the Rise of Liberalism* (Abingdon, 1987).

Field, Sandra Leonie, *Potentia: Hobbes and Spinoza on Power and Popular Politics* (Oxford, 2020).

Fix, Andrew C., *Prophecy and Reason: The Dutch Collegiants in the Early Enlightenment* (Princeton, 1991).

Fix, Andrew C., "Comets in the Early Dutch Enlightenment," in Wiep van Bunge (ed.), *The Early Enlightenment in the Dutch Republic, 1650–1750* (Leiden, 2003), 157–72.

Floss, Pavel, "The Problem of Comenius' Sensualism," in M. Kyralova and J. Privratska (eds.), *Symposium Comenianum 1982: The Impact of J.A. Comenius on Educational Thinking and Practice* (Uhersky Brod, 1984), 102–7.

Forclaz, Bertrand, "Rather French than Subject to the Prince of Orange: The Conflicting Loyalties of the Utrecht Catholics during the French Occupation (1672–73)," *CHRC* 87 (2007), 509–33.

Franco, Paul, *Nietzsche's Enlightenment: The Free-Spirit Trilogy of the Middle Period* (Chicago, 2011).

Fraenkel, Carlos, "Maimonides' God and Spinoza's *Deus sive Natura*," *JHPh* 44 (2006), 169–215.

Fraenkel, Carlos, "Could Spinoza Have Presented the *Ethics* as the True Content of the Bible?," in Dan Garber and Steven Nadler (eds.), *OEMPh* 4 (2008), 1–50.

Fraenkel, Carlos, "Hasdai Crescas on God as the Place of the World and Spinoza's Notion of God extensa," *Aleph* 91 (2009), 77–111.

Fraenkel, Carlos, *Philosophical Religions from Plato to Spinoza: Reason, Religion and Autonomy* (Cambridge, 2012).

Fraenkel, Carlos, "Reconsidering the Case of Elijah Delmedigo's Averroism and its Impact on Spinoza," in Anna Akasoy and G. Guiglioni (eds.), *Renaissance Averroism and its Aftermath* (Dordrecht, 2013), 213–36.

Fraenkel, Carlos, "Spinoza's Philosophy of Religion," in Michael Della Rocca (ed.), *The Oxford Handbook of Spinoza* (Oxford, 2018), 377–407.

Frampton, Travis, *Spinoza and the Rise of Historical Criticism of the Bible* (New York-London, 2006).

Francès, Madeline, "Un gazetier français en Hollande: Gabriel de Saint Glen, traducteur de Spinoza," *Revue des sciences humaines* 79 (1955), 407–20.

Frankel, Steven, "Spinoza's Rejection of Maimonideism," in Steven Nadler (ed.), *Spinoza and Medieval Jewish Philosophy* (Cambridge, 2014), 79–95.

Freeman, David, *A Silver River in a Silver World: Dutch Trade in the Rio de la Plata, 1648–1678* (Cambridge, 2018).

Friedenwald, Herbert, "Material for the History of the Jews in the British West Indies," PAJHS V (1897), 45–95.

Friedmann, Georges, *Leibniz et Spinoza* (1946; 2nd edn., Paris, 1962).

Frijhoff, Willem, "Religious Toleration in the United Provinces: From 'Case' to 'Model'," in R. Po-Chia Hsia and H. van Nierop (eds.), *Calvinism and Religious Toleration in the Dutch Golden Age* (Cambridge, 2002), 27–52.

Fuks, L., "Een rechtsstrijd onder Amsterdamse Sefardim in de 17^e eeuw," in *'T Exempel dwinght. Opstellen angeboden aan I. Kisch ter gelegenheid van zijn zeventigste verjaardag* (Zwolle, 1975), 175–89.

Fuks-Mansfeld, R. G., *Sefardim in Amsterdam tot 1795. Aspecten van een joodse minderheid in een Hollandse stad* (Hilversum, 1989).

Fukuoka, Atsuko, *The Sovereign and the Prophets: Spinoza on Groatian and Hobbesian Biblical Argumentation* (Leiden, 2018).

Funkenstein, Amos, *Theology and the Scientific Imagination from the Middle Ages to the Seventeenth Century* (Princeton, 1986).

Gabbey, Alan, "A Disease Incurable: Scepticism and the Cambridge Platonists," in R. H. Popkin and A. Vanderjagt (eds.), *Scepticism and Irreligion in the Seventeenth and Eighteenth Centuries* (Leiden, 1993), 71–91.

Gabbey, Alan, "Spinoza's Natural Science and Methodology," in Don Garrett (ed.), *The Cambridge Companion to Spinoza* (Cambridge, 1996), 142–91.

Gabbey, Alan, "Spinoza on Natural Science and Methodology" in Don Garrett (ed.), *The Cambridge Companion to Spinoza* (2nd edn., Cambridge, 2022), 187–233.

Gafni, Isaiah, "The Historical Background," in M. Stone (ed.), *The Literature of the Jewish People in the Period of the Second Temple and the Talmud*, vol.2 (Leiden, 1984), 1–31.

Gans, Mozes H., *Memorboek. Platenatlas van het leven der joden in Nederland van de middeleeuwen tot 1940* (Baarn, 1940).

Garber, Dan, *Descartes' Metaphysical Physics* (Chicago, 1992).

Garber, Dan, *Leibniz: Body, Substance, Monad* (Oxford, 2009).

Garber, Dan, "Spinoza's Cartesian Dualism in the *Korte Verhandeling*," in Yitzhak Melamed (ed.), *The Young Spinoza: A Metaphysician in the Making* (Oxford, 2015), 121–32.

Garber, Dan, "Superheroes in the History of Philosophy: Spinoza, Super-Rationalist," *JHPh* 53 no. 3 (2015), 507–22.

Garber, Dan, "Religion and the Civil State in the *Tractatus Politicus*," in Yitzhak Melamed and H. Sharp (eds.), *Spinoza's Political Treatise: A Critical Guide* (Cambridge, 2018), 128–45.

García-Arenal, Mercedes, "Conexiones entre los judíos marroquíes y la comunidad de Amsterdam," in Jaime Contreras, B. J. García García, and Ignacio Pulido (eds.), *Familia, Religión y negocio. El sefardismo en las relaciones entre el mundo ibérico y los Países Bajos en la Edad Moderna* (Madrid, 2002), 173–205.

García-Arenal, Mercedes and G. Wiegers, *Entre el Islam y Occidente. Vida de Samuel Pallache, judío de Fez* (Madrid, 1999).

García-Arenal, Mercedes and G. Wiegers, *Un hombre en tres mundos: Samuel Pallache, un judío marroquí en la Europa protestante y en la católica* (Madrid, 2006).

Garrett, Aaron, "The Virtues of Geometry," in Michael Della Rocca (ed.), *The Oxford Handbook of Spinoza* (Oxford, 2018), 18–44.

Garrett, Don, "Spinoza's Ethical Theory," in Don Garrett (ed.), *The Cambridge Companion to Spinoza* (Cambridge, 1996), 267–314.

Garrett, Don, "'Promising' Ideas: Hobbes and Contract in Spinoza's Political Philosophy," in Y. Y. Melamed and M. A. Rosenthal (eds.), *Spinoza's* Theological-Political Treatise: *A Critical Guide* (Cambridge, 2010), 192–209.

Garrett, Don, *Nature and Necessity in Spinoza's Philosophy* (Oxford, 2018).

Garrett, Don, "Representation, Misrepresentation, and Error in Spinoza's Philosophy of Mind," in Michael Della Rocca (ed.), *The Oxford Handbook of Spinoza* (Oxford, 2018), 190–203.

Gascón Pérez, Jesús, *Aragón en la monarquía de Felipe II* (2 vols., Zaragoza, 2007).

Gatens, Moira, *Spinoza's Hard Path to Freedom* (Assen, 2011).

Gatens, Moira, "Benedict Spinoza and George Eliot: *Daniel Deronda* as Heretical Text," *MeSp* 99 (2015).

Gatens, Moira, "The Condition of Human Nature," in Yitzhak Melamed and H. Sharp (eds.), *Spinoza's* Political Treatise: *A Critical Guide* (Cambridge, 2018), 47–60.

Gatens, Moira and Genevieve Lloyd, *Collective Imaginings: Spinoza, Past and Present* (London, 1999).

Gaukroger, Stephen, *Descartes, an Intellectual Biography* (Oxford, 1995).

Gaukroger, Stephen, *Francis Bacon and the Transformation of Early-Modern Philosophy* (Cambridge, 2001).

Gaukroger, Stephen, *Descartes' System of Natural Philosophy* (2002).

Gaukroger, Stephen, *The Failures of Philosophy: A Historical Essay* (Princeton, 2020).

Gebhardt, Carl, "Juan de Prado," *Chronicon Spinozanum* iii (1923), 269–91.

Gebhardt, Carl, "Spinoza gegen Clapmarius," *Chronicon Spinozanum* iii (1923), 334–7.

Geldersblom, A. J., "The Publisher of Hobbes' Dutch *Leviathan*," in S. Roach (ed.), *Across the Narrow Seas: Studies in the History and Bibliography of the Low Countries* (London, 1991), 162–6.

Gengoux, N., P. Girard, and M. Laerke (eds.), *Libertinage et philosophie à l'époque classique (XVIe–XVIIIe siècle). Les Libertins néerlandais* (Paris, 2022).

Gerritsen, Johan, "Printing Spinoza: Some Questions," in Fokke Akkerman and Piet Steenbakkers (eds.), *Spinoza to the Letter: Studies in Words, Texts and Books* (Leiden, 2005), 251–62.

Gerson, Horst, *Rembrandt's Paintings* (New York, 1968).

Giancotti Boscherini, Emilia, "Nota sulla diffusione dellla filosofia di Spinoza in Italia," *Giornale critico della filosofía italiana* 42 (1963) 339–62.

Giancotti Boscherini, Emilia, *Lexicon Spinozanum* (2 vols., The Hague, 1970).

Goetschel, Willi, *Spinoza's Modernity: Mendelssohn, Lessing and Heine* (Madison, WI, 2004).

Goldenbaum, Ursula, "Die Philosophische Methodendiskussion des 17. Jahrhunderts in ihrer Bedeutung für den Modernisierungsschub in der Historiographie," in W. Küttler,

J. Rüsen, and E. Schulin (eds.), *Geschichtsdiskurs*, vol. 2, *Anfänge modernen historischen Denkens* (Frankfurt, 1994), 148-61.

Goldenbaum, Ursula, "Der historische Ansatz des Theologisch-politischen Traktats Baruch Spinozas als ein Ausweg aus den religionsphilosophischen Debatten des 17. Jahrhunderts," in Thomas Brose (ed.), *Religionsphilosophie. Europäische Denker zwischen philosophischer Theologie und Religionskritik* (Würzburg 1998), 83-112.

Goldenbaum, Ursula, "Leibniz as a Lutheran," in A. P. Coudert, R. H. Popkin, and G. M. Weiner (eds.), *Leibniz, Mysticism and Religion* (Dordrecht, 1998), 169-92.

Goldenbaum, Ursula, "Die *Commentatiuncula de judice* als Leibnizens erste philosophische Auseinandersetzung mit Spinoza," *Studia Leibnitiana* Sonderheft 29 (Stuttgart, 1999), 60-106.

Goldenbaum, Ursula, "Zwischen Bewunderung und Entsetzen. Leibniz' frühe Faszination durch Spinoza's *Tractatus Theologico-Politicus*," *MeSp* 80 (2001).

Goldenbaum, Ursula, "Spinoza's Parrot, Socinian Syllogisms and Leibniz's Metaphysics: Leibniz's Three Strategies for Defending the Christian Mysteries," *American Catholic Philosophical Quarterly* 76 (2002), 551-74.

Goldfarb, Michael, *Emancipation: How Liberating Europe's Jews from the Ghetto Led to Revolution and Renaissance* (Melbourne, 2009).

Gómez-Centurión Jiménez, Carlos, *Felipe II, La Empresa de Inglaterra y el comercio septentrional (1566-1609)* (Madrid, 1988).

González Diéguez, Guadalupe, "Spinoza and the Grammar of the Hebrew Language," in Yitzhak Melamed (ed.), *A Companion to Spinoza* (Hoboken, NJ, 2021), 483-91.

Gootjes, Albert, "Le Réseau cartésien d'Utrecht face au *Tractatus Theologico-Politicus* esquisses d'une campagne anti-spinoziste," *Bulletin annuel de l'Institut d'histoire de la Réformation* 36 (2015), 49-54.

Gootjes, Albert, "The First Orchestrated Attack on Spinoza: Johannes Melchioris and the Cartesian Network in Utrecht," *JHI* 79 (2018), 23-43.

Gootjes, Albert, "Spinoza between French Libertines and Dutch Cartesians: The 1673 Utrecht Visit," *Modern Intellectual History* (published online 16 Nov. 2018).

Gootjes, Albert, "The Collegie der Sçavanten: A Seventeenth-Century Scholarly Society in Utrecht," in Joke Spaans and Jetze Touber (eds.), *Enlightened Religion: From Confessional Churches to Polite Piety in the Dutch Republic* (Leiden, 2019), 156-82.

Gootjes, Albert, "Tussen vriendschap en vijandschap: Spinoza en de Cartesianen in Utrecht," in B. Posthuma (ed.), *Spinoza en zijn kring. Een balans van veertig jaar onderzoek* (Uitgeverij Spinozahuis, The Hague, 2019), 19-29.

Gottlieb, Micah, "The Serpent and the Dove: Spinoza's Two Paths to Enlightenment," in Yitzhak Melamed (ed.), *A Companion to Spinoza* (Hoboken, NJ, 2021), 338-48.

Goudriaan, Aza, *Reformed Orthodoxy and Philosophy, 1625-1750: Gisbertus Voetius, Petrus van Mastricht, and Anthonius Driessen* (Leiden, 2006).

Grafton, Anthony, "Isaac Vossius, Chronologer," in Eric Jorink and Dirk van Miert (eds.), *Isaac Vossius (1618-1689): Between Science and Scholarship* (Leiden, 2012), 43-84.

Grafton, Anthony, "Spinoza's Hermeneutics: Some Heretical Thoughts," in Dirk van Miert, Henk Nellen, Piet Steenbakkers, and Jetze Touber (eds.), *Scriptural Authority and Biblical Criticism in the Dutch Golden Age* (Oxford, 2017), 177-96.

Green, Alexander, "A Portrait of Spinoza as a Maimonidean Reconsidered," *Shofar* 34 (2015), 81-106.

Grigoropolou, Vasiliki, "Steno's Critique of Descartes and Louis de La Forge's Response," in R. Andrault and M. Laerke (eds.), *Steno and the Philosophers* (Leiden, 2018), 113-37.

Gros, Jean-Michel, *Les dissidences de la philosophie à l'âge classique* (Paris, 2009).

Grunwald, Max, *Spinoza in Deutschland* (Berlin, 1897).
Gullan-Whur, Margaret, *With Reason: A Life of Spinoza* (London, 1998).
Hagoort, Lydia, "Persons of a Restless Disposition: Conflicts between the Jewish Merchants Lopo Ramires and Manuel Dias Henriques and the Parnassim," *SR* 32 (1998), 156–74.
Hagoort, Lydia, *Het Beth Haim in Ouderkerk aan de Amstel* (Hilversum, 2005).
Hainsworth, Roger and Christine Churches, *The Anglo-Dutch Naval Wars 1652–1674* (Fayetteville, TX, 1998).
Haitsma Mulier, E. O. G., "Spinoza en Tacitus: de filosoof en de geschiedschrijver," in E. O. G. Haitsma Mulier, L. H. Maas, and J. Vogel (eds.), *Het beeld in de spiegel. Historiografische verkenningen* (Hilversum, 2000), 67–78.
Haitsma Mulier, E. O. G. and W. R. E. Velema (eds.), *Vrijheid. Een geschiedenis van de vijftiende tot de twintigste eeuw* (Amsterdam, 1999).
Haley, K. H. D., *An English Diplomat in the Low Countries: Sir William Temple and John de Witt 1665–1672* (Oxford, 1986).
Hamel, Frank, *Famous French Salons* (New York, 1908).
Hamilton, Alastair, *The Apocryphal Apocalypse: The Reception of the Second Book of Esdras (4 Ezra) from the Renaissance to the Enlightenment* (Oxford, 1999).
Hamilton, Alastair, "The Quran in Early Modern Europe," in J. Schaeps, K. van Ommen, and A. Vrolijk (eds.), *Oostersche weelde: de Orient in westerse kunst en cultuur* (Leiden, 2005), 131–43.
Hammer, P. E. J., "New Light on the Cadiz Expedition of 1596," *Historical Research* 70 (1997), 182–202.
Hampshire, Stuart, *Spinoza* (Harmondsworth, 1951).
Hardt, Michael, *Gilles Deleuze: An Apprenticeship in Philosophy* (London, 1993).
Harlow, V. T., *A History of Barbados, 1625–1685* (Oxford, 1926).
Harmsen, A. J. E., *Onderwijs in de Toneel-poëzy. De opvattingen over toneel van het kunstgenootschap Nil Volentibus Arduum* (Rotterdam, 1989).
Harris, Erol E., *Salvation from Despair: A Reappraisal of Spinoza's Philosophy* (Dordrecht, 1973).
Harris, Tim, *Restoration: Charles II and his Kingdoms, 1660–1685* (London, 2005).
Harrison, John and Peter Laslett, *The Library of John Locke* (Oxford, 1971).
Harrison, Peter, *The Territories of Science and Religion* (Chicago, 2015).
Harvey, Warren Zev, "Hasdai Crescas's Critique of the Theory of the Acquired Intellect," (Columbia University, New York Ph.D. thesis, 1973).
Harvey, Warren Zev, "A Portrait of Spinoza as a Maimonidean," *JHPh* 19 (1981), 151–72.
Harvey, Warren Zev, *Physics and Metaphysics in Hasdai Crescas* (Amsterdam, 1998).
Harvey, Warren Zev, "Spinoza's Metaphysical Hebraism," in H. M. Ravven and L. E. Goodman (eds.), *Jewish Themes in Spinoza's Philosophy* (Albany, NY, 2002), 207–14.
Harvey, Warren Zev, "Spinoza on Ibn Ezra's 'Secret of the Twelve'," in Y. Y. Melamed and M. A. Rosenthal (eds.), *Spinoza's* Theological-Political Treatise: *A Critical Guide* (Cambridge, 2010), 41–55.
Harvey, Warren Zev, "Spinoza and Maimonides on True Religion," in Yitzhak Melamed (ed.), *A Companion to Spinoza* (Hoboken, NJ, 2021), 41–6.
Hattendorf, John B., "Competing Navies: Anglo-Dutch Naval Rivalry, 1652–88," in D. Ormrod and G. Rommelse (eds.), *War, Trade and the State: Anglo-Dutch Conflict, 1652–89* (Woodbridge, 2020), 92–116.
Hautz, Johann Friedrich, *Geschichte der Universität Heidelberg* (2 vols., 1862–4; repr. Hildesheim, 1980).

Heijbroek, J. F., *Met Huygens op reis. Tekeningen en dagboeknotities van Constantijn Huygens jr (1628-1697)* (Amsterdam, 1982).
Hell, Maarten, "A Walk around the Block on Vlooienburg," *SR* 48 (2002), 53-79.
Hengstermann, Christian, "God or Space and Nature? Henry More's Panentheism of Space and Panpsychism of Life and Nature," in Godehard Brüntrup, Benedikt Paul Göcke, and Ludwig Jaskolla (eds.), *Panentheism and Panpsychism: Philosophy of Religion Meets Philosophy of Mind* (Leiden, 2020), 157-89.
Henry, John, "A Cambridge Platonist's Materialism: Henry More and the Concept of the Soul," *Journal of the Warburg and Courtauld Institutes* 49 (1986), 172-95.
Henry, Julie, "Freedom of Conscience in Spinoza's *Political Treatise*," *Reformation and Renaissance Review* 14 (2012), 8-22.
Hermann, Jacqueline, "An Undesired King: Some Notes on the Political Trajectory of D. Antonio, Prior do Crato," *Revista Brasileira de Historia* 30 (2010), 139-64.
Herrero Sánchez, Manuel, "La Monarquía hispánica y el Tratado de La Haya de 1673," *Diálogos Hispánicos* 16 (1995), 103-18.
Herrero Sánchez, Manuel, *Acercamiento hispano-neerlandés (1648-1678)* (Madrid, 2000).
Hes, Hindle S., *Jewish Physicians in the Netherlands, 1600-1940* (Assen, 1980).
Hirschman, Albert, *The Passions and the Interests* (1977; Princeton, 1996).
Hoekstra, Kinch, "A Lion in the House: Hobbes and Democracy," in A. Brett and James Tully (eds.), *Rethinking the Foundations of Modern Political Thought* (Cambridge, 2007), 191-218.
Hollewand, Karen, *The Banishment of Beverland: Sex, Sin and Scholarship in the Seventeenth-Century Dutch Republic* (Leiden, 2019).
Holton, Geoffrey, "Einstein's Third Paradise," *Daedalus* (Fall, 2003), 26-34.
Holzhey, Tanja, *"Als gy maar scherp wordt, zo zyn wy voldaan." Rationalistische ideën van het kunstgenootschap Nil Volentibus Arduum, 1669-1680* (Amsterdam, 2014).
Hope, Quentin M., *Saint-Évremond and His Friends* (Geneva, 1999).
Horn, Hendrik J., *The Golden Age Revisited: Arnold Houbraken's Great Theatre of Netherlandish Painters and Paintresses*, 2 vols. (Doornspijk, 2000).
Hornäk, Sara, *Spinoza und Vermeer. Immanenz in Philosophie und Malerei* (Würzburg, 2004).
Hubbeling, H. G., *Spinoza* (Baarn, 1966).
Hubbeling, H. G., "Zur frühen Spinozarezeption in der Niederlanden," in K. Gründer and W. Schmidt-Biggemann (eds.), *Spinoza in der Frühzeit seiner religiösen Wirkung* (Heidelberg, 1984), 149-200.
Hudson, Wayne, *The English Deists: Studies in Early Enlightenment* (London, 2009).
Hudson, Wayne, *Enlightenment and Modernity: The English Deists and Reform* (London, 2009).
Huenemann, Charles, *Spinoza's Radical Theology: The Metaphysics of the Infinite* (Abingdon, 2013).
Huisman, Gerda. "Bibliothecae instructissimae: geleerd boekenbezit in Groningen in de 17e en 18e eeuw," in A. H. Huussen (ed.), *Onderwijs en onderzoek. Studie en wetenschap aan de academie van Groningen in de 17e en 18e eeuw* (Hilversum, 2003), 299-328.
Huizinga, J. H., *Dutch Civilization in the Seventeenth Century* (London, 1968).
Hunter, Graeme, *Radical Protestantism in Spinoza's Thought* (Abingdon, 2005).
Hunter, Michael, "Early Problems in Professionalizing Scientific Research: Nathanial Grew (1641-172) and the Royal Society," *Notes and Records of the Royal Society of London* 36 (1982), 189-209.
Hutton, Sarah, "Science, Philosophy and Atheism: Edward Stillingfleet's Defense of Religion," in R. H. Popkin and J. Vanderjagt (eds.), *Scepticism and Irreligion in the Seventeenth and Eighteenth Centuries* (Leiden, 1993), 102-20.

Hutton, Sarah, "Henry Oldenburg (1617/20-1677) and Spinoza," in Paolo Cristofolini (ed.), *L'hérésie spinoziste. Actes du colloque international de Cortona* (Amsterdam, 1995), 106-22.
Hutton, Sarah, "Edward Stillingfleet and Spinoza," in W. van Bunge and W. Klever (eds.), *Disguised and Overt Spinozism around 1700* (Leiden, 1996), 261-74.
Hutton, Sarah, *Benjamin Furly (1646-1714): A Quaker Merchant and His Milieu* (Florence, 2007).
Iliffe, Rob, "Jesus Nazarenus Legislator: Adam Boreel's Defense of Christianity," in S. Berti, F. Charles-Daubert, and R. H. Popkin (eds.), *Heterodoxy, Spinozism and Free Thought in Early Eighteenth-Century Europe* (Dordrecht, 1996), 365-96.
Iofrida, M., "Linguaggio e verità in Lodewijk Meyer," in Paolo Cristofolini (ed.), *L'hérésie spinoziste. Actes du colloque international de Cortona* (Amsterdam, 1995), 29-35.
Israel, Jonathan I., *Race, Class and Politics in Colonial Mexico, 1610-1670* (Oxford, 1975).
Israel, Jonathan I., "Spain and the Dutch Sephardim, 1609-1660," *SR* 12 (1978), 1-61.
Israel, Jonathan I., "Some Further Data on the Amsterdam Sephardim and their Trade with Spain during the 1650s," *SR* 14 (1980), 7-19.
Israel, Jonathan, *The Dutch Republic and the Hispanic World, 1606-1661* (Oxford, 1982).
Israel, Jonathan I., "The Economic Contribution of Dutch Sephardi Jewry to Holland's Golden Age, 1595-1713," *Tijdschrift voor Geschiedenis* 96 (1983), 505-35.
Israel, Jonathan I., "An Amsterdam Jewish Merchant of the Golden Age: Jeronimo Nunes da Costa (1620-1697), Agent of Portugal in the United Provinces," *SR* 18 (1984), 21-40.
Israel, Jonathan I., "Duarte Nunes da Costa (Jacob Curiel), of Hamburg, Sephardi Nobleman and Communal Leader (1585-1664)," *SR* 21 (1987), 14-34.
Israel, Jonathan I., *Dutch Primacy in World Trade, 1585-1740* (Oxford, 1989).
Israel, Jonathan I., "Menasseh ben Israel and the Dutch Sephardic Colonization Movement of the mid-Seventeenth Century (1645-1657), in Yosef Kaplan, H. Méchoulan, and R. Popkin (eds.), *Menasseh ben Israel and His World* (Leiden, 1989), 139-63.
Israel, Jonathan I., "The Amsterdam Stock Exchange and the English Revolution of 1688," *Tijdschrift voor Geschiedenis* 103 (1990), 412-40.
Israel, Jonathan I., "The Dutch Role in the Glorious Revolution," in J. I. Israel (ed.), *The Anglo-Dutch Moment* (Cambridge, 1991), 105-62.
Israel, Jonathan I., *The Dutch Republic: Its Rise, Greatness, and Fall, 1477-1806* (Oxford, 1995).
Israel, Jonathan I., "Spinoza, King Solomon and Frederik van Leenhof's Spinozistic Republicanism," *SS* 11 (1995), 303-17.
Israel, Jonathan I., "The Banning of Spinoza's Works in the Dutch Republic," in W. van Bunge and W. Klever (eds.), *Disguised and Overt Spinozism around 1700* (Leiden, 1996), 3-14.
Israel, Jonathan I., *Conflicts of Empires: Spain, the Low Countries and the Struggle for World Supremacy, 1585-1713* (London, 1997).
Israel, Jonathan I., *European Jewry in the Age of Mercantilism, 1550-1750* (1985; 2nd edn., London, 1998).
Israel, Jonathan I., Review article "De belangrijkste nederlander," on Steven Nadler, *Spinoza: A Life*, and Margaret Gullen-Whur, *Within Reason: A Life of Spinoza*, in *NRC Handelsblad: Boeken, Overzicht en kritiek* (9 March 1999), 31.
Israel, Jonathan I., "Maurits en de wording van de buitenlandse politiek," in Kees Zandvliet (ed.), *Maurits, Prins van Oranje* (Zwolle, 2000), 65-75.
Israel, Jonathan I., *Radical Enlightenment: Philosophy and the Making of Modernity 1650-1750* (Oxford, 2001).

Israel, Jonathan I., *Diasporas within a Diaspora: Jews, Crypto-Jews and the World Maritime Empires (1540-1740)* (Leiden, 2002).
Israel, Jonathan I., "Philosophy, Commerce, and the Synagogue: Spinoza's Expulsion from the Portuguese Jewish Community in 1656," in Jonathan I. Israel and Reinier Salverda (eds.), *Dutch Jewry: Its History and Secular Culture (1500-2000)* (Leiden, 2002), 125-40.
Israel, Jonathan I., "The Early Dutch Enlightenment as a Factor in the Spread of the Wider European Enlightenment," in Wiep van Bunge (ed.), *The Early Enlightenment in the Dutch Republic, 1650-1750* (Leiden, 2003), 215-30.
Israel, Jonathan I., *Empires and Entrepots: Dutch, the Spanish Monarchy and the Jews, 1585-1713* (London, 2003).
Israel, Jonathan I., "Meyer, Koerbagh and the Radical Enlightenment Critique of Socinianism," *GWND* 14 (2003), 197-208.
Israel, Jonathan I., "The Intellectual Origins of Modern Democratic Republicanism (1660-1720)," *European Journal of Political Theory* 3 (2004), 7-36.
Israel, Jonathan I., *Enlightenment Contested: Philosophy, Modernity, and the Emancipation of Man 1670-1752* (Oxford, 2006).
Israel, Jonathan I., "Spinoza as an Expounder, Critic and 'Reformer' of Descartes," *IHR* 17 (2007), 41-53.
Israel, Jonathan I., "Dr Cornelis Bontekoe's Views on Spinoza and the Spread of Spinozism Published in the Year 1680," *SS* 16 (2008), 221-41.
Israel, Jonathan I., "Philosophy, Deism and the Early Jewish Enlightenment (1655-1740)," in Y. Kaplan (ed.), *The Dutch Intersection: The Jews and the Netherlands in Modern History* (Leiden, 2008), 173-202.
Israel, Jonathan I., "The Early Dutch and German Reaction to the *Tractatus Theologico-Politicus*," in Y. Y. Melamed and M. A. Rosenthal (eds.), *Spinoza's* Theological-Political Treatise: *A Critical Guide* (Cambridge, 2010), 72-100.
Israel, Jonathan I., *Democratic Enlightenment: Philosophy, Revolution, and Human Rights 1750-1790* (Oxford, 2011).
Israel, Jonathan I., "The Philosophical Context of Hermann Samuel Reimarus' Radical Bible Criticism," in Martin Mulsow (ed.), *Between Philology and Radical Enlightenment: Hermann Samuel Reimarus (1694-1768)* (Leiden, 2011).
Israel, Jonathan I., "Spain's Empire, 'superstitio' and 'Enlightened' Networks in Spinoza's Philosophical System of Subversion," in Juan Carlos Garavaglia, Jacques Poloni-Simard, and Gilles Rivière (eds.), *Au miroir de l'Anthropologie historique. Mélanges offerts à Nathan Wachtel* (Rennes, 2013), 75-94.
Israel, Jonathan I., "Spinozistic Popular Radicalism in the Dutch Art World of the Later Golden Age," in Hanno Brand (ed.), *De tienduizend dingen. Feestbundel voor Reinier Salverda* (Leeuwarden, 2013), 129-44.
Israel, Jonathan I., "Grotius and the Rise of Christian 'Radical Enlightenment'," *Grotiana* 35 (2014), 19-31.
Israel, Jonathan I., "Leibniz's Theodicy as a Critique of Spinoza and Bayle—and Blueprint for the Philosophy Wars of the Eighteenth Century," in L. M. Jorgensen and S. Newlands (eds.), *New Essays on Leibniz's* Theodicy (Oxford, 2014), 233-44.
Israel, Jonathan I., "Dutch Golden Age Politics and the Rise of the Radical Enlightenment," in S. Lavaert and W. Schröder (eds.), *The Dutch Legacy: Radical Thinkers in the 17th Century and the Enlightenment* (Leiden, 2017), 35-60.
Israel, Jonathan I., "How Did Spinoza Declare War on Theology and the Theologians?," in Dirk van Miert, Henk Nellen, Piet Steenbakkers, and Jetze Touber (eds.), *Scriptural Authority and Biblical Criticism in the Dutch Golden Age* (Oxford, 2017), 197-216.

Israel, Jonathan I., "'Radical Enlightenment': A Game-Changing Concept," in Steffen Ducheyne (ed.), *Reassessing the Radical Enlightenment* (Abingdon, 2017), 15–47.

Israel, Jonathan I., "Spinozism and the Erotic: Hadrianus Beverland's Suppressed Writings," in Chr. Bahier-Porte, P.-F. Moreau, and D. Reguig (eds.), *Liberté de conscience et arts de penser (XVIe–XIIIe Siècle. Mélanges en l'Honneur d'Antony McKenna* (Paris, 2017), 385–406.

Israel, Jonathan I., "King Philip II of Spain as a Symbol of 'Tyranny' in Spinoza's Political Writings," *Co-herencia* 15 (2018), 137–54.

Israel, Jonathan I., *The Enlightenment that Failed: Ideas, Revolution, and Democratic Defeat, 1748–1830* (Oxford, 2019).

Israel, Jonathan I., "Pierre Bayle's Correspondence and Its Significance for the History of Ideas," *JHI* 80 (2019), 479–500.

Israel, Jonathan I., "Popularizing Radical Ideas in the Dutch Art World of the Early Eighteenth Century: Willem Goeree (1635–1711) and Arnold Houbraken (1660–1719)," in Joke Spaans and Jetze Touber (eds.), *Enlightened Religion: From Confessional Churches to Polite Piety in the Dutch Republic* (Leiden, 2019), 268–89.

Israel, Jonathan I., "Spinoza's Formulation of the Radical Enlightenment's Two Foundational Concepts: How Much Did He Owe to the Dutch Golden Age?," in Jack Stetter and Charles Ramond (eds.), *Spinoza in Twenty-First Century American and French Philosophy* (London, 2019), 335–49.

Israel, Jonathan I., "Spinoza, Radical Enlightenment and the General Reform of the Arts in the Later Dutch Golden Age: The Aims of *Nil Volentibus Arduum*," *IHR* 30 (2020), 387–409.

Israel, Jonathan I., "How Does Spinoza's 'Democracy' Differ from that of Hobbes?," *Hobbes Studies* 34 (2021), 227–40.

Israel, Jonathan I., *Revolutionary Jews from Spinoza to Marx: The Fight for a Secular World of Universal and Equal Rights* (Seattle, 2021).

Israel, Jonathan I. and Reinier Salverda (eds.), *Dutch Jewry: Its History and Secular Culture (1500–2000)* (Leiden, 2002).

Jacob, Alexander, *Henry More's Refutation of Spinoza* (Hildesheim, 1991).

Jagersma, Rindert and Trude Dijkstra, "Uncovering Spinoza's Printers by Means of Bibliographical Research," *Quaerendo* 43 (2013), 278–310.

James, Susan, "Spinoza the Stoic," in T. Sorrell (ed.), *The Rise of Modern Philosophy* (Oxford, 1993), 289–316.

James, Susan, "Freedom, Slavery and the Passions," in Olli Koistinen (ed.), *The Cambridge Companion to Spinoza's* Ethics (Cambridge, 2009), 223–41.

James, Susan, *Spinoza on Philosophy, Religion, and Politics* (Oxford, 2012).

James, Susan, "Politically Mediated Affects: Envy in Spinoza's *Tractatus Politicus*," in Yitzhak Melamed and H. Sharp (eds.), *Spinoza's* Political Treatise: *A Critical Guide* (Cambridge, 2018), 61–77.

James, Susan, *Spinoza on Learning to Live Together* (Oxford, 2020).

Jammer, Max, *Einstein and Religion: Physics and Theology* (Princeton, 1999).

Janet, Paul, "Spinoza et le spinozisme," *Revue des deux mondes* 70 (1867), 470–98.

Janssen, Geert, *Princely Power in the Dutch Republic: Patronage and William Frederick of Nassau (1613–64)* (Manchester, 2008).

Japikse, N., *Johan de Witt* (Amsterdam, 1915).

Japikse, N., "Spinoza en De Witt," in *Bijdragen voor vaderlandsche geschiedenis en oudheidkunde*, 6th series vi (1928), 1–16.

Jaquet, Chantal, "L'Actualité du *Traité Politique* de Spinoza," in Chantal Jaquet, P. Sévérac, and A. Suhamy (eds.), *La Multitude libre. Nouvelles lectures du* Traité Politique (Paris, 2008), 13–26.

Jaquet, Chantal, "From Parallelism to Equality: The Nature of the Union of Mind and Body in Spinoza," *MeSp* 104.
Jaquet, Chantal, *Spinoza à l'oeuvre. Composition des corps et force des idées* (Paris, 2017).
Jaquet, Chantal, "Longing (Desiderium) for Vengeance as the Foundation of the Commonwealth," in Yitzhak Melamed and H. Sharp (eds.), *Spinoza's Political Treatise: A Critical Guide* (Cambridge, 2018), 78–92.
Jaumann, Herbert, "Einleitung," in La Peyrère, *Praedamitae* i, pp. vii–lxxxviii.
Jautze, K., L. Álvarez Francés, and F. R. E. Blom, "Spaans Theater in de Amsterdamse Schouwburg (1638-1672)," *De Zeventiende Eeuw* 32 (2016), 12–39.
Jesseph, Douglas, "Hobbes on 'Conatus': A Study in the Foundations of Hobbesian Philosophy," *Hobbes Studies* 29 (2016), 66–85.
Jessurun-ten Dam Ham, S. C. J., *Utrecht in 1672 en 1673* (Utrecht, 1934).
Jones, J. R., *The Anglo-Dutch Wars of the Seventeenth Century* (Harlow, 1996).
Jongeneelen, G., "An Unknown Pamphlet of Adriaen Koerbagh," *SS* 3 (1987), 405–15.
Jongeneelen, G., "La Philosophie politique d'Adrien Koerbagh," *CS* 6 (1991), 247–67.
Jorink, Eric, "Outside God there is Nothing: Swammerdam, Spinoza, and the Janus-Face of the Early Dutch Enlightenment," in Wiep van Bunge (ed.), *The Early Enlightenment in the Dutch Republic, 1650-1750* (Leiden, 2003), 81–107.
Jorink, Eric, *Het Boeck der Natuere. Nederlandse geleerden en de wonderen van Gods schepping 1575-1715* (Leiden, 2007).
Jorink, Eric, "Horrible and Blasphemous: Isaac la Peyrère, Isaac Vossius, and the Emergence of Radical Biblical Criticism in the Dutch Republic," in J. M. van der Meer and Scott Mandelbrote (eds.), *Nature and Scripture in the Abrahamic Religions up to 1700*, vol. 2 (Leiden, 2008), 429–50.
Jorink, Eric, *Reading the Book of Nature in the Dutch Golden Age, 1575-1715* (Leiden, 2010).
Jorink, Eric, "In the Twilight Zone: Isaac Vossius and the Scientific Communities in France, England and the Dutch Republic," in Eric Jorink and Dirk van Miert (eds.), *Isaac Vossius (1618-1689): Between Science and Scholarship* (Leiden, 2012), 119–56.
Jorink, Eric, "Modus Politicus Vivendi: Nicolaus Steno and the Dutch (Spinoza, Swammerdam and other Friends) 1660–1664," in R. Andrault and M. Laerke (eds.), *Steno and the Philosophers* (Leiden, 2018), 13–44.
Jorink, Eric and Dirk van Miert (eds.), *Isaac Vossius (1618-1689): Between Science and Scholarship* (Leiden, 2012).
Juffermans, Paul, *Drie perspectiven op religie in het denken van Spinoza: een onderzoek naar de verschillende betekenissen van religie in het oeuvre van Spinoza* (Budel, 2003).
Jütte, Daniel, *The Age of Secrecy: Jews, Christians, and the Economy of Secrets, 1400-1800* (New Haven, CT, 2015).
Kambouchner, Denis, "Spinoza and Descartes," in Yitzhak Melamed (ed.), *A Companion to Spinoza* (Hoboken, NJ, 2021), 56–67.
Kamen, Henry, *Philip of Spain* (New Haven, CT, 1997).
Kannegieter, J. Z., *Geschiedenis van de vroegere Quakergemeenschap to Amsterdam* (Amsterdam, 1971).
Kaplan, Gregory B., "Morteira's Democratic Hebrew Republic and Amsterdam's Converso Legacy," in David J. Wertheim (ed.), "Tradition and Modernity in *Ets Haim*," *Menasseh ben Israel Instituut Studies* 14 (2017), 7–17.
Kaplan, Yosef, "The Social Functions of the 'Herem' in the Portuguese Jewish Community of Amsterdam in the Seventeenth Century," in Jozeph Michman (ed.), *Dutch Jewish History, Vol. 1* (Jerusalem, 1984), 111–55.

Kaplan, Yosef, *From Christianity to Judaism: The Story of Isaac Orobio de Castro* (Oxford, 1989).
Kaplan, Yosef, "Political Concepts in the World of the Portuguese Jews of Amsterdam during the Seventeenth Century," in Y. Kaplan, H. Méchoulan, and R. H. Popkin (eds.), *Menasseh ben Israel and His World* (Leiden, 1989), 45–62.
Kaplan, Yosef, "Karaites in Early Eighteenth-Century Amsterdam," in David S. Katz and Jonathan I. Israel (eds.), *Sceptics, Millenarians and Jews* (Leiden, 1990), 196–236.
Kaplan, Yosef, "The Intellectual Ferment in the Spanish-Portuguese Community of Seventeenth-Century Amsterdam," in Haim Beinart (ed.), *Moreshet Sepharad: The Sephardi Legacy*, vol. 2 (Jerusalem, 1992), 288–314.
Kaplan, Yosef, *Judíos nuevos en Amsterdam. Estudios sobre la historia social y intelectual del judaísmo sefardí en el siglo XVII* (Barcelona, 1996).
Kaplan, Yosef, *An Alternative Path to Modernity: The Sephardi Diaspora in Western Europe* (Leiden, 2000).
Kaplan, Yosef, "The Jews in the Republic until about 1750: Religious, Cultural and Social Life," in J. C. H. Blom, R. G. Fuks-Mansfeld, and Ivo Schöffer (eds.), *The History of the Jews in the Netherlands* (2002; new edn., Liverpool, 2019), 116–63.
Kaplan, Yosef, "Foi et skepticisme dans la diaspora des nouveaux-chrétiens des débuts de l'Europe moderne," *Arquivos do Centro Cultural Calouste Gulbenkian* 48 (2004), 21–40.
Kaplan, Yosef, "Amsterdam, the Forbidden Lands and the Dynamics of the Sephardi Diaspora," in Y. Kaplan (ed.), *The Dutch Intersection: The Jews and the Netherlands in Modern History* (Leiden, 2008), 33–62.
Kaplan, Yosef, "Religion, Politics and Freedom of Conscience: Excommunication in Early Modern Jewish Amsterdam," *Menasseh ben Israel Studies* 5 (Amsterdam, 2010).
Kaplan, Yosef, "Spinoza in the Library of an Early Modern Dutch Sephardi Rabbi," in C. Hermanin and L. Simonutti (eds.), *La Centralità del dubbio. Un progetto di Antonio Rotondò* (2 vols., Florence, 2011) ii, 641–64.
Kaplan, Yosef, "Amsterdam's Jewry as Perceived by English Tourists and other Christian Visitors in the Seventeenth Century," *Frankfurter Judaistische Studien* 40 (2015), 259–83.
Kaplan, Yosef, "This Thing Alone will Preserve their Nation Forever: Circumcision and Conversion in Early Modern Western Sephardic Communities," in K. Ingram and J. Ignacio Pulido Serrano (eds.), *Conversos and Moriscos in Late Medieval Spain and Beyond*, vol. 3, *Displaced Persons* (Leiden, 2015), 218–43.
Kaplan, Yosef, "On the Burial of Spinoza's Grandfather and Grandmother," *Zutot: Perspectives on Jewish Culture* 13 (2016), 26–39.
Kaplan, Yosef, "Between Religion and Ethnicity: Shaping the Western Sephardic Diaspora," in Y. Kaplan (ed.), *Early Modern Ethnic and Religious Communities in Exile* (Newcastle upon Tyne, 2017), 189–205.
Kaplan, Yosef, "De joden in de Republiek tot omstreeks 1750: Religieus cultureel en social leven," in J. C. H. Blom, R. G. Fuks-Mansfeld, and Ivo Schöffer (eds.), *Geschiedenis van de joden in Nederland* (Amsterdam, 2017), 131–96, 518–30.
Kasher, Asa and Shlomo Biderman, "Why was Baruch de Spinoza Excommunicated?," in David S. Katz and Jonathan I. Israel (eds.), *Sceptics, Millenarians and Jews* (Leiden, 1990), 98–141.
Kato, Yoshi, "Petrus van Mastricht and Descartes's New Philosophy," in A. C. Neele (ed.), *Petrus van Mastricht (1630–1706): Text, Context, and Interpretation* (Göttingen, 2020), 127–41.
Katz, David S., "Quakers and Jews: A Hebrew Appeal from George Fox," in J. van den Berg and E. van der Wall (eds.), *Jewish-Christian Relations in the Seventeenth Century* (Dordrecht, 1988), 201–5.

Kaufmann, Walter, *Nietzsche: Philosopher, Psychologist, Antichrist* (1950; 4th edn., Princeton, 1974).

Kayserling, M., "Une histoire de la littérature juive de Daniel Levi de Barrios," *REJ* 18 (1889), 276–89.

Kayserling, M., "The Jews in Jamaica and David Lopez Laguna," *The Jewish Quarterly Review* 12 (1900), 708–17.

Keesing, Elisabeth, "Les frères Huygens et Spinoza," *CS* 5 (1985), 109–28.

Kemmer, Claus, "In Search of Classical Form: Gerard de Lairesse's *Groot-Schilderboek* and Seventeenth-Century Dutch Genre Painting," *Simiolus: Netherlands Quarterly for the History of Art* 26 (1998), 87–115.

Kerkhof, Maxim P. A. M., "Préstamos en el portugués de los judíos hispano-portugueses de Ámsterdam en la primera mitad del siglo XVII," *Sefarad* 71 (2011), 413–34.

Kerkhof, Maxim P. A. M., *Het Portugeees en het Spaans van de Sefardische Joden van Amsterdam in 17de, 18de en 19e eeuw* (2003; revised edn., Maastricht, 2013).

Kermit, Hans, "The Oneness in Niels Stensen's Life," in K. Ascani, H. Kermit, and G. Skytte (eds.), *Niccolo Stenone (1638–1686). Anatomista, geologo, vescovo* (Rome, 2002), 24–7.

Kingma, J., "Spinoza in zijn Haagse periode," *Die Haghe Jaarboek* (The Hague, 1977), 117–33.

Kingma, J. and A. K. Offenberg, "Bibliography of Spinoza's Works up to 1800," *SR* 11 (1977), 1–32.

Kishlansky, Mark, *A Monarchy Transformed: Britain, 1603–1714* (London, 1996).

Kisner, Matthew, *Spinoza on Human Freedom: Reason, Autonomy and the Good Life* (Cambridge, 2011).

Klein, Julie R., "Philosophizing Historically/Historizing Philosophy: Some Spinozistic Reflections," in Mogens Laerke, Justin Smith, and Eric Schliesser (eds.), *Philosophy and Its History: Aims and Methods in the Study of Early Modern Philosophy* (Oxford, 2013), 134–58.

Klever, Wim (W. N. A), "Burchardus de Volder (1643–1709)," *Lias* 15 (1988), 191–241.

Klever, Wim, "Spinoza Interviewed by Willem van Blijenbergh," *SS* 4 (1988), 317–21.

Klever, Wim, "Spinoza and Van den Enden in Borch's Diary in 1661 and 1662," *SR* 5 (1989), 311–25.

Klever, Wim, "Insignis opticus. Spinoza in de geschiedenis van de optica," *De Zeventiende Eeuw* vi (1990), 47–63.

Klever, Wim, "Proto-Spinoza Franciscus van den Enden," *SS* 6 (1990), 281–9.

Klever, Wim, "Steno's Statements on Spinoza and Spinozism," *SS* 6 (1990), 303–13.

Klever, Wim, "La Clé d'un nom: Petrus van Gent et Schuller à partir d'une correspondance," *CS* 6 (1991), 189–94.

Klever, Wim, "A New Source of Spinozism: Franciscus van den Enden," *JHPh* 29 (1991), 613–31.

Klever, Wim, "Inleiding" to Franciscus van den Enden, *Vrije politijke stellingen* (Amsterdam, 1992), 13–119.

Klever, Wim, "De spoken van Hugo Boxel," *Bulletin. Literair Magazine* 22 (1992/93), 53–64.

Klever, Wim, "Qui était l'homunculus?" *Bulletin de l'association des amis de Spinoza* 29 (1993), 24–6.

Klever, Wim, *Een nieuwe Spinoza in veertig facetten* (Amsterdam, 1995).

Klever, Wim, "Omtrent Spinoza. Openbaar College gehouden op 15 November 1995" (Rotterdam, Erasmus Universiteit, 1995).

Klever, Wim, *Ethicom. Spinoza's Ethica vertolkt in tekst en commentaar* (Delft, 1996).

Klever, Wim, "Spinoza's Life and Works," in Don Garrett (ed.), *The Cambridge Companion to Spinoza* (Cambridge, 1996), 13–60.
Klever, Wim, *Mannen rond Spinoza. Presentatie van een emanciperende generatie* (Hilversum, 1997).
Klever, Wim, "Spinoza en Huygens. Een geschakeerde relatie tussen twee fysici," *Gewina* 20 (1997), 14–31.
Klever, Wim, *Definitie van het Christendom. Spinoza's Tractatus Theologico-Politicus opnieuw vertaald en toegelicht* (Delft, 1999).
Klever, Wim, *The Sphinx: Spinoza Reconsidered in Three Essays* ("Vrijstad," 2000).
Klever, Wim, "Hoe men wijs wordt. Een gespannen doch vruchtbare relatie tussen Spinoza en Bouwmeester in het licht van een nieuw document," *De Zeventiende Eeuw* 21 (2005), 335–53.
Klever, Wim, *Spinoza Classicus. Antike bronnen van een moderne denker* (Budel, 2005).
Klever, Wim, "Jan Hendrickz Glasemaker: The Addressee of Letter 84?," in North American Spinoza Society (NASS) *Monograph* 13 (2007), 25–31.
Klibansky, R. and J. Gough, "Introduction" to John Locke, *Epistola de Tolerantia* (Oxford, 1968).
Klijnsmit, Anthony J., "Gerardus Joannes Vossius on Hebrew," *SR* 32 (1998), 8–23.
Klooster, Wim, *The Dutch Moment: War, Trade, and Settlement in the Seventeenth-Century Atlantic World* (Ithaca, NY, 2016).
Knol, Jan, "Waarom hield Spinoza zijn *Korte Verhandeling* voor gezien?," *MeSp* 96 (2009).
Knolle, Paul, "Een goede kunstwerk-plaats. De Haarlemse tekenschool," in H. van Nierop, E. Grabowsky, A. Janssen, H. Leeflang, and G. Verhoeven (eds.), *Romeyn de Hooghe: De verbeelding van de late Gouden Eeuw* (Zwolle, 2008), 184–9.
Knuttel, W. P. C., *Verboden boeken in de Republiek der Verenigde Nederlanden* (The Hague, 1914).
Knuttel, W. P. C., *Balthasar Bekker, de bestrijder van het bijgeloof* (Groningen, 1979).
Koch, Hans-Reinhard and K. R. Koch, "Borri, the Prophet, on the 'Restitutio Humorum' and on Lens Aspiration in the 17th Century," *Sudhoff's Archiv* 101 (2017), 160–83.
Koen, E. M., "Duarte Fernandes, Koopman van de Portugese Natie te Amsterdam," *SR* 2 (1968), 178–93.
Koistinen, Olli, "On Steno's Letter to Spinoza," in V. Oittinen (ed.), *Spinoza in Nordic Countries* (Helsinki, 2004), 13–28.
Koistinen, Olli (ed.), *The Cambridge Companion to Spinoza's Ethics* (Cambridge, 2009).
Koistinen, Olli, "Spinoza on Action," in Olli Koistinen (ed.), *The Cambridge Companion to Spinoza's Ethics* (Cambridge, 2009), 167–87.
Kolakowski, Leszek, *Chrétiens sans église* (new edn., Paris, 1987).
Kooi, Christine, "Paying off the Sheriff: Strategies of Catholic Toleration in Golden Age Holland," in R. Po-Chia Hsia and H. van Nierop (eds.), *Calvinism and Religious Toleration in the Dutch Golden Age* (Cambridge, 2002), 87–101.
Kooijmans, Luuc, *Frederik Ruysch (1638-1731). Op het snijvlak van kunsten en wetenschap* (Amsterdam, 2018).
Kors, Alan, *Epicureans and Atheists in France, 1650–1720* (Cambridge, 2016).
Kors, Alan, *Naturalism and Unbelief in France, 1650–1729* (Cambridge, 2016).
Korsten, Frans-Willem, *A Dutch Republican Baroque: Theatricality, Dramatization, Moment and Event* (Amsterdam, 2017).
Kossmann, Ernst, *Political Thought in the Dutch Republic* (Amsterdam, 2000).
Kraemer, Joel, *Maimonides: The Life and World of One of Civilization's Greatest Minds* (Chicago, 2008).

Kronenburg, Albertus Jacob, *Het kunstgenootschap Nil Volentibus Arduum* (Deventer, 1875).
Krop, Henri, "Spinoza's Library: The Mathematical and Scientific Works," *IHR* 23 (2013), 25–43.
Krop, Henri, *Spinoza, een paradoxale icoon van Nederland* (Amsterdam, 2014).
Krop, Henri, "Spinoza en Amsterdam," *MeSp* 117, 11–22.
Krop, Henri, "The Secularism of Spinoza and his Circle," in A. Tomaszewska and H. Hämäläinen (eds.), *The Sources of Secularism* (London, 2017), 73–99.
Krop, Henri (ed.), *Spinoza en zijn kring. Een balans van veertig jaar onderzoek* (Uitgeverij Spinozahuis, The Hague, 2019).
Krop, Henri, "The Tractatus Theologico-Politicus and the Dutch," in Henri Krop and Pooyan Tamimi Arab (eds.), *Spinoza's Theological Political Treatise (1670–2020): Commemorating A Long-Forgotten Masterpiece* (Basel, 2021), 25–39.
Krop, Henri and Pooyan Tamimi Arab (eds.), *Spinoza's Theological Political Treatise (1670–2020): Commemorating A Long-Forgotten Masterpiece* (Basel, 2021).
Krop, Henri, J. A. van Ruler, and A. J. Vanderjagt (eds.), *Zeer kundige professoren. Beoefening van de filosofie in Groningen van 1614 tot 1996* (Hilversum, 1997).
Krul, R., "Haagsche en Amersfoortse krukkendans. Bijdrage tot het leven van Johann Friedrich Schweitzer (Helvetius)," *Haagsch Jaarboekje voor 1893* (The Hague, 1893), 4–32.
Kuchlbauer, Simon, *Johannes Amos Comenius' anti-sozinianische Schriften. Entwurf eines integrativen Konzepts von Aufklärung* (Dresden, 2001).
Kühler, W. J., *Het Socinanisme in Nederland* (1912; repr., Leeuwarden, 1980).
Kulstad, Mark, "Leibniz et Spinoza sur Dieu comme nature ou essence des choses," in R. Andrault, M. Laerke, and Pierre-François Moreau (eds.), *Spinoza/Leibniz. Rencontres, controverses, réceptions* (Paris, 2014), 21–35.
Kuyper, W., *Dutch Classicist Architecture* (Delft, 1980).
Labrousse, Elizabeth, "Jean-Baptiste Stouppe," in E. Labrousse, *Conscience et conviction. Études sur le XVIIe siècle* (Paris-Oxford, 1996), 60–8.
Laerke, Mogens, "À la Recherche d'un homme égal à Spinoza. G. W. Leibniz et la *Demonstratio evangelica* de Pierre-Daniel Huet," *Dix-septième Siècle* 232 (2006), 387–410.
Laerke, Mogens, *Leibniz lecteur de Spinoza. La Genèse d'une opposition complexe* (Paris, 2008).
Laerke, Mogens, "G. W. Leibniz's Two Readings of the *Tractatus Theologico-Politicus*," in Y. Y. Melamed and M. A. Rosenthal (eds.), *Spinoza's Theological-Political Treatise: A Critical Guide* (Cambridge, 2010), 121–7.
Laerke, Mogens, "Leibniz on Spinoza's Political Philosophy," in D. Garber and D. Rutherford (eds.), *OEMPh* 4 (Oxford, 2012), 105–34.
Laerke, Mogens, "Leibniz, Spinoza et le controverse sur le *terminus extensionis*," in R. Andrault, M. Laerke, and Pierre-François Moreau (eds.), *Spinoza/Leibniz. Rencontres, controverses, réceptions* (Paris, 2014), 219–43.
Laerke, Mogens, "Leibniz and Steno, 1675–1680," in R. Andrault and M. Laerke (eds.), *Steno and the Philosophers* (Leiden, 2018), 63–84.
Laerke, Mogens, "*De Summa Rerum*," in Paul Lodge and L. Strickland (eds.), *Leibniz's Key Philosophical Writings: A Guide* (Oxford, 2020), 35–50.
Laerke, Mogens, "Spinoza in France, ca. 1670–1970," in Yitzhak Melamed (ed.), *A Companion to Spinoza* (Hoboken, NJ, 2021), 506–16.
Laerke, Mogens, *Spinoza and the Freedom of Philosophizing* (Oxford, 2021).

Laerke, Mogens, "*Homo Politicus*: Spinoza, Oldenburger and the Politics of Envy and Friendship," in N. Gengoux, P. Girard, and M. Laerke (eds.), *Libertinage et philosophie à l'époque Classique (XVIe–XVIIIe siècle). Les Libertins néerlandais* (Paris, 2022), 137–65.
Laerke, Mogens, Justin Smith, and Eric Schliesser (eds.), *Philosophy and Its History: Aims and Methods in the Study of Early Modern Philosophy* (Oxford, 2013).
Lagrée, Jaqueline, "Louis Meyer et la 'Philosophia S. Scripturae Interpres'," *Revue des sciences philosophiques et théologiques* 71 (1987), 31–43.
Lagrée, Jaqueline, "Sens et vérité. Philosophie et théologie chez L. Meyer et Spinoza," *SS* 4 (1988), 75–92.
Lagrée, Jacqueline, "Le thème des deux livres de la nature et de l'Écriture," *Groupe de Recherches Spinozistes, travaux et documents* no. 4 (Paris, 1992), 9–37.
Lagrée, Jacqueline, *Spinoza et le débat religieux* (Rennes, 2004).
Lamont, William M., *Richard Baxter and the Millennium* (Totowa, NJ, 1979).
Langermann, Tzvi, "Proclus Revenant: The (Re-)integration of Proclus into the Creationism-Eternalism Debate in Joseph Solomon Delmedigo's (1591–1655) *Novelot Hokhma*," in D. A. Layne and D. D. Butorac (eds.), *Proclus and his Legacy* (Berlin, 2017), 375–89.
Langton, Daniel, "Modern Jewish Philosophical Responses to the Apostle Paul: Spinoza, Shestov and Taubes," *Studies in Jewish-Christian Relations* 2 (2007), 114–39.
Lasker, Daniel J., "Reflections of the Medieval Jewish-Christian Debate in the *Theological-Political Treatise* and the Epistles," in Y. Y. Melamed and M. A. Rosenthal (eds.), *Spinoza's* Theological-Political Treatise: *A Critical Guide* (Cambridge, 2010), 56–71.
Laurens, Hannah, *De rede: bron van geluk voor iedereen. Inleiding tot de filosofie van Adriaan Koerbagh (1633–1669)* (Nijmegen, 2019).
Laursen, John Christian, "Impostors and Liars: Clandestine Manuscripts and the Limits of Freedom of the Press in the Huguenot Netherlands," in J. Chr. Laursen (ed.), *New Essays on the Political Thought of Huguenots of the Refuge* (Leiden, 1994), 73–100.
Lavaert, Sonja, "Lieutenants of the Commonwealth. A Political Reading of *De Jure Ecclesiasticorum*," in S. Lavaert and W. Schröder (eds.), *The Dutch Legacy: Radical Thinkers in the 17th Century and the Enlightenment* (Leiden, 2017), 150–64.
Lavaert, Sonja, "Entre clandestinité et sphère publique. Le cas Koerbagh," *La Lettre Clandestine* 26 (2018), 33–48.
Lavaert, Sonja, "Prelude voor een demokratische revolutie: het politiek-filosofische project van Frans van den Enden," in B. Posthuma (ed.), *Spinoza en zijn kring. Een balans van veertig jaar onderzoek* (Uitgeverij Spinozahuis, The Hague, 2019), 65–76.
Lavaert, Sonja, "Adriaan Koerbagh: An Excellent Mathematician but a Wicked Fellow," *CHRC* 100 (2020), 255–71.
Lavaert, Sonja, *Vrijheid, gelijkheid, veelheid. Het moderne democratie-denken van Machiavelli tot Spinoza en zijn kring* (Brussels, 2020).
Lavaert, Sonja, "Le renversement de Spinoza, dans l'esprit de Machiavel," in S. Lavaert and P.-F. Moreau (eds.), *Spinoza et la politique de la multitude* (Paris, 2021), 35–55.
Lavaert, Sonja and Pierre-François Moreau (eds.), *Spinoza et la politique de la multitude* (Paris, 2021).
Lavaert, Sonja and Winfried Schröder (eds.), *The Dutch Legacy: Radical Thinkers of the 17th Century and the Enlightenment* (Leiden, 2017).
Lazarus-Yafeh, Hava, *Intertwined Worlds: Medieval Islam and Bible Criticism* (Princeton, 1992).
LeBuffe, Michael, "Why Spinoza Tells People to Try to Preserve their Being," *Archiv für Geschichte der Philosophie* 86 (2004), 119–45.

LeBuffe, Michael, "The Anatomy of the Passions," in Olli Koistinen (ed.), *The Cambridge Companion to Spinoza's Ethics* (Cambridge, 2009), 188-222.
LeBuffe, Michael, *From Bondage to Freedom: Spinoza on Human Excellence* (Oxford, 2010).
LeBuffe, Michael, *Spinoza on Reason* (Oxford, 2018).
LeBuffe, Michael, "Spinoza and Hobbes," in Yitzhak Melamed (ed.), *A Companion to Spinoza* (Hoboken, NJ, 2021), 81-91.
Leemans, Inger, *Het Woord is aan de onderkant: Radicale ideeen in Nederlandse pornografische romans, 1670-1700* (Utrecht, 2002).
Leemans, Inger, "De weg naar de hel is geplaveid met boeken over de bijbel. Vrijgeest en veelschrijver Willem Goeree (1635-1700)," *Nederlandse Letterkunde* 9 (2004), 255-73.
Leeuwenburgh, Bart B., "Meten is weten: Pierre Bayles populariteit in de Republiek," *GWND* 13 (2002), 81-93.
Leeuwenburgh, Bart, B., *Het Noodlot van een ketter. Adriaan Koerbagh (1633-69)* (Nijmegen, 2013).
Leezenberg, Michiel, "How Comparative Should a Comparative History of the Humanities Be? The Case of the Dutch Spinoza Circle," in Rens Bod, Jaap Maat, and Thijs Weststeijn (eds.), *The Making of the Humanities, Vol. 1: Early Modern Europe* (Amsterdam, 2010), 17-37.
Lennon, Thomas M., *The Plain Truth: Descartes, Huet, and Skepticism* (Leiden, 2008).
Leo, Russ, "Spinoza's Calvin: Reformed Theology in the *Korte Verhandeling van God, de Mensch en Deszelfs Welstand*," in Yitzhak Melamed (ed.), *The Young Spinoza: A Metaphysician in the Making* (Oxford, 2015), 144-59.
Leo, Russ, "Nil Volentibus Arduum, Baruch Spinoza and the Reason of Tragedy," in Blair Hoxby (ed.), *Darkness Visible: Tragedy in the Enlightenment* (Columbus, OH, 2022), 125-52.
Levene, Nancy, "Spinoza the Radical," in Steffen Ducheyne (ed.), *Reassessing the Radical Enlightenment* (Abingdon, 2017), 107-26.
Levie Bernfeld, Tirtsah, "De Financiering van de armenzorg van de Spaans-Portugees joodse gemeenschap in Amsterdam in de zeventiende en achttiende eeuw," *Tijdschrift voor Sociale Geschiedenis* 23 (1997), 428-58.
Levie Bernfeld, Tirtsah, "Financing Poor Relief in the Spanish-Portuguese Jewish Community in Amsterdam in the Seventeenth and Eighteenth Centuries," in Jonathan I. Israel and Reinier Salverda (eds.), *Dutch Jewry: Its History and Secular Culture (1500-2000)* (Leiden, 2002), 63-102.
Levie Bernfeld, Tirtsah, *Poverty and Welfare Among the Portuguese Jews in Early Modern Amsterdam* (Liverpool, 2012).
Levine, George, "Determinism and Responsibility in the Works of George Eliot," *Publications of the Modern Language Association* 77 (1962), 268-79.
Levitin, Dmitri, "From Sacred History to the History of Religion," *Historical Journal* 55 (2012), 1117-60.
Levitin, Dmitri, *Ancient Wisdom in the Age of the New Science* (Cambridge, 2015).
Levy, Ze'ev, *Baruch or Benedict? On Some Jewish Aspects of Spinoza's Philosophy* (New York, 1989).
Lewes, George Henry, "Spinoza," *Fortnightly Review* 22 (1 April 1866), 385-406.
Licata, Giovanni, "La Nature de la langue hébraïque chez Spinoza," in Jean Baumgarten, I. Rosier-Catach, and Pina Totaro (eds.), *Spinoza, philosophe grammairien. Le Compendium grammatices linguae hebraeae* (Paris, 2019), 47-62.
Licata, Giovanni, "The Law Inscribed in the Mind: On the Meaning of a Biblical Image in Spinoza's Theological-Political Treatise," in A. del Prete, A. L. Schino, and P. Totaro (eds.), *The Philosophers and the Bible* (Leiden, 2022), 196-214.

Liedtke, Walter, *Vermeer and the Delft School* (New York, 2001).
Lindeboom, G. A., "A Short Biography of Jan Swammerdam (1637–1680)," in *The Letters of Jan Swammerdam to Melchisedec Thévenot*, (ed.) G. A. Lindeboom (Amsterdam, 1975), 1–34.
Lindeboom, Gerrit, "Jan Swammerdam (1637–1680) and his *Bibliae Naturae*," *Clio medica. Acta Academiae Internationalis Historiae Medicinae* 17 (1982), 113–31.
Lindeboom, J., *Stiefkinderen van het Christendom* (Arnhem, 1973).
Lloyd, Genevieve, *Part of Nature: Self-Knowledge in Spinoza's* Ethics (Ithaca, NY, 1994).
Lloyd, Genevieve, "Spinoza and the Idea of the Secular," *MeSp* 102, 3–22.
Lodge, Paul (ed.), *Leibniz and His Correspondents* (Cambridge, 2004).
Lomba, Pedro, "Pierre Bayle, Spinoza's Reader," in António Bento and José Maria da Silva Rosa (eds.), *Revisiting Spinoza's Theological-Political Treatise* (Hildesheim, 2013), 213–35.
Long, A. A., "Stoicism in the Philosophical Tradition: Spinoza, Lipsius, Butler," in Brad Inwood (ed.), *The Cambridge Companion to Stoicism* (Cambridge, 2003), 365–92.
Look, Brandon, "Becoming Who One Is in Spinoza and Nietzsche," *Iyyun* (2001), 327–38.
López-Salazar Codes, Ana Isabel, *Inquisición y política. El gobierno del Santo Oficio en el Portugal de los Austrias (1578–1653)* (Lisbon, 2011).
Lucci, Diego, *Scripture and Deism: The Biblical Criticism of the Eighteenth-Century British Deists* (Bern, 2008).
Lucci, Diego, *John Locke's Christianity* (Cambridge, 2021).
Lucio de Azevedo, João, *História dos Cristãos Novos portugueses* (Lisbon, 1921).
Lupoli, Agostino, "Boyle's Influence on Locke's 'Study of the Way to Salvation'," in L. Simonutti (ed.), *Locke and Biblical Hermeneutics: Conscience and Scripture* (Berlin, 2019), 21–54.
Lyons, Henry, *The Royal Society, 1660–1940: A History of its Administration* (Cambridge, 1944).
Macherey, Pierre, "Spinoza lecteur et critique de Boyle," *Revue du Nord* 77 (1995), 733–4.
McKie, Douglas, "The Arrest and Imprisonment of Henry Oldenburg," *Notes and Records of the Royal Society* 6 (1948), 28–47.
MacMillan, Alissa, "Exorcising Demons: Thomas Hobbes and Balthasar Bekker on Spirits and Demons," *Philosophica* 89 (2014), 13–48.
McShea, R. J., *The Political Philosophy of Spinoza* (New York, 1968).
Maia Nieto, José M., "The Struggle against Unbelief in the Portuguese Jewish Community of Amsterdam after Spinoza's Excommunication," in S. Berti, F. Charles-Daubert, and R. H. Popkin (eds.), *Heterodoxy, Spinozism and Free Thought in Early Eighteenth-Century Europe* (Dordrecht, 1996), 425–37.
Malcolm, Noel, "A Summary Biography of Hobbes," in Tom Sorell (ed.), *The Cambridge Companion to Hobbes* (Cambridge, 1996), 13–44.
Malcolm, Noel, *Aspects of Hobbes* (Oxford, 2002).
Malcolm, Noel, "Hobbes, Ezra, and the Bible: The History of a Subversive Idea," in N. Malcolm, *Aspects of Hobbes* (Oxford, 2002), 383–431.
Malcolm, Noel, "Leibniz, Oldenburg and Spinoza in the Light of Leibniz's Letter to Oldenburg of 18/28 November 1676," *Studia Leibnitiana* 35 (2003), 225–43.
Malcolm, Noel, "The Library of Henry Oldenburg," *The Electronic British Library Journal* eBLJ 2005, article 7.
Malcolm, Noel, *Editorial Introduction*. Volume 1 of Thomas Hobbes, *Leviathan*, (ed.) N. Malcolm (3 vols., Oxford, 2012).
Malinowski-Charles, Syliane, *Affects et conscience chez Spinoza: l'automatisme dans le progrès éthique* (Hildesheim, 2004).

Mandelbrote, Scott, "Isaac Vossius and the Septuagint," in *Isaac Vossius (1618-1689): Between Science and Scholarship* (Leiden, 2012), 85-117.
Mangold, Matthias, "Salomon van Til (1643-1713): His Appropriation of Cartesian Tenets in his Compendium of Natural Theology," *CHRC* 94 (2014), 337-57.
Manekin, Charles H., "Spinoza and the Determinist Tradition in Medieval Jewish philosophy," in Steven Nadler (ed.), *Spinoza and Medieval Jewish Philosophy* (Cambridge, 2014), 36-58.
Manning, David, "Accusations of Blasphemy in English anti-Quaker Polemic c.1660-1701," *Quaker Studies* 14 (2010), 27-56.
Manusov-Verhage, Clarina G., "Jan Rieuwertsz, marchand libraire et éditeur de Spinoza," in Fokke Akkerman and Piet Steenbakkers (eds.), *Spinoza to the Letter: Studies in Words, Texts and Books* (Leiden, 2005), 237-50.
Manzini, Frederic, "When Was Spinoza Not Young Any More?," in Yitzhak Melamed (ed.), *The Young Spinoza: A Metaphysician in the Making* (Oxford, 2015), 196-204.
Marburg, Clara, *Sir William Temple: A Seventeenth Century "Libertin"* (New Haven, CT, 1932).
Marshall, John, *John Locke, Toleration and Early Enlightenment Culture* (Cambridge, 2006).
Martin, C. and Geoffrey Parker, *The Spanish Armada* (Harmondsworth, 1988).
Maryks, Robert A., *The Jesuit Order as a Synagogue of Jews* (Leiden, 2009).
Mason, Richard, *The God of Spinoza: A Philosophical Study* (Cambridge, 1997).
Masson, Gustav, "Graevius et le duc de Montpensier d'après des lettres inédites," *Le Cabinet historique* 13 (1867), 217-38.
Matheron, Alexandre, *Le Christ et le salut des ignorants chez Spinoza* (Paris, 1971).
Matheron, Alexandre, *Individu et communauté chez Spinoza* (Paris, 1988).
Mathorez, Jules, "Notes sur l'histoire de la colonie portugaise de Nantes," *Bulletin Hispanique* 15 (1913), 316-39.
Maury, Alfred, "Une conspiration républicaine sous Louis XIV," *Revue des deux mondes* 76 (1886, July-August), 376-406 and 756-84.
Méchoulan, Henry, "Spinoza lecteur d'Antonio Pérez," *Ethno-psychologie. Revue de psychologie des peuples* 29 (1974), 289-301.
Méchoulan, Henry, "Le *Herem* à Amsterdam et 'l'excommunication' de Spinoza," *CS* 3 (1980), 117-34.
Méchoulan, Henry, "Un Regard sur la pensée juive à Amsterdam au temps de Spinoza," *CS* 3 (1980), 51-66.
Méchoulan, Henry, *Hispanidad y Judaísmo en tiempos de Espinoza* (Salamanca, 1987).
Meihuizen, H. W., *Galenus Abrahamsz, 1622-1706* (Haarlem, 1954).
Meijer, Willem, "De Ioanne Caseario," *Chronicon Spinozanum* iii (1923), 232-52.
Meininger, Jan V. and Guido van Suchtelen, *Liever met wercken als met woorden. De levensreis van Doctor Franciscus van den Enden, leermeester van Spinoza, complotteur tegen Lodewijk de Veertiende* (Weesp, 1980).
Meinsma, K. O., *Spinoza et son cercle. Étude critique historique sur les hétérodoxes hollandais* (1896; expanded French edn., Paris, 1983).
Melamed, Yitzhak, "Charitable Interpretations and the Political Domestication of Spinoza, or, Benedict in the Land of the Secular Imagination," in Mogens Laerke, Justin Smith, and Eric Schliesser (eds.), *Philosophy and Its History: Aims and Methods in the Study of Early Modern Philosophy* (Oxford, 2013), 258-77.
Melamed, Yitzhak, *Spinoza's Metaphysics: Substance and Thought* (Oxford, 2013).
Melamed, Yitzhak (ed.), *The Young Spinoza: A Metaphysician in the Making* (Oxford, 2015).

Melamed, Yitzhak, "Spinozism, Acosmism, and Hasidism: A Closed Circle," in A. Kravitz and J. Noller (eds.), *Der Begriff des Judentums in der klassischen deutschen Philosophie* (Tűbingen, 2018), 75–85.
Melamed, Yitzhak (ed.), *A Companion to Spinoza* (Hoboken, NJ, 2021).
Melamed, Yitzhak and H. Sharp (eds.), *Spinoza's Political Treatise: A Critical Guide* (Cambridge, 2018).
Melles, J., *Joachim Oudaan. Heraut der verdraagzaamheid, 1628–1692* (Utrecht, 1958).
Mellor, Ronald, *Tacitus* (London, 1993).
Mendes dos Remedios, Joaquim, *Os judeus portugueses em Amsterdam* (Coimbra, 1911).
Mercer, Christia, "Leibniz and His Master: The Correspondence with Thomasius," in Paul Lodge (ed.), *Leibniz and His Correspondents* (Cambridge, 2004), 10–46.
Mertens, Frank, "Spinoza's Amsterdamse vriendenkring: studievriendschappen, zakenrelaties en familiebanden," in Cis van Heertum (ed.), *Libertas philosophandi. Spinoza als gids voor een vrije wereld* (Amsterdam, 2009), 69–81.
Mertens, Frank, "Johannes Koerbagh's Lost *Album Amicorum* Seen through the Eyes of Pieter de la Rue," *Lias* 38 (2011), 59–127.
Mertens, Frank, *Van den Enden en Spinoza* (Voorschoten: Uigeverij Spinozahuis, 2012).
Mertens, Frank, "Van den Enden and Religion," in S. Lavaert and W. Schröder (eds.), *The Dutch Legacy: Radical Thinkers in the 17th Century and the Enlightenment* (Leiden, 2017), 62–89.
Mertens, Frank, "All in the Family: Verwantschap en vriendschap in de kring van Spinoza," in B. Posthuma (ed.), *Spinoza en zijn kring. Een balans van veertig jaar onderzoek* (Uitgeverij Spinozahuis, The Hague, 2019), 47–64.
Mertens, Frank, "Where Thou Dwellest: The Abodes of Spinoza's Early Amsterdam Friends" (forthcoming).
Meschonnic, Henri, *Spinoza. Poème de la pensée* (2002; new edn., Paris, 2017).
Mignini, Filippo, "Nuovi contributi per la datazione e l'interpretazione del *Tractatus de Intellectus Emendatione*," in E. Giancotti (ed.), *Spinoza nel 350° anniversario della nascità* (Naples, 1985), 515–25.
Mignini, Filippo, "Données et problèmes de la chronologie spinozienne entre 1656 et 1665," *Revue des Sciences philosophiques et théologiques* 71 (1987), 9–21.
Mignini, Filippo, "La Dottrina spinoziana della religione," *SS* 11 (1995), 53–80.
Mignini, Filippo, "Le texte du *Tractatus de intellectus emendatione* et sa transmission," in Fokke Akkerman and Piet Steenbakkers (eds.), *Spinoza to the Letter: Studies in Words, Texts and Books* (Leiden, 2005), 189–207.
Mignini, Filippo, "*Fictio/Verziering (e)* in Spinoza's Early Writings," in Yitzhak Melamed (ed.), *The Young Spinoza: A Metaphysician in the Making* (Oxford, 2015), 33–51.
Mignini, Filippo, "Introduction au *Tractatus de Intellectus Emendatione*," in Spinoza, *Oeuvres* (ed. Moreau) i, 21–58.
Mignini, Filippo, "Introduction au *Court Traité*," in Spinoza, *Oeuvres* (ed. Moreau) i, 159–80.
Mijnhardt, Wijnand, *Tot heil van't Menschdom. Culturele genootschappen in Nederland, 1750–1800* (Amsterdam, 1987).
Miller, Jon, *Spinoza and the Stoics* (Cambridge, 2015).
Montag, Warren, *Bodies, Masses, Power: Spinoza and his Contemporaries* (London, 1999).
Montag, Warren, "That Hebrew Word: Spinoza and the Concept of *Shekhinah*," in H. M. Ravven and L. E. Goodman (eds.), *Jewish Themes in Spinoza's Philosophy* (Albany, NY, 2002), 131–44.

Moreau, Pierre-François, "Les Principes de la lecture de l'Écriture dans le TTP," in *Groupe de Recherches Spinozistes. Travaux et documents* iv (1992), 119–31.
Moreau, Pierre-François, *Spinoza, L'expérience et l'éternité* (1994; 2nd edn., Paris, 2009).
Moreau, Pierre-François, "Spinoza's Reception and Influence," in Don Garrett (ed.), *The Cambridge Companion to Spinoza* (Cambridge, 1996), 408–33.
Moreau, Pierre-François, *Spinoza et le spinozisme* (Paris, 2003).
Moreau, Pierre-François, *Spinoza. État et religion* (Paris, 2005).
Moreau, Pierre-François, "Traduire Spinoza: l'exemple d'Émile Saisset," in André Tosel, Pierre-François Moreau, and Jean Salem (eds.), *Spinoza au XIXe siècle* (Paris, 2007), 221–30.
Moreau, Pierre-François, "A-t-on raison de se révolter? Spinoza, la multitude et l'insurrection," in Sonja Lavaert and Pierre-François Moreau (eds.), *Spinoza et la politique de la multitude* (Paris, 2021), 11–33.
Moreau, Pierre-François and Mogens Laerke, "Spinoza's Reception," in Don Garrett (ed.), *The Cambridge Companion to Spinoza* (2nd edn., Cambridge, 2022), 405–43.
Moreau, Pierre-François and Piet Steenbakkers, "L'historique du texte," introduction to Spinoza, *Oeuvres* iv *Ethica*, (trans.) P. F. Moreau (Paris, 2020), 13–66.
Moreau, Pierre-François and L. Vinciguerra (eds.), *Spinoza et les arts* (Paris, 2020).
Mori, Gianluca, *Bayle philosophe* (Paris, 1999).
Mori, Gianluca, "Bayle, Saint-Évremond and Fideism," *JHI* 65 (2004), 323–34.
Mori, Gianluca, *L'ateismo dei moderni. Filosofia e negazione di Dio da Spinoza a d'Holbach* (Rome, 2016).
Mori, Giuliano, "Ancient Theology and New Philosophies: Pierre-Daniel Huet against Descartes and Spinoza," *Erudition and the Republic of Letters* 4 (2019), 167–98.
Mori, Gianluca, *Athéisme et dissimulation au XVII siècle* (Paris, 2022).
Mosbah, Salah, "Ultimi Barbarorum: Spinoza et la tradition républicaine," in P.-F. Moreau, C. Cohen-Boulakia, and M. Delbraccio (eds.), *Lectures contemporaines de Spinoza* (Paris, 2012), 311–30.
Muchnik, Natalia, *Une Vie Marrane. Les pérégrinations de Juan de Prado dans l'Europe du XVIIe siècle* (Paris, 2005).
Muchnik, Natalia, "Orobio contra Prado: A Trans-European Controversy," in Carsten Wilke (ed.), *Isaac Orobio: The Jewish Argument with Dogma and Doubt* (Berlin, 2018), 31–56.
Muhana, Adma, "António Vieira: A Jesuit Missionary to the Portuguese Jews of Amsterdam," *Journal of Jesuit Studies* 8 (2021), 233–49.
Mulsow, Martin, "The 'New Socinians': Intertextuality and Cultural Exchange in Late Socinianism," in M. Mulsow and J. Rohls (eds.), *Socinianism and Arminianism: Antitrinitarians, Calvinists and Cultural Exchange in Seventeenth-Century Europe* (Leiden, 2005), 49–78.
Mulsow, Martin, *Enlightenment Underground: Radical Germany, 1680–1720* (Charlottesville, 2015).
Mulsow, Martin, *Radikale Frühaufklärung in Deutschland 1680–1720* (2 vols., Göttingen, 2018).
Munt, Annette, "The Impact of the *Rampjaar* on Dutch Golden Age Culture," *Dutch Crossing* 21 (1997), 3–51.
Munt, Annette, "The Impact of Dutch Medical Authors in German Translation (1680–1720)," in Lotte Hellinga, Elaine Paintin, and Alastair Duke (eds.), *The Bookshop of the World: The Role of the Low Countries in the Book-Trade, 1473–1941* ('t Goy-Houten, 2001), 219–31.

Munt, Annette, "The Impact of Dutch Cartesian Medical Reformers in Early Enlightenment Germany (1680–1720)" (University of London Ph.D. thesis, 2004).
Nachtomy, Ohad, "Infinité de l'être et infinité du nombre chez Leibniz et Spinoza," in R. Andrault, M. Laerke, and Pierre-François Moreau (eds.), *Spinoza/Leibniz. Rencontres, controverses, réceptions* (Paris, 2014), 121–43.
Nadler, Steven, "Spinoza as a Jewish Philosopher," *SS* 13 (1997), 64–80.
Nadler, Steven, *Spinoza: A Life* (1999; 2nd edn., Cambridge, 2018).
Nadler, Steven, *Spinoza's Heresy: Immortality and the Jewish Mind* (Oxford, 2001).
Nadler, Steven, *Rembrandt's Jews* (Chicago, 2003).
Nadler, Steven, "Spinoza's Theory of Divine Providence," *MeSp* 87 (2005).
Nadler, Steven, "The Jewish Spinoza," *JHI* 70 (2009), 491–510.
Nadler, Steven, *A Book Forged in Hell: Spinoza's Scandalous Treatise and the Birth of the Secular Age* (Princeton, 2011).
Nadler, Steven (ed.), *Spinoza and Medieval Jewish Philosophy* (Cambridge, 2014).
Nadler, Steven, "Spinoza on the Divinity of Scripture," in *Spinoza Research: To Be Continued* (Uitgeverij Spinozahuis, 2016), 35–47.
Nadler, Steven, "*Aliquid remanet*: What Are We to Do with Spinoza's Compendium of Hebrew Grammar?," *JHPh* 56 (2018), 155–67.
Nadler, Steven, *Menasseh ben Israel: Rabbi of Amsterdam* (New Haven, CT, 2018).
Nadler, Steven, *Think Least of Death: Spinoza on How to Live and How to Die* (Princeton, 2020).
Nahon, Gérard, *Métropoles et périphéries sefarades* (Paris, 1993).
Nauta, D., *Samuel Maresius* (Amsterdam, 1935).
Nauta, D., "Gijsbertus Voetius," in *Biografisch Lexicon voor de Geschiedenis van het Nederlandse Protestantisme* (6 vols., 1978–2006) ii, 443–9.
Negri, Antonio, *Spinoza for our Time* (2003; English trans., New York, 2013).
Nellen, Henk and Piet Steenbakkers, "Biblical Philology in the Long Seventeenth Century: New Orientations," in Dirk van Miert, Henk Nellen, Piet Steenbakkers, and Jetze Touber (eds.), *Scriptural Authority and Biblical Criticism in the Dutch Golden Age* (Oxford, 2017), 16–57.
Neuman, Els, "Aller steden pronkjuweel. Den Haag in de 17de eeuw," in Edwin Buijsen, *Haagse Schilders in de Gouden Eeuw. Het Hoogsteder Lexicon van alle schilders werkzaam in Den Haag 1600–1700* (The Hague-Zwolle, 1998), 15–25.
Neveu, Bruno, *Sebastien Joseph du Cambout de Pontchâteau, 1634–1690* (Paris, 1969).
Nord, David Paul, "Teleology and News," *The Journal of American History* 77 (1990), 9–38.
Norris, Christopher, *Spinoza and the Origins of Modern Critical Theory* (Oxford, 1991).
Nourrisson, J. F., *Spinoza et le naturalisme contemporain* (Paris, 1866).
Novak, David, "Spinoza and the Doctrine of the Election of Israel," *SS* 13 (1997), 81–99.
Nuovo, Victor, "Locke's Proof of the Divine Authority of Scripture," in R. Savage (ed.), *Philosophy and Religion in Enlightenment Britain* (Oxford, 2012), 56–76.
Nuovo, Victor, *John Locke: The Philosopher as Christian Virtuoso* (Oxford, 2017).
Nusteling, H. P. H., *Welvaart and werkgelegenheid in Amsterdam, 1540–1860* (Amsterdam, 1985).
Nusteling, H. P. H., "The Jews in the Republic of the United Provinces: Origin, Numbers and Dispersion," in Jonathan I. Israel and Reinier Salverda (eds.), *Dutch Jewry: Its History and Secular Culture (1500–2000)* (Leiden, 2002), 43–62.
Offenberg, A. K., "Spinoza's Library: The Story of a Reconstruction," *Quaerendo* 3 (1973), 309–21.

Offenberg, A. K., "Jacob Jehuda Leon(1602–1675) and his Model of the Temple," in J. van den Berg and E. G. E. van der Wall (eds.), *Jewish-Christian Relations in the Seventeenth Century: Studies and Documents* (Dordrecht, 1988), 95–115.

Oldewelt, W. F. H., "De Bevolking van 's Gravenhage omstreeks 1674," *Jaarboek Die Haghe* (1948/49), 11–17.

Oravetz Albert, Anne, "The Rabbi and the Rebels: A Pamphlet on the Herem by Rabbi Isaac Aboab da Fonseca," *Jewish Quarterly Review* 104 (2014), 171–91.

Orcibal, Jean, "Les Jansénistes face à Spinoza," *Revue de littérature comparée* 23 (1949), 441–68.

Osier, Jean-Pierre, *D'Uriel da Costa à Spinoza* (Paris, 1983).

Osier, Jean-Pierre, "L'Hermeneutique de Hobbes et Spinoza," *SS* 3 (1987), 319–47.

Ottaviani, Octavio, "Divine Wisdom and Possible Worlds: Leibniz's Notes to the Spinoza-Oldenburg Correspondence and the Development of His Metaphysics," *Studia Leibnitiana* 48 (2016), 15–41.

Otterspeer, Willem, *Groepsportret met Dame*, vol. 2: *De Leidse Universiteit, 1673–1775* (Amsterdam, 2000).

Otto, Rüdiger, *Studien zur Spinozarezeption in Deutschland im 18. Jahrhundert* (Frankfurt, 1994).

Paganini, Gianni, "Enlightenment before the Enlightenment: Clandestine Philosophy," *Etica e Politica/Ethics and Politics* 20 (2018), 183–200.

Parker, Geoffrey, *The Grand Strategy of Philip II* (New Haven, CT, 1998).

Parker, Jon, "The Reception of Hobbes' *Leviathan*," *JHI* 76 (2015), 289–300.

Parker, Kim Ian, "Spinoza, Locke and Biblical Interpretation," in Luisa Simonutti (ed.), *Locke and Biblical Hermeneutics: Conscience and Scripture* (Cham, 2019), 163–88.

Parkinson, G. H. R., "Leibniz's Paris Writings in Relation to Spinoza," *Studia Leibnitiana Supplementa* 18 (1978), 73–90.

Parkinson, G. H. R., "Editor's Introduction," to Spinoza, *Ethics*, (trans.) G. H. R. Parkinson (Oxford, 2000), 5–50.

Patoir, Jean-Baptiste, "Polemic Pamphleteering: Confession, Politics and Reformed Internationalism during the Dutch War, 1672–1678," online article (2011), 63 pp.

Pelham, Lipika, *Jerusalem on the Amstel: The Quest for Zion in the Dutch Republic* (London, 2019).

Peña, Javier, "República, libertad y democracia en Spinoza," *Co-herencia. Revista de Humanidades* (Colombia) 15 (2018), 155–80.

Peterman, Alison, "Spinoza on the 'Principles of Natural Things'," *The Leibniz Review* 22 (2012), 37–65.

Peterman, Alison, "Spinoza's Physics," in Yitzhak Melamed (ed.), *A Companion to Spinoza* (Hoboken, NJ, 2021), 240–50.

Peterman, Alison, "Newton and Spinoza," in Eric Schliesser and Chr. Smeenk (eds.), *The Oxford Handbook of Newton* (published online 6 Feb. 2017).

Petram, Lodewijk, *The World's First Stock Exchange* (New York, 2014).

Petry, Michael and Guido van Suchtelen, "Spinoza and the Military," *SS* 1 (1985), 359–69.

Pettegree, Andrew and Arthur der Weduwen, *The Bookshop of the World: Making and Trading Books in the Dutch Golden Age* (New Haven, CT, 2018).

Pieterse, Wilhelmina, *Daniel Levi de Barrios als geschiedschrijver van de Portugees-Israelietische gemeente te Amsterdam in zijn 'Triumpho del Govierno Popular'* (Amsterdam, 1969).

Pieterse, Wilhelmina, "Introduction" to *Livro de Bet Haim* (1970), pp. ix–xvi.

Pines, Shlomo, "Spinoza's *Tractatus Theologico-Politicus* and the Jewish Philosophical Tradition," in Isidore Twersky and B. Septimus (eds.), *Jewish Thought in the Seventeenth Century* (Cambridge, MA, 1987), 499–521.

Pitassi, Maria-Cristina, "Un manuscrit genevois du XVIIIe siècle: la 'Réfutation du système de Spinosa,' par Mr Turretini," *Nederlands Archief voor kerkgeschiedenis* 68 (1988), 180-212.
Popkin, Richard H., "Spinoza and La Peyrère," *The Southwestern Journal of Philosophy* 8 (1977), 177-95.
Popkin, Richard H., *History of Scepticism from Erasmus to Spinoza* (Berkeley and Los Angeles, 1979).
Popkin, Richard H., "Introduction" to Margaret Fell, *A Loving Salutation* (Assen, 1987), 1-20.
Popkin, Richard H., *Isaac La Peyrère (1596-1676): His Life, Work and Influence* (Leiden, 1987).
Popkin, Richard H., "Some Aspects of Jewish-Christian Theological Interchanges in Holland and England, 1640-1700," in J. van den Berg and E. van der Wall (eds.), *Jewish-Christian Relations in the Seventeenth Century* (Dordrecht, 1988), 3-32.
Popkin, Richard H., "Spinoza's Earliest Philosophical Years (1655-61)," *SS* 4 (1988), 37-55.
Popkin, Richard H., *The Third Force in Seventeenth-Century Thought* (Leiden, 1992).
Popkin, Richard H., "Image of the Jew in Clandestine Literature circa 1700," in Guido Canziani (ed.), *Filosofia e religione nella letteratura clandestina* (Milan, 1994), 13-34.
Popkin, Richard H., "Another Spinoza," *JHPh* 34 (1996), 133-4.
Popkin, Richard H., "Spinoza and Bible Criticism," in Don Garrett (ed.), *The Cambridge Companion to Spinoza* (Cambridge, 1996), 383-407.
Popkin, Richard H., "Spinoza's Excommunication," in H. M. Ravven and L. E. Goodman (eds.), *Jewish Themes in Spinoza's Philosophy* (Albany, NY, 2002), 263-79.
Popkin, Richard H., *Spinoza* (Oxford, 2004).
Pozzi, Patricia, "Un libro misterioso nella biblioteca di Spinoza," *Rivista di Storia della Filosofia* 53 (1998), 681-708.
Prak, Maarten and L. Hesselink, "Stad en gevestigden, 1650-1730," in W. Frijhoff and M. Prak (eds.), *Geschiedenis van Amsterdam. Zelfbewuste stadstaat, 1615-1813* (Amsterdam, 2005), 89-149.
Préposiet, Jean, *Spinoza (1632-1677)* (Paris, 2007).
Preus, J. Samuel, "A Hidden Opponent in Spinoza's 'Tractatus'," *The Harvard Theological Review* 88 (1995), 361-88.
Preus, J. Samuel, *Spinoza and the Irrelevance of Biblical Authority* (Cambridge, 2001).
Prince, M. B., *The Shortest Way with Defoe: Robinson Crusoe, Deism and the Novel* (Charlottesville, VA, 2020).
Proietti, Omero, "Il 'Satyricon' di Petronio e la datazione della 'Grammatica ebraica' Spinoziana," *SS* 5 (1989), 253-72.
Proietti, Omero, "Spinoza et le 'Conciliador' de Menasseh ben Israel," *SS* 13 (1997), 48-63.
Proietti, Omero, *La Città Divisa. Flavio Giuseppe, Spinoza e i farisei* (Rome, 2003).
Proietti, Omero, *Uriel da Costa e l'Exemplar Humanae Vitae* (Macerata, 2005).
Proietti, Omero, "Vita e opere di Francescus van den Enden," in Van den Enden, *Philedonius* (Macerata, 2010), 15-140.
Prokhovnik, Raia, *Spinoza and Republicanism* (Basingstoke, 2004).
Prud'homme van Reine, Ronald, *Moordenaars van Jan De Witt: de zwartste bladzijde van de Gouden Eeuw* (Amsterdam, 2013).
Putnam, Lodewijk, "The World's First Stock Exchange" (University of Amsterdam Ph.D. thesis, 2011).
Quatrini, Francesco, *Adam Boreel (1602-1665): A Collegiant's Attempt to Reform Christianity* (Leiden, 2021).

Ramond, Charles, *Qualité et quantité dans la philosophie de Spinoza* (Paris, 1995).
Ramond, Charles, "Introduction: La Loi du nombre (ou la démocratie comme 'régime absolue'" to B. De Spinoza, *Traité Politique*, (ed.) O. Proietti and Ch. Ramond (Paris, 2005), 7-43.
Ranalli, Brent, "Unity of Brethren Tradition and Comenius's Pansophy," *Journal of Moravian History* 20 (2020), 1-29.
Rapetti, Elen, *Pierre-Daniel Huet: erudizione, filosofia, apologetica* (Milan, 1999).
Raphael, Frederic, *A Jew among the Romans: The Life and Legacy of Flavius Josephus* (New York, 2013).
Rediehs, Laura, "Candlestick Mysteries," *Quaker Studies* 18 (2014), 151-69.
Redondi, Pietro, "Spinoza, Critic of Galileo," *IHR* 23 (2013), 109-18.
Reid, Jasper, "Henry More and Nicolas Malebranche's Critiques of Spinoza," *European Journal of Philosophy* 23 (2013), 764-92.
Renz, Ursula, "Spinoza's Epistemology," in Don Garrett (ed.), *The Cambridge Companion to Spinoza* (Cambridge, 1996), 141-86.
Renz, Ursula, *The Explainability of Experience: Realism and Subjectivity in Spinoza's Theory of the Human Mind* (Oxford, 2018).
Rester, Todd M., "Petrus van Mastricht on Theoretical-Practical Theology, Saving Faith, and the Ministry of the Word," in A. C. Neele (ed.), *Petrus Van Mastricht (1630-1706): Text, Context, and Interpretation* (Göttingen, 2020), 89-108.
Révah, I. S., "Le Premier établissement des Marranes portugais à Rouen (1603-1609)," *Mélanges Isidore Levy. Annuaire de l'Institut de Philologie et d'Histoire orientales et slaves XIII* (1953), 539-52.
Révah, I. S., "Les Marranes," *REJ* 118 (1959), 29-77.
Révah, I. S., *Spinoza et Dr Juan de Prado* (Paris-The Hague, 1959).
Révah, I. S., "Pour l'histoire des Nouveaux-Chrétiens Portugais. La Relation généalogique d'I. de M. Aboab," *Boletim Internacional de Bibliografía Luso-Brasileira* 2 (1961), 276-312.
Révah, I. S., "Pour l'histoire des Marranes à Anvers: recensements de la 'nation portugaise' de 1571 à 1666," *REJ* 122 (1963), 123-47.
Révah, I. S., "Le premier règlement imprimé de la santa companhia de dotar orfans e donzelas pobres," *Boletim Internacional de Bibliografía Luso-Brasileira* 4 (1963), 650-91.
Révah, I. S., "Aux origines de la rupture spinozienne," *REJ* 123 (1964), 359-431.
Révah, I. S., *Des Marranes à Spinoza* (Paris, 1995).
Rice, L. C. and Fr. Pastijn, "Introduction" to L. Meyer, *Philosophy as the Interpreter*, 1-19.
Rogier, L. J., *Geschiedenis van het katholicisme in Noord-Nederland in de 16e en 17e eeuw* (3 vols., Amsterdam, 1945-7).
Roitman, J. V., *The Same but Different? Inter-Cultural Trade and the Sephardim, 1595-1640* (Leiden, 2011).
Rommelse, Gijs, *The Second Anglo-Dutch War (1665-1667): International* Raison d'État, *Mercantilism and Maritime Strife* (Hilversum, 2006).
Rood, Wilhelmus, *Comenius and the Low Countries* (Leiden, 1970).
Rooden, P. T. van, "Spinoza's Bijbeluitleg," *SR* 18 (1984), 120-33.
Roodenburg, Herman, *Onder censuur. De kerkelijke tucht in de reformeerde gemeente van Amsterdam, 1578-1700* (Hilversum, 1990).
Roorda, D. J., "Prins Willem III en het Utrechtse regeringsreglement," in *Van Standen tot Staten, Stichtse Historische Reeks* 1 (Utrecht, 1975), 91-133.
Roorda, D. J., *Parti en factie. De oproeren van 1672 in de steden van Holland en Zeeland* (Groningen, 1978).

Rosenberg, Abraham, "Op welke school leerde Spinoza?' in Cis van Heertum (ed.), *Libertas philosophandi. Spinoza als gids voor een vrije wereld* (Amsterdam, 2009), 55–67.
Rosenthal, Michael, "Why Spinoza Chose the Hebrews: The Exemplary Function of Prophecy in the *Theological-Political Treatise*," in H. M. Ravven and L. E. Goodman (eds.), *Jewish Themes in Spinoza's Philosophy* (Albany, NY, 2002), 225–60.
Rosenthal, Michael, "Miracles, Wonder and the State in Spinoza's *Theological-Political Treatise*," in Y. Y. Melamed and M. A. Rosenthal (eds.), *Spinoza's* Theological-Political Treatise: *A Critical Guide* (Cambridge, 2010), 231–49.
Rosenthal, Michael, "Why Spinoza is Intolerant of Atheists: God and the Limits of Early Modern Liberalism," *The Review of Metaphysics* 65 (2012), 813–39.
Rosenthal, Michael, "The Siren Song of Revolution," *Crossmark Graduate Faculty Philosophy Journal* 34 (2013), 11–32.
Rosenthal, Michael, "What is Real about 'Ideal Constitutions'? Spinoza on Political Explanation," in Yitzhak Melamed and H. Sharp (eds.), *Spinoza's* Political Treatise: *A Critical Guide* (Cambridge, 2018), 12–28.
Rosenthal, Michael, "Spinoza's 'Republican Idea of Freedom'," in Yitzhak Melamed (ed.), *A Companion to Spinoza* (Hoboken, NJ, 2021), 402–9.
Roth, Cecil, "Abraham Nuñez Bernal et autres martyrs contemporains de l'Inquisition," *REJ* (1936), 32–51.
Roth, Cecil, "The Strange Case of Hector Mendes Bravo," *Hebrew Union College Annual* 18 (1943/44), 221–45.
Roth, Norman, "Forgery and Abrogation of the Torah: A Theme in Muslim and Christian Polemic in Spain," *Proceedings of the American Academy for Jewish Research* 54 (1987), 203–36.
Rothkamm, Jan, *Institutio Oratoria: Bacon, Descartes, Hobbes, Spinoza* (Leiden, 2009).
Rothkrug, Lionel, *Opposition to Louis XIV: The Political and Social Origins of the French Enlightenment* (Princeton, 1965).
Rotthier, Rudi, *De naakte perenboom. Op reis met Spinoza* (Amsterdam-Antwerp, 2013).
Rovere, Maxime, "Avoir commerce: Spinoza et les modes de l'échange," *Astérion: Philosophie, histoire des idées, pensée politique* 5 (2007), online publication.
Rovere, Maxime, *Spinoza. Méthodes pour exister* (2010; repr. Paris, 2019).
Rovere, Maxime, *Le Clan Spinoza. Amsterdam 1677. L'Invention de la liberté* (Paris, 2017).
Rovere, Maxime, "Présentation de l'*Index Rerum* (1677)," in M. Rovere (ed.), *Spinoza par ses amis* (Paris, 2017), 81–205.
Rovere, Maxime (ed.), *Spinoza par ses amis* (Paris, 2017).
Rovere, Maxime, "Honors and Theater in Spinoza's Pedagogical Experience and His Relation to Van den Enden," *Educational Philosophy and Theory* 50 (2018), 809–18.
Rovere, Maxime, "Spinoza et les langues," in Jean Baumgarten, I. Rosier-Catach, and Pina Totaro (eds.), *Spinoza, philosophe grammairien. Le* Compendium grammatices linguae hebraeae (Paris, 2019), 21–45.
Rovere, Maxime, "Spinoza au théâtre," in Pierre-François Moreau and L. Vinciguerra (eds.), *Spinoza et les arts* (Paris, 2020), 76–89.
Rovere, Maxime, "Shaping the Freedom of Speech, Toleration and Intimacy in Pieter Balling's *Light Upon the Candlestick*," in N. Gengoux, P. Girard, and M. Laerke (eds.), *Libertinage et philosophie à l'époque Classique (XVIe–XVIIIe siècle). Les Libertins néerlandais* (Paris, 2022), 103–36.
Rowen, Herbert, *John de Witt, Grand Pensionary of Holland (1625–1672)* (Princeton, 1978).
Roy, Alain, *Gérard de Lairesse (1640–1711)* (Paris, 1992).

Rudavsky, T. M., "The Science of Scripture Ibn Ezra and Spinoza on Biblical Hermeneutics," in Steven Nadler (ed.), *Spinoza and Medieval Jewish Philosophy* (Cambridge, 2014), 59–78.

Ruestow, E. G., *Physics in Seventeenth- and Eighteenth-Century Leiden* (The Hague, 1973).

Ruspio, Federica, "La presenza portoghese a Venezia (fine del XVI—metà del XVII secolo)" (Università di Ca' Foscari di Venezia, Venice, Ph.D. thesis, 2006).

Russo, Raffaele, "The Thread of Discourse," in Luisa Simonutti (ed.), *Locke and Biblical Hermeneutics: Conscience and Scripture* (Cham, 2019), 121–41.

Saar, Martin, *Die Immanenz der Macht* (Berlin, 2013).

Saar, Martin, "The Immanence of Power: From Spinoza to 'Radical Democracy'," *MeSp* 106 (2014).

Sadler, J., "The Collegiants," in L. Hunt, M. Jacob, and W. Mijnhardt (eds.), *Bernard Picart and the First Global Vision of Religion* (Los Angeles, 2010), 59–74.

Salatowsky, Sascha, "Socinian Headaches: Adriaan Koerbagh and the Antitrinitarians," in S. Lavaert and W. Schröder (eds.), *The Dutch Legacy: Radical Thinkers in the 17th Century and the Enlightenment* (Leiden, 2017), 165–203.

Salomon, H. P., "Haham Saul Levi Morteira en de Portugese Nieuw-Christenen," *SR* 10 (1976), 127–41.

Salomon, H. P., *Portrait of a New Christian: Fernão Alvares Melo (1569–1632)* (Paris, 1982).

Salomon, H. P., "La vraie excommunication de Spinoza," in H. Bots and M. Kerkhof (eds.), *Forum Litterarum. Miscelânea de estudos literários, linguísticos e históricos oferecida a J.J. Van de Besselaar* (Amsterdam, 1984), 181–99.

Salomon, H. P., "Introdução" to Mortera, *Tratado da Verdade da Lei de Moisés* (Coimbra, 1988), pp. xxxv–cxxvii.

Samuel, Edgar, *At the End of the Earth: Essays on the History of the Jews in England and Portugal* (London, 2004).

Sangiacomo, Andrea, "Adam's Sin in Spinoza's Correspondence with Willem van Blijenbergh," *MeSp* 108 (2015).

Sangiacomo, Andrea, "Dichters en Profeten: Lodewijk Meyer's Leer van de Hartstochten in het Onderwijs in de Toneel-Poëzy," in B. Posthuma (ed.), *Spinoza en zijn kring. Een balans van veertig jaar onderzoek* (Uitgeverij Spinozahuis, The Hague, 2019), 99–108.

Sangiacomo, Andrea, *Spinoza on Reason, Passions and the Supreme Good* (Oxford, 2019).

Santana Pérez, Germán, "Los Holandeses y la utilización de la Canarias como puerta atlántica durante los siglos XVI–XVIII," in R. Vermeir, M. Ebben, and R. Fagel (eds.), *Agentes e Indentidades en movimiento. España y los Paises Bajos Siglos XVI–XVIII* (Madrid, 2011), 329–49.

Santinelli, Cristina, "À partir de *Spinoza in Italia*. Quelques notes historico-critiques et quelques remarques de méthode," in Chantal Jaquet and Pierre-François Moreau (eds.), *Spinoza Transalpin* (Paris, 2012), 23–45.

Saperstein, Marc, *Exile in Amsterdam: Saul Levi Morteira's Sermons to a Congregation of "New Jews"* (Cincinnati, 2005).

Saraiva, António José, *Inquisição e Cristãos-Novos* (1969; new edn., Porto, 1985).

Saraiva, António José, "António Vieira, Menasseh ben Israel et le Cinquième Empire," *SR* 6 (1972), 23–57.

Sassen, Ferd, *Geschiedenis van de wijsbegeerte in Nederland* (Amsterdam, 1959).

Sassen, Ferd, *Het wijsgerig onderwijs aan de Illustre School, te 's-Hertogenbosch* (Amsterdam, 1963).

Schacht, Richard, "Nietzsche's Gay Science, Or, How to Naturalize Cheerfully," in R. C. Solomon and K. M. Higgins (eds.), *Reading Nietzsche* (Oxford, 1988), 68–86.

Scherz, Gustav, *Pionier der Wissenschaft. Niels Stensen in seinen Schriften* (Copenhagen, 1963).
Scherz, Gustav, *Niels Stensen. Forscher und Denker im Barock* (Stuttgart, 1964).
Scherz, Gustav, "Biography of Nicolaus Steno," trans. P. Maquet, in Troels Kardel and P. Maquet (eds.), *Nicolaus Steno: Biography and Original Papers of a 17th Century Scientist* (Berlin, 2013), 7-344.
Schierbeek, A., *Jan Swammerdam, zijn leven en zij werken* (Lochem, 1946).
Schliesser, Eric, "Newton and Spinoza on Motion and Matter (and God, of course)," *The Southern Journal of Philosophy* 50 (2002), 436-58.
Schliesser, Eric, "Angels and Philosophers with a New Interpretation of Spinoza's 'Common Notions'," *Proceedings of the Aristotelian Society* 11 (2011), 497-518.
Schliesser, Eric, "Spinoza and the Philosophy of Science: Mathematics, Motion and Being," in Michael Della Rocca (ed.), *The Oxford Handbook of Spinoza* (Oxford, 2018), 155-89.
Schmaltz, Tad M., *Radical Cartesianism: The French Reception of Descartes* (Cambridge, 2002).
Schmaltz, Tad M., "Spinoza on Eternity and Duration," in Yitzhak Melamed (ed.), *The Young Spinoza: A Metaphysician in the Making* (Oxford, 2015), 205-20.
Schmaltz, Tad M., "Spinoza and Descartes," in Michael Della Rocca (ed.), *The Oxford Handbook of Spinoza* (Oxford, 2018), 63-83.
Schmidt-Biggemann, W., "Edifying versus Rational Hermeneutics," in M. Mulsow (ed.), *Between Philology and Radical Enlightenment: Hermann Samuel Reimarus (1694-1768)* (Leiden, 2011), 41-74.
Schnepf, Robert, "Enlightened Radicals: A Possible Difference between Spinoza and Van den Enden," in Frank Grunert (ed.), *Concepts of (Radical) Enlightenment* (Halle, 2014), 95-111.
Scholberg, K. R., "Miguel de Barrios and the Amsterdam Sephardic Community," *Jewish Quarterly Review* 53 (1962), 120-59.
Scholder, Klaus, *The Birth of Modern Critical Theology* (1966; London, 1990).
Scholem, Gershom, *Sabbatai Sevi: The Mystical Messiah, 1626-1676* (1973, new edn., Princeton, 2016).
Schreuder, Ida, *Amsterdam's Sephardic Merchants and the Atlantic Sugar Trade in the Seventeenth Century* (n.p., 2019).
Schröder, Winfried, "Spinozam tota armenta in Belgio sequi ducem: The Reception of the Early Dutch Spinozists in Germany," in W. van Bunge and W. Klever (eds.), *Disguised and Overt Spinozism around 1700* (Leiden, 1996), 157-70.
Schröder, Winfried, *Ursprünge des Atheismus* (Stuttgart, 1998).
Schröder, Winfried, "Spinozismus in der deutschen Frühaufklärung?," in Eva Schürmann, Norbert Waszek, and Frank Weinreich (eds.), *Spinoza im Deutschland des achtzehnten Jahrhunderts* (Stuttgart 2002), 121-38.
Schröder, Winfried, "Einleitung" to Matthias Knutzen, *Schriften* (Stuttgart, 2010), 7-32.
Schuyt, Kees, *Spinoza en de vreugde van het inzicht* (Amsterdam, 2017).
Schwartz, Gary, *Rembrandt, his Life, his Paintings* (New York, 1985).
Schwarz, Simon, *Uriel da Costa—Ahnherr der Aufklärung und Vorläufer von Spinoza* (Saarbrücken, 2011).
Sclar, David, "A Communal Tree of Life: Western Sephardic Jewry and the Library of the Ets Haim Yesiba in Early Modern Amsterdam," *Book History* 22 (2019), 43-65.
Scott McClure, Christopher, "Hell and Anxiety in Hobbes's *Leviathan*," *The Review of Politics* 73 (2011), 1-27.
Scribano, Emanuela, "Johannes Bredenburg (1643-1691) confutatore di Spinoza," in Paolo Cristofolini (ed.), *L'hérésie spinoziste. Actes du colloque international de Cortona* (Amsterdam, 1995), 66-76.

Scribano, Emanuela, "La connaissance du bien et du mal. Du *Court Traité* à l'*Ethique*," in Chantal Jaquet and Pierre-François Moreau (eds.), *Spinoza transalpin* (Paris, 2012), 59–74.
Scruton, Roger, *Spinoza* (Oxford, 1986).
Secrétan, Catherine, "Qu'est-ce qu'être libertin dans les Pays-Bas au 'Siècle d'Or'," in N. Gengoux, P. Girard, and M. Laerke (eds.), *Libertinage et philosophie à l'époque Classique (XVIe–XVIIIe siècle). Les Libertins néerlandais* (Paris, 2022), 19–46.
Seeskin, Kenneth, "From Maimonides to Spinoza," in Michael Della Rocca (ed.), *The Oxford Handbook of Spinoza* (Oxford, 2018), 45–62.
Servaas de Rooijen, A. J., *Inventaire des livres formant la bibliothèque de Benedict Spinoza* (Paris-The Hague, 1888).
Shapin, Stevin and Simon Schaffer, *Leviathan and the Air-Pump: Hobbes, Boyle and the Experimental Life* (1985; new edn., Princeton, 2011).
Sharp, Hasana, *Spinoza and the Politics of Renaturalization* (Chicago, 2011).
Sharp, Hasana, "Family Quarrels and Mental Harmony: Spinoza's *Oikos-Polis* Analogy," in Yitzhak Melamed and H. Sharp (eds.), *Spinoza's Political Treatise: A Critical Guide* (Cambridge, 2018), 93–110.
Sharp, Hasana, "Spinoza and Feminism," in Yitzhak Melamed (ed.), *A Companion to Spinoza* (Hoboken, NJ, 2021), 422–30.
Shaw, Jane, *Miracles in Enlightenment England* (New Haven, CT, 2006).
Shelford, April, *Transforming the Republic of Letters: Pierre-Daniel Huet and European Intellectual Life, 1650–1720* (Rochester, NY, 2007).
Shelford, April, "The Quest for Certainty in Fact and Faith: Piere-Daniel Huet and Josephus' *Testimonium*," in A. Frazer and P. Nold (eds.), *Essays in Renaissance Thought and Letters* (Leiden, 2015), 217–40.
Siebrand, H. J., *Spinoza and the Netherlanders* (Assen-Maastricht, 1988).
Silva Rosa, José Maria da, "That the *Catholica religio* Does [Not] Need a Pontiff," in António Bento and José Maria da Silva Rosa (eds.), *Revisiting Spinoza's Theological-Political Treatise* (Hildesheim, 2013), 55–71.
Silva Rosa, J. S. da, *Geschiedenis der Portugeesche Joden te Amsterdam, 1593–1925* (Amsterdam, 1925).
Silvério Lima, Luis Felipe, "Prophetic Hopes, New World Experiences and Imperial Expectations: Menasseh ben Israel, António Vieira, Fifth-Monarchy Men and Millenarian Connections in the Seventeenth Century," *Anais de História de Além-Mar* 17 (Lisbon, 2016), 359–408.
Simonutti, Luisa, *Arminianesimo e tolleranza nel seicento olandese* (Florence, 1984).
Simonutti, Luisa, "Premières réactions anglaises au *Traité Théologico-Politique*," in Paolo Cristofolini (ed.), *L'hérésie spinoziste. Actes du colloque international de Cortona* (Amsterdam, 1995), 123–37.
Simonutti, Luisa, "Spinoza and the English Thinkers," in W. van Bunge and W. Klever (eds.), *Disguised and Overt Spinozism around 1700* (Leiden, 1996), 191–211.
Simonutti, Luisa, "English Guests at De Lantaarn," in S. Hutton (ed.), *Benjamin Furly (1646–1714): A Quaker Merchant and his Milieu* (Florence, 2007), 31–66.
Simonutti, Luisa, "Vindiciae Miraculorum. I Rimostranti e Spinoza," in C. Hermanin and L. Simonutti (eds.), *La Centralità del dubbio. Un progetto di Antonio Rotondò* (2 vols., Florence, 2011) ii, 613–37.
Simonutti, Luisa (ed.), *Locke and Biblical Hermeneutics: Conscience and Scripture* (Cham, 2019).
Sleigh, R. C., *Leibniz and Arnauld: A Commentary on their Correspondence* (New Haven, CT, 1990).

Slive, Seymour, *Rembrandt and his Critics 1630–1730* (The Hague, 1953).
Smith, Nigel, "The Politics of Tragedy in the Dutch Republic: Joachim Oudaen's Martyr Drama in Context," in K. Gozdeva, T. Korneeva, and K. Ospovat (eds.), *Dramatic Experience: The Politics of Drama and the Public Sphere in Early Modern Europe and Beyond* (Leiden, 2016), 220–49.
Snyder, Laura, *Eye of the Beholder: Johannes Vermeer, Antoni van Leeuwenhoek, and the Reinvention of Seeing* (New York, 2015).
Socher, Abraham P., *The Radical Enlightenment of Solomon Maimon* (Stanford, CA, 2006).
Sonnino, Paul, *Louis XIV and the Origins of the Dutch War* (Cambridge, 1988).
Sorkin, David, *The Religious Enlightenment: Protestants, Jews and Catholics from London to Vienna* (Princeton, 2008).
Spaans, Joke, "Between the Catechism and the Microscope: The World of Johannes Duijkerius," in Joke Spaans and Jetze Touber (eds.), *Enlightened Religion: From Confessional Churches to Polite Piety in the Dutch Republic* (Leiden, 2019), 316–45.
Spaans, Joke and Jetze Touber (eds.), *Enlightened Religion: From Confessional Churches to Polite Piety in the Dutch Republic* (Leiden, 2019).
Spiertz, M. G., *L'Église catholique des Provinces-Unies et le Saint-Siège pendant la deuxième moitié du XVIIe siècle* (Louvain, 1975).
Spiertz, M. G., "Jansénisme in en rond de Nederlanden 1640–1690," *Tijdschrift voor de geschiedenis van het katholiek leven in de Nederlanden* 1 (1992), 144–67.
Spies, Marijke, "Lodewijk Meijer en de hartstochten," in P. Hoftijzer and Theo Verbeek (eds.), *Leven na Descartes. Zeven opstellen over de ideeëngeschiedenis in Nederland in de tweede helft van de zeventiende eeuw* (Hilversum, 2005), 39–53.
Springborg, Patricia, "The Enlightenment of Thomas Hobbes," *British Journal for the History of Philosophy* 12 (2004), 513–34.
Spruit, Leen, "Intruduzione" to Jelles, *Belydenisse*, pp. xiii–lxiii.
Spruit, Leen, "Un cristianesimo ragionevole: la cristologia de Jarig Jelles," in C. Hermanin and L. Simonutti (eds.), *La Centralità del dubbio. Un progetto di Antonio Rotondò* (2 vols., Florence, 2011) ii, 525–42.
Spruit, Leen and Pina Totaro, "Introduction" to L. Spruit and P. Totaro (eds.), *The Vatican Manuscript of Spinoza's* Ethica (Leiden, 2011), 1–47.
Steenbakkers, Piet, *Spinoza's* Ethica *from Manuscript to Print: Studies on the Text, Form and Related Topics* (Assen, 1994).
Steenbakkers, Piet, "Johannes Braun (1628–1708), Cartesian in Groningen," *Nederlands Archief voor Kerkgeschiedenis* 77 (1997), 196–210.
Steenbakkers, Piet, "De Nederlandse vertalingen van Spinoza's *Ethica*," *MeSp* 74 (1997), 3–40.
Steenbakkers, Piet, "Een vijandige overname: Spinoza over *natura naturans* en *natura naturata*," in G. Coppens (ed.), *Spinoza en de scholastiek* (Louvain, 2003), 35–52.
Steenbakkers, Piet, "Jean-Maximilien Lucas," in *DDPhil* ii, 643–4.
Steenbakkers, Piet, "Spinoza over vrijheid, dwang en noodzaak," in Cis van Heertum (ed.), *Libertas philosophandi. Spinoza als gids voor een vrije wereld* (Amsterdam, 2009), 113–23.
Steenbakkers, Piet, "The Textual History of Spinoza's *Ethics*," in Olli Koistinen (ed.), *The Cambridge Companion to Spinoza's* Ethics (Cambridge, 2009), 26–41.
Steenbakkers, Piet, "La Mort de Spinoza: une rumeur inconnue," *Archives de Philosophie* 73 (2010), 733–64.
Steenbakkers, Piet, "Spinoza in the History of Biblical Scholarship," in Rens Bod, Jaap Maat, and Thijs Weststeijn (eds.), *The Making of the Humanities, Vol. 1: Early Modern Europe* (Amsterdam, 2010), 313–26.

Steenbakkers, Piet, "The Text of Spinoza's *Tractatus Theologico-Politicus*," in Y. Y. Melamed and M. A. Rosenthal (eds.), *Spinoza's* Theological-Political Treatise: *A Critical Guide* (Cambridge, 2010), 29–40.
Steenbakkers, Piet, "Spinoza, beyond the Legends," in *Spinoza Research: To Be Continued* (Uitgeverij Spinozahuis, 2016), 9–24.
Steenbakkers, Piet, "Spinoza's Correspondentie," in B. Posthuma (ed.), *Spinoza en zijn kring. Een balans van veertig jaar onderzoek* (Uitgeverij Spinozahuis, The Hague, 2019), 7–17.
Steenbakkers, Piet, "Spinoza's Life," in Don Garrett (ed.), *The Cambridge Companion to Spinoza* (2nd edn., Cambridge, 2022), 12–60.
Steenbakkers, Piet and R. Bordoli, "Lodewijk Meijer's Tribute to Johannes Bouwmeester, 4 November 1673," *SS* 13 (1997), 241–57.
Stein, Ludwig, *Leibniz und Spinoza* (Berlin, 1890).
Stein, Yoram, "The Coherence of Spinoza's Theological-Political Treatise," in Henri Krop and Pooyan Tamimi Arab (eds.), *Spinoza's* Theological Political Treatise *(1670–2020): Commemorating a Long-Forgotten Masterpiece* (Basel, 2021), 87–98.
Steinberg, Diane, "Knowledge in Spinoza's *Ethics*," in Olli Koistinen (ed.), *The Cambridge Companion to Spinoza's* Ethics (Cambridge, 2009), 140–66.
Steinberg, Justin, "Spinoza's Curious Defense of Toleration," in Y. Y. Melamed and M. A. Rosenthal (eds.), *Spinoza's* Theological-Political Treatise: *A Critical Guide* (Cambridge, 2010), 210–30.
Steinberg, Justin, *Spinoza's Political Psychology* (Cambridge, 2018).
Steinberg, Justin and V. Viljanen, *Spinoza* (Cambridge, 2021).
Stern, Jill, *Orangism in the Dutch Republic in Word and Image, 1650–75* (Manchester, 2010).
Stewart, Matthew, *The Courtier and the Heretic: Leibniz, Spinoza and the Fate of God in the Modern World* (New Haven, CT, 2005).
Stilianou, Aristotelis, "Spinoza et l'histoire antique," *SS* 12 (1996) 121–37.
Stone, Michael E. (ed.), *Jewish Writings of the Second Temple Period* (Assen, 1984).
Stracenski, I., "Spinoza's *Compendium* of the Grammar of the Hebrew Language, *Parrhesia* 32 (2020), 122–44.
Strauss, Leo, *Spinoza's Critique of Religion* (Chicago, 1965).
Strazzoni, Andrea, *Burchard de Volder and the Age of Scientific Revolution* (Cham, 2019).
Stroumsa, Sarah, *Andalus and Sefarad: On Philosophy and Its History in Islamic Spain* (Princeton, 2019).
Strum, Daniel, *The Sugar Trade: Brazil, Portugal and the Netherlands (1595–1630)* (Stanford, CA, 2013).
Swetschinski, Daniel M., *Reluctant Cosmopolitans: The Portuguese Jews of Seventeenth-Century Amsterdam* (London, 2000).
Swetschinski, Daniel M., "Vestiging, verdraagzaamheid en vereniging tot 1639," in J. C. H. Blom, R. G. Fuks-Mansfeld, and Ivo Schöffer (eds.), *Geschiedenis van de Joden in Nederland* (Amsterdam, 2017), 55–130.
Sytsma, David S., *Richard Baxter and the Mechanical Philosophers* (Oxford, 2017).
Tatián, Diego, *Spinoza, filosofía terrena* (Buenos Aires, 2014).
Taylor, Dan, "The Reasonable Republic? Statecraft, Affects and the Highest Good," *History of European Ideas* 45 (2019), 645–60, published online 21 March 2019.
Taylor, Paul, *Dutch Flower Painting 1600–1720* (New Haven, CT, 1995).
Thijssen-Schoute, C. Louise, "Lodewijk Meyer en diens verhouding tot Descartes en Spinoza," *MeSp* 11 (Leiden, 1954).

Thijssen-Schoute, C. Louise, *Nederlands Cartesianisme* (1954; repr. Utrecht, 1989).
Thijssen-Schoute, C. L., *Uit de Republiek der Letteren* (The Hague, 1967).
Thomas, Werner, "Jerónimo Gracián de la Madre de Dios, la Corte de Bruselas y la política religiosa en los Países Bajos meridianales, 1609–1614," in R. Vermeir, M. A. Ebben, and R. P. Fagel (eds.), *Agentes y identidades en movimiento. España y los Países Bajos, siglos XVI–XVIII* (Madrid, 2011), 289–312.
Tiribás, Victor, "Mobility, Clandestine Literature and Censorship: A Case-Study in the Transatlantic Diaspora of a Migrant Circle," *Rivista Storica Italiana* 131 (2019), 1050–83.
Tolmer, Leon, *Pierre-Daniel Huet (1630–1721). Humaniste-physicien* (Bayeux, 1949).
Tomalin, Claire, *Samuel Pepys: The Unequalled Self* (New York, 2002).
Tomasoni, Francesco, "Il 'sistema Intellectuale' di Cudworth fra l'edizione originale e la tradizione Latina di Mosheim," *Rivista critica di storia della filosofia* 46 (1991), 629–60.
Tosel, André, "La Théorie de la pratique et la fonction de l'opinion publique dans la philosophie politique de Spinoza," *SS* 1 (1985), 184–208.
Tosel, André, "Le *Discours sur l'histoire universelle* de Bossuet: une stratégie de dénégration du *Traité théologico- politique*," in Paolo Cristofolini (ed.), *L'hérésie spinoziste. Actes du colloque international de Cortona* (Amsterdam, 1995), 97–105.
Tosel, André, *Spinoza, ou l'autre (in)finitude* (Paris, 2009).
Tosel, André, "La Figure du Christ et la vérité de la religion," in António Bento and José Maria da Silva Rosa (eds.), *Revisiting Spinoza's Theological-Political Treatise* (Hildesheim, 2013), 123–96.
Totaro, Pina (Giuseppina), "Nota su due manoscritti delle 'Adnotationes' al *Tractatus Theologico-Politicus* di Spinoza," *Nouvelles de la Republique des Lettres* 10 (1990), 107–15.
Totaro, Pina, "Niels Stensen (1638–1686) e la prima diffusione della filosofia di Spinoza nella Firenze di Cosimo III," in Paolo Cristofolini (ed.), *L'hérésie spinoziste. Actes du colloque international de Cortona* (Amsterdam, 1995), 147–68.
Totaro, Pina, "La Congrégation de l'Index et la censure des oeuvres de Spinoza," in W. van Bunge and W. Klever (eds.), *Disguised and Overt Spinozism around 1700* (Leiden, 1996), 353–76.
Totaro, Pina, "Documenti su Spinoza nell' archivio del Sant' Uffizio dell'Inquisizione," *Nouvelles de la Republique des Lettres* 20 (2000), 95–128.
Totaro, Pina, "Ho certi amici in Ollandia: Stensen and Spinoza – Science and Faith," in K. Ascani, H. Kermit, and G. Skytte (eds.), *Niccolò Stenone (1638–1686). Anatomista, geologo, vescovo* (Rome, 2002), 27–36.
Totaro, Pina, "L'Enigme du nom: Spinoza et les noms propres," *Corpus: Revue de Philosophie* 50 (2006), 169–84.
Totaro, Pina, "Note" to P. Totaro (ed.) *Spinoza, Tractatus Theologico-Politicus* (Naples, 2007), 499–719.
Totaro, Pina, "Introduzione" to Spinoza, *Trattato Teologico Politico* (Naples, 2007), pp. xix–xlvii.
Totaro, Pina, "La Religion catholique ou universelle. Philosophie, théologie et politique chez Spinoza," in Chantal Jaquet and Pierre-François Moreau (eds.), *Spinoza Transalpin* (Paris, 2012), 97–112.
Totaro, Pina, "The Young Spinoza and the Vatican Manuscript of the *Ethics*," in Yitzhak Melamed (ed.), *The Young Spinoza: A Metaphysician in the Making* (Oxford, 2015), 319–31.
Totaro, Pina, "Steno in Italy from Florence to Rome," in R. Andrault and M. Laerke (eds.), *Steno and the Philosophers* (Leiden, 2018), 270–87.
Totaro, Pina, "Le *Compendium grammatices linguae hebraeae* dans le contexte des ouevres de Spinoza," in Jean Baumgarten, I. Rosier-Catach, and Pina Totaro (eds.), *Spinoza,*

philosophe grammairien. Le Compendium grammatices linguae hebraeae (Paris, 2019), 63-89.
Totaro, Pina, "Masaniello, la Hollande et un autoportrait de Spinoza?," in Pierre-François Moreau and L. Vinciguerra (eds.), *Spinoza et les arts* (Paris, 2020), 19-34.
Totaro, Pina, "More on Spinoza and the Authorship of the Pentateuch," in A. Del Prete, A. L. Schino, and Pina Totaro (eds.), *The Philosophers and the Bible* (Leiden, 2022), 42-7.
Touber, Jetze, "Biblical Philology and Hermeneutical Debate in the Dutch Republic in the Second Half of the Seventeenth Century," in Dirk van Miert, Henk Nellen, Piet Steenbakkers, and Jetze Touber (eds.), *Scriptural Authority and Biblical Criticism in the Dutch Golden Age* (Oxford, 2017), 325-47.
Touber, Jetze, *Spinoza and Biblical Philology in the Dutch Republic, 1660-1710* (Oxford, 2018).
Trevor, Meriol, *The Shadow of a Crown: The Life Story of James II of England and VII of Scotland* (London, 1988).
Trevor-Roper, Hugh, *One Hundred Letters from Hugh Trevor-Roper*, (eds.) R Davenport-Hines and A. Sisman (Oxford, 2014).
Troost, Wouter, "William III, Brandenburg, and the Construction of the Anti-French Coalition," in Jonathan I. Israel (ed.), *The Anglo-Dutch Moment* (Cambridge, 1991), 299-333.
Troost, Wout, *William III, the Stadholder-King: A Political Biography* (Abingdon, 2005).
Twining, T., "Richard Simon and the Remaking of Seventeenth-Century Biblical Criticism," *Erudition and the Republic of Letters* 3 (2018), 421-87.
Uhlmann, Anthony and Moira Gatens, "Spinoza on Art and the Cultivation of a Disposition toward Joyful Living," *IHR* 30 (2020), 429-45.
Valladares, Rafael, *La Conquista de Lisboa. Violencia militar y comunidad política en Portugal, 1578-1583* (Madrid, 2008).
Van Berkel, K., "Intellectuals against Leeuwenhoek," in L. C. Palm and H. A. M. Sneders (eds.), *Antoni van Leeuwenhoek 1632-1723* (Amsterdam, 1982), 187-209.
Van Berkel, Klaas, *Universiteit van het noorden: Vier Eeuwen Academisch Leven in Groningen, Volume 1: De Oude Universiteit, 1614-1876* (Hilversum, 2014).
Van Boheemen, F. and R. Bosscher, "Daniel Harmensz Tijdeman (1630-1677). Schilder van huis uit, querulant van nature," in *Spinoza in Voorburg*, in *Historisch Voorburg* 28 (2022), 32-53.
Van Bunge, Wiep, "Johannes Bredenburg and the *Korte Verhandeling*," *SS* 4 (1988), 321-8.
Van Bunge, Wiep, "A Tragic Idealist: Jacob Ostens (1630-1678)," *SS* 4 (1988), 263-79.
Van Bunge, Wiep, "On the Early Dutch Reception of the *Tractatus Theologico-Politicus*," *SS* 5 (1989), 225-51.
Van Bunge, Wiep, *Johannes Bredenburg (1643-1691). Een Rotterdamse Collegiant in de ban van Spinoza* (Rotterdam, 1990).
Van Bunge, Wiep, "De Rotterdamse Collegiant Jacob Ostens (1630-1678)," *De Zeventiende Eeuw* 6 (1990), 65-77.
Van Bunge, Wiep, "Spinoza's atheïsme," in E. Kuypers (ed.), *Sporen van Spinoza* (Leuven, 1993), 89-113.
Van Bunge, Wiep, *Baruch of Benedictus? Spinoza en de "Marranen,"* MeSp 81 (2001).
Van Bunge, Wiep, *From Stevin to Spinoza: An Essay on Philosophy in the Seventeenth-Century Dutch Republic* (Leiden, 2001).
Van Bunge, Wiep (ed.), *The Early Enlightenment in the Dutch Republic, 1650-1750* (Leiden, 2003).

Van Bunge, Wiep, "De bibliotheek van Jacob Ostens: spinozana en sociniana," *Doopsgezinde Bijdragen* nieuwe reeks 30 (2004), 125–40.
Van Bunge, Wiep, *Philosopher of Peace: Spinoza, Resident of The Hague* (The Hague, 2008).
Van Bunge, Wiep, "Spinoza's filosofische achtergronden," in Cis van Heertum (ed.), *Libertas philosophandi. Spinoza als gids voor een vrije wereld* (Amsterdam, 2008), 95–111.
Van Bunge, Wiep, "Introduction" to A. Koerbagh, *A Light Shining in Dark Places* (ed.), M. Wielema (Leiden, 2011), 1–40.
Van Bunge, Wiep, *Spinoza Past and Present: Essays on Spinoza, Spinozism and Spinoza Scholarship* (Leiden, 2012).
Van Bunge, Wiep, "Spinoza's Friendships," in Chr. Bahier-Porte, Pierre-François Moreau, and Delphine Reguig (eds.), *Liberté de conscience et arts de penser (XVIe–XVIIIe siècle). Melanges en l'honneur d'Antony McKenna* (Paris, 2017), 371–84.
Van Bunge, Wiep, "Spinoza's Life, 1677–1802," *JHI* 78 (2017), 211–31.
Van Bunge, Wiep, "Geografie en filosofie: Olfert Dapper (1636–1689) en de kring van Spinoza," in Spinozahuis symposium *Spinoza en zijn kring*, 75–95.
Van Burg, Elco, "Petrus van Mastricht and the External and Internal Call," in A. C. Neele (ed.), *Petrus van Mastricht (1630–1706): Text, Context and Interpretation* (Göttingen, 2020), 55–70.
Van Cauter, Jo, "Spinoza on History, Christ and Lights Untamable" (University of Ghent Ph.D. thesis, 2016).
Van Cauter, Jo, "Another Dialogue in the 'Tractatus': Spinoza on 'Christ's Disciples' and the Religious Society of Friends," in D. Edelstein and A. Matytsin (eds.), *Let there be Enlightenment: The Religious and Mystical Sources of the Enlightenment* (Baltimore, 2018), 131–52.
Van Cauter, Jo and D. Schneider, "A Baconian in the *TTP*, but not in the *Ethics*?' in Henri Krop and Pooyan Tamimi Arab (eds.), *Spinoza's Theological Political Treatise (1670–2020): Commemorating a Long-Forgotten Masterpiece* (Basel, 2021), 55–74.
Van Dalen, J. L., "Willem Laurensz. van Blijenbergh," *De Tijdspiegel* 65 (1908), 344–71.
Van de Kamp, J. L. J., *Emanuel van Portugal en Emilia van Nassau* (Assen, 1980).
Van de Klashorst, "De ware vrijheid, 1650–1672," in E. O. G. Haitsma Mulier and W. R. E. Velema (eds.), *Vrijheid. Een geschiedenis van de vijftiende tot de twintigste eeuw* (Amsterdam, 1999), 157–85.
Van de Ven, Jeroen, "Life. Spinoza's Life and Time: An Annotated Chronology Based Upon Historical Documents," in Wiep van Bunge, Henri Krop, and Piet Steenbakkers (eds.), *The Bloomsbury Companion to Spinoza* (London: Bloomsbury, 2014), 1–57.
Van de Ven, Jeroen, "Crastina die loquar cum celsissimo principe de Spinosa: New Perspectives on Spinoza's Visit to the French Army Headquarters in Utrecht in late July 1673," *IHR* 25 (2015), 147–65.
Van de Ven, Jeroen, "Van bittere galle by een gebonden: over de laat zeventiende-eeuwse Nederlandse vertalingen van Spinoza's *Tractatus Theologico-Politicus*," in B. Posthuma (ed.), *Spinoza en zijn kring. Een balans van veertig jaar onderzoek* (Uitgeverij Spinozahuis, The Hague, 2019), 109–20.
Van de Ven, Jeroen, *Printing Spinoza: A Descriptive Bibliography of the Works Published in the Seventeenth Century* (Leiden, 2022).
Van de Ven, Jeroen, *Documenting Spinoza: A Biographical History of his Life and Time* (forthcoming).
Van de Wetering, Ernst, *Rembrandt: The Painter at Work* (Amsterdam, 2000).
Van Delft, Dirk, *Antoni van Leeuwenhoek en de wondere wereld van de microbiologie* (Amsterdam, 2022).
Van den Besselaar, *António Vieira en Holland (1624–1649)* (Nijmegen, 1967).

Vandenbossche, H., "Adriaan en Jan Koerbagh," in H. Dethier and Hubert Vandenbossche (eds.), *Woordenboek van Belgische en Nederlandse Vrijdenkers* (2 vols., Brussels, 1979) i, 167–92.
Van den End, G., *Guiljelmus Saldenus (1627–1694). Een praktisch en irenisch theoloog uit de Nadere Reformatie* (Leiden, 1991).
Van den Hoven, M. J., "Inleiding" to Petrus van Balen, *De Verbetering der gedachten* (Baarn, 1988).
Van der Bijl, M., "Utrechts weerstand tegen de oorlogspolitiek tijdens de Spaanse Successieoorlog," in *Van Standen tot Staten. Stichtse Historische Reeks* 1 (Utrecht, 1975), 135–99.
Van der Deijl, Lucas, "The Dutch Translation and Circulation of Spinoza's *Tractatus Theologico-Politicus* in Manuscript and Print (1670–1694)," *Quaerendo* 50 (2020), 207–37.
Van der Deijl, Lucas, "A New Language for the Natural Light: Translating the New Philosophy in the Early Dutch Enlightenment" (University of Amsterdam Ph.D. thesis, 2022).
Van der Leer, Kees, "Een speurtocht naar het Spinozahuis in de Kerkstraat," in *Spinoza in Voorburg*, in *Historisch Voorburg* 28 (2022), 54–103.
Van der Leer, Kees and Henk Boers, *Huygens and Hofwijck: The Inventive World of Constantijn and Christiaan Huygens* (Voorburg, 2022).
Van der Tak, W. G., "Spinoza's Payments to the Portuguese-Israelitic Community, and the Language in Which He Was Raised," *SR* 16 (1982), 190–5.
Van der Tak, W. G., "Jellesz' Life and Business," *MeSp* 59 (1989), 11–22.
Van der Tak, W. G. and Leon Brunschvicg, *Spinoza* (The Hague, 1931).
Van der Tang, Aad, "Spinoza en Schiedam," *Scyedam* 10 (1984), 159–84.
Van der Wall, Ernestine, *De Mystieke Chiliast Petrus Serrarius (1600–1669) en zijn wereld* (Leiden, 1987).
Van der Wall, Ernestine, "The Amsterdam Millenarian Petrus Serrarius (1600–1669) and the Anglo-Dutch Circle of Philo-Judaists," in J. van den Berg and E. van der Wall (eds.), *Jewish-Christian Relations in the Seventeenth Century* (Dordrecht, 1988), 73–94.
Van der Wall, Ernestine, "Petrus Serrarius and Menasseh ben Israel: Christian Millenarianism and Jewish Messianism in Seventeenth-Century Amsterdam," in Yosef Kaplan, H. Méchoulan, and R. Popkin (eds.), *Menasseh ben Israel and His World* (Leiden, 1989), 164–90.
Van der Wall, Ernestine, "The *Tractatus Theologico-Politicus* and Dutch Calvinism, 1670–1700," *SS* 11 (1995), 201–26.
Van der Wall, Ernestine, "The Religious Context of the Early Dutch Enlightenment: Moral Religion and Society," in Wiep van Bunge (ed.), *The Early Enlightenment in the Dutch Republic, 1650–1750* (Leiden, 2003), 39–57.
Van der Welle, J. A., *Dryden and Holland* (Groningen, 1962).
Van Dillen, J. G., "Vreemdelingen te Amsterdam in de eerste helft van de zeventiende eeuw 1: de portugeesche joden," *Tijdschrift voor geschiedenis* 1 (1935), 4–35.
Van Eeghen, I. H., *De Amsterdamse boekhandel 1680–1725* (5 vols., Amsterdam, 1963).
Van Gelder, H. A. Enno, *Getemperde vrijheid* (Groningen, 1972).
Van Gelder, H. E., "Schutterij en Magistraat in 1672," *Jaarboekje Die Haghe* (1937), 58–80.
Van Gelderen, Maarten, "Turning Swiss? Discord in Dutch debates," in A. Holenstein, Th. Maissen, and M. Prak (eds.), *The Republican Alternative: The Netherlands and Switzerland Compared* (Amsterdam, 2008), 151–70.

Van Hardeveld, Idalina, "Lodewijk Meijer (1629–1681) als lexicograaf" (University of Leiden Ph.D. thesis, 2000).
Van Heertum, Cis (ed.), *Libertas philosophandi. Spinoza als gids voor en vrije wereld* (Amsterdam, 2008).
Van Heertum, Cis, "Reading the Career of Johannes Koerbagh: The Auction Catalogue of His Library," *Lias* 38 (2011), 1–57.
Van Heertum, Cis, "A Not So Harmless Drudge: Koerbagh's *Bloemhof van allerley liefliykheid* (1668)," *Quaerendo* 50 (2020), 395–426.
Van Kleveren, G., "Utrecht zonder regering 1673/4," *Jaarboekje van 'Oud-Utrecht'* (1925), 93–109.
Van Lieburg, F. A., *De Nadere Reformatie in Utrecht ten tijde van Voetius* (Rotterdam, 1989).
Van Malssen, P. J. W., *Louis XIV d'après les pamphlets répandus en Hollande* (Paris, 1936).
Van Miert, Dirk, *Humanism in an Age of Science: The Amsterdam Athenaeum in the Golden Age, 1632–1704* (Leiden, 2009).
Van Miert, Dirk, *The Emancipation of Biblical Philology in the Dutch Republic 1590–1670* (Oxford, 2018).
Van Miert, Dirk, H. Nellen, Piet Steenbakkers, and J. Touber (eds.), *Scriptural Authority and Biblical Criticism in the Dutch Golden Age* (Oxford, 2017).
Van Nierop, Henk, *The Life of Romeyn de Hooghe (1645–1708)* (Amsterdam, 2018).
Van Rees, O., *Verhandeling over de Aanwijsing der Politike Gronden van Pieter de La Court* (Utrecht, 1851).
Van Ruler, Han, *The Crisis of Causality: Voetius and Descartes on God, Nature and Change* (Leiden, 1995).
Van Ruler, Han, "Calvinisme, cartesianisme, spinosisme," in G. Coppens (ed.), *Spinoza en het Nederlands Cartesianisme* (Leuven, 2004), 23–37.
Van Ruler, Han, "Spinoza in Leiden," in Spinozahuis symposium *Spinoza en zijn kring*, 33–46.
Van Slee, J. C., *De Rijnsburger Collegianten* (1895, repr. Utrecht, 1980).
Van Sluis, Jacob and T. Musschenga, *De Boeken van Spinoza* (n.p., 2009).
Van Strien, C. D., *British Travellers in Holland during the Stuart Period* (Leiden, 1993).
Van Suchtelen, Guido, "The Spinoza Houses at Rijnsburg and The Hague," in S. Hessing (ed.), *Speculum Spinozanum 1677–1977* (London, 1977), 475–8.
Van Suchtelen, Guido, "Nil Volentibus Arduum; les amis de Spinoza au travail," *SS* 3 (1987), 391–404.
Van Suchtelen, Guido, *Spinoza's sterfhuis aan de Paviljoensgracht* (The Hague, 1997).
Van Vloten, Johan, *Benedictus de Spinoza, naar leven en werken in verband met zijnen en onzen tijd geschetst* (Schiedam, 1871).
Van Vugt, Ingeborg, "The Structure and Dynamics of Scholarly Networks between the Dutch Republic and the Grand Duchy of Tuscany" (University of Amsterdam Ph.D. thesis, 2019).
Vaz Diaz, A. M. and W. G. van der Tak (eds.), *Spinoza Mercator et Autodidactus: Oorkonden en andere authentieke documenten betreffende des wijsgeers jeugd en diens betrekkingen* (The Hague, 1932).
Vaz Diaz, A. M. and W. G. van der Tak, "Spinoza Merchant and Autodidact," *SR* 16 (1982), 109–195.
Vega, L. A., *Het Beth Haim van Ouderkerk* (3rd edn., n.p., 1994).
Verbeek, Theo, *Descartes and the Dutch* (Carbondale, IL, 1992).
Verbeek, Theo, *Spinoza's Theologico-Political Treatise: Exploring "the Will of God"* (Aldershot, 2003).

Verbeek, Theo, "Spinoza on Aristocratic and Democratic Government," in Yitzhak Melamed and H. Sharp (eds.), *Spinoza's Political Treatise: A Critical Guide* (Cambridge, 2018), 145–60.
Vercruysse, Jérôme, *Bibliographie descriptive des écrits du Baron d'Holbach* (Paris, 1971), section 1770.
Verhoeven, G., *De derde stad van Holland: geschiedenis van Delft tot 1795* (Zwolle, 2015).
Vermeir, René, *In Staat van oorlog: Felips IV en de Zuiderlijke Nederlanden (1629–1648)* (Maastricht, 2001).
Vermij, Rink, "Le Spinozisme en Hollande: le cercle de Tschirnhaus," *CS* 6 (1991), 145–68.
Vermij, Rink, "Bijdrage tot de bio-bibliografie van Johannes Hudde," *Gewina* 18 (1995), 25–35, 78.
Vermij, Rink, *The Calvinist Copernicans: The Reception of the New Astronomy in the Dutch Republic, 1575–1750* (Amsterdam, 2002).
Vernière, Paul, *Spinoza et la pensée française avant la Révolution* (1954; 2nd edn., Paris, 1982).
Villani, Stefano, "'A Man of Intrigue but of no Virtue': Jean-Baptiste Stouppe (1623–1692), a Libertine between Raison d'État and Religion," *CHRC* 101 (2021), 306–23.
Villaverde, José María, *Rousseau y el pensamiento de Las Luces* (Madrid, 1987).
Villaverde, José María, "Rousseau, lecteur de Spinoza," *Studies on Voltaire and the Eighteenth Century* 369 (1999), 107–39.
Vinciguerra, Lorenzo, *Spinoza et le signe. La Genèse de l'imagination* (Paris, 2005).
Visser, H. B., *De geschiedenis van den sabbatsstrijd en de Gereformeerden in de zeventiende eeuw* (Utrecht, 1939).
Visser, Piet, "Kritisch commentaar van een Collegiantische kwelgeest," *Doopsgezinde Bijdragen* 38 (2012), 285–350.
Vlessing, Odette, "The Portuguese-Jewish Merchant Community in Seventeenth-Century Amsterdam," in A. Lesger and L. Noordegraaf (eds.), *Entrepreneurs and Entrepreneurship in Early Modern Times* (The Hague, 1995), 223–43.
Vlessing, Odette, "The Excommunication of Baruch Spinoza: A Conflict between Jewish and Dutch Law," *SS* 13 (1997), 15–47.
Vlessing, Odette, "The Excommunication of Baruch Spinoza: The Birth of a Philosopher," in Jonathan I. Israel and Reinier Salverda (eds.), *Dutch Jewry: Its History and Secular Culture (1500–2000)* (Leiden, 2002), 141–72.
Vlessing, Odette, "Twee bijzondere klanten van de Amsterdamse Wisselbank: Baruch Spinoza en Francisco Lopes Suasso," *Amstelodamum* 96 (2009), 155–68.
Waardt, Hans de, "Academic Careers and Scholarly Networks," in Wiep van Bunge (ed.), *The Early Enlightenment in the Dutch Republic, 1650–1750* (Leiden, 2003), 17–37.
Wade, Ira, *The Clandestine Organization and Diffusion of Philosophic Ideas in France from 1700 to 1750* (Princeton, 1967).
Wade, Ira, *The Intellectual Development of Voltaire* (Princeton, 1969).
Wagenaar, Lodewijk, *Een Toscaanse Prins bezoekt Nederland. De twee reizen van Cosimo de' Medici 1667–1669* (Amsterdam, 2014).
Waite, Gary K., "Menno and Muhammed: Anabaptists and Mennonites reconsider Islam, 1525–1657," *The Sixteenth Century Journal* 41 (2010), 995–1016.
Waite, Gary K., "The Drama of the Two-Word Debate among Liberal Dutch Mennonites," in B. Heal and A. Kremers (eds.), *Radicalism and Dissent in the World of Protestant Reform* (Göttingen, 2017), 118–35.
Waite, Gary K., *Jews and Muslims in Seventeenth-Century Discourse* (Abingdon, 2019).

Wallet, Bart and Irene Zwiep, "Locals: Jews in the Early Modern Dutch Republic," in Jonathan Karp and Adam Sutcliffe (eds.), *The Cambridge History of Judaism, Vol. 7: The Early Modern World, 1500-1815* (Cambridge, 2018), 894–922.

Walther, Manfred, "Biblische Hermeneutik und/oder theologische Politik bei Hobbes und Spinoza: Historische Studie zur Theorie der Ausdifferenzierung von Religion und Politik in der Neuzeit," in D. Bostrenghi (ed.), *Spinoza e Hobbes: Atti del Convegno Urbino, 14-17 ottobre, 1988* (Naples, 1992), 623–69.

Walther, Manfred, "Spinoza's Critique of Miracles: A Miracle of Criticism?," in Graeme Hunter (ed.), *Spinoza: The Enduring Questions* (Toronto, 1994), 100–12.

Walther, Manfred, "Biblische Hermeneutik und historische Erklärung: Lodewijk Meyer und Benedikt de Spinoza über Norm, Methode und Ergebnis wissenschaftlicher Bibelauslegung," *SS* 11 (1995), 227–300.

Walther, Manfred, "Machina civilis oder von deutscher Freiheit," in Paolo Cristofolini (ed.), *L'hérésie spinoziste. Actes du colloque international de Cortona* (Amsterdam, 1995), 184–221.

Walther, Manfred, "Spinoza in seiner Welt: Neuere Forschungsergebnisse," *Zeitschrift für Religions- und Geistesgeschichte* 47 (1995), 73–80.

Walther, Manfred, "Was/is Spinoza a 'Jewish Philosopher'? Spinoza in the Struggle for a Modern Jewish Cultural Identity in Germany: A Meta-Reflection," *SS* 13 (1997), 207–37.

Walther, Manfred, *Spinoza Studien* (3 vols., Heidelberg, 2018).

Watson, Richard, *The Breakdown of Cartesian Metaphysics* (Atlantic Highlands, NJ, 1987).

Wauters, Tim, "*Libertinage érudit* and Isaac Vossius," *The Journal of Early Modern Cultural Studies* 12 (2012), 37–53.

Weekhout, Ingrid, *Boekencensuur in de Noordelijke Nederlanden. De vrijheid van drukpers in de zeventiende eeuw* (The Hague, 1998).

Weisz, George, "Remembering Eliahu de Luna Montalto (1567–1616)," *Rambam Maimonides Medical Journal* 8 (2017), online article.

Wesselius, J. W., "Spinoza's Excommunication and Related Matters," *SR* 24 (1990), 43–63.

Weststeijn, Arthur, *Commercial Republicanism in the Dutch Golden Age: The Political Thought of Johan and Pieter De La Court* (Leiden, 2012).

Weststeijn, Arthur, *De radicale Republiek: Johan en Pieter de la Court, dwarse denkers uit de Gouden Eeuw* (Amsterdam, 2013).

Weststeijn, Thijs, *The Visible World: Samuel van Hoogstraten's Art Theory and the Legitimation of Painting in the Dutch Golden Age* (Amsterdam, 2008).

Whitebook, Joel, *Freud: An Intellectual Biography* (Cambridge, 2017).

Whittingham, Martin, "Ezra as the Corrupter of the Torah? Re-Assessing Ibn Hazm's Role in the Long History of an Idea," *Intellectual History of the Islamic World* 1 (2013), 253–71.

Wielema, Michiel, *Filosofen aan de Maas. Kroniek van vijfhonderd jaar wijsgerig denken in Rotterdam* (Baarn, 1991).

Wielema, Michiel, "Een onbekende aanhanger van Spinoza, Antony van Dalen," *GWND* 4 (1993), 21–40.

Wielema, Michiel, "The Two Faces of Adriaan Koerbagh," *GWND* 12 (2001), 57–75.

Wielema, Michiel, "Adriaan Koerbagh: Biblical Criticism and Enlightenment," in Wiep van Bunge (ed.), *The Early Enlightenment in the Dutch Republic, 1650–1750* (Leiden, 2003), 61–80.

Wielema, Michiel, *The March of the Libertines: Spinozists and the Dutch Reformed Church (1660-1750)* (Hilversum, 2004).

Wielema, Michiel, "Abraham van Berkel's Translations as Contributions to the Dutch Radical Enlightenment," in S. Lavaert and W. Schröder (eds.), *The Dutch Legacy: Radical Thinkers in the 17th Century and the Enlightenment* (Leiden, 2017), 204–26.

Wigelsworth, J. R., *Deism in Enlightenment England* (Manchester, 2009).

Wilke, Carsten, "Le 'Messie mystique' et la Bourse d'Amsterdam, le 3 mai 1666," *Sefarad* 67 (2007), 191–211.

Wilke, Carsten, "Clandestine Classics: Isaac Orobio and the Polemical Genre among the Dutch Sephardim," in Carsten Wilke (ed.), *Isaac Orobio: The Jewish Argument with Dogma and Doubt* (Berlin, 2018), 57–76.

Wilke, Carsten (ed.), *Isaac Orobio: The Jewish Argument with Dogma and Doubt* (Berlin, 2018).

Williams, D. L., "Spinoza and the General Will," in J. Farr and D. L. Williams (eds.), *The General Will: The Evolution of a Concept* (Cambridge, 2015), 115–46.

Willis, Robert, *Benedict de Spinoza: His Life, Correspondence and Ethics* (London, 1870).

Winn, James Anderson, *John Dryden and His World* (New Haven, CT, 1987).

Wiznitzer, Arnold, "Isaac de Castro, Brazilian Jewish Martyr," PAJHS 47 (1957), 63–75.

Woldring, H. E. S., *Jan Amos Comenius. Zijn leven, missie en erfenis* (Budel, 2014).

Woldring, H. E. S., *De pansofie van Comenius. Zijn zoektocht naar allesomvattende wijsheid* (Budel, 2016).

Wolf, Lucien, *Jews in the Canary Islands* (London, 1926).

Wolloch, Nathaniel, *Moderate and Radical Liberalism: The Enlightenment Sources of Liberal Thought* (Leiden, 2022).

Woolf, M., "Foreign Trade of London Jews in the Seventeenth Century," *Transactions of the Jewish Historical Society of England* 24 (1970/73), 35–58.

Wootton, David, *The Invention of Science: A New History of the Scientific Revolution* (London, 2016).

Wurtz, Jean-Paul, "Introduction" to E. W. Von Tschirnhaus, *Médecine de l'esprit* (Paris, 1980).

Wurtz, Jean-Paul, "Tschirnhaus und die B. de Spinozabeschuldigung: die Polemik mit Christian Thomasius," *Studia Leibnitiana* 13 (1981), 61–75.

Wurtz, Jean-Paul, "La théorie de la connaissance de Tschirnhaus," in R. Bouveresse (ed.), *Spinoza, Science et religion* (Paris, 1982), 123–40.

Wurtz, Jean-Paul, "Un disciple hérétique de Spinoza: Ehrenfried Walther von Tschirnhaus," *CS* 6 (1991), 111–43.

Yasuhira, Genji, "Confessional Coexistence and Perceptions of the 'Public': Catholics in Negotiations on Poverty and Charity in Utrecht 1620–1670," *BMGN* 132 (2017), 3–24.

Yerushalmi, Y. H., *From Spanish Court to Italian Ghetto* (1971; repr. Seattle, 1981).

Yonover, Jason, "Nietzsche and Spinoza," in Yitzhak Melamed (ed.), *A Companion to Spinoza* (Hoboken, NJ, 2021), 527–37.

Young, Julian, *Friedrich Nietzsche: A Philosophical Biography* (Cambridge, 2010).

Yovel, Y., *Spinoza and Other Heretics*, vol. 1 (Princeton, 1989).

Zahedieh, Nuala, "The Second Anglo-Dutch War in the Caribbean," in D. Ormrod and G. Rommelse (eds.), *War, Trade and the State: Anglo-Dutch Conflict 1652–89* (Woodbridge, 2020), 185–202.

Zaunick, Rudolf, "Einführung" zu Tschirnhaus, Medicina Mentis (Leipzig, 1963), 5–28.

Zaunick, Rudolf, *Ehrenfried Walther von Tshirnhaus* (Dresden, 2001).

Zenker, Kay, *Denkfreiheit. Libertas Philosophandi in der deutschen Aufklärung* (Hamburg, 2012).

Zwarts, Jacques, "De eerste rabbijnen en synagogen van Amsterdam naar archivalische bronnen," *Bijdragen en Mededeelingen van het Genootschap voor Joodsche Wetenschap in Nederland* 4 (1928), 145–271.

Zwiep, Irene, "Ceci n'est pas une grammaire: Le *Compendium grammatices linguae hebraeae* de Spinoza," in Jean Baumgarten, I. Rosier-Catach, and Pina Totaro (eds.), *Spinoza, philosophe grammairien. Le* Compendium grammatices linguae hebraeae (Paris, 2019), 159–81.

Index

For the benefit of digital users, indexed terms that span two pages (e.g., 52–53) may, on occasion, appear on only one of those pages.

Abbadie, Jacques (1654–1727), Huguenot theologian 46n62, 697, 1103
Aboab da Fonseca, Isaac (1605–93), rabbi at Amsterdam 78, 152, 153, 162–3, 176–7, 180–1, 309
"above reason" 30, 391, 555, 559–60, 612–13, 722–3
Académie Royale des Sciences, *see* Paris
Accademia del Cimento, *see* Florence
Adam, Eve and "the Fall" 387–8, 390–1, 430–1, 646, 1017, 1028–9, 1075, 1077–9
Aeltz, Herman (1621–96), Amsterdam printer 616, 620–1, 772
"affects", passions, controlling our emotions 367–8, 413–14, 449–54, 630, 636–7, 641–2, 755–6, 768, 802–3, 1116
  inadequacy of Descartes' theory 449, 636–8, 802–3
Akkerman, Fokke, Spinoza scholar 327–8, 495–6, 495n27, 1221–2
Alcalá de Henares University 304–7, 312–13, 324
alchemy 9, 395–6, 400, 662–3, 1049, 1151–2
Alting, Jacob (1618–79), Reformed theologian and Hebrew philologist 784–6, 1082–3
Alva, Don Fernando Álvarez de Toledo, Duke of (1507–82) 92, 94–5, 103–4, 1007
Alvares, Antonio, Amsterdam Sephardic jeweler 215–16
Ames, William (d. 1662), Quaker leader 274–8, 280–1, 334–5
Amsterdam 4–5, 115–18, 129, 665–6, 876–7, 885–6, 888–9, 898–9, 999, 1052–3,
  air quality 117–18, 352–3, 605–6
  Athenaeum Illustre 185–7, 244–6, 250–1, 518, 1078
  city government 65–6, 70–1, 120–1, 137, 140, 160, 164–5, 193, 237–8, 617–18, 620–2, 778–9, 871, 1052–3
  civic theatre (Schouwburg) 253, 256, 627–31, 640–1, 865–6, 1050
  Collegiants, *see* Collegiants
  Collegium medicum 307, 315
  Collegium Privatim Amtelodamsense 244–5, 368–70
  Dam Square 140, 206, 214, 616–17
  epidemics 117–18, 352–3, 492–6, 499–503, 517–18, 663–4
  Exchange 191–2, 199–200, 230, 264–5, 489–90, 492–3, 503–4, 571–2, 865–6
  Exchange Bank (Wisselbank) 140, 165, 190–1, 194–5, 205–6, 214
  Lutheran community 241, 264–6, 470–3, 548–9, 715
  Moravian Brethren 261, 265–6, 273–4, 276, 284, 286–7, 358
  Orphans' Chamber 65–6, 220–4
  population 117–18, 494
  Portuguese Jewish community, *see* Portuguese Jewish community of Amsterdam
  Quakers, *see* Quakers
  Reformed consistory (kerkeraad) 119–20, 253, 256, 263, 280–1, 543–5, 608–9, 622, 781–2, 1200
  Remonstrant community (Arminians), *see* Remonstrants
  Singel 241, 543–4, 599, 622–4, 649
  toleration, model for 70–1, 114–15, 119–21, 124–5, 265–7, 665–6, 796–7, 811, 1047–8
  town hall (stadhuis) 192, 206, 617, 651
  Vlooienburg 115–17, 121, 128–9, 145, 171–2
  Willige Rasphuis 622, 1200–1
  see also synagogues
angels and spirits 9, 31, 413–14, 419–20, 445–6, 507, 557–8, 581–2, 610–11, 646, 661–3, 684–5, 715–16, 791–3, 809, 816–17, 829–30, 898–901, 912, 947–8, 1008, 1014–15, 1121–3, 1130
Anglican Church (Church of England) 36–9, 258–9, 532–3, 722, 743–4, 747
  Latitudinarianism 37–9, 952
Anglo-Dutch Wars, the First (1652–54) 195–202, 206–8, 213, 239–40, 502, 510, 586, 654–5
  Second (1664–67) 487–93, 505–8, 510, 512–18, 520–1, 526–7, 529–32, 564–71, 580–92, 594–5, 770

Anglo-Dutch Wars, the First (1652–54) *(cont.)*
Third (1672–74) 861–3, 947–8, 981–2, 993, 1000, 1039–40
animals and humans 369–73, 419–20, 424–5, 442–4, 802–3
Anti-Socinian decrees (blasphemy laws) 262, 273, 276, 290–1, 610, 670–1, 778–9, 783–4, 1047–8, 1206
António, Prior of Crato, Dom (1531–95), pretender to the Portuguese throne 93–9, 101, 104–6, 165–6
Antonianismo (movement supporting Dom Antonio's claims to the Portuguese throne) 95–7, 106, 165–6
Antwerp, crypto-Jewish community in 112–13, 118–19, 122–4, 127, 133–4
Apostles 13–14, 541, 577, 645, 689–90, 723–5, 820–1, 909–10, 1085–6, 1088–9
contradict each other 910–11
Aragon, as medieval monarchy 102–5, 109–10, 1090
Aragonese Revolt against Philip II (1590–91) 92–3, 101, 104–5, 108–10
Aramaic 689–90, 704
"argument from design," physico-theology 369–70, 1119, 1142, 1190–1
aristocracy rejected 9, 482–3, 591–2, 670–1, 679–80, 740–2, 752–3, 756–7, 887, 892–6
aristocratic republicanism rejected 9, 679–80, 682–3, 737–8, 742–3, 745–6, 877–8, 894–6, 1148
Aristotle (384–322 BC.), Aristotelianism 155, 173–4, 186–7, 302–3, 306, 324, 366–7, 400–1, 425–6, 519–20, 531–2, 541, 796–7, 799
Spinoza's dismissive view of 155, 178–9, 186–7, 302–3, 306, 324, 420, 435–6, 541, 661–2, 731, 771–2, 907–9, 912, 1017
Arlington, Lord Henry Bennet, first earl of (1618–85), advisor to Charles II 488–9, 493–4, 510–11, 570–1, 583–4, 589, 592, 837–8, 863, 892–3, 1041
Arminianism, *see* Remonstrants
Arnauld, Antoine (1612–84), "le grand Arnauld," Jansenist theologian 41, 44–5, 966–7, 1098–9, 1113–14, 1117–18, 1136–9, 1141–2
atheism 259–60, 333–5, 339, 346–7, 349, 378–80, 394, 424–6, 432–3, 440–1, 474–7, 537, 545, 558–9, 578–9, 606–7, 612, 616–17, 662, 748, 772, 783–4, 791–3, 815–16, 840, 879–80, 918, 987, 1117–18, 1123–4, 1190–1, 1194–5
redefined by Spinoza 17–18, 368, 440–1, 826–7, 1169–70
atoms 428–9, 802–3, 908–9

Aubert de Versé, Noel (c.1642–1714), French religious dissident and advocate of toleration 964, 1009–10, 1013–14, 1023, 1034
Auzout, Adrien (1622–91), French astronomer 530–1, 533–4
Averroes (Ibn Rushd)(1126–98), Averroism, crypto-Averroism, neo-Averroism 155–7, 174–5, 299–300, 303–4, 306–8, 336, 343–4, 350–1, 539–40, 624, 670–1
Azores Islands (Terceira, São Miguel and Santa Maria) 88, 91, 94–6, 100–2, 165

Babylonian Captivity, the (c.598–539 BC) 702, 1076–7, 1079, 1082–3, 1090–1, 1140–1
Bacon, Francis (1561–1626), English philosopher 15, 284, 363–5, 367, 385–91, 393–5, 398–401, 404, 409, 412–13, 415–16, 418–19, 456–7, 559, 563–4, 720, 727, 729–30, 747, 1059
and the Bible 389–90, 688, 722–3, 727, 747, 806, 809
Spinoza's critique of 386–7, 390–1, 395, 412–13, 415–16, 729–30, 1169–70
venerated by the Royal Society 386–7, 400, 1119
Balen, Petrus van (1643–92), Spinozist philosopher at Rotterdam 32, 875–6, 1023, 1025–30, 1032–4, 1208
Balling, Pieter (d.1664), Collegiant friend of Spinoza 76, 262–4, 273–4, 276–8, 280–3, 285–8, 333–4, 342, 354, 356, 427, 435–6, 495–6, 615–16, 711–12, 726, 779, 814, 822–3, 1203
translates Spinoza from Latin into Dutch 328, 330, 427, 440, 457–8, 495, 506, 1168–9
Light on the Candlestick (1662) 282, 817
Balmes, Abraham de (c.1440–1523), Italian Jewish scholar 1076–7
Balzac, Jean-Louis Guez de (1597–1654), French essayist 677–8
Barbados 196, 209–10, 490–1, 516–17
Barrios, Daniel Levi (Miguel) de (c.1625–1701), Sephardic poet and historian 5, 65, 67–70, 88–9, 122, 138–9, 172–3, 180–1, 189, 218–19
Flor de Apolo (1665) 65
Triumpho del gobierno popular (1682) 67, 307
Basnage, Jacques (1653–1723), Huguenot pastor and historian 61–2, 73–4, 964, 1004, 1037–8
Batelier (also Batalerius), Jacobus Johannes (1593–1672), Remonstrant preacher at The Hague 45–6, 830–2
Vindiciae miraculorum (1673) 830–2

Baumgarten, Siegmund Jacob (1706–57), Wolffian Pietist bibliographer 436, 484–5
Baxter, Richard (1615–91), Puritan theologian 33–41, 44–6, 750, 951–3, 969, 1120, 1122–3, 1126–9, 1194
 Catholick Theologie (1675–76) 34, 38n40
 Second part of the Nonconformists Plea for Peace (April 1680) 34
 Church-History (1681) 36–41
Baxterites 33–4, 36–8, 1125–6, 1206
Bayle, Pierre (1647–1706), philosopher 4–5, 7–9, 42, 44–6, 76–7, 269–70, 328–9, 464–5, 551, 558–9, 587, 819–20, 830, 837–9, 842, 845, 901, 957, 978–9, 1057, 1101, 1110–11, 1132–5, 1140–1, 1147, 1152, 1187–8, 1205
 correspondence 5, 269n24, 838–9, 842, 849, 1133–4
 profiles Spinozism as a movement 830, 853–4, 937–8, 984, 1011, 1013–14, 1016, 1018–19, 1038
 reads Spinoza 23–4, 853–4, 1132–6, 1194–5
 researches Spinoza's life and circle 63–5, 75–7, 218–19, 227, 236, 242–3, 269–70, 290, 319, 483–5, 537–8, 558–9, 615–16, 843, 937–8, 991–2, 1013, 1023, 1038, 1153, 1196–7
 "Spinozismus ante Spinozam" topos 730–1, 1013, 1207
 superstition 518–19, 531–2, 901, 1194–5
 transforms "Spinoza" into an iconic mythical figure 1195–7, 1206, 1208–9, 1213–14, 1216
 Pensées diverses (1682) 518–19, 531–2, 837, 1152, 1188–9, 1194–5
 Dictionnaire historique et critique (1697) 29–30, 64–5, 240–1, 484, 984, 1013, 1196–7, 1207
Beelthouwer, Jan Pietersz (c.1603–c.1669), Amsterdam Socinian Collegiant 549–50, 556–7, 617–19, 716
Beiser, Frederick, historian 7–8, 12, 15
Beja, and "conjura de Beja [conspiracy of Beja]," (1570–72) 85–7, 97–8, 300
Bekker, Balthasar (1634–98), Reformed minister and pro-Cartesian theologian 322–3, 337, 518, 551–2, 555–6, 635, 643–5, 898–900, 1004, 1015–16, 1023, 1197–8
 profiles Spinozism as a sect 1010–11, 1013, 1018–19, 1211
Bentley, Richard (1662–1742), classical scholar 1190–1, 1193
Bergen (Norway), Battle of, 12 August 1665 504–5

Berkel, Abraham van (1639–89), ally of the Koerbaghs 545, 547–8, 599–602, 612, 614, 616, 618–20, 622–3, 720–2, 727, 730–2, 740, 742, 769
Bernard, Jacques (1658–1718), Huguenot Reformed preacher at The Hague 236, 901
Beverland, Hadrianus (1650–1716), Dutch freethinker 32, 545, 551–2, 635–6, 646, 661, 1021, 1023, 1025, 1028–32, 1044–5, 1154
Bible chronology 308, 659–61, 684–5, 697–8, 703–4, 718–19, 923, 1087–8
Bible criticism, *see* Grotius, Hobbes, Spinoza, *and* Isaac Vossius
Bibliotheca Anglesiana auctioned in 1686 1130–1
Bibliotheca Fratrum Polonorum quos Unitarios vocant (Library of the Polish Brothers called Unitarians), clandestinely published (Amsterdam, 1665–68) 779–80, 815–16, 867–8, 948
Blasius, Gerardus (1627–82), Amsterdam "city physician" and Athenaeum professor 244–5, 247, 368–70
blasphemy laws, *see* Anti-Socinian decrees
Blijenbergh, Willem van (1613–94), Dordrecht regent and Cartesian 28–30, 33, 45–6, 429–37, 448, 496, 709, 957–9, 1004, 1025–6, 1122–3
 confers with Spinoza, in Voorburg 432–3, 496
 The Truth of the Christian Religion and Authority of Holy Scripture (1674) 28–9, 432–3, 957–8
 Refutation of the Ethica *or Moral Science of Benedictus de Spinosa* [*Wederlegging van de* Ethica *of Zede-kunst van Benedictus van Spinosa*] (Dordrecht, 1682) 29–30, 957–8, 1183
Blijenburgh, Adriaan van (1616–82), Dordrecht Orangist regent 874, 884, 1044–5
Block, Ameldonck (c.1651–1702), Collegiant savant 1184–5
Blount, Charles (1654–93), deist philosopher and translator of Spinoza into English 729, 747, 1018, 1129–30, 1189–92
 Miracles, No Violations of the Laws of Nature (1683) 728, 1129–30
Bodegraven, sack of (1672) 886–90, 915–16, 968
Boeckelman, Andries (d.1679), Amsterdam physician 632–3
Bontekoe, Cornelis (1647–85), Cartesian medical reformer 361–2, 411, 433–5, 663–4, 1021–6, 1030, 1059, 1150, 1153–4, 1162
 profiles Spinoza's following 362, 1018–21
 ties to Van Balen 1026–30, 1034
Bontemantel, Hans (1613–88), Amsterdam regent 617–21, 782

Borch, Ole (Olaus) (1626–90), Danish
   savant 250, 259–60, 334–5, 338, 344–9, 352,
   359–61, 364, 367–9
Boreel, Adam (1603–67), and Boreelists,
   Collegiant group 171–2, 270–3, 276–82,
   285, 287–8, 334, 346–7, 352–3, 363–4,
   493, 567–70, 576–7, 582, 594, 684, 750,
   982–3, 985–6
Borelli, Giovanni Alfonso (1608–79), Neapolitan
   physiologist and astronomer 329, 516–17,
   519–20, 578–9
Borri, Giuseppe Francesco (1627–95),
   alchemist 344–9
Bossuet, Jacques Benigne (1627–1704), French
   bishop, courtier and theologian 23–4, 41–2,
   44–5, 1101–2, 1104, 1135, 1137–8, 1140–1,
   1188–9, 1193–4
Boulainvilliers, Henri de (1659–1722), clandestine
   French Spinozist 857, 1004, 1208
Bourignon, Antoinette (1616–80), mystic
   and leader of an ultra-austere
   Christian sect 370
Bouwmeester, Johannes (1634–80), physician,
   freethinker, and friend of Spinoza 231–2,
   248, 342, 347–8, 352–4, 379, 382, 426–7,
   435–6, 484–6, 501–2, 506, 537–42, 547–8,
   556–7, 563, 575, 588–9, 644, 770–1,
   825, 827, 941–2, 1075, 1103–4, 1146–7,
   1183–4
   assists Spinoza 426–7, 607, 634–5, 825–6,
   955–6, 963, 972–3, 987–9, 993–5, 1057–8,
   1074, 1166–70
   complex personality 382, 605–7, 632–6, 642
   Nil Volentibus Arduum 624, 627–8, 630–3,
   636–7, 639
   ties with the Koerbaghs 333–4, 606–7,
   609–10, 614–15
   Hai Ebn Yokhdan (1672) 631–2, 1047
Boxel, Hugo (1607–80), regent of Gorcum 871,
   901–3, 1122–3
Boyle, Robert (1627–91), Anglo-Irish scientist
   and theologian 15, 33–4, 363–8, 370–1,
   375–6, 385–6, 388–9, 392–4, 456–7, 505,
   508, 512, 528–9, 563, 589–91, 900–1,
   1041–2, 1148
   avoids engaging directly with Spinoza 387–8,
   393–4, 402, 405, 407–8, 508, 510–13, 525–6,
   528–9, 947
   defense of faith and miracles 391–3, 532–4,
   559, 568–70, 582, 688–9, 722–3, 900–1,
   931, 947–8, 951–3, 1119–20, 1188–90, 1193
   discusses Spinoza with Oldenburg 394, 407–8,
   493–4, 499–501, 507–8, 528–9
   outraged by the *TTP* 1042–3, 1066, 1068, 1096
   researches saltpeter and nitre 395–8, 400–1,
   405, 505
   Spinoza's critique of 389–92, 396–8, 400–4,
   507, 533–4
   *Experiments and considerations touching
   colours* (London, 1664) 499–501, 529
   *Free Enquiry into the vulgarly received Notion
   of Nature* (1686) 394, 1119–20
Boyle Lectures 1190–1
Braun (Brun), Jean (1631–1708),
   Walloon pastor and author 654, 790–1,
   971, 1202
   La Véritable religion des Hollandois
   (1675) 985–7, 993, 995–6
Brazil, *Companhia do comercio para o Brasil*
   established in 1649 169–70
   Dutch zone (1645–65) 50, 56–7, 74–5, 113,
   120, 153–4, 165–70, 194–5
   Sephardic communities in Brazil 133, 153–4,
   165, 170
   Sephardic soldiers fighting for the
   WIC 153–4, 318
Breda Peace Negotiations (1667) 588–9,
   594–5, 649
   Polaroon 649
Bredenburg, Johannes (1643–91), Rotterdam
   Collegiant philosopher-theologian 45–6,
   817–20, 822
   Enervatio Tractatus Theologico-Politici
   (1674) 818–20
   *Verhandeling, van de oorsprong van de
   kennisse Gods* [Treatise on the Origin of the
   Knowledge of God] (1684) 818
Brouncker William 2nd Viscount, (1620–84),
   Anglo-Irish nobleman, the Royal Society's
   first President 365, 503, 507–8, 512–13,
   588–9
Browne, Thomas (c1654–1721), Cambridge
   Nonjuror 728, 1129–30
   Miracles Work's Above and Contrary to Nature
   (1683) 1129
"Bruitists", meaning philosophical
   atheists 34–40
Brun Antoine (1599–1654), Spanish envoy at The
   Hague 192–3, 198, 211, 224–6
Brun, Jean, *see* Braun
Buissière, Paul, Huguenot apothecary to Condé at
   Utrecht 991–2
Burgersdijk, Pieter (1623–91), pensionary of
   Leiden 25–6
Burgh, Albert Coenraedsz. (c.1648–1708),
   former disciple of Spinoza 88–9, 92, 233,
   235, 243, 276–7, 827–8, 931, 1006–8,
   1113–14, 1168–9

Burman, Frans (Franciscus) (1628–79), Utrecht theologian 6–7, 471, 517, 534, 551, 553–4, 557–8, 715–16, 771, 779–80, 784–6, 788, 809–11, 829, 971–2, 976–7, 1062–3
Buxtorf, Johannes, the Elder (1564–1629), professor of Hebrew at Basel 620, 703, 809–10, 1077, 1080–3, 1090–1

"Cabal, the," at court in Whitehall 488–9, 493–4, 892–3, 1040–1
Caceres (or Casseres), Benjamin de, son of Spinoza's sister Rebecca 184–5, 1159–61
Caceres (Casseres), Daniel de (dates unknown), son of Spinoza's sister, Miriam 184–5, 1055, 1159–60, 1161n63, 1164
Caceres, Michael de (d. 1695), Rebecca's son 1161
Caceres (or Casseres), Samuel de (1628–60), Spinoza's brother-in-law, Sephardic community *sopher* in Amsterdam 142, 180–1, 184–5, 187–8, 1055
calendar, switching between Julian and Gregorian 867, 981, 998, 1143
Cambridge University 368–9, 944–7, 952–3
  Christ's College 561, 1043, 1124
  Neo-Platonism 952, 1124
  St John's College 728
Campen, Jacob van (1596–1657), Dutch architect, disciple of Palladio 253, 460–1
Camphuysen, Dirk Rafaelsz (1586–1627), Remonstrant minister and poet 354–6, 1103–4
Canary Islands 168–9, 194–9, 201, 217, 311–12
  Michael d'Espinoza's trade with 168, 190, 194–5
  see also Inquisition
Cappel, Louis (1585–1658), Huguenot professor of Hebrew at Saumur 686, 703, 1076, 1078, 1090–1, 1139–40
Carlisle, Clare 10n16
Cartesians, Cartesianism, Cartesian philosophy 5, 15, 44–5, 71–2, 162, 187, 229–30, 236, 238, 245–51, 253–4, 283–6, 291–2, 299–300, 332, 338–9, 351, 367, 374, 424, 540–1, 659–60
  alleged source of Spinozism 29, 380–2, 663, 777, 787–8, 791–3, 798, 957–8, 1021–2, 1025, 1034, 1060–4, 1099, 1183
  astronomy transformed 249–50, 468, 518–22, 532–4, 563–4, 658, 973
  Cartesians rarely attack Spinoza by name 424–6, 429–33, 437–8, 787–9, 791, 794, 799, 811, 1059, 1063–4
  divisive impact on Dutch universities 290, 292, 362, 382–4, 548, 799, 1010–11, 1046
  medical reformism 370–1, 374–5, 631–2, 663–4
  mind/body divide 250–1, 284, 374–6, 381–2, 415–17, 420, 639, 903–4, 1021–2
  motion external to matter 420, 525, 1021–2
  pseudo-Cartesiani (Bastaard-Cartesiaanen) 552, 557–8, 711–12, 715–16, 717–18, 792–5, 799, 1022, 1047–8
  Spinoza "reforms" and subverts 229–30, 244, 250–1, 290, 293, 301–3, 324, 360–2, 367, 380–2, 385–6, 391, 395, 409–12, 415–20, 433–7, 456–7, 461, 521–2, 525, 563–4, 576, 639, 717–18, 748
  see also, Descartes
Carvajal, Antonio Fernández (Abraham Israel), Michael d'Espinoza's London agent 196–7
Casearius, Johannes (1642–77), student of Spinoza, later a Reformed preacher at Cochin 333–4, 342–3, 379, 434
Cassini, Gian Domenico (1625–1712), Savoyard astronomer 500–1, 516–17, 1113–14
Castro Tartas, David de (1630–98), Amsterdam printer, brother of Isaac 315–16
Castro Tartas, Isaac de (c.1623–47), burnt at the stake in Lisbon 153–5, 315–16, 318
Catholic League (la Sainte Ligue, founded in 1576), French anti-Protestant, pro-Spanish coalition 88, 93–6, 98–9
Caton, William (1636–65), Quaker leader in Amsterdam 277–80, 285
cercle spinoziste, see Spinozists
Charles I, king of England (reigned: 1625–49) (executed 30 January 1649) 163–4, 893, 920–1
Charles II, king of England (1630–85; reigned: 1660–85) 11–12, 38–9, 105–6, 275, 386–7, 457, 489–91, 530–1, 564–5, 575–6, 580, 591–3, 680–1, 893, 969
  anti-Dutch strategies 488–91, 493–4, 496, 499, 504, 514, 566, 664–5, 861, 993
  court of, *see* "Cabal"
  personality 588–90, 726–7, 863
  alliance with Louis XIV 583–4, 587–8, 861–3, 1040–1
Chevreau, Urbain (1613–1701), French savant 921–3, 925
  Histoire du Monde (*History of the World*) (1686) 921–3
  Chevraeana (1697) 922
China, Chinese antiquity and monuments 131–2, 294–6, 299, 659–62
Christ, *see* Jesus Christ

Christianity, "true" 13–14, 270, 280–1, 342, 361, 1067, 1087
Christ's divinity denied, just a pre-eminent teacher of men 263–4, 266–8, 270, 287, 339–40, 346, 350, 354, 417, 430, 543–4, 555, 569–70, 608–9, 611, 614–16, 622, 712–13, 723, 775–6, 784, 810–11, 815–16, 819–20, 948, 1020, 1066–7, 1086–90, 1103–4, 1127–8, 1199
churches, falsify "religion" and church history, reject the "true universal church,' 39–40, 90, 266–7, 270–1, 726, 771, 911, 1017, 1086–7, 1103–4
Church Fathers 13–14, 90, 273, 306–7, 644–5, 703–4, 1095, 1110–11
circumcision and uncircumcision, and Spinoza's views on 114, 128–9, 131, 138–9, 159, 313, 573
citizens categorized into four kinds 757
civil religion and its ceremonies 432–3, 757–8, 764–5, 877–8, 1014–15
Clapmarius (Klapmeier), Arnold (1574–1634), Altdorf law professor 575–6
Clarke, Samuel (1675–1729), Anglican theologian 45–6, 964, 1191, 1208–9
Cocceians, Cocceianism, as liberal tendency in the Dutch Reformed Church 230 661, 1082, 1196–7
  linked to Cartsianism 383–4, 470–2, 879–80, 973–4
Cocceius, Johannes (1603–69), Reformed Church theologian 292, 334, 364–6, 373, 383–4, 469–70, 472–3, 534, 547–8, 575, 809–10, 973–4, 1027, 1046
Coenerding, Jan (1632–1705), Amsterdam surgeon and theatre director 632–3
Cohen Herrera, Rabbi Abraham (c.1570–c.1635), Kabbalist 176–8
Colbert, Jean-Baptiste (1619–83), Louis XIV's "first minister of state," 88, 365, 511–12, 927–8, 967–8, 1096–7, 1140
Colerus, Johannes (1647–1707), Lutheran preacher and biographer of Spinoza 21–2, 61–3, 73–5, 78, 230, 236–7, 241–2, 328–9, 348–9, 461, 466–7, 484, 648–9, 652, 813–14, 840, 997, 1143, 1146, 1154–5, 1208–9
Collegiants, at Amsterdam 53, 171–2, 248–9, 261–6, 268–71, 273–4, 276–8, 285–7, 293, 807–8, 1203
  Anti-Trinitarian philosophical Collegiants," 269, 273, 277, 549, 814–18, 820, 822–3

Bible literalist Anti-Trinitarian Collegiants 272, 280–4, 287–8, 822
Rokin gatherings 608–9, 615–16, 622–3
Rotterdam, see Rotterdam
Spiritualist Collegiants 270, 277, 750, 817–18, 822
toleration and "reason" exalted 817–18, 820, 822–3, 845–6, 1087
Trinitarian Collegiants 272, 280–4, 287–8, 549, 814–15
see also Rijnsburg
Cologne, archbishop-electorate 460, 786–7, 863
Comenius (or Komensky), Jan Amos (1592–1670), head of the Moravian Brethren in Holland 265–8, 270–1, 283–5, 334, 346, 573–4, 594
  critique of Descartes 265–6, 283–5, 550–1
  pansophia 266–7, 283–5, 550, 750
  De Irenico Irenicorum Admonitio (1660) 266–8
comets and the great comet controversy (1664–5) 516–19, 521–2, 526, 531–2, 534, 566–7, 587, 658–9, 1194–5
  comets purely natural phenomena 175, 177–8, 400, 468, 518–19, 553–4
common good (*salus populi*), the "supreme law" 12, 336, 361, 454, 482, 592–3, 645–6, 675–6, 679–82, 733–5, 740–3, 745–6, 750–1, 759–63, 769, 876, 893; see also "general will"
conatus, striving, will to live, innate tendency of a thing to exist and enhance itself 450–1, 453, 732–3, 908, 1030–1, 1185–6
  see also Hobbes
Condé, Louis II de Bourbon, Prince de (le grand Condé) (1621–86) 294–6, 969, 978–81, 984, 987, 990, 997, 1135
  alleged discussions with Spinoza (1673) 843, 850, 990–2, 1003
  unwilling to invite Spinoza to Utrecht in his own name 979–80, 982, 990–1
Confucius (trad. 551–479 BC.), Chinese philosopher 574–5, 662, 838
consensus gentium, consensus omnium (consensus of all) 901, 907, 1008–9, 1119
[Constans, Lucius Antistius (pseud.)] *De Jure Ecclesiasticorum* (On the Rights of Ecclesiastics) (1665), anonymous radical text 32, 480–5, 556–7, 560–1, 612, 667, 776–7, 798, 975–6, 1108–9
  misattributed to Spinoza 483–5
  Spinoza denies being its author 484–5
Constantine, Roman emperor (reigned A.D. 306–337) 668–9, 694–5
Constantinople (Istanbul) 175, 567–9, 571

contingency, ruled out by Spinoza 448, 757, 905–6, 908, 1069–71
Conway, Anne (1631–79), English philosopher 45–6, 816–17, 1122, 1127–8
  combats "Spinosian philosophy" 1127–8
Conversos, see New Christians
Copernicanism (heliocentrism),
  Copernican-Galilean system of astronomy, as religious and cultural divide 249–50, 386–7, 412–13, 463, 467–8, 470–1, 522, 531, 534, 658, 793, 799, 1060–2
Cosimo III, penultimate Medici Grand Duke of Tuscany (reigned: 1670–1712) 590, 658–9, 840, 916–19
Costa, Uriel (Gabriel) da (1585–1640), Portuguese Jewish philosopher 55, 61, 70–2, 78, 89–90, 159–62, 174–5, 178, 220, 227, 294, 299, 571–2
  Exame das Tradições Phariseas [Examination of the Pharisaic Traditions] (1623) 160–1, 701
  Exemplar humanae vitae, 160–1
Craanen, Theodore (1620–88?), Leiden medical professor 776–7, 927–8, 1093, 1108, 1113–14
Craeijers (Crayer), Louis (d.1668), Spinoza's legal guardian (1655–56) 220–3
Creation, date of 659–60
Creation from nothing, or creation as a continuous process 31, 156–7, 174–5, 177–8, 302–3, 419, 428–9, 435–7, 440, 442, 545–6, 582, 609–10, 613, 617, 621–2, 659–60, 703–4, 827, 923, 1010, 1012, 1144–5
Crescas, Rabbi Hasdai (c.1340–c.1410), Catalan Jewish philosopher 174–6, 301–3, 1071–2
  Or Hashem [Light of the Lord] (1410) 302–3, 1071–2
Cromwell, Oliver (1599–1658), Lord Protector of England (1653–58) 11–12, 35, 163–5, 196–7, 240, 272, 275–6, 507–8, 679, 739, 969
  "king" without the name 679
Cudworth, Ralph (1617–88), Cambridge Neoplatonist philosopher 33, 900–1, 1043, 1066, 1123–5, 1127–8, 1130, 1190
  True Intellectual System of the Universe (1678) 1043, 1124–5
Cuffeler, Abraham Johannes (c.1637–94), Spinozist jurist and philosopher 32, 1021, 1023, 1028–30, 1047, 1208
Culemborg, province of Utrecht 600, 612, 616–20
Cumberland, Richard (1631–1718), Anglican ecclesiastic 34–5, 945–7
Curaçao (Dutch Antilles) 185, 209–10, 1161

Dale, Antonie van (1638–1708), Mennonite physician and scholar 75–6, 551–2, 644–5, 1193–4
Dalen, Antonie van, Spinozist at The Hague 30–2
Danforth, Samuel (1626–74), New England Puritan minister and astronomer 516–20
David, Biblical king (reigned: 1010–970 BC.) 669, 1065–6
De Bie, Alexander (1623–90), professor at the Amsterdam Athenaeum 186–7, 249, 251, 518
De Hooghe, Romeyn (1645–1708), Dutch engraver 129–30, 1055
  Mirror of the French Tyranny (1673) 889–90
deism, deists 34–6, 42–3, 806, 822, 1181, 1192, 1199–200
  New Christian (Marrano) deists 293, 304–6, 321–2
De Raey, Johannes (1622–1702), philosophy professor 360, 373, 427–8, 465
determinism 9–10, 236, 302, 403–4, 818–19, 822, 1020, 1068–9, 1071–2, 1199–200, 1216
Delft 458–60, 471–2, 474–6, 653–4, 871, 874–5, 884–6, 913–14
  Reformed Church consistory 476–8, 880–1
Delmedigo, Elijah (c.1458–c.1492), of Crete, Averroist philosopher 174–5, 350–1, 539–40
  "sages" and the multitude 101, 751–2
Delmedigo, Yoseph Shlomo (1591–1655), of Crete, rabbi, philosopher, and astronomer 173–9, 220, 253, 301, 304
  epistemology and science 177–9
  Sefer Elim (1629) 173, 175–9
  Abscondita Sapientiae [Ta'ahmoth Hochma] 173
  Novelat Hokhmah [Fallen Fruit of Wisdom] (1631) 177, 1079–80
democratic republicanism, Spinoza's variant 15, 36–7, 108, 171–2, 481–2, 591–3, 676, 679, 681–3, 730, 732, 736–47, 750, 753–4, 757, 760, 763–6, 768–9, 796–7, 878, 894–6
  democratic republics prize peace above war 482, 592–3, 676, 740, 763–7, 876, 881–2, 893–5
Democritus (c.460 B.C.–370), Greek pre-Socratic philosopher 508, 908–9
demons, devils and the Devil 9, 322–3, 336–7, 413–14, 440–1, 558, 582, 644–6, 793, 809, 816, 829–30, 898–901, 903–4, 912, 947–8, 1008, 1122–3, 1197–8, 1201
Denmark-Norway, kingdom of 497–8, 504–5, 510–11, 566

Denmark-Norway, kingdom of (*cont.*)
   Spinozism in 1005–6, 1176–7
Descartes, René (1596–1650), French
   philosopher 4–5, 7–8, 58–9, 62, 232–3,
   244–50, 262–3, 283–5, 290, 345, 367, 383,
   410–15, 434–5, 566–7, 626–7, 658, 823
   correspondence 5
   death in Stockholm 658, 996
   departs from his own principles 285, 371–2,
      375–6, 378, 380, 415–20, 436–7, 520
   doctrine of the (immortal) soul 430–1, 434–5,
      443–4, 793
   laws of motion, *see* motion
   legacy 1205, 1213, 1217
   matter is inert 420, 1020, 1122
   revolutionizes astronomy with
      vortices 249–50, 517–22, 563–4, 973
   revolutionizes philosophy 285, 410, 412–13,
      538–9, 548, 561–2, 578, 625, 685, 717–18,
      996, 1118
   Spinoza "reforms" in the sense of
      subverts 29–30, 250, 360–1, 381–2, 385–6,
      391, 416–20, 433–6, 449, 526, 543, 556–7,
      657–8, 729–30, 757, 802–3, 823–4, 1143–4,
      1172, 1209
   two-substance doctrine (substance
      dualism) 30, 415–17, 420, 560, 637, 639,
      794, 818–19, 823–4, 1063–4, 1199
   Letter to Voetius (1648) 339
   De Homine ed. Fl. Schuyl (1662) 424–6
   see also Cartesianism *and* motion
Desmaizeaux (or Des Maizeaux), Pierre
   (1666–1745), Huguenot editor and
   biographer of Saint-Évremond and
   Bayle 835–7, 840–3, 849, 853–4
determinism 40, 10, 236, 302, 403–4, 755–7,
   1020, 1068–72, 1115–17, 1199–200
Diderot, Denis (1713–84), French
   philosophe 4–5, 625, 740–2, 757–8, 763–8,
   857, 1017–18, 1214–16
Disaster Year (Rampjaar)(1672) 240, 655–6, 673,
   766–7, 789, 809–10, 861–75, 877–8, 882–3,
   885–6, 894, 965–6, 971–2, 977–8
   anti De Witt pamphlet offensive 870–5,
      879–81
divine providence 244, 330, 505–6, 621–2,
   663–4, 689, 721–2, 822–4, 829–30, 875–6,
   995, 1012, 1116–17, 1128, 1136–7
   Spinoza redefines 236–7, 330, 335, 420–1, 442,
      811, 1116
divinity of Christ, *see* Jesus
Doiley, Oliver (1616–63), Cambridge don 944–5,
   947, 951–2
Dordrecht 429, 847–8, 874, 884, 957–8

Downing, Sir George (c.1625–84), English
   ambassador at The Hague (1657–65)
   358 488–91, 494, 496–7, 499, 503, 592
Dryden, John (1631–1700), English poet 457,
   488–90, 493–4, 504–5, 531–2
   Annus Mirabilis (poem; 1667) 505, 531–2,
      566, 580–1, 585–6
Du Bois, Jacobus, anti-Cartesian Voetian
   preacher in Utrecht 384
Duijkerius, Johannes (c.1661–1702), Amsterdam
   schoolmaster and writer 1197–8, 1200–3
Du Ryer, André (c.1580–c. 1660), French
   translator of the Koran 340–1
Dutch East India Company (VOC) 199–200,
   488–90, 496–7, 504, 649
   and Japan 763–4
   share price movements 199–200, 489–90,
      503–4, 865–6, 1040
Dutch Republic
   Catholic minority 564–5, 800, 868, 891–2,
      964–7, 982–3, 985–6, 995–6
   defects identified by Spinoza 682–3, 741–2,
      762–3, 877–8, 882
   individual freedom and general liberty 11–12,
      109–10, 341, 650–1, 666, 672, 680–1, 738–9,
      877, 894, 1194, 1217–18
   inner political instability 12, 470–1, 341, 543,
      672, 681–2, 768–9, 804, 864–5, 878–9, 885
   Jewish prayers and vows of allegiance 164–5,
      891–2, 995–6
   religious toleration 12, 649–51, 680–1, 768–9,
      983, 985–6
   treatment of Jews 120–1, 970, 995–6
   vilified by French propaganda
      (1672–3) 969–70
Dutch Revolt against Spain (1572–1609),
   Spinoza's perspective 51–2, 103–6, 108–10,
   116, 124–5, 163–4, 666, 671–2, 676, 683
Dutch West India Company (WIC) 167–9,
   489–90, 492–3

Earbury, Mathias (1658–c.1730), Kent
   schoolmaster 722, 805, 807–8, 1192
   Deism Examin'd and Confuted (1697)
      807–8, 1192
Eede, Johannes van, Utrecht publisher 616, 618
Eighty Years War (1568-1648) 121–2, 190–1,
   233–6, 674–5, 863–4
Einstein, Albert (1879–1955), German-Jewish
   physicist 9–11, 14, 403–4, 527
Eliot, George (Mary Anne Evans), English novelist
   and translator of Spinoza 7–8, 14–15, 155,
   341, 638–9, 646–7, 735, 1205, 1219
   Silas Marner (1861) 14–15

Daniel Deronda (1876) 14–15
Middlemarch (1871–72) 14–15
Elizabeth 1, Queen of England (1533–1603; reigned 1558–1603) 93–6, 104–6
Elogios, que zelosos dedicaron a la Felice Memoria de Abraham Nuñez Bernal (1655) 315–18
Emmanuel "of Portugal," Dom (c. 1588–1636), heir of Dom António 96–7, 118
empiricism, *philosophia experimentalis* 284, 367–8, 373–4, 378, 380, 388–91, 393, 398–404, 420–1, 456–7, 510–11, 527–8, 532–3, 559, 578–9, 728–9, 900–1, 1004
English Revolution and Civil War (1642–51) 163–4, 266, 358, 679–80, 744–5
Enlightenment 3–5, 7–9, 23, 42–3, 270, 284, 367–8, 538, 563–4, 621–2, 667, 675, 730, 745–7, 754, 756, 857, 900–1, 938, 984, 1003–4, 1017–18, 1020, 1163, 1186–8, 1190, 1195–7, 1206–7
  Counter-Enlightenment 746, 1007–8, 1211–12
  see also Radical Enlightenment
Epicurus (341–270 BC), Epicureans and Epicureanism 4, 15, 34–40, 332, 350, 394, 538–9, 661–2, 730–1, 835, 837–8, 845–6, 908–9, 1017, 1117–18, 1187–8
  Spinoza rejects Epicurean non-activism 454, 1003
epistemology 329, 388–92, 410, 415–16
  Spinoza's three kinds of knowledge 179, 301, 376, 446–7
Erasmus of Rotterdam (1469–1536), Dutch humanist 203, 684–7
Ernst Augustus, Elector of Hannover (1629–98), husband of Sophia 932–3
espinas and *pardos*, *see* "thorns and meadows,"
Espiritu Santo, Fray Martín del, crypto-Jewish friar and political intermediary 123–5, 678
Evelyn, John (1620–1706), English diarist 204, 386–7
Eusebius (c. 260–340 A.D.), bishop of Caesarea 694–5
"evil" eliminated, *see* good and evil
Ezra the Scribe (480–440 B.C.), "editor" of the Old Testament 574, 691, 693, 697–702, 1030–1, 1082–4, 1106, 1120, 1133–4, 1139–40
Ezra thesis, *see* Porphyry, Ibn Hazm, Spinoza, La Peyrère, Koerbagh and Hobbes

Fabricius, Johann Ludwig (1644–1729), Swiss-German Reformed theologian 922–6, 928–9, 1168–9

Fabricius, Johann Seobald (1622–97), Heidelberg professor, brother of the above 924
Fagel, Gaspar (1634–88), Pensionary of Holland (1672–88) 25–8, 914, 992–3, 1001, 1047
Farar, David (1573–1624) (alias Francisco Lopes Henriques), Amsterdam Sephardic community leader 136–7
Fell, Margaret (1614–1702), "mother of Quakerism" 274–5, 278–9, 285
  For Menasseh-Ben Israel, the Call of the Jews out of Babylon (1656) 278
  A Loving Salutation to the Seed of Abraham (1656) 279
Ferdinand, the Cardinal-Infante (1609–41), Philip IV of Spain's younger brother, governor of the Spanish Netherlands: 1635–41) 233–6
Ferdinand II of Aragon (1452–1516), king of Aragon (and from 1475) Castile 102–3, 106, 164–5
Fernandes, Duarte (Joshua Habilho) (d.c1623), Spinoza's maternal great-grandfather 112, 114, 118–27, 133–6, 190, 678
fig and almond importing from Portugal, Spinoza family business 135, 194, 200–1, 214, 282
final causes 657–8, 1115, 1122–3, 1191
Finch, Sir John (1626–82), anatomist, physician and English resident at Florence 570–1, 578–9
First Temple Era (Temple of Solomon) (c.B.C. 950–c.586) 329–30, 334, 669, 697–8, 702, 923, 1053–4
  no divisive sects evident 700–2
Fisher, Samuel (1605–65), English Quaker leader 279–80, 285–6
Florence, Accademia di Cimento (1657–67) 244–5, 499–501, 570–1, 578–9, 916–19, 1172
  Florentine Republic 481–2, 658–9
Four Days' Battle, near the Thames Estuary (11–14 June 1666) 580–1
Fraenkel, Carlos 174–5, 709n97, 1010n18
Franco-Dutch war (1672–78) 42–3, 850, 861–8, 963–5, 1000, 1003, 1005, 1051–2, 1101–2
Franco Mendes, David (1713–92), chronicler of the Amsterdam Sephardi community 59, 61–2, 73–4, 77–8, 218–19
Franeker University 547–8, 600–1, 935, 976–7, 1064
Frederik Hendrik, Prince of Orange, (Stadholder: 1625–47) 51–2, 162–3, 233–4, 237–8, 671–2, 920–1

"freedom [libertas]" in Spinoza contrasted with the "freedom" of Hobbes 591, 726–7, 729–31, 734–8, 740–2, 749–51, 754–7, 763–4, 767, 877, 1071–2, 1216
freedom of expression and to criticize 743, 746–7, 754–5, 772, 796–7
freedom of thought (to philosophize) 17–18, 341, 474, 741, 743, 746–7, 753–5, 772, 778, 796, 924–5,
  States of Holland regulates (1656 and 1675) imposing limits Cartesians accept 789, 810–11, 826
freedom to publish 143, 330–1, 405–6, 650–1, 735–6, 935–6
Free Will, Descartes on 391, 418–21, 430–2, 435, 448, 755, 757, 1094, 1199
  eliminated by Spinoza 418–19, 430, 432, 435, 442–3, 448–9, 606–7, 757, 1020, 1093–5
Freud, Sigmund (1856–1939), founder of psychology 9–10
Freudenthal, Jacob (1839–1907), Silesian Jewish Spinoza scholar 1035–6, 1221–2
Friesland 149, 238, 384, 515, 564–5, 681, 782
  provincial States 471–2, 547–8, 1199
  Reformed Church Synod 948–50, 1064, 1200–1
Froude, James Anthony (1818–94), English historian 1219–20
Fullana, Don Nicolau D'Oliver y (Daniel Judah) (1623–c.1698), Sephardic senior military officer, assisted by Spinoza 875, 882–3, 887–92
"Further Reformation" (De Nadere Reformatie) 290–1, 506, 867, 1039, 1050, 1052

Galen, Christoph Bernhard von (1606–78), prince-bishop of Münster (1650–78) 513–14, 529–30, 566, 575–6, 591–2, 739, 863, 963–4
Galenus Abrahamsz de Haan (1622–1706), Collegiant leader 268–73, 277, 280–1, 285–6, 814, 822–3, 1051
Galileo Galilei (1564–1642), astronomer 173, 175–9, 412–13, 464, 519–20, 522, 532–4, 553–4, 563–4, 578–9, 625, 630, 658–9, 686
Gallois, Abbé Jean (1632–1707), French scholar and editor 41–2, 44, 1108–9, 1113–14
Garces, Henrique (Baruch Senior) (d.1619), Spinoza's maternal grandfather after whom he was named "Baruch" 83–5, 112–15, 122–5, 127–9, 131–2, 142, 144, 678
Gelderland, province 980–2, 1000
  Reformed Synod 962, 1014–15, 1200–1

general will 341, 349–50, 482, 681–3, 726–7, 730, 740–2, 744–5, 760, 763–4, 768, 876, 896–7, 1148
Geneva 106–7, 682–3, 742–3, 762–3, 983
Genoa, as defective aristocratic republic 109, 481–2, 682–3, 737–8, 762–3, 877
Gent, Pieter van (1640–95), assistant editor of Spinoza's works 52–3, 379, 1042–3, 1049, 1057–8, 1093–4, 1165–6, 1168–70, 1175, 1185
Gentman, Cornelis (1616–96), Voetian preacher 429–30, 472–3, 998–1000
geometric order (*ordo geometricus*) 329, 333, 336–7, 361–2, 410, 415–16, 433, 439, 461–2, 578–9, 614–15, 657–8, 716, 799–800, 1026
Gersonides (or Levi ben Gershom)(1288–1344), Jewish philosopher 156–7, 175–6, 178, 301, 306–7, 479, 537, 1217
Geulincx, Arnold (1624–69), Cartesian philosopher at Leiden 362, 1019–20, 1023–4
ghosts and apparitions 9, 816, 902–7, 1017, 1122–3
Gijsen, Alewijn (d.1683), patron of Spinoza, husband of Trijntje 498–9, 648–9, 1150
Glazemaker, Jan Hendriksz. (c.1619–82), ex-Collegiant freethinker and translator of Descartes 236–7, 247–51, 299, 354, 359–60, 506, 538n8, 636–7, 640, 865–6, 937, 955–61, 1057–8, 1160, 1165–9, 1199–200
"Glorious Revolution" of 1688–91 in Britain and Ireland 11–12, 276, 768–9, 807–8, 1018, 1036–7, 1129, 1188–90, 1192
God or Nature (Deus sive natura) 30–1, 250–1, 302, 331, 335, 361, 439–40, 452–3, 619, 707, 755–7, 811, 818–19, 1010, 1034–5, 1048–9, 1066–7, 1069, 1085–6
Goeree, Willem (1635–1711), antiquarian and writer on art 545, 622, 642–6
Goethals, Johannes (1611–73), Voetian Reformed preacher at Delft 476–7, 486, 874
Goethe, Johann Wolfgang von (1749–1832) 4–5, 7–10, 1205
good and bad, or good and evil 6–7, 283, 335–6, 421–2, 426–7, 453–4, 510, 613, 732–3, 758, 1016, 1122–3
good citizens rare 760
good works 802, 910–11
Gorcum (Gorinchem) 901–3, 915
Gospels, *see* New Testament
Goyen, Jan van (1596–1656), artist 467, 654–6
Graevius, Johann Georg (1632–1703), German classical scholar and Utrecht professor 353–4, 517–18, 771, 776–7, 783–4, 786–9, 793–4, 800–1, 804–5, 809, 963, 971–4, 1000, 1002, 1005, 1045–6, 1110–11

invites Spinoza to Utrecht 978–80, 982, 988–9, 992–4, 996–8
Oratio de Cometis [About Comets] (1665) 517–18, 553–4, 973
"Great Assembly [Knesset ha-Godolah]," of 120 scribes, sages and prophets (5th or 4th century BC.) 699–701
"Great Jewish Revolt" against Rome of 66–74 A.D 77–8, 698–9
Gregorian Calendar, replaces Julian Calendar, *see* calendar
Grew, Nehemiah (1641–1712), English microscopist and botanist 1162–3, 1193
Cosmologia sacra (1701) 1162–3, 1193–4
Groningen, city 557, 942–4
Province 199–200, 384, 515, 564–5, 600–1, 782
Reformed Synod 782, 1200–1
University 272–3, 384, 543–5, 557–8, 791–4, 799, 865–6, 976–7
Gronovius, Johann Friedrich (1611–71), classical philologist and editor 334, 360, 373, 575, 800
Grotius, Hugo (1583–1645), Dutch humanist, jurist and Bible critic 120–1, 297, 599–600, 671–2, 681
Bible criticism 684–8, 703, 706–7, 720, 731, 820–2, 1090–1
God's justice 689, 722–3, 735–6
Socinian leanings 688–9, 817–18, 820, 879–80
Guadaleste, marqués de, Philip III's minister in Brussels 119–22, 125–7
Guerra, Don Joseph, Canary Islands merchant in Amsterdam 310–12, 314–15
Guez de Balzac, Jean Louis (1597–1654), French writer 677–8
Gundling, Niklaus Hieronymus (1671–1729), German savant 832–3

Haarlem 780, 866–7, 1051
Hague, The, 264 478, 495, 502, 648, 654–7, 663, 665–6, 681, 837, 883–4, 889–90, 915–16, 993–4, 1024, 1028, 1058, 1164
air quality 352–3, 652–4
apothecaries 654, 1150
Binnenhof 652–3, 892
bookshops 24, 654, 812, 892
civic militia 654, 880–1, 884
Heilige Geesthofje [Holy Ghost court] 654–5, 1150
Hof van Holland 24, 296, 477–8, 777–8, 782–4
Hooge Raad 221–2
Huygens' town house (Mauritshuis) 652–4
murder of the De Witts (20 Aug. 1672) 883–4
New Church (Nieuwe Kerk) 652–3, 1156–8

Noordeinde Palace 477–8, 653–4, 1027–8
Paviljoensgracht 652–5, 1021, 1059, 1150, 1161–2, 1164, 1220–1
population 654
Reformed consistory 24, 291, 780–1, 880–1, 1027–8, 1043–6, 1059, 1171
Stille Veerkade 652
Walloon Church 847–8
Halevi, Judah (1075–1141) of Toledo, poet and Hebraist 1077–8
Sefer ha-Kuzari (c.1140) 1077–8, 1081–2
Halma, François (1653–1722), Utrecht publisher 63–5, 227, 315, 319, 964, 984, 1152–3, 1197, 1199–200
Het Leven van B. de Spinoza, (1698) 63, 991–2, 1194, 1197
"happiness" and "sadness," 7, 100–1, 109, 216, 289–90, 336, 343–4, 361, 373–4, 378, 387, 391, 448–9, 451–3, 457–8, 562, 611, 613–14, 626, 638–9, 647, 673–4, 678–9, 730–1, 735–7, 758, 1028, 1208
Hanover, court of 921–2, 926–8, 930–1
Hasmonaean Jewish Republic (c. 165–63 B.C.) 163–4, 760–2
hatred is never good 13–16, 278, 287, 359–60, 367–8, 505–6, 508–9, 765
Heaven redefined 361, 440–1, 543–4, 608, 613, 663, 816
Hebrew alphabet, Paleo-Hebrew 1080–3
Hebrew studies (Christian) 784–5, 804–5, 808–10, 1075–6, 1082–3, 1090–1, 1103
Hebrew monarchy (ancient Israelite kings), commencing with Saul 575, 592–4, 669–70, 745, 760–1
Hebrew Republic, ancient, political Hebraism 172–3, 574–5, 592–3, 668–70, 680, 737, 743–5, 760–1, 1056, 1074–5, 1089–91
free from divisive sects 760–1
Heereboord, Adriaan (1614–61), Leiden philosophy professor 283–4, 385–6, 420, 427–8, 435, 600–1, 1046
Heidanus (van Heiden), Abraham (1597–1678), Leiden theology professor 283–4, 373, 383–4, 429–30, 435, 437, 471, 557, 575, 600–1, 810–11, 976, 1027, 1046–7, 1060
Heidegger, Johann Heinrich (1633–98), Swiss Reformed theologian 550, 695–6, 922–3, 925
Heidelberg University 791–2, 915–16, 919–22, 924–6
Heinsius, Daniel (1580–1655), historian and exegete 703–4, 837, 941–2
"Hell" redefined 354–5, 361, 440–1, 543–4, 608, 663, 816, 912, 1201

Helmont, Francis Mercurius van (1614–99), Flemish alchemist and Christian Kabbalist 1127
Helvetius, Johannes Fridericus (Johann Friedrich Schweitzer)(1630–1709), anti- Cartesian physician and alchemist 662–4, 1024–6
Henri IV, king of France (reigned: 1589–1610) 88, 93–9, 104–5, 123–4
Henrietta Maria, Queen of England (1609–69) 51, 162–4
Henríquez, Enrique (1536–1608), Jesuit professor at Salamanca 90–2, 128–9, 678
herem, in Dutch Sephardic society 70–1, 77–8, 140–1, 161, 179–80, 225–7, 312, 571–3, 832
   Juan de Prado under 55, 78, 227, 308–9, 315
   Lopo Ramires (David Curiel) 65–7, 225–6
   Uriel da Costa 78, 159–61, 303
   Spinoza (July 1656) 55, 67, 71–5, 77–8, 148–9, 184–5, 209–11, 226–7, 229–30, 303, 1011
Hevelius, Johann (1611–87), astronomer at Danzig 285, 516–17, 520, 526
"highest good (summum bonum)" 259, 343–4, 374, 733–6, 739, 741–2, 762–4, 767, 1014–15, 1017
highest happiness [summa felicitas] 336, 343–4, 373–4, 387, 562, 611, 613, 638, 750–1
highest human perfection [suma humana perfectionis] 322, 343–4
Hobbes, Thomas (1588–1679) 4, 7–9, 23–4, 34–5, 37, 40, 42–4, 336–7, 494, 543–5, 602, 616–17, 679–82, 729–31, 736–41, 743–4, 794, 900, 937–8, 952, 1092
   anti-experimentalism 400–1, 559
   Bible criticism 9, 298, 602, 610–11, 684–5, 688–9, 691–3, 695–6, 701–2, 705–8, 720–3, 725–8, 900, 912, 1090–1, 1187–8, 1191–2
   bracketed in notoriety with Spinoza 720–2, 729–31, 776–7, 794, 796–7, 1130, 1195–6
   censorship 721–2, 729–30, 733–4, 747, 768
   church doctrine fixed by the sovereign 721–2, 725–30, 733–4, 740, 743–4, 747, 833
   conatus 450–1, 732–3
   considered Spinoza's chief source 34, 694, 701–2, 721–2, 732, 776–7, 804–5, 945–7, 1021, 1103–4, *see also* Leibniz
   education, views on 258–9, 727–9, 734
   Ezra thesis 691–3, 695–7, 701–2
   miracles 727–9, 1129–30
   monarchy 35–6, 38–9, 575–6, 602–4, 679–80, 686–7, 730–1, 733–4, 738–40, 742, 768, 839–40, 875
   psychology of perception and ideas 445–6, 450–1, 482–3, 722–3, 726–7, 732–3, 899–900
   political theory 104–5, 576, 675–6, 722, 725–6, 729–30, 740–3, 745–7
   social contract 736–7, 749–50
   Spinoza subverts 104–5, 301, 681–2, 720, 729–30, 738, 742, 746–7, 751–4, 768, 805, 876, 892–4, 900, 912
   De Cive 720, 731–2, 738
   Leviathan, Dutch language version (1667) 28n18, 480, 599–600, 720–2, 731–2, 738–9, 741, 783–4, 867–8, 872, 912, 1051, 1130–1
Holmes, Sir Robert (1622–92), English naval commander 489–90, 492, 520–1
"Holmes Bonfire" at Terschelling (19 and 20 August 1666) 582–5
Holy Ghost (Sanctus Spiritus), as guide to true understanding 267, 270, 548–51, 554, 663, 710–11, 716, 816–17, 831–2
Holy Land (Palestine) 146–7, 163–4, 207, 271–2, 294–6, 572–3, 660–1, 698, 1054, 1090, 1135, 1140–1
Hooke, Robert (1635–1703), English astronomer 387–9, 393, 499–501, 566–7
Horowitz, Rabbi Shabtai Sheftel (1592–1660) 150–2
Horn, Ignác (1825–75), Hungarian-Jewish scholar and revolutionary 1217
Houbraken, Arnold (1666–1719) Dutch artist and writer on art 640–1, 645–6
Howe, John (1630–1705), English Puritan (Baxterite) theologian 35, 37, 45–6, 1125–6, 1206
Hudde, Johannes (1628–1704), Amsterdam burgomaster, mathematician and optics expert 248–51, 383–6, 406–7, 468, 521–5, 590–1, 618, 640, 657, 659, 927–8, 1052–3, 1057–8, 1107–8, 1113–14
"great telescope" (forty-foot) constructed with Spinoza's help 521–3
Huet, Pierre-Daniel (1630–1721), French churchman and savant 23–4, 42, 44–6, 202–3, 244–5, 695, 846–7, 921–2, 927–8, 930, 1099–103, 1107, 1134–5, 1141, 1147
   accuses Spinoza of plagiarizing from Hobbes and La Peyrère 1103–4, 1110
   Demonstratio evangelica (1679) 42 644–5, 1073, 1102–6, 1110–12, 1134–5, 1193–4
humility, not a virtue 223–4, 453–4, 638–9, 758–9, 1090
Huygens, Christiaan (1629–95), Dutch scientist 41–2, 249–51, 365–8, 415–16, 457, 462–4, 525, 591, 652–3, 656, 659, 915–16, 927–8, 1096–8, 1168–9

astronomical telescopes 358-9, 366, 462-3, 522-5
condescending towards Spinoza 464-6, 523-5
dialogue with Spinoza 460-1, 463-5, 468, 500-1, 517, 528-9, 1049
pendulums, longitude research 511-13, 516, 520-1, 1113-14
revises Descartes' "laws of motion,", *see*, motion, laws of
Spinoza considers self-promoting 464-5, 510-11
Huygens, Constantijn (the Younger) (1628-97), brother of Christiaan, optics expert 32-3, 358-9, 462-3, 524-5, 914, 979-80, 988-9, 1066-7, 1113-14
Huygens, Lodewijk (1631-99), younger brother of Christiaan and Constantijn the Younger 462-3, 915

Ibn Ezra, Abraham (1089-1167), medieval Andalusian Jewish Bible commentator 156-7, 304, 479, 696-7, 1080, 1103
Ibn Hazm, Abu Muhammed of Córdoba (994-1064), Jewish convert to Islam, Bible critic 693-4
ignorance, as basis of servitude and despotism 8, 12, 16, 18, 20, 99-101, 105-8, 278, 284, 323-4, 339, 483, 611, 626, 675-6
imagination, Spinoza on 495-6, 906, 1085-6
Immaculate Conception 31, 266-7, 344-5, 611, 663, 1088
immortality of the soul 160, 162, 294, 306-7, 322-3, 376, 508-9, 701, 792-3, 928-9, 1116-17, 1121-2, 1186, 1199-201
Incarnation, in Christian theology 358, 811, 1066-8, 1088, 1107-8
Inquisition, the 12, 83-6, 93, 95-6, 100, 108, 127, 157, 165-7, 169-70, 192-3, 267-8, 299, 313, 680-1, 739, 1008, 1174-8, 1187
 regional tribunals 85-6, 114, 153-4, 184, 380, 1005-6, 1171, 1175, 1181
Islam, Spinoza's view of 13-14, 287-8, 577, 708, 827-8, 846-7, 1014-15
Isaiah, the Prophet (8th cent. BC) 706, 832-3, 1055-6
Israelites, *see* Hebrew Republic

Jamaica 491, 1055, 1161
James the Apostle 910-11, 1086-7
Janet, Paul (1823-99), French philosophy professor 1217-18
Jelles (or Jellesz), Jarig (c.1620-83), Spinoza's Collegiant friend and editor 217, 248, 262-4, 268-70, 278, 280-1, 285-7, 333-4,
350, 354, 356, 362, 461, 601-2, 615-16, 651, 662-3, 711-12, 726, 732, 738-9, 822, 955-7, 1112, 1203
 assists with publishing Spinoza's works 956-8, 1166
 backs Spinoza and Spinozists financially 427, 1166, 1185
 'Preface' to the *Opera Posthuma* 62, 223, 262, 352, 385, 850, 944, 1167-8, 1170
Jenkes, Henry (d. 1697), Cambridge don 950-2
Jenichen, Gottlob Friedrich (1680-1735), Lutheran theologian at Leipzig 45-6
Jesuits 35, 38-9, 90-2, 170, 232, 238, 954, 965-7, 981, 1098, 1122
Jesus Christ (c. 4BC-c.AD 33) 10, 44, 90, 273, 417, 541, 543-4, 569-70, 639, 646, 671, 793-4, 909
 did not expiate men's sins 266-7, 614, 689-90, 723, 811, 827-8, 1008-9, 1034-5, 1069
 established no theology, church, or ceremonies 266-8, 277, 281, 480-1, 543-4, 577, 611, 723, 725, 779, 872, 910-11, 1089, 1132
 used untruth against superstition 645, 911-12
 First Coming 827-8, 1138, 1193-4
 illegitimate birth, father unknown 611, 619, 775-6, 1049, 1065-6
 nowhere foretold in the Hebrew Bible 614-16, 619, 775-6, 1102-3, 1105-6
 "redeemer" of men, but purely by teaching 611, 721-3, 725
 Second Coming 167, 551, 568-70, 573-4, 817
 and "Three Impostors" legend 317
 see also "spirit of Christ"
Jews, Jewish people, not "chosen" or elected by God 131-2, 287-8, 359-60, 573, 699, 1008-9
 military prowess lost but recoverable 131-2, 888, 891-2
João IV, king of Portugal (reigned: 1640-56) 165-8, 170, 175
Johann Friedrich, Duke of Brunswick-Lüneburg (1625-79: ruled: 1665-79), Leibniz's employer after his Paris period 926-31, 1113-15, 1117, 1147
Josephus, Titus Flavius (Joseph ben Matthias) (Yosef ben Mattityahu)(c.37-c.100 AD.) 171-2, 479, 697-701, 1053-4, 1106, 1110-11, 1114, 1135, 1139
 Antiquities (93-94 A.D.) 697-8, 701-2, 1111
 De Bello Judaico 698
 Testimonium Flavium 1102-3, 1111, 1135

Joshua (d.c 1250 B.C.), Moses' successor 72–3, 294–6, 387–8, 533, 695–6, 706, 745, 996
Judaism and Jewish history, in Spinoza's thought 13–14, 317, 320–1, 359–60, 699–700, 1056, 1067, 1087–9
Judas Maccabeus (190 B.C.–160), leader of the Maccabean Revolt against the Seleucids 51–2, 163–4, 660–1, 702
Julian "the Apostate (331–63 AD.)," Roman emperor (ruled: 361–63 AD.) 485, 1134
Julius Caear (B.C. 100–44) 906–7, 1008–9
Justel, Henri (1619–93), French Huguenot scholar 44–5, 237–8, 837, 1102, 1112, 1115, 1141
justice and charity, as basis of "true religion" 17–18, 155, 264–5, 277, 826–7, 837, 840, 1088, 1116–17, 1123–4, 1169–70
Juvenal (Decimus Junius Juvenalis)(late 1st century -early 2nd century AD), Roman poet and satirist 29, 788–9

Kabbalah (Cabbala) 136, 177–8, 203, 844–5, 1127
Christian Kabbalism 1127
Kakotegnus, picaresque novel by J. Roodenpoort 1201–2
Kaplan, Yosef, historian of Dutch Sephardi Jewry 61–2, 128–9, 131, 321–2
Karaites, Karaism, medieval-early modern Jewish sect 156, 173–4, 177, 304, 320–1
Karl Ludwig, Elector Palatine (1617–80; ruled: 1648–80) 915–16, 919–25
Kepler, Johannes, (1571–1630) German astronomer 400, 404, 412–13, 517, 520–2, 531–4, 611
Kerckring (also Kerckrinck), Theodor (1638–93), Amsterdam physician and anatomist 243, 259–60, 347–9, 352–3, 359, 368–9, 385–6
eye dissections 345, 348–9
marries Van den Enden's daughter, *see* Clara Maria van den Enden
Specilegium anatomicum (1670) 345, 348–9
Ketteringh, Ida Margareta, Van der Spijck's wife, Spinoza's landlady during his last years 187–8, 1149–50, 1152, 1155
Kidder, Richard (1633–1703), bishop of Bath and Wells 9, 1141, 1190–1
Klever, Wim, Spinoza scholar 254–5, 293, 424, 710, 719
Knol, Jan (d.1672), Amsterdam Anti-Trinitarian Collegiant preacher 263–4, 277, 286–8, 779
Knorr, Christian Friedrich (1646–1704), German Lutheran theologian 812–13
Knutzen, Matthias (1646–?), German atheist author 813

Koekoecx-Zangh van de Nachtuylen (1677), polemical pamphlet 606–7, 632–5, 825–6
Koelman, Jacobus (1632–95), Voetian theologian 548, 691–2, 1210–11
Koerbagh, Adriaan ("Vreederijk Waarmond [Peaceful Mouth of Truth]" (1633–69), physician and Spinoza disciple 248, 263–4, 269–70, 285, 350, 373, 381–2, 537, 543, 546–7, 560–3, 581–2, 600–18, 644–5, 670–1, 718, 747, 827, 1034–5, 1146–7, 1183–4
antipathy to nobility and elites 602–4, 807
critique of Socinianism 545–6, 615–16
Ezra thesis 691–3, 1030–1
no existing church is the "true universal church," 287, 725
publishes key elements of Spinoza's philosophy 350, 447, 562, 581–2, 600, 610, 613–14, 621–2, 1030
Spinoza's complicity 545, 619–20
trial, imprisonment and death 617–18, 620–3, 772–3, 786, 1044–5
unHobbesian perspectives 336–7, 602–4, 610, 616–17, 747
Bloemhof van allerley Lieflijkheid (1668) 427, 432–3, 602–4, 609–13, 618, 691–2, 772, 778, 898–9
Een Licht schijnende in duystere plaatsen [A Light Shining in Dark Places] (1668) 447, 572–3, 581–2, 608, 610–12, 670–1, 695, 778–9, 898–9
Koerbagh, Johannes (1634–72), brother and ally of Adriaan 245, 263–4, 269–70, 285, 287–8, 350, 373, 379, 381–2, 537, 543–5, 600, 607–9, 612–13, 616, 618, 620, 644
complicity in Adriaan' books 618–21
converted to Spinozism 543–6, 607–9
Königsmarck, Kurt Christoph von (1634–73), Swedish general 886–9
Koran (Quran) 340–1, 351, 359–60, 693, 825, 954
Kortholt, Christian (1633–94), theologian at Kiel, designates Spinoza "impostor omnium maximum [the greatest impostor of all]," 328–9, 1164
Kortholt, Sebastian (1675–1760), Kiel University professor and biographer of Spinoza 187–8, 328–9, 1145, 1167, 1208–9
Kossmann, Ernst, intellectual historian 8
Kuyper, Frans (1629–92), anti-philosophical Collegiant leader 45–6, 285–6, 814–20, 899, 1132
Arcana Atheismi (1676) 816–17, 952–3
Den Philosopherenden Boer [The Philosophizing Farmer](1676–77) 815–16, 1008, 1010

Labadie, Jean de (1610–74), Huguenot theologian 552–3, 555–7
La Court, Johan de (1622–60), Dutch political thinker 259, 481–3, 732, 742, 769, 1194
  Consideratien van staat ofte poityke weeg-schaal (1661) 481–2
La Court, Pieter de (1618–85), Dutch political thinker 259, 382, 481–6, 590, 729–31, 734–5, 737–8, 740, 742, 769, 1108
  monarchy rejected, the democratic republic embraced 481–3, 590, 599–600, 664–7, 682, 730–1, 1194
  Interest van Holland (1662) 483–4, 879–80
  Aanwysing der heilsame politike Gronden (1669) 664–5, 1047–8
Lairesse, Gérard de (1640–1711), artist in Amsterdam 630, 640–1, 645–6
Lamy, Dom François (1636–1711), French Benedictine theologian 44–6, 1142
Land, J.P.N. (1834–97), edited the 1882 edition of Spinoza's Collected Works 944, 1220–1
Lantman, Thaddeus de (also De Landman) (1622–81), Reformed preacher at Delft and The Hague 476–8, 486, 530–1, 822–3, 1029–30, 1050
  incites the common people against the De Witt regime 478, 486, 866–7, 872–4, 998–1000
  targets Spinoza 476–7, 486–7, 1045, 1059
La Peyrère, Isaac (1596–76), Bible commentator 9, 44, 227–8, 293–9, 301, 612, 658–61, 685, 691–3, 701–4, 725, 806, 820–1, 990–1, 1103
  Ezra thesis 691–2, 695–6, 701–2
  Prae-Adamitae, [Men before Adam](1655) 9, 294–6, 773–5, 806
"large governing councils" rather than "small councils," recommended 736, 742–3, 745–6, 762–3, 861–3, 876, 882, 886–7, 893–5
Latitudinarianism, *see* Anglican Church
Lavater, Ludwig (1527–86), Swiss theologian 904–7
Le Boë Sylvius, Franciscus De (1614–72), Leiden professor of medicine 334, 347, 370–1, 373, 575, 800, 939–42
Le Clerc, Jean (1657–1736), Remonstrant theologian and Bible critic 3–4, 45–6, 559, 686–9, 1017–18, 1057, 1103, 1131, 1135, 1195–6
  veiled anti-Spinoza strategy 830, 1131, 1141, 1188–9, 1208–9, 1213–14
  Sentiments de Quelques Théologiens de Hollande (1685) 688, 1131

Leenhof, Frederik van (1647–1715), crypto-Spinozist Reformed preacher 76–7, 642, 832–3, 1004, 1016–17, 1208
Leeuwenhoek, Antonie van (1632–1723), microscopist, discoverer of bacteria, sperm cells and blood cells, 525 659, 927–8, 1107–8, 1113–14, 1191, 1193
Leibniz, Gottfried Wilhelm (1646–1716), German philosopher 4–5, 7–8, 21–2, 41, 45, 236, 427–8, 483–4, 537–8, 551, 558–9, 926–9, 1073, 1112, 1117–18, 1136, 1147, 1151
  ambivalent on censorship 809, 930, 1117
  anti-Cartesianism 809, 929–30, 932–3, 1101, 1105, 1108, 1116–17, 1147
  correspondence 5, 1092, 1099, 1113–14, 1118, 1166, 1213–14
  corresponds with Spinoza 657, 773–5, 784, 928–9, 1112, 1166–7, 1178–80
  defends Christian Trinity and "mysteries" 808, 927–31, 1092–3, 1100–1, 1107–8, 1115–16, 1149, 1205
  encounter with Oldenburg (1676) 1107–8, 1112–13
  encounter with Spinoza at The Hague (1676) 314, 1098, 1108–10, 1113
  encounter with Steno 801–2, 920, 928–30, 1115
  encounter with Van den Enden 1098–9
  fascination for Spinoza's *Ethics* 930, 1097–9, 1110, 1115–16, 1171–2, 1178–9
  fascination for the TTP 23–4, 773–7, 804–6, 808–10, 830, 927–8, 1068, 1102–3
  God chooses what is best 302–3, 421, 657–8, 931, 1115–17
  innovative conservatism 808–9, 1118
  rejects Spinoza's Ezra thesis 697
  researches Spinoza and his circle 483–4, 537–8, 552, 558–9, 609–10, 704–5, 776–7, 785–6, 789, 795, 801–2, 1092–3, 1097–8, 1111–13
  ties Spinoza to Hobbes 1112–13
  visits Holland (1676) 538, 662–3, 884, 927–30
  New Essays (1704) 1115
  Theodicy (1710) 537–8, 1097–8, 1109–10, 1147
Leiden 120–1, 357–8, 368–9, 373, 495, 580, 654, 1050
  anatomical theatre 368–9, 371–4
  bookshops 25, 780
  city government 25, 192, 292, 356–8, 486, 780, 783, 885–6, 913–14
  hortus botanicus 368–9, 372–3, 424

Leiden (*cont.*)
  Reformed Church consistory 24–5, 780, 1050, 1059
  Spinoza at 242–3, 245, 247, 264, 354, 356, 363, 372–3, 380, 382–3, 425–6, 545, 559
  student body and accommodation 368–9, 600
  University 291–2, 368–9, 371–2, 378–9, 382–4, 425–6, 600–1, 989, 1020, 1046–9, 1059–60, 1201–2
Leipzig University 795, 804
Leon Templo, Rabbi Judah (1603–75) 163–4, 172–3, 271–2, 334, 346–7, 549–50, 1055
  Retrato del Templo de Selomoh (1642) 171–3
  Sefer Tavnit Hekhal [Book of the Image of the Temple](1650) 1055
Leopold I (1658–1705), Holy Roman Emperor 850, 963–5, 981–2, 1000, 1039–40
Lessing, Gotthold Ephraim (1729–81) 4–5, 9–10, 1017–18, 1205, 1216, 1219
Leupenius, Petrus (1607–70), Reformed minister at Amsterdam 543–4, 607–8
Le Vassor, Father Michel (c.1648–1718), French Oratorian who converted to Anglicanism 43–6, 842, 1073, 1141–2, 1152
  De la Véritable Religion (1689) 1141–2
Levita, Elia (1468–1549) doyen of Hebrew grammarians 703, 1075–7, 1081, 1139–40
  Sefer ha-Dikduk [Book of Grammar] 1075–6
Lewes, George Henry (1817–78), philosopher, critic and partner of George Eliot 1219-21
Leydekker, Melchior (1642–1721), Reformed theologian 291–2, 322–3, 1004
Limborch, Philippus van (1633–1712), Remonstrant theologian 25, 560, 621–2, 686–7, 832–3, 840, 846–7, 1034–5, 1131, 1197–8
  Dutch toleration excessive 945, 1057
  orchestrates Remonstrant campaign against Spinoza 830–2, 944–5, 950–3, 1057
  Theologia Christiana (1686) 1057
limpieza de sangre [purity of blood] statutes, in Spain, Portugal and Ibero-America 80–2, 90–1
Lipsius, Justus (1547–1607), Flemish Catholic Renaissance humanist scholar 566–7, 751–2
Livorno (Tuscany) 151, 199–200, 208–10, 316–18, 570–1, 579–80, 918
Locke, John (1632–1704), English philosopher 30, 39, 284, 390–1, 427–8, 555, 559–60, 708, 814, 830, 901, 946–7, 964–5, 1004
  legacy 1205, 1213–14

supra rationem (above reason) 555, 560, 722–3, 727, 900–1, 1213–14
Loevesteiners, "Loevestein faction," 483–4, 672–3, 681, 867, 870–1, 879–80, 883, 965, 982, 1001
London 38, 193–4, 196–7, 206, 332, 488–9, 502–3, 580, 585, 649–50, 1053
  book shops and book distribution 585, 948
  coffee houses 359, 457, 495, 1192
  Covent Garden 457, 512–13
  Exchange 497, 586, 590
  "Great Fire" (2-7 September 1666) 584–5, 649–50
  Great Plague (1665–66) 501, 503, 564–5, 580–1
  London Bridge 1052
  Royal Society 363–7, 386–91, 393, 405, 492–3, 503–4, 511–12, 563, 565–6, 577–8
  St Paul's Cathedral 584–5
  Tower of London 582–3, 588–9
  Whitehall 196–7, 516, 584–5
Lopes Suasso, Antonio (Isaac Israel) (1614-85), Baron Avernas le Gras 213–14, 571–2
Louis XIV, king of France (1638–1715; reigned: 1643–1715) 11–12, 105–7, 575–6, 580–1, 591–3, 649, 664–5, 680–1, 752, 848–9, 861–3, 887, 986, 995, 1136–7
  contempt for the Dutch Republic 566, 849, 861–3, 871
  forbids teaching of Cartesianism in France 1105
  invades the Dutch Republic (1672–3) 838–9, 850, 863–5, 868–70, 978–9, 982, 1000
  invades the Spanish Netherlands (1667–8) 587–8, 590–1, 594–5, 649–50, 861–3
  persecutes Huguenots 88, 839, 863, 1194–5, 1211–12
  persecutes Jansenists 863, 1136–7
Lowestoft, Battle of (13 June (O.S. 3 June) 1665 502–4
Lucas, Jean-Maximilien (d.1697), French journalist designated the "first biographer" of Spinoza 63, 179, 231, 352–3, 484, 846n39, 849–51, 857, 1058
  La Vie de Monsieur Benoit de Spinosa 850, 853–4
Lucian of Samosata, (c.Ad. 125- after 180), ancient satirist 1031–2
Lucretius (Titus Lucretius Carus)(c.99–c.55 B.C.), Roman philosopher-poet 908–9, 1187–8, 1190–1, 1195–6
Luxembourg, François Henri de Montmorency, duc de (1628–95), French commander 889–90, 968, 988, 1051–2

Machiavelli, Niccolò (1469-1527), Florentine
political thinker 9, 29, 67-8, 107, 485-6,
558, 575, 592, 625, 673-6, 731
citizen soldiers 882
Roman Republic admired 575, 679-80
Magalotti, Lorenzo (1637-1712), secretary of the
Florentine Accademia del Cimento 658-9,
916-19, 928-9
magic, and sorcery 9, 413-14, 440-2, 644-6,
899-900, 1197-8
Mahamad, Sephardic community board of
governors (*parnasim*) 73-4, 129-30, 135-7,
144, 162, 168, 206-7, 209-12, 214-15, 218,
224, 226-7, 293, 308, 317-19, 571-2
Maimonides (Moses ben Maimon) (1138-1204)
medieval Jewish philosopher 18-19, 101,
155-7, 301-3, 350-1, 539-40, 542, 670-1,
676, 700, 1217
concept of God 155-6
sages and the multitude 675-6, 751-2
Spinoza criticizes 155-6, 700, 706, 716-17,
825-6
Malebranche, Nicolas (1638-1715),
philosopher 44-5, 1137, 1141-2
Mansvelt, Regnerus van (1639-1671), Cartesian
philosophy professor at Utrecht 45-6, 534,
786-9, 791-4, 820, 976
Adversus anonymum Theologico-politicum
(1674) 789, 794, 809-12, 986, 996-7,
1025-6, 1046-8, 1093, 1146-7
Maresius (Des Marets), furore Samuel
(1599-1673), Reformed theologian at
Groningen 199-200, 272-3, 296-8, 545, 552,
557-8, 575, 600-1, 784-5, 791-4, 811-12
feud with Cartesians 791-3, 799, 976-7, 1093
reconciliation with Voetius 557-8, 792-3, 799
De Abusu philosophiae Cartesianae
(1670) 557, 799
martyrdom, Spinoza's perspective 11-12, 88-9,
100-1, 121, 153-4, 157, 315-16, 509, 577,
615, 804-5, 931
Mary, mother of Jesus, Mariology or study of
Mary 234-6, 339-40, 344-5, 646, 663,
912, 1049
Masaniello (1642-47), leader of the 1647
Neapolitan popular revolt 285, 466-8, 630-1
Masoretic Era, Jewish scribal tradition of 6th to
10th century AD., 297 660-1, 693n29,
702-3, 809-10, 1081-3
Mastricht, Petrus van (1630-1706) 538-9,
710-11, 715-16, 777, 779, 785, 798,
"Spinosa Cartesianus" 1063-4
Novitatum Cartesianarum Gangraena [The
Gangrene of Cartesian Novelties]
(1677) 829-30, 1060-4

Maurits (Maurice) of Nassau, Prince of Orange
(Stadholder, 1585-1625) 51-2, 97, 124-5,
138-9, 672-3
Meinsma, K.O. (1865-1929), archivist, and
Spinoza scholar 544n31, 605, 1018-19,
1221-2
Melchior, Johannes (1646-89), Reformed preacher
on the Lower Rhine 786-9, 796, 830-1
announces Spinoza as "Zinospa" and
"Xinospa" 787-8
Menasseh ben Israel (Manoel Dias Soeiro)
(1604-57), Amsterdam rabbi 50-3, 65-6,
70, 74-5, 125, 138-9, 154-5, 157, 161-7,
170-2, 179-81, 184, 204-5, 209-10, 212,
227, 278, 282, 318, 658, 923
as community book publisher 50-1, 173,
176-7, 271
debates with Christian scholars 186, 203,
270-3, 297-8, 322-3, 549-50, 658, 1101-3
El Conciliador (3 vols., 1632-51) 52-3, 165-6,
171, 376-7, 821-2
Mikveh Israel (*Hope of Israel*) (1650) 125, 139,
154-5, 167, 189, 196-7
Thesouro dos denim (1647) 181-2
Mendelssohn, Moses (1729-86) 4-5, 1017-18,
1216, 1219
Mertens, Frank, Spinoza scholar 237, 247-8,
254-5, 349, 1221-2
Meyer (also Meijer), Lodewijk (c.1629-81),
Amsterdam physician, theatre director 32,
231-2, 248, 250, 302, 329, 333-4, 342,
347-8, 350, 353-4, 373, 381-2, 403-4,
415-16, 424-7, 484-6, 535-7, 538n8,
539-41, 545-7, 556-61, 563, 600-2,
606, 615-16, 632-6, 639, 642, 710-11,
718, 747, 771, 828, 930, 957, 1108-9,
1146-7, 1150
Bible criticism 389-90, 479, 542-3, 547, 561,
613, 702-3, 706-19, 825, 833-4
edits Spinoza's works 409-12, 417-18,
422-4, 426-9, 433-4, 458, 461, 485-6,
958-9, 1049, 1166, 1169-70
guided by Spinoza 332, 716, 718, 825-6
Nil Volentibus Arduum 624, 627-8, 630-2,
636, 640, 642-3, 1076-7, 1083-4
theory of the emotions 635-8, 635n51,
640-2
'Preface' to Spinoza's book on Descartes'
"Principles" 329, 410, 417-20, 426-31, 433,
526, 560
Philosophia S. Scripturae Interpres (1666)
See *Philosophia S. Scripturae Interpres*
L. Meijers Woordenschat [L.Meijer's
Dictionary](1669) 546-7, 604, 610, 628,
640-1

microscopes and microscopy 228, 243, 247–9, 251, 264, 328, 347–8, 352, 358–9, 366–7, 380, 398–9, 466–7, 525, 659, 1107–8
microscopes made by Spinoza 251, 264, 366–7, 443–4
varieties of construction and lenses 358–9, 522–5, 659
Mignini, Filippo, Italian historian of philosophy 57, 274n48, 1221–2
mind-body divide 250–1, 373, 393–4, 415, 639, 1199
miracles, denied, 26, 35, 37, 44, 100–1, 156–7, 335, 374, 532–3, 569–70, 572–3, 582, 667–8, 684–5, 721–3, 727–8, 802, 805, 809, 811, 813–16, 831–2, 947–8, 952–3, 995, 1016, 1057, 1067–71, 1128, 1138
Modena, Leone da (Yehudah Aryeh mi-Modena) (1571–1648), Venetian rabbi and hazzan 159–60, 176, 1139
monarchy, Spinoza's antipathy to 99–101, 109–10, 467–8, 510, 515, 592–3, 674–6, 682–3, 741, 745–6, 752–4, 756–7, 796, 892–3, 895–6, 1090, 1148, 1194, 1212–13
monarchies incline to war, republics to peace 482, 592–3, 681, 745, 760–1
money-making no path to virtue or happiness 368, 478–9, 752–3, 756–7, 1169–70
monism, all reality one substance 236, 284, 333, 386, 390–1, 415–17, 436, 439–42, 602, 619, 636–7, 937–8, 1006, 1016–17, 1110, 1116, 1121–3, 1127–8
Monnikhoff, Johannes (1707–87), Amsterdam physician and biographer of Spinoza 242–3, 315, 335, 354–6, 465–6, 652, 959–61, 1200
Montalto, Elijah (Eliahu or Elias) (1567–1616), personal physician to Marie de Medici 134–5, 138–9, 157, 173–4, 273, 306
Montbas, Jean de Barton, vicomte de (1613–96) 863–4, 872–4, 889, 990
Montausier 973–4, 978, 1101–2, 1132
Moravian Brethren 265–6
Moray, Sir Robert (c.1609–73), founder member of the Royal Society 365–6, 507–8, 512–14, 520–1, 528–9, 564–7
More, Henry (1614–87), Cambridge Neoplatonist philosopher 33, 45–6, 364, 561, 621–2, 816–17, 900–1, 945–7, 1007–8, 1120–1, 1125–8, 1188–90
reforms Descartes 1121–2
Spinoza assailed 952–3, 1043, 1066, 1120–2
Ad V.C. Epistola altera (1677) 952–4, 1120
Confutatio (1678) 1120–2

Morelli, Dr (Henriquez Morales)(d.1715), Sephardic physician 842–9, 855–7, 991–2
claims to have known Spinoza well 843
Morocco, Spinoza family ties with 114–15, 118, 121–3, 125–7, 140
Mortera (or Morteira) Rabbi Saul Levi (c.1596–1660), senior rabbi at Amsterdam 50–3, 55, 65–6, 71–2, 117–18, 134–7, 149–51, 154–5, 157, 162, 167, 195–6, 205, 273
and ancient Hebrew 'republic' 171–3
clashes with Spinoza 55, 68–9, 74–5, 179–81, 231, 307
and "heretics" within Judaism 55–6, 68–70, 159, 161, 185, 308, 316–17
ties to Spinoza's family 74–5, 111, 134–7, 139–42, 148, 1161
O Tratatdo da Verdade da lei de Moises [Treatise of the Truth of the Law of Moses] 70, 172–3
Mosaic Law 55–6, 67, 70, 73–4, 83–5, 162, 220, 226–7, 308, 312–13, 696, 701, 760–1, 1089–90
Moses 67–8, 76, 155–6, 177–8, 280, 307–8, 602, 660–1, 669, 684–7, 696–7, 700, 702, 704–5, 743–4, 760, 923
authored the Pentateuch (the Five Books), or not 156, 294–6, 602, 659–60, 684–5, 691–2, 743–4, 1025–6, 1080, 1104–6, 1120, 1138, 1147, 1193
motion, innate in matter, motion and rest 368, 393–4, 396–7, 420–2, 544, 802–3, 1143–5
motion, laws of, revising Descartes' attempts to formulate 414–15, 464, 528–9, 1020
Huygens' revision of 464–5, 500–1, 512–13, 525–6, 528–9, 566–7
Spinoza's revision of 409–10, 419–20, 500–1, 525–6, 528–9, 566–7, 651, 1109–10
Muhammed (570–632 A.D.) 207, 340–1, 351, 825, 827
Mulay Zaydan, Sultan (ruled southern Morocco: 1603–27) 125
"multitude" (*vulgus*), the 18–19, 105–6, 108–10, 269–70, 343–4, 350–1, 359–60, 488–9, 509–10, 541–2, 629, 674, 676, 678–9, 709, 735–6, 745, 750–2, 754, 756–7, 760–2, 806–8, 835–6, 894–7, 1006, 1148–9
Münsterite invasions of the Netherlands, in 1666 513–30, 564–5, 580–1, 590
in 1672–73 865–6, 869–70, 965–6, 1040
Musaeus, Johannes (1613–91), Jena Lutheran theologian 45–6, 538, 812–14

Muslims, see Islam
myth (posthumous) of Spinoza the secular saint "wise and pious" 1195–6, 1201, 1203, 1206–7, 1215–16, 1218–19

Nadler, Steven, biographer of Spinoza 152, 183–4, 187–8, 294, 424–5, 1221–2
Nantes, Portuguese Marranos in 86–8, 94–9, 110, 112, 114–15, 132–4, 139, 207
natura naturans, natura naturata 174–5, 289, 336, 419, 421–2, 428–9, 436–7, 442, 818–19, 1123
"natural right", quashed by Hobbes reconstituted by Spinoza 736–9, 749–50, 765, 881
necessitarianism, see determinism
Neercassel, Johannes van (1626–86), 'Vicar Apostolic' of the Dutch Catholic Church 41, 964–5, 970–2, 977–8, 989–90, 998–9, 1005–6, 1136–7, 1203
  pro-French policy 965–6, 970–1, 973–4, 981
  tries to prevent publication of Spinoza's Ethics 1177–9, 1181
New Christians" [cristãos novos], or Marranos (or conversos) 79, 81–2, 86–8, 90–1, 94–7, 112, 114, 118–19, 121–2, 127, 129–30, 132, 134–5, 138–9, 153–4, 166–7, 170, 190–3, 195–6, 212, 273, 319–20
  subversive intellectual tradition 55–7, 299–300, 303, 306–7, 320–1
New Netherland (present-day New York, New Jersey and Delaware) 259, 490–2, 496, 990, 1040–1
New Testament, essentially Hebraic in origin and meanings 266–7, 332, 610–11, 704, 712–13, 723–5, 752, 898, 900, 908–9, 1065–6, 1079–80, 1088–9, 1134–5
  Apostles diverge in doctrine 724–5, 909–11, 1086
  established no church, institutions or Trinitarian theology 267, 910–11, 975–6
  no true fulfilment of the Old Testament 1134–5, 1147
  "teaching" not "prophesying" 909–11
  written long after Jesus' death 725
Newton, Isaac (1643–1727), scientist 390–1, 399–401, 404, 463–4, 527–8, 559, 722–3, 901, 964–5, 1004, 1010, 1190–1
Nicaean Council of AD. 325 266–7, 270–1, 273, 833–4, 1111
Nicolson, William (1655–1727), English churchman, linguist and antiquarian 652–4, 989, 1052
Nietzsche, Friedrich (1844–1900) 7–10, 223–4, 756, 758, 1205, 1215–16, 1220

Nieuwstad (or Nieustad), Joachim (c.1623–96), Utrecht regent, friend of Spinoza 871, 988, 992, 997–8, 1001, 1045–6, 1059, 1064–5, 1165–6
Nieuwentijt, Bernard van (1654–1718), polemicizes against Spinoza's philosophy 431–2, 964–5, 1023, 1046, 1059, 1155–6
Nil Volentibus Arduum, theatre and arts society in Amsterdam 1184–5; see also Meyer and Bouwmeester
Noahide Laws (Seven Laws of Noah) 155
nobility and "the ignoble" 101, 592, 602–4, 670–1
North Holland (Reformed) Synod 780–3, 962, 1021, 1051
Nourrison, J.F., nineteenth-century French philosopher 1217–19
Nunes da Costa, Jeronimo (Moses Curiel) (1620–97), Sephardic merchant-diplomat 165–9, 933–4, 1055–7
Nuñez Bernal, Manuel (alias Abraham) (c.1612–55), judaizer burnt in the Córdoba Auto-da-fé of 3 May 1655 315–17

Oldenbarnevelt, Johan van (1547–1619), Pensionary of Holland, executed by Maurice of Nassau, in 1619 104–5, 123–7, 240, 650–1, 671–3, 877, 879–80
Oldenburg, Henry (1619–77), secretary of the London Royal Society 33, 330–1, 333, 352–4, 363–8, 393–4, 404–8, 433–4, 456–7, 465, 487, 492, 499–500, 505, 507–8, 512–13, 520–1, 525–6, 528, 564, 566–7, 582, 590–1, 672, 839, 944–5, 948, 1073, 1112–13, 1162–3, 1168–9
  Anglophilia 492–4, 499–500, 513–16, 529–30, 564–5
  imprisoned in the Tower of London (1667) 588–90
  interrupts correspondence with Spinoza 457, 487, 499–500, 566–7, 1041
  millenarianism 364, 567–71
  shocked by the TTP 839, 950–1, 1006–7, 1041–3, 1066–8, 1070–3, 1096
  visits Spinoza in Rijnsburg (1661) 363–8, 385–6
Oldenburger, Philipp Andreas (1617–78), German political writer 677–8
olive oil imports from Portugal and the Spinoza family 194, 197, 201
Opera Posthuma, published in 1677 4, 21–4, 41–2, 64, 289, 327–8, 337, 1094–5, 1106–7, 1112
  clandestine team editing project 1165–70, 1177–9, 1183

Opera Posthuma, published in 1677 (*cont.*)
  editing ruses 251, 1168–9, 1179–80
  Index rerum 1164–5, 1169–70
  Nagelate Schriften (1677) 21, 327–8, 904–5, 958, 1112, 1168
  portrait of Spinoza 1181–3
  prohibited 41–2, 1181, 1214–15
optics and optical theory 228, 245, 380, 385–6, 524–5, 657–9, 501
oracles of ancient Greece and Rome 75–6, 644–5, 722–3, 1138, 1193–4
Orangists, Orangism, as Dutch ideological and political faction 12, 240, 331, 355–8, 468–9, 471–2, 476–9, 486, 506, 530, 664–7, 671–2, 682–3, 1045–8
Original Sin 263, 270, 430, 710–13, 758, 1017, 1028–9, 1031
Orobio de Castro, Isaac (c.1617–87), Sephardic physician and polemicist 22–3, 56–7, 304–6, 311–12, 319–22, 911, 933–4
  strategy against Spinoza 321–2, 1011–12
  Certamen philosophicum (1684) 306, 1012
  Epistola invectiva 56–7, 67–8, 320–1, 562
Ostens, Jacob (1630–78), Rotterdam surgeon, Anti-Trinitarian Collegiant leader 286–8, 429–30, 498–9, 817–18, 822–3, 825–7, 880–1, 1112
Oudaen, Frans Joachim (1628–1692), Rotterdam Collegiant poet 817–18, 992–3
Ouderkerk, village and Sephardic cemetery near Amsterdam 114–15, 128–30, 132, 134, 137–9, 141–2, 185, 204–5, 226, 352, 1055
Overkamp, Hedentrijk (1651–94), Dutch Spinozist physician 1020–3
Overijssel 515, 530, 612, 681, 785–6, 981–2, 1000
Oxford 368–9, 373, 393, 503–4, 654, 946–7, 1120, 1129

Pacheco, Samuel, Amsterdam Sephardic confectioner 311–12, 314
Pain-et-Vin, Moïse (c.1620–73), Huguenot general in Dutch service 890–1
Pallache, Don Samuel (c.1550–1616), diplomatic agent of the Moroccan sultan 114, 122–7, 138–9
Pantheismusstreit 1017–18, 1216
Papacy 169–70, 668, 802, 1086–8, 1090
  condemns Spinoza and Spinoza 1177–8, 1181
Paraíba (Brazil) 154, 318
Pardo, David (c.1591–1657), Amsterdam rabbi 50, 136–7
Pardo, Josiah (1626–84), rabbi in Curaçao and Port Royal, Jamaica 50, 136, 1161

Paris 376–7, 843, 927–8, 990–1, 1050, 1053
  Académie française 628, 1101
  Académie des sciences 365, 376–7
  Bastille 42–3, 836–9, 1098–9
  Bibliothèque du Roi 1100–1
  discussing Spinoza in the 1670s 376–7, 1099, 1102, 1107
  Observatoire 526, 1113–14
  Sorbonne 45, 1105
Passover Service 206–7, 744–5, 760
Paul of Tarsus (c. 5 B.C.–64 A.D.) 131, 541, 723–4, 909–12, 1067, 1072, 1086–9
Paull, Israel Abrahamsz. de (1632–80), Amsterdam printer 772–3, 1170, 1177–8
Paz, Elias and Juan de (alias "Simão Barbosa Homem", and "Simão de Dias Nunes"), Sephardic firm trading with Spain 194–5, 213–14, 216–17
Peixoto, Captain Diogo (alias Moíses Cohen), Sephardic army officer in Brazil 318
Pels, Andries (1631–81), founder member of *Nil Volentibus Arduum* 627, 630–1, 640–2
Pepys, Samuel (1633–1703), English diarist 457, 493–5, 497, 501–4, 580–1, 584, 586–90
Pereyra, Abraham Israel (Tomas Rodriguez Pereyra) (d.1699), merchant, *parnas* and author 170–1, 211–12, 572–3
  Certeza del Camino (1666) 67–8
Pereyra, Isaac and Abraham Israel (alias Francisco and Antonio da Gurre), Amsterdam firm trading with Spain 67–8, 194–5, 198, 211–12
Pérez, Antonio (1540–1611), secretary to and later opponent of Philip II, and historian 79–80, 102–7, 107n79, 238
  Spinoza's admiration for 104–7
  Las obras y relaciones del Ant. Pérez secretario que fue del rey de España 106–7
Pérez de Maltranilla, Captain Miguel, Spanish infantry officer 313–16
Perizonius, Anthony (1626–72), theology professor at the Deventer Illustre School 785–6
Perizonius, Jacobus (1651–1715), Leiden professor of Greek 785–6, 832
"Perpetual Edict [Eeuwig Edict]" (5 Aug. 1667) 486, 664–8, 872–5, 894
Persian Empire (B.C. 550–BC. 330) 694–7, 699–700, 923, 1053–4
Pharisees, Pharisaic 152, 160, 698–701, 1056, 1067, 1076, 1081–2, 1086, 1140
  as key term in Spinoza's Bible criticism 670–1, 699–702, 761–2, 1169–70

Philip II, king of Spain (reigned: 1555–98) 3, 11–12, 88, 92–8, 100, 104–7, 110, 131–2, 680–1, 739, 752
  as "Count of Holland," 105, 108–9, 671–2, 878
Philip III, king of Spain (reigned: 1598–1621) 118–19, 124–7
Philip IV, king of Spain (reigned: 1621–65) 165, 193–4, 225, 233
Philopater (1697), clandestine Spinozistic novel 798, 955–9, 961–2, 1010–11, 1013, 1197–203
  profiles Spinozism as a sect 1197–9
Philosophia S. Scripturae Interpres (1666) 27–8, 32, 332, 480, 670, 709, 717–18, 773–5, 777–9, 783–4, 791, 794, 806, 825–6, 829–30, 867–8, 977–8, 1022, 1051, 1060
  announces Spinoza's philosophy and "sect" 556–7, 561–2
  attributed to "pseudo-Cartesiani" subverting true Cartesian principles 552, 554, 557–8, 792–4
  attributed wrongly to Spinoza 538, 719, 776–7, 1093
  authorship concealed 537–9, 549, 551–2, 798
  exalts Cartesianism "reformed" as evident truth 540–1, 550–1, 556–7, 1122
  Christology demolished 711–12, 813
  Critique of Socinianism 548–59, 708–11, 717–19
  Meyer identified as likely principal author 537–8, 560–1, 1113
  octavo edition (1674) bound with the TTP 538
  religious divisions healed by (true) philosophy 540–1, 825
  theology wholly subsumed into philosophy 550–1, 810–11, 815–16, 825, 828
piety and impiety found in every organized religion 17–18, *see also* Spinozists
Pinto Delgado, João (Moshe) (1580–1653), Sephardic poet 110
Placcius, Vincent (1642–99), professor at the Hamburg Gymnasium 1116
Plato (c.424–348BC.), and Platonists 18–19, 34–5, 302–3, 425–6, 541, 661–2, 731, 771–2, 907, 912, 952, 1017, 1106, 1122–4
Pliny the Younger (Gaius Plinius Caecilius) (A.D. 61–113), Roman administrator and letter-writer 425–6, 904–5
Polish Brethren, *see* Socinians
Pontchâteau, Sebastien du Cambout, sieur de (1634–90), Jansenist nobleman at the French court 41, 966–7
Popkin, Richard H., historian 57n19, 58–9, 61, 274–5, 691–2

Porphyry (c234–c.305 A.D.), late Roman, Platonist anti-Christian philosopher 692–5
Portugal 51–2, 104–5, 108–9, 118–19, 121, 123–4, 163–9
  crypto-Judaism 11–12, 79–87, 101–2, 113, 165
  revolt against Philip II (1580) 100–3, 165
  secession from Spain (1640) 165–7, 193–4
  see also Inquisition
Portuguese Jewish Community of Amsterdam
  Bikur Holim society for care of the sick 210
  "buen gobierno" 226–7
  burial society 135–6, 138–9
  cemetery, *see* Ouderkerk
  demographic development 114–15, 190–2, 208–10
  donations to the Holy Land, Terra Santa [Holy Land] society 146–7, 207, 865–6
  Dotar, marriage dowry society 132–4, 146
  Ets Haim school library 137, 150–2, 157, 184, 206–7
  evening classes and groups (academias) 68–9, 179–81, 185, 212
  finta assessments, for communal tax 60–1, 135, 139–40, 142, 195–6, 206–9, 213, 218
  imposta, communal tax 192, 195–6, 206–10, 213, 218
  "Keter Torah [Crown of the Law]" *yeshivah*, evening discussion circle 50, 68–9, 179–81, 307
  kosher meat provision 113, 121, 135–6, 139–40, 206–7
  Mahamad See *Mahamad* and *parnasim*
  poor relief 139–40, 195–6, 206–10
  prayers for the sovereign, or ruler 163–5
  rabbinic book censorship 143, 176–7, 317–18
  schooling 52–4, 137, 139–40, 148–55, 157–9, 170–1, 180–1, 206–7
  Sabbataean furore 152, 1053–4
  Senhores Quinze 137–8, 143, 160, 176
  Spanish and Portuguese language usage 125–6, 143, 151, 157, 164–5, 167, 180–1, 273
  see also *Mahamad*, Ouderkerk, and synagogues
Prado, Juan (Daniel) de (1612–70), Sephardic deist physician and freethinker 54–8, 61–2, 65, 67–9, 241–2, 303–6, 312–14, 317, 319–22, 571–2
  feud with Orobio de Castro 305–6, 319–22
  financial difficulties 314–15
  physical appearance 313–14
  Elogios, que zelosos dedicaron a la Felice Memoria de Abraham Nuñez Bernal, 315–17

Pre-Adamite sect 297–8
priestcraft 760–2
Prophets, prophecy 335, 592–3, 700, 716–17, 759, 805, 823–4, 952–3
　role of imagination, according to Spinoza 669–70, 690, 706, 809, 1085–6
"Public Prayers" controversy of 1663–64 471–3, 486
Pufendorf, Samuel (1632–94), German jurist 360, 735–6

Quakers, Quakerism, in Amsterdam 40, 273–82, 815–16, 1122
　Anti-Trintarianism 275–6

Radical Enlightenment 251, 259, 339–41, 403–4, 483–5, 600, 730–1, 746, 767, 769, 833–4, 838–9, 896, 900, 1186–7, 1189–90, 1206, 1211–13
"Raid on the River Medway" (19–24 June 1667) 586–8, 649
'Rakow (Racovian) Catechism' of the Socinian Polish Brethren 263–4
Ramirez, Lopo (alias David Curiel), Sephardic merchant in Amsterdam 65–7, 140, 194–5, 224–6
Rappolt, Friedrich (1615–76), Leipzig Lutheran theologian 45–6, 797–8, 809
Rashi (acronym for Shlomo Yitzhaki) (1040–1105), Hebrew Bible commentator 155, 1080
Ravensteyn, Johannes van (1618–81), Amsterdam publisher 601–2, 606–7
Ray, John (1627–1705), English parson, naturalist and traveler 357–8, 368–9, 373
　Observations topographical, moral and physiological (1673) 989, 1053
reason, the exclusive route to individual and collective improvement 12, 15–16, 19–20, 453–4, 483, 591, 725
Regius, Johannes (1656–1738), Franeker professor 9, 380–1, 402–3, 1060–2
Reimarus, Hermann Samuel (1694–1768), German deist and Bible critic 687–8
Rembrandt van Rijn (1606–69), artist 50–1, 116–17, 163, 222–3, 239, 383, 640–1, 646
Remonstrants (Arminians) 25, 185–6, 267–8, 285–6, 380, 470–1, 477–8, 549, 599–600, 621–2, 650–1, 673, 777, 815–16, 830–2, 877–8, 944–5, 982–3, 1050–2
　views on toleration 549, 832, 1047–8, 1050
representation, government by Spinoza's "great councils" 893–6

Restoration (1660), monarchy re-established in England 35–6, 253, 275, 358, 773, 969, 1125–6
Resurrection, of Christ denied 26, 37, 262, 270, 275, 277, 539, 569, 611, 621, 569–70, 689–90, 723, 819–20, 827–8, 912, 1020, 1049, 1069–73, 1088, 1169–70
Révah, Israel Salvator (1917–73), French hispanicist and historian 55, 56n15, 58–9, 61–2, 73, 110, 293
Reynoso, Dr Miguel (Abraham Israel), Sephardic physician at Amsterdam 310–16, 324
Ribera, Daniel de (José Carreras y Coligo) (c.1616–94), Catalan convert to, and apostate from, Judaism 56–7, 70, 231–2, 296–8, 307–9, 312, 316–21
Riddle (or Secret) of the Twelve 696–7
Rieuwertsz, Jan, the Elder (1617–87), Spinoza's publisher 24, 64–5, 263–5, 273–4, 277–8, 285, 333–4, 336–7, 355–6, 422–3, 458, 719, 817–18, 865–6, 1150, 1160
　Collegiant meetings in his shop 262–5, 268–9, 297–8, 364, 640
　publishes Collegiant texts 262–3, 282, 779, 1103–4
　publishes Descartes works 247–8, 262–3, 338–9, 640
　publishes radical works 535–8, 612, 631–2, 719, 772
　publishes Spinoza clandestinely 422, 537, 640, 719, 772–3, 775, 780–1, 842, 851, 930, 938–41, 947–8, 956–7, 1057–8, 1112, 1164–5, 1170–1, 1178–9, 1181
　Spinoza participates in clandestine distribution 948, 955–6
Rieuwertsz, Jan, the Younger (c.1651–1723), continues his father's publishing business 63–5, 229, 264, 333–4, 336–7, 356, 461, 537–8, 545, 957, 1035–7, 1164, 1185, 1203–4
Rijnsburg 327–9, 363–4, 418–19, 439, 456, 656–7
　abbey 356–7
　Collegiants 354, 356–7, 1103–4
　jurisdiction 356–7
　Spinoza's lodgings, 354–5, 358–9, 366–8, 372, 401–2
　walking path to Leiden 354–6, 372
Ríos y Alarcón, Bartolomé de los (1580–1652) 232–6
Rodrigues de Morais, Antonio, New Christian merchant in Rouen 201–2, 206, 214, 222
Rodrigues Lamego, Duarte (c.1590–c.1655), New Christian merchant in Rouen 206, 214, 222
Rohan, Louis Chevalier de (1635–74), noble conspirator against Louis XIV 838–9, 926, 1098–9

Roman Republic, suppressed by the Emperor Augustus 575, 679–80, 839–40, 1008–9
  Spinoza's analysis of its ills 109, 575–6, 735, 744–5, 894
Rome under the popes 120–1, 240–1, 344–5, 516–17, 1056–7, 1171, 1176
  Vatican Library 912, 1175, 1208
  see also Inquisition and Papacy
Rotterdam 112, 117–18, 134, 193, 203, 266, 280, 652–3, 880, 1047–8
  city government 193, 880, 884, 913–14, 1198–9
  Collegiants 286, 358, 498–9, 815–19, 822–3, 832, 880–1, 954–5, 985–6
  Reformed Church and Walloon consistories 280–1, 847–8, 1198–9
  Remonstrant community 286, 822–3
Rouen, Portuguese New Christian community 87–8, 110, 123–4, 133–4, 219–20
Rousseau, Jean-Jacques (1712–78), philosopher and political thinker 7–8, 730–1, 740, 746, 749–50, 757–8, 763–8, 896–7, 1008
Royal Society, see London,
Ruyter, Admiral Michiel de (1607–76), Dutch admiral 492–3, 497, 581–3, 586–7, 592, 864–5, 882–3, 964, 993–5, 997–8
Ryckius, Theodorus (1640–90), Leiden history professor 1044–5, 1047–8

Sadducees, ancient Jewish sect of the Second Temple era 70, 699–702, 761–2, 1056, 1140
Saint-Évremond, Charles de Marguetel de Saint-Denis, seigneur de (1613–1703), French
  essayist, critic and wit 656–7, 661–2, 835–40, 842–6, 848–9, 857, 917–18
  assessment of Spinoza 840–1
Saint-Glain, Chevalier Gabriel de (c.1620–84) 842, 848–51, 855–7, 1065
Saisset, Émile (1814–63), translator of Spinoza into French 1217
salaries and incomes 149, 173, 181, 499, 506, 521, 866–7, 914, 1162
Saldenus, Willem (Guilielmus)(1627–94), Reformed preacher 33, 476–8, 822–3, 866–7, 957
Saleh (Morocco) 121–2, 126–7, 140, 181
salus populi (welfare of the people) 336, 681–2, 741–6, 751, 760, 876, 893; *see also* general will
Salvation (Redemption) redefined 287–8, 305, 361, 510, 562, 611, 613–14, 633–4, 689–90, 721–2

Samuel, biblical prophet 1193–4
Sandius (or Sand), Christoph)(1644–80), Antitrinitarian historian and editor 684, 1103–4, 1106–7, 1110–11, 1135
  Nucleus historiae ecclesiasticae (Amsterdam, 1669) 1103–4, 1110–11
Sandwich, Lady Elizabeth Wilmot, countess of 842–5
Satan, see demons and devils,
Saul, King (c.1021–1000 BC.) and the ancient Israelite monarchy 670, 696–9, 745, 1090
Scaliger, Joseph Justus (1540–1609), humanist and Bible critic 684–8, 703–4, 809–10
Schelling, Friedrich Wilhelm Joseph (1775–1854), German philosopher 4–5, 1205, 1216
Scheveningen 653–4, 993–4
Schiedam 228, 429, 648–9
Schuller, Georg Hermann (c.1650–79), physician, friend of Spinoza, 1042–3, 1048–9, 1068, 1093–4, 1111–12, 1148–52, 1165–9, 1171–2, 1178–9
Schuyl, Florentius (1619–69), Cartesian professor of medicine and botany 424–6, 437
Second Anglo-Dutch War (1664–67), see Anglo-Dutch Wars
Second Temple Era (516 B.C.–A.D. 70), era of priests, theology and divisive sects 271, 699–702, 760–1, 1053–4, 1056
Seneca, Lucius Annaeus (4 BC–65 AD.), first of the three great philosophers of Córdoba (Seneca, Averroes and Maimonides) 252–4, 1017
  Trojan Women 252, 254
  Moral Letters to Lucilius 254
Senior, Baruch, see Garces, Henrique
Senior, Joshua, Spinoza's uncle 129, 131
Senior, Miriam (Maria Nunes (Garces), (1577–1638), Spinoza's maternal grandmother 83, 89–90, 111, 113, 124, 129–31, 144–5
Septuagint, Greek version of the Old Testament (3rd century BC.) 296–7, 659–62, 703–4, 1065–6, 1139–40
Serrarius, Pieter (1600–69), Millenarian Collegiant theologian 262–3, 265–6, 278, 282, 285, 334, 500–1, 550–1, 567, 710–11, 817–18
  chiliastic spiritualism, 282, 285–6, 522, 550–1, 567–8, 750, 814
  messianic philosemitism 346–7, 364, 493, 567–8, 573–4
Simon, Richard (1638–1712), French Catholic Bible critic 44–6, 686–7, 830, 1135, 1138–41

Simon, Richard (1638–1712), French Catholic Bible critic (*cont.*)
  and the Ezra thesis 1134–5, 1139–40
  Histoire critique du Vieux Testament (1678) 1140–1, 1213–14
Sinsheim battle of (16 June 1674), near Heidelberg 926
scepticism 156–7, 299, 304, 366, 412–13, 444–5, 813, 818, 1101, 1123, 1138, 1147
"social contract" of Hobbes, contrasted with that of Spinoza 736, 749–50
Socinianism, Socinians 261–4, 267, 272–3, 276, 290–1, 339–40, 354, 358, 430, 477–8, 535, 538–9, 543, 545–6, 548–50, 554–5, 559, 615–16, 708–10, 725, 797–8, 810–11, 814–16, 983, 987, 1050–2, 1068, 1092–3, 1202
  Dutch anti-Socinian decrees (1653 and 1656) 670, 779
  "Socinian books" banned 27–8, 32, 548, 775, 778–9, 783–4
Solano y Robles, Fray Tomás, Augustinian friar (c.1627-c.1659) 294, 310–15, 319
Solebay, naval battle on 6 June 1672 865, 882–3, 889
Solms, Amalia van (1602–75), wife of Frederik Hendrik and grandmother of William III 1027–8, 1045
Solomon, Biblical king (reigned: c.970–931 BC.) 171–2, 697–8, 718–19, 1055–6, 1086–7
Sophia, Princess Palatine and Duchess of Hanover (1630–1714), mother of George II of England 920–2, 926–7, 930–2
  reads Spinoza 920–3, 931–4
  freethinking inclinations 932–4
  Hanoverian Succession 933
South Holland (Reformed) Synod 24, 27–8, 290–2, 470–1, 780–2, 1051
sovereignty lodged in the "common good," via reason 730–1, 735–9, 741, 744–5, 760, 764–5, 768
Spain, crypto-Judaism and underground intellectual culture 21–2, 51–2, 80–2, 101–3, 121, 125, 165–6, 238, 299–301, 304–6, 319
  forms alliance with the Dutch Republic (1672-78) 963, 981–2, 1001, 1039–40
  crypto-Averroism, *see* Averroes
  see also Inquisition
Spanheim, Ezekiel (1629–1710), Calvinist scholar-diplomat 1138–41
Spijck, Hendrik van der (d.1715), Spinoza's landlord during his last years 648–9, 652, 654–6, 846–7, 884, 888, 997, 1150, 1155–6, 1159–62, 1164–5

Spinoza, Abraham (Manoel Rodrigues d'Espinoza) (d.1637), Spinoza's paternal uncle 87–8, 98, 111, 127, 132–5, 137–40, 181–2
Spinoza, Benedict de (Baruch)(1632–77)
  abhors quarrels 343, 386, 661–2, 801–2, 1006–7, 1205
  aborts the 1671 Dutch language edition of the TTP 955–7
  abstemiousness, loathing of greed 216, 352, 358–9, 648–9, 838–9, 987–8
  activism 109–10, 666–7, 835, 847–8, 857, 1003–6, 1013–14, 1025–6, 1205, 1220–1
  anti-Catholic bias 157, 264–5, 276
  aspiring to "reform the world," mocked as an insane ambition 7, 18–19, 49, 100, 285, 289–90, 387, 570, 1002, 1010
  attempts to publish his *Ethics* 772, 804, 1041–4, 1048–9, 1051–2, 1057–8, 1066–7, 1145, 1149, 1172–3
  auction of belongings (Nov. 1677) 1158–62
  Bible criticism, *verus sensus* seprated from *veritas rei* 389–90, 415, 665, 685–6, 689–90, 704–9, 711–12, 714–19, 728–9, 746–7, 820–2, 833–4, 1142
  bracketed conventionally with Hobbes 34, 722, 729–30, 776–7, 945–7, 1187–8
  bravado and heroic codes downgraded 505–6, 509–10
  breaks with Sephardic community 69–78, 218–28
  career as merchant (1654–56) 205–18
  "caute [caution]," guidance for himself and his sect 840–2, 846, 899–900, 957, 1057
  considered emigrating (1672-3) 861–3, 916–19, 922–5
  conversational style and courtesy 363–4, 840–1, 846–7, 984–5
  correspondence 353–4, 556–7, 566–7, 580, 589–90, 619, 902, 1049, 1094–5, 1122–3, 1143–5, 1179–80
  died unrepentant, in tranquility 1152–6, 1159
  early group strategy, *see* Spinozists
  embraces experimental science and optics 399, 442–3, 651, 661–2, 846, 908
  empiricism, critique of Baconian *philosophia experimentalis* 396–400, 402–5, 728–9, 908
  experiments in chemistry 396–400, 402, 406–8, 651
  Ezra thesis 691–8, 701–2, 786
  "free man" and his qualities 452–3, 508–10
  Greek studies 661–2, 687–9, 1204
  health and illnesses 138, 352–3, 605–6, 869–70, 1143, 1148–51

Hebrew studies after 1656 479, 689, 705–6, 805, 1074–9, 1083–4, 1088–9, 1091
herem See *herem*
"honour and wealth" 57–9, 158, 189–90, 209–10
mass spontaneous revolts against despots repudiated 105, 107–10, 631, 646–7, 683, 698
mathematics as model for philosophy and the sciences 412–13, 444–5, 533–4, 705–6
military organization, views on 574–5, 592, 882–3, 885–6, 888–9
mockery condemned as harmful 337, 626–7, 638
"mocks all religions," 360, 476–7, 846–7
nighttime labours by lamplight 158–9, 328–9, 993–4
outdoor costume 840
personal library 106–7, 110, 151, 173, 254, 339, 347–8, 704, 812
physical appearance 313–14, 840, 846–7, 917–18, 1006–7
polemics avoided 1107, 1146–7, 1205
politics envisaged as a science 673–4
portrait sketching 465–6, 656
reclusiveness 328–9, 639, 846, 1146–7, 1165–6, 1205, 1220–1
sarcastic humour 131, 667–8, 904–5, 1031–2, 1090
schooling, *see* Portuguese Jewish Community, schooling
shrewdness as political observer 127, 988
studied at Leiden, *see* Leiden
switches from divinity to Cartesianism and natural philosophy (mid-1650s) 63, 231–2, 243–51, 262, 309, 327, 333, 378–80
synagogue attendance (pre-1656) 52, 111, 157–8, 210–11, 217–19
teaching 228–9, 252–3, 256–9, 269–70
three orders of knowledge, culminating in *scientia intuitiva*, *see* epistemology
use of Spanish and Portuguese 49–50, 52, 63–5, 111, 145–6, 151, 159, 300, 495–6, 1160
Apologia (1656) 63–5, 67–8, 78, 296–7, 691–2, 825, 1072
On the Emendation of the Understanding (c.1657–58) 22, 190, 219–20, 247–8, 253–4, 259, 289–90, 301, 322, 327, 332–3, 389, 398, 404, 1095, 1166, 1169, 1219
Korte Verhandeling (c.1659–60) 247–8, 289, 301, 330, 332–6, 346, 370–1, 395–6, 398, 407, 439, 442, 446–7, 450–1, 456–7, 602, 732–3, 818–19, 899, 1167, 1217–18

Principia philosophiae cartesianae (Principles of Cartesian Philosophy)(1663) 39, 329, 361–2, 407, 409–24, 426–9, 496, 922–3, 1015, 1025–6, 1036–7, 1050, 1178, 1186, 1202–3
Cogitata metaphysica (1663) 416–17, 419–20, 426–7, 429, 432–4, 541–2, 756–7, 832–3
Treatise on the Rainbow (lost) 461, 1145, 1167
Tractatus Theologico-Politicus (1670) 14, 17–20, 27–9, 35, 39, 45, 64–5, 74, 108–10, 253–4, 454–5, 458–60, 474, 477–9, 483–4, 507–8, 522–3, 535–7, 560–2, 564, 623, 633–4, 665, 681–2, 684–719, 722, 742–3, 745–6, 750–1, 753–4, 762–3, 770; see also *Tractatus Theologico-Politicus*, refutations
Ethics (1677) 5–6, 9–10, 14, 17–20, 22–3, 35, 178–9, 253–4, 258, 301, 327–30, 335–6, 341, 343, 361, 376, 398, 410–11, 428–9, 434, 439–55, 458–60, 474, 487, 505–8, 522–3, 535–7, 562, 564, 607, 626–7, 637, 706, 750–1, 762–3, 770, 1036, 1074, 1165–6, 1171–3, 1175, 1208
Tractatus Politicus (1678) 4, 103, 105–7, 109–10, 253–4, 575, 592, 681–3, 736, 742–3, 745–6, 750–1, 753–4, 762–3, 765–6, 876, 878, 881, 894, 1148, 1166, 1169
Compendium Grammatices Linguae Hebraeae [Grammatical Compendium of the Hebrew Language](1678) 376–7, 1075, 1077, 1079–80, 1083–4, 1169, 1177–8
Adnotationes to the TTP 700, 850–1, 1036, 1064–6, 1069, 1080
Old Testament translation project (into Latin?) 1145–6
Spinoza, Esther de (Solis), Spinoza's step-mother 145, 159, 203–4, 204n51
Spinoza (d'Espinoza), Gabriel (Abraham), Spinoza's younger brother 59, 84, 145, 148–9, 157–8, 182–3, 201–2, 205–8, 213–14, 218, 490–1, 586, 1055
Spinoza, Hanna Deborah (Senior) (d.1638), Spinoza's mother 83–5, 90–1, 111–17, 144–5, 183, 205, 220–3
Spinoza, Isaac de Pedro Rodrigues d'Espinosa (Spinoza's paternal grandfather) 79, 82–4, 86–8, 96–7, 112, 132, 135, 139, 141–2
Spinoza, Isaac de (d.1649), Spinoza's elder brother 59, 83–4, 111, 129–31, 145, 148–9, 182–3, 190, 242–3
Spinoza, Jacob de, son of Abraham, uncle of Spinoza 137–8, 140–2, 146, 181–2

Spinoza, Michael (Miguel) (Gabriel Álvares d'Espinoza) (c.1587–1654), Spinoza's father 59, 73–4, 83, 87–8, 111, 129–31, 138, 140, 158, 176–7, 183–4, 191–2, 242–3
  career as *parnas* 73–4, 110, 142–4, 148, 157–8, 170, 189–90, 1055
  death and funeral 203–5, 214
  as merchant 59, 140–2, 168–9, 190–1, 194–5, 200–2
  quarrels with family members 158–9, 180–3, 220–2
  tense relationship with Spinoza 158–9, 187–8, 205, 222, 753
Spinoza, Miriam de (de Caceres) (1629–51), Spinoza's elder sister 83–4, 142, 145, 182–5, 203–4
Spinoza, Rachel de (d.1627) daughter of Abraham, Michael's first wife 83–4, 134, 137–8, 140–2, 181
Spinoza, Rebecca (Ribca)(de Caceres) (d.1695), Spinoza's younger sister 84, 145, 173, 182–5, 203–4, 211, 319, 1055, 1159–61, 1164
Spinozists [*Spinozistas*], identified as a "sect 251, 322, 380, 435–6, 537–8, 546–7, 551, 556–7, 560, 582, 606–7, 1106–7, 1217–18
  all religions considered on the same level 287–8, 359, 825, 954, 1014–15, 1067–8, 1201
  alleged arrogance 1005–6, 1201–2
  blessedness (salvation), by the Spinozist sect rendered remote from the uneducated (scorn for the ignorant) 614, 782–3, 1006, 1009–10, 1017–18, 1055–6, 1084
  "mockers of faith " scorned as 816, 825–6, 847–8
  "mockers of men" (Lucianists) 1017–18, 1031–2
  early group strategy 346–7, 349–51, 380–2, 418, 435–6, 456–8, 506, 537, 594, 619–25, 711, 847–9, 1018–19, 1034–5, 1057
  "Spinozist" label often, falsely applied 1010–11
  "sect" variously designated *Spinozismus*, *Spinozisterij*, *Spinosistendom*, *Spinosisme* 1014–17, 1202
  spreading in the 1670s 803, 849, 935–7, 1117–18, 1126, 1131, 1174–7
  "sect" spreading after 1680 844–5, 1011–13, 1016, 1034–5, 1037–8, 1117–18, 1142, 1174–7, 1198–203, 1206

label "Spinozist" displaces the terms "Socinian" and "Hobbist" (after 1680) 1191–2, 1195–6
subversive methods 76, 349–51, 457–8, 725, 817, 827–8, 1011, 1018, 1067, 1072, 1088–90, 1122, 1176–7, 1201, 1207, 1210–11
"spirit of Christ [spiritus Christi]", in Spinoza's thought 155, 269–70, 276, 280–1, 569–70, 576–7, 723–5, 817, 827–8, 1067, 1072, 1088–90, 1122
Spitzel, Gottlieb (1639–91), Lutheran Hebraist and Bible commentator 809, 1100–1
St James Day Fight (Battle) (25 July 1666 OS; 4 August 1666 NS). 582
stadholderate 664–5, 674–5, 874–5, 879, 883, 885–7, 892–3, 1041, 1194
  Spinoza's view of 666, 671–2, 875–9, 881, 885–7, 892–4
"States Bible" (Calvinist) 684–5, 712–13, 784–5, 799, 1082
Steen, Jan (1626–79) Dutch artist 654–6
Steenbakkers, Piet, Spinoza scholar 293, 330n13, 352–3
Steno (Stensen), Nicolas (1638–86), Danish anatomist, geologist and churchman 23–4, 41–2, 45–6, 244–7, 346, 361, 369–73, 375–80, 424, 434–5, 570–1, 582, 800
  abandons science 380, 918–19, 929–30, 1171–2, 1176
  converts to Catholicism 372, 380–1, 579–80, 801, 917–18, 1005–6
  disillusionment with Cartesianism 245–7, 371–82, 424, 434–5, 437, 578–9, 802–3, 1176
  early friendship with Spinoza 244–5, 368–9, 372, 375, 380, 801, 929, 1005–6, 1172, 1174
  exhorts Spinoza to abandon his philosophy 434–5, 801–3, 930
  heart, muscle and brain dissections 244–5, 372–5, 578, 929
  in Italy 570–1, 579–80, 658–9, 916–19, 1170, 1173
  mobilizes Roman Inquisition against Spinoza, 244 375, 380, 918–19, 1005–6, 1008, 1171–8
  pioneer of geology and fossil science 579–80, 917, 929–30
  profiles Spinozism as a movement 935, 1005–8, 1010, 1013, 1021–2, 1174–7, 1183
  religious fervour 377–8, 579–85, 750, 759, 802
  residence at Hanover 932, 1115, 1171–2

Stillingfleet, Edward (1635-99), English theologian and bishop 37-40, 946-7, 951-2, 1043, 1103, 1126-7, 1188-9
  Origenes sacrae (1662) 39
  Letter to a Deist (1675) 951-2, 1043
Stoicism, Stoics 4, 58-9, 236-7, 251-3, 541, 624, 661-2, 730-1, 748, 756, 907, 1106
Stolle, Gottlieb (1673-1744), Jena philosophy professor 75-7, 229-31, 264, 336-8, 461, 538, 538n8, 545, 1034-7, 1164, 1199-200
storms and tempests 444, 674, 999-1000
Stouppe, Jean-Baptiste (Giovanni Battista Stoppa), (1623-1692), Swiss Lieutenant-Colonel, intelligence officer and propagandist for Louis XIV 790-1, 799-800, 963, 966-9, 973-4, 982, 992, 998, 1000, 1009
  profiles Spinozism as a "sect" 935-6, 967-8, 970, 982-5, 987, 1005-6, 1013
  Spinoza's host in Utrecht (1673) 967-8, 971-3, 987, 992, 997-8
  La religion des Hollandois (1673) 790, 811-12, 841, 964-5, 969-71, 979, 982-5, 1000, 1004-5, 1178
Stouppe, Pierre-Alexandre, military governor of Utrecht (1672-73), older brother of the above 869-70, 889, 968, 978-9, 990, 997-8
Strato of Lampsacus (335-269 B.C.), Greek philosopher 1124-5
substance, Spinoza (and the Koerbaghs) on 24-5, 236, 250-1, 284, 333, 336, 386, 390-1, 393, 414-17, 420, 434-6, 439-42, 445, 602, 617, 1012, 1127-8
Suetonius (Gaius Suetonius Tranquillus) (A.D.69-c.130), biographer of the Roman emperors 904-5
supernatural agency 663-4, 898-901
  rejected by Spinoza 809, 813-14, 898-901
Swaen, Martinus de (1651-1713), Catholic priest in Amsterdam 1178
Swammerdam, Jan (1637-80), Dutch naturalist and expert on insects 245, 366-9, 799-800, 802-3, 918-19, 1191
Switzerland, Swiss canton republics, Swiss republicanism 557-8, 762-3, 768-9, 878, 969-70, 976-7, 982-3, 1064
synagogues, at Amsterdam
  Ashkenazic 138-9
  Beth Neve Shalom [Synagogue: House of Peace] 119-20, 122, 125-6, 135-6
  Beth Ya'acob (Jacob), first house synagogue 116-17, 125-6, 134-7, 139-40
  Beth Yisrael (Bet Israel)(1618-39) 135-7, 143, 173
  Talmud Torah united congregation formed (1639) 129-30, 137, 189
  united congregation's new synagogue (1675) 865-6, 1053-4, 1056-7
  visiting Christian scholars and dignitaries 162-3, 169, 171-2

Tacitus, Publius Cornelius (56-c.120 AD), Roman historian 575, 751-2, 896, 1148-9
Talmud 74, 150, 152, 155, 304, 320-1, 340-1, 436-7, 954
Talmudic Era (A.D. 70-c. 500), in Jewish history 702-3, 1079-80
teaching, in schools and universities, Spinoza's critique 243, 256-7, 259, 361-2, 411, 451-2, 734, 755, 879
teleology, Spinoza rejects 443-4, 706
telescopes revolutionizing astronomy 148-9, 205, 228, 358-9, 366, 462-3, 500-1, 517, 520-2
Temple of Solomon *see* Jerusalem
Temple, Sir William (1628-99), English diplomat and writer 352-3, 469, 493-4, 566, 580, 594-5, 649-50, 656-7, 661-2, 999, 1041
  on Dutch 'liberty' 465, 469-71, 651, 672, 845-6
  Epicurean outlook 394, 662, 835, 845-6
  Lettre d'un Marchand de Londres (1666) 583-4
Terence (Publius Terentius Afer)(c.195-159 BC), Roman playwright 252-4
  Andria 252-4
  Eunuchus 252-4
Texel, naval battle of (or Kijkduin), on 21 August 1673 993, 997-8
Thales of Miletus (c. BC 620-c.BC 548), first of the Greek philosophers 216, 677, 1030
theatre and the arts 239 252-4, 624-31, 636, 641-2, 646-7, 656, 755, 1174-6
  theatre, condemned by Calvinists 253, 256, 290-1, 470-1, 1050
  see also Nil Volentibus Arduum
Theodosius the Great, Roman emperor (ruled: AD.379-95) 644-5, 667
  suppresses the ancient oracles 75-6, 644-5
Thévenot, Melchisédec (c.1620-92), French scientist, traveler, and orientalist 7, 49, 100, 365, 376-8, 385-6, 800, 916-17, 927-8, 965, 973-4, 978, 1002, 1005, 1113-14
Third Anglo-Dutch War (1672-74), *see* Anglo-Dutch Wars

Thirty Years' War (1618-48) 266, 284, 516-17, 541, 616, 674-5, 920-1, 1211-12
Thomasius Christian (1655-1728), German jurist and philosopher 360, 1035-6, 1186-7
Thomasius, Jacob (1622-84), Leipzig philosopher and historian of philosophy 45-6, 427-8, 795-8, 804, 807-9, 812-13
"thorns and meadows" (espinas, or espinos, y prados), espinoso or Espinosa as thorny 67-9, 68n53, 82, 185, 425-6
Tienen (Tirlemont), sack of (8 May 1635) 233-5, 243
Tijdeman (or Tydeman), Daniel Harmensz (d.1677), Spinoza's landlord in Voorburg 458-60, 465-9, 475-9, 477n67
Tindal, Matthew (1657-1733), English "deist" and Spinozist 485, 1192
  The Rights of the Christian Church Asserted (1706) 485
Tisha b'Av [9th of Av], Jewish Fast Day commemorating destruction of the First Temple by the
  Babylonians in 587 BC and subsequent disasters 77-8, 1053-4
Toland, John (1670-1722), Anglo-Irish deist and Spinozist 4-5, 18-19, 328-9, 728-9, 747, 1143-5, 1192, 1206-9, 1213-14, 1216
  Letters to Serena (1704) 1145
toleration, "moderate" versus "radical" 3-4, 21-2, 36-40, 109, 276, 302, 331, 341, 354, 469-73, 479, 493-4, 515, 621-2, 649, 665-6, 671-2, 676, 681-2, 708, 735-6, 743, 746-7, 768-9, 773, 796, 811-14, 817-18, 823, 970-1, 1186-7, 1206, 1212-13
Tower of Babel, *lingua adamica* 5, 1075, 1077-9
Tractatus Theologico-Politicus, controversy, refutations, and translations 773-6, 789-91, 795-7, 804, 810-11
  banned 772, 775-81, 790-1
  Dutch translation 955-6, 1199-200
  English translation (1689) 1189-90
  French translation (1678) 841, 849-57, 1132-4
  paucity and inadequacy of early refutations 806, 809-10, 828-9, 947-8, 984-6, 996-7, 1128, 1135-6, 1138-9, 1141
  Spinoza distributes copies 784
  see also, Spinoza, *Tractatus Theologico-Politicus*
Tremellius, Immanuel (1510-80), Hebrew and Syriac scholar, Jewish convert to Christianity 704, 909
Trinity, the (*Drie-Eenheid*), church doctrine, and Anti-Trinitarianism 263, 265-8, 270, 275, 339-40, 430, 539-40, 549, 608, 610, 612-13, 619-21, 645, 712-13, 775-6, 784, 832, 948, 983, 1100-1, 1110-11, 1123-4, 1200-1
  nowhere established in Scripture 543-4, 609-10, 612-13, 689-90, 1092-3, 1132
"true Christianity," 13-14, 40-1, 270, 280-1, 342, 361, 1067, 1087, 1089, 1204
"True Freedom", the, in Dutch politics 472-3, 481-2, 486, 530-1, 593, 634, 650-1, 664-5, 671-3, 679, 682-3, 766-7, 770, 773, 799-800, 865-7, 881, 977-8
"true religion," 10-11, 14, 155, 264-5, 342, 351, 359-61, 363, 725-7, 747, 826-7, 1086-90
Tschirnhaus, Ehrenfried Walther von (1651-1708), German philosopher and friend of Spinoza 1042-3, 1110, 1112, 1149, 1151, 1159, 1165-6, 1183-4, 1208
  and the *cercle spinoziste* 1048-9, 1093-4, 1168-9, 1184-6
  discussions and correspondence with Spinoza 1093-6, 1143-5, 1179-80, 1186
  encounter with Leibniz 1096-8, 1102, 1106-7, 1185-6
  encounter with Steno 1171-5, 1177-8, 1184-5
  in Paris 1050, 1095-8
  Medecina Mentis (1687) 1099-100, 1168-9, 1184-7
Twelve Years' Truce (1609-21), between Spain and the Dutch Republic, 99 119, 121-2, 132, 190-1, 468-9

universal grammar (*grammatica universalis*) 639, 1083-4, 1183-4
"universal religion", universalism (*religio catolica universalis*) 562, 569-70, 826-8, 833, 1017, 1090
university teaching, needs reforming 878-9
Utrecht, 120 286, 298-9, 518, 864, 868-70, 1001
  bookshops 27-8, 612, 779-81
  cathedral (Dom) 863, 869, 989-90, 994-5, 998-1000
  Catholic minority 869, 980-1, 995-6, 1001
  city government 27-8, 471, 548, 551-4, 556, 616, 779-80, 870, 975-6, 1001
  coffee-shops and taverns, for meetings 971, 1021, 1023
  Collegie van Sçavanten, 377-8, 517, 534, 553, 557-8, 785-6, 798, 800, 971-3, 977-80, 988-9, 1001
  French occupation (1672-3) 864, 869-70, 967-74, 977-8, 980-1, 998-9
  Provincial States 27-8, 299, 298-9, 471, 548, 779-80, 879-80, 1001

INDEX 1311

Reformed consistory 27–8, 548, 551, 548, 556, 779–80, 879–80, 973, 975–6
Reformed Church Synod 27–8, 779–80, 975
Spinoza's visit (1673) 841, 843, 935, 980, 988–9, 994, 997
University 294–6, 382–4, 411, 471, 553–4, 989, 994–5

Vallan, Jacob (1637–1720), Dutch physician and friend of Spinoza 379–82, 545, 575, 601–2, 605–7, 627–8, 635–6
Van Bunge, Wiep, Spinoza scholar 293, 1221–2
Van de Ven, Jeroen, bibliographer and Spinoza expert 57, 200, 211n70, 352–3, 382, 405, 424–5, 427, 632n39, 649n2, 853, 1177–8, 1221–2
Van Dyck, Anthony (1599–1641), Flemish painter 238–9
Vanini, Lucio (1585–1619), anti-Christian philosopher burnt at the stake 9 February 33, 40, 43–4, 600, 612, 633, 792–3, 937–8, 952–3, 1009, 1117–18, 1187–8, 1195–6
Van Dale, Anthonie (1638–1708) 75–6, 1193–4
Van den Enden, Clara Maria 259–60, 348–9, 1097–8
Van den Enden, Franciscus (1602–74), Spinoza's Latin teacher 42–3, 54, 227–45, 247–8, 251–60, 285, 293–4, 303, 327, 333–5, 346–50, 378–80, 545, 634–5, 642–3, 838–9, 926–7, 1031–2, 1097–9, 1181
  anti-university bias 258–9, 269–70
  art dealing 238–41
  "converted" the Koerbaghs 545, 1031
  democratic republicanism in political theory 242, 251, 256–7, 259, 590–1, 664–5, 682, 732, 734–5, 740, 742, 747, 764, 769, 1098–9, 1194
  equality (evengelijkheid) extolled 257–9
  excluded from Collegiant meetings (early 1660s) 346–7
  influence on Spinoza 258–60
  in Paris (1671–4) 259–60, 634–5, 838–9, 926–7
  propagates "atheism" 236–7, 244, 246–8, 256, 293–4, 303, 334–5, 339, 346, 368–9
  teaching methods 241–2, 252, 254–5, 258–9
  Philedonius (1656) 252, 254–7
  Vrije Politieke Stellingen [Free Political Propositions] (1665) 259, 740, 764
Van den Enden, Martinus (1605–73?), brother of Franciscus, Antwerp art dealer 237–8

Van Schooten, Frans (1615–60), Dutch mathematician 248–50, 373, 416–17, 525
Van Staveren, Petrus (1632–83), Leiden Reformed preacher 24–5
Van Til, Salomon (1643–1713), Dutch Reformed theologian 45–6, 64–5, 229–30, 236, 433–4, 691–2, 695–6, 841–2, 964, 1209–10
Van Velthuysen, Lambert (1622–85), Utrecht regent and philosopher 39, 45–6, 249–50, 368, 383–4, 406–7, 517, 534, 538, 540–1, 547–8, 551, 553–4, 715–16, 729–30, 771, 776–7, 784–7, 822–7, 870, 973–4, 976–7
  becomes a friend of Spinoza 979–80, 982, 988, 992, 997–8, 1001–2, 1045–6
  corresponds with Spinoza 1064–5, 1165–6
  discussions with Spinoza 871, 1001–2, 1004–5
  feud with Utrecht Reformed consistory 872, 972
  Gospels founded no church, church doctrines or sacraments 975–7
  promotes Cartesianism 823–4, 828–9
  targeted by Voetians and Orangists 776–7, 829–30, 972, 1000, 1062–3
  Tractaet van Afgodery en Superstitie [Treatise of Idolatry and Superstition](1669) 780–1, 975–6
Van Vloten, Johannes (1818–83), Dutch biographer of Spinoza, 330 1220–1
  Benedictus de Spinoza (1862) 1220–1
Venice as aristocratic republic 109, 481–2, 682–3, 737–8, 742–3, 762–3, 877–8, 1056–7, 1194
  Sephardic community 114–17, 120–1, 124–6, 132–3, 135–6, 159–60
Vermeer, Johannes (1632–75), artist 525, 866
Vidigueira, town and wine-growing district in southern Portugal 82–7, 97–8, 168
Vieira, Father António (1608–97), Portuguese Jesuit Millenarian missionary 166–70, 189
Vila Nova (Algarve) 194, 200–1
Villacorta, Franciscus Henriquez (1616–80), Spanish medical professor 942–4
virtue, Spinoza redefines 5–7, 448–9, 453–4, 637–9, 681–2, 758–9, 762–3, 802, 825–7, 992–3, 1185–6, 1195–6
"virtuous atheist" topos 837–8, 1194–6, 1207–8
Vitringa, Campegius (1659–1722), theologian and Hebraist at Franeker 832–3
Vlooswijk, Cornelis van (1601–1687), Amsterdam burgomaster 255–6

VOC share price index, *see* Dutch East India Company

Voetius, Gijsbertus (1589-1676), Dutch Reformed theologian opposing Descartes and Cartesianism 294-7, 322-3, 339, 383, 471, 473, 534, 554, 558, 575, 710-11, 770-1, 792-3, 798, 823, 831-2, 973, 977, 998-9, 1028

Voetians, Voetsianism, theological faction of the Dutch Reformed Church 383-4, 472-3, 486, 553-6, 661, 666-7, 792-3, 973-4, 1046-8, 1052-3, 1064, 1197

Volder, Burchardus de (1643-1709), Leiden physics professor 75-7, 250-1, 378, 468, 800, 976, 996, 1037, 1042, 1046-7, 1060, 1062-3, 1147, 1165-6
  perceptions of Spinoza and Spinozism 1199-200, 1202-3

Voltaire, François-Marie Arouet de (1694-1778) 4-5, 18-19, 625, 849, 857, 964-5, 1004, 1017-18, 1215-16
  Questions sur l'Encyclopédie (1770-72) 1017-18, 1205, 1215

Vondel, Joost van den (1587-1679), Dutch poet and playwright 254-5

Voorburg 31, 186, 264, 352-3, 409, 412, 439, 456, 458-61, 467-8, 471-2, 474-9, 495-6, 498-9, 515, 525, 535-7, 648, 651, 656-9, 665-6
  Huygens' country retreat (Hofwijck) 460-6, 510-11
  rift within the Reformed Church consistory (1665-6) 468-9, 475-8, 480, 535-7
  Spinoza's decision to reside there 456, 460, 1025-6
  under Delft's jurisdiction 476-8

vortices, *see* Descartes

Vossius, Gerardus Joannes (1577-1649), Dutch philologist 161, 202-3, 658, 1081, 1090-1
  Bible hermeneutics 684, 686
  De Arte grammatica [On the Art of Grammar] (1635) 1078, 1080-1

Vossius, Isaac (1618-89), Dutch freethinker 656-64, 835, 837-8, 857, 915-17, 921-2, 996, 1101-3
  clashes with Richard Simon 1139-41
  credulity 661-2
  encounter with Descartes 658-9
  the Flood local not universal 659-61
  rates the Septuagint above the Hebrew Bible, *see* Septuagint
  Sinophilia 339-40, 662, 814, 837-8
  De Vera Aetate Mundi (1659) 296-7, 659-60, 685, 703-4

Variarum observatrionum liber (London, 1685) 662

Vries, Simon Joosten de (c.1633-67), Collegiant friend and patron of Spinoza 262-3, 277, 285-6, 327-8, 333-4, 409, 498-9, 506, 607, 648-9, 1158, 1184-5

Vries, Trijntje Joosten de, sister of the above 498-9, 648-9, 1158, 1184-5

Wade, Ira O. (1896-1983) historian of clandestine philosophical literature 1214-15

Walloon Reformed Church Synod 555-6, 847-8, 1158-9, 1171

Wars of Religion, in France (1562-98) 88, 93-4, 98-100, 616

water-line (1672-73)(Dutch strategic defense line) 864, 868, 870-1, 887-90, 901-2, 963-4, 981-2, 988

Westerneyn, Eduardus (1632-1674), Reformed preacher at Voorburg 475-6, 478-9, 535-7

Weyer, Johan(1515-88), Dutch physician and opponent of witchcraft trials 904-5, 907

William the Silent (Stadholder, 1559-84) 665, 672-3, 981

William II, Prince of Orange (Stadholder: 1647-50) 162-3, 171-2, 240, 483-4, 673

William III (1650-1702), from 1672 Dutch Stadholder, from 1689 also king of England 463-4, 466-7, 471-2, 476, 483-5, 535, 664, 666-7, 863-4, 874-5, 879, 914-15, 992-3, 1039-40
  anti-Orangists try to weaken 971-2, 1052-3
  as the new "David 875-6, 914-15, 1051-2
  expands the States' army 882, 979-82, 1052-3
  purges States of Holland 885-6, 901-2, 913-14, 979-80, 1045-6
  purges states of Utrecht, Gelderland and Overijssel 1039-40, 1045-6
  rebuffs French and English offers 885, 889
  revived anti-Orangist sentiment 979-80
  strengthens stadholder's powers 890-1, 913, 965, 979-80, 1000, 1039-40
  and toleration 914-15, 964-5, 1039-40

Willis, Robert (1799-1878), Scots physician, librarian and translator of Spinoza 1218-19

Wilson, John (dates unknown), English divine 45-6, 953-4
  The Scripture's Genuine Interpreter (1678) 708-10, 713-14, 953-4

"wise, the," "sages" or "elect few," against the "multitude" 18–19, 269–70, 675–9, 750–3, 1006, 1055–6, 1175–6, 1198, 1201
Wiszowaty, Andrzej, Polish Socinian leader in Amsterdam 555, 563, 779, 814–15
witches, witchcraft 643–4, 899–905, 1008, 1015, 1122–3, 1197–8
see also Blount, Toland, and Tindal
Witt, Johan de (1625–72), Pensionary of Holland: 1653–72 292, 384, 468–75, 480–2, 486, 490–1, 496, 502, 530, 634, 651, 664–7, 681, 766–7, 863–4, 866–7, 882
anti-De Witt pamphlets, *see* Disaster Year
colluded with Spinoza alleged Orangist propaganda 634, 777–8, 782–4
downfall and murder 587–8, 673, 867, 874–8, 881, 886–7, 976–7, 1064, 1109
personal library 870–4
pro-Cartesian and pro-Arminian 474–5, 483–4, 872, 1046–7
republican political philosophy, *see* True Freedom
Spinoza criticizes 481–2, 590, 666, 671–2, 679, 682–3, 770, 877, 882–3
Wittichius (Wittich)(1625–87), Christopher, Reformed theologian 45–6, 383–4, 540–1, 547–8, 553–4, 714–16, 771, 792–3, 810–11, 825, 829–30, 1046–7, 1060, 1062–3, 1165–6, 1202–3
Anti-Spinoza (1695) 1012–13, 1062–3, 1202–3
principles of Bible exegesis 540–1, 560, 714–16, 771, 829–30, 1062–3
Wolff, Christian (1679–1754), German philosopher 1207–8, 1211
Wolsgryn, Aert (dates unknown), Spinozist publisher 1200–1
Wolzogen, Ludwig (Louis)(1633–90), Austro-Dutch Reformed theologian 708–9, 712, 714–16, 829–30, 1062–3
women in politics, Spinoza's view 895–6
wonder, rooted in ignorance 629–30, 635–8, 689–90

Zevi, Sabbatai (Mehmed Pasha)(1626–76), Jewish false Messiah, and the Sabbataean frenzy 493, 567–74, 586–7, 1053–4, 1161
Zwicker, Daniel (1612–78), Anti-Trinitarian Collegiant theologian 266–8, 277, 287–8, 779, 797–8, 1111
Irenicum Irenicorum (1658) 266–7
Zwolle Reformed consistory 1016–17